S0-BCP-866

AMERICA IN LITERATURE

Volume
II

AMERICA IN LITERATURE

General Editor: Theodore L. Gross

VOLUME I
PART I.   THE FIRST TWO CENTURIES

David Levin
The University of Virginia

PART II.   THE ROMANTIC ERA

Theodore L. Gross
The City College of New York

VOLUME II
PART III.   THE AGE OF REALISM

Alan Trachtenberg
Yale University

PART IV.   THE TWENTIETH CENTURY

Benjamin DeMott
Amherst College

AMERICA IN LITERATURE

VOLUME II

Alan Trachtenberg
YALE UNIVERSITY

Benjamin DeMott
AMHERST COLLEGE

JOHN WILEY & SONS
NEW YORK   SANTA BARBARA   LONDON   SYDNEY   TORONTO

CREDITS

Goddard Frederick Tuckerman: From *The Sonnets of Frederick Goddard Tuckerman* by Frederick Goddard Tuckerman. Copyright 1931, by Alfred A. Knopf, and renewed 1959 by Witter Bynner. Reprinted by permission of Alfred A. Knopf.

Frederick Goddard Tuckerman: From "The Cricket" by Frederick Goddard Tuckerman. Originally published by Cummington Press. Copyright 1950, by Margaret Tuckerman Clark.

Frederick Goddard Tuckerman: From "Oh, Lovely Appearance of Death," "John Henry," "Hard Times in the Country," "The Rising Sun Blues," and "The Little Black Train." Collected, adapted, and arranged by John A. Lomax and Alan Lomax. Copyright 1941, by Tro and renewed 1969, by Ludlow Music, New York. Used by permission.

(Acknowledgments are continued on page 1713.)

COPYRIGHT © 1978, BY JOHN WILEY & SONS, INC.

ALL RIGHTS RESERVED. PUBLISHED SIMULTANEOUSLY IN CANADA.

NO PART OF THIS BOOK MAY BE REPRODUCED BY ANY MEANS, NOR TRANSMITTED, NOR TRANSLATED INTO A MACHINE LANGUAGE WITHOUT THE WRITTEN PERMISSION OF THE PUBLISHER.

LIBRARY OF CONGRESS CATALOGING IN PUBLICATION DATA:
MAIN ENTRY UNDER TITLE:

AMERICA IN LITERATURE.

BIBLIOGRAPHY: V. 1, P.   ; V. 2, P.
INCLUDES INDEXES.
1. AMERICAN LITERATURE.   2. UNITED STATES—
LITERARY COLLECTIONS.   3. UNITED STATES—CIVILIZATION.
I. GROSS, THEODORE L.
PS509.U52A38   810'.9   76-49486
ISBN 0-471-32808-1 (V. 1)
ISBN 0-471-32809-X (V. 2)

PRINTED IN THE UNITED STATES OF AMERICA

10 9 8 7 6 5 4 3 2 1

Preface

America is a civilization whose literature cannot be fully understood apart from the culture that has helped to shape it. When the achievement of a novelist or poet is viewed in the context of his time, the work assumes a meaning it can never possess alone; it becomes a dominant feature in the social and literary record of the nation rather than an isolated artifact. *America in Literature* is an attempt to reflect organically the most urgent ideas of our nation as they have risen from the roots of the American soil and issued through the American mind and imagination.

In form, *America in Literature* is as interdisciplinary as the culture itself. Although the dominant expression is literary and is represented by the essential authors who must be included in any record of artistic achievement, other disciplines illuminate a common heritage. As Bryant, Cooper, Whitman, and Twain draw verbal landscapes of the American scene, their contemporaries, Cole, Mount, Heade, and Bingham, create paintings of the same land, nourished by similar concepts of nature, and man, and God, and society. As Emerson, Thoreau, and Hawthorne write literary masterpieces concerned with the reformation of the human heart, others seek to translate these ideas into social action: Horace Mann in education; Margaret Fuller in woman's rights; Dorothea Dix in prison reform; and Frederick Douglass through the abolition of slavery. F. Scott Fitzgerald shows the reader how the American rich are different from the American poor, but Edward Dahlberg and Robert Coles speak intimately and powerfully of "bottom dogs" in a democracy, even though their voices may be less conventionally artistic; they, too, must be included in a record of American civilization. Artemus Ward satirizes Lincoln's thought in words less reverential than those of Whitman and Lincoln himself. The autobiographies of Elizabeth Ashbridge, Benjamin Franklin, Charlotte Forten, and Randolph Bourne; the spirituals of blacks and Indians; the architecture of Horatio Greenough, Louis Sullivan, and Frank Lloyd Wright; the historical documents of John Adams, Thomas Jefferson, James Madison, and Abraham Lincoln; the photographs of Matthew Brady and Walker Evans—these various forms of expression help to create the mosaic of a complex culture and involve us in the real texture of actual American lives.

The interdisciplinary approach of *America in Literature* depends upon a view of national culture that is organic. If Puritanism is the primary force of early American civilization, how may we represent it most vividly and comprehensively? Should we restrict ourselves to a few poems and sermons, or should we include diaries, histories, paintings, and architectural reproductions of homes and landscapes in order to recreate the full sense of life as it was lived in the seventeenth and eighteenth centuries? Can we truly understand slavery by reading only Thoreau, Whitman, and Twain, or might we not have a deeper sense of its complexity and cutting edge by also hearing John C. Calhoun and Daniel Webster, looking at contemporary cartoons and photographs, listening to songs and battle hymns, and reading the journalism of William Lloyd Garrison and Wendell Phillips, the slave narratives, and the sociological treatises and tracts of the time? In the modern period, technocracy can be interpreted not only by artists like Norman Mailer and James Baldwin, but also by those who affect all of us in our daily lives: practitioners of film and television, creators of photographs and posters, the participants in interviews, and voices in tape recordings.

Clearly American civilization is more complex than the traditional and almost exclusively literary presentation it has been accorded. As authors who have participated in the general critical attempt to view literature in the fullest cultural context, we have sought to redress the balance, to present a record of American civilization as well as of American literature, "to come to a hard bottom and rocks in place," as Thoreau admonished us to do, "which we can call *reality*"—an *American reality*.

In order to broaden the range of our selections, we have been compelled to make certain arbitrary decisions regarding space. We are deeply aware that no account of American civilization would be complete without the inclusion of major creations of considerable length, and we urge the reader to possess the following books as a minimal list of masterpieces: *The Pioneers, The Scarlet Letter, Walden, Moby Dick, Huckleberry Finn, The Portrait of a Lady, The Rise of Silas Lapham, An American Tragedy, The Sun Also Rises, The Sound and the Fury, The Great Gatsby,* and *Invisible Man.* It did not seem a wise use of space to reprint these or other comparable works, since they are readily available in paperback editions, but they obviously should have a primary place in any discussion of the materials presented in American civilization.

Inevitably, certain ideas have dominated our record: democratization and its effect on the poor, the wealthy, and minorities; the conflict between nature and technocracy; the myth of the West that has shaped the imagination of writers, painters, and humorists; the artistic response to evil and sin that is so central to our most deeply creative authors. But if one theme has seemed of special urgency at the end of

vii
PREFACE

America's fourth century, it has been the tension between personal expression and mutual dependency, announced in Whitman's famous inscription, "One's-self I sing, a simple separate person,/Yet utter the word Democratic, the word En-Masse," and repeated for the twentieth century in John Dewey's reminder that a democracy is a "conjoint communicated experience." Many have profited from this land; too many have been excluded from its riches and its power. And, together with the record of artistic achievement in America, we have sought to reflect this tension that preoccupies us—to borrow a word from William Carlos Williams—in the "dailiness" of our lives.

Within the limits of two volumes, we have attempted to view American civilization contextually, and the reader will discover that much of the writing is arranged in clusters of experience. Thus the pamphlets and tracts of black authors like Jupiter Hammond, Absalom Jones, and William Hamilton are grouped together as early commentaries on slavery; Emerson's "Divinity School Address" is seen in the context of transcendentalist expression, and Thoreau's "Civil Disobedience" is placed with other works concerning reform; the observations of Frederick Jackson Turner, Henry Adams, William James, Thorstein Veblen, and George Santayana are grouped together in "Expressions of Social Thought"; the essays of John Dewey, Randolph Bourne, and Van Wyck Brooks are juxtaposed in a section entitled "The Case for Cultural Revolution"; the writings of Jane Addams, W. E. B. DuBois, Edward Dahlberg, James Agee, Richard Wright, Ralph Ellison, James Baldwin, Robert Coles, and N. Scott Momaday point toward the possibility of a "new society" in which we care more about all of the Americans who constitute, in Gwendolyn Brooks' image, "our mutual estate." Great authors naturally transcend movements, and their writings are presented as the expression of their unique sensibilities; but we have also introduced the social and historical record without which their works of art lose meaning.

While we share the principles of *America in Literature*, as four discrete editors we have individual approaches to these principles, reflected in our own quite personal idioms. It would be a contradiction of purpose to suppress or deny our individual voices, and we have not done so; we have allowed ourselves the freedom of personal expression, even of idiosyncrasy. Although we present the fundamental documents of American civilization—certainly those major literary works of prose, poetry, and drama—and are as informative as space will allow, we always interpret these materials, hoping to provoke the reader into his own interpretation. There is one vision in *America in Literature*, but four distinct angles of that vision. We invite the reader to provide his own angle of vision, to make our book complete.

The shifting patterns of democracy and the contradictory elements of a mobile society do not yield readily to any formal structure and, through this formidable record, we have followed the natural direction of those who have articulated the meaning of America. The result, we hope, is a reflection of our nation that will persuade the reader who touches this book that he touches not merely a book, but a culture— the whole way of life of a people.

Theodore L. Gross

Acknowledgments

During the many years in which this manuscript was developing, a number of people have given the editors invaluable help, ranging from scholarly advice and research concerning texts and biography to collation and proofreading. We are grateful to these people and regret that space does not allow us to mention all of their names. Certain individuals, however, have been so helpful that they must be mentioned.

In terms of the sort of book that would seem appropriate to the contemporary student, we received significant advice from Elizabeth Wooten Cowan, Texas A & M University; Carl H. Klaus, The University of Iowa; James A. Parrish, University of South Florida, Tampa; Louis D. Rubin, Jr., University of North Carolina at Chapel Hill; Michael F. Shugrue, The Staten Island College, CUNY; Eugene Soules, Sonoma State College; and Neal Woodruff, Coe College.

Alan Trachtenberg wishes to thank Robert Byer for his generosity in commenting on the contents and introduction to Part I of Volume 2; Patricia Shepherd for her research assistance; and Laura Wexler for her invaluable and sensitive help in preparing the notes and the manuscript in general.

Benjamin DeMott wishes to thank his research assistant Marian Simpson, for her invaluable contributions to his section of Volume 2. He is especially indebted also, to the general editor, Professor Gross, for selecting and editing, as a specialist, the works by black writers included in Volume 2.

As general editor, I wish to express my personal appreciation to the staff at John Wiley who worked on *America in Literature:* Vivian Kahane for her final editing; Debra Schwartz for her production supervision; and Andrea Stingelin for her extensive work on permissions. My deepest gratitude to Thomas O. Gay, without whom *America in Literature* would not have been realized. From conception to reality, and at every stage of development, Mr. Gay monitored the progress of this anthology. He exhibited a rare sensitivity to a complex task, and I am grateful for his devotion to the project and for his continuous support.

Although the individual sections are the responsibility of their respective editors, I should note that certain selections were handled by another editor within the project; in this sense as well as in the continual discussions we have had with one another, *America in Literature* expresses the common view of the four editors. David Levin wrote the headnote to William Ellery Channing; Theodore Gross wrote the head-

ACKNOWLEDGMENTS

notes to the Southern Agrarians, James Weldon Johnson, Claude McKay, Jean Toomer, Countee Cullen, Langston Hughes, Adrienne Rich, Michael Harper, Don Lee, Melvin Tolson, and Gwendolyn Brooks.

Theodore L. Gross

Contents

PART III: THE AGE OF REALISM, 1860-1900
1

FREDERICK GODDARD TUCKERMAN (1821–1873)   421

II. The Triumph of Realism
428

III. Toward Naturalism
599

II. The Life of the Imagination
1110

ROBERT FROST (1874-1963) 1138

WALLACE STEVENS (1879-1955) 1162

MARIANNE MOORE (1887-1972) 1186

MELVIN TOLSON (1900-1960) 1189

GWENDOLYN BROOKS (1917-   ) 1194

PART III

THE AGE OF REALISM

1860-1900

1.

A sense of sudden, vast, and bewildering change appeared in American life after the Civil War. Mark Twain and his collaborator Charles Dudley Warner expressed a popular feeling when they wrote in their novel *The Gilded Age* (1873) that "the eight years in America from 1860 to 1868 uprooted institutions that were centuries old, changed the politics of a people, transformed the social life of half the country, and wrought so profoundly upon the entire national character that the influence cannot be measured short of two or three generations." The new scene, according to the novel, was ridden with corruption in politics and business, with an inflamed greed for wealth, a fever for the quick turnover and the fast buck, dishonesty and meanness in public and private life, and almost total debasement of national ideals. The *Gilded Age* is a satire and a melodrama, as if to say that the age itself deserved no better treatment. And, far from offending readers, the book's title gave the period one of its most eloquent descriptive tags.

The Gilded Age, the Great Barbeque, the Chromo Civilization, the Age of Negation—these familiar phrases headline a common interpretation of the three decades following the Northern victory in 1865. The country seemed under siege to a different set of values and ideals from those associated with the Founding Fathers and the major literary figures of the antebellum years: the hopeful, idealistic, and democratic ideals of Jefferson and Washington, of Emerson and Melville and Whitman. The new pace was set by shady politicians working glove in hand with a new breed of businessmen, of crude money-men and plunderers, bankers, financiers, and speculators. The country watched as if helpless before the spectacle of President Grant's ineptitude, the Credit Mobilier scandal, and the Black Fridays on the stock market. City and national politics threatened to become the fiefdoms of "bosses" like Tweed in New York and Roscoe Conklin and Mark Hanna in the Republican Party. Financiers like Daniel Drew, Jim Fisk, and Jay Gould manipulated stocks and aggressively seized control of railroads and other companies (Mark Twain said about Jay Gould: "The people had *desired* money before his day, but *he* taught them to fall down and worship it."). Industrial titans or, as Matthew Josephson dubbed them, Robber Barons, like Rockefeller, Carnegie, Vanderbilt, Armour, Pillsbury, and Stanford wrested their giant fortunes (and founded families of inherited wealth that still figure prominently in American life) through swindles of mind-staggering proportions, plunder and outright theft of public funds and natural resources, and ruthless suppression of competition. It is no wonder that many Americans felt depressed and angered at the state of the union.

To a New England aristocrat like Henry Adams, the new order was distasteful in the extreme: the lords of politics and business were hardly gentlemen of the old genteel cut, the sort who would appeal to the Adamses, the Cabots, the Lodges, and the Lowells. The ascendent leaders posed a menace to Henry Adams; they were, like Grant, men for whom "the intellect counted for nothing; only the energy counted. The type was pre-industrial, archaic, and would have seemed so even to the cave-dwellers." Speaking as a patrician displaced from power—he had hoped for a cabinet appointment under Grant—Adams wondered what confidence one could have in such men to organize and control the new energies unleashed by science and industry and exploited by business. But even a democrat like Whitman stood appalled before the "dry and flat Sahara" of public life in the early 1870's. "Genuine belief seems to have left us," he wrote, and the "underlying principles" of the country were disrespected at every turn. "The depravity of the business classes of our country is not less than has been supposed, but infinitely greater. The official services of America, national, state, and municipal, in all their branches and departments, except the judiciary, are saturated in corruption, bribery, falsehood, mal-administration; and the judiciary is tainted."

American society had clearly entered a new phase, one in which it was no longer possible to think of America as a relatively simple and harmonious world, exempt from the evils of the older European societies. Complication had set in, and even though many Americans persisted in their belief in traditional morality and in the democratic ideals of equal opportunity and just rewards for labor—indeed, the conflict between such ideals and the harsh, sometimes brutal realities of the new industrial and urban world is a major theme in the literature of the period—time was running out for the older way of life. The Civil War had permanently damaged the once credible world of a predominantly agricultural society pursuing its divinely endorsed goals of peace and plenty. Henry James arrived at just such a recognition in his study of an earlier American writer, Nathaniel Hawthorne. James wrote in 1879 that the war had "rudely dispelled" the "illusions" of an "earlier and simpler generation."

The subsidence of that great convulsion has left a different tone from the tone it found, and one may say that the Civil War marks an era in the history of the American mind. It introduced in the national consciousness a certain sense of proportion and relation, of the world being a more complicated place than it had hitherto seemed, the future more treacherous, success more difficult.

But illusions die hard. The scope of the change—it amounted to the total transformation of a mainly rural into a mainly urban, industrial, and corporate society—left disorientation and uncertainty in its wake. The war had ushered in a period of transition.

The writing of the period shared the ambiance of an age of transition. Most of the literature is interesting and valuable as attempts to delineate and understand the new shapes of American experience, but only Henry James, Mark Twain, and Emily Dickinson emerge as writers of the first rank. It was not a period in which literature flourished, as it had in the 1850's with Emerson, Thoreau, Hawthorne, Melville, and Whitman. Short in masterpieces, the period nevertheless was rich in literary activity, in the development of new outlooks and styles, in the winning of new audiences, and in the discovery of new veins of common experience for literary treatment. Under the aegis of "realism"— the major literary theory of the period—writers broke new ground and prepared the soil for another flowering of American literature early in the twentieth century. And they did so by observing in fuller detail and with sharper specificity than earlier generations of writers the commonplace actualities of American life.

2.

The "great convulsion" of the Civil War affected the commonplace, and not so commonplace, activities of Americans in many ways. The war itself was fought with astonishing ferocity. The combined Union and Confederate deaths surpassed 600,000, excluding victims of epidemics and starvation in the South, and a countless number were maimed and injured. The South bore the brunt of the devastation, suffering the destruction of its economic system—not only its agriculture based on slavery, but its industries and its banking system. Confederate casualties amounted to a fifth of the white male population otherwise able to work productively. Physical destruction was widespread in the South, where most of the war was fought. According to a typical Southern account, the Union armies "destroyed everything which the most infernal Yankee ingenuity could devise means to destroy; hands, hearts, fire, gunpowder, and behind everything the spirit of hell, were the agencies which they used." The war left the South impoverished, its social system based on chattel slavery destroyed, its economy dependent on Northern investments, and its white ruling groups demoralized. Moreover, its black population, although technically "freed" through the Emancipation Proclamation, was allowed only meager political and social means to assure its freedom; before long federal troops were withdrawn, Reconstruction ended (in 1877), white supremacy was restored, and the blacks again found themselves subject to white rule.

The defeat of the South, on the other hand, allowed the North to clothe itself in superior moral garments. Victory was seen as vindication of the cause of Union (except for the minority of abolitionists, the cause of emancipation was secondary). In its commemoration rhetoric the North saw the outcome as a mark that Providence supported the Union, that the cause was just, and that the nation might now continue its benign course, purged of the evils of secession and slavery. The moral advantage would have counted for naught, however, without the superior fire-power, the military might of the North, backed by an industrial plant that flexed its muscles during the war and discovered its enormous capacity for mobilizing finances and organizing production. The Union government had spent close to $4 billion executing the war, much of the money providing a tremendous spur of capital investment in basic industries. To judge by the results, Northern captains of industry and finance were the real victors; to them went the choicest spoils, and insofar as their outlook prevailed in public life, they occupied the field without serious opposition. Through the Republican Party the business interests were able to take charge immediately after the war, winning subsidies for railroad construction in the West, increasing the protective tariff against foreign goods, manipulating the war debt in favor of financial interests, and picking off, free of charge, large chunks of the public domain for railroad, mining, cattle-raising, and lumbering enterprises. During the war itself, Judge Thomas Mellon of Pittsburgh, who built a fortune in the aluminum business, observed that "such opportunities for making money had never existed before," and the outcome proved him right.

In somewhat different terms Herman Melville also observed that the war had opened new and, for him, ominous potentialities. One of the portentous facts about the war itself was the change in the nature of warfare that came with mechanization. And these changes—conscript armies fighting often blindly, and armour holding the balance of power—prefigured a wholly novel way of life. Many of Melville's poems in *Battle Pieces* (1866) reflect his concern that the war had unleashed new and menacing forces. "A Utilitarian's View of the Monitor's Battle" is a dire prophecy. In the famous battle of the armour-clad warships the Monitor and the Merrimac, Melville envisions the war as an industrial operation: "plain mechanic power/ Plied cogently in War now placed—/ Where War belongs—/ Among the trades and artisans." This may signal a welcome degradation of warfare—Melville is not shedding any tears over the loss of the chance for battlefield heroics—but now that war is made commonplace, nothing more than a trade, a business, its real terror stands forth. Impersonal warfare impersonalizes the combatants. In place of traditional warriors fighting for love and honor we now find "operatives" (a common word for factory workers): "no passion; all went on by crank,/ Pivot, and screw,/ And calculations of caloric." The mechanization of warfare obscures the great issues of the war (at least from a "utilitarian's" point of view); it marks the end of an era and the threshold of a world in which "calculations of caloric" might turn incalculable changes on human life.

Melville perceived that the war had amplified the birth pangs of the industrial world itself, and also that this world would be a radically different place from what it replaced. The difference would lie in the domination of crank, pivot, and screw and of the appropriate "utilitarian" outlook—in the fact that the sources of behavior and the determinations of value would derive from impersonal, abstract, and ultimately indifferent "calculations" of energy and profit.

And, to be sure, the sheer scale, speed, and thoroughness of industrialization after the war proved to be staggering. Exploiting the favorable circumstance of the defeat of the Southern planter class and overriding the Western agrarian interests, Northern business proceeded at breakneck speed to transform the American physical, social, and ultimately moral landscape. The defeat of the Confederacy was a victory for the national state which, freed of the drag of an agrarian opposition, now committed itself decisively through the Republican majority to industrial capitalism. The war had given a tremendous impetus to the formation of corporations, which made possible the accumulation of huge amounts of capital for investment into single industries and eventually led to the rise of giant monopolies in basic industries such as steel, meat-packing, railroads, and oil. A financial newspaper described the situation just after the war as follows: "There is an increasing tendency in our capital to move in larger masses than formerly. Small business firms compete at more disadvantage with richer houses, and are gradually being absorbed into them." This movement toward the concentration of economic power corresponded to the increasing power of the national state itself which, in the 30 years after Appomattox extended its control across the entire continent (the frontier and the era of free land were officially declared "closed" in 1893). The aggregation of distinct sections that gave the nation its character before the war was now tied more and more into a national system, with the South, the Midwest, and the West clearly subordinate to the economic control of Northeastern finance and industry.

It was difficult to distinguish the interests of capitalist development from the interests of the government in this period. The West was "won" by military might against the Indians and the economic might of the railroad titans. Military action against the Indian inhabitants of Western lands began in earnest even during the war, and continued with a savagery only recently brought to light through the 1870's and 1880's, culminating in the massacre of Wounded Knee in 1889. The defeat of the Indians opened the Western plains to the great herds of the cattle kingdom which, in turn, depended on the railroad for links with the meat-packing centers in Chicago and Kansas City. The very rapid settlement of the West typified the energies and themes of the period: a "romance" of exploration, adventure, high excitement, based on an underlying process of military, economic, and political expansion. The drama of settlement seemed to be over as soon as it started and, by the end of the century, the Old West was already a legend shorn of the troublesome facts of greed, aggrandizement, and expropriation.

The new national unity counted on both transportation and communication, and these in turn developed from the new inventions and new industries of the period. American "know-how" came into its own in these years; and whether or not Americans were better endowed than others in inventiveness, their swift application of technological improvements led to impressive results. The war was a great proving ground for business organization and industrial management, and the lessons carried over. A key instrument of expansion and of development of new regions, the railroad improved its speed, safety, and convenience throughout these years. After the hookup of the first transcontinental line in 1869, the railroad became the essential element in the national system: carrying raw materials to processing centers and carrying finished mass-produced goods to markets. Improvements in basic industrial processes contributed to enormous increases in productivity—in steel, for example, the Bessemer process led to an increase in production of steel ingots between 1860 and 1890 from about 17,000 to 7,000,000 tons per year. With new farm machinery, such as the McCormick reaper, the annual crops of wheat and cotton tripled in this period.

Measured in these terms, progress seemed tangible and unmistakable. From one point of view these were, indeed, the significant events in American life: so many miles of railroad track put down, so many tons of steel produced, so many telephones and telegraph units installed (by 1898 the United States had twice as many telephones as all of Europe), so many cities and towns and homes connected in a spreading intricate system. By the end of the century the transformation was nearly complete. By 1890 the value of manufactured goods surpassed that of agricultural products. Most of the population now lived in areas classified as cities, in close daily contact with the physical products of the new industrial society, and more and more dependent on the modern technologies of electricity for the basic features of their lives: light, heat, travel, and communication. Electricity typified

Construction of St. Paul-Minneapolis and Manitoba railroad, 1887.
Minnesota Historical Society.

Grand opening of the Brooklyn Bridge, May 24, 1883. *Museum of the City of New York, The J. Clarence Davies Collection.*

the new forces that the wonders of civilization held in store for modern America. In about a generation, in less than half a normal lifetime, America had become an industrial giant, surpassing Great Britain in wealth and sea power, replacing it as the world's workshop, and ready to plunge into imperial ventures overseas in competition with Western Europe for new sources of raw materials and cheap labor and additional markets. The Columbian Exposition in Chicago in 1893, with its neoclassical buildings and design and its first full-scale use of electric lighting proclaimed the new imperial stance.

3.

The new American world was a world made largely by industry and capitalism—a world of shapes and things (crowded cities, tall buildings, massive factories, packaged goods), but also a world of values and ideas. The business classes themselves subscribed to an outlook that had wide currency in the period, that can be summarized as "what is good for business is good for America." It was a philosophy that justified unrestricted business enterprise, aggressive profit-making, and ruthless competition. Private wealth, argued the English social philosopher Herbert Spencer, was a legitimate reward for the "fittest" who survived in the "struggle for existence." Spencer, who had a large following among American clergymen, college presidents and professors, and businessmen, drew his analogies from Darwin's discoveries in natural science; he insisted that "there cannot be more good done than that of letting social progress go on unhindered; and immensity of mischief may be done in . . . the artificial preservation of those least able to care for themselves." Of course, this doctrine did not hinder the government from *aiding* business in all sorts of visible and invisible ways and, in general, a doctrine of *laissez faire* seemed a bit hypocritical in an age of the Beef Trust, the Sugar Trust, the Oil Trust, and the United States Steel Corporation (founded in 1901 as the first billion dollar corporation in the world, controlling 60 percent of the market). But the "survival of the fittest" seemed to make sense to many Americans who were raised on the twin notions of economic individualism and the Protestant equation of worldly goods with godliness. In sermons, college lectures, moral essays, and the voluminous "rags to riches" literature, of which the Horatio Alger stories are best known, the values supporting the behavior of the business classes took hold with a tight grip. Andrew Carnegie, the Pittsburgh steel-maker of legendary wealth and brutal labor policies, found a large following for his gospel of wealth among the hundreds of thousands of would-be millionaires who filled the commercial centers of the big cities.

The world created by the Robber Barons was hardly one of peace and contentment, nor did it fit their doctrine that left to themselves, businessmen would create a prosperous, harmonious society. In fact, these years were ridden with conflict, struggle, and anxiety. Carnegie adopted for his motto, "All is well since all grows better." Yet the period was torn by bitter and violent strikes that often became pitched battles between workers and federal troops that were called out to protect the private interests of the railroad and steel corporations. Industrialization had created an urban working class, much of it composed of newly arrived immigrants who were encouraged by the hopes of economic and social opportunities in the expanding American economy, but most of whom found themselves instead recruited into the industrial army of laborers. Poorly organized (in 1898 only 500,000 out of 17 million factory workers belonged to unions), the laws stacked against them, public opinion frequently inflamed by the spectre of anarchy and revolution, the workers found themselves rather defenseless against the power of the corporations, which could count on the police and the army to intervene on their side. Industrial workers, like farmers, were particularly vulnerable during the frequent economic crises, when starvation loomed as the alternative to accepting decreased income and depressed living conditions. Out of this situation arose the several bloody strikes of the period: the railroad strikes of 1877; the McCormick Harvester strike in 1886; the accompanying Haymarket Riot in Chicago, which resulted in the arrest and execution of several anarchists for allegedly throwing a bomb that killed a policeman; the Homestead steel strike in 1892; and the Pullman strike in 1894, led by Eugene V. Debs, who later became the national leader of the Socialist Party. Although unionization advanced slowly, two national unions emerged in these years, the Noble Order of the Knights of Labor, which originated in 1869 under the leadership of Uriah S. Stephens, and, in 1881, the American Federation of Labor, founded by Samuel Gompers.

The predicament of farmers in the South and the Midwest was also severe and led to protest and opposition movements. Squeezed by the railroads, by large landowners (in the South especially, where the sharecropper system was widespread), by suppliers and middlemen and packagers, and by the fluctuations of the market (increasingly sensitive to international pressures and stock market speculations), farmers experienced a particular bafflement and frustration in the new society. They had been, after all, the pillars of the republic not many years back, the "noble husbandman," according to Jefferson, on whom the virtue of the country rested. Now they were suffering impoverishment and unrewarding toil, and the rest of the country seemed not to care. Agrarian distress increased during the period and burst into the revolt

Anarchist riot in Chicago. *Library of Congress.*

known as Populism in the 1880's and 1890's, a revolt fired by resentment and bitterness against the "system" symbolized by Wall Street. The aim of the movement, which was absorbed by the Democratic Party with the nomination of William Jennings Bryan in 1896, was to win government intervention on behalf of the farmer against the monopolies, and especially against the gold standard, which Bryan and most of the Populists believed was the cause of much of their misery.

4.

The period, in short, was agitated by social conflicts arising from uncontrolled capitalism. Against Carnegie's motto must be placed the evidence that all was not well, as the radical reformer Henry George suggested in *Social Problems* (1883):

> That the rapid changes now going on are bringing up problems that demand the most earnest attention may be seen on every hand. Symptoms of danger, premonitions of violence, are appearing all over the civilized world. Creeds are dying, beliefs are changing; the old forces of conservatism are melting away. Political institutions are falling, as clearly in democratic America as in monarchical Europe. There is growing unrest and bitterness among the masses, whatever be the form of government, a blind groping for escape from conditions becoming intolerable. To attribute all this to the teachings of demogogues is like attributing the fever to the quickening pulse.

A full account of the new world of modern America must include the symptoms of strain, the buried as well as the overt anxieties, the feeling of displacement, of disorientation, of disequilibrium. It must also include the positive responses and signs of resistance to the new order, not only in the labor and farmer movements and in the varieties of socialism and anarchism that were widely discussed and that appealed to many writers, but also in the political reform movements, in the feminist movement, and in the "social gospel" movement in the churches. In spite of the fact that the economic and political energies of the country were centralizing and consolidating—or perhaps because of it—the intellectual life of the period, especially in the late 1880's and 1890's, was agitated with talk of reform, with radical alternatives and utopian visions. Edward Bellamy's *Looking Backward: 2000-1887* (1888) launched a popular movement for a rational society that would end extremes of poverty and wealth by abolishing private property and turning over the control of production and distribution

Family in front of Minneapolis house, 1891. *Minnesota Historical Society.*

to the state. Socialism, albeit of a mild, nonrevolutionary kind, seemed a reasonable and possible alternative to many Americans, including the most prominent literary figure of the 1880's and 1890's, William Dean Howells.

At the same time, faced with bewildering changes and with novel demands on their lives, Americans in the middle classes looked for material and psychological security above all else. Working-çlass turbulence frightened them, just as the new immigration filled them with unease. Thomas Bailey Aldrich, a poet in the tradition of genteel, aristocratic values, expressed the common feelings of the older Americans in *"Unguarded Gates"* (1895):

> Wide open and unguarded stand our gates,
> And through them passes a wild motley throng—
> Men from the Volga and the Tartar steppes,
> Featureless figures of the Hoang-Ho,
> Malayan, Scythian, Teuton, Kelt, and Slav,
> Flying the Old World's poverty and scorn;
> These bringing with them unknown gods and rites,
> Those, tiger passions, here to stretch their claws,
> In street and alley what strange tongues are loud,
> Accents of menace alien to our air,
> Voices that once the Tower of Babel knew!
>
> O Liberty, white Goddess! is it well
> To leave the gates unguarded? . . .

Some indication of the basis of this alarm comes from the fact that between 1870 and 1910 more than 20 million new Americans arrived from Europe alone (the majority arrived toward the close of the period from Southern and Eastern Europe), and that in 1910 two-thirds of the labor force of the top 20 industries consisted of recent immigrants and blacks. (As late as 1920 an established historian of immigration included Negroes among "Our Foreigners.")

Anxiety and a sense of threat were inescapable in the new American world. In large part it was implicit in the creed that formulated the most common middle-class aspirations—a creed that became a dominant feature of the culture of the new society. At a time of severe social and economic conflict, the creed insisted on the fundamental health and benevolence of American life. Speaking on July 4, 1876, Henry Ward Beecher, the ever-popular preacher of assurances, embraced the entire nation in the mantle of progress. While admitting "mischiefs and troubles" in public life, he asserted in reassuring phrases that "on the whole there has been a steady ascent in intelligence, in conscience, in purity, in industry, in happiness." Stressing advances in education, publishing, sanitation, and humanitarianism (the freeing of the slaves and, as he saw it, the coming suffrage for women), he assured his audience that "there never was a time . . . when the conditions of life were so wholesome, the conditions of happiness so universally diffused, as they are today in this great land." Optimism about unlimited opportunities was his keynote, and the essentials of the creed were addressed directly to the most problematic figure in American life, the industrial worker:

> The laborer ought to be ashamed of himself—or to find fault with Providence that stinted him when he was endowed—who in 20 years does not own the ground on which his house stands, and that, too, an unmortgaged house; who has not in that house provided carpets for his rooms, who has not his China plates, who has not his chromos, who has not some books nestling on the shelf, who has not there a household that he can call his home, the sweetest place upon the earth. This is not a picture of some future time, but the picture of to-day, a picture of the homes of the workingmen of America.

The creed projected a norm of basic economic security, a middle-class norm of family comfort and cultivation. What lay outside the image of the household was precisely that, *outside* the accepted definition of "American." The authority of this image of aspiration, which defined for the poor, the immigrant, and the nonwhite what they were missing, is indicated by its pervasiveness in the period and, indeed, since then. For example, Whitman admits in *Democratic Vistas* that although the business classes are depraved and making money is a corruption of ideals, nevertheless "a more universal ownership of property, general homesteads, general comfort," is essential for his theory of democracy. "My theory includes riches, and the getting of riches." In part it is a matter of security: the "safety and endurance" of the republic depends on "the aggregate of its middling property owners." "Democracy looks with suspicious, ill-satisfied eye upon the very poor, the ignorant, and on those out of business. She asks for men and women with occupations, well-off, owners of homes and acres, and with cash in the bank—and with some cravings for literature, too." Whitman confesses that the idea is paradoxical, in light of his condemnation of the "almost maniacal appetite for wealth prevalent in the United States," and "ungracious" in its exclusion of "the very poor, the ignorant, and those out of business" (the very outcasts, it should be said, he embraces as brothers and sisters in his poetry), but nevertheless necessary in the process of "amelioration and progress" that underlies his theory.

The image, then, was projected against the threat of a large class of the dispossessed and dissatisfied. In Beecher's version of the creed protection lay not simply in the mortgage-free house that all Americans should feel ashamed not to own, but in the "culture" of the household, in the China plates, the carpets, the chromos, the few books scattered about. The hidden presence in Beecher's picture of the happy home is, of course, the presiding woman; the tokens of cultivation betoken her particular realm. The country is safe as long as the spirit of womanhood prevails; she is "god's own," the household legislator, the educator, the merciful judge who forgives and atones for the transgression of children. A champion of woman's suffrage (although his grounds might be questionable in the eyes of the militant suffragettes), Beecher wrote: "You that live long enough will see women vote, and when you see women vote, you will see less fraud, less selfishness, less brutality, and more public spirit and rectitude and harmony in the administration of public affairs." Ultimate protection against the besetting dangers of the new American world—corrupt politicians, selfish businessmen, grinding and demoralizing poverty, and nagging dissent—lay in the redemptive powers of the American woman.

The creed assigned roles, defined conventional outlooks, and took a generally cozy view of human existence. It assumed that the universe was in the hands of a divine providence, that human hearts were more good than bad, that decent behavior would be rewarded, and that "purity" of manners, speech, and thoughts was a sure guarantee that providence would smile on Americans. The role of "culture" in this vision—of the feminine cultivation associated with books and China plates—was to uphold the existence of a realm of "higher" values. "Culture" gave some assurance that the economic struggle for survival was not an end in itself; it also allowed the middle classes to hold themselves together against the gaudy and vulgar display of outrageous wealth in the Fifth Avenue and "Upper Tenth" crowd, and to draw a line of safety above the demoralized, downtrodden poor. Beecher's examples of "culture" were a diluted and democratized version of what had earlier been the exclusive domain of the European aristocracy and the very rich, now universally open to all people above the poverty line. It is not exactly what Whitman had in mind as a democratic culture, which would be manly, strenuous, and radically egalitarian, but neither is it merely a shadow of gentility. The middle-class creed sought a middle path among the embattled extremes of American life; it rejected the crude Robber Barons along with the volatile foreign anarchists; and it projected an optimistic future for all the temporarily disenchanted groups at the bottom of the American system. It was a point of view that emerged in response to the new cleavages and the undercurrents of even more treacherous dangers in the new America—a point of view compounded of the older work ethic, of liberal Protestantism, of sentimental domesticity. The middling property owner was its commonplace hero, and education, stability, and a sweet benevolence were its chief values. The vision provided comfort for all those within its boundaries, but left many Americans out in the cold.

5.

The strain between the vision of the popular creed and the actual report of the eyesight as it witnessed the conflicts and contrasts of the times provided perhaps the single most important theme of the imaginative writing of the period. The word atmosphere might be a better word than theme, since most of the writing in the decades after the Civil War more or less explicitly evoked a sense of tension, of misdirection in personal life, of an uneasy fit between ideals and aspirations and practical realities. No generalization about the writing of a period will be accurate enough to cover every case, but it is generally true that a feeling of vague discontent (sometimes, of course, quite specific discontent, as in outright protest literature like Hamlin Garland's stories of Midwest farm life), of uncertainty, of dislocation, fills the pages of the stories and novels of these years. The pervasive mood was rebellious, but not outwardly so until the more pointed social fiction of the 1890's. Instead, rebellion took the form of mockery of outmoded values, in some cases the form of nostalgia for the lost past, and also the form of a campaign for "realism," addressed chiefly against the standards of polite and sentimental fiction that ruled in the periodicals and publishing houses.

We might venture further with this generalization and suggest that along with rebellion and criticism of established social and literary values, the writing of the period conveys an undercurrent of loss, of unspecified and vague failure—loss and failure especially of the ability to *act* in the bold, decisive manner of the earlier Romantic writing. If we compare the heroes of, say, Howells and James with Cooper's frontiersmen, Melville's men of worldly action, Whitman's all-encompassing self, Emerson's self-reliant hero, or Thoreau's man of principle, we feel a falling off in the range of human experience, a diminished sense of possibility as well as a lowered tone of voice, a sense even of victimization at the hands of rather dimly perceived social and psychological forces. Indeed, impoverishment and a hunger for experience is a prominent theme throughout the period, notably in the poetry of Emily Dickinson and the fiction of Henry James, Harold Frederic, and Kate Chopin. Taken in the aggregate, the writing of the period records a growing sense of inadequacy to human need in the social patterns and the prevailing values of the new America. We find little praise, little boisterous affirmation; instead, there is much analysis, criticism, introspection, and quest.

The writing of these years seems very much in transition. At the beginning of the period just after the war, the leading literary figures were still the "household" or "fireside" poets, Longfellow and Holmes and Lowell, poets of conscience, feeling, and moral elevation. They remained the best selling and most popular writers throughout the period, and their literary values—cultured, Brahmin, polite—exercised a major influence on editors and publishers and, therefore, on young aspiring writers. Literary culture was associated with the East, with Boston, with *Atlantic Monthly, Harper's,* and *Century Magazine,* and young writers from the South and West, like William Dean Howells and Mark Twain, came East to find their acceptance and fame. In the older poets and in their followers among the influential critics and editors, such as the "genteel" Edmund Clarence Stedman, Richard Watson Gilder, George William Curtis, Charles Eliot Norton, and the younger writers Thomas Bailey Aldrich and Bayard Taylor, the middle-class creed of virtue and "culture" found its literary expression. They were defenders of ideality, as one recent critic put it, and they stood guard over the province of literature to preserve its purity. Edith Wharton recounted that one editor warned her away from certain topics— "religion, love, politics, alcohol or fairies."

The impulse toward realism was largely provoked by the tepid quality of the poetry and fiction appearing in the major Eastern (New York and Boston) journals—the best paying and most influential outlets for new writing. Whitman had these journals and their literary folk in mind when he asked in *Democratic Vistas,* "Do you call those genteel little creatures American poets?" This is how he described the breed:

> . . . a parcel of dandies and ennuyees, dapper little gentlemen from abroad, who flood us with their thin sentiment of parlors, parasols, piano songs, tinkling rhymes, the five-hundreth importation—or whimpering and crying about something, chasing one aborted conceit after another, and forever occupied in dyspeptic amours with dyspeptic women.

The audience for Whitman's poetry was confined to a handful of eccentric intellectuals and Bohemians—he himself was dismissed from a job in Washington for possessing a copy of his own book, *Leaves of Grass,* known as a dirty and disreputable work. And the most important and original poet of the following generation, Emily Dickinson, lived as a recluse, her work mostly unknown and misunderstood when it was known. Early in the twentieth century the Harvard philosopher

George Santayana characterized the prevailing poetry in this period as "simple, sweet, humane, Protestant literature, grandmotherly in that sedate, spectacled wonder with which it gazed at this terrible world and said how beautiful and how interesting it all was." It was "realism" simply to say it was not so.

The term "realism" can be deceptive, however, and must be understood as it was understood in the period itself. Although the term derives from its appearance in France a generation earlier where *realisme* designated a literary method of detached, objective description of what exists, in the United States it came to mean less an aesthetic objective than an outlook toward life, a moral point of view. Flaubert, the chief exponent of realism in the French novel, insisted that the aim of art was no longer beauty but truth, and that the artist must deal with the facts of everyday life with the detachment of a scientist, impersonally and without moral judgment (although not with indifference: Flaubert also confessed an abiding identification with his best known character, Emma Bovary). On the other hand, Howells' realism was an attitude toward experience—less a matter of craft than of moral awareness. In his criticism and his fiction he sought a kind of writing that would honor the commonplace realities of everyday middle-class life, courtship, and family realities and the quotidian, undramatic dilemmas of the business and working worlds. "Realism," he wrote (somewhat reassuringly to an audience perhaps concerned about the questionable effect of French manners on American morals), "is nothing more and nothing less than the truthful treatment of material." For Howells realism was democracy in fiction:

> But let fiction cease to lie about life; let it portray men and women as they are, actuated by the motives and the passions in the measure we all know; let it leave off painting dolls and working them by springs and wires; let it show the different interests in their true proportions . . . let it not put on fine literary airs; let it speak the dialect, the language, that most Americans know— the language of unaffected people everywhere.

The words "measure" and "proportion" point to the major limits in Howells's own practice of realism, which never exceeds bounds of decorum, especially sexual decorum, even when it treats controversial social and economic themes.

One of Howells's worthy services to American letters was his funneling of European ideas into American literary and intellectual life. His notion of realism was derived from reading Balzac, Tolstoy, Ibsen, and Verga, as well as from his own reading of the American scene, a scene that seemed to him fundamentally "smiling" in its major aspects and thus not appropriate for a tragic literature. The currents that flowed in his criticism joined other currents in the changing American world to form a composite conception of realism. These included new kinds of expression coming from the West, a new emphasis on place, local, and regional experience, and new winds of thought in philosophy and social science.

The contributions of Western humor—the humor of the oral tradition, the tall tale, and the deadpan comedian—were manifold and subtle. They included a general attitude of skepticism toward inflated statements, an uncanny quickness to spot the fake and the fraudulent, and implicit in its sniping against fools an affirmation of the good sense of common unpretentious people. The attitude was inseparable from the characteristic language of frontier humor, a language of common speech: rough, unpolished, rich in homely and sometimes rude figures of speech, vulgarities, and near-obscenities. Mark Twain was, of course, the master of this mode, but behind him was a major tradition of storytellers, black and white, including some who became well-known lecturer-comedians, like Artemus Ward and Josh Billings. The relation of Western humorous language to realism can be glimpsed negatively in the outraged comments of New York critic Edmund C. Stedman in the 1870's; he said that "the whole country . . . is flooded, deluged, swamped, beneath a muddy tide of slang, vulgarity . . . impertinence, and buffoonery that is not wit." Wit was acceptable to literary gentlemen; buffoonery was not. The troubles Mark Twain faced reconciling his background in the West with his success among the literati in the East trace to this conflict. His own contribution to defining realism lay in his fusion of the Western vernacular language with the shrewd outlook, the apparently fumbling wisdom that never misses its mark, of the comic storyteller. In *Adventures of Huckleberry Finn* the social criticism latent in this point of view comes to the surface, as do the humanist affirmations.

The vogue of Western writers like Mark Twain, Bret Harte, and others indicated a vast popular audience ready for literary experiences closer to the appetites of their own lives than the fare laid out by the genteel writers and critics. The popularity of regional writing, stories about specific locales and their traditions and customs, suggested a wide interest in the day-by-day lives of common people, and particularly in ways of life that were passing away in the expansive rush of American life. In this period schools of writers were identified by region and place—Mary Wilkins Freeman and Sarah Orne Jewett in New England; Edward Eggleston, E. W. Howe, Joseph Kirkland, and Hamlin Garland in the Middle West; and George Washington Cable, Joel Chandler Harris, Thomas Nelson Page, Kate Chopin, Paul Lawrence Dunbar, and Charles W. Chesnutt in the South. Accurate renderings of speech, manners, and environment made this regional literature critically important in the development of realism. Moreover, regionalist stories were mainly unglamorized accounts of the small daily problems and conflicts of country life at times of large historical changes; they contain some of the most vivid and exact accounts of the texture of life of blacks, women, farmers, fishermen, and plain working people in the period.

In regional and local color writings we find for the first time the presence of the illiterate, the uncultivated, the criminal, and the outcasts of American society. This was obviously a rich vein of native experience, and it made its contribution to the break with Howellsian realism in the 1890's, in the novels and stories of Stephen Crane, Frank Norris and, later, Theodore Dreiser. Regionalist literature stressed the crucial role of upbringing and environment on character, for example, and thus helped prepare for literary naturalism. But, on the whole, this mode of writing itself generally remained within the bounds of literary safety by assuming a condescending or picturesque point of view toward its "low" characters or by devising plots (Bret Harte and O'Henry are the best examples) that would reveal an acceptable "heart of gold" under the disreputable exteriors of prostitutes, criminals, and the socially undesirable.

Particularly in the 1880's and 1890's literary realism came to share important attitudes with other currents in American life, currents of political radicalism—socialism and anarchism—and currents of scientific thinking in philosophy and social science. Pragmatists like William James and John Dewey, social thinkers like the economist Thorstein Veblen and the historian Frederick Jackson Turner are also realists in their revolt against idealized patterns of thinking, their new regard for empirical methods of research, and their critical stance toward American values and social institutions. In the literary movement known as "naturalism" science and literary method join in fashioning a kind of writing that will move beyond the moral outlook of Howells and the psychological realism of James, a writing that took for granted that American society had already become a closed system, victimizing its lower classes and driving its individuals to confusion and despair. Dreiser was the most powerful voice of this new turn of realism, which launched American writing into the twentieth century with a far different attitude toward the chances for freedom, for the fulfillment of the democratic ideals, from that of the post-Civil War years. In *Jennie Gerhardt* (1911) Dreiser explained the new outlook:

> We live in an age in which the impact of materialized forces is well-nigh irresistible; the spiritual nature is overwhelmed by the shock. The tremendous and complicated development of our material civilization, the multiplicity and variety of our social forms, the depth, subtlety, and sophistry of our imaginative impressions, gathered, remultiplied, and disseminated by such

agencies as the railroad, the express and the post-office, the telephone, the telegraph, the newspaper, and, in short, the whole
machinery of social intercourse—these elements of existence
combine to produce what may be termed a kaleidoscopic glitter,
a dazzling and confusing phantasmagoria of life that wearies and
stultifies the mental and moral nature. It induces a sort of intellectual fatigue through which we see the ranks of the victims of
insomnia, melancholia, and insanity constantly recruited.

In short, naturalism was a response to a late phase of the aquisitive
industrial society, a phase in which the subordination of man to system was almost complete, abetted by an array of machinery—a phase,
moreover, in which sheer passive surrender, or insanity, seemed the
only alternatives.

6.

An age reveals itself most clearly and powerfully in its conflicts. From
the Civil War to the present, American society has been torn in a
dozen different directions: by race, class, generation, ethnic grouping,
and sex. The literature from 1865 to 1900 is an integral part of the
history of these years; it was created in the ambiance of a transforming
society, a society rushing headlong toward the closed corporate organization that has become the staple of recent social criticism. The
culture, too, was in a state of transition—that is, the reflective expressions of the period, in art and literature, in popular fiction, in philosophy and social thought, and in religion all suggested uncertainty,
quest, and growing dissatisfaction with the emerging order. Yet the
culture was attached to that order, committed to it either by shared
values or social and economic connections. Criticism often became
crabbed, nagging, either trivial or utopian, as if it could not work itself
free to a fully independent position. Intellectuals discussed socialism
and anarchism and feminism; disgruntled liberals set out to reform the
most glaring kinds of political corruption and inefficiency; utopian
visions like Bellamy's aroused many readers to wish for a better state of
affairs. Yet apart from the slowly emerging labor movement—and from
abortive quixotic movements such as Henry George's Single Tax
Party—no grand plans to implement an alternative captured the imagination of writers or plain people.

In fact much of the thinking and writing in the period was contradictory and suffered from the familiar American (and modern) malaise
of ambivalence. The inner conflicts, the contradictions within established values, the fissures in group and personal consciousness are as
crucial in characterizing the period and its literature as the more manifest conflicts they reflected. Consider some of the more obvious con-

An elderly female vagrant with her plank bed at the Eldridge Street police station, c. 1890. *Photo by Jacob A. Riis. The Granger Collection.*

A Jewish cobbler preparing for the sabbath in a Ludlow Street coal cellar, c. 1890. Photo by Jacob A. Riis, The Granger Collection.

traditions—some still unresolved in American life: public optimism about the future, along with clinging nostalgia about the past; confidence in the bigness of the industrial machine and of the state, along with anxiety about loss of control, about submergence of the self in the system; increasing demands for government control and intervention, for more bigness to solve problems created by bigness, along with increasingly fierce jealousy about personal freedom and local authority. The case, or what Van Wyck Brooks called the "ordeal" of Mark Twain, typifies an important strain in the period: his hatred of hypocrisy and deceit on one hand, his deep attraction to wealth and power and ostentatious display on the other. He seemed unable to reconcile the values of his Western background and frontier experience with his success in the East and around the world. Fame and wealth seemed to struggle with something we might call "authenticity" for mastery of his life. At the end, the conflict resolved itself into personal bitterness but, along the way, his personal dilemma led to a masterpiece like *Adventures of Huckleberry Finn,* which speaks to several of the deep issues of American life.

Ambivalence was a mark that Americans had not reached an accord with the collective issues of their lives, with the far-reaching and unfathomed changes in their expanding world. Realism itself shared this pervasive ambivalence: on one hand its strategies helped to confirm the middle-class creed of a fundamentally healthy and smiling society; on the other, it cleared away obstructions of vision and became the leading instrument of interpretation and criticism of the new society. The culture was feeling its way from inherited values to new formations. Realism expressed the process because it was part of it. The dominant creed did not allow that any unsolvable problems existed; it did not allow that the conflict between strikers and factory owners was a conflict of class that had no easy settlement in store. It did not allow that the unemployed, the very poor, and the nonwhites had a legitimate place and legitimate claims. Realism helped to bring excluded realities to light, and thus played an essential role in preparing for the reenlightenment of American culture that has occurred at several turbulent junctures in the twentieth century. The realists's enterprise of recording the details of everyday life was itself a significant response to the age; the commonplace assumed special importance at a time of swift and thorough change, of disruptions in the familiar patterns of life. But this is not to say that the writing of the period was merely a mirror of the times. Borrowing an expression from Henry James, we can speak of the best writing as constituting a kind of chamber in which the texture of lived experience, the feel and timbre of actual life, is registered with a clarity and sharpness of focus and insight not available elsewhere. The period's dilemmas, conflicts, and uncertainties left a permanent trace in its stories, novels, and poems.

I
New Forms of Literary Expression

WALT WHITMAN

(1819–1892)

Of all the major Romantic writers in America Walt Whitman seems the easiest to know, the most familiar, and the most accessible to readers. He insisted that his poetry not be read as a "literary performance" and,

The standard edition, which presently includes nine published volumes, is *The Collected Writings of Walt Whitman,* General Editors: Gay Wilson Allen and Sculley Bradley, 1966–. Eighteen volumes are projected. This edition includes *Leaves of Grass,* Comprehensive Reader's Edition, ed. Harold Blodgett and Sculley Bradley, 1965. Until superseded by this edition, the most useful text is *Leaves of Grass,* ed. Emory Holloway, 1924, 1954. Another complete edition is *The Complete Writings of Walt Whitman,* 10 vols., ed. R. W. Bucke and others, 1902.

The standard biography is Gay Wilson Allen, *The Solitary Singer, A Critical Biography of Walt Whitman,* 1955. Allen has also published two other important studies: *Walt Whitman Handbook,* 1957, and *A Reader's Guide to Walt Whitman,* 1970. The best early biographies are Emory Holloway, *Whitman, An Interpretation in*

Narrative, 1926; Newton Arving, *Whitman,* 1938, and H. S. Canby, *Walt Whitman, An American,* 1943.

Recent biographies and criticism include the translation of Gay Wilson Allen, ed., *Walt Whitman Abroad,* 1955; Roger Asselineau, *The Evolution of Walt Whitman,* 2 vols., 1960, 1962; Richard Chase, *Walt Whitman Reconsidered,* 1955, and the pamphlet, "Walt Whitman," 1961; Milton Hindus, ed., *Leaves of Grass, One Hundred Years After,* 1955; J. E. Miller, *A Critical Guide to Leaves of Grass,* 1957; Roy Harvey Pearce, *Whitman, A Collection of Critical Essays,* 1962; H. J. Waskow, *Whitman, Explorations in Form,* 1966; E. H. Miller, *Walt Whitman's Poetry,* 1968; E. H. Miller, ed., *A Century of Whitman Criticism.*

The texts from *Leaves of Grass* are those of the edition of 1891–1892.

Walt Whitman. *The Granger Collection.*

indeed, his verse does seem free and open, inviting the casual reader to poke along at his ease. The notion is deceptive, however, one of a host of deceptions practiced by Whitman on the unwary; with all his apparent spontaneity and bluff good nature, he is often covert, devious, furtive, and sly. Late in life, particularly after his disabling stroke at the age of 54, Whitman cultivated a view of himself as the Good Grey Poet, a homespun bard and prophet. The image has unhappily remained, for with all its validity in terms of his fervent attachment to democracy, it has mislead readers into expecting a poetry of doctrine, of slogan, of trumpeted celebration. There is this quality in his poetry, to be sure, but few readers have been prepared for the special difficulties of his best works, which arise from the double nature of his successful verse, its startling immediacy, and its refusal to yield a definite meaning. The poetry is a beguiling assault of the reader's conventional sense of himself as a reader. To all readers who take the Good Grey Poet at face value, he issues a warning, in "Whoever You Are Holding Me Now in Hand":

But these leaves conning you con at peril,
For these leaves and me you will not understand,
They will elude you at first and still more afterward, I will certainly
    elude you,
Even while you should think you had unquestionably caught me,
    behold!
Already you see I have escaped from you.

With calculation he plots against the security of readers who feel "proud to get at the meaning of poems." His is a book, wrote Robert Lewis Stevenson, only for those with "the gift of reading." He demands participation; his "you" is the name of a presence for each reader to experience as himself. "The process of reading," Whitman writes in *Democratic Vistas,* "is not a half-sleep, but, in the highest sense, an exercise, a gymnast's struggle." The reader "is to do something for himself, must be on the alert, must himself or herself construct indeed the poem . . .—the text furnishing the hints, the clue, the start of frame-work."

Whitman's radical spirit is embodied most exactingly in this conception of the active reader, the emergent "you" who will stand in equality with the poet, for whom the poem is less a finished thing than a beginning, a new channel into richer, deeper experience. Herein lies his significant break with what George Santayana called the Genteel Tradition, a tradition that cherishes "art," specifically of the European past, over rough and brute contemporary life. "In Walt Whitman," Santayana wrote, "democracy is carried into psychology and morals.

The various sights, moods, and emotions are given each one vote; they are declared to be all free and equal, and the innumerable commonplace moments of life are suffered to speak like the others. Those moments formerly reputed great are not excluded, but they are made to march in the ranks with their companions—plain foot-soldiers and servants of the hour." D. H. Lawrence makes a similar point in describing Whitman's poetry as "the unrestful, ungraspable poetry of the sheer present, poetry whose very permanency lies in its wind-like transit. . . . The clue to all his utterances lies in the sheer appreciation of the instant moment, life surging into utterance at its very well-head."

Whitman's is a poetry of *sources,* in the root sense of engendering acts: uttering, naming, and reconstituting a world of named things and feelings. We sense a fresh world, freshly encountered and perceived. It is a poetry of plenitude, of the "amplitude of time," of an abundance that in its cumulative surge sometimes forces the self (the uttering, generative voice) to step back, retreat, and reconstitute itself on different grounds. Identity is central to the ebb and flow movements of Whitman's poetry, because at bottom the principle is the endless challenge posed by experience to any provisional version of reality. Thus the elusiveness, the rhythms of contraction and expansion, the patterns of contradiction, all serve to maintain a fragile, ineffable sense of life, of *livingness.* The poetry lives, in short, as long as the dialectic between self and world, self and Other, remains tense, taut with potential, as in the crucial inscription, "One's-Self I sing, a simple separate person, / Yet utter the word Democratic, the word En-Masse."

For Whitman the poem is not a vehicle of abstract meaning but the reader's opportunity for a personal liberation, a transformation—or, to use a term Whitman appropriated from his master Emerson, a *translation* of experience into truth. Emerson wrote that the poet is essential to the very being of a culture, since he "represents" the fullness of being: "The man is only half himself, the other half is his expression." The poet, the "sayer," is a liberating god, Emerson writes in his essay "The Poet." "He is the only teller of news, for he was present and privy to the appearance which he describes"; "he unlocks our chains and admits us to a new scene."

How well these epithets fit Whitman; no wonder Emerson saw immediately the value of the slim green volume titled *Leaves of Grass* that he received from the author, previously unknown to him, in 1855. "I find it the most extraordinary piece of wit and wisdom that America has yet contributed," he wrote to Whitman, adding: "I greet you at the beginning of a great career, which yet must have had a long foreground somewhere, for such a start." He must have recognized precisely the "tyrannous eye" he had called for in "The Poet": "We have had yet no genius in America, with tyrannous eye, which knew the value of our incomparable materials, and saw, in the barbarism and materialism of the times, another carnival of the same gods whose picture he so much admires in Homer." The emphasis falls here on the act of seeing, which precedes and remains part and parcel of the act of saying. Emerson's poet knows what the average man has forgotten, that "every sensuous fact" has manifold meanings, is an emblem or symbol, if properly seen. The poet endows facts with "a power" and "puts eyes and a tongue into every dumb and inanimate object." And, by thus turning "the world to glass," the poet endows his adept reader with equal powers of seeing, saying, and being. In such manner, by "an ulterior intellectual perception," vivifying experience by detaching fixed meanings from things, poets "make free." "To be is just as great as to perceive or tell," echoes Whitman in his 1855 preface.

Whitman recorded late in life that he had been simmering and that Emerson had brought him to a boil. One can well imagine the effect of the Emersonian rhapsody of self-reliance on a young man like Whitman, whose early years read like a quest for selfhood as well as vocation. Emerson sanctioned individual experience above formal schooling, and this fit exactly the needs of a young man who, until his creation of "Walt Whitman, a kosmos," had by turn tried his hand at school teaching, printing, typesetting, reporting, editing, and carpentry, whose life from his birth on rural Long Island had been one of movement in and out of jobs and places, and a variety of "roles": political campaigner, man about town, dandy, one of the roughs. In retrospect Whitman wrote that the purpose of *Leaves of Grass* (the title of the book that contained all his poems) was "to put *a Person,* a human being (myself, in the latter half of the Nineteenth Century, in America,) freely, fully and truly on record." The intention is perhaps comparable to Wordsworth's in *The Prelude,* except that Whitman's effort was not a reflection on experience but an attempt to give a voice to experience itself. Traces of his many vocations, his travels (including a trip to New Orleans with his brother in 1848), his family life (one brother died in an insane asylum, another was a congenital idiot, the wife of another became a prostitute, a sister suffered from melancholia, the father was ill-tempered, and the mother of Dutch and Quaker background, the chief source of strength in the family) take many forms in the poetry, as does the cosmopolitanism of New York in this period, where he had access to music, opera, museums, galleries, and books. Whitman tapped a novel resource for poetry—common experience. His route to poetry fell not through the colleges where most of the eminent literary figures of his day had received their training, but through printing shops and newspaper offices, political stumps and city streets. Whitman himself emerged from the "incomparable materials" Emerson spoke of; he was raised in and gave expression to their ambiance.

During the late 1830's and 1840's Whitman had contributed highly "literary" pieces to the New York press, conventional essays, poems, and sentimental fiction. After a series of editorial positions in the 1840's, ending with his being fired from the editorship of the prominent Brooklyn *Eagle* (the reason was his too-fervent commitment to the Free Soil movement), Whitman began keeping a notebook in which the first edition of *Leaves* germinated. After 1848 he worked mainly as a free-lance writer, odd-jobber, and house-builder with his father. His book appeared in 1855, appropriately enough on July 4, privately printed and anonymous, the author identified not by name but by image (a visual emblem), in a photographic frontispiece of a bearded young man in workman's clothes. This unique large-sized volume in a green cover held 12 untitled poems. In 1856 an expanded second edition appeared, again at the author's own expense (neither edition sold many copies). By 1860 yet a third edition reached print, much expanded, this time printed commercially. All in all Whitman issued nine editions of his book, each enlarged and revised. The final or "death bed" edition (1891) is generally considered definitive, though scholars and critics argue that the earliest version of specific poems is usually the best.

It is clear that the years between the late 1840's when the first poems were in composition and 1860, when the book achieved its characteristic form, represent Whitman's most fertile period. Judging from the evidence of the superb sensual and covertly homosexual lyrics of "Children of Adam" and "Calamus" and the great longer poems, "Crossing Brooklyn Ferry," "Out of the Cradle Endlessly Rocking," and "As I Ebb'd with the Ocean of Life" (all composed between 1855 and 1860), Whitman must have experienced a profound crisis in these years. The 1855 edition also held poems of the underside of life, most notably the Baudelairean "The Sleepers," along with the heady poems of self-discovery and venturing forth; the poems of 1860 introduce a deeper note of loss, even of despair and self-loathing. Their preoccupation is with death and the discovery of the outlet of poetry in the awareness of mortality.

The Civil War was another sort of crisis. At first Whitman seems to have paid little serious attention to the outbreak of hostilities after the secession but, in 1862, his brother George was wounded and Whitman traveled to the front in Virginia, beginning a momentous phase of his life as nurse and wound-dresser. The issue of these years was *Drum-Taps* (1865), a book of often restrained death-ridden etchings of battle scenes, fed by a compassion that reaches moving heights in poems such as "The Wound-Dresser," and the stark, evocative prose sketches of *Specimen Days* (1882). In 1866 a sequel to *Drum-Taps* appeared, including what many readers consider his greatest single poem, "When Lilacs Last in the Dooryard Bloom'd," an elegy on the death of

Lincoln. After the war Whitman held a clerkship in the Bureau of Indian Affairs, but was dismissed after six months as the author of disreputable works; he found another government position in the Attorney General's office, and continued to revise his *Leaves* and make additions. In 1873 he suffered the stroke that left him paralyzed the rest of his life. He moved to Camden where he lived first with his brother, then in the famous Mickle Street house, living close to the edge of poverty, surrounded by a band of disciples and admirers, carrying on a vast correspondence, still revising and polishing, and making occasional public appearances. In 1879 he traveled west as far as Nevada; he died in Camden on March 26, 1892.

Much of Whitman's prose writings in his last period was retrospective. In the preface to the 1855 edition he had written that the "proof of a poet is that his country absorbs him as affectionately as he has absorbed it." Except for a handful of Bohemians, off-beats and transcendentalists, few of his countrymen were ready to take his work into their system, although he was sometimes enthusiastically received by prominent writers in England. Moreover, the Civil War and its aftermath, especially the erosion of public morality and the emergence of a fashionable cynicism, posed a challenge to his commitment to democracy. Typically, out of personal doubt and crisis, Whitman created a major literary work, this time, in 1870, the long essay *Democratic Vistas*. In this difficult, part-satiric, part-prophetic work, Whitman gives free rein to his disappointments yet, in the end, transcends his doubts and concludes affirmatively. What emerges from the shifting perpsectives, the dialectics of belief and doubt, is an illuminating sense of what democracy, equality, and America mean for Whitman, and of the relation of the poet to these concepts. The main argument of the essay is that if democracy denotes only a political system, if it does not, in Santayana's words, enter psychology and morals, if it remains a political system without becoming a culture (a way of life), then it fails in its historic mission. We learn in this remarkable essay that at the deepest level Whitman's poetry is inseparable from his vision of a culture of free men and women, living in mutuality and self-respect. We learn too that the American reality was in his eyes extremely difficult and problematic. It raises the existential question of what any man has to do with others, or the individual with the mass. Poetry plays the role of a mediation, the vehicle through which the democratic synthesis of the interests of the self and the interests of the mass can take place. It is a high order for poetry, but Whitman insists on it. Here, too, we find his clearest statements about the methods of poetry, its necessary indirection, its teaching through hints and clues instead of didactic message.

Much of Whitman has been and remains enigmatic for audiences who do not share his abiding conviction in the relationship between poetry, the soul, and the way people live with each other. Surely Whitman is a "presence" in modern poetry—his influence is felt in almost all twentieth-century American poets, from Pound and Eliot to Hart Crane, Wallace Stevens, and William Carlos Williams—but perhaps, as Hart Crane wrote, his "bequest" is "still to be realized in all its implications."

Preface to Leaves of Grass[1]

1855

America does not repel the past or what it has produced under its forms or amid other politics or the idea of castes or the old religions . . . accepts the lesson with calmness . . . is not so impatient as has been supposed that the slough still sticks to opinions and manners and literature while the life which served its requirements has passed into the new life of the new forms . . . perceives that the corpse is slowly borne from the eating and sleeping rooms of the house . . . perceives that it waits a little while in the door . . . that it was fittest for its days . . . that its action has descended to the stalwart and well-shaped heir who approaches . . . and that he shall be fittest for his days.

The Americans of all nations at any time upon the earth have probably the fullest poetical nature. The United States themselves are essentially the greatest poem. In the history of the earth hitherto the largest and most stirring appear tame and orderly to their ampler largeness and stir. Here at last is something in the doings of man that corresponds with the broadcast doings of the day and night. Here is not merely a nation but a teeming nation of nations. Here is action untied from strings necessarily blind to particulars and details magnificently moving in vast masses. Here is the hospitality which forever indicates heroes. . . . Here are the roughs and beards and space and ruggedness and nonchalance that the soul loves. Here the performance disdaining the trivial unapproached in the tremendous audacity of its crowds and groupings and the push of its perspective spreads with crampless and flowing breadth and showers its prolific and splendid extravagance. One sees it must indeed own the riches of the summer and winter, and need

---

[1] This preface, which appeared in the first edition of *Leaves of Grass* in 1855, contains Whitman's earliest statement of a democracy. It has the epigrammatic quality of Emerson's essays, which strongly influenced the writing, and the power of the poem, "Song of Myself," which followed.

never be bankrupt while corn grows from the ground or the orchards drop apples or the bays contain fish or men beget children upon women.

Other states indicate themselves in their deputies . . . but the genius of the United States is not best or most in its executives or legislatures, nor in its ambassadors or authors or colleges or churches or parlors, nor even in its newspapers or inventors . . . but always most in the common people. Their manners speech dress friendships—the freshness and candor of their physiognomy—the picturesque looseness of their carriage . . . their deathless attachment to freedom—their aversion to anything indecorous or soft or mean—the practical acknowledgment of the citizens of one state by the citizens of all other states—the fierceness of their roused resentment—their curiosity and welcome of novelty—their self-esteem and wonderful sympathy—their susceptibility to a slight—the air they have of persons who never knew how it felt to stand in the presence of superiors—the fluency of their speech—their delight in music, the sure symptom of manly tenderness and native elegance of soul . . . their good temper and openhandedness—the terrible significance of their elections—the President's taking off his hat to them not they to him—these too are unrhymed poetry. It awaits the gigantic and generous treatment worthy of it.

The largeness of nature or the nation were monstrous without a corresponding largeness and generosity of the spirit of the citizen. Not nature nor swarming states nor streets and steamships nor prosperous business nor farms nor capital nor learning may suffice for the ideal of man . . . nor suffice the poet. No reminiscences may suffice either. A live nation can always cut a deep mark and can have the best authority the cheapest . . . namely from its own soul. This is the sum of the profitable uses of individuals or states and of present action and grandeur and of the subjects of poets.—As if it were necessary to trot back generation after generation to the eastern records! As if the beauty and sacredness of the demonstrable must fall behind that of the mythical! As if men do not make their mark out of any times! As if the opening of the western continent by discovery and what has transpired since in North and South America were less than the small theatre of the antique or the aimless sleepwalking of the middle ages! The pride of the United States leaves the wealth and finesse of the cities and all returns of commerce and agriculture and all the magnitude of geography or shows of exterior victory to enjoy the breed of full-sized men or one full-sized man unconquerable and simple.

The American poets are to enclose old and new for America is the race of races. Of them a bard is to be commensurate with a people. To him the other continents arrive as contributions . . . he gives them reception for their sake and his own sake. His spirit responds to his country's spirit . . . he incarnates its geography and natural life and rivers and lakes. Mississippi with annual freshets and changing chutes, Missouri and Columbia and Ohio and Saint Lawrence with the falls and beautiful masculine Hudson, do not embouchure where they spend themselves more than they embouchure into him. The blue breadth over the inland sea of Virginia and Maryland and the sea off Massachusetts and Maine and over Manhattan bay and over Champlain and Erie and over Ontario and Huron and Michigan and Superior, and over the Texan and Mexican and Floridian and Cuban seas and over the seas off California and Oregon, is not tallied by the blue breadth of the waters below more than the breadth of above and below is tallied by him. When the long Atlantic coast stretches longer and the Pacific coast stretches longer he easily stretches with them north or south. He spans between them also from east to west and reflects what is between them. On him rise solid growths that offset the growths of pine and cedar and hemlock and live oak and locust and chestnut and cypress and hickory and lime tree and cottonwood and tulip tree and cactus and wild vine and tamarind and persimmon . . . and tangles as tangled as any cane brake or swamp . . . and forests coated with transparent ice and icicles hanging from the boughs and crackling in the wind . . . and sides and peaks of mountains . . . and pasturage sweet and free as savannah or upland or prairie . . . with flights and songs and screams that answer those of the wild pigeon and highhole and orchard oriole and coot and surf duck and red-shouldered hawk and fish hawk and white ibis and Indian hen and cat owl and water pheasant and quabird and pied sheldrake and blackbird and mockingbird and buzzard and condor and night heron and eagle. To him the hereditary countenance descends both mother's and father's. To him enter the essences of the real things and past and present events—of the enormous diversity of temperature and agriculture and mines—the tribes of red aborigines—the weatherbeaten vessels entering new ports or making landings on rocky coasts—the first settlements north or south—the rapid stature and muscle—the haughty defiance of '76, and the war and peace and formation of the constitution . . . the union always surrounded by blatherers and always calm and impregnable—the perpetual coming of immigrants—the wharf-hem'd cities and superior marine—the unsurveyed interior—the loghouses and clearings and wild animals and hunters and trappers . . . the free commerce—the fisheries and whaling and golddigging—the endless gestation of new states—the convening of Congress every December, the members duly coming up from all climates and the uttermost parts . . . the noble character of the young mechanics and of all free American workmen and workwomen . . . the general ardor and friendliness and enterprise—the perfect equality of the female with the male . . . the large amativeness—the fluid movement of the population—the factories and mercantile life and laborsaving machinery—the Yankee swap—the New York firemen and the target excursion—the southern plantation life—the character of the northeast and of the northwest and southwest—slavery and the tremulous spreading of hands to protect it, and the stern opposition to it which shall never cease till it ceases or the speaking of tongues and the moving of lips cease. For such the expression of the American poet is to be transcendant and new. It is to be indirect and not direct or descriptive or epic. Its quality goes through these to much more. Let the age and wars of other nations be chanted and let their eras and characters be illustrated and that finish the verse. Not so the great psalm of the republic. Here the theme is creative and has vista. Here comes one among the well-beloved stonecutters and plans with decision and science and sees the solid and beautiful forms of the future where there are now no solid forms.

Of all nations the United States with veins full of poetical stuff most need poets and will doubtless have the greatest and use them the greatest. Their Presidents shall not be their common referee so much as their poets shall. Of all mankind the great poet is the equable man. Not in him but off from him things are grotesque or eccentric or fail of their sanity. Nothing out of its place is good and nothing in its place is bad. He bestows on every object or quality its fit proportions neither more nor less. He is the arbiter of the diverse and he is the key. He is the equalizer of his age and land . . . he supplies what wants supplying and checks what wants checking. If peace is the routine, out of him speaks the spirit of peace, large, rich, thrifty, building vast and populous cities, encouraging agriculture and the arts and commerce—lighting the study of man, the soul, immortality—federal, state or municipal government, marriage, health, free trade, intertravel by land and sea . . . nothing too close, nothing too far off . . . the stars not too far off. In war he is the most deadly force of the war. Who recruits him recruits horse and foot . . . he fetches parks of artillery the best that engineer ever knew. If the time becomes slothful and heavy he knows how to arouse it . . . he can make every word he speaks draw blood. Whatever stagnates in the flat of custom or obedience or legislation he never stagnates. Obedience does not master him, he masters it. High up out of reach he stands turning a concentrated light . . . he turns the pivot with his finger . . . he baffles the swiftest runners as he stands and easily overtakes and envelops them. The time straying toward infidelity and confections and persiflage he withholds by his steady faith . . . he spreads out his dishes . . . he offers the sweet firm-fibred meat that grows men and women. His brain is the ultimate brain. He is no arguer . . . he is judgment. He judges not as the judge judges but as the sun falling around a helpless thing. As he sees the farthest he has the most faith. His thoughts are the hymns of the praise of things. In the talk on the soul and eternity and God off of his equal plane he is silent. He sees eternity less like a play with a prologue and denouement . . . he sees eternity in men and women . . . he does not see men and women as dreams or dots. Faith is the antiseptic of the soul . . . it pervades the common people and preserves them . . . they never give up believing and expecting and trusting. There is that indescribable freshness and unconsciousness about an illiterate person that humbles and mocks the power of the noblest expressive genius. The poet sees for a certainty how one not a great artist may be just as sacred and

perfect as the greatest artist. . . . The power to destroy or remold is freely
used by him but never the power of attack. What is past is past. If he does
not expose superior models and prove himself by every step he takes he is
not what is wanted. The presence of the greatest poet conquers . . . not
parleying or struggling or any prepared attempts. Now he has passed that
way see after him! There is not left any vestige of despair or misanthropy or
cunning or exclusiveness or the ignominy of a nativity or color or delusion of
hell or the necessity of hell . . . and no man thenceforward shall be degraded
for ignorance or weakness or sin.

The greatest poet hardly knows pettiness or triviality. If he breathes into
any thing that was before thought small it dilates with the grandeur and life
of the universe. He is a seer . . . he is individual . . . he is complete in himself
. . . the others are as good as he, only he sees it and they do not. He is not one
of the chorus . . . he does not stop for any regulations . . . he is the president
of regulation. What the eyesight does to the rest he does to the rest. Who
knows the curious mystery of the eyesight? The other senses corroborate
themselves, but this is removed from any proof but its own and foreruns the
identities of the spiritual world. A single glance of it mocks all the investiga-
tions of man and all the instruments and books of the earth and all reasoning.
What is marvelous? what is unlikely? what is impossible or baseless or vague?
after you have once just opened the space of a peach pit and given audience
to far and near and to the sunset and had all things enter with electric
swiftness softly and duly without confusion or jostling or jam.

The land and sea, the animals fishes and birds, the sky of heaven and the
orbs, the forests mountains and rivers, are not small themes . . . but folks
expect of the poet to indicate more than the beauty and dignity which
always attach to dumb real objects . . . they expect him to indicate the path
between reality and their souls. Men and women perceive the beauty well
enough . . . probably as well as he. The passionate tenacity of hunters,
woodmen, early risers, cultivators of gardens and orchards and fields, the
love of healthy women for the manly form, seafaring persons, drivers of
horses, the passion for light and the open air, all is an old varied sign of the
unfailing perception of beauty and of a residence of the poetic in outdoor
people. They can never be assisted by poets to perceive . . . some may but
they never can. The poetic quality is not marshalled in rhyme or uniformity
or abstract addresses to things nor in melancholy complaints or good precepts, but is the life of these and much else and is in the soul. The profit of
rhyme is that it drops seeds of a sweeter and more luxuriant rhyme, and of
uniformity that it conveys itself into its own roots in the ground out of sight.
The rhyme and uniformity of perfect poems show the free growth of metri-
cal laws and bud from them as unerringly and loosely as lilacs or roses on a
bush, and take shapes as compact as the shapes of chestnuts and oranges and
melons and pears, and shed the perfume impalpable to form. The fluency
and ornaments of the finest poems or music or orations or recitations are not

independent but dependent. All beauty comes from beautiful blood and a beautiful brain. If the greatnesses are in conjunction in a man or woman it is enough . . . the fact will prevail through the universe . . . but the gaggery and gilt of a million years will not prevail. Who troubles himself about his ornaments or fluency is lost. This is what you shall do: Love the earth and sun and the animals, despise riches, give alms to everyone that asks, stand up for the stupid and crazy, devote your income and labor to others, hate tyrants, argue not concerning God, have patience and indulgence toward the people, take off your hat to nothing known or unknown or to any man or number of men, go freely with powerful uneducated persons and with the young and with the mothers of families, read these leaves in the open air every season of every year of your life, re-examine all you have been told at school or church or in any book, dismiss whatever insults your own soul, and your very flesh shall be a great poem and have the richest fluency not only in its words but in the silent lines of its lips and face and between the lashes of your eyes and in every motion and joint of your body . . . The poet shall not spend his time in unneeded work. He shall know that the ground is always ready plowed and manured . . . others may not know it but he shall. He shall go directly to the creation. His trust shall master the trust of everything he touches . . . and shall master all attachment.

The known universe has one complete lover and that is the greatest poet. He consumes an eternal passion and is indifferent which chance happens and which possible contingency of fortune or misfortune and persuades daily and hourly his delicious pay. What balks or breaks others is fuel for his burning progress to contact and amorous joy. Other proportions of the reception of pleasure dwindle to nothing to his proportions. All expected from heaven or from the highest he is rapport with in the sight of the daybreak or a scene of the winter woods or the presence of children playing or with his arm around the neck of a man or woman. His love above all love has leisure and expanse . . . he leaves room ahead of himself. He is no irresolute or suspicious lover . . he is sure . . . he scorns intervals. His experience and the showers and thrills are not for nothing. Nothing can jar him . . . suffering and darkness cannot—death and fear cannot. To him complaint and jealousy and envy are corpses buried and rotten in the earth . . . he saw them buried. The sea is not surer of the shore or the shore of the sea than he is of the fruition of his love and of all perfection and beauty.

The fruition of beauty is no chance of hit or miss . . . it is inevitable as life . . . it is exact and plumb as gravitation. From the eyesight proceeds another eyesight and from the hearing proceeds another hearing and from the voice proceeds another voice eternally curious of the harmony of things with man. To these respond perfections not only in the committees that were supposed to stand for the rest but in the rest themselves just the same. These understand the law of perfection in masses and floods . . . that its finish is to each for itself and onward from itself . . . that it is profuse and impartial . . . that there is not a minute of the light or dark nor an acre of the earth or sea without it—nor any direction of the sky nor any trade or employment nor any turn of events. This is the reason that about the proper expression of beauty there is precision and balance . . . one part does not need to be thrust above another. The best singer is not the one who has the most lithe and powerful organ . . . the pleasure of poems is not in them that take the handsomest measure and similes and sound.

Without effort and without exposing in the least how it is done the greatest poet brings the spirit of any or all events and passions and scenes and persons some more and some less to bear on your individual character as you hear or read. To do this well is to compete with the laws that pursue and follow time. What is the purpose must surely be there and the clue of it must be there . . . and the faintest indication is the indication of the best and then becomes the clearest indication. Past and present and future are not disjoined but joined. The greatest poet forms the consistence of what is to be from what has been and is. He drags the dead out of their coffins and stands them again on their feet . . . he says to the past, Rise and walk before me that I may realize you. He learns the lesson . . . he places himself where the future becomes present. The greatest poet does not only dazzle his rays over character and scenes and passions . . . he finally ascends and finishes all . . . he exhibits the pinnacles that no man can tell what they are for or what is beyond . . . he glows a moment on the extremest verge. He is most wonderful in his last half-hidden smile or frown . . . by that flash of the moment of parting the one that sees it shall be encouraged or terrified afterwards for many years. The greatest poet does not moralize or make applications of morals . . . he knows the soul. The soul has that measureless pride which consists in never acknowledging any lessons but its own. But it has sympathy as measureless as its pride and the one balances the other and neither can stretch too far while it stretches in company with the other. The inmost secrets of art sleep with the twain. The greatest poet has lain close betwixt both and they are vital in his style and thoughts.

The art of art, the glory of expression and the sunshine of the light of letters is simplicity. Nothing is better than simplicity . . . nothing can make up for excess or for the lack of definiteness. To carry on the heave of impulse and pierce intellectual depths and give all subjects their articulations are powers neither common nor very uncommon. But to speak in literature with the perfect rectitude and insouciance of the movements of animals and the unimpeachableness of the sentiment of trees in the woods and grass by the roadside is the flawless triumph of art. If you have looked on him who has achieved it you have looked on one of the masters of the artists of all nations and times. You shall not contemplate the flight of the graygull over the bay or the mettlesome action of the blood horse or the tall leaning of sunflowers on their stalk or the appearance of the sun journeying through heaven or the appearance of the moon afterward with any more satisfaction than you shall contemplate him. The greatest poet has less a marked style and is more the channel of thoughts and things without increase or diminution, and is the free channel of himself. He swears to his art, I will not be meddlesome, I will not have in my writing any elegance or effect or originality to hang in the way between me and the rest like curtains. I will have nothing hang in the way, not the richest curtains. What I tell I tell for precisely what it is. Let who may exalt or startle or fascinate or sooth I will have purposes as health or heat or snow has and be as regardless of observation. What I experience or portray shall go from my composition without a shred of my composition. You shall stand by my side and look in the mirror with me.

The old red blood and stainless gentility of great poets will be proved by their unconstraint. A heroic person walks at his ease through and out of that custom or precedent or authority that suits him not. Of the traits of the brotherhood of writers savants musicians inventors and artists nothing is finer than silent defiance advancing from new free forms. In the need of poems philosophy politics mechanism science behavior, the craft of art, an appropriate native grand opera, shipcraft, or any craft, he is greatest forever and forever who contributes the greatest original practical example. The cleanest expression is that which finds no sphere worthy of itself and makes one.

The messages of great poets to each man and woman are, Come to us on equal terms, Only then can you understand us, We are no better than you, What we enclose you enclose, What we enjoy you may enjoy. Did you suppose there could be only one Supreme? We affirm there can be unnumbered Supremes, and that one does not countervail another any more than one eyesight countervails another . . . and that men can be good or grand only of the consciousness of their supremacy within them. What do you think is the grandeur of storms and dismemberments and the deadliest battles and wrecks and the wildest fury of the elements and the power of the sea and the motion of nature and of the throes of human desires and dignity and hate and love? It is that something in the soul which says, Rage on, Whirl on, I tread master here and everywhere, Master of the spasms of the sky and of the shatter of the sea, Master of nature and passion and death, And of all terror and all pain.

The American bards shall be marked for generosity and affection and for encouraging competitors. . . . They shall be kosmos . . . without monopoly or secrecy . . . glad to pass any thing to any one . . . hungry for equals night and day. They shall not be careful of riches and privilege they shall be riches and privilege . . . they shall perceive who the most affluent man is. The most affluent man is he that confronts all the shows he sees by equivalents out of the stronger wealth of himself. The American bard shall delineate no class of persons nor one or two out of the strata of interests nor love most nor truth most nor the soul most nor the body most . . . and not be for the eastern states more than the western or the northern states more than the southern.

Exact science and its practical movements are no checks on the greatest poet but always his encouragement and support. The outset and remembrance are there . . . there are the arms that lifted him first and brace him best . . . there he returns after all his goings and comings. The sailor and traveler . . . the anatomist chemist astronomer geologist phrenologist spiritualist mathematician historian and lexicographer are not poets, but they are the lawgivers of poets and their construction underlies the structure of every perfect poem. No matter what rises or is uttered they sent the seed of the conception of it . . . of them and by them stand the visible proofs of souls . . . always of their father-stuff must be begotten the sinewy races of bards. If there shall be love and content between the father and the son and if the greatness of the son is the exuding of the greatness of the father there shall be love between the poet and the man of demonstrable science. In the beauty of poems are the tuft and final applause of science.

Great is the faith of the flush of knowledge and of the investigation of the depths of qualities and things. Cleaving and circling here swells the soul of the poet yet is president of itself always. The depths are fathomless and therefore calm. The innocence and nakedness are resumed . . . they are neither modest nor immodest. The whole theory of the special and supernatural and all that was twined with it or educed out of it departs as a dream. What has ever happened . . . what happens and whatever may or shall happen, the vital laws enclose all . . . they are sufficient for any case and for all cases . . . none to be hurried or retarded . . . any miracle of affairs or persons inadmissible in the vast clear scheme where every motion and every spear of grass and the frames and spirits of men and women and all that concerns them are unspeakably perfect miracles all referring to all and each distinct and in its place. It is also not consistent with the reality of the soul to admit that there is anything in the known universe more divine than men and women.

Men and women and the earth and all upon it are simply to be taken as they are, and the investigation of their past and present and future shall be unintermitted and shall be done with perfect candor. Upon this basis philosophy speculates ever looking toward the poet, ever regarding the eternal tendencies of all toward happiness never inconsistent with what is clear to the senses and to the soul. For the eternal tendencies of all toward happiness make the only point of sane philosophy. Whatever comprehends less than that . . . whatever is less than the laws of light and of astronomical motion . . . or less than the laws that follow the thief the liar the glutton and the drunkard through this life and doubtless afterward . . . or less than vast stretches of time or the slow formation of density or the patient upheaving of strata—is of no account. Whatever would put God in a poem or system of philosophy as contending against some being or influence, is also of no account. Sanity and ensemble characterize the great master . . . spoilt in one principle all is spoilt. The great master has nothing to do with miracles. He sees health for himself in being one of the mass . . . he sees the hiatus in singular eminence. To the perfect shape comes common ground. To be under the general law is great for that is to correspond with it. The master knows that he is unspeakably great and that all are unspeakably great . . . that nothing for instance is greater than to conceive children and bring them up well . . . that to be is just as great as to perceive or tell.

In the make of the great masters the idea of political liberty is indispensable. Liberty takes the adherence of heroes wherever men and women exist . . . but never takes any adherence or welcome from the rest more than from poets. They are the voice and exposition of liberty. They out of ages are worthy the grand idea . . . to them it is confided and they must sustain it. Nothing has precedence of it and nothing can warp or degrade it. The attitude of great poets is to cheer up slaves and horrify despots. The turn of their necks, the sound of their feet, the motions of their wrists, are full of hazard to the one and hope to the other. Come nigh them awhile and though they neither speak or advise you shall learn the faithful American lesson. Liberty is poorly served by men whose good intent is quelled from one failure or two failures or any number of failures, or from the casual indifference or ingratitude of the people, or from the sharp show of the tushes of power, or the bringing to bear soldiers and cannon or any penal statutes. Liberty relies upon itself, invites no one, promises nothing, sits in calmness and light, is positive and composed, and knows no discouragement. The battle rages with many a loud alarm and frequent advance and retreat . . . the enemy triumphs . . . the prison, the handcuffs, the iron necklace and anklet, the scaffold, garrote and lead balls do their work . . . the cause is asleep . . . the strong throats are choked with their own blood . . . the young men drop their eyelashes toward the ground when they pass each other . . . and is liberty gone out of that place? No never. When liberty goes it is not the first to go nor the second nor third to go . . . it waits for all the rest to go . . . it is the last. . . . When the memories of the old martyrs are faded utterly away . . . when the large names of patriots are laughed at in the public halls from the lips of the orators . . . when the boys are no more christened after the same but christened after tyrants and traitors instead . . . when the laws of the free are grudgingly permitted and laws for informers and blood money are sweet to the taste of the people . . . when I and you walk abroad upon the earth stung with compassion at the sight of numberless brothers answering our equal friendship and calling no man master—and when we are elated with noble joy at the sight of slaves . . . when the soul retires in the cool communion of the night and surveys its experience and has much extasy over the word and deed that put back a helpless innocent person into the gripe of the gripers or into any cruel inferiority . . . when those in all parts of these states who could easier realize the true American character but do not yet— when the swarms of cringers, suckers, doughfaces, lice of politics, planners of sly involutions for their own preferment to city offices or state legislatures or the judiciary or congress or the presidency, obtain a response of love and natural deference from the people whether they get the offices or no . . . when it is better to be bound booby and rogue in office at a high salary than the poorest free mechanic or farmer with his hat unmoved from his head and firm eyes and a candid and generous heart . . . and when servility by town or state or the federal government or any oppression on a large scale or small scale can be tried on without its own punishment following duly after in exact proportion against the smallest chance of escape . . . or rather when all life and all the souls of men and women are discharged from any part of the earth—then only shall the instinct of liberty be discharged from that part of the earth.

As the attributes of the poets of the kosmos concenter in the real body and soul and in the pleasure of things they possess the superiority of genuineness over all fiction and romance. As they emit themselves facts are showered over with light . . . the daylight is lit with more volatile light . . . also the deep between the setting and rising sun goes deeper many fold. Each precise object or condition or combination or process exhibits a beauty . . . the multiplication table its—old age its—the carpenter's trade its—the grand opera its . . . the huge hulled clean-shaped New York clipper at sea under steam or full sail gleams with unmatched beauty . . . the American circles and large harmonies of government gleam with theirs . . . and the commonest definite intentions and actions with theirs. The poets of the kosmos advance through all interpositions and coverings and turmoils and stratagems to first principles. They are of use . . . they dissolve poverty from its need and riches from its conceit. You large proprietor they say shall not realize or perceive more than anyone else. The owner of the library is not he who holds a legal title to it having bought and paid for it. Anyone and everyone is owner of the library who can read the same through all the varieties of tongues and subjects and styles, and in whom they enter with ease and take residence and force toward paternity and maternity, and make supple and powerful and rich and large . . . These American states strong and healthy and accomplished shall receive no pleasure from violations of natural models and must not permit them. In paintings or moldings or carvings in mineral or wood, or in the illustrations of books or newspapers, or in any comic or tragic prints, or in the patterns of woven stuffs or anything to beautify rooms or furniture or costumes, or to put upon cornices or monuments or on the prows or sterns of ships, or to put anywhere before the human eye indoors or out, that which distorts honest shapes or which creates unearthly beings or places or contingencies is a nuisance and revolt. Of the human form especially it is so great it must never be made ridiculous. Of ornaments to a work nothing outre can be allowed . . . but those ornaments can be allowed that conform to the perfect facts of the open air and that flow out of the nature of the work and come irrepressibly from it and are necessary to the completion of the work. Most works are most beautiful without ornament. . . . Exaggerations will be revenged in human physiology. Clean and vigorous children are jetted and conceived only in those communities where the models of natural forms are public every day. . . . Great genius and the people of these states must never be demeaned to romances. As soon as histories are properly told there is no more need of romances.

The great poets are also to be known by the absence in them of tricks and by the justification of perfect personal candor. Then folks echo a new cheap joy and a divine voice leaping from their brains: How beautiful is candor! All faults may be forgiven of him who has perfect candor. Henceforth let no man of us lie, for we have seen that openness wins the inner and outer world and that there is no single exception, and that never since our earth gathered itself in a mass have deceit or subterfuge or prevarication attracted its smallest particle or the faintest tinge of a shade—and that through the enveloping wealth and rank of a state or the whole republic of states a sneak or sly person shall be discovered and despised . . . and that the soul has never been once fooled and never can be fooled . . . and thrift without the loving nod of the soul is only a fetid puff . . . and there never grew up in any of the continents of the globe nor upon any planet or satellite or star, nor upon the asteroids, nor in any part of ethereal space, nor in the midst of density, nor under the fluid wet of the sea, nor in that condition which precedes the birth of babes, nor at any time during the changes of life, nor in that condition that follows what we term death, nor in any stretch of abeyance or action afterward of vitality, nor in any process of formation or reformation anywhere, a being whose instinct hated the truth.

Extreme caution or prudence, the soundest organic health, large hope and comparison and fondness for women and children, large alimentiveness and destructiveness and causality, with a perfect sense of the oneness of nature and the propriety of the same spirit applied to human affairs . . . these are called up of the float of the brain of the world to be parts of the greatest poet from his birth out of his mother's womb and from her birth out of her mother's. Caution seldom goes far enough. It has been thought that the prudent citizen was the citizen who applied himself to solid gains and did well for himself and his family and completed a lawful life without debt or crime. The greatest poet sees and admits these economies as he sees the economies of food and sleep, but has higher notions of prudence than to think he gives much when he gives a few slight attentions at the latch of the gate. The premises of the prudence of life are not the hospitality of it or the ripeness and harvest of it. Beyond the independence of a little sum laid aside for burial money, and of a few clapboards around and shingles overhead on a lot of American soil owned, and the easy dollars that supply the year's plain clothing and meals, the melancholy prudence of the abandonment of such a great being as a man is to the toss and pallor of years of moneymaking with all their scorching days and icy nights and all their stifling deceits and under-

handed dodgings, or infinitesimals of parlors, or shameless stuffing while
others starve . . . and all the loss of the bloom and odor of the earth and of
the flowers and atmosphere and of the sea and of the true taste of the
women and men you pass or have to do with in youth or middle age, and the
issuing sickness and desperate revolt at the close of a life without elevation
or naïveté, and the ghastly chatter of a death without serenity or majesty, is
the great fraud upon modern civilization and forethought, blotching the
surface and system which civilization undeniably drafts, and moistening with
tears the immense features it spreads and spreads with such velocity before
the reached kisses of the soul. . . . Still the right explanation remains to be
made about prudence. The prudence of the mere wealth and respectability
of the most esteemed life appears too faint for the eye to observe at all when
little and large alike drop quietly aside at the thought of the prudence suitable for immortality. What is wisdom that fills the thinness of a year or
seventy or eighty years to wisdom spaced out by ages and coming back at a
certain time with strong reinforcements and rich presents and the clear faces
of wedding guests as far as you can look in every direction running gaily
toward you? Only the soul is of itself . . . all else has reference to what
ensues. All that a person does or thinks is of consequence. Not a move can a
man or woman make that affects him or her in a day or a month or any part
of the direct lifetime or the hour of death but the same affects him or her
onward afterward through the indirect lifetime. The indirect is always as
great and real as the direct. The spirit receives from the body just as much as
it gives to the body. Not one name of word or deed . . . not of venereal sores
or discolorations . . . not the privacy of the onanist . . . not of the putrid veins
of gluttons or rum drinkers . . . not peculation or cunning or betrayal or
murder . . . no serpentine poison of those that seduce women . . . not the
foolish yielding of women . . . not prostitution . . . not of any depravity of
young men . . . not of the attainment of gain by discreditable means . . . not
any nastiness of appetite . . . not any harshness of officers to men or judges to
prisoners or fathers to sons or sons to fathers or husbands to wives or bosses
to their boys . . . not of greedy looks or malignant wishes . . . nor any of the
wiles practiced by people upon themselves . . . ever is or ever can be
stamped on the program but it is duly realized and returned, and that returned in further performances . . . and they returned again. Nor can the
push of charity or personal force ever be anything else than the profoundest
reason, whether it brings arguments to hand or no. No specification is necessary . . . to add or subtract or divide is in vain. Little or big, learned or
unlearned, white or black, legal or illegal, sick or well, from the first inspiration down the windpipe to the last expiration out of it, all that a male or
female does that is vigorous and benevolent and clean is so much sure profit
to him or her in the unshakable order of the universe and through the whole
scope of it forever. If the savage or felon is wise it is well . . . if the greatest
poet or savant is wise it is simply the same . . . if the President or chief justice

is wise it is the same . . . if the young mechanic or farmer is wise it is no more or less . . . if the prostitute is wise it is no more or less. The interest will come round . . . all will come round. All the best actions of war and peace . . . all help given to relatives and strangers and the poor and old and sorrowful and young children and widows and the sick, and to all shunned persons . . . all furtherance of fugitives and of the escape of slaves . . . all the self-denial that stood steady and aloof on wrecks and saw others take the seats of the boats . . . all offering of substance or life for the good old cause, or for a friend's sake or opinion's sake . . . all pains of enthusiasts scoffed at by their neighbors . . . all the vast sweet love and precious suffering of mothers . . . all honest men baffled in strifes recorded or unrecorded . . . all the grandeur and good of the few ancient nations whose fragments of annals we inherit . . . and all the good of the hundreds of far mightier and more ancient nations unknown to us by name or date or location . . . all that was ever manfully begun, whether it succeeded or not . . . all that has at any time been well suggested out of the divine heart of man or by the divinity of his mouth or by the shaping of his great hands . . . and all that is well thought or done this day on any part of the surface of the globe . . . or on any of the wandering stars or fixed stars by those there as we are here . . . or that is henceforth to be well thought or done by you whoever you are, or by anyone—these singly and wholly inured at their time and inure now and will inure always to the identities from which they sprung or shall spring. . . . Did you guess any of them lived only its moment? The world does not so exist . . . no parts palpable or impalpable so exist . . . no result exists now without being from its long antecedent result, and that from its antecedent, and so backward without the farthest mentionable spot coming a bit nearer to the beginning than any other spot. . . . Whatever satisfies the soul is truth. The prudence of the greatest poet answers at last the craving and glut of the soul, is not contemptuous of less ways of prudence if they conform to its ways, puts off nothing, permits no let-up for its own case or any case, has no particular sabbath or judgment day, divides not the living from the dead or the righteous from the unrighteous, is satisfied with the present, matches every thought or act by its correlative, knows no possible forgiveness or deputed atonement . . . knows that the young man who composedly periled his life and lost it has done exceeding well for himself, while the man who has not periled his life and retains it to old age in riches and ease has perhaps achieved nothing for himself worth mentioning . . . and that only that person has no great prudence to learn who has learnt to prefer real long-lived things, and favors body and soul the same, and perceives the indirect assuredly following the direct, and what evil or good he does leaping onward and waiting to meet him again—and who in his spirit in any emergency whatever neither hurries or avoids death.

The direct trial of him who would be the greatest poet is today. If he does not flood himself with the immediate age as with vast oceanic tides . . . and if he does not attract his own land body and soul to himself and hang on its neck with incomparable love and plunge his semitic muscle into its merits and demerits . . . and if he be not himself the age transfigured . . . and if to him is not opened the eternity which gives similitude to all periods and locations and processes and animate and inanimate forms, and which is the bond of time, and rises up from its inconceivable vagueness and infiniteness in the swimming shape of today, and is held by the ductile anchors of life, and makes the present spot the passage from what was to what shall be, and commits itself to the representation of this wave of an hour and this one of the sixty beautiful children of the wave—let him merge in the general run and wait his development. . . . Still the final test of poems or any character or work remains. The prescient poet projects himself centuries ahead and judges performer or performance after the changes of time. Does it live through them? Does it still hold on untired? Will the same style and the direction of genius to similar points be satisfactory now? Has no new discovery in science or arrival at superior planes of thought and judgment and behavior fixed him or his so that either can be looked down upon? Have the marches of tens and hundreds and thousands of years made willing detours to the right hand and the left hand for his sake? Is he beloved long and long after he is buried? Does the young man think often of him? and the young woman think often of him? and do the middle-aged and the old think of him?

A great poem is for ages and ages in common and for all degrees and complexions and all departments and sects and for a woman as much as a man and a man as much as a woman. A great poem is no finish to a man or woman but rather a beginning. Has anyone fancied he could sit at last under some due authority and rest satisfied with explanations and realize and be content and full? To no such terminus does the greatest poet bring . . . he brings neither cessation or sheltered fatness and ease. The touch of him tells in action. Whom he takes he takes with firm sure grasp into live regions previously unattained . . . thenceforward is no rest . . . they see the space and ineffable sheen that turn the old spots and lights into dead vacuums. The companion of him beholds the birth and progress of stars and learns one of the meanings. Now there shall be a man cohered out of tumult and chaos . . . the elder encourages the younger and shows him how . . . they two shall launch off fearlessly together till the new world fits an orbit for itself and looks unabashed on the lesser orbits of the stars and sweeps through the ceaseless rings and shall never be quiet again.

There will soon be no more priests. Their work is done. They may wait awhile . . . perhaps a generation or two . . . dropping off by degrees. A superior breed shall take their place . . . the gangs of kosmos and prophets en masse shall take their place. A new order shall arise and they shall be the priests of man, and every man shall be his own priest. The churches built under their umbrage shall be the churches of men and women. Through the divinity of themselves shall the kosmos and the new breed of poets be interpreters of men and women and of all events and things. They shall find their inspiration in real objects today, symptoms of the past and future. . . . They shall not deign to defend immortality or God or the perfection of things or liberty or the exquisite beauty and reality of the soul. They shall arise in America and be responded to from the remainder of the earth.

The English language befriends the grand American expression . . . it is brawny enough and limber and full enough. On the tough stock of a race who through all change of circumstances was never without the idea of political liberty, which is the animus of all liberty, it has attracted the terms of daintier and gayer and subtler and more elegant tongues. It is the powerful language of resistance . . . it is the dialect of common sense. It is the speech of the proud and melancholy races and of all who aspire. It is the chosen tongue to express growth faith self-esteem freedom justice equality friendliness amplitude prudence decision and courage. It is the medium that shall well nigh express the inexpressible.

No great literature nor any like style of behavior or oratory or social intercourse or household arrangements or public institutions or the treatment by bosses of employed people, nor executive detail or detail of the army or navy, nor spirit of legislation or courts or police or tuition or architecture or songs or amusements or the costumes of young men, can long elude the jealous and passionate instinct of American standards. Whether or no the sign appears from the mouths of the people, it throbs a live interrogation in every freeman's and freewoman's heart after that which passes by or this built to remain. Is it uniform with my country? Are its disposals without ignominious distinctions? Is it for the evergrowing communes of brothers and lovers, large, well united, proud beyond the old models, generous beyond all models? Is it something grown fresh out of the fields or drawn from the sea for use to me today here? I know that what answers for me an American must answer for any individual or nation that serves for a part of my materials. Does this answer? or is it without reference to universal needs? or sprung of the needs of the less developed society of special ranks? or old needs of pleasure overlaid by modern science and forms? Does this acknowledge liberty with audible and absolute acknowledgment, and set slavery at naught for life and death? Will it help breed one good shaped and well hung man, and a woman to be his perfect and independent mate? Does it improve manners? Is it for the nursing of the young of the republic? Does it solve readily with the sweet milk of the nipples of the breasts of the mother of many children? Has it too the old ever-fresh forbearance and impartiality? Does it look with the same love on the last born and those hardening toward stature, and on the errant, and on those who disdain all strength of assault outside of their own?

The poems distilled from other poems will probably pass away. The coward will surely pass away. The expectation of the vital and great can only be satisfied by the demeanor of the vital and great. The swarms of the polished

deprecating and reflectors and the polite float off and leave no remembrance. America prepares with composure and good will for the visitors that
have sent word. It is not intellect that is to be their warrant and welcome.
The talented, the artist, the ingenious, the editor, the statesman, the erudite
. . . they are not unappreciated . . . they fall in their place and do their work.
The soul of the nation also does its work. No disguise can pass on it . . . no
disguise can conceal from it. It rejects none, it permits all. Only toward as
good as itself and toward the like of itself will it advance half-way. An
individual is as superb as a nation when he has the qualities which make a
superb nation. The soul of the largest and wealthiest and proudest nation
may well go half-way to meet that of its poets. The signs are effectual. There
is no fear of mistake. If the one is true the other is true. The proof of a poet
is that his country absorbs him as affectionately as he has absorbed it.

Song of Myself [1]

1 I celebrate myself, and sing myself,
   And what I assume you shall assume,
   For every atom belonging to me as good belongs to you.

   I loafe and invite my soul,
   I lean and loafe at my ease observing a spear of summer grass.   5

   My tongue, every atom of my blood, form'd from this soil, this air,
   Born here of parents born here from parents the same,
     and their parents the same,
   I, now thirty-seven years old in perfect health begin,
   Hoping to cease not till death.

   Creeds and schools in abeyance,   10
   Retiring back a while sufficed at what they are, but never
     forgotten,
   I harbor for good or bad, I permit to speak at every hazard,
   Nature without check with original energy.

2 Houses and rooms are full of perfumes, the shelves are crowded
     with perfumes,
   I breathe the fragrance myself and know it and like it,   15
   The distillation would intoxicate me also, but I shall not let it.

[1] The poem is Whitman's most brilliant early
expression of his "barbaric yawp," the exaltation of the individual man and his physical
nature.
   The first version, printed in 1855 with the
Preface, was untitled; in 1856 it was called
"A Poem of Walt Whitman, an American";
in 1860 and 1867, "Walt Whitman"; and, in
1881, "Song of Myself."

The atmosphere is not a perfume, it has no taste of the distillation,
   it is odorless,
It is for my mouth forever, I am in love with it,
I will go to the bank by the wood and become undisguised and
   naked,
I am mad for it to be in contact with me.   20

The smoke of my own breath,
Echoes, ripples, buzz'd whispers, love-root, silk-thread, crotch and
   vine,
My respiration and inspiration, the beating of my heart,
   the passing of blood and air through my lungs,
The sniff of green leaves and dry leaves, and of the shore
   and dark-color'd sea-rocks, and of hay in the barn,
The sound of the belch'd words of my voice loos'd to the eddies of
   the wind,   25
A few light kisses, a few embraces, a reaching around of arms,
The play of shine and shade on the trees as the supple boughs wag,
The delight alone or in the rush of the streets, or along the fields
   and hill-sides,
The feeling of health, the full-noon trill, the song of me rising from
   bed and meeting the sun.

Have you reckon'd a thousand acres much? have you reckon'd the
   earth much?   30
Have you practis'd so long to learn to read?
Have you felt so proud to get at the meaning of poems?

Stop this day and night with me and you shall possess the origin of
   all poems,
You shall possess the good of the earth and sun, (there are millions
   of suns left,)
You shall no longer take things at second or third hand, nor look
   through the eyes of the dead, nor feed on the spectres in books,   35
You shall not look through my eyes either, nor take things from me,
You shall listen to all sides and filter them from your self.

3 I have heard what the talkers were talking, the talk of the
   beginning and the end,
But I do not talk of the beginning or the end.

There was never any more inception than there is now,   40
Nor any more youth or age than there is now,
And will never be any more perfection than there is now,
Nor any more heaven or hell than there is now.

Urge and urge and urge,
Always the procreant urge of the world.   45

Out of the dimness opposite equals advance, always substance
    and increase, always sex,
Always a knit of identity, always distinction, always a breed of life.

To elaborate is no avail, learn'd and unlearn'd feel that it is so.

Sure as the most certain sure, plumb in the uprights, well
    entretied,[2] braced in the beams,
Stout as a horse, affectionate, haughty, electrical,   50
I and this mystery here we stand.

Clear and sweet is my soul, and clear and sweet is all that is not
    my soul.

Lack one lacks both, and the unseen is proved by the seen,
Till that becomes unseen and receives proof in its turn.

Showing the best and dividing it from the worst age vexes age,   55
Knowing the perfect fitness and equanimity of things,
    while they discuss I am silent, and go bathe and admire myself.

Welcome is every organ and attribute of me, and of any man
    hearty and clean,
Not an inch nor a particle of an inch is vile, and none
    shall be less familiar than the rest.

I am satisfied—I see, dance, laugh, sing;
As the hugging and loving bed-fellow sleeps at my side through the
    night, and withdraws at the peep of the day with stealthy tread,   60
Leaving me baskets cover'd with white towels swelling the house
    with their plenty,
Shall I postpone my acceptation and realization and scream at my
    eyes,
That they turn from gazing after and down the road,
And forthwith cipher and show me to a cent,
Exactly the value of one and exactly the value of two, and which is
    ahead?   65

4 Trippers and askers surround me,
    People I meet, the effect upon me of my early life or the ward and
        city I live in, or the nation,
    The latest dates, discoveries, inventions, societies, authors old and
        new,

2 Cross braced.

My dinner, dress, associates, looks, compliments, dues,
The real or fancied indifference of some man or woman I love,   70
The sickness of one of my folks or of myself, or ill-doing or loss
   or lack of money, or depressions or exaltations,
Battles, the horrors of fratricidal war, the fever of doubtful news,
   the fitful events;
These come to me days and nights and go from me again,
But they are not the Me myself.

Apart from the pulling and hauling stands what I am,   75
Stands amused, complacent, compassionating, idle, unitary,
Looks down, is erect, or bends an arm on an impalpable certain
   rest,
Looking with side-curved head curious what will come next,
Both in and out of the game and watching and wondering at it.

Backward I see in my own days where I sweated through fog
   with linguists and contenders,   80
I have no mockings or arguments, I witness and wait.

5 I believe in you my soul, the other I am must not abase itself to
   you,
And you must not be abased to the other.

Loafe with me on the grass, loose the stop from your throat,
Not words, not music or rhyme I want, not custom or lecture, not
   even the best,   85
Only the lull I like, the hum of your valved voice.

I mind how once we lay such a transparent summer morning,
How you settled your head athwart my hips and gently turn'd over
   upon me,
And parted the shirt from my bosom-bone, and plunged your
   tongue to my bare-stript heart,
And reach'd till you felt my beard, and reach'd till you held my
   feet.   90

Swiftly arose and spread around me the peace and knowledge
   that pass all the argument of the earth,
And I know that the hand of God is the promise of my own,
And I know that the spirit of God is the brother of my own,
And that all the men ever born are also my brothers,
   and the women my sisters and lovers,
And that a kelson[3] of the creation is love,   95

[3] A timber or girder placed parallel with and
bolted to the keel for additional strength.

And limitless are leaves stiff or drooping in the fields,
And brown ants in the little wells beneath them,
And mossy scabs of the worm fence, heap'd stones, elder,
  mullein and poke-weed.

6 A child said What is the grass? fetching it to me with full hands;
How could I answer the child? I do not know what it is any more
  than he.   100

I guess it must be the flag of my disposition, out of hopeful green
  stuff woven.

Or I guess it is the handkerchief of the Lord,
A scented gift and remembrancer designedly dropt,
Bearing the owner's name someway in the corners, that we may
  see and remark, and say Whose?

Or I guess the grass is itself a child, the produced babe of the
  vegetation.   105

Or I guess it is a uniform hieroglyphic,
And it means, Sprouting alike in broad zones and narrow zones,
Growing among black folks as among white,
Kanuck, Tuckahoe, Congressman, Cuff,[4] I give them the same,
  I receive them the same.

And now it seems to me the beautiful uncut hair of graves.   110

Tenderly will I use you curling grass,
It may be you transpire from the breasts of young men,
It may be if I had known them I would have loved them,
It may be you are from old people, or from offspring taken soon
  out of their mothers' laps,
And here you are the mothers' laps.   115

This grass is very dark to be from the white heads of old mothers,
Darker than the colorless beards of old men,
Dark to come from under the faint red roofs of mouths.

O I perceive after all so many uttering tongues,
And I perceive they do not come from the roofs of mouths for
  nothing.   120

I wish I could translate the hints about the dead young men and
  women,
And the hints about old men and mothers, and the offspring taken
  soon out of their laps.

[4] "Kanuck" is a French Canadian; "Tuckahoe" is a poor Virginian in the tidewater; and
"Cuff" is a black man.

What do you think has become of the young and old men?
And what do you think has become of the women and children?

They are alive and well somewhere,   125
The smallest sprout shows there is really no death,
And if ever there was it led forward life, and does not wait
    at the end to arrest it,
And ceas'd the moment life appear'd.

All goes onward and outward, nothing collapses,
And to die is different from what any one supposed, and luckier.   130

7 Has any one supposed it lucky to be born?
  I hasten to inform him or her it is just as lucky to die, and I know
      it.

  I pass death with the dying and birth with the new-wash'd babe,
      and am not contain'd between my hat and boots,
  And peruse manifold objects, no two alike and every one good,
  The earth good and the stars good, and their adjuncts all good.   135

  I am not an earth nor an adjunct of an earth,
  I am the mate and companion of people, all just as immortal
      and fathomless as myself,
  (They do not know how immortal, but I know.)

  Every kind for itself and its own, for me mine male and female,
  For me those that have been boys and that love women,   140
  For me the man that is proud and feels how it stings to be slighted,
  For me the sweet-heart and the old maid, for me mothers
      and the mothers of mothers,
  For me lips that have smiled, eyes that have shed tears,
  For me children and the begetters of children.

  Undrape! you are not guilty to me, nor stale nor discarded,   145
  I see through the broadcloth and gingham whether or no,
  And am around, tenacious, acquisitive, tireless, and cannot be
      shaken away.

8 The little one sleeps in its cradle,
  I lift the gauze and look a long time, and silently brush away flies
      with my hand.

  The youngster and the red-faced girl turn aside up the bushy hill,   150
  I peeringly view them from the top.

  The suicide sprawls on the bloody floor of the bedroom,
  I witness the corpse with its dabbled hair, I note where the pistol
      has fallen.

The blab of the pave, tires of carts, sluff of boot-soles, talk of the
    promenaders,
The heavy omnibus, the driver with his interrogating thumb, the
    clank of the shod horses on the granite floor,   155
The snow-sleighs, clinking, shouted jokes, pelts of snow-balls,
The hurrahs for popular favorites, the fury of rous'd mobs,
The flap of the curtain'd litter, a sick man inside borne to the
    hospital,
The meeting of enemies, the sudden oath, the blows and fall,
The excited crowd, the policeman with his star quickly working
    his passage to the centre of the crowd,   160
The impassive stones that receive and return so many echoes,
What groans of over-fed or half-starv'd who fall sunstruck or in fits,
What exclamations of women taken suddenly who hurry home
    and give birth to babes,
What living and buried speech is always vibrating here,
    what howls restrain'd by decorum,
Arrests of criminals, slights, adulterous offers made, acceptances,
    rejections with convex lips,   165
I mind them or the show or resonance of them—I come and I
    depart.

9 The big doors of the country barn stand open and ready,
The dried grass of the harvest-time loads the slow-drawn wagon,
The clear light plays on the brown gray and green intertinged,
The armfuls are pack'd to the sagging mow.   170

I am there, I help, I came stretch'd atop of the load,
I felt its soft jolts, one leg reclined on the other,
I jump from the cross-beams and seize the clover and timothy,
And roll head over heels and tangle my hair full of wisps.

10 Alone far in the wilds and mountains I hunt,   175
Wandering amazed at my own lightness and glee,
In the late afternoon choosing a safe spot to pass the night,
Kindling a fire and broiling the fresh-kill'd game,
Falling asleep on the gather'd leaves with my dog and gun by my
    side.

The Yankee clipper is under her sky-sails, she cuts the sparkle and
    scud,   180
My eyes settle the land, I bend at her prow or shout joyously from
    the deck.

The boatmen and clam-diggers arose early and stopt for me,
I tuck'd my trouser-ends in my boots and went and had a good
    time;
You should have been with us that day round the chowder-kettle.

I saw the marriage of the trapper in the open air in the far west,
    the bride was a red girl,   185
Her father and his friends sat near cross-legged and dumbly
    smoking, they had moccasins to their feet and large thick
    blankets hanging from their shoulders,
On a bank lounged the trapper, he was drest mostly in skins,
    his luxuriant beard and curls protected his neck,
    he held his bride by the hand,
She had long eyelashes, her head was bare, her coarse straight
    locks descended upon her voluptuous limbs and reach'd to her
    feet.

The runaway slave came to my house and stopt outside,
I heard his motions crackling the twigs of the woodpile,   190
Through the swung half-door of the kitchen I saw him limpsy and
    weak,
And went where he sat on a log and led him in and assured him,
And brought water and fill'd a tub for his sweated body and
    bruis'd feet,
And gave him a room that enter'd from my own, and gave him
    some coarse clean clothes,
And remember perfectly well his revolving eyes and his
    awkwardness,   195
And remember putting plasters on the galls of his neck and ankles;
He staid with me a week before he was recuperated and pass'd
    north,
I had him sit next me at table, my fire-lock lean'd in the corner.

11 Twenty-eight young men bathe by the shore,
Twenty-eight young men and all so friendly;   200
Twenty-eight years of womanly life and all so lonesome.

She owns the fine house by the rise of the bank,
She hides handsome and richly drest aft the blinds of the window.

Which of the young men does she like the best?
Ah the homeliest of them is beautiful to her.   205

Where are you off to, lady? for I see you,
You splash in the water there, yet stay stock still in your room.

Dancing and laughing along the beach came the twenty-ninth
    bather,
The rest did not see her, but she saw them and loved them.

The beards of the young men glisten'd with wet,
    it ran from their long hair,   210
Little streams pass'd all over their bodies.

An unseen hand also pass'd over their bodies,
It descended tremblingly from their temples and ribs.

The young men float on their backs, their white bellies bulge to the
    sun, they do not ask who seizes fast to them,
They do not know who puffs and declines with pendant and
    bending arch,   215
They do not think whom they souse with spray.

¹² The butcher-boy puts off his killing-clothes, or sharpens his knife
    at the stall in the market,
I loiter enjoying his repartee and his shuffle and break-down.⁵

Blacksmiths with grimed and hairy chests environ the anvil,
Each has his main-sledge, they are all out, there is a great heat in
    the fire.   220

From the cinder-stew'd threshold I follow their movements,
The lithe sheer of their waists plays even with their massive arms,
Overhand the hammers swing, overhand so slow, overhand so sure,
They do not hasten, each man hits in his place.

¹³ The negro holds firmly the reins of his four horses, the block swags
    underneath on its tied-over chain,   225
The negro that drives the long dray of the stone-yard, steady and
    tall he stands pois'd on one leg on the string-piece,
His blue shirt exposes his ample neck and breast and loosens over
    his hip-band,
His glance is calm and commanding, he tosses the slouch of his hat
    away from his forehead,
The sun falls on his crispy hair and mustache, falls on the black
    of his polish'd and perfect limbs.

I behold the picturesque giant and love him, and I do not stop
    there,   230
I go with the team also.

In me the caresser of life wherever moving, backward as well as
    forward sluing
To niches aside and junior bending, not a person or object missing,
Absorbing all to myself and for this song.

Oxen that rattle the yoke and chain or halt in the leafy shade,
    what is that you express in your eyes?   235
It seems to be more than all the print I have read in my life.

⁵ The "shuffle" is a sliding dance; the "breakdown" a festive and noisy dance.

My tread scares the wood-drake and wood-duck on my distant
   and day-long ramble,
They rise together, they slowly circle around.

I believe in those wing'd purposes,
And acknowledge red, yellow, white, playing within me,   240
And consider green and violet and the tufted crown intentional,
And do not call the tortoise unworthy because she is not something
   else,
And the jay in the woods never studied the gamut, yet trills pretty
   well to me,
And the look of the bay mare shames silliness out of me.

14 The wild gander leads his flock through the cool night,   245
Ya-honk, he says, and sounds it down to me like an invitation,
The pert may suppose it meaningless, but I listening close,
Find its purpose and place up there toward the wintry sky.

The sharp-hoof'd moose of the north, the cat on the house-sill,
   the chickadee, the prairie-dog,
The litter of the grunting sow as they tug at her teats,   250
The brood of the turkey-hen and she with her half-spread wings,
I see in them and myself the same old law.

The press of my foot to the earth springs a hundred affections,
They scorn the best I can do to relate them.

I am enamour'd of growing out-doors,   255
Of men that live among cattle or taste of the ocean or woods,
Of the builders and steerers of ships and the wielders of axes and
   mauls, and the drivers of horses,
I can eat and sleep with them week in and week out.

What is commonest, cheapest, nearest, easiest, is Me,
Me going in for my chances, spending for vast returns,   260
Adorning myself to bestow myself on the first that will take me,
Not asking the sky to come down to my good will,
Scattering it freely forever.

15 The pure contralto sings in the organ loft,
The carpenter dresses his plank, the tongue of his foreplane
   whistles its wild ascending lisp,   265
The married and unmarried children ride home to their
   Thanksgiving dinner,
The pilot seizes the king-pin, he heaves down with a strong arm,
The mate stands braced in the whale-boat, lance and harpoon are
   ready,
The duck-shooter walks by silent and cautious stretches,

The deacons are ordain'd with cross'd hands at the altar,   270
The spinning-girl retreats and advances to the hum of the big
    wheel,
The farmer stops by the bars as he walks on a First-day[6] loafe
    and looks at the oats and rye,
The lunatic is carried at last to the asylum a confirm'd case,
(He will never sleep any more as he did in the cot
    in his mother's bed-room;)
The jour printer with gray head and gaunt jaws works at his case,[7]   275
He turns his quid of tobacco while his eyes blurr with the
    manuscript;
The malform'd limbs are tied to the surgeon's table,
What is removed drops horribly in a pail;
The quadroon girl is sold at the auction-stand, the drunkard nods
    by the bar-room stove,
The machinist rolls up his sleeves, the policeman travels his beat,
    the gate-keeper marks who pass,   280
The young fellow drives the express-wagon, (I love him,
    though I do not know him;)
The half-breed straps on his light boots to compete in the race,
The western turkey-shooting draws old and young,
    some lean on their rifles, some sit on logs,
Out from the crowds steps the marksman, takes his position, levels
    his piece;
The groups of newly-come immigrants cover the wharf or levee,   285
As the woolly-pates hoe in the sugar-field, the overseer views them
    from his saddle,
The bugle calls in the ball-room, the gentlemen run for their
    partners, the dancers bow to each other,
The youth lies awake in the cedar-roof'd garret and harks to the
    musical rain,
The Wolverine[8] sets traps on the creek that helps fill the Huron,
The squaw wrapt in her yellow-hemm'd cloth is offering moccasins
    and bead-bags for sale,   290
The connoisseur peers along the exhibition-gallery with half-shut
    eyes bent sideways,
As the deck-hand makes fast the steamboat the plank is thrown
    for the shore-going passengers,
The young sister holds out the skein while the elder sister winds it
    off in a ball, and stops now and then for the knots,

[6] The Quaker term for Sunday.   [8] A native of Michigan.

[7] The box that holds type.

The one-year wife is recovering and happy having a week ago
   borne her first child,
The clean-hair'd Yankee girl works with her sewing-machine
   or in the factory or mill,   295
The paving-man leans on his two-handed rammer, the reporter's
   lead flies swiftly over the note-book, the sign-painter is lettering
   with blue and gold,
The canal boy trots on the tow-path, the book-keeper counts at his
   desk, the shoemaker waxes his thread,
The conductor beats time for the band and all the performers
   follow him,
The child is baptized, the convert is making his first professions,
The regatta is spread on the bay, the race is begun,
   (how the white sails sparkle!)   300
The drover watching his drove sings out to them that would stray,
The pedler sweats with his pack on his back,
   (the purchaser higgling about the odd cent;)
The bride unrumples her white dress, the minute-hand of the clock
   moves slowly,
The opium-eater reclines with rigid head and just-open'd lips,
The prostitute draggles her shawl, her bonnet bobs
   on her tipsy and pimpled neck,   305
The crowd laugh at her blackguard oaths, the men jeer and wink
   to each other,
(Miserable! I do not laugh at your oaths nor jeer you;)
The President holding a cabinet council is surrounded by the great
   Secretaries,
On the piazza walk three matrons stately and friendly with twined
   arms,
The crew of the fish-smack pack repeated layers of halibut in the
   hold,   310
The Missourian crosses the plains toting his wares and his cattle,
As the fare-collector goes through the train he gives notice
   by the jingling of loose change,
The floor-men are laying the floor, the tinners are tinning the roof,
   the masons are calling for mortar,
In single file each shouldering his hod pass onward the laborers;
Seasons pursuing each other the indescribable crowd is gather'd,
   it is the fourth of Seventh-month,[9] (what salutes
   of cannon and small arms!)   315
Seasons pursuing each other the plougher ploughs, the mower
   mows, and the winter-grain falls in the ground;

[9] The Quaker term for the Fourth of July.

Off on the lakes the pike-fisher watches and waits
    by the hole in the frozen surface,
The stumps stand thick round the clearing, the squatter strikes
    deep with his axe,
Flatboatmen make fast towards dusk near the cotton-wood or
    pecan-trees,
Coon-seekers go through the regions of the Red river or through
    those drain'd by the Tennessee, or through those of the
    Arkansas,   320
Torches shine in the dark that hangs on the Chattahoochee or
    Altamahaw,
Patriarchs sit at supper with sons and grandsons and great-
    grandsons around them,
In walls of adobie,[10] in canvas tents, rest hunters and trappers
    after their day's sport,
The city sleeps and the country sleeps,
The living sleep for their time, the dead sleep for their time,   325
The old husband sleeps by his wife and the young husband sleeps
    by his wife,
And these tend inward to me and I tend outward to them,
And such as it is to be of these more or less I am,
And of these one and all I weave the song of myself.

[16] I am of old and young, of the foolish as much as the wise,   330
Regardless of others, ever regardful of others,
Maternal as well as paternal, a child as well as a man,
Stuff'd with the stuff that is coarse and stuff'd with the stuff that is
    fine,
One of the Nation of many nations, the smallest the same and the
    largest the same,
A Southerner soon as a Northerner, a planter nonchalant and
    hospitable down by the Oconee[11] I live,   335
A Yankee bound my own way ready for trade, my joints the
    limberest joints on earth and the sternest joints on earth,
A Kentuckian walking the vale of the Elkhorn in my deer-skin
    leggings, a Louisianian or Georgian,
A boatman over lakes or bays or along coasts, a Hoosier, Badger,
    Buckeye;[12]
At home on Kanadian snow-shoes or up in the bush,
    or with fishermen off Newfoundland,

---

[10] A sun-dried, unburned brick of clay and straw—used for a Spanish house.

[11] Oconee is a river in Northeast Georgia.

[12] Slang for Indiana, Wisconsin, Ohio.

Max Schmitt in a Single Scull, 1871. Thomas Eakins, The Metropolitan Museum of Art, Alfred N. Punnet Fund and Gift of George D. Pratt.

At home in the fleet of ice-boats, sailing with the rest and tacking,
At home on the hills of Vermont or in the woods of Maine, or the
    Texan ranch,
Comrade of Californians, comrade of free North-Westerners,
    (loving their big proportions,)
Comrade of raftsmen and coalmen, comrade of all who shake
    hands and welcome to drink and meat,
A learner with the simplest, a teacher of the thoughtfullest,
A novice beginning yet experient of myriads of seasons,
Of every hue and caste am I, of every rank and religion,
A farmer, mechanic, artist, gentleman, sailor, quaker,
Prisoner, fancy-man, rowdy, lawyer, physician, priest.

I resist any thing better than my own diversity,
Breathe the air but leave plenty after me,
And am not stuck up, and am in my place.

(The moth and the fish-eggs are in their place,
The bright suns I see and the dark suns I cannot see are in their
    place,
The palpable is in its place and the impalpable is in its place.)

17 These are really the thoughts of all men in all ages and lands,
    they are not original with me,
If they are not yours as much as mine they are nothing, or next to
    nothing,
If they are not the riddle and the untying of the riddle they are
    nothing,
If they are not just as close as they are distant they are nothing.

This is the grass that grows wherever the land is and the water is,
This the common air that bathes the globe.

18 With music strong I come, with my cornets and my drums,
I play not marches for accepted victors only, I play marches
    for conquer'd and slain persons.

Have you heard that it was good to gain the day?
I also say it is good to fall, battles are lost in the same spirit
    in which they are won.

I beat and pound for the dead,
I blow through my embouchures[13] my loudest and gayest for them.

Vivas to those who have fail'd!
And to those whose war-vessels sank in the sea!
And to those themselves who sank in the sea!

---

[13] Mouthpieces of instruments.

And to all generals that lost engagements, and all overcome heroes!   370
And the numberless unknown heroes equal to the greatest heroes
  known!

19 This is the meal equally set, this the meat for natural hunger,
It is for the wicked just the same as the righteous, I make
  appointments with,
I will not have a single person slighted or left away,
The kept-woman, sponger, thief, are hereby invited,   375
The heavy-lipp'd slave is invited, the venerealee is invited;
There shall be no difference between them and the rest.

This is the press of a bashful hand, this the float and odor of hair,
This the touch of my lips to yours, this the murmur of yearning,
This the far-off depth and height reflecting my own face,   380
This the thoughtful merge of myself, and the outlet again.

Do you guess I have some intricate purpose?
Well I have, for the Fourth-month[14] showers have,
  and the mica on the side of a rock has.

Do you take it I would astonish?
Does the daylight astonish? does the early redstart twittering
  through the woods?   385
Do I astonish more than they?

This hour I tell things in confidence,
I might not tell everybody, but I will tell you.

20 Who goes there? hankering, gross, mystical, nude;
How is it I extract strength from the beef I eat?   390

What is a man anyhow? what am I? what are you?

All I mark as my own you shall offset it with your own,
Else it were time lost listening to me.

I do not snivel that snivel the world over,
That months are vacuums and the ground but wallow and filth.   395

Whimpering and truckling fold with powders for invalids,
  conformity goes to the fourth-remov'd,
I wear my hat as I please indoors or out.

Why should I pray? why should I venerate and be ceremonious?

Having pried through the strata, analyzed to a hair,
  counsel'd with doctors and calculated close,
I find no sweeter fat than sticks to my own bones.   400

[14] April.

In all people I see myself, none more and not one a barley-corn
    less,
And the good or bad I say of myself I say of them.

I know I am solid and sound,
To me the converging objects of the universe perpetually flow,
All are written to me, and I must get what the writing means.   4(

I know I am deathless,
I know this orbit of mine cannot be swept by a carpenter's
    compass,
I know I shall not pass like a child's carlacue cut
    with a burnt stick at night.

I know I am august,
I do not trouble my spirit to vindicate itself or be understood,   410
I see that the elementary laws never apologize,
(I reckon I behave no prouder than the level I plant my house by,
    after all.)

I exist as I am, that is enough,
If no other in the world be aware I sit content,
And if each and all be aware I sit content.   415

One world is aware and by far the largest to me, and that is
    myself,
And whether I come to my own to-day or in ten thousand or ten
    million years,
I can cheerfully take it now, or with equal cheerfulness I can wait.

My foothold is tenon'd and mortis'd in granite,
I laugh at what you call dissolution,   420
And I know the amplitude of time.

21 I am the poet of the Body and I am the poet of the Soul,
The pleasures of heaven are with me and the pains of hell are with
    me,
The first I graft and increase upon myself, the latter I translate
    into a new tongue.

I am the poet of the woman the same as the man,   425
And I say it is as great to be a woman as to be a man,
And I say there is nothing greater than the mother of men.

I chant the chant of dilation or pride,
We have had ducking and deprecating about enough,
I show that size is only development.   430

Have you outstript the rest? are you the President?
It is a trifle, they will more than arrive there every one, and still
    pass on.

I am he that walks with the tender and growing night,
I call to the earth and sea half-held by the night.

Press close bare-bosom'd night—press close magnetic nourishing
    night!   435 •
Night of south winds—night of the large few stars!
Still nodding night—mad naked summer night.

Smile O voluptuous cool-breath'd earth!
Earth of the slumbering and liquid trees!
Earth of departed sunset—earth of the mountains misty-topt!   440
Earth of the vitreous[15] pour of the full moon just tinged with blue!
Earth of shine and dark mottling the tide of the river!
Earth of the limpid gray of clouds brighter and clearer for my
    sake!
Far-swooping elbow'd earth—rich apple-blossom'd earth!
Smile, for your lover comes.   445

Prodigal, you have given me love—therefore I to you give love!
O unspeakable passionate love.

22 You sea! I resign myself to you also—I guess what you mean,
I behold from the beach your crooked inviting fingers,
I believe you refuse to go back without feeling of me,   450
We must have a turn together, I undress, hurry me out of sight of
    the land,
Cushion me soft, rock me in billowy drowse,
Dash me with amorous wet, I can repay you.

Sea of stretch'd ground-swells,
Sea breathing broad and convulsive breaths,   455
Sea of the brine of life and of unshovell'd yet always-ready graves,
Howler and scooper of storms, capricious and dainty sea,
I am integral with you, I too am of one phase and of all phases.

Partaker of influx and efflux I, extoller of hate and conciliation,
Extoller of amies and those that sleep in each others' arms.   460

I am he attesting sympathy,
(Shall I make my list of things in the house and skip the house
    that supports them?)

I am not the poet of goodness only, I do not decline to be
    the poet of wickedness also.

---

[15] Pertaining to glass.

What blurt is this about virtue and about vice?
Evil propels me and reform of evil propels me, I stand indifferent,   465
My gait is no fault-finder's or rejecter's gait,
I moisten the roots of all that has grown.

Did you fear some scrofula[16] out of the unflagging pregnancy?
Did you guess the celestial laws are yet to be work'd over and
    rectified?

I find one side a balance and the antipodal side a balance,   470
Soft doctrine as steady help as stable doctrine,
Thoughts and deeds of the present our rouse and early start.

This minute that comes to me over the past decillions,[17]
There is no better than it and now.

What behaved well in the past or behaves well to-day is not such a
    wonder,   475
The wonder is always and always how there can be a mean man or
    an infidel.

23 Endless unfolding of words of ages!
And mine a word of the modern, the word En-Masse.

A word of the faith that never balks,
Here or henceforward it is all the same to me, I accept Time
    absolutely.   480

It alone is without flaw, it alone rounds and completes all,
That mystic baffling wonder alone completes all.

I accept Reality and dare not question it,
Materialism first and last imbuing.

Hurrah for positive science! long live exact demonstration!   485
Fetch stonecrop mixt with cedar and branches of lilac,
This is the lexicographer, this the chemist, this made a grammar
    of the old cartouches,[18]
These mariners put the ship through dangerous unknown seas,
This is the geologist, this works with the scalpel, and this is a
    mathematician.

Gentlemen, to you the first honors always!   490
Your facts are useful, and yet they are not my dwelling,
I but enter by them to an area of my dwelling.

[16] Predisposition to tuberculosis and respiratory catarrhs.

[17] One followed by 33 zeroes, 10^{33}.

[18] A scroll-like tablet used to provide space
for an inscription.

Less the reminders of properties told my words,
And more the reminders they of life untold, and of freedom
    and extrication,
And make short account of neuters and geldings,[19] and favor men
    and women fully equipt,   495
And beat the gong of revolt, and stop with fugitives
    and them that plot and conspire.

[24] Walt Whitman, a kosmos, of Manhattan the son,
Turbulent, fleshy, sensual, eating, drinking and breeding,
No sentimentalist, no stander above men and women or apart from
    them,
No more modest than immodest.   500

Unscrew the locks from the doors!
Unscrew the doors themselves from their jambs!

Whoever degrades another degrades me,
And whatever is done or said returns at last to me.

Through me the afflatus[20] surging and surging, through me
    the current and index.   505

I speak the pass-word primeval, I give the sign of democracy,
By God! I will accept nothing which all cannot have their
    counterpart of on the same terms.

Through me many long dumb voices,
Voices of the interminable generations of prisoners and slaves,
Voices of the diseas'd and despairing and of thieves and dwarfs,   510
Voices of cycles of preparation and accretion,
And of the threads that connect the stars, and of wombs
    and of the father-stuff,
And of the rights of them the others are down upon,
Of the deform'd, trivial, flat, foolish, despised,
Fog in the air, beetles rolling balls of dung.   515

Through me forbidden voices,
Voices of sexes and lusts, voices veil'd and I remove the veil,
Voices indecent by me clarified and transfigur'd.

I do not press my fingers across my mouth,
I keep as delicate around the bowels as around the head and heart, 520
Copulation is no more rank to me than death is.

I believe in the flesh and the appetites,
Seeing, hearing, feeling, are miracles, and each part and tag of me
    is a miracle.

[19] Castrated animals.   [20] A creative impulse.

Divine am I inside and out, and I make holy whatever I touch or
    am touch'd from,
The scent of these arm-pits aroma finer than prayer,   525
This head more than churches, bibles, and all the creeds.

If I worship one thing more than another it shall be the spread of
    my own body, or any part of it,
Translucent mould of me it shall be you!
Shaded ledges and rests it shall be you!
Firm masculine colter it shall be you!   530
Whatever goes to the tilth[21] of me it shall be you!
You my rich blood! your milky stream pale strippings of my life!
Breast that presses against other breasts it shall be you!
My brain it shall be your occult convolutions!
Root of wash'd sweet-flag! timorous pond-snipe! nest of guarded
    duplicate eggs! it shall be you!   535
Mix'd tussled hay of head, beard, brawn, it shall be you!
Trickling sap of maple, fibre of manly wheat, it shall be you!
Sun so generous it shall be you!
Vapors lighting and shading my face it shall be you!
You sweaty brooks and dews it shall be you!   540
Winds whose soft-tickling genitals rub against me it shall be you!
Broad muscular fields, branches of live oak, loving lounger
    in my winding paths, it shall be you!
Hands I have taken, face I have kiss'd, mortal I have ever touch'd,
    it shall be you.

I dote on myself, there is that lot of me and all so luscious,
Each moment and whatever happens thrills me with joy,   545
I cannot tell how my ankles bend, nor whence the cause of my
    faintest wish,
Nor the cause of the friendship I emit, nor the cause of the
    friendship I take again.

That I walk up my stoop, I pause to consider if it really be,
A morning-glory at my window satisfies me more than the
    metaphysics of books.

To behold the day-break!   550
The little light fades the immense and diaphanous shadows,
The air tastes good to my palate.

Hefts of the moving world at innocent gambols silently rising,
    freshly exuding,
Scooting obliquely high and low.

21 The tilled earth.

Something I cannot see puts upward libidinous prongs, 555
Seas of bright juice suffuse heaven.

The earth by the sky staid with, the daily close of their junction,
The heav'd challenge from the east that moment over my head,
The mocking taunt, See then whether you shall be master!

25 Dazzling and tremendous how quick the sun-rise would kill me, 560
If I could not now and always send sun-rise out of me.

We also ascend dazzling and tremendous as the sun,
We found our own O my soul in the calm and cool of the day-
      break.

My voice goes after what my eyes cannot reach,
With the twirl of my tongue I encompass worlds and volumes of
      worlds. 565

Speech is the twin of my vision, it is unequal to measure itself,
It provokes me forever, it says sarcastically,
Walt you contain enough, why don't you let it out then?

Come now I will not be tantalized, you conceive too much of
      articulation,
Do you not know O speech how the buds beneath you are folded? 570
Waiting in gloom, protected by frost,
The dirt receding before my prophetical screams,
I underlying causes to balance them at last,
My knowledge my live parts, it keeping tally with the meaning of
      all things,
Happiness, (which whoever hears me let him or her
      set out in search of this day.) 575

My final merit I refuse you, I refuse putting from me what I really
      am,
Encompass worlds, but never try to encompass me,
I crowd your sleekest and best by simply looking toward you.

Writing and talk do not prove me,
I carry the plenum of proof and every thing else in my face, 580
With the hush of my lips I wholly confound the skeptic.

26 Now I will do nothing but listen,
To accrue what I hear into this song, to let sounds contribute
      toward it.

I hear bravuras of birds, bustle of growing wheat, gossip of flames,
      clack of sticks cooking my meals,
I hear the sound I love, the sound of the human voice, 585

I hear all sounds running together, combined, fused or following,
Sounds of the city and sounds out of the city, sounds of the day
    and night,
Talkative young ones to those that like them,
    the loud laugh of work-people at their meals,
The angry base of disjointed friendship, the faint tones of the sick,
The judge with hands tight to the desk, his pallid lips   590
    pronouncing a death-sentence,
The heave'e'yo of stevedores unlading ships by wharves,
    the refrain of the anchor-lifters,
The ring of alarm-bells, the cry of fire, the whirr of swift-streaking
    engines and hose-carts with premonitory tinkles and color'd
    lights,
The steam-whistle, the solid roll of the train of approaching cars,
The slow march play'd at the head of the association marching two
    and two,
(They go to guard some corpse, the flag-tops are draped with black   595
    muslin.)

I hear the violoncello, ('tis the young man's heart's complaint,)
I hear the key'd cornet, it glides quickly in through my ears,
It shakes mad-sweet pangs through my belly and breast.

I hear the chorus, it is a grand opera,   600
Ah this indeed is music—this suits me.

A tenor large and fresh as the creation fills me,
The orbic flex of his mouth is pouring and filling me full.

I hear the train'd soprano (what work with hers is this?)
The orchestra whirls me wider than Uranus[22] flies,   605
It wrenches such ardors from me I did not know I possess'd them,
It sails me, I dab with bare feet, they are lick'd by the indolent
    waves,
I am cut by bitter and angry hail, I lose my breath,
Steep'd amid honey'd morphine, my windpipe throttled in fakes of
    death,
At length let up again to feel the puzzle of puzzles,   610
And that we call Being.

27 To be in any form, what is that?
(Round and round we go, all of us, and ever come back thither,)
If nothing lay more develop'd the quahaug[23] in its callous shell
    were enough.

---

22 The seventh planet from the sun, an early
supreme god in Greek mythology, the personification of the sky.

23 An edible, hard-shelled clam.

Mine is no callous shell,
I have instant conductors all over me whether I pass or stop,   615
They seize every object and lead it harmlessly through me.

I merely stir, press, feel with my fingers, and am happy,
To touch my person to some one else's is about as much as I can
  stand.

28 Is this then a touch? quivering me to a new identity,
Flames and ether making a rush for my veins,   620
Treacherous tip of me reaching and crowding to help them,
My flesh and blood playing out lightning to strike
  what is hardly different from myself,
On all sides prurient provokers stiffening my limbs,
Straining the udder of my heart for its withheld drip,
Behaving licentious toward me, taking no denial,   625
Depriving me of my best as for a purpose,
Unbuttoning my clothes, holding me by the bare waist,
Deluding my confusion with the calm of the sunlight and pasture-
  fields,
Immodestly sliding the fellow-senses away,
They bribed to swap off with touch and go and graze at the edges
  of me,   630
No consideration, no regard for my draining strength or my anger,
Fetching the rest of the herd around to enjoy them a while,
Then all uniting to stand on a headland and worry me.

The sentries desert every other part of me,
They have left me helpless to a red marauder,   635
They all come to the headland to witness and assist against me.

I am given up by traitors,
I talk wildly, I have lost my wits, I and nobody else am the
  greatest traitor,
I went myself first to the headland, my own hands carried me
  there.

You villain touch! what are you doing? my breath is tight in its
  throat,
Unclench your floodgates, you are too much for me.   640

29 Blind loving wrestling touch, sheath'd hooded sharp-tooth'd touch!
Did it make you ache so, leaving me?

Parting track'd by arriving, perpetual payment of perpetual loan,
Rich showering rain, and recompense richer afterward.   645

Sprouts take and accumulate, stand by the curb prolific and vital,
Landscapes projected masculine, full-sized and golden.

30 All truths wait in all things,
They neither hasten their own delivery nor resist it,
They do not need the obstetric forceps of the surgeon,   650
The insignificant is as big to me as any,
(What is less or more than a touch.)

Logic and sermons never convince,
The damp of the night drives deeper into my soul.

(Only what proves itself to every man and woman is so,   655
Only what nobody denies is so.)

A minute and a drop of me settle my brain,
I believe the soggy clods shall become lovers and lamps,
And a compend of compends is the meat of a man or woman,
And a summit and flower there is the feeling they have for each
    other,   660
And they are to branch boundlessly out of that lesson until it
    becomes omnific,
And until one and all shall delight us, and we them.

31 I believe a leaf of grass is no less than the journey-work of the
    stars,
And the pismire[24] is equally perfect, and a grain of sand, and the
    egg of the wren,
And the tree-toad is a chef-d'œuvre for the highest,   665
And the running blackberry would adorn the parlors of heaven,
And the narrowest hinge in my hand puts to scorn all machinery,
And the cow crunching with depress'd head surpasses any statue,
And a mouse is miracle enough to stagger sextillions[25] of infidels.

I find I incorporate gneis,[26] coal, long-threaded moss, fruits, grains,
    esculent[27] roots,   670
And am stucco'd with quadrupeds and birds all over,
And have distanced what is behind me for good reasons,
But call any thing back again when I desire it.

In vain the speeding or shyness,
In vain the plutonic rocks send their old heat against my approach,   675
In vain the mastodon retreats beneath its own powder'd bones,
In vain objects stand leagues off and assume manifold shapes,
In vain the ocean settling in hollows and the great monsters lying
    low,
In vain the buzzard houses herself with the sky,

---

[24] An ant.   [27] Edible.
[25] One followed by 21 zeroes, 10^{21}.
[26] A kind of granite, in which the minerals
are arranged in layers.

In vain the snake slides through the creepers and logs,   680
In vain the elk takes to the inner passes of the woods,
In vain the razor-bill'd auk sails far north to Labrador,
I follow quickly, I ascend to the nest in the fissure of the cliff.

32 I think I could turn and live with animals, they are so placid and
       self-contain'd,
   I stand and look at them long and long.   685

They do not sweat and whine about their condition,
They do not lie awake in the dark and weep for their sins,
They do not make me sick discussing their duty to God,
Not one is dissatisfied, not one is demented with the mania of
   owning things,
Not one kneels to another, nor to his kind that lived thousands of
   years ago,   690
Not one is respectable or unhappy over the whole earth.

So they show their relations to me and I accept them,
They bring me tokens of myself, they evince them plainly in their
   possession.

I wonder where they get those tokens,
Did I pass that way huge times ago and negligently drop them?   695
Myself moving forward then and now and forever,
Gathering and showing more always and with velocity,
Infinite and omnigenous, and the like of these among them,
Not too exclusive toward the reachers of my remembrancers,
Picking out one that I love, and now go with him on brotherly
   terms.   700

A gigantic beauty of a stallion, fresh and responsive to my caresses,
Head high in the forehead, wide between the ears,
Limbs glossy and supple, tail dusting the ground,
Eyes full of sparkling wickedness, ears finely cut, flexibly moving.

His nostrils dilate as my heels embrace him,   705
His well-built limbs tremble with pleasure as we race around and
   return.

I but use you a minute, then I resign you, stallion,
Why do I need your paces when I myself out-gallop them?
Even as I stand or sit passing faster than you.

33 Space and Time! now I see it is true, what I guess'd at,   710
   What I guess'd when I loaf'd on the grass,
   What I guess'd while I lay alone in my bed,
   And again as I walk'd the beach under the paling stars of the
      morning.

My ties and ballasts leave me, my elbows rest in sea-gaps,
I skirt sierras, my palms cover continents,   715
I am afoot with my vision.
By the city's quadrangular houses—in log huts, camping with
  lumbermen,
Along the ruts of the turnpike, along the dry gulch and rivulet bed,
Weeding my onion-patch or hoeing rows of carrots and parsnips,
  crossing savannas,[28] trailing in forests,
Prospecting, gold-digging, girdling the trees of a new purchase,   720
Scorch'd ankle-deep by the hot sand, hauling my boat
  down the shallow river,
Where the panther walks to and fro on a limb overhead,
  where the buck turns furiously at the hunter,
Where the rattlesnake suns his flabby length on a rock,
  where the otter is feeding on fish,
Where the alligator in his tough pimples sleeps by the bayou,
Where the black bear is searching for roots or honey, where the
  beaver pats the mud with his paddle-shaped tail;   725
Over the growing sugar, over the yellow-flower'd cotton plant,
  over the rice in its low moist field,
Over the sharp-peak'd farm house, with its scallop'd scum
  and slender shoots from the gutters,
Over the western persimmon, over the long-leav'd corn,
  over the delicate blue-flower flax,
Over the white and brown buckwheat, a hummer and buzzer
  there with the rest,
Over the dusky green of the rye as it ripples and shades in the
  breeze;   730
Scaling mountains, pulling myself cautiously up,
  holding on by low scragged limbs,
Walking the path worn in the grass and beat through the leaves of
  the brush,
Where the quail is whistling betwixt the woods and the wheat-lot,
Where the bat flies in the Seventh-month eve, where the great
  gold-bug drops through the dark,
Where the brook puts out of the roots of the old tree and flows to
  the meadow,   735
Where cattle stand and shake away flies with the tremulous
  shuddering of their hides,
Where the cheese-cloth hangs in the kitchen, where andirons
  straddle the hearth-slab, where cobwebs fall in festoons from
  the rafters;

[28] Flat, treeless grassland in the tropics.

Where trip-hammers crash, where the press is whirling its
    cylinders,
Wherever the human heart beats with terrible throes under its ribs,
Where the pear-shaped balloon is floating aloft,
    (floating in it myself and looking composedly down,) 740
Where the life-car is drawn on the slip-noose, where the heat
    hatches pale-green eggs in the dented sand,
Where the she-whale swims with her calf and never forsakes it,
Where the steam-ship trails hind-ways its long pennant of smoke,
Where the fin of the shark cuts like a black chip out of the water,
Where the half-burn'd brig is riding on unknown currents, 745
Where shells grow to her slimy deck, where the dead are
    corrupting below;
Where the dense-starr'd flag is borne at the head of the regiments,
Approaching Manhattan up by the long-stretching island,
Under Niagara, the cataract falling like a veil over my
    countenance,
Upon a door-step, upon the horse-block of hard wood outside, 750
Upon the race-course, or enjoying picnics or jigs or a good game of
    base-ball,
At he-festivals, with blackguard gibes, ironical license, bull-dances,
    drinking, laughter,
At the cider-mill tasting the sweets of the brown mash,
    sucking the juice through a straw,
At apple-peelings wanting kisses for all the red fruit I find,
At musters, beach-parties, friendly bees, huskings, house-raisings; 755
Where the mocking-bird sounds his delicious gurgles, cackles,
    screams, weeps,
Where the hay-rick stands in the barn-yard, where the dry-stalks
    are scatter'd, where the brood-cow waits in the hovel,
Where the bull advances to do his masculine work, where the stud
    to the mare, where the cock is treading the hen,
Where the heifers browse, where geese nip their food with short
    jerks,
Where sun-down shadows lengthen over the limitless and lonesome
    prairie, 760
Where herds of buffalo make a crawling spread of the square miles
    far and near,
Where the humming-bird shimmers, where the neck of the long-
    lived swan is curving and winding,
Where the laughing-gull scoots by the shore, where she laughs her
    near-human laugh,
Where bee-hives range on a gray bench in the garden
    half hid by the high weeds,

Where band-neck'd partridges roost in a ring on the ground
    with their heads out,   765
Where burial coaches enter the arch'd gates of a cemetery,
Where winter wolves bark amid wastes of snow and icicled trees,
Where the yellow-crown'd heron comes to the edge of the marsh
    at night and feeds upon small crabs,
Where the splash of swimmers and divers cools the warm noon,
Where the katy-did works her chromatic reed on the walnut-tree
    over the well,   770
Through patches of citrons and cucumbers with silver-wired leaves,
Through the salt-lick or orange glade, or under conical firs,
Through the gymnasium, through the curtain'd saloon,
    through the office or public hall;
Pleas'd with the native and pleas'd with the foreign,
    pleas'd with the new and old,
Pleas'd with the homely woman as well as the handsome,   775
Pleas'd with the quakeress as she puts off her bonnet and talks
    melodiously,
Pleas'd with the tune of the choir of the whitewash'd church,
Pleas'd with the earnest words of the sweating Methodist preacher,
    impress'd seriously at the camp-meeting;
Looking in at the shop-windows of Broadway the whole forenoon,
    flatting the flesh of my nose on the thick plate glass,
Wandering the same afternoon with my face turn'd up to the
    clouds, or down a lane or along the beach,   780
My right and left arms round the sides of two friends, and I in the
    middle;
Coming home with the silent and dark-cheek'd bush-boy,
    (behind me he rides at the drape of the day,)
Far from the settlements studying the print of animals' feet,
    or the moccasin print,
By the cot in the hospital reaching lemonade to a feverish patient,
Nigh the coffin'd corpse when all is still, examining with a candle;   785
Voyaging to every port to dicker and adventure,
Hurrying with the modern crowd as eager and fickle as any,
Hot toward one I hate, ready in my madness to knife him,
Solitary at midnight in my back yard, my thoughts gone from me a
    long while,
Walking the old hills of Judæa with the beautiful gentle God by
    my side,   790
Speeding through space, speeding through heaven and the stars,
Speeding amid the seven satellites and the broad ring,
    and the diameter of eighty thousand miles,
Speeding with tail'd meteors, throwing fire-balls like the rest,

Carrying the crescent child that carries its own full mother in its
    belly,
Storming, enjoying, planning, loving, cautioning,   795
Backing and filling, appearing and disappearing,
I tread day and night such roads.

I visit the orchards of spheres and look at the product,
And look at quintillions[29] ripen'd and look at quintillions green.

I fly those flights of a fluid and swallowing soul,   800
My course runs below the soundings of plummets.

I help myself to material and immaterial,
No guard can shut me off, no law prevent me.

I anchor my ship for a little while only,
My messengers continually cruise away or bring their returns to
    me.   805

I go hunting polar furs and the seal, leaping chasms with a pike-
    pointed staff, clinging to topples of brittle and blue.

I ascend to the foretruck,
I take my place late at night in the crow's-nest,
We sail the arctic sea, it is plenty light enough,
Through the clear atmosphere I stretch around on the wonderful
    beauty,   810
The enormous masses of ice pass me and I pass them,
    the scenery is plain in all directions,
The white-topt mountains show in the distance,
    I fling out my fancies toward them,
We are approaching some great battle-field in which we are soon
    to be engaged,
We pass the colossal outposts of the encampment,
    we pass with still feet and caution,
Or we are entering by the suburbs some vast and ruin'd city,   815
The blocks and fallen architecture more than all the living cities of
    the globe.

I am a free companion, I bivouac by invading watchfires,
I turn the bridegroom out of bed and stay with the bride myself,
I tighten her all night to my thighs and lips.

My voice is the wife's voice, the screech by the rail of the stairs,   820
They fetch my man's body up dripping and drown'd.

I understand the large hearts of heroes,
The courage of present times and all times,

---

[29] One followed by eighteen zeroes, 10^{18}.

How the skipper saw the crowded and rudderless wreck of the
    steam-ship, and Death chasing it up and down the storm,
How he knuckled tight and gave not back an inch, and was faithful
    of days and faithful of nights,   825
And chalk'd in large letters on a board, Be of good cheer, we will
    not desert you;
How he follow'd with them and tack'd with them three days
    and would not give it up,
How he saved the drifting company at last,
How the lank loose-gown'd women look'd when boated
    from the side of their prepared graves,
How the silent old-faced infants and the lifted sick,
    and the sharp-lipp'd unshaved men;   830
All this I swallow, it tastes good, I like it well, it becomes mine,
I am the man, I suffer'd, I was there.

The disdain and calmness of martyrs,
The mother of old, condemn'd for a witch, burnt with dry wood,
    her children gazing on,
The hounded slave that flags in the race, leans by the fence,
    blowing, cover'd with sweat,   835
The twinges that sting like needles his legs and neck,
    the murderous buckshot and the bullets,
All these I feel or am.

I am the hounded slave, I wince at the bite of the dogs,
Hell and despair are upon me, crack and again crack the
    marksmen,
I clutch the rails of the fence, my gore dribs, thinn'd with the ooze
    of my skin,   840
I fall on the weeds and stones,
The riders spur their unwilling horses, haul close,
Taunt my dizzy ears and beat me violently over the head with
    whip-stocks.

Agonies are one of my changes of garments,
I do not ask the wounded person how he feels,
   I myself become the wounded person,   845
My hurts turn livid upon me as I lean on a cane and observe.

I am the mash'd fireman with breast-bone broken,
Tumbling walls buried me in their debris,
Heat and smoke I inspired, I heard the yelling shouts of my
    comrades,
I heard the distant click of their picks and shovels,   850
They have clear'd the beams away, they tenderly lift me forth.

I lie in the night air in my red shirt, the pervading hush is for my
    sake,
Painless after all I lie exhausted but not so unhappy,
White and beautiful are the faces around me,
    the heads are bared of their fire-caps,
The kneeling crowd fades with the light of the torches.   855

Distant and dead resuscitate,
They show as the dial or move as the hands of me, I am the clock
    myself.

I am an old artillerist, I tell of my fort's bombardment,
I am there again.

Again the long roll of the drummers,   860
Again the attacking cannon, mortars,
Again to my listening ears the cannon responsive.

I take part, I see and hear the whole,
The cries, curses, roar, the plaudits for well-aim'd shots,
The ambulanza slowly passing trailing its red drip,   865
Workmen searching after damages, making indispensable repairs,
The fall of grenades through the rent roof, the fan-shaped
    explosion,
The whizz of limbs, heads, stone, wood, iron, high in the air.

Again gurgles the mouth of my dying general, he furiously waves
    with his hand,
He gasps through the clot, Mind not me—mind—the
    entrenchments.   870

34 Now I tell what I knew in Texas in my early youth,
(I tell not the fall of Alamo,[30]
Not one escaped to tell the fall of Alamo,
The hundred and fifty are dumb yet at Alamo,)
'Tis the tale of the murder in cold blood
    of four hundred and twelve young men.   875

Retreating they had form'd in a hollow square with their baggage
    for breastworks,
Nine hundred lives out of the surrounding enemies, nine times their
    number was the price they took in advance,
Their colonel was wounded and their ammunition gone,
They treated for an honorable capitulation, receiv'd writing and
    seal, gave up their arms and march'd back prisoners of war.

[30] A Franciscan mission in San Antonio,
Texas; the site of the massacre of Texans by
Mexican forces in 1836.

They were the glory of the race of rangers, 880
Matchless with horse, rifle, song, supper, courtship,
Large, turbulent, generous, handsome, proud, and affectionate,
Bearded, sunburnt, drest in the free costume of hunters,
Not a single one over thirty years of age.

The second First-day morning they were brought out in squads and
 massacred, it was beautiful early summer, 885
The work commenced about five o'clock and was over by eight.

None obey'd the command to kneel,
Some made a mad and helpless rush, some stood stark and straight,
A few fell at once, shot in the temple or heart, the living and dead
 lay together,
The maim'd and mangled dug in the dirt, the new-comers saw
 them there, 890
Some half-kill'd attempted to crawl away,
These were despatch'd with bayonets or batter'd with the blunts of
 muskets,
A youth not seventeen years old seiz'd his assassin till two more
 came to release him,
The three were all torn and cover'd with the boy's blood.

At eleven o'clock began the burning of the bodies; 895
That is the tale of the murder of the four hundred and twelve
 young men.

35 Would you hear of an old-time sea-fight?
Would you learn who won by the light of the moon and stars?
Last to the yarn, as my grandmother's father the sailor told it to
 me.[31]

Our foe was no skulk in his ship I tell you, (said he,) 900
His was the surly English pluck, and there is no tougher or truer,
 and never was, and never will be;
Along the lower'd eve he came horribly raking us.

We closed with him, the yards entangled, the cannon touch'd,
My captain lash'd fast with his own hands.

We had receiv'd some eighteen pound shots under the water, 905
On our lower-gun-deck two large pieces had burst at the first fire,
 killing all around and blowing up overhead.

[31] The yarn is of John Paul Jones (1747–1792), a Scottish-born American naval officer in the Revolutionary War whose ship, *Bonhomme Richard*, was triumphant over the British *Seraphs* in the sea fight of September 23, 1779.

Fighting at sun-down, fighting at dark,
Ten o'clock at night, the full moon well up, our leaks on the gain,
    and five feet of water reported,
The master-at-arms loosing the prisoners confined in the after-hold
    to give them a chance for themselves.

The transit to and from the magazine is now stopt by the sentinels,   910
They see so many strange faces they do not know whom to trust.

Our frigate takes fire,
The other asks if we demand quarter?
If our colors are struck and the fighting done?

Now I laugh content, for I hear the voice of my little captain,   915
We have not struck, he composedly cries, we have just begun
    our part of the fighting.

Only three guns are in use,
One is directed by the captain himself against the enemy's main-
    mast,
Two well serv'd with grape and canister silence his musketry
    and clear his decks.
The tops alone second the fire of this little battery, especially the
    main-top,   920
They hold out bravely during the whole of the action.

Not a moment's cease,
The leaks gain fast on the pumps, the fire eats toward the powder-
    magazine.

One of the pumps has been shot away, it is generally thought we
    are sinking.

Serene stands the little captain,   925
He is not hurried, his voice is neither high nor low,
His eyes give more light to us than our battle-lanterns.

Toward twelve there in the beams of the moon they surrender to
    us.

36 Stretch'd and still lies the midnight,
Two great hulls motionless on the breast of the darkness,   930
Our vessel riddled and slowly sinking, preparations to pass to the
    one we have conquer'd,
The captain on the quarter-deck coldly giving his orders
    through a countenance white as a sheet,
Near by the corpse of the child that serv'd in the cabin,
The dead face of an old salt with long white hair and carefully
    curl'd whiskers,

The flames spite of all that can be done flickering aloft and below,   935
The husky voices of the two or three officers yet fit for duty,
Formless stacks of bodies and bodies by themselves,
    dabs of flesh upon the masts and spars,
Cut of cordage, dangle of rigging, slight shock of the soothe of
    waves,
Black and impassive guns, litter of powder-parcels, strong scent,
A few large stars overhead, silent and mournful shining,   940
Delicate sniffs of sea-breeze, smells of sedgy grass and fields by the
    shore, death-messages given in charge to survivors,
The hiss of the surgeon's knife, the gnawing teeth of his saw,
Wheeze, cluck, swash of falling blood, short wild scream, and long,
    dull, tapering groan,
These so, these irretrievable.

37 You laggards there on guard! look to your arms!   945
In at the conquer'd doors they crowd! I am possess'd!
Embody all presences outlaw'd or suffering,
See myself in prison shaped like another man,
And feel the dull unintermitted pain.

For me the keepers of convicts shoulder their carbines and keep
    watch,   950
It is I let out in the morning and barr'd at night.

Not a mutineer walks handcuff'd to jail but I am handcuff'd to him
    and walk by his side,
(I am less jolly one there, and more the silent one with sweat on
    my twitching lips.)

Not a youngster is taken for larceny but I go up too, and am tried
    and sentenced.

Not a cholera patient lies at the last gasp but I also lie at the last
    gasp,   955
My face is ash-color'd, my sinews gnarl, away from me people
    retreat.

Askers embody themselves in me and I am embodied in them,
I project my hat, sit shame-faced, and beg.

38 Enough! enough! enough!
Somehow I have been stunn'd. Stand back!   960
Give me a little time beyond my cuff'd head, slumbers, dreams,
    gaping,
I discover myself on the verge of a usual mistake.

That I could forget the mockers and insults!
That I could forget the trickling tears and the blows
  of the bludgeons and hammers!
That I could look with a separate look on my own crucifixion
  and bloody crowning.   965

I remember now,
I resume the overstaid fraction,
The grave of rock multiplies what has been confided to it, or to
  any graves,
Corpses rise, gashes heal, fastenings roll from me.

I troop forth replenish'd with supreme power, one of an average
  unending procession,   970
Inland and sea-coast we go, and pass all boundary lines,
Our swift ordinances on their way over the whole earth,
The blossoms we wear in our hats the growth of thousands of
  years.

Eleves,[32] I salute you! come forward!
Continue your annotations, continue your questionings.   975

[39] The friendly and flowing savage, who is he?
Is he waiting for civilization, or past it and mastering it?

Is he some Southwesterner rais'd out-doors? is he Kanadian?
Is he from the Mississippi country? Iowa, Oregon, California?
The mountains? prairie-life, bush-life? or sailor from the sea?   980

Wherever he goes men and women accept and desire him,
They desire he should like them, touch them, speak to them, stay
  with them.

Behavior lawless as snow-flakes, words simple as grass,
  uncomb'd head, laughter, and naïvetè,
Slow-stepping feet, common features, common modes and
  emanations,
They descend in new forms from the tips of his fingers,   985
They are wafted with the odor of his body or breath,
  they fly out of the glance of his eyes.

[40] Flaunt of the sunshine I need not your bask—lie over!
You light surfaces only, I force surfaces and depths also.

Earth! you seem to look for something at my hands,
Say, old top-knot, what do you want?   990

[32] Students.

Man or woman, I might tell how I like you, but cannot,
And might tell what it is in me and what it is in you, but cannot,
And might tell that pining I have, that pulse of my nights and days.

Behold, I do not give lectures or a little charity,
When I give I give myself.   995

You there, impotent, loose in the knees,
Open your scarf'd chops till I blow grit within you,
Spread your palms and lift the flaps of your pockets,
I am not to be denied, I compel, I have stores plenty and to spare,
And any thing I have I bestow.   1000

I do not ask who you are, that is not important to me,
You can do nothing and be nothing but what I will infold you.

To cotton-field drudge or cleaner of privies I lean,
On his right cheek I put the family kiss,
And in my soul I swear I never will deny him.   1005

On women fit for conception I start bigger and nimbler babes,
(This day I am jetting the stuff of far more arrogant republics.)

To any one dying, thither I speed and twist the knob of the door,
Turn the bed-clothes toward the foot of the bed,
Let the physician and the priest go home.   1010

I seize the descending man and raise him with resistless will,
O despairer, here is my neck,
By God, you shall not go down! hang your whole weight upon me.

I dilate you with tremendous breath, I buoy you up,
Every room of the house do I fill with an arm'd force,   1015
Lovers of me, bafflers of graves.

Sleep—I and they keep guard all night,
Not doubt, not decease shall dare to lay finger upon you,
I have embraced you, and henceforth possess you to myself,
And when you rise in the morning you will find what I tell you is   1020
    so.

41 I am he bringing help for the sick as they pant on their backs,
And for strong upright men I bring yet more needed help.

I heard what was said of the universe,
Heard it and heard it of several thousand years;
It is middling well as far as it goes—but is that all?   1025

Magnifying and applying come I,
Outbidding at the start the old cautious hucksters,
Taking myself the exact dimensions of Jehovah,

Lithographing Kronos, Zeus his son, and Hercules his grandson,
Buying drafts of Osiris, Isis, Belus, Brahma, Buddha,   1030
In my portfolio placing Manito loose, Allah on a leaf, the crucifix
    engraved,
With Odin and the hideous-faced Mexitli[33] and every idol and
    image,
Taking them all for what they are worth and not a cent more,
Admitting they were alive and did the work of their days,
(They bore mites as for unfledg'd birds who have now to rise
    and fly and sing for themselves,)   1035
Accepting the rough deific sketches to fill out better in myself,
    bestowing them freely on each man and woman I see,
Discovering as much or more in a framer framing a house,
Putting higher claims for him there with his roll'd-up sleeves
    driving the mallet and chisel,
Not objecting to special revelations, considering a curl of smoke or
    a hair on the back of my hand just as curious as any revelation,
Lads ahold of fire-engines and hook-and-ladder ropes no less to me
    than the gods of the antique wars,   1040
Minding their voices peal through the crash of destruction,
Their brawny limbs passing safe over charr'd laths, their white
    foreheads whole and unhurt out of the flames;
By the mechanic's wife with her babe at her nipple interceding for
    every person born,
Three scythes at harvest whizzing in a row from three lusty angels
    with shirts bagg'd out at their waists,
The snag-tooth'd hostler with red hair redeeming sins past and to
    come,   1045
Selling all he possesses, traveling on foot to fee lawyers for his
    brother and sit by him while he is tried for forgery;
What was strewn in the amplest strewing the square rod about me,
    and not filling the square rod then,
The bull and the bug never worshipp'd half enough,
Dung and dirt more admirable than was dream'd,
The supernatural of no account, myself waiting my time
    to be one of the supremes,   1050
The day getting ready for me when I shall do as much good as the
    best, and be as prodigious;
By my life-lumps! becoming already a creator,
Putting myself here and now to the ambush'd womb of the
    shadows.

[33] The gods of many different faiths.

42   A call in the midst of the crowd,
     My own voice, orotund sweeping and final.   1055

Come my children,
Come my boys and girls, my women, household and intimates,
Now the performer launches his nerve,
     he has pass'd his prelude on the reeds within.

Easily written loose-finger'd chords—I feel the thrum of your
     climax and close.

My head slues[34] round on my neck,   1060
Music rolls, but not from the organ,
Folks are around me, but they are no household of mine.

Ever the hard unsunk ground,
Ever the eaters and drinkers, ever the upward and downward sun,
     ever the air and the ceaseless tides,
Ever myself and my neighbors, refreshing, wicked, real,   1065
Ever the old inexplicable query, ever that thorn'd thumb, that
     breath of itches and thirsts,
Ever the vexer's hoot! hoot! till we find where the sly one hides
     and bring him forth,
Ever love, ever the sobbing liquid of life,
Ever the bandage under the chin, ever the trestles of death.

Here and there with dimes on the eyes walking,   1070
To feed the greed of the belly the brains liberally spooning,
Tickets buying, taking, selling, but in to the feast never once going,
Many sweating, ploughing, thrashing, and then the chaff
     for payment receiving,
A few idly owning, and they the wheat continually claiming.

This is the city and I am one of the citizens,   1075
Whatever interests the rest interests me, politics, wars, markets,
     newspapers, schools,
The mayor and councils, banks, tariffs, steamships, factories, stocks,
     stores, real estate and personal estate.

The little plentiful manikins skipping around in collars and tail'd
     coats,
I am aware who they are, (they are positively not worms or fleas,)
I acknowledge the duplicates of myself, the weakest and shallowest
     is deathless with me,   1080
What I do and say the same waits for them,
Every thought that flounders in me the same flounders in them.

[34] Twists sideways.

I know perfectly well my own egotism,
Know my omnivorous lines and must not write any less,
And would fetch you whoever you are flush with myself.   1085

Not words of routine this song of mine,
But abruptly to question, to leap beyond yet nearer bring;
This printed and bound book—but the printer and the printing-
    office boy?
The well-taken photographs—but your wife or friend
    close and solid in your arms?
The black ship mail'd with iron, her mighty guns in her turrets—
    but the pluck of the captain and engineers?   1090
In the houses the dishes and fare and furniture—but the host and
    hostess, and the look out of their eyes?
The sky up there—yet here or next door, or across the way?
The saints and sages in history—but you yourself?
Sermons, creeds, theology—but the fathomless human brain,
And what is reason? and what is love? and what is life?   1095

43 I do not despise you priests, all time, the world over,
My faith is the greatest of faiths and the least of faiths,
Enclosing worship ancient and modern and all between ancient
    and modern,
Believing I shall come again upon the earth after five thousand
    years,
Waiting responses from oracles, honoring the gods, saluting the sun,   1100
Making a fetich[35] of the first rock or stump, powowing with sticks
    in the circle of obis,[36]
Helping the llama or brahmin as he trims the lamps of the idols,
Dancing yet through the streets in a phallic procession,
    rapt and austere in the woods a gymnosophist,[37]
Drinking mead from the skull-cup, to Shastas and Vedas admirant,
    minding the Koran,[38]
Walking the teokallis,[39] spotted with gore from the stone and knife,
    beating the serpent-skin drum,   1105
Accepting the Gospels, accepting him that was crucified,
    knowing assuredly that he is divine,

[35] A material object believed among primitive cultures to have magical powers.

[36] A form of religious belief, of African origin, involving witchcraft.

[37] One of an ancient sect of Hindu ancestors, as reported in classical antiquity.

[38] In the Hindu religion, Shastas are the lessons, Vedas the holy writings, and the Koran the sacred text, which contains the revelations made by Allah to Mohammed.

[39] Teocallis is a temple of ancient Mexico and Central America, built on a mound of truncated pyramidal shape. Whitman refers to the mound itself.

To the mass kneeling or the puritan's prayer rising, or sitting
    patiently in a pew,
Ranting and frothing in my insane crisis, or waiting dead-like
    till my spirit arouses me,
Looking forth on pavement and land, or outside of pavement and
    land,
Belonging to the winders of the circuit of circuits.   1110

One of that centripetal and centrifugal gang I turn and talk
    like a man leaving charges before a journey.

Down-hearted doubters dull and excluded,
Frivolous, sullen, moping, angry, affected, dishearten'd, atheistical,
I know every one of you, I know the sea of torment, doubt, despair
    and unbelief.

How the flukes splash!   1115
How they contort rapid as lightning, with spasms and spouts of
    blood!

Be at peace bloody flukes of doubters and sullen mopers,
I take my place among you as much as among any,
The past is the push of you, me, all, precisely the same,
And what is yet untried and afterward is for you, me, all, precisely
    the same.   1120

I do not know what is untried and afterward,
But I know it will in its turn prove sufficient, and cannot fail.

Each who passes is consider'd, each who stops is consider'd,
    not a single one can it fail.

It cannot fail the young man who died and was buried,
Nor the young woman who died and was put by his side,   1125
Nor the little child that peep'd in at the door, and then drew back
    and was never seen again,
Nor the old man who has lived without purpose,
    and feels it with bitterness worse than gall,
Nor him in the poor house tubercled by rum and the bad disorder,
Nor the numberless slaughter'd and wreck'd, nor the brutish
    koboo[40] call'd the ordure of humanity,
Nor the sacs merely floating with open mouths for food to slip in,   1130
Nor any thing in the earth, or down in the oldest graves of the
    earth,

[40] A native of Palembang on the east coast of
Sumatra.

Nor any thing in the myriads of spheres, nor the myriads of
    myriads that inhabit them,
Nor the present, nor the least wisp that is known.

44 It is time to explain myself—let us stand up.

What is known I strip away, 1135
I launch all men and women forward with me into the Unknown.

The clock indicates the moment—but what does eternity, indicate?

We have thus far exhausted trillions of winters and summers,
There are trillions ahead, and trillions ahead of them.

Births have brought us richness and variety, 1140
And other births will bring us richness and variety.

I do not call one greater and one smaller,
That which fills its period and place is equal to any.

Were mankind murderous or jealous upon you, my brother, my
    sister?
I am sorry for you, they are not murderous or jealous upon me, 1145
All has been gentle with me, I keep no account with lamentation,
(What have I to do with lamentation?)

I am an acme of things accomplish'd, and I an encloser of things to
    be.

My feet strike an apex of the apices of the stairs,
On every step bunches of ages, and larger bunches between the
    steps, 1150
All below duly travel'd, and still I mount and mount.

Rise after rise bow the phantoms behind me,
Afar down I see the huge first Nothing, I know I was even there,
I waited unseen and always, and slept through the lethargic mist,
And took my time, and took no hurt from the fetid carbon. 1155

Long I was hugg'd close—long and long.

Immense have been the preparations for me,
Faithful and friendly the arms that have help'd me.

Cycles ferried my cradle, rowing and rowing like cheerful
    boatmen,
For room to me stars kept aside in their own rings, 1160
They sent influences to look after what was to hold me.

Before I was born out of my mother generations guided me,
My embryo has never been torpid, nothing could overlay it.

For it the nebula cohered to an orb,
The long slow strata piled to rest it on,   1165
Vast vegetables gave it sustenance,
Monstrous sauroids[41] transported it in their mouths and deposited it
    with care.

All forces have been steadily employ'd to complete and delight me,
Now on this spot I stand with my robust soul.

45 O span of youth! ever-push'd elasticity!   1170
O manhood, balanced, florid and full.

My lovers suffocate me,
Crowding my lips, thick in the pores of my skin,
Jostling me through streets and public halls, coming naked to me at
    night,
Crying by day, Ahoy! from the rocks of the river,
    swinging and chirping over my head,   1175
Calling my name from flower-beds, vines, tangled underbrush,
Lighting on every moment of my life,
Bussing my body with soft balsamic busses,
Noiselessly passing handfuls out of their hearts and giving them to
    be mine.

Old age superbly rising! O welcome, ineffable grace of dying days!   1180

Every condition promulges not only itself,
    it promulges what grows after and out of itself,
And the dark hush promulges as much as any.

I open my scuttle at night and see the far-sprinkled systems,
And all I see, multiplied as high as I can cypher, edge but the rim
    of the farther systems.

Wider and wider they spread, expanding, always expanding,   1185
Outward and outward and forever outward.

My sun has his sun and round him obediently wheels,
He joins with his partners a group of superior circuit,
And greater sets follow, making specks of the greatest inside them.

There is no stoppage and never can be stoppage,   1190
If I, you, and the words, and all beneath or upon their surfaces,
    were this moment reduced back to a pallid float,
    it would not avail in the long run,
We should surely bring up again where we now stand,
And surely go as much farther, and then farther and farther.

41 Lizards.

A few quadrillions of eras, a few octillions of cubic leagues,
  do not hazard the span or make it impatient,
They are but parts, anything is but a part. 1195

See ever so far, there is limitless space outside of that,
Count ever so much, there is limitless time around that.

My rendezvous is appointed, it is certain,
The Lord will be there and wait till I come on perfect terms,
The great Camerado, the lover true for whom I pine will be there. 1200

46 I know I have the best of time and space, and was never measured
  and never will be measured.

I tramp a perpetual journey, (come listen all!)
My signs are a rain-proof coat, good shoes, and a staff cut from the
  woods,
No friend of mine takes his ease in my chair,
I have no chair, no church, no philosophy, 1205
I lead no man to a dinner-table, library, exchange,
B ıt each man and each woman of you I lead upon a knoll,
My left hand hooking you round the waist,
My right hand pointing to landscapes of continents and the public
  road.

Not I, not any one else can travel that road for you, 1210
You must travel it for yourself.

It is not far, it is within reach,
Perhaps you have been on it since you were born and did not
  know,
Perhaps it is everywhere on water and on land.

Shoulder your duds dear son, and I will mine, and let us hasten
  forth, 1215
Wonderful cities and free nations we shall fetch as we go.

If you tire, give me both burdens, and rest the chuff of your hand
  on my hip,
And in due time you shall repay the same service to me,
For after we start we never lie by again.

This day before dawn I ascended a hill and look'd at the crowded
  heaven, 1220
And I said to my spirit, When we become the enfolders of those
  orbs, and the pleasure and knowledge of every thing in them,
  shall we be fill'd and satisfied then?
And my spirit said, No, we but level that lift to pass and continue
  beyond.

You are also asking me questions and I hear you,
I answer that I cannot answer, you must find out for yourself.

Sit a while dear son, 1225
Here are biscuits to eat and here is milk to drink,
But as soon as you sleep and renew yourself in sweet clothes, I kiss
    you with a good-by kiss and open the gate for your egress hence.

Long enough have you dream'd contemptible dreams,
Now I wash the gum from your eyes,
You must habit yourself to the dazzle of the light and of every
    moment of your life. 1230

Long have you timidly waded holding a plank by the shore,
Now I will you to be a bold swimmer,
To jump off in the midst of the sea, rise again, nod to me, shout,
    and laughingly dash with your hair.

47 I am the teacher of athletes,
He that by me spreads a wider breast than my own proves the
    width of my own, 1235
He most honors my style who learns under it to destroy the
    teacher.

The boy I love, the same becomes a man not through derived
    power, but in his own right,
Wicked rather than virtuous out of conformity or fear,
Fond of his sweetheart, relishing well his steak,
Unrequited love or a slight cutting him worse than sharp steel cuts, 1240
First-rate to ride, to fight, to hit the bull's eye, to sail a skiff,
    to sing a song or play on the banjo,
Preferring scars and the beard and faces pitted with small-pox
    over all latherers,
And those well-tann'd to those that keep out of the sun.

I teach straying from me, yet who can stray from me?
I follow you whoever you are from the present hour, 1245
My words itch at your ears till you understand them.

I do not say these things for a dollar or to fill up the time
    while I wait for a boat,
(It is you talking just as much as myself, I act as the tongue of you,
Tied in your mouth, in mine it begins to be loosen'd.)

I swear I will never again mention love or death inside a house, 1250
And I swear I will never translate myself at all, only to him or her
    who privately stays with me in the open air.

If you would understand me go to the heights or water-shore,
The nearest gnat is an explanation, and a drop or motion of waves
    a key,
The maul, the oar, the hand-saw, second my words.

No shutter'd room or school can commune with me,   1255
But roughs and little children better than they.

The young mechanic is closest to me, he knows me well,
The woodman that takes his axe and jug with him shall take me
    with him all day,
The farm-boy ploughing in the field feels good at the sound of my
    voice,
In vessels that sail my words sail, I go with fishermen and seamen
    and love them.   1260

The soldier camp'd or upon the march is mine,
On the night ere the pending battle many seek me, and I do not
    fail them,
On that solemn night (it may be their last) those that know me seek
    me.

My face rubs to the hunter's face when he lies down alone in his
    blanket,
The driver thinking of me does not mind the jolt of his wagon,   1265
The younger mother and old mother comprehend me,
The girl and the wife rest the needle a moment and forget where
    they are,
They and all would resume what I have told them.

48 I have said that the soul is not more than the body,
    And I have said that the body is not more than the soul,   1270
    And nothing, not God, is greater to one than one's self is,
    And whoever walks a furlong[42] without sympathy walks to his own
        funeral drest in his shroud,
    And I or you pocketless of a dime may purchase the pick of the
        earth,
    And to glance with an eye or show a bean in its pod
        confounds the learning of all times,
    And there is no trade or employment but the young man following
        it may become a hero,   1275
    And there is no object so soft but it makes a hub for the wheel'd
        universe,
    And I say to any man or woman, Let your soul stand cool and
        composed before a million universes.

[42] ⅛th of a mile or 220 yards.

And I say to mankind, Be not curious about God,
For I who am curious about each am not curious about God,
(No array of terms can say how much I am at peace about God
    and about death.)   1280

I hear and behold God in every object, yet understand God not in
    the least,
Nor do I understand who there can be more wonderful than
    myself.

Why should I wish to see God better than this day?

I see something of God each hour of the twenty-four,
    and each moment then,
In the faces of men and women I see God, and in my own face
    in the glass,   1285
I find letters from God dropt in the street, and every one is sign'd
    by God's name,
And I leave them where they are, for I know that wheresoe'er I
    go,
Others will punctually come for ever and ever.

49 And as to you Death, and you bitter hug of mortality,
    it is idle to try to alarm me.

To his work without flinching the accoucheur[43] comes,   1290
I see the elder-hand pressing, receiving, supporting,
I recline by the sills of the exquisite flexible doors,
And mark the outlet, and mark the relief and escape.

And as to you Corpse I think you are good manure,
    but that does not offend me,
I smell the white roses sweet-scented and growing,   1295
I reach to the leafy lips, I reach to the polish'd breasts of melons.

And as to you Life I reckon you are the leavings of many deaths,
(No doubt I have died myself ten thousand times before.)

I hear you whispering there O stars of heaven,
O suns—O grass of graves—O perpetual transfers and promotions,   1300
If you do not say any thing how can I say any thing?

Of the turbid pool that lies in the autumn forest,
Of the moon that descends the steeps of the soughing twilight,
Toss, sparkles of day and dusk—toss on the black stems that decay
    in the muck,
Toss to the moaning gibberish of the dry limbs.   1305

---

[43] The midwife.

I ascend from the moon, I ascend from the night,
I perceive that the ghastly glimmer is noonday sunbeams reflected,
And debouch[44] to the steady and central from the offspring great or
small.

50 There is that in me—I do not know what it is—but I know it is in
me.

Wrench'd and sweaty—calm and cool then my body becomes,   1310
I sleep—I sleep long.

I do not know it—it is without name—it is a word unsaid,
It is not in any dictionary, utterance, symbol.

Something it swings on more than the earth I swing on,
To it the creation is the friend whose embracing awakes me.   1315

Perhaps I might tell more. Outlines! I plead for my brothers and
sisters.

Do you see O my brothers and sisters?
It is not chaos or death—it is form, union, plan—it is eternal life—
it is Happiness.

51 The past and present wilt—I have fill'd them, emptied them,
And proceed to fill my next fold of the future.   1320

Listener up there! what have you to confide to me?
Look in my face while I snuff the sidle of evening,
(Talk honestly, no one else hears you, and I stay only a minute
longer.)

Do I contradict myself?
Very well then I contradict myself,   1325
(I am large, I contain multitudes.)

I concentrate toward them that are nigh, I wait on the door-slab.

Who has done his day's work? who will soonest be through
with his supper?
Who wishes to walk with me?

Will you speak before I am gone? will you prove already too late?   1330

52 The spotted hawk swoops by and accuses me, he complains of my
gab and my loitering.

I too am not a bit tamed, I too am untranslatable,
I sound my barbaric yawp over the roofs of the world.

[44] To come out.

The last scud of day holds back for me,
It flings my likeness after the rest and true as any on the shadow'd
    wilds,   1335
It coaxes me to the vapor and the dusk.

I depart as air, I shake my white locks at the runaway sun,
I effuse[45] my flesh in eddies, and drift it in lacy jags.

I bequeath myself to the dirt to grow from the grass I love,
If you want me again look for me under your boot-soles.   1340

You will hardly know who I am or what I mean,
But I shall be good health to you nevertheless,
And filter and fibre your blood.

Failing to fetch me at first keep encouraged,
Missing me one place search another,   1345
I stop somewhere waiting for you.

          1855

[45] To spread out or exude.

The Sleepers[1]

[1] I wander all night in my vision,
    Stepping with light feet, swiftly and noiselessly stepping and
        stopping,
    Bending with open eyes over the shut eyes of sleepers,
    Wandering and confused, lost to myself, ill-assorted, contradictory,
    Pausing, gazing, bending, and stopping.   5

    How solemn they look there, stretch'd and still,
    How quiet they breathe, the little children in their cradles.

    The wretched features of ennuyés,[2] the white features of corpses,
        the livid faces of drunkards, the sick-gray faces of onanists,[3]
    The gash'd bodies on battle-fields, the insane in their strong-door'd
        rooms, the sacred idiots, the new-born emerging from gates, and
        the dying emerging from gates,
    The night pervades them and infolds them.   10

[1] This poem is Whitman's attempt to project himself as a spirit among the sleepers of all lands and is one of the few surrealist verses of the nineteenth century. The poem was called "Night Poem" in 1856, "Sleep-Chasings" in 1860 and 1867, and "The Sleepers" since 1871.

[2] Bored ones.

[3] Male masturbators.

The married couple sleep calmly in their bed, he with his palm on
    the hip of the wife, and she with her palm on the hip of the
    husband.

The sisters sleep lovingly side by side in their bed,
The men sleep lovingly side by side in theirs,
And the mother sleeps with her little child carefully wrapt.

The blind sleep, and the deaf and dumb sleep,   15
The prisoner sleeps well in the prison, the runaway son sleeps,
The murderer that is to be hung next day, how does he sleep?
And the murder'd person, how does he sleep?

The female that loves unrequited sleeps,
And the male that loves unrequited sleeps,   20
The head of the money-maker that plotted all day sleeps,
And the enraged and treacherous dispositions, all, all sleep.

I stand in the dark with drooping eyes by the worst-suffering
    and the most restless,
I pass my hands soothingly to and fro a few inches from them,
The restless sink in their beds, they fitfully sleep.   25

Now I pierce the darkness, new beings appear,
The earth recedes from me into the night,
I saw that it was beautiful, and I see that what is not the earth is
    beautiful.

I go from bedside to bedside, I sleep close with the other sleepers
    each in turn,
I dream in my dream all the dreams of the other dreamers,   30
And I become the other dreamers.

I am a dance—play up there! the fit is whirling me fast!

I am the ever-laughing—it is new moon and twilight,
I see the hiding of douceurs,[4] I see nimble ghosts whichever way I
    look,
Cache and cache[5] again deep in the ground and sea,
    and where it is neither ground nor sea.   35

Well do they do their jobs those journeymen divine,
Only from me can they hide nothing, and would not if they could,
I reckon I am their boss and they make me a pet besides,
And surround me and lead me and run ahead when I walk,
To lift their cunning covers to signify me with stretch'd arms,
    and resume the way;   40
Onward we move, a gay gang of blackguards! with mirth-shouting
    music and wild-flapping pennants of joy!

[4] Sweetnesses.   [5] Hide.

I am the actor, the actress, the voter, the politician,
The emigrant and the exile, the criminal that stood in the box,
He who has been famous and he who shall be famous after to-day,
The stammerer, the well-form'd person, the wasted or feeble
    person.   45

I am she who adorn'd herself and folded her hair expectantly,
My truant lover has come, and it is dark.

Double yourself and receive me darkness,
Receive me and my lover too, he will not let me go without him.

I roll myself upon you as upon a bed, I resign myself to the dusk.   50

He whom I call answers me and takes the place of my lover,
He rises with me silently from the bed.

Darkness, you are gentler than my lover, his flesh was sweaty and
    panting,
I feel the hot moisture yet that he left me.

My hands are spread forth, I pass them in all directions,   55
I would sound up the shadowy shore to which you are journeying.

Be careful darkness! already what was it touch'd me?
I thought my lover had gone, else darkness and he are one,
I hear the heart-beat, I follow, I fade away.

2 I descend my western course, my sinews are flaccid,   60
Perfume and youth course through me and I am their wake.

It is my face yellow and wrinkled instead of the old woman's,
I sit low in a straw-bottom chair and carefully darn my grandson's
    stockings.

It is I too, the sleepless widow looking out on the winter midnight,
I see the sparkles of starshine on the icy and pallid earth.   65

A shroud I see and I am the shroud, I wrap a body and lie in the
    coffin,
It is dark here under ground, it is not evil or pain here,
    it is blank here, for reasons.

(It seems to me that every thing in the light and air ought to be
    happy,
Whoever is not in his coffin and the dark grave
    let him know he has enough.)

3 I see a beautiful gigantic swimmer swimming naked
    through the eddies of the sea,   70
His brown hair lies close and even to his head, he strikes out with
    courageous arms, he urges himself with his legs,

I see his white body, I see his undaunted eyes,
I hate the swift-running eddies that would dash him
head-foremost on the rocks.

What are you doing you ruffianly red-trickled waves?
Will you kill the courageous giant?
will you kill him in the prime of his middle age? 75

Steady and long he struggles,
He is baffled, bang'd, bruis'd, he holds out while his strength holds
out,
The slapping eddies are spotted with his blood, they bear him away,
they roll him, swing him, turn him,
His beautiful body is borne in the circling eddies,
it is continually bruis'd on rocks,
Swiftly and out of sight is borne the brave corpse. 80

4 I turn but do not extricate myself,
Confused, a past-reading, another, but with darkness yet.

The beach is cut by the razory ice-wind, the wreck-guns sound,
The tempest lulls, the moon comes floundering through the drifts.

I look where the ship helplessly heads end on, I hear the burst as
she strikes, I hear the howls of dismay, they grow fainter and
fainter. 85

I cannot aid with my wringing fingers,
I can but rush to the surf and let it drench me and freeze upon me.

I search with the crowd, not one of the company is wash'd to us
alive,
In the morning I help pick up the dead and lay them in rows in a
barn.

5 Now of the older war-days, the defeat at Brooklyn,[6] 90
Washington stands inside the lines, he stands on the intrench'd hills
amid a crowd of officers,
His face is cold and damp, he cannot repress the weeping drops,
He lifts the glass perpetually to his eyes, the color is blanch'd from
his cheeks,
He sees the slaughter of the southern braves confided to him by
their parents.

The same at last and at last when peace is declared, 95
He stands in the room of the old tavern,
the well-belov'd soldiers all pass through,

[6] The battle of Brooklyn Heights, August 27,
1776.

The officers speechless and slow draw near in their turns,
The chief encircles their necks with his arm
   and kisses them on the cheek,
He kisses lightly the wet cheeks one after another,
   he shakes hands and bids good-by to the army.

6 Now what my mother told me one day as we sat at dinner together,   100
  Of when she was a nearly grown girl living home with her parents
     on the old homestead.

A red squaw came one breakfast-time to the old homestead,
On her back she carried a bundle of rushes for rush-bottoming
   chairs,
Her hair, straight, shiny, coarse, black, profuse, half-envelop'd her
   face,
Her step was free and elastic, and her voice sounded exquisitely as
   she spoke.   105

My mother look'd in delight and amazement at the stranger,
She look'd at the freshness of her tall-borne face
   and full and pliant limbs,
The more she look'd upon her she loved her,
Never before had she seen such wonderful beauty and purity,
She made her sit on a bench by the jamb of the fireplace,
   she cook'd food for her,   110
She had no work to give her, but she gave her remembrance and
   fondness.

The red squaw staid all the forenoon,
   and toward the middle of the afternoon she went away,
O my mother was loth to have her go away,
All the week she thought of her, she watch'd for her many a month,
She remember'd her many a winter and many a summer,   115
But the red squaw never came nor was heard of there again.

7 A show of the summer softness—a contact of something unseen—an
   amour of the light and air,
I am jealous and overwhelm'd with friendliness,
And will go gallivant with the light and air myself.

O love and summer, you are in the dreams and in me,   120
Autumn and winter are in the dreams, the farmer goes with his
   thrift,
The droves and crops increase, the barns are well-fill'd.

Elements merge in the night, ships make tacks in the dreams,
The sailor sails, the exile returns home,
The fugitive returns unharm'd, the immigrant is back beyond
   months and years,   125

The poor Irishman lives in the simple house of his childhood
   with the well-known neighbors and faces,
They warmly welcome him, he is barefoot again, he forgets he is
   well off,
The Dutchman voyages home, and the Scotchman and Welshman
   voyage home, and the native of the Mediterranean voyages
   home,
To every port of England, France, Spain, enter well-fill'd ships,
The Swiss foots it toward his hills, the Prussian goes his way,
   the Hungarian his way, and the Pole his way,   130
The Swede returns, and the Dane and Norwegian return.

The homeward bound and the outward bound,
The beautiful lost swimmer, the ennuyé, the onanist,
   the female that loves unrequited, the money-maker,
The actor and actress, those through with their parts
   and those waiting to commence,
The affectionate boy, the husband and wife, the voter,
   the nominee that is chosen and the nominee that has fail'd,   135
The great already known and the great any time after to-day,
The stammerer, the sick, the perfect-form'd, the homely,
The criminal that stood in the box, the judge that sat and sentenced
   him, the fluent lawyers, the jury, the audience,
The laugher and weeper, the dancer, the midnight widow, the red
   squaw,
The consumptive, the erysipalite,[7] the idiot, he that is wrong'd,   140
The antipodes, and every one between this and them in the dark,
I swear they are averaged now—one is no better than the other,
The night and sleep have liken'd them and restored them.

I swear they are all beautiful,
Every one that sleeps is beautiful, every thing in the dim light is
   beautiful,   145
The wildest and bloodiest is over, and all is peace.

Peace is always beautiful,
The myth of heaven indicates peace and night.

The myth of heaven indicates the soul,
The soul is always beautiful, it appears more or it appears less,
   it comes or it lags behind,   150
It comes from its embower'd garden and looks pleasantly on itself
   and encloses the world,

[7] One who has an acute disease of the skin,
commonly called "St. Anthony's fire."

Perfect and clean the genitals previously jetting,
    and perfect and clean the womb cohering,
The head well-grown proportion'd and plumb,
    and the bowels and joints proportion'd and plumb.

The soul is always beautiful,
The universe is duly in order, every thing is in its place,   155
What has arrived is in place and what waits shall be in its place,
The twisted skull waits, the watery or rotten blood waits,
The child of the glutton or venerealee waits long, and the child
    of the drunkard waits long, and the drunkard himself waits long,
The sleepers that lived and died wait, the far advanced are to go on
    in their turns, and the far behind are to come on in their turns,
The diverse shall be no less diverse, but they shall flow and unite—
    they unite now.   160

8 The sleepers are very beautiful as they lie unclothed,
  They flow hand in hand over the whole earth from east to west
    as they lie unclothed,
  The Asiatic and African are hand in hand,
    the European and American are hand in hand,
  Learn'd and unlearn'd are hand in hand, and male and female are
    hand in hand,
  The bare arm of the girl crosses the bare breast of her lover,
    they press close without lust, his lips press her neck,   165
  The father holds his grown or ungrown son in his arms with
    measureless love, and the son holds the father in his arms with
    measureless love,
  The white hair of the mother shines on the white wrist of the
    daughter,
  The breath of the boy goes with the breath of the man, friend is
    inarm'd by friend,
  The scholar kisses the teacher and the teacher kisses the scholar,
    the wrong'd is made right,
  The call of the slave is one with the master's call, and the master
    salutes the slave,   170
  The felon steps forth from the prison, the insane becomes sane,
    the suffering of sick persons is reliev'd,
  The sweatings and fevers stop, the throat that was unsound is
    sound, the lungs of the consumptive are resumed, the poor
    distress'd head is free,
  The joints of the rheumatic move as smoothly as ever, and smoother
    than ever,
  Stiflings and passages open, the paralyzed become supple,

The swell'd and convuls'd and congested awake to themselves in
   condition,   175
They pass the invigoration of the night
   and the chemistry of the night, and awake.

I too pass from the night,
I stay a while away O night, but I return to you again and love you.

Why should I be afraid to trust myself to you?
I am not afraid, I have been well brought forward by you,   180
I love the rich running day, but I do not desert her in whom I lay
   so long,
I know not how I came of you and I know not where I go with
   you, but I know I came well and shall go well.

I will stop only a time with the night, and rise betimes,
I will duly pass the day O my mother, and duly return to you.

                           1855

Scented Herbage of My Breast[1]

Scented herbage of my breast,
Leaves from you I glean, I write, to be perused best afterwards,
Tomb-leaves, body-leaves growing up above me above death,
Perennial roots, tall leaves, O the winter shall not freeze you delicate
   leaves,
Every year shall you bloom again, out from where you retired
   you shall emerge again;   5
O I do not know whether many passing by will discover you
   or inhale your faint odor, but I believe a few will;
O slender leaves! O blossoms of my blood! I permit you to tell
   in your own way of the heart that is under you,
O I do not know what you mean there underneath yourselves,
   you are not happiness,
You are often more bitter than I can bear, you burn and sting me,
Yet you are beautiful to me you faint tinged roots, you make me think
   of death,   10
Death is beautiful from you, (what indeed is finally beautiful
   except death and love?)

[1] The poem is the second in the volume
called *Calamus*, poems of manly attachment.

SCENTED HERBAGE OF MY BREAST

O I think it is not for life I am chanting here my chant of lovers,
  I think it must be for death,
For how calm, how solemn it grows to ascend to the atmosphere of
  lovers,
Death or life I am then indifferent, my soul declines to prefer,
(I am not sure but the high soul of lovers welcomes death most,)   15
Indeed O death, I think now these leaves mean precisely the same as
  you mean,
Grow up taller sweet leaves that I may see! grow up out of my
  breast!
Spring away from the conceal'd heart there!
Do not fold yourself so in your pink-tinged roots timid leaves!
Do not remain down there so ashamed, herbage of my breast!   20
Come I am determin'd to unbare this broad breast of mine, I have
  long enough stifled and choked;
Emblematic and capricious blades I leave you, now you serve me not,
I will say what I have to say by itself,
I will sound myself and comrades only, I will never again utter a call
  only their call,
I will raise with it immortal reverberations through the States,   25
I will give an example to lovers to take permanent shape and will
  through the States,

Through me shall the words be said to make death exhilarating,
Give me your tone therefore O death, that I may accord with it,
Give me yourself, for I see that you belong to me now above all, and
  are folded inseparably together, you love and death are,
Nor will I allow you to balk me any more with what I was calling
  life,   30
For now it is convey'd to me that you are the purports[2] essential,
That you hide in these shifting forms of life, for reasons, and that they
  are mainly for you,
That you beyond them come forth to remain, the real reality,
That behind the mask of materials you patiently wait, no matter how
  long,   35
That you will one day perhaps take control of all,
That you will perhaps dissipate this entire show of appearance,
That may-be you are what it is all for, but it does not last so very
  long,
But you will last very long.

                            1860

---

[2] The apparent meanings.

Whoever You Are Holding Me Now in Hand

Whoever you are holding me now in hand,
Without one thing all will be useless,
I give you fair warning before you attempt me further,
I am not what you supposed, but far different.

Who is he that would become my follower? 5
Who would sign himself a candidate for my affections?

The way is suspicious, the result uncertain, perhaps destructive,
You would have to give up all else, I alone would expect to be your
    sole and exclusive standard,
Your novitiate[1] would even then be long and exhausting,
The whole past theory of your life and all conformity to the lives
    around you would have to be abandon'd, 10
Therefore release me now before troubling yourself any further, let
    go your hand from my shoulders,
Put me down and depart on your way.

Or else by stealth in some wood for trial,
Or back of a rock in the open air,
(For in any roof'd room of a house I emerge not, nor in company, 15
And in libraries I lie as one dumb, a gawk, or unborn, or dead,)
But just possibly with you on a high hill, first watching lest any person
    for miles around approach unawares,

Or possibly with you sailing at sea, or on the beach of the sea or some
    quiet island,
Here to put your lips upon mine I permit you,
With the comrade's long-dwelling kiss or the new husband's kiss, 20
For I am the new husband and I am the comrade.

Or if you will, thrusting me beneath your clothing,
Where I may feel the throbs of your heart or rest upon your hip,
Carry me when you go forth over land or sea;
For thus merely touching you is enough, is best, 25
And thus touching you would I silently sleep and be carried eternally.

But these leaves conning you con at peril,
For these leaves and me you will not understand,
They will elude you at first and still more afterward, I will certainly
    elude you,

---

[1] A beginner.

Even while you should think you had unquestionably caught me,
    behold! 30
Already you see I have escaped from you.

For is it not for what I have put into it that I have written this book,
Nor is it by reading it you will acquire it,
Nor do those know me best who admire me and vauntingly praise
    me,
Nor will the candidates for my love (unless at most a very few) prove
    victorious, 35
Nor will my poems do good only, they will do just as much evil,
    perhaps more,
For all is useless without that which you may guess at many times and
    not hit, that which I hinted at;
Therefore release me and depart on your way.

1860

I Saw in Louisiana a Live-Oak Growing

I saw in Louisiana a live-oak growing,
All alone stood it and the moss hung down from the branches,
Without any companion it grew there uttering joyous leaves of dark
    green,
And its look, rude, unbending, lusty, made me think of myself,
But I wonder'd how it could utter joyous leaves standing alone there
    without its friend near, for I knew I could not, 5
And I broke off a twig with a certain number of leaves upon it, and
    twined around it a little moss,
And brought it away, and I have placed it in sight in my room,
It is not needed to remind me as of my own dear friends,
(For I believe lately I think of little else than of them,)
Yet it remains to me a curious token, it makes me think of manly
    love; 10
For all that, and though the live-oak glistens there in Louisiana
    solitary in a wide flat space,
Uttering joyous leaves all its life without a friend a lover near,
I know very well I could not.

1860

Out of the Cradle Endlessly Rocking[1]

Out of the cradle endlessly rocking,
Out of the mocking-bird's throat, the musical shuttle,
Out of the Ninth-month[2] midnight,
Over the sterile sands and the fields beyond, where the child leaving
  his bed wander'd alone, bareheaded, barefoot,
Down from the shower'd halo,   5
Up from the mystic play of shadows twining and twisting as if they
  were alive,
Out from the patches of briers and blackberries,
From the memories of the bird that chanted to me,
From your memories sad brother, from the fitful risings and fallings I
  heard,
From under that yellow half-moon late-risen and swollen as I with
  tears,   10
From those beginning notes of yearning[3] and love there in the mist,
From the thousand responses of my heart never to cease,
From the myriad thence-arous'd words,
From the word stronger and more delicious than any,
From such as now they start the scene revisiting,   15
As a flock, twittering, rising, or overhead passing,
Borne hither, are all eludes me, hurriedly,
A man, yet by these tears a little boy again,
Throwing myself on the sand, confronting the waves,
I, chanter of pains and joys, uniter of here and hereafter,   20
Taking all hints to use them, but swiftly leaping beyond them,
A reminiscence sing.

Once Paumanok,[4]
When the lilac-scent was in the air and Fifth-month[5] grass was
  growing,
Up this seashore in some briers,   25
Two feather'd guests from Alabama, two together,
And their nest, and four light-green eggs spotted with brown,
And every day the he-bird to and fro near at hand,
And every day the she-bird crouch'd on her nest, silent, with bright
  eyes,

[1] The poem revisits Whitman's childhood in Long Island. The setting moves Whitman to write about the search for the origins of the poet's song and of the origins of poetry itself. It first appeared as "A Child's Reminiscence" on December 24, 1859 in the New York *Saturday Press*.

[2] The Quaker term for September.
[3] Sickness.
[4] The Indian term for Long Island.
[5] The Quaker term for May.

And every day I, a curious boy, never too close, never disturbing
   them,   30
Cautiously peering, absorbing, translating.

Shine! shine! shine!
Pour down your warmth, great sun!
While we bask, we two together.

Two together!   35
Winds blow south, or winds blow north,
Day come white, or night come black,
Home, or rivers and mountains from home,
Singing all time, minding no time,
While we two keep together.   40

Till of a sudden,
May-be kill'd, unknown to her mate,
One forenoon the she-bird crouch'd not on the nest,
Nor return'd that afternoon, nor the next,
Nor ever appear'd again.   45

And thenceforward all summer in the sound of the sea,
And at night under the full of the moon in calmer weather,
Over the hoarse surging of the sea,
Or flitting from brier to brier by day,
I saw, I heard at intervals the remaining one, the he-bird,   50
The solitary guest from Alabama.

Blow! blow! blow!
Blow up sea-winds along Paumanok's shore;
I wait and I wait till you blow my mate to me.

Yes, when the stars glisten'd,   55
All night long on the prong of a moss-scallop'd stake,
Down almost amid the slapping waves,
Sat the lone singer wonderful causing tears.

He call'd on his mate,
He pour'd forth the meanings which I of all men know.   60

Yes my brother I know,
The rest might not, but I have treasur'd every note,
For more than once dimly down to the beach gliding,
Silent, avoiding the moonbeams, blending myself with the shadows,
Recalling now the obscure shapes, the echoes, the sounds and sights
   after their sorts,   65
The white arms out in the breakers tirelessly tossing,
I, with bare feet, a child, the wind wafting my hair,
Listen'd long and long.

Listen'd to keep, to sing, now translating the notes,
Following you my brother.   70

Soothe! soothe! soothe!
Close on its wave soothes the wave behind,
And again another behind embracing and lapping, every one close,
But my love soothes not me, not me.

Low hangs the moon, it rose late,   75
It is lagging—O I think it is heavy with love, with love.

O madly the sea pushes upon the land,
With love, with love.

O night! do I not see my love fluttering out among the breakers?
What is that little black thing I see there in the white?   80

Loud! loud! loud!
Loud I call to you, my love!
High and clear I shoot my voice over the waves,
Surely you must know who is here, is here,
You must know who I am, my love.   85

Low-hanging moon!
What is that dusky spot in your brown yellow?
O it is the shape, the shape of my mate!
O moon do not keep her from me any longer.

Land! land! O land!   90
Whichever way I turn, O I think you could give me my mate back
     again if you only would,
For I am almost sure I see her dimly whichever way I look.

O rising stars!
Perhaps the one I want so much will rise, will rise with some of you.

O throat! O trembling throat!   95
Sound clearer through the atmosphere!
Pierce the woods, the earth,
Somewhere listening to catch you must be the one I want.

Shake our carols!
Solitary here, the night's carols!   100
Carols of lonesome love! death's carols!
Carols under that lagging, yellow, waning moon!
O under that moon where she droops almost down into the sea!
O reckless despairing carols.

But soft! sink low!   105
Soft! let me just murmur,
And do you wait a moment you husky-nois'd sea,
For somewhere I believe I heard my mate responding to me,
So faint, I must be still, be still to listen,
But not altogether still, for then she might not come immediately to
    me.   110

Hither my love!
Here I am! here!
With this just-sustain'd note I announce myself to you,
This gentle call is for you my love, for you.

Do not be decoy'd elsewhere,   115
That is the whistle of the wind, it is not my voice,
That is the fluttering, the fluttering of the spray,
Those are the shadows of leaves.

O darkness! O in vain!
O I am very sick and sorrowful.   120

O brown halo in the sky near the moon, drooping upon the sea!
O troubled reflection in the sea!
O throat! O throbbing heart!
And I singing uselessly, uselessly all the night.

O past! O happy life! O songs of joy!   125
In the air, in the woods, over fields,
Loved! loved! loved! loved! loved!
But my mate no more, no more with me!
We two together no more.

The aria sinking,   130
All else continuing, the stars shining,
The winds blowing, the notes of the bird continuous echoing,
With angry moans the fierce old mother incessantly moaning,
On the sands of Paumanok's shore gray and rustling,
The yellow half-moon enlarged, sagging down, drooping, the face of
    the sea almost touching,   135
The boy ecstatic, with his bare feet the waves, with his hair the
    atmosphere dallying,
The love in the heart long pent, now loose, now at last tumultuously
    bursting,
The aria's meaning, the ears, the soul, swiftly depositing,
The strange tears down the cheeks coursing,
The colloquy there, the trio, each uttering,   140

The undertone, the savage old mother incessantly crying,
To the boy's soul's questions sullenly timing, some drown'd secret
   hissing,
To the outsetting bard.

Demon or bird! (said the boy's soul,)
Is it indeed toward your mate you sing? or is it really to me?   145
For I, that was a child, my tongue's use sleeping, now I have heard
   you,
Now in a moment I know what I am for, I awake,
And already a thousand singers, a thousand songs, dearer, louder and
   more sorrowful than yours,
A thousand warbling echoes have started to life within me, never to
   die.

O you singer solitary, singing by yourself, projecting me,   150
O solitary me listening, never more shall I cease perpetuating you,
Never more shall I escape, never more the reverberations,
Never more the cries of unsatisfied love be absent from me,
Never again leave me to be the peaceful child I was before what
   there in the night,
By the sea under the yellow and sagging moon,   155
The messenger there arous'd, the fire, the sweet hell within,
The unknown want, the destiny of me.

O give me the clue! (it lurks in the night here somewhere,)
O if I am to have so much, let me have more!

A word then, (for I will conquer it,)   160
The word final, superior to all,
Subtle, sent up—what is it?—I listen;
Are you whispering it, and have been all the time, you sea-waves?
Is that it from your liquid rims and wet sands?

Whereto answering, the sea,   165
Delaying not, hurrying not,
Whisper'd me through the night, and very plainly before daybreak,
Lisp'd to me the low and delicious word death,
And again death, death, death, death,
Hissing melodious, neither like the bird nor like my arous'd child's
   heart,   170
But edging near as privately for me rustling at my feet,
Creeping thence steadily up to my ears and laving me softly all over,
Death, death, death, death, death.

Which I do not forget,
But fuse the song of my dusky demon and brother,   175

That he sang to me in the moonlight on Paumanok's gray beach,
With the thousand responsive songs at random,
My own songs awaked from that hour,
And with them the key, the word up from the waves,
The word of the sweetest song and all songs,   180
That strong and delicious word which, creeping to my feet,
(Or like some old crone rocking the cradle, swathed in sweet
    garments, bending aside,)
The sea whisper'd me.

                                                               1859

As I Ebb'd with the Ocean of Life

1 As I ebb'd with the ocean of life,
  As I wended the shores I know,
  As I walk'd where the ripples continually wash you Paumanok,
  Where they rustle up hoarse and sibilant,
  Where the fierce old mother endlessly cries for her castaways,   5
  I musing late in the autumn day, gazing off southward,
  Held by this electric self out of the pride of which I utter poems,
  Was seiz'd by the spirit that trails in the lines underfoot,
  The rim, the sediment that stands for all the water and all the land
    of the globe.

  Fascinated, my eyes reverting from the south, dropt, to follow those
    slender windrows,   10
  Chaff, straw, splinters of wood, weeds, and the sea-gluten,[1]
  Scum, scales from shining rocks, leaves of salt-lettuce, left by the
    tide,
  Miles walking, the sound of breaking waves the other side of me,
  Paumanok there and then as I thought the old thought of likenesses,
  These you presented to me you fish-shaped island,   15
  As I wended the shores I know,
  As I walk'd with that electric self seeking types.

2 As I wend to the shores I know not,
  As I list to the dirge, the voices of men and women wreck'd,
  As I inhale the impalpable breezes that set in upon me,   20
  As the ocean so mysterious rolls toward me closer and closer,

---

[1] Adhesive.

I too but signify at the utmost a little wash'd-up drift,
A few sands and dead leaves to gather,
Gather, and merge myself as part of the sands and drift.

O baffled, balk'd, bent to the very earth,   25
Oppress'd with myself that I have dared to open my mouth,
Aware now that amid all that blab whose echoes recoil upon me I
    have not once had the least idea who or what I am,
But that before all my arrogant poems the real Me stands yet
    untouch'd, untold, altogether unreach'd,
Withdrawn far, mocking me with mock-congratulatory signs and
    bows,
With peals of distant ironical laughter at every word I have written,   30
Pointing in silence to these songs, and then to the sand beneath.

I perceive I have not really understood any thing, not a single
    object, and that no man ever can,
Nature here in sight of the sea taking advantage of me to dart upon
    me and sting me,
Because I have dared to open my mouth to sing at all.

³ You oceans both, I close with you,   35
We murmur alike reproachfully rolling sands and drift, knowing not
    why,
These little shreds indeed standing for you and me and all.

You friable² shore with trails of debris,
You fish-shaped island, I take what is underfoot,
What is yours is mine my father.   40

I too Paumanok,
I too have bubbled up, floated the measureless float, and been
    wash'd on your shores,
I too am but a trail of drift and debris,
I too leave little wrecks upon you, you fish-shaped island.

I throw myself upon your breast my father,   45
I cling to you so that you cannot unloose me,
I hold you so firm till you answer me something.

Kiss me my father,
Touch me with your lips as I touch those I love,
Breathe to me while I hold you close the secret of the murmuring I
    envy.   50

² Readily crumbled, brittle.

⁴ Ebb, ocean of life, (the flow will return,)
Cease not your moaning you fierce old mother,
Endlessly cry for your castaways, but fear not, deny not me,
Rustle not up so hoarse and angry against my feet as I touch you or
    gather from you.

I mean tenderly by you and all,   55
I gather for myself and for this phantom looking down where we
    lead, and following me and mine.

Me and mine, loose windrows, little corpses,
Froth, snowy white, and bubbles,
(See, from my dead lips the ooze exuding at last,
See, the prismatic colors glistening and rolling,)   60
Tufts of straw, sands, fragments,
Buoy'd hither from many moods, one contradicting another,
From the storm, the long calm, the darkness, the swell,
Musing, pondering, a breath, a briny tear, a dab of liquid or soil,
Up just as much out of fathomless workings fermented and thrown,   65
A limp blossom or two, torn, just as much over waves floating,
    drifted at random,
Just as much for us that sobbing dirge of Nature,
Just as much whence we come that blare of the cloud-trumpets,
We, capricious, brought hither we know not whence, spread out
    before you,
You up there walking or sitting,   70
Whoever you are, we too lie in drifts at your feet.³

1860

³ Gay Wilson Allen, in *The Whitman Hand-book* (1956), calls attention to the pessimistic quality of these lines. Whitman was suffering at the time from depression and brooding.

The Dalliance of the Eagles¹

Skirting the river road, (my forenoon walk, my rest,)
Skyward in air a sudden muffled sound, the dalliance of the eagles,
The rushing amorous contact high in space together,
The clinching interlocking claws, a living, fierce, gyrating wheel,
Four beating wings, two beaks, a swirling mass tight grappling,   5
In tumbling turning clustering loops, straight downward falling,

¹ The poem first appeared in the November
1880 issue of *Cope's Tobacco Plant*.

Till o'er the river pois'd, the twain yet one, a moment's lull,
A motionless still balance in the air, then parting, talons loosing,
Upward again on slow-firm pinions slanting, their separate diverse
    flight,
She hers, he his, pursuing.   10

1880

Cavalry Crossing a Ford[1]

A line in long array where they wind betwixt green islands,
They take a serpentine course, their arms flash in the sun—hark to
    the musical clank,
Behold the silvery river, in it the splashing horses loitering stop to
    drink,
Behold the brown-faced men, each group, each person a picture, the
    negligent rest on the saddles,
Some emerge on the opposite bank, others are just entering the
    ford—while,   5
Scarlet and blue and snowy white,
The guidon flags[2] flutter gayly in the wind.

1865

[1] This and the next two poems were included in *Drum Taps* (1865), Whitman's poetic record of the Civil War.

[2] The standard for a military unit.

Vigil Strange I Kept on the Field One Night

Vigil strange I kept on the field one night;
When you my son and my comrade dropt at my side that day,
One look I but gave which your dear eyes return'd with a look I shall
    never forget,
One touch of your hand to mine O boy, reach'd up as you lay on the
    ground,
Then onward I sped in the battle, the even-contested battle,   5
Till late in the night reliev'd to the place at last again I made my
    way,
Found you in death so cold dear comrade, found your body son of
    responding kisses, (never again on earth responding,)

Bared your face in the starlight, curious the scene, cool blew the
    moderate night-wind,
Long there and then in vigil I stood, dimly around me the battle-field
    spreading,
Vigil wondrous and vigil sweet there in the fragrant silent night,   10
But not a tear fell, not even a long-drawn sigh, long, long I gazed,
Then on the earth partially reclining sat by your side leaning my chin
    in my hands,
Passing sweet hours, immortal and mystic hours with you dearest
    comrade—not a tear, not a word,
Vigil of silence, love and death, vigil for you my son and my soldier,
As onward silently stars aloft, eastward new ones upward stole,   15
Vigil final for you brave boy, (I could not save you, swift was your
    death,
I faithfully loved you and cared for you living, I think we shall surely
    meet again,)
Till at latest lingering of the night, indeed just as the dawn appear'd,
My comrade I wrapt in his blanket, envelop'd well his form,
Folded the blanket well, tucking it carefully over head and carefully
    under feet.   20
And there and then and bathed by the rising sun, my son in his grave,
    in his rude-dug grave I deposited,
Ending my vigil strange with that, vigil of night and battle-field dim,
Vigil for boy of responding kisses, (never again on earth responding,)
Vigil for comrade swiftly slain, vigil I never forget, how as day
    brighten'd,
I rose from the chill ground and folded my soldier well in his blanket,   25
And buried him where he fell.

1865

A Sight in Camp in the Daybreak Gray and Dim[1]

A sight in camp in the daybreak gray and dim,
As from my tent I emerge so early sleepless,
As slow I walk in the cool fresh air the path near by the hospital tent,

[1] The source of this poem is in Whitman's notebook of 1862–1863: "Sight at daybreak in camp in front of the hospital tent. Three dead men lying, each with a blanket spread over him—I lift up one and look at the young man's face, calm and yellow. 'Tis strange (Young man: I think this face of yours is the face of my 'dead Christ')."

Three forms I see on stretchers lying, brought out there untended
  lying,
Over each the blanket spread, ample brownish woolen blanket,   5
Gray and heavy blanket, folding, covering all.

Curious I halt and silent stand,
Then with light fingers I from the face of the nearest the first just lift
  the blanket;
Who are you elderly man so gaunt and grim, with well-gray'd hair,
  and flesh all sunken about the eyes?
Who are you my dear comrade?   10

Then to the second I step—and who are you my child and darling?
Who are you sweet boy with cheeks yet blooming?

Then to the third—a face nor child nor old, very calm, as of beautiful
  yellow-white ivory;
Young man I think I know you—I think this face is the face of the
  Christ himself,
Dead and divine and brother of all, and here again he lies.   15

1865

When Lilacs Last in the Dooryard Bloom'd

1 When lilacs[1] last in the dooryard bloom'd,
  And the great star[2] early droop'd in the western sky in the night,
  I mourn'd, and yet shall mourn with ever-returning spring.

  Ever-returning spring, trinity sure to me you bring,
  Lilac blooming perennial and drooping star in the west,   5
  And thought of him I love.

2 O powerful western fallen star!
  O shades of night—O moody, tearful night!
  O great star disappear'd—O the black murk that hides the star!
  O cruel hands that hold me powerless—O helpless soul of me!   10
  O harsh surrounding cloud that will not free my soul.

---

[1] The lilacs are associated with memories of Abraham Lincoln.

[2] President Lincoln, whose death was the occasion of the poem.

3 In the dooryard fronting an old farm-house near the white-wash'd
  palings,
  Stands the lilac-bush tall-growing with heart-shaped leaves of rich
  green,
  With many a pointed blossom rising delicate, with the perfume
  strong I love,

  With every leaf a miracle—and from this bush in the dooryard,   15
  With delicate-color'd blossoms and heart-shaped leaves of rich
  green,
  A sprig with its flower I break.

4 In the swamp in secluded recesses,
  A shy and hidden bird[3] is warbling a song.

  Solitary the thrush,   20
  The hermit withdrawn to himself, avoiding the settlements,
  Sings by himself a song.

  Song of the bleeding throat,
  Death's outlet song of life, (for well dear brother I know,
  If thou wast not granted to sing thou would'st surely die.)   25

5 Over the breast of the spring, the land, amid cities,
  Amid lanes and through old woods, where lately the violets peep'd
    from the ground, spotting the gray debris,
  Amid the grass in the fields each side of the lanes, passing the
    endless grass,
  Passing the yellow-spear'd wheat, every grain from its shroud in the
    dark-brown fields uprisen,
  Passing the apple-tree blows of white and pink in the orchards,   30
  Carrying a corpse to where it shall rest in the grave,
  Night and day journeys a coffin.[4]

6 Coffin that passes through lanes and streets,
  Through day and night with the great cloud darkening the land,
  With the pomp of the inloop's flags with the cities draped in black,   35
  With the show of the States themselves as of crape-veil'd women
    standing,
  With processions long and winding and the flambeaus of the night,
  With the countless torches lit, with the silent sea of faces and the
    unbared heads,
  With the waiting depot, the arriving coffin, and the sombre faces,

[3] The poet.
[4] The coffin holds the immortal character of

Lincoln, whose body was taken to Springfield, Illinois, where it was buried.

With dirges through the night, with the thousand voices rising
  strong and solemn,   40
With all the mournful voices of the dirges pour'd around the coffin,
The dim-lit churches and the shuddering organs—where amid these
  you journey,
With the tolling tolling bells' perpetual clang,
Here, coffin that slowly passes,
I give you my sprig of lilac.   45

7 (Not for you, for one alone,
Blossoms and branches green to coffins all I bring,
For fresh as the morning, thus would I chant a song for you O sane
  and sacred death.

All over bouquets of roses,
O death, I cover you over with roses and early lilies,   50
But mostly and now the lilac that blooms the first,
Copious I break, I break the sprigs from the bushes,
With loaded arms I come, pouring for you,
For you and the coffins all of you O death.)

8 O western orb sailing the heaven,   55
Now I know what you must have meant as a month since I walk'd,
As I walk'd in silence the transparent shadowy night,
As I saw you had something to tell as you bent to me night after
  night,
As you droop'd from the sky low down as if to my side, (while the
  other stars all look'd on,)
As we wander'd together the solemn night, (for something I know
  not what kept me from sleep,)   60
As the night advanced, and I saw on the rim of the west how full
  you were of woe,
As I stood on the rising ground in the breeze in the cool
  transparent night,
As I watch'd where you pass'd and was lost in the netherward
  black of the night,
As my soul in its trouble dissatisfied sank, as where you sad orb,
Concluded, dropt in the night, and was gone.   65

9 Sing on there in the swamp,
O singer bashful and tender, I hear your notes, I hear your call,
I hear, I come presently, I understand you,
But a moment I linger, for the lustrous star has detain'd me,
The star my departing comrade holds and detains me.   70

¹⁰ O how shall I warble myself for the dead one there I loved?
And how shall I deck my song for the large sweet soul that has
    gone?
And what shall my perfume be for the grave of him I love?

Sea-winds blown from east and west,
Blown from the Eastern sea and blown from the Western sea, till
    there on the prairies meeting,   75
These and with these and the breath of my chant,
I'll perfume the grave of him I love.

¹¹ O what shall I hang on the chamber walls?
And what shall the pictures be that I hang on the walls,
To adorn the burial-house of him I love?   80

Pictures of growing spring and farms and homes,
With the Fourth-month⁵ eve at sundown, and the gray smoke lucid
    and bright,
With floods of the yellow gold of the gorgeous, indolent, sinking
    sun, burning, expanding the air,
With the fresh sweet herbage under foot, and the pale green leaves
    of the trees prolific,
In the distance the flowing glaze, the breast of the river, with a
    wind-dapple here and there,   85
With ranging hills on the banks, with many a line against the sky,
    and shadows,
And the city at hand with dwellings so dense, and stacks of
    chimneys,
And all the scenes of life and the workshops, and the workmen
    homeward returning.

¹² Lo, body and soul—this land,
My own Manhattan with spires, and the sparkling and hurrying
    tides, and the ships,   90
The varied and ample land, the South and the North in the light,
    Ohio's shores and flashing Missouri,
And ever the far-spreading prairies cover'd with grass and corn.

Lo, the most excellent sun so calm and haughty,
The violet and purple morn with just-felt breezes,
The gentle soft-born measureless light,   95
The miracle spreading bathing all, the fulfill'd noon,
The coming eve delicious, the welcome night and the stars,
Over my cities shining all, enveloping man and land.

⁵ The Quaker term for April.

13 Sing on, sing on you gray-brown bird,
Sing from the swamps, the recesses, pour your chant from the 100
bushes,
Limitless out of the dusk, out of the cedars and pines.

Sing on dearest brother, warble your reedy song,
Loud human song, with voice of uttermost woe.

O liquid, and free and tender! 105
O wild and loose to my soul—O wondrous singer!
You only I hear—yet the star holds me, (but will soon depart,)
Yet the lilac with mastering odor holds me.

14 Now while I sat in the day and look'd forth,
In the close of the day with its light and the fields of spring, and
the farmers preparing their crops,
In the large unconscious scenery of my land with its lakes and
forests, 110
In the heavenly aerial beauty, (after the perturb'd winds and the
storms,)
Under the arching heavens of the afternoon swift passing, and the
voices of children and women,
The many-moving sea-tides, and I saw the ships how they sail'd,
And the summer approaching with richness, and the fields all busy
with labor,
And the infinite separate houses, how they all went on, each with
its meals and minutia of daily usages, 115
And the streets how their throbbings throbb'd, and the cities
pent—lo, then and there,
Falling upon them all and among them all, enveloping me with the
rest,
Appear'd the cloud, appear'd the long black trail,
And I knew death, its thought, and the sacred knowledge of death.

Then with the knowledge of death as walking one side of me, 120
And the thought of death close-walking the other side of me,
And I in the middle as with companions, and as holding the hands
of companions,
I fled forth to the hiding receiving night that talks not,
Down to the shores of the water, the path by the swamp in the
dimness,
To the solemn shadowy cedars and ghostly pines so still. 125

And the singer so shy to the rest receiv'd me,
The gray-brown bird I know receiv'd us comrades three,
And he sang the carol of death, and a verse for him I love.

From deep secluded recesses,
From the fragrant cedars and the ghostly pines so still,   130
Came the carol of the bird.

And the charm of the carol rapt me,
As I held as if by their hands my comrades in the night,
And the voice of my spirit tallied the song of the bird.

Come lovely and soothing death,   135
Undulate round the world, serenely arriving, arriving,
In the day, in the night, to all, to each,
Sooner or later delicate death.

Prais'd be the fathomless universe,
For life and joy, and for objects and knowledge curious,   140
And for love, sweet love—but praise! praise! praise!
For the sure-enwinding arms of cool-enfolding death.

Dark mother always gliding near with soft feet,
Have none chanted for thee a chant of fullest welcome?
Then I chant it for thee, I glorify thee above all,   145
I bring thee a song that when thou must indeed come, come
unfalteringly.

Approach strong deliveress,
When it is so, when thou hast taken them I joyously sing the dead,
Lost in the loving floating ocean of thee,
Laved in the flood of thy bliss O death.   150

From me to thee glad serenades,
Dances for thee I propose saluting thee, adornments and feastings
for thee,
And the sights of the open landscape and the high-spread sky are
fitting,
And life and the fields, and the huge and thoughtful night.

The night in silence under many a star,   155
The ocean shore and the husky whispering wave whose voice I
know,
And the soul turning to thee O vast and well-veil'd death,
And the body gratefully nestling close to thee.

Over the tree-tops I float thee a song,
Over the rising and sinking waves, over the myriad fields and the
prairies wide,   160
Over the dense-pack'd cities all and the teeming wharves and ways,
I float this carol with joy, with joy to thee O death.

15 To the tally of my soul,
Loud and strong kept up the gray-brown bird,
With pure deliberate notes spreading filling the night.   165

Loud in the pines and cedars dim,
Clear in the freshness moist and the swamp-perfume,
And I with my comrades there in the night.

While my sight that was bound in my eyes unclosed,
As to long panoramas of visions.   170

And I saw askant the armies,
I saw as in noiseless dreams hundreds of battle-flags,
Borne through the smoke of the battles and pierc'd with missiles I
    saw them,
And carried hither and yon through the smoke, and torn and
    bloody,
And at last but a few shreds left on the staffs, (and all in silence,)   175
And the staffs all splinter'd and broken.

I saw battle-corpses, myriads of them,
And the white skeletons of young men, I saw them,
I saw the debris and debris of all the slain soldiers of the war,
But I saw they were not as was thought,   180
They themselves were fully at rest, they suffer'd not,
The living remain'd and suffer'd, the mother suffer'd,
And the wife and the child and the musing comrade suffer'd,
And the armies that remain'd suffer'd.

16 Passing the visions, passing the night,   185
Passing, unloosing the hold of my comrades' hands,
Passing the song of the hermit bird and the tallying song of my
    soul,
Victorious song, death's outlet song, yet varying ever-altering song,
As low and wailing, yet clear the notes, rising and falling, flooding
    the night,
Sadly sinking and fainting, as warning and warning,
    and yet again bursting with joy,   190

Covering the earth and filling the spread of the heaven,
As that powerful psalm in the night I heard from recesses,
Passing, I leave thee lilac with heart-shaped leaves,
I leave thee there in the door-yard, blooming, returning with
    spring.

I cease from my song for thee,   195
From my gaze on thee in the west, fronting the west, communing
    with thee,
O comrade lustrous with silver face in the night.

Yet each to keep and all, retrievements out of the night,
The song, the wondrous chant of the gray-brown bird,
And the tallying chant, the echo arous'd in my soul,   200
With the lustrous and drooping star with the countenance full of
  woe,
With the holders holding my hand nearing the call of the bird,
Comrades mine and I in the midst, and their memory ever to keep,
  for the dead I loved so well,
For the sweetest, wisest soul of all my days and lands—
  and this for his dear sake,
Lilac and star and bird twined with the chant of my soul,   205
There in the fragrant pines and the cedars dusk and dim.

                                                    1865–1866

Sparkles from the Wheel

Where the city's ceaseless crowd moves on the livelong day,
Withdrawn I join a group of children watching, I pause aside with
  them.

By the curb toward the edge of the flagging,
A knife-grinder works at his wheel sharpening a great knife,
Bending over he carefully holds it to the stone, by foot and knee,   5
With measur'd tread he turns rapidly, as he presses with light but
  firm hand,
Forth issue then in copious golden jets,
Sparkles from the wheel.

The scene and all its belongings, how they seize and affect me,
The sad sharp-chinn'd old man with worn clothes
  and broad shoulder-band of leather,   10
Myself effusing and fluid, a phantom curiously floating,
  now here absorb'd and arrested,
The group, (an unminded point set in a vast surrounding,)
The attentive, quiet children, the loud, proud, restive base of the
  streets,
The low hoarse purr of the whirling stone, the light-press'd blade,
Diffusing, dropping, sideways-darting, in tiny showers of gold,   15
Sparkles from the wheel.

                                                    1871

[1] This poem was first published as "Poem of
Wonder at the Resurrection of the Wheat."

Passage to India[1]

1 Singing my days,
  Singing the great achievements of the present,
  Singing the strong light works of engineers,
  Our modern wonders, (the antique ponderous Seven outvied,)
  In the Old World the east the Suez canal,   5
  The New by its mighty railroad spann'd,
  The seas inlaid with eloquent gentle wires;
  Yet first to sound, and ever sound, the cry with thee O soul,
  The Past! the Past! the Past!

  The Past—the dark unfathom'd retrospect!   10
  The teeming gulf—the sleepers and the shadows!
  The past—the infinite greatness of the past!
  For what is the present after all but a growth out of the past?
  (As a projectile form'd, impell'd, passing a certain line, still keeps
    on,
  So the present, utterly form'd, impell'd by the past.)   15

2 Passage O soul to India!
  Eclaircise[2] the myths Asiatic, the primitive fables.

  Not you alone proud truths of the world,
  Nor you alone ye facts of modern science,
  But myths and fables of eld, Asia's, Africa's fables,   20
  The far-darting beams of the spirit, the unloos'd dreams,
  The deep diving bibles and legends,
  The daring plots of the poets, the elder religions;
  O you temples fairer than lilies pour'd over by the rising sun!
  O you fables spurning the known, eluding the hold of the known,
    mounting to heaven!   25
  You lofty and dazzling towers, pinnacled, red as roses,
    burnish'd with gold!
  Towers of fables immortal fashion'd from mortal dreams!
  You too I welcome and fully the same as the rest!
  You too with joy I sing.

  Passage to India!   30
  Lo, soul, seest thou not God's purpose from the first?
  The earth to be spann'd, connected by network,

[1] The poem is an expression of Whitman's universalism, inspired by the opening of the Suez Canal (1869), linking Asia and Europe; the completion of a transcontinental railroad in the United States (1869), and the Atlantic Cable, linking Europe and America.
[2] Clarify.

The races, neighbors, to marry and be given in marriage,
The oceans to be cross'd, the distant brought near,
The lands to be welded together. 35

A worship new I sing,
You captains, voyagers, explorers, yours,
You engineers, you architects, machinists, yours,
You, not for trade or transportation only,
But in God's name, and for thy sake O soul. 40

3 Passage to India!
Lo soul for thee of tableaus twain,
I see in one the Suez canal initiated, open'd,
I see the procession of steamships, the Empress Eugenie's leading
    the band,
I mark from on deck the strange landscape, the pure sky,
    the level sand in the distance, 45
I pass swiftly the picturesque groups, the workmen gather'd,
The gigantic dredging machines.

In one again, different, (yet thine, all thine, O soul, the same,)
I see over my own continent the Pacific railroad surmounting every
    barrier,
I see continual trains of cars winding along the Platte
    carrying freight and passengers, 50
I hear the locomotives rushing and roaring, and the shrill steam-
    whistle,
I hear the echoes reverberate through the grandest scenery in the
    world,
I cross the Laramie plains, I note the rocks in grotesque shapes, the
    buttes,
I see the plentiful larkspur and wild onions, the barren, colorless,
    sage-deserts, 55
I see in glimpses afar or towering immediately above me the great
    mountains, I see the Wind river and the Wahsatch mountains,
I see the Monument mountain and the Eagle's Nest, I pass the
    Promontory, I ascend the Nevadas,
I scan the noble Elk mountain and wind around its base,
I see the Humboldt range, I thread the valley and cross the river,
I see the clear waters of lake Tahoe, I see forests of majestic pines, 60
Or crossing the great desert, the alkaline plains, I behold enchanting
    mirages of waters and meadows,
Marking through these and after all, in duplicate slender lines,
Bridging the three or four thousand miles of land travel,

Tying the Eastern to the Western sea,
The road between Europe and Asia.   65

(Ah Genoese[3] thy dream! thy dream!
Centuries after thou art laid in thy grave,
The shore thou foundest verifies thy dream.)

[4] Passage to India!
Struggles of many a captain, tales of many a sailor dead,   70
Over my mood stealing and spreading they come,
Like clouds and cloudlets in the unreach'd sky.

Along all history, down the slopes,
As a rivulet running, sinking now, and now again to the surface
    rising,
A ceaseless thought, a varied train—lo, soul, to thee, thy sight, they
    rise,   75
The plans, the voyages again the expeditions;
Again Vasco de Gama[4] sails forth,
Again the knowledge gain'd, the mariner's compass,
Lands found and nations born, thou born America,
For purpose vast, man's long probation fill'd,   80
Thou rondure of the world at last accomplish'd.

[5] O vast Rondure, swimming in space,
Cover'd all over with visible power and beauty,
Alternate light and day and the teeming spiritual darkness,
Unspeakable high processions of sun and moon and countless stars
    above,   85
Below, the manifold grass and waters, animals, mountains, trees,
With inscrutable purpose, some hidden prophetic intention,
Now first it seems my thought begins to span thee.

Down from the gardens of Asia descending radiating,
Adam and Eve appear, then their myriad progeny after them,   90
Wandering, yearning, curious, with restless explorations,
With questionings, baffled, formless, feverish, with never-happy
    hearts,
With that sad incessant refrain, Wherefore unsatisfied soul? and
    Whither O mocking life?

Ah who shall soothe these feverish children?
Who justify these restless explorations?   95
Who speak the secret of impassive earth?
Who bind it to us? what is this separate Nature so unnatural?

---

[3] Christopher Columbus.
[4] Vasco de Gama (1469?-1524) was a Portu-
guese explorer and colonial administrator,
the first to reach India by the sea.

What is this earth to our affections? (unloving earth,
    without a throb to answer ours,
Cold earth, the place of graves.)

Yet soul be sure the first intent remains, and shall be carried out,   100
Perhaps even now the time has arrived.

After the seas are all cross'd, (as they seem already cross'd,)
After the great captains and engineers have accomplish'd their
    work,
After the noble inventors, after the scientists, the chemist,
    the geologist, ethnologist,
Finally shall come the poet worthy that name,   105
The true son of God shall come singing his songs.

Then not your deeds only O voyagers, O scientists and inventors,
    shall be justified,
All these hearts as of fretted children shall be sooth'd,
All affection shall be fully responded to, the secret shall be told,
All these separations and gaps shall be taken up and hook'd
    and link'd together,   110
The whole earth, this cold, impassive, voiceless earth,
    shall be completely justified,
Trinitas divine shall be gloriously accomplish'd and compacted
    by the true son of God, the poet,
(He shall indeed pass the straits and conquer the mountains,
He shall double the cape of Good Hope to some purpose.)
Nature and Man shall be disjoin'd and diffused no more,   115
The true son of God shall absolutely fuse them.

6 Year at whose wide-flung door I sing!
Year of the purpose accomplish'd!
Year of the marriage of continents, climates and oceans!
(No mere doge of Venice now wedding the Adriatic,)   120
I see O year in you the vast terraqueous globe given and giving all,
Europe to Asia, Africa join'd, and they to the New World,
The lands, geographies, dancing before you, holding a festival
    garland,
As brides and bridegrooms hand in hand.

Passage to India!   125
Cooling airs from Caucasus far, soothing cradle of man,
The river Euphrates[5] flowing, the past lit up again.

[5] A river of southwestern Asia, flowing some
2235 miles from east-central Turkey, through
northeastern Syria and central Iraq, to the
Tigris River. It was thought to be the "cradle" of the West.

Lo soul, the retrospect brought forward,
The old, most populous, wealthiest of earth's lands,
The streams of the Indus and the Ganges[6] and their many affluents,   130
(I my shores of America walking to-day behold, resuming all,)
The tale of Alexander[7] on his warlike marches suddenly dying,
On one side China and on the other side Persia and Arabia,
To the south the great seas and the bay of Bengal,
The flowing literatures, tremendous epics, religions, castes,   135
Old occult Brahma interminably far back, the tender and junior
    Buddha,
Central and southern empires and all their belongings, possessors,
The wars of Tamerlane,[8] the reign of Aurungzebe,[9]
The traders, rulers, explorers, Moslems, Venetians, Byzantium,
    the Arabs, Portuguese,
The first travelers famous yet, Marco Polo,[10] Batouta the Moor,[11]   140
Doubts to be solv'd, the map incognita, blanks to be fill'd,
The foot of man unstay'd, the hands never at rest,
Thyself O soul that will not brook a challenge.

The mediæval navigators rise before me,
The world of 1492, with its awaken'd enterprise,   145
Something swelling in humanity now like the sap of the earth in
    spring,
The sunset splendor of chivalry declining.

And who are thou sad shade?
Gigantic, visionary, thyself a visionary,
With majestic limbs and pious beaming eyes,   150
Spreading around with every look of thine a golden world,
Enhuing it with gorgeous hues.

As the chief histrion,[12]
Down to the footlights walks in some great scene,
Dominating the rest I see the Admiral[13] himself,   155
(History's type of courage, action, faith,)

[6] Indus is a river rising in southwestern Tibet and flowing through Tibet and Pakistan to the Arabian Sea. The Ganges is a river in northern India and East Pakistan, flowing from the Himalayas to the Bay of Bengal. It is sacred to the Hindus.

[7] Alexander the Great (356-323 B.C.) was king of Macedonia and conqueror of Greece, the Persian Empire, and Egypt. He died on his return from India.

[8] Tamerlane (1336?-1405) was an Islamic conqueror of central Asia and eastern Europe.

[9] A seventeenth-century emperor of Hindustan.

[10] A Venetian traveler (1254?-1324?) at the court of Kublai Khan who traveled to Cathay.

[11] Baboutsh (1303-1377) went to Asia and Africa.

[12] Performer.

[13] Christopher Columbus.

Behold him sail from Palos[14] leading his little fleet,
His voyage behold, his return, his great fame,
His misfortunes, calumniators, behold him a prisoner, chain'd,
Behold his dejection, poverty, death.   160

(Curious in time I stand, noting the efforts of heroes,
Is the deferment long? bitter the slander, poverty, death?
Lies the seed unreck'd for centuries in the ground? lo, to God's due
   occasion,
Uprising in the night, it sprouts, blooms,
And fills the earth with use and beauty.)   165

7 Passage indeed O soul to primal thought,
Not lands and seas alone, thy own clear freshness,
The young maturity of brood and bloom,
To realms of budding bibles.

O soul, repressless, I with thee and thou with me,   170
Thy circumnavigation of the world begin,
Of man, the voyage of his mind's return,
To reason's early paradise,
Back, back to wisdom's birth, to innocent intuitions,
Again with fair creation.   175

8 O we can wait no longer,
We too take ship O soul,
Joyous we too launch out on trackless seas,
Fearless for unknown shores on waves of ecstasy to sail,
Amid the wafting winds, (thou pressing me to thee, I thee to me, O
   soul,)   180
Caroling free, singing our song of God,
Chanting our chant of pleasant exploration.

With laugh and many a kiss,
(Let others deprecate, let others weep for sin, remorse, humiliation,)
O soul thou pleasest me, I thee.   185

Ah more than any priest O soul we too believe in God,
But with the mystery of God we dare not dally.

O soul thou pleasest me, I thee,
Sailing these seas or on the hills, or waking in the night,
Thoughts, silent thoughts, of Time and Space and Death, like waters
   flowing,   190
Bear me indeed as through the regions infinite,
Whose air I breathe, whose ripples heat, lave me all over,

---

[14] Columbus sailed from this Spanish seaport.

Bathe me O God in thee, mounting to thee,
I and my soul to range in range of thee.

O Thou transcendent,   195
Nameless, the fibre and the breath,
Light of the light, shedding forth universes, thou centre of them,
Thou mightier centre of the true, the good, the loving,
Thou moral, spiritual fountain—affection's source—thou reservoir,
(O pensive soul of me—O thirst unsatisfied—waitest not there?   200
Waitest not haply for us somewhere there the Comrade perfect?)
Thou pulse—thou motive of the stars, suns, systems,
That, circling, move in order, safe, harmonious,
Athwart the shapeless vastnesses of space,
How should I think, how breathe a single breath, how speak, if, out
    of myself,   205
I could not launch, to those, superior universes?

Swiftly I shrivel at the thought of God,
At Nature and its wonders, Time and Space and Death,
But that I, turning, call to thee O soul, thou actual Me,
And lo, thou gently masterest the orbs,   210
Thou matest Time, smilest content at Death,
And fillest, swellest full the vastnesses of Space.

Greater than stars or suns,
Bounding O soul thou journeyest forth;
What love than thine and ours could wider amplify?   215
What aspirations, wishes, outvie thine and ours O soul?
What dreams of the ideal? what plans of purity, perfection,
    strength?
What cheerful willingness for others' sake to give up all?
For others' sake to suffer all?

Reckoning ahead O soul, when thou, the time achiev'd,   220
The seas all cross'd, weather'd the capes, the voyage done,
Surrounded, copest, frontest God, yieldest, the aim attain'd,
As fill'd with friendship, love complete, the Elder Brother found,
The Younger melts in fondness in his arms.

9 Passage to more than India!   225
Are thy wings plumed indeed for such far flights?
O soul, voyagest thou indeed on voyages like those?
Disportest thou on waters such as those?
Soundest below the Sanscrit and the Vedas?[15]
Then have thy bent unleash'd.   230

[15] The oldest sacred writings of Hinduism,
written in Sanskrit.

Passage to you, your shores, ye aged fierce enigmas!
Passage to you, to mastership of you, ye strangling problems!
You, strew'd with the wrecks of skeletons, that, living,
    never reach'd you.

Passage to more than India!
O secret of the earth and sky! 235
Of you O waters of the sea! O winding creeks and rivers!
Of you O woods and fields! of you strong mountains of my land!
Of you O prairies! of you gray rocks!
O morning red! O clouds! O rain and snows!
O day and night, passage to you! 240

O sun and moon and all you stars! Sirius and Jupiter![16]
Passage to you!

Passage, immediate passage! the blood burns in my veins!
Away O soul! hoist instantly the anchor!
Cut the hawsers—haul out—shake out every sail! 245
Have we not stood here like trees in the ground long enough?
Have we not grovel'd here long enough, eating and drinking like
    mere brutes?
Have we not darken'd and dazed ourselves with books long
    enough?

Sail forth—steer for the deep waters only,
Reckless O soul, exploring, I with thee, and thou with me, 250
For we are bound where mariner has not yet dared to go,
And we will risk the ship, ourselves and all.

O my brave soul!
O farther farther sail!
O daring joy, but safe! are they not all the seas of God? 255
O farther, farther, farther sail!

1871

[16] Sirius is the brightest star in the sky; Jupiter is the fifth planet from the sun, the largest in the solar system.

Whispers of Heavenly Death

Whispers of heavenly death murmur'd I hear,
Labial gossip of night, sibilant chorals,
Footsteps gently ascending, mystical breezes wafted soft and low,
Ripples of unseen rivers, tides of a current flowing, forever flowing,
(Or is it the plashing of tears? the measureless waters of human tears?) 5

I see, just see skyward, great cloud-masses,
Mournfully slowly they roll, silently swelling and mixing,
With at times a half-dimm'd sadden'd far-off star,
Appearing and disappearing.

(Some parturition[1] rather, some solemn immortal birth;
On the frontiers to eyes impenetrable,
Some soul is passing over.)

10

1868

[1] Childbirth.

A Noiseless Patient Spider

A noiseless patient spider,
I mark'd where on a little promontory it stood isolated,
Mark'd how to explore the vacant vast surrounding,
It launch'd forth filament, filament, filament, out of itself,
Ever unreeling them, ever tirelessly speeding them.

5

And you O my soul where you stand,
Surrounded, detached, in measureless oceans of space,
Ceaselessly musing, venturing, throwing, seeking the spheres to
    connect them,
Till the bridge you will need be form'd, till the ductile anchor hold,
Till the gossamer thread you fling catch somewhere, O my soul.

10

1868

From Democratic Vistas

1871

As the greatest lessons of Nature through the universe are perhaps the lessons of variety and freedom, the same present the greatest lessons also in New World politics and progress. If a man were asked, for instance, the distinctive points contrasting modern European and American political and other life with the old Asiatic cultus, as lingering-bequeathed yet in China and Turkey, he might find the amount of them in John Stuart Mill's profound essay on Liberty[1] in the future, where he demands two main constituents, or sub-strata, for a truly grand nationality—1st, a large variety of character— and 2nd, full play for human nature to expand itself in numberless and even conflicting directions—(seems to be for general humanity much like the influences that make up, in their limitless field, that perennial health-action of the air we call the weather—an infinite number of currents and forces, and contributions, and temperatures, and cross purposes, whose ceaseless play of counterpart upon counterpart brings constant restoration and vitality). With this thought—and not for itself alone, but all it necessitates, and draws after it—let me begin my speculations.

America, filling the present with greatest deeds and problems, cheerfully accepting the past, including feudalism (as, indeed, the present is but the legitimate birth of the past, including feudalism), counts, as I reckon, for her justification and success (for who, as yet, dare claim success?) almost entirely on the future. Nor is that hope unwarranted. Today, ahead, though dimly yet, we see, in vistas, a copious, sane, gigantic offspring. For our New World I consider far less important for what it has done, or what it is, than for results to come. Sole among nationalities, these States have assumed the task to put in forms of lasting power and practicality, on areas of amplitude rivaling the operations of the physical kosmos, the moral political speculations of ages, long, long deferred, the democratic republican principle, and the theory of development and perfection by voluntary standards, and self-reliance. Who else, indeed, except the United States, in history, so far, have accepted in unwitting faith, and, as we now see, stand, act upon, and go security for, these things?

But preluding no longer, let me strike the keynote of the following strain. First premising that, though the passages of it have been written at widely different times (it is, in fact, a collection of memoranda, perhaps for future designers, comprehenders), and though it may be open to the charge of one part contradicting another—for there are opposite sides to the great question of democracy, as to every great question—I feel the parts harmoniously blended in my own realization and convictions, and present them to be read only in such oneness, each page and each claim and assertion modified and tempered by the others. Bear in mind, too, that they are not the result of studying up in political economy, but of the ordinary sense, observing, wandering among men, these States, these stirring years of war and peace. I will not gloss over the appalling dangers of universal suffrage in the United States. In fact, it is to admit and face these dangers I am writing. To him or her within whose thought rages the battle, advancing, retreating, between democracy's convictions, aspirations, and the people's crudeness, vice, ca-

[1] John Stuart Mill (1806-1873), English economist, philosopher, and political theorist published *On Liberty* in 1859.

prices, I mainly write this essay. I shall use the words America and democracy as convertible terms. Not an ordinary one is the issue. The United States are destined either to surmount the gorgeous history of feudalism, or else prove the most tremendous failure of time. Not the least doubtful am I on any prospects of their material success. The triumphant future of their business, geographic and productive departments, on larger scales and in more varieties than ever, is certain. In those respects the republic must soon (if she does not already) outstrip all examples hitherto afforded, and dominate the world.

Admitting all this, with the priceless value of our political institutions, general suffrage (and fully acknowledging the latest, widest opening of the doors), I say that, far deeper than these, what finally and only is to make of our Western world a nationality superior to any hither known, and outtopping the past, must be vigorous, yet unsuspected Literatures, perfect personalities and sociologies, original, transcendental, and expressing (what, in highest sense, are not yet expressed at all) democracy and the modern. With these, and out of these, I promulgate new races of Teachers, and of perfect Women, indispensable to endow the birth-stock of a New World. For feudalism, caste, the ecclesiastic traditions, though palpably retreating from political institutions, still hold essentially, by their spirit, even in this country, entire possession of the more important fields, indeed the very subsoil, of education, and of social standards and literature.

I say that democracy can never prove itself beyond cavil, until it founds and luxuriantly grows its own forms of art, poems, schools, theology, displacing all that exists, or that has been produced anywhere in the past, under opposite influences. It is curious to me that while so many voices, pens, minds, in the press, lecture rooms, in our Congress, etc., are discussing intellectual topics, pecuniary dangers, legislative problems, the suffrage, tariff and labor questions, and the various business and benevolent needs of America, with propositions, remedies, often worth deep attention, there is one need, a hiatus the profoundest, that no eye seems to perceive, no voice to state. Our fundamental want today in the United States, with closest, amplest reference to present conditions, and to the future, is of a class, and the clear idea of a class, of native authors, literatures, far different, far higher in grade, than any yet known, sacerdotal, modern, fit to cope with our occasions, lands, permeating the whole mass of American mentality, taste, belief, breathing into it a new breath of life, giving it decision, affecting politics far more than the popular superficial suffrage, with results inside and underneath the elections of Presidents or Congresses—radiating, begetting appropriate teachers, schools, manners, and, as its grandest result, accomplishing (what neither the schools nor the churches and their clergy have hitherto accomplished, and without which this nation will no more stand, permanently, soundly, than a house will stand without a sub-stratum), a religious and moral character beneath the political and productive and intellectual bases of the States. For know you not, dear, earnest reader, that the people of our land may all read and write, and may all possess the right to vote—and yet the main things may be entirely lacking?—(and this to suggest them).

Viewed, today, from a point of view sufficiently over-arching, the problem of humanity all over the civilized world is social and religious, and is to be finally met and treated by literature. The priest departs, the divine literatus comes. Never was anything more wanted than, today, and here in the States, the poet of the modern is wanted, or the great literatus of the modern. At all times, perhaps, the central point in any nation, and that whence it is itself really swayed the most and whence it sways others, is its national literature, especially its archetypal poems. Above all previous lands, a great original literature is surely to become the justification and reliance, (in some respects the sole reliance) of American democracy.

Few are aware how the great literature penetrates all, gives hue to all, shapes aggregates and individuals, and, after subtle ways, with irresistible power, constructs, sustains, demolishes at will. Why tower, in reminiscence, above all the nations of the earth, two special lands, petty in themselves, yet inexpressibly gigantic, beautiful, columnar? Immortal Judah lives, and Greece immortal lives, in a couple of poems.

Nearer than this. It is not generally realized, but it is true, as the genius of Greece, and all the sociology, personality, politics, and religion of those wonderful states, resided in their literature or aesthetics, that what was afterwards the main support of European chivalry, the feudal, ecclesiastical, dynastic world over there—forming its osseous structure, holding it together for hundreds, thousands of years, preserving its flesh and bloom, giving it form, decision, rounding it out, and so saturating it in the conscious and unconscious blood, breed, belief, and intuitions of men, that it still prevails powerful to this day, in defiance of the mighty changes of time—was its literature, permeating to the very marrow, especially that major part, its enchanting songs, ballads, and poems.

. . .

I say we had best look our times and lands searchingly in the face, like a physician diagnosing some deep disease. Never was there, perhaps, more hollowness at heart than at present, and here in the United States. Genuine belief seems to have left us. The underlying principles of the States are not honestly believed in (for all this hectic glow, and these melodramatic screamings), nor is humanity itself believed in. What penetrating eye does not everywhere see through the mask? The spectacle is appalling. We live in an atmosphere of hypocrisy throughout. The men believe not in the women, nor the women in the men. A scornful superciliousness rules in literature. The aim of all the *littérateurs* is to find something to make fun of. A lot of churches, sects, etc., the most dismal phantasms I know, usurp the name of religion. Conversation is a mass of badinage. From deceit in the spirit, the mother of all false deeds, the offspring is already incalculable. An acute and candid person, in the revenue department in Washington, who is led by the course of his employment to regularly visit the cities, north, south, and west, to investigate frauds, has talked much with me about his discoveries. The depravity of the business classes of our country is not less than has been supposed, but infinitely greater. The official services of America, national, state, and municipal, in all their branches and departments, except the judiciary, are saturated in corruption, bribery, falsehood, maladministration; and the judiciary is tainted. The great cities reek with respectable as much as non-respectable robbery and scoundrelism. In fashionable life, flippancy, tepid amours, weak infidelism, small aims, or no aims at all, only to kill time. In business (this all-devouring modern word, business), the one sole object is, by any means, pecuniary gain. The magician's serpent in the fable ate up all the other serpents; and moneymaking is our magician's serpent, remaining today sole master of the field. The best class we show, is but a mob of fashionably dressed speculators and vulgarians. True, indeed, behind this fantastic farce, enacted on the visible stage of society, solid things and stupendous labors are to be discovered, existing crudely and going on in the background, to advance and tell themselves in time. Yet the truths are none the less terrible. I say that our New World democracy, however great a success in uplifting the masses out of their sloughs, in materialistic development, products, and in a certain highly deceptive superficial popular intellectuality, is, so far, an almost complete failure in its social aspects, and in really grand religious, moral, literary, and aesthetic results. In vain do we march with unprecedented strides to empire so colossal, outvying the antique, beyond Alexander's, beyond the proudest sway of Rome. In vain have we annexed Texas, California, Alaska, and reach north for Canada and south for Cuba. It is as if we were somehow being endowed with a vast and more and more thoroughly appointed body, and then left with little or no soul.

· · ·

The purpose of democracy—supplanting old belief in the necessary absoluteness of established dynastic rulership, temporal, ecclesiastical, and scholastic, as furnishing the only security against chaos, crime, and ignorance—is, through many transmigrations and amid endless ridicules, arguments, and ostensible failures, to illustrate, at all hazards, this doctrine or theory that man, properly trained in sanest, highest freedom, may and must become a law, and series of laws, unto himself, surrounding and providing for, not only his own personal control, but all his relations to other individuals, and to the State; and that, while other theories, as in the past histories of nations, have proved wise enough, and indispensable perhaps for their conditions, *this*, as matters now stand in our civilized world, is the only scheme worth working from, as warranting results like those of Nature's laws, reliable, when once established, to carry on themselves.

The argument of the matter is extensive, and, we admit, by no means all on one side. What we shall offer will be far, far from sufficient. But while leaving unsaid much that should properly even prepare the way for the treatment of this many-sided question of political liberty, equality, or republicanism—leaving the whole history and consideration of the feudal plan and its products, embodying humanity, its politics and civilization, through the retrospect of past time (which plan and products, indeed, make up all of the past, and a large part of the present)—leaving unanswered, at least by any specific and local answer, many a well-wrought argument and instance, and many a conscientious declamatory cry and warning—as, very lately, from an eminent and venerable person abroad[2]—things, problems, full of doubt, dread, suspense (not new to me, but old occupiers of many an anxious hour in city's din, or night's silence), we still may give a page or so, whose drift is opportune. Time alone can finally answer these things. But as a substitute in passing, let us, even if fragmentarily, throw forth a short direct or indirect suggestion of the premises of that other plan, in the new spirit, under the new forms, started here in our America.

As to the political section of Democracy, which introduces and breaks ground for further and vaster sections, few probably are the minds, even in these republican States, that fully comprehend the aptness of that phrase, "the government of the people, by the people, for the people," which we inherit from the lips of Abraham Lincoln; a formula whose verbal shape is homely wit, but whose scope includes both the totality and all minutiæ of the lesson.

The People! Like our huge earth itself, which, to ordinary scansion, is full of vulgar contradictions and offense, man, viewed in the lump, displeases, and is a constant puzzle and affront to the merely educated classes. The rare, cosmical, artist-mind, lit with the Infinite, alone confronts his manifold and oceanic qualities—but taste, intelligence and culture (so-called), have been against the masses, and remain so. There is plenty of glamour about the most damnable crimes and hoggish meannesses, special and general, of the feudal and dynastic world over there, with its *personnel* of lords and queens and courts, so well dressed and so handsome. But the People are ungrammatical, untidy, and their sins gaunt and ill bred.

Literature, strictly considered, has never recognized the People, and, whatever may be said, does not today. Speaking generally, the tendencies of literature, as hitherto pursued, have been to make mostly critical and queru-

[2] Shooting Niagara.—*I was at first roused to much anger and abuse by this essay from Mr. Carlyle, so insulting to the theory of America—but happening to think afterwards how I had more than once been in the like mood, during which his essay was evidently cast, and seen persons and things in the same light (indeed, some might say there are signs of the same feeling in these Vistas)—I have since read it again, not only as a study, expressing as it does certain judgments from the highest feudal point of view, but have read it with respect as coming from an earnest soul, and as contributing certain sharp-cutting metallic grains, which, if not gold or silver, may be good, hard, honest iron.* [Whitman's note.]

lous men. It seems as if, so far, there were some natural repugnance between a literary and professional life, and the rude rank spirit of the democracies. There is, in later literature, a treatment of benevolence, a charity business, rife enough it is true; but I know nothing more rare, even in this country, than a fit scientific estimate and reverent appreciation of the People—of their measureless wealth of latent power and capacity, their vast, artistic contrasts of lights and shades—with, in America, their entire reliability in emergencies, and a certain breadth of historic grandeur, of peace or war, far surpassing all the vaunted samples of book-heroes, or any *haut ton* coteries, in all the records of the world.

. . .

I say the mission of government, henceforth, in civilized lands, is not repression alone, and not authority alone, not even of law, nor by that favorite standard of the eminent writer, the rule of the best men, the born heroes and captains of the race (as if such ever, or one time out of a hundred, get into the big places, elective or dynastic)—but higher than the highest arbitrary rule, to train communities through all their grades, beginning with individuals and ending there again, to rule themselves. What Christ appeared for in the moral-spiritual field for human-kind, namely, that in respect to the absolute soul, there is in the possession of such by each single individual, something so transcendent, so incapable of gradations (like life), that, to that extent, it places all beings on a common level, utterly regardless of the distinctions of intellect, virtue, station, or any height or lowliness whatever—is tallied in like manner, in this other field, by democracy's rule that men, the nation, as a common aggregate of living identities, affording in each a separate and complete subject for freedom, worldly thrift and happiness, and for a fair chance for growth, and for protection in citizenship, etc., must, to the political extent of the suffrage or vote, if no further, be placed, in each and in the whole, on one broad, primary, universal, common platform.

The purpose is not altogether direct; perhaps it is more indirect. For it is not that democracy is of exhaustive account in itself. Perhaps, indeed, it is (like Nature), of no account in itself. It is that, as we see, it is the best, perhaps only, fit and full means, formulater, general caller-forth, trainer, for the million, not for grand material personalities only, but for immortal souls. To be a voter with the rest is not so much; and this, like every institute, will have its imperfections. But to become an enfranchised man, and now, impediments removed, to stand and start without humiliation, and equal with the rest; to commence, or have the road cleared to commence, the grand experiment of development, whose end (perhaps requiring several generations), may be the forming of a full-grown man or woman—that *is* something. To ballast the State is also secured, and in our times is to be secured, in no other way.

We do not (at any rate I do not), put it either on the ground that the People, the masses, even the best of them, are, in their latent or exhibited qualities, essentially sensible and good—nor on the ground of their rights; but that good or bad, rights or no rights, the democratic formula is the only safe and preservative one for coming times. We endow the masses with the suffrage for their own sake, no doubt; then, perhaps still more, from another point of view, for community's sake. Leaving the rest to the sentimentalists, we present freedom as sufficient in its scientific aspect, cold as ice, reasoning, deductive, clear and passionless as crystal.

Democracy too is law, and of the strictest, amplest kind. Many suppose (and often in its own ranks the error), that it means a throwing aside of law, and running riot. But, briefly, it is the superior law, not alone that of physical force, the body, which, adding to, it supersedes with that of the spirit. Law is the unshakable order of the universe forever; and the law over all, and law of laws, is the law of successions; that of the superior law, in time, gradually supplanting and overwhelming the inferior one. (While, for myself, I would cheerfully agree—first covenanting that the formative tendencies shall be administered in favor, or at least not against it, and that this reservation be closely construed—that until the individual or community show due signs, or be so minor and fractional as not to endanger the State, the condition of authoritative tutelage may continue, and self-government must abide its time.) Nor is the aesthetic point, always an important one, without fascination for highest aiming souls. The common ambition strains for elevations, to become some privileged exclusive. The master sees greatness and health in being part of the mass; nothing will do as well as common ground. Would you have in yourself the divine, vast, general law? Then merge yourself in it.

And, topping democracy, this most alluring record, that it alone can bind, and ever seeks to bind, all nations, all men, of however various and distant lands, into a brotherhood, a family. It is the old, yet ever-modern dream of earth, out of her eldest and her youngest, her fond philosophers and poets. Not that half only, individualism, which isolates. There is another half, which is adhesiveness or love, that fuses, ties, and aggregates, making the races comrades, and fraternizing all. Both are to be vitalized by religion (sole worthiest elevator of man or State), breathing into the proud, material tissues, the breath of life. For I say at the core of democracy, finally, is the religious element. All the religions, old and new, are there. Nor may the scheme step forth, clothed in resplendent beauty and command, till these, bearing the best, the latest fruit, the spiritual, shall fully appear.

A portion of our pages we might indite with reference toward Europe, especially the British part of it, more than our own land, perhaps not absolutely needed for the home reader. But the whole question hangs together, and fastens and links all peoples. The liberalist of today has this advantage over antique or medieval times, that his doctrine seeks not only to individualize but to universalize. The great word Solidarity has arisen. Of all dangers to a nation, as things exist in our day, there can be no greater one than having certain portions of the people set off from the rest by a line drawn—they not privileged as others, but degraded, humiliated, made of no account. Much quackery teems, of course, even on democracy's side, yet does not really affect the orbic quality of the matter. To work in, if we may so term it, and justify God, His divine aggregate, the People (or, the veritable horned and sharp-tailed Devil, *His* aggregate, if there be who convulsively insist upon it)—this, I say, is what democracy is for; and this is what our America means, and is doing—may I not say, has done? If not, she means nothing more, and does nothing more, than any other land. And, as by virtue of its cosmical, antiseptic power, Nature's stomach is fully strong enough not only to digest the morbific matter always presented, not to be turned aside, and perhaps, indeed, intuitively gravitating thither—but even to change such contributions into nutriment for highest use and life—so American democracy's. That is the lesson we, these days, send over to European lands by every western breeze.

And truly, whatever may be said, in the way of abstract argument, for or against the theory of a wider democratizing of institutions in any civilized country, much trouble might well be saved to all European lands by recognizing this palpable fact (for a palpable fact it is), that some form of such democratizing is about the only resource now left. *That,* or chronic dissatisfaction continued, mutterings which grow annually louder and louder, till, in due course, and pretty swiftly in most cases, the inevitable crisis, crash, dynastic ruin. Anything worthy to be called statesmanship in the Old World, I should say, among the advanced students, adepts, or men of any brains, does not debate today whether to hold on, attempting to lean back and monarchize, or to look forward and democratize—but *how,* and in what degree and part, most prudently to democratize.

. . .

I submit, therefore, that the fruition of democracy, on aught like a grand scale, resides altogether in the future. As, under any profound and comprehensive view of the gorgeous-composite feudal world, we see in it, through the long ages and cycles of ages, the results of a deep, integral, human and divine principle, or fountain, from which issued laws, ecclesia, manners, institutes, costumes, personalities, poems (hitherto unequaled), faithfully partaking of their source, and indeed only arising either to betoken it, or to furnish parts of that varied-flowing display, whose center was one and absolute—so, long ages hence, shall the due historian or critic make at least an equal retrospect, an equal history for the democratic principle. It too must be adorned, credited with its results—then, when it, with imperial power, through amplest time, has dominated mankind—has been the source and test of all the moral, aesthetic, social, political, and religious expressions and institutes of the civilized world—has begotten them in spirit and in form, and has carried them to its own unprecedented heights—has had (it is possible) monastics and ascetics, more numerous, more devout than the monks and priests of all previous creeds—has swayed the ages with a breadth and rectitude tallying Nature's own—has fashioned, systematized, and triumphantly finished and carried out, in its own interest, and with unparalleled success, a new earth and a new man.

Thus we presume to write, as it were, upon things that exist not, and travel by maps yet unmade, and a blank. But the throes of birth are upon us; and we have something of this advantage in seasons of strong formations, doubts, suspense—for then the afflatus of such themes haply may fall upon us, more or less; and then, hot from surrounding war and revolution, our speech, though without polished coherence, and a failure by the standard called criticism, comes forth, real at least as the lightnings.

And maybe we, these days, have, too, our own reward—(for there are yet some, in all lands, worthy to be so encouraged). Though not for us the joy of entering at the last the conquered city—not ours the chance ever to see with our own eyes the peerless power and splendid *éclat* of the democratic principle, arrived at meridian, filling the world with effulgence and majesty far beyond those of past history's kings, or all dynastic sway—there is yet, to whoever is eligible among us, the prophetic vision, the joy of being tossed in the brave turmoil of these times—the promulgation and the path, obedient, lowly reverent to the voice, the gesture of the god, or holy ghost, which others see not, hear not—with the proud consciousness that amid whatever clouds, seductions, or heart-wearying postponements, we have never deserted, never despaired, never abandoned the faith.

So much contributed, to be conned well, to help prepare and brace our edifice, our planned Idea—we still proceed to give it in another of its aspects—perhaps the main, the high façade of all. For to democracy, the leveler, the unyielding principle of the average, surely joined another principle, equally unyielding, closely tracking the first, indispensable to it, opposite (as the sexes are opposite), and whose existence, confronting and ever modifying the other, often clashing, paradoxical, yet neither of highest avail without the other, plainly supplies to these grand cosmic politics of ours, and to the launched forth mortal dangers of republicanism, today, or any day, the counterpart and offset whereby Nature restrains the deadly original relentlessness of all her first-class laws. This second principle is individuality, the pride and centripetal isolation of a human being in himself—identity—personalism. Whatever the name, its acceptance and thorough infusions through the organizations of political commonalty now shooting Aurora-like about the world, are of utmost importance, as the principle itself is needed for very life's sake. It forms, in a sort, or is to form, the compensating balance-wheel of the successful working machinery of aggregate America.

And, if we think of it, what does civilization itself rest upon—and what object has it, what its religions, arts, schools, etc., but rich, luxuriant, varied

personalism? To that, all bends; and it is because toward such result democracy alone, on anything like Nature's scale, breaks up the limitless fallows of
human-kind, and plants the seed, and gives fair play, that its claims now
precede the rest. The literature, songs, aesthetics, etc., of a country are of
importance principally because they furnish the materials and suggestions of
personality for the women and men of that country, and enforce them in a
thousand effective ways. As the topmost claim of a strong consolidating of
the nationality of these States is, that only by such powerful compaction can
the separate States secure that full and free swing within their spheres,
which is becoming to them, each after its kind, so will individuality, and
unimpeded branchings, flourish best under imperial republican forms.

Assuming Democracy to be at present in its embryo condition, and that
the only large and satisfactory justification of it resides in the future, mainly
through the copious production of perfect characters among the people, and
through the advent of a sane and pervading religiousness, it is with regard to
the atmosphere and spaciousness fit for such characters, and of certain nutriment and cartoon-draftings proper for them, and indicating them for New
World purposes, that I continue the present statement—an exploration, as of
new ground, wherein, like other primitive surveyors, I must do the best I
can, leaving it to those who come after me to do much better. (The service,
in fact, if any, must be to break a sort of first path or track, no matter how
rude and ungeometrical.)

We have frequently printed the word Democracy. Yet I cannot too often
repeat that it is a word the real gist of which still sleeps, quite unawakened,
notwithstanding the resonance and the many angry tempests out of which its
syllables have come, from pen or tongue. It is a great word, whose history, I
suppose, remains unwritten, because that history has yet to be enacted. It is,
in some sort, younger brother of another great and often-used word, Nature,
whose history also waits unwritten. As I perceive, the tendencies of our day,
in the States (and I entirely respect them), are toward those vast and sweeping movements, influences, moral and physical, of humanity, now and always
current over the planet, on the scale of the impulses of the elements. Then it
is also good to reduce the whole matter to the consideration of a single self,
a man, a woman, on permanent grounds. Even for the treatment of the
universal, in politics, metaphysics, or anything, sooner or later we come
down to one single, solitary soul.

There is, in sanest hours, a consciousness, a thought that rises, independent, lifted out from all else, calm, like the stars, shining eternal. This is the
thought of identity—yours for you, whoever you are, as mine for me. Miracle
of miracles, beyond statement, most spiritual and vaguest of earth's dreams,
yet hardest basic fact, and only entrance to all facts. In such devout hours, in
the midst of the significant wonders of heaven and earth (significant only
because of the Me in the center), creeds, conventions, fall away and become
of no account before this simple idea. Under the luminousness of real vision,

it alone takes possession, takes value. Like the shadowy dwarf in the fable, once liberated and looked upon, it expands over the whole earth, and spreads to the roof of heaven.

The quality of Being, in the object's self, according to its own central idea and purpose, and of growing therefrom and thereto—not criticism by other standards, and adjustments thereto—is the lesson of Nature. True, the full man wisely gathers, culls, absorbs; but if, engaged disproportionately in that, he slights or overlays the precious idiocrasy and special nativity and intention that he is, the man's self, the main thing, is a failure, however wise his general cultivation. Thus, in our times, refinement and delicatesse are not only attended to sufficiently, but threaten to eat us up, like a cancer. Already, the democratic genius watches, ill-pleased, these tendencies. Provision for a little healthy rudeness, savage virtue, justification of what one has in one's self, whatever it is, is demanded. Negative qualities, even deficiencies, would be a relief. Singleness and normal simplicity and separation, amid this more and more complex, more and more artificialized state of society—how pensively we yearn for them! how we would welcome their return!

In some such direction, then—at any rate enough to preserve the balance—we feel called upon to throw what weight we can, not for absolute reasons, but current ones. To prune, gather, trim, conform, and ever cram and stuff, and be genteel and proper, is the pressure of our days. While aware that much can be said even in behalf of all this, we perceive that we have not now to consider the question of what is demanded to serve a half-starved and barbarous nation, or set of nations, but what is most applicable, most pertinent, for numerous congeries of conventional, overcorpulent societies, already becoming stifled and rotten with flatulent, infidelistic literature, and polite conformity and art. In addition to established sciences, we suggest a science as it were of healthy average personalism, on original-universal grounds, the object of which should be to raise up and supply through the States a copious race of superb American men and women, cheerful, religious, ahead of any yet known.

America has yet morally and artistically originated nothing. She seems singularly unaware that the models of persons, books, manners, etc., appropriate for former conditions and for European lands, are but exiles and exotics here. No current of her life, as shown on the surfaces of what is authoritatively called her society, accepts or runs into social or aesthetic democracy; but all the currents set squarely against it. Never, in the Old World, was thoroughly upholstered exterior appearance and show, mental and other, built entirely on the idea of caste, and on the sufficiency of mere outside acquisition—never were glibness, verbal intellect more the test, the emulation—more loftily elevated as head and sample—than they are on the surface of our republican States this day. The writers of a time hint the mottoes of its gods. The word of the modern, say these voices, is the word Culture.

We find ourselves abruptly in close quarters with the enemy. This word Culture, or what it has come to represent, involves, by contrast, our whole theme, and has been, indeed, the spur, urging us to engagement. Certain questions arise. As now taught, accepted and carried out, are not the processes of culture rapidly creating a class of supercilious infidels, who believe in nothing? Shall a man lose himself in countless masses of adjustments, and be so shaped with reference to this, that, and the other, that the simply good and healthy and brave parts of him are reduced and clipped away, like the bordering of box in a garden? You can cultivate corn and roses and orchards—but who shall cultivate the mountain peaks, the ocean, and the tumbling gorgeousness of the clouds? Lastly—is the readily given reply that culture only seeks to help, systematize, and put in attitude, the elements of fertility and power, a conclusive reply?

I do not so much object to the name, or word, but I should certainly insist, for the purposes of these States, on a radical change of category, in the distribution of precedence. I should demand a program of culture, drawn out, not for a single class alone, or for the parlors or lecture rooms, but with an eye to practical life, the west, the workingmen, the facts of farms and jackplanes and engineers, and of the broad range of the women also of the middle and working strata, and with reference to the perfect equality of women, and of a grand and powerful motherhood. I should demand of this program or theory a scope generous enough to include the widest human area. It must have for its spinal meaning the formation of a typical personality of character, eligible to the uses of the high average of men—and *not* restricted by conditions ineligible to the masses. The best culture will always be that of the manly and courageous instincts, and loving perceptions, and of self-respect—aiming to form, over this continent, an idiocrasy of universalism, which, true child of America, will bring joy to its mother, returning to her in her own spirit, recruiting myriads of offspring, able, natural, perceptive, tolerant, devout believers in her, America, and with some definite instinct why and for what she has arisen, most vast, most formidable of historic births, and is, now and here, with wonderful step, journeying through Time.

The problem, as it seems to me, presented to the New World, is, under permanent law and order, and after preserving cohesion (ensemble-Individuality), at all hazards, to vitalize man's free play of special Personalism, recognizing in it something that calls ever more to be considered, fed, and adopted as the sub-stratum for the best that belongs to us (government indeed is for it), including the new aesthetics of our future.

To formulate beyond this present vagueness—to help line and put before us the species, or a specimen of the species, of the democratic ethnology of the future, is a work toward which the genius of our land, with peculiar encouragement, invites her well-wishers. Already certain limnings, more or less grotesque, more or less fading and watery, have appeared. We too (repressing doubts and qualms) will try our hand.

Attempting, then, however crudely, a basic model or portrait of personality for general use for the manliness of the States (and doubtless that is most useful which is most simple and comprehensive for all, and toned low enough), we should prepare the canvas well beforehand. Parentage must consider itself in advance. (Will the time hasten when fatherhood and motherhood shall become a science—and the noblest science?) To our model, a clear-blooded, strong-fibered physique is indispensable; the questions of food, drink, air, exercise, assimilation, digestion, can never be intermitted. Out of these we descry a well-begotten selfhood—in youth, fresh, ardent, emotional, aspiring, full of adventure; at maturity, brave, perceptive, under control, neither too talkative nor too reticent, neither flippant nor somber; of the bodily figure, the movements easy, the complexion showing the best blcod, somewhat flushed, breast expanded, an erect attitude, a voice whose sound outvies music, eyes of calm and steady gaze, yet capable also of flashing—and a general presence that holds its own in the company of the highest. (For it is native personality, and that alone, that endows a man to stand before presidents or generals, or in any distinguished collection, with *aplomb*—and *not* culture, or any knowledge or intellect whatever.)

With regard to the mental-educational part of our model, enlargement of intellect, stores of cephalic knowledge, etc., the concentration thitherward of all the customs of our age, especially in America, is so overweening, and provides so fully for that part, that, important and necessary as it is, it really needs nothing from us here—except, indeed, a phrase of warning and restraint. Manners, costumes, too, though important, we need not dwell upon here. Like beauty, grace of motion, etc., they are results. Causes, original things, being attended to, the right manners unerringly follow. Much is said, among artists, of "the grand style," as if it were a thing by itself. When a man, artist or whoever, has health, pride, acuteness, noble aspirations, he has the motive-elements of the grandest style. The rest is but manipulation (yet that is no small matter).

Leaving still unspecified several sterling parts of any model fit for the future personality of America, I must not fail, again and ever, to pronounce myself on one, probably the least attended to in modern times—a hiatus, indeed, threatening its gloomiest consequences after us. I mean the simple, unsophisticated Conscience, the primary moral element. If I were asked to specify in what quarter lie the grounds of darkest dread, respecting the America of our hopes, I should have to point to this particular. I should demand the invariable application to individuality, this day and any day, of that old, ever-true plumb-rule of persons, eras, nations. Our triumphant modern civilizee, with its all-schooling and his wondrous appliances, will still show himself but an amputation while this deficiency remains. Beyond (assuming a more hopeful tone), the vertebration of the manly and womanly personalism of our Western world, can only be, and is, indeed, to be (I hope), its all penetrating Religiousness.

The ripeness of Religion is doubtless to be looked for in this field of individuality, and is a result that no organization or church can ever achieve. As history is poorly retained by what the technists call history, and is not given out from their pages, except the learner has in himself the sense of the well-wrapt, never yet written, perhaps impossible to be written, history—so Religion, although casually arrested, and, after a fashion, preserved in the churches and creeds, does not depend at all upon them, but is a part of the identified soul, which, when greatest, knows not bibles in the old way, but in new ways—the identified soul, which can really confront Religion when it extricates itself entirely from the churches, and not before.

Personalism fuses this, and favors it. I should say, indeed, that only in the perfect uncontamination and solitariness of individuality may the spirituality of religion positively come forth at all. Only here, and on such terms, the meditation, the devout ecstasy, the soaring flight. Only here, communion with the mysteries, the eternal problems, whence? whither? Alone, and identity, and the mood—and the soul emerges, and all statements, churches, sermons, melt away like vapors. Alone, and silent thought and awe, and aspiration—and then the interior consciousness, like a hitherto unseen inscription, in magic ink, beams out its wondrous lines to the sense. Bibles may convey, and priests expound, but it is exclusively for the noiseless operation of one's isolated Self, to enter the pure ether of veneration, reach the divine levels, and commune with the unutterable.

. . .

Then there are mutterings (we will not now stop to heed them here, but they must be heeded), of something more revolutionary. The day is coming when the deep questions of woman's entrance amid the arenas of practical life, politics, the suffrage, etc., will not only be argued all around us, but may be put to decision, and real experiment.

Of course, in these States, for both man and woman, we must entirely recast the types of highest personality from what the oriental, feudal, ecclesiastical worlds bequeath us, and which yet possess the imaginative and aesthetic fields of the United States, pictorial and melodramatic, not without use as studies, but making sad work, and forming a strange anachronism upon the scenes and exigencies around us. Of course, the old undying elements remain. The task is, to successfully adjust them to new combinations, our own days. Nor is this so incredible. I can conceive a community, today and here, in which, on a sufficient scale, the perfect personalities, without noise meet; say in some pleasant western settlement or town, where a couple of hundred best men and women, of ordinary worldly status, have by luck been drawn together, with nothing extra of genius or wealth, but virtuous, chaste, industrious, cheerful, resolute, friendly and devout. I can conceive such a community organized in running order, powers judiciously delegated—farming, building, trade, courts, mails, schools, elections, all attended to; and then the rest of life, the main thing, freely branching and blossoming in each individual, and bearing golden fruit. I can see there, in every young and old man, after his kind, and in every woman after hers, a true personality, developed, exercised proportionately in body, mind, and spirit. I can imagine this case as one not necessarily rare or difficult, but in buoyant accordance with the municipal and general requirements of our times. And I can realize in it the culmination of something better than any stereotyped *éclat* of history or poems. Perhaps unsung, undramatized, unput in essays or biographies—perhaps even some such community already exists, in Ohio, Illinois, Missouri, or somewhere, practically fulfilling itself, and thus outvying, in cheapest vulgar life, all that has been hitherto shown in best ideal pictures.

In short, and to sum up, America, betaking herself to formative action (as it is about time for more solid achievement, and less windy promise), must, for her purposes, cease to recognize a theory of character grown of feudal aristocracies, or formed by merely literary standards, or from any ultramarine full-dress formulas of culture, polish, caste, etc., and must sternly promulgate her own new standard, yet old enough, and accepting the old, the perennial elements, and combining them into groups, unities, appropriate to the modern, the democratic, the west, and to the practical occasions and needs of our own cities, and of the agricultural regions. Ever the most precious in the common. Ever the fresh breeze of field, or hill or lake, is more than any palpitation of fans, though of ivory, and redolent with perfume; and the air is more than the costliest perfumes.

.   .   .

In the prophetic literature of these States (the reader of my speculations will miss their principal stress unless he allows well for the point that a new Literature, perhaps a new Metaphysics, certainly a new Poetry, are to be, in my opinion, the only sure and worthy supports and expressions of the American Democracy), Nature, true Nature, and the true idea of Nature, long absent, must, above all, become fully restored, enlarged, and must furnish the pervading atmosphere to poems, and the test of all high literary and aesthetic compositions. I do not mean the smooth walks, trimmed hedges, posys and nightingales of the English poets, but the whole orb, with its geologic history, the cosmos, carrying fire and snow, that rolls through the illimitable areas, light as a feather, though weighing billions of tons. Furthermore, as by what we now partially call Nature is intended, at most, only what is entertainable by the physical conscience, the sense of matter, and of good animal health—on these it must be distinctly accumulated, incorporated, that man, comprehending these, has, in towering superaddition, the moral and spiritual consciences, indicating his destination beyond the ostensible, the mortal.

To the heights of such estimate of Nature indeed ascending, we proceed to make observations for our Vistas, breathing rarest air. What is I believe called Idealism seems to me to suggest (guarding against extravagance, and ever modified even by its opposite) the course of inquiry and desert of favor for our New World metaphysics, their foundation of and in literature, giving hue to all.

The elevating and etherealizing ideas of the unknown and of unreality must be brought forward with authority, as they are the legitimate heirs of the known, and of reality, and at least as great as their parents. Fearless of scoffing, and of the ostent,[3] let us take our stand, our ground, and never desert it, to confront the growing excess and arrogance of realism. To the cry, now victorious—the cry of sense, science, flesh, incomes, farms, merchandise, logic, intellect, demonstrations, solid perpetuities, buildings of brick and iron, or even the facts of the shows of trees, earth, rocks, etc., fear not, my brethren, my sisters, to sound out with equally determined voice, that conviction brooding within the recesses of every envisioned soul—illusions! apparitions! figments all! True, we must not condemn the show, neither absolutely deny it, for the indispensability of its meanings; but how clearly we see that, migrate in soul to what we can already conceive of superior and spiritual points of view, and palpable as it seems under present relations, it all and several might, nay certainly would, fall apart and vanish.

. . .

In the future of these States must arise poets immenser far, and make great poems of death. The poems of life are great, but there must be the poems of the purports of life, not only in itself, but beyond itself. I have eulogized Homer, the sacred bards of Jewry, Aeschylus, Juvenal, Shakespeare, etc., and acknowledged their inestimable value. But (with perhaps the exception in some, not all respects, of the second-mentioned) I say there must, for future and democratic purposes, appear poets (dare I to say so?) of higher class even than any of those—poets not only possessed of the religious fire and abandon of Isaiah, luxuriant in the epic talent of Homer, or for proud characters as in Shakespeare, but consistent with the Hegelian formulas, and consistent with modern science.[4] America needs, and the world needs, a class of bards who will, now and ever, so link and tally the rational physical being of man, with the ensembles of time and space, and with this

---

[3] In the archaic sense, an act of showing or exhibition.

[4] Homer (850–800 B.C.), the Greek epic poet of *The Iliad* and *The Odyssey;* Juvenal (A.D. 60?–140?), Roman lawyer and satirist. Hegelianism is the philosophy of George Wilhelm Friedrich Hegel (1770-1831), German philosopher whose doctrine of phenomenology attempts by dialectical method to make scientific the final truths of religion.

Divine Maternity

vast and multiform show, Nature, surrounding him, ever tantalizing him, equally a part, and yet not a part of him, as to essentially harmonize, satisfy, and put at rest. Faith, very old, now scared away by science, must be restored, brought back by the same power that caused her departure—restored with new sway, deeper, wider, higher than ever. Surely, this universal ennui, this coward fear, this shuddering at death, these low, degrading views, are not always to rule the spirit pervading future society, as it has the past, and does the present. What the Roman Lucretius[5] sought most nobly, yet all too blindly, negatively to do for his age and its successors, must be done positively by some great coming literatus, especially poet, who, while remaining fully poet, will absorb whatever science indicates, with spiritualism, and out of them, and out of his own genius, will compose the great poem of death. Then will man indeed confront Nature, and confront time and space, both with science, and *con amore*, and take his right place, prepared for life, master of fortune and misfortune. And then that which was long wanted will be supplied, and the ship that had it not before in all her voyages, will have an anchor.

There are still other standards, suggestions, for products of high literatuses. That which really balances and conserves the social and political world is not so much legislation, police, treaties, and dread of punishment, as the latent eternal intuitional sense, in humanity, of fairness, manliness, decorum, etc. Indeed, this perennial regulation, control, and oversight, by self-suppliance, is *sine qua non* to democracy; and a highest, widest aim of democratic literature may well be to bring forth, cultivate, brace, and strengthen this sense, in individuals and society. A strong mastership of the general inferior self by the superior self, is to be aided, secured, indirectly, but surely, by the literatus, in his works, shaping, for individual or aggregate democracy, a great passionate body, in and along with which goes a great masterful spirit.

.   .   .

Investigating here, we see, not that it is a little thing we have, in having the bequeathed libraries, countless shelves of volumes, records, etc.; yet how serious the danger, depending entirely on them, of the bloodless vein, the nerveless arm, the false application, at second or third hand. We see that the real interest of this people of ours in the theology, history, poetry, politics, and personal models of the past (the British islands, for instance, and indeed all the past), is not necessarily to mold ourselves or our literature upon them, but to attain fuller, more definite comparisons, warnings, and the insight to ourselves, our own present, and our own far grander, different, future history, religion, social customs, etc. We see that almost everything that has

[5] Lucretius Caius (96?–55 B.C.) was a Roman philosophical poet and a disciple of Epicu-rus. His great work was *De Rerum Natura* (in six books).

Belief in sexual equality

been written, sung, or stated, of old, with reference to humanity under the feudal and oriental institutes, religions, and for other lands, needs to be rewritten, resung, restated, in terms consistent with the institution of these States, and to come in range and obedient uniformity with them.

We see, as in the universes of the material cosmos, after meteorological, vegetable, and animal cycles, man at last arises, born through them, to prove them, concentrate them, to turn upon them with wonder and love—to command them, adorn them, and carry them upward into superior realms—so, out of the series of the preceding social and political universes, now arise these States. We see that while many were supposing things established and completed, really the grandest things always remain; and discover that the work of the New World is not ended, but only fairly begun.

We see our land, America, her literature, aesthetics, etc., as, substantially, the getting in form, or effusement and statement, of deepest basic elements and loftiest final meanings, of history and man—and the portrayal (under the eternal laws and conditions of beauty) of our own physiognomy, the subjective tie and expression of the objective, as from our own combination, continuation, and points of view—and the deposit and record of the national mentality, character, appeals, heroism, wars, and even liberties—where these, and all, culminate in native literary and artistic formulation, to be perpetuated; and not having which native, first-class formulation, she will flounder about, and her other, however imposing, eminent greatness, prove merely a passing gleam; but truly having which, she will understand herself, live nobly, nobly contribute, emanate, and, swinging, poised safely on herself, illumined and illuming, become a full-formed world, and divine Mother not only of material but spiritual worlds, in ceaseless succession through time—the main thing being the average, the bodily, the concrete, the democratic, the popular, on which all the superstructures of the future are to permanently rest.

LOCALE AND REGION: THE BEGINNINGS OF REALISM

American writing after the Civil War turned toward the new preoccupations of a rapidly changing society. The foremost facts of life were to be found in the sprawling railroad empires that accelerated the defeat of the Indian nations and opened the fantastic natural resources of the Far West to exploitation, and in the new centralized economy of corporations and monopolies that brought even backwoods villages and mountain communities under the domain of modern life. The idea of "Union" seemed to prevail in politics, in the economy, and in culture. To be sure, the period witnessed extreme conflicts and much violence, in the wars against the Indians, in labor struggles, and in the unsettling influx of masses of new immigrants. These conflicts and antagonisms would eventually find their way into literature; by the 1890's "naturalism" would appear as the banner under which young writers such as Frank Norris and Stephen Crane would open their fiction to the realities of violence, sexual passion, poverty, and greed. But in the decades just after the war, when talk of unification and the healing of wounds was uppermost, the most popular literary works were those that dealt not with the "nation," but with the region and the locale, with the peculiarities of custom, dialect, and mannerisms associated with distinct places such as the tidewater and piedmont South, the Maine coast, and the Far West mining camps and ranches. The phenomenon came to be known as regionalism or local color, and examples filled the pages of the growing number of nationally circulating periodicals that emerged in these years.

A feeling for place had never been absent from American writing, and earlier in the nineteenth century, in the works of Irving, Cooper, Sims, and Hawthorne, we often find specific locales portrayed in loving detail. Antebellum humor, the frontier and downeast comedy of Longstreet, Thorpe, Smith, and others, also was steeped in local traits of speech, habits, and landscape. The call for a national literature in the criticism before the war made much of the value of native materials; writers like Emerson and Lowell urged their fellows to discover the unique beauties of the everyday actualities around them. When Emerson asked writers to explore "the near, the low, the common," when

Man with horse-drawn plow, c. 1880's. *Bureau of Reclamation National Archives.*

Pioneer home of Nels Wickstrom family, Fence, Wisconsin, 1893. *State Historical Society of Wisconsin.*

he tried to win American poets away from "the remote, the romantic" in favor of "the meal in the firkin; the milk in the pan; the ballad in the street," he called for what was, in effect, a literature of regional characteristics.

But regionalism did not emerge as a movement until after the Civil War. It was stimulated in part by the swift changes occurring in American life, changes that provoked a need for roots and knowledge of local connections. The regional aspects in the writings of figures such as Harriet Beecher Stowe in *Oldtown Folks,* James Russell Lowell in *Bigelow Papers,* and the authors included in this section offered a much-needed orientation by evoking what seemed to be unchanging patterns of life at the local level, in village gossip, in family affairs, in the very speech and customs of common folk. Moreover, regionalism was related to the emerging literary movement known as realism, which also stressed the commonplace, the broad doings of relatively simple, unremarkable people. For both movements, the prewar ideal of the "common man" was a guiding principle. Regionalism focused on homespun characters in tucked-away corners of American life. It frequently chose to describe, and occasionally to analyze with remarkable psychological astuteness (Sarah Orne Jewett's work is a case in point), idiosyncracies of character associated with a particular landscape, a particular local history, or particular folkways and ways of speech. Although dialect had appeared earlier in American writing—in frontier humor, for example—regionalist writers prided themselves on the accuracy of their imitation, and thus preservation, of native speech habits.

"Regionalism" and "local color" are often used interchangeably, but it is useful to distinguish between them. Regionalism emphasizes character in relation to a specific community and history, as in Cable's New Orleans stories, while local color often dramatizes the eccentric, the picturesque, the colorful. Bret Harte, often credited with inventing local color fiction, offers the best examples of the genre. While "realistic" in their portrayal of "low" characters such as gamblers, miners, and prostitutes, Harte's stories are also suffused with "romantic" feeling in their neat plot structures and their sentimental endings, which often affirm the universal goodness of mankind in general by revealing a "heart of gold" under the most disreputable and even immoral exterior. Local color stories are often costume dramas, while regionalist fiction, as in the works of a brilliant group of women writers such as Kate Chopin, Mary Wilkins Freeman, and Sarah Orne Jewett, is less dependent on formulaic plots, less clever in contriving neat endings, and more engaging in their psychological insight and character analysis.

The regionalist impulse represents an enduring strain in American writing, one that will reappear in the twentieth century most notably among Southern writers. The stress on the local and the regional says implicitly that reality in America cannot be summed up in abstractions about a national character. While it appeared in a period of national consolidation after the breach of the Civil War, and while it may have reinforced the idea of national unity simply by spreading information about the many parts of the country and their quaint, odd habits to a national readership, regionalist literature still can be seen as a resistance to the fiction of a homogeneous national culture. It is significant, too, that much of this writing dealt with the recent past, keeping alive a sense of history and local tradition at a time of rapid change. Idealization and nostalgia for simpler, more predictable times also crept into regionalist writing, notably in Southern plantation fiction, which enjoyed an astonishing popularity in the North after the war. Was regionalism a form of escapist literature? This element was present, especially in the fact that regionalist subjects were mainly rural, just at the time of the most intense expansion of cities in American history. But the mode attracted some of the most talented young writers in the years after the war. With its insistence on commonplace subjects and its use of the actual speech of common people, it fed the springs of realism that would flow through the novels of William Dean Howells, Henry James, Harold Frederick, E. B. Fuller, and Edith Wharton. To be sure, much of the writing that goes by the name of regionalism and local color retains more of a historical than a genuinely literary interest, but the movement was able to boast several writers of high order and, in Mark Twain, one of the authentic geniuses of American literature.

BRET HARTE

(1836–1902)

The local color story will always be associated with Bret Harte. On the weight of his tales of California mining camps, Harte enjoyed a dazzling success for a few years in the late 1860's; he was sought after with handsome contracts by Eastern publishers and was acclaimed by the likes of Charles Dickens. His stories about the rough and ready ways of picturesque, slangy, and lovable characters established a style that many writers, unfortunately including Harte himself, proceeded to imitate. The style easily became a formula, and Harte's subsequent career became a lesson in the dangers of too much success too soon.

Harte was neither a native Californian nor a longtime resident. He arrived in California in 1854 from Albany, where he had grown up. He was the son of a Dutch-American mother and a Jewish father (who seems to have deserted the family about the time of Bret's birth). While living in northern California frontier towns, the youngster tried his hand at prospecting, typesetting, teaching, and newspaper writing. Because he was rather learned and cultivated, he was not exactly a frontier type, and he was nearly run out of one town for writing a straightforward account of a massacre of local Indians, including many women and children. He moved to San Francisco and quickly established himself as a literary figure. In 1864 he won a sinecure as secretary to the mint. His first important publication came in 1867 with *Condensed Novels,* a group of parodies of popular romantic writers. Next came a stint as editor of the influential *Overland Monthly.* Harte opened the journal to the brilliant new writing appearing in the West, such as Mark Twain's early pieces, and his own stories and poems. His status and influence in these days were enviable; he held sway over a

The standard text is *The Writings of Bret Harte,* 20 vols., 1896–1914. See also *The Works of Bret Harte,* 25 vols., 1914. Geoffrey Bret Harte has edited the *Letters,* 1926.

A definitive biography is George R. Stewart, *Bret Harte, Argonaut in Exile,* 1931. An early treatment is T. Edgar Pemberton, *The Life of Bret Harte,* 1903. Criticism may be found in Van Wyck Brooks, *The Times of Melville and Whitman,* 1947; Josiah Royce, *California, From the Conquest in* 1846 to the Second Vigilance Committee in San Francisco: A Study in American Character, 1948; Everett Carter, *Howells and the Age of Realism,* 1950; Guy Cardwell, *Twins of Genius,* 1953; Margaret Duckett, *Mark Twain and Bret Harte,* 1964.

For Harte's historical role as an American short story writer, see Fred Lewis Pattee, *The Development of the American Short Story,* 1923, and Arthur Hobson Quinn, *American Fiction,* 1936.

Cowboy at the B.T. Ranch, North Dakota, summer of 1887. *The Metropolitan Museum of Art, Gift of Charles Bregler, 1961.*

group of writers that included at one time Mark Twain (his closest friend for a few years), Joaquin Miller, and Ambrose Bierce.

Meteoric personal success arrived with the publication of "The Luck of Roaring Camp" in 1868, followed by "The Outcasts of Poker Flat" 1869. His collection, *The Luck of Roaring Camp and Other Sketches* (1870) was another smashing success and, in 1871 *The Atlantic Monthly* rushed him a contract for $10,000 for 12 contributions (he had meanwhile been appointed Professor of Literature at the University of California).

Harte left California on a triumphant trip to Boston in 1871. But his career had already peaked; he would never live up to his initial success. In the following years, most of them spent abroad, he repeated over and again the formula of his early tales, but without the freshness that came from his contact with the California atmosphere. Harte's work proved to be sentimental at its core, always idealizing gestures of sacrifice that revealed the true but hidden worth of apparently disreputable and outcast characters. Without Mark Twain's genius for invention or genuine feeling for his material, Harte eventually lost his popularity, although he continued to grind out stories at a regular pace. He spent the last 24 years of his life in minor diplomatic positions in Germany, Scotland, and England, and died in London shortly after completing several volumes of a collected work.

The Society Upon the Stanislaus[1]

I reside at Table Mountain, and my name is Truthful James;
I am not up to small deceit or any sinful games;
And I'll tell in simple language what I know about the row
That broke up our Society[2] upon the Stanislow.[3]

[1] The poem was first published in the "San Francisco News Letter and California Advertiser" in 1868 with the title "Proceedings of the Academy of Natural Sciences at Smith's Crossing, Tuolumne County." It was collected into *Poems*, published in 1871, with the present title.

[2] The California Academy of Natural Science in San Francisco, one of the literary and scientific societies often satirized by Pacific Slope humorists.

[3] Stanislaus Peak in northeastern California.

But first I would remark, that it is not a proper plan   5
For any scientific gent to whale his fellow-man,
And, if a member don't agree with his peculiar whim,
To lay for that same member for to "put a head" on him.

Now nothing could be finer or more beautiful to see
Than the first six months' proceedings of that same Society,   10
Till Brown of Calaveras[4] brought a lot of fossil bones
That he found within a tunnel near the tenement of Jones.

Then Brown he read a paper, and he reconstructed there,
From those same bones, an animal that was extremely rare;
And Jones then asked the Chair for a suspension of the rules,   15
Till he could prove that those same bones was one of his lost mules.

Then Brown he smiled a bitter smile, and said he was at fault.
It seemed he had been trespassing on Jones's family vault;
He was a most sarcastic man, this quiet Mr. Brown,
And on several occasions he had cleaned out the town.   20

Now I hold it is not decent for a scientific gent
To say another is an ass,—at least, to all intent;
Nor should the individual who happens to be meant
Reply by heaving rocks at him, to any great extent.

Then Abner Dean of Angel's[5] raised a point of order, when   25
A chunk of old red sandstone took him in the abdomen,
And he smiled a kind of sickly smile, and curled up on the floor,
And the subsequent proceedings interested him no more.

For, in less time than I write it, every member did engage
In a warfare with the remnants of a palæozoic age;   30
And the way they heaved those fossils in their anger was a sin,
Till the skull of an old mammoth caved the head of Thompson in.

And this is all I have to say of these improper games,
For I live at Table Mountain, and my name is Truthful James;
And I've told in simple language what I know about the row   35
That broke up our Society upon the Stanislow.

1868, 1871

---

[4] Calaveras County is east of San Francisco.   [5] Angel's Camp, near Stanislaus Peak.

The Outcasts of Poker Flat[1]

As Mr. John Oakhurst, gambler, stepped into the main street of Poker Flat on the morning of the 23d of November, 1850, he was conscious of a change in its moral atmosphere since the preceding night. Two or three men, conversing earnestly together, ceased as he approached, and exchanged significant glances. There was a Sabbath lull in the air, which, in a settlement unused to Sabbath influences, looked ominous.

Mr. Oakhurst's calm, handsome face betrayed small concern in these indications. Whether he was conscious of any predisposing cause, was another question. "I reckon they're after somebody," he reflected; "likely it's me." He returned to his pocket the handkerchief with which he had been whipping away the red dust of Poker Flat from his neat boots, and quietly discharged his mind of any further conjecture.

In point of fact, Poker Flat was "after somebody." It had lately suffered the loss of several thousand dollars, two valuable horses, and a prominent citizen. It was experiencing a spasm of virtuous reaction, quite as lawless and ungovernable as any of the acts that had provoked it. A secret committee had determined to rid the town of all improper persons. This was done permanently in regard of two men who were then hanging from the boughs of a sycamore in the gulch, and temporarily in the banishment of certain other objectionable characters. I regret to say that some of these were ladies. It is but due to the sex, however, to state that their impropriety was professional, and it was only in such easily established standards of evil that Poker Flat ventured to sit in judgment.

Mr. Oakhurst was right in supposing that he was included in this category. A few of the committee had urged hanging him as a possible example, and a sure method of reimbursing themselves from his pockets of the sums he had won from them. "It's agin justice," said Jim Wheeler, "to let this yer young man from Roaring Camp—an entire stranger—carry away our money." But a crude sentiment of equity residing in the breasts of those who had been fortunate enough to win from Mr. Oakhurst overruled this narrower local prejudice.

Mr. Oakhurst received his sentence with philosophic calmness, none the less coolly that he was aware of the hesitation of his judges. He was too much of a gambler not to accept fate. With him life was at best an uncertain game, and he recognized the usual percentage in favor of the dealer.

A body of armed men accompanied the deported wickedness of Poker Flat to the outskirts of the settlement. Besides Mr. Oakhurst, who was known to be a coolly desperate man, and for whose intimidation the armed escort was intended, the expatriated party consisted of a young woman fa-

---

[1] The story was first published in the "Overland Monthly" in January 1869 and then collected in *The Luck of Roaring Camp and Other Sketches*, published in 1870.

miliarly known as "The Duchess"; another, who had won the title of "Mother Shipton"; and "Uncle Billy," a suspected sluice-robber[2] and confirmed drunkard. The cavalcade provoked no comments from the spectators, nor was any word uttered by the escort. Only when the gulch which marked the uttermost limit of Poker Flat was reached, the leader spoke briefly and to the point. The exiles were forbidden to return at the peril of their lives.

As the escort disappeared, their pent-up feelings found vent in a few hysterical tears from the Duchess, some bad language from Mother Shipton, and a Parthian volley of expletives from Uncle Billy. The philosophic Oakhurst alone remained silent. He listened calmly to Mother Shipton's desire to cut somebody's heart out, to the repeated statements of the Duchess that she would die in the road, and to the alarming oaths that seemed to be bumped out of Uncle Billy as he rode forward. With the easy good humor characteristic of his class, he insisted upon exchanging his own riding-horse, "Five-Spot," for the sorry mule which the Duchess rode. But even this act did not draw the party into any closer sympathy. The young woman readjusted her somewhat draggled plumes with a feeble, faded coquetry; Mother Shipton eyed the possessor of "Five-Spot" with malevolence, and Uncle Billy included the whole party in one sweeping anathema.

The road to Sandy Bar—a camp that, not having as yet experienced the regenerating influences of Poker Flat, consequently seemed to offer some invitation to the emigrants—lay over a steep mountain range. It was distant a day's severe travel. In that advanced season, the party soon passed out of the moist, temperate regions of the foothills into the dry, cold, bracing air of the Sierras. The trail was narrow and difficult. At noon the Duchess, rolling out of her saddle upon the ground, declared her intention of going no farther, and the party halted.

The spot was singularly wild and impressive. A wooded amphitheatre, surrounded on three sides by precipitous cliffs of naked granite, sloped gently toward the crest of another precipice that overlooked the valley. It was, undoubtedly, the most suitable spot for a camp, had camping been advisable. But Mr. Oakhurst knew that scarcely half the journey to Sandy Bar was accomplished, and the party were not equipped or provisioned for delay. This fact he pointed out to his companions curtly, with a philosophic commentary on the folly of "throwing up their hand before the game was played out." But they were furnished with liquor, which in this emergency stood them in place of food, fuel, rest, and prescience. In spite of his remonstrances, it was not long before they were more or less under its influence. Uncle Billy passed rapidly from a bellicose state into one of stupor, the Duchess became maudlin, and Mother Shipton snored. Mr. Oakhurst alone remained erect, leaning against a rock, calmly surveyed them.

---

[2] A trough for washing gold from gravel and sand.

Mr. Oakhurst did not drink. It interfered with a profession which required coolness, impassiveness, and presence of mind, and, in his own language, he "couldn't afford it." As he gazed at his recumbent fellow exiles, the loneliness begotten of his pariah trade, his habits of life, his very vices, for the first time seriously oppressed him. He bestirred himself in dusting his black clothes, washing his hands and face, and other acts characteristic of his studiously neat habits, and for a moment forgot his annoyance. The thought of deserting his weaker and more pitiable companions never perhaps occurred to him. Yet he could not help feeling the want of that excitement which, singularly enough, was most conducive to that calm equanimity for which he was notorious. He looked at the gloomy walls that rose a thousand feet sheer above the circling pines around him, at the sky ominously clouded, at the valley below, already deepening into shadow; and, doing so, suddenly he heard his own name called.

heart of gold

A horseman slowly ascended the trail. In the fresh, open face of the newcomer Mr. Oakhurst recognized Tom Simson, otherwise known as "The Innocent," of Sandy Bar. He had met him some months before over a "little game," and had, with perfect equanimity, won the entire fortune—amounting to some forty dollars—of the guileless youth. After the game was finished, Mr. Oakhurst drew the youthful speculator behind the door and thus addressed him: "Tommy, you're a good little man, but you can't gamble worth a cent. Don't try it ever again." He then handed him his money back, pushed him gently from the room, and so made a devoted slave of Tom Simson.   *circumstance*

There was a remembrance of this in his boyish and enthusiastic greeting of Mr. Oakhurst. He had started, he said, to go to Poker Flat to seek his fortune. "Alone?" No, not exactly alone; in fact (a giggle), he had run away with Piney Woods. Didn't Mr. Oakhurst remember Piney? She that used to wait on the table at the Temperance House? They had been engaged a long time, but old Jake Woods had objected, and so they had run away, and were going to Poker Flat to be married, and here they were. And they were tired out, and how lucky it was they had found a place to camp, and company. All this the Innocent delivered rapidly, while Piney, a stout, comely damsel of fifteen, emerged from behind the pine-tree, where she had been blushing unseen, and rode to the side of her lover.

Mr. Oakhurst seldom troubled himself with sentiment, still less with propriety; but he had a vague idea that the situation was not fortunate. He retained, however, his presence of mind sufficiently to kick Uncle Billy, who was about to say something, and Uncle Billy was sober enough to recognize in Mr. Oakhurst's kick a superior power that would not bear trifling. He then endeavored to dissuade Tom Simson from delaying further, but in vain. He *whore with a heart of gold.*

even pointed out the fact that there was no provision, nor means of making a camp. But, unluckily, the Innocent met this objection by assuring the party that he was provided with an extra mule loaded with provisions, and by the discovery of a rude attempt at a log house near the trail. "Piney can stay with Mrs. Oakhurst," said the Innocent, pointing to the Duchess, "and I can shift for myself."

Nothing but Mr. Oakhurst's admonishing foot saved Uncle Billy from bursting into a roar of laughter. As it was, he felt compelled to retire up the cañon until he could recover his gravity. There he confided the joke to the tall pine-trees, with many slaps of his leg, contortions of his face, and the usual profanity. But when he returned to the party, he found them seated by a fire—for the air had grown strangely chill and the sky overcast—in apparently amicable conversation. Piney was actually talking in an impulsive girlish fashion to the Duchess, who was listening with an interest and animation she had not shown for many days. The Innocent was holding forth, apparently with equal effect, to Mr. Oakhurst and Mother Shipton, who was actually relaxing into amiability. "Is this yer a d——d picnic?" said Uncle Billy, with inward scorn, as he surveyed the sylvan group, the glancing firelight, and the tethered animals in the foreground. Suddenly an idea mingled with the alcoholic fumes that disturbed his brain. It was apparently of a jocular nature, for he felt impelled to slap his leg again and cram his fist into his mouth.

As the shadows crept slowly up the mountain, a slight breeze rocked the tops of the pine-trees and moaned through their long and gloomy aisles. The ruined cabin, patched and covered with pine boughs, was set apart for the ladies. As the lovers parted, they unaffectedly exchanged a kiss, so honest and sincere that it might have been heard above the swaying pines. The frail Duchess and the malevolent Mother Shipton were probably too stunned to remark upon this last evidence of simplicity, and so turned without a word to the hut. The fire was replenished, the men lay down before the door, and in a few minutes were asleep.

Mr. Oakhurst was a light sleeper. Toward morning he awoke benumbed and cold. As he stirred the dying fire, the wind, which was now blowing strongly, brought to his cheek that which caused the blood to leave it,— snow!

He started to his feet with the intention of awakening the sleepers, for there was no time to lose. But turning to where Uncle Billy had been lying, he found him gone. A suspicion leaped to his brain, and a curse to his lips. He ran to the spot where the mules had been tethered—they were no longer there. The tracks were already rapidly disappearing in the snow.

The momentary excitement brought Mr. Oakhurst back to the fire with his usual calm. He did not waken the sleepers. The Innocent slumbered peacefully, with a smile on his good-humored, freckled face; the virgin Piney slept beside her frailer sisters as sweetly as though attended by celestial guardians; and Mr. Oakhurst, drawing his blanket over his shoulders, stroked his mustaches and waited for the dawn. It came slowly in a whirling mist of snowflakes that dazzled and confused the eye. What could be seen of the landscape appeared magically changed. He looked over the valley, and summed up the present and future in two words, "Snowed in!"

A careful inventory of the provisions, which, fortunately for the party, had been stored within the hut, and so escaped the felonious fingers of Uncle Billy, disclosed the fact that with care and prudence they might last ten days longer. "That is," said Mr. Oakhurst *sotto voce* to the Innocent, "if you're willing to board us. If you ain't—and perhaps you'd better not—you can wait till Uncle Billy gets back with provisions." For some occult reason, Mr. Oakhurst could not bring himself to disclose Uncle Billy's rascality, and so offered the hypothesis that he had wandered from the camp and had accidentally stampeded the animals. He dropped a warning to the Duchess and Mother Shipton, who of course knew the facts of their associate's defection. "They'll find out the truth about us *all* when they find out anything," he added significantly, "and there's no good frightening them now."

Tom Simson not only put all his worldly store at the disposal of Mr. Oakhurst, but seemed to enjoy the prospect of their enforced seclusion. "We'll have a good camp for a week, and then the snow'll melt, and we'll all go back together." The cheerful gayety of the young man and Mr. Oakhurst's calm infected the others. The Innocent, with the aid of pine boughs, extemporized a thatch for the roofless cabin, and the Duchess directed Piney in the rearrangement of the interior with a taste and tact that opened the blue eyes of that provincial maiden to their fullest extent. "I reckon now you're used to fine things at Poker Flat," said Piney. The Duchess turned away sharply to conceal something that reddened her cheeks through their professional tint, and Mother Shipton requested Piney not to "chatter." But when Mr. Oakhurst returned from a weary search for the trail, he heard the sound of happy laughter echoed from the rocks. He stopped in some alarm, and his thoughts first naturally reverted to the whiskey, which he had prudently cachéd. "And yet it don't somehow sound like whiskey," said the gambler. It was not until he caught sight of the blazing fire through the still blinding storm, and the group around it, that he settled to the conviction that it was "square fun."

Whether Mr. Oakhurst had cachéd his cards with the whiskey as something debarred the free access of the community, I cannot say. It was certain that, in Mother Shipton's words, he "didn't say 'cards' once" during that evening. Haply the time was beguiled by an accordion, produced somewhat ostentatiously by Tom Simson from his pack. Notwithstanding some difficulties attending the manipulation of this instrument, Piney Woods managed to pluck several reluctant melodies from its keys, to an accompaniment by the

Innocent on a pair of bone castanets. But the crowning festivity of the evening was reached in a rude camp-meeting hymn, which the lovers, joining hands, sang with great earnestness and vociferation. I fear that a certain defiant tone and Covenanter's[3] swing to its chorus, rather than any devotional quality, caused it speedily to infect the others, who at last joined in the refrain:

> "I'm proud to live in the service of the Lord,
> And I'm bound to die in His army."

The pines rocked, the storm eddied and whirled above the miserable group, and the flames of their altar leaped heavenward, as if in token of the vow.

At midnight the storm abated, the rolling clouds parted, and the stars glittered keenly above the sleeping camp. Mr. Oakhurst, whose professional habits had enabled him to live on the smallest possible amount of sleep, in dividing the watch with Tom Simson somehow managed to take upon himself the greater part of that duty. He excused himself to the Innocent by saying that he had "often been a week without sleep." "Doing what?" asked Tom. "Poker!" replied Oakhurst sententiously. "When a man gets a streak of luck,—nigger-luck,—he don't get tired. The luck gives in first. Luck," continued the gambler reflectively, "is a mighty queer thing. All you know about it for certain is that it's bound to change. And it's finding out when it's going to change that makes you. We've had a streak of bad luck since we left Poker Flat,—you come along, and slap you get into it, too. If you can hold your cards right along you're all right. For," added the gambler, with cheerful irrelevance—

> " 'I'm proud to live in the service of the Lord,
> And I'm bound to die in His army.' "

The third day came, and the sun, looking through the white-curtained valley, saw the outcasts divide their slowly decreasing store of provisions for the morning meal. It was one of the peculiarities of that mountain climate that its rays diffused a kindly warmth over the wintry landscape, as if in regretful commiseration of the past. But it revealed drift on drift of snow piled high around the hut,—a hopeless, uncharted, trackless sea of white lying below the rocky shores to which the castaways still clung. Through the marvelously clear air the smoke of the pastoral village of Poker Flat rose miles away. Mother Shipton saw it, and from a remote pinnacle of her rocky fastness hurled in that direction a final malediction. It was her last vituperative attempt, and perhaps for that reason was invested with a certain degree

[3] The Scottish Covenanters, separatists from the Church of England in the seventeenth century, who sang with a stirring martial beat.

of sublimity. It did her good, she privately informed the Duchess. "Just you go out there and cuss, and see." She then set herself to the task of amusing "the child," as she and the Duchess were pleased to call Piney. Piney was no chicken, but it was a soothing and original theory of the pair thus to account for the fact that she didn't swear and wasn't improper.

When night crept up again through the gorges, the reedy notes of the accordion rose and fell in fitful spasms and long-drawn gasps by the flickering campfire. But music failed to fill entirely the aching void left by insufficient food, and a new diversion was proposed by Piney,—story-telling. Neither Mr. Oakhurst nor his female companions caring to relate their personal experiences, this plan would have failed too, but for the Innocent. Some months before he had chanced upon a stray copy of Mr. Pope's ingenious translation of the Iliad. He now proposed to narrate the principal incidents of that poem—having thoroughly mastered the argument and fairly forgotten the words—in the current vernacular of Sandy Bar. And so for the rest of that night the Homeric demigods again walked the earth. Trojan bully and wily Greek wrestled in the winds, and the great pines in the cañon seemed to bow to the wrath of the son of Peleus.[4] Mr. Oakhurst listened with quiet satisfaction. Most especially was he interested in the fate of "Ashheels," as the Innocent persisted in denominating the "swift-footed Achilles."

So, with small food and much of Homer and the accordion, a week passed over the heads of the outcasts. The sun again forsook them, and again from leaden skies the snowflakes were sifted over the land. Day by day closer around them drew the snowy circle, until at last they looked from their prison over drifted walls of dazzling white, that towered twenty feet above their heads. It became more and more difficult to replenish their fires, even from the fallen trees beside them, now half hidden in the drifts. And yet no one complained. The lovers turned from the dreary prospect and looked into each other's eyes, and were happy. Mr. Oakhurst settled himself coolly to the losing game before him. The Duchess, more cheerful than she had been, assumed the care of Piney. Only Mother Shipton—once the strongest of the party—seemed to sicken and fade. At midnight on the tenth day she called Oakhurst to her side. "I'm going," she said, in a voice of querulous weakness, "but don't say anything about it. Don't waken the kids. Take the bundle from under my head, and open it." Mr. Oakhurst did so. It contained Mother Shipton's rations for the last week, untouched. "Give 'em to the child," she said, pointing to the sleeping Piney. "You've starved yourself," said the gambler. "That's what they call it," said the woman querulously, as she lay down again, and, turning her face to the wall, passed quietly away.

The accordion and the bones were put aside that day, and Homer was forgotten. When the body of Mother Shipton had been committed to the

[4] Achilles.

snow, Mr. Oakhurst took the Innocent aside, and showed him a pair of snowshoes, which he had fashioned from the old pack-saddle. "There's one chance in a hundred to save her yet," he said, pointing to Piney; "but it's there," he added, pointing toward Poker Flat. "If you can reach there in two days she's safe." "And you?" asked Tom Simson. "I'll stay here," was the curt reply.

The lovers parted with a long embrace. "You are not going, too?" said the Duchess, as she saw Mr. Oakhurst apparently waiting to accompany him. "As far as the cañon," he replied. He turned suddenly and kissed the Duchess, leaving her pallid face aflame, and her trembling limbs rigid with amazement.

Night came, but not Mr. Oakhurst. It brought the storm again and the whirling snow. Then the Duchess, feeding the fire, found that some one had quietly piled beside the hut enough fuel to last a few days longer. The tears rose to her eyes, but she hid them from Piney.

The women slept but little. In the morning, looking into each other's faces, they read their fate. Neither spoke, but Piney, accepting the position of the stronger, drew near and placed her arm around the Duchess's waist. They kept this attitude for the rest of the day. That night the storm reached its greatest fury, and, rending asunder the protecting pines, invaded the very hut.

Toward morning they found themselves unable to feed the fire, which gradually died away. As the embers slowly blackened, the Duchess crept closer to Piney, and broke the silence of many hours: "Piney, can you pray?" "No, dear," said Piney simply. The Duchess, without knowing exactly why, felt relieved, and, putting her head upon Piney's shoulder, spoke no more. And so reclining, the younger and purer pillowing the head of her soiled sister upon her virgin breast, they fell asleep.

The wind lulled as if it feared to waken them. Feathery drifts of snow, shaken from the long pine boughs, flew like white-winged birds, and settled about them as they slept. The moon through the rifted clouds looked down upon what had been the camp. But all human stain, all trace of earthly travail, was hidden beneath the spotless mantle mercifully flung from above.

They slept all that day and the next, nor did they waken when voices and footsteps broke the silence of the camp. And when pitying fingers brushed the snow from their wan faces, you could scarcely have told, from the equal peace that dwelt upon them, which was she that had sinned. Even the law of Poker Flat recognized this, and turned away, leaving them still locked in each other's arms.

But at the head of the gulch, on one of the largest pinetrees, they found the deuce of clubs pinned to the bark with a bowie-knife. It bore the following, written in pencil in a firm hand:

†
BENEATH THIS TREE
LIES THE BODY
OF
JOHN OAKHURST,
WHO STRUCK A STREAK OF BAD LUCK
ON THE 23D OF NOVEMBER, 1850,
AND
HANDED IN HIS CHECKS
ON THE 7TH DECEMBER, 1850
†

And pulseless and cold, with a Derringer by his side and a bullet in his heart, though still calm as in life, beneath the snow lay he who was at once the strongest and yet the weakest of the outcasts of Poker Flat.

1869, 1870

SAMUEL LANGHORNE CLEMENS (MARK TWAIN)

(1835–1910)

If Whitman seemed to be a direct answer to Emerson's call in "The Poet," Mark Twain, in turn, seems to embody the democratic ethos evoked in *Democratic Vistas*. There is no question of discipleship—

The standard edition of the works and papers of Mark Twain is now being published by The University of California Press. Until that edition appears, the most useful collection is *The Writings of Mark Twain,* 1899–1910. Twain's most important works are *The Innocents Abroad,* 1869; *Roughing It,* 1872; *The Gilded Age,* 1873; *The Adventures of Tom Sawyer,* 1876; *The Prince and the Pauper,* 1882; *Life on the Mississippi,* 1883; *The Adventures of Huckleberry Finn,* 1885; *A Connecticut Yankee in King Arthur's Court,* 1889; *Personal Recollections of Joan of Arc,* 1896; *The Man That Corrupted Had-* *leyburg and Other Stories and Essays,* 1900.

Albert Bigelow Paine wrote the first important biography, *Mark Twain, A Biography,* 3 vols., 1912, 1935. He also edited *Mark Twain's Autobiography,* 1925; *Mark Twain's Letters,* 1917; and *Mark Twain's Notebooks,* 1935. Biographical treatments include Clara Clemens, *My Father, Mark Twain,* 1931; DeLancey Ferguson, *Mark Twain: Man and Legend,* 1943; Dixon Wecter, *Sam Clemens of Hannibal,* 1952; and Justin Kaplan, *Mr. Clemens and Mark Twain,* 1966.

(Footnote continued next page.)

Mark Twain's masters were Mississippi riverboat men and Pacific slope humorists—but his roots in the oral traditions of the frontier and his brilliant command of a popular audience, as a writer and lecturer, represent Whitman's "main thing": "the average, the bodily, the concrete, the democratic, the popular, on which all the superstructures of the future are to permanently rest." The authentic goings and comings of native scenes achieve in his work what Whitman would call an "autochthonic" expression: sense of place, turn of speech, habit of mind, and atmosphere of feeling; in his prose these have a concreteness never before achieved in American fiction. Mark Twain broke the soil later tilled by the most important twentieth-century writers—Anderson, Hemingway, Faulkner, and their followers. But his talent lay not only in his resources but in his resourcefulness, not only in his possession of folk materials but in his literary imagination, his genius in grasping the essentials of story-telling, and his ability to speak on many levels at once. As the most famous writer of America and probably the world, Mark Twain held audiences on all scales, high and low, fulfilling the role of a truly *popular* artist.

Mark Twain was hardly a simple folk poet. His art is, at its best, complex and demanding, and very much a part of the *literary* tradition of Europe and America. In fact, the very literariness of Mark Twain's

In addition to Bigelow's edition of the letters, see *The Love Letters of Mark Twain,* ed. Dixon Wecter, 1949; *Mark Twain—Howells' Letters,* 2 vols., ed. Henry Nash Smith and William M. Gibson, 1900; *Mark Twain's Letters from Hawaii,* ed. A. Grove Day, 1966.

Criticism includes William Dean Howells, *My Mark Twain,* 1910; Van Wyck Brooks, *The Ordeal of Mark Twain,* 1920; Constance Rourke, *American Humor: A Study of the National Character,* 1931; Bernard DeVoto, *Mark Twain at Work,* 1942; and *Mark Twain's America,* 1932; Edward Wagenknecht, *Mark Twain, The Man and His Work,* 1935, rev. 1967; Lionel Trilling, "Introduction," *The Adventures of Huckleberry Finn,* 1948; T. S. Eliot, "Introduction," *The Adventures of Huckleberry Finn,* 1950; Gladys Carmen Bellamy, *Mark Twain as a Literary Artist,* 1950; Dixon Wecter, *Sam Clemens of Hannibal,* 1952; Leo Marx, "Mr. Eliot, Mr. Trilling, and Huckleberry Finn," *American Scholar* (Fall 1955); Philip S. Foner, *Mark Twain:* *Social Critic,* 1958; Daniel G. Hoffman, *Form and Fable in American Fiction,* 1961; Kenneth S. Lynn, *Mark Twain and Southwestern Humor,* 1959; Roger B. Salomon, *Twain and the Image of History,* 1961; Walter Blair, *Mark Twain and Huck Finn,* 1960; Henry Nash Smith, *Mark Twain: The Development of a Writer,* 1961, *Mark Twain's Fable of Progress,* 1964; Albert E. Stone, *The Innocent Eye,* 1961; Louis Budd, *Mark Twain: Social Philosopher,* 1962; Pascal Covici, *Mark Twain's Humor: The Image of a World,* 1962; Douglas Grant, *Mark Twain,* 1963; Robert Wiggins, *Mark Twain: Jackleg Novelist,* 1964; Margaret Duckett, *Mark Twain and Bret Harte,* 1965; Leslie A. Fiedler, *Love and Death in the American Novel,* 1966; Robert Ryan, *Uncompromising Heroes: Mark Twain and His Characters,* 1966; James M. Cox, *Mark Twain: The Fate of Humor,* 1966; Fred W. Lorch, *The Trouble Begins at Eight: Mark Twain's Lecture Tours,* 1968; Maxwell Geismar, *Mark Twain: An American Prophet,* 1970.

Mark Twain or Samuel Clemens. *The Granger Collection.*

work, the wealth of allusion and skilled use of earlier writers (consider the range of allusion in *Huck Finn* alone, including the Bible, Shakespeare, Cervantes, Bunyan, Scott, and others), points to a central characteristic of both his life and his work: his attempt to reconcile, to harmonize, disparate styles of speech and writing, concepts of "the writer," and ideals of personal behavior. This attempt was the source of great tension in his life; after his initial success he became a more and more troubled and divided man. His troubles were partly representative of the age. This was a period of rapid modernization, of change, and Mark Twain, son of the frontier who came East into fame and wealth, was touched by most of the chief issues of the times. In his work and in his life the question of identity, of uneasiness and ambivalence toward any single role (or name: his own shifts from Mark Twain to Sam Clemens) stands as a major signal to an underlying distress.

Few writers in America have revealed so much of their lives in their books as Mark Twain, and yet revelations often seem to be calculated concealments. His own life seemed to puzzle him, and he mulled it over endlessly. In its external detail it is one of the most exciting, adventuresome of literary lives, anticipating the career of followers such as Hemingway. Born in a small frontier settlement called Florida, Missouri (where his parents had just recently arrived from Tennessee), he moved with his family four years later to Hannibal, a river town where he spent his youth. Memories of this time and place fill his books, especially those dealing with Tom Sawyer and Huck Finn, whose St. Petersberg is a fictional version of Hannibal. His rather unsuccessful father died in 1847, and Sam Clemens left school to work in local printing offices, including that of his brother Orion, who ran a newspaper. Clemens left home in 1853 at the age of 18 and traveled for several years as a journeyman printer to St. Louis, New York, Philadelphia, and Cincinnati. His first literary efforts took the form of comic travel letters about this period on the road; the letters were published in Orion's paper. In 1857 Clemens met Horace Bixby on a Mississippi riverboat (the young adventurer thought he was on his way to South America), became an apprentice ("cub") pilot and then a pilot on the river until the Civil War halted river traffic in 1861. After a very brief spell in an irregular Confederate unit, Clemens turned West with Orion, who had been appointed secretary of the Nevada Territory, and he began a period of traveling about, prospecting, mining, speculating, and reporting for the Virginia City (Nevada) *Territorial Enterprise* and for papers in San Francisco. Clemens became an adept practitioner of popular modes of newspaper writing in the West, chiefly humorous sketches, burlesque news stories, travel letters, and lectures. The predominant style was based on a laconic comic character—an "inspired idiot"—who did not reveal by his deadpan manner that he realized anything he said was funny. Many of the writers who used this style adopted comic names, such as Artemus Ward and Josh Billings, to represent their stage or literary "character." The name Mark Twain begins to appear in this period and received national attention first with the publication of "The Celebrated Frog of Calaveras County"—the classic instance of the Western tall tale in deadpan manner—in a New York journal in 1865. In 1866 Clemens was in Hawaii as a correspondent, and he turned east in 1867, when he journeyed to New York by way of the Isthmus of Panama in order to accompany a group of tourists, as a paid correspondent for a California paper, to Europe and the Holy Land. Out of this trip came his first book-length narrative and bestseller, *The Innocents Abroad* (1869).

The following years were ones of crucial change and personal development. In 1867 Clemens had boasted of himself as "The Wild Humorist of the Pacific Slope." By 1870 he had married the very respectable Olivia Langdon of Elmira, New York, and by 1871 they had moved to Nook Farm, near Hartford, Connecticut, a community of eminent New England writers, intellectuals, and clergymen. His lifelong friendship with William Dean Howells began in this period, as did his self-conception as "author," which both Howells and wife Livy did much to shape. At the time Howells was editor of the genteel *Atlantic Monthly;* he reviewed and praised Clemens' work, and served as a kind of literary "conscience" to the side of Mark Twain that wished for approval from established literary figures. In the 1870's he won wide and enthusiastic acclaim for his writings and his lectures (although never without reservation from the New England Brahmins, who were uneasy about the credentials of any "humorist"). With the exception of *The Gilded Age* (1873), a satire of contemporary political life and the spirit of speculation, written in collaboration with Charles Dudley Warner, his books mined the rich vein of his childhood and youthful experiences on the river and in the West. These works include *Roughing It* (1872), which covers the Nevada and California and Hawaii period; *The Adventures of Tom Sawyer* (1876), a boyhood idyll in a pre-Civil War Mississippi River town; *A Tramp Abroad* (1880), a book of comic travel adventures in Europe; *Life on the Mississippi* (1883), which recounts his experiences as riverboat pilot, and then, many years later, as passenger and observer of a much-changed river culture; and his masterpiece, *The Adventures of Huckleberry Finn* (1884), a first-person account by a river waif of his adventures with Jim, a runaway slave.

By the mid-1880's Mark Twain had established himself as a world-famous figure, the bushy-headed, mustachioed, white-clad American humorist. The role fit only one side of his complicated life, however, and while writing and lecturing his way to much desired fame, he also involved himself in a number of ultimately disastrous business schemes. He seemed in a way afflicted by the same get-rich-quick fever he satirized in the figure of Colonel Sellers in *The Gilded Age.* Beginning in 1880 he had backed the ill-fated Paige typesetter, an enterprise that drained energy and funds for close to 15 years, with the promise of success and wealth always just around the corner. In 1884, he had established his own publishing house, under the management of his nephew Charles L. Webster. The firm failed in 1894, along with the Paige machine, and Clemens found himself bankrupt. With the help of the financial wizardry of Henry H. Rogers, a Standard Oil executive, and a worldwide lecture tour from 1895 to 1896, he was able to free himself from debt. On the heels of these complications came severe personal losses: the death of daughter Susy in 1896 from spinal meningitis; the diagnosis the same year of daughter Jean's ailments as epilepsy; and the death of his wife Livy in 1904 and of Jean in 1909.

These events were no doubt partly responsible for the bitterness of tone of much of Mark Twain's later work. Signs of pessimism, however, of skepticism about man's capacity for honesty and decency within society, appear even in the earlier works. These elements come forward and virtually dominate works such as *A Connecticut Yankee in King Arthur's Court* (1889), where the full signs of disillusion with the idea of progress begin to show themselves; *Pudd'nhead Wilson* (1894); "The Mysterious Stranger" (written in 1898 and published posthumously); and the brilliant satire, "The Man That Corrupted Hadleyburg" (1889). In his last years his fame widened, yet his anger and bitterness deepened—especially anger over the hypocrisy, cynicism, and jingoism that accompanied the imperialist adventures in Cuba and the Philippines. An international celebrity, awarded honorary degrees at Yale and Oxford, Mark Twain spent his last years pretty much in gloom and exasperation, writing fables, many of them only for posthumous publication, of the "damned human race."

Mark Twain's importance to literature lies in the fact that, as T. S. Eliot (a fellow Missourian) put it, he "discovered a new way of writing." Out of common speech and the body of tales, lore, and verbal games storied within it, Mark Twain developed a supple and graceful literary language, an elevation of the colloquial without loss of its cardinal virtues: vividness, honesty, and playfulness. More than a technical achievement, Mark Twain's discovery was of a language that articulated a major vision, what Henry Nash Smith has called a "vernacular perspective," one that sees through the pretenses and conceit of high-flown diction and that, by its own indirections, affirms straightness, decency, and the wisdom of common experience. It is an unconventional, nonconformist perspective, the perspective, in short, of Huck Finn, the greatest creation of Mark Twain's "new way of writing." Hemingway points to the larger range of meaning and possibility within Huck's vernacular language when he writes, in a famous passage, that "all modern American literature comes from one book by Mark Twain called *Huckleberry Finn*." In that book Huck's voice becomes the subtle register of a growing and, in its form, typically American, awareness of the conflict between "natural" and socially conditioned feelings and actions, and of the blind, self-defeating violence within society. The values implicit within Huck's voice, within the very structure of his language, are realized as a virtual way of life in his relationship with Jim, the escaped slave. The book contains a rich and living panorama of Southern slave society along the river in the 1840's, and it is proper to speak of the reach of the book as mythic. It presents essential ingredients of American experience, the initiation of a child into the sorrows and failures of adult life, and the evocation of a powerful if idyllic source of saving feelings, in the community of child and black slave, of outsiders, undeceived by the facades of respectable society. In Mark Twain's subsequent work the perspective of Huck and Jim, of the raft, recedes in favor of a more overtly satiric excoriation, usually performed by a "stranger," like Hank Morgan in *Connecticut Yankee,* Satan in *Mysterious Stranger,* or the visitor in "The Man That Corrupted Hadleyburg." This figure is generally immune to the self-deceptions that he exposes at the heart of society. He is above as well as outside the world he attacks and usually destroys. In *Huck Finn,* however, the poignant vulnerability of Huck and Jim, and especially Huck's own innocent susceptibility to society's delusions, open a channel of sympathy between reader and character sacrificed in the later works. In *Huck Finn* more than any other work Mark Twain earns his position as, in H. L. Mencken's words, "the true father of our national literature."

The Notorious Jumping Frog of Calaveras County[1]

In compliance with the request of a friend of mine who wrote me from the East, I called on good-natured, garrulous old Simon Wheeler and inquired after my friend's friend, Leonidas W. Smiley, as requested to do, and I hereunto append the result. I have a lurking suspicion that *Leonidas W. Smiley* is a myth, that my friend never knew such a personage, and that he only conjectured that if I asked old Wheeler about him, it would remind him of his infamous *Jim* Smiley and he would go to work and bore me to death with some exasperating reminiscence of him as long and as tedious as it should be useless to me. If that was the design, it succeeded.

I found Simon Wheeler dozing comfortably by the barroom stove of the dilapidated tavern in the decayed mining camp of Angel's, and I noticed that he was fat and bald-headed and had an expression of winning gentleness and simplicity upon his tranquil countenance. He roused up and gave me good day. I told him that a friend of mine had commissioned me to make some inquiries about a cherished companion of his boyhood named *Leonidas W. Smiley—Rev. Leonidas W.* Smiley, a young minister of the Gospel, who he had heard was at one time a resident of Angel's Camp. I added that if Mr. Wheeler could tell me anything about this Rev. Leonidas W. Smiley, I would feel under many obligations to him.

Simon Wheeler backed me into a corner and blockaded me there with his chair, and then sat down and reeled off the monotonous narrative which follows this paragraph. He never smiled, he never frowned, he never changed his voice from the gentle-flowing key to which he tuned his initial sentence, he never betrayed the slightest suspicion of enthusiasm, but all through the interminable narrative there ran a vein of impressive earnestness and sincerity which showed me plainly that, so far from his imagining that there was anything ridiculous or funny about his story, he regarded it as a really important matter and admired its two heroes as men of transcendent genius in *finesse*. I let him go on in his own way and never interrupted him once.

"Rev. Leonidas W. H'm, Reverend Le—— Well, there was a feller here once by the name of *Jim* Smiley, in the winter of '49—or maybe it was the spring of '50—I don't recollect exactly, somehow, though what makes me think it was one or the other is because I remember the big flume warn't finished when he first come to the camp; but anyway, he was the curiousest man about always betting on anything that turned up you ever see, if he could get anybody to bet on the other side, and if he couldn't he'd change

[1] This story was first published in 1865 with the title "Jim Smiley and His Jumping Frog."

"Pronounced Cal-e-*va*-ras" [Twain's note].

sides. Any way that suited the other man would suit *him*—any way just so's he got a bet, *he* was satisfied. But still he was lucky, uncommon lucky; he most always come out winner. He was always ready and laying for a chance; there couldn't be no solit'ry thing mentioned but that feller'd offer to bet on it and take any side you please, as I was just telling you. If there was a horse-race, you'd find him flush or you'd find him busted at the end of it; if there was a dog-fight, he'd bet on it; if there was a cat-fight, he'd bet on it; if there was a chicken-fight, he'd bet on it; why, if there was two birds setting on a fence, he would bet you which one would fly first; or if there was a camp-meeting, he would be there reg'lar to bet on Parson Walker, which he judged to be the best exhorter about here, and so he was too, and a good man. If he even see a straddle-bug start to go anywheres, he would bet you how long it would take him to get to—to wherever he was going to, and if you took him up, he would foller that straddle-bug to Mexico but what he would find out where he was bound for and how long he was on the road. Lots of the boys here has seen that Smiley and can tell you about him. Why, it never made no difference to *him*—he'd bet on *any* thing—the dangdest feller. Parson Walker's wife laid very sick once for a good while, and it seemed as if they warn't going to save her; but one morning he come in and Smiley up and asked him how she was, and he said she was considerable better—thank the Lord for his inf'nite mercy—and coming on so smart that with the blessing of Prov'dence she'd get well yet; and Smiley, before he thought, says, 'Well, I'll resk two-and-a-half she don't anyway.'

"Thish-yer Smiley had a mare—the boys called her the fifteen-minute nag but that was only in fun, you know, because of course she was faster than that—and he used to win money on that horse, for all she was so slow and always had the asthma, or the distemper, or the consumption, or something of that kind. They used to give her two or three hundred yards' start and then pass her under way, but always at the fag end of the race she'd get excited and desperate like, and come cavorting and straddling up and scattering her legs around limber, sometimes in the air and sometimes out to one side among the fences, and kicking up m-o-r-e dust and raising m-o-r-e racket with her coughing and sneezing and blowing her nose—and *always* fetch up at the stand just about a neck ahead, as near as you could cipher it down.

"And he had a little small bull-pup, that to look at him you'd think he warn't worth a cent but to set around and look ornery and lay for a chance to steal something. But as soon as money was up on him he was a different dog; his under-jaw'd begin to stick out like the fo'castle of a steamboat and his teeth would uncover and shine like the furnaces. And a dog might tackle him and bully-rag him, and bite him and throw him over his shoulder two or three times, and Andrew Jackson—which was the name of the pup—Andrew Jackson would never let on but what *he* was satisfied and hadn't expected nothing else—and the bets being doubled and doubled on the other side all the time, till the money was all up; and then all of a sudden he would grab that other dog jest by the j'int of his hind leg and freeze to it—not chaw, you understand, but only just grip and hang on till they throwed up the sponge, if it was a year. Smiley always come out winner on that pup till he harnessed a dog once that didn't have no hind legs, because they'd been sawed off in a circular saw, and when the thing had gone along far enough and the money was all up and he come to make a snatch for his pet holt, he see in a minute how he'd been imposed on and how the other dog had him in the door, so to speak, and he 'peared surprised, and then he looked sorter discouraged-like and didn't try no more to win the fight, and so he got shucked out bad. He give Smiley a look, as much as to say his heart was broke, and it was *his* fault for putting up a dog that hadn't no hind legs for him to take holt of, which was his main dependence in a fight, and then he limped off a piece and laid down and died. It was a good pup, was that Andrew Jackson, and would have made a name for hisself if he'd lived, for the stuff was in him and he had genius—I know it, because he hadn't no opportunities to speak of, and it don't stand to reason that a dog could make such a fight as he could under them circumstances if he hadn't no talent. It always makes me feel sorry when I think of that last fight of his'n and the way it turned out.

"Well, thish-yer Smiley had rat-tarriers, and chicken cocks, and tomcats and all them kind of things till you couldn't rest, and you couldn't fetch nothing for him to bet on but he'd match you. He ketched a frog one day and took him home, and said he cak'lated to educate him; and so he never done nothing for three months but set in his back yard and learn that frog to jump. And you bet you he *did* learn him, too. He'd give him a little punch behind, and the next minute you'd see that frog whirling in the air like a doughnut—see him turn one summerset, or maybe a couple if he got a good start, and come down flat-footed and all right, like a cat. He got him up so in the matter of ketching flies, and kep' him in practice so constant, that he'd nail a fly every time as fur as he could see him. Smiley said all a frog wanted was education and he could do 'most anything—and I believe him. Why, I've seen him set Dan'l Webster down here on this floor—Dan'l Webster was the name of the frog—and sing out, 'Flies, Dan'l, flies!' and quicker'n you could wink he'd spring straight up and snake a fly off'n the counter there, and flop down on the floor ag'in as solid as a gob of mud, and fall to scratching the side of his head with his hind foot as indifferent as if he hadn't no idea he'd been doin' any more'n any frog might do. You never see a frog so modest and straight-for'ard as he was, for all he was so gifted. And when it come to fair and square jumping on a dead level, he could get over more ground at one straddle than any animal of his breed you ever see. Jumping on a dead level was his strong suit, you understand; and when it come to that, Smiley would ante up money on him as long as he had a red. Smiley was monstrous proud of his frog, and well he might be for fellers that had traveled and been everywheres all said he laid over any frog that ever *they* see.

"Well, Smiley kep' the beast in a little lattice box, and he used to fetch him down-town sometimes and lay for a bet. One day a feller—a stranger in the camp, he was—come acrost him with his box and says:

" 'What might it be that you've got in the box?'

"And Smiley says, sorter indifferent-like, 'It might be a parrot, or it might be a canary, maybe, but it ain't—it's only just a frog.'

"And the feller took it and looked at it careful, and turned it around this way and that, and says, 'H'm—so 'tis. Well, what's *he* good for?'

" 'Well,' Smiley says, easy and careless, 'he's good enough for *one* thing, I should judge—he can outjump any frog in Calaveras County.'

"The feller took the box again and took another long, particular look, and give it back to Smiley and says, very deliberate, 'Well,' he says, 'I don't see no p'ints about that frog that's any better'n any other frog.'

" 'Maybe you don't,' Smiley says. 'Maybe you understand frogs and maybe you don't understand 'em; maybe you've had experience and maybe you ain't only a amature, as it were. Anyways, I've got *my* opinion, and I'll resk forty dollars that he can outjump any frog in Calaveras County.'

"And the feller studied a minute and then says, kinder sad-like, 'Well, I'm only a stranger here and I ain't got no frog; but if I had a frog, I'd bet you.'

"And then Smiley says, 'That's all right—that's all right—if you'll hold my box a minute, I'll go and get you a frog.' And so the feller took the box and put up his forty dollars along with Smiley's, and set down to wait.

"So he set there a good while thinking and thinking to himself, and then he got the frog out and prized his mouth open and took a teaspoon and filled him full of quail-shot—filled him pretty near up to his chin—and set him on the floor. Smiley he went to the swamp and slopped around in the mud for a long time, and finally he ketched a frog and fetched him in and give him to this feller, and says:

" 'Now, if you're ready, set him alongside of Dan'l, with his forepaws just even with Dan'l's, and I'll give the word.' Then he says, 'One—two—three—*git!*' and him and the feller touched up the frogs from behind, and the new frog hopped off lively, but Dan'l give a heave and hysted up his shoulders—so—like a Frenchman but it warn't no use—he couldn't budge; he was planted as solid as a church, and he couldn't no more stir than if he was anchored out. Smiley was a good deal surprised, and he was disgusted too, but he didn't have no idea what the matter was, of course.

"The feller took the money and started away, and when he was going out at the door, he sorter jerked his thumb over his shoulder—so—at Dan'l and says again, very deliberate, 'Well,' he says, '*I* don't see no p'ints about that frog that's any better'n any other frog.'

"Smiley he stood scratching his head and looking down at Dan'l a long time, and at last he says, 'I do wonder what in the nation that frog throw'd off for—I wonder if there ain't something the matter with him—he 'pears to look mighty baggy, somehow.' And he ketched Dan'l by the nap of the neck and hefted him, and says, 'Why, blame my cats if he don't weigh five pound!' and turned him upside down and he belched out a double handful of shot. And then he see how it was, and he was the maddest man—he set the frog down and took out after that feller, but he never ketched him. And—"

(Here Simon Wheeler heard his name called from the front yard and got up to see what was wanted.) And turning to me as he moved away, he said: "Just set where you are, stranger, and rest easy—I ain't going to be gone a second."

But, by your leave, I did not think that a continuation of the history of the enterprising vagabond *Jim* Smiley would be likely to afford me much information concerning the Rev. *Leonidas W.* Smiley and so I started away.

At the door I met the sociable Wheeler returning, and he buttonholed me and recommenced:

"Well, thish-yer Smiley had a yaller one-eyed cow that didn't have no tail, only just a short stump like a bannanner, and—"

However, lacking both time and inclination, I did not wait to hear about the afflicted cow but took my leave.   *1865/1867, 1875*

From Roughing It

A GENUINE MEXICAN PLUG[1]

I resolved to have a horse to ride. I had never seen such wild, free, magnificent horsemanship outside of a circus as these picturesquely clad Mexicans, Californians and Mexicanized Americans displayed in Carson streets every day. How they rode! Leaning just gently forward out of the perpendicular, easy and nonchalant, with broad slouch-hat brim blown square up in front, and long *riata*[2] swinging above the head, they swept through the town like the wind! The next minute they were only a sailing puff of dust on the far desert. If they trotted, they sat up gallantly and gracefully, and seemed part of the horse; did not go jiggering up and down after the silly Miss Nancy fashion of the riding-schools. I had quickly learned to tell a horse from a cow, and was full of anxiety to learn more. I was resolved to buy a horse.

[1] The story was first published in *Roughing It*   [2] Lasso.
in 1872.

While the thought was rankling in my mind, the auctioneer came skurrying through the plaza on a black beast that had as many humps and corners on him as a dromedary, and was necessarily uncomely; but he was "going, going, at twenty-two!—horse, saddle and bridle at twenty-two dollars, gentlemen!" and I could hardly resist.

A man whom I did not know (he turned out to be the auctioneer's brother) noticed the wistful look in my eye, and observed that that was a very remarkable horse to be going at such a price; and added that the saddle alone was worth the money. It was a Spanish saddle, with ponderous *tapidaros*,[3] and furnished with the ungainly sole-leather covering with the unspellable name. I said I had half a notion to bid. Then this keen-eyed person appeared to me to be "taking my measure;" but I dismissed the suspicion when he spoke, for his manner was full of guileless candor and truthfulness. Said he:

"I know that horse—know him well. You are a stranger, I take it, and so you might think he was an American horse, maybe, but I assure you he is not. He is nothing of the kind; but—excuse my speaking in a low voice, other people being near—he is, without the shadow of a doubt, a Genuine Mexican Plug!"

I did not know what a Genuine Plug was, but there was something about this man's way of saying it that made me swear inwardly that I would own a Genuine Mexican Plug or die.

"Has he any other—er advantages?" I inquired, suppressing what eagerness I could.

He hooked his forefinger in the pocket of my army-shirt, led me to one side, and breathed in my ear impressively these words:

"He can out-buck anything in America!"

"Going, going, going—at *twen-ty*-four dollars and a half, gen—'

"Twenty-seven!" I shouted, in a frenzy.

"And sold!" said the auctioneer, and passed over the Genuine Mexican Plug to me.

I could scarcely contain my exultation. I paid the money, and put the animal in a neighboring livery-stable to dine and rest himself.

In the afternoon I brought the creature into the plaza, and certain citizens held him by the head, and others by the tail, while I mounted him. As soon as they let go, he placed all his feet in a bunch together, lowered his back, and then suddenly arched it upward, and shot me straight into the air a matter of three or four feet! I came as straight down again, lit in the saddle, went instantly up again, came down almost on the high pommel, shot up again, and came down on the horse's neck—all in the space of three or four seconds. Then he rose and stood almost straight up on his hind feet, and I,

[3] Decorated leather covering for stirrups.

clasping his lean neck desperately, slid back into the saddle, and held on. He came down, and immediately hoisted his heels into the air, delivering a vicious kick at the sky, and stood on his forefeet. And then down he came once more, and began the original exercise of shooting me straight up again. The third time I went up I heard a stranger say:

"Oh, *don't* he buck, though!"

While I was up, somebody struck the horse a sounding thwack with a leathern strap, and when I arrived again the Genuine Mexican Plug was not there. A Californian youth chased him up and caught him, and asked if he might have a ride. I granted him that luxury. He mounted the Genuine, got lifted into the air once, but sent his spurs home as he descended, and the horse darted away like a telegram. He soared over three fences like a bird, and disappeared down the road toward the Washoe Valley.

I sat down on a stone with a sigh, and by a natural impulse one of my hands sought my forehead, and the other the base of my stomach. I believe I never appreciated, till then, the poverty of the human machinery—for I still needed a hand or two to place elsewhere. Pen cannot describe how I was jolted up. Imagination cannot conceive how disjointed I was—how internally, externally and universally I was unsettled, mixed up and ruptured. There was a sympathetic crowd around me, though.

One elderly looking comforter said:

"Stranger, you've been taken in. Everybody in this camp knows that horse. Any child, any Injun, could have told you that he'd buck; he is the very worst devil to buck on the continent of America. You hear *me*. I'm Curry. *Old* Curry. Old *Abe* Curry. And moreover, he is a simon-pure, out-and-out, genuine d——d Mexican plug, and an uncommon mean one at that, too. Why, you turnip, if you had laid low and kept dark, there's chances to buy an *American* horse for mighty little more than you paid for that bloody old foreign relic."

I gave no sign; but I made up my mind that if the auctioneer's brother's funeral took place while I was in the Territory I would postpone all other recreations and attend it.

After a gallop of sixteen miles the Californian youth and the Genuine Mexican Plug came tearing into town again, shedding foam-flakes like the spume-spray that drives before a typhoon, and, with one final skip over a wheelbarrow and a Chinaman, cast anchor in front of the "ranch."

Such panting and blowing! Such spreading and contracting of the red equine nostrils, and glaring of the wild equine eye! But was the imperial beast subjugated? Indeed he was not. His lordship the Speaker of the House thought he was, and mounted him to go down to the Capitol; but the first dash the creature made was over a pile of telegraph poles half as high as a church; and his time to the Capitol—one mile and three-quarters—remains unbeaten to this day. But then he took an advantage—he left out the mile, and only did three-quarters. That is to say, he made a straight cut across-lots, preferring fences and ditches to a crooked road; and when the Speaker got to the Capitol he said he had been in the air so much he felt as if he had made the trip on a comet.

In the evening the Speaker came home afoot for exercise, and got the Genuine towed back behind a quartz wagon. The next day I loaned the animal to the Clerk of the House to go down to the Dana silver mine, six miles, and *he* walked back for exercise, and got the horse towed. Everybody I loaned him to always walked back; they never could get enough exercise any other way. Still, I continued to loan him to anybody who was willing to borrow him, my idea being to get him crippled, and throw him on the borrower's hands, or killed, and make the borrower pay for him. But somehow nothing ever happened to him. He took chances that no other horse ever took and survived, but he always came out safe. It was his daily habit to try experiments that had always before been considered impossible, but he always got through. Sometimes he miscalculated a little, and did not get his rider through intact, but *he* always got through himself. Of course I had tried to sell him; but that was a stretch of simplicity which met with little sympathy. The auctioneer stormed up and down the streets on him for four days, dispersing the populace, interrupting business, and destroying children, and never got a bid—at least never any but the eighteen dollar one he hired a notoriously substanceless bummer to make. The people only smiled pleasantly, and restrained their desire to buy, if they had any. Then the auctioneer brought in his bill, and I withdrew the horse from the market. We tried to trade him off at private vendue next, offering him at a sacrifice for second-hand tombstones, old iron, temperance tracts—any kind of property. But holders were stiff, and we retired from the market again. I never tried to ride the horse any more. Walking was good enough exercise for a man like me, that had nothing the matter with him except ruptures, internal injuries, and such things. Finally I tried to *give* him away. But it was a failure. Parties said earthquakes were handy enough on the Pacific coast—they did not wish to own one. As a last resort I offered him to the Governor for the use of the "Brigade." His face lit up eagerly at first, but toned down again, and he said the thing would be too palpable.

Just then the livery-stable man brought in his bill for six weeks' keeping—stall-room for the horse, fifteen dollars; hay for the horse, two hundred and fifty! The Genuine Mexican Plug had eaten a ton of the article, and the man said he would have eaten a hundred if he had let him.

I will remark here, in all seriousness, that the regular price of hay during that year and a part of the next was really two hundred and fifty dollars a ton. During a part of the previous year it had sold at five hundred a ton, in gold, and during the winter before that, there was such scarcity of the article that in several instances small quantities had brought eight hundred dollars a ton in coin! The consequence might be guessed without my telling it: people turned their stock loose to starve, and before the spring arrived Carson and

Eagle valleys were almost literally carpeted with their carcasses! Any old settler there will verify these statements.

I managed to pay the livery bill, and that same day I gave the Genuine Mexican Plug to a passing Arkansas emigrant whom fortune delivered into my hand. If this ever meets his eye, he will doubtless remember the donation.

Now whoever has had the luck to ride a real Mexican plug will recognize the animal depicted in this chapter, and hardly consider him exaggerated— but the uninitiated will feel justified in regarding his portrait as a fancy sketch, perhaps.

1888

From Life on the Mississippi[1]

CUB-PILOT

CHAPTER IV   THE BOYS' AMBITION

When I was a boy, there was but one permanent ambition among my comrades in our village[2] on the west bank of the Mississippi River. That was, to be a steamboatman. We had transient ambitions of other sorts, but they were only transient. When a circus came and went, it left us all burning to become clowns; the first negro minstrel show that ever came to our section left us all suffering to try that kind of life; now and then we had a hope that, if we lived and were good, God would permit us to be pirates. These ambitions faded out, each in its turn; but the ambition to be a steamboatman always remained.

Once a day a cheap, gaudy packet arrived upward from St. Louis, and another downward from Keokuk.[3] Before these events, the day was glorious with expectancy; after them, the day was a dead and empty thing. Not only the boys, but the whole village, felt this. After all these years I can picture that old time to myself now, just as it was then: the white town drowsing in the sunshine of a summer's morning; the streets empty, or pretty nearly so; one or two clerks sitting in front of the Water Street stores, with their splint-bottomed chairs tilted back against the walls, chins on breasts, hats slouched over their faces, asleep—with shingle-shavings enough around to show what broke them down; a sow and a litter of pigs loafing along the sidewalk, doing

---

[1] These chapters were first published in the *Atlantic Monthly* in 1875 and were later incorporated into *Life on the Mississippi*, published in 1883.

[2] "Hannibal, Mo." [Twain's note.]

[3] In southeastern Iowa.

a good business in watermelon rinds and seeds; two or three lonely little freight piles scattered about the "levee";[4] a pile of "skids"[5] on the slope of the stone-paved wharf, and the fragrant town drunkard asleep in the shadow of them; two or three wood flats at the head of the wharf, but nobody to listen to the peaceful lapping of the wavelets against them; the great Mississippi, the majestic, the magnificent Mississippi, rolling its mile-wide tide along, shining in the sun; the dense forest away on the other side; the "point" above the town, and the "point" below, bounding the river-glimpse and turning it into a sort of sea, and withal a very still and brilliant and lonely one. Presently a film of dark smoke appears above one of those remote "points"; instantly a negro drayman, famous for his quick eye and prodigious voice, lifts up the cry, "S-t-e-a-m-boat a-comin!" and the scene changes! The town drunkard stirs, the clerks wake up, a furious clatter of drays follows, every house and store pours out a human contribution, and all in a twinkling the dead town is alive and moving. Drays, carts, men, boys, all go hurrying from many quarters to a common center, the wharf. Assembled there, the people fasten their eyes upon the coming boat as upon a wonder they are seeing for the first time. And the boat *is* rather a handsome sight, too. She is long and sharp and trim and pretty; she has two tall, fancy-topped chimneys, with a gilded device of some kind swung between them; a fanciful pilot-house, all glass and "gingerbread," perched on top of the "texas"[6] deck behind them; the paddle-boxes are gorgeous with a picture or with gilded rays above the boat's name; the boiler deck, the hurricane deck, and the texas deck are fenced and ornamented with clean white railings; there is a flag gallantly flying from the jack-staff; the furnace doors are open and the fires glaring bravely; the upper decks are black with passengers; the captain stands by the big bell, calm, imposing, the envy of all; great volumes of the blackest smoke are rolling and tumbling out of the chimneys—a husbanded grandeur created with a bit of pitch pine just before arriving at a town; the crew are grouped on the forecastle; the broad stage is run far out over the port bow, and an envied deck-hand stands picturesquely on the end of it with a coil of rope in his hand; the pent steam is screaming through the gauge-cocks; the captain lifts his hand, a bell rings, the wheels stop; then they turn back, churning the water to foam, and the steamer is at rest. Then such a scramble as there is to get aboard, and to get ashore, and to take in freight and to discharge freight, all at one and the same time; and such a yelling and cursing as the mates facilitate it all with! Ten minutes later the steamer is under way again, with no flag on the jack-staff and no black smoke issuing from the chimneys. After ten more minutes the town is dead again, and the town drunkard asleep by the skids once more.

---

[4] An embankment to prevent flooding.
[5] Timbers on which a heavy object is placed to be shoved along on rollers or slid.

[6] Because they were the largest on the boat, the officers' quarters were called the "texas" and the deck above them the "texas" deck.

My father was a justice of the peace, and I supposed he possessed the power of life and death over all men, and could hang anybody that offended him. This was distinction enough for me as a general thing; but the desire to be a steamboatman kept intruding, nevertheless. I first wanted to be a cabin-boy, so that I could come out with a white apron on and shake a table-cloth over the side, where all my old comrades could see me; later I thought I would rather be the deck-hand who stood on the end of the stage-plank with the coil of rope in his hand, because he was particularly conspicuous. But these were only day-dreams—they were too heavenly to be contemplated as real possibilities. By and by one of our boys went away. He was not heard of for a long time. At last he turned up as apprentice engineer or "striker" on a steamboat. This thing shook the bottom out of all my Sunday-school teachings. That boy had been notoriously worldly, and I just the reverse; yet he was exalted to this eminence, and I left in obscurity and misery. There was nothing generous about this fellow in his greatness. He would always manage to have a rusty bolt to scrub while his boat tarried at our town, and he would sit on the inside guard and scrub it, where we all could see him and envy him and loathe him. And whenever his boat was laid up he would come home and swell around the town in his blackest and greasiest clothes, so that nobody could help remembering that he was a steamboatman; and he used all sorts of steamboat technicalities in his talk, as if he were so used to them that he forgot common people could not understand them. He would speak of the "labboard" side of a horse in an easy, natural way that would make one wish he was dead. And he was always talking about "St. Looy" like an old citizen; he would refer casually to occasions when he was "coming down Fourth street," or when he was "passing by the Planter's House," or when there was a fire and he took a turn on the brakes of "the old Big Missouri"; and then he would go on and lie about how many towns the size of ours were burned down there that day. Two or three of the boys had long been persons of consideration among us because they had been to St. Louis once and had a vague general knowledge of its wonders, but the day of their glory was over now. They lapsed into a humble silence, and learned to disappear when the ruthless "cub"-engineer approached. This fellow had money, too, and hair-oil. Also an ignorant silver watch and a showy brass watch-chain. He wore a leather belt and used no suspenders. If ever a youth was cordially admired and hated by his comrades, this one was. No girl could withstand his charms. He "cut out" every boy in the village. When his boat blew up at last, it diffused a tranquil contentment among us such as we had not known for months. But when he came home the next week, alive, renowned, and appeared in church all battered up and bandaged, a shining hero, stared at and wondered over by everybody, it seemed to us that the partiality of Providence for an undeserving reptile had reached a point where it was open to criticism.

This creature's career could produce but one result, and it speedily followed. Boy after boy managed to get on the river. The minister's son became an engineer. The doctor's and the postmaster's sons became "mud clerks"; the wholesale liquor dealer's son became a barkeeper on a boat; four sons of the chief merchant, and two sons of the county judge, became pilots. Pilot was the grandest position of all. The pilot, even in those days of trivial wages, had a princely salary—from a hundred and fifty to two hundred and fifty dollars a month, and no board to pay. Two months of his wages would pay a preacher's salary for a year. Now some of us were left disconsolate. We could not get on the river—at least our parents would not let us.

So, by and by, I ran away. I said I would never come home again till I was a pilot and could come in glory. But somehow I could not manage it. I went meekly aboard a few of the boats that lay packed together like sardines at the long St. Louis wharf, and humbly inquired for the pilots, but got only a cold shoulder and short words from mates and clerks. I had to make the best of this sort of treatment for the time being, but I had comforting day-dreams of a future when I should be a great and honored pilot, with plenty of money, and could kill some of these mates and clerks and pay for them.

CHAPTER V   I WANT TO BE A CUB-PILOT

Months afterward the hope within me struggled to a reluctant death, and I found myself without an ambition. But I was ashamed to go home. I was in Cincinnati, and I set to work to map out a new career. I had been reading about the recent exploration of the river Amazon by an expedition sent out by our government. It was said that the expedition, owing to difficulties, had not thoroughly explored a part of the country lying about the headwaters, some four thousand miles from the mouth of the river. It was only about fifteen hundred miles from Cincinnati to New Orleans, where I could doubtless get a ship. I had thirty dollars left; I would go and complete the exploration of the Amazon. This was all the thought I gave to the subject. I never was great in matters of detail. I packed my valise, and took passage on an ancient tub called the *Paul Jones* for New Orleans. For the sum of sixteen dollars I had the scarred and tarnished splendors of "her" main saloon principally to myself, for she was not a creature to attract the eye of wiser travelers.

When we presently got under way and went poking down the broad Ohio, I became a new being, and the subject of my own admiration. I was a traveler! A word never had tasted so good in my mouth before. I had an exultant sense of being bound for mysterious lands and distant climes which I never have felt in so uplifting a degree since. I was in such a glorified condition that all ignoble feelings departed out of me, and I was able to look down and pity the untraveled with a compassion that had hardly a trace of contempt in it. Still, when we stopped at villages and wood-yards, I could not help lolling carelessly upon the railings of the boiler-deck to enjoy the envy of the country boys on the bank. If they did not seem to discover me, I presently sneezed to attract their attention, or moved to a position where they could not help seeing me. And as soon as I knew they saw me I gaped and stretched, and gave other signs of being mightily bored with traveling.

I kept my hat off all the time, and stayed where the wind and the sun could strike me, because I wanted to get the bronzed and weather-beaten look of an old traveler. Before the second day was half gone I experienced a joy which filled me with the purest gratitude; for I saw that the skin had begun to blister and peel off my face and neck. I wished that the boys and girls at home could see me now.

We reached Louisville in time—at least the neighborhood of it. We stuck hard and fast on the rocks in the middle of the river, and lay there four days. I was now beginning to feel a strong sense of being a part of the boat's family, a sort of infant son to the captain and younger brother to the officers. There is no estimating the pride I took in this grandeur, or the affection that began to swell and grow in me for those people. I could not know how the lordly steamboatman scorns that sort of presumption in a mere landsman. I particularly longed to acquire the least trifle of notice from the big stormy mate, and I was on the alert for an opportunity to do him a service to that end. It came at last. The riotous powwow of setting a spar[7] was going on down on the forecastle, and I went down there and stood around in the way—or mostly skipping out of it—till the mate suddenly roared a general order for somebody to bring him a capstan bar.[8] I sprang to his side and said: "Tell me where it is—I'll fetch it!"

If a rag-picker had offered to do a diplomatic service for the Emperor of Russia, the monarch could not have been more astounded than the mate was. He even stopped swearing. He stood and stared down at me. It took him ten seconds to scrape his disjointed remains together again. Then he said impressively: "Well, if this don't beat h——l!" and turned to his work with the air of a man who had been confronted with a problem too abstruse for solution.

I crept away, and courted solitude for the rest of the day. I did not go to dinner; I stayed away from supper until everybody else had finished. I did not feel so much like a member of the boat's family now as before. However, my spirits returned, in installments, as we pursued our way down the river. I was sorry I hated the mate so, because it was not in (young) human nature not to admire him. He was huge and muscular, his face was bearded and whiskered all over; he had a red woman and a blue woman tattooed on his

[7] Adjusting a mast, yard, boom, gaff, or the like.

[8] A long lever for turning a capstan by hand.

A capstan is a post that is rotated for winding in ropes and cables.

right arm—one on each side of a blue anchor with a red rope to it; and in the matter of profanity he was sublime. When he was getting out cargo at a landing, I was always where I could see and hear. He felt all the majesty of his great position, and made the world feel it, too. When he gave even the simplest order, he discharged it like a blast of lightning, and sent a long, reverberating peal of profanity thundering after it. I could not help contrasting the way in which the average landsman would give an order with the mate's way of doing it. If the landsman should wish the gang-plank moved a foot farther forward, he would probably say: "James, or William, one of you push that plank forward, please;" but put the mate in his place, and he would roar out: "Here, now, start that gang-plank for'ard! Lively, now! What're you about! Snatch it! *snatch* it! There! there! Aft again! aft again! Don't you hear me? Dash it to dash! are you going to *sleep* over it! 'Vast heaving. 'Vast heaving, I tell you! Going to heave it clear astern! WHERE're you going with that barrel *for'ard* with it 'fore I make you swallow it, you dash-dash-dash-*dashed* split between a tired mud-turtle and a crippled hearse-horse!"

I wished I could talk like that.

When the soreness of my adventure with the mate had somewhat worn off, I began timidly to make up to the humblest official connected with the boat—the night watchman. He snubbed my advances at first, but I presently ventured to offer him a new chalk pipe, and that softened him. So he allowed me to sit with him by the big bell on the hurricane deck, and in time he melted into conversation. He could not well have helped it, I hung with such homage on his words and so plainly showed that I felt honored by his notice. He told me the names of dim capes and shadowy islands as we glided by them in the solemnity of the night, under the winking stars, and by and by got to talking about himself. He seemed over-sentimental for a man whose salary was six dollars a week—or rather he might have seemed so to an older person than I. But I drank in his words hungrily, and with a faith that might have moved mountains if it had been applied judiciously. What was it to me that he was soiled and seedy and fragrant with gin? What was it to me that his grammar was bad, his construction worse, and his profanity so void of art that it was an element of weakness rather than strength in his conversation? He was a wronged man, a man who had seen trouble, and that was enough for me. As he mellowed into his plaintive history, his tears dripped upon the lantern in his lap, and I cried, too, from sympathy. He said he was the son of an English nobleman—either an earl or an alderman, he could not remember which, but believed was both; his father, the nobleman, loved him, but his mother hated him from the cradle; and so while he was still a little boy he was sent to "one of them old, ancient colleges"—he couldn't remember which; and by and by his father died and his mother seized the property and "shook" him, as he phrased it. After his mother shook him, members of the nobility with whom he was acquainted used their influence to get him the position of "loblolly-boy in a ship";[9] and from that point my watchman threw off all trammels of date and locality and branched out into a narrative that bristled all along with incredible adventures; a narrative that was so reeking with bloodshed, and so crammed with hair-breadth escapes and the most engaging and unconscious personal villainies, that I sat speechless, enjoying, shuddering, wondering, worshiping.

It was a sore blight to find out afterward that he was a low, vulgar, ignorant, sentimental, half-witted humbug, an untraveled native of the wilds of Illinois, who had absorbed wildcat literature and appropriated its marvels, until in time he had woven odds and ends of the mess into this yarn, and then gone on telling it to fledglings like me, until he had come to believe it himself.

CHAPTER VI   A CUB-PILOT'S EXPERIENCE

What with lying on the rocks four days at Louisville, and some other delays, the poor old *Paul Jones* fooled away about two weeks in making the voyage from Cincinnati to New Orleans. This gave me a chance to get acquainted with one of the pilots, and he taught me how to steer the boat, and thus made the fascination of river life more potent than ever for me.

It also gave me a chance to get acquainted with a youth who had taken deck passage—more's the pity; for he easily borrowed six dollars of me on a promise to return to the boat and pay it back to me the day after we should arrive. But he probably died or forgot, for he never came. It was doubtless the former, since he had said his parents were wealthy, and he only traveled deck passage because it was cooler.[10]

I soon discovered two things. One was that a vessel would not be likely to sail for the mouth of the Amazon under ten or twelve years; and the other was that the nine or ten dollars still left in my pocket would not suffice for so impossible an exploration as I had planned, even if I could afford to wait for a ship. Therefore it followed that I must contrive a new career. The *Paul Jones* was now bound for St. Louis. I planned a siege against my pilot, and at the end of three hard days he surrendered. He agreed to teach me the Mississippi River from New Orleans to St. Louis for five hundred dollars, payable out of the first wages I should receive after graduating. I entered upon the small enterprise of "learning" twelve or thirteen hundred miles of the great Mississippi River with the easy confidence of my time of life. If I had really known what I was about to require of my faculties, I should not have had the courage to begin. I supposed that all a pilot had to do was to keep his boat in the river, and I did not consider that that could be much of a trick, since it was so wide.

---

[9] An assistant to the surgeon on board ship. The term is obsolete.

[10] "Deck" passage—i.e., steerage passage. (Twain's note.)

The boat backed out from New Orleans at four in the afternoon, and it was "our watch" until eight. Mr. Bixby, my chief, "straightened her up," ploughed her along past the sterns of the other boats that lay at the Levee, and then said, "Here, take her; shave those steamships as close as you'd peel an apple." I took the wheel, and my heart-beat fluttered up into the hundreds; for it seemed to me that we were about to scrape the side off every ship in the line, we were so close. I held my breath and began to claw the boat away from the danger; and I had my own opinion of the pilot who had known no better than to get us into such peril, but I was too wise to express it. In half a minute I had a wide margin of safety intervening between the *Paul Jones* and the ships; and within ten seconds more I was set aside in disgrace, and Mr. Bixby was going into danger again and flaying me alive with abuse of my cowardice. I was stung, but I was obliged to admire the easy confidence with which my chief loafed from side to side of his wheel, and trimmed the ships so closely that disaster seemed ceaselessly imminent. When he had cooled a little he told me that the easy water was close ashore and the current outside, and therefore we must hug the bank, up-stream, to get the benefit of the former, and stay well out, down-stream, to take advantage of the latter. In my own mind I resolved to be a down-stream pilot and leave the up-streaming to people dead to prudence.

Now and then Mr. Bixby called my attention to certain things. Said he, "This is Six-Mile Point." I assented. It was pleasant enough information, but I could not see the bearing of it. I was not conscious that it was a matter of any interest to me. Another time he said, "This is Nine-Mile Point." They were all about level with the water's edge; they all looked about alike to me; they were monotonously unpicturesque. I hoped Mr. Bixby would change the subject. But no; he would crowd up around a point, hugging the shore with affection, and then say: "The slack water ends here, abreast this bunch of China-trees; now we cross over." So he crossed over. He gave me the wheel once or twice, but I had no luck. I either came near chipping off the edge of a sugar plantation, or I yawed too far from shore, and so dropped back into disgrace again and got abused.

The watch was ended at last, and we took supper and went to bed. At midnight the glare of a lantern shone in my eyes, and the night watchman said:

"Come, turn out!"

And then he left. I could not understand this extraordinary procedure; so I presently gave up trying to, and dozed off to sleep. Pretty soon the watchman was back again, and this time he was gruff. I was annoyed. I said:

"What do you want to come bothering around here in the middle of the night for? Now, as like as not, I'll not get to sleep again to-night."

The watchman said:

"Well, if this ain't good. I'm blessed."

The "off-watch" was just turning in, and I heard some brutal laughter from them, and such remarks as "Hello, watchman! ain't the new cub turned out yet? He's delicate, likely. Give him some sugar in a rag, and send for the chambermaid to sing 'Rock-a-by-Baby,' to him."

About this time Mr. Bixby appeared on the scene. Something like a minute later I was climbing the pilot-house steps with some of my clothes on and the rest in my arms. Mr. Bixby was close behind, commenting. Here was something fresh—this thing of getting up in the middle of the night to go to work. It was a detail in piloting that had never occurred to me at all. I knew that boats ran all night, but somehow I had never happened to reflect that somebody had to get up out of a warm bed to run them. I began to fear that piloting was not quite so romantic as I had imagined it was; there was something very real and worklike about this new phase of it.

It was a rather dingy night, although a fair number of stars were out. The big mate was at the wheel, and he had the old tub pointed at a star and was holding her straight up the middle of the river. The shores on either hand were not much more than half a mile apart, but they seemed wonderfully far away and ever so vague and indistinct. The mate said:

"We've got to land at Jones' plantation, sir."

The vengeful spirit in me exulted. I said to myself, "I wish you joy of your job, Mr. Bixby; you'll have a good time finding Mr. Jones' plantation such a night as this; and I hope you never *will* find it as long as you live."

Mr. Bixby said to the mate:

"Upper end of the plantation, or the lower?"

"Upper."

"I can't do it. The stumps there are out of water at this stage. It's no great distance to the lower, and you'll have to get along with that."

"All right sir. If Jones don't like it, he'll have to lump it, I reckon."

And then the mate left. My exultation began to cool and my wonder to come up. Here was a man who not only proposed to find this plantation on such a night, but to find either end of it you preferred. I dreadfully wanted to ask a question, but I was carrying about as many short answers as my cargo-room would admit of, so I held my peace. All I desired to ask Mr. Bixby was the simple question whether he was ass enough to really imagine he was going to find that plantation on a night when all plantations were exactly alike and all of the same color. But I held in. I used to have fine inspirations of prudence in those days.

Mr. Bixby made for the shore and soon was scraping it, just the same as if it had been daylight. And not only that, but singing:

"Father in heaven, the day is declining," etc.

It seemed to me that I had put my life in the keeping of a peculiarly reckless outcast. Presently he turned on me and said:

"What's the name of the first point above New Orleans?"

I was gratified to be able to answer promptly, and I did. I said I didn't know.

"Don't *know?*"

This manner jolted me. I was down at the foot again, in a moment. But I had to say just what I had said before.

"Well, you're a smart one!" said Mr. Bixby. "What's the name of the *next* point?"

Once more I didn't know.

"Well, this beats anything. Tell me the name of *any* point or place I told you."

I studied a while and decided that I couldn't.

"Look here! What do you start out from, above Twelve-Mile Point, to cross over?"

"I—I—don't know."

"You—you—don't know!" mimicking my drawling manner of speech. "What *do* you know?"

"I—I—nothing, for certain."

"By the great Caesar's ghost, I believe you! You're the stupidest dunderhead I ever saw or ever heard of, so help me Moses! The idea of *you* being a pilot—*you!* Why, you don't know enough to pilot a cow down a lane."

Oh, but his wrath was up! He was a nervous man, and he shuffled from one side of his wheel to the other as if the floor was hot. He would boil a while to himself, and then overflow and scald me again.

"Look here! What do you suppose I told you the names of those points for?"

I tremblingly considered a moment, and then the devil of temptation provoked me to say:

"Well—to—to—be entertaining, I thought."

This was a red rag to the bull. He raged and stormed so (he was crossing the river at the time) that I judge it made him blind, because he ran over the steering-oar of a trading-scow. Of course the traders sent up a volley of red-hot profanity. Never was a man so grateful as Mr. Bixby was; because he was brimful, and here were subjects who could *talk back*. He threw open a window, thrust his head out, and such an irruption followed as I never had heard before. The fainter and farther away the scowmen's curses drifted, the higher Mr. Bixby lifted his voice and the weightier his adjectives grew. When he closed the window he was empty. You could have drawn a seine through his system and not caught curses enough to disturb your mother with. Presently he said to me in the gentlest way:

"My boy, you must get a little memorandum-book; and every time I tell you a thing, put it down right away. There's only one way to be a pilot, and that is to get this entire river by heart. You have to know it just like A B C."

That was a dismal revelation to me; for my memory was never loaded with anything but blank cartridges. However, I did not feel discouraged long. I judged that it was best to make some allowances, for doubtless Mr. Bixby was "stretching." Presently he pulled a rope and struck a few strokes on the big bell. The stars were all gone now, and the night was as black as ink. I could hear the wheels churn along the bank, but I was not entirely certain that I could see the shore. The voice of the invisible watchman called up from the hurricane deck:

"What's this, sir?"

"Jones' plantation."

I said to myself, "I wish I might venture to offer a small bet that it isn't." But I did not chirp. I only waited to see. Mr. Bixby handled the engine-bells, and in due time the boat's nose came to the land, a torch glowed from the forecastle, a man skipped ashore, a darkey's voice on the bank said, "Gimme de k'yarpet-bag, Mass' Jones," and the next moment we were standing up the river again, all serene. I reflected deeply a while, and then said—but not aloud—"Well, the finding of that plantation was the luckiest accident that ever happened; but it couldn't happen again in a hundred years." And I fully believed it *was* an accident, too.

By the time we had gone seven or eight hundred miles up the river, I had learned to be a tolerably plucky up-stream steersman, in daylight, and before we reached St. Louis I had made a trifle of progress in night-work, but only a trifle. I had a note-book that fairly bristled with the names of towns, "points," bars, islands, bends, reaches, etc.; but the information was to be found only in the note-book—none of it was in my head. It made my heart ache to think I had only got half of the river set down; for as our watch was four hours off and four hours on, day and night, there was a long four-hour gap in my book for every time I had slept since the voyage began.

My chief was presently hired to go on a big New Orleans boat, and I packed my satchel and went with him. She was a grand affair. When I stood in her pilot-house I was so far above the water that I seemed perched on a mountain; and her decks stretched so far away, fore and aft, below me, that I wondered how I could ever have considered the little *Paul Jones* a large craft. There were other differences, too. The *Paul Jones'* pilot-house was a cheap, dingy, battered rattle-trap, cramped for room; but here was a sumptuous glass temple; room enough to have a dance in; showy red and gold window-curtains; an imposing sofa; leather cushions and a back to the high bench where visiting pilots sit, to spin yarns and "look at the river"; bright, fanciful "cuspadores," instead of a broad wooden box filled with sawdust; nice new oil-cloth on the floor; a hospitable big stove for winter; a wheel as high as my head, costly with inlaid work; a wire tiller-rope; bright brass knobs for the bells; and a tidy, white-aproned, black "texas-tender," to bring up tarts and ices and coffee during mid-watch, day and night. Now this was "something like"; and so I began to take heart once more to believe that piloting was a romantic sort of occupation after all. The moment we were under way I began to prowl about the great steamer and fill myself with joy. She was as clean and as dainty as a drawing-room; when I looked down her long-gilded saloon, it was like gazing through a splendid tunnel; she had an oil-picture, by some gifted sign-painter, on every state-room door; she glittered with no end of prism-fringed chandeliers; the clerk's office was elegant, the bar was marvelous, and the barkeeper had been barbered and upholstered at incredible cost. The boiler-deck (*i.e.*, the second story of the boat, so to speak), was as spacious as a church, it seemed to me; so with the forecastle; and there was no pitiful handful of deck-hands, firemen, and roustabouts down there, but a whole battalion of men. The fires were fiercely glaring from a long row of furnaces, and over them were eight huge boilers. This was unutterable pomp. The mighty engines—but enough of this. I had never felt so fine before. And when I found that the regiment of natty servants respectfully "sir'd" me, my satisfaction was complete.

1875/1883

How To Tell a Story[1]

(1895)

The Humorous Story, an American Development.—
Its Difference from Comic and Witty Stories.

I do not claim that I can tell a story as it ought to be told. I only claim to know how a story ought to be told, for I have been almost daily in the company of the most expert storytellers for many years.

There are several kinds of stories, but only one difficult kind—the humorous. I will talk mainly about that one. The humorous story is American, the comic story is English, the witty story is French. The humorous story depends for its effect upon the *manner* of the telling; the comic story and the witty story upon the *matter*.

The humorous story may be spun out to great length, and may wander around as much as it pleases, and arrive nowhere in particular; but the comic and witty stories must be brief and end with a point. The humorous story bubbles gently along, the others burst.

[1] First published in "The Youth's Companion," October 1895 and later collected in *How To Tell a Story and Other Essays*, published in 1897.

The humorous story is strictly a work of art—high and delicate art—and only an artist can tell it; but no art is necessary in telling the comic and the witty story; anybody can do it. The art of telling a humorous story—understand, I mean by word of mouth, not print—was created in America, and has remained at home.

The humorous story is told gravely; the teller does his best to conceal the fact that he even dimly suspects that there is anything funny about it; but the teller of the comic story tells you beforehand that it is one of the funniest things he has ever heard, then tells it with eager delight, and is the first person to laugh when he gets through. And sometimes, if he has had good success, he is so glad and happy that he will repeat the "nub" of it and glance around from face to face, collecting applause, and then repeat it again. It is a pathetic thing to see.

Very often, of course, the rambling and disjointed humorous story finishes with a nub, point, snapper, or whatever you like to call it. Then the listener must be alert, for in many cases the teller will divert attention from that nub by dropping it in a carefully casual and indifferent way, with the pretense that he does not know it is a nub.

Artemus Ward used that trick a good deal; then when the belated audience presently caught the joke he would look up with innocent surprise, as if wondering what they had found to laugh at. Dan Setchell used it before him, Nye and Riley[2] and others use it to-day.

But the teller of the comic story does not slur the nub; he shouts it at you—every time. And when he prints it, in England, France, Germany, and Italy, he italicizes it, puts some whooping exclamation-points after it, and sometimes explains it in a parenthesis. All of which is very depressing, and makes one want to renounce joking and lead a better life.

Let me set down an instance of the comic method, using an anecdote which has been popular all over the world for twelve or fifteen hundred years. The teller tells it in this way:

THE WOUNDED SOLDIER

In the course of a certain battle a soldier whose leg had been shot off appealed to another soldier who was hurrying by to carry him to the rear, informing him at the same time of the loss which he had sustained; whereupon the generous son of Mars, shouldering the unfortunate, proceeded to carry out his desire. The bullets and cannon-balls were flying in all directions, and presently one of the latter took the wounded man's head off—without, however, his deliverer being aware of it. In no long time he was hailed by an officer, who said:

[2] Artemus Ward was the pen name of Charles Farrar Browne (1834-1867). Dan Setchell, Edgar W. Nye (1850-1896) and James Whitcomb Riley (1849-1916) were other well-known humorists.

"Where are you going with that carcass?"

"To the rear, sir—he's lost his leg!"

"His leg, forsooth?" responded the astonished officer; "you mean his head, you booby."

Whereupon the soldier dispossessed himself of his burden, and stood looking down upon it in great perplexity. At length he said:

"It is true, sir, just as you have said." Then after a pause he added, "*But he* TOLD *me* IT WAS HIS LEG! ! ! ! !"

Here the narrator bursts into explosion after explosion of thunderous horse-laughter, repeating that nub from time to time through his gaspings and shriekings and suffocatings.

It takes only a minute and a half to tell that in its comic-story form; and isn't worth the telling, after all. Put into the humorous-story form it takes ten minutes, and is about the funniest thing I have ever listened to—as James Whitcomb Riley tells it.

He tells it in the character of a dull-witted old farmer who has just heard it for the first time, thinks it is unspeakably funny, and is trying to repeat it to a neighbor. But he can't remember it; so he gets all mixed up and wanders helplessly round and round, putting in tedious details that don't belong in the tale and only retard it; taking them out conscientiously and putting in others that are just as useless; making minor mistakes now and then and stopping to correct them and explain how he came to make them; remembering things which he forgot to put in in their proper place and going back to put them in there; stopping his narrative a good while in order to try to recall the name of the soldier that was hurt, and finally remembering that the soldier's name was not mentioned, and remarking placidly that the name is of no real importance, anyway—better, of course, if one knew it, but not essential, after all—and so on, and so on, and so on.

The teller is innocent and happy and pleased with himself, and has to stop every little while to hold himself in and keep from laughing outright; and does hold in, but his body quakes in a jelly-like way with interior chuckles; and at the end of the ten minutes the audience have laughed until they are exhausted, and the tears are running down their faces.

The simplicity and innocence and sincerity and unconsciousness of the old farmer are perfectly simulated, and the result is a performance which is thoroughly charming and delicious. This is art—and fine and beautiful, and only a master can compass it; but a machine could tell the other story.

To string incongruities and absurdities together in a wandering and sometimes purposeless way, and seem innocently unaware that they are absurdities, is the basis of the American art, if my position is correct. Another feature is the slurring of the point. A third is the dropping of a studied remark apparently without knowing it, as if one were thinking aloud. The fourth and last is the pause.

Artemus Ward dealt in numbers three and four a good deal. He would begin to tell with great animation something which he seemed to think was wonderful; then lose confidence, and after an apparently absent-minded pause add an incongruous remark in a soliloquizing way; and that was the remark intended to explode the mine—and it did.

For instance, he would say eagerly, excitedly, "I once knew a man in New Zealand who hadn't a tooth in his head"—here his animation would die out; a silent, reflective pause would follow, then he would say dreamily, and as if to himself, "and yet that man could beat a drum better than any man I ever saw."

The pause is an exceedingly important feature in any kind of story, and a frequently recurring feature, too. It is a dainty thing, and delicate, and also uncertain and treacherous; for it must be exactly the right length—no more and no less—or it fails of its purpose and makes trouble. If the pause is too short the impressive point is passed, and the audience have had time to divine that a surprise is intended—and then you can't surprise them, of course.

On the platform I used to tell a negro ghost story that had a pause in front of the snapper on the end, and that pause was the most important thing in the whole story. If I got it the right length precisely, I could spring the finishing ejaculation with effect enough to make some impressible girl deliver a startled little yelp and jump out of her seat—and that was what I was after. This story was called "The Golden Arm," and was told in this fashion. You can practise with it yourself—and mind you look out for the pause and get it right.

THE GOLDEN ARM

Once 'pon a time dey wuz a monsus mean man, en he live 'way out in de prairie all 'lone by hisself, 'cep'n he had a wife. En bimeby she died, en he tuck en toted her way out dah in de prairie en buried her. Well, she had a golden arm—all solid gold, fum de shoulder down. He wuz pow'ful mean— pow'ful; en dat night he couldn't sleep, caze he want dat golden arm so bad.

When it come midnight, he couldn't stan' it no mo'; so he git up, he did, en tuck his lantern en shoved out thoo de storm en dug her up en got de golden arm; en he bent his head down 'gin de win', en plowed en plowed en plowed thoo de snow. Den all on a sudden he stop (make a considerable pause here, and look startled, and take a listening attitude) en say: "My *lan'*, what's dat!"

En he listen—en listen—en de win' say (set your teeth together and imitate the wailing and wheezing singsong of the wind), "Bzzz-z-zzz"—en den, way back yonder whah de grave is, he hear a *voice!*—he hear a voice all mix' up in de win'—cain't hardly tell 'em 'part— "Bzzz-zzz—W-h-o—g-o-

t—m-y—g-o-l-d-e-n *arm?*—zzz—zzz—W-h-o g-o-t m-y g-o-l-d-e-n *arm?*"
(You must begin to shiver violently now.)

En he begin to shiver en shake, en say, "Oh, my! *Oh*, my lan'!" en de win'
blow de lantern out, en de snow en sleet blow in his face en mos' choke him,
en he start a-plowin' knee-deep towards home mos' dead, he so sk'yerd—en
pooty soon he hear de voice agin, en (pause) it 'us comin' *after* him! "Bzzz—
zzz—zzz—W-h-o—g-o-t—m-y—g-o-l-d-e-n—*arm?*"

When he git to de pasture he hear it agin—closter now, en *a-comin'!*—a-
comin' back dah in de dark en de storm—(repeat the wind and the voice).
When he git to de house he rush up-stairs en jump in de bed en kiver up,
head and years, en lay dah shiverin' en shakin'—en den way out dah he hear
it *agin!*—en a-*comin'!* En bimeby he hear (pause—awed, listening attitude)—pat—pat—pat—*hit's a-comin' up-stairs!* Den he hear de latch, en he
know it's in de room!

Den pooty soon he know it's a-*stannin' by de bed!* (Pause.) Den—he know
it's a-*bendin' down over him*—en he cain't skasely git his breath! Den—
den—he seem to feel someth'n *c-o-l-d*, right down 'most agin his head!
(Pause.)

Den de voice say, *right at his year*— "W-h-o—g-o-t—m-y—g-o-l-d-e-n
arm?" (You must wail it out very plaintively and accusingly; then you stare
steadily and impressively into the face of the farthest-gone auditor—a girl,
preferably—and let that awe-inspiring pause begin to build itself in the deep
hush. When it has reached exactly the right length, jump suddenly at the girl
and yell, "*You've* got it!"

If you've got the *pause* right, she'll fetch a dear little yelp and spring right
out of her shoes. But you *must* get the pause right; and you will find it the
most troublesome and aggravating and uncertain thing you ever undertook.)

Fenimore Cooper's Literary Offences[1]

(1895)

The Pathfinder and *The Deerslayer* stand at the head of Cooper's novels
as artistic creations. There are others of his works which contain parts as
perfect as are to be found in these, and scenes even more thrilling. Not
one can be compared with either of them as a finished whole.

The defects in both of these tales are comparatively slight. They were
pure works of art.—*Prof. Lounsbury.*[2]

---

[1] First published in 1895. James Fenimore
Cooper (1789-1851) was a highly regarded
American novelist who wrote the five *Leath-
erstocking Tales,* including *The Deerslayer*

(1841), *The Last of the Mohicans* (1826), *The
Pathfinder* (1840), *The Pioneers* (1823), and
The Prairie (1827).

[2] Thomas R. Lounsbury (1838-1915).

The five tales reveal an extraordinary fulness of invention.
. . . One of the very greatest characters in fiction, Natty Bumppo . . .
The craft of the woodsman, the tricks of the trapper, all the delicate art of the forest, were familiar to Cooper from his youth up.—*Prof. Brander Matthews.*[3]

Cooper is the greatest artist in the domain of romantic fiction yet produced by America.—*Wilkie Collins.*[4]

It seems to me that it was far from right for the Professor of English Literature in Yale, the Professor of English Literature in Columbia, and Wilkie Collins to deliver opinions on Cooper's literature without having read some of it. It would have been much more decorous to keep silent and let persons talk who have read Cooper.

Cooper's art has some defects. In one place in *Deerslayer,* and in the restricted space of two-thirds of a page, Cooper has scored 114 offences against literary art out of a possible 115. It breaks the record.

There are nineteen rules governing literary art in the domain of romantic fiction—some say twenty-two. In *Deerslayer* Cooper violated eighteen of them. These eighteen require:

1. That a tale shall accomplish something and arrive somewhere. But the *Deerslayer* tale accomplishes nothing and arrives in the air.
2. They require that the episodes of a tale shall be necessary parts of the tale, and shall help to develop it. But as the *Deerslayer* tale is not a tale, and accomplishes nothing and arrives nowhere, the episodes have no rightful place in the work, since there was nothing for them to develop.
3. They require that the personages in a tale shall be alive, except in the case of corpses, and that always the reader shall be able to tell the corpses from the others. But this detail has often been overlooked in the *Deerslayer* tale.
4. They require that the personages in a tale, both dead and alive, shall exhibit a sufficient excuse for being there. But this detail also has been overlooked in the *Deerslayer* tale.
5. They require that when the personages of a tale deal in conversation, the talk shall sound like human talk, and be talk such as human beings would be likely to talk in the given circumstances, and have a discoverable meaning, also a discoverable purpose, and a show of relevancy, and remain in the neighborhood of the subject in hand, and be interesting to the reader, and help out the tale, and stop when the people cannot think of anything more to say. But this requirement has been ignored from the beginning of the *Deerslayer* tale to the end of it.

[3] Brander Matthews (1852–1929).   [4] English novelist (1824–1899).

6. They require that when the author describes the character of a personage in his tale, the conduct and conversation of that personage shall justify said description. But this law gets little or no attention in the *Deerslayer* tale, as Natty Bumppo's case will amply prove.
7. They require that when a personage talks like an illustrated, gilt-edged, tree-calf, hand-tooled, seven-dollar Friendship's Offering[5] in the beginning of a paragraph, he shall not talk like a negro minstrel in the end of it. But this rule is flung down and danced upon in the *Deerslayer* tale.
8. They require that crass stupidities shall not be played upon the reader as "the craft of the woodsman, the delicate art of the forest," by either the author or the people in the tale. But this rule is persistently violated in the *Deerslayer* tale.
9. They require that the personages of a tale shall confine themselves to possibilities and let miracles alone; or, if they venture a miracle, the author must so plausibly set it forth as to make it look possible and reasonable. But these rules are not respected in the *Deerslayer* tale.
10. They require that the author shall make the reader feel a deep interest in the personages of his tale and in their fate; and that he shall make the reader love the good people in the tale and hate the bad ones. But the reader of the *Deerslayer* tale dislikes the good people in it, is indifferent to the others, and wishes they would all get drowned together.
11. They require that the characters in a tale shall be so clearly defined that the reader can tell beforehand what each will do in a given emergency. But in the *Deerslayer* tale this rule is vacated.

In addition to these large rules there are some little ones. These require that the author shall

12. Say what he is proposing to say, not merely come near it.
13. Use the right word, not its second cousin.
14. Eschew surplusage.
15. Not omit necessary details.
16. Avoid slovenliness of form.
17. Use good grammar.
18. Employ a simple and straightforward style.

Even these seven are coldly and persistently violated in the *Deerslayer* tale.

Cooper's gift in the way of invention was not a rich endowment; but such as it was he liked to work it, he was pleased with the effects, and indeed he

---

[5] A splendidly ornamented gift book, usually filled with sentimental stories and poems in high flown language and given to young ladies.

did some quite sweet things with it. In his little box of stage properties he kept six or eight cunning devices, tricks, artifices for his savages and woodsmen to deceive and circumvent each other with, and he was never so happy as when he was working these innocent things and seeing them go. A favorite one was to make a moccasined person tread in the tracks of the moccasined enemy, and thus hide his own trail. Cooper wore out barrels and barrels of moccasins in working that trick. Another stage-property that he pulled out of his box pretty frequently was his broken twig. He prized his broken twig above all the rest of his effects, and worked it the hardest. It is a restful chapter in any book of his when somebody doesn't step on a dry twig and alarm all the reds and whites for two hundred yards around. Every time a Cooper person is in peril, and absolute silence is worth four dollars a minute, he is sure to step on a dry twig. There may be a hundred handier things to step on, but that wouldn't satisfy Cooper. Cooper requires him to turn out and find a dry twig; and if he can't do it, go and borrow one. In fact, the Leather Stocking Series ought to have been called the Broken Twig Series.

I am sorry there is not room to put in a few dozen instances of the delicate art of the forest, as practised by Natty Bumppo and some of the other Cooperian experts. Perhaps we may venture two or three samples. Cooper was a sailor—a naval officer; yet he gravely tells us how a vessel, driving towards a lee shore in a gale, is steered for a particular spot by her skipper because he knows of an *undertow* there which will hold her back against the gale and save her. For just pure woodcraft, or sailorcraft, or whatever it is, isn't that neat? For several years Cooper was daily in the society of artillery, and he ought to have noticed that when a cannon-ball strikes the ground it either buries itself or skips a hundred feet or so; skips again a hundred feet or so—and so on, till finally it gets tired and rolls. Now in one place he loses some "females"—as he always calls women—in the edge of a wood near a plain at night in a fog, on purpose to give Bumppo a chance to show off the delicate art of the forest before the reader. These mislaid people are hunting for a fort. They hear a cannon-blast, and a cannon-ball presently comes rolling into the wood and stops at their feet. To the females this suggests nothing. The case is very different with the admirable Bumppo. I wish I may never know peace again if he doesn't strike out promptly and *follow the track* of that cannon-ball across the plain through the dense fog and find the fort. Isn't it a daisy? If Cooper had any real knowledge of Nature's ways of doing things, he had a most delicate art in concealing the fact. For instance: one of his acute Indian experts, Chingachgook (pronounced Chicago, I think), has lost the trail of a person he is tracking through the forest. Apparently that trail is hopelessly lost. Neither you nor I could ever have guessed out the way to find it. It was very different with Chicago. Chicago was not stumped for long. He turned a running stream out of its course, and there, in the slush in its old bed, were that person's moccasin-tracks. The current did not wash them away, as it would have done in all other like cases—no, even the eternal laws of Nature have to vacate when Cooper wants to put up a delicate job of woodcraft on the reader.

We must be a little wary when Brander Matthews tells us that Cooper's books "reveal an extraordinary fulness of invention." As a rule, I am quite willing to accept Brander Matthews's literary judgments and applaud his lucid and graceful phrasing of them; but that particular statement needs to be taken with a few tons of salt. Bless your heart, Cooper hadn't any more invention than a horse; and I don't mean a high-class horse, either; I mean a clothes-horse. It would be very difficult to find a really clever "situation" in Cooper's books, and still more difficult to find one of any kind which he has failed to render absurd by his handling of it. Look at the episodes of "the caves"; and at the celebrated scuffle between Maqua[6] and those others on the table-land a few days later; and at Hurry Harry's[7] queer water-transit from the castle to the ark; and at Deerslayer's half-hour with his first corpse; and at the quarrel between Hurry Harry and Deerslayer later; and at—but choose for yourself; you can't go amiss.

If Cooper had been an observer his inventive faculty would have worked better; not more interestingly, but more rationally, more plausibly. Cooper's proudest creations in the way of "situations" suffer noticeably from the absence of the observer's protecting gift. Cooper's eye was splendidly inaccurate. Cooper seldom saw anything correctly. He saw nearly all things as through a glass eye, darkly. Of course a man who cannot see the commonest little every-day matters accurately is working at a disadvantage when he is constructing a "situation." In the *Deerslayer* tale Cooper has a stream which is fifty feet wide where it flows out of a lake; it presently narrows to twenty as it meanders along for no given reason, and yet when a stream acts like that it ought to be required to explain itself. Fourteen pages later the width of the brook's outlet from the lake has suddenly shrunk thirty feet, and become "the narrowest part of the stream." This shrinkage is not accounted for. The stream has bends in it, a sure indication that it has alluvial banks and cuts them; yet these bends are only thirty and fifty feet long. If Cooper had been a nice and punctilious observer he would have noticed that the bends were oftener nine hundred feet long than short of it.

Cooper made the exit of that stream fifty feet wide, in the first place, for no particular reason; in the second place, he narrowed it to less than twenty to accommodate some Indians. He bends a "sapling" to the form of an arch over this narrow passage, and conceals six Indians in its foliage. They are "laying" for a settler's scow or ark which is coming up the stream on its way to the lake; it is being hauled against the stiff current by a rope whose stationary end is anchored in the lake; its rate of progress cannot be more

---

[6] A Huron chief in *The Last of the Mohicans*, and an evil character.

[7] A violent white hunter with two lovely daughters in *The Deerslayer*.

than a mile an hour. Cooper describes the ark, but pretty obscurely. In the matter of dimensions "it was little more than a modern canal-boat." Let us guess, then, that it was about one hundred and forty feet long. It was of "greater breadth than common." Let us guess, then, that it was about sixteen feet wide. This leviathan had been prowling down bends which were but a third as long as itself, and scraping between banks where it had only two feet of space to spare on each side. We cannot too much admire this miracle. A low-roofed log dwelling occupies "two-thirds of the ark's length"—a dwelling ninety feet long and sixteen feet wide, let us say—a kind of vestibule train. The dwelling has two rooms—each forty-five feet long and sixteen feet wide, let us guess. One of them is the bedroom of the Hutter girls, Judith and Hetty; the other is the parlor in the daytime, at night it is papa's bedchamber. The ark is arriving at the stream's exit now, whose width has been reduced to less than twenty feet to accommodate the Indians—say to eighteen. There is a foot to spare on each side of the boat. Did the Indians notice that there was going to be a tight squeeze there? Did they notice that they could make money by climbing down out of that arched sapling and just stepping aboard when the ark scraped by? No, other Indians would have noticed these things, but Cooper's Indians never notice anything. Cooper thinks they are marvelous creatures for noticing, but he was almost always in error about his Indians. There was seldom a sane one among them.

The ark is one hundred and forty feet long; the dwelling is ninety feet long. The idea of the Indians is to drop softly and secretly from the arched sapling to the dwelling as the ark creeps along under it at the rate of a mile an hour, and butcher the family. It will take the ark a minute and a half to pass under. It will take the ninety foot dwelling a minute to pass under. Now, then, what did the six Indians do? It would take you thirty years to guess, and even then you would have to give it up, I believe. Therefore, I will tell you what the Indians did. Their chief, a person of quite extraordinary intellect for a Cooper Indian, warily watched the canal-boat as it squeezed along under him, and when he had got his calculations fined down to exactly the right shade, as he judged, he let go and dropped. And *missed the house!* That is actually what he did. He missed the house, and landed in the stern of the scow. It was not much of a fall, yet it knocked him silly. He lay there unconscious. If the house had been ninety-seven feet long he would have made the trip. The fault was Cooper's, not his. The error lay in the construction of the house. Cooper was no architect.

There still remained in the roost five Indians. The boat has passed under and is now out of their reach. Let me explain what the five did—you would not be able to reason it out for yourself. No. 1 jumped for the boat, but fell in the water astern of it. Then No. 2 jumped for the boat, but fell in the water still farther astern of it. Then No. 3 jumped for the boat, and fell a good way astern of it. Then No. 4 jumped for the boat, and fell in the water *away* astern. Then even No. 5 made a jump for the boat—for he was a Cooper Indian. In the matter of intellect, the difference between a Cooper Indian and the Indian that stands in front of the cigar-shop is not spacious. The scow episode is really a sublime burst of invention; but it does not thrill, because the inaccuracy of the details throws a sort of air of fictitiousness and general improbability over it. This comes of Cooper's inadequacy as an observer.

The reader will find some examples of Cooper's high talent for inaccurate observation in the account of the shooting-match in *The Pathfinder*.

> "A common wrought nail was driven lightly into the target, its head having been first touched with paint."

The color of the paint is not stated—an important omission, but Cooper deals freely in important omissions. No, after all, it was not an important omission; for this nail-head is *a hundred yards from* the marksmen, and could not be seen by them at that distance, no matter what its color might be. How far can the best eyes see a common house-fly? A hundred yards? It is quite impossible. Very well; eyes that cannot see a house-fly that is a hundred yards away cannot see an ordinary nail-head at that distance, for the size of the two objects is the same. It takes a keen eye to see a fly or a nailhead at fifty yards—one hundred and fifty feet. Can the reader do it?

The nail was lightly driven, its head painted, and game called. Then the Cooper miracles began. The bullet of the first marksman chipped an edge of the nail-head; the next man's bullet drove the nail a little way into the target—and removed all the paint. Haven't the miracles gone far enough now? Not to suit Cooper; for the purpose of this whole scheme is to show off his prodigy, Deerslayer-Hawkeye-Long-Rifle-Leather-Stocking-Pathfinder-Bumppo before the ladies.

> " 'Be all ready to clench it, boys!' cried out Pathfinder, stepping into his friend's tracks the instant they were vacant. 'Never mind a new nail; I can see that, though the paint is gone, and what I can see I can hit at a hundred yards, though it were only a mosquito's eye. Be ready to clench!'
>
> "The rifle cracked, the bullet sped its way, and the head of the nail was buried in the wood, covered by the piece of flattened lead."

There, you see, is a man who could hunt flies with a rifle, and command a ducal salary in a Wild West show to-day if we had him back with us.

The recorded feat is certainly surprising just as it stands; but it is not surprising enough for Cooper. Cooper adds a touch. He has made Pathfinder do this miracle with another man's rifle; and not only that, but Pathfinder did not have even the advantage of loading it himself. He had everything against him, and yet he made that impossible shot; and not only made it, but did it with absolute confidence, saying, "Be ready to clench." Now a person like that would have undertaken that same feat with a brickbat, and with Cooper to help he would have achieved it, too.

Pathfinder showed off handsomely that day before the ladies. His very first feat was a thing which no Wild West show can touch. He was standing with the group of marksmen, observing—a hundred yards from the target, mind; one Jasper raised his rifle and drove the center of the bull's-eye. Then the Quartermaster fired. The target exhibited no result this time. There was a laugh. "It's a dead miss," said Major Lundie. Pathfinder waited an impressive moment or two; then said, in that calm, indifferent, know-it-all way of his, "No, Major, he has covered Jasper's bullet, as will be seen if any one will take the trouble to examine the target."

Wasn't it remarkable! How *could* he see that little pellet fly through the air and enter that distant bullet-hole? Yet that is what he did; for nothing is impossible to a Cooper person. Did any of those people have any deep-seated doubts about this thing? No; for that would imply sanity, and these were all Cooper people.

"The respect for Pathfinder's skill and for his *quickness and accuracy of sight*" (the italics are mine) "was so profound and general, that the instant he made this declaration the spectators began to distrust their own opinions, and a dozen rushed to the target in order to ascertain the fact. There, sure enough, it was found that the Quartermaster's bullet had gone through the hole made by Jasper's, and that, too, so accurately as to require a minute examination to be certain of the circumstance, which, however, was soon clearly established by discovering one bullet over the other in the stump against which the target was placed."

They made a "minute" examination; but never mind, how could they know that there were two bullets in that hole without digging the latest one out? for neither probe nor eyesight could prove the presence of any more than one bullet. Did they dig? No; as we shall see. It is the Pathfinder's turn now; he steps out before the ladies, takes aim, and fires.

But, alas! here is a disappointment; an incredible, an unimaginable disappointment—for the target's aspect is unchanged; there is nothing there but that same old bullet-hole!

" 'If one dared to hint at such a thing,' cried Major Duncan, 'I should say that the Pathfinder has also missed the target!' "

As nobody had missed it yet, the "also" was not necessary; but never mind about that, for the Pathfinder is going to speak.

> " 'No, no, Major,' said he, confidently, 'that *would* be a risky declaration. I didn't load the piece, and can't say what was in it; but if it was lead, you will find the bullet driving down those of the Quartermaster and Jasper, else is not my name Pathfinder.'
> "A shout from the target announced the truth of his assertion."

Is the miracle sufficient as it stands? Not for Cooper. The Pathfinder speaks again, as he "now slowly advances towards the stage occupied by the females":

> " 'That's not all, boys, that's not all; if you find the target touched at all, I'll own to a miss. The Quartermaster cut the wood, but you'll find no wood cut by that last messenger.' "

The miracle is at last complete. He knew—doubtless *saw*—at the distance of a hundred yards—that his bullet had passed into the hole *without fraying the edges.* There were now three bullets in that one hole—three bullets embedded processionally in the body of the stump back of the target. Everybody knew this—somehow or other—and yet nobody had dug any of them out to make sure. Cooper is not a close observer, but he is interesting. He is certainly always that, no matter what happens. And he is more interesting when he is not noticing what he is about than when he is. This is a considerable merit.

The conversations in the Cooper books have a curious sound in our modern ears. To believe that such talk really ever came out of people's mouths would be to believe that there was a time when time was of no value to a person who thought he had something to say; when it was the custom to spread a two-minute remark out to ten; when a man's mouth was a rolling-mill, and busied itself all day long in turning four-foot pigs of thought into thirty-foot bars of conversational railroad iron by attenuation; when subjects were seldom faithfully stuck to, but the talk wandered all around and arrived nowhere; when conversations consisted mainly of irrelevancies, with here and there a relevancy, a relevancy with an embarrassed look, as not being able to explain how it got there.

Cooper was certainly not a master in the construction of dialogue. Inaccurate observation defeated him here as it defeated him in so many other enterprises of his. He even failed to notice that the man who talks corrupt English six days in the week must and will talk it on the seventh, and can't help himself. In the *Deerslayer* story he lets Deerslayer talk the showiest kind of book-talk sometimes, and at other times the basest of base dialects.

For instance, when some one asks him if he has a sweetheart, and if so, where she abides, this is his majestic answer:

> " 'She's in the forest—hanging from the boughs of the trees, in a soft rain—in the dew on the open grass—the clouds that float about in the blue heavens—the birds that sing in the woods—the sweet springs where I slake my thirst—and in all the other glorious gifts that come from God's Providence!' "

And he preceded that, a little before, with this:

> " 'It consarns me as all things that touches a fri'nd consarns a fri'nd.' "

And this is another of his remarks:

> " 'If I was Injin born, now, I might tell of this, or carry in the scalp and boast of the expl'ite afore the whole tribe; or if my inimy had only been a bear' "—and so on.

We cannot imagine such a thing as a veteran Scotch Commander-in-Chief comporting himself in the field like a windy melodramatic actor, but Cooper could. On one occasion Alice and Cora were being chased by the French through a fog in the neighborhood of their father's fort:

> " *'Point de quartier aux coquins!'*[8] cried an eager pursuer, who seemed to direct the operations of the enemy.
> " 'Stand firm and be ready, my gallant 60ths!' suddenly exclaimed a voice above them; 'wait to see the enemy; fire low, and sweep the glacis.'
> " 'Father! father!' exclaimed a piercing cry from out the mist; 'it is I! Alice! thy own Elsie! spare, O! save your daughters!'
> " 'Hold!' shouted the former speaker, in the awful tones of parental agony, the sound reaching even to the woods, and rolling back in solemn echo. ' 'Tis she! God has restored me my children! Throw open the sally-port; to the field, 60ths, to the field! pull not a trigger, lest ye kill my lambs! Drive off these dogs of France with your steel!' "

Cooper's word-sense was singularly dull. When a person has a poor ear for music he will flat and sharp right along without knowing it. He keeps near the tune, but it is *not* the tune. When a person has a poor ear for words, the result is a literary flatting and sharping; you perceive what he is intending to say, but you also perceive that he doesn't *say* it. This is Cooper. He was not

---

[8] Show the rascals no mercy!

a word-musician. His ear was satisfied with the *approximate* word. I will furnish some circumstantial evidence in support of this charge. My instances are gathered from half a dozen pages of the tale called *Deerslayer*. He uses "verbal," for "oral"; "precision," for "facility"; "phenomena," for "marvels"; "necessary," for "predetermined"; "unsophisticated," for "primitive"; "preparation," for "expectancy"; "rebuked," for "subdued"; "dependent on," for "resulting from"; "fact," for "condition"; "fact," for "conjecture"; "precaution," for "caution"; "explain," for "determine"; "mortified," for "disappointed"; "meretricious," for "factitious"; "materially," for "considerably"; "decreasing," for "deepening"; "increasing," for "disappearing"; "embedded," for "enclosed"; "treacherous," for "hostile"; "stood," for "stooped"; "softened," for "replaced"; "rejoined," for "remarked"; "situation," for "condition"; "different," for "differing"; "insensible," for "unsentient"; "brevity," for "celerity"; "distrusted," for "suspicious"; "mental imbecility," for "imbecility"; "eyes," for "sight"; "counteracting," for "opposing"; "funeral obsequies," for "obsequies."

There have been daring people in the world who claimed that Cooper could write English, but they are all dead now—all dead but Lounsbury. I don't remember that Lounsbury makes the claim in so many words, still he makes it, for he says that *Deerslayer* is a "pure work of art." Pure, in that connection, means faultless—faultless in all details—and language is a detail. If Mr. Lounsbury had only compared Cooper's English with the English which he writes himself—but it is plain that he didn't; and so it is likely that he imagines until this day that Cooper's is as clean and compact as his own. Now I feel sure, deep down in my heart, that Cooper wrote about the poorest English that exists in our language, and that the English of *Deerslayer* is the very worst that even Cooper ever wrote.

I may be mistaken, but it does seem to me that *Deerslayer* is not a work of art in any sense; it does seem to me that it is destitute of every detail that goes to the making of a work of art; in truth, it seems to me that *Deerslayer* is just simply a literary *delirium tremens*.

A work of art? It has no invention; it has no order, system, sequence, or result; it has no life-likeness, no thrill, no stir, no seeming of reality; its characters are confusedly drawn, and by their acts and words they prove that they are not the sort of people the author claims that they are; its humor is pathetic; its pathos is funny; its conversations are—oh! indescribable; its love-scenes odious; its English a crime against the language.

Counting these out, what is left is Art. I think we must all admit that.

Twain *What is Man* — *philosophy of human nature*
share assumptions of naturalists — *fate*

From On "The Damned Human Race"[1]

Man is a machine — *personality / training!*

THE MAN THAT CORRUPTED HADLEYBURG

I

It was many years ago. Hadleyburg was the most honest and upright town in all the region round about it. It had kept that reputation unsmirched during three generations, and was prouder of it than of any other of its possessions. It was so proud of it, and so anxious to insure its perpetuation, that it began to teach the principles of honest dealing to its babies in the cradle, and made the like teachings the staple of their culture thenceforward through all the years devoted to their education. Also, throughout the formative years temptations were kept out of the way of the young people, so that their honesty could have every chance to harden and solidify, and became a part of their very bone. The neighboring towns were jealous of this honorable supremacy and affected to sneer at Hadleyburg's pride in it and call it vanity; but all the same they were obliged to acknowledge that Hadleyburg was in reality an incorruptible town; and if pressed they would also acknowledge that the mere fact that a young man hailed from Hadleyburg was all the recommendation he needed when he went forth from his natal town to seek for responsible employment.

But at last, in the drift of time, Hadleyburg had the ill luck to offend a passing stranger—possibly without knowing it, certainly without caring, for Hadleyburg was sufficient unto itself, and cared not a rap for strangers or their opinions. Still, it would have been well to make an exception in this one's case, for he was a bitter man and revengeful. All through his wanderings during a whole year he kept his injury in mind, and gave all his leisure moments to trying to invent a compensating satisfaction for it. He contrived many plans, and all of them were good, but none of them was quite sweeping enough; the poorest of them would hurt a great many individuals, but what he wanted was a plan which would comprehend the entire town, and not let so much as one person escape unhurt. At last he had a fortunate idea, and when it fell into his brain it lit up his whole head with an evil joy. He began to form a plan at once, saying to himself, "That is the thing to do—I will corrupt the town."

Six months later he went to Hadleyburg, and arrived in a buggy at the house of the old cashier of the bank about ten at night. He got a sack out of the buggy, shouldered it, and staggered with it through the cottage yard, and knocked at the door. A woman's voice said "Come in," and he entered, and

[1] First published in *Harper's Magazine* for December 1899. Later collected in *The Man That Corrupted Hadleyburg and Other Stories and Essays*, published in 1900.

set his sack behind the stove in the parlor, saying politely to the old lady who sat reading the *Missionary Herald* by the lamp:

"Pray keep your seat, madam, I will not disturb you. There—now it is pretty well concealed; one would hardly know it was there. Can I see your husband a moment, madam?"

No, he was gone to Brixton, and might not return before morning.

"Very well, madam, it is no matter. I merely wanted to leave that sack in his care, to be delivered to the rightful owner when he shall be found. I am a stranger; he does not know me; I am merely passing through the town to-night to discharge a matter which has been long in my mind. My errand is now completed, and I go pleased and a little proud, and you will never see me again. There is a paper attached to the sack which will explain everything. Goodnight, madam."

The old lady was afraid of the mysterious big stranger, and was glad to see him go. But her curiosity was roused, and she went straight to the sack and brought away the paper. It began as follows:

> "TO BE PUBLISHED; or, the right man sought out by private inquiry—either will answer. This sack contains gold coin weighing a hundred and sixty pounds four ounces—"

"Mercy on us, and the door not locked!"

Mrs. Richards flew to it all in a tremble and locked it, then pulled down the window-shades and stood frightened, worried, and wondering if there was anything else she could do toward making herself and the money more safe. She listened awhile for burglars, then surrendered to curiosity and went back to the lamp and finished reading the paper:

> "I am a foreigner, and am presently going back to my own country, to remain there permanently. I am grateful to America for what I have received at her hands during my long stay under her flag; and to one of her citizens—a citizen of Hadleyburg—I am especially grateful for a great kindness done me a year or two ago. Two great kindnesses, in fact. I will explain. I was a gambler. I say I WAS. I was a ruined gambler. I arrived in this village at night, hungry and without a penny. I asked for help—in the dark; I was ashamed to beg in the light. I begged of the right man. He gave me twenty dollars—that is to say, he gave me life, as I considered it. He also gave me fortune; for out of that money I have made myself rich at the gaming-table. And finally, a remark which he made to me has remained with me to this day, and has at last conquered me; and in conquering has saved the remnant of my morals: I shall gamble no more. Now I have no idea who that man was, but I want him found, and I want him to have this money, to give

away, throw away, or keep, as he pleases. It is merely my way of testifying my gratitude to him. If I could stay, I would find him myself; but no matter, he will be found. This is an honest town, an incorruptible town, and I know I can trust it without fear. This man can be identified by the remark which he made to me; I feel persuaded that he will remember it.

"And now my plan is this: If you prefer to conduct the inquiry privately, do so. Tell the contents of this present writing to any one who is likely to be the right man. If he shall answer, 'I am the man; the remark I made was so-and-so,' apply the test—to wit: open the sack, and in it you will find a sealed envelope containing that remark. If the remark mentioned by the candidate tallies with it, give him the money, and ask no further questions, for he is certainly the right man.

"But if you shall prefer a public inquiry, then publish this present writing in the local paper—with these instructions added, to wit: Thirty days from now, let the candidate appear at the town-hall at eight in the evening (Friday), and hand his remark, in a sealed envelope, to the Rev. Mr. Burgess (if he will be kind enough to act); and let Mr. Burgess there and then destroy the seals of the sack, open it, and see if the remark is correct; if correct, let the money be delivered, with my sincere gratitude, to my benefactor thus identified."

Mrs. Richards sat down, gently quivering with excitement, and was soon lost in thinkings—after this pattern: "What a strange thing it is! . . . And what a fortune for that kind man who set his bread afloat upon the waters! . . . If it had only been my husband that did it!—for we are so poor, so old and poor! . . ." Then, with a sigh—"But it was not my Edward; no, it was not he that gave a stranger twenty dollars. It is a pity too; I see it now. . . ." Then, with a shudder—"But it is *gambler's* money! the wages of sin; we couldn't take it; we couldn't touch it. I don't like to be near it; it seems a defilement." She moved to a farther chair. . . . "I wish Edward would come, and take it to the bank; a burglar might come at any moment; it is dreadful to be here all alone with it."

At eleven Mr. Richards arrived, and while his wife was saying, "I am *so* glad you've come!" he was saying, "I'm so tired—tired clear out; it is dreadful to be poor, and have to make these dismal journeys at my time of life. Always at the grind, grind, grind, on a salary—another man's slave, and he sitting at home in his slippers, rich and comfortable."

"I am so sorry for you, Edward, you know that; but be comforted; we have our livelihood; we have our good name—"

"Yes, Mary, and that is everything. Don't mind my talk—it's just a moment's irritation and doesn't mean anything. Kiss me—there, it's all gone now, and I am not complaining any more. What have you been getting? What's in the sack?"

Then his wife told him the great secret. It dazed him for a moment; then he said:

"It weighs a hundred and sixty pounds? Why, Mary, it's for-ty thou-sand dollars—think of it—a whole fortune! Not ten men in this village are worth that much. Give me the paper."

He skimmed through it and said:

"Isn't it an adventure! Why, it's a romance; it's like the impossible things one reads about in books, and never sees in life." He was well stirred up now; cheerful, even gleeful. He tapped his old wife on the cheek, and said, humorously, "Why, we're rich, Mary, rich; all we've got to do is to bury the money and burn the papers. If the gambler ever comes to inquire, we'll merely look coldly upon him and say: 'What is this nonsense you are talking? We have never heard of you and your sack of gold before;' and then he would look foolish, and—"

"And in the mean time, while you are running on with your jokes, the money is still here, and it is fast getting along toward burglar-time."

"True. Very well, what shall we do—make the inquiry private? No, not that; it would spoil the romance. The public method is better. Think what a noise it will make! And it will make all the other towns jealous; for no stranger would trust such a thing to any town but Hadleyburg, and they know it. It's a great card for us. I must get to the printing office now, or I shall be too late."

"But stop—stop—don't leave me here alone with it, Edward!"

But he was gone. For only a little while, however. Not far from his own house he met the editor-proprietor of the paper, and gave him the document, and said, "Here is a good thing for you, Cox—put it in."

"It may be too late, Mr. Richards, but I'll see."

At home again he and his wife sat down to talk the charming mystery over; they were in no condition for sleep. The first question was, Who could the citizen have been who gave the stranger the twenty dollars? It seemed a simple one; both answered it in the same breath—

"Barclay Goodson."

"Yes," said Richards, "he could have done it, and it would have been like him, but there's not another in the town."

"Everybody will grant that, Edward—grant it privately, anyway. For six months, now, the village has been its own proper self once more—honest, narrow, self-righteous, and stingy."

"It is what he always called it, to the day of his death—said it right out publicly, too."

"Yes, and he was hated for it."

"Oh, of course; but he didn't care. I reckon he was the best-hated man among us, except the Reverend Burgess."

"Well, Burgess deserves it—he will never get another congregation here. Mean as the town is, it knows how to estimate *him*. Edward, doesn't it seem odd that the stranger should appoint Burgess to deliver the money?"

"Well, yes—it does. That is—that is—"

"Why so much that-*is*-ing? Would *you* select him?"

"Mary, maybe the stranger knows him better than this village does."

"Much *that* would help Burgess!"

The husband seemed perplexed for an answer; the wife kept a steady eye upon him, and waited. Finally Richards said, with the hesitancy of one who is making a statement which is likely to encounter doubt.

"Mary, Burgess is not a bad man."

His wife was certainly surprised.

"Nonsense!" she exclaimed.

"He is not a bad man. I know. The whole of his unpopularity had its foundation in that one thing—the thing that made so much noise."

"That 'one thing,' indeed! As if that 'one thing' wasn't enough, all by itself."

"Plenty. Plenty. Only he wasn't guilty of it."

"How you talk! Not guilty of it! Everybody knows he *was* guilty."

"Mary, I give you my word—he was innocent."

"I can't believe it, and I don't. How do you know?"

"It is a confession. I am ashamed, but I will make it. I was the only man who knew he was innocent. I could have saved him, and—well, you know how the town was wrought up—I hadn't the pluck to do it. It would have turned everybody against me. I felt mean, ever so mean; but I didn't dare; I hadn't the manliness to face that."

Mary looked troubled, and for a while was silent. Then she said, stammeringly:

"I—I didn't think it would have done for you to—to—One mustn't—er— public opinion—one has to be so careful—so—" It was a difficult road, and she got mired; but after a little she got started again. "It was a great pity, but—Why, we couldn't afford it, Edward—we couldn't indeed. Oh, I wouldn't have had you do it for anything!"

"It would have lost us the good-will of so many people, Mary; and then— and then—"

"What troubles me now is, what *he* thinks of us, Edward."

"He? *He* doesn't suspect that I could have saved him."

"Oh," exclaimed the wife, in a tone of relief, "I am glad of that. As long as he doesn't know that you could have saved him, he—he—well, that makes it a great deal better. Why, I might have known he didn't know, because he is always trying to be friendly with us, as little encouragement as we give him. More than once people have twitted me with it. There's the

Wilsons, and the Wilcoxes, and the Harknesses, they take a mean pleasure in saying, 'Your friend Burgess,' because they know it pesters me. I wish he wouldn't persist in liking us so; I can't think why he keeps it up."

"I can explain it. It's another confession. When the thing was new and hot, and the town made a plan to ride him on a rail, my conscience hurt me so that I couldn't stand it, and I went privately and gave him notice, and he got out of the town and staid out till it was safe to come back."

"Edward! If the town had found it out—"

"*Don't!* It scares me yet, to think of it. I repented of it the minute it was done; and I was even afraid to tell you, lest your face might betray it to somebody. I didn't sleep any that night, for worrying. But after a few days I saw that no one was going to suspect me, and after that I got to feeling glad I did it. And I feel glad yet, Mary—glad through and through."

"So do I, now, for it would have been a dreadful way to treat him. Yes, I'm glad; for really you did owe him that, you know. But Edward, suppose it should come out yet, some day!"

"It won't."

"Why?"

"Because everybody thinks it was Goodson."

"Of course they would!"

"Certainly. And of course *he* didn't care. They persuaded poor old Sawlsberry to go and charge it on him, and he went blustering over there and did it. Goodson looked him over, like as if he was hunting for a place on him that he could despise the most, then he says, 'So you are the Committee of Inquiry, are you?' Sawlsberry said that was about what he was. 'Hm. Do they require particulars, or do you reckon a kind of a *general* answer will do?' 'If they require particulars, I will come back, Mr. Goodson; I will take the general answer first.' 'Very well, then, tell them to go to hell—I reckon that's general enough. And I'll give you some advice, Sawlsberry; when you come back for the particulars, fetch a basket to carry the relics of yourself home in.'"

"Just like Goodson; it's got all the marks. He had only one vanity; he thought he could give advice better than any other person."

"It settled the business, and saved us, Mary. The subject was dropped."

"Bless you, I'm not doubting *that*."

Then they took up the gold-sack mystery again, with strong interest. Soon the conversation began to suffer breaks—interruptions caused by absorbed thinkings. The breaks grew more and more frequent. At last Richards lost himself wholly in thought. He sat long, gazing vacantly at the floor, and by-and-by he began to punctuate his thoughts with little nervous movements of his hands that seemed to indicate vexation. Meantime his wife too had relapsed into a thoughtful silence, and her movements were beginning to show a troubled discomfort. Finally Richards got up and strode aimlessly about the room, ploughing his hands through his hair, much as a somnambulist

might do who was having a bad dream. Then he seemed to arrive at a
definite purpose; and without a word he put on his hat and passed quickly
out of the house. His wife sat brooding, with a drawn face, and did not seem
to be aware that she was alone. Now and then she murmured, "Lead us not
into t. . . . but—but—we are so poor, so poor! . . . Lead us not into. . . . Ah,
who would be hurt by it?—and no one would ever know. . . . Lead us. . . ." .
The voice died out in mumblings. After a little she glanced up and muttered
in a half-frightened, half-glad way—

"He is gone! But, oh dear, he may be too late—too late. . . . Maybe not—
maybe there is still time." She rose and stood thinking, nervously clasping
and unclasping her hands. A slight shudder shook her frame, and she said,
out of a dry throat, "God forgive me—it's awful to think such things—but.
. . . Lord, how we are made—how strangely we are made!"

She turned the light low, and slipped stealthily over and kneeled down by
the sack and felt of its ridgy sides with her hands, and fondled them lovingly;
and there was a gloating light in her poor old eyes. She fell into fits of
absence; and came half out of them at times to mutter, "If we had only
waited!—oh, if we had only waited a little, and not been in such a hurry!"

Meantime Cox had gone home from his office and told his wife all about
the strange thing that had happened, and they had talked it over eagerly, and
guessed that the late Goodson was the only man in the town who could have
helped a suffering stranger with so noble a sum as twenty dollars. Then there
was a pause, and the two became thoughtful and silent. And by-and-by
nervous and fidgety. At last the wife said, as if to herself,

"Nobody knows this secret but the Richardses . . . and us . . . nobody."

The husband came out of his thinkings with a slight start, and gazed
wistfully at his wife, whose face was becoming very pale; then he hesitatingly rose, and glanced furtively at his hat, then at his wife—a sort of mute
inquiry. Mrs. Cox swallowed once or twice, with her hand at her throat, then
in place of speech she nodded her head. In a moment she was alone, and
mumbling to herself.

And now Richards and Cox were hurrying through the deserted streets,
from opposite directions. They met, panting, at the foot of the printing-office
stairs; by the night-light where they read each other's face. Cox whispered,

"Nobody knows about this but us?"

The whispered answer was,

"Not a soul—on honor, not a soul!"

"If it isn't too late to—"

The men were starting up-stairs; at this moment they were overtaken by
a boy, and Cox asked,

"Is that you, Johnny?"

"Yes, sir."

"You needn't ship the early mail—nor *any* mail; wait till I tell you."

"It's already gone, sir."

"Gone?" It had the sound of an unspeakable disappointment in it.

"Yes, sir. Time-table for Brixton and all the towns beyond changed to-day, sir—had to get the papers in twenty minutes earlier than common. I had to rush; if I had been two minutes later—"

The men turned and walked slowly away, not waiting to hear the rest. Neither of them spoke during ten minutes; then Cox said, in a vexed tone,

"What possessed you to be in such a hurry, *I* can't make out."

The answer was humble enough:

"I see it now, but somehow I never thought, you know, until it was too late. But the next time—"

"Next time be hanged! It won't come in a thousand years."

Then the friends separated without a good-night, and dragged themselves home with the gait of mortally stricken men. At their homes their wives sprang up with an eager "Well?"—then saw the answer with their eyes and sank down sorrowing, without waiting for it to come in words. In both houses a discussion followed of a heated sort—a new thing; there had been discussions before, but not heated ones, not ungentle ones. The discussions to-night were a sort of seeming plagiarisms of each other. Mrs. Richards said,

"If you had only waited, Edward—if you had only stopped to think; but no, you must run straight to the printing-office and spread it all over the world."

"It *said* publish it."

"That is nothing; it also said do it privately, if you liked. There, now—is that true, or not?"

"Why, yes—yes, it is true; but when I thought what a stir it would make, and what a compliment it was to Hadleyburg that a stranger should trust it so—"

"Oh, certainly, I know all that; but if you had only stopped to think, you would have seen that you *couldn't* find the right man, because he is in his grave, and hasn't left chick nor child nor relation behind him; and as long as the money went to somebody that awfully needed it, and nobody would be hurt by it, and—and—"

She broke down, crying. Her husband tried to think of some comforting thing to say, and presently came out with this:

"But after all, Mary, it must be for the best—it *must* be; we know that. And we must remember that it was so ordered—"

"Ordered! Oh, everything's *ordered*, when a person has to find some way out when he has been stupid. Just the same, it was *ordered* that the money should come to us in this special way, and it was you that must take it on yourself to go meddling with the designs of Providence—and who gave you the right? It was wicked, that is what it was—just blasphemous presumption, and no more becoming to a meek and humble professor of—"

"But, Mary, you know how we have been trained all our lives long, like the whole village, till it is absolutely second nature to us to stop not a single moment to think when there's an honest thing to be done—"

"Oh, I know it, I know it—it's been one everlasting training and training and training in honesty—honesty shielded, from the very cradle, against every possible temptation, and so it's *artificial* honesty, and weak as water when temptation comes, as we have seen this night. God knows I never had shade nor shadow of a doubt of my petrified and indestructible honesty until now—and now, under the very first big and real temptation, I—Edward, it is my belief that this town's honesty is as rotten as mine is; as rotten as yours is. It is a mean town, a hard, stingy town, and hasn't a virtue in the world but this honesty it is so celebrated for and so conceited about; and so help me, I do believe that if ever the day comes that its honesty falls under great temptation, its grand reputation will go to ruin like a house of cards. There, now, I've made confession, and I feel better; I am a humbug, and I've been one all my life, without knowing it. Let no man call me honest again—I will not have it."

"I—well, Mary, I feel a good deal as you do; I certainly do. It seems strange, too, so strange. I never could have believed it—never."

A long silence followed; both were sunk in thought. At last the wife looked up and said,

"I know what you are thinking, Edward."

Richards had the embarrassed look of a person who is caught.

"I am ashamed to confess it, Mary but—"

"It's no matter, Edward, I was thinking the same question myself."

"I hope so. State it."

"You were thinking, if a body could only guess out *what the remark was* that Goodson made to the stranger."

"It's perfectly true. I feel guilty and ashamed. And you?"

"I'm past it. Let us make a pallet here; we've got to stand watch till the bank vault opens in the morning and admits the sack. . . . Oh, dear, oh, dear—if we hadn't made the mistake!"

The pallet was made, and Mary said:

"The open sesame—what could it have been? I do wonder what that remark could have been? But come; we will get to bed now."

"And sleep?"

"No; think."

"Yes, think."

By this time the Coxes too had completed their spat and their reconciliation, and were turning in—to think, to think, and toss, and fret, and worry over what the remark could possibly have been which Goodson made to the stranded derelict: that golden remark; that remark worth forty thousand dollars, cash.

The reason that the village telegraph-office was open later than usual that night was this: The foreman of Cox's paper was the local representative of the Associated Press. One might say its honorary representative, for it wasn't four times a year that he could furnish thirty words that would be accepted. But this time it was different. His despatch stating what he had caught got an instant answer:

Send the whole thing—all the details—twelve hundred words.

A colossal order! The foreman filled the bill; and he was the proudest man in the State. By breakfast-time the next morning the name of Hadleyburg the Incorruptible was on every lip in America, from Montreal to the Gulf, from the glaciers of Alaska to the orange-groves of Florida; and millions and millions of people were discussing the stranger and his money-sack, and wondering if the right man would be found, and hoping some more news about the matter would come soon—right away.

II

Hadleyburg village woke up world-celebrated—astonished—happy—vain. Vain beyond imagination. Its nineteen principal citizens and their wives went about shaking hands with each other, and beaming, and smiling, and congratulating, and saying *this* thing adds a new word to the dictionary—*Hadleyburg*, synonym for *incorruptible*—destined to live in dictionaries forever! And the minor and unimportant citizens and their wives went around acting in much the same way. Everybody ran to the bank to see the gold-sack; and before noon grieved and envious crowds began to flock in from Brixton and all neighboring towns; and that afternoon and next day reporters began to arrive from everywhere to verify the sack and its history and write the whole thing up anew, and make dashing free-hand pictures of the sack, and of Richards's house, and the bank, and the Presbyterian church, and the Baptist church, and the public square, and the town-hall where the test would be applied and the money delivered; and damnable portraits of the Richardses, and Pinkerton the banker, and Cox, and the foreman, and Reverend Burgess, and the postmaster—and even of Jack Halliday, who was the loafing, good-natured, no-account, irreverent fisherman, hunter, boys' friend, stray-dogs' friend, typical "Sam Lawson"[2] of the town. The little mean, smirking, oily Pinkerton showed the sack to all comers, and rubbed his sleek palms together pleasantly, and enlarged upon the town's fine old reputation for honesty and upon this wonderful endorsement of it, and hoped and

[2] A Yankee character in Harriet Beecher Stowe's *Oldtown Folks* (1869) and *Sam Lawson's Oldtown Fireside Stories* (1872).

believed that the example would now spread far and wide over the American world, and be epoch-making in the matter of moral regeneration. And so on, and so on.

By the end of a week things had quieted down again; the wild intoxication of pride and joy had sobered to a soft, sweet, silent delight—a sort of deep, nameless, unutterable content. All faces bore a look of peaceful, holy happiness.

Then a change came. It was a gradual change: so gradual that its beginnings were hardly noticed; maybe were not noticed at all, except by Jack Halliday, who always noticed everything; and always made fun of it, too, no matter what it was. He began to throw out chaffing remarks about people not looking quite so happy as they did a day or two ago; and next he claimed that the new aspect was deepening to positive sadness; next, that it was taking on a sick look; and finally he said that everybody was become so moody, thoughtful, and absent-minded that he could rob the meanest man in town of a cent out of the bottom of his breeches pocket and not disturb his revery.

At this stage—or at about this stage—a saying like this was dropped at bedtime—with a sigh, usually—by the head of each of the nineteen principal households:

"Ah, what *could* have been the remark that Goodson made!"

And straightway—with a shudder—came this, from the man's wife:

"Oh, *don't!* What horrible thing are you mulling in your mind? Put it away from you, for God's sake!"

But that question was wrung from those men again the next night—and got the same retort. But weaker.

And the third night the men uttered the question yet again—with anguish, and absently. This time—and the following night—the wives fidgeted feebly, and tried to say something. But didn't.

And the night after that they found their tongues and responded—longingly,

"Oh, if we *could* only guess!"

Halliday's comments grew daily more and more sparkingly disagreeable and disparaging. He went diligently about, laughing at the town, individually and in mass. But his laugh was the only one left in the village: it fell upon a hollow and mournful vacancy and emptiness. Not even a smile was findable anywhere. Halliday carried a cigar-box around on a tripod, playing that it was a camera, and halted all passers and aimed the thing and said, "Ready!— now look pleasant, please," but not even this capital joke could surprise the dreary faces into any softening.

So three weeks passed—one week was left. It was Saturday evening— after supper. Instead of the aforetime Saturday-evening flutter and bustle and shopping and larking, the streets were empty and desolate. Richards and his old wife sat apart in their little parlor—miserable and thinking. This was become their evening habit now: the life-long habit which had preceded it, of reading, knitting, and contented chat, or receiving or paying neighborly calls, was dead and gone and forgotten, ages ago—two or three weeks ago; nobody talked now, nobody read, nobody visited—the whole village sat at home, sighing, worrying, silent. Trying to guess out that remark.

The postman left a letter. Richards glanced listlessly, at the superscription and the post-mark—unfamiliar, both—and tossed the letter on the table and resumed his might-have-beens and his hopeless dull miseries where he had left them off. Two or three hours later his wife got wearily up and was going away to bed without a good-night—custom now—but she stopped near the letter and eyed it awhile with a dead interest, then broke it open, and began to skim it over. Richards, sitting there with his chair tilted back against the wall and his chin between his knees, heard something fall. It was his wife. He sprang to her side, but she cried out:

"Leave me alone, I am too happy. Read the letter—read it!"

He did. He devoured it, his brain reeling. The letter was from a distant State, and it said:

> "I am a stranger to you, but no matter: I have something to tell. I have just arrived home from Mexico, and learned about that episode. Of course you do not know who made that remark, but I know, and I am the only person living who does know. It was GOODSON. I knew him well, many years ago. I passed through your village that very night, and was his guest till the midnight train came along. I overheard him make that remark to the stranger in the dark—it was in Hale Alley. He and I talked of it the rest of the way home, and while smoking in his house. He mentioned many of your villagers in the course of his talk—most of them in a very uncomplimentary way, but two or three favorably: among these latter yourself. I say "favorably"—nothing stronger. I remember his saying he did not actually LIKE any person in the town—not one; but that you—I THINK he said you—am almost sure—had done him a very great service once, possibly without knowing the full value of it, and he wished he had a fortune, he would leave it to you when he died, and a curse apiece for the rest of the citizens. Now, then, if it was you that did him that service, you are his legitimate heir, and entitled to the sack of gold. I know that I can trust to your honor and honesty, for in a citizen of Hadleyburg these virtues are an unfailing inheritance, and so I am going to reveal to you the remark, well satisfied that if you are not the right man you will seek and find the right one and see that poor Goodson's debt of gratitude for the service referred to is paid. This is the remark: 'YOU ARE FAR FROM BEING A BAD MAN: GO, AND REFORM.'
>
> "Howard L. Stephenson."

"Oh, Edward, the money is ours, and I am so grateful, *oh*, so grateful—kiss me, dear, it's forever since we kissed—and we needed it so—the money— and now you are free of Pinkerton and his bank, and nobody's slave any more; it seems to me I could fly for joy."

It was a happy half-hour that the couple spent there on the settee caressing each other; it was the old days come again—days that had begun with their courtship and lasted without a break till the stranger brought the deadly money. By-and-by the wife said:

"Oh, Edward, how lucky it was you did him that grand service, poor Goodson! I never liked him, but I love him now. And it was fine and beautiful of you never to mention it or brag about it." Then, with a touch of reproach, "But you ought to have told *me*, Edward, you ought to have told your wife, you know."

"Well, I—er—well, Mary, you see—"

"Now stop hemming and hawing, and tell me about it, Edward. I always loved you, and now I'm proud of you. Everybody believes there was only one good generous soul in this village, and now it turns out that you— Edward, why don't you tell me?"

"Well—er—er—— Why, Mary, I can't!"

"You *can't? Why* can't you?"

"You see, he—well, he—he made me promise I wouldn't."

The wife looked him over, and said, very slowly,

"Made—you—promise? Edward, what do you tell me that for?"

"Mary, do you think I would lie?"

She was troubled and silent for a moment, then she laid her hand within his and said:

"No . . . no. We have wandered far enough from our bearings—God spare us that! In all your life you have never uttered a lie. But now—now that the foundations of things seem to be crumbling from under us, we— we—" She lost her voice for a moment, then said, brokenly, "Lead us not into temptation. . . . I think you made the promise, Edward. Let it rest so. Let us keep away from that ground. Now—that is all gone by; let us be happy again; it is no time for clouds."

Edward found it something of an effort to comply, for his mind kept wandering—trying to remember what the service was that he had done Goodson.

The couple lay awake the most of the night, Mary happy and busy, Edward busy, but not so happy. Mary was planning what she would do with the money. Edward was trying to recall that service. At first his conscience was sore on account of the lie he had told Mary—if it was a lie. After much reflection—suppose it *was* a lie? What then? Was it such a great matter? Aren't we always *acting* lies? Then why not *tell* them? Look at Mary—look what she had done. While he was hurrying off on his honest errand, what was she doing? Lamenting because the papers hadn't been destroyed and the money kept! Is theft better than lying?

That point lost its sting—the lie dropped into the background and left comfort behind it. The next point came to the front: *had* he rendered that service? Well, here was Goodson's own evidence as reported in Stephenson's letter; there could be no better evidence than that—it was even *proof* that he had rendered it. Of course. So that point was settled. . . . No, not quite. He recalled with a wince that this unknown Mr. Stephenson was just a trifle unsure as to whether the performer of it was Richards or some other—and, oh dear, he had put Richards on his honor! He must himself decide whither that money must go—and Mr. Stephenson was not doubting that if he was the wrong man he would go honorably and find the right one. Oh, it was odious to put a man in such a situation—ah, why couldn't Stephenson have left out that doubt! What did he want to intrude that for?

Further reflection. How did it happen that *Richards's* name remained in Stephenson's mind as indicating the right man, and not some other man's name? That looked good. Yes, that looked very good. In fact, it went on looking better and better, straight along—until by-and-by it grew into positive *proof*. And then Richards put the matter at once out of his mind, for he had a private instinct that a proof once established is better left so.

He was feeling reasonably comfortable now, but there was still one other detail that kept pushing itself on his notice: of course he had done that service—that was settled; but what *was* that service? He must recall it—he would not go to sleep till he had recalled it; it would make his peace of mind perfect. And so he thought and thought. He thought of a dozen things—possible services, even probable services—but none of them seemed adequate, none of them seemed large enough, none of them seemed worth the money—worth the fortune Goodson had wished he could leave in his will. And besides, he couldn't remember having done them, anyway. Now, then—now, then—what *kind* of a service would it be that would make a man so inordinately grateful? Ah—the saving of his soul! That must be it. Yes, he could remember, now, how he once set himself the task of converting Goodson, and labored at it as much as—he was going to say three months; but upon closer examination it shrunk to a month, then to a week, then to a day, then to nothing. Yes, he remembered now, and with unwelcome vividness, that Goodson had told him to go to thunder and mind his own business—*he* wasn't hankering to follow Hadleyburg to heaven!

So that solution was a failure—he hadn't saved Goodson's soul. Richards was discouraged. Then after a little came another idea: had he saved Goodson's property? No, that wouldn't do—he hadn't any. His life? That is it! Of course. Why, he might have thought of it before. This time he was on the right track, sure. His imagination-mill was hard at work in a minute, now.

Thereafter during a stretch of two exhausting hours he was busy saving Goodson's life. He saved it in all kinds of difficult and perilous ways. In every case he got it saved satisfactorily up to a certain point; then, just as he was beginning to get well persuaded that it had really happened, a troublesome detail would turn up which made the whole thing impossible. As in the matter of drowning, for instance. In that case he had swum out and tugged Goodson ashore in an unconscious state with a great crowd looking on and applauding, but when he had got it all thought out and was just beginning to remember all about it a whole swarm of disqualifying details arrived on the ground: the town would have known of the circumstance, Mary would have known of it, it would glare like a limelight in his own memory instead of being an inconspicuous service which he had possibly rendered "without knowing its full value." And at this point he remembered that he couldn't swim, anyway.

Ah—*there* was a point which he had been overlooking from the start: it had to be a service which he had rendered "possibly without knowing the full value of it." Why, really, that ought to be an easy hunt—much easier than those others. And sure enough, by-and-by he found it. Goodson, years and years ago, came near marrying a very sweet and pretty girl named Nancy Hewitt, but in some way or other the match had been broken off; the girl died, Goodson remained a bachelor, and by-and-by became a soured one and a frank despiser of the human species. Soon after the girl's death the village found out, or thought it had found out, that she carried a spoonful of negro blood in her veins. Richards worked at these details a good while, and in the end he thought he remembered things concerning them which must have gotten mislaid in his memory through long neglect. He seemed to dimly remember that it was *he* that found out about the negro blood; that it was he that told the village; that the village told Goodson where they got it; that he thus saved Goodson from marrying the tainted girl; that he had done him this great service "without knowing the full value of it," in fact without knowing that he *was* doing it; but that Goodson knew the value of it, and what a narrow escape he had had, and so went to his grave grateful to his benefactor and wishing he had a fortune to leave him. It was all clear and simple now, and the more he went over it the more luminous and certain it grew; and at last, when he nestled to sleep satisfied and happy, he remembered the whole thing just as if it had been yesterday. In fact, he dimly remembered Goodson's *telling* him his gratitude once. Meantime Mary had spent six thousand dollars on a new house for herself and a pair of slippers for her pastor, and then had fallen peacefully to rest.

That same Saturday evening the postman had delivered a letter to each of the other principal citizens—nineteen letters in all. No two of the envelopes were alike, and no two of the superscriptions were in the same hand, but the letters inside were just like each other in every detail but one. They were exact copies of the letter received by Richards—handwriting and all—and were all signed by Stephenson, but in place of Richards's name each receiver's own name appeared.

All night long eighteen principal citizens did what their caste-brother
Richards was doing at the same time—they put in their energies trying to
remember what notable service it was that they had unconsciously done
Barclay Goodson. In no case was it a holiday job; still they succeeded.

And while they were at this work, which was difficult, their wives put in
the night spending the money, which was easy. During that one night the
nineteen wives spent an average of seven thousand dollars each out of the
forty thousand in the sack—a hundred and thirty-three thousand altogether.

Next day there was a surprise for Jack Halliday. He noticed that the faces
of the nineteen chief citizens and their wives bore that expression of peaceful and holy happiness again. He could not understand it, neither was he able
to invent any remarks about it that could damage it or disturb it. And so it
was his turn to be dissatisfied with life. His private guesses at the reasons for
the happiness failed in all instances, upon examination. When he met Mrs.
Wilcox and noticed the placid ecstasy in her face, he said to himself, "Her
cat has had kittens"—and went and asked the cook; it was not so; the cook
had detected the happiness, but did not know the cause. When Halliday
found the duplicate ecstasy in the face of "Shadbelly" Billson (village nickname), he was sure some neighbor of Billson's had broken his leg, but inquiry
showed that this had not happened. The subdued ecstasy in Gregory Yates's
face could mean but one thing—he was a mother-in-law short; it was another mistake. "And Pinkerton—Pinkerton—he has collected ten cents that
he thought he was going to lose." And so on, and so on. In some cases the
guesses had to remain in doubt, in the others they proved distinct errors. In
the end Halliday said to himself, "Anyway it foots up that there's nineteen
Hadleyburg families temporarily in heaven: I don't know how it happened;
I only know Providence is off duty to-day."

An architect and builder from the next State had lately ventured to set up
a small business in this unpromising village, and his sign had now been
hanging out a week. Not a customer yet; he was a discouraged man, and
sorry he had come. But his weather changed suddenly now. First one and
then another chief citizen's wife said to him privately:

"Come to my house Monday week—but say nothing about it for the
present. We think of building."

He got eleven invitations that day. That night he wrote his daughter and
broke off her match with her student. He said she could marry a mile higher
than that.

Pinkerton the banker and two or three other well-to-do men planned
country-seats—but waited. That kind don't count their chickens until they
are hatched.

The Wilsons devised a grand new thing—a fancy-dress ball. They made
no actual promises, but told all their acquaintanceship in confidence that
they were thinking the matter over and thought they should give it—"and if
we do, you will be invited, of course." People were surprised, and said, one

to another, "Why, they are crazy, those poor Wilsons, they can't afford it."
Several among the nineteen said privately to their husbands, "It is a good
idea, we will keep still till their cheap thing is over, then *we* will give one
that will make it sick."

The days drifted along, and the bill of future squanderings rose higher
and higher, wilder and wilder, more and more foolish and reckless. It began
to look as if every member of the nineteen would not only spend his whole
forty thousand dollars before receiving-day, but be actually in debt by the
time he got the money. In some cases light-headed people did not stop with
planning to spend, they really spent—on credit. They bought land, mortgages, farms, speculative stocks, fine clothes, horses, and various other
things, paid down the bonus, and made themselves liable for the rest—at ten
days. Presently the sober second thought came, and Halliday noticed that a
ghastly anxiety was beginning to show up in a good many faces. Again he was
puzzled, and didn't know what to make of it. "The Wilcox kittens aren't
dead, for they weren't born; nobody's broken a leg; there's no shrinkage in
mother-in-laws; *nothing* has happened—it is an insolvable mystery."

There was another puzzled man, too—the Rev. Mr. Burgess. For days,
wherever he went, people seemed to follow him or to be watching out for
him; and if he ever found himself in a retired spot, a member of the nineteen
would be sure to appear, thrust an envelope privately into his hand, whisper
"To be opened at the town-hall Friday evening," then vanish away like a
guilty thing. He was expecting that there might be one claimant for the
sack—doubtful, however, Goodson being dead—but it never occurred to
him that all this crowd might be claimants. When the great Friday came at
last, he found that he had nineteen envelopes.

III

The town-hall had never looked finer. The platform at the end of it was
backed by a showy draping of flags; at intervals along the walls were festoons
of flags; the gallery fronts were clothed in flags; the supporting columns were
swathed in flags; all this was to impress the stranger, for he would be there
in considerable force, and in a large degree he would be connected with the
press. The house was full. The 412 fixed seats were occupied; also the 68
extra chairs which had been packed into the aisles; the steps of the platform
were occupied; some distinguished strangers were given seats on the platform; at the horseshoe of tables which fenced the front and sides of the
platform sat a strong force of special correspondents who had come from
everywhere. It was the best-dressed house the town had ever produced.
There were some tolerably expensive toilets there, and in several cases the
ladies who wore them had the look of being unfamiliar with that kind of
clothes. At least the town thought they had that look, but the notion could
have arisen from the town's knowledge of the fact that these ladies had
never inhabited such clothes before.

The gold-sack stood on a little table at the front of the platform where all the house could see it. The bulk of the house gazed at it with a burning interest, a mouth-watering interest, a wistful and pathetic interest; a minority of nineteen couples gazed at it tenderly, lovingly, proprietarily, and the male half of this minority kept saying over to themselves the moving little impromptu speeches of thankfulness for the audience's applause and congratulations which they were presently going to get up and deliver. Every now and then one of these got a piece of paper out of his vest pocket and privately glanced at it to refresh his memory.

Of course there was a buzz of conversation going on—there always is, but at last when the Rev. Mr. Burgess rose and laid his hand on the sack he could hear his microbes gnaw, the place was so still. He related the curious history of the sack, then went on to speak in warm terms of Hadleyburg's old and well-earned reputation for spotless honesty, and of the town's just pride in this reputation. He said that this reputation was a treasure of priceless value; that under Providence its value had now become inestimably enhanced, for the recent episode had spread this fame far and wide, and thus had focussed the eyes of the American world upon this village, and made its name for all time, as he hoped and believed, a synonym for commercial incorruptibility. [*Applause.*] "And who is to be the guardian of this noble treasure—the community as a whole?" No! The responsibility is individual, not communal. From this day forth each and every one of you is in his own person its special guardian, and individually responsible that no harm shall come to it. Do you—does each of you—accept this great trust? [*Tumultuous assent.*] Then all is well. Transmit it to your children and to your children's children. To-day your purity is beyond reproach—see to it that it shall remain so. To-day there is not a person in your community who could be beguiled to touch a penny not his own—see to it that you abide in this grace. ["*We will! we will!*"] This is not the place to make comparisons between ourselves and other communities—some of them ungracious toward us; they have their ways, we have ours; let us be content. [*Applause.*] I am done. Under my hand, my friends, rests a stranger's eloquent recognition of what we are: through him the world will always henceforth know what we are. We do not know who he is, but in your name I utter your gratitude, and ask you to raise your voices in indorsement."

The house rose in a body and made the walls quake with the thunders of its thankfulness for the space of a long minute. Then it sat down, and Mr. Burgess took an envelope out of his pocket. The house held its breath while he slit the envelope open and took from it a slip of paper. He read its contents—slowly and impressively—the audience listening with tranced attention to this magic document, each of whose words stood for an ingot of gold:

" '*The remark which I made to the distressed stranger was this: "You are very far from being a bad man: go, and reform.' "* Then he continued:

"We shall know in a moment now whether the remark here quoted corresponds with the one concealed in the sack; and if that shall prove to be so—and it undoubtedly will—this sack of gold belongs to a fellow-citizen who will henceforth stand before the nation as the symbol of the special virtue which has made our town famous throughout the land—Mr. Billson!"

The house had gotten itself all ready to burst into the proper tornado of applause; but instead of doing it, it seemed stricken with a paralysis; there was a deep hush for a moment or two, then a wave of whispered murmurs swept the place—of about this tenor: *"Billson!* oh, come, this is *too* thin! Twenty dollars to a stranger—or *anybody*—*Billson!* Tell it to the marines!" And now at this point the house caught its breath all of a sudden, in a new access of astonishment, for it discovered that whereas in one part of the hall Deacon Billson was standing up with his head meekly bowed, in another part of it Lawyer Wilson was doing the same. There was a wondering silence now for a while. Everybody was puzzled, and nineteen couples were surprised and indignant.

Billson and Wilson turned and stared at each other. Billson asked, bitingly,

"Why do *you* rise, Mr. Wilson?"

"Because I have a right to. Perhaps you will be good enough to explain to the house why *you* rise?"

"With great pleasure. Because I wrote that paper."

"It is an impudent falsity! I wrote it myself." It was Burgess's turn to be paralyzed. He stood looking vacantly at first one of the men and then the other, and did not seem to know what to do. The house was stupefied. Lawyer Wilson spoke up, now, and said,

"I ask the Chair to read the name signed to that paper."

That brought the Chair to itself, and it read out the name,

" 'John Wharton *Billson.*' "

"There!" shouted Billson, "what have you got to say for yourself, now? And what kind of apology are you going to make to me and to this insulted house for the imposture which you have attempted to play here?"

"No apologies are due, sir; and as for the rest of it, I publicly charge you with pilfering my note from Mr. Burgess and substituting a copy of it signed with your own name. There is no other way by which you could have gotten hold of the test-remark; I alone, of living men, possessed the secret of its wording."

There was likely to be a scandalous state of things if this went on; everybody noticed with distress that the short-hand scribes were scribbling like mad; many people were crying "Chair, Chair! Order! order!" Burgess rapped with his gavel, and said:

"Let us not forget the proprieties due. There has evidently been a mistake somewhere, but surely that is all. If Mr. Wilson gave me an envelope—and I remember now that he did—I still have it."

He took one out of his pocket, opened it, glanced at it, looked surprised and worried, and stood silent a few moments. Then he waved his hand in a wandering and mechanical way, and made an effort or two to say something, then gave it up, despondently. Several voices cried out:

"Read it! read it! What is it?"

So he began in a dazed and sleep-walker fashion:

" *'The remark which I made to the unhappy stranger was this: "You are far from being a bad man.* [The house gazed at him, marvelling.] *Go, and reform.'* " [*Murmurs:* "Amazing! what can this mean?"] "This one," said the Chair, "is signed Thurlow G. Wilson."

"There!" cried Wilson, "I reckon that settles it! I knew perfectly well my note was purloined."

"Purloined!" retorted Billson. "I'll let you know that neither you nor any man of your kidney must venture to—"

The Chair. "Order, gentlemen, order! Take your seats, both of you, please."

They obeyed, shaking their heads and grumbling angrily. The house was profoundly puzzled; it did not know what to do with this curious emergency. Presently Thompson got up. Thompson was the hatter. He would have liked to be a Nineteener; but such was not for him; his stock of hats was not considerable enough for the position. He said:

"Mr. Chairman, if I may be permitted to make a suggestion, can both of these gentlemen be right? I put it to you, sir, can both have happened to say the very same words to the stranger? It seems to me—"

The tanner got up and interrupted him. The tanner was a disgruntled man; he believed himself entitled to be a Nineteener, but he couldn't get recognition. It made him a little unpleasant in his ways and speech. Said he:

"Sho, *that's* not the point! *That* could happen—twice in a hundred years—but not the other thing. *Neither* of them gave the twenty dollars!" [*A ripple of applause.*]

Billson. "*I* did!"

Wilson. "*I* did!"

Then each accused the other of pilfering.

The Chair. "Order! Sit down, if you please—both of you. Neither of the notes has been out of my possession at any moment."

A Voice. "Good—that settles *that!*"

The Tanner. "Mr. Chairman, one thing is now plain: one of these men has been eavesdropping under the other one's bed, and filching family secrets. If it is not unparliamentary to suggest it, I will remark that both are equal to it. [*The Chair.* "Order! order!"] I withdraw the remark, sir, and will confine myself to suggesting that *if* one of them has overheard the other reveal the test-remark to his wife, we shall catch him now."

A Voice. "How?"

The Tanner. "Easily. The two have not quoted the remark in exactly the same words. You would have noticed that, if there hadn't been a considerable stretch of time and an exciting quarrel inserted between the two readings."

A Voice. "Name the difference."

The Tanner. "The word *very* is in Billson's note, and not in the other."

Many Voices. "That's so—he's right!"

The Tanner. "And so, if the Chair will examine the test-remark in the sack, we shall know which of these two frauds—[*The Chair.* "Order!"]—which of these adventures—[*The Chair.* "Order! Order!"]—which of these two gentlemen—[*laughter and applause*]—is entitled to wear the belt as being the first dishonest blatherskite ever bred in this town—which he has dishonored, and which will be a sultry place for him from now out!" [*Vigorous applause.*]

Many Voices. "Open it!—open the sack!"

Mr. Burgess made a slit in the sack, slid his hand in and brought out an envelope. In it were a couple of folded notes. He said:

"One of these is marked, 'Not to be examined until all written communications which have been addressed to the Chair—if any—shall have been read.' The other is marked '*The Test.*' Allow me. It is worded—to wit:

" 'I do not require that the first half of all the remark which was made to me by my benefactor shall be quoted with exactness, for it was not striking, and could be forgotten; but its closing fifteen words are quite striking, and I think easily rememberable; unless *these* shall be accurately reproduced, let the applicant be regarded as an impostor. My benefactor began by saying he seldom gave advice to any one, but that it always bore the hall-mark of high value when he did give it. Then he said this—and it has never faded from my memory: *"You are far from being a bad man—"* ' "

Fifty Voices. "That settles it—the money's Wilson's! Wilson! Wilson! Speech! Speech!"

People jumped up and crowded around Wilson, wringing his hand and congratulating fervently—meantime the Chair was hammering with the gavel and shouting:

"Order, gentlemen! Order! Order! Let me finish reading, please." When quiet was restored, the reading was resumed—as follows:

" ' *"Go, and reform—or, mark my words—some day, for your sins, you will die and go to hell or Hadleyburg—*TRY AND MAKE IT THE FORMER." ' "

A ghastly silence followed. First an angry cloud began to settle darkly upon the faces of the citizenship; after a pause the cloud began to rise, and a tickled expression tried to take its place; tried so hard that it was only kept under with great and painful difficulty; the reporters, the Brixtonites, and other strangers bent their heads down and shielded their faces with their hands, and managed to hold in by main strength and heroic courtesy. At this most inopportune time burst upon the stillness the roar of a solitary voice— Jack Halliday's:

"*That's* got the hall-mark on it!"

Then the house let go, strangers and all. Even Mr. Burgess's gravity broke down presently, then the audience considered itself officially absolved from all restraint, and it made the most of its privilege. It was a good long laugh, and a tempestuously whole-hearted one, but it ceased at last—long enough for Mr. Burgess to try to resume, and for the people to get their eyes partially wiped; then it broke out again; and afterward yet again; then at last Burgess was able to get out these serious words:

"It is useless to try to disguise the fact—we find ourselves in the presence of a matter of grave import. It involves the honor of your town, it strikes at the town's good name. The difference of a single word between the test-remarks offered by Mr. Wilson and Mr. Billson was itself a serious thing, since it indicated that one or the other of these gentlemen had committed a theft—"

The two men were sitting limp, nerveless, crushed; but at these words both were electrified into movement, and started to get up—

"Sit down!" said the Chair, sharply, and they obeyed. "That, as I have said, was a serious thing. And it was—but for only one of them. But the matter has become graver; for the honor of *both* is now in formidable peril. Shall I go even further, and say in inextricable peril? *Both* left out the crucial fifteen words." He paused. During several moments he allowed the pervading stillness to gather and deepen its impressive effects, then added: "There would seem to be but one way whereby this could happen. I ask these gentlemen—Was there *collusion?—agreement?*"

A low murmur sifted through the house; its import was, "He's got them both."

Billson was not used to emergencies; he sat in a helpless collapse. But Wilson was a lawyer. He struggled to his feet, pale and worried, and said:

"I ask the indulgence of the house while I explain this most painful matter. I am sorry to say what I am about to say, since it must inflict irreparable injury upon Mr. Billson, whom I have always esteemed and respected until now, and in whose invulnerability to temptation I entirely believed—as did you all. But for the preservation of my own honor I must speak—and with frankness. I confess with shame—and I now beseech your pardon for it—that I said to the ruined stranger all of the words contained in the test-remark, including the disparaging fifteen. [*Sensation.*] When the late publication was made I recalled them, and I resolved to claim the sack of coin, for by every right I was entitled to it. Now I will ask you to consider this point, and weigh it well: that stranger's gratitude to me that night knew no bounds; he said himself that he could find no words for it that were adequate, and that if he should ever be able he would repay me a thousandfold. Now, then, I ask you this: could I expect—could I believe—could I even remotely imagine—that, feeling as he did, he would do so ungrateful a thing as to add those quite unnecessary fifteen words to his test?—set a trap for me?—

expose me as a slanderer of my own town before my own people assembled in a public hall? It was preposterous; it was impossible. His test would contain only the kindly opening clause of my remark. Of that I had no shadow of doubt. You would have thought as I did. You would not have expected a base betrayal from one whom you had befriended and against whom you had committed no offence. And so, with perfect confidence, perfect trust, I wrote on a piece of paper the opening words—ending with 'Go, and reform,'—and signed it. When I was about to put it in an envelope I was called into my back office, and without thinking I left the paper lying open on my desk." He stopped, turned his head slowly toward Billson, waited a moment, then added: "I ask you to note this: when I returned, a little later, Mr. Billson was retiring by my street door." [*Sensation.*]

In a moment Billson was on his feet shouting:

"It's a lie! It's an infamous lie!"

The Chair. "Be seated, sir! Mr. Wilson has the floor."

Billson's friends pulled him into his seat and quieted him, and Wilson went on:

"Those are the simple facts. My note was now lying in a different place on the table from where I had left it. I noticed that, but attached no importance to it, thinking a draught had blown it there. That Mr. Billson would read a private paper was a thing which could not occur to me; he was an honorable man, and he would be above that. If you will allow me to say it, I think his extra word '*very*' stands explained; it is attributable to a defect of memory. I was the only man in the world who could furnish here any detail of the test-mark—by *honorable* means. I have finished."

There is nothing in the world like a persuasive speech to fuddle the mental apparatus and upset the convictions and debauch the emotions of an audience not practised in the tricks and delusions of oratory. Wilson sat down victorious. The house submerged him in tides of approving applause; friends swarmed to him and shook him by the hand and congratulated him, and Billson was shouted down and not allowed to say a word. The Chair hammered and hammered with its gavel, and kept shouting,

"But let us proceed, gentlemen, let us proceed!"

At last there was a measurable degree of quiet, and the hatter said,

"But what is there to proceed with, sir, but to deliver the money?"

Voices. "That's it! That's it! Come forward, Wilson!"

The Hatter. "I move three cheers for Mr. Wilson, Symbol of the special virtue which—"

The cheers burst forth before he could finish; and in the midst of them— and in the midst of the clamor of the gavel also—some enthusiasts mounted Wilson on a big friend's shoulder and were going to fetch him in triumph to the platform. The Chair's voice now rose above the noise—

"Order! To your places! You forget that there is still a document to be read." When quiet had been restored he took up the document, and was going to read it, but laid it down again, saying, "I forgot; this is not to be read until all written communications received by me have first been read." He took an envelope out of his pocket, removed its enclosure, glanced at it— seemed astonished—held it out and gazed at it—stared at it.

Twenty or thirty voices cried out:

"What is it? Read it! read it!"

And he did—slowly, and wondering:

" 'The remark which I made to the stranger—[*Voices.* "Hello! how's this?"]—was this: "You are far from being a bad man. [*Voices.* "Great Scott!"] Go, and reform." ' [*Voice.* "Oh, saw my leg off!"] Signed by Mr. Pinkerton the banker."

The pandemonium of delight which turned itself loose now was of a sort to make the judicious weep. Those whose withers were unwrung laughed till the tears ran down; the reporters, in throes of laughter, set down disordered pot-hooks which would never in the world be decipherable; and a sleeping dog jumped up, scared out of its wits, and barked itself crazy at the turmoil. All manner of cries were scattered through the din: "We're getting rich— *two* Symbols of Incorruptibility!—without counting Billson!" "*Three!*— count Shadbelly in—we can't have too many!" "All right—Billson's elected!" "Alas, poor Wilson—victim of *two* thieves!"

A Powerful Voice. "Silence! The Chair's fished up something more out of its pocket."

Voices. "Hurrah! Is it something fresh? Read it! read! read!"

The Chair [*reading*]. " 'The remark which I made,' etc. 'You are far from being a bad man. Go,' etc. Signed, 'Gregory Yates.' "

Tornado of Voices. "Four Symbols!" "Rah for Yates!" "Fish again!"

The house was in a roaring humor now, and ready to get all the fun out of the occasion that might be in it. Several Nineteeners, looking pale and distressed, got up and began to work their way toward the aisles, but a score of shouts went up:

"The doors, the doors—close the doors; no Incorruptible shall leave this place! Sit down, everybody!"

The mandate was obeyed.

"Fish again! Read! read!"

The Chair fished again, and once more the familiar words began to fall from its lips—" 'You are far from being a bad man—' "

"Name! name! What's his name?"

" 'L. Ingoldsby Sargent'."

"Five elected! Pile up the Symbols! Go on, go on!"

" 'You are far from being a bad—' "

"Name! name!"

" 'Nicholas Whitworth.' "

"Hooray! hooray! it's a symbolical day!"

Somebody wailed in, and began to sing this rhyme (leaving out "it's") to the lovely "Mikado"[3] tune of "When a man's afraid of a beautiful maid"; the audience joined in, with joy; then, just in time, somebody contributed another line—

"And don't you this forget—"

The house roared it out. A third line was at once furnished—

"Corruptibles far from Hadleyburg are—"

The house roared that one too. As the last note died, Jack Halliday's voice rose high and clear, freighted with a final line—

"But the Symbols are here, you bet!"

That was sung, with booming enthusiasm. Then the happy house started in at the beginning and sang the four lines through twice, with immense swing and dash, and finished up with a crashing three-times-three and a tiger for "Hadleyburg the Incorruptible and all Symbols of it which we shall find worthy to receive the hall-mark to-night."

Then the shoutings at the Chair began again, all over the place:

"Go on! go on! Read! read some more! Read all you've got!"

"That's it—go on! We are winning eternal celebrity"

A dozen men got up now and began to protest. They said that this farce was the work of some abandoned joker, and was an insult to the whole community. Without a doubt these signatures were all forgeries—

"Sit down! sit down! Shut up! You are confessing. We'll find *your* names in the lot."

"Mr. Chairman, how many of those envelopes have you got?"

The Chair counted.

"Together with those that have been already examined, there are nineteen."

A storm of derisive applause broke out.

"Perhaps they will contain the secret. I move that you open them all and read every signature that is attached to a note of that sort—and read also the first eight words of the note."

"Second the motion!"

It was put and carried—uproariously. Then poor old Richards got up, and his wife rose and stood at his side. Her head was bent down, so that none

---

[3] "When a man's afraid,/ A beautiful maid/ is a cheering sight to see." Gilbert and Sullivan, "The Mikado," Act II, 1885.

might see that she was crying. Her husband gave her his arm, and so supporting her, he began to speak in a quavering voice;

"My friends, you have known us two—Mary and me—all our lives, and I think you have liked us and respected us—"

The Chair interrupted him:

"Allow me. It is quite true—that which you are saying, Mr. Richards; this town *does* know you two; it *does* like you; it *does* respect you; more—it honors you and *loves* you—"

Halliday's voice rang out:

"That the hall-marked truth, too! If the Chair is right, let the house speak up and say it. Rise! Now, then—hip! hip! hip—all together!"

The house rose in mass, faced toward the old couple eagerly, filled the air with a snow-storm of waving handkerchiefs, and delivered the cheers with all its affectionate heart.

The Chair then continued:

"What I was going to say is this: We know your good heart, Mr. Richards, but this is not a time for the exercise of charity toward offenders. [Shouts of "Right right!"] I see your generous purpose in your face, but I cannot allow you to plead for these men—"

"But I was going to—"

"Please take your seat, Mr. Richards. We must examine the rest of these notes—simple fairness to the men who have already been exposed requires this. As soon as that has been done—I give you my word for this—you shall be heard."

Many Voices. "Right!—the Chair is right—no interruption can be permitted at this stage! Go on!—the names! the names!—according to the terms of the motion!"

The old couple sat reluctantly down, and the husband whispered to the wife, "It is pitifully hard to have to wait; the shame will be greater than ever when they find we were only going to plead for *ourselves.*"

Straightway the jollity broke loose again with the reading of the names.

" 'You are far from being a bad man—' Signature, 'Robert J. Titmarsh.'

" 'You are far from being a bad man—' Signature, 'Eliphalet Weeks.'

" 'You are far from being a bad man—' Signature, 'Oscar B. Wilder.' "

At this point the house lit upon the idea of taking the eight words out of the Chairman's hands. He was not unthankful for that. Thenceforward he held up each note in its turn, and waited. The house droned out the eight words in a massed and measured and musical deep volume of sound (with a daringly close resemblance to a well-known church chant)—" 'You are f-a-r from being a b-a-a-d man.' " Then the Chair said, "Signature, 'Archibald Wilcox.' " And so on, and so on, name after name, and everybody had an increasingly and gloriously good time except the wretched Nineteen. Now and then, when a particularly shining name was called, the house made the Chair wait while it chanted the whole of the test-remark from the beginning to the closing words, "And go to hell or Hadleyburg—try and make it the for-or-m-e-r!" and in these special cases they added a grand and agonized and imposing "A-a-a-a-*men!*"

The list dwindled, dwindled, dwindled, poor old Richards keeping tally of the count, wincing when a name resembling his own was pronounced, and waiting in miserable suspense for the time to come when it would be his humiliating privilege to rise with Mary and finish his plea, which he was intending to word thus: ". . . for until now we have never done any wrong thing, but have gone our humble way unreproached. We are very poor, we are old, and have no chick nor child to help us; we were sorely tempted, and we fell. It was my purpose when I got up before to make confession and beg that my name might not be read out in this public place, for it seemed to us that we could not bear it; but I was prevented. It was just; it was our place to suffer with the rest. It has been hard for us. It is the first time we have ever heard our name fall from any one's lips—sullied. Be merciful—for the sake of the better days; make our shame as light to bear as in your charity you can." At this point in his revery Mary nudged him, perceiving that his mind was absent. The house was chanting, "You are f-a-r," etc.

"Be ready," Mary whispered. "Your name comes now; he has read eighteen."

The chant ended.

"Next! next! next!" came volleying from all over the house.

Burgess put his hand into his pocket. The old couple, trembling, began to rise. Burgess fumbled a moment, then said,

"I find I have read them all."

Faint with joy and surprise, the couple sank into their seats, and Mary whispered.

"Oh, bless God, we are saved!—he has lost ours—I wouldn't give this for a hundred of those sacks!"

The house burst out with its "Mikado" travesty, and sang it three times with ever-increasing enthusiasm, rising to its feet when it reached for the third time the closing line—

"But the Symbols are here, you bet!"

and finishing up with cheers and a tiger for "Hadleyburg purity and our eighteen immortal representatives of it."

Then Wingate, the saddler, got up and proposed cheers "for the cleanest man in town, the one solitary important citizen in it who didn't try to steal that money—Edward Richards."

They were given with great and moving heartiness; then somebody proposed that Richards "be elected sole Guardian and Symbol of the now Sacred Hadleyburg Tradition, with power and right to stand up and look the whole sarcastic world in the face."

Passed, by acclamation; then they sang the "Mikado" again, and ended it with,

"And there's *one* Symbol left, you bet!"

There was a pause; then—
A Voice. "Now, then, who's to get the sack?"
The Tanner (with bitter sarcasm). "That's easy. The money has to be divided among the eighteen Incorruptibles. They gave the suffering stranger twenty dollars apiece—and that remark—each in his turn—it took twenty-two minutes for the procession to move past. Staked the stranger—total contribution, $360. All they want is just the loan back—and interest—forty thousand dollars altogether."
Many Voices [derisively]. "That's it! Divvy! divvy! Be kind to the poor—don't keep them waiting!"
The Chair. "Order! I now offer the stranger's remaining document. It says: 'If no claimant shall appear [*grand chorus of groans*], I desire that you open the sack and count out the money to the principal citizens of your town, they to take it in trust [*cries of "Oh! Oh! Oh!"*], and use it in such ways as to them shall seem best for the propagation and preservation of your community's noble reputation for incorruptible honesty [*more cries*]—a reputation to which their names and their efforts will add a new and far-reaching lustre.' [*Enthusiastic outburst of sarcastic applause.*] That seems to be all. No—here is a postscript:
" 'P.S.—CITIZENS OF HADLEYBURG: There *is* no test-remark—nobody made one. [*Great sensation*] There wasn't any pauper stranger, nor any twenty-dollar contribution, nor any accompanying benediction and compliment—these are all inventions. [*General buzz and hum of astonishment and delight.*] Allow me to tell my story—it will take but a word or two. I passed through your town at a certain time, and received a deep offence which I had not earned. Any other man would have been content to kill one or two of you and call it square, but to me that would have been a trivial revenge, and inadequate; for the dead do not *suffer*. Besides, I could not kill you all—and, anyway, made as I am, even that would not have satisfied me. I wanted to damage every man in the place, and every woman—and not in their bodies or in their estate, but in the vanity—the place where feeble and foolish people are most vulnerable. So I disguised myself and came back and studied you. You were easy game. You had an old and lofty reputation for honesty, and naturally you were proud of it—it was your treasure of treasures, the very apple of your eye. As soon as I found out that you carefully and vigilantly kept yourselves and your children *out of temptation*, I knew how to proceed. Why, you simple creatures, the weakest of all weak things is a virtue which has not been tested in the fire. I laid a plan, and gathered a list of names. My project was to corrupt Hadleyburg the Incorruptible. My

idea was to make liars and thieves of nearly half a hundred smirchless men and women who had never in their lives uttered a lie or stolen a penny. I was afraid of Goodson. He was neither born nor reared in Hadleyburg. I was afraid that if I started to operate my scheme by getting my letter laid before you, you would say to yourselves, "Goodson is the only man among us who would give away twenty dollars to a poor devil"—and then you might not bite at my bait. But Heaven took Goodson; then I knew I was safe, and I set my trap and baited it. It may be that I shall not catch all the men to whom I mailed the pretended test secret, but I shall catch the most of them, if I know Hadleyburg nature. [*Voices.* "Right—he got every last one of them."] I believe they will even steal ostensible *gamble*-money, rather than miss, poor, tempted, and mistrained fellows. I am hoping to eternally and everlastingly squelch your vanity and give Hadleyburg a new renown—one that will *stick*—and spread far. If I have succeeded, open the sack and summon the Committee on Propagation and Preservation of the Hadleyburg Reputation.' "

A Cyclone of Voices. "Open it! Open it! The Eighteen to the front! Committee on Propagation of the Tradition! Forward—the Incorruptibles!"

The chair ripped the sack wide, and gathered up a handful of bright, broad yellow coins, shook them together, then examined them—

"Friends, they are only gilded disks of lead!"

There was a crashing outbreak of delight over this news, and when the noise had subsided, the tanner called out:

"By right of apparent seniority in this business, Mr. Wilson is Chairman of the Committee on Propagation of the Tradition. I suggested that he step forward on behalf of his pals, and receive in trust the money."

A Hundred Voices. "Wilson! Wilson! Wilson! Speech! Speech!"

Wilson [*in a voice trembling with anger*]. "You will allow me to say, and without apologies for my language, *damn* the money!"

A Voice. "Oh, and him a Baptist!"

A Voice. "Seventeen Symbols left! Step up, gentlemen, and assume your trust!"

There was a pause—no response.

The Saddler. "Mr. Chairman, we've got *one* clean man left, anyway, out of the late aristocracy; and he needs money, and deserves it. I move that you appoint Jack Halliday to get up there and auction off that sack of gilt twenty-dollar pieces, and give the result to the right man—the man whom Hadleyburg delights to honor—Edward Richards."

This was received with great enthusiasm, the dog taking a hand again; the saddler started the bids at a dollar, the Brixton folk and Barnum's[4] repre-

---

[4] P.T. Barnum (1810-1891), an impressario who became famous for his exhibitions of oddities and freaks.

sentative fought hard for it, the people cheered every jump that the bids made, the excitement climbed moment by moment higher and higher, the bidders got on their mettle and grew steadily more and more daring, more and more determined, the jumps went from a dollar up to five, then to ten, then to twenty, then fifty, then to a hundred, then—

At the beginning of the auction Richards whispered in distress to his wife: "Oh, Mary, can we allow it? It—it—you see, it is an honor-reward, a testimonial to purity of character, and—and—can we allow it? Hadn't I better get up and—Oh, Mary, what ought we to do?—what do you think we—" [*Halliday's voice. "Fifteen I'm bid!—fifteen for the sack!—twenty!—ah, thanks!—thirty—thanks again! Thirty, thirty, thirty—do I hear forty?—forty it is! Keep the ball rolling, gentlemen, keep it rolling!—fifty!—thanks, noble Roman!—going at fifty, fifty, fifty!—seventy!—ninety!—splendid!—a hundred!—pile it up, pile it up!—hundred and twenty—forty!—just in time!—hundred and fifty;—*TWO *hundred!—superb! Do I hear two h—thanks!—two hundred and fifty!—"*] "It is another temptation, Edward—I'm all in a tremble—but, oh, we've escaped *one* temptation, and that ought to warn us, to [*"Six did I hear?—thanks!—six fifty, six f—*SEVEN *hundred!"*] And yet, Edward, when you think—nobody susp— [*"Eight hundred dollars!—hurrah!—make it nine!—Mr. Parsons, did I hear you say—thanks!—nine!—this noble sack of virgin lead going at only nine hundred dollars, gilding and all—come! do I hear—a thousand!—gratefully yours!—did some one say eleven?—a sack which is going to be the most celebrated in the whole Uni—"*] Oh, Edward" (beginning to sob), "we are *so* poor!—but—but—do as you think best—do as you think best."

Edward fell—that is, he sat still; sat with a conscience which was not satisfied, but which was overpowered by circumstances.

Meantime a stranger, who looked like an amateur detective gotten up as an impossible English earl, had been watching the evening's proceedings with manifest interest, and with a contented expression in his face; and he had been privately commenting to himself. He was now soliloquizing somewhat like this: "None of the Eighteen are bidding; that is not satisfactory; I must change that—the dramatic unities require it; they must buy the sack they tried to steal; they must pay a heavy price, too—some of them are rich. And another thing, when I make a mistake in Hadleyburg nature the man that puts that error upon me is entitled to a high honorarium, and some one must pay it. This poor old Richards has brought my judgment to shame; he is an honest man:—I don't understand it, but I acknowledge it. Yes, he saw my deuces *and* with a straight flush, and by rights the pot is his. And it shall be a jack-pot, too, if I can manage it. He disappointed me, but let that pass."

He was watching the bidding. At a thousand, the market broke; the prices tumbled swiftly. He waited—and still watched. One competitor dropped out; then another, and another. He put in a bid or two, now. When the bids had sunk to ten dollars, he added a five; some one raised him a three; he waited a moment, then flung in a fifty-dollar jump, and the sack was his—at $1282. The house broke out in cheers—then stopped; for he was on his feet, and had lifted his hand. He began to speak.

"I desire to say a word, and ask a favor. I am a speculator in rarities, and I have dealings with persons interested in numismatics all over the world. I can make a profit on this purchase, just as it stands; but there is a way, if I can get your approval, whereby I can make every one of these leaden twenty-dollar pieces worth its face in gold, and perhaps more. Grant me that approval, and I will give part of my gains to your Mr. Richards, whose invulnerable probity you have so justly and so cordially recognized to-night; his share will be ten thousand dollars, and I will hand him the money to-morrow. [*Great applause from the house.* But the "invulnerable probity" made the Richardses blush prettily; however, it went for modesty, and did no harm.] If you will pass my proposition by a good majority—I would like a two-thirds vote—I will regard that as the town's consent, and that is all I ask. Rarities are always helped by any device which will rouse curiosity and compel remark. Now if I may have your permission to stamp upon the faces of each of these ostensible coins the names of the eighteen gentlemen who—"

Nine-tenths of the audience were on their feet in a moment—dog and all—and the proposition was carried with a whirlwind of approving applause and laughter.

They sat down, and all the Symbols except "Dr." Clay Harkness got up, violently protesting against the proposed outrage, and threatening to—

"I beg you not to threaten me," said the stranger, calmly. "I know my legal rights, and am not accustomed to being frightened at bluster." [*Applause.*] He sat down. "Dr." Harkness saw an opportunity here. He was one of the two very rich men of the place, and Pinkerton was the other. Harkness was proprietor of a mint; that is to say, a popular patent medicine. He was running for the Legislature on one ticket, and Pinkerton on the other. It was a close race and a hot one, and getting hotter every day. Both had strong appetites for money; each had bought a great tract of land, with a purpose; there was going to be a new railway, and each wanted to be in the Legislature and help locate the route to his own advantage; a single vote might make the decision, and with it two or three fortunes. The stake was large, and Harkness was a daring speculator. He was sitting close to the stranger. He leaned over while one or another of the other Symbols was entertaining the house with protests and appeals, and asked, in a whisper,

"What is your price for the sack?"

"Forty thousand dollars."

"I'll give you twenty."

"No."

"Twenty-five."

"No."

"Say thirty."

"The price is forty thousand dollars; not a penny less."

"All right, I'll give it. I will come to the hotel at ten in the morning. I don't want it known; will see you privately."

"Very good." Then the stranger got up and said to the house:

"I find it late. The speeches of these gentlemen are not without merit, not without interest, not without grace; yet if I may be excused I will take my leave. I thank you for the great favor which you have shown me in granting my petition. I ask the Chair to keep the sack for me until to-morrow, and to hand these three five-hundred-dollar notes to Mr. Richards." They were passed up to the Chair. "At nine I will call for the sack, and at eleven will deliver the rest of the ten thousand to Mr. Richards in person, at his home. Good-night."

Then he slipped out, and left the audience making a vast noise, which was composed of a mixture of cheers, the "Mikado" song, dog-disapproval, and the chant. "You are f-a-r from being a b-a-a-d man—a-a-a-a-men!"

IV

At home the Richardses had to endure congratulations and compliments until midnight. Then they were left to themselves. They looked a little sad, and they sat silent and thinking. Finally Mary sighed and said,

"Do you think we are to blame, Edward—*much* to blame?" and her eyes wandered to the accusing triplet of big bank-notes lying on the table, where the congratulators had been gloating over them and reverently fingered them. Edward did not answer at once; then he brought out a sigh, and said hesitatingly:

"We—we couldn't help it, Mary. It—well, it was ordered. *All* things are."

Mary glanced up and looked at him steadily; but he didn't return the look. Presently she said:

"I thought congratulations and praises always tasted good. But—it seems to me, now—Edward?"

"Well?"

"Are you going to stay in the bank?"

"N-no."

"Resign?"

"In the morning—by note."

"It does seem best."

Richards bowed his head in his hands and muttered:

"Before, I was not afraid to let oceans of people's money pour through my hands, but—Mary, I am so tired, so tired—"

"We will go to bed."

At nine in the morning the stranger called for the sack and took it to the hotel in a cab. At ten Harkness had a talk with him privately. The stranger asked for and got five checks on a metropolitan bank—drawn to "Bearer,"—four for $1,500 each, and one for $34,000. He put the former in his pocketbook, and the remainder, representing $38,500, he put in an envelope, and with these he added a note, which he wrote after Harkness was gone. At eleven he called at the Richards house and knocked. Mrs. Richards peeped through the shutters, then went and received the envelope, and the stranger disappeared without a word. She came back flushed and a little unsteady on her legs, and gasped out:

"I am sure I recognized him! Last night it seemed to me that maybe I had seen him somewhere before."

"He is the man that brought the sack here?"

"I am almost sure of it."

"Then he is the ostensible Stephenson too, and sold every important citizen in this town with his bogus secret. Now if he has sent checks instead of money, we are sold too, after we thought we had escaped. I was beginning to feel fairly comfortable once more, after my night's rest, but the look of that envelope makes me sick. It isn't fat enough; $8500 in even the largest banknotes makes more bulk than that."

"Edward, why do you object to checks?"

"Checks signed by Stephenson! I am resigned to take the $8500 if it could come in bank-notes—for it does seem that it was so ordered, Mary—but I have never had much courage, and I have not the pluck to try to market a check signed with that disastrous name. It would be a trap. That man tried to catch me; we escaped somehow or other; and now he is trying a new way. If it is checks—"

"Oh, Edward, it is *too* bad!" and she held up the checks and began to cry.

"Put them in the fire! quick! we mustn't be tempted. It is a trick to make the world laugh at *us*, along with the rest, and—Give them to *me*, since you can't do it!" He snatched them and tried to hold his grip till he could get to the stove; but he was human, he was a cashier, and he stopped a moment to make sure of the signature. Then he came near to fainting.

"Fan me, Mary, fan me! They are the same as gold!"

"Oh, how lovely, Edward! Why?"

"Signed by Harkness. What can the mystery of that be, Mary?"

"Edward, do you think—"

"Look here—look at this! Fifteen—fifteen—fifteen—thirty-four. Thirty-eight thousand five hundred! Mary, the sack isn't worth twelve dollars, and Harkness—apparently—has paid about par for it."

"And does it all come to us, do you think—instead of the ten thousand?"

"Why, it looks like it. And the checks are made to 'Bearer,' too."

"Is that good, Edward? What is it for?"

"A hint to collect them at some distant bank, I reckon. Perhaps Harkness doesn't want the matter known. What is that—a note?"

"Yes. It was with the checks."

It was in the "Stephenson" handwriting, but there was no signature. It said:

> *"I am a disappointed man. Your honesty is beyond the reach of temptation. I had a different idea about it, but I wronged you in that, and I beg pardon, and do it sincerely. I honor you—and that is sincere, too. This town is not worthy to kiss the hem of your garment. Dear sir, I made a square bet with myself that there were nineteen debauchable men in your self-righteous community. I have lost. Take the whole pot, you are entitled to it."*

Richards drew a deep sigh, and said:

"It seems written with fire—it burns so. Mary—I am miserable again."

"I, too. Ah, dear, I wish—"

"To think, Mary——he *believes* in me."

"Oh, don't Edward—I can't bear it."

"If those beautiful words were deserved, Mary—and God knows I believed I deserved them once—I think I could give the forty thousand dollars for them. And I would put that paper away, as representing more than gold and jewels, and keep it always. But now—We could not live in the shadow of its accusing presence, Mary."

He put it in the fire.

A messenger arrived and delivered an envelope. Richards took from it a note and read it; it was from Burgess.

> *"You saved me, in a difficult time. I saved you last night. It was at cost of a lie, but I made the sacrifice freely, and out of a grateful heart. None in this village knows so well as I know how brave and good and noble you are. At bottom you cannot respect me, knowing as you do of that matter of which I am accused, and by the general voice condemned; but I beg that you will at least believe that I am a grateful man; it will help me to bear my burden.*
>
> *[Signed]*   *BURGESS."*

"Saved, once more. And on such terms!" He put the note in the fire. "I—I wish I were dead, Mary, I wish I were out of it all."

"Oh, these are bitter, bitter days, Edward. The stabs, through their very generosity, are so deep—and they come so fast!"

Three days before the election each of two thousand voters suddenly found himself in possession of a prized momento—one of the renowned bogus double-eagles. Around one of its faces was stamped these words: "THE REMARK I MADE TO THE POOR STRANGER WAS—" Around the other face was stamped these "GO, AND REFORM. [SIGNED] PINKERTON." Thus the entire remaining refuse of the renowned joke was emptied upon a single head, and with calamitous effect. It revived the recent vast laugh and concentrated it upon Pinkerton; and Harkness's election was a walk-over.

Within twenty-four hours after the Richardses had received their checks their consciences were quieting down, discouraged; the old couple were learning to reconcile themselves to the sin which they had committed. But they were to learn, now, that a sin takes on new and real terrors when there seems a chance that it is going to be found out. This gives it a fresh and most substantial and important aspect. At church the morning sermon was of the usual pattern; it was the same old things said in the same old way; they had heard them a thousand times and found them innocuous, next to meaningless, and easy to sleep under; but now it was different: the sermon seemed to bristle with accusations; it seemed aimed straight and specially at people who were concealing deadly sins. After church they got away from the mob of congratulators as soon as they could and hurried homeward, chilled to the bone as they did not know what—vague, shadowy, indefinite fears. And by chance they caught a glimpse of Mr. Burgess as he turned a corner. He paid no attention to their nod of recognition! He hadn't seen it; but they did not know that. What could his conduct mean? It might mean—it might mean—oh, a dozen dreadful things. Was it possible that he knew that Richards could have cleared him of guilt in that bygone time, and had been silently waiting for a chance to even up accounts? At home, in their distress they got to imagining that their servant might have been in the next room listening when Richards revealed the secret to his wife that he knew of Burgess's innocence; next Richards began to imagine that he had heard the swish of a gown in there at that time; next, he was sure he *had* heard it. They would call Sarah in, on a pretext, and watch her face: if she had been betraying them to Mr. Burgess, it would show in her manner. They asked her some questions—questions which were so random and incoherent and seemingly purposeless that the girl felt sure that the old people's minds had been affected by their sudden good fortune; the sharp and watchful gaze which they bent upon her frightened her, and that completed the business. She blushed, she became nervous and confused, and to the old people these were plain signs of guilt—guilt of some fearful sort or other—without doubt she was a spy and a traitor. When they were alone again they began to piece many unrelated things together and get horrible results out of the combination. When things had got about to the worst, Richards was delivered of a sudden gasp, and his wife asked,

"Oh, what is it?—what is it?"

"The note—Burgess's note! Its language was sarcastic, I see it now." He quoted: " 'At bottom you cannot respect me, *knowing* as you do, of *that matter* of which I am accused'—oh, it is perfectly plain, now, God help me! He knows that I know! You see the ingenuity of the phrasing. It was a trap—and like a fool, I walked into it. And Mary—?"

"Oh, it is dreadful—I know what you are going to say—he didn't return your transcript of the pretended test-remark."

"No—kept it to destroy us with. Mary, he has exposed us to some already. I know it—I know it well. I saw it in a dozen faces after church. Ah, he wouldn't answer our nod of recognition—*he* knew what he had been doing!"

In the night the doctor was called. The news went around in the morning that the old couple were rather seriously ill—prostrated by the exhausting excitement growing out of their great windfall, the congratulations, and the late hours, the doctor said. The town was sincerely distressed; for these old people were about all it had left to be proud of, now.

Two days later the news was worse. The old couple were delirious, and were doing strange things. By witness of the nurses, Richards had exhibited checks—for $8,500? No—for an amazing sum—$38,500! What could be the explanation of this gigantic piece of luck?

The following day the nurses had more news—and wonderful. They had concluded to hide the checks, lest harm come to them; but when they searched they were gone from under the patient's pillow—vanished away. The patient said:

"Let the pillow alone; what do you want?"

"We thought it best that the checks—"

"You will never see them again—they are destroyed. They came from Satan. I saw the hell-brand on them, and I knew they were sent to betray me to sin." Then he fell to gabbling strange and dreadful things which were not clearly understandable, and which the doctor admonished them to keep to themselves.

Richards was right; the checks were never seen again.

A nurse must have talked in her sleep, for within two days the forbidden gabblings were the property of the town; and they were of a surprising sort. They seemed to indicate that Richards had been a claimant for the sack himself, and that Burgess had concealed that fact and then maliciously betrayed it.

Burgess was taxed with this and stoutly denied it. And he said it was not fair to attach weight to the chatter of a sick old man who was out of his mind. Still, suspicion was in the air, and there was much talk.

After a day or two it was reported that Mrs. Richards's delirious deliveries were getting to be duplicates of her husband's. Suspicion flamed up into conviction now, and the town's pride in the purity of its one undiscredited important citizen began to dim down and flicker toward extinction.

Six days passed, then came more news. The old couple were dying. Richards's mind cleared in his latest hour, and he sent for Burgess. Burgess said:

"Let the room be cleared. I think he wishes to say something in privacy."

"No!" said Richards; "I want witnesses. I want you all to hear my confession, so that I may die a man, and not a dog. I was clean—artificially—like the rest; and like the rest I fell when temptation came. I signed a lie, and claimed the miserable sack. Mr. Burgess remembered that I had done him a service, and in gratitude (and ignorance) he suppressed my claim and saved me. You know the thing that was charged against Burgess years ago. My testimony, and mine alone, could have cleared him, and I was a coward, and left him to suffer disgrace—"

"No—no—Mr. Richards, you—"

"My servant betrayed my secret to him—"

"No one has betrayed anything to me—"

"—and then he did a natural and justifiable thing, he repented of the saving kindness which he had done me, and he *exposed* me—as I deserved—"

"Never!—I make oath—" true

"Out of my heart I forgive him."

Burgess's impassioned protestations fell upon deaf ears; the dying man passed away without knowing that once more he had done poor Burgess a wrong. The old wife died that night.

The last of the sacred Nineteen had fallen a prey to the fiendish sack; the town was stripped the last rag of its ancient glory. Its mourning was not showy, but it was deep.

By act of the Legislature—upon prayer and petition—Hadleyburg was allowed to change its name to (never mind what—I will not give it away), and leave one word out of the motto that for many generations had graced the town's official seal. "not lead us into temptation"

It is an honest town once more, and the man will have to rise early that catches it napping again.

Milton "distrust a cloistered virtue"   1899; 1900

From Europe and Elsewhere[1]

TO THE PERSON SITTING IN DARKNESS

NEWS

Christmas will dawn in the United States over a people full of hope and aspiration and good cheer. Such a condition means contentment and happiness. The carping grumbler who may here and there go forth will find few to listen to him. The majority will wonder what is the matter with him and pass on.—New York *Tribune*, on Christmas Eve.

[1] First published in the *North American Review* in February 1901.

Things not so good at home ...

SAMUEL LANGHORNE CLEMENS (MARK TWAIN)

From the *Sun*, of New York:

The purpose of this article is not to describe the terrible offenses against humanity committed in the name of Politics in some of the most notorious East Side districts. *They could not be described, even verbally.* But it is the intention to let the great mass of more or less careless citizens of this beautiful metropolis of the New World get some conception of the havoc and ruin wrought to man, woman, and child in the most densely populated and least-known section of the city. Name, date, and place can be supplied to those of little faith—or to any man who feels himself aggrieved. It is a plain statement of record and observation, written without license and without garnish.

Imagine, if you can, a section of the city territory completely dominated by one man, without whose permission neither legitimate nor illegitimate business can be conducted; *where illegitimate business is encouraged and legitimate business discouraged;* where the respectable residents have to fasten their doors and windows summer nights and sit in their rooms with asphyxiating air and 100-degree temperature, rather than try to catch the faint whiff of breeze in their natural breathing places, the stoops of their homes; *where naked women dance by night in the streets, and unsexed men prowl like vultures through the darkness on "business"* not only permitted but encouraged by the police; *where the education of infants begins with the knowledge of prostitution* and the training of little girls is training in the arts of Phryne;[2] where *American* girls brought up with the refinements of *American* homes are imported from small towns up-state, Massachusetts, Connecticut, and New Jersey, and kept as virtually prisoners as if they were locked up behind jail bars until they have lost all semblance of womanhood; *where small boys are taught to solicit for the women of disorderly houses;* where there is an organized society of young men *whose sole business in life is to corrupt young girls and turn them over to bawdy houses;* where men walking with their wives along the street are openly insulted; *where children that have adult diseases are the chief patrons of the hospitals and dispensaries;* where it is the rule, rather than the exception, that *murder, rape, robbery, and theft go unpunished*—in short where the Premium of the most awful forms of Vice is the Profit of the politicians.

The following news from China appeared in the *Sun*, of New York, on Christmas Eve. The italics are mine:

[2] A notorious courtesan of Ancient Greece.

The Rev. Mr. Ament, of the American Board of Foreign Missions, has returned from a trip which he made for the purpose of collecting indemnities for damages done by Boxers.[3] *Everywhere he went he compelled the Chinese to pay.* He says that all his native Christians are now provided for. He had 700 of them under his charge, and 300 were killed. He has *collected 300 taels for each* of these murders, and has *compelled full payment for all the property belonging to Christians* that was destroyed. He also assessed *fines* amounting to THIRTEEN TIMES the amount of the indemnity. *This money will be used for the propagation of the Gospel.*

Mr. Ament declares that the compensation he has collected is *moderate* when compared with the amount secured by the Catholics, who demand, in addition to money, *head for head.* They collect 500 taels for each murder of a Catholic. In the Wenchiu country, 680 Catholics were killed, and for this the European Catholics here demand 750,000 strings of cash and 680 *heads.*

In the course of a conversation, Mr. Ament referred to the attitude of the missionaries toward the Chinese. He said:

"I deny emphatically that the missionaries are *vindictive,* that they *generally* looted, or that they have done anything *since* the siege that *the circumstances did not demand.* I criticize the Americans. *The soft hand of the Americans is not as good as the mailed fist of the Germans.* If you deal with the Chinese with a soft hand they will take advantage of it.

"The statement that the French government will return the loot taken by the French soldiers is the source of the greatest amusement here. The French soldiers were more systematic looters than the Germans, and it is a fact that to-day *Catholic Christians,* carrying French flags and armed with modern guns, *are looting villages* in the Province of Chili."

By happy luck, we get all these glad tidings on Christmas Eve—just in time to enable us to celebrate the day with proper gaiety and enthusiasm. Our spirits soar, and we find we can even make jokes: Taels, I win, Heads you lose.

Our Reverend Ament is the right man in the right place. What we want of our missionaries out there is, not that they shall merely represent in their acts and persons the grace and gentleness and charity and loving-kindness of our religion, but that they shall also represent the American spirit. The oldest Americans are the Pawnees. Macallum's *History* says:[4]

---

[3] The name attached to Chinese patriots—members of Righteous Harmony Bands (or Fists)—who participated in an uprising against Europeans in China in 1900.

[4] Twain made up this quotation.

When a white Boxer kills a Pawnee and destroys his property, the other Pawnees do not trouble to seek *him* out, they kill any white person that comes along; also, they make some white village pay deceased's heirs the full cash value of deceased, together with full cash value of the property destroyed; they also make the village pay, in addition, *thirteen times* the value of that property into a fund for the dissemination of the Pawnee religion, which they regard as the best of all religions for the softening and humanizing of the heart of man. It is their idea that it is only fair and right that the innocent should be made to suffer for the guilty, and that it is better that ninety and nine innocent should suffer than that one guilty person should escape.

Our Reverend Ament is justifiably jealous of those enterprising Catholics who not only get big money for each lost convert but get "head for head" besides. But he should soothe himself with the reflections that the entirety of their exactions are for their own pockets, whereas he, less selfishly, devotes only 300 taels per head to that service, and gives the whole vast thirteen repetitions of the property-indemnity to the service of propagating the Gospel. His magnanimity has won him the approval of his nation and will get him a monument. Let him be content with these rewards. We all hold him dear for manfully defending his fellow missionaries from exaggerated charges which were beginning to distress us, but which his testimony has so considerably modified that we can now contemplate them without noticeable pain. For now we know that, even before the siege, the missionaries were not "generally" out looting, and that "since the siege" they have acted quite handsomely, except when "circumstances" crowded them. I am arranging for the monument. Subscriptions for it can be sent to the American Board, designs for it can be sent to me. Designs must allegorically set forth the Thirteen Reduplications of the Indemnity and the Object for which they were exacted; as Ornaments the designs must exhibit 680 Heads, so disposed as to give a pleasing and pretty effect, for the Catholics have done nicely, and are entitled to notice in the monument. Mottoes may be suggested, if any shall be discovered that will satisfactorily cover the ground.

Mr. Ament's financial feat of squeezing a thirteen-fold indemnity out of the pauper peasants to square other people's offenses, thus condemning them and their women and innocent little children to inevitable starvation and lingering death, in order that the blood money so acquired might be *"used for the propagation of the Gospel,"* does not flutter my serenity; although the act and the words, taken together, concrete a blasphemy so hideous and so colossal that without doubt its mate is not findable in the history of this or of any other age. Yet if a layman had done that thing and justified it with those words, I should have shuddered, I know. Or if I had done the thing and said the words myself—However, the thought is unthinkable, irreverent as some imperfectly informed people think me. Sometimes an ordained minister sets out to be blasphemous. When this happens the layman is out of the running; he stands no chance.

We have Mr. Ament's impassioned assurance that the missionaries are not "vindictive." Let us hope and pray that they will never become so, but will remain in the almost morbidly fair and just and gentle temper which is affording so much satisfaction to their brother and champion today.

The following is from the New York *Tribune* of Christmas Eve. It comes from that journal's Tokyo correspondent. It has a strange and impudent sound, but the Japanese are but partially civilized as yet. When they become wholly civilized they will not talk so:

> The missionary question, of course, occupies a foremost place in the discussion. It is now felt as essential that the Western Powers take cognizance of the sentiment here, that religious invasions of Oriental countries by powerful Western organizations are tantamount to filibustering expeditions, and should not only be discountenanced, but that stern measures should be adopted for their suppression. The feeling here is that the missionary organizations constitute a constant menace to peaceful international relations.

Shall we? That is, shall we go on conferring our Civilization upon the peoples that sit in darkness, or shall we give those poor things a rest? Shall we bang right ahead in our old-time, loud, pious way, and commit the new century to the game; or shall we sober up and sit down and think it over first? Would it not be prudent to get our Civilization tools together and see how much stock is left on hand in the way of Glass Beads and Theology, and Maxim Guns[5] and Hymn Books, and Trade Gin and Torches of Progress and Enlightenment (patent adjustable ones, good to fire villages with, upon occasion), and balance the books and arrive at the profit and loss, so that we may intelligently decide whether to continue the business or sell out the property and start a new Civilization Scheme on the proceeds?

Extending the Blessings of Civilization to our Brother who Sits in Darkness has been a good trade and has paid well, on the whole; and there is money in it yet, if carefully worked—but not enough, in my judgment, to make any considerable risk advisable. The People that Sit in Darkness are getting to be too scarce—too scarce and too shy. And such darkness as is now left is really of but an indifferent quality, and not dark enough for the game. The most of those People that Sit in Darkness have been furnished with more light than was good for them or profitable for us. We have been injudicious.

[5] Machine guns invented by Hiram Maxim (1840–1916).

The Blessings-of-Civilization Trust, wisely and cautiously administered, is a Daisy. There is more money in it, more territory, more sovereignty and other kinds of emolument, than there is in any other game that is played. But Christendom has been playing it badly of late years and must certainly suffer by it, in my opinion. She has been so eager to get every stake that appeared on the green cloth that the People who Sit in Darkness have noticed it—they have noticed it and have begun to show alarm. They have become suspicious of the Blessings of Civilization. More—they have begun to examine them. This is not well. The Blessings of Civilization are all right, and a good commercial property; there could not be a better, in a dim light. In the right kind of a light and at a proper distance, with the goods a little out of focus, they furnish this desirable exhibit to the Gentlemen who Sit in Darkness:

LOVE	LAW AND ORDER
JUSTICE	LIBERTY
GENTLENESS	EQUALITY
CHRISTIANITY	HONORABLE DEALING
PROTECTION TO THE WEAK	MERCY
TEMPERANCE	EDUCATION

—and so on.

There. Is it good? Sir, it is pie. It will bring into camp any idiot that sits in darkness anywhere. But not if we adulterate it. It is proper to be emphatic upon that point. This brand is strictly for Export—apparently. *Apparently.* Privately and confidentially, it is nothing of the kind. Privately and confidentially, it is merely an outside cover, gay and pretty and attractive, displaying the special patterns of our Civilization which we reserve for Home Consumption, while *inside* the bale is the Actual Thing that the Customer Sitting in Darkness buys with his blood and tears and land and liberty. That Actual Thing is indeed Civilization, but it is only for Export. Is there a difference between the two brands? In some of the details, yes.

We all know that the Business is being ruined. The reason is not far to seek. It is because our Mr. McKinley, and Mr. Chamberlain, and the Kaiser and the Tsar[6] and the French have been exporting the Actual Thing *with the outside cover left off.* This is bad for the Game. It shows that these new players of it are not sufficiently acquainted with it.

It is a distress to look on and note the mismoves, they are so strange and so awkward. Mr. Chamberlain manufactures a war[7] out of materials so inad-

---

[6] William McKinley (1840-1901), U.S. President (1897-1901); Joseph Chamberlain (1836-1914), an English imperialist statesman; Kaiser William II (1888-1918) was a German emperor, and Czar Nicholas II (1894-1917) was Emperor of Russia.

[7] The South African, or Boer War (1899-1902) between Britain and the Boer Republics.

equate and so fanciful that they make the boxes grieve and the gallery laugh, and he tries hard to persuade himself that it isn't purely a private raid for cash but has a sort of dim, vague respectability about it somewhere, if he could only find the spot; and that by and by he can scour the flag clean again after he has finished dragging it through the mud, and make it shine and flash in the vault of heaven once more as it had shone and flashed there a thousand years in the world's respect until he laid his unfaithful hand upon it. It is bad play—bad. For it exposes the Actual Thing to Them that Sit in Darkness, and they say: "What! Christian against Christian? And only for money? Is *this* a case of magnanimity, forbearance, love, gentleness, mercy, protection of the weak—this strange and overshowy onslaught of an elephant upon a nest of field mice, on the pretext that the mice had squeaked an insolence at him—conduct which 'no self-respecting government could allow to pass unavenged'? as Mr. Chamberlain said. Was that a good pretext in a small case, when it had not been a good pretext in a large one?—for only recently Russia had affronted the elephant three times and survived alive and unsmitten. Is this Civilization and Progress? Is it something better than we already possess? These harryings and burnings and desert-makings in the Transvaal[8]—is this an improvement on our darkness? Is it, perhaps, possible that there are two kinds of Civilization—one for home consumption and one for the heathen market?"

Then They that Sit in Darkness are troubled, and shake their heads, and they read this extract from a letter of a British private, recounting his exploits in one of Methuen's victories some days before the affair of Magersfontein,[9] and they are troubled again:

> We tore up the hill and into the intrenchments, and the Boers saw we had them; so they dropped their guns and went down on their knees and put up their hands clasped, and begged for mercy. And we gave it them—*with the long spoon.*

The long spoon is the bayonet. See *Lloyd's Weekly*, London, of those days. The same number—and the same column—contained some quite unconscious satire in the form of shocked and bitter upbraidings of the Boers for their brutalities and inhumanities!

Next, to our heavy damage, the Kaiser went to playing the game without first mastering it. He lost a couple of missionaries in a riot in Shantung, and in his account he made an overcharge for them. China had to pay a hundred thousand dollars apiece for them in money; twelve miles of territory, containing several millions of inhabitants and worth twenty million dollars; and to build a monument and also a Christian church; whereas the people of

---

[8] The Republic of South Africa.
[9] Lord Methuen (1845–1932), was a British general who was beaten by the Boers in the Battle of Magersfontein.

China could have been depended upon to remember the missionaries without the help of these expensive memorials. This was all bad play. Bad, because it would not, and will not now or ever, deceive the Person Sitting in Darkness. He knows that it was an overcharge. He knows that a missionary is like any other man: he is worth merely what you can supply his place for and no more. He is useful, but so is a doctor, so is a sheriff, so is an editor; but a just Emperor does not charge war prices for such. A diligent, intelligent, but obscure missionary, and a diligent, intelligent country editor are worth much, and we know it; but they are not worth the earth. We esteem such an editor and we are sorry to see him go, but when he goes, we should consider twelve miles of territory and a church and a fortune overcompensation for his loss. I mean, if he was a Chinese editor and we had to settle for him. It is no proper figure for an editor or a missionary; one can get shop-worn kings for less. It was bad play on the Kaiser's part. It got this property, true; but it *produced the Chinese revolt*, the indignant uprising of China's traduced patriots, the Boxers. The results have been expensive to Germany and to the other Disseminators of Progress and the Blessings of Civilization.

The Kaiser's claim was paid, yet it was bad play, for it could not fail to have an evil effect upon Persons Sitting in Darkness in China. They would muse upon the event and be likely to say: "Civilization is gracious and beautiful, for such is its reputation, but can we afford it? There are rich Chinamen, perhaps they can afford it; but this tax is not laid upon them, it is laid upon the peasants of Shantung; it is they that must pay this mighty sum and their wages are but four cents a day. Is this a better civilization than ours, and holier and higher and nobler? Is not this rapacity? Is not this extortion? Would Germany charge America two hundred thousand dollars for two missionaries, and shake the mailed fist in her face and send warships and send soldiers, and say, 'Seize twelve miles of territory, worth twenty millions of dollars, as additional pay for the missionaries, and make those peasants build a monument to the missionaries, and a costly Christian church to remember them by?' And later would Germany say to her soldiers, 'March through America and slay, *giving no quarter;* make the German face there, as has been our Hun-face here, a terror for a thousand years; march through the Great Republic and slay, slay, slay, carving a road for our offended religion through its heart and bowels?' Would Germany do like this to America, to England, to France, to Russia? Or only to China, the helpless—imitating the elephant's assault upon the field mice? Had we better invest in this Civilization—this Civilization which called Napoleon a buccaneer for carrying off Venice's bronze horses, but which steals our ancient astronomical instruments from our walls and goes looting like common bandits—that is, all the alien soldiers except America's; and (Americans again excepted) storms frightened villages and cables the result to glad journals at home every day: 'Chinese losses, 450 killed; ours, *one officer and two men wounded*. Shall proceed against neighboring village tomorrow, where a *massacre* is reported.' Can we afford Civilization?"

Great world power bully

And next Russia must go and play the game injudiciously. She affronts England once or twice—with the Person Sitting in Darkness observing and noting; by moral assistance of France and Germany, she robs Japan of her hard-earned spoil, all swimming in Chinese blood—Port Arthur—with the Person again observing and noting; then she seizes Manchuria, raids its villages, and chokes its great river with the swollen corpses of countless massacred peasants—that astonished Person still observing and noting. And perhaps he is saying to himself, "It is yet *another* Civilized Power, with its banner of the Prince of Peace in one hand and its loot basket and its butcher knife in the other. Is there no salvation for us but to adopt Civilization and lift ourselves down to its level?"

And by and by comes America, and our Master of the Game plays it badly—plays it as Mr. Chamberlain was playing it in South Africa. It was a mistake to do that; also, it was one which was quite unlooked for in a Master who was playing it so well in Cuba. In Cuba, he was playing the usual and regular *American* game and it was winning, for there is no way to beat it. The Master, contemplating Cuba, said, "Here is an oppressed and friendless little nation which is willing to fight to be free; we go partners, and put up the strength of seventy million sympathizers and the resources of the United States: play!" Nothing but Europe combined could call that hand, and Europe cannot combine on anything. There in Cuba he was following our great traditions in a way which made us very proud of him, and proud of the deep dissatisfaction which his play was provoking in continental Europe. Moved by a high inspiration, he threw out those stirring words which proclaimed that forcible annexation would be "criminal aggression," and in that utterance fired another "shot heard round the world." The memory of that fine saying will be outlived by the remembrance of no act of his but one—that he forgot it within the twelvemonth, and its honorable gospel along with it.

For presently came the Philippine temptation. It was strong, it was too strong, and he made that bad mistake: he played the European game, the Chamberlain game. It was a pity, it was a great pity, that error—that one grievous error, that irrevocable error. For it was the very place and time to play the American game again. And at no cost. Rich winnings to be gathered in, too, rich and permanent, indestructible, a fortune transmissible forever to the children of the flag. Not land, not money, not dominion—no, something worth many times more than that dross: our share, the spectacle of a nation of long harassed and persecuted slaves set free through our influence; our posterity's share, the golden memory of that fair deed. The game was in our hands. If it had been played according to the American rules, Dewey[10] would have sailed away from Manila as soon as he had destroyed the Spanish fleet—after putting up a sign on shore guaranteeing foreign property and life

[10] George Dewey (1837–1917), Commander of the U.S. Asiatic Fleet, who defeated the Spanish in the Battle of Manilla (May 1898).

against damage by the Filipinos, and warning the Powers that interference with the emancipated patriots would be regarded as an act unfriendly to the United States. The Powers cannot combine in even a bad cause, and the sign would not have been molested.

Dewey could have gone about his affairs elsewhere and left the competent Filipino army to starve out the little Spanish garrison and send it home, and the Filipino citizens to set up the form of government they might prefer and deal with the friars and their doubtful acquisitions according to Filipino ideas of fairness and justice—ideas which have since been tested and found to be of as high an order as any that prevail in Europe or America.

But we played the Chamberlain game and lost the chance to add another Cuba and another honorable deed to our good record.

The more we examine the mistake, the more clearly we perceive that it is going to be bad for the Business. The Person Sitting in Darkness is almost sure to say, "There is something curious about this—curious and unaccountable. There must be two Americas, one that sets the captive free, and one that takes a once-captive's new freedom away from him, and picks a quarrel with him with nothing to found it on, then kills him to get his land."

The truth is, the Person Sitting in Darkness *is* saying things like that, and for the sake of the Business we must persuade him to look at the Philippine matter in another and healthier way. We must arrange his opinions for him. I believe it can be done, for Mr. Chamberlain has arranged England's opinion of the South African matter and done it most cleverly and successfully. He presented the facts—some of the facts—and showed those confiding people what the facts meant. He did it statistically, which is a good way. He used the formula: "Twice 2 are 14, and 2 from 9 leaves 35." Figures are effective; figures will convince the elect.

Now, my plan is a still bolder one than Mr. Chamberlain's, though apparently a copy of it. Let us be franker than Mr. Chamberlain; let us audaciously present the whole of the facts, shirking none, then explain them according to Mr. Chamberlain's formula. This daring truthfulness will astonish and dazzle the Person Sitting in Darkness, and he will take the Explanation down before his mental vision has had time to get back into focus. Let us say to him:

"Our case is simple. On the first of May, Dewey destroyed the Spanish fleet. This left the Archipelago in the hands of its proper and rightful owners, the Filipino nation. Their army numbered 30,000 men and they were competent to whip out or starve out the little Spanish garrison; then the people could set up a government of their own devising. Our traditions required that Dewey should now set up his warning sign and go away. But the Master of the Game happened to think of another plan—the European plan. He acted upon it. This was to send out an army—ostensibly to help the native patriots put the finishing touch upon their long and plucky struggle for independence, but really to take their land away from them and keep it. That is, in the interest of Progress and Civilization. The plan developed stage by stage, and quite satisfactorily. We entered into a military alliance with the trusting Filipinos and they hemmed in Manila on the land side, and by their valuable help the place, with its garrison of 8,000 or 10,000 Spaniards, was captured—a thing which we could not have accomplished unaided at that time. We got their help by—by ingenuity. We knew they were fighting for their independence and that they had been at it for two years. We knew they supposed that we also were fighting in their worthy cause—just as we had helped the Cubans fight for Cuban independence—and we allowed them to go on thinking so. *Until Manila was ours and we could get along without them.* Then we showed our hand. Of course, they were surprised— that was natural, surprised and disappointed, disappointed and grieved. To them it looked un-American, uncharacteristic, foreign to our established traditions. And this was natural, too, for we were only playing the American Game in public—in private it was the European. It was neatly done, very neatly, and it bewildered them. They could not understand it, for we had been so friendly—so affectionate, even—with those simple-minded patriots! We, our own selves, had brought back out of exile their leader, their hero, their hope, their Washington—Aguinaldo[11]; brought him in a warship, in high honor, under the sacred shelter and hospitality of the flag; brought him back and restored him to his people and got their moving and eloquent gratitude for it. Yes, we had been so friendly to them and had heartened them up in so many ways! We had lent them guns and ammunition; advised with them; exchanged pleasant courtesies with them; placed our sick and wounded in their kindly care; intrusted our Spanish prisoners to their humane and honest hands; fought shoulder to shoulder with them against "the common enemy" (our own phrase); praised their courage, praised their gallantry, praised their mercifulness, praised their fine and honorable conduct; borrowed their trenches, borrowed strong positions which they had previously captured from the Spaniards; petted them, lied to them—officially proclaiming that our land and naval forces came to give them their freedom and displace the bad Spanish Goverment—fooled them, used them until we needed them no longer, then derided the sucked orange and threw it away. We kept the positions which we had beguiled them of, by and by we moved a force forward and overlapped patriot ground—a clever thought, for we needed trouble and this would produce it. A Filipino soldier, crossing the ground, where no one had a right to forbid him, was shot by our sentry. The badgered patriots resented this with arms, without waiting to know whether Aguinaldo, who was absent, would approve or not. Aguinaldo did not approve, but that availed nothing. What we wanted in the interest of Progress and Civilization was the Archipelago, unencumbered by patriots struggling

[11] Emilia Aguinaldo (1869–1964), the leader
of a Philipino rebellion against Spain in 1896.

for independence; and War was what we needed. We clinched our opportunity. It is Mr. Chamberlain's case over again—at least in its motive and intention; and we played the game as adroitly as he played it himself."

At this point in our frank statement of fact to the Person Sitting in Darkness, we should throw in a little trade taffy about the Blessings of Civilization—for a change, and for the refreshment of his spirit—then go on with our tale:

"We and the patriots having captured Manila, Spain's ownership of the Archipelago and her sovereignty over it were at an end—obliterated—annihilated—not a rag or shred of either remaining behind. It was then that we conceived the divinely humorous idea of *buying* both of these specters from Spain! [It is quite safe to confess this to the Person Sitting in Darkness, since neither he nor any other sane person will believe it.] In buying those ghosts for twenty millions, we also contracted to take care of the friars and their accumulations. I think we also agreed to propagate leprosy and smallpox, but as to this there is doubt. But it is not important, persons afflicted with the friars do not mind other diseases.

"With our Treaty ratified, Manila subdued, and our Ghosts secured, we had no further use for Aguinaldo and the owners of the Archipelago. We forced a war and we have been hunting America's guest and ally through the woods and swamps ever since."

At this point in the tale, it will be well to boast a little of our war work and our heroisms in the field, so as to make our performance look as fine as England's in South Africa, but I believe it will not be best to emphasize this too much. We must be cautious. Of course, we must read the war telegrams to the Person, in order to keep up our frankness, but we can throw an air of humorousness over them and that will modify their grim eloquence a little, and their rather indiscreet exhibitions of gory exultation. Before reading to him the following display heads of the dispatches of November 18, 1900, it will be well to practice on them in private first, so as to get the right tang of lightness and gayety into them:

"ADMINISTRATION WEARY OF PROTRACTED HOSTILITIES!"

"REAL WAR AHEAD FOR FILIPINO REBELS!"[12]

"WILL SHOW NO MERCY!"

"KITCHENER'S[13] PLAN ADOPTED!"

[12] "Rebels—"Mumble that funny word—don't let the Person catch it distinctly." [Twain's note.]

[13] Horatio Herbert, Lord Kitchiner (1850-1916), was the British commander during the Boer War. By his orders, the families of the Boer soldiers were gathered up into concentration camps where more than 20,000 died.

Kitchener knows how to handle disagreeable people who are fighting for their homes and their liberties, and we must let on that we are merely imitating Kitchener and have no national interest in the matter, further than to get ourselves admired by the Great Family of Nations, in which august company our Master of the Game has brought a place for us in the back row.

Of course, we must not venture to ignore our General MacArthur's[14] reports—oh, why do they keep on printing those embarrassing things?—we must drop them trippingly from the tongue and take the chances:

> During the last ten months our losses have been 268 killed and 750 wounded; Filipino loss, *three thousand two hundred and twenty-seven killed,* and 694 wounded.

Killed ratio higher than wounded — unprovoked [handwritten annotation]

We must stand ready to grab the Person Sitting in Darkness, for he will swoon away at this confession, saying, "Good God! those 'niggers' spare their wounded, and the Americans massacre theirs!"

We must bring him to and coax him and coddle him, and assure him that the ways of Providence are best and that it would not become us to find fault with them; and then, to show him that we are only imitators, not originators, we must read the following passage from the letter of an American soldier lad in the Philippines to his mother, published in *Public Opinion,* of Decorah, Iowa, describing the finish of a victorious battle:

"WE NEVER LEFT ONE ALIVE. IF ONE WAS WOUNDED, WE WOULD RUN OUR BAYONETS THROUGH HIM." *explains casually figures* [handwritten annotation]

Having now laid all the historical facts before the Person Sitting in Darkness, we should bring him to again and explain them to him. We should say to him:

"They look doubtful but in reality they are not. There have been lies, yes, but they were told in a good cause. We have been treacherous, but that was only in order that real good might come out of apparent evil. True, we have crushed a deceived and confiding people; we have turned against the weak and the friendless who trusted us; we have stamped out a just and intelligent and well-ordered republic; we have stabbed an ally in the back and slapped the face of a guest; we have bought a Shadow from an enemy that hadn't it to sell; we have robbed a trusting friend of his land and his liberty; we have invited our clean young men to shoulder a discredited musket and do bandits' work under a flag which bandits have been accustomed to fear, not to follow; we have debauched America's honor and blackened her face before the world; but each detail was for the best. We know this. The Head of

---

[14] Arthur MacArthur (1845–1912), American General in the Spanish-American War and later military governor of the Philippines, from 1900-1901.

every State and Sovereignty in Christendom and 90 per cent of every legislative body in Christendom, including our Congress and our fifty state legislatures, are members not only of the church but also of the Blessings-of-Civilization Trust. This world-girdling accumulation of trained morals, high principles, and justice cannot do an unright thing, an unfair thing, an ungenerous thing, an unclean thing. It knows what it is about. Give yourself no uneasiness; it is all right."

Now then, that will convince the Person. You will see. It will restore the Business. Also, it will elect the Master of the Game to the vacant place in the Trinity of our national gods, and there on their high thrones the Three will sit, age after age, in the people's sight, each bearing the Emblem of his service: Washington, the Sword of the Liberator; Lincoln, the Slave's Broken Chains; the Master, the Chains Repaired.

It will give the Business a splendid new start. You will see.

Everything is prosperous, now; everything is just as we should wish it. We have got the Archipelago, and we shall never give it up. Also, we have every reason to hope that we shall have an opportunity before very long to slip out of our congressional contract with Cuba and give her something better in the place of it. It is a rich country and many of us are already beginning to see that the contract was a sentimental mistake. But now—right now—is the best time to do some profitable rehabilitating work—work that will set us up and make us comfortable, and discourage gossip. We cannot conceal from ourselves that, privately, we are a little troubled about our uniform. It is one of our prides, it is acquainted with honor, it is familiar with great deeds and noble, we love it, we revere it, and so this errand it is on makes us uneasy. And our flag—another pride of ours, our chiefest! We have worshipped it so, and when we have seen it in far lands—glimpsing it unexpectedly in that strange sky, waving its welcome and benediction to us—we have caught our breaths and uncovered our heads and couldn't speak for a moment, for the thought of what it was to us and the great ideals it stood for. Indeed, we *must* do something about these things; it is easily managed. We can have a special one—our states do it: we can have just our usual flag, with the white stripes painted black and the stars replaced by the skull and crossbones.

And we do not need that Civil Commission out there. Having no powers, it has to invent them, and that kind of work cannot be effectively done by just anybody; an expert is required. Mr. Croker[15] can be spared. We do not want the United States represented there, but only the Game.

By help of these suggested amendments, Progress and Civilization in that country can have a boom, and it will take in the Persons who are Sitting in Darkness, and we can resume Business at the old stand.

[15] Richard Croker (1841–1922), New York City political boss.

THE SOUTHERN EXPERIENCE

GEORGE WASHINGTON CABLE

(1844–1925)

Regionalism dominated Southern writing in the decades after the Civil War. Before the war the South had appeared in literature either as a plantation society with the aura of romance and gentility, or as a raw frontier. Now, curiosity was aroused about the variety of peoples and ways of life in the defeated region, about the folkways and customs of blacks, of poor mountain folk, about dispossessed planter-gentlemen and their womenfolk, and about exotic subcultures such as that of the Creoles who inhabited the bayous of Louisiana. Much of the writing that addressed this curiosity reached back into the antebellum period, culled old traditions and legends and, all in all, portrayed a complex and fascinating way of life, one ridden with the curse of racial separation just as it aspired to an ideal of social perfection. A good deal of such writing was filled with nostalgia for an idealized plantation society, but a strain of realistic character study and even of anthropological preservation of old tales and traditions was interfused with the romance and sentimentality.

Both strains are apparent in the skillful, evocative tales about New Orleans Creoles by George Washington Cable. Cable emerged as the chief portraitist of his polyglot city, where the atmospheres of the old and the new worlds mingled. A native of New Orleans, he had fought in the Civil War as a boy of 15 and then worked for a while as a writer for the New Orleans *Picayune* before joining a cotton firm as a book-

The most important works are *Old Creole Days,* 1879; *The Grandissimes,* 1880, rev. 1883; *Madame Delphine,* 1881; *The Creoles of Louisiana,* 1884; *The Silent South,* 1885, enlarged edition, 1889; *The Negro Question,* 1890, enlarged edition, ed. Arlin Turner, 1958.

The definitive biography is Arlin Turner, *George Washington Cable,* 1956. An early account is Lucy Leffingwell Cable Bikle, *George W. Cable: His Life and Letters,* 1928.

Criticism appears in K. Ekström, *George Washington Cable: A Study of His Early Life and Work,* 1950; Guy Cardwell, *Twins of Genius,* 1953; Philip Butcher, *George W. Cable: The Northampton Years,* 1959; C. Vann Woodward, *The Strange Career of Jim Crow,* 1957; Arlin Turner, *Mark Twain and George W. Cable,* 1960; Edmund Wilson, *Patriotic Gore: Studies in the American Civil War,* 1962; Louis D. Rubin, *George W. Cable: The Life and Times of a Southern Heretic,* 1969.

keeper. During his free time he began to dip into the city archives and to pour over old newspapers, steeping himself in the colorful past of the city, particularly the life of the Creoles (American-born descendants of French and Spanish settlers, sometimes with mixed white and black ancestry).

Cable's sketches of the old French Quarter in antebellum days soon attracted attention, and his work began to appear in the prominent Northern journal, *Scribner's Monthly*. The appeal of these tales, collected as *Old Creole Days* (1879), lay in their charming glimpse of a passing way of life, one full of exotic hints and tantalizing mystery. Cable wrote partly in the spirit of high romance, filling his stories with complicated love situations (often tortured by suggestions of mixed blood), with beautiful quadroon women, handsome, dashing young heroes, feuds and stolen inheritances, the separation of families by an intensely strict caste system, and the pathos of disappointed love and lost family honor. But a critical spirit is present in the tales as well; the stubborn pride of the Creoles is often exposed as narrow and cruel, and their code is revealed as often bizarrely unbending. He continued his narratives of old New Orleans in two longer works, *The Grandissimes* (1880) and *Madame Delphine* (1881).

Cable himself became more and more disenchanted with the racial situation in the South and, as his opposition to white supremacy became more open, he decided to move with his family to Northampton, Massachusetts in the 1880's. He spent the last 40 years of his life there, denying that he had been driven from New Orleans because of his Creole portraits and his essays that were sympathetic to the plight of blacks, which were collected in *The Silent South* (1885) and *The Negro Question* (1890). From 1884 to 1886 he had enjoyed a very successful lecture tour with Mark Twain.

Belles Demoiselles Plantation[1]

The original grantee was Count——, assume the name to be DeCharleu; the old Creoles never forgive a public mention. He was the French king's commissary. One day, called to France to explain the lucky accident of the commissariat having burned down with his account-books inside, he left his wife, a Choctaw Comptesse, behind.

[1] First published in *Scribner's Monthly* for April 1874, and later collected in *Old Creole Days*, published in 1879.

Arrived at court, his excuses were accepted, and that tract granted him where afterwards stood Belles Demoiselles Plantation. A man cannot remember every thing! In a fit of forgetfulness he married a French gentlewoman, rich and beautiful, and "brought her out." However, "All's well that ends well;" a famine had been in the colony, and the Choctaw Comptesse had starved, leaving nought but a half-caste orphan family lurking on the edge of the settlement, bearing our French gentlewoman's own new name, and being mentioned in Monsieur's will.

And the new Comptesse—she tarried but a twelve-month, left Monsieur a lovely son, and departed, led out of this vain world by the swamp-fever.

From this son sprang the proud Creole family of De Charleu. It rose straight up, up, up, generation after generation, tall, branchless, slender, palm-like; and finally, in the time of which I am to tell, flowered with all the rare beauty of a century-plant, in Artemise, Innocente, Felicité, the twins Marie and Martha, Leontine and little Septima; the seven beautiful daughters for whom their home had been fitly named Belles Demoiselles.

The Count's grant had once been a long Pointe,[2] round which the Mississippi used to whirl, and seethe, and foam, that it was horrid to behold. Big whirlpools would open and wheel about in the savage eddies under the low bank, and close up again, and others open, and spin, and disappear. Great circles of muddy surface would boil up from hundreds of feet below, and gloss over, and seem to float away,—sink, come back again under water, and with only a soft hiss surge up again, and again drift off, and vanish. Every few minutes the loamy bank would tip down a great load of earth upon its besieger, and fall back a foot,—sometimes a yard,—and the writhing river would press after, until at last the Pointe was quite swallowed up, and the great river glided by in a majestic curve, and asked no more; the bank stood fast, the "caving" became a forgotten misfortune, and the diminished grant was a long, sweeping, willowy bend, rustling with miles of sugar-cane.

Coming up the Mississippi in the sailing craft of those early days, about the time one first could descry the white spires of the old St. Louis Cathedral, you would be pretty sure to spy, just over to your right under the levee, Belles Demoiselles Mansion, with its broad veranda and red painted cypress roof, peering over the embankment, like a bird in the nest, half hid by the avenue of willows which one of the departed De Charleus,—he that married a Marot,—had planted on the levee's crown.

The house stood unusually near the river, facing eastward, and standing four-square, with an immense veranda about its sides, and a flight of steps in front spreading broadly downward, as we open arms to a child. From the veranda nine miles of river were seen; and in their compass, near at hand, the shady garden full of rare and beautiful flowers; farther away broad fields

---

[2] An arrow-shaped cape.

of cane and rice, and the distant quarters of the slaves, and on the horizon everywhere a dark belt of cypress forest.

The master was old Colonel De Charleu,—Jean Albert Henri Joseph De Charleu-Marot, and "Colonel" by the grace of the first American governor. Monsieur,—he would not speak to any one who called him "Colonel,"—was a hoary-headed patriarch. His step was firm, his form erect, his intellect strong and clear, his countenance classic, serene, dignified, commanding, his manners courtly, his voice musical,—fascinating. He had had his vices,—all his life; but had borne them, as his race do, with a serenity of conscience and a cleanness of mouth that left no outward blemish on the surface of the gentleman. He had gambled in Royal Street, drank hard in Orleans Street, run his adversary through in the duelling-ground at Slaughter-house Point, and danced and quarrelled at the St. Philippe-street-theatre quadroon[3] balls. Even now, with all his courtesy and bounty, and a hospitality which seemed to be entertaining angels, he was bitter-proud and penurious, and deep down in his hard-finished heart loved nothing but himself, his name, and his motherless children. But these!—their ravishing beauty was all but excuse enough for the unbounded idolatry of their father. Against these seven goddesses he never rebelled. Had they even required him to defraud old De Carlos— I can hardly say.

Old De Carlos was his extremely distant relative on the Choctaw side. With this single exception, the narrow thread-like line of descent from the Indian wife, diminished to a mere stand by injudicious alliances, and deaths in the gutters of old New Orleans, was extinct. The name, by Spanish contact, had become De Carlos; but this one surviving bearer of it was known to all, and known only, as Injin Charlie.

One thing I never knew a Creole to do. He will not utterly go back on the ties of blood, no matter what sort of knots those ties may be. For one reason, he is never ashamed of his or his father's sins; and for another,—he will tell you—he is "all heart!"

So the different heirs of the De Charleu estate had always strictly regarded the rights and interests of the De Carlos, especially their ownership of a block of dilapidated buildings in a part of the city, which had once been very poor property, but was beginning to be valuable. This block had much more than maintained the last De Carlos through a long and lazy lifetime, and, as his household consisted only of himself, and an aged and crippled negress, the inference was irresistible that he "had money." Old Charlie, though by *alias* an "Injin," was plainly a dark white man, about as old as Colonel De Charleu, sunk in the bliss of deep ignorance, shrewd, deaf, and, by repute at least, unmerciful.

[3] One-fourth Negro. Wealthy white men often "kept" quadroon women, who were forbidden by law to marry white men.

The Colonel and he always conversed in English. This rare accomplishment, which the former had learned from his Scotch wife,—the latter from up-river traders,—they found an admirable medium of communication, answering, better than French could, a similar purpose to that of the stick which we fasten to the bit of one horse and breast-gear of another, whereby each keeps his distance. Once in a while, too, by way of jest, English found its way among the ladies of Belles Demoiselles, always signifying that their sire was about to have business with old Charlie.

Now a long-standing wish to buy out Charlie troubled the Colonel. He had no desire to oust him unfairly; he was proud of being always fair; yet he did long to engross the whole estate under one title. Out of his luxurious idleness he had conceived this desire, and thought little of so slight an obstacle as being already somewhat in debt to old Charlie for money borrowed, and for which Belles Demoiselles was, of course, good, ten times over. Lots, buildings, rents, all, might as well be his, he thought, to give, keep, or destroy. "Had he but the old man's heritage. Ah! he might bring that into existence which his *belles demoiselles* had been begging for, 'since many years;' a home,—and such a home,—in the gay city. Here he should tear down this row of cottages, and make his garden wall; there that long rope-walk should give place to vine-covered arbors; the bakery yonder should make way for a costly conservatory; that wine warehouse should come down, and the mansion go up. It should be the finest in the State. Men should never pass it, but they should say—'the palace of the De Charleus; a family of grand descent, a people of elegance and bounty, a line as old as France, a fine old man, and seven daughters as beautiful as happy; whoever dare attempt to marry there must leave his own name behind him!'

"The house should be of stones fitly set, brought down in ships from the land of 'les Yankees,' and it should have an airy belvedere,[4] with a gilded image tip-toeing and shining on its peak, and from it you should see, far across the gleaming folds of the river, the red roof of Belles Demoiselles, the country-seat. At the big stone gate there should be a porter's lodge, and it should be a privilege even to see the ground."

Truly they were a family fine enough, and fancy-free enough to have fine wishes, yet happy enough where they were, to have had no wish but to live there always.

To those, who, by whatever fortune, wandered into the garden of Belles Demoiselles some summer afternoon as the sky was reddening towards evening, it was lovely to see the family gathered out upon the tiled pavement at the foot of the broad front steps, gayly chatting and jesting, with that ripple of laughter that comes so pleasingly from a bevy of girls. The father would be found seated in their midst, the centre of attention and compliment,

[4] A kind of veranda on top of a house built as a place to sit and admire the view.

witness, arbiter, umpire, critic, by his beautiful children's unanimous appointment, but the single vassal, too, of seven absolute sovereigns.

Now they would draw their chairs near together in eager discussion of some new step in the dance, or the adjustment of some rich adornment. Now they would start about him with excited comments to see the eldest fix a bunch of violets in his button-hole. Now the twins would move down a walk after some unusual flower, and be greeted on their return with the high-pitched notes of delighted feminine surprise.

As evening came on they would draw more quietly about their paternal centre. Often their chairs were forsaken, and they grouped themselves on the lower steps, one above another, and surrendered themselves to the tender influences of the approaching night. At such an hour the passer on the river, already attracted by the dark figures of the broad-roofed mansion, and its woody garden standing against the glowing sunset, would hear the voices of the hidden group rise from the spot in the soft harmonies of an evening song; swelling clearer and clearer as the thrill of music warmed them into feeling, and presently joined by the deeper tones of the father's voice; then, as the daylight passed quite away, all would be still, and he would know that the beautiful home had gathered its nestlings under its wings.

And yet, for mere vagary, it pleased them not to be pleased.

"Arti!" called one sister to another in the broad hall, one morning,—mock amazement in her distended eyes,—"something is goin' to took place!"

"*Comm-e-n-t?*"[5]—long-drawn perplexity.

"Papa is goin' to town!"

The news passed up stairs.

"Inno!"—one to another meeting in a doorway,—"something is goin' to took place!"

"*Qu'est-ce-que c'est!*"[6]—vain attempt at gruffness.

"Papa is goin' to town!"

The unusual tidings were true. It was afternoon of the same day that the Colonel tossed his horse's bridle to his groom, and stepped up to old Charlie, who was sitting on his bench under a China-tree, his head, as was his fashion, bound in a Madras handkerchief. The "old man" was plainly under the effect of spirits, and smiled a deferential salutation without trusting himself to his feet.

"Eh, well Charlie!"—the Colonel raised his voice to suit his kinsman's deafness,—"how is those times with my friend Charlie?"

"Eh?" said Charlie, distractedly.

"Is that goin' well with my friend Charlie?"

"In de house,—call her,"—making a pretence of rising.

"*Non, non!* I don't want,"—the speaker paused to breathe—"ow is collection?"

5 What?

6 What is it?

"Oh!" said Charlie, "every day he make me more poorer!"

"What do you hask for it?" asked the planter indifferently, designating the house by a wave of his whip.

"Ask for w'at?" said Injin Charlie.

"De *house!* What you ask for it?"

"I don't believe," said Charlie.

"What you would *take* for it!" cried the planter.

"Wait for w'at?"

"What you would *take* for the whole block?"

"I don't want to sell him!"

"I'll give you *ten thousand dollah* for it."

"Ten t'ousand dollah for dis house? Oh, no, dat is no price. He is blame good old house,—dat old house." (Old Charlie and the Colonel never swore in presence of each other.) "Forty years dat old house didn't had to be paint! I easy can get fifty t'ousand dollah for dat old house."

"Fifty thousand picayunes;[7] yes," said the Colonel.

"She's a good house. Can make plenty money," pursued the deaf man.

"That's what make you so rich, eh, Charlie?"

"*Non,* I don't make nothing. Too blame clever, me, dat's de troub'. She's a good house,—make money fast like a steamboat,—make a barrel full in a week! Me, I lose money all de days. Too blame clever."

"Charlie!"

"Eh?"

"Tell me what you'll take."

"Make? I don't make *nothing.* Too blame clever."

"What will you *take?*"

"Oh! I got enough already,—half drunk now."

"What will you take for the 'ouse?"

"You want to buy her?"

"I don't know,"—(shrug),—"may*be,*—if you sell it cheap."

"She's a bully old house."

There was a long silence. By and by old Charlie commenced—

"Old Injin Charlie is a low-down dog."

"*C'est vrai, oui!*"[8] retorted the Colonel in an undertone.

"He's got Injin blood in him."

The Colonel nodded assent.

"But he's got some blame good blood, too, ain't it?"

The Colonel nodded impatiently.

"*Bien!* Old Charlie's Injin blood says, 'sell de house, Charlie, you blame old fool!' *Mais,*[9] old Charlie's good blood says, 'Charlie if you sell dat old house, Charlie, you low-down old dog, Charlie, what de Compte De Char-

[7] A Spanish coin worth 6¼ cents.
[8] Yes, that's true.
[9] But.

leu make for you grace-gran'-muzzer, de dev' can eat you, Charlie, I don't care.' "

"But you'll sell it anyhow, won't you, old man?"

"No!" And the *no* rumbled off in muttered oaths like thunder out on the Gulf. The incensed old Colonel wheeled and started off .

"Curl!" (Colonel) said Charlie, standing up unsteadily.

The planter turned with an inquiring frown.

"I'll trade with you!" said Charlie.

The Colonel was tempted. " 'Ow'l you trade?" he asked.

"My house for yours!"

The old Colonel turned pale with anger. He walked very quickly back, and came close up to his kinsman.

"Charlie!" he said.

"Injin Charlie,"—with a tipsy nod.

But by this time self-control was returning. "Sell Belles Demoiselles to you?" he said in a high key, and then laughed "Ho, ho, ho!" and rode away.

A cloud, but not a dark one, overshadowed the spirits of Belles Demoiselles' plantation. The old master, whose beaming presence had always made him a shining Saturn, spinning and sparkling within the bright circle of his daughters, fell into musing fits, started out of frowning reveries, walked often by himself, and heard business from his overseer fretfully.

No wonder. The daughters knew his closeness in trade, and attributed to it his failure to negotiate for the Old Charlie buildings,—so to call them. They began to depreciate Belles Demoiselles. If a north wind blew, it was too cold to ride. If a shower had fallen, it was too muddy to drive. In the morning the garden was wet. In the evening the grasshopper was a burden. *Ennui* was turned into capital; every headache was interpreted a premonition of ague; and when the native exuberance of a flock of ladies without a want or a care burst out in laughter in the father's face, they spread their French eyes, rolled up their little hands, and with rigid wrists and mock vehemence vowed and vowed again that they only laughed at their misery, and should pine to death unless they could move to the sweet city. "Oh! the theatre! Oh! Orleans Street! Oh! the masquerade! the Place d'Armes! the ball!" and they would call upon Heaven with French irreverence, and fall into each other's arms, and whirl down the hall singing a waltz, end with a grand collision and fall, and, their eyes streaming merriment, lay the blame on the slippery floor, that would some day be the death of the whole seven.

Three times more the fond father, thus goaded, managed, by accident,—business accident,—to see old Charlie and increase his offer; but in vain. He finally went to him formally.

"Eh?" said the deaf and distant relative. "For what you want him, eh? Why you don't stay where you halways be 'appy? Dis is a blame old rat-hole,—good for old Injin Charlie,—da's all. Why you don't stay where you be halways 'appy? Why you don't buy somewheres else?"

"That's none of your business," snapped the planter. Truth was, his reasons were unsatisfactory even to himself.

A sullen silence followed. Then Charlie spoke:

"Well, now, look here; I sell you old Charlie's house."

"*Bien!* and the whole block," said the Colonel.

"Hold on," said Charlie. "I sell you de 'ouse and de block. Den I go and git drunk, and go to sleep; de dev' comes along and says, 'Charlie! old Charlie, you blame low-down old dog, wake up! What you doin' here? Where's de 'ouse what Monsieur le Compte give your grace-gran-muzzer?' Don't you see dat fine gentyman, De Charleu, done gone and tore him down and make him over new, you blame old fool, Charlie, you low-down old Injin dog!' "

"I'll give you forty thousand dollars," said the Colonel.

"For de 'ouse?"

"For all."

The deaf man shook his head.

"Forty-five!" said the Colonel.

"What a lie? For what you tell me 'What a lie?' I don't tell you no lie."

"*Non, non!* I give you *forty-five!*" shouted the Colonel.

Charlie shook his head again.

"Fifty!"

He shook it again.

The figures rose and rose to—

"Seventy-five!"

The answer was an invitation to go away and let the owner alone, as he was, in certain specified respects, the vilest of living creatures, and no company for a fine gentyman.

The "fine gentyman" longed to blaspheme,—but before old Charlie!—in the name of pride, how could he? He mounted and started away.

"Tell you what I'll make wid you," said Charlie.

The other, guessing aright, turned back without dismounting, smiling.

"How much Belles Demoiselles hoes me now?" asked the deaf one.

"One hundred and eighty thousand dollars," said the Colonel, firmly.

"Yass," said Charlie. "I don't want Belles Demoiselles."

The old Colonel's quiet laugh intimated it made no difference either way.

"But me," continued Charlie, "me,—I'm got le Compte De Charleu's blood in me, any'ow,—a litt' bit, any'ow, ain't it?"

The Colonel nodded that it was.

"*Bien!* If I go out of dis place and don't go to Belles Demoiselles, de peoples will say,—dey will say, 'Old Charlie he been all doze time tell a blame *lie!* He ain't no kin to his old grace-gran-muzzer, not a blame bit! He don't got nary drop of De Charleu blood to save his blame low-down old Injin soul! No, sare! What I want wid money, den? No, sare! My place for yours!"

He turned to go into the house, just too soon to see the Colonel make an ugly whisk at him with his riding-whip. Then the Colonel, too, moved off.

Two or three times over, as he ambled homeward, laughter broke through his annoyance, as he recalled old Charlie's family pride and the presumption of his offer. Yet each time he could but think better of—not the offer to swap, but the preposterous ancestral loyalty. It was so much better than he could have expected from his "low-down" relative, and not unlike his own whim withal—the proposition which went with it was forgiven.

This last defeat bore so harshly on the master of Belles Demoiselles, that the daughters, reading chagrin in his face, began to repent. They loved their father as daughters can, and when they saw their pretended dejection harassing him seriously they restrained their complaints, displayed more than ordinary tenderness, and heroically and ostentatiously concluded there was no place like Belles Demoiselles. But the new mood touched him more than the old, and only refined his discontent. Here was a man, rich without the care of riches, free from any real trouble, happiness as native to his house as perfume to his garden, deliberately, as it were with premeditated malice, taking joy by the shoulder and bidding her be gone to town, whither he might easily have followed, only that the very same ancestral nonsense that kept Injin Charlie from selling the old place for twice its value prevented him from choosing any other spot for a city home.

But by and by the charm of nature and the merry hearts around him prevailed; the fit of exalted sulks passed off, and after a while the year flared up at Christmas, flickered, and went out.

New Year came and passed; the beautiful garden of Belles Demoiselles put on its spring attire; the seven fair sisters moved from rose to rose; the cloud of discontent had warmed into invisible vapor in the rich sunlight of family affection, and on the common memory the only scar of last year's wound was old Charlie's sheer impertinence in crossing the caprice of the De Charleus. The cup of gladness seemed to fill with the filling of the river.

How high that river was! Its tremendous current rolled and tumbled and spun along, hustling the long funeral flotillas of drift,—and how near shore it came! Men were out day and night, watching the levee. On windy nights even the old Colonel took part, and grew light-hearted with occupation and excitement, as every minute the river threw a white arm over the levee's top, as though it would vault over. But all held fast, and, as the summer drifted in, the water sunk down into its banks and looked quite incapable of harm.

On a summer afternoon of uncommon mildness, old Colonel Jean Albert Henri Joseph De Charleu-Marot, being in a mood for revery, slipped the custody of his feminine rulers and sought the crown of the levee, where it was his wont to promenade. Presently he sat upon a stone bench,—a favorite seat. Before him lay his broad-spread fields; near by, his lordly mansion; and being still,—perhaps by female contact,—somewhat sentimental, he fell to musing on his past. It was hardly worthy to be proud of. All its morning was reddened with mad frolic, and far toward the meridian it was marred with elegant rioting. Pride had kept him well-nigh useless, and despised the honors won by valor; gaming had dimmed prosperity; death had taken his heavenly wife; voluptuous ease had mortgaged his lands; and yet his house still stood, his sweet-smelling fields were still fruitful, his name was fame enough; and yonder and yonder, among the trees and flowers, like angels walking in Eden, were the seven goddesses of his only worship.

Just then a slight sound behind him brought him to his feet. He cast his eyes anxiously to the outer edge of the little strip of bank between the levee's base and the river. There was nothing visible. He paused, with his ear toward the water, his face full of frightened expectation. Ha! There came a single plashing sound, like some great beast slipping into the river, and little waves in a wide semicircle came out from under the bank and spread over the water!

"My God!"

He plunged down the levee and bounded through the low weeds to the edge of the bank. It was sheer, and the water about four feet below. He did not stand quite on the edge, but fell upon his knees a couple of yards away, wringing his hands, moaning and weeping, and staring through his watery eyes at a fine, long crevice just discernible under the matted grass, and curving outward on either hand toward the river.

"My God!" he sobbed aloud; "my God!" and even while he called, his God answered: the tough Bermuda grass stretched and snapped, the crevice slowly became a gape, and softly, gradually, with no sound but the closing of the water at last, a ton or more of earth settled into the boiling eddy and disappeared.

At the same instant a pulse of the breeze brought from the garden behind, the joyous, thoughtless laughter of the fair mistresses of Belles Demoiselles.

The old Colonel sprang up and clambered over the levee. Then forcing himself to a more composed movement, he hastened into the house and ordered his horse.

"Tell my children to make merry while I am gone," he left word.

"I shall be back to-night," and the horse's hoofs clattered down a by-road leading to the city.

"Charlie," said the planter, riding up to a window, from which the old man's nightcap was thrust out, "what you say, Charlie,—my house for yours, eh, Charlie—what you say?"

"Ello!" said Charlie; "from where you come from dis time of to-night?"

"I come from the Exchange[10] in St. Louis Street." (A small fraction of the truth.)

[10] In New Orleans the saloons were called "exchanges."

"What you want?" said matter-of-fact Charlie.

"I come to trade."

The low-down relative drew the worsted[11] off his ears. "Oh! yass," he said with an uncertain air.

"Well, old man Charlie, what you say: my house for yours,—like you said,—eh, Charlie?"

"I dunno," said Charlie; "it's nearly mine now. Why you don't stay dare youse'f?"

"*Because I don't want!*" said the Colonel savagely. "Is dat reason enough for you? You better take me in de notion, old man, I tell you,—yes!"

Charlie never winced; but how his answer delighted the Colonel! Quoth Charlie:

"I don't care—I take him!—*mais*, possession give right off."

"Not the whole plantation, Charlie; only"—

"I don't care," said Charlie; "we easy can fix dat. *Mais*, what for you don't want to keep him? I don't want him. You better keep him."

"Don't you try to make no fool of me, old man," cried the planter.

"Oh, no!" said the other. "Oh, no! but you make a fool of yourself, ain't it?"

The dumbfounded Colonel stared; Charlie went on:

"Yass! Belles Demoiselles is more wort' dan tree block like dis one. I pass by dare since two weeks. Oh, pritty Belles Demoiselles! De cane was wave in de wind, de garden smell like a bouquet, de white-cap was jump up and down on de river; seven *belles demoiselles* was ridin' on horses. 'Pritty, pritty, pritty!' says old Charlie. Ah! *Monsieur le père*, 'ow 'appy, 'appy, 'appy!"

"Yass!" he continued—the Colonel still staring—"le Compte De Charleu have two familie. One was low-down Choctaw, one was high up *noblesse*. He gave the low-down Choctaw dis old rat-hole; he give Belles Demoiselles to you gran-fozzer; and now you don't be *satisfait*. What I'll do wid Belles Demoiselles? She'll break me in two years, yass. And what you'll do wid old Charlie's house, eh? You'll tear her down and make you'se'f a blame old fool. I rather wouldn't trade!"

The planter caught a big breathful of anger, but Charlie went straight on:

"I rather wouldn't, *mais* I will do it for you;—just the same, like Monsieur le Compte would say, 'Charlie, you old fool, I want to shange houses wid you.'"

So long as the Colonel suspected irony he was angry, but as Charlie seemed, after all, to be certainly in earnest, he began to feel conscience-stricken. He was by no means a tender man, but his lately discovered misfortune had unhinged him, and this strange, undeserved, disinterested family fealty on the part of Charlie touched his heart. And should he still try to lead

[11] Night cap.

him into the pitfall he had dug? He hesitated;—no, he would show him the place by broad daylight, and if he chose to overlook the "caving bank," it would be his own fault;—a trade's a trade.

"Come," said the planter, "come at my house to-night; to-morrow we look at the place before breakfast, and finish the trade."

"For what?" said Charlie.

"Oh, because I got to come in town in the morning."

"I don't want," said Charlie. "How I'm goin' to come dere?"

"I git you a horse at the liberty stable."

"Well—anyhow—I don't care—I'll go." And they went.

When they had ridden a long time, and were on the road darkened by hedges of Cherokee rose, the Colonel called behind him to the "low-down" scion:

"Keep the road, old man."

"Eh?"

"Keep the road."

"Oh, yes all right; I keep my word; we don't goin' to play no tricks, eh?"

But the Colonel seemed not to hear. His ungenerous design was beginning to be hateful to him. Not only old Charlie's unprovoked goodness was prevailing; the eulogy on Belles Demoiselles had stirred the depths of an intense love for his beautiful home. True, if he held to it, the caving of the bank, at its present fearful speed, would let the house into the river within three months; but were it not better to lose it so, than sell his birthright? Again,—coming back to the first thought,—to betray his own blood! It was only Injin Charlie; but had not the De Charleu blood just spoken out in him? Unconsciously he groaned.

After a time they struck a path approaching the plantation in the rear, and a little after, passing from behind a clump of live-oaks, they came in sight of the villa. It looked so like a gem, shining through its dark grove, so like a great glow-worm in the dense foliage, so significant of luxury and gayety, that the poor master, from an overflowing heart, groaned again.

"What?" asked Charlie.

The Colonel only drew his rein, and, dismounting mechanically, contemplated the sight before him. The high, arched doors and windows were thrown wide to the summer air; from every opening the bright light of numerous candelabra darted out upon the sparkling foliage of magnolia and bay, and here and there in the spacious verandas a colored lantern swayed in the gentle breeze. A sound of revel fell on the ear, the music of harps; and across one window, brighter than the rest, flitted, once or twice, the shadows of dancers. But oh! the shadows flitting across the heart of the fair mansion's master!

"Old Charlie," said he, gazing fondly at his house, "You and me is both old, eh?"

"Yaas," said the stolid Charlie.

"And we has both been bad enough in our time, eh, Charlie?"

Charlie, surprised at the tender tone, repeated "Yaas."

"And you and me is might close?"

"Blame close, yaas."

"But you never know me to cheat, old man!"

"No,"—impassively.

"And do you think I would cheat you now?"

"I dunno," said Charlie. "I don't believe."

"Well, old man, old man,"—his voice began to quiver,—"I sha'n't cheat you now. My God!—old man, I tell you—you better not make the trade!"

"Because for what?" asked Charlie in plain anger; but both looked quickly toward the house! The Colonel tossed his hands wildly in the air, rushed forward a step or two, and giving one fearful scream of agony and fright, fell forward on his face in the path. Old Charlie stood transfixed with horror. Belles Demoiselles, the realm of maiden beauty, the home of merriment, the house of dancing, all in the tremor and glow of pleasure, suddenly sank, with one short, wild wail of terror—sunk, sunk, down, down, down, into the merciless, unfathomable flood of the Mississippi.

Twelve long months were midnight to the mind of the childless father; when they were only half gone, he took his bed; and every day, and every night, old Charlie, the "low-down," the "fool," watched him tenderly, tended him lovingly, for the sake of his name, his misfortunes, and his broken heart. No woman's step crossed the floor of the sick-chamber, whose western dormer-windows overpeered the dingy architecture of old Charlie's block; Charlie and a skilled physician, the one all interest, the other all gentleness, hope, and patience—these only entered by the door; but by the window came in a sweet-scented evergreen vine, transplanted from the caving bank of Belles Demoiselles. It caught the rays of sunset in its flowery net and let them softly in upon the sick man's bed; gathered the glancing beams of the moon at midnight, and often wakened the sleeper to look, with his mindless eyes, upon their pretty silvery fragments strewn upon the floor.

By and by there seemed—there was—a twinkling dawn of returning reason. Slowly, peacefully, with an increase unseen from day to day, the light of reason came into the eyes, and speech became coherent; but withal there came a failing of the wrecked body, and the doctor said that monsieur was both better and worse.

One evening, as Charlie sat by the vine-clad window with his fireless pipe in his hand, the old Colonel's eyes fell full upon his own, and rested there.

"Charl—," he said with an effort, and his delighted nurse hastened to the bedside and bowed his best ear. There was an unsuccessful effort or two, and then he whispered, smiling with sweet sadness,—

"We didn't trade."

The truth, in this case, a secondary matter to Charlie; the main point was to give a pleasing answer. So he nodded his head decidedly, as who should say—"Oh yes, we did, it was a bonafide swap!" but when he saw the smile vanish, he tried the other expedient and shook his head with still more vigor, to signify that they had not so much as approached a bargain; and the smile returned.

Charlie wanted to see the vine recognized. He stepped backward to the window with a broad smile, shook the foliage, nodded and looked smart.

"I know," said the Colonel, with beaming eyes, "—many weeks."

The next day—

"Charl—"

The best ear went down.

"Send for a priest."

The priest came, and was alone with him a whole afternoon. When he left, the patient was very haggard and exhausted, but smiled and would not suffer the crucifix to be removed from his breast.

One more morning came. Just before dawn Charlie, lying on a pallet in the room, thought he was called, and came to the bedside.

"Old man," whispered the failing invalid, "is it caving yet?"

Charlie nodded.

"It won't pay you out."

"Oh, dat makes not'ing," said Charlie. Two big tears rolled down his brown face. "Dat makes not'in."

The Colonel whispered once more:

"*Mes belles demoiselles!* in paradise;—in the garden—I shall be with them at sunrise;" and so it was.

1874, 1879

The Freedman's Case In Equity[1]

The greatest social problem before the American people to-day is, as it has been for a hundred years, the presence among us of the negro.

No comparable entanglement was ever drawn round itself by any other modern nation with so serene a disregard of its ultimate issue, or with a more distinct national responsibility. The African slave was brought here by cruel force, and with everybody's consent except his own. Everywhere the practice was favored as a measure of common aggrandizement. When a few men and women protested, they were mobbed in the public interest, with the public consent. There rests, therefore, a moral responsibility on the whole nation never to lose sight of the results of African-American slavery until they cease to work mischief and injustice.

[1] First published in *The Silent South,* C. Scribner's Sons, New York, 1885.

It is true these responsibilities may not fall everywhere with the same weight; but they are nowhere entirely removed. The original seed of trouble was sown with the full knowledge and consent of the nation. The nation was to blame; and so long as evils spring from it, the correction must be the nation's duty.

The late Southern slave has within two decades risen from slavery to freedom, from freedom to citizenship, passed on to political ascendency, and fallen again from that eminence. The amended Constitution holds him up in his new political rights as well as a mere constitution can. On the other hand, certain enactments of Congress, trying to reach further, have lately been made void by the highest court of the nation.[2] And another thing has happened. The popular mind in the old free States, weary of strife at arm's length, bewildered by its complications, vexed by many a blunder, eager to turn to the cure of other evils, and even tinctured by that race feeling whose grosser excesses it would so gladly see suppressed, has retreated from its uncomfortable dictational attitude and thrown the whole matter over to the States of the South. Here it rests, no longer a main party issue, but a group of questions which are to be settled by each of these States separately in the light of simple equity and morals, and which the genius of American government does not admit of being forced upon them from beyond their borders. Thus the whole question, become secondary in party contest, has yet reached a period of supreme importance.

Before slavery ever became a grave question in the nation's politics— when it seemed each State's private affair, developing unmolested,—it had two different fates in two different parts of the country. In one, treated as a question of public equity, it withered away. In the other, overlooked in that aspect, it petrified and became the corner-stone of the whole social structure; and when men sought its overthrow as a national evil, it first brought war upon the land, and then grafted into the citizenship of one of the most intelligent nations in the world six millions of people from one of the most debased races of the globe.

And now this painful and wearisome question, sown in the African slave-trade, reaped in our civil war, and garnered in the national adoption of millions of an inferior race, is drawing near a second seed-time. For this is what the impatient proposal to make it a dead and buried issue really means. It means to recommit it to the silence and concealment of the covered furrow. Beyond that incubative retirement no suppressed moral question can be pushed; but all such questions, ignored in the domain of private morals, spring up and expand once more into questions of public equity; neglected

---

[2] The "second civil rights bill" of 1875 was declared unconstitutional by the U.S. Supreme Court in 1883. It had sought to enforce Negro equality in railways, hotels, the-aters, and public places and, as a result of the Supreme Court ruling, Jim Crow laws were passed in almost every Southern state.

as matters of public equity, they blossom into questions of national interest; and, despised in that guise, presently yield the red fruits of revolution.

This question must never again bear the fruit. There must arise, nay, there has arisen, in the South itself, a desire to see established the equity of the issue; to make it no longer a question of endurance between one group of States and another, but between the moral debris of an exploded evil and the duty, necessity, and value of planting society firmly upon universal justice and equity. This, and this only, can give the matter final burial. True, it is still a question between States; but only secondarily, as something formerly participated in, or as it concerns every householder to know that what is being built against his house is built by level and plummet. It is the interest of the Southern States first, and *consequently* of the whole land, to discover clearly these equities and the errors that are being committed against them.

If we take up this task, the difficulties of the situation are plain. We have, first, a revision of Southern State laws which has forced into them the recognition of certain human rights discordant with the sentiments of those who have always called themselves the community; second, the removal of the entire political machinery by which this forcing process was effected; and, third, these revisions left to be interpreted and applied under the domination of these antagonistic sentiments. These being the three terms of the problem, one of three things must result. There will arise a system of vicious evasions eventually ruinous to public and private morals and liberty, or there will be a candid reconsideration of the sentiments hostile to these enactments, or else there will be a division, some taking one course and some the other.

·   ·   ·

It will be wise to remember that these were the acts [of persecution] of an enlightened, God-fearing people, the great mass of whom have passed beyond all earthly accountability. They were our fathers. I am the son and grandson of the slave-holders. These were their faults; posterity will discover ours; but these things must be frankly, fearlessly taken into account if we are ever to understand the true interests of our peculiar state of society.

Why, then, did this notion, that the man of color must always remain an alien, stand so unshaken? We may readily recall how, under ancient systems, he rose not only to high privileges, but often to public station and power. Singularly, with us the trouble lay in a modern principle of liberty. The whole idea of American government rested on all men's equal, inalienable right to secure their life, liberty, and the pursuit of happiness by governments founded in their own consent. Hence, our Southern forefathers, shedding their blood, or ready to shed it, for this principle, yet proposing in equal good conscience to continue holding the American black man and mulatto and quadroon in slavery, had to anchor that conscience, their conduct, and their laws in the conviction that the man of African tincture was, not by his master's arbitrary assertion merely, but by nature and unalterably, an alien. If that hold should break, one single wave of irresistible inference would lift our whole Southern social fabric and dash it upon the rocks of negro emancipation and enfranchisement. How was it made secure? Not by books, though they were written among us from every possible point of view, but, with the mass of our slave-owners, by the calm hypothesis of a positive, intuitive knowledge. To them the statement was an axiom. They abandoned · the methods of moral and intellectual reasoning, and fell back upon this assumption of a God-given instinct, nobler than reason, and which it was an insult to a freeman to ask him to prove on logical grounds.

Yet it was found not enough. The slave multiplied. Slavery was a dangerous institution. Few in the South to-day have any just idea how often the slave plotted for his freedom. Our Southern ancestors were a noble, manly people, springing from some of the most highly intelligent, aspiring, upright, and refined nations of the modern world; from the Hugenot,[3] the French Chevalier, the Old Englander, the New Englander. Their acts were not always right; whose are? But for their peace of mind they had to believe them so. They therefore spoke much of the negro's contentment with that servile condition for which nature had designed him. Yet there was no escaping the knowledge that we dared not trust the slave caste with any power that could be withheld from them. So the perpetual alien was made also a perpetual menial, and the belief became fixed that this, too, was nature's decree, not ours.

Thus we stood at the close of the civil war. There were always a few Southerners who did not justify slavery, and many who cared nothing whether it was just or not. But what we have described was the general sentiment of good Southern people. There was one modifying sentiment. It related to the slave's spiritual interests. Thousands of pious masters and mistresses flatly broke the shameful laws that stood between their slaves and the Bible. Slavery was right; but religion, they held, was for the alien and menial as well as for the citizen and master. They could be alien and citizen, menial and master, in church as well as out; and they were.

Yet over against this lay another root of to-day's difficulties. This perpetuation of the alien, menial relation tended to perpetuate the vices that naturally cling to servility, dense ignorance and a hopeless separation from true liberty; and as we could not find it in our minds to blame slavery with this perpetuation, we could only assume as a further axiom that there was, by nature, a disqualifying moral taint in every drop of negro blood. The testimony of an Irish, German, Italian, French, or Spanish beggar in a court of justice was taken on its merits; but the colored man's was excluded by law

[3] A French Protestant persecuted during the religious wars of the sixteenth and seventeenth centuries.

wherever it weighed against a white man. The colored man was a prejudged culprit. The discipline of the plantation required that the difference between master and slave be never lost sight of by either. It made our master caste a solid mass, and fixed a common masterhood and subserviency between the ruling and the serving race.[4] Every one of us grew up in the idea that he had, by birth and race, certain broad powers of police over any and every person of color.

.   .   .

Thus we reach the ultimate question of fact. Are the freedman's liberties suffering any real abridgment? The answer is easy. The letter of the laws, with a few exceptions, recognizes him as entitled to every right of an American citizen; and to some it may seem unimportant that there is scarcely one public relation of life in the South where he is not arbitrarily and unlawfully compelled to hold toward the white man the attitude of an alien, a menial, and a probable reprobate, by reason of his race and color. One of the marvels of future history will be that it was counted a small matter, by a majority of our nation, for six millions of people within it, made by its own decree a component part of it, to be subjected to a system of oppression so rank that nothing could make it seem small except the fact that they had already been ground under it for a century and a half.

Examine it. It proffers to the freedman a certain security of life and property, and then holds the respect of the community, that dearest of earthly boons, beyond his attainment. It gives him certain guarantees against thieves and robbers, and then holds him under the unearned contumely of the mass of good men and women. It acknowledges in constitutions and statutes his title to an American's freedom and aspirations, and then in daily practice heaps upon him in every public place the most odious distinctions, without giving ear to the humblest plea concerning mental or moral character. It spurns his ambition, tramples upon his languishing self-respect, and indignantly refuses to let him either buy with money, or earn by any excellence of inner life or outward behavior, the most momentary immunity from these public indignities even for his wife and daughters. Need we cram these pages with facts in evidence, as if these were charges denied and requiring to be proven? They are simply the present avowed and defended state of affairs peeled of its exteriors.

Nothing but the habit, generations old, of enduring it could make it endurable by men not in actual slavery. Were we whites of the South to remain

---

[4] The old Louisiana Black Code says, "That free people of color ought never to . . . presume to conceive themselves equal to the white; but, on the contrary, that they ought to yield to them in every occasion, and never speak or answer to them but with respect, under the penalty of imprisonment according to the nature of the offense." (*Section 21*, p. 164.)

every way as we are, and our six million blacks to give place to any sort of whites exactly their equals, man for man, in mind, morals, and wealth, provided only that they had tasted two years of American freedom, and were this same system of tyrannies attempted upon them, there would be as bloody an uprising as this continent has ever seen. We can say this quietly. There is not a scruple's weight of present danger. These six million freedmen are dominated by nine million whites immeasurably stronger than they, backed by the virtual consent of thirty odd millions more. Indeed, nothing but the habit of oppression could make such oppression possible to a people of the intelligence and virtue of our Southern whites, and the invitation to practice it on millions of any other than the children of former slaves would be spurned with a noble indignation.

Suppose, for a moment, the tables turned. Suppose the courts of our Southern States, while changing no laws requiring the impaneling of jurymen without distinction as to race, etc., should suddenly begin to draw their thousands of jurymen all black, and well-nigh every one of them counting not only himself, but all his race, better than any white man. Assuming that their average of intelligence and morals should be not below that of jurymen as now drawn, would a white man, for all that, choose to be tried in one of those courts? Would he suspect nothing? Could one persuade him that his chances of even justice were all that they should be, or all they would be were the court not evading the law in order to sustain an outrageous distinction against him because of the accidents of his birth? Yet only read white man for black man, and black man for white man, and that—I speak as an eye-witness—has been the practice for years, and is still so to-day; an actual emasculation, in the case of six million people both as plaintiff and defendant, of the right of trial by jury.

· · ·

See its every-day working. Any colored man gains unquestioned admission into innumerable places the moment he appears as the menial attendant of some white person, where he could not cross the threshold in his own right as a well-dressed and well-behaved master of himself. The contrast is even greater in the case of colored women. There could not be a system which when put into practice would more offensively condemn itself. It does more: it actually creates the confusion it pretends to prevent. It blunts the sensibilities of the ruling class themselves. It waives all strict demand for painstaking in either manners or dress of either master or menial, and, for one result, makes the average Southern railway coach more uncomfortable than the average of railway coaches elsewhere. It prompts the average Southern white passenger to find less offense in the presence of a profane, boisterous, or unclean white person than in that of a quiet, well-behaved colored man or woman attempting to travel on an equal footing with him without a white master or mistress. The holders of the old sentiments hold the opposite choice in scorn. It is only when we go on to say that there are regions where the riotous expulsion of a decent and peaceable colored person is preferred to his inoffensive company, that it may seem necessary to bring in evidence. And yet here again it is *prima facie* evidence; for the following extract was printed in the Selma (Alabama) "Times" not six months ago, and not as a complaint, but as a boast:

> A few days since, a negro minister, of this city, boarded the east-bound passenger train on the E.T., V. and G. Railway and took a seat in the coach occupied by white passengers. Some of the passengers complained to the conductor and brakemen, and expressed considerable dissatisfaction that they were forced to ride alongside of a negro. The railroad official informed the complainants that they were not authorized to force the colored passenger into the coach set apart for negroes, and they would lay themselves liable should they do so. The white passengers then took the matter in their own hands and ordered the ebony-hued minister to take a seat in the next coach. He positively refused to obey orders, whereupon the white men gave him a sound flogging and forced him to a seat among his own color and equals. We learned yesterday that the vanquished preacher was unable to fill his pulpit on account of the severe chastisement inflicted upon him. Now [says the delighted editor] the query that puzzles is, "Who did the flogging?"

And as good an answer as we can give is that likely enough they were some of the men for whom the whole South has come to a halt to let them get over the "feelings engendered by the war." Must such men, such acts, such sentiments, stand alone to represent us of the South before an enlightened world? No. I say, as a citizen of an extreme Southern State, a native of Louisiana, an ex-Confederate soldier, and a lover of my home, my city, and my State, as well as of my country, that this is not the best sentiment in the South, nor the sentiment of her best intelligence; and that it would not ride up and down that beautiful land dominating and domineering were it not for its tremendous power as the *traditional* sentiment of a conservative people. But is not silent endurance criminal? I cannot but repeat my own words, spoken near the scene and about the time of this event. Speech may be silver and silence golden; but if a lump of gold is only big enough, it can drag us to the bottom of the sea and hold us there while all the world sails over us.

. . .

A far pleasanter aspect of our subject shows itself when we turn from courts and prisons to the school-house. And the explanation is simple. Were our educational affairs in the hands of that not high average of the community commonly seen in jury-boxes, with their transient sense of accountability and their crude notions of public interests, there would most likely be no such pleasant contrast. But with us of the South, as elsewhere, there is a fairly honest effort to keep the public-school interests in the hands of the State's most highly trained intelligence. Hence our public educational work is a compromise between the unprogressive prejudices of the general mass of the whites and the progressive intelligence of their best minds. Practically, through the great majority of our higher education officers, we are fairly converted to the imperative necessity of elevating the colored man intellectually, and are beginning to see very plainly that the whole community is sinned against in every act or attitude of oppression, however gross or however refined.

Yet one thing must be said. I believe it is wise that all have agreed not to handicap education with the race question, but to make a complete surrender of that issue, and let it find adjustment elsewhere first and in the schools last. And yet, in simple truth and justice and in the kindest spirit, we ought to file one exception for that inevitable hour when the whole question must be met. There can be no more real justice in pursuing the freedman's children with humiliating arbitrary distinctions and separations in the schoolhouses than in putting them upon him in other places. If, growing out of their peculiar mental structure, there are good and just reasons for their isolation, by all means let them be proved and known; but it is simply tyrannous to assume them without proof. I know that just here looms up the huge bugbear of Social Equality. Our eyes are filled with absurd visions of all Shanty-town pouring its hordes of unwashed imps into the company and companionship of our sunny-headed darlings. What utter nonsense! As if our public schools had no gauge of cleanliness, decorum, or moral character! Social Equality! What a godsend it would be if the advocates of the old Southern regime could only see that the color line points straight in the direction of social equality by tending toward the equalization of all whites on one side and all blacks on the other. We may reach the moon some day, not social equality; but the only class that really effects anything toward it are the makers and holders of arbitrary and artificial social distinctions interfering with society's natural self-distribution. Even the little children everywhere are taught, and begin to learn almost with their A B C, that they will find, and must be guided by, the same variations of the social scale in the public school as out of it; and it is no small mistake to put them or their parents off their guard by this cheap separation on the line of color.

But some will say that this is not a purely artifical distinction. We hear much about race instinct. The most of it, I fear, is pure twaddle. It may be there is no such thing. We do not know. It is not proved. And even if it were established, it would not necessarily be a proper moral guide. We subordinate instinct to society's best interests as apprehended in the light of reason.

If there is such a thing, it behaves with strange malignity toward the remnants of African blood in individuals principally of our own race, and with singular indulgence to the descendants of—for example—Pocahontas.[5] Of mere race *feeling* we all know there is no scarcity. Who is a stranger to it? And as another man's motive of private preference no one has a right to forbid it or require it. But as to its being an instinct, one thing is plain: if there is such an instinct, so far from excusing the malignant indignities practiced in its name, it furnishes their final condemnation; for it stands to reason that just in degree as it is a real thing it will take care of itself.

It has often been seen to do so, whether it is real or imaginary. I have seen in New Orleans a Sunday-school of white children every Sunday afternoon take possession of its two rooms immediately upon their being vacated by a black school of equal or somewhat larger numbers. The teachers of the colored school are both white and black, and among the white teachers are young ladies and gentlemen of the highest social standing. The pupils of the two schools are alike neatly attired, orderly, and in every respect inoffensive to each other. I have seen the two races sitting in the same public high-school and grammar-school rooms, reciting in the same classes and taking recess on the same ground at the same time, without one particle of detriment that any one ever pretended to discover, although the fiercest enemies of the system swarmed about it on every side. And when in the light of these observations I reflect upon the enormous educational test our Southern States have before them, the inadequacy of their own means for performing it, the hoped-for beneficence of the general Government, the sparseness with which so much of our Southern population is distributed over the land, the thousands of school districts where, consequently, the multiplication of schools must involve both increase of expense and reductions of efficiency, I must enter some demurrer to the enforcement of the tyrannous sentiments of the old régime until wise experiments have established better reasons than I have yet heard given.

What need to say more? The question is answered. Is the freedman a free man? No. We have considered his position in a land whence nothing can, and no man has a shadow of right to drive him, and where he is being multiplied as only oppression can multiply a people. We have carefully analyzed his relations to the finer and prouder race, with which he shares the ownership and citizenship of a region large enough for ten times the number of both. Without accepting one word of his testimony, we have shown that the laws made for his protection against the habits of suspicion and oppres-

---

[5] An Indian princess who, legend has it, saved the life of Captain John Smith when he had been made an Indian prisoner. She was converted to Christianity and married an English gentleman, John Rolfe, at Jamestown in 1614. She was received by the King and Queen of England in London in 1616, and some people are proud to claim her as an ancestor.

Charleston mammy with her charge, c. 1889. *Library of Congress.*

sion in his late master are being constantly set aside, not for their defects, but for such merit as they possess. We have shown that the very natural source of these oppressions is the surviving sentiments of an extinct and now universally execrated institution; sentiments which no intelligent or moral people should harbor a moment after the admission that slavery was a moral mistake. We have shown the outrageousness of these tyrannies in some of their workings, and how distinctly they antagonize every State and national interest involved in the elevation of the colored race. Is it not well to have done so? For, I say again, the question has reached a moment of special importance. The South stands on her honor before the clean equities of the issue. It is no longer whether constitutional amendments, but whether the eternal principles of justice, are violated. And the answer must—it shall—come from the South. And it shall be practical. It will not cost much. We have had a strange experience: the withholding of simple rights has cost much blood; such concessions of them as we have made have never yet cost a drop. The answer is coming. Is politics in the way? Then let it clear the track or get run over, just as it prefers. But, as I have said over and over to my brethren in the South, I take upon me to say again here, that there is a moral and intellectual intelligence there which is not going to be much longer beguiled out of its moral right of way by questions of political punctilio, but will seek that plane of universal justice and equity which it is every people's duty before God to seek, not along the line of politics,—God forbid!—but across it and across it and across it as many times as it may lie across its path, until the whole people of every once slaveholding State can stand up as one man, saying, "Is the freedman a free man?" and the whole world shall answer, "Yes."

1885

JOEL CHANDLER HARRIS

(1848–1908)

Outside of the work of Mark Twain, the portrayal of black characters by white writers in this period rarely succeeded in getting beyond the level of stereotype. Set most often in antebellum days, many of the stories that appeared in the South after the war showed plantation life in a romantic and idealized light, with black people as ignorant, shiftless, and content with their lot as slaves. Harris also placed his very popular Uncle Remus tales in a romantic plantation world free of any sign of conflict or of the harsh realities of slavery. By drawing on the rich traditions of legend and folklore among blacks and by effectively impersonating the dialect of the black storyteller, he gave his stories an air of authenticity. Harris himself grew up as a poor boy in rural Georgia and called on his childhood memories in creating Uncle Remus, the wise old house servant with a bag full of tales about personified animals like Brer Rabbit, Brer Fox, and Brer B'ar. The tales are clearly parables about human life and convey the folk wisdom and shrewdness through which the underdog (usually the cunning Brer Rabbit) outwits his larger, usually dim-witted persecutors. In other works such as "Free Joe and the Rest of the World" Harris reveals that he well understood that cruelty and hardship were common facts in the life of the slave.

Harris had little schooling as a youth. He worked as a printer, and eventually joined the influential Atlanta *Constitution,* where his first Uncle Remus story appeared in 1879. Although best known for his works based on collections and retellings of folklore, legend, and proverbs, he also wrote a considerable body of fiction portraying a wide range of social types in the postwar South, including stories

The major works are *Uncle Remus: His Sons and His Sayings,* 1881; *Nights with Uncle Remus,* 1883; *Uncle Remus and His Friends,* 1892; *Told by Uncle Remus,* 1905; *Uncle Remus and the Little Boy,* 1910; *Free Joe and Other Georgian Sketches,* 1887; *Balaam and His Master,* 1891; *Tales of the Home Folks in Peace and War,* 1898; *The Chronicles of Aunt Minervy Ann,* 1899.

The most complete biography is Julia F. C. Harris, *The Life and Letters of Joel Chandler Harris,* 1918. A recent treatment is Paul M. Cousins, *Joel Chandler Harris, A Biography,* 1968; see also Robert L. Wiggins, *The Life of Joel Chandler Harris,* 1918, and *Joel Chandler Harris (Uncle Remus): Plantation Storyteller,* 1941.

Criticism includes Stella B. Brookes, *Joel Chandler Harris: Folklorist,* 1950; Darwin T. Turner, "Daddy Joel Harris and His Old-Time Darkies," *Southern Literary Journal* (1968).

about poor whites and aristocrats. He remained with the *Constitution,* which advocated a progressive policy of reconciliation with the North, until 1900.

From Uncle Remus: His Songs and His Sayings

OLD MR. RABBIT, HE'S A GOOD FISHERMAN[1]

"Brer Rabbit en Brer Fox wuz like some chilluns w'at I knows un," said Uncle Remus, regarding the little boy, who had come to hear another story, with an affectation of great solemnity. "Bofe un um wuz allers atter wunner nudder, a prankin' en a pester'n 'roun', but Brer Rabbit did had some peace, kaze Brer Fox done got skittish 'bout puttin' de clamps on Brer Rabbit.

"One day, w'en Brer Rabbit, en Brer Fox, en Brer Coon, en Brer B'ar, en a whole lot un um wuz clearin' up a new groun' fer ter plant a roas'n'year patch, de sun 'gun ter git sorter hot, en Brer Rabbit he got tired; but he didn't let on, kaze he 'fear'd de balance un um'd call 'im lazy, en he keep on totin' off trash en pilin' up bresh, twel bimeby he holler out dat he gotter brier in his han', en den he take'n slip off, en hunt fer cool place fer ter res'. Atter w'ile he come 'crosst a well wid a bucket hangin' in it.

" 'Dat look cool,' sez Brer Rabbit, sezee, 'en cool I speck she is. I'll des 'bout git in dar en take a nap,' en wid dat in he jump, he did, en he ain't no sooner fix hisse'f dan de bucket 'gun ter go down."

"Wasn't the Rabbit scared, Uncle Remus?" asked the little boy.

"Honey, dey ain't no wusser skeer'd beas' sence de worril begin dan dish yer same Brer Rabbit. He fa'rly had a ager.[2] He know whar he cum fum, but he dunner whar he gwine. Dreckly he feel de bucket hit de water, en dar she sot, but Brer Rabbit he keep mighty still, kaze he dunner w'at minnit gwineter be de nex'. He des lay dar en shuck en shiver.

"Brer Fox allers got one eye on Brer Rabbit, en w'en he slip off fum de new groun', Brer Fox he sneak atter 'im. He know Brer Rabbit wuz atter some projick er nudder, en he tuck'n crope off, he did, en watch 'im. Brer Fox see Brer Rabbit come to de well en stop, en den he sees 'im jump in de bucket, en den, lo en beholes, he see 'im go down outer sight. Brer Fox wuz de mos' 'stonish Fox dat you ever laid eyes on. He sot off dar in de bushes en study en study, but he don't make no head ner tails ter dis kinder bizness. Den he say ter hisse'f, sezee:

" 'Well, ef dis don't bang my times.' sezee, 'den Joe's dead en Sal's a

---

[1] First published in *Uncle Remus: His Songs and His Sayings* in 1880

[2] Ague; a fit of trembling.

widder. Right down dar in dat well Brer Rabbit keep his money hid, en ef 'tain't dat den he done gone en 'skiver'd a gole-mine, en ef 'tain't dat, den I'm a gwineter see w'at's in dar,' sezee.

"Brer Fox crope up a little nigher, he did, en lissen, but he don't year no fuss, en he keep on gittin' higher, en yit he don't year nuthin'. Bimeby he git up close en peep down, but he don't see nuthin' en he don't year nuthin'. All dis time Brer Rabbit mighty nigh skeer'd outen his skin, en he fear'd fer ter move kaze de bucket might keel over en spill him out in de water. W'ile he sayin' his pra'rs over like a train er kyars runnin', old Brer Fox holler out:

" 'Heyo, Brer Rabbit! Who you wizzitin' down dar?' sezee.

" 'Who? Me? Oh, I'm des a fishin', Brer Fox,' sez Brer Rabbit, sezee. 'I des sayter myse'f dat I'd sorter sprize you wid a mess er fishes fer dinner, en so here I is, en dar's de fishes. I'm a fishin' fer suckers, Brer Fox,' sez Brer Rabbit, sezee.

" 'Is dey many un um down dar, Brer Rabbit?' sez Brer Fox, sezee.

" 'Lots un um, Brer Fox; scoze en scoze un um. De water is natally live wid um. Come down en he'p me haul um in, Brer Fox,' sez Brer Rabbit, sezee.

" 'How I gwineter git down, Brer Rabbit?'

" 'Jump inter de bucket, Brer Fox. Hit'll fetch you down all safe en soun'.'

"Brer Rabbit talk so happy en talk so sweet dat Brer Fox he jump in de bucket, he did, en, ez he went down, co'se his weight pull Brer Rabbit up. W'en dey pass one nudder on de half-way groun', Brer Rabbit he sing out:

'Good-by, Brer Fox, take keer yo' cloze,
Fer dis is de way de worril goes;
Some goes up en some goes down,
You'll git ter der bottom all safe en soun'.'[3]

"W'en Brer Rabbit got out, he gallop off en tole de fokes w'at de well b'long ter dat Brer Fox wuz down in dar muddyin' up de drinkin' water, en den he gallop back ter de well, en holler down ter Brer Fox:

'Yer come a man wid a great big gun—
W'en he haul you up, you jump en run.' "

"What then, Uncle Remus?" asked the little boy, as the old man paused.

"In des 'bout half n'our, honey, bofe un um wuz back in de new groun' wukkin des like dey never heer'd er no well, ceppin' dat eve'y now'n den Brer Rabbit'd bust out in er laff, en old Brer Fox, he'd git a spell er de dry grins."

[3] As a Northern Friend suggests that this story may be somewhat obscure, it may be as well to state that the well is supposed to be supplied with a rope over a wheel, or pulley, with a bucket at each end. [Harris's note.]

Free Joe and the Rest of the World [1]

Suspect

The name of Free Joe strikes humorously upon the ear of memory. It is impossible to say why, for he was the humblest, the simplest, and the most serious of all God's living creatures, sadly lacking in all those elements that suggest the humorous. It is certain, moreover, that in 1850 [2] the sober-minded citizens of the little Georgian village of Hillsborough were not inclined to take a humorous view of Free Joe, and neither his name nor his presence provoked a smile. He was a black atom, drifting hither and thither without an owner, blown about by all the winds of circumstance, and given over to shiftlessness.

The problems of one generation are the paradoxes of a succeeding one, particularly if war, or some such incident, intervenes to clarify the atmosphere and strengthen the understanding. Thus, in 1850, Free Joe represented not only a problem of large concern, but, in the watchful eyes of Hillsborough, he was the embodiment of that vague and mysterious danger that seemed to be forever lurking on the outskirts of slavery, ready to sound a shrill and ghostly signal in the impenetrable swamps, and steal forth under the midnight stars to murder, rapine, and pillage—a danger always threatening, and yet never assuming shape; intangible, and yet real; impossible, and yet not improbable. Across the serene and smiling front of safety, the pale outlines of the awful shadow of insurrection sometimes fell. With this invisible panorama as a background, it was natural that the figure of Free Joe, simple and humble as it was, should assume undue proportions. Go where he would, do what he might, he could not escape the finger of observation and the kindling eye of suspicion. His lightest words were noted, his slightest actions marked.

Under all the circumstances it was natural that his peculiar condition should reflect itself in his habits and manners. The slaves laughed loudly day by day, but Free Joe rarely laughed. The slaves sang at their work and danced at their frolics, but no one ever heard Free Joe sing or saw him dance. There was something painfully plaintive and appealing in his attitude, something touching in his anxiety to please. He was of the friendliest nature, and seemed to be delighted when he could amuse the little children who had made a playground of the public square. At times he would please them by making his little dog Dan perform all sorts of curious tricks, or he would tell them quaint stories of the beasts of the field and birds of the air; and frequently he was coaxed into relating the story of his own freedom. That story was brief, but tragical.

Stacks cards in favour of racial justice

[1] First published in *Free Joe and Other Sketches* in 1887.
[2] The Fugitive Slave Act of 1850—requiring that escaped slaves be returned to their masters in the South—enflamed already existing tensions, North and South.

In the year of our Lord 1840, when a negro speculator of a sportive turn of mind reached the little village of Hillsborough on his way to the Mississippi region, with a caravan of likely negroes of both sexes, he found much to interest him. In that day and at that time there were a number of young men in the village who had not bound themselves over to repentance for the various misdeeds of the flesh. To these young men the negro speculator (Major Frampton was his name) proceeded to address himself. He was a Virginian, he declared; and, to prove the statement, he referred all the festively inclined young men of Hillsborough to a barrel of peach-brandy in one of his covered wagons. In the minds of these young men there was less doubt in regard to the age and quality of the brandy than there was in regard to the negro trader's birthplace. Major Frampton might or might not have been born in the Old Dominion—that was a matter for consideration and inquiry—but there could be no question as to the mellow pungency of the peach-brandy.

In his own estimation, Major Frampton was one of the most accomplished of men. He had summered at the Virginia Springs; he had been to Philadelphia, to Washington, to Richmond, to Lynchburg, and to Charleston, and had accumulated a great deal of experience which he found useful. Hillsborough was hid in the woods of Middle Georgia, and its general aspect of innocence impressed him. He looked on the young men who had shown their readiness to test his peach-brandy as overgrown country boys who needed to be introduced to some of the arts and sciences he had at his command. Thereupon the major pitched his tents, figuratively speaking, and became, for the time being, a part and parcel of the innocence that characterized Hillsborough. A wiser man would doubtless have made the same mistake.

The little village possessed advantages that seemed to be providentially arranged to fit the various enterprises that Major Frampton had in view. There was the auction block in front of the stuccoed court-house, if he desired to dispose of a few of his negroes; there was a quarter-track, laid out to his hand and in excellent order, if he chose to enjoy the pleasures of horse-racing; there were secluded pine thickets within easy reach, if he desired to indulge in the exciting pastime of cock-fighting; and variously lonely and unoccupied rooms in the second story of the tavern, if he cared to challenge the chances of dice or cards.

Major Frampton tried them all with varying luck, until he began his famous game of poker with Judge Alfred Wellington, a stately gentleman with a flowing white beard and mild blue eyes that gave him the appearance of a benevolent patriarch. The history of the game in which Major Frampton and Judge Alfred Wellington took part is something more than a tradition in Hillsborough, for there are still living three or four men who sat around the table and watched its progress. It is said that at various stages of the game Major Frampton would destroy the cards with which they were playing, and send for a new pack, but the result was always the same. The mild blue eyes of Judge Wellington, with few exceptions, continued to overlook "hands" that were invincible—a habit they had acquired during a long and arduous course of training from Saratoga to New Orleans. Major Frampton lost his money, his horses, his wagons, and all his negroes but one, his body-servant. When his misfortune had reached this limit, the major adjourned the game. The sun was shining brightly, and all nature was cheerful. It is said that the major also seemed to be cheerful. However this may be, he visited the court-house, and executed the papers that gave his body-servant his freedom. This being done, Major Frampton sauntered into a convenient pine thicket, and blew out his brains.

The negro thus freed came to be known as Free Joe. Compelled, under the law, to choose a guardian, he chose Judge Wellington, chiefly because his wife Lucinda was among the negroes won from Major Frampton. For several years Free Joe had what may be called a jovial time. His wife Lucinda was well provided for, and he found it a comparatively easy matter to provide for himself; so that, taking all the circumstances into consideration, it is not matter for astonishment that he became somewhat shiftless.

When Judge Wellington died, Free Joe's troubles began. The judge's negroes, including Lucinda, went to his half-brother, a man named Calderwood, who was a hard master and a rough customer generally—a man of many eccentricities of mind and character. His neighbors had a habit of alluding to him as "Old Spite"; and the name seemed to fit him so completely that he was known far and near as "Spite" Calderwood. He probably enjoyed the distinction the name gave him, at any rate he never resented it, and it was not often that he missed an opportunity to show that he deserved it. Calderwood's place was two or three miles from the village of Hillsborough, and Free Joe visited his wife twice a week, Wednesday and Saturday nights.

One Sunday he was sitting in front of Lucinda's cabin, when Calderwood happened to pass that way.

"Howdy, marster?" said Free Joe, taking off his hat.

"Who are you?" exclaimed Calderwood abruptly, halting and staring at the negro.

"I'm name' Joe, marster. I'm Lucindy's ole man."

"Who do you belong to?"

"Marse John Evans is my gyardeen, marster."

"Big name—gyardeen. Show your pass."

Free Joe produced that document, and Calderwood read it aloud slowly, as if he found it difficult to get at the meaning:

"To whom it may concern: This is to certify that the boy Joe Frampton has my permission to visit his wife Lucinda."

This was dated at Hillsborough, and signed "John W. Evans."

Calderwood read it twice, and then looked at Free Joe, elevating his eyebrows, and showing his discolored teeth.

"Some mighty big words in that there. Evans owns this place, I reckon. When's he comin' down to take hold?"

Free Joe fumbled with his hat. He was badly frightened.

"Lucindy say she speck you wouldn't min' my comin', long ez I behave, marster."

Calderwood tore the pass in pieces and flung it away.

"Don't want no free niggers 'round here," he exclaimed. "There's the big road. It'll carry you to town. Don't let me catch you here no more. Now, mind what I tell you."

Free Joe presented a shabby spectacle as he moved off with his little dog Dan slinking at his heels. It should be said in behalf of Dan, however, that his bristles were up, and that he looked back and growled. It may be that the dog had the advantage of insignificance, but it is difficult to conceive how a dog bold enough to raise his bristles under Calderwood's very eyes could be as insignificant as Free Joe. But both the negro and his little dog seemed to give a new and more dismal aspect to forlornness as they turned into the road and went toward Hillsborough.

After this incident Free Joe appeared to have clearer ideas concerning his peculiar condition. He realized the fact that though he was free he was more helpless than any slave. Having no owner, every man was his master. He knew that he was the object of suspicion, and therefore all his slender resources (ah! how pitifully slender they were!) were devoted to winning, not kindness and appreciation, but toleration; all his efforts were in the direction of mitigating the circumstances that tended to make his condition so much worse than that of the negroes around him—negroes who had friends because they had masters.

So far as his own race was concerned, Free Joe was an exile. If the slaves secretly envied him his freedom (which is to be doubted, considering his miserable condition), they openly despised him, and lost no opportunity to treat him with contumely. Perhaps this was in some measure the result of the attitude which Free Joe chose to maintain toward them. No doubt his instinct taught him that to hold himself aloof from the slaves would be to invite from the whites the toleration which he coveted, and without which even his miserable condition would be rendered more miserable still.

His greatest trouble was the fact that he was not allowed to visit his wife; but he soon found a way out of his difficulty. After he had been ordered away from the Calderwood place, he was in the habit of wandering as far in that direction as prudence would permit. Near the Calderwood place, but not on Calderwood's land, lived an old man named Micajah Staley and his sister Becky Staley. These people were old and very poor. Old Micajah had a palsied arm and hand; but, in spite of this, he managed to earn a precarious living with his turning-lathe.

When he was a slave Free Joe would have scorned these representatives of a class known as poor white trash, but now he found them sympathetic and helpful in various ways. From the back door of their cabin he could hear the Calderwood negroes singing at night, and he sometimes fancied he could distinguish Lucinda's shrill treble rising above the other voices. A large poplar grew in the woods some distance from the Staley cabin, and at the foot of this tree Free Joe would sit for hours with his face turned toward Calderwood's. His little dog Dan would curl up in the leaves near by, and the two seemed to be as comfortable as possible.

One Saturday afternoon Free Joe, sitting at the foot of this friendly poplar, fell asleep. How long he slept, he could not tell; but when he awoke little Dan was licking his face, the moon was shining brightly, and Lucinda his wife stood before him laughing. The dog, seeing that Free Joe was asleep, had grown somewhat impatient, and he concluded to make an excursion to the Calderwood place on his own account. Lucinda was inclined to give the incident a twist in the direction of superstition.

"I 'uz settn' down front er de fireplace," she said, "cookin' me some meat, w'en all of a sudden I year sumpin at de do'—scratch, scratch. I tuck'n tu'n de meat over, en make out I ain't year it. Bimeby it come dar 'gin—scratch, scratch. I up en open de do', I did, en, bless de Lord! dar wuz little Dan, en it look like ter me dat his ribs done grow terge'er. I gin 'im some bread, en den, w'en he start out, I tuck'n foller 'im, kaze, I say ter myse'f, maybe my nigger man mought be some'rs 'roun'. Dat ar little dog got sense, mon."

Free Joe laughed and dropped his hand lightly on Dan's head. For a long time after that he had no difficulty in seeing his wife. He had only to sit by the poplar tree until little Dan could run and fetch her. But after a while the other negroes discovered that Lucinda was meeting Free Joe in the woods, and information of the fact soon reached Calderwood's ears. Calderwood was what is called a man of action. He said nothing; but one day he put Lucinda in his buggy, and carried her to Macon, sixty miles away. He carried her to Macon, and came back without her; and nobody in or around Hillsborough, or in that section, ever saw her again.

For many a night after that Free Joe sat in the woods and waited. Little Dan would run merrily off and be gone a long time, but he always came back without Lucinda. This happened over and over again. The "willis-whistlers" would call and call, like fantom huntsmen wandering on a far-off shore; the screech-owl would shake and shiver in the depths of the woods; the night-hawks, sweeping by on noiseless wings, would snap their beaks as though they enjoyed the huge joke of which Free Joe and little Dan were the victims; and the whip-poor-wills would cry to each other through the gloom. Each night seemed to be lonelier than the preceding, but Free Joe's patience was proof against loneliness. There came a time, however, when little Dan refused to go after Lucinda. When Free Joe motioned him in the direction of the Calderwood place, he would simply move about uneasily and whine; then he would curl up in the leaves and make himself comfortable.

One night, instead of going to the poplar tree to wait for Lucinda, Free Joe went to the Staley cabin, and, in order to make his welcome good, as he expressed it, he carried with him an armful of fat-pine splinters. Miss Becky Staley had a great reputation in those parts as a fortune-teller, and the schoolgirls, as well as older people, often tested her powers in this direction, some in jest and some in earnest. Free Joe placed his humble offering of light-wood in the chimney corner, and then seated himself on the steps, dropping his hat on the ground outside.

"Miss Becky," he said presently, "whar in de name er gracious you reckon Lucindy is?"

"Well, the Lord he'p the nigger!" exclaimed Miss Becky, in a tone that seemed to reproduce, by some curious agreement of sight with sound, her general aspect of peakedness. "Well, the Lord he'p the nigger! hain't you been a-seein' her all this blessed time? She's over at old Spite Calderwood's, if she's anywheres, I reckon."

"No'm, dat I ain't, Miss Becky. I ain't seen Lucindy in now gwine on mighty nigh a mont'."

"Well, it hain't a-gwine to hurt you," said Miss Becky, somewhat sharply. "In my day an' time it wuz allers took to be a bad sign when niggers got to honeyin' 'roun' an' gwine on."

"Yessum," said Free Joe, cheerfully assenting to the proposition— "yessum, dat's so, but me an' my ole 'oman, we 'uz raise terge'er, en dey ain't bin many days w'en we 'uz 'way fum one 'n'er like we is now."

"Maybe she's up an' took up wi' some un else," said Micajah Staley from the corner. "You know what the sayin' is: 'New master, new nigger.'"

"Dat's so, dat's de sayin', but tain't wid my ole 'oman like 'tis wid yuther niggers. Me en her wuz des natally raise up terge'er. Dey's lots likelier niggers dan w'at I is," said Free Joe, viewing his shabbiness with a critical eye, "but I knows Lucindy mos' good ez I does little Dan dar—dat I does."

There was no reply to this, and Free Joe continued:

"Miss Becky, I wish you please, ma'am, take en run yo' kyards en see sump'n n'er 'bout Lucindy; kaze ef she sick, I'm gwine dar. Dey ken take me up en gimme a stroppin', but I'm gwine dar."

Miss Becky got her cards, but first she picked up a cup, in the bottom of which were some coffee-grounds. These she whirled slowly round and round, ending finally by turning the cup upside down on the hearth and allowing it to remain in that position.

"I'll turn the cup first," said Miss Becky, "and then I'll run the cards and see what they say."

As she shuffled the cards the fire on the hearth burned low, and in its fitful light the gray-haired, thin-featured woman seemed to deserve the weird reputation which rumor and gossip had given her. She shuffled the cards for some moments, gazing intently in the dying fire; then, throwing a piece of pine on the coals, she made three divisions of the pack, disposing them about in her lap. Then she took the first pile, ran the cards slowly through her fingers, and studied them carefully. To the first she added the second pile. The study of these was evidently not satisfactory. She said nothing, but frowned heavily; and the frown deepened as she added the rest of the cards until the entire fifty-two had passed in review before her. Though she frowned, she seemed to be deeply interested. Without changing the relative position of the cards, she ran them all over again. Then she threw a larger piece of pine on the fire, shuffled the cards afresh, divided them into three piles, and subjected them to the same careful and critical examination.

"I can't tell the day when I've seed the cards run this a-way," she said after a while. "What is an' what ain't, I'll never tell you; but I know what the cards sez."

"W'at does dey say, Miss Becky?" the negro inquired, in a tone the solemnity of which was heightened by its eagerness.

"They er runnin' quare. These here that I'm a-lookin' at," said Miss Becky, "they stan' for the past. Them there, they er the present; and the t'others, they er the future. Here's a bundle"—tapping the ace of clubs with her thumb—"an' here's a journey as plain as the nose on a man's face. Here's Lucinda—"

"Whar she, Miss Becky?"

"Here she is—the queen of spades."

Free Joe grinned. The idea seemed to please him immensely.

"Well, well, well!" he exclaimed. "Ef dat don't beat my time! De queen er spades! W'en Lucindy year dat hit'll tickle 'er, sho'!"

Miss Becky continued to run the cards back and forth through her fingers.

"Here's a bundle an' a journey, and here's Lucinda. An' here's ole Spite Calderwood."

She held the cards toward the negro and touched the king of clubs.

"De Lord he'p my soul!" exclaimed Free Joe with a chuckle. "De faver's[3] dar. Yesser, dat's him! W'at de matter 'long wid all un um, Miss Becky?"

The old woman added the second pile of cards to the first, and then the third, still running them through her fingers slowly and critically. By this time the piece of pine in the fireplace had wrapped itself in a mantle of flame, illuminating the cabin and throwing into strange relief the figure of Miss Becky as she sat studying the cards. She frowned ominously at the cards and mumbled a few words to herself. Then she dropped her hands in her lap and gazed once more into the fire. Her shadow danced and capered on the wall and floor behind her, as if, looking over her shoulder into the future, it could behold a rare spectacle. After a while she picked up the cup that had

---

[3] Resembled.

been turned on the hearth. The coffee grounds, shaken around, presented what seemed to be a most intricate map.

"Here's the journey," said Miss Becky, presently; "here's the big road, here's rivers to cross, here's the bundle to tote." She paused and sighed. "They hain't no names writ here, an' what it all means I'll never tell you. Cajy, I wish you'd be so good as to han' me my pipe."

"I hain't no hand wi' the kyards," said Cajy, as he handed the pipe, "but I reckon I can patch out your misinformation, Becky, bekaze the other day, whiles I was a-finishin' up Mizzers Perdue's rollin'-pin, I hearn a rattlin' in the road. I looked out, an' Spite Calderwood was a-drivin' by in his buggy, an' thar sot Lucinda by him. It'd in-about drapt out er my min'."

Free Joe sat on the door-sill and fumbled at his hat, flinging it from one hand to the other.

"You ain't see um gwine back, is you, Mars Cajy?" he asked after a while.

"Ef they went back by this road," said Mr. Staley, with the air of one who is accustomed to weigh well his words, "it must 'a' bin endurin' of the time whiles I was asleep, bekaze I hain't bin no furder from my shop than to yon bed."

"Well, sir!" exclaimed Free Joe in an awed tone, which Mr. Staley seemed to regard as a tribute to his extraordinary powers of statement.

"Ef it's my beliefs you want," continued the old man, "I'll pitch 'em at you fair and free. My beliefs is that Spite Calderwood is gone an' took Lucindy outen the county. Bless your heart and soul! when Spite Calderwood meets the Old Boy[4] in the road they'll be a turrible scuffle. You mark what I tell you."

Free Joe, still fumbling with his hat, rose and leaned against the door-facing. He seemed to be embarrassed. Presently he said:

"I speck I better be gittin' 'long. Nex' time I see Lucindy, I'm gwine tell 'er w'at Miss Becky say 'bout de queen er spades—dat I is. Ef dat don't tickle 'er, dey ain't no nigger 'oman never bin tickle'."

He paused a moment, as though waiting for some remark or comment, some confirmation of misfortune, or, at the very least, some endorsement of his suggestion that Lucinda would be greatly pleased to know that she had figured as the queen of spades; but neither Miss Becky nor her brother said anything.

"One minnit ridin' in the buggy 'longside er Mars Spite, en de nex' high-falutin' 'roun' playin' de queen er spades. Mon, deze yer nigger gals gittin' up in de pictur's; dey sholy is."

With a brief "Good night, Miss Becky, Mars Cajy," Free Joe went out into the darkness, followed by little Dan. He made his way to the poplar, where Lucinda had been in the habit of meeting him, and sat down. He sat there a long time; he sat there until little Dan, growing restless, trotted off in

[4] The Devil.

the direction of the Calderwood place. Dozing against the poplar, in the gray dawn of the morning, Free Joe heard Spite Calderwood's fox-hounds in full cry a mile away.

"Shoo!" he exclaimed, scratching his head, and laughing to himself, "dem ar dogs is des a-warmin' dat old fox up."

But it was Dan the hounds were after, and the little dog came back no more. Free Joe waited and waited, until he grew tired of waiting. He went back the next night and waited, and for many nights thereafter. His waiting was in vain, and yet he never regarded it as in vain. Careless and shabby as he was, Free Joe was thoughtful enough to have his theory. He was convinced that little Dan had found Lucinda, and that some night when the moon was shining brightly through the trees, the dog would rouse him from his dreams as he sat sleeping at the foot of the poplar tree, and he would open his eyes and behold Lucinda standing over him, laughing merrily as of old; and then he thought what fun they would have about the queen of spades. *sentimentality* [handwritten]

How many long nights Free Joe waited at the foot of the poplar tree for Lucinda and little Dan no one can ever know. He kept no account of them, and they were not recorded by Micajah Staley nor by Miss Becky. The season ran into summer and then into fall. One night he went to the Staley cabin, cut the two old people an armful of wood, and seated himself on the doorsteps, where he rested. He was always thankful—and proud, as it seemed—when Miss Becky gave him a cup of coffee, which she was sometimes thoughtful enough to do. He was especially thankful on this particular night.

"You er still layin' off for to strike up wi' Lucindy out thar in the woods, I reckon," said Micajah Staley, smiling grimly. The situation was not without its humorous aspects.

"Oh, dey er comin', Mars Cajy, dey er comin', sho," Free Joe replied. "I boun' you dey'll come; en w'en dey does come, I'll des take en fetch um yer, whar you kin see um wid you own eyes, you en Miss Becky."

"No," said Mr. Staley, with a quick and emphatic gesture of disapproval. "Don't! don't fetch 'em anywheres. Stay right wi' 'em as long as may be."

Free Joe chuckled, and slipped away into the night, while the two old people sat gazing in the fire. Finally Micajah spoke.

"Look at that nigger; look at 'im. He's pine-blank as happy now as a killdee by a mill-race. You can't faze 'em. I'd in-about give up my t'other hand ef I could stan' flatfooted, an' grin at trouble like that there nigger."

"Niggers is niggers," said Miss Becky, smiling grimly, "an' you can't rub it out; yit I lay I've seed a heap of white people lots meaner'n Free Joe. He grins—an' that's nigger—but I've ketched his under jaw a-tremblin' when Lucindy's name uz brung up. An' I tell you," she went on, bridling up a little, and speaking with almost fierce emphasis, "the Old Boy's done sharpened his claws for Spite Calderwood. You'll see it."

devil [handwritten]

"Me, Rebecca?" said Mr. Staley, hugging his palsied arm; "me? I hope not."

"Well, you'll know it then," said Miss Becky, laughing heartily at her brother's look of alarm.

The next morning Micajah Staley had occasion to go into the woods after a piece of timber. He saw Free Joe sitting at the foot of the poplar, and the sight vexed him somewhat.

"Git up from there," he cried, "an' go an' arn your livin'. A mighty purty pass it's come to, when great big buck niggers can lie a-snorin' in the woods all day, when t'other folks is got to be up an' a-gwine. Git up from there!"

Receiving no response, Mr. Staley went to Free Joe, and shook him by the shoulder; but the negro made no response. He was dead. His hat was off, his head was bent, and a smile was on his face. It was as if he had bowed and smiled when death stood before him, humble to the last. His clothes were ragged; his hands were rough and callous; his shoes were literally tied together with strings; he was shabby in the extreme. A passer-by, glancing at him, could have no idea that such a humble creature had been summoned as a witness before the Lord God of Hosts.

condemnation

1887

Sentimentality - poor wretched creature
shunned outcast, loses wife, dog
yet goes to heave

does no good at all
got poor + old

SIDNEY LANIER

(1842–1881)

Lanier was a richly talented but unfulfilled figure, a scholar and a musician as well as a poet, whose work combines strains of social criticism with romantic aestheticism. Like Poe, he was drawn to science at

The standard edition is Charles R. Anderson, ed., *Centennial Edition of the Works of Sidney Lanier*, 10 vols., 1945. An edition of the letters was compiled by Henry Lanier, *The Letters of Sidney Lanier, 1866–1881*, 1899; see also Mary Day Lanier, ed., *Letters of Sidney Lanier*, 1907. For a complete listing of Lanier's work, see *A Concordance to the Poems of Sidney Lanier*, 1939, eds. Philip Graham and Joseph Jones.

The standard biography is Aubrey Starke, *Sidney Lanier*, 1933. See also Edwin Mims,

Sidney Lanier, 1905; Lincoln Lorenz, *The Life of Sidney Lanier*, 1935, and Jack DeBellis, *Sidney Lanier*, 1972.

For criticism see Allen Tate, "A Southern Romantic," *New Republic*, LXXVI (August 30, 1933); Robert Penn Warren, "The Blind Poet: Sidney Lanier," *American Review*, II (November 1933); John Crowe Ransom, "Hearts and Heads," *American Review*, II (March 1934); Gay Wilson Allen, "Sidney Lanier," *American Prosody* (1935), pp. 277–306; Stanley T. Williams, (Footnote continued next page.)

the same time that he decried abstract rationality and a society based on commerce. Regionalism was not his major literary goal, but he wrote very much as a Southerner, and his native Georgia landscape is a real presence in poems such as "Corn" and "The Marshes of Glynn." A variety of motives and interests, intellectual, social, aesthetic, occupied him during his brief life—he died at the age of 39—and his erudition is not always beneficial to his writing. Yet his poetic voice is original and authentic, and his fine musical ear is always apparent, even if he sometimes strives for effects that are more appropriate to pure music than to poetry.

Born in Macon, Georgia, Lanier was torn between a career in law and one in music during his student days at Oglethorpe University, but the Civil War removed the necessity of an immediate choice. He served as a private in the Confederate Army, was captured and imprisoned for several months at Point Lookout, Maryland, where he developed the tuberculosis that caused his early death. Finding a regular career after the war proved difficult; in the 1870's he moved with his family to Baltimore, where he pieced together an income by playing the flute in the Peabody Orchestra, lecturing on literature and versification at the Johns Hopkins University, and writing. He published an effusive, melodramatic Civil War novel, *Tiger-Lilies* (1867), but he did not receive any recognition until his poems began to appear in Northern journals in the 1870's. He was commissioned to compose a cantata for the Centennial Exhibition in Philadelphia in 1876; the cantata was performed and won him a wider audience.

In *Tiger-Lilies* Lanier had proclaimed an ideal of chivalric behavior against what he described as the degrading influence of commerce or "trade." "Trade" reappears throughout his later work as an evil against which he opposes a rather eclectic ideal of agrarian idealism (anticipating the Southern Agrarians of the 1930's), emotionalism (as opposed to the cold calculations of the marketplace), and aestheticism. The conflict between the natural and nourishing crop of corn, and the market crop of cotton, in the poem "Corn," is a good example of his point of view, indicating the strain of social criticism that runs through his work.

Another strain is represented by the title of his treatise, *The Science of English Verse*, written in 1880 shortly before his death. In this work he attempted a reconciliation of science and art, searching for a scien-

"Experiments in Poetry: Sidney Lanier and Emily Dickinson," *A Literary History of the United States,* eds. Robert Spiller et al. 1948; Darrell Abel, "Sidney Lanier," *American Literature,* II (1963); Philip Graham, "Sidney Lanier and the Pattern of Contrast," *American Quarterly,* XI (Winter 1956); Roy Harvey Pearce, *The Continuity of American Poetry,* 1961.

tific foundation for prosody. Like Poe, he believed that poetry is essentially a form of music and, in the spirit of scientific experimentation, he tried to uncover laws of identity between the two kinds of expression. His efforts to fuse poetry and music in his own verse often result in lush but overwrought, misty lines. At his best, he is capable of delicate melodies and sensitive, evocative imagery. Lanier was never able to bring all of his talents and interests together in a single lasting work; his early death cut him off from any major literary effort. Yet his poems remain valuable expressions of both a regional and a cosmopolitan sensibility in Southern writing in this period.

The Marshes of Glynn[1]

Glooms of the live-oaks, beautiful-braided and woven
With intricate shades of the vines that myriad-cloven
   Clamber the forks of the multiform boughs,—
      Emerald twilights,—
      Virginal shy lights,   5

Wrought of the leaves to allure to the whisper of vows,
When lovers pace timidly down through the green colonnades
Of the dim sweet woods, of the dear dark woods,
   Of the heavenly woods and glades,
That run to the radiant marginal sand-beach within   10
   The wide sea-marshes of Glynn;—

Beautiful glooms, soft dusks in the noon-day fire,—
Wildwood privacies, closets of lone desire,
Chamber from chamber parted with wavering arras[2] of leaves,—
Cells for the passionate pleasure of prayer to the soul that grieves,   15
Pure with a sense of the passing of saints through the wood,
Cool for the dutiful weighing of ill with good;—

O braided dusks of the oak and woven shades of the vine,
While the riotous noon-day sun of the June-day long did shine
Ye held me fast in your heart and I held you fast in mine;   20
But now when the noon is no more, and riot is rest,
And the sun is a-wait at the ponderous gate of the West,
And the slant yellow beam down the wood-aisle doth seem
Like a lane into heaven that leads from a dream,—
Ay, now, when my soul all day hath drunken the soul of the oak,—   25

[1] First published in *A Masque of Poets* in 1878.   [2] Tapestries.

And my heart is at ease from men, and the wearisome sound of the
    stroke
  Of the scythe of time and the trowel of trade is low,
  And belief overmasters doubt, and I know that I know,
  And my spirit is grown to a lordly great compass within,
That the length and the breadth and the sweep of the marshes of
    Glynn   30
Will work me no fear like the fear they have wrought me of yore
When length was fatigue, and when breadth was but bitterness sore,
And when terror and shrinking and dreary unnamable pain
Drew over me out of the merciless miles of the plain,—

Oh, now, unafraid, I am fain to face   35
  The vast sweet visage of space.
To the edge of the wood I am drawn, I am drawn,
Where the gray beach glimmering runs, as a belt of the dawn,
  For a mete and a mark
  To the forest-dark:—   40
             So:

Affable live-oak, leaning low,—
Thus—with your favor—soft, with a reverent hand,
(Not lightly touching your person, Lord of the land!)
Bending your beauty aside, with a step I stand   45
On the firm-packed sand,
            Free
By a world of marsh that borders a world of sea.
  Sinuous southward and sinuous northward the shimmering band
Of the sand-beach fastens the fringe of the marsh to the folds of the
    land.   50
Inward and outward to northward and southward the beach-lines
    linger and curl
As a silver-wrought garment that clings to and follows the firm sweet
    limbs of a girl.
Vanishing, swerving, evermore curving again into sight,
Softly the sand-beach wavers away to a dim gray looping of light.
And what if behind me to westward the wall of the woods stands
    high?   55
The world lies east: how ample, the marsh and the sea and the sky!
A league and a league of marsh-grass, waist-high, broad in the blade,
Green, and all of a height, and unflecked with a light or a shade,
Stretch leisurely off, in a pleasant plain,
To the terminal blue of the main.   60

Oh, what is abroad in the marsh and the terminal sea?
  Somehow my soul seems suddenly free
From the weighing of fate and the sad discussion of sin,
By the length and the breadth and the sweep of the marshes of
    Glynn.

Ye marshes, how candid and simple and nothing-withholding and free 65
Ye publish yourselves to the sky and offer yourselves to the sea!
Tolerant plains, that suffer the sea and the rains and the sun,
Ye spread and span like the catholic[3] man who hath mightily won
God out of knowledge and good out of infinite pain
And sight out of blindness and purity out of a stain. 70

As the marsh-hen secretly builds on the watery sod,
Behold I will build me a nest on the greatness of God:
I will fly in the greatness of God as the marsh-hen flies
In the freedom that fills all the space 'twixt the marsh and the skies:
By so many roots as the marsh-grass sends in the sod 75
I will heartily lay me a-hold on the greatness of God:
Oh, like to the greatness of God is the greatness within
The range of the marshes, the liberal marshes of Glynn.

And the sea lends large, as the marsh: lo, out of his plenty the sea
Pours fast: full soon the time of the flood-time must be: 80
Look how the grace of the sea doth go
About and about through the intricate channels that flow
      Here and there,
                        Everywhere,
Till his waters have flooded the uttermost creeks and the low-lying
    lanes, 85
And the marsh is meshed with a million veins,
That like as with rosy and silvery essences flow
  In the rose-and-silver evening glow.
          Farewell, my lord Sun!
The creeks overflow: a thousand rivulets run 90
'Twixt the roots of the sod; the blades of the marsh-grass stir;
Passeth a hurrying sound of wings that westward whirr;
Passeth, and all is still; and the currents cease to run;
And the sea and the marsh are one.

How still the plains of the waters be! 95
The tide is in his ecstasy.
The tide is at his highest height:
          And it is night.

And now from the Vast of the Lord will the waters of sleep

[3] Worldly.

Roll in on the souls of men, 100
But who will reveal to our waking ken
The forms that swim and the shapes that creep
　　　Under the waters of sleep?
And I would I could know what swimmeth below when the tide
　　　comes in
On the length and the breadth of the marvellous marshes of Glynn. 105

1878, 1884

The Symphony[1]

'O Trade! O Trade! would thou wert dead!
The Time needs heart—'tis tired of head:
We're all for love,' the violins said.
'Of what avail the rigorous tale
Of bill for coin and box for bale? 5
Grant thee, O Trade! thine uttermost hope:
Level red gold with blue sky-slope,
And base it deep as devils grope:
When all's done, what hast thou won
Of the only sweet that's under the sun? 10
Ay, canst thou buy a single sigh
Of true love's least, least ecstasy?'
Then, with a bridegroom's heart-beats trembling,
All the mightier strings assembling
Ranged them on the violin's side 15
As when the bridegroom leads the bride,
And, heart in voice, together cried:
'Yea, what avail the endless tale
Of gain by cunning and plus by sale?
Look up the land, look down the land, 20
The poor, the poor, the poor, they stand
Wedged by the pressing of Trade's hand
Against an inward-opening door
That pressure tightens evermore:
They sigh a monstrous foul-air sigh 25
For the outside leagues of liberty,
Where Art, sweet lark, translates the sky
Into a heavenly melody.

[1] First published in *Lippincott's* for June
1875 and later collected in *Poems* in 1877.

"Each day, all day" (these poor folks say),
"In the same old year-long, drear-long way,   30
We weave in the mills and heave in the kilns,
We sieve mine-meshes under the hills,
And thieve much gold from the Devil's bank tills,
To relieve, O God, what manner of ills?—
The beasts, they hunger, and eat, and die;   35
And so do we, and the world's a sty;
Hush, fellow-swine: why nuzzle and cry?
Swinehood hath no remedy
Say many men, and hasten by,
Clamping the nose and blinking the eye.   40
But who said once, in the lordly tone,
Man shall not live by bread alone
But all that cometh from the Throne?[2]
    Hath God said so?
    But Trade saith *No:*   45
And the kilns and the curt-tongued mills say *Go!*
There's plenty that can, if you can't: we know.
Move out, if you think you're underpaid.
The poor are prolific; we're not afraid;
"Trade is trade." '   50
Thereat this passionate protesting
Meekly changed, and softened till
It sank to sad requesting
And suggesting sadder still:
'And oh, if men might some time see   55
How piteous-false the poor decree
That trade no more than trade must be!
Does business mean, *Die, you—live, I?*
Then "Trade is trade" but sings a lie:
'Tis only war grown miserly.   60
If business is battle, name it so:
War-crimes less will shame it so,
And widows less will blame it so.
Alas, for the poor to have some part
In yon sweet living lands of Art,   65
Makes problem not for head, but heart,
Vainly might Plato's brain revolve it:
Plainly the heart of a child could solve it.'

[2] Luke iv:4.

And then, as when from words that seem but rude
We pass to silent pain that sits abrood   70
Back in our heart's great dark and solitude,
So sank the strings to gentle throbbing
Of long chords change-marked with sobbing—
Motherly sobbing, not distinctlier heard
Than half wing-openings of the sleeping bird,   75
Some dream of danger to her young hath stirred.
Then stirring and demurring ceased, and lo!
Every least ripple of the strings' song-flow
Died to a level with each level bow
And made a great chord tranquil-surfaced so,   80
As a brook beneath his curving bank doth go
To linger in the sacred dark and green
Where many boughs the still pool overlean
And many leaves make shadow with their sheen.
   But presently   85
A velvet flute-note fell down pleasantly
Upon the bosom of that harmony,
And sailed and sailed incessantly,
As if a petal from a wild-rose blown
Had flubbered down upon that pool of tone   90
And boatwise dropped o' the convex side
And floated down the glassy tide
And clarified and glorified
The solemn spaces where the shadows bide.
From the warm concave of that fluted note   95
Somewhat, half song, half odor, forth did float,
As if a rose might somehow be a throat.
'When Nature from her far-off glen
Flutes her soft messages to men,
   The flute can say them o'er again;   100
   Yea, Nature, singing sweet and lone,
Breathes through life's strident polyphone[3]
The flute-voice in the world of tone.
   Sweet friends,
   Man's love ascends   105
To finer and diviner ends
Than man's mere thought e'er comprehends,

---

[3] From "polyphony," a musical term for
more than one independent but related voice
parts sounding at once.

For I, e'en I,
As here I lie,
A petal on a harmony,   110
Demand of Science whence and why
Man's tender pain, man's inward cry,
When he doth gaze on earth and sky?
I am not overbold:
    I hold   115
Full powers from Nature manifold.
I speak for each no-tongued tree
That, spring by spring, doth nobler be,
And dumbly and most wistfully
His mighty prayerful arms outspreads   120
Above men's oft-unheeding heads,
And his big blessing downward sheds.
I speak for all-shaped blooms and leaves,
Lichens on stones and moss on eaves,
Grasses and grains in ranks and sheaves;   125
Broad-fronded ferns and keen-leaved canes,
And briery mazes bounding lanes,
And marsh-plants, thirsty-cupped for rains,
And milky stems and sugary veins,
For every long-armed woman-vine   130
That round a piteous tree doth twine;
For passionate odors, and divine
Pistils, and petals crystalline;
All purities of shady springs,
All shynesses of film-winged things   135
That fly from tree-trunks and bark-rings;
All modesties of mountain-fawns
That leap to covert from wild lawns,
And tremble if the day but dawns;
All sparklings of small beady eyes   140
Of birds, and sidelong glances wise
Wherewith the jay hints tragedies;
All piquancies of prickly burs,
And smoothnesses of downs and furs,
Of eiders[4] and of minivers;[5]   145
All limpid honeys that do lie
At stamen-bases, nor deny

[4] Soft feathers from the eider duck.
[5] A lavish white fur used on medieval court
costumes.

The humming-birds' fine roguery,
Bee-thighs, nor any butterfly;
All gracious curves of slender wings,   150
Bark-mottlings, fibre-spiralings,
Fern-wavings and leaf-flickerings;
Each dial-marked leaf and flower-bell
Wherewith in every lonesome dell
Time to himself his hours doth tell;   155
All tree-sounds, rustlings of pine-cones,
Wind-sighings, doves' melodious moans,
And night's unearthly under-tones;
All placid lakes and waveless deeps,
All cool reposing mountain-steeps,   160
Vale-calms and tranquil lotos-sleeps;—
Yea, all fair forms, and sounds, and lights,
And warmths, and mysteries, and mights,
Of Nature's utmost depths and heights.
—These doth my timid tongue present,   165
Their mouthpiece and leal[6] instrument
And servant, all love-eloquent.
I heard, when *All for love* the violins cried:
So, Nature calls through all her system wide,
Give me thy love, O man, so long denied.   170
Much time is run, and man hath changed his ways,
Since Nature, in the antique fable-days,
Was hid from man's true love by proxy fays,
False fauns and rascal gods that stole her praise.
The nymphs, cold creatures of man's colder brain,   175
Chilled Nature's streams till man's warm heart was fain
Never to lave its love in them again.
Later, a sweet Voice *Love thy neighbor* said;
Then first the bounds of neighborhood outspread
Beyond all confines of old ethnic dread.   180
Vainly the Jew might wag his covenant head:
All men are neighbors, so the sweet Voice said.
So, when man's arms had circled all man's race,
The liberal compass of his warm embrace
Stretched bigger yet in the dark bounds of space;   185
With hands a-grope he felt smooth Nature's grace,
Drew her to breast and kissed her sweetheart face:
Yea, man found neighbors in great hills and trees
And streams and clouds and suns and birds and bees,

[6] Loyal.

And throbbed with neighbor-loves in loving these.   190
But oh, the poor! the poor! the poor!
That stand by the inward-opening door
Trade's hand doth tighten ever more,
And sigh their monstrous foul-air sigh
For the ouside hills of liberty,   195
Where Nature spreads her wild blue sky
For Art to make into melody!
Thou Trade! thou king of the modern days!
     Change thy ways,
     Change thy ways: 200
Let the sweaty laborers file
     A little while,
     A little while,
Where Art and Nature sing and smile,
Trade! is thy heart all dead, all dead?   205
And hast thou nothing but a head?
I'm all for heart,' the flute-voice said,
And into sudden silence fled,
Like as a blush that while 'tis red
Dies to a still, still white instead.   210

    Thereto a thrilling calm succeeds,
Till presently the silence breeds
A little breeze among the reeds
That seems to blow by sea-marsh weeds:
Then from the gentle stir and fret   215
Sings out the melting clarionet,
Like as a lady sings while yet
Her eyes with salty tears are wet.
'O Trade! O Trade!' the Lady said,
'I too will wish thee utterly dead   220
If all thy heart is in thy head.
For O my God! and O my God!
What shameful ways have women trod
At beckoning of Trade's golden rod!
Alas when sighs are traders' lies,   225
And heart's-ease eyes and violet eyes
     Are merchandise!
O purchased lips that kiss with pain!
O cheeks coin-spotted with smirch and stain!
O trafficked hearts that break in twain!   230
—And yet what wonder at my sisters' crime?
So hath Trade withered up Love's sinewy prime,

Men love not women as in olden time.
Ah, not in these cold merchantable days
Deem men their life an opal gray, where plays   235
The one red Sweet of gracious ladies'-praise.
Now, comes a suitor with sharp prying eye—
Says, *Here, you Lady, if you'll sell, I'll buy:*
Come, heart for heart—a trade? What! weeping? why?
Shame on such wooers' dapper mercery![7]   240
I would my lover kneeling at my feet
In humble manliness should cry, *O sweet!*
I know not if thy heart my heart will greet:
I ask not if thy love my love can meet:
Whate'er thy worshipful soft tongue shall say,   245
I'll kiss thine answer, be it yea or nay:
I do but know I love thee, and I pray
To be thy knight until my dying day.
Woe him that cunning trades in hearts contrives!
Base love good women to base loving drives   250
If men loved larger, larger were our lives;
And wooed they nobler, won they nobler wives.'
There thrust the bold straightforward horn
To battle for that lady lorn,
With heartsome voice of mellow scorn,   255
Like any knight in knighthood's morn.
        'Now comfort thee,' said he,
                'Fair Lady.
For God shall right thy grievous wrong,
And man shall sing thee a true-love song,   260
Voiced in act his whole life long,
        Yea, all thy sweet life long,
                Fair Lady.
Where's he that craftily hath said,
The day of chivalry is dead?   265
I'll prove that lie upon his head,
        Or I will die instead,
                Fair Lady.
Is Honor gone into his grave?
Hath Faith become a caitiff knave,   270
And Selfhood turned into a slave
        To work in Mammon's cave,[8]
                Fair Lady?

[7] The goods of a mercer (a dealer in textiles).
[8] Mammon personifies selfish greed. Cf. Edmund Spenser's *Faerie Queen*, Book II, Canto vii.

Will Truth's long blade ne'er gleam again?
Hath Giant Trade in dungeons slain   275
All great contempts of mean-got gain
    And hates of inward stain,
        Fair Lady?
For aye shall name and fame be sold,
And place be hugged for the sake of gold,   280
And smirch-robed Justice feebly scold
    At Crime all money-bold,
        Fair Lady?
Shall self-wrapt husbands aye forget
Kiss-pardons for the daily fret   285
Wherewith sweet wifely eyes are wet—
    Blind to lips kiss-wise set—
        Fair Lady?
Shall lovers higgle, heart for heart,
Till wooing grows a trading mart   290
Where much for little, and all for part,
    Make love a cheapening art,
        Fair Lady?
Shall woman scorch for a single sin
That her betrayer may revel in,   295
And she be burnt, and he but grin
    When that the flames begin,
        Fair Lady?
Shall ne'er prevail the woman's plea,
We maids would far, far whiter be   300
If that our eyes might sometimes see
    Men maids in purity,
        Fair Lady?
Shall Trade aye salve his conscience-aches
With jibes at Chivalry's old mistakes—   305
The wars that o'erhot knighthood makes
    For Christ's and ladies' sakes,
        Fair Lady?
Now by each knight that e'er hath prayed
To fight like a man and love like a maid,   310
Since Pembroke's[9] life, as Pembroke's blade,
    I' the scabbard, death, was laid,
        Fair Lady,

[9] William Herbert, Third Earl of Pembroke,
a nephew of Sir Phillip Sidney.

I dare avouch my faith is bright
That God doth right and God hath might.   315
Nor time hath changed His hair to white,
    Nor His dear love to spite,
        Fair Lady.
I doubt no doubts: I strive, and shrive my clay,
And fight my fight in the patient modern way   320
For true love and for thee—ah me! and pray
    To be thy knight until my dying day,
        Fair Lady.'
Made end that knightly horn, and spurred away
Into the thick of the melodious fray.   325

And then the hautboy[10] played and smiled,
And sang like any large-eyed child,
Cool-hearted and all undefiled.
    'Huge Trade!' he said,
'Would thou wouldst life me on thy head   330
And run where'er my finger led!
Once said a Man—and wise was He—
Never shalt thou the heavens see,
Save as a little child thou be.'
Then o'er sea-lashings of commingling tunes   335
The ancient wise bassoons,
        Like weird,
        Gray-beard
Old harpers sitting on the high sea-dunes,
        Chanted runes:[11]   340
'Bright-waved gain, gray-waved loss,
The sea of all doth lash and toss,
One wave forward and one across:
But now 'twas trough, now 'tis crest,
And worst doth foam and flash to best,   345
        And curst to blest.

'Life! Life! thou sea-fugue, writ from east to west,
        Love, Love alone can pore
        On thy dissolving score
        Of harsh half-phrasings,   350
            Blotted ere writ,
        And double erasings
            Of chords most fit.

[10] Oboe.
[11] Secret mystery writing or signs; also means
a poem or song.

Yea, Love, sole music-master blest.
May read thy weltering palimpsest.[12]   355
To follow Time's dying melodies through,
And never to lose the old in the new,
And ever to solve the discords true—
    Love alone can do.
And ever Love hears the poor-folks' crying,   360
And ever Love hears the woman's sighing,
And ever sweet knighthood's death-defying,
And ever wise childhood's deep implying,
But never a trader's glozing and lying.

'And yet shall Love himself be heard,   365
Though long deferred, though long deferred:
O'er the modern waste a dove[13] hath whirred:
Music is Love in search of a word.'

                    1875, 1877

[12] A writing tablet or parchment that is being used again after the original message has been erased or scraped off.

[13] A reference to the dove in Genesis 8:8-11 that Noah sent forth from the ark at the end of the flood and that returned bearing an olive branch in its beak to signify the existence of dry land. The dove is a traditional symbol for the restoration of peace and harmony.

Corn[1]

To-day the woods are trembling through and through
With shimmering forms, that flash before my view,
Then melt in green as dawn-stars melt in blue.
    The leaves that wave against my cheek caress
    Like women's hands; the embracing boughs express   5
        A subtlety of mighty tenderness;
    The copse[2]-depths into little noises start,
That sound anon like beatings of a heart,
Anon like talk 'twixt lips not far apart.
The beech dreams balm, as a dreamer hums a song;   10
Through that vague wafture, expirations strong
Throb from young hickories breathing deep and long
With stress and urgence bold of prisoned spring
        And ecstasy of burgeoning.

[1] First published in *Lippincotts* in February 1875.

[2] A small thicket of trees or bushes.

Now, since the dew-plashed road of morn is dry,   15
Forth venture odors of more quality
And heavenlier giving. Like Jove's locks awry,
    Long muscadines[3]
Rich-wreathe the spacious foreheads of great pines,
And breathe ambrosial passion from their vines.   20
  I pray with mosses, ferns and flowers shy
  That hide like gentle nuns from human eye
  To life adoring perfumes to the sky.
I hear faint bridal-sighs of brown and green
Dying to silent hints of kisses keen   25
As far lights fringe into a pleasant sheen.
  I start at fragmentary whispers, blown
  From undertalks of leafy souls unknown.
  Vague purports sweet, of inarticulate tone.
Dreaming of gods, men, nuns and brides, between   30
Old companies of oaks that inward lean
To join their radiant amplitudes of green
  I slowly move, with ranging looks that pass
  Up from the matted miracles of grass
Into yon veined complex of space   35
Where sky and leafage interlace
  So close, the heaven of blue is seen
  Inwoven with a heaven of green.

I wander to the zigzag-corner fence
Where sassafras, intrenched in brambles dense,   40
Contests with stolid vehemence
  The march of culture, setting limb and thorn
  As pikes against the army of the corn.

There, while I pause, my fieldward-faring eyes
Take harvests, where the stately corn-ranks rise,   45
  Of inward dignities
And large benignities and insights wise,
  Graces and modest majesties.
Thus, without theft, I reap another's field;
Thus, without tilth, I house a wondrous yield,   50
And heap my heart with quintuple crops concealed.

Look, out of line one tall corn-captain stands
Advanced beyond the foremost of his bands,

[3] A grape from the southern United States
that has a dull purple, thick-skinned musky
fruit.

And waves his blades upon the very edge
And hottest thicket of the battling hedge.   55
Thou lustrous stalk, that ne'er mayst walk nor talk,
   Still shall thou type[4] the poet-soul sublime
   That leads the vanward[5] of his timid time
   And sings up cowards with commanding rhyme—
Soul calm, like thee, yet fain, like thee, to grow   60
By double increment, above, below;
   Soul homely, as thou art, yet rich in grace like thee,
   Teaching the yeomen selfless chivalry
   That moves in gentle curves of courtesy;
Soul filled like thy long veins with sweetness tense,   65
     By every godlike sense
Transmuted from the four wild elements.
     Drawn to high plans,
   Thou lift'st more stature than a mortal man's,
Yet ever piercest downard in the mould   70
     And keepest hold
   Upon the reverend and steadfast earth
     That gave thee birth;
   Yea, standest smiling in thy future grave,
     Serene and brave,   75
   With unremitting breath
   Inhaling life from death,
Thine epitaph writ fair in fruitage eloquent,
     Thyself thy monument.

     As poets should,   80
Thou hast built up thy hardihood
With universal food,
   Drawn in select proportion fair
   From honest mould and vagabond air;
From darkness of the dreadful night,   85
     And joyful light;
   From antique ashes, whose departed flame
   In thee has finer life and longer flame;
From wounds and balms,
From storms and calms,   90
From potsherds and dry bones
     And ruin-stones.

[4] A theological term meaning to represent   [5] Front.
symbolically and prophetically.

Into thy vigorous substance thou hast wrought
Whate'er the hand of Circumstance hath brought;
   Yea, into cool solacing green hast spun   95
   While radiance hot from out the sun.
So thou dost mutually leaven
Strength of earth with grace of heaven;
   So thou dost marry new and old
   Into a one of higher mould;   100
   So thou dost reconcile the hot and cold,
      The dark and bright,
And many a heart-perplexing opposite,
      And so,
   Akin by blood to high and low,   105
Fitly thou playest out thy poet's part,
Richly expending thy much-bruised heart
   In equal care to nourish lord in hall,
      Or beast in stall:
   Thou took'st from all that thou mighst give to all.   110

O steadfast dweller on the selfsame spot
Where thou wast born, that still repinest not—
Type of the home-fond heart, the happy lot!—
   Deeply thy mild content rebukes the land
   Whose flimsy homes, built on the shifting sand   115
Of trade, for ever rise and fall
With alternation whimsical,
   Enduring scarce a day,
   Then swept away
By swift engulfments of incalculable tides   120
Whereon capricious Commerce rides.
Look, thou substantial spirit of content!
Across this little vale, thy continent,
   To where, beyond the mouldering mill,
   Yon old deserted Georgian hill   125
Bares to the sun his piteous aged crest
      And seamy breast,
   By restless-hearted children left to lie
   Untended there beneath the heedless sky,
   As barbarous folk expose their old to die.   130
Upon that generous-rounding side,
      With gullies scarified
   Where keen Neglect his lash hath plied,
Dwelt one I knew of old, who played at toil,
And gave to coquette Cotton soul and soil.   135

Scorning the slow reward of patient grain,
He sowed his heart with hopes of swifter gain,
Then sat him down and waited for the rain.
He sailed in borrowed ships of usury—
A foolish Jason on a treacherous sea, 140
Seeking the Fleece and finding misery.
    Lulled by smooth-rippling loans, in idle trance
    He lay, content that unthrift Circumstance
    Should plough for him the stony field of Chance.
Yea, gathering crops whose worth no man might tell, 145
He staked his life on games of Buy-and-Sell,
And turned each field into a gambler's hell.
    Aye, as each year began,
    My farmer to the neighboring city ran;
Passed with a mournful anxious face 150
Into the banker's inner place;
Parleyed, excused, pleaded for longer grace;
    Railed at the drought, the worm, the rust, the grass;
    Protested ne'er again 'twould come to pass;
    With many an *oh* and *if* and *but alas* 155
Parried or swallowed searching questions rude,
And kissed the dust to soften Dives's[6] mood.
At last, small loans by pledges great renewed,
    He issues smiling from the fatal door,
    And buys with lavish hand his yearly store 160
    Till his small borrowings will yield no more.
Aye, as each year declined,
With bitter heart and ever-brooding mind
He mourned his fate unkind.
    In dust, in rain, with might and main, 165
    He nursed his cotton, cursed his grain,
    Fretted for news that made him fret again,
Snatched at each telegram of Future Sale,
And thrilled with Bulls' or Bears' alternate wail—
In hope or fear alike for ever pale. 170
    And thus from year to year, through hope and fear,
    With many a curse and many a secret tear,
    Striving in vain his cloud of debt to clear,
        At last
He woke to find his foolish dreaming past, 175
    And all his best-of-life the easy prey

[6] The rich man of the parable, in Luke
16:19-31.

Of squandering scamps and quacks that lined his way
    With vile array,
From rascal statesman down to petty knave;
Himself, at best, for all his bragging brave,   180
A gamester's catspaw and a banker's slave.
Then, worn and gray, and sick with deep unrest,
He fled away into the oblivious West,
    Unmourned, unblest.

Old hill! old hill! thou gashed and hairy Lear   185
Whom the divine Cordelia of the year,
E'en pitying Spring, will vainly strive to cheer—
    King, that no subject man nor beast may own,
    Discrowned, undaughtered and alone—
Yet shall the great God turn thy fate,   190
And bring thee back into thy monarch state
    And majesty immaculate.
Lo, through hot waverings of the August morn,
Thou givest from thy vasty sides forlorn
Visions of golden treasures of corn—   195
Ripe largesse lingering for some bolder heart
That manfully shall take thy part,
    And tend thee,
    And defend thee,
With antique sinew and with modern art.   200

1875

KATE CHOPIN

(1851–1904)

Although she was born outside the South, Kate Chopin portrayed Creole and Acadian (or "Cajun") life in Louisiana with remarkable intimacy and certainty. Born in St. Louis as Kate O'Flaherty (her father was

The writings have been collected in Per Seyersted, ed., *The Complete Works of Kate Chopin*, 2 Vols., 1969. Seyersted has also written *Kate Chopin: A Critical Biography*, 1969. A one-volume edition is Daniel S. Rankin, *Kate Chopin and Her Creole Stories*, 1932.

Criticism includes Edmund Wilson, *Patriotic Gore: Studies in the Literature of the American Civil War*, 1962: George Arms, "Kate Chopin's *The Awakening* in the Perspective of Her Literary Career," *Essays in American Literature in Honor of J. B. Hubbell*, ed. Clarence Gohdes, 1969.

Irish and her mother French), she married a Creole banker in 1870 and moved with him to New Orleans and a plantation near Nachitoches. She returned to St. Louis with her six children after her husband died of swamp fever in 1882, and she began to write fiction based on her Southern experiences and observations. She published a novel, *At Fault,* in 1890, and two collections of short stories, *Bayou Folk* (1894) and *A Night in Acadia* (1897).

Chopin's stories mark her as a local colorist, yet she transcends the mode with her superior talent for characterization and her sensitivity to emotional conflict. Partly through her study of Flaubert and Maupassant, she developed a taut, restrained style, capable of telling details and subtle evocations of feelings. Her manner is cool and finished. Her tales are less drenched in the aura of tradition and romance than Cable's; they are more sharply focused on situations of conflict between desire and moral codes. Delicate social moments are her speciality and reveal her acute sensitivity to the nuances of behavior among a people whose lives are strictly guided by moral principles.

Unhappiness within marriage is one of Kate Chopin's most powerful themes. Her best work, a minor masterpiece of psychological realism, is *The Awakening* (1899), a book only recently rediscovered by readers. It deals with sexual passion, conflict, adultery, despair, and suicide in a convincing and moving manner. Chopin is especially successful in this work in portraying the predicament of a married woman within Creole society. While it is clearly her most successful literary effort, it is also the book that virtually ended her career. The novel raised a storm of criticism for its frankness about a woman's sexual feelings and her infidelity. One critic wrote that the book "should be labeled poison." As a result, Chopin found herself ostracized by St. Louis society, where she had earlier had a place as a woman of means and social connections. Hurt and baffled by the response (the book is relatively mild by today's standards), she never again published, and she died a few years later.

Désirée's Baby[1]

As the day was pleasant, Madame Valmondé drove over to L'Abri to see Désirée and the baby.

It made her laugh to think of Désirée with a baby. Why, it seemed but yesterday that Désirée was little more than a baby herself; when Monsieur in

[1] First published in *Vogue* magazine on January 14, 1893, then collected in *Bayou Folk,* published in 1894

riding through the gateway of Valmondé had found her lying asleep in the shadow of the big stone pillar.

The little one awoke in his arms and began to cry for "Dada." That was as much as she could do or say. Some people thought she might have strayed there of her own accord, for she was of the toddling age. The prevailing belief was that she had been purposely left by a party of Texans, whose canvas-covered wagon, late in the day, had crossed the ferry that Coton Maïs kept, just below the plantation. In time Madame Valmondé abandoned every speculation but the one that Désirée had been sent to her by a beneficent Providence to be the child of her affection, seeing that she was without child of the flesh. For the girl grew to be beautiful and gentle, affectionate and sincere—the idol of Valmondé.

It was no wonder, when she stood one day against the stone pillar in whose shadow she had lain asleep, eighteen years before, that Armand Aubigny riding by and seeing her there, had fallen in love with her. That was the way all the Aubignys fell in love, as if struck by a pistol shot. The wonder was that he had not loved her before; for he had known her since his father brought him home from Paris, a boy of eight, after his mother died there. The passion that awoke in him that day, when he saw her at the gate, swept along like an avalanche, or like a prairie fire, or like anything that drives headlong over all obstacles.

Monsieur Valmondé grew practical and wanted things well considered: that is, the girl's obscure origin. Armand looked into her eyes and did not care. He was reminded that she was nameless. What did it matter about a name when he could give her one of the oldest and proudest in Louisiana? He ordered the *corbeille*[2] from Paris, and contained himself with what patience he could until it arrived; then they were married.

Madame Valmondé had not seen Désirée and the baby for four weeks. When she reached L'Abri she shuddered at the first sight of it, as she always did. It was a sad-looking place, which for many years had not known the gentle presence of a mistress, old Monsieur Aubigny having married and buried his wife in France, and she having loved her own land too well ever to leave it. The roof came down steep and black like a cowl, reaching out beyond the wide galleries that encircled the yellow stuccoed house. Big, solemn oaks grew close to it, and their thick-leaved, far-reaching branches shadowed it like a pall. Young Aubigny's rule was a strict one, too, and under it his negroes had forgotten how to be gay, as they had been during the old master's easy-going and indulgent lifetime.

The young mother was recovering slowly, and lay full length, in her soft white muslins and laces, upon a couch. The baby was beside her, upon her arm, where he had fallen asleep, at her breast. The yellow nurse woman sat beside a window fanning herself.

[2] Basket.

Madame Valmondé bent her portly figure over Désirée and kissed her, holding her an instant tenderly in her arms. Then she turned to the child. "This is not the baby!" she exclaimed, in startled tones. French was the language spoken at Valmondé in those days.

"I knew you would be astonished!" laughed Désirée, "at the way he has grown. The little *cochon de lait!*[3] Look at his legs, mamma, and his hands and finger-nails—real finger-nails. Zandrine had to cut them this morning. Isn't it true, Zandrine?"

The woman bowed her turbaned head majestically, *Mais si, Madame.*"[4]

"And the way he cries," went on Désirée, "is deafening. Armand heard him the other day as far away as La Blanche's cabin."

Madame Valmondé had never removed her eyes from the child. She lifted it and walked with it over to the window that was lightest. She scanned the baby narrowly, then looked as searchingly at Zandrine, whose face was turned to gaze across the fields.

"Yes, the child has grown, has changed," said Madame Valmondé, slowly, as she replaced it beside its mother. "What does Armand say?"

Désirée's face became suffused with a glow that was happiness itself.

"Oh, Armand is the proudest father in the parish, I believe, chiefly because it is a boy, to bear his name; though he says not—that he would have loved a girl as well. But I know it isn't true. I know he says that to please me. And mamma," she added, drawing Madame Valmondé's head down to her, and speaking in a whisper, "he hasn't punished one of them—not one of them—since baby is born. Even Négrillon, who pretended to have burnt his leg that he might rest from work—he only laughed, and said Négrillon was a great scamp. Oh, mamma, I'm so happy; it frightens me."

What Désirée said was true. Marriage, and later the birth of his son, had softened Armand Aubigny's imperious and exacting nature greatly. This was what made the gentle Désirée so happy, for she loved him desperately. When he frowned she trembled, but loved him. When he smiled, she asked no greater blessing of God. But Armand's dark, handsome face had not often been disfigured by frowns since the day he fell in love with her.

When the baby was about three months old, Désirée awoke one day to the conviction that there was something in the air menacing her peace. It was at first too subtle to grasp. It had only been a disquieting suggestion; an air of mystery among the blacks; unexpected visits from far-off neighbors who could hardly account for their coming. Then a strange, an awful change in her husband's manner, which she dared not ask him to explain. When he spoke to her, it was with averted eyes, from which the old love-light seemed to have gone out. He absented himself from home; and when there, avoided her presence and that of her child, without excuse. And the very spirit of

---

[3] Little pig about milk.　　　　　　　　　　[4] But yes, Madame.

Satan seemed suddenly to take hold of him in his dealings with the slaves. Désirée was miserable enough to die.

She sat in her room, one hot afternoon, in her *peignoir*,[5] listlessly drawing through her fingers the strands of her long, silky brown hair that hung about her shoulders. The baby, half naked, lay asleep upon her own great mahogany bed, that was like a sumptuous throne, with its satin-lined half-canopy. One of La Blanche's little quadroon boys—half naked too—stood fanning the child slowly with a fan of peacock feathers. Désirée's eyes had been fixed absently and sadly upon the baby, while she was striving to penetrate the threatening mist that she felt closing about her. She looked from her child to the boy who stood beside him, and back again; over and over. "Ah!" It was a cry that she could not help; which she was not conscious of having uttered. The blood turned like ice in her veins, and a clammy moisture gathered upon her face.

She tried to speak to the little quadroon boy; but no sound would come, at first. When he heard his name uttered, he looked up, and his mistress was pointing to the door. He laid aside the great, soft fan, and obediently stole away, over the polished floor, on his bare tiptoes.

She stayed motionless, with gaze riveted upon her child, and her face the picture of fright.

Presently her husband entered the room, and without noticing her, went to a table and began to search among some papers which covered it.

"Armand," she called to him, in a voice which must have stabbed him, if he was human. But he did not notice, "Armand," she said again. Then she rose and tottered towards him. "Armand," she panted once more, clutching his arm, "look at our child. What does it mean? tell me."

He coldly but gently loosened her fingers from about his arm and thrust the hand away from him. "Tell me what it means!" she cried despairingly.

"It means," he answered lightly, "that the child is not white; it means that you are not white."

A quick conception of all that this accusation meant for her nerved her with unwonted courage to deny it. "It is a lie; it is not true, I am white! Look at my hair, it is brown; and my eyes are gray, Armand, you know they are gray. And my skin is fair," seizing his wrist. "Look at my hand; whiter than yours, Armand," she laughed hysterically.

"As white as La Blanche's," he returned cruelly; and went away leaving her alone with their child.

When she could hold a pen in her hand, she sent a despairing letter to Madame Valmondé.

"My mother, they tell me I am not white. Armand has told me I am not white. For God's sake tell them it is not true. You must know it is not true. I shall die. I must die. I cannot be so unhappy, and live."

[5] Dressing gown.

The answer that came was as brief:

"My own Désirée: Come home to Valmondé; back to your mother who loves you. Come with your child."

When the letter reached Désirée she went with it to her husband's study, and laid it opened upon the desk before which he sat. She was like a stone image: silent, white, motionless after she placed it there.

In silence he ran his cold eyes over the written words. He said nothing. "Shall I go, Armand?" she asked in tones sharp with agonized suspense.

"Yes, go."

"Do you want me to go?"

"Yes, I want you to go."

He thought Almighty God had dealt cruelly and unjustly with him; and felt, somehow, that he was paying Him back in kind when he stabbed thus into his wife's soul. Moreover he no longer loved her, because of the unconscious injury she had brought upon his home and his name.

She turned away like one stunned by a blow, and walked slowly towards the door, hoping he would call her back.

"Good-by, Armand," she moaned.

He did not answer her. That was his last blow at fate.

Désirée went in search of her child. Zandrine was pacing the sombre gallery with it. She took the little one from the nurse's arms with no word of explanation, and descending the steps, walked away, under the live-oak branches.

It was an October afternoon; the sun was just sinking. Out in the still fields the negroes were picking cotton.

Désirée had not changed the thin white garment nor the slippers which she wore. Her hair was uncovered and the sun's rays brought a golden gleam from its brown meshes. She did not take the broad, beaten road which led to the far-off plantation of Valmondé. She walked across a deserted field, where the stubble bruised her tender feet, so delicately shod, and tore her thin gown to shreds.

She disappeared among the reeds and willows that grew thick along the banks of the deep, sluggish bayou; and she did not come back again.

Some weeks later there was a curious scene enacted at L'Abri. In the centre of the smoothly swept back yard was a great bonfire. Armand Aubigny sat in the wide hallway that commanded a view of the spectacle; and it was he who dealt out to a half dozen negroes the material which kept this fire ablaze.

A graceful cradle of willow, with all its dainty furbishings, was laid upon the pyre, which had already been fed with the richness of a priceless *layette.*[6] Then there were silk gowns, and velvet and satin ones added to these;

---

[6] The baby's outfit.

laces, too, and embroideries; bonnets and gloves; for the *corbeille* had been of rare quality.

The last thing to go was a tiny bundle of letters; innocent little scribblings that Désirée had sent to him during the days of their espousal. There was the remnant of one back in the drawer from which he took them. But it was not Désirée's; it was part of an old letter from his mother to his father. He read it. She was thanking God for the blessing of her husband's love:

"But, above all," she wrote, "night and day, I thank the good God for having so arranged our lives that our dear Armand will never know that his mother, who adores him, belongs to the race that is cursed with the brand of slavery."

CHARLES WADDELL CHESNUTT

(1858–1932)

The presence of black figures in Southern fiction—their folklore, their speech rhythms and imagery, their religion and customs—is hardly surprising. In many regions of the South blacks outnumbered whites by sizable majorities, and it was a rare piece of land where daily contacts between blacks and whites was not a common occurrence. After the end of Reconstruction in 1877, however, the gulf between the races widened dramatically as newly restored white governments in the Southern states introduced laws establishing segregation and depriving blacks of their right to vote. A color line was, of course, one of the vestiges of slavery; the Jim Crow laws toughened the line and made any attempt to cross it a very dangerous matter. The rarity of anything like equal relations or friendship between blacks and whites in the literature of the closing decades of the nineteenth century reflects the increasingly rigid barriers, often enforced by Ku Klux Klan terror, between the races.

The literary portraits of blacks were most frequently the products of white writers, some of whom, like Harris and Twain, had absorbed the folklore and superstitions of blacks. Not until the late 1880's, with the

The writings include *The Wife of His Youth and Other Stories of the Color Line*, 1899; *The Conjure Woman*, 1899; *The House Behind the Cedars*, 1900; *The Marrow of Tradition*, 1901; *The Colonel's Dream*, 1905.

A biography is Helen M. Chesnutt, *Charles Waddell Chesnutt: Pioneer of the Color Line*, 1952.

appearance of the poems of Paul Laurence Dunbar and the stories of Chesnutt in journals like *The Atlantic Monthly,* did black regionalist writers emerge before a national audience. Neither of these writers were Southerners by birth, nor does their work derive directly from black folk traditions. Both are talented professional writers, whose rendering of the experiences of blacks appears in the conventional literary forms of written story and poem. They are both, in short, regionalist writers who deal with the experiences of black people with more intimacy and sympathy than their white colleagues.

Chesnutt was born in Cleveland but raised in the South. After the War (his father had served in the Union Army), his parents returned to their native North Carolina. During Reconstruction Chesnutt managed to educate himself well enough to find work as a schoolteacher and a journalist. Back in Cleveland in the 1880's, he studied law, and he won a degree and a job as a court stenographer. He began to write fiction in these years, published his stories in *The Atlantic Monthly* and other national journals and, in 1899, published a collection of tales called *The Conjure Woman.* Like many other regionalists he drew on legends of antebellum times and, in this collection, he created an elderly black storyteller, Uncle Julius McAdoo, who resembles Harris's Uncle Remus.

Also in 1899 he published a biography of the distinguished black leader, Frederick Douglass, and another collection of stories, *The Wife of his Youth,* which deals with racial feelings and prejudice in contemporary times. William Dean Howells bestowed high praise on his work, comparing it to that of Turgenev and Henry James. The personal consequences of prejudice and the color line dominate Chesnutt's later work, which consists almost entirely of three novels: *The House Behind the Cedars* (1900), *The Marrow of Tradition* (1901), and *The Colonel's Dream* (1905), which portrays the efforts of an idealistic white Southerner to combat prejudice in a small Southern town. Apparently disillusioned by continuing racial injustice, he abandoned fiction, although he remained a prominent figure in the black community of Cleveland.

The Wife of His Youth[1]

Mr. Ryder was going to give a ball. There were several reasons why this was an opportune time for such an event.

Mr. Ryder might aptly be called the dean of the Blue Veins. The original

[1] First published in 1899 in a collection of stories called *The Wife of His Youth and Other Stories of the Color Line.*

Blue Veins were a little society of colored persons organized in a certain Northern city shortly after the war. Its purpose was to establish and maintain correct social standards among a people whose social condition presented almost unlimited room for improvement. By accident, combined perhaps with some natural affinity, the society consisted of individuals who were, generally speaking, more white than black. Some envious outsider made the suggestion that no one was eligible for membership who was not white enough to show blue veins. The suggestion was readily adopted by those who were not of the favored few, and since that time the society, though possessing a longer and more pretentious name, had been known far and wide as the "Blue Vein Society," and its members as the "Blue Veins."

The Blue Veins did not allow that any such requirement existed for admission to their circle, but, on the contrary, declared that character and culture were the only things considered; and that if most of their members were light-colored, it was because such persons, as a rule, had had better opportunities to qualify themselves for membership. Opinions differed, too, as to the usefulness of the society. There were those who had been known to assail it violently as a glaring example of the very prejudice from which the colored race had suffered most; and later, when such critics had succeeded in getting on the inside, they had been heard to maintain with zeal and earnestness that the society was a life-boat, an anchor, a bulwark and a shield—a pillar of cloud by day and of fire by night, to guide their people through the social wilderness. Another alleged prerequisite for Blue Vein membership was that of free birth: and while there was really no such requirement, it is doubtless true that very few of the members would have been unable to meet it if there had been. If there were one or two of the older members who had come up from the South and from slavery, their history presented enough romantic circumstances to rob their servile origin of its grosser aspects.

While there were no such tests of eligibility, it is true that the Blue Veins had their notions on these subjects, and that not all of them were equally liberal in regard to the things they collectively disclaimed. Mr. Ryder was one of the most conservative. Though he had not been among the founders of the society, but had come in later, his genius for social leadership was such that he had speedily become its recognized adviser and head, the custodian of its standards, and the preserver of its traditions. He shaped its social policy, was active in providing for its entertainment, and when the interest fell off, as it sometimes did, he fanned the embers until they burst again into a cheerful flame.

There were still other reasons for his popularity. While he was not as white as some of the Blue Veins, his appearance was such as to confer distinction upon them. His features were of a refined type, his hair was almost straight; he was always neatly dressed; his manners were irreproachable, and his morals above suspicion. He had come to Groveland a young man, and obtaining employment in the office of a railroad company as messenger had in time worked himself up to the position of stationery clerk, having charge of the distribution of the office supplies for the whole company. Although the lack of early training had hindered the orderly development of a naturally fine mind, it had not prevented him from doing a great deal of reading or from forming decidedly literary tastes. Poetry was his passion. He could repeat whole pages of the great English poets; and if his pronunciation was sometimes faulty, his eye, his voice, his gestures, would respond to the changing sentiment with a precision that revealed a poetic soul and disarmed criticism. He was economical, and had saved money; he owned and occupied a very comfortable house on a respectable street. His residence was handsomely furnished, containing among other things a good library, especially rich in poetry, a piano, and some choice engravings. He generally shared his house with some young couple, who looked after his want and were company for him; for Mr. Ryder was a single man. In the early days of his connection with the Blue Veins he had been regarded as quite a catch, and young ladies and their mothers had maneuvered with much ingenuity to capture him. Not, however, until Mrs. Molly Dixon visited Groveland had any woman ever made him wish to change his condition to that of a married man.

Mrs. Dixon had come to Groveland from Washington in the spring, and before the summer was over she had won Mr. Ryder's heart. She possessed many attractive qualities. She was much younger than he; in fact, he was old enough to have been her father, though no one knew exactly how old he was. She was whiter than he, and better educated. She had moved in the best colored society of the country, at Washington, and had taught in the schools of that city. Such a superior person had been eagerly welcomed to the Blue Vein Society, and had taken a leading part in its activities. Mr. Ryder had at first been attracted by her charms of person, for she was very good-looking and not over twenty-five; then by her refined manners and the vivacity of her wit. Her husband had been a government clerk, and at his death had left a considerable life insurance. She was visiting friends in Groveland, and, finding the town and the people to her liking, had prolonged her stay indefinitely. She had not seemed displeased at Mr. Ryder's attentions, but on the contrary had given him every proper encouragement; and indeed, a younger and less cautious man would long since have spoken. But he had made up his mind, and had only to determine the time when he would ask her to be his wife. He decided to give a ball in her honor, and at some time during the evening of the ball to offer her his heart and hand. He had no special fears about the outcome, but, with a little touch of romance, he wanted the surroundings to be in harmony with his own feelings when he should have received the answer he expected.

Mr. Ryder resolved that this ball should mark an epoch in the social history of Groveland. He knew, of course—no one could know better—the entertainments that had taken place in past years, and what must be done to surpass them. His ball must be worthy of the lady in whose honor it was to be given, and must, by the quality of its guests, set an example for the future. He had observed of late a growing liberality, almost a laxity, in social matters, even among members of his own set, and had several times been forced to meet in a social way persons whose complexions and callings in life were hardly up to the standard which he considered proper for the society to maintain. He had a theory of his own.

"I have no race prejudice," he would say, "but we people of mixed blood are ground between the upper and the nether millstone. Our fate lies between absorption by the white race and extinction in the black. The one doesn't want us yet, but may take us in time. The other would welcome us, but it would be for us a backward step. 'With malice towards none, with charity for all,' we must do the best we can for ourselves and those who are to follow us. Self-preservation is the first law of nature."

His ball would serve by its exclusiveness to counteract leveling tendencies, and his marriage with Mrs. Dixon would help to further the upward process of absorption he had been wishing and waiting for.

2

The ball was to take place on Friday night. The house had been put in order, the carpets covered with canvas, the halls and stairs decorated with palms and potted plants; and in the afternoon Mr. Ryder sat on his front porch, which the shade of a vine running up over a wire netting made a cool and pleasant lounging place. He expected to respond to the toast "The Ladies" at the supper, and from a volume of Tennyson—his favorite poet—was fortifying himself with apt quotations. The volume was open at "A Dream of Fair Women." His eyes fell on these lines, and he read them aloud to judge better of their effect:

> At length I saw a lady within call,
>   Stiller than chisell'd marble, standing there;
> A daughter of the gods, divinely tall,
>   And most divinely fair.

He remarked the verse, and turning the page read the stanza beginning

> O sweet pale Margaret,
> O rare pale Margaret.

He weighed the passage a moment, and decided that it would not do. Mrs. Dixon was the palest lady he expected at the ball, and she was of a rather ruddy complexion, and of lively disposition and buxom build. So he ran over the leaves until his eyes rested on the description of Queen Guinevere:

> She seem'd a part of joyous Spring:
> A gown of grass-green silk she wore,
> Buckled with golden clasps before;
> A light-green tuft of plumes she bore
> Closed in a golden ring.

> .   .   .

> She look'd so lovely, as she sway'd
> The rein with dainty finger-tips,
> A man had given all other bliss,
> And all his worldly worth for this,
> To waste his whole heart in one kiss
> Upon her perfect lips.

As Mr. Ryder murmured these words audibly, with an appreciative thrill, he heard the latch of his gate click, and a light footfall sounding on the steps. He turned his head, and saw a woman standing before his door.

She was a little woman, not five feet tall, and proportioned to her height. Although she stood erect, and looked around her with very bright and restless eyes, she seemed quite old; for her face was crossed and recrossed with a hundred wrinkles, and around the edges of her bonnet could be seen protruding here and there a tuft of short gray wool. She wore a blue calico gown of ancient cut, a little red shawl fastened around her shoulders with an old-fashioned brass brooch, and a large bonnet profusely ornamented with faded red and yellow artificial flowers. And she was very black, so that her toothless gums, revealed when she opened her mouth to speak, were not red, but blue. She looked like a bit of the old plantation life, summoned up from the past by the wave of a magician's wand, as the poet's fancy had called into being the gracious shapes of which Mr. Ryder had just been reading.

He rose from his chair and came over to where she stood. "Good afternoon, madam," he said.

"Good evenin', suh," she answered, ducking suddenly with a quaint curtsy. Her voice was shrill and piping, but softened somewhat by age. "Is dis yere whar Mistuh Ryduh lib, suh?" she asked, looking around her doubtfully, and glancing into the open windows, through which some of the preparations for the evening were visible.

"Yes," he replied, with an air of kingly patronage, unconsciously flattered by her manner, "I am Mr. Ryder. Did you want to see me?"

"Yas, suh, ef I ain't 'sturbin' of you too much."

"Not at all. Have a seat over here behind the vine, where it is cool. What can I do for you?"

"'Scuse me, suh," she continued, when she had sat down on the edge of a chair. "'Scuse me, suh, I's lookin' for my husban'. I heerd you wuz a big man an' had libbed heah a long time, an' I 'lowed you would n't min' if I'd come roun' an' ax you ef you'd ever heerd of a merlatter man by de name er Sam Taylor 'quirin' 'round' in de chu'ches ermongs' de people fer his wife 'Liza Jane?"

Mr. Ryder seemed to think for a moment.

"There used to be many such cases right after the war," he said, "but it has been so long that I have forgotten them. There are very few now. But tell me your story, and it may refresh my memory."

She sat back farther in her chair so as to be more comfortable, and folded her withered hands in her lap.

"My name's 'Liza," she began, "'Liza Jane. W'en I wuz young I us'ter b'long ter Marse Bob Smif, down in ole Missoura. I wuz bawn down dere. W'en I wuz a gal I wuz married ter a man named Jim. But Jim died, an' after dat I married a merlatter man named Sam Taylor. Sam wuz frebawn, but his mammy and daddy died, an' de w'ite folks 'prenticed him ter my marster fer ter work fer 'im 'tel he wuz growed up. Sam worked in de fiel', an' I wuz de cook. One day Ma'y Ann, ole miss's maid, came rushin' out ter de kitchen, an' says she, 'Liza Jane, old marse gwine sell yo' Sam down de ribber.' "

" 'Go way f'm yere,' says I; 'my husban's free!' "

" 'Don' make no diff'ence. I heard ole marse tell ole miss he wuz gwine take yo' Sam wid 'im termorrow, fer he needed money, an' he knowed whar he could get a t'ousan' dollars fer Sam an' no questions axed.' "

"W'en Sam come home f'm de fiel' dat night, I tole him 'bout ole marse gwine steal 'im, an' Sam run erway. His time wuz mos' up, an' he swo' dat w'en he wuz twenty-one he would come back an' he'p me run erway, er else save up de money ter buy my freedom. An I know he'd 'a' done it, fer he thought a heap er me, Sam did. But w'en he come back he did n' fin' me, fer I wuzn' dere. Ole marse had heerd dat I warned Sam, so he had me whip' an' sol' down de ribber.

"Den de wah broke out, an' w'en it wuz ober de cullud folks wuz scattered. I went back ter de ole home; but Sam wuzn' dere, an' I could n' l'arn nuffin' 'bout 'im. But I knowed he'd be'n dere to look fer me an' had n' foun' me an' had gone erway ter hunt fer me.

"I's be'n lookin' fer 'im eber sence," she added simply, as though twenty-five years were but a couple of weeks, "an' I knows he's be'n lookin' fer me. Fer he sot a heap er sto' by me, Sam did, an' I know he's be'n huntin' fer me all dese years—'les'n he's be'n sick er sump'n, so he could n' work, er out'n his head, so he could n' 'member his promise. I went back down de ribber, fer I 'lowed he'd gone down dere lookin' fer me. I's be'n ter Noo Orleens, an' Atlanty, an' Charleston, an' Richmon'; an' w'en I'd be'n all ober de Souf I come ter de Norf. Fer I knows I'll fin' 'im some er dese days," she said softly, "er he'll fin' me, an' den we'll bofe be as happy in freedom as we wuz in de ole days befo' de wah." A smile stole over her withered countenance as she paused a moment, and her bright eyes softened into a far-away look.

This was the substance of the old woman's story. She had wandered a. little here and there. Mr. Ryder was looking at her curiously when she finished.

"How have you lived all these years?" he asked.

"Cookin', suh. I's a good cook. Does you know anybody w'at needs a good cook, suh? I's stoppin' wid a cullud fam'ly roun' de corner yonder 'tel I kin git a place."

"Do you really expect to find your husband? He may be dead long ago."

She shook her head emphatically. "Oh, no, he ain' dead. De signs an' de tokens tells me. I dremp three nights runnin' on'y dis las' week dat I foun' him."

"He may have married another woman. Your slave marriage would not have prevented him, for you never lived with him after the war, and without that your marriage doesn't count."

"Wouldn' make no diff'ence wid Sam. He would n' marry no yuther 'ooman 'tel he foun' out 'bout me. I knows it," she added. "Sump'n's be'n tellin' me all dese years dat I's gwine fin' Sam 'fo' I dies."

"Perhaps he's outgrown you, and climbed up on the world where he wouldn't care to have you find him."

"No, indeed suh," she replied, "Sam ain' dat kin' er man. He wuz good ter me, Sam wuz, but he wuzn' much good ter nobody e'se, fer he wuz one er de triflin'es' han's on de plantation. I 'spec's ter haf ter suppo't 'im w'en I fin' 'im, fer he nebber would work 'less'n he had ter. But den he wuz free, an' he did n' git no pay fer his work, an' I don' blame 'im much. Mebbe he's done better sence he run erway, but I ain' 'spectin' much."

"You may have passed him on the street a hundred times during the twenty-five years, and not have known him; time works great changes."

She smiled incredulously. "I'd know 'im 'mongs' a hund'ed men. Fer dey wuzn' no yuther merlatter man like my man Sam, an' I could n' be mistook. I's toted his picture roun' wid me twenty-five years."

"May I see it?" asked Mr. Ryder. "It might help me to remember whether I have seen the original."

As she drew a small parcel from her bosom he saw that it was fastened to a string that went around her neck. Removing several wrappers, she brought to light an old-fashioned daguerreotype in a black case. He looked long and intently at the portrait. It was faded with time, but the features were still distinct, and it was easy to see what manner of man it had represented.

He closed the case, and with a slow movement handed it back to her.

"I don't know of any man in town who goes by that name," he said, "nor have I heard of any one making such inquiries. But if you will leave me your address, I will give the matter some attention, and if I find anything I will let you know."

She gave him the number of a house in the neighborhood and went away, after thanking him warmly.

He wrote the address on the fly-leaf of the volume of Tennyson, and, when she had gone, rose to his feet and stood looking after her curiously. As she walked down the street with mincing step, he saw several persons whom she passed turn and look back at her with a smile of kindly amusement. When she had turned the corner, he went upstairs to his bedroom, and stood for a long time before the mirror of his dressing-case, gazing thoughtfully at the reflection of his own face.

3

At eight o'clock the ballroom was a blaze of light and the guests had begun to assemble; for there was a literary programme and some routine business of the society to be gone through with before the dancing. A black servant in evening dress waited at the door and directed the guests to the dressing-rooms.

The occasion was long memorable among the colored people of the city; not alone for the dress and display, but for the high average of intelligence and culture that distinguished the gathering as a whole. There were a number of school teachers, several young doctors, three or four lawyers, some professional singers, an editor, a lieutenant in the United States Army spending his furlough in the city, and others in various polite callings; these were colored, though most of them would not have attracted even a casual glance because of any marked difference from white people. Most of the ladies were in evening costume, and dress coats and dancing pumps were the rule among the men. A band of string music, stationed in an alcove behind a row of palms, played popular airs while the guests were gathering.

The dancing began at half past nine. At eleven o'clock supper was served. Mr. Ryder had left the ballroom some little time before the intermission, but reappeared at the supper table. The spread was worthy of the occasion, and the guests did full justice to it. When the coffee had been served, the toast-master, Mr. Solomon Sadler, rapped for order. He made a brief introductory speech, complimenting host and guests, and then presented in their order the toasts of the evening. They were responded to with a very fair display of after-dinner wit.

"The last toast," said the toastmaster, when he reached the end of the list, "is one which must appeal to us all. There is no one of us of the sterner sex who is not at some time dependent upon woman—in infancy for protection, in manhood for companionship, in old age for care and comforting. Our good host has been trying to live alone, but the fair faces I see around me tonight prove that he is too largely dependent upon the gentler sex for most that makes life worth living—the society and love of friends—and rumor is at fault if he does not soon yield entire subjection to one of them. Mr. Ryder will now respond to the toast—'The Ladies.' "

There was a pensive look in Mr. Ryder's eyes as he took the floor and adjusted his eye-glasses. He began by speaking of woman as the gift of Heaven to man, and after some general observations on the relations of the sexes he said: "But perhaps the quality which most distinguishes woman is her fidelity and devotion to those she loves. History is full of examples, but has recorded none more striking than one which only today came under my notice."

He then related, simply but effectively, the story told by his visitor of the afternoon. He gave it in the same soft dialect, which came readily to his lips, while the company listened attentively and sympathetically. For the story had awakened a responsive thrill in many hearts. There were some present who had seen, and others who had heard their fathers and grandfathers tell, the wrongs and sufferings of this past generation, and all of them still felt, in their darker moments, the shadow hanging over them. Mr. Ryder went on:

"Such devotion and confidence are rare even among women. There are many who would have searched a year, some who would have waited five years, a few who might have hoped ten years; but for twenty-five years this woman has retained her affection for and her faith in a man she has not seen or heard of in all that time.

"She came to me today in hope that I might be able to help her find this long-lost husband. And when she was gone I gave my fancy rein, and imagined a case I will put to you.

"Suppose that this husband, soon after his escape, had learned that his wife had been sold away, and that such inquiries as he could make brought no information of her whereabouts. Suppose that he was young, and she much older than he; that he was light, and she was black; that their marriage was a slave marriage, and legally binding ·only if they chose to make it so after the war. Suppose, too, that he made his way to the North, as some of us have done, and there, where he had larger opportunities, had improved them, and had in the course of all these years grown to be as different from the ignorant boy who ran away from fear of slavery as the day is from the night. Suppose, even, that he had qualified himself, by industry, by thrift, and by study, to win the friendship and be considered worthy of the society of such people as these I see around me to-night, gracing my board and filling my heart with gladness; for I am old enough to remember the day when such a gathering would not have been possible in this land. Suppose, too, that, as the years went by, this man's memory of the past grew more and more indistinct, until at last it was rarely, except in his dreams, that any image of this bygone period rose before his mind. And then suppose that accident should bring to his knowledge the fact that the wife of his youth, the wife he had left behind him—not one who had walked by his side and kept pace with him in his upward struggle, but one upon whom advancing years and a laborious life had set their mark—was alive and seeking him, but that he was absolutely safe from recognition or discovery, unless he chose to reveal himself. My friends, what would the man do? I will presume that he was one who loved honor, and tried to deal justly with all men. I will even carry the case further, and suppose that perhaps he had set his heart upon another, whom he had hoped to call his own. What would he do, or rather what ought he to do, in such a crisis of a lifetime?

"It seemed to me that he might hesitate, and I imagined that I was an old friend, a near friend, and that he had come to me for advice; and I argued the case with him. I tried to discuss it impartially. After we had looked upon the matter from every point of view, I said to him, in words that we all know

> This above all: to thine own self be true,
> And it must follow, as the night the day,
> Thou canst not then be false to any man.

Then, finally, I put the question to him, 'Shall you acknowledge her?'

"And now, ladies and gentlemen, friends and companions, I ask you, what should he have done?"

There was something in Mr. Ryder's voice that stirred the hearts of those who sat around him. It suggested more than mere sympathy with an imaginary situation; it seemed rather in the nature of a personal appeal. It was observed, too, that his look rested more especially upon Mrs. Dixon, with a mingled expression of renunciation and inquiry.

She had listened, with parted lips and streaming eyes. She was the first to speak: "He should have acknowledged her."

"Yes," they all echoed, "he should have acknowledged her."

"My friends and companions," responded Mr. Ryder, "I thank you, one and all. It is the answer I expected, for I knew your hearts."

He turned and walked toward the closed door of an adjoining room, while every eye followed him in wondering curiosity. He came back in a moment, leading by the hand his visitor of the afternoon, who stood startled and trembling at the sudden plunge into this scene of brilliant gayety. She was neatly dressed in gray, and wore the white cap of an elderly woman.

"Ladies and gentlemen," he said, "this is the woman, and I am the man, whose story I have told you. Permit me to introduce to you the wife of my youth."

PAUL LAURENCE DUNBAR

(1872–1906)

Dunbar had earned a brilliant reputation before his death at the age of 34. Taken primarily as a writer of black dialect poems, he was compared to Robert Burns and James Whitcomb Riley. Booker T. Washington hailed him as the "Poet Laureate of the Negro race." William Dean Howells and others responded with great enthusiasm to his humorous poems of black life in the rural South. No black writer before Dunbar received so wide and so encouraging a recognition.

Dunbar was born in Dayton, Ohio, son of a former slave who had fought on the side of the Union. He began his literary career while still in high school, where he was the only black in the class. He edited the school paper and was president of the literary society; instead of going to college, he went right to work after graduation. He worked as an elevator operator, and he continued to write poems; in 1893 he published his first volume, *Oak and Ivy,* at his own expense. His poetry attracted almost immediate attention. In 1894 Frederick Douglass arranged for the young poet to present a reading during "Negro Day" at the Chicago World's Fair. In 1895 Dunbar published *Majors and Minors,* which won an enthusiastic review from Howells in *Harper's Weekly.* Howells detected a talent in the young black similar to that of the Scot Robert Burns, and he wrote an admiring introduction to Dunbar's next and best-known book, *Lyrics of Lowly Life* (1896).

The folk humor represented by a poem such as "Chrismus on the Plantation" seemed to Howells and other admirers of Dunbar to be his richest vein. In addition to dialect and local color and sentimental humor, protest also appeared in Dunbar's work, as in "We Wear the Mask." The mode of humor prevails, however, in the astonishingly prolific years that remained to Dunbar. In addition to several volumes of poetry he published four novels, including *The Sports of the Gods* (1902), considered the first novel that described the city life of black

The poems have been reprinted from *The Complete Poems of Paul Laurence Dunbar,* 1913, 1938, 1965. For a bibliography, see Andrew Burris, "A Bibliography of Works by Paul Laurence Dunbar . . .," *American Collector,* V (1927). A good one-volume edition of the stories is Benjamin G. Brawley, ed., *The Best Stories of Paul Laurence Dunbar,* 1938. Brawley has also written a biography, *Paul Laurence Dunbar: Poet of His People,* 1936, and a study, *Negro Builders and Heroes,* 1937.

Other studies include Vernon Loggins, *The Negro Author,* 1931; Jay Saunders Redding, *To Make a Poet Black,* 1939; Virginia Cunningham, *Paul Laurence Dunbar and His Son,* 1947. A recent account is Addison Gayle, *Oak and Ivy: A Biography of Paul Laurence Dunbar,* 1971.

migrants from the South, and three collections of short fiction, including a group of local color stories in *Folks from Dixie* (1898). Like Sidney Lanier and Stephen Crane before him, Dunbar died of tuberculosis.

Accountability[1]

Folks ain't got no right to censuah othah folks about dey habits;
Him dat giv' de squir'ls de bushtails made de bobtails fu' de rabbits.
Him dat built de gread big mountains hollered out de little valleys,
Him dat made de streets an' driveways wasn't shamed to make de
alleys.

We is all constructed diff'ent, d'ain't no two of us de same;   5
We cain't he'p ouah likes an' dislikes, ef we'se bad we ain't to blame.
Ef we'se good, we needn't show off, cose you bet it ain't ouah doin'
We gits into su'ttain channels dat we jes' cain't he'p pu'suin'.

But we all fits into places dat no othah ones could fill,
An' we does the things we has to, big er little, good er ill.   10
John cain't tek de place o' Henry, Su an' Sally ain't alike;
Bass ain't nuthin' like a suckah,[2] chub ain't nuthin' like a pike.

When you come to think about it, how it's all planned out it's
splendid.
Nuthin's done er evah happens, 'dout hit's somefin' dat's intended;
Don't keer whut you does, you has to, an' hit sholy beats de
dickens—   15
Viney, go put on de kittle, I got one o' mastah's chickens.

1895

[1] First published in *Lyrics of Lowly Life* in   [2] A kind of small fish.
1895.

We Wear the Mask[1]

We wear the mask that grins and lies,
It hides our cheeks and shades our eyes—
This debt we pay to human guile;
With torn and bleeding hearts we smile,
And mouth with myriad subtleties.   5

[1] First published in *Lyrics of Lowly Life* in
1895.

Why should the world be overwise,
In counting all our tears and sighs?
Nay, let them only see us, while
    We wear the mask.

We smile, but, O great Christ, our cries   10
To thee from tortured souls arise.
We sing, but oh the clay is vile
Beneath our feet, and long the mile;
But let the world dream otherwise,
    We wear the mask!   15

Chrismus on the Plantation[1]

It was Chrismus Eve, I mind hit fu' a mighty gloomy day—
Bofe de weathah an' de people—not a one of us was gay;
Cose you'll t'ink dat's mighty funny 'twell I try to mek hit cleah,
Fu' a da'ky's allus happy when de holidays is neah.
But we wasn't, fu' dat mo'nin' Mastah'd tol' us we mus' go,   5
He'd been payin' us sence freedom, but he couldn't pay no mo';
He wa'n't nevah used to plannin' fo' he got so po' an' ol',
So he gwine to give up tryin', an' de homestead mus' be sol'.

I kin see him stan'in' now erpon de step ez cleah ez day,
Wid de win' a-kind o' fondlin' thoo his haih all thin an' gray;   10
An' I 'membah how he trimbled when he said, "It's ha'd fu' me,
Not to mek yo' Chrismus brightah, but I 'low it wa'n't to be."

All de women was a-cryin' an' de men, too, on de sly,
An' I noticed somep'n shinin' even in ol' Mastah's eye.
But we all stood still to listen ez ol' Ben come f'om de crowd   15
An' spoke up, a-try'n' to steady down his voice and mek it loud:—

"Look hyeah, Mastah, I's been servin' you' fu' lo! dese many yeahs,
An' now, sence we's got freedom an' you's kind o' po', hit 'pears
Dat you want us all to leave you 'cause you don't t'ink you can pay.
Ef my membry hasn't fooled me, seem dat whut I hyead you say.   20

"Er in othah wo'ds, you wants us to fu'git dat you's been kin',
An' ez soon ez you is he'pless, we's to leave you hyeah behin'.
Well, ef dat's de way dis freedom ac's on people, white er black,
You kin jes' tell Mistah Lincum fu' to tek his freedom back.

[1] First published in *Lyrics of the Hearthside*
in 1899.

"We gwine wo'k dis ol' plantation fu' whatevah we kin git,   25
Fu' I know hit did suppo't us, an' de place kin do it yit.
Now de land is yo's, de hands is ouahs, an' I reckon we'll be brave,
An' we'll bah ez much ez you do w'en we has to scrape an' save."
Ol' Mastah stood dah trimblin', but a-smilin' thoo his teahs,
An' den hit seemed jes' nachul-like, de place fah rung wid cheahs,   30
An' soon ez dey was quiet, some one sta'ted sof' an' low:
"Praise God," an' den we all jined in, "from whom all blessin's flow!"

Well, dey wasn't no use tryin', ouah min's was sot to stay,
An' po' ol' Mastah,couldn't plead ner baig, ner drive us 'way,
An' all at once, hit seemed to us, de day was bright agin,   35
So evahone was gay dat night, an' watched de Chrismus in.

BOOKER T. WASHINGTON

(1856–1915)

Up From Slavery (1901) is a classic narrative of the black experience in
America. The autobiography of one of the most influential and controversial leaders of Afro-Americans, it begins in slavery and recounts
Washington's rise to worldly success and eminence. As the title intimates, the force of his famous work derives from its bringing together
two separate strains in American popular writing: the slave narrative of
oppression and escape, typified by Frederick Douglass's *My Bondage
and My Freedom* (1855), and the "rags to riches" story of the self-made

The major works are *Sowing and Reap-
ing*, 1900; *Up from Slavery*, 1901; *Character Building*, 1902; *Putting the Most into
Life*, 1906; *Frederick Douglass: The Negro
in Business*, 1907; *The Story of the Negro*,
1909; *My Larger Education*, 1911; *The Man
Farthest Down*, 1912.
A recent biography is E. L. Thornbrough,
Booker T. Washington, 1969. Critical estimates appear in Gunnar Myrdal, *An
American Dilemma*, 1940; Basil Matthews,
*Booker T. Washington: Educator and In-
terracial Interpreter*, 1948; C. Vann Woodward, *Origins of the New South*,

1877–1910, 1951; G. R. Spencer, *Booker T.
Washington and the Negro's Place in
American Life*, 1955; L. R. Horton,
"Booker T. Washington and the White
Man's Burden," *American Historical Re-
view*, 1961; Hugh Hawkins, *Booker T.
Washington and His Critics: The Prob-
lems of Negro Leadership*, 1962; August
Meier, *Negro Thought in America*,
1880–1915, 1963; Francis L. Broderick and
August Meier, *Negro Protest Thought in
the Twentieth Century*, 1965; John Hope
Franklin, *From Slavery to Freedom: A His-
tory of American Negroes*, 1967.

man, of which Benjamin Franklin's *Autobiography* is the earliest example, and the best-selling novels of Horatio Alger, Jr., in the post-Civil War period, another very popular instance. Washington's story is pre-eminently a success story, but one that formed itself under the special conditions of a racially divided society. Hardly typical of the experience of most black Americans, it nevertheless presented a model of aspiration.

Washington was born a slave on a Virginia plantation; his father, as best as he could determine, was a white man who lived in the neighborhood. Emancipation came when the boy was 5 years old. At 9 he was working in a West Virginia coal mine. But he managed to get some schooling, and he eventually found his way, in 1872, to the Hampton Institute in Virginia. Hampton was established during Reconstruction as a vocational school for blacks and Indians, one that stressed social manners and decorum as well as book learning and crafts. After his graduation in 1875, Washington taught school in the South for a few years and then became the head of a newly founded Normal and Industrial Institute for blacks in Tuskegee, Alabama. In the next 20 years, because of his driving determination to improve the conditions of the life of blacks, he rose to international fame; he won many honors including an invitation to the White House under Theodore Roosevelt.

Washington was convinced that the future of Afro-Americans rested with their ability to learn practical skills in trades and business, rather than with social and political campaigns against discrimination. In 1895 he was invited to deliver a speech in Atlanta at the Cotton States and International Exposition, and there he proclaimed his doctrine of self-help for blacks. "The wisest among my race," he argued, "understand that the agitation of questions of social equality is the extremest folly." Instead, he continued, "the enjoyment of all the privileges that will come to us must be the result of severe and constant struggle rather than artificial forcing." Hailed by influential whites as a "Negro Moses," Washington soon alienated a growing number of younger black intellectuals, including W.E.B. DuBois, who charged him with betrayal of his race by conformity to the "spirit and thought of triumphant commercialism." In 1909 DuBois helped found the National Association for the Advancement of Colored People (NAACP) which, in opposition to Washington's doctrine of accommodation, pledged itself to winning full civil rights and social justice. By the time of his death in 1915, Washington's once enormous influence and prestige had begun to wane significantly.

From Up from Slavery[1]

CHAPTER 1
A SLAVE AMONG SLAVES

I was born a slave on a plantation in Franklin County, Virginia. I am not quite sure of the exact place or exact date of my birth, but at any rate I suspect I must have been born somewhere and at some time. As nearly as I have been able to learn, I was born near a cross-roads postoffice called Hale's Ford, and the year was 1858 or 1859. I do not know the month or the day. The earliest impressions I can now recall are of the plantation and the slave quarters—the latter being the part of the plantation where the slaves had their cabins.

My life had its beginning in the midst of the most miserable, desolate, and discouraging surroundings. This was so, however, not because my owners were especially cruel, for they were not, as compared with many others. I was born in a typical log cabin, about fourteen by sixteen feet square. In this cabin I lived with my mother and a brother and sister till after the Civil War, when we were all declared free.

Of my ancestry I know almost nothing. In the slave quarters, and even later, I heard whispered conversations among the coloured people of the tortures which the slaves, including, no doubt, my ancestors on my mother's side, suffered in the middle passage of the slave ship while being conveyed from Africa to America. I have been unsuccessful in securing any information that would throw any accurate light upon the history of my family beyond my mother. She, I remember, had a half-brother and a half-sister. In the days of slavery not very much attention was given to family history and family records—that is, black family records. My mother, I suppose, attracted the attention of a purchaser who was afterward my owner and hers. Her addition to the slave family attracted about as much attention as the purchase of a new horse or cow. Of my father I know even less than of my mother. I do not even know his name. I have heard reports to the effect that he was a white man who lived on one of the near-by plantations. Whoever he was, I never heard of his taking the least interest in me or providing in any way for my rearing. But I do not find especial fault with him. He was simply another unfortunate victim of the institution which the Nation unhappily had engrafted upon it at that time.

The cabin was not only our living-place, but was also used as the kitchen for the plantation. My mother was the plantation cook. The cabin was without glass windows; it had only openings in the side which let in the light, and

[1] First published in 1901, by Doubleday, Page, & Co., New York.

also the cold, chilly air of winter. There was a door to the cabin—that is, something that was called a door—but the uncertain hinges by which it was hung, and the large cracks in it, to say nothing of the fact that it was too small, made the room a very uncomfortable one. In addition to these openings there was, in the lower right-hand corner of the room, the "cat-hole,"— a contrivance which almost every mansion or cabin in Virginia possessed during the ante-bellum period. The "cat-hole" was a square opening, about seven by eight inches, provided for the purpose of letting the cat pass in and out of the house at will during the night. In the case of our particular cabin I could never understand the necessity for this convenience, since there were at least a half-dozen other places in the cabin that would have accommodated the cats. There was no wooden floor in our cabin, the naked earth being used as a floor. In the centre of the earthen floor there was a large, deep opening covered with boards, which was used as a place in which to store sweet potatoes during the winter. An impression of this potato-hole is very distinctly engraved upon my memory, because I recall that during the process of putting the potatoes in or taking them out I would often come into possession of one or two, which I roasted and thoroughly enjoyed. There was no cooking-stove on our plantation, and all the cooking for the whites and slaves my mother had to do over an open fireplace, mostly in pots and "skillets." While the poorly built cabin caused us to suffer with cold in the winter, the heat from the open fireplace in summer was equally trying.

The early years of my life, which were spent in the little cabin, were not very different from those of thousands of other slaves. My mother, of course, had little time in which to give attention to the training of her children during the day. She snatched a few moments for our care in the early morning before her work began, and at night after the day's work was done. One of my earliest recollections is that of my mother cooking a chicken late at night, and awakening her children for the purpose of feeding them. How or where she got it I do not know. I presume, however, it was procured from our owner's farm. Some people may call this theft. If such a thing were to happen now, I should condemn it as theft myself. But taking place at the time it did, and for the reason that it did, no one could ever make me believe that my mother was guilty of thieving. She was simply a victim of the system of slavery. I cannot remember having slept in a bed until after our family was declared free by the Emancipation Proclamation. Three children— John, my older brother, Amanda, my sister, and myself—had a pallet on the dirt floor, or, to be more correct, we slept in and on a bundle of filthy rags laid upon the dirt floor.

I was asked not long ago to tell something about the sports and pastimes that I engaged in during my youth. Until that question was asked it had never occurred to me that there was no period of my life that was devoted to play. From the time that I can remember anything, almost every day of my life has been occupied in some kind of labour; though I think I would now be a more useful man if I had had time for sports. During the period that I spent in slavery I was not large enough to be of much service, still I was occupied most of the time in cleaning the yards, carrying water to the men in the fields, or going to the mill, to which I used to take the corn, once a week, to be ground. The mill was about three miles from the plantation. This work I always dreaded. The heavy bag of corn would be thrown across the back of the horse, and the corn divided about evenly on each side; but in some way, almost without exception, on these trips, the corn would so shift as to become unbalanced and would fall off the horse, and often I would fall with it. As I was not strong enough to reload the corn upon the horse, I would have to wait, sometimes for many hours, till a chance passer-by came along who would help me out of my trouble. The hours while waiting for some one were usually spent in crying. The time consumed in this way made me late in reaching the mill, and by the time I got my corn ground and reached home it would be far into the night. The road was a lonely one, and often led through dense forests. I was always frightened. The woods were said to be full of soldiers who had deserted from the army, and I had been told that the first thing a deserter did to a Negro boy when he found him alone was to cut off his ears. Besides, when I was late in getting home I knew I would always get a severe scolding or a flogging.

I had no schooling whatever while I was a slave, though I remember on several occasions I went as far as the schoolhouse door with one of my young mistresses to carry her books. The picture of several dozen boys and girls in a schoolroom engaged in study made a deep impression upon me, and I had the feeling that to get into a schoolhouse and study in this way would be about the same as getting into paradise.

So far as I can now recall, the first knowledge that I got of the fact that we were slaves, and that freedom of the slaves was being discussed, was early one morning before day, when I was awakened by my mother kneeling over her children and fervently praying that Lincoln and his armies might be successful, and that one day she and her children might be free. In this connection I have never been able to understand how the slaves throughout the South, completely ignorant as were the masses so far as books or newspapers were concerned, were able to keep themselves so accurately and completely informed about the great National questions that were agitating the country. From the time that Garrison, Lovejoy, and others began to agitate for freedom, the slaves throughout the South kept in close touch with the progress of the movement. Though I was a mere child during the preparation for the Civil War and during the war itself, I now recall the many late-at-night whispered discussions that I heard my mother and the other slaves on the plantation indulge in. These discussions showed that they understood the situation, and that they kept themselves informed of events by what was termed the "grape-vine" telegraph.

During the campaign when Lincoln was first a candidate for the Presidency, the slaves on our far-off plantation, miles from any railroad or large city or daily newspaper, knew what the issues involved were. When war was begun between the North and the South, every slave on our plantation felt and knew that, though other issues were discussed, the primal one was that of slavery. Even the most ignorant members of my race on the remote plantations felt in their hearts, with a certainty that admitted of no doubt, that the freedom of the slaves would be the one great result of the war, if the Northern armies conquered. Every success of the Federal armies and every defeat of the Confederate forces was watched with the keenest and most intense interest. Often the slaves got knowledge of the results of great battles before the white people received it. This news was usually gotten from the coloured man who was sent to the post-office for the mail. In our case the post-office was about three miles from the plantation and the mail came once or twice a week. The man who was sent to the office would linger about the place long enough to get the drift of the conversation from the group of white people who naturally congregated there, after receiving their mail, to discuss the latest news. The mail-carrier on his way back to our master's house would as naturally retail the news that he had secured among the slaves, and in this way they often heard of important events before the white people at the "big house," as the master's house was called.

I cannot remember a single instance during my childhood or early boyhood when our entire family sat down to the table together, and God's blessing was asked, and the family ate a meal in a civilized manner. On the plantation in Virginia, and even later, meals were gotten by the children very much as dumb animals get theirs. It was a piece of bread here and a scrap of meat there. It was a cup of milk at one time and some potatoes at another. Sometimes a portion of our family would eat out of the skillet or pot, while someone else would eat from a tin plate held on the knees, and often using nothing but the hands with which to hold the food. When I had grown to sufficient size, I was required to go to the "big house" at meal-times to fan the flies from the table by means of a large set of paper fans operated by a pulley. Naturally much of the conversation of the white people turned upon the subject of freedom and the war, and I absorbed a good deal of it. I remember that at one time I saw two of my young mistresses and some lady visitors eating ginger-cakes, in the yard. At that time those cakes seemed to me to be absolutely the most tempting and desirable things that I had ever seen; and I then and there resolved that, if I ever got free, the height of my ambition would be reached if I could get to the point where I could secure and eat ginger-cakes in the way that I saw those ladies doing.

Of course as the war was prolonged the white people, in many cases, often found it difficult to secure food for themselves. I think the slaves felt the deprivation less than the white, because the usual diet for the slaves was corn bread and pork, and these could be raised on the plantation; but coffee, tea, sugar, and other articles which the whites had been accustomed to use could not be raised on the plantation, and the conditions brought about by the war frequently made it impossible to secure these things. The whites were often in great straits. Parched corn was used for coffee, and a kind of black molasses was used instead of sugar. Many times nothing was used to sweeten the so-called tea and coffee.

The first pair of shoes that I recall wearing were wooden ones. They had rough leather on the top, but the bottoms, which were about an inch thick, were of wood. When I walked they made a fearful noise, and besides this they were very inconvenient, since there was no yielding to the natural pressure of the foot. In wearing them one presented an exceedingly awkward appearance. The most trying ordeal that I was forced to endure as a slave boy, however, was the wearing of a flax shirt. In the portion of Virginia where I lived it was common to use flax as part of the clothing for the slaves. That part of the flax from which our clothing was made was largely the refuse, which of course was the cheapest and roughest part. I can scarcely imagine any torture, except, perhaps, the pulling of a tooth, that is equal to that caused by putting on a new flax shirt for the first time. It is almost equal to the feeling that one would experience if he had a dozen or more chestnut burrs, or a hundred small pinpoints, in contact with his flesh. Even to this day I can recall accurately the tortures that I underwent when putting on one of these garments. The fact that my flesh was soft and tender added to the pain. But I had no choice. I had to wear the flax shirt or none; and had it been left to me to choose, I should have chosen to wear no covering. In connection with the flax shirt, my brother John, who is several years older than I am, performed one of the most generous acts that I ever heard of one slave relative doing for another. On several occasions when I was being forced to wear a new flax shirt, he generously agreed to put it on in my stead and wear it for several days, till it was "broken in." Until I had grown to be quite a youth this single garment was all that I wore.

One may get the idea from what I have said, that there was bitter feeling toward the white people on the part of my race, because of the fact that most of the white population was away fighting in a war which would result in keeping the Negro in slavery if the South was successful. In the case of the slaves on our place this was not true, and it was not true of any large portion of the slave population in the South where the Negro was treated with anything like decency. During the Civil War one of my young masters was killed, and two were severely wounded. I recall the feeling of sorrow which existed among the slaves when they heard of the death of "Mars' Billy." It was no sham sorrow but real. Some of the slaves had nursed "Mars' Billy"; others had played with him when he was a child. "Mars' Billy" had begged for mercy in the case of others when the overseer or master was thrashing them. The sorrow in the slave quarter was only second to that in the "big house." When the two young masters were brought home wounded, the sympathy of the slaves was shown in many ways. They were just as anxious to assist in the nursing as the family relatives of the wounded. Some of the slaves would even beg for the privilege of sitting up at night to nurse their wounded masters. This tenderness and sympathy on the part of those held in bondage was a result of their kindly and generous nature. In order to defend and protect the women and children who were left on the plantations when the white males went to war, the slaves would have laid down their lives. The slave who was selected to sleep in the "big house" during the absence of the males was considered to have the place of honour. Any one attempting to harm "young Mistress" or "old Mistress" during the night would have had to cross the dead body of the slave to do so. I do not know how many have noticed it, but I think that it will be found to be true that there are few instances, either in slavery or freedom, in which a member of my race has been known to betray a specific trust.

As a rule, not only did the members of my race entertain no feelings of bitterness against the whites before and during the war, but there are many instances of Negroes tenderly caring for their former masters and mistresses who for some reason have become poor and dependent since the war. I know of instances where the former masters of slaves have for years been supplied with money by their former slaves to keep them from suffering. I have known of still other cases in which the former slaves have assisted in the education of the descendants of their former owners. I know of a case on a large plantation in the South in which a young white man, the son of the former owner of the estate, has become so reduced in purse and self-control by reason of drink that he is a pitiable creature; and yet, notwithstanding the poverty of the colored people themselves on this plantation, they have for years supplied this young white man with the necessities of life. One sends him a little coffee or sugar, another a little meat, and so on. Nothing that the colored people possess is too good for the son of "old Mars' Tom," who will perhaps never be permitted to suffer while any remain on the place who knew directly or indirectly of "old Mars' Tom."

I have said that there are few instances of a member of my race betraying a specific trust. One of the best illustrations of this which I know of is in the case of an ex-slave from Virginia whom I met not long ago in a little town in the state of Ohio. I found that this man had made a contract with his master, two or three years previous to the Emancipation Proclamation, to the effect that the slave was to be permitted to buy himself, by paying so much per year for his body; and while he was paying for himself, he was to be permitted to labor where and for whom he pleased. Finding that he could secure better wages in Ohio, he went there. When freedom came, he was still in debt to his master some three hundred dollars. Notwithstanding that the Emancipation Proclamation freed him from any obligation to his master, this black man walked the greater portion of the distance back to where his old master lived in Virginia, and placed the last dollar, with interest, in his hands.

In talking to me about this, the man told me that he knew he did not have to pay the debt, but that he had given his word to his master, and his word he had never broken. He felt that he could not enjoy his freedom till he had fulfilled his promise.

From some things that I have said one may get the idea that some of the slaves did not want freedom. This is not true. I have never seen one who did not want to be free, or one who would return to slavery.

I pity from the bottom of my heart any nation or body of people that is so unfortunate as to get entangled in the net of slavery. I have long since ceased to cherish any spirit of bitterness against the Southern white people on account of the enslavement of my race. No one section of our country was wholly responsible for its introduction, and, besides, it was recognized and protected for years by the General Government. Having once got its tentacles fastened on to the economic and social life of the Republic, it was no easy matter for the country to relieve itself of the institution. Then, when we rid ourselves of prejudice, or racial feeling, and look facts in the face, we must acknowledge that, notwithstanding the cruelty and moral wrong of slavery, the ten million Negroes inhabiting this country, who themselves or whose ancestors went through the school of American slavery, are in a stronger and more hopeful condition, materially, intellectually, morally, and religiously, than is true of an equal number of black people in any other portion of the globe. This is so to such an extent that Negroes in this country, who themselves or whose forefathers went through the school of slavery, are constantly returning to Africa as missionaries to enlighten those who remained in the fatherland. This I say, not to justify slavery—on the other hand, I condemn it as an institution, as we all know that in America it was established for selfish and financial reasons, and not from a missionary motive—but to call attention to a fact, and to show how Providence so often uses men and institutions to accomplish a purpose. When persons ask me in these days how, in the midst of what sometimes seem hopelessly discouraging conditions, I can have such faith in the future of my race in this country, I remind them of the wilderness through which and out of which, a good Providence has already led us.

Ever since I have been old enough to think for myself, I have entertained the idea that, not withstanding the cruel wrongs inflicted upon us, the black man got nearly as much out of slavery as the white man did. The hurtful influences of the institution were not by any means confined to the Negro. This was fully illustrated by the life upon our own plantation. The whole machinery of slavery was so constructed as to cause labor, as a rule, to be looked upon as a badge of degradation, of inferiority. Hence labor was something that both races on the slave plantation sought to escape. The slave system on our place, in a large measure, took the spirit of self-reliance and self-help out of the white people. My old master had many boys and girls, but not one, so far as I know, ever mastered a single trade or special line of productive industry. The girls were not taught to cook, sew, or to take care of the house. All of this was left to the slaves. The slaves, of course, had little personal interest in the life of the plantation, and their ignorance prevented them from learning how to do things in the most improved and thorough manner. As a result of the system, fences were out of repair, gates were hanging half off the hinges, doors creaked, window-panes were out, plastering had fallen but was not replaced, weeds grew in the yard. As a rule, there was food for whites and blacks, but inside the house, and on the dining-room table, there was wanting that delicacy and refinement of touch and finish which can make a home the most convenient, comfortable, and attractive place in the world. Withal there was a waste of food and other materials which was sad. When freedom came, the slaves were almost as well fitted to begin life anew as the master, except in the matter of book-learning and ownership of property. The slave owner and his sons had mastered no special industry. They unconsciously had imbibed the feeling that manual labor was not the proper thing for them. On the other hand, the slaves, in many cases, had mastered some handicraft, and none were ashamed, and few unwilling, to labor.

Finally the war closed, and the day of freedom came. It was a momentous and eventful day to all upon our plantation. We had been expecting it. Freedom was in the air, and had been for months. Deserting soldiers returning to their homes were to be seen every day. Others who had been discharged, or whose regiments had been paroled, were constantly passing near our place. The "grape-vine telegraph" was kept busy night and day. The news and mutterings of great events were swiftly carried from one plantation to another. In the fear of "Yankee" invasions, the silverware and other valuables were taken from the "big house," buried in the woods, and guarded by trusted slaves. Woe be to any one who would have attempted to disturb the buried treasure. The slaves would give the Yankee soldiers food, drink, clothing—anything but that which had been specifically intrusted to their care and honour. As the great day drew nearer, there was more singing in the slave quarters than usual. It was bolder, had more ring, and lasted later into the night. Most of the verses of the plantation songs had some reference to freedom. True, they had sung those same verses before, but they had been careful to explain that the "freedom" in these songs referred to the next world, and had no connection with life in this world. Now they gradually threw off the mask; and were not afraid to let it be known that the "freedom" in their songs meant freedom of the body in this world. The night before the eventful day, word was sent to the slave quarters to the effect that something unusual was going to take place at the "big house" the next morning. There was little, if any, sleep that night. All was excitement and expectancy. Early the next morning word was sent to all the slaves, old and young, to gather at the house. In company with my mother, brother, and sister, and a large number of other slaves, I went to the master's house. All of our master's family were either standing or seated on the veranda of the house, where they could see what was to take place and hear what was said. There was a feeling of deep interest, or perhaps sadness, on their faces, but not bitterness. As I now recall the impression they made upon me, they did not at the moment seem to be sad because of the loss of property, but rather because of parting with those whom they had reared and who were in many ways very close to them. The most distinct thing that I now recall in connection with the scene was that some man who seemed to be a stranger (a United States officer, I presume) made a little speech and then read a rather long paper—the Emancipation Proclamation, I think. After the reading we were told that we were all free, and could go when and where we pleased. My mother, who was standing by my side, leaned over and kissed her children, while tears of joy ran down her cheeks. She explained to us what it all meant, that this was the day for which she had been so long praying, but fearing that she would never live to see.

For some minutes there was great rejoicing, and thanksgiving, and wild scenes of ecstasy. But there was no feeling of bitterness. In fact, there was pity among the slaves for our former owners. The wild rejoicing on the part of the emancipated colored people lasted but for a brief period, for I noticed that by the time they returned to their cabins there was a change in their feelings. The great responsibility of being free, of having charge of themselves, of having to think and plan for themselves and their children, seemed to take possession of them. It was very much like suddenly turning a youth of ten or twelve years out into the world to provide for himself. In a few hours the great questions with which the Anglo-Saxon race had been grappling for centuries had been thrown upon these people to be solved. These were the questions of a home, a living, the rearing of children, education, citizenship, and the establishment and support of churches. Was it any wonder that within a few hours the wild rejoicing ceased and a feeling of deep gloom seemed to pervade the slave quarters? To some it seemed that, now that they were in actual possession of it, freedom was a more serious thing than they had expected to find it. Some of the slaves were seventy or eighty years old; their best days were gone. They had no strength with which to earn a living in a strange place and among strange people, even if they had been sure where to find a new place of abode. To this class the problem seemed especially hard. Besides, deep down in their hearts there was a strange and peculiar attachment to "old Master" and "old Missus," and to their children, which they found it hard to think of breaking off. With these they had spent in some cases nearly a half-century, and it was no light thing to think of parting. Gradually, one by one, stealthily at first, the older slaves began to wander from the slave quarters back to the "big house" to have a whispered conversation with their former owners as to the future.

FOLK SONGS AND BALLADS

While it has been a matter of argument among some scholars whether or not America has a genuine folk tradition, there is no question about the wealth of folk materials—tales, songs, ballads—present in American life. Some purists insist that the majority of the songs and ballads discovered in regions like the Appalachian Mountains or the Southern Black Belt derive from traditions rooted elsewhere, in Europe or Africa. It is true that many strains have appeared in American folk literature, but evidence indicates significant modifications of traditional lyrics, music, and, most significantly, singing and story-telling style. The interaction among Anglo-Saxon, ethnic (German, Scandinavian, Italian, Slavic, Jewish), Afro-American, and Indian cultures has produced forms and styles unique to this land. The "blues" are one example, and the white "country and western" another. The adaption of the "spiritual" by blacks in the South resulted in another major alteration of a traditional form.

American folk literature reflects the great diversity of life better than the "high" or sophisticated novels and poems and short stories in the same period. An oral literature, subject to daily modifications as each performer adds or subtracts or changes words and details of melodies, is much more sensitive to the temperature of feelings and currents of popular thought than published writing. Many serious writers were familiar with the oral literatures of the folk; Whitman, Mark Twain, and the local color regionalists incorporated themes and styles in their own work. Also reflected in a more immediate and spontaneous way than in "high" literature are the deep changes occurring in the lives of common Americans in this period. The experiences of farmers and cowboys in the West, of railroad workers, of "outlaws" who pitted themselves against the power of the railroad companies, of prostitutes and prisoners, all these appear in the folk songs that emerged in this period and continue to be sung and appreciated to the present day. With the arrival of millions of new immigrants, and with the tumultu-

For a general introduction see Richard M. Dorson, ed., *Folklore and Folklife: An Introduction*, 1972. Tristram P. Coffin, ed., *Our Living Traditions: An Introduction*, 1968, is also useful. On folk songs specifically, see Evelyn K. Wells, *The Ballad Tree*, 1950, and Tristram P. Coffin, *The British Traditional Ballad in North America*, 1963.

Valuable general collections of folk songs and ballads can be found in Carl Sandburg, *An American Songbag*, 1927, and John A. Lomax and Alan Lomax, *Our Singing Country*, 1941. Many studies and collections of regional, ethnic, and topical songs are also available. Especially important is Howard W. Odum and Guy B. Johnson, *The Negro and His Songs*, 1925.

ous changes unsettling American life in the years after the Civil War,
this period was something of a golden age of folk invention, surely
one of the notable heritages of the writing of the age.

Frankie and Johnny[1]

1 Frankie and Johnny were lovers, O lordy how they could love.
 Swore to be true to each other, true as the stars above;
 He was her man but he done her wrong, so wrong.

2 Johnny's mother told him, and she was mighty wise,
 Don't spend Frankie's money on that parlor Ann Eliz;
 You're Frankie's man, and you're doin' her wrong, so wrong.

3 Frankie and Johnny went walking, Johnny in his bran' new suit,
 "O good Lawd," says Frankie, "Don't my Johnny look cute?"
 He was her man but he done her wrong, so wrong.

4 Frankie went down to the corner, to buy a glass of beer;
 She says to the fat bartender, "Has my lovinest man been here?
 He was my man but he's done me wrong, so wrong."

5 Frankie went down to the pawn shop, she bought herself a little forty-
 four
 She aimed it at the ceiling, shot a big hole in the floor;
 "Where is my man, he's doin' me wrong, so wrong?"

6 Frankie went back to the hotel, she didn't go there for fun,
 'Cause under her long red kimono she toted a forty-four gun.
 He was her man but he done her wrong, so wrong.

7 Frankie went down to the hotel, looked in the window so high,
 There she saw her lovin' Johnny a-lovin' up Alice Bly;
 He was her man but he done her wrong, so wrong.

8 Frankie went down to the hotel, she rang that hotel bell,
 "Stand back all of you floozies or I'll blow you all to hell,
 I want my man, he's doin' me wrong, so wrong."

9 Frankie threw back her kimono, she took out her forty-four.
 Root-a-toot-toot, three times she shot, right through the hardwood floor,
 She shot her man, cause he done her wrong, so wrong.

---

[1] "Frankie and Johnnie" has been called "America's classic gutter song." There are many versions of the song—Frankie and Johnny, Frankie and Albert, Annie and Johnny, Lillie and Albert. There are many tunes as well, and the number of verses is infinite. But the story remains always the same: one of desire, betrayal, and death.

10 Johnny grabbed off his Stetson, "O good Lawd, Frankie, don't shoot."
But Frankie put her finger on the trigger, and the gun went roota-toot-toot,
He was her man but she shot him down.

11 Johnny saw Frankie a comin', down the backstairs he did scoot;
Frankie had the little gun out, let him have it rooty-de-toot;
For he was her man, but she shot him down.

12 Johnny he mounted the staircase, cried, "O Frankie don't shoot!"
Three times she pulled the forty-four gun a rooty-toot-toot-toot-toot,
She nailed the man what threw her down.

13 "Roll me over easy, roll me over slow,
Roll me over easy, boys, 'cause my wounds they hurt me so,
But I was her man, and I done her wrong, so wrong."

14 "Oh my baby, kiss me once before I go.
Turn me over on my right side, doctor, where de bullet hurt me so.
I was her man but I done her wrong, so wrong."

15 Johnny he was a gambler, he gambled for the gain.
The very last words he ever said were, "High-low Jack and the game."
He was her man but he done her wrong, so wrong.

16 Bring out your long black coffin, bring out your funeral clo'es;
Bring back Johnny's mother; to the churchyard Johnny goes.
He was her man but he done her wrong, so wrong.

17 Frankie went to his coffin, she looked down on his face.
She said, "O Lawd, have mercy on me, I wish I could take his place,
He was my man, and I done him wrong, so wrong."

18 Oh bring on your rubber-tired hearses, bring on your rubber-tired hacks,
They're takin' Johnny to the buryin' groun' an' they won't bring a bit of him back;
He was her man but he done her wrong, so wrong.

19 Frankie stood on the corner to watch the funeral go by;
"Bring back my poor dead Johnny to me," to the undertaker she did say,
"He was my man, but he done me wrong, so wrong."

20 Frankie heard a rumbling away down in the ground,
Maybe it was little Johnny where she had shot him down.
He was her man and she done him wrong, so wrong.

21 Frankie went to Mrs. Halcomb, she fell down on her knees,
She said, "Mrs. Halcomb, forgive me, forgive me, if you please,
For I've killed my man what done me wrong, so wrong."

22 "Forgive you, Frankie darling, forgive you I never can.
Forgive you, Frankie darling, for killing your only man,
Oh he was your man tho' he done you wrong, so wrong."

23 Frankie said to the warden, "What are they goin' to do?"
The warden he said to Frankie, "It's the electric chair for you,
You shot your man tho' he done you wrong, so wrong."

24 The sheriff came around in the morning, said it was all for the best,
He said her lover Johnny was nothin' but a doggone pest.
He was her man but he done her wrong, so wrong."

25 The judge said to the jury, "It's as plain as plain can be;
This woman shot her lover, it's murder in the second degree,
He was her man tho' he done her wrong, so wrong."

26 Now it was not murder in the second degree, and was not murder in
the third,
The woman simply dropped her man, like a hunter drops a bird.
He was her man but he done her wrong, so wrong.

27 "Oh bring a thousand policemen, bring 'em around today,
Oh lock me in that dungeon, and throw the keys away,
I shot my man, 'cause he done me wrong, so wrong."

28 "Yes, put me in that dungeon, oh put me in that cell,
Put me where the northeast wind blows from the southeast corner of
hell.
I shot my man, 'cause he done me wrong, so wrong."

29 Frankie mounted to the scaffold as calm as a girl can be,
And turning her eyes to heaven, she said, "Good Lord, I am coming to
Thee.
He was my man, but he done me wrong, so wrong."

Midnight Special[1]

[1] If you evah go to Houston,
You better walk right;
You better not gamble
And you better not fight.
T. Bentley will arrest you,
He'll surely take you down;
Judge Nelson'll sentence you,
Then you're jailhouse bound.

[1] The Midnight Special is any good fast train;
it means escape from prison.

Refrain:
O let the Midnight Special
Shine a light on me,
Let the Midnight Special
Shine a evah lovin' light on me!

2 Every Monday mawnin',
When the ding-dong rings,
You go to the table,
See the same damn things;
And on the table,
There's a knife an' pan,
Say anything about it,
Have trouble with a man.

3 Yondah come Miss Rosy;
Oh, how do you know?
By th' umbrella on her shoulder
An' the dress that she woah!
Straw hat on her head,
Piece of paper in her hand,
Says, "Look here, Mr. Jailer,
I want's my life-time man."

As I Walked Out in the Streets of Laredo[1]

1 As I walked out in the streets of Laredo,
As I walked out in Laredo one day,
I spied a poor cowboy wrapped up in white linen,
Wrapped up in white linen and cold as the clay.

2 "I see by your outfit that you are a cowboy,"
These words he did say as I boldly stepped by.
"Come sit down beside me and hear my sad story;
I was shot in the breast and I know I must die.

[1] There are many tunes and verses to this cowboy song. Many of the verses printed here are Irish and come from fond memories of the broadsides of Dublin.

3 "Let sixteen gamblers come handle my coffin,
   Let sixteen cowboys come sing me a song,
   Take me to the graveyard and lay the sod o'er me,
   For I'm a poor cowboy and I know I've done wrong.

4 "It was once in the saddle I used to go dashing,
   It was once in the saddle I used to go gay.
   'Twas first to drinking and then to card playing,
   Got shot in the breast, I am dying today.

5 "Get six jolly cowboys to carry my coffin,
   Get six pretty girls to carry my pall;
   Put bunches of roses all over my coffin,
   Put roses to deaden the clods as they fall.

6 "O beat the drum slowly and play the fife lowly
   And play the dead march as you carry me along,
   Take me to the green valley and lay the sod o'er me,
   For I'm a young cowboy and I know I've done wrong."

7 We beat the drum slowly and played the fife lowly,
   And bitterly wept as we bore him along;
   For we all loved our comrade, so brave, young, and handsome,
   We all loved our comrade although he'd done wrong.

Casey Jones[1]

1 Come all you rounders, for I want you to hear,
   The story of a brave engineer.
   Casey Jones was the rounder's name,
   On a big eight wheeler of a mighty fame.

[1] In the Santa Fe Railway Station in Dodge City, Kansas, there is a white wooden post that carries the painted message, "Lest We Forget." Nailed onto it is an old fashioned link-and-pin coupler. Casey Jones was a real man, named John Luther Jones, born in Missouri in 1864. He was an expert engineer on the Chicago-New Orleans run of the Illinois Central Railroad. On April 29, 1900, substituting for a sick engineer, he took charge of the southbound Cannonball run. Outside of the small town of Vaughn some cars of four trains that were on a side track waiting for the Cannonball to pass were overlapping Casey's track. Casey ordered his fireman to jump and, in a heroic effort to save lives, he stayed at his post, sounding the warning whistle and trying to slow the train down. In the crash, no life was lost but his own.

2 Caller called Casey 'bout half-past four,
   He kissed his wife at the station door,
   Climbed to the cab with the orders in his hand,
   He says, "This is my trip to the holy land."

3 Out of South Memphis yard on the fly,
   Heard the fireman say, "You got a white eye."
   Well, the switchmen knew by the engine moan
   That the man at the throttle was Casey Jones.

4 The rain was comin' down five or six weeks.
   The railroad track was like the bed of a creek.
   They slowed her down to a thirty mile gait
   And the south-bound mail was eight hours late.

5 Fireman says, "Casey, you're runnin' too fast,
   You run that block board the last station you passed."
   Casey says, "I believe we'll make it though,
   For she steams a lot better than I ever know."

6 Casey says, "Fireman, don't you fret,
   Keep knockin' at the fire door, don't give up yet,
   I'm going to run her till she leaves the rail,
   Or make it on time with south-bound mail."

7 Around the curve and down the dump,
   Two locomotives was bound to jump,
   Fireman hollered, "Casey, it's just ahead,
   We might jump and make it but we'll all be dead."

8 Around the curve comes a passenger train,
   Casey blows the whistle, tells the fireman, "Ring the bell,"
   Fireman jumps and says "Good-by,
   Casey Jones, You're bound to die."

9 Well Casey Jones was all right.
   He stuck to his duty day and night.
   They loved his whistle and his ring number three,
   And he came into Memphis on the old I. C.

10 Fireman goes down the depot track,
   Begging his honey to take him back,
   She says, "Oranges on the table, peaches on the shelf,
   You're a goin' to get tired sleepin' by yourself."

¹¹ Mrs. Casey Jones was a sittin' on the bed.
Telegram comes that Casey is dead.
She says, "Children, go to bed, and hush your cryin',
'Cause you got another papa on the Frisco line."

¹² Headaches and heartaches and all kinds of pain.
They ain't apart from a railroad train.
Stories of brave men, noble and grand,
Belong to the life of a railroad man.

Jesse James[1]

[1] It was on a Wednesday night, the moon was shining bright,
    They robbed the Glendale train.
And the people they did say, for many miles away,
    'Twas the outlaws Frank and Jesse James.

Refrain—Jesse had a wife to mourn all her life,
        The children they are brave.
    'Twas a dirty little coward shot Mister Howard,
        And laid Jesse James in his grave.

[2] It was Robert Ford, the dirty little coward,
    I wonder how he does feel,
For he ate of Jesse's bread and he slept in Jesse's bed,
    Then he laid Jesse James in his grave.—*Refrain*

[3] It was his brother Frank that robbed the Gallatin bank,
    And carried the money from the town.
It was in this very place that they had a little race,
    For they shot Captain Sheets to the ground.—*Refrain*

[1] The legend of Jesse James the outlaw speaks for itself, as do those of Paul Bunyan, Davy Crockett, Mike Fink, and John Henry. Jesse James was living quietly in Missouri under the assumed name of Howard when he was shot in the back of the head by a young man, Robert Ford, whom he had thought a friend.

4 They went to the crossing not very far from there,
   And there they did the same;
 And the agent on his knees he delivered up the keys
   To the outlaws Frank and Jesse James.—*Refrain*

5 It was on a Saturday night, Jesse was at home
   Talking to his family brave,
 When the thief and the coward, little Robert Ford,
   Laid Jesse James in his grave.—*Refrain*

6 How people held their breath when they heard of Jesse's death,
   And wondered how he ever came to die.
 'Twas one of the gang, dirty Robert Ford,
   That shot Jesse James on the sly.—*Refrain*

7 Jesse went to his rest with his hand on his breast.
   The devil will be upon his knee.
 He was born one day in the county of Clay,
   And came from a solitary race.—*Refrain*

Oh, Lovely Appearance of Death[1]

1 Oh, lovely appearance of death,
   What sight upon earth is so fair?
   Not all the gay pageants that breathe
   Can with a dead body compare.
   In solemn delight I survey
   A corpse when the spirit is fled,
   In love with the beautiful clay,
   And longing to lie in its stead.

2 Its languishing pain is at rest,
   Its aching and aching are o'er;
   The quiet immovable breast
   Is pained by affliction no more.
   The heart it no longer receives
   Of trouble and torturing pain;
   It ceases to flutter and beat,
   It never shall flutter again.

[1] Reverend George Whitfield, the English minister, possessed a powerful and inspiring manner of preaching. He came several times to the American colonies in order to preach up and down the eastern seaboard during the religious revival known as the Great Awakening. Ten years before he died in 1770, Whitfield wrote this song to be sung at his own funeral.

John Henry[1]

1 Well, every Monday mornin'
When the bluebirds begin to sing,
You can hear those hammers a mile or mo',
You can hear John Henry's hammer ring, oh, Lawdy,
Hear John Henry's hammer ring.

2 John Henry told his old lady,
"Will you fix my supper soon?
Got ninety miles o' track I've got to line,
Got to line it by the light of the moon, oh, Lawdy,
Line it by the light o' the moon."

3 John Henry had a little baby,
He could hold him out in his hand;
But the last word I heard that po' child say,
"My dad is a steel-drivin' man, oh, Lawdy,
Daddy is a steel-drivin' man."

4 John Henry told his old capt'in,
Said, "A man ain't nothin' but a man,
Before I let yo' steel gang down
I will die with the hammer in my hand, oh, Lawdy,
Die with the hammer in my hand."

5 John Henry told his capt'in,
"Next time you go to town
A-jes' bring me back a ten-pound maul
Fer to beat yo' steel-drivin' down, oh, Lawdy,
Beat yo' steel-drivin' down."

6 John Henry had a old lady,
An' her name was Polly Ann.
John Henry tuck sick an' he had to go to bed;
Pauline drove steel like a man, oh, Lawdy,
P'line drove steel like a man.

7 John Henry had a old lady,
An' the dress she wo' was red;
Well, she started up the track an' she never looked back,
"Gwine where my man fell dead, oh, Lawdy,
Where my man fell dead."

[1] It is unclear whether a particular man named John Henry ever lived and then died in an apochryphal race against a steam drill. But the song, which first appeared in a 1905 Tennessee mountain ballad, was adopted by the black pick-and-shovel man who labored for his livelihood against other men and machines and for whom the story carried truth.

8 Well, they taken John Henry to Wash'n'ton,
   An' they bury him in the san',
   There's people from the East an' there's people from the West
   Come to see such a steel-drivin' man, oh, Lawdy,
   See such a steel-drivin' man.

9 Well, some say he's fum England,
   Well, an' some say he's fum Spain,
   But I say he's nothin' but a Lou's'ana man,
   Jes' the leader of a steel-drivin' gang, oh, Lawdy,
   Leader of a steel-drivin' gang.

The Little Black Train[1]

Chorus (intermittent through the song):
       There's a little black train a-comin'—
       Get all your business right;
       There's a little black train a-comin',
       An' it may be here tonight.

1 Oh, the little black train is a-comin',
   I know it's goin' to slack;
   You can tell it by its rumblin'—,
   It's all draped in black.

2 The train we are singin' about,
   It has no whistle or bell,
   And when you find your station
   You are in heaven or hell.

3 There's a little black train and an engine,
   And one small baggage car;
   You won't need to have much baggage
   To come to the judgment bar.

[1] This is a song of the "Holiness" people, a sect of people in poor and rural America. The Holiness preachers believe that God means his people to rejoice at the altar. Thus they play guitars, banjos, saxaphones, fiddles, and pianos during the lively services. There is group singing, dancing, and praying, and often there is speaking in tongues, snake handling, and playing with fire. Holiness meetings are usually the only form of diversion available to the people who attend, and the spiritual and emotional uplift they receive is precious to them.

4 O Death, why don't you spare me?
I see my wicked plight.
Have mercy, Lord, to hear me,
Come and set me right.

5 Oh, Death had fixed the shackles
Around his throat so tight,
Before he got his business fixed,
The train rolled in that night.

6 They are men and women
What love their sport and game,
Yet Death is ridin' with them
Will take them just the same.

7 Go tell that barroom lady,
All filled with worldly pride,
That Death's black train's a-coming—
Prepare to take a ride.

8 There's a rich old man in his darkness
Says: "I have no such fears—
I'll build my barns a little larger,
For I'll live a million years."

9 So while he sat there plannin',
The God of power and might
Took the old fool to the judgment bar,
So his soul's in the fire tonight.

INDIAN SONGS

Indian poetry is almost the last bridge to the original mind and culture of the native American. Although it is read in translation, its power and beauty communicate an entire world, vastly different from the European culture but common in some indefinable sense to all men. One must be careful, however, not to presume comprehension of the Indian mind without a great deal of study. American Indian culture was ancient and sophisticated, and it is not easily reconstructable.

For an excellent introduction, collection, and useful bibliography of original sources, see Margot Astrov, ed., *American Indian Prose and Poetry,* 1946. Standard works on the history and culture of North American Indians are Paul Radin, *The Story of the American Indians,* 1944, and John J. Collier, *The Indians of the Americas,* 1947.

Young Honey Wolf, c. 1903. *Photo by Edward Curtis. Library of Congress.*

Pueblo Sun Dance. *Library of Congress*

Silence, to the Indian, is the sign of equilibrium in the world. Therefore, when he speaks he uses words purposefully and feels the power
of them. He sings ancient songs in order to restore to nature a lost
balance, to heal, to encourage, to console. He composes his own new
songs to interpret messages from his Creator and, at the crisis points of
his life, he sings personal songs that seem to express and embody his
essential spirit.

The following selection is not meant to be comprehensive, but it
suggests the scope of the Indian's art. Some Indian poems are long,
based on repetition, metaphoric device, and parallel rhythm. Others
include none of these elements, but depend instead on short phrases
that evoke familiar trains of thought for both the singer and the listeners. These short poems are usually not complete in themselves, but rely
on myth, ritual, and history. A Papago Indian once explained, "The
song is short because we know so much."

Dream Song[1]

(CHIPPEWA)

In the Sky
I am walking,
A Bird
I accompany.

[1] The dream song of an Indian is sacred to him and guides him throughout his life. Only after he has fasted and suffered bodily pain that accentuates his contact with the supernatural does his individual song occur to him. In future years he can renew his close contact with the supernatural by singing this song. From Frances Densmore, *Chippewa Music I*, (Washington, 1910) p. 95.

A Woman's Song[1]

(CHIPPEWA)

You are walking around
Trying to remember
What you promised,
But you can't remember.

[1] Chippewa songs are short and cryptic, like the Japanese haiku. They depend on the associations of the hearer for the fullness of their meaning; sometimes the singer must in-terpret the song before it is sung. This song, however, speaks freely. From Frederick R. Burton, *American Primitive Music* (New York, 1909), p. 277.

Love Song[1]

(CHIPPEWA)

A loon I thought it was
But it was
My love's
Splashing oar.

[1] Indian songs are subtle and delicate; the love songs are exquisitely so. Sometimes the singer is simply expressing feelings of joy, but sometimes the singer is hoping that the song will warm the beloved's cold heart. From Densmore. *op. cit.* p. 89.

A Sequence of Songs of the Ghost Dance Religion[1]

1.

My children,
When at first I liked the whites,
I gave them fruits,
I gave them fruits.

2.

Father have pity on me,
I am crying for thirst,
All is gone,
I have nothing to eat.

3.

The father will descend,
The earth will tremble,
Everybody will arise,
Stretch out your hands.

4.

The Crow—*Ehe' eye!*
I saw him when he flew down,
To the earth, to the earth.
He has renewed our life,
He has taken pity on us.

[1] The Plains Indians were eloquent in their statements of what the white man had meant to their people. In 1890, at the point of annihilation, they experienced a great religious revival movement, expressed by the songs of the Ghost Dance. From James Mooney, *The Ghost Dance Religion* (Washington, 1896), *passim.*

5.

I circle around
The boundaries of the earth,
Wearing the long wing feathers,
As I fly.

6.

I'yehé! my children—
My children,
We have rendered them desolate.
The whites are crazy—Ahe'yuhe'yu!

7.

We shall live again,
We shall live again.

A Prayer of the Night Chant[1]

(NAVAJO)

Tségihi.
House made of dawn.
House made of evening light.
House made of the dark cloud.
House made of male rain.
House made of dark mist.
House made of female rain.
House made of pollen.
House made of grasshoppers.
Dark cloud is at the door.
The trail out of it is dark cloud.
The zigzag lightning stands high upon it.
Male deity!
Your offering I make.
I have prepared a smoke for you.
Restore my feet for me.
Restore my legs for me.
Restore my body for me.
Restore my mind for me.
This very day take out your spell for me.
Your spell remove for me.

---

[1] The Navajo are known today as superb weavers and silversmiths. Their songs also are outstanding in the vitality they manifest.

From Washington Matthews, *Navajo Myths, Prayers, and Songs* (Berkeley, 1907), pp. 54–55.

You have taken it away for me.
Far off it has gone.
Happily I recover.
Happily my interior becomes cool.
Happily I go forth.
My interior feeling cool, may I walk.
No longer sore, may I walk.
Impervious to pain, may I walk.
With lively feelings may I walk.
As it used to be long ago, may I walk.
Happily may I walk.
Happily, with abundant dark clouds, may I walk.
Happily, with abundant showers, may I walk.
Happily, with abundant plants, may I walk.
Happily, on a trail of pollen, may I walk.
Happily may I walk.
Being as it used to be long ago, may I walk.
May it be beautiful before me.
May it be beautiful behind me.
May it be beautiful below me.
May it be beautiful above me.
May it be beautiful all around me.
In beauty it is finished.

Song of the Black Bear

(NAVAJO)

My moccasins are black obsidian,
My leggings are black obsidian,
My shirt is black obsidian.
I am girded with a black arrowsnake.
Black snakes go up from my head.
With zigzag lightning darting from the ends of my feet I step,
With zigzag lightning streaming out from my knees I step,
With zigzag lightning streaming from the tip of my tongue I speak.
Now a disk of pollen rests on the crown of my head.
Gray arrowsnakes and rattlesnakes eat it.
Black obsidian and zigzag lightning streams out from me in four ways,
Where they strike the earth, bad things, bad talk does not like it.
It causes the missiles to spread out.
Long Life, something frightful I am.
Now I am.

There is danger where I move my feet.
I am whirlwind.
There is danger when I move my feet.
I am a gray bear.
When I walk, where I step, lightning flies from me,
Where I walk, one to be feared [I am].

Rain Song[1]

(SIA)

White floating clouds.
Clouds like the plains
Come and water the earth.
Sun, embrace the earth
That she may be fruitful.
Moon, lion of the north,
Bear of the west,
Badger of the South,
Wolf of the east,
Eagle of the heavens, shrew of the earth,
Elder war hero,
Warriors of the six mountains of the world,
Intercede with the cloud people for us,
That they may water the earth.
Medicine bowl, cloud bowl, and water vase,
Give us your hearts,
That the earth may be watered.
I make the ancient road of meal,
That my song may straight pass over it—the ancient road.
White shell bead woman,
Who lives where the sun goes down,
Mother whirlwind, mother Sûs'sistumako,
Mother Ya-ya, creator of good thoughts,
Yellow woman of the north, blue woman of the west,
Red woman of the south, white woman of the east,
Slightly yellow woman of the zenith,
And dark woman of the nadir,
I ask your intercession with the cloud people.

[1] From Mathilde Stevenson, *The Sia* (Washington, 1864) p. 130.

THE NEW ENGLAND SPIRIT

MARY E. WILKINS FREEMAN

(1852–1930)

Freeman writes of a declining rural New England. Her predominant subject is the deteriorating fabric of New England village life in the closing years of the nineteenth century. Grim, deprived, stunted lives fill her pages, such as that of Louisa Ellis in "A New England Nun."

Born in western Massachusetts, her own life seemed to prefigure the pattern of many of her stories; ill-health curtailed her education, family deaths left her alone to nurse an invalid father, and then stranded her with an aged aunt. In the 1880's she took up writing as a source of income. Two collections of stories, *A Humble Romance* (1887) and *A New England Nun and Other Stories* (1891), established her among the regionalist writers as an artist with a unique vision.

Her stories have the grainy force of direct, unpretty renderings of wasted lives, frustration, and unhappiness. Sexual sublimation is often close to the surface of her tales. Her characters, especially her women, are frequently victims of both circumstance and restrictive, dehumanizing moral codes. Yet Freeman is not entirely without a sense of the comic, even if her situations seem awful and hopeless. Her language is tough, austere, and gritty.

At the age of 50 she married a doctor (who later went insane), moved to Metuchen, New Jersey, and turned out several novels, none very successful. On the whole, her later work does not match the special character of suffering in her earlier stories.

The most important works are *A Humble Romance,* 1887; *A New England Nun and Other Stories,* 1891; *Pembroke,* 1894.

A biography is Edward Foster, *Mary E. Wilkins Freeman,* 1956. Criticism includes William Dean Howells, *Heroines of Fiction,* II (1901); Vernon L. Parrington, *The Beginnings of Critical Realism in America,* 1930, and F. O. Matthiessen, "New England Stories," *American Writers on American Literature,* ed. John Macy, 1931.

The Morning Bell, c. 1866, Winslow Homer. *Yale University Art Gallery, Bequest of Stephen Carlton Clark.*

A New England Nun[1]

It was late in the afternoon, and the light was waning. There was a difference in the look of the tree shadows out in the yard. Somewhere in the distance cows were lowing and a little bell was tinkling; now and then a farm-wagon tilted by, and the dust flew; some blue-shirted laborers with shovels over their shoulders plodded past; little swarms of flies were dancing up and down before the people's faces in the soft air. There seemed to be a gentle stir arising over everything for the mere sake of subsidence—a very premonition of rest and hush and night.

This soft diurnal commotion was over Louisa Ellis also. She had been peacefully sewing at her sitting-room window all the afternoon. Now she quilted her needle carefully into her work, which she folded precisely, and laid in a basket with her thimble and thread and scissors. Louisa Ellis could not remember that ever in her life she had mislaid one of these little feminine appurtenances, which had become, from long use and constant association, a very part of her personality.

Louisa tied a green apron round her waist, and got out a flat straw hat with a green ribbon. Then she went into the garden with a little blue crockery bowl, to pick some currants for her tea. After the currants were picked she sat on the back door-step and stemmed them, collecting the stems carefully in her apron, and afterwards throwing them into the hen-coop. She looked sharply at the grass beside the step to see if any had fallen there.

Louisa was slow and still in her movements; it took her a long time to prepare her tea; but when ready it was set forth with as much grace as if she had been a veritable guest to her own self. The little square table stood exactly in the centre of the kitchen, and was covered with a starched linen cloth whose border pattern of flowers glistened. Louisa had a damask napkin on her tea-tray, where were arranged a cut-glass tumbler full of teaspoons, a silver cream-pitcher, a china sugar-bowl, and one pink china cup and saucer. Louisa used china every day—something which none of her neighbors did. They whispered about it among themselves. Their daily tables were laid with common crockery, their sets of best china stayed in the parlor closet, and Louisa Ellis was no richer nor better bred than they. Still she would use the china. She had for her supper a glass dish full of sugared currants, a plate of little cakes, and one of light white biscuits. Also a leaf or two of lettuce, which she cut up daintily. Louisa was very fond of lettuce, which she raised to perfection in her little garden. She ate quite heartily, though in a delicate, pecking way; it seemed almost surprising that any considerable bulk of the food should vanish.

[1] First published in *A New England Nun and Other Stories* in 1891.

After tea she filled a plate with nicely baked thin corn-cakes, and carried them out into the back-yard.

"Caesar!" she called. "Caesar! Caesar!"

There was a little rush, and the clank of a chain, and a large yellow-and-white dog appeared at the door of his tiny hut, which was half hidden among the tall grasses and flowers. Louisa patted him and gave him the corn-cakes. Then she returned to the house and washed the tea-things, polishing the china carefully. The twilight had deepened; the chorus of the frogs floated in at the open window wonderfully loud and shrill, and once in a while a long sharp drone from a tree-toad pierced it. Louisa took off her green gingham apron, disclosing a shorter one of pink-and-white print. She lighted her lamp, and sat down again with her sewing.

In about half an hour Joe Dagget came. She heard his heavy step on the walk, and rose and took off her pink-and-white apron. Under that was still another—white linen with a little cambric edging on the bottom; that was Louisa's company apron. She never wore it without her calico sewing apron over it unless she had a guest. She had barely folded the pink-and-white one with methodical haste and laid it in a table-drawer when the door opened and Joe Dagget entered.

He seemed to fill up the whole room. A little yellow canary that had been asleep in his green cage at the south window woke up and fluttered wildly, beating his little yellow wings against the wires. He always did so when Joe Dagget came into the room.

"Good-evening," said Louisa. She extended her hand with a kind of solemn cordiality.

"Good-evening, Louisa," returned the man, in a loud voice.

She placed a chair for him, and they sat facing each other, with the table between them. He sat bolt-upright, toeing out his heavy feet squarely, glancing with a good-humored uneasiness around the room. She sat gently erect, folding her slender hands in her white-linen lap.

"Been a pleasant day," remarked Dagget.

"Real pleasant," Louisa assented, softly. "Have you been haying?" she asked, after a little while.

"Yes, I've been haying all day, down in the ten-acre lot. Pretty hot work."

"It must be."

"Yes, it's pretty hot work in the sun."

"Is your mother well to-day?"

"Yes, mother's pretty well."

"I suppose Lily Dyer's with her now?"

Dagget colored. "Yes, she's with her," he answered, slowly.

He was not very young, but there was a boyish look about his large face. Louisa was not quite as old as he, her face was fairer and smoother, but she gave people the impression of being older.

"I suppose she's a good deal of help to your mother," she said, further.

"I guess she is; I don't know how mother'd get along without her," said Dagget, with a sort of embarrassed warmth.

"She looks like a real capable girl. She's pretty-looking too," remarked Louisa.

"Yes, she is pretty fair looking."

Presently Dagget began fingering the books on the table. There was a square red autograph album, and a Young Lady's Gift-Book which had belonged to Louisa's mother. He took them up one after the other and opened them; then laid them down again, the album on the Gift-Book.

Louisa kept eyeing them with mild uneasiness. Finally she rose and changed the position of the books, putting the album underneath. That was the way they had been arranged in the first place.

Dagget gave an awkward little laugh. "Now what difference did it make which book was on top?" said he.

Louisa looked at him with a deprecating smile. "I always keep them that way," murmured she.

"You do beat everything," said Dagget, trying to laugh again. His large face was flushed.

He remained about an hour longer, then rose to take leave. Going out, he stumbled over a rug, and trying to recover himself, hit Louisa's work-basket on the table, and knocked it on the floor.

He looked at Louisa, then at the rolling spools; he ducked himself awkwardly toward them, but she stopped him. "Never mind," said she; "I'll pick them up after you're gone."

She spoke with a mild stiffness. Either she was a little disturbed, or his nervousness affected her, and made her seem constrained in her effort to reassure him.

When Joe Dagget was outside he drew in the sweet evening air with a sigh, and felt much as an innocent and perfectly well-intentioned bear might after his exit from a china shop.

Louisa, on her part, felt much as the kind-hearted, long-suffering owner of the china shop might have done after the exit of the bear.

She tied on the pink, then the green apron, picked up all the scattered treasures and replaced them in her work-basket, and straightened the rug. Then she set the lamp on the floor, and began sharply examining the carpet. She even rubbed her fingers over it, and looked at them.

"He's tracked in a good deal of dust," she murmured. "I thought he must have."

Louisa got a dust-pan and brush, and swept Joe Dagget's track carefully.

If he could have known it, it would have increased his perplexity and uneasiness, although it would not have disturbed his loyalty in the least. He came twice a week to see Louisa Ellis, and every time, sitting there in her delicately sweet room, he felt as if surrounded by a hedge of lace. He was afraid to stir lest he should put a clumsy foot or hand through the fairy web, and he had always the consciousness that Louisa was watching fearfully lest he should.

Still the lace and Louisa commanded perforce his perfect respect and patience and loyalty. They were to be married in a month, after a singular courtship which had lasted for a matter of fifteen years. For fourteen out of the fifteen years the two had not once seen each other, and they had seldom exchanged letters. Joe had been all those years in Australia, where he had gone to make his fortune, and where he had stayed until he made it. He would have stayed fifty years if it had taken so long, and come home feeble and tottering, or never come home at all, to marry Louisa.

But the fortune had been made in the fourteen years, and he had come home now to marry the woman who had been patiently and unquestioningly waiting for him all that time.

Shortly after they were engaged he had announced to Louisa his determination to strike out into new fields, and secure a competency before they should be married. She had listened and assented with the sweet serenity which never failed her, not even when her lover set forth on that long and uncertain journey. Joe, buoyed up as he was by his sturdy determination, broke down a little at the last, but Louisa kissed him with a mild blush, and said good-by.

"It won't be for long," poor Joe had said, huskily; but it was for fourteen years.

In that length of time much had happened. Louisa's mother and brother had died, and she was all alone in the world. But greatest happening of all— a subtle happening which both were too simple to understand—Louisa's feet had turned into a path, smooth maybe under a calm, serene sky, but so straight and unswerving that it could only meet a check at her grave, and so narrow that there was no room for any one at her side.

Louisa's first emotion when Joe Dagget came home (he had not apprised her of his coming) was consternation, although she would not admit it to herself, and he never dreamed of it. Fifteen years ago she had been in love with him—at least she considered herself to be. Just at that time, gently acquiescing with and falling into the natural drift of girlhood, she had seen marriage ahead as a reasonable feature and a probable desirability of life. She had listened with calm docility to her mother's views upon the subject. Her mother was remarkable for her cool sense and sweet, even temperament. She talked wisely to her daughter when Joe Dagget presented himself, and Louisa accepted him with no hesitation. He was the first lover she had ever had.

She had been faithful to him all these years. She had never dreamed of the possibility of marrying any one else. Her life, especially for the last seven years, had been full of a pleasant peace; she had never felt discontented nor impatient over her lover's absence; still she had always looked forward to his return and their marriage as the inevitable conclusion of things. However, she had fallen into a way of placing it so far in the future that it was almost equal to placing it over the boundaries of another life.

When Joe came she had been expecting him, and expecting to be married for fourteen years, but she was as much surprised and taken aback as if she had never thought of it.

Joe's consternation came later. He eyed Louisa with an instant confirmation of his old admiration. She had changed but little. She still kept her pretty manner and soft grace, and was, he considered, every whit as attractive as ever. As for himself, his stint was done; he had turned his face away from fortune-seeking, and the old winds of romance whistled as loud and sweet as ever through his ears. All the song which he had been wont to hear in them was Louisa; he had for a long time a loyal belief that he heard it still, but finally it seemed to him that although the winds sang always that one song, it had another name. But for Louisa the wind had never more than murmured; now it had gone down, and everything was still. She listened for a little while with half-wistful attention; then she turned quietly away and went to work on her wedding clothes.

Joe had made some extensive and quite magnificent alterations in his house. It was the old homestead; the newly-married couple would live there, for Joe could not desert his mother, who refused to leave her old home. So Louisa must leave hers. Every morning, rising and going about among her neat maidenly possessions, she felt as one looking her last upon the faces of dear friends. It was true that in a measure she could take them with her, but, robbed of their old environments, they would appear in such new guises that they would almost cease to be themselves. Then there were some peculiar features of her happy solitary life which she would probably be obliged to relinquish altogether. Sterner tasks than these graceful but half-needless ones would probably devolve upon her. There would be a large house to care for; there would be company to entertain; there would be Joe's rigorous and feeble old mother to wait upon; and it would be contrary to all thrifty village traditions for her to keep more than one servant.

Louisa had a little still, and she used to occupy herself pleasantly in summer weather with distilling the sweet and aromatic essences from roses and peppermint and spearmint. By-and-by her still must be laid away. Her store of essences was already considerable, and there would be no time for her to distil for the mere pleasure of it. Then Joe's mother would think it foolishness; she had already hinted her opinion in the matter.

Louisa dearly loved to sew a linen seam, not always for use, but for the simple, mild pleasure which she took in it. She would have been loath to confess how more than once she had ripped a seam for the mere delight of sewing it together again. Sitting at her window during long sweet afternoons, drawing her needle gently through the dainty fabric, she was peace itself. But there was small chance of such foolish comfort in the future. Joe's mother, domineering, shrewd old matron that she was even in her old age, and very likely even Joe himself, with his honest masculine rudeness, would laugh and frown down all these pretty but senseless old maiden ways.

Louisa had almost the enthusiasm of an artist over the mere order and cleanliness of her solitary home. She had throbs of genuine triumph at the sight of the window-panes which she had polished until they shone like jewels. She gloated gently over her orderly bureau-drawers, with their exquisitely folded contents redolent with lavender and sweet clover and every purity. Could she be sure of the endurance of even this? She had visions, so startling that she half repudiated them as indelicate, of coarse masculine belongings strewn about in endless litter; of dust and disorder arising necessarily from a coarse masculine presence in the midst of all this delicate harmony.

Among her forebodings of disturbance, not the least was with regard to Caesar. Caesar was a veritable hermit of a dog. For the greater part of his life he had dwelt in his secluded hut, shut out from the society of his kind and all innocent canine joys. Never had Caesar since his early youth watched at a woodchuck's hole; never had he known the delights of a stray bone at a neighbor's kitchen door. And it was all on account of a sin committed when hardly out of his puppyhood. No one knew the possible depth of remorse of which this mild-visaged, altogether innocent-looking old dog might be capable; but whether or not he had encountered remorse, he had encountered a full measure of righteous retribution. Old Caesar seldom lifted up his voice in a growl or a bark; he was fat and sleepy; there were yellow rings which looked like spectacles around his dim old eyes; but there was a neighbor who bore on his hand the imprint of several of Caesar's sharp white youthful teeth, and for that he had lived at the end of a chain, all alone in a little hut, for fourteen years. The neighbor, who was choleric and smarting with the pain of his wound, had demanded either Caesar's death or complete ostracism. So Louisa's brother, to whom the dog had belonged, had built him his little kennel and tied him up. It was now fourteen years since, in a flood of youthful spirits, he had inflicted that memorable bite, and with the exception of short excursions, always at the end of the chain, under the strict guardianship of his master or Louisa, the old dog had remained a close prisoner. It is doubtful if, with his limited ambition, he took much pride in the fact, but it is certain that he was possessed of considerable cheap fame. He was regarded by all the children in the village and by many adults as a very monster of ferocity. St. George's dragon could hardly have surpassed in evil repute Louisa Ellis's old yellow dog. Mothers charged their children with solemn emphasis not to go too near to him, and the children listened and believed greedily, with a fascinated appetite for terror, and ran by Louisa's house stealthily, with many sidelong and backward glances at the terrible dog. If perchance he sounded a hoarse bark, there was a panic. Wayfarers chancing into Louisa's yard eyed him with respect, and inquired if the chain were stout. Caesar at large might have seemed a very ordinary dog, and excited no comment whatever; chained, his reputation overshadowed him, so that he lost his own proper outlines and looked darkly vague and enormous. Joe Dagget, however, with his good-humored sense and shrewdness, saw him as he was. He strode valiantly up to him and patted him on the head, in spite of Louisa's soft clamor of warning, and even attempted to set him loose. Louisa grew so alarmed that he desisted, but kept announcing his opinion in the matter quite forcibly at intervals. "There ain't a better-natured dog in town," he would say, "and it's downright cruel to keep him tied up there. Some day I'm going to take him out."

Louisa had very little hope that he would not, one of these days, when their interests and possessions should be more completely fused in one. She pictured to herself Caesar on the rampage through the quiet and unguarded village. She saw innocent children bleeding in his path. She was herself very fond of the old dog, because he had belonged to her dead brother, and he was always very gentle with her; still she had great faith in his ferocity. She always warned people not to go too near him. She fed him on ascetic fare of corn-mush and cakes, and never fired his dangerous temper with heating and sanguinary diet of flesh and bones. Louisa looked at the old dog munching his simple fare, and thought of her approaching marriage and trembled. Still no anticipation of disorder and confusion in lieu of sweet peace and harmony, no forebodings of Caesar on the rampage, no wild fluttering of her little yellow canary, were sufficient to turn her a hair's-breadth. Joe Dagget had been fond of her and working for her all these years. It was not for her, whatever came to pass, to prove untrue and break his heart. She put the exquisite little stitches into her wedding-garments, and the time went on until it was only a week before her wedding-day. It was a Tuesday evening, and the wedding was to be a week from Wednesday.

There was a full moon that night. About nine o'clock Louisa strolled down the road a little way. There were harvest-fields on either hand, bordered by low stone walls. Luxuriant clumps of bushes grew beside the wall, and trees—wild cherry and old apple-trees—at intervals. Presently Louisa sat down on the wall and looked about her with mildly sorrowful reflectiveness. Tall shrubs of blueberry and meadow-sweet, all woven together and tangled with blackberry vines and horsebriers, shut her in on either side. She had a little clear space between them. Opposite her, on the other side of the road, was a spreading tree; the moon shone between its boughs, and the leaves twinkled like silver. The road was bespread with a beautiful shifting dapple of silver and shadow; the air was full of a mysterious sweetness. "I wonder if it's wild grapes?" murmured Louisa. She sat there some time. She was just thinking of rising, when she heard footsteps and low voices, and remained quiet. It was a lonely place, and she felt a little timid. She thought she would keep still in the shadow and let the persons, whoever they might be, pass her.

But just before they reached her the voices ceased, and the footsteps. She understood that their owners had also found seats upon the stone wall. She was wondering if she could not steal away unobserved, when the voice broke the stillness. It was Joe Dagget's. She sat still and listened.

The voice was announced by a loud sigh, which was as familiar as itself. "Well," said Dagget, "you've made up your mind, then, I suppose?"

"Yes," returned another voice; "I'm going day after to-morrow."

"That's Lily Dyer," thought Louisa to herself. The voice embodied itself in her mind. She saw a girl tall and full-figured, with a firm, fair face, looking fairer and firmer in the moonlight, her strong yellow hair braided in a close knot. A girl full of a calm rustic strength and bloom with a masterful way which might have beseemed a princess. Lily Dyer was a favorite with the village folk; she had just the qualities to arouse the admiration. She was good and handsome and smart. Louisa had often heard her praises sounded.

"Well," said Joe Dagget, "I ain't got a word to say."

"I don't know what you could say," returned Lily Dyer.

"Not a word to say," repeated Joe, drawing out the words heavily. Then there was a silence. "I ain't sorry," he began at last, "that that happened yesterday—that we kind of let on how we felt to each other. I guess it's just as well we knew. Of course I can't do anything any different. I'm going right on an' get married next week. I ain't going back on a woman that's waited for me fourteen years, an' break her heart."

"If you should jilt her to-morrow, I wouldn't have you," spoke up the girl, with sudden vehemence.

"Well, I ain't going to give you the chance," said he; "but I don't believe you would, either."

"You'd see I wouldn't. Honor's honor, an' right's right. An' I'd never think anything of any man that went against 'em for me or any other girl; you'd find that out, Joe Dagget."

"Well, you'll find out fast enough that I ain't going against 'em for you or any other girl," returned he. Their voices sounded almost as if they were angry with each other. Louisa was listening eagerly.

"I'm sorry you feel as if you must go away," said Joe, "but I don't know but it's best."

"Of course it's best. I hope you and I have got common-sense."

"Well, I suppose you're right." Suddenly Joe's voice got an undertone of tenderness. "Say, Lily," said he, "I'll get along well enough myself, but I can't bear to think—You don't suppose you're going to fret much over it?"

"I guess you'll find out I sha'n't fret much over a married man."

"Well, I hope you won't—I hope you won't, Lily. God knows I do. And— I hope—one of these days—you'll—come across somebody else—"

"I don't see any reason why I shouldn't." Suddenly her tone changed. She spoke in a sweet, clear voice, so loud that she could have been heard across the street. "No, Joe Dagget," said she, "I'll never marry any other man as long as I live. I've got good sense, an' I ain't going to break my heart nor make a fool of myself; but I'm never going to be married, you can be sure of that. I ain't that sort of girl to feel this way twice."

Louisa heard an exclamation and a soft commotion behind the bushes; then Lily spoke again—the voice sounded as if she had risen. "This must be put a stop to," said she. "We've stayed here long enough. I'm going home."

Louisa sat there in a daze, listening to their retreating steps. After a while she got up and slunk softly home herself. The next day she did her housework methodically; that was as much a matter of course as breathing; but she did not sew on her wedding-clothes. She sat at her window and meditated. In the evening Joe came. Louisa Ellis had never known that she had any diplomacy in her, but when she came to look for it that night she found it, although meek of its kind, among her little feminine weapons. Even now she could hardly believe that she had heard aright, and that she would not do Joe a terrible injury should she break her trothplight. She wanted to sound him without betraying too soon her own inclinations in the matter. She did it successfully, and they finally came to an understanding; but it was a difficult thing, for he was as afraid of betraying himself as she.

She never mentioned Lily Dyer. She simply said that while she had no cause of complaint against him, she had lived so long in one way that she shrank from making a change.

"Well, I never shrank, Louisa," said Dagget. "I'm going to be honest enough to say that I think maybe it's better this way; but if you'd wanted to keep on, I'd have stuck to you till my dying day. I hope you know that."

"Yes, I do," said she.

That night she and Joe parted more tenderly than they had done for a long time. Standing in the door, holding each other's hands, a last great wave of regretful memory swept over them.

"Well, this ain't the way we've thought it was all going to end, is it, Louisa?" said Joe.

She shook her head. There was a little quiver on her placid face.

"You let me know if there's ever anything I can do for you," said he. "I ain't ever going to forget you, Louisa." Then he kissed her, and went down the path.

Louisa, all alone by herself that night, wept a little, she hardly knew why; but the next morning, on waking, she felt like a queen who, after fearing lest her domain be wrested away from her, sees it firmly insured in her possession.

Now the tall weeds and grasses might cluster around Caesar's little hermit hut, the snow might fall on its roof year in and year out, but he never would go on a rampage through the unguarded village. Now the little canary might turn itself into a peaceful yellow ball night after night, and have no need to wake and flutter with wild terror against its bars. Louisa could sew linen seams, and distil roses, and dust and polish and fold away in lavender, as long as she listed. That afternoon she sat with her needle-work at the window, and felt fairly steeped in peace. Lily Dyer, tall and erect and blooming, went past; but she felt no qualm. If Louisa Ellis had sold her birthright she did not know it; the taste of the pottage was so delicious, and had been her sole satisfaction for so long. Serenity and placid narrowness had become to her as the birthright itself. She gazed ahead through a long reach of future days strung together like pearls in a rosary, every one like the others, and all smooth and flawless and innocent, and her heart went up in thankfulness. Outside was the fervid summer afternoon; the air was filled with the sounds of the busy harvest of men and birds and bees; there were halloos, metallic clatterings, sweet calls, and long hummings. Louisa sat, prayerfully numbering her days, like an uncloistered nun.

SARAH ORNE JEWETT

(1849–1909)

The desire simply to record ways of life that were passing away inspired much regionalist writing. Sarah Orne Jewett's region, in and around her hometown of South Berwick, Maine, was precisely such an area of decline and stagnation. Once the home of prosperous and proud families of farmers, sailors, and shipbuilders, the region now had lost its standing and had given way to new patterns. Children left home, seeking better times in the larger cities, and mostly older folk remained behind, still proud, still stubborn in their devotion to their ways and their land.

Raised as the daughter of a doctor and Professor of Medicine at Bowdoin College, Jewett came to know her region and its people with a special intimacy as a result of accompanying her father on his coun-

There is a seven-volume edition, *Stories and Tales,* 1910. See also *The Best Short Stories of Sarah Orne Jewett,* ed., with an introduction by Willa Cather, 2 vols. 1925. The most recent edition of letters has been edited by Richard Cary, *Sarah Orne Jewett Letters,* 1947; but see also *Letters of Sarah Orne Jewett,* ed., Annie Fields, 1911, and *Letters of Sarah Orne Jewett,* ed., Carl J. Weber, 1947.

The major works are *Deephaven,* 1877; *Old Friends and New,* 1879; *Country By-Ways,* 1881; *A Country Doctor,* 1884; *A Marsh Island,* 1885; *A White Heron and Other Stories,* 1886; *The King of Folly Island and Other People,* 1888; *Tales of New England,* 1890; *A Native of Winby, and Other Stories,* 1893; *Strangers and Wayfarers,* 1890; *The Country of the Pointed Firs,* 1896; *The Queen's Twins, and Other Stories,* 1889.

For criticism see F. O. Matthiessen, *Sarah Orne Jewett,* 1929; Warner Berthoff, "The Art of Jewett's Pointed Firs," *New England Quarterly,* XXXII (March 1959); and Richard Cary, *Sarah Orne Jewett,* 1971.

try and island rounds (she fictionalized him as a woman doctor in *A Country Doctor*, 1884). A learned and sympathetic man, her father shared with her his wide and detailed knowledge of the locale and its history; he also encouraged her to read the classics of world literature and supported her own desires to write. Jewett was inspired by Harriet Beecher Stowe's *The Pearl of Orr's Island* (1862) to try her own hand at a literary rendering of the peculiar ways of life, speech habits, and personal relations that prevailed in her section of the Maine coast and, by the later 1860's, was already publishing stories in *The Atlantic Monthly*. She found a very receptive audience for her elegant, evocative stories, and between 1877 and 1901 she published more than a dozen books.

Jewett soon held the attention of the literary world as the most distinguished of the regional writers. Many of her books, like her first, *Deephaven* (1877), and her masterpiece, *The Country of the Pointed Firs* (1896), are collections unified more by mood than plot. Her hallmark is delicacy of description and characterization. Her touch is tender, and she captures elusive and subtle nuances of a way of life noted for its closed and tight-lipped demeanor to outsiders. Jewett's style can be described as analogous to both music and painting; it is a style of direct impression, of evocations drawn out of lovingly rendered details. The faithful representation of a scene or a dramatic moment always takes precedence in her work over judgment, analysis, or editorial interpretation. "The White Heron," one of her greatest stories, reveals her talents at their best; place and character make a single whole, and the young girl's conflict of feelings between the charming young scientist and the white heron emerges convincingly.

Although the Maine coast exercised a powerful hold on her and her imagination, Jewett traveled a good deal and could boast of many literary friendships, including world-famous writers such as Tennyson, Kipling, Henry James, Howells, and Whittier. She developed a close friendship with a younger writer destined to fame in her own right, Willa Cather. After a serious injury resulting from a fall in 1902, she curtailed her work, and she died of a stroke in 1909.

A White Heron[1]

The woods were already filled with shadows one June evening, just before eight o'clock, though a bright sunset still glimmered faintly among the trunks of the trees. A little girl was driving home her cow, a plodding, dilatory,

[1] First published in *A White Heron and Other Stories* in 1886.

provoking creature in her behavior, but a valued companion for all that. They were going away from the western light, and striking deep into the dark woods, but their feet were familiar with the path, and it was no matter whether their eyes could see it or not.

There was hardly a night the summer through when the old cow could be found waiting at the pasture bars; on the contrary, it was her greatest pleasure to hide herself away among the high huckleberry bushes, and though she wore a loud bell she had made the discovery that if one stood perfectly still it would not ring. So Sylvia had to hunt for her until she found her, and call Co'! Co'! with never an answering Moo, until her childish patience was quite spent. If the creature had not given good milk and plenty of it, the case would have seemed very different to her owners. Besides, Sylvia had all the time there was, and very little use to make of it. Sometimes in pleasant weather it was a consolation to look upon the cow's pranks as an intelligent attempt to play hide and seek, and as the child had no playmates she lent herself to this amusement with a good deal of zest. Though this chase had been so long that the wary animal herself had given an unusual signal of her whereabouts, Sylvia had only laughed when she came upon Mistress Moolly at the swamp-side, and urged her affectionately homeward with a twig of birch leaves. The old cow was not inclined to wander farther, she even turned in the right direction for once as they left the pasture, and stepped along the road at a good pace. She was quite ready to be milked now, and seldom stopped to browse. Sylvia wondered what her grandmother would say because they were so late. It was a great while since she had left home at half past five o'clock, but eveybody knew the difficulty of making this errand a short one. Mrs. Tilley had chased the hornèd torment too many summer evenings herself to blame any one else for lingering, and was only thankful as she waited that she had Sylvia, nowadays, to give such valuable assistance. The good woman suspected that Sylvia loitered occasionally on her own account; there never was such a child for straying about out-of-doors since the world was made! Everybody said that it was a good change for a little maid who had tried to grow for eight years in a crowded manufacturing town, but, as for Sylvia herself, it seemed as if she never had been alive before she came to live at the farm. She thought often with wistful compassion of a wretched dry geranium that belonged to a town neighbor.

" 'Afraid of folks,' " old Mrs. Tilley said to herself, with a smile, after she had made the unlikely choice of Sylvia from her daughter's houseful of children, and was returning to the farm. " 'Afraid of folks,' they said! I guess she won't be troubled no great with 'em up to the old place!" When they reached the door of the lonely house and stopped to unlock it, and the cat came to purr loudly, and rub against them, a deserted pussy, indeed, but fat with young robins, Sylvia whispered that this was a beautiful place to live in, and she never should wish to go home.

The companions followed the shady woodroad, the cow taking slow steps, and the child very fast ones. The cow stopped long at the brook to drink, as if the pasture were not half a swamp, and Sylvia stood still and waited, letting her bare feet cool themselves in the shoal water, while the great twilight moths struck softly against her. She waded on through the brook as the cow moved away, and listened to the thrushes with a heart that beat fast with pleasure. There was a stirring in the great boughs overhead. They were full of little birds and beasts that seemed to be wide-awake, and going about their world, or else saying goodnight to each other in sleepy twitters. Sylvia herself felt sleepy as she walked along. However, it was not much farther to the house, and the air was soft and sweet. She was not often in the woods so late as this, and it made her feel as if she were a part of the gray shadows and the moving leaves. She was just thinking how long it seemed since she first came to the farm a year ago, and wondering if everything went on in the noisy town just the same as when she was there; the thought of the great red-faced boy who used to chase and frighten her made her hurry along the path to escape from the shadow of the trees.

Suddenly this little woods-girl is horror-stricken to hear a clear whistle not very far away. Not a bird's whistle, which would have a sort of friendliness, but a boy's whistle, determined, and somewhat aggressive. Sylvia left the cow to whatever sad fate might await her, and stepped discreetly aside into the bushes, but she was just too late. The enemy had discovered her, and called out in a very cheerful and persuasive tone, "Halloa, little girl, how far is it to the road?" and trembling Sylvia answered almost inaudibly, "A good ways."

She did not dare to look boldly at the tall young man, who carried a gun over his shoulder, but she came out of her bush and again followed the cow, while he walked alongside.

"I have been hunting for some birds," the stranger said kindly, "and I have lost my way, and need a friend very much. Don't be afraid," he added gallantly. "Speak up and tell me what your name is, and whether you think I can spend the night at your house, and go out gunning early in the morning."

Sylvia was more alarmed than before. Would not her grandmother consider her much to blame? But who could have foreseen such an accident as this? It did not appear to be her fault, and she hung her head as if the stem of it were broken, but managed to answer "Sylvy," with much effort when her companion again asked her name.

Mrs. Tilley was standing in the doorway when the trio came into view. The cow gave a loud moo by way of explanation.

"Yes, you'd better speak up for yourself, you old trial! Where'd she tuck herself away this time, Sylvy?" Sylvia kept an awed silence; she knew by instinct that her grandmother did not comprehend the gravity of the situation. She must be mistaking the stranger for one of the farmer-lads of the region.

The young man stood his gun beside the door, and dropped a heavy game-bag beside it; then he bade Mrs. Tilley good-evening, and repeated his wayfarer's story, and asked if he could have a night's lodging.

"Put me anywhere you like," he said. "I must be off early in the morning, before day; but I am very hungry, indeed. You can give me some milk at any rate, that's plain."

"Dear sakes, yes" responded the hostess, whose long slumbering hospitality seemed to be easily awakened. "You might fare better if you went out on the main road a mile or so, but you're welcome to what we've got. I'll milk right off, and you make yourself at home. You can sleep on husks or feathers," she proffered graciously. "I raised them all myself. There's good pasturing for geese just below here towards the ma'sh. Now step round and set a plate for the gentleman, Sylvy!" and Sylvia promptly stepped. She was glad to have something to do, and she was hungry herself.

It was a surprise to find so clean and comfortable a little dwelling in this New England wilderness. The young man had known the horrors of its most primitive housekeeping, and the dreary squalor of that level of society which does not rebel at the companionship of hens. This was the best thrift of an old-fashioned farmstead, though on such a small scale that it seemed like a hermitage. He listened eagerly to the old woman's quaint talk, he watched Sylvia's pale face and shining gray eyes with ever growing enthusiasm, and insisted that this was the best supper he had eaten for a month; then, afterward, the new-made friends sat down in the doorway together while the moon came up.

Soon it would be berry-time, and Sylvia was a great help at picking. The cow was a good milker, though a plaguy thing to keep track of, the hostess gossiped frankly, adding presently that she had buried four children, so that Sylvia's mother, and a son (who might be dead) in California were all the children she had left. "Dan, my boy, was a great hand to go gunning," she explained sadly. "I never wanted for pa'tridges or gray squer'ls while he was to home. He's been a great wand'rer, I expect, and he's no hand to write letters. There, I don't blame him, I'd ha' seen the world myself if it had been so I could.

"Sylvia takes after him," the grandmother continued affectionately, after a minute's pause. "There ain't a foot o'ground she don't know her way over, and the wild creatur's counts her one o' themselves. Squer'ls she'll tame to come an' feed right out o' her hands, and all sorts o' birds. Last winter she got the jay-birds to bangeing here, and I believe she'd 'a' scanted herself of her own meals to have plenty to throw out amongst 'em, if I hadn't kep' watch. Anything but crows, I tell her, I'm willin' to help support,—though Dan he went an' tamed one o' them that did seem to have reason same as folks. It was round here a good spell after he went away. Dan an' his father they didn't hitch—but he never held up his head ag'in after Dan had dared him an' gone off."

The guest did not notice this hint of family sorrows in his eager interest in something else.

"So Sylvy knows all about birds, does she?" he exclaimed, as he looked round at the little girl who sat, very demure but increasingly sleepy, in the moonlight. "I am making a collection of birds myself. I have been at it ever since I was a boy." (Mrs. Tilley smiled.) "There are two or three very rare ones I have been hunting for these five years. I mean to get them on my own grounds if they can be found."

"Do you cage 'em up?" asked Mrs. Tilley doubtfully, in response to this enthusiastic announcement.

"Oh, no, they're stuffed and preserved, dozens and dozens of them," said the ornithologist, "and I have shot or snared every one myself. I caught a glimpse of a white heron three miles from here on Saturday, and I have followed it in this direction. They have never been found in this district at all. The little white heron, it is," and he turned again to look at Sylvia with the hope of discovering that the rare bird was one of her acquaintances.

But Sylvia was watching a hop-toad in the narrow footpath.

"You would know the heron if you saw it," the stranger continued eagerly. "A queer tall white bird with soft feathers and long thin legs.

"And it would have a nest perhaps in the top of a high tree, made of sticks, something like a hawk's nest."

Sylvia's heart gave a wild beat; she knew that strange white bird, and had once stolen softly near where it stood in some bright green swamp grass, away over at the other side of the woods. There was an open place where the sunshine always seemed strangely yellow and hot, where tall, nodding rushes grew, and her grandmother had warned her that she might sink in the soft black mud underneath and never be heard of more. Not far beyond were the salt marshes and beyond those was the sea, the sea which Sylvia wondered and dreamed about, but never had looked upon, though its great voice could often be heard above the noise of the woods on stormy nights.

"I can't think of anything I should like so much as to find the heron's nest," the handsome stranger was saying. "I would give ten dollars to anybody who could show it to me," he added desperately, "and I mean to spend my whole vacation hunting for it if need be. Perhaps it was only migrating, or had been chased out of its own region by some bird of prey."

Mrs. Tilley gave amazed attention to all this, but Sylvia still watched the toad, not diving, as she might have done at some calmer time, that the creature wished to get to its hole under the doorstep, and was much hindered by the unusual spectators at that hour of the evening. No amount of thought, that night, could decide how many wished-for treasures the ten dollars, so lightly spoken of, would buy.

The next day the young sportsman hovered about the woods, and Sylvia kept him company, having lost her first fear of the friendly lad, who proved to be most kind and sympathetic. He told her many things about the birds

and what they knew and where they lived and what they did with themselves. And he gave her a jack-knife, which she thought as great a treasure as
if she were a desert-islander. All day long he did not once make her troubled
or afraid except when he brought down some unsuspecting singing creature
from its bough. Sylvia would have liked him vastly better without his gun;
she could not understand why he killed the very birds he seemed to like so
much. But as the day waned, Sylvia still watched the young man with loving
admiration. She had never seen anybody so charming and delightful; the
woman's heart, asleep in the child, was vaguely thrilled by a dream of love.
Some premonition of that great power stirred and swayed these young for-
esters who traversed the solemn woodlands with soft-footed silent care.
They stopped to listen to a bird's song; they pressed forward again eagerly,
parting the branches—speaking to each other rarely and in whispers; the
young man going first and Sylvia following, fascinated, a few steps behind,
with her gray eyes dark with excitement.

She grieved because the longed-for white heron was elusive, but she did
not lead the guest, she only followed, and there was no such thing as speaking first. The sound of her own unquestioned voice would have terrified
her—it was hard enough to answer yes or no when there was need of that.
At last, evening began to fall, and they drove the cow home together, and
Sylvia smiled with pleasure when they came to the place where she heard
the whistle and was afraid only the night before.

II

Half a mile from home, at the farther edge of the woods, where the land was
highest, a great pine-tree stood, the last of its generation. Whether it was left
for a boundary mark, or for what reason, no one could say; the woodchop-
pers who had felled its mates were dead and gone long ago, and a whole
forest of sturdy trees, pines and oaks and maples, had grown again. But the
stately head of this old pine towered above them all and made a landmark
for sea and shore miles and miles away. Sylvia knew it well. She had always
believed that whoever climbed to the top of it could see the ocean; and the
little girl had often laid her hand on the great rough trunk and looked up
wistfully at those dark boughs that the wind always stirred, no matter how
hot and still the air might be below. Now she thought of the tree with a new
excitement, for why, if one climbed it at break of day, could not one see all
the world, and easily discover from whence the white heron flew, and mark
the place, and find the hidden nest?

What a spirit of adventure, what wild ambition! What fancied triumph
and delight and glory for the later morning when she could make known the
secret! It was almost too real and too great for the childish heart to bear.

All night the door of the little house stood open, and the whippoorwills
came and sang upon the very step. The young sportsman and his old hostess

were sound asleep, but Sylvia's great design kept her broad awake and watching. She forgot to think of sleep. The short summer night seemed as long as the winter darkness, and at last when the whippoorwills ceased, and she was afraid the morning would after all come too soon, she stole out of the house and followed the pasture path through the woods, hastening toward the open ground beyond, listening with a sense of comfort and companionship to the drowsy twitter of a half-awakened bird, whose perch she had jarred in passing. Alas, if the great wave of human interest which flooded for the first time this dull little life should sweep away the satisfactions of an existence heart to heart with nature and the dumb life of the forest!

There was the huge tree asleep yet in the paling moonlight, and small and hopeful Sylvia began with utmost bravery to mount to the top of it, with tingling, eager blood coursing the channels of her whole frame, with her bare feet and fingers, that pinched and held like bird's claws to the monstrous ladder reaching up, up, almost to the sky itself. First she must mount the white oak tree that grew alongside, where she was almost lost among the dark branches and green leaves heavy and wet with dew; a bird fluttered off its nest, and a red squirrel ran to and fro and scolded pettishly at the harmless housebreaker. Sylvia felt her way easily. She had often climbed there, and knew that higher still one of the oak's upper branches chafed against the pine trunk, just where its lower boughs were set close together. There, when she made the dangerous pass from one tree to the other, the great enterprise would really begin.

She crept out along the swaying oak limb at last, and took the daring step across into the old pine-tree. The way was harder than she thought; she must reach far and hold fast, the sharp dry twigs caught and held her and scratched her like angry talons, the pitch made her thin little fingers clumsy and stiff as she went round and round the tree's great stem, higher and higher upward. The sparrows and robins in the woods were beginning to wake and twitter to the dawn, yet it seemed much lighter there aloft in the pine-tree, and the child knew that she must hurry if her project were to be of any use.

The tree seemed to lengthen itself out as she went up, and to reach farther and farther upward. It was like a great main-mast to the voyaging earth; it must truly have been amazed that morning through all its ponderous frame as it felt this determined spark of human spirit creeping and climbing from high branch to branch. Who knows how steadily the least twigs held themselves to advantage this light, weak creature on her way! The old pine must have loved his new dependent. More than all the hawks, and bats, and moths, and even the sweet-voiced thrushes, was the brave beating heart of the solitary gray-eyed child. And the tree stood still and held away the winds that June morning while the dawn grew bright in the east.

Sylvia's face was like a pale star, if one had seen it from the ground, when the last thorny bough was past, and she stood trembling and tired but wholly triumphant, high in the tree-top. Yes, there was the sea with the dawning sun making a golden dazzle over it, and toward that glorious east flew two hawks with slow-moving pinions. How low they looked in the air from that height when before one had only seen them far up, and dark against the blue sky. Their gray feathers were as soft as moths; they seemed only a littly way from the tree; and Sylvia felt as if she too could go flying away among the clouds. Westward, the woodlands and farms reached miles and miles into the distance; here and there were church steeples, and white villages; truly it was a vast and awesome world.

The birds sang louder and louder. At last the sun came up bewilderingly bright. Sylvia could see the white sails of ships out at sea, and the clouds that were purple and rose-colored and yellow at first began to fade away. Where was the white heron's nest in the sea of green branches, and was this wonderful sight and pageant of the world the only reward for having climbed to such a giddy height? Now look down again, Sylvia, where the green marsh is set among the shining birches and dark hemlocks; there where you saw the white heron once you will see him again; look, look! a white spot of him like a single floating feather comes up from the dead hemlock and grows larger, and rises, and comes close at last, and goes by the landmark pine with steady sweep of wing and outstretched slender neck and crested head. And wait! wait! do not move a foot or a finger, little girl, do not send an arrow of light and consciousness from your two eager eyes, for the heron has perched on a pine bough not far beyond yours, and cries back to his mate on the nest, and plumes his feathers for the new day!

The child gives a long sigh a minute later when a company of shouting cat-birds comes also to the tree, and vexed by their fluttering and lawlessness the solemn heron goes away. She knows his secret now, the wild, light, slender bird that floats and wavers, and goes back like an arrow presently to his home in the green world beneath. Then Sylvia, well satisfied, makes her perilous way down again, not daring to look far below the branch she stands on, ready to cry sometimes because her fingers ache and her lamed feet slip. Wondering over and over again what the stranger would say to her, and what he would think when she told him how to find his way straight to the heron's nest.

"Sylvy, Sylvy!" called the busy old grandmother again and again, but nobody answered, and the small husk bed was empty, and Sylvia had disappeared.

The guest waked from a dream, and remembering his day's pleasure hurried to dress himself that it might sooner begin. He was sure from the way the shy little girl looked once or twice yesterday that she had at least seen the white heron, and now she must really be persuaded to tell. Here she comes now, paler than ever, and her worn old frock is torn and tattered, and smeared with pine pitch. The grandmother and the sportsman stand in the door together and question her, and the splendid moment has come to speak of the dead hemlock-tree by the green marsh.

But Sylvia does not speak after all, though the old grandmother fretfully rebukes her, and the young man's kind appealing eyes are looking straight in her own. He can make them rich with money; he has promised it, and they are poor now. He is so well worth making happy, and he waits to hear the story she can tell.

No, she must keep silence! What is it that suddenly forbids her and makes her dumb? Has she been nine years growing, and now, when the great world for the first time puts out a hand to her, must she thrust it aside for a bird's sake? The murmur of the pine's green branches is in her ears, she remembers how the white heron came flying through the golden air and how they watched the sea and the morning together, and Sylvia cannot speak; she cannot tell the heron's secrets and give its life away.

Dear loyalty, that suffered a sharp pang as the guest went away disappointed later in the day, that could have served and followed him and loved him as a dog loves! Many a night Sylvia heard the echo of his whistle haunting the pasture path as she came home with the loitering cow. She forgot even her sorrow at the sharp report of his gun and the piteous sight of thrushes and sparrows dropping silent to the ground, their songs hushed and their pretty feathers stained and wet with blood. Were the birds better friends than their hunter might have been—who can tell? Whatever treasures were lost to her, woodlands and summer-time, remember! Bring your gifts and graces and tell your secrets to this lonely country child!

1886

EMILY DICKINSON

(1830–1886)

Emily Dickinson's poems are unlike any others written at her time; they are a unique body of verse in American and world literature. Intense, often cryptic, eccentric in syntax and prosody, the poems

The standard edition is Thomas Johnson, ed., *The Poems of Emily Dickinson,* 3 vols., 1955. Johnson has also edited *Final Harvest: Emily Dickinson's Poems,* 1961; with Theodora Ward, eds., *The Letters of Dickinson,* 3 vols. 1958, and *Emily Dickinson: Selected Letters,* 1971. Earlier edi-

tions are *Poems by Emily Dickinson,* 1890; *Poems by Emily Dickinson,* 1891; *Letters of Emily Dickinson,* 1894; *Poems by Emily Dickinson,* 1896. A *Concordance to the Poems of Emily Dickinson* has been edited by S. O. Rosenbaum, 1964.

(Footnote continued next page.)

seem odd, secretive communications, as if, like riddles, they are delib-erately teasing and baffling the mind. They seem at times to be pure acts of intelligence, yet they contain a great range of feeling from anguish to exultation. The poems have about them, too, the aura of legend, of the poet's own peculiar life of isolation, hiding her poems, hardly ever allowing publication. The legend and the poems together make up a curiosity and a mystery: out of what experiences, what background, did such expressions come?

Dickinson was born in Amherst, Massachusetts, and lived all her life in her father's house, with her sister Lavinia and her brother Austin, who lived next door after his marriage. Her father, Edward, was a suc-cessful lawyer: at one time he was treasurer of Amherst College. It was a cultivated Calvinist household, where intelligent conversation might be expected with interesting visitors, and with a library of standard English and New England writers. Emily Dickinson was a normally ac-tive, high-spirited, sometimes comical child; she attended school in town and later attended Mount Holyoke Female Seminary in nearby South Hadley. But in her early thirties she settled into a secluded pat-tern of life, never leaving Amherst (except twice to Boston for eye care), like an eccentric spinster seeing fewer and fewer people beyond her family and close friends.

Her deliberately cloistered life—she took to wearing only white—and her self-willed exile have aroused much conjecture, as can be expected. It seems certain that she was deeply affected by two losses of

Early biographies include Genevieve Tag-gard, The Life and Mind of Emily Dickin-son, 1930; George Whicher, This Was a Poet, A Critical Biography of Emily Dick-inson, 1938, and a series of books by Mil-icent Todd Bingham: Ancestors' Bro-cades: The Literary Debut of Emily Dickinson, 1945; Emily Dickinson: A Rev-elation, 1954; Emily Dickinson's Home, 1955. Thomas H. Johnson has also written a solid biography, Emily Dickinson: An Interpretive Biography, 1955. Richard B. Sewall's The Life of Emily Dickinson (2 volumes), 1974, is a definitive study.

Some of the more important critical esti-mates include Henry W. Wells, Introduc-tion to Emily Dickinson, 1947; Richard Chase, Emily Dickinson, 1951; R. P. Black-mur, Language as Gesture and "Emily Dickinson's Notation," Kenyon Review (Spring, 1956); Austin Warren, "Emily Dickinson," Sewanee Review (Autumn, 1957); John Crowe Ransom, "Emily Dick-inson, A Poet Restored," Perspectives USA (Spring 1956); Allen Tate, Collected Essays, 1959; Jay Leyda, The Years and Hours of Emily Dickinson, 1960; Richard Sewall, Emily Dickinson, A Collection of Critical Essays, 1963, and Emily Dickinson, 1975; Clark Griffith, The Long Shadow: Emily Dickinson's tragic poetry, 1964; Charles R. Anderson, Emily Dickinson's Poetry: Stairway of Surprise, 1960; Albert Gelpi, Emily Dickinson, The Mind of the Poet, 1965; Caesar Blake and Carlton Wills, The Recognition of Emily Dickin-son, 1965; David T. Porter, The Art of Em-ily Dickinson's Poetry, 1966; David Hig-gins, Portrait of Emily Dickinson, 1967; John B. Pickars, Emily Dickinson: An In-troduction and Interpretation, 1967; Ruth Miller, The Poetry of Emily Dickinson, 1968.

Emily Dickinson. The Granger Collection.

friendship with older men: the first by death, the second by departure. Benjamin Franklin Newton, nine years her senior, worked in her father's office, and was, she wrote, "a gentle, yet grave Preceptor, teaching me what to read, what authors to admire, what was most grand & beautiful in nature, and that sublime lesson, faith in things unseen, and in a life again, nobler, and much more blessed." He died in 1853. She met the Reverend Charles Wadsworth the following year and developed a close and perhaps romantic attachment, thwarted by the fact of his being married and by his departure for San Francisco in 1862. She began her withdrawal about then. In later years her few intimate friends were Samuel Bowles, editor of the Springfield *Daily Republican,* which published one of her early poems, Judge Otis P. Lord, and the well-known writer Helen Hunt Jackson, who also lived in Amherst. These were the only people along with members of her family, and most significantly Thomas Wentworth Higginson, to whom she occasionally showed her poems.

Rarely more than 20 lines in length, the poems were scrawled on backs of envelopes, on brown paper bags, and on scraps of newspaper: they were then sewn together into packets. Many appear in her letters. One of the most famous of her letters was to Higginson in 1862. A Civil War colonel, a liberal, and a writer who appeared often in the *Atlantic Monthly,* he received from her a few poems and a note inquiring whether the verses "breathed." This initiated a correspondence, her only connection with the literary world; it led to two visits with Higginson, and may be responsible for her work being saved. Although he was bewildered and overwhelmed, Higginson recognized an original talent and gave her encouragement. After her death, Higginson helped to bring out the first edition of her poems.

Higginson's difficulties in comprehending the poetry are a useful indicator of the special, unconventional qualities of her verse. He admonished her to correct her grammar, her meter, and her rhyme and, in the editions of 1890 and 1891, he polished diction and regularized punctuation up to current standards. He spoke of her verses as "poetry torn up by the roots," an effective image that evokes the jolting, breath-taking effect of her best poems. Higginson glimpsed the unorthodox intentions but responded uneasily. In reply to his suggestions she wrote: "If I read a book, and it makes my whole body so cold no fire ever can warm me, I know *that* is poetry. If I feel physically as if the top of my head were taken off, I know *that* is poetry. These are the only ways I know it. Is there any other way?" As a statement of her "way," this is, of course, incomplete, but we do get insight into the primacy of sharp feelings, of the intense unexpected experience, of the entrancement she herself felt and wished to communicate. Clearly she did not intend a poetry of moral wisdom dressed up in rhyme, or of "poetic" emotions passing for true feelings.

Her means were as idiosyncratic as her deeper intentions. Dashes and capitals make do for punctuation, which is actually a system of musical notation indicating pauses and points of emphasis. Her rhyming is often imperfect, oblique or "slant" or suspended, as in woodroad, tree-die, thing-along. Her commonest stanza form is, on the other hand, usually fairly regular, derived from the New England hymnals that were an integral feature of village life. In fact, the poems draw a good deal of their substance from the ordinary life of her village and family: a steady awareness of the details of domestic life, of the change of seasons, of neighbors; this lends a homespun quality to her verse as in "A Bird came down the Walk" (#328) or "There's been a Death, in the Opposite House" (#389). But it is her extraordinary uses of the ordinary that matter, as she testifies in these stanzas (#448).

> This was a Poet—It is That
> Distills amazing sense
> From ordinary Meanings—
> And Attar so immense
>
> From the familiar species
> That perished by the Door—
> We wonder it was not Ourselves
> Arrested it—before—

Her characteristic way of distilling the unusual, the precious scents from commonplace experience, lies through indirection: "Tell all the Truth but tell it slant" (#1129). Thus such unexpectedly yoked-together images as in "As imperceptibly as Grief/The Summer lapsed away—" (#1540), linking the perception of time's passage in the seasons with the sensation of a feeling, and associating both with loss, with a decline from intensity, with a lapsing away, comments on both grief and summer and on the ambiguous effect of time which, while curing grief, betrays the authentic moment of strong feeling.

An expansion of meaning, a sense of arrestment before the moment of disclosure or revelation: these are typical occurrences in many poems occasioned by ostensibly ordinary events, like the appearance of a butterfly or a bird or a snake, the death of a neighbor, the departure of a friend. "There's a certain Slant of Light" (#258) is an example of her power to invest familiar experiences, such as the appearance of a quality of sunlight on winter afternoons in New England, with enlarged meaning; the moment becomes an immensity:

> When it comes, the Landscape listens—
> Shadows—hold their breath—
> When it goes, 'tis like the Distance
> On the look of Death—

The magnitude and intensity of emotion in many of the poems belie their frail look. Although often enough she gives way to sheer cleverness, to a cloying verbal brilliance, at her best she can change her register with great subtlety, moving from the mundane to the breathtaking, as in "I felt a Funeral, in my Brain" (#280), "A Bird came down the Walk" (#328), "I started Early—Took my Dog" (#520), and "A narrow fellow in the Grass" (#986). The need for strong feeling, for a kind of transport, as evidence of life, is often her theme: "Tis so appalling—it exhilarates" (#281). We feel this even in her many light, irreverent, daringly ingenuous poems such as "I taste a liquor never brewed" (#214), or in the satiric "What Soft—Cherubic Creatures" (#401). Her poetic voice appeared in a variety of guises, from the impishly mocking to the stoically accepting, but throughout we feel at the bottom a hunger for experience, an affirmation of the world's body even as, in one sense, it is being renounced.

The variety and abundancy of Dickinson's verse have caused difficulty in discovering exactly where her center lies. Certainly there are large clusters of poems in which death, love, deprivation, and poetry itself are main themes. Her most moving poems concern suffering, but not so much as a direct experience as the apprehension of the experience in its trace left on consciousness. Thus the stately lyric "After great pain a formal feeling comes" (#341) deals not with the pain but with the reaction to it, with the experience of having suffered. While she hungers for direct experience, she realizes, as we see in "I Had been hungry, all the Years" (#579), that it is not the having of experience that matters so much as the hunger; it is in the act of wanting, or in the after effects, that the mind and feelings are most alive. Experience is an "Angled Road," which the mind paradoxically prefers *against* itself, even while "presuming" to lead in an opposite direction (#910). She characteristically locates herself at the angle, inside the paradox of the mind's wanting even as it recognizes that it cannot have, or as she puts it in one of the quasi riddles of intelligence she often writes: "Perception of an object costs/Precise the Object's loss—" (#1071). In this sense she is very much a poet of consciousness, of the mind's many acts of self-apprehension in the process of its most acute states of feeling. One of her most common words is "circumference," the outer edge of the circle of awareness, the boundary of knowing and enduring. She is finely aware in her best poems that all experiencing occurs within the circumference of consciousness, where the most complex and subtle transactions occur between mind and the world.

These qualities place her in a revealing relation to the New England tradition. Many of her concerns derive from tradition and concerns with God, faith, and nature. But she is neither a religious nor a nature poet in any traditional sense. Although we may hear certain Wordsworthian or Emersonian notes in her nature poems, they are deceptive; nature is chiefly a source of terror, threat, and affliction, for which her major symbol is death. Unlike Whitman, who found consolation in the natural process of death and rebirth, Dickinson could think of death only as loss, as blankness; the traditional Christian concepts of immortality and redemption appear often in her verse, but they are almost invariably tinged with skepticism, as taunting reminders of an earlier age of confident faith. Hers is a poetry of questioning, of probings, as Melville wrote of Hawthorne, at the axis of reality; in place of God she faces "The Missing All" (#985). In her skeptical relation to the absolutes of heritage she is, then, very much of her times. As R. P. Blackmur said of her, "All her life she was looking for a subject, and the looking *was* her subject, in life as in poetry." Her importance as a forerunner of modern consciousness is made clear in this restless but self-sufficing quest.

49

I never lost as much but twice,
And that was in the sod.
Twice have I stood a beggar
Before the door of God!

Angels—twice descending   5
Reimbursed my store—
Burglar! Banker—Father!
I am poor once more!

c. 1858   1890

67

Success is counted sweetest
By those who ne'er succeed.
To comprehend a nectar
Requires sorest need.

Not one of all the purple Host   5
Who took the Flag today
Can tell the definition
So clear of Victory

As he defeated—dying—
On whose forbidden ear   10
The distant strains of triumph
Burst agonized and clear!

c. 1859   *1878*

130

These are the days when Birds come back—
A very few—a Bird or two—
To take a backward look.

These are the days when skies resume
The old—old sophistries of June—   5
A blue and gold mistake.

Oh fraud that cannot cheat the Bee—
Almost thy plausibility
Induces my belief.

Till ranks of seeds their witness bear—   10
And softly thro' the altered air
Hurries a timid leaf.

Oh Sacrament of summer days,
Oh Last Communion in the Haze—
Permit a child to join.   15

Thy sacred emblems to partake—
Thy consecrated bread to take
And thine immortal wine!

c. 1859   *1890*

158

Dying! Dying in the night!
Won't somebody bring the light
So I can see which way to go
Into the everlasting snow?

And "Jesus!" Where is *Jesus* gone?   5
They said that Jesus—always came—
Perhaps he doesn't know the House—
This way, Jesus, Let him pass!

Somebody run to the great gate
And see if Dollie's coming! Wait!   10
I hear her feet upon the stair!
Death won't hurt—now Dollie's here!

c. 1860

1945

160

Just lost, when I was saved!
Just felt the world go by!
Just girt me for onset with Eternity,
When breath blew back,
And on the other side   5
I heard recede the disappointed tide!

Therefore, as One returned, I feel
Odd secrets of the line to tell!
Some Sailor, skirting foreign shores—
Some pale Reporter from the awful doors   10
Before the Seal!

Next time, to stay!
Next time, the things to see
By Ear unheard,
Unscrutinized by Eye—   15

Next time, to tarry,
While the Ages steal—
Slow tramp the Centuries,
And the Cycles wheel!

c. 1860

1891

167

To learn the Transport by the Pain—
As Blind Men learn the sun!
To die of thirst—suspecting
That Brooks in Meadows run!

398

## EMILY DICKINSON

To stay the homesick—homesick feet
Upon a foreign shore—
Haunted by native lands, the while—
And blue—beloved air!

This is the Sovereign Anguish!
This—the signal woe!
These are the patient "Laureates"
Whose voices—trained—below—

Ascend in ceaseless Carol—
Inaudible, indeed,
To us—the duller scholars
Of the Mysterious Bard!

c. 1860   *1891*

199

I'm "wife"—I've finished that—
That other state—
I'm Czar—I'm "Woman" now—
It's safer so—

How odd the Girl's life looks
Behind this soft Eclipse—
I think that Earth feels so
To folks in Heaven—now—

This being comfort—then
That other kind—was pain
But why compare?
I'm "Wife"! Stop there!

c. 1860   *1890*

214

I taste a liquor never brewed—
From Tankards scooped in Pearl—
Not all the Vats upon the Rhine
Yield such an Alcohol!

EMILY DICKINSON

Inebriate of Air—am I—
And Debauchee of Dew—
Reeling—thro endless summer days—   5
From inns of Molten Blue—

When "Landlords" turn the drunken Bee
Out of the Foxglove's door—   10
When Butterflies—renounce their "drams"—
I shall but drink the more!

Till Seraphs swing their snowy Hats—
And Saints—to windows run—
To see the little Tippler   15
Leaning against the—Sun—

c. 1860   *1861*

241

I like a look of Agony,
Because I know it's true—
Men do not sham Convulsion,
Nor simulate, a Throe—

The Eyes glaze once—and that is Death—   5
Impossible to feign
The beads upon the Forehead
By homely Anguish strung.

c. 1861   *1890*

249

Wild Nights—Wild Nights!
Were I with thee
Wild Nights should be
Our luxury!

Futile—the Winds—   5
To Heart in port—
Done with the Compass—
Done with the Chart!

Rowing in Eden—
Ah, the Sea!
Might I but moor—Tonight—
In Thee!

c. 1861   1891

258

There's a certain Slant of light,
Winter Afternoons—
That oppresses, like the Heft
Of Cathedral Tunes—

Heavenly Hurt, it gives us—   5
We can find no scar,
But internal difference,
Where the Meanings, are—

None may teach it—Any—   10
'Tis the Seal Despair—
An imperial affliction
Sent us of the Air—

When it comes, the Landscape listens—
Shadows—hold their breath
When it goes, 'tis like the Distance   15
On the look of Death—

c. 1861   1890

280

I felt a Funeral, in my Brain,
And Mourners to and fro
Kept treading—treading—till it seemed
That Sense was breaking through—

And when they all were seated,   5
A Service, like a Drum—
Kept beating—beating—till I thought
My Mind was going numb—

And then I heard them lift a Box
And creak across my Soul   10
With those same Boots of Lead, again,
Then Space—began to toll,

As all the Heavens were a Bell,
And Being, but an Ear,
And I, and Silence, some strange Race   15
Wrecked, solitary, here—

And then a Plank in Reason, broke,
And I dropped down, and down—
And hit a World, at every plunge,
And Finished knowing—then—   20

c. 1861   1896

281

'Tis so appalling—it exhilarates—
So over Horror, it half Captivates—
The Soul stares after it, secure—
A Sepulchre, fears frost, no more—

To scan a Ghost, is faint—   5
But grappling, conquers it—
How easy, Torment, now—
Suspense kept sawing so—

The Truth, is Bald, and Cold—
But that will hold—   10
If any are not sure—
We show them—prayer—
But we, who know,
Stop hoping, now—

Looking at Death, is Dying—   15
Just let go the Breath—
And not the pillow at your Cheek
So Slumbereth—

Others, Can wrestle—
Yours, is done—   20
And so of Woe, bleak dreaded—come,
It sets the Fright at liberty—
And Terror's free—
Gay, Ghastly, Holiday!

c. 1861   *1935*

287

A Clock stopped—
Not the Mantel's—
Geneva's farthest skill
Can't put the puppet bowing—
That just now dangled still—   5

An awe came on the Trinket!
The Figures hunched, with pain—
Then quivered out of Decimals—
Into Degreeless Noon—

It will not stir for Doctors—   10
This Pendulum of snow—
This Shopman importunes it—
While cool—concernless No—

Nods from the Gilded pointers:
Nods from the Seconds slim—   15
Decades of Arrogance between
The Dial life—
And Him—

c. 1861   *1896*

288

I'm Nobody! Who are you?
Are you—Nobody—Too?
Then there's a pair of us?
Don't tell! they'd advertise—you know!

How dreary—to be—Somebody!   5
How public—like a Frog—
To tell one's name—the livelong June—
To an admiring Bog!

c. 1861   *1891*

303

The Soul selects her own Society—
Then—shuts the Door—   *E.D withdraw*
To her divine Majority—   *from society.*
Present no more—

Unmoved—she notes the Chariots—pausing—   5
At her low Gate—   *courtship*
Unmoved—an Emperor be kneeling
Upon her Mat—   *unmoved by pomp*
World has nothing   *& ceremony.*
I've known her—from an ample nation—
Choose One—   *shellfish / heart*   10
Then—close the Valves of her attention—
Like Stone—
            potentially
            harmful
            world

c. 1862   *1890*

327

Before I got my eye put out
I liked as well to see—
As other Creatures, that have Eyes
And know no other way—

But were it told to me—Today—   5
That I might have the sky
For mine—I tell you that my Heart
Would split, for size of me—

The Meadows—mine—
The Mountains—mine—   10
All Forests—Stintless Stars—
As much of Noon as I could take
Between my finite eyes—

The Motions of the Dipping Birds—
The Morning's Amber Road—   15
For mine—to look at when I liked—
The News would strike me dead—

So safer—guess—with just my soul
Upon the Window pane—
Where other Creatures put their eyes—   20
Incautious—of the Sun—

c. 1862   *1891*

328

A Bird came down the Walk—
He did not know I saw—
He bit an Angleworm in halves
And ate the fellow, raw,

And then he drank a Dew   5
From a convenient Grass—
And then hopped sidewise to the Wall
To let a Beetle pass—

He glanced with rapid eyes
That hurried all around—   10
They looked like frightened Beads, I thought—
He stirred his Velvet Head

Like one in danger, Cautious,
I offered him a Crumb
And he unrolled his feathers   15
And rowed him softer home—

Than Oars divide the Ocean,
Too silver for a seam—
Or Butterflies, off Banks of Noon
Leap, plashless as they swim.   20

c. 1862   *1891*

341

After great pain, a formal feeling comes—
The Nerves sit ceremonious, like Tombs—
The stiff Heart questions was it He, that bore,
And Yesterday, or Centuries before?

The Feet, mechanical, go round—   5
Of Ground, or Air, or Ought—
A Wooden way
Regardless grown,
A Quartz contentment, like a stone—

This is the Hour of Lead—   10
Remembered, if outlived,
As Freezing persons, recollect the Snow—
First—Chill—then Stupor—then the letting go—

c. 1862   1929

383

Exhilaration—is within—
There can no Outer Wine
So royally intoxicate
As that diviner Brand

The Soul achieves—Herself—   5
To drink—or set away
For Visitor—Or Sacrament—
'Tis not of Holiday

To stimulate a Man
Who hath the Ample Rhine   10
Within his Closet—Best you can
Exhale in offering.

c. 1862   1935

389

There's been a Death, in the Opposite House,
As lately as Today—
I know it, by the numb look
Such Houses have—alway—

The Neighbors rustle in and out—
The Doctor—drives away—
A Window opens like a Pod—
Abrupt—mechanically—

Somebody flings a Mattress out—
The Children hurry by—
They wonder if it died—on that—
I used to—when a Boy—

The Minister—goes stiffly in—
As if the House were His—
And He owned all the Mourners—now—
And little Boys—besides—

And then the Milliner—and the Man
Of the Appalling Trade—
To take the measure of the House—
There'll be that Dark Parade—

Of Tassels—and of Coaches—soon—
It's easy as a Sign—
The Intuition of the News—
In just a Country Town—

c. 1862   *1896*

401

What Soft—Cherubic Creatures—
These Gentlewomen are—
One would as soon assault a Plush—
Or violate a Star—

Such Dimity[1] Convictions—
A Horror so refined
Of freckled Human Nature—
Of Deity—ashamed—

It's such a common—Glory—
A Fisherman's—Degree—
Redemption—Brittle Lady—
Be so—ashamed of Thee—

c. 1862   *1896*

[1] A sheer dainty cotton fabric in checks or stripes.

society determines norm

435

knows how to look

Much Madness is divinest Sense—
To a discerning Eye—
Much Sense—the starkest Madness—
'Tis the Majority
In this, as All, prevail—   go along - normal ?   5
Assent—and you are sane— non conformist - nuts
Demur—you're straightway dangerous—
And handled with a Chain—

society

c. 1862   What is norm in insane society ?   *1890*
A. Huxley

441

This is my letter to the World
That never wrote to Me—
The simple News that Nature told—
With tender Majesty

Her Message is committed   5
To Hands I cannot see—
For love of Her—Sweet—countrymen—
Judge tenderly—of Me

c. 1862   *1890*

448

This was a Poet—It is That
Distills amazing sense
From ordinary Meanings—
And Attar[1] so immense

From the familiar species   5
That perished by the Door—
We wonder it was not Ourselves
Arrested it—before—

[1] A fragrant essential oil.

Of Pictures, the Discloser—
The Poet—it is He— 10
Entitles Us—by Contrast—
To ceaseless Poverty—

Of Portion—so unconscious—
The Robbing—could not harm—
Himself—to Him—a Fortune— 15
Exterior—to Time—

c. 1862   *1929*

449

I died for Beauty—but was scarce
Adjusted in the Tomb
When One who died for Truth, was lain
In an adjoining Room—

He questioned softly "Why I failed"? 5
"For Beauty", I replied—
"And I—for Truth—Themself are One—
We Brethren, are", He said—

And so, as Kinsmen, met a Night—
We talked between the Rooms— 10
Until the Moss had reached our lips—
And covered up—our names—

c. 1862   *1890*

465

I heard a Fly buzz—when I died—
The Stillness in the Room
Was like the Stillness in the Air—
Between the Heaves of Storm—

The Eyes around—had wrung them dry— 5
And Breaths were gathering firm
For that last Onset—when the King
Be witnessed—in the Room—

I willed my Keepsakes—Signed away
What portion of me be   *dying awile*   10
Assignable—and then it was   *taken care of all*
There interposed a Fly—
                            describe
With Blue—uncertain stumbling Buzz—
Between the light—and me—
And then the Windows failed—and then   15
I could not see to see—
                    died

c. 1862   *1896*

510

It was not Death, for I stood up,
And all the Dead, lie down—
It was not Night, for all the Bells
Put out their Tongues, for Noon.

It was not Frost, for on my Flesh   5
I felt Siroccos[1]—crawl—
Nor Fire—for just my Marble feet
Could keep a Chancel, cool—

And yet, it tasted, like them all,
The Figures I have seen   10
Set orderly, for Burial,
Reminded me, of mine—

As if my life were shaven,
And fitted to a frame,
And could not breathe without a key,   15
And 'twas like Midnight, some—

When everything that ticked—has stopped—
And Space stares all around—
Or Grisly frosts—first Autumn morns,
Repeal the Beating Ground—   20

[1] A hot dusty wind from the Libyan desert
that blows on the northern Mediterranean
coast, chiefly in Italy, Malta, and Sicily.

But, most, like Chaos—Stopless—cool—
Without a Chance, or Spar—
Or even a Report of Land—
To justify—Despair.

c. 1862   1891

520

I started Early—Took my Dog—
And visited the Sea—
The Mermaids in the Basement
Came out to look at me—

And Frigates—in the Upper Floor   5
Extended Hempen Hands—
Presuming Me to be a Mouse—
Aground—upon the Sands—

But no Man moved Me—till the Tide
Went past my simple Shoe—   10
And past my Apron—and my Belt
And past my Bodice—too—

And made as He would eat me up—
As wholly as a Dew
Upon a Dandelion's Sleeve—   15
And then—I started—too—

And He—He followed—close behind—
I felt His Silver Heel
Upon my Ankle—Then my Shoes
Would overflow with Pearl—   20

Until We met the Solid Town—
No One He seemed to know—
And bowing—with a Mighty look—
At me—The Sea withdrew—

c. 1862   1891

Calvinist — salvation given by god to select few

related to C.D.'s
withdrawal

528

Mine—by the Right of the White Election!
Mine—by the Royal Seal!
Mine—by the Sign in the Scarlet prison—
Bars—cannot conceal!

Mine—here—in Vision—and in Veto!   5
Mine—by the Grave's Repeal—
Titled—Confirmed—
Delirious Charter!
Mine—long as Ages steal!

her
suffering
loneliness
memories

c. 1862   *1890*

547

I've seen a Dying Eye
Run round and round a Room—
In search of Something—as it seemed—
Then Cloudier become—
And then—obscure with Fog—   5
And then—be soldered down
Without disclosing what it be
'Twere blessed to have seen—

c. 1862   *1890*

579

I had been hungry, all the Years—
My Noon had Come—to dine—
I trembling drew the Table near—
And touched the Curious Wine—

'Twas this on Tables I had seen—   5
When turning, hungry, Home
I looked in Windows, for the Wealth
I could not hope—for Mine—

I did not know the ample Bread—
'Twas so unlike the Crumb
The Birds and I, had often shared
In Nature's—Dining Room—

The Plenty hurt me—'twas so new—
Myself felt ill—and odd—
As Berry—of a Mountain Bush—
Transplanted—to the Road—

Nor was I hungry—so I found
That Hunger—was a way
Of Persons outside Windows—
The Entering—takes away—

c. 1862   *1891*

585

I like to see it lap the Miles—
And lick the Valleys up—
And stop to feed itself at Tanks—
And then—prodigious step

Around a Pile of Mountains—
And supercilious peer
In Shanties—by the sides of Roads—
And then a Quarry pare

To fit its Ribs
And crawl between
Complaining all the while
In horrid—hooting stanza—
Then chase itself down Hill—

And neigh like Boanerges[1]—
Then—punctual as a Star
Stop—docile and omnipotent
As its own stable door—

c. 1862   *1891*

[1] A vociferous preacher or orator.

640

[handwritten: Cannot live with / g-d — locked away]

[handwritten: Compares / g-d to a sexton]

I cannot live with You—
It would be Life—
And Life is over there—
Behind the Shelf

The Sexton keeps the Key to—   5
Putting up
Our Life—His Porcelain—
Like a Cup—   *[handwritten: w.]*

Discarded of the Housewife—
Quaint—or Broke—   10
A newer Sevres pleases—
Old Ones crack—

I could not die—with You—
For One must wait
To shut the Other's Gaze down—   15
You—could not—

And I—Could I stand by
And see You—freeze—
Without my Right of Frost—
Death's privilege?   20

Nor could I rise—with You—
Because Your Face
Would put out Jesus'—
That New Grace

Glow plain—and foreign   25
On my homesick Eye—
Except that You than He
Shone closer by—

They'd judge Us—How—
For You—served Heaven—You know,   *[handwritten: Something to be about / Rev?]*   30
Or sought to—
I could not—

Because You saturated Sight—
And I had no more Eyes
For sordid excellence   35
As Paradise

She changes her perspective of death several times. Usually it is seen as an extention of life.

And were You lost, I would be—
Though My Name
Rang loudest
On the Heavenly fame—   40

And were You—saved—
And I—condemned to be
Where You were not—
That self—were Hell to Me—

So We must meet apart—   45
You there—I—here—
With just the Door ajar
That Oceans are—and Prayer—
And that White Sustenance—
Despair—   50

c. 1862   1890

657

I dwell in Possibility—
A fairer House than Prose—
More numerous of Windows—
Superior—for Doors—

Of Chambers as the Cedars—   5
Impregnable of Eye—
And for an Everlasting Roof
The Gambrels of the Sky—

Of Visitors—the fairest—
For Occupation—This—   10
The spreading wide my narrow Hands
To gather Paradise—

c. 1862   1929

Meditation on death

712

Because I could not stop for Death—
He kindly stopped for me—
The Carriage held but just Ourselves—
And Immortality.

For suffering people death is welcome

Keeps her own ID in death
another stage in being

415

EMILY DICKINSON

We slowly drove—He knew no haste
And I had put away
My labor and my leisure too,
For His Civility—

We passed the School, where Children strove
At Recess—in the Ring—
We passed the Fields of Gazing Grain—
We passed the Setting Sun—

Or rather—He passed Us—
The Dews drew quivering and chill—
For only Gossamer, my Gown—
My Tippet[1]—only Tulle—

We paused before a House that seemed
A Swelling of the Ground—
The Roof was scarcely visible—
The Cornice—in the Ground—

Since then—'tis Centuries—and yet
Feels shorter than the Day
I first surmised the Horses' Heads
Were toward Eternity—

c. 1863 1890

754

My Life had stood—a Loaded Gun—
In Corners—till a Day
The Owner passed—identified—
And carried Me away—

And now We roam in Sovereign Woods—
And now We hunt the Doe—
And every time I speak for Him—
The Mountains straight reply—

And do I smile, such cordial light
Upon the Valley glow—
It is as a Vesuvian face
Had let its pleasure through—

[1] A shawl for covering the neck and shoulders, usually of fur or wool.

And when at Night—Our good Day done—
I guard My Master's Head—
'Tis better than the Eider-Duck's 15
Deep Pillow—to have shared—

To foe of His—I'm deadly foe—
None stir the second time—
On whom I lay a Yellow Eye—
Or an emphatic Thumb— 20

Though I than He—may longer live
He longer must—than I—
For I have but the power to kill,
Without—the power to die—

c. 1863 1929

910

Experience is the Angled Road
Preferred against the Mind
By—Paradox—the Mind itself—
Presuming it to lead ·

Quite Opposite—How Complicate 5
The Discipline of Man—
Compelling Him to Choose Himself
His Preappointed Pain—

c. 1864 1929

959

A loss of something ever felt I—
The first that I could recollect
Bereft I was—of what I knew not
Too young that any should suspect

A Mourner walked among the children 5
I notwithstanding went about
As one bemoaning a Dominion
Itself the only Prince cast out—

Elder, Today, a session wiser
And fainter, too, as Wiseness is—   10
I find myself still softly searching
For my Delinquent Palaces—

And a Suspicion, like a Finger
Touches my Forehead now and then
That I am looking oppositely   15
For the site of the Kingdom of Heaven—

c. 1864   *1945*

963

A nearness to Tremendousness—
An Agony procures—
Affliction ranges Boundlessness—
Vicinity to Laws

Contentment's quiet Suburb—   5
Affliction cannot stay
In Acres—Its Location
Is Illocality—

c. 1864   *1935*

985

The Missing All—prevented Me
From missing minor Things.
If nothing larger than a World's
Departure from a Hinge—
Or Sun's extinction, be observed—   5
'Twas not so large that I
Could lift my Forehead from my work
For Curiosity.

c. 1865   *1914*

Extremely acute powers of observation.

986

A narrow Fellow in the Grass
Occasionally rides—
You may have met Him—did you not
His notice sudden is—

The Grass divides as with a Comb—   5
A spotted shaft is seen—
And then it closes at your feet
And opens further on—

He likes a Boggy Acre   *cool, moist*
A Floor too cool for Corn—   10
Yet when a Boy, and Barefoot—
I more than once at Noon
Have passed, I thought, a Whip lash
Unbraiding in the Sun
When stooping to secure it   15
It wrinkled, and was gone—

Several of Nature's People
I know, and they know me—
I feel for them a transport   *favorable
Of cordiality—   emotional*   20
                                  reaction

But never met this Fellow
Attended, or alone
Without a tighter breathing *gives a*
And Zero at the Bone—   *chill*

c. 1865   *1866*

1068

Further in Summer than the Birds
Pathetic from the Grass
A minor Nation celebrates
Its unobtrusive Mass.

No Ordinance be seen   5
So gradual the Grace
A pensive Custom it becomes
Enlarging Loneliness.

Antiquest felt at Noon
When August burning low   10
Arise this spectral Canticle[2]
Repose to typify[3]

Remit as yet no Grace
No Furrow on the Glow
Yet a Druidic Difference   15
Enhances Nature now

c. 1866   1891

1071

Perception of an object costs
Precise the Object's loss—
Perception in itself a Gain
Replying to its Price—

The Object Absolute—is nought—   5
Perception sets it fair
And then upbraids a Perfectness
That situates so far—

c. 1866   1914

1129

Tell all the Truth but tell it slant—
Success in Circuit lies
Too bright for our infirm Delight
The Truth's superb surprise

As Lightning to the Children eased   5
With explanation kind
The Truth must dazzle gradually
Or every man be blind—

c. 1868   1945

---

[2] A nonmetrical hymn or chant from the
Bible used in Church services.

[3] To serve as the symbol or emblem of.

1207

He preached upon "Breadth" till it argued him narrow—
The Broad are too broad to define
And of "Truth" until it proclaimed him a Liar—
The Truth never flaunted a Sign—

Simplicity fled from his counterfeit presence   5
As Gold the Pyrites would shun—
What confusion would cover the innocent Jesus
To meet so enabled a Man!

c. 1872   *1891*

1540

As imperceptibly as Grief
The Summer lapsed away—
Too imperceptible at last
To seem like Perfidy—
A Quietness distilled   5
As Twilight long begun,
Or Nature spending with herself
Sequestered Afternoon—
The Dusk drew earlier in—
The Morning foreign shone—   10
A courteous, yet harrowing Grace,
As Guest, that would be gone—
And thus, without a Wing
Or service of a Keel
Our Summer made her light escape   15
Into the Beautiful.

c. 1865   *1891*

FREDERICK GODDARD TUCKERMAN

(1821–1873)

Like Emily Dickinson, Tuckerman lived and wrote in seclusion, only his was an isolation even more solitary than hers. Both represent a deliberate inward turning of the New England literary imagination, a turning back from the more public posture of an Emerson, a Lowell, and a Longfellow, to the line of introspection that begins in the Seventeenth century in the meditations of Anne Bradstreet and Edward Taylor.

Tuckerman's poetry has even less apparent touch with his day than Emily Dickinson's. Born into a very prominent New England family of writers and scientists, and Harvard-bred, he gave up a career of law in Boston and moved with his wife to Greenfield, in western Massachusetts, not far from Amherst. His wife died in 1857, and he lived the rest of his life a recluse, writing poetry, and studying astronomy (and publishing occasional papers on eclipses) and botany. He wrote sonnet sequences in journal fashion—anticipating, curiously, recent works by the contemporary New England poet Robert Lowell—as if in communion with his dead wife, whose presence haunts most of his verse. He published a volume of sonnets in 1860, with new editions in 1864 and 1869, but he was virtually unknown in his day (although admired by Tennyson) and rediscovered only in 1931 by the poet Witter Bynner, who published *The Sonnets of Frederick Goddard Tuckerman*. Bynner was struck by the original innovations in sonnet form achieved by this obscure New Englander, and he emphasized his experimentation, his search for a more personal mode within conventional verse. Tuckerman's absorption of Romantic poetry is beautifully manifest in "The Cricket," a poem printed for the first time in 1950.

A strange coincidence is that Emily Dickinson knew well members of Tuckerman's family: his brother, who taught at Amherst, and his son. Moreover, Tuckerman had been a classmate at Harvard of Thomas Wentworth Higginson, who befriended Emily Dickinson. Yet there is no evidence that these two poets who lived within miles of each other knew of each other's secret vocation of poetry.

An authoritative edition is N. Scott Momaday, ed., *The Complete Poems of Frederick Goddard Tuckerman*. Other editions of the Poems were published in 1860, 1863, 1864, 1869. Witter Bynner has edited *The Sonnets of Frederick Goddard Tuckerman, 1931.*

A biography is Samuel A. Golden, *Frederick Goddard Tuckerman: An American Sonneteer, 1952.*

From Poems

X[1]

An upper chamber in a darkened house,
Where, ere his footsteps reached ripe manhood's brink,
Terror and anguish were his lot to drink;
I cannot rid the thought nor hold it close
But dimly dream upon that man alone:⁵
Now though the autumn clouds most softly pass,
The cricket chides beneath the doorstep stone
And greener than the season grows the grass.
Nor can I drop my lids nor shade my brows,
But there he stands beside the lifted sash;¹⁰
And with a swooning of the heart, I think
Where the black shingles slope to meet the boughs
And, shattered on the roof like smallest snows,
The tiny petals of the mountain ash.

1860

[1] First appeared in the 1860 edition of *Poems*
by Tuckerman, published by John Wilson &
Son, Boston.

XVIII[1]

And change with hurried hand has swept these scenes:
The woods have fallen, across the meadow-lot
The hunter's trail and trap-path is forgot,
And fire has drunk the swamps of evergreens;
Yet for a moment let my fancy plant⁵
These autumn hills again: the wild dove's haunt,
The wild deer's walk. In golden umbrage shut,
The Indian river runs, Quonecktacut![2]
Here, but a lifetime back, where falls tonight
Behind the curtained pane a sheltered light¹⁰
On buds of rose or vase of violet
Aloft upon the marble mantel set,
Here in the forest-heart, hung blackening
The wolfbait on the bush beside the spring.

1860

[1] First published in the 1860 Wilson edition.
[2] Tuckerman's Indian spelling for Connecticut.

XXIV[1]

Each common object too, the house, the grove,
The street, the face, the ware in the window, seems
Alien and sad, the wreck of perished dreams;
Painfully present, yet remote in love.
The day goes down in rain, the winds blow wide.   5
I leave the town; I climb the mountain side,
Striving from stumps and stones to wring relief,
And in the senseless anger of my grief,
I rave and weep, I roar to the unmoved skies;
But the wild tempest carries away my cries.   10
Then back I turn to hide my face in sleep,
Again with dawn the same dull round to sweep,
And buy and sell and prate and laugh and chide,
As if she had not lived, or had not died.

1860

[1] First published in the 1860 Wilson edition.

THE CRICKET[1]

I

The humming bee purrs softly o'er his flower;
   From lawn and thicket
The dogday locust singeth in the sun
   From hour to hour:
Each has his bard, and thou, ere day be done,   5
   Shalt have no wrong.
So bright that murmur mid the insect crowd,
Muffled and lost in bottom-grass, or loud
   By pale and picket:
Shall I not take to help me in my song   10
   A little cooing cricket?

II

The afternoon is sleepy; let us lie
Beneath these branches whilst the burdened brook,
Muttering and moaning to himself, goes by;

[1] First published in 1950 by the editors of the
Cummington Press, over 70 years after Tuckerman's death.

And mark our minstrel's carol whilst we look   15
Toward the faint horizon swooning blue.
    Or in a garden bower,
Trellised and trammeled with deep drapery
    Of hanging green,
    Light glimmering through—   20
There let the dull hop be,
Let bloom, with poppy's dark refreshing flower:
Let the dead fragrance round our temples beat,
Stunning the sense to slumber, whilst between
The falling water and fluttering wind   25
    Mingle and meet,
    Murmur and mix,
No few faint pipings from the glades behind,
    Or alder-thicks:
But louder as the day declines,   30
From tingling tassel, blade, and sheath,
Rising from nets of river vines,
    Winrows and ricks,
    Above, beneath,
    At every breath,   35
At hand, around, illimitably
Rising and falling like the sea,
    Acres of cricks!

III

Dear to the child who hears thy rustling voice
Cease at his footstep, though he hears thee still,   40
Cease and resume with vibrance crisp and shrill,
Thou sittest in the sunshine to rejoice.
Night lover too; bringer of all things dark
And rest and silence; yet thou bringest to me
Always that burthen of the unresting Sea,   45
The moaning cliffs, the low rocks blackly stark;
These upland inland fields no more I view,
But the long flat seaside beach, the wild seamew,
    And the overturning wave!
Thou bringest too, dim accents from the grave   50
To him who walketh when the day is dim,
Dreaming of those who dream no more of him,
With edged remembrances of joy and pain;
And heyday looks and laughter come again:

Forms that in happy sunshine lie and leap,   55
With faces where but now a gap must be,
Renunciations, and partitions deep
And perfect tears, and crowning vacancy!
And to thy poet at the twilight's hush,
No chirping touch of lips with laugh and blush,   60
But wringing arms, hearts wild with love and woe,
Closed eyes, and kisses that would not let go!

IV

So wert thou loved in that old graceful time
    When Greece was fair,
While god and hero hearkened to thy chime;   65
    Softly astir
Where the long grasses fringed Caÿster's[2] lip;
Long-drawn, with glimmering sails of swan and ship,
    And ship and swan;
    Or where   70
    Reedy Eurotas[3] ran.
Did that low warble teach thy tender flute
    Xenaphyle?[4]
Its breathings mild? say! did the grasshopper
Sit golden in thy purple hair   75
    O Psammathe?[5]
    Or wert thou mute,
Grieving for Pan amid the alders there?
And by the water and along the hill
That thirsty tinkle in the herbage still,   80
Though the lost forest wailed to horns of Arcady?

[2] A river in ancient Greece that is famous for bountiful waterfowl, now as in Homer's days. The valley of the Cayster is called "the Asian meadow" by Homer.

[3] The chief river of the valley of Laconia, where Sparta stood.

[4] Xenophilus was a Pythagorean philosopher who lived for 170 years in good health. Since he wrote about music, he was called "the musician."

[5] Psammathe was a princess, daughter of King Argos and, by Apollo, the mother of Linos. She abandoned Linos to be brought up by shepherds, but dogs tore him apart. Psammathe grieved so deeply that her father, King Argos, found out all and condemned her to death. Apollo became angry at the cruelty of the father and sent a plague on him and his kingdom. The people tried to beg for mercy by offering sacrifices and singing dirges for the dead son; these were called lini, or linos-songs. The name Linos is usually taken to stand for an old Greek nature god, as is the name Pan.

V

Like the Enchanter old—
Who sought mid the dead water's weeds and scum
For evil growths beneath the moonbeam cold,
    Or mandrake or dorcynium;   85
And touched the leaf that opened both his ears,
So that articulate voices now he hears
In cry of beast, or bird, or insect's hum,—
Might I but find thy knowledge in thy song!
    That twittering tongue,   90
Ancient as light, returning like the years.
    So might I be,
Unwise to sing, thy true interpreter
Through denser stillness and in sounder dark,
Than ere thy notes have pierced to harrow me.   95
    So might I stir
    The world to hark
    To thee my lord and lawgiver,
    And cease my quest:
Content to bring thy wisdom to the world;   100
Content to gain at last some low applause,
    Now low, now lost
Like thine from mossy stone, amid the stems and straws,
    Or garden gravemound tricked and dressed—
    Powdered and pearled   105
    By stealing frost—
In dusky rainbow beauty of euphorbias![6]
For larger would be less indeed, and like
The ceaseless simmer in the summer grass
To him who toileth in the windy field,   110
    Or where the sunbeams strike,
Naught in innumerable numerousness.
    So might I much possess,
    So much must yield;
But failing this, the dell and grassy dike,   115
The water and the waste shall still be dear,
And all the pleasant plots and places
    Where thou hast sung, and I have hung
    To ignorantly hear.
Then Cricket, sing thy song! or answer mine!   120

[6] A species of plant, some of which have a
beautiful scarlet flower.

Thine whispers blame, but mine has naught but praises.
It matters not. Behold! the autumn goes,
   The shadow grows,
The moments take hold of eternity;
Even while we stop to wrangle or repine   125
   Our lives are gone—
   Like thinnest mist,
Like yon escaping color in the tree;
Rejoice! rejoice! whilst yet the hours exist—
Rejoice or mourn, and let the world swing on   130
Unmoved by cricket song of thee or me.

II
The Triumph of Realism

WILLIAM DEAN HOWELLS

(1837–1920)

An advocate and practitioner of literary realism, William Dean Howells enjoyed a long productive career of nearly 70 years. His role in the movement to ground the novel in the real experiences of the contemporary world was large and generous. As an editor and critic, he championed the works of his close friends Henry James and Mark Twain; he

The Indiana Press is now putting together a 41-volume edition of Howell's writings, which will become the standard edition. The important works, most of which are available in inexpensive paperbacks, are *Venetian Life*, 1866; *Italian Journals*, 1867; *Their Wedding Journey*, 1872; *A Chance Acquaintance*, 1873; *A Modern Instance*, 1882; *The Rise of Silas Lapham*, 1885; *Indian Summer*, 1886; *A Hazard of New Fortunes*, 1890; *A Traveler From Altruria*, 1894; *The Landlord at Lion's Head*, 1897; *Literary Friends and Acquaintances*, 1900; *My Mark Twain*, 1910. *Selected Writings of William Dean Howells*, ed. Henry Steele Commager, 1950, includes *The Rise of Silas Lapham, A Modern Instance, A Boy's Town,* and *My Mark Twain.*

Biographies are Edwin H. Cady, *The Road to Realism*, 1956, and *The Realist at War*, 1958; Kenneth S. Lynn, W. D. Howells, 1971; See also O. W. Farkins, *William Dean Howells*, 1929, and Mildred How- ells, ed., *Life and Letters of William Dean Howells*, 2 vols., 1928.

For criticism see Everett Carter, *Howells and the Age of Realism*, 1954; A. Olov W. Fryckstedt, *In Quest of America: A Study of Howells' Early Development as a Novelist*, 1958; George N. Bennett, *William Dean Howells: The Development of a Novelist*, 1959; Van Wyck Brooks, *Howells: His Life and World*, 1959; R. L. Hough, *Quiet Rebel*, 1959; Kenneth E. Eble, ed., *Howells: A Century of Criticism*, 1961; Edwin H. Cady and David L. Frazier, eds., *The War of the Critics Over William Dean Howells*, 1962; Clara M. Kirk and Rudolf Kirk, *William Dean Howells*, 1962; George Carrington, *The Immense Complex Drama*, 1966; William M. Gibson, *William Dean Howells*, 1967; Kermit Vanderbilt, *The Achievement of William Dean Howells: A Reinterpretation*, 1968; Edward Wagenknecht, *William Dean Howells: The Friendship*, 1969.

gave sympathetic encouragement to many younger writers like Hamlin Garland, Stephen Crane, Henry Blake Fuller, Harold Frederic, and Frank Norris. He was an ardent reader of European writers such as Tolstoy, Dostoevski, Turgenev, Zola, and Verga; he reviewed their works and drew lessons from them in his campaign to deprovincialize American literature. He was also open to European social thought, and he took up the unpopular cause of socialism in the 1890's. Howells played a significant role, then, in the widening of horizons, literary and social, in this period, and it is difficult to imagine the literary scene from 1870 to 1900 without him.

Yet no leading American writer has had more abuse directed against him by younger figures. In the revolt against the past during World War I Howells became a particular target, perhaps because he was still alive and had become by then a venerable figure, the "Dean of American Letters." Even earlier, Ambrose Bierce and others had sneered at his "smug personality and his factory of little wooden men and women." Later, Mencken dismissed him as having "nothing to say," and Van Wyck Brooks charged him with acting the prissy, genteel censor of Mark Twain's manuscripts. Ironically, Howells was now identified with many of the literary prejudices and social attitudes he himself had earlier assaulted and often antagonized. By the 1920's, in short, he had come to seem the incarnation of the "genteel tradition."

A more accurate and balanced picture of this complex figure began to emerge in the 1940's and 1950's. Howells was, indeed, open to some of the condemnations, but they erred seriously in their excess. They do point to ambiguities in his work and career, however: an incompleteness in his own rebelliousness, and a sometimes desperate clinging to a traditional idea of a "moral universe" controlling the affairs of men. Like others of his generation he was torn by ambivalent relations with the older New England Brahman tradition, with wealth, and with the idea of progress. He survived basically as optimistic and confident in a period of strife, but not without cost: nagging currents of doubt and despair persist, and there is evidence of at least one serious nervous collapse.

The external facts of his career hint at a pattern of conflict, just as they point to his strategic place in the changing forms of American life. He was, to begin with, a poor boy from the rural Midwest who made the incredible passage from backwoods Ohio, with little formal schooling but much experience as a printer (he had started setting type at age nine) to the summits of acceptance by the literary elite of Boston. He had read a great deal in his teens, studied languages, wrote poetry and, by the late 1850's, was an editor of an Ohio paper. The *Atlantic Monthly* accepted some of his poems, and he published a volume of verse. A turning point was a campaign biography of Lincoln,

The White Girl (Symphony in White, No. 1), James McNeill Whistler.
Harris Whittemore Collection, National Gallery of Art, Washington, D.C.

Madame X, John Singer Sargent. *The Metropolitan Museum of Art, The Arthur H. Hearn Fund, 1916.*

which earned him enough money for a visit to Boston, where he met Lowell, Hawthorne, Emerson, and Thoreau, and to New York, where he encountered Whitman. The biography also won him a consulship in Venice where he spent the Civil War years (1861–1865) and wrote two books of travel observations: *Venetian Life* (1866) and *Italian Journey* (1866). A major plum for his literary ambitions came in 1867 when he was offered the editorship of the prestigious *Atlantic Monthly,* which he edited for the next 15 years, living in Boston as an adopted son of the fading New England culture. His career as a novelist begins in this period with several light books that follow the descriptive travel narrative, interwoven with courtship plots and a comedy of social contrasts. But his chief impact appeared in the pages of the *Atlantic,* where he published early stories of Henry James and lavishly praised Mark Twain. This period ended when he resigned the editorship in 1881. His fiction now turned to the contemporary scene, to studies of character and of social problems, particularly in cities.

In the 1880's Howells had his most creative decade, producing his best known and most important novels. Leaving the thin travel and courtship themes, he now addressed weightier issues, filling his narratives with more characters and widening his scope toward a social panorama. Social and moral conflicts dominate the works of this period, conflicts rooted chiefly in character and class, in the new situations that modern industrial society had created. In *A Modern Instance* (1882), the issue is moral irresponsibility and fervent passion, leading to a divorce. The novel has its force in the contrast between an earlier village culture of moral certainty and Calvinistic righteousness and modern urban life of more casual relations and behavior. *The Rise of Silas Lapham* (1885) examines a similar conflict from another point of view. It focuses on the crisis of values in the life of a self-made millionaire, a simple and crude but sympathetic Vermont farmer who struck it rich in the paint business. He tries to rise in Boston society for the sake of his daughters. His social failures are coupled with a serious financial setback he refuses to protect himself against by underhanded means, and this leads to a moral success, a "rise" that justifies his behavior and equalizes the distance between himself and the Boston Brahman caste that had snubbed him. In these and other novels in the decade Howells persistently worked with materials he called "the commonplace," aiming to treat average sorts of people and their likely dilemmas and predicaments in a changing social world. These works represent his deliberate effort to break with "the romance" and its extravagant emphasis on love stories and implausible situations. Howells attacked the problem of faithfully representing average lives with a moral fervor, arguing that the realistic novel was a major force for social improvement in a democratic society. He became in this period an extremely accomplished novelist of social life, of the daily affairs of marriage, family, and business, and of the solid realities of middle-class life. His farce, *The Unexpected Guest,* is typical of these concerns.

Later in the 1880's Howells moved to New York, became an editor of *Harper's,* took up the cause of realism more militantly and, in his fiction, confronted questions of social and economic injustice. His new interests reflect the unrest of the period, the many strikes, industrial violence typified by the Haymarket Riot in Chicago in 1886 for which several anarchist leaders were sentenced to death (Howells risked his position by coming to their defense, arguing that they had been unfairly tried). His fiction shifts to a broader, more historical form. *The Minister's Charge* (1887) and *Annie Kilburn* (1889)—the latter set in a Massachusetts mill town—undertake more pointed portraits of social types and conflicts than before. Howells now urged on his readers the notion of "moral complicity," that all shared in the guilt of social injustice. The best of these books, and his most ambitious book, is *A Hazard of New Fortunes* (1890), which assembles a large cast of representative characters in New York City and brings them to a crisis turning on a streetcar strike that results in a killing. The central character is Basil March, a figure much like Howells himself: literary, an editor, kindly, somewhat ineffectual yet well-intentioned, a liberal with leanings toward socialism. In the social contrasts and conflicts of the novel March serves as a center of humane sanity, yet is without much hope of altering either the social structure or the headlong passions of others.

Howells's works of direct social concern culminate in his utopian novel, *A Traveler from Altruria* (1894). His later novels have a diminished scale, but continue his project of social realism. In all, he wrote 35 novels, about the same number of plays, and several books of criticism, travel, and literary reminiscence, including the masterful *My Mark Twain* (1910). Several leading convictions pervade all his work as essential ingredients of his outlook, although they are not always perfectly realized in his fiction. For all his hobnobbing with aristocrats, he remained a steady democrat, an egalitarian prepared to trespass the boundaries of his own class in support of justice for anarchists and in behalf of radical social change. His democratic commitments appear in his literary criticism as well; realism represented for him a decisive force for education and for constructive change. Not that he wrote or supported novels of outright propaganda; he felt, instead, that the true delineation of the commonplace activities and patterns of society would enhance the reader's self-regard and moral growth. He believed in the health of a democratic people and was capable of writing "the more smiling aspects of life are the more American." But the unfortunate line should be read in the context of his own refusal to flinch at or blink away less smiling features in the tumult of the closing decades of the century. Even in the area where he seems most vulnerable to a post-Freudian audience, his depiction of sexual emotions, his courage in facing themes such as divorce and miscegenation and prostitution should be taken into account with his sometimes annoying reticence. To be sure, he held the young American girl in too high a regard as an arbiter of morals in fiction, and his own taste rejected the much more thorough realism of Dreiser. But, at his best, Howells sought to widen and deepen the sympathies and capacities of his readers for experiences less conventional than those appearing in popular romances and standard magazine fiction. He deserves to be read and admired as a critical force in the development of the American novel and to be judged against his own ideals.

The Rise of Silas Lapham[1]

CHAPTER XIV

[The Coreys, Boston aristocrats, have asked the Laphams to dinner at the behest of young Corey, who is in love with Penelope Lapham. Colonel Lapham is the owner of a prosperous paint factory in Vermont with offices in Boston, and is, at this point in the story, building a new home on Beacon Street for the sake of his daughters' social careers. Both the Coreys and the Laphams think it is the beautiful daughter, Irene, with whom Tom is in love, and both families are struggling unavailingly to overcome the social differences between them. Penelope, the clever daughter, whom Tom really loves, senses the whole situation, and wisely decides to stay at home from the dinner party. See Introduction, pp. cvii–cxi]

The Coreys were one of the few old families who lingered in Bellingham Place, the handsome, quiet old street which the sympathetic observer must grieve to see abandoned to boarding-houses. The dwellings are stately and tall, and the whole place wears an air of aristocratic seclusion, which Mrs. Corey's father might well have thought assured when he left her his house there at his death. It is one of two evidently designed by the same architect who built some houses in a characteristic taste on Beacon Street opposite the Common. It has a wooden portico, with slender fluted columns, which have always been painted white, and which, with the delicate moldings of the cornice, form the sole and sufficient decoration of the street front; nothing could be simpler, and nothing could be better. Within, the architect has

[1] First published in 1885.

again indulged his preference for the classic; the roof of the vestibule, wide and low, rests on marble columns, slim and fluted like the wooden columns without, and an ample staircase climbs in a graceful, easy curve from the tesselated pavement. Some carved Venetian *scrigni*[2] stretched along the wall; a rug lay at the foot of the stairs; but otherwise the simple adequacy of the architectural intention had been respected, and the place looked bare to the eyes of the Laphams when they entered. The Coreys had once kept a man, but when young Corey began his retrenchments the man had yielded to the neat maid who showed the Colonel into the reception-room and asked the ladies to walk up two flights.

He had his charges from Irene not to enter the drawing-room without her mother, and he spent five minutes in getting on his gloves, for he had desperately resolved to wear them at last. When he had them on, and let his large fists hang down on either side, they looked, in the saffron tint which the shop-girl said his gloves should be of, like canvassed hams. He perspired with doubt as he climbed the stairs, and while he waited on the landing for Mrs. Lapham and Irene to come down from above before going into the drawing-room, he stood staring at his hands, now open and now shut, and breathing hard. He heard quiet talking beyond the *portière*[3] within, and presently Tom Corey came out.

"Ah, Colonel Lapham! Very glad to see you."

Lapham shook hands with him and gasped, "Waiting for Mis' Lapham," to account for his presence. He had not been able to button his right glove, and he now began, with as much indifference as he could assume, to pull them both off, for he saw that Corey wore none. By the time he had stuffed them into the pocket of his coat-skirt his wife and daughter descended.

Corey welcomed them very cordially too, but looked a little mystified. Mrs. Lapham knew that he was silently inquiring for Penelope, and she did not know whether she ought to excuse her to him first or not. She said nothing, and after a glance toward the regions where Penelope might conjecturably be lingering, he held aside the *portière* for the Laphams to pass, and entered the room with them.

Mrs. Lapham had decided against low-necks on her own responsibility, and had entrenched herself in the safety of a black silk, in which she looked very handsome. Irene wore a dress of one of those shades which only a woman or an artist can decide to be green or blue, and which to other eyes looks both or neither, according to their degrees of ignorance. If it was more like a ball dress than a dinner dress, that might be excused to the exquisite effect. She trailed, a delicate splendour, across the carpet in her mother's sombre wake, and the consciousness of success brought a vivid smile to her face. Lapham, pallid with anxiety lest he should somehow disgrace himself, giving thanks to God that he should have been spared the shame of wearing

---

[2] Ornately carved chests.   [3] A door curtain.

gloves where no one else did, but at the same time despairing that Corey should have seen him in them, had an unwonted aspect of almost pathetic refinement.

Mrs. Corey exchanged a quick glance of surprise and relief with her husband as she started across the room to meet her guests, and in her gratitude to them for being so irreproachable, she threw into her manner a warmth that people did not always find there. "General Lapham?" she said, shaking hands in quick succession with Mrs. Lapham and Irene, and now addressing herself to him.

"No, ma'am, only Colonel," said the honest man, but the lady did not hear him. She was introducing her husband to Lapham's wife and daughter, and Bromfield Corey was already shaking his hand and saying he was very glad to see him again, while he kept his artistic eye on Irene, and apparently could not take it off. Lily Corey gave the Lapham ladies a greeting which was physically rather than socially cold, and Nanny stood holding Irene's hand in both of hers a moment, and taking in her beauty and her style with a generous admiration which she could afford, for she was herself faultlessly dressed in the quiet taste of her city, and looking very pretty. The interval was long enough to let every man present confide his sense of Irene's beauty to every other; and then, as the party was small, Mrs. Corey made everybody acquainted. When Lapham had not quite understood, he held the person's hand, and leaning urbanely forward, inquired, "What name?" He did that because a great man to whom he had been presented on the platform at a public meeting had done so to him, and he knew it must be right.

A little lull ensued upon the introductions, and Mrs. Corey said quietly to Mrs. Lapham, "Can I send any one to be of use to Miss Lapham?" as if Penelope must be in the dressing-room.

Mrs. Lapham turned fire-red, and the graceful forms in which she had been intending to excuse her daughter's absence went out of her head. "She isn't upstairs," she said, at her bluntest, as country people are when embarrassed. "She didn't feel just like coming tonight. I don't know as she's feeling very well."

Mrs. Corey emitted a very small "O!"—very small, very cold,—which began to grow larger and hotter and to burn into Mrs. Lapham's soul before Mrs. Corey could add, "I'm very sorry. It's nothing serious, I hope?"

Robert Chase, the painter, had not come, and Mrs. James Bellingham was not there, so that the table really balanced better without Penelope; but Mrs. Lapham could not know this, and did not deserve to know it. Mrs. Corey glanced round the room, as if to take account of her guests, and said to her husband, "I think we are all here, then," and he came forward and gave his arm to Mrs. Lapham. She perceived then that in their determination not to be the first to come they had been the last, and must have kept the others waiting for them.

Lapham had never seen people go down to dinner arm-in-arm before, but he knew that his wife was distinguished in being taken out by the host, and he waited in jealous impatience to see if Tom Corey would offer his arm to Irene. He gave it to that big girl they called Miss Kingsbury, and the handsome old fellow whom Mrs. Corey had introduced as her cousin took Irene out. Lapham was startled from the misgiving in which this left him by Mrs. Corey's passing her hand through his arm, and he made a sudden movement forward, but felt himself gently restrained. They went out the last of all; he did not know why, but he submitted, and when they sat down he saw that Irene, although she had come in with that Mr. Bellingham, was seated beside young Corey, after all.

He fetched a long sigh of relief when he sank into his chair and felt himself safe from error if he kept a sharp lookout and did only what the others did. Bellingham had certain habits which he permitted himself, and one of these was tucking the corner of his napkin into his collar; he confessed himself an uncertain shot with a spoon, and defended his practice on the ground of neatness and common-sense. Lapham put his napkin into his collar too, and then, seeing that no one but Bellingham did it, became alarmed and took it out again slyly. He never had wine on his table at home, and on principle he was a prohibitionist; but now he did not know just what to do about the glasses at the right of his plate. He had a notion to turn them all down, as he had read of a well-known politician's doing at a public dinner, to show that he did not take wine; but, after twiddling with one of them a moment, he let them be, for it seemed to him that would be a little too conspicuous, and he felt that every one was looking. He let the servant fill them all, and he drank out of each, not to appear odd. Later, he observed that the young ladies were not taking wine, and he was glad to see that Irene had refused it, and that Mrs. Lapham was letting it stand untasted. He did not know but he ought to decline some of the dishes, or at least leave most of some on his plate, but he was not able to decide; he took everything and ate everything.

He noticed that Mrs. Corey seemed to take no more trouble about the dinner than anybody, and Mr. Corey rather less; he was talking busily to Mrs. Lapham, and Lapham caught a word here and there that convinced him she was holding her own. He was getting on famously himself with Mrs. Corey, who had begun with him about his new house; he was telling her all about it, and giving her his ideas. Their conversation naturally included his architect across the table; Lapham had been delighted and secretly surprised to find the fellow there; and at something Seymour said the talk spread suddenly, and the pretty house he was building for Colonel Lapham became the general theme. Young Corey testified to its loveliness, and the architect said laughingly that if he had been able to make a nice thing of it, he owed it to the practical sympathy of his client.

"Practical sympathy is good," said Bromfield Corey; and, slanting his head confidentially to Mrs. Lapham, he added, "Does he bleed your husband, Mrs. Lapham? He's a terrible fellow for appropriations!"

Mrs. Lapham laughed, reddening consciously, and said she guessed the Colonel knew how to take care of himself. This struck Lapham, then draining his glass of sauterne, as wonderfully discreet in his wife.

Bromfield Corey leaned back in his chair a moment. "Well, after all, you can't say, with all your modern fuss about it, that you do much better now than the old fellows who built such houses as this."

"Ah," said the architect, "nobody can do better than well. Your house is in perfect taste; you know I've always admired it; and I don't think it's at all the worse for being old-fashioned. What we've done is largely to go back of the hideous style that raged after they forgot how to make this sort of house. But I think we may claim a better feeling for structure. We use better material, and more wisely; and by and by we shall work out something more characteristic and original."

"With your chocolates and olives, and your clutter of bric-a-brac?"

"All that's bad, of course, but I don't mean that. I don't wish to make you envious of Colonel Lapham, and modesty prevents my saying that his house is prettier,—though I may have my convictions,—but it's better built. All the new houses are better built. Now, your house—"

"Mrs. Corey's house," interrupted the host, with a burlesque haste in disclaiming responsibility for it that made them all laugh. "*My* ancestral halls are in Salem, and I'm told you couldn't drive a nail into their timbers; in fact, I don't know that you would want to do it."

"I should consider it a species of sacrilege," answered Seymour, "and I shall be far from pressing the point I was going to make against a house of Mrs. Corey's."

This won Seymour the easy laugh, and Lapham silently wondered that the fellow never got off any of those things to him.

"Well," said Corey, "you architects and the musicians are the true and only artistic creators. All the rest of us, sculptors, painters, novelists, and tailors, deal with forms that we have before us; we try to imitate, we try to represent. But you two sorts of artists create form. If you represent, you fail. Somehow or other you do evolve the camel out of your inner consciousness."

"I will not deny the soft impeachment," said the architect, with a modest air.

"I dare say. And you'll own that it's very handsome of me to say this, after your unjustifiable attack on Mrs. Corey's property."

Bromfield Corey addressed himself again to Mrs. Lapham, and the talk subdivided itself as before. It lapsed so entirely away from the subject just in hand, that Lapham was left with rather a good idea, as he thought it, to perish in his mind, for want of a chance to express it. The only thing like a recurrence to what they had been saying was Bromfield Corey's warning

Mrs. Lapham, in some connection that Lapham lost, against Miss Kingsbury. "She's worse," he was saying, "when it comes to appropriations than Seymour himself. Depend upon it, Mrs. Lapham, she will give you no peace of your mind, now she's met you, from this out. Her tender mercies are cruel; and I leave you to supply the context from your own scriptural knowledge. Beware of her, and all her works. She calls them works of charity; but heaven knows whether they are. It don't stand to reason that she gives the poor *all* the money she gets out of people. I have my own belief"—he gave it in a whisper for the whole table to hear—"that she spends it for champagne and cigars."

Lapham did not know about that kind of talking; but Miss Kingsbury seemed to enjoy the fun as much as anybody, and he laughed with the rest.

"You shall be asked to the very next debauch of the committee, Mr. Corey; then you won't dare expose us," said Miss Kingsbury.

"I wonder you haven't been down upon Corey to go to the Chardon Street home and talk with your indigent Italians in their native tongue," said Charles Bellingham. "I saw in the *Transcript* the other night that you wanted some one for the work."

"We did think of Mr. Corey," replied Miss Kingsbury; "but we reflected that he probably wouldn't talk with them at all; he would make them keep still to be sketched, and forget all about their wants."

Upon the theory that this was a fair return for Corey's pleasantry, the others laughed again.

"There is one charity," said Corey, pretending superiority to Miss Kingsbury's point, "that is so difficult, I wonder it hasn't occurred to a lady of your courageous invention."

"Yes?" said Miss Kingsbury. "What is that?"

"The occupation, by deserving poor of neat habits, of all the beautiful, airy, wholesome houses that stand empty the whole summer long, while their owners are away in their lowly cots beside the sea."

"Yes, that is terrible," replied Miss Kingsbury, with quick earnestness, while her eyes grew moist. "I have often thought of our great, cool houses standing useless here, and the thousands of poor creatures stifling in their holes and dens, and the little children dying for wholesome shelter. How cruelly selfish we are!"

"That is a very comfortable sentiment, Miss Kingsbury," said Corey, "and must make you feel almost as if you had thrown open No. 31 to the whole North End. But I am serious about this matter. I spend my summers in town, and I occupy my own house, so that I can speak impartially and intelligently; and I tell you that in some of my walks on the Hill and down on the Back Bay, nothing but the surveillance of the local policeman prevents my offering personal violence to those long rows of close-shuttered, handsome, brutally insensible houses. If I were a poor man, with a sick child pining in some garret or cellar at the North End, I should break into one of them, and camp out on the grand piano."

"Surely, Bromfield," said his wife, "you don't consider what havoc such people would make with the furniture of a nice house!"

"That is true," answered Corey, with meek conviction. "I never thought of that."

"And if you were a poor man with a sick child, I doubt if you'd have so much heart for burglary as you have now," said James Bellingham.

"It's wonderful how patient they are," said the minister. "The spectacle of the hopeless comfort the hard-working poor man sees must be hard to bear."

Lapham wanted to speak up and say that he had been there himself, and knew how such a man felt. He wanted to tell them that generally a poor man was satisfied if he could make both ends meet; that he didn't envy any one his good luck, if he had earned it, so long as he wasn't running under himself. But before he could get the courage to address the whole table, Sewell added, "I suppose he don't always think of it."

"But some day he *will* think about it," said Corey. "In fact, we rather invite him to think about it, in this country."

"My brother-in-law," said Charles Bellingham, with the pride a man feels in a mentionably remarkable brother-in-law, "has no end of fellows at work under him out there at Omaha, and he says it's the fellows from countries where they've been kept from thinking about it that are discontented. The Americans never make any trouble. They seem to understand that so long as we give unlimited opportunity, nobody has a right to complain."

"What do you hear from Leslie?" asked Mrs. Corey, turning from these profitless abstractions to Mrs. Bellingham.

"You know," said the lady in a lower tone, "that there is another baby?"

"No! I hadn't heard of it!"

"Yes; a boy. They have named him after his uncle."

"Yes," said Charles Bellingham, joining in. "He is said to be a noble boy, and to resemble me."

"All boys of that tender age are noble," said Corey, "and look like anybody you wish them to resemble. Is Leslie still homesick for the bean-pots of her native Boston?"

"She is getting over it, I fancy," replied Mrs. Bellingham. "She's very much taken up with Mr. Blake's enterprises, and leads a very exciting life. She says she's like people who have been home from Europe three years; she's past the most poignant stage of regret, and hasn't reached the second, when they feel that they *must* go again."

Lapham leaned a little toward Mrs. Corey, and said of a picture which he saw on the wall opposite, "Picture of your daughter, I presume?"

"No; my daughter's grandmother. It's a Stewart Newton; he painted a great many Salem beauties. She was a Miss Polly Burroughs. My daughter *is* like her, don't you think?" They both looked at Nanny Corey and then at the portrait. "Those pretty old-fashioned dresses are coming in again. I'm not surprised you took it for her. The others"—she referred to the other portraits more or less darkling on the walls—"are my people; mostly Copleys."

These names, unknown to Lapham, went to his head like the wine he was drinking; they seemed to carry light for the moment, but a film of deeper darkness followed. He heard Charles Bellingham telling funny stories to Irene and trying to amuse the girl; she was laughing, and seemed very happy. From time to time Bellingham took part in the general talk between the host and James Bellingham and Miss Kingsbury and that minister, Mr. Sewell. They talked of people mostly; it astonished Lapham to hear with what freedom they talked. They discussed these persons unsparingly; James Bellingham spoke of a man known to Lapham for his business success and great wealth as not a gentleman; his cousin Charles said he was surprised that the fellow had kept from being governor so long.

When the latter turned from Irene to make one of these excursions into the general talk, young Corey talked to her; and Lapham caught some words from which it seemed that they were speaking of Penelope. It vexed him to think she had not come; she could have talked as well as any of them; she was just as bright; and Lapham was aware that Irene was not as bright, though when he looked at her face, triumphant in its young beauty and fondness, he said to himself that it did not make any difference. He felt that he was not holding up his end of the line, however. When some one spoke to him he could only summon a few words of reply, that seemed to lead to nothing; things often came into his mind appropriate to what they were saying, but before he could get them out they were off on something else; they jumped about so, he could not keep up; but he felt, all the same, that he was not doing himself justice.

At one time the talk ran off upon a subject that Lapham had never heard of before; but again he was vexed that Penelope was not there, to have her say; he believed that her say would have been worth hearing.

Miss Kingsbury leaned forward and asked Charles Bellingham if he had read *Tears, Idle Tears,* the novel that was making such a sensation; and when he said no, she said she wondered at him. "It's perfectly heart-breaking, as you'll imagine from the name; but there's such a dear old-fashioned hero and heroine in it, who keep dying for each other all the way through, and making the most wildly satisfactory and unnecessary sacrifices for each other. You feel as if you'd done them yourself."

"Ah, that's the secret of its success," said Bromfield Corey. "It flatters the reader by painting the characters colossal, but with his limp and stoop, so that he feels himself of their supernatural proportions. You've read it, Nanny?"

"Yes," said his daughter. "It ought to have been called *Slop, Silly Slop.*"

"Oh, not quite *slop,* Nanny," pleaded Miss Kingsbury.

"It's astonishing," said Charles Bellingham, "how we do like the books that go for our heart-strings. And I really suppose that you can't put a more popular thing than self-sacrifice into a novel. We do like to see people suffering sublimely."

"There was talk some years ago," said James Bellingham, "about novels going out."

"They're just coming in!" cried Miss Kingsbury.

"Yes," said Mr. Sewell, the minister. "And I don't think there ever was a time when they formed the whole intellectual experience of more people. They do greater mischief than ever."

"Don't be envious, parson," said the host.

"No," answered Sewell. "I should be glad of their help. But those novels with old-fashioned heroes and heroines in them—excuse me, Miss Kingsbury—are ruinous!"

"Don't you feel like a moral wreck, Miss Kingsbury?" asked the host.

But Sewell went on: "The novelists might be the greatest possible help to us if they painted life as it is, and human feelings in their true proportion and relation, but for the most part they have been and are altogether noxious."

This seemed sense to Lapham; but Bromfield Corey asked: "But what if life as it is isn't amusing? Aren't we to be amused?"

"Not to our hurt," sturdily answered the minister. "And the self-sacrifice painted in most novels like this—"

"*Slop, Silly Slop?*" suggested the proud father of the inventor of the phrase.

"Yes—is nothing but psychical suicide, and is as wholly immoral as the spectacle of a man falling upon his sword."

"Well, I don't know but you're right, parson," said the host; and the minister, who had apparently got upon a battle-horse of his, careered onward in spite of some tacit attempts of his wife to seize the bridle.

"Right? To be sure I am right. The whole business of love, and love-making and marrying, is painted by the novelists in a monstrous disproportion to the other relations of life. Love is very sweet, very pretty—"

"Oh, *thank you*, Mr. Sewell," said Nanny Corey, in a way that set them all laughing.

"But it's the affair, commonly, of very young people, who have not yet character and experience enough to make them interesting. In novels it's treated, not only as if it were the chief interest of life, but the sole interest of the lives of two ridiculous young persons; and it is taught that love is perpetual, that the glow of a true passion lasts for ever; and that it is sacrilege to think or act otherwise."

"Well, but isn't that true, Mr. Sewell?" pleaded Miss Kingsbury.

"I have known some most estimable people who had married a second time," said the minister, and then he had the applause with him. Lapham wanted to make some open recognition of his good sense, but could not.

"I suppose the passion itself has been a good deal changed," said Bromfield Corey, "since the poets began to idealise it in the days of chivalry."

"Yes; and it ought to be changed again," said Mr. Sewell.

"What! Back?"

"I don't say that. But it ought to be recognised as something natural and mortal, and divine honours, which belong to righteousness alone, ought not to be paid it."

"Oh, you ask too much, parson," laughed his host, and the talk wandered away to something else.

It was not an elaborate dinner; but Lapham was used to having everything on the table at once, and this succession of dishes bewildered him; he was afraid perhaps he was eating too much. He now no longer made any pretence of not drinking his wine, for he was thirsty, and there was no more water, and he hated to ask for any. The ice-cream came, and then the fruit. Suddenly Mrs. Corey rose, and said across the table to her husband, "I suppose you will want your coffee here." And he replied, "Yes; we'll join you at tea."

The ladies all rose, and the gentlemen got up with them. Lapham started to follow Mrs. Corey, but the other men merely stood in their places, except young Corey, who ran and opened the door for his mother. Lapham thought with shame that it was he who ought to have done that; but no one seemed to notice, and he sat down again gladly, after kicking out one of his legs which had gone to sleep.

They brought in cigars with coffee, and Bromfield Corey advised Lapham to take one that he chose for him. Lapham confessed that he liked a good cigar about as well as anybody, and Corey said: "These are new. I had an Englishman here the other day who was smoking old cigars in the superstition that tobacco improved with age, like wine."

"Ah," said Lapham, "anybody who had ever lived off a tobacco country could tell him better than that." With the fuming cigar between his lips he felt more at home than he had before. He turned sidewise in his chair and, resting one arm on the back, intertwined the fingers of both hands, and smoked at large ease.

James Bellingham came and sat down by him. "Colonel Lapham, weren't you with the 96th Vermont when they charged across the river in front of Pickensburg, and the rebel battery opened fire on them in the water?"

Lapham slowly shut his eyes and slowly dropped his head for assent, letting out a white volume of smoke from the corner of his mouth.

"I thought so," said Bellingham. "I was with the 85th Massachusetts, and I sha'n't forget that slaughter. We were all new to it still. Perhaps that's why it made such an impression."

"I don't know," suggested Charles Bellingham. "Was there anything much more impressive afterward? I read of it out in Missouri, where I was stationed at the time, and I recollect the talk of some old army men about it.

They said that death-rate couldn't be beaten. I don't know that it ever was."

"About one in five of us got out safe," said Lapham, breaking his cigar-ash off on the edge of a plate. James Bellingham reached him a bottle of Apollinaris. He drank a glass, and then went on smoking.

They all waited, as if expecting him to speak, and then Corey said: "How incredible those things seem already! You gentlemen *know* that they happened; but are you still able to believe it?"

"Ah, nobody *feels* that anything happened," said Charles Bellingham. "The past of one's experience doesn't differ a great deal from the past of one's knowledge. It isn't more probable; it's really a great deal less vivid than some scenes in a novel that one read when a boy."

"I'm not sure of that," said James Bellingham.

"Well, James, neither am I," consented his cousin, helping himself from Lapham's Apollinaris bottle. "There would be very little talking at dinner if one only said the things that one was sure of."

The others laughed, and Bromfield Corey remarked thoughtfully, "What astonishes the craven civilian in all these things is the abundance—the superabundance—of heroism. The cowards were the exception; the men that were ready to die, the rule."

"The woods were full of them," said Lapham, without taking his cigar from his mouth.

"That's a nice little touch in *School*," interposed Charles Bellingham, "where the girl says to the fellow who was at Inkerman, 'I should think you would be so proud of it,' and he reflects a while, and says, 'Well, the fact is, you know, there were so many of us.' "

"Yes, I remember that," said James Bellingham, smiling for pleasure in it. "But I don't see why you claim the credit of being a craven civilian, Bromfield," he added, with a friendly glance at his brother-in-law, and with the willingness Boston men often show to turn one another's good points to the light in company; bred so intimately together at school and college and in society, they all know these points. "A man who was out with Garibaldi in '48," continued James Bellingham.

"Oh, a little amateur red-shirting," Corey interrupted in deprecation. "But even if you choose to dispute my claim, what has become of all the heroism? Tom, how many club men do you know who would think it sweet and fitting to die for their country?"

"I can't think of a great many at the moment, sir," replied the son, with the modesty of his generation.

"And I couldn't in '61," said his uncle. "Nevertheless they were there."

"Then your theory is that it's the occasion that is wanting," said Bromfield Corey. "But why shouldn't civil service reform, and the resumption of specie payment, and a tariff for revenue only, inspire heroes? They are all good causes."

"It's the occasion that's wanting," said James Bellingham, ignoring the *persiflage*.[4] "And I'm very glad of it."

"So am I," said Lapham, with a depth of feeling that expressed itself in spite of the haze in which his brain seemed to float. There was a great deal of the talk that he could not follow; it was too quick for him; but here was something he was clear of. "I don't want to see any more men killed in my time." Something serious, something sombre must lurk behind these words, and they waited for Lapham to say more; but the haze closed round him again, and he remained silent, drinking Apollinaris.

"We non-combatants were notoriously reluctant to give up fighting," said Mr. Sewell, the minister; "but I incline to think Colonel Lapham and Mr. Bellingham may be right. I dare say we shall have the heroism again if we have the occasion. Till it comes, we must content ourselves with the everyday generosities and sacrifices. They make up in quantity what they lack in quality, perhaps."

"They're not so picturesque," said Bromfield Corey. "You can paint a man dying for his country, but you can't express on canvas a man fulfilling the duties of a good citizen."

"Perhaps the novelists will get at him by and by," suggested Charles Bellingham. "If I were one of these fellows, I shouldn't propose to myself anything short of that."

"What? the commonplace?" asked his cousin.

"Commonplace? The commonplace is just that light, impalpable, aërial essence which they've never got into their confounded books yet. The novelist who could interpret the common feelings of commonplace people would have the answer to 'the riddle of the painful earth' on his tongue."

"Oh, not so bad as that, I hope," said the host; and Lapham looked from one to the other, trying to make out what they were at. He had never been so up a tree before.

"I suppose it isn't well for us to see human nature at white heat habitually," continued Bromfield Corey, after a while. "It would make us vain of our species. Many a poor fellow in that war and in many another has gone into battle simply and purely for his country's sake, not knowing whether, if he laid down his life, he should ever find it again, or whether, if he took it up hereafter, he should take it up in heaven or hell. Come, parson!" he said, turning to the minister, "what has ever been conceived of omnipotence, of omniscience, so sublime, so divine as that?"

"Nothing," answered the minister quietly. "God has never been imagined at all. But if you suppose such a man as that was Authorised, I think it will help you to imagine what God must be."

"There's sense in that," said Lapham. He took his cigar out of his mouth, and pulled his chair a little toward the table, on which he placed his ponderous fore-arms. "I want to tell you about a fellow I had in my own company

[4] Banter.

when we first went out. We were all privates to begin with; after a while they elected me captain—I'd had the tavern stand, and most of 'em knew me. But Jim Millon never got to be anything more than corporal; corporal when he was killed." The others arrested themselves in various attitudes of attention, and remained listening to Lapham with an interest that profoundly flattered him. Now, at last, he felt that he was holding up his end of the rope. "I can't say he went into the thing from the highest motives, altogether; our motives are always pretty badly mixed, and when there's such a hurrah-boys as there was then, you can't tell which is which. I suppose Jim Millon's wife was enough to account for his going, herself. She was a pretty bad assortment," said Lapham, lowering his voice and glancing round at the door to make sure that it was shut, "and she used to lead Jim *one* kind of life. Well, sir," continued Lapham, synthetising his auditors in that form of address, "that fellow used to save every cent of his pay and send it to that woman. Used to get me to do it for him. I tried to stop him. 'Why, Jim,' said I, 'you know what she'll do with it.' 'That's so, Cap,' says he, 'but I don't know what she'll do without it.' And it did keep her straight—straight as a string—as long as Jim lasted. Seemed as if there was something mysterious about it. They had a little girl,—about as old as my oldest girl,—and Jim used to talk to me about her. Guess he done it as much for her as for the mother; and he said to me before the last action we went into, 'I should like to turn tail and run, Cap. I ain't comin' out o' this one. But I don't suppose it would do.' 'Well, not for you, Jim,' said I. 'I want to live,' he says; and he bust out crying right there in my tent. 'I want to live for poor Molly and Zerrilla'— that's what they called the little one; I dunno where they got the name. 'I ain't ever had half a chance; and now she's doing better, and I believe we should get along after this.' He set there cryin' like a baby. But he wan't no baby when he went into action. I hated to look at him after it was over, not so much because he'd got a ball that was meant for me by a sharpshooter— he saw the devil takin' aim, and he jumped to warn me—as because he didn't look like Jim; he looked like—fun; all desperate and savage. I guess he died hard."

The story made its impression, and Lapham saw it. "Now I say," he resumed, as if he felt that he was going to do himself justice, and say something to heighten the effect his story had produced. At the same time he was aware of a certain want of clearness. He had the idea, but it floated vague, elusive, in his brain. He looked about as if for something to precipitate it in tangible shape.

"Apollinaris?" asked Charles Bellingham, handing the bottle from the other side. He had drawn his chair closer than the rest to Lapham's, and was listening with great interest. When Mrs. Corey asked him to meet Lapham, he accepted gladly. "You know I go in for that sort of thing, Anna. Since Leslie's affair we're rather bound to do it. And I think we meet these practical fellows too little. There's always something original about them." He might naturally have believed that the reward of his faith was coming.

"Thanks, I will take some of this wine," said Lapham, pouring himself a glass of Madeira from a black and dusty bottle caressed by a label bearing the date of the vintage. He tossed off the wine, unconscious of its preciousness, and waited for the result. That cloudiness in his brain disappeared before it, but a mere blank remained. He not only could not remember what he was going to say, but he could not recall what they had been talking about. They waited, looking at him, and he stared at them in return. After a while he heard the host saying, "Shall we join the ladies?"

Lapham went, trying to think what had happened. It seemed to him a long time since he had drunk that wine.

Miss Corey gave him a cup of tea, where he stood aloof from his wife, who was talking with Miss Kingsbury and Mrs. Sewell; Irene was with Miss Nancy Corey. He could not hear what they were talking about; but if Penelope had come, he knew that she would have done them all credit. He meant to let her know how he felt about her behavior when he got home. It was a shame for her to miss such a chance. Irene was looking beautiful, as pretty as all the rest of them put together, but she was not talking, and Lapham perceived that at a dinner-party you ought to talk. He was himself conscious of having talked very well. He now wore an air of great dignity, and, in conversing with the other gentlemen, he used a grave and weighty deliberation. Some of them wanted him to go into the library. There he gave his ideas of books. He said he had not much time for anything but the papers; but he was going to have a complete library in his new place. He made an elaborate acknowledgment to Bromfield Corey of his son's kindness in suggesting books for his library; he said that he had ordered them all, and that he meant to have pictures. He asked Mr. Corey who was about the best American painter going now. "I don't set up to be a judge of pictures, but I know what I like," he said. He lost the reserve which he had maintained earlier, and began to boast. He himself introduced the subject of his paint, in a natural transition from pictures; he said Mr. Corey must take a run up to Lapham with him some day, and see the Works; they would interest him, and he would drive him round the country; he kept most of his horses up there, and he could show Mr. Corey some of the finest Jersey grades in the country. He told about his brother William, the judge at Dubuque; and a farm he had out there that paid for itself every year in wheat. As he cast off all fear, his voice rose, and he hammered his arm-chair with the thick of his hand for emphasis. Mr. Corey seemed impressed; he sat perfectly quiet, listening, and Lapham saw the other gentlemen stop in their talk every now and then to listen. After this proof of his ability to interest them, he would have liked to have Mrs. Lapham suggest again that he was unequal to their society, or to the society of anybody else. He surprised himself by his ease among men whose names had hitherto overawed him. He got to calling Bromfield Corey by his surname alone. He did not understand why young Corey seemed so preoccupied, and he took occasion to tell the company how he had said to his wife the first time he saw that fellow that he could make a man of him if he had him in the business; and he guessed he was not mistaken. He began to tell stories of the different young men he had in his employ. At last he had the talk altogether to himself; no one else talked, and he talked unceasingly. It was a great time; it was a triumph.

He was in this successful mood when word came to him that Mrs. Lapham was going; Tom Corey seemed to have brought it, but he was not sure. Anyway, he was not going to hurry. He made cordial invitations to each of the gentlemen to drop in and see him at his office, and would not be satisfied till he had exacted a promise from each. He told Charles Bellingham that he liked him, and assured James Bellingham that it had always been his ambition to know him, and that if any one had said when he first came to Boston that in less than ten years he should be hobnobbing with Jim Bellingham, he should have told the person he lied. He would have told anybody he lied that had told him ten years ago that a son of the Bromfield Corey would have come and asked him to take him into the business. Ten years ago he, Silas Lapham, had come to Boston a little worse off than nothing at all, for he was in debt for half the money that he had bought out his partner with, and here he was now worth a million, and meeting you gentlemen like one of you. And every cent of that was honest money,—no speculation,—every copper of it for value received. And here, only the other day, his old partner, who had been going to the dogs ever since he went out of the business, came and borrowed twenty thousand dollars of him! Lapham lent it because his wife wanted him to: she had always felt bad about the fellow's having to go out of the business.

He took leave of Mr. Sewell with patronising affection, and bade him come to him if he ever got into a tight place with his parish work; he would let him have all the money he wanted; he had more money than he knew what to do with. "Why, when your wife sent to mine last fall," he said, turning to Mr. Corey, "I drew my cheque for five hundred dollars, but my wife wouldn't take more than one hundred; said she wasn't going to show off before Mrs. Corey. I call that a pretty good joke on Mrs. Corey. I must tell her how Mrs. Lapham done her out of a cool four hundred dollars."

He started toward the door of the drawing-room to take leave of the ladies; but Tom Corey was at his elbow, saying, "I think Mrs. Lapham is waiting for you below, sir," and in obeying the direction Corey gave him toward another door he forgot all about his purpose, and came away without saying good-night to his hostess.

Mrs. Lapham had not known how soon she ought to go, and had no idea that in her quality of chief guest she was keeping the others. She stayed till eleven o'clock, and was a little frightened when she found what time it was; but Mrs. Corey, without pressing her to stay longer, had said it was not at all late. She and Irene had had a perfect time. Everybody had been very polite; on the way home they celebrated the amiability of both the Miss Coreys and Miss Kingsbury. Mrs. Lapham thought that Mrs. Bellingham was about the pleasantest person she ever saw; she had told her all about her married daughter who had married an inventor and gone to live in Omaha—a Mrs. Blake.

"If it's that car-wheel Blake," said Lapham proudly, "I know all about him. I've sold him tons of the paint."

"Pooh, papa! How you do smell of smoking!" cried Irene.

"Pretty strong, eh?" laughed Lapham, letting down a window of the carriage. His heart was throbbing wildly in the close air, and he was glad of the rush of cold that came in, though it stopped his tongue, and he listened more and more drowsily to the rejoicings that his wife and daughter exchanged. He meant to have them wake Penelope up and tell her what she had lost; but when he reached home he was too sleepy to suggest it. He fell asleep as soon as his head touched the pillow, full of supreme triumph.

But in the morning his skull was sore with the unconscious, nightlong ache; and he rose cross and taciturn. They had a silent breakfast. In the cold grey light of the morning the glories of the night before showed poorer. Here and there a painful doubt obtruded itself and marred them with its awkward shadow. Penelope sent down word that she was not well, and was not coming to breakfast, and Lapham was glad to go to his office without seeing her.

He was severe and silent all day with his clerks, and peremptory with customers. Of Corey he was slyly observant, and as the day wore away he grew more restively conscious. He sent out word by his office-boy that he would like to see Mr. Corey for a few minutes after closing. The type-writer girl had lingered too, as if she wished to speak to him, and Corey stood in abeyance as she went toward Lapham's door.

"Can't see you to-night, Zerrilla," he said bluffly, but not unkindly. "Perhaps I'll call at the house, if it's important."

"It is," said the girl, with a spoiled air of insistence.

"Well," said Lapham, and, nodding to Corey to enter, he closed the door upon her. Then he turned to the young man and demanded: "Was I drunk last night?"

From Criticism and Fiction

THE SMILING ASPECTS OF AMERICAN LIFE[1]

M. Vogüé writes with perhaps too breathless a fervor, but his article is valuable for the light it casts upon the origins of Dostoïevsky's work, and its inspirations and motives. It was the natural expression of such a life and such conditions. But it is useful to observe that while *The Crime and the Punish-*

[1] First published in *Harper's* magazine, September 1886 and later included in *Criticism and Fiction* in 1891.

ment may be read with the deepest sympathy and interest, and may enforce with unique power the lessons which it teaches, it is to be praised only in its place, and its message is to be received with allowances by readers exterior to the social and political circumstances in which it was conceived. It used to be one of the disadvantages of the practice of romance in America, which Hawthorne more or less whimsically lamented, that there were so few shadows and inequalities in our broad level of prosperity; and it is one of the reflections suggested by Dostoïevsky's book that whoever struck a note so profoundly tragic in American fiction would do a false and mistaken thing—as false and as mistaken in its way as dealing in American fiction with certain nudities which the Latin peoples seem to find edifying. Whatever their deserts, very few American novelists have been led out to be shot, or finally exiled to the rigors of a winter at Duluth; one might make Herr Most the hero of a labor-question romance with perfect impunity; and in a land where journeyman carpenters and plumbers strike for four dollars a day the sum of hunger and cold is certainly very small, and the wrong from class to class is almost inappreciable. We invite our novelists, therefore, to concern themselves with the more smiling aspects of life, which are the more American, and to seek the universal in the individual rather than the social interests. It is worth while, even at the risk of being called commonplace, to be true to our well-to-do actualities; the very passions themselves seem to be softened and modified by conditions which cannot be said to wrong any one, to cramp endeavor, or to cross lawful desire. Sin and suffering and sham there must always be in the world, we suppose, but we believe that in this new world of ours it is mainly from one to another one, and oftener still from one to one's self. We have death too in America, and a great deal of disagreeable and painful disease, which the multiplicity of our patent medicines does not seem to cure; but this is tragedy that comes in the very nature of things, and is not peculiarly American, as the large, cheerful average of health and success and happy life is. It will not do to boast, but it is well to be true to the facts, and to see that, apart from these purely mortal troubles, the race here enjoys conditions in which most of the ills that have darkened its annals may be averted by honest work and unselfish behavior.

It is only now and then, when some dark shadow of our shameful past appears, that we can believe there ever was a tragic element in our prosperity. Even then, when we read such an artlessly impressive sketch as Mrs. Sarah Bradford writes of Harriet Tubman—once famous as the Moses of her people—the self-freed bondwoman who led three hundred of her brethren out of slavery, and with a price set upon her head, risked her life and liberty nineteen times in this cause; even then it affects us like a tale

> "Of old, unhappy, far-off things,
> And battles long ago,"

and nothing within the date of actual history. We cannot realize that most of the men and women now living were once commanded by the law of the land to turn and hunt such fugitives back into slavery, and to deliver such an outlaw as Harriet over to her owner; that those who abetted such outlaws were sometimes mulcted[2] to the last dollar of their substance in fines. We can hardly imagine such things now for the purposes of fiction; all troubles that now hurt and threaten us are as crumpled rose leaves in our couch. But we may nevertheless read Dostoïevsky, and especially our novelists may read him, to advantage, for in spite of his terrible picture of a soul's agony he is hopeful and wholesome, and teaches in every page patience, merciful judgment, humble helpfulness, and that brotherly responsibility, that duty of man to man, from which not even the Americans are emancipated.

[2] Fined.

PERNICIOUS FICTION[1]

It must have been a passage from Vernon Lee's *Baldwin*, claiming for the novel an indefinitely vast and subtle influence on modern character, which provoked the following suggestive letter from one of our readers:

"—, — Co., Md., Sept. 18, 1886.

"Dear Sir,—With regard to article IV, in the Editor's Study in the September *Harper*, allow me to say that I have very grave doubts as to the whole list of magnificent things that you seem to think novels have done for the race, and can witness in myself many evil things which they have done for me. Whatever in my mental make-up is wild and visionary, whatever is untrue, whatever is injurious, I can trace to the perusal of some work of fiction. Worse than that, they beget such high-strung and supersensitive ideas of life that plain industry and plodding perseverance are despised, and matter-of-fact poverty, or everyday commonplace distress, meets with no sympathy, if indeed noticed at all, by one who has wept over the impossibly accumulated sufferings of some gaudy hero or heroine.

"Hoping you will pardon the liberty I have taken in addressing you, I remain,

"Most respectfully yours,

We are not sure that we have the controversy with the writer which he seems to suppose, and we should perhaps freely grant the mischievous effects which he says novel-reading has wrought upon him, if we were not afraid that he had possibly reviewed his own experience with something of

[1] First published April 1887 in *Harper's Magazine*.

the inaccuracy we find in his report of our opinions. By his confession he is himself proof that Vernon Lee is right in saying, "The modern human being has been largely fashioned by those who have written about him, and most of all by the novelist," and there is nothing in what he urges to conflict with her claim that "the chief use of the novel" is "to make the shrewd and tolerant a little less shrewd and tolerant, and to make the generous and austere a little more skeptical and easy-going." If he will look more closely at these postulates, we think he will see that in the one she deals with the effect of the novel in the past, and in the other with its duty in the future. We still think that there "is sense if not final wisdom" in what she says, and we are quite willing to acknowledge something of each in our correspondent.

But novels are now so fully accepted by every one pretending to culti- vated taste—and they really form the whole intellectual life of such im- mense numbers of people, without question of their influence, good or bad, upon the mind—that it is refreshing to have them frankly denounced, and to be invited to revise one's ideas and feelings in regard to them. A little hon- esty, or a great deal of honesty, in this quest will do the novel, as we hope yet to have it, and as we have already begun to have it, no harm; and for our own part we will confess that we believe fiction in the past to have been largely injurious, as we believe the stage play to be still almost wholly injuri- ous, through its falsehood, its folly, its wantonness, and its aimlessness. It may be safely assumed that most of the novel-reading which people fancy is an intellectual pastime is the emptiest dissipation, hardly more related to thought or the wholesome exercise of the mental faculties than opium-eat- ing; in either case the brain is drugged, and left weaker and crazier for the debauch. If this may be called the negative result of the fiction habit, the positive injury that most novels work is by no means so easily to be measured in the case of young men whose character they help so much to form and deform, and the women of all ages whom they keep so much in ignorance of the world they misrepresent. Grown men have little harm from them, but in the other cases, which are the vast majority, they hurt because they are not true—not because they are malevolent, but because they are idle lies about human nature and the social fabric, which it behooves us to know and to understand, that we may deal justly with ourselves and with one another. One need not go so far as our correspondent, and trace to the fiction habit "whatever is wild and visionary, whatever is untrue, whatever is injurious," in one's life; bad as the fiction habit is, it is probably not responsible for the whole sum of evil in its victims, and we believe that if the reader will use care in choosing from this fungus-growth with which the fields of literature teem every day, he may nourish himself as with the true mushroom, at no risk from the poisonous species.

The tests are very plain and simple, and they are perfectly infallible. If a novel flatters the passions, and exalts them above the principles, it is poisonous; it may not kill, but it will certainly injure; and this test will alone exclude an entire class of fiction, of which eminent examples will occur to all. Then the whole spawn of so-called un-moral romances, which imagine a world where the sins of sense are unvisited by the penalties following, swift or slow, but inexorably sure, in the real world, are deadly poison: these do kill. The novels that merely tickle our prejudices and lull our judgment, or that coddle our sensibilities, or pamper our gross appetite for the marvellous, are not so fatal, but they are innutritious, and clog the soul with unwholesome vapors of all kinds. No doubt they too help to weaken the mental fibre, and make their readers indifferent to "plodding perseverance and plain industry," and to "matter-of-fact poverty and commonplace distress."

Without taking them too seriously, it still must be owned that the "gaudy hero and heroine" are to blame for a great deal of harm in the world. That heroine long taught by example, if not precept, that Love, or the passion or fancy she mistook for it, was the chief interest of a life which is really concerned with a great many other things; that it was lasting in the way she knew it; that it was worthy of every sacrifice, and was altogether a finer thing than prudence, obedience, reason; that love alone was glorious and beautiful, and these were mean and ugly in comparison with it. More lately she has begun to idolize and illustrate Duty, and she is hardly less mischievous in this new rôle, opposing duty, as she did love, to prudence, obedience, and reason. The stock hero, whom, if we met him, we could not fail to see was a most deplorable person, has undoubtedly imposed himself upon the victims of the fiction habit as admirable. With him, too, love was and is the great affair, whether in its old romantic phase of chivalrous achievement or manifold suffering for love's sake, or its more recent development of the "virile," the bullying, and the brutal, or its still more recent agonies of self-sacrifice, as idle and useless as the moral experiences of the insane asylums. With his vain posturings and his ridiculous splendor he is really a painted barbarian, the prey of his passions, and his delusions, full of obsolete ideals, and the motives and ethics of a savage, which the guilty author of his being does his best—or his worst—in spite of his own light and knowledge, to foist upon the reader as something generous and noble. We are not merely bringing this charge against that sort of fiction which is beneath literature and outside of it, "the shoreless lakes of ditch-water," whose miasms[2] fill the air below the empyrean where the great ones sit; but we are accusing the work of some of the most famous, who have, in this instance or in that, sinned against the truth, which can alone exalt and purify men. We do not say that they have constantly done so, or even commonly done so; but that they have done so at all marks them as of the past, to be read with the due historical allowance for

---

[2] A noxious atmosphere from rotting organic matter.

moral order in universe

their epoch and their conditions. For we believe that, while inferior writers will and must continue to imitate them in their foibles and their errors, no one hereafter will be able to achieve greatness who is false to humanity, either in its facts or its duties. The light of civilization has already broken even upon the novel, and no conscientious man can now set about painting an image of life without perpetual question of the verity of his work, and without feeling bound to distinguish so clearly that no reader of his may be misled, between what is right and what is wrong, what is noble and what is base, what is health and what is perdition, in the actions and the characters he portrays.

The fiction that aims merely to entertain—the fiction that is to serious fiction as the opéra bouffe,[3] the ballet, and the pantomime are to the true drama—need not feel the burden of this obligation so deeply; but even such fiction will not be gay or trivial to any reader's hurt, and criticism will hold it to account if it passes from painting to teaching folly.

More and more not only the criticism which prints its opinions, but the infinitely vaster and powerfuler criticism which thinks and feels them merely, will make this demand. For our own part we confess that we do not care to judge any work of the imagination without first of all applying this test to it. We must ask ourselves before we ask anything else, Is it true?—true to the motives, the impulses, the principles that shape the life of actual men and women? This truth, which necessarily includes the highest morality and the highest artistry—this truth given, the book *cannot* be wicked and cannot be weak; and without it all graces of style and feats of invention and cunning of construction are so many superfluities of naughtiness. It is well for the truth to have all these, and shine in them, but for falsehood they are merely meretricious, the bedizenment of the wanton; they atone for nothing, they count for nothing. But in fact they come naturally of truth, and grace it without solicitation; they are added unto it. In the whole range of fiction we know of no *true* picture of life—that is, of human nature—which is not also a masterpiece of literature, full of divine and natural beauty. It may have no touch or tint of this special civilization or of that; it had *better* have this local color well ascertained; but the truth is deeper and finer than aspects, and if the book is true to what men and women know of one another's souls it will be true enough, and it will be great and beautiful. It is the conception of literature as something apart from life, superfinely aloof, which makes it really unimportant to the great mass of mankind, without a message or a meaning for them; and it is the notion that a novel may be false in its portrayal of causes and effects that makes literary art contemptible even to those whom it amuses, that forbids them to regard the novelist as a serious or right-minded person. If they do not in some moment of indignation cry out against all novels, as our correspondent does, they remain besotted in the

---

[3] Comic opera.

fume of the delusions purveyed to them, with no higher feeling for the author than such maudlin affection as the *habitué* of an opium-joint perhaps knows for the attendant who fills his pipe with the drug.

An Opportunity for American Fiction.[1]

FIRST PAPER

One of the most interesting books which has fallen in my way since I read "The Workers" of Mr. Wyckoff is Mr. Thorstein Veblen's "Theory of a Leisure Class" (Macmillan's). It does for the Idlers in terms of cold, scientific analysis the office which Mr. Wyckoff's book dramatically performs for the Workers; and I think that it is all the more important because it deals, like that book, with a class newly circumstanced rather than newly conditioned. The workers and the idlers of America are essentially the same as the workers and the idlers of occidental civilisation everywhere; but there is a novelty in their environment peculiarly piquant to the imagination. In the sociological region the spectacle has for the witness some such fascination as geological stratification would have for the inquirer if he could look on at its processes; and it is apparently with as strong a zest as this would inspire that Mr. Veblen considers the nature and the growth of the leisure class among us.

His name is newer to me than it should be, or than it will hereafter be to any student of our status; but it must be already well known to those whose interests or pleasures have led them into the same field of inquiry. To others, like myself, the clear method, the graphic and easy style, and the delightful accuracy of characterisation will be part of the surprise which the book has to offer. In the passionless calm with which the author pursues his investigation, there is apparently no animus for or against a leisure class. It is his affair simply to find out how and why and what it is. If the result is to leave the reader with a feeling which the author never shows, that seems to be solely the effect of the facts. But I have no purpose, as I doubt if I have the qualification, to criticise the book, and it is only with one of its manifold suggestions that this notice will concern itself.

The suggestion, which is rather a conclusion, is the curious fact, noted less securely and less scientifically before, that the flower of the American leisure class does not fruit in its native air, and perhaps cannot yet perpetuate itself in our soil. In other words, the words of Mr. Veblen, "the English leisure class being for purposes of reputable usage, the upper leisure class of this

---

[1] First published in April and May 1899 in *Literature, An International Gazette of Criticism.*

country," the extraordinary impulse among us toward the aristocraticisation of society can as yet fulfil itself only in monarchical conditions. A conspicuous proof of this is the frequent intermarriage of our moneyed bourgeoisie with the English aristocracy, and another proof, less conspicuous, is the frequent absenteeism of our rich people. The newspapers from time to time make a foolish and futile clamor about both these things, as if they were abnormal, or as if they were not the necessary logic of great wealth and leisure in a democracy. Such things result as infallibly from wealth and leisure as indigence and servility, and are in no wise to be deprecated. They are only representations on a wider stage of the perpetual and universal drama of our daily life. The man who makes money in a small town goes into the nearest large town to spend it—that is, to waste it; waste in some form or other being the corollary of wealth; and he seeks to marry his children into rich and old families. He does this from the instinct of self-preservation, which is as strong in classes as in individuals; if he has made his money in a large town, he goes to some such inland metropolis as Chicago to waste his wealth and to marry his children above him. The Chicago, and San Francisco, and St. Louis, and Cleveland millionaires come to New York with the same ambitions and purposes.

But these are all intermediate stages in the evolution of the American magnate. At every step he discovers that he is less in his own country, that he is living in a provisional exile, and that his true home is in monarchical conditions, where his future establishes itself often without his willing it, and sometimes against his willing it. The American life is the life of labor, and he is now of the life of leisure, or if he is not, his wife is, his daughters and his sons are. The logic of their existence, which they cannot struggle against, and on which all the fatuous invective of pseudo public spirit launches itself effectlessly, is intermarriage with the European aristocracies, and residence abroad. Short of this there is no rest, and can be none for the American leisure class. This may not be its ideal, but it is its destiny.

It is far the most dramatic social fact of our time, and if some man of creative imagination were to seize upon it, he would find in it the material of that great American novel which after so much travail has not yet seen the light. It is, above all our other facts, synthetic; it sums up and includes in itself the whole American story: the relentless will, the tireless force, the vague ideal, the inexorable destiny, the often bewildered acquiescence. If the novelist were a man of very great imagination indeed, he might forecast a future in which the cycle would round itself, and our wealth would return from European sojourn, and dwell among us again, bringing its upper class with it, so that we should have a leisure class ultimated and established on our own ground. But for my part I should prefer the novel which kept itself entirely to the actualities, and studied in them the most profoundly interesting spectacle which life has ever offered to the art of fiction, with elements of equal tragedy and comedy, and a pathos through all which must be expressed, if the full significance of the spectacle were to be felt.

SECOND PAPER

Mr. Thorstein Veblen does not evolve his Theory of a Leisure Class from his knowledge of that class in America alone. Until very lately we had no such class, and we rather longed for it. We thought it would edify us, or, if not that, at least ornament us; but now that we have got it, on certain terms, we can hardly be sure that it does either. The good things that we expected of it have not come to pass, and perhaps it is too soon; but in Mr. Veblen's analysis our leisure class does not seem essentially different from any of the older aristocracies, which seem not to have brought to pass the good things expected of them and often attributed to them. As with these, "pecuniary emulation" and "conspicuous leisure" are the first evidences of its superiority, and "conspicuous consumption," direct or delegated in the splendid apparelling and housing of its women and its dependents, is one of the gross means of striking the popular imagination. The "pecuniary standard of living" is really the only standard, and the "pecuniary canons of taste" are finally the only canons; for if the costly things are not always beautiful, all beautiful things which are cheap must be rejected because they are not costly. "Dress as an expression of pecuniary culture" is left in our day mostly to women by the leisure class; but the men of that class share in it at least as fully as in the "devout observances" and "the higher learning." Both sexes in our leisure class, as in the European aristocracies, are distinguished by the love of sport, in which they prolong their own childhood and the childhood of the race, and they are about equally devoted to the opera and the fine arts, as these minister to their magnificence. It would be hard, in fact, to draw the line between our leisure class and any aristocracy in the traits of piety, predacity, courage, prowess, charity, luxury, conservatism, authority, and the other virtues and vices which have characterised the patricians in all times.

The most notable difference, and the difference which would most invite the study of the novelist, is that hitherto our leisure class has had no political standing. It has had no place in the civic mechanism; but we seem to be at the moment when this is ceasing to be less apparently so. It is idle to suppose because the leisure class, which with us is the moneyed class, does not hold public offices that it does not control public affairs; and possibly it has always controlled them more than we have imagined. The present proof is in the fact that the industrial classes, with all the means of power in their hands, are really powerless in any contest with a group of rich man; it is almost impossible for the people to balk the purpose of such a group; to undo what money has done has been so impossible, with all the apparatus of the elections, the legislatures, the courts, that there is hardly yet an instance of the kind in our history.

All this, however, makes the situation the more attractive to a novelist of imaginative force. This is the most dramatic moment, the most psychological moment which has ever offered itself to fiction; this is the supreme opportunity of the American novelist. Hitherto our politics have repelled the artist by their want of social complexity, by their rude simplicity, as a fight between parties. But if he can look at the situation from the point of view suggested, as an inevitable result from the nature of the class which Mr. Veblen has studied, I believe he will find it full of charm. If he is psychologist enough he will be fascinated by the operation of the silent forces which are, almost unconsciously, working out the permanency of a leisure class, and preparing for it in our own circumstance the ultimation it now seeks elsewhere.

But I should be content if he would portray the life of our leisure class without an eye to such implications, with an eye merely to its superficial facts. If he did this he would appeal to the widest general interest in our reading public. Our appetite for everything that relates to the life removed from the life of work, from the simple republican ideal, is almost insatiable. It strives to satisfy itself, in plays and romances, with the doings of princes and nobles in realms as surely fictitious as Lilliput and Brobdignag; it gluts itself, in the newspapers, with fables almost as gross as Gulliver's concerning the social affairs of our leisure class.

Seen truly and reproduced faithfully these would be extremely interesting, and the field they offer to inquiry is almost wholly unexplored. Our fiction has brought pretty fully into literature the country and village life of the Americans of all sections. We know this through our short stories in New England, in the South, in the middle and farther West, and on the Pacific Slope; and in a certain measure our novels have acquainted us with the lower and upper middle-class life in the minor and even the greater cities. But the attempts to deal with the life of fashion, of luxury, of leisure, have been so insufficient that they cannot be considered. This life can hardly be studied by one who is a part of it, not merely because that sort of life is not fruitful in talent, but because the procession cannot very well look on at itself. The observer must have some favorable position on the outside, and must regard it neither "with a foolish face of praise," nor with a satiric scorn. Like every other phase of life, it has its seriousness, its importance, and one who studies it rightly will find in it the old elements of interest so newly compounded that they will merit his most intelligent scrutiny, often his most sympathetic scrutiny. It would be easy to burlesque it, but to burlesque it would be intolerable, and the witness who did this would be bearing false testimony where the whole truth and nothing but the truth is desirable. A democracy, the proudest, the most sincere, the most ardent that history has ever known, has evolved here a leisure class which has all the distinguishing traits of a patriciate, and which by the chemistry of intermarriage with European aristocracies is rapidly acquiring antiquity. Is not this a phenomenon worthy the highest fiction?

Mr. Veblen has brought to its study the methods and habits of scientific inquiry. To translate these into dramatic terms would form the unequalled triumph of the novelist who had the seeing eye and the thinking mind, not to mention the feeling heart. That such a thing has not been done hitherto is all the stranger, because fiction, in other countries, has always employed itself with the leisure class, with the aristocracy; and our own leisure class now offers not only as high an opportunity as any which fiction has elsewhere enjoyed, but by its ultimation in the English leisure class, it invites the American imagination abroad on conditions of unparalleled advantage.

HENRY JAMES

(1843-1916)

Henry James is the commanding figure in American fiction in this period: in his hands the American novel comes into its maturity. But his stature has also been a matter of some controversy. He has never been

"The New York Edition," with the Prefaces written by James, is standard: *The Novels and Tales of Henry James*, 26 vol. 1907-1917. The most comprehensive edition is *The Novels and Stories of Henry James*, 35 vols. 1921-1923. Other original work is Henry James, *The American Scene*, 1907: *Henry James, Autobiography*, 1956; F. O. Matthiessen and Kenneth B. Murdock, eds., *The Notebooks of Henry James*, 1947; Leon Edel, ed., *The Ghostly Tales of Henry James*, 1948; *The Complete Plays of Henry James*, 1949; *The Selected Letters of Henry James*, 1956; and *Complete Tales*, 1964.

The definitive biography is the 5-volume life by Leon Edel, *The Life of Henry James: I. The Untried Years; II. The Conquest of London; III. The Middle Years; IV. The Treacherous Years; V. The Master*, (1953-1972).

Some of the major critical estimates include J. W. Beach, *The Method of Henry James*, 1918, rev., 1954; R. P. Blackmur, *The Art of the Novel*, 1935; F. O. Matthiessen, *Henry James; The Major Phase*, 1944, and *The James Family*, 1947; R. P. Blackmur, "Henry James," in *Literary History of the United States*, ed., R. E. Spiller et al., 1948; F. W. Dupee, ed., *The Question of Henry James: A Collection of Critical Essays*, 1947, and *Henry James*, 1951; Allan Wade, ed., *The Scenic Art: Notes on Acting and the Drama, 1872-1901*, 1949; Marius Bewley, *The Complex Fate*, 1952, 1954, and *The Eccentric Design: Form In the Classic American Novel*, 1959; Quentin Anderson, *The American Henry James*, 1958; Dorothea Krook, *The Ordeal of Consciousness in Henry James*, 1962; Maxwell Geismar,

(Footnote continued next page.)

as popular as Twain or Howells, except perhaps for a short spell early
in his career when his tales of American girls abroad gave him a vogue.
Because he spent most of his mature years outside the United States, it
is sometimes questioned whether or not he can be classified as an
American author: indeed, he is sometimes listed as an English novelist.
After his death, younger writers such as Van Wyck Brooks upbraided
him for an excessive concern with the private lives of the very wealthy
in international society and for his apparent desertion of his native
culture (he became a British subject shortly before he died). A revival
occurred during World War II, as European travel became more common among Americans, and as literary and intellectual interests after
the war turned away from public matters toward private life and the
complications and limits of personal awareness. As preeminently a
writer of the private relation and of the process of perception that
governs friendships, courtships, and family entaglements, and with his
central concern with art itself, James enjoyed a very large audience,
particularly among students. More recently the taste for introspection
and the scruples of personal behavior have given way to the much
different excitement of social conflict, of challenges to systems of belief and power, and James's standing seems to have suffered.

His is, then, what R. P. Blackmur calls a "special case," a writer "in
whom succeeding ages find differing values and to whom each age
assigns a different rank." He makes great demands on his reader; his
language requires extraordinary attention. James has appealed to most
readers not so much for his literal subject matter but for what he does
with his subject, for the rendering of his tales. His major achievement
as a technician of fiction is his method of telling his stories through the
minds of the participating characters. In his novels, for example, the
omniscient author eventually disappears from the narrative, and the
reader is left to rely on the often unreliable accounts and character
that arrive filtered through a particular character's consciousness. In his
mature work there is little story as such, only *someone's* story, one or
several versions of the world refracted in particular minds. His realism
is primarily psychological, based on private reactions, individual perceptions. The highest value is placed on the quality of a person's

Henry James and The Jacobins, 1963; Millicent Bell, *Edith Wharton and Henry
James: The Story of a Friendship,* 1965;
Van Wyck Brooks, *The Pilgrimage of Henry James,* 1966; John A. Clair, *The Ironic
Dimension in the Fiction of Henry James,*
1966; Samuel Gorley Putt, *Henry James: A
Reader's Guide,* 1966; Christof Wegelin,
The Image of Europe in Henry James,
1968; Sallie Sears, *The Negative Imagination: Form and Perspective in the Novels
of Henry James,* 1969; Ora Segal, *The Lucid Reflector: The Observer in Henry
James' Fiction,* 1969; Peter Buitenhuis,
*The Grasping Imagination: The American
Writings of Henry James;* Philip Wein-
stein, *Henry James and the Requirements
of the Imagination,* 1971.

Henry James, c. 1905. *The Granger Collection.*

awareness, the fineness of his recognitions. In this sense James's central characters are often similar to artists themselves, persons "upon whom nothing is lost," as James described the kind of person best equipped to be a novelist.

Although James generally takes the social order for granted, in his emphasis on the psychological, he is still very much a social realist. As T. S. Eliot remarked, "the real hero, in any of James's stories, is a social entity of which men and women are constituents." He does not focus on the larger structure of society, but on the minute interactions that comprise a social world, a milieu. True, his social entities are usually confined to drawing rooms, gardens, dinner tables, and resort hotels instead of to streets, business offices, or factories, but the setting matters less than the author's conviction that society is the communication of individuals, the exchange of thoughts and feelings, the constant play of awareness in the give and take of relationships. For this reason he held that experience is always and inevitably social, always some specific person's experience, colored by time and place and context. Moreover, the social drama that James repeatedly creates is one in which "innocents" face manipulation and exploitation, in a challenge to their ability to *see* as well as to their pocket books or persons.

The social experience that provided James with the richest vein of his fiction was that of the American abroad. Essentially a comedy of contrasts, the "international theme" had been long established in American literature, at least from the time of Washington Irving and James Fenimore Cooper, and practiced by Hawthorne, Twain, and Howells. But James deepened and extended and refined the theme in original ways, using the contrasts of two kinds of society to explore differences of character and, eventually, in his "major phase," converting the theme into a symbolic drama in which New World innocence and Old World experience and worldliness engage each other in unexpected and mutually illuminating and corrective ways. James always felt a potential tragedy within the American–European comedy, of a naiveté leading his Americans blindly into the fascinating corruption of European high society. Tempted by the expectations of a richer, deeper experience than was available in America, such characters are often passionate pilgrims who find themselves unexpectedly enmeshed in alien societies. The situation became for James his greatest symbol of the sensitive consciousness itself, confronting dense, intractable experience. The test is whether the innocent characters can muster enough intelligence to survive.

James's international vision grew from his own wide personal experience on both sides of the Atlantic. European travel was not uncommon among American writers, but none absorbed Old World culture and came to feel as intimate with it as James, who knew especially well the major capitals of London, Paris, and Rome. Along with New York, Boston, Newport, Florence, and Venice, these cities are the settings for most of his fiction. He was born in New York in 1843 the brother of William James, and son of Henry James, Sr., an unorthodox religious and social philosopher who devoted his considerable wealth to travel and an eclectic private education for his sons. James made several extended trips to Europe during his childhood and adolescence, studying with tutors, visiting galleries and museums and monuments, gathering impressions, and reading novels inveterately. He lived much of his childhood in Washington Square, New York, and shortly before the Civil War the family settled in Newport, Rhode Island, where James developed a close friendship with the artist John Lafarge. He injured his back early in the war years, and this "obscure hurt," as he later referred to it, kept him out of military service. Instead, he entered Harvard Law School in 1862, but he soon withdrew and, until his death, he devoted his life entirely to writing: 20 novels, 100 tales, and much criticism, travel books, and memoirs. In the late 1860's and 1870's he divided his time between Boston and New York, with extended stays abroad. In England and France he met a number of literary figures, including Flaubert and Turgenev, from whom he learned of the exacting demands of the vocation of the artist. Early in the 1880's, after his father's death in 1882, he settled in England for good, first in London, then at Lamb House, Rye. He did not visit the United States again for 20 years.

James' career can be divided conveniently into three periods. In the first, from about 1865 to 1882, he establishes the basic lineaments of his theme of the innocent American abroad and develops a characteristic treatment. His earliest stories, written for periodicals in America, were influenced chiefly by Hawthorne and Dickens and presented reflective, cultivated young men as heroes. His first popular success was the novella *Daisy Miller* (1878), in which a vibrant, fresh young American girl scandalizes both Europeans and Americans by her naive flirtation with an Italian in Rome. She is at the end destroyed, the victim of a fever but also of the social uproar she had unwittingly and ingenuously provoked. A key character is a sophisticated American expatriate who might have helped Daisy handle her embarrassing situation, but he is himself too ironic, too detached, no longer in touch with American realities and not wholly assimilated to the culture in which he drifts rather aimlessly. This type of character reappears in later works, and is one of James's more complex creations. Several stories in this period, including "Madame de Mauves," treat the international theme similarly. The theme is expanded in the novels of the 1870's. In *Roderick Hudson* (1875), the American abroad is a Byronic artist who destroys himself in Rome; in *The American* (1877) he is a businessman, a self-made millionaire who comes to Paris in search of a wife and finds himself entangled in a plot of treachery beyond his comprehension. Also in this period James wrote his brief study of Hawthorne, which indirectly explains his own relations to America and his own artistic intentions. He speaks here of the difficulties facing the novelist in a society with so brief a past, so thin a layer of social life, so many associations, manners, institutions—the rich materials of the English realists—missing. Apart from his tribute to an earlier writer, the study suggests a defense for James's own search abroad for denser fields for fiction.

The crowning work of this period is *The Portrait of a Lady* (1881). The heroine, Isabel Archer, comes to England from a dull provincial life in Albany and, finding herself an heiress, has the world virtually at her feet. Europe and wealth represent freedom, and the question is what she will make of it. Isabel's idealism and pride lead her into a scheme by an adventurer and his mistress, who manipulate her and her wealth into a bleak marriage. She is the victim of her own generous impulses as well as of a calculated plot and, in realizing the full truth of her predicament, Isabel rises to moving heights of courage, honesty, and endurance.

The Portrait of a Lady was the last book of James to find a popular audience and, in the next or "middle" period, his art entered a phase of experimentation, with new subjects and new forms. First came two attempts at more naturalistic social realism, without the American-European contrast. In *The Bostonians* (1886) he portrayed, mainly satirically, a group of figures obsessed with reform, especially feminism. In the process, he probes the sources of radical ideas in personal psychology. The anarchist movement, its dark urges and its conspiracies, is the subject of the almost Dickensian *The Princess Cassamassima* (1886). Politics, passion, and art are the issues in another venture in this more public vein, *The Tragic Muse* (1889). All were failures from the point of view of sales, and James turned next to an ill-fated enterprise of writing drama for the popular stage in London. He abandoned this profitless line for which he had no real love, after being hissed off the stage at the opening performance of one of his plays. His following works focus on English upper-middle-class society and its country houses. Several of these works develop the point of view of childhood, a variant of innocence, confronting the mysterious adult behavior that often ineffectively disguises corruption, greed, lust, and cruelty. James's social vision in these predominantly English books, *The Spoils of Poynton* (1897), *What Maisie Knew* (1897), *The Awkward Age* (1899), and *The Sacred Fount* (1901), is increasingly occupied with violations of privacy and the horrors accompanying dawning recognitions of betrayal and exploitation.

In his "major phase," from about 1900 to World War I, James brings to fruition the lessons of his entire career in three masterful novels that return to the international theme on a much more subtle and refined scale. In *The Ambassadors* (written in 1899–1901; published 1903), *The Wings of the Dove* (1902), and *The Golden Bowl* (1904), James's narrative techniques reach new intensities; sentences expand, grow more supple, and register greater nuances of meaning and feeling. These are the most tightly woven of his fictions, and the most demanding. The first two are in a sense new versions of *The American* and *Portrait of a Lady:* in *The Ambassadors* he brings to Europe a middle-aged New Englander, Lambert Strether, who discovers there how inhibiting and emotionally barren his life has been; he also learns that he cannot easily shake off American moral strictures for Parisian sophistication; in *Wings of the Dove* Milly Theale is a young American heiress who arrives in Europe with a fatal disease and is immediately caught up in a scheme to exploit her fierce desire for life by arranging a marriage that would profit the schemers after her death. The most elaborately wrought of the three books is *The Golden Bowl,* which is considered James's "ultimate" novel. Here the international drama yields its greatest complications, since the destiny of the Americans, Maggie Verver and her father Adam, is enmeshed in a European situation of adultery, betrayal, and deceit. In the end the Americans triumph by extending their capacity to see clearly and to receive the revealed vision of impurity without loss of integrity. Their moral growth vindicates the superiority of their chastened innocence.

The triumph of Maggie Verver is in many ways the triumph of art itself, of the ability to experience the world as one of those on whom nothing is lost. Throughout James's work affirmation of existence has competed with renunciation from a world too complex, too evil. In the end the figure of the artist points the way to a transcendence. This figure is itself the subject of many of James's finest tales, in which he explores both the nature of art and the vocation of artist, as in "The Figure in the Carpet" (1896). Now, after completing his major novels, he found opportunities to test his art and expound his critical ideas in two unique enterprises. The first is a remarkable book, *The American Scene* (1907), which records his impressions of America in his first visit after 20 years, a "restless analysis" of a society given over to material expansion without critical consciousness of its direction and the costs of its "progress." The other works are the prefaces to a selection of novels published as the "New York Edition" (1907–1909), in which James makes his fullest, most reasoned statements about the art of the novel. Both stand as monuments, as it were, to the rigorous "ordeal of consciousness," in the words of one critic, which characterizes all his major work.

Daisy Miller[1]

I

At the little town of Vevey in Switzerland, there is a particularly comfortable hotel; there are indeed many hotels, since the entertainment of tourists is the business of the place, which, as many travellers will remember, is seated upon the edge of a remarkably blue lake[2]—a lake that it behoves every tourist to visit. The shore of the lake presents an unbroken array of establishments of this order, of every category, from the "grand hotel" of the newest fashion, with a chalk-white front, a hundred balconies, and a dozen flags flying from its roof, to the small Swiss pension of an elder day, with its name inscribed in German-looking lettering upon a pink or yellow wall and an awkward summer-house in the angle of the garden. One of the hotels at Vevey, however, is famous, even classical, being distinguished from many of its upstart neighbours by an air both of luxury and of maturity. In this region, through the month of June, American travellers are extremely numerous; it may be said indeed that Vevey assumes at that time some of the characteristics of an American watering-place. There are sights and sounds that evoke a vision, an echo, of Newport and Saratoga. There is a flitting hither and thither of "stylish" young girls, a rustling of muslin flounces, a rattle of dance-music in the morning hours, a sound of high-pitched voices at all times. You receive an impression of these things at the excellent inn of the "Trois Couronnes," and are transported in fancy to the Ocean House or to Congress Hall.[3] But at the "Trois Couronnes," it must be added, there are other features much at variance with these suggestions: neat German waiters who look like secretaries of legation; Russian princesses sitting in the garden; little Polish boys walking about, held by the hand, with their governors; a view of the snowy crest of the Dent du Midi[4] and the picturesque towers of the Castle of Chillon.[5]

I hardly know whether it was the analogies or the differences that were uppermost in the mind of a young American, who, two or three years ago, sat in the garden of the "Trois Couronnes," looking about him rather idly at some of the graceful objects I have mentioned. It was a beautiful summer morning, and in whatever fashion the young American looked at things they must have seemed to him charming. He had come from Geneva the day before, by the little steamer, to see his aunt, who was staying at the hotel—Geneva having been for a long time his place of residence. But his aunt had a headache—his aunt had almost always a headache—and she was now shut

[1] First published in *Cornhill Magazine* in June-July 1878; published in book form in 1879.

[2] Lake Geneva.

[3] Newport and Saratoga Hotels.

[4] A Swiss Alp.

[5] A castle of the 1400's. Lord Byron wrote a poem, "The Prisoner of Chillon" (1816), using the castle for his setting.

up in her room smelling camphor, so that he was at liberty to wander about. He was some seven-and-twenty years of age; when his friends spoke of him they usually said that he was at Geneva "studying." When his enemies spoke of him they said—but after all he had no enemies: he was extremely amiable and generally liked. What I should say is simply that when certain persons spoke of him they conveyed that the reason of his spending so much time at Geneva was that he was extremely devoted to a lady who lived there—a foreign lady, a person older than himself. Very few Americans—truly I think none—had ever seen this lady, about whom there were some singular stories. But Winterbourne had an old attachment for the little capital of Calvinism,[6] he had been put to school there as a boy and had afterwards even gone, on trial—trial of the grey old "Academy" on the steep and stony hillside—to college there; circumstances which had led to his forming a great many youthful friendships. Many of these he had kept, and they were a source of great satisfaction to him.

After knocking at his aunt's door and learning that she was indisposed he had taken a walk about the town and then he had come in to his breakfast. He had now finished that repast, but was enjoying a small cup of coffee which had been served him on a little table in the garden by one of the waiters who looked like *attachés*. At last he finished his coffee and lit a cigarette. Presently a small boy came walking along the path—an urchin of nine or ten. The child, who was diminutive for his years, had an aged expression of countenance, a pale complexion and sharp little features. He was dressed in knickerbockers and had red stockings that displayed his poor little spindle-shanks; he also wore a brilliant red cravat. He carried in his hand a long alpenstock,[7] the sharp point of which he thrust into everything he approached—the flower-beds, the garden-benches, the trains of the ladies' dresses. In front of Winterbourne he paused, looking at him with a pair of bright and penetrating little eyes.

"Will you give me a lump of sugar?" he asked in a small sharp hard voice—a voice immature and yet somehow not young.

Winterbourne glanced at the light table near him, on which his coffee-service rested, and saw that several morsels of sugar remained. "Yes, you may take one," he answered; "but I don't think too much sugar good for little boys."

This little boy stepped forward and carefully selected three of the coveted fragments, two of which he buried in the pocket of his knickerbockers, depositing the other as promptly in another place. He poked his alpenstock, lance-fashion, into Winterbourne's bench and tried to crack the lump of sugar with his teeth.

---

[6] John Calvin, Protestant theologian (1509-1564) lived in Geneva from 1541 until he died.

[7] A long iron-pointed staff used for mountain climbing.

"Oh blazes; it's har-r-d!" he exclaimed, divesting vowel and consonants, pertinently enough, of any taint of softness.

Winterbourne had immediately gathered that he might have the honour of claiming him as a countryman. "Take care you don't hurt your teeth," he said paternally.

"I have n't got any teeth to hurt. They've all come out. I've only got seven teeth. Mother counted them last night, and one came out right afterwards. She said she'd slap me if any more came out. I can't help it. It's this old Europe. It's the climate that makes them come out. In America they didn't come out. It's these hotels."

Winterbourne was much amused. "If you eat three lumps of sugar your mother will certainly slap you," he ventured.

"She's got to give me some candy then," rejoined his young interlocutor. "I can't get any candy here—any American candy. American candy's the best candy."

"And are American little boys the best little boys?" Winterbourne asked.

"I don't know. *I'm* an American boy," said the child.

"I see you're one of the best!" the young man laughed.

"Are you an American man?" pursued this vivacious infant. And then on his friend's affirmative reply, "American men are the best," he declared with assurance.

His companion thanked him for the compliment, and the child, who had now got astride of his alpenstock, stood looking about him while he attacked another lump of sugar. Winterbourne wondered if he himself had been like this in his infancy, for he had been brought to Europe at about the same age.

"Here comes my sister!" cried his young compatriot. "She's an American girl, you bet!"

Winterbourne looked along the path and saw a beautiful young lady advancing. "American girls are the best girls," he thereupon cheerfully remarked to his visitor.

"My sister ain't the best!" the child promptly returned. "She's always blowing at me."

"I imagine that's your fault, not hers," said Winterbourne. The young lady meanwhile had drawn near. She was dressed in white muslin, with a hundred frills and flounces and knots of pale-coloured ribbon. Bareheaded, she balanced in her hand a large parasol with a deep border of embroidery; and she was strikingly, admirably pretty. "How pretty they are!" thought our friend, who straightened himself in his seat as if he were ready to rise.

The young lady paused in front of his bench, near the parapet of the garden, which overlooked the lake. The small boy had now converted his alpenstock into a vaulting-pole, by the aid of which he was springing about in the gravel and kicking it up not a little. "Why Randolph," she freely began, "what *are* you doing?"

"I'm going up the Alps!" cried Randolph. "This is the way!" And he gave another extravagant jump, scattering the pebbles about Winterbourne's ears.
"That's the way they come down," said Winterbourne.
"He's an American man!" proclaimed Randolph in his harsh little voice.
The young lady gave no heed to this circumstance, but looked straight at her brother. "Well, I guess you'd better be quiet," she simply observed.
It seemed to Winterbourne that he had been in a manner presented. He got up and stepped slowly toward the charming creature, throwing away his cigarette. "This little boy and I have made acquaintance," he said with great civility. In Geneva, as he had been perfectly aware, a young man was n't at liberty to speak to a young unmarried lady save under certain rarely-occurring conditions; but here at Vevey what conditions could be better than these?—a pretty American girl coming to stand in front of you in a garden with all the confidence in life. This pretty American girl, whatever that might prove, on hearing Winterbourne's observation simply glanced at him; she then turned her head and looked over the parapet, at the lake and the opposite mountains. He wondered whether he had gone too far, but decided that he must gallantly advance rather than retreat. While he was thinking of something else to say the young lady turned again to the little boy, whom she addressed quite as if they were alone together. "I should like to know where you got that pole."
"I bought it!" Randolph shouted.
"You don't mean to say you're going to take it to Italy!"
"Yes, I'm going to take it t' Italy!" the child rang out.
She glanced over the front of her dress and smoothed out a knot or two of ribbon. Then she gave her sweet eyes to the prospect again. "Well, I guess you'd better leave it somewhere," she dropped after a moment.
"Are you going to Italy?" Winterbourne now decided very respectfully to enquire.
She glanced at him with lovely remoteness. "Yes, sir," she then replied. And she said nothing more.
"And are you—a—thinking of the Simplon?"[8] he pursued with a slight drop of assurance.
"I don't know," she said. "I suppose it's some mountain. Randolph, what mountain are we thinking of?"
"Thinking of?"—the boy stared.
"Why going right over."
"Going to where?" he demanded.
"Why right down to Italy"—Winterbourne felt vague emulations.

[8] An Alpine pass between Switzerland and Italy.

"I don't know," said Randolph. "I don't want to go t' Italy. I want to go to America."

"Oh Italy's a beautiful place!" the young man laughed.

"Can you get candy there?" Randolph asked of all the echoes.

"I hope not," said his sister. "I guess you've had enough candy, and mother thinks so too."

"I have n't had any for ever so long—for a hundred weeks!" cried the boy, still jumping about.

The young lady inspected her flounces and smoothed her ribbons again; and Winterbourne presently risked an observation on the beauty of the view. He was ceasing to be in doubt, for he had begun to perceive that she was really not in the least embarrassed. She might be cold, she might be austere, she might even be prim; for that was apparently—he had already so generalised—what the most "distant" American girls did: they came and planted themselves straight in front of you to show how rigidly unapproachable they were. There had n't been the slightest flush in her fresh fairness however; so that she was clearly neither offended nor fluttered. Only she was composed—he had seen that before too—of charming little parts that did n't match and that made no *ensemble;* and if she looked another way when he spoke to her, and seemed not particularly to hear him, this was simply her habit, her manner, the result of her having no idea whatever of "form" (with such a tell-tale appendage as Randolph where in the world would she have got it?) in any such connexion. As he talked a little more and pointed out some of the objects of interest in the view, with which she appeared wholly unacquainted, she gradually, none the less, gave him more of the benefit of her attention; and then he saw that act unqualified by the faintest shadow of reserve. It was n't however what would have been called a "bold" front that she presented, for her expression was as decently limpid as the very cleanest water. Her eyes were the very prettiest conceivable and indeed Winterbourne had n't for a long time seen anything prettier than his fair countrywoman's various features—her complexion, her nose, her ears, her teeth. He took a great interest generally in that range of effects and was addicted to noting and, as it were, recording them; so that in regard to this young lady's face he made several observations. It was n't at all insipid, yet at the same time was n't pointedly—what point, on earth, could she ever make?—expressive; and though it offered such a collection of small finenesses and neatnesses he mentally accused it—very forgivingly—of a want of finish. He thought nothing more likely than that its wearer would have had her own experience of the action of her charms, as she would certainly have acquired a resulting confidence; but even should she depend on this for her main amusement her bright sweet superficial little visage gave out neither mockery or irony. Before long it became clear that, however these things might be, she was much disposed to conversation. She remarked to Winterbourne that they were going to Rome for the winter—she and her mother and

Randolph. She asked him if he was a "real American"; she would n't have taken him for one; he seemed more like a German—this flower was gathered as from a large field of comparison—especially when he spoke. Winterbourne, laughing, answered that he had met Germans who spoke like Americans, but not, so far as he remembered, any American with the resemblance she noted. Then he asked her if she might n't be more at ease should she occupy the bench he had just quitted. She answered that she liked hanging round, but she none the less resignedly, after a little, dropped to the bench. She told him she was from New York State—"if you know where that is"; but our friend really quickened this current by catching hold of her small slippery brother and making him stand a few minutes by his side.

"Tell me your honest name, my boy." So he artfully proceeded.

In response to which the child was indeed unvarnished truth. "Randolph C. Miller. And I'll tell you hers." With which he levelled his alpenstock at his sister.

"You had better wait till you're asked!" said this young lady quite at her leisure.

"I should like very much to know *your* name," Winterbourne made free to reply.

"Her name's Daisy Miller!" cried the urchin.

"But that ain't her real name; that ain't her name on her cards."

"It's a pity you have n't got one of my cards!" Miss Miller quite as naturally remarked.

"Her real name's Annie P. Miller," the boy went on.

It seemed, all amazingly, to do her good. "Ask him *his* now"—and she indicated their friend.

But to this point Randolph seemed perfectly indifferent; he continued to supply information with regard to his own family. "My father's name is Ezra B. Miller. My father ain't in Europe—he's in a better place than Europe." Winterbourne for a moment supposed this the manner in which the child had been taught to intimate that Mr. Miller had been removed to the sphere of celestial rewards. But Randolph immediately added: "My father's in Schenectady. He's got a big business. My father's rich, you bet."

"Well!" ejaculated Miss Miller, lowering her parasol and looking at the embroidered border. Winterbourne presently released the child, who departed, dragging his alpenstock along the path. "He don't like Europe," said the girl as with an artless instinct for historic truth. "He wants to go back."

"To Schenectady, you mean?"

"Yes, he wants to go right home. He has n't got any boys here. There's one boy here, but he always goes round with a teacher. They won't let him play."

"And your brother has n't any teacher?" Winterbourne enquired.

It tapped, at a touch, the spring of confidence. "Mother thought of getting him one—to travel round with us. There was a lady told her of a very good

teacher; an American lady—perhaps you know her—Mrs. Sanders. I think
she came from Boston. She told her of this teacher, and we thought of
getting him to travel round with us. But Randolph said he did n't want a
teacher travelling round with us. He said he would n't have lessons when he
was in the cars. And we *are* in the cars about half the time. There was an
English lady we met in the cars—I think her name was Miss Featherstone;
perhaps you know her. She wanted to know why I did n't give Randolph
lessons—give him 'instruction,' she called it. I guess he could give me more
instruction than I could give him. He's very smart."

"Yes," said Winterbourne; "he seems very smart."

"Mother's going to get a teacher for him as soon as we get t' Italy. Can
you get good teachers in Italy?"

"Very good, I should think," Winterbourne hastened to reply.

"Or else she's going to find some school. He ought to learn some more.
He's only nine. He's going to college." And in this way Miss Miller continued
to converse upon the affairs of her family and upon other topics. She sat
there with her extremely pretty hands, ornamented with very brilliant rings,
folded in her lap, and with her pretty eyes now resting upon those of Winterbourne, now wandering over the garden, the people who passed before her
and the beautiful view. She addressed her new acquaintance as if she had
known him a long time. He found it very pleasant. It was many years since
he had heard a young girl talk so much. It might have been said of this
wandering maiden who had come and sat down beside him upon a bench
that she chattered. She was very quiet, she sat in a charming tranquil attitude; but her lips and her eyes were constantly moving. She had a soft
slender agreeable voice, and her tone was distinctly sociable. She gave Winterbourne a report of her movements and intentions, and those of her
mother and brother, in Europe, and enumerated in particular the various
hotels at which they had stopped. "That English lady in the cars," she said—
"Miss Featherstone—asked me if we didn't all live in hotels in America. I
told her I had never been in so many hotels in my life as since I came to
Europe. I've never seen so many—it's nothing but hotels." But Miss Miller
made this remark with no querulous accent; she appeared to be in the best
humour with everything. She declared that the hotels were very good when
once you got used to their ways and that Europe was perfectly entrancing.
She wasn't disappointed—not a bit. Perhaps it was because she had heard so
much about it before. She had ever so many intimate friends who had been
there ever so many times, and that way she had got thoroughly posted. And
then she had had ever so many dresses and things from Paris. Whenever she
put on a Paris dress she felt as if she were in Europe.

"It was a kind of a wishing-cap," Winterbourne smiled.

"Yes," said Miss Miller at once and without examining this analogy; "it
always made me wish I was here. But I need n't have done that for dresses.
I'm sure they send all the pretty ones to America; you see the most frightful

things here. The only thing I don't like," she proceeded, "is the society. There ain't any society—or if there is I don't know where it keeps itself. Do you? I suppose there's some society somewhere, but I have n't seen anything of it. I'm very fond of society and I've always had plenty of it. I don't mean only in Schenectady, but in New York. I used to go to New York every winter. In New York I had lots of society. Last winter I had seventeen dinners given me, and three of them were by gentlemen," added Daisy Miller. "I've more friends in New York than in Schenectady—more gentlemen friends; and more young lady friends too," she resumed in a moment. She paused again for an instant; she was looking at Winterbourne with all her prettiness in her frank gay eyes and in her clear rather uniform smile. "I've always had," she said, "a great deal of gentlemen's society."

Poor Winterbourne was amused and perplexed—above all he was charmed. He had never yet heard a young girl express herself in just this fashion; never at least save in cases where to say such things was to have at the same time some rather complicated consciousness about them. And yet was he to accuse Miss Daisy Miller of an actual or a potential *arrière-pen-sée*,[9] as they said at Geneva? He felt he had lived at Geneva so long as to have got morally muddled; he had lost the right sense for the young American tone. Never indeed since he had grown old enough to appreciate things had he encountered a young compatriot of so "strong" a type as this. Certainly she was very charming, but how extraordinarily communicative and how tremendously easy! Was she simply a pretty girl from New York State— were they all like that, the pretty girls who had had a good deal of gentlemen's society? Or was she also a designing, an audacious, in short an expert young person? Yes, his instinct for such a question had ceased to serve him, and his reason could but mislead. Miss Daisy Miller looked extremely innocent. Some people had told him that after all American girls *were* exceedingly innocent, and others had told him that after all they were n't. He must on the whole take Miss Daisy Miller for a flirt—a pretty American flirt. He had never as yet had relations with representatives of that class. He had known here in Europe two or three women—persons older than Miss Daisy Miller and provided, for respectability's sake, with husbands—who were great coquettes; dangerous terrible women with whom one's light commerce might indeed take a serious turn. But this charming apparition was n't a coquette in that sense; she was very unsophisticated; she was only a pretty American flirt. Winterbourne was almost grateful for having found the formula that applied to Miss Daisy Miller. He leaned back in his seat; he remarked to himself that she had the finest little nose he had ever seen; he wondered what were the regular conditions and limitations of one's intercourse with a pretty American flirt. It presently became apparent that he was on the way to learn.

[9] Mental reservation.

"Have you been to that old castle?" the girl soon asked, pointing with her parasol to the far-shining walls of the Château de Chillon.

"Yes, formerly, more than once," said Winterbourne. "You too, I suppose, have seen it?"

"No, we haven't been there. I want to go there dreadfully. Of course I mean to go there. I would n't go away from here without having seen that old castle."

"It's a very pretty excursion," the young man returned, "and very easy to make. You can drive, you know, or you can go by the little steamer."

"You can go in the cars," said Miss Miller.

"Yes, you can go in the cars," Winterbourne assented.

"Our courier says they take you right up to the castle," she continued. "We were going last week, but mother gave out. She suffers dreadfully from dyspepsia. She said she could n't any more go—!" But this sketch of Mrs. Miller's plea remained unfinished. "Randolph would n't go either; he says he don't think much of old castles. But I guess we'll go this week if we can get Randolph."

"Your brother isn't interested in ancient monuments?" Winterbourne indulgently asked.

He now drew her, as he guessed she would herself have said, every time. "Why no, he says he don't care much about old castles. He's only nine. He wants to stay at the hotel. Mother's afraid to leave him alone, and the courier won't stay with him; so we have n't been to many places. But it will be too bad if we don't go up there." And Miss Miller pointed again at the Château de Chillon.

"I should think it might be arranged," Winterbourne was thus emboldened to reply. "Could n't you get some one to stay—for the afternoon—with Randolph?"

Miss Miller looked at him a moment, and then with all serenity, "I wish *you'd* stay with him!" she said.

He pretended to consider it. "I'd much rather go to Chillon with you."

"With me?" she asked without a shadow of emotion.

She did n't rise blushing, as a young person at Geneva would have done; and yet, conscious that he had gone very far, he thought it possible she had drawn back. "And with your mother," he answered very respectfully.

But it seemed that both his audacity and his respect were lost on Miss Daisy Miller. "I guess mother would n't go—for *you*," she smiled. "And she ain't much *bent* on going, anyway. She don't like to ride round in the afternoon." After which she familiarly proceeded: "But did you really mean what you said just now—that you'd like to go up there?"

"Most earnestly I meant it," Winterbourne declared.

"Then we may arrange it. If mother will stay with Randolph I guess Eugenio will."

"Eugenio?" the young man echoed.

"Eugenio's our courier.[10] He does n't like to stay with Randolph—he's the most fastidious man I ever saw. But he's a splendid courier. I guess he'll stay at home with Randolph if mother does, and then we can go to the castle."

Winterbourne reflected for an instant as lucidly as possible: "we" could only mean Miss Miller and himself. This prospect seemed almost too good to believe; he felt as if he ought to kiss the young lady's hand. Possibly he would have done so,—and quite spoiled his chance; but at this moment another person—presumably Eugenio—appeared. A tall handsome man, with superb whiskers and wearing a velvet morning-coat and a voluminous watch-guard, approached the young lady, looking sharply at her companion. "Oh Eugenio!" she said with the friendliest accent.

Eugenio had eyed Winterbourne from head to foot; he now bowed gravely to Miss Miller. "I have the honour to inform Mademoiselle that luncheon's on table."

Mademoiselle slowly rose. "See here, Eugenio, I'm going to that old castle anyway."

"To the Château de Chillon, Mademoiselle?" the courier enquired. "Mademoiselle has made arrangements?" he added in a tone that struck Winterbourne as impertinent.

Eugenio's tone apparently threw, even to Miss Miller's own apprehension, a slightly ironical light on her position. She turned to Winterbourne with the slightest blush. "You won't back out?"

"I shall not be happy till we go!" he protested.

"And you're staying in this hotel?" she went on. "And you're really American?"

The courier still stood there with an effect of offence for the young man so far as the latter saw in it a tacit reflexion on Miss Miller's behaviour and an insinuation that she "picked up" acquaintances. "I shall have the honour of presenting to you a person who'll tell you all about me," he said, smiling, and referring to his aunt.

"Oh well, we'll go some day," she beautifully answered; with which she gave him a smile and turned away. She put up her parasol and walked back to the inn beside Eugenio. Winterbourne stood watching her, and as she moved away, drawing her muslin furbelows over the walk, he spoke to himself of her natural elegance.

II

He had, however, engaged to do more than proved feasible in promising to present his aunt, Mrs. Costello, to Miss Daisy Miller. As soon as that lady had got better of her headache he waited on her in her apartment and, after a

[10] A servant who manages travelers' arrangements.

show of the proper solicitude about her health, asked if she had noticed in the hotel an American family—a mamma, a daughter and an obstreperous little boy.

"An obstreperous little boy and a preposterous big courier?" said Mrs. Costello. "Oh yes, I've noticed them. Seen them, heard them and kept out of their way." Mrs. Costello was a widow of fortune, a person of much distinction and who frequently intimated that if she hadn't been so dreadfully liable to sick-headaches she would probably have left a deeper impress on her time. She had a long pale face, a high nose and a great deal of very striking white hair, which she wore in large puffs and over the top of her head. She had two sons married in New York and another who was now in Europe. This young man was amusing himself at Homburg and, though guided by his taste, was rarely observed to visit any particular city at the moment selected by his mother for her appearance there. Her nephew, who had come to Vevey expressly to see her, was therefore more attentive than, as she said, her very own. He had imbibed at Geneva the idea that one must be irreproachable in all such forms. Mrs. Costello had n't seen him for many years and was now greatly pleased with him, manifesting her approbation by initiating him into many of the secrets of social sway which, as he could see she would like him to think, she exerted from her stronghold in Forty-Second Street. She admitted that she was very exclusive, but if he had been better acquainted with New York he would see that one had to be. And her picture of the minutely hierarchical constitution of the society of that city, which she presented to him in many different lights, was, to Winterbourne's imagination, almost oppressively striking.

He at once recognised from her tone that Miss Daisy Miller's place in the social scale was low. "I'm afraid you don't approve of them," he pursued in reference to his new friends.

"They're horribly common"—it was perfectly simple. "They're the sort of Americans that one does one's duty by just ignoring."

"Ah you just ignore them?"—the young man took it in.

"I can't *not*, my dear Frederick. I would n't if I had n't to, but I have to."

"The little girl's very pretty," he went on in a moment.

"Of course she's very pretty. But she's of the last crudity."

"I see what you mean of course," he allowed after another pause.

"She has that charming look they all have," his aunt resumed. "I can't think where they pick it up; and she dresses in perfection—no, you don't know how well she dresses. I can't think where they get their taste."

"But, my dear aunt, she's not, after all, a Comanche savage."

"She is a young lady," said Mrs. Costello, "who has an intimacy with her mamma's courier?"

"An 'intimacy' with him?" Ah there it was!

"There's no other name for such a relation. But the skinny little mother's just as bad! They treat the courier as a familiar friend—as a gentleman and a scholar. I should n't wonder if he dines with them. Very likely they've never seen a man with such good manners, such fine clothes, *so like* a gentleman— or a scholar. He probably corresponds to the young lady's idea of a count. He sits with them in the garden of an evening. I think he smokes in their faces."

Winterbourne listened with interest to these disclosures; they helped him to make up his mind about Miss Daisy. Evidently she was rather wild. "Well," he said, "I'm not a courier and I did n't smoke in her face, and yet she was very charming to me."

"You had better have mentioned at first," Mrs. Costello returned with dignity, "that you had made her valuable acquaintance."

"We simply met in the garden and talked a bit."

"By appointment—no? Ah that's still to come! Pray what did you say?"

"I said I should take the liberty of introducing her to my admirable aunt."

"Your admirable aunt's a thousand times obliged to you."

"It was to guarantee my respectability."

"And pray who's to guarantee hers?"

"Ah you're cruel!" said the young man. "She's a very innocent girl."

"You don't say that as if you believed it," Mrs. Costello returned.

"She's completely uneducated," Winterbourne acknowledged, "but she's wonderfully pretty, and in short she's very nice. To prove I believe it I'm going to take her to the Château de Chillon."

Mrs. Costello made a wondrous face. "You two are going off there together? I should say it proved just the contrary. How long had you known her, may I ask, when this interesting project was formed? You have n't been twenty-four hours in the house."

"I had known her half an hour!" Winterbourne smiled.

"Then she's just what I supposed."

"And what do you suppose?"

"Why that she's a horror."

Our youth was silent for some moments. "You really think then," he presently began, and with a desire for trustworthy information, "you really think that—" But he paused again while his aunt waited.

"Think what, sir?"

"That she's the sort of young lady who expects a man sooner or later to— well, we'll call it carry her off?"

"I haven't the least idea what such young ladies expect a man to do. But I really consider you had better not meddle with little American girls who are uneducated, as you mildly put it. You've lived too long out of the country. You'll be sure to make some great mistake. You're too innocent."

"My dear aunt, not so much as that comes to!" he protested with a laugh and a curl of his moustache.

"You're too guilty then!"

He continued all thoughtfully to finger the ornament in question. "You won't let the poor girl know you then?" he asked at last.

"Is it literally true that she's going to the Château de Chillon with you?"

"I've no doubt she fully intends it."

"Then, my dear Frederick," said Mrs. Costello, "I must decline the honour of her acquaintance. I'm an old woman, but I'm not too old—thank heaven—to be honestly shocked!"

"But don't they all do these things—the little American girls at home?" Winterbourne enquired.

Mrs. Costello stared a moment. "I should like to see my granddaughters do them!" she then grimly returned.

This seemed to throw some light on the matter, for Winterbourne remembered to have heard his pretty cousins in New York, the daughters of this lady's two daughters, called "tremendous flirts." If therefore Miss Daisy Miller exceeded the liberal licence allowed to these young women it was probable she did go even by the American allowance rather far. Winterbourne was impatient to see her again, and it vexed, it even a little humiliated him, that he should n't by instinct appreciate her justly.

Though so impatient to see her again he hardly knew what ground he should give for his aunt's refusal to become acquainted with her; but he discovered promptly enough that with Miss Daisy Miller there was no great need of walking on tiptoe. He found her that evening in the garden, wandering about in the warm starlight after the manner of an indolent sylph and swinging to and fro the largest fan he had ever beheld. It was ten o'clock. He had dined with his aunt, had been sitting with her since dinner, and had just taken leave of her till the morrow. His young friend frankly rejoiced to renew their intercourse; she pronounced it the stupidest evening she had ever passed.

"Have you been all alone?" he asked with no intention of an epigram and no effect of her perceiving one.

"I've been walking round with mother. But mother gets tired walking round," Miss Miller explained.

"Has she gone to bed?"

"No, she does n't like to go to bed. She does n't sleep scarcely any—not three hours. She says she does n't know how she lives. She's dreadfully nervous. I guess she sleeps more than she thinks. She's gone somewhere after Randolph; she wants to try to get him to go to bed. He does n't like to go to bed."

The soft impartiality of her *constatations*,[11] as Winterbourne would have termed them, was a thing by itself—exquisite little fatalist as they seemed to make her. "Let us hope she'll persuade him," he encouragingly said.

[11] Statements.

"Well, she'll talk to him all she can—but he does n't like her to talk to him": with which Miss Daisy opened and closed her fan. "She's going to try to get Eugenio to talk to him. But Randolph ain't afraid of Eugenio. Eugenio's a splendid courier, but he can't make much impression on Randolph! I don't believe he'll go to bed before eleven." Her detachment from any invidious judgement of this was, to her companion's sense, inimitable; and it appeared that Randolph's vigil was in fact triumphantly prolonged, for Winterbourne attended her in her stroll for some time without meeting her mother. "I've been looking round for that lady you want to introduce me to," she resumed—"I guess she's your aunt." Then on his admitting the fact and expressing some curiosity as to how she had learned it, she said she had heard all about Mrs. Costello from the chambermaid. She was very quiet and very *comme il faut*; [12] she wore white puffs; she spoke to no one and she never dined at the common table. Every two days she had a headache. "I think that's a lovely description, headache and all!" said Miss Daisy, chattering along in her thin gay voice. "I want to know her ever so much. I know just what *your* aunt would be; I know I'd like her. She'd be very exclusive. I like a lady to be exclusive; I'm dying to be exclusive myself. Well, I guess we *are* exclusive, mother and I. We don't speak to any one—or they don't speak to us. I suppose it's about the same thing. Anyway, I shall be ever so glad to meet your aunt."

Winterbourne was embarrassed—he could but trump up some evasion. "She'd be most happy, but I'm afraid those tiresome headaches are always to be reckoned with."

The girl looked at him through the fine dusk. "Well, I suppose she does n't have a headache every day."

He had to make the best of it. "She tells me she wonderfully does." He didn't know what else to say.

Miss Miller stopped and stood looking at him. Her prettiness was still visible in the darkness; she kept flapping to and fro her enormous fan. "She doesn't want to know me!" she then lightly broke out. "Why don't you say so? You needn't be afraid. *I'm* not afraid!" And she quite crowed for the fun of it.

Winterbourne distinguished however a wee false note in this: he was touched, shocked, mortified by it. "My dear young lady, she knows no one. She goes through life immured. It's her wretched health."

The young girl walked on a few steps in the glee of the thing. "You need n't be afraid," she repeated. "Why should she want to know me?" Then she paused again; she was close to the parapet of the garden, and in front of her was the starlit lake. There was a vague sheen on its surface, and in the distance were dimly-seen mountain forms. Daisy Miller looked out at these great lights and shades and again proclaimed a gay indifference—"Gracious!

[12] Proper.

she *is* exclusive!" Winterbourne wondered if she were seriously wounded and for a moment almost wished her sense of injury might be such as to make it becoming in him to reassure and comfort her. He had a pleasant sense that she would be all accessible to a respectful tenderness at that moment. He felt quite ready to sacrifice his aunt—conversationally; to acknowledge she was a proud rude woman and to make the point that they need n't mind her. But before he had time to commit himself to this questionable mixture of gallantry and impiety, the young lady, resuming her walk, gave an exclamation in quite another tone. "Well, here's mother! I guess she *has n't* got Randolph to go to bed." The figure of a lady appeared, at a distance, very indistinct in the darkness; it advanced with a slow and wavering step and then suddenly seemed to pause.

"Are you sure it's your mother? Can you make her out in this thick dusk?" Winterbourne asked.

"Well," the girl laughed, "I guess I know my own mother! And when she has got on my shawl too. She's always wearing my things."

The lady in question, ceasing now to approach, hovered vaguely about the spot at which she had checked her steps.

"I'm afraid your mother doesn't see you," said Winterbourne. "Or perhaps," he added—thinking, with Miss Miller, the joke permissible—"perhaps she feels guilty about your shawl."

"Oh, it's a fearful old thing!" his companion placidly answered. "I told her she could wear it if she did n't mind looking like a fright. She won't come here because she sees you."

"Ah then," said Winterbourne, "I had better leave you."

"Oh no—come on!" the girl insisted.

"I'm afraid your mother does n't approve of my walking with you."

She gave him, he thought, the oddest glance. "It is n't for me; it's for you—that is it's for *her*. Well, I don't know who it's for! But mother does n't like any of my gentlemen friends. She's right down timid. She always makes a fuss if I introduce a gentleman. But I *do* introduce them—almost always. If I did n't introduce my gentlemen friends to mother," Miss Miller added, in her small falt monotone, "I should n't think I was natural."

"Well, to introduce me," Winterbourne remarked, "you must know my name." And he proceeded to pronounce it.

"Oh my—I can't say all that!" cried his companion, much amused. But by this time they had come up to Mrs. Miller, who, as they drew near, walked to the parapet of the garden and leaned on it, looking intently at the lake and presenting her back to them. "Mother!" said the girl in a tone of decision—upon which the elder lady turned round. "Mr. Frederick Forsyth Winterbourne," said the latter's young friend, repeating his lesson of a moment before and introducing him very frankly and prettily. "Common" she might be, as Mrs. Costello had pronounced her; yet what provision was made by that epithet for her queer little native grace?

Her mother was a small spare light person, with a wandering eye, a scarce perceptible nose, and, as to make up for it, an unmistakeable forehead, decorated—but too far back, as Winterbourne mentally described it—with thin much-frizzled hair. Like her daughter Mrs. Miller was dressed with extreme elegance; she had enormous diamonds in her ears. So far as the young man could observe, she gave him no greeting—she certainly was n't looking at him. Daisy was near her, pulling her shawl straight. "What are you doing, poking round here?" this young lady enquired—yet by no means with the harshness of accent her choice of words might have implied.

"Well, I don't know"—and the new-comer turned to the lake again.

"I should n't think you'd want that shawl!" Daisy familiarly proceeded.

"Well—I do!" her mother answered with a sound that partook for Winterbourne of an odd strain between mirth and woe.

"Did you get Randolph to go to bed?" Daisy asked.

"No, I could n't induce him"—and Mrs. Miller seemed to confess to the same mild fatalism as her daughter. "He wants to talk to the waiter. He *likes* to talk to that waiter."

"I was just telling Mr. Winterbourne," the girl went on; and to the young man's ear her tone might have indicated that she had been uttering his name all her life.

"Oh yes!" he concurred—"I've the pleasure of knowing your son."

Randolph's mamma was silent; she kept her attention on the lake. But at last a sigh broke from her. "Well, I don't see how he lives!"

"Anyhow, it is n't so bad as it was at Dover," Daisy at least opined.

"And what occurred at Dover?" Winterbourne desired to know.

"He would n't go to bed at all. I guess he sat up all night—in the public parlour. He was n't in bed at twelve o'clock: it seemed as if he could n't budge."

"It was half-past twelve when *I* gave up," Mrs. Miller recorded with passionless accuracy.

It was of great interest to Winterbourne. "Does he sleep much during the day?"

"I guess he doesn't sleep *very* much," Daisy rejoined.

"I wish he just *would!*" said her mother. "It seems as if he *must* make it up somehow."

"Well, I guess it's we that make it up. I think he's real tiresome," Daisy pursued.

After which, for some moments, there was silence. "Well, Daisy Miller," the elder lady then unexpectedly broke out, "I shouldn't think you'd want to talk against your own brother!"

"Well, he *is* tiresome, mother," said the girl, but with no sharpness of insistence.

"Well, he's only nine," Mrs. Miller lucidly urged.

"Well, he wouldn't go up to that castle, anyway," her daughter replied as for accomodation. "I'm going up there with Mr. Winterbourne."

To this announcement, very placidly made, Daisy's parent offered no response. Winterbourne took for granted on this that she opposed such a course; but he said to himself at the same time that she was a simple easily-managed person and that few deferential protestations would modify her attitude. "Yes," he therefore interposed, "your daughter has kindly allowed me the honour of being her guide."

Mrs. Miller's wandering eyes attached themselves with an appealing air to her other companion, who, however, strolled a few steps further, gently humming to herself. "I presume you'll go in the cars," she then quite colourlessly remarked.

"Yes, or in the boat," said Winterbourne.

"Well, of course I don't know," Mrs. Miller returned. "I've never been up to that castle."

"It is a pity you should n't go," he observed, beginning to feel reassured as to her opposition. And yet he was quite prepared to find that as a matter of course she meant to accompany her daughter.

It was on this view accordingly that light was projected for him. "We've been thinking ever so much about going, but it seems as if we could n't. Of course Daisy—she wants to go round everywhere. But there's a lady here—I don't know her name—she says she should n't think we'd want to go to see castles *here*; she should think we'd want to wait till we got t' Italy. It seems as if there would be so many there," continued Mrs. Miller with an air of increasing confidence. "Of course we only want to see the principal ones. We visited several in England," she presently added.

"Ah, yes, in England there are beautiful castles," said Winterbourne. "But Chillon here is very well worth seeing."

"Well, if Daisy feels up to it—" said Mrs. Miller in a tone that seemed to break under the burden of such conceptions. "It seems as if there's nothing she won't undertake."

"Oh I'm pretty sure she'll enjoy it!" Winterbourne declared. And he desired more and more to make it a certainty that he was to have the privilege of a *tête-à-tête* with the young lady who was still strolling along in front of them and softly vocalising. "You're not disposed, madam," he enquired, "to make the so interesting excursion yourself?"

So addressed Daisy's mother looked at him an instant with a certain scared obliquity and then walked forward in silence. Then, "I guess she had better go alone," she said simply.

It gave him occasion to note that this was a very different type of maternity from that of the vigilant matrons who massed themselves in the forefront of social intercourse in the dark old city at the other end of the lake. But his meditations were interrupted by hearing his name very distinctly pronounced by Mrs. Miller's unprotected daughter. "Mr. Winterbourne!" she piped from a considerable distance.

"Mademoiselle!" said the young man.

"Don't you want to take me out in a boat?"

"At present?" he asked.

"Why of course!" she gaily returned.

"Well, Annie Miller!" exclaimed her mother.

"I beg you, madam, to let her go," he hereupon eagerly pleaded; so instantly had he been struck with the romantic side of this chance to guide through the summer starlight a skiff freighted with a fresh and beautiful young girl.

"I should n't think she'd want to," said her mother. "I should think she'd rather go indoors."

"I'm sure Mr. Winterbourne wants to *take* me," Daisy declared. "He's so awfully devoted!"

"I'll row you over to Chillon under the stars."

"I don't believe it!" Daisy laughed.

"Well!" the elder lady again gasped, as in rebuke of this freedom.

"You haven't spoken to me for half an hour," her daughter went on.

"I've been having some very pleasant conversation with your mother," Winterbourne replied.

"Oh pshaw! I want you to take me out in a boat!" Daisy went on as if nothing else had been said. They had all stopped and she had turned round and was looking at her friend. Her face wore a charming smile, her pretty eyes gleamed in the darkness, she swung her great fan about. No, he felt, it was impossible to be prettier than that.

"There are half a dozen boats moored at that landing-place," and he pointed to a range of steps that descended from the garden to the lake. "If you'll do me the honour to accept my arm we'll go and select one of them."

She stood there smiling; she threw back her head; she laughed as for the drollery of this. "I like a gentleman to be formal!"

"I assure you it's a formal offer."

"I was bound I'd make you say something," Daisy agreeably mocked.

"You see it's not very difficult," said Winterbourne. "But I'm afraid you're chaffing me."

"I think not, sir," Mrs. Miller shyly pleaded.

"Do then let me give you a row," he persisted to Daisy.

"It's quite lovely, the way you say that!" she cried in reward.

"It will be still more lovely to do it."

"Yes, it would be lovely!" But she made no movement to accompany him; she only remained an elegant image of free light irony.

"I guess you'd better find out what time it is," her mother impartially contributed.

"It's eleven o'clock, Madam," said a voice with a foreign accent out of the neighbouring darkness; and Winterbourne, turning, recognised the florid personage he had already seen in attendance. He had apparently just approached.

"Oh Eugenio," said Daisy, "I'm going out with Mr. Winterbourne in a boat!"

Eugenio bowed. "At this hour of the night, Mademoiselle?"

"I'm going with Mr. Winterbourne," she repeated with her shining smile. "I'm going this very minute."

"Do tell her she can't, Eugenio," Mrs. Miller said to the courier.

"I think you had better not go out in a boat, Mademoiselle," the man declared.

Winterbourne wished to goodness this pretty girl were not on such familiar terms with her courier; but he said nothing, and she meanwhile added to his ground. "I suppose you don't think it's proper! My!" she wailed; "Eugenio does n't think anything's proper."

"I'm nevertheless quite at your service," Winterbourne hastened to remark.

"Does Mademoiselle propose to go alone?" Eugenio asked of Mrs. Miller.

"Oh no, with this gentleman!" cried Daisy's mamma for reassurance.

"I *meant* alone with the gentleman." The courier looked for a moment at Winterbourne—the latter seemed to make out in his face a vague presumptuous intelligence as at the expense of their companions—and then solemnly and with a bow, "As Mademoiselle pleases!" he said.

But Daisy broke off at this. "Oh I hoped you'd make a fuss! I don't care to go now."

"Ah but I myself shall make a fuss if you don't go," Winterbourne declared with spirit.

"That's all I want—a little fuss!" With which she began to laugh again.

"Mr. Randolph has retired for the night!" the courier hereupon importantly announced.

"Oh Daisy, now we can go then!" cried Mrs. Miller.

Her daughter turned away from their friend, all lighted with her odd perversity. "Good-night—I hope you're disappointed or disgusted or something!"

He looked at her gravely, taking her by the hand she offered. "I'm puzzled, if you want to know!" he answered.

"Well, I hope it won't keep you awake!" she said very smartly; and, under the escort of the privilegd Eugenio, the two ladies passed toward the house.

Winterbourne's eyes followed them; he was indeed quite mystified. He lingered beside the lake a quarter of an hour, baffled by the question of the girl's sudden familiarities and caprices. But the only very definite conclusion he came to was that he should enjoy deucedly "going off" with her some-where.

Two days later he went off with her to the Castle of Chillon. He waited for her in the large hall of the hotel, where the couriers, the servants, the foreign tourists were lounging about and staring. It wasn't the place he would have chosen for a tryst, but she had placidly appointed it. She came tripping downstairs, buttoning her long gloves, squeezing her folded parasol against her pretty figure, dressed exactly in the way that consorted best, to his fancy, with their adventure. He was a man of imagination and, as our ancestors used to say, of sensibility; as he took in her charming air and caught from the great staircase her impatient confiding step the note of some small sweet strain of romance, not intense but clear and sweet, seemed to sound for their start. He could have believed he was *really* going "off" with her. He led her out through all the idle people assembled—they all looked at her straight and hard: she had begun to chatter as soon as she joined him. His preference had been that they should be conveyed to Chillon in a carriage, but she expressed a lively wish to go in the little steamer—there would be such a lovely breeze upon the water and they should see such lots of people. The sail was n't long, but Winterbourne's companion found time for many characteristic remarks and other demonstrations, not a few of which were, from the extremity of their candour, slightly disconcerting. To the young man himself their small excursion showed so for delightfully irregular and incongruously intimate that, even allowing for her habitual sense of freedom, he had some expectation of seeing her appear to find in it the same savour. But it must be confessed that he was in this particular rather disappointed. Miss Miller was highly animated, she was in the brightest spirits; but she was clearly not at all in a nervous flutter—as she should have been to match *his* tension; she avoided neither his eyes nor those of any one else; she neither coloured from an awkward consciousness when she looked at him nor when she saw that people were looking at herself. People continued to look at her a great deal, and Winterbourne could at least take pleasure in his pretty companion's distinguished air. He had been privately afraid she would talk loud, laugh overmuch, and even perhaps desire to move extravagantly about the boat. But he quite forgot his fears; he sat smiling with his eyes on her face while, without stirring from her place, she delivered herself of a great number of original reflexions. It was the most charming innocent prattle he had ever heard, for, by his own experience hitherto, when young persons were so ingenuous they were less articulate and when they were so confident were more sophisticated. If he had assented to the idea that she was "common," at any rate, *was* she proving so, after all, or was he simply getting used to her commonness? Her discourse was for the most part of what immediately and superficially surrounded them, but there were moments when it threw out a longer look or took a sudden straight plunge.

"What on *earth* are you so solemn about?" she suddenly demanded, fixing her agreeable eyes on her friend's.

"*Am* I solemn?" he asked. "I had an idea I was grinning from ear to ear."

"You look as if you were taking me to a prayer-meeting or a funeral. If that's a grin your ears are very near together."

"Should you like me to dance a hornpipe on the deck?"

"Pray do, and I'll carry round your hat. It will pay the expenses of our journey."

"I never was better pleased in my life," Winterbourne returned.

She looked at him a moment, then let it renew her amusement. "I like to make you say those things. You're a queer mixture!"

In the castle, after they had landed, nothing could exceed the light independence of her humor. She tripped about the vaulted chambers, rustled her skirts in the corkscrew staircases, flirted back with a pretty littly cry and a shudder from the edge of the oubliettes[13] and turned a singularly well-shaped ear to everything Winterbourne told her about the place. But he saw she cared little for mediaeval history and that the grim ghosts of Chillon loomed but faintly before her. They had the good fortune to have been able to wander without other society than that of their guide; and Winterbourne arranged with this companion that they shouldn't be hurried—that they should linger and pause wherever they chose. He interpreted the bargain generously—Winterbourne on his side had been generous—and ended by leaving them quite to themselves. Miss Miller's observations were marked by no logical consistency; for anything she wanted to say she was sure to find a pretext. She found a great many, in the tortuous passages and rugged embrasures of the place, for asking her young man sudden questions about himself, his family, his previous history, his tastes, his habits, his designs, and for supplying information on corresponding points in her own situation. Of her own tastes, habits and designs the charming creature was prepared to give the most definite and indeed the most favourable account.

"Well, I hope you know enough!" she exclaimed after Winterbourne had sketched for her something of the story of the unhappy Bonnivard.[14] "I never saw a man that knew so much!" The history of Bonnivard had evidently, as they say, gone into one ear and out of the other. But this easy erudition struck her none the less as wonderful, and she was soon quite sure she wished Winterbourne would travel with them and "go round" with them: they too in that case might learn something about something. "Don't you want to come and teach Randolph?" she asked; "I guess he'd improve with a gentleman teacher." Winterbourne was certain that nothing could possibly please him so much, but that he had unfortunately other occupa-

[13] French dungeon cells; holes in the ground with grillwork tops.

[14] The hero of Byron's "The Prisoner of Chillon," Francois de Bonivard (1496?-1570) was a Swiss patriot held prisoner in the Castle of Chillon.

tions. "Other occupations? I don't believe a speck of it!" she protested. "What do you mean now? You're not in business." The young man allowed that he was not in business, but he had engagements which even within a day or two would necessitate his return to Geneva. "Oh bother!" she panted, "I don't believe it!" and she began to talk about something else. But a few moments later, when he was pointing out to her the interesting design of an antique fireplace, she broke out irrelevantly: "You don't mean to say you're going back to Geneva?"

"It is a melancholy fact that I shall have to report myself there to-morrow."

She met it with a vivacity that could only flatter him. "Well, Mr. Winterbourne, I think you're horrid!"

"Oh don't say such dreadful things!" he quite sincerely pleaded—"just at the last."

"The last?" the girl cried; "I call it the very first! I've half a mind to leave you here and go straight back to the hotel alone." And for the next ten minutes she did nothing but call him horrid. Poor Winterbourne was fairly bewildered; no young lady had as yet done him the honour to be so agitated by the mention of his personal plans. His companion, after this, ceased to pay any attention to the curiosities of Chillon or the beauties of the lake; she opened fire on the special charmer in Geneva whom she appeared to have instantly taken it for granted that he was hurrying back to see. How did Miss Daisy Miller know of that agent of his fate in Geneva? Winterbourne, who denied the existence of such a person, was quite unable to discover; and he was divided between amazement at the rapidity of her induction and amusement at the directness of her criticism. She struck him afresh, in all this, as an extraordinary mixture of innocence and crudity. "Does she never allow you more than three days at a time?" Miss Miller wished ironically to know. "Does n't she give you a vacation in summer? there's no one so hard-worked but they can get leave to go off somewhere at this season. I suppose if you stay another day she'll come right after you in the boat. Do wait over till Friday and I'll go down to the landing to see her arrive!" He began at last even to feel he had been wrong to be disappointed in the temper in which his young lady had embarked. If he had missed the personal accent, the personal accent was now making its appearance. It sounded very distinctly, toward the end, in her telling him she'd stop "teasing" him if he'd promise her solemnly to come down to Rome that winter.

"That's not a difficult promise to make," he hastened to acknowledge. "My aunt has taken an apartment in Rome from January and has already asked me to come and see her."

"I don't want you to come for your aunt," said Daisy; "I want you just to come for me." And this was the only allusion he was ever to hear her make again to his invidious kinswoman. He promised her that at any rate he would certainly come, and after this she forbore from teasing. Winterbourne took a carriage and they drove back to Vevey in the dusk; the girl at his side, her animation a little spent, was now quite distractingly passive.

In the evening he mentioned to Mrs. Costello that he had spent the afternoon at Chillon with Miss Daisy Miller.

"The Americans—of the courier?" asked this lady.

"Ah happily the courier stayed at home."

"She went with you all alone?"

"All alone."

Mrs. Costello sniffed a little at her smelling-bottle. "And that," she exclaimed, "is the little abomination you wanted me to know!"

III

Winterbourne, who had returned to Geneva the day after his excursion to Chillon, went to Rome toward the end of January. His aunt had been established there a considerable time and he had received from her a couple of characteristic letters. "Those people you were so devoted to last summer at Vevey have turned up here, courier and all," she wrote. "They seem to have made several acquaintances, but the courier continues to be the most *intime*. The young lady, however, is also very intimate with various third-rate Italians, with whom she rackets about in a way that makes much talk. Bring me that pretty novel of Cherbuliez's[15]—'Paule Méré'—and don't come later than the 23d."

Our friend would in the natural course of events, on arriving in Rome, have presently ascertained Mrs. Miller's address at the American banker's and gone to pay his compliments to Miss Daisy. "After what happened at Vevey I certainly think I may call upon them," he said to Mrs. Costello.

"If after what happens—at Vevey and everywhere—you desire to keep up the acquaintance, you're very welcome. Of course you're not squeamish—a man may know every one. Men are welcome to the privilege!"

"Pray what is it then that 'happens'—here for instance?" Winterbourne asked.

"Well, the girl tears about alone with her unmistakeably low foreigners. As to what happens further you must apply elsewhere for information. She has picked up half a dozen of the regular Roman fortune-hunters of the inferior sort and she takes them about to such houses as she may put *her* nose into. When she comes to a party—such a party as she can come to—she brings with her a gentleman with a good deal of manner and a wonderful moustache."

"And where's the mother?"

"I have n't the least idea. They're very dreadful people."

[15] Victor Cherbuliez's (1829–1899).

Winterbourne thought them over in these new lights. "They're very ignorant—very innocent only, and utterly uncivilised. Depend on it they're not 'bad.'"

"They're hopelessly vulgar," said Mrs. Costello. "Whether or no being hopelessly vulgar is being 'bad' is a question for the metaphysicians. They're bad enought to blush for, at any rate; and for this short life that's quite enough."

The news that his little friend the child of nature of the Swiss lakeside was now surrounded by half a dozen wonderful moustaches checked Winterbourne's impulse to go straightway to see her. He had perhaps not definitely flattered himself that he had made an ineffaceable impression upon her heart, but he was annoyed at hearing of a state of affairs so little in harmony with an image that had lately flitted in and out of his own meditations; the image of a very pretty girl looking out of an old Roman window and asking herself urgently when Mr. Winterbourne would arrive. If, however, he determined to wait a little before reminding this young lady of his claim to her faithful remembrance, he called with more promptitude on two or three other friends. One of these friends was an American lady who had spent several winters at Geneva, where she had placed her children at school. She was a very accomplished woman and she lived in Via Gregoriana. Winterbourne found her in a little crimson drawing-room on a third floor; the room was filled with southern sunshine. He had n't been there ten minutes when the servant, appearing in the doorway, announced complacently "Madame Mila!" This announcement was presently followed by the entrance of little Randolph Miller, who stopped in the middle of the room and stood staring at Winterbourne. An instant later his pretty sister crossed the threshold; and then, after a considerable interval, the parent of the pair slowly advanced.

"I guess I know you!" Randolph broke ground without delay.

"I'm sure you know a great many things"—and his old friend clutched him all interestedly by the arm. "How's your education coming on?"

Daisy was engaged in some pretty babble with her hostess, but when she heard Winterbourne's voice she quickly turned her head with a "Well, I declare!" which he met smiling. "I told you I should come, you know."

"Well, I did n't believe it," she answered.

"I'm much obliged to you for that," laughed the young man.

"You might have come to see me then," Daisy went on as if they had parted the week before.

"I arrived only yesterday."

"I don't believe any such thing!" the girl declared afresh.

Winterbourne turned with a protesting smile to her mother, but this lady evaded his glance and, seating herself, fixed her eyes on her son. "We've got a bigger place than this," Randolph hereupon broke out. "It's all gold on the walls."

chair. "I told you if I was to bring you you'd say something!" she stated as for the benefit of such of the company as might hear it.

"I told *you!*" Randolph retorted. "I tell *you,* sir!" he added jocosely, giving Winterbourne a thump on the knee. "It *is* bigger too!"

As Daisy's conversation with her hostess still occupied her Winterbourne judged it becoming to address a few words to her mother—such as "I hope you've been well since we parted at Vevey."

Mrs. Miller now certainly looked at him—at his chin. "Not very well, sir," she answered.

"She's got the dyspepsia," said Randolph. "I've got it too. Father's got it bad. But I've got it worst!"

This proclamation, instead of embarrassing Mrs. Miller, seemed to soothe her by reconstituting the environment to which she was most accustomed. "I suffer from the liver," she amiably whined to Winterbourne. "I think it's this climate; it's less bracing than Schenectady, especially in the winter season. I don't know whether you know we reside at Schenectady. I was saying to Daisy that I certainly had n't found any one like Dr. Davis and I did n't believe I *would.* Oh up in Schenectady, he stands first; they think everything of Dr. Davis. He has so much to do, and yet there was nothing he would n't do for *me.* He said he never saw anything like my dyspepsia, but he was bound to get at it. I'm sure there was nothing he would n't try, and I did n't care what he did to me if he only brought me relief. He was just going to try something new, and I just longed for it, when we came right off. Mr. Miller felt as if he wanted Daisy to see Europe for herself. But I couldn't help writing the other day that I supposed it was all right for Daisy, but that I didn't know as I *could* get on much longer without Dr. Davis. At Schenectady he stands at the very top; and there's a great deal of sickness there too. It affects my sleep."

Winterbourne had a good deal of pathological gossip with Dr. Davis's patient, during which Daisy chattered unremittingly to her own companion. The young man asked Mrs. Miller how she was pleased with Rome. "Well, I must say I'm disappointed," she confessed. "We had heard so much about it—I suppose we had heard too much. But we could n't help that. We had been led to expect something different."

Winterbourne, however, abounded in reassurance. "Ah wait a little, and you'll grow very fond of it."

"I hate it worse and worse every day!" cried Randolph.

"You're like the infant Hannibal," his friend laughed.

"No I ain't—like any infant!" Randolph declared at a venture.

"Well, that's so—and you never *were!*" his mother concurred. "But we've seen places," she resumed, "that I'd put a long way ahead of Rome." And in reply to Winterbourne's interrogation, "There's Zürich—up there in the mountains," she instanced; "I think Zürich's real lovely, and we had n't heard half so much about it."

"The best place we've seen's the *City of Richmond!*" said Randolph. "He means the ship," Mrs. Miller explained. "We crossed in that ship. Randolph had a good time on the *City of Richmond.*"

"It's the best place *I've* struck," the child repeated. "Only it was turned the wrong way."

"Well, we've got to turn the right way sometime," said Mrs. Miller with strained but weak optimism. Winterbourne expressed the hope that her daughter at least appreciated the so various interests of Rome, and she declared with some spirit that Daisy was quite carried away. "It's on account of the society—the society's splendid. She goes round everywhere; she has made a great number of acquaintances. Of course she goes round more than I do. I must say they've all been very sweet—they've taken her right in. And then she knows a great many gentlemen. Oh she thinks there's nothing like Rome. Of course it's a great deal pleasanter for a young lady if she knows plenty of gentlemen."

By this time Daisy had turned her attention again to Winterbourne, but in quite the same free form. "I've been telling Mrs. Walker how mean you were!"

"And what's the evidence you've offered?" he asked, a trifle disconcerted, for all his superior gallantry, by her inadequate measure of the zeal of an admirer who on his way down to Rome had stopped neither at Bologna nor at Florence, simply because of a certain sweet appeal to his fond fancy, not to say to his finest curiosity. He remembered how a cynical compatriot had once told him that American women—the pretty ones, and this gave a largeness to the axiom—were at once the most exacting in the world and the least endowed with a sense of indebtedness.

"Why you were awfully mean up at Vevey," Daisy said. "You would n't do most anything. You would n't stay there when I asked you."

"Dearest young lady," cried Winterbourne, with generous passion, "have I come all the way to Rome only to be riddled by your silver shafts?"

"Just hear him say that!"—and she gave an affectionate twist to a bow on her hostess's dress. "Did you ever hear anything so quaint?"

"So 'quaint,' my dear?" echoed Mrs. Walker more critically—quite in the tone of a partisan of Winterbourne.

"Well, I don't know"—the girl continued to finger her ribbons. "Mrs. Walker, I want to tell you something."

"Say, mother-r," broke in Randolph with his rough ends to his words, "I tell you you've got to go. Eugenio'll raise something!"

"I'm not afraid of Eugenio," said Daisy with a toss of her head. "Look here, Mrs. Walker," she went on, "you know I'm coming to your party."

"I'm delighted to hear it."

"I've got a lovely dress."

"I'm sure of that."

"But I want to ask a favour—permission to bring a friend."

"I shall be happy to see any of your friends," said Mrs. Walker, who turned with a smile to Mrs. Miller.

"Oh they 're not friends," cried that lady, squirming in shy repudiation. "It seems as if they did n't take to *me*—I never spoke to one of them!"

"It's an intimate friend of mine, Mr. Giovanelli," Daisy pursued without a tremor in her young clearness or a shadow on her shining bloom.

Mrs. Walker had a pause and gave a rapid glance at Winterbourne. "I shall be glad to see Mr. Giovanelli," she then returned.

"He's just the finest kind of Italian," Daisy pursued with the prettiest serenity. "He's a great friend of mine and the handsomest man in the world—except Mr. Winterbourne! He knows plenty of Italians, but he wants to know some Americans. It seems as if he was crazy about Americans. He's tremendously bright. He's perfectly lovely!"

It was settled that this paragon should be brought to Mrs. Walker's party, and then Mrs. Miller prepared to take her leave. "I guess we'll go right back to the hotel," she remarked with a confessed failure of the larger imagination.

"You may go back to the hotel, mother," Daisy replied, "but I'm just going to walk round."

"She's going to go it with Mr. Giovanelli," Randolph unscrupulously commented.

"I'm going to go it on the Pincio,"[16] Daisy peaceably smiled, while the way that she "condoned" these things almost melted Winterbourne's heart.

"Alone, my dear—at this hour?" Mrs. Walker asked. The afternoon was drawing to a close—it was the hour for the throng of carriages and of contemplative pedestrians. "I don't consider it's safe, Daisy," her hostess firmly asserted.

"Neither do I then," Mrs. Miller thus borrowed confidence to add. "You'll catch the fever as sure as you live. Remember what Dr. Davis told you!"

"Giver her some of that medicine before she starts in," Randolph suggested.

The company had risen to its feet; Daisy, still showing her pretty teeth, bent over and kissed her hostess. "Mrs. Walker, you're too perfect," she simply said. "I'm not going alone; I'm going to meet a friend."

"Your friend won't keep you from catching the fever even if it *is* his own second nature," Mrs. Miller observed.

"Is it Mr. Giovanelli that's the dangerous attraction?" Mrs. Walker asked without mercy.

Winterbourne was watching the challenged girl; at this his attention quickened. She stood there smiling and smoothing her bonnet-ribbons; she

---

[16] One of the hills of Rome with a splendid view of the city.

glanced at Winterbourne. Then, while she glanced and smiled, she brought out all affirmatively and without a shade of hesitation: "Mr. Giovanelli—the beautiful Giovanelli."

"My dear young friend"—and, taking her hand, Mrs. Walker turned to pleading—"don't prowl off to the Pincio at this hour to meet a beautiful Italian."

"Well, he speaks first-rate English," Mrs. Miller incoherently mentioned.

"Gracious me," Daisy piped up, "I don't want to do anything that's going to affect my health—or my character either! There's an easy way to settle it." Her eyes continued to play over Winterbourne. "The Pincio's only a hundred yards off, and if Mr. Winterbourne were as polite as he pretends he'd offer to walk right in with me!"

Winterbourne's politeness hastened to proclaim itself, and the girl gave him gracious leave to accompany her. They passed downstairs before her mother, and at the door he saw Mrs. Miller's carriage drawn up, with the ornamental courier whose acquaintance he had made at Vevey seated within. "Good-bye, Eugenio," cried Daisy; "I'm going to take a walk!" The distance from Via Gregoriana to the beautiful garden at the other end of the Pincian Hill is in fact rapidly traversed. As the day was splendid, however, and the concourse of vehicles, walkers and loungers numerous, the young Americans found their progress much delayed. This fact was highly agreeable to Winterbourne, in spite of his consciousness of his singular situation. The slow-moving, idly-gazing Roman crowd bestowed much attention on the extremely pretty young woman of English race who passed through it, with some difficulty, on his arm; and he wondered what on earth had been in Daisy's mind when she proposed to exhibit herself unattended to its appreciation. His own mission, to her sense, was apparently to consign her to the hands of Mr. Giovanelli; but, at once annoyed and gratified, he resolved that he would do no such thing.

"Why have n't you been to see me?" she meanwhile asked. "You can't get out of that."

"I've had the honour of telling you that I've only just stepped out of the train."

"You must have stayed in the train a good while after it stopped!" she derisively cried. "I suppose you were asleep. You've had time to go to see Mrs. Walker."

"I knew Mrs. Walker—" Winterbourne began to explain.

"I know where you knew her. You knew her at Geneva. She told me so. Well, you knew me at Vevey. That's just as good. So you ought to have come." She asked him no other question than this; she began to prattle about her own affairs. "We've got splendid rooms at the hotel; Eugenio says they 're the best in Rome. We're going to stay all winter—if we don't die of the fever; and I guess we'll stay then! It's a great deal nicer than I thought; I thought it would be fearfully quiet—in fact I was sure it would be deadly pokey. I foresaw we should be going round all the time with one of those dreadful old men who explain about the pictures and things. But we only had about a week of that, and now I'm enjoying myself. I know ever so many people, and they're all so charming. The society's extremely select. There are all kinds—English and Germans and Italians. I think I like the English best. I like their style of conversation. But there are some lovely Americans. I never saw anything so hospitable. There's something or other every day. There's not much dancing—but I must say I never thought dancing was everything. I was always fond of conversation. I guess I'll have plenty at Mrs. Walker's—her rooms are so small." When they had passed the gate of the Pincian Gardens Miss Miller began to wonder where Mr. Giovanelli might be. "We had better go straight to that place in front, where you look at the view."

Winterbourne at this took a stand. "I certainly shan't help you to find him."

"Then I shall find him without you," Daisy said with spirit.

"You certainly won't leave me!" he protested.

She burst into her familiar little laugh. "Are you afraid you'll get lost—or run over? But there's Giovanelli leaning against that tree. He's staring at the women in the carriages: did you ever see anything so cool?"

Winterbourne descried hereupon at some distance a little figure that stood with folded arms and nursing its cane. It had a handsome face, a hat artfully poised, a glass in one eye and a nosegay in its buttonhole. Daisy's friend looked at it a moment and then said: "Do you mean to speak to that thing?"

"Do I mean to speak to him? Why you don't suppose I mean to communicate by signs!"

"Pray understand then," the young man returned, "that I intend to remain with you."

Daisy stopped and looked at him without a sign of troubled consciousness, with nothing in her face but her charming eyes, her charming teeth and her happy dimples. "Well, she's a cool one!" he thought.

"I don't like the way you say that," she declared. "It's too imperious."

"I beg your pardon if I say it wrong. The main point's to give you an idea of my meaning."

The girl looked at him more gravely, but with eyes that were prettier than ever. "I've never allowed a gentleman to dictate to me or to interfere with anything I do."

"I think that's just where your mistake has come in," he retorted. "You should sometimes listen to a gentleman—the right one."

At this she began to laugh again. "I do nothing but listen to gentlemen! Tell me if Mr. Giovanelli is the right one."

The gentleman with the nosegay in his bosom had now made out our two friends and was approaching Miss Miller with obsequious rapidity. He bowed to Winterbourne as well as to the latter's compatriot; he seemed to shine, in his coxcombical way, with the desire to please and the fact of his own intelligent joy, though Winterbourne thought him not a bad-looking fellow. But he nevertheless said to Daisy: "No, he's not the right one."

She had clearly a natural turn for free introductions; she mentioned with the easiest grace the name of each of her companions to the other. She strolled forward with one of them on either hand; Mr. Giovanelli, who spoke English very cleverly—Winterbourne afterwards learned that he had practised the idiom upon a great many American heiresses—addressed her a great deal of very polite nonsense. He had the best possible manners, and the young American, who said nothing, reflected on that depth of Italian subtlety, so strangely opposed to Anglo-Saxon simplicity, which enables people to show a smoother surface in proportion as they're more acutely displeased. Giovanelli of course had counted upon something more intimate—he had not bargained for a party of three; but he kept his temper in a manner that suggested far-stretching intentions. Winterbourne flattered himself he had taken his measure. "He's anything but a gentleman," said the young American; "he is n't even a plausible imitation of one. He's a music-master or a penny-a-liner[17] or a third-rate artist. He's awfully on his good behaviour, but damn his fine eyes!" Mr. Giovanelli had indeed great advantages; but it was deeply disgusting to Daisy's other friend that something in her should n't have instinctively discriminated against such a type. Giovanelli chattered and jested and made himself agreeable according to his honest Roman lights. It was true that if he was an imitation the imitation was studied. "Nevertheless," Winterbourne said to himself, "a nice girl ought to know!" And then he came back to the dreadful question of whether this *was* in fact a nice girl. Would a nice girl—even allowing for her being a little American flirt—make a rendezvous with a presumably low-lived foreigner? The rendezvous in this case indeed had been in broad daylight and in the most crowded corner of Rome; but was n't it possible to regard the choice of these very circumstances as a proof more of vulgarity than of anything else? Singular though it may seem, Winterbourne was vexed that the girl, in joining her *amoroso*,[18] should n't appear more impatient of his own company, and he was vexed precisely because of his inclination. It was impossible to regard her as a wholly unspotted flower—she lacked a certain indispensable fineness; and it would therefore much simplify the situation to be able to treat her as the subject of one of the visitations known to romancers as "lawless passions." That she should seem to wish to get rid of him would have helped him to think more lightly of her, just as to be able to think more lightly of her would have made her less perplexing. Daisy at any rate continued on this occasion to present herself as an inscrutable combination of audacity and innocence.

[17] A hack writer. [18] Suitor.

She had been walking some quarter of an hour, attended by her two cavaliers and responding in a tone of very childish gaiety, as it after all struck one of them, to the pretty speeches of the other, when a carriage that had detached itself from the revolving train drew up beside the path. At the same moment Winterbourne noticed that his friend Mrs. Walker—the lady whose house he had lately left—was seated in the vehicle and was beckoning to him. Leaving Miss Miller's side, he hastened to obey her summons—and all to find her flushed, excited, scandalised. "It's really too dreadful"—she earnestly appealed to him. "That crazy girl must n't do this sort of thing. She mus n't walk here with you two men. Fifty people have remarked her."

Winterbourne—suddenly and rather oddly rubbed the wrong way by this—raised his grave eyebrows. "I think it's a pity to make too much fuss about it."

"It's a pity to let the girl ruin herself!"

"She's very innocent," he reasoned in his own troubled interest.

"She's very reckless," cried Mrs. Walker, "and goodness knows how far— left to itself—it may go. Did you ever," she proceeded to enquire, "see anything so blatantly imbecile as the mother? After you had all left me just now I could n't sit still for thinking of it. It seemed too pitiful not even to attempt to save them. I ordered the carriage and put on my bonnet and came here as quickly as possible. Thank heaven I've found you!"

"What do you propose to do with us?" Winterbourne uncomfortably smiled.

"To ask her to get in, to drive her about here for half an hour—so that the world may see she's not running absolutely wild—and then take her safely home."

"I don't think it's a very happy thought," he said after reflexion, "but you're at liberty to try."

Mrs. Walker accordingly tried. The young man went in pursuit of their young lady who had simply nodded and smiled, from her distance, at her recent patroness in the carriage and then had gone her way with her own companion. On learning, in the event, that Mrs. Walker had followed her, she retraced her steps, however, with a perfect good grace and with Mr. Giovanelli at her side. She professed herself "enchanted" to have a chance to present this gentleman to her good friend, and immediately achieved the introduction; declaring with it, and as if it were of as little importance, that she had never in her life seen anything so lovely as that lady's carriage-rug.

"I'm glad you admire it," said her poor pursuer, smiling sweetly. "Will you get in and let me put it over you?"

"Oh no, thank you!"—Daisy knew her mind. "I'll admire it ever so much more as I see you driving round with it."

"Do get in and drive round *with* me," Mrs. Walker pleaded.

"That would be charming, but it's so fascinating just as I am!"—with which the girl radiantly took in the gentlemen on either side of her.

"It may be fascinating, dear child, but it's not the custom here," urged the lady of the victoria,[19] leaning forward in this vehicle with her hands devoutly clasped.

"Well, it ought to be then!" Daisy imperturbably laughed. "If I did n't walk I'd expire."

"You should walk with your mother, dear," cried Mrs. Walker with a loss of patience.

"With my mother dear?" the girl amusedly echoed. Winterbourne saw she scented interference. "My mother never walked ten steps in her life. And then, you know," she blandly added, "I'm more than five years old."

"You're old enough to be more reasonable. You're old enough, dear Miss Miller, to be talked about."

Daisy wondered to extravagance. "Talked about? What do you mean?"

"Come into my carriage and I'll tell you."

Daisy turned shining eyes again from one of the gentlemen beside her to the other. Mr. Giovanelli was bowing to and fro, rubbing down his gloves and laughing irresponsibly; Winterbourne thought the scene the most unpleasant possible. "I don't think I want to know what you mean," the girl presently said. "I don't think I should like it."

Winterbourne wished Mrs. Walker would tuck up her carriage-rug and drive away; but this lady, as she afterwards told him, did n't feel she could "rest there." "Should you prefer being thought a very reckless girl?" she accordingly asked.

"Gracious me!" exclaimed Daisy. She looked again at Mr. Giovanelli, then she turned to her other companion. There was a small pink flush in her cheek; she was tremendously pretty. "Does Mr. Winterbourne think," she put to him with a wonderful bright intensity of appeal, "that—to save my reputation—I ough to get into the carriage?"

It really embarrassed him; for an instant he cast about—so strange was it to hear her speak that way of her "reputation." But he himself in fact had to speak in accordance with gallantry. The finest gallantry here was surely just to tell her the truth; and the truth, for our young man, as the few indications I have been able to give have made him known to the reader, was that his charming friend should listen to the voice of civilised society. He took in again her exquisite prettiness and then said the more distinctly: "I think you should get into the carriage."

Daisy gave the rein to her amusement. "I never heard anything so stiff! If this is improper, Mrs. Walker," she pursued, "then I'm *all* improper, and you had better give me right up. Good-bye; I hope you'll have a lovely ride!"— and with Mr. Giovanelli, who made a triumphantly obsequious salute, she turned away.

---

[19] A carriage.

Mrs. Walker sat looking after her, and there were tears in Mrs. Walker's eyes. "Get in here, sir," she said to Winterbourne, indicating the place beside her. The young man answered that he felt bound to accompany Miss Miller; whereupon the lady of the victoria declared that if he refused her this favour she would never speak to him again. She was evidently wound up. He accordingly hastened to overtake Daisy and her more faithful ally, and, offering her his hand, told her that Mrs. Walker had made a stringent claim on his presence. He had expected her to answer with something rather free, something still more significant of the perversity from which the voice of society, through the lips of their distressed friend, had so earnestly endeavoured to dissuade her. But she only let her hand slip, as she scarce looked at him, through his slightly awkward grasp; while Mr. Giovanelli, to make it worse, bade him farewell with too emphatic a flourish of the hat.

Winterbourne was not in the best possible humour as he took his seat beside the author of his sacrifice. "That was not clever of you," he said candidly, as the vehicle mingled again with the throng of carriages.

"In such a case," his companion answered, "I don't want to be clever—I only want to be *true!*"

"Well, your truth has only offended the strange little creature—it has only put her off."

"It has happened very well"—Mrs. Walker accepted her work. "If she's so perfectly determined to compromise herself the sooner one knows it the better—one can act accordingly."

"I suspect she meant no great harm, you know," Winterbourne maturely opined.

"So I thought a month ago. But she has been going too far."

"What has she been doing?"

"Everything that's not done here. Flirting with any man she can pick up; sitting in corners with mysterious Italians; dancing all the evening with the same partners; receiving visits at eleven o'clock at night. Her mother melts away when the visitors come."

"But her brother," laughed Winterbourne, "sits up till two in the morning."

"He must be edified by what he sees. I'm told that at their hotel every one's talking about her and that a smile goes round among the servants when a gentleman comes and asks for Miss Miller."

"Ah we need n't mind the servants!" Winterbourne compassionately signified. "The poor girl's only fault," he presently added, "is her complete lack of education."

"She's naturally indelicate," Mrs. Walker, on her side, reasoned. "Take that example this morning. How long had you known her at Vevey?"

"A couple of days."

"Imagine then the taste of her making it a personal matter that you should have left the place!"

He agreed that taste wasn't the strong point of the Millers—after which he was silent for some moments; but only at last to add: "I suspect, Mrs. Walker, that you and I have lived too long at Geneva!" And he further noted that he should be glad to learn with what particular design she had made him enter her carriage.

"I wanted to enjoin on you the importance of your ceasing your relations with Miss Miller; that of your not appearing to flirt with her; that of your giving her no further opportunity to expose herself; that of your in short letting her alone."

"I'm afraid I can't do anything quite so enlightened as *that*," he returned. "I like her awfully, you know."

"All the more reason you should n't help her to make a scandal."

"Well, there shall be nothing scandalous in my attentions to her," he was willing to promise.

"There certainly will be in the way she takes them. But I've said what I had on my conscience," Mrs. Walker pursued. "If you wish to rejoin the young lady I'll put you down. Here, by the way, you have a chance."

The carriage was engaged in that part of the Pincian drive which over-hangs the wall of Rome and overlooks the beautiful Villa Borghese. It is bordered by a large parapet, near which are several seats. One of these, at a distance, was occupied by a gentleman and a lady, toward whom Mrs. Walker gave a toss of her head. At the same moment these persons rose and walked to the parapet. Winterbourne had asked the coachman to stop; he now descended from the carriage. His companion looked at him a moment in silence and then, while he raised his hat, drove majestically away. He stood where he had alighted; he had turned his eyes toward Daisy and her cavalier. They evidently saw no one; they were too deeply occupied with each other. When they reached the low garden-wall they remained a little looking off at the great flat-topped pine-clusters of Villa Borghese; then the girl's attendant admirer seated himself familiarly on the broad ledge of the wall. The western sun in the opposite sky sent out a brilliant shaft through a couple of cloud-bars; whereupon the gallant Giovanelli took her parasol out of her hands and opened it. She came a little nearer and he held the parasol over her; then, still holding it, he let it so rest on her shoulder that both of their heads were hidden from Winterbourne. This young man stayed but a moment longer; then he began to walk. But he walked—not toward the couple united beneath the parasol, rather toward the residence of his aunt Mrs. Costello.

IV

He flattered himself on the following day that there was no smiling among the servants when he at least asked for Mrs. Miller at her hotel. This lady and her daughter, however, were not at home; and on the next day after, repeating his visit, Winterbourne again was met by a denial. Mrs. Walker's party took place on the evening of the third day, and in spite of the final reserves that had marked his last interview with that social critic our young man was among the guests. Mrs. Walker was one of those pilgrims from the younger world who, while in contract with the elder, make a point, in their own phrase, of studying European society; and she had on this occasion collected several specimens of diversely-born humanity to serve, as might be, for text-books. When Winterbourne arrived the little person he desired most to find was n't there; but in a few moments he saw Mrs. Miller come in alone, very shyly and ruefully. This lady's hair, above the dead waste of her temples, was more frizzled than ever. As she approached their hostess Winterbourne also drew near.

"You see I've come all alone," said Daisy's unsupported parent. "I'm so frightened I don't know what to do; it's the first time I've ever been to a party alone—especially in this country. I wanted to bring Randolph or Eugenio or some one, but Daisy just pushed me off by myself. I ain't used to going round alone."

"And does n't your daughter intend to favour us with her society?" Mrs. Walker impressively enquired.

"Well, Daisy's all dressed," Mrs. Miller testified with that accent of the dispassionate, if not of the philosophic, historian with which she always recorded the current incidents of her daughter's career. "She got dressed on purpose before dinner. But she has a friend of hers there; that gentleman—the handsomest of the Italians—that she wanted to bring. They've got going at the piano—it seems as if they could n't leave off. Mr. Giovanelli does sing splendidly. But I guess they'll come before very long," Mrs. Miller hopefully concluded.

"I'm sorry she should come—in that particular way," Mrs. Walker permitted herself to observe.

"Well, I told her there was no use in her getting dressed before dinner if she was going to wait three hours," returned Daisy's mamma. "I did n't see the use of her putting on such a dress as that to sit round with Mr. Giovanelli."

"This is most horrible!" said Mrs. Walker, turning away and addressing herself to Winterbourne. "*Elle s'affiche, la malheureuse.*[20] It's her revenge for my having ventured to remonstrate with her. When she comes I shan't speak to her."

Daisy came after eleven o'clock, but she was n't, on such an occasion, a young lady to be spoken to. She rustled forward in radiant loveliness, smiling and chattering, carrying a large bouquet and attended by Mr. Giovanelli. Every one stopped talking and turned and looked at her while she floated up

[20] She makes a spectacle of herself, the poor girl.

to Mrs. Walker. "I'm afraid you thought I never was coming, so I sent mother off to tell you. I wanted to make Mr. Giovanelli practise some things before he came; you know he sings beautifully, and I want you to ask him to sing. This is Mr. Giovanelli; you know I introduced him to you; he's got the most lovely voice and he knows the most charming set of songs. I made him go over them this evening on purpose; we had the greatest time at the hotel." Of all this Daisy delivered herself with the sweetest brightest loudest confidence, looking now at her hostess and now at all the room, while she gave a series of little pats, round her very white shoulders, to the edges of her dress. "Is there any one I know?" she as undiscourageably asked.

"I think every one knows you!" said Mrs. Walker as with a grand intention; and she gave a very cursory greeting to Mr. Giovanelli. This gentleman bore himself gallantly; he smiled and bowed and showed his white teeth, he curled his moustaches and rolled his eyes and performed all the proper functions of a handsome Italian at an evening party. He sang, very prettily, half a dozen songs, though Mrs. Walker afterwards declared that she had been quite unable to find out who asked him. It was apparently not Daisy who had set him in motion—this young lady being seated a distance from the piano and though she had publicly, as it were, professed herself his musical patroness or guarantor, giving herself to gay and audible discourse while he warbled.

"It's a pity these rooms are so small; we can't dance," she remarked to Winterbourne as if she had seen him five minutes before.

"I'm not sorry we can't dance," he candidly returned. "I'm incapable of a step."

"Of course you're incapable of a step," the girl assented. "I should think your legs *would* be stiff cooped in there so much of the time in that victoria."

"Well, they were very restless there three days ago," he amicably laughed; "all they really wanted was to dance attendance on you."

"Oh my other friend—my friend in need—stuck to me; he seems more at one with his limbs than you are—I'll say that for him. But did you ever hear anything so cool," Daisy demanded, "as Mrs. Walker's wanting me to get into her carriage and drop poor Mr. Giovanelli, and under the pretext that it was proper? People have different ideas! It would have been most unkind; he had been talking about that walk for ten days."

"He should n't have talked about it at all," Winterbourne decided to make answer on this: "he would never have proposed to a young lady of this country to walk about the streets of Rome with him."

"About the streets?" she cried with her pretty stare. "Where then would he have proposed to her to walk? The Pincio ain't the streets either, I guess; and I besides, thank goodness, am not a young lady of this country. The young ladies of this country have a dreadfully pokey time of it, by what I can discover; I don't see why I should change my habits for *such* stupids."

"I'm afraid your habits are those of ruthless flirt," said Winterbourne with studied severity.

"Of course they are!"—and she hoped, evidently, by the manner of it, to take his breath away. "I'm a fearful frightful flirt! Did you ever hear of a nice girl that was n't? But I suppose you'll tell me now I'm not a nice girl."

He remained grave indeed under the shock of her cynical profession. "You're a very nice girl, but I wish you'd flirt with me, and me only."

"Ah thank you, thank you very much: you're the last man I should think of flirting with. As I've had the pleasure of informing you, you're too stiff."

"You say that too often," he resentfully remarked.

Daisy gave a delighted laugh. "If I could have the sweet hope of making you angry I'd say it again."

"Don't do that—when I'm angry I'm stiffer than ever. But if you won't flirt with me do cease at least to flirt with your friend at the piano. They don't," he declared as in full sympathy with "them," "understand that sort of thing here."

"I thought they understood nothing else!" Daisy cried with startling world-knowledge.

"Not in young unmarried women."

"It seems to me much more proper in young unmarried than in old married ones," she retorted.

"Well," said Winterbourne, "when you deal with natives you must go by the custom of this country. American flirting is a purely American silliness; it has—in its ineptitude of innocence—no place in *this* system. So when you show yourself in public with Mr. Giovanelli and without your mother—"

"Gracious, poor mother!"—and she made it beautifully unspeakable.

Winterbourne had a touched sense for this, but it did n't alter his attitude. "Though *you* may be flirting Mr. Giovanelli is n't—he means something else."

"He is n't preaching at any rate," she returned. "And if you want very much to know, we're neither of us flirting—not a little speck. We're too good friends for that. We're real intimate friends."

He was to continue to find her thus at moments inimitable. "Ah," he then judged, "if you're in love with each other it's another affair altogether!"

She had allowed him up to this point to speak so frankly that he had not thought of shocking her by the force of his logic; yet she now none the less immediately rose, blushing visibly and leaving him mentally to exclaim that the name of little American flirts was incoherence. "Mr. Giovanelli at least," she answered, sparing but a single small queer glance for it, a queerer small glance, he felt, than he had ever yet had from her—"Mr. Giovanelli never says to me such very disagreeable things."

It had an effect on him—he stood staring. The subject of their contention had finished singing; he left the piano, and his recognition of what—a little awkwardly—did n't take place in celebration of this might nevertheless have been an acclaimed operatic tenor's series of repeated ducks before the curtain. So he bowed himself over to Daisy. "Won't you come to the other room and have some tea?" he asked—offering Mrs. Walker's slightly thin refreshment as he might have done all the kingdoms of the earth.

Daisy at last turned on Winterbourne a more natural and calculable light. He was but the more muddled by it, however, since so inconsequent a smile made nothing clear—it seemed at the most to prove in her a sweetness and softness that reverted instinctively to the pardon of offences. "It has never occurred to Mr. Winterbourne to offer me any tea," she said with her finest little intention of torment and triumph.

"I've offered you excellent advice," the young man permitted himself to growl.

"I prefer weak tea!" cried Daisy, and she went off with the brilliant Giovanelli. She sat with him in the adjoining room, in the embrasure of the window, for the rest of the evening. There was an interesting performance at the piano, but neither of these conversers gave heed to it. When Daisy came to take leave of Mrs. Walker this lady conscientiously repaired the weakness of which she had been guilty at the moment of the girl's arrival—she turned her back straight on Miss Miller and left her to depart with what grace she might. Winterbourne happened to be near the door; he saw it all. Daisy turned very pale and looked at her mother, but Mrs. Miller was humbly unconscious of any rupture of any law or of any deviation from any custom. She appeared indeed to have felt an incongruous impulse to draw attention to her own striking conformity. "Good-night, Mrs. Walker," she said; "we've had a beautiful evening. You see if I let Daisy come to parties without me I don't want her to go away without me." Daisy turned away, looking with a small white prettiness, a blighted grace, at the circle near the door: Winterbourne saw that for the first moment she was too much shocked and puzzled even for indignation. He on his side was greatly touched.

"That was very cruel," he promptly remarked to Mrs. Walker.

But this lady's face was also as a stone. "She never enters my drawing-room again."

Since Winterbourne then, hereupon, was not to meet her in Mrs. Walker's drawing-room he went as often as possible to Mrs. Miller's hotel. The ladies were rarely at home, but when he found them the devoted Giovanelli was always present. Very often the glossy little Roman, serene in success, but not unduly presumptuous, occupied with Daisy alone the florid salon enjoyed by Eugenio's care, Mrs. Miller being apparently ever of the opinion that discretion is the better part of solicitude. Winterbourne noted, at first with surprise, that Daisy on these occasions was neither embarrassed nor annoyed by his own entrance; but he presently began to feel that she had no more surprises for him and that he really liked, after all, not making out what she was "up to." She showed no displeasure for the interruption of her tête-à-tête with Giovanelli; she could chatter as freshly and freely with two gentlemen as with one, and this easy flow had ever the same anomaly for her earlier friend that it was so free without availing itself of its freedom. Winterbourne reflected that if she was seriously interested in the Italian it was odd she should n't take more trouble to preserve the sanctity of their interviews, and he liked her the better for her innocent-looking indifference and her inexhaustible gaiety. He could hardly have said why, but she struck him as a young person not formed for a troublesome jealousy. Smile at such a betrayal though the reader may, it was a fact with regard to the women who had hitherto interested him that, given certain contingencies, Winterbourne could see himself afraid—literally afraid—of these ladies. It pleased him to believe that even were twenty other things different and Daisy should love him and he should know it and like it, he would still never be afraid of Daisy. It must be added that this conviction was not altogether flattering to her: it represented that she was nothing every way if not light.

But she was evidently very much interested in Giovanelli. She looked at him whenever he spoke; she was perpetually telling him to do this and to do that; she was constantly chaffing and abusing him. She appeared completely to have forgotten that her other friend had said anything to displease her at Mrs. Walker's entertainment. One Sunday afternoon, having gone to Saint Peter's with his aunt, Winterbourne became aware that the young woman held in horror by that lady was strolling about the great church under escort of her coxcomb of the Corso. It amused him, after a debate, to point out the exemplary pair—even at the cost, as it proved, of Mrs. Costello's saying when she had taken them in through her eye-glass: "That's what makes you so pensive in these days, eh?"

"I had n't the least idea I was pensive," he pleaded.

"You're very much preoccupied; you're always thinking of something."

"And what is it," he asked, "that you accuse me of thinking of?"

"Of that young lady's, Miss Baker's, Miss Chandler's—what's her name?—Miss Miller's intrigue with that little barber's block."

"Do you call it an intrigue," he asked—"an affair that goes on with such peculiar publicity?"

"That's their folly," said Mrs. Costello, "it's not their merit."

"No," he insisted with a hint perhaps of the preoccupation to which his aunt had alluded—"I don't believe there's anything to be called an intrigue."

"Well"—and Mrs. Costello dropped her glass—"I've heard a dozen people speak of it: they say she's quite carried away by him."

"They're certainly as thick as thieves," our embarrassed young man allowed.

Mrs. Costello came back to them, however, after a little; and Winterbourne recognised in this a further illustration—than that supplied by his own condition—of the spell projected by the case. "He's certainly very handsome. One easily sees how it is. She thinks him the most elegant man in the world, the finest gentleman possible. She has never seen anything like him—he's better even than the courier. It was the courier probably who introduced him, and if he succeeds in marrying the young lady the courier will come in for a magnificent commission."

"I don't believe she thinks of marrying him," Winterbourne reasoned, "and I don't believe he hopes to marry her."

"You may be very sure she thinks of nothing at all. She romps on from day to day, from hour to hour, as they did in the Golden Age. I can imagine nothing more vulgar," said Mrs. Costello, whose figure of speech scarcely went on all fours. "And at the same time," she added, "depend upon it she may tell you any moment that she is 'engaged.'"

"I think that's more than Giovanelli really expects," said Winterbourne.

"And who is Giovanelli?"

"The shiny—but, to do him justice, not greasy—little Roman. I've asked questions about him and learned something. He's apparently a perfectly respectable little man. I believe he's in a small way a *cavaliere avvocato*.[21] But he doesn't move in what are called the first circles. I think it really not absolutely impossible the courier introduced him. He's evidently immensely charmed with Miss Miller. If she thinks him the finest gentleman in the world, he, on his side, has never found himself in personal contact with such splendour, such opulence, such personal daintiness, as this young lady's. And then she must seem to him wonderfully pretty and interesting. Yes, he can't really hope to pull it off. That must appear to him too impossible a piece of luck. He has nothing but his handsome face to offer, and there's a substantial, a possibly explosive Mr. Miller in that mysterious land of dollars and six-shooters. Giovanelli's but too conscious that he has n't a title to offer. If he were only a count or a *marchese*![22] What on earth can he make of the way they've taken him up?"

"He accounts for it by his handsome face and thinks Miss Miller a young lady *qui se passe ses fantaisies!*"[23]

"It's very true," Winterbourne pursued, "that Daisy and her mamma haven't yet risen to that stage of—what shall I call it?—of culture, at which the idea of catching a count or a *marchese* begins. I believe them intellectually incapable of that conception."

"Ah but the *cavaliere avvocato* doesn't believe them!" cried Mrs. Costello.

Of the observation excited by Daisy's "intrigue" Winterbourne gathered that day at Saint Peter's sufficient evidence. A dozen of the American colonists in Rome came to talk with his relative, who sat on a small portable stool at the base of one of the great pilasters. The vesper-service was going forward in splendid chants and organ-tones in the adjacent choir, and mean-

---

[21] A lawyer of low rank and degree.
[22] An Italian rank of nobility.
[23] Who gives in to her own whims.

while, between Mrs. Costello and her friends, much was said about poor little Miss Miller's going really "too far." Winterbourne was not pleased with what he heard; but when, coming out upon the great steps of the church, he saw Daisy, who had emerged before him, get into an open cab with her accomplice and roll away through the cynical streets of Rome, the measure of her course struck him as simply there to take. He felt very sorry for her— not exactly that he believed she had completely lost her wits, but because it was painful to see so much that was pretty and undefended and natural sink so low in human estimation. He made an attempt after this to give a hint to Mrs. Miller. He met one day in the Corso a friend—a tourist like himself— who had just come out of the Doria Palace, where he had been walking through the beautiful gallery. His friend "went on" for some moments about the great portrait of Innocent X, by Velasquez,[24] suspended in one of the cabinets of the palace, and then said: "And in the same cabinet, by the way, I enjoyed sight of an image of a different kind; that little American who's so much more a work of nature than of art and whom you pointed out to me last week." In answer to Winterbourne's enquiries his friend narrated that the little American—prettier now than ever—was seated with a companion in the secluded nook in which the papal presence is enshrined.

"All alone?" the young man heard himself disingenuously ask.

"Alone with a little Italian who sports in his button-hole a stack of flowers. The girl's a charming beauty, but I thought I understood from you the other day that she's a young lady *du meilleur monde.*"[25]

"So she is!" said Winterbourne; and having assured himself that his informant had seen the interesting pair but ten minutes before, he jumped into a cab and went to call on Mrs. Miller. She was at home, but she apologised for receiving him in Daisy's absence.

"She's gone out somewhere with Mr. Giovanelli. She's always going round with Mr. Giovanelli."

"I've noticed they're intimate indeed," Winterbourne concurred.

"Oh it seems as if they couldn't live without each other!" said Mrs. Miller. "Well, he's a real gentleman anyhow. I guess I have the joke on Daisy—that she *must* be engaged!"

"And how does your daughter *take* the joke?"

"Oh she just says she ain't. But she might as *well* be!" this philosophic parent resumed. "She goes on as if she was. But I've made Mr. Giovanelli promise to tell me if Daisy don't. I'd want to write to Mr. Miller about it— would n't you?"

Winterbourne replied that he certainly should; and the state of mind of Daisy's mamma struck him as so unprecedented in the annuals of parental

---

[24] Diego Rodriguez de Silva y Velasquez (1599-1660) was a Spanish painter whose portrait of Pope Innocent X (1649) hangs in the Doria gallery.

[25] Of the best society.

vigilance that he recoiled before the attempt to educate at a single interview either her conscience or her wit.

After this Daisy was never at home and he ceased to meet her at the houses of their common acquaintance, because, as he perceived, these shrewd people had quite made up their minds as to the length she must have gone. They ceased to invite her, intimating that they wished to make, and make strongly, for the benefit of the observant Europeans, the point that though Miss Daisy Miller was a pretty American girl all right, her behaviour was n't pretty at all—was in fact regarded by her compatriots as quite monstrous. Winterbourne wondered how she felt about all the cold shoulders that were turned upon her, and sometimes found himself suspecting with impatience that she simply did n't feel and did n't know. He set her down as hopelessly childish and shallow, as such mere giddiness and ignorance incarnate as was powerless either to heed or to suffer. Then at other moments he couldn't doubt that she carried about in her elegant and irresponsible little organism a defiant, passionate, perfectly observant consciousness of the impression she produced. He asked himself whether the defiance would come from the consciousness of innocence or from her being essentially a young person of the reckless class. Then it had to be admitted, he felt, that holding fast to a belief in her "innocence" was more and more but a matter of gallantry too fine-spun for use. As I have already had occasion to relate, he was reduced without pleasure to this chopping of logic and vexed at his poor fallibility, his want of instinctive certitude as to how far her extravagance was generic and national and how far it was crudely personal. Whatever it was he had helplessly missed her, and now it was too late. She was "carried away" by Mr. Giovanelli.

A few days after his brief interview with her mother he came across her at that supreme seat of flowering desolation known as the Palace of the Cæsars. The early Roman spring had filled the air with bloom and perfume, and the rugged surface of the Palatine was muffled with tender verdure. Daisy moved at her ease over the great mounds of ruin that are embanked with mossy marble and paved with monumental inscriptions. It seemed to him he had never known Rome so lovely as just then. He looked off at the enchanting harmony of line and colour that remotely encircles the city—he inhaled the softly humid odours and felt the freshness of the year and the antiquity of the place reaffirm themselves in deep interfusion. It struck him also that Daisy had never showed to the eye for so utterly charming; but this had been his conviction on every occasion of their meeting. Giovanelli was of course at her side, and Giovanelli too glowed as never before with something of the glory of his race.

"Well," she broke out upon the friend it would have been such mockery to designate as the latter's rival, "I should think you'd be quite lonesome!"

"Lonesome?" Winterbourne resignedly echoed.

"You're always going round by yourself. Can't you get any one to walk with you?"

"I'm not so fortunate," he answered, "as your gallant companion."

Giovanelli had from the first treated him with distinguished politeness; he listened with a deferential air to his remarks; he laughed punctiliously at his pleasantries; he attached such importance as he could find terms for to Miss Miller's cold compatriot. He carried himself in no degree like a jealous wooer; he had obviously a great deal of tact; he had no objection to any one's expecting a little humility of him. It even struck Winterbourne that he almost yearned at times for some private communication in the interest of his character for common sense; a chance to remark to him as another intelligent man that, bless him, *he* knew how extraordinary was their young lady and didn't flatter himself with confident—at least *too* confident and too delusive—hopes of matrimony and dollars. On this occasion he strolled away from his charming charge to pluck a sprig of almond-blossom which he carefully arranged in his button-hole.

"I know why you say that," Daisy meanwhile observed. "Because you think I go round too much with *him!*" And she nodded at her discreet attendant.

"Every one thinks so—if you care to know," was all Winterbourne found to reply.

"Of course I care to know!"—she made this point with much expression. "But I don't believe a word of it. They're only pretending to be shocked. They don't really care a straw what I do. Besides, I don't go round so much."

"I think you'll find they do care. They'll show it—disagreeably," he took on himself to state.

Daisy weighed the importance of that idea. "How—disagreeably?"

"Have n't you noticed anything?" he compassionately asked.

"I've noticed *you*. But I noticed you've no more 'give' than a ramrod the first time ever I saw you."

"You'll find at least that I've more 'give' than several others," he patiently smiled.

"How shall I find it?"

"By going to see the others."

"What will they do to me?"

"They'll show you the cold shoulder. Do you know what that means?"

Daisy was looking at him intently; she began to colour. "Do you mean as Mrs. Walker did the other night?"

"Exactly as Mrs. Walker did the other night."

She looked away at Giovanelli, still titivating with his almond-blossom. Then with her attention again on the important subject: "I should n't think you'd let people be so unkind!"

"How can I help it?"

"I should think you'd want to say something."

"I do want to say something"—and Winterbourne paused a moment. "I want to say that your mother tells me she believes you engaged."

"Well, I guess she does," said Daisy very simply.

The young man began to laugh. "And does Randolph believe it?"

"I guess Randolph does n't believe anything." This testimony to Randolph's scepticism excited Winterbourne to further mirth, and he noticed that Giovanelli was coming back to them. Daisy, observing it as well, addressed herself again to her countryman. "Since you've mentioned it," she said, "I *am* engaged." He looked at her hard—he had stopped laughing. "You don't believe it!" she added.

He asked himself, and it was for a moment like testing a heart-beat; after which, "Yes, I believe it!" he said.

"Oh no, you don't," she answered. "But *if* you possibly do," she still more perversely pursued—"well, I ain't!"

Miss Miller and her constant guide were on their way to the gate of the enclosure, so that Winterbourne, who had but lately entered, presently took leave of them. A week later on he went to dine at a beautiful villa on the Cælian Hill,[26] and, on arriving, dismissed his hired vehicle. The evening was perfect and he promised himself the satisfaction of walking home beneath the Arch of Constantine[27] and past the vaguely-lighted monuments of the Forum.[28] Above was a moon half-developed, whose radiance was not brilliant but veiled in a thin cloud-curtain that seemed to diffuse and equalise it. When on his return from the villa at eleven o'clock he approached the dusky circle of the Colosseum the sense of romantic in him easily suggested that the interior, in such an atmosphere, would well repay a glance. He turned aside and walked to one of the empty arches, near which, as he observed, an open carriage—one of the little Roman street-cabs—was stationed. Then he passed in among the cavernous shadows of the great structure and emerged upon the clear and silent arena. The place had never seemed to him more impressive. One half of the gigantic circus was in deep shade while the other slept in the luminous dusk. As he stood there he began to murmur Byron's famous lines out of "Manfred";[29] but before he had finished his quotation he remembered that if nocturnal meditation thereabouts was the fruit of a rich literary culture it was none the less deprecated by medical science. The air of other ages surrounded one; but the air of other ages, coldly analysed, was no better than a villainous miasma. Winterbourne sought, however, toward the middle of the arena, a further reach of vision, intending the next moment a hasty retreat. The great cross in the centre was almost obscured; only as he drew near did he make it out distinctly. He thus also distinguished two

[26] One of the hills of Rome.

[27] Roman victory arch, built A.D. 312.

[28] Business and administrative center of ancient Rome.

[29] From "Manfred" (1817) Act III; scene iv; lines 8-11

upon such a night
I stood within the Coliseum's wall
'Midst the chief relics of almighty Rome.

persons stationed on the low steps that formed its base. One of these was a woman seated; her companion hovered before her.

Presently the sound of the woman's voice came to him distinctly in the warm night-air. "Well, he looks at us as one of the old lions or tigers may have looked at the Christian martyrs!" These words were winged with their accent, so that they fluttered and settled about him in the darkness like vague white doves. It was Miss Daisy Miller who had released them from flight.

"Let us hope he's not very hungry"—the bland Giovanelli fell in with her humor. "He'll have to take *me* first; you'll serve for dessert."

Winterbourne felt himself pulled up with final horror now—and, it must be added, with final relief. It was as if a sudden clearance had taken place in the ambiguity of the poor girl's appearances and the whole riddle of her contradictions had grown easy to read. She was a young lady about the *shades* of whose perversity a foolish puzzled gentleman need no longer trouble his head or his heart. That once questionable quantity *had* no shades—it was a mere black little blot. He stood there looking at her, looking at her companion too, and not reflecting that though he saw them vaguely he himself must have been more brightly presented. He felt angry at all his shiftings of view—he felt ashamed of all his tender little scruples and all his witless little mercies. He was about to advance again, and then again checked himself; not from the fear of doing her injustice, but from a sense of the danger of showing undue exhilaration for this disburdenment of cautious criticism. He turned away toward the entrance of the place; but as he did so he heard Daisy speak again.

"Why it was Mr. Winterbourne! He saw me and he cuts me dead!"

What a clever little reprobate she was, he was amply able to reflect at this, and how smartly she feigned, how promptly she sought to play off on him, a surprised and injured innocence! But nothing would induce him to cut her either "dead" or to within any measurable distance even of the famous "inch" of her life. He came forward again and went toward the great cross. Daisy had got up and Giovanelli lifted his hat. Winterbourne had now begun to think simply of the madness, on the ground of exposure and infection, of a frail young creature's lounging away such hours in a nest of malaria. What if she *were* the most plausible of little reprobates? That was no reason for her dying of the *perniciosa*.[30] "How long have you been 'fooling round here?'" he asked with conscious roughness.

Daisy, lovely in the sinister silver radiance, appraised him a moment, roughness and all. "Well, I guess all the evening." She answered with spirit, and he could see even then, with exaggeration. "I never saw anything so quaint."

---

[30] Malaria; the Roman Fever.

"I'm afraid," he returned, "you'll not think a bad attack of Roman fever very quaint. This is the way people catch it. I wonder," he added to Giovanelli, "that you, a native Roman, should countenance such extraordinary rashness."

"Ah," said this seasoned subject, "for myself I have no fear."

"Neither have I—for you!" Winterbourne retorted in French. "I'm speaking for this young lady."

Giovanelli raised his well-shaped eyebrows and showed his shining teeth, but took his critic's rebuke with docility. "I assure Mademoiselle it was a grave indiscretion, but when was Mademoiselle ever prudent?"

"I never was sick, and I don't mean to be!" Mademoiselle declared. "I don't look like much, but I'm healthy! I was bound to see the Coliseum by moonlight—I would n't have wanted to go home without *that;* and we've had the most beautiful time, have n't we, Mr. Giovanelli? If there has been any danger Eugenio can give me some pills. Eugenio has got some splendid pills."

"I should advise you then," said Winterbourne, "to drive home as fast as possible and take one!"

Giovanelli smiled as for the striking happy thought. "What you say is very wise. I'll go and make sure the carriage is at hand." And he went forward rapidly.

Daisy followed with Winterbourne. He tried to deny himself the small fine anguish of looking at her, but his eyes themselves refused to spare him, and she seemed moreover not in the least embarrassed. He spoke no word; Daisy chattered over the beauty of the place: "Well, I *have* seen the Colosseum by moonlight—that's one thing I can rave about!" Then noticing her companion's silence she asked him why he was so stiff—it had always been her great word. He made no answer, but he felt his laugh an immense negation of stiffness. They passed under one of the dark archways; Giovanelli was in front with the carriage. Here Daisy stopped a moment, looking at her compatriot. "*Did* you believe I was engaged the other day?"

"It does n't matter now what I believed the other day!" he replied with infinite point.

It was a wonder how she didn't wince for it. "Well, what do you believe now?"

"I believe it makes very little difference whether you're engaged or not!"

He felt her lighted eyes fairly penetrate the thick gloom of the vaulted passage—as if to seek some access to him she had n't yet compassed. But Giovanelli, with a graceful inconsequence, was at present all for retreat. "Quick, quick; if we get in by midnight we're quite safe!"

Daisy took her seat in the carriage and the fortunate Italian placed himself beside her. "Don't forget Eugenio's pills!" said Winterbourne as he lifted his hat.

"I don't care," she unexpectedly cried out for this, "whether I have Roman fever or not!" On which the cab-driver cracked his whip and they rolled across the desultory patches of antique pavement.

Winterbourne—to do him justice, as it were—mentioned to no one that he had encountered Miss Miller at midnight in the Colosseum with a gentleman; in spite of which deep discretion, however, the fact of the scandalous adventure was known a couple of days later, with a dozen vivid details, to every member of the little American circle, and was commented on accordingly. Winterbourne judged thus that the people about the hotel had been thoroughly empowered to testify, and that after Daisy's return there would have been an exchange of jokes between the porter and the cab-driver. But the young man became aware at the same moment of how thoroughly it had ceased to ruffle him that the little American flirt should be "talked about" by low-minded menials. These sources of current criticism a day or two later abounded still further: the little American flirt was alarmingly ill and the doctors now in possession of the scene. Winterbourne, when the rumour came to him, immediately went to the hotel for more news. He found that two or three charitable friends had preceded him and that they were being entertained in Mrs. Miller's salon by the all-efficient Randolph.

"It's going round at night that way, you bet—that's what has made her so sick. She's always going round at night. I should n't think she'd want to—it's so plaguey dark over here. You can't see anything over here without the moon's right up. In America they don't go round by the moon!" Mrs. Miller meanwhile wholly surrendered to her genius for unapparent uses; her salon knew her less than ever, and she was presumably now at least giving her daughter the advantage of society. It was clear that Daisy was dangerously ill.

Winterbourne constantly attended for news from the sick-room, which reached him, however, but with worrying indirectness, though he once had speech, for a moment, of the poor girl's physician and once saw Mrs. Miller, who, sharply alarmed, struck him as thereby more happily inspired than he could have conceived and indeed as the most noiseless and lighthanded of nurses. She invoked a good deal the remote shade of Dr. Davis, but Winterbourne paid her the compliment of taking her after all for less monstrous a goose. To this indulgence indeed something she further said perhaps even more insidiously disposed him. "Daisy spoke of you the other day quite pleasantly. Half the time she does n't know what she's saying, but that time I think she did. She gave me a message—she told me to tell you. She wanted you to know she never was engaged to that handsome Italian who was always round. I'm sure I'm very glad; Mr. Giovanelli has n't been near us since she was taken ill. I thought he was so much of a gentleman, but I don't call that very polite! A lady told me he was afraid I had n't approved of his being round with her so much evenings. Of course it ain't as if their evenings were as pleasant as ours—since *we* don't seem to feel that way about the poison. I guess I *don't* see the point now; but I suppose he knows I'm a lady and I'd scorn to raise a fuss. Anyway, she wants you to realise she ain't engaged. I don't know why she makes so much of it, but she said to me three times 'Mind you tell Mr. Winterbourne.' And then she told me to ask if you remembered the time you went up to that castle in Switzerland. But I said I would n't give any such messages as *that*. Only if she ain't engaged I guess I'm glad to realise it too."

But, as Winterbourne had originally judged, the truth on this question had small actual relevance. A week after this the poor girl died; it had been indeed a terrible case of the *perniciosa*. A grave was found for her in the little Protestant cemetery, by an angle of the wall of imperial Rome, beneath the cypresses and the thick spring-flowers. Winterbourne stood there beside it with a number of other mourners; a number larger than the scandal excited by the young lady's career might have made probable. Near him stood Giovanelli, who came nearer still before Winterbourne turned away. Giovanelli, in decorous mourning, showed but a whiter face; his button-hole lacked its nosegay and he had visibly something urgent—and even to distress—to say, which he scarce knew how to "place." He decided at last to confide it with a pale convulsion to Winterbourne. "She was the most beautiful young lady I ever saw, and the most amiable." To which he added in a moment: "Also—naturally!—the most innocent."

Winterbourne sounded him with hard dry eyes, but presently repeated his words, "The most innocent?"

"The most innocent!"

It became somehow so much too late that our friend could only glare at its having come at all. "Why the devil," he asked, "did you take her to that fatal place?"

Giovanelli raised his neat shoulders and eyebrows to within suspicion of a shrug. "For myself I had no fear; and *she*—she did what she liked."

Winterbourne's eyes attached themselves to the ground. "She did what she liked!"

It determined on the part of poor Giovanelli a further pious, a further candid, confidence. "If she had lived I should have got nothing. She never would have married me."

It had been spoken as if to attest, in all sincerity, his disinterestedness, but Winterbourne scarce knew what welcome to give it. He said, however, with a grace inferior to his friend's: "I dare say not."

The latter was even by this not discouraged. "For a moment I hoped so. But no. I'm convinced."

Winterbourne took it in; he stood staring at the raw protuberance among the April daisies. When he turned round again his fellow mourner had stepped back.

He almost immediately left Rome, but the following summer he again met his aunt Mrs. Costello at Vevey. Mrs. Costello extracted from the charming

? — In Winterbourne's mind
— Does she or doesn't she
Decides she is innocent

HENRY JAMES

old hotel there a value that the Miller family had n't mastered the secret of. In the interval Winterbourne had often thought of the most interesting member of that trio—of her mystifying manners and her queer adventure. One day he spoke of her to his aunt—said it was on his conscience he had done her injustice.

"I'm sure I don't know"—that lady showed caution. "How did your injustice affect her?"

"She sent me a message before her death which I did n't understand at the time. But I've understood it since. She would have appreciated one's esteem." *didn't cultivate it*

"She took an odd way to gain it! But do you mean by what you say," Mrs. Costello asked, "that she would have reciprocated one's affection?"

As he made no answer to this she after a little looked round at him—he had n't been directly within sight; but the effect of that wasn't to make her repeat her question. He spoke, however, after a while. "You were right in that remark that you made last summer. I was booked to make a mistake. I've lived too long in foreign parts." *Europe* And this time she herself said nothing.

Nevertheless he soon went back to live at Geneva, whence there continue to come the most contradictory accounts of his motives of sojourn: a report that he's "studying" hard—an intimation that he's much interested in a very clever foreign lady.

The Pupil[1]

I

The poor young man hesitated and procrastinated: it cost him such an effort to broach the subject of terms, to speak of money to a person who spoke only of feelings and, as it were, of the aristocracy. Yet he was unwilling to take leave, treating his engagement as settled, without some more conventional glance in that direction than he could find an opening for in the manner of the large affable lady who sat there drawing a pair of soiled *gants de Suède*[2] through a fat jewelled hand and, at once pressing and gliding, repeated over and over everything but the thing he would have liked to hear. He would have liked to hear the figure of his salary; but just as he was nervously about to sound that note the little boy came back—the little boy Mrs. Moreen had sent out of the room to fetch her fan. He came back

[1] First published in *Longman's Magazine* in March and April 1891; in book form in *The Lesson of the Master and Other Tales* in 1892.

[2] Suede gloves.

without the fan, only with the casual observation that he couldn't find it. As he dropped this cynical confession he looked straight and hard at the candidate for the honour of taking his education in hand. This personage reflected somewhat grimly that the first thing he should have to teach his little charge would be to appear to address himself to his mother when he spoke to her— especially not to make her such an improper answer as that.

When Mrs. Moreen bethought herself of this pretext for getting rid of their companion Pemberton supposed it was precisely to approach the delicate subject of his remuneration. But it had been only to say some things about her son that it was better a boy of eleven shouldn't catch. They were extravagantly to his advantage save when she lowered her voice to sigh, tapping her left side familiarly, "And all overclouded by *this*, you know; all at the mercy of a weakness—!" Pemberton gathered that the weakness was in the region of the heart. He had known the poor child was not robust: this was the basis on which he had been invited to treat, through an English lady, an Oxford acquaintance, then at Nice, who happened to know both his needs and those of the amiable American family looking out for something really superior in the way of a resident tutor.

The young man's impression of his prospective pupil, who had come into the room as if to see for himself the moment Pemberton was admitted, was not quite the soft solicitation the visitor had taken for granted. Morgan Moreen was somehow sickly without being "delicate," and that he looked intelligent—it is true Pemberton would have enjoyed his being stupid—only added to the suggestion that, as with his big mouth and big ears he really couldn't be called pretty, he might too utterly fail to please. Pemberton was modest, was even timid; and the chance that his small scholar would prove cleverer than himself had quite figured, to his anxiety, among the dangers of an untried experiment. He reflected, however, that these were risks one had to run when one accepted a position, as it was called, in a private family; when as yet one's university honours had, pecuniarily speaking, remained barren. At any rate when Mrs. Moreen got up as to intimate that, since it was understood he would enter upon his duties within the week she would let him off now, he succeeded, in spite of the presence of the child, in squeezing out a phrase about the rate of payment. It was not the fault of the conscious smile which seemed a reference to the lady's expensive identity, it was not the fault of this demonstration, which had, in a sort, both vagueness and point, if the allusion didn't sound rather vulgar. This was exactly because she became still more gracious to reply: "Oh I can assure you that all that will be quite regular."

Pemberton only wondered, while he took up his hat, what "all that" was to amount to—people had such different ideas. Mrs. Moreen's words, however, seemed to commit the family to a pledge definite enough to elicit from the child a strange little comment in the shape of the mocking foreign ejaculation "Oh la-la!"

Pemberton, in some confusion, glanced at him as he walked slowly to the window with his back turned, his hands in his pockets and the air in his elderly shoulders of a boy who didn't play. The young man wondered if he should be able to teach him to play, though his mother had said it would never do and that this was why school was impossible. Mrs. Moreen exhibited no discomfiture; she only continued blandly: "Mr. Moreen will be delighted to meet your wishes. As I told you, he has been called to London for a week. As soon as he comes back you shall have it out with him."

This was so frank and friendly that the young man could only reply, laughing as his hostess laughed: "Oh I don't imagine we shall have much of a battle."

"They'll give you anything you like," the boy remarked unexpectedly, returning from the window. "We don't mind what anything costs—we live awfully well."

"My darling, you're too quaint!" his mother exclaimed, putting out to caress him a practised but ineffectual hand. He slipped out of it, but looked with intelligent innocent eyes at Pemberton, who had already had time to notice that from one moment to the other his small satiric face seemed to change its time of life. At this moment it was infantine, yet it appeared also to be under the influence of curious intuitions and knowledges. Pemberton rather disliked precocity and was disappointed to find gleams of it in a disciple not yet in his teens. Nevertheless he divined on the spot that Morgan wouldn't prove a bore. He would prove on the contrary a source of agitation. This idea held the young man, in spite of a certain repulsion.

"You pompous little person! We're not extravagant!" Mrs. Moreen gaily protested, making another unsuccessful attempt to draw the boy to her side. "You must know what to expect," she went on to Pemberton.

"The less you expect the better!" her companion interposed. "But we *are* people of fashion."

"Only so far as *you* make us so!" Mrs. Moreen tenderly mocked. "Well then, on Friday—don't tell me you're superstitious—and mind you don't fail us. Then you'll see us all. I'm so sorry the girls are out. I guess you'll like the girls. And, you know, I've another son, quite different from this one."

"He tries to imitate me," Morgan said to their friend.

"He tries? Why he's twenty years old!" cried Mrs. Moreen.

"You're very witty," Pemberton remarked to the child—a proposition his mother echoed with enthusiasm, declaring Morgan's sallies to be the delight of the house.

The boy paid no heed to this; he only enquired abruptly of the visitor, who was surprised afterwards that he hadn't struck him as offensively forward: "Do you *want* very much to come?"

"Can you doubt it after such a description of what I shall hear?" Pemberton replied. Yet he didn't want to come at all; he was coming because he had to go somewhere, thanks to the collapse of his fortune at the end of a year abroad spent on the system of putting his scant patrimony into a single full wave of experience. He had had his full wave but couldn't pay the score at his inn. Moreover he had caught in the boy's eyes the glimpse of a far-off appeal.

"Well, I'll do the best I can for you," said Morgan; with which he turned away again. He passed out of one of the long windows; Pemberton saw him go and lean on the parapet of the terrace. He remained there while the young man took leave of his mother, who, on Pemberton's looking as if he expected a farewell from him, interposed with: "Leave him, leave him; he's so strange!" Pemberton supposed her to fear something he might say. "He's a genius—you'll love him," she added. "He's much the most interesting person in the family." And before he could invent some civility to oppose to this she wound up with: "But we're all good, you know!"

"He's a genius—you'll love him!" were words that recurred to our aspirant before the Friday, suggesting among many things that geniuses were not invariably loveable. However, it was all the better if there was an element that would make tutorship absorbing: he had perhaps taken too much for granted it would only disgust him. As he left the villa after his interview he looked up at the balcony and saw the child leaning over it. "We shall have great larks!" he called up.

Morgan hung fire a moment and then gaily returned: "By the time you come back I shall have thought of something witty!"

This made Pemberton say to himself "After all he's rather nice."

II

On the Friday he saw them all, as Mrs. Moreen had promised, for her husband had come back and the girls and the other son were at home. Mr. Moreen had a white moustache, a confiding manner and, in his buttonhole, the ribbon of a foreign order—bestowed, as Pemberton eventually learned, for services. For what services he never clearly ascertained: this was a point—one of a larger number—that Mr. Moreen's manner never confided. What it emphatically did confide was that he was even more a man of the world than you might first make out. Ulick, the firstborn, was in visible training for the same profession—under the disadvantage as yet, however, of a buttonhole but feebly floral and a moustache with no pretensions to type. The girls had hair and figures and manners and small fat feet, but had never been out alone. As for Mrs. Moreen, Pemberton saw on a nearer view that her elegance was intermittent and her parts didn't always match. Her husband, as she had promised, met with enthusiasm Pemberton's ideas in regard to a salary. The young man had endeavoured to keep these stammerings modest, and Mr. Moreen made it no secret that *he* found them wanting in "style." He further mentioned that he aspired to be intimate with his children, to be their best friend, and that he was always looking out for them.

That was what he went off for, to London and other places—to look out; and this vigilance was the theory of life, as well as the real occupation, of the whole family. They all looked out, for they were very frank on the subject of its being necessary. They desired it to be understood that they were earnest people, and also that their fortune, though quite adequate for earnest people, required the most careful administration. Mr. Moreen, as the parent bird, sought sustenance for the nest. Ulick invoked support mainly at the club, where Pemberton guessed that it was usually served on green cloth. The girls used to do up their hair and their frocks themselves, and our young man felt appealed to to be glad, in regard to Morgan's education, that, though it must naturally be of the best, it didn't cost too much. After a little he *was* glad, forgetting at times his own needs in the interest inspired by the child's character and culture and the pleasure of making easy terms for him.

During the first weeks of their acquaintance Morgan had been as puzzling as a page in an unknown language—altogether different from the obvious little Anglo-Saxons who had misrepresented childhood to Pemberton. Indeed the whole mystic volume in which the boy had been amateurishly bound demanded some practice in translation. Today, after a considerable interval, there is something phantasmagoric, like a prismatic reflexion or a serial novel, in Pemberton's memory of the queerness of the Moreens. If it were not for a few tangible tokens—a lock of Morgan's hair cut by his own hand, and the half-dozen letters received from him when they were disjoined—the whole episode and the figures peopling it would seem too inconsequent for anything but dreamland. Their supreme quaintness was their success—as it appeared to him for a while at the time; since he had never seen a family so brilliantly equipped for failure. Wasn't it success to have kept him so hatefully long? Wasn't it success to have drawn him in that first morning at déjeuner, the Friday he came—it was enough to *make* one superstitious—so that he utterly committed himself, and this not by calculation or on a signal, but from a happy instinct which made them, like a band of gipsies, work so neatly together? They amused him as much as if they had really been a band of gipsies. He was still young and had not seen much of the world—his English years had been properly arid; therefore the reversed conventions of the Moreens—for they had *their* desperate properties—struck him as topsy-turvy. He had encountered nothing like them at Oxford; still less had any such note been struck to his younger American ear during the four years at Yale in which he had richly supposed himself to be reacting against a Puritan strain. The reaction of the Moreens, at any rate, went ever so much further. He had thought himself very sharp that first day in hitting them all off in his mind with the "cosmopolite" label. Later it seemed feeble and colourless—confessedly helplessly provisional.

He yet when he first applied it felt a glow of joy—for an instructor he was still empirical—rise from the apprehension that living with them would really be to see life. Their sociable strangeness was an imitation of that—

their chatter of tongues, their gaiety and good humour, their infinite dawdling (they were always getting themselves up, but it took for ever, and
Pemberton had once found Mr. Moreen shaving in the drawing-room), their
French, their Italian and, cropping up in the foreign fluencies, their cold
tough slices of American. They lived on macaroni and coffee—they had
these articles prepared in perfection—but they knew recipes for a hundred
other dishes. They overflowed with music and song, were always humming
and catching each other up, and had a sort of professional acquaintance with
Continental cities. They talked of "good places" as if they had been pick-
pockets or strolling players. They had at Nice a villa, a carriage, a piano and
a banjo, and they went to official parties. They were a perfect calendar of
the "days" of their friends, which Pemberton knew them, when they were
indisposed, to get out of bed to go to, and which made the week larger than
life when Mrs. Moreen talked of them with Paula and Amy. Their initiations
gave their new inmate at first an almost dazzling sense of culture. Mrs.
Moreen had translated something at some former period—an author whom
it made Pemberton feel *borné*[3] never to have heard of. They could imitate
Venetian and sing Neapolitan, and when they wanted to say something very
particular communicated with each other in an ingenious dialect of their
own, an elastic spoken cipher which Pemberton at first took for some *patois*[4]
of one of their countries, but which he "caught on to" as he would not have
grasped provincial development of Spanish or German.

"It's the family language—Ultramoreen," Morgan explained to him drolly
enough; but the boy rarely condescended to use it himself, though he dealt
in colloquial Latin as if he had been a little prelate.

Among all the "days" with which Mrs. Moreen's memory was taxed she
managed to squeeze in one of her own, which her friends sometimes forgot.
But the house drew a frequented air from the number of fine people who
were freely named there and from several mysterious men with foreign titles
and English clothes whom Morgan called the Princes and who, on sofas with
the girls, talked French very loud—though sometimes with some oddity of
accent—as if to show they were saying nothing improper. Pemberton wondered how the Princes could ever propose in that tone and so publicly: he
took for granted cynically that this was what was desired of them. Then he
recognised that even for the chance of such an advantage Mrs. Moreen
would never allow Paula and Amy to receive alone. These young ladies were
not at all timid, but it was just the safeguards that made them so candidly
free. It was a houseful of Bohemians who wanted tremendously to be Philistines.

In one respect, however, certainly, they achieved no rigour—they were
wonderfully amiable and ecstatic about Morgan. It was a genuine tenderness, an artless admiration, equally strong in each. They even praised his

[3] Narrow and limited, gauche.   [4] Provincial dialect.

beauty, which was small, and were as afraid of him as if they felt him of finer clay. They spoke of him as a little angel and a prodigy—they touched on his want of health with long, vague faces. Pemberton feared at first an extravagance that might make him hate the boy, but before this happened he had become extravagant himself. Later, when he had grown rather to hate the others, it was a bribe to patience for him that they were at any rate nice about Morgan, going on tiptoe if they fancied he was showing symptoms, and even giving up somebody's "day" to procure him a pleasure. Mixed with this too was the oddest wish to make him independent, as if they had felt themselves not good enough for him. They passed him over to the new members of their circle very much as if wishing to force some charity of adoption on so free an agent and get rid of their own charge. They were delighted when they saw Morgan take so to his kind playfellow, and could think of no higher praise for the young man. It was strange how they contrived to reconcile the appearance, and indeed the essential fact, of adoring the child with their eagerness to wash their hands of him. Did they want to get rid of him before he should find them out? Pemberton was finding them out month by month. The boy's fond family, however this might be, turned their backs with exaggerated delicacy, as if to avoid the reproach of interfering. Seeing in time how little he had in common with them—it was by *them* he first observed it; they proclaimed it with complete humility—his companion was moved to speculate on the mysteries of transmission, the far jumps of heredity. Where his detachment from most of the things they represented had come from was more than an observer could say—it certainly had burrowed under two or three generations.

As for Pemberton's own estimate of his pupil, it was a good while before he got the point of view, so little had he been prepared for it by the smug young barbarians to whom the tradition of tutorship, as hitherto revealed to him, had been adjusted. Morgan was scrappy and surprising, deficient in many properties supposed common to the *genus* and abounding in others that were the portion only of the supernaturally clever. One day his friend made a great stride: it cleared up the question to perceive that Morgan *was* supernaturally clever and that, though the formula was temporarily meagre, this would be the only assumption on which one could successfully deal with him. He had the general quality of a child for whom life had not been simplified by school, a kind of homebred sensibility which might have been bad for himself but was charming for others, and a whole range of refinement and perception—little musical vibrations as taking as picked-up airs—begotten by wandering about Europe at the tail of his migratory tribe. This might not have been an education to recommend in advance, but its results with so special a subject were as appreciable as the marks on a piece of fine porcelain. There was at the same time in him a small strain of stoicism, doubtless the fruit of having had to begin early to bear pain, which counted for pluck and made it of less consequence that he might have been thought at school rather a polyglot little beast. Pemberton indeed quickly found himself rejoicing that school was out of the question: in any million of boys it was probably good for all but one, and Morgan was that millionth. It would have made him comparative and superior—it might have made him really require kicking. Pemberton would try to be school himself—a bigger seminary than five hundred grazing donkeys, so that, winning no prizes, the boy would remain unconscious and irresponsible and amusing—amusing, because though life was already intense in his childish nature, freshness still made there a strong draught for jokes. It turned out that even in the still air of Morgan's various disabilities jokes flourished greatly. He was a pale lean acute undeveloped little cosmopolite, who liked intellectual gymnastics and who also, as regards the behavior of mankind, had noticed more things than you might suppose, but who nevertheless had his proper playroom of superstitions, where he smashed a dozen toys a day.

III

At Nice once, toward evening, as the pair rested in the open air after a walk, and looked over the sea at the pink western lights, he said suddenly to his comrade: "Do you like it, you know—being with us all in this intimate way?"

"My dear fellow, why should I stay if I didn't?"

"How do I know you'll stay? I'm almost sure you won't, very long."

"I hope you don't mean to dismiss me," said Pemberton.

Morgan debated, looking at the sunset, "I think if I did right I ought to."

"Well, I know I'm supposed to instruct you in virtue; but in that case don't do right."

"You're very young—fortunately," Morgan went on, turning to him again.

"Oh yes, compared with you!"

"Therefore it won't matter so much if you do lose a lot of time."

"That's the way to look at it," said Pemberton accommodatingly.

They were silent a minute; after which the boy asked: "Do you like my father and my mother very much?"

"Dear me, yes. Charming people."

Morgan received this with another silence; then unexpectedly, familiarly, but at the same time affectionately, he remarked: "You're a jolly old humbug!"

For a particular reason the words made our young man change colour. The boy noticed in an instant that he had turned red, whereupon he turned red himself and pupil and master exchanged a longish glance in which there was a consciousness of many more things than are usually touched upon, even tacitly, in such a relation. It produced for Pemberton an embarrassment; it raised in a shadowy form a question—this was the first glimpse of it—destined to play a singular and, as he imagined, owing to the altogether peculiar conditions, an unprecedented part in his intercourse with his little

companion. Later, when he found himself talking with the youngster in a
way in which few youngsters could ever have been talked with, he thought
of that clumsy moment on the bench at Nice as the dawn of an understanding that had broadened. What had added to the clumsiness then was that he
thought it his duty to declare to Morgan that he might abuse him, Pemberton, as much as he liked, but must never abuse his parents. To this Morgan
had the easy retort that he hadn't dreamed of abusing them; which appeared
to be true: it put Pemberton in the wrong.

"Then why am I a humbug for saying *I* think them charming?" the young
man asked, conscious of a certain rashness.

"Well—they're not your parents."

"They love you better than anything in the world—never forget that,"
said Pemberton.

"Is that why you like them so much?"

"They're very kind to me," Pemberton replied evasively.

"You *are* a humbug!" laughed Morgan, passing an arm into his tutor's. He
leaned against him looking off at the sea again and swinging his long thin legs.

"Don't kick my shins," said Pemberton while he reflected "Hang it, I
can't complain of them to the child!"

"There's another reason too," Morgan went on, keeping his legs still.

"Another reason for what?"

"Besides their not being your parents."

"I don't understand you," said Pemberton.

"Well, you will before long. All right!"

He did understand fully before long, but he made a fight even with
himself before he confessed it. He thought it the oddest thing to have a
struggle with the child about. He wondered he didn't hate the hope of the
Moreens for bringing the struggle on. But by the time it began any such
sentiment for that scion was closed to him. Morgan was a special case, and to
know him was to accept him on his own odd terms. Pemberton had spent his
aversion to special cases before arriving at knowledge. When at last he did
arrive his quandary was great. Against every interest he had attached himself. They would have to meet things together. Before they went home that
evening at Nice the boy had said, clinging to his arm:

"Well, at any rate you'll hang on to the last."

"To the last?"

"Till you're fairly beaten."

"*You* ought to be fairly beaten!" cried the young man, drawing him
closer.

IV

A year after he had come to live with them Mr. and Mrs. Moreen suddenly
gave up the villa at Nice. Pemberton had got used to suddenness, having

seen it practised on a considerable scale during two jerky little tours—one in Switzerland the first summer, and the other late in the winter, when they all ran down to Florence and then, at the end of ten days, liking it much less than they had intended, straggled back in mysterious depression. They had returned to Nice "for ever," as they said; but this didn't prevent their squeezing, one rainy muggy May night, into a second-class railway-carriage—you could never tell by which class they would travel—where Pemberton helped them to stow away a wonderful collection of bundles and bags. The explanation of this manœuvre was that they had determined to spend the summer "in some bracing place"; but in Paris they dropped into a small furnished apartment—a fourth floor in a third-rate avenue, where there was a smell on the staircase and the *portier* was hateful—and passed the next four months in blank indigence.

The better part of this baffled sojourn was for the preceptor and his pupil, who, visiting the Invalides and Notre Dame, the Conciergerie and all the museums, took a hundred remunerative rambles. They learned to know their Paris, which was useful, for they came back another year for a longer stay, the general character of which in Pemberton's memory to-day mixes pitiably and confusedly with that of the first. He sees Morgan's shabbly knickerbockers—the everlasting pair that didn't match his blouse and that as he grew longer could only grow faded. He remembers the particular holes in his three or four pair of coloured stockings.

Morgan was dear to his mother, but he never was better dressed than was absolutely necessary—partly, no doubt, by his own fault, for he was as indifferent to his appearance as a German philosopher. "My dear fellow, you *are* coming to pieces," Pemberton would say to him in sceptical remonstrance; to which the child would reply, looking at him serenely up and down: "My dear fellow, so are you! I don't want to cast you in the shade." Pemberton could have no rejoinder for this—the assertion so closely represented the fact. If however the deficiencies of his own wardrobe were a chapter by themselves he didn't like his little charge to look too poor. Later he used to say "Well, if we're poor, why, after all, shouldn't we look it?" and he consoled himself with thinking there was something rather elderly and gentlemanly in Morgan's disrepair—it differed from the untidiness of the urchin who plays and spoils his things. He could trace perfectly the degrees by which, in proportion as her little son confined himself to his tutor for society, Mrs. Moreen shrewdly forbore to renew his garments. She did nothing that didn't show, neglected him because he escaped notice, and then, as he illustrated this clever policy, discouraged at home his public appearances. Her position was logical enough—those members of her family who did show had to be showy.

During this period and several others Pemberton was quite aware of how he and his comrade might strike people; wandering languidly through the Jardin des Plantes as if they had nowhere to go, sitting on the winter days in the galleries of the Louvre, so splendidly ironical to the homeless, as if for the advantage of the *calorifère*.[5] They joked about it sometimes: it was the sort of joke that was perfectly within the boy's compass. They figured themselves as part of the vast vague hand-to-mouth multitude of the enormous city and pretended they were proud of their position in it—it showed them "such a lot of life" and made them conscious of a democratic brotherhood. If Pemberton couldn't feel a sympathy in destitution with his small companion—for after all Morgan's fond parents would never have let him really suffer—the boy would at least feel it with him, so it came to the same thing. He used sometimes to wonder what people would think they were—to fancy they were looked askance at, as if it might be a suspected case of kidnapping. Morgan wouldn't be taken for a young patrician with a preceptor—he wasn't smart enough; though he might pass for his companion's sickly little brother. Now and then he had a five-franc piece, and except once, when they bought a couple of lovely neckties, one of which he made Pemberton accept, they laid it out scientifically in old books. This was sure to a great day, always spent on the quays, in a rummage of the dusty boxes that garnish the parapets. Such occasions helped them to live, for their books ran low very soon after the beginning of their acquaintance. Pemberton had a good many in England, but he was obliged to write to a friend and ask him kindly to get some fellow to give him something for them.

If they had to relinquish that summer the advantage of the bracing climate the young man couldn't but suspect this failure of the cup when at their very lips to have been the effect of a rude jostle of his own. This had represented his first blow-out, as he called it, with his patrons; his first successful attempt—though there was little other success about it—to bring them to a consideration of his impossible position. As the ostensible eve of a costly journey the moment had struck him as favourable to an earnest protest, the presentation of an ultimatum. Ridiculous as it sounded, he had never yet been able to compass an uninterrupted private interview with the elder pair or with either of them singly. They were always flanked by their elder children, and poor Pemberton usually had his own little charge at his side. He was conscious of its being a house in which the surface of one's delicacy got rather smudged; nevertheless he had preserved the bloom of his scruple against announcing to Mr. and Mrs. Moreen with publicity that he shouldn't be able to go on longer without a little money. He was still simple enough to suppose Ulick and Paula and Amy might not know that since his arrival he had only had a hundred and forty francs; and he was magnanimous enough to wish not to compromise their parents in their eyes. Mr. Moreen now listened to him, as he listened to every one and to every thing, like a man of the world, and seemed to appeal to him—though not of course too grossly—to try and be a little more of one himself. Pemberton recognised in

[5] Central heating.

fact the importance of the character—from the advantage it gave Mr. Moreen. He was not even confused or embarrassed, whereas the young man in his service was more so than there was any reason for. Neither was he surprised—at least any more than a gentleman had to be who freely confessed himself a little shocked—though not perhaps strictly at Pemberton.

"We must go into this, mustn't we, dear?" he said to his wife. He assured his young friend that the matter should have his very best attention; and he melted into space as elusively as if, at the door, he were taking an inevitable but deprecatory precedence. When, the next moment, Pemberton found himself alone with Mrs. Moreen it was to hear her say "I see, I see"—stroking the roundness of her chin and looking as if she were only hesitating between a dozen easy remedies. If they didn't make their push Mr. Moreen could at least disappear for several days. During his absence his wife took up the subject again spontaneously, but her contribution to it was merely that she had thought all the while they were getting on so beautifully. Pemberton's reply to this revelation was that unless they immediately put down something on account he would leave them on the spot and for ever. He knew she would wonder how he would get away, for a moment expected her to enquire. She didn't, for which he was almost grateful to her, so little was he in a position to tell.

"You won't, you *know* you won't—you're too interested," she said. "You *are* interested, you know you are, you dear kind man!" She laughed with almost condemnatory archness, as if it were a reproach—though she wouldn't insist; and flirted a soiled pocket-handkerchief at him.

Pemberton's mind was fully made up to take his step the following week. This would give him time to get an answer to a letter he had dispatched to England. If he did in the event nothing of the sort—that is if he stayed another year and then went away only for three months—it was not merely because before the answer to his letter came (most unsatisfactory when it did arrive) Mr. Moreen generously counted out to him, and again with the sacrifice to "form" of a marked man of the world, three hundred francs in elegant ringing gold. He was irritated to find that Mrs. Moreen was right, that he couldn't at the pinch bear to leave the child. This stood out clearer for the very reason that, the night of his desperate appeal to his patrons, he had seen fully for the first time where he was. Wasn't it another proof of the success with which those patrons practised their arts that they had managed to avert for so long the illuminating flash? It descended on our friend with a breadth of effect which perhaps would have struck a spectator as comical, after he had returned to his little servile room, which looked into a close court where a bare dirty opposite wall took with the sound of shrill clatter, the reflexion of lighted back windows. He had simply given himself away to a band of adventurers. The idea, the word itself, wore a romantic horror for him—he had always lived on such safe lines. Later it assumed a more interesting, almost a soothing, sense: it pointed a moral, and Pemberton could enjoy a moral. The Moreens were adventurers not merely because they didn't pay their debts, because they lived on society, but because their whole view of life, dim and confused and instinctive, like that of clever colour-blind animals, was speculative and rapacious and mean. Oh they were "respectable," and that only made them more *immondes!*[6] The young man's analysis, while he brooded, put it at last very simply—they were adventurers because they were toadies and snobs. That was the completest account of them—it was the law of their being. Even when this truth became vivid to their ingenious inmate he remained unconscious of how much his mind had been prepared for it by the extraordinary little boy who had now become such a complication in his life. Much less could he then calculate on the information he was still to owe the extraordinary little boy.

V

But it was during the ensuing time that the real problem came up—the problem of how far it was excusable to discusss the turpitude of parents with a child of twelve, of thirteen, of fourteen. Absolutely inexcusable and quite impossible it of course at first appeared; and indeed the question didn't press for some time after Pemberton had received his three hundred francs. They produced a temporary lull, a relief from the sharpest pressure. The young man frugally amended his wardrobe and even had a few francs in his pocket. He thought the Moreens looked at him as if he were almost too smart, as if they ought to take care not to spoil him. If Mr. Moreen hadn't been such a man of the world he would perhaps have spoken of the freedom of such neckties on the part of a subordinate. But Mr. Moreen was always enough a man of the world to let things pass—he had certainly shown that. It was singular how Pemberton guessed that Morgan, though saying nothing about it, knew something had happened. But three hundred francs, especially when one owed money, couldn't last for ever; and when the treasure was gone—the boy knew when it had failed—Morgan did break ground. The party had returned to Nice at the beginning of the winter, but not to the charming villa. They went to an hotel, where they stayed three months, and then moved to another establishment, explaining that they had left the first because, after waiting and waiting, they couldn't get the rooms they wanted. These apartments, the rooms they wanted, were generally very splendid; but fortunately they never *could* get them—fortunately, I mean, for Pemberton, who reflected always that if they had got them there would have been a still scanter educational fund. What Morgan said at last was said suddenly, irrelevantly, when the moment came, in the middle of a lesson, and consisted of the apparently unfeeling words: "You ought to *filer*, you know—you really ought."

[6] Impure.

Pemberton stared. He had learnt enough French slang from Morgan to know that to *filer* meant to cut sticks. "Ah my dear fellow, don't turn me off!"

Morgan pulled a Greek lexicon toward him—he used a Greek-German— to look out a word, instead of asking it of Pemberton. "You can't go on like this, you know."

"Like what, my boy?"

"You know they don't pay you up," said Morgan, blushing and turning his leaves.

"Don't pay me?" Pemberton stared again and feigned amazement. "What on earth put that into your head?"

"It has been there a long time," the boy replied rummaging his book.

Pemberton was silent, then he went on: "I say, what are you hunting for? They pay me beautifully."

"I'm hunting for the Greek for awful whopper," Morgan dropped.

"Find that rather for gross impertinence and disabuse your mind. What do I want of money?"

"Oh that's another question!"

Pemberton wavered—he was drawn in different ways. The severely correct thing would have been to tell the boy that such a matter was none of his business and bid him go on with his lines. But they were really too intimate for that; it was not the way he was in the habit of treating him; there had been no reason it should be. On the other hand Morgan had quite lighted on the truth—he really shouldn't be able to keep it up much longer; therefore why not let him know one's real motive for forsaking him? At the same time it wasn't decent to abuse to one's pupil the family of one's pupil; it was better to misrepresent than to do that. So in reply to his comrade's last exclamation he just declared, to dismiss the subject, that he had received several payments.

"I say—I say!" the boy ejaculated, laughing.

"That's all right," Pemberton insisted. "Give me your written rendering."

Morgan pushed a copybook across the table, and he began to read the page, but with something running in his head that made it no sense. Looking up after a minute or two he found the child's eyes fixed on him and felt in them something strange. Then Morgan said: "I'm not afraid of the stern reality."

"I haven't yet seen the thing you *are* afraid of—I'll do you that justice!"

This came out with a jump—it was perfectly true—and evidently gave Morgan pleasure. "I've thought of it a long time," he presently resumed.

"Well, don't think of it any more."

The boy appeared to comply, and they had a comfortable and even an amusing hour. They had a theory that they were very thorough, and yet they seemed always to be in the amusing part of lessons, the intervals between the dull dark tunnels, where there were waysides and jolly views. Yet the morn-

ing was brought to a violent end by Morgan's suddenly leaning his arms on
the table, burying his head in them and bursting into tears: at which Pemberton was the more startled that, as it then came over him, it was the first time
he had ever seen the boy cry and that the impression was consequently quite
awful.

The next day, after much thought, he took a decision and, believing it to
be just, immediately acted on it. He cornered Mr. and Mrs. Moreen again
and let them know that if on the spot they didn't pay him all they owed him
he wouldn't only leave their house but would tell Morgan exactly what had
brought him to it.

"Oh, you *haven't* told him?" cried Mrs. Moreen with a pacifying hand on
her well-dressed bosom.

"Without warning you? For what do you take me?" the young man returned.

Mr. and Mrs. Moreen looked at each other; he could see that they appreciated, as tending to their security, his superstition of delicacy, and yet that
there was a certain alarm in their relief. "My dear fellow," Mr. Moreen
demanded, "what use *can* you have, leading the quiet life we all do, for such
a lot of money?"—a question to which Pemberton made no answer, occupied as he was in noting that what passed in the mind of his patrons was
something like: "Oh then, if we've felt that the child, dear little angel, has
judged us and how he regards us, and we haven't been betrayed, he must
have guessed—and in short it's *general!*" an inference that rather stirred up
Mr. and Mrs. Moreen, as Pemberton had desired it should. At the same time,
if he had supposed his threat would do something towards bringing them
round, he was disappointed to find them taking for granted—how vulgar
their perception *had* been!—that he had already given them away. There
was a mystic uneasiness in their parental breasts, and that had been the
inferior sense of it. None the less, however, his threat did touch them; for if
they had escaped it was only to meet a new danger. Mr. Moreen appealed to
him, on every precedent, as a man of the world; but his wife had recourse,
for the first time since his domestication with them, to a fine *hauteur*,[7]
reminding him that a devoted mother, with her child, had arts that protected
her against gross misrepresentation.

"I should misrepresent you grossly if I accused you of common honesty!"
our friend replied; but as he closed the door behind him sharply, thinking he
had not done himself much good, while Mr. Moreen lighted another cigarette, he heard his hostess shout after him more touchingly:

"Oh you do, you *do*, put the knife to one's throat!"

The next morning, very early, she came to his room. He recognised her
knock, but had no hope she brought him money; as to which he was wrong,
for she had fifty francs in her hand. She squeezed forward in her dressing-

[7] Haughtiness.

gown, and he received her in his own, between his bath-tub and his bed. He had been tolerably schooled by this time to the "foreign ways" of his hosts. Mrs. Moreen was ardent, and when she was ardent she didn't care what she did; so she now sat down on his bed, his clothes being on the chairs, and, in her preoccupation, forgot, as she glanced round, to be ashamed of giving him such a horrid room. What Mrs. Moreen's ardour now bore upon was the design of persuading him that in the first place she was very good-natured to bring him fifty francs, and that in the second, if he would only see it, he was really too absurd to expect to be *paid*. Wasn't he paid enough without perpetual money—wasn't he paid by the comfortable luxurious home he enjoyed with them all, without a care, an anxiety, a solitary want? Wasn't he sure of his position, and wasn't that everything to a young man like him, quite unknown, with singularly little to show, the ground of whose exorbitant pretensions it had never been easy to discover? Wasn't he paid above all by the sweet relation he had established with Morgan—quite ideal as from master to pupil—and by the simple privilege of knowing and living with so amazingly gifted a child; than whom really (and she meant literally what she said) there was no better company in Europe? Mrs. Moreen herself took to appealing to him as a man of the world; she said "Voyons, mon cher," and "My dear man, look here now"; and urged him to be reasonable, putting it before him that it was truly a chance for him. She spoke as if, according as he *should* be reasonable, he would prove himself worthy to be her son's tutor and of the extraordinary confidence they had placed in him.

After all, Pemberton reflected, it was only a difference of theory and the theory didn't matter much. They had hitherto gone on that of remunerated, as now they would go on that of gratuitous, service; but why should they have so many words about it? Mrs. Moreen at all events continued to be convincing; sitting there with her fifty francs she talked and reiterated as women reiterate, and bored and irritated him, while he leaned against the wall with his hands in the pockets of his wrapper, drawing it together round his legs and looking over the head of his visitor at the grey negations of his window. She wound up with saying: "You see I bring you a definite proposal."

"A definite proposal?"

"To make our relations regular, as it were—to put them on a comfortable footing."

"I see—it's a system," said Pemberton. "A kind of organised blackmail."

Mrs. Moreen bounded up, which was exactly what he wanted. "What do you mean by that?"

"You practice on one's fears—one's fears about the child if one should go away."

"And pray what would happen to him in that event?" she demanded with majesty.

"Why he'd be alone with *you*."

"And pray with whom *should* a child be but with those whom he loves most?"

"If you think that, why don't you dismiss me?"

"Do you pretend he loves you more than he loves *us*?" cried Mrs. Moreen.

"I think he ought to. I make sacrifices for him. Though I've heard of those *you* make I don't see them."

Mrs. Moreen stared a moment; then with emotions she grasped her inmate's hand. "*Will* you make it—the sacrifice?"

He burst out laughing. "I'll see. I'll do what I can. I'll stay a little longer. Your calculation's just—I *do* hate intensely to give him up; I'm fond of him and he thoroughly interests me, in spite of the inconvenience I suffer. You know my situation perfectly. I haven't a penny in the world and, occupied as you see me with Morgan, am unable to earn money."

Mrs. Moreen tapped her undressed arm with her folded bank-note. "Can't you write articles? Can't you translate as *I* do?"

"I don't know about translating; it's wretchedly paid."

"I'm glad to earn what I can," said Mrs. Moreen with prodigious virtue.

"You ought to tell me who you do it for." Pemberton paused a moment, and she said nothing; so he added: "I've tried to turn off some little sketches, but the magazines won't have them—they're declined with thanks."

"You see then you're not such a phœnix," his visitor pointedly smiled—"to pretend to abilities you're sacrificing for our sake."

"I haven't time to do things properly," he ruefully went on. Then as it came over him that he was almost abjectly good-natured to give these explanations he added: "If I stay on longer it must be on one condition—that Morgan shall know distinctly on what footing I am."

Mrs. Moreen demurred. "Surely you don't want to show off to a child?"

"To show *you* off, do you mean?"

Again she cast about, but this time it was to produce a still finer flower. "And *you* talk of blackmail!"

"You can easily prevent it," said Pemberton.

"And *you* talk of practising on fears!" she bravely pushed on.

"Yes, there's no doubt I'm a great scoundrel."

His patroness met his eyes—it was clear she was in straits. Then she thrust out her money at him. "Mr. Moreen desired me to give you this on account."

"I'm much obliged to Mr. Moreen, but we *have* no account."

"You won't take it?"

"That leaves me more free," said Pemberton.

"To poison my darling's mind?" groaned Mrs. Moreen.

"Oh your darling's mind—!" the young man laughed.

She fixed him a moment, and he thought she was going to break out tormentedly, pleadingly: "For God's sake, tell me what *is* in it!" But she checked this impulse—another was stronger. She pocketed the money—the crudity of the alternative was comical—and swept out of the room with the desperate concession: "You may tell him any horror you like!"

VI

A couple of days after this, during which he had failed to profit by so free a permission, he had been for a quarter of an hour walking with his charge in silence when the boy became sociable again with the remark: "I'll tell you how I know it; I know it through Zénobie."

"Zénobie? Who in the world is *she?*"

"A nurse I used to have—ever so many years ago. A charming woman. I liked her awfully, and she liked me."

"There's no accounting for tastes. What is it you know through her?"

"Why what their idea is. She went away because they didn't fork out. She did like me awfully, and she stayed two years. She told me all about it—that at last she could never get her wages. As soon as they saw how much she liked me they stopped giving her anything. They thought she'd stay for nothing—just *because*, don't you know?" And Morgan had a queer little conscious lucid look. "She did stay ever so long—as long as she could. She was only a poor girl. She used to send money to her mother. At last she couldn't afford it any longer, and went away in a fearful rage one night—I mean of course in a rage against *them*. She cried over me tremendously, she hugged me nearly to death. She told me all about it," the boy repeated. "She told me it was their idea. So I guessed, ever so long ago, that they have had the same idea with you."

"Zénobie was very sharp," said Pemberton. "And she made you so."

"Oh that wasn't Zénobie; that was nature. And experience!" Morgan laughed.

"Well, Zénobie was a part of your experience."

"Certainly I was a part of hers, poor dear!" the boy wisely sighed. "And I'm part of yours."

"A very important part. But I don't see how you know I've been treated like Zénobie."

"Do you take me for the biggest dunce you've known?" Morgan asked. "Haven't I been conscious of what we've been through together?"

"What we've been through?"

"Our privations—our dark days."

"Oh our days have been bright enough."

Morgan went on in silence for a moment. Then he said: "My dear chap, you're a hero!"

"Well, you're another!" Pemberton retorted.

"No I'm not, but I ain't a baby. I won't stand it any longer. You must get some occupation that pays. I'm ashamed, I'm ashamed!" quavered the boy with a ring of passion, like some high silver note from a small cathedral chorister, that deeply touched his friend.

"We ought to go off and live somewhere together," the young man said. "I'll go like a shot if you'll take me."

"I'd get some work that would keep us both afloat," Pemberton continued.

"So would I. Why shouldn't *I* work? I ain't such a beastly little muff as *that* comes to."

"The difficulty is that your parents wouldn't hear of it. They'd never part with you; they worship the ground you tread on. Don't you see the proof of it?" Pemberton developed. "They don't dislike me; they wish me no harm; they're very amiable people; but they're perfectly ready to expose me to any awkwardness in life for your sake."

The silence in which Morgan received his fond sophistry struck Pemberton somehow as expressive. After a moment the child repeated: "You *are* a hero!" Then he added: "They leave me with you altogether. You've all the responsibility. They put me off on you from morning till night. Why then should they object to my taking up with you completely? I'd help you."

"They're not particularly keen about my being helped, and they delight in thinking of you as *theirs*. They're tremendously proud of you."

"I'm not proud of *them*. But you know that," Morgan returned.

"Except for the little matter we speak of they're charming people," said Pemberton, not taking up the point made for his intelligence, but wondering greatly at the boy's own, and especially at this fresh reminder of something he had been conscious of from the first—the strangest thing in his friend's large little composition, a temper, a sensibility, even a private ideal, which made him as privately disown the stuff his people were made of. Morgan had in secret a small loftiness which made him acute about betrayed meanness; as well as a critical sense for the manners immediately surrounding him that was quite without precedent in a juvenile nature, especially when one noted that it had not made this nature "old-fashioned," as the word is of children— quaint or wizened or offensive. It was as if he had been a little gentleman and had paid the penalty by discovering that he was the only such person in his family. This comparison didn't make him vain, but it could make him melancholy and a trifle austere. While Pemberton guessed at these dim young things, shadows of shadows, he was partly drawn on and partly checked, as for a scruple, by the charm of attempting to sound the little cool shallows that were so quickly growing deeper. When he tried to figure to himself the morning twilight of childhood, so as to deal with it safely, he saw it was never fixed, never arrested, that ignorance, at the instant he touched it, was already flushing faintly into knowledge, that there was nothing that at a given moment you could say an intelligent child didn't know. It seemed to him that he himself knew too much to imagine Morgan's simplicity and too little to disembroil his tangle.

The boy paid no heed to his last remark; he only went on: "I'd have spoken to them about their idea, as I call it, long ago, if I hadn't been sure what they'd say."

"And what would they say?"

"Just what they said about what poor Zénobie told me—that it was a horrid dreadful story, that they had paid her every penny they owed her."

"Well, perhaps they had," said Pemberton.

"Perhaps they've paid you!"

"Let us pretend they have, and *n'en parlons plus.*"[8]

"They accused her of lying and cheating"—Morgan stuck to historic truth. "That's why I don't want to speak to them."

"Lest they should accuse me too?" To this Morgan made no answer, and his companion, looking down at him—the boy turned away his eyes, which had filled—saw that he couldn't have trusted himself to utter. "You're right. Don't worry them," Pemberton pursued. "Except for that, they *are* charming people."

"Except for *their* lying and *their* cheating?"

"I say—I say!" cried Pemberton, imitating a little tone of the lad's which was itself an imitation.

"We must be frank, at the last; we *must* come to an understanding," said Morgan with the importance of the small boy who lets himself think he is arranging great affairs—almost playing at shipwreck or at Indians. "I know all about everything."

"I dare say your father has his reasons," Pemberton replied, but too vaguely, as he was aware.

"For lying and cheating?"

"For saving and managing and turning his means to the best account. He has plenty to do with his money. You're an expensive family."

"Yes, I'm very expensive," Morgan concurred in a manner that made his preceptor burst out laughing.

"He's saving for *you*," said Pemberton. "They think of you in everything they do."

"He might, while he's about it, save a little—" The boy paused, and his friend waited to hear what. Then Morgan brought out oddly: "A little reputation."

"Oh there's plenty of that. That's all right!"

"Enough of it for the people they know, no doubt. The people they know are awful."

"Do you mean the princes? We mustn't abuse the princes."

"Why not? They haven't married Paula—they haven't married Amy. They only clean out Ulick."

"You *do* know everything!" Pemberton declared.

---

[8] Let's not mention it anymore.

"No I don't after all. I don't know what they live on, or how they live, or *why* they live! What have they got and how did they get it? Are they rich, are they poor, or have they a *modeste aisance?*[9] Why are they always chivey-ing me about—living one year like ambassadors and the next like paupers? Who are they, anyway, and what are they? I've thought of all that—I've thought of a lot of things. They're so beastly worldly. That's what I hate most—oh I've *seen* it! All they care about is to make an appearance and to pass for something or other. What the dickens do they want to pass for? What *do* they, Mr. Pemberton?

"You pause for a reply," said Pemberton, treating the question as a joke, yet wondering too and greatly struck with his mate's intense if imperfect vision. "I haven't the least idea."

"And what good does it do? Haven't I seen the way people treat them—the 'nice' people, the ones they want to know? They'll take anything from them—they'll lie down and be trampled on. The nice ones hate that—they just sicken them. You're the only really nice person we know."

"Are you sure? They don't lie down for me!"

"Well, you shan't lie down for them. You've got to go—that's what you've got to do," said Morgan.

"And what will become of you?"

"Oh I'm growing up. I shall get off before long. I'll see you later."

"You had better let me finish you," Pemberton urged, lending himself to the child's strange superiority.

Morgan stopped in their walk, looking up at him. He had to look up much less than a couple of years before—he had grown, in his loose leanness, so long and high. "Finish me?" he echoed.

"There are such a lot of jolly things we can do together yet. I want to turn you out—I want you to do me credit."

Morgan continued to look at him. "To give you credit—do you mean?"

"My dear fellow, you're too clever to live."

"That's just what I'm afraid you think. No, no; it isn't fair—I can't endure it. We'll separate next week. The sooner it's over the sooner to sleep."

"If I hear of anything—any other chance—I promise to go," Pemberton said.

Morgan consented to consider this. "But you'll be honest," he demanded; "you won't pretend you haven't heard?"

"I'm much more likely to pretend I have."

"But what can you hear of, this way, stuck in a hole with us? You ought to be on the spot, to go to England—you ought to go to America."

"One would think you were *my* tutor!" said Pemberton.

Morgan walked on and after a little had begun again: "Well, now that you

---

[9] Moderate income.

know I know and that we look at the facts and keep nothing back—it's much more comfortable, isn't it?"

"My dear boy, it's so amusing, so interesting, that it will surely be quite impossible for me to forego such hours as these."

This made Morgan stop once more. "You *do* keep something back. Oh you're not straight—*I* am!"

"How am I not straight?"

"Oh you've got your idea!"

"My idea?"

"Why that I probably shan't make old—make older—bones, and that you can stick it out till I'm removed."

"You *are* too clever to live!" Pemberton repeated.

"I call it a mean idea," Morgan pursued. "But I shall punish you by the way I hang on."

"Look out or I'll poison you!" Pemberton laughed.

"I'm stronger and better every year. Haven't you noticed that there hasn't been a doctor near me since you came?"

"*I'm* your doctor," said the young man, taking his arm and drawing him tenderly on again.

Morgan proceeded and after a few steps gave a sigh of mingled weariness and relief. "Ah now that we look at the facts it's all right!"

VII

They looked at the facts a good deal after this; and one of the first consequences of their doing so was that Pemberton stuck it out, in his friend's parlance, for the purpose. Morgan made the facts so vivid and so droll, and at the same time so bald and so ugly, that there was fascination in talking them over with him, just as there would have been heartlessness in leaving him alone with them. Now that the pair had such perceptions in common it was useless for them to pretend they didn't judge such people; but the very judgment and the exchange of perceptions created another tie. Morgan had never been so interesting as now that he himself was made plainer by the sidelight of these confidences. What came out in it most was the small fine passion of his pride. He had plenty of that, Pemberton felt—so much that one might perhaps wisely wish for it some early bruises. He would have liked his people to have a spirit and had waked up to the sense of their perpetually eating humble-pie. His mother would consume any amount, and his father would consume even more than his mother. He had a theory that Ulick had wriggled out of an "affair" at Nice; there had once been a flurry at home, a regular panic, after which they all went to bed and took medicine, not to be accounted for on any other supposition. Morgan had a romantic imagination, fed by poetry and history, and he would have liked those who "bore his name"—as he used to say to Pemberton with the humour that made his queer delicacies manly—to carry themselves with an air. But their one idea was to get in with people who didn't want them and to take snubs as if they were honourable scars. Why people didn't want them more he didn't know—that was people's own affair; after all they weren't superficially repulsive, they were a hundred times cleverer than most of the dreary grandees, the "poor swells" they rushed about Europe to catch up with. "After all they *are* amusing—they are!" he used to pronounce with the wisdom of the ages. To which Pemberton always replied: "Amusing—the great Moreen troupe? Why they're altogether delightful; and if it weren't for the hitch that you and I (feeble performers!) make in the *ensemble* they'd carry everything before them."

What the boy couldn't get over was the fact that this particular blight seemed, in a tradition of self-respect, so undeserved and so arbitrary. No doubt people had a right to take the line they liked; but why should *his* people have liked the line of pushing and toadying and lying and cheating? What had their forefathers—all decent folk, so far as he knew—done to them, or what had *he* done to them? Who had poisoned their blood with the fifth-rate social ideal, the fixed idea of making smart acquaintances and getting into the *monde chic*, especially when it was foredoomed to failure and exposure? They showed so what they were after; that was what made the people they wanted not want *them*. And never a wince for dignity, never a throb of shame at looking each other in the face, never any independence or resentment or disgust. If his father or his brother would only knock someone down once or twice a year! Clever as they were they never guessed the impression they made. They were good-natured, yes—as good-natured as Jews at the doors of clothing-shops! But was that the model one wanted one's family to follow? Morgan had dim memories of an old grandfather, the maternal, in New York, whom he had been taken across the ocean at the age of five to see: a gentleman with a high neck-cloth and a good deal of pronunciation, who wore a dress-coat in the morning, which made one wonder what he wore in the evening, and had, or was supposed to have, "property" and something to do with the Bible Society. It couldn't have been but that *he* was a good type. Pemberton himself remembered Mrs. Clancy, a widowed sister of Mr. Moreen's, who was as irritating as a moral tale and had paid a fortnight's visit to the family at Nice shortly after he came to live with them. She was "pure and refined," as Amy said over the banjo, and had the air of not knowing what they meant when they talked, and of keeping something rather important back. Pemberton judged that what she kept back was an approval of many of their ways; therefore it was to be supposed that she too was of a good type, and that Mr. and Mrs. Moreen and Ulick and Paula and Amy might easily have been of a better one if they would.

But that they wouldn't was more and more perceptible from day to day. They continued to "chivey," as Morgan called it, and in due time became aware of a variety of reasons for proceeding to Venice. They mentioned a great many of them—they were always strikingly frank and had the brightest friendly chatter, at the late foreign breakfast in especial, before the ladies had made up their faces, when they leaned their arms on the table, had something to follow the *demi-tasse*, [10] and, in the heat of familiar discussion as to what they "really ought" to do, fell inevitably into the languages in which they could *tutoyer*. [11] Even Pemberton liked them then; he could endure even Ulick when he heard him give his little flat voice for the "sweet sea-city." That was what made him have a sneaking kindness for them—that they were so out of the workaday world and kept him so out of it. The summer had waned when, with cries of ecstasy, they all passed out on the balcony that overhung the Grand Canal. The sunsets then were splendid and the Dorringtons had arrived. The Dorringtons were the only reason they hadn't talked of at breakfast; but the reasons they didn't talk of at breakfast always came out in the end. The Dorringtons on the other hand came out very little; or else when they did they stayed—as was natural—for hours, during which periods Mrs. Moreen and the girls sometimes called at their hotel (to see if they had returned) as many as three times running. The gondola was for the ladies, as in Venice too there were "days," which Mrs. Moreen knew in their order an hour after she arrived. She immediately took one herself, to which the Dorringtons never came, though on a certain occasion when Pemberton and his pupil were together at Saint Mark's—where, taking the best walks they had ever had and haunting a hundred churches, they spent a great deal of time—they saw the old lord turn up with Mrs. Moreen and Ulick, who showed him the dim basilica as if it belonged to them. Pemberton noted how much less, among its curiosities, Lord Dorrington carried himself as a man of the world; wondering too whether, for such services, his companions took a fee from him. The autumn at any rate waned, the Dorringtons departed, and Lord Verschoyle, the eldest son, had proposed neither for Amy nor for Paula.

One sad November day, while the wind roared round the old palace and the rain lashed the lagoon, Pemberton, for exercise and even somewhat for warmth—the Moreens were horribly frugal about fires; it was a cause of suffering to their inmate—walked up and down the big bare *sala* [12] with his pupil. The scagliola [13] floor was cold, the high battered casements shook in the storm, and the stately decay of the place was unrelieved by a particle of furniture. Pemberton's spirits were low, and it came over him that the fortune of the Moreens was now even lower. A blast of desolation, a portent of disgrace and disaster, seemed to draw through the comfortless hall. Mr. Moreen and Ulick were in the Piazza, looking out for something, strolling drearily, in mackintoshes, under the arcades; but still, in spite of mackin-

---

[10] A half cup of coffee served in small cups.
[11] To speak in the familiar case.

[12] Large room.
[13] Imitation marble.

toshes, unmistakeable men of the world. Paula and Amy were in bed—it might have been thought they were staying there to keep warm. Pemberton looked askance at the boy at his side, to see to what extent he was conscious of these dark omens. But Morgan, luckily for him, was now mainly conscious of growing taller and stronger and indeed of being in his fifteenth year. This fact was intensely interesting to him and the basis of a private theory—which, however, he had imparted to his tutor—that in a little while he should stand on his own feet. He considered that the situation would change—that in short he should be "finished," grown up, producible in the world of affairs and ready to prove himself of sterling ability. Sharply as he was capable at times of analysing, as he called it, his life, there were happy hours when he remained, as he also called it—and as the name, really, of their right ideal—"jolly" superficial; the proof of which was his fundamental assumption that he should presently go to Oxford, to Pemberton's college, and aided and abetted by Pemberton, do the most wonderful things. It depressed the young man to see how little in such a project he took account of ways and means; in other connexions he mostly kept to the measure. Pemberton tried to imagine the Moreens at Oxford and fortunately failed; yet unless they were to adopt it as a residence there would be no *modus vivendi*[14] for Morgan. How could he live without an allowance, and where was the allowance to come from? He, Pemberton, might live on Morgan; but how could Morgan live on *him?* What was to become of him anyhow? Somehow the fact that he was a big boy now, with better prospects of health, made the question of his future more difficult. So long as he was markedly frail the great consideration he inspired seemed enough of an answer to it. But at the bottom of Pemberton's heart was the recognition of his probably being strong enough to live and not yet strong enough to struggle or to thrive. Morgan himself at any rate was in the first flush of the rosiest consciousness of adolescence, so that the beating of the tempest seemed to him after all but the voice of life and the challenge of fate. He had on his shabby little overcoat, with the collar up, but was enjoying his walk.

It was interrupted at last by the appearance of his mother at the end of the *sala*. She beckoned him to come to her, and while Pemberton saw him, complaisant, pass down the long vista and over the damp false marble, he wondered what was in the air. Mrs. Moreen said a word to the boy and made him go into the room she had quitted. Then, having closed the door after him, she directed her steps swiftly to Pemberton. There *was* something in the air, but his wildest flight of fancy wouldn't have suggested what it proved to be. She signified that she had made a pretext to get Morgan out of the way, and then she enquired—without hesitation—if the young man could favour her with the loan of three louis. While, before bursting into a laugh,

[14] Means of living.

he stared at her with surprise, she declared that she was awfully pressed for the money; she was desperate for it—it would save her life.

"Dear lady, *c'est trop fort!*"[15] Pemberton laughed in the manner and with the borrowed grace of idiom that marked the best colloquial, the best anecdotic, moments of his friends themselves. "Where in the world do you suppose I should get three louis, *du train dont vous allez?*"[16]

"I thought you worked—wrote things. Don't they pay you?"

"Not a penny."

"Are you such a fool as to work for nothing?"

"You ought surely to know that."

Mrs. Moreen stared, then she coloured a little. Pemberton saw she had quite forgotten the terms—if "terms" they could be called—that he had ended by accepting from herself; they had burdened her memory as little as her conscience. "Oh yes, I see what you mean—you've been very nice about that; but why drag it in so often?" She had been perfectly urbane with him ever since the rough scene of explanation in his room the morning he made her accept *his* "terms"—the necessity of his making his case known to Morgan. She had felt no resentment after seeing there was no danger Morgan would take the matter up with her. Indeed, attributing this immunity to the good taste of his influence with the boy, she had once said to Pemberton "My dear fellow, it's an immense comfort you're a gentleman." She repeated this in substance now. "Of course you're a gentleman—that's a bother the less!" Pemberton reminded her that he had not "dragged in" anything that wasn't already in as much as his foot was in his shoe; and she also repeated her prayer that, somewhere and somehow, he would find her sixty francs. He took the liberty of hinting that if he could find them it wouldn't be to lend them to *her*—as to which he consciously did himself injustice, knowing that if he had them he would certainly put them at her disposal. He accused himself, at bottom and not unveraciously, of a fantastic, a demoralised sympathy with her. If misery made strange bed-fellows it also made strange sympathies. It was moreover a part of the abasement of living with such people that one had to make vulgar retorts, quite out of one's own tradition of good manners. "Morgan, Morgan, to what pass have I come for you?" he groaned while Mrs. Moreen floated voluminously down the *sala* again to liberate the boy, wailing as she went that everything was too odious.

Before their young friend was liberated there came a thump at the door communicating with the staircase, followed by the apparition of a dripping youth who poked in his head. Pemberton recognised him as the bearer of a telegram and recognised the telegram as addressed to himself. Morgan came back as, after glancing at the signature—that of a relative in London—he was reading the words: "Found jolly job for you, engagement to coach opulent youth on own terms. Come at once." The answer happily was paid and

---

[15] This is too much. [16] The way you carry on.

the messenger waited. Morgan, who had drawn near, waited too and looked hard at Pemberton; and Pemberton, after a moment, having met his look, handed him the telegram. It was really by wise looks—they knew each other so well now—that, while the telegraph-boy, in his waterproof cape, made a great puddle on the floor, the thing was settled between them. Pemberton wrote the answer with a pencil against the frescoed wall, and the messenger departed. When he had gone the young man explained himself.

"I'll make a tremendous charge; I'll earn a lot of money in a short time, and we'll live on it."

"Well, I hope the opulent youth will be a dismal dunce—he probably will," Morgan parenthesised—"and keep you a long time a-hammering of it in."

"Of course the longer he keeps me the more we shall have for our old age."

"But suppose *they* don't pay you!" Morgan awfully suggested.

"Oh, there are not two such—!" But Pemberton pulled up; he had been on the point of using too invidious a term. Instead of this he said "Two such fatalities."

Morgan flushed—the tears came to his eyes. "*Dites toujours*[17] two such rascally crews!" Then in a different tone he added: "Happy opulent youth!"

"Not if he's a dismal dunce."

"Oh they're happier then. But you can't have everything, can you?" the boy smiled.

Pemberton held him fast, hands on his shoulders—he had never loved him so. "What will become of *you*, what will you do?" He thought of Mrs. Moreen, desperate for sixty francs.

"I shall become an *homme fait*."[18] And then as if he recognised all the bearings of Pemberton's allusion: "I shall get on with them better when you're not here."

"Ah don't say that—it sounds as if I set you against them!"

"You do—the sight of you. It's all right; you know what I mean. I shall be beautiful. I'll take their affairs in hand; I'll marry my sisters."

"You'll marry yourself!" joked Pemberton; as high, rather tense pleasantry would evidently be the right, or the safest, tone for their separation.

It was, however, not purely in this strain that Morgan suddenly asked: "But I say—how will you get to your jolly job? You'll have to telegraph to the opulent youth for money to come on."

Pemberton bethought himself. "They won't like that, will they?"

"Oh look out for them!"

Then Pemberton brought out his remedy. "I'll go to the American Consul; I'll borrow some money of him—just for the few days, on the strength of the telegram."

---

[17] Let's hear it anyway.　　　　[18] A self-made man.

Morgan was hilarious. "Show him the telegram—then collar the money and stay!"

Pemberton entered into the joke sufficiently to reply that for Morgan he was really capable of that; but the boy, growing more serious, and to prove he hadn't meant what he said, not only hurried him off to the Consulate—since he was to start that evening, as he had wired to his friend—but made sure of their affair by going with him. They splashed through the tortuous perforations and over the humpbacked bridges, and they passed through the Piazza, where they saw Mr. Moreen and Ulick go into a jeweller's shop. The Consul proved accommodating—Pemberton said it wasn't the letter, but Morgan's grand air—and on their way back they went into Saint Mark's for a hushed ten minutes. Later they took up and kept up the fun of it to the very end; and it seemed to Pemberton a part of that fun that Mrs. Moreen, who was very angry when he had announced her his intention, should charge him, grotesquely and vulgarly and in reference to the loan she had vainly endeavoured to effect, with bolting lest they should "get something out" of him. On the other hand he had to do Mr. Moreen and Ulick the justice to recognise that when on coming in *they* heard the cruel news they took it like perfect men of the world.

VIII

When he got at work with the opulent youth, who was to be taken in hand for Balliol, he found himself unable to say if this aspirant had really such poor parts or if the appearance were only begotten of his own long association with an intensely living little mind. From Morgan he heard half a dozen times: the boy wrote charming young letters, a patchwork of tongues, with indulgent postscripts in the family Volapuk and, in little squares and rounds and crannies of the text, the drollest illustrations—letters that he was divided between the impulse to show his present charge as a vain, a wasted incentive, and the sense of something in them that publicity would profane. The opulent youth went up in due course and failed to pass; but it seemed to add to the presumption that brilliancy was not expected of him all at once that his parents, condoning the lapse, which they good-naturedly treated as little as possible as if it were Pemberton's, should have sounded the rally again, begged the young coach to renew the siege.

The young coach was now in a position to lend Mrs. Moreen three louis, and he sent her a post-office order even for a larger amount. In return for his favour he received a frantic scribbled line from her: "Implore you to come back instantly—Morgan dreadfully ill." They were on the rebound, once more in Paris—often as Pemberton had seen them depressed he had never seen them crushed—and communication was therefore rapid. He wrote to the boy to ascertain the state of his health, but awaited the answer in vain.

He accordingly, after three days, took an abrupt leave of the opulent youth and, crossing the Channel, alighted at the small hotel, in the quarter of the Champs Élysées, of which Mrs. Moreen had given him the address. A deep if dumb dissatisfaction with this lady and her companions bore him company: they couldn't be vulgarly honest, but they could live at hotels, in velvety *entresols*,[19] amid a smell of burnt pastilles,[20] surrounded by the most expensive city in Europe. When he had left them in Venice it was with an irrepressible suspicion that something was going to happen; but the only thing that could have taken place was again their masterly retreat. "How is he? where is he?" he asked of Mrs. Moreen; but before she could speak these questions were answered by the pressure round his neck of a pair of arms, in shrunken sleeves, which still were perfectly capable of an effusive young foreign squeeze.

"Dreadfully ill—I don't see it!" the young man cried. And then to Morgan: "Why on earth didn't you relieve me? Why didn't you answer my letter?"

Mrs. Moreen declared that when she wrote he was very bad, and Pemberton learned at the same time from the boy that he had answered every letter he had received. This led to the clear inference that Pemberton's note had been kept from him so that the game to be practised should not be interfered with. Mrs. Moreen was prepared to see the fact exposed, as Pemberton saw the moment he faced her that she was prepared for a good many other things. She was prepared above all to maintain that she had acted from a sense of duty, that she was enchanted she had got him over, whatever they might say, and that it was useless of him to pretend he didn't know in all his bones that his place at such a time was with Morgan. He had taken the boy away from them and now had no right to abandon him. He had created for himself the gravest responsibilities and must at least abide by what he had done.

"Taken him away from you?" Pemberton exclaimed indignantly.

"Do it—do it for pity's sake; that's just what I want. I can't stand *this*—and such scenes. They're awful frauds—poor dears!" These words broke from Morgan, who had intermitted his embrace, in a key which made Pemberton turn quickly to him and see that he had suddenly seated himself, was breathing in great pain and was very pale.

"*Now* do you say he's not ·in a state, my precious pet?" shouted his mother, dropping on her knees before him with clasped hands, but touching him no more than if he had been a gilded idol. "It will pass—it's only for an instant; but don't say such dreadful things!"

"I'm all right—all right," Morgan panted to Pemberton, whom he sat looking up at with a strange smile, his hands resting on either side of the sofa.

[19] Mezzanines.
[20] A roll or small cone of paste containing aromatic substances; when burnt, it smells like incense.

"Now do you pretend I've been dishonest, that I've deceived?" Mrs. Moreen flashed at Pemberton as she got up.

"It isn't *he* says it, it's I!" the boy returned, apparently easier but sinking back against the wall; while his restored friend, who had sat down beside him, took his hand and bent over him.

"Darling child, one does what one can; there are so many things to consider," urged Mrs. Moreen. "It's his *place*—his only place. You see *you* think it is now."

"Take me away—take me away," Morgan went on, smiling to Pemberton with his white face.

"Where shall I take you, and how—oh *how*, my boy?" the young man stammered, thinking of the rude way in which his friends in London held that, for his convenience, with no assurance of prompt return, he had thrown them over; of the just resentment with which they would already have called in a successor, and of the scant help to finding fresh employment that resided for him in the grossness of his having failed to pass his pupil.

"Oh we'll settle that. You used to talk about it," said Morgan. "If we can only go all the rest's a detail."

"Talk about it as much as you like, but don't think you can attempt it. Mr. Moreen would never consent—it would be so *very* hand-to-mouth," Pemberton's hostess beautifully explained to him. Then to Morgan she made it clearer: "It would destroy our peace, it would break our hearts. Now that he's back it will be all the same again. You'll have your life, your work and your freedom, and we'll all be happy as we used to be. You'll bloom and grow perfectly well, and we won't have any more silly experiments, will we? They're too absurd. It's Mr. Pemberton's place—every one in his place. You in yours, your papa in his, me in mine—*n'est-ce pas, chéri?* We'll all forget how foolish we've been and have lovely times."

She continued to talk and to surge vaguely about the little draped stuffy salon while Pemberton sat with the boy, whose colour gradually came back; and she mixed up her reasons, hinting that there were going to be changes, that the other children might scatter (who knew?—Paula had her ideas) and that then it might be fancied how much the poor old parent-birds would want the little nestling. Morgan looked at Pemberton, who wouldn't let him move; and Pemberton knew exactly how he felt at hearing himself called a little nestling. He admitted that he had had one or two bad days, but he protested afresh against the wrong of his mother's having made them the ground of an appeal to poor Pemberton. Poor Pemberton could laugh now, apart from the comicality of Mrs. Moreen's mustering so much philosophy for her defence—she seemed to shake it out of her agitated petticoats, which knocked over the light gilt chairs—so little did their young companion, *marked*, unmistakeably marked at the best, strike him as qualified to repudiate any advantage.

He himself was in for it at any rate. He should have Morgan on his hands again indefinitely; though indeed he saw the lad had a private theory to produce which would be intended to smooth this down. He was obliged to him for it in advance; but the suggested amendment didn't keep his heart rather from sinking, any more than it prevented him from accepting the prospect on the spot, with some confidence moreover that he should do even better if he could have a little supper. Mrs. Moreen threw out more hints about the changes that were to be looked for, but she was such a mixture of smiles and shudders—she confessed she was very nervous—that he couldn't tell if she were in high feather or only in hysterics. If the family was really at last going to pieces why shouldn't she recognise the necessity of pitching Morgan into some sort of lifeboat? This presumption was fostered by the fact that they were established in luxurious quarters in the capital of pleasure; that was exactly where they naturally *would* be established in view of going to pieces. Moreover, didn't she mention that Mr. Moreen and the others were enjoying themselves at the opera with Mr. Granger, and wasn't *that* also precisely where one would look for them on the eve of a smash? Pemberton gathered that Mr. Granger was a rich vacant American—a big bill with a flourishy heading and no items; so that one of Paula's "ideas" was probably that this time she hadn't missed fire—by which straight shot indeed she would have shattered the general cohesion. And if the cohesion was to crumble what would become of poor Pemberton? He felt quite enough bound up with them to figure to his alarm as a dislodged block in the edifice.

It was Morgan who eventually asked if no supper had been ordered for him; sitting with him below, later, at the dim delayed meal, in the presence of a great deal of corded green plush, a plate of ornamental biscuit and an aloofness marked on the part of the waiter. Mrs. Moreen had explained that they had been obliged to secure a room for the visitor out of the house; and Morgan's consolation—he offered it while Pemberton reflected on the nastiness of luke-warm sauces—proved to be, largely, that this circumstance would facilitate their escape. He talked of their escape—recurring to it often afterwards—as if they were making up a "boy's book" together. But he likewise expressed his sense that there was something in the air, that the Moreens couldn't keep it up much longer. In point of fact, as Pemberton was to see, they kept it up for five or six months. All the while, however, Morgan's contention was designed to cheer him. Mr. Moreen and Ulick, whom he had met the day after his return, accepted that return like perfect men of the world. If Paula and Amy treated it even with less formality an allowance was to be made for them, inasmuch as Mr. Granger hadn't come to the opera after all. He had only placed his box at their service, with a bouquet for each of the party; there was even one apiece, embittering the thought of his profusion, for Mr. Moreen and Ulick. "They're all like that," was Morgan's comment; "at the very last, just when we think we've landed them they're back in the deep sea!"

Morgan's comments in these days were more and more free; they even included a large recognition of the extraordinary tenderness with which he had been treated while Pemberton was away. Oh yes, they couldn't do enough to be nice to him, to show him they had him on their mind and make up for his loss. That was just what made the whole thing so sad and caused him to rejoice after all in Pemberton's return—he had to keep thinking of their affection less, had less sense of obligation. Pemberton laughed out at this last reason, and Morgan blushed and said "Well, dash it, you know what I mean." Pemberton knew perfectly what he meant; but there were a good many things that—dash it too!—it didn't make any clearer. This episode of his second sojourn in Paris stretched itself out wearily, with their resumed readings and wanderings and maunderings, their potterings on the quays, their hauntings of the museums, their occasional lingerings in the Palais Royal when the first sharp weather came on and there was a comfort in warm emanations, before Chevet's wonderful succulent window. Morgan wanted to hear all about the opulent youth—he took an immense interest in him. Some of the details of his opulence—Pemberton could spare him none of them—evidently fed the boy's appreciation of all his friend had given up to come back to him; but in addition to the greater reciprocity established by that heroism he had always his little brooding theory, in which there was a frivolous gaiety too, that their long probation was drawing to a close. Morgan's conviction that the Moreens couldn't go on much longer kept pace with the unexpended impetus with which, from month to month, they did go on. Three weeks after Pemberton had rejoined them they went on to another hotel, a dingier one than the first; but Morgan rejoiced that his tutor had at least still not sacrificed the advantage of a room outside. He clung to the romantic utility of this when the day, or rather the night, should arrive for their escape.

For the first time, in this complicated connexion, our friend felt his collar gall him. It was, as he had said to Mrs. Moreen in Venice, *trop fort*[21]— everything was *trop fort*. He could neither really throw off his blighting burden nor find in it the benefit of a pacified conscience or of a rewarded affection. He had spent all the money accruing to him in England, and he saw his youth going and that he was getting nothing back for it. It was all very well of Morgan to count it for reparation that he should now settle on him permanently—there was an irritating flaw in such a view. He saw what the boy had in his mind; the conception that as his friend had had the generosity to come back he must show his gratitude by giving him his life. But the poor friend didn't desire the gift—what could he do with Morgan's dreadful little life? Of course at the same time that Pemberton was irritated he remembered the reason, which was very honourable to Morgan and which dwelt simply in his making one so forget that he was no more than a

[21] Too much.

patched urchin. If one dealt with him on a different basis one's misadventures were one's own fault. So Pemberton waited in a queer confusion of yearning and alarm for the catastrophe which was held to hang over the house of Moreen, of which he certainly at moments felt the symptoms brush his cheek and as to which he wondered much in what form it would find its liveliest effect.

Perhaps it would take the form of sudden dispersal—a frightened *sauve qui peut*,[22] a scuttling into selfish corners. Certainly they were less elastic than of yore; they were evidently looking for something they didn't find. The Dorringtons hadn't re-appeared, the princes had scattered; wasn't that the beginning of the end? Mrs. Moreen had lost her reckoning of the famous "days"; her social calendar was blurred—it had turned its face to the wall. Pemberton suspected that the great, the cruel discomfiture had been the unspeakable behaviour of Mr. Granger, who seemed not to know what he wanted, or, what was much worse, what *they* wanted. He kept sending flowers, as if to bestrew the path of his retreat, which was never the path of a return. Flowers were all very well, but—Pemberton could complete the proposition. It was now positively conspicuous that in the long run the Moreens were a social failure; so that the young man was almost grateful the run had not been short. Mr. Moreen indeed was still occasionally able to get away on business and, what was more surprising, was likewise able to get back. Ulick had no club, but you couldn't have discovered it from his appearance, which was as much as ever that of a person looking at life from the window of such an institution; therefore Pemberton was doubly surprised at an answer he once heard him make his mother in the desperate tone of a man familiar with the worst privations. Her question Pemberton had not quite caught; it appeared to be an appeal for a suggestion as to whom they might get to take Amy. "Let the Devil take her!" Ulick snapped; so that Pemberton could see that they had not only lost their amiability but had ceased to believe in themselves. He could also see that if Mrs. Moreen was trying to get people to take her children she might be regarded as closing the hatches for the storm. But Morgan would be the last she would part with.

One winter afternoon—it was a Sunday—he and the boy walked far together in the Bois de Boulogne. The evening was so splendid, the cold lemon-coloured sunset so clear, the stream of carriages and pedestrians so amusing and the fascination of Paris so great, that they stayed out later than usual and became aware that they should have to hurry home to arrive in time for dinner. They hurried accordingly, arm-in-arm, good-humoured and hungry, agreeing that there was nothing like Paris after all and that after everything too that had come and gone they were not yet sated with innocent pleasures. When they reached the hotel they found that, though scandalously late, they were in time for all the dinner they were likely to sit down to. Confusion reigned in the apartments of the Moreens—very shabby

---

[22] Every man for himself.

ones this time, but the best in the house—and before the interrupted service of the table, with objects displaced almost as if there had been a scuffle and a great winestain from an overturned bottle, Pemberton couldn't blink the fact that there had been a scene of the last proprietary firmness. The storm had come—they were all seeking refuge. The hatches were down, Paula and Amy were invisible—they had never tried the most casual art upon Pemberton, but he felt they had enough of an eye to him not to wish to meet him as young ladies whose frocks had been confiscated—and Ulick appeared to have jumped overboard. The host and his staff, in a word, had ceased to "go on" at the pace of their guests, and the air of embarrassed detention, thanks to a pile of gaping trunks in the passage, was strangely commingled with the air of indignant withdrawal.

When Morgan took all this in—and he took it in very quickly—he coloured to the roots of his hair. He had walked from his infancy among difficulties and dangers, but he had never seen a public exposure. Pemberton noticed in a second glance at him that the tears had rushed into his eyes and that they were tears of a new and untasted bitterness. He wondered an instant, for the boy's sake, whether he might successfully pretend not to understand. Not successfully, he felt, as Mr. and Mrs. Moreen, dinnerless by their extinguished hearth, rose before him in their little dishonoured salon, casting about with glassy eyes for the nearest port in such a storm. They were not prostrate but were horribly white, and Mrs. Moreen had evidently been crying. Pemberton quickly learned however that her grief was not for the loss of her dinner, much as she usually enjoyed it, but the fruit of a blow that struck even deeper, as she made all haste to explain. He would see for himself, so far as that went, how the great change had come, the dreadful bolt had fallen, and how they would now all have to turn themselves about. Therefore cruel as it was to them to part with their darling she must look to him to carry a little further the influence he had so fortunately acquired with the boy—to induce his young charge to follow him into some modest retreat. They depended on him—that was the fact—to take their delightful child temporarily under his protection: it would leave Mr. Moreen and herself so much more free to give the proper attention (too little, alas! had been given) to the readjustment of their affairs.

"We trust you—we feel we *can*," said Mrs. Moreen, slowly rubbing her plump white hands and looking with compunction hard at Morgan, whose chin, not to take liberties, her husband stroked with a tentative paternal forefinger.

"Oh yes—we feel that we *can*. We trust Mr. Pemberton fully, Morgan," Mr. Moreen pursued.

Pemberton wondered again if he might pretend not to understand; but everything good gave way to the intensity of Morgan's understanding. "Do you mean he may take me to live with him for ever and ever?" cried the boy. "May take me away, away, anywhere he likes?"

"For ever and ever? *Comme vous-y-allez?*"[23] Mr. Moreen laughed indulgently. "For as long as Mr. Pemberton may be so good."

"We've struggled, we've suffered," his wife went on; "but you've made him so your own that we've already been through the worst of the sacrifice."

Morgan had turned away from his father—he stood looking at Pemberton with a light in his face. His sense of shame for their common humiliated state had dropped; the case had another side—the thing was to clutch at *that*. He had a moment of boyish joy, scarcely mitigated by the reflexion that with this unexpected consecration of his hope—too sudden and too violent; the turn taken was away from a *good* boy's book—the "escape" was left on their hands. The boyish joy was there an instant, and Pemberton was almost scared at the rush of gratitude and affection that broke through his first abasement. When he stammered "My dear fellow, what do you say to *that?*" how could one not say something enthusiastic? But there was more need for courage at something else that immediately followed and that made the lad sit down quickly on the nearest chair. He had turned quite livid and had raised his hand to his left side. They were all three looking at him, but Mrs. Moreen suddenly bounded forward. "Ah his darling little heart!" she broke out; and this time, on her knees before him and without respect for the idol, she caught him ardently in her arms. "You walked him too far, you hurried him too fast!" she hurled over her shoulder at Pemberton. Her son made no protest, and the next instant, still holding him, she sprang up with her face convulsed and with the terrified cry "Help, help! he's going, he's gone!" Pemberton saw with equal horror, by Morgan's own stricken face, that he was beyond their wildest recall. He pulled him half out of his mother's hands, and for a moment, while they held him together, they looked all their dismay into each other's eyes. "He couldn't stand it with his weak organ," said Pemberton—"the shock, the whole scene, the violent emotion."

"But I thought he *wanted* to go to you!" wailed Mrs. Moreen.

"I *told* you he didn't my dear," her husband made answer. Mr. Moreen was trembling all over and was in his way as deeply affected as his wife. But after the very first he took his bereavement as a man of the world.

1891

[23] How you take to it.

The Art of Fiction[1]

I should not have affixed so comprehensive a title to these few remarks, necessarily wanting in any completeness upon a subject the full consider-

[1] Originally published in *Longman's Magazine* for September 1884 and included in *Partial Portraits*, 1888.

ation of which would carry us far, did I not seem to discover a pretext for my temerity in the interesting pamphlet lately published under this name by Mr. Walter Besant.[2] Mr. Besant's lecture at the Royal Institution—the original form of his pamphlet—appears to indicate that many persons are interested in the art of fiction, and are not indifferent to such remarks, as those who practise it may attempt to make about it. I am therefore anxious not to lose the benefit of this favourable association, and to edge in a few words under cover of the attention which Mr. Besant is sure to have excited. There is something very encouraging in his having put into form certain of his ideas on the mystery of story-telling.

It is a proof of life and curiosity—curiosity on the part of the brotherhood of novelists as well as on the part of their readers. Only a short time ago it might have been supposed that the English novel was not what the French call *discutable*.[3] It had no air of having a theory, a conviction, a consciousness of itself behind it—of being the expression of an artistic faith, the result of choice and comparison. I do not say it was necessarily the worse for that: it would take much more courage than I possess to intimate that the form of the novel as Dickens and Thackeray (for instance) say it had any taint of incompleteness. It was, however, *naïf* (if I may help myself out with another French word); and evidently if it be destined to suffer in any way for having lost its *naïveté* it has now an idea of making sure of the corresponding advantages. During the period I have alluded to there was a comfortable, good-humoured feeling abroad that a novel is a novel, as a pudding is a pudding, and that our only business with it could be to swallow it. But within a year or two, for some reason or other, there have been signs of returning animation—the era of discussion would appear to have been to a certain extent opened. Art lives upon discussion, upon experiment, upon curiosity, upon variety of attempt, upon the exchange of views and the comparison of standpoints; and there is a presumption that those times when no one has anything particular to say about it, and has no reason to give for practice or preference, though they may be times of honour, are not times of development—are times, possibly even, a little of dulness. The successful application of any art is a delightful spectacle, but the theory too is interesting; and though there is a great deal of the latter without the former I suspect there has never been a genuine success that has not had a latent core of conviction. Discussion, suggestion, formulation, these things are fertilising when they are frank and sincere. Mr. Besant has set an excellent example in saying what he thinks, for his part, about the way in which fiction should be written, as well as about the way in which it should be published; for his view of the "art," carried on into an appendix, covers that too. Other labourers in the same field will doubtless take up the argument, they will give it the light of their experience, and the effect will surely be to make our interest in the novel a

[2] An English historian, critic, and novelist (1836-1901).   [3] A good topic for discussion.

little more what it had for some time threatened to fail to be—a serious, active, inquiring interest, under protection of which this delightful study may, in moments of confidence, venture to say a little more what it thinks of itself.

It must take itself seriously for the public to take it so. The old superstition about fiction being "wicked" has doubtless died out in England; but the spirit of it lingers in a certain oblique regard directed toward any story which does not more or less admit that it is only a joke. Even the most jocular novel feels in some degree the weight of the proscription that was formerly directed against literary levity; the jocularity does not always succeed in passing for orthodoxy. It is still expected, though perhaps people are ashamed to say it, that a production which is after all only a "make-believe" (for what else is a "story"?) shall be in some degree apologetic—shall renounce the pretension of attempting really to represent life. This, of course, any sensible, wide-awake story declines to do, for it quickly perceives that the tolerance granted to it on such a condition is only an attempt to stifle it disguised in the form of generosity. The old evangelical hostility to the novel, which was as explicit as it was narrow, and which regarded it as little less favourable to our immortal part than a stage-play, was in reality far less insulting. The only reason for the existence of a novel is that it does attempt to represent life. When it relinquishes this attempt, the same attempt that we see on the canvas of the painter, it will have arrived at a very strange pass. It is not expected of the picture that it will make itself humble in order to be forgiven; and the analogy between the art of the painter and the art of the novelist is, so far as I am able to see, complete. Their inspiration is the same, their process (allowing for the different quality of the vehicle), is the same, their success is the same. They may learn from each other, they may explain and sustain each other. Their cause is the same, and the honour of one is the honour of another. The Mahometans think a picture an unholy thing, but it is a long time since any Christian did, and it is therefore the more odd that in the Christian mind the traces (dissimulated though they may be) of a suspicion of the sister art should linger to this day. The only effectual way to lay it to rest is to emphasise the analogy to which I just alluded—to insist on the fact that as the picture is reality, so the novel is history. That is the only general description (which does it justice) that we may give of the novel. But history also is allowed to represent life; it is not, any more than painting, expected to apologise. The subject-matter of fiction is stored up likewise in documents and records, and if it will not give itself away, as they say in California, it must speak with assurance, with the tone of the historian. Certain accomplished novelists have a habit of giving themselves away which must often bring tears to the eyes of people who take their fiction seriously. I was lately struck, in reading over many pages of Anthony Trollope,[4] with

[4] English novelist, author of *The Warden*, and *Barchester Towers* (1815-1882).

his want of discretion in this particular. In a digression, a parenthesis or an aside, he concedes to the reader that he and this trusting friend are only "making believe." He admits that the events he narrates have not really happened, and that he can give his narrative any turn the reader may like best. Such a betrayal of a sacred office seems to me, I confess, a terrible crime; it is what I mean by the attitude of apology, and it shocks me every whit as much in Trollope as it would have shocked me in Gibbon or Macaulay.[5] It implies that the novelist is less occupied in looking for the truth (the truth, of course, I mean, that he assumes, the premises that we must grant him, whatever they may be), than the historian, and in doing so it deprives him at a stroke of all his standing-room. To represent and illustrate the past, the actions of men, is the task of either writer, and the only difference that I can see is, in proportion as he succeeds, to the honour of the novelist, consisting as it does in his having more difficulty in collecting his evidence, which is so far from being purely literary. It seems to me to give him a great character, the fact that he has at once so much in common with the philosopher and the painter; this double analogy is a magnificent heritage.

It is of all this evidently that Mr. Besant is full when he insists upon the fact that fiction is one of the *fine* arts, deserving in its turn of all the honours and emoluments that have hitherto been reserved for the successful profession of music, poetry, painting, architecture. It is impossible to insist too much on so important a truth, and the place that Mr. Besant demands for the work of the novelist may be represented, a trifle less abstractly, by saying that he demands not only that it shall be reputed artistic, but that it shall be reputed very artistic indeed. It is excellent that he should have struck this note, for his doing so indicates that there was need of it, that his proposition may be to many people a novelty. One rubs one's eyes at the thought; but the rest of Mr. Besant's essay confirms the revelation. I suspect in truth that it would be possible to confirm it still further, and that one would not be far wrong in saying that in addition to the people to whom it has never occurred that a novel ought to be artistic, there are a great many others who, if this principle were urged upon them, would be filled with an indefinable mistrust. They would find it difficult to explain their repugnance, but it would operate strongly to put them on their guard. "Art," in our Protestant communities, where so many things have got so strangely twisted about, is supposed in certain circles to have some vaguely injurious effect upon those who make it an important consideration, who let it weigh in the balance. It is assumed to be opposed in some mysterious manner to morality, to amusement, to instruction. When it is embodied in the work of the painter (the sculptor is another affair!) you know what it is: it stands there before you, in

[5] Edward Gibbon (1737-1794), English historian, author of *The Decline and Fall of the Roman Empire*. Thomas Babington Macaulay, (1800-1959) English historian, author of *History of England from the Accession of James II*.

the honesty of pink and green and a gilt frame; you can see the worst of it at a glance, and you can be on your guard. But when it is introduced into literature it becomes more insidious—there is danger of its hurting you before you know it. Literature should be either instructive or amusing, and there is in many minds an impression that these artistic preoccupations, the search for form, contribute to neither end, interfere indeed with both. They are too frivolous to be edifying, and too serious to be diverting; and they are moreover priggish and paradoxical and superfluous. That, I think, represents the manner in which the latent thought of many people who read novels as an exercise in skipping would explain itself if it were to become articulate. They would argue, of course, that a novel ought to be "good," but they would interpret this term in a fashion of their own, which indeed would vary considerably from one critic to another. One would say that being good means representing virtuous and aspiring characters, placed in prominent positions; another would say that it depends on a "happy ending," on a distribution at the last of prizes, pensions, husbands, wives, babies, millions, appended paragraphs, and cheerful remarks. Another still would say that it means being full of incident and movement, so that we shall wish to jump ahead, to see who was the mysterious stranger, and if the stolen will was ever found, and shall not be distracted from this pleasure by any tiresome analysis or "description." But they would all agree that the "artistic" idea would spoil some of their fun. One would hold it accountable for all the description, another would see it revealed in the absence of sympathy. Its hostility to a happy ending would be evident, and it might even in some cases render any ending at all impossible. The "ending" of a novel is, for many persons, like that of a good dinner, a course of desert and ices, and the artist in fiction is regarded as a sort of meddlesome doctor who forbids agreeable aftertastes. It is therefore true that this conception of Mr. Besant's of the novel as a superior form encounters not only a negative but a positive indifference. It matters little that as a work of art it should really be as little or as much of its essence to supply happy endings, sympathetic characters, and an objective tone, as if it were a work of mechanics: the association of ideas, however incongruous, might easily be too much for it if an eloquent voice were not sometimes raised to call attention to the fact that it is at once as free and as serious a branch of literature as any other.

Certainly this might sometimes be doubted in the presence of an enormous number of works of fiction that appeal to the credulity of our generation, for it might easily seem that there could be no great character in a commodity so quickly and easily produced. It must be admitted that good novels are much compromised by bad ones, and that the field at large suffers discredit from overcrowding. I think, however, that this injury is only superficial, and that the superabundance of written fiction proves nothing against the principle itself. It has been vulgarised, like all other kinds of literature, like everything else to-day, and it has proved more than some kinds accessible to vulgarisation. But there is as much difference as there ever was between a good novel and a bad one: the bad is swept with all the daubed canvases and spoiled marble into some unvisited limbo, or infinite rubbish-yard beneath the back-windows of the world, and the good subsists and emits its light and stimulates our desire for perfection. As I shall take the liberty of making but a single criticism of Mr. Besant, whose tone is so full of the love of his art, I may as well have done with it at once. He seems to me to mistake in attempting to say so definitely beforehand what sort of an affair the good novel will be. To indicate the danger of such an error as that has been the purpose of these few pages; to suggest that certain traditions of the subject applied *a priori*, have already had much to answer for, and that the good health of an art which undertakes so immediately to reproduce life must demand that it be perfectly free. It lives upon exercise, and the very meaning of exercise is freedom. The only obligation to which in advance we may hold a novel, without incurring the accusation of being arbitrary, is that it be interesting. That general responsibility rests upon it, but it is the only one I can think of. The ways in which it is at liberty to accomplish this result (of interesting us) strike me as innumerable, and such as can only suffer from being marked out or fenced in by prescription. They are as various as the temperament of man, and they are successful in proportion as they reveal a particular mind, different from others. A novel is in its broadest definition a personal, a direct impression of life; that, to begin with, constitutes its value, which is greater or less according to the intensity of the impression. But there will be no intensity at all, and therefore no value, unless there is freedom to feel and say. The tracing of a line to be followed, of a tone to be taken, of a form to be filled out, is a limitation of that freedom and a suppression of the very thing that we are most curious about. The form it seems to me, is to be appreciated after the fact: then the author's choice has been made, his standard has been indicated; then we can follow lines and directions and compare tones and resemblances. Then in a word we can enjoy one of the most charming of pleasures, we can estimate quality, we can apply the test of execution. The execution belongs to the author alone; it is what is most personal to him, and we measure him by that. The advantage, the luxury, as well as the torment and responsibility of the novelist, is that there is no limit to what he may attempt as an executant—no limit to his possible experiments, efforts, discoveries, successes. Here it is especially that he works, step by step, like his brother of the brush, of whom we may always say that he has painted his picture in a manner best known to himself. His manner is his secret, not necessarily a jealous one. He cannot disclose it as a general thing if he would; he would be at a loss to teach it to others. I say this with a due recollection of having insisted on the community of method of the artist who paints a picture and the artist who writes a novel. The painter *is* able to teach the rudiments of his practice, and it is possible, from the study of good work (granted the aptitude), both to learn how to paint and to learn how to write. Yet it remains true, without injury to the *rap-*

prochement,[6] that the literary artist would be obliged to say to his pupil much more than the other, "Ah, well, you must do it as you can!" It is a question of degree, a matter of delicacy. If there are exact sciences, there are also exact arts, and the grammar of painting is so much more definite that it makes the difference.

I ought to add, however, that if Mr. Besant says at the beginning of his essay that the "laws of fiction may be laid down and taught with as much precision and exactness as the laws of harmony, perspective, and proportion," he mitigates what might appear to be an extravagance by applying his remark to "general" laws, and by expressing most of these rules in a manner with which it would certainly be unaccommodating to disagree. That the novelist must write from his experience, that his "characters must be real and such as might be met with in actual life"; that "a young lady brought up in a quiet country village should avoid descriptions of garrison life," and "a writer whose friends and personal experiences belong to the lower middle-class should carefully avoid introducing his characters into society"; that one should enter one's notes in a common-place book; that one's figures should be clear in outline; that making them clear by some trick of speech or of carriage is a bad method, and "describing them at length" is a worse one; that English Fiction should have a "conscious moral purpose"; that "it is almost impossible to estimate too highly the value of careful workmanship—that is, of style"; that "the most important point of all is the story," that "the story is everything": these are principles with most of which it is surely impossible not to sympathise. That remark about the lower middle-class writer and his knowing his place is perhaps rather chilling; but for the rest I should find it difficult to dissent from any one of these recommendations. At the same time, I should find it difficult positively to assent to them, with the exception, perhaps, of the injunction as to entering one's notes in a common-place book. They scarcely seem to me to have the quality that Mr. Besant attributes to the rules of the novelist—the "precision and exactness" of "the laws of harmony, perspective, and proportion." They are suggestive, they are even inspiring, but they are not exact, though they are doubtless as much so as the case admits of: which is a proof of that liberty of interpretation for which I just contended. For the value of these different injunctions—so beautiful and so vague—is wholly in the meaning one attaches to them. The characters, the situation, which strike one as real will be those that touch and interest one most, but the measure of reality is very difficult to fix. The reality of Don Quixote or of Mr. Micawber[7] is a very delicate shade; it is a reality so coloured by the author's vision that, vivid as it may be, one would hesitate to propose it as a model: one would expose one's self to some very embarrassing questions on the part of a pupil. It goes without saying that you will not write a good novel unless you possess the sense of reality; but it will

---

[6] Analogy.   [7] Character in Dickens' *David Copperfield.*

be difficult to give you a recipe for calling that sense into being. Humanity is immense, and reality has myriad forms; the most one can affirm is that some of the flowers of fiction have the odour of it, and others have not; as for telling you in advance how your nosegay should be composed, that is another affair. It is equally excellent and inconclusive to say that one must write from experience; to our supposititious aspirant such a declaration might savour of mockery. What kind of experience is intended, and where does it begin and end? Experience is never limited, and it is never complete; it is an immense sensibility, a kind of huge spider-web of the finest silken threads suspended in the chamber of consciousness, and catching every airborne particle in its tissue. It is the very atmosphere of the mind; and when the mind is·imaginative—much more when it happens to be that of a man of genius—it takes to itself the faintest hints of life, it converts the very pulses of the air into revelations. The young lady living in a village has only to be a damsel upon whom nothing is lost to make it quite unfair (as it seems to me) to declare to her that she shall have nothing to say about the military. Greater miracles have been seen than that, imagination assisting, she should speak the truth about some of these gentlemen. I remember an English novelist, a woman of genius, telling me that she was much commended for the impression she had managed to give in one of her tales of the nature and the way of life of the French Protestant youth. She had been asked where she learned so much about this recondite being, she had been congratulated on her peculiar opportunities. These opportunities consisted in her having once, in Paris, as she ascended a staircase, passed an open door where, in the household of a *pasteur*,[8] some of the young Protestants were seated at table round a finished meal. The glimpse made a picture; it lasted only a moment, but that moment was experience. She had got her direct personal impression, and she turned out her type. She knew what youth was, and what Protestantism; she also had the advantage of having seen what it was to be French, so that she converted these ideas into a concrete image and produced a reality. Above all, however, she was blessed with the faculty which when you give it an inch takes an ell, and which for the artist is a much greater source of strength than any accident of residence or of place in the social scale. The power to guess the unseen from the seen, to trace the implication of things, to judge the whole piece by the pattern, the condition of feeling life in general so completely that you are well on your way to knowing any particular corner of it—this cluster of gifts may almost be said to constitute experience, and they occur in country and in town, and in the most differing stages of education. If experience consists of impressions, it may be said that impressions *are* experience, just as (have we not seen it?), they are the very air we breathe. Therefore, if I should certainly say to a novice, "Write from experience and experience only," I should feel that this was rather a tantalising monition if I

[8] Clergyman.

were not careful immediately to add, "Try to be one of the people on whom nothing is lost!"

I am far from intending by this to minimise the importance of exactness—of truth of detail. One can speak best from one's own taste, and I may therefore venture to say that the air of reality (solidity of specification) seems to me to be the supreme virtue of a novel—the merit on which all its other merits (including that conscious moral purpose of which Mr. Besant speaks) helplessly and submissively depend. If it be not there they are all as nothing, and if these be there, they owe their effect to the success with which the author has produced the illusion of life. The cultivation of this success, the study of this exquisite process, form, to my taste, the beginning and the end of the art of the novelist. They are his inspiration, his despair, his reward, his torment, his delight. It is here in very truth that he competes with life; it is here that he competes with his brother the painter in *his* attempt to render the look of things, the look that conveys their meaning, to catch the colour, the relief, the expression, the surface, the substance of the human spectacle. It is in regard to this that Mr. Besant is well inspired when he bids him take notes. He cannot possibly take too many, he cannot possibly take enough. All life solicits him, and to "render" the simplest surface, to produce the most momentary illusion, is a very complicated business. His case would be easier, and the rule would be more exact, if Mr. Besant had been able to tell him what notes to take. But this, I fear, he can never learn in any manual; it is the business of his life. He has to take a great many in order to select a few, he has to work them up as he can, and even the guides and philosophers who might have most to say to him must leave him alone when it comes to the application of precepts, as we leave the painter in communion with his palette. That his characters "must be clear in outline," as Mr. Besant says— he feels that down to his boots; but how he shall make them so is a secret between his good angel and himself. It would be absurdly simple if he could be taught that a great deal of "description" would make them so, or that on the contrary the absence of description and the cultivation of dialogue, or the absence of dialogue and the multiplication of "incident," would rescue him from his difficulties. Nothing, for instance, is more possible than that he be of a turn of mind for which this odd, literal opposition of description and dialogue, incident and description, has little meaning and light. People often talk of these things as if they had a kind of internecine distinctness, instead of melting into each other at every breath, and being intimately associated parts of one general effort of expression. I cannot imagine composition existing in a series of blocks, nor conceive, in any novel worth discussing at all, of a passage of description that is not in its intention narrative, a passage of dialogue, that is not in its intention descriptive, a touch of truth of any sort that does not partake of the nature of incident, or an incident that derives its interest from any other source than the general and only source of the success of a work of art—that of being illustrative. A novel is a living thing, all one and continuous, like any other organism, and in proportion as it lives will it be found, I think, that in each of the parts there is something of each of the other parts. The critic who over the close texture of a finished work shall pretend to trace a geography of items will mark some frontiers as artificial, I fear, as any that have been known to history. There is an old-fashioned distinction between the novel of character and the novel of incident which must have cost many a smile to the intending fabulist who was keen about his work. It appears to me as little to the point as the equally celebrated distinction between the novel and the romance—to answer as little to any reality. There are bad novels and good novels, as there are bad pictures and good pictures; but that is the only distinction in which I see any meaning, and I can as little imagine speaking of a novel of character as I can imagine speaking of a picture of character. When one says picture one says of character, when one says novel one says of incident, and the terms may be transposed at will. What is character but the determination of incident? What is incident but the illustration of character? What is either a picture or a novel that is *not* of character? What else do we seek in it and find in it? It is an incident for a woman to stand up with her hand resting on a table and look out at you in a certain way; or if it be not an incident I think it will be hard to say what it is. At the same time it is an expression of character. If you don't see it (characters in *that—allons donc.*[9]), this is exactly what the artist who has reasons of his own for thinking he *does* see it undertakes to show you. When a young man makes up his mind that he has not faith enough after all to enter the church as he intended, that is an incident, though you may not hurry to the end of the chapter to see whether perhaps he doesn't change once more. I do not say that these are extraordinary or startling incidents. I do not pretend to estimate the degree of interest proceeding from them, for this will depend upon the skill of the painter. It sounds almost puerile to say that some incidents are intrinsically much more important than others, and I need not take this precaution after having professed my sympathy for the major ones in remarking that the only classification of the novel that I can understand is into that which has life and that which has it not.

The novel and the romance, the novel of incident and that of character— these clumsy separations appear to me to have been made by critics and reader for their own convenience, and to help them out of some of their occasional queer predicaments, but to have little reality or interest for the producer, from whose point of view it is of course that we are attempting to consider the art of fiction. The case is the same with another shadowy category which Mr. Besant apparently is disposed to set up—that of the "modern English novel"; unless indeed it be that in this matter he has fallen into an accidental confusion of stand-points. It is not quite clear whether he intends the remarks in which he alludes it to be didactic or historical. It is as difficult to suppose a person intending to write a modern English as to sup-

---

[9] Come on, now!

pose him writing an ancient English novel: that is a label which begs the question. One writes the novel, one paints the picture, of one's language and of one's time, and calling it modern English will not, alas! make the difficult task any easier. No more, unfortunately, will calling this or that work of one's fellow-artist a romance—unless it be, of course, simply for the pleasantness of the thing, as for instance when Hawthorne gave this heading to his story of *Blithedale*. The French, who have brought the theory of fiction to remarkable completeness, have but one name for the novel, and have not attempted smaller things in it, that I can see, for that. I can think of no obligation to which the "romancer" would not be held equally with the novelist; the standard of execution is equally high for each. Of course it is of execution that we are talking—that being the only point of a novel that is open to contention. This is perhaps too often lost sight of, only to produce interminable confusions and cross-purposes. We must grant the artist his subject, his idea, his *donnée:*[10] our criticism is applied only to what he makes of it. Naturally I do not mean that we are bound to like it or find it interesting: in case we do not our course is perfectly simple—to let it alone. We may believe that of a certain idea even the most sincere novelist can make nothing at all, and the event may perfectly justify our belief; but the failure will have been a failure to execute, and it is in the execution that the fatal weakness is recorded. If we pretend to respect the artist at all, we must allow him his freedom of choice, in the face, in particular cases, of innumerable presumptions that the choice will not fructify. Art derives a considerable part of its beneficial exercise from flying in the face of presumptions, and some of the most interesting experiments of which it is capable are hidden in the bosom of common things, Gustave Flaubert[11] has written a story about the devotion of a servant-girl to a parrot,[12] and the production, highly finished as it is, cannot on the whole be called a success. We are perfectly free to find it flat, but I think it might have been interesting; and I, for my part, am extremely glad he should have written it; it is a contribution to our knowledge of what can be done—or what cannot. Ivan Turgenieff[13] has written a tale about a deaf and dumb serf and a lap-dog, and the thing is touching, loving, a little masterpiece. He struck the note of life where Gustave Flaubert missed it—he flew in the face of a presumption and achieved a victory.

Nothing, of course, will ever take the place of the good old fashion of "liking" a work of art or not liking it: the most improved criticism will not abolish that primitive, that ultimate test. I mention this to guard myself from the accusation of intimating that the idea, the subject, of a novel or a picture, does not matter. It matters to my sense, in the highest degree, and if I might

---

[10] What is given.

[11] Gustave Flaubert, French novelist (1821–1880).

[12] "A Simple Heart."

[13] Russian author (1818–1883).

put up a prayer it would be that artists should select none but the richest. Some, as I have already hastened to admit, are much more remunerative than others, and it would be a world happily arranged in which persons intending to treat them should be exempt from confusions and mistakes. This fortunate condition will arrive only, I fear, on the same day that critics become purged from error. Meanwhile, I repeat, we do not judge the artist with fairness unless we say to him, "Oh, I grant you your starting-point, because if I did not I should seem to prescribe to you, and heaven forbid I should take that responsibility. If I pretend to tell you what you must not take, you will call upon me to tell you then what you must take; in which case I shall be prettily caught. Moreover, it isn't till I have accepted your data that I can begin to measure you. I have the standard, the pitch; I have no right to tamper with your flute and then criticise your music. Of course I may not care for your idea at all; I may think it silly, or stale, or unclean; in which case I wash my hands of you altogether. I may content myself with believing that you will not have succeeded in being interesting, but I shall, of course, not attempt to demonstrate it, and you will be as indifferent to me as I am to you. I needn't remind you that there are all sorts of tastes: who can know it better? Some people, for excellent reasons, don't like to read about carpenters; others, for reasons even better, don't like to read about courtesans. Many object to Americans. Others (I believe they are mainly editors and publishers) won't look at Italians. Some readers don't like quiet subjects; other's don't like bustling ones. Some enjoy a complete illusion, others the consciousness of large concessions. They choose their novels accordingly, and if they don't care about your idea they won't, *a fortiori*,[14] care about your treatment."

So that it comes back very quickly, as I have said, to the liking: in spite of M. Zola, who reasons less powerfully than he represents,[15] and who will not reconcile himself to this absoluteness of taste, thinking that there are certain things that people ought to like, and that they can be made to like. I am quite at a loss to imagine anything (at any rate in this matter of fiction) that people *ought* to like or to dislike. Selection will be sure to take care of itself, for it has a constant motive behind it. That motive is simply experience. As people feel life, so they will feel the art that is most closely related to it. This closeness of relation is what we should never forget in talking of the effort of the novel. Many people speak of it as a factitious, artificial form, a product of ingenuity, the business of which is to alter and arrange the things that surround us, to translate them into conventional, traditional moulds. This, however, is a view of the matter which carries us but a very short way, condemns the art to an eternal repetition of a few familiar *clichés*, cuts short its development, and leads us straight up to a dead wall. Catching the very note and

[14] For a stronger reasons.
[15] Emile Zola, French novelist. He explained his "naturalistic" theory of the novel in *Le Roman Experimental* (1840–1902).

trick, the strange irregular rhythm of life, this is the attempt whose strenuous force keeps Fiction upon her feet. In proportion as in what she offers us we see life *without* rearrangement do we feel that we are touching the truth; in proportion as we see it *with* rearrangement do we feel that we are being put off with a substitute, a compromise and convention. It is not uncommon to hear an extraordinary assurance of remark in regard to this matter of rearranging, which is often spoken of as if it were the last word of art. Mr. Besant seems to me in danger of falling into the great error with his rather unguarded talk about "selection." Art is essentially selection, but it is a selection whose main care is to be typical, to be inclusive. For many people art means rose-coloured window-panes, and selection means picking a bouquet for Mrs. Grundy.[16] They will tell you glibly that artistic considerations have nothing to do with the disagreeable, with the ugly; they will rattle off shallow commonplaces about the province of art and the limits of art till you are moved to some wonder in return as to the province and the limits of ignorance. It appears to me that no one can ever have made a seriously artistic attempt without becoming conscious of an immense increase—a kind of revelation—of freedom. One perceives in that case—by the light of a heavenly ray—that the province of art is all life, all feeling, all observation, all vision. As Mr. Besant so justly intimates, it is all experience. That is a sufficient answer to those who maintain that it must not touch the sad things of life, who stick into its divine unconscious bosom little prohibitory inscriptions on the end of sticks, such as we see in public gardens—"It is forbidden to walk on the grass; it is forbidden to touch the flowers; it is not allowed to introduce dogs or to remain after dark; it is requested to keep to the right." The young aspirant in the line of fiction whom we continue to imagine will do nothing without taste, for in that case his freedom would be of little use to him; but the first advantage of his taste will be to reveal to him the absurdity of the little sticks and tickets. If he have taste, I must add, of course he will have ingenuity, and my disrespectful reference to that quality just now was not meant to imply that it is useless in fiction. But it is only a secondary aid; the first is a capacity for receiving straight impressions.

Mr. Besant has some remarks on the question of "the story" which I shall not attempt to criticise, though they "seem to me to contain a singular ambiguity, because I do not think I understand them. I cannot see what is meant by talking as if there were a part of a novel which is the story and part of it which for mystical reasons is not—unless indeed the distinction be made in a sense in which it is difficult to suppose that any one should attempt to convey anything. "The story," if it represents anything, represents the subject, the idea, the *donnée* of the novel; and there is surely no "school"—Mr. Besant speaks of a school—which urges that a novel should be all treatment

---

[16] Generic name for a prude, from Thomas Morton's *Speed the Plough* (1798).

and no subject. There must assuredly be something to treat; every school is intimately conscious of that. This sense of the story being the idea, the starting-point, of the novel, is the only one that I see in which it can be spoken of as something different from its organic whole; and since in proportion as the work is successful the idea permeates and penetrates it, informs and animates it, so that every word and every punctuation-point contribute directly to the expression, in that proportion do we lose our sense of the story being a blade which may be drawn more or less out of its sheath. The story and the novel, the idea and the form, are the needle and thread, and I never heard of a guild of tailors who recommended the use of the thread without the needle, or the needle without the thread. Mr. Besant is not the only critic who may be observed to have spoken as if there were certain things in life which constitute stories, and certain others which do not. I find the same odd implication in an entertaining article in the *Pall Mall Gazette*, devoted, as it happens, to Mr. Besant's lecture. "The story is the thing!" says this graceful writer, as if with a tone of opposition to some other idea. I should think it was, as every painter who, as the time for "sending in" his picture looms in the distance, finds himself still in quest of a subject—as every belated artist not fixed about his theme will heartily agree. There are some subjects which speak to us and others which do not, but he would be a clever man who should undertake to give a rule—an index expurgatorius[17]—by which the story and the no-story should be known apart. It is impossible (to me at least) to imagine any such rule which shall not be altogether arbitrary. The writer in the *Pall Mall* opposes the delightful (as I suppose) novel of *Margot la Balafrée*[18] to certain tales in which "Bostonian nymphs" appear to have "rejected English dukes for psychological reasons."[19] I am not acquainted with the romance just designated, and can scarcely forgive the *Pall Mall* critic for not mentioning the name of the author, but the title appears to refer to a lady who may have received a scar in some heroic adventure. I am inconsolable at not being acquainted with this episode, but am utterly at a loss to see why it is a story when the rejection (or acceptance) of a duke is not, and why a reason, psychological or other, is not a subject when a cicatrix[20] is. They are all particles of the multitudinous life with which the novel deals, and surely no dogma which pretends to make it lawful to touch the one and unlawful to touch the other will stand for a moment on its feet. It is the special picture that must stand or fall, according as it seem to possess truth or to lack it. Mr. Besant does not, to my sense, light up the subject by intimating that a story must, under penalty of not being a story, consist of "adventures." Why of adventures

[17] An allusion to the Catholic "index" of forbidden books.

[18] A novel written by Fortune du Boisgobey, French Romantic novelist (1821-1891).

[19] James is speaking about his own novels, cf. *An International Episode* and *The Portrait of a Lady*.

[20] Scar.

more than of green spectacles? He mentions a category of impossible things, and among them he places "fiction without adventure." Why without adventure, more than without matrimony, or celibacy, or parturition, or cholera, or hydropathy, or Jansenism? This seems to me to bring the novel back to the hapless little *rôle* of being an artificial, ingenious thing—bring it down from its large, free character of an immense and exquisite correspondence with life. And what *is* adventure, when it comes to that, and by what sign is the listening pupil to recognise it? It is an adventure—an immense one—for me to write this little article; and for a Bostonian nymph to reject an English duke is an adventure only less stirring, I should say, than for an English duke to be rejected by a Bostonian nymph. I see dramas within dramas in that, and innumerable points of view. A psychological reason is, to my imagination, an object adorably pictorial; to catch the tint of its complexion—I feel as if that idea might inspire one to Titianesque efforts.[21] There are few things more exciting to me, in short, than a psychological reason, and yet, I protest, the novel seems to me the most magnificent form of art. I have just been reading, at the same time, the delightful story of *Treasure Island*, by Mr. Robert Louis Stevenson and, in a manner less consecutive, the last tale from M. Edmond de Goncourt, which is entitled *Chérie*. One of these works treats of murders, mysteries, islands of dreadful renown, hairbreadth escapes, miraculous coincidences and buried doubloons. The other treats of a little French girl who lived in a fine house in Paris, and died of wounded sensibility because no one would marry her. I call *Treasure Island* delightful, because it appears to me to have succeeded wonderfully in what it attempts; and I venture to bestow no epithet upon *Chérie*, which strikes me as having failed deplorably in what it attempts—that is in tracing the development of the moral consciousness of a child. But one of these productions strikes me as exactly as much of a novel as the other, and as having a "story" quite as much. The moral consciousness of a child is as much a part of life as the islands of the Spanish Main, and the one sort of geography seems to me to have those "surprises" of which Mr. Besant speaks quite as much as the other. For myself (since it comes back in the last resort, as I say, to the preference of the individual), the picture of the child's experience has the advantage that I can at successive steps (an immense luxury, near to the "sensual pleasure" of which Mr. Besant's critic in the *Pall Mall* speaks) say Yes or No, as it may be, to what the artist puts before me. I have been a child in fact, but I have been on a quest for a buried treasure only in supposition, and it is a simple accident that with M. de Goncourt I should have for the most part to say No. With George Eliot, when she painted that country with a far other intelligence, I always said Yes.

[21] Titian, sixteenth-century Venetian painter, who painted heroic historical and mythological scenes in vivid realism (1487?–1576).

The most interesting part of Mr. Besant's lecture is unfortunately the briefest passage—his very cursory allusion to the "conscious moral purpose" of the novel. Here again it is not very clear whether he be recording a fact or laying down a principle; it is a great pity that in the latter case he should not have developed his idea. This branch of the subject is of immense importance, and Mr. Besant's few words point to considerations of the widest reach, not to be lightly disposed of. He will have treated the art of fiction but superficially who is not prepared to go every inch of the way that these considerations will carry him. It is for this reason that at the beginning of these remarks I was careful to notify the reader that my reflections on so large a theme have no pretension to be exhaustive. Like Mr. Besant, I have left the question of the morality of the novel till the last, and at the last I find I have used up my space. It is a question surrounded with difficulties, as witness the very first that meets us, in the form of a definite question, on the threshold. Vagueness, in such a discussion, is fatal, and what is the meaning of your morality and your conscious moral purpose? Will you not define your terms and explain how (a novel being a picture) a picture can be either moral or immoral? You wish to paint a moral picture or carve a moral statue: will you not tell us how you would set about it? We are discussing the Art of Fiction; questions of art are questions (in the widest sense) of execution; questions of morality are quite another affair, and will you not let us see how it is that you find it so easy to mix them up? These things are so clear to Mr. Besant that he has deduced from them a law which he sees embodied in English Fiction, and which is "a truly admirable thing and a great cause for congratulation." It is a great cause for congratulation indeed when such thorny problems become as smooth as silk. I may add that in so far as Mr. Besant perceives that in point of fact English Fiction has addressed itself preponderantly to these delicate questions he will appear to many people to have made a vain discovery. They will have been positively struck, on the contrary, with the moral timidity of the usual English novelist; with his (or with her) aversion to face the difficulties with which on every side the treatment of reality bristles. He is apt to be extremely shy (whereas the picture that Mr. Besant draws is a picture of boldness), and the sign of his work, for the most part, is a cautious silence on certain subjects. In the English novel (by which of course I mean the American as well), more than in any other, there is a traditional difference between that which people know and that which they agree to admit that they know, that which they see and that which they speak of, that which they feel to be a part of life and that which they allow to enter into literature. There is the great difference, in short, between what they talk of in conversation and what they talk of in print. The essence of moral energy is to survey the whole field, and I should directly reverse Mr. Besant's remark and say not that the English novel has a purpose, but that it has a diffidence. To what degree a purpose in a work of art is a source of corruption I shall not attempt to inquire; the one that seems to me least dangerous is the purpose of making a perfect work. As for our novel, I may say lastly on this score that as we find it in England to-day it strikes me as addressed in a large degree to "young people," and that this in itself constitutes a presumption that it will be rather shy. There are certain things which it is generally agreed not to discuss, not even to mention, before young people. That is very well, but the absence of discussion is not a symptom of the moral passion. The purpose of the English novel—"a truly admirable thing, and a great cause for congratulation"—strikes me therefore as rather negative.

There is one point at which the moral sense and the artistic sense lie very near together; that is in the light of the very obvious truth that the deepest quality of a work of art will always be the quality of the mind of the producer. In proportion as that intelligence is fine will the novel, the picture, the statue partake of the substance of beauty and truth. To be constituted of such elements is, to my vision, to have purpose enough. No good novel will ever proceed from a superficial mind; that seems to me an axiom which, for the artist in fiction, will cover all needful moral ground: if the youthful aspirant take it to heart it will illuminate for him many of the mysteries of "purpose." There are many other useful things that might be said to him, but I have come to the end of my article, and can only touch them as I pass. The critic in the *Pall Mall Gazette*, whom I have already quoted, draws attention to the danger, in speaking of the art of fiction, of generalising. The danger that he has in mind is rather, I imagine, that of particularising, for there are some comprehensive remarks which, in addition to those embodied in Mr. Besant's suggestive lecture, might without fear of misleading him be addressed to the ingenuous student. I should remind him first of the magnificence of the form that is open to him, which offers to sight so few restrictions and such innumerable opportunities. The other arts, in comparison, appear confined and hampered; the various conditions under which they are exercised are so rigid and definite. But the only condition that I can think of attaching to the composition of the novel is, as I have already said, that it is sincere. This freedom is a splendid privilege, and the first lesson of the young novelist is to learn to be worthy of it. "Enjoy it as it deserves," I should say to him; "take possession of it, explore it to its utmost extent, publish it, rejoice in it. All life belongs to you, and do not listen either to those who would shut you up into corners of it and tell you that it is only here and there that art inhabits, or to those who would persuade you that this heavenly messenger wings her way outside of life altogether, breathing a superfine air, and turning away her head from the truth of things. There is no impression of life, no manner of seeing it and feeling it, to which the plan of the novelist may not offer a place; you have only to remember that talents so dissimilar as those of Alexandre Dumas and Jane Austen, Charles Dickens and Gustave Flaubert have worked in this field with equal glory. Do not think too much about optimism and pessimism; try and catch the colour of life itself. In

France to-day we see a prodigious effort (that of Emile Zola, to whose solid and serious work no explorer of the capacity of the novel can allude without respect), we see an extraordinary effort vitiated by a spirit of pessimism on a narrow basis. M. Zola is magnificent, but he strikes an English reader as ignorant; he has an air of working in the dark; if he had as much light as energy, his results would be of the highest value. As for the aberrations of a shallow optimism, the ground (of English fiction especially) is strewn with their brittle particles as with broken glass. If you must indulge in conclusions, let them have the taste of a wide knowledge. Remember that your first duty is to be as complete as possible—to make as perfect a work. Be generous and delicate and pursue the prize."

1884/1888

From the American Scene

NEW YORK AND THE HUDSON
A SPRING IMPRESSION[1]

I

It was a concomitant, always, of the down-town hour that it could be felt as *most* playing into the surrendered consciousness and making the sharpest impression; yet, since the up-town hour was apt, in its turn, to claim the same distinction, I could only let each of them take its way with me as it would. The oddity was that they seemed not at all to speak of different things—by so quick a process does any one aspect, in the United States, in general, I was to note, connect itself with the rest; so little does any link in the huge looseness of New York, in especial, appear to come as a whole, or as final, out of the fusion. The fusion, as of elements in solution in a vast hot pot, is always going on, and one stage of the process is as typical or as vivid as another. Whatever I might be looking at, or be struck with, the object or the phase was an item in the pressing conditions of the place, and as such had more in common with its sister items than it had in difference from them. It mattered little, moreover, whether this might be a proof that New York, among cities, most deeply languishes and palpitates, or vibrates and flourishes (whichever way one may put it) under the breath of her conditions, or whether, simply, this habit of finding a little of *all* my impressions reflected in any one of them testified to the enjoyment of a real relation with the subject. I like indeed to think of my relation to New York as, in that manner, almost inexpressibly intimate, and as hence making, for daily sensation, a keyboard as continuous, and as free from hard transitions, as if swept

[1] First published by Harper & Bros., 1907.

by the fingers of a master-pianist. You cannot, surely, say more for your sense of the underlying unity of an occasion than that the taste of each dish in the banquet recalls the taste of most of the others; which is what I mean by the "continuity," not to say the affinity, on the island of Manhattan, between the fish and the sweets, between the soup and the game. The whole feast affects one as eaten—that is the point—with the general queer sauce of New York; a preparation as freely diffused, somehow, on the East side as on the West, in the quarter of Grand Street as in the quarter of Murray Hill. No fact, I hasten to add, would appear to make the place more amenable to delineations of the order that may be spoken of as hanging together.

I must confess, notwithstanding, to not being quite ready to point directly to the common element in the dense Italian neighbourhoods of the lower East side, and in the upper reaches of Fifth and of Madison Avenues; though indeed I wonder at this inability in recollecting two or three of those charming afternoons of early summer, in Central Park, which showed the fruit of the foreign tree as shaken down there with a force that smothered everything else. The long residential vistas I have named were within a quarter of an hour's walk, but the alien was as truly in possession, under the high "aristocratic" nose, as if he had had but three steps to come. If it be asked why, the alien still striking you so as an alien, the singleness of impression, throughout the place, should still be so marked, the answer, close at hand, would seem to be that the alien himself fairly *makes* the singleness of impression. Is not the universal sauce essentially *his* sauce, and do we not feel ourselves feeding, half the time, from the ladle, as greasy as he chooses to leave it for us, that he holds out? Such questions were in my ears, at all events, with the cheerful hum of that babel of tongues established in the vernal Park, and they supplied, beyond doubt, the livelier interest of any hour of contemplation there. I hate to drift into dealing with them at the expense of a proper tribute, kept distinct and vivid, to the charming bosky[2] precinct itself, the great field of recreation with which they swarmed; but it could not be the fault of the brooding visitor, and still less that of the restored absentee, if he was conscious of the need of mental adjustment to phenomena absolutely fresh. He could remember still how, months before, a day or two after his restoration, a noted element of one of his first impressions had been this particular revealed anomaly. He had been, on the Jersey shore, walking with a couple of friends through the grounds of a large new rural residence, where groups of diggers and ditchers were working, on those lines of breathless haste which seem always, in the United States, of the essence of any question, toward an expensive effect of landscape gardening. To pause before them, for interest in their labour, was, and would have been everywhere, instinctive; but what came home to me on the spot was that whatever *more* would have been anywhere else involved had here inevitably to lapse.

[2] Woody, covered with bushes.

What lapsed, on the spot, was the element of communication with the workers, as I may call it for want of a better name; that element which, in a European country, would have operated, from side to side, as the play of mutual recognition, founded on old familiarities and heredities, and involving, for the moment, some impalpable exchange. The men, in the case I speak of, were Italians, of superlatively southern type, and any impalpable exchange struck me as absent from the air to positive intensity, to mere unthinkability. It was as if contact were out of the question and the sterility of the passage between us recorded, with due dryness, in our staring silence. This impression was for one of the party a shock—a member of the party for whom, on the other side of the world, the imagination of the main furniture, as it might be called, of any rural excursion, of *the* rural in particular, had been, during years, the easy sense, for the excursionist, of a social relation with any encountered type, from whichever end of the scale proceeding. Had that not ever been, exactly, a part of the vague warmth, the intrinsic colour, of any honest man's rural walk in his England or his Italy, his Germany or his France, and was not the effect of its so suddenly dropping out, in the land of universal brotherhood—for I was to find it drop out again and again—rather a chill, straightway, for the heart, and rather a puzzle, not less, for the head? Shortly after the spring of this question was first touched for me I found it ring out again with a sharper stroke. Happening to have lost my way, during a long ramble among the New Hampshire hills, I appealed, for information, at a parting of the roads, to a young man whom, at the moment of my need, I happily saw emerge from a neighbouring wood. But his stare was blank, in answer to my inquiry, and, seeing that he failed to understand me and that he had a dark-eyed "Latin" look, I jumped to the inference of his being a French Canadian. My repetition of my query in French, however, forwarded the case as little, and my trying him with Italian had no better effect. "What *are* you then?" I wonderingly asked—on which my accent loosened in him the faculty of speech. "I'm an Armenian," he replied, as if it were the most natural thing in the world for a wage-earning youth in the heart of New England to be—so that all I could do was to try and make my profit of the lesson. I could have made it better, for the occasion, if, even on the Armenian basis, he had appeared to expect brotherhood; but this had been as little his seeming as it had been that of the diggers by the Jersey shore.

To inquire of these things on the spot, to betray, that is, one's sense of the "chill" of which I have spoken, is of course to hear it admitted, promptly enough, that there is no claim to brotherhood with aliens in the first grossness of their alienism. The material of which they consist is being dressed and prepared, at this stage, for brotherhood, and the consummation, in respect to many of them, will not be, can not from the nature of the case be, in any lifetime of their own. Their children are another matter—as in fact the children throughout the United States, are an immense matter, are almost the greatest matter of all; it is the younger generation who will fully profit, rise to the occasion and enter into the privilege. The machinery is colossal—nothing is more characteristic of the country than the development of this machinery, in the form of the political and social habit, the common school and the newspaper; so that there are always millions of little transformed strangers growing up in regard to whom the idea of intimacy of relation may be as freely cherished as you like. *They* are the stuff of whom brothers and sisters are made, and the making proceeds on a scale that really need leave nothing to desire. All this you take in, with a wondering mind, and in the light of it the great "ethnic" question rises before you on a corresponding scale and with a corresponding majesty. Once it has set your observation, to say nothing of your imagination, working, it becomes for you, as you go and come, the wonderment to which everything ministers and that is quickened well-nigh to madness, in some places and on some occasions, by every face and every accent that meet your eyes and ears. The sense of the elements in the cauldron—the cauldron of the "American" character—becomes thus about as vivid a thing as you can at all quietly manage, and the question settles into a form which makes the intelligible answer further and further recede. "What meaning, in the presence of such impressions, can continue to attach to such a term as the 'American' character?—what type, as the result of such a prodigious amalgam, such a hotch-potch of racial ingredients, is to be conceived as shaping itself?" The challenge to speculation, fed thus by a thousand sources, is so intense as to be, as I say, irritating; but practically, beyond doubt, I should also say, you take refuge from it— since your case would otherwise be hard; and you find your relief not in the least in any direct satisfaction or solution, but absolutely in that blest general drop of the immediate need of conclusions, or rather in that blest general feeling for the impossibility of them, to which the philosophy of any really fine observation of the American spectacle must reduce itself, and the large intellectual, quite even the large æsthetic, margin supplied by which accompanies the spectator as his one positively complete comfort.

It is more than a comfort to him, truly, in all the conditions, this accepted vision of the too-defiant scale of numerosity and quantity—the effect of which is so to multiply the possibilities, so to open, by the million, contingent doors and windows: he rests in it at last as an absolute luxury, converting it even into a substitute, into *the* constant substitute, for many luxuries that are absent. He doesn't *know*, he can't *say*, before the facts, and he doesn't even want to know or to say; the facts themselves loom, before the understanding, in too large a mass for a mere mouthful: it is as if the syllables were too numerous to make a legible word. The *il*legible word, accordingly, the great inscrutable answer to questions, hangs in the vast American sky, to his imagination, as something fantastic and *abracadabrant*, belonging to no known language, and it is under this convenient ensign that he travels and considers and contemplates, and, to the best of his ability, enjoys. The interesting point, in the connection, is moreover that this particular effect of the scale of things is the only effect that, throughout the land, is not directly adverse to joy. Extent and reduplication, the multiplication of cognate items and the continuity of motion, are elements that count, there, in general, for fatigue and satiety, prompting the earnest observer, overburdened perhaps already a little by his earnestness, to the reflection that the country is too large for any human convenience, that it can scarce, in the scheme of Providence, have been meant to be dealt with as we are trying, perhaps all in vain, to deal with it, and that its very possibilities of population themselves cause one to wince in the light of the question of intercourse and contact. That relation to its superficies and content—the relation of flat fatigue—is, with the traveller, a constant quantity; so that he feels himself justified of the inward, the philosophic, escape into the immensity. And as it is the restored absentee, with his acquired habit of nearer limits and shorter journeys and more muffled concussions, who is doubtless most subject to flat fatigue, so it is this same personage who most avails himself of the liberty of waiting to see. It is an advantage—acting often in the way of a compensation, or of an appeal from the immediate—that he becomes, early in his period of inquiry, conscious of intimately invoking, in whatever apparent inconsistency it may lodge him. There is too much of the whole thing, he sighs, for the personal relation with it; and yet he would desire no inch less for the relation that he describes to himself best perhaps either as the provisionally-imaginative or as the distantly-respectful. Diminution of quantity, even by that inch, might mark the difference of his having to begin to recognize from afar, as through a rift in the obscurity, the gleam of some propriety of opinion. What would a man make, many things still being as they are, he finds himself asking, of a *small* America?—and what may a big one, on the other hand, still not make of itself? Goodness be thanked, accordingly, for the bigness. The state of flat fatigue, obviously, is not an opinion, save in the sense attributed to the slumber of the gentleman of the anecdote who had lost consciousness during the reading of the play—it belongs to the order of mere sensation and impression; and as to these the case is quite different: he may have as many of each as he can carry.

II

The process of the mitigation and, still more, of the conversion of the alien goes on, meanwhile, obviously, not by leaps and bounds or any form of easy magic, but under its own mystic laws and with an outward air of quite declining to be unduly precipitated. How little it may be thought of in New York as a quick business we readily perceive as the effect of merely remembering the vast numbers of their kind that the arriving reinforcements, from whatever ends of the earth, find already in possession in the field. There awaits the disembarked Armenian, for instance, so warm and furnished an

Armenian corner that the need of hurrying to get rid of the sense of it must become less and less a pressing preliminary. The corner growing warmer and warmer, it is to be supposed, by rich accretions, he may take his time, more and more, for becoming absorbed in the surrounding element, and he may in fact feel more and more that he can do so on his own conditions. I seem to find indeed in this latter truth a hint for the best expression of a whole side of New York—the best expression of much of the medium in which one consciously moves. It is formed by this fact that the alien is taking his time, and that you go about with him meanwhile, sharing, all respectfully, in his deliberation, waiting on his convenience, watching him at his interesting work. The vast foreign quarters of the city present him as thus engaged in it, and they are curious and portentous and "picturesque" just by reason of their doing so. You recognize in them, freely, those elements that are not elements of swift convertibility, and you lose yourself in the wonder of what becomes, as it were, of the obstinate, the unconverted residuum. The country at large, as you cross it in different senses, keeps up its character for you as the hugest thinkable organism for successful "assimilation"; but the assimilative force itself has the residuum still to count with. The operation of the immense machine, identical after all with the total of American life, trembles away into mysteries that are beyond our present notation and that reduce us in many a mood to renouncing analysis.

Who and what is an alien, when it comes to that, in a country peopled from the first under the jealous eye of history?—peopled, that is, by migrations at once extremely recent, perfectly traceable and urgently required. They are still, it would appear, urgently required—if we look about far enough for the urgency; though of that truth such a scene as New York may well make one doubt. Which is the American, by these scant measures?— which is *not* the alien, over a large part of the country at least, and where does one put a finger on the dividing line, or, for that matter, "spot" and identify any particular phase of the conversion, any one of its successive moments? The sense of the interest of so doing is doubtless half the interest of the general question—the possibility of our seeing lucidly presented some such phenomenon, in a given group of persons, or even in a felicitous individual, as the dawn of the American spirit while the declining rays of the Croatian, say, or of the Calabrian, or of the Lusitanian, still linger more or less pensively in the sky. Fifty doubts and queries come up, in regard to any such possibility, as one circulates in New York, with the so ambiguous element in the *launched* foreign personality always in one's eyes; the wonder, above all, of whether there be, comparatively, in the vastly greater number of the representatives of the fresh contingent, any spirit that the American does not find an easy prey. Repeatedly, in the electric cars, one seemed invited to take that for granted—there being occasions, days and weeks together, when the electric cars offer you nothing else to think of. The carful, again and again, is a foreign carful; a row of faces, up and down, testifying, without exception, to alienism unmistakable, alienism undisguised and unashamed. You do here, in a manner perhaps, discriminate; the launched condition, as I have called it, is more developed in some types than in others; but I remember observing how, in the Broadway and the Bowery conveyances in especial, they tended, almost alike, to make the observer gasp with the sense of isolation. It was not for this that the observer on whose behalf I more particularly write had sought to take up again the sweet sense of the natal air.

The great fact about his companions was that, foreign as they might be, newly inducted as they might be, they were *at home*, really more at home, at the end of their few weeks or months or their year or two, than they had ever in their lives been before; and that *he* was at home too, quite with the same intensity: and yet that it was this very equality of condition that, from side to side, made the whole medium so strange. Here again, however, relief may be sought and found—and I say this at the risk of perhaps picturing the restored absentee as too constantly requiring it; for there is fascination in the study of the innumerable ways in which this sense of being at home, on the part of all the types, may show forth. New York offers to such a study a well-nigh unlimited field, but I seem to recall winter days, harsh, dusky, sloshy winter afternoons, in the densely-packed East-side street-cars, as an especially intimate surrender to it. It took its place thus, I think, under the general American law of *all* relief from the great equalizing pressure: it took on that last disinterestedness which consists of one's getting away from one's subject by plunging into it, for sweet truth's sake, still deeper. If I speak, moreover, of this general first grossness of alienism as presented in "types," I use that word for easy convenience and not in respect to its indicating marked variety. There are many different ways, certainly, in which obscure fighters of the battle of life may look, under new high lights, queer and crude and unwrought; but the striking thing, precisely, in the crepuscular, tunnel-like avenues that the "Elevated" overarches—yet without quenching, either, that constant power of any American exhibition rather luridly to light itself—the striking thing, and the beguiling, was always the manner in which figure after figure and face after face already betrayed the common consequence and action of their whereabouts. Face after face, unmistakably, was "low"—particularly in the men, squared all solidly in their new security and portability, their vague but growing sense of many unprecedented things; and as signs of the reinforcing of a large local conception of manners and relations it was difficult to say if they most affected one as promising or as portentous.

The great thing, at any rate, was that they were all together so visibly on the new, the lifted level—that of consciously not being what they *had* been, and that this immediately glazed them over as with some mixture, of indescribable hue and consistency, the wholesale varnish of consecration, that might have been applied, out of a bottomless receptacle, by a huge white-washing brush. Here, perhaps, was the nearest approach to a seizable step in the evolution of the oncoming citizen, the stage of his no longer being for you—for any complacency of the romantic, or even verily of the fraternizing, sense in you—the foreigner of the quality, of the kind, that he might have been *chez lui*.[3] Whatever he might see himself becoming, he was never to see himself that again, any more than you were ever to see him. He became then, to my vision (which I have called fascinated for want of a better description of it), a creature promptly despoiled of those "manners" which were the grace (as I am again reduced to calling it) by which one had best known and, on opportunity, best liked him. He presents himself thus, most of all, to be plain—and not only in New York, but throughout the country—as wonderingly conscious that his manners of the other world, that everything you have there known and praised him for, have been a huge mistake: to that degree that the sense of this luminous discovery is what we mainly imagine his weighted communications to those he has left behind charged with; those rich letters home as to the number and content of which the Post Office gives us so remarkable a statistic. If there are several lights in which the great assimilative organism itself may be looked at, does it not still perhaps loom largest as an agent for revealing to the citizen-to-be the error in question? He hears it, under this ægis, proclaimed in a thousand voices, and it is as listening to these and as, according to the individual, more or less swiftly, but always infallibly, penetrated and convinced by them, that I felt myself see him go about his business, see him above all, for some odd reason, sit there in the street-car, and with a slow, brooding gravity, a dim calculation of bearings, which yet never takes a backward step, expand to the full measure of it.

So, in New York, largely, the "American" value of the immigrant who arrives at all mature is restricted to the enjoyment (all prepared to increase) of that important preliminary truth; which makes him for us, we must own, till more comes of it, a tolerably neutral and colourless image. He resembles for the time the dog who sniffs round the freshly-acquired bone, giving it a push and a lick, betraying a sense of its possibilities, but not—and quite as from a positive deep tremor of consciousness—directly attacking it. There are categories of foreigners, truly, meanwhile, of whom we are moved to say that only a mechanism working with scientific force could have performed this feat of making them colourless. The Italians, who, over the whole land, strike us, I am afraid, as, after the Negro and the Chinaman, the human value most easily produced, the Italians meet us, at every turn, only to make us ask what has become of that element of the agreeable address in *them* which has, from far back, so enhanced for the stranger the interest and pleasure of a visit to their beautiful country. They shed it utterly, I couldn't but observe, on their advent, after a deep inhalation or two of the clear native air; shed it

[3] At home.

with a conscientious completeness which leaves one looking for any faint trace of it. "Colour," of that pleasant sort, was what they had appeared, among the races of the European family, most to have; so that the effect I speak of, the rapid action of the ambient air, is like that of the tub of hot water that reduces a piece of bright-hued stuff, on immersion, to the proved state of not "washing": the only fault of my image indeed being that if the stuff loses its brightness the water of the tub at least is more or less agreeably dyed with it. That is doubtless not the case for the ambient air operating after the fashion I here note—since we surely fail to observe that the property washed out of the new subject begins to tint with its pink or its azure his fellow-soakers in the terrible tank. If this property that has quitted him—the general amenity of attitude in the absence of provocation to its opposite— could be accounted for by its having rubbed off on any number of surrounding persons, the whole process would be easier and perhaps more comforting to follow. It will not have been his first occasion of taking leave of short-sighted comfort in the United States, however, if the patient inquirer postpones that ideal to the real solicitation of the question I here touch on.

What *does* become of the various positive properties, on the part of certain of the installed tribes, the good manners, say, among them, as to which the process of shedding and the fact of eclipse come so promptly into play? It has taken long ages of history, in the other world, to produce them, and you ask yourself, with independent curiosity, if they may really be thus extinguished in an hour. And if they are not extinguished, into what pathless tracts of the native atmosphere do they virtually, do they provisionally, and so all undiscoverably, melt? Do they burrow underground, to await their day again?—or in what strange secret places are they held in deposit and in trust? The "American" identity that has profited by their sacrifice has meanwhile acquired (in the happiest cases) all apparent confidence and consistency; but may not the doubt remain of whether the extinction of qualities ingrained in generations is to be taken for quite complete? Isn't it conceivable that, for something like a final efflorescence, the business of slow comminglings and makings-over at last ended, they may rise again to the surface, affirming their vitality and value and playing their part? It would be for them, of course, in this event, to attest that they had been worth waiting so long for; but the speculation, at any rate, irresistibly forced upon us, is a sign of the interest, in the American world, of what I have called the "ethnic" outlook. The cauldron, for the great stew, has such circumference and such depth that we can only deal here with ultimate syntheses, ultimate combinations and possibilities. Yet I am well aware that if these vague evocations of them, in their nebulous remoteness, may charm the ingenuity of the student of the scene, there are matters of the foreground that they have no call to supplant. Any temptation to let them do so is meanwhile, no doubt, but a proof of that impulse irresponsibly to escape from the formidable foreground which so often, in the American world, lies in wait for the spirit of intellectual dalliance.

III

New York really, I think, is all formidable foreground; or, if it be not, there is more than enough of this pressure of the present and the immediate to cut out the close sketcher's work for him. These things are a thick growth all round him, and when I recall the intensity of the material picture in the dense Yiddish quarter, for instance, I wonder at its not having forestalled, on my page, mere musings and, as they will doubtless be called, moonings. There abides with me, ineffaceably, the memory of a summer evening spent there by invitation of a high public functionary domiciled on the spot—to the extreme enhancement of the romantic interest his visitor found him foredoomed to inspire—who was to prove one of the most liberal of hosts and most luminous of guides. I can scarce help it if this brilliant personality, on that occasion the very medium itself through which the whole spectacle showed, so colours my impressions that if I speak, by intention, of the facts that played into them I may really but reflect the rich talk and the general privilege of the hour. That accident moreover must take its place simply as the highest value and the strongest note in the total show—so much did it testify to the quality of appealing, surrounding life. The sense of this quality was already strong in my drive, with a companion, through the long, warm June twilight, from a comparatively conventional neighborhood; it was the sense, after all, of a great swarming, a swarming that had begun to thicken, infinitely, as soon as we had crossed to the East side and long before we had got to Rutgers Street. There is no swarming like that of Israel when once Israel has got a start, and the scene here bristled, at every step, with the signs and sounds, immitigable, unmistakable, of a Jewry that had burst all bounds. That it has burst all bounds in New York, almost any combination of figures or of objects taken at hazard sufficiently proclaims; but I remember how the rising waters, on this summer night, rose, to the imagination, even above the housetops and seemed to sound their murmur to the pale distant stars. It was as if we had been thus, in the crowded, hustled roadway, where multiplication, multiplication of everything, was the dominant note, at the bottom of some vast sallow aquarium in which innumerable fish, of over-developed proboscis, were to bump together, for ever, amid heaped spoils of the sea.

The children swarmed above all—here was multiplication with a vengeance; and the number of very old persons, of either sex, was almost equally remarkable; the very old persons being in equal vague occupation of the doorstep, pavement, curbstone, gutter, roadway, and every one alike using the street for overflow. As overflow, in the whole quarter, is the main fact of life—I was to learn later on that, with the exception of some shy corner of Asia, no district in the world known to the statistician has so many

inhabitants to the yard—the scene hummed with the human presence beyond any I had ever faced in quest even of refreshment; producing part of
the impression, moreover, no doubt, as a direct consequence of the intensity
of the Jewish aspect. This, I think, makes the individual Jew more of a
concentrated person, savingly possessed of everything that is in him, than
any other human, noted at random—or is it simply, rather, that the unsur-
passed strength of the race permits of the chopping into myriads of fine
fragments without loss of race-quality? There are small strange animals,
known to natural history, snakes or worms, I believe, who, when cut into
pieces, wriggle away contentedly and live in the snippet as completely as in
the whole. So the denizens of the New York Ghetto, heaped as thick as the
splinters on the table of a glass-blower, had each, like the fine glass particle,
his or her individual share of the whole hard glitter of Israel. This diffused
intensity, as I have called it, causes any array of Jews to resemble (if I may be
allowed another image) some long nocturnal street where every window in
every house shows a maintained light. The advanced age of so many of the
figures, the ubiquity of the children, carried out in fact this analogy; they
were all there for race, and not, as it were, for reason: that excess of lurid
meaning, in some of the old men's and old women's faces in particular,
would have been absurd, in the conditions, as a really directed attention—it
could only be the gathered past of Israel mechanically pushing through. The
way, at the same time, this chapter of history did, all that evening, seem to
push, was a matter that made the "ethnic" apparition again sit like a skeleton
at the feast. It was fairly as if I could see the spectre grin while the talk of
the hour gave me, across the board, facts and figures, chapter and verse, for
the extent of the Hebrew conquest of New York. With a reverence for
intellect, one should doubtless have drunk in tribute to an intellectual people; but I remember being at no time more conscious of that merely portentous element, in the aspects of American growth, which reduces to inanity
any marked dismay quite as much as any high elation. The portent is one of
too many—you always come back, as I have hinted, with your easier gasp, to
that: it will be time enough to sigh or to shout when the relation of the
particular appearance to all the other relations shall have cleared itself up.
Phantasmagoric for me, accordingly, in a high degree, are the interesting
hours I here glance at content to remain—setting in this respect, I recognize,
an excellent example to all the rest of the New York phantasmagoria. Let me
speak of the remainder only as phantasmagoric too, so that I may both the
more kindly recall it and the sooner have done with it.

I have not done, however, with the impression of that large evening in the
Ghetto; there was too much in the vision, and it has left too much the sense
of a rare experience. For what did it all really come to but that one had seen
with one's eyes the New Jerusalem on earth? What less than that could it all
have been, in its far-spreading light and its celestial serenity of multiplication? There it was, there it is, and when I think of the dark, foul, stifling

Ghettos of other remembered cities, I shall think by the same stroke of the city of redemption, and evoke in particular the rich Rutgers Street perspective—rich, so peculiarly, for the eye, in that complexity of fire-escapes with which each house-front bristles and which gives the whole vista so modernized and appointed a look. Omnipresent in the "poor" regions, this neat applied machinery has, for the stranger, a common side with the electric light and the telephone, suggests the distance achieved from the old Jerusalem. (These frontal iron ladders and platforms, by the way, so numerous throughout New York, strike more New York notes than can be parenthetically named—and among them perhaps most sharply the note of the ease with which, in the terrible town, on opportunity, "architecture" goes by the board; but the appearance to which they often most conduce is that of the spaciously organized cage for the nimbler class of animals in some great zoological garden. This general analogy is irresistible—it seems to offer, in each district, a little world of bars and perches and swings for human squirrels and monkeys. The very name of architecture perishes, for the fire-escapes look like abashed afterthoughts, staircases and communications forgotten in the construction; but the inhabitants lead, like the squirrels and monkeys, all the merrier life.) It was while I hung over the prospect from the windows of my friend, however, the presiding genius of the district, and it was while, at a later hour, I proceeded in his company, and in that of a trio of contributive fellow-pilgrims, from one "characteristic" place of public entertainment to another: it was during this rich climax, I say, that the city of redemption was least to be taken for anything less than it was. The windows, while we sat at meat, looked out on a swarming little square in which an ant-like population darted to and fro; the square consisted in part of a "district" public garden, or public lounge rather, one of those small backwaters or refuges, artfully economized for rest, here and there, in the very heart of the New York whirlpool, and which spoke louder than anything else of a Jerusalem disinfected. What spoke loudest, no doubt, was the great overtowering School which formed a main boundary and in the shadow of which we all comparatively crouched.

But the School must not lead me on just yet—so colossally has its presence still to loom for us; that presence which profits so, for predominance, in America, by the failure of concurrent and competitive presences, the failure of any others looming at all on the same scale save that of Business, those in particular of a visible Church, a visible State, a visible Society, a visible Past; those of the many visibilities, in short, that warmly cumber the ground in older countries. Yet it also spoke loud that my friend was quartered, for the interest of the thing (from his so interesting point of view), in a "tenement-house"; the New Jerusalem would so have triumphed, had it triumphed nowhere else, in the fact that this charming little structure *could* be ranged, on the wonderful little square, under that invidious head. On my asking to what latent vice it owed its stigma, I was asked in return if it didn't sufficiently pay for its name by harbouring some five-and-twenty families. But this, exactly, was the way it testified—this circumstance of the simultaneous enjoyment by five-and-twenty families, on "tenement" lines, of conditions so little sordid, so highly "evolved." I remember the evolved fire-proof staircase, a thing of scientific surfaces, impenetrable to the microbe, and above all plated, against side friction, with white marble of a goodly grain. The white marble was surely the New Jerusalem note, and we followed that note, up and down the district, the rest of the evening, through more happy changes than I may take time to count. What struck me in the flaring streets (over and beyond the everywhere insistent, defiant, unhumorous, exotic face) was the blaze of the shops addressed to the New Jerusalem wants and the splendour with which these were taken for granted; the only thing indeed a little ambiguous was just this look of the trap too brilliantly, too candidly baited for the wary side of Israel itself. It is not *for* Israel, in general, that Israel so artfully shines—yet its being moved to do so, at last, in that luxurious style, might be precisely the grand side of the city of redemption. Who can ever tell, moreover, in any conditions and in presence of any apparent anomaly, what the genius of Israel may, or may not, really be "up to"?

The grateful way to take it all, at any rate, was with the sense of its coming back again to the inveterate rise, in the American air, of every value, and especially of the lower ones, those most subject to multiplication; such a wealth of meaning did this keep appearing to pour into the value and function of the country at large. Importances are all strikingly shifted and reconstituted, in the United States, for the visitor attuned, from far back, to "European" importances; but I think of no other moment of my total impression as so sharply working over my own benighted vision of them. The scale, in this light of the New Jerusalem, seemed completely rearranged; or, to put it more simply, the wants, the gratifications, the aspirations of the "poor," as expressed in the shops (which were the shops of the "poor"), denoted a new style of poverty; and this new style of poverty, from street to street, stuck out of the possible purchasers, one's jostling fellow-pedestrians, and made them, to every man and woman, individual throbs in the larger harmony. One can speak only of what one has seen, and there were grosser elements of the sordid and the squalid that I doubtless never saw. That, with a good deal of observation and of curiosity, I should have failed of this, the country over, affected me as by itself something of an indication. To miss that part of the spectacle, or to know it only by its having so unfamiliar a pitch, was an indication that made up for a great many others. It is when this one in particular is forced home to you—this immense, vivid *general* lift of poverty and general appreciation of the living unit's paying property in himself—that the picture seems most to clear and the way to jubilation most to open. For it meets you there, at every turn, as the result most definitely attested. You are as constantly reminded, no doubt, that these rises in enjoyed value shrink and dwindle under the icy breath of Trusts and the weight of the new remorseless monopolies that operate as no madnesses of ancient personal power thrilling us on the historic page ever operated; the living unit's property in himself becoming more and more merely such a property as may consist with a relation to properties overwhelmingly greater and that allow the asking of no questions and the making, for co-existence with them, of no conditions. But that, in the fortunate phrase, is another story, and will be altogether, evidently, a new and different drama. There is such a thing, in the United States, it is hence to be inferred, as freedom to grow up to be blighted, and it may be the only freedom in store for the smaller fry of future generations. If it is accordingly of the smaller fry I speak, and of how large they massed on that evening of endless admonitions, this will be because I caught them thus in their comparative humility and at an early stage of their American growth. The life-thread has, I suppose, to be of a certain thickness for the great shears of Fate to feel for it. Put it, at the worst, that the Ogres were to devour them, they were but the more certainly to fatten into food for the Ogres.

Their dream, at all events, as I noted it, was meanwhile sweet and undisguised—nowhere sweeter than in the half-dozen picked beer-houses and cafés in which our ingenuous *enquête*,[4] that of my fellow-pilgrims and I, wound up. These establishments had each been selected for its playing off some facet of the jewel, and they wondrously testified, by their range and their individual colour, to the spread of that lustre. It was a pious rosary of which I should like to tell each bead, but I must let the general sense of the adventure serve. Our successive stations were in no case of the "seamy" order, an inquiry into seaminess having been unanimously pronounced futile, but each had its separate social connotation, and it was for the number and variety of these connotations, and their individual plenitude and prosperity, to set one thinking. Truly the Yiddish world was a vast world, with its own deeps and complexities, and what struck one above all was that it sat there at its cups (and in no instance vulgarly the worse for them) with a sublimity of good conscience that took away the breath, a protrusion of elbow never aggressive, but absolutely proof against jostling. It was the incurable man of letters under the skin of one of the party who gasped, I confess; for it was in the light of letters, that is in the light of our language as literature has hitherto known it, that one stared at this all-unconscious impudence of the agency of future ravage. The man of letters, in the United States, has his own difficulties to face and his own current to stem—for dealing with which his liveliest inspiration may be, I think, that they are still very much his own, even in an Americanized world, and that more than elsewhere they press him to intimate communion with his honour. For that honour, the honour that sits astride of the consecrated English tradition, to his mind, quite as old

[4] Investigation.

knighthood astride of its caparisoned charger, the dragon most rousing, over the land, the proper spirit of St. George, is just this immensity of the alien presence climbing higher and higher, climbing itself into the very light of publicity.

I scarce know why, but I saw it that evening as in some dim dawn of that promise to its own consciousness, and perhaps this was precisely what made it a little exasperating. Under the impression of the mere mob the question doesn't come up, but in these haunts of comparative civility we saw the mob sifted and strained, and the exasperation was the sharper, no doubt, because what the process had left most visible was just the various possibilities of the waiting spring of intelligence. Such elements constituted the germ of a "public," and it was impossible (possessed of a sensibility worth speaking of) to be exposed to them without feeling how new a thing under the sun the resulting public would be. That was where one's "lettered" anguish came in—in the turn of one's eye from face to face for some betrayal of a prehensile hook for the linguistic tradition as one had known it. Each warm lighted and supplied circle, each group of served tables and smoked pipes and fostered decencies and unprecedented accents, beneath the extravagant lamps, took on thus, for the brooding critic, a likeness to that terrible modernized and civilized room in the Tower of London, haunted by the shade of Guy Fawkes, which had more than once formed part of the scene of the critic's taking tea there. In this chamber of the present urbanities the wretched man had been stretched on the rack, and the critic's ear (how else should it have been a critic's?) could still always catch, in pauses of talk, the faint groan of his ghost. Just so the East side cafés—and increasingly as their place in the scale was higher—showed to my inner sense, beneath their bedizenment, as torture-rooms of the living idiom; the piteous gasp of which at the portent of lacerations to come could reach me in any drop of the surrounding Accent of the Future. The accent of the very ultimate future, in the States, may be destined to become the most beautiful on the globe and the very music of humanity (here the "ethnic" synthesis shrouds itself thicker than ever); but whatever we shall know it for, certainly, we shall not know it for English—in any sense for which there is an existing literary measure.

EDITH WHARTON

(1862-1937)

Edith Wharton was perhaps the most accomplished novelist of manners of her generation. Somewhat of a disciple of her older friend, Henry James, Wharton took as her subject the moral drama of sensitive individuals caught in the tangles of a social world they could neither accept entirely nor resist decisively. *The House of Mirth* (1909), *The Custom of the Country* (1913), and *The Age of Innocence* (1920) are sharp eyed, partly satiric, partly tragic portraits set in an exclusive segment of American life, the posh upper-class world of New York, Newport, and international society. Wharton was herself part of this world and knew its details and textures intimately. She understood well the effects of its pretensions and its hypocrisies on nonconformists, and no one has portrayed more convincingly the capacity of the wealthy, especially the newly rich, for rationalizing objectionable personal behavior. Obtuseness enforced by rigid codes of behavior and social cruelty masking as polite respectability were her particular objects of scorn. Her leading theme might be described as the moral ambiguities of the fashionable world.

Wharton was born into this society, herself a well-bred daughter of the upper crust. Her memoir, *A Backward Glance* (1934), recalls the old New York burgher class of merchants and lawyers, jealous of their style of life and suspicious of outsiders. She was privately educated, traveled widely abroad and, at 23, married a prosperous man 13 years her

The major works include *The Decoration of Houses*, together with Ogden Codman, 1897; *The Greater Inclination*, 1899; *The Valley of Decision*, 1902; *The House of Mirth*, 1905; *Ethan Frome*, 1911; *The Custom of the Country*, 1913; *Summer*, 1917; *The Age of Innocence*, 1920; *Old New York*, 1926; *A Backward Glance*, 1934.

Louis Auchincloss has edited, with an introduction, *The Edith Wharton Reader*, 1965. R. W. B. Lewis edited *The Collected Stories of Edith Wharton*, 2 vols., 1968. See also *An Edith Wharton Treasury*, 1950, ed. Arthur Hobson Quinn, and *Best Short Stories of Edith Wharton*, ed. Wayne Andrews, 1958.

Biographies are Percy Lubbock, *Portrait of Edith Wharton*, 1947, Grace Kellogg, *The Two Lives of Edith Wharton, The Woman and Her Work*, 1965, and R. W. B. Lewis, *Edith Wharton*, 1976.

Criticism includes K. F. Gerould, *Edith Wharton, A Critical Study*, 1922; R. M. Lovett, *Edith Wharton*, 1925; Blake Nevius, *Edith Wharton: A Study of Her Fiction*, 1953; Marilyn Jones Lyde, *Edith Wharton: Convention and Morality in the Work of a Novelist*, 1959; Millicent Bell, *Edith Wharton and Henry James: The Story of Their Friendship*, 1965; Olivia Coolidge, *Edith Wharton, 1862-1937*, 1964.

senior. The marriage was an unhappy and frustrating affair for Edith Wharton; it ended in divorce in 1913. Wharton had begun writing at about the age of 40. In fiction she found a kind of release from her personal trying predicament; entrapment, victimization, and waste of talent, beauty, and capacity for love were leading themes in her work. She departed from her usual settings among the country houses and salons of the wealthy and comfortable in her best-known and most widely admired work, *Ethan Frome* (1911), a tragic tale of simple people in rural New England. In addition to her novels she produced a steady stream of short stories, including masterful ghost stories, a genre that she (like Henry James) transformed into a mode of psychological analysis.

The Other Two[1]

I

Waythorn, on the drawing-room hearth, waited for his wife to come down to dinner.

It was their first night under his own roof, and he was surprised at his thrill of boyish agitation. He was not so old, to be sure—his glass gave him little more than the five-and-thirty years to which his wife confessed—but he had fancied himself already in the temperate zone; yet here he was listening for her step with a tender sense of all it symbolized, with some old trail of verse about the garlanded nuptial doorposts floating through his enjoyment of the pleasant room and the good dinner just beyond it.

They had been hastily recalled from their honeymoon by the illness of Lily Haskett, the child of Mrs. Waythorn's first marriage. The little girl, at Waythorn's desire, had been transferred to his house on the day of her mother's wedding, and the doctor, on their arrival, broke the news that she was ill with typhoid, but declared that all the symptoms were favorable. Lily could show twelve years of unblemished health, and the case promised to be a light one. The nurse spoke as reassuringly, and after a moment of alarm Mrs. Waythorn had adjusted herself to the situation. She was very fond of Lily—her affection for the child had perhaps been her decisive charm in Waythorn's eyes—but she had the perfectly balanced nerves which her little girl had inherited, and no woman ever wasted less tissue in unproductive worry. Waythorn was therefore quite prepared to see her come in presently, a little late because of a last look at Lily, but as serene and well-appointed as if her good-night kiss had been laid on the brow of health. Her composure

[1] First published in 1904 in *The Descent of Man and Other Stories*, Charles Scribner's Sons, New York.

was restful to him; it acted as ballast to his somewhat unstable sensibilities. As he pictured her bending over the child's bed he thought how soothing her presence must be in illness: her very step would prognosticate recovery.

His own life had been a gray one, from temperament rather than circumstance, and he had been drawn to her by the unperturbed gaiety which kept her fresh and elastic at an age when most women's activities are growing either slack or febrile. He knew what was said about her; for, popular as she was, there had always been a faint undercurrent of detraction. When she had appeared in New York, nine or ten years earlier, as the pretty Mrs. Haskett whom Gus Varick had unearthed somewhere—was it in Pittsburg or Utica?—society, while promptly accepting her, had reserved the right to cast a doubt on its own indiscrimination. Inquiry, however, established her undoubted connection with a socially reigning family, and explained her recent divorce as the natural result of a runaway match at seventeen; and as nothing was known of Mr. Haskett it was easy to believe the worst of him.

Alice Haskett's remarriage with Gus Varick was a passport to the set whose recognition she coveted, and for a few years the Varicks were the most popular couple in town. Unfortunately the alliance was brief and stormy, and this time the husband had his champions. Still, even Varick's stanchest supporters admitted that he was not meant for matrimony, and Mrs. Varick's grievances were of a nature to bear the inspection of the New York courts. A New York divorce is in itself a diploma of virtue, and in the semiwidowhood of this second separation Mrs. Varick took on an air of sanctity, and was allowed to confide her wrongs to some of the most scrupulous ears in town. But when it was known that she was to marry Waythorn there was a momentary reaction. Her best friends would have preferred to see her remain in the role of the injured wife, which was as becoming to her as crepe to a rosy complexion. True, a decent time had elapsed, and it was not even suggested that Waythorn had supplanted his predecessor. People shook their heads over him, however, and one grudging friend, to whom he affirmed that he took the step with his eyes open, replied oracularly: "Yes— and with your ears shut."

Waythorn could afford to smile at these innuendoes. In the Wall Street phrase, he had "discounted" them. He knew that society has not yet adapted itself to the consequences of divorce, and that till the adaptation takes place every woman who uses the freedom the law accords her must be her own social justification. Waythorn had an amused confidence in his wife's ability to justify herself. His expectations were fulfilled, and before the wedding took place Alice Varick's group had rallied openly to her support. She took it all imperturbably: she had a way of surmounting obstacles without seeming to be aware of them, and Waythorn looked back with wonder at the trivialities over which he had worn his nerves thin. He had the sense of having found refuge in a richer, warmer nature than his own, and his satisfaction, at the moment, was humorously summed up in the thought that his wife, when she had done all she could for Lily, would not be ashamed to come down and enjoy a good dinner.

The anticipation of such enjoyment was not, however, the sentiment expressed by Mrs. Waythorn's charming face when she presently joined him. Though she had put on her most engaging tea gown she had neglected to assume the smile that went with it, and Waythorn thought he had never seen her look so nearly worried.

"What is it?" he asked. "Is anything wrong with Lily?"

"No; I've just been in and she's still sleeping." Mrs. Waythorn hesitated. "But something tiresome has happened."

He had taken her two hands, and now perceived that he was crushing a paper between them.

"This letter?"

"Yes—Mr. Haskett has written—I mean his lawyer has written."

Waythorn felt himself flush uncomfortably. He dropped his wife's hands. "What about?"

"About seeing Lily. You know the courts—"

"Yes, yes," he interrupted nervously.

Nothing was known about Haskett in New York. He was vaguely supposed to have remained in the outer darkness from which his wife had been rescued, and Waythorn was one of the few who were aware that he had given up his business in Utica and followed her to New York in order to be near his little girl. In the days of his wooing, Waythorn had often met Lily on the doorstep, rosy and smiling, on her way "to see papa."

"I am so sorry," Mrs. Waythorn murmured.

He roused himself. "What does he want?"

"He wants to see her. You know she goes to him once a week."

"Well—he doesn't expect her to go to him now, does he?"

"No—he has heard of her illness; but he expects to come here."

"*Here?*"

Mrs. Waythorn reddened under his gaze. They looked away from each other.

"I'm afraid he has the right. . . . You'll see. . . ." She made a proffer of the letter.

Waythorn moved away with a gesture of refusal. He stood staring about the softly-lighted room, which a moment before had seemed so full of bridal intimacy.

"I'm so sorry," she repeated. "If Lily could have been moved—"

"That's out of the question," he returned impatiently.

"I suppose so."

Her lip was beginning to tremble, and he felt himself a brute.

"He must come, of course," he said. "When is—his day?"

"I'm afraid—tomorrow."

"Very well. Send a note in the morning."

The butler entered to announce dinner.

Waythorn turned to his wife. "Come—you must be tired. It's beastly, but try to forget about it," he said, drawing her hand through his arm.

"You're so good, dear. I'll try," she whispered back.

Her face cleared at once, and as she looked at him across the flowers, between the rosy candleshades, he saw her lips waver back into a smile.

"How pretty everything is!" she sighed luxuriously.

He turned to the butler. "The champagne at once, please. Mrs. Waythorn is tired."

In a moment or two their eyes met above the sparkling glasses. Her own were quite clear and untroubled: he saw that she had obeyed his injunction and forgotten.

II

Waythorn, the next morning, went downtown earlier than usual. Haskett was not likely to come till the afternoon, but the instinct of flight drove him forth. He meant to stay away all day—he had thoughts of dining at his club. As his door closed behind him he reflected that before he opened it again it would have admitted another man who had as much right to enter it as himself, and the thought filled him with a physical repugnance.

He caught the elevated at the employees' hour, and found himself crushed between two layers of pendulous humanity. At Eighth Street the man facing him wriggled out, and another took his place. Waythorn glanced up and saw that it was Gus Varick. The men were so close together that it was impossible to ignore the smile of recognition on Varick's handsome overblown face. And after all—why not? They had always been on good terms, and Varick had been divorced before Waythorn's attentions to his wife began. The two exchanged a word on the perennial grievance of the congested trains, and when a seat at their side was miraculously left empty the instinct of self-preservation made Waythorn slip into it after Varick.

The latter drew the stout man's breath of relief. "Lord—I was beginning to feel like a pressed flower." He leaned back, looking unconcernedly at Waythorn. "Sorry to hear that Sellers is knocked out again."

"Sellers?" echoed Waythorn, starting at his partner's name.

Varick looked surprised. "You didn't know he was laid up with the gout?"

"No. I've been away—I only got back last night." Waythorn felt himself reddening in anticipation of the other's smile.

"Ah—yes; to be sure. And Sellers' attack came on two days ago. I'm afraid he's pretty bad. Very awkward for me, as it happens, because he was just putting through a rather important thing for me."

"Ah?" Waythorn wondered vaguely since when Varick had been dealing in "important things." Hitherto he had dabbled only in the shallow pools of speculation, with which Waythorn's office did not usually concern itself.

It occurred to him that Varick might be talking at random, to relieve the strain of their propinquity. That strain was becoming momentarily more apparent to Waythorn, and when, at Cortlandt Street, he caught sight of an acquaintance and had a sudden vision of the picture he and Varick must present to an initiated eye, he jumped up with a muttered excuse.

"I hope you'll find Sellers better," said Varick civilly, and he stammered back: "If I can be of any use to you—" and let the departing crowd sweep him to the platform.

At his office he heard that Sellers was in fact ill with the gout, and would probably not be able to leave the house for some weeks.

"I'm sorry it should have happened so, Mr. Waythorn," the senior clerk said with affable significance. "Mr. Sellers was very much upset at the idea of giving you such a lot of extra work just now."

"Oh, that's no matter," said Waythorn hastily. He secretly welcomed the pressure of additional business, and was glad to think that, when the day's work was over, he would have to call at his partner's on the way home.

He was late for luncheon, and turned in at the nearest restaurant instead of going to his club. The place was full, and the waiter hurried him to the back of the room to capture the only vacant table. In the cloud of cigar smoke Waythorn did not at once distinguish his neighbors: but presently, looking about him, he saw Varick seated a few feet off. This time, luckily, they were too far apart for conversation, and Varick, who faced another way, had probably not even seen him; but there was an irony in their renewed nearness.

Varick was said to be fond of good living, and as Waythorn sat dispatching his hurried luncheon he looked across half enviously at the other's leisurely degustation of his meal. When Waythorn first saw him he had been helping himself with critical deliberation to a bit of Camembert at the ideal point of liquefaction, and now, the cheese removed, he was just pouring his *café double* from its little two-storied earthen pot. He poured slowly, his ruddy profile bent over the task, and one beringed white hand steadying the lid of the coffeepot; then he stretched his other hand to the decanter of cognac at his elbow, filled a liqueur glass, took a tentative sip, and poured the brandy into his coffee cup.

Waythorn watched him in a kind of fascination. What was he thinking of—only of the flavor of the coffee and the liqueur? Had the morning's meeting left no more trace in his thoughts than on his face? Had his wife so completely passed out of his life that even this odd encounter with her present husband, within a week after her remarriage, was no more than an incident in his day? And as Waythorn mused, another idea struck him: had Haskett ever met Varick as Varick and he had just met? The recollection of Haskett perturbed him, and he rose and left the restaurant, taking a circuitous way out to escape the placid irony of Varick's nod.

It was after seven when Waythorn reached home. He thought the footman who opened the door looked at him oddly.

"How is Miss Lily?" he asked in haste.

"Doing very well, sir. A gentleman—"

"Tell Barlow to put off dinner for half an hour," Waythorn cut him off, hurrying upstairs.

He went straight to his room and dressed without seeing his wife. When he reached the drawing room she was there, fresh and radiant. Lily's day had been good; the doctor was not coming back that evening.

At dinner Waythorn told her of Sellers' illness and of the resulting complications. She listened sympathetically, adjuring him not to let himself be overworked, and asking vague feminine questions about the routine of the office. Then she gave him the chronicle of Lily's day; quoted the nurse and doctor, and told him who had called to inquire. He had never seen her more serene and unruffled. It struck him, with a curious pang, that she was very happy in being with him, so happy that she found a childish pleasure in rehearsing the trivial incidents of her day.

After dinner they went to the library, and the servant put the coffee and liqueurs on a low table before her and left the room. She looked singularly soft and girlish in her rosy-pale dress, against the dark leather of one of his bachelor armchairs. A day earlier the contrast would have charmed him.

He turned away now, choosing a cigar with affected deliberation.

"Did Haskett come?" he asked, with his back to her.

"Oh, yes—he came."

"You didn't see him, of course?"

She hesitated a moment. "I let the nurse see him."

That was all. There was nothing more to ask. He swung round toward her, applying a match to his cigar. Well, the thing was over for a week, at any rate. He would not try to think of it. She looked up at him, a trifle rosier than usual, with a smile in her eyes.

"Ready for your coffee, dear?"

He leaned against the mantelpiece, watching her as she lifted the coffeepot. The lamplight struck a gleam from her bracelets and tipped her soft hair with brightness. How light and slender she was, and how each gesture flowed into the next! She seemed a creature all compact of harmonies. As the thought of Haskett receded, Waythorn felt himself yielding again to the joy of possessorship. They were his, those white hands with their flitting motions, his the light haze of hair, the lips and eyes. . . .

She set down the coffeepot, and reaching for the decanter of cognac, measured off a liqueur glass and poured it into his cup.

Waythorn uttered a sudden exclamation.

"What is the matter?" she said, startled.

"Nothing; only—I don't take cognac in my coffee."

"Oh, how stupid of me," she cried.
Their eyes met, and she blushed a sudden agonized red.

III

Ten days later, Mr. Sellers, still housebound, asked Waythorn to call on his way downtown.

The senior partner, with his swaddled foot propped up by the fire, · greeted his associate with an air of embarrassment.

"I'm sorry, my dear fellow; I've got to ask you to do an awkward thing for me."

Waythorn waited, and the other went on, after a pause apparently given to the arrangement of his phrases: "The fact is, when I was knocked out I had just gone into a rather complicated piece of business for—Gus Varick."

"Well?" said Waythorn, with an attempt to put him at his ease.

"Well—it's this way: Varick came to me the day before my attack. He had evidently had an inside tip from somebody, and had made about a hundred thousand. He came to me for advice, and I suggested his going in with Vanderlyn."

"Oh, the deuce!" Waythorn exclaimed. He saw in a flash what had happened. The investment was an alluring one, but required negotiation. He listened quietly while Sellers put the case before him, and, the statement ended, he said: "You think I ought to see Varick?"

"I'm afraid I can't as yet. The doctor is obdurate. And this thing can't wait. I hate to ask you, but no one else in the office knows the ins and outs of it."

Waythorn stood silent. He did not care a farthing for the success of Varick's venture, but the honor of the office was to be considered, and he could hardly refuse to oblige his partner.

"Very well," he said, "I'll do it."

That afternoon, apprised by telephone, Varick called at the office. Waythorn, waiting in his private room, wondered what the others thought of it. The newspapers, at the time of Mrs. Waythorn's marriage, had acquainted their readers with every detail of her previous matrimonial ventures, and Waythorn could fancy the clerks smiling behind Varick's back as he was ushered in.

Varick bore himself admirably. He was easy without being undignified, and Waythorn was conscious of cutting a much less impressive figure. Varick had no experience of business, and the talk prolonged itself for nearly an hour while Waythorn set forth with scrupulous precision the details of the proposed transaction.

"I'm awfully obliged to you," Varick said as he rose. "The fact is I'm not used to having much money to look after, and I don't want to make an ass of myself—" He smiled, and Waythorn could not help noticing that there was something pleasant about his smile. "It feels uncommonly queer to have enough cash to pay one's bills. I'd have sold my soul for it a few years ago!" Waythorn winced at the allusion. He had heard it rumored that a lack of funds had been one of the determining causes of the Varick separation, but it did not occur to him that Varick's words were intentional. It seemed more likely that the desire to keep clear of embarrassing topics had fatally drawn him into one. Waythorn did not wish to be outdone in civility.

"We'll do the best we can for you," he said. "I think this is a good thing you're in."

"Oh, I'm sure it's immense. It's awfully good of you—" Varick broke off, embarrassed. "I suppose the thing's settled now—but if—"

"If anything happens before Sellers is about, I'll see you again," said Waythorn quietly. He was glad, in the end, to appear the more self-possessed of the two.

The course of Lily's illness ran smooth, and as the days passed Waythorn grew used to the idea of Haskett's weekly visit. The first time the day came round, he stayed out late, and questioned his wife as to the visit on his return. She replied at once that Haskett had merely seen the nurse downstairs, as the doctor did not wish anyone in the child's sickroom till after the crisis.

The following week Waythorn was again conscious of the recurrence of the day, but had forgotten it by the time he came home to dinner. The crisis of the disease came a few days later, with a rapid decline of fever, and the little girl was pronounced out of danger. In the rejoicing which ensued the thought of Haskett passed out of Waythorn's mind, and one afternoon, letting himself into the house with a latchkey, he went straight to his library without noticing a shabby hat and umbrella in the hall.

In the library he found a small effaced-looking man with a thinnish gray beard sitting on the edge of a chair. The stranger might have been a piano tuner, or one of those mysteriously efficient persons who are summoned in emergencies to adjust some detail of the domestic machinery. He blinked at Waythorn through a pair of gold-rimmed spectacles and said mildly: "Mr. Waythorn, I presume? I am Lily's father."

Waythorn flushed. "Oh—" he stammered uncomfortably. He broke off, disliking to appear rude. Inwardly he was trying to adjust the actual Haskett to the image of him projected by his wife's reminiscences. Waythorn had been allowed to infer that Alice's first husband was a brute.

"I am sorry to intrude," said Haskett, with his over-the-counter politeness.

"Don't mention it," returned Waythorn, collecting himself. "I suppose the nurse has been told?"

"I presume so. I can wait," said Haskett. He had a resigned way of speaking, as though life had worn down his natural powers of resistance.

Waythorn stood on the threshold, nervously pulling off his gloves.

"I'm sorry you've been detained. I will send for the nurse," he said; and as he opened the door he added with an effort: "I'm glad we can give you a good report of Lily." He winced as the *we* slipped out, but Haskett seemed not to notice it.

"Thank you, Mr. Waythorn, It's been an anxious time for me."

"Ah, well, that's past. Soon she'll be able to go to you." Waythorn nodded and passed out.

In his own room he flung himself down with a groan. He hated the womanish sensibility which made him suffer so acutely from the grotesque chances of life. He had known when he married that his wife's former husbands were both living, and that amid the multiplied contacts of modern existence there were a thousand chances to one that he would run against one or the other, yet he found himself as much disturbed by his brief encounter with Haskett as though the law had not obligingly removed all difficulties in the way of their meeting.

Waythorn sprang up and began to pace the room nervously. He had not suffered half as much from his two meetings with Varick. It was Haskett's presence in his own house that made the situation so intolerable. He stood still, hearing steps in the passage.

"This way, please," he heard the nurse say. Haskett was being taken upstairs, then: not a corner of the house but was open to him. Waythorn dropped into another chair, staring vaguely ahead of him. On his dressing table stood a photograph of Alice, taken when he had first known her. She was Alice Varick then—how fine and exquisite he had thought her! Those were Varick's pearls about her neck. At Waythorn's instance they had been returned before her marriage. Had Haskett ever given her any trinkets—and what had become of them, Waythorn wondered? He realized suddenly that he knew very little of Haskett's past or present situation; but from the man's appearance and manner of speech he could reconstruct with curious precision the surroundings of Alice's first marriage. And it startled him to think that she had, in the background of her life, a phase of existence so different from anything with which he had connected her. Varick, whatever his faults, was a gentleman, in the conventional, traditional sense of the term: the sense which at that moment seemed, oddly enough, to have most meaning to Waythorn. He and Varick had the same social habits, spoke the same language, understood the same allusions. But this other man . . . it was grotesquely uppermost in Waythorn's mind that Haskett had worn a made-up tie attached with an elastic. Why should that ridiculous detail symbolize the whole man? Waythorn was exasperated by his own paltriness, but the fact of the tie expanded, forced itself on him, became as it were the key to Alice's past. He could see her, as Mrs. Haskett, sitting in a "front parlor" furnished in plush, with a pianola, and copy of *Ben Hur* on the center table. He could see her going to the theater with Haskett—or perhaps even to a "Church

Sociable"—she in a "picture hat" and Haskett in a black frock coat, a little creased, with a made-up tie on an elastic. On the way home they would stop and look at the illuminated shop windows, lingering over the photographs of New York actresses. On Sunday afternoons Haskett would take her for a walk, pushing Lily ahead of them in a white enameled perambulator, and Waythorn had a vision of the people they would stop and talk to. He could fancy how pretty Alice must have looked, in a dress adroitly constructed from the hints of a New York fashion paper, and how she must have looked down on the other women, chafing at her life, and secretly feeling that she belonged in a bigger place.

For the moment his foremost thought was one of wonder at the way in which she had shed the phase of existence which her marriage with Haskett implied. It was as if her whole aspect, every gesture, every inflection, every allusion, were a studied negation of that period of her life. If she had denied being married to Haskett she could hardly have stood more convicted of duplicity than in this obliteration of the self which had been his wife.

Waythorn started up, checking himself in the analysis of her motives. What right had he to create a fantastic effigy of her and then pass judgment on it? She had spoken vaguely of her first marriage as unhappy, had hinted, with becoming reticence, that Haskett had wrought havoc among her young illusions. . . . It was a pity for Waythorn's peace of mind that Haskett's very inoffensiveness shed a new light on the nature of those illusions. A man would rather think that his wife had been brutalized by her first husband than that the process has been reversed.

IV

"Mr. Waythorn, I don't like that French governess of Lily's."

Haskett, subdued and apologetic, stood before Waythorn in the library, revolving his shabby hat in his hand.

Waythorn, surprised in his armchair over the evening paper, stared back perplexedly at his visitor.

"You'll excuse my asking to see you," Haskett continued. "But this is my last visit, and I thought if I could have a word with you it would be a better way than writing to Mrs. Waythorn's lawyer."

Waythorn rose uneasily. He did not like the French governess either; but that was irrelevant.

"I am not so sure of that," he returned stiffly; "but since you wish it I will give your message to—my wife." He always hesitated over the possessive pronoun in addressing Haskett.

The latter sighed. "I don't know as that will help much. She didn't like it when I spoke to her."

Waythorn turned red. "When did you see her?" he asked.

"Not since the first day I came to see Lily—right after she was taken sick. I remarked to her then that I didn't like the governess."

Waythorn made no answer. He remembered distinctly that, after that first visit, he had asked his wife if she had seen Haskett. She had lied to him then, but she had respected his wishes since; and the incident cast a curious light on her character. He was sure she would not have seen Haskett that first day if she had divined that Waythorn would object, and the fact that she did not divine it was almost as disagreeable to the latter as the discovery that she had lied to him.

"I don't like the woman," Haskett was repeating with mild persistency. "She ain't straight, Mr. Waythorn—she'll teach the child to be underhand. I've noticed a change in Lily—she's too anxious to please—and she don't always tell the truth. She used to be the straightest child, Mr. Waythorn—" He broke off, his voice a little thick. "Not but what I want her to have a stylish education," he ended.

Waythorn was touched. "I'm sorry, Mr. Haskett; but frankly, I don't quite see what I can do."

Haskett hesitated. Then he laid his hat on the table, and advanced to the hearthrug, on which Waythorn was standing. There was nothing aggressive in his manner, but he had the solemnity of a timid man resolved on a decisive measure.

"There's just one thing you can do, Mr. Waythorn," he said. "You can remind Mrs. Waythorn that, by the decree of the courts, I am entitled to have a voice in Lily's bringing-up." He paused, and went on more deprecatingly: "I'm not the kind to talk about enforcing my rights, Mr. Waythorn. I don't know as I think a man is entitled to rights he hasn't known how to hold on to; but this business of the child is different. I've never let go there—and I never mean to."

The scene left Waythorn deeply shaken. Shamefacedly, in indirect ways, he had been finding out about Haskett; and all that he had learned was favorable. The little man, in order to be near his daughter, had sold out his share in a profitable business in Utica, and accepted a modest clerkship in a New York manufacturing house. He boarded in a shabby street and had few acquaintances. His passion for Lily filled his life. Waythorn felt that this exploration of Haskett was like groping about with a dark lantern in his wife's past; but he saw now that there were recesses his lantern had not explored. He had never inquired into the exact circumstances of his wife's first matrimonial rupture. On the surface all had been fair. It was she who had obtained the divorce, and the court had given her the child. But Waythorn knew how many ambiguities such a verdict might cover. The mere fact that Haskett retained a right over his daughter implied an unsuspected compromise. Waythorn was an idealist. He always refused to recognize unpleasant contingencies till he found himself confronted with them, and then he saw them followed by a spectral train of consequences. His next days were thus haunted, and he determined to try to lay the ghosts by conjuring them up in his wife's presence.

When he repeated Haskett's request a flame of anger passed over her face; but she subdued it instantly and spoke with a slight quiver of outraged motherhood.

"It is very ungentlemanly of him," she said.

The word grated on Waythorn. "That is neither here nor there. It's a bare question of rights."

She murmured: "It's not as if he could ever be a help to Lily—"

Waythorn flushed. This was even less to his taste. "The question is," he repeated, "what authority has he over her?"

She looked downward, twisting herself a little in her seat. "I am willing to see him—I thought you objected," she faltered.

In a flash he understood that she knew the extent of Haskett's claims. Perhaps it was not the first time she had resisted them.

"My objecting has nothing to do with it," he said coldly; "if Haskett has a right to be consulted you must consult him."

She burst into tears, and he saw that she expected him to regard her as a victim.

Haskett did not abuse his rights. Waythorn had felt miserably sure that he would not. But the governess was dismissed, and from time to time the little man demanded an interview with Alice. After the first outburst she accepted the situation with her usual adaptability. Haskett had once reminded Waythorn of the piano tuner, and Mrs. Waythorn, after a month or two, appeared to class him with that domestic familiar. Waythorn could not but respect the father's tenacity. At first he had tried to cultivate the suspicion that Haskett might be "up to" something, that he had an object in securing a foothold in the house. But in his heart Waythorn was sure of Haskett's single-mindedness; he even guessed in the latter a mild contempt for such advantages as his relation with the Waythorns might offer. Haskett's sincerity of purpose made him invulnerable, and his successor had to accept him as an alien on the property.

Mr. Sellers was sent to Europe to recover from his gout, and Varick's affairs hung on Waythorn's hands. The negotiations were prolonged and complicated; they necessitated frequent conferences between the two men, and the interests of the firm forbade Waythorn's suggesting that his client should transfer his business to another office.

Varick appeared well in the transaction. In moments of relaxation his coarse streak appeared, and Waythorn dreaded his geniality; but in the office he was concise and clear-headed, with a flattering deference to Waythorn's judgment. Their business relations being so affably established, it would have been absurd for the two men to ignore each other in society. The first time they met in a drawing room, Varick took up their intercourse in the same easy key, and his hostess' grateful glance obliged Waythorn to respond to it. After that they ran across each other frequently, and one evening at a ball

Waythorn, wandering through the remoter rooms, came upon Varick seated beside his wife. She colored a little, and faltered in what she was saying; but Varick nodded to Waythorn without rising, and the latter strolled on.

In the carriage, on the way home, he broke out nervously: "I didn't know you spoke to Varick."

Her voice trembled a little. "It's the first time—he happened to be standing near me; I didn't know what to do. It's so awkward, meeting everywhere—and he said you had been very kind about some business."

"That's different," said Waythorn.

She paused a moment. "I'll do just as you wish," she returned pliantly. "I thought it would be less awkward to speak to him when we meet."

Her pliancy was beginning to sicken him. Had she really no will of her own—no theory about her relation to these men? She had accepted Haskett—did she mean to accept Varick? It was "less awkward," as she had said, and her instinct was to evade difficulties or to circumvent them. With sudden vividness Waythorn saw how the instinct had developed. She was "as easy as an old shoe"—a shoe that too many feet had worn. Her elasticity was the result of tension in too many different directions. Alice Haskett—Alice Varick—Alice Waythorn—she had been each in turn, and had left hanging to each name a little of her privacy, a little of her personality, a little of the inmost self where the unknown god abides.

"Yes—it's better to speak to Varick," said Waythorn wearily.

V

The winter wore on, and society took advantage of the Waythorns' acceptance of Varick. Harassed hostesses were grateful to them for bridging over a social difficulty, and Mrs. Waythorn was held up as a miracle of good taste. Some experimental spirits could not resist the diversion of throwing Varick and his former wife together, and there were those who thought he found a zest in the propinquity. But Mrs. Waythorn's conduct remained irreproachable. She neither avoided Varick nor sought him out. Even Waythorn could not but admit that she had discovered the solution of the newest social problem.

He had married her without giving much thought to that problem. He had fancied that a woman can shed her past like a man. But now he saw that Alice was bound to hers both by the circumstances which forced her into continued relation with it, and by the traces it had left on her nature. With grim irony Waythorn compared himself to a member of a syndicate. He held so many shares in his wife's personality and his predecessors were his partners in the business. If there had been any element of passion in the transaction he would have felt less deteriorated by it. The fact that Alice took her change of husbands like a change of weather reduced the situation to mediocrity. He could have forgiven her for blunders, for excesses; for resisting

Hackett, for yielding to Varick; for anything but her acquiescence and her tact. She reminded him of a juggler tossing knives; but the knives were blunt and she knew they would never cut her.

And then, gradually, habit formed a protecting surface for his sensibilities. If he paid for each day's comfort with the small change of his illusions, he grew daily to value the comfort more and set less store upon the coin. He had drifted into a dulling propinquity with Haskett and Varick and he took refuge in the cheap revenge of satirizing the situation. He even began to reckon up the advantages which accrued from it, to ask himself if it were not better to own a third of a wife who knew how to make a man happy than a whole one who had lacked opportunity to acquire the art. For it *was* an art, and made up, like all others, of concessions, eliminations and embellishments; of lights judiciously thrown and shadows skillfully softened. His wife knew exactly how to manage the lights, and he knew exactly to what training she owed her skill. He even tried to trace the source of his obligations, to discriminate between the influences which had combined to produce his domestic happiness: he perceived that Haskett's commonness had made Alice worship good breeding, while Varick's liberal construction of the marriage bond had taught her to value the conjugal virtues; so that he was directly indebted to his predecessors for the devotion which made his life easy if not inspiring.

From this phase he passed into that of complete acceptance. He ceased to satirize himself because time dulled the irony of the situation and the joke lost its humor with its sting. Even the sight of Haskett's hat on the hall table had ceased to touch the springs of epigram. The hat was often seen there now, for it had been decided that it was better for Lily's father to visit her than for the little girl to go to his boardinghouse. Waythorn, having acquiesced in this arrangement, had been surprised to find how little difference it made. Haskett was never obtrusive, and the few visitors who met him on the stairs were unaware of his identity. Waythorn did not know how often he saw Alice, but with himself Haskett was seldom in contact.

One afternoon, however, he learned on entering that Lily's father was waiting to see him. In the library he found Haskett occupying a chair in his usual provisional way. Waythorn always felt grateful to him for not leaning back.

"I hope you'll excuse me, Mr. Waythorn," he said rising. "I wanted to see Mrs. Waythorn about Lily, and your man asked me to wait here till she came in."

"Of course," said Waythorn, remembering that a sudden leak had that morning given over the drawing room to the plumbers.

He opened his cigar case and held it out to his visitor, and Haskett's acceptance seemed to make a fresh stage in their intercourse. The spring evening was chilly, and Waythorn invited his guest to draw up his chair to the fire. He meant to find an excuse to leave Haskett in a moment; but he was tired and cold, and after all the little man no longer jarred on him.

The two were enclosed in the intimacy of their blended cigar smoke when the door opened and Varick walked into the room. Waythorn rose abruptly. It was the first time that Varick had come to the house, and the surprise of seeing him, combined with the singular inopportuneness of his arrival, gave a new edge to Waythorn's blunted sensibilities. He stared at his visitor without speaking.

Varick seemed too preoccupied to notice his host's embarrassment.

"My dear fellow," he exclaimed in his most expansive tone, "I must apologize for tumbling in on you in this way, but I was too late to catch you downtown, and so I thought—"

He stopped short, catching sight of Haskett, and his sanguine color deepened to a flush which spread vividly under his scant blond hair. But in a moment he recovered himself and nodded slightly. Haskett returned the bow in silence, and Waythorn was still groping for speech when the footman came in carrying a tea table.

The intrusion offered a welcome vent to Waythorn's nerves. "What the deuce are you bringing this here for?" he said sharply.

"I beg your pardon, sir, but the plumbers are still in the drawing room, and Mrs. Waythorn said she would have tea in the library." The footman's perfectly respectful tone implied a reflection on Waythorn's reasonableness.

"Oh, very well," said the latter resignedly, and the footman proceeded to open the folding tea table and set out its complicated appointments. While this interminable process continued the three men stood motionless, watching it with a fascinated stare, till Waythorn, to break the silence, said to Varick, "Won't you have a cigar?"

He held out the case he had just tendered to Haskett, and Varick helped himself with a smile. Waythorn looked about for a match, and finding none, proffered a light from his own cigar. Haskett, in the background, held his ground mildly, examining his cigar tip now and then, and stepping forward at the right moment to knock its ashes into the fire.

The footman at last withdrew, and Varick immediately began: "If I could just say half a word to you about this business—"

"Certainly," stammered Waythorn; "in the dining room—"

But as he placed his hand on the door it opened from without, and his wife appeared on the threshold.

She came in fresh and smiling, in her street dress and hat, shedding a fragrance from the boa which she loosened in advancing.

"Shall we have tea in here, dear?" she began; and then she caught sight of Varick. Her smile deepened, veiling a slight tremor of surprise.

"Why, how do you do?" she said with a distinct note of pleasure.

As she shook hands with Varick she saw Haskett standing behind him. Her smile faded for a moment, but she recalled it quickly, with a scarcely perceptible side glance at Waythorn.

Steelworkers at Noontime, Thomas Anschutz. *Kennedy Galleries, Inc.*

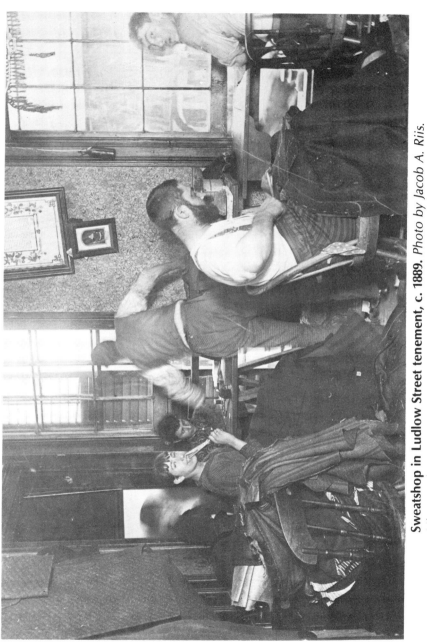

Sweatshop in Ludlow Street tenement, c. 1889. *Photo by Jacob A. Riis. Library of Congress.*

"How do you do, Mr. Haskett?" she said, and shook hands with him a shade less cordially.

The three men stood awkwardly before her, till Varick, always the most self-possessed, dashed into an explanatory phrase.

"We—I had to see Waythorn a moment on business," he stammered, brick-red from chin to nape.

Haskett stepped forward with his air of mild obstinacy. "I am sorry to intrude; but you appointed five o'clock—" he directed his resigned glance to the timepiece on the mantel.

She swept aside their embarrassment with a charming gesture of hospitality.

"I'm so sorry—I'm always late; but the afternoon was so lovely." She stood drawing off her gloves, propitiatory and graceful, diffusing about her a sense of ease and familiarity in which the situation lost its grotesqueness. "But before talking business," she added brightly, "I'm sure everyone wants a cup of tea."

She dropped into her low chair by the tea table, and the two visitors, as if drawn by her smile, advanced to receive the cups she held out.

She glanced about for Waythorn, and he took the third cup with a laugh.

III
Toward Naturalism

AMBROSE GWINNETT BIERCE

(1842-?1914)

Disillusion was common among writers in the 1890's, and many embraced a detached, "scientific," and often cynical point of view toward American life. One of the motives in American literary naturalism was simply to register a personal sense of outrage against the popular pieties that disguised fundamental facts of life, including the glaring facts of corruption and deceit. Although he was neither a realist nor a naturalist in his fiction—his stories are more on the mold of Gothic suspense and horror tales—Bierce reflected in an extreme way the current of bitterness that flowed in much of the serious writing at the end of the century. His notorious disgust with respectability, moralism, and patriotism appeared in *The Devil's Dictionary* (1906): "Commerce, *n*. A kind of transaction in which A plunders from B the goods of C, and for compensation B picks the pocket of D of money belonging to E"; "Diplomacy, *n*. The patriotic art of lying for one's country." "My country 'tis of thee, sweet land of felony," begins his parody, the "Rational Anthem."

Born into a large, poor farming family in Ohio, Bierce had only a spotty education before enlisting to fight in the Civil War. He was 19, and before the end of his service, had seen action in some of the bloodiest battles of the war, including Shiloh and Chickamauga. "Bitter Bierce's" disillusion with politicians, patriots, and businessmen

The standard edition is *The Collected Works of Ambrose Bierce,* 12 vols. ed. Walter Neale, 1909-1912.

Early biographies are C. Hartley Grattan, *Bitter Bierce*, 1929; Vincent Starrett, *Ambrose Bierce*, 1929; Carey McWilliams, *Ambrose Bierce*, 1929. A fuller study is Paul Fatout, *Ambrose Bierce, The Devil's Lexicographer*, 1951.

probably stemmed from his war experiences. After the war he became a journalist in England and America, eventually settled in San Francisco where he worked for years for Hearst's *Examiner* and wrote several pot-boilers. His stories of the Civil War, however, revealed a talent for laconic, ironic statement and an obsession with the grim physical and psychological horrors of battle. Most of these stories appeared in *Tales of Soldiers and Civilians* (1891), later reissued as *In the Midst of Life*. Although he personally scorned naturalists such as Stephen Crane "who think they get close to nature by depicting the sterile lives and limited emotions of the gowks and sodhoppers," his work shares a sense of man as trapped in nature, a helpless animal before impersonal forces, and prone to pathetically false illusions about his importance. Bierce left America in 1913, at the age of 70, presumably to search for a better world in Mexico. He was reported to have joined Pancho Villa, and he was never heard of again.

AN OCCURRENCE AT OWL CREEK BRIDGE[1]

I

A man stood upon a railroad bridge in northern Alabama, looking down into the swift water twenty feet below. The man's hands were behind his back, the wrists bound with a cord. A rope loosely encircled his neck. It was attached to a stout cross-timber above his head, and the slack fell to the level of his knees. Some loose boards laid upon the sleepers supporting the metals of the railway supplied a footing for him and his executioners—two private soldiers of the Federal army, directed by a sergeant, who in civil life may have been a deputy sheriff. At a short remove upon the same temporary platform was an officer in the uniform of his rank, armed. He was a captain. A sentinel at each end of the bridge stood with his rifle in the position known as "support," that is to say, vertical in front of the left shoulder, the hammer resting on the forearm thrown straight across the chest—a formal and un- natural position, enforcing an erect carriage of the body. It did not appear to be the duty of these two men to know what was occurring at the center of the bridge; they merely blockaded the two ends of the foot plank which traversed it.

---

[1] The story first appeared in *Tales of Soldiers and Civilians* in 1891; it was published in 1898 as *In The Midst of Life.*

Beyond one of the sentinels, nobody was in sight; the railroad ran straight away into a forest for a hundred yards, then, curving, was lost to view. Doubtless there was an outpost farther along. The other bank of the stream was open ground—a gentle acclivity crowned with a stockade of vertical tree trunks, loopholed for rifles, with a single embrasure through which protruded the muzzle of a brass cannon commanding the bridge. Midway of the slope between bridge and fort were the spectators—a single company of infantry in line, at "parade rest," the butts of the rifles on the ground, the barrels inclining slightly backward against the right shoulder, the hands crossed upon the stock. A lieutenant stood at the right of the line, the point of his sword upon the ground, his left hand resting upon his right. Excepting the group of four at the center of the bridge, not a man moved. The company faced the bridge, staring stonily, motionless. The sentinels, facing the banks of the stream, might have been statues to adorn the bridge. The captain stood with folded arms, silent, observing the work of his subordinates, but making no sign. Death is a dignitary, who when he comes announced is to be received with formal manifestations of respect, even by those most familiar with him. In the code of military etiquette silence and fixity are forms of deference.

The man who was engaged in being hanged was apparently about thirty-five years of age. He was a civilian, if one might judge from his dress, which was that of a planter. His features were good—a straight nose, firm mouth, broad forehead, from which his long, dark hair was combed straight back, falling behind his ears to the collar of his well-fitting frock coat. He wore a mustache and pointed beard, but no whiskers; his eyes were large and dark gray, and had a kindly expression which one would hardly have expected in one whose neck was in the hemp. Evidently this was no vulgar assassin. The liberal military code makes provision for hanging many kinds of people, and gentlemen are not excluded.

The preparations being complete, the two private soldiers stepped aside and each drew away the plank upon which he had been standing. The sergeant turned to the captain, saluted, and placed himself immediately behind that officer, who in turn moved apart one pace. These movements left the condemned man and the sergeant standing on the two ends of the same plank, which spanned three of the crossties of the bridge. The end upon which the civilian stood almost, but not quite, reached a fourth. This plank had been held in place by the weight of the captain; it was now held by that of the sergeant. At a signal from the former, the latter would step aside, the plank would tilt, and the condemned man go down between two ties. The arrangement commended itself to his judgment as simple and effective. His face had not been covered nor his eyes bandaged. He looked a moment at his "unsteadfast footing," then let his gaze wander to the swirling water of the stream racing madly beneath his feet. A piece of dancing driftwood caught his attention and his eyes followed it down the current. How slowly it appeared to move! What a sluggish stream!

He closed his eyes in order to fix his last thoughts upon his wife and children. The water, touched to gold by the early sun, the brooding mists under the banks at some distance down the stream, the fort, the soldiers, the piece of drift—all had distracted him. And now he became conscious of a new disturbance. Striking through the thought of his dear ones was a sound which he could neither ignore nor understand, a sharp, distinct, metallic percussion like the stroke of a blacksmith's hammer upon the anvil; it had the same ringing quality. He wondered what it was, and whether immeasurably distant or near by—it seemed both. Its recurrence was regular, but as slow as the tolling of a death knell. He awaited each stroke with impatience and—he knew not why—apprehension. The intervals of silence grew progressively longer; the delays became maddening. With their greater infrequency the sounds increased in strength and sharpness. They hurt his ear like the thrust of a knife; he feared he would shriek. What he heard was the ticking of his watch.

He unclosed his eyes and saw again the water below him. "If I could free my hands," he thought, "I might throw off the noose and spring into the stream. By diving I could evade the bullets, and, swimming vigorously, reach the bank, take to the woods, and get away home. My home, thank God, is as yet outside their lines; my wife and little ones are still beyond the invader's farthest advance."

As these thoughts, which have here to be set down in words, were flashed into the doomed man's brain rather than evolved from it, the captain nodded to the sergeant. The sergeant stepped aside.

II

Peyton Farquhar was a well-to-do planter of an old and highly respected Alabama family. Being a slave owner and like other slave owners a politician, he was naturally an original secessionist and ardently devoted to the Southern cause. Circumstances of an imperious nature, which it is unnecessary to relate here, had prevented him from taking service with the gallant army which had fought the disastrous campaigns ending with the fall of Corinth, and he chafed under the inglorious restraint, longing for the release of his energies, the larger life of the soldier, the opportunity for distinction. That opportunity, he felt, would come, as it comes to all in war time. Meanwhile he did what he could. No service was too humble for him to perform in aid of the South, no adventure too perilous for him to undertake if consistent with the character of a civilian who was at heart a soldier, and who in good faith and without too much qualification assented to at least a part of the frankly villainous dictum that all is fair in love and war.

One evening while Farquhar and his wife were sitting on a rustic bench near the entrance to his grounds, a gray-clad soldier rode up to the gate and asked for a drink of water. Mrs. Farquhar was only too happy to serve him with her own white hands. While she was gone to fetch the water, her husband approached the dusty horseman and inquired eagerly for news from the front.

"The Yanks are repairing the railroads," said the man, "and are getting ready for another advance. They have reached the Owl Creek bridge, put it in order, and built a stockade on the north bank. The commandant has issued an order, which is posted everywhere, declaring that any civilian caught interfering with the railroad, its bridges, tunnels, or trains will be summarily hanged. I saw the order."

"How far is it to the Owl Creek bridge?" Farquhar asked.

"About thirty miles."

"Is there no force on this side the creek?"

"Only a picket post half a mile out, on the railroad, and a single sentinel at this end of the bridge."

"Suppose a man—a civilian and student of hanging—should elude the picket post and perhaps get the better of the sentinel," said Farquhar, smiling, "what could he accomplish?"

The soldier reflected. "I was there a month ago," he replied. "I observed that the flood of last winter had lodged a great quantity of driftwood against the wooden pier at this end of the bridge. It is now dry and would burn like tow."

The lady had now brought the water, which the soldier drank. He thanked her ceremoniously, bowed to her husband, and rode away. An hour later, after nightfall, he repassed the plantation, going northward in the direction from which he had come. He was a Federal scout.

III

As Peyton Farquhar fell straight downward through the bridge he lost consciousness and was as one already dead. From this state he was awakened—ages later, it seemed to him—by the pain of a sharp pressure upon his throat, followed by a sense of suffocation. Keen, poignant agonies seemed to shoot from his neck downward through every fiber of his body and limbs. These pains appeared to flash along well-defined lines a ramification and to beat with an inconceivably rapid periodicity. They seemed like streams of pulsating fire heating him to an intolerable temperature. As to his head, he was conscious of nothing but a feeling of fullness—of congestion. These sensations were unaccompanied by thought. The intellectual part of his nature was already effaced; he had power only to feel, and feeling was torment. He was conscious of motion. Encompassed in a luminous cloud, of which he was now merely the fiery heart, without material substance, he swung through unthinkable arcs of oscillation, like a vast pendulum. Then all at once, with terrible suddenness, the light about him shot upward with the noise of a loud plash; a frightful roaring was in his ears, and all was cold and dark. The power of thought was restored; he knew that the rope had broken and he had fallen into the stream. There was no additional strangulation; the noose about his neck was already suffocating him and kept the water from his lungs. To die of hanging at the bottom of a river!—the idea seemed to him ludicrous. He opened his eyes in the darkness and saw above him a gleam of light, but how distant, how inaccessible! He was still sinking, for the light became fainter and fainter until it was a mere glimmer. Then it began to grow and brighten, and he knew that he was rising toward the surface—knew it with reluctance, for he was now very comfortable. "To be hanged and drowned," he thought, "that is not so bad; but I do not wish to be shot. No, I will not be shot, that is not fair."

He was not conscious of an effort, but a sharp pain in his wrist apprised him that he was trying to free his hands. He gave the struggle his attention, as an idler might observe the feat of a juggler, without interest in the outcome. What splendid effort!—what magnificent, what super-human strength! Ah, that was a fine endeavor! Bravo! The cord fell away; his arms parted and floated upward, the hands dimly seen on each side in the growing light. He watched them with a new interest as first one and then the other pounced upon the noose at his neck. They tore it away and thrust it fiercely aside, its undulations resembling those of a water snake. "Put it back, put it back!" He thought he shouted these words to his hands, for the undoing of the noose had been succeeded by the direst pang that he had yet experienced. His neck ached horribly; his brain was on fire; his heart, which had been fluttering faintly, gave a great leap, trying to force itself out at his mouth. His whole body was racked and wrenched with an insupportable anguish! But his disobedient hands gave no heed to the command. They beat the water vigorously with quick, downward strokes, forcing him to the surface. He felt his head emerge; his eyes were blinded by the sunlight; his chest expanded convulsively, and with a supreme and crowning agony his lungs engulfed a great draught of air, which instantly he expelled in a shriek!

He was now in full possession of his physical senses. They were, indeed, preternaturally keen and alert. Something in the awful disturbance of his organic system had so exalted and refined them that they made record of things never before perceived. He felt the ripples upon his face and heard their separate sounds as they struck. He looked at the forest on the bank of the stream, saw the individual trees, the leaves and the veining of each leaf—saw the very insects upon them: the locusts, the brilliant-bodied flies, the gray spiders stretching their webs from twig to twig. He noted the prismatic colors in all the dewdrops upon a million blades of grass. The humming of the gnats that danced above the eddies of the stream, the beating of the dragonflies' wings, the strokes of the water spiders' legs, like oars which had lifted their boat—all these made audible music. A fish slid along beneath his eyes and he heard the rush of its body parting the water.

He had come to the surface facing down the stream; in a moment the visible world seemed to wheel slowly round, himself the pivotal point, and he saw the bridge, the fort, the soldiers upon the bridge, the captain, the sergeant, the two privates, his executioners. They were in silhouette against the blue sky. They shouted and gesticulated, pointing at him. The captain had drawn his pistol, but did not fire; the others were unarmed. Their movements were grotesque and horrible, their forms gigantic.

Suddenly he heard a sharp report and something struck the water smartly within a few inches of his head, spattering his face with spray. He heard the second report, and saw one of the sentinels with his rifle at his shoulder, a light cloud of blue smoke rising from the muzzle. The man in the water saw the eye of the man on the bridge gazing into his own through the sights of the rifle. He observed that it was a gray eye and remembered having read that gray eyes were keenest, and that all famous marksmen had them. Nevertheless, this one had missed.

A counterswirl had caught Farquhar and turned him half round; he was again looking into the forest on the bank opposite the fort. The sound of a clear, high voice in a monotonous singsong now rang out behind him and came across the water with distinctness that pierced and subdued all other sounds, even the beating of the ripples in his ears. Although no soldier, he had frequented camps enough to know the dread significance of that deliberate, drawling, aspirated chant; the lieutenant on shore was taking part in the morning's work. How coldly and pitilessly—with what an even, calm intonation, presaging and enforcing tranquillity in the men—with what accurately measured intervals fell those cruel words:

"Attention, company! . . . Shoulder arms! . . . Ready! . . . Aim! . . . Fire!"

Farquhar dived—dived as deeply as he could. The water roared in his ears like the voice of Niagara, yet he heard the dulled thunder of the volley and, rising again toward the surface, met shining bits of metal, singularly flattened, oscillating slowly downward. Some of them touched him on the face and hands, then fell away, continuing their descent. One lodged between his collar and his neck; it was uncomfortably warm and he snatched it out.

As he rose to the surface, gasping for breath, he saw that he had been a long time under water; he was perceptibly farther downstream—nearer to safety. The soldiers had almost finished reloading; the metal ramrods flashed all at once in the sunshine as they were drawn from the barrels, turned in the air, and thrust into their sockets. The two sentinels fired again, independently and ineffectually.

The hunted man saw all this over his shoulder; he was now swimming vigorously with the current. His brain was as energetic as his arms and legs; he thought with the rapidity of lightning.

"The officer," he reasoned, "will not make that martinet's error a second time. It is as easy to dodge a volley as a single shot. He has probably already given the command to fire at will. God help me, I cannot dodge them all!"

An appalling plash within two yards of him was followed by a loud, rushing sound, *diminuendo*, which seemed to travel back through the air to the fort and died in an explosion which stirred the very river to its deeps! A rising sheet of water, which curved over him, fell down upon him, blinded him, strangled him! The cannon had taken a hand in the game. As he shook his head free from the commotion of the smitten water, he heard the deflected shot humming through the air ahead, and in an instant it was cracking and smashing the branches in the forest beyond.

"They will not do that again," he thought; "the next time they will use a charge of grape. I must keep my eye upon the gun; the smoke will apprise me—the report arrives too late; it lags behind the missile. That is a good gun."

Suddenly he felt himself whirled round and round—spinning like a top. The water, the banks, the forests, the now distant bridge, fort, and men—all were commingled and blurred. Objects were represented by their colors only; circular horizontal streaks of color—that was all he saw. He had been caught in a vortex and was being whirled on with a velocity of advance and gyration which made him giddy and sick. In a few moments he was flung upon the gravel at the foot of the left bank of the stream—the southern bank—and behind a projecting point which concealed him from his enemies. The sudden arrest of his motion, the abrasion of one of his hands on the gravel, restored him, and he wept with delight. He dug his fingers into the sand, threw it over himself in handfuls, and audibly blessed it. It looked like gold, like diamonds, rubies, emeralds; he could think of nothing beautiful which it did not resemble. The trees upon the bank were giant garden plants; he noted a definite order in their arrangement, inhaled the fragrance of their blooms. A strange, roseate light shone through the spaces among their trunks and the wind made in their branches the music of aeolian harps. He had no wish to perfect his escape—was content to remain in that enchanting spot until retaken.

A whiz and rattle of grapeshot among the branches high above his head roused him from his dream. The baffled cannoneer had fired him a random farewell. He sprang to his feet, rushed up the sloping bank, and plunged into the forest.

All that day he traveled, laying his course by the rounding sun. The forest seemed interminable; nowhere did he discover a break in it, not even a woodman's road. He had not known that he lived in so wild a region. There was something uncanny in the revelation.

By nightfall he was fatigued, footsore, famishing. The thought of his wife and children urged him on. At last he found a road which led him in what he knew to be the right direction. It was wide and straight as a city street, yet it seemed untraveled. No fields bordered it, no dwelling anywhere. Not so much as the barking of a dog suggested human habitation. The black bodies of the great trees formed a straight wall on both sides, terminating on the horizon in a point, like a diagram in a lesson in perspective. Overhead, as he looked up through this rift in the wood, shone great golden stars looking unfamiliar and grouped in strange constellations. He was sure they were arranged in some order which had a secret and malign significance. The wood on either side was full of singular noises, among which—once, twice, and again—he distinctly heard whispers in an unknown tongue.

His neck was in pain and lifting his hand to it he found it horribly swollen. He knew that it had a circle of black where the rope had bruised it. His eyes felt congested; he could no longer close them. His tongue was swollen with thirst; he relieved its fever by thrusting it forward from between his teeth into the cool air. How softly the turf had carpeted the untraveled avenue— he could no longer feel the roadway beneath his feet!

Doubtless, despite his suffering, he had fallen asleep while walking, for now he sees another scene—perhaps he has merely recovered from a delirium. He stands at the gate of his own home. All is as he left it, and all bright and beautiful in the morning sunshine. He must have traveled the entire night. As he pushes open the gate and passes up the wide white walk, he sees a flutter of female garments; his wife, looking fresh and cool and sweet, steps down from the veranda to meet him. At the bottom of the steps she stands waiting, with a smile of ineffable joy, an attitude of matchless grace and dignity. Ah, how beautiful she is! He springs forward with extended arms. As he is about to clasp her, he feels a stunning blow upon the back of the neck; a blinding white light blazes all about him with a sound like the shock of a cannon—then all is darkness and silence!

Peyton Farquhar was dead; his body, with a broken neck, swung gently from side to side beneath the timbers of the Owl Creek bridge.

illusion vs reality

1891

HAMLIN GARLAND

(1860–1940)

Local color stories of the 1860's and 1870's often idealized frontier and farm life in the West. Although these stories contributed to a growing taste for realistic portrayal of character and setting, they remained bound to sentimental plots and themes. In the 1880's and 1890's another view emerged, particularly in the works of Edward Eggleston, E. W. Howe, Joseph Kirkland, and Hamlin Garland. All of them were Midwesterners and wrote out of a desire to expose the myth of happy rural life, to show the underlying meanness of existence that resulted from social isolation and economic insecurity. In Garland's stories the outrage becomes more pointed, sharpened by a definite political outlook.

Born into a farming family that had homesteaded unluckily in Wisconsin, Iowa, and South Dakota, Hamlin Garland managed to get to Boston in his youth, met Howells and Whitman, read the social evolutionist Herbert Spencer, and fell under the influence of Henry George's solution of a "single tax" as a cure to social injustice and poverty. His interests leaned to Populist politics and oratory but, on his return to South Dakota in the late 1880's, he turned to fiction as a way of expressing the bleak, draining life he found there.

Garland's first stories, published as *Main-Travelled Roads* (1891), are mainly unrelieved tales of disappointment; they are protests against social conditions and, despite their often clumsy and excessively literary treatment, they have a certain power. He tends to state rather than dramatize his meaning, subordinating character to his political ideas. "Under the Lion's Paw" is virtually an illustration of Henry George's argument against unearned increment in land rents; at the same time the story is a credible parable of farm life, rendered with realistic detail. In *Crumbling Idols* (1894) Garland defined his literary approach as "veritism," a pretentious term for Howellsian realism conceived as an instrument of protest and social change.

The major works are *Main-Travelled Roads*, 1891: *Rose of Dutcher's Coolly*, 1895: *A Son of the Middle Border*, 1917: *A Daughter of the Middle Border*, 1921.

Two recent biographies are Jean Holloway, *Hamlin Garland: A Biography*, 1960, and D. Pizer, *Hamlin Garland's Early Work and Career*, 1960. Background studies include Walter Fuller Taylore, *The Economic Novel in America*, 1942, pp. 148–183: Arthur Hobson Quinn, *American Fiction*, 1936, pp. 454–59: Larzer Ziff, *The American 1890's*, 1966.

The Veteran in a New Field, Winslow Homer. *The Metropolitan Museum of Art, Bequest of Adelaide Milton de Groot.*

Under the Lion's Paw[1]

"Along this main-travelled road trailed an endless line of prairie schooners, coming into sight at the east, and passing out of sight over the swell to the west. We children used to wonder where they were going and why they went."

It was the last of autumn and first day of winter coming together. All day long the plowmen on their prairie farms had moved to and fro in their wide level fields through the falling snow, which melted as it fell, wetting them to the skin—all day, notwithstanding the frequent squalls of snow, the dripping, desolate clouds, and the muck of the furrows, black and tenacious as tar.

Under their dripping harness the horses swung to and fro silently, with that marvelous uncomplaining patience which marks the horse. All day the wild geese, honking wildly as they sprawled sidewise down the wind, seemed to be fleeing from an enemy behind, and with neck outthrust and wings extended, sailed down the wind, soon lost to sight.

Yet the plowman behind his plow, though the snow lay on his ragged greatcoat and the cold clinging mud rose on his heavy boots, fettering him like gyves[2] whistled in the very beard of the gale. As day passed, the snow, ceasing to melt, lay along the plowed land and lodged in the depth of the stubble, till on each slow round the last furrow stood out black and shining as jet between the plowed land and the gray stubble.

When night began to fall, and the geese, flying low, began to alight invisibly in the near cornfield, Stephen Council was still at work "finishing a land." He rode on his sulky-plow when going with the wind, but walked when facing it. Sitting bent and cold but cheery under his slouch hat, he talked encouragingly to his four-in-hand.

"Come round there, boys!—round agin! We got t' finish this land. Come in there, Dan! *Stiddy*, Kate!—stiddy! None o' y'r tantrums, Kittie. It's purty tuff, but gotta be did. *Tchk! tchk!* Step along, Pete! Don't let Kate git y'r single tree on the wheel. *Once* more!"

They seemed to know what he meant, and that this was the last round, for they worked with greater vigor than before.

"Once more, boys, an' then sez I oats, an' a nice warm stall, an' sleep f'r all."

By the time the last furrow was turned on the land it was too dark to see the house, and the snow was changing to rain again. The tired and hungry man could see the light from the kitchen shining through the leafless hedge, and lifted a great shout, "Sup*per* f'r a half a dozen!"

---

[1] The story was first published in 1889 and was collected in *Main-Travelled Roads*, in 1891.

[2] Shackles.

It was nearly eight o'clock by the time he had finished his chores and started for supper. He was picking his way carefully through the mud when the tall form of a man loomed up before him with a premonitory cough. "Waddy ye want?" was the rather startled question of the farmer.

"Well, ye see," began the stranger in a deprecating tone, "we'd like t' git in f'r the night. We've tried every house f'r the last two miles, but they hadn't any room f'r us. My wife's jest about sick, 'n' the children are cold and hungry—"

"Oh, y' want a stay all night, eh?"

"Yes, sir; it 'ud be a great accom—"

"Waal, I don't make it a practice t' turn anybuddy away hungry, not on sech nights as this. Drive right in. We ain't got much, but sech as it is—"

But the stranger had disappeared. And soon his teaming, weary team, with drooping heads and swinging single trees, moved past the well to the block beside the path. Council stood at the side of the "schooner" and helped the children out—two little half-sleeping children—and then a small woman with a babe in her arms.

"There ye go!" he shouted jovially to the children. "*Now* we're all right. Run right along to the house there, an' tell M'am Council you wants sumpthin' t' eat. Right this way, Mis'—keep right off t' the right there I'll go an' git a lantern. Come," he said to the dazed and silent group at his side.

"Mother," he shouted as he neared the fragrant and warmly lighted kitchen, "here are some wayfarers an' folks who need sumpthin' t' eat an' a place t'snooze." He ended by pushing them all in.

Mrs. Council, a large, jolly, rather coarse-looking woman, took the children in her arms. "Come right in, you little rabbits. 'Most asleep, hey? Now here's a drink o' milk f'r each o' ye. I'll have s'm tea in a minute. Take off y'r things and set up t' the fire."

While she set the children to drinking milk, Council got out his lantern and went out to the barn to help the stranger about his team, where his loud, hearty voice could be heard as it came and went between the haymow and the stalls.

The woman came to light as a small, timid, and discouraged-looking woman, but still pretty, in a thin and sorrowful way.

"Land sakes! An' you've travelled all the way from Clear Lake t'day in this mud! Waal! waal! No wonder you're all tired out. Don't wait f'r the men, Mis'—" She hesitated, waiting for the name.

"Haskins."

"Mis' Haskins, set right up to the table an' take a good swig o' tea, whilst I make y' s'm toast. It's green tea, an' it's good. I tell Council as I git older I don't seem t' enjoy Young Hyson n'r Gunpowder. I want the reel green tea, jest as it comes off'n the vines. Seems t' have more heart in it some way. Don't s'pose it has. Council says it's all in m' eye."

Going on in this easy way, she soon had the children filled with bread and milk and the woman thoroughly at home, eating some toast and sweet-melon pickles and sipping the tea.

"See the little rats!" she laughed at the children. "They're full as they can stick now, and they want to go to bed. Now don't git up, Mis' Haskins; set right where you are an' let me look after 'em. I know all about young ones, though I'm all alone now. Jane went an' married last fall. But, as I tell Council, it's lucky we keep our health. Set right there, Mis' Haskins; I won't have you stir a finger."

It was an unmeasured pleasure to sit there in the warm, homely kitchen, the jovial chatter of the housewife driving out and holding at bay the growl of the impotent, cheated wind.

The little woman's eyes filled with tears which fell down upon the sleeping baby in her arms. The world was not so desolate and cold and hopeless, after all.

"Now I hope Council won't stop out there and talk politics all night. He's the greatest man to talk politics an' read the *Tribune*. How old is it?"

She broke off and peered down at the face of the babe.

"Two months 'n' five days," said the mother, with a mother's exactness.

"Ye don't say! I want t' know! The dear little pudzy-wudzy!" she went on, stirring it up in the neighborhood of the ribs with her fat forefinger.

"Pooty tough on 'oo to go gallivant'n' 'cross lots this way."

"Yes, that's so; a man can't lift a mountain," said Council, entering the door. "Sarah, this is Mr. Haskins from Kansas. He's been eat up 'n' drove out by grasshoppers."

"Glad t' see yeh! Pa, empty that washbasin 'n' give him a chance t' wash."

Haskins was a tall man with a thin, gloomy face. His hair was a reddish brown, like his coat, and seemed equally faded by the wind and sun. And his sallow face, though hard and set, was pathetic somehow. You would have felt that he had suffered much by the line of his mouth showing under his thin, yellow mustache.

"Hain't Ike got home yet, Sairy?"

"Hain't seen 'im."

"W-a-a-l, set right up, Mr. Haskins; wade right into what we've got; 'tain't much, but we manage to live on it—she gits fat on it," laughed Council, pointing his thumb at his wife.

After supper, while the women put the children to bed, Haskins and Council talked on, seated near the huge cooking stove, the steam rising from their wet clothing. In the Western fashion, Council told as much of his own life as he drew from his guest. He asked but few questions; but by and by the story of Haskins' struggles and defeat came out. The story was a terrible one, but he told it quietly, seated with his elbows on his knees, gazing most of the time at the hearth.

"I didn't like the looks of the country, anyhow," Haskins said, partly rising and glancing at his wife. "I was ust t' northern Ingyannie, where we have lots a timber 'n' lots o' rain, 'n' I didn't like the looks o' that dry prairie. What galled me the worst was goin' s' far away acrosst so much fine land layin' all through here vacant."

"And the 'hoppers eat ye four years hand runnin', did they?"

"Eat! They wiped us out. They chawed everything that was green. They jest set around waitin' f'r us to die t' eat us, too. My God! I ust t' dream of 'em sitt'n' 'round on the bedpost, six feet long, workin' their jaws. They eet the fork handles. They got worse 'n' worse till they jest rolled on one another, piled up like snow in winter. Well, it ain't no use; if I was t' talk all winter I couldn't tell nawthin'. But all the while I couldn't help thinkin' of all that land back here that nobuddy was usin', that I ought a had 'stead o' bein' out there in that cussed country."

"Waal, why didn't ye stop an' settle here?" asked Ike, who had come in and was eating his supper.

"Fer the simple reason that you fellers wantid ten 'r fifteen dollars an acre fer the bare land, and I hadn't no money fer that kind o' thing."

"Yes, I do my own work," Mrs. Council was heard to say in the pause which followed. "I'm a-gettin' purty heavy t' be on m' laigs all day, but we can't afford t' hire, so I keep rackin' around somehow, like a foundered horse. S' lame—I tell Council he can't tell how lame I am f'r I'm jest as lame in one laig as t'other." And the good soul laughed at the joke on herself as she took a handful of flour and dusted the biscuit board to keep the dough from sticking.

"Well, I hain't *never* been very strong," said Mrs. Haskins. "Our folks was Canadians an' small-boned, and then since my last child I hain't got up again fairly. I don't like t' complain—Tim has about all he can bear now—but they was days this week when I jest wanted to lay right down an' die."

"Waal, now, I'll tell ye," said Council from his side of the stove, silencing everybody with his good-natured roar, "I'd go down and *see* Butler, *anyway*, if I was you. I guess he'd let you have his place purty cheap; the farm's all run down. He's ben anxious t' let t' somebuddy next year. It 'ud be a good chance fer you. Anyhow, you go to bed and sleep like a babe. I've got some plowin' t' do anyhow, an' we'll see if somethin' can't be done about your case. Ike, you go out an' see if the horses is all right, an' I'll show the folks t' bed."

When the tired husband and wife were lying under the generous quilts of the spare bed, Haskins listened a moment to the wind in the eaves, and then said with a slow and solemn tone:

"There are people in this world who are good enough t' be angels, an' only haff t' die to *be* angels."

II

Jim Butler was one of those men called in the West "land poor." Early in the history of Rock River he had come into the town and started in the grocery business in a small way, occupying a small building in a mean part of the town. At this period of his life he earned all he got, and was up early and late, sorting beans, working over butter, and carting his goods to and from the station. But a change came over him at the end of the second year, when he sold a lot of land for four times what he paid for it. From that time forward he believed in land speculation as the surest way of getting rich. Every cent he could save or spare from his trade he put into land at forced sale, or mortgages on land, which were "just as good as the wheat," he was accustomed to say.

Farm after farm fell into his hands, until he was recognized as one of the leading landowners of the county. His mortgages were scattered all over Cedar County, and as they slowly but surely fell in he sought usually to retain the former owner as tenant.

He was not ready to foreclose; indeed, he had the name of being one of the "easiest" men in the town. He let the debtor off again and again, extending the time whenever possible.

"I don't want y'r land," he said. "All I'm after is the int'rest on my money—that's all. Now if y' want 'o stay on the farm, why, I'll give y' a good chance. I can't have the land layin' vacant." And in many cases the owner remained as tenant.

In the meantime he had sold his store; he couldn't spend time in it; he was mainly occupied now with sitting around town on rainy days, smoking and "gassin' with the boys," or in riding to and from his farms. In fishing time he fished a good deal. Doc Grimes, Ben Ashley, and Cal Cheatham were his cronies on these fishing excursions or hunting trips in the time of chickens or partridges. In winter they went to northern Wisconsin to shoot deer.

In spite of all these signs of easy life, Butler persisted in saying he "hadn't money enough to pay taxes on his land," and was careful to convey the impression that he was poor in spite of his twenty farms. At one time he was said to be worth fifty thousand dollars, but land had been a little slow of sale of late, so that he was not worth so much. A fine farm, known as the Higley place, had fallen into his hands in the usual way the previous year, and he had not been able to find a tenant for it. Poor Higley, after working himself nearly to death on it, in the attempt to lift the mortgage, had gone off to Dakota, leaving the farm and his curse to Butler.

This was the farm which Council advised Haskins to apply for; and the next day Council hitched up his team and drove down town to see Butler.

"You jest let *me* do the talkin'," he said. "We'll find him wearin' out his pants on some salt barrel somew'er's; and if he thought you *wanted* a place, he'd sock it to you hot and heavy. You jest keep quiet; I'll fix'im."

Butler was seated in Ben Ashley's store, telling "fish yarns," when Council sauntered in casually.

"Hello, But; lyin' agin, hey?"

"Hello, Steve! how goes it?"

"Oh, so-so. Too dang much rain these days. I thought it was goin' t' freeze up f'r good last night. Tight sqeak if I git m' plowin done. How's farmin with *you* these days?"

"Bad. Plowin' ain't half done."

"It 'ud be a religious idee f'r you t' go out an' take a hand y'rself."

"I don't haff to," said Butler with a wink.

"Got anybody on the Higley place?"

"No. Know of anybody?"

"Waal, no; not eggsackly. I've got a relation back t' Michigan who's b'en hot an' cold on the idee o' comin' West f'r some time. *Might* come if he could get a good layout. What do you talk on the farm?"

"Well, I d' know. I'll rent it on shares, or I'll rent it money rent."

"Waal, how much money, say?"

"Well, say ten per cent on the price—two-fifty."

"Waal, that ain't bad. Wait on 'im til l'e thrashes?"

Haskins listened eagerly to his important question, but Council was cool y eating a dried apple which he had speared out of a barrel with his knife. Butler studied him carefully.

"Well, knocks me out of twenty-five dollars interest."

"My relation'll need all he's got t' git his crops in," said Council in the same indifferent way.

"Well, all right; *say* wait," concluded Butler.

"All right, this is the man. Haskins, this is Mr. Butler—no relation to Ben—the hardest working man in Cedar county."

On the way home Haskins said: "I ain't much better off. I'd like that farm; it's a good farm, but it's all run down, an' so'm I. I could make a good farm of it if I had half a show. But I can't stock it n'r seed it."

"Waal, now, don't you worry," roared Council in his ear. "We'll pull y' through somehow till next harvest. He's agreed t' hire it plowed, an' you can earn a hundred dollars ploughin', an' y' c'n git the seed o' me, an' pay me back when y' can."

Haskins was silent with emotion, but at last he said, "I ain't got nothin' t' live on."

"Now, don't you worry 'bout that. You jest make your headquarters at ol' Steve Council's. Mother 'll take a pile o' comfort in havin' y'r wife an' children 'round. Y' see Jane's married off lately, an' Ike's away a good 'eal, so we'll be darn glad t' have ye stop with us this winter. Nex' spring we'll see if y' can't git a start agin." And he chirruped to the team, which sprang forward with the rumbling, clattering wagon.

"Say, looky here, Council, you can't do this. I never saw—" shouted Haskins in his neighbor's ear.

Council moved about uneasily in his seat and stopped his stammering gratitude by saying: "Hold on, now; don't make such a fuss over a little thing. When I see a man down, an' things all on top of 'im, I jest like t' kick em off an' help 'm up. That's the kind of religion I got, an' it's about the *only* kind."

They rode the rest of the way home in silence. And when the red light of the lamp shone out into the darkness of the cold and windy night, and he thought of this refuge for his children and wife, Haskins could have put his arm around the neck of his burly companion and squeezed him like a lover; but he contented himself with saying: "Steve Council, you'll git y'r pay f'r this some day."

"Don't want any pay. My religion ain't run on such business principles."

The wind was growing colder, and the ground was covered with a white frost, as they turned into the gate of the Council farm, and the children came rushing out, shouting "Papa's come!" They hardly looked like the same children who had sat at the table the night before. Their torpidity under the influence of sunshine and Mother Council had given way to a sort of spasmodic cheerfulness, as insects in winter revive when laid on the hearth.

III

Haskins worked like a fiend, and his wife, like the heroic woman that she was, bore also uncomplainingly the most terrible burdens. They rose early and toiled without intermission till the darkness fell on the plain, then tumbled into bed, every bone and muscle aching with fatigue, to rise with the sun next morning to the same round of the same ferocity of labor.

The eldest boy, now nine years old, drove a team all through the spring, plowing and seeding, milked the cows, and did chores innumerable, in most ways taking the place of a man; an infinitely pathetic but common figure— this boy—on the American farm, where there is no law against child labor. To see him in his coarse clothing, his huge boots, and his ragged cap, as he staggered with a pail of water from the well, or trudged in the cold and cheerless dawn out into the frosty field behind his team, gave the city-bred visitor a sharp pang of sympathetic pain. Yet Haskins loved his boy, and would have saved him from this if he could, but he could not.

By June the first year the result of such Herculean toil began to show on the farm. The yard was cleaned up and sown to grass, the garden plowed and planted, and the house mended. Council had given them four of his cows.

"Take 'em an' run 'em on shares. I don't want a milk s' many. Ike's away s' much now, Sat'd'ys an' Sund'ys, I can't stand the bother anyhow."

Other men, seeing the confidence of Council in the newcomer, had sold him tools on time; and as he was really an able farmer, he soon had round him many evidences of his care and thrift. At the advice of Council he had taken the farm for three years, with the privilege of re-renting or buying at the end of the term.

"It's a good bargain, an' y' want 'o nail it," said Council. "If you have any kind ov a crop, you can pay y'r debts an' keep seed an' bread."

The new hope which now sprang up in the heart of Haskins and his wife grew great almost as a pain by the time the wide field of wheat began to wave and rustle and swirl in the winds of July. Day after day he would snatch a few moments after supper to go and look at it.

"Have ye seen the wheat t'day, Nettie?" he asked one night as he rose from supper.

"No, Tim, I ain't had time."

"Well, take time now. Le's go look at it."

She thew an old hat on her head—Tommy's hat—and looking almost pretty in her thin sad way, went out with her husband to the hedge.

"Ain't it grand, Nettie? Just look at it."

It was grand. Level, russet here and there, heavy-headed, wide as a lake, and full of multitudinous whispers and gleams of wealth, it stretched away before the gazers like the fabled field of the cloth of gold.

"Oh, I think—I hope we'll have a good crop, Tim; and oh, how good the people have been to us!"

"Yes; I don't know where we'd be t'day if it hadn't ben f'r Council and his wife."

"They're the best people in the world," said the little woman with a great sob of gratitude.

"We'll be in the field on Monday, sure," said Haskins, gripping the rail on the fence as if already at the work of the harvest.

The harvest came, bounteous, glorious, but the winds came and blew it into tangles, and the rain matted it here and there close to the ground, increasing the work of gathering it threefold.

Oh, how they toiled in those glorious days! Clothing dripping with sweat, arms aching, filled with briers, fingers raw and bleeding, backs broken with the weight of heavy bundles, Haskins and his man toiled on. Tommy drove the harvester while his father and a hired man bound on the machine. In this way they cut ten acres every day, and almost every night after supper, when the hand went to bed, Haskins returned to the field, shocking the bound grain in the light of the moon. Many a night he worked till his anxious wife came out at ten o'clock to call him in to rest and lunch.

At the same time she cooked for the men, took care of the children, washed and ironed, milked the cows at night, made the butter, and sometimes fed the horses and watered them while her husband kept at the shocking. No slave in the Roman galleys could have toiled so frightfully and lived, for this man thought himself a free man, and that he was working for his wife and babes.

When he sank into his bed with a deep groan of relief, too tired to change his grimy, dripping clothing, he felt that he was getting nearer and nearer to a home of his own, and pushing the wolf of want a little farther from his door.

There is no despair so deep as the despair of a homeless man or woman. To roam the roads of the country or the streets of the city, to feel there is no rood of ground on which the feet can rest, to halt weary and hungry outside lighted windows and hear laughter and song within—these are the hungers and rebellions that drive men to crime and women to shame.

It was the memory of this homelessness, and the fear of its coming again that spurred Timothy Haskins and Nettie, his wife, to such ferocious labor during that first year.

IV

" 'M, yes; 'm, yes; first-rate," said Butler as his eyes took in the neat garden, the pigpen, and the well-filled barnyard. "You're git'n' quite a stock around yeh. Done well, eh?"

Haskins was showing Butler around the place. He had not seen it for a year, having spent the year in Washington and Boston with Ashley, his brother-in-law, who had been elected to Congress.

"Yes, I've laid out a good deal of money durin' the last three years. I've paid out three hundred dollars f'r fencin'."

"Um—h'm! I see, I see," said Butler while Haskins went on.

"The kitchen there cost two hundred; the barn ain't cost much in money, but I've put a lot o' time on it. I've dug a new well, and I—"

"Yes, yes. I see! You've done well. Stock worth a thousand dollars," said Butler, picking his teeth with a straw.

"About that," said Haskins modestly. "We begin to feel's if we wuz git'n' a home f'r ourselves; but we've worked hard. I tell ye we begin to feel it, Mr. Butler, and we're goin' t' begin t' ease up purty soon. We've been kind o' plannin' a trip back t' *her* folks after the fall plowin's done."

"*Eggs-*actly!" said Butler, who was evidently thinking of something else. "I suppose you've kind o' calc'lated on stayin' here three years more?"

"Well, yes. Fact is, I think I c'n buy the farm this fall, if you'll give me a reasonable show."

"Um—m! What do you call a reasonable show?"

"Waal; say a quarter down and three years' time."

Butler looked at the huge stacks of wheat which filled the yard, over which the chickens were fluttering and crawling, catching grasshoppers, and out of which the crickets were singing innumerably. He smiled in a peculiar way as he said, "Oh, I won't be hard on yeh. But what did you expect to pay f'r the place?"

"Why, about what you offered it for before, two thousand five hundred, or *possibly* the three thousand dollars," he added quickly as he saw the owner shake his head.

"This farm is worth five thousand and five hundred dollars," said Butler in a careless but decided voice.

"*What!*" almost shrieked the astounded Haskins. "What's that? Five thousand? Why, that's double what you offered it for three years ago."

"Of course; and it's worth it. It was all run down then; now it's in good shape. You've laid out fifteen hundred dollars in improvements, according to your own story."

"But *you* had nothin' t' do about that. It's my work an' my money."

"You bet it was; but it's my land."

"But what's to pay me for all my—?"

"Ain't you had the use of 'em?" replied Butler, smiling calmly into his face.

Haskins was like a man struck on the head with a sandbag; he couldn't think; he stammered as he tried to say: "But—I never'd git the use—You'd rob me. More'n that: you agreed—you promised that I could buy or rent at the end of three years at—"

"That's all right. But I didn't say I'd let you carry off the improvements, nor that I'd go on renting the farm at two-fifty. The land is doubled in value, it don't matter how; it don't enter into the question; an' now you can pay me five hundred dollars a year rent, or take it on your own terms at fifty-five hundred, or—git out."

He was turning away when Haskins, the sweat pouring from his face, fronted him, saying again:

"But *you've* done nothing to make it so. You hain't added a cent. I put it all there myself, expectin' to buy. I worked an' sweat to improve it. I was workin' f'r myself an' babes—"

"Well, why didn't you buy when I offered to sell? What y' kickin' about?"

"I'm kickin' about payin' you twice f'r my own things—my own fences, my own kitchen, my own garden."

Butler laughed. "You're too green t' eat, young feller. *Your* improvements! The law will sing another tune."

"But I trusted your word."

"Never trust anybody, my friend. Besides, I didn't promise not to do this thing. Why, man, don't look at me like that. Don't take me for a thief. It's the law. The reg'lar thing. Everybody does it."

"I don't care if they do. It's stealin' jest the same. You take three thousand dollars of my money. The work o' my hands and my wife's." He broke down at this point. He was not a strong man mentally. He could face hardship, ceaseless toil, but he could not face the cold and sneering face of Butler.

"But I don't take it," said Butler coolly. "All you've got to do is to go on jest as you've been a-doin', or give me a thousand dollars down and a mortgage at ten per cent on the rest."

Haskins sat down blindly on a bundle of oats nearby and, with staring eyes and drooping head, went over the situation. He was under the lion's paw. He felt a horrible numbness in his heart and limbs. He was hid in a mist, and there was no path out.

Butler walked about, looking at the huge stacks of grain and pulling now and again a few handfuls out, shelling the heads in his hands and blowing the chaff away. He hummed a little tune as he did so. He had an accommodating air of waiting.

Haskins was in the midst of the terrible toil of the last year. He was walking again in the rain and the mud behind his plow; he felt the dust and dirt of the threshing. The ferocious husking time, with its cutting wind and biting, clinging snows, lay hard upon him. Then he thought of his wife, how she had cheerfully cooked and baked, without holiday and without rest.

"Well, what do you think of it?" inquired the cool, mocking, insinuating voice of Butler.

"I think you're a thief and a liar!" shouted Haskins, leaping up. "A black-hearted houn'!" Butler's smile maddened him; with a sudden leap he caught a fork in his hands and whirled it in the air. "You'll never rob another man, damn ye!" he grated through his teeth, a look of pitiless ferocity in his accusing eyes.

Butler shrank and quivered, expecting the blow; stood, held hypnotized by the eyes of the man he had a moment before despised—a man transformed into an avenging demon. But in the deadly hush between the lift of the weapon and its fall there came a gush of faint, childish laughter, and then across the range of his vision, far away and dim, he saw the sunbright head of his baby girl as, with the pretty tottering run of a two-year-old, she moved across the grass of the dooryard. His hands relaxed; the fork fell to the ground; his head lowered.

"Make out y'r deed an' mor'gage, an' git off'n my land, an' don't ye never cross my line agin; if y' do, I'll kill ye."

Butler backed away from the man in wild haste and, climbing into his buggy with trembling limbs, drove off down the road, leaving Haskins seated dumbly on the sunny pile of sheaves, his head sunk into his hands.

1889

STEPHEN CRANE

(1871–1900)

Although his life was tragically brief—he died of tuberculosis at the age of 29—Stephen Crane made an indelible impression on American literature. The original genius among the naturalists of the 1890's, he broke new ground in subject matter and experimented with new possibilities in narrative style. Others had written of "low life" in city slums before Crane, but none made his attempt to capture the inner point of view of the slums along with the outer sights and sounds, the picturesque exterior. In *Maggie: A Girl of the Streets* (1893), written when he was 22 years old, Crane brought naturalism to American fiction; the novel is the first American effort at a completely deterministic vision, in which environment is an unrelenting, controlling force, a trap that destroys the innocent and defenseless Maggie. In his later work Crane radically changed the very conception of warfare as a literary theme, beginning with his masterpiece, *The Red Badge of Courage* (1895) and continuing with tales, sketches, and dispatches concerning

A 10-volume standard edition of Crane's work is being completed by the University Press of Virginia. See also Wilson Follett, ed., *The Works of Stephen Crane*, 13 vols. 1925-1927. The letters have been edited by Robert W. Stallman, 1960. See also Olov W. Fryckstedt, ed., *Stephen Crane: Uncollected Writings*, 1963; Thomas Gullason, ed., *The Complete Short Stories and Sketches*, 1963, and *The Complete Novels*, 1967; Melvin Schoberlin, ed., *The Sullivan County Sketches of Stephen Crane*, 1949; Joseph Katz, *The Poems of Stephen Crane: A Critical Edition*, 1966. The major works are *Maggie: A Girl of The Streets*, 1893; *The Red Badge of Courage*, 1894; *The Black Riders*, 1895; *George's Mother*, 1896; *The Open Boat and Other Tales of Adventure*, 1898; *The Monster and Other Stories*, 1899; *War is Kind*, 1899; *Active Service*, 1899; *Whilomville Stories*, 1900; *Wounds in the Rain*, 1900.

Biographies are Thomas Beer, *Stephen Crane*, 1923; John Berryman, *Stephen Crane*, 1950; E. H. Cady, *Stephen Crane*, 1962; Robert W. Stallman, *Stephen Crane*, 1968.

Interesting commentaries may be found in James B. Colvert, "Structure and Theme in Stephen Crane's Fiction," *Modern Fiction Studies* (Fall 1959); Joseph Conrad, *Notes on Life and Letters*, 1921, Maxwell Geismar, *Rebels and Ancestors: The American Novel, 1890-1915*, 1953; Daniel G. Hoffman, *The Poetry of Stephen Crane*, 1957; Lillian Gilkes, *Cora Crane*, 1960; Eric Solomon, *Stephen Crane in England; A Portrait of the Artist*, 1965, and *Stephen Crane: From Parody to Realism*, 1966; Marston LaFrance, *A Reading of Stephen Crane*, 1971; Milne Holton, *The Fiction and Journalistic Writing of Stephen Crane*, 1972.

One-volume editions are James B. Colvert, ed., *The Great Short Works of Stephen Crane*, 1968; Robert W. Stallman, ed., *Stephen Crane: An Omnibus*, 1952, and *The Red Badge of Courage*, 1960; Daniel Hoffman, *The Poetry of Stephen Crane*, 1960.

men at war. And in his poetry Crane introduced a new manner of laconic, epigrammatic statement, a manner that would reappear in the next decade in the experimental work of the Imagists. While it is true that none of Crane's books ranks with first-order works such as *Moby Dick* or *Adventures of Huckleberry Finn*, his work as a whole is a remarkable achievement, one that virtually begins the era of modern writing in America.

Experimentation was the hallmark of Crane's writing, and the same can be said of his life. His writings represent a clean break with the belief of his elders in a well-ordered and morally guided universe; his vision, perhaps most powerfully represented by "The Open Boat," is of a universe essentially indifferent to man. The detached, ironic point of view toward fear-ridden yet eternally hopeful man we find in his stories has roots in Crane's own existence. He was born into an old, respected New Jersey family, full of the pieties of religious and cultural orthodoxy. His father was a reputable Methodist minister, and his mother, the daughter of a clergyman, was an enthusiastic socialite crusader for temperance. The family moved a good deal, especially after the father's death in 1880, and Crane grew up in small towns, where he developed a love and talent for sports, especially baseball. After a spell at a New York military school, he switched to an engineering curriculum at Lafayette College; he failed after a term, then tried Syracuse University, but withdrew in 1891 before his first year was up. At Syracuse Crane did some writing as a correspondent for the New York *Herald* (his brother ran a news agency in Asbury Park, New Jersey), became acquainted with the slums and saloons of the city and, in two days before Christmas in 1891, he completed the first draft of *Maggie* in a fraternity house.

Defiance of convention and contempt for easy pieties seemed to govern Crane's own choices in these years. His motives in writing his tale of the degradation of a Bowery prostitute from a completely impersonal and amoral point of view probably included a personal rebellion against the complacencies of his own respectable middle-class background. But his chief motive was to tell an honest story, "to show people as they seemed to me," as he put it. He was undoubtedly influenced by the French naturalist novelists; Emile Zola, especially, by his novel of slum life, *L'Assomoir*. But Crane was never a theorist of or spokesman for naturalism, his reading of figures such as Charles Darwin and Herbert Spencer was neither deep nor wide. For him naturalism came to consist mainly of writing out of first hand experience and observation; he was drawn to his persistent themes of poverty, violence, fear, and shame less out of a doctrinaire conviction concerning the significance of these themes than out of a desire to write about those areas of modern experience that had been excluded from literature or blanketed with moralistic attitudes. He learned of the falseness of the moralistic and the sentimental from his encounters with "unrespectable" life.

The next several years were difficult and frustrating. He moved to New York, lived near the slums of the East Side and Bowery, and wrote freelance pieces that he occasionally placed with New York newspapers, but he was unable to find a steady position. Absorbing the Bohemian atmosphere of art students and saloon companions and prostitutes, he was in part acquiring experiences for his city stories, but more important was the value of this period in the evolution of his unique style of detached, impressionistic observation. Unable to place *Maggie* with a publisher, he published it privately in 1893 with money borrowed from his brother; the book appeared in yellow paper wrappers under the pseudonym of Johnston Smith. Crane's fortunes changed when Hamlin Garland, then living in New York, responded enthusiastically to the novel, sent to him by Crane; the older writer introduced Crane to Howells, who also admired the novel and wrote a preface for its regular publication in 1896 in which he likened the story of the fated prostitute to Greek tragedy. In the same year Crane published his second Bowery novel, *George's Mother*.

But Crane's greatest success occurred in 1895 with the publication of *The Red Badge of Courage*. Here Crane emerged as the promising writer of his generation. In part the book is an astonishing and brilliant *tour de force*: an account of the Civil War Battle of Chancellorsville written with the vividness and terror of an eye witness. Crane drew on the tales of veterans and on the stark, grim photographs by Matthew Brady to portray the battle as a realistic experience. But his main interest was not the war itself; the Civil War is never mentioned by name. Instead, he brought forward a psychological theme of an inexperienced youth winning a sense of manhood through courge in violent battle against the overwhelming odds of his own fear. War itself is stripped of any noble or romantic associations; it is simply fierce, violent, and senseless combat. In Henry Fleming's struggles with his fear and shame, war emerges as typical of the human condition, both in nature and in society; the hero confronts the elemental forces that challenge human survival. Crane portrays the struggle without sentimentality, merely as the given facts of life that, in the end, turn out to be no more significant than the facts themselves seem to be. It is a novel without any transcendent values for the reader who yearns for the comfort of some moral lesson in the youth's anguish. As in the sharply etched poems of *The Black Riders and Other Lines* (1895) and *War is Kind* (1899), Crane regards the insignificance of man in an alien universe with a cool and distant eye.

After 1895 and the immediate worldwide success of *The Red Badge of Courage*, Crane spent most of his remaining few years as a traveling correspondent. He toured the West and Mexico for a newspaper syndicate in 1895, and he produced some of his finest stories out of the experience, such as "The Blue Hotel." From Florida in the same year he joined a gun-running expedition to Cuba, was shipwrecked, and wrote his best-known story, "The Open Boat," out of that adventure. Whether by assignment or inclination or both, he was drawn to situations of extremity, in which human capacities were faced with ultimate tests of endurance and nerve. In this sense, and in his mature style of bare, taut notations of sense experience, he is a forerunner of Ernest Hemingway, who acknowledged the influence of Crane.

During his Florida expedition Crane met and fell in love with Cora Stewart, the "hostess" of a brothel in Jacksonville. Together they moved to England in 1897, settled in an old manor in Sussex called Brede, and lived in an extravagant and expensive style, forcing Crane to work at a feverish pace to keep up with their debts. He covered the Greco-Turkish War in 1897 and the Spanish-American War in Cuba in 1898; he returned to England in declining health in 1899. His tuberculosis took a severe turn, and he sought a cure in a German sanitorium, but he died there in 1900. In his last years in England Crane enjoyed the friendship of Henry James, Joseph Conrad, Ford Madox Ford, and H. G. Wells, all of whom admired his unique genius.

An Episode of War[1]

The lieutenant's rubber blanket lay on the ground, and upon it he had poured the company's supply of coffee. Corporals and other representatives of the grimy and hot-throated men who lined the breastwork had come for each squad's portion.

The lieutenant was frowning and serious at this task of division. His lips pursed as he drew with his sword various crevices in the heap until brown squares of coffee, astoundingly equal in size, appeared on the blanket. He was on the verge of a great triumph in mathematics, and the corporals were thronging forward, each to reap a little square, when suddenly the lieutenant cried out and looked quickly at a man near him as if he suspected it was a case of personal assault. The others cried out also when they saw blood upon the lieutenant's sleeve.

[1] First published in "The Gentlewoman," (Christmas 1899) and later collected in *Men,* *Women and Boats*, edited by Vincent Starrett, N.Y., in 1921.

He had[2] winced like a man stung, swayed dangerously, and then straightened. The sound of his hoarse breathing was plainly audible. He looked sadly, mystically, over the breastwork at the green face of a wood, where now were many little puffs of white smoke. During this moment the men about him gazed statue-like and silent, astonished and awed by this catastrophe which happened when catastrophes were not expected—when they had leisure to observe it.

As the lieutenant stared at the wood, they too swung their heads, so that for another instant all hands, still silent, contemplated the distant forest as if their minds were fixed upon the mystery of a bullet's journey.

The officer had, of course, been compelled to take his sword into his left hand. He did not hold it by the hilt. He gripped it at the middle of the blade, awkwardly. Turning his eyes from the hostile wood, he looked at the sword as he held it there, and seemed puzzled as to what to do with it, where to put it. In short, this weapon had of a sudden become a strange thing to him. He looked at it in a kind of stupefaction, as if he had been endowed with a trident, a sceptre, or a spade.

Finally he tried to sheath it. To sheath a sword held by the left hand, at the middle of the blade, in a scabbard hung at the left hip, is a feat worthy of a sawdust ring. This wounded officer engaged in a desperate struggle with the sword and the wobbling scabbard, and during the time of it he breathed like a wrestler.

But at this instant the men, the spectators, awoke from their stone-like poses and crowded forward sympathetically. The orderly-sergeant took the sword and tenderly placed it in the scabbard. At the time, he leaned nervously backward, and did not allow even[3] his fingers to brush the body of the lieutenant. A wound gives strange dignity to him who bears it. Well men shy from this new and terrible majesty. It is as if the wounded man's hand is upon the curtain which hangs before the revelations of all existence—the meaning cf ants, potentates, wars, cities, sunshine, snow, a feather dropped from a bird's wing; and the power of it sheds radiance upon a bloody form, and makes the other men understand sometimes that they are little. His comrades look at him with large eyes thoughtfully. Moreover, they fear vaguely that the weight of a finger upon him might send him headlong, precipitate the tragedy, hurl him at once into the dim, grey unknown. And so the orderly-sergeant, while sheathing the sword, leaned nervously backward.

There were others who proffered assistance. One timidly presented his shoulder and asked the lieutenant if he cared to lean upon it, but the latter waved him away mournfully. He wore the look of one who knows he is the victim of a terrible disease and understands his helplessness. He again stared over the breastwork at the forest, and then turning went slowly rearward.

---

[2] The source reads "has."   [3] The source reads "een."

He held his right wrist tenderly in his left hand as if the wounded arm was made of very brittle glass.

And the men in silence stared at the wood, then at the departing lieutenant—then at the wood, then at the lieutenant.

As the wounded officer passed from the line of battle, he was enabled to see many things which as a participant in the fight were unknown to him. He saw a general on a black horse gazing over the lines of blue infantry at the green woods which veiled his problems. An aide galloped furiously, dragged his horse suddenly to a halt, saluted, and presented a paper. It was, for a wonder, precisely like an historical painting.

To the rear of the general and his staff a group, composed of a bugler, two or three orderlies, and the bearer of the corps standard, all upon maniacal horses, were working like slaves to hold their ground, preserve their respectful interval, while the shells boomed in the air about them, and caused their chargers to make furious quivering leaps.

A battery, a tumultuous and shining mass, was swirling toward the right. The wild thud of hoofs, the cries of the riders shouting blame and praise, menace and encouragement, and, last, the roar of the wheels, the slant of the glistening guns, brought the lieutenant to an intent pause. The battery swept in curves that stirred the heart; it made halts as dramatic as the crash of a wave on the rocks, and when it fled onward, this aggregation of wheels, levers, motors, had a beautiful unity, as if it were a missile. The sound of it was a war-chorus that reached into the depths of man's emotion.

The lieutenant, still holding his arm as if it were of glass, stood watching this battery until all detail of it was lost, save the figures of the riders, which rose and fell and waved lashes over the black mass.

Later, he turned his eyes toward the battle where the shooting sometimes crackled like bush-fires, sometimes sputtered with exasperating irregularity, and sometimes reverberated like the thunder. He saw the smoke rolling upward and saw crowds of men who ran and cheered, or stood and blazed away at the inscrutable distance.

He came upon some stragglers, and they told him how to find the field hospital. They described its exact location. In fact, these men, no longer having part in the battle, knew more of it than others. They told the performance of every corps, every division, the opinion of every general. The lieutenant, carrying his wounded arm rearward, looked upon them with wonder.

At the roadside a brigade was making coffee and buzzing with talk like a girls' boarding-school. Several officers came out to him and inquired concerning things of which he knew nothing. One, seeing his arm, began to scold. "Why, man, that's no way to do. You want to fix that thing." He appropriated the lieutenant and the lieutenant's wound. He cut the sleeve and laid bare the arm, every nerve of which softly fluttered under his touch.

He bound his handkerchief over the wound, scolding away in the meantime. His tone allowed one to think that he was in the habit of being wounded every day. The lieutenant hung his head, feeling, in this presence, that he did not know how to be correctly wounded.

The low white tents of the hospital were grouped around an old school-house. There was here a singular commotion. In the foreground two ambulances interlocked wheels in the deep mud. The drivers were tossing the blame of it back and forth, gesticulating and berating, while from the ambulances, both crammed with wounded, there came an occasional groan. An interminable crowd of bandaged men were coming and going. Great numbers sat under the trees nursing heads or arms or legs. There was a dispute of some kind raging on the steps of the school-house. Sitting with his back against a tree a man with a face as grey as a new army blanket was serenely smoking a corn-cob pipe. The lieutenant wished to rush forward and inform him that he was dying.

A busy surgeon was passing near the lieutenant. "Good-morning," he said, with a friendly smile. Then he caught sight of the lieutenant's arm and his face at once changed. "Well, let's have a look at it." He seemed possessed suddenly of a great contempt for the lieutenant. This wound evidently placed the latter on a very low social plane. The doctor cried out impatiently, "What mutton-head had tied it up that way anyhow?" The lieutenant answered, "Oh, a man."

When the wound was disclosed the doctor fingered it disdainfully. "Humph," he said. "You come along with me and I'll tend to you." His voice contained the same scorn as if he were saying, "You will have to go to jail."

The lieutenant had been very meek, but now his face flushed, and he looked into the doctor's eyes. "I guess I won't have it amputated," he said.

"Nonsense, man! Nonsense! Nonsense!" cried the doctor. "Come along, now. I won't amputate it. Come along. Don't be a baby."

"Let go of me," said the lieutenant, holding back wrathfully, his glance fixed upon the door of the old school-house, as sinister to him as the portals of death.

And this is the story of how the lieutenant lost his arm. When he reached home, his sisters, his mother, his wife, sobbed for a long time at the sight of the flat sleeve. "Oh, well," he said, standing shamefaced amid these tears, "I don't suppose it matters so much as all that."

The Open Boat

A Tale Intended to be after the Fact:
Being the Experience of Four Men from the Sunk Steamer Commodore[1]

I

None of them knew the color of the sky. Their eyes glanced level, and were fastened upon the waves that swept toward them. These waves were of the hue of slate, save for the tops, which were of foaming white, and all of the men knew the colors of the sea. The horizon narrowed and widened, and dipped and rose, and at all times its edge was jagged with waves that seemed thrust up in points like rocks.

Many a man ought to have a bathtub larger than the boat which here rode upon the sea. These waves were most wrongfully and barbarously abrupt and tall, and each frothtop was a problem in small-boat navigation.

The cook squatted in the bottom, and looked with both eyes at the six inches of gunwale[2] which separated him from the ocean. His sleeves were rolled over his fat forearms, and the two flaps of his unbuttoned vest dangled as he bent to bail out the boat. Often he said, "Gawd! that was a narrow clip." As he remarked it he invariably gazed eastward over the broken sea.

The oiler,[3] steering with one of the two oars in the boat, sometimes raised himself suddenly to keep clear of water that swirled in over the stern. It was a thin little oar, and it seemed often ready to snap.

The correspondent, pulling at the other oar, watched the waves and wondered why he was there.

The injured captain, lying in the bow, was at this time buried in the profound dejection and indifference which comes, temporarily at least, to even the bravest and most enduring when, willy-nilly, the firm fails, the army loses, the ship goes down.

The mind of the master of a vessel is rooted deep in the timbers of her, though he command for a day or a decade; and this captain had on him the stern impression of a scene in the grays of dawn of seven turned faces, and later a stump of a topmast with a white ball on it, that slashed to and fro at the waves, went low and lower, and down.

---

[1] First published in Scribner's Magazine, June 1897, and later collected in *The Open Boat and Other Tales of Adventure* in 1898. Crane accepted an assignment as a newspaper reporter on the Cuban Revolution. On January 1, 1897, he left for Cuba on the "Commodore," which was loaded with arms for the Cuban rebels. The ship sank before

morning. The *New York Press* announced news of Crane's death but, on January 4, the headline read, "Young New York Writer Astonishes the Sea Dogs by His Courage in the Face of Death."

[2] The sides of the boat.

[3] A ship's crew member who works in the engine room.

Thereafter there was something strange in his voice. Although steady, it was deep with mourning, and of a quality beyond oration or tears.

"Keep 'er a little more south, Billie," said he.

"A little more south, sir," said the oiler in the stern.

A seat in this boat was not unlike a seat upon a bucking broncho, and by the same token a broncho is not much smaller. The craft pranced and reared and plunged like an animal. As each wave came, and she rose for it, she seemed like a horse making at a fence outrageously high. The manner of her scramble over these walls of water is a mystic thing, and, moreover, at the top of them were ordinarily these problems in white water, the foam racing down from the summit of each wave requiring a new leap, and a leap from the air. Then, after scornfully bumping a crest, she would slide and race and splash down a long incline, and arrive bobbing and nodding in front of the next menace.

A singular disadvantage of the sea lies in the fact that after successfully surmounting one wave you discover that there is another behind it just as important and just as nervously anxious to do something effective in the way of swamping boats. In a ten-foot dinghy one can get an idea of the resources of the sea in the line of waves that is not probable to the average experience which is never at sea in a dinghy. As each slaty wall of water approached, it shut all else from the view of the men in the boat, and it was not difficult to imagine that this particular wave was the final outburst of the ocean, the last effort of the grim water. There was a terrible grace in the move of the waves, and they came in silence, save for the snarling of the crests.

In the wan light the faces of the men must have been gray. Their eyes must have glinted in strange ways as they gazed steadily astern. Viewed from a balcony, the whole thing would doubtless have been weirdly picturesque. But the men in the boat had no time to see it, and if they had had leisure, there were other things to occupy their minds. The sun swung steadily up the sky, and they knew it was broad day because the color of the sea changed from slate to emerald green streaked with amber lights, and the foam was like tumbling snow. The process of the breaking day was unknown to them. They were aware only of this effect upon the color of the waves that rolled toward them.

In disjointed sentences the cook and the correspondent argued as to the difference between a life-saving station and a house of refuge. The cook had said: "There's a house of refuge just north of the Mosquito Inlet Light, and as soon as they see us they'll come off in their boat and pick us up."

"As soon as who see us?" said the correspondent.

"The crew," said the cook.

"Houses of refuge don't have crews," said the correspondent. "As I understand them, they are only places where clothes and grub are stored for the benefit of shipwrecked people. They don't carry crews."

"Oh, yes, they do," said the cook.

"No, they don't," said the correspondent.

"Well, we're not there yet, anyhow," said the oiler, in the stern.

"Well," said the cook, "perhaps it's not a house of refuge that I'm thinking of as being near Mosquito Inlet Light; perhaps it's a life-saving station."

"We're not there yet," said the oiler in the stern.

II

As the boat bounced from the top of each wave the wind tore through the hair of the hatless men, and as the craft plopped her stern down again the spray slashed past them. The crest of each of these waves was a hill, from the top of which the men surveyed for a moment a broad tumultuous expanse, shining and wind-riven. It was probably splendid, it was probably glorious, this play of the free sea, wild with lights of emerald and white and amber.

"Bully good thing it's an on-shore wind," said the cook. "If not, where would we be? Wouldn't have a show."

"That's right," said the correspondent.

The busy oiler nodded his assent.

Then the captain, in the bow, chuckled in a way that expressed humor, contempt, tragedy, all in one. "Do you think we've got much of a show now, boys?" said he.

Whereupon the three were silent, save for a trifle of hemming and hawing. To express any particular optimism at this time they felt to be childish and stupid, but they all doubtless possessed this sense of the situation in their minds. A young man thinks doggedly at such times. On the other hand, the ethics of their condition was decidedly against any open suggestion of hopelessness. So they were silent.

"Oh, well," said the captain, soothing his children, "we'll get ashore all right."

But there was that in his tone which made them think; so the oiler quoth, "Yes! if this wind holds."

The cook was bailing. "Yes! if we don't catch hell in the surf."

Canton-flannel[4] gulls flew near and far. Sometimes they sat down on the sea, near patches of brown seaweed that rolled over the waves with a movement like carpets on a line in a gale. The birds sat comfortably in groups, and they were envied by some in the dinghy, for the wrath of the sea was no more to them than it was to a covey of prairie chickens a thousand miles inland. Often they came very close and stared at the men with black bead-like eyes. At these times they were uncanny and sinister in their unblinking scrutiny, and the men hooted angrily at them, telling them to be gone. One came, and evidently decided to alight on the top of the captain's head. The bird flew parallel to the boat and did not circle, but made short sidelong

[4] Cotton flannel.

jumps in the air in chicken-fashion. His black eyes were wistfully fixed upon the captain's head. "Ugly brute," said the oiler to the bird. "You look as if you were made with a jackknife." The cook and the correspondent swore darkly at the creature. The captain naturally wished to knock it away with the end of the heavy painter,[5] but he did not dare do it, because anything resembling an emphatic gesture would capsize this freighted boat; and so, with his open hand, the captain gently and carefully waved the gull away. After it had been discouraged from the pursuit the captain breathed easier on account of his hair, and others breathed easier because the bird struck their minds at this time as being somehow gruesome and ominous.

In the meantime the oiler and the correspondent rowed. And also they rowed. They sat together in the same seat, and each rowed an oar. Then the oiler took both oars; then the correspondent took both oars; then the oiler; then the correspondent. They rowed and they rowed. The very ticklish part of the business was when the time came for the reclining one in the stern to take his turn at the oars. By the very last star of truth, it is easier to steal eggs from under a hen than it was to change seats in the dinghy. First the man in the stern slid his hand along the thwart[6] and moved with care, as if he were of Sèvres.[7] Then the man in the rowing-seat slid his hand along the other thwart. It was all done with the most extraordinary care. As the two sidled past each other, the whole party kept watchful eyes on the coming wave, and the captain cried: "Look out, now! Steady, there!"

The brown mats of seaweed that appeared from time to time were like islands, bits of earth. They were travelling, apparently, neither one way nor the other. They were, to all intents, stationary. They informed the men in the boat that it was making progress slowly toward the land.

The captain, rearing cautiously in the bow after the dinghy soared on a great swell, said that he had seen the lighthouse at Mosquito Inlet. Presently the cook remarked that he had seen it. The correspondent was at the oars then, and for some reason he too wished to look at the lighthouse; but his back was toward the far shore, and the waves were important, and for some time he could not seize an opportunity to turn his head. But at last there came a wave more gentle than the others, and when at the crest of it he swiftly scoured the western horizon.

"See it?" said the captain.

"No," said the correspondent, slowly; "I didn't see anything."

"Look again," said the captain. He pointed. "It's exactly in that direction."

At the top of another wave the correspondent did as he was bid, and this time his eyes chanced on a small, still thing on the edge of the swaying

[5] Rope.
[6] Seat.

[7] Fine china, very fragile, made in Sèvres, France.

horizon. It was precisely like the point of a pin. It took an anxious eye to find a lighthouse so tiny.

"Think we'll make it, Captain?"

"If this wind holds and the boat don't swamp, we can't do much else," said the captain.

The little boat, lifted by each towering sea and splashed viciously by the crests, made progress that in the absence of seaweed was not apparent to those in her. She seemed just a wee thing wallowing, miraculously top up, at the mercy of five oceans. Occasionally a great spread of water, like white flames, swarmed into her.

"Bail her, cook," said the captain, serenely.

"All right, Captain," said the cheerful cook.

III

It would be difficult to describe the subtle brotherhood of men that was here established on the seas. No one said that it was so. No one mentioned it. But it dwelt in the boat, and each man felt it warm him. They were a captain, an oiler, a cook, and a correspondent, and they were friends—friends in a more curiously iron-bound degree than may be common. The hurt captain, lying against the water-jar in the bow, spoke always in a low voice and calmly; but he could never command a more ready and swiftly obedient crew than the motley three of the dinghy. It was more than a mere recognition of what was best for the common safety. There was surely in it a quality that was personal and heart-felt. And after this devotion to the commander of the boat, there was this comradeship, that the correspondent, for instance, who had been taught to be cynical of men, knew even at the time was the best experience of his life. But no one said that it was so. No one mentioned it.

"I wish we had a sail," remarked the captain. "We might try my overcoat on the end of an oar, and give you two boys a chance to rest." So the cook and the correspondent held the mast and spread wide the overcoat; the oiler steered; and the little boat made good way with her new rig. Sometimes the oiler had to scull[8] sharply to keep a sea from breaking into the boat, but otherwise sailing was a success.

Meanwhile the lighthouse had been growing slowly larger. It had now almost assumed color, and appeared like a little gray shadow on the sky. The man at the oars could not be prevented from turning his head rather often to try for a glimpse of this little gray shadow.

At last, from the top of each wave, the men in the tossing boat could see land. Even as the lighthouse was an upright shadow on the sky, this land

[8] To propel a small boat forward by means of an oar mounted on a fulcrum at the stern and moved from side to side.

seemed but a long black shadow on the sea. It certainly was thinner than paper. "We must be about opposite New Smyrna," said the cook, who had coasted this shore often in schooners. "Captain, by the way, I believe they abandoned that life-saving station there about a year ago."

"Did they?" said the captain.

The wind slowly died away. The cook and the correspondent were not now obliged to slave in order to hold high the oar. But the waves continued their old impetuous swooping at the dinghy, and the little craft, no longer under way, struggled woundily over them. The oiler or the correspondent took the oars again.

Shipwrecks are apropos of nothing. If men could only train for them and have them occur when the men had reached pink condition, there would be less drowning at sea. Of the four in the dinghy none had slept any time worth mentioning for two days and two nights previous to embarking in the dinghy, and in the excitement of clambering about the deck of a foundering ship they had also forgotten to eat heartily.

For these reasons, and for others, neither the oiler nor the correspondent was fond of rowing at this time. The correspondent wondered ingenuously how in the name of all that was sane could there be people who thought it amusing to row a boat. It was not an amusement; it was a diabolical punishment, and even a genius of mental aberrations could never conclude that it was anything but a horror to the muscles and crime against the back. He mentioned to the boat in general how the amusement of rowing struck him, and the weary-faced oiler smiled in full sympathy. Previously to the foundering, by the way, the oiler had worked double watch in the engine-room of the ship.

"Take her easy now, boys," said the captain. "Don't spend yourselves. If we have to run a surf you'll need all your strength, because we'll sure have to swim for it. Take your time."

Slowly the land arose from the sea. From a black line it became a line of black and a line of white—trees and sand. Finally the captain said that he could make out a house on the shore. "That's the house of refuge, sure," said the cook. "They'll see us before long, and come out after us."

The distant lighthouse reared high. "The keeper ought to be able to make us out now, if he's looking through a glass," said the captain. "He'll notify the life-saving people."

"None of those other boats could have got ashore to give word of the wreck," said the oiler, in a low voice, "else the life-boat would be out hunting us."

Slowly and beautifully the land loomed out of the sea. The wind came again. It had veered from the north-east to the south-east. Finally a new sound struck the ears of the men in the boat. It was the low thunder of the surf on the shore. "We'll never be able to make the lighthouse now," said the captain. "Swing her head a little more north, Billie."

"A little more north, sir," said the oiler.

Whereupon the little boat turned her nose once more down the wind, and all but the oarsman watched the shore grow. Under the influence of this expansion doubt and direful apprehension were leaving the minds of the men. The management of the boat was still most absorbing, but it could not prevent a quiet cheerfulness. In an hour, perhaps, they would be ashore.

Their backbones had become thoroughly used to balancing in the boat, and they now rode this wild colt of a dinghy like circus men. The correspondent thought that he had been drenched to the skin, but happening to feel in the top pocket of his coat, he found therein eight cigars. Four of them were soaked with sea-water; four were perfectly scatheless. After a search, somebody produced three dry matches; and thereupon the four waifs rode impudently in their little boat and, with an assurance of an impending rescue shining in their eyes, puffed at the big cigars, and judged well and ill of all men. Everybody took a drink of water.

Concrete

IV

"Cook," remarked the captain, "there don't seem to be any signs of life about your house of refuge."

"No," replied the cook. "Funny they don't see us!"

A broad stretch of lowly coast lay before the eyes of the men. It was of low dunes topped with dark vegetation. The roar of the surf was plain, and sometimes they could see the white lip of a wave as it spun up the beach. A tiny house was blocked out black upon the sky. Southward, the slim lighthouse lifted its little gray length.

Tide, wind, and waves were swinging the dinghy northward. "Funny they don't see us," said the men.

The surf's roar was here dulled, but its tone was nevertheless thunderous and mighty. As the boat swam over the great rollers the men sat listening to this roar. "We'll swamp sure," said everybody.

It is fair to say here that there was not a life-saving station within twenty miles in either direction; but the men did not know this fact, and in consequence they made dark and opprobrious remarks concerning the eyesight of the nation's life-savers. Four scowling men sat in the dinghy and surpassed records in the invention of epithets.

"Funny they don't see us."

The light-heartedness of a former time had completely faded. To their sharpened minds it was easy to conjure pictures of all kinds of incompetency and blindness and, indeed, cowardice. There was the shore of the populous land, and it was bitter and bitter to them that from it came no sign.

"Well," said the captain, ultimately, "I suppose we'll have to make a try for ourselves. If we stay out here too long, we'll none of us have strength left to swim after the boat swamps."

And so the oiler, who was at the oars, turned the boat straight for the shore. There was a sudden tightening of muscles. There was some thinking.

"If we don't all get ashore," said the captain—"if we don't all get ashore, I suppose you fellows know where to send news of my finish?"

They then briefly exchanged some addresses and admonitions. As for the reflections of the men, there was a great deal of rage in them. Perchance they might be formulated thus: "If I am going to be drowned—if I am going to be drowned—if I am going to be drowned, why, in the name of the seven mad gods who rule the sea, was I allowed to come thus far and contemplate sand and trees? Was I brought here merely to have my nose dragged away as I was about to nibble the sacred cheese of life? It is preposterous. If this old ninny-woman, Fate, cannot do better than this, she should be deprived of the management of men's fortunes. She is an old hen who knows not her intention. If she has decided to drown me, why did she not do it in the beginning and save me all this trouble? The whole affair is absurd.—But no; she cannot mean to drown me. She dare not drown me. She cannot drown me. Not after all this work." Afterward the man might have had an impulse to shake his fist at the clouds. "Just you drown me, now, and then hear what I call you!"

The billows that came at this time were more formidable. They seemed always just about to break and roll over the little boat in a turmoil of foam. There was a preparatory and long growl in the speech of them. No mind unused to the sea would have concluded that the dinghy could ascend these sheer heights in time. The shore was still afar. The oiler was a wily surfman. "Boys," he said swiftly, "she won't live three minutes more, and we're too far out to swim. Shall I take her to sea again, Captain?"

"Yes; go ahead!" said the captain.

This oiler, by a series of quick miracles and fast and steady oarsmanship, turned the boat in the middle of the surf and took her safely to sea again.

There was a considerable silence as the boat bumped over the furrowed sea to deeper water. Then somebody in gloom spoke: "Well, anyhow, they must have seen us from the shore by now."

The gulls went in slanting flight up the wind toward the gray, desolate east. A squall, marked by dingy clouds and clouds brick-red like smoke from a burning building, appeared from the south-east.

"What do you think of those life-saving people? Ain't they peaches?"

"Funny they haven't seen us."

"Maybe they think we're out here for sport! Maybe they think we're fishin'. Maybe they think we're damned fools."

It was a long afternoon. A changed tide tried to force them southward, but wind and wave said northward. Far ahead, where coast-line, sea, and sky formed their mighty angle, there were little dots which seemed to indicate a city on the shore.

"St. Augustine?"

The captain shook his head. "Too near Mosquito Inlet."

And the oiler rowed, and then the correspondent rowed; then the oiler rowed. It was a weary business. The human back can become the seat of more aches and pains than are registered in books for the composite anatomy of a regiment. It is a limited area, but it can become the theatre of innumerable muscular conflicts, tangles, wrenches, knots, and other comforts.

"Did you ever like to row, Billie?" asked the correspondent.

"No," said the oiler; "hang it!"

When one exchanged the rowing-seat for a place in the bottom of the boat, he suffered a bodily depression that caused him to be careless of everything save an obligation to wiggle one finger. There was cold sea-water swashing to and fro in the boat, and he lay in it. His head, pillowed on a thwart, was within an inch of the swirl of a wave-crest, and sometimes a particularly obstreperous sea came inboard and drenched him once more. But these matters did not annoy him. It is almost certain that if the boat had capsized he would have tumbled comfortably out upon the ocean as if he felt sure that it was a great soft mattress.

"Look! There's a man on the shore!"

"Where?"

"There! See 'im?"

"Yes, sure! He's walking along."

"Now he's stopped. Look! He's facing us!"

"He's waving at us!"

"So he is! By thunder!"

"Ah, now we're all right! Now we're all right! There'll be a boat out here for us in half an hour."

"He's going on. He's running. He's going up to that house there."

The remote beach seemed lower than the sea, and it required a searching glance to discern the little black figure. The captain saw a floating stick, and they rowed to it. A bath towel was by some weird chance in the boat, and tying this on the stick, the captain waved it. The oarsman did not dare turn his head, so he was obliged to ask questions.

"What's he doing now?"

"He's standing still again. He's looking, I think. . . . There he goes again—toward the house. . . . Now he's stopped again."

"Is he waving at us?"

"No, not now; he was, though."

"Look! There comes another man!"

"He's running."

"Look at him go, would you!"

"Why, he's on a bicycle. Now he's met the other man. They're both waving at us. Look!"

"There comes something up the beach."

"What the devil is that thing?"

"Why, it looks like a boat."

"Why, certainly, it's a boat."

"No, it's on wheels."

"Yes, so it is. Well, that must be the life-boat. They drag them along shore on a wagon."

"That's the life-boat sure."

"No, by——, it's—it's an omnibus."

"I tell you it's a life-boat."

"It is not! It's an omnibus. I can see it plain. See? One of these big hotel omnibuses."

"By thunder, you're right. It's an omnibus, sure as fate. What do you suppose they are doing with an omnibus? Maybe they are going around collecting the life-crew, hey?"

"That's it, likely. Look! There's a fellow waving a little black flag. He's standing on the steps of the omnibus. There come those other two fellows. Now they're all talking together. Look at the fellow with the flag. Maybe he ain't waving it!"

"That ain't a flag, is it? That's his coat. Why, certainly, that's his coat."

"So it is; it's his coat. He's taken it off and is waving it around his head. But would you look at him swing it!"

"Oh, say, there isn't any life-saving station there. That's just a winter-resort hotel omnibus that has brought over some of the boarders to see us drown."

"What's that idiot with the coat mean? What's he signalling, anyhow?"

"It looks as if he were trying to tell us to go north. There must be a life-saving station up there."

"No; he thinks we're fishing. Just giving us a merry hand. See? Ah, there, Willie!"

"Well, I wish I could make something out of those signals. What do you suppose he means?"

"He don't mean anything; he's just playing."

"Well, if he'd just signal us to try the surf again, or to go to sea and wait, or go north, or go south, or go to hell, there would be some reason in it. But look at him! He just stands there and keeps his coat revolving like a wheel. The ass!"

"There come more people."

"Now there's quite a mob. Look! Isn't that a boat?"

"Where? Oh, I see where you mean. No, that's no boat."

"That fellow is still waving his coat."

"He must think we like to see him do that. Why don't he quit it? It don't mean anything."

"I don't know. I think he is trying to make us go north. It must be that there's a life-saving station there somewhere."

"Say, he ain't tired yet. Look at 'im wave!"

"Wonder how long he can keep that up. He's been revolving his coat ever since he caught sight of us. He's an idiot. Why aren't they getting men to bring a boat out? A fishingboat—one of those big yawls—could come out here all right. Why don't he do something?"

"Oh, it's all right now."

"They'll have a boat out here for us in less than no time, now that they've seen us."

A faint yellow tone came into the sky over the low land. The shadows on the sea slowly deepened. The wind bore coldness with it, and the men began to shiver.

"Holy smoke!" said one, allowing his voice to express his impious mood, "if we keep on monkeying out here! If we've got to flounder out here all night!"

"Oh, we'll never have to stay here all night! Don't you worry. They've seen us now, and it won't be long before they'll come chasing out after us."

The shore grew dusky. The man waving a coat blended gradually into this gloom, and it swallowed in the same manner the omnibus and the group of people. The spray, when it dashed uproariously over the side, made the voyagers shrink and swear like men who were being branded.

"I'd like to catch the chump who waved the coat. I feel like socking him one, just for luck."

"Why? What did he do?"

"Oh, nothing, but then he seemed so damned cheerful."

In the meantime the oiler rowed, and then the correspondent rowed, and then the oiler rowed. Gray-faced and bowed forward, they mechanically, turn by turn, plied the leaden oars. The form of the lighthouse had vanished from the southern horizon, but finally a pale star appeared, just lifting from the sea. The streaked saffron in the west passed before the all-merging darkness, and the sea to the east was black. The land had vanished, and was expressed only by the low and drear thunder of the surf.

"If I am going to be drowned—if I am going to be drowned—if I am going to be drowned, why, in the name of the seven mad gods who rule the sea, was I allowed to come thus far and contemplate sand and trees? Was I brought here merely to have my nose dragged away as I was about to nibble the sacred cheese of life?"

The patient captain, drooped over the water-jar, was sometimes obliged to speak to the oarsman.

"Keep her head up! Keep her head up!"

"Keep her head up, sir." The voices were weary and low.

This was surely a quiet evening. All save the oarsman lay heavily and listlessly in the boat's bottom. As for him, his eyes were just capable of noting the tall black waves that swept foward in a most sinister silence, save for an occasional subdued growl of a crest.

The cook's head was on a thwart, and he looked without interest at the water under his nose. He was deep in other scenes. Finally he spoke. "Billie," he murmured, dreamfully, "what kind of pie do you like best?"

V

"Pie!" said the oiler and the correspondent, agitatedly. "Don't talk about those things, blast you!"

"Well," said the cook, "I was just thinking about ham sandwiches, and—"

A night on the sea in an open boat is a long night. As darkness settled finally, the shine of the light, lifting from the sea in the south, changed to full gold. On the northern horizon a new light appeared, a small bluish gleam on the edge of the waters. These two lights were the furniture of the world. Otherwise there was nothing but waves.

Two men huddled in the stern, and distances were so magnificent in the dinghy that the rower was enabled to keep his feet partly warm by thrusting them under his companions. Their legs indeed extended far under the rowing-seat until they touched the feet of the captain forward. Sometimes, despite the efforts of the tired oarsman, a wave came piling into the boat, an icy wave of the night, and the chilling water soaked them anew. They would twist their bodies for a moment and groan, and sleep the dead sleep once more, while the water in the boat gurgled about them as the craft rocked.

The plan of the oiler and the correspondent was for one to row until he lost the ability, and then arouse the other from his sea-water couch in the bottom of the boat.

The oiler plied the oars until his head drooped forward and the overpowering sleep blinded him; and he rowed yet afterward. Then he touched a man in the bottom of the boat, and called his name. "Will you spell me for a little while?" he said meekly.

"Sure, Billie," said the correspondent, awaking and dragging himself to a sitting position. They exchanged places carefully, and the oiler, cuddling down in the sea-water at the cook's side, seemed to go to sleep instantly.

The particular violence of the sea had ceased. The waves came without snarling. The obligation of the man at the oars was to keep the boat headed so that the tilt of the rollers would not capsize her, and to preserve her from filling when the crests rushed past. The black waves were silent and hard to be seen in the darkness. Often one was almost upon the boat before the oarsman was aware.

In a low voice the correspondent addressed the captain. He was not sure that the captain was awake, although this iron man seemed to be always awake. "Captain, shall I keep her making for that light north, sir?"

The same steady voice answered him. "Yes. Keep it about two points off the port bow."

The cook had tied a life-belt around himself in order to get even the warmth which this clumsy cork contrivance could donate, and he seemed almost stove-like when a rower, whose teeth invariably chattered wildly as soon as he ceased his labor, dropped down to sleep.

The correspondent, as he rowed, looked down at the men sleeping underfoot. The cook's arm was around the oiler's shoulders, and, with their fragmentary clothing and haggard faces, they were the babes of the sea—a grotesque rendering of the old babes in the wood.

Later he must have grown stupid at his work, for suddenly there was a growling of water, and a crest came with a roar and a swash into the boat, and it was a wonder that it did not set the cook afloat in his life-belt. The cook continued to sleep, but the oiler sat up, blinking his eyes and shaking with the new cold.

"Oh, I'm awful sorry, Billie," said the correspondent, contritely.

"That's all right, old boy," said the oiler, and lay down again and was asleep.

Presently it seemed that even the captain dozed, and the correspondent thought that he was the one man afloat on all the oceans. The wind had a voice as it came over the waves, and it was sadder than the end.

There was a long, loud swishing astern of the boat, and a gleaming trail of phosphorescence, like blue flame, was furrowed on the black waters. It might have been made by a monstrous knife.

Then there came a stillness, while the correspondent breathed with open mouth and looked at the sea.

Suddenly there was another swish and another flash of bluish light, and this time it was alongside the boat, and might almost have been reached with an oar. The correspondent saw an enormous fin speed like a shadow through the water, hurling the crystalline spray and leaving the long glowing trail.

The correspondent looked over his shoulder at the captain. His face was hidden, and he seemed to be asleep. He looked at the babes of the sea. They certainly were asleep. So, being bereft of sympathy, he leaned a little way to one side and swore softly into the sea.

But the thing did not then leave the vicinity of the boat. Ahead or astern, on one side or the other, at intervals long or short, fled the long sparkling streak, and there was to be heard the *whirroo* of the dark fin. The speed and power of the thing was greatly to be admired. It cut the water like a gigantic and keen projectile.

The presence of this biding thing did not affect the man with the same horror that it would if he had been a picnicker. He simply looked at the sea dully and swore in an undertone.

Nevertheless, it is true that he did not wish to be alone with the thing. He wished one of his companions to awake by chance and keep him company with it. But the captain hung motionless over the water-jar, and the oiler and the cook in the bottom of the boat were plunged in slumber.

VI

"If I am going to be drowned—if I am going to be drowned—if I am going to be drowned, why, in the name of the seven mad gods who rule the sea, was I allowed to come thus far and contemplate sand and trees?"

During this dismal night, it may be remarked that a man would conclude that it was really the intention of the seven mad gods to drown him, despite the abominable injustice of it. For it was certainly an abominable injustice to drown a man who had worked so hard, so hard. The man felt it would be a crime most unnatural. Other people had drowned at sea since galleys swarmed with painted sails, but still—

When it occurs to a man that nature does not regard him as important, and that she feels she would not maim the universe by disposing of him, he at first wishes to throw bricks at the temple, and he hates deeply the fact that there are no bricks and no temples. Any visible expression of nature would surely be pelleted with his jeers.

Then, if there be no tangible thing to hoot, he feels, perhaps, the desire to confront a personification and indulge in pleas, bowed to one knee, and with hands supplicant, saying, "Yes, but I love myself."

A high cold star on a winter's night is the word he feels that she says to him. Thereafter he knows the pathos of his situation.

The men in the dinghy had not discussed these matters, but each had, no doubt, reflected upon them in silence and according to his mind. There was seldom any expression upon their faces save the general one of complete weariness. Speech was devoted to the business of the boat.

To chime the notes of his emotion, a verse mysteriously entered the correspondent's head. He had even forgotten that he had forgotten this verse, but it suddenly was in his mind.

A soldier of the Legion lay dying in Algiers;
There was lack of woman's nursing, there was dearth of woman's tears;
But a comrade stood beside him, and he took that comrade's hand,
And he said, "I never more shall see my own, my native land."[9]

In his childhood the correspondent had been made acquainted with the fact that a soldier of the Legion lay dying in Algiers, but he had never regarded the fact as important. Myriads of his school-fellows had informed him of the soldier's plight, but the dinning had naturally ended by making him perfectly indifferent. He had never considered it his affair that a soldier of the Legion lay dying in Algiers, nor had it appeared to him as a matter for sorrow. It was less to him than the breaking of a pencil's point.

[9] From "Bingen on the Rhine" by Carolyn E. S. Norton (1808-1877).

Now, however, it quaintly came to him as a human, living thing. It was no longer merely a picture of a few throes in the breast of a poet, meanwhile drinking tea and warming his feet at the grate; it was an actuality—stern, mournful, and fine.

The correspondent plainly saw the soldier. He lay on the sand with his feet out straight and still. While his pale left hand was upon his chest in an attempt to thwart the going of his life, the blood came between his fingers. In the far Algerian distance, a city of low square forms was set against a sky that was faint with the last sunset hues. The correspondent, plying the oars and dreaming of the slower movements of the lips of the soldier, was moved by a profound and perfectly impersonal comprehension. He was sorry for the soldier of the Legion who lay dying in Algiers.

The thing which had followed the boat and waited evidently grown bored at the delay. There was no longer to be heard the slash of the cutwater, and there was no longer the flame of the long trail. The light in the north still glimmered, but it was apparently no nearer to the boat. Sometimes the boom of the surf rang in the correspondent's ears, and he turned the craft seaward then and rowed harder. Southward, some one had evidently built a watch-fire on the beach. It was too low and too far to be seen, but it made a shimmering, roseate reflection upon the bluff in back of it, and this could be discerned from the boat. The wind came stronger, and sometimes a wave suddenly raged out like a mountain cat, and there was to be seen the sheen and sparkle of a broken crest.

The captain, in the bow, moved on his water-jar and sat erect. "Pretty long night," he observed to the correspondent. He looked at the shore. "Those life-saving people take their time."

"Did you see that shark playing around?"

"Yes, I saw him. He was a big fellow, all right."

"Wish I had known you were awake."

Later the correspondent spoke into the bottom of the boat.

"Billie!" There was a slow and gradual disentanglement.

"Billie, will you spell me?"

"Sure," said the oiler.

As soon as the correspondent touched the cold, comfortable sea-water in the bottom of the boat and had huddled close to the cook's life-belt he was deep in sleep, despite the fact that his teeth played all the popular airs. This sleep was so good to him that it was but a moment before he heard a voice call his name in a tone that demonstrated the last stages of exhaustion. "Will you spell me?"

"Sure, Billie."

The light in the north had mysteriously vanished, but the correspondent took his course from the wide-awake captain.

Later in the night they took the boat farther out to sea, and the captain directed the cook to take one oar at the stern and keep the boat facing the seas. He was to call out if he should hear the thunder of the surf. This plan enabled the oiler and the correspondent to get respite together. "We'll give those boys a chance to get into shape again," said the captain. They curled down and, after a few preliminary chatterings and trembles, slept once more the dead sleep. Neither knew they had bequeathed to the cook the company of another shark, or perhaps the same shark.

As the boat caroused on the waves, spray occasionally bumped over the side and gave them a fresh soaking, but this had no power to break their repose. The ominous slash of the wind and the water affected them as it would have affected mummies.

"Boys," said the cook, with the notes of every reluctance in his voice, "she's drifted in pretty close. I guess one of you had better take her to sea again." The correspondent, aroused, heard the crash of the toppled crests.

As he was rowing, the captain gave him some whisky-and-water, and this steadied the chills out of him. "If I ever get ashore and anybody shows me even a photograph of an oar—"

At last there was a short conversation.

"Billie!—Billie, will you spell me?"

"Sure," said the oiler.

VII

When the correspondent again opened his eyes, the sea and the sky were each of the gray hue of the dawning. Later, carmine and gold was painted upon the waters. The morning appeared finally, in its splendor, with a sky of pure blue, and the sunlight flamed on the tips of the waves.

On the distant dunes were set many little black cottages, and a tall white windmill reared above them. No man, nor dog, nor bicycle appeared on the beach. The cottages might have formed a deserted village.

The voyagers scanned the shore. A conference was held in the boat. "Well," said the captain, "if no help is coming, we might better try a run through the surf right away. If we stay out here much longer we will be too weak to do anything for ourselves at all." The others silently acquiesced in this reasoning. The boat was headed for the beach. The correspondent wondered if none ever ascended the tall wind-tower, and if then they never looked seaward. This tower was a giant, standing with its back to the plight of the ants. It represented in a degree, to the correspondent, the serenity of nature amid the struggles of the individual—nature in the wind, and nature in the vision of men. She did not seem cruel to him then, nor beneficent, nor treacherous, nor wise. But she was indifferent, flatly indifferent. It is, perhaps, plausible that a man in this situation, impressed with the unconcern of the universe, should see the innumerable flaws of his life, and have them taste wickedly in his mind, and wish for another chance. A distinction between right and wrong seems absurdly clear to him, then, in this new ignorance of the grave-edge, and he understands that if he were given another opportunity he would mend his conduct and his words, and be better and brighter during an introduction or at a tea.

"Now boys," said the captain, "she is going to swamp sure. All we can do is to work her in as far as possible, and then when she swamps, pile out and scramble for the beach. Keep cool now, and don't jump until she swamps sure."

The oiler took the oars. Over his shoulders he scanned the surf. "Captain," he said, "I think I'd better bring her about and keep her head-on to the seas and back her in."

"All right, Billie," said the captain. "Back her in." The oiler swung the boat then, and, seated in the stern, the cook and the correspondent were obliged to look over their shoulders to contemplate the lonely and indifferent shore.

The monstrous inshore rollers heaved the boat high until the men were again enabled to see the white sheets of water scudding up the slanted beach. "We won't get in very close," said the captain. Each time a man could wrest his attention from the rollers, he turned his glance toward the shore, and in the expression of the eyes during this contemplation there was a singular quality. The correspondent, observing the others, knew that they were not afraid, but the full meaning of their glances was shrouded.

As for himself, he was too tired to grapple fundamentally with the fact. He tried to coerce his mind into thinking of it, but the mind was dominated at this time by the muscles, and the muscles said they did not care. It merely occurred to him that if he should drown it would be a shame.

There were no hurried words, no pallor, no plain agitation. The men simply looked at the shore. "Now, remember to get well clear of the boat when you jump," said the captain.

Seaward the crest of a roller suddenly fell with a thunderous crash, and the long white comber came roaring down upon the boat.

"Steady now," said the captain. The men were silent. They turned their eyes from the shore to the comber and waited. The boat slid up the incline, leaped at the furious top, bounced over it, and swung down the long back of the wave. Some water had been shipped, and the cook bailed it out.

But the next crest crashed also. The tumbling, boiling flood of white water caught the boat and whirled it almost perpendicular. Water swarmed in from all sides. The correspondent had his hands on the gunwale at this time, and when the water entered at that place he swiftly withdrew his fingers, as if he objected to wetting them.

The little boat, drunken with this weight of water, reeled and snuggled deeper into the sea.

"Bail her out, cook! Bail her out!" said the captain.

"All right, Captain," said the cook.

"Now, boys, the next one will do for us sure," said the oiler. "Mind to jump clear of the boat."

The third wave moved forward, huge, furious, implacable. It fairly swallowed the dinghy, and almost simultaneously the men tumbled into the sea. A piece of the life-belt had lain in the bottom of the boat, and as the correspondent went overboard he held this to his chest with his left hand.

The January water was icy, and he reflected immediately that it was colder than he had expected to find it off the coast of Florida. This appeared to his dazed mind as a fact important enough to be noted at the time. The coldness of the water was sad; it was tragic. This fact was somehow mixed and confused with his opinion of his own situation, so that it seemed almost a proper reason for tears. The water was cold.

When he came to the surface he was conscious of little but the noisy water. Afterward he saw his companions in the sea. The oiler was ahead in the race. He was swimming strongly and rapidly. Off to the correspondent's left, the cook's great white and corked back bulged out of the water; and in the rear the captain was hanging with his one good hand to the keel of the overturned dinghy.

There is a certain immovable quality to a shore, and the correspondent wondered at it amid the confusion of the sea.

It seemed also very attractive; but the correspondent knew that it was a long journey, and he paddled leisurely. The piece of life-preserver lay under him, and sometimes he whirled down the incline of a wave as if he were on a hand-sled.

But finally he arrived at a place in the sea where travel was beset with difficulty. He did not pause swimming to inquire what manner of current had caught him, but there his progress ceased. The shore was set before him like a bit of scenery on a stage, and he looked at it and understood with his eyes each detail of it.

As the cook passed, much farther to the left, the captain was calling to him, "Turn over on your back, cook! Turn over on your back and use the oar."

"All right, sir." The cook turned on his back, and, paddling with an oar, went ahead as if he were a canoe.

Presently the boat also passed to the left of the correspondent, with the captain clinging with one hand to the keel. He would have appeared like a man raising himself to look over a board fence if it were not for the extraordinary gymnastics of the boat. The correspondent marvelled that the captain could still hold to it.

They passed on nearer to shore—the oiler, the cook, the captain—and following them went the water-jar, bouncing gaily over the seas.

The correspondent in the grip of this strange new enemy—a current. The shore, with its white slope of sand and its green bluff topped with little silent cottages, was spread like a picture before him. It was very near to him then, but he was impressed as one who, in a gallery, looks at a scene from Brittany or Algiers.

He thought: "I am going to drown? Can it be possible? Can it be possible? Can it be possible?" Perhaps an individual must consider his own death to be the final phenomenon of nature.

But later a wave perhaps whirled him out of this small deadly current, for he found suddenly that he could again make progress toward the shore. Later still he was aware that the captain, clinging with one hand to the keel of the dinghy, had his face turned away from the shore and toward him, and was calling his name. "Come to the boat! Come to the boat!"

In his struggle to reach the captain and the boat, he reflected that when one gets properly wearied drowning must really be a comfortable arrangement—a cessation of hostilities accompanied by a large degree of relief; and he was glad of it, for the main thing in his mind for some moments had been horror of the temporary agony. He did not wish to be hurt.

Presently he saw a man running along the shore. He was undressing with most remarkable speed. Coat, trousers, shirt, evrything flew magically off him.

"Come to the boat!" called the captain.

"All right, Captain." As the correspondent paddled, he saw the captain let himself down to the bottom and leave the boat. Then the correspondent performed his one marvel of the voyage. A large wave caught him and flung him with ease and supreme speed completely over the boat and far beyond it. It struck him even then as an event in gymnastics and a true miracle of the sea. An overturned boat in the surf is not a plaything to a swimming man.

The correspondent arrived in water that reached only to his waist, but his condition did not enable him to stand for more than a moment. Each wave knocked him into a heap, and the undertow pulled at him.

Then he saw the man who had been running and undressing, and undress-. ing and running, come bounding into the water. He dragged ashore the cook, and then waded toward the captain; but the captain waved him away and sent him to the correspondent. He was naked—naked as a tree in winter; but a halo was about his head, and he shone like a saint. He gave a strong pull, and a long drag, and a bully heave at the correspondent's hand. The correspondent, schooled in the minor formulae, said, "Thanks, old man." But suddenly the man cried, "What's that?" He pointed a swift finger. The correspondent said, "Go."

In the shallows, face downward, lay the oiler. His forehead touched sand that was periodically, between each wave, clear of the sea.

The correspondent did not know all that transpired afterward. When he achieved safe ground he fell, striking the sand with each particular part of his body. It was as if he had dropped from a roof, but the thud was grateful to him.

It seems that instantly the beach was populated with men with blankets, clothes, and flasks, and women with coffee-pots and all the remedies sacred to their minds. The welcome of the land to the men from the sea was warm and generous; but a still and dripping shape was carried slowly up the beach, and the land's welcome for it could only be the different and sinister hospitality of the grave.

When it came night, the white waves paced to and fro in the moonlight, and the wind brought the sound of the great sea's voice to the men on the shore, and they felt that they could then be interpreters.

feel sea says: nothing indifferent

1897/1898

The Blue Hotel[1]

I

The Palace Hotel at Fort Romper was painted a light blue, a shade that is on the legs of a kind of heron, causing the bird to declare its position against any background. The Palace Hotel, then, was always screaming and howling in a way that made the dazzling winter landscape of Nebraska seem only a gray swampish hush. It stood alone on the prairie, and when the snow was falling the town two hundred yards away was not visible. But when the traveler alighted at the railway station he was obliged to pass the Palace Hotel before he could come upon the company of low clap-board houses which composed Fort Romper, and it was not to be thought that any traveler could pass the Palace Hotel without looking at it. Pat Scully, the proprietor, had proved himself a master of strategy when he chose his paints. It is true that on clear days, when the great trans-continental expresses, long lines of swaying Pullmans, swept through Fort Romper, passengers were overcome at the sight, and the cult that knows the brown-reds and the subdivisions of the dark greens of the East expressed shame, pity, horror, in a laugh.[2] But to the citizens of this prairie town, and to the people who would naturally stop there, Pat Scully had performed a feat. With this opulence and splendor, these creeds, classes, egotisms, that streamed through Romper on the rails day after day, they had no color in common.

[1] Stephen Crane, *Tales of Adventure*, ed. Fredson Bowers, with an Introduction by J. C. Levenson (The University Press of Virginia, Charlottesville, 1970), 143–170. An Approved Text, Center for Editions of American Authors, Modern Language Association of America.

[2] Crane refers here to the "genteel tradition" of the East and its snobbery toward the West in matters of culture, especially architecture and interior design.

As if the displayed delights of such a blue hotel were not sufficiently enticing, it was Scully's habit to go every morning and evening to meet the leisurely trains that stopped at Romper and work his seductions upon any man that he might see wavering, gripsack in hand.

One morning, when a snow-crusted engine dragged its long string of freight cars and its one passenger coach to the station, Scully performed the marvel of catching three men. One was a shaky and quick-eyed Swede, with a great shining cheap valise; one was a tall bronzed cowboy, who was on his way to a ranch near the Dakota line; one was a little silent man from the East, who didn't look it, and didn't announce it. Scully practically made them prisoners. He was so nimble and merry and kindly that each probably felt it would be the height of brutality to try to escape. They trudged off over the creaking board sidewalks in the wake of the eager little Irishman. He wore a heavy fur cap squeezed tightly down on his head. It caused his two red ears to stick out stiffly, as if they were made of tin.

At last, Scully, elaborately, with boisterous hospitality, conducted them through the portals of the blue hotel. The room which they entered was small. It seemed to be merely a proper temple for an enormous stove, which, in the center, was humming with god-like violence. At various points on its surface the iron had become luminous and glowed yellow from the heat. Beside the stove Scully's son Johnnie was playing High-Five with an old farmer who had whiskers both gray and sandy. They were quarreling. Frequently the old farmer turned his face toward a box of sawdust—colored brown from tobacco juice—that was behind the stove, and spat with an air of great impatience and irritation. With a loud flourish of words Scully destroyed the game of cards, and bustled his son upstairs with part of the baggage of the new guests. He himself conducted them to three basins of the coldest water in the world. The cowboy and the Easterner burnished themselves fiery red with this water, until it seemed to be some kind of a metal polish. The Swede, however, merely dipped his fingers gingerly and with trepidation. It was notable that throughout this' series of small ceremonies the three travelers were made to feel that Scully was very benevolent. He was conferring great favors upon them. He handed the towel from one to the other with an air of philanthropic impulse.

Afterward they went to the first room, and, sitting about the stove, listened to Scully's officious clamor at his daughters, who were preparing the midday meal. They reflected in the silence of experienced men who tread carefully amid new people. Nevertheless, the old farmer, stationary, invincible in his chair near the warmest part of the stove, turned his face from the sawdust box frequently and addressed a glowing commonplace to the strangers. Usually he was answered in short but adequate sentences by either the cowboy or the Easterner. The Swede said nothing. He seemed to be occupied in making furtive estimates of each man in the room. One might have thought that he had the sense of silly suspicion which comes to guilt. He resembled a badly frightened man.

Later, at dinner, he spoke a little, addressing his conversation entirely to Scully. He volunteered that he had come from New York, where for ten years he had worked as a tailor. These facts seemed to strike Scully as fascinating, and afterward he volunteered that he had lived at Romper for fourteen years. The Swede asked about the crops and the price of labor. He seemed barely to listen to Scully's extended replies. His eyes continued to rove from man to man.

Finally, with a laugh and a wink, he said that some of these Western communities were very dangerous; and after his statement he straightened his legs under the table, tilted his head, and laughed again, loudly. It was plain that the demonstration had no meaning to the others. They looked at him wondering and in silence.

II

As the men trooped heavily back into the front room, the two little windows presented views of a turmoiling sea of snow. The huge arms of the wind were making attempts—mighty, circular, futile—to embrace the flakes as they sped. A gate-post like a still man with a blanched face stood aghast amid this profligate fury. In a hearty voice Scully announced the presence of a blizzard. The guests of the blue hotel, lighting their pipes, assented with grunts of lazy masculine contentment. No island of the sea could be exempt in the degree of this little room with its humming stove. Johnnie, son of Scully, in a tone which defined his opinion of his ability as a card-player, challenged the old farmer of both gray and sandy whiskers to a game of High-Five. The farmer agreed with a contemptuous and bitter scoff. They sat close to the stove, and squared their knees under a wide board. The cowboy and the Easterner watched the game with interest. The Swede remained near the window, aloof, but with a countenance that showed signs of an inexplicable excitement.

The play of Johnnie and the gray-beard was suddenly ended by another quarrel. The old man arose while casting a look of heated scorn at his adversary. He slowly buttoned his coat, and then stalked with fabulous dignity from the room. In the discreet silence of all other men the Swede laughed. His laughter rang somehow childish. Men by this time had begun to look at him askance, as if they wished to inquire what ailed him.

A new game was formed jocosely. The cowboy volunteered to become the partner of Johnnie, and they all then turned to ask the Swede to throw in his lot with the little Easterner. He asked some questions about the game, and learning that it wore many names, and that he had played it when it was under an alias, he accepted the invitation. He strode toward the men nervously, as if he expected to be assaulted. Finally, seated, he gazed from face to face and laughed shrilly. This laugh was so strange that the Easterner looked up quickly, the cowboy sat intent and with his mouth open, and Johnnie paused, holding the cards with still fingers.

Afterward there was a short silence. Then Johnnie said: "Well, let's get at it. Come on now!" They pulled their chairs forward until their knees were bunched under the board. They began to play, and their interest in the game caused the others to forget the manner of the Swede.

The cowboy was a board-whacker. Each time that he held superior cards he whanged them, one by one, with exceeding force, down upon the improvised table, and took the tricks with a glowing air of prowess and pride that sent thrills of indignation into the hearts of his opponents. A game with a board-whacker in it is sure to become intense. The countenances of the Easterner and the Swede were miserable whenever the cowboy thundered down his aces and kings, while Johnnie, his eyes gleaming with joy, chuckled and chuckled.

Because of the absorbing play none considered the strange ways of the Swede. They paid strict heed to the game. Finally, during a lull caused by a new deal, the Swede suddenly addressed Johnnie: "I suppose there have been a good many men killed in this room." The jaws of the others dropped and they looked at him.

"What in hell are you talking about?" said Johnnie.

The Swede laughed again his blatant laugh, full of a kind of false courage and defiance. "Oh, you know what I mean all right," he answered.

"I'm a liar if I do!" Johnnie protested. The card was halted, and the men stared at the Swede. Johnnie evidently felt that as the son of the proprietor he should make a direct inquiry. "Now, what might you be drivin' at, mister?" he asked. The Swede winked at him. It was a wink full of cunning. His fingers shook on the edge of the board. "Oh, maybe you think I have been to nowheres. Maybe you think I'm a tenderfoot?"

"I don't know nothin' about you," answered Johnnie, "and I don't give a damn where you've been. All I got to say is that I don't know what you're driving at. There hain't never been nobody killed in this room."

The cowboy, who had been steadily gazing at the Swede, then spoke. "What's wrong with you, mister?"

Apparently it seemed to the Swede that he was formidably menaced. He shivered and turned white near the corners of his mouth. He sent an appealing glance in the direction of the little Easterner. During these moments he did not forget to wear his air of advanced pot-valor. "They say they don't know what I mean," he remarked mockingly to the Easterner.

The latter answered after prolonged and cautious reflection. "I don't understand you," he said, impassively.

The Swede made a movement then which announced that he thought he had encountered treachery from the only quarter where he had expected sympathy if not help. "Oh, I see you are all against me. I see——"

The cowboy was in a state of deep stupefaction. "Say," he cried, as he tumbled the deck violently down upon the board. "Say, what are you gittin' at, hey?"

The Swede sprang up with the celerity of a man escaping from a snake on the floor. "I don't want to fight!" he shouted. "I don't want to fight!"

The cowboy stretched his long legs indolently and deliberately. His hands were in his pockets. He spat into the sawdust box. "Well, who the hell thought you did?" he inquired.

The Swede backed rapidly toward a corner of the room. His hands were out protectingly in front of his chest, but he was making an obvious struggle to control his fright. "Gentlemen," he quavered, "I suppose I am going to be killed before I can leave this house! I suppose I am going to be killed before I can leave this house!" In his eyes was the dying swan look. Through the windows could be seen the snow turning blue in the shadow of dusk. The wind tore at the house and some loose thing beat regularly against the clapboards like a spirit tapping.

A door opened, and Scully himself entered. He paused in surprise as he noted the tragic attitude of the Swede. Then he said: "What's the matter here?"

The Swede answered him swiftly and eagerly: "These men are going to kill me."

"Kill you!" ejaculated Scully. "Kill you! What are you talkin'?"

The Swede made the gesture of a martyr.

Scully wheeled sternly upon his son. "What is this, Johnnie?"

The lad had grown sullen. "Damned if I know," he answered. "I can't make no sense to it." He began to shuffle the cards, fluttering them together with an angry snap. "He says a good many men have been killed in this room, or something like that. And he says he's goin' to be killed here too. I don't know what ails him. He's crazy, I shouldn't wonder."

Scully then looked for explanation to the cowboy, but the cowboy simply shrugged his shoulders.

"Kill you?" said Scully again to the Swede. "Kill you? Man, you're off your nut."

"Oh, I know," burst out the Swede. "I know what will happen. Yes, I'm crazy—yes. Yes, of course, I'm crazy—yes. But I know one thing——" There was a sort of sweat of misery and terror upon his face. "I know I won't get out of here alive."

The cowboy drew a deep breath, as if his mind was passing into the last stages of dissolution. "Well, I'm dog-goned," he whispered to himself.

Scully wheeled suddenly and faced his son. "You've been troublin' this man!"

Johnnie's voice was loud with its burden of grievance. "Why, good Gawd, I ain't done nothin' to 'im."

The Swede broke in. "Gentlemen, do not disturb yourselves. I will leave this house. I will go 'way because——" He accused them dramatically with his glance. "Because I do not want to be killed."

Scully was furious with his son. "Will you tell me what is the matter, you young divil? What's the matter, anyhow? Speak out!"

"Blame it," cried Johnnie in despair, "don't I tell you I don't know. He—he says we want to kill him, and that's all I know. I can't tell what ails him."

The Swede continued to repeat: "Never mind, Mr. Scully, never mind. I will leave this house. I will go away, because I do not wish to be killed. Yes, of course, I am crazy—yes. But I know one thing! I will go away. I will leave this house. Never mind, Mr. Scully, never mind. I will go away."

"You will not go 'way," said Scully. "You will not go 'way until I hear the reason of this business. If anybody has troubled you I will take care of him. This is my house. You are under my roof, and I will not allow any peaceable man to be troubled here." He cast a terrible eye upon Johnnie, the cowboy, and the Easterner.

"Never mind, Mr. Scully, never mind. I will go 'way. I do not wish to be killed." The Swede moved toward the door, which opened upon the stairs. It was evidently his intention to go at once for his baggage.

"No, no," shouted Scully peremptorily; but the white-faced man slid by him and disappeared. "Now," said Scully severely, "what does this mean?"

Johnnie and the cowboy cried together: "Why, we didn't do nothin' to 'im!"

Scully's eyes were cold. "No," he said, "you didn't?"

Johnnie swore a deep oath. "Why, this the wildest loon I ever see. We didn't do nothin' at all. We were jest sittin' here playin' cards and he——"

The father suddenly spoke to the Easterner. "Mr. Blanc," he asked, "what has these boys been doin'?"

The Easterner reflected again. "I didn't see anything wrong at all," he said at last slowly.

Scully began to howl. "But what does it mean?" He stared ferociously at his son. "I have a mind to lather you for this, me boy."

Johnnie was frantic. "Well, what have I done?" he bawled at his father.

III

"I think you are tongue-tied," said Scully finally to his son, the cowboy and the Easterner, and at the end of this scornful sentence he left the room.

Upstairs the Swede was swiftly fastening the straps of his great valise. Once his back happened to be half-turned toward the door, and hearing a noise there, he wheeled and sprang up, uttering a loud cry. Scully's wrinkled visage showed grimly in the light of the small lamp he carried. This yellow effulgence, streaming upward, colored only his prominent features, and left his eyes, for instance, in mysterious shadow. He resembled a murderer.

"Man, man!" he exclaimed, "have you gone daffy?"

"Oh, no! Oh, no!" rejoined the other. "There are people in this world who know pretty nearly as much as you do—understand?"

For a moment they stood gazing at each other. Upon the Swede's deathly pale cheeks were two spots brightly crimson and sharply edged, as if they had been carefully painted. Scully placed the light on the table and sat himself on the edge of the bed. He spoke ruminatively. "By cracky, I never heard of such a thing in my life. It's a complete muddle. I can't for the soul of me think how you ever got this idea into your head." Presently he lifted his eyes and asked: "And did you sure think they were going to kill you?"

The Swede scanned the old man as if he wished to see into his mind. "I did," he said at last. He obviously suspected that this answer might precipitate an outbreak. As he pulled on a strap his whole arm shook, the elbow wavering like a bit of paper.

Scully banged his hand impressively on the foot-board of the bed. "Why, man, we're goin' to have a line of ilictric street-cars in this town next spring."

"'A line of electric street-cars,'" repeated the Swede stupidly.

"And," said Scully, "there's a new railroad goin' to be built down from Broken Arm to here. Not to mintion the four churches and the smashin' big brick school-house. Then there's the big factory, too. Why, in two years Romper'll be a met-tro-*pol*-is."

Having finished the preparation of his baggage, the Swede straightened himself. "Mr. Scully," he said with sudden hardihood, "how much do I owe you?"

"You don't owe me anythin'," said the old man angrily.

"Yes, I do," retorted the Swede. He took seventy-five cents from his pocket and tendered it to Scully; but the latter snapped his fingers in disdainful refusal. However, it happened that they both stood gazing in a strange fashion at three silver pieces on the Swede's open palm.

"I'll not take your money," said Scully at last. "Not after what's been goin' on here." Then a plan seemed to strike him. "Here," he cried, picking up his lamp and moving toward the door. "Here! Come with me a minute."

"No," said the Swede in overwhelming alarm.

"Yes," urged the old man. "Come on! I want you to come and see a picter—just across the hall—in my room."

The Swede must have concluded that his hour was come. His jaw dropped and his teeth showed like a dead man's. He ultimately followed Scully across the corridor, but he had the step of one hung in chains.

Scully flashed the light high on the wall of his own chamber. There was revealed a ridiculous photograph of a little girl. She was leaning against a balustrade of gorgeous decoration, and the formidable bang to her hair was prominent. The figure was as graceful as an upright sled-stake, and, withal, it was of the hue of lead. "There," said Scully tenderly. "That's the picter of my little girl that died. Her name was Carrie. She had the purtiest hair you ever saw! I was that fond of her, she——"

Turning then he saw that the Swede was not contemplating the picture at all, but, instead, was keeping keen watch on the gloom in the rear.

"Look, man!" shouted Scully heartily. "That's the picter of my little gal that died. Her name was Carrie. And then here's the picter of my oldest boy, Michael. He's a lawyer in Lincoln an' doin' well. I gave that boy a grand eddycation, and I'm glad for it now. He's a fine boy. Look at 'im now. Ain't he bold as blazes, him there in Lincoln, an honored an' respicted gintleman. An honored an' respicted gintleman," concluded Scully with a flourish. And so saying, he smote the Swede jovially on the back.

The Swede faintly smiled.

"Now," said the old man, "there's only one more thing." He dropped suddenly to the floor and thrust his head beneath the bed. The Swede could hear his muffled voice. "I'd keep it under me piller if it wasn't for that boy Johnnie. Then there's the old woman—— Where is it now? I never put it twice in the same place. Ah, now come out with you!"

Presently he backed clumsily from under the bed, dragging with him an old coat rolled into a bundle. "I've fetched him," he muttered. Kneeling on the floor he unrolled the coat and extracted from its heart a large yellow-brown whisky bottle.

His first maneuver was to hold the bottle up to the light. Reassured, apparently, that nobody had been tampering with it, he thrust it with a generous movement toward the Swede.

The weak-kneed Swede was about to eagerly clutch this element of strength, but he suddenly jerked his hand away and cast a look of horror upon Scully.

"Drink," said the old man affectionately. He had arisen to his feet, and now stood facing the Swede.

There was a silence. Then again Scully said: "Drink!"

The Swede laughed wildly. He grabbed the bottle, put it to his mouth, and as his lips curled absurdly around the opening and his throat worked, he kept his glance burning with hatred upon the old man's face.

IV

After the departure of Scully the three men, with the card-board still upon their knees, preserved for a long time an astounded silence. Then Johnnie said: "That's the dod-dangest Swede I ever see."

"He ain't no Swede," said the cowboy scornfully.

"Well, what is he then?" cried Johnnie. "What is he then?"

"It's my opinion," replied the cowboy deliberately, "he's some kind of a Dutchman." It was a venerable custom of the country to entitle as Swedes all light-haired men who spoke with a heavy tongue. In consequence the idea of the cowboy was not without its daring. "Yes, sir," he repeated. "It's my opinion this feller is some kind of a Dutchman."

"Well, he says he's a Swede, anyhow," muttered Johnnie sulkily. He turned to the Easterner: "What do you think, Mr. Blanc?"

"Oh, I don't know," replied the Easterner.

"Well, what do you think makes him act that way?" asked the cowboy.

"Why, he's frightened!" The Easterner knocked his pipe against a rim of the stove. "He's clear frightened out of his boots."

"What at?" cried Johnnie and cowboy together.

The Easterner reflected over his answer.

"What at?" cried the others again.

"Oh, I don't know, but it seems to me this man has been reading dime-novels, and he thinks he's right out in the middle of it—the shootin' and stabbin' and all."

"But," said the cowboy, deeply scandalized, "this ain't Wyoming, ner none of them places. This is Nebrasker."

"Yes," added Johnnie, "an' why don't he wait till he gits *out West?*"

The traveled Easterner laughed. "It isn't different there even—not in these days. But he thinks he's right in the middle of hell."

Johnnie and the cowboy mused long.

"It's awful funny," remarked Johnnie at last.

"Yes," said the cowboy. "This is a queer game. I hope we don't git snowed in, because then we'd have to stand this here man bein' around with us all the time. That wouldn't be no good."

"I wish pop would throw him out," said Johnnie.

Presently they heard a loud stamping on the stairs, accompanied by ringing jokes in the voice of old Scully, and laughter, evidently from the Swede. The men around the stove stared vacantly at each other. "Gosh," said the cowboy. The door flew open, and old Scully, flushed and anecdotal, came into the room. He was jabbering at the Swede, who followed him, laughing bravely. It was the entry of two roysterers from a banquet hall.

"Come now," said Scully sharply to the three seated men, "move up and give us a chance at the stove." The cowboy and the Easterner obediently sidled their chairs to make room for the newcomers. Johnnie, however, simply arranged himself in a more indolent attitude, and then remained motionless.

"Come! Git over, there," said Scully.

"Plenty of room on the other side of the stove," said Johnnie.

"Do you think we want to sit in the draught?" roared the father.

But the Swede here interposed with a grandeur of confidence. "No, no. Let the boy sit where he likes," he cried in a bullying voice to the father.

"All right! All right!" said Scully deferentially. The cowboy and the Easterner exchanged glances of wonder.

The five chairs were formed in a crescent about one side of the stove. The Swede began to talk; he talked arrogantly, profanely, angrily. Johnnie, the cowboy and the Easterner maintained a morose silence, while old Scully appeared to be receptive and eager, breaking in constantly with sympathetic ejaculations.

Finally the Swede announced that he was thirsty. He moved in his chair, and said that he would go for a drink of water.

"I'll git it for you," cried Scully at once.

"No," said the Swede contemptuously. "I'll get it for myself." He arose and stalked with the air of an owner off into the executive parts of the hotel.

As soon as the Swede was out of hearing Scully sprang to his feet and whispered intensely to the others. "Upstairs he thought I was tryin' to poison 'im."

"Say," said Johnnie, "this makes me sick. Why don't you throw 'im out in the snow?"

"Why, he's all right now," declared Scully. "It was only that he was from the East and he thought this was a tough place. That's all. He's all right now."

The cowboy looked with admiration upon the Easterner. "You were straight," he said. "You were on to that there Dutchman."

"Well," said Johnnie to his father, "he may be all right now, but I don't see it. Other time he was scared, and now he's too fresh."

Scully's speech was always a combination of Irish brogue and idiom, Western twang and idiom, and scraps of curiously formal diction taken from the story-books and newspapers. He now hurled a strange mass of language at the head of his son. "What do I keep? What do I keep? What do I keep?" he demanded in a voice of thunder. He slapped his knee impressively, to indicate that he himself was going to make reply, and that all should heed. "I keep a hotel," he shouted. "A hotel, do you mind? A guest under my roof has sacred privileges. He is to be intimidated by none. Not one word shall he hear that would prijudice him in favor of goin' away. I'll not have it. There's no place in this here town where they can say they iver took in a guest of mine because he was afraid to stay here." He wheeled suddenly upon the cowboy and the Easterner. "Am I right?"

"Yes, Mr. Scully," said the cowboy, "I think you're right."

"Yes, Mr. Scully," said the Easterner, "I think you're right."

V

At six-o'clock supper, the Swede fizzed like a fire-wheel. He sometimes seemed on the point of bursting into riotous song, and in all his madness he was encouraged by old Scully. The Easterner was incased in reserve; the cowboy sat in wide-mouthed amazement, forgetting to eat, while Johnnie wrathly demolished great plates of food. The daughters of the house when they were obliged to replenish the biscuits approached as warily as Indians, and, having succeeded in their purposes, fled with ill-concealed trepidation. The Swede domineered the whole feast, and he gave it the appearance of a cruel bacchanal.[3] He seemed to have grown suddenly taller; he gazed, brutally disdainful, into every face. His voice rang through the room. Once when he jabbed out harpoon-fashion with his fork to pinion a biscuit the weapon nearly impaled the hand of the Easterner which had been stretched quietly out for the same biscuit.

After supper, as the men filed toward the other room, the Swede smote Scully ruthlessly on the shoulder. "Well, old boy, that was a good square meal." Johnnie looked hopefully at his father; he knew that shoulder was tender from an old fall; and indeed it appeared for a moment as if Scully was going to flame out over the matter, but in the end he smiled a sickly smile and remained silent. The others understood from his manner that he was admitting his responsibility for the Swede's new viewpoint.

Johnnie, however, addressed his parent in an aside. "Why don't you license somebody to kick you downstairs?" Scully scowled darkly by way of reply.

When they were gathered about the stove, the Swede insisted on another game of High-Five. Scully gently deprecated the plan at first, but the Swede turned a wolfish glare upon him. The old man subsided, and the Swede canvassed the others. In his tone there was always a great threat. The cowboy and the Easterner both remarked indifferently that they would play. Scully said that he would presently have to go to meet the 6.58 train, and so the Swede turned menacingly upon Johnnie. For a moment their glances crossed like blades, and then Johnnie smiled and said: "Yes, I'll play."

They formed a square with the little board on their knees. The Easterner and the Swede were again partners. As the play went on, it was noticeable that the cowboy was not board-whacking as usual. Meanwhile, Scully, near the lamp, had put on his spectacles and, with an appearance curiously like an old priest, was reading a newspaper. In time he went out to meet the 6.58 train, and, despite his precautions, a gust of polar wind whirled into the room as he opened the door. Besides scattering the cards, it chilled the players to the marrow. The Swede cursed frightfully. When Scully returned, his entrance disturbed a cozy and friendly scene. The Swede again cursed. But presently they were once more intent, their heads bent forward and their hands moving swiftly. The Swede had adopted the fashion of board-whacking.

Scully took up his paper and for a long time remained immersed in matters which were extraordinarily remote from him. The lamp burned badly, and once he stopped to adjust the wick. The newspaper as he turned from

[3] A drunken revelry; the word derives from the name, Bacchus, the god of wine.

page to page rustled with a slow and comfortable sound. Then suddenly he heard three terrible words: "You are cheatin'!"

Such scenes often prove that there can be little of dramatic import in environment. Any room can present a tragic front; any room can be comic. This little den was now hideous as a torture-chamber. The new faces of the men themselves had changed it upon the instant. The Swede held a huge fist in front of Johnnie's face, while the latter looked steadily over it into the blazing orbs of his accuser. The Easterner had grown pallid; the cowboy's jaw had dropped in that expression of bovine amazement which was one of his important mannerisms. After the three words, the first sound in the room was made by Scully's paper as it floated forgotten to his feet. His spectacles had also fallen from his nose, but by a clutch he had saved them in air. His hand, grasping the spectacles, now remained poised awkwardly and near his shoulder. He stared at the card-players.

Probably the silence was while a second elapsed. Then, if the floor had been suddenly twitched out from under the men they could not have moved quicker. The five had projected themselves headlong toward a common point. It happened that Johnnie in rising to hurl himself upon the Swede had stumbled slightly because of his curiously instinctive care for the cards and the board. The loss of the moment allowed time for the arrival of Scully, and also allowed the cowboy time to give the Swede a great push which sent him staggering back. The men found tongue together, and horse shouts of rage, appeal or fear burst from every throat. The cowboy pushed and jostled feverishly at the Swede, and the Easterner and Scully clung wildly to Johnnie; but, through the smoky air, above the swaying bodies of the peace-compellers, the eyes of the two warriors ever sought each other in glances of challenge that were at once hot and steely.

Of course the board had been overturned, and now the whole company of cards was scattered over the floor, where the boots of the men trampled the fat and painted kings and queens as they gazed with their silly eyes at the war that was waging above them.

Scully's voice was dominating the yells. "Stop now! Stop, I say! Stop, now——"

Johnnie, as he struggled to burst through the rank formed by Scully and the Easterner, was crying: "Well, he says I cheated! He says I cheated! I won't allow no man to say I cheated! If he says I cheated, he's a—— ——!"

The cowboy was telling the Swede: "Quit, now! Quit, d'ye hear——"

The screams of the Swede never ceased. "He did cheat! I saw him! I saw him——"

As for the Easterner, he was importuning in a voice that was not heeded. "Wait a moment, can't you? Oh, wait a moment. What's the good of a fight over a game of cards? Wait a moment——"

In this tumult no complete sentences were clear. "Cheat"—"Quit"—"He says"—These fragments pierced the uproar and rang out sharply. It was remarkable that whereas Scully undoubtedly made the most noise, he was the least heard of any of the riotous band.

Then suddenly there was a great cessation. It was as if each man had paused for breath, and although the room was still lighted with the anger of men, it could be seen that there was no danger of immediate conflict, and at once Johnnie, shouldering his way forward, almost succeeded in confronting the Swede. "What did you say I cheated for? What did you say I cheated for? I don't cheat and I won't let no man say I do!"

The Swede said: "I saw you! I saw you!"

"Well," cried Johnnie, "I'll fight any man what says I cheat!"

"No, you won't," said the cowboy. "Not here."

"Ah, be still, can't you?" said Scully, coming between them.

The quiet was sufficient to allow the Easterner's voice to be heard. He was repeating: "Oh, wait a moment, can't you? What's the good of a fight over a game of cards? Wait a moment."

Johnnie, his red face appearing above his father's shoulder, hailed the Swede again. "Did you say I cheated?"

The Swede showed his teeth. "Yes."

"Then," said Johnnie, "we must fight."

"Yes, fight," roared the Swede. He was like a demoniac. "Yes, fight! I'll show you what kind of a man I am! I'll show you who you want to fight! Maybe you think I can't fight! Maybe you think I can't! I'll show you, you skin, you card-sharp! Yes, you cheated! You cheated! You cheated!"

"Well, let's git at it, then, mister," said Johnnie coolly.

The cowboy's brow was beaded with sweat from his efforts in intercepting all sorts of raids. He turned in despair to Scully. "What are you goin' to do now?"

A change had come over the Celtic visage of the old man. He now seemed all eagerness; his eyes glowed.

"We'll let them fight," he answered stalwartly. "I can't put up with it any longer. I've stood this damned Swede till I'm sick. We'll let them fight."

VI

The men prepared to go out of doors. The Easterner was so nervous that he had great difficulty in getting his arms into the sleeves of his new leather-coat. As the cowboy drew his fur-cap down over his ears his hands trembled. In fact, Johnnie and old Scully were the only ones who displayed no agitation. These preliminaries were conducted without words.

Scully threw open the door. "Well, come on," he said. Instantly a terrific wind caused the flame of the lamp to struggle at its wick, while a puff of black smoke sprang from the chimney-top. The stove was in mid-current of the blast, and its voice swelled to equal the roar of the storm. Some of the scarred and bedabbled cards were caught up from the floor and dashed helplessly against the further wall. The men lowered their heads and plunged into the tempest as into a sea.

No snow was falling, but great whirls and clouds of flakes, swept up from the ground by the frantic winds, were streaming southward with the speed of bullets. The covered land was blue with the sheen of an unearthly satin, and there was no other hue save where at the low black railway station—which seemed incredibly distant—one light gleamed like a tiny jewel. As the men floundered into a thigh-deep drift, it was known that the Swede was bawling out something. Scully went to him, put a hand on his shoulder and projected an ear. "What's that you say?" he shouted.

"I say," bawled the Swede again, "I won't stand much show against this gang. I know you'll all pitch on me."

Scully smote him reproachfully on the arm. "Tut, man," he yelled. The wind tore the words from Scully's lips and scattered them far a-lee.

"You are all a gang of——" boomed the Swede, but the storm also seized the remainder of this sentence.

Immediately turning their backs upon the wind, the men had swung around a corner to the sheltered side of the hotel. It was the function of the little house to preserve here, amid this great devastation of snow, an irregular V-shape of heavily-incrusted grass, which crackled beneath the feet. One could imagine the great drifts piled against the windward side. When the party reached the comparative peace of this spot it was found that the Swede was still bellowing.

"Oh, I know what kind of a thing this is! I know you'll all pitch on me. I can't lick you all!"

Scully turned upon him panther-fashion. "You'll not have to whip all of us. You'll have to whip my son Johnnie. An' the man what troubles you durin' that time will have me to dale with."

The arrangements were swiftly made. The two men faced each other, obedient to the harsh commands of Scully, whose face, in the subtly luminous gloom, could be seen set in the austere impersonal lines that are pictured on the countenances of the Roman veterans. The Easterner's teeth were chattering, and he was hopping up and down like a mechanical toy. The cowboy stood rock-like.

The contestants had not stripped off any clothing. Each was in his ordinary attire. Their fists were up, and they eyed each other in a calm that had the elements of leonine cruelty in it.

During the pause, the Easterner's mind, like a film, took lasting impressions of three men—the iron-nerved master of the ceremony; the Swede, pale, motionless, terrible; and Johnnie, serene yet ferocious, brutish yet heroic. The entire prelude had in it a tragedy greater than the tragedy of action, and this aspect was accentuated by the long mellow cry of the blizzard, as it sped the tumbling and wailing flakes into the black abyss of the south.

"Now!" said Scully.

The two combatants leaped forward and crashed together like bullocks. There was heard the cushioned sound of blows, and of a curse squeezing out from between the tight teeth of one.

As for the spectators, the Easterner's pent-up breath exploded from him with a pop of relief, absolute relief from the tension of the preliminaries. The cowboy bounded into the air with a yowl. Scully was immovable as from supreme amazement and fear at the fury of the fight which he himself had permitted and arranged.

For a time the encounter in the darkness was such a perplexity of flying arms that it presented no more detail than would a swiftly-revolving wheel. Occasionally a face, as if illumined by a flash of light, would shine out, ghastly and marked with pink spots. A moment later, the men might have been known as shadows, if it were not for the involuntary utterance of oaths that came from them in whispers.

Suddenly a holocaust of warlike desire caught the cowboy, and he bolted forward with the speed of a broncho. "Go it, Johnnie; go it! Kill him! Kill him!"

Scully confronted him. "Kape back," he said; and by his glance the cowboy could tell that this man was Johnnie's father.

To the Easterner there was a monotony of unchangeable fighting that was an abomination. This confused mingling was eternal to his sense, which was concentrated in a longing for the end, the priceless end. Once the fighters lurched near him, and as he scrambled hastily backward, he heard them breathe like men on the rack.

"Kill him, Johnnie! Kill him! Kill him! Kill him!" The cowboy's face was contorted like one of those agony-masks in museums.

"Keep still," said Scully icily.

Then there was a sudden loud grunt, incomplete, cut-short, and Johnnie's body swung away from the Swede and fell with sickening heaviness to the grass. The cowboy was barely in time to prevent the mad Swede from flinging himself upon his prone adversary. "No, you don't," said the cowboy, interposing an arm. "Wait a second."

Scully was at his son's side. "Johnnie! Johnnie, me boy?" His voice had a quality of melancholy tenderness. "Johnnie? Can you go on with it?" He looked anxiously down into the bloody pulpy face of his son.

There was a moment of silence, and then Johnnie answered in his ordinary voice: "Yes, I—it—yes."

Assisted by his father he struggled to his feet. "Wait a bit now till you git your wind," said the old man.

A few paces away the cowboy was lecturing the Swede. "No, you don't! Wait a second!"

The Easterner was plucking at Scully's sleeve. "Oh, this is enough," he pleaded. "This is enough! Let it go as it stands. This is enough!"

"Bill," said Scully, "git out of the road." The cowboy stepped aside. "Now." The combatants were actuated by a new caution as they advanced toward collision. They glared at each other, and then the Swede aimed a lightning blow that carried with it his entire weight. Johnnie was evidently half-stupid from weakness, but he miraculously dodged, and his fist sent the over-balanced Swede sprawling.

The cowboy, Scully and the Easterner burst into a cheer that was like a chorus of triumphant soldiery, but before its conclusion the Swede had scuffled agilely to his feet and come in berserk abandon at his foe. There was another perplexity of flying arms, and Johnnie's body again swung away and fell, even as a bundle might fall from a roof. The Swede instantly staggered to a little wind-waved tree and leaned upon it, breathing like an engine, while his savage and flame-lit eyes roamed from face to face as the men bent over Johnnie. There was a splendor of isolation in his situation at this time which the Easterner felt once when, lifting his eyes from the man on the ground, he beheld that mysterious and lonely figure, waiting.

"Are you any good yet, Johnnie?" asked Scully in a broken voice.

The son gasped and opened his eyes languidly. After a moment he answered: "No—I ain't—any good—any—more." Then, from shame and bodily ill, he began to weep, the tears furrowing down through the blood-stains on his face. "He was too—too—too heavy for me."

Scully straightened and addressed the waiting figure. "Stranger," he said, evenly, "it's all up with our side." Then his voice changed into that vibrant huskiness which is commonly the tone of the most simple and deadly announcements. "Johnnie is whipped."

Without replying, the victor moved off on the route to the front door of the hotel.

The cowboy was formulating new and unspellable blasphemies. The Easterner was startled to find that they were out in a wind that seemed to come direct from the shadowed arctic floes. He heard again the wail of the snow as it was flung to its grave in the south. He knew now that all this time the cold had been sinking into him deeper and deeper, and he wondered that he had not perished. He felt indifferent to the condition of the vanquished man.

"Johnnie, can you walk?" asked Scully.

"Did I hurt—hurt him any?" asked the son.

"Can you walk, boy? Can you walk?"

Johnnie's voice was suddenly strong. There was a robust impatience in it. "I asked you whether I hurt him any!"

"Yes, yes, Johnnie," answered the cowboy consolingly; "he's hurt a good deal."

They raised him from the ground, and as soon as he was on his feet he went tottering off, rebuffing all attempts at assistance. When the party rounded the corner they were fairly blinded by the pelting of the snow. It burned their faces like fire. The cowboy carried Johnnie through the drift to the door. As they entered some cards again rose from the floor and beat against the wall.

The Easterner rushed to the stove. He was so profoundly chilled that he almost dared to embrace the glowing iron. The Swede was not in the room. Johnnie sank into a chair, and folding his arms on his knees, buried his face in them. Scully, warming one foot and then the other at a rim of the stove, muttered to himself with Celtic mournfulness. The cowboy had removed his fur-cap, and with a dazed and rueful air he was now running one hand through his tousled locks. From overhead they could hear the creaking of boards, as the Swede tramped here and there in his room.

The sad quiet was broken by the sudden flinging open of a door that led toward the kitchen. It was instantly followed by an inrush of women. They precipitated themselves upon Johnnie amid a chorus of lamentation. Before they carried their prey off to the kitchen, there to be bathed and harangued with that mixture of sympathy and abuse which is a feat of their sex, the mother straightened herself and fixed old Scully with an eye of stern reproach. "Shame be upon you, Patrick Scully!" she cried. "Your own son, too. Shame be upon you!"

"There, now! Be quite, now!" said the old man weakly.

"Shame be upon you, Patrick Scully!" The girls, rallying to this slogan, sniffed disdainfully in the direction of those trembling accomplices, the cowboy and the Easterner. Presently they bore Johnnie away, and left the three men to dismal reflection.

VII

"I'd like to fight this here Dutchman myself," said the cowboy, breaking a long silence.

Scully wagged his head sadly. "No, that wouldn't do. It wouldn't be right. It wouldn't be right."

"Well, why wouldn't it?" argued the cowboy. "I don't see no harm in it."

"No," answered Scully with mournful heroism. "It wouldn't be right. It was Johnnie's fight, and now we mustn't whip the man just because he whipped Johnnie."

"Yes, that's true enough," said the cowboy; "but—he better not get fresh with me, because I couldn't stand no more of it."

"You'll not say a word to him," commanded Scully, and even then they heard the tread of the Swede on the stairs. His entrance was made theatric. He swept the door back with a bang and swaggered to the middle of the room. No one looked at him. "Well," he cried, insolently, at Scully, "I s'pose you'll tell me now how much I owe you?"

The old man remained stolid. "You don't owe me nothin'."

"Huh!" said the Swede, "huh! Don't owe 'im nothin'."

The cowboy addressed the Swede. "Stranger, I don't see how you come to be so gay around here."

Old Scully was instantly alert. "Stop!" he shouted, holding his hand forth, fingers upward. "Bill, you shut up!"

The cowboy spat carelessly into the sawdust box. "I didn't say a word, did I?" he asked.

"Mr. Scully," called the Swede, "how much do I owe you?" It was seen that he was attired for departure, and that he had his valise in his hand.

"You don't owe me nothin'," repeated Scully in his same imperturbable way.

"Huh!" said the Swede. "I guess you're right. I guess if it was any way at all, you'd owe me somethin'. That's what I guess." He turned to the cowboy. "'Kill him! Kill him! Kill him!'" he mimicked, and then guffawed victoriously. "'Kill him!'" He was convulsed with ironical humor.

But he might have been jeering the dead. The three men were immovable and silent, staring with glassy eyes at the stove.

The Swede opened the door and passed into the storm, giving one derisive glance backward at the still group.

As soon as the door was closed, Scully and the cowboy leaped to their feet and began to curse. They trampled to and fro, waving their arms and smashing into the air with their fists. "Oh, but that was a hard minute!" wailed Scully. "That was a hard minute! Him there leerin' and scoffin'! One bang at his nose was worth forty dollars to me that minute! How did you stand it, Bill?"

"How did I stand it?" cried the cowboy in a quivering voice. "How did I stand it? Oh!"

The old man burst into sudden brogue. "I'd loike to take that Swade," he wailed, "and hould 'im down on a shtone flure and bate 'im to a jelly wid a shtick!"

The cowboy groaned in sympathy. "I'd like to git him by the neck and ha-ammer him"—he brought his hand down on a chair with a noise like a pistol-shot—"hammer that there Dutchman until he couldn't tell himself from a dead coyote!"

"I'd bate 'im until he——"

"I'd show *him* some things——"

And then together they raised a yearning fanatic cry. "Oh-o-oh! if we only could——"

"Yes!"

"Yes!"

"And then I'd——"

"O-o-oh!"

VIII

The Swede, tightly gripping his valise, tacked across the face of the storm as if he carried sails. He was following a line of little naked gasping trees, which he knew must mark the way of the road. His face, fresh from the pounding of Johnnie's fists, felt more pleasure than pain in the wind and the driving snow. A number of square shapes loomed upon him finally, and he knew them as the houses of the main body of the town. He found a street and made travel along it, leaning heavily upon the wind whenever, at a corner, a terrific blast caught him.

He might have been in a deserted village. We picture the world as thick with conquering and elate humanity, but here, with the bugles of the tempest pealing, it was hard to imagine a peopled earth. One viewed the existence of man then as a marvel, and conceded a glamour of wonder to these lice which were caused to cling to a whirling, fire-smote, ice-locked, disease-stricken, space-lost bulb. The conceit of man was explained by this storm to be the very engine of life. One was a coxcomb not to die in it. However, the Swede found a saloon.

In front of it an indomitable red light was burning, and the snow-flakes were made blood-color as they flew through the circumscribed territory of the lamp's shining. The Swede pushed open the door of the saloon and entered. A sanded expanse was before him, and at the end of it four men sat about a table drinking. Down one side of the room extended a radiant bar, and its guardian was leaning upon his elbows listening to the talk of the men at the table. The Swede dropped his valise upon the floor, and, smiling fraternally upon the barkeeper, said: "Gimme some whisky, will you?" The man placed a bottle, a whisky-glass, and a glass of ice-thick water upon the bar. The Swede poured himself an abnormal portion of whisky and drank it in three gulps. "Pretty bad night," remarked the bartender indifferently. He was making the pretension of blindness, which is usually a distinction of his class; but it could have been seen that he was furtively studying the half-erased blood-stains on the face of the Swede. "Bad night," he said again.

"Oh, it's good enough for me," replied the Swede, hardily, as he poured himself some more whisky. The barkeeper took his coin and maneuvered it through its reception by the highly-nickeled cash-machine. A bell rang; a card labled "20 cts." had appeared.

"No," continued the Swede, "this isn't too bad weather. It's good enough for me."

"So?" murmured the barkeeper languidly.

The copious drams made the Swede's eyes swim, and he breathed a trifle heavier. "Yes, I like this weather. I like it. It suits me." It was apparently his design to impart a deep significance to these words.

"So?" murmured the bartender again. He turned to gaze dreamily at the scroll-like birds and bird-like scrolls which had been drawn with soap upon the mirrors back of the bar.

"Well, I guess I'll take another drink," said the Swede presently. "Have something?"

"No, thanks; I'm not drinkin'," answered the bartender. Afterward he asked: "How did you hurt your face?"

The Swede immediately began to boast loudly. "Why, in a fight. I thumped the soul out of a man down here at Scully's hotel."

The interest of the four men at the table was at last aroused.

"Who was it?" said one.

"Johnnie Scully," blustered the Swede. "Son of the man what runs it. He will be pretty near dead for some weeks, I can tell you. I made a nice thing of him, I did. He couldn't get up. They carried him in the house. Have a drink?"

Instantly the men in some subtle way incased themselves in reserve. "No, thanks," said one. The group was of curious formation. Two were prominent local business men; one was the district-attorney; and one was a professional gambler of the kind known as "square." But a scrutiny of the group would not have enabled an observer to pick the gambler from the men of more reputable pursuits. He was, in fact, a man so delicate in manner, when among people of fair class, and so judicious in his choice of victims, that in the strictly masculine part of the town's life he had come to be explicitly trusted and admired. People called him a thoroughbred. The fear and contempt with which his craft was regarded was undoubtedly the reason that his quiet dignity shone conspicuous above the quiet dignity of men who might be merely hatters, billiard-markers or grocery clerks. Beyond an occasional unwary traveler, who came by rail, this gambler was supposed to prey solely upon reckless and senile farmers, who, when flush with good crops, drove into town in all the pride and confidence of an absolutely invulnerable stupidity. Hearing at times in circuitous fashion of the despoilment of such a farmer, the important men of Romper invariably laughed in contempt of the victim, and if they thought of the wolf at all, it was with a kind of pride at the knowledge that he would never dare think of attacking their wisdom and courage. Besides, it was popular that this gambler had a real wife and two real children in a neat cottage in a suburb, where he led an exemplary home life, and when any one even suggested a discrepancy in his character, the crowd immediately vociferated descriptions of this virtuous family circle. Then men who led exemplary home lives, and men who did not lead exemplary home lives, all subsided in a bunch, remarking that there was nothing more to be said.

However, when a restriction was placed upon him—as, for instance, when a strong clique of members of the new Pollywog Club refused to permit him, even as a spectator, to appear in the rooms of the organization— the candor and gentleness with which he accepted the judgment disarmed many of his foes and made his friends more desperately partisan. He invariably distinguished between himself and a respectable Romper man so quickly and frankly that his manner actually appeared to be a continual broadcast compliment.

And one must not forget to declare the fundamental fact of his entire position in Romper. It is irrefutable that in all affairs outside of his business, in all matters that occur eternally and commonly between man and man, this thieving card-player was so generous, so just, so moral, that, in a contest, he could have put to flight the consciences of nine-tenths of the citizens of Romper.

And so it happened that he was seated in this saloon with the two prominent local merchants and the district-attorney.

The Swede continued to drink raw whisky, meanwhile babbling at the barkeeper and trying to induce him to indulge in potations. "Come on. Have a drink. Come on. What—no? Well, have a little one then. By gawd, I've whipped a man to-night, and I want to celebrate. I whipped him good, too. Gentlemen," the Swede cried to the men at the table, "have a drink?"

"Ssh!" said the barkeeper.

The group at the table, although furtively attentive, had been pretending to be deep in talk, but now a man lifted his eyes toward the Swede and said shortly: "Thanks. We don't want any more."

At this reply the Swede ruffled out his chest like a rooster. "Well," he exploded, "it seems I can't get anybody to drink with me in this town. Seems so, don't it? Well!"

"Ssh!" said the barkeeper.

"Say," snarled the Swede, "don't you try to shut me up. I won't have it. I'm a gentleman, and I want people to drink with me. And I want 'em to drink with me now. *Now*—do you understand?" He rapped the bar with his knuckles.

Years of experience had calloused the bartender. He merely grew sulky. "I hear you," he answered.

"Well," cried the Swede, "listen hard then. See those men over there? Well, they're going to drink with me, and don't you forget it. Now you watch."

"Hi!" yelled the barkeeper, "this won't do!"

"Why won't it?" demanded the Swede. He stalked over to the table, and by chance laid his hand upon the shoulder of the gambler. "How about this?" he asked, wrathfully. "I asked you to drink with me."

The gambler simply twisted his head and spoke over his shoulder. "My friend, I don't know you."

"Oh, hell!" answered the Swede, "come and have a drink."

"Now, my boy," advised the gambler kindly, "take your hand off my shoulder and go 'way and mind your own business." He was a little slim man, and it seemed strange to hear him use this tone of heroic patronage to the burly Swede. The other men at the table said nothing.

"What? You won't drink with me, you little dude! I'll make you then! I'll make you!" The Swede had grasped the gambler frenziedly at the throat, and was dragging him from his chair. The other men sprang up. The bar-keeper dashed around the corner of his bar. There was a great tumult, and then was seen a long blade in the hand of the gambler. It shot forward, and a human body, this citadel of virtue, wisdom, power, was pierced as easily as if it had been a melon. The Swede fell with a cry of supreme astonishment.

The prominent merchants and the district-attorney must have at once tumbled out of the place backward. The bartender found himself hanging limply to the arm of a chair and gazing into the eyes of a murderer.

"Henry," said the latter, as he wiped his knife on one of the towels that hung beneath the bar-rail, "you tell 'em where to find me. I'll be home, waiting for 'em." Then he vanished. A moment afterward the barkeeper was in the street dinning through the storm for help, and, moreover, companion-ship.

The corpse of the Swede, alone in the saloon, had its eyes fixed upon a dreadful legend that dwelt a-top of the cash-machine. "This registers the amount of your purchase."

IX

Months later, the cowboy was frying pork over the stove of a little ranch near the Dakota line, when there was a quick thud of hoofs outside, and, presently, the Easterner entered with the letters and the papers.

"Well," said the Easterner at once, "the chap that killed the Swede has got three years. Wasn't much, was it?"

"He has? Three years?" The cowboy poised his pan of pork, while he ruminated upon the news. "Three years. That ain't much."

"No. It was a light sentence," replied the Easterner as he unbuckled his spurs. "Seems there was a good deal of sympathy for him in Romper."

"If the bartender had been any good," observed the cowboy thoughtfully, "he would have gone in and cracked that there Dutchman on the head with a bottle in the beginnin' of it and stopped all this here murderin'."

"Yes, a thousand things might have happened," said the Easterner tartly.

The cowboy returned his pan of pork to the fire, but his philosophy continued. "It's funny, ain't it? If he hadn't said Johnnie was cheatin' he'd be alive this minute. He was an awful fool. Game played for fun, too. Not for money. I believe he was crazy."

"I feel sorry for that gambler," said the Easterner.

"Oh, so do I," said the cowboy. "He don't deserve none of it for killin' who he did."

"The Swede might not have been killed if everything had been square."

"Might not have been killed?" exclaimed the cowboy. "Everythin' square? Why, when he said that Johnnie was cheatin' and acted like such a jackass? And then in the saloon he fairly walked up to git hurt?" With these arguments the cowboy browbeat the Easterner and reduced him to rage.

"You're a fool!" cried the Easterner viciously. "You're a bigger jackass than the Swede by a million majority. Now let me tell you one thing. Let me tell you something. Listen! Johnnie *was* cheating!"

" 'Johnnie,' " said the cowboy blankly. There was a minute of silence, and then he said robustly: "Why, no. The game was only for fun."

"Fun or not," said the Easterner, "Johnnie was cheating. I saw him. I know it. I saw him. And I refused to stand up and be a man. I let the Swede fight it out alone. And you—you were simply puffing around the place and wanting to fight. And then old Scully himself! We are all in it! This poor gambler isn't even a noun. He is kind of an adverb. Every sin is the result of a collaboration. We, five of us, have collaborated in the murder of this Swede. Usually there are from a dozen to forty women really involved in every murder, but in this case it seems to be only five men—you, I, Johnnie, old Scully, and that fool of an unfortunate gambler came merely as a culmination, the apex of a human movement, and gets all the punishment."

The cowboy, injured and rebellious, cried out blindly into this fog of mysterious theory. "Well, I didn't do anythin', did I?"

Poems from The Black Riders and Other Lines[1]

1 Black riders came from the sea.
There was clang and clang of spear and shield,
And clash and clash of hoof and heel,
Wild shouts and the wave of hair
In the rush upon the wind: 5
Thus the ride of Sin.[2]

3 In the desert
I saw a creature, naked, bestial,
Who, squatting upon the ground,
Held his heart in his hands,
And ate of it.   5
I said: "Is it good, friend?"
"It is bitter—bitter," he answered;
"But I like it
Because it is bitter,
And because it is my heart."   10

[1] From Crane's first book of poems, entitled *The Black Riders and Other Lines*, published in 1895

[2] Compare Revelations 6:2, 4, 5, 8.

6 God fashioned the ship of the world carefully.
   With the infinite skill of an all-master
   Made He the hull and the sails,
   Held He the rudder
   Ready for adjustment.   5
   Erect stood He, scanning His work proudly.
   Then—at fateful time—a wrong called,
   And God turned, heeding.
   Lo, the ship, at this opportunity, slipped slyly,
   Making cunning noiseless travel down the ways.   10
   So that, forever rudderless, it went upon the seas
   Going ridiculous voyages,
   Making quaint progress,
   Turning as with serious purpose
   Before stupid winds.   15
   And there were many in the sky
   Who laughed at this thing.

9 I stood upon a high place,
   And saw, below, many devils
   Running, leaping,
   And carousing in sin.
   One looked up, grinning,   5
   And said: "Comrade! Brother!"

10 Should the wide world roll away,
    Leaving black terror,
    Limitless night,
    Nor God, nor man, nor place to stand
    Would be to me essential,   5
    If thou and thy white arms were there,
    And the fall to doom a long way.

12 "And the sins of the fathers shall be visited upon
        the heads of the children, even unto the third
        and fourth generation of them that hate me."³

    Well, then, I hate Thee, unrighteous picture;
    Wicked image, I hate Thee;
    So, strike with Thy vengeance
    The heads of those little men
    Who come blindly.   5
    It will be a brave thing.

³ Exodus 20:5.

24 I saw a man pursuing the horizon;
Round and round they sped.
I was disturbed at this;
I accosted the man.
"It is futile," I said,   5
"You can never—"

"You lie," he cried,
And ran on.

27 A youth in apparel that glittered
Went to walk in a grim forest.
There he met an assassin
Attired all in garb of old days;
He, scowling through the thickets,   5
And dagger poised quivering,
Rushed upon the youth.
"Sir," said this latter,
"I am enchanted, believe me,
To die, thus,   10
In this medieval fashion,
According to the best legends;
Ah, what joy!"
Then took he the wound, smiling,
And died, content.   15

45 Tradition, thou are for suckling children,
Thou art the enlivening milk for babes;
But no meat for men is in thee.
Then—
But, alas, we all are babes.   5

67 God lay dead in Heaven;
Angels sang the hymn of the end;
Purple winds went moaning,
Their wings drip-dripping
With blood   5
That fell upon the earth.
It, groaning thing,
Turned black and sank.
Then from the far caverns
Of dead sins   10
Came monsters, livid with desire,
They fought,
Wrangled over the world,

A morsel.
But of all sadness this was sad,— 15
A woman's arms tried to shield
The head of a sleeping man
From the jaws of the final beast.

1895

Poems from War Is Kind[1]

76 Do not weep, maiden, for war is kind.
Because your lover threw wild hands toward the sky
And the affrighted steed ran on alone,
Do not weep.
War is kind. 5

 Hoarse, booming drums of the regiment,
 Little souls who thirst for fight,
 These men were born to drill and die.
 The unexplained glory flies above them,
 Great is the Battle-God, great, and his Kingdom— 10
 A field where a thousand corpses lie.

Do not weep, babe, for war is kind.
Because your father tumbled in the yellow trenches,
Raged as his breast, gulped and died,
Do not weep. 15
War is kind.

 Swift blazing flag of the regiment,
 Eagle with crest of red and gold,
 These men were born to drill and die.
 Point for them the virtue of slaughter, 20
 Make plain to them the excellence of killing
 And a field where a thousand corpses lie.

Mother whose heart hung humble as a button
On the bright splendid shroud of your son,
Do not weep. 25
War is kind.

86 On the desert
A silence from the moon's deepest valley.
Fire-rays fall athwart the robes
Of hooded men, squat and dumb.
Before them, a woman 5
Moves to the blowing of shrill whistles
And distant-thunder of drums

[1] From *War Is Kind*, published in 1899

While slow things, sinuous, dull with terrible color
Sleepily fondle her body
Or move at her will, swishing stealthily over the sand.   10
The snakes whisper softly;
The whispering, whispering snakes
Dreaming and swaying and staring
But always whispering, softly whispering.
The wind streams from the lone reaches   15
Of Arabia, solemn with night,
And the wild fire makes shimmer of blood
Over the robes of the hooded men
Squat and dumb.
Bands of the moving bronze, emerald, yellow   20
Circle the throat and the arms of her
And over the sands serpents move warily
Slow, menacing and submissive,
Swinging to the whistles and drums,
The whispering, whispering snakes,   25
Dreaming and swaying and staring
But always whispering, softly whispering.
The dignity of the accurséd;
The glory of slavery, despair, death
Is in the dance of the whispering snakes.   30

[87] A newspaper is a collection of half-injustices
Which, bawled by boys from mile to mile,
Spreads its curious opinion
To a million merciful and sneering men,
While families cuddle the joys of the fireside   5
When spurred by tale of dire lone agony.
A newspaper is a court
Where every one is kindly and unfairly tried
By a squalor of honest men.
A newspaper is a market   10
Where wisdom sells its freedom
And melons are crowned by the crowd.
A newspaper is a game
Where his error scores the plàyer victory.
While another's skill wins death.   15
A newspaper is a symbol;
It is fetless life's chronicle,
A collection of loud tales
Concentrating eternal stupidities
That in remote ages lived unhaltered,   20
Roaming through a fenceless world.

96 A man said to the universe:
"Sir, I exist!"
"However," replied the universe,
"The fact has not created in me
A sense of obligation."   5

                                                        1899

FRANK NORRIS

(1870-1902)

In his brief career Frank Norris changed dramatically from a precocious schoolboy writer of medieval romances to the leading American exponent of literary naturalism. The shift was not so much a change in direction as an enlargement of his initial literary impulse. Norris came to conceive of his naturalist novels as themselves romances on a large scale, taking in social, economic, and natural forces. He read Emile Zola while a student at the University of California in the early 1890's (earlier he had studied art at Paris after finishing a prep school in San Francisco) and, under Zola's influence, began his first serious fiction. While at Harvard for a year (1894-1895) he worked on *McTeague* (1899), a novel of passion, greed, and violence set in San Francisco. In the following years Norris traveled as far as South Africa, covered the Spanish-American War in Cuba (he and Stephen Crane met there but apparently did not care for each other), and published a number of stories and essays explaining his literary credo (collected in *The Responsibilities of the Novelist*, 1903).

At the end of the 1890's Norris turned his attention to an "epic of the West," which was to consist of three novels, of which he completed only two before his untimely death: *The Octopus* (1901), which concerns the growing of wheat and the conflicts between farmers and the railroad, and *The Pit* (1903), which deals with speculation and

The standard edition is *The Complete Works of Frank Norris,* 10 vol., 1928. Biographies are F. Walker, *Frank Norris: A Biography,* 1932; E. Marchand, *Frank Norris: A Study,* 1942. Criticism includes W. D. Howells, "Frank Norris," *North American Review,* CLXXV, 1902; W. Taylor, *The Economic Novel in America,* 1942; L. Ahnebrink, *The Influence of Emile Zola on Frank Norris,* 1947; M. Geismar, *Rebels and Ancestors: The American Novel, 1890-1910,* 1953; Charles Walcutt, *American Literary Naturalism, A Divided Stream,* 1956.

power in the "pit" of the Chicago grain market. The third novel, *The Wolf*, was to have portrayed the effect of American wheat around the world. The conception of the trilogy, some hint of which is present in "A Deal in Wheat," embodied Norris's program for the American novel: an epic drama of struggle, of the clash of mighty interests, of the warfare for control of land and wealth, and of the futile efforts of the human actors to comprehend the meaning of the huge forces shaping their lives. Norris died suddenly in 1902 after an appendix operation.

A Deal in Wheat[1]

I. THE BEAR[2]—WHEAT AT SIXTY-TWO

As Sam Lewiston backed the horse into the shafts of his buckboard and began hitching the tugs to the whiffletree,[3] his wife came out from the kitchen door of the house and drew near, and stood for some time at the horse's head, her arms folded and her apron rolled around them. For a long moment neither spoke. They had talked over the situation so long and so comprehensively the night before that there seemed to be nothing more to say.

The time was late in the summer, the place a ranch in southwestern Kansas, and Lewiston and his wife were two of a vast population of farmers, wheat growers, who at that moment were passing through a crisis—a crisis that at any moment might culminate in tragedy. Wheat was down to sixty-six.

At length Emma Lewiston spoke.

"Well," she hazarded, looking vaguely out across the ranch toward the horizon, leagues distant; "well, Sam, there's always that offer of brother Joe's. We can quit—and go to Chicago—if the worst comes."

"And give up!" exclaimed Lewiston, running the lines through the torets.[4] "Leave the ranch! Give up! After all these years!"

His wife made no reply for the moment. Lewiston climbed into the buckboard and gathered up the lines. "Well, here goes for the last try, Emmie," he said. "Good-bye, girl. Maybe things will look better in town to-day."

---

[1] From *A Deal in Wheat*, published in 1903 by Doubleday & Co., Inc.

[2] In the language of the stock market, a bear profits from a falling market (Bear Market) and a bull profits from a rising market (Bull Market).

[3] A pivoting bar to which horse's traces (tugs) are tied.

[4] Harness rings.

"Maybe," she said gravely. She kissed her husband good-bye and stood for some time looking after the buckboard travelling toward the town in a moving pillar of dust.

"I don't know," she murmured at length; "I don't know just how we're going to make out."

When he reached town, Lewiston tied the horse to the iron railing in front of the Odd Fellows' Hall, the ground floor of which was occupied by the post-office, and went across the street and up the stairway of a building of brick and granite—quite the most pretentious structure of the town—and knocked at a door upon the first landing. The door was furnished with a pane of frosted glass, on which, in gold letters, was inscribed, "Bridges & Co., Grain Dealers."

Bridges himself, a middle-aged man who wore a velvet skullcap and who was smoking a Pittsburg stogie, met the farmer at the counter and the two exchanged perfunctory greetings.

"Well," said Lewiston, tentatively, after a while.

"Well, Lewiston," said the other, "I can't take that wheat of yours at any better than sixty-two."

"Sixty-*two!*"

"It's the Chicago price that does it, Lewiston. Truslow is bearing the stuff for all he's worth. It's Truslow and the bear clique that stick the knife into us. The price broke again this morning. We've just got a wire."

"Good heavens," murmured Lewiston, looking vaguely from side to side. "That—that ruins me. I *can't* carry my grain any longer—what with storage charges and—and—— Bridges, I don't see just how I'm going to make out. Sixty-two cents a bushel! Why, man, what with this and with that it's cost me nearly a dollar a bushel to raise that wheat, and now Truslow——."

He turned away abruptly with a quick gesture of infinite discouragement.

He went down the stairs, and making his way to where his buckboard was hitched, got in, and, with eyes vacant, the reins slipping and sliding in his limp, half-open hands, drove slowly back to the ranch. His wife had seen him coming, and met him as he drew up before the barn.

"Well?" she demanded.

"Emmie," he said as he got out of the buckboard, laying his arm across her shoulder, "Emmie, I guess we'll take up with Joe's offer. We'll go to Chicago. We're cleaned out!"

II. THE BULL—WHEAT AT A DOLLAR-TEN

. . . ——*and said Party of the Second Part further covenants and agrees to merchandise such wheat in foreign ports, it being understood and agreed between the Party of the First Part and the Party of the Second Part that the wheat hereinbefore mentioned is released and sold to the Party of the Second*

Part for export purposes only, and not for consumption or distribution within the boundaries of the United States of America or of Canada.

"Now, Mr. Gates, if you will sign for Mr. Truslow I guess that'll be all," remarked Hornung when he had finished reading.

Hornung affixed his signature to the two documents and passed them over to Gates, who signed for his principal and client, Truslow—or, as he had been called ever since he had gone into the fight against Hornung's corner— the Great Bear. Hornung's secretary was called in and witnessed the signatures, and Gates thrust the contract into his Gladstone bag and stood up, smoothing his hat.

"You will deliver the warehouse receipts for the grain," began Gates.

"I'll send a messenger to Truslow's office before noon," interrupted Hornung. "You can pay by certified check through the Illinois Trust people."

When the other had taken himself off, Hornung sat for some moments gazing abstractedly toward his office windows, thinking over the whole matter. He had just agreed to release to Truslow, at the rate of one dollar and ten cents per bushel, one hundred thousand out of the two million and odd bushels of wheat that he, Hornung, controlled, or actually owned. And for the moment he was wondering if, after all, he had done wisely in not goring the Great Bear to actual financial death. He had made him pay one hundred thousand dollars. Truslow was good for this amount. Would it not have been better to have put a prohibitive figure on the grain and forced the bear into bankruptcy? True, Hornung would then be without his enemy's money, but Truslow would have been eliminated from the situation, and that—so Hornung told himself—was always a consummation most devoutly, strenuously, and diligently to be striven for. Truslow once dead was dead, but the Bear was never more dangerous than when desperate.

"But so long as he can't get *wheat*," muttered Hornung at the end of his reflections, "he can't hurt me. And he can't get it. That I *know*."

For Hornung controlled the situation. So far back as the February of that year an "unknown bull" had been making his presence felt on the floor of the Board of Trade. By the middle of March the commercial reports of the daily press had begun to speak of "the powerful bull clique"; a few weeks later that legendary condition of affairs implied and epitomized in the magic words "Dollar Wheat" had been attained, and by the first of April, when the price had been boosted to one dollar and ten cents a bushel, Hornung had disclosed his hand, and in place of mere rumours, the definite and authoritative news that May wheat had been cornered in the Chicago pit went flashing around the world from Liverpool to Odessa and from Duluth to Buenos Ayres.

It was—so the veteran operators were persuaded—Truslow himself who had made Hornung's corner possible. The Great Bear had for once overreached himself, and, believing himself all-powerful, had hammered the price just the fatal fraction too far down. Wheat had gone to sixty-two—for the time, and under the circumstances, an abnormal price. When the reaction came it was tremendous. Hornung saw his chance, seized it, and in a few months had turned the tables, had cornered the product, and virtually driven the bear clique out of the pit.

On the same day that the delivery of the hundred thousand bushels was made to Truslow, Hornung met his broker at his lunch club.

"Well," said the latter, "I see you let go that line of stuff to Truslow."

Hornung nodded; but the broker added:

"Remember, I was against it from the very beginning. I know we've cleared up over a hundred thou'. I would have fifty times preferred to have lost twice that and *smashed Truslow dead*. Bet you what you like he makes · us pay for it somehow."

"Huh!" grunted his principal. "How about insurance, and warehouse charges, and carrying expenses on that lot? Guess we'd have had to pay those, too, if we'd held on."

But the other put up his chin, unwilling to be persuaded. "I won't sleep easy," he declared, "till Truslow is busted."

III. THE PIT[5]

Just as Going mounted the steps on the edge of the pit the great gong struck, a roar of a hundred voices developed with the swiftness of successive explosions, the rush of a hundred men surging downward to the centre of the pit filled the air with the stamp and grind of feet, a hundred hands in eager, strenuous gestures tossed upward from out the brown of the crowd, the official reporter in his cage on the margin of the pit leaned far forward with straining ear to catch the opening bid, and another day of battle was begun.

Since the sale of the hundred thousand bushels of wheat to Truslow the "Hornung crowd" had steadily shouldered the price higher until on this particular morning it stood at one dollar and a half. That was Hornung's price. No one else had any grain to sell.

But not ten minutes after the opening, Going was surprised out of all countenance to hear shouted from the other side of the pit these words: "Sell May at one-fifty."

Going was for the moment touching elbows with Kimbark on one side and with Merriam on the other, all three belonging to the "Hornung crowd." Their answering challenge of "*Sold*" was as the voice of one man. They did not pause to reflect upon the strangeness of the circumstance. (That was for afterward.) Their response to the offer was as unconscious as reflex action and almost as rapid, and before the pit was well aware of what had happened the transaction of one thousand bushels was down upon Going's trad-

[5] The space where the actual trading takes place.

ing-card and fifteen hundred dollars had changed hands. But here was a marvel—the whole available supply of wheat cornered, Hornung master of the situation, invincible, unassailable; yet behold a man willing to sell, a bear bold enough to raise his head.

"That was Kennedy, wasn't it, who made that offer?" asked Kimbark, as Going noted down the trade—"Kennedy, that new man?"

"Yes; who do you suppose he's selling for; who's willing to go short at this stage of the game?"

"Maybe he ain't short."

"Short! Great heavens, man; where'd he get the stuff?"

"Blamed if I know. We can account for every handful of May. Steady! Oh, there he goes again."

"Sell a thousand May at one-fifty," vociferated the bear-broker, throwing out his hand, one finger raised to indicate the number of "contracts" offered. This time it was evident that he was attacking the Hornung crowd deliberately, for, ignoring the jam of traders that swept toward him, he looked across the pit to where Going and Kimbark were shouting "*Sold! Sold!*" and nodded his head.

A second time Going made memoranda of the trade, and either the Hornung holdings were increased by two thousand bushels of May wheat or the Hornung bank account swelled by at least three thousand dollars of some unknown short's money.

Of late—so sure was the bull crowd of its position—no one had even thought of glancing at the inspection sheet on the bulletin board. But now one of Going's messengers hurried up to him with the announcement that this sheet showed receipts at Chicago for that morning of twenty-five thousand bushels, and not credited to Hornung. Someone had got hold of a line of wheat overlooked by the "clique" and was dumping it upon them.

"Wire the Chief," said Going over his shoulder to Merriam. This one struggled out of the crowd, and on a telegraph blank scribbled:

"Strong bear movement—New man—Kennedy—Selling in lots of five contracts—Chicago receipts twenty-five thousand."

The message was despatched, and in a few moments the answer came back, laconic, of military terseness:

"Support the market."

And Going obeyed, Merriam and Kimbark following, the new broker fairly throwing the wheat at them in thousand-bushel lots.

"Sell May at 'fifty; sell May; sell May." A moment's indecision, an instant's hesitation, the first faint suggestion of weakness, and the market would have broken under them. But for the better part of four hours they stood their ground, taking all that was offered, in constant communication with the Chief, and from time to time stimulated and steadied by his brief, unvarying command:

"Support the market."

At the close of the session they had bought in the twenty-five thousand bushels of May. Hornung's position was as stable as a rock, and the price closed even with the opening figure—one dollar and a half.

But the morning's work was the talk of all La Salle Street. Who was back of the raid? What was the meaning of this unexpected selling? For weeks the pit trading had been merely nominal. Truslow, the Great Bear, from whom the most serious attack might have been expected, had gone to his country seat at Geneva Lake, in Wisconsin, declaring himself to be out of the market entirely. He went bass-fishing every day.

IV. THE BELT LINE

On a certain day toward the middle of the month, at a time when the mysterious Bear had unloaded some eighty thousand bushels upon Hornung, a conference was held in the library of Hornung's home. His broker attended it, and also a clean-faced, bright-eyed individual whose name of Cyrus Ryder might have been found upon the pay-roll of a rather well-known detective agency. For upward of half an hour after the conference began the detective spoke, the other two listening attentively, gravely.

"Then, last of all," concluded Ryder, "I made out I was a hobo, and began stealing rides on the Belt Line Railroad. Know the road? It just circles Chicago. Truslow owns it. Yes? Well, then I began to catch on. I noticed that cars of certain numbers—thirty-one nought thirty-four, thirty-two one ninety—well, the numbers don't matter, but anyhow, these cars were always switched onto the sidings by Mr. Truslow's main elevator D soon as they came in. The wheat was shunted in, and they were pulled out again. Well, I spotted one car and stole a ride on her. Say, look here, *that car went right around the City on the Belt, and came back to D again, and the same wheat in her all the time.* The grain was reinspected—it was raw, I tell you—and the warehouse receipts made out just as though the stuff had come in from Kansas or Iowa."

"The same wheat all the time!" interrupted Hornung.

"The same wheat—your wheat, that you sold to Truslow."

"Great snakes!" ejaculated Hornung's broker: "Truslow never took it abroad at all."

"Took it abroad! Say, he's just been running it around Chicago, like the supers in 'Shenandoah,'[6] round an' round, so you'd think it was a new lot, an' selling it back to you again."

---

[6] The extras in the Civil War play, "Shenandoah" (1888) marched in a circle on the stage to make it appear that a great Army was present.

istration, which was to make the national domain the inexhaustible fund for progressive and unceasing internal improvement, has failed." The reason is obvious: a system of administration was not what the West demanded; it wanted land. Adams states the situation as follows: "The slaveholders of the South have bought the cooperation of the western country by the bribe of the western lands, abandoning to the new Western States their own proportion of the public property and aiding them in the design of grasping all the lands into their own hands. Thomas H. Benton was the author of this system, which he brought forward as a substitute for the American system of Mr. Clay, and to supplant him as the leading statesman of the West. Mr. Clay, by his tariff compromise with Mr. Calhoun, abandoned his own American system. At the same time he brought forward a plan for distributing among all the States of the Union the proceeds of the sales of the public lands. His bill for that purpose passed both Houses of Congress, but was vetoed by President Jackson, who, in his annual message of December, 1832, formally recommended that all public lands should be gratuitously given away to individual adventurers and to the States in which the lands are situated."

"No subject," said Henry Clay, "which has presented itself to the present, or perhaps any preceding Congress, is of greater magnitude than that of the public lands." When we consider the far-reaching effects of the government's land policy upon political, economic, and social aspects of American life, we are disposed to agree with him. But this legislation was framed under frontier influences, and under the lead of Western statesmen like Benton and Jackson. Said Senator Scott of Indiana in 1841: "I consider the preemption law merely declaratory of the custom or common law of the settlers."

It is safe to say that the legislation with regard to land, tariff, and internal improvements—the American system of the nationalizing Whig party—was conditioned on frontier ideas and needs. But it was not merely in legislative action that the frontier worked against the sectionalism of the coast. The economic and social characteristics of the frontier worked against sectionalism. The men of the frontier had closer resemblances to the Middle region than to either of the other sections. Pennsylvania had been the seed-plot of frontier emigration, and although she passed on her settlers along the Great Valley into the west of Virginia and the Carolinas, yet the industrial society of these Southern frontiersmen was always more like that of the Middle region than like that of the tide-water portion of the South, which later came to spread its industrial type throughout the South.

The Middle region, entered by New York harbor, was an open door to all Europe. The tide-water part of the South represented typical Englishmen, modified by a warm climate and servile labor, and living in baronial fashion on great plantations; New England stood for a special English movement—Puritanism. The Middle region was less English than the other sections. It had a wide mixture of nationalities, a varied society, the mixed town and county system of local government, a varied economic life, many religious sects. In short, it was a region mediating between New England and the South, and the East and the West. It represented that composite nationality which the contemporary United States exhibits, that juxtaposition of non-English groups, occupying a valley or a little settlement, and presenting reflections of the map of Europe in their variety. It was democratic and non-sectional, if not national; "easy, tolerant, and contented"; rooted strongly in material property. It was typical of the modern United States. It was least sectional, not only because it lay between North and South, but also because with no barriers to shut out its frontiers from its settled region, and with a system of connecting waterways, the Middle region mediated between East and West as well as between North and South. Thus it became the typically American region. Even the New Englander, who was shut out from the frontier by the Middle region, tarrying in New York or Pennsylvania on his westward march, lost the acuteness of his sectionalism on the way.

The spread of cotton culture into the interior of the South finally broke down the contrast between the "tide-water" region and the rest of the State, and based Southern interests on slavery. Before this process revealed its results the western portion of the South, which was akin to Pennsylvania in stock, society, and industry, showed tendencies to fall away from the faith of the fathers into internal improvement legislation and nationalism. In the Virginia convention of 1829–30, called to revise the constitution, Mr. Leigh, of Chesterfield, one of the tide-water counties, declared:

> One of the main causes of discontent which led to this convention, that which had the strongest influence in overcoming our veneration for the work of our fathers, which taught us to contemn the sentiments of Henry and Mason and Pendleton, which weaned us from our reverence for the constituted authorities of the State, was an overweening passion for internal improvement. I say this with perfect knowledge, for it has been avowed to me by gentlemen from the West over and over again. And let me tell the gentleman from Albemarle (Mr. Gordon) that it has been another principal object of those who set this ball of revolution in motion, to overturn the doctrine of State rights, of which Virginia has been the very pillar, and to remove the barrier she has interposed to the interference of the Federal Government in that same work of internal improvement, by so reorganizing the legislature that Virginia, too, may he hitched to the Federal car.

It was this nationalizing tendency of the West that transformed the democracy of Jefferson into the national republicanism of Monroe and the democracy of Andrew Jackson. The West of the War of 1812, the West of Clay, and Benton and Harrison, and Andrew Jackson, shut off by the Middle States and the mountains from the coast sections, had a solidarity of its own with national tendencies. On the tide of the Father of Waters, North and South met and mingled into a nation. Interstate migration went steadily on—a process of cross-fertilization of ideas and institutions. The fierce struggle of the sections over slavery on the western frontier does not diminish the truth of this statement; it proves the truth of it. Slavery was a sectional trait that would not down, but in the West it could not remain sectional. It was the greatest of frontiersmen who declared: "I believe this Government can not endure permanently half slave and half free. It will become all of one thing or all of the other."[12] Nothing works for nationalism like intercourse within the nation. Mobility of population is death to localism, and the western frontier worked irresistibly in unsettling population. The effect reached back from the frontier and affected profoundly the Atlantic coast and even the Old World.

But the most important effect of the frontier has been in the promotion of democracy here and in Europe. As has been indicated, the frontier is productive of individualism. Complex society is precipitated by the wilderness into a kind of primitive organization based on the family. The tendency is anti-social. It produces antipathy to control, and particularly to any direct control. The tax-gatherer is viewed as a representative of oppression. Prof. Osgood, in an able article, has pointed out that the frontier conditions prevalent in the colonies are important factors in the explanation of the American Revolution, where individual liberty was sometimes confused with absence of all effective government. The same conditions aid in explaining the difficulty of instituting a strong government in the period of the confederacy. The frontier individualism has from the beginning promoted democracy.

The frontier States that came into the Union in the first quarter of a century of its existence came in with democratic suffrage provisions, and had reactive effects of the highest importance upon the older States whose peoples were being attracted there. An extension of the franchise became essential. It was *western* New York that forced an extension of suffrage in the constitutional convention of that State in 1821; and it was *western* Virginia that compelled the tide-water region to put a more liberal suffrage provision in the constitution framed in 1830, and to give to the frontier region a more nearly proportionate representation with the tide-water aristocracy. The rise of democracy as an effective force in the nation came in with western preponderance under Jackson and William Henry Harrison, and it meant the triumph of the frontier—with all of its good and with all of its evil elements. An interesting illustration of the tone of frontier democracy in 1830 comes from the same debates in the Virginia convention already referred to. A representative from western Virginia declared:

> But, sir, it is not the increase of population in the West which this gentleman ought to fear. It is the energy which the mountain breeze and western habits impart to those emigrants. They are regenerated,

[12] Lincoln.

politically I mean, sir. They soon become *working politicians;* and the difference, sir, between a *talking* and a *working* politician is immense. The Old Dominion has long been celebrated for producing great orators; the ablest metaphysicians in policy; men that can split hairs in all abstruse questions of political economy. But at home, or when they return from Congress, they have negroes to fan them asleep. But a Pennsylvania, a New York, an Ohio, or a western Virginia statesman, though far inferior in logic, metaphysics, and rhetoric to an old Virginia statesman, has this advantage, that when he returns home he takes off his coat and takes hold of the plow. This gives him bone and muscle, sir, and preserves his republican principles pure and uncontaminated.

So long as free land exists, the opportunity for a competency exists, and economic power secures political power. But the democracy born of free land, strong in selfishness and individualism, intolerant of administrative experience and education, and pressing individual liberty beyond its proper bounds, has its dangers as well as its benefits. Individualism in America has allowed a laxity in regard to governmental affairs which has rendered possible the spoils system and all the manifest evils that follow from the lack of a highly developed civic spirit. In this connection may be noted also the influence of frontier conditions in permitting lax business honor, inflated paper currency and wild-cat banking. The colonial and revolutionary frontier was the region whence emanated many of the worst forms of an evil currency. The West in the War of 1812 repeated the phenomenon on the frontier of that day, while the speculation and wild-cat banking of the period of the crisis of 1837 occurred on the new frontier belt of the next tier of States. Thus each one of the periods of lax financial integrity coincides with periods when a new set of frontier communities had arisen, and coincides in area with these successive frontiers, for the most part. The recent Populist agitation is a case in point. Many a State that now declines any connection with the tenets of the Populists,[13] itself adhered to such ideas in an earlier stage of the development of the State. A primitive society can hardly be expected to show the intelligent appreciation of the complexity of business interests in a developed society. The continual recurrence of these areas of paper-money agitation is another evidence that the frontier can be isolated and studied as a factor in American history of the highest importance.

The East has always feared the result of an unregulated advance of the frontier, and has tried to check and guide it. The English authorities would have checked settlement at the headwaters of the Atlantic tributaries and allowed the "savages to enjoy their deserts in quiet lest the peltry trade should decrease." This called out Burke's[14] splendid protest:

---

[13] Also called the "People's Party." A political organization formed in the United States in 1891 with a platform calling for an increase in currency, free silver, public control of the railroads, an income tax, and land ownership limitations.

[14] Edmund Burke (1782–1858) a British orator, writer, and statesman.

If you stopped your grants, what would be the consequence? The people would occupy without grants. They have already so occupied in many places. You can not station garrisons in every part of these deserts. If you drive the people from one place, they will carry on their annual tillage and remove with their flocks and herds to another. Many of the people in the back settlements are already little attached to particular situations. Already they have topped the Appalachian Mountains. From thence they behold before them an immense plain, one vast, rich level meadow; a square of five hundred miles. Over this they would wander without a possibility of restraint; they would change their manners with their habits of life; would soon forget a government by which they were disowned; would become hordes of English Tartars; and pouring down upon your unfortified frontiers a fierce and irresistible cavalry, become masters of your governors and your counselers, your collectors and comptrollers, and of all the slaves that adhered to them. Such would, and in no long time must, be the effect of attempting to forbid as a crime and to suppress as an evil the command and blessing of Providence, "Increase and multiply." Such would be the happy result of an endeavor to keep as a lair of wild beasts that earth which God, by an express charter, has given to the children of men.

But the English Government was not alone in its desire to limit the advance of the frontier and guide its destinies. Tide-water Virginia and South Carolina gerrymandered those colonies to insure the dominance of the coast in their legislatures. Washington desired to settle a State at a time in the Northwest; Jefferson would reserve from settlement the territory of his Louisiana Purchase north of the thirty-second parallel, in order to offer it to the Indians in exchange for their settlements east of the Mississippi. "When we shall be full on this side," he writes, "we may lay off a range of States on the western bank from the head to the mouth, and so range after range, advancing compactly as we multiply." Madison went so far as to argue to the French minister that the United States had no interest in seeing population extend itself on the right bank of the Mississippi, but should rather fear it. When the Oregon question was under debate, in 1824, Smyth, of Virginia, would draw an unchangeable line for the limits of the United States at the outer limit of two tiers of States beyond the Mississippi, complaining that the seaboard States were being drained of the flower of their population by the bringing of too much land into market. Even Thomas Benton,[15] the man of widest views of the destiny of the West, at this stage of his career declared that along the ridge of the Rocky Mountains "the western limits of the Republic should be

---

[15] Thomas Hart Benton (1782-1858) was a senator who long championed the cause of settlement of the West.

drawn, and the statue of the fabled god Terminus should be raised upon its highest peak, never to be thrown down." But the attempts to limit the boundaries, to restrict land sales and settlement, and to deprive the West of its share of political power were all in vain. Steadily the frontier of settlement advanced and carried with it individualism, democracy, and nationalism, and powerfully affected the East and the Old World.

The most effective efforts of the East to regulate the frontier came through its educational and religious activity, exerted by interstate migration and by organized societies. Speaking in 1835, Dr. Lyman Beecher[16] declared: "It is equally plain that the religious and political destiny of our nation is to be decided in the West," and he pointed out that the population of the West "is assembled from all the States of the Union and from all the nations of Europe, and is rushing in like the waters of the flood, demanding for its moral preservation the immediate and universal action of those institutions which discipline the mind and arm the conscience and the heart. And so various are the opinions and habits, and so recent and imperfect is the acquaintance, and so sparse are the settlements of the West, that no homogeneous public sentiment can be formed to legislate immediately into being the requisite institutions. And yet they are all needed immediately in their utmost perfection and power. A nation is being 'born in a day'. . . . But what will become of the West if her prosperity rushes up to such a majesty of power, while those great institutions linger which are necessary to form the mind and the conscience and the heart of that vast world? It must not be permitted. . . . Let no man at the East quiet himself and dream of liberty, whatever may become of the West. . . . Her destiny is our destiny."

With the appeal to the conscience of New England, he adds appeals to her fears lest other religious sects anticipate her own. The New England preacher and school-teacher left their mark on the West. The dread of Western emancipation from New England's political and economic control was paralleled by her fears lest the West cut loose from her religion. Commenting in 1850 on reports that settlement was rapidly extending northward in Wisconsin, the editor of the *Home Missionary* writes: "We scarcely know whether to rejoice or mourn over this extension of our settlements. While we sympathize in whatever tends to increase the physical resources and prosperity of our country, we can not forget that with all these dispersions into remote and still remoter corners of the land the supply of the means of grace is becoming relatively less and less." Acting in accordance with such ideas, home missions were established and Western colleges were erected. As seaboard cities like Philadelphia, New York, and Baltimore strove for the mastery of Western trade, so the various denominations strove for the possession of the West. Thus an intellectual stream from New England sources fertil-

---

[16] Dr. Lyman Beecher (1775-1863) was a Presbyterian clergyman.

ized the West. Other sections sent their missionaries; but the real struggle was between sects. The contest for power and the expansive tendency furnished to the various sects by the existence of a moving frontier must have had important results on the character of religious organization in the United States. The multiplication of rival churches in the little frontier towns had deep and lasting social effects. The religious aspects of the frontier make a chapter in our history which needs study.

From the conditions of frontier life came intellectual traits of profound importance. The works of travelers along each frontier from colonial days onward describe certain common traits, and these traits have, while softening down, still persisted as survivals in the place of their origin, even when a higher social organization succeeded. The result is that to the frontier the American intellect owes its striking characteristics. That coarseness and strength combined with acuteness and inquisitiveness; that practical, inventive turn of mind, quick to find expedients; that masterful grasp of material things, lacking in the artistic but powerful to effect great ends; that restless, nervous energy; that dominant individualism, working for good and for evil, and withal that buoyancy and exuberance which comes with freedom—these are traits of the frontier, or traits called out elsewhere because of the existence of the frontier. Since the days when the fleet of Columbus sailed into the waters of the New World, America has been another name for opportunity, and the people of the United States have taken their tone from the incessant expansion which has not only been open but has even been forced upon them. He would be a rash prophet who should assert that the expansive character of American life has now entirely ceased. Movement has been its dominant fact, and, unless this training has no effect upon a people, the American energy will continually demand a wider field for its exercise. But never again will such gifts of free land offer themselves. For a moment, at the frontier, the bonds of custom are broken and unrestraint is triumphant. There is not *tabula rasa*. The stubborn American environment is there with its imperious summons to accept its conditions; the inherited ways of doing things are also there; and yet, in spite of environment, and in spite of custom each frontier did indeed furnish a new field of opportunity, a gate of escape from the bondage of the past; and freshness, and confidence, and scorn of olden society, impatience of its restraints and its ideas, and indifference to its lessons have accompanied the frontier. What the Mediterranean Sea was to the Greeks breaking the bond of custom, offering new experiences, calling out new institutions and activities, that, and more, the ever retreating frontier has been to the United States directly, and to the nations of Europe more remotely. And now, four centuries from the discovery of America, at the end of a hundred years of life under the Constitution, the frontier has gone, and with its going has closed the first period of American history.

HENRY ADAMS

(1838-1918)

Historian, journalist, editor, teacher, and man of letters, Henry Adams touched at many points the significant cultural and political realities of his day. He was throughout a sensitive and creative historian, registering the profound changes in form and substance in modern American life. In his best-known work, *The Education of Henry Adams* (1907), he makes of his own restless career a model of historical experience, a way of testing his culture by examining his education, but formal and "accidental," against the needs of an age dominated by industrial capitalism. It is a book of ironic reflection and gloomy prediction about the progressive loss of control over events he perceived in American political, economic, social, and intellectual life.

Adams was born into a family of patrician rulers, the makers of history. Great-grandson and grandson of presidents (John and John Quincy Adams), son of Charles Francis Adams, famed as ambassador to England during the Civil War, it is no wonder that Henry Adams was plagued with the problem of choosing a vocation, particularly since, after the Civil War, national politics seemed less hospitable to the traditional conservative statesmanship of the Adams line. Educated at Harvard and in Germany, he began with expectations of a political career, accompanying his father in London as his secretary. While

The major works are *Democracy, an American Novel,* 1880: *Esther, A Novel,* 1884: *History of the United States During the Administrations of Jefferson and Madison,* 9 vols. 1889-1891, condensed by Herbert Agar as *The Formative Years,* 1947: *Mont Saint-Michel and Chartres,* 1904: *The Education of Henry Adams,* 1918: *The Degradation of Democratic Dogma,* 1919: *Travels in Tahiti,* ed. Robert Spiller, 1947.

Worthington C. Ford edited *A Cycle of Adams Letters, 1861-1865,* 2 vols. 1920, *Letters of Henry Adams, 1858-1891,* 1930, and *Letters of Henry Adams, 1892-1918,* 1938: Harold D. Cater edited *Henry Adams and His Friends,* 1947: Newton Arvin edited *The Selected Letters of Henry Adams,* 1951.

The definitive biography is by E. Samuels:

Young Henry Adams, 1948; *Henry Adams: The Middle Years, 1877-1891,* 1958: and *Henry Adams: The Major Phase,* 1964. See also James Truslow Adams, *Henry Adams,* 1933.

Studies include Robert. A. Hume, *Runaway Star: An Appreciation of Henry Adams,* 1951; W. H. Jordy, *Henry Adams: Scientific Historian,* 1952; Elizabeth Stevenson, *Henry Adams, A Biography,* 1955; J. C. Levenson, *The Mind and Art of Henry Adams,* 1958; George Hochfield, *Henry Adams, an Interpretation and Introduction,* 1962; Vern Wagner, *The Suspension of Henry Adams: A Study of Manners and Matter,* 1969, John Condor, *A Formula of His Own: Henry Adams Literary Experiment,* 1970; and Melvin Lyon, *Symbol and Idea in Henry Adams,* 1970.

there he contributed reviews and articles on historical and scientific subjects to journals; on his return to the United States in 1868 he gave up entirely the notion of a political career.

Adams left Washington again in 1870 to take a post teaching history at Harvard, at the same time serving as editor of the prestigious *North American Review.* He left both positions in 1877, to return to Washington and the companionship of a small number of political figures he respected, such as John Hay and Clarence King (both writers as well as government servants). Early in the 1880's he embarked on a major work in American history, and also wrote two novels: *Democracy* (1880), dealing with scandal, corruption, and romance in Washington, and *Esther* (1884), a novel of romance and ideas set in New York society. In 1885 his wife committed suicide, driving Adams into a despair that colors the rest of his work. He made a long trip to the Orient and returned to Washington to complete his magisterial *History of the United States During the Administrations of Jefferson and Madison* (nine volumes, 1889–1891). He continued to travel widely, studying medieval culture in Europe, and visiting the South Seas.

In these later years Adams was influenced in his thinking about history by developments in science and technology. He decided that history is governed by measurable forces, including human will. In "A Letter to American Teachers of History" (1910) he argues that history needs to be understood in light of the Second Law of Thermodynamics, which presupposes a universal tendency of energy to dissipate itself, to run down. He pointed out that the popular nineteenth-century belief in history as a movement toward an eventual perfection could not stand against a dynamic theory of history based on analogy to physics. Terms like acceleration, force, attraction, energy, and inertia became critical terms of historical explanation for him.

Adams's two masterpieces of his late years are both premised on such a theory of historical change. The first, *Mont St. Michel and Chartres* (1904), is subtitled "A Study of Thirteenth-Century Unity." The book is a wonderfully detailed account of the architecture, literature, and philosophy of the period from 1150 to 1250 in Western Europe, and concludes that the great cathedrals, the systematic philosophy of Aquinas, the romances and the courtly poetry all testify to the presence of a single unifying focal point for emotion, intellect, and technical skill. The governing image or force was the Virgin, who elicited love from her devotees and whose power converted love to an energy of extraordinary creativity. Adams wrote that the period was "the point of history when man held the highest idea of himself as a unit in a unified universe," and thus the period could serve to "measure motion" down to contemporary times.

The *Education* is a complementary work, a "study of twentieth-century multiplicity." As in the first book, Adams again places himself at the center, here speaking of himself in the third person, presenting himself as a kind of mannikin, as he explains his method in the preface, on which various educations are draped "in order to show the fit or misfit of the clothes." The theme here is failure: the personal failure of an offspring of presidents, and the larger failure of a society blind to its own sources of intellectual energy. Modern society is a "multiverse," typified by the externalizing energies of the dynamo, whose religious and moral qualities reveal themselves to Adams in contrast with the Virgin in the most familiar chapter of the book. As an autobiography the book is seriously deficient, leaving a gap between 1871 and 1892, years of great private strain and loss. And in its explicit political and social attitudes the work expresses often corrosively the bitterness of Adams's personal failures, generalized as the displacement of his class of educated, politically intelligent, and disinterested statesmen by a new breed of party bosses and hacks. But the book is unique in its intense, thorough self-consciousness of a mind seeing itself acted on by the vast forces of modern life: the coming of the railroad, the Civil War, steam power, electrical power, Darwinism, Marxism, the discovery of radium, and imperialism. A difficult reading experience, especially for readers unprepared for Adams's persistent irony, the book ranks high among American inventions in literature.

From History of the United States During the Jefferson and Madison Administrations

AMERICAN IDEALS[1]

Nearly every foreign traveller who visited the United States during these early years, carried away an impression sober if not sad. A thousand miles of desolate and dreary forest, broken here and there by settlements; along the sea-coast a few flourishing towns devoted to commerce; no arts, a provincial literature, a cancerous disease of negro slavery, and differences of political theory fortified within geographical lines,—what could be hoped for such a country except to repeat the story of violence and brutality which the world

---

[1] First published in *History of the United States during the Jefferson and Madison Administrations*.

already knew by heart, until repetition for thousands of years had wearied and sickened mankind? Ages must probably pass before the interior could be thoroughly settled; even Jefferson, usually a sanguine man, talked of a thousand years with acquiescence, and in his first Inaugural Address, at a time when the Mississippi River formed the Western boundary, spoke of the country as having "room enough for our descendants to the hundredth and thousandth generation." No prudent person dared to act on the certainty that when settled, one government could comprehend the whole; and when the day of separation should arrive, and America should have her Prussia, Austria, and Italy, as she already had her England, France, and Spain, what else could follow but a return to the old conditions of local jealousies, wars, and corruption which had made a slaughter-house of Europe?

The mass of Americans were sanguine and self-confident, partly by temperament, but partly also by reason of ignorance; for they knew little of the difficulties which surrounded a complex society. The Duc de Liancourt,[2] like many critics, was struck by this trait. Among other instances, he met with one in the person of a Pennsylvania miller, Thomas Lea, "a sound American patriot, persuading himself that nothing good is done, and that no one has any brains, except in America; that the wit, the imagination, the genius of Europe are already in decrepitude"; and the duke added: "This error is to be found in almost all Americans,—legislators, administrators, as well as millers, and is less innocent there." In the year 1796 the House of Representatives debated whether to insert in the Reply to the President's Speech a passing remark that the nation was "the freest and most enlightened in the world,"—a nation as yet in swaddling-clothes, which had neither literature, arts, sciences, nor history; nor even enough nationality to be sure that it was a nation. The moment was peculiarly ill-chosen for such a claim, because Europe was on the verge of an outburst of genius. Goethe and Schiller, Mozart and Haydn, Kant and Fichte, Cavendish and Herschel were making way for Walter Scott, Wordsworth, and Shelley, Heine and Balzac, Beethoven and Hegel, Oersted and Cuvier, great physicists, biologists, geologists, chemists, mathematicians, metaphysicians, and historians by the score. Turner was painting his earliest landscapes, and Watt completing his latest steam-engine; Napoleon was taking command of the French armies, and Nelson of the English fleets; investigators, reformers, scholars, and philosophers swarmed, and the influence of enlightenment, even amid universal war, was working with an energy such as the world had never before conceived. The idea that Europe was in her decrepitude proved only ignorance and want of enlightenment, if not of freedom, on the part of Americans who could only excuse their error by pleading that notwithstanding these objections, in matters which for the moment most concerned themselves Europe

---

[2] François de La Rochefoucauld-Liancourt (1747–1827), liberal French author of *Travels*   *Through the United States of America* (1799).

was a full century behind America. If they were right in thinking that the
next necessity of human progress was to lift the average man upon an intellectual and social level with the most favored, they stood at least three
generations nearer than Europe to their common goal. The destinies of the
United States were certainly staked, without reserve or escape, on the
soundness of this doubtful and even improbable principle, ignoring or overthrowing the institutions of church, aristocracy, family, army, and political
intervention, which long experience had shown to be needed for the safety
of society. Europe might be right in thinking that without such safeguards
society must come to an end; but even Europeans must concede that there
was a chance, if no greater than one in a thousand, that America might, at
least for a time, succeed. If this stake of temporal and eternal welfare stood
on the winning card; if man actually should become more virtuous and
enlightened, by mere process of growth, without church or paternal authority; if the average human being could accustom himself to reason with the
logical processes of Descartes and Newton!—what then?

Then, no one could deny that the United States would win a stake such as
defied mathematics. With all the advantages of science and capital, Europe
must be slower than America to reach the common goal. American society
might be both sober and sad, but except for negro slavery it was sound and
healthy in every part. Stripped for the hardest work, every muscle firm and
elastic, every ounce of brain ready for use, and not a trace of superfluous
flesh on his nervous and supple body, the American stood in the world a new
order of man. From Maine to Florida, society was in this respect the same,
and was so organized as to use its human forces with more economy than
could be approached by any society of the world elsewhere. Not only were
artificial barriers carefully removed, but every influence that could appeal to
ordinary ambition was applied. No brain or appetite active enough to be
conscious of stimulants could fail to answer the intense incentive. Few human beings, however sluggish, could long resist the temptation to acquire
power; and the elements of power were to be had in America almost for the
asking. Reversing the old-world system, the American stimulant increased in
energy as it reached the lowest and most ignorant class, dragging and whirling them upward as in the blast of a furnace. The penniless and homeless
Scotch or Irish immigrant was caught and consumed by it; for every stroke
of the axe and the hoe made him a capitalist, and made gentlemen of his
children. Wealth was the strongest agent for moving the mass of mankind;
but political power was hardly less tempting to the more intelligent and
better-educated swarms of American-born citizens, and the instinct of activity, once created, seemed heritable and permanent in the race.

Compared with this lithe young figure, Europe was actually in decrepitude. Mere class distinctions, the *patois* or dialect of the peasantry, the fixity
of residence, the local costumes and habits marking a history that lost itself
in the renewal of identical generations, raised from birth barriers which

paralyzed half the population. Upon this mass of inert matter rested the Church and the State, holding down activity of thought. Endless wars withdrew many hundred thousand men from production, and changed them into agents of waste; huge debts, the evidence of past wars and bad government, created interests to support the system and fix its burdens on the laboring class; courts, with habits of extravagance that shamed common-sense, helped to consume private economies. All this might have been borne; but behind this stood aristocracies, sucking their nourishment from industry, producing nothing themselves, employing little or no active capital or intelligent labor, but pressing on the energies and ambition of society with the weight of an incubus. Picturesque and entertaining as these social anomalies were, they were better fitted for the theatre or for a museum of historical costumes than for an active workshop preparing to compete with such machinery as America would soon command. From an economical point of view, they were as incongruous as would have been the appearance of a mediæval knight in helmet and armor, with battle-axe and shield, to run the machinery of Arkwright's[3] cotton-mill; but besides their bad economy they also tended to prevent the rest of society from gaining a knowledge of its own capacities. In Europe, the conservative habit of mind was fortified behind power. During nearly a century Voltaire[4] himself—the friend of kings, the wit and poet, historian and philosopher of his age—had carried on, in daily terror, in exile and excommunication, a protest against an intellectual despotism contemptible even to its own supporters. Hardly was Voltaire dead, when Priestley,[5] as great a man if not so great a wit, trying to do for England what Voltaire tried to do for France, was mobbed by the people of Birmingham and driven to America. Where Voltaire and Priestly failed, common men could not struggle; the weight of society stifled their thought. In America the balance between conservative and liberal forces was close; but in Europe conservatism held the physical power of government. In Boston a young Buckminster[6] might be checked for a time by his father's prayers or commands in entering that path that led toward freer thought; but youth beckoned him on, and every reward that society could offer was dangled before his eyes. In London or Paris, Rome, Madrid, or Vienna, he must have sacrificed the worldly prospects of his life.

Granting that the American people were about to risk their future on a new experiment, they naturally wished to throw aside all burdens of which they could rid themselves. Believing that in the long run interest, not violence, would rule the world, and that the United States must depend for

---

[3] Sir Richard Arkwright (1732-1792), an English cotton manufacturer who invented the spinning jenny.

[4] Francois Marie Arouet de Voltaire (1694-1778), French author.

[5] Joseph Priestly (1733-1804), an English scientist and theologian who discovered oxygen.

[6] Joseph Stevens Buckminster (1784-1812), a Unitarian clergyman who was a great preacher and scholar.

safety and success on the interests they could create, they were tempted to look upon war and preparations for war as the worst of blunders; for they were sure that every dollar capitalized in industry was a means of overthrowing their enemies more effective than a thousand dollars spent on frigates or standing armies. The success of the American system was, from this point of view, a question of economy. If they could relieve themselves from debts, taxes, armies, and government interference with industry, they must succeed in outstripping Europe in economy of production; and Americans were even then partly aware that if their machine were not so weakened by these economies as to break down in the working, it must of necessity break down every rival. If their theory was sound, when the day of competition should arrive, Europe might choose between American and Chinese institutions, but there would be no middle path; she might become a confederated democracy, or a wreck.

Whether these ideas were sound or weak, they seemed self-evident to those Northern democrats who, like Albert Gallatin[7] were comparatively free from slave-owning theories, and understood the practical forces of society. If Gallatin wished to reduce the interference of government to a minimum, and cut down expenditures to nothing, he aimed not so much at saving money as at using it with the most certain effect. The revolution of 1800 was in his eyes chiefly political, because it was social; but as a revolution of society, he and his friends hoped to make it the most radical that had occurred since the downfall of the Roman empire. Their ideas were not yet cleared by experience, and were confused by many contradictory prejudices, but wanted neither breadth nor shrewdness.

Many apparent inconsistencies grew from this undeveloped form of American thought, and gave rise to great confusion in the different estimates of American character that were made both at home and abroad.

That Americans should not be liked was natural; but that they should not be understood was more significant by far. After the downfall of the French republic they had no right to expect a kind word from Europe, and during the next twenty years they rarely received one. The liberal movement of Europe was cowed, and no one dared express democratic sympathies until the Napoleonic tempest had passed. With this attitude Americans had no right to find fault, for Europe cared less to injure them than to protect herself. Nevertheless, observant readers could not but feel surprised that none of the numerous Europeans who wrote or spoke about America seemed to study the subject seriously. The ordinary traveller was apt to be little more reflective than a bee or an ant, but some of these critics possessed powers far from ordinary; yet Talleyrand[8] alone showed that had he but

---

[7] Albert Gallatin (1701-1849), a financier, statesman, and diplomat who signed the treaty of peace with Britain at Ghent in 1814, and who was later minister to France.

[8] Talleyrand (1754-1838) a French statesman.

seen America a few years later than he did, he might have suggested some sufficient reason for apparent contradictions that perplexed him in the national character. The other travellers—great and small, from the Duc de Liancourt to Basil Hall,[9] a long and suggestive list—were equally perplexed. They agreed in observing the contradictions, but all, including Talleyrand, saw only sordid motives. Talleyrand expressed extreme astonishment at the apathy of Americans in the face of religious sectarians; but he explained it by assuming that the American ardor of the moment was absorbed in money-making. The explanation was evidently insufficient, for the Americans were capable of feeling and showing excitement, even to their great pecuniary injury, as they frequently proved; but in the foreigner's range of observation, love of money was the most conspicuous and most common trait, of American character. "There is, perhaps, no civilized country in the world," wrote Félix de Beaujour, soon after 1800, "where there is less generosity in the souls, and in the heads fewer of those illusions which make the charm or the consolation of life. Man here weighs everything, calculates everything, and sacrifices everything to his interest." An Englishman named Fearon, in 1818, expressed the same idea with more distinctness: "In going to America, I would say generally, the emigrant must expect to find, not an economical or cleanly people; not a social or generous people; not a people of enlarged ideas; not a people of liberal opinions, or toward whom you can express your thoughts free as air; not a people friendly to the advocates of liberty in Europe; not a people who understand liberty from investigation and principle; not a people who comprehend the meaning of the words 'honor' and 'generosity.' " Such quotations might be multiplied almost without limit. Rapacity was the accepted explanation of American peculiarities; yet every traveller was troubled by inconsistencies that required explanations of a different kind. "It is not in order to hoard that the Americans are rapacious," observed Liancourt as early as 1796. The extravagance, or what economical Europeans thought extravagance, with which American women were allowed and encouraged to spend money, was as notorious in 1790 as a century later; the recklessness with which Americans often risked their money, and the liberality with which they used it, were marked even then, in comparison with the ordinary European habit. Europeans saw such contradictions, but made no attempt to reconcile them. No foreigner of that day—neither poet, painter, nor philosopher—could detect in American life anything higher than vulgarity; for it was something beyond the range of their experience, which education and culture had not framed a formula to express. Moore[10] came to Washington, and found there no loftier inspiration than any Federalist rhymester of Dennie's[11] school.

[9] Basil Hall (1788-1844) a British naval officer who wrote a three-volume *Travel in North America* (1829), which incensed Americans because of its disdain for the new country.

[10] Thomas Moore (1779-1852), an Irish poet.

[11] Joseph Dennie (1768-1812), an essayist, editor, and pioneer American man of letters.

"Take Christians, Mohawks, democrats and all,
From the rude wigwam to the congress hall,—
From man the savage, whether slaved or free,
To man the civilized, less tame than he:
T' is one dull chaos, one unfertile strife,
Betwixt half-polished and half-barbarous life;
Where every ill the ancient world can brew
Is mixed with every grossness of the new;
Where all corrupts, though little can entice,
And nothing 's known of luxury but vice."

Moore's two small volumes of Epistles, printed in 1807, contained much more so-called poetry of the same tone,—poetry more polished and less respectable than that of Barlow and Dwight;[12] while, as though to prove that the Old World knew what grossness was, he embalmed in his lines the slanders which the Scotch libeller Callender[13] invented against Jefferson:—

"The weary statesman for repose hath fled
From halls of council to his negro's shed;
Where, blest, he woos some black Aspasia's grace;
And dreams of freedom in his slave's embrace."

To leave no doubt of his meaning, he explained in a footnote that his allusion was to the President of the United States; and yet even Moore, trifler and butterfly as he was, must have seen, if he would, that between the morals of politics and society in America and those then prevailing in Europe, there was no room for comparison,—there was room only for contrast.

Moore was but an echo of fashionable England in his day. He seldom affected moral sublimity; and had he in his wanderings met a race of embodied angels, he would have sung of them or to them in the slightly erotic notes which were so well received in the society he loved to frequent and flatter. His remarks upon American character betrayed more temper than truth; but even in this respect he expressed only the common feeling of Europeans, which was echoed by the Federalist society of the United States. Englishmen especially indulged in unbounded invective against the sordid character of American society, and in shaping their national policy on this contempt they

[12] Joel Barlow (1754-1812), one of the "Connecticut Wits," a political thinker, and an American epic poet. Barlow wrote "The Columbiad" in 1807 to celebrate the glories of the new country. Timothy Dwight (1752-1817) was the author of the first epic poem to appear in America, "The Conquest of Canaan" (1785). He was another of the "Con-

necticut Wits" and wrote satiric verse as well. He was President of Yale College from 1795 to his death.

[13] James Callender (1758-1803) was a political writer at first patronized by Thomas Jefferson, whom he treated viciously. He was the author of *History of the United States for 1796* (1797) and other tracts.

carried their theory into practice with so much energy as to produce its own refutation. To their astonishment and anger, a day came when the Americans, in defiance of self-interest and in contradiction of all the qualities ascribed to them, insisted on declaring war; and readers of this narrative will be surprised at the cry of incredulity, not unmixed with terror, with which Englishmen started to their feet when they woke from their delusion on seeing what they had been taught to call the meteor flag of England, which had burned terrific at Copenhagen and Trafalgar, suddenly waver and fall on the bloody deck of the "Guerriere." Fearon and Beaujour, with a score of other contemporary critics, could see neither generosity, economy, honor, nor ideas of any kind in the American breast; yet the obstinate repetition of these denials itself betrayed a lurking fear of the social forces whose strength they were candid enough to record. What was it that, as they complained, turned the European peasant into a new man within half an hour after landing at New York? Englishmen were never at a loss to understand the poetry of more prosaic emotions. Neither they nor any of their kindred failed in later times to feel the "large excitement" of the country boy, whose "spirit leaped within him to be gone before him," when the lights of London first flared in the distance; yet none seemed ever to feel the larger excitement of the American immigrant. Among the Englishmen who criticised the United States was one greater than Moore,—one who thought himself at home only in the stern beauty of a moral presence. Of all poets, living or dead, Wordsworth felt most keenly what he called the still, sad music of humanity; yet the highest conception he could create of America was not more poetical than that of any Cumberland beggar he might have met in his morning walk:—

> "Long-wished-for sight, the Western World appeared;
> And when the ship was moored, I leaped ashore
> Indignantly,—resolved to be a man,
> Who, having o'er the past no power, would live
> No longer in subjection to the past,
> With abject mind—from a tyrannic lord
> Inviting penance, fruitlessly endured.
> So, like a fugitive whose feet have cleared
> Some boundary which his followers may not cross
> In prosecution of their deadly chase,
> Respiring, I looked round. How bright the sun,
> The breeze how soft! Can anything produced
> In the Old World compare, thought I, for power
> And majesty, with this tremendous stream
> Sprung from the desert? And behold a city
> Fresh, youthful, and aspiring! . . .
>   Sooth to say,

On nearer view, a motley spectacle
Appeared, of high pretensions—unreproved
But by the obstreperous voice of higher still;
Big passions strutting on a petty stage,
Which a detached spectator may regard
Not unamused. But ridicule demands
Quick change of objects; and to laugh alone,
. . . in the very centre of the crowd
To keep the secret of a poignant scorn,
           . . . is least fit
For the gross spirit of mankind."

Thus Wordsworth, although then at his prime, indulging in what sounded like a boast that he alone had felt the sense sublime of something interfused, whose dwelling is the light of setting suns, and the round ocean, and the living air, and the blue sky, and in the mind of man,—even he, to whose moods the heavy and the weary weight of all this unintelligible world was lightened by his deeper sympathies with nature and the soul, could do no better, when he stood in the face of American democracy, than "keep the secret of a poignant scorn."

Possibly the view of Wordsworth and Moore, of Weld,[14] Dennie, and Dickens[15] was right. The American democrat possessed little art of expression, and did not watch his own emotions with a view of uttering them either in prose or verse; he never told more of himself than the world might have assumed without listening to him. Only with diffidence could history attribute to such a class of men a wider range of thought or feeling than they themselves cared to proclaim. Yet the difficulty of denying or even ignoring the wider range was still greater, for no one questioned the force or the scope of an emotion which caused the poorest peasant in Europe to see what was invisible to poet and philosopher,—the dim outline of a mountain-summit across the ocean, rising high above the mist and mud of American democracy. As though to call attention to some such difficulty, European and American critics, while affirming that Americans were a race without illusions or enlarged ideas, declared in the same breath that Jefferson was a visionary whose theories would cause the heavens to fall upon them. Year after year, with endless iteration, in every accent of contempt, rage, and despair, they repeated this charge against Jefferson. Every foreigner and Federalist agreed that he was a man of illusions, dangerous to society and unbounded in power of evil; but if this view of his character was right, the

[14] Theodore Dwight Weld (1803–1895), an abolitionist who had high hopes for his country and great personal modesty.

[15] Charles Dickens (1812–1870) English novelist who described his first tour of America in *American Notes* (1842) and *Martin Chuzzlewit* (1843–4).

same visionary qualities seemed also to be a national trait, for every one admitted that Jefferson's opinions, in one form or another, were shared by a majority of the American people.

Illustrations might be carried much further, and might be drawn from every social class and from every period in national history. Of all presidents, Abraham Lincoln has been considered the most typical representative of American society, chiefly because his mind, with all its practical qualities, also inclined, in certain directions, to idealism. Lincoln was born in 1809, the moment when American character stood in lowest esteem. Ralph Waldo Emerson, a more distinct idealist, was born in 1803. William Ellery Channing, another idealist, was born in 1780. Men like John Fitch, Oliver Evans, Robert Fulton, Joel Barlow, John Stevens, and Eli Whitney[16] were all classed among visionaries. The whole society of Quakers belonged in the same category. The records of the popular religious sects abounded in examples of idealism and illusion to such an extent that the masses seemed hardly to find comfort or hope in any authority, however old or well established. In religion as in politics, Americans seemed to require a system which gave play to their imagination and their hopes.

Some misunderstanding must always take place when the observer is at cross-purposes with the society he describes. Wordsworth might have convinced himself by a moment's thought that no country could act on the imagination as America acted upon the instincts of the ignorant and poor, without some quality that deserved better treatment than poignant scorn; but perhaps this was only one among innumerable cases in which the unconscious poet breathed an atmosphere which the self-conscious poet could not penetrate. With equal reason he might have taken the opposite view,—that the hard, practical, money-getting American democrat, who had neither generosity nor honor nor imagination, and who inhabited cold shades where fancy sickened and where genius died, was in truth living in a world of dream, and acting a drama more instinct with poetry than all the avators of the East, walking in gardens of emerald and rubies, in ambition already ruling the world and guiding Nature with a kinder and wiser hand than had ever yet been felt in human history. From this point his critics never ap-

[16] Ralph Waldo Emerson (1803-1882) was a world-famous essayist, poet, lecturer, and founder of the American transcendentalist movement. See p.840 William Ellery Channing (1780-1842) was one of the first Unitarian clergymen, and an abolitionist and a pacifist. See p.1561.John Fitch (1743-1798) was a metal craftsman, inventor, and a developer of the passenger steamboat. Oliver Evans (1755-1819) was an inventor and the first steam-engine builder in America. Robert Fulton (1765-1815) was an artist, civil engi-neer, inventor, and the builder of one of the first successful steamboats, the "Clermont," although not the inventor of the steamboat, as is commonly thought. John Stevens (1749-1838) was an engineer and inventor in the steamboat field. He also built the first American steam locomotive. Eli Whitney (1765-1825) invented the cotton gin and mass produced precision guns with interchangeable parts (his idea) in his factory in New Haven, Connecticut.

proached him,—they stopped at a stone's throw; and at the moment when they declared that the man's mind had no illusions, they added that he was a knave or a lunatic. Even on his practical and sordid side, the American might easily have been represented as a victim to illusion. If the Englishman had lived as the American speculator did,—in the future,—the hyperbole of enthusiasm would have seemed less monstrous. "Look at my wealth!" cried the American to his foreign visitor. "See these solid mountains of salt and iron, of lead, copper, silver, and gold! See these magnificent cities scattered broadcast to the Pacific! See my cornfields rustling and waving in the summer breeze from ocean to ocean, so far that the sun itself is not high enough to mark where the distant mountains bound my golden seas! Look at this continent of mine, fairest of created worlds, as she lies turning up to the sun's never-failing caress her broad and exuberant breasts, overflowing with milk for her hundred million children! See how she glows with youth, health, and love!" Perhaps it was not altogether unnatural that the foreigner, on being asked to see what needed centuries to produce, should have looked about him with bewilderment and indignation. "Gold! cities! cornfields! continents! Nothing of the sort! I see nothing but tremendous wastes, where sickly men and women are dying of home-sickness or are scalped by savages! mountain-ranges a thousand miles long, with no means of getting to them, and nothing in them when you get there! swamps and forests choked with their own rotten ruins! nor hope of better for a thousand years! Your story is a fraud, and you are a liar and swindler!"

Met in this spirit, the American, half perplexed and half defiant, retaliated by calling his antagonist a fool, and by mimicking his heavy tricks of manner. For himself he cared little, but his dream was his whole existence. The men who denounced him admitted that they left him in his forest-swamp quaking with fever, but clinging in the delirium of death to the illusions of his dazzled brain. No class of men could be required to support their convictions with a steadier faith, or pay more devotedly with their persons for the mistakes of their judgment. Whether imagination or greed led them to describe more than actually existed, they still saw no more than any inventor or discoverer must have seen in order to give him the energy of success. They said to the rich as to the poor, "Come and share our limitless riches! Come and help us bring to light these unimaginable stores of wealth and power!" The poor came, and from them were seldom heard complaints of deception or delusion. Within a moment, by the mere contact of a moral atmosphere, they saw the gold and jewels, the summer cornfields and the glowing continent. The rich for a long time stood aloof,—they were timid and narrow-minded; but this was not all,—between them and the American democrat was a gulf.

The charge that Americans were too fond of money to win the confidence of Europeans was a curious inconsistency; yet this was a common belief. If the American deluded himself and led others to their death by baseless speculations; if he buried those he loved in a gloomy forest where they quaked and died while he persisted in seeing there a splendid, healthy, and well-built city,—no one could deny that he sacrificed wife and child to his greed for gain, that the dollar was his god, and a sordid avarice his demon. Yet had this been the whole truth, no European capitalist would have hesitated to make money out of his grave; for, avarice against avarice, no more sordid or meaner type existed in America than could be shown on every 'Change in Europe. With much more reason Americans might have suspected that in America Englishmen found everywhere a silent influence, which they found nowhere in Europe, and which had nothing to do with avarice or with the dollar, but, on the contrary, seemed likely at any moment to sacrifice the dollar in a cause and for an object so illusory that most Englishmen could not endure to hear it discussed. European travellers who passed through America noticed that everywhere, in the White House at Washington and in log-cabins beyond the Alleghenies, except for a few Federalists, every American, from Jefferson and Gallatin down to the poorest squatter, seemed to nourish an idea that he was doing what he could to overthrow the tyranny which the past had fastened on the human mind. Nothing was easier than to laugh at the ludicrous expressions of this simple-minded conviction, or to cry out against its coarseness, or grow angry with its prejudices; to see its nobler side, to feel the beatings of a heart underneath the sordid surface of a gross humanity, was not so easy. Europeans seemed seldom or never conscious that the sentiment could possess a noble side, but found only matter for complaint in the remark that every American democrat believed himself to be working for the overthrow of tyranny, aristocracy, hereditary privilege, and priesthood, wherever they existed. Even where the American did not openly proclaim this conviction in words, he carried so dense an atmosphere of the sentiment with him in his daily life as to give respectable Europeans an uneasy sense of remoteness.

Of all historical problems, the nature of a national character is the most difficult and the most important. Readers will be troubled, at almost every chapter of the coming narrative, [17] by the want of some formula to explain what share the popular imagination bore in the system pursued by government. The acts of the American people during the administrations of Jefferson and Madison were judged at the time by no other test. According as bystanders believed American character to be hard, sordid, and free from illusion, they were severe and even harsh in judgement. This rule guided the governments of England and France. Federalists in the United States, knowing more of the circumstances, often attributed to the democratic instinct a visionary quality which they regarded as sentimentality, and charged with many bad consequences. If their view was correct, history could occupy

[17] "The coming narrative" here refers to the complete work [from which these six chapters are excerpted.] (publisher's note).

itself to no better purpose than in ascertaining the nature and force of the quality which was charged with results so serious; but nothing was more elusive than the spirit of American democracy. Jefferson, the literary representative of the class, spoke chiefly for Virginians, and dreaded so greatly his own reputation as a visionary that he seldom or never uttered his whole thought. Gallatin and Madison were still more cautious. The press in no country could give shape to a mental condition so shadowy. The people themselves, although millions in number, could not have expressed their finer instincts had they tried, and might not have recognized them if expressed by others,

In the early days of colonization, every new settlement represented an idea and proclaimed a mission. Virginia was founded by a great, liberal movement aiming at the spread of English liberty and empire. The Pilgrims of Plymouth, the Puritans of Boston, the Quakers of Pennsylvania, all avowed a moral purpose, and began by making institutions that consciously reflected a moral idea. No such character belonged to the colonization of 1800. From Lake Erie to Florida, in long, unbroken line, pioneers were at work, cutting into the forests with the energy of so many beavers, and with no more express moral purpose than the beavers they drove away. The civilization they carried with them was rarely illumined by an idea; they sought room for no new truth, and aimed neither at creating, like the Puritans, a government of saints, nor, like the Quakers, one of love and peace; they left such experiments behind them, and wrestled only with the hardest problems of frontier life. No wonder that foreign observers, and even the educated, well-to-do Americans of the sea-coast, could seldom see anything to admire in the ignorance and brutality of frontiersmen, and should declare that virtue and wisdom no longer guided the United States! What they saw was not encouraging. To a new society, ignorant and semi-barbarous, a mass of demagogues insisted on applying every stimulant that could inflame its worst appetites, while at the same instant taking away every influence that had hitherto helped to restrain its passions. Greed for wealth, lust for power, yearning for the blank void of savage freedom such as Indians and wolves delighted in,—these were the fires that flamed under the caldron of American society, in which, as conservatives believed, the old, well-proven, conservative crust of religion, government, family, and even common respect for age, education, and experience was rapidly melting away, and was indeed already broken into fragments, swept about by the seething mass of scum ever rising in greater quantities to the surface.

Against this Federalist and conservative view of democratic tendencies, democrats protested in a thousand forms, but never in any mode of expression which satisfied them all, or explained their whole character. Probably Jefferson came nearest to the mark, for he represented the hopes of science as well as the prejudices of Virginia; but Jefferson's writings may be searched from beginning to end without revealing the whole measure of the man, far less of the movement. Here and there in his letters a suggestion was thrown out, as though by chance, revealing larger hopes,—as in 1815, at a moment of despondency, he wrote: "I fear from the experience of the last twenty-five years that morals do not of necessity advance hand in hand with the sciences." In 1800, in the flush of triumph, he believed that his task in the world was to establish a democratic republic, with the sciences for an intellectual field, and physical and moral advancement keeping pace with their advance. Without an excessive introduction of more recent ideas, he might be imagined to define democratic progress, in the somewhat affected precision of his French philosophy: "Progress is either physical or intellectual. If we can bring it about that men are on the average an inch taller in' the next generation than in this; if they are an inch larger round the chest; if their brain is an ounce or two heavier, and their life a year or two longer,—that is progress. If fifty years hence the average man shall invariably argue from two ascertained premises where he now jumps to a conclusion from single supposed revelation,—that is progress! I expect it to be made here, under our democratic stimulants, on a great scale, until every man is potentially an athlete in body and an Aristotle in mind." To this doctrine the New Englander replied, "What will you do for moral progress?" Every possible answer to this question opened a chasm. No doubt Jefferson held the faith that men would improve morally with their physical and intellectual growth; but he had no idea of any moral improvement other than that which came by nature. He could not tolerate a priesthood, a state church, or revealed religion. Conservatives, who could tolerate no society without such pillars of order, were, from their point of view, right in answering, "Give us rather the worst despotism of Europe,—there our souls at least may have a chance of salvation!" To their minds vice and virtue were not relative, but fixed terms. The Church was a divine institution. How could a ship hope to reach port when the crew threw overboard sails, spars, and compass, unshipped their rudder, and all the long day thought only of eating and drinking? Nay, even should the new experiment succeed in a worldly sense, what was a man profited if he gained the whole world, and lost his own soul? The Lord God was a jealous God, and visited the sins of the parents upon the children; but what worse sin could be conceived than for a whole nation to join their chief in chanting the strange hymn with which Jefferson, a new false prophet, was deceiving and betraying his people: "It does me no injury for my neighbor to say there are twenty Gods or no God!"

On this ground conservatism took its stand, as it had hitherto done with success in every similar emergency in the world's history, and fixing its eyes on moral standards of its own, refused to deal with the subject as further open to argument. The two parties stood facing opposite ways, and could see no common ground of contact.

Yet even then one part of the American social system was proving itself to be rich in results. The average American was more intelligent than the average European, and was becoming every year still more active-minded as the new movement of society caught him up and swept him through a life of more varied experiences. On all sides the national mind responded to its stimulants. Deficient as the American was in the machinery of higher instruction; remote, poor; unable by any exertion to acquire the training, capital, or even the elementary text-books he needed for a fair development of his natural powers,—his native energy and ambition already responded to the spur applied to them. Some of his triumphs were famous throughout the world; for Benjamin Franklin had raised high the reputation of American printers, and the actual President of the United States, who signed with Franklin the treaty of peace with Great Britain, was the son of a small farmer, and had himself kept a school in his youth. In both these cases social recognition followed success; but the later triumphs of the American mind were becoming more and more popular. John Fitch was not only one of the poorest, but one of the least-educated Yankees who ever made a name, he could never spell with tolerable correctness, and his life ended as it began,—in the lowest social obscurity. Eli Whitney was better educated than Fitch, but had neither wealth, social influence, nor patron to back his ingenuity. In the year 1800 Eli Terry, another Connecticut Yankee of the same class, took into his employ two young men to help him make wooden clocks, and this was the capital on which the greatest clock-manufactory in the world began its operations. In 1797 Asa Whittemore, a Massachusetts Yankee, invented a machine to make cards for carding wool, which "operated as if it had a soul," and became the foundation for a hundred subsequent patents. In 1790 Jacob Perkins, of Newburyport, invented a machine capable of cutting and turning out two hundred thousand nails a day; and then invented a process for transferring engraving from a very small steel cylinder to copper, which revolutionized cotton-printing. The British traveller Weld, passing through Wilmington, stopped, as Liancourt had done before him, to see the great flour-mills on the Brandywine. "The improvements," he said, "which have been made in the machinery of the flour-mills in America are very great. The chief of these consist in a new application of the screw, and the introduction of what are called elevators, the idea of which was evidently borrowed from the chain-pump." This was the invention of Oliver Evans, a native of Delaware, whose parents were in very humble life, but who was himself, in spite of every disadvantage, an inventive genius of the first order. Robert Fulton, who in 1800 was in Paris with Joel Barlow, sprang from the same source in Pennsylvania. John Stevens, a native of New York, belonged to a more favored class, but followed the same impulses. All these men were the outcome of typical American society, and all their inventions transmuted the democratic instinct into a practical and tangible shape. Who would undertake to say that there was a limit to the fecundity of this teeming source?

Who that saw only the narrow, practical, money-getting nature of the devices could venture to assert that as they wrought their end and raised the standard of millions, they would not also raise the creative power of those millions to a higher plane? If the priests and barons who set their names to Magna Charta had been told that in a few centuries every swine-herd and cobbler's apprentice would write and read with an ease such as few kings could then command, and reason with better logic than any university could then practise, the priest and baron would have been more incredulous than any man who was told in 1800 that within another five centuries the plough-boy would go a-field whistling a sonata of Beethoven, and figure out in quaternions[18] the relation of his furrows. The American democrat knew so little of art that among his popular illusions he could not then nourish artistic ambition; but leaders like Jefferson, Gallatin, and Barlow might without extravagance count upon a coming time when the diffused ease and education should bring the masses into familiar contact with higher forms of human achievement, and their vast creative power, turned toward a nobler culture, might rise to the level of that democratic genius which found expression in the Parthenon; might revel in the delights of a new Buonarotti[19] and a richer Titian,[20] might create for five hundred million people the America of thought and art which alone could satisfy their omnivorous ambition.

Whether the illusions, so often affirmed and so often denied to the American people, took such forms or not, these were in effect the problems that lay before American society: Could it transmute its social power into the higher forms of thought? Could it provide for the moral and intellectual needs of mankind? Could it take permanent political shape? Could it give new life to religion and art? Could it create and maintain in the mass of mankind those habits of mind which had hitherto belonged to men of science alone? Could it physically develop the convolutions of the human brain? Could it produce, or was it compatible with, the differentiation of a higher variety of the human race? Nothing less than this was necessary for its complete success.

[18] A term in calculus.

[19] The full name of Michelangelo (1475-1564), Italian sculptor, painter, architect, and poet, was Michelangelo Buonarroti.

[20] Tiziano Vecellio, or Titian (1477-1576) was a Venetian painter.

From The Education of Henry Adams

CHAPTER XXV
THE DYNAMO AND THE VIRGIN (1900)[1]

Until the Great Exposition of 1900[2] closed its doors in November, Adams haunted it, aching to absorb knowledge, and helpless to find it. He would have liked to know how much of it could have been grasped by the best-informed man in the world. While he was thus meditating chaos, Langley[3] came by, and showed it to him. At Langley's behest, the Exhibition dropped its superfluous rags and stripped itself to the skin, for Langley knew what to study, and why, and how; while Adams might as well have stood outside in the night, staring at the Milky Way. Yet Langley said nothing new, and taught nothing that one might not have learned from Lord Bacon,[4] three hundred years before; but though one should have known the "Advancement of Science" as well as one knew the "Comedy of Errors,"[5] the literary knowledge counted for nothing until some teacher should show how to apply it. Bacon took a vast deal of trouble in teaching King James I and his subjects, American or other, towards the year 1620, that true science was the development or economy of forces; yet an elderly American in 1900 knew neither the formula nor the forces; or even so much as to say to himself that his historical business in the Exposition concerned only the economies or developments of force since 1893, when he began the study at Chicago.[6]

Nothing in education is so astonishing as the amount of ignorance it accumulates in the form of inert facts. Adams had looked at most of the accumulations of art in the storehouses called Art Museums; yet he did not know how to look at the art exhibits of 1900. He had studied Karl Marx[7] and his doctrines of history with profound attention, yet he could not apply them at Paris. Langley, with the ease of a great master of experiment, threw out of the field every exhibit that did not reveal a new application of force, and naturally threw out, to begin with, almost the whole art exhibit. Equally, he

---

[1] From *The Education of Henry Adams*, printed privately in 1906. It was first published in 1918 by the Massachusetts Historical Society, and then in 1918 by Houghton Mifflin, in Boston.

[2] The Exposition of 1900 was in Paris.

[3] Samuel Pierpont Langley (1834–1906) was an American astrophysicist and investigator of the solar spectrum.

[4] Francis Bacon (1561–1626), English statesman and philosopher of science, author of *The Advancement of Learning* (1605) and

Novum Organum (1620). Bacon started the movement toward modern inductive scientific reasoning.

[5] Shakespeare's play, 1594.

[6] In 1893 there was a large technological display at The Columbian Exposition in Chicago that Adams saw.

[7] Karl Marx (1818–1883) German revolutionary thinker who, in *Das Kapital* (1867), explained his theory of the economic forces governing history.

ignored almost the whole industrial exhibit. He led his pupil directly to the forces. His chief interest was in new motors to make his airship feasible, and he taught Adams the astonishing complexities of the new Daimler[8] motor, and of the automobile, which, since 1893, had become a nightmare at a hundred kilometres an hour, almost as destructive as the electric tram which was only ten years older; and threatening to become as terrible as the locomotive steam-engine itself, which was almost exactly Adams's own age.

Then he showed his scholar the great hall of dynamos, and explained how little he knew about electricity or force of any kind, even of his own special sun, which spouted heat in inconceivable volume, but which, as far as he knew, might spout less or more, at any time, for all the certainty he felt in it. To him, the dynamo itself was but an ingenious channel for conveying somewhere the heat latent in a few tons of poor coal hidden in a dirty engine-house carefully kept out of sight; but to Adams the dynamo became a symbol of infinity. As he grew accustomed to the great gallery of machines, he began to feel the forty-foot dynamos as a moral force, much as the early Christians felt the Cross. The planet itself seemed less impressive, in its old-fashioned, deliberate, annual or daily revolution, than this huge wheel, revolving within arm's-length at some vertiginous speed, and barely murmuring—scarcely humming an audible warning to stand a hair's-breadth further for respect of power—while it would not wake the baby lying close against its frame. Before the end, one began to pray to it; inherited instinct taught the natural expression of man before silent and infinite force. Among the thousand symbols of ultimate energy, the dynamo was not so human as some, but it was the most expensive.

Yet the dynamo, next to the steam-engine, was the most familiar of exhibits. For Adams's objects its value lay chiefly in its occult mechanism. Between the dynamo in the gallery of machines and engine-house outside, the break of continuity amounted to abysmal fracture for a historian's objects. No more relation could he discover between the steam and the electric current than between the Cross and the cathedral. The forces were interchangeable if not reversible, but he could see only an absolute *fiat* in electricity as in faith. Langley could not help him. Indeed, Langley seemed to be worried by the same trouble, for he constantly repeated that the new forces were anarchical, and specially that he was not responsible for the new rays, that were little short of parricidal in their wicked spirit towards science. His own rays, with which he had doubled the solar spectrum, were altogether harmless and beneficent; but Radium denied its God—or, what was to Langley the same thing, denied the truths of his Science. The force was wholly new.[9]

---

[8] Gottlieb Daimler (1834–1900) was the German inventor of the internal-combustion engine.

[9] The discovery of radium in 1898 led to the discovery of the disintegration of the atom and to modern nuclear physics.

A historian who asked only to learn enough to be as futile as Langley or Kelvin,[10] made rapid progress under this teaching, and mixed himself up in the tangle of ideas until he achieved a sort of Paradise of ignorance vastly consoling to his fatigued senses. He wrapped himself in variations and rays which were new, and he would have hugged Marconi and Branly[11] had he met them, as he hugged the dynamo; while he lost his arithmetic in trying to figure out the equation between the discoveries and the economies of force. The economies, like the discoveries, were absolute, supersensual, occult; incapable of expression in horse-power. What mathematical equivalent could he suggest as the value of a Branly coherer? Frozen air, or the electric furnace, had some scale of measurement, no doubt, if somebody could invent a thermometer adequate to the purpose; but X-rays had played no part whatever in man's consciousness, and the atom itself had figured only as a fiction of thought. In these seven years man had translated himself into a new universe which had no common scale of measurement with the old. He had entered a supersensual world, in which he could measure nothing except by chance collisions of movements imperceptible to his senses, perhaps even imperceptible to his instruments, but perceptible to each other, and so to some known ray at the end of the scale. Langley seemed prepared for anything, even for an indeterminable number of universes interfused—physics stark mad in metaphysics.

Historians undertake to arrange sequences,—called stories, or histories— assuming in silence a relation of cause and effect. These assumptions, hidden in the depths of dusty libraries, have been astounding, but commonly unconscious and childlike; so much so, that if any captious critic were to drag them to light, historians would probably reply, with one voice, that they had never supposed themselves required to know what they were talking about. Adams, for one, had toiled in vain to find out what he meant. He had even published a dozen volumes of American history for no other purpose than to satisfy himself whether, by the severest process of stating, with the least possible comment, such facts as seemed sure, in such order as seemed rigorously consequent, he could fix for a familiar moment a necessary sequence of human movement. The result has satisfied him as little as at Harvard College. Where he saw sequence, other men saw something quite different, and no one saw the same unit of measure. He cared little about his experiments and less about his statesmen, who seemed to him quite as ignorant as himself and, as a rule, no more honest; but he insisted on a relation of sequence, and if he could not reach it by one method, he would try as many methods as science knew. Satisfied that the sequence of men led to nothing and that the

---

[10] William Thomson, Lord Kelvin (1824–1907), British physicist who worked with electrodynamics and transatlantic telegraphy.

[11] Guglielmo Marconi (1874–1937) invented the wireless telegraph. Edouard Branly (1846–1940) invented the first detector for radio waves.

sequence of their society could lead no further, while the mere sequence of time was artificial, and the sequence of thought was chaos, he turned at last to the sequence of force; and thus it happened that, after ten years' pursuit, he found himself lying in the Gallery of Machines at the Great Exposition of 1900, his historical neck broken by the sudden irruption of forces totally new.

Since no one else showed much concern, an elderly person without other cares had no need to betray alarm. The year 1900 was not the first to upset schoolmasters. Copernicus and Galileo[12] had broken many professorial necks about 1600; Columbus had stood the world on its head towards 1500; but the nearest approach to the revolution of 1900 was that of 310, when Constantine set up the Cross.[13] The rays that Langley disowned, as well as those which he fathered, were occult, supersensual, irrational; they were a revelation of mysterious energy like that of the Cross; they were what, in terms of mediæval science, were called immediate modes of the divine substance.

The historian was thus reduced to his last resources. Clearly if he was bound to reduce all these forces to a common value, this common value could have no measure but that of their attraction of his own mind. He must treat them as they had been felt; as convertible, reversible, interchangeable attractions on thought. He made up his mind to venture it; he would risk translating rays into faith. Such a reversible process would vastly amuse a chemist, but the chemist could not deny that he, or some of his fellow physicists, could feel the force of both. When Adams was a boy in Boston, the best chemist in the place had probably never heard of Venus except by way of scandal, or of the Virgin except as idolatry; neither had he heard of dynamos or automobiles or radium; yet his mind was ready to feel the force of all, though the rays were unborn and the women were dead.

Here opened another totally new education, which promised to be by far the most hazardous of all. The knife-edge along which he must crawl, like Sir Lancelot in the twelfth century,[14] divided two kingdoms of force which had nothing in common but attraction. They were as different as a magnet is from gravitation, supposing one knew what a magnet was, or gravitation, or love. The force of the Virgin was still felt at Lourdes,[15] and seemed to be as potent as X-rays; but in America neither Venus nor Virgin ever had value as force—at most as sentiment. No American had ever been truly afraid of either.

---

[12] Copernicus (1473-1543) and Galileo (1564-1642) affirmed that the earth circled the sun.

[13] The Emperor Constantine (288?-337) legalized and proclaimed Christianity in the Roman Empire after having seen a vision of a cross bearing the words "In this sign conquer."

[14] A test Sir Lancelot had to undergo in order to free Guinevere who was being held captive in a castle, in Chretien de Troyes' *Chevalier de la Charratte.*

[15] A French shrine to the Virgin Mary that has a spring of healing waters and thus attracts many pilgrims.

This problem in dynamics gravely perplexed an American historian. The Woman had once been supreme; in France she still seemed potent, not merely as a sentiment, but as a force. Why was she unknown in America? For evidently America was ashamed of her, and she was ashamed of herself, otherwise they would not have strewn fig-leaves so profusely all over her. When she was a true force, she was ignorant of fig-leaves, but the monthly-magazine-made American female had not a feature that would have been recognized by Adam. The trait was notorious, and often humorous, but any one brought up among Puritans knew that sex was sin. In any previous age, sex was strength. Neither art nor beauty was needed. Every one, even among Puritans, knew that neither Diana of the Ephesians[16] nor any of the Oriental goddesses was worshipped for her beauty. She was goddess because of her force; she was the animated dynamo; she was reproduction—the greatest and most mysterious of all energies; all she needed was to be fecund. Singularly enough, not one of Adams' many schools of education had ever drawn his attention to the opening lines of Lucretius, though they were perhaps the finest in all Latin literature, where the poet invoked Venus exactly as Dante invoked the Virgin:—

"Quae quoniam rerum naturam *sola* gubernas."[17]

The Venus of Epicurean philosophy survived in the Virgin of the Schools:—

"Donna, sei tanto grande, e tanto vali,
Che qual vuol grazia, e a te non ricorre,
Sua disianza vuol volar senz' ali."[18]

All this was to American thought as though it had never existed. The true American knew something of the facts, but nothing of the feelings; he read the letter, but he never felt the law. Before this historical chasm, a mind like that of Adams felt itself helpless; he turned from the Virgin to the Dynamo as though he were a Branly coherer. On one side, at the Louvre and at Chartres, as he knew by the record of work actually done and still before his eyes, was the highest energy ever known to man, the creator of four-fifths of his noblest art, exercising vastly more attraction over the human mind than all the steam-engines and dynamos ever dreamed of; and yet this energy was unknown to the American mind. An American Virgin would never dare command; an American Venus would never dare exist.

The question, which to any plain American of the nineteenth century seemed as remote as it did to Adams, drew him almost violently to study,

---

[16] Fertility goddess.

[17] "Since thou alone dost govern the nature of things." From *De Rerum Natura*, Book I, 21, by Lucretius, a Roman poet (95-51? B.C.)

[18] "Lady, thou are so great in all things/That he who wishes grace, and seeks not thee,/ Would have his wish fly upwards without wings." (Dante, *Paradiso* xxxiii, 13-15.)

once it was posed; and on this point Langleys were as useless as though they were Herbert Spencers[19] or dynamos. The idea survived only as art. There one turned as naturally as though the artist were himself a woman. Adams began to ponder, asking himself whether he knew of an American artist who had ever insisted on the power of sex, as every classic had always done; but he could think only of Walt Whitman; Bret Harte, as far as the magazines would let him venture; and one or two painters, for the flesh-tones. All the rest had used sex for sentiment, never for force; to them, Eve was a tender . flower, and Herodias[20] an unfeminine horror. American art, like the American language and American education, was as far as possible sexless. Society regarded this victory over sex as its greatest triumph, and the historian readily admitted it, since the moral issue, for the moment, did not concern one who was studying the relations of unmoral force. He cared nothing for the sex of the dynamo until he could measure its energy.

Vaguely seeking a clue, he wandered through the art exhibit, and, in his stroll, stopped almost every day before St. Gaudens's General Sherman,[21] which had been given the central post of honor. St. Gaudens himself was in Paris, putting on the work his usual interminable last touches, and listening to the usual contradictory suggestions of brother sculptors. Of all the American artists who gave to American art whatever life it breathed in the seventies, St. Gaudens was perhaps the most sympathetic, but certainly the most inarticulate. General Grant or Don Cameron[22] had scarcely less instinct of rhetoric than he. All the others—the Hunts, Richardson, John La Farge, Stanford White[23]—were exuberant; only St. Gaudens could never discuss or dilate on an emotion, or suggest artistic arguments for giving to his work the forms that he felt. He never laid down the law, or affected the despot, or became brutalized like Whistler[24] by the brutalities of his world. He required no incense; he was no egoist; his simplicity of thought was excessive; he could not imitate, or give any form but his own to the creations of his hand. No one felt more strongly than he the strength of other men, but the idea that they could affect him never stirred an image in his mind.

[19] Herbert Spencer (1820-1903), British philosopher and Social Darwinist.

[20] King Herod's lustful wife who caused the death of John the Baptist, Cf. Mark vi:17-28.

[21] Augustus Saint-Gaudens (1848-1907) was an American sculptor whose statue under discussion here stands now on the Fifth Avenue Plaza in New York City. Saint-Gaudens created the memorial that Henry Adams erected for his wife in Rock Creek Cemetery, Washington, D.C.

[22] James Donald Cameron (1833-1918) was Secretary of War in President Grant's cabinet and a friend of Henry Adams.

[23] William Morris Hunt (1824-1879) was a Vermont painter. Richard Morris Hunt, his brother, (1828-1895) was an architect, as were Henry Hobson Richardson (1838-1886) and Stanford White (1853-1906). John La Farge (1835-1910) was an artist and author who went with Adams to the South Seas in 1886.

[24] James Abbott McNeill Whistler (1834-1903) was an American portrait and landscape painter with a nasty personality.

This summer his health was poor and his spirits were low. For such a temper, Adams was not the best companion, since his own gaiety was not *folle;*[25] but he risked going now and then to the studio on Mont Parnasse[26] to draw him out for a stroll in the Bois de Boulogne,[27] or dinner as pleased his moods, and in return St. Gaudens sometimes let Adams go about in his company.

Once St. Gaudens took him down to Amiens, with a party of Frenchmen, to see the cathedral. Not until they found themselves actually studying the sculpture of the western portal, did it dawn on Adams's mind that, for his purposes, St. Gaudens on that spot had more interest to him than the cathedral itself. Great men before great monuments express great truths, provided they are not taken too solemnly. Adams never tired of quoting the supreme phrase of his idol Gibbon,[28] before the Gothic cathedrals: "I darted a contemptuous look on the stately monuments of superstition." Even in the footnotes of his history, Gibbon had never inserted a bit of humor more human than this, and one would have paid largely for a photograph of the fat little historian, on the background of Notre Dame of Amiens, trying to persuade his readers—perhaps himself—that he was darting a contemptuous look on the stately monument, for which he felt in fact the respect which every man of his vast study and active mind always feels before objects worthy of it; but besides the humor, one felt also the relation. Gibbon ignored the Virgin, because in 1789 religious monuments were out of fashion. In 1900 his remark sounded fresh and simple as the green fields to ears that had heard a hundred years of other remarks, mostly no more fresh and certainly less simple. Without malice, one might find it more instructive than a whole lecture of Ruskin.[29] One sees what one brings, and at that moment Gibbon brought the French Revolution. Ruskin brought reaction against the Revolution. St. Gaudens had passed beyond all. He liked the stately monuments much more than he liked Gibbon or Ruskin; he loved their dignity; their unity; their scale; their lines; their lights and shadows; their decorative sculpture; but he was even less conscious than they of the force that created it all—the Virgin, the Woman—by whose genius "the stately monuments of superstition" were built, through which she was expressed. He would have seen more meaning in Isis[30] with the cow's horns, at Edfoo, who expressed the same thought. The art remained, but the energy was lost even upon the artist.

Yet in mind and person St. Gaudens was a survival of the 1500's; he bore the stamp of the Renaissance, and should have carried an image of the Virgin

[25] Crazy.
[26] Parisian artist's quarter.
[27] A large wooded park in Paris.
[28] Edward Gibbon (1737-1794), English historian, author of *The Decline and Fall of the Roman Empire* (1776-1788).
[29] John Ruskin (1819-1900), English art and architecture critic.
[30] Egyptian fertility goddess whose statue at Edfu, a city on the upper Nile, had impressed Adams.

round his neck, or stuck in his hat, like Louis XI.[31] In mere time he was a lost soul that had strayed by chance into the twentieth century, and forgotten where it came from. He writhed and cursed at his ignorance, much as Adams did at his own, but in the opposite sense. St. Gaudens was a child of Benvenuto Cellini,[32] smothered in an American cradle. Adams was a quintessence of Boston, devoured by curiosity to think like Benvenuto. St. Gaudens's art was starved from birth, and Adams's instinct was blighted from babyhood. Each had but half of a nature, and when they came together before the Virgin of Amiens they ought both to have felt in her the force that made them one; but it was not so. To Adams she became more than ever a channel of force; to St. Gaudens she remained as before a channel of taste.

For a symbol of power, St. Gaudens instinctively preferred the horse, as was plain in his horse and Victory of the Sherman monument. Doubtless Sherman also felt it so. The attitude was so American that, for at least forty years, Adams had never realized that any other could be in sound taste. How many years had he taken to admit a notion of what Michael Angelo and Rubens[33] were driving at? He could not say; but he knew that only since 1895 had he begun to feel the Virgin or Venus as force, and not everywhere even so. At Chartres—perhaps at Lourdes—possibly at Cnidos if one could still find there the divinely naked Aphrodite of Praxiteles[34]—but otherwise one must look for force to the goddesses of Indian mythology. The idea died out long ago in the German and English stock. St. Gaudens at Amiens was hardly less sensitive to the force of the female energy than Matthew Arnold at the Grande Chartreuse.[35] Neither of them felt goddesses as power—only as reflected emotion, human expression, beauty, purity, taste, scarcely even as sympathy. They felt a railway train as power; yet they, and all other artists, constantly complained that the power embodied in a railway train could never be embodied in art. All the steam in the world could not, like the Virgin, build Chartres.

Yet in mechanics, whatever the mechanicians might think, both energies acted as interchangeable forces on man, and by action on man all known force may be measured. Indeed, few men of science measured force in any other way. After once admitting that a straight line was the shortest distance between two points, no serious mathematician cared to deny anything that suited his convenience, and rejected no symbol, unproved or unproveable,

---

[31] King of France (1423-1483) who was very superstitious in his later years.

[32] Benvenuto Cellini (1500-1571), an Italian goldsmith and sculptor who celebrates sexuality in his *Autobiography*.

[33] Michelangelo (1475-1564), an Italian artist and Peter Paul Rubens (1577-1640), a Flemish painter.

[34] Greek sculptor of the fourth century B.C.

whose statue of Aphrodite stood in the temple at Cnidos and whose statue of a faun Nathaniel Hawthorne wrote *The Marble Faun* about in 1860.

[35] In "Stanzas from the Grand Chartreuse" (1855), the English Victorian critic and poet Matthew Arnold (1822-1888) described his religious experiences and his feeling of "Wandering between two worlds, one dead,/The other powerless to be born."

that helped him to accomplish work. The symbol was force, as a compass-needle or a triangle was force, as the mechanist might prove by losing it, and nothing could be gained by ignoring their value. Symbol or energy, the Virgin had acted as the greatest force the Western world ever felt, and had drawn man's activities to herself more strongly than any other power, natural or supernatural, had ever done; the historian's business was to follow the track of the energy; to find where it came from and where it went to; its complex source and shifting channels; its values, equivalents, conversions. It could scarcely be more complex than radium; it could hardly be deflected, diverted, polarized, absorbed more perplexingly than other radiant matter. Adams knew nothing about any of them, but as a mathematical problem of influence on human progress, though all were occult, all reacted on his mind, and he rather inclined to think the Virgin easiest to handle.

The pursuit turned out to be long and tortuous, leading at last into the vast forests of scholastic science. From Zeno[36] to Descartes, hand in hand with Thomas Aquinas, Montaigne, and Pascal, one stumbled as stupidly as though one were still a German student in 1860. Only with the instinct of despair could one force one's self into this old thicket of ignorance after having been repulsed at a score of entrances more promising and more popular. Thus far, no path had led anywhere, unless perhaps to an exceedingly modest living. Forty-five years of study had proved to be quite futile for the pursuit of power; one controlled no more force in 1900 than in 1850, although the amount of force controlled by society had enormously increased. The secret of education still hid itself somewhere behind ignorance, and one fumbled over it as feebly as ever. In such labyrinths, the staff is a force almost more necessary than the legs; the pen becomes a sort of blind-man's dog, to keep him from falling into the gutters. The pen works for itself, and acts like a hand, modelling the plastic material over and over again to the form that suits it best. The form is never arbitrary, but is a sort of growth like crystallization, as any artist knows too well; for often the pencil or pen runs into side-paths and shapelessness, loses its relations, stops or is bogged. Then it has to return on its trail, and recover, if it can, its line of force. The result of a year's work depends more on what is struck out than on what is left in; on the sequence of the main lines of thought, than on their play or variety. Compelled once more to lean heavily on this support, Adams covered more thousands of pages with figures as formal as though they were algebra, laboriously striking out, altering, burning, experimenting, until the year had expired, the Exposition had long been closed, and winter drawing to its end, before he sailed from Cherbourg, on January 19, 1901, for home.

[36] Zeno of Elea (fifth century B.C.) was a Greek philosopher who used paradoxes; Rene Descartes (1596-1650) was a French philosopher and mathematician; St. Thomas Aquinas (1225?-1274) was an Italian theologian and philosopher; Michel de Montaigne (1533-1592) was a brilliant French essayist who invented the form; Blaise Pascal (1623-1662) was a French physicist, mathematician, and moralist.

WILLIAM JAMES

(1842-1910)

A pivotal figure in American thought, William James led a revolt in philosophy against the hold of theology and idealism, toward an application of scientific method to philosophical, social, and personal problems. Instead of simply opposing religion, James offered a method of harmonizing the conflicting claims of experience and faith. He rejected dogmatism of any kind, standing for confidence in human capacity, and hope in an improved future. The name he chose for his outlook and method, "Pragmatism," indicates its central proposition that truth is a relation between ideas and practical consequences, or as he sometimes put it with coy bluntness, the truth of an idea is its cash value. In a period when traditional beliefs were collapsing, when the need for personal certainty as well as for workable social policies was great, James proposed testing propositions by their practical workableness as a way out of crippling dilemmas. In the spirit of Emerson's "self-reliance" and Whitman's "be althymindedness" (James's own term), he refused to accept defeat by circumstances or by the nature of things, insisting that the universe was still open, an unfinished experiment, adventure.

It is significant that James arrived at philosophy by way of experimental science. He was born in New York, the son of Henry James, Sr., and the brother of Henry James. He graduated from Harvard in 1864 and enrolled in Harvard Medical School where, after a year on a zoological expedition in Brazil he earned a medical degree. He did not practice medicine, however, but began his long and distinguished teaching career at Harvard in 1872 as an instructor of physiology. In 1876 he established a pioneering laboratory for psychological research and, in 1890, he published his groundbreaking *Principles of Psychology,* based on empirical studies, and arguing that "mind" is essentially

The major works are *Principles of Psychology,* 1890; *The Will To Believe and Other Essays in Popular Philosophy,* 1897; *The Varieties of Religious Experience,* 1902, reprinted 1936; *Pragmatism,* 1907. John D. McDermott edited *The Writings of William James: A Comprehensive Edition,* 1967.

A solid biography is Gay Wilson Allen, *William James: A Biography,* 1967. See also Ralph Barton Perry, *The Thought and Character of William James,* 2 vol., 1935; Edward C. Moore, *William James,* 1965; Lloyd Morris, *William James, The Message of a Modern Mind,* 1951; Bernard P. Brennan, *William James,* 1968.

Observations by important thinkers are George Santayana, *Character and Opinion in the United States,* 1920; John Dewey, *Character and Events,* 1929.

the organism's instrument of adjustment to its environment. He began to publish philosophical essays in the middle 1890's and, in 1898, he adopted the term "pragmatism." In 1902 he published his brilliant *Varieties of Religious Experience,* which treated religious states and ideas as psychological facts. He expounded his "radical empiricist" position in philosophy in *Pragmatism* (1907), and continued to write and lecture after his retirement from Harvard in the same year. As a public figure, James often took unpopular stands, opposing the Spanish-American war as well as war and imperialism in general. His influence has been of a major magnitude, notably in educational and social theory through the work of his follower, John Dewey.

What Makes a Life Significant[1]

In my previous talk, 'On a Certain Blindness,' I tried to make you feel how soaked and shot-through life is with values and meanings which we fail to realize because of our external and insensible point of view. The meanings are there for the others, but they are not there for us. There lies more than a mere interest of curious speculation in understanding this. It has the most tremendous practical importance. I wish that I could convince you of it as I feel it myself. It is the basis of all our tolerance, social, religious, and political. The forgetting of it lies at the root of every stupid and sanguinary mistake that rulers over subject-peoples make. The first thing to learn in intercourse with others is non-interference with their own peculiar ways of being happy, provided those ways do not assume to interfere by violence with ours. No one has insight into all the ideals. No one should presume to judge them off-hand. The pretension to dogmatize about them in each other is the root of most human injustices and cruelties, and the trait in human character most likely to make the angels weep.

Every Jack sees in his own particular Jill charms and perfections to the enchantment of which we stolid onlookers are stone-cold. And which has the superior view of the absolute truth, he or we? Which has the more vital insight into the nature of Jill's existence, as a fact? Is he in excess, being in this matter a maniac? or are we in defect, being victims of a pathological anæsthesia as regards Jill's magical importance? Surely the latter; surely to Jack are the profounder truths revealed; surely poor Jill's palpitating little life-throbs *are* among the wonders of creation, *are* worthy of this sympathetic interest; and it is to our shame that the rest of us cannot feel like Jack. For Jack realizes Jill concretely, and we do not. He struggles toward a union

[1] From *Talks to Teachers on Psychology,* 1899.

with her inner life, divining her feelings, anticipating her desires, understanding her limits as manfully as he can, and yet inadequately, too; for he is also afflicted with some blindness, even here. Whilst we, dead clods that we are, do not even seek after these things, but are contented that that portion of eternal fact named Jill should be for us as if it were not. Jill, who knows her inner life, knows that Jack's way of taking it—so importantly—is the true and serious way; and she responds to the truth in him by taking him truly and seriously, too. May the ancient blindness never wrap its clouds about either of them again! Where would any of *us* be, were there no one willing to know us as we really are or ready to repay us for *our* insight by making recognizant return? We ought, all of us, to realize each other in this intense, pathetic, and important way.

If you say that this is absurd, and that we cannot be in love with everyone at once, I merely point out to you that, as a matter of fact, certain persons do exist with an enormous capacity for friendship and for taking delight in other people's lives; and that such persons know more of truth than if their hearts were not so big. The vice of ordinary Jack and Jill affection is not its intensity, but its exclusions and its jealousies. Leave those out, and you see that the ideal I am holding up before you, however impracticable to-day, yet contains nothing intrinsically absurd.

We have unquestionably a great cloud-bank of ancestral blindness weighing down upon us, only transiently riven here and there by fitful revelations of the truth. It is vain to hope for this state of things to alter much. Our inner secrets must remain for the most part impenetrable by others, for beings as essentially practical as we are necessarily short of sight. But, if we cannot gain much positive insight into one another, cannot we at least use our sense of our own blindness to make us more cautious in going over the dark places? Cannot we escape some of those hideous ancestral intolerances and cruelties, and positive reversals of the truth?

For the remainder of this hour I invite you to seek with me some principle to make our tolerance less chaotic. And, as I began my previous lecture by a personal reminiscence, I am going to ask your indulgence for a similar bit of egotism now.

A few summers ago I spent a happy week at the famous Assembly Grounds on the borders of Chautauqua Lake.[2] The moment one treads that sacred enclosure, one feels one's self in an atmosphere of success. Sobriety and industry, intelligence and goodness, orderliness and ideality, prosperity and cheerfulness, pervade the air. It is a serious and studious picnic on a gigantic scale. Here you have a town of many thousands of inhabitants, beautifully laid out in the forest and drained, and equipped with means for

[2] A famous summer resort and educational institute in western New York state on Lake Chautauqua.

satisfying all the necessary lower and most of the superfluous higher wants of man. You have a first-class college in full blast. You have magnificent music—a chorus of seven hundred voices, with possibly the most perfect open-air auditorium in the world. You have every sort of athletic exercise from sailing, rowing, swimming, bicycling, to the ball-field and the more artificial doings which the gymnasium affords. You have kindergartens and model secondary schools. You have general religious services and special club-houses for the several sects. You have perpetually running soda-water fountains, and daily popular lectures by distinguished men. You have the best of company, and yet no effort. You have no zymotic[3] diseases, no poverty, no drunkenness, no crime, no police. You have culture, you have kindness, you have cheapness, you have equality, you have the best fruits of what mankind has fought and bled and striven for under the name of civilization for centuries. You have, in short, a foretaste of what human society might be, were it all in the light, with no suffering and no dark corners.

I went in curiosity for a day. I stayed for a week, held spell-bound by the charm and ease of everything, by the middle-class paradise, without a sin, without a victim, without a blot, without a tear.

And yet what was my own astonishment, on emerging into the dark and wicked world again, to catch myself quite unexpectedly and involuntarily saying: "Ouf! what a relief! Now for something primordial and savage, even though it were as bad as an Armenian massacre, to set the balance straight again. This order is too tame, this culture too second-rate, this goodness too uninspiring. This human drama without a villain or a pang; this community so refined that ice-cream soda-water is the utmost offering it can make to the brute animal in man; this city simmering in the tepid lakeside sun; this atrocious harmlessness of all things,—I cannot abide with them. Let me take my chances again in the big outside worldly wilderness with all its sins and sufferings. There are the heights and depths, the precipices and the steep ideals, the gleams of the awful and the infinite; and there is more hope and help a thousand times than in this dead level and quintessence of every mediocrity."

Such was the sudden right-about-face performed for me by my lawless fancy! There had been spread before me the realization—on a small, sample scale of course—of all the ideals for which our civilization has been striving: security, intelligence, humanity, and order; and here was the instinctive hostile reaction, not of the natural man, but of a so-called cultivated man upon such a Utopia. There seemed thus to be a self-contradiction and paradox somewhere, which I, as a professor drawing a full salary, was in duty bound to unravel and explain, if I could.

So I meditated. And, first of all, I asked myself what the thing was that was so lacking in this Sabbatical city, and the lack of which kept one forever falling short of the higher sort of contentment. And I soon recognized that it

[3] Contagious or infectious bacterial diseases.

was the element that gives to the wicked outer world all its moral style, expressiveness and picturesqueness,—the element of precipitousness, so to call it, of strength and strenuousness, intensity and danger. What excited and interests the looker-on at life, what the romances and the statues celebrate and the grim civic monuments remind us of, is the everlasting battle of the powers of light with those of darkness; with heroism, reduced to its bare chance, yet ever and anon snatching victory from the jaws of death. But in this unspeakable Chautauqua there was no potentiality of death in sight anywhere, and no point of the compass visible from which danger might possibly appear. The ideal was so completely victorious already that no sign of any previous battle remained, the place just resting on its oars. But what our human emotions seem to require is the sight of the struggle going on. The moment the fruits are being merely eaten, things become ignoble. Sweat and effort, human nature strained to its uttermost and on the rack, yet getting through alive, and then turning its back on its success to pursue another more rare and arduous still—this is the sort of thing the presence of which inspires us, and the reality of which it seems to be the function of all the higher forms of literature and fine art to bring home to us and suggest. At Chautauqua there were no racks, even in the place's historical museum; and no sweat, except possibly the gentle moisture on the brow of some lecturer, or on the sides of some player in the ball-field.

Such absence of human nature in *extremis* anywhere seemed, then, a sufficient explanation for Chautauqua's flatness and lack of zest.

But was not this a paradox well calculated to fill one with dismay? It looks indeed, thought I, as if the romantic idealists with their pessimism about our civilization were, after all, quite right. An irremediable flatness is coming over the world. Bourgeoisie and mediocrity, church sociables and teachers' conventions, are taking the place of the old heights and depths and romantic chiaroscuro.[4] And, to get human life in its wild intensity, we must in future turn more and more away from the actual, and forget it, if we can, in the romancer's or the poet's pages. The whole world, delightful and sinful as it may still appear for a moment to one just escaped from the Chautauquan enclosure, is nevertheless obeying more and more just those ideals that are sure to make of it in the end a mere Chautauqua Assembly on an enormous scale. *Was im Gesang soll leben muss im Leben untergehn.*[5] Even now, in our own country, correctness, fairness, and compromise for every small advantage are crowding out all other qualities. The higher heroisms and the old rare flavors are passing out of life.[6]

With these thoughts in my mind, I was speeding with the train toward Buffalo, when, near that city, the sight of workman doing something on the

[4] The treatment of lights and darks in a picture to give special dramatic effect.
[5] Who passes his life in song must sink his life in ruin.
[6] This address was composed before the Cuban and Philippine wars. Such outbursts of the passion of mastery are, however, only episodes in a social process which in the long run seems everywhere tending toward the Chautauquan ideals. (Author's note.)

dizzy edge of a sky-scaling iron construction brought me to my senses very suddenly. And now I perceived, by a flash of insight, that I had been steeping myself in pure ancestral blindness, and looking at life with the eyes of a remote spectator. Wishing for heroism and the spectacle of human nature on the rack, I had never noticed the great fields of heroism lying round about me, I had failed to see it present and alive. I could only think of it as dead and embalmed, labelled and costumed, as it is in the pages of romance. And yet there it was before me in the daily lives of the laboring classes. Not in clanging fights and desperate marches only is heroism to be looked for, but on every railway bridge and fire-proof building that is going up to-day. On freight-trains, on the decks of vessels, in cattleyards and mines, on lumber-rafts, among the firemen and the policemen, the demand for courage is incessant; and the supply never fails. There, ever day of the year somewhere, is human nature *in extremis* for you. And wherever a scythe, an axe, a pick, or a shovel is wielded, you have it sweating and aching and with its powers of patient endurance racked to the utmost under the length of hours of the strain.

As I awoke to all this unidealized heroic life around me, the scales seemed to fall from my eyes; and a wave of sympathy greater than anything I had ever before felt with the common life of common men began to fill my soul. It began to seem as if virtue with horny hands and dirty skin were the only virtue genuine and vital enough to take account of. Every other virtue poses; none is absolutely unconscious and simple, and unexpectant of decoration or recognition, like this. These are our soldiers, thought I, these our sustainers, there the very parents of our life.

Many years ago, when in Vienna, I had had a similar feeling of awe and reverence in looking at the peasant-women, in from the country on their business at the market for the day. Old hags many of them were, dried and brown and wrinkled, kerchiefed and short-petticoated, with thick wool stockings on their bony shanks, stumping through the glittering thorough-fares, looking neither to the right nor the left, bent on duty, envying nothing, humble-hearted, remote;—and yet at bottom, when you came to think of it, bearing the whole fabric of the splendors and corruptions of that city on their laborious backs. For where would any of it have been without their unremitting, unrewarded labor in the fields? And so with us: not to our generals and poets, I thought, but to the Italian and Hungarian laborers in the Subway, rather, ought the monuments of gratitude and reverence of a city like Boston to be reared.

If any of you have been readers of Tolstoï,[7] you will see that I passed into a vein of feeling similar to his, with its abhorrence of all that conventionally

---

[7] Count Leo Nikolaevich Tolstoy (1828–1910), a great Russian novelist and social reformer.

passes for distinguished, and its exclusive deification of the bravery, patience, kindliness, and dumbness of the unconscious natural man.

Where now is *our* Tolstoï, I said, to bring the truth of all this home to our American bosoms, fill us with a better insight, and wean us away from that spurious literary romanticism on which our wretched culture—as it calls itself—is fed? Divinity lies all about us, and culture is too hide-bound to even suspect the fact. Could a Howells[8] or a Kipling[9] be enlisted in this mission? or are they still too deep in the ancestral blindness, and not humane enough for the inner joy and meaning of the laborer's existence to be really revealed? Must we wait for some one born and bred and living as a laborer himself, but who, by grace of Heaven, shall also find a literary voice?

And there I rested on that day, with a sense of widening of vision, and with what it is surely fair to call an increase of religious insight into life. In God's eyes the differences of social position, of intellect, of culture, of cleanliness, of dress, which different men exhibit, and all the other rarities and exceptions on which they so fantastically pin their pride, must be so small as practically quite to vanish; and all that should remain is the common fact that here we are, a countless multitude of vessels of life, each of us pent in to peculiar difficulties, with which we must severally struggle by using whatever of fortitude and goodness we can summon up. The exercise of the courage, patience, and kindness, must be the significant portion of the whole business; and the distinctions of position can only be a manner of diversifying the phenomenal surface upon which these underground virtues may manifest their effects. At this rate, the deepest human life is everwhere, is eternal. And, if any human attributes exist only in particular individuals, they must belong to the mere trapping and decoration of the surface-show.

Thus are men's lives levelled up as well as levelled down,—levelled up in their common inner meaning, levelled down in their outer gloriousness and show. Yet always, we must confess, this levelling insight tends to be obscured again; and always the ancestral blindness returns and wraps us up, so that we end once more by thinking that creation can be for no other purpose than to develop remarkable situations and conventional distinctions and merits. And then always some new leveller in the shape of a religious prophet has to arise—the Buddha, the Christ, or some Saint Francis, some Rousseau[10] or Tolstoï—to redispel our blindness. Yet, little by little, there comes some stable gain; for the world does get more humane, and the religion of democracy tends toward permanent increase.

---

[8] William Dean Howells (1837-1920), editor, critic, and author a *A Modern Instance* (1882) and *The Rise of Silas Lapham* (1885), among other novels.

[9] Rudyard Kipling (1865-1936), English poet of verses such as "Gunga Din."

[10] Jean Jacques Rousseau (1712-1778) was a French philosopher and author of *The Confessions* (1781).

This, as I said, became for a time my consolation, and gave me great content. I have put the matter into the form of a personal reminiscence, so that I might lead you into it more directly and completely, and so save time. But now I am going to discuss the rest of it with you in a more impersonal way.

Tolstoï's levelling philosophy began long before he had the crisis of melancholy commemorated in that wonderful document of his entitled 'My Confession,' which led the way to his more specifically religious works. In his masterpiece 'War and Peace,'—assuredly the greatest of human novels,—the rôle of the spiritual hero is given to a poor little soldier named Karataïeff, so helpful, so cheerful, and so devout that, in spite of his ignorance and filthiness, the sight of him opens the heavens, which have been closed, to the mind of the principal character of the book; and his example evidently is meant by Tolstoï to let God into the world again for the reader. Poor little Karataïeff is taken prisoner by the French; and, when too exhausted by hardship and fever to march, is shot as other prisoners were in the famous retreat from Moscow. The last view one gets of him is his little figure leaning against a white birch-tree, and uncomplainingly awaiting the end.

"The more," writes Tolstoï in the work 'My Confession,' "the more I examined the life of these laboring folks, the more persuaded I became that they veritably have faith, and get from it alone the sense and the possibility of life. . . . Contrariwise to those of our own class, who protest against destiny and grow indignant at its rigor, these people receive maladies and misfortunes without revolt, without opposition, and with a firm and tranquil confidence that all had to be like that, could not be otherwise, and that it is all right so. . . . The more we live by our intellect, the less we understand the meaning of life. We see only a cruel jest in suffering and death, whereas these people live, suffer, and draw near to death with tranquillity, and oftener than not with joy. . . . There are enormous multitudes of them happy with the most perfect happiness, although deprived of what for us is the sole good of life. Those who understand life's meaning, and know how to live and die thus, are to be counted not by twos, threes, tens, but by hundreds, thousands, millions. They labor quietly, endure privations and pains, live and die, and throughout everything see the good without seeing the vanity. I had to love these people. The more I entered into their life, the more I loved them; and the more it became possible for me to live, too. It came about not only that the life of our society, of the learned and of the rich, disgusted me—more than that, it lost all semblance of meaning in my eyes. All our actions, our deliberations, our sciences, our arts, all appeared to me with a new significance. I understood that these things might be charming pastimes, but that one need seek in them no depth, whereas the life of the hardworking populace, of that multitude of human beings who really contribute to existence, appeared to me in its true light. I understood that there veritably is life, that the meaning which life there receives is the truth; and I accepted it."

In a similar way does Stevenson[11] appeal to our piety toward the elemental virtue of mankind.

"What a wonderful thing," he writes, "is this Man! How surprising are his attributes! Poor soul, here for so little, cast among so many hardships, savagely surrounded, savagely descended, irremediably condemned to prey upon his fellow-lives,—who should have blamed him, had he been of a piece with his destiny and a being merely barbarous? . . . [Yet] it matters not where we look, under what climate we observe him, in what stage of society, in what depth of ignorance, burdened with what erroneous morality; in ships at sea, a man inured to hardship and vile pleasures, his brightest hope a fiddle in a tavern, and a bedizened trull[12] who sells herself to rob him, and he, for all that, simple, innocent, cheerful, kindly like a child, constant to toil, brave to drown, for others; . . . in the slums of cities, moving among indifferent millions to mechanical employments, without hope of change in the future, with scarce a pleasure in the present, and yet true to his virtues, honest up to his lights, kind to his neighbors, tempted perhaps in vain by the bright gin-palace, . . . often repaying the world's scorn with service, often standing firm upon a scruple; . . . everywhere some virtue cherished or affected, everywhere some decency of thought and courage, everywhere the ensign of man's ineffectual goodness,—ah! if I could show you this! If I could show you these men and women all the world over, in every stage of history, under every abuse of error, under every circumstance of failure, without hope, without help, without thanks, still obscurely fighting the lost fight of virtue, still clinging to some rag of honor, the poor jewel of their souls."

All this is as true as it is splendid, and terribly do we need our Tolstoïs and Stevensons to keep our sense for it alive. Yet you remember the Irishman, who, when asked, "Is not one man as good as another?" replied, "Yes; and a great deal better, too!" Similarly (it seems to me) does Tolstoï overcorrect our social prejudices, when he makes his love of the peasant so exclusive, and hardens his heart toward the educated man as absolutely as he does. Grant that at Chautauqua there was little moral effort, little sweat or muscular strain in view. Still, deep down in the souls of the participants we may be sure that something of the sort was hid, some inner stress, some vital virtue not found wanting when required. And, after all, the question recurs, and forces itself upon us, Is it so certain that the surroundings and circumstances of the virtue do make so little difference in the importance of the result? Is the functional utility, the worth to the universe of a certain definite amount of courage, kindliness, and patience, no greater if the possessor of these virtues is in an educated situation, working out far-reaching tasks, than if he be an illiterate nobody, hewing wood and drawing water, just to keep himself alive? Tolstoï's philosophy, deeply enlightening though it certainly is,

---

[11] Robert Louis Stevenson (1850-1894) was a Scottich novelist, and the author of *Treasure Island*, and poems for children.

[12] A prostitute.

remains a false abstraction. It savors too much of that Oriental pessimism and nihilism of his, which declares the whole phenomenal world and its facts and their distinctions to be a cunning fraud.

A mere bare fraud is just what our Western common sense will never believe the phenomenal world to be. It admits fully that the inner joys and virtues are the *essential* part of life's business, but it is sure that *some* positive part is also played by the adjuncts of the show. If it is idiotic in romanticism to recognize the heroic only when it sees it labelled and dressed-up in books, it is really just as idiotic to see it only in the dirty boots and sweaty shirt of some one in the fields. It is with us really under every disguise: at Chautauqua; here in your college; in the stock-yards and on the freight-trains; and in the czar of Russia's court. But, instinctively, we make a combination of two things in judging the total significance of a human being. We feel it to be some sort of a product (if such a product only could be calculated) of his inner virtue *and* his outer place,—neither singly taken, but both conjoined. If the outer differences had no meaning for life, why indeed should all this immense variety of them exist? They *must* be significant elements of the world as well.

Just test Tolstoï's deification of the mere manual laborer by the facts. This is what Mr. Walter Wyckoff, after working as an unskilled laborer in the demolition of some buildings at West Point, writes of the spiritual condition of the class of men to which he temporarily chose to belong:—

"The salient features of our condition are plain enough. We are grown men, and are without a trade. In the labor-market we stand ready to sell to the highest bidder our mere muscular strength for so many hours each day. We are thus in the lowest grade of labor. And, selling our muscular strength in the open market for what it will bring, we sell it under peculiar conditions. It is all the capital that we have. We have no reserve means of subsistence, and cannot, therefore, stand off for a 'reserve price.' We sell under the necessity of satisfying imminent hunger. Broadly speaking, we must sell our labor or starve; and, as hunger is a matter of a few hours, and we have no other way of meeting this need, we must sell at once for what the market offers for our labor.

"Our employer is buying labor in a dear market, and he will certainly get from us as much work as he can at the price. The gang-boss is secured for this purpose, and thoroughly does he know his business. He has sole command of us. He never saw us before, and he will discharge us all when the débris is cleared away. In the mean time he must get from us, if he can, the utmost of physical labor which we, individually and collectively, are capable of. If he should drive some of us to exhaustion, and we should not be able to continue at work, he would not be the loser; for the market would soon supply him with others to take our places.

"We are ignorant men, but so much we clearly see,—that we have sold our labor where we could sell it dearest, and our employer has bought it where he could buy it cheapest. He has paid high, and he must get all the labor that he can; and, by a strong instinct which possesses us, we shall part with as little as we can. From work like ours there seems to us to have been eliminated every element which constitutes the nobility of labor. We feel no personal pride in its progress, and no community of interest with our employer. There is none of the joy of responsibility, none of the sense of achievement, only the dull monotony of grinding toil, with the longing for the signal to quit work, and for our wages at the end.

"And being what we are, the dregs of the labor-market, and having no certainty of permanent employment, and no organization among ourselves, we must expect to work under the watchful eye of a gang-boss, and be driven, like the wage-slaves that we are, through our tasks.

"All this is to tell us, in effect, that our lives are hard, barren, hopeless lives."

And such hard, barren, hopeless lives, surely, are not lives in which one ought to be willing permanently to remain. And why is this so? Is it because they are so dirty? Well, Nansen[13] grew a great deal dirtier on his polar expedition; and we think none the worse of his life for that. Is it the insensibility? Our soldiers have to grow vastly more insensible, and we extol them to the skies. Is it the poverty? Poverty has been reckoned the crowning beauty of many a heroic career. Is it the slavery to a task, the loss of finer pleasures? Such slavery and loss are of the very essence of the higher fortitude, and are always counted to its credit,—read the records of missionary devotion all over the world. It is not any one of these things, then, taken by itself,—no, nor all of them together,—that make such a life undesirable. A man might in truth live like an unskilled laborer, and do the work of one, and yet count as one of the noblest of God's creatures. Quite possibly there were some such persons in the gang that our author describes; but the current of their souls ran underground; and he was too steeped in the ancestral blindness to discern it.

If there *were* any such morally exceptional individuals, however, what made them different from the rest? It can only have been this,—that their souls worked and endured in obedience to some inner *ideal*, while their comrades were not actuated by anything worthy of that name. These ideals of other lives are among those secrets that we can almost never penetrate, although something about the man may often tell us when they are there. In Mr. Wyckoff's own case we know exactly what the self-imposed ideal was. Partly he had stumped himself, as the boys say, to carry through a strenuous achievement; but mainly he wished to enlarge his sympathetic insight into

---

[13] Fridtjof Nansen (1861-1930), a Norwegian Arctic explorer and naturalist.

fellow-lives. For this his sweat and toil acquire a certain heroic significance, and make us accord to him exceptional esteem. But it is easy to imagine his fellows with various other ideals. To say nothing of wives and babies, one may have been a convert of the Salvation Army, and had a nightingale singing of expiation and forgiveness in his heart all the while he labored. Or there might have been an apostle like Tolstoï himself, or his compatriot Bondareff, in the gang, voluntarily embracing labor as their religious mission. Class-loyalty was undoubtedly an ideal with many. And who knows how much of that higher manliness of poverty, of which Phillips Brooks[14] has spoken so penetratingly, was or was not present in that gang?

"A rugged, barren land," says Phillips Brooks, "is poverty to live in,—a land where I am thankful very often if I can get a berry or a root to eat. But living in it really, letting it bear witness to me of itself, not dishonoring it all the time by judging it after the standard of the other lands, gradually there come out its qualities. Behold! no land like this barren and naked land of poverty could show the moral geology of the world. See how the hard ribs . . . stand out strong and solid. No life like poverty could so get one to the heart of things and make men know their meaning, could so let us feel life and the world with all the soft cushions stripped off and thrown away. . . . Poverty makes men come very near each other, and recognize each other's human hearts; and poverty, highest and best of all, demands and cries out for faith in God. . . . I know how superficial and unfeeling, how like mere mockery, words in praise of poverty may seem. . . . But I am sure that the poor man's dignity and freedom, his self-respect and energy, depend upon his cordial knowledge that his poverty is a true region and kind of life, with its own chances of character, its own springs of happiness and revelations of God. Let him resist the characterlessness which often goes with being poor. Let him insist on respecting the condition where he lives. Let him learn to love it, so that by and by, [if] he grows rich, he shall go out of the low door of the old familiar poverty with a true pang of regret, and with a true honor for the narrow home in which he has lived so long."

The barrenness and ignobleness of the more usual laborer's life consist in the fact that it is moved by no such ideal inner springs. The backache, the long hours, the danger, are patiently endured—for what? To gain a quid of tobacco, a glass of beer, a cup of coffee, a meal, and a bed, and to begin again the next day and shirk as much as one can. This really is why we raise no monument to the laborers in the Subway, even though they be our conscripts, and even though after a fashion our city is indeed based upon thir patient hearts and enduring backs and shoulders. And this is why we do raise monuments to our soldiers, whose outward conditions were even brutaller

---

[14] Phillips Brooks (1835-1893) was an Episcopal clergyman and outstanding pulpit orator. Phillips Brooks House at Harvard is named after him.

still. The soldiers are supposed to have followed an ideal, and the laborers are supposed to have followed none.

You see, my friends, how the plot now thickens; and how strangely the complexities of this wonderful human nature of ours begin to develop under our hands. We have seen the blindness and deadness to each other which are our natural inheritance; and, in spite of them, we have been led to acknowledge an inner meaning which passeth show, and which may be present in the lives of others where we least descry it. And now we are led to say that such inner meaning can be *complete* and *valid for us also,* only when the inner joy, courage, and endurance are joined with an ideal.

But what, exactly, do we mean by an ideal? Can we give no definite account of such a word?

To a certain extent we can. An ideal, for instance, must be something intellectually conceived, something of which we are not unconscious, if we have it; and it must carry with it that sort of outlook, uplift, and brightness that go with all intellectual facts. Secondly, there must be *novelty* in an ideal,—novelty at least for him who the ideal grasps. Sodden routine is incompatible with ideality, although what is sodden routine for one person may be ideal novelty for another. This shows that there is nothing absolutely ideal: ideals are relative to the lives that entertain them. To keep out of the gutter is for us here no part of consciousness at all, yet for many of our brethren it is the most legitimately engrossing of ideals.

Now, taken nakedly, abstractly, and immediately, you see that mere ideals are the cheapest things in life. Everybody has them in some shape or other, personal or general, sound or mistaken, low or high; and the most worthless sentimentalists and dreamers, drunkards, shirks and versemakers, who never show a grain of effort, courage, or endurance, possibly have them on the most copious scale. Education, enlarging as it does our horizon and perspective, is a means of multiplying our ideals, of bringing new ones into view. And your college professor, with a starched shirt and spectacles, would, if a stock of ideals were all alone by itself enough to render a life significant, be the most absolutely and deeply significant of men. Tolstoï would be completely blind in despising him for a prig, a pedant and a parody; and all our new insight into the divinity of muscular labor would be altogether off the track of truth.

But such consequences as this, you instinctively feel, are erroneous. The more ideals a man has, the more contemptible, on the whole, do you continue to deem him, if the matter ends there for him, and if none of the laboring man's virtues are called into action on his part,—no courage shown, no privations undergone, no dirt or scars contracted in the attempt to get them realized. It is quite obvious that something more than the mere possession of ideals is required to make a life significant in any sense that claims the spectator's admiration. Inner joy, to be sure, it may *have*, with its ideals; but that is its own private sentimental matter. To extort from us, outsiders as we are, with our own ideals to look after, the tribute of our grudging recognition, it must back its ideal visions with what the laborers have, the sterner stuff of manly virtue; it must multiply their sentimental surface by the dimension of the active will, if we are to have *depth*, if we are to have anything cubical and solid in the way of character.

The significance of a human life for communicable and publicly recognizable purposes is thus the offspring of a marriage of two different parents, either of whom alone is barren. The ideals taken by themselves give no reality, the virtues by themselves no novelty. And let the orientalists and pessimists say what they will, the thing of deepest—or, at any rate, of comparatively deepest—significance in life does seem to be its character of *progress*, or that strange union of reality with ideal novelty which it continues from one moment to another to present. To recognize ideal novelty is the task of what we call intelligence. Not every one's intelligence can tell which novelties are ideal. For many the ideal thing will always seem to cling still to the older more familiar good. In this case character, though not significant totally, may be still significant pathetically. So, if we are to choose which is the more essential factor of human character, the fighting virtue or the intellectual breadth, we must side with Tolstoï, and choose that simple faithfulness to his light or darkness which any common unintellectual man can show.

But, with all this beating and tacking on my part, I fear you take me to be reaching a confused result. I seem to be just taking things up and dropping them again. First I took up Chautauqua, and dropped that; then Tolstoï and the heroism of common toil, and dropped them; finally, I took up ideals, and seem now almost dropping those. But please observe in what sense it is that I drop them. It is when they pretend *singly* to redeem life from insignificance. Culture and refinement all alone are not enough to do so. Ideal aspirations are not enough, when uncombined with pluck and will. But neither are pluck and will, dogged endurance and insensibility to danger enough, when taken all alone. There must be some sort of fusion, some chemical combination among these principles, for a life objectively and thoroughly significant to result.

Of course, this is a somewhat vague conclusion. But in a question of significance, of worth, like this, conclusions can never be precise. The answer of appreciation, of sentiment, is always a more or a less, a balance struck by sympathy, insight, and good will. But it is an answer, all the same, a real conclusion. And, in the course of getting it, it seems to me that our eyes have been opened to many important things. Some of you are perhaps, more livingly aware than you were an hour ago of the depths of worth that lie around you, hid in alien lives. And, when you ask how much sympathy you ought to bestow, although the amount is, truly enough, a matter of ideal on your own part, yet in this notion of the combination of ideals with active virtues you have a rough standard for shaping your decision. In any case, your imagination is extended. You divine in the world about you matter for a little more humility on your own part, and tolerance, reverence, and love for others; and you gain a certain inner joyfulness at the increased importance of our common life. Such joyfulness is a religious inspiration and an element of spiritual health, and worth more than large amounts of that sort of technical and accurate information which we professors are supposed to be able to impart.

To show the sort of thing I mean by these words, I will just make one brief practical illustration and then close.

We are suffering to-day in America from what is called the labor-question; and, when you go out into the world, you will each and all of you be caught up in its perplexities. I use the brief term labor-question to cover all sorts of anarchistic discontents and socialistic projects, and the conservative resistances which they provoke. So far as this conflict is unhealthy and regrettable,—and I think it is so only to a limited extent,—the unhealthiness consists solely in the fact that one-half of our fellow-countrymen remain entirely blind to the internal significance of the lives of the other half. They miss the joys and sorrows, they fail to feel the moral virtue, and they do not guess the presence of the intellectual ideals. They are at cross-purposes all along the line, regarding each other as they might regard a set of dangerously gesticulating automata, or, if they seek to get at the inner motivation, making the most horrible mistakes. Often all that the poor man can think of in the rich man is a cowardly greediness for safety, luxury, and effeminacy, and a boundless affectation. What he is, is not a human being, but a pocket-book, a bank-account. And a similar greediness, turned by disappointment into envy, is all that many rich men can see in the state of mind of the dissatisfied poor. And, if the rich man begins to do the sentimental act over the poor man, what senseless blunders does he make, pitying him for just those very duties and those very immunities which, rightly taken, are the condition of his most abiding and characteristic joys! Each, in short, ignores the fact that happiness and unhappiness and significance are a vital mystery; each pins them absolutely on some ridiculous feature of the external situation; and everybody remains outside of everybody else's sight.

Society has, with all this, undoubtedly got to pass toward some newer and better equilibrium, and the distribution of wealth has doubtless slowly got to change: such changes have always happened, and will happen to the end of time. But if, after all that I have said, any of you expect that they will make any *genuine vital difference* on a large scale, to the lives of our descendants, you will have missed the significance of my entire lecture. The solid meaning of life is always the same eternal thing,—the marriage, namely, of some unhabitual ideal, however special, with some fidelity, courage, and endurance; with some man's or woman's pains.—And, whatever or wherever life may be, there will always be the chance for that marriage to take place.

Fitz-James Stephen[15] wrote many years ago words to this effect more eloquent than any I can speak: "The 'Great Eastern,'[16] or some of her successors," he said, "will perhaps defy the roll of the Atlantic, and cross the seas without allowing their passengers to feel that they have left the firm land. The voyage from the cradle to the grave may come to be performed with similar facility. Progress and science may perhaps enable untold millions to live and die without a care, without a pang, without an anxiety. They will have a pleasant passage and plenty of brilliant conversation. They will wonder that men ever believed at all in clanging fights and blazing towns and sinking ships and praying hands; and, when they come to the end of their course, they will go their way, and the place thereof will know them no more. But it seems unlikely that they will have such a knowledge of the great ocean on which they sail, with its storms and wrecks, its currents and icebergs, its huge waves and mighty winds, as those who battled with it for years together in the little craft, which, if they had few other merits, brought those who navigated them full into the presence of time and eternity, their maker and themselves, and forced them to have some definite view of their relations to them and to each other."

In this solid and tridimensional sense, so to call it, those philosophers are right who contend that the world is a standing thing, with no progress, no real history. The changing conditions of history touch only the surface of the show. The altered equilibriums and redistributions only diversify our opportunities and open chances to us for new ideals. But, with each new ideal that comes into life, the chance for a life based on some old ideal will vanish; and he would needs be a presumptuous calculator who should with confidence say that the total sum of significances is positively and absolutely greater at any one epoch than at any other of the world.

I am speaking broadly, I know, and omitting to consider certain qualifications in which I myself believe. But one can only make one point in one lecture, and I shall be well content if I have brought my point home to you this evening in even a slight degree. *There are compensations:* and no outward changes of condition in life can keep the nightingale of its eternal meaning from singing in all sorts of different men's hearts. That is the main fact to remember. If we could not only admit it with our lips, but really and truly believe it, how our convulsive insistencies, how our anitpathies and dreads of each other, would soften down! If the poor and the rich could look at each other in this way, *sub specie æternatis,* how gentle would grow their disputes! what tolerance and good humor, what willingness to live and let live, would come into the world!

---

[15] Fitz-James Stephen (1882–1950), Irish poet and novelist.

[16] A large early cross-Atlantic steamship that excited great interest in New York City when at the dock.

THORSTEIN VEBLEN

(1857–1929)

Thorstein Veblen has a significant place in American writing as a severe and acid critic of modern business civilization. A professional academic economist, Veblen wrote many works exposing the illusions and inefficiencies of American industrial capitalism and its culture, but none is so popular nor as directly critical of the Gilded Age as his first work, *The Theory of the Leisure Class* (1899). In that book he coined the expressions "conspicuous consumption" and "pecuniary emulation," terms that in many ways fit the view of the monied classes and their middle-class imitators that we find in the critical fiction of the period. Embodying a new spirit of realism in the social sciences, Veblen spared no feature of modern American life. In *The Higher Learning in America* (1918) he made a still trenchant attack on the "conduct of universities by business men."

Born of poor Norwegian immigrant parents in Wisconsin, Veblen made his way through a complete formal education, including a Ph.D. from Yale University (1884). He held faculty positions at the University of Chicago, Stanford University, The University of Missouri, and The New School for Social Research. Yet he remained essentially an outsider, more and more radical in his criticism of capitalism. His manner was eccentric, prickly, proud, and his intellectual powers and erudition profound. The style of his writing carries the impress of his personality: complex, knotty, ironic. He viewed the behavior of the new business classes as a satirist, with both moral outrage and bemused, detached, scientific commentary.

The major works are *The Theory of the Leisure Class,* 1899; *The Theory of Business Enterprise,* 1904; *The Instinct of Workmanship and the State of the Industrial Arts,* 1914; *The Higher Learning in America,* 1918; *The Place of Science in Modern Civilization,* 1919;

Two important studies are Joseph Dorfman, *Thorstein Veblen and His America,* 1934; David Reisman, *Thorstein Veblen, A Critical Interpretation,* 1953.

From The Theory of the Leisure Class

CHAPTER V
THE PECUNIARY STANDARD OF LIVING[1]

For the great body of the people in any modern community, the proximate ground of expenditure in excess of what is required for physical comfort is not a conscious effort to excel in the expensiveness of their visible consumption, so much as it is a desire to live up to the conventional standard of decency in the amount and grade of goods consumed. This desire is not guided by a rigidly invariable standard, which must be lived up to, and beyond which there is no incentive to go. The standard is flexible; and especially it is indefinitely extensible, if only time is allowed for habituation to any increase in pecuniary ability and for acquiring facility in the new and larger scale of expenditure that follows such an increase. It is much more difficult to recede from a scale of expenditure once adopted than it is to extend the accustomed scale in response to an accession of wealth. Many items of customary expenditure prove on analysis to be almost purely wasteful, and they are therefore honorific only, but after they have once been incorporated into the scale of decent consumption, and so have become an integral part of one's scheme of life, it is quite as hard to give up these as it is to give up many items that conduce directly to one's physical comfort, or even that may be necessary to life and health. That is to say, the conspicuously wasteful honorifc expenditure that confers spiritual well-being may become more indispensable than much of that expenditure which ministers to the "lower" wants of physical well-being or sustenance only. It is notoriously just as difficult to recede from a "high" standard of living as it is to lower a standard which is already relatively low; although in the former case the difficulty is a moral one, while in the latter it may involve a material deduction from the physical comforts of life.

But while retrogression is difficult, a fresh advance in conspicuous expenditure is relatively easy; indeed, it takes place almost as a matter of course. In the rare cases where it occurs, a failure to increase one's visible consumption when the means for an increase are at hand is felt in popular apprehension to call for explanation, and unworthy motives of miserliness are imputed to those who fall short in this respect. A prompt response to the stimulus, on the other hand, is accepted as the moral effect. This suggests that the standard of expenditure which commonly guides our efforts is not the average, ordinary expenditure already achieved; it is an ideal of consumption that lies just beyond our reach, or to reach which requires some strain. The motive is emulation—the stimulus of an invidious comparison which prompts us to

[1] First published in *The Theory of the Leisure Class*, 1899.

outdo those with whom we are in the habit of classing ourselves. Substantially the same proposition is expressed in the commonplace remark that each class envies and emulates the class next above it in the social scale, while it rarely compares itself with those below or with those who are considerably in advance. That is to say, in other words, our standard of decency in expenditure, as in other ends of emulation, is set by the usage of those next above us in reputability; until, in this way, especially in any community where class distinctions are somewhat vague, all canons of reputability and decency, and all standards of consumption, are traced back by insensible gradations to the usages and habits of thought of the highest social and pecuniary class—the wealthy leisure class.

It is for this class to determine, in general outline, what scheme of life the community shall accept as decent or honorific; and it is their office by precept and example to set forth this scheme of social salvation in its highest, ideal form. But the higher leisure class can exercise this quasi-sacerdotal[2] office only under certain material limitations. The class cannot at discretion effect a sudden revolution or reversal of the popular habits of thought with respect to any of these ceremonial requirements. It takes time for any change to permeate the mass and change the habitual attitude of the people; and especially it takes time to change the habits of those classes that are socially more remote from the radiant body. The process is slower where the mobility of the population is less or where the intervals between the several classes are wider and more abrupt. But if time be allowed, the scope of the discretion of the leisure class as regards questions of form and detail in the community's scheme of life is large; while as regards the substantial principles of reputability, the changes which it can effect lie within a narrow margin of tolerance. Its example and precept carries the force of prescription for all classes below it; but in working out the precepts which are handed down as governing the form and method of reputability—in shaping the usages and the spiritual attitude of the lower classes—this authoritative prescription constantly works under the selective guidance of the canon of conspicuous waste, tempered in varying degree by the instinct of workmanship. To these norms is to be added another broad principle of human nature—the predatory animus—which in point of generality and of psychological content lies between the two just named. The effect of the latter in shaping the accepted scheme of life is yet to be discussed.

The canon of reputability, then, must adapt itself to the economic circumstances, the traditions, and the degree of spiritual maturity of the particular class whose scheme of life it is to regulate. It is especially to be noted that however high its authority and however true to the fundamental requirements of reputability it may have been at its inception, a specific formal

[2] As if pertaining to or believing in a priest or priesthood.

observance can under no circumstances maintain itself in force if with the lapse of time or on its transmission to a lower pecuniary class it is found to run counter to the ultimate ground of decency among civilised peoples, namely, serviceability for the purpose of an invidious comparison in pecuniary success.

It is evident that these canons of expenditure have much to say in determining the standard of living for any community and for any class. It is no less evident that the standard of living which prevails at any time or at any given social altitude will in its turn have much to say as to the forms which honorific expenditure will take, and as to the degree to which this "higher" need will dominate a people's consumption. In this respect the control exerted by the accepted standard of living is chiefly of a negative character; it acts almost solely to prevent recession from a scale of conspicuous expenditure that has once become habitual.

A standard of living is of the nature of habit. It is an habitual scale and method of responding to given stimuli. The difficulty in the way of receding from an accustomed standard is the difficulty of breaking a habit that has once been formed. The relative facility with which an advance in the standard is made means that the life process is a process of unfolding activity and that it will readily unfold in a new direction whenever and wherever the resistance to self-expression decreases. But when the habit of expression along such a given line of low resistance has once been formed, the discharge will seek the accustomed outlet even after a change has taken place in the environment whereby the external resistance has appreciably risen. That heightened facility of expression in a given direction which is called habit may offset a considerable increase in the resistance offered by external circumstances to the unfolding of life in the given direction. As between the various habits, or habitual modes and directions of expression, which go to make up an individual's standard of living, there is an appreciable difference in point of persistence under counteracting circumstances and in point of the degree of imperativeness with which the discharge seeks a given direction.

That is to say, in the language of current economic theory, while men are reluctant to retrench their expenditures in any direction, they are more reluctant to retrench in some directions than in others; so that while any accustomed consumption is reluctantly given up, there are certain lines of consumption which are given up with relatively extreme reluctance. The articles or forms of consumption to which the consumer clings with the greatest tenacity are commonly the so-called necessaries of life, or the subsistence minimum. The subsistence minimum is of course not a rigidly determined allowance of goods, definite and invariable in kind and quantity; but for the purpose in hand it may be taken to comprise a certain, more or less definite, aggregate of consumption required for the maintenance of life. This minimum, it may be assumed, is ordinarily given up last in case of a progressive retrenchment of expenditure. That is to say, in a general way, the most ancient and ingrained of the habits which govern the individual's life—those habits that touch his existence as an organism—are the most persistent and imperative. Beyond these come the higher wants—later-formed habits of the individual or the race—in a somewhat irregular and by no means invariable gradation. Some of these higher wants, as for instance the habitual use of certain stimulants, or the need of salvation (in the eschatological sense),[3] or of good repute, may in some cases take precedence of the lower or more elementary wants. In general, the longer the habituation, the more unbroken the habit and the more nearly it coincides with previous habitual forms of the life process, the more persistently will the given habit assert itself. The habit will be stronger if the particular traits of human nature which its action involves, or the particular aptitudes that find exercise in it, are traits or aptitudes that are already largely and profoundly concerned in the life process or that are intimately bound up with the life history of the particular racial stock.

The varying degrees of ease with which different habits are formed by different persons, as well as the varying degrees of reluctance with which different habits are given up, goes to say that the formation of specific habits is not a matter of length of habituation simply. Inherited aptitudes and traits of temperament count for quite as much as length of habituation in deciding what range of habits will come to dominate any individual's scheme of life. And the prevalent type of transmitted aptitudes, or in other words the type of temperament belonging to the dominant ethnic element in any community, will go far to decide what will be the scope and form of expression of the community's habitual life process. How greatly the transmitted idiosyncrasies of aptitude may count in the way of a rapid and definitive formation of habit in individuals is illustrated by the extreme facility with which an all-dominating habit of alcoholism is sometimes formed; or in the similar facility and the similarly inevitable formation of a habit of devout observances in the case of persons gifted with a special aptitude in that direction. Much the same meaning attaches to that peculiar facility of habituation to a specific human environment that is called romantic love.

Men differ in respect of transmitted aptitudes, or in respect of the relative facility with which they unfold their life activity in particular directions; and the habits which coincide with or proceed upon a relatively strong specific aptitude or a relatively great specific facility of expression become of great consequence to the man's well-being. The part played by this element of aptitude in determining the relative tenacity of the several habits which constitute the standard of living goes to explain the extreme reluctance with which men give up any habitual expenditure in the way of conspicuous

[3] The theology of death, resurrection, the end of the world, immortality, the final judgement, and the future.

consumption. The aptitudes or propensities to which a habit of this kind is to be referred as its ground are those aptitudes whose exercise is comprised in emulation; and the propensity for emulation—for invidious comparison—is of ancient growth and is a pervading trait of human nature. It is easily called into vigorous activity in any new form, and it asserts itself with great insistence under any form under which it has once found habitual expression. When the individual has once formed the habit of seeking expression in a given line of honorific expenditure,—when a given set of stimuli have come to be habitually responded to in activity of a given kind and direction under the guidance of these alert and deep-reaching propensities of emulation,—it is with extreme reluctance that such an habitual expenditure is given up. And on the other hand, whenever an accession of pecuniary strength puts the individual in a position to unfold his life process in larger scope and with additional reach, the ancient propensities of the race will assert themselves in determining the direction which the new unfolding of life is to take. And those propensities which are already actively in the field under some related form of expression, which are aided by the pointed suggestions afforded by a current accredited scheme of life, and for the exercise of which the material means and opportunities are readily available,—these will especially have much to say in shaping the form and direction in which the new accession to the individual's aggregate force will assert itself. That is to say, in concrete terms, in any community where conspicuous consumption is an element of the scheme of life, an increase in an individual's ability to pay is likely to take the form of an expenditure for some accredited line of conspicuous consumption.

With the exception of the instinct of self-preservation, the propensity for emulation is probably the strongest and most alert and persistent of the economic motives proper. In an industrial community this propensity for emulation expresses itself in pecuniary emulation; and this, so far as regards the Western civilised communities of the present, is virtually equivalent to saying that it expresses itself in some form of conspicuous waste. The need of conspicuous waste, therefore, stands ready to absorb any increase in the community's industrial efficiency or output of goods, after the most elementary physical wants have been provided for. Where this result does not follow, under modern conditions, the reason for the discrepancy is commonly to be sought in a rate of increase in the individual's wealth too rapid for the habit of expenditure to keep abreast of it; or it may be that the individual in question defers the conspicuous consumption of the increment to a later date—ordinarily with a view to heightening the spectacular effect of the aggregate expenditure contemplated. As increased industrial efficiency makes it possible to procure the means of livelihood with less labour, the energies of the industrious members of the community are bent to the compassing of a higher result in conspicuous expenditure, rather than slackened to a more comfortable pace. The strain is not lightened as industrial efficiency increases and makes a lighter strain possible, but the increment of output is turned to use to meet this want, which is indefinitely expansible, after the manner commonly imputed in economic theory to higher or spiritual wants. It is owing chiefly to the presence of this element in the standard of living that J. S. Mill[4] was able to say that "hitherto it is questionable if all the mechanical inventions yet made have lightened the day's toil of any human being."

The accepted standard of expenditure in the community or in the class to which a person belongs largely determines what his standard of living will be. It does this directly by commending itself to his common sense as right and good, through his habitually contemplating it and assimilating the scheme of life in which it belongs; but it does so also indirectly through popular insistence on conformity to the accepted scale of expenditure as a matter of propriety, under pain of disesteem and ostracism. To accept and practice the standard of living which is in vogue is both agreeable and expedient, commonly to the point of being indispensable to personal comfort and to success in life. The standard of living of any class, so far as concerns the element of conspicuous waste, is commonly as high as the earning capacity of the class will permit—with a constant tendency to go higher. The effect upon the serious activities of men is therefore to direct them with great singleness of purpose to the largest possible acquisition of wealth, and to discountenance work that brings no pecuniary gain. At the same time the effect on consumption is to concentrate it upon the lines which are most patent to the observers whose good opinion is sought; while the inclinations and aptitudes whose exercise does not involve an honorific expenditure of time or substance tend to fall into abeyance through disuse.

Through this discrimination in favour of visible consumption it has come about that the domestic life of most classes is relatively shabby, as compared with the éclat of that overt portion of their life that is carried on before the eyes of observers. As a secondary consequence of the same discrimination, people habitually screen their private life from observation. So far as concerns that portion of their consumption that may without blame be carried on in secret, they withdraw from all contact with their neighbours. Hence the exclusiveness of people, as regards their domestic life, in most of the industrially developed communities; and hence, by remoter derivation, the habit of privacy and reserve that is so large a feature in the code of proprieties of the better classes in all communities. The low birthrate of the classes upon whom the requirements of reputable expenditure fall with great urgency is likewise traceable to the exigencies of a standard of living based on conspicuous waste. The conspicuous consumption, and the consequent increased expense, required in the reputable maintenance of a child is very

[4] John Stuart Mill (1806-1873), English philosopher and political economist.

considerable and acts as a powerful deterrent. It is probably the most effectual of the Malthusian[5] prudential checks.

The effect of this factor of the standard of living, both in the way of retrenchment in the obscurer elements of consumption that go to physical comfort and maintenance, and also in the paucity or absence of children, is perhaps seen at its best among the classes given to scholarly pursuits. Because of presumed superiority and scarcity of the gifts and attainments that characterise their life, these classes are by convention subsumed under a higher social grade than their pecuniary grade should warrant. The scale of decent expenditure in their case is pitched correspondingly high, and it consequently leaves an exceptionally narrow margin disposable for the other ends of life. By force of circumstances, their own habitual sense of what is good and right in these matters, as well as the expectations of the community in the way of pecuniary decency among the learned, are excessively high—as measured by the prevalent degree of opulence and earning capacity of the class, relatively to the non-scholarly classes whose social equals they nominally are. In any modern community where there is no priestly monopoly of these occupations, the people of scholarly pursuits are unavoidably thrown into contact with classes that are pecuniarily their superiors. The high standard of pecuniary decency in force among these superior classes is transfused among the scholarly classes with but little mitigation of its rigour; and as a consequence there is no class of the community that spends a larger proportion of its substance in conspicuous waste than these.

[5] Pertaining to the theory of Thomas Robert Malthus (1766-1834) that population increases faster than food, shelter and jobs so that when it is not limited by sexual restraint, it is restricted by famine, disease, and war.

GEORGE SANTAYANA

(1863-1952)

Spanish-born, urbane, Catholic by "sympathy and traditional allegiance," Santayana had the point of view of a somewhat displaced person in American life at the end of the century. Although he was

The major works are *The Sense of Beauty*, 1896; *Lucifer, A Poetic Drama*, 1899; *Interpretations of Poetry and Religion*, 1900; *The Life of Reason*, 1905-06; *Three Philosophical Poets*, 1910; *Winds of Doctrine*, 1913; *Character and Opinion in the United States*, 1920; *Skepticism and Animal Faith*, 1923; *The Last Puritan*, 1935; *Person and Places*, 1944.

(Footnote continued next page.)

raised in Boston, attended Harvard, and then taught there in the same department with his former teachers Josiah Royce and William James, he retained and cultivated the perspective of an alien, looking out on the predominantly Protestant and Anglo-Saxon culture of New England with a bemused, cosmopolitan eye. He left the United States for good in 1914. Yet he wrote, "It is as an American that I must be counted, if I am counted at all."

Philosophically Santayana stood apart from both idealism and pragmatism, calling himself a "Platonic materialist." He had little interest in scientific method; his approach to philosophy as to life was humanistic, literary, aesthetic. Early in the 1890's he was part of a circle of young poets at Harvard that included Trumbull Stickney and William Vaughn Moody. He brought out several volumes of verse in these years, including *Sonnets and Other Verses* (1894) and *Lucifer: A Theological Tragedy* (1899). Much of his writing was literary criticism, in works such as *Interpretations of Poetry and Religion* (1900) and *Three Philosophical Poets* (1910). His major philosophical treatises in these years, which stress man's materiality and object to all abstracting ideologies, are *The Sense of Beauty* (1896) and *The Life of Reason* (five volumes, 1905–1906).

Santayana's incisive observations on American life and culture appear in many essays and in *Character and Opinion in the United States* (1920). His essay, "The Genteel Tradition in American Philosophy," first delivered as a lecture in California in 1910, combines philosophical insight with cultural criticism and provides a comprehensive overview of the relation between American thought and literature with cultural patterns. Although its view of America leaves much out, and its detached tone suggests a perhaps unwarranted immunity on his own part to the phenomenon he describes, the essay's description of a split in American life between a business culture and a literary culture, and its analysis of the dominant Anglo-Saxon Protestant outlook, anticipates the attack on Puritanism and commercialism launched by younger writers in the same years.

Daniel Cory has edited *Letters*, 1963. Studies include Irving Singer, *Santayana's Aesthetics: A Critical Introduction*, 1957; M. M. Kirkwood, *Santayana: Saint of the Imagination*, 1961; Richard Colton Lyon, *Santayana on America*, 1968.

The Gross Clinic, Thomas Eakins. *Courtesy Public Relations Department, Thomas Jefferson University, Philadelphia, Pennsylvania.*

The Genteel Tradition in American Philosophy[1]

Ladies and Gentlemen,—The privilege of addressing you today is very welcome to me, not merely for the honour of it, which is great, nor for the pleasures of travel, which are many, when it is California that one is visiting for the first time, but also because there is something I have long wanted to say which this occasion seems particularly favourable for saying. America is still a young country, and this part of it is especially so; and it would have been nothing extraordinary if, in this young country, material preoccupations had altogether absorbed people's minds, and they had been too much engrossed in living to reflect upon life, or to have any philosophy. The opposite, however, is the case. Not only have you already found time to philosophise in California, as your society proves, but the eastern colonists from the very beginning were a sophisticated race. As much as in clearing the land and fighting the Indians they were occupied, as they expressed it, in wrestling with the Lord. The country was new, but the race was tried, chastened, and full of solemn memories. It was an old wine in new bottles; and America did not have to wait for its present universities, with their departments of academic philosophy, in order to possess a living philosophy—to have a distinct vision of the universe and definite convictions about human destiny.

Now this situation is a singular and remarkable one, and has many consequences, not all of which are equally fortunate. America is a young country with an old mentality: it has enjoyed the advantages of a child carefully brought up and thoroughly indoctrinated; it has been a wise child. But a wise child, an old head on young shoulders, always has a comic and an unpromising side. The wisdom is a little thin and verbal, not aware of its full meaning and grounds; and physical and emotional growth may be stunted by it, or even deranged. Or when the child is too vigorous for that, he will develop a fresh mentality of his own, out of his observations and actual instincts; and this fresh mentality will interfere with the traditional mentality, and tend to reduce it to something perfunctory, conventional, and perhaps secretly despised. A philosophy is not genuine unless it inspires and expresses the life of those who cherish it. I do not think the hereditary philosophy of America has done much to atrophy the natural activities of the inhabitants; the wise child has not missed the joys of youth or of manhood; but what has happened is that the hereditary philosophy has grown stale, and that the academic philosophy afterwards developed has caught the stale odour from it. America is not simply, as I said a moment ago, a young country with an old mentality: it is a country with two mentalities, one a survival of the beliefs and standards

[1] First given as a lecture at the University of California on August 15, 1911 and then collected in *The Genteel Tradition at Bay*, C. Scribner's Sons, New York 1931.

of the fathers, the other an expression of the instincts, practice, and discoveries of the younger generations. In all the higher things of the mind—in religion, in literature, in the moral emotions—it is the hereditary spirit that still prevails, so much so that Mr. Bernard Shaw[2] finds that America is a hundred years behind the times. The truth is that one-half of the American mind, that not occupied intensely in practical affairs, has remained, I will not say high-and-dry, but slightly becalmed; it has floated gently in the backwater, while, alongside, in invention and industry and social organisation, the other half of the mind was leaping down a sort of Niagara Rapids. This division may be found symbolised in American architecture: a neat reproduction of the colonial mansion—with some modern comforts introduced surreptitiously—stands beside the sky-scraper. The American Will inhabits the sky-scraper; the American Intellect inhabits the colonial mansion. The one is the sphere of the American man; the other, at least predominantly, of the American woman. The one is all aggressive enterprise; the other is all genteel tradition.

Now, with your permission, I should like to analyse more fully how this interesting situation has arisen, how it is qualified, and whither it tends. And in the first place we should remember what, precisely, that philosophy was which the first settlers brought with them into the country. In strictness there was more than one; but we may confine our attention to what I will call Calvinism, since it is on this that the current academic philosophy has been grafted. I do not mean exactly the Calvinism of Calvin,[3] or even of Jonathan Edwards,[4] for in their systems there was much that was not pure philosophy, but rather faith in the externals and history of revelation. Jewish and Christian revelation was interpreted by these men, however, in the spirit of a particular philosophy, which might have arisen under any sky, and been associated with any other religion as well as with Protestant Christianity. In fact, the philosophical principle of Calvinism appears also in the Koran,[5] in Spinoza,[6] and in Cardinal Newman;[7] and persons with no very distinctive Christian belief, like Carlyle[8] or like Professor Royce,[9] may be nevertheless,

[2] George Bernard Shaw (1856-1950), Irish dramatist, critic, novelist, and misogynist.

[3] John Calvin (1509-1564) was a Protestant reformer who emphasized the depravity and helplessness of man and the utter sovereignty of God.

[4] Jonathan Edwards (1703-1758), a great Calvinist theologian and scholar who was a powerful revivalist preacher and led a religious "awakening" in the 1740s in New England. See p. 310.

[5] Moslem sacred book.

[6] Baruch Spinoza (1632-1677), a Jewish philosopher who regarded the whole universe as one with God, of which space and mind are attributes and specific things, ideas, and states are modes.

[7] Cardinal John Henry Newman (1801-1890), an English theologian and author.

[8] Thomas Carlyle (1795-1881) was a British writer and personality. He wrote *Sartor Resartus.*

[9] Professor Josiah Royce (1855-1916) was a leading American philosopher and follower of post-Kantian idealism. He was a professor at Harvard and a friend of William James.

philosophically, perfect Calvinists. Calvinism, taken in this sense, is an expression of the agonised conscience. It is a view of the world which an agonised conscience readily embraces, if it takes itself seriously, as, being agonised, of course it must. Calvinism, essentially, asserts three things: that sin exists, that sin is punished, and that it is beautiful that sin should exist to be punished. The heart of the Calvinist is therefore divided between tragic concern at his own miserable condition, and tragic exultation about the universe at large. He oscillates between a profound abasement and a paradoxical elation of the spirit. To be a Calvinist philosophically is to feel a fierce pleasure in the existence of misery, especially of one's own, in that this misery seems to manifest the fact that the Absolute is irresponsible or infinite or holy. Human nature, it feels, is totally depraved: to have the instincts and motives that we necessarily have is a great scandal, and we must suffer for it; but that scandal is requisite, since otherwise the serious importance of being as we ought to be would not have been vindicated.

To those of us who have not an agonised conscience this system may seem fantastic and even unintelligible; yet it is logically and intently thought from its emotional premises. It can take permanent possession of a deep mind here and there, and under certain conditions it can become epidemic. Imagine, for instance, a small nation with an intense vitality, but on the verge of ruin, ecstatic and distressful, having a strict and minute code of laws, that paints life in sharp and violent chiaroscuro, [10] all pure righteousness and black abominations, and exaggerating the consequences of both perhaps to infinity. Such a people were the Jews after the exile, and again the early Protestants. If such a people is philosophical at all, it will not improbably be Calvinistic. Even in the early American communities many of these conditions were fulfilled. The nation was small and isolated; it lived under pressure and constant trial; it was acquainted with but a small range of goods and evils. Vigilance over conduct and an absolute demand for personal integrity were not merely traditional things, but things that practical sages, like Franklin and Washington, recommended to their countrymen, because they were virtues that justified themselves visibly by their fruits. But soon these happy results themselves helped to relax the pressure of external circumstances, and indirectly the pressure of the agonised conscience within. The nation became numerous; it ceased to be either ecstatic or distressful; the high social morality which on the whole it preserved took another colour; people remained honest and helpful out of good sense and good will rather than out of scrupulous adherence to any fixed principles. They retained their instinct for order, and often created order with surprising quickness; but the sanctity of law, to be obeyed for its own sake, began to escape them; it seemed too

---

[10] The way the lights and darks in a painting or drawing are treated so that they produce a dramatic illusion of depth.

unpractical a notion, and not quite serious. In fact, the second and native-born American mentality began to take shape. The sense of sin totally evaporated. Nature, in the words of Emerson, was all beauty and commodity; and while operating on it laboriously, and drawing quick returns, the American began to drink in inspiration from it æsthetically. At the same time, in so broad a continent, he had elbow-room. His neighbours helped more than they hindered him; he wished their number to increase. Good will became the great American virtue; and a passion arose for counting heads, and square miles, and cubic feet, and minutes saved—as if there had been anything to save them for. How strange to the American now that saying of Jonathan Edwards, that men are naturally God's enemies! Yet that is an axiom to any intelligent Calvinist, though the words he uses may be different. If you told the modern American that he is totally depraved, he would think you were joking, as he himself usually is. He is convinced that he always has been, and always will be, victorious and blameless.

Calvinism thus lost its basis in American life. Some emotional natures, indeed, reverted in their religious revivals or private searchings of heart to the sources of the tradition; for any of the radical points of view in philosophy may cease to be prevalent, but none can cease to be possible. Other natures, more sensitive to the moral and literary influences of the world, preferred to abandon parts of their philosophy, hoping thus to reduce the distance which should separate the remainder from real life.

Meantime, if anybody arose with a special sensibility or a technical genius, he was in great straits; not being fed sufficiently by the world, he was driven in upon his own resources. The three American writers whose personal endowment was perhaps the finest—Poe, Hawthorne, and Emerson—had all a certain starved and abstract quality. They could not retail the genteel tradition; they were too keen, too perceptive, and too independent for that. But life offered them little digestible material, nor were they naturally voracious. They were fastidious, and under the circumstances they were starved. Emerson, to be sure, fed on books. There was a great catholicity in his reading; and he showed a fine tact in his comments, and in his way of appropriating what he read. But he read transcendentally, not historically, to learn what he himself felt, not what others might have felt before him. And to feed on books, for a philosopher or a poet, is still to starve. Books can help him to acquire form, or to avoid pitfalls; they cannot supply him with substance, if he is to have any. Therefore the genius of Poe and Hawthorne, and even of Emerson, was employed on a sort of inner play, or digestion of vacancy. It was a refined labour, but it was in danger of being morbid, or tinkling, or self-indulgent. It was a play of intra-mental rhymes. Their mind was like an old music-box, full of tender echoes and quaint fancies. These fancies expressed their personal genius sincerely, as dreams may; but they were arbitrary fancies in comparison with what a real observer would have said in the premises. Their manner, in a word, was subjective. In their own persons they escaped the mediocrity of the genteel tradition, but they supplied nothing to supplant it in other minds.

The churches, likewise, although they modified their spirit, had no philosophy to offer save a new emphasis on parts of what Calvinism contained. The theology of Calvin, we must remember, had much in it besides philosophical Calvinism. A Christian tenderness, and a hope of grace for the individual, came to mitigate its sardonic optimism; and it was these evangelical elements that the Calvinistic churches now emphasised, seldom and with blushes referring to hell-fire or infant damnation. Yet philosophic Calvinism, with a theory of life that would perfectly justify hell-fire and infant damnation if they happened to exist, still dominates the traditional metaphysics. It is an ingredient, and the decisive ingredient, in what calls itself idealism. But in order to see just what part Calvinism plays in current idealism, it will be necessary to distinguish the other chief element in that complex system, namely, transcendentalism.

Transcendentalism is the philosophy which the romantic era produced in Germany, and independently, I believe, in America also. Transcendentalism proper, like romanticism, is not any particular set of dogmas about what things exist; it is not a system of the universe regarded as a fact, or as a collection of facts. It is a method, a point of view, from which any world, no matter what it might contain, could be approached by a self-conscious observer. Transcendentalism is systematic subjectivism. It studies the perspectives of knowledge as they radiate from the self; it is a plan of those avenues of inference by which our ideas of things must be reached, if they are to afford any systematic or distant vistas. In other words, transcendentalism is the critical logic of science. Knowledge, it says, has a station, as in a watchtower; it is always seated here and now, in the self of the moment. The past and the future, things inferred and things conceived, lie around it, painted as upon a panorama. They cannot be lighted up save by some centrifugal ray of attention and present interest, by some active operation of the mind.

This is hardly the occasion for developing or explaining this delicate insight; suffice it to say, lest you should think later that I disparage transcendentalism, that as a method I regard it as correct and, when once suggested, unforgettable. I regard it as the chief contribution made in modern times to speculation. But it is a method only, an attitude we may always assume if we like and that will always be legitimate. It is no answer, and involves no particular answer, to the question: What exists; in what order is what exists produced; what is to exist in the future? This question must be answered by observing the object, and tracing humbly the movement of the object. It cannot be answered at all by harping on the fact that this object, if discovered, must be discovered by somebody, and by somebody who has an interest in discovering it. Yet the Germans who first gained the full transcendental insight were romantic people; they were more or less frankly poets; they were colossal egotists, and wished to make not only their own knowledge but the whole universe centre about themselves. And full as they were of their romantic isolation and romantic liberty, it occurred to them to imagine that all reality might be a transcendental self and a romantic dreamer like themselves; nay, that it might be just their own transcendental self and their own romantic dreams extended indefinitely. Transcendental logic, the method of discovery for the mind, was to become also the method of evolution in nature and history. Transcendental method, so abused, produced transcendental myth. A conscientious critique of knowledge was turned into a sham system of nature. We must therefore distinguish sharply the transcendental grammar of the intellect, which is significant and potentially correct, from the various transcendental systems of the universe, which are chimeras.

In both its parts, however, transcendentalism had much to recommend it to American philosophers, for the transcendental method appealed to the individualistic and revolutionary temper of their youth, while transcendental myths enabled them to find a new status for their inherited theology, and to give what parts of it they cared to preserve some semblance of philosophical backing. This last was the use to which the transcendental method was put by Kant[11] himself, who first brought it into vogue, before the terrible weapon had got out of hand, and become the instrument of pure romanticism. Kant came, he himself said, to remove knowledge in order to make room for faith, which in his case meant faith in Calvinism. In other words, he applied the transcendental method to matters of fact, reducing them thereby to human ideas, in order to give to the Calvinistic postulates of conscience a metaphysical validity. For Kant had a genteel tradition of his own, which he wished to remove to a place of safety, feeling that the empirical world had become too hot for it; and this place of safety was the region of transcendental myth. I need hardly say how perfectly this expedient suited the needs of philosophers in America, and it is no accident if the influence of Kant soon became dominant here. To embrace this philosophy was regarded as a sign of profound metaphysical insight, although the most mediocre minds found no difficulty in embracing it. In truth it was a sign of having been brought up in the genteel tradition, of feeling it weak, and of wishing to save it.

But the transcendal method, in its way, was also sympathetic to the American mind. It embodied, in a radical form, the spirit of Protestantism as distinguished from its inherited doctrines; it was autonomous, undismayed, calmly revolutionary; it felt that Will was deeper than Intellect; it focussed everything here and now, and asked all things to show their credentials at the bar of the young self, and to prove their value for this latest born moment. These things are truly American; they would be characteristic of any young society with a keen and discursive intelligence, and they are strikingly

[11] Immanuel Kant (1724-1804) was a major German idealist philosopher who wrote *Critique of Pure Reason* (1781).

exemplified in the thought and in the person of Emerson. They constitute what he called self-trust. Self-trust, like other transcendental attitudes, may be expressed in metaphysical fables. The romantic spirit may imagine itself to be an absolute force, evoking and moulding the plastic world to express its varying moods. But for a pioneer who is actually a world-builder this metaphysical illusion has a partial warrant in historical fact; far more warrant than it could boast of in the fixed and articulated society of Europe, among the moonstruck rebels and sulking poets of the romantic era. Emerson was a shrewd Yankee, by instinct on the winning side; he was a cheery, child-like soul, impervious to the evidence of evil, as of everything that it did not suit his transcendental individuality to appreciate or to notice. More, perhaps, than anybody that has ever lived, he practised the transcendental method in all its purity. He had no system. He opened his eyes on the world every morning with a fresh sincerity, marking how things seemed to him then, or what they suggested to his spontaneous fancy. This fancy, for being spontaneous, was not always novel; it was guided by the habits and training of his mind, which were those of a preacher. Yet he never insisted on his notions so as to turn them into settled dogmas; he felt in his bones that they were myths. Sometimes, indeed, the bad example of other transcendentalists, less true than he to their method, or the pressing questions of unintelligent people, or the instinct we all have to think our ideas final, led him to the very verge of system-making; but he stopped short. Had he made a system out of his notion of compensation, or the over-soul, or spiritual laws, the result would have been as thin and forced as it is in other transcendental systems. But he coveted truth; and he returned to experience, to history, to poetry, to the natural science of his day, for new starting-points and hints toward fresh transcendental musings.

To covet truth is a very distinguished passion. Every philosopher says he is pursuing the truth, but this is seldom the case. As Mr. Bertrand Russell[12] has observed, one reason why philosophers often fail to reach the truth is that often they do not desire to reach it. Those who are genuinely concerned in discovering what happens to be true are rather the men of science, the naturalists, the historians; and ordinarily they discover it, according to their lights. The truths they find are never complete, and are not always important; but they are integral parts of the truth, facts and circumstances that help to fill in the picture, and that no later interpretation can invalidate or afford to contradict. But professional philosophers are usually only apologists: that is, they are absorbed in defending some vested illusion or some eloquent idea. Like lawyers or detectives, they study the case for which they are retained, to see how much evidence or semblance of evidence they can

[12] Bertrand Russell, Third Earl Russell (1872-1970), was a British philosopher, mathematician, and writer.

gather for the defence, and how much prejudice they can raise against the witnesses for the prosecution; for they know they are defending prisoners suspected by the world, and perhaps by their own good sense, of falsification. They do not covet truth, but victory and the dispelling of their own doubts. What they defend is some system, that is, some view about the totality of things, of which men are actually ignorant. No system would have ever been framed if people had been simply interested in knowing what is true, whatever it may be. What produces systems is the interest in maintaining against all comers that some favourite or inherited idea of ours is sufficient and right. A system may contain an account of many things which, in detail, are true enough; but as a system, covering infinite possibilities that neither our experience nor our logic can prejudge, it must be a work of imagination and a piece of human soliloquy. It may be expressive of human experience, it may be poetical; but how should any one who really coveted truth suppose that it was true?

Emerson had no system; and his coveting truth had another exceptional consequence: he was detached, unworldly, contemplative. When he came out of the conventicle[13] or the reform meeting, or out of the rapturous close atmosphere of the lecture-room, he heard Nature whispering to him: "Why so hot, little sir?" No doubt the spirit or energy of the world is what is acting in us, as the sea is what rises in every little wave; but it passes through us, and cry out as we may, it will move on. Our privilege is to have perceived it as it moves. Our dignity is not in what we do, but in what we understand. The whole world is doing things. We are turning in that vortex; yet within us is silent observation, the speculative eye before which all passes, which bridges the distances and compares the combatants. On this side of his genius Emerson broke away from all conditions of age or country and represented nothing except intelligence itself.

There was another element in Emerson, curiously combined with transcendentalism, namely, his love and respect for Nature. Nature, for the transcendentalist, is precious because it is his own work, a mirror in which he looks at himself and says (like a poet relishing his own verses), "What a genius I am! Who would have thought there was such stuff in me?" And the philosophical egotist finds in his doctrine a ready explanation of whatever beauty and commodity Nature actually has. No wonder, he says to himself, that Nature is sympathetic, since I made it. And such a view, one-sided and even fatuous as it may be, undoubtedly sharpens the vision of a poet and a moralist to all that is inspiring and symbolic in the natural world. Emerson was particularly ingenious and clear-sighted in feeling the spiritual uses of fellowship with the elements. This is something in which all Teutonic poetry is rich and which forms, I think, the most genuine and spontaneous part of

[13] A secret religious assembly or the place where it is held.

modern taste, and especially of American taste. Just as some people are naturally enthralled and refreshed by music, so others are by landscape. Music and landscape make up the spiritual resources of those who cannot or dare not express their unfulfilled ideals in words. Serious poetry, profound religion (Calvinism, for instance), are the joys of an unhappiness that confesses itself; but when a genteel tradition forbids people to confess that they are unhappy, serious poetry and profound religion are closed to them by that; and since human life, in its depths, cannot then express itself openly, imagination is driven for comfort into abstract arts, where human circumstances are lost sight of, and human problems dissolve in a purer medium. The pressure of care is thus relieved, without its quietus being found in intelligence. To understand oneself is the classic form of consolation; to elude oneself is the romantic. In the presence of music or landscape human experience eludes itself; and thus romanticism is the bond between transcendental and naturalistic sentiment. The winds and clouds come to minister to the solitary ego.

Have there been, we may ask, any unsuccessful efforts to escape from the genteel tradition, and to express something worth expressing behind its back? This might well not have occurred as yet; but America is so precocious, it has been trained by the genteel tradition to be so wise for its years, that some indications of a truly native philosophy and poetry are already to be found. I might mention the humourists, of whom you here in California have had your share. The humourists, however, only half escape the genteel tradition; their humour would lose its savour if they had wholly escaped it. They point to what contradicts it in the facts; but not in order to abandon the genteel tradition, for they have nothing solid to put in its place. When they point out how ill many facts fit into it, they do not clearly conceive that this militates against the standard, but think it a funny perversity in the facts. Of course, did they earnestly respect the genteel tradition, such an incongruity would seem to them sad, rather than ludicrous. Perhaps the prevalence of humour in America, in and out of season, may be taken as one more evidence that the genteel tradition is present pervasively, but everywhere weak. Similarly in Italy, during the Renaissance, the Catholic tradition could not be banished from the intellect, since there was nothing articulate to take its place; yet its hold on the heart was singularly relaxed. The consequence was that humourists could regale themselves with the foibles of monks and of cardinals, with the credulity of fools, and the bogus miracles of the saints; not intending to deny the theory of the church, but caring for it so little at heart that they could find it infinitely amusing that it should be contradicted in men's lives and that no harm should come of it. So when Mark Twain says, "I was born of poor but dishonest parents," the humour depends on the parody of the genteel Anglo-Saxon convention that it is disreputable to be poor; but to hint at the hollowness of it would not be amusing if it did not remain at bottom one's habitual conviction.

The one American writer who has left the genteel tradition entirely behind is perhaps Walt Whitman. For this reason educated Americans find him rather an unpalatable person, who they sincerely protest ought not to be taken for a representative of their culture; and he certainly should not, because their culture is so genteel and traditional. But the foreigner may sometimes think otherwise, since he is looking for what may have arisen in America to express, not the polite and conventional American mind, but the spirit and the inarticulate principles that animate the community, on which its own genteel mentality seems to sit rather lightly. When the foreigner opens the pages of Walt Whitman, he thinks that he has come at last upon something representative and original. In Walt Whitman democracy is carried into psychology and morals. The various sights, moods, and emotions are given each one vote; they are declared to be all free and equal, and the innumerable commonplace moments of life are suffered to speak like the others. Those moments formerly reputed great are not excluded, but they are made to march in the ranks with their companions—plain foot-soldiers and servants of the hour. Nor does the refusal to discriminate stop there; we must carry our principle further down, to the animals, to inanimate nature, to the cosmos as a whole. Whitman became a pantheist; but his pantheism, unlike that of the Stoics[14] and of Spinoza, was unintellectual, lazy, and self-indulgent; for he simply felt jovially that everything real was good enough, and that he was good enough himself. In him Bohemia rebelled against the genteel tradition; but the reconstruction that alone can justify revolution did not ensue. His attitude, in principle, was utterly disintegrating; his poetic genius fell back to the lowest level, perhaps, to which it is possible for poetic genius to fall. He reduced his imagination to a passive sensorium for the registering of impressions. No element of construction remained in it, and therefore no element of penetration. But his scope was wide; and his lazy, desultory apprehension was poetical. His work, for the very reason that it is so rudimentary, contains a beginning, or rather many beginnings, that might possibly grow into a noble moral imagination, a worthy filling for the human mind. An American in the nineteenth century who completely disregarded the genteel tradition could hardly have done more.

But there is another distinguished man, lately lost to this country, who has given some rude shocks to this tradition and who, as much as Whitman, may be regarded as representing the genuine, the long silent American mind—I mean William James.[15] He and his brother Henry[16] were as tightly swaddled in the genteel tradition as any infant geniuses could be, for they were born

[14] A school of Greek philosophy founded by Xeno around 308 B.C. that believes that men should follow virtue only and be oblivious to the external world and passive to emotion.
[15] William James (1842-1910) was a psychologist and philosophy professor at Harvard; a brilliant talker and writer.
[16] Henry James (1843-1916) was the brother of William James, and a major American writer and critic.

before 1850, and in a Swedenborgian[17] household. Yet they burst those bands almost entirely. The ways in which the two brothers freed themselves, however, are interestingly different. Mr. Henry James has done it by adopting the point of view of the outer world, and by turning the genteel American tradition, as he turns everything else, into a subject-matter for analysis. For him it is a curious habit of mind, intimately comprehended, to be compared with other habits of mind, also well known to him. Thus he has overcome the genteel tradition in the classic way, by understanding it. With William James too this infusion of worldly insight and European sympathies was a potent influence, especially in his earlier days; but the chief source of his liberty was another. It was his personal spontaneity, similar to that of Emerson, and his personal vitality, similar to that of nobody else. Convictions and ideas came to him, so to speak, from the subsoil. He had a prophetic sympathy with the dawning sentiments of the age, with the moods of the dumb majority. His scattered words caught fire in many parts of the world. His way of thinking and feeling represented the true America, and represented in a measure the whole ultra-modern, radical world. Thus he eluded the genteel tradition in the romantic way, by continuing it into its opposite. The romantic mind, glorified in Hegel's[18] dialectic (which is not dialectic at all, but a sort of tragi-comic history of experience), is always rendering its thoughts unrecognisable through the infusion of new insights, and through the insensible transformation of the moral feeling that accompanies them, till at last it has completely reversed its old judgments under cover of expanding them. Thus the genteel tradition was led a merry dance when it fell again into the hands of a genuine and vigorous romanticist like William James. He restored their revolutionary force to its neutralised elements, by picking them out afresh, and emphasising them separately, according to his personal predilections.

For one thing, William James kept his mind and heart wide open to all that might seem, to polite minds, odd, personal, or visionary in religion and philosophy. He gave a sincerely respectful hearing to sentimentalists, mystics, spiritualists, wizards, cranks, quacks, and impostors—for it is hard to draw the line, and James was not willing to draw it prematurely. He thought, with his usual modesty, that any of these might have something to teach him. The lame, the halt, the blind, and those speaking with tongues could come to him with the certainty of finding sympathy; and if they were not healed, at least they were comforted, that a famous professor should take them so

[17] Emanuel Swedenborg (1688-1772) was a Swedish scientist, mystic, and religious philosopher. James' father was a Swedenborgian.
[18] Georg Wilhelm Friedrich Hegel (1770-1831) was a German philosopher, author of *The Phenomenology of Mind* (1807). His principle is called dialectic, which enables a thinker to arrange all the categories of reason in an order of development that corresponds to the actual order, in development, of all reality. Hegelianism is characterized as "absolute idealism."

seriously; and they began to feel that after all to have only one leg, or one hand, or one eye, or to have three, might be in itself no less beauteous than to have just two, like the stolid majority. Thus William James became the friend and helper of those groping, nervous, half-educated, spiritually disinherited, passionately hungry individuals of which America is full. He became, at the same time, their spokesman and representative before the learned world; and he made it a chief part of his vocation to recast what the learned world has to offer, so that as far as possible it might serve the needs and interests of these people.

Yet the normal practical masculine American, too, had a friend in William James. There is a feeling abroad now, to which biology and Darwinism lend some colour, that theory is simply an instrument for practice, and intelligence merely a help toward material survival. Bears, it is said, have fur and claws, but poor naked man is condemned to be intelligent, or he will perish. This feeling William James embodied in that theory of thought and of truth which he called pragmatism. Intelligence, he thought, is no miraculous, idle faculty, by which we mirror passively any or everything that happens to be true, reduplicating the real world to no purpose. Intelligence has its roots and its issue in the context of events; it is one kind of practical adjustment, an experimental act, a form of vital tension. It does not essentially serve to picture other parts of reality, but to connect them. This view was not worked out by William James in its psychological and historical details; unfortunately he developed it chiefly in controversy against its opposite, which he called intellectualism, and which he hated with all the hatred of which his kind heart was capable. Intellectualism, as he conceived it, was pure pedantry; it impoverished and verbalised everything, and tied up nature in red tape. Ideas and rules that may have been occasionally useful it put in the place of the full-blooded irrational movement of life which had called them into being; and these abstractions, so soon obsolete, it strove to fix and to worship for ever. Thus all creeds and theories and all formal precepts sink in the estimation of the pragmatist to a local and temporary grammar of action; a grammar that must be changed slowly by time, and may be changed quickly by genius. To know things as a whole, or as they are eternally, if there is anything eternal in them, is not only beyond our powers, but would prove worthless, and perhaps even fatal to our lives. Ideas are not mirrors, they are weapons; their function is to prepare us to meet events, as future experience may unroll them. Those ideas that disappoint us are false ideas; those to which events are true are true themselves.

This may seem a very utilitarian view of the mind; and I confess I think it a partial one, since the logical force of beliefs and ideas, their truth or falsehood as assertions, has been overlooked altogether, or confused with the vital force of the material processes which these ideas express. It is an external view only, which marks the place and condition of the mind in nature, but neglects its specific essence; as if a jewel were defined as a round hole in a ring. Nevertheless, the more materialistic the pragmatist's theory of the mind is, the more vitalistic his theory of nature will have to become. If the intellect is a device produced in organic bodies to expedite their processes, these organic bodies must have interests and a chosen direction in their life; otherwise their life could not be expedited, nor could anything be useful to it. In other words—and this is a third point at which the philosophy of William James has played havoc with the genteel tradition, while ostensibly defending it—nature must be conceived anthropomorphically and in psychological terms. Its purposes are not to be static harmonies, self-unfolding destinies, the logic of spirit, the spirit of logic, or any other formal method and abstract law; its purposes are to be concrete endeavours, finite efforts of souls living in an environment which they transform and by which they, too, are affected. A spirit, the divine spirit as much as the human, as this new animism conceives it, is a romantic adventurer. Its future is undetermined. Its scope, its duration, and the quality of its life are all contingent. This spirit grows; it buds and sends forth feelers, sounding the depths around for such other centres of force or life as may exist there. It has a vital momentum, but no predetermined goal. It uses its past as a stepping-stone, or rather as a diving-board, but has an absolutely fresh will at each moment to plunge this way or that into the unknown. The universe is an experiment; it is unfinished. It has no ultimate or total nature, because it has no end. It embodies no formula or statable law; any formula is at best a poor abstraction, describing what, in some region and for some time, may be the most striking characteristic of existence; the law is a description *a posteriori* of the habit things have chosen to acquire, and which they may possibly throw off altogether. What a day may bring forth is uncertain; uncertain even to God. Omniscience is impossible; time is real; what had been omniscience hitherto might discover something more to-day. "There shall be news," William James was fond of saying with rapture, quoting from the unpublished poem of an obscure friend, "there shall be news in heaven!" There is almost certainly, he thought, a God now; there may be several gods, who might exist together, or one after the other. We might, by our conspiring sympathies, help to make a new one. Much in us is doubtless immortal; we survive death for some time in a recognisable form; but what our career and transformations may be in the sequel we cannot tell, although we may help to determine them by our daily choices. Observation must be continual if our ideas are to remain true. Eternal vigilance is the price of knowledge; perpetual hazard, perpetual experiment keep quick the edge of life.

This is, so far as I know, a new philosophical vista; it is a conception never before presented, although implied, perhaps, in various quarters, as in Norse and even Greek mythology. It is a vision radically empirical and radically romantic; and as William James himself used to say, the visions and not the arguments of a philosopher are the interesting and influential things about him. William James, rather too generously, attributed this vision to M. Bergson,[19] and regarded him in consequence as a philosopher of the first rank, whose thought was to be one of the turning-points in history. M. Bergson had killed intellectualism. It was his book on creative evolution, said James with humourous emphasis, that had come at last to *"écraser l'infâme."*[20] We may suspect, notwithstanding, that intellectualism, infamous and crushed, will survive the blow; and if the author of the Book of Ecclesiastes were now alive, and heard that there shall be news in heaven, he would doubtless say that there may possibly be news there, but that under the sun there is nothing new—not even radical empiricism or radical romanticism, which from the beginning of the world has been the philosophy of those who as yet had had little experience; for to the blinking little child it is not merely something in the world that is new daily, but everything is new all day.

I am not concerned with the rights and wrongs of that controversy; my point is only that William James, in this genial evolutionary view of the world, has given a rude shock to the genteel tradition. What! The world a gradual improvisation? Creation unpremeditated? God a sort of young poet or struggling artist? William James is an advocate of theism; pragmatism adds one to the evidences of religion; that is excellent. But is not the cool abstract piety of the genteel getting more than it asks for? This empirical naturalistic God is too crude and positive a force; he will work miracles, he will answer prayers, he may inhabit distinct places, and have distinct conditions under which alone he can operate; he is a neighbouring being, whom we can act upon, and rely upon for specific aids, as upon a personal friend, or a physician, or an insurance company. How disconcerting! Is not this new theology a little like superstition? And yet how interesting, how exciting, if it should happen to be true! I am far from wishing to suggest that such a view seems to me more probable than conventional idealism or than Christian orthodoxy. All three are in the region of dramatic system-making and myth to which probabilities are irrelevant. If one man says the moon is sister to the sun, and another that she is his daughter, the question is not which notion is more probable, but whether either of them is at all expressive. The so-called evidences are devised afterwards, when faith and imagination have prejudged the issue. The force of William James's new theology, or romantic cosmology, lies only in this: that it has broken the spell of the genteel tradition, and enticed faith in a new direction, which on second thoughts may prove no less alluring than the old. The important fact is not that the new fancy might possibly be true—who shall know that?—but that it has entered the heart of a leading American to conceive and to cherish it. The genteel tradition cannot be dislodged by these insurrections; there are circles to

[19] Henri Bergson (1859-1941) was a French philosopher who held that the world is in constant flux, novelty, and evolution and that reality is the expression of the creative vital force of the universe. Knowledge of it comes through intuition rather than through analytic intellectualization.

[20] To squelch the unspeakable.

which it is still congenial, and where it will be preserved. But it has been challenged and (what is perhaps more insidious) it has been discovered. No one need be browbeaten any longer into accepting it. No one need be afraid, for instance, that his fate is sealed because some young prig may call him a dualist; the pint would call the quart a dualist, if you tried to pour the quart into him. We need not be afraid of being less profound, for being direct and sincere. The intellectual world may be traversed in many directions; the whole has not been surveyed; there is a great career in it open to talent. That is a sort of knell, that tolls the passing of the genteel tradition. Something else is now in the field; something else can appeal to the imagination, and be a thousand times more idealistic than academic idealism, which is often simply a way of white-washing and adoring things as they are. The illegitimate monopoly which the genteel tradition had established over what ought to be assumed and what ought to be hoped for has been broken down by the first-born of the family, by the genius of the race. Henceforth there can hardly be the same peace and the same pleasure in hugging the old proprieties. Hegel will be to the next generation what Sir William Hamilton was to the last. Nothing will have been disproved, but everything will have been abandoned. An honest man has spoken, and the cant of the genteel tradition has become harder for young lips to repeat.

With this I have finished such a sketch as I am here able to offer you of the genteel tradition in American philosophy. The subject is complex, and calls for many an excursus and qualifying footnote; yet I think the main outlines are clear enough. The chief fountains of this tradition were Calvinism and transcendentalism. Both were living fountains; but to keep them alive they required, one an agonised conscience, and the other a radical subjective criticism of knowledge. When these rare metaphysical preoccupations disappeared—and the American atmosphere is not favourable to either of them—the two systems ceased to be inwardly understood; they subsisted as sacred mysteries only; and the combination of the two in some transcendental system of the universe (a contradiction in principle) was doubly artificial. Besides, it could hardly be held with a single mind. Natural science, history, the beliefs implied in labour and invention, could not be disregarded altogether; so that the transcendental philosopher was condemned to a double allegiance, and to not letting his left hand know the bluff that his right hand was making. Nevertheless, the difficulty in bringing practical inarticulate convictions to expression is very great, and the genteel tradition has subsisted in the academic mind for want of anything equally academic to take its place.

The academic mind, however, has had its flanks turned. On the one side came the revolt of the Bohemian temperament, with its poetry of crude naturalism; on the other side came an impassioned empiricism, welcoming popular religious witnesses to the unseen, reducing science to an instrument of success in action, and declaring the universe to be wild and young, and not to be harnessed by the logic of any school.

This revolution, I should think, might well find an echo among you, who live in a thriving society, and in the presence of a virgin and prodigious world. When you transform nature to your uses, when you experiment with her forces, and reduce them to industrial agents, you cannot feel that nature was made by you or for you, for then these adjustments would have been pre-established. Much less can you feel it when she destroys your labour of years in a momentary spasm. You must feel, rather, that you are an offshoot of her life; one brave little force among her immense forces. When you escape, as you love to do, to your forests and your sierras, I am sure again that you do not feel you made them, or that they were made for you. They have grown, as you have grown, only more massively and more slowly. In their non-human beauty and peace they stir the sub-human depths and the superhuman possibilities of your own spirit. It is no transcendental logic that they teach; and they give no sign of any deliberate morality seated in the world. It is rather the vanity and superficiality of all logic, the needlessness of argument, the relativity of morals, the strength of time, the fertility of matter, the variety, the unspeakable variety, of possible life. Everything is measurable and conditioned, indefinitely repeated, yet, in repetition, twisted somewhat from its old form. Everywhere is beauty and nowhere permanence, everywhere an incipient harmony, nowhere an intention, nor a responsibility, nor a plan. It is the irresistible suasion of this daily spectacle, it is the daily discipline of contact with things, so different from the verbal discipline of the schools, that will, I trust, inspire the philosophy of your children. A Californian whom I had recently the pleasure of meeting observed that, if the philosophers had lived among your mountains their systems would have been different from what they are. Certainly, I should say, very different from what those systems are which the European genteel tradition has handed down since Socrates; for these systems are egotistical; directly or indirectly they are anthropocentric, and inspired by the conceited notion that man, or human reason, or the human distinction between good and evil, is the centre and pivot of the universe. That is what the mountains and the woods should make you at last ashamed to assert. From what, indeed, does the society of nature liberate you, that you find it so sweet? It is hardly (is it?) that you wish to forget your past, or your friends, or that you have any secret contempt for your present ambitions. You respect these, you respect them perhaps too much; you are not suffered by the genteel tradition to criticise or to reform them at all radically. No; it is the yoke of this genteel tradition itself that these primeval solitudes lift from your shoulders. They suspend your forced sense of your own importance not merely as individuals, but even as men. They allow you, in one happy moment, at once to play and to worship, to take yourselves simply, humbly, for what you are, and to salute the wild, indifferent, non-censorious infinity of nature. You are admonished that what you can do avails little materially, and in the end nothing. At the same time, through wonder and pleasure, you are taught speculation. You learn what you are really fitted to do, and where lie your natural dignity and joy, namely, in representing many things, without being them, and in letting your imagination, through sympathy, celebrate and echo their life. Because the peculiarity of man is that his machinery for reaction on external things has involved an imaginative transcript of these things, which is preserved and suspended in his fancy; and the interest and beauty of this inward landscape, rather than any fortunes that may await his body in the outer world, constitute his proper happiness. By their mind, its scope, quality, and temper, we estimate men, for by the mind only do we exist as men, and are more than so many storage-batteries for material energy. Let us therefore be frankly human. Let us be content to live in the mind.

PART IV

THE TWENTIETH CENTURY

1900-1976

"A democracy is more than a form of government," John Dewey wrote in 1914, "it is primarily a mode of associated living, of conjoint communicated experience." Explaining himself, the philosopher enlarged on democracy as a psychological as well as political state—a condition of mutual sympathy. The advance of democracy, he declared, amounts in essence to an "extension in space of the number of individuals who participate in an interest so that each has to refer his own action to that of others, and to consider the action of others to give point and direction to his own. . . ." And he added that the real goal of "breaking down barriers of class and national territory which [keep] men from perceiving the full import of their activity" is precisely to achieve extended participation, for all people, in interests not immediately their own.

Assessed for achievements in participation and mutual sympathy, the period to which the writing in this book belongs is uneven: worse than could have been hoped, better than fashionable opinion just now allows. Dewey's remarks about sympathy were composed as World War I began—and since then America has repeatedly bloodied itself (and others) in ferocious international assault. The country has also been less attentive in action than in rhetoric to the concerns of those embraced as "little men," "common men," "minorities," or "working people." And in matters involving relations among groups, "domestic policy" has been consistently wrongheaded. Dogmas of Americanization and homogenization held sway in the early decades when we might have been committing ourselves to belief in the bracing effects of interaction among cultural strangers. (Tocqueville once claimed that the basis of the professed American faith in "individualism" was the conviction that if everyone were free to choose in accordance with his or her own tastes and beliefs, everyone would choose exactly the same thing.) Later, as the concept of assimilation lost favor and as ethnic groups came to assert (properly) the right to honor their own cultural legacy, the threat of an intensified cultural enclaveism arose: people peering out at each other from suburbs, exurbs, ghettoes, perceiving not fellow human creatures in their individuality, but stereotyped persecutors—or layabouts—or animals. Constructing the Deweyan community wherein widely differing interests are shared and pursued by groups significantly various in themselves has obviously not been a conscious national goal.

Yet the key resource necessary to the creation of that community— the energy and will to democratization, that is—hasn't been depleted in this century, and may even have increased. And no trivial portion of credit for this belongs, it is clear, to American letters. The phrase "energy of democratization" has its home in a vocabulary of idealism, and it's proper to note at once that this vocabulary—together with all other modes of overt moral optimism—has had little vogue in books of the modern period. Recent American writing is perhaps not as unrelievedly blackish as reputed to be; some great names had strong appetites for pleasure. Theodore Dreiser liked a good restaurant.

> (Fitzgerald and Moy's) was . . . ornamented with a blaze of incandescent lights, held in handsome chandeliers. The floors were of brightly coloured tiles, the walls a composition of rich, dark, polished wood, which reflected the light, and coloured stucco-work, which gave the place a very sumptuous appearance. The long bar was a blaze of lights, polished wood-work, coloured and cut glassware, and many fancy bottles. It was a truly swell saloon, with rich screens, fancy wines, and a line of bar goods unsurpassed in the country. (*Sister Carrie*)

Scott Fitzgerald loved a good party.

> There were fireflies riding on the dark air and a dog baying on some low and far-away ledge of the cliff. The table seemed to have risen a little toward the sky like a mechanical dancing platform, giving the people around it a sense of being alone with each other in the dark universe, nourished by its only food, warmed by its only lights. And, as if a curious hushed laugh from Mrs. McKisco were a signal that such a detachment from the world had been attained, the two Divers began suddenly to warm and glow and expand, as if to make up to their guests, already so subtly assured of their importance, so flattered with politeness, for anything they might still miss from that country well left behind. Just for a moment they seemed to speak to everyone at the table, singly and together, assuring them of their friendliness, their affection. And for the moment the faces turned up toward them were like the faces of poor children at a Christmas tree. (*Tender is the Night*)

Reading Hemingway on trout fishing is like spending an afternoon in Utopia.

> I did not feel the first trout strike. When I started to pull up I felt that I had one and brought him, fighting and bending the rod almost double, out of the boiling water at the foot of the falls, and swung him up and onto the dam. He was a good trout, and I banged his head against the timber so that he quivered out straight, and then slipped him into my bag.

While I had him on, several trout had jumped at the falls. As soon as I baited up and dropped in again I hooked another and brought him in the same way. In a little while I had six. They were all about the same size. I laid them out, side by side, all their heads pointing the same way, and looked at them. They were beautifully colored and firm and hard from the cold water. It was a hot day, so I slit them all and shucked out the insides, gills and all, and tossed them over across the river. I took the trout ashore, washed them in the cold, smoothly heavy water above the dam, and then picked some ferns and packed them all in the bag, three trout on a layer of ferns, then another layer of ferns, then three more trout, and then covered them with ferns. They looked nice in the ferns, and now the bag was bulky, and I put it in the shade of the tree. (*The Sun Also Rises*)

And once or twice in the period—most notably, when William Faulkner delivered his Nobel Prize acceptance speech, replete with a declaration of faith in the survival of human kind—a traditional language of hope issued from the lips of a major writer.

On the whole, though, tones of despair are dominant in twentieth-century writing; statements of affirmation are extremely rare; discomfort with "abstractions"—democracy, justice, lasting peace, and the like—is virtually universal. Which is to say that the contribution of letters to the nourishment of the will to democratize is indirect—not a matter of exhortation or speechifying on "the wonders of our Constitution" or on "the beauties of our form of government."

It is proper also to note that the fact that such a contribution has been made, one that is far from negligible, in no way implies the existence of a consensus, political or stylistic, among literary men. Politically speaking, the literary landscape of the present century is a chaos. Here are two giants, T. S. Eliot and Theodore Dreiser; the former lables himself a classicist in letters, Anglican in religion, and royalist in politics; the latter declares himself a communist. Here is a major innovator, John Dos Passos, who begins on the left and ends on the right; here is another, Norman Mailer, whose fluctuations of political belief are so frequent and eccentric as to be nearly untrackable. And here at all hours disputes rage between "schools," and within schools . . . "Proletarians" abuse "aesthetes" (Michael Gold versus Thornton Wilder); writers oriented toward public affairs belabor self-involved colleagues for ivory towerism (Archibald MacLeish versus "the irresponsibles"); modern Hamiltonians and Jeffersonians renew old wars—Southern writers of the so-called agrarian school (John Crowe Ransom, Allen Tate, and others) taking out after assorted urban wits; black writers assail each other for failures of militancy (Eldridge Cleaver savaging James Baldwin in *Soul on Ice*). . . . All that is certain, in the political arenas of letters, is that *no* fundamental harmony of assumption can be discerned: these are, to a man and to a woman, individualists.

And individualism ceaselessly erupts as "personal style." The gap between the royalist and the communist is wide, but no more so than the gap between the kinky haughtiness of Wallace Stevens:

> Poetry is the supreme fiction, madame.
> Take the moral law and make a nave of it
> And from the nave build haunted heaven. Thus
> The conscience is converted into psalms,
> Like windy citherns hankering for hymns.
> We agree in principle. That's clear . . .

> THIS IS JUST TO SAY
>
> I have eaten
> the plums
> that were in
> the icebox
>
> and which
> you were probably
> saving
> for breakfast.
>
> Forgive me
> they were delicious
> so sweet
> and so cold

The period bent briefly beneath one or two stylistic influences. (On the writing of prose the strongest influence in the middle of the century was Hemingway; thereafter the ascendant influence was Faulkner.) But there was and is no period style: the cultural impact of the writing of our time cannot be explained as a consequence of deep-running, shared assumptions about "how to write."

Yet there has been cultural impact—an influence simultaneously moral and political. This lies beyond doubt. And there are sound reasons for believing that the node of this influence lies in the emergent, already remarked participational ethos.

Not the least of the reasons is that central figures of the period— writers of measurable cultural force—spent and continue to spend themselves in contests, subtle or otherwise, with authority. Poets and novelists whose manner and preoccupations are, on their face, wholly dissimilar nevertheless have made common cause throughout the period—by, to begin with, refusals of deference, determined disrespect for the established and the authorized. The health of this common cause—it may as well be termed the cause of presumption or of Uppitiness—is no small factor in the future of democratic will. Admittedly, the "backers" do not declare themselves as that, do not count themselves part of a movement, would scoff at the very notion of being "grouped" in any so-called school of disrespect. And admittedly the differences of idiom, of nuance, of subject are huge—almost sufficient to defeat flat categorization. Yet when these and other appropriate qualifications have been offered, the force of the point remains: (1) the vitality of the Contemporary American participational ethos depends heavily (not solely) on a continual infusion of stimulants to irreverence—religious, political, and literary; (2) given the rates of literacy and advanced education in America, the influence of such stimulants cannot be restricted to high culture even though barriers to wider diffusion appear to exist; and (3) American letters throughout this period has been marvelously rich in stimulants of the kind specified.

The quietest, weightiest, and most elegant irreverence among them is, predictably, that which says unsaddened farewell to established religious orthodoxy—the example of the poet Wallace Stevens is pertinent. The noisy preening gestures of village atheists have no echo in Stevens' poetry. This man's "hero" is notable not for the disposition to taunt, but for a grave readiness to wear the dignity of loneliness—a dignity too long postponed by history and by the temptations of self-deception. Stevens' grand theme is the obligation of human beings to exercise the full powers of imagination, to grasp that when the gods are dead and the religions are seen to be empty, people have to create meaning on their own.

> . . . in an age of disbelief, when the gods have come to an end, when we think of them as the aesthetic projections of a time that has passed, men turn to a fundamental glory of their own and from that create a style of bearing themselves in reality. (*Opus Posthumous*)

The power to do this, Stevens asserts, lies within us, and the discovery that we do not have any choice except to use it should not diminish anyone: to rise to consciousness that poetry is what there is (no other meanings to be vouchsafed) is to achieve serious elevation. The pride of Stevens' poetry lies in art and argument, not in "common men." But everywhere implicit is the theme that beyond superstition lies the prospect of a more distinguished humanity, an added dimension of possibility replacing the evasions of religious dependence. Stevens' "Sunday Morning" ends with stanzas summoning a nobility achievable not by social ascent to official honor or rank, but by a new consciousness, a facing of fact.

> Supple and turbulent, a ring of men
> Shall chant in orgy on a summer morn
> Their boisterous devotion to the sun,
> Not as a god, but as a god might be,
> Naked among them, like a savage source.
> Their chant shall be a chant of paradise,
> Out of their blood, returning to the sky;
> And in their chant shall enter, voice by voice, . . .
>
> The windy lake wherein their lord delights,
> The trees, like serafin, and echoing hills,
> That choir among themselves along afterward.
> They shall know well the heavenly fellowship
> Of men that perish and of summer morn.
> And whence they came and whither they shall go
> The dew upon their feet shall manifest. . . .
>
> She hears, upon that water without sound,
> A voice that cries, "The tomb in Palestine
> Is not the porch of spirits lingering.
> It is the grave of Jesus, where he lay."
> We live in an old chaos of the sun,
> Or old dependency of day and night,
> Or island solitude, unsponsored, free,
> Of that wide water, inescapable.
> Deer walk upon our mountains, and the quail
> Whistle about us their spontaneous cries;
> Sweet berries ripen in the wilderness;
> And, in the isolation of the sky,
> At evening, casual flocks of pigeons make
> Ambiguous undulations as they sink,
> Downward to darkness, on extended wings.

The mode of "presumption" here is heroic.

As may or may not go without saying, the refusal of deference of which we are speaking often produces tawdrier sights than that of "extended wings" sinking downward to darkness. When the context is literary, rage at the governors occasionally seems a shade inconsequential or mannered, even comical. A writer embraces the accents of a thug as a way of establishing his imperviousness to the pretensions of his "betters." His behavior aims to clear away—how regularly this demolition work is undertaken in American culture!—the encrustations of gentility that hide things as they are, interposing "poetic diction" or "general ideas" or "approved manners" between writers and truth. And often the writer behaves thus because he is an anti-egalitarian himself, convinced that the "insufferable" "rising middle class" has been ruinous to letters, taste, the *echt* American tradition. (The gesture against strictly literary authority in American letters has been a complicated affair at least since the time of Whitman and Twain.)

Yet the act of "antiliterary" protest continues to have more marginal significance. In twentieth-century letters the best performance in this line has been by all odds Ezra Pound's.

A major poet, a great translator and critic, and a selfless promoter of the reputations of gifted contemporaries (Eliot, Frost, Williams, and many others had his aid at crucial moments in their careers), Pound played publicist of art, and simultaneously adopted the manners of a cornball Yankee. The intention was partly to mock cornballs, mainly to mock people of "high breeding" who would assume that cornball manners were proof of vulgarity. (Their own tastes in art were, in Pound's mind, the truly damning evidence of vulgarity. Here is a sample of this poet's joking, mocking, leveling ways.

To T. S. Eliot

Rapallo, 14 December (1937)

Waaal my able an sable ole Crepuscule: It tain't often I has the chanct ter invite yer, but there izza bloke, as they say here, "IN GAMBA," and he wanssa rouse all the mudfrawgz of the Camasco an he sez: Will the Possum rite a piece saying just and *plain* wot he fink a styge (notta stooge) playe orter be.

He pays somfink, not much acc. Threadneedle standards, but you cd. sell the piece later in the orryginal wiff the kudos of its havin been requested an published nearer the centres of European culture. Dew yew git me? It needn't be *long,* as I know you're lazy. But also it needn't be in that keerful Criterese which so successfully protekks you in the stinking and foggy climik agin the bare-boreians. Dew yew git meh?? I spose the answer is: lanwidg of Agon sustained thru a lively and brefftakink to a Tomthunderink KlimuXX. However, you can say wot you lik in epistolary, cause they cdn't translate *that* wiffaht losink somfink, Queen Eliz's and the Pos's English).----

The coarseness, the pretended cynicism, the seeming rejection of proprieties—these expressed, in addition to hostility to the fake culture of
"nice- people," an awkward reaching out after common speech and
plain "genuine" opinion. The o.k. types who ran the government, the
salons, the magazines, and the universities—especially the universities—were remote from genuine response. (They were especially ob-
noxious in the university environment, in Pound's view. The academic
culture ritually certified, from generation to generation, sentimental
canons of "greatness," yet had long ago ceased to seek out what was
fresh and pertinent and enhancing to the health of the language). Obstreperous "old Ez," as Pound signed himself, mocked "approved"
characters and their pretensions and, before the third decade of this
century, forged in company with others an influential, lay-it-on-the-
line style, grainy and brisk. But his hatred of authority drew him on to
political madness—an abhorrent, Jew-baiting viciousness—and to
study his life is to discover again the price, in human terms, of the
posture of eternal unremitting disrespect and, in addition, the ambiguities of egalitarianism when reduced to a mere stylistic device. Yet the
Poundian way (half the "age" represented in this volume has been
declared, by a subtle critic, the Age of Pound) was a momentous cultural innovation. Its undeviating assurance that language and society
both must be made new and that newness can only begin in acts of
scorn for the proprieties of the classy illiterates at the top sustained a
skepticism of the establishment that is now a norm, and that probably
is essential to the maintenance of open cultural air.

A comparable influence is exerted by the most effective recent
baiter of political (as opposed to literary or religious) authority: Norman Mailer. The Mailer version of the writer (a socker, an athlete, an
infantryman, the friend of pugs, a dangerous chap at parties, a *macho*
caesar) derives from a romantic literary past whose shapers were Byron
and Hemingway. (The novelist's own qualifications as a bottom dog
are shaky: a cosseted Harvard boy, he was subsidized into the life of
letters—*à Paris*—by loving parents after World War II.) And the
avowed attitudes in his books toward the weak and unlucky of this
society are hostile. Yet, as an embodiment and an endorsement of the
national refusal of deference, Mailer has exceptional value. His posture
as a journalist, his mode of address to the great and near great in
politics, is furiously participational. Nixons, Kennedys, Goldwaters,
Kissingers—all our Chiefs—are perceived as small potatoes, figures
commanding no awe, people to be accepted putatively or socially as
one's equals (maybe), but under no circumstances as anybody's superiors. And this manner of address, filtering through the media and into
the attitudes of university teachers and students alike, has nourished a
trilling nerve of impertinence in the culture, encouraging leaders to

retain at least some frail sense of their possible imperfection. At its worst the power of presumption in Mailer's writing issues in loutishness, and it produces only dreams of glory that are bad poison when diffused in men and women unprepared to bear the responsibilities of governors. But when this power produces a portrait like that of Henry Cabot Lodge—a person recognized by Mailer as understanding himself to be in some way *"necessarily* superb"—it is difficult to overvalue it. And, as must be added, there are moments in Mailer's writing—especially in his account of the Apollo mission, called *Of a Fire on the Moon*—that lift off toward true eloquence, approaching (not conquering) the summits of Wallace Stevens' mountains.

2.

The refusal to bow down is one thing, the capacity to become truly comprehensive is another. If Dewey's "conjoint communicated experience" cannot occur save in a nation of proud hearts (persons persuaded that those "above" me can learn from me as well as teach me), it asks of people more than pride, more than presumption. It asks new forms of intellectual awareness—a new kind of mind, really, models of unprecedented imaginative mobility, as yet underdeveloped aptitudes for interplay with "interests not our own." As it happens, one function of the most famous poem of the century—T. S. Eliot's "The Waste Land"—was to body forth such a mind, and to persuade a whole culture of its interest, value, and possibilities. The poem told a "story"— yet had no definable narrative sequence; it developed a whole set of historical, cultural, and religious themes—yet eschewed explanation, qualification, announcements of purpose, and all other helpful hints; and it appeared to accomplish these tasks simply by behaving as though contemporary readers had taken (the day before the poem was published) a leap forward into extraordinary sophistication. People can (and ought to) think faster than they've been thinking, the poem seemed to insist. People can (and ought to) translate several languages at once, can and ought to link up—in a second—multiple, "unrelated" perspectives, and can and ought to find grounds of comfort among astonishing densities of allusion.

The initial public reaction to all this wasn't universally positive, needless to say. Not every reader thought that it could or should be easy for him to inhabit a variety of times and places simultaneously, or to recognize instantly differences *and* resemblances between manners of the cosmopolitan rich and manners of the urban poor, or to grasp in every value-laden gesture of the present culture the significant contrast with earlier values. The mind Eliot envisaged—Pound envisaged it too, for in editing Eliot's poem (as he did) he was utterly remorseless about

deleting passages of explanation and amplification—was simultaneously anthropological, novelistic, journalistic, psychoanalytic, everything by turns, nothing long, troutlike in its movement, shuttling in
sensation between then and now, the Thames in 1600, the Thames in
1921. . . . And the poem was not an overnight triumph. People said (in
the 1920's) that the vision was brain-breaking: they held that no such
mind was feasible, argued that the aptitudes blithely assumed to be
just around the historical corner in fact would never be natural to
anybody, and that, in truth, "The Waste Land" was just another outbreak of "obscurity."

But ultimately the poem did triumph. In concert with other aesthetic influences of the earlier decades of this century—movements in
painting and film, particularly—it exacted acceptance of its model of
feasible intellectual competencies. And soon enough the "new mind"
was functioning everywhere. With practice the job of reading "wild
juxtapositions" became less onerous: people learned how to negotiate
the opening frames of a film showing a helicopter in midair, a statue of
Christ hanging beneath it, Rome below—or how to interpret when
another film cut suddenly from a lover's mind to the burning of Hiroshima—or what to conclude when Herzog, a character in a novel by
Saul Bellow, raced from private anguish to public letters to the philosopher Heidegger. Nonpoetic influences were important, naturally, in
nurturing and schooling the emergent skills. But in the history of those
skills the appearance of Eliot's poem was the dramatic and seminal
moment: it not only defined the characteristics of the new mind
(speed, mobility, complication), it figured them forth in an exciting,
substantive experience.

Viewed in a Deweyan perspective, "The Waste Land" has a negative
as well as positive charge. For there was a model of feeling as well as of
thought in the poem, and the effect of the former model was to lessen
the potency of the latter by cutting it off from social and humane
functions. "The Waste Land," on its "affective" side, is a poem confined in wary emotions—foreboding, distaste, detachment. It mocks,
teases, warns, chides, chokes in torment, but only once—and then
only briefly—does it fully enter a moment of human time, breathe with
a person at the borders of hope or communion or ecstasy. The ideal
reader of the poem is a person intellectually alert to alien standards
and values, but disinclined to link himself in sympathy with them,
indisposed to fathom understanding at class levels different from his
own, and skeptical about social or cultural reconstruction. Accustomed to seeing from above, from a distance, this reader never springs
toward what he observes, is touched from within by no force save that
of religious despair. Dominated on the one hand by habitual distaste
and on the other by expectation of doom, he neither wants nor is able

to adapt his complex intelligence to social need as ordinarily conceived: he lives in a world beyond politics, beyond significant social interaction, beyond "possibility" other than religious redemption.

For Eliot and all others suffering a comparable confinement of sympathies, that location is crippling: and thereby hangs social loss and deprivation. But the mind Eliot "invented" is an uncommon social resource nevertheless—it is at least capable of staying in touch simultaneously with opposing or contrasting values and beliefs. And this talent does have definable contemporary functions. It can become the means by which men carry through without disaster the negotiations that open an established culture to excluded influences, energies, and beliefs in the way Dewey spoke about; the means by which new standards of democratization, new moral and cultural values, are articulated. To be thoroughly functional, the talent needs the support of an essentially optimistic and embracing temperament. When complexity feeds on itself, multiplying perceptions of interdependence and interrelationship as though for their own sake; when the ruling conviction is that interactions of value—out there, in the social world, between, say, the rich and poor—lead to corruption of the best, not to improvement of the whole, then sterility is the risk. But while it is undeniable that the complex, admirable alertness to apparent conflicts of values, hidden correspondencies of values, which emerged in "The Waste Land" is diminished in usefulness by the atmosphere of the poem—its polluting pessimism, sniffishness, terror of the future—the work as a whole remains indispensable. You grasp as you read it that here at intervals is a kind of incarnation of the intellectual talents necessary for a human future—a model of human power to perceive, order, and compare in complex situations, a guide to ways of advancing beyond sexual, geographical, and historical limits. The promise is immense, so it still seems: escaping cultural bonds could move us toward the growth point wherein effective caring for otherness, true mutuality with our successors, could begin. The will to participate gains a mirror of mobility, also an inkling of how to prepare for its future part.

3.

In the end, of course, it is the voice of compassion more than any other that energizes belief in democratic possibility. And, in letters, the equivalent of compassion is quite simply the discovery of details of feeling within uncelebrated, lost, or "minor" persons that possess value and beauty. Discoveries of this sort in twentieth-century American writing are, to speak flatly, unmatched in earlier bodies of literature. And as often as not they have been achieved by writers who have allowed themselves to stand at an angle of closeness to "the unlet-

tered" or "the lost" hitherto seldom imagined by litterateurs: an angle
permitting instruction through interplay. Robert Frost, who often
adopted the voice of the plain man or the countryman, more importantly often succeeded in locating significant bases for a critique of
middle-class cant by touching unspoken feelings and understandings
within the "underclass." In a poem called "The Axe-Helve," Frost tells
of a farmer-neighbor of French descent who interrupts him as he's
chopping firewood—interrupts to point out imperfections in the ma-
chine-made handle of Frost's axe. The neighbor [his name is Baptiste]
invites Frost to his house, promising him a decent axe-handle; the poet
visits in the evening.

> Needlessly soon he had his axe-helves out,
> A quiverful to choose from, since he wished me
> To have the best he had, or had to spare—
> Not for me to ask which, when what he took
> Had beauties he had to point me out at length
> To insure their not being wasted on me.
> He liked to have it slender as a whipstock,
> Free from the least knot, equal to the strain
> Of bending like a sword across the knee.
> He showed me that the lines of a good helve
> Were native to the grain before the knife
> Expressed them, and its curves were no false curves
> Put on it from without. And there its strength lay
> For the hard work. He chafed its long white body
> From end to end with his rough hand shut round it.
> He tried it at the eye-hole in the axe-head.
> 'Hahn, hahn,' he mused, 'don't need much taking down.'
> Baptiste knew how to make a short job long
> For love of it, and yet not waste time either.
>
> Do you know, what we talked about was knowledge?
> Baptiste on his defence about the children
> He kept from school, or did his best to keep—
> Whatever school and children and our doubts
> Of laid-on education had to do
> With the curves of his axe-helves and his having
> Used these unscrupulously to bring me
> To see for once the inside of his house.
> Was I desired in friendship, partly as some one
> To leave it to, whether the right to hold
> Such doubts of education should depend
> Upon the education of those who held them?

But now he brushed the shavings from his knee
And stood the axe there on its horse's hoof,
Erect, but not without its waves, as when
The snake stood up for evil in the Garden,—
Top-heavy with a heaviness his short,
Thick hand made light of, steel-blue chin drawn down
And in a little—a French touch in that.
Baptiste drew back and squinted at it, pleased;
'See how she's cock her head!'

The Frenchman's attitudes are, as the phrase goes, "anti-intellectual."
But the action of the poem reveals—in passing—that the phrase
doesn't go very far. The poet shows how an opinion about schooling
sits within a total mind, where it fits in a whole configuration of values,
motives, feelings. And, in the process of disclosing this to himself, the
poet enters a subtle interplay of "classes" and advances beyond stock
pros and cons about booklearning. "The Axe-Helve" has other themes
besides that of an encounter between literacy and illiteracy but, in
course of exploring them, it reveals how the former can learn from the
latter without reducing itself, without companionable "slumming" or
loss of self-respect. (Consider the meanings of that "laid-on" education.) And the revelation carries within it an unsentimental warning
against impoverishing yourself by dismissing opinions before touching
them from inside.

For levels of understanding comparable to that occupied by Frost's
Baptiste, respect flows fairly easily "from above." The man is, after all,
not only an able craftsman, but somebody disposed to link up his
attitudes about work with his attitudes about educating his children—
a "New England character," a figure whose individual personhood appears tangible, unpolluted by admass cliché. Liking him, learning from
him, is unembarrassing—and morally undemanding. The distinction of
American letters in this age is that time and again our writers have
tested their power of penetration in more demanding situations. Can a
human truth worth notice be pieced out where the mind and heart
under scrutiny possess no craft, no opinions not derived from advertising copy, no language save that of cliché?

It can indeed. The piecing out, true enough, is sometimes a process
lacking in aesthetic beauty. The writer who undertakes it is as likely as
not to appear clumsy, unfastidious, indelicate. Early in Dreiser's *An
American Tragedy,* the hero, Clyde Griffiths, goes on a date with a girl
who works with him in a shirt factory and whom he is later to victim-
ize. The lad Griffiths is normally selfish, opportunistic, hopeful, appetitive, and uncruel. He is "out to get what he can." The talk that Dreiser
reports is utterly banal ("You know, Roberta, I'm crazy about you. I

really am. I think you're the dearest, sweetest thing. Oh, say! Do you mind my telling you? Ever since you showed up there, I haven't been able to sleep, nearly. That's the truth—honest it is. I think and think of you. You've got such nice eyes and hair. Tonight you look just too cute—lovely, I think"). The gestures are described in an idiom as graceless as instructions for assembling a bicycle. ("He squeezed her arm affectionately, then stopped suddenly and, disengaging his arm from hers, put both his about her.") The scene seems endless, a pass is made, rejected, tried again; the girl Roberta chastizes herself miserably ("What would people think—say—if they knew? She was a bad girl, really, and yet she wanted to be this way—near him—now as never before.").The blend of opportunism, disingenuousness, sexual appetite, and half-truths becomes almost unbearably painful. Yet see how the chapter ends.

> "Oh Roberta, dearest, please, please say that you love me. Please do! I know that you do, Roberta. I can tell. Please, tell me now. I'm so crazy about you. We have so little time."
>
> He kissed her again upon the cheek and mouth, and suddenly he felt her relax. She stood quite still and unresisting in his arms. He felt a wonder of something—he could not tell what. All of a sudden he felt tears upon her face, her head sunk to his shoulder, and then he heard her say: "Yes, yes, yes. I do love you. Yes, yes. I do. I do."
>
> There was a sob—half of misery, half of delight—in her voice and Clyde caught that. He was so touched by her honesty and simplicity that tears sprang to his own eyes. "It's all right, Roberta. It's all right. Please don't cry. Oh, I think you're so sweet. I do. I do, Roberta."
>
> He looked up and before him in the east over the low roofs of the city was the thinnest, yellowest topmost arc of the rising July moon. It seemed at the moment as though life had given him all—all—that he could possibly ask of it.

The material of these four paragraphs is "low" and the way in which it is worked is still ungainly. But the sentences are irradiated even so—by an eruption of the poetic and the generous that momentarily clears away meanness and baseness. The writer does not announce the truth he breaks through to, merely by his tone acknowledges it—acknowledges, that is, that what is "low" can be transformed. What is mean or exploitative can open suddenly on a healing prospect beyond itself; *any* human creature can awake all at once to awareness of the inner goodness and helplessness of the person opposite him. And that awareness is ennobling.

It is not merely the assertion of this truth—the truth of momentary human moral possibility—that elevates our best writing; it is the warmth of welcome for it. Conscious that he is face to face with significant matter, Dreiser feels no sense of shame, no impulse to cut out of the place with some piece of wit or show of sophistication. He waits and watches, as though before a miracle and, watching with him, you catch sight of something yourself, grasp that "miraculous" may not be an extravagant label. Is not this power that of the weakest to instruct the strong?

Whatever the sound label, it is a power that surfaces everywhere in our letters. It is present in a half dozen of Faulkner's novels, in the "interior monologues" of the helpless and uneducated and "retarded," convicts, serving women, exploited Negro retainers. . . . You feel it in the extraordinary pages of James Agee's *Let us Now Praise Famous Men* where the writer argues that the walls of a suffering tenant farmer's family shack, in the great depression, possess a meaning and dignity not inferior to that of a work of high art. It is there in certain simple acts of witnessing, appreciative witnessing, in the stories and poems of William Carlos Williams.

> At ten A.M. the young housewife
> moves about in negligee behind
> the wooden walls of her husband's house.
> I pass solitary in my car.
>
> Then again she comes to the curb
> to call the ice-man, fish-man, and stands
> shy, uncorseted, tucking in
> stray ends of hair, and I compare her
> to a fallen leaf.
>
> The noiseless wheels of my car
> rush with a crackling sound over
> dried leaves as I bow and pass smiling.

And it is most vivid and most moving, perhaps, in the great protest against American *antidemocracy* echoing through the line of black writers from DuBois to Baldwin and Cleaver. To mention that line is to be reminded again that the case for "conjoint communicated experience," as built up by imaginative writers, has hardly begun to create, in the live reality of society, true mutuality or full interplay. And from this it follows that the proper praise of letters is limited, as we began by saying—a matter of having nourished an energy, not of having completed a task. It is a question, though, whether the nature of the task would be as evident as it is, and whether the perception of need would be as piercing as now and then it still becomes, if there had been no "modern American letters." The individual contributions are far too various for summary. This writer charges the democratizing will by rousing fury at social injustice; this writer makes his effect subtly, creating images of the kind of sensibility necessary in a fully participational society; this writer calls his reader back to the roughest skepticism (teaching him again how to say, "Who do you think you are, God?"); this writer shows that, in the smallest among us, there is that which alone can help the greatest find his own best self. And rare indeed is the voice that says: Now, let everyone shut the door on the rest. Let each man shut out humanity.

One word more. The quality of any given moment of writing cannot ever be represented adequately by moral or political formula. Pages can be composed on the moral tact and self-respecting poise of Frost's speaker in the presence of the craftsman, but the poem is most magical—and most astonishing—when it comes on an image that cannot be nicely accommodated in talk about the relations of classes.

> The axe there on its horse's hoof,
> Erect, but not without its waves, as when
> The snake stood up for evil in the Garden—

To speak of the issues of sympathy and mutuality and openness to experience is not to step forth with a touchstone by which every achievement can be assessed. It is only to register—what for this reader is the truth—that the climate in the strongest twentieth-century writing in America (as in much that came before) often is one of social daring, and that this climate is invariably worth considering as an element of any given aesthetic achievement. Again and again the promise of interruption . . . the refusal of quick confirmation . . . the hint that everything could be otherwise than it is. . . . And again and again a spirit like that which Learned Hand had in mind when, years ago, he remarked that "the spirit of liberty is the spirit which seeks to understand the minds of other men and women."

PHOTO JOURNALISM

Twentieth century American history has been, for most of those living through it, a picture story—an age made known to itself by stunning images of crisis fixed forever by photographers. Many men and women of letters remained skeptical of the camera eye; some—John Dos Passos in *USA,* for one—mimicked its ways in prose. The early achievements in photo news were, of course, those of the daily press; a kind of summit of journalistic photographic brilliance was reached in the glossy pages of *Life* magazine.

A New York tenement family, c. 1910. *(The Granger Collection)*

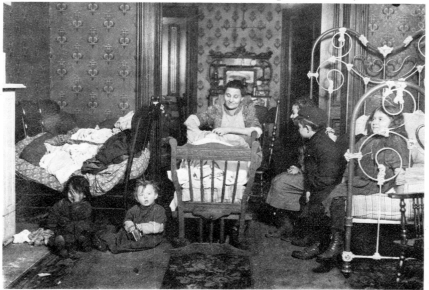

Depression bread line.
(U.S. Information Agency, The National Archives)

**Migrant mother and children in
California, 1938.** *(F.S.A. photo by Dorothea Lange,
The Granger Collection)*

Flag raising on Mount Suribachi (Iwo Jima).
(Courtesy of Defense Department, Marine Corps)

Selma march, 1963; Martin Luther King, Jr., in center. *(Bob Adelman/Magnum)*

Antiwar protest, Washington, D.C., 1965. *(Charles Harbutt/Magnum)*

Walking on the moon. *(Courtesy of NASA)*

I

Cultural Revolution

THE CASE FOR
CULTURAL REVOLUTION

RANDOLPH BOURNE

(1886-1918)

Born on May 30, 1886, in Bloomfield, New Jersey, Randolph Bourne studied under Charles A. Beard, John Dewey, and Franz Boas at Columbia University. After his graduation in 1913 he published three books and a number of articles and reviews in the remainder of his short life, but what he meant to his contemporaries, the young radical intellectuals in the period of World War I, and what he has come to mean today, would seem to be impossible to explain by a purely literary assessment of his achievement. Two of Bourne's books are about schools. The other, *Youth and Life* (1913), is a collection of essays; a sampling of titles includes "The Adventure of Life," "The Dodging of

The principal works are *Youth and Life,* (1913); *The Gary Schools* (1916); *Towards an Enduring Peace,* (1916); *Education and Living,* (1917); *Untimely Papers,* ed. James Oppenheim, (1919); *The History of a Literary Radical and Other Essays,* ed. Van Wyck Brooks, 1920, revised and changed slightly, 1956.

Louis Filler edited a bibliography, *Randolph Bourne,* 1943. A recent biography is John A. Moreau, *Randolph Bourne: Legend and Reality,* 1966. Lillian Schlissel has edited *The World of Randolph Bourne,* 1965. Sherman Paul has written a pamphlet in the University of Minnesota series, *Randolph Bourne,* 1966.

Pressures," "A Philosophy of Handicap." He wrote about politics, economics, literature, and philosophy, but whatever the subject at hand he stood against authority, rigidity, pedantry, and on the side of the irreverent and the fresh. This led him into some excesses—the claim that youth is never wrong and age is never right; "Youth is the incarnation of reason pitted against the rigidity of tradition." But such declarations were witness to his faith in the young and in the new age that they were to forge, and his passionate optimism appealed strongly to the rising generation of dissidents from a provincial, complacent society. In short, Bourne was, for an America no longer young, the voice of hope for renewal.

At the center of this hope lay a belief in individual authenticity as a key—and neglected—resource. The task for youth, Bourne argued, was to stay true to itself; for him growing up meant learning how to dodge familial, social, economic, and authoritarian pressures and to maintain one's true nature, "the priceless jewel of selfhood." The art of resisting the culture must be learned and practiced; people must refuse "to let a system submerge . . . real and direct reactions to . . . observation and experience." By the same token the task for ethnic, national, and other groups is to resist "Americanization," to preserve and toughen their sense of distinctness, to avoid engulfment in the insipid, bland homogeneity of the cultural majority. "America is a unique sociological fabric, and it bespeaks poverty of imagination not to be thrilled at the incalculable potentialities of so novel a union of men."

One of his contemporaries, Van Wyck Brooks, wrote after Bourne's death that had he lived, "his criticism would have concentrated more and more on the problem of evoking and shaping an American literature as the nucleus of that rich, vital and independent national life he had been seeking in so many ways to promote." One reason that Bourne might have moved in this direction is that he connected literary stances and tones with social attitudes and policies. Irony, for instance, was not in his mind simply a double-edged way of writing or talking; it was a possible new way of living—a means of achieving mobility, of releasing oneself from encapsulation in a single viewpoint or vocabulary and enlarging one's range of sympathies, one's capacity to hold within himself harmonies and frequencies different from those of one's "proper" race or class.

It is, though, as a prod to new hope that Bourne mattered most to his own age. He had no time to become a recognized authority—how he would have hated the label—in a "field"; he had many contemporaries with better credentials as theorists on radical politics, education, art, or letters. But his writing is unified, expressive of a clear and passionate personal philosophy that held that a new fellowship of Americans could create a free, literate, and generous society. His tone is sometimes prophetic and his strength lies in a nearly religious purity of faith; he was a man with a joyous gospel. "You felt that in him the new America had suddenly found itself and was all astir with the excitement of its first maturity," said his friend Brooks. "To have known Randolph Bourne is indeed to have surprised some of the finest secrets of the American future."

The History Of a Literary Radical

For a man of culture, my friend Miro began his literary career in a singularly unpromising way. Potential statesmen in log-cabins might miraculously come in touch with all the great books of the world, but the days of Miro's young school life were passed in innocence of Homer or Dante[1] or Shakespeare, or any of the other traditional mind-formers of the race. What Miro had for his nourishment, outside the Bible, which was a magical book that you must not drop on the floor, or his school-readers, which were like lightning flashes of unintelligible scenes, was the literature that his playmates lent him—exploits of British soldiers in Spain and the Crimea, the death-defying adventures of young filibusters in Cuba and Nicaragua. Miro gave them a languid perusing, and did not criticize their literary style. Huckleberry Finn and Tom Sawyer somehow eluded him until he had finished college, and no fresher tale of adventure drifted into his complacent home until the era of "Richard Carvel" and "Janice Meredith"[2] sharpened his wits and gave him a vague feeling that there was such a thing as literary art. The classics were stiffly enshrined behind glass doors that were very hard to open—at least Hawthorne and Irving and Thackeray were there, and Tennyson's and Scott's poems—but nobody ever discussed them or looked at them. Miro's busy elders were taken up with the weekly *Outlook* and *Independent* and *Christian Work*, and felt they were doing much for Miro when they provided him and his sister with *St. Nicholas* and *The Youth's Companion*. It was only that Miro saw the black books looking at him accusingly from the case, and a rudimentary conscience, slipping easily over from Calvinism to culture, forced him solemnly to grapple with "The Scarlet Letter" or "Marmion." All he remembers is that the writers of these books he browsed among used a great many words and made a great fuss over shadowy offenses and conflicts and passions that did not even stimulate his imagination with sufficient force to cause him to ask his elders what it was all about. Certainly the filibusters were easier.

---

[1] Dante Alighieri (1265-1321), Italian poet, author of the *Divine Comedy*.

[2] *Richard Carvel* (1899), a novel written by

Winston Churchill (1871-1947), American historical novelist.

At school Miro was early impressed with the vast dignity of the literary works and names he was compelled to learn. Shakespeare and Goethe[3] and Dante lifted their plaster heads frowningly above the teacher's, as they perched on shelves about the room. Much was said of the greatness of literature. But the art of phonetics and the complications of grammar swamped Miro's early school years. It was not until he reached the High School that literature began really to assume that sacredness which he had heretofore felt only for Holy Scripture. His initiation into culture was made almost a religious mystery by the conscientious and harassed teacher. As the Deadwood Boys and Henty and David Harum slipped away from Miro's soul in the presence of Milton's "Comus" and Burke "On Conciliation,"[4] a cultural devoutness was engendered in him that never really died. At first it did not take Miro beyond the stage where your conscience is strong enough to make you uncomfortable, but not strong enough to make you do anything about it. Miro did not actually become an omnivorous reader of great books. But he was filled with a rich grief that the millions pursued cheap and vulgar fiction instead of the best that has been thought and said in the world. Miro indiscriminately bought cheap editions of the English classics and read them with a certain patient incomprehension.

As for the dead classics, they came to Miro from the hands of his teachers with a prestige even vaster than the books of his native tongue. No doubt ever entered his head that four years of Latin and three years of Greek, an hour a day, were the important preparation he needed for his future as an American citizen. No doubt ever hurt him that the world into which he would pass would be a world where, as his teacher said, Latin and Greek were a solace to the aged, a quickener of taste, a refreshment after manual labor, and a clue to the general knowledge of all human things. Miro would as soon have doubted the rising of the sun as have doubted the wisdom of these serious, puckered women who had the precious manipulation of his cultural upbringing in their charge. Miro was a bright, if a rather vague, little boy, and a fusion of brightness and docility gave him high marks in the school where we went together.

No one ever doubted that these marks expressed Miro's assimilation of the books we pored over. But he told me later that he had never really known what he was studying. Cæsar, Virgil, Cicero, Xenophon, Homer,[5] were veiled and misty experiences to him. His mind was a moving present,

[3] Johann Wolfgang Goethe (1749-1832), German poet, dramatist, scientist, and court official.

[4] John Milton (1608-1674), English poet. *Comus* (1634), the libretto of a masque written by Milton. Edmund Burke (1729-1797) delivered his speech on "Conciliation with America" in 1775.

[5] Gaius Julius Caesar (100 B.C.-44 B.C.), Roman statesman, general, historian, and dictator; Virgil (70-19 B.C.), Roman poet, author of the epic poem "Aeneid"; Cicero (106-43 B.C.), Roman statesman and orator; Zenephon (430?-355 B.C.), Greek general, historian, and author of *Anabasis*, among other works: Homer, Greek epic poet, believed to be the author of the *Iliad* and the *Odyssey*.

obliterating each day what it had read the day before, and piercing into a no more comprehended future. He could at no time have given any intelligible account of Æneas's wanderings or what Cicero was really inveighing against. The Iliad was even more obscure. The only thing which impressed him deeply was an expurgated passage, which he looked up somewhere else and found to be about Mars and Venus caught in the golden bed. Cæsar seemed to be at war, and Xenophon wandering somewhere in Asia Minor, with about the same lengthiness and hardship as Miro suffered in reading him. The trouble, Miro thought afterwards, was that these books were to his mind flickering lights in a vast jungle of ignorance. He does not remember marvelling at the excessive dullness of the stories themselves. He plodded his faithful way, using them as his conscientious teachers did, as exercises in language. He looked on Virgil and Cicero as essentially problems in disentangling words which had unaccountably gotten into a bizarre order, and in recognizing certain rather amusing and ingenious combinations, known as "constructions." Why these words took so irritating an order Miro never knew, but he always connected the problem with those algebraic puzzles he had elsewhere to unravel. Virgil's words were further complicated by being arranged in lines which one had to "scan." Miro was pleased with the rhythm, and there were stanzas that had a roll of their own. But the inexorable translating that had to go on tore all this fabric of poetry to pieces. His translations were impeccable, but, as he never wrote them down, he had never before his eyes the consecutive story.

Translations Miro never saw. He knew that they were implements of deadly sin that boys used to cheat with. His horror of them was such as a saint might feel towards a parody of the Bible. Just before Miro left school, his sister in a younger class began to read a prose translation of the Odyssey, and Miro remembers the scorn with which he looked down on so sneaking an entrance into the temple of light. He knew that not everyone could study Latin and Greek, and he learned to be proud of his knowledge. When at last he had passed his examinations for college—his Latin composition and grammar, his syntax and his sight-reading, and his Greek composition and grammar, his Greek syntax and sight-reading, and his translation of Gallic battles and Anabatic frosts, and Dido's farewell[6] and Cicero's objurgations—his zealous rage did not abate. He even insisted on reading the Bucolics,[7] while he was away on his vacation, and a book or two in the Odyssey. His family was a little chilled by his studiousness, but he knew well that he was laying

[6] The *Anabasis* was the Greek expedition across Asia Minor (401 B.C.), led by Cyrus the younger of Persia, described by Xenephon in his *Anabasis*. Anabasis now refers to any large-scale military advance. In Roman mythology, Dido was the Queen of Carthage.

[7] The *Bucolics* or *Eclogues*, pastoral poems, were written by Virgil.

up cultural treasures in heaven, where moth and rust do not corrupt, neither do thieves break in and steal.

Arrived at college, Miro expanded his cultural interests on the approved lines. He read Horace and Plato, Lysias and Terence,[8] impartially, with faithful conscience. Horace was the most exciting because of the parodies that were beginning to appear in the cleverer newspapers. Miro scarcely knew whether to be amused or shocked at "Odi Persicos" or "Integer Vitæ"[9] done into current slang. The professors, mild-mannered men who knew their place and kept it, never mentioned these impudent adventures, but for Miro it was the first crack in his Ptolemaic system of reverences. There came a time when his mind began to feel replete, when this heavy pushing through the opaque medium of dead language began to fatigue him. He should have been able to read fluently, but there were always turning up new styles, new constructions, to plague him. Latin became to him like a constant diet of beefsteak, and Greek like a constant diet of fine wheaten bread. They lost their taste. These witty poets and ostentatious orators—what were they all about? What was their background? Where did they fit into Miro's life? The professors knew some history, but what did that history mean? Miro found himself surfeited and dissatisfied. He began to look furtively at translations to get some better English than he was able to provide. The hair-splittings of Plato began to bore him when he saw them in crystal-clear English, and not muffled in the original Greek. His apostasy had begun.

It was not much better in his study of English literature. Miro was given a huge anthology, a sort of press-clipping bureau of *belles-lettres*, from Chaucer to Arthur Symons.[10] Under the direction of a professor who was laying out a career for himself as poet—or "modern singer," as he expressed it— the class went briskly through the centuries sampling their genius and tasting the various literary flavors. The enterprise reminded Miro of those books of woollen samples which one looks through when one is to have a suit of clothes made. But in this case, the student did not even have the pleasure of seeing the suit of clothes. All that was expected of him, apparently, was that he should become familiar, from these microscopic pieces, with the different textures and patterns. The great writers passed before his mind like figures in a crowded street. There was no time for preferences. Indeed the professor strove diligently to give each writer his just due. How was one to appreciate the great thoughts and the great styles if one began to choose violently between them, or attempt any discrimination on grounds of their peculiar congeniality for one's own soul? Criticism had to spurn such subjectivity,

---

[8] Horace (65-8 B.C.), Roman poet and satirist. *The Odes* is his most famous work. Plato (427?-347 B.C.), Greek philosopher; Lysias (c.450-380 B.C.), Greek orator. Terence (185-159 B.C.), Roman author of comedies.

[9] I hate the Persians. The man upright in life.
[10] Arthur Symons (1865-1945), English poet and literary critic.

scholarship could not be wilful. The neatly arranged book of "readings," with its medicinal doses of inspiration, became the symbol of Miro's education.

These early years of college did not deprive Miro of his cultural loyalty, but they deadened his appetite. Although almost inconceivably docile, he found himself being bored. He had come from school a serious boy, with more than a touch of priggishness in him, and a vague inspiration to be a "man of letters." He found himself becoming a collector of literary odds-and-ends. If he did not formulate this feeling clearly, he at least knew. He found that the literary life was not as interesting as he had expected. He sought no adventures. When he wrote, it was graceful lyrics of polite criticisms of William Collins or Charles Lamb.[11] These canonized saints of culture still held the field for Miro, however. There was nothing between them and that popular literature of the day that all good men bemoaned. Classic or popular, "highbrow" or "lowbrow," this was the choice, and Miro unquestioningly took the orthodox heaven. In 1912 the most popular of Miro's English professors had never heard of Galsworthy,[12] and another was creating a flurry of scandal in the department by recommending Chesterton[13] to his classes. It would scarcely have been in college that Miro would have learned of an escape from the closed dichotomy of culture. Bored with the "classic," and frozen with horror at the "popular," his career as a man of culture must have come to a dragging end if he had not been suddenly liberated by a chance lecture which he happened to hear while he was at home for the holidays.

The literary radical who appeared before the Lyceum Club of Miro's village was none other than Professor William Lyon Phelps, and it is to that evening of cultural audacity Miro thinks he owes all his later emancipation. The lecturer grappled with the "modern novel," and tossed Hardy, Tolstoi, Turgenev, Meredith, even Trollope, into the minds of the charmed audience with such effect that the virgin shelves of the village library were ravished for days to come by the eager minds upon whom these great names dawned for the first time. "Jude the Obscure" and "Resurrection" were of course kept officially away from the vulgar, but Miro managed to find "Smoke" and "Virgin Soil" and "Anna Karenina" and "The Warden" and "A Pair of Blue Eyes" and "The Return of the Native." Later at college he explored the forbidden realms. It was as if some devout and restless saint had suddenly been introduced to the Apocrypha. A new world was opened to Miro that was neither "classic" nor "popular," and yet which came to one under the most unimpeachable auspices. There was, at first, it is true, an air of illicit

[11] William Collins (1721-1759), English poet of odes. Charles Lamb (1775-1834), English essayist.

[12] John Galsworthy (1867-1933), English novelist and playwright whose most famous work is *The Forsyte Saga*.

[13] Gilbert Keith Chesterton (1874-1936), English journalist, novelist, poet, and critic.

adventure about the enterprise. The lecturer who made himself the missionary of such vigorous and piquant doctrine had the air of being a heretic, or at least a boy playing out of school. But Miro himself returned to college a cultural revolutionist. His orthodoxies crumbled. He did not try to reconcile the new with the old. He applied pick and dynamite to the whole structure of the canon. Irony, humor, tragedy, sensuality, suddenly appeared to him as literary qualities in forms that he could understand. They were like oxygen to his soul.

If these qualities were in the books he had been reading, he had never felt them. The expurgated sample-books he had studied had passed too swiftly over the Elizabethans to give him a sense of their lustiness. Miro immersed himself voluptuously in the pessimism of Hardy. He fed on the poignant torture of Tolstoi. While he was reading "Resurrection," his class in literature was making an "intensive" study of Tennyson. It was too much. Miro rose in revolt. He forswore literary courses forever, dead rituals in which anaemic priests mumbled their trite critical commentary. Miro did not know that to naughtier critics even Mr. Phelps might eventually seem a pale and timid Gideon, himself stuck in moral sloughs. He was grateful enough for that blast of trumpets which made his own scholastic walls fall down.

The next stage in Miro's cultural life was one of frank revolt. He became as violent as a heretic as he had been docile as a believer. Modern novels merely started the rift that widened into modern ideas. The professors were of little use. Indeed, when Miro joined a group of radicals who had started a new college paper, a relentless vendetta began with the teachers. Miro and his friends threw over everything that was mere literature. Social purpose must shine from any writing that was to rouse their enthusiasm. Literary flavor was to be permissible only where it made vivid high and revolutionary thought. Tolstoi became their god, Wells their high priest. Chesterton infuriated them. They wrote violent assaults upon him which began in imitation of his cool paradoxicality and ended in incoherent ravings. There were so many enemies to their new fervor that they scarcely knew where to begin. There were not only the old tables of stone to destroy, but there were new and threatening prophets of the eternal verities who had to be exposed. The nineteenth century which they had studied must be weeded of its nauseous moralists. The instructors consulted together how they might put down the revolt, and bring these sinners back to the faith of cultural scripture.

It was of no avail. In a short time Miro had been converted from an aspiration for the career of a cultivated "man of letters" to a fiery zeal for artistic and literary propaganda in the service of radical ideas. One of the results of this conversion was the discovery that he really had no standards of critical taste. Miro had been reverential so long that he had felt no preferences. Everything that was classic had to be good to him. But now that he had thrown away the books that were stamped with the mark of the classic mint, and was dealing with the raw materials of letters, he had to become a critic and make selection. It was not enough that a book should be radical. Some of the books he read, though impeccably revolutionary as to ideas, were clearly poor as literature. His muffled taste began to assert itself. He found himself impressionable where before he had been only mildly acquisitive. The literature of revolt and free speculation fired him into a state of spiritual explosiveness. All that he read now stood out in brighter colors and in sharper outlines than before. As he reached a better balance, he began to feel the vigor of literary form, the value of sincerity and freshness of style. He began to look for them keenly in everything he read. It was long before Miro realized that enthusiasm not docility had made him critical. He became a little proud of his sensitive and discriminating reactions to the modern and the unsifted.

This pursuit had to take place without any help from the college. After Miro graduated, it is true that it became the fashion to study literature as the record of ideas and not merely as a canon of sacred books to be analyzed, commented upon, and absorbed. But no dent was made upon the system in Miro's time, and, the inventory of English criticism not going beyond Stevenson. The Elizabethans had been exhumed and fumigated, but the most popular attention went to the gallery of Victorians, who combined moral soundness with literary beauty, and were therefore considered wholesome food for young men. The instructors all remained in the state of reverence which saw all things good that had been immemorially taught. Miro's own teacher was a fragile, earnest young man, whose robuster parents had evidently seized upon his nature as a fortunate pledge of what the family might produce in the way of an intellectual flower that should surpass in culture and gentility the ambitions of his parents. His studiousness, hopeless for his father's career as grocer, had therefore been capitalized into education.

The product now shone forth as one of the most successful and promising younger instructors in the department. He knew his subject. Card-indexes filled his room, covering in detail the works, lives, and deaths of the illustrious persons whom he expounded, as well as everything that had been said about them in the way of appreciation or interpretation. An endless number of lectures and courses could be made from this bountiful store. He never tried to write himself, but he knew all about the different kinds of writing, and when he corrected the boys' themes he knew infallibly what to tell them to avoid. Miro's vagaries scandalized his teacher all the more because during his first year in college Miro had been generally noticed as one with the proper sobriety and scholarly patience to graduate into a similar priestly calling. Miro found scant sympathy in the young man. To the latter literary studies were a science not an art, and they were to be treated with somewhat the same cold rigor of delimitation and analysis as any other science. Miro felt his teacher's recoil at the idea that literature was significant only as the expression of personality or as interpretation of some social movement. Miro saw how uneasy he became when he was confronted with current literature. It was clear that Miro's slowly growing critical sense had not a counterpart in the scholastic mind.

When Miro and his friends abandoned literary studies, they followed after the teachers of history and philosophy, intellectual arenas of which the literary professors seemed scandalously ignorant. At this ignorance Miro boiled with contempt. Here were the profitable clues that would give meaning to dusty literary scholarship, but the scholars had not the wits to seize them. They lived along, playing what seemed to Miro a rather dreary game, when they were not gaping reverently at ideas and forms which they scarcely had the genuine personality to appreciate. Miro felt once and for all free of these mysteries and reverences. He was to know the world as it has been and as it is. He was to put literature into its proper place, making all "culture" serve its apprenticeship for him as interpretation of things larger than itself, of the course of individual lives and the great tides of society.

Miro's later cultural life is not without interest. When he had finished college and his architectural course, and was making headway in his profession, his philosophy of the intellectual life began to straighten itself out. Rapid as his surrender of orthodoxy had been, it had taken him some time to live down that early education. He found now that he would have to live down his heresies also, and get some coherent system of tastes that was his own and not the fruit of either docility or the zeal of propaganda.

The old battles that were still going on helped Miro to realize his modern position. It was a queer, musty quarrel, but it was enlisting minds from all classes and of all intellectual fibers. The "classics" were dying hard, as Miro recognized whenever he read, in the magazines, attacks on the "new education." He found that professors were still taken seriously who declared in passion that without the universal study of the Latin language in American schools all conceptions of taste, standards, criticism, the historic sense itself, would vanish from the earth. He found that even as late as 1917 professional men were gathering together in solemn conclave and buttressing the "value of the classics" with testimonials from "successful men" in a variety of vocations. Miro was amused at the fact that the mighty studies once pressed upon him so uncritically should now require, like the patent medicines, testimonials as to their virtue. Bank presidents, lawyers, and editors had taken the Latin language regularly for years, and had found its effects painless and invigorating. He could not escape the unconscious satire that such plump and prosperous Americans expressed when they thought it admirable to save their cherished intellectual traditions in any such fashion.

Other conservatives Miro saw to be abandoning the line of opposition to science, only to fall back on the line of a defensive against "pseudo-science," as they seemed to call whatever intellectual interests had not yet become indubitably reputable. It was a line which would hold them rather strongly for a time, Miro thought, because so many of the cultural revolutionists agreed with them in hating some of these arrogant and mechanical psychologies and sociologies that reduced life to figures or organisms. But Miro felt also how obstructive was their fight. If the "classics" had done little for him except to hold his mind in an uncomprehending prison, and fetter his spontaneous taste, they seemed to have done little more for even the thorough scholars. When professors had devoted scholarly lives to the "classics" only to exhibit in their own polemics none of the urbanity and intellectual command which were supposed by the believer somehow to rub off automatically on the faithful student, Miro had to conclude an absence of causal connection between the "classics" and the able modern mind. When, moreover, critical power or creative literary work became almost extinct among these defenders of the "old education," Miro felt sure that a revolution was needed in the materials and attitudes of "culture."

The case of the defenders was all the weaker because their enemies were not wanton infidels, ignorant of the holy places they profaned. They were rather cultural "Modernists," reforming the church from within. They had the classic background, these young vandals, but they had escaped from its flat and unoriented surface. Abreast of the newer objective, impersonal standards of thinking, they saw the weakness of these archaic minds which could only appeal to vested interests in culture and testimonials from successful men.

The older critics had long since disavowed the intention of discriminating among current writers. These men, who had to have an Academy to protect them, lumped the younger writers of verse and prose together as "anarchic" and "naturalistic," and had become, in these latter days, merely peevish and querulous, protesting in favor of standards that no longer represented our best values. Every one, in Miro's time, bemoaned the lack of critics, but the older critics seemed to have lost all sense of hospitality and to have become tired and a little spitefully disconsolate, while the newer ones were too intent on their crusades against puritanism and philistinism to have time for a constructive pointing of the way.

Miro had a very real sense of standing at the end of an era. He and his friends had lived down both their old orthodoxies of the classics and their new orthodoxies of propaganda. Gone were the priggishness and self-consciousness which had marked their teachers. The new culture would be more personal than the old, but it would not be held as a personal property. It would be democratic in the sense that is would represent each person's honest spontaneous taste. The old attitude was only speciously democratic. The assumption was that if you pressed your material long enough and winningly enough upon your culturable public, they would acquire it. But the material was sometimes handed down, not grown in the garden of their own appreciations. Under these conditions the critic and appreciator became a mere impersonal register of orthodox opinion. The cultivated person, in confronting his judgments to what was authoritatively taught him, was really a member of the herd—a cultivated herd, it is true, but still a herd. It was the mass that spoke through the critic and not his own discrimination. These authoritative judgments might, of course, have come—probably had come— to the herd through discerning critics, but in Miro's time judgment in the schools had petrified. One believed not because one felt the original discernment, but because one was impressed by the weight and reputability of opinion. At least so it seemed to Miro.

Now just as the artists had become tired of conventions and were breaking through into new and personal forms, so Miro saw the younger critics breaking through these cultural conventions. To the elders the result would seem mere anarchy. But Miro's attitude did not want to destroy, it merely wanted to arrange the materials. He wanted no more second-hand appreciations. No one's cultural store was to include anything that one could not be enthusiastic about. One's acquaintance with the best that had been said and thought should be encouraged—in Miro's ideal school—to follow the lines of one's temperament. Miro, having thrown out the old gods, found them slowly and properly coming back to him. Some would always repel him, others he hoped to understand eventually. But if it took wisdom to write the great books, did it not also take wisdom to understand them? Even the Latin writers he hoped to recover, with the aid of translations. But why bother with Greek when you could get Euripides in the marvellous verse of Gilbert Murray? Miro was willing to believe that no education was complete without at least an inoculation of the virus of the two orthodoxies that he was transcending.

As Miro looked around the American scene, he wondered where the critics were to come from. He saw, on the one hand, Mr. Mencken and Mr. Dreiser and their friends, going heavily forth to battle with the Philistines, glorying in pachydermatous[14] vulgarisms that hurt the polite and cultivated young men of the old school. And he saw these violent critics, in their rage against puritanism, becoming themselves moralists, with the same bigotry and tastelessness as their enemies. No, these would never do. On the other hand, he saw Mr. Stuart P. Sherman, in his youthful if somewhat belated ardor, revolting so conscientiously against the "naturalism" and crude expression of current efforts that, in his defense of *belles-lettres*, of the fine tradition of literary art, he himself became a moralist of the intensest brand, and as critic plumped for Arnold Bennett, because that clever man had a feeling for the proprieties of human conduct. No, Mr. Sherman would do even less adequately. His fine sympathies were as much out of the current as was the specious classicism of Professor Shorey. He would have to look for the critics among the young men who had an abounding sense of life, as well as a feeling for literary form. They would be men who had not been content to live on their cultural inheritance, but had gone out into the modern world and amassed a fresh fortune of their own. They would be men who were not

---

[14] Thick-skinned.

squeamish, who did not feel the delicate differences between "animal" and "human" conduct, who were enthusiastic about Mark Twain and Gorki as well as Romain Rolland, and at the same time were thrilled by Copeau's theater.[15]

Where was a better program for culture, for any kind of literary art? Culture as a living effort, a driving attempt both at sincere expression and at the comprehension of sincere expression wherever it was found! Appreciation to be as far removed from the "I know what I like!" as from the textbook impeccability of taste! If each mind sought its own along these lines, would not many find themselves agreed? Miro insisted on liking Amy Lowell's attempt to outline the tendencies in American poetry in a form which made clear the struggles of contemporary men and women with the tradition and against "every affectation of the mind." He began to see in the new class consciousness of poets the ending of that old division which "culture" made between the chosen people and the gentiles. We were now to form little pools of workers and appreciators of similar temperaments and tastes. The little magazines that were starting up became voices for these new communities of sentiment. Miro thought that perhaps at first it was right to adopt a tentative superciliousness towards the rest of the world, so that both Mr. Mencken with his shudders at the vulgar Demos and Mr. Sherman with his obsession with the sanely and wholesomely American might be shut out from influence. Instead of fighting the Philistine in the name of freedom, or fighting the vulgar iconoclast in the name of wholesome human notions, it might be better to write for one's own band of comprehenders, in order that one might have something genuine with which to appeal to both the mob of the "bourgeois" and the ferocious vandals who had been dividing the field among them. Far better a quarrel among these intensely self-conscious groups than the issues that had filled *The Atlantic* and *The Nation* with their dreary obsolescence. Far better for the mind that aspired towards "culture" to be told not to conform or worship, but to search out its group, its own temperamental community of sentiment, and there deepen appreciations through sympathetic contact.

It was no longer a question of being hospitable towards the work of other countries. Miro found the whole world open to him, in these days, through the enterprise of publishers. He and his friends felt more sympathetic with certain groups in France and Russia than they did with the variegated "prominent authors" of their own land. Winston Churchill as a novelist came to seem more of an alien than Artzybashev.[16] The fact of culture being international had been followed by a sense of its being. The old cultural

---

[15] Jacques Copeau (1879-1949), French theatrical manager, cofounder of the *Nouvelle Revue Francaise* in 1908 and manager of the Théâtre de Vieux-Columbier.

[16] Artzybasheff (1899-1965), an American illustrator and writer.

attitude had been hospitable enough, but it had imported its alien culture in the form of "comparative literature." It was hospitable only in trying to mould its own taste to the orthodox canons abroad. The older American critic was mostly interested in getting the proper rank and reverence for what he borrowed. The new critic will take what suits his community of sentiment. He will want to link up not with the foreign canon, but with that group which is nearest in spirit with the effort he and his friends are making. The American has to work to interpret and portray the life he knows. He cannot be international in the sense that anything but the life in which he is saturated, with its questions and its colors, can be the material for his art. But he can be international—and must be—in the sense that he works with a certain hopeful vision of a "young-world," and with certain ideal values upon which the younger men, stained and revolted by war, in all countries are agreeing.

Miro wonders sometimes whether the direction in which he is tending will not bring him around the circle again to a new classicism. The last stage in the history of the man of culture will be that "classic" which he did not understand and which his mind spent its youth in overthrowing. But it will be a classicism far different from that which was so unintelligently handed down to him in the American world. It will be something worked out and lived into. Looking into the future he will have to do what Van Wyck Brooks calls "inventing a usable past." Finding little in the American tradition that is not tainted with sweetness and light and burdened with the terrible patronage of bourgeois society, the new classicist will yet rescue Thoreau and Whitman and Mark Twain and try to tap through them a certain eternal human tradition of abounding vitality and moral freedom, and so build out the future. If the classic means power with restraint, vitality with harmony, a fusion of intellect and feeling, and a keen sense of the artistic conscience, then the revolutionary world is coming out into the classic. When Miro sees behind the minds of *The Masses* group a desire for form and for expressive beauty, and sees the radicals following Jacques Copeau and reading Chekhov, he smiles at the thought of the American critics, young and old, who do not know yet that they are dead.

VAN WYCK BROOKS

(1886-1963)

Van Wyck Brooks struggled all his writing life with an issue that had interested Randolph Bourne before him and that is still central in this country's cultural and political life—how to connect the parts, how to open up lines of communication from enclave to enclave, how to insure that the rulers and the ruled participate fully and equally in a democratic society reality. In *America's Coming of Age* (1915) he wrote that:

> Twenty, even ten years, ago, it would have been universally as-
> sumed that the only hope for American society lay in somehow
> lifting the "Lowbrow" elements in it to the level of the "High-
> brow" elements. But that quickening realism which belongs to
> contemporary thought makes it plain on the one hand that the
> mere idealism of university ethics, the mere loftiness of what is
> called culture, the mere purity of so-called Good Government,
> left to themselves, not only produce a glassy inflexible priggish-
> ness on the upper levels which paralyses life; but that the lower
> levels have a certain humanity, flexibility, tangibility which are
> indispensable in any programme: that Tammany has quite as
> much to teach Good Government as Good Government has to
> teach Tammany, that slang has quite as much in store for so-
> called culture as culture has for slang—that the universities, while

Brooks' critical studies include *The Wine of the Puritans: A Study of Present Day America*, 1908; *The Soul: An Essay Towards a Point of View*, 1910; *The Malady of the Ideal: Obermann, Maurice de Guerin and Amiel*, 1913; *John Addington Symonds: A Biographical Study*, 1914; *The World of H. G. Wells*, 1915; *America's Coming of Age*, 1915; *The Ordeal of Mark Twain*, 1920; *The Pilgrimage of Henry James*, 1925; *Emerson and Others*, 1927; *Sketches in Criticism*, 1932; *The Life of Emerson*, 1932; *Three Essays on America*, 1934; *The Flowering of New England*, 1936; *New England: Indian Summer (1865-1915)*, 1940; *On Literature Today*,

1941; *Opinions of Oliver Allston*, 1941; *The World of Washington Irving*, 1944; *The Times of Melville and Whitman*, 1947; *The Confident Years: 1885-1915*, 1952; *The Writer in America*, 1953; *From a Writer's Notebook*, 1958.

Brooks has written of his life in *An Autobiography*, with a foreword by John Hall Wheelock, 1965. He has also edited many volumes, among them *Randolph Bourne, the History of a Literary Radical*, 1920.

Recent studies of Brooks are James R. Vitelli, *Van Wyck Brooks*, 1969 and William Wasserstrom, *The Legacy of Van Wyck Brooks*, 1971.

emphatically not becoming more "practical," must base their disinterestedness on human, moral, social, artistic, and personal needs, impulses, and experience.

The problem was, on one view, that of fostering a sense of mutuality and common adventure in a general population in danger of losing, as it pursued personal profit, its feeling for the unique oneness of the nation as a whole. On another view the problem was that of encouraging a special group—writers, teachers, intellectuals—to resist the temptation to withdraw into an aestheticism remote from ordinary life. Addressing these issues, Brooks tried to speak to literary people, businessmen, intelligent average citizens in a single voice, and he often gave offense to one interest or another in the process. The frustrations of attempting to articulate standards of moral and cultural health for society in the large at a time when each group seemed chiefly preoccupied with its own welfare, sometimes induced extravagance, oversimplification, shrillness and floridity of style. At his best, however, Brooks was that rarity among Americans—an unsentimental patriot whose noble aspirations for his country had firm underpinnings in wit and historical understanding.

His characteristic way of dramatizing the matters that concerned him was by probing conflicts in individual American lives—usually writers' lives—that had clear bearing on broad cultural issues. In *The Ordeal of Mark Twain* (1920), for example, he sought to show how "upper middle class" gentility and poor boy dreams of business success edged the author of *Huckleberry Finn* away from his true literary mission as a unifying voice for American society. In *The Pilgrimage of Henry James* (1925) he chastised the great novelist for taking flight from American reality, immuring himself in a palace of art remote from common realities. Brooks' American heroes were Whitman and Emerson and, as a model of right relationships between literature and society, he held up—in *The Flowering of New England* (1936)—the early nineteenth-century Cambridge and Concord worlds of Emerson and Thoreau.

Educated at Harvard, Brooks led a bookman's life for close to six decades—publishing poetry as early as 1905, when he was 19, and working thereafter, with few interruptions, as author, reviewer, culture critic, and magazine editor (*Seven Arts,* the *Dial,* the *Freeman,* the *New Republic*), and earning many honors. In the decade before his death in 1963 the positions he had held throughout his career were treated by many as irrelevant; more recently his books have been winning fresh regard among younger critics.

America's Coming of Age

CHAPTER I
"HIGHBROW" AND "LOWBROW"

I

At the time when he was trying to release humanity from the cross of gold on which, as he said, it was crucified, the Apostle of Free Silver—in this manner, at least, representing the old American frame of mind—announced that the opinion of all the professors in the United States would not affect his opinions in the least. Now this, plainly, was a very formidable dilemma. For on the one hand stood a body of supposed experts in economic theory, on the other a man whose profession it was to change and reform economic practice,—the one knowing, the other doing; and not only was there no compatibility between them but an openly avowed and cynical contempt of theory on the part of practice was a principal element in the popularity of a popular hero. Was Mr. Bryan,[1] however, to blame for it? To know anything of the economic theory which is taught in American universities—in many cases compulsorily taught—is to confess that blame is not the right word. For this economic theory is at the least equally cynical. It revolves round and round in its tree-top dream of the economic man; and no matter how much the wind blows political economy never comes down. Incompatibility, mutual contempt between theory and practice, is in the very nature of things.

One might extend the illustration to literature, merely substituting one professor for another and putting any typical best-selling novelist in the place of Mr. Bryan. It is a peculiar twist in the academic mind to suppose that a writer belongs to literature only when he is dead; living he is, vaguely, something else; and an habitual remoteness from the creative mood has made American professors quite peculiarly academic. "Literature," as distinguished from excellent writing, is, in the American universities, a thing felt to have been done, and while for all one knows it may continue to be done the quality in it which makes it literature only comes out, like the quality in wines, with age.

Now I suppose that most of the American novelists in our day are university men; they have learned to regard literature as an august compound of Browning, Ben Jonson, and Hesiod;[2] and consequently when they themselves begin to write it is in a spirit of real humility that they set themselves to the composition of richly rewarded trash. I am sure of this: it is modesty that lies behind the "best-seller"; and there is an aspect in which the specta-

---

[1] William Jennings Bryan (1860-1925), American statesman and lawyer, three times Presidential candidate (1896, 1900, 1908).

[2] Robert Browning (1812-1889), English poet of 300 works, including dramatic monologues. Ben Jonson (1573-1673), English poet and dramatist. Hesiod, Greek poet of the eighth century B.C.

cle of writers regarding themselves as humble tradesfolk has a certain charm. But the conception of literature as something, so to speak, high and dry, gives to the craft of authorship in America a latitude like that of morality in Catholic countries: so long as the heavenly virtues are upheld mundane virtues may shift as they will. In a word, writers are relieved of responsibility, and while their ethical conscience remains quite sound they absolve themselves from any artistic conscience whatsoever. And the worst of it is that precisely these writers of inmitigable trash are often the bright, vigorous, intuitive souls who *could* make literature out of American life. Has it ever been considered how great a knowledge of men, what psychological gifts of the first order their incomparable achievement of popularity implies?

These two attitudes of mind have been phrased once for all in our vernacular as "Highbrow" and "Lowbrow." I have proposed these terms to a Russian, and Englishman, and a German, asking each in turn whether in his country there was anything to correspond with the conceptions implied in them. In each case they have been returned to me as quite American, authentically our very own, and, I should add, highly suggestive.

What side of American life is not touched by this antithesis? What explanation of American life is more central or more illuminating? In everything one finds this frank acceptance of twin values which are not expected to have anything in common: on the one hand a quite unclouded, quite unhypocritical assumption of transcendent theory ("high ideals"); on the other a simultaneous acceptance of catchpenny realities. Between university ethics and business ethics; between American culture and American humor, between Good Government and Tammany, between academic pedantry and pavement slang, there is no community, no genial middle ground.

The very accent of the words "Highbrow" and "Lowbrow" implies an instinctive perception that this is a very unsatisfactory state of affairs. For both are used in a derogatory sense. The "Highbrow" is the superior person whose virtue is admitted but felt to be an inept unpalatable virtue; while the "Lowbrow" is a good fellow one readily takes to, but with a certain scorn for him and all his works. And what is true of them as personal types is true of what they stand for. They are equally undesirable, and they are incompatible; but they divide American life between them.

II

They always have divided American life between them; and to understand them one has to go back to the beginning of things,—for without doubt the Puritan Theocracy is the all-influential fact in the history of the American mind. It was the Puritan conception of the Deity as not alone all-determining but precisely responsible for the practical affairs of the race, as constituting, in fact, the State itself, which precluded in advance any central bond, any responsibility, any common feeling in American affairs and which justified the unlimited centrifugal expediency which has always marked American life. And the same instinct that made against centrality in government made against centrality in thought, against common standards of any kind. The imminent eternal issues the Puritans felt so keenly, the equally imminent practical issues they experienced so monotonously threw almost no light on one another; there was no middle ground between to mitigate, combine, or harmonize them.

So it is that from the beginning we find two main currents in the American mind running side by side but rarely mingling—a current of overtones and a current of undertones—and both equally unsocial: on the one hand, the current of Transcendentalism, originating in the piety of the Puritans, becoming a philosophy in Jonathan Edwards, passing through Emerson, producing the fastidious refinement and aloofness of the chief American writers, and, as the coherent ideals and beliefs of Transcendentalism gradually faded out, resulting in the final unreality of most contemporary American culture; and on the other hand the current of catchpenny opportunism, originating in the practical shifts of Puritan life, becoming a philosophy in Franklin, passing through the American humorists, and resulting in the atmosphere of contemporary business life.

Thus the literature of the seventeenth century in America is composed in equal parts, one may fairly say, of piety and advertisement; and the revered chronicles of New England had the double effect of proving how many pilgrim souls had been elected to salvation and of populating with hopeful immigrants a land where heaven had proved so indulgent.

For three generations the prevailing American character was compact in one type, the man of action who was also the man of God. Not until the eighteenth century did the rift appear and with it the essential distinction between "Highbrow" and "Lowbrow." It appeared in the two philosophers, Jonathan Edwards and Benjamin Franklin, who share the eighteenth century between them. In their amazing purity of type and in the apparent incompatibility of their aims they determined the American character as a racial fact, and after them the Revolution became inevitable. Channing, Lincoln, Emerson, Whitman, Grant, Webster, Garrison, Edison, Mr. Rockefeller, Mrs. Eddy[3] are all, in one way or another, permutations and combinations of these two grand progenitors of the American character.

Strange that at the very outset two men should have arisen so aptly side by side and fixed the poles of our national life! For no one has ever more

---

[3] All of these writers are represented in this anthology except for Ulysses Grant (1822-1885), eighteenth president; Thomas A. Edison (1847-1931), American inventor; John D. Rockefeller (1839-1937), American industrialist and philanthropist; and Mrs. Mary Baker Eddy (1821-1910), American religious leader, founder of the Church of Christ, Scientist.

fully and typically than Jonathan Edwards displayed the infinite inflexibility of the upper levels of the American mind, nor any one more typically than Franklin the infinite flexibility of its lower levels.

The intellect of Jonathan Edwards was like the Matterhorn, steep, icy, and pinnacled. At its base were green slopes and singing valleys filled with all sorts of little tender wild-flowers—for he was the most lovable of men; but as soon as the ground began to rise in good earnest all this verdurous life came to an abrupt end: not one green or living thing could subsist in that frozen soil, on those pale heights. It was the solitude of logic that led him to see in destiny only a wrathful tyrant and a viper's trail in the mischievous ways of little boys and girls.

I confess to an old-time and so to speak aboriginal affection for this man, so gently solicitous to make up in his daily walk and conversation for the ferocious impulsions of that brain of his. He was even the most romantic of men, as I thought once, and I well remember that immense old musty book of his theology, covered with mildew, with its desert of tiny print, which I carried out with me into the fields and read, in the intervals of birdnesting, under the hedgerows and along the borders of the wood: the sun fell for the first time on those clammy old pages and the pallid thoughts that lay in them, and the field-sparrows all about were twittering in a language which, to tell the truth, was no more unintelligible to me. But everything that springs from solitude shines by a light of its own, and Manfred among the Alps[4] was not more lonely than this rapt scholar in his parsonage among the Indians.

There are, however, solitudes and solitudes. Great poets and fruitful thinkers live apart themselves, perhaps, but they have society and the ways of men in their blood. They recollect in tranquillity, as it were, gestate, live again, and reveal the last significance of active generations rich in human stuff, in experience, in emotion, in common reason. Nothing like this existed in the background of Jonathan Edwards, no profound and complex race-life. Intellect in him, isolated and not responsible to the other faculties, went on its way unchecked; and he was able to spin those inept sublimities of his by subtracting from his mind every trace of experience, every touch of human nature as it really was among his innocent country-folk.

Notoriously, of course, our great Dr. Franklin simplified existence in precisely the opposite way; for the opposite of unmitigated theory is unmitigated practice. Who can deny that in *Poor Richard* the "Lowbrow" point of view for the first time took definite shape, stayed itself with axioms, and found a sanction in the idea of "policy"? It emerges there full-fledged, in its classical form, a two-dimensional wisdom, a wisdom shorn of overtones, the most accommodating wisdom in the world.

[4] Manfred is the hero of Byron's poem of the same name. Manfred was king of Naples and Sicily (1258–1266).

Were ever two views of life more incompatible than these? What indeed could Poor Richard have in common with an Angry God?

And what can Mr. Bryan have in common with political economy?

III

"Our people," said Emerson, "have their intellectual culture from one country and their duties from another." In how many spheres that phrase can be applied! Desiccated culture at one end and stark utility at the other have created a deadlock in the American mind, and all our life drifts chaotically between the two extremes. Consider, for example, our use of the English language. Literary English in England is naturally a living speech, which occupies the middle of the field and expresses the flesh and blood of an evolving race. Literary English with us is a tradition, just as Anglo-Saxon law with us is a tradition. They persist not as the normal expressions of a race, the essential fibre of which is permanently Anglo-Saxon, but through prestige and precedent and the will and habit of a dominating class largely out of touch with a national fabric unconsciously taking form "out of school." No wonder that our literary style is "pure," that our literary tradition, our tradition especially in oratory and political prose, retains the spirit of the eighteenth century. But at what a cost! At the cost of expressing a popular life which bubbles with energy and spreads and grows and slips away ever more and more from the control of tested ideas, a popular life "with the lid off," which demands an intellectual outlet and finds one in slang, journalism, and unmannerly fiction.

After seventy years Carlyle's well-known appeal to Emerson still applies to the spirit of American culture: "For the rest, I have to object still (what you will call objecting against the Law of Nature) that we find you a speaker indeed, but as it were a *Soliloquizer* on the eternal mountain-tops only, in vast solitudes where men and their affairs lie all hushed in a very dim remoteness; and only *the man* and the stars and the earth are visible—whom, so fine a fellow seems he, we could perpetually punch into, and say, 'Why won't you come and help us then? We have terrible need of one man like you down among us! It is cold and vacant up there; nothing paintable but rainbows and emotions; come down and you shall do life-pictures, passions, facts. . . .' "

And what a comment on the same utterance that at this very moment an amiable New Englander should have been painting in Parson Wilbur and Hosea Biglow,[5] respectively, unconscious of any tragic symbolism of things to come, the unbridgeable chasm between literate and illiterate America!

[5] Parson Wilbur and Hosea Bigelow are figures in James Russell Lowell's *The Bigelow Papers* (1846).

Morally, no doubt, in Jaalam, they understood one another and got along very well, as Yankees will. But in Chicago?

IV

To pass now from the social to the personal question, since the question is at bottom a personal one, let us figure to ourselves how this divergence comes about and how it is that our educational system, instead of creating what President Eliot calls a "serviceable fellowship" between theory and practice, tends to set them apart and to confirm us all either in the one extreme or in the other.

Let us figure to ourselves a typical American who has grown up, as an American typically does grow up, in a sort of orgy of lofty examples, moralized poems, national anthems, and baccalaureate sermons; until he is charged with all manner of ideal purities, ideal honorabilities, ideal femininities, flagwavings and skyscrapings of every sort;—until he comes to feel in himself the hovering presence of all manner of fine potentialities, remote, vaporous, and evanescent as a rainbow. All this time, it can fairly be said, he has not been taught to associate himself personally with ends even much lower than these, he has not been taught that life is a legitimate progress toward spiritual or intellectual ends at all, his instincts of acquisition, pleasure, enterprise, and desire have in no way been linked and connected with disinterested ends; he has had it very firmly embedded in his mind that the getting of a living is not a necessity incidental to some higher and more disinterested end, but that it is the prime and central end in things, and as a corollary to this he has been encouraged to assume that the world is a stamping-ground for every untrained, greedy, and aggressive impulse in him, that, in short, society is fair prey for what he can get out of it.

Let us imagine that, having grown up in this way, he is sent to college. And here, in order to keep the case a typical one, we shall have to exercise a little discrimination in the choice of a university.

It will not be Harvard, because the ideal of Harvard, as I shall point out, is not a typically modern American ideal. Nor will it be one of the modern utilitarian universities, which have no ideal at all. It will be any one of the others; and when I say this I mean that each of the others is in one way or another a development of the old American country college; its ideal, its experience, its tradition spring out of and lead one back to that. Now among these old colleges Harvard might have been figured as an ever-developing, ever-liberalizing catholicism, of which they were all sectarian offshoots, established on a principle of progressive theological fragmentation, each one

[6] Charles W. Eliot (1834-1926), American educator and editor, was president of Harvard (1869-1909).

defending an orthodoxy its predecessors had outworn or violently setting up in defense of some private orthodoxy of its own. They founded themselves each on a remote dogma or system of dogma as their central and sufficient basis, and all their wheels turned in relation to the central theological dynamo. In a sense of course this was true also of Harvard, but with a marked difference. For the theologians who founded Harvard were men of action as well; in the seventeenth century a New England minister was also a politician, and the education of ministers for which Harvard was mainly established implied an education for public affairs as well, as education for society, so far as the word society can be used in connection with the early Puritans at all. Thus at the outset the founders of Harvard drove in the wedge of secularism: Harvard had from the beginning a sort of national basis, at least among New Englanders, and its dogmatic structure consequently reflected and shifted with and accommodated itself to the currents of national thought. Remaining in touch with society, it educated to a certain extent, relatively to an extraordinary extent, the social function of its students; and it is thus no accident that so large a proportion of the political, the literary, and the scientific life of America has sprung from it. But in the eighteenth century the conditions under which Harvard was established had ceased to be true. The minister was no longer a man of affairs,—he was a stark theologian, and usually of a type which the majority of his flock had outgrown. Yale, Princeton, and virtually all the other typically American colleges were founded by men of this type. Jonathan Edwards may figure for them all; the motive which led him to become the president of Princeton being precisely that his flock in Connecticut could no longer see the anger of God eye to eye with him. Already in his time the fathers and mothers of young America had submitted to the charms of *Poor Richard's Almanac*— they had themselves for the most part become inveterately "Lowbrow"; but they seem to have believed that an Angry God might still be a good influence over young America himself.

To return now to the typical case with whom we began, let us imagine that he makes a typical choice and goes to a typical university. Having arrived there will he be confronted with an Angry God, or any sort of direct theological dogma? By no means. But there will have remained in the air a certain fragrance and vibration, as if an ideal had passed that way and not stayed, there will be intangible whispers and seductions, there will be a certain faint, rarified, remote, but curiously pervasive and insistent influence—like the sound of an Æolian harp or the recollection of Plato in some uncouth slum; there will be memories and portraits of many an old metaphysician, white, unearthly, fragile. It will all seem very much as if, the significance of these remote dogmas having evaporated, only the remoteness, in a way, had remained.

One would have to be very insensitive not to feel the quite unbalancing charm of this quality—so different from its comparatively robust Oxford parallel—in the old New England colleges, as in Princeton, Yale, and the other universities which have developed out of them; but one cannot help feeling also, I think, something vaguely Circean in it. And in fact, given the preliminary method of bringing up which I have sketched, what will be its effect in the case we are considering? Suddenly confronted during four years with just this remote influence of ideals, out of which the intellectual structure has evaporated and which never possessed a social structure, will he not find them too vague, too intangible, too unprepared for to be incorporated into his nature? Certainly ideals of this kind, in this way presented, in this way prepared for, cannot enrich life, because they are wanting in all the elements of personal contact. Wholly dreamlike and vaporous, they end by breeding nothing but cynicism and chagrin; and in becoming permanently catalogued in the mind as impracticable they lead to a belief in the essential unreality of ideas as well.

Indeed there is nothing so tragic and so ominous as the familiar saying that college is the happiest time of one's life. Yet perhaps a majority of college men think of their college life in this way. They deliberately put their Golden Age behind them—and, as things are, they know it is behind them. But consider what a comment this is on the American university itself,—a place, one can fairly say, where ideals are cherished precisely because they are ineffectual, because they are ineptly and mournfully beautiful, because they make one cynical, because they make life progressively uninteresting, because, practically and in effect, they are illusions and frauds and infinitely charming lies. There surely is the last and the most impenetrable stronghold of Puritanism, refined to the last degree of intangibility, which persists in making the world a world inevitably sordid, basely practical, and whose very definition of the ideal consequently is, that which has no connection with the world!

Thus far then for our typical university graduate. He has been consistently educated in twin values which are incompatible. The theoretical atmosphere in which he has lived is one that bears no relation to society, the practical atmosphere in which he has lived bears no relation to ideals. Theory has become for him permanently a world in itself, a kind of *ding an sich;* practice has become simply a world of dollars.

Now supposing he has already become interested in the study, let us say, of economics, three paths are open to him: either he can give himself once for all to economics, or he can go the way of all flesh, i.e., into business, or he can hesitate between the two, becoming an economist for the time being and eventually going into business.

It is just here, at the moment of choice, that the want of ballast in his education becomes manifest. There is nothing for him but to lurch violently to the one extreme or the other; and this, according as there is in his nature a crude preponderance either of intellect or of the sense of action, he does. If he is preponderantly intellectual he adopts the first course; that is to say, he dedicates himself to the service of a type of economic theory that bears no relation to this wicked world at all, leaving all the good people who are managing the economic practice of society (and, for the want of him, chiefly muddling it)—leaving all these good people to talk nonsense in the wilderness. If he is preponderantly a man of action, he adopts the second course; that is to say, he dedicates himself to the service of a private end which knows nothing of theory, which is most cynically contemptuous of ideals, flatulent or other, and which is precisely as indifferent to the economic life of society as the professor of economics himself.

Well, good riddance to both of them, one might be inclined to say, except that on second thought the professor and the business man between them hold in their hands so great a part of human destiny. It is the third case that is really interesting and really tragic. For just so far as our typical student is a normal man, just so far as he shares the twin elements of intellect and action in equal parts, just so far will he be on the fence. The probability is that in this case he will become a professor for as long as he can stand it and then burst into business and become a first-rate millionaire as quickly as possible. The sense of action in him will rebel against the sense of theory and finding in theory no basis for action, no relation to action, will press him into a fresh life where the theoretical side of his nature will at least be of some slight use in furthering his own aggrandizement, and that alone.

V

Naturally the question of economics is only typical. Any branch of human activity which is represented by professors at all—and which is not?—would serve as well. Human nature itself in America exists on two irreconcilable planes, the plane of stark theory and the plane of stark business; and in the back of its mind is heaven knows what world of poetry, hidden away, too inaccessible, too intangible, too unreal in fact ever to be brought into the open, or to serve, as the poetry of life rightly should serve, in harnessing thought and action together, turning life into a disinterested adventure.

Argue which way you will, from the individual to society or from society to the individual, it is the same. Just as the American attitude toward the State has been the attitude of an oratorical and vague patriotism which has not based itself on a concrete interest in public affairs; just as, in consequence of this, the "invisible government" of business has swept in and taken possession of the field and become the actual government under which we live, overgrowing and supplanting the government we recognize: so also in the case of the individual; the cherishing of ideals that are simply unmapped regions to which nobody has the least intention of building roads, the baccalaureate sermons that are no just, organic comment on the educational system that precedes them—precisely these themselves strengthen the forces from below; the invisible government of self-interest, built up carefully from the beginning by maxim and example, fills the vacuum a disinterested purpose ought to have occupied.

Twenty, even ten years, ago, it would have been universally assumed that the only hope for American society lay in somehow lifting the "Lowbrow" elements in it to the level of the "Highbrow" elements. But that quickening realism which belongs to contemporary thought makes it plain on the one hand that the mere idealism of university ethics, the mere loftiness of what is called culture, the mere purity of so-called Good Government, left to themselves, not only produce a glassy inflexible priggishness on the upper levels which paralyzes life; but that the lower levels have a certain humanity, flexibility, tangibility which are indispensable in any programme: that Tammany has quite as much to teach Good Government as Good Government has to teach Tammany, that slang has quite as much in store for so-called culture as culture has for slang—that the universities, while emphatically not becoming more "practical," must base their disinterestedness on human, moral, social, artistic, and personal needs, impulses, and experience.

But society cannot become humane of itself; and it is for this reason that the movements of Reform are so external and so superficial. The will to reform springs from a conviction *ex post facto,* and is strictly analogous to the frame of mind of business men who retire at sixty and collect pictures. Nothing so exemplifies it as the spectacle of Mr. Carnegie spending three quarters of his life in providing steel for battleships and the last quarter of it in trying to abolish war. He himself surely has not been conscious of any inward revolution; plainly with him as with others the will to create disorder and the will to reform it spring from the same inner condition of mind. The impetus of Reform is evidently derived from the hope that a sufficient number of reformers can be trained and brought into the field to match the forces of business—the one group cancelling the other group. The ideal of Reform, in short, is the attainment of zero.

Nothing is more absurd than to attack business as such. But the motives and circumstances of business vary from age to age, and there is a world of difference between industry conceived as a social process and trade conceived as a private end. A familiar distinction between the nineteenth century and the twentieth is that the problem of civilization is no longer the problem of want but the problem of surplus. Roughly speaking, the hereditary American class—the prevailing class, I mean—is faced with the problem not of making money but of spending it; the prevailing American class is in a position of relative, but relatively great, economic freedom, and under these conditions it is plain that in them economic self-assertion ("enterprise") has become to a large extent a vicious anachronism. But force of habit, the sheer impetus and groundswell of an antiquated pioneering spirit finds them with no means of personal outlet except a continued economic self-assertion on the one hand, and on the other a reckless and essentially impersonal overflow of surplus wealth which takes the form of doing what everybody else does, and doing it as much more so as possible.

Because it was for so long the law of the tribe economic self-assertion still remains to most Americans a sort of moral obligation; while self-fulfillment still looks like a pretty word for selfishness. Yet self-fulfillment through science, or literature, or mechanics, or industry itself—the working out of one's own personality, one's own inventiveness through forms of activity that are directly social, as all these activities *are* directly social, gives a man, through his very sociality, through the feeling he has that as a good workman he is coöperating with all other good workmen, a life-interest apart from his rewards. And just as this principle becomes generally diffused and understood the incentive is withdrawn from economic self-assertion, a relative competence being notoriously satisfying to the man whose prime end is the fulfilling of his own creative instincts; and the wealth of the world is already socialized.

You cannot have personality, you cannot have the expressions of personality so long as the end of society is an impersonal end like the accumulation of money. For the individual whose personal end varies too greatly from the end of the mass of men about him not only suffers acutely and becomes abnormal, he actually cannot accomplish anything healthily fine at all. The best and most disinterested individual can only express the better intuitions and desires of his age and place;—there must be some sympathetic touch between him and some visible or invisible host about him, since the mind is a flower that has an organic connection with the soil it springs from.

The only serious approach to society is the personal approach, and what I have called the quickening realism of contemporary social thought is at bottom simply a restatement for the mass of commercialized men, and in relation to issues which directly concern the mass of men as a whole, of those personal instincts that have been the essence of art, religion, literature—the essence of personality itself—since the beginning of things. It will remain of the least importance to patch up politics, to become infected with social consciousness, or to do any of the other easy popular contemporary things unless, in some way, personality can be made to release itself on a middle plane between vaporous idealism and self-interested practicality; unless, in short, self-fulfillment as an ideal can be substituted for self-assertion as an ideal. On the economic plane that implies socialism; on every other plane it implies something which a majority of Americans in our day certainly do not possess—an object in living.

VI

It is perhaps just as well that Cervantes lived and died in Spain three hundred years ago. Had he been born an American of the twentieth century he might have found the task of satire an all too overwhelming one. Yet his fable, which has its personal bearing in all men always, has in America a social bearing that is perhaps unique. Don Quixote is the eternal "Highbrow" under a polite name, just as Sancho Panza is the eternal "Lowbrow"; and if the adorable Dulcinea is not a vision of the night and a daily goal in the mind of our professors, then there is no money in Wall Street. One admits the charm of both extremes, the one so fantastically above, the other so fantastically below the level of right reason; to have any kind of relish for muddled humanity is necessarily to feel the charm of both extremes. But where is all that is real, where is personality and all its works, if it is not essentially somewhere, somehow, in some not very vague way, between?

CHAPTER III
THE PRECIPITANT

I have been trying to show in what way a survey of American literature would inevitably lead us to certain general facts about American life. I opened the survey with a statement which I think no one will contradict, that in American literature something has always been wanting, that a certain density, weight, and richness, a certain poignancy, a "something far more deeply interfused," simply is not there. Beginning with this clue and reaching an axiom to which it seemed to me inevitably to lead, I suggested a certain practical conclusion as the result of our inquiry: that those of our writers who have possessed a vivid personal talent have been paralyzed by the want of a social background, while those who have possessed a vivid social talent have been equally unable to develop their personalities.

There is, I think, something in some not very vague way unsatisfactory about each of the writers we have been examining. Taken as a whole the most characteristic fact about them is a certain delicacy which arrives in literature almost in the degree to which it stands remote from life, achieves its own salvation (after the Puritan fashion) by avoiding contact with actuality. Almost all the greater American writers, placed beside their English contemporaries, have a certain all too unworldly refinement. Purity of style and delicacy of touch at once distinguish Emerson from Carlyle and Hawthorne from any Victorian novelist; but the abyss between their writings and the world in which they lived is immeasurably greater. The American character speaks through them, of course, but it is the American character only in its most sublimated form, carefully cleansed as it were and highly rarified. Nothing is more marked than their disinclination to take a plunge, reckless and complete, as Carlyle and Dickens did, into the rudest and grossest actualities. The poet Camoens on his deathbed observed that his whole life had been spent in trying to keep himself afloat in a stormy sea, and his only care had been to exercise his left hand with double energy so that his right hand might be free to hold his *Luciad* aloft, uncontaminated by the waves. This is the whole story of American literature: in a more than usually difficult and sordid world it has applied its principal energies to being uncontaminated itself. It has held aloof, as a consciously better part, like all American idealism. The talent is there, high and dry; and if it is not always too high, it is very often a great deal too dry.

In fact, we have in America two publics, the cultivated public and the business public, the public of theory and the public of action, the public that reads Maeterlinck and the public that accumulates money: the one largely feminine, the other largely masculine. Wholly incompatible in their ideals they still pull together, as the ass and the ox must. But the ass shows no disposition to convert the ox, nor the ox the ass. They do not mitigate one another;—they are, in biological phrase, infertile with one another.

But it happens that we have the rudiments of a middle tradition, a tradition which effectively combines theory and action, a tradition which is just as fundamentally American as either flag-waving or money-grabbing, one which is visibly growing but which has already been grossly abused; and this is the tradition which begins with Walt Whitman. The real significance of Walt Whitman is that he, for the first time, gave us the sense of something organic in American life.

Whitman was himself a great vegetable of a man, all of a piece in roots, flavor, substantiality, and succulence, well-ripened in the common sunshine. In him the hitherto incompatible extremes of the American temperament were fused. The exquisite refinement of the Puritan tradition, summed up as an original type in Jonathan Edwards, able to make nothing of a life so rude in its actuality, turned for its outlet to a perfectly disembodied world, the shadow-world of Emerson, Hawthorne, and Poe, a world fastidiously intellectual in which only two colors exist, white and black. Whitman was the Antæus[7] of this tradition who touched earth with it and gave it hands and feet. For having all the ideas of New England, being himself saturated with Emersonianism, he came up from the other side with everything New England did not possess: quantities of rude emotion and a faculty of gathering humane experience almost as great as that of the hero of the Odyssey. Living habitually among world ideas, world emotions, world impulses and having experienced life on a truly grand scale, this extraordinary person, innocent as a pioneer of what is called urbanity, became nevertheless a man of the world in a sense in which ambassadors are not; and there is every reason to suppose that he would have been perfectly at home in the company of Achilles, or Erasmus, or Louis XIV.

This fact is full of meaning, and if any one doubts it let him dwell on the following record in *Specimen Days*. Whitman is describing what he did in the military hospitals at Washington during the war:

[7] Antæus, in Greek mythology, was a giant, invincible while touching the ground, who was lifted into the air by Hercules and crushed to death.

"For reading I generally have some old pictorial magazines or story papers—they are always acceptable. . . . In these wards, or on the field, as I thus continue to go round, I have come to adapt myself to each emergency, after its kind or call, however trivial, however solemn, every one justified and made real under its circmstances—not only visits and cheering talk and little gifts—not only washing and dressing wounds . . . but passages from the Bible, expounding them, . . . etc. (I think I see my friends smiling at this confession, but I was never more in earnest in my life.) In camp and elsewhere, I was in the habit of reading or giving recitations to the men. They were very fond of it, and liked declamatory pieces. We would gather in a large group by ourselves after supper, and spend the time in such readings, or in talking, and occasionally by an amusing game called the game of twenty questions."

This passage will serve very well to mark the distinction between Whitman and all the other American men of letters of his time. Could Emerson have recited "declamatory pieces," even if it was at the moment the one tactful thing to do? Could Bryant have led a game of twenty questions? Could Edgar Allan Poe have expounded the Bible? Could Whittier have juggled with oranges? Could Lowell have pointed out the felicities that lurk in the pictorial adventures of Nick Carter and the Wharf Rats? Could any one of them, in short, have entered so fully and many-sidedly into the spirit of a great human situation? But allowing for certain inevitable differences in the *milieu* (orange-juggling and the adventures of Nick Carter being peculiarly democratic and modern), I am sure that Achilles, or Erasmus, or Louis XIV could have done so; and this is why I have called Whitman a man of the world.

It was in these ways that he gained his experience, in these ways that he shared it. And it is the more remarkable since he had sprung from the most provincial, inadaptable, homespun stock, his aspect being, as Edmund Gosse remembers it, like that of a plain old deal table, scrubbed and scrubbed and scrubbed. He let in the air of a wider world on those inadequate decencies; he came home to his own traditions like a prodigal son, visiting for a while, mingling an element of indulgent pity in his new sense of the limited old ways, aware of a few confidences that could not be shared any more and of so many things, human, too, which could find no place there. To compare the particular homeliness of Whitman with the homeliness, for example, of *Snow-Bound* is at once to recall his line "There was a child went forth."

And he challenged the abnormal dignity of American letters. The dignity of letters! It is a question how much dignity letters can afford to have. No doubt in the perennial indignity of our world a considerable emphasis on that becomes all too easily the price of self-preservation. The possession of culture with us has always been rather a jealous possession, it has the nature of a right which has been earned, an investment which might have been a yacht, a country-house, or a collection of Rembrandts instead.

All this was especially true of the New York men of letters who formed the background of Whitman: Stedman, Stoddard, and their group. The eighteenth century was never so meticulous about form, style, presentableness as were these men. Style to them was a quite sacred thing, bought and paid for, as it were; and for them the essence of literature lay in its remoteness from Wall Street. Witness the poem in which Stedman, in order to lift the scene of his daily avocations to the level of literature, achieved the incredible ineptitude of getting the god Pan into it. They had the temperament of collectors, viveurs, connoisseurs of one generation; they understood and they emulated the fragile and the far-sought; and Whitman came in upon them thundering and with his coat off, like an inconvenient country uncle, puddling their artistic expectations. Could anything have been more disconcerting than his Olympian summary of what he calls the "endless supply of small coin . . . the dandies and ennuyées who flood us with their thin sentiment of parlors, parasols, piano-songs, tinkling rhymes, the five-hundredth importation—or whimpering and crying about something, chasing one aborted conceit after another, and forever occupied in dyspeptic amours with dyspeptic women"—when, faced with this, he dwells only on a certain substantial grandeur in the mountains of white paper and the crashing, ten-cylinder presses which turn them out?

Whitman—how else can I express it?—precipitated the American character. All those things which had been separate, self-sufficient, incoördinate—action, theory, idealism, business—he cast into a crucible; and they emerged, harmonious and molten, in a fresh democratic ideal, which is based upon the whole personality. Every strong personal impulse, every coöperating and unifying impulse, everything that enriches the social background, everything that enriches the individual, everything that impels and clarifies in the modern world owes something to Whitman. And especially of those American writers who have written preëminently for young men—and which has not?—Whitman alone, it seems to me, has pitched his tone to the real spring of action in them.

All this indicates a function quite different from that of a poet in any but the most radical and primitive sense of the word (the sense in which it was held by Whitman himself), a man, that is to say, who first gives to a nation a certain focal centre in the consciousness of its own character. Virgil did this. Mazzini did this, Björnson did this; and it was the main work of Whitman to make fast what he called "the idea and fact of American Totality," an idea and fact summed up with singular completeness in his own character and way of life. Emerson before him had provided a kind of skeleton outline; but what Emerson drew in black and white Whitman filled in with color and set in three dimensions.

A *focal centre*—that is the first requisite of a great people. And by this I do not mean the sense of national or imperial destiny which has consolidated the great temporal Powers of history. I mean that national "point of rest," to adopt a phrase in which Coleridge indicated that upon which the harmony of a work of art is founded and to which everything in the composition is more or less unconsciously referred; that secure and unobtrusive element of national character, taken for granted, and providing a certain underlying coherence and background of mutual understanding which Rome, for example, had in everything the name of Cato called up, or England in her great remembered worthies, or the elder Germany in Martin Luther. "National culture," to speak in the dialect of our own time, is only the perhaps too-conscious equivalent of this element in which everything admirably characteristic of a people sums itself up, which creates everywhere a kind of spiritual team-work, which radiates outward and articulates the entire living fabric of a race.

For us, it seems to me, Whitman laid the cornerstone of a national ideal capable in this way of releasing personality and of retrieving for our civilization, originally deficient in the richer juices of human nature, and still further bled and flattened out by the Machine Process, the only sort of "place in the sun" really worth having.

But at this point one has to discriminate. The social ideal of Whitman is essentially a collection of raw materials, molten and malleable, which take shape only in an emotional form. This emotional attitude is at bottom the attitude of a perfectly free personality, naturally affirmative, naturally creative; the rude material of right personal instinct, which is, however, antecedent to the direction personality it is to adopt and to the ideas that are to inform it.

To ignore this distinction, as most of the direct disciples of Whitman have done, is to go wrong utterly. And in fact Whitman himself ignored the distinction, and himself went wrong. Perfectly right in all his instincts, perfectly right so long as he kept to the plane of instinct, he was lost on the plane of ideas. He lacked a sure sense of his own province and limitations. Influenced no doubt by his disciples, he began in later years to assume functions not properly his own, and the greatness and sweetness of his character were increasingly marred by much pomposity and fatuousness. He was led to speak not as a poet but as an authority, the painful results of which may be seen in his newspaper interviews.

All this was probably inevitable. Whitman's instinct was to affirm everything, to accept everything, to relish the personal and human elements in everything. For himself he accepted "sustenance, clothing, shelter, and continuity." As regards the world he was equally catholic and passive. Soldiers being the strapping upright animals they are he accepts armies because armies breed them. He enjoys an old restauranteur because he knows how to select champagne, likes to look at nursemaids because they are so trim and wholesome and at fashionable women because they are so pretty and gay, likes money because of a certain strength it implies and business because it is so active, nimble, and adventurous. On the plane of instinct where he properly belongs he is right in each case: on the plane of ideas the practical effect is that, in accepting everything, he accepts the confusion of things and the *fait accompli*.

It is, in fact, the simple corollary of his thorough-going mood of affirmation on the personal, instinctive, emotional plane, that his ideas should be perfectly conventional. In ideas he is just an old-fashioned Jacksonian democrat. Except for a certain amount of uncommonly vigorous criticism, of the stock type, on American abuses, he never questions the old institutions. He takes for granted "the unform'd and nebulous state of many things, not yet permanently settled, but agreed on all hands to be the preparations of an infinitely greater future." He talks the greatest amount of nonsense about the "feudalism" of a contemporary Europe whose principal artists have been men like Tolstoi, Dostoievski, Millet, Thomas Hardy. He is never able to release himself from the vicious comparative; he is morbid about geography. Not being satisfied by the greatness of anything as a positive fact he has to prove its greatness by belittling something else. A fertile plain strikes him at once as more fertile than any other plain on earth, a grand scene "outvies all the historic places of note," and an American general is more of a general than Napoleon, an American poem has to be better than any poem hitherto.

All this is just what Mr. Bryan says,—it is just our fun. And the funniest thing of all, from this point of view, is to find Whitman solemnly posed, as he records it, before a vast canvas twenty feet by twelve, representing "Custer's Last Rally," the work of one John Mulvany; finding its "physiognomy realistic and Western," with an "almost entire absence of the stock traits of European war pictures," and recommending that it be sent to Paris "to show Messieur Crapeau [*sic*] that some things can be done in America as well as others." Perhaps one has to be an American to feel the lovableness of that scene. But if it demonstrates once for all any one thing it is that Whitman was never intended to be an authority, even on democracy.

An opportunity and in certain respects also a faculty Whitman had, in his own time and place, very similar to those of Montaigne.[8] I mean by this, on the one hand, a malleable and still incoherent race to be interpreted to itself, to be articulated, to be brought into focus, and on the other a temperament archetypical of that race, a range of sympathy co-incidental with it, and a power of revealing and in a sense fixing the racial norm. "I look within myself, I am only concerned with myself, I reflect on myself, I examine myself, I take pleasure in myself," said Montaigne; and all France for the first time saw itself in a looking-glass and fell together in a common discipline.

The raw materials of a racial norm Whitman provided; but—and in this he resembled Emerson—he was too passive to go further. He assembled in himself and his writings the characteristics of America,—with him originated

[8] Michel de Montaigne (1533-1592), French author of three books of essays.

the most contagious, the most liberating, the most unifying of native impulses; but he failed to react upon them, to mould them, and to drive them home. He had no ideas and he was satisfied to have none. He wanted, above all, intensity. He was too complacent. He was incapable of discipline and he did not see that discipline is, for Americans, the condition of all forward movement.

But the conventionality of Whitman's intellectual equipment is not, for us, a necessary part of the personal attitude which he originated. History is filled with instances of men who, having been called upon to originate fresh points of view, have had, in order to establish these points of view, to adopt a severely conventional position toward most of the phenomena of their time. Each of these men has had his disciples in the letter and his disciples in the spirit,—Martin Luther,[9] for example, especially in questions economic and social. The direct and immediate children of Luther, those who have laid apostolic hands on one another from generation to generation, are simply the bourgeoisie of the world; but the true Lutherans are those who, in every age, have thought keenly and honestly and independently and have, in so doing, contributed stone by stone to the great catholicism of the future. So also with Whitman and the children of Whitman. It was inevitable, in the America of his time, that he should have been so much of an outrageous egoist (consider the provocation!), inevitable that he should, in Emerson's phrase, have swallowed the universe like a cake, inevitable that he should have been indiscriminating, confused, and a little fatuous. To affirm sufficiently, he had to affirm everything.

We are in a different position, and we have different responsibilities. On the philosophical side, the simple doctrine of evolution, in its crude form the last word in Whitman's cosmos, has been refined and ripened. Above all, we have no excuse not to see that affirmation, in the most real sense, proceeds to a certain extent through rejection, by merely dropping off most of the old clothes that Whitman found quite good enough. To keep these old clothes, to affirm that since everything is good they must be good also, to embroider them and make them over and stalk about in them, loudly affirming one's own ego and the indiscriminate grandeur of all creation, with particular reference to the Whole Crowd of Good Americans—all this is not to continue and to reaffirm the right Whitmanian tradition; but it is, in a way, to have the sanction of Whitman's own character and experience, and it is above all to do what the typical contemporary Whitmanian does.

In some way—and primarily by returning upon Whitman as Whitman returned upon Emerson, not, as in that case, by adding emotion to intellect, but by adding intellect to emotion—the social ideal the raw materials of

[9] Martin Luther (1483-1546), German monk, a founder of Protestantism.

which have been provided by Whitman must be formulated and driven home.

The Whitmanians, meanwhile, have made haste to formulate out of these materials a certain number of spurious social ideals, the more dangerous the more plausible, and even the more "American," they are. Of these the one that seems to me most typical will have to be examined.

JOHN DEWEY

(1859–1952)

John Dewey achieved greatest fame as the "father of progressive schools" and, partly because of this, the nature and value of his most significant contributions to American life have often been misunderstood. "Progressive schools" at the height of their fad (the late 1920's and early 1930's) were popularly identified with escape from restriction, inhibition, Victorian severity. When the fad was over, the same schools were identified with permissivism, absence of discipline, immorality, and laxness. Dewey, as the philosopher and teacher unlucky enough to have his name coupled with the progressive education movement at its worst, as well as at its best, suffered in succession uninformed idolatry and uninformed abuse.

It was not only for his alleged role in fostering a "breakdown of discipline among the young" that Dewey was excoriated in his life-

A bibliography has been compiled by M. H. Thomas, ed., *John Dewey: A Centennial Bibliography*, 1962.

Dewey's works include *The School and Society*, 1899; *Studies in Logical Theory*, 1903; *Ethics*, 1908; *How We Think*, 1910; *The Influence of Darwin on Philosophy*, 1910; *Democracy and Education*, 1916; *Essays in Experimental Logic*, 1916; *Reconstruction in Philosophy*, 1920; *Human Nature and Conduct*, 1922; *Experience and Nature*, 1925; *The Public and Its Problems*, 1927; *Characters and Events*, 1929; *The Quest for Certainty*, 1929; *Individualism, Old and New*, 1930; *Philosophy and Civilization*, 1931; *Art as Experience*, 1934; *A Common Faith*, 1934; *Liberalism and Social Action*, 1935; *Logic: The Theory of Inquiry*, 1938; *Freedom and Culture*, 1939; *Problems of Men*, 1946, and *Knowing and the Known*, 1949.

An early study of Dewey is Sidney Hook, *John Dewey: An Intellectual Portrait*, 1939. Recent works include Joseph Ratner, ed., *Intelligence in the Modern World: John Dewey's Philosophy;* George M. Gutzke, *John Dewey's Thought and Its Implication for Christian Education*, 1956; George R. Geiger, *John Dewey in Perspective*, 1958; Richard Bernstein, ed., *John Dewey: Our Experience, Nature, and Freedom*, 1960; and Harry M. Campbell, *John Dewey*, 1971.

time. For longer than half a century he served as the intellectual center for liberalism and the left; time and again when outrage was committed against the weak, the oppressed, the jobless, his quick and passionate protest became the rallying point for the rightminded, the cry that did most to awaken public consciousness of wrongdoing, cruelty, and obliviousness among the privileged. Naturally the latter did not take kindly to this. They attacked Dewey as an irresponsible radical, vilified him as a Bolshevik when he spoke up for communism (after a visit to Russia in 1928). They chided him, too, for "godless atheism" and immorality because, as a philosopher, Dewey insisted on the primacy of experience and nature, sustained a lifetime interest in moral experiment, and dismissed as delusory all concepts of transcendent deity and moral absolutes. And many also criticized him throughout his career as an ungainly writer—a fairer charge than most of the others.

In recent years Dewey has been freshly perceived as a remarkable social theorist whose great theme, the democratization of mind, became the foundation of a unified ethics, politics, aesthetics, and pedagogy. Democracy for many commentators is a matter of universal suffrage; Dewey saw it as, ideally, a unique way of experiencing human life, a special mode of communication and association, implying extraordinary culture-wide achievements and adjusting individual interests and talents to each other. In his opinion the groundwork for these hoped-for achievements could only be laid in school itself—but "the school" he had in mind was rather different from those existing either then or now. The school, as he argued, must not be separate from life, a scene of drill and rote learning; it would have to be continuous with real-life activity, less a set of classrooms than a series of projects enlisting young and old, skilled and unskilled, professionals and tradesmen in a common endeavor directed at meeting social needs. In course of that endeavor all participants would be engaged in learning the truths of human mutuality and the necessity of shared concern.

Sharing and communication between people of different gifts and interests are key concepts for this philosopher, and at moments—the close of *Reconstruction in Philosophy* (1920), for example—he rises to uncommon intensity in defining them: " . . . when the emotional force, the mystic force one might say, of communication, of the miracle of shared life and shared experience is spontaneously felt, the hardness and crudeness of contemporary life will be bathed in the light that never was on land or sea." The key resource for diffusing a sense of the ideal of perfected communication throughout society is, not surprisingly, aesthetic experience: art is "communication in its pure and undefiled form," Dewey declared in *Art as Experience* (1934). It "breaks through barriers that divide human beings which are impermeable in ordinary association." At the center of the entire vision stands a superbly moving faith in human possibility, a force enabling Dewey to imagine a time when "every human being might become great, and Humanity instead of being a wide heath of furze and briars with here and there a remote Pine or Oak, would become a grand democracy of Forest Trees!"

A teacher all his adult life, Dewey was born in Vermont, educated at the University of Vermont (B.A., 1879) and at Johns Hopkins (Ph.D., 1884), and taught at the universities of Minnesota, Michigan, and Chicago. He then joined the faculty at Columbia in 1904 and remained there until 1930. He was founder of the teacher's union movement; president of the Peoples Lobby (a nonpartisan political movement on the left founded in the year of the Great Wall Street crash), the American Psychological Association, the American Philosophical Association, the American Association of University Professors, and chairman of the commission of inquiry into the charges against the revolutionist Leon Trotsky.

The Democratic Conception in Education

For the most part, save incidentally, we have hitherto been concerned with education as it may exist in any social group. We have now to make explicit the differences in the spirit, material, and method of education as it operates in different types of community life. To say that education is a social function, securing direction and development in the immature through their participation in the life of the group to which they belong, is to say in effect that education will vary with the quality of life which prevails in a group. Particularly is it true that a society which not only changes but which has the ideal of such change as will improve it, will have different standards and methods of education from one which aims simply at the perpetuation of its own customs. To make the general ideas set forth applicable to our own educational practice, it is, therefore, necessary to come to closer quarters with the nature of present social life.

1. **The Implications of Human Association.**—Society is one word, but many things. Men associate together in all kinds of ways and for all kinds of purposes. One man is concerned in a multitude of diverse groups, in which his associates may be quite different. It often seems as if they had nothing in common except that they are modes of associated life. Within every larger social organization there are numerous minor groups: not only political subdivisions, but industrial, scientific, religious, associations. There are political

parties with differing aims, social sets, cliques, gangs, corporations, partnerships, groups bound closely together by ties of blood, and so in endless variety. In many modern states, and in some ancient, there is great diversity of populations, of varying languages, religions, moral codes, and traditions. From this standpoint, many a minor political unit, one of our large cities, for example, is a congeries of loosely associated societies, rather than an inclusive and permeating community of action and thought.

The terms society, community, are thus ambiguous. They have both a eulogistic or normative sense, and a descriptive sense; a meaning *de jure* and a meaning *de facto*. In social philosophy, the former connotation is almost always uppermost. Society is conceived as one by its very nature. The qualities which accompany this unity, praiseworthy community of purpose and welfare, loyalty to public ends, mutuality of sympathy, are emphasized. But when we look at the facts which the term *denotes* instead of confining our attention to its intrinsic *connotation*, we find not unity, but a plurality of societies, good and bad. Men banded together in a criminal conspiracy, business aggregations that prey upon the public while serving it, political machines held together by the interest of plunder, are included. If it is said that such organizations are not societies because they do not meet the ideal requirements of the notion of society, the answer, in part, is that the conception of society is then made so "ideal" as to be of no use, having no reference to facts; and in part, that each of these organizations, no matter how opposed to the interests of other groups, has something of the praiseworthy qualities of "Society" which hold it together. There is honor among thieves, and a band of robbers has a common interest as respects its members. Gangs are marked by fraternal feeling, and narrow cliques by intense loyalty to their own codes. Family life may be marked by exclusiveness, suspicion, and jealousy as to those without, and yet be a model of amity and mutual aid within. Any education given by a group tends to socialize its members, but the quality and value of the socialization depends upon the habits and aims of the group.

Hence, once more, the need of a measure for the worth of any given mode of social life. In seeking this measure, we have to avoid two extremes. We cannot set up, out of our heads, something we regard as an ideal society. We must base our conception upon societies which actually exist, in order to have any assurance that our ideal is a practicable one. But, as we have just seen, the ideal cannot simply repeat the traits which are actually found. The problem is to extract the desirable traits of forms of community life which actually exist, and employ them to criticize undesirable features and suggest improvement. Now in any social group whatever, even in a gang of thieves, we find some interest held in common, and we find a certain amount of interaction and coöperative intercourse with other groups. From these two traits we derive our standard. How numerous and varied are the interests which are consciously shared? How full and free is the interplay with other forms of association? If we apply these considerations to, say, a criminal band, we find that the ties which consciously hold the members together are few in number, reducible almost to a common interest in plunder; and that they are of such a nature as to isolate the group from other groups with respect to give and take of the values of life. Hence, the education such a society gives is partial and distorted. If we take, on the other hand, the kind of family life which illustrates the standard, we find that there are material, intellectual, aesthetic interests in which all participate and that the progress of one member has worth for the experience of other members—it is readily communicable—and that the family is not an isolated whole, but enters intimately into relationships with business groups, with schools, with all the agencies of culture, as well as with other similar groups, and that it plays a due part in the political organization and in return receives support from it. In short, there are many interests consciously communicated and shared; and there are varied and free points of contact with other modes of association.

I. Let us apply the first element in this criterion to a despotically governed state. It is not true there is no common interest in such an organization between governed and governors. The authorities in command must make some appeal to the native activities of the subjects, must call some of their powers into play. Talleyrand[1] said that a government could do everything with bayonets except sit on them. This cynical declaration is at least a recognition that the bond of union is not merely one of coercive force. It may be said, however, that the activities appealed to are themselves unworthy and degrading—that such a government calls into functioning activity simply capacity for fear. In a way, this statement is true. But it overlooks the fact that fear need not be an undesirable factor in experience. Caution, circumspection, prudence, desire to foresee future events so as to avert what is harmful, these desirable traits are as much a product of calling the impulse of fear into play as is cowardice and abject submission. The real difficulty is that the appeal to fear is *isolated*. In evoking dread and hope of specific tangible reward—say comfort and ease—many other capacities are left untouched. Or rather, they are affected, but in such a way as to pervert them. Instead of operating on their own account they are reduced to mere servants of attaining pleasure and avoiding pain.

This is equivalent to saying that there is no extensive number of common interests; there is no free play back and forth among the members of the social group. Stimulation and response are exceedingly one sided. In order to have a large number of values in common, all the members of the group must have an equable opportunity to receive and to take from others. There must be a large variety of shared undertakings and experiences. Otherwise,

[1] Charles Maurice de Talleyrand-Perigord (1754-1838), French statesman and diplo- mat, author of *Memories* edited in 1891-1892.

the influences which educate some into masters, educate others into slaves. And the experience of each party loses in meaning, when the free interchange of varying modes of life-experience is arrested. A separation into a privileged and a subject-class prevents social endosmosis. The evils thereby affecting the superior class are less material and less perceptible, but equally real. Their culture tends to be sterile, to be turned back to feed on itself; their art becomes a showy display and artificial; their wealth luxurious; their knowledge overspecialized; their manners fastidious rather than humane.

Lack of the free and equitable intercourse which springs from a variety of shared interests makes intellectual stimulation unbalanced. Diversity of stimulation means novelty, and novelty means challenge to thought. The more activity is restricted to a few definite lines—as it is when there are rigid class lines preventing adequate interplay of experiences—the more action tends to become routine on the part of the class at a disadvantage, and capricious, aimless, and explosive on the part of the class having the materially fortunate position. Plato defined a slave as one who accepts from another the purposes which control his conduct. This condition obtains even where there is no slavery in the legal sense. It is found wherever men are engaged in activity which is socially serviceable, but whose service they do not understand and have no personal interest in. Much is said about scientific management of work. It is a narrow view which restricts the science which secures efficiency of operation to movements of the muscles. The chief opportunity for science is the discovery of the relations of a man to his work—including his relations to others who take part—which will enlist his intelligent interest in what he is doing. Efficiency in production often demands division of labor. But it is reduced to a mechanical routine unless workers see the technical, intellectual, and social relationships involved in what they do, and engage in their work because of the motivation furnished by such perceptions. The tendency to reduce such things as efficiency of activity and scientific management to purely technical externals is evidence of the one-sided stimulation of thought given to those in control of industry—those who supply its aims. Because of their lack of all-round and well-balanced social interest, there is not sufficient stimulus for attention to the human factors and relationships in industry. Intelligence is narrowed to the factors concerned with technical production and marketing of goods. No doubt, a very acute and intense intelligence in these narrow lines can be developed, but the failure to take into account the significant social factors means none the less an absence of mind, and a corresponding distortion of emotional life.

II. This illustration (whose point is to be extended to all associations lacking reciprocity of interest) brings us to our second point. The isolation and exclusiveness of a gang or clique brings its antisocial spirit into relief. But this same spirit is found wherever one group has interests "of its own" which shut it out from full interaction with other groups, so that its prevailing purpose is the protection of what it has got, instead of reorganization and progress through wider relationships. It marks nations in their isolation from one another; families which seclude their domestic concerns as if they had no connection with a larger life; schools when separated from the interest of home and community; the divisions of rich and poor; learned and unlearned. The essential point is that isolation makes for rigidity and formal institutionalizing of life, for static and selfish ideals within the group. That savage tribes regard aliens and enemies as synonymous is not accidental. It springs from the fact that they have identified their experience with rigid adherence to their past customs. On such a basis it is wholly logical to fear intercourse with others, for such contact might dissolve custom. It would certainly occasion reconstruction. It is a commonplace that an alert and expanding mental life depends upon an enlarging range of contact with the physical environment. But the principle applies even more significantly to the field where we are apt to ignore it—the sphere of social contacts.

Every expansive era in the history of mankind has coincided with the operation of factors which have tended to eliminate distance between peoples and classes previously hemmed off from one another. Even the alleged benefits of war, so far as more than alleged, spring from the fact that conflict of peoples at least enforces intercourse between them and thus accidentally enables them to learn from one another, and thereby to expand their horizons. Travel, economic and commercial tendencies, have at present gone far to break down external barriers; to bring peoples and classes into closer and more perceptible connection with one another. It remains for the most part to secure the intellectual and emotional significance of this physical annihilation of space.

2. The Democratic Ideal.—The two elements in our criterion both point to democracy. The first signifies not only more numerous and more varied points of shared common interest, but greater reliance upon the recognition of mutual interests as a factor in social control. The second means not only freer interaction between social groups (once isolated so far as intention could keep up a separation) but change in social habit—its continuous readjustment through meeting the new situations produced by varied intercourse. And these two traits are precisely what characterize the democratically constituted society.

Upon the educational side, we note first that the realization of a form of social life in which interests are mutually interpenetrating, and where progress, or readjustment, is an important consideration, makes a democratic community more interested than other communities have cause to be in deliberate and systematic education. The devotion of democracy to education is a familiar fact. The superficial explanation is that a government resting upon popular suffrage cannot be successful unless those who elect and who obey their governors are educated. Since a democratic society repudiates the principle of external authority, it must find a substitute in voluntary disposition and interest; these can be created only by education. But there is a deeper explanation. A democracy is more than a form of government; it is primarily a mode of associated living, of conjoint communicated experience. The extension in space of the number of individuals who participate in an interest so that each has to refer his own action to that of others, and to consider the action of others to give point and direction to his own, is equivalent to the breaking down of those barriers of class, race, and national territory which kept men from perceiving the full import of their activity. These more numerous and more varied points of contact denote a greater diversity of stimuli to which an individual has to respond; they consequently put a premium on variation in his action. They secure a liberation of powers which remain suppressed as long as the incitations to actions are partial, as they must be in a group which in its exclusiveness shuts out many interests.

The widening of the area of shared concerns, and the liberation of a greater diversity of personal capacities which characterize a democracy, are not of course the product of deliberation and conscious effort. On the contrary, they were caused by the development of modes of manufacture and commerce, travel, migration, and intercommunication which flowed from the command of science over natural energy. But after greater individualization on one hand, and a broader community of interest on the other have come into existence, it is a matter of deliberate effort to sustain and extend them. Obviously a society to which stratification into separate classes would be fatal, must see to it that intellectual opportunities are accessible to all on equable and easy terms. A society marked off into classes need be specially attentive only to the education of its ruling elements. A society which is mobile, which is full of channels for the distribution of a change occurring anywhere, must see to it that its members are educated to personal initiative and adaptability. Otherwise, they will be overwhelmed by the changes in which they are caught and whose significance or connections they do not perceive. The result will be a confusion in which a few will appropriate to themselves the results of the blind and externally directed activities of others.

3. **The Platonic Educational Philosophy.**—Subsequent chapters will be devoted to making explicit the implications of the democratic ideas in education. In the remaining portions of this chapter, we shall consider the educational theories which have been evolved in three epochs when the social import of education was especially conspicuous. The first one to be considered is that of Plato. No one could better express than did he the fact that a society is stably organized when each individual is doing that for which he has aptitude by nature in such a way as to be useful to others (or to contribute to the whole to which he belongs); and that it is the business of education to discover these aptitudes and progressively to train them for social use. Much which has been said so far is borrowed from what Plato first consciously taught the world. But conditions which he could not intellectually

control led him to restrict these ideas in their application. He never got any conception of the indefinite plurality of activities which may characterize an individual and a social group, and consequently limited his view to a limited number of *classes* of capacities and of social arrangements.

Plato's starting point is that the organization of society depends ultimately upon the knowledge of the end of existence. If we do not know its end, we shall be at the mercy of accident and caprice. Unless we know the end, the good, we shall have no criterion for rationally deciding what the possibilities are which should be promoted, nor how social arrangments are to be ordered. We shall have no conception of the proper limits and distribution of activities—what he called justice—as a trait of both individual and social organization. But how is the knowledge of the final and permanent good to be achieved? In dealing with this question we come upon the seemingly insuperable obstacle that such knowledge is not possible save in a just and harmonious social order. Everywhere else the mind is distracted and misled by false valuations and false perspectives. A disorganized and factional society sets up a number of different models and standards. Under such conditions it is impossible for the individual to attain consistency of mind. Only a complete whole is fully self-consistent. A society which rests upon the supremacy of some factor over another irrespective of its rational or proportionate claims, inevitably leads thought astray. It puts a premium on certain things and slurs over others, and creates a mind whose seeming unity is forced and distorted. Education proceeds ultimately from the patterns furnished by institutions, customs, and laws. Only in a just state will these be such as to give the right education; and only those who have rightly trained minds will be able to recognize the end, and ordering principle of things. We seem to be caught in a hopeless circle. However, Plato suggested a way out. A few men, philosophers or lovers of wisdom—or truth—may by study learn at least in outline the proper patterns of true existence. If a powerful ruler should form a state after these patterns, then its regulations could be preserved. An education could be given which would shift individuals, discovering what they were good for, and supplying a method of assigning each to the work in life for which his nature fits him. Each doing his own part, and never transgressing, the order and unity of the whole would be maintained.

It would be impossible to find in any scheme of philosophic thought a more adequate recognition on one hand of the educational significance of social arrangements and, on the other, of the dependence of those arrangements upon the means used to educate the young. It would be impossible to find a deeper sense of the function of education in discovering and developing personal capacities, and training them so that they would connect with the activities of others. Yet the society in which the theory was propounded was so undemocratic that Plato could not work out a solution for the problem whose terms he clearly saw.

While he affirmed with emphasis that the place of the individual in society should not be determined by birth or wealth or any conventional status, but by his own nature as discovered in the process of education, he had no perception of the uniqueness of individuals. For him they fall by nature into classes, and into a very small number of classes at that. Consequently the testing and sifting function of education only shows to which one of three classes an individual belongs. There being no recognition that each individual constitutes his own class, there could be no recognition of the infinite diversity of active tendencies and combinations of tendencies of which an individual is capable. There were only three types of faculties or powers in the individual's constitution. Hence education would soon reach a static limit in each class, for only diversity makes change and progress.

In some individuals, appetites naturally dominate; they are assigned to the laboring and trading class, which expresses and supplies human wants. Others reveal, upon education, that over and above appetites, they have a generous, outgoing, assertively courageous disposition. They become the citizen-subjects of the state; its defenders in war; its internal guardians in peace. But their limit is fixed by their lack of reason, which is a capacity to grasp the universal. Those who possess this are capable of the highest kind of education, and become in time the legislators of the state—for laws are the universals which control the particulars of experience. Thus it is not true that in intent, Plato subordinated the individual to the social whole. But it is true that lacking the perception of the uniqueness of every individual, his incommensurability with others, and consequently not recognizing that a society might change and yet be stable, his doctrine of limited powers and classes came in net effect to the idea of the subordination of individuality.

We cannot better Plato's conviction that an individual is happy and society well organized when each individual engages in those activities for which he has a natural equipment, nor his conviction that it is the primary office of education to discover this equipment to its possessor and train him for its effective use. But progress in knowledge has made us aware of the superficiality of Plato's lumping of individuals and their original powers into a few sharply marked-off classes; it has taught us that original capacities are indefinitely numerous and variable. It is but the other side of this fact to say that in the degree in which society has become democratic, social organization means utilization of the specific and variable qualities of individuals, not stratification by classes. Although his educational philosophy was revolutionary, it was none the less in bondage to static ideals. He thought that change or alteration was evidence of lawless flux; that true reality was unchangeable. Hence while he would radically change the existing state of society, his aim was to construct a state in which change would subsequently have no place. The final end of life is fixed; given a state framed with this end in view, not even minor details are to be altered. Though they might not be inherently important, yet if permitted they would inure the minds of men to

858
JOHN DEWEY

the idea of change, and hence be dissolving and anarchic. The breakdown of his philosophy is made apparent in the fact that he could not trust to gradual improvements in education to bring about a better society which should then improve education, and so on indefinitely. Correct education could not come into existence until an ideal state existed, and after that education would be devoted simply to its conservation. For the existence of this state he was obliged to trust to some happy accident by which philosophic wisdom should happen to coincide with possession of ruling power in the state.

4. **The "Individualistic" Ideal of the Eighteenth Century.**—In the eighteenth-century philosophy we find ourselves in a very different circle of ideas. "Nature" still means something antithetical to existing social organization; Plato exercised a great influence upon Rousseau.[2] But the voice of nature now speaks for the diversity of individual talent and for the need of free development of individuality in all its variety. Education in accord with nature furnishes the goal and the method of instruction and discipline. Moreover, the native or original endowment was conceived, in extreme cases, as nonsocial or even as antisocial. Social arrangements were thought of as mere external expedients by which these nonsocial individuals might secure a greater amount of private happiness for themselves.

Nevertheless, these statements convey only an inadequate idea of the true significance of the movement. In reality its chief interest was in progress and in social progress. The seeming antisocial philosophy was a somewhat transparent mask for an impetus toward a wider and freer society—towards cosmopolitanism. The positive ideal was humanity. In membership in humanity, as distinct from a state, man's capacities would be liberated; while in existing political organizations his powers were hampered and distorted to meet the requirements and selfish interests of the rulers of the state. The doctrine of extreme individualism was but the counterpart, the obverse, of ideals of the indefinite perfectibility of man and of a social organization having a scope as wide as humanity. The emancipated individual was to become the organ and agent of a comprehensive and progressive society.

The heralds of this gospel were acutely conscious of the evils of the social estate in which they found themselves. They attributed these evils to the limitations imposed upon the free powers of man. Such limitation was both distorting and corrupting. Their impassioned devotion to emancipation of life from external restrictions which operated to the exclusive advantage of the class to whom a past feudal system consigned power, found intellectual formulation in a worship of nature. To give "Nature" full swing was to replace an artificial, corrupt, and inequitable social order by a new and better kingdom of humanity. Unrestrained faith in "Nature" as both a model

[2] Jean Jacques Rousseau (1712–1778), French author of works on political philosophy, education, and morality like *The Social* *Contract* (1762), *Émile* (1762), and the *Confessions* (1781).

and a working power was strengthened by the advances of natural science. Inquiry freed from prejudice and artificial restraints of church and state had revealed that the world is a scene of law. The Newtonian solar system,[3] which expressed the reign of natural law, was a scene of wonderful harmony, where every force balanced with every other. Natural law would accomplish the same result in human relations, if men would only get rid of the artificial man-imposed coercive restrictions.

Education in accord with "Nature" was thought to be the first step in insuring this more social society. It was plainly seen that economic and political limitations were ultimately dependent upon limitations of thought and feeling. The first step in freeing men from external chains was to emancipate them from the internal chains of false beliefs and ideals. What was called social life, existing institutions, were too false and corrupt to be intrusted with this work. How could it be expected to undertake it when the undertaking meant its own destruction? "Nature" must then be the power to which the enterprise was to be left. Even the extreme sensationalistic theory of knowledge which was current derived itself from this conception. To insist that mind is originally passive and empty was one way of glorifying the possibilities of education. If the mind was a wax tablet to be written upon by objects, there were no limits to the possibility of education by means of the natural environment. And since the natural world of objects is a scene of harmonious "truth," this education would infallibly produce minds filled with truth.

5. **Education as National and as Social.**—As soon as the first enthusiasm for freedom waned, the weakness of the theory upon the constructive side became obvious. Merely to leave everything to "Nature" was, after all, but to negate the very idea of education; it was to trust to the accidents of circumstance. Not only was some method required but also some positive organ, some administrative agency for carrying on the process of instruction. The "complete and harmonious development of all powers," having as its social counterpart an enlightened and progressive humanity, required definite organization for its realization. Private individuals here and there could proclaim the gospel; they could not execute the work. A Pestalozzi[4] could try experiments and exhort philanthropically inclined persons having wealth and power to follow his example. But even Pestalozzi saw that any effective pursuit of the new educational ideal required the support of the state. The realization of the new education destined to produce a new society was,

---

[3] Newtonian solar system refers to the work of Sir Isaac Newton (1642-1727), English mathematician, scientist, and philosopher who developed theories of universal gravitation, theoretical mechanics, and color, and the invention of differential calculus.

[4] Johann Heinrich Pestalozzi (1746-1827), Swiss educationalist whose theory was that the development of human nature should be in dependence on natural laws.

after all, dependent upon the activities of existing states. The movement for the democratic idea inevitably became a movement for publicly conducted and administered schools.

So far as Europe was concerned, the historic situation identified the movement for a state-supported education with the nationalistic movement in political life—a fact of incalculable significance for subsequent movements. Under the influence of German thought in particular, education became a civic function and the civic function was identified with the realization of the ideal of the national state. The "state" was substituted for humanity; cosmopolitanism gave way to nationalism. To form the citizen, not the "man," became the aim of education.[5] The historic situation to which reference is made is the after-effects of the Napoleonic conquests, especially in Germany. The German states felt (and subsequent events demonstrate the correctness of the belief) that systematic attention to education was the best means of recovering and maintaining their political integrity and power. Externally they were weak and divided. Under the leadership of Prussian statesmen they made this condition a stimulus to the development of an extensive and thoroughly grounded system of public education.

This change in practice necessarily brought about a change in theory. The individualistic theory receded into the background. The state furnished not only the instrumentalities of public education but also its goal. When the actual practice was such that the school system, from the elementary grades through the university faculties, supplied the patriotic citizen and soldier and the future state official and administrator and furnished the means for military, industrial, and political defense and expansion, it was impossible for theory not to emphasize the aim of social efficiency. And with the immense importance attached to the nationalistic state, surrounded by other competing and more or less hostile states, it was equally impossible to interpret social efficiency in terms of a vague cosmopolitan humanitarianism. Since the maintenance of a particular national sovereignty required subordination of individuals to the superior interests of the state both in military defense and in struggles for international supremacy in commerce, social efficiency was understood to imply a like subordination. The educational process was taken to be one of disciplinary training rather than of personal development. Since, however, the ideal of culture as complete development of personality persisted, educational philosophy attempted a reconciliation of the two ideas. The reconciliation took the form of the conception of the "organic" charac-

[5] There is a much neglected strain in Rousseau tending intellectually in this direction. He opposed the existing state of affairs on the ground that it formed *neither* the citizen nor the man. Under existing conditions, he preferred to try for the latter rather than for the former. But there are many sayings of his which point to the information of the citizen as ideally the higher, and which indicate that his own endeavor, as embodied in the "Émile," was simply the best makeshift the corruption of the times permitted him to sketch. [Dewey's note].

ter of the state. The individual in his isolation is nothing; only in and through an absorption of the aims and meaning of organized institutions does he attain true personality. What appears to be his subordination to political authority and the demand for sacrifice of himself to the commands of his superiors is in reality but making his own the objective reason manifested in the state—the only way in which he can become truly rational. The notion of development which we have seen to be characteristic of institutional idealism (as in the Hegelian philosophy) was just such a deliberate effort to combine the two ideas of complete realization of personality and thoroughgoing "disciplinary" subordination to existing institutions.

The extent of the transformation of educational philosophy which occured in Germany in the generation occupied by the struggle against Napoleon for national independence, may be gathered from Kant,[6] who well expresses the earlier individual-cosmopolitan ideal. In his treatise on Pedagogics, consisting of lectures given in the later years of the eighteenth century, he defines education as the process by which man becomes man. Mankind begins its history submerged in nature—not as Man who is a creature of reason, while nature furnishes only instinct and appetite. Nature offers simply the germs which education is to develop and perfect. The peculiarity of truly human life is that man has to create himself by his own voluntary efforts; he has to make himself a truly moral, rational, and free being. This creative effort is carried on by the educational activities of slow generations. Its acceleration depends upon men consciously striving to educate their successors not for the existing state of affairs but so as to make possible a future better humanity. But there is the great difficulty. Each generation is inclined to educate its young so as to get along in the present world instead of with a view to the proper end of education: the promotion of the best possible realization of humanity as humanity. Parents educate their children so that they may get on; princes educate their subjects as instruments of their own purposes.

Who, then, shall conduct education so that humanity may improve? We must depend upon the efforts of enlightened men in their private capacity. "All culture begins with private men and spreads outward from them. Simply through the efforts of persons of enlarged inclinations, who are capable of grasping the ideal of a future better condition, is the gradual approximation of human nature to its end possible. . . . Rulers are simply interested in such training as will make their subjects better tools for their own intentions." Even the subsidy by rulers of privately conducted schools must be carefully safeguarded. For the rulers' interest in the welfare of their own nation instead of in what is best for humanity, will make them, if they give money for the schools, wish to draw their plans. We have in this view an express statement of the points characteristic of the eighteenth century in-

[6] Imannuel Kant (1724–1804), German philosopher of idealism.

dividualistic cosmopolitanism. The full development of private personality is identified with the aims of humanity as a whole and with the idea of progress. In addition we have an explicit fear of the hampering influence of a state-conducted and state-regulated education upon the attainment of these ideas. But in less than two decades after this time, Kant's philosophic successors, Fichte and Hegel,[7] elaborated the idea that the chief function of the state is educational; that in particular the regeneration of Germany is to be accomplished by an education carried on in the interests of the state, and that the private individual is of necessity an egoistic, irrational being, enslaved to his appetites and to circumstances unless he submits voluntarily to the educative discipline of state institutions and laws. In this spirit, Germany was the first country to undertake a public, universal, and compulsory system of education extending from the primary school through the university, and to submit to jealous state regulation and supervision all private educational enterprises.

Two results should stand out from this brief historical survey. The first is that such terms as the individual and the social conceptions of education are quite meaningless taken at large, or apart from their context. Plato had the ideal of an education which should equate individual realization and social coherency and stability. His situation forced his ideal into the notion of a society organized in stratified classes, losing the individual in the class. The eighteenth century educational philosophy was highly individualistic in form, but this form was inspired by a noble and generous social ideal: that of a society organized to include humanity, and providing for the indefinite perfectibility of mankind. The idealistic philosophy of Germany in the early nineteenth century endeavored again to equate the ideals of a free and complete development of cultured personality with social discipline and political subordination. It made the national state an intermediary between the realization of private personality on one side and of humanity on the other. Consequently, it is equally possible to state its animating principle with equal truth either in the classic terms of "harmonious development of all the powers of personality" or in the more recent terminology of "social efficiency." All this reënforces the statement which opens this chapter: The conception of education as a social process and function has no definite meaning until we define the kind of society we have in mind.

These considerations pave the way for our second conclusion. One of the fundamental problems of education in and for a democratic society is set by the conflict of a nationalistic and a wider social aim. The earlier cosmopolitan and "humanitarian" conception suffered both from vagueness and from lack of definite organs of execution and agencies of administration. In Europe, in the Continental states particularly, the new idea of the importance

[7] Johann Gottlieb Fichte (1762-1814), German philosopher. Georg W. F. Hegel (1770-1831), German philosopher of phenomenology.

of education for human welfare and progress was captured by national interests and harnessed to do a work whose social aim was definitely narrow and exclusive. The social aim of education and its national aim were identified, and the result was a marked obscuring of the meaning of a social aim.

This confusion corresponds to the existing situation of human intercourse. On the one hand, science, commerce, and art transcend national boundaries. They are largely international in quality and method. They involve interdependencies and coöperation among the peoples inhabiting different countries. At the same time, the idea of national sovereignty has never been as accentuated in politics as it is at the present time. Each nation lives in a state of suppressed hostility and incipient war with its neighbors. Each is supposed to be the supreme judge of its own interests, and it is assumed as matter of course that each has interests which are exclusively its own. To question this is to question the very idea of national sovereignty which is assumed to be basic to political practice and political science. This contradiction (for it is nothing less) between the wider sphere of associated and mutually helpful social life and the narrower sphere of exclusive and hence potentially hostile pursuits and purposes, exacts of educational theory a clearer conception of the meaning of "social" as a function and test of education than has yet been attained.

Is it possible for an educational system to be conducted by a national state and yet the full social ends of the educative process not be restricted, constrained, and corrupted? Internally, the question has to face the tendencies, due to present economic conditions, which split society into classes some of which are made merely tools for the higher culture of others. Externally, the question is concerned with the reconciliation of national loyalty, of patriotism, with superior devotion to the things which unite men in common ends, irrespective of national political boundaries. Neither phase of the problem can be worked out by merely negative means. It is not enough to see to it that education is not actively used as an instrument to make easier the exploitation of one class by another. School facilities must be secured of such amplitude and efficiency as will in fact and not simply in name discount the effects of economic inequalities, and secure to all the wards of the nation equality of equipment for their future careers. Accomplishment of this end demands not only adequate administrative provision of school facilities, and such supplementation of family resources as will enable youth to take advantage of them, but also such modification of traditional ideals of culture, traditional subjects of study and traditional methods of teaching and discipline as will retain all the youth under educational influences until they are equipped to be masters of their own economic and social careers. The ideal may seem remote of execution, but the democratic ideal of education is a farcical yet tragic delusion except as the ideal more and more dominates our public system of education.

The same principle has application on the side of the considerations which concern the relations of one nation to another. It is not enough to teach the horrors of war and to avoid everything which would stimulate international jealousy and animosity. The emphasis must be put upon whatever binds people together in coöperative human pursuits and results, apart from geographical limitations. The secondary and provisional character of national sovereignty in respect to the fuller, freer, and more fruitful association and intercourse of all human beings with one another must be instilled as a working disposition of mind. If these applications seem to be remote from a consideration of the philosophy of education, the impression shows that the meaning of the idea of education previously developed has not been adequately grasped. This conclusion is bound up with the very idea of education as a freeing of individual capacity in a progressive growth directed to social aims. Otherwise a democratic criterion of education can only be inconsistently applied.

Summary.—Since education is a social process, and there are many kinds of societies, a criterion for educational criticism and construction implies a *particular* social ideal. The two points selected by which to measure the worth of a form of social life are the extent in which the interests of a group are shared by all its members, and the fullness and freedom with which it interacts with other groups. An undesirable society, in other words, is one which internally and externally sets up barriers to free intercourse and communication of experience. A society which makes provision for participation in its good of all its members on equal terms and which secures flexible readjustment of its institutions through interaction of the different forms of associated life is in so far democratic. Such a society must have a type of education which gives individuals a personal interest in social relationships and control, and the habits of mind which secure social changes without introducing disorder.

Three typical historic philosophies of education were considered from this point of view. The Platonic was found to have an ideal formally quite similar to that stated, but which was compromised in its working out by making a class rather than an individual the social unit. The so-called individualism of the eighteenth-century enlightenment was found to involve the notion of a society as broad as humanity, of whose progress the individual was to be the organ. But it lacked any agency for securing the development of its ideal as was evidenced in its falling back upon "Nature." The institutional idealistic philosophies of the nineteenth century supplied this lack by making the national state the agency, but in so doing narrowed the conception of the social aim to those who were members of the same political unit, and reintroduced the idea of the subordination of the individual to the institution.

JOHN CROWE RANSOM
DONALD DAVIDSON
FRANK LAWRENCE OWSLEY
JOHN GOULD FLETCHER
LYLE H. LANIER
ALLEN TATE
HERMAN CLARENCE NIXON
ANDREW NELSON LYTLE
ROBERT PENN WARREN
JOHN DONALD WADE
HENRY BLUE KLINE
STARK YOUNG

In 1930, twelve Southerners published a collection of essays entitled *I'll Take My Stand*. This book represented one of the strongest indictments of an industrial and commercial age that the writers felt had infected American culture. In their view, Americans—especially those in the Northeast—had become so driven by acquisitiveness and ostensible progress that they had lost the essential values of art, religion, and civilization. In the South, where industrialism had not yet turned the landscape into the utilitarian purposes of man, there was still time for leisure and spiritual reflection.

The Southerners, who became known as the Agrarians, were among the most important twentieth-century poets, novelists, and historians. John Crowe Ransom, Allen Tate, Robert Penn Warren, and Donald Davidson—all from Vanderbilt University—formed a group of poets who had published the *Fugitive* and made a considerable impact on the study and structure of poetry. Stark Young and Andrew Nelson Lytle wrote fiction; Frank Lawrence Owsley was an historian of considerable distinction; and others—John Gould Fletcher, John Donald Wade, Herman Clarence Nixon, Henry Blue Kline, and Lyle Lanier—were poets, historians, journalists, and psychologists.

Although many of the essays in *I'll Take My Stand* seem narrowly conservative, especially in the light of subsequent racial developments and the rapid industrialization of the South, they are an historical landmark. They recall a Southern way of life that had produced a distinctive culture and they portend the serious re-examination of that culture by William Faulkner, Eudora Welty, Flannery O'Connor, Carson McCullers, William Styron, Truman Capote, and many others.

The collective introduction to the volume is a clear celebration of the individual man in nature as these writers thought he had existed and could continue to exist in the South. But the introduction and essays that follow it are more than a defense of the South and of a way of life. They criticize man's mindless pursuit of possessions and thus become a defense of humanism in the broadest possible terms.

From I'll Take My Stand

INTRODUCTION:
A STATEMENT OF PRINCIPLES

The authors contributing to this book are Southerners, well acquainted with one another and of similar tastes, though not necessarily living in the same physical community, and perhaps only at this moment aware of themselves as a single group of men. By conversation and exchange of letters over a number of years it had developed that they entertained many convictions in common, and it was decided to make a volume in which each one should furnish his views upon a chosen topic. This was the general background. But background and consultation as to the various topics were enough; there was to be no further collaboration. And so no single author is responsible for any view outside his own article. It was through the good fortune of some deeper agreement that the book was expected to achieve its unity. All the articles bear in the same sense upon the book's title-subject: all tend to support a Southern way of life against what may be called the American or prevailing way; and all as much as agree that the best terms in which to represent the distinction are contained in the phrase, Agrarian *versus* Industrial.

But after the book was under way it seemed a pity if the contributors, limited as they were within their special subjects, should stop short of showing how close their agreements really were. On the contrary, it seemed that they ought to go on and make themselves known as a group already consolidated by a set of principles which could be stated with a good deal of particularity. This might prove useful for the sake of future reference, if they should undertake any further joint publication. It was then decided to prepare a general introduction for the book which would state briefly the common convictions of the group. This is the statement. To it every one of the contributors in this book has subscribed.

Nobody now proposes for the South, or for any other community in this country, an independent political destiny. That idea is thought to have been finished in 1865. But how far shall the South surrender its moral, social, and economic autonomy to the victorious principle of Union? That question remains open. The South is a minority section that has hitherto been jealous of its minority right to live its own kind of life. The South scarcely hopes to determine the other sections, but it does propose to determine itself, within the utmost limits of legal action. Of late, however, there is the melancholy fact that the South itself has wavered a little and shown signs of wanting to join up behind the common or American industrial ideal. It is against that tendency that this book is written. The younger Southerners, who are being converted frequently to the industrial gospel, must come back to the support of the Southern tradition. They must be persuaded to look very critically at the advantages of becoming a "new South" which will be only an undistinguished replica of the usual industrial community.

But there are many other minority communities opposed to industrialism, and wanting a much simpler economy to live by. The communities and private persons sharing the agrarian tastes are to be found widely within the Union. Proper living is a matter of the intelligence and the will, does not depend on the local climate or geography, and is capable of a definition which is general and not Southern at all. Southerners have a filial duty to discharge to their own section. But their cause is precarious and they must seek alliances with sympathetic communities everywhere. The members of the present group would be happy to be counted as members of a national agrarian movement.

Industrialism is the economic organization of the collective American society. It means the decision of society to invest its economic resources in the applied sciences. But the word science has acquired a certain sanctitude. It is out of order to quarrel with science in the abstract, or even with the applied sciences when their applications are made subject to criticism and intelligence. The capitalization of the applied sciences has now become extravagant and uncritical; it has enslaved our human energies to a degree now clearly felt to be burdensome. The apologists of industrialism do not like to meet this charge directly; so they often take refuge in saying that they are devoted simply to science! They are really devoted to the applied sciences and to practical production. Therefore it is necessary to employ a certain skepticism even at the expense of the Cult of Science, and to say, It is an Americanism, which looks innocent and disinterested, but really is not either.

The contribution that science can make to a labor is to render it easier by the help of a tool or a process, and to assure the laborer of his perfect economic security while he is engaged upon it. Then it can be performed with leisure and enjoyment. But the modern laborer has not exactly received this benefit under the industrial regime. His labor is hard, its tempo is fierce, and his employment is insecure. The first principle of a good labor is that it must be effective, but the second principle is that it must be enjoyed. Labor is one of the largest items in the human career; it is a modest demand to ask that it may partake of happiness.

The regular act of applied science is to introduce into labor a labor-saving device or a machine. Whether this is a benefit depends on how far it is advisable to save the labor. The philosophy of applied science is generally quite sure that the saving of labor is a pure gain, and that the more of it the better. This is to assume that labor is an evil, that only the end of labor or the material product is good. On this assumption labor becomes mercenary and servile, and it is no wonder if many forms of modern labor are accepted without resentment though they are evidently brutalizing. The act of labor as one of the happy functions of human life has been in effect abandoned, and is practiced solely for its rewards.

Even the apologists of industrialism have been obliged to admit that some economic evils follow in the wake of the machines. These are such as over-production, unemployment, and a growing inequality in the distribution of wealth. But the remedies proposed by the apologists are always homeo-pathic. They expect the evils to disappear when we have bigger and better machines, and more of them. Their remedial programs, therefore, look forward to more industrialism. Sometimes they see the system righting itself spontaneously and without direction: they are Optimists. Sometimes they rely on the benevolence of capital, or the militancy of labor, to bring about a fairer division of the spoils: they are Coöperationists or Socialists. And sometimes they expect to find super-engineers, in the shape of Boards of Control, who will adapt production to consumption and regulate prices and guarantee business against fluctuations: they are Sovietists. With respect to these last it must be insisted that the true Sovietists or Communists—if the term may be used here in the European sense—are the Industrialists them-selves. They would have the government set up an economic super-organiza-tion, which in turn would become the government. We therefore look upon the Communist menace as a menace indeed, but not as a Red one; because it is simply according to the blind drift of our industrial development to expect in America at last much the same economic system as that imposed by violence upon Russia in 1917.

Turning to consumption, as the grand end which justifies the evil of modern labor, we find that we have been deceived. We have more time in which to consume, and many more products to be consumed. But the tempo of our labors communicates itself to our satisfactions, and these also become brutal and hurried. The constitution of the natural man probably does not permit him to shorten his labor-time and enlarge his consuming-time indefinitely. He has to pay the penalty in satiety and aimlessness. The modern man has lost his sense of vocation.

Religion can hardly expect to flourish in an industrial society. Religion is our submission to the general intention of a nature that is fairly inscrutable; it is the sense of our rôle as creatures within it. But nature industrialized, transformed into cities and artificial habitations, manufactured into commodities, is no longer nature but a highly simplified picture of nature. We receive the illusion of having power over nature, and lose the sense of nature as something mysterious and contingent. The God of nature under these conditions is merely an amiable expression, a superfluity, and the philosophical understanding ordinarily carried in the religious experience is not there for us to have.

Nor do the arts have a proper life under industrialism, with the general decay of sensibility which attends it. Art depends, in general, like religion, on a right attitude to nature; and in particular on a free and disinterested observation of nature that occurs only in leisure. Neither the creation nor the understanding of works of art is possible in an industrial age except by some local and unlikely suspension of the industrial drive.

The amenities of life also suffer under the curse of a strictly-business or industrial civilization. They consist in such practices as manners, conversation, hospitality, sympathy, family life, romantic love—in the social exchanges which reveal and develop sensibility in human affairs. If religion and the arts are founded on right relations of man-to-nature, these are founded on right relations of man-to-man.

Apologists of industrialism are even inclined to admit that its actual processes may have upon its victims the spiritual effects just described. But they think that all can be made right by extraordinary educational efforts, by all sorts of cultural institutions and endowments. They would cure the poverty of the contemporary spirit by hiring experts to instruct it in spite of itself in the historic culture. But salvation is hardly to be encountered on that road. The trouble with the life-pattern is to be located at its economic base, and we cannot rebuild it by pouring in soft materials from the top. The young men and women in colleges, for example, if they are already placed in a false way of life, cannot make more than an inconsequential acquaintance with the arts and humanities transmitted to them. Or else the understanding of these arts and humanities will but make them the more wretched in their own destitution.

The "Humanists" are too abstract. Humanism, properly speaking, is not an abstract system, but a culture, the whole way in which we live, act, think, and feel. It is a kind of imaginatively balanced life lived out in a definite social tradition. And, in the concrete, we believe that this, the genuine humanism, was rooted in the agrarian life of the older South and of other parts of the country that shared in such a tradition. It was not an abstract moral "check" derived from the classics—it was not soft material poured in from the top. It was deeply founded in the way of life itself—in its tables, chairs, portraits, festivals, laws, marriage customs. We cannot recover our native humanism by adopting some standard of taste that is critical enough to question the contemporary arts but not critical enough to question the social and economic life which is their ground.

The tempo of the industrial life is fast, but that is not the worst of it; it is accelerating. The ideal is not merely some set form of industrialism, with so many stable industries, but industrial progress, or an incessant extension of industrialization. It never proposes a specific goal; it initiates the infinite series. We have not merely capitalized certain industries; we have capitalized the laboratories and inventors, and undertaken to employ all the labor-saving devices that come out of them. But a fresh labor-saving device introduced into an industry does not emancipate the laborers in that industry so much as it evicts them. Applied at the expense of agriculture, for example, the new processes have reduced the part of the population supporting itself upon the soil to a smaller and smaller fraction. Of course no single labor-saving process is fatal; it brings on a period of unemployed labor and unemployed capital, but soon a new industry is devised which will put them both to work again, and a new commodity is thrown upon the market. The laborers were sufficiently embarrassed in the meantime, but, according to the theory, they will eventually be taken care of. It is now the public which is embarrassed; it feels obligated to purchase a commodity for which it had expressed no desire, but it is invited to make its budget equal to the strain. All might yet be well, and stability and comfort might again obtain, but for this: partly because of industrial ambitions and partly because the repressed creative impulse must break out somewhere, there will be a stream of further labor-saving devices in all industries, and the cycle will have to be repeated over and over. The result is an increasing disadjustment and instability.

It is an inevitable consequence of industrial progress that production greatly outruns the rate of natural consumption. To overcome the disparity, the producers, disguised as the pure idealists of progress, must coerce and wheedle the public into being loyal and steady consumers, in order to keep the machines running. So the rise of modern advertising—along with its twin, personal salesmanship—is the most significant development of our industrialism. Advertising means to persuade the consumers to want exactly what the applied sciences are able to furnish them. It consults the happiness of the consumer no more than it consulted the happiness of the laborer. It is the great effort of a false economy of life to approve itself. But its task grows more difficult every day.

It is strange, of course, that a majority of men anywhere could ever as with one mind become enamored of industrialism: a system that has so little regard for individual wants. There is evidently a kind of thinking that rejoices in setting up a social objective which has no relation to the individual. Men are prepared to sacrifice their private dignity and happiness to an abstract social ideal, and without asking whether the social ideal produces the welfare of any individual man whatsoever. But this is absurd. The responsibility of men is for their own welfare and that of their neighbors; not for the hypothetical welfare of some fabulous creature called society.

Opposed to the industrial society is the agrarian, which does not stand in particular need of definition. An agrarian society is hardly one that has no use at all for industries, for professional vocations, for scholars and artists, and for the life of cities. Technically, perhaps, an agrarian society is one in which agriculture is the leading vocation, whether for wealth, for pleasure, or for prestige—a form of labor that is pursued with intelligence and leisure, and that becomes the model to which the other forms approach as well as they may. But an agrarian regime will be secured readily enough where the superfluous industries are not allowed to rise against it. The theory of agrarianism is that the culture of the soil is the best and most sensitive of vocations, and that therefore it should have the economic preference and enlist the maximum number of workers.

These principles do not intend to be very specific in proposing any practical measures. How may the little agrarian community resist the Chamber of Commerce of its county seat, which is always trying to import some foreign industry that cannot be assimilated to the life-pattern of the community? Just what must the Southern leaders do to defend the traditional Southern life? How may the Southern and the Western agrarians unite for effective action? Should the agrarian forces try to capture the Democratic party, which historically is so closely affiliated with the defense 'of individualism, the small community, the state, the South? Or must the agrarians—even the Southern ones—abandon the Democratic party to its fate and try a new one? What legislation could most profitably be championed by the powerful agrarians in the Senate of the United States? What anti-industrial measures might promise to stop the advances of industrialism, or even undo some of them, with the least harm to those concerned? What policy should be pursued by the educators who have a tradition at heart? These and many other questions are of greatest importance, but they cannot be answered here.

For, in conclusion, this much is clear: If a community, or a section, or a race, or an age, is groaning under industrialism, and well aware that it is an evil dispensation, it must find the way to throw it off. To think that this cannot be done is pusillanimous. And if the whole community, section, race, or age thinks it cannot be done, then it has simply lost its political genius and doomed itself to impotence.

JOHN CROWE RANSOM

(1888-1974)

John Crowe Ransom established himself at Vanderbilt University where he taught Robert Penn Warren, Allen Tate, Donald Davidson, and other figures in what came to be known as the Fugitive Movement. Ransom edited *The Fugitive,* a magazine devoted to a conservative tradition in politics and literature, and then *The Kenyon Review.* Ransom was a minor poet whose wit and irony inform several interesting books of poetry: *Poems About God* (1919), *Chills and Fever* (1924), and *Two Gentlemen in Bonds* (1926); his influence was pervasive as a teacher, a critic, and an editor.

The third and final edition of *Selected Poems* was published in 1969. The prose appears in *Beating the Bushes: Selected Essays, 1941-1970,* 1972.

For Ransom's place among the Fugitives see Louise Cowan, *The Fugitive Group: A Literary History,* 1959 and John L. Stewart, *The Burden of Time: The Fugitive and Agrarians,* 1965. Individual studies include Robert Buffington, *The Equilibrist: A Study of John Crowe Ransom's Poems, 1916-1963,* 1967; Thomas H. Parsons, *John Crowe Ransom,* 1969, and Miller Williams, *The Poetry of John Crowe Ransom,* 1972. Thomas Daniel Young edited *John Crowe Ransom: Critical Essays and a Bibliography,* 1968.

Born on April 30, 1888, in Pulaski, Tennessee, Ransom studied at Vanderbilt University. After graduating in 1909, he attended Christ Church College, Oxford, as a Rhodes scholar, and returned to teach at Vanderbilt. He stayed at the university until 1937, when he went to Kenyon College, edited the highly influential *Kenyon Review,* and began to write literary criticism. In 1938, *The World's Body* appeared and, in 1941, *The New Criticism,* which was a consideration of the work of I. A. Richards, T. S. Eliot, Yvor Winters, and William Empson. His *Selected Poems* appeared in 1945 and his *Poems and Essays* in 1955.

Ransom's leadership in the Agrarian and Fugitive movements and his conservative point of view are well articulated in "Reconstructed but Unregenerate," the first essay in the book, *I'll Take My Stand.*

Reconstructed But Unregenerate

I

It is out of fashion in these days to look backward rather than forward. About the only American given to it is some unreconstructed Southerner, who persists in his regard for a certain terrain, a certain history, and a certain inherited way of living. He is punished as his crime deserves. He feels himself in the American scene as an anachronism, and knows he is felt by his neighbors as a reproach.

Of course he is a tolerably harmless reproach. He is like some quaint local character of eccentric but fixed principles who is thoroughly and almost pridefully accepted by the village as a rare exhibit in the antique kind. His position is secure from the interference of the police, but it is of a rather ambiguous dignity.

I wish now that he were not so entirely taken for granted, and that as a reproach he might bear a barb and inflict a sting. I wish that the whole force of my own generation in the South would get behind his principles and make them an ideal which the nation at large would have to reckon with. But first I will describe him in the light of the position he seems now to occupy actually before the public.

His fierce devotion is to a lost cause—though it grieves me that his contemporaries are so sure it is lost. They are so far from fearing him and his example that they even in the excess of confidence offer him a little honor, a little petting. As a Southerner I have observed this indulgence and I try to be

NOTE—This article is made up largely from articles of the author's that have appeared in the *Sewanee Review* and *Harper's Magazine.*

grateful. Obviously it does not constitute a danger to the Republic; distinctly it is not treasonable. They are good enough to attribute a sort of glamour to the Southern life as it is defined for them in a popular tradition. They like to use the South as the nearest available locus for the scenes of their sentimental songs, and sometimes they send their daughters to the Southern seminaries. Not too much, of course, is to be made of this last gesture, for they do not expose to this hazard their sons, who in our still very masculine order will have to discharge the functions of citizenship, and who must accordingly be sternly educated in the principles of progress at progressive institutions of learning. But it does not seem to make so much difference what principles of a general character the young women acquire, since they are not likely to be impaired by principles in their peculiar functions, such as virtue and the domestic duties. And so, at suitable seasons, and on the main-line trains, one may see them in some numbers, flying south or flying north like migratory birds; and one may wonder to what extent their philosophy of life will be affected by two or three years in the South. One must remember that probably their parents have already made this calculation and are prepared to answer, Not much.

The Southerner must know, and in fact he does very well know, that his antique conservatism does not exert a great influence against the American progressivist doctrine. The Southern idea today is down, and the progressive or American idea is up. But the historian and the philosopher, who take views that are thought to be respectively longer and deeper than most, may very well reverse this order and find that the Southern idea rather than the American has in its favor the authority of example and the approval of theory. And some prophet may even find it possible to expect that it will yet rise again.

I will propose a thesis which seems to have about as much cogency as generalizations usually have: The South is unique on this continent for having founded and defended a culture which was according to the European principles of culture; and the European principles had better look to the South if they are to be perpetuated in this country.

II

The nearest of the European cultures which we could examine is that of England; and this is of course the right one in the case, quite aside from our convenience. England was actually the model employed by the South, in so far as Southern culture was not quite indigenous. And there is in the South even today an Anglophile sentiment quite anomalous in the American scene.

England differs from America doubtless in several respects, but most notably in the fact that England did her pioneering an indefinite number of centuries ago, did it well enough, and has been living pretty tranquilly on her establishment ever since, with infrequent upheavals and replacements. The customs and institutions of England seem to the American observer very fixed and ancient. There is no doubt that the English tradition expresses itself in many more or less intangible ways, but it expresses itself most importantly in a material establishment; and by this I mean the stable economic system by which Englishmen are content to take their livelihood from the physical environment. The chief concern of England's half-mythical pioneers, as with pioneers anywhere, was with finding the way to make a living. Evidently they found it. But fortunately the methods they worked out proved transmissible, proved, in fact, the main reliance of the succeeding generations. The pioneers explored the soil, determined what concessions it might reasonably be expected to make them, housed themselves, developed all their necessary trades, and arrived by painful experiment at a thousand satisfactory recipes by which they might secure their material necessities. Their descendants have had the good sense to consider that this establishment was good enough for them. They have elected to live their comparatively easy and routine lives in accordance with the tradition which they inherited, and they have consequently enjoyed a leisure, a security, and an intellectual freedom that were never the portion of pioneers.

The pioneering life is not the normal life, whatever some Americans may suppose. It is not, if we look for the meaning of European history. The lesson of each of the European cultures now extant is in this—that European opinion does not make too much of the intense practical enterprises, but is at pains to define rather narrowly the practical effort which is prerequisite to the reflective and aesthetic life. Boys are very well pleased to employ their muscles almost exclusively, but men prefer to exercise their minds. It is the European intention to live materially along the inherited line of least resistance, in order to put the surplus of energy into the free life of the mind. Thus is engendered that famous, or infamous, European conservatism, which will appear stupid, necessarily, to men still fascinated by materialistic projects, men in a state of arrested adolescence; for instance, to some very large if indefinite fraction of the population of these United States.

I have in mind here the core of unadulterated Europeanism, with its self-sufficient, backward-looking, intensely provincial communities. The human life of English provinces long ago came to terms with nature, fixed its roots somewhere in the spaces between the rocks and in the shade of the trees, founded its comfortable institutions, secured its modest prosperity—and then willed the whole in perpetuity to the generations which should come after, in the ingenuous confidence that it would afford them all the essential human satisfactions. For it is the character of a seasoned provincial life that it is realistic, or successfully adapted to its natural environment, and that as a consequence it is stable, or hereditable. But it is the character of our urbanized, anti-provincial, progressive, and mobile American life that it is in a condition of eternal flux. Affections, and long memories, attach to the ancient bowers of life in the provinces; but they will not attach to what is always changing. Americans, however, are peculiar in being somewhat averse to these affections for natural objects, and to these memories.

Memories of the past are attended with a certain pain called nostalgia. It is hardly a technical term in our sociology or our psychiatry, but it might well be. Nostalgia is a kind of growing-pain, psychically speaking. It occurs to our sorrow when we have decided that it is time for us, marching to some magnificent destiny, to abandon an old home, an old provincial setting, or an old way of living to which we had become habituated. It is the complaint of human nature in its vegetative aspect, when it is plucked up by the roots from the place of its origin and transplanted in foreign soil, or even left dangling in the air. And it must be nothing else but nostalgia, the instinctive objection to being transplanted, that chiefly prevents the deracination of human communities and their complete geographical dispersion as the casualties of an insatiable wanderlust.

Deracination in our Western life is the strange discipline which individuals turn upon themselves, enticed by the blandishments of such fine words as Progressive, Liberal, and Forward-looking. The progressivist says in effect: Do not allow yourself to feel homesick; form no such powerful attachments that you feel a pain in cutting them loose; prepare your spirit to be always on the move. According to this gospel, there is no rest for the weary, not even in heaven. The poet Browning expresses an ungrateful intention, the moment he shall enter into his reward, to "fight onward, there as here." The progressivist H. G. Wells has outlined very neatly his scheme of progress, the only disheartening feature being that he had to revise it a good many times, and that the state to which he wants us to progress never has any finality or definition. Browning and Wells would have made very good Americans, and I am sure they have got the most of their disciples on this side of the Atlantic; they have not been good Europeans. But all the true progressivists intend to have a program so elastic that they can always propose new worlds to conquer. If his Utopia were practicable really, and if the progressivist should secure it, he would then have to defend it from further progress, which would mean his transformation from a progressivist into a conservative. Which is unthinkable.

The gospel of Progress is a curious development, which does not reflect great credit on the supposed capacity of our species for formulating its own behavior. Evidently the formula may involve its practitioners in self-torture and suicide just as readily as in the enjoyment of life. In most societies man has adapted himself to environment with plenty of intelligence to secure easily his material necessities from the graceful bounty of nature. And then, ordinarily, he concludes a truce with nature, and he and nature seem to live on terms of mutual respect and amity, and his loving arts, religions, and philosophies come spontaneously into being: these are the blessings of peace. But the latter-day societies have been seized—none quite so violently as our American one—with the strange idea that the human destiny is not to secure an honorable peace with nature, but to wage an unrelenting war on nature. Men, therefore, determine to conquer nature to a degree which is quite beyond reason so far as specific human advantage is concerned, and which enslaves them to toil and turnover. Man is boastfully declared to be a natural scientist essentially, whose strength is capable of crushing and making over to his own desires the brute materiality which is nature; but in his infinite contention with this materiality he is really capitulating to it. His engines transform the face of nature—a little—but when they have been perfected, he must invent new engines that will perform even more heroically. And always the next engine of his invention, even though it be that engine which is to invade the material atom and exploit the most secret treasury of nature's wealth, will be a physical engine; and the man who uses it will be engaged in substantially the same struggle as was the primitive Man with the Hoe.

This is simply to say that Progress never defines its ultimate objective, but thrusts its victims at once into an infinite series. Our vast industrial machine, with its laboratory centers of experimentation, and its far-flung organs of mass production, is like a Prussianized state which is organized strictly for war and can never consent to peace. Or, returning to the original figure, our progressivists are the latest version of those pioneers who conquered the wilderness, except that they are pioneering on principle, or from force of habit, and without any recollection of what pioneering was for.

III

Along with the gospel of Progress goes the gospel of Service. They work beautifully as a team.

Americans are still dreaming the materialistic dreams of their youth. The stuff these dreams were made on was the illusion of preëminent personal success over a material opposition. Their tone was belligerence, and the euphemism under which it masqueraded was ambition. But men are not lovely, and men are not happy, for being too ambitious. Let us distinguish two forms under which ambition drives men on their materialistic projects; a masculine and a feminine.

Ambitious men fight, first of all, against nature; they propose to put nature under their heel; this is the dream of scientists burrowing in their cells, and then of the industrial men who beg of their secret knowledge and go out to trouble the earth. But after a certain point this struggle is vain, and we only use ourselves up if we prolong it. Nature wears out man before man can wear out nature; only a city man, a laboratory man, a man cloistered from the normal contacts with the soil, will deny that. It seems wiser to be moderate in our expectations of nature, and respectful; and out of so simple a thing as respect for the physical earth and its teeming life comes a primary joy, which is an inexhaustible source of arts and religions and philosophies.

Ambitious men are belligerent also in the way they look narrowly and enviously upon one another; and I do not refer to such obvious disasters as wars and the rumors of wars. Ambition of the first form was primary and masculine, but there is a secondary form which is typically feminine, though the distribution between the sexes may not be without the usual exceptions. If it is Adam's curse to will perpetually to work his mastery upon nature, it is Eve's curse to prompt Adam every morning to keep up with the best people in the neighborhood in taking the measure of his success. There can never be stability and establishment in a community whose every lady member is sworn to see that her mate is not eclipsed in the competition for material advantages; that community will fume and ferment, and every constituent part will be in perpetual physical motion. The good life depends on leisure, but leisure depends on an establishment, and the establishment depends on a prevailing magnanimity which scorns personal advancement at the expense of the free activity of the mind.

The masculine form is hallowed by Americans, as I have said, under the name of Progress. The concept of Progress is the concept of man's increasing command, and eventually perfect command, over the forces of nature; a concept which enhances too readily our conceit, and brutalizes our life. I believe there is possible no deep sense of beauty, no heroism of conduct, and no sublimity of religion, which is not informed by the humble sense of man's precarious position in the universe. The feminine form is likewise hallowed among us under the name of Service. The term has many meanings, but we come finally to the one which is critical for the moderns; service means the function of Eve, it means the seducing of laggard men into fresh struggles with nature. It has special application to the apparently stagnant sections of mankind, it busies itself with the heathen Chinee, with the Roman Catholic Mexican, with the "lower" classes in our own society. Its motive is missionary. Its watchwords are such as Protestantism, Individualism, Democracy, and the point of its appeal is a discontent, generally labeled "divine."

Progress and Service are not European slogans, they are Americanisms. We alone have devoted our lives to ideals which are admirable within their proper limits, but which expose us to slavery when pursued without critical intelligence. Some Europeans are taken in by these ideals, but hardly the American communities on the whole. Herr Spengler, with a gesture of defeat, glorifies the modern American captain of industry when he compares his positive achievements with the futilities of modern poets and artists. Whereupon we may well wish to save Europe from even so formidable a European as Spengler, hoping that he may not convert Europe to his view. And it is hardly likely; Europe is founded on a principle of conservatism, and is deeply scornful of the American and pioneer doctrine of the strenuous life. In 1918 there was danger that Europe might ask to be Americanized, and American missionaries were quite prepared to answer the call. But since then there has been a revulsion in European opinion, and this particular missionary enterprise confronts now an almost solid barrier of hostility. Europe is not going to be Americanized through falling suddenly in love with strenuousness. It only remains to be seen whether Europe may not be Americanized after all through envy, and through being reminded ceaselessly of our superior prosperity. That is an event to be determined by the force of European magnanimity; Europe's problem, not ours.

IV

The Southern states were settled, of course, by miscellaneous strains. But evidently the one which determined the peculiar tradition of the South was the one which came out of Europe most convinced of the virtues of establishment, contrasting with those strains which seem for the most part to have dominated the other sections, and which came out of Europe feeling rebellious toward all establishments. There are a good many faults to be found with the old South, but hardly the fault of being intemperately addicted to work and to gross material prosperity. The South never conceded that the whole duty of man was to increase material production, or that the index to the degree of his culture was the volume of his material production. His business seemed to be rather to envelop both his work and his play with a leisure which permitted the activity of intelligence. On this assumption the South pioneered her way to a sufficiently comfortable and rural sort of establishment, considered that an establishment was something stable, and proceeded to enjoy the fruits thereof. The arts of the section, such as they were, were not immensely passionate, creative, and romantic; they were the eighteenth-century social arts of dress, conversation, manners, the table, the hunt, politics, oratory, the pulpit. These were arts of living and not arts of escape; they were also community arts, in which every class of society could participate after its kind. The South took life easy, which is itself a tolerably comprehensive art.

But so did other communities in 1850, I believe. And doubtless some others do so yet; in parts of New England, for example. If there are such communities, this is their token, that they are settled. Their citizens are comparatively satisfied with the life they have inherited, and are careful to look backward quite as much as they look forward. Before the Civil War there must have been many such communities this side of the frontier. The difference between the North and the South was that the South was constituted by such communities and made solid. But solid is only a comparative term here. The South as a culture had more solidity than another section, but there were plenty of gaps in it. The most we can say is that the Southern establishment was completed in a good many of the Southern communities, and that this establishment was an active formative influence on the spaces between, and on the frontier spaces outlying, which had not yet perfected their organization of the economic life.

The old Southern life was of course not so fine as some of the traditional-ists like to believe. It did not offer serious competition against the glory that was Greece or the grandeur that was Rome. It hardly began to match the finish of the English, or any other important European civilization. It is quite enough to say that it was a way of life which had been considered and authorized. The establishment had a sufficient economic base, it was meant to be stable rather than provisional, it had got beyond the pioneering stage, it provided leisure, and its benefits were already being enjoyed. It may as well be admitted that Southern society was not an institution of very showy elegance, for the so-called aristocrats were mostly home-made and countri-fied. Aristocracy is not the word which defines this social organization so well as squirearchy, which I borrow from a recent article by Mr. William Frierson in the *Sewanee Review*. And even the squires, and the other classes, too, did not define themselves very strictly. They were loosely graduated social orders, not fixed as in Europe. Their relations were personal and friendly. It was a kindly society, yet a realistic one; for it was a failure if it could not be said that people were for the most part in their right places. Slavery was a feature monstrous enough in theory, but, more often than not, humane in practice; and it is impossible to believe that its abolition alone could have effected any great revolution in society.

The fullness of life as it was lived in the ante-bellum South by the differ-ent social orders can be estimated today only by the application of some difficult sociological technique. It is my thesis that all were committed to a form of leisure, and that their labor itself was leisurely. The only Southerners who went abroad to Washington and elsewhere, and put themselves into the record, were those from the top of the pyramid. They held their own with their American contemporaries. They were not intellectually as seasoned as good Europeans, but then the Southern culture had had no very long time to grow, as time is reckoned in these matters: it would have borne a better fruit eventually. They had a certain amount of learning, which was not as formi-dable as it might have been: but at least it was classical and humanistic learning, not highly scientific, and not wildly scattered about over a variety of special studies.

V

Then the North and the South fought, and the consequences were disastrous to both. The Northern temper was one of jubilation and expansiveness, and now it was no longer shackled by the weight of the conservative Southern tradition. Industrialism, the latest form of pioneering and the worst, pres-ently overtook the North, and in due time has now produced our present American civilization. Poverty and pride overtook the South; poverty to bring her institutions into disrepute and to sap continually at her courage; and a false pride to inspire a distaste for the thought of fresh pioneering projects, and to doom her to an increasing physical enfeeblement.

It is only too easy to define the malignant meaning of industrialism. It is the contemporary form of pioneering; yet since it never consents to define its goal, it is a pioneering on principle, and with an accelerating speed. Industrialism is a program under which men, using the latest scientific paraphernalia, sacrifice comfort, leisure, and the enjoyment of life to win Pyrrhic victories from nature at points of no strategic importance. Ruskin and Carlyle feared it nearly a hundred years ago, and now it may be said that their fears have been realized partly in England, and with almost fatal completeness in America. Industrialism is an insidious spirit, full of false promises and generally fatal to establishments since, when it once gets into them for a little renovation, it proposes never again to leave them in peace. Industrialism is rightfully a menial, of almost miraculous cunning but no intelligence; it needs to be strongly governed or it will destroy the economy of the household. Only a community of tough conservative habit can master it.

The South did not become industrialized; she did not repair the damage to her old establishment, either, and it was in part because she did not try hard enough. Hers is the case to cite when we would show how the good life depends on an adequate pioneering, and how the pioneering energy must be kept ready for call when the establishment needs overhauling. The Southern tradition came to look rather pitiable in its persistence when the twentieth century had arrived, for the establishment was quite depreciated. Unregenerate Southerners were trying to live the good life on a shabby equipment, and they were grotesque in their effort to make an art out of living when they were not decently making the living. In the country districts great numbers of these broken-down Southerners are still to be seen in patched blue-jeans, sitting on ancestral fences, shotguns across their laps and hound-dogs at their feet, surveying their unkempt acres while they comment shrewdly on the ways of God. It is their defect that they have driven a too easy, an unmanly bargain with nature, and that their æstheticism is based on insufficient labor.

But there is something heroic, and there may prove to be yet something very valuable to the Union, in their extreme attachment to a certain theory of life. They have kept up a faith which was on the point of perishing from this continent.

Of course it was only after the Civil War that the North and the South came to stand in polar opposition to each other. Immediately after Appomattox it was impossible for the South to resume even that give-and-take of ideas which had marked her ante-bellum relations with the North. She was offered such terms that acquiescence would have been abject. She retired within her borders in rage and held the minimum of commerce with the enemy. Persecution intensified her tradition, and made the South more solid and more Southern in the year 1875, or thereabouts, than ever before. When the oppression was left off, naturally her guard relaxed. But though the period of persecution had not been long, nevertheless the Southern tradition found itself then the less capable of uniting gracefully with the life of the Union; for that life in the meantime had been moving on in an opposite direction. The American progressive principle was like a ball rolling down the hill with an increasing momentum, and by 1890 or 1900 it was clear to any intelligent Southerner that it was a principle of boundless aggression against nature which could hardly offer much to a society devoted to the arts of peace.

But to keep on living shabbily on an insufficient patrimony is to decline, both physically and spiritually. The South declined.

VI

And now the crisis in the South's decline has been reached.

Industrialism has arrived in the South. Already the local chambers of commerce exhibit the formidable data of Southern progress. A considerable party of Southern opinion, which might be called the New South party, is well pleased with the recent industrial accomplishments of the South and anxious for many more. Southerners of another school, who might be said to compose an Old South party, are apprehensive lest the section become completely and uncritically devoted to the industrial ideal precisely as the other sections of the Union are. But reconstruction is actually under way. Tied politically and economically to the Union, her borders wholly violable, the South now sees very well that she can restore her prosperity only within the competition of an industrial system.

After the war the Southern plantations were often broken up into small farms. These have yielded less and less of a living, and it [is] said that they will never yield a good living until once more they are integrated into large units. But these units will be industrial units, controlled by a board of directors or an executive rather than a squire, worked with machinery, and manned not by farmers living at home, but by "labor." Even so they will not, according to Mr. Henry Ford, support the population that wants to live on them. In the off seasons the laborers will have to work in factories, which henceforth are to be counted on as among the charming features of Southern landscape. The Southern problem is complicated, but at its center is the farmer's problem, and this problem is simply the most acute version of that general agrarian problem which inspires the despair of many thoughtful Americans today.

The agrarian discontent in America is deeply grounded in the love of the tiller for the soil, which is probably, it must be confessed, not peculiar to the Southern specimen, but one of the more ineradicable human attachments, be the tiller as progressive as he may. In proposing to wean men from this foolish attachment, industrialism sets itself against the most ancient and the most humane of all the modes of human livelihood. Do Mr. Hoover and the distinguished thinkers at Washington see how essential is the mutual hatred between the industrialists and the farmers, and how mortal is their conflict?

The gentlemen at Washington are mostly preaching and legislating to secure the fabulous "blessings" of industrial progress; they are on the industrial side. The industrialists have a doctrine which is monstrous, but they are not monsters personally; they are forward-lookers with nice manners, and no American progressivist is against them. The farmers are boorish and inarticulate by comparison. Progressivism is against them in their fight, though their traditional status is still so strong that soft words are still spoken to them. All the solutions recommended for their difficulties are really enticements held out to them to become a little more coöperative, more mechanical, more mobile—in short, a little more industrialized. But the farmer who is not a mere laborer, even the farmer of the comparatively new places like Iowa and Nebraska, is necessarily among the more stable and less progressive elements of society. He refuses to mobilize himself and become a unit in the industrial army, because he does not approve of army life.

I will use some terms which are hardly in his vernacular. He identifies himself with a spot of ground, and this ground carries a good deal of meaning; it defines itself for him as nature. He would till it not too hurriedly and not too mechanically to observe in it the contingency and the infinitude of nature; and so his life acquires its philosophical and even its cosmic consciousness. A man can contemplate and explore, respect and love, an object as substantial as a farm or a native province. But he cannot contemplate nor explore, respect nor love, a mere turnover, such as an assemblage of "natural resources," a pile of money, a volume of produce, a market, or a credit system. It is into precisely these intangibles that industrialism would translate the farmer's farm. It means the dehumanization of his life.

However that may be, the South at last, looking defensively about her in all directions upon an industrial world, fingers the weapons of industrialism. There is one powerful voice in the South which, tired of a long status of disrepute, would see the South made at once into a section second to none in wealth, as that is statistically reckoned, and in progressiveness, as that might be estimated by the rapidity of the industrial turnover. This desire offends those who would still like to regard the South as, in the old sense, a home; but its expression is loud and insistent. The urban South, with its heavy importation of regular American ways and regular American citizens, has nearly capitulated to these novelties. It is the village South and the rural South which supply the resistance, and it is lucky for them that they represent a vast quantity of inertia.

Will the Southern establishment, the most substantial exhibit on this continent of a society of the European and historic order, be completely crumbled by the powerful acid of the Great Progressive Principle? Will there be no more looking backward but only looking forward? Is our New World to be dedicated forever to the doctrine of newness?

It is in the interest of America as a whole, as well as in the interest of the South, that these questions press for an answer. I will enter here the most important items of the situation as well as I can; doubtless they will appear a little over-sharpened for the sake of exhibition.

(1) The intention of Americans at large appears now to be what it was always in danger of becoming: an intention of being infinitely progressive. But this intention cannot permit of an established order of human existence, and of that leisure which conditions the life of intelligence and the arts.

(2) The old South, if it must be defined in a word, practiced the contrary and European philosophy of establishment as the foundation of the life of the spirit. The ante-bellum Union possessed, to say the least, a wholesome variety of doctrine.

(3) But the South was defeated by the Union on the battlefield with remarkable decisiveness, and the two consequences have been dire: the Southern tradition was physically impaired, and has ever since been unable to offer an attractive example of its philosophy in action; and the American progressive principle has developed into a pure industrialism without any check from a Southern minority whose voice ceased to make itself heard.

(4) The further survival of the Southern tradition as a detached local remnant is now unlikely. It is agreed that the South must make contact again with the Union. And in adapting itself to the actual state of the Union, the Southern tradition will have to consent to a certain industrialization of its own.

(5) The question at issue is whether the South will permit herself to be so industrialized as to lose entirely her historic identity, and to remove the last substantial barrier that has stood in the way of American progressivism; or will accept industrialism, but with a very bad grace, and will manage to maintain a good deal of her traditional philosophy.

VII

The hope which is inherent in the situation is evident from the terms in which it is stated. The South must be industrialized—but to a certain extent only, in moderation. The program which now engages the Southern leaders is to see how the South may handle this fire without being burnt badly. The South at last is to be physically reconstructed; but it will be fatal if the South should conceive it as her duty to be regenerated and get her spirit reborn with a totally different orientation toward life.

Fortunately, the Southern program does not have to be perfectly vague. There are at least two definite lines, along either of which an intelligent Southern policy may move in the right general direction; it may even move back and forth between them and still advance.

The first course would be for the Southern leaders to arouse the sectional feeling of the South to its highest pitch of excitement in defense of all the old ways that are threatened. It might seem ungrateful to the kind industrialists to accept their handsome services in such a churlish spirit. But if one thing is more certain than another, it is that these gentlemen will not pine away in their discouragement; they have an inextinguishable enthusiasm for their rôle. The attitude that needs artificial respiration is the attitude of resistance on the part of the natives to the salesmen of industrialism. It will be fiercest and most effective if industrialism is represented to the Southern people as— what it undoubtedly is for the most part—a foreign invasion of Southern soil, which is capable of doing more devastation than was wrought when Sherman marched to the sea. From this point of view it will be a great gain if the usually peaceful invasion forgets itself now and then, is less peaceful, and commits indiscretions. The native and the invader will be sure to come to an occasional clash, and that will offer the chance to revive ancient and almost forgotten animosities. It will be in order to proclaim to Southerners that the carpet-baggers are again in their midst. And it will be well to seize upon and advertise certain Northern industrial communities as horrible examples of a way of life we detest—not failing to point out the human catastrophe which occurs when a Southern village or rural community becomes the cheap labor of a miserable factory system. It will be a little bit harder to impress the people with the fact that the new so-called industrial "slavery" fastens not only upon the poor, but upon the middle and better classes of society, too. To make this point it may be necessary to revive such an antiquity as the old Southern gentleman and his lady, and their scorn for the dollar-chasers.

Such a policy as this would show decidedly a sense of what the Germans call *Realpolitik*. It could be nasty and it could be effective.

Its net result might be to give to the South eventually a position in the Union analogous more or less to the position of Scotland under the British crown—a section with a very local and peculiar culture that would, nevertheless, be secure and respected. And Southern traditionalists may take courage from the fact that it was Scottish stubbornness which obtained this position for Scotland; it did not come gratuitously; it was the consequence of an intense sectionalism that fought for a good many years before its fight was won.

That is one policy. Though it is not the only one, it may be necessary to employ it, with discretion, and to bear in mind its Scottish analogue. But it is hardly handsome enough for the best Southerners. Its methods are too easily abused; it offers too much for the professional demagogue; and one would only as a last resort like to have the South stake upon it her whole chance of survival. After all, the reconstruction may be undertaken with some imagination, and not necessarily under the formula of a literal restoration. It does not greatly matter to what extent the identical features of the old Southern establishment are restored; the important consideration is that there be an establishment for the sake of stability.

The other course may not be so easily practicable, but it is certainly more statesmanlike. That course is for the South to reënter the American political field with a determination and an address quite beyond anything she has exhibited during her half-hearted national life of the last half a century. And this means specifically that she may pool her own stakes with the stakes of other minority groups in the Union which are circumstanced similarly. There is in active American politics already, to start with, a very belligerent if somewhat uninformed Western agrarian party. Between this party and the South there is much community of interest; both desire to defend home, stability of life, the practice of leisure, and the natural enemy of both is the insidious industrial system. There are also, scattered here and there, numerous elements with the same general attitude which would have some power if united: the persons and even communities who are thoroughly tired of progressivism and its spurious benefits, and those who have recently acquired, or miraculously through the generations preserved, a European point of view—sociologists, educators, artists, religionists, and ancient New England townships. The combination of these elements with the Western farmers and the old-fashioned South would make a formidable bloc. The South is numerically much the most substantial of these three groups, but has done next to nothing to make the cause prevail by working inside the American political system.

The unifying effective bond between these geographically diverse elements of public opinion will be the clean-cut policy that the rural life of America must be defended, and the world made safe for the farmers. My friends are often quick to tell me that against the power of the industrial spirit no such hope can be entertained. But there are some protests in these days rising against the industrial ideal, even from the centers where its grip is the stoutest; and this would indicate that our human intelligence is beginning again to assert itself. Of course this is all the truer of the European countries, which have required less of the bitter schooling of experience. Thus Dean Inge declares himself in his Romanes Lecture on "The Idea of Progress":

> I believe that the dissatisfaction with things as they are is caused not only by the failure of nineteenth-century civilization, but partly also by its success. We no longer wish to progress on those lines if we could. Our apocalyptic dream is vanishing into thin air. It may be that the industrial revolution which began in the reign of George the Third has produced most of its fruits, and has had its day. We may have to look forward to such a change as is imagined by Anatole France at the end of his *Isle of the Penguins,* when, after an orgy of revolution and destruction, we shall slide back into the quiet rural life of the early modern period. If so, the authors of the revolution will have cut their own throats, for there can be no great manufacturing towns in such a society. Their disappearance will be no great loss. The race will have tried a great experiment, and will have rejected it as unsatisfying.

The South has an important part to play, if she will, in such a counter-revolution. But what pitiful service have the inept Southern politicians for many years been rendering to the cause! Their Southern loyalty at Washington has rarely had any more imaginative manifestation than to scramble vigorously for a Southern share in the federal pie. They will have to be miraculously enlightened.

I get quickly beyond my depth in sounding these political possibilities. I will utter one last fantastic thought.

No Southerner ever dreams of heaven, or pictures his Utopia on earth, without providing room for the Democratic party. Is it really possible that the Democratic party can be held to a principle, and that the principle can now be defined as agrarian, conservative, anti-industrial? It may not be impossible, after all. If it proves possible, then the South may yet be rewarded for a sentimental affection that has persisted in the face of many betrayals.

PRECIPITANTS: INVENTING THE TERMS OF LIBERATION

THEODORE DREISER

(1871–1945)

Theodore Dreiser was the son of an immigrant German weaver who married the daughter of an immigrant Moravian farmer; the couple had 12 children. There was a moment of relative affluence in the 1860s, but a series of accidents and disasters wiped the family out financially in 1870, and the town of Terre Haute, where Dreiser was born, was a place of desperate retreat. The novelist-to-be grew up in miserably

The novels are *Sister Carrie,* 1900; *Jennie Gerhardt,* 1911; *The Financier,* 1912; *The Titan,* 1914; *The "Genius",* 1915; *An American Tragedy,* 1925; *The Bulwark,* 1946; and *The Stoic,* 1947. Collections of short stories are *Free, and Other Stories,* 1918; *Chains,* 1927; *Fine Furniture,* 1930; *The Best Short Stories of Theodore Dreiser,* ed. Howard Fast, 1947; *The Best Short Stories of Theodore Dreiser,* ed. James T. Farrell, 1956. Dreiser has written several autobiographies: *A Traveler at Forty,* 1913; *A Hoosier Holiday,* 1916; *A Book About Myself,* 1922; and *Drawn,* 1931. Nonfiction includes *Twelve Men,* 1919; *Hey, Rub-a-Dub-Dub: A Book of The Mystery and Wonder and Terror of Life,* 1920; *The Color of a Great City,* 1923; *Dreiser Looks at Russia,* 1928; *A Gallery of Women,* 1929; *Tragic America,* 1931; *America is Worth Saving,* 1941. There is a book of poems, *Moods, Cadenced, and Declaimed,* 1928, rev. 1935, and dramas:

Plays of the Natural and Supernatural, 1916; *The Hand of the Potter,* 1918. The *Letters of Theodore Dreiser,* 3 vols., has been edited by Robert H. Elias.

A reliable biography is Robert Elias, *Theodore Dreiser: Apostle of Nature,* 1949. Recent critical studies include F. O. Matthiessen, *Theodore Dreiser,* 1951; Charles Shapiro, *Theodore Dreiser: Our Bitter Patriot,* 1962; Philip L. Gerber, *Theodore Dreiser,* 1964; William A. Swanberg, *Dreiser,* 1965; Marguerite Tjader, *Theodore Dreiser: A New Dimension,* 1965; *The Stature of Theodore Dreiser,* 1955, ed. Alfred Kazin and Charles Shapiro. See also John J. McAleer, *Theodore Dreiser: An Introduction and Interpretation,* 1968; Richard Lehan, *Theodore Dreiser: His World and His Novels,* 1969: Ellen Moers, *Two Dreisers,* 1969; and Robert Penn Warren, *Homage to Theodore Dreiser,* 1971.

straitened circumstances, his father often jobless, his mother obliged to work as a scrubwoman, his brothers and sisters reduced to stealing coal from railway cars; the family survived finally only by breaking up into several separate households. The lad was further tormented in youth by what he perceived as religious fanaticism in his father and "medievalism" in his teachers (Dreiser regarded the parochial schools he attended as prisons).

While he was often in despair, though, the young Dreiser seems seldom to have been without an imagination of possibility. His mother was generous and loving. An older brother, Paul, successful in show business as an entertainer (as Paul Dresser, he composed and promoted "My Gal Sal" and other hits of the day), bailed out the family periodically and lent some light of hope about the future. Theodore's own fantasies were immensely stimulated when, at 12, he and several siblings moved to Chicago with his mother, where he had his first thrilling vision of Metropolis. And he was lucky enough in high school to win the interest of a teacher who, recognizing his promise, paid his way through a year of study at the University of Indiana.

Before that interval Dreiser worked as a common laborer, then as a hardware clerk in Chicago. Afterward he held a succession of jobs as a reporter on papers in Chicago, Toledo, Cleveland, Pittsburgh, and New York. In his mid-20s he began a career as editor for popular magazines that he pursued simultaneously with his own writing for the next 15 years. His reputation as a novelist was not made overnight and, at many points in his writing life, he was an embattled man. His first novel, *Sister Carrie* (1900), was suppressed by its own publisher almost immediately after publication. Controversy burgeoned about the frankness of his treatment of sex in *An American Tragedy* (1925). *The Financier* (1912), the first volume of *A Trilogy of Desire,* made common cause with the muckrakers in its analysis of the Machiavellianism of its hero, a financial wizard modeled on an 1890's moneyman named Charles T. Yerkes. There was a battle with Hollywood about the movie version of *An American Tragedy* (Dreiser despised it); there were domestic troubles, a controversial trip to Russia 1927–1928 and, at the very end, a few months before his death, a decision to apply for membership in the Communist Party.

Yet for all his embattlement Dreiser stayed at his last. The composition of his major novels was often interrupted in midcourse, but articles and books flowed steadily from his pen for four decades, and the large projects in the fiction that he launched were all, without exception, brought to completion. Several collections of stories and sketches, a book about Russia, a remarkable volume of biographical narratives (*Twelve Men,* 1919), two memorable autobiographical volumes [*Dawn* (1931) and *A Book About Myself* (1931), later reprinted as

Newspaper Days], a book of poems, a play, an interesting speculative work about philosophical implications of advances in biochemical knowledge [*Hey, Rub-a-Dub-Dub* (1920)], several volumes of criticism of American culture. . . . These were minor works, to be sure, when compared with the books first mentioned, or with *Jennie Gerhardt* (1911), a novel about the Dreiser family or even with *The "Genius,"* an attempt at an autobiographical novel. But they are evidence of the personal characteristics—breadth of sympathetic interest and huge energy—that, together with one or two major literary influences (Balzac and Zola) and some amateur yet serious study in the fields of evolution, shaped his permanent achievements.

About those achievements various not wholly edifying critical squabbles have occurred over the years. One charge against the novelist is that he is a bad writer, clumsy in his address to the sentence, continuously offensive to the ear, lacking in genuinely aesthetic instincts. One defense is that the scope of his themes, the power of his work to rouse the emotions, render "stylistic" considerations trivial; his stories of the pitiable rise to climaxes that drive from the mind all reservations about literary inelegance. Like many bookish arguments, disputes about Dreiser have produced more oversimplification than understanding. If it is hard to read Dreiser without a certain measure of embarrassment at his taste, it is no less difficult to read him without a sense of shame that errors of taste can turn the eye from matters that count infinitely more than such errors. The author's overt theme is the pollution flowing from the dream of success; he is preoccupied by class divisions, by the arrogance of economic power, by the inability of those caught up in success religion to rise—even when superficially they seem to have beaten the system—into a world of decently humane values. His deeper theme is the mystery of the nonhuman—the operation within the universe of forces infinitely more potent than human will and wholly oblivious to human social or moral concern. His exploration of these themes—the most powerful books are *Sister Carrie* and *An American Tragedy*—takes the reader deep into the confusion and pain suffered by those imprisoned by success religion.

And neither work is clear of embarrassments, for the author participates fully and vulnerably in the dreams and frustration of their hero and heroine. Putting it another way, the authenticity of both books derives directly from that author's intimate awareness of what it would be like to be in the vulgar man's shoes—and thereby lies embarrassment. For while the writer sees the thinness of the idols that enslave his people, while he lectures his audience on the unworthiness of such idols, and while he reaches for metaphysical or scientific overviews that will restore a proportioned estimate of the significance of his characters, there is nevertheless much evidence that he himself was by no means among the unenslaved. The sense communicated over and over in Dreiser's fiction is that the vulgar object that awakens wonder in a character—a "swell" restaurant, a "gorgeous" rug—awakens like wonder in their creator; indeed, the very capacity of the novelist to show us what it is like to prize and hunger after glamor stimulates doubt about the authenticity of his own detachment, his own freedom from the pervasive corruption, his own commitment to philosophic thought. *These victims of his, they matter so much to him,* a voice whispers, *because he is still one of them.*

Implicit in this response is, as is obvious, justification for treating a writer's intellectual powers lightly. Dreiser was undervalued in his own time; he should have been the first American to win the Nobel Prize, yet that honor went, in 1930, to Sinclair Lewis, and his claims were ignored thereafter. What is more, the undervaluing has not yet ceased. There are critics who have allowed their contempt for his "determinism" and his fascination with "chemisms" to blind them to the relative sophistication of Dreiser's approach to these matters. (The author was a shrewd reader not only of Freud but of such works as Jacques Loeb's *Mechanistic Conception of Life.*) Yet it must be added that it is not finally as a thinker that Dreiser endures. A "naturalist" by intention, an author committed to fact and objective realities (most of Dreiser's fiction was based either on his own experience or on extensive field research into the lives of other "real" human beings), a hero in recent days of certain antihumanistic literary schools, Dreiser never reached that condition of pure intellectuality toward which he seemed sometimes to aspire. An intense and continuous responsiveness to inner human feeling is the core of his best books; it is the flood of heart's longing realized in his pages that alone assures their permanence.

From An American Tragedy

CHAPTER XLIII

Yet a thought such as that of the lake, connected as it was with the predicament by which he was being faced, and shrink from it though he might, was not to be dismissed as easily as he desired. Born as it was of its accidental relation to this personal problem that was shaking and troubling and all but disarranging his own none-too-forceful mind, this smooth, seemingly blameless, if dreadful, blotting out of two lives at Pass Lake, had its weight. That girl's body—as some peculiar force in his own brain now still compelled him to think—being found, but the man's not. In that interesting fact—and this quite in spite of himself—lurked a suggestion that insisted upon obtruding itself on his mind—to wit, that it might be possible that the man's body was not in that lake at all. For, since evil-minded people did occasionally desire to get rid of other people, might it not be possible that the man had gone there with that girl in order to get rid of her? A very smooth and devilish trick, of course, but one which, in this instance at least, seemed to have succeeded admirably.

But as for him accepting such an evil suggestion and acting upon it . . . never! Yet here was his own problem growing hourly more desperate, since every day, or at least every other day, brought him either letters from Roberta or a note from Sondra—their respective missives maintaining the same relative contrast between ease and misery, gayety of mood and the somberness of defeat and uncertainty.

To Roberta, since he would not write her, he was telephoning briefly and in as non-committal a manner as possible. How was she? He was so glad to hear from her and to know that she was out in the country and at home, where it must be much nicer than in the factory here in this weather. Everything was going smoothly, of course, and except for a sudden rush of orders which made it rather hard these last two days, all was as before. He was doing his best to save a certain amount of money for a certain project about which she knew, but otherwise he was not worrying about anything—and she must not. He had not written before because of the work, and could not write much—there were so many things to do—but he missed seeing her in her old place, and was looking forward to seeing her again soon. If she were coming down toward Lycurgus as she said, and really thought it important to see him, well, that could be arranged maybe—but was it necessary right now? He was so very busy and expected to see her later, of course.

But at the same time he was writing Sondra that assuredly on the eighteenth, and the week-end following, if possible, he would be with her.

So, by virtue of such mental prestidigitation and tergiversation, inspired and animated as it was by his desire for Sondra, his inability to face the facts in connection with Roberta, he achieved the much-coveted privilege of again seeing her, over one week-end at least, and in such a setting as never before in his life had he been privileged to witness.

For as he came down to the public dock at Sharon, adjoining the veranda of the inn at the foot of Twelfth Lake, he was met by Bertine and her brother as well as Sondra, who, in Grant's launch, had motored down the Chain to pick him up. The bright blue waters of the Indian Chain. The tall, dark spear pines that sentineled the shores on either side and gave to the waters at the west a band of black shadow where the trees were mirrored so clearly. The small and large, white and pink and green and brown lodges on every hand, with their boathouses Pavilions by the shore. An occasional slender pier reaching out from some spacious and at times stately summer lodge, such as those now owned by the Cranstons, Finchleys and others. The green and blue canoes and launches. The gay hotel and pavilion at Pine Point already smartly attended by the early arrivals here! And then the pier and boathouse of the Cranston Lodge itself, with two Russian wolfhounds recently acquired by Bertine lying on the grass near the shore, apparently awaiting her return, and a servant John, one of a half dozen who attended the family here, waiting to take the single bag of Clyde, his tennis racquet and golf sticks. But most of all he was impressed by the large rambling and yet smartly-designed house, with its bright geranium-bordered walks, its wide, brown, wicker-studded veranda commanding a beautiful view of the lake; the cars and personalities of the various guests, who in golf, tennis or lounging clothes were to be seen idling here and there.

At Bertine's request, John at once showed him to a spacious room overlooking the lake, where it was his privilege now to bathe and change for tennis with Sondra, Bertine and Grant. After dinner, as explained by Sondra, who was over at Bertine's for the occasion, he was to come over with Bertine and Grant to the Casino, where he would be introduced to such as all here knew. There was to be dancing. To-morrow, in the morning early, before breakfast, if he chose—he should ride with her and Bertine and Stuart along a wonderful woodland trail through the forests to the west which led to Inspiration Point and a more distant view of the lake. And, as he now learned, except for a few such paths as this, the forest was trackless for forty miles. Without a compass or guide, as he was told, one might wander to one's death even—so evasive were directions to those who did not know. And after breakfast and a swim she and Bertine and Nina Temple would demonstrate their new skill with Sondra's aquaplane. After that, lunch, tennis, or golf, a trip to the Casino for tea. After dinner at the lodge of the Brookshaws of Utica across the lake, there was to be dancing.

Within an hour after his arrival, as Clyde could see, the program for the week-end was already full. But that he and Sondra would contrive not only moments but possibly hours together he well knew. And then he would see what new delight, in connection with her many-faceted temperament, the wonderful occasion would provide. To him, in spite of the dour burden of Roberta, which for this one week-end at least he could lay aside, it was as though he were in Paradise.

And on the tennis grounds of the Cranstons, it seemed as though never before had Sondra, attired in a short, severe white tennis skirt and blouse, with a yellow-and-green dotted handkerchief tied about her hair, seemed so gay, graceful and happy. The smile that was upon her lips! The gay, laughing light of promise that was in her eyes whenever she glanced at him! And now and then, in running to serve him, it was as though she were poised bird-like in flight—her racquet arm high, a single toe seeming barely to touch the ground, her head thrown back, her lips parted and smiling always. And in calling twenty love, thirty love, forty love, it was always with a laughing accent on the word love, which at once thrilled and saddened him, as he saw, and rejoiced in from one point of view, she was his to take, if only he were free to take her now. But this other black barrier which he himself had built!

And then this scene, where a bright sun poured a flood of crystal light upon a greensward that stretched from tall pines to the silver rippling waters of a lake. And off shore in a half dozen different directions the bright white sails of small boats—the white and green and yellow splashes of color, where canoes paddled by idling lovers were passing in the sun! Summertime—leisure—warmth—color—ease—beauty—love—all that he had dreamed of the summer before, when he was so very much alone.

At moments it seemed to Clyde that he would reel from very joy of the certain fulfillment of a great desire, that was all but immediately within his control; at other times (the thought of Roberta sweeping down upon him as an icy wind), as though nothing could be more sad, terrible, numbing to the dreams of beauty, love and happiness than this which now threatened him. That terrible item about the lake and those two people drowned. The probability that in spite of his wild plan within a week, or two or three at most, he would have to leave all this forever. And then of a sudden he would wake to realize that he was fumbling or playing badly—that Bertine or Sondra or Grant was calling: "Oh, Clyde, what are you thinking of, anyhow?" And from the darkest depths of his heart he would have answered, had he spoken, "Roberta."

At the Brookshaws', again that evening, a smart company of friends of Sondra's, Bertine's and others. On the dance floor a reëncounter with Sondra, all smiles, for she was pretending for the benefit of others here—her mother and father in particular—that she had not seen Clyde before—did not even know that he was here.

"You up here? That's great. Over at the Cranstons'? Oh, isn't that dandy? Right next door to us. Well, we'll see a lot of each other, what? How about a canter to-morrow before seven? Bertine and I go nearly every day. And we'll have a picnic to-morrow, if nothing interferes, canoeing and motoring. Don't worry about not riding well. I'll get Bertine to let you have Jerry—he's just a sheep. And you don't need to worry about togs, either. Grant has scads of things. I'll dance the next two dances with others, but you sit out the third one with me, will you? I know a peach of a place outside on the balcony."

She was off with fingers extended but with a "we-understand-each-other" look in her eye. And outside in the shadow later she pulled his face to hers when no one was looking and kissed him eagerly, and, before the evening was over, they had managed, by strolling along a path which led away from the house along the lake shore, to embrace under the moon.

"Sondra so glad Clydie here. Misses him so much." She smoothed his hair as he kissed her, and Clyde, bethinking him of the shadow which lay so darkly between them, crushed her feverishly, desperately. "Oh, my darling baby girl," he exclaimed. "My beautiful, beautiful Sondra! If you only knew how much I love you! If you only knew! I wish I could tell you *all*. I wish I could."

But he could not now—or ever. He would never dare to speak to her of even so much as a phase of the black barrier that now lay between them. For, with her training, the standards of love and marriage that had been set for her, she would never understand, never be willing to make so great a sacrifice for love, as much as she loved him. And he would be left, abandoned on the instant, and with what horror in her eyes! '

Yet looking into his eyes, his face white and tense, and the glow of the moon above making small white electric sparks in his eyes, she exclaimed as he gripped her tightly: "Does he love Sondra so much? Oh, sweetie boy! Sondra loves him, too." She seized his head between her hands and held it tight, kissing him swiftly and ardently a dozen times. "And Sondra won't give her Clydie up either. She won't. You just wait and see! It doesn't matter what happens now. It may not be so very easy, but she won't." Then as suddenly and practically, as so often was her way, she exclaimed: "But we must go now, right away. No, not another kiss now. No, no, Sondra says no, now. They'll be missing us." And straightening up and pulling him by the arm she hurried him back to the house in time to meet Palmer Thurston, who was looking for her.

The next morning, true to her promise, there was the canter to Inspiration Point, and that before seven—Bertine and Sondra in bright red riding coats and white breeches and black boots, their hair unbound and loose to the wind, and riding briskly on before for the most part, then racing back to where he was. Or Sondra halloing gaily for him to come on, or the two of them laughing and chatting a hundred yards ahead in some concealed chapel of the aisled trees where he could not see them. And because of the interest which Sondra was so obviously manifesting in him these days—an interest which Bertine herself had begun to feel might end in marriage, if no family complications arose to interfere—she, Bertine, was all smiles, the very soul of cordiality, winsomely insisting that he should come up and stay for the summer and she would chaperon them both so that no one would have a chance to complain. And Clyde thrilling, and yet brooding too—by turns—occasionally—and in spite of himself drifting back to the thought that the item in the paper had inspired—and yet fighting it—trying to shut it out entirely.

And then at one point, Sondra, turning down a steep path which led to a stony and moss-lipped spring between the dark trees, called to Clyde to "Come on down. Jerry knows the way. He won't slip. Come and get a drink. If you do, you'll come back again soon—so they say."

And once he was down and had dismounted to drink, she exclaimed: "I've been wanting to tell you something. You should have seen Mamma's face last night when she heard you were up here. She can't be sure that I had anything to do with it, of course, because she thinks that Bertine likes you, too. I made her think that. But just the same she suspects that I had a hand in it, I guess, and she doesn't quite like it. But she can't say anything more than she has before. And I had a talk with Bertine just now and she's agreed to stick by me and help me all she can. But we'll have to be even more careful than ever now, because I think if Mamma got too suspicious I don't know what she might do—want us to leave here, even now maybe, just so I couldn't see you. You know she feels that I shouldn't be interested in any one except some one she likes. You know how it is. She's that way with Stuart, too. But if you'll take care not to show that you care for me so much whenever we're around any one of our crowd, I don't think she'll do anything—not now, anyhow. Later on, in the fall, when we're back in Lycurgus, things will be different. I'll be of age then, and I'm going to see what I can do. I never loved any one before, but I do love you, and, well, I won't give you up, that's all. I won't. And they can't make me, either!"

She stamped her foot and struck her boot, the while the two horses looked idly and vacantly about. And Clyde, enthused and astonished by this second definite declaration in his behalf, as well as fired by the thought that now, if ever, he might suggest the elopement and marriage and so rid himself of the sword that hung so threateningly above him, now gazed at Sondra, his eyes filled with a nervous hope and a nervous fear. For she might refuse, and change, too, shocked by the suddenness of his suggestion. And he had no money and no place in mind where they might go either, in case she accepted his proposal. But she had, perhaps, or she might have. And having once consented, might she not help him? Of course. At any rate, he felt that he must speak, leaving luck or ill luck to the future.

And so he said "Why couldn't you run away with me now, Sondra, darling? It's so long until fall and I want you so much. Why couldn't we? Your mother's not likely to want to let you marry me then, anyhow. But if we went away now, she couldn't help herself, could she? And afterwards, in a few months or so, you could write her and then she wouldn't mind. Why couldn't we, Sondra?" His voice was very pleading, his eyes full of a sad dread of refusal—and of the future that lay unprotected behind that.

And by now so caught was she by the tremor with which his mood invested him, that she paused—not really shocked by the suggestion at all— but decidedly moved, as well as flattered by the thought that she was able to evoke in Clyde so eager and headlong a passion. He was so impetuous—so blazing now with a flame of her own creating, as she felt, yet which she was incapable of feeling as much as he, as she knew—such a flame as she had never seen in him or any one else before. And would it not be wonderful if she could run away with him now—secretly—to Canada or New York or Boston, or anywhere? The excitement her elopement would create here and elsewhere—in Lycurgus, Albany, Utica! The talk and feeling in her own family as well as elsewhere! And Gilbert would be related to her in spite of him—and the Griffiths, too, whom her mother and father so much admired.

For a moment there was written in her eyes the desire and the determination almost, to do as he suggested—run away—make a great lark of this, her intense and true love. For, once married, what could her parents do? And was not Clyde worthy of her and them, too? Of course—even though nearly all in her set fancied that he was not quite all he should be, just because he didn't have as much money as they had. But he would have—would he not—after he was married to her—and get as good a place in her father's business as Gil Griffiths had in his father's?

Yet a moment later, thinking of her life here and what her going off in such a way would mean to her father and mother just then—in the very beginning of the summer season—as well as how it would disrupt her own plans and cause her mother to feel especially angry and perhaps even to bring about the dissolution of the marriage on the ground that she was not of age, she paused—that gay light of adventure replaced by a marked trace of the practical and the material that so persistently characterized her. What difference would a few months make, anyhow? It might, and no doubt would, save Clyde from being separated from her forever, whereas their present course might insure their separation.

Accordingly she now shook her head in a certain, positive and yet affectionate way, which by now Clyde had come to know spelled defeat—the most painful and irremediable defeat that had yet come to him in connection with all this. She would not go! Then he was lost—lost—and she to him forever maybe. Oh God! For while her face softened with a tenderness which was not usually there—even when she was most moved emotionally—she said "I would, honey, if I did not think it best not to, now. It's too soon. Mamma isn't going to do anything right now. I know she isn't. Besides she has made all her plans to do a lot of entertaining here this summer, and for my particular benefit. She wants me to be nice to—well, you know who I mean. And I can be, without doing anything to interfere with us in any way, I'm sure—so long as I don't do anything to really frighten her." She paused to smile a reassuring smile. "But you can come up here as often as you choose, don't you see, and she and these others won't think anything of it, because you won't be our guest, don't you see? I've fixed all that with Bertine. And that means that we can see each other all summer long up here, just about as much as we want to, don't you see? Then in the fall, when I come back, and if I find that I can't make her be nice to you at all, or consider our being engaged, why, I will run away with you. Yes, I will, darling—really and truly."

Darling! The fall!

She stopped, her eyes showing a very shrewd conception of all the practical difficulties before them, while she took both of his hands in hers and looked up into his face. Then, impulsively and conclusively, she threw both arms about his neck and, pulling his head down, kissed him.

"Can't you see, dearie? Please don't look so sad, darling. Sondra loves her Clyde so much. And she'll do anything and everything to make things come out right. Yes, she will. And they will, too. Now you wait and see. She won't give him up ever—ever!"

And Clyde, realizing that he had not one moving argument wherewith to confront her, really—not one that might not cause her to think strangely and suspiciously of his intense anxiety, and that this, because of Roberta's demand, and unless—unless—well—, unless Roberta let him go it all spelled defeat for him, now looked gloomily and even desperately upon her face. The beauty of her! The completeness of this world! And yet not to be allowed to possess her or it, ever. And Roberta with her demand and his promise in the immediate background! And no way of escape save by flight! God!

At this point it was that a nervous and almost deranged look—never so definite or powerful at any time before in his life—the border-line look between reason and unreason, no less—so powerful that the quality of it was even noticeable to Sondra—came into his eyes. He looked sick, broken, unbelievably despairing. So much so that she exclaimed, "Why, what is it, Clyde, dearie—you look so—oh, I can't say just how—forlorn or—Does he love me so much? And can't he wait just three or four months? But, oh, yes he can, too. It isn't as bad as he thinks. He'll be with me most of the time— the lovekins will. And when he isn't, Sondra'll write him every day—every day."

"But, Sondra! Sondra! If I could just tell you. If you knew how much it were going to mean to me——"

He paused here, for as he could see at this point, into the expression of Sondra came a practical inquiry as to what it was that made it so urgent for her to leave with him at once. And immediately, on his part, Clyde sensing how enormous was the hold of this world on her—how integral a part of it she was—and how, by merely too much insistence here and now, he might so easily cause her to doubt the wisdom of her primary craze for him, was moved to desist, sure that if he spoke it would lead her to questioning him in such a way as might cause her to change—or at least to modify her enthusiasm to the point where even the dream of the fall might vanish.

And so, instead of explaining further why he needed a decision on her part, he merely desisted, saying: "It's because I need you so much now, dear—all of the time. That's it, just that. It seems at times as though I could never be away from you another minute any more. Oh, I'm so hungry for you all of the time."

And yet Sondra, flattered as she was by this hunger, and reciprocating it in part at least, merely repeated the various things she had said before. They must wait. All would come out all right in the fall. And Clyde, quite numb because of his defeat, yet unable to forego or deny the delight of being with her now, did his best to recover his mood—and think, think, think that in some way—somehow—maybe via that plan of that boat or in some other way!

But what other way?

But no, no, no—not that. He was not a murderer and never could be. He was not a murderer—never—never—never.

And yet this loss.

This impending disaster.

This impending disaster.

How to avoid that and win to Sondra after all.

How, how, how?

CHAPTER XLIV

And then on his return to Lycurgus early Monday morning, the following letter from Roberta,

DEAR CLYDE:

My dear, I have often heard the saying, "it never rains but it pours," but I never knew what it meant until to-day. About the first person I saw this morning was Mr. Wilcox, a neighbor of ours, who came to say that Mrs. Anse would not be out to-day on account of some work she had to do for Mrs. Dinwiddie in Biltz, although when she left yesterday everything had been prepared for her so that I could help her a little with the sewing and so hurry things up a bit. And now she won't be here until to-morrow. Next word came that Mother's sister, Mrs. Nichols, is very ill and Mother had to go over to her house at Baker's Pond, which is about twelve miles east of here, Tom driving her, although he ought to be here to help father with all the work that there is to do about the farm. And I don't know if Mother will be able to get back before Sunday. If I were better and didn't have all this work of my own on my hands I would have to go too, I suppose, although Mother insists not.

Next, Emily and Tom, thinking all is going so well with me and that I might enjoy it, were having four girls and four boys come here to-night for a sort of June moon-party, with ice cream and cake to be made by Emily and Mother and myself. But now, poor dear, she has to do a lot of telephoning over Mr. Wilcox's phone, which we share, in order to put it off some day next week, if possible. And she's just heartsick and gloomy, of course.

As for myself, I'm trying to keep a stiff upper lip, as the saying is. But it's pretty hard, dear, I'll tell you. For so far I have only had three small telephone talks with you, saying that you didn't think you would have the necessary money before July fifth. And to put the finishing touches on it, as I only learned to-day, Mamma and Papa have about decided to go to my Uncle Charlie's in Hamilton for over the fourth (from the fourth to the fifteenth) and take me with them, unless I decide to return to Lycurgus, while Tom and Emily visit with my sister at Homer. But, dear, I can't do that, as you know. I'm too sick and worried. Last night I vomited dreadful and have been half dead on my feet all day, and I am just about crazy to-night.

Dear, what can we do? Can't you come for me before July third, which will be the time they will be going? You will have to come for me before then, really, because I just can't go up there with them. It's fifty miles from here. I could say I would go up there with them if only you would be sure to come for me before they start. But I must be absolutely sure that you are coming—absolutely.

Clyde, I have done nothing but cry since I got here. If you were only here I wouldn't feel so badly. I do try to be brave, dear, but how can I help thinking at times that you will never come for me when you haven't written me one single note and have only talked to me three times since I've been up here. But then I say to myself you couldn't be so mean as that, and especially since you have promised. Oh, you will come, won't you? Everything worries me so now, Clyde, for some reason and I'm so frightened, dear. I think of last summer and then this one, and all my dreams. It won't make any real difference to you about your coming a few days sooner than you intended, will it, dear? Even if we have to get along on a little less. I know that we can. I can be very saving and economical. I will try to have my dresses made by then. If not, I will do with what I have and finish them later. And I will try and be brave, dear, and not annoy you much, if only you will come. You must, you know, Clyde. It can't be any other way, although for your sake now I wish it could.

Please, please, Clyde, write and tell me that you will be here at the end of the time that you said. I worry so and get so lonesome off here all by myself. I will come straight back to you if you don't come by the time you said. I know you will not like me to say this, but, Clyde, I can't stay here and that's all there is to it. And I can't go away with Mamma and Papa either, so there is only one way out. I don't believe I will sleep a wink to-night, so please write me and in your letter tell me over and over not to worry about your not coming for me. If you could only come to-day, dear, or this week-end, I wouldn't feel so blue. But nearly two weeks more! Every one is in bed and the house is still, so I will stop.

But please write me, dear, right away, or if you won't do that call me up sure to-morrow, because I just can't rest one single minute until I do hear from you.

Your miserable ROBERTA.

P.S.: This is a horrid letter, but I just can't write a better one, I'm so blue.

But the day this letter arrived in Lycurgus Clyde was not there to answer it at once. And because of that, Roberta being in the darkest and most hysterical mood and thought, sat down on Saturday afternoon and, half-convinced as she was that he might already have departed for some distant point without any word to her, almost shrieked or screamed, if one were to properly characterize the mood that animated the following:

Biltz, Saturday, June 14th.

MY DEAR CLYDE:

I am writing to tell you that I am coming back to Lycurgus. I simply can't stay here any longer. Mamma worries and wonders why I cry so much, and I am just about sick. I know I promised to stay until the 25th or 26th, but then you said you would write me, but you never have—only an occasional telephone message when I am almost crazy. I woke up this morning and couldn't help crying right away and this afternoon my headache is dreadful.

I'm so afraid you won't come and I'm so frightened, dear. Please come and take me away some place, anywhere, so I can get out of here and not worry like I do. I'm so afraid in the state that I'm in that Papa and Mamma may make me tell the whole affair or that they will find it out for themselves.

Oh, Clyde, you will never know. You have said you would come, and sometimes I just know you will. But at other times I get to thinking about other things and I'm just as certain you won't, especially when you don't write or telephone. I wish you would write and say that you will come just so I can stand to stay here. Just as soon as you get this, I wish you would write me and tell me the exact day you can come—not later than the first, really, because I know I cannot stand to stay here any longer than then. Clyde, there isn't a girl in the whole world as miserable as I am, and you have made me so. But I don't mean that, either, dear. You were good to me once, and you are now, offering to come for me. And if you will come right away I will be so grateful. And when you read this, if you think I am unreasonable, please do not mind it, Clyde, but just think I am crazy with grief and worry and that I just don't know what to do. Please write me, Clyde. If you only knew how I need a word.

ROBERTA.

This letter, coupled as it was with a threat to come to Lycurgus, was sufficient to induce in Clyde a state not unlike Roberta's. To think that he had no additional, let alone plausible, excuse to offer Roberta whereby she could be induced to delay her final and imperative demand. He racked his brains. He must not write her any long and self-incriminating letters. That would be foolish in the face of his determination not to marry her. Besides his mood at the moment, so fresh from the arms and kisses of Sondra, was not for anything like that. He could not, even if he would.

At the same time, something must be done at once, as he could see, in order to allay her apparently desperate mood. And ten minutes after he had finished reading the last of these two letters, he was attempting to reach Roberta over the telephone. And finally getting her after a troublesome and impatient half-hour, he heard her voice, thin and rather querulous as it seemed to him at first, but really only because of a poor connection, saying: "Hello, Clyde, hello. Oh, I'm so glad you called. I've been terribly nervous. Did you get my two letters? I was just about to leave here in the morning if I didn't hear from you by then. I just couldn't stand not to hear anything. Where have you been, dear? Did you read what I said about my parents going away? That's true. Why don't you write, Clyde, or call me up anyhow? What about what I said in my letter about the third? Will you be sure and come then? Or shall I meet you somewhere? I've been so nervous the last three or four days, but now that I hear you again, maybe I'll be able to quiet down some. But I do wish you would write me a note every few days anyhow. Why won't you, Clyde? You haven't even written me once since I've been here. I can't tell you what a state I'm in and how hard it is to keep calm now."

Plainly Roberta was very nervous and fearsome as she talked. As a matter of fact, except that the home in which she was telephoning was deserted at the moment she was talking very indiscreetly, it seemed to Clyde. And it aided but little in his judgment for her to explain that she was all alone and that no one could hear her. He did not want her to use his name or refer to letters written to him.

Without talking too plainly, he now tried to make it clear that he was very busy and that it was hard for him to write as much as she might think necessary. Had he not said that he was coming on the 28th or thereabouts if he could? Well, he would if he could, only it looked now as though it might be necessary for him to postpone it for another week or so, until the seventh or eighth of July—long enough for him to get together an extra fifty for which he had a plan, and which would be necessary for him to have. But really, which was the thought behind this other, long enough for him to pay one more visit to Sondra as he was yearning to do, over the next week-end. But this demand of hers, now! Couldn't she go with her parents for a week or so and then let him come for her there or she come to him? It would give him more needed time, and——

But at this Roberta, bursting forth in a storm of nervous disapproval— saying that most certainly if that were the case she was going back to her room at the Gilpins', if she could get it, and not waste her time up there getting ready and waiting for him when he was not coming—he suddenly decided that he might as well say that he was coming on the third, or that if he did not, that at least by then he would have arranged with her where to meet him. For even by now, he had not made up his mind as to how he was to do. He must have a little more time to think—more time to think.

And so now he altered his tone greatly and said: "But listen, Bert. Please don't be angry with me. You talk as though I didn't have any troubles in connection with all this, either. You don't know what this may be going to cost me before I'm through with it, and you don't seem to care much. I know you're worried and all that, but what about me? I'm doing the very best I can now, Bert, with all I have to think about. And won't you just be patient now until the third, anyhow? Please do. I promise to write to you and if I don't, I'll call you up every other day. Will that be all right? But I certainly don't want you to be using my name like you did a while ago. That will lead to trouble, sure. Please don't. And when I call again, I'll just say it's Mr. Baker asking, see, and you can say it's any one you like afterwards. And then, if by any chance anything should come up that would stop our starting exactly on the third, why you can come back here if you want to, see, or somewhere near here, and then we can start as soon as possible after that."

His tone was so pleading and soothing, infused as it was—but because of his present necessity only with a trace of that old tenderness and seeming helplesness which, at times, had quite captivated Roberta, that even now it served to win her to a bizarre and groundless gratitude. So much so that at once she had replied, warmly and emotionally, even: "Oh, no, dear. I don't want to do anything like that. You know I don't. It's just because things are so bad as they are with me and I can't help myself now. You know that, Clyde, don't you? I can't help loving you. I always will, I suppose. And I don't want to do anything to hurt you, dear, really I don't if I can help it."

And Clyde, hearing the ring of genuine affection, and sensing anew his old-time power over her, was disposed to reënact the rôle of lover again, if only in order to dissuade Roberta from being too harsh and driving with him now. For while he could not like her now, he told himself, and could not think of marrying her, still in view of this other dream he could at least be gracious to her—could he not?—Pretend! And so this conversation ended with a new peace based on this agreement.

The preceding day—a day of somewhat reduced activities on the lakes from which he had just returned—he and Sondra and Stuart and Bertine, together with Nina Temple and a youth named Harley Baggott, then visiting the Thurstons, had motored first from Twelfth Lake to Three Mile Bay, a small lakeside resort some twenty-five miles north, and from thence, between towering walls of pines, to Big Bittern and some other small lakes lost in the recesses of the tall pines of the region to the north of Trine Lake. And en route, Clyde, as he now recalled, had been most strangely impressed at moments and in spots by the desolate and for the most part lonely character of the region. The narrow and rain-washed and even rutted nature of the dirt roads that wound between tall, silent and darksome trees—forests in the largest sense of the word—that extended for miles and miles apparently on either hand. The decadent and weird nature of some of the bogs and tarns on either side of the only comparatively passable dirt roads which here and there were festooned with funereal or viperous vines, and strewn like deserted battlefields with soggy and decayed piles of fallen and criss-crossed logs—in places as many as four deep—one above the other—in the green slime that an undrained depression in the earth had accumulated. The eyes and backs of occasional frogs that, upon lichen or vine or moss-covered stumps and rotting logs in this warm June weather, there sunned themselves apparently undisturbed; the spirals of gnats, the solitary flick of a snake's tail as disturbed by the sudden approach of the machine, one made off into the muck and the poisonous grasses and water-plants which were thickly imbedded in it.

And in seeing one of these Clyde, for some reason, had thought of the accident at Pass Lake. He did not realize it, but at the moment his own subconscious need was contemplating the loneliness and the usefulness at times of such a lone spot as this. And at one point it was that a wier-wier, one of the solitary water-birds of this region, uttered its ouphe and barghest cry, flying from somewhere near into some darker recess within the woods. And at this sound it was that Clyde had stirred nervously and then sat up in the car. It was so very different to any bird-cry he had ever heard anywhere.

"What was that?" he asked of Harley Baggott, who sat next him.

"What?"

"Why, that bird or something that just flew away back there just now?"

"I didn't hear any bird."

"Gee! That was a queer sound. It makes me feel creepy."

As interesting and impressive as anything else to him in this almost tenantless region had been the fact that there were so many lonesome lakes, not one of which he had ever heard of before. The territory through which they were speeding as fast as the dirt roads would permit, was dotted with them in these deep forests of pine. And only occasionally in passing near one, were there any signs indicating a camp or lodge, and those to be reached only by some half-blazed trail or rutty or sandy road disappearing through darker trees. In the main, the shores of the more remote lakes passed, were all but untenanted, or so sparsely that a cabin or a distant lodge to be seen across the smooth waters of some pine-encircled gem was an object of interest to all.

Why must he think of that other lake in Massachusetts! That boat! The body of that girl found—but not that of the man who accompanied her! How terrible, really!

He recalled afterwards,—here in his room, after his last conversation with Roberta—that the car, after a few more miles, had finally swung into an open space at the north end of a long narrow lake—the south prospect of which appeared to be divided by a point or an island suggesting a greater length and further windings or curves than were visible from where the car had stopped. And except for the small lodge and boathouse at this upper end it had appeared so very lonesome—not a launch or canoe on it at the time their party arrived. And as in the case of all the other lakes seen this day, the

banks to the very shore line were sentineled with those same green pines—
tall, spear-shaped—their arms widespread like one outside his window here
in Lycurgus. And beyond them in the distance, to the south and west, rose
the humped and still smooth and green backs of the nearer Adirondacks.
And the water before them, now ruffled by a light wind and glowing in the
afternoon sun, was of an intense Prussian blue, almost black, which suggested, as was afterwards confirmed by a guide who was lounging upon the
low veranda of the small inn—that it was very deep—"all of seventy feet not
more than a hundred feet out from that boathouse."

And at this point Harley Baggott, who was interested to learn more about
the fishing possibilities of this lake in behalf of his father, who contemplated
coming to this region in a few days, had inquired of the guide who appeared
not to look at the others in the car: "How long is this lake, anyhow?"

"Oh, about seven miles." "Any fish in it?" "Throw a line in and see. The
best place for black bass and the like of that almost anywhere around here.
Off the island down yonder, or just to the south of it round on the other side
there, there's a little bay that's said to be one of the best fishin' holes in any
of the lakes up this way. I've seen a coupla men bring back as many as
seventy-five fish in two hours. That oughta satisfy anybody that ain't tryin' to
ruin the place for the rest of us."

The guide, a thinnish, tall and wizened type, with a long, narrow head
and small, keen, bright blue eyes laughed a yokelish laugh as he studied the
group. "Not thinkin' of tryin' your luck to-day?"

"No, just inquiring for my dad. He's coming up here next week, maybe. I
want to see about accommodations."

"Well, they ain't what they are down to Racquette, of course, but then
the fish down there ain't what they are up here, either." He visited all with
a sly and wry and knowing smile.

Clyde had never seen the type before. He was interested by all the
anomalies and contrarities of this lonesome world as contrasted with cities he
had known almost exclusively, as well as the decidedly exotic and material
life and equipment with which, at the Cranstons' and elsewhere, he was then
surrounded. The strange and comparatively deserted nature of this region as
contrasted with the brisk and vigorous life of Lycurgus, less than a hundred
miles to the south.

"The country up here kills me," commented Stuart Finchley at this point.
"It's so near the Chain and yet it's so different, scarcely any one living up
here at all, it seems."

"Well, except for the camps in summer and the fellows that come up to
hunt moose and deer in the fall, there ain't much of anybody or anything
around here after September first," commented the guide. "I've been guidin'
and trappin' for nigh onto seventeen years now around here and 'cept for
more and more people around some of the lakes below here—the Chain
principally in summer—I ain't see much change. You need to know this

country purty well if yer goin't strike out anywhere away from the main roads, though o' course about five miles to the west o' here is the railroad. Gun Lodge is the station. We bring 'em by bus from there in the summer. And from the south end down there is a sorta road leadin' down to Greys Lake and Three Mile Bay. You musta come along a part of it, since it's the only road up into this country as yet. They're talkin' of cuttin' one through to Long Lake sometime, but so far it's mostly talk. But from most of these other lakes around here, there's no road at all, not that an automobile could make. Just trails and there's not even a decent camp on some o' 'em. You have to bring your own outfit. But Ellis and me was over to Gun Lake last summer—that's thirty miles west o' here and we had to walk every inch of the way and carry our packs. But, oh, say, the fishin' and moose and deer come right down to the shore in places to drink. See 'em as plain as that stump across the lake."

And Clyde remembered that, along with the others, he had carried away the impression that for solitude and charm—or at least mystery—this region could scarcely be matched. And to think it was all so comparatively near Lycurgus—not more than a hundred miles by road; not more than seventy by rail, as he eventually came to know.

But now once more in Lycurgus and back in his room after just explaining to Roberta, as he had, he once more encountered on his writing desk, the identical paper containing the item concerning the tragedy at Pass Lake. And in spite of himself, his eye once more followed nervously and yet unwaveringly to the last word all the suggestive and provocative details. The uncomplicated and apparently easy way in which the lost couple had first arrived at the boathouse; the commonplace and entirely unsuspicious way in which they had hired a boat and set forth for a row; the manner in which they had disappeared to the north end; and the then the upturned boat, the floating oars and hats near the shore. He stood reading in the still strong evening light. Outside the windows were the dark boughs of the fir tree of which he had thought the preceding day and which now suggested all those firs and pines about the shores of Big Bittern.

But, good God! What was he thinking of anyhow? He, Clyde Griffiths! The nephew of Samuel Griffiths! What was "getting into" him? Murder! That's what it was. This terrible item—this devil's accident or machination that was constantly putting it before him! A most horrible crime, and one for which they electrocuted people if they were caught. Besides, he could not murder anybody—not Roberta, anyhow. Oh, no! Surely not after all that had been between them. And yet—this other world!—Sondra—which he was certain to lose now unless he acted in some way——

His hands shook, his eyelids twitched—then his hair at the roots tingled and over his body ran chill nervous titillations in waves. Murder! Or upsetting a boat at any rate in deep water, which of course might happen anywhere, and by accident, as at Pass Lake. And Roberta could not swim. He

knew that. But she might save herself at that—scream—cling to the boat—
and then—if there were any to hear—and she told afterwards! An icy perspiration now sprang to his forehead; his lips trembled and suddenly his throat
felt parched and dry. To prevent a thing like that he would have to—to—
but no—he was not like that. He could not do a thing like that—hit any
one—a girl—Roberta—and when drowning or struggling. Oh, no, no—no
such thing as that! Impossible.

He took his straw hat and went out, almost before any one heard him
think, as he would have phrased it to himself, such horrible, terrible
thoughts. He could not and would not think them from now on. He was no
such person. And yet—and yet—these thoughts. The solution—if he wanted
one. The way to stay here—not leave—marry Sondra—be rid of Roberta
and all—all—for the price of a little courage or daring. But no!

He walked and walked—away from Lycurgus—out on a road to the
southeast which passed through a poor and decidedly unfrequented rural
section, and so left him alone to think—or, as he felt, not to be heard in his
thinking.

Day was fading into dark. Lamps were beginning to glow in the cottages
here and there. Trees in groups in fields or along the road were beginning to
blur or smokily blend. And although it was warm—the air lifeless and lethargic—he walked fast, thinking, and perspiring as he did so, as though he were
seeking to outwalk and outthink or divert some inner self that preferred to
be still and think.

That gloomy, lonely lake up there!

That island to the south!

Who would see?

Who could hear?

That station at Gun Lodge with a bus running to it at this season of the
year. (Ah, he remembered that, did he? The deuce!) A terrible thing, to
remember a thing like that in connection with such a thought as this! But if
he were going to think of such a thing as this at all, he had better think
well—he could tell himself that—or stop thinking about it now—once and
forever—forever. But Sondra! Roberta! If ever he were caught—electrocuted! And yet the actual misery of his present state. The difficulty! The
danger of losing Sondra. And yet, murder—

He wiped his hot and wet face, and paused and gazed at a group of trees
across a field which somehow reminded him of the trees of . . . well . . . he
didn't like this road. It was getting too dark out here. He had better turn and
go back. But that road at the south and leading to Three Mile Bay and Greys
Lake—if one chose to go that way—to Sharon and the Cranston Lodge—
whither he would be going afterwards if he did go that way. God! Big
Bittern—the trees along there after dark would be like that—blurred and
gloomy. It would have to be toward evening, of course. No one would think
of trying to . . . well . . . in the morning, when there was so much light. Only

a fool would do that. But at night, toward dusk, as it was now, or a little later. But, damn it, he would not listen to such thoughts. Yet no one would be likely to see him or Roberta either—would they—there? It would be so easy to go to a place like Big Bittern—for an alleged wedding trip—would it not—over the Fourth, say—or after the fourth or fifth, when there would be fewer people. And to register as some one else—not himself—so that he could never be traced that way. And then, again, it would be so easy to get back to Sharon and the Cranstons' by midnight, or the morning of the next day, maybe, and then, once there he could pretend also that he had come north on that early morning train that arrived about ten o'clock. And then . . .

Confound it—why should his mind keep dwelling on this idea? Was he actually planning to do a thing like this? But he was not! He could not be! He, Clyde Griffiths, could not be serious about a thing like this. That was not possible. He could not be. Of course! It was all too impossible, too wicked, to imagine that he, Clyde Griffiths, could bring himself to execute a deed like that. And yet . . .

And forthwith an uncanny feeling of wretchedness and insufficiency for so dark a crime insisted on thrusting itself forward. He decided to retrace his steps toward Lycurgus, where at least he could be among people.

CHAPTER XLV

There are moments when in connection with the sensitively imaginative or morbidly anachronistic—the mentality assailed and the same not of any great strength and the problem confronting it of sufficient force and complexity— the reason not actually toppling from its throne, still totters or is warped or shaken—the mind befuddled to the extent that for the time being, at least, unreason or disorder and mistaken or erroneous counsel would appear to hold against all else. In such instances the will and the courage confronted by some great difficulty which it can neither master not endure, appears in some to recede in precipitate flight, leaving only panic and temporary unreason in its wake.

And in this instance, the mind of Clyde might well have been compared to a small and routed army in full flight before a major one, yet at various times in its precipitate departure, pausing for a moment to meditate on some way of escaping complete destruction and in the coincident panic of such a state, resorting to the weirdest and most haphazard of schemes of escaping from an impending and yet wholly unescapable fate. The strained and bedeviled look in his eyes at moments—the manner in which, from moment to moment and hour to hour, he went over and over his hitherto poorly balanced actions and thoughts but with no smallest door of escape anywhere. And yet again at moments the solution suggested by the item in *The Times-*

Union again thrusting itself forward, psychogenetically, born of his own turbulent, eager and disappointed seeking. And hence persisting.

Indeed, it was now as though from the depths of some lower or higher world never before guessed or plumbed by him . . . a region otherwhere than in life or death and peopled by creatures otherwise than himself . . . there had now suddenly appeared, as the genii at the accidental rubbing of Aladdin's lamp—as the efrit emerging as smoke from the mystic jar in the net of the fisherman—the very substance of some leering and diabolic wish or wisdom concealed in his own nature, and that now abhorrent and yet compelling, leering and yet intriguing, friendly and yet cruel, offered him a choice between an evil which threatened to destroy him (and against his deepest opposition) and a second evil which, however it might disgust or sear or terrify, still provided for freedom and success and love.

Indeed the center or mentating section of his brain at this time might well have been compared to a sealed and silent hall in which alone and undisturbed, and that in spite of himself, he now sat thinking on the mystic or evil and terrifying desires or advice of some darker or primordial and unregenerate nature of his own, and without the power to drive the same forth or himself to decamp, and yet also without the courage to act upon anything.

For now the genii of his darkest and weakest side was speaking. And it said: "And would you escape from the demands of Roberta that but now and unto this hour have appeared unescapable to you? Behold! I bring you a way. It is the way of the lake—Pass Lake. This item that you have read—do you think it was placed in your hands for nothing? Remember Big Bittern, the deep, blue-black water, the island to the south, the lone road to Three Mile Bay? How suitable to your needs! A rowboat or a canoe upset in such a lake and Roberta would pass forever from your life. She cannot swim! The lake—the lake—that you have seen—that I have shown you—is it not ideal for the purpose? So removed and so little frequented and yet comparatively near—but a hundred miles from here. And how easy for you and Roberta to go there—not directly but indirectly—on this purely imaginative marriage-trip that you have already agreed to. And all that you need do now is to change your name—and hers—or let her keep her own and you use yours. You have never permitted her to speak of you and this relationship, and she never has. You have written her but formal notes. And now if you should meet her somewhere as you have already agreed to, and without any one seeing you, you might travel with her, as in the past to Fonda, to Big Bittern—or some point near there."

"But there is no hotel at Big Bittern," at once corrected Clyde. "A mere shack that entertains but few people and that not very well."

"All the better. The less people are likely to be there."

"But we might be seen on the train going up together. I would be identified as having been with her."

"Were you seen at Fonda, Gloversville, Little Falls? Have you not ridden in separate cars or seats before and could you not do so now? Is it not presumably to be a secret marriage? Then why not a secret honeymoon?"

"True enough—true enough."

"And once you have arranged for that and arrive at Big Bittern or some lake like it—there are so many there—how easy to row out on such a lake? No questions. No registry under your own name or hers. A boat rented for an hour or half-day or day. You saw the island far to the south on that lone lake. Is it not beautiful? It is well worth seeing. Why should you not go there on such a pleasure trip before marriage? Would she not be happy, so to do—as weary and distressed as she is now—an outing—a rest before the ordeal of the new life? Is not that sensible—plausible? And neither of you will ever return presumably. You will both be drowned, will you not? Who is to see? A guide or two—the man who rents you the boat—the innkeeper once, as you go. But how are they to know who you are? Or who she is? And you heard the depth of the water."

"But I do not want to kill her. I do not want to kill her. I do not want to injure her in any way. If she will but let me go and she go her own way, I will be so glad and so happy never to see her more."

"But she will not let you go or go her way unless you accompany her. And if you go yours, it will be without Sondra and all that she represents, as well as all this pleasant life here—your standing with your uncle, his friends, their cars, the dances, visits to the lodges on the lakes. And what then? A small job! Small pay! Another such period of wandering as followed that accident at Kansas City. Never another chance like this anywhere. Do you prefer that?"

"But might there not be some accident here, destroying all my dreams—my future—as there was in Kansas City?"

"An accident, to be sure—but not the same. In this instance the plan is in your hands. You can arrange it all as you will. And how easy! So many boats upsetting every summer—the occupants of them drowning, because in most cases they cannot swim. And will it ever be known whether the man who was with Roberta Alden on Big Bittern could swim? And of all deaths, drowning is the easiest—no noise—no outcry—perhaps the accidental blow of an oar—the side of a boat. And then silence! Freedom—a body that no one may ever find. Or if found and identified, will it not be easy, if you but trouble to plan, to make it appear that you were elsewhere, visiting at one of the other lakes before you decided to go to Twelfth Lake. What is wrong with it? Where is the flaw?"

"But assuming that I should upset the boat and that she should not drown, then what? Should cling to it, cry out, be saved and relate afterward that . . . But no, I cannot do that—will not do it. I will not hit her. That would be too terrible . . . too vile."

"But a little blow—any little blow under such circumstances would be sufficient to confuse and complete her undoing. Sad, yes, but she has an opportunity to go her own way, has she not? And she will not, nor let you go yours. Well, then, is this so terribly unfair? And do not forget that afterwards there is Sondra—the beautiful—a home with her in Lycurgus—wealth, a high position such as elsewhere you may never obtain again—never—never. Love and happiness—the equal of any one here—superior even to your cousin Gilbert."

The voice ceased temporarily, trailing off into shadow,—silence, dreams.

And Clyde, contemplating all that had been said, was still unconvinced. Darker fears or better impulses supplanted the counsel of the voice in the great hall. But presently thinking of Sondra and all that she represented, and then of Roberta, the dark personality would as suddenly and swiftly return and with amplified suavity and subtlety.

"Ah, still thinking on the matter. And you have not found a way out and you will not. I have truly pointed out to you and in all helpfulness the only way—the only way—It is a long lake. And would it not be easy in rowing about to eventually find some secluded spot—some invisible nook near that south shore where the water is deep? And from here how easy to walk through the woods to Three Mile Bay and Upper Greys Lake? And from here to the Cranstons'? There is a boat from there, as you know. Pah—how cowardly—how lacking in courage to win the thing that above all things you desire—beauty—wealth—position—the solution of your every material and spiritual desire. And with poverty, commonplace, hard and poor work as the alternative to all this."

"But you must choose—choose! And then act. You must! You must! You must!

Thus the voice in parting, echoing from some remote part of the enormous chamber.

And Clyde, listening at first with horror and in terror, later with a detached and philosophic calm as one who, entirely apart from what he may think or do, is still entitled to consider even the wildest and most desperate proposals for his release, at last, because of his own mental and material weakness before pleasures and dreams which he could not bring himself to forego, psychically intrigued to the point where he was beginning to think that it might be possible. Why not? Was it not even as the voice said—a possible and plausible way—all his desires and dreams to be made real by this one evil thing? Yet in his case, because of flaws and weaknesses in his own unstable and highly variable will, the problem was not to be solved by thinking thus—then—nor for the next ten days for that matter.

He could not really act on such a matter for himself and would not. It remained as usual for him to be forced either to act or to abandon this most *wild* and terrible thought. Yet during this time a series of letters—seven from Roberta, five from Sondra—in which in somber tones in so far as Roberta was concerned—in gay and colorful ones in those which came from Sondra—was painted the now so sharply contrasting phases of the black rebus which lay before him. To Roberta's pleadings, argumentative and threatening as they were, Clyde did not trust himself to reply, not even by telephone. For now he reasoned that to answer would be only to lure Roberta to her doom—or to the attempted drastic conclusion of his difficulties as outlined by the tragedy at Pass Lake.

At the same time, in several notes addressed to Sondra, he gave vent to the most impassioned declaration of love—his darling—his wonder girl—how eager he was to be at Twelfth Lake by the morning of the Fourth, if he could, and so thrilled to see her there again. Yet, alas, as he also wrote now, so uncertain was he, even now, as to how he was to do, there were certain details in connection with his work here that might delay him a day or two or three—he could not tell as yet—but would write her by the second at the latest, when he would know positively. Yet saying to himself as he wrote this, if she but knew what those details were—if she but knew. Yet in penning this, and without having as yet answered the last importunate letter from Roberta, he was also saying to himself that this did not mean that he was planning to go to Roberta at all, or that if he did, it did not mean that he was going to attempt to kill her. Never once did he honestly, or to put it more accurately, forthrightly and courageously or coldly face the thought of committing so grim a crime. On the contrary, the nearer he approached a final resolution or the need for one in connection with all this, the more hideous and terrible seemed the idea—hideous and difficult, and hence the more improbable it seemed that he should ever commit it. It was true that from moment to moment—arguing with himself as he constantly was—sweating mental sweats and fleeing from moral and social terrors in connection with it all, he was thinking from time to time that he might go to Big Bittern in order to quiet her in connection with these present importunities and threats and hence (once more evasion—tergiversation with himself) give himself more time in which to conclude what his true course must be.

The way of the Lake.

The way of the Lake.

But once there—whether it would then be advisable so to do—or not—well who could tell. He might even yet be able to convert Roberta to some other point of view. For, say what you would, she was certainly acting very unfairly and captiously in all this. She was, as he saw it in connection with his very vital dream of Sondra, making a mountain—an immense terror—out of a state that when all was said and done, was not so different from Esta's. And Esta had not compelled any one to marry her. And how much better were the Aldens to his own parents—poor farmers as compared to poor preachers. And why should he be so concerned as to what they would think when Esta had not troubled to think what her parents would feel?

In spite of all that Roberta had said about blame, was she so entirely lacking in blame herself? To be sure, he had sought to entice or seduce her, as you will, but even so, could she be held entirely blameless? Could she not have refused, if she was so positive at the time that she was so very moral?

But she had not. And as to all this, all that he had done, had he not done all he could to help her out of it? And he had so little money, too. And was placed in such a difficult position. She was just as much to blame as he was. And yet now she was so determined to drive him this way. To insist on his marrying her, whereas if she would only go her own way—as she could with his help—she might still save both of them all this trouble.

But no, she would not, and he would not marry her and that was all there was to it. She need not think that she could make him. No, no, no! At times, when in such moods, he felt that he could do anything—drown her easily enough, and she would only have herself to blame.

Then again his more cowering sense of what society would think and do, if it knew, what he himself would be compelled to think of himself afterwards, fairly well satisfied him that as much as he desired to stay, he was not the one to do anything at all and in consequence must flee.

And so it was that Tuesday, Wednesday and Thursday following Roberta's letter received on Monday, had passed. And then, on Thursday night, following a most torturesome mental day on his and Roberta's part for that matter, this is what he received:

Biltz, Wednesday, June 30th.

DEAR CLYDE:

This to to tell you that unless I hear from you either by telephone or letter before noon, Friday, I shall be in Lycurgus that same night, and the world will know how you have treated me. I cannot and will not wait and suffer one more hour. I regret to be compelled to take this step, but you have allowed all this time to go in silence really, and Saturday is the third, and without any plans of any kind. My whole life is ruined and so will yours be in a measure, but I cannot feel that I am entirely to blame. I have done all I possibly could to make this burden as easy for you as possible and I certainly regret all the misery it will cause my parents and friends and all whom you know and hold dear. But I will not wait and suffer one hour more.

ROBERTA.

And with this in his hands, he was finally all but numbed by the fact that now decidedly he must act. She was actually coming! Unless he could soothe or restrain her in some manner she would be here to-morrow—the second. And yet the second, or the third, or any time until after the Fourth, was no time to leave with her. The holiday crowds would be too great. There would be too many people to see—to encounter. There must be more secrecy. He must have at least a little more time in which to get ready. He must think now quickly and then act. Great God! Get ready. Could he not telephone her and say that he had been sick or so worried on account of the necessary money or something that he could not write—and that besides his uncle had sent for him to come to Greenwood Lake over the Fourth. His uncle! His uncle! No, that would not do. He had used his name too much. What difference should it make to him or her now, whether he saw his uncle once more or not? He was leaving once and for all, or so he had been telling her, on her account, was he not? And so he had better say that he was going to his uncle, in order to give reason why he was going away so that, possibly, he might be able to return in a year or so. She might believe that. At any rate he must tell her something that would quiet her until after the Fourth—make her stay up there until at least he could perfect some plan—bring himself to the place where he could do one thing or the other. One thing or the other.

Without pausing to plan anything more than just this at this time, he hurried to the nearest telephone where he was least likely to be overheard. And, getting her once more, began one of those long and evasive and, in this instance, ingratiating explanations which eventually, after he had insisted that he had actually been sick—confined to his room with a fever and hence not able to get to a telephone—and because, as he now said, he had finally decided that it would be best if he were to make some explanation to his uncle, so that he might return some time in the future, if necessary—he, by using the most pleading, if not actually affectionate, tones and asking her to consider what a state he had been in, too, was able not only to make her believe that there was some excuse for his delay and silence, but also to introduce the plan that he now had in mind; which was if only she could wait until the sixth, then assuredly, without fail as to any particular, he would meet her at any place she would choose to come—Homer, Fonda, Lycurgus, Little Falls—only since they were trying to keep everything so secret, he would suggest that she come to Fonda on the morning of the sixth in order to make the noon train for Utica. There they could spend the night since they could not very well discuss and decide on their plans over the telephone, now, and then they could act upon whatever they had decided. Besides he could tell her better then just how he thought they ought to do. He had an idea—a little trip maybe, somewhere before they got married or after, just as she wished, but—something nice anyhow—(his voice grew husky and his knees and hands shook slightly as he said this, only Roberta could not detect the sudden perturbation within him). But she must not ask him now. He could not tell her over the phone. But as sure as anything, at noon on the sixth, he would be on the station platform at Fonda. All she had to do after seeing him was to buy her ticket to Utica and get in one coach, and he would buy his separately and get in another—the one just ahead or behind hers. On the way down, if she didn't see him at the station beforehand, he would pass through her car for a drink so that she could see that he was there—no more than that—but she mustn't speak to him. Then once in Utica, she should check her bag and he would follow her out to the nearest quiet corner. After that he would go and get her bag, and then they could go to some little hotel and he would take care of all the rest.

But she must do this. Would she have that much faith in him? If so, he would call her up on the third—the very next day—and on the morning of the sixth—sure, so that both he and she would know that everything was all right—that she was starting and that he would be there. What was that? Her trunk? The little one? Sure. If she needed it, certainly bring it. Only, if he were she, he would not trouble to try to bring too much now, because once she was settled somewhere, it would be easy enough to send for anything else that she really needed.

As Clyde stood at the telephone in a small outlying drug store and talked—the lonely proprietor buried in a silly romance among his pots and phials at the back—it seemed as though the Giant Efrit that had previously materialized in the silent halls of his brain, was once more here at his elbow—that he himself, cold and numb and fearsome, was being talked through—not actually talking himself.

Go to the lake which you visited with Sondra!

Get travel folders of the region there from either the Lycurgus House here or the depot.

Go to the south end of it and from there walk south, afterwards.

Pick a boat that will upset easily—one with a round bottom, such as those you have seen here at Crum Lake and up there.

Buy a new and different hat and leave that on the water—one that cannot be traced to you. You might even tear the lining out of it so that it cannot be traced.

Pack all of your things in your trunk here, but leave it, so that swiftly, in the event that anything goes wrong, you can return here and get it and depart.

And take only such things with you as will make it seem as though you were going for an outing to Twelfth Lake—not away, so that should you be sought at Twelfth Lake, it will look as though you had gone only there, not elsewhere.

Tell her that you intend to marry her, but *after* you return from this outing, not before.

And if necessary strike a light blow, so as to stun her—no more—so that falling in the water, she will drown the more easily.

Do not fear!

Do not be weak!

Walk through the woods by night, not by day—so that when seen again you will be in Three Mile Bay or Sharon—and can say that you came from Racquette or Long Lake south, or from Lycurgus north.

Use a false name and alter your handwriting as much as possible.

Assume that you will be successful.

And whisper, whisper—let your language be soft, your tone tender, loving, even. It must be, if you are to win her to your will now.

So the Efrit of his own darker self.

EZRA POUND

(1885-1970)

Born in Hailey, Idaho (his father was a gold assayer), Ezra Pound spent his childhood in a Philadelphia suburb, entered the University of Pennsylvania at 15, transferred to Hamilton College from which he graduated, returned to Penn for an M.A. degree in Romance Languages, and set out on a conventional academic career in a teaching job at Wabash College in Indiana. The career was over almost before it began, for Pound quickly offended local proprieties. He smoked, he entertained women in his apartment, and he was fired. At once the poet-to-be left for Europe on a cattle boat, made his way to Venice, and set up a volume of poems called *A Lume Spento* (1908). A year later, in London, he was immersed in the round of activities—writing

Individual volumes of poetry include *A Lume Spento,* 1908: *A Quinzaine for This Yule,* 1908; *Personae,* 1909, enlarged from 1913 to 1926; *Exultations,* 1909; *Provenca,* 1910; *Canzoni,* 1911; *The Sonnets and Ballate of Guido Calvacanti,* 1912; *Ripostes,* 1912, rev., 1915; *Personae and Exultations,* 1913; *Cathay,* 1915; *Lustra,* 1916; *Quiz Pauper Amavi,* c. 1919; *Hugh Selwyn Mauberley,* 1920; *Umbra,* 1920; *Poems 1918-1921,* 1921; *Personae; The Collected Poems,* 1926; *Homage to Sextus Propertius,* 1934. Selected editions of the poems are *Selected Poems,* ed. T. S. Eliot, 1928, 1959, and *Selected Poems,* 1957. *The Cantos* appeared in 1964 and *Selected Cantos* in 1970.

Pound's criticism includes *Gaudier-Brzeska,* 1910: *Pavannes and Divisions,* 1918; *Instigations,* 1920; *Indiscretions, An Autobiography,* 1923; *The ABC of Reading,* 1934; *Culture,* 1938; *Money Pamphlets by Pound,* 1950-1952; *Pavannes and Divagations,* 1958; *The Literary Essays of Ezra Pound,* ed. T. S. Eliot. D. D. Paige edited *The Letters of Ezra Pound,* 1950 and Forest Read edited *Pound/Joyce: Letters and Essays,* 1967.

The bibliographies are Donald Gallup,

ed., *A Bibliography of Ezra Pound,* 1963 and Gary Lane, ed., *A Concordance to Personae: The Shorter Poems of Ezra Pound,* 1972. Two biographies are Charles Norman, *Ezra Pound,* 1960, rev., 1969 and Noel Stock, *The Life of Ezra Pound.* Mary di Rachewiltz's *Discretions* is a more personal account.

Critical studies are T. S. Eliot's *Ezra Pound: His Metric and Poetry,* 1917; R. P. Blackmur, "Masks of Ezra Pound" in *The Double Agent,* 1935; Alice Admur, *The Poetry of Ezra Pound, 1936;* Peter Russell, ed., *The Examination of Ezra Pound,* 1950; John Espey, *Ezra Pound's Mauberley,* 1955; George Dekker, *The Cantos of Ezra Pound: A Critical Study,* 1963; Noel Stock, *Poet in Exile,* 1964; N. Christoph de Nagy, *Ezra Pound's Poetics and Literary Tradition: The Critical Decade, 1966;* Daniel P. Pearlman, *The Barb of Time: On the Unity of Ezra Pound's "Cantos," 1969.* Good general criticism may be found in Hugh Kenner, *The Poetry of Ezra Pound,* 1951; Walter Sutton, ed., *Ezra Pound: A Collection of Critical Essays,* 1963; K. L. Godwin, *The Influence of Ezra Pound,* 1966; Christine Brooke-Rose, *An ABC of Ezra Pound,* 1971; Hugh Kenner, *The Pound Era,* 1972.

poems, reviews, essays, manifestoes, founding "movements," pressing the claims of gifted contemporaries—that resulted in a literary revolution in English.

Pound's interests from the start were linguistic, historical, and theoretical. His first published critical writing, *The Spirit of Romance* (1910), was a survey of medieval and later literature in the Romance languages. Even as it appeared he was promulgating, enthusiastically, the doctrines of Imagism. (As summarized by a colleague at the time, Pound's imagistic principles called for: "1. Direct treatment of the thing, whether subjective or objective. 2. [The use of] absolutely no word that did not contribute to the presentation. 3. [Composition] in sequence of the musical phrase, not in sequence of a metronome.") Speculation about the image in poetry led on to speculation about fundamental affinities among the arts of music, literature, painting, and sculpture; Pound joined with the writer and painter Wyndham Lewis to found a new multidimensional aesthetic movement called Vorticism. The motives and aspirations shaping these enterprises were continuous with those that stimulated Pound to begin translating Japanese Noh plays and Chinese poems (1912–1913) and to work over the Japanese translations and manuscripts of Ernest Fenellosa, a Harvard-educated "gentleman-scholar" who, before his death in 1908, had been Commissioner of Arts for the Imperial Japanese Government. Pound was never one to shed interests; he perceived new relationships among them, worked as with a map of felt cultural unities. In the second decade of the twentieth century his literary studies—pursued in London, Paris, Northern Italy, the South of France—embraced music, Provencal poetry, Chinese and Japanese letters, nineteenth-century symbolist poetry and criticism, ninth-century Anglo-Saxon poetry, and the great translators of the Elizabethan era. And it was these literary and cultural studies that served as the genesis of his most ambitious poetic work, *The Cantos,* which was also begun in this period.

In many respects the decisive moment of Pound's life came in the 1920's when he and his wife moved to Rapallo, Italy. He was soon to be engaged in producing work of culture criticism influenced by the ideas about money, credit, and economic history advanced by Major C. H. Douglas, theorist of "Social Credit." And the combination of these ideas, a powerful feeling of self-worth sanctified by art, and some shrewd flattery of the poet by Mussolini himself teased Pound on toward treachery. During World War II he broadcast for Rome Radio a series of talks developing his ideas about usury; more than once he descended into anti-Semitism; he was subsequently indicted as a traitor by the United States, imprisoned in a barbed wire cage near Pisa by the U.S. Army; at length, in the winter of 1945, on the eve of his trial as a traitor, he was pronounced insane and incarcerated in St. Elizabeth's Hospital in Washington. A few years later he was awarded the important Bollingen Poetry Prize by the Fellows of the Library of Congress, an event that triggered one of this country's noisiest literary squabbles. The noise diminished and Pound was forgotten almost for a decade. A well-judged approach to President Eisenhower by the poet Archibald MacLeish, aided by Frost, Hemingway, and others, finally won his release in 1958. The poet returned to Rapallo where he lived on in relative silence, receiving an occasional literary pilgrim, and dying at 85.

Critics hostile to Ezra Pound usually focus first on his moral and political offenses—his embrace of Fascism, his anti-Semitism, the mean arrogance toward "inferiors" that seems to lie close to the very center of his character. But moral complaints are by no means the only kind that have been registered. A number of his earlier major poems— "Hugh Selwyn Mauberley," for one—have been harshly treated for structural failures. The wilful obscurantism of *The Cantos,* their assumption that every reader will, of course, possess the layered knowledge of Italian art, Chinese philosophy, money and banking in the American federalist and later periods, and a dozen other subjects (matters Pound himself learned of through a lifetime of study) has been much berated. So, too, have various howlers Pound committed as a translator of Latin and Anglo-Saxon texts insufficiently conversant with the original tongues.

The case for Pound begins with his services to the great writers of his age, some of whom conceivably might never have surfaced had it not been for his advocacy. It was Pound who fought for a hearing for Eliot and Joyce, finding publishers for both and financial backing for Joyce. It was Pound who, by an act of genius, editing and persuasion, transformed Eliot's "The Waste Land" from a loose-limbed, tonally uncertain, autobiographical ramble into a perfectly controlled work of poetic art. It was Pound who, almost simultaneously, taught W. B. Yeats how to disengage from the abstractions of Celtic twilight, how to talk straight, from a genuine center of feeling, in a poem. It was Pound who helped Frost and Hemingway, who energized the hopes and talents of a dozen important writers and artists of his time, and who won the battle for public acceptance of these talents as chief voices of their age. (Marshall McLuhan once wrote that "Mr. Pound brought to letters the evangelical public spirit of the American town-meeting.")

A different line of praise stresses Pound's claim as a prophet. A half century before the Zen generation, Pound had turned his eyes (and those of many other artists) eastward. A half-century before the notion of the translator as seeker-out of the spirit of the original instead of as a mere word-for-word literalist won acceptance, Pound was freely recreating the ancients. A half-century before open poetic forms were commonplace, Pound had launched his own immensely ambitious experiment in the field. The poet's best and subtlest modern critic, Professor Hugh Kenner, has remarked that Pound is "very likely, in ways controversy still hides, the contemporary of our grandchildren." Many "men of the future," from Frank Lloyd Wright to Buckminster Fuller, have spoken admiringly of him.

More important than any of this perhaps is Pound's capacity, as poet, critic, historian, musician, artisan (in youth and in old age this "maker" designed and built his own furniture) to communicate passion for the well-made thing, certainty that decent work is the surest redeemer. There is sadness, and worse, in the spectacle of Pound in the labyrinth, struggling to put together a version of cultural history that would allow him to claim for "quality of labor" all that he knew should be claimed for it—struggling, declining all too quickly into barely coherent polemics against usury, ending in Jew-baiting both disgusting and cruel. There is sadness, too, that a man who burst on his moment as an incredible surge of energy on behalf of the new, the emergent, should have become, in his best poetry, an elegist, a voice of lament for the death of the best: "Tudor indeed is gone and every rose. . . ." In truth the work of Ezra Pound is an infested ruin, grandeur enclosing ponds of sick air. Line on line come extraordinary purities of sound, perfected continuities, language matchlessly sculptured, to use a verb lately put in play by a sympathetic critic. Superb bits of historical reconstruction show themselves forth at a hundred turns. And the entire edifice is somehow not rotten, despite all, in its foundations. Belief that the whole way of life of a society finds expression in every verse, every artifact, every transaction; belief that the hope of human dignity is best nourished by honorable labor honorably paid; belief that money-madness is the most fearful killer on earth: these are the roots of Pound's ultimate argument, and they are not diseased. A dramatic monologist in his early years, an inventor of personae, this poet was moving on from the example of Browning, who had invented a character certain of the desirability that man's reach should exceed his grasp. Pound's grasp was overambitious, and his arrogance hateful, but the man did make a revolution, and there is only a little in this ruin that no longer can instruct.

Mauberley[1]

"Vacuos exercet in aera morsus."[2]

I

Turned from the "eau-forte
Par Jacquemart"[3]
To the strait head
Of Messalina:

"His true Penelope   5
Was Flaubert,"[4]
And his tool
The engraver's.

Firmness,
Not the full smile,   10
His art, but an art
In profile;

Colourless
Pier Francesca,[5]
Pisanello[6] lacking the skill   15
To forge Achaia.[7]

1920

[1] See also "Hugh Selwyn Mauberley, Life and Contacts," written a year earlier in 1919.

[2] He expends ineffective bites into the air.

[3] Strong water (or whiskey).

[4] Penelope was the wife of Odysseus (Ulysses) and the mother of Telemachus in *The Odyssey*, celebrated for her constancy. She waited at Messaline for the return of her husband. A French novelist, Flaubert (1821–1880) was noted for his precision of detail.

[5] Piero della Francesca (1420?–1492) was a Florentine religious painter and leader of the Umbrian school, known especially for his frescoes.

[6] Voltaire or Antonio Pisanello (c. 1395–c. 1455) born at San Visilio, was a noted fresco-painter and medallist.

[7] The administrative unit of Greece on the northern Peloponnesus, bounded by the Gulfs of Corinth and Patras.

Mr. Housman's Message[1]

O woe, woe,
People are born and die,
We also shall be dead pretty soon
Therefore let us act as if we were
        dead already.   5

The bird sits on the hawthorn tree
But he dies also, presently.
Some lads get hung, and some get shot.
Woeful is this human lot.
        Woe! woe, etcetera. . . .   10
London is a woeful place,
Shropshire[2] is much pleasanter.
Then let us smile a little space
Upon fond nature's morbid grace.
        Oh, Woe, woe, woe, etcetera. . . .   15

                       1911

[1] A. E. Housman (1859-1936), the English scholar and poet of *The Shropshire Lad* (1896).

[2] Shropshire is a county of 1337 square miles in western England.

A Girl

The tree has entered my hands,
The sap has ascended my arms,
The tree has grown in my breast—
Downward,
The branches grow out of me, like arms.   5

Tree you are,
Moss you are,
You are violets with wind above them.
A child—*so* high—you are,
And all this is folly to the world.   10

                       1912

Salutation

O generation of the thoroughly smug
    and thoroughly uncomfortable,
I have seen fishermen picnicking in the sun,
I have seen them with untidy families,
I have seen their smiles full of teeth
    and heard ungainly laughter.
And I am happier than you are,   5
And they were happier than I am;
And the fish swim in the lake
    and do not even own clothing.

1913

1916

Salutation the Second

You were praised, my books,
    because I had just come from the country;
I was twenty years behind the times
    so you found an audience ready.
I do not disown you,   5
    do not you disown your progeny.

Here they stand without quaint devices,
Here they are with nothing archaic about them.
Observe the irritation in general:

"Is this," they say, "the nonsense   10
    that we expect of poets?"
"Where is the Picturesque?"
    "Where is the vertigo of emotion?"
"No! his first work was the best."
    "Poor Dear! he has lost his illusions."

Go, little naked and impudent songs,   15
Go with a light foot!
(Or with two light feet, if it please you!)
Go and dance shamelessly!
Go with an impertinent frolic!

Greet the grave and the stodgy,   20
Salute them with your thumbs at your noses.

Here are your bells and confetti.
Go! rejuvenate things!
Rejuvenate even "The Spectator."
      Go! and make cat calls!   25
Dance and make people blush,
Dance the dance of the phallus
      and tell anecdotes of Cybele![1]
Speak of the indecorous conduct of the Gods!
      (Tell it to Mr. Strachey)[2]

Ruffle the skirts of prudes,   30
      speak of their knees and ankles.
But, above all, go to practical people—
      go! jangle their door-bells!
Say that you do no work
      and that you will live forever.

1913

                             1916

[1] The Phrygian goddess of nature, the consort of Attis (a god of fertilty).

[2] Lytton Strachey (1880–1942), English biographer, famous for his *Eminent Victorians* (1918), which mocked Victorian smugness.

Salutation the Third

Let us deride the smugness of "The Times":
GUFFAW!
      So much for the gagged reviewers,
It will pay them when the worms are wriggling in their vitals;
These are they who objected to newness,   5
Here are their tomb-stones.
      They supported the gag and the ring:
A little BLACK BOX contains them.
      So shall you be also,
You slut-bellied obstructionist,   10
You sworn foe to free speech and good letters,
You fungus, you continuous gangrene.

Come, let us on with the new deal,
      Let us be done with pandars and jobbery,
Let us spit upon those who pat the big-bellies for profit,   15
Let us go out in the air a bit.

Or perhaps I *will* die at thirty?
Perhaps you will have the pleasure of defiling my pauper's grave;
I wish you joy, I proffer you all my assistance.
It has been your habit for long   20
   to do away with good writers,
You either drive them mad, or else you blink at their suicides,
Or else you condone their drugs,
   and talk of insanity and genius,
But I will not go mad to please you,   25
   I will not flatter you with an early death,
Oh, no, I will stick it out,
   Feel your hates wriggling about my feet
As a pleasant tickle,
   to be observed with derision,   30
Though many move with suspicion,
   Afraid to say that they hate you;
The taste of my boot?
   Here is the taste of my boot,
Caress it,   35
   lick off the blacking.

 1914

                1926

A Pact

I make a pact with you, Walt Whitman—[1]
I have detested you long enough.
I come to you as a grown child
Who has had a pig-headed father;
I am old enough now to make friends.   5
It was you that broke the new wood,
Now is a time for carving.
We have one sap and one root—
Let there be commerce between us.

 1913

                1916

[1] Walt Whitman (1819–1892). See p. 989.

Further Instructions

Come, my songs, let us express our baser passions,
Let us express our envy of the man with a steady job and no worry
    about the future.
You are very idle, my songs.
I fear you will come to a bad end.
You stand about in the streets,   5
You loiter at the corners and bus-stops,
You do next to nothing at all.

You do not even express our inner nobilities,
You will come to a very bad end.

And I?   10
I have gone half cracked,
I have talked to you so much that
                    I almost see you about me,
Insolent little beasts, shameless, devoid of clothing!

But you, newest song of the lot,   15
You are not old enough to have done much mischief,
I will get you a green coat out of China
With dragons worked upon it,
I will get you the scarlet silk trousers
From the statue of the infant Christ in Santa Maria Novella,   20
Lest they say we are lacking in taste,
Or that there is no caste in this family.

    1913

                                      1916

Les Millwin

The little Millwins attend the Russian Ballet.
The mauve and greenish souls of the little Millwins
Were seen lying along the upper seats
Like so many unused boas.[1]

The turbulent and undisciplined host of art students—   5
The rigorous deputation from "Slade"—
Was before them.

[1] Long, fluffy scarfs.

With arms exalted, with fore-arms
Crossed in great futuristic X's, the art students
Exulted, they beheld the splendours of *Cleopatra*.   10

And the little Millwins beheld these things;
With their large and anæmic eyes they looked out upon this
   configuration.

Let us therefore mention the fact,
For it seems to us worthy of record.

  1913

                1916

The Bath Tub

As a bathtub lined with white porcelain,
When the hot water gives out or goes tepid,
So is the slow cooling of our chivalrous passion,
O my much praised but-not-altogether-satisfactory lady.

  1913

                1916

The Encounter

All the while they were talking the new morality
Her eyes explored me.
And when I arose to go
Her fingers were like the tissue
Of a Japanese paper napkin.   5

  1913

                1916

Ancient Music

Winter is icummen in,
Lhude sing Goddamm,
Raineth drop and staineth slop,
And how the wind doth ramm!
          Sing: Goddamm.   5

Skiddeth bus and sloppeth us,
An ague hath my ham.
Freezeth river, turneth liver,
   Damn you, sing: Goddamm.
Goddamm, Goddamm, 'tis why I am, Goddamm,   10
   So 'gainst the winter's balm.
Sing goddamm, damm, sing Goddamm,
Sing goddamm, sing goddamm, DAMM.

1915

            1917

NOTE.—This is not folk music, but Dr. Ker
writes that the tune is to be found under the
Latin words of a very ancient canon.

The River-Merchant's Wife: A Letter

While my hair was still cut straight across my forehead
I played about the front gate, pulling flowers.
You came by on bamboo stilts, playing horse,
You walked about my seat, playing with blue plums.
And we went on living in the village of Chōkan: 5
Two small people, without dislike or suspicion.

At fourteen I married My Lord you.
I never laughed, being bashful.
Lowering my head, I looked at the wall.
Called to, a thousand times, I never looked back.   10

At fifteen I stopped scowling,
I desired my dust to be mingled with yours
Forever and forever and forever.
Why should I climb the look out?

At sixteen you departed,   15
You went into far Ku-tō-en, by the river of swirling eddies,
And you have been gone five months.
The monkeys make sorrowful noise overhead.
You dragged your feet when you went out.
By the gate now, the moss is grown, the different mosses,   20
Too deep to clear them away!
The leaves fall early this autumn, in wind.
The paired butterflies are already yellow with August
Over the grass in the West garden;

They hurt me. I grow older. 25
If you are coming down through the narrows of the river Kiang,
Please let me know beforehand,
And I will come out to meet you
       As far as Chō-fū-Sa.

By Rihaku (Li T'ai Po)

1915

CANTICO DEL SOLE[1]

    The thought of what America would be like
    If the Classics had a wide circulation
        Troubles my sleep,
    The thought of what America,
    The thought of what America,
    The thought of what America would be like 5
    If the Classics had a wide circulation
        Troubles my sleep.
    Nunc dimittis,[2] now lettest thou thy servant,
    Now lettest thou thy servant
        Depart in peace.
    The thought of what America,
    The thought of what America, 10
    The thought of what America would be like
    If the Classics had a wide circulation . . .
        Oh well!
        It troubles my sleep.

1918

1920

[1] Song of the Soul.   [2] Now you send down.

T. S. ELIOT

(1888-1965)

A variety of writers—models of literary achievement—seem to have composed themselves into the single person of Thomas Stearns Eliot. There are poets who earn their honor by distinctiveness of voice: the timbre and rhythm is unmistakable, and you have only to call to your ear a single phrase or two from a poem for the entire work to flood the mind with remembered progressions of sound and tone (Eliot is such a poet). There are writers like Samuel Johnson who command by virtue of comprehensive intelligence, repeatedly forcing their reader to shed lulling clichés and launch on a stimulating voyage of thought (Eliot is such a writer). And there are literary careers whose ultimate meaning extends beyond the compass even of their best single poem or play or

The Complete Poems and Plays of T. S. Eliot, 1952, contains all the significant work except "The Confidential Clerk," 1954 and The Elder Statesman, 1958. Eliot's widow has published Poems Written in Early Youth, 1967; Collected Plays includes Murder in the Cathedral, The Family Reunion, The Cocktail Party, The Confidential Clerk, and The Elder Statesman. Eliot's essays have been printed in Selected Essays, 1917-1932, 1932, 1951; Essays, Ancient and Modern, 1936; Selected Essays, 1950; Essays on Elizabethan Drama, 1956; On Poetry and Poets, 1957; and To Criticize the Critic and Other Writings, 1965. Individual volumes of criticism are The Idea of a Christian Society, 1939; The Music of Poetry, 1942; Notes Toward the Definition of a Culture, 1948; The Three Voices of Poetry, 1953; and The Frontiers of Criticism, 1956.

Donald L. Gallup has edited T. S. Eliot: A Bibliography, 1953, rev., 1969. An early attempt at a biography was Herbert Howarth, Notes on Some Figures Behind T. S. Eliot, 1964; more recent are Bernard Bergonzi, T. S. Eliot, 1971 and Robert Sencourt, T. S. Eliot: A Memoir, 1971.

Early studies of the poetry are George Williamson, The Talent of T. S. Eliot, 1929;

Edmund Wilson, Axel's Castle, 1931; F. O. Matthiessen, The Achievement of T. S. Eliot , 1935, rev., 1947; Clive Sansom, The Poetry of T. S. Eliot, 1947; Elizabeth A. Drew, T. S. Eliot: The Design of His Poetry, 1949; Leonard Unger, The Art of T. S. Eliot, 1949; George Williamson, A Reader's Guide to T. S. Eliot, 1953; Hugh Kenner, The Invisible Poet: T. S. Eliot, 1959; Séan Lucy, T. S. Eliot and the Idea of Tradition, 1960; and Philip Headings, T. S. Eliot, 1964.

Eliot's work has been studied by many critics concerned with modern poetry including Cleanth Brooks, Modern Poetry and the Tradition, 1930; F. R. Leavis, New Bearings on English Poetry, 1932; Allen Tate, Reactionary Essays on Poetry and Ideas, 1936.

Recent criticism includes Northrop Frye, T. S. Eliot, 1963; Allen Tate, ed., T. S. Eliot: The Man and His Work, 1966; Leonard Unger, T. S. Eliot: Moments and Patterns, 1966; E. Martin Browne, The Making of T. S. Eliot's Plays, 1969; Marion Montgomery, T. S. Eliot: An Essay on the American Magus, 1969; Russell Kirk, Eliot and His Age, 1971; Roger Kojecky, T. S. Eliot's Social Criticism, 1971; John D. Margolis, T. S. Eliot's Intellectual Development: 1922-1939, 1972.

essay, and resides in an overarching moral drama, a faring forward toward general understanding independent of this or that individual text; arguably, Eliot's literary career—the movement from "The Waste Land" through "Four Quartets" to *The Elder Statesman*—has meaning of this kind. Inevitably there are critical quarrels about the ultimate stature of this poet. But it is already clear that few twentieth-century writers in any language have exerted greater influence on their contemporaries than Eliot has exerted, and it is altogether possible that none in English has written poetry with a surer claim to regard as imperishable.

Not astonishingly, the writer who was to become literary dictator of the English-speaking nations, set apart from and above most writers of his day, was well-acquainted from youth with the experience of separateness and detachment—indeed, he may never have been able to take for granted his relation either to place or to community. Born in St. Louis, Missouri, he was in theory a Southerner, but his family lived in Missouri as embattled, displaced New Englanders; Eliot's grandfather campaigned against slavery, established a Unitarian church, and founded—in Washington University—an institution of learning with definite Northeastern leanings. As for his father: the man was in the brick business in St. Louis, but built a vacation house near Gloucester, Mass., no short journey for holidays, and the family went often to this place. In consequence, Eliot, as a Harvard undergraduate (1906–1910), was a Southerner (with a drawl) in New England and, later, at the Sorbonne University in Paris (1911), in Germany at the University of Marburg (1913), at Merton College, Oxford (1914), and London, teaching, working in a bank, writing the poems that brought him world fame, he was the other kind of stranger—an "American abroad." And while he married an English woman in 1916 and became a British citizen in 1927, joined the Church of England, edited a major English literary periodical *(The Criterion),* and worked as a partner in a major English publishing house (Faber and Faber) for well over three decades, Eliot felt himself to be, knew himself to be—for all his affected English forms of dress and address—a foreigner in spirit for life. The sense of removal from ordinary human and social solidarities derived not alone from the luck, good or bad, of life circumstance, but from pride and other features of personal psychology, and from a natural superiority of intelligence, which laid on him an imperative to reckon critically, with detachment, of others. No force was more potent in shaping the themes of his art than the sense of enclosure within personal "difference," an awareness of interior and impermeable scrims of thought and feeling forbidding open human connection.

But there were, of course, a variety of other influences shaping this creative mind. As a graduate student in philosophy at Harvard

(1911–1913) and then as an auditor of lectures by Bergson in Paris, he not only developed his aptitude for speculative thought but put himself in possession of the concepts of "reality" and "the mind"—the modern, rational approach to man—that lay at the center of early twentieth-century thought in its scientific dimension. Earlier, as an undergraduate attending the lectures of Professor Irving Babbit, he felt for the first time the exhilarating pleasure of firm-mindedness in the dismissal of romantic self-indulgence (he was soon to become the spokesman for this new probity). An aesthetic of poetry asserting suggestiveness as a prime value had emerged from the French symbolists (most importantly, from Mallarmé); Eliot absorbed this and at the same time was moved, by the example of certain Imagist poets and by the teachings of his friend Ezra Pound, in the direction of terse colloquialism, relish of immediacy, delight in striking juxtapositions. Then, beyond all this, but in no way separable, stood the weight of the age itself—a world war attesting to the breakup of traditional hierarchies and securities, an overnight obliteration of an "approved" culture by a commercial, mass communications machine, and the emergence of the astonishing new lines of scientific thought summoned by the names of Freud and Einstein. None of the poetic influences on Eliot is negligible; none begins to match in power the dawning sense of values and beliefs undergoing sudden wrenching unopposable transformation.

While significant continuities are discernible in the *Collected Poems,* Eliot's poetry can conveniently be sorted into three periods. *Prufrock and Other Observations* (1917) contains urban pieces, exercises in craft, and humorous bits, together with two extraordinary dramatic monologues—"The Love-Song of J. Alfred Prufrock" and "Portrait of a Lady"—each in its way an accounting, not without sympathy, of pretentious inauthenticity. A dark period follows [*Poems (1920)* and, in 1922, "The Waste Land"]; the poet broods bleakly on civilization in collapse, on the death of potency, on universal desiccation. In the mid-1920's there is a silence, ended by a series of poems wherein the dominant feeling and imagery is clearly religious—"The Ariel Poems" and "Ash Wednesday." Thereafter the poet works almost exclusively with religious themes, although in a variety of tones. The bulk of his writing is done for the theater—*The Rock* (a pageant written in collaboration with E. Martin Browne); *Murder in the Cathedral* (1935) about the martyrdom of Thomas à Becket; *The Family Reunion* (1939); *The Cocktail Party* (1949); *The Confidential Clerk* (1953); and *The Elder Statesman* (1957). The summit of his achievement as a religious poet is a series of long speculative poems composed over a period of a decade and published as *Four Quartets* in 1943.

No small measure of Eliot's authority as literary man derived from his capacity to create the taste by which he would be judged. And essential to its creation were the dozen or so volumes of literary and cultural criticism that he published in his lifetime. (There was also a quantity of influential reviews and shorter critical pieces that he chose not to reprint.) The major volumes in this series include *Selected Essays* (3rd ed., 1951), *The Use of Poetry and The Use of Criticism* (1933), *Notes Toward a Definition of Culture* (1948), and *The Function of Criticism* (1956). The most consequential achievements were the redirection of attention to seventeenth-century English poetry (especially Donne and Marvell), and the brilliant clarification of relations between literary tradition and original genius. (With characteristic antiromanticism, Eliot scaled down "original genius" to "individual talent" in his famous essay on this matter.)

Hostility to T. S. Eliot springs from many sources. He has been mocked as a Tory—a self-proclaimed "classicist in literature, royalist in politics, and Anglo-Catholic in religion." Critics have read his use of Semitic proper names in "The Waste Land" and elsewhere as evidence of a Jew-baiting impulse. It has been intimated in print that at the center of his most famous poems lies a homosexual experience. And it has been charged, publicly, that the deepest of this poet's feelings— that which shaped his vision of "things as they are"—was nothing other than self-contempt.

In time the wars of reputation will work out, through critical negotiation, their peace-making settlements. For the present it seems safe to place T. S. Eliot with this century's invaluable literary men of the West. Arriving at a moment when "things fell apart," lacking qualities of warmth, openness, generosity of political view, he nevertheless showed his age what was happening, undertook to explain why, and, at the level of most intense feeling, made the disintegration matter. In the process he invented (or presupposed) levels of awareness of self and of culture that asked a certain height of his readers; he presumed the existence of a mind equal to the task of comprehending his poem "The Waste Land" and thereby helped to extend human intellectual agility. The mind of the ideal reader of this poem is prepared to uncreate itself, more or less, ready to explore the content of the unconscious, the inner directing forces of myth, the pressures of historical awareness, the never-stilled human longing for coherence and fullness of relationship. It was a new style of mind—at once "foreign" and exhilarating, richer and more positive in its hint of our possibilities than the poet may have meant it to be. Tormented continually in his early and middle years, Eliot seemed to have reached an extraordinary creative tranquility as an elder literary statesman, revered in his 60s, his full intellectual powers intact. He was awarded the Nobel Prize for Literature in 1948.

The Love Song
of J. Alfred Prufrock

S'io credesse che mia risposta fosse
A persona che mai tornasse al mondo,
Questa fiamma staria senza piu scosse.
Ma perciocche giammai di questo fondo
Non torno vivo alcun, s'i'odo il vero,
Senza tema d'infamia ti rispondo. [1]

Let us go then, you and I,
When the evening is spread out against the sky
Like a patient etherised upon a table;
Let us go, through certain half-deserted streets,
The muttering retreats   5
Of restless nights in one-night cheap hotels
And sawdust restaurants with oyster-shells:
Streets that follow like a tedious argument
Of insidious intent
To lead you to an overwhelming question. . . .   10
Oh, do not ask, "What is it?"
Let us go and make our visit.

In the room the women come and go
Talking of Michelangelo.

The yellow fog that rubs its back upon the window-panes,   15
The yellow smoke that rubs its muzzle on the window-panes
Licked its tongue into the corners of the evening,
Lingered upon the pools that stand in drains,
Let fall upon its back the soot that falls from chimneys,
Slipped by the terrace, made a sudden leap,   20
And seeing that it was a soft October night,
Curled once about the house, and fell asleep.

And indeed there will be time
For the yellow smoke that slides along the street,
Rubbing its back upon the window-panes;   25
There will be time, there will be time
To prepare a face to meet the faces that you meet;
There will be time to murder and create,

[1] "If I believed my answer were being made to one who could ever return to the world, this flame would gleam no more; but since, if what I hear is true, never from this abyss did living man return, I answer thee without fear of infamy." (Dante, *Inferno*, xxvii, 61-66.)

And time for all the works and days[2] of hands
That lift and drop a question on your plate;   30
Time for you and time for me,
And time yet for a hundred indecisions,
And for a hundred visions and revisions,
Before the taking of a toast and tea.

   In the room the women come and go   35
Talking of Michelangelo.

   And indeed there will be time
To wonder, "Do I dare?" and, "Do I dare?"
Time to turn back and descend the stair,[3]
With a bald spot in the middle of my hair—   40
[They will say: "How his hair is growing thin!"]
My morning coat, my collar mounting firmly to the chin,
My necktie rich and modest, but asserted by a simple pin—
[They will say: "But how his arms and legs are thin!"]
Do I dare   45
Disturb the universe?
In a minute there is time
For decisions and revisions which a minute will reverse.

   For I have known them all already, known them all:—[4]
Have known the evenings, mornings, afternoons,   50
I have measured out my life with coffee spoons;
I know the voices dying with a dying fall[5]
Beneath the music from a farther room.
   So how should I presume?

   And I have known the eyes already, known them all—   55
The eyes that fix you in a formulated phrase,
And when I am formulated, sprawling on a pin,
When I am pinned and wriggling on the wall,
Then how should I begin
To spit out all the butt-ends of my days and ways?   60
   And how should I presume?

[2] *Works and Days* by Hesiod, a Greek poet who lived in the eighth-century B.C. and whose work of moral maxims deals with husbandry.

[3] See Dante, *Purgatorio*, xxvi, 11, 145-148, in which he describes the stairway from Hell to Heaven.

[4] See Laforgue's *Le Concile féerique* (11. 54, 62).

[5] See Shakespeare, *Twelfth Night*, I, 1, 11. 1-4

And I have known the arms already, known them all—
Arms that are braceleted and white and bare
[But in the lamplight, downed with light brown hair!]
Is it perfume from a dress   65
That makes me so digress?
Arms that lie along a table, or wrap about a shawl.
   And should I then presume?
   And how should I begin?

        . . . . .

Shall I say, I have gone at dusk through narrow streets   70
And watched the smoke that rises from the pipes
Of lonely men in shirt-sleeves, leaning out of windows? . . .

   I should have been a pair of ragged claws
Scuttling across the floors of silent seas.

        . . . . .

And the afternoon, the evening, sleeps so peacefully!   75
Smoothed by long fingers,
Asleep . . . tired . . . or it malingers,
Stretched on the floor, here beside you and me.
Should I, after tea and cakes and ices,
Have the strength to force the moment to its crisis?   80
But though I have wept and fasted, wept and prayed,
Though I have seen my head [grown slightly bald] brought in upon a
   platter,
I am no prophet[6]—and here's no great matter;
I have seen the moment of my greatness flicker,
And I have seen the eternal Footman hold my coat, and snicker, 85
And in short, I was afraid.

   And would it have been worth it, after all,
After the cups, the marmalade, the tea,
Among the porcelain, among some talk of you and me,
Would it have been worth while,   90
To have bitten off the matter with a smile,
To have squeezed the universe into a ball[7]
To roll it toward some overwhelming question,
To say: "I am Lazarus,[8] come from the dead,
Come back to tell you all, I shall tell you all"—   95

[6] Cf. Matthew xiv: 3-11, in which the head
of John the Baptist was taken to Queen Herodias.

[7] Cf. Andrew Marvell's "To A Coy Mistress."

[8] See John xi: 1-44 in which the resurrection
of Lazarus is described. Lazarus was the
brother of Mary and Martha of Bethany,
whom Jesus raised from the dead.

If one, settling a pillow by her head,
   Should say: "That is not what I meant at all.
That is not it, at all."

  And would it have been worth it, after all,
Would it have been worth while,   100
After the sunsets and the dooryards and the sprinkled streets,
After the novels, after the teacups, after the skirts that trail along the
    floor—
And this, and so much more?—
It is impossible to say just what I mean!
But as if a magic lantern threw the nerves in patterns on a screen: 105
Would it have been worth while
If one, settling a pillow or throwing off a shawl,
And turning toward the window, should say:
   "That is not it at all,
   That is not what I meant, at all."   110

                  . . . . .

No! I am not Prince Hamlet, nor was meant to be;
Am an attendant lord, one that will do
To swell a progress, start a scene or two,
Advise the prince; no doubt, an easy tool,
Deferential, glad to be of use,   115
Politic, cautious, and meticulous;
Full of high sentence, but a bit obtuse;
At times, indeed, almost ridiculous—
Almost, at times, the Fool.

  I grow old . . . I grow old . . .   120
I shall wear the bottoms of my trousers rolled.

  Shall I part my hair behind? Do I dare to eat a peach?
I shall wear white flannel trousers, and walk upon the beach.
I have heard the mermaids singing, each to each.

  I do not think that they will sing to me.   125

  I have seen them riding seaward on the waves
Combing the white hair of the waves blown back
When the wind blows the water white and black.

  We have lingered in the chambers of the sea
By sea-girls wreathed with seaweed red and brown   130
Till human voices wake us, and we drown.

    1915

                                             1917

Portrait of a Lady[1]

Thou has committed—
Fornication: but that was in another country,
And besides, the wench is dead.
                        THE JEW OF MALTA.[2]

I

Among the smoke and fog of a December afternoon
You have the scene arrange itself—as it will seem to do—
With "I have saved this afternoon for you";
And four wax candles in the darkened room,
Four rings of light upon the ceiling overhead,   5
An atmosphere of Juliet's tomb[3]
Prepared for all the things to be said, or left unsaid.
We have been, let us say, to hear the latest Pole
Transmit the Preludes, through his hair and fingertips.
"So intimate, this Chopin,[4] that I think his soul   10
Should be resurrected only among friends
Some two or three, who will not touch the bloom
That is rubbed and questioned in the concert room."
—And so the conversation slips
Among velleities and carefully caught regrets   15
Through attenuated tones of violins
Mingled with remote cornets
And begins.
"You do not know how much they mean to me, my friends,
And how, how rare and strange it is, to find   20
In a life composed so much, so much of odds and ends,
[For indeed I do not love it . . . you knew? you are not blind!
How keen you are!]
To find a friend who has these qualities,
Who has, and gives   25
Those qualities upon which friendship lives.
How much it means that I say this to you—
Without these friendships—life, what *cauchemar!*"[5]

---

[1] The title is taken from the novel by Henry James, *A Portrait of a Lady.*

[2] *The Jew of Malta* (1588-1592) by Christopher Marlowe. See Act IV, Scene 1, ll 43-44. The lines are spoken by Barobos.

[3] See *Romeo and Juliet,* Act V, Sc. 3.

[4] Frederic Chopin (1810-1849), Polish composer.

[5] A nightmare.

Among the windings of the violins
And the ariettes[6]   30
Of cracked cornets
Inside my brain a dull tom-tom begins
Absurdly hammering a prelude of its own,
Capricious monotone
That is at least one definite "false note."   35
—Let us take the air, in a tobacco trance,
Admire the monuments,
Discuss the late events,
Correct our watches by the public clocks.
Then sit for half an hour and drink our bocks.   40

II

Now that lilacs are in bloom
She has a bowl of lilacs in her room
And twists one in her fingers while she talks.
"Ah, my friend, you do not know, you do not know
What life is, you who hold it in your hands";   45
(Slowly twisting the lilac stalks)
"You let it flow from you, you let it flow,
And youth is cruel, and has no remorse
And smiles at situations which it cannot see."
I smile, of course,   50
And go on drinking tea.
"Yet with these April sunsets, that somehow recall
My buried life, and Paris in the Spring,
I feel immeasurably at peace, and find the world
To be wonderful and youthful, after all."   55

The voice returns like the insistent out-of-tune
Of a broken violin on an August afternoon:
"I am always sure that you understand
My feelings, always sure that you feel,
Sure that across the gulf you reach your hand.   60

You are invulnerable, you have no Achilles' heel.
You will go on, and when you have prevailed
You can say: at this point many a one has failed.
But what have I, but what have I, my friend,
To give you, what can you receive from me?   65
Only the friendship and the sympathy
Of one about to reach her journey's end.

[6] Ariettes are short arias.

I shall sit here, serving tea to friends. . . ."

I take my hat: how can I make a cowardly amends
For what she has said to me?   70
You will see me any morning in the park
Reading the comics and the sporting page.
Particularly I remark
An English countess goes upon the stage.
A Greek was murdered at a Polish dance,   75
Another bank defaulter has confessed.
I keep my countenance,
I remain self-possessed
Except when a street piano, mechanical and tired
Reiterates some worn-out common song   80
With the smell of hyacinths across the garden
Recalling things that other people have desired.
Are these ideas right or wrong?

III

The October night comes down; returning as before
Except for a slight sensation of being ill at ease   85
I mount the stairs and turn the handle of the door
And feel as if I had mounted on my hands and knees.
"And so you are going abroad; and when do you return?
But that's a useless question.
You hardly know when you are coming back,   90
You will find so much to learn."
My smile falls heavily among the bric-à-brac.

"Perhaps you can write to me."
My self-possession flares up for a second;
This is as I had reckoned.   95
"I have been wondering frequently of late
(But our beginnings never know our ends!)
Why we have not developed into friends."
I feel like one who smiles, and turning shall remark
Suddenly, his expression in a glass.   100
My self-possession gutters; we are really in the dark.

"For everybody said so, all our friends,
They all were sure our feelings would relate
So closely! I myself can hardly understand.
We must leave it now to fate.   105
You will write, at any rate.
Perhaps it is not too late.
I shall sit here, serving tea to friends."

And I must borrow every changing shape
To find expression . . . dance, dance   110
Like a dancing bear,
Cry like a parrot, chatter like an ape.
Let us take the air, in a tobacco trance—

Well! and what if she should die some afternoon,
Afternoon grey and smoky, evening yellow and rose;   115
Should die and leave me sitting pen in hand
With the smoke coming down above the housetops;
Doubtful, for a while
Not knowing what to feel or if I understand
Or whether wise or foolish, tardy or too soon . . .   120
Would she not have the advantage, after all?
This music is successful with a "dying fall"
Now that we talk of dying—
And should I have the right to smile?

1915

1917

Aunt Helen

Miss Helen Slingsby was my maiden aunt,
And lived in a small house near a fashionable square
Cared for by servants to the number of four.
Now when she died there was silence in heaven
And silence at her end of the street.   5
The shutters were drawn and the undertaker wiped his feet—
He was aware that this sort of thing had occurred before.
The dogs were handsomely provided for,
But shortly afterwards the parrot died too.
The Dresden clock continued ticking on the mantelpiece,   10
And the footman sat upon the dining-table
Holding the second housemaid on his knees—
Who had always been so careful while her mistress lived.

1915

1917

Sweeney Erect

> *And the trees about me,*
> *Let them be dry and leafless; let the rocks*
> *Groan with continual surges; and behind me*
> *Make all a desolation. Look, look, wenches!*[1]

Paint me a cavernous waste shore
  Cast in the unstilled Cyclades,[2]
Paint me the bold anfractuous rocks
  Faced by the snarled and yelping seas.

Display me Aeolus[3] above   5
  Reviewing the insurgent gales
Which tangle Ariadne's hair
  And swell with haste the perjured sails.

Morning stirs the feet and hands
  (Nausicaa and Polypheme).[4]   10
Gesture of orang-outang[5]
  Rises from the sheets in stream.

This withered root of knots of hair
  Slitted below and gashed with eyes,
This oval O cropped out with teeth: 15
  The sickle motion from the thighs

---

[1] *The Maid's Tragedy*, Act II, Sc. 2, ll. 74-77, by Francis Beaumont and John Fletcher, who were late Elizabethan dramatists. Queen Aspatia is telling her maid, whom she has asked to design a tapestry after the character of Ariadne, how she would like the scene to look. Her remarks are carried into the first two stanzas of the poem.

[2] Theseus deserted Ariadne at the coast of the Cyclades, after she had saved his life and he had lived with her. Jupiter felt sorrow for the deserted Ariadne and stopped Theseus from changing his sails (see line 8) from black to white, which was Theseus' signal to his father, King Aegeus, that he had survived. When Aegeus saw the black sails, he killed himself. See Catullus, *Carmine*, LXIV.

[3] In classical mythology, the one who controlled the winds.

[4] Nausicaa, who was princess of Phaeacia, rescued Ulysses and loved him futilely. She then helped him leave on a ship provided by her father. Polyphemus was a one-eyed, man-eating monster, the head of the Cyclops, whose eye was burned out by Ulysses as he escaped.

[5] An anthropoid ape with shaggy hair, long arms, and no tail.

Jackknifes upward at the knees
   Then straightens out from heel to hip
Pushing the framework of the bed
   And clawing at the pillow slip.   20

Sweeney addressed full length to shave
   Broadbottomed, pink from nape to base,
Knows the female temperament
   And wipes the suds around his face.

(The lengthened shadow of a man   25
   Is history, said Emerson[6]
Who had not seen the silhouette
   Of Sweeney straddled in the sun.)

Tests the razor on his leg
   Waiting until the shriek subsides.   30
The epileptic on the bed
   Curves backward, clutching at her sides.

The ladies of the corridor
   Find themselves involved, disgraced,
Call witness to their principles   35
   And deprecate the lack of taste

Observing that hysteria
   Might easily be misunderstood;
Mrs. Turner intimates
   It does the house no sort of good.   40

But Doris, towelled from the bath,
   Enters padding on broad feet,
Bringing sal volatile
   And a glass of brandy neat.

1919

1920

[6] See Emerson's "Self-Reliance": "An institution is the lengthened shadow of one man . . . and all history resolves itself very easily into the biography of a few stout and earnest persons."

The Waste Land[1]

"Nam Sibyllam quidem Cumis ego ipse oculis meis vidi in ampulla pendere, et cum illi pueri dicerent Σίβυλλα τί θέλεις; respondebat illa: ἀποθανεῖν θέλω."[2]

For Ezra Pound
il miglior fabbro.[3]

I. THE BURIAL OF THE DEAD

April is the cruellest month, breeding
Lilacs out of the dead land, mixing
Memory and desire, stirring
Dull roots with spring rain.
Winter kept us warm, covering
Earth in forgetful snow, feeding
A little life with dried tubers.   5
Summer surprised us, coming over the Starnbergersee[4]
With a shower of rain; we stopped in the colonnade,
And went on in sunlight, into the Hofgarten,[5]   10
And drank coffee, and talked for an hour.
Bin gar keine Russin, stamm' aus Litauen, echt deutsch.[6]
And when we were children, staying at the archduke's,
My cousin's, he took me out on a sled,
And I was frightened. He said, Marie,   15
Marie, hold on tight. And down we went.
In the mountains, there you feel free.
I read, much of the night, and go south in the winter.

[1] "The Waste Land" first appeared in *The Criterion* in October 1922, after having been revised by Ezra Pound (hence Eliot's tribute to Pound: *il miglior fabbro* (the better craftsman). Eliot's own introductory note explains his sources: "Not only the title, but the plan and a good deal of the incidental symbolism of the poem were suggested by Miss Jessie L. Weston's book on the Grail legend: *From Ritual to Romance* (Cambridge). Indeed, so deeply am I indebted, Miss Weston's book will elucidate the difficulties of the poem much better than my notes can do; and I recommend it (apart from the great interest of the book itself) to any who think such elucidation of the poem worth the trouble. To another work of anthropology I am indebted in general, one which has influenced our generation profoundly; I mean *The Golden Bough* [by Sir James Frazer]; I have used especially the two volumes *Adonis, Attis, Osiris*. Anyone who is acquainted with these works will immediately recognize in the poem certain references to vegetation ceremonies."

[2] "For I myself, with my own eyes, saw the Sibyl of Cumae hanging in an ampule (or jug), and when the boys said to her, 'Sibyl, what do you want,' she answered, 'I want to die.'" (Petronius, *Satyricon*, Chapter 48).

[3] "The better craftsman," from Dante, *Purgatoria*, xxvi, 117.

[4] A lake resort outside Munich.

[5] An outdoor cafe.

[6] I am no Russian, I come from Lithuania, true German.

What are the roots that clutch, what branches grow
Out of this stony rubbish? Son of man,[7]   20
You cannot say, or guess, for you know only
A heap of broken images, where the sun beats,
And the dead tree gives no shelter, the cricket no relief,[8]
And the dry stone no sound of water. Only
There is shadow under this red rock,   25
(Come in under the shadow of this red rock),[9]
And I will show you something different from either
Your shadow at morning striding behind you
Or your shadow at evening rising to meet you;
I will show you fear in a handful of dust.   30

     Frisch weht der Wind
     Der Heimat zu
     Mein Irisch Kind,
     Wo weilest du?[10]

"You gave me hyacinths first a year ago;   35
"They called me the hyacinth girl."
—Yet when we came back, late, from the Hyacinth garden,[11]
Your arms full, and your hair wet, I could not
Speak, and my eyes failed, I was neither
Living nor dead, and I knew nothing,   40
Looking into the heart of light, the silence.
Oed' und leer das Meer.[12]

    Madame Sosostris, famous clairvoyante,
Had a bad cold, nevertheless
Is known to be the wisest woman in Europe,   45
With a wicked pack of cards.[13] Here, said she,
Is your card, the drowned Phoenician Sailor,
(Those are pearls that were his eyes.[14] Look!)

[7] Cf. Ezekiel, II, i. [Eliot's note.]

[8] Cf. Ecclesiastes XII. v. [Eliot's note.]

[9] Cf. Ecclesiastes xii: 7, l. 23.

[10] *Tristan and Isolde*, I, verses 5-8. [Eliot's note.] The lines are translated: "Fresh blows the wind/from off the bow,/My Irish maid,/where lingerest thou?"

[11] The boy Hyacinthus was loved by Apollo and slain by Zephyrus (Ovid, *Metamorphoses*, X). After he died, he was reborn in the flower.

[12] Id. III, verse 24 [Eliot's note.] Desolate and deserted the sea.

[13] I am not familiar with the exact constitution of the Tarot pack of cards, from which I have obviously departed to suit my own convenience. The Hanged Man, a member of the traditional pack, fits my purpose in two ways: because he is associated in my mind with the Hanged God of Frazer, and because I associate him with the hooded figure in the passage of the disciples to Emmaus in Part V. The Phoenician Sailor and the Merchant appear later; also the 'crowds of people,' and Death by Water is executed in Part IV. The Man with Three Staves (an authentic member of the Tarot pack) I associate, quite arbitrarily, with the Fisher King himself." [Eliot's note.]

[14] From Ariel's song in *The Tempest*, Act 1, Sc. 2, 398.

Here is Belladonna, the Lady of the Rocks,
The lady of situations.   50
Here is the man with three staves, and here the Wheel,
And here is the one-eyed merchant, and this card,
Which is blank, is something he carries on his back,
Which I am forbidden to see. I do not find
The Hanged Man. Fear death by water.   55
I see crowds of people, walking round in a ring.
Thank you. If you see dear Mrs. Equitone,
Tell her I bring the horoscope myself:
One must be so careful these days.

   Unreal City,[15]   60
Under the brown fog of a winter dawn,
A crowd flowed over London Bridge, so many,
I had not thought death had undone so many.[16]
Sighs, short and infrequent, were exhaled,[17]
And each man fixed his eyes before his feet.   65
Flowed up the hill and down King William Street,
To where Saint Mary Woolnoth kept the hours
With a dead sound on the final stroke of nine.[18]
There I saw one I knew, and stopped him, crying: "Stetson!
"You who were with me in the ships at Mylae![19]   70
"That corpse you planted last year in your garden,
"Has it begun to sprout? Will it bloom this year?
"Or has the sudden frost disturbed its bed?
"Oh keep the Dog far hence, that's friend to men,
"Or with his nails he'll dig it up again![20]   75
"You! hypocrite lecteur!—mon semblable,—mon frère!"[21]

---

[15] Baudelaire: "*Fourmillante cité, cité pleine de rêves,/Ou le spectre en plein jour raccroche le passant.*" [Eliot's note.] This means "Swarming city, city full of dreams,/Where the ghost in full daylight greets the passersby."

[16] Cf. *Inferno*, III, 55–57 "si lunga tratta/di gente, ch'io non avrei mai creduto/che morte tanta n'avesse disfatta." [Eliot's note]: "So long a train of people: I never should have believed Death had undone so many."

[17] Cf. Inferno IV, 25–27: "Quivi, secondo che per ascoltare,/"non avea pianto, ma' che di sospiri,/"che l'aura eterna facevan tremare." [Eliot's note.] "Here, not a sound of lamentation was to be heard, except for sighs which made the eternal air tremble."

[18] A phenomenon, which I have often noticed. [Eliot's note.]

[19] A reference to the Punic War (260 B.C.).

[20] Eliot refers to "the Dirge in Webster's *White Devil*." V, 4, ll. 97–98. "But keep the wolf far thence, that's foe to men,/For with his nails he'll dig them up again."

[21] See Baudelaire, *Preface to Fleurs du Mal.* [Eliot's note.] The line means: "hypocritical reader!—my double,—my brother!"

II. A GAME OF CHESS[22]

The Chair she sat in, like a burnished throne,[23]
Glowed on the marble, where the glass
Held up by standards wrought with fruited vines
From which a golden Cupidon peeped out   80
(Another hid his eyes behind his wing)
Doubled the flames of sevenbranched candelabra
Reflecting light upon the table as
The glitter of her jewels rose to meet it,
From satin cases poured in rich profusion;   85
In vials of ivory and coloured glass
Unstoppered, lurked her strange synthetic perfumes,
Unguent, powdered, or liquid—troubled, confused
And drowned the sense in odours; stirred by the air
That freshened from the window, these ascended   90
In fattening the prolonged candle-flames,
Flung their smoke into the laquearia,[24]
Stirring the pattern on the coffered ceiling.
Huge sea-wood fed with copper
Burned green and orange, framed by the coloured stone,   95
In which sad light a carved dolphin swam.
Above the antique mantel was displayed
As though a window gave upon the sylvan scene[25]
The change of Philomel,[26] by the barbarous king
So rudely forced; yet there the nightingale[27]   100
Filled all the desert with inviolable voice
And still she cried, and still the world pursues,
"Jug Jug" to dirty ears.
And other withered stumps of time
Were told upon the walls; staring forms   105
Leaned out, leaning, hushing the room enclosed.
Footsteps shuffled on the stair.

[22] Thomas Middleton's play, *A Game of Chess* (1624) is a satire of a marriage based on political expediency.

[23] Cf. *Antony and Cleopatra*, II, ii, l. 190. [Eliot's note.]

[24] Eliot's note refers to the "*Aeneid*, I, 726: dependent lychni laquearibus aureis incensi, et noctem flammis funalia vincunt." The lines may be translated: "Lighted lamps hang from the golden laquearia [an elaborate ceiling], and flaming torches dispel the night."

[25] Milton, *Paradise Lost*, IV, 140. [Eliot's note.]

[26] Cf. Ovid, *Metamorphoses*, VI, Philomela. [Eliot's note.] Philomela was raped by Tereus, the husband of her sister Procne. In revenge Procne killed his son and gave the heart to the king. The gods saved Philomela and Procne by changing them respectively into a nightingale and a swallow.

[27] Cf. Part III, l. 204. [Eliot's note.]

Under the firelight, under the brush, her hair
Spread out in fiery points
Glowed into words, then would be savagely still.   110

   "My nerves are bad to-night. Yes, bad. Stay with me.
"Speak to me. Why do you never speak. Speak.
  "What are you thinking of? What thinking? What?
"I never know what you are thinking. Think."

   I think we are in rats' alley[28]   115
Where the dead men lost their bones.

   "What is that noise?"
             The wind under the door.[29]
"What is that noise now? What is the wind doing?"
             Nothing again nothing.   120
"Do."
"You know nothing? Do you see nothing? Do you remember
"Nothing?"

    I remember
Those are pearls that were his eyes.[30]
"Are you alive, or not? Is there nothing in your head?"   125
                    But

O O O O that Shakespeherian Rag—
It's so elegant
So intelligent   130
"What shall I do now? What shall I do?"
"I shall rush out as I am, and walk the street
"With my hair down, so. What shall we do to-morrow?
"What shall we ever do?"
          The hot water at ten.   135
And if it rains, a closed car at four.
And we shall play a game of chess,
Pressing lidless eyes and waiting for a knock upon the door.[31]

   When Lil's husband got demobbed, I said—[32]
I didn't mince my words, I said to her myself,   140

---

[28] Cf. Part III, l. 195. [Eliot's note.]

[29] "Cf. Webster: 'Is the wind in that door still?' " [Eliot's note.] Eliot is referring to John Webster, *The Devil's Law Case*, 1623.

[30] Cf. Part I, ll. 37, 48. [Eliot's note.] The line is taken from *The Tempest*.

[31] "Cf. the game of chess in Middleton's *Women beware Women*." [Eliot's note.] In the play (II, 2), a widow is kept occupied in a chess game while her daughter-in-law is being raped.

[32] This scene is of two cockney women in a London pub discussing love and abortion. Demobbed is British slang for "demobilized" from the army.

Hurry up please its time[33]
Now Albert's coming back, make yourself a bit smart.
He'll want to know what you done with that money he gave you
To get yourself some teeth. He did, I was there.
You have them all out, Lil, and get a nice set,   145
He said, I swear, I can't bear to look at you.
And no more can't I, I said, and think of poor Albert,
He's been in the army four years, he wants a good time,
And if you don't give it him, there's others will, I said.
Oh is there, she said. Something o' that, I said.   150
Then I'll know who to thank, she said, and give me a straight look.
Hurry up please its time
If you don't like it you can get on with it, I said.
Others can pick and choose if you can't.
But if Albert makes off, it won't be for lack of telling.   155
You ought to be ashamed, I said, to look so antique.
(And her only thirty-one.)
I can't help it, she said, pulling a long face,
It's them pills I took, to bring it off, she said.
(She's had five already, and nearly died of young George.)   160
The chemist[34] said it would be all right, but I've never been the
    same.
You are a proper fool, I said.
Well, if Albert won't leave you alone, there it is, I said,
What you get married for if you don't want children?
Hurry up please its time   165
Well, that Sunday Albert was home, they had a hot gammon,[35]
And they asked me in to dinner, to get the beauty of it hot—
Hurry up please its time
Hurry up please its time
Goodnight Bill. Goodnight Lou. Goodnight May. Goodnight.   170
Ta ta. Goodnight. Goodnight.
Good night, ladies, good night, sweet ladies, good night, good night.[36]

III. THE FIRE SERMON

The river's tent is broken: the last fingers of leaf
Clutch and sink into the wet bank. The wind
Crosses the brown land, unheard. The nymphs are departed.   175
Sweet Thames, run softly, till I end my song.[37]

---

[33] The bartender's warning that it is legal closing time.

[34] The British word for druggist.

[35] British word for ham.

[36] Cf. *Hamlet* IV, v, l. 73.

[37] "V. Spenser, *Prothalamion.*" [Eliot's note.]

The river bears no empty bottles, sandwich papers,
Silk handkerchiefs, cardboard boxes, cigarette ends
Or other testimony of summer nights. The nymphs are departed.
And their friends, the loitering heirs of city directors;   180
Departed, have left no addresses.
By the waters of Leman I sat down and wept . . .[38]
Sweet Thames, run softly till I end my song,
Sweet Thames, run softly, for I speak not loud or long.
But at my back in a cold blast I hear   185
The rattle of the bones, and chuckle spread from ear to ear.
A rat crept softly through the vegetation
Dragging its slimy belly on the bank
While I was fishing in the dull canal
On a winter evening round behind the gashouse   190
Musing upon the king my brother's wreck
And on the king my father's death before him.[39]
White bodies naked on the low damp ground
And bones cast in a little low dry garret,
Rattled by the rat's foot only, year to year.   195
But at my back from time to time I hear[40]
The sound of horns[41] and motors, which shall bring
Sweeney to Mrs. Porter in the spring.
O the moon shone bright on Mrs. Porter[42]
And on her daughter   200
They wash their feet in soda water
Et O ces voix d'enfants, chantant dans la coupole![43]

   Twit twit twit
Jug jug jug jug jug jug
So rudely forc'd.   205
Tereu

   Unreal City
Under the brown fog of a winter noon
Mr. Eugenides, the Smyrna merchant

[38] Cf. Psalms cxxxvii: l. 4.

[39] Cf. *The Tempest*, I, ii. [Eliot's note.]

[40] Cf. Marvell, *To His Coy Mistress.* [Eliot's note.]

[41] "Cf. Day, *Parliament of Bees:* When of the sudden, listening, you shall hear,/A noise of horns and hunting, which shall bring/Actaeon to Diana in the spring/Where all shall see her naked skin. . . ." [Eliot's note.]

[42] "I do not know the origin of the ballad from which these lines are taken: It was reported to me from Sydney, Australia." [Eliot's note.] A song of World War I.

[43] "V. Verlaine, *Parsifal.*" [Eliot's note.] "And O those children's voices, singing in the cupola."

Unshaven, with a pocket full of currants[44]   210
C.i.f. London: documents at sight
Asked me in demotic[45] French
To luncheon at the Cannon Street Hotel
Followed by a weekend at the Metropole.

At the violet hour, when the eyes and back   215
Turn upward from the desk, when the human engine waits
Like a taxi throbbing waiting,
I Tiresias,[46] though blind, throbbing between two lives,
Old man with wrinkled female breasts, can see
At the violet hour, the evening hour that strives   220
Homeward, and brings the sailor home from sea,[47]
The typist home at teatime, clears her breakfast, lights
Her stove, and lays out food in tins.
Out of the window perilously spread
Her drying combinations touched by the sun's last rays,   225
On the divan are piled (at night her bed)
Stockings, slippers, camisoles, and stays.

[44] "The currants were quoted at a price 'carriage and insurance free to London'; and the Bill of Lading, etc., were to be handed to the buyer upon payment of the sight draft." [Eliot's note.]

[45] The vulgar language, spoken by the people.

[46] "Tiresias, although a mere spectator and not indeed a 'character,' is yet the most important personage in the poem, uniting all the rest. Just as the one-eyed merchant, seller of currants, melts into the Phoenician Sailor, and the latter is not wholly distinct from Ferdinand Prince of Naples [in *The Tempest*], so all the women are one woman, and the two sexes meet in Tiresias. What Tiresias *sees*, in fact, is the substance of the poem. The whole passage from Ovid is of great anthropological interest: 'Cum Iunone iocos et maior vestra profecto est/Quam, quae contingit maribus,' dixisse, 'voluptas.'/Illa negat; placuit quae sit sententia docti/Quaerere Tiresiae; venus huic erat utraque nota./Nam duo magnorum viridi coeuntia silva/Corpora serpentum baculi violaverat ictu/Deque viro factus, mirabile, femina septem/Egerat autumnos; octavo rursus eosdem/Vidit et 'est vestrae si tanta potentia plagae,'/Dixit 'ut auctoris sortem in contraria mutet,/Nunc quoque vos feriam!' percussis anguibus isdem/Forma prior rediit genetivaque venit imago/Arbiter hic igitur sumptus de lite iocosa/Dicta Iovis firmat; gravius Saturnia iusto/Nec pro materia fertur doluisse suique/Iudicis aeterna damnavit lumina nocte,/At pater omnipotens (neque enim licet inrita cuiquam/Facta dei fecisse deo) pro lumine adempto/Scire futura dedit poenamque levavit honore. Metamorphoses, III, 320–328. This passage recounts a dispute between Jove and Juno: Jove claims that those of Juno's sex receive more pleasure from the act of love than do the male gods, while Juno asserts the opposite. They decide to ask Tiresias for a judgment since he has known "both sides of love," for once Tiresias had angered two mating serpents, and had been immediately changed into a woman. Eight years later he struck the same serpents and was transformed into man again. Tiresias decides the dispute in favor of Jove, whereupon the angered Juno condemns Tiresias to eternal blindness. In compensation, Jove gives him the power to know the future." [Eliot's note.]

[47] "This may not appear as exact as Sappho's lines, but I had in mind the 'longshore' or 'dory' fisherman, who returns at nightfall." [Eliot's note.]

I Tiresias, old man with wrinkled dugs
Perceived the scene, and foretold the rest—
I too awaited the expected guest.   230
He, the young man carbuncular, arrives,
A small house agent's clerk, with one bold stare,
One of the low on whom assurance sits
As a silk hat on a Bradford millionaire.
The time is now propitious, as he guesses,   235
The meal is ended, she is bored and tired,
Endeavours to engage her in caresses
Which still are unreproved, if undesired.
Flushed and decided, he assaults at once;
Exploring hands encounter no defence;   240
His vanity requires no response,
And makes a welcome of indifference.
(And I Tiresias have foresuffered all
Enacted on this same divan or bed;
I who have sat by Thebes below the wall   245
And walked among the lowest of the dead.)
Bestows one final patronising kiss,
And gropes his way, finding the stairs unlit . . .

    She turns and looks a moment in the glass,
Hardly aware of her departed lover;   250
Her brain allows one half-formed thought to pass:
"Well now that's done: and I'm glad it's over."
When lovely woman stoops to folly[48] and
Paces about her room again, alone,
She smoothes her hair with automatic hand,   255
And puts a record on the gramophone.

    "This music crept by me upon the waters"[49]
And along the Strand, up Queen Victoria Street.
O City city, I can sometimes hear
Beside a public bar in Lower Thames Street,   260
The pleasant whining of a mandoline
And a clatter and a chatter from within
Where fishmen lounge at noon: where the walls
Of Magnus Martyr hold[50]
Inexplicable splendour of Ionian white and gold.   265

[48] "V. Goldsmith, the song in *The Vicar of Wakefield*." [Eliot's note.]
[49] "V. *The Tempest*, as above [l. 48]." [Eliot's note.]
[50] "The interior of St. Magnus Martyr is to my mind one of the finest among Wren's interiors. See *The Proposed Demolition of Nineteen City Churches: (P.S. King & Son, Ltd.).*" [Eliot's note.]

The river sweats[51]
Oil and tar
The barges drift
With the turning tide
Red sails   270
Wide
To leeward, swing on the heavy spar.
The barges wash
Drifting logs
Down Greenwich reach   275
Past the Isle of Dogs.
      Weialala leia
      Wallala leialala

Elizabeth and Leicester[52]
Beating oars   280
The stern was formed
A gilded shell
Red and gold
The brisk swell
Rippled both shores   285
Southwest wind
Carried down stream
The peal of bells
White towers
      Weialala leia   290
      Wallala leialala

"Trams and dusty trees.
Highbury bore me. Richmond and Kew[53]
Undid me. By Richmond I raised my knees
Supine on the floor of a narrow canoe."   295

"My feet are at Moorgate,[54] and my heart
Under my feet. After the event
He wept. He promised 'a new start.'
I made no comment. What should I resent?"

[Handwritten annotations in right margin: "Rhine maidens", "stolen golden ball", "lovers used Thames"]

---

[51] "The Song of the (three) Thames-daughters begins here. From line 292 to 306 inclusive they speak in turn. V. _Götterdämmerung_, III, i: the Rhine-daughters." [Eliot's note.]

[52] "V. Froude, _Elizabeth_, Vol. I, ch. iv, letter of De Quadra to Philip of Spain: 'In the afternoon we were in a barge, watching the games on the river. (The queen) was alone with Lord Robert and myself on the poop, when they began to talk nonsense, and went so far that Lord Robert at last said, as I was on the spot there was no reason why they should not be married if the queen pleased.'" [Eliot's note.]

[53] "Cf. _Purgatorio_, V, 133: _Ricorditi di me, che son la Pia;/Siena mi fé, disfecemi Maremma._" [Eliot's note:] "Remember me, who am la Pia,/Siena made me, Maremma unmade me."

[54] Moorgate is a London slum.

"On Margate[55] Sands.
I can connect
Nothing with nothing.
The broken fingernails of dirty hands.
My people humble people who expect
Nothing."   305

                    la la
To Carthage then I came[56]

Burning burning burning burning[57]
O Lord Thou pluckest me out[58]
O Lord Thou pluckest   310

burning

IV. DEATH BY WATER

Phlebas the Phoenician, a fortnight dead
Forgot the cry of gulls, and the deep sea swell
And the profit and loss.
                    A current under sea   315
Picked his bones in whispers. As he rose and fell
He passed the stages of his age and youth
Entering the whirlpool.
                    Gentile or Jew
O you who turn the wheel and look to windward,   320
Consider Phlebas, who was once handsome and tall as you.

V. WHAT THE THUNDER SAID[59]

After the torchlight red on sweaty faces
After the frosty silence in the gardens

[55] Margate is a seaside resort of Londoners.

[56] "V. St. Augustine's *Confessions*": 'to Carthage then I came, where a cauldron of unholy loves sang all about mine ears.' " [Eliot's note.]

[57] "The complete text of the Buddha's Fire Sermon (which corresponds in importance to the Sermon on the Mount) from which these words are taken, will be found translated in the late Henry Clarke Warren's *Buddhism in Translation* (Harvard Oriental Series). Mr. Warren was one of the great pioneers of Buddhist studies in the occident." [Eliot's note.]

[58] "From St. Augustine's *Confessions* again. The collocation of these two representatives of eastern and western asceticism [Buddha and St. Augustine], as the culmination of this part of the poem, is not an accident." [Eliot's note.]

[59] "In the first part of Part V three themes are employed: the journey to Emmaus, the approach to the Chapel Perilous (see Miss Weston's book) and the present decay of eastern Europe." [Eliot's note.]

After the agony in stony places
The shouting and the crying   325
Prison and palace and reverberation
Of thunder of spring over distant mountains
He who was living is now dead
We who are living are now dying
With a little patience   330

   Here is no water but only rock
Rock and no water and the sandy road
The road winding above among the mountains
Which are mountains of rock without water
If there were water we should stop and drink   335
Amongst the rock one cannot stop or think
Sweat is dry and feet are in the sand
If there were only water amongst the rock
Dead mountain mouth of carious teeth that cannot spit
Here one can neither stand nor lie nor sit   340
There is not even silence in the mountains
But dry sterile thunder without rain
There is not even solitude in the mountains
But red sullen faces sneer and snarl
From doors of mudcracked houses   345
               If there were water
   And no rock
   If there were rock
   And also water
   And water   350
   A spring

   A pool among the rock
   If there were the sound of water only
   Not the cicada[60]
   And dry grass singing   355
   But sound of water over a rock
   Where the hermit-thrush sings in the pine trees[61]
   Drip drop drip drop drop drop drop
   But there is no water

[60] A locust or cricket.

[61] "This is *Turdus aonalaschkae pallasii*, the hermit-thrush which I have heard in Quebec Province. Chapman says *(Handbook of Birds of Eastern North America)* 'it is most at home in secluded woodland and thickety retreats. . . . Its notes are not remarkable for variety or volume, but in purity and sweetness of tone and exquisite modulation they are unequalled.' Its 'water-dripping song' is justly celebrated." [Eliot's note.]

Who is the third who walks always beside you?[62]   360
When I count, there are only you and I together
But when I look ahead up the white road
There is always another one walking beside you
Gliding wrapt in a brown mantle, hooded
I do not know whether a man or a woman   365
—But who is that on the other side of you?

What is that sound high in the air[63]
Murmur of maternal lamentation
Who are those hooded hordes swarming
Over endless plains, stumbling in cracked earth   370
Ringed by the flat horizon only
What is the city over the mountains
Cracks and reforms and bursts in the violet air
Falling towers
Jerusalem Athens Alexandria   375
Vienna London
Unreal

A woman drew her long black hair out tight
And fiddled whisper music on those strings
And bats with baby faces in the violet light   380
Whistled, and beat their wings
And crawled head downward down a blackened wall
And upside down in air were towers
Tolling reminiscent bells, that kept the hours
And voices singing out of empty cisterns and exhausted wells.   385

In this decayed hole among the mountains
In the faint moonlight, the grass is singing
Over the tumbled graves, about the chapel
There is the empty chapel, only the wind's home.
It has no windows, and the door swings,   390

[62] "The following lines were stimulated by the account of one of the Antarctic expeditions (I forget which, but I think one of Shackleton's): it was related that the party of explorers, at the extremity of their strength, had the constant delusion that there was *one more member* than could actually be counted." [Eliot's note.]

[63] "Cf. Hermann Hesse, *Blick ins Chaos:* 'Schon ist halb Europa, schon ist zumindest der halbe Osten Europas auf dem Wege zum Chaos, fährt betrunken im heiligem Wahn am Abgrund entlang und singt dazu, singt betrunken und hymnisch wie Dritri Karamasoff sang. Ueber diese Lieder lacht der Bürger beleidigt, der Heilige und Seher hört sie mit Tranen.' " [Eliot's note.] "Already half of Europe, already at least half of Eastern Europe is on the way to Chaos, drives drunkenly in spiritual frenzy along the edge of the abyss, and sings hymns drunkenly, as Dmitri Karamazov sang. The offended bourgeois laughs at the songs; the saint and seer hear them with tears."

Dry bones can harm no one.
Only a cock stood on the rooftree
Co co rico co co rico
In a flash of lightning. Then a damp gust
Bringing rain   395

    Ganga[64] was sunken, and the limp leaves
Waited for rain, while the black clouds
Gathered far distant, over Himavant.
The jungle crouched, humped in silence.
Then spoke the thunder   400
DA
Datta:[65] what have we given?
My friend, blood shaking my heart
The awful daring of a moment's surrender
Which an age of prudence can never retract   405
By this, and this only, we have existed
Which is not to be found in our obituaries
Or in memories draped by the beneficent spider[66]
Or under seals broken by the lean solicitor
In our empty rooms   410
DA
Dayadhvam: I have heard the key[67]
Turn in the door once and turn once only
We think of the key, each in his prison
Thinking of the key, each confirms a prison   415
Only at nightfall, aethereal rumours
Revive for a moment a broken Coriolanus[68]
DA
Damyata: The boat responded

[64] The Ganges. The Himavant is the personification of the Himalayas.

[65] " 'Datta, dayadhvam, damyata' (Give, sympathise, control). The fable of the meaning of the Thunder is found in the Brihadaranyaka—Upanishad, 5, 1. A translation is found in Deussen's Sechzig Upanishads Des Veda, p. 489." [Eliot's note.]

[66] "Cf. Webster, The White Devil, V, vi: '. . . they'll remarry/Ere the worm pierce your winding-sheet, ere the spider/Make a thin curtain for your epitaphs.' " [Eliot's note.]

[67] "Cf. Inferno, XXXIII, 46: ed lo sentii chiavar l'uscio di sotto/all' orrible torre." ["And I heard the door of the horrible tower being locked below me."]

"Also F. H. Bradley, Appearance and Reality, p. 346. 'My external sensations are no less private to myself than are my thoughts or my feelings. In either case my experience falls within my circle, a circle closed on the outside; and, with all its elements alike, every sphere is opaque to the others which surround it. . . . In brief, regarded as an existence which appears in a soul, the whole world for each is peculiar and private to that soul.' " [Eliot's note.]

[68] Gnaeus Marcius Coriolanus, the fifth-century patrician leader of Rome and the central figure in Shakespeare's Coriolanus.

Gaily, to the hand expert with sail and oar   420
The sea was calm, your heart would have responded
Gaily, when invited, beating obedient
To controlling hands

                    I sat upon the shore   *not gas house*
Fishing,[69] with the arid plain behind me   425
Shall I at least set my lands in order?[70]   *save myself*
London Bridge is falling down falling down falling down
Poi s'ascose nel foco che gli affina[71]
Quando fiam uti chelidon[72]—O swallow swallow   *Has lessons*
Le Prince d'Aquitaine à la tour abolie[73]   430
These fragments I have shored against my ruins
Why then Ile fit you. Hieronymo's mad againe.[74]
Datta. Dayadhvam. Damyata.
      Shantih shantih shantih[75]

Few years late enters Anglo-Catholic faith
                                  1922

[69] "V. Weston: *From Ritual to Romance,* chapter on the Fisher King." [Eliot's note.]

[70] Isaiah xxviii: "Thus saith the Lord, Set thine house in order: for thou shalt die, and not live."

[71] "V. *Purgatorio,* XXVI, 148. 'Ara vos prec per aquella/valor/'que vos guida al some de l'escalina,/'sovegna vos a temps de ma dolor.'/poi s 'ascose nel foco che gli affina.' *[Eliot's note]*": "I pray you now, by the Goodness that guides you to the summit of this staircase, bethink you in due season of my suffering."

[72] "V. *Pervigilium Veneris.* Cf. Philomela in Parts II and III." [Eliot's note.] "When shall I be [able to sing] like the swallow."

[73] "V. Gerard de Nerval, Sonnet *El Desdichado.*" [Eliot's note.] "The Prince of Aquitane at the ruined tower."

[74] "V. Kyd's *Spanish Tragedy.*" [Eliot's note.] In the play, the king asks Hieronymo to write a play, and he creates one in which he, as an actor, kills the murderers of his son and then himself.

[75] "Shantih. Repeated as here, a formal ending to an Upanishad. 'The Peace which passeth understanding' is our equivalent to this word." [Eliot's note.] The Upanishads are the theological works in Hindu Vedas, sacred literature.

Journey of the Magi[1]

'A cold coming we had of it,
Just the worst time of the year
For a journey, and such a long journey:
The ways deep and the weather sharp,

[1] The Magi are the "wise men from the East" who traveled to Bethlehem to pay homage to the infant Jesus. See Matthew ii: 1–12.

The very dead of winter.'[2]   5
And the camels galled, sore-footed, refractory,
Lying down in the melting snow.
There were times we regretted
The summer palaces on slopes, the terraces,
And the silken girls bringing sherbet.   10
Then the camel men cursing and grumbling
And running away, and wanting their liquor and women,
And the night-fires going out, and the lack of shelters,
And the cities hostile and the towns unfriendly
And the villages dirty and charging high prices: 15
A hard time we had of it.
At the end we preferred to travel all night,
Sleeping in snatches,
With the voices singing in our ears, saying
That this was all folly.   20

    Then at dawn we came down to a temperate valley,
Wet, below the snow line, smelling of vegetation;
With a running stream and a water-mill beating the darkness,
And three trees on the low sky,
And an old white horse galloped away in the meadow.   25
Then we came to a tavern with vine-leaves over the lintel,
Six hands at an open door dicing for pieces of silver,
And feet kicking the empty wine-skins.
But there was no information, and so we continued
And arrived at evening, not a moment too soon   30
Finding the place; it was (you may say) satisfactory.

    All this was a long time ago, I remember,
And I would do it again, but set down
This set down
This: were we led all that way for   35
Birth or Death? There was a Birth, certainly,
We had evidence and no doubt. I had seen birth and death,
But had thought they were different; this Birth was
Hard and bitter agony for us, like Death, our death.
We returned to our places, these Kingdoms,   40
But no longer at ease here, in the old dispensation,
With an alien people clutching their gods.
I should be glad of another death.

                                                            1927

<hr>

[2] These lines are taken from Lancelot Andrewes. See Eliot's essay on Andrewes.

East Coker[1]

I

In my beginning is my end. In succession
Houses rise and fall, crumble, are extended,
Are removed, destroyed, restored, or in their place
Is an open field, or a factory, or a by-pass.
Old stone to new building, old timber to new fires,   5
Old fires to ashes, and ashes to the earth
Which is already flesh, fur and faeces,
Bone of man and beast, cornstalk and leaf.
Houses live and die: there is a time for building
And a time for living and for generation   10
And a time for the wind to break the loosened pane
And to shake the wainscot where the field-mouse trots
And to shake the tattered arras woven with a silent motto.[2]

   In my beginning is my end. Now the light falls
Across the open field, leaving the deep lane   15
Shuttered with branches, dark in the afternoon,
Where you lean against a bank while a van passes,
And the deep lane insists on the direction
Into the village, in the electric heat
Hypnotised. In a warm haze the sultry light   20
Is absorbed, not refracted, by grey stone.
The dahlias sleep in the empty silence.
Wait for the early owl.
               In that open field
If you do not come too close, if you do not come too close,   25
On a Summer midnight, you can hear the music
Of the weak pipe and the little drum
And see them dancing around the bonfire
The association of man and woman
In daunsinge, signifying matrimonie—   30
A dignified and commodious sacrament.
Two and two, necessarye coniunction,
Holding eche other by the hand or the arm

---

[1] Coker is a small village near Yeovil (Dorestshire and Somersetshire in England), the birthplace of Thomas Elyot (?-1546).

[2] The inscription that Mary Queen of Scots had on her cloth.

Whiche betokeneth concorde.[3] Round and round the fire
Leaping through the flames, or joined in circles,   35
Rustically solemn or in rustic laughter
Lifting heavy feet in clumsy shoes,
Earth feet, loam feet, lifted in country mirth
Mirth of those long since under earth
Nourishing the corn. Keeping time,   40
Keeping the rhythm in their dancing
As in their living in the living seasons
The time of the seasons and the constellations
The time of milking and the time of harvest
The time of the coupling of man and woman   45
And that of beasts. Feet rising and falling.
Eating and drinking. Dung and death.

   Dawn points, and another day
Prepares for heat and silence. Out at sea the dawn wind
Wrinkles and slides. I am here   50
Or there, or elsewhere. In my beginning.

II

What is the late November doing
With the disturbance of the spring
And creatures of the summer heat,
And snowdrops writhing under feet   55
And hollyhocks that aim too high
Red into grey and tumble down
Late roses filled with early snow?
Thunder rolled by the rolling stars
Simulates triumphal cars   60
Deployed in constellated wars
Scorpion fights against the Sun
Until the Sun and Moon go down
Comets weep and Leonids fly
Hunt the heavens and the plains   65
Whirled in a vortex that shall bring
The world to that destructive fire
Which burns before the ice-cap reigns.

[3] These lines are from Thomas Elyot's *The Boke Named the Gouvernour* (I, 21). Elyot's work is concerned with political education and suggests for his period a pattern of harmonious living based on Renaissance Platonism.

That was a way of putting it—not very satisfactory:
A periphrastic study in a worn-out poetical fashion,   70
Leaving one still with the intolerable wrestle
With words and meanings. The poetry does not matter.
It was not (to start again) what one had expected.
What was to be the value of the long looked forward to,
Long hoped for calm, the autumnal serenity   75
And the wisdom of age? Had they deceived us
Or deceived themselves, the quiet-voiced elders,
Bequeathing us merely a receipt for deceit?
The serenity only a deliberate hebetude,[4]
The wisdom only the knowledge of dead secrets   80
Useless in the darkness into which they peered
Or from which they turned their eyes. There is, it seems to us,
At best, only a limited value
In the knowledge derived from experience.
The knowledge imposes a pattern, and falsifies,   85
For the pattern is new in every moment
And every moment is a new and shocking
Valuation of all we have been. We are only undeceived
Of that which, deceiving, could no longer harm.
In the middle, not only in the middle of the way   90
But all the way, in a dark wood, in a bramble,
On the edge of a grimpen, where is no secure foothold,
And menaced by monsters, fancy lights,
Risking enchantment. Do not let me hear
Of the wisdom of old men, but rather of their folly,[5]   95
Their fear of fear and frenzy, their fear of possession,
Of belonging to another, or to others, or to God.
The only wisdom we can hope to acquire
Is the wisdom of humility: humility is endless.

The houses are all gone under the sea.   100

The dancers are all gone under the hill.[6]

III

O dark dark dark. They all go into the dark,
The vacant interstellar spaces, the vacant into the vacant,

---

[4] Dullness of mind or mental lethargy.   [6] From Steven's requiem.

[5] Their vanity.

The captains, merchant bankers, eminent men of letters,
The generous patrons of art, the statesmen and the rulers,   105
Distinguished civil servants, chairmen of many committees,
Industrial lords and petty contractors, all go into the dark,
And dark the Sun and Moon, and the Almanach de Gotha[7]
And the Stock Exchange Gazette, the Directory of Directors,
And cold the sense and lost the motive of action.   110
And we all go with them, into the silent funeral,
Nobody's funeral, for there is no one to bury.
I said to my soul, be still, and let the dark come upon you
Which shall be the darkness of God.   As, in a theatre,
The lights are extinguished, for the scene to be changed   115
With a hollow rumble of wings, with a movement of darkness on
    darkness,
And we know that the hills and the trees, the distant panorama
And the bold imposing façade are all being rolled away—
Or as, when an underground train, in the tube, stops too long
    between stations
And the conversation rises and slowly fades into silence   120
And you see behind every face the mental emptiness deepen
Leaving only the growing terror of nothing to think about;
Or when, under ether, the mind is conscious but conscious of
    nothing—
I said to my soul, be still, and wait without hope
For hope would be hope for the wrong thing; wait without love   125
For love would be love of the wrong thing; there is yet faith
But the faith and the love and the hope are all in the waiting.
Wait without thought, for you are not ready for thought:
So the darkness shall be the light, and the stillness the dancing.

  Whisper of running streams, and winter lightning.   130
The wild thyme unseen and the wild strawberry,
The laughter in the garden, echoed ecstasy
Not lost, but requiring, pointing to the agony
Of death and birth.
                    You say I am repeating   135
Something I have said before. I shall say it again.
Shall I say it again? In order to arrive there,
To arrive where you are, to get from where you are not,
    You must go by a way wherein there is no ecstasy.
In order to arrive at what you do not know   140
    You must go by a way which is the way of ignorance.

---

[7] A genealogical almanac of the world.

In order to possess what you do not possess
  You must go by the way of dispossession.
In order to arrive at what you are not
  You must go through the way in which you are not.   145
And what you do not know is the only thing you know
And what you own is what you do not own
And where you are is where you are not.

IV

The wounded surgeon plies the steel
That questions the distempered part;   150
Beneath the bleeding hands we feel
The sharp compassion of the healer's art
Resolving the enigma of the fever chart.

  Our only health is the disease
If we obey the dying nurse   155
Whose constant care is not to please
But to remind of our, and Adam's curse,
And that, to be restored, our sickness must grow worse.

  The whole earth is our hospital
Endowed by the ruined millionaire,   160
Wherein, if we do well, we shall
Die of the absolute paternal care
That will not leave us, but prevents us everywhere.

  The chill ascends from feet to knees,
The fever sings in mental wires.   165
If to be warmed, then I must freeze
And quake in frigid purgatorial fires
Of which the flame is roses, and the smoke is briars.

  The dripping blood our only drink,
The bloody flesh our only food: 170
In spite of which we like to think
That we are sound, substantial flesh and blood—
Again, in spite of that, we call this Friday good.

V

So here I am, in the middle way, having had twenty years—
Twenty years largely wasted, the years of *l'entre deux guerres*—[8]   175

---

[8] Between the two wars.

Trying to learn to use words, and every attempt
Is a wholly new start, and a different kind of failure
Because one has only learnt to get the better of words
For the thing one no longer has to say, or the way in which
One is no longer disposed to say it. And so each venture   180
Is a new beginning, a raid on the inarticulate
With shabby equipment always deteriorating
In the general mess of imprecision of feeling,
Undisciplined squads of emotion. And what there is to conquer
By strength and submission, has already been discovered   185
Once or twice, or several times, by men whom one cannot hope
To emulate—but there is no competition—
There is only the fight to recover what has been lost
And found and lost again and again: and now, under conditions
That seem unpropitious. But perhaps neither gain nor loss.   190
For us, there is only the trying. The rest is not our business.

   Home is where one starts from. As we grow older
The world becomes stranger, the pattern more complicated
Of dead and living. Not the intense moment
Isolated, with no before and after,   195
But a lifetime burning in every moment
And not the lifetime of one man only
But of old stones that cannot be deciphered.
There is a time for the evening under starlight,
A time for the evening under lamplight   200
(The evening with the photograph album).
Love is most nearly itself
When here and now cease to matter.
Old men ought to be explorers
Here and there does not matter   205
We must be still and still moving
Into another intensity
For a further union, a deeper communion
Through the dark cold and the empty desolation,
The wave cry, the wind cry, the vast waters   210
Of the petrel and the porpoise.   In my end is my beginning.

                                                    1940

WILLIAM CARLOS WILLIAMS

(1883-1963)

For the better part of a lifetime William Carlos Williams waged war against reductiveness—the tendency of human beings to mistake the part for the whole or the explanation for the reality. He wrote lyric poems, an epic, short stories, novels, essays, and a remarkable volume of American history (*In the American Grain,* 1925), invariably reshaping these literary forms in the hope of engaging readers more directly with experience in its fullness. The standard poetic line seemed to him overintimidating—armored black print marching across the page in impregnable rhythmic order; he broke the line to create spaces—white spaces—wherein the reader could gather himself into the moment of each word or phrase, penetrating the poetic design with his own counterenergy and counterresponse, freshening the speaker-audience relationship with his own immediacy. In history the usual structures

The poems are in *Complete Collected Poems, 1906-1938,* 1938; *Selected Poems,* 1949; *Collected Later Poetry of William Carlos Williams,* 1950; *Paterson, 1946-1951,* 4 vols., 1951; *The Desert Music and Other Poems,* 1954; and *Journey To Love,* 1955. *Paterson, Book V* was published in 1958 and *Pictures from Brueghel* in 1962. *Paterson* (Books I to V as well as part of Book VI) appeared in 1963. Collections of stories are *The Knife of the Times,* 1932; *Life Along the Passaic River,* 1938; *Make Light of It,* 1950. Williams' novels are *A Voyage to Pagany,* 1928; *White Mule,* 1937; *In The Money,* 1940; and *The Build-Up,* 1952. His essays appear in *The Great American Novel,* 1923; *In the American Grain,* 1925, 1940; and *Selected Essays of William Carlos Williams,* 1954. He has written a play, *Loves,* produced in 1958. J. C. Thirlwall edited *The Selected Letters of William Carlos Williams,* 1950. Webster Schott edited *Imaginations: Collected Early Prose,* 1970. In 1951 *The Autobiography of William Carlos Williams* appeared. Recollections are in *I Wanted To Write a Poem,* ed. Edith Heal, 1958. Emily M. Wallace has is-

sued *A Bibliography of William Carlos Williams,* 1968.

Criticism includes Vivienne Koch, *William Carlos Williams,* 1950: John M. Brinnin, *William Carlos Williams,* 1963; Linda W. Wagner, *The Poems of William Carlos Williams: A Critical Study,* 1964 and *The Prose of William Carlos Williams,* 1970; J. Hillis Miller, *Poets of Reality,* 1965; James Guimond, *The Art of William Carlos Williams,* 1968; Sherman Paul, *The Music of Survival: A Biography of a Poem by William Carlos Williams,* 1968; Thomas Whitaker, *William Carlos Williams,* 1968; James E. Breslin, *William Carlos Williams: An American Artist,* 1970; Joel Conarroe, *William Carlos Williams' "Paterson": Language and Landscape,* 1970; Mike Weaver, *William Carlos Williams: The American Background,* 1971; Benjamin Sankey, *A Companion to William Carlos Williams' "Paterson",* 1971. Two studies that see Williams in relationship to his contemporaries and to the history of American poetry are M. L. Rosenthal, *The Modern Poets: A Critical Introduction,* 1960 and Roy Harvey Pearce, *The Continuity of American Poetry,* 1961.

and methodological pieties seemed, in Williams' view, to smother the vitality of life as lived, transforming Columbus or Cotton Mather or whomever into juiceless nonbeings, stripped of presence in the here-and-now of their own time; accordingly, Williams wrote history "from inside," laying out probabilities of confusion and feeling within historical personages as those confusions could be intuited or imagined by generations looking backward. In fiction the poise, clarity, and competence of the knowing narrator, sure of the meaning of the tale he told, struck Williams as repressive if not duplicitous; in story after story he stepped forth as an *un*comprehending narrator, uncertain about meanings, wholly vulnerable. The consequence of these gestures is a literary world sometimes messy, opaque, or even chaotic, but often fresh, various, multivalent, delicately-spontaneously alive.

The chief marvel of that world is the warmth, kindness, and courtesy of its creator. Williams had a power of rage inside him at the meanness of the values cut into the American grain over the centuries. Self-containment, watchfulness, canniness, petty greed, lack of responsiveness to the beautiful, fear of connection—these presented themselves repeatedly to the poet in his public professional life. (Williams practiced general medicine in Rutherford, New Jersey, for nearly 40 years.) He did not turn away from them or pretend that these human traits were mere protective covers for natural goodness and tenderness. Neither, though, did he perceive them as "purely personal" defects, grounds for blame or damnation. Meanness and narrowness within persons were traceable to culturewide denials of freedom and excessive preoccupation with system, order, structure, and "practicality"; no individual could accept responsibility for them, but vitality, wherever found, would inevitably struggle to overcome them. ("We should have a revolution of some sort in America every ten years," Williams wrote.) For openness, gaiety, friendliness, an absence of fuss and puritannical judgmental airs, and ease of sympathy, Williams has few peers in American letters.

Perhaps partly because his training and service as a medical man regularly recharged his belief in the capacity of ordinary men and women in ordinary roles to help each other, perhaps partly because of the evident satisfactions of his life as husband and father, Williams neither saw himself, nor was seen by others, as a haunted or tragic artist.

Born in Rutherford, New Jersey, Williams was the son of parents of foreign origins (an English father, a Puerto Rican mother). He attended Horarce Mann High School in New York and went on to the University of Pennsylvania, where he received a medical degree in 1906. After graduate work in pediatrics at the University of Leipzig, he settled in

Rutherford in 1910 and opened a medical practice. His first volume, *Poems* (1909), was largely imitative, but he soon published poetry that was characteristic of his later work and that he termed "objectivitism." He was "discovered" early as a poet by Ezra Pound, and the two men were lifelong friends. The cultural impact of Williams' achievements was registered more slowly than was the case with his famous contemporary, T. S. Eliot; Williams' Pulitzer Prize and Gold Medal from the National Institute of Arts and Letters, for example, were awarded posthumously. But his influence on major poets of the succeeding generation—Allen Ginsberg and Robert Lowell among them—has been pivotal, and a sense of the importance of his example continues to increase.

From Spring and All

By the road to the contagious hospital
under the surge of the blue
mottled clouds driven from the
northeast—a cold wind. Beyond, the
waste of broad, muddy fields   5
brown with dried weeds, standing and fallen

patches of standing water
the scattering of tall trees

All along the road the reddish
purplish, forked, upstanding, twiggy   10
stuff of bushes and small trees
with dead, brown leaves under them
leafless vines—

Lifeless in appearance, sluggish
dazed spring approaches—   15

They enter the new world naked,
cold, uncertain of all
save that they enter. All about them
the cold, familiar wind—

Now the grass, tomorrow   20
the stiff curl of wildcarrot leaf
One by one objects are defined—
It quickens: clarity, outline of leaf

But now the stark dignity of
entrance—Still, the profound change   25
has come upon them: rooted, they
grip down and begin to awaken

1923

Fine Work with Pitch and Copper

Now they are resting
in the fleckless light
separately in unison

like the sacks
of sifted stone stacked   5
regularly by twos

about the flat roof
ready after lunch
to be opened and strewn

The copper in eight   10
foot strips has been
beaten lengthwise

down the center at right
angles and lies ready
to edge the coping   15

One still chewing
picks up a copper strip
and runs his eye along it

1936

The Widow's Lament in Springtime

Sorrow is my own yard
where the new grass
flames as it has flamed
often before but not
with the cold fire   5
that closes round me this year.

Thirty-five years
I lived with my husband.
The plumtree is white today
with masses of flowers.   10
Masses of flowers
load the cherry branches
and color some bushes
yellow and some red
but the grief in my heart   15
is stronger than they
for though they were my joy
formerly, today I notice them
and turned away forgetting.
Today my son told me   20
that in the meadows,
at the edge of the heavy woods
in the distance, he saw
trees of white flowers.
I feel that I would like   25
to go there
and fall into those flowers
and sink into the marsh near them.

1921

Queen-Ann's-Lace

Her body is not so white as
anemone petals nor so smooth—nor
so remote a thing. It is a field
of the wild carrot taking
the field by force; the grass   5
does not raise above it.
Here is no question of whiteness,
white as can be, with a purple mole
at the center of each flower.
Each flower is a hand's span   10
of her whiteness. Wherever
his hand has lain there is
a tiny purple blemish. Each part
is a blossom under his touch
to which the fibres of her being   15

stem one by one, each to its end,
until the whole field is a
white desire, empty, a single stem,
a cluster, flower by flower,
a pious wish to whiteness gone over—   20
or nothing.

1921

To Waken An Old Lady

Old age is
a flight of small
cheeping birds
skimming
bare trees   5
above a snow glaze.
Gaining and failing
they are buffeted
by a dark wind—
But what?   10
On harsh weedstalks
the flock has rested,
the snow
is covered with broken
seedhusks   15
and the wind tempered
by a shrill
piping of plenty.

1951

The Young Housewife

At ten A.M. the young housewife
moves about in negligee behind
the wooden walls of her husband's house.
I pass solitary in my car.

Then again she comes to the curb 5
to call the ice-man, fish-man, and stands
shy, uncorseted, tucking in
stray ends of hair, and I compare her
to a fallen leaf.

The noiseless wheels of my car 10
rush with a crackling sound over
dried leaves as I bow and pass smiling.

1917

Asphodel: That Greeny Flower

Inseparable from the fire
    its light
        takes precedence over it.
Then follows
    what we have dreaded— 5
        but it can never
overcome what has gone before.
    In the huge gap
        between the flash
and the thunderstroke 10
    spring has come in
        or a deep snow fallen.
Call it old age.
    In that stretch
        we have lived to see 15
a colt kick up his heels.
    Do not hasten
        laugh and play
in an eternity
    the heat will not overtake the light 20
        That's sure.
That gelds the bomb,
    permitting
        that the mind contain it.
This is that interval, 25
    that sweetest interval,
        when love will blossom,

come early, come late
    and give itself to the lover.
Only the imagination is real!   30
    I have declared it
        time without end.
If a man die
    it is because death
        has first   35
possessed his imagination.
    But if he refuse death—
        no greater evil
can befall him
    unless it be the death of love   40
        meet him
in full career.
    Then indeed
        for him
the light has gone out   45
But love and the imagination
    are of a piece,
        swift as the light
to avoid destruction.
    So we come to watch time's flight   50
        as we might watch
summer lightning
    or fireflies, secure,
        by grace of the imagination.
safe in its care.   55
    For if
        the light itself
has escaped,
    the whole edifice opposed to it
        goes down   60
Light, the imagination
    and love,
        in our age,
by natural law,
    which we worship,   65
        maintain
all of a piece
    their dominance.

So let us love
        confident as is the light   70
                in its struggle with darkness
that there is as much to say
        and more
                for the one side
and that not the darker   75
        which John Donne
                for instance
among many men
        presents to us.
                In the controversy   80
touching the younger
        and the older Tolstoi,
                Villon, St. Anthony, Kung [Confucius],
Rimbaud, Buddha
        and Abraham Lincoln   85
                the palm goes
always to the light;
        Who most shall advance the light
                call it what you may!
The light   90
        for all time shall outspeed
                the thunder crack.
Medieval pageantry
        is human and we enjoy
                the rumor of it   95
as in our world we enjoy
        the reading of Chaucer,
                likewise
a priest's raiment
        (or that of a savage chieftain)   100
                It is all
a celebration of the light.
        All the pomp and ceremony
                of weddings,
"Sweet Thames, run softly   105
        till I end
                my song," —
are of an equal sort.
For our wedding, too,
        the light was wakened   110
                and shone, The light!

the light stood before us
　　　　waiting!
　　　　　　　　I thought the world
stood still.
　　　　At the altar
　　　　　　　　so intent was I
before my vows,
　　　　so moved by your presence
　　　　　　　　a girl so pale　　　　　　　　　　　120
and ready to faint
　　　　that I pitied
　　　　　　　　and wanted to protect you.
As I think of it now,
　　　　after a lifetime,　　　　　　　　　　　　125
　　　　　　　　it is as if
a sweet-scented flower
　　　　were poised
　　　　　　　　and for me did open.
Asphodel　　　　　　　　　　　　　　　　　130
　　　　had no odor
　　　　　　　　save to the imagination
but it too
　　　　celebrates the light.
　　　　　　　　It is late　　　　　　　　　　　135
but an odor
　　　　as from our wedding
　　　　　　　　has revived for me
and begun again to penetrate
　　　　into all crevices　　　　　　　　　　　140
　　　　　　　　of my world.

　　　　　　　　　　　　　　　　　　1955

JAMES WELDON JOHNSON

(1871–1938)

James Weldon Johnson was the first significant black poet to attempt a union of dialect and conventional literary style. He sensed that the dialect poems of Paul L. Dunbar were limited, but he also felt that whenever the black poet wrote conventionally for a white audience, he betrayed the organic nature of his own life-style. As he noted in the introduction to *The Book of American Negro Poetry,*

> Negro dialect poetry had its origin in the minstrel traditions, and a persisting pattern was set. When the individual writer attempted to get away from that pattern, the fixed conventions allowed him only to slip over into a slough of sentimentality. These conventions were not broken for the simple reason that the individual writers wrote chiefly to entertain an outside audience, and in concord with its stereotyped ideas about the Negro.

Johnson was deeply influenced by Whitman's *Leaves of Grass,* which he thought was a splendid expression of folk poetry in literary language. His own first attempt at shaping the actual speech of blacks to the forms of poetry was in "The Creation," first published in 1920 and then in *God's Trombones* (1927). Although Johnson never really went beyond this book of poems, he pointed a significant direction for later black poets by giving the black idiom a greater range of expression.

Johnson's other significant work was *The Autobiography of an Ex-Coloured Man* (1912), an interesting novel that traces the migration of a mulatto from the South to black social circles in New York and concentrates realistically on the central figure's racial ambivalence. In its subject matter and thematic concerns, *The Autobiography* anticipates much of the fiction of the Harlem Renaissance.

In addition to his roles as poet and novelist, Johnson led a very active life as a black leader in the first four decades of the twentieth century. Born in 1871, in Jacksonville, Florida, he studied law, worked on newspapers in Jacksonville, and then collaborated with his brother John Rosamond in the creation of songs for Tin Pan Alley. Johnson later became a leader in the NAACP, serving as field secretary from

Johnson's works include *The Autobiography of an Ex-Coloured Man,* 1912; *Fifty Years and Other Poems,* 1917; *God's Trombones, Seven Negro Sermons in Verse,* 1927; *Black Manhattan,* 1930; *Along This Way,* 1933; *Negro Americans, What Now?,* 1934; and *St. Peter Relates an Incident,* 1935. His work is analyzed by Stephen H. Bronz in *Roots of Negro Racial Consciousness,* 1964.

1916 to 1920 and as general secretary from 1920 to 1930; he was an essayist on political and literary matters and a professor of Creative Literature at Fisk University until his death in an auto accident in 1938. Johnson's autobiography, *Along This Way* (1933), is an engaging account of his complex and successful life.

From all that he wrote, two poems seem most representative: "O Black and Unknown Bards" and the first sermon of "The Creation." They are different in tone and style from anything written by a black poet before Johnson's time, and they anticipate the literary awakening that has come to be known as the Harlem Renaissance.

O Black and Unknown Bards

O black and unknown bards of long ago,
How came your lips to touch the sacred fire?
How, in your darkness, did you come to know
The power and beauty of the minstrel's lyre?
Who first from midst his bonds lifted his eyes?   5
Who first from out the still watch, lone and long,
Feeling the ancient faith of prophets rise
Within his dark-kept soul, burst into song?

Heart of what slave poured out such melody
As "Steal away to Jesus"? On its strains   10
His spirit must have nightly floated free,
Though still about his hands he felt his chains.
Who heard great "Jordan roll"? Whose starward eye
Saw chariot "swing low"? And who was he
That breathed that comforting, melodic sigh,   15
"Nobody knows de trouble I see"?

What merely living clod, what captive thing,
Could up toward God through all its darkness grope,
And find within its deadened heart to sing
These songs of sorrow, love and faith, and hope?   20
How did it catch that subtle undertone,
That note in music heard not with the ears?
How sound the elusive reed so seldom blown,
Which stirs the soul or melts the heart to tears.

Not that great German master in his dream   25
Of harmonies that thundered amongst the stars
At the creation, ever heard a theme
Nobler than "Go down, Moses." Mark its bars
How like a mighty trumpet-call they stir
The blood. Such are the notes that men have sung   30
Going to valorous deeds; such tones there were
That helped make history when Time was young.

There is a wide, wide wonder in it all,
That from degraded rest and servile toil
The fiery spirit of the seer should call   35
These simple children of the sun and soil.

O black slave singers, gone, forgot, unfamed,
You—you alone, of all the long, long line
Of those who've sung untaught, unknown, unnamed,
Have stretched out upward, seeking the divine.   40

You sang not deeds of heroes or of kings;
No chant of bloody war, no exulting paean
Of arms-won triumphs; but your humble strings
You touched in chord with music empyrean.
You sang far better than you knew; the songs   45
That for your listeners' hungry hearts sufficed
Still live,—but more than this to you belongs:
You sang a race from wood and stone to Christ.

1908

1917

The Creation

A Negro Sermon

And God stepped out on space,
And He looked around and said,
"I'm lonely—.
I'll make me a world."

And far as the eye of God could see   5
Darkness covered everything,
Blacker than a hundred midnights
Down in a cypress swamp.

Then God smiled.
And the light broke,   10
And the darkness rolled up on one side,
And the light stood shining on the other,
And God said, *"That's good!"*

Then God reached out and took the light in His hands,
And God rolled the light around in His hands,   15
Until He made the sun;
And He set that sun a-blazing in the heavens.
And the light that was left from making the sun
God gathered up in a shining ball
And flung against the darkness,   20
Spangling the night with the moon and stars.

Then down between
The darkness and the light
He hurled the world;
And God said, *"That's good!"*   25

Then God himself stepped down—
And the sun was on His right hand,
And the moon was on His left;
The stars were clustered about His head,
And the earth was under His feet.   30
And God walked, and where He trod
His footsteps hollowed the valleys out
And bulged the mountains up.

Then He stopped and looked and saw
That the earth was hot and barren.   35
So God stepped over to the edge of the world
And He spat out the seven seas;
He batted His eyes, and the lightnings flashed;
He clapped His hands, and the thunders rolled;
And the waters above the earth came down,   40
The cooling waters came down.

Then the green grass sprouted,
And the little red flowers blossomed,
The pine-tree pointed his finger to the sky,
And the oak spread out his arms;   45

The lakes cuddled down in the hollows of the ground,
And the rivers ran down to the sea;
And God smiled again,
And the rainbow appeared.
And curled itself around His shoulder.   50

Then God raised His arm and He waved His hand
Over the sea and over the land.
And He said, *"Bring forth! Bring forth!"*
And quicker than God could drop his hand,
Fishes and fowls   55
And beast and birds
Swam the rivers and the seas.
Roamed the forests and the woods,
And split the air with their wings,
And God said, *"That's good!"*   60

Then God walked around
And God looked around
On all that He had made.
He looked at His sun,
And He looked at His moon,   65
And He looked at His little stars;
He looked on His world
With all its living things,
And God said, *"I'm lonely still."*

Then God sat down   70
On the side of a hill where He could think;
By a deep, wide river He sat down;
With His head in His hands,
God thought and thought,
Till He thought, *"I'll make me a man!"*   75

Up from the bed of the river
God scooped the clay;
And by the bank of the river
He kneeled Him down;
And there the great God Almighty,   80
Who lit the sun and fixed it in the sky,
Who flung the stars to the most far corner of the night,
Who rounded the earth in the middle of His hand—
This Great God,

Like a mammy bending over her baby,   85
Kneeled down in the dust
Toiling over a lump of clay
Till He shaped it in His own image;

Then into it He blew the breath of life,
And man became a living soul.   90
Amen. Amen.

1920

1927

CLAUDE McKAY

(1890-1948)

Of all the significant authors associated with the Harlem Renaissance, Claude McKay is the most militant. He can lament the illicit, pagan lover of Negro prostitutes, "the sacred brown feet of [his] fallen race," as in "Harlem Shadows," "The Harlem Dancers," or "On Broadway"; he can explore economic and social evils, as in "White Houses" or "In Bondage"; and he can create dialect poems of pastoral beauty about his birthplace in Jamaica. But there is a strain of frustration and bitterness in McKay that finds expression in some of his powerful poems— "Baptism," "The White City," and "If We Must Die"—where he speaks of his "lifelong hate" and urges black people to protest their common suffering, assert their dignity and "like men . . . face the murderous cowardly pack,/Pressed to the wall, dying, but fighting back!" McKay models his poems on the polemical sonnets of Milton and Wordsworth and uses the controlled artistic form to rebel against the racism he has confronted in white America.

McKay's early life would not have suggested his militancy. Born in the Clarendon Hills of Jamaica on September 15, 1890, he received a

Claude McKay's work includes *Constab Ballads*, 1912; *Songs From Jamaica*, 1912; *Spring in New Hampshire, and Other Poems*, 1920; *Harlem Shadows*, 1922; *Home to Harlem*, 1928; *Banjo*, 1929; *Gingertown*, 1932; *Banana Bottom*, 1933; *A Long Way from Home*, 1937; and *Harlem: Negro Metropolis*, 1940.

His most important poems are collected in *Selected Poems*, 1953. Wayne Cooper has an essay on McKay's work: "Claude McKay and the New Negro of the 1920's," *Phylon*, XXV (Third Quarter, 1964), 297-306. The following poems are reprinted from *Selected Poems of Claude McKay*, 1953.

thorough training in British and American literature and developed a technical authority that is evident even in his earliest verse. Through the influence of an English squire, McKay became interested in Jamaican dialects, and his first book of poems, *Song from Jamaica* (1912), has a strong native flavor in style and setting. Indeed, McKay became known as "a kind of Robert Burns among his own people."

McKay came to the United States in 1912 and studied at Tuskegee Institute and the Kansas State University. He pursued a career as an agriculturist, but he soon saw that his own future was as a poet; within a short time he migrated to Harlem in search of sympathetic artists. He could not earn a living as a poet and took jobs as a porter, houseman, longshoreman, barman, and waiter. But finally "The Harlem Dancer" was published in 1917; his volume of poems, *Spring in New Hampshire and Other Poems,* appeared in 1920, and his most important volume, *Harlem Shadows,* was published in 1922. As an associate editor of *The Liberator* and *The Masses,* McKay had become attached politically to communism, and he traveled throughout Russia, representing the American Worker's Party and protesting the lynching of Negroes in the United States. When he returned to New York, he published a number of prose works: *Home to Harlem* (1928) describes the night life of Harlem; *Banjo* (1929) is concerned with harbor life at Marseilles; *Gingertown* (1932), is a collection of stories; *Banana Bottom* (1933) and *A Long Way from Home* (1937), autobiographies, recall McKay's youth and some of the racial tensions in his native island; and *Harlem: Negro Metropolis* (1940) is a sociological study of the black community in New York.

Of all these books, *Harlem Shadows* remains McKay's most impressive, a slender volume of lyrics and sonnets reflecting the poet's two most distinctive qualities: a poignant lyricism that projects McKay's sensuousness, paganism, and romanticism, and the social realism that rises to a level of protest. McKay disturbed many of the older black critics and scholars who were content with the way life should be instead of the way life actually was. These critics did not want black life in America represented realistically. With the publication of McKay's *Harlem Shadows*—followed by the poems of Langston Hughes and Countee Cullen, the stories of Jean Toomer, Rudolph Fisher, and Z. N. Hurstom—the Harlem Renaissance began, and the older critics found themselves incapable of repressing the spontaneous outburst of creativity among black artists. Among these writers, Claude McKay has a permanent place as a poet of considerable vitality and accomplishment. He helped to create what was being called during the Harlem Renaissance the image of the "New Negro."

The White House

Your door is shut against my tightened face,
And I am sharp as steel with discontent;
But I possess the courage and the grace
To bear my anger proudly and unbent.
The pavement slabs burn loose beneath my feet,   5
A chafing savage, down the decent street;
And passion rends my vitals as I pass,
Where boldly shines your shuttered door of glass.

Oh, I must search for wisdom every hour,
Deep in my wrathful bosom sore and raw,   10
And find in it the superhuman power
To hold me to the letter of your law!
Oh, I must keep my heart inviolate
Against the potent poison of your hate.

1922

Harlem Dancer

Applauding youths laughed with young prostitutes
And watched her perfect, half-clothed body sway;
Her voice was like the sound of blended flutes
Blown by black players on a picnic day.
She sang and danced on gracefully and calm,   5
The light gauze hanging loose about her form;
To me she seemed a proudly-swaying palm
Grown lovelier for passing through a storm.
Upon her swarthy neck black shiny curls
Luxuriant fell; and tossing coins in praise,   10
The wine-flushed, bold-eyed boys, and even girls,
Devoured her shape with eager, passionate gaze;
But looking at her falsely-smiling face,
I knew her self was not in that strange place.

1917

1922

Harlem Shadows

I hear the halting footsteps of a lass
  In Negro Harlem when the night lets fall
Its veil. I see the shapes of girls who pass
  To bend and barter at desire's call.
Ah, little dark girls, who in slippered feet   5
Go prowling through the night from street to street!
Through the long night until the silver break
  Of day the little gray feet know no rest;
Through the lone night until the last snow-flake
  Has dropped from heaven upon the earth's white breast,   10
The dusky, half-clad girls of tired feet
Are trudging, thinly shod, from street to street.
Ah, stern harsh world, that in the wretched way
  Of poverty, dishonor and disgrace,
Has pushed the timid little feet of clay,   15
  The sacred brown feet of my fallen race!
Ah, heart of me, the weary, weary feet
In Harlem wandering from street to street.

  1918

              1922

If We Must Die

If we must die, let it not be like hogs
Hunted and penned in an inglorious spot,
While round us bark the mad and hungry dogs,
Making their mock at our accursed lot.
If we must die, O let us nobly die,   5
So that our precious blood may not be shed
In vain; then even the monsters we defy
Shall be constrained to honor us though dead!
O kinsmen! we must meet the common foe!
Though far outnumbered let us show us brave.   10
And for their thousand blows deal one death-blow!
What though before us lies the open grave?
Like men we'll face the murderous, cowardly pack,
Pressed to the wall, dying, but fighting back!

1919

              1922

JEAN TOOMER

(1894–1967)

When Jean Toomer's *Cane* was published in 1923, the Harlem Renaissance had scarcely begun. James Weldon Johnson had prefigured the movement in his novel, *The Autobiography of an Ex-Coloured Man* (1912); Langston Hughes had begun his career with "The Negro Speaks of Rivers" in *The Crisis* in 1920; Claude McKay had issued *Harlem Shadows* (1922). In a few years, Countee Cullen would publish *Color* (1925), Rudolph Fisher his stories of life in Harlem, and Eric Walrond the fiction that appeared in *Tropic Death* (1926). The Negro was undergoing a metamorphosis, the sociologist Alain Locke maintained, "achieving something like a spiritual emancipation." Whereas the old Negro had always been "a type" in the fiction of white authors and had seen himself in "the distorted perspective of a social problem," the new Negro was "shaking off the psychology of imitation and implied inferiority. . . . The American mind must reckon with a fundamentally changed Negro." Nowhere was the spirit of this "new Negro" more lyrically and powerfully expressed than in the remarkable volume, *sui generis,* entitled *Cane.*

Cane is a potpourri of stories and poems, a gallery of fictional portraits and highly impressionistic poems. The stories—"Becky," "Fern," "Esther," "Blood-Burning Moon," and "Avey"—depict young people in moments of intense and primitive passion, frustrated by their sensuality, caught in crises of violence, murder, and human misery. Toomer does not judge his characters, even though they may murder (in "Blood-Burning Moon"), commit adultery (in "Carma"), or turn to prostitution (in "Karintha"). His attitude is one of compassion and understanding, and his style is lyrical. Like so many of the works of the Harlem Renaissance, *Cane* celebrates feeling, sensuality, and spirit, and questions conventional living. The 13 brief poems that are interwoven in the text are similar evocations of passion and racial consciousness.

The setting of *Cane* is Washington, D.C., where Toomer was born in 1894 and educated, and in Georgia, where he taught in the schools after briefly attending the University of Wisconsin (1914–1915). Toomer never published another full-length work, although a short

Other works include "Winter on Earth," *The Second American Caravan,* ed. Alfred Kreymbourg, 1928; "Race Problems and Modern Society," *Problems of Civilization,* 1929; "York Beach," *The New American Caravan,* ed. Alfred Kreym-

The Flavor of Man, 1949.

For an overview of *Cane,* see Arna Bontemps' introduction to the paperback reprint (1951). See also Robert Bone's *The Negro in America.*

novel, *York Beach,* appeared in *The New American Caravan* in 1929, "Race Problems and Modern Society" was published in 1929, and a book of meditations, *Essentials,* was published shortly before his death in 1967. Toomer had drifted into mysticism during the 1920's and later associated himself with the Society of Friends in Philadelphia. He had come to feel, as he said in *Essentials,* that "Walt Whitman's average man had turned out to be Babbitt, and that his generation had two emblems, namely the machine gun and the contraceptive."

Toomer did not write a significant work of literature after *Cane.* His first volume, which now is widely available, remains a classic of black literature. "No earlier volume of poetry or fiction, or both," as Arna Bontemps has said, "had come closer to expressing the ethos of the Negro in the Southern setting as *Cane* did."

Song of the Son

Pour O pour that parting soul in song,
O pour it in the sawdust glow of night,
Into the velvet pine-smoke air to-night,
And let the valley carry it along.
And let the valley carry it along.   5

O land and soil, red soil and sweet-gum tree,
So scant of grass, so profligate of pines,
Now just before an epoch's sun declines
Thy son, in time, I have returned to thee,
Thy son, I have in time returned to thee.   10

In time, for though the sun is setting on
A song-lit race of slaves, it has not set;
Though late, O soil, it is not too late yet
To catch thy plaintive soul, leaving, soon gone,
Leaving, to catch thy plaintive soul soon gone.   15

O Negro slaves, dark purple ripened plums,
Squeezed, and bursting in the pine-wood air,
Passing, before they stripped the old tree bare
One plum was saved for me, one seed becomes

An everlasting song, a singing tree,   20
Caroling softly souls of slavery,
What they were, and what they are to me,
Caroling softly souls of slavery.

1923

Portrait in Georgia

Hair—braided chestnut,
     coiled like a lyncher's rope,
Eyes—fagots,
Lips—old scars, or the first red blisters,
Breath—the last sweet scent of cane,   5
And her slim body, white as the ash
     of black flesh after flame.

1923

Her Lips Are Copper Wire

whisper of yellow globes
gleaming on lamp-posts that sway
like bootleg licker drinkers in the fog

and let your breath be moist against me
like bright beads on yellow globes   5

telephone the power-house
that the main wires are insulate

(her words play softly up and down
dewy corridors of billboards)

then with your tongue remove the tape   10
and press your lips to mine
till they are incandescent

1923

ESTHER

1

NINE.

Esther's hair falls in soft curls about her high-cheek-boned chalk-white face. Esther's hair would be beautiful if there were more gloss to it. And if her face were not prematurely serious, one would call it pretty. Her cheeks are too flat and dead for a girl of nine. Esther looks like a little white child, starched, frilled, as she walks slowly from her home towards her father's grocery store. She is about to turn in Broad from Maple Street. White and black men loafing on the corner hold no interest for her. Then a strange thing happens. A clean-muscled, magnificent, black-skinned Negro, whom she had heard her father mention as King Barlo, suddenly drops to his knees on a spot called the Spittoon. White men, unaware of him, continue squirting tobacco juice in his direction. The saffron fluid splashes on his face. His smooth black face begins to glisten and to shine. Soon, people notice him, and gather round. His eyes are rapturous upon the heavens. Lips and nostrils quiver. Barlo is in a religious trance. Town folks know it. They are not startled. They are not afraid. They gather round. Some beg boxes from the grocery stores. From old McGregor's notion shop. A coffin-case is pressed into use. Folks line the curb-stones. Business men close shop. And Banker Warply parks his car close by. Silently, all await the prophet's voice. The sheriff, a great florid fellow whose leggings never meet around his bulging calves, swears in three deputies. "Wall, y cant never tell what a nigger like King Barlo might be up t." Soda bottles, five fingers full of shine, are passed to those who want them. A couple of stray dogs start a fight. Old Goodlow's cow comes flopping up the street. Barlo, still as an Indian fakir, has not moved. The town bell strikes six. The sun slips in behind a heavy mass of horizon cloud. The crowd is hushed and expectant. Barlo's under jaw relaxes, and his lips begin to move.

"Jesus has been awhisperin strange words deep down, O way down deep, deep in my ears."

Hums of awe and of excitement.

"He called me to His side an said, 'Git down on your knees beside me, son, Ise gwine t whisper in your ears.' "

An old sister cries, "Ah, Lord."

"Ise agwine t whisper in your ears," he said, an I replied 'Thy will be done on earth as it is in heaven.' "

"Ah, Lord. Amen. Amen."

"An Lord Jesus whispered strange good words deep down O way down deep, deep in my ears. An He said, 'Tell em till you feel your throat on fire.' I saw a vision. I saw a man arise, an he was big an black an powerful—"

Some one yells, "Preach it, preacher, preach it!"

"—but his head was caught up in th clouds. An while he was agazin at th heavens, heart filled up with th Lord, some little white-ant biddies came an tied his feet to chains. They led him t th coast, they led him t th sea, they led him across th ocean an they didnt set him free. The old coast didnt miss him, an th new coast wasnt free, he left the old-coast brothers, t give birth t you an me. O Lord, great God Almighty, t give birth t you an me."

Barlo pauses. Old gray mothers are in tears. Fragments of melodies are being hummed. White folks are touched and curiously awed. Off to themselves, white and black preachers confer as to how best to rid themselves of the vagrant, usurping fellow. Barlo looks as though he is struggling to continue. People are hushed. One can hear weevils work. Dusk is falling rapidly and the customary store lights fail to throw their feeble glow across the gray dust and flagging of the Georgia town. Barlo rises to his full height. He is immense. To the people he assumes the outlines of his visioned African. In a mighty voice he bellows:

"Brothers an sisters, turn your faces t th sweet face of the Lord, an fill your hearts with glory. Open your eyes an see th dawnin of the mornin light. Open your ears—"

Years afterwards Esther was told that at that very moment a great, heavy, rumbling voice actually was heard. That hosts of angels and of demons paraded up and down the streets all night. That King Barlo rode out of town astride a pitch-black bull that had a glowing gold ring in its nose. And that old Limp Underwood, who hated niggers, woke up next morning to find that he held a black man in his arms. This much is certain: an inspired Negress, of wide reputation for being sanctified, drew a portrait of a black madonna on the court-house wall. And King Barlo left town. He left his image indelibly upon the mind of Esther. He became the starting point of the only living patterns that her mind was to know.

2

SIXTEEN.

Esther begins to dream. The low evening sun sets the windows of McGregor's notion shop aflame. Esther makes believe that they really are aflame. The town fire department rushes madly down the road. It ruthlessly shoves black and white idlers to one side. It whoops. It clangs, It rescues from the second-story window a dimpled infant which she claims for her own. How had she come by it? She thinks of it immaculately. It is a sin to think of it immaculately. She must dream no more. She must repent her sin. Another dream comes. There is no fire department. There are no heroic men. The fire starts. The loafers on the corner form a circle, chew their tobacco faster, and squirt juice just as fast as they can chew. Gallons on top of gallons they squirt upon the flames. The air reeks with the stench of scorched tobacco juice. Women, fat chunky Negro women, lean scrawny white women, pull their skirts up above their heads and display the most ludicrous underclothes. The women scoot in all directions from the danger zone. She alone is left to take the baby in her arms. But what a baby! Black, singed, woolly, tobacco-juice baby—ugly as sin. Once held to her breast, miraculous thing: its breath is sweet and its lips can nibble. She loves it frantically. Her joy in it changes the town folks' jeers to harmless jealousy, and she is left alone.

TWENTY-TWO.

Esther's schooling is over. She works behind the counter of her father's grocery store. "To keep the money in the family," so he said. She is learning to make distinctions between the business and the social worlds. "Good business comes from remembering that the white folks dont divide the niggers, Esther. Be just as black as any man who has a silver dollar." Esther listlessly forgets that she is near white, and that her father is the richest colored man in town. Black folk who drift in to buy lard and snuff and flour of her, call her a sweet-natured, accommodating girl. She learns their names. She forgets them. She thinks about men. "I dont appeal to them. I wonder why." She recalls an affair she had with a little fair boy while still in school. It had ended in her shame when he as much as told her that for sweetness he preferred a lollipop. She remembers the salesman from the North who wanted to take her to the movies that first night he was in town. She refused, of course. And he never came back, having found out who she was. She thinks of Barlo. Barlo's image gives her a slightly stale thrill. She spices it by telling herself his glories. Black. Magnetically so. Best cotton picker in the county, in the state, in the whole world for that matter. Best man with his fists, best man with dice, with a razor. Promoter of church benefits. Of colored fairs. Vagrant preacher. Lover of all the women for miles and miles around. Esther decides that she loves him. And with a vague sense of life slipping by, she resolves that she will tell him so, whatever people say, the next time he comes to town. After the making of this resolution which becomes a sort of wedding cake for her to tuck beneath her pillow and go to sleep upon, she sees nothing of Barlo for five years. Her hair thins. It looks like the dull silk on puny corn ears. Her face pales until it is the color of the gray dust that dances with dead cotton leaves.

3

ESTHER IS TWENTY-SEVEN.

Esther sells lard and snuff and flour to vague black faces that drift in her store to ask for them. Her eyes hardly see the people to whom she gives change. Her body is lean and beaten. She rests listlessly against the counter, too weary to sit down. From the street some one shouts, "King Barlo has come back to town." He passes her window, driving a large new car. Cutout open. He veers to the curb, and steps out. Barlo has made money on cotton during the war. He is as rich as anyone. Esther suddenly is animate. She goes to her door. She sees him at a distance, the center of a group of credulous men. She hears the deep-bass rumble of his talk. The sun swings low. McGregor's windows are aflame again. Pale flame. A sharply dressed white girl passes by. For a moment Esther wishes that she might be like her.

Not white: she has no need for being that. But sharp, sporty, with get-up about her. Barlo is connected with that wish. She mustnt wish. Wishes only make you restless. Emptiness is a thing that grows by being moved. "I'll not think. Not wish. Just set my mind against it." Then the thought comes to her that those purposeless, easy-going men will possess him, if she doesnt. Purpose is not dead in her, now that she comes to think of it. That loose women will have their arms around him at Nat Bowle's place to-night. As if her veins are full of fired sun-bleached southern shanties, a swift heat sweeps them. Dead dreams, and a forgotten resolution are carried upward by the flames. Pale flames. "They shant have him. Oh, they shall not. Not if it kills me they shant have him." Jerky, aflutter, she closes the store and starts home. Folks lazing on store window-sills wonder what on earth can be the matter with Jim Crane's gal, as she passes them. "Come to remember, she always was a little off, a little crazy, I reckon." Esther seeks her own room, and locks the door. Her mind is a pink mesh-bag filled with baby toes.

Using the noise of the town clock striking twelve to cover the creaks of her departure, Esther slips into the quiet road. The town, her parents, most everyone is sound asleep. This fact is a stable thing that comforts her. After sundown a chill wind came up from the west. It is still blowing, but to her it is a steady, settled thing like the cold. She wants her mind to be like that. Solid, contained, and blank as a sheet of darkened ice. She will not permit herself to notice the peculiar phosphorescent glitter of the sweet-gum leaves. Their movement would excite her. Exciting too, the recession of the dull familiar homes she knows so well. She doesnt know them at all. She closes her eyes, and holds them tightly. Wont do. Her being aware that they are closed recalls her purpose. She does not want to think of it. She opens them. She turns now into the deserted business street. The corrugated iron canopies and mule- and horse-gnawed hitching posts bring her a strange composure. Ghosts of the commonplaces of her daily life take stride with her and become her companions. And the echoes of her heels upon the flagging are rhythmically monotonous and soothing. Crossing the street at the corner of McGregor's notion shop, she thinks that the windows are a dull flame. Only a fancy. She walks faster. Then runs. A turn into a side street brings her abruptly to Nat Bowle's place. The house is squat and dark. It is always dark. Barlo is within. Quietly she opens the outside door and steps in. She passes through a small room. Pauses before a flight of stairs down which people's voices, muffled, come. The air is heavy with fresh tobacco smoke. It makes her sick. She wants to turn back. She goes up the steps. As if she were mounting to some great height, her head spins. She is violently dizzy. Blackness rushes to her eyes. And then she finds that she is in a large room. Barlo is before her.

"Well, I'm sholy damned—skuse me, but what, what brought you here, lil milk-white gal?"

"You." Her voice sounds like a frightened child's that calls homeward from some point miles away.

"Me?"

"Yes, you Barlo."

"This aint th place fer y. This aint th place fer y."

"I know. I know. But I've come for you."

"For me for what?"

She manages to look deep and straight into his eyes. He is slow at understanding. Guffaws and giggles break out from all around the room. A coarse woman's voice remarks, "So thats how th dictie niggers does it." Laughs. "Mus give em credit fo their gall."

Esther doesn't hear. Barlo does. His faculties are jogged. She sees a smile, ugly and repulsive to her, working upward through thick licker fumes. Barlo seems hideous. The thought comes suddenly, that conception with a drunken man must be a mighty sin. She draws away, frozen. Like a somnambulist she wheels around and walks stiffly to the stairs. Down them. Jeers and hoots pelter bluntly upon her back. She steps out. There is no air, no street, and the town has completely disappeared.

COUNTEE CULLEN

(1903–1946)

"In spite of myself," Countee Cullen wrote in 1926. "I find that I am actuated by a strong sense of race consciousness. This grows upon me, I find, as I grow older, and although I struggle against it, it colors my writing, I fear, in spite of everything I can do. There have been many things in my life that have hurt me, and I find that the surest relief from these hurts is in writing."

Although Countee Cullen accepted the complexity of his blackness, he also wished to go beyond the role of being only black so that he could become a poet like John Keats, whom he admired and emulated. Cullen's early childhood in Harlem and his experiences at DeWitt High School and New York University would not allow him to forget his

Cullen's books of poetry are *Color*, 1925; *Ballad of The Brown Girl*, 1927; *Copper Sun*, 1927; *The Black Christ and Other Poems*, 1929; and *The Medea and Other Poems*, 1935.

He collected his best poems in *On These*

I Stand, from which the following poems are reprinted.

The only full-length study is Blanche Ferguson, *Countee Cullen and the Negro Renaissance*, 1966.

race; some of his most important verse—"I Have a Rendezvous with Life," "The Ballad of the Brown Girl," "The Shroud of Color"—was included in his first important book of poetry, *Color* (1925). Cullen went on for his Master's Degree at Harvard, but he returned to become assistant editor of *Opportunity, Journal of Negro Life,* and became in time a well-known figure in the Harlem Renaissance. In 1927 he published *Copper Sun* and *The Brown Girl.*

Cullen's marriage to the daughter of W. E. B. DuBois failed in 1928, and he went to Paris to live quietly. When he returned, he took a position in the New York public schools and remained there until his death in 1946. Cullen continued to publish verse—*The Medea and Other Poems* (1935); *The Lost Zoo* (1940), a children's book; and *My Nine Lives and How I Lost Them* (1942)—, a novel; *One Way to Heaven* (1932), a satire on elite blacks in Harlem; and a musical play, *St. Louis Woman.* But Cullen never really developed beyond the poignant lyricism of *Color,* and his best poems, published in *On These I Stand* (1947), are from this early volume.

Yet Do I Marvel

I doubt not God is good, well-meaning, kind,
And did He stoop to quibble could tell why
The little buried mole continues blind,
Why flesh that mirrors Him must some day die,
Make plain the reason tortured Tantalus   5
Is baited by the fickle fruit, declare
If merely brute caprice dooms Sisyphus
To struggle up a never-ending stair.
Inscrutable His ways are, and immune
To catechism by a mind too strewn   10
With petty cares to slightly understand
What awful brain compels His awful hand.
Yet do I marvel at this curious thing:
To make a poet black, and bid him sing!

1925

For Paul Laurence Dunbar

Born of the sorrowful of heart,
    Mirth was a crown upon his head;
Pride kept his twisted lips apart
    In jest, to hide a heart that bled.

1925

Incident

Once riding in old Baltimore,
    Heart-filled, head-filled with glee,
I saw a Baltimorean
Keep looking straight at me.

Now I was eight and very small,   5
    And he was no whit bigger,
And so I smiled, but he poked out
    His tongue and called me, "Nigger."

I saw the whole of Baltimore
    From May until December: 10
Of all the things that happened there
    That's all that I remember.

1925

Scottsboro, Too, Is Worth Its Song
(A poem to American poets)

I said:
Now will the poets sing,—
Their cries go thundering
Like blood and tears
Into the nation's ears,   5
Like lightning dart
Into the nation's heart.

Against disease and death and all things fell,
And war,
Their strophes rise and swell   10
To jar
The foe smug in his citadel.

Remembering their sharp and pretty
Tunes for Sacco and Vanzetti,
I said: 15
Here too's a cause divinely spun
For those whose eyes are on the sun,
Here in epitome
Is all disgrace
And epic wrong,   20
Like wine to brace
The minstrel heart, and blare it into song.

Surely, I said,
Now will the poets sing.
   But they have raised no cry.   25
   I wonder why.

                                              1935

MUSICAL CULTURE

At many moments in recent American history the power of the musical giants of popular culture equaled or even perhaps exceeded that of elected officialdom. The language of the civil rights movement and of war protest, for example, was a musical language at its core, spoken fluently by such artists as Bob Dylan. The greatest achievements of American musical culture remain those of its jazz musicians; matchless among the latter both as singer and trumpeter was Louis Armstrong—a major original genius of modern cultural times.

Billie Holiday.
(Dennis Stock/Magnum)

Louis Armstrong. *(Henri Dauman/Magnum)*

Thelonius Monk at the piano. *(Henri Dauman/Magnum)*

Bob Dylan performing. *(E. Landy/Magnum)*

LANGSTON HUGHES

(1902–1967)

More comprehensively and intimately than any other black author, Langston Hughes expressed the everyday life-style of black people. Born on February 1, 1902, in Joplin, Missouri, he was taken to Buffalo, Topeka, Colorado Springs, and Mexico City early in his life as a result of the separation of his parents. This constant movement became a restless pattern in later life that is reflected in his work. In 1921 he traveled to New York, studied briefly and unhappily at Columbia University, and became a central figure in the Harlem Renaissance. Later he was a mess boy on a ship bound for 30 West African ports; then he was in Paris as a dish washer, in Genoa as a beachcomber, and in Cuba, Haiti, Russia, Korea, Tokyo, Shanghai, and finally New York, where he lived on East 127th Street in Harlem for the last 20 years of his life.

Hughes achieved his early and perhaps his most enduring reputation in poetry. *The Weary Blues* (1926) and *Fine Clothes to the Jew* (1927) drew on rhythms of the gospel, jazz, bebop, boogie woogie, and the blues. In eight subsequent volumes of poetry he continued to interweave these folk materials into poems that were distinctively colloquial and yet were rendered as sophisticated lyrics. *Shakespeare in Harlem* (1942), *Fields of Wonder* (1947), *One Way Ticket* (1949) and, finally, his *Selected Poems* (1959) contain a range of poetic experimentation and an achievement rarely equaled in black American literature.

Hughes was, of course, far more than a poet. He wrote in every genre, and he was a dominant literary figure, as a creator and a guide to younger writers, from the 1920's until his death in 1967. His early collection of stories, *The Ways of White Folks* (1934), is filled with an irony that arises from the social perspective of blacks who are not generally heard. His plays—*Troubled Island* (1936), *Don't You Want To Be Free?* (1938), *Mulatto* (1935), and 17 others—were modest efforts

Hughes' collections of poems include *The Weary Blues,* 1926; *Shakespeare in Harlem,* 1942; and *Montage of a Dream Deferred,* 1951. His best poems are in *Selected Poems of Langston Hughes,* 1959. His short stories are in *The Ways of White Folks,* 1934; and *Something in Common and Other Stories,* 1963; his satire in *The Best of Simple,* 1961; and his plays in *Five*

Plays by Langston Hughes, 1963. Hughes has written several autobiographies: *The Big Sea,* 1940, 1963; and *I Wonder as I Wander,* 1964. A good representation of Hughes' work is in *The Langston Hughes Reader,* 1966.

James Emanuel has written *Langston Hughes,* 1967.

that had modest success; his novel, *Not Without Laughter* (1930), his autobiographies—*The Big Sea* (1940) and *I Wonder as I Wander* (1956)—and his musicals—*The Sun Do Move* (1942), *Tambourines to Glory* (1963), and others—testify to a restlessly creative mind. Hughes also created the famous folk character of Simple, who expressed the special form of irony and fresh diction for which Hughes has become noted. First appearing in *The Chicago Defender,* the "Simple" articles were gathered in *Simple Speaks His Mind* (1950), *Simple Takes a Wife* (1953), *Simple Stakes a Claim* (1957), and the Broadway musical comedy, *Simply Heavenly.*

Toward the end of his life, Hughes became especially sensitive to the state of black culture in America and Africa. He published children's books, *The First Book of Negroes* (1952), and *The First Book of Jazz* (1955); he brought out historical studies celebrating black achievement—*Famous Negro Music Makers* (1955) and *Famous Negro Heroes of America* (1958); he published *The First Book of Africa* (1960) and *Poems from Black Africa* (1963); he publicized the work of young black poets in the *New Negro Poets, U. S. A.* (1964) and of fictionists in *The Best Short Stories by Negro Writers* (1967).

Hughes is clearly one of those writers whose total achievement and deep influence cannot be expressed in a few works. He remains among black writers, as Blyden Jackson has recently remarked, The Great Impressionist. Yet it is fair to say that his early lyrics represent him at his most poignant, characterized as they are by simplicity, irony, and melancholy, and drawing upon the deepest sources of black folk. The short story "Jazz, Jive, and Jam" takes the reader into the center of Jesse B. Simple's comic sensibility—and that is a revelation that cannot be ignored in any consideration of Langston Hughes and of American culture.

The Negro Speaks of Rivers

I've known rivers:
I've known rivers ancient as the world and older than the flow of
 human blood in human veins.

My soul has grown deep like the rivers.

I bathed in the Euphrates when dawns were young.

I built my hut near the Congo and it lulled me to sleep. 5
I looked upon the Nile and raised the pyramids above it.
I heard the singing of the Mississippi when Abe Lincoln went down
  to New Orleans, and I've seen its muddy bosom turn all golden in
  the sunset.

I've known rivers:
Ancient, dusky rivers.

My soul has grown deep like the rivers. 10

    1921

    1926

Evenin' Air Blues

Folks, I come up North
Cause they told me de North was fine.
I come up North
Cause they told me de North was fine.
Been up here six months— 5
I'm about to lose my mind.

This mornin' for breakfast
I chawed de morning' air.
This mornin' for breakfast
Chawed de mornin' air. 10

But this evenin' for supper,
I got evenin' air to spare.

Believe I'll do a little dancin'
Just to drive my blues away—
A little dancin' 15
To drive my blues away,
Cause when I'm dancin'
De blues forget to stay.

But if you was to ask me
How de blues they come to be, 20
Says if you was to ask me
How de blues they come to be—
You wouldn't need to ask me:
Just look at me and see!

    1942

Dream Boogie

Good morning, daddy!
Ain't you heard
The boogie-woogie rumble
Of a dream deferred?

Listen closely: 5
You'll hear their feet
Beating out and beating out a—

    You think
    It's a happy beat?

Listen to it closely: 10
Ain't you heard
something underneath
like a—

    What did I say?

Sure,   15
I'm happy!
Take it away!

    Hey, pop!
    Re-bop!
    Mop!   20

    Y-e-a-h!

1951

Jazz, Jive, and Jam

"It being Negro History Week," said Simple, "Joyce took me to a pay lecture to hear some Negro hysterian——"

"Historian," I corrected.

"—hysterian speak," continued Simple, "and he laid our Negro race low. He said he was misbred, misread, and misled, also losing our time good-timing. Instead of time-taking and money-making, we are jazz-shaking. Oh, he enjoyed his self at the expense of the colored race—and him black as me. He really delivered a lecture—in which, no doubt, there is some truth."

"Constructive criticism, I gather—a sort of tearing down in order to build up."

"He tore us down good," said Simple. "Joyce come out saying to me, her husband, that he had really got my number. I said, " 'Baby, he did not miss you, neither.' But Joyce did not consider herself included in the bad things he said.

"She come telling me on the way home by subway, 'Jess Simple, I have been pursuing culture since my childhood. But you, when I first met you, all you did was drape yourself over some beer bar and argue with the barflies. The higher things of life do not come out of a licker trough.'

"I replied, 'But, Joyce, how come culture has got to be so dry?'

"She answers me back, 'How come your gullet has got to be so wet? You are sitting in this subway right now looking like you would like to have a beer.'

" 'Solid!' I said. 'I would. How did you guess it?'

" 'Married to you for three years, I can read your mind,' said Joyce. 'We'll buy a couple of cans to take home. I might even drink one myself.'

" 'Joyce, baby,' I said, 'in that case, let's buy three cans.'

"Joyce says, 'Remember the budget, Jess.'

"I says, 'Honey, you done busted the budget going to that lecture program which cost One Dollar a head, also we put some small change in the collection to help Negroes get ahead.'

" 'Small change?' says Joyce, 'I put a dollar.'

" 'Then our budget is busted real good,' I said, 'so we might as well dent it some more. Let's get six cans of beer.'

" 'All right,' says Joyce, 'go ahead, drink yourself to the dogs—instead of saving for that house we want to buy!'

" 'Six cans of beer would not pay for even the bottom front step,' I said. 'But they would lift my spirits this evening. That Negro high-speaking doctor done tore my spirits down. I did not know before that the colored race was so misled, misread, and misbred. According to him there is hardly a pure black man left. But I was setting in the back, so I guess he did not see me.'

" 'Had you not had to go to sleep in the big chair after dinner,' says Joyce, 'we would have been there on time and had seats up front.'

" 'I were near enough to that joker,' I said. 'Loud as he could holler, we did not need to set no closer. And he certainly were nothing to look at!'

" 'Very few educated men look like Harry Belafonte,' said Joyce.

" 'I am glad I am handsome instead of wise,' I said. But Joyce did not crack a smile. She had that lecture on her mind.

" 'Dr. Conboy is smart,' says Joyce. 'Did you hear him quoting Aristotle?'

" 'Who were Harry Stottle?' I asked.

" 'Some people are not even misread,' said Joyce. 'Aristotle was a Greek philosopher like Socrates, a great man of ancient times.'

" 'He must of been before Booker T. Washington then,' I said, 'because, to tell the truth, I has not heard of him at all. But tonight being *Negro History Week*, how come Dr. Conboy has to quote some Greek?'

" 'There were black Greeks,' said Joyce. 'Did you not hear him say that Negroes have played a part in all history, throughout all time, from Eden to now?'

" 'Do you reckon Eve was brownskin?' I requested.

" 'I do not know about Eve,' said Joyce, 'but Cleopatra was of the colored race, and the Bible says Sheba, beloved of Solomon, was black but comely.'

" 'I wonder would she come to me?' I says.

" 'Solomon also found Cleopatra comely. He was a king.' says Joyce.

" 'And I am Jesse B. Simple,' I said.

"But by that time the subway had got to our stop. At the store Joyce broke the budget again, opened up her pocket purse, and bought us six cans of beer. So it were a good evening. It ended well—except that I ain't for going to any more meetings—especially interracial meetings."

"Come now! Don't you want to improve race relations?"

"Sure," said Simple, "but in my opinion, jazz, jive, and jam would be better for race relations than all this high-flown gab, gaff, and gas the orators put out. All this talking that white folks do at meetings, and big Negroes, too, about how to get along together—just a little jam session would have everybody getting along fine without having to listen to so many speeches. Why, last month Joyce took me to a Race Relations Seminar which her club and twenty other clubs gave, and man, it lasted three days! It started on a Friday night and it were not over until Sunday afternoon. They had sessions' mammy! Joyce is a fiend for culture."

"And you sat through all that?"

"I did not set," said Simple. "I stood. I walked in and walked out. I smoked on the corner and snuck two drinks at the bar. But I had to wait for Joyce, and I thought them speeches would never get over! My wife were a delegate from her club, so she had to stay, although I think Joyce got tired her own self. But she would not admit it. Joyce said, 'Dr. Hillary Thingabod was certainly brilliant, were he not?'

"I said, 'He were not.'

"Joyce said, 'What did you want the man to say?'

"I said, 'I wish he had sung, instead of *said*. That program needed some music to keep folks awake.'

"Joyce said, 'Our forum was not intended for a musical. It was intended to see how we can work out integration.'

"I said, 'With a jazz band, they could work out integration in ten minutes. Everybody would have been dancing together like they all did at the Savoy—colored and white—or down on the East Side at them Casinos on a Friday night where jam holds forth—and we would have been integrated.'

"Joyce said, 'This was a serious seminar, aiming at facts, not fun.'

" 'Baby,' I said, 'what is more facts than acts? Jazz makes people get into action, move! Didn't nobody move in that hall where you were—except to jerk their head up when they went to sleep, to keep anybody from seeing that they was nodding. Why, that chairman, Mrs. Maxwell-Reeves, almost lost her glasses off her nose, she jerked her head up so quick one time when that man you say was so brilliant were speaking!' "

" 'Jess Simple, that is not so!' yelled Joyce. 'Mrs. Maxwell-Reeves were just lost in the thought. And if you think you saw *me* sleeping——'

" 'You was too busy trying to look around and see where I was,' I said. 'Thank God, I did not have to set up there like you with the delegation. I would not be a delegate to no such gabfest for nothing on earth.'

" 'I thought you was so interested in saving the race!' said Joyce. 'Next time I will not ask you to accompany me to no cultural events, Jesse B., because I can see you do not appreciate them. That were a discussion of ways and means. And you are talking about jazz bands!'

" 'There's more ways than one to skin a cat,' I said. 'A jazz band like Duke's or Hamp's or Basie's sure would of helped that meeting. At least on Saturday afternoon, they could have used a little music to put some pep into the proceedings. Now, just say for instant, baby, they was to open with jazz and close with jam—and do the talking in between. Start out, for example, with "The St. Louis Blues," which is a kind of colored national anthem. That would put every human in a good humor. Then play "Why Don't You Do Right?" which could be addressed to white folks. They could pat their feet to that. Then for a third number before introducing the speaker, let some guest star like Pearl Bailey sing "There'll Be Some Changes Made"—which, as I understand it, were the theme of the meeting, anyhow—and all the Negroes could say *Amen!*

" 'Joyce, I wish you would let me plan them interracial seminaries next time. After the music, let the speechmaking roll for a while—with maybe a calypso between speeches. Then, along about five o'clock, bring on the jam session, extra-special. Start serving tea to "Tea for Two," played real cool. Whilst drinking tea and dancing, the race relationers could relate, the integraters could integrate, and desegregators desegregate. Joyce, you would not have to beg for a crowd to come out and support your efforts then. Jam—and the hall would be jammed! Even I would stick around, and not be outside sneaking a smoke, or trying to figure how I can get to the bar before the resolutions are voted on. *Resolved: that we solve* the race problem! Strike up the band! Hit it, men! Aw, play that thing! "How High the Moon!" How high! Wheee-ee-e!' "

"What did Joyce say to that?" I demanded.

"Joyce just thought I was high," said Simple.

Theme for English B

The instructor said,

> *Go home and write*
> *a page tonight,*
> *And let that page come out of you—* 5
> *Then, it will be true.*

I wonder if it's that simple?

I am twenty-two, colored, born in Winston-Salem.
I went to school there, then Durham, then here
to this college on the hill above Harlem. 10
I am the only colored student in my class.
The steps from the hill lead down into Harlem,
through a park, then I cross St. Nicholas,
Eighth Avenue, Seventh, and I come to the Y,
the Harlem Branch Y, where I take the elevator 15
up to my room, sit down, and write this page:

It's not easy to know what is true for you or me
at twenty-two, my age. But I guess I'm what
I feel and see and hear, Harlem, I hear you:
hear, you, hear me—we two—you, me, talk on this page. 20
(I hear New York, too.) Me—who?
Well, I like to eat, sleep, drink, and be in love.
I like to work, read, learn, and understand life.
I like a pipe for a Christmas present,
or records—Bessie, bop, or Bach. 25
I guess being colored doesn't make me *not* like
the same things other folks like who are other races.
So will my page be colored that I write?
Being me, it will not be white.
But it will be 30
a part of you, instructor.
You are white—
yet a part of me, as I am a part of you.
That's American.
Sometimes perhaps you don't want to be a part of me. 35
Nor do I often want to be a part of you.
But we are, that's true!

As I learn from you,
I guess you learn from me—
although you're older—and white—   40
and somewhat more free.

This is my page for English B.

1951

Harlem

What happens to a dream deferred?

   Does it dry up
like a raisin in the sun?
Or fester like a sore—
And then run?   5
Does it stink like rotten meat?
Or crust and sugar over—
like a syrupy sweet?

   Maybe it just sags
like a heavy load   10

   Or does it explode?

1951

NORMAN MAILER

(1923-   )

Saul Bellow once said, unkindly, about Norman Mailer that he wished "to be the Joe Louis of American letters." The comment points most immediately at Mailer's avowed ambition—to be champ—and at his fascination with fights and fighters. Less obviously and more interestingly the comment suggests Mailer's impatience with the "merely literary." Although he went to Harvard, read English and American literature (he originally meant to become an aeronautical engineer), and worked on the traditional literary periodicals of that highly literary university, the life of the bookman—slightly apart from the mainstream, quiet and composed—had not the slightest attraction for this writer. Mailer launched himself in letters as a war novelist—*The Naked and the Dead* (1948)—whose knowledge of combat agony was firsthand. And from that time to the present he has driven himself to explore a succession of roles and functions usually excluded from literary careers.

It is true, of course, that the author of *Marilyn* (an essay on Marilyn Monroe published in 1973) is not the first American writer to work in Hollywood as a screenwriter. (Mailer went to Hollywood in 1949 to produce an original screenplay for Samuel Goldwyn; he lasted only a single summer at the job.) Neither is he the first American writer to write about sports, to fantasize about becoming President (see the essays collected as *The Presidential Papers* in 1963), or to work as a political journalist (see his reports on the 1968 party conventions published that year in *Miami and the Siege of Chicago*). But the variety of Mailer's activities over three decades of a writing life extends well beyond these limits. In 1955 he founded, with two others, a newspa-

Mailer's novels are *The Naked and the Dead*, 1948; *Barbary Shore*, 1951; *The Deer Park*, 1955; *An American Dream*, 1965; and *Why Are We In Vietnam?*, 1967. Collections of essays, miscellanies, and narrative journals are *Advertisements for Myself*, 1959; *The Presidential Papers*, 1963; *Cannibals and Christians*, 1966; *The Armies of the Night*, 1968; *Miami and the Siege of Chicago*, 1968; *Of a Fire on The Moon*, 1970; *The Prisoner of Sex*, 1971; and *Existential Errands*, 1972. His poetry is in *Deaths For the Ladies (And Other Di-* sasters)*, 1962; his drama is *The Deer Park, a Play*, 1967; his films are *Wild 90*, 1967; *Beyond the Law*, 1967; *Maidstone: A Mystery*, 1971. Some studies of Mailer are Richard Foster, *Norman Mailer*, 1968; Donald L. Kaufmann, *Norman Mailer: The Countdown (The First Twenty Years)*, 1969; Barry Leeds, *The Structural Vision of Norman Mailer*, 1969; Robert Lucid, ed., *Norman Mailer: The Man and His Work*, 1971; and Richard Poirier, *Norman Mailer*, 1972.

per—*The Village Voice.* In 1969 he campaigned in the New York mayoral primaries, proposing that the city "secede" and become the fifty-first state. (A decade before he had talked of running for the same job—on an "Existentialist ticket.") In 1960 he stabbed his second wife after a party and spent 17 days in Bellevue hospital under observation. In 1967 he published a new novel (*Why Are We in Vietnam?*), put an older one, *The Deer Park* (1955), on stage as a play, produced, directed and acted in a movie (*Wild 90*), orated at peace demonstrations on the quality of his urine and other matters, marched on the Pentagon (with tens of thousands of others), and finished the first published version of his account of that march—a work (*The Armies of the Night*) that was ultimately to win a National Book Award and a share of a Pulitzer prize (1969). In a word, Mailer, although on occasion crude, foolish, or vicious, got around.

It is exactly this sense of a man in motion that is most striking in his books. Whether reporting a moonshot [*Of a Fire on the Moon* (1970)], imitating, in a novel, the voice of a hip disk jockey (*Why Are We in Vietnam?*), studying the art of a counterpuncher, or attempting, as in *The Armies of the Night,* to recreate the texture of mass protest in a democratic society, Mailer is most impressive as an incarnation of literary energy. Force is his passion; even in those works in which his quirky but by no means negligible intelligence works through a complex line of reasoning, the impression is that the wrestling—the pell-mell, nearly physical penetration and marshaling of concepts, images, and observations—somehow counts for more, ranks as a higher value in itself, than any individual conclusion or thesis.

About the overall quality of Mailer's theses—his views of technological reality, "plastic civilization," cancer as the universal lot, birth control as mental disease, violence and diabolism as deep human needs—judgment cannot be generous. In course of developing them, the writer invariably offers many delights—extraordinarily evocative descriptions (the U.S. Marshall in *The Armies of the Night;* midflight cabin sounds on the moon-bent Apollo). And his characterizations of public men are at once marvelously irreverent and telling. But the theses and themes themselves rarely seem either subtle or especially fresh and, under the writer's hyperbolic hammering, they grow wearing. Mailer himself, though, does not. The bunched force of his best pages jerks the nerves alert, heightens consciousness of the worth of appetite, muscle, vibrancy itself, works as a powerfully energizing stimulant.

And there are some finely finished achievements among his works. If, aside from a perfected story like "The Man Who Invented Yoga," Mailer has not yet produced a thoroughly well-ordered and moving work of fiction, he has invented standards of journalistic performance that have had major cultural consequences. Humor, metaphorical brilliance, unremitting self-awareness, mastery of both the relevant history and the relevant mysteries of national character conjoin repeatedly in his work to produce genuine clarifications of contemporary experience. The body of work this writer is in process of creating hopes to be—and perhaps deserves to be—understood as quintessentially American.

The White Negro
Superficial Reflections on the Hipster

Our search for the rebels of the generation led us to the hipster. The hipster is an *enfant terrible* turned inside out. In character with his time, he is trying to get back at the conformists by lying low. . . . You can't interview a hipster because his main goal is to keep out of a society which, he thinks, is trying to make everyone over in its own image. He takes marijuana because it supplies him with experiences that can't be shared with "squares." He may affect a broadbrimmed hat or a zoot suit, but usually he prefers to skulk unmarked. The hipster may be a jazz musician; he is rarely an artist, almost never a writer. He may earn his living as a petty criminal, a hobo, a carnival roustabout or a free-lance moving man in Greenwich Village, but some hipsters have found a safe refuge in the upper income brackets as television comics or movie actors. (The late James Dean, for one, was a hipster hero.). . . It is tempting to describe the hipster in psychiatric terms as infantile, but the style of his infantilism is a sign of the times. He does not try to enforce his will on others, Napoleon-fashion, but contents himself with a magical omnipotence never disproved because never tested. . . . As the only extreme nonconformist of his generation, he exercises a powerful if underground appeal for conformists, through newspaper accounts of his delinquencies, his structureless jazz, and his emotive grunt words.

—*"Born 1930: The Unlost Generation"*
by Caroline Bird
Harper's Bazaar, *Feb. 1957*

Probably, we will never be able to determine the psychic havoc of the concentration camps and the atom bomb upon the unconscious mind of almost everyone alive in these years. For the first time in civilized history, perhaps for the first time in all of history, we have been forced to live with the suppressed knowledge that the smallest facets of our personality or the most minor projection of our ideas, or indeed the absence of ideas and the absence of personality could mean equally well that we might still be doomed to die as a cipher in some vast statistical operation in which our teeth would be counted, and our hair would be saved, but our death itself would be unknown, unhonored, and unremarked, a death which could not follow with dignity as a possible consequence to serious actions we had chosen, but rather a death by *deus ex machina* in a gas chamber or a radioactive city; and so if in the midst of civilization—that civilization founded upon the Faustian urge to dominate nature by mastering time, mastering the links of social cause and effect—in the middle of an economic civilization founded upon the confidence that time could indeed be subjected to our will, our psyche was subjected itself to the intolerable anxiety that death being causeless, life was causeless as well, and time deprived of cause and effect had come to a stop.

The Second World War presented a mirror to the human condition which blinded anyone who looked into it. For if tens of millions were killed in concentration camps out of the inexorable agonies and contractions of super-states founded upon the always insoluble contradictions of injustice, one was then obliged also to see that no matter how crippled and perverted an image of man was the society he had created, it was nonetheless his creation, his collective creation (at least his collective creation from the past) and if society was so murderous, then who could ignore the most hideous of questions about his own nature?

Worse. One could hardly maintain the courage to be individual, to speak with one's own voice, for the years in which one could complacently accept oneself as part of an elite by being a radical were forever gone. A man knew that when he dissented, he gave a note upon his life which could be called in any year of overt crisis. No wonder then that these have been the years of conformity and depression. A stench of fear has come out of every pore of American life, and we suffer from a collective failure of nerve. The only courage, with rare exceptions, that we have been witness to, has been the isolated courage of isolated people.

2.

It is on this bleak scene that a phenomenon has appeared: the American existentialist—the hipster, the man who knows that if our collective condition is to live with instant death by atomic war, relatively quick death by the State as *l'univers concentrationnaire,* or with a slow death by conformity with every creative and rebellious instinct stifled (at what damage to the mind and the heart and the liver and the nerves no research foundation for cancer will discover in a hurry), if the fate of twentieth-century man is to live with death from adolescence to premature senescence, why then the only life-giving answer is to accept the terms of death, to live with death as immediate danger, to divorce oneself from society, to exist without roots, to set out on that uncharted journey into the rebellious imperatives of the self. In short, whether the life is criminal or not, the decision is to encourage the psychopath in oneself, to explore that domain of experience where security is boredom and therefore sickness, and one exists in the present, in that enormous present which is without past or future, memory or planned intention, the life where a man must go until he is beat, where he must gamble with his energies through all those small or large crises of courage and unforeseen situations which beset his day, where he must be with it or doomed not to swing. The unstated essense of Hip, its psychopathic brilliance, quivers with the knowledge that new kinds of victories increase one's power for new kinds of perception; and defeats, the wrong kind of defeats, attack the body and imprison one's energy until one is jailed in the prison air of other people's habits, other people's defeats, boredom, quiet desperation, and muted icy self-destroying rage. One is Hip or one is Square (the alternative which each new generation coming into American life is beginning to feel), one is a rebel or one conforms, one is a frontiersman in the Wild West of American night life, or else a Square cell, trapped in the totalitarian tissues of American society, doomed willy-nilly to conform if one is to succeed.

A totalitarian society makes enormous demands on the courage of men, and partially totalitarian society makes even greater demands, for the general anxiety is greater. Indeed if one is to be a man, almost any kind of unconventional action often takes disproportionate courage. So it is no accident that the source of Hip is the Negro for he has been living on the margin between totalitarianism and democracy for two centuries. But the presence of Hip as a working philosophy in the sub-worlds of American life is probably due to jazz, and its knifelike entrance into culture, its subtle but so penetrating influence on an avant-garde generation—that postwar generation of adventurers who (some consciously, some by osmosis) had absorbed the lessons of disillusionment and disgust of the twenties, the depression, and the war. Sharing a collective disbelief in the words of men who had too much money and controlled too many things, they knew almost as powerful a disbelief in the socially monolithic ideas of the single mate, the solid family and the respectable love life. If the intellectual antecedents of this generation can be traced to such separate influences as D. H. Lawrence,[1] Henry Miller,[2] and Wilhelm Reich,[3] the viable philosophy of Hemingway fit most of their facts: in a bad world, as he was to say over and over again (while taking time out from his parvenu snobbery and dedicated gourmandize), in a bad world there is no love nor mercy nor charity nor justice unless a man can keep his courage, and this indeed fitted some of the facts. What fitted the need of the adventurer even more precisely was Hemingway's categorical imperative that what made him feel good became therefore The Good.

So no wonder that in certain cities of America, in New York of course, and New Orleans, in Chicago and San Francisco and Los Angeles, in such American cities as Paris and Mexico, D. F., this particular part of a genera-

[1] D.H. Lawrence (1885-1930), English novelist and one of the important writers of early twentieth-century literature.

[2] Henry Miller (1891–   ), the novelist whose early works (*Tropic of Cancer*, 1943; *Tropic of Capricorn*, 1938) attacked modern society and called for sexual liberation.

[3] Wilhelm Reich, psychoanalytical thinker.

tion was attracted to what the Negro had to offer. In such places as Greenwich Village, a ménage-à-trois was completed—the bohemian and the juvenile delinquent came face-to-face with the Negro, and the hipster was a fact in American life. If marijuana was the wedding ring, the child was the language of Hip for its argot gave expression to abstract states of feeling which all could share, at least all who were Hip. And in this wedding of the white and the black it was the Negro who brought the cultural dowry. Any Negro who wishes to live must live with danger from his first day, and no experience can ever be casual to him, no Negro can saunter down a street with any real certainty that violence will not visit him on his walk. The cameos of security for the average white: mother and the home, job and the family, are not even a mockery to millions of Negroes; they are impossible. The Negro has the simplest of alternatives: live a life of constant humility or ever-threatening danger. In such a pass where paranoia is as vital to survival as blood, the Negro had stayed alive and begun to grow by following the need of his body where he could. Knowing in the cells of his existence that life was war, nothing but war, the Negro (all exceptions admitted) could rarely afford the sophisticated inhibitions of civilization, and so he kept for his survival the art of the primitive, he lived in the enormous present, he subsisted for his Saturday night kicks, relinquishing the pleasures of the mind for the more obligatory pleasures of the body, and in his music he gave voice to the character and quality of his existence, to his rage and the infinite variations of joy, lust, languor, growl, cramp, pinch, scream and despair of his orgasm. For jazz is orgasm, it is the music of orgasm, good orgasm and bad, and so it spoke across a nation, it had the communication of art even where it was watered, perverted, corrupted, and almost killed, it spoke in no matter what laundered popular way of instantaneous existential states to which some whites could respond, it was indeed a communication by art because it said, "I feel this, and now you do too."

So there was a new breed of adventurers, urban adventurers who drifted out at night looking for action with a black man's code to fit their facts. The hipster had absorbed the existentialist synapses of the Negro, and for practical purposes could be considered a white Negro.

To be an existentialist, one must be able to feel oneself—one must know one's desires, one's rages, one's anguish, one must be aware of the character of one's frustration and know what would satisfy it. The overcivilized man can be an existentialist only if it is chic, and deserts it quickly for the next chic. To be a real existentialist (Satre[4] admittedly to the contrary) one must be religious, one must have one's sense of the "purpose"—whatever the purpose may be—but a life which is directed by one's faith in the necessity

[4] Jean Paul Sartre (1905-   ), French philosopher, dramatist, and novelist, a prominent exponent of atheistic existentialism.

of action is a life committed to the notion that the substratum of existence is the search, the end meaningful but mysterious; it is impossible to live such a life unless one's emotions provide their profound conviction. Only the French, alienated beyond alienation from their unconscious could welcome an existential philosophy without ever feeling it at all; indeed only a Frenchman by declaring that the unconscious did not exist could then proceed to explore the delicate involutions of consciousness, the microscopically sensuous and all but ineffable *frissons*[5] of mental becoming, in order finally to create the theology of atheism and so submit that in a world of absurdities the existential absurdity is most coherent.

In the dialogue between the atheist and the mystic, the atheist is on the side of life, rational life, undialectical life—since he conceives of death as emptiness, he can, no matter how weary or despairing, wish for nothing but more life; his pride is that he does not transpose his weakness and spiritual fatigue into a romantic longing for death, for such appreciation of death is then all too capable of being elaborated by his imagination into a universe of meaningful structure and moral orchestration.

Yet this masculine argument can mean very little for the mystic. The mystic can accept the atheist's description of his weakness, he can agree that his mysticism was a response to despair. And yet . . . and yet his argument is that he, the mystic, is the one finally who has chosen to live with death, and so death is his experience and not the atheist's, and the atheist by eschewing the limitless dimensions of profound despair has rendered himself incapable to judge the experience. The real argument which the mystic must always advance is the very intensity of his private vision—his argument depends from the vision precisely because what was felt in the vision is so extraordinary that no rational argument, no hypotheses of "oceanic feelings" and certainly no skeptical reductions can explain away what has become for him the reality more real than the reality of closely reasoned logic. His inner experience of the possibilities within death is his logic. So, too, for the existentialist. And the psychopath. And the saint and the bullfighter and the lover. The common denominator for all of them is their burning consciousness of the present, exactly that incandescent consciousness which the possibilities within death has opened for them. There is a depth of desperation to the condition which enables one to remain in life only by engaging death, but the reward is their knowledge that what is happening at each instant of the electric present is good or bad for them, good or bad for their cause, their love, their action, their need.

It is this knowledge which provides the curious community of feeling in the world of the hipster, a muted cool religious revival to be sure, but the element which is exciting, disturbing, nightmarish perhaps, is that incompatibles have come to bed, the inner life and the violent life, the orgy and the

---

[5] Thrills.

dream of love, the desire to murder and the desire to create, a dialectical conception of existence with a lust for power, a dark, romantic, and yet undeniably dynamic view of existence for it sees every man and woman as moving individually through each moment of life forward into growth or backward into death.

3.

It may be fruitful to consider the hipster a philosophical psychopath, a man interested not only in the dangerous imperatives of his psychopathy but in codifying, at least for himself, the suppositions on which his inner universe is constructed. By this premise the hipster is a psychopath, for he possesses the narcissistic detachment of the philosopher, that absorption in the recessive nuances of one's own motive which is so alien to the unreasoning drive of the psychopath. In this country where new millions of psychopaths are developed each year, stamped with the mint of our contradictory popular culture (where sex is sin and yet sex is paradise), it is as if there has been room already for the development of the antithetical psychopath who extrapolates from his own condition, from the inner certainty that his rebellion is just, a radical vision of the universe which thus separates him from the general ignorance, reactionary prejudice, and self-doubt of the more conventional psychopath. Having converted his unconscious experience into much conscious knowledge, the hipster has shifted the focus of his desire from immediate gratification toward that wider passion for future power which is the mark of civilized man. Yet with an irreducible difference. For Hip is the sophistication of the wise primitive in a giant jungle, and so its appeal is still beyond the civilized man. If there are ten million Americans who are more or less psychopathic (and the figure is most modest), there are probably not more than one hundred thousand men and women who consciously see themselves as hipsters, but their importance is that they are an elite with the potential ruthlessness of an elite, and a language most adolescents can understand instinctively, for the hipster's intense view of existence matches their experience and their desire to rebel.

Before one can say more about the hipster, there is obviously much to be said about the psychic state of the psychopath—or, clinically, the psychopathic personality. Now, for reasons which may be more curious than the similarity of the words, even many people with a psychoanalytical orientation often confuse the psychopath with the psychotic. Yet the terms are polar. The psychotic is legally insane, the psychopath is not; the psychotic is almost always incapable of discharging in physical acts the rage of his frustration, while the psychopath at his extreme is virtually as incapable of restraining his violence. The psychotic lives in so misty a world that what is happening at each moment of his life is not very real to him whereas the psychopath seldom knows any reality greater than the face, the voice, the being of the particular people among whom he may find himself at any moment. Sheldon and Eleanor Glueck describe him as follows:

> The psychopath . . . can be distinguished from the person sliding into or clambering out of a "true psychotic" state by the long tough persistence of his anti-social attitude and behaviour and the absence of hallucinations, delusions, manic flight of ideas, confusion, disorientation, and other dramatic signs of psychosis.

The late Robert Lindner, one of the few experts on the subject, in his book *Rebel Without a Cause—The Hypnoanalysis of a Criminal Psychopath* presented part of his definition in this way:

> . . . the psychopath is a rebel without a cause, an agitator without a slogan, a revolutionary without a program: in other words, his rebelliousness is aimed to achieve goals satisfactory to himself alone; he is incapable of exertions for the sake of others. All his efforts, hidden under no matter what disguise, represent investments designed to satisfy his immediate wishes and desires. . . . The psychopath, like the child, cannot delay the pleasures of gratification; and this trait is one of his underlying, universal characteristics. He cannot wait upon erotic gratification which convention demands should be preceded by the chase before the kill: he must rape. He cannot wait upon the development of prestige in society: his egoistic ambitions lead him to leap into headlines by daring performances. Like a red thread the predominance of this mechanism for immediate satisfaction runs through the history of every psychopath. It explains not only his behaviour but also the violent nature of his acts.

Yet even Lindner who was the most imaginative and most sympathetic of the psychoanalysts who have studied the psychopathic personality was not ready to project himself into the essential sympathy—which is that the psychopath may indeed be the perverted and dangerous front-runner of a new kind of personality which could become the central expression of human nature before the twentieth century is over. For the psychopath is better adapted to dominate those mutually contradictory inhibitions upon violence and love which civilization has exacted of us, and if it be remembered that not every psychopath is an extreme case, and that the condition of psychopathy is present in a host of people including many politicians, professional soldiers, newspaper columnists, entertainers, artists, jazz musicians, callgirls, promiscuous homosexuals and half the executives of Hollywood, television, and advertising, it can be seen that there are aspects of psychopathy which already exert considerable cultural influence.

What characterizes almost every psychopath and part-psychopath is that they are trying to create a new nervous system for themselves. Generally we are obliged to act with a nervous system which has been formed from infancy, and which carries in the style of its circuits the very contradictions of our parents and our early milieu. Therefore, we are obliged, most of us, to meet the tempo of the present and the future with reflexes and rhythms which come from the past. It is not only the "dead weight of the institutions of the past" but indeed the inefficient and often antiquated nervous circuits of the past which strangle our potentiality for responding to new possibilities which might be exciting for our individual growth.

Through most of modern history, "sublimation" was possible: at the expense of expressing only a small portion of oneself, that small portion could be expressed intensely. But sublimation depends on a reasonable tempo to history. If the collective life of a generation has moved too quickly, the "past" by which particular men and women of that generation may function is not, let us say, thirty years old, but relatively a hundred or two hundred years old. And so the nervous system is overstressed beyond the possibility of such compromises as sublimation, especially since the stable middle-class values so prerequisite to sublimation have been virtually destroyed in our time, at least as nourishing values free of confusion or doubt. In such a crisis of accelerated historical tempo and deteriorated values, neurosis tends to be replaced by psychopathy, and the success of psychoanalysis (which even ten years ago gave promise of becoming a direct major force) diminishes because of its inbuilt and characteristic incapacity to handle patients more complex, more experienced, or more adventurous than the analyst himself. In practice, psychoanalysis has by now become all too often no more than a psychic blood-letting. The patient is not so much changed as aged, and the infantile fantasies which he is encouraged to express are condemned to exhaust themselves against the analyst's nonresponsive reactions. The result for all too many patients is a diminution, a "tranquilizing" of their most interesting qualities and vices. The patient is indeed not so much altered as worn out— less bad, less good, less bright, less willful, less destructive, less creative. He is thus able to conform to that contradictory and unbearable society which first created his neurosis. He can conform to what he loathes because he no longer has the passion to feel loathing so intensely.

The psychopath is notoriously difficult to analyze because the fundamental decision of his nature is to try to live the infantile fantasy, and in this decision (given the dreary alternative of psychoanalysis) there may be a certain instinctive wisdom. For there is a dialectic to changing one's nature, the dialectic which underlies all psychoanalytic method: it is the knowledge that if one is to change one's habits, one must go back to the source of their creation, and so the psychopath exploring backward along the road of the homosexual, the orgiast, the drug-addict, the rapist, the robber and the murderer seeks to find those violent parallels to the violent and often hopeless contradictions he knew as an infant and as a child. For if he has the courage to meet the parallel situation at the moment when he is ready, then he has a chance to act as he has never acted before, and in satisfying the frustration— if he can succeed—he may then pass by symbolic substitute through the locks of incest. In thus giving expression to the buried infant in himself, he can lessen the tension of those infantile desires and so free himself to remake a bit of his nervous system. Like the neurotic he is looking for the opportunity to grow up a second time, but the psychopath knows instinctively that to express a forbidden impulse actively is far more beneficial to him than merely to confess the desire in the safety of a doctor's room. The psychopath is ordinately ambitious, too ambitious ever to trade his warped brilliant conception of his possible victories in life for the grim if peaceful attrition of the analyst's couch. So his associational journey into the past is lived out in the theatre of the present, and he exists for those charged situations where his senses are so alive that he can be aware actively (as the analysand is aware passively) of what his habits are, and how he can change them. The strength of the psychopath is that he knows (where most of us can only guess) what is good for him and what is bad for him at exactly those instants when an old crippling habit has become so attacked by experience that the potentiality exists to change it, to replace a negative and empty fear with an outward action, even if—and here I obey the logic of the extreme psychopath—even if the fear is of himself, and the action is to murder. The psychopath murders—if he has the courage—out of the necessity to purge his violence, for if he cannot empty his hatred then he cannot love, his being is frozen with implacable self-hatred for his cowardice. (It can of course be suggested that it takes little courage for two strong eighteen-year-old hoodlums, let us say, to beat in the brains of a candy-store keeper, and indeed the act—even by the logic of the psychopath—is not likely to prove very therapeutic, for the victim is not an immediate equal. Still, courage of a sort is necessary, for one murders not only a weak fifty-year-old man but an institution as well, one violates private property, one enters into a new relation with the police and introduces a dangerous element into one's life. The hoodlum is therefore daring the unknown, and so no matter how brutal the act, it is not altogether cowardly.)

At bottom, the drama of the psychopath is that he seeks love. Not love as the search for a mate, but love as the search for an orgasm more apocalyptic than the one which preceded it. Orgasm is his therapy—he knows at the seed of his being that good orgasm opens his possibilities and bad orgasm imprisons him. But in this search, the psychopath becomes an embodiment of the extreme contradictions of the society which formed his character, and the apocalyptic orgasm often remains as remote as the Holy Grail, for there are clusters and nests and ambushes of violence in his own necessities and in the imperatives and retaliations of the men and women among whom he lives his life, so that even as he drains his hatred in one act or another, so the conditions of his life create it anew in him until the drama of his movements bears a sardonic resemblance to the frog who climbed a few feet in the well only to drop back again.

Yet there is this to be said for the search after the good orgasm: when one lives in a civilized world, and still can enjoy none of the cultural nectar of such a world because the paradoxes on which civilization is built demand that there remain a cultureless and alienated bottom of exploitable human material, then the logic of becoming a sexual outlaw (if one's psychological roots are bedded in the bottom) is that one has at least a running competitive chance to be physically healthy so long as one stays alive. It is therefore no accident that psychopathy is most prevalent with the Negro. Hated from outside and therefore hating himself, the Negro was forced into the position of exploring all those moral wildernesses of civilized life which the Square automatically condemns as delinquent or evil or immature or morbid or self-destructive or corrupt. (Actually the terms have equal weight. Depending on the telescope of the cultural clique from which the Square surveys the universe, "evil" or "immature" are equally strong terms of condemnation.) But the Negro, not being privileged to gratify his self-esteem with the heady satisfactions of categorical condemnation, chose to move instead in that other direction where all situations are equally valid, and in the worst of perversion, promiscuity, pimpery, drug addiction, rape, razor-slash, bottle-break, what-have-you, the Negro discovered and elaborated a morality of the bottom, an ethical differentiation between the good and the bad in every human activity from the go-getter pimp (as opposed to the lazy one) to the relatively dependable pusher or prostitute. Add to this, the cunning of their language, the abstract ambiguous alternatives in which from the danger of their oppression they learned to speak ("Well, now, man, like I'm looking for a cat to turn me on . . ."), add even more the profound sensitivity of the Negro jazzman who was the cultural mentor of a people, and it is not too difficult to believe that the language of Hip which evolved was an artful language, tested and shaped by an intense experience and therefore different in kind from white slang, as different as the special obscenity of the soldier, which in its emphasis upon "ass" as the soul and "shit" as circumstance, was able to express the existential states of the enlisted man. What makes Hip a special language is that it cannot really be taught—if one shares none of the experiences of elation and exhaustion which it is equipped to describe, then it seems merely arch or vulgar or irritating. It is a pictorial language, but pictorial like non-objective art, imbued with the dialectic of small but intense change, a language for the microcosm, in this case man, for it takes the immediate experiences of any passing man and magnifies the dynamic of his movements, not specifically but abstractly so that he is seen more as a vector in a network of forces than as a static character in a crystallized field. (Which latter is the practical view of the snob.) For example, there is real difficulty in trying to find a Hip substitute for "stubborn." The best possibility I can come up with is: "That cat will never come off his groove, dad." But groove implies movement, narrow movement but motion nonetheless. There is really no way to describe someone who does not move at all. Even a creep does move—if at a pace exasperatingly more slow than the pace of the cool cats.

4.

Like children, hipsters are fighting for the sweet, and their language is a set of subtle indications of their success or failure in the competition for pleasure. Unstated but obvious is the social sense that there is not nearly enough sweet for everyone. And so the sweet goes only to the victor, the best, the most, the man who knows the most about how to find his energy and how not to lose it. The emphasis is on energy because the psychopath and the hipster are nothing without it since they do not have the protection of a position or a class to rely on when they have overextended themselves. So the language of Hip is a language of energy, how it is found, how it is lost.

But let us see. I have jotted down perhaps a dozen words, the Hip perhaps most in use and most likely to last with the minimum of variation. The words are man, go, put down, make, beat, cool, swing, with it, crazy, dig, flip, creep, hip, square. They serve a variety of purposes and the nuance of the voice uses the nuance of the situation to convey the subtle contextual difference. If the hipster moves through his life on a constant search with glimpses of Mecca in many a turn of his experience (Mecca being the apocalyptic orgasm) and if everyone in the civilized world is at least in some small degree a sexual cripple, the hipster lives with the knowledge of how he is sexually crippled and where he is sexually alive, and the faces of experience which life presents to him each day are engaged, dismissed or avoided as his need directs and his lifemanship makes possible. For life is a contest between people in which the victor generally recuperates quickly and the loser takes long to mend, a perpetual competition of colliding explorers in which one must grow or else pay more for remaining the same (pay in sickness, or depression, or anguish for the lost opportunity), but pay or grow.

Therefore one finds words like go, and make it, and with it, and swing: "Go" with its sense that after hours or days or months or years of monotony, boredom, and depression one has finally had one's chance, one has amassed enough energy to meet an exciting opportunity with all one's present talents for the flip (up or down) and so one is ready to go, ready to gamble. Movement is always to be preferred to inaction. In motion a man has a chance, his body is warm, his instincts are quick, and when the crisis comes, whether of love or violence, he can win, he can release a little more energy for himself since he hates himself a little less, he can make a little better nervous system, make it a little more possible to go again, to go faster next time and so make more and thus find more people with whom he can swing. For to swing is to communicate, is to convey the rhythms of one's own being to a lover, a friend, or an audience, and—equally necessary—be able to feel the rhythms of their response. To swing with the rhythms of another is to enrich oneself—the conception of the learning process as dug by Hip is that one cannot really learn until one contains within oneself the implicit rhythm of the subject or the person. As an example, I remember once hearing a Negro friend have an intellectual discussion at a party for half an hour with a white girl who was a few years out of college. The Negro literally could not read or write, but he had an extraordinary ear and a fine sense of mimicry. So as the girl spoke, he would detect the particular formal uncertainties in her argument, and in a pleasant (if slightly Southern) English accent, he would respond to one or another facet of her doubts. When she would finish what she felt was a particularly well-articulated idea, he would smile privately and say, "Other-direction . . . do you really believe in that?"

"Well . . . No," the girl would stammer, "now that you get down to it, there is something disgusting about it to me," and she would be off again for five more minutes.

Of course the Negro was not learning anything about the merits and demerits of the argument, but he was learning a great deal about a type of girl he had never met before, and that was what he wanted. Being unable to read or write, he could hardly be interested in ideas nearly as much as in lifemanship, and so he eschewed any attempt to obey the precision or lack of precision in the girl's language, and instead sensed her character (and the values of her social type) by swinging with the nuances of her voice.

So to swing is to be able to learn, and by learning take a step toward making it, toward creating. What is to be created is not nearly so important as the hipster's belief that when he really makes it, he will be able to turn his hand to anything, even to self-discipline. What he must do before that is find his courage at the moment of violence, or equally make it in the act of love, find a little more between his woman and himself, or indeed between his mate and himself (since many hipsters are bisexual), but paramount, imperative, is the necessity to make it because in making it, one is making the new habit, unearthing the new talent which the old frustration denied.

Whereas if you goof (the ugliest word in Hip), if you lapse back into being a frightened stupid child, or if you flip, if you lose your control, reveal the buried weaker more feminine part of your nature, then it is more difficult to swing the next time, your ear is less alive, your bad and energy-wasting habits are further confirmed, you are farther away from being with it. But to be with it is to have grace, is to be closer to the secrets of that inner unconscious life which will nourish you if you can hear it, for you are then nearer to that God which every hipster believes is located in the senses of his body, that trapped, mutilated and nonetheless megalomaniacal God who is It, who is energy, life, sex, force, the Yoga's *prana*, the Reichian's orgone, Lawrence's "blood," Hemingway's "good," the Shavian life-force; "It"; God; not the God of the churches but the unachievable whisper of mystery within the sex, the paradise of limitless energy and perception just beyond the next wave of the next orgasm.

To which a cool cat might reply, "Crazy, man!"

Because, after all, what I have offered above is an hypothesis, no more, and there is not the hipster alive who is not absorbed in his own tumultuous hypotheses. Mine is interesting, mine is way out (on the avenue of the mystery along the road to "It") but still I am just one cat in a world of cool cats, and everything interesting is crazy, or at least so the Squares who do not know how to swing would say.

(And yet crazy is also the self-protective irony of the hipster. Living with questions and not with answers, he is so different in his isolation and in the far reach of his imagination from almost everyone with whom he deals in the outer world of the Square, and meets generally so much enmity, competition, and hatred in the world of Hip, that his isolation is always in danger of turning upon itself, and leaving him indeed just that, crazy.)

If however, you agree with my hypothesis, if you as a cat are way out too, and we are in the same groove (the universe now being glimpsed as a series of ever-extending radii from the center), why then you say simply, "I dig," because neither knowledge nor imagination comes easily, it is buried in the pain of one's forgotten experience, and so one must work to find it, one must occasionally exhaust oneself by digging into the self in order to perceive the outside. And indeed it is essential to dig the most, for if you do not dig you lose your superiority over the Square, and so you are less likely to be cool (to be in control of a situation because you have swung where the Square has not, or because you have allowed to come to consciousness a pain, a guilt, a shame or a desire which the other has not had the courage to face). To be cool is to be equipped, and if you are equipped it is more difficult for the next cat who comes along to put you down. And of course one can hardly afford to be put down too often, or one is beat, one has lost one's confidence, one has lost one's will, one is impotent in the world of action and so closer to the demeaning flip of becoming a queer, or indeed closer to dying, and therefore it is even more difficult to recover enough energy to try to make it again, because once a cat is beat he has nothing to give, and no one is interested any longer in making it with him. This is the terror of the hipster—to be beat—because once the sweet of sex has deserted him, he still cannot give up the search. It is not granted to the hipster to grow old gracefully—he has been captured too early by the oldest dream of power, the gold fountain of Ponce de León, the fountain of youth where the gold is in the orgasm.

To be beat is therefore a flip, it is a situation beyond one's experience, impossible to anticipate—which indeed in the circular vocabulary of Hip is still another meaning for flip, but then I have given just a few of the connotations of these words. Like most primitive vocabularies each word is a prime symbol and serves a dozen or a hundred functions of communication in the instinctive dialectic through which the hipster perceives his experience, that dialectic of the instantaneous differentials of existence in which one is forever moving forward into more or retreating into less.

5.

It is impossible to conceive a new philosophy until one creates a new language, but a new popular language (while it must implicitly contain a new philosophy) does not necessarily present its philosophy overtly. It can be asked then what really is unique in the life-view of Hip which raises its argot above the passing verbal whimsies of the bohemian or the lumpenproletariat.

The answer would be in the psychopathic element of Hip which has almost no interest in viewing human nature, or better, in judging human nature, from a set of standards conceived a priori to the experience, standards inherited from the past. Since Hip sees every answer as posing immediately a new alternative, a new question, its emphasis is on complexity rather than simplicity (such complexity that its language without the illumination of the voice and the articulation of the face and body remains hopelessly incommunicative). Given its emphasis on complexity, Hip abdicates from any conventional moral responsibility because it would argue that the results of our actions are unforeseeable, and so we cannot know if we do good or bad, we cannot even know (in the Joycean sense of the good and the bad) whether we have given energy to another, and indeed if we could, there would still be no idea of what ultimately the other would do with it.

Therefore, men are not seen as good or bad (that they are good-and-bad is taken for granted) but rather each man is glimpsed as a collection of possibilities, some more possible than others (the view of character implicit in Hip) and some humans are considered more capable than others of reaching more possibilities within themselves in less time, provided, and this is the dynamic, provided the particular character can swing at the right time. And here arises the sense of context which differentiates Hip from a Square view of character. Hip sees the context as generally dominating the man, dominating him because his character is less significant than the context in which he must function. Since it is arbitrarily five times more demanding of one's energy to accomplish even an inconsequential action in an unfavorable context than a favorable one, man is then not only his character but his context, since the success or failure of an action in a given context reacts upon the character and therefore affects what the character will be in the next context. What dominates both character and context is the energy available at the moment of intense context.

Character being thus seen as perpetually ambivalent and dynamic enters then into an absolute relativity where there are no truths other than the isolated truths of what each observer feels at each instant of his existence. To take a perhaps unjustified metaphysical extrapolation, it is as if the universe which has usually existed conceptually as a Fact (even if the Fact were Berkeley's[6] God) but a Fact which it was the aim of all science and philosophy to reveal, becomes instead a changing reality whose laws are remade at each instant by everything living, but most particularly man, man raised to a neo-medieval summit where the truth is not what one has felt yesterday or what one expects to feel tomorrow but rather truth is no more nor less than what one feels at each instant in the perpetual climax of the present.

What is consequent therefore is the divorce of man from his values, the liberation of the self from the Super-Ego of society. The only Hip morality (but of course it is an ever-present morality) is to do what one feels whenever and wherever it is possible, and—this is how the war of the Hip and the Square begins—to be engaged in one primal battle: to open the limits of the possible for oneself, for oneself alone, because that is one's need. Yet in widening the arena of the possible, one widens it reciprocally for others as well, so that the nihilistic fulfillment of each man's desire contains its antithesis of human co-operation.

If the ethic reduces to Know Thyself and Be Thyself, what makes it radically different from Socratic moderation with its stern conservative respect for the experience of the past is that the Hip ethic is immoderation, childlike in its adoration of the present (and indeed to respect the past means that one must also respect such ugly consequences of the past as the collective murders of the State). It is this adoration of the present which contains the affirmation of Hip, because its ultimate logic surpasses even the unforgettable solution of the Marquis de Sade[7] to sex, private property, and the family, that all men and women have absolute but temporary rights over the bodies of all other men and women—the nihilism of Hip proposes as its final tendency that every social restraint and category be removed, and the affirmation implicit in the proposal is that man would then prove to be more creative than murderous and so would not destroy himself. Which is exactly what separates Hip from the authoritarian philosophies which now appeal to the conservative and liberal temper—what haunts the middle of the twentieth century is that faith in man has been lost, and the appeal of authority has been that it would restrain us from ourselves. Hip, which would return us to ourselves, at no matter what price in individual violence, is the affirmation of the barbarian, for it requires a primitive passion about human nature to believe that individual acts of violence are always to be preferred to the collective violence of the State; it takes literal faith in the creative possibilities of the human being to envisage acts of violence as the catharsis which prepares growth.

[6] George Berkeley (1685-1753), Irish philosopher and idealist.

[7] Marquis de Sade (1740-1814), French author who wrote *Justine* (1791), *Juliette* (1798), and other works.

Whether the hipster's desire for absolute sexual freedom contains any genuinely radical conception of a different world is of course another matter, and it is possible, since the hipster lives with his hatred, that many of them are the material for an elite of storm troopers ready to follow the first truly magnetic leader whose view of mass murder is phrased in a language which reaches their emotions. But given the desperation of his condition as a psychic outlaw, the hipster is equally a candidate for the most reactionary and most radical of movements, and so it is just as possible that many hipsters will come—if the crisis deepens—to a radical comprehension of the horror of society, for even as the radical has had his incommunicable dissent confirmed in his experience by precisely the frustration, the denied opportunities, and the bitter years which his ideas have cost him, so the sexual adventurer deflected from his goal by the implacable animosity of a society constructed to deny the sexual radical as well, may yet come to an equally bitter comprehension of the slow relentless inhumanity of the conservative power which controls him from without and from within. And in being so controlled, denied, and starved into the attrition of conformity, indeed the hipster may come to see that his condition is no more than an exaggeration of the human condition, and if he would be free, then everyone must be free. Yes, this is possible too, for the heart of Hip is its emphasis upon courage at the moment of crisis, and it is pleasant to think that courage contains within itself (as the explanation of its existence) some glimpse of the necessity of life to become more than it has been.

It is obviously not very possible to speculate with sharp focus on the future of the hipster. Certain possibilities must be evident, however, and the most central is that the organic growth of Hip depends on whether the Negro emerges as a dominating force in American life. Since the Negro knows more about the ugliness and danger of life than the white, it is possible that if the Negro can win his equality, he will possess a potential superiority, a superiority so feared that the fear itself has become the underground drama of domestic politics. Like all conservative political fear it is the fear of unforeseeable consequences, for the Negro's equality would tear a profound shift into the psychology, the sexuality, and the moral imagination of every white alive.

With this possible emergence of the Negro, Hip may erupt as a psychically armed rebellion whose sexual impetus may rebound against the antisexual foundation of every organized power in America, and bring into the air such animosities, antipathies, and new conflicts of interest that the mean empty hypocrisies of mass conformity will no longer work. A time of violence, new hysteria, confusion and rebellion will then be likely to replace the time of conformity. At that time, if the liberal should prove realistic in his belief that there is peaceful room for every tendency in American life, then Hip would end by being absorbed as a colorful figure in the tapestry. But if this is not the reality, and the economic, the social, the psychological, and finally the moral crises accompanying the rise of the Negro should prove insupportable, then a time is coming when every political guidepost will be gone, and millions of liberals will be faced with political dilemmas they have so far succeeded in evading, and with a view of human nature they do not wish to accept. To take the desegregation of the schools in the South as an example, it is quite likely that the reactionary sees the reality more closely than the liberal when he argues that the deeper issue is not desegregation but miscegenation. (As a radical I am of course facing in the opposite direction from the White Citizen's Councils—obviously I believe it is the absolute human right of the Negro to mate with the white, and matings there will undoubtedly be, for there will be Negro high school boys brave enough to chance their lives.) But for the average liberal whose mind has been dulled by the committee-ish cant of the professional liberal, miscegenation is not an issue because he has been told that the Negro does not desire it. So, when it comes, miscegenation will be a terror, comparable perhaps to the derangement of the American Communists when the icons to Stalin came tumbling down. The average American Communist held to the myth of Stalin for reasons which had little to do with the political evidence and everything to do with their psychic necessities. In this sense it is equally a psychic necessity for the liberal to believe that the Negro and even the reactionary Southern white are eventually and fundamentally people like himself, capable of becoming good liberals too if only they can be reached by good liberal reason. What the liberal cannot bear to admit is the hatred beneath the skin of a society so unjust that the amount of collective violence buried in the people is perhaps incapable of being contained, and therefore if one wants a better world one does well to hold one's breath, for a worse world is bound to come first, and the dilemma may well be this: given such hatred, it must either vent itself nihilistically or become turned into the cold murderous liquidations of the totalitarian state.

6.

No matter what its horrors the twentieth century is a vastly exciting century for its tendency is to reduce all of life to its ultimate alternatives. One can well wonder if the last war of them all will be between the blacks and the whites, or between the women and the men, or between the beautiful and ugly, the pillagers and managers, or the rebels and the regulators. Which of course is carrying speculation beyond the point where speculation is still serious, and yet despair at the monotony and bleakness of the future have become so engrained in the radical temper that the radical is in danger of abdicating from all imagination. What a man feels is the impulse for his creative effort, and if an alien but nonetheless passionate instinct about the meaning of life has come so unexpectedly from a virtually illiterate people, come out of the most intense conditions of exploitation, cruelty, violence, frustration, and lust, and yet has succeeded as an instinct in keeping this tortured people alive, then it is perhaps possible that the Negro holds more of the tail of the expanding elephant of truth than the radical, and if this is so, the radical humanist could do worse than to brood upon the phenomenon. For if a revolutionary time should come again, there would be a crucial difference if someone had already delineated a neo-Marxian calculus aimed at comprehending every circuit and process of society from ukase to kiss as the communications of human energy—a calculus capable of translating the economic relations of man into his psychological relations and then back again, his productive relations thereby embracing his sexual relations as well, until the crises of capitalism in the twentieth century would yet be understood as the unconscious adaptations of a society to solve its economic imbalance at the expense of a new mass psychological imbalance. It is almost beyond the imagination to conceive of a work in which the drama of human energy is engaged, and a theory of its social currents and dissipations, its imprisonments, expressions, and tragic wastes are fitted into some gigantic synthesis of human action where the body of Marxist thought, and particularly the epic grandeur of *Das Kapital* (that first of the major *psychologies* to approach the mystery of social cruelty so simply and practically as to say that we are a collective body of humans whose life-energy is wasted, displaced, and procedurally stolen as it passes from one of us to another)—where particularly the epic grandeur of *Das Kapital* would find its place in an even more God-like view of human justice and injustice, in some more excruciating vision of those intimate and institutional processes which lead to our creations and disasters, our growth, our attrition, and our rebellion.

1957

The Marshal and the Nazi

They put him in the rear seat of a Volkswagen camper and he welcomed the opportunity to relax. Soon they would drive him, he guessed, to some nearby place where he would be arraigned, fined, and released. He kept searching the distance for sight of Lowell and Macdonald whom he assumed would be following any minute. The thought that they might not have been picked up was depressing, for he could only guess at the depths of Lowell's dejection if he had botched his arrest, and now, with each twenty seconds, he became more gloomily certain that Lowell and Macdonald had been turned back, had failed to get arrested, and blamed himself now for the rush with which he had set out—he should have warned them the arrest might not be automatic, that one might have to steal it—he felt somehow incompetent at not having properly prepared them.

Now a new man entered the Volkswagen. Mailer took him at first for a Marshal or an official, since he was wearing a dark suit and a white motorcycle helmet, and had a clean-cut stubborn face with short features. But he was carrying something which looked like a rolled-up movie screen over five feet long, and he smiled in the friendliest fashion, sat down next to Mailer, and took off his helmet. Mailer thought he was about to be interrogated and he looked forward to that with this friendly man, no less! (of course the prisoner often looks forward to his interrogation) but then another man carrying a clipboard came up to them, and leaning through the wide double door of the camper, asked questions of them both. When Mailer gave his name, the man with the clipboard acted as if he had never heard of him, or at least pretended never to have heard of him, the second possibility seeming possible since word traveled quickly from reporters.

"How do you spell it?"

"M.A.I.L.E.R."

"Why were you arrested, Mr. Miller?"

"For transgressing a police line as a protest against the war in Vietnam."

The Clipboard then asked a question of the man sitting next to him. "And why were *you* arrested?"

"As an act of solidarity with oppressed forces fighting for liberty against this country in Southeast Asia."

The Clipboard nodded drily, as if to say, "Yeah, we're all crazy here." Then he asked, pointing to the object which looked like a rolled-up movie screen. "You want that with you?"

"Yessir," said the man next to Mailer. "I'd like to take it along."

The Clipboard gave a short nod, and walked off. Mailer would never see him again. If the History has therefore spent a pointless exchange with him, it is to emphasize that the first few minutes of an arrest such as this are without particular precedent, and so Mailer, like a visitor from Mars, or an adolescent entering polite society, had no idea of what might be important next and what might not. This condition of innocence was not, however, particularly disagreeable since it forced him to watch everything with the attention, let us say, of a man like William Buckley spending his first hour in a Harlem bar—no, come! things are far safer for Mailer at the Pentagon.

He chatted with his fellow prisoner, Teague, Walter Teague was the name, who had been in the vanguard of the charge Mailer had seen from the parking lot. But before any confused impressions were to be sorted, they were interrupted by the insertion of the next prisoner put into the Volkswagen, a young man with straight blond hair and a Nazi armband on his sleeve. He was installed in the rear, with a table between, but Mailer was not happy, for his eyes and the Nazi's bounced off each other like two heads colliding—the novelist discovered he was now in a hurry for them to get this stage of the booking completed. He was also privately indignant at the U.S. Army (like a private citizen, let us say, who writes a letter to his small-town newspaper) at the incredible stupidity of putting a Nazi in the same Volks-wagen camper with Pentagon demonstrators—there were two or three other cars available, at least!—next came the suspicion that this was not an accident, but a provocation in the making. If the Nazi started trouble, and there was a fight, the newspaper accounts would doubtless state that Norman Mailer had gotten into an altercation five minutes after his arrest. (Of course, they would not say with whom.) This is all doubtless most paranoid of Mailer, but then he had had nearly twenty years of misreporting about himself, and the seed of paranoia is the arrival of the conviction that the truth about oneself is never told. (Mailer might have done better to pity the American populace—receiving misinformation in systematic form tends to create mass schizophrenia: poor America—Eddie and Debbie are True Love.)

Now they were moved out of the camper and over to an Army truck. There was Teague, and the novelist, and another arrestee—a tall Hungarian who quickly told Mailer how much he liked his books and in much the same breath that he was a Freedom Fighter—there was also a new U.S. Marshal, and the Nazi. The prisoners climbed one by one over the high tailgate, Mailer finding it a touch awkward for he did not wish to dirty his dark blue pinstripe suit, and then they stood in the rear of the truck, a still familiar $2\frac{1}{2}$ ton 6-by of a sort which the novelist hadn't been in for twenty-one years, not since his Army discharge.

Standing in the truck, a few feet apart from each other, all prisoners regarding one another, the Nazi fixed on Mailer. Their eyes locked like magnets coming into line, and for perhaps twenty seconds they stared at each other. Mailer looked into a pair of yellow eyes so compressed with hate that back of his own eyes he could feel the echo of such hatred ringing. The Nazi was taller than Mailer, well-knit, and with neatly formed features and a shock of blond hair, would have been handsome but for the ferocity of his yellow eyes which were sunk deep in their sockets. Those eyes made him look like an eagle.

Yet Mailer had first advantage in this eye-staring contest. Because he had been prepared for it. He had been getting into such confrontations for years, and rarely lost them, even though he sometimes thought they were costing him eyesight. Still, some developed instinct had made him ready an instant before the Nazi. Every bit of intensity he possessed—with the tremors of the March and the Marshal's arm still pent in him—glared forth into the other's eyes: he was nonetheless aghast at what he saw. The American Nazis were all fanatics, yes, poor mad tormented fanatics, their psyches twisted like burning leaves in the fire of their hatreds, yes, indeed! but this man's conviction stood in his eyes as if his soul had been focused to a single point of light. Mailer could feel violence behind violence rocking through his head. If the two of them were ever alone in an alley, one of them might kill the other in a fight—it was not unlike holding an electric wire in the hand. And the worst of it was that he was not even feeling violent himself—whatever violence he possessed had gone to his eyes—by that route had he projected himself on the Nazi.

After the first five seconds of the shock had passed, he realized he might be able to win—the Nazi must have taken too many easy contests, and had been too complacent in the first moment, yes it was like wrestlers throwing themselves on each other: one knuckle of one finger a little better able to be worked on a grip could make the difference—now he could feel the hint of force ebbing in the other's eyes, and could wonder at his own necessity to win. He did not hate the Nazi nearly so much as he was curious about him, yet the thought of losing had been intolerable as if he had been *obliged* not to lose, as if the duty of his life at this particular moment must have been to look into that Nazi's eye, and say with his own, "You claim you have a philosophical system which comprehends all—you know nothing! My eyes encompass yours. My philosophy contains yours. You have met the wrong man!" And the Nazi looked away, and was hysterical with fury on the instant.

"You Jew bastard," he shouted. "Dirty Jew with kinky hair."

They didn't speak that way. It was too corny. Yet he could only answer, "You filthy Kraut."

"Dirty Jew."

"Kraut pig."

A part of his mind could actually be amused at this choice—he didn't even hate Germans any more. Indeed Germans fascinated him now. Why they liked his books more than Americans did. Yet here he could think of nothing better to return than "Kraut-pig."

"I'm not a Kraut," said the Nazi, "I'm a Norwegian." And then as if the pride of his birth had tricked him into communication with an infidel, thus into sacrilege, the Nazi added quickly, "Jew bastard red," then cocked his fists. "Come here, you coward," he said to Mailer, "I'll kill you."

"Throw the first punch, baby," said Mailer, "you'll get it all."

They were both absolutely right. They had a perfect sense of the other. Mailer was certainly not brave enough to advance on the Nazi—it would be like springing an avalanche on himself. But he also knew that if the Nazi jumped him, one blond youth was very likely to get massacred. In retrospect, it would appear not uncomic—two philosophical monomaniacs with the same flaw—they could not help it, they were counterpunchers.

"Jew coward! Red bastard!"

"Go fuck yourself, Nazi baby."

But now a tall U.S. Marshal who had the body and insane look of a very good rangy defensive end in professional football—that same hard high-muscled build, same coiled spring of wrath, same livid conviction that everything opposing the team must be wrecked, sod, turf, grass, uniforms, helmets, bodies, yes even bite the football if it will help—now leaped into the truck and jumped between them. "Shut up," he said, "or I'll wreck both of you." He had a long craggy face somewhere in the physiognomical land between Steve McQueen and Robert Mitchum, but he would never have made Hollywood, for his skin was pocked with the big boiling craters of a red lunar acne, and his eyes in Cinemascope would have blazed an audience off their seat for such gray-green flame could only have issued from a blowtorch. Under his white Marshal's helmet, he was one impressive piece of gathered wrath.

Speaking to the Marshal at this point would have been dangerous. The Marshal's emotions had obviously been marinating for a week in the very special bile waters American Patriotism reserves for its need. His feelings were now caustic as a whip—too gentle the simile!—he was in agonies of frustration because the honor of his profession kept him from battering every prisoner's head to a Communist pulp. Mailer looked him over covertly to see what he could try if the Marshal went to work on him. All reports: negative. He would not stand a chance with this Marshal—there seemed no place to hit him where he'd be vulnerable; stone larynx, leather testicles, ice cubes for eyes. And he had his Marshal's club in his hand as well. Brother! Bring back the Nazi!

Whether the Marshal had been once in the Marine Corps, or in Vietnam, or if half his family were now in Vietnam, or if he just hated the sheer Jew York presumption of that slovenly, drug-ridden weak contaminating America-hating army of termites outside this fortress' walls, he was certainly any upstanding demonstrator's nightmare. Because he was full of American rectitude and was fearless, and savage, savage as the exhaust left in the wake of a motorcycle club, gasoline and cheap perfume were one end of his spectrum, yeah, this Marshal loved action, but he was also in that no man's land between the old frontier and the new ranch home—as they, yes *they*—the enemies of the Marshal—tried to pass bills to limit the purchase of hunting rifles, so did *they* try to kill America, inch by inch, all the forces of evil, disorder, mess and chaos in the world, and *cowardice!* and city ways, and slick shit, and despoliation of national resources, all the subtle invisible creeping paralyses of Communism which were changing America from a land where blood was red to a land where water was foul—yes in this Marshal's mind—no lesser explanation could suffice for the Knight of God light in the flame of his eye—the evil was without, America was threatened by a foreign disease and the Marshal was threatened to the core of his sanity by any one of the first fifty of Mailer's ideas which would insist that the evil was within, that the best in America was being destroyed by what in itself seemed next best, yes American heroism corrupted by American know-how—no wonder murder stood out in his face as he looked at the novelist—for the Marshal to lose his sanity was no passing psychiatric affair: think rather of a rifleman on a tower in Texas and a score of his dead on the street.

But now the Nazi began to play out the deepest of ceremonies. The truck standing still, another Marshal at the other end of the van (the one indeed who had arrested Mailer) and Teague and the Hungarian to different sides, everyone had their eyes on the Norwegian. He now glared again at Mailer, but then whipped away his eyes before a second contest could begin, and said, "All right, Jew, come over here if you want a fight."

The Marshal took the Nazi and threw him against the side-wall of the truck. As he bounced off, the Marshal gave him a rap below the collarbone with the butt of his club. "I told you to shut up. Now, just shut up." His rage was intense. The Nazi looked back at him sullenly, leaned on the butt of the club almost defiantly as if the Marshal didn't know what foolish danger he was in to treat the Nazi so, the Nazi had a proud curved hint of a smile, as if he were recording the features of this Marshal forever in the history of his mind, the Nazi's eyes seemed to say to the Marshal, "You are really on my side although you do not admit it—you would like to beat me now because in the future you know you will yet kiss my boots!" And the Marshal traveling a high edge of temper began to slam the Nazi against the wall of the truck with moderate force, but rhythmically, as if he would pacify them both by this act, bang, and bang, step by step, the imaginary dialogue of the Marshal to the Nazi now sounding in Mailer's ear somewhat like this, "Listen, Nazi, you're nothing but a rat fart who makes my job harder, and gives the scum around me room to breathe, cause they look at you and feel righteous. You just keep me diverted from the real danger."

And the Nazi looked back with a full sullen pouting defiance as if from deep in himself he was all unconsciously saying to the Marshal, "You know I am beautiful, and you are frightened of me. I have a cause, and I am ready to die for it, and you are just ready to die for a uniform. Join me where the real war is. Already the strongest and wildest men in America wear our symbol on their motorcycle helmets."

And the Marshal, glaring back at the Nazi, butt of his club transfixing him against the wall of the van, gave a contemptuous look, as if to drop him with the final unspoken word. "Next to strong wild men, you're nothing but a bitch."

Then the truck began to move, and the Marshal calmer now, stood silently between Mailer and the Nazi; and the Nazi also quiet now, stood in place looking neither at the Marshal nor Mailer. Some small storm of hysteria seemed to have worked itself out of the van.

ALLEN GINSBERG

(1926-   )

In 1956 Allen Ginsberg, then leader (with the novelist Jack Kerouac) of a group of peripatetic youngish writers known as "Beats," published a poem called "Howl," thereby provoking a noisy cultural controversy that culminated in an obscenity trial. The Beats were born in the Great Depression; they grew up with World War II and came to maturity in the midst of anticommunist hysteria; they were sick of placid, money-grabbing, ambition-ridden 1950's America; Ginsberg's poem vented their fury and despair. It also used bad words (in the 1950's these were a lot less acceptable than they are now) and a verse form so loose that some critics denied it the status of "verse form," and it drew much abuse as mindless raving passing itself off as poetry. The poet himself was then 30, a graduate of Columbia who had worked briefly as a market researcher after college and then left the East for California. A short time after the publication of "Howl," Ginsberg was world famous, launched on a series of readings that took him all over the world—Boston, Prague, Moscow, Warsaw, London, and elsewhere.

One reason that abuse of his most famous poem no longer seems appropriate is that some important features of both poem and poet have become at once clearer and easier to value with the passage of the years. "Howl" is a protest poem in one of its dimensions, a ferocious indictment of the destructive forces of a competitive, industrial, property-maddened society. And that protest echoes and reechoes throughout Ginsberg's work. (In the middle section of "Howl" America is hailed as "Moloch the vast stone of war! . . . Moloch whose love is endless oil and stone! Moloch whose soul is electricity and banks!" Ten years later in *The Fall of America* the poet still rails at a country where "Violence floods the State from above" and "Earth pollution [is] identical with Mind pollution.") It is also, though, a summons to generosity, openness, fraternity, love. "Above all," said the novelist John Clellon Holmes about Ginsberg in the 1950's, "I heard in his obsessed monologue the howl of the divided spirit of our time, times (as he would describe them later) of 'tenderness denied.' " And this theme— a demand for an end to human division—ceaselessly resurfaces

Allen Ginsberg's poems are included in *Howl, and Other Poems*, with an introduction by William Carlos Williams, 1956; *Empty Mirror*, 1961; *Kaddish, and Other Poems: 1958-1960*, 1969; *Reality Sandwiches, 1953-1960*, 1963; *Ankor-Wat*, 1968; and *T. V. Baby Poems*, 1968.

Critical studies are Jane Kramer, *Allen Ginsberg in America*, 1969; and Thomas Merrill, *Allen Ginsberg*, 1969.

throughout the poet's career. Sometimes the poet addresses himself to "separate identity" as an abstract problem—a false belief or illusion needing correction. Sometimes, as in "Howl," he celebrates his own love for a friend in terms that imply that this quality of feeling deserves standing as a model. Sometimes he engages the "issue" of division by adopting modes of address to "friends" (the dead novelist Dostoevsky for one: "I call him Dusty now") that reject the notion that we are cut off from each other by barriers of time or place. And sometimes Ginsberg's dream of universal openness emerges in homelier form, with the poet functioning as a one-man committee of correspondence. (John Holmes recalls him " . . . writing endless, chaotic, relentlessly cheerful letters to everyone, imprecating them to care for each other, to *know* more extravagantly, to be braver than they are . . . ")

The American literary example most inspiring to Ginsberg is Walt Whitman; he is saluted in more than one Ginsberg poem, and words of his serve as preface to one of Ginsberg's books.

> Intense and loving comradeship, the personal and passionate attachment of man to man . . . seems to promise, when thoroughly develop'd, cultivated and recognised in manners and literature, the most substantial hope and safety of the future of these States . . It is to the development, identification, and general prevalence of that fervid comradeship . . . that I look for the counterbalance and offset of our materialistic and vulgar American democracy . . . . I say democracy infers such loving comradeship, as its most inevitable twin or counterpart, without which it will be incomplete, in vain, and incapable of perpetuating itself.

The assumption here is that political forms and traits of character are directly connected. And the trait that matters most—as Ginsberg sees it—is sincerity; no breakthrough of the barriers that enforce human isolation is conceivable without it—and no decent writing, either, Ginsberg argued in a 1965 interview:

> . . . what happens if you make a distinction between what you tell your friends and what you tell your Muse? The problem is to break down that distinction: when you approach the Muse to talk as frankly as you would talk with yourself or with your friends . . . . It's the ability to commit to writing, to *write*, the same way that you . . . are! . . . there should be no distinction between what we write down, and what we really know, to begin with. As we know it every day, with each other.

Some corollaries of this faith—enthusiasm for the unrevised, the unretouched, the chaotic—are of ambiguous worth. But the faith is at least partly responsible for Ginsberg's charm—his complete absence of self-protectiveness, his disarming (and fearful and daring) assumption that readers will know, understand, receive him with the same generosity of spirit that moves him to offer himself. In Ginsberg's eyes writing is a gift of self (he once marveled at William Burroughs, who had been going through a bad personal crisis: " . . . it was a very generous thing of him to do, to start writing all of a sudden"). And the kindness, even sweetness, that is implicit in this view is seldom wholly absent from his work.

While the Whitmanian vision of universal merging of egos is central in Ginsberg, he is by no means a one-dimensional writer. Much of his work is marked by a sly, teasing humor. He is, by his own lights, an *engaged* artist—a presence at peace rallies and protest marches, a dogged articulate advocate of revised drug laws (at one point he proposed, provocatively, that "existing marijuana statutes violate the legal rights of artists to the necessary materials of their trade"). And as a cultural influence—shaper of attitudes among the Flower Generation, popularizer of all things "mystical," "Eastern," far-out—he is conceivably among the two or three most consequential literary figures of his generation.

Howl
for Carl Solomon

I

I saw the best minds of my generation destroyed by madness, starving
    hysterical naked,
dragging themselves through the negro streets at dawn looking for an
    angry fix,
angelheaded hipsters burning for the ancient heavenly connection to
    the starry dynamo in the machinery of night,
who poverty and tatters and hollow-eyed and high sat up smoking in
    the supernatural darkness of cold-water flats floating across the
    tops of cities contemplating jazz,
who bared their brains to Heaven under the El[1] and saw
    Mohammedan angels staggering on tenement roofs illuminated,   5
who passed through universities with radiant cool eyes hallucinating
    Arkansas and Blake-light tragedy among the scholars of war,
who were expelled from the academies for crazy & publishing
    obscene odes on the windows of the skull,
who cowered in unshaven rooms in underwear, burning their money
    in wastebaskets and listening to the Terror through the wall,

---

[1] The elevated railway.

who got busted in their pubic beards returning through Laredo with a
    belt of marijuana for New York,
who ate fire in paint hotels or drank turpentine in Paradise Alley,
    death, or purgatoried their torsos night after night   10
with dreams, and drugs, with waking nightmares, alcohol and cock
    and endless balls,
incomparable blind streets of shuddering cloud and lightning in the
    mind leaping toward poles of Canada & Paterson, illuminating all
    the motionless world of Time between,
Peyote solidities of halls, backyard green tree cemetery dawns, wine
    drunkenness over the rooftops, storefront boroughs of teahead
    joyride neon blinking traffic light, sun and moon and tree vibrations
    in the roaring winter dusks of Brooklyn, ashcan rantings and kind
    king light of mind,
who chained themselves to subways for the endless ride from Battery
    to holy Bronx on benzedrine until the noise of wheels and children
    brought them down shuddering mouth-wracked and battered bleak
    of brain all drained of brilliance in the drear light of Zoo,[2]
who sank all night in submarine light of Bickford's[3] floated out and
    sat through the stale beer afternoon in desolate Fugazzi's,[4] listening
    to the crack of doom on the hydrogen jukebox,   15
who talked continuously seventy hours from park to pad to bar to
    Bellevue[5] to museum to the Brooklyn Bridge,
lost battalion of platonic conversationalists jumping down the stoops
    off fire escapes off windowsills off Empire State out of the moon,
yacketayakking screaming vomiting whispering facts and memories
    and anecdotes and eyeball kicks and shocks of hospitals and jails
    and wars,
whole intellects disgorged in total recall for seven days and nights
    with brilliant eyes, meat for the Synagogue cast on the pavement,
who vanished into nowhere Zen[6] New Jersey leaving a trail of
    ambiguous picture postcards of Atlantic City Hall,   20
suffering Eastern sweats and Tangerian bone-grindings and migraines
    of China under junk-withdrawal in Newark's bleak furnished room,
who wandered around and around at midnight in the railroad yard
    wondering where to go, and went, leaving no broken hearts,
who lit cigarettes in boxcars boxcars boxcars racketing through snow
    toward lonesome farms in grandfather night,
who studied Plotinus Poe St. John of the Cross[7] telepathy and bop

[2] The Bronx Zoo.
[3] A chain restaurant in New York.
[4] A Greenwich Village bar.
[5] A hospital in Manhattan with a psychiatric clinic.
[6] Zen Buddhism, an Eastern form of religion, fashionable with the Beat Generation in the 1950's.
[7] Plotinus, Roman philosopher (205?-270 A.D.; EDGAR ALLAN POE 1809-1849; ST. JOHN OF THE CROSS 1542-1591, SPANISH POET.

kaballa because the cosmos instinctively vibrated at their feet in
 Kansas,
who loned it through the streets of Idaho seeking visionary indian
 angels who were visionary indian angels, 25
who thought they were only mad when Baltimore gleamed in
 supernatural ecstasy,
who jumped in limousines with the Chinaman of Oklahoma on the
 impulse of winter midnight streetlight smalltown rain,
who lounged hungry and lonesome through Houston seeking jazz or
 sex or soup, and followed the brilliant Spaniard to converse about
 America and Eternity, a hopeless task, and so took ship to Africa,
who disappeared into the volcanoes of Mexico leaving behind nothing
 but the shadow of dungarees and the lava and ash of poetry
 scattered in fireplace Chicago,
who reappeared on the West Coast investigating the F.B.I. in beards
 and shorts with big pacifist eyes sexy in their dark skin passing out
 incomprehensible leaflets, 30
who burned cigarette holes in their arms protesting the narcotic
 tobacco haze of Capitalism,
who distributed Supercommunist pamphlets in Union Square[8]
 weeping and undressing while the sirens of Los Alamos wailed
 them down, and wailed down Wall, and the Staten Island ferry
 also wailed,
who broke down crying in white gymnasiums naked and trembling
 before the machinery of other skeletons,
who bit detectives in the neck and shrieked with delight in policecars
 for committing no crime but their own wild cooking pederasty and
 intoxication,
who howled on their knees in the subway and were dragged off the
 roof waving genitals and manuscripts, 35
who let themselves be fucked in the ass by saintly motorcyclists, and
 screamed with joy,
who blew and were blown by those human seraphim, the sailors,
 caresses of Atlantic and Caribbean love,
who balled in the morning in the evenings in rosegardens, and the
 grass of public parks and cemeteries scattering their semen freely
 to whomever come who may,
who hiccupped endlessly trying to giggle but wound up with a sob
 behind a partition in a Turkish Bath when the blonde & naked
 angel came to pierce them with a sword,
who lost their loveboys to the three old shrews of fate the one eyed
 shrew of the heterosexual dollar the one eyed shrew that winks out
 of the womb and the one eyed shrew that does nothing but sit on

[8] 14th Street and 5th Avenue, New York.

her ass and snip the intellectual golden threads of the craftsman's
loom, 40
who copulated ecstatic and insatiate with a bottle of beer a
sweetheart a package of cigarettes a candle and fell off the bed,
and continued along the floor and down the hall and ended
fainting on the wall with a vision of ultimate cunt and come
eluding the last gyzym of consciousness,
who sweetened the snatches of a million girls trembling in the sunset,
and were red eyed in the morning but prepared to sweeten the
snatch of the sunrise, flashing buttocks under barns and naked in
the lake,
who went out whoring through Colorado in myriad stolen night-cars,
N.C.,[9] secret hero of these poems, cocksman and Adonis of
Denver—joy to the memory of his innumerable lays of girls in
empty lots & diner backyards, moviehouses' rickety rows, on
mountaintops in caves or with gaunt waitresses in familiar roadside
lonely petticoat upliftings & especially secret gas-station solipisisms
of johns, & hometown alleys too,
who faded out in vast sordid movies, were shifted in dreams, woke on
a sudden Manhattan, and picked themselves up out of basements
hungover with heartless Tokay and horrors of Third Avenue iron
dreams & stumbled to unemployment offices,
who walked all night with their shoes full of blood on the snowbank
docks waiting for a door in the East River to open to a room full
of steamheat and opium, 45
who created great suicidal dramas on the apartment cliff-banks of the
Hudson under the wartime blue floodlight of the moon & their
heads shall be crowned with laurel in oblivion,
who ate the lamb stew of the imagination or digested the crab at the
muddy bottom of the rivers of Bowery,
who wept at the romance of the streets with their pushcarts full of
onions and bad music,
who sat in boxes breathing in the darkness under the bridge, and rose
up to build harpsichords in their lofts,
who coughed on the sixth floor of Harlem crowned with flame under
the tubercular sky surrounded by orange crates of theology, 50
who scribbled all night rocking and rolling over lofty incantations
which in the yellow morning were stanzas of gibberish,
who cooked rotten animals lung heart feet tail borsht & tortillas
dreaming of the pure vegetable kingdom,

[9] Neal Cassady, a hero of the Beat generation
and the model for characters in several novels.

who plunged themselves under meat trucks looking for an egg, who
threw their watches off the roof to cast their ballot for Eternity
outside of Time, & alarm clocks fell on their heads every day for
the next decade,

who cut their wrists three times successively unsuccessfully, gave up
and were forced to open antique stores where they thought they
were growing old and cried,   55

who were burned alive in their innocent flannel suits on Madison
Avenue amid blasts of leaden verse & the tanked-up clatter of the
iron regiments of fashion & the nitroglycerine shrieks of the fairies
of advertising & the mustard gas of sinister intelligent editors, or
were run down by the drunken taxicabs of Absolute Reality,

who jumped off the Brooklyn Bridge this actually happened and
walked away unknown and forgotten into the ghostly daze of
Chinatown soup alleyways & firetrucks, not even one free beer,

who sang out of their windows in despair, fell out of the subway
window, jumped in the filthy Passaic, leaped on negroes, cried all
over the street, danced on broken wineglasses barefoot smashed
phonograph records of nostalgic European 1930's German jazz
finished the whiskey and threw up groaning into the bloody toilet,
moans in their ears and the blast of colossal steamwhistles,

who barreled down the highways of the past journeying to each
other's hotrod-Golgotha[10] jail-solitude watch or Birmingham jazz
incarnation,

who drove crosscountry seventytwo hours to find out if I had a vision
or you had a vision or he had a vision to find out Eternity,   60

who journeyed to Denver, who died in Denver, who came back to
Denver & waited in vain, who watched over Denver & brooded &
loned in Denver and finally went away to find out the Time, &
now Denver is lonesome for her heroes,

who fell on their knees in hopeless cathedrals praying for each other's
salvation and light and breasts, until the soul illuminated its hair for
a second,

who crashed through their minds in jail waiting for impossible
criminals with golden heads and the charm of reality in their hearts
who sang sweet blues to Alcatraz,

who retired to Mexico to cultivate a habit, or Rocky Mount to tender
Buddha or Tangiers to boys or Southern Pacific to the black
locomotive or Harvard to Narcissus to Woodlawn[11] to the
daisychain or grave.

who demanded sanity trials accusing the radio of hypnotism & were
left with their insanity & their hands & a hung jury,   65

[10] The place where Christ was crucified.   [11] A cemetery in the Bronx.

who threw potato salad at CCNY lecturers on Dadaism[12] and
   subsequently presented themselves on the granite steps of the
   madhouse with shaven heads and harlequin speech of suicide,
   demanding instantaneous lobotomy,
and who were given instead the concrete void of insulin metrasol
   electricity hydrotherapy psychotherapy occupational therapy
   pingpong & amnesia,
who in humorless protest overturned only one symbolic pingpong
   table, resting briefly in catatonia,
returning years later truly bald except for a wig of blood, and tears
   and fingers, to the visible madman doom of the wards of the
   madtowns of the East,
Pilgrim State's Rockland's and Greystone's[13] foetid halls, bickering
   with the echoes of the soul, rocking and rolling in the midnight
   solitude-bench dolmen-realms of love, dream of life a nightmare,
   bodies turned to stone as heavy as the moon, with mother finally
   °°°°°°, and the last fantastic book flung out of the tenement
   window, and the last door closed at 4 AM and the last telephone
   slammed at the wall in reply and the last furnished room emptied
   down to the last piece of mental furniture, a yellow paper rose
   twisted on a wire hanger in the closet, and even that imaginary,
   nothing but a hopeful little bit of hallucination—   70
ah, Carl, while you are not safe I am not safe, and now you're really
   in the total animal soup of time—
and who therefore ran through the icy streets obsessed with a sudden
   flash of the alchemy of the use of the ellipse the catalog the meter
   & the vibrating plane,
who dreamt and made incarnate gaps in Time & Space through
   images juxtaposed, and trapped the archangel of the soul between
   a visual image and joined the elemental verbs and set the noun and
   dash of consciousness together jumping with sensation of Pater
   Omnipotens Acterna Deus[14]
to recreate the syntax and measure of poor human prose and stand
   before you speechless and intelligent and shaking with shame,
   rejected yet confessing out the soul to conform to the rhythm of
   thought in his naked and endless head,   75
the madman bum and angel beat in Time, unknown, yet putting
   down here what might be left to say in time come after death,
and rose reincarnate in the ghostly clothes of jazz in the goldhorn

---

[12] Dadaism, a form of art popular in the 1920's.
[13] Mental hospitals in New York and New Jersey.
[14] Father omnipotent eternal God.

shadow of the band and blew the suffering of America's naked
  mind for love into an eli eli lamma lamma sabactham[15] saxophone
  cry that shivered the cities down to the last radio
with the absolute heart of the poem of life butchered out of their
  own bodies good to eat a thousand years.

II

What sphinx of cement and aluminum bashed open their skulls and
  ate up their brains and imagination?
Moloch! Solitude! Filth! Ugliness! Ashcans and unobtainable dollars!
  Children screaming under the stairways! Boys sobbing in armies!
  Old men weeping in the parks!   80
Moloch! Moloch! Nightmare of Moloch! Moloch the loveless!
Mental Moloch! Moloch the heavy judger of men!
Moloch the incomprehensible prison! Moloch the crossbone soulless
  jailhouse and Congress of sorrows! Moloch whose buildings are
  judgement! Moloch the vast stone of war! Moloch the stunned
  governments!
Moloch whose mind is pure machinery! Moloch whose blood is
  running money! Moloch whose fingers are ten armies! Moloch
  whose breast is a cannibal dynamo! Moloch whose ear is a smoking
  tomb!
Moloch whose eyes are a thousand blind windows! Moloch whose
  skyscrapers stand in the long streets like endless Jehovahs! Moloch
  whose factories dream and croak in the fog! Moloch whose
  smokestacks and antennae crown the cities!
Moloch whose love is endless oil and stone! Moloch whose soul is
  electricity and banks! Moloch whose poverty is the specter of
  genius! Moloch whose fate is a cloud of sexless hydrogen! Moloch
  whose name is the Mind!   85
Moloch in whom I sit lonely! Moloch in whom I dream Angels! Crazy
  in Moloch! Cocksucker in Moloch! Lacklove and manless in
  Moloch!
Moloch who entered my soul early! Moloch in whom I am a
  consciousness without a body! Moloch who frightened me out of
  my natural ecstasy! Moloch whom I abandon! Wake up in Moloch!
  Light streaming out of the sky!
Moloch! Moloch! Robot apartments! invisible suburbs! skeleton
  treasuries! blind capitals! demonic industries! spectral nations!
  invincible madhouses! granite cocks! monstrous bombs!

---

[15] "My God, my God, why has thou forsaken
me." Christ spoke these words on the Cross.
(Matthew xxvii: 46, Mark vx: 34.)

They broke their backs lifting Moloch to Heaven! Pavements, trees,
radios, tons! lifting the city to Heaven which exists and is
everywhere about us!

Visions! omens! hallucinations! miracles! ecstasies! gone down the
American river!   90

Dreams! adorations! illuminations! religions! the whole boatload of
sensitive bullshit!

Breakthroughs! over the river! flips and cruxifixions! gone down the
flood! High! Epiphanies! Despairs! Ten years' animal screams and
suicides! Minds! New loves! Mad generation! down on the rocks of
Time!

Real holy laughter in the river! They saw it all! the wild eyes! the
holy yells! They bade farewell! They jumped off the roof! to
solitude! waving! carrying flowers! Down to the river! into the
street!

III

Carl Solomon! I'm with you in Rockland[16]
  where you're madder than I am

I'm with you in Rockland
  where you must feel very strange   95

I'm with you in Rockland
  where you imitate the shade of my mother

I'm with you in Rockland
  where you've murdered your twelve secretaries

I'm with you in Rockland
  where you laugh at this invisible humor

I'm with you in Rockland
  where we are great writers on the same dreadful typewriter

I'm with you in Rockland
  where your condition has become serious and is reported on the
    radio   100

I'm with you in Rockland
  where the faculties of the skull no longer admit the worms of the
    senses

I'm with you in Rockland
  where you drink the tea of the breasts of the spinsters of Utica

I'm with you in Rockland
  where you pun on the bodies of your nurses the harpies of the
    Bronx

I'm with you in Rockland
  where you scream in a straightjacket that you're losing the game of
    the actual pingpong of the abyss

[16] New York psychiatric hospital.

I'm with you in Rockland
    where you bang on the catatonic piano the soul is innocent and
       immortal it should never die ungodly in an armed madhouse   105
I'm with you in Rockland
    where fifty more shocks will never return your soul to its body
       again from its pilgrimage to a cross in the void
I'm with you in Rockland
    where you accuse your doctors of insanity and plot the Hebrew
       socialist revolution against the fascist national Golgotha
I'm with you in Rockland
    where you will split the heavens of Long Island and resurrect your
       living human Jesus from the superhuman tomb
I'm with you in Rockland
    where there are twentyfive-thousand mad comrades all together
       singing the final stanzas of the Internationale[17]
I'm with you in Rockland
    where we hug and kiss the United States under our bedsheets the
       United States that coughs all night and won't let us sleep   110
I'm with you in Rockland
    where we wake up electrified out of the coma by our own souls'
       airplanes roaring over the roof they've come to drop angelic
       bombs the hospital illuminates itself imaginary walls collapse O
       skinny legions run outside O starry-spangled shock of mercy the
       eternal war is here O victory forget your underwear we're free
I'm with you in Rockland
    in my dreams you walk dripping from a sea-journey on the
       highway across America in tears to the door of my cottage in
       the Western night

                                                              1956

[17] Communist anthem.

A Supermarket in California

What thoughts I have of you tonight, Walt Whitman, for I walked
    down the sidestreets under the trees with a headache self-
    conscious looking at the full moon.
In my hungry fatigue, and shopping for images, I went into the neon
    fruit supermarket, dreaming of your enumerations!

What peaches and what penumbras! Whole families shopping at
    night! Aisles full of husbands! Wives in the avocados, babies in the
    tomatoes!—and you, Garcia Lorca,[1] what were you doing down by
    the watermelons?

I saw you, Walt Whitman, childless, lonely old grubber, poking
    among the meats in the refrigerator and eyeing the grocery boys.
I heard you asking questions of each: Who killed the pork chops?
    What price bananas? Are you my Angel?   5
I wandered in and out of the brilliant stacks of cans following you,
    and followed in my imagination by the store detective.
We strode down the open corridors together in our solitary fancy
    tasting artichokes, possessing every frozen delicacy, and never
    passing the cashier.
Where are we going, Walt Whitman? The doors close in an hour.
    Which way does your beard point tonight?
(I touch your book and dream of our odyssey in the supermarket and
    feel absurd.)
Will we walk all night through solitary streets? The trees add shade to
    shade, lights out in the houses, we'll both be lonely.   10
Will we stroll dreaming of the lost America of love past blue
    automobiles in driveways, home to our silent cottage?
Ah, dear father, graybeard, lonely old courage-teacher, what America
    did you have when Charon[2] quit poling his ferry and you got out
    on a smoking bank and stood watching the boat disappear on the
    black waters of Lethe?[3]

1956

[1] Federico Garcia Lorca (1899-1936), a Spanish poet.

[2] The ferryman in Greek mythology who brought dead souls across the river Styx in Hades.

[3] The river of forgetfulness in Hades.

To Aunt Rose

Aunt Rose—now—might I see you
with your thin face and buck tooth smile and pain
        of rheumatism—and a long black heavy shoe
           for your bony left leg
  limping down the long hall in Newark on the running carpet   5
        past the black grand piano
          in the day room
            where the parties were

and I sang Spanish loyalist songs
    in a high squeaky voice   10
        (hysterical) the committee listening
    while you limped around the room
        collected the money—
Aunt Honey, Uncle Sam, a stranger with a cloth arm
    in his pocket   15
        and huge young bald head
        of Abraham Lincoln Brigade

—your long sad face
    your tears of sexual frustration
        (what smothered sobs and bony hips   20
            under the pillows of Osborne Terrace)
—the time I stood on the toilet seat naked
    and you powdered my thighs with Calomine
        against the poison ivy—my tender
            and shamed first black curled hairs   25
what were you thinking in secret heart then
        knowing me a man already—
and I an ignorant girl of family silence on the thin pedestal
        of my legs in the bathroom—Museum of Newark.
Hitler is dead, Hitler is in Eternity; Hitler is with   30
    Tamburlane and Emily Brontë

Though I see you walking still, a ghost on Osborne Terrace
        down the long dark hall to the front door
    limping a little with a pinched smile
        in what must have been a silken   35
        flower dress
welcoming my father, the Poet, on his visit to Newark
    —see you arriving in the living room
        dancing on your crippled leg
        and clapping hands his book   40
        had been accepted by Liveright

Hitler is dead and Liveright's gone out of business
The Attic of the Past and Everlasting Minute are out of print
    Uncle Harry sold his last silk stocking
    Claire quit interpretive dancing school   45
        Buba sits a wrinkled monument in Old
        Ladies Home blinking at new babies

last time I saw you was the hospital
    pale skull protruding under ashen skin
        blue veined unconscious girl   50
            in an oxygen tent
    the war in Spain has ended long ago
        Aunt Rose

1958

                          1961

ROBERT LOWELL

(1917-   )

Robert Traill Spence Lowell's best book of poems, *Life Studies* (1959), includes a memoir in prose ("91 Revere Street") about his childhood in Boston. The story it tells is of taut nerves and unfulfillment: a notable New England family fallen into decline, elders possessing more charm and grace of speech than energy ("We are barely perched," Lowell reports his mother saying, "on the outer rim of the hub of decency"), the father a mumbling, ineffective naval officer (second in command at the Boston Navy Yard), the mother a witty, cultivated, more or less domineering head of the house, and the only child, Robert himself, "absorbing cold and anxiety" from complicated family Sunday dinners, repeatedly hearing grown-ups speak scornfully of his father, bemusing himself with toy soldiers. "I bored my parents, they bored me."

The young Lowell was sent to St. Marks School at age 13 (he had been enrolled since birth; his great-grandfather had served a term as the school's headmaster), and later to Harvard. He transferred to Ken-

The volumes of poetry include *Land of Unlikeness,* . 1944; *Lord Weary's Castle,* 1946; *The Mills of the Kavanaughs,* 1951; *Poems: 1938-1949,* 1950; *Life Studies,* 1959; *For the Union Dead,* 1964; *Selected Poems,* 1965; *Near the Ocean,* 1967; *Voyage, and Other Versions of Poems by Baudelaire,* 1968; *Notebook 1967-68,* 1969; *Notebooks, Revised and Expanded,* 1970; *History,* 1973; *For Lizzie and Harriet,* 1973; and *The Dolphin,* 1973.

The plays are *Phaedra,* a translation, 1961; *The Old Glory,* 1965; and *Prometheus Bound,* 1969.

For criticism, see Jerome Mazzaro, *The Poetic Themes of Robert Lowell,* 1965; Thomas Parkinson, ed., *Robert Lowell: A Collection of Critical Essays,* 1968; and Patrick Cosgrave, *The Public Poetry of Robert Lowell,* 1972.

yon after 2 years and became a student of John Crowe Ransom's; he graduated *summa cum laude* in classics in 1940. In 1943, after some teaching and a job in a publishing house, and after an unsuccessful attempt at the start of the war to enlist in the Navy, Lowell was indicted for failure to register for the draft. At his trial he sought the status of conscientious objector, arguing that the saturation bombing by the Allies of European cities was criminal; his sentence was a year and a day in a federal prison, of which he served 5 months. Thereafter, in a space of 7 years, came the three volumes of poetry—*Land of Unlikeness* (1944), *Lord Weary's Castle* (1946), and *The Mills of the Kavanaughs* (1951)—that won him rank among the country's four or five best younger poets.

Periodically Lowell has taught at various universities—Boston, Harvard, Essex in England—but he has perceived himself as a writer, not as a teacher, and no American poet of reputation has been more prolific. His volumes of poetry include, in addition to *Life Studies, For the Union Dead* (1964), *Near the Ocean* (1967), *Notebook* (1969, expanded and reissued in 1970, redone again as *History* in 1973), and *The Dolphin* and *For Lizzie and Harriet* (1973). Three plays based on Hawthorne and Melville stories were collected in *The Old Glory* (1965); *Prometheus Bound* appeared in 1969. Among the volumes of translations are *Phaedra* and *Imitations* (1961) and *The Voyage and Other Versions of Baudelaire* (1968). The quantity of Lowell's production suggests a tranquil, safely ordered life, but the suggestion is misleading. The poet's struggles with mental illness have more than once led him through breakdown and convalescences in mental hospitals; his domestic life has twice erupted in divorce; from 1965 he was an active protester against this country's intervention in Vietnam.

One reason for Lowell's preeminence among living American poets is that his career shows a striking development both in style and in substance. The air of the early Lowell books is turbulent; there are imposing sonorities of theme and sound, as in "The Quaker Graveyard at Nantucket," a sense of huge ambition grappling with first and last things, intimidating sin, death, and the chaos of nature with powerful rhythms and the symbols of a tortured Christianity. (Lowell became a convert to Catholicism in 1940.) Late in the 1950's, however, in *Life Studies,* he moved on to a manner enormously less pretentious; the speaking voice was now hesitant, random, intimate, casual, more disposed to confess than to command, moved on occasion to intensities of revulsion but concentrated everywhere on particulars, fragments that delivered few moral or spiritual messages, but stood for themselves—charged moments of feeling precisely observed and embodied. The conversational as opposed to high rhetorical mode still persists but, more recently, in such poems as "Waking Early Sunday

Morning" *(Near The Ocean)*, Lowell has seemed to conjoin personal longing and concern for the fate of the state; the result is a voice that is less than public, that does not shed particulars in the name of portentous philosophical systems, but that nevertheless can range beyond the limits of personal psyche.

As is often the case with a poet whose reputation far exceeds those of most of his generation (critics have actually spoken of the present period as "The Age of Lowell"), there is more than a little resistance to the notion that the author of *For the Union Dead* qualifies as a great poet. The frequent charge is that, in his pursuit of an unassuming manner, in his search for a telling Chekhovian flatness, and, above all, in his assumption that in the late twentieth century personal despair must be unquestioningly accepted as the only remotely appropriate response to the age, Lowell has abdicated from the responsibilities of the artist. He has ceased, that is, to function as a meaning-maker, an adversary of confusion, a shaper of forms that renew awareness that human beings in the worst of times can produce more and better than a "savage servility [that] slides by on grease." It is possible that judgment from this perspective will at length reduce estimates of Lowell's importance; it is unlikely that it will markedly diminish for many readers the sad charm of his reminiscences of his elders or the poignance of his reaching out—to wife, child, departed friends, trusted teachers—for heart's ease in hours of blackish beaten strain.

Lowell won the Pulitzer Prize for *Lord Weary's Castle* in 1947 and the National Book Award for *Life Studies* in 1960.

The Old Flame

My old flame, my wife!
Remember our lists of birds?
One morning last summer, I drove
by our house in Maine. It was still
on top of its hill—   5

Now a red ear of Indian maize
was splashed on the door.
Old Glory was thirteen stripes
hung on a pole. The clapboard
was old-red schoolhouse red.   10

Inside, a new landlord,
a new wife, a new broom!
Atlantic seaboard antique shop
pewter and plunder
shone in each room.   15

A new frontier!
No running next door
now to phone the sheriff
for his taxi to Bath
and the State Liquor Store!   20

No one saw your ghostly
imaginary lover
stare through the window,
and tighten
the scarf at his throat.   25

Health to the new people,
health to their flag, to their old
restored house on the hill!
Everything had been swept bare,
furnished, garnished and aired.   30

Everything's changed for the best—
how quivering and fierce we were,
there snowbound together,
simmering like wasps
in our tent of books!   35

Poor ghost, old love, speak
with your old voice
of flaming insight
that kept us awake all night.
In one bed and apart,   40

we heard the plow
groaning up hill—
a red light, then a blue,
as it tossed off the snow
to the side of the road.   45

1964

Mr. Edwards and the Spider

Jonathan Edwards (1703-1758) was the last great American defender of Calvinism. At the age of eleven, he wrote an essay called "The Flying Spider," in which he observed that the flight of the spider ended in death. In such sermons as "Sinners in the Hands of an Angry God," he described in vivid detail the fate of the dammed— "The God that holds you over the pit of hell, much as one holds a spider, or some loathsome insect over the fire, abhors you, and is dreadfully provoked." To the "Narrative of Surprising Conversions," an account of a religious revival and reawakening in Northampton, Mass., beginning around 1734, Edwards added a postscript describing the suicide of "my Uncle Hawley" (the Josiah Hawley of Lowell's last stanza), caused by "melancholly" and despair. Edwards attributed Hawley's suicide not to the terror of his sermons, of course, but to the devil, stirred to action because of the religious revival.

I saw the spiders marching through the air,
Swimming from tree to tree that mildewed day
  In latter August when the hay
  Came creaking to the barn. But where
    The wind is westerly, 5
Where gnarled November makes the spiders fly
Into the apparitions of the sky,
They purpose nothing but their ease and die
Urgently beating east to sunrise and the sea;

What are we in the hands of the great God? 10
It was in vain you set up thorn and briar
  In battle array against the fire
  And treason crackling in your blood;
    For the wild thorns grow tame
And will do nothing to oppose the flame; 15
Your lacerations tell the losing game
Your play against a sickness past your cure.
How will the hands be strong? How will the heart endure?

A very little thing, a little worm,
Or hourglass-blazoned spider, it is said, 20
  Can kill a tiger. Will the dead
  Hold up his mirror and affirm
    To the four winds the smell
And flash of his authority? It's well
If God who holds you to the pit of hell, 25
  Much as one holds a spider, will destroy,
Baffle and dissipate your soul. As a small boy

On Windsor Marsh, I saw the spider die
When thrown into the bowels of fierce fire:
   There's no long struggle, no desire   30
   To get up on its feet and fly—
      It stretches out its feet
And dies. This is the sinner's last retreat;
Yes, and no strength exerted on the heat
Then sinews the abolished will, when sick   35
And full of burning, it will whistle on a brick.

But who can plumb the sinking of that soul?
Josiah Hawley, picture yourself cast
   Into a brick-kiln where the blast
   Fans your quick vitals to a coal—   40
      If measured by a glass.
How long would it seem burning! Let there pass
A minute, ten, ten trillion; but the blaze
Is infinite, eternal: this is death,
To die and know it. This is the Black Widow, death.   45

                        1946

The Quaker Graveyard in Nantucket
(FOR WARREN WINSLOW, DEAD AT SEA)

Let man have dominion over the fishes of the sea and the fowls of the air and the beasts and the whole earth, and every creeping creature that moveth upon the earth.

1

A brackish reach of shoal off Madaket,—
The sea was still breaking violently and night
Had steamed into our North Atlantic Fleet,
When the drowned sailor clutched the dragnet. Light
Flashed from his matted head and marble feet,   5
He grappled at the net
With the coiled, hurdling muscles of his thighs:
The corpse was bloodless, a botch of reds and whites,
Its open, staring eyes
were lustreless dead-lights   10
Or cabin-windows on a stranded hulk
Heavy with sand. We weight the body, close
Its eyes and heave it seaward whence it came,
Where the heel-headed dogfish barks its nose
On Ahab's void and forehead; and the name   15

Is blocked in yellow chalk.
Sailors, who pitch this portent at the sea
Where dreadnaughts shall confess
Its hell-bent deity,
When you are powerless   20
To sand-bag this Atlantic bulwark, faced
By the earth-shaker, green, unwearied, chaste
In his steel scales: ask for no Orphean lute
To pluck life back. The guns of the steeled fleet
Recoil and then repeat   25
The hoarse salute.

2

Whenever winds are moving and their breath
Heaves at the roped-in bulwarks of this pier,
The terns and sea-gulls tremble at your death
In these home waters. Sailors, can you hear   30
The Pequod's sea wings, beating landward, fall
Headlong and break on our Atlantic wall
Off 'Sconset, where the yawing S-boats splash
The bellbuoy, with ballooning spinnakers,
As the entangled, screeching mainsheet clears   35
The blocks: off Madaket, where lubbers lash
The heavy surf and throw their long lead squids
For blue-fish? Sea-gulls blink their heavy lids
Seaward. The winds' wings beat upon the stones,
Cousin, and scream for you and the claws rush   40
At the sea's throat and wing it in the slush
Of this old Quaker graveyard where the bones
Cry out in the long night for the hurt beast
Bobbing by Ahab's whaleboats in the East.

3

All you recovered from Poseidon died   45
With you, my cousin, and the harrowed brine
Is fruitless on the blue beard of the god,
Stretching beyond us to the castles in Spain,
Nantucket's westward haven. To Cape Cod
Guns, cradled on the tide,   50
Blast the eelgrass about a waterclock
Of bilge and backwash, roil the salt and sand
Lashing earth's scaffold, rock
Our warships in the hand
Of the great God, where time's contrition blues   55
Whatever it was these Quaker sailors lost
In the mad scramble of their lies. They died

When time was open-eyed,
Wooden and childish; only bones abide
There, in the nowhere, where their boats were tossed   60
Sky-high, where mariners had fabled news
Of IS, the whited monster. What it cost
Them is their secret. In the sperm-whale's slick
I see the Quakers drown and hear their cry:
"If God himself had not been on our side.   65
If God himself had not been on our side,
When the Atlantic rose against us, why,
Then it had swallowed us up quick."

4

This is the end of the whaleroad and the whale
Who spewed Nantucket bones on the thrashed swell   70
And stirred the troubled waters to whirlpools
To send the Pequod packing off to hell:
This is the end of them, three-quarters fools,
Snatching at straws to sail
Seaward and seaward on the turntail whale,   75
Spouting out blood and water as it rolls,
Sick as a dog to these Atlantic shoals:
Clamavimus, O depths. Let the sea-gulls wail
For water, for the deep where the high tide
Mutters to its hurt self, mutters and ebbs.   80
Waves wallow in their wash, go out and out,
Leave only the death-rattle of the crabs,
The beach increasing, its enormous snout
Sucking the ocean's side.
This is the end of running on the waves;   85
We are poured out like water. Who will dance
The mast-lashed master of Leviathans
Up from this field of Quakers in their unstoned graves?

5

When the whale's viscera go and the roll
Of its corruption overruns the world   90
Beyond tree-swept Nantucket and Wood's Hole
And Martha's Vineyard, Sailor, will your sword
Whistle and fall and sink into the fat?
In the great ash-pit of Jehoshaphat
The bones cry for the blood of the white whale.   95
The fat flukes arch and whack about its ears.
The death-lance churns into the sanctuary, tears
The gun-blue swingle, heaving like a flail,
And hacks the coiling life out: it works and drags

And rips the sperm-whale's midriff into rags,   100
Gobbets of blubber spill to wind and weather,
Sailor, and gulls go round the stoven timbers
Where the morning stars sing out together
And thunder shakes the white surf and dismembers
The red flag hammered in the mast-head. Hide,   105
Our steel, Jonas Messias, in Thy side.

1945

1946

In Memory of Arthur Winslow[1]

I. DEATH FROM CANCER

This Easter, Arthur Winslow, less than dead,
Your people set you up in Phillips' House
To settle off your wrestling with the crab—
The claws drop flesh upon your yachting blouse
Until longshoreman Charon[2] come and stab   5
Through your adjusted bed
And crush the crab. On Boston Basin, shells
Hit water by the Union Boat Club wharf:
You ponder why the coxes[3] squeakings dwarf
The *resurrexit dominus*[4] of all the bells.   10

Grandfather Winslow, look, the swanboats coast
That island in the Pacific Gardens, where
The bread-stuffed ducks are brooding, where with tub
And strainer the mid-Sunday Irish scare
The sun-struck shallows for the dusky chub[5]   15
This Easter, and the ghost
Of risen Jesus walks the waves to run[6]
Arthur upon a trumpeting black swan
Beyond Charles River to the Acheron[7]
Where the wide waters and their voyager are one.   20

[1] Arthur Winslow was Lowell's grandfather
on his mother's side. See "91 Revere Street"
[2] The ferryman who conveyed the dead to
Hades over the river Styx.
[3] Coxwains are people who steer the boat
and are in charge of the crews.

[4] God has risen.
[5] Fresh water fish.
[6] See Matthew, XIV: 25.
[7] The Charles River flows into Boston Harbor and separates the city of Boston from
Cambridge. Acheron was a river in Hades.

II. DUNBARTON[8]

The stones are yellow and the grass is gray
Past Concord by the rotten lake and hill
Where crutch and trumpet meet the limousine
And half-forgotten Starks and Winslows fill
The granite plot and the dwarf pines are green   25
From watching for the day
When the great year of the little yeomen come
Bringing its landed Promise and the faith
That made the Pilgrim Makers take a lathe
And point their wooden steeples lest the Word be dumb.   30

O fearful witnesses, your day is done:
The minister from Boston waves your shades,
Like children, out of sight and out of mind.
The first selectman of Dunbarton spreads
Wreaths of New Hampshire pine cones on the lined   35
Casket where the cold sun
Is melting. But, at last, the end is reached;
We started our cars. The preacher's mouthings still
Deafen my poor relations on the hill:
Their sunken landmarks echo what our fathers preached. 40

III. FIVE YEARS LATER

This Easter, Arthur Winslow, five years gone
I came to mourn you, not to praise the craft
That netted you a million dollars, late
Hosing out gold in Colorado's waste,
Then lost it all in Boston real estate.   45
Now from the train, at dawn
Leaving Columbus in Ohio, shell
On shell of our stark culture strikes the sun
To fill my head with all our fathers won
When Cotton Mather wrestled with the fiends from hell.[9] 50

You must have hankered for our family's craft:
The block-house Edward made, the Governor,[10]

[8] Dunbarton, New Hampshire is the seat of the Starks, the maternal ancestors of Arthur Winslow.

[9] Cotton Mather (1663-1728) was a fierce opponent of witchcraft. See Volume I, pp. 229.

[10] Edward Winslow (1595-1655), Lowell's ancestor, was an English Puritan colonist in America who was elected governor of Plymouth Colony (1633-1644) three times.

At Marshfield, and the slight coin-silver spoons
The Sheriff beat to shame the gaunt Revere,[11]
And General Stark's[12] coarse bas-relief in bronze   55
Set on your granite shaft
In rough Dunbarton; for what else could bring
You, Arthur, to the veined and alien West
But devil's notions that your gold at least
Could give back life to men who whipped or backed the King?   60

IV. A PRAYER FOR MY GRANDFATHER TO OUR LADY

Mother, for these three hundred years or more
Neither our clippers nor our slavers reached
The haven of your peace in this Bay State:
Neither my father nor his father. Beached
On these dry flats of fishy real estate,   65
O Mother, I implore
Your scorched, blue thunderbreasts of love to pour
Buckets of blessings on my burning head
Until I rise like Lazarus from the dead:[13]
Lavabis nos et super nivem dealbabor.[14]   70

"On Copley Square,[15] I saw you hold the door
To Trinity, the costly Church, and saw
The painted Paradise of harps and lutes
Sink like Atlantis[16] in the Devil's jaw
And know the Devil's teeth out by the roots;   75
But when I strike for shore
I find no painted idols to adore:
Hell is burned out, heaven's harp-strings are slack.
Mother, run to the chalice, and bring back
Blood on your finger-tips for Lazarus who was poor."   80

1946

[11] The American silversmith, engraver, and Revolutionary patriot who rode (1775) from Charleston to Lexington to warn colonists of the British advance.
[12] General John Stark (1728-1822), Lowell's ancestor, was a Revolutionary hero from New Hampshire.
[13] Lazarus was raised from the dead by Jesus. See John 11:1-44.
[14] "Wash us and I will be whiter than snow."
[15] An old square in the center of Boston.
[16] A legendary island in the Atlantic, west of Gibraltar, said by Plato to have sunk into the sea.

For the Union Dead

"Relinquunt Omnia Servare Rem Publicam."[1]

The old South Boston Aquarium stands
in a Sahara of snow now. Its broken windows are boarded.
The bronze weathervane cod has lost half its scales.
The airy tanks are dry.

Once my nose crawled like a snail on the glass;   5
my hand tingled
to burst the bubbles
drifting from the noses of the cowed, compliant fish.

My hand draws back. I often sigh still
for the dark downward and vegetating kingdom   10
of the fish and reptile. One morning last March,
I pressed against the new barbed and galvanized

fence on the Boston Common. Behind their cage,
yellow dinosaur steamshovels were grunting
as they cropped up tons of mush and grass   15
to gouge their underworld garage.

Parking spaces luxuriate like civic
sandpiles in the heart of Boston.
A girdle of orange, Puritan-pumpkin colored girders
braces the tingling Statehouse,   20

shaking over the excavations, as it faces Colonel Shaw[2]
and his bell-cheeked Negro infantry
on St. Gaudens' shaking Civil War relief,
propped by a plank splint against the garage's earthquake.

Two months after marching through Boston,   25
half the regiment was dead;
at the dedication,
William James could almost hear the bronze Negroes breathe.

Their monument sticks like a fishbone
in the city's throat.   30
Its Colonel is as lean
as a compass needle.

---

[1] They relinquished all to serve the State.
[2] Robert Gould Shaw (1837-1963) was the first leader of the Negro regiment in the Civil War. Augustus Saint-Gaudens' tribute to him is on the Boston Common, facing the State House.

He has an angry wrenlike vigilance,
a greyhound's gentle tautness;
he seems to wince at pleasure,   35
and suffocate for privacy.

He is out of bounds now. He rejoices in man's lovely,
peculiar power to choose life and die—
when he leads his black soldiers to death,
he cannot bend his back.   40

On a thousand small town New England greens,
the old white churches hold their air
of sparse, sincere rebellion; frayed flags
quilt the graveyards of the Grand Army of the Republic.

The stone statues of the abstract Union Soldier   45
grow slimmer and younger each year—
wasp-waisted, they doze over muskets
and muse through their sideburns . .

Shaw's father wanted no monument
except the ditch,   50
where his son's body was thrown
and lost with his "niggers."[3]

The ditch is nearer.
There are no statues for the last war here;
on Boylston Street, a commercial photograph   55
shows Hiroshima boiling

over a Mosler Safe,[4] the "Rock of Ages"
that survived the blast. Space is nearer.
When I crouch to my television set,
the drained faces of Negro school-children rise like balloons.   60

Colonel Shaw
is riding on his bubble,
he waits
for the blesséd break.

The Aquarium is gone. Everywhere,   65
giant finned cars nose forward like fish;
a savage servility
slides by on grease.

                                                          1959

[3] Shaw was buried with his soldiers.
[4] The Mosler safe survived the bombing of
Hiroshima and was photographed.

Skunk Hour
(For Elizabeth Bishop)

Nautilus Island's hermit
heiress still lives through winter in her Spartan[1] cottage;
her sheep still graze above the sea.
Her son's a bishop. Her farmer
is first selectman in our village;   5
she's in her dotage.

Thirsting for
the hierarchic privacy
of Queen Victoria's century,
she buys up all   10
the eyesores facing her shore,
and lets them fall.

The season's ill—
we've lost our summer millionaire.
who seemed to leap from an L.L. Bean   15
catalogue. His nine-knot yawl
was auctioned off to lobstermen.
A red fox stain covers Blue Hill.

And now our fairy
decorator brightens his shop for fall;   20
his fishnet's filled with orange cork,
orange, his cobbler's bench and awl;
there is no money in his work,
he'd rather marry.

One dark night,   25
my Tudor Ford climbed the hill's skull;
I watched for love-cars. Lights turned down,
they lay together, hull to hull,
where the graveyard shelves on the town. . . .
My mind's not right.   30

A car radio bleats,
"Love, O careless Love. . . ." I hear
my ill-spirit sob in each blood cell,
as if my hand were at its throat. . . .
I myself am hell;   35
nobody's here—

[1] Austere and rigorous.

only skunks, that search
in the moonlight for a bite to eat.
They march on their soles up Main Street:
while stripes, moonstruck eyes' red fire   40
under the chalk-dry and spar spire
of the Trinitarian Church.

I stand on top
of our back steps and breathe the rich air—
a mother skunk with her column of kittens swills the garbage pail.   45
She jabs her wedge-head in a cup
of sour cream, drops her ostrich tail,
and will not scare.

1958

                                                            1959

Beyond the Alps

(On the train from Rome to Paris. 1950, the year Pius XII defined the dogma of Mary's bodily assumption.)[1]

Reading how even the Swiss had thrown the sponge
in once again and Everest[2] was still
unscaled, I watched our Paris pullman lunge
mooning across the fallow Alpine snow.
O bella Roma! I saw our stewards go   5
forward on tiptoe banging on their gongs.
Life changed to landscape. Much against my will
I left the City of God where it belongs.
There the skirt-mad Mussolini[3] unfurled
the eagle of Caesar.[4] He was one of us   10
only, pure prose. I envy the conspicuous
waste of our grandparents on their grand tours—
long-haired Victorian sages accepted the universe,
while breezing on their trust funds through the world.

[1] The dogma that asserts the bodily taking up of the Virgin Mary into heaven after her death.

[2] Mount Everest in the Himalayas on the border of Nepal and Tibet, the highest peak in the world (29,028 feet).

[3] Benito Mussolini (1883-1945), Fascist dictator of Italy from 1923 to 1943.

[4] Julius Caesar (100-44 B.C.), Roman statesman, general, dictator from 49 to 44 B.C.

When the Vatican made Mary's Assumption dogma,   15
the crowds at San Pietro screamed *Papa*.
The Holy Father dropped his shaving glass,
and listened. His electric razor purred,
his pet canary chirped on his left hand.
The lights of science couldn't hold a candle   20
to Mary risen—at one miraculous stroke,
angel-wing'd, gorgeous as a jungle bird!
But who believed this? Who could understand?
Pilgrims still kissed Saint Peter's[5] brazen sandal.
The Duce's lynched, bare, booted skull still spoke.   25
God herded his people to the *coup de grâce*—[6]
the costumed Switzers sloped their pikes to push,
O Pius, through the monstrous human crush. . . .

Our mountain-climbing train had come to earth.
Tired of the querulous hush-hush of the wheels,   30
the blear-eyed ego kicking in my berth
lay still, and saw Apollo plant his heels
on terra firma through the morning's thigh . . .
each backward, wasted Alp, a Parthenon,[7]
fire-branded socket of the Cyclops'[8] eye.   35
There were no tickets for that altitude
once held by Hellas,[9] when the Goddess stood,
prince, pope, philosopher and golden bough,
pure mind and murder at the scything prow—
Minerva,[10] the miscarriage of the brain.   40
Now Paris,[11] our black classic, breaking up
like killer kings on an Etruscan[12] cup.

1953

1959

---

[5] Chief of the Apostles.
[6] The mortal or finishing stroke.
[7] The Parthenon was the Greek senate.
[8] In Homer's *Odyssey*, a one-eyed giant.
[9] Greece.

[10] The goddess of wisdom, invention, the arts, and martial powers.
[11] The prince of Troy whose abduction of Helen provoked the Trojan War.
[12] Pre-Roman.

From Life Studies

91 REVERE STREET

The account of him is platitudinous, worldly and fond, but he has no Christian name and is entitled merely Major *M.* Myers in my Cousin Cassie Mason Myers Julian-James's privately printed *Biographical Sketches: A Key to a Cabinet of Heirlooms in the Smithsonian Museum.* The name-plate under his portrait used to spell out his name bravely enough: he was Mordecai Myers. The artist painted Major Myers in his sanguine War of 1812 uniform with epaulets, white breeches, and a scarlet frogged waistcoat. His right hand played with the sword "now to be seen in the Smithsonian cabinet of heirlooms." The pose was routine and gallant. The full-lipped smile was good-humoredly pompous and embarrassed.

Mordecai's father, given neither name nor initial, is described with an air of hurried self-congratulation by Cousin Cassie as "a friend of the Reverend Ezra Styles, afterward President of Yale College." As a very young man the son, Mordecai, studied military tactics under a French émigré, "the Bourbons' celebrated Colonel De la Croix." Later he was "matured" by six years' practical experience in a New York militia regiment organized by Colonel Martin Van Buren. After "the successful engagement against the British at Chrysler's Field, thirty shrapnel splinters were extracted from his shoulder." During convalescence, he wooed and won Miss Charlotte Bailey, "thus proving himself a better man than his rivals, the united forces of Plattsburg." He fathered ten children, sponsored an enlightened law exempting Quakers from military service in New York State, and died in 1870 at the age of ninety-four, "a Grand Old Man, who impressed strangers with the poise of his old-time manners."

Undoubtedly Major Mordecai had lived in a more ritualistic, gaudy, and animal world then twentieth-century Boston. There was something undecided, Mediterranean, versatile, almost double-faced about his bearing which suggested that, even to his contemporaries, he must have seemed gratuitously both *ci-devant* and *parvenu.* He was a dark man, a German Jew—no downright Yankee, but maybe such a fellow as Napoleon's mad, pomaded son-of-an-innkeeper-general, Junot, Duc D'Abrantes; a man like mad George III's pomaded, disreputable son, "Prinny," the Prince Regent. Or he was one of those Moorish-looking dons painted by his contemporary, Goya[1]—some leader of Spanish guerrillas against Bonaparte's occupation, who fled to

[1] Lucientes y Goya (1746-1828), Spanish artist.

South America. Our Major's suffering almond eye rested on his luxurious dawn-colored fingers ruffling an off-white glove.

Bailey-Mason-Myers! Easy-going, Empire State patricians, these relatives of my Grandmother Lowell seemed to have given my father his character. For he likewise lacked that granite *back-countriness* which Grandfather Arthur Winslow attributed to his own ancestors, the iconoclastic, mulish Dunbarton New Hampshire Starks. On the joint Mason-Myers bookplate, there are two merry and naked mermaids—lovely marshmallowy, boneless, Rubensesque butterballs, all burlesque-show bosoms and Flemish smiles. Their motto, *malo frangere quam flectere*, reads "I prefer to bend than to break."

Mordecai Myers was my Grandmother Lowell's grandfather. His life was tame and honorable. He was a leisured squire and merchant, a member of the state legislature, a mayor of Schenectady, a "president" of Kinderhook village. Disappointingly, his famous "blazing brown eye" seems in all things to have shunned the outrageous. After his death he was remembered soberly as a New York State gentleman, the friend and host of worldly men and politicians with Dutch names: De Witt Clinton, Vanderpoel, Hoes, and Schuyler.[2] My mother was roused to warmth by the Major's scarlet vest and exotic eye. She always insisted that he was the one properly dressed and dieted ancestor in the lot we had inherited from my father's Cousin Cassie. Great-great-Grandfather Mordecai! Poor sheepdog in wolf's clothing! In the anarchy of my adolescent war on my parents, I tried to make him a true wolf, the wandering Jew! *Homo lupus homini!*

Major Mordecai Myers' portrait has been mislaid past finding, but out of my memories I often come on it in the setting of our Revere Street house, a setting now fixed in the mind, where it survives all the distortions of fantasy, all the blank befogging of forgetfulness. There, the vast number of remembered *things* remains rocklike. Each is in its place, each has its function, its history, its drama. There, all is preserved by that motherly care that one either ignored or resented in his youth. The things and their owners come back urgent with life and meaning—because finished, they are endurable and perfect.

Cousin Cassie only became a close relation in 1922. In that year she died. After some unpleasantness between Mother and a co-heiress, Helen Bailey, the estate was divided. Mother used to return frozen and thrilled from her property disputes, and I, knowing nothing of the rights and wrongs, would half-perversely confuse Helen Bailey with Helen of Troy and harden my mind against the monotonous *parti pris* of Mother's voice. Shortly after our move to Boston in 1924, a score of unwanted Myers portraits were delivered

[2] De Witt Clinton (1769-1828) was an American politician; Vanderpoel (1746-1793), an inventor; Hoes (1784-1833), the manufacturer of the printing press; Philip Schuyler (1733-1804), a leader of the American revolution.

to our new house on Revere Street. These were later followed by "their dowry"—four moving vans groaning with heavy Edwardian furniture. My father began to receive his first quarterly payments from the Mason-Myers Julian-James Trust Fund, sums "not grand enough to corrupt us," Mother explained, "but sufficient to prevent Daddy from being entirely at the mercy of his salary." The Trust sufficed: our lives became tantalized with possibilities, and my father felt encouraged to take the risk—a small one in those boom years—of resigning from the Navy on the gamble of doubling his income in business.

I was in the third grade and for the first time becoming a little more popular at school. I was afraid Father's leaving the Navy would destroy my standing. I was a churlish, disloyal, romantic boy, and quite without hero worship for my father, whose actuality seemed so inferior to the photographs in uniform he once mailed to us from the Golden Gate. My real *love*, as Mother used to insist to all new visitors, was toy soldiers. For a few months at the flood tide of this infatuation, people were ciphers to me—valueless except as chances for increasing my armies of soldiers. Roger Crosby, a child in the second grade of my Brimmer Street School, had thousands—not mass-produced American stereotypes, but hand-painted solid lead soldiers made to order in Dijon, France. Roger's father had a still more artistic and adult collection; its ranks—each man at least six inches tall—marched in glass cases under the eyes of recognizable replicas of mounted Napoleonic captains: Kleber, Marshall Ney, Murat, King of Naples.[3] One delirious afternoon Mr. Crosby showed me his toys and was perhaps the first grownup to talk to me not as a child but as an equal when he discovered how feverishly I followed his ancedotes on uniforms and the evolution of tactical surprise. Afterwards, full of high thoughts, I ran up to Roger's play room and hoodwinked him into believing that his own soldiers were "ballast turned out by central European sweatshops." He agreed I was being sweetly generous when I traded twenty-four worthless Jordan Marsh papier-mâché doughboys for whole companies of his gorgeous, imported Old Guards, Second Empire "red-legs," and modern *chasseurs d'Alpine* with sky-blue berets. The haul was so huge that I had to take a child's wheelbarrow to Roger's house at the top of Pinckney Street. When I reached home with my last load, Mr. Crosby was talking with my father on our front steps. Roger's soldiers were all returned; I had only the presence of mind to hide a single soldier, a peely-nosed black sepoy wearing a Shriner's fez.

Nothing consoled me for my loss, but I enjoyed being allowed to draw Father's blunt dress sword, and I was proud of our Major Mordecai. I used to stand dangerously out in the middle of Revere Street in order to see

[3] Jean B. Kleber (1753–1800), Michel Ney (1769–1815), and Joachim Murat (1767–1815) served under Napoleon.

through our windows and gloat on this portrait's scarlet waistcoat blazing in the bare, Spartan whiteness of our den-parlor. Mordecai Myers lost his glory when I learned from my father that he was only a "major *pro tem.*" On a civilian, even a civilian soldier, the flamboyant waistcoat was stuffy and no more martial than officers' costumes in our elementary school musicals.

In 1924 people still lived in cities. Late that summer, we bought the 91 Revere Street house, looking out on an unbuttoned part of Beacon Hill bounded by the North End slums, though reassuringly only four blocks away from my Grandfather Winslow's brown pillared house at 18 Chestnut Street. In the decades preceding and following the First World War, old Yankee families had upset expectation by regaining this section of the Hill from the vanguards of the lace-curtain Irish. This was bracing news for my parents in that topsy-turvy era when the Republican Party and what were called "people of the right sort" were no longer dominant in city elections. Still, even in the palmy, laissezfaire '20s, Revere Street refused to be a straightforward, immutable residential fact. From one end to the other, houses kept being sanded down, repainted, or abandoned to the flaking of decay. Houses, changing hands, changed their language and nationality. A few doors to our south the householders spoke "Beacon Hill British" or the flat *nay nay* of the Boston Brahmin. The parents of the children a few doors north spoke mostly in Italian.

My mother felt a horrified giddiness about the adventure of our address. She once said, "We are barely perched on the outer rim of the hub of decency." We were less than fifty yards from Louisburg Square, the cynosure of old historic Boston's plain-spoken, cold roast elite—the Hub of the Hub of the Universe. Fifty yards!

As a naval ensign, Father had done postgraduate work at Harvard. He had also done postgraduate work at M.I.T., preferred the purely scientific college, and condescended to both. In 1924, however, his tone began to change; he now began to speak warmly of Harvard as his second alma mater. We went to football games at the Harvard Stadium, and one had the feeling that our lives were now being lived in the brutal, fashionable expectancy of the stadium: we had so many downs, so many minutes, and so many yards to go for a winning touchdown. It was just such a winning financial and social advance that my parents promised themselves would follow Father's resignation from the Navy and his acceptance of a sensible job offered him at the Cambridge branch of Lever Brothers' Soap.

The advance was never to come. Father resigned from the service in 1927, but he never had a civilian *Career;* he instead had merely twenty-two years of the civilian *life.* Almost immediately he bought a larger and more stylish house; he sold his ascetic, stove-black Hudson and bought a plump brown Buick; later the Buick was exchanged for a high-toned, as-good-as-new Packard with a custom-designed royal blue and mahogany body. Without drama, his earnings more or less decreased from year to year.

But so long as we were on Revere Street, Father tried to come to terms with it and must have often wondered whether he on the whole liked or disliked the neighborhood's lack of side. He was still at this time rather truculently democratic in what might be described as an upper middle-class, naval, and Masonic fashion. He was a mumbler. His opinions were almost morbidly hesitant, but he considered himself a matter-of-fact man of science and had an unspoiled faith in the superior efficiency of northern nations. He modeled his allegiances and humor on the cockney imperialism of Rudyard Kipling's swearing Tommies, who did their job. Autochthonous Boston snobs, such as the Winslows or members of Mother's reading club, were alarmed by the brassy callousness of our naval visitors, who labeled the Italians they met on Revere Street as "grade-A" and "grade-B wops." The Revere Street "grade-B's" were Sicilian Catholics and peddled crummy second-hand furniture on Cambridge Street, not far from the site of Great-great-Grandfather Charles Lowell's disused West Church, praised in an old family folder as "a haven from the Sodom and Gomorrah of Trinitarian orthodoxy and the tyranny of the letter." Revere Street "grade-A's," good North Italians, sold fancy groceries and Colonial heirlooms in their shops near the Public Garden. Still other Italians were Father's familiars; they sold him bootleg Scotch and *vino rosso* in teacups.

The outside of our Revere Street house was a flat red brick surface unvaried by the slightest suggestion of purple panes, delicate bay, or triangular window-cornice—a sheer wall formed by the seamless conjunction of four inseparable façades, all of the same commercial and purgatorial design. Though placed in the heart of Old Boston, it was ageless and artless, an epitome of those "leveler" qualities Mother found most grueling about the naval service. 91 Revere Street was mass-produced, *regulation-issue,* and yet struck Boston society as stupidly out of the ordinary, like those white elephants—a mother-of-pearl scout knife or a tea-kettle barometer—which my father used to pick up on sale at an Army-Navy store.

The walls of Father's minute Revere Street den-parlor were bare and white. His bookshelves were bare and white. The den's one adornment was a ten-tube home-assembled battery radio set, whose loudspeaker had the shape and color of a Mexican sombrero. The radio's speciality was getting programs from Australia and New Zealand in the early hours of the morning.

My father's favorite piece of den furniture was his oak and "rhinoceros hide" armchair. It was ostentatiously a masculine, or rather a bachelor's, chair. It had a notched, adjustable back; it was black, cracked, hacked, scratched, splintered, gouged, initialed, gunpowder-charred and tumbler-ringed. It looked like pale tobacco leaves laid on dark tobacco leaves. I doubt if Father, a considerate man, was responsible for any of the marring.

The chair dated from his plebe days at the Naval Academy, and had been bought from a shady, shadowy, roaring character, midshipman "Beauty" Burford. Father loved each disfigured inch.

My father had been born two months after his own father's death. At each stage of his life, he was to be forlornly fatherless. He was a deep boy brought up entirely by a mild widowed mother and an intense widowed grandmother. When he was fourteen and a half, he became a deep young midshipman. By the time he graduated from Annapolis, he had a high sense of abstract form, which he beclouded with his humor. He had reached, perhaps, his final mental possibilities. He was deep—not with profundity, but with the dumb depth of one who trusted in statistics and was dubious of personal experience. In his forties, Father's soul went underground: as a civilian he kept his high sense of form, his humor, his accuracy, but this accuracy was henceforth unimportant, recreational, *hors de combat*. His debunking grew myopic; his shyness grew evasive; he argued with a fumbling languor. In the twenty-two years Father lived after he resigned from the Navy, he never again deserted Boston and never became Bostonian. He survived to drift from job to job, to be displaced, to be grimly and literally that old cliché, a fish out of water. He gasped and wheezed with impotent optimism, took on new ideals with each new job, never ingeniously enjoyed his leisure, never even hid his head in the sand.

Mother hated the Navy, hated naval society, naval pay, and the triphammer rote of settling and unsettling a house every other year when Father was transferred to a new station or ship. She had been married nine or ten years and still suspected that her husband was savorless, unmasterful, merely considerate. Unmasterful—Father's specialized efficiency lacked utterly the flattering bossiness she so counted on from her father, my Grandfather Winslow. It was not Father's absence on sea-duty that mattered; it was the eroding necessity of moving *with* him, of keeping in step. When he was far away on the Pacific, she had her friends, her parents, a house to herself—Boston! Fully conscious of her uniqueness and normality she basked in the refreshing stimulation of dreams in which she imagined Father as suitably sublimed. She used to describe such a sublime man to me over tea and English muffins. He was Siegfried carried lifeless through the shining air by Brunnhilde to Valhalla, and accompanied by the throb of my Great Aunt Sarah playing his leitmotif in the released manner taught her by the Abbé Liszt. Or Mother's hero dove through the grottoes of the Rhine and slaughtered the homicidal and vulgar dragon coiled about the golden hoard. Mother seemed almost lightheaded when she retold the romance of Sarah Bernhardt in *L'Aiglon,* the Eaglet, the weakling! She would speak the word *weakling* with such amused vehemence that I formed a grandiose and false image of L'Aiglon's Father, the *big* Napoleon: he was a strong man who scratched under his paunchy little white vest a torso all hair, muscle, and manliness. Instead of the dreams, Mother now had the insipid fatigue of keeping house. Instead of the *Eagle*, she had a twentieth-century naval commander interested in steam, radio, and "the fellows." To avoid naval yards, steam, and "the fellows," Mother had impulsively bought the squalid, impractical Revere Street house. Her marriage daily forced her to squander her subconsciously hoarded energies.

"*Weelawaugh, we-ee-eeelawaugh, weelawaugh,*" shrilled Mother's high voice. "*But-and, but-and, but-and!*" Father's low mumble would drone in answer. Though I couldn't be sure that I had caught the meaning of the words, I followed the sounds as though they were a movie. I felt drenched in my parents' passions.

91 Revere Street was the setting for those arthritic spiritual pains that troubled us for the two years my mother spent in trying to argue my father into resigning from the Navy. When the majestic, hollow boredom of the second year's autumn dwindled to the mean boredom of a second winter, I grew less willing to open my mouth. I bored my parents, they bored me. "Weelawaugh, we-ee-eelawaugh, weelawaugh!" "But-and, but-and, but-and!"

During the week ends I was at home much of the time. All day I used to look forward to the nights when my bedroom walls would once again vibrate, when I would awake with rapture to the rhythm of my parents arguing, arguing one another to exhaustion. Sometimes, without bathrobe or slippers, I would wriggle out into the cold hall on my belly and ambuscade myself behind the banister. I could often hear actual words. "Yes, yes, yes," Father would mumble. He was "backsliding" and "living in the fool's paradise of habitual retarding and retarded do-nothing inertia." Mother had violently set her heart on the resignation. She was hysterical even in her calm, but like a patient and forbearing strategist, she tried to pretend her neutrality. One night she said with murderous coolness, "Bobby and I are leaving for Papá's." This was an ultimatum to force Father to sign a deed placing the Revere Street house in Mother's name.

I writhed with disappointment on the nights when Mother and Father only lowed harmoniously together like cows, as they criticized Helen Bailey or Admiral De Stahl. Once I heard my mother say, "A *man* must make up his *own* mind. Oh, Bob, if you are going to resign, do it *now* so I can at least plan for your son's *survival* and education on a single continent."

About this time I was being sent for my *survival* to Dr. Dane, a Quaker chiropractor with an office on Marlborough Street. Dr. Dane wore an old-fashioned light tan druggist's smock; he smelled like a healthy old-fashioned drugstore. His laboratory was free of intimidating technical equipment, and had only the conservative lay roughness and toughness that was so familiar and disarming to us in my Grandfather Winslow's country study or bedroom.

Dr. Dane's rosy hands wrenched my shoulders with tremendous éclat and made me feel a hero; I felt unspeakable joy whenever an awry muscle fell back into serenity. My mother, who had no curiosity or imagination for cranky occultism, trusted Dr. Dane's clean, undrugged manliness—so like home. She believed that chiropractic had cured me of my undiagnosed asthma, which had defeated the expensive specialists.

"A penny for your thoughts, Schopenhauer," my mother would say.
"I am thinking about pennies," I'd answer.
"When *I* was a child I used to love telling Mamá everything I had done," Mother would say.
"But you're not a child," I would answer.
I used to enjoy dawdling and humming "Anchors Aweigh" up Revere Street after a day at school. "Anchors Aweigh," the official Navy song, had originally been the song composed for my father's class. And yet my mind always blanked and seemed to fill with a clammy hollowness when Mother asked prying questions. Like other tongue-tied, difficult children, I dreamed I was a master of cool, stoical repartee. "What have you been doing, Bobby?" Mother would ask. "I haven't," I'd answer. At home I thus saved myself from emotional exhaustion.
At school, however, I was extreme only in my conventional mediocrity, my colorless, distracted manner, which came from restless dreams of being admired. My closest friend was Eric Burckhard, the son of a professor of architecture at Harvard. The Burckhards came from Zurich and were very German, not like Ludendorff, but in the kindly, comical, nineteenth-century manner of Jo's German husband in *Little Men*, or in the manner of the crusading *sturm und drang* liberal scholars in second year German novels. "Eric's mother and father are *both* called Dr. Burckhard," my mother once said, and indeed there was something endearingly repellent about Mrs. Burckhard with her doctor's degree, her long, unstylish skirts, and her dramatic, dulling blond braids. Strangely the Burckhards' sober continental bourgeois house was without golden mean—everything was either hilariously old Swiss or madly modern. The Frau Doctor Burckhard used to serve midmorning hot chocolate with rosettes of whipped cream, and receive her friends in a long, uncarpeted hall-drawing room with lethal ferns and a yellow beeswaxed hardwood floor shining under a central skylight. On the wall there were large expert photographs of what at a distance appeared to be Mont Blanc—they were in reality views of Frank Lloyd Wright's Japanese hotel.
I admired the Burckhards and felt at home in their house, and these feelings were only intensified when I discovered that my mother was always ill at ease with them. The heartiness, the enlightenment, and the bright, ferny greenhouse atmosphere were too much for her.

Eric and I were too young to care for books or athletics. Neither of our houses had absorbing toys or an elevator to go up and down in. We were inseparable, but I cannot imagine what we talked about. I loved Eric because he was more popular than I and yet absolutely *sui generis* at the Brimmer School. He had a chalk-white face and limp, fine, white-blond hair. He was frail, elbowy, started talking with an enthusiastic Mount Blanc chirp and would flush with bewilderment if interrupted. All the other boys at Brimmer wore little tweed golf suits and knickerbockers, but Eric always arrived in a black suit coat, a Byronic collar, and cuffless gray flannel trousers that almost hid his shoes. The long trousers were replaced on warm days by gray flannel shorts, such as were worn by children still in kindergarten. Eric's unenviable and freakish costumes were too old or too young. He accepted the whims of his parents with a buoyant tranquility that I found unnatural.

My first and terminating quarrel with Eric was my fault. Eventually almost our whole class at Brimmer had whooping cough, but Eric's seizure was like his long trousers—untimely: he was sick a month too early. For a whole month he was in quarantine and forced to play by himself in a removed corner of the Public Garden. He was certainly conspicuous as he skiproped with his Swiss nurse under the out-of-the-way Ether Memorial Fountain far from the pond and the swan boats. His parents had decided that this was an excellent opportunity for Eric to brush up on his German, and so the absoluteness of his quarantine was monstrously exaggerated by the fact that child and nurse spoke no English but only a guttural, British-sounding, Swiss German. Round and round and round the Fountain, he played intensely, frailly, obediently, until I began to tease him. Though motioned away by him, I came close. I had attracted some of the most popular Brimmer School boys. For the first time I had gotten favorable attention from several little girls. I came close. I shouted. Was Eric afraid of girls? I imitated his German. *Ein, swei, drei, BEER.* I imitated Eric's coughing. "He is afraid he will give you whooping cough if he talks or lets you come nearer," the nurse said in her musical Swiss-English voice. I came nearer. Eric flushed, grew white, bent double with coughing. He began to cry, and had to be led away from the Public Garden. For a whole week I routed Eric from the Garden daily, and for two or three days I was a center of interest. "Come see the Lake Geneva spider monkey!" I would shout. I don't know why I couldn't stop. Eric never told his father, I think, but when he recovered we no longer spoke. The breach was so unspoken and intense that our classmates were actually horrified. They even devised a solemn ritual for our reconciliation. We crossed our hearts, mixed spit, mixed blood. The reconciliation was hollow.

My parents' confidences and quarrels stopped each night at ten or eleven o'clock, when my father would hang up his tuxedo, put on his commander's uniform, and take a trolley back to the naval yard at Charlestown. He had just broken in a new car. Like a chauffeur, he watched this car, a Hudson, with an informed vigilance, always giving its engine hair-trigger little tinkerings of adjustment or friendship, always fearful lest the black body, unbeautiful as his boiled shirts, should lose its outline and gloss. He drove with flawless, almost instrumental, monotony. Mother, nevertheless, was forever encouraging him to walk or take taxis. She would tell him that his legs were growning vestigial from disuse and remind him of the time a jack had slipped and he had broken his leg while shifting a tire. "Alone and at night," she would say, "an amateur driver is unsafe in a car." Father sighed and obeyed—only, putting on a martyred and penny-saving face, he would keep his self-respect by taking the trolley rather than a taxi. Each night he shifted back into his uniform, but his departures from Revere Street were so furtive that several months passed before I realized what was happening—we had *two* houses! Our second house was the residence in the Naval Yard assigned to the third in command. It was large, had its own flagpole, and screen porches on three levels—yet it was something to be ashamed of. Whatever pomp or distinction its possession might have had for us was destroyed by an eccentric humiliation inflicted on Father by his superior, Admiral De Stahl, the commandant at Charlestown. De Stahl had not been consulted about our buying the 91 Revere Street house. He was outraged, stormed about "flaunting private fortunes in the face of naval tradition," and ordered my father to sleep on bounds at the Yard in the house provided for that purpose.

On our first Revere Street Christmas Eve, the telephone rang in the middle of dinner; it was Admiral De Stahl demanding Father's instant return to the Navy Yard. Soon Father was back in his uniform. In taking leave of my mother and grandparents he was, as was usual with him under pressure, a little evasive and magniloquent. "A woman works from sun to sun," he said, "but a sailor's watch is never done." He compared a naval officer's hours with a doctor's, hinted at surprise maneuvers, and explained away the uncommunicative arrogance of Admiral De Stahl: "The Old Man has to be hush-hush." Later that night, I lay in bed and tried to imagine that my father was leading his engineering force on a surprise maneuver through arctic wastes. A forlorn hope! "Hush-hush, hush-hush," whispered the snowflakes as big as street lamps as they broke on Father—broke and buried. Outside, I heard real people singing carols, shuffling snow off their shoes, opening and shutting doors. I worried at the meaning of a sentence I had heard quoted from the *Boston Evening Transcript:* "On this Christmas Eve, as usual, the whole of Beacon Hill can be expected to become a single old-fashioned open house—the names of mine host the Hill, and her guests will read like the contents of the Social Register." I imagined Beacon Hill changed to the snow queen's palace, as vast as the north pole. My father pressed a cold finger to his lip: "hush-hush," and led his surprise squad of sailors around an altar, but the altar was a tremendous cash register, whose roughened nickel surface was cheaply decorated with trowels, pyramids, and Arabic swirls. A great drawer helplessly chopped back and forth, unable to shut because choked with greenbacks. "Hush-hush!" My father's engineers wound about me with their eye-patches, orange sashes, and curtain-ring earrings, like the Gilbert and Sullivan pirates' chorus. . . . Outside on the streets of Beacon Hill, it was night, it was dismal, it was raining. Something disturbing had befallen the familiar and honorable Salvation Army band; its big drum and accordion were now accompanied by drunken voices howling: *The Old Gray Mare, she ain't what she used to be, when Mary went to milk the cow.* A sound of a bosun's whistle. Women laughing. Someone repeatedly rang our doorbell. I heard my mother talking on the telephone. "Your inebriated sailors have littered my doorstep with the dregs of Scollay Square." There was a gloating panic in her voice that showed she enjoyed the drama of talking to Admiral De Stahl. "Sir," she shrilled, "you have compelled my husband to leave me alone and defenseless on Christmas Eve!" She ran into my bedroom. She hugged me. She said, "Oh Bobby, it's such a comfort to have a man in the house." "I am not a man," I said, "I am a boy."

Boy—at that time this word had private associations for me; it meant weakness, outlawry, and yet was a status to be held onto. Boys were a sideline at my Brimmer School. The eight superior grades were limited to girls. In these grades, moreover, scholarship was made subservient to discipline, as if in contempt of the male's two idols: career and earning power. The school's tone, its *ton*, was a blend of the feminine and the military, a bulky reality governed in turn by stridency, smartness, and steadiness. The girls wore white jumpers, black skirts, stockings, and rectangular low-heeled shoes. An ex-West Pointer had been appointed to teach drill; and, at the moment of my enrollment in Brimmer, our principal, the hitherto staid Miss Manice, was rumored to be showing signs of age and of undermining her position with the school trustees by girlish, quite out of character, rhapsodies on the varsity basketball team, winner of two consecutive championships. The lower four grades, peaceful and lackadaisical, were, on the other hand, almost a separate establishment. Miss Manice regarded these "coeducated" classes with amused carelessness, allowed them to wear their ordinary clothes, and . . . carelessness, however, is incorrect—Miss Manice, in her administration of the lower school, showed the inconsistency and euphoria of a dual personality. Here she mysteriously shed all her Prussianism. She quoted Emerson and Mencken, disparaged the English, threatened to break with the past, and boldly coquetted with the non-military American genuis by displaying movies illustrating the careers of Edison and Ford. Favored lower school teachers were permitted to use us as guinea pigs for mildly radical experiments. At Brimmer I *un*learned writing. The script that I had mastered with much agony at my first school was denounced as illegible: I was taught to print according to the Dalton Plan—to this day, as a result, I have to print even my two middle names and can only really *write* two words: "Robert" and "Lowell." Our instruction was subject to bewildering leaps. The usual fall performance by the Venetian glass-blowers was followed by a tour of the Riverside Press. We heard Rudy Vallee, then heard spirituals sung by the Hampton Institute choir. We studied grammar from a formidable, unreconstructed textbook written by Miss Manice's father. There I battled with figures of speech and Greek terminology: *Chiásmus*, the arrangement of corresponding words in opposite order; *Brachyology*, the failure to repeat an element that is supplied in more or less modified form. Then all this pedantry was nullified by the introduction of a new textbook which proposed to lift the face of syntax by using game techniques and drawings.

Physical instruction in the lower school was irregular, spontaneous, and had nothing of that swept and garnished barrack-room camaraderie of the older girls' gymnasium exercises. On the roof of our school building, there was an ugly concrete area that looked as if it had been intended for the top floor of a garage. Here we played tag, drew lines with chalk, and chose up sides for a kind of kids' soccer. On bright spring days, Mr. Newell, a submerged young man from Boston University, took us on botanical hikes through the Arboretum. He had an eye for inessentials—read us Martha Washington's poems at the Old State House, pointed out the roof of Brimmer School from the top of the Custom House, made us count the steps of the Bunker Hill Monument, and one rainy afternoon broke all rules by herding us into the South Boston Aquarium in order to give an unhealthy, eager, little lecture on the sewage-consumption of the conger eel. At last Miss Manice seemed to have gotten wind of Mr. Newell's moods. For an afternoon or two she herself served as his substitute. We were walked briskly past the houses of Parkman and Dana, and assigned themes on the spunk of great persons who have overcome physical handicaps and risen to the top of the ladder. She talked about Elizabeth Barrett, Helen Keller; her pet theory, however, was that "women simply are not the equals of men." I can hear Miss Manice browbeating my white and sheepish father, "How can we stand up to you? Where are our Archimedeses, our Wagners, our Admiral Simses?" Miss Manice adored "Sir Walter Scott's *big bow-wow*," wished "Boston had banned the tubercular novels of the Brontës," and found nothing in the world "so simpatico" as the "strenuous life" lived by President Roosevelt. Yet the extravagant hysteria of Miss Manice's philanthropy meant nothing; Brimmer was entirely a woman's world—*dumkopf*, perhaps, but not in the least Quixotic, Brimmer was ruled by a woman's obvious aims and by her naive pragmatism. The quality of this regime, an extension of my mother's, shone out in full glory at general assemblies or when I sat with a handful of other boys on the bleachers of Brimmer's new Manice Hall. In unison our big girls sang "America"; back and forth our amazons tramped— their brows were wooden, their dress was black and white, and their columns followed standard-bearers holding up an American flag, the white flag of the Commonwealth of Massachusetts, and the green flag of Brimmer. At basketball games against Miss Lee's or Miss Winsor's, it was our upper-school champions who rushed onto the floor, as feline and fateful in their pace as lions. This was our own immediate and daily spectacle; in comparison such masculine displays as trips to battle cruisers commanded by comrades of my father seemed eyewash—the Navy moved in a realm as ghostlike and removed from my life as the elfin acrobatics of Douglas Fairbanks or Peter Pan. I wished I were an older girl. I wrote Santa Claus for a field hockey stick. To be a boy at Brimmer was to be small, denied, and weak.

I was promised an improved future and taken on Sunday afternoon drives through the suburbs to inspect the boys' schools: Rivers, Dexter, Country Day. These expeditions were stratagems designed to give me a chance to know my father; Mother noisily stayed behind and amazed me by pretending that I had forbidden her to embark on "men's work." Father, however, seldom insisted, as he should have, on seeing the headmasters in person, yet he made an astonishing number of friends; his trust begat trust, and something about his silences encouraged junior masters and even school janitors to pour out small talk that was detrimental to rival institutions. At each new school, however, all this gossip was easily refuted; worse still Mother was always ready to cross-examine Father in a manner that showed that she was asking questions for the purpose of giving, not of receiving, instruction; she expressed astonishment that a wishy-washy desire to be everything to everybody had robbed a naval man of any reliable concern for his son's welfare. Mother regarded the suburban schools as "gerrymandered" and middle-class; after Father had completed his round of inspections, she made her own follow-up visits and told Mr. Dexter and Mr. Rivers to their faces that she was looking for a "respectable stop-gap" for her son's "three years between Brimmer and Saint Mark's." Saint Mark's was the boarding school for which I had been enrolled at birth, and was due to enter in 1930. I distrusted change, knew each school since kindergarten had been more constraining and punitive than its predecessor, and believed the suburban country day schools were flimsily disguised fronts for reformatories. With the egotistic, slightly paranoid apprehensions of an only child, I wondered what became of boys graduating from Brimmer's fourth grade, feared the worst—we were darkly imperiled, like some annual bevy of Athenian youths destined for the Minotaur. And to judge from my father, men between the ages of six and sixty did nothing but meet new challenges, take on heavier responsibilities, and lose all freedom to explode. A ray of hope in the far future was my white-haired Grandfather Winslow, whose unchecked commands and demands were always upsetting people for their own good—he was all I could ever want to be: the bad boy, the problem child, the commodore of his household.

When I entered Brimmer I was eight and a half. I was distracted in my studies, assented to whatever I was told, picked my nose whenever no one was watching, and worried our third-grade teacher by organizing creepy little gangs of boys at recess. I was girl-shy. Thick-witted, narcissistic, thuggish, I had the conventional prepuberty character of my age; whenever a girl came near me, my whole person cringed like a sponge wrung dry by a clenching fist. I was less rather than more bookish than most children, but the girl I dreamed about continually had wheel-spoke black and gold eyelashes, double-length page-boy blond hair, a little apron, a bold, blunt face, a saucy, shivery way of talking, and . . . a paper body—she was the girl in John Tenniel's illustrations to *Alice in Wonderland*. The invigorating and symmetrical aplomb of my ideal Alice was soon enriched and nullified by a second face, when my father took me to the movies on the afternoon of one of Mother's headaches. An innocuous child's movie, the bloody, all-male *Beau Geste* had been chosen, but instead my father preferred a nostalgic tour of places he had enjoyed on shore leave. We went to the Majestic Theater where he had first seen Pola Negri—where we too saw Pola Negri, sloppy-haired, slack, yawning, ravaged, unwashed . . . an Anti-Alice.

Our class belles, the Norton twins, Elie and Lindy, fell far short of the Nordic Alice and the foreign Pola. Their prettiness, rather fluffy, freckled, bashful, might have escaped notice if they had been one instead of two, and if their manners had been less goodhumored, entertaining, and reliable. What mattered more than sex, athletics, or studies to us at Brimmer was our popularity; each child had an unwritten class-popularity poll inside his head. Everyone was ranked, and all day each of us mooned profoundly on his place, as it quivered like our blood on a compass needle with a thousand revisions. At nine character is, perhaps, too much *in ovo* for a child to be strongly disliked, but sitting next to Elie Norton, I glanced at her and gulped prestige from her popularity. We were not close at first; then nearness made us closer friends, for Elie had a gracious gift, the gift of gifts, I suppose, in a child: she forgot all about the popularity-rank of the classmate she was talking to. No moron could have seemed so uncritical as this airy, chatty, intelligent child, the belle of our grade. She noticed my habit of cocking my head on one side, shutting my eyes, and driving like a bull through opposition at soccer—wishing to amuse without wounding, she called me Buffalo Bull. At general assembly she would giggle with contented admiration at the upper-school girls in their penal black and white. "What bruisers, what beefeaters! Dear girls," she would sigh, parroting her sophisticated mother, "we shall all become fodder for the governess classes before graduating from Brimmer." I felt that Elie Norton understood me better than anyone except my playful little Grandmother Winslow.

One morning there was a disaster. The boy behind me, no friend, had been tapping at my elbow for over a minute to catch my attention before I consented to look up and see a great golden puddle spreading toward me from under Elie's chair. I dared not speak, smile, or flicker an eyelash in her direction. She ran bawling from the classroom. Trying to catch every eye, yet avoid commitment, I gave sidelong and involuntary smirks at space. I began to feel manic with superiority to Elie Norton and struggled to swallow down a feeling of goaded hollowness—was I deserting her? Our teacher left us on our honor and ran down the hall. The class milled about in a hesitant hush. The girls blushed. The boys smirked. Miss Manice, the principal, appeared. She wore her whitish-brown dress with darker brown spots. Shimmering in the sunlight and chilling us, she stood mothlike in the middle of the classroom. We rushed to our seats. Miss Manice talked about how there was "nothing laughable about a malaise." She broke off. Her face took on an expression of invidious disguise. She was staring at me. . . . In the absent-mindedness of my guilt and excitement, I had taken the nearest chair, the chair that Elie Norton had just left. "Lowell," Miss Manice shrieked, "are you going to soak there all morning like a bump on a log?"

When Elie Norton came back, there was really no break in her friendliness toward me, but there was something caved in, something crippled in the way I stood up to her and tried to answer her disengaging chatter. I thought about her all the time; seldom meeting her eyes now, I felt rich and raw in her nearness. I wanted passionately to stay on at Brimmer, and told my mother a fib one afternoon late in May of my last year. "Miss Manice has begged me to stay on," I said, "and enter the fifth grade." Mother pointed out that there had never been a boy in the fifth grade. Contradicted, I grew excited. "If Miss Manice has begged me to stay," I said, "why can't I stay?" My voice rose, I beat on the floor with my open hands. Bored and bewildered, my mother went upstairs with a headache. "If you won't believe me," I shouted after her, "why don't you telephone Miss Manice or Mrs. Norton?"

Brimmer School was thrown open on sunny March and April afternoons and our teachers took us for strolls on the polite, landscaped walks of the Public Garden. There I'd loiter by the old iron fence and gape longingly across Charles Street at the historic Boston Common, a now largely wrong-side-of-the-tracks park. On the Common there were mossy bronze reliefs of Union soldiers, and a captured German tank filled with smelly wads of newspaper. Everywhere there were grit, litter, gangs of Irish, Negroes, Latins. On Sunday afternoons orators harangued about Sacco and Vanzetti, while others stood about heckling and blocking the sidewalks. Keen young policemen, looking for trouble, lolled on the benches. At nightfall a police lieutenant on horseback inspected the Common. In the Garden, however, there was only Officer Lever, a single white-haired and mustached dignitary, who had once been the doorman at the Union Club. He now looked more like a member of the club. "Lever's a man about town," my Grandfather Winslow would say. "Give him Harris tweeds and a glass of Scotch, and I'd take him for Cousin Herbert." Officer Lever was without thoughts or deeds, but Back Bay and Beacon Hill parents loved him just for being. No one asked this hollow and leonine King Log to be clairvoyant about children.

One day when the saucer magnolias were in bloom, I bloodied Bulldog Binney's nose against the pedestal of George Washington's statue in full view of Commonwealth Avenue; then I bloodied Dopey Dan Parker's nose; then I stood in the center of a sundial tulip bed and pelted a little enemy ring of third-graders with wet fertilizer. Officer Lever was telephoned. Officer Lever telephoned my mother. In the presence of my mother and some thirty nurses and children, I was expelled from the Public Garden. I was such a bad boy, I was told, "that *even* Officer Lever had been forced to put his foot down."

New England winters are long. Sunday mornings are long. Ours were often made tedious by preparations for dinner guests. Mother would start airing at nine. Whenever the air grew so cold that it hurt, she closed the den windows; then we were attacked by sour kitchen odors winding up a clumsily rebuilt dumb-waiter shaft. The windows were again thrown open. We sat in an atmosphere of glacial purity and sacrifice. Our breath puffed whitely. Father and I wore sleeveless cashmere jerseys Mother had bought at Filene's Basement. A do-it-yourself book containing diagrams for the correct carving of roasts lay on the arm of Father's chair. At hand were Big Bill Tilden on tennis, Capablanca on chess, newspaper clippings from Sidney Lenz's bridge column, and a magnificent tome with photographs and some American's nationalist sketch of Sir Thomas Lipton's errors in the Cup Defender races. Father made little progress in these diversions, and yet one of the authors assured him that mastery demanded only willing readers who understood the meaning of English words. Throughout the winter a gray-whiteness glared through the single den window. In the apoplectic brick alley, a fire escape stood out against our sooty plank fence. Father believed that churchgoing was undignified for a naval man; his Sunday mornings were given to useful acts such as lettering his three new galvanized garbage cans: R.T.S. Lowell—U.S.N.

Our Sunday dinner guests were often naval officers. Naval officers were not Mother's sort; very few people *were* her sort in those days, and that was her trouble—a very authentic, human, and plausible difficulty, which made Mother's life one of much suffering. She did not have the self-assurance for wide human experience; she needed to feel liked, admired, surrounded by the approved and familiar. Her haughtiness and chilliness came from apprehension. She would start talking like a *grande dame* and then stand back rigid and faltering, as if she feared being crushed by her own massively intimidating offensive.

Father's old Annapolis roomate, Commander Billy "Battleship Bilge" Harkness, was a frequent guest at Revere Street and one that always threw Mother off balance. Billy was a rough diamond. He made jokes about his "all-American family tree," and insisted that his name, pronounced Harkness, should be spelled Herkness. He came from Louisville, Kentucky, drank whiskey to "renew his Bourbon blood," and still spoke with an accent that sounded—so his colleagues said—"like a bran-fed stallion." Like my father, however, Commander Billy had entered the Naval Academy when he was a boy of fourteen; his Southernisms had been thoroughly rubbed away. He was teased for knowing nothing about race horses, mountaineers, folk ballads, hams, sour mash, tobacco . . . Kentucky Colonels. Though hardly an officer and a gentleman in the old Virginian style, he was an unusual combination of clashing virtues: he had led his class in the sciences and yet was what his superiors called "a *mathmaddition* with the habit of command." He and my father, the youngest men in their class, had often been shipmates. Bilge's executive genius had given color and direction to Father's submissive tenacity. He drank like a fish at parties, but was a total abstainer on duty. With reason Commander Harkness had been voted the man most likely to make a four-star admiral in the class of '07.

Billy called his wife *Jimmy* or *Jeems*, and had a rough friendly way of saying, "Oh Jimmy's bright as a penny." Mrs. Harkness was an unpleasant rarity: she was the only naval officer's wife we knew who was also a college graduate. She had a flat flapper's figure, and hid her intelligence behind a nervous twitter of vulgarity and toadyism. "Charlotte," she would almost scream at Mother, "is this mirAGE, this MIRacle your *own* dining room!"

Then Mother might smile and answer in a distant, though cosy and amused, voice, "I usually manage to make myself pretty comfortable."

Mother's comfort was chic, romantic, impulsive. If her silver service shone, it shone with hectic perfection to rebuke the functional domesticity of naval wives. She had determined to make her *ambiance* beautiful and luxurious, but wanted neither her beauty nor her luxury unaccompanied. Beauty pursued too exclusively meant artistic fatuity of a kind made farcical by her Aunt Sarah Stark Winslow, a beauty too lofty and original ever to marry, a prima donna on the piano, too high-strung ever to give a public recital. Beauty alone meant the maudlin ignominy of having one's investments managed by interfering relatives. Luxury alone, on the other hand, meant for Mother the "paste and fool's-gold polish" that one met with in the foyer of the new Statler Hotel. She loathed the "undernourishment" of Professor Burckhard's Bauhaus modernism, yet in moments of pique she denounced our pompous Myers mahoganies as "suitable for politicians at the Bellevue Hotel." She kept a middle-of-the-road position, and much admired Italian pottery with its fresh peasant colors and puritanical, clean-cut lines. She was fond of saying, "The French *do* have taste," but spoke with a double-edged irony which implied the French, with no moral standards to support their finish, were really no better than naval yahoos. Mother's beautiful house was dignified by a rich veneer of the useful.

"I have always believed carving to be *the* gentlemanly talent," mother used to proclaim. Father, faced with this opinion, pored over his book of instructions or read the section on table carving in the Encyclopaedia Britannica. Eventually he discovered among the innumerable small, specialized Boston "colleges" an establishment known as a carving school. Each Sunday from then on he would sit silent and erudite before his roast. He blinked, grew white, looked winded, and wiped beads of perspiration from his eyebrows. His purpose was to reproduce stroke by stroke his last carving lesson, and he worked with all the formal rightness and particular error of some shaky experiment in remote control. He enjoyed quiet witticisms at the expense of his carving master—"a philosopher who gave himself all the airs of a Mahan!" He liked to pretend that the carving master had stated that "No two cuts are identical," *ergo:* "each offers original problems for the *executioner.*" Guests were appeased by Father's saying, "I am just a plebe at this guillotine. Have a hunk of my roast beef hash."

What angered Father was Mrs. Harkness's voice grown merciless with excitement, as she studied his hewing and hacking. She was sure to say something tactless about how Commander Billy was "a stingy artist at carving who could shave George Washington off the dollar bill."

Nothing could stop Commander Billy, that born carver, from reciting verses:

> *"By carving my way*
> *I lived on my pay;*
> *This reeward, though small,*
> *Beats none at all . . .*
>
> *My carving paper-thin*
> *Can make a guinea hin,*
> *All giblets, bones, and skin,*
> *Canteen a party of tin."*

And I, furious for no immediate reason, blurted out, "Mother, how much does Grandfather Winslow have to fork up to pay for Daddy's carving school?"

These Sunday dinners with the Harknesses were always woundingly boisterous affairs. Father, unnaturally outgoing, would lead me forward and say, "Bilge, I want you to meet my first coupon from the bond of matrimony."

Commander Billy would answer, "So this is the range-finder you are raising for future wars!" They would make me salute, stand at attention, stand at ease. "Angel-face," Billy would say to me, "you'll skipper a flivver."

"Jimmy" Harkness, of course, knew that Father was anxiously negotiating with Lever Brothers' Soap, and arranging for his resignation from the service, but nothing could prevent her from proposing time and again her "hens' toast to the drakes." Dragging Mother to her feet, Jimmy would scream, "To Bob and Bilgy's next battleship together!"

What Father and Commander Billy enjoyed talking about most was their class of '07. After dinner, the ladies would retire to the upstairs sitting room. As a special privilege I was allowed to remain at the table with the men. Over and over, they would talk about their ensigns' cruise around the world, escaping the "reeport," gunboating on the upper Yangtse during the Chinese Civil War, keeping sane and sanitary at Guantanamo,[4] patroling the Golfo del Papayo during the two-bit Nicaraguan Revolution, when water to wash in cost a dollar a barrel and was mostly "alkali and wrigglers." There were the class casualties: Holden and Holcomb drowned in a foundered launch off Hampton Roads; "Count" Bowditch, killed by the Moros and famous for his dying words to Commander Harkness: "I'm all right. Get on the job, Bilge."

They would speak about the terrible 1918 influenza epidemic, which had killed more of their classmates than all the skirmishes or even the World War. It was an honor, however, to belong to a class which included "Chips" Carpender, whose destroyer, the *Fanning*, was the only British or American warship to force a German submarine to break water and surrender. It was a feather in their caps that three of their classmates, Bellinger, Reade, and another, should have made the first trans-Atlantic seaplane flight. They put their faith in teamwork, and Lindbergh's solo hop to Paris struck them as unprofessional, a newspaper trick. What made Father and Commander Billy mad as hornets was the mare's-nest made of naval administration by "deserving Democrats." Hadn't Secretary of State Bryan ordered their old battle-wagon the *Idaho* to sail on a goodwill mission to Switzerland? "Bryan, Bryan, Bryan," Commander Billy would boom, "the pious swab had been told that Lake Geneva had annexed the Adriatic." Another "guy with false gills," Josephus Daniels, "ordained by Divine Providence Secretary of the Navy," had refused to send Father and Billy to the war zone. "You are looking," Billy would declaim, "at martyrs in the famous victory of red tape. Our names are rubric." A man they had to take their hats off to was Theodore Roosevelt; Billy had been one of the lucky ensigns who had helped "escort the redoubtable Teddy to Panama." Perhaps because of his viciously inappropriate nickname, "Bilge," Commander Harkness always spoke with brutal facetiousness against the class *bilgers*, officers whose services were no longer required by the service." In more Epicurean moods, Bilge would announce that he "meant to accumulate a lot of dough from complacent, well-meaning, although misguided West Point officers gullible enough to bet their shirts on the Army football team."

"Let's have a squint at your *figger* and waterline, Bob," Billy would say. He'd admire Father's trim girth and smile familiarly at his bald spot. "Bob," he'd say, "you've maintained your displacement and silhouette unmodified, except for somewhat thinner top chafing gear."

[4] A city in southeastern Cuba.

Commander Billy's drinking was a "pain in the neck." He would take possession of Father's sacred "rhino" armchair, sprawl legs astraddle, make the tried and true framework groan, and crucify Mother by roaring out verbose toasts in which he called "me boozy cockney-h'Irish." He would drink to our cocktail shaker. "'Ere's to the 'older of the Lowelldom nectar," he would bellow. "Hip, hip, horray for senor Martino, h'our h'old hipmate, 'elpmate, and honorary member of '07—h'always h'able to navigate and never say dry." We never got through a visit without one of Billy's "Bottoms up to the 'ead of the Nation. 'Ere's to herb-garden 'Erb." This was a swaggering dig at Herbert Hoover's notoriously correct, but insular, refusal to "imbibe anything more potent than Bromo-Seltzer" at a war-relief banquet in Brussels. Commander Billy's bulbous, water-on-the-brain forehead would glow and trickle with fury. Thinking on Herbert Hoover and Prohibition, he was unable to contain himself. "What a hick! We haven't been steered by a gentleman of parts since the redoubtable Teddy." He recited *wet* verses, such as the following inserted in Father's class book:

> *"I tread the bridge with measured pace;*
> *Proud, yet anguish marks my face—*
> *What worries me like crushing sin*
> *Is where on the sea can I buy dry gin?"*

In his cups, Commander Bilge acted as though he owned us. He looked like a human ash-heap. Cigar ashes buried the heraldic hedgehog on the ash tray beside him; cigar ashes spilled over and tarnished the golden stork embroidered on the table-cover; cigar ashes littered his own shiny blue-black uniform. Greedily Mother's eyes would brighten, drop and brighten. She would say darkly, "I was brought up by Papá to be like a naval officer, to be ruthlessly neat."

Once Commander Billy sprawled back so recklessly that the armchair began to come apart. "You see, Charlotte," he said to Mother, "at the height of my *climacteric* I am breaking Bob's chair."

Harkness went in for tiresome, tasteless harangues against Amy Lowell, which he seemed to believe necessary for the enjoyment of his after-dinner cigar. He would point a stinking baby stogie at Mother. "'Ave a peteeto cigareeto, Charlotte," he would crow. "Puff on this whacking black cheroot, and you'll be a match for any reeking senorita *femme fatale* in the spiggotty republics, where blindness from Bob's bathtub hooch is still unknown. When you go up in smoke, Charlotte, remember the *Maine*. Remember Amy Lowell, that cigar-chawing, guffawing, senseless and meterless, multimillion-heiress, heavyweight mascot on a floating fortress. Damn the *Patterns!* Full speed ahead on a cigareeto!"

Amy Lowell was never a welcome subject in our household. Of course, no one spoke disrespectfully of Miss Lowell. She had been so plucky, *so formidable, so beautifully and unblushingly immense,* as Henry James might have said. And yet, though irreproachably decent herself apparently, like Mae West she seemed to provoke indecorum in others. There was an anecdote which I was too young to understand: it was about Amy's getting her migraine headaches from being kept awake by the exercises of honeymooners in an adjacent New York hotel room. Amy's relatives would have liked to have honored her as a *personage,* a personage a little *outrée* perhaps, but perfectly within the natural order, like Amy's girlhood idol, the Duse.[5] Or at least she might have been unambiguously tragic, short-lived, and a classic, like her last idol, John Keats. My parents piously made out a case for Miss Lowell's *Life of Keats,* which had killed its author and was so much more manly and intelligible than her poetry. Her poetry! But was *poetry* what one could call Amy's loud, bossy, unladylike *chinoiserie*[6]—her free verse! For those that could understand it, her matter was, no doubt, blameless, but the effrontery of her manner made my parents relish Robert Frost's remark that "writing free verse was like playing tennis without a net."

Whenever Amy Lowell was mentioned Mother bridled. Not distinguishing, not caring whether her relative were praised or criticized, she would say, "Amy had the courage of her convictions. She worked like a horse." Mother would conclude characteristically, "Amy did insist on doing everything the *hard* way. I think, perhaps, that her brother, the President of Harvard, did more for *other* people."

Often Father seemed to pay little attention to the conversation of his guests. He would smack his lips, and beam absentmindedly and sensuously, as if he were anticipating the comforts of civilian life—a perpetual shore leave in Hawaii. The Harknesses, however, cowed him. He would begin to feel out the subject of his resignation and observe in a wheedle obscurely loaded with significance that "certain *cits,* no brighter than you or I, pay income taxes as large as a captain's yearly salary."

Commander Harkness, unfortunately, was inclined to draw improper conclusions from such remarks. Disregarding the "romance of commerce," he would break out into ungentlemanly tirades against capital. "Yiss, old Bob," he would splutter, "when I consider the ungodly hoards garnered in by the insurance and broking gangs, it breaks my heart. Riches, reaches, overreaches! If Bob and I had half the swag that Harkness of Yale has just given Lowell of Harvard to build Georgian houses for Boston quee-eers with British accents!" He rumbled on morosely about retired naval officers "forced to live like coolies on their half-pay. Hurrah for the Bull Moose Party!" he'd shout. "Hurrah for Boss Curley! Hurrah for the Bolshies!"

Nothing prevented Commander Billy from telling about his diplomatic mission in 1918, when "his eyes had seen the Bolshie on his native heath."

---

[5] Eleonora Duse (1859–1924), Italian actress.
[6] A style in art reflecting Chinese influence through the use of elaborate decoration and intricate pattern.

He had been in Budapest "during the brief sway of Béla Kun-Whon. Béla was giving those Hunkyland money-bags and educators the boot into the arms of American philanthropy!"

Then Mother would say, hopefully, "Mamá always said that the *old* Hungarians *did* have taste. Billy, your reference to Budapest makes me heartsick for Europe. I am dying for Bob and Bobby's permission to spend next summer at Etretat."

Commander Billy Harkness specialized in verses like "The Croix de Guerre":

> *"I toast the guy, who, crossing over,*
> *Abode in London for a year,*
> *The guy who to his wife and lover*
> *Returned with conscience clean and clear,*
> *Who nightly prowling Piccadilly*
> *Gave icy stares to floozies wild,*
> *And when approached said, 'Bilgy Billy*
> *Is mama's darling angel child—'*
> *Now he's the guy who rates the croy dee geer!"*

Mother, however, smiled mildly. "Billy," she would say, "my cousin, Admiral Ledyard Atkinson, always has a twinkle in his eye when he asks after your *vers de société*."

" 'Tommy' Atkins!" snorted Commander Billy. "I know Tommy better than my own mother. He's the first chapter in a book I'm secretly writing and leaving to the archives called *Wild Admirals I Have Known*. And now my bodily presence may no longer grace the inner sanctum of the Somerset Club, for fear Admiral Tommy'll assault me with five new chapters of his *Who Won the Battle of Jutland?*"

After the heat and push of Commander Billy, it was pleasant to sit in the shade of the Atkinsons. Cousin Ledyard wasn't exactly an admiral: he had been promoted to this rank during the World War and had soon reverted back to his old rank of captain. In 1926 he was approaching the retiring age and was still a captain. He was in charge of a big, stately, comfortable, but anomalous warship, which seldom sailed further than hailing distance from its Charlestown drydock. He was himself stately and anomalous. Serene, silver-maned, and Spanish-looking, Cousin Ledyard liked full-dress receptions and crowed like a rooster in his cabin crowded with liveried Filipinos, Cuban trophies, and racks of experimental firearms, such as pepper-box pistols and a machine gun worked by electric batteries. He rattled off Spanish phrases, told first-hand adventure stories about service with Admiral Schley, and reminded one of some landsman and diplomat commanding a galleon in Philip II's Armada. With his wife's money he had bought a motor launch which had a teak deck and a newfangled diesel engine. While his warship perpetually rode at anchor, Cousin Ledyard was forever hurrying about the harbor in his launch. "Oh, Led Atkinson has dash and his own speedboat!" This was about the best my father could bring himself to say for his relative. Commander Billy, himself a man of action, was more sympathetic: "Tommy's about a hundred horse and buggy power." Such a dinosaur, however, had little to offer an '07 Annapolis graduate. Billy's final judgment was that Cousin Ledyard knew less *trig* than a schoolgirl, had been promoted through mistaken identity or merely as "window-dressing," and "was really plotting to put airplane carriers in square sails to stem the tide of our declining Yankee seamanship." Mother lost her enthusiasm for Captain Atkinson's stately chatter—he was "unable to tell one woman from another."

Cousin Ledyard's wife, a Schenectady Hoes distantly related to my still living Great-Grandmother Myers, was twenty years younger than her husband. This made her a trying companion; with the energy of youth she demanded the homage due to age. Once while playing in the Mattapoisett tennis tournament, she had said to her opponent, a woman her own age but married to a young husband, "I believe I'll call you Ruth; you can call me Mrs. Atkinson." She was a radiant Christian Scientist, darted about in smart serge suits and blouses frothing with lace. She filled her purse with Science literature and boasted without irony of "Boston's greatest grand organ" in the Christian Science mother temple on Huntington Avenue. As a girl, she had grown up with our Myers furniture. We dreaded Mrs. Atkinson's descents on Revere Street. She pooh-poohed Mother's taste, snorted at our ignorance of Myers family history, treated us as mere custodians of the Myers furniture, resented alterations, and had the memory of a mastodon for Cousin Cassie's associations with each piece. She wouldn't hear of my mother's distress from neuralgia, dismissed my asthma as "growing-pains," and sought to rally us by gossiping about healers. She talked a prim, sprightly babble. Like many Christian Scientists, she had a bloodless, euphoric, inexhaustible interest in her own body. In a discourse which lasted from her first helping of roast beef through her second demitasse, Mrs. Atkinson held us spellbound by telling how her healer had "surprised and evaporated a cyst inside a sac" inside her "major intestine."

I can hear my father trying to explain his resignation from the Navy to Cousin Ledyard or Commander Billy. Talking with an unnatural and importunate jocularity, he would say, "Billy Boy, it's a darned shame, but this State of Massachusetts doesn't approve of the service using its franchise and voting by mail. I haven't had a chance to establish residence since our graduation in '07. I think I'll put my blues in mothballs and become a *cit* just to prove I still belong to the country. The directors of Lever Brothers' Soap in Cambridge . . . I guess for *cits*, Billy, they've really got something on the ball, because they tell me they want me on their team."

Or Father, Cousin Ledyard, Commander Billy, and I would be sitting on after dinner at the dining-room table and talking man to man. Father would say, "I'm afraid I'll grow dull and drab with all this goldbricking ashore. I am too old for tennis singles, but too young for that confirmed state of senility known as golf."

Cousin Ledyard and Commander Billy would puff silently on their cigars. Then Father would try again and say pitifully, "I don't think a naval man can ever on the *outside* replace the friends he made during his years of wearing the blue."

Then Cousin Ledyard would give Father a polite, funereal look and say, "Speaking of golf, Bob, you've hit me below the belt. I've been flubbing away at the game for thirty years without breaking ninety."

Commander Billy was blunter. He would chaff Father about becoming a "beachcomber" or "purser for the Republican junior chamber of commerce." He would pretend that Father was in danger of being jailed for evading taxes to support "Uncle Sam's circus." *Circus* was Commander Billy's slang for the Navy. The word reminded him of a comparison, and once he stood up from the table and bellowed solemnly: "Oyez, oyez! Bob Lowell, our bright boy, our class baby, is now on a par with 'Rattle-Ass Rats' Richardson, who resigned from us to become press agent for Sells-Floto Circus, and who writes me: 'Bilgy Dear—Beating the drum ahead of the elephants and the spangled folk, I often wonder why I run into so few of my classmates.' "

Those dinners, those apologies! Perhaps I exaggerate their embarrassment because they hover so grayly in recollection and seem to anticipate ominously my father's downhill progress as a civilian and Bostonian. It was to be expected, I suppose, that Father should be in irons for a year or two, while becoming detached from his old comrades and interests, while waiting for the new life.

I used to sit through the Sunday dinners absorbing cold and anxiety from the table. I imagined myself hemmed in by our new, inherited Victorian Myers furniture. In the bleak Revere Street dining room, none of these pieces had at all that air of unhurried condescension that had been theirs behind the summery veils of tissue paper in Cousin Cassie Julian-James's memorial volume. Here, table, highboy, chairs, and screen—mahogany, cherry, teak—looked nervous and disproportioned. They seemed to wince, touch elbows, shift from foot to foot. High above the highboy, our gold National Eagle stooped forward, plastery and doddering. The Sheffield silver-plate urns, more precious than solid sterling, peeled; the bodies of the heraldic mermaids on the Mason-Myers crest blushed a metallic copper tan. In the harsh New England light, the bronze sphinxes supporting our sideboard looked as though manufactured in Grand Rapids. All too clearly no one had worried about synchronizing the grandfather clock's minutes, days, and months with its mellow old Dutch seascape-painted discs for showing the phases of the moon. The stricken, but still striking gong made sounds like steam banging through pipes. Colonel Myers' monumental Tibetan screen had been impiously shortened to fit it for a low Yankee ceiling. And now, rough and gawky, like some Hindu water buffalo killed in mid-rush but still alive with mad momentum, the screen hulked over us . . . and hid the pantry sink.

Our real blue-ribbon-winning *bête noire* was of course the portrait of Cousin Cassie's father, Mordecai Myers' fourth and most illustrious son: Colonel Theodorus Bailey Myers. The Colonel, like half of our new portraits, was merely a collateral relation; though really as close to us as James Russell Lowell, no one called the Colonel "Great Grand Uncle," and Mother playfully pretended that her mind was overstrained by having to remember his full name, rank, and connection. In the portrait, Colonel Theodorus wore a black coat and gray trousers, an obsequiously conservative costume which one associated with undertakers and the musicians at Symphony Hall. His spats were pearl gray plush with pearl buttons. His mustache might have been modeled on the mustache of a bartender in a Western. The majestic Tibetan screen enclosed him as though he were an ancestor-god from Lhasa, a blasphemous yet bogus attitude. Mr. Myers' colonel's tabs were crudely stitched to a civilian coat; his New York Yacht Club button glowed like a carnation; his vainglorious picture frame was a foot and a half wide. Forever, his right hand hovered over a glass dome that covered a model locomotive. He was vaguely Middle-Eastern and waiting. A lady in Mother's sewing circle had pertly interpreted this portrait as, "King Solomon about to receive the Queen of Sheba's shares in the Boston and Albany Railroad." Gone now was the Colonel's place of honor at Cousin Cassie's Washington mansion; gone was his charming satire on the belles of 1850, entitled, *Nothing to Wear,* which had once been quoted "throughout the length and breadth of the land as generally as was Bret Harte's *Heathen Chinee";* gone was his priceless collection of autographed letters of *all* the Signers of the Declaration of Independence—he had said once, "my letters will be my tombstone." Colonel Theodorus Bailey Myers had never been a New Englander. His family tree reached to no obscure Somersetshire yeoman named Winslowe or Lowle. He had never even, like his father, Mordecai, gloried in a scarlet War of 1812 waistcoat. His portrait was an indifferent example from a dull, bad period. The Colonel's only son had sheepishly changed his name from Mason-Myers to Myers-Mason.

Waiting for dinner to end and for the guests to leave, I used to lean forward on my elbows, support each cheekbone with a thumb, and make my fingers meet in a clumsy Gothic arch across my forehead. I would stare through this arch and try to make life stop. Out in the alley the sun shone irreverently on our three garbage cans lettered: R. T. S. Lowell—U.S.N. When I shut my eyes to stop the sun, I saw first an orange disc, then a red disc, then the portrait of Major Myers apotheosized, as it were, by the sunlight lighting the blood smear of his scarlet waistcoat. Still there was no *coup de théatre* about the Major as he looked down on us with his portly young man's face of a comfortable upper New York State patroon and the friend of Robert Livingston and Martin Van Buren. Great-great-Grandfather Myers had never frowned down in judgment on a Salem witch. There was no allegory in his eyes, no *Mayflower*. Instead he looked peacefully at his sideboard, his cut-glass decanters, his cellaret[7]—the worldly bosom of the Mason-Myers mermaid engraved on a silver-plated urn. If he could have spoken, Mordecai would have said, "My children, my blood, accept graciously the loot of your inheritance. We are all dealers in used furniture."

The man who seems in my memory to sit under old Mordecai's portrait is not my father, but Commander Billy—*the* Commander after Father had thrown in his commission. There Billy would sit glowing, perspiring, bragging. Despite his rowdiness, he even then breathed the power that would make him a vice-admiral and hero in World War II. I can hear him boasting in lofty language of how he had stood up for democracy in the day of Lenin and Béla Kun;[8] of how he "practiced the sport of kings" (i.e., commanded a destroyer) and combed the Mediterranean, Adriatic, and Black Seas like gypsies—seldom knowing what admiral he served under or where his next meal or load of fuel oil was coming from.

It always vexed the Commander, however, to think of the strings that had been pulled to have Father transferred from Washington to Boston. He would ask Mother, "Why in God's name should a man with Bob's brilliant cerebellum go and mess up his record by actually *begging* for that impotent field nigger's job of second in command at the defunct Boston Yard!"

I would squirm. I dared not look up because I knew that the Commander abhorred Mother's dominion over my father, thought my asthma, supposedly brought on by the miasmal damp of Washington, a myth, and considered our final flight to Boston a scandal.

My mother, on the other hand, would talk back sharply and explain to Billy that there was nothing second-string about the Boston Yard except its commandant, Admiral De Stahl, who had gone into a frenzy when he learned that my parents, supposed to live at the naval yard, had set themselves up without his permission at 91 Revere Street. The Admiral had *commanded* Father to reside at the yard, but Mother had bravely and stubbornly held on at Revere Street.

"A really great person," she would say, "knows how to be courteous to his superiors."

---

[7] A cabinet used for storing wine.

[8] Nikolai Lenin (1870–1924) was the Russian revolutionary statesman and the first premier of Russia (1918–1924). Béla Kun (1886–c.1937) was a communist leader who set up a Soviet republic for 6 months in Hungary.

Then Commander Harkness would throw up his hands in despair and make a long buffoonish speech. "Would you believe it?" he'd say. "De Stahl, the anile slob, would make Bob Lowell sleep seven nights a week and twice on Sundays in that venerable twenty-room pile provided for his third in command at the yard. 'Bobby me boy,' the Man says, 'henceforth I will that you sleep wifeless. You're to push your beauteous mug into me boudoir each night at ten-thirty and each morn at six. And don't mind me laying to along-side the Missus De Stahl,' the old boy squeaks; 'we're just two oldsters as weak as babies. But Robbie Boy,' he says, 'don't let me hear of you hanging on your telephone wire and bending off the ear of that forsaken frau of yours sojourning on Revere Street. I might have to phone you in a hurry, if I should happen to have me stroke.' "

Taking hold of the table with both hands, the Commander tilted his chair backwards and gaped down at me with sorrowing Gargantuan wonder: "I know why Young Bob is an only child."

ADRIENNE RICH

(1929-   )

Adrienne Rich has been a productive poet since her graduation from Radcliffe College in 1951. That year she published *A Change of World,* since then seven other books: *The Diamond Cutters* (1955); *Snapshots of a Daughter-in-Law* (1963); *Necessities of Life* (1966); *Selected Poems* (1967); *Leaflets: Poems 1965-1968* (1969); *The Will to Change, Poems 1968-1970* (1971); and *Diving into the Wreck, Poems 1971-1972* (1973), which won the National Book Award in 1974.[1] Adrienne Rich's poetry has always been a "reading of history," as Richard Howard has said, "that will include herself, a perspective that will contain not only what she knows herself to be *now,* the present woman who is an anthology of her wounds and wanderings . . . she wants to be able to say: . . . 'I, too, have lived in history.' " As she has related herself to the political world, she has explored the tensions between her private self and the society. The poetry in her recent book, *Diving into the Wreck,* is, in her own words,

a coming-home to the darkest and richest source of my poetry: sex, sexuality, sexual wounds, sexual identity, sexual politics;

---

[1] Rich has also published *Poems: Selected and New, 1950-1974,* 1974.

many names for pieces of one whole. I feel this book continues the work I've been trying to do—breaking down the artificial barriers between private and public, between Vietnam and the lovers' bed, between the deepest images we carry out of our dreams and the most daylight events "out in the world." This is the intention and longing behind everything I write.

In addition to her poetry, she has written essays on sexual politics and is completing a history of the feminist movement in America.

Living in Sin

She had thought the studio would keep itself;
no dust upon the furniture of love.
Half heresy, to wish the taps less vocal,
the panes relieved of grime. A plate of pears,
a piano with a Persian shawl, a cat   5
stalking the picturesque amusing mouse
had risen at his urging.
Not that at five each separate stair would writhe
under the milkman's tramp; that morning light
so coldly would delineate the scraps   10
of last night's cheese and three sepulchral bottles;
that on the kitchen shelf among the saucers
a pair of beetle-eyes would fix her own—
envoy from some black village in the mouldings . . .
Meanwhile he, with a yawn,   15
sounded a dozen notes upon the keyboard,
declared it out of tune, shrugged at the mirror,
rubbed at his beard, went out for cigarettes;
while she, jeered by the minor demons,
pulled back the sheets and made the bed and found   20
a towel to dust the table-top,
and let the coffee-pot boil over on the stove.
By evening she was back in love again,
though not so wholly but throughout the night
she woke sometimes to feel the daylight coming   25
like a relentless milkman up the stairs.

1955

Rape

There is a cop who is both prowler and father:
he comes from your block, grew up with your brothers,
had certain ideals.
You hardly know him in his boots and silver badge,
on horseback, one hand touching his gun.   5

You hardly know him but you have to get to know him:
he has access to machinery that could kill you.
He and his stallion clop like warlords among the trash,
his ideals stand in the air, a frozen cloud
from between his unsmiling lips.   10

And so, when the time comes, you have to turn to him,
the maniac's sperm still greasing your thighs,
your mind whirling like crazy. You have to confess
to him, you are guilty of the crime
of having been forced.   15

And you see his blue eyes, the blue eyes of all the family
whom you used to know, grow narrow and glisten,
his hand types out the details
and he wants them all
but the hysteria in your voice pleases him best.   20

You hardly know him but now he thinks he knows you:
he has taken down your worst moment
on a machine and filed it in a file.
He knows, or thinks he knows, how much you imagined;
he knows, or thinks he knows, what you secretly wanted.   25
He has access to machinery that could get you put away;
and if, in the sickening light of the precinct,
and if, in the sickening light of the precinct,
your details sound like a portrait of your confessor,
will you swallow, will you deny them, will you lie your way home?   30

1972

1973

A Valediction Forbidding Mourning

My swirling wants. Your frozen lips.
The grammar turned and attacked me.
Themes, written under duress.
Emptiness of the notations.

They gave me a drug that slowed the healing of wounds.　　5

I want to see this before I leave:
the experience of repetition as death
the failure of criticism to locate the pain
the poster in the bus that said:
my bleeding is under control.　　10

A red plant in a cemetery of plastic wreaths.

A last attempt: the language is a dialect called metaphor.
These images go unglossed: hair, glacier, flashlight.
When I think of a landscape I am thinking of a time.
When I talk of taking a trip I mean forever.　　15
I could say: those mountains have a meaning
but further than that I could not say.

To do something very common, in my own way.

1970

1971

Peeling Onions

Only to have a grief
equal to all these tears!

There's not a sob in my chest.
Dry-hearted as Peer Gynt
I pare away, no hero,　　5
merely a cook.

Crying was labor, once
when I'd good cause.
Walking, I felt my eyes like wounds
raw in my head,   10
so postal-clerks, I thought, must stare.
A dog's look, a cat's, burnt to my brain—
yet all that stayed
stuffed in my lungs like smog.

These old tears in the chopping-bowl.

1961

1963

SYLVIA PLATH

(1932–1963)

During her life Sylvia Plath published only one book, *The Colossus* (1960); however, with the posthumous publication of *Ariel* (1965), *Crossing the Water* (1971), *Winter Trees* (1971), and the autobiographical novel *The Bell Jar* (1963), her work—and inevitably her life, so intensely described in her work—has been more available to readers and has become a more and more popular subject of discussion and criticism.

Sylvia Plath was born in Boston, the child of teachers. Her father, who was apparently domineering, died when she was only 10; his death had a traumatic effect on her sensibility, and she was to refer to it recurrently in her poetry. She graduated *summa cum laude,* from Smith College, in 1955, and went on a Fulbright Fellowship to Newnham College, where she received her Master's Degree in 1957. She married the British poet Ted Hughes and had a son and daughter.

Before going to England, Plath studied with Robert Lowell at Boston University and, although she never imitated his style, she found in him a great liberating force. "I've been very excited by what I feel is the new breakthrough that came with, say, Robert Lowell's *Life Studies.*

For criticism, see Charles Newman, *The Art of Sylvia Plath,* 1970; and the pertinent sections in M. L. Rosenthal, *Poetry and the Common Life,* 1975.

This intense breakthrough into very serious, very personal emotional experience, which I feel has been partly taboo. Robert Lowell's poems about his experiences in a mental hospital, for example, interest me very much. These peculiar private and taboo subjects I feel have been explored in recent American poetry. . . ." These qualities inform Plath's poetry to an extraordinary degree and make the reading of her work particularly personal and immediate, implacable and painful.

"The passion for destruction is also a creative passion." So comments A. Alvarez, who has written movingly of Sylvia Plath's suicide in *The Savage God.* "She turned anger, implacability, and her roused, needle-sharp sense of trouble into a kind of celebration. . . . Her intensity was of the nerves, something urban and near screaming point."

Daddy

You do not do, you do not do
Any more, black shoe
In which I have lived like a foot
For thirty years, poor and white,
Barely daring to breathe or Achoo.   5

Daddy, I have had to kill you.
You died before I had time—
Marble-heavy, a bag full of God,
Ghastly statue with one grey toe
Big as a Frisco seal   10

And a head in the freakish Atlantic
Where it pours bean green over blue
In the waters off beautiful Nauset.
I used to pray to recover you.
Ach, du.   15

In the German tongue, in the Polish town
Scraped flat by the roller
Of wars, wars, wars.
But the name of the town is common.
My Polack friend   20

Says there are a dozen or two.
So I never could tell where you
Put your foot, your root,
I never could talk to you.
The tongue stuck in my jaw.   25

It stuck in a barb wire snare.
Ich, ich, ich, ich,
I could hardly speak.
I thought every German was you.
And the language obscene   30

An engine, an engine
Chuffing me off like a Jew.
A Jew to Dachau, Auschwitz, Belsen.
I began to talk like a Jew.
I think I may well be a Jew.   35

The snows of the Tyrol, the clear beer of Vienna
Are not very pure or true.
With my gypsy ancestress and my weird luck
And my Taroc pack and my Taroc pack
I may be a bit of a Jew.   40
I have always been scared of *you,*
With your Luftwaffe, your gobbledygoo.
And your neat moustache
And your Aryan eye, bright blue.
Panzer-man, panzer-man, O You——   45

Not God but a swastika
So black no sky could squeak through.
Every woman adores a Fascist,
The boot in the face, the brute
Brute heart of a brute like you.   50

You stand at the blackboard, daddy,
In the picture I have of you,
A cleft in your chin instead of your foot
But no less a devil for that, no not
Any less the black man who   55

Bit my pretty red heart in two.
I was ten when they buried you.
At twenty I tried to die
And get back, back, back to you.
I thought even the bones would do.   60

But they pulled me out of the sack,
And they stuck me together with glue.
And then I knew what to do.
I made a model of you.
A man in black with a Meinkampf look   65

And a love of the rack and the screw.
And I said I do, I do.
So daddy, I'm finally through.   70
The black telephone's off at the root.
The voices just can't worm through.

If I've killed one man. I've killed two——
The vampire who said he was you
And drank my blood for a year,

Seven years, if you want to know.
Daddy, you can lie back now.   75

There's a stake in your fat black heart
And the villagers never liked you.
They are dancing and stamping on you.
They always *knew* it was you.
Daddy, daddy, you bastard, I'm through.   80

1965

The Applicant

First, are you our sort of a person?
Do you wear
A glass eye, false teeth or a crutch,
A brace or a hook,
Rubber breasts or a rubber crotch,   5

Stitches to show-something's missing? No, no? Then
How can we give you a thing?
Stop crying.
Open your hand.
Empty? Empty. Here is a hand   10

To fill it and willing
To bring teacups and roll away headaches
And do whatever you tell it.
Will you marry it?
It is guaranteed   15

To thumb shut your eyes at the end
And dissolve of sorrow.
We make new stock from the salt.
I notice you are stark naked.
How about this suit—   20

Black and stiff, but not a bad fit.
Will you marry it?

It is waterproof, shatterproof, proof
Against fire and bombs through the roof.
Believe me, they'll bury you in it.   25

Now your head, excuse me, is empty.
I have the ticket for that.
Come here, sweetie, out of the closet.
Well, what do you think of *that?*
Naked as paper to start   30

But in twenty-five years she'll be silver,
In fifty, gold.
A living doll, everywhere you look.
It can sew, it can cook,
It can talk, talk, talk.   35

It works, there is nothing wrong with it.
You have a hole, it's a poultice.
You have an eye, it's an image.
My boy, it's your last resort.
Will you marry it, marry it, marry it.   40

1965

Lady Lazarus

I have done it again.
One year in every ten
I manage it——

A sort of walking miracle, my skin
Bright as a Nazi lampshade,   5
My right foot

A paperweight,
My face a featureless, fine
Jew linen.

Peel off the napkin   10
O my enemy.
Do I terrify?——

The nose, the eye pits, the full set of teeth?
The sour breath
Will vanish in a day.   15

Soon, soon the flesh
The grave cave ate will be
At home on me

And I a smiling woman.
I am only thirty.   20
And like the cat I have nine times to die.

This is Number Three.
What a trash
To annihilate each decade.

What a million filaments.   25
The peanut-crunching crowd
Shoves in to see

Them unwrap me hand and foot——
The big strip tease.
Gentleman, ladies,   30

These are my hands,
My knees.
I may be skin and bone,

Nevertheless, I am the same, identical woman.
The first time it happened I was ten.   35
It was an accident.

The second time I meant
To last it out and not come back at all.
I rocked shut

As a seashell.   40
They had to call and call
And pick the worms off me like sticky pearls.

Dying
Is an art, like everything else.
I do it exceptionally well.   45

I do it so it feels like hell.
I do it so it feels real.
I guess you could say I've a call.

It's easy enough to do it in a cell.
It's easy enough to do it and stay put.   50
It's the theatrical

Comeback in broad day
To the same place, the same face, the same brute
Amused shout:

"A miracle!"   55
That knocks me out.
There is a charge

For the eyeing of my scars, there is a charge
For the hearing of my heart——
It really goes.   60

And there is a charge, a very large charge,
For a word or a touch
Or a bit of blood

Or a piece of my hair or my clothes,
So, so Herr Doktor.   65
So, Herr Enemy.

I am your opus,
I am your valuable,
The pure gold baby

That melts to a shriek.   70
I turn and burn.
Do not think I underestimate your great concern.

Ash, ash——
You poke and stir.
Flesh, bone, there is nothing there——   75

A cake of soap,
A wedding ring,
A gold filling.

Herr God, Herr Lucifer,
Beware   80
Beware.

Out of the ash
I rise with my red hair
And I eat men like air.

1963

1965

Ariel

Stasis in darkness.
Then the substanceless blue
Pour of tor and distances.

God's lioness,
How one we grow,   5
Pivot of heels and knees!—The furrow

Splits and passes, sister to
The brown arc
Of the neck I cannot catch,

Nigger-eye   10
Berries cast dark
Hooks——

Black sweet blood mouthfuls,
Shadows.
Something else   15

Hauls me through air——
Thighs, hair;
Flakes from my heels.

White
Godiva, I unpeel——   20
Dead hands, dead stringencies.

And now I
Foam to wheat, a glitter of seas.
The child's cry

Melts in the wall.   25
And I
Am the arrow,

The dew that flies,
Suicidal, at one with the drive
Into the red   30

Eye, the cauldron of morning.

1963

1965

Death & Co.

Two, of course there are two.
It seems perfectly natural now——
The one who never looks up, whose eyes are lidded
And balled, like Blake's,
Who exhibits

The birthmarks that are his trademark——
The scald scar of water,
The nude
Verdigris of the condor.
I am red meat. His beak   10

Claps sidewise: I am not his yet.
He tells me how badly I photograph.
He tells me how sweet
The babies look in their hospital
Icebox, a simple   15

Frill at the neck,
Then the flutings of their Ionian
Death-gowns,
Then two little feet.
He does not smile or smoke.   20

The other does that,
His hair long and plausive.

1965

IMAMU AMIRI BARAKA (LEROI JONES)

(1934-   )

During the 1960's, LeRoi Jones emerged as the dominant figure of black literature in America. The stridency that had been predicted by Baldwin in *The Fire Next Time* (1962) was represented by Jones, who

Jones' essays appear in *Home: Social Essays*, 1966. A critical study is Theodore R. Hudson, *From LeRoi Jones to Amiri Baraka: The Literary Works*, 1973.

grew more militant with each published volume until he found it almost impossible to write literature at all. His gifts have been turned to the political battles of Newark, New Jersey, where he has taken a hard line in the racial warfare that erupted in the late 1960's and has continued throughout the 1970's. As a black nationalist, Jones has changed his name to Imamu Amiri Baraka, has sought to bring blacks together as an economic force, has urged the study of African and Arabic languages, and has inveighed against almost all things white.

Jones was born in Newark of a middle-class black family—his father was a postal supervisor and his mother a social worker. He began his education at Rutgers, but felt alienated and transferred to Howard University, from which he graduated in 1954. He went on to Columbia University and the New School for Social Research, where he taught poetry. During the late 1950's, Jones lived in Greenwich Village and established his reputation as a poet by publishing in a variety of magazines. His verse was collected in *Preface to a Twenty Volume Suicide Note* (1961), *The Dead Lecturer* (1964), the mimeographed *Black Art* (1968), and *Black Magic* (1969). In the same period his short plays gave him a wide popularity: *Baptism, The 8th Ditch, Home on the Range, Arm Yrself or Harm Yrself, Dutchman, The Slave,* and *The Toilet.* The *Dutchman* won the Obie Award in 1964 as the best off-Broadway play.

In addition to poetry and drama, Jones has written a semiautobiographical novel, *The System of Dante's Hell* (1965); stories that were collected in *Tales* (1967); and essays and reviews on black music, published in two volumes, *Blues People: Negro Music in White America* (1963) and *Black Music* (1967). Jones' view of black literature is sharply dramatized in the anthology that he edited with Larry Neal, *Black Fire: An Anthology of Afro-American Writing* (1968).

In recent years Jones, now known as Baraka, has devoted himself almost completely to militant politics in Newark, New Jersey. Whereas he was considered the most popular and influential figure of black literature in the 1960's, his following has shrunk as his political position has become more rigidly radical. But he remains as the most accomplished poet of black militancy and as the playwright who expresses most eloquently the rage in the hearts of many black people.

"Preface to a Twenty Volume Suicide Note" is a lyrical poem of quiet intensity. "A Poem for Black Hearts" is Jones' tribute to Malcolm X, the symbol of manly black pride with which he is identified so closely. *Dutchman* captures the tension of urban living as whites and blacks confront one another in a conflict that too often has resulted in riot or death.

Preface to a Twenty Volume Suicide Note

Lately, I've become accustomed to the way
The ground opens up and envelops me
Each time I go out to walk the dog.
Or the broad edged silly music the wind
Makes when I run for a bus——   5

Things have come to that.

And now, each night I count the stars,
And each night I get the same number.
And when they will not come to be counted
I count the holes they leave.   10

Nobody sings anymore.

And then last night, I tiptoed up
To my daughter's room and heard her
Talking to someone, and when I opened
The door, there was no one there . . .   15
Only she on her knees.
Peeking into her own clasped hands.

1961

A Poem for Black Hearts

For Malcolm's eyes, when they broke
the face of some dumb white man. For
Malcolm's hands raised to bless us
all black and strong in his image
of ourselves, for Malcolm's words   5
fire darts, the victor's tireless
thrusts, words hung above the world
change as it may, he said it, and
for this he was killed, for saying,
and feeling, and being, change, all   10
collected hot in his heart. For Malcolm's
heart, raising us above our filthy cities,

for his stride, and his beat, and his address
to the grey monsters of the world, For Malcolm's
pleas for your dignity, black men, for your life,   15
black men, for the filling of your minds
with righteousness, For all of him dead and
gone and vanished from us, and all of him which
clings to our speech black god of our time.
For all of him, and all of yourself, look up,   20
black man, quit stuttering and shuffling, look up,
black man, quit whining and stooping, for all of him,
For Great Malcolm a prince of the earth, let nothing in us rest
until we avenge ourselves for his death, stupid animals
that killed him, let us never breathe a pure breath if   25
we fail, and white men call us faggots till the end of
the earth.

1965

MICHAEL HARPER

(1938-   )

Michael Harper's poetry is strongly rooted in black music and speech.
In his first two books, *Dear John, Dear Coltrane* and *History is Your
Own Heartbeat,* he draws on the rhythms of jazz musicians like John
Coltrane, McCoy Tyner, Bud Powell, Miles Davis, Dizzie Gillespie,
Leadbelly, Charles Parker, Theolonius Monk, Billie Holiday. For him
"poetry is to be spoken or sung." In addition, he is deeply sensitive to
black history and literature in America, and a recent book, *Debridement,* reminds the reader of John Brown, Nat Turner, Harriet Tubman,
Frederick Douglass, and Richard Wright. But history for Harper is always made personal—history is your own heartbeat, "an hallucination," as he says in one poem, or "a nightmare" in which responsibility
begins.

Harper was born in Brooklyn in 1938 and grew up in Los Angeles. He
studied at Los Angeles State College and the University of Iowa Writers
Workshop, and has taught at a variety of colleges—the University of
Illinois, Reed, Lewis and Clark, Contra Costa, and California State at
Hayward. At present he is at Brown University. Harper's first book,
Dear John, Dear Coltrane, was published in 1970, and since then he
has published five others: *History is Your Own Heartbeat* (1971), *Pho-*

tographs, Negatives, History as Apple Tree (1972), Song: I Want a Witness (1972), Debridement (1973), and Nightmare Begins Responsibility (1973).

Running through Harper's work is the sense, as he puts it, "that man is basically spiritual." He is particularly concerned with a "wholistic concept of the universe," with a "modality" that unifies man and his environment and that is captured in the music of someone like John Coltrane.

> This means that the universe is not fragmented, that man has a place in it, that man is a reflection of the environment, and that the environment is a reflection of man. John Coltrane was a model musician. One of the things that is important about Coltrane's music is the energy and passion with which he approached his instrument and music. Such energy was perhaps akin to the nature of oppression generally and the kind of energy it takes to break oppressive conditions, oppressive music strictures, and oppressive societal situations.

Myths, for Harper, must be open-ended. He retains an abiding respect for the possibility, combination, and diversity "of human beings"; but he indicts white Americans for viewing

> history as myth as lie, . . . Of course the fantasy of white supremist America with its closed myths has always been a fantasy of a white country. Out of that kind of fantasy came genocide, Indian massacres, fugitive slave laws, manifest destiny, open-door policies, Vietnam, Detroit, East Saint Louis, Watts, the Mexican War, Chicago and the Democratic Convention of 1968. So one ought to be careful about myth as lie, when it's stereotyped, when it's reductive, when it freezes experience and denies freedom. Myths are true when they suggest new arrangements of human essentials confirmed by past experience, when they invoke modes of connotation and implication, when they are open-ended."

With this kind of understanding, Harper has created a remarkable body of poetry within only a few years. Music and history are informative, shaping forces in all of his work, as Harper attempts to locate the individual human experience in its mythical and universal context. "The dream of every poem is to become a myth." His recent works, Song: I Want a Witness and Debridement "direct themselves to the concept of fragmentation that results from a reductive vision of complexity in a historical context. Dominion has functioned as aesthetics through the modicum of a specialized, reductive language without the reactive imagery connected to a true picture of history, national and personal. The first act of liberation is always to destroy one's own cage."

Reuben, Reuben

I reach from pain
to music great enough
to bring me back.
swollenhead, madness.
lovefruit, a pickle of hate   5
so sour my mouth twicked
up and would not sing;
there's nothing in the beat
to hold it in
melody and turn human skin;   10
a brown berry gone
to rot just two days on the branch;
we've lost a son,
the music, *jazz*, comes in.

1970

Dear John, Dear Coltrane

a love supreme, a love supreme
a love supreme, a love supreme

Sex fingers toes
in the marketplace
near your father's church
in Hamlet, North Carolina:
witness to this love   5
in this calm fallow
of these minds.
there is no substitute for pain:
genitals gone or going,
seed burned out,   10
you tuck the roots in the earth,
turn back, and move
by river through the swamps,
singing: *a love supreme, a love supreme;*
what does it all mean?   15
Loss, so great each black
woman expects your failure
in mute change, the seed gone.
You plod up into the electric city—

your song now crystal and   20
the blues. You pick up the horn
with some will and blow
into the freezing night:
a love supreme, a love supreme—

Dawn comes and you cook   25
up the thick sin 'tween
impotence and death, fuel
the tenor sax cannibal
heart, genitals and sweat
that makes you clean—   30
a love supreme, a love supreme—

Why you so black?
cause I am
why you so funky?
cause I am   35
why you so black?
cause I am
why you so sweet?
cause I am
why you so black?   40
cause I am.
a love supreme, a love supreme:

So sick
you couldn't play *Naima,*
so flat we ached   45
for song you'd concealed
with your own blood,
your diseased liver gave
out its purity,
the inflated heart   50
pumps out, the tenor kiss,
tenor love:
a love supreme, a love supreme—
a love supreme, a love supreme—

1970

DON L. LEE

(1942-   )

Don Lee is a vigorous spokesman for the view that black people should protect themselves against the dominant white culture and should come to understand the sources of power in America. Blacks have "ceased to be a responsible people," because they adapt themselves to a white America, seeking "position, status, and power" without the primary criterion needed for achievement—whiteness.

> Our problem, too, is one of identification. We *do not consider ourselves a people*—an Afrikan people. We identify ourselves as black Christians, black Muslims, negro NAACP'ers, black business-men, black teachers, Afro-doctors, colored musicians, or black this-and-that. What we've done, in most cases, is take the European definition and put black in front of it and still work within a European Frame of Reference. However, if we define ourselves as a people, as an Afrikan people, and set up the necessary mechanisms and institutions that will re-educate people to such, we will then begin to act and not re-act in the best interests of Afrika and Afrikan people, which is what *all* other ethnic groups do naturally. Will it take Afrikan pogroms to move us into this position?
> We are Afrikan people in America, defining ourselves from the positive (Afrikan) toward the negative (American).

All of Lee's work has centered on this fundamental principle. He sees his role as a poet in the larger political context of his role as an Afrikan in America, and he writes for black audiences. He was, as he says, "born into slavery in Feb. of 1942. In the spring of that same year 110,000 persons of Japanese descent were placed in protective custody by the white people of the United States." His militant position was established early in his career, when he published *Think Black* (1967), *Black Pride* (1968), and *Don't Cry, Scream* (1969). Since then he has continually published poetry and essays: *We Walk the Way of the New World* (1970), *Directionscore: Selected and New Poems* (1971), *Dynamite Voices: Black Poets of the 1960's* (1971), and *From Plan to Planet, Life Studies: The Need for Afrikan Minds and Institutions* (1973). Two of his most recent books are *Enemy Defined: Political and Literary Essays, 1965–1973* and *Dynamite Voices II*.

Lee, who makes his home in Chicago, is also an activist in the publishing, education, and politics of black people. He is publisher and editor of Third World Press, has been Executive Director of the Institute of Positive Education, and a member of the Congress of Afrikan People. He lectures and reads his poetry widely and has taught at Howard University.

The New Integrationist

i
seek
integration
of
negroes   5
with
black
people.

1968

The negro
(a pure product of americanism)

Swinging, Swinging,
     thru cotton fields,
     small southern towns,
     big ghetto darkness where
     his mind was blown,   5
Swinging, Swinging,
     to assimilation into whi
     te madness called civilization
     by those who have the
     power to define,   10
Swinging, Swinging,
     with power to define, whi
     te power; indians were never
     the victors—they massacred/
     black history was booker t.   15
     & george c. & a whi-te lie
     over black truth,

THE NEGRO (A PURE PRODUCT OF AMERICANISM)

Swinging, Swinging,
>   with ray charles singing
>   the star spangle banner/   20
>   all his soul didn't change the
>   colors/red, white & light blue,

Swinging, Swinging,
>   working, saving all year/
>   working, saving to buy   25
>   christmas gifts for children/
>   just to tell them a whi
>   te santa claus brought them.

Swinging, Swinging,
>   into aberration where there   30
>   is a black light trying
>   to penetrate that whi-teness
>   called mr. clean,

Swinging, Swinging,
>   into blackness/away from   35
>   negroness/to Self to
>   awareness of basic color/
>   my color, i found it,

Swinging, Swinging,
>   by   40
>   his
>   neck. (nigger)

II
The Life of the Imagination

FIGURES OF THE POET

EDWIN ARLINGTON ROBINSON

(1869–1935)

Frost once wrote that Robinson's prime subject is "immedicable woes—woes that nothing can be done for—woes flat and final." And it is a fact that Robinson knew a good deal, early on, about such woes.

The editions since *Collected Poems,* 1921 show continued changes; the edition of 1937 is complete. Three collections of letters are *Selected Letters of Edwin Arlington Robinson,* 1940, with an introduction by Robinson's friend Ridgely Torrence; *Untriangulated Stars: Letters of Edwin Arlington Robinson to Harry De Forest Smith, 1890–1905,* 1947, ed. Denham Sutcliffe; and *Edwin Arlington Robinson's Letters to Edith Brower,* 1968, ed. Richard Cary.

A reliable bibliography is Charles Beecher Hogan. *A Bibliography of Edwin Arlington Robinson,* 1936. An early biography is Hermann Hagedorn, *Edwin Arlington Robinson, A Biography,* 1938. Emery Neff's *Edwin Arlington Robinson* (1948) is a mixture of biography and criticism.

Critical studies include Lloyd Morris, *The Poetry of Edwin Arlington Robinson,* 1923; Mark Van Doren, *Edwin Arlington Robinson,* 1927; Yvor Winters, *Edwin Arlington Robinson,* 1946; Elsworth Barnard, *Edwin Arlington Robinson: A Critical Study,* 1948; Edwin G. Fussell, *Edwin Arlington Robinson: The Literary Background of a Traditional Poet,* 1954; Louis Untermeyer, *Edwin Arlington Robinson: A Reappraisal,* 1963; Hoyt C. Franchere, *Edwin Arlington Robinson,* 1968; and Louis Coxe, *Edwin Arlington Robinson: The Life of Poetry,* 1968. See also Richard Cary, ed., *Appreciation of Edwin Arlington Robinson,* 1969; and Ellsworth Barnard, ed., *Edwin Arlington Robinson: Centenary Essays,* 1969.

1111
FIGURES OF THE POET

Born in 1869, an unwanted third son, he escaped only briefly to college
from a declining industrial town in Maine, and was called home from
Harvard by the death of his father. Financial catastrophe followed,
then the death of his mother from "black diptheria," then the gradual
disintegration and death of his elder brothers, one by drugs and one
by drink. The pattern of the experience announced, in other words,
that existence was both lonely and tragic, made bearable chiefly by
acts of self-deception. The pattern of his poetry conforms.

It does so, however, with a curious absence of posturing, despair,
and moralizing and, while it is true that Robinson's humor is grim, it is,
nevertheless, humor—the real thing, not mere sardonics. The poet's
idiom is plain; more important, it's the problems of plain people that
most interest him—lost, "minor" persons, instead of the grand or bizarre or sordid. The figures in question are, almost invariably, pathetic
or absurd. The aim sometimes is to show forth hidden qualities in
obscure lives ("Richard Cory," "Clavering"), sometimes to gently mock
a pretension ("Miniver Cheevy"), sometimes to place a failed individual life against the backdrop of community ("Flammonde", "Mr.
Flood's Party," "Eros Turannos"). And as often as not we are made to
understand the complicity of the community in individual failure—
something arising not from viciousness, but simply from self-absorp-
tion and "conventional" unconcern.

In other writers passivity before the inevitabilities of failure and
self-delusion seems a weakness. In Robinson the coolness and poise of
the acceptance embodies a value. It makes it possible for him to attend
patiently and caringly to the details of doomed aspirations without
claiming too much significance for them, yet without casting them
brutally aside as trivial. In "The Gift of God," a poem about a mother's
hopes for her son, there's no suggestion that these hopes are better
than misconceived; everybody in town knows the boy isn't a winner.

> Perchance a canvass of the town
> Would find him far from flags and shouts,
> And leave him only the renown
> Of many smiles and many doubts . . .

But Robinson knows that the delusion itself, the mother's "faith and
praise," is no fair object for scorn: who could endure a world unsoft-
ened by love or dream?

> And should the gift of God be less
> In him than in her motherhood,
> His fame, though vague, will not be small,
> As upward through her dream he fares,
> Half clouded with a crimson fall
> Of roses thrown on marble stairs.

Bleak in its beginning—his first two books of poems, *The Torrent and The Night Before* (1889) and *The Children of the Night* (1897) were published at his own expense and were unsuccessful—Robinson's life had several golden turns. In 1905 he was "discovered" by President Theodore Roosevelt, who liked *The Children of the Night* and offered Robinson a position in the New York custom house. He spent regular summers at the MacDowell Colony in New Hampshire, wrote voluminously, enjoyed remarkable popularity in his own time, and won the Pulitzer Prize three times before his death in 1935.

Some of Robinson's later works are *The Town Down the River* (1910), which includes "Miniver Cheevy," and *The Man Against the Sky* (1916), which includes "Cassandra." His early lyrics are mostly dramatic in form and recount the lives of the residents in "Tilbury Town," modeled after Robinson's native Gardiner. In 1921, *Collected Poems* appeared. Other books include *Merlin* (1917), *Lancelot* (1920), and *Tristram* (1927), concerned with Arthurian legend; *The Three Taverns* (1920); *Roman Bartholow* (1923); *The Man Who Died Twice* (1924); *Dionysus in Doubt* (1925); *Cavender's House* (1929); *Matthias at the Door* (1931); *Amaranth* (1934); and *King Jasper* (1935). His plays include *Van Zorn* (1914) and *The Porcupine* (1915).

Mr. Flood's Party

Old Eben Flood, climbing alone one night
Over the hill between the town below
And the forsaken upland hermitage
That held as much as he should ever know
On earth again of home, paused warily.   5
The road was his with not a native near;
And Eben, having leisure, said aloud,
For no man else in Tilbury Town to hear:

"Well, Mr. Flood, we have the harvest moon
Again, and we may not have many more;   10
The bird is on the wing, the poet says,
And you and I have said it here before.
Drink to the bird." He raised up to the light
The jug that he had gone so far to fill,
And answered huskily: "Well, Mr. Flood,   15
Since you propose it, I believe I will."

Alone, as if enduring to the end
A valiant armor of scarred hopes outworn,
He stood there in the middle of the road
Like Roland's[1] ghost winding a silent horn.   20
Below him, in the town among the trees,
Where friends of other days had honored him,
A phantom salutation of the dead
Rang thinly till old Eben's eyes were dim.

Then, as a mother lays her sleeping child   25
Down tenderly, fearing it may awake,
He set the jug down slowly at his feet
With trembling care, knowing that most things break;
And only when assured that on firm earth
It stood, as the uncertain lives of men   30
Assuredly did not, he paced away,
And with his hand extended paused again:

"Well, Mr. Flood, we have not met like this
In a long time; and many a change has come
To both of us, I fear, since last it was   35
We had a drop together. Welcome home!"
Convivially returning with himself,
Again he raised the jug up to the light;
And with an acquiescent quaver said:
"Well, Mr. Flood, if you insist, I might.   40

"Only a very little, Mr. Flood—
For auld lang syne, No more, sir; that will do."
So, for the time, apparently it did,
And Eben evidently thought so too;
For soon amid the silver loneliness   45
Of night he lifted up his voice and sang,
Secure, with only two moons listening,
Until the whole harmonious landscape rang—

"For auld lang syne." The weary throat gave out,
The last word wavered, and the song was done.   50
He raised again the jug regretfully
And shook his head, and was again alone.

[1] In "The Song of Roland" (11th century), Roland, nephew of Charlemagne and the ideal Christian knight, had a horn that he played when beginning battle.

There was not much that was ahead of him,
And there was nothing in the town below—
Where strangers would have shut the many doors   55
That many friends had opened long ago.

1920

1921

George Crabbe

Give him the darkest inch your shelf allows,
Hide him in lonely garrets, if you will,—
But his hard, human pulse is throbbing still
With the sure strength that fearless truth endows.
In spite of all fine science disavows,   5
Of his plain excellence and stubborn skill
There yet remains what fashion cannot kill,
Though years have thinned the laurel from his brows.

Whether or not we read him, we can feel
From time to time the vigor of his name   10
Against us like a finger for the shame
And emptiness of what our souls reveal
In books that are as altars where we kneel
To consecrate the flicker, not the flame.

1897

Richard Cory

Whenever Richard Cory went down town,
We people on the pavement looked at him:
He was a gentleman from sole to crown,
Clean favored, and imperially slim.

And he was always quietly arrayed,   5
And he was always human when he talked;
But still he fluttered pulses when he said,
"Good-morning," and he glittered when he walked.

And he was rich—yes, richer than a king—
And admirably schooled in every grace: 10
In fine, we thought that he was everything
To make us wish that we were in his place.

So on we worked, and waited for the light,
And went without the meat, and cursed the bread;
And Richard Cory, one calm summer night, 15
Went home and put a bullet through his head. ,

1897

Miniver Cheevy

Miniver Cheevy, child of scorn,
  Grew lean while he assailed the seasons;
He wept that he was ever born,
  And he had reasons.

Miniver loved the days of old 5
  When swords were bright and steeds were prancing;
The vision of a warrior bold
  Would set him dancing.

Miniver sighed for what was not,
  And dreamed, and rested from his labors; 10
He dreamed of Thebes and Camelot,
  And Priam's neighbors.[1]

Miniver mourned the ripe renown
  That made so many a name so fragrant;
He mourned Romance, now on the town, 15
  And Art, a vagrant.

Miniver loved the Medici,[2]
  Albeit he had never seen one;
He would have sinned incessantly
  Could he have been one. 20

[1] Thebes, an ancient city of Greece, destroyed by Alexander the Great in 336 B.C.; Camelot, the legendary town where Arthur had his court; Priam, in Greek mythology, was King of Troy, father of Paris and Hector; he was killed when his city fell to the Greeks.
[2] An Italian family that dominated Florence and Tuscany during the Renaissance.

Miniver cursed the commonplace
  And eyed a khaki suit with loathing;
He missed the mediæval grace
  Of iron clothing.

Miniver scorned the gold he sought,   25
  But sore annoyed was he without it;
Miniver thought, and thought, and thought,
  And thought about it.

Miniver Cheevy, born too late,
  Scratched his head and kept on thinking;   30
Miniver coughed, and called it fate,
  And kept on drinking.

1907

                                                    1910

Bewick Finzer

Time was when his half million drew
  The breath of six per cent:
But soon the worm of what-was-not
  Fed hard on his content;
And something crumbled in his brain   5
  When his half million went.

Time passed, and filled along with his
  The place of many more;
Time came, and hardly one of us
  Had credence to restore,   10
From what appeared one day, the man
  Whom we had known before.

The broken voice, the withered neck,
  The coat worn out with care,
The cleanliness of indigence,   15
  The brilliance of despair,
The fond imponderable dreams
  Of affluence,—all were there.

Poor Finzer, with his dreams and schemes,
   Faces hard now in the race,   20
With heart and eye that have a task
   When he looks in the face
Of one who might so easily
   Have been in Finzer's place.

He comes unfailing for the loan   25
   We give and then forget;
He comes, and probably for years
   Will he be coming yet,—
Familiar as an old mistake,
   And futile as regret.   30

1916

Cassandra[1]

I heard one who said: "Verily,
   What word have I for children here?
Your Dollar is your only Word.
   The wrath of it your only fear.

"You build it altars tall enough   5
   To make you see, but you are blind;
You cannot leave it long enough
   To look before you or behind.

"When Reason beckons you to pause,
   You laugh and say that you know best;   10
But what it is you know, you keep
   As dark as ingots in a chest.

"You laugh and answer, 'We are young;
   O leave us now, and let us grow.'—
Not asking how much more of this   15
   Will Time endure or Fate bestow.

[1] Cassandra, the daughter of Priam, King of Troy, was endowed with the gift of prophecy but fated by Apollo never to be believed.

"Because a few complacent years
　　Have made your peril of your pride,
Think you that you are to go on
　　Forever pampered and untried?　　　　　　　　20

"What lost eclipse of history,
　　What bivouac of the marching stars,
Has given the sign for you to see
　　Millenniums and last great wars?

"What unrecorded overthrow　　　　　　　　　　　25
　　Of all the world has ever known,
Or ever been, has made itself
　　So plain to you, and you alone?

"Your Dollar, Dove and Eagle make
　　A Trinity that even you　　　　　　　　　　　30
Rate higher than you rate yourselves;
　　It pays, it flatters, and it's new.

"And though your very flesh and blood
　　Be what your Eagle eats and drinks,
You'll praise him for the best of birds,　　　　　　35
　　Not knowing, what the Eagle thinks.

"The power is yours, but not the sight;
　　You see not upon what you tread;
You have the ages for your guide,
　　But not the wisdom to be led.　　　　　　　　40

"Think you to tread forever down
　　The merciless old verities?
And are you never to have eyes
　　To see the world for what it is?

"Are you to pay for what you have　　　　　　　　45
　　With all you are?"—No other word
We caught, but with a laughing crowd
　　Moved on. None heeded, and few heard.

1914

1916

Flammonde

The man Flammonde, from God knows where,
With firm address and foreign air,
With news of nations in his talk
And something royal in his walk,
With glint of iron in his eyes,   5
But never doubt, nor yet surprise,
Appeared, and stayed, and held his head
As one by kings accredited.

Erect, with his alert repose
About him, and about his clothes,   10
He pictured all tradition hears
Of what we owe to fifty years.
His cleansing heritage of taste
Paraded neither want nor waste;
And what he needed for his fee   15
To live, he borrowed graciously.

He never told us what he was,
Or what mischance, or other cause,
Had banished him from better days
To play the Prince of Castaways.   20
Meanwhile he played surpassing well
A part, for most, unplayable;
In fine, one pauses, half afraid
To say for certain that he played.

For that, one may as well forego   25
Conviction as to yes or no;
Nor can I say just how intense
Would then have been the difference
To several, who, having striven
In vain to get what he was given,   30
Would see the stranger taken on
By friends not easy to be won.

Moreover, many a malcontent
He soothed and found munificent;
His courtesy beguiled and foiled   35
Suspicion that his years were soiled;

His mien distinguished any crowd,
His credit strengthened when he bowed;
And women, young and old, were fond
Of looking at the man Flammonde.   40

There was a woman in our town
Of whom the fashion was to frown;
But while our talk renewed the tinge
Of a long-faded scarlet fringe,
The man Flammonde saw none of that,   45
And what he saw we wondered at—
That none of us, in her distress,
Could hide or find our littleness.

There was a boy that all agreed
Had shut within him the rare seed   50
Of learning. We could understand,
But none of us could lift a hand.
The man Flammonde appraised the youth,
And told a few of us the truth;
And thereby, for a little gold,   55
A flowered future was unrolled.

There were two citizens who fought
For years and years, and over nought;
They made life awkward for their friends,
And shortened their own dividends,   60
The man Flammonde said what was wrong
Should be made right; nor was it long
Before they were again in line,
And had each other in to dine.

And these I mention are but four   65
Of many out of many more.
So much for them. But what of him—
So firm in every look and limb?
What small satanic sort of kink
Was in his brain? What broken link   70
Withheld him from the destinies
That came so near to being his?

What was he, when we came to sift
His meaning, and to note the drift
Of incommunicable ways   75
That make us ponder while we praise?

Why was it that his charm revealed
Somehow the surface of a shield?
What was it that we never caught?
What was he, and what was he not?   80

How much it was of him we met
We cannot ever know; nor yet
Shall all he gave us quite atone
For what was his, and his alone;
Nor need we now, since he knew best,   85
Nourish an ethical unrest:
Rarely at once will nature give
The power to be Flammonde and live.

We cannot know how much we learn
From those who never will return,   90
Until a flash of unforeseen
Remembrance falls on what has been.
We've each a darkening hill to climb;
And this is why, from time to time
In Tilbury Town, we look beyond   95
Horizons for the man Flammonde.

1915

1916

Reuben Bright

Because he was a butcher and thereby
Did earn an honest living (and did right),
I would not have you think that Reuben Bright
Was any more a brute than you or I;
For when they told him that his wife must die,   5
He stared at them, and shook with grief and fright,

And cried like a great baby half that night,
And made the women cry to see him cry.

And after she was dead, and he had paid
The singers and the sexton and the rest,   10
He packed a lot of things that she had made
Most mournfully away in an old chest
Of hers, and put some chopped-up cedar boughs
In with them, and tore down the slaughter-house.

1897

Eros Turannos

She fears him, and will always ask
    What fated her to choose him;
She meets in his engaging mask
    All reasons to refuse him;
But what she meets and what she fears   5
Are less than are the downward years,
Drawn slowly to the foamless weirs
    Of age, were she to lose him.

Between a blurred sagacity
    That once had power to sound him,   10
And Love, that will not let him be
    The Judas that she found him,
Her pride assuages her almost,
As if it were alone the cost.—
He sees that he will not be lost,   15
    And waits and looks around him.

A sense of ocean and old trees
    Envelops and allures him;
Tradition, touching all he sees,
    Beguiles and reassures him;   20
And all her doubts of what he says
Are dimmed with what she knows of days—
Till even prejudice delays
    And fades, and she secures him.

The falling leaf inaugurates   25
    The reign of her confusion;
The pounding wave reverberates
    The dirge of her illusion;

And home, where passion lived and died,
Becomes a place where she can hide,   30
While all the town and harbor side
    Vibrate with her seclusion.

We tell you, tapping on our brows,
    The story as it should be,—
As if the story of a house   35
    Were told, or ever could be;
We'll have no kindly veil between
Her visions and those we have seen,—
As if we guessed what hers have been,
    Or what they are or would be.   40

Meanwhile we do no harm; for they
    That with a god have striven,
Not hearing much of what we say,
    Take what the god has given;
Though like waves breaking it may be   45
Or like a changed familiar tree,
Or like a stairway to the sea
    Where down the blind are driven.

1914

                                              1916

Clavering

I say no more for Clavering
    Than I should say of him who fails
To bring his wounded vessel home
    When reft of rudder and of sails;

I say no more than I should say   5
    Of any other one who sees
Too far for guidance of to-day,
    Too near for the eternities.

I think of him as I should think
    Of one who for scant wages played,   10
And faintly, a flawed instrument
    That fell while it was being made;

I think of him as one who fared,
  Unfaltering and undeceived,
Amid mirages of renown   15
  And urgings of the unachieved;

I think of him as one who gave
  To Lingard[1] leave to be amused,
And listened with a patient grace
  That we, the wise ones, had refused;   20

I think of metres that he wrote
  For Cubit, the ophidian guest:
"What Lilith, or Dark Lady" . . . Well,
  Time swallows Cubit with the rest.

I think of last words that he said   25
  One midnight over Calvery:
"Goodbye—good man." He was not good;
  So Clavering was wrong, you see.

I wonder what had come to pass
  Could he have borrowed for a spell   30
The fiery-frantic indolence
  That made a ghost of Leffingwell;

I wonder if he pitied us
  Who cautioned him till he was gray
To build his house with ours on earth   35
  And have an end of yesterday;

I wonder what it was we saw
  To make us think that we were strong;
I wonder if he saw too much,
  Or if he looked one way too long.   40

But when were thoughts or wonderings
  To ferret out the man within?
Why prate of what he seemed to be,
  And all that he might not have been?

He clung to phantoms and to friends,   45
  And never came to anything.
He left a wreath on Cubit's grave.
  I say no more for Clavering.

                                              1910

---

[1] John Lingard (1771–1851), English historian, author of *A History of England to 1866*,
8 vol. (1819–1830).

CARL SANDBURG

(1878–1967)

Born in Galesburg, Illinois, Carl Sandburg lived in youth the working life often thought of as essential for American writers. He was by turns a porter in a barbershop, a truckhandler in a brickyard, a dishwasher, a designer, a harvester in the Kansas wheatfields, a newspaper correspondent during the Spanish-American War, and, for 3 years, at Lombard College in Galesburg, a student. Although he remained a wanderer even in later years, and did one longish stint as a newspaper editor in Milwaukee, the center of his life from the first decade of this century onward was Chicago. He became a leader, together with the poets Vachel Lindsay and Edgar Lee Masters, of a Chicago-based movement of regional bardism. His first volume of poetry, which appeared in 1916, was entitled *The Chicago Poems* and took as its focus the quality of life in that city. From 1918 until 1933 Sandburg was editor of The *Chicago Daily News,* and the volumes of poetry that he published during this period—most notably *Cornhuskers* (1918), which contains several of his most famous poems, including "Cool Tombs," "Grass," and "Fog," *Smoke and Steel* (1920), which won a Pulitzer Prize, and *Slabs of the Sunburnt West* (1922), which opens with a long poem celebrating "The Windy City"—found their ruling images and preoccupations in that place.

From the first, Sandburg's poems were often loose-limbed, the lines of the longer works tending to ravel out into the rhythms and structure of prose. [*The People, Yes* (1936), Sandburg's best-known work, is a collection of fables, tall tales, and protests at social injustice, which frequently announce themselves as poems and end as prose monologues.] And this poet did in fact make his reputation partly as a historian and biographer. He published two impressionistic volumes on Lincoln—*Abraham Lincoln: The Prairie Years* (1928) and *Abraham Lincoln: The War Years* (1940)—the second of which won the Pulitzer Prize in 1940 and, in addition, a mixture of history and fiction about this country's past, *Remembrance Rock* (1948).

To many modern critics Sandburg's chief interest is as a figure in cultural history who combined populist social themes, the myth of the

Two recent studies of Sandburg are Richard Crowder, *Carl Sandburg,* 1963, and Hazell Durnell, *The America of Carl Sandburg,* 1965. Other studies include Karl Detzer's *Carl Sandburg: A Study in Personality and Background,* 1941; and North Callahan, *Carl Sandburg: A Study in Personality and Background,* 1941.

The standard text is *The Complete Poems of Carl Sandburg,* 1950, new and expanded in 1970; Herbert Mitgang edited *The Letters of Carl Sandburg,* 1968.

bard, and America mongering in a fashion that brought him fame and kept alive the idea of the poet as consequential public man for an age that was otherwise perfectly agreeable to burying the idea for good. And it is true that much of Sandburg's windy city rhetoric is very windy indeed, and that much of his Walt Whitmanizing rhapsody reads today like pretentious posturing. There is, however, a more valuable and more satisfying Sandburg, a poet whose eye for the rawness and bleakness of human relationships on the American landscape and cityscape, our brutal indifference to each other, has something in common with E. A. Robinson's. And the directness and unashamedness of the compassion for the helpless that appears in a handful of Sandburg's best poems is worthy of Theodore Dreiser.

Chicago

Hog Butcher for the World,
Tool Maker, Stacker of Wheat,
Player with Railroads and the Nation's Freight Handler;
Stormy, husky, brawling,
City of the Big Shoulders: 5

They tell me you are wicked and I believe them, for I have seen your
    painted women under the gas lamps luring the farm boys.
And they tell me you are crooked and I answer: Yes, it is true I have
    seen the gunman kill and go free to kill again.
And they tell me you are brutal and my reply is: On the faces of
    women and children I have seen the marks of wanton hunger.
And having answered so I turn once more to those who sneer at this
    my city, and I give them back the sneer and say to them:
Come and show me another city with lifted head singing so proud to
    be alive and coarse and strong and cunning.   10

Flinging magnetic curses amid the toil of piling job on job, here is a
    tall bold slugger set vivid against the little soft cities;
Fierce as a dog with tongue lapping for action, cunning as a savage
    pitted against the wilderness,
        Bareheaded,
        Shoveling,
        Wrecking,   15
        Planning,
        Building, breaking, rebuilding,
Under the smoke, dust all over his mouth, laughing with white teeth,
Under the terrible burden of destiny laughing as a young man laughs,

Laughing even as an ignorant fighter laughs who has never lost a
    battle,   20
Bragging and laughing that under his wrist is the pulse, and under his
    ribs the heart of the people,
                    Laughing!
Laughing the stormy, husky, brawling laughter of Youth, half-naked,
    sweating, proud to be Hog Butcher, Tool Maker, Stacker of
Wheat, Player with Railroads and Freight Handler to the Nation.

    1914

                                                     1916

Grass

Pile the bodies high at Austerlitz and Waterloo.
Shovel them under and let me work—
        I am the grass; I cover all.

And pile them high at Gettysburg
And pile them high at Ypres and Verdun.   5

Shovel them under and let me work.
Two years, ten years, and passengers ask the conductor:
        What place is this?
        Where are we now?

        I am the grass.   10
        Let me work.

                                                       1918

Washerwoman

The washerwoman is a member of the Salvation Army.
And over the tub of suds rubbing underwear clean
She sings that Jesus will wash her sins away
And the red wrongs she has done God and man
Shall be white as driven snow.   5
Rubbing underwear she sings of the Last Great Washday.

                                                        1918

Waiting for the Chariot
(Mrs. Peter Cartwright)

Can bare fact make the cloth of a shining poem?
In Sangamon County, Illinois, they remembered how
The aged widow walked a mile from home to Bethel Chapel
Where she heard the services and was called on
"To give her testimony," rising to speak freely, ending: 5
　　"The past three weeks have been the happiest
　of all my life; I am waiting for the chariot."
The pastor spoke the benediction; the members rose and moved
Into the aisles toward the door, and looking back
They saw the widow of the famous circuit rider   10
Sitting quiet and pale in an inviolable dignity
And they heard the pastor: "The chariot has arrived."

1960

Cool Tombs

When Abraham Lincoln was shoveled into the tombs, he forgot the
　copperheads and the assassin . . . in the dust, in the cool tombs.

And Ulysses Grant lost all thought of con men and Wall Street, cash and
　collateral turned ashes . . . in the dust, in the cool tombs.

Pocahontas' body, lovely as a poplar, sweet as a red haw in November or
　a pawpaw in May, did she wonder? Does she remember? . . . in the
　dust, in the cool tombs?

Take any streetful of people buying clothes and groceries, cheering a hero
　or throwing confetti and blowing tin horns . . . tell me if the lovers are
　losers . . . tell me if any get more than the lovers . . . in the dust . . . in
　the cool tombs.

1918

HART CRANE

(1899–1932)

In the ordinary sense of the words, Harold Hart Crane was an incompetent thinker, a poorly educated poet, and a wretchedly unhappy man. He was born in Garrettsville, Ohio, the son of a successful businessman and a woman of flighty religiosity. His parents, estranged from each other, fought for "possession" of him (Crane was an only child); his mother, whose maiden name was Grace Hart, won, and dropping "Harold" from his name was, for the poet, a significant gesture. After placing a poem in a tiny literary magazine in Greenwich Village, Crane left home for New York at 17 and made his living in a succession of odd jobs, returning to Ohio on occasion to work in one of his father's candy shops, in an advertising agency, or (during World War I) in defense plants. For no brief portion of his life he was jobless and down and out in a hell of alcoholic homosexuality; once or twice he was helped by a philanthropist or a foundation, and there was a period of relative peace and uninterrupted composition in 1926, on the Isle of Pines, Cuba, where his grandmother owned a plantation. His first book, *White Buildings,* appeared in 1926; his last, *The Bridge,* in 1930. The latter volume won him a Guggenheim Fellowship, and he traveled to Mexico, planning new poems, but sinking swiftly into new excesses. One night in the spring of 1932, bound from Vera Cruz to New York on an ocean liner, he was beaten in a brawl involving sailors; the following morning he dove to his death from the ship's stern.

Critics of this poet have found numberless defects in his work. His poems are obscure. He lacks anything resembling a philosophical system that could lend general meaning to his symbols or provide him with a basis for coherent organization of his experience. He is a pantheist, committed to a feverish antirationality masquerading as reli-

Brom Weber edited *The Complete Poems and Selected Letters and Prose of Hart Crane,* 1966; he also edited *The Letters of Hart Crane, 1916–1932,* 1952; and wrote *Hart Crane: A Biographical and Critical Study,* 1948. Other biographies are Philip Horton, *Hart Crane: The Life of an American Poet,* 1937; and John Unterecker, *Voyager: A Life of Hart Crane,* 1969.

Early criticism includes Gorham Munson, "Hart Crane: Young Titan in the Sacred Wood," in *Destinations,* 1928; R. P. Blackmur, *The Double Agent,* 1935; and Allen Tate, *Reactionary Essays,* 1936. In recent years the following works have appeared: Vincent Quinn, *Hart Crane,* 1963; Samuel Hazo, *Hart Crane: An Introduction and Interpretation,* 1963; R. W. B. Lewis, *The Poetry of Hart Crane,* 1967; Alan Trachtenberg, *Brooklyn Bridge: Fact and Symbol,* 1965; Herbert A. Leibowitz, *Hart Crane: An Introduction to the Poetry,* 1968; and R. W. Butterfield, *The Broken Arc: A Study of Hart Crane,* 1969.

For a bibliographical aid, see H. D. Rowe, ed., *Hart Crane: A Bibliography,* 1955.

gion. He is a slavish Whitmanite, celebrating America without possessing his master's essential understanding of its import in human history. He is lacking in taste, with the result that in his "epic," *The Bridge,* passages that splendidly evoke American land- and riverscapes alternate with Hollywood-style pasteups of pioneer women saluting—at a seemly distance, to be sure—their sisters among the native Americans, mothers together in the end.

It is clear that Crane asks more of his symbols of the march of industrial civilization—Brooklyn Bridge, the subway tunnel, the Pullman car, the airplane—than they can deliver, in the absence of any fully thought-out perspective on cultural history. And about the chaos of this poet's inner mind there cannot be any doubt. Neither, though, is it possible to deny him an intuitive vision—an idea of a subject of extraordinary depth and grandeur, solid at its core. There were times when, in framing this subject in expository language, Crane vulgarized it—spoke of "refuting" pessimists like T. S. Eliot. But in the best sections of *The Bridge* the subject stands well beyond vulgarization. Crane is speaking to—and creating in his speech—the wonder of human movement in time, the impactment of all the gone generations in the deed of the present. He is asking for the kind of reverent attentiveness to the public scene that strips it of its taken-for-grantedness, of those veils that coat made and natural objects, hiding from view the complex processes in time that brought them into being. To imagine the mode of consciousness necessary for an adequate reading of "The River," a writer needs knowledge at levels of intensity that neither sound systems nor schooling can provide. Ruined lives beyond counting fill the histories of art, and far fewer than might be hoped yielded work worth its cost; Crane's life is one of them.

From The Bridge
Poem: To Brooklyn Bridge

How many dawns, chill from his rippling rest
The seagull's wings shall dip and pivot him,
Shedding white rings of tumult, building high
Over the chained bay waters Liberty—

Then, with inviolate curve, forsake our eyes   5
As apparitional as sails that cross
Some page of figures to be filed away;
—Till elevators drop us from our day . . .

I think of cinemas, panoramic sleights
With multitudes bent toward some flashing scene   10
Never disclosed, but hastened to again,
Foretold to other eyes on the same screen;

And Thee, across the harbor, silver-paced
As though the sun took step of thee, yet left
Some motion ever unspent in thy stride,—   15
Implicitly thy freedom staying thee!

Out of some subway scuttle, cell or loft
A bedlamite speeds to thy parapets,
Tilting there momently, shrill shirt ballooning.
A jest falls from the speechless caravan.   20

Down Wall, from girder into street noon leaks,
A rip-tooth of the sky's acetylene;
All afternoon the cloud-flown derricks turn . . .
Thy cables breathe the North Atlantic still.

And obscure as that heaven of the Jews,   25
Thy guerdon . . . Accolade thou dost bestow
Of anonymity time cannot raise:
Vibrant reprieve and pardon thou dost show.

O harp and altar, of the fury fused,
(How could mere toil align thy choiring strings!)   30
Terrific threshold of the prophet's pledge,
Prayer of pariah, and the lover's cry,—

Again the traffic lights that skim thy swift
Unfractioned idiom, immaculate sigh of stars,
Beading thy path—condense eternity: 35
And we have seen night lifted in thine arms.

Under thy shadow of the piers I waited;
Only in darkness is thy shadow clear.
The City's fiery parcels all undone,
Already snow submerges an iron year . . .   40

O Sleepless as the river under thee,
Vaulting the sea, the prairies' dreaming sod,
Unto us lowliest sometime sweep, descend
And of the curveship lend a myth to God.

The River

Stick your patent name on a signboard
brother—all over—going west—young man
Tintex—Japalac—Certain-teed Overalls ads
and lands sakes! under the new playbill ripped
in the guaranteed corner—see Bert Williams[1] what?   5

Minstrels when you steal a chicken just
save me the wing, for if it isn't
Erie it ain't for miles around a
Mazda—and the telegraphic night coming on Thomas

a Ediford—and whistling down the tracks   10
a headlight rushing with the sound—can you
imagine—while an EXPRESS makes time like
SCIENCE—COMMERCE and the HOLYGHOST
RADIO ROARS IN EVERY HOME WE HAVE THE NORTHPOLE
WALLSTREET AND VIRGINBIRTH WITHOUT STONES OR   15
WIRES OR EVEN RUNNING brooks connecting ears
and no more sermons windows flashing roar
Breathtaking—as you like it . . . eh?

                    So the 20th Century—so
whizzed the Limited—roared by and left   20
three men, still hungry on the tracks, ploddingly
watching the tail lights wizen and converge,
slipping gimleted and neatly out of sight.

The last bear, shot drinking in the Dakotas,
Loped under wires that span the mountain stream.   25
Keen instruments, strung to a vast precision
Bind town to town and dream to ticking dream.
But some men take their liquor slow—and count—
Though they'll confess no rosary nor clue—
The river's minute by the far brook's year.   30
Under a world of whistles, wires and steam
Caboose-like they go ruminating through
Ohio, Indiana—blind baggage—
To Cheyenne tagging . . . Maybe Kalamazoo.

Time's renderings, time's blendings they construe   35
As final reckonings of fire and snow;
Strange bird-wit, like the elemental gist
Of unwalled winds they offer, singing low

[1] A Negro comedian in the early part of the
twentieth-century.

My Old Kentucky Home and *Casey Jones,*
Some Sunny Day. I heard a road-gang chanting so.   40
And afterwards, who had a colt's eyes—one said,
"Jesus! Oh I remember watermelon days!" And sped
High in a cloud of merriment, recalled
"—And when my Aunt Sally Simpson smiled," he drawled—
"It was almost Louisiana, long ago."   45

"There's no place like Booneville though, Buddy,"
One said, excising a last burr from his vest,
"—For early trouting." Then peering in the can,
"—But I kept on the tracks." Possessed, resigned,
He trod the fire down pensively and grinned,   50
Spreading dry shingles of a beard. . . .
                                        Behind
My father's cannery works I used to see
Rail-squatters ranged in nomad raillery,
The ancient men—wifeless or runaway   55
Hobo-trekkers that forever search
An empire wilderness of freight and rails.
Each seemed a child, like me, on a loose perch,
Holding to childhood like some termless play.
John, Jake, or Charley, hopping the slow freight   60
—Memphis to Tallahassee—riding the rods,
Blind fists of nothing, humpty-dumpty clods.

Yet they touch something like a key perhaps.
From pole to pole across the hills, the states
—They know a body under the wide rain;   65
Youngsters with eyes like fjords, old reprobates
With racetrack jargon,—dotting immensity
They lurk across her, knowing her yonder breast
Snow-silvered, sumac-stained or smoky blue,
Is past the valley-sleepers, south or west.   70
—As I have trod the rumorous midnights, too.

And past the circuit of the lamp's thin flame
(O Nights that brought me to her body bare!)
Have dreamed beyond the print that bound her name.
Trains sounding the long blizzards out—I heard   75
Wail into distances I knew were hers.
Papooses crying on the wind's long mane
Screamed redskin dynasties that fled the brain,
—Dead echoes! But I knew her body there,
Time like a serpent down her shoulder dark   80
And space, an eaglet's wing, laid on her hair.

Under the Ozarks, domed by Iron Mountain,
The old gods of the rain lie wrapped in pools
Where eyeless fish curvet a sunken fountain
And re-descend with corn from querulous crows.   85
Such pilferings make up their timeless eatage,
Propitiate them for their timber torn
By iron, iron—always the iron dealt cleavage!
They doze now, below axe and powder horn.

And Pullman breakfasters glide glistening steel   90
From tunnel into field—iron strides the dew—
Straddles the hill, a dance of wheel on wheel.
You have a half-hour's wait at Siskiyou,
Or stay the night and take the next train through.
Southward, near Cairo passing, you can see   95
The Ohio merging,—borne down Tennessee;
And if it's summer and the sun's in dusk
Maybe the breeze will lift the River's musk
—As though the waters breathed that you might know
Memphis Johnny, Steamboat Bill, Missouri Joe.   100
Oh, lean from the window, if the train slows down,
As though you touched hands with some ancient clown,
—A little while gaze absently below
And hum *Deep River* with them while they go.

Yes, turn again and sniff once more—look see,   105
O Sheriff, Brakeman and Authority—
Hitch up your pants and crunch another quid,
For you, too, feed the River timelessly.
And few evade full measure of their fate;
Always they smile out eerily what they seem.   110
I could believe he joked at heaven's gate—
Dan Midland—jolted from the cold brake-beam.

Down, down—born pioneers in time's despite,
Grimed tributaries to an ancient flow—
They win no frontier by their wayward plight,   115
But drift in stillness, as from Jordan's brow.

You will not hear it as the sea; even stone
Is not more hushed by gravity . . . But slow,
As loth to take more tribute—sliding prone
Like one whose eyes were buried long ago   120

The River, spreading, flows—and spends your dream.
What are you, lost within this tideless spell?
You are your father's father, and the stream—
A liquid theme that floating niggers swell.

Damp tonnage and alluvial march of days—   125
Nights turbid, vascular with silted shale
And roots surrendered down of moraine clays:
The Mississippi drinks the farthest dale.

O quarrying passion, undertowed sunlight!
The basalt surface drags a jungle grace   130
Ochreous and lynx-barred in lengthening might;
Patience! and you shall reach the biding place!

Over De Soto's bones the freighted floors
Throb past the City storied of three thrones.[2]
Down two more turns the Mississippi pours   135
(Anon tall ironsides up from salt lagoons)

And flows within itself, heaps itself free.
All fades but one thin skyline 'round . . . Ahead
No embrace opens but the stinging sea;
The River lifts itself from its long bed.   140

Poised wholly on its dream, a mustard glow,
Tortured with history, its one will—flow!
—The Passion spreads in wide tongues, choked and slow,
Meeting the Gulf, hosannas silently below.

                                                     1930

[2] De Soto's men buried him in the Mississippi near New Orleans so that the Indians would not find him. The three thrones refer to Spain, France, and England.

Cutty Sark

O, the navies old and oaken,
O, the Temeraire no more!
                    —MELVILLE[1]

I met a man in South Street, tall—
a nervous shark tooth swung on his chain.

[1] The last two lines from Melville's poem, "The Temeraire." The Temeraire means "one who dares."

His eyes pressed through green grass
—green glasses, or bar lights made them
so—   5
    shine—
        GREEN—
            eyes—
stepped out—forgot to look at you
or left you several blocks away—   10

in the nickel-in-the-slot piano jogged
"Stamboul Nights"—weaving somebody's nickel—
        sang—

    O Stamboul Rose—dreams weave the rose!

    Murmurs of Leviathan he spoke,   15
    and rum was Plato in our heads . . .

"It's S.S., *Ala*—Antwerp—now remember kid
to put me out at three she sails on time.

I'm not much good at time any more keep
weakeyed watches sometimes snooze—" his bony hands   20
got to beating time . . . "A whaler once—
I ought to keep time and get over it—I'm a
Democrat—I know what time it is—No
I don't want to know what time it is—that
damned white Arctic killed my time . . ."   25

    O Stamboul Rose—drums weave—

"I ran a donkey engine down there on the Canal
in Panama—got tired of that—
then Yucatan selling kitchenware—beads—
have you seen Popocatepetl[2]—birdless mouth   30
with ashes sifting down—?
                and then the coast again . . ."

    Rose of Stamboul O coral Queen—
    teased remnants of the skeletons of cities—
    and galleries, galleries of watergutted lava   35
    snarling stone—green—drums—drown—

[2] Popocatepetl is a dormant volcano in Mexico, in Puebla State, 43 miles southeast of Mexico City.

Sing!
"—that spiracle!" he shot a finger out the door . . .
"O life's a geyser—beautiful—my lungs—
No—I can't live on land—!"   40

I saw the frontiers gleaming of his mind;
or are there frontiers—running sands sometimes
running sands—somewhere—sands running . . .

Or they may start some white machine that sings.
Then you may laugh and dance the axletree—   45
steel—silver—kick the traces—and know—

    ATLANTIS ROSE drums wreathe the rose,
    the star floats burning in a gulf of tears
    and sleep another thousand—

                            interminably   50
long since somebody's nickel—stopped—
playing—

A wind worried those wicker-neat lapels, the
swinging summer entrances to cooler hells . . .
Outside a wharf truck nearly ran him down   55
—he lunged up Bowery way while the dawn
was putting the Statue of Liberty out—that
torch of hers you know—

I started walking home across the Bridge . . .

                     °

Blithe Yankee vanities, turreted sprites, winged   60
                         British repartees, skil-
ful savage sea-girls
that bloomed in the spring—Heave, weave
those bright designs the trade winds drive . . .

    Sweet opium and tea, Yo-ho!
    Pennies for porpoises that bank the keel!   65
    Fins whip the breeze around Japan!

Bright skysails ticketing the Line, wink round the Horn
to Frisco, Melbourne . . .

Pennants, parabolas— 70
clipper dreams indelible and ranging,
baronial white on lucky blue!

Perennial-*Cutty*-trophied-*Sark!*

Thermopylae,[3] *Black Prince, Flying Cloud* through Sunda
—scarfed of foam, their bellies veered green esplanades,
locked in wind-humors, ran their eastings down; 75

   at Java Head freshened the nip
   (sweet opium and tea!)
   and turned and left us on the lee . . .

Buntlines tusseling (91 days, 20 hours and anchored!)
                         Rainbow, Leander 80
(last trip a tragedy)—where can you be
Nimbus? and you rivals two—

      a long tack keeping—

                  Taeping?
                  Ariel? 85

1930

[3] A locality in eastern Greece, a navigation route. It is the site of the heroic but unsuccessful defense by the Spartans against the Persians (480 B.C.)

ROBERT FROST

(1874–1963)

Robert Frost was born in San Francisco, the son of an eccentric and sporadically improvident newspaperman from Massachusetts. His mother left her husband and took the child back to New England

Edward Connery Lathem has edited the standard edition of Frost's poetry, *The Poetry of Robert Frost,* 1969. A handy volume of selected poetry, with an introduction by the author, is *The Poems of Robert Frost,* 1946, Modern Library edition.

Louis Untermeyer has edited *The Letters of Robert Frost to Louis Untermeyer,* 1963. Other editions of letters are Lawrance R. Thompson, ed., *Selected Letters,* 1964; and Arnold Grade, ed., *Family Letters of Robert and Elinor Frost,* 1972. Books of conversations, reminiscences, and interviews include Louis Mertins, *Robert Frost: Life and Talks-Walking,* 1965; E. C. Lathem, ed., *Interviews with Robert Frost,* 1966; Robert Francis, *Frost: a time to talk: conversations and indiscretions,* 1972; and Elaine Barry, ed., *Robert Frost on Writing,* 1973. E. C. Lathem compiled *A Concordance to the Poetry of Robert Frost,* 1966.

(Footnote continued next page.)

when he was two, but the family was eventually reunited in San Francisco; it was not until his father's death, in Frost's eleventh year, that he moved permanently to the region with which he is usually—often simplistically—identified. He studied for a period at Dartmouth and at Harvard, but finding standard-form higher education uncongenial, took no degrees. After leaving Harvard in 1899, he farmed, wrote poetry, and taught school in New Hampshire for a time. From 1912 to 1915 he lived in England, and it was there, owing partly to the intervention of Ezra Pound, that his poetry received initial attention and praise; his first book, *A Boy's Will,* was published in London in 1913. A second volume, *North of Boston* (1915), made his name known at home.

More often than not commentary on Frost invites the reader to focus on the poet through one or the other of two somewhat distorting lenses. Through the first Frost appears as a homey American institution—a "people's poet." It is not an unaccountable image. Many who found all poetry difficult and modern poetry impenetrable managed to "understand" Frost. Reading selectively, they made the poet as a kindly New England curmudgeon, wise, lovable, shrewd, a celebrant of pastoral life for which it was pleasing to feel nostalgia, a "character" fascinated by "characters" (downhome Yankees, bewhiskered, quick) and, most importantly, a dispenser of instant proverbs: "Choose something like a star," "Good fences make good neighbors," "Earth's the right place for love." Frost was by no means above exploiting the homespun image—indeed at exploitation he was a master. He found it possible to write about the country in the first person plural—dared, in other words, the role of patriot-historian-spokesman (see "The Gift Outright"). A reading of this poem on a public platform, combined with acerb remarks about contemporary public leaders, the death of American individuality, independence, and the like, could not fail to charm. And did not fail. Frost's poetry readings around the country were enormously successful public events. He was periodically poet-in-residence, lecturer, teacher at a number of colleges and universities, including Harvard, the University of Michigan, Dartmouth, and Amherst;

The most reliable biography is by Lawrance Thompson, *Robert Frost: The Early Years, 1874-1915,* 1966; and *Robert Frost: The Years of Triumph, 1915-1938,* 1970. Other biographies include Elizabeth S. Sergeant, *Robert Frost: The Trial by Existence,* 1960; Jean Gould, *Robert Frost: The Aim was Song,* 1964; and Louis Mertins, *Robert Frost,* 1965.

Early criticism includes Caroline Ford, *The Less Traveled Road, A Study of Robert Frost,* 1935; Lawrance R. Thompson, *Fire and Ice: The Art and Thought of Robert Frost,* 1942; Sidney Cox, *Swinger of Birches,* 1957; and Reginald L. Cook, *The Dimensions of Robert Frost,* 1958. More recently J. F. Lynan has written *The Pastoral Art of Robert Frost,* 1964; Reuben Brower, *The Poetry of Robert Frost,* 1963; Radcliff Squires, *The Major Themes of Robert Frost,* 1963; and Philip Gerber, *Robert Frost,* 1966.

he was almost ceaselessly on the road as bardic entertainer. Lionel Trilling, speaking on Frost's eighty-fifth birthday, called him "a national fact . . . virtually a symbol of America . . . not unlike an articulate, an actually poetic, Bald Eagle." He won four Pulitzers and a profusion of other prizes and honorary degrees, was awarded a Congressional Medal, served as Consultant to the Library of Congress, and remains the only poet in America's history to have read his work at a Presidential inauguration (John F. Kennedy's in 1961).

Is Frost as people's poet nothing but myth? It is undeniable that this poet wrote many a tale of deprived or injured folk, allowing his figures to speak in plain regional idioms, seldom scolding their whimsey or their unsophistication. Its also undeniable that he himself more than once spoke the bitter wisdom—cynically self-serving—of the underside, those who cannot afford illusions about the quantity of unselfishness in this world (see "Provide, Provide"). And there seems no reason whatever for denying that Frost's "natural feeling" was genuine: American writers, Emerson in particular, shaped his thought, styles of cosmopolitan hauteur never drew him and, when fame opened up opportunities to get an American message across (as, for example, a visit to Khrushchev in Russia), he took the openings seriously.

Yet there are aspects of Frost that cannot be neatly packaged in the image in question; therefore a second Frost is often proposed. This alternative figure is clothed in black and wounded with woes. Commentary that insists on this dimension of the poet is inclined to point to rural narratives like "Home Burial" and "A Servant to Servants," which speak of the breaking of human ties and of the lives of people who find their days unbearable. It cites "Provide, Provide" as a fiercely amoral piece, certain of the nonexistence of goodness. It remarks the frequency with which the kindly nature poet presents nature itself as inimical, part of "a design of darkness to appall."

And everywhere it is struck by what it perceives as Frost's indifference, his ability to report bad news with equanimity. In "Out, Out–" the reader experiences three waves of shock; first at the boy's death, then at the calm of the bereaved—"And they, since they/Were not the one dead, turned to their affairs"—and then at the flatness with which the statement is made, a flatness hinting (so some say) at contempt. In "Neither Out Far Nor In Deep," the statements of human limitation (what people can or should know they don't care about, what they'd like to know they can't know, what ought to bother them they're scarcely aware of) seem to some ears to carry a half-jubilant taunt. And in the poet's life—so this line of commentary asserts—there is evidence of a will to control personal feeling, or to bury it, or to insist on his own callousness that is in some sense inhumane. Frost experienced a series of appalling personal calamities—the deaths of his wife and three of his children, a daughter's mental illness, a son's suicide—yet once wrote in a personal letter:

> . . . I suppose I am a brute in that my nature refuses to carry sympathy to the point of going crazy just because someone else goes crazy, or of dying just because someone else dies. As I get older I find it easier to lie awake nights over other people's troubles. But that's as far as I go to date.

As both these critical versions of the poet attest, the root of the "Frost problem" lies elsewhere than in the writer himself: it is the normal human problem of what to make of a complicated thing. Part of the truth, no doubt, is that Frost was a selfish man; another part is that, knowing selfishness from inside, he knew what it exacts from those nearby, and obliged himself, as penance for his own exactings, to the severest moral realism in his art. Part of the truth, no doubt, is that Frost can be seen, in some poems, to be in a measure heartened by his own capacity to confront the unbearable—the limits of human intelligence, the mad ferocity and the cycles of growth and decay; another part is that this satisfaction flows from consciousness of his own awful inner delicacy and vulnerability—the power that alone can produce such a poem as "The Silken Tent," the curse that alone can force into life such a drama of shame as "The Subverted Flower." To know this very great poet well is to have an inkling of wars of sensitivity from which the strongest might well wish to flee—even into bardic posturings or the gestures of the Tory hardnose. It is a question whether the true interior of a man's love for a woman, the inner weather made in him by his belief that she transforms the world, has been more precisely rendered in letters than it is in "Never Again Would Birds' Song Be The Same." The ineluctable sweetness of full human connection, man to woman and woman to man, whole ranges of mind as well as feeling opening to each other, is present as nowhere else in "West-Running Brook."

And these *are*, first and last, triumphs of *response:* they are what they are because of the richness, quickness, waywardness, and incredible variousness of this poet's feelings. A way of saying it is that this poet had extraordinary wealth in his emotions, hence terrible vulnerability; he was not writing idly in these lines.

> The present
> Is too much for the senses,
> Too crowding, too confusing—
> Too present to imagine.   ("Carpe Diem")

His poems set the inner crowds and confusion in order in their world; the outer world persists, however, and in it there is need for the posturing, the fantasies, the gauchery that produce—Frost as a "critical problem."

As a solver of critical problems, incidentally, the poet himself was by no means negligible. His literary criticism was largely informal—snippets in letters to friends, or casual, conversation pronouncements—but invariably stimulating. The most interesting essay, "The Figure a Poem Makes," is included in *Complete Poems* (1949), which collects the first 14 volumes of poetry. Frost's last book, *In The Clearing,* was published in 1962.

Neither Out Far Nor in Deep

The people along the sand
All turn and look one way.
They turn their back on the land.
They look at the sea all day.

As long as it takes to pass   5
A ship keeps raising its hull;
The wetter ground like glass
Reflects a standing gull.

The land may vary more;
But wherever the truth may be—   10
The water comes ashore,
And the people look at the sea.

They cannot look out far.
They cannot look in deep.
But when was that ever a bar   15
To any watch they keep?

1934

1936

Directive

Back out of all this now too much for us,
Back in a time made simple by the loss

Of detail, burned, dissolved, and broken off
Like graveyard marble sculpture in the weather,
There is a house that is no more a house   5
Upon a farm that is no more a farm
And in a town that is no more a town.
The road there, if you'll let a guide direct you
Who only has at heart your getting lost,
May seem as if it should have been a quarry—   10
Great monolithic knees the former town
Long since gave up pretense of keeping covered.
And there's a story in a book about it:
Besides the wear of iron wagon wheels
The ledges show lines ruled southeast-northwest,   15
The chisel work of an enormous Glacier
That braced his feet against the Arctic Pole.
You must not mind a certain coolness from him
Still said to haunt this side of Panther Mountain.
Nor need you mind the serial ordeal   20
Of being watched from forty cellar holes
As if by eye pairs out of forty firkins.
As for the woods' excitement over you
That sends light rustle rushes to their leaves,
Charge that to upstart inexperience.   25
Where were they all not twenty years ago?
They think too much of having shaded out
A few old pecker-fretted apple trees.
Make yourself up a cheering song of how
Someone's road home from work this once was,   30
Who may be just ahead of you on foot
Or creaking with a buggy load of grain.
The height of the adventure is the height
Of country where two village cultures faded
Into each other. Both of them are lost.   35
And if you're lost enough to find yourself
By now, pull in your ladder road behind you
And put a sign up CLOSED to all but me.
Then make yourself at home. The only field
Now left's no bigger than a harness gall.   40
First there's the children's house of make-believe,
Some shattered dishes underneath a pine,
The playthings in the playhouse of the children.
Weep for what little things could make them glad.
Then for the house that is no more a house,   45
But only a belilaced cellar hole,

Now slowly closing like a dent in dough.
This was no playhouse but a house in earnest.
Your destination and your destiny's
A brook that was the water of the house,   50
Cold as a spring as yet so near its source,
Too lofty and original to rage.
(We know the valley streams that when aroused
Will leave their tatters hung on barb and thorn.)
I have kept hidden in the instep arch   55
Of an old cedar at the waterside
A broken drinking goblet like the Grail
Under a spell so the wrong ones can't find it,
So can't get saved, as Saint Mark says they mustn't.
(I stole the goblet from the children's playhouse.)   60
Here are your waters and your watering place.
Drink and be whole again beyond confusion.

                                                    1947

West-Running Brook

'Fred, where is north?'

                          'North? North is there, my love.
The brooks runs west.'

                              'West-running Brook then call it.'
(West-running Brook men call it to this day.)   5
'What does it think it's doing running west
When all the other country brooks flow east
To reach the ocean? It must be the brook
Can trust itself to go by contraries
The way I can with you—and you with me—   10
Because we're—we're—I don't know what we are.
What are we?'

                    'Young or new?'

                                        'We must be something,
We've said we two. Let's change that to we three.   15
As you and I are married to each other,
We'll both be married to the brook. We'll build
Our bridge across it, and the bridge shall be
Our arm thrown over it asleep beside it.

Look, look, it's waving to us with a wave   20
To let us know it hears me.'

               'Why, my dear,
That wave's been standing off this jut of shore—'
(The black stream, catching on a sunken rock,
Flung backward on itself in one white wave,   25
And the white water rode the black forever,
Not gaining but not losing, like a bird
White feathers from the struggle of whose breast
Flecked the dark stream and flecked the darker pool
Below the point, and were at last driven wrinkled   30
In a white scarf against the far shore alders.)
'That wave's been standing off this jut of shore
Ever since rivers, I was going to say,
Were made in heaven. It wasn't waved to us.'

'It wasn't, yet it was. If not to you   35
It was to me—in an annunciation.'

'Oh, if you take it off to lady-land,
As't were the country of the Amazons
We men must see you to the confines of
And leave you there, ourselves forbid to enter,—   40
It is your brook! I have no more to say.'

'Yes, you have, too. Go on. You thought of something.'

'Speaking of contraries, see how the brook
In that white wave runs counter to itself.
It is from that in water we were from   45
Long, long before we were from any creature.
Here we, in our impatience of the steps,
Get back to the beginning of beginnings,
The stream of everything that runs away.
Some say existence like a Pirouot   50
And Pirouette, forever in one place,
Stands still and dances, but it runs away,
It seriously, sadly, runs away
To fill the abyss' void with emptiness.
It flows beside us in this water brook,   55
But it flows over us. It flows between us
To separate us for a panic moment.
It flows between us, over us, and *with* us.
And it is time, strength, tone, light, life and love—
And even substance lapsing unsubstantial;   60

The universal cataract of death
That spends to nothingness—and unresisted,
Save by some strange resistance in itself,
Not just a swerving, but a throwing back,
As if regret were in it and were sacred.   65
It has this throwing backward on itself
So that the fall of most of it is always
Raising a little, sending up a little.
Our life runs down in sending up the clock.
The brook runs down in sending up our life.   70
The suns runs down in sending up the brook.
And there is something sending up the sun.
It is this backward motion toward the source,
Against the stream, that most we see ourselves in,
The tribute of the current to the source.   75
It is from this in nature we are from
It is most us.'

              'Today will be the day   80
You said so.'

             'No, today will be the day
You said the brook was called West-running Brook.'

'Today will be the day of what we both said.'

                                  1928

The Subverted Flower

She drew back; he was calm:
"It is this that had the power."
And he lashed his open palm
With the tender-headed flower.
He smiled for her to smile,   5
But she was either blind
Or wilfully unkind.
He eyed her for a while
For a woman and a puzzle.
He flicked and flung the flower,   10
And another sort of smile
Caught up like finger tips
The corners of his lips
And cracked his ragged muzzle.

She was standing to the waist 15
In goldenrod and brake,
Her shining hair displaced.
He stretched her either arm
As if she made it ache
To clasp her—not to harm; 20
As if he could not spare
To touch her neck and hair.
"If this has come to us
And not to me alone—"
So she thought she heard him say; 25
Though with every word he spoke
His lips were sucked and blown
And the effort made him choke
Like a tiger at a bone.
She had to lean away. 30
She dared not stir a foot,
Lest movement should provoke
The demon of pursuit
That slumbers in a brute.
It was then her mother's call 35
From inside the garden wall
Made her steal a look of fear
To see if he could hear
And would pounce to end it all
Before her mother came. 40
She looked and saw the shame:
A hand hung like a paw,
An arm worked like a saw
As if to be persuasive,
An ingratiating laugh 45
That cut the snout in half,
An eye become evasive.
A girl could only see
That a flower had marred a man,
But what she could not see 50
Was that the flower might be
Other than base and fetid:
That the flower had done but part,
And what the flower began
Her own too meagre heart 55
Had terribly completed.
She looked and saw the worst.
And the dog or what it was,
Obeying bestial laws,

A coward save at night,   60
Turned from the place and ran.
She heard him stumble first
And use his hands in flight.
She heard him bark outright.
And oh for one so young   65
The bitter words she spit
Like some tenacious bit
That will not leave the tongue.
She plucked her lips for it,
And still the horror clung.   70
Her mother wiped the foam
From her chin, picked up her comb
And drew her backward home.

1942

The Silken Tent

She is as in a field a silken tent
At midday when a sunny summer breeze
Has dried the dew and all its ropes relent,
So that in guys it gently sways at ease,
And its supporting central cedar pole,   5
That is its pinnacle to heavenward
And signifies the sureness of the soul,
Seems to owe naught to any single cord,
But strictly held by none, is loosely bound
By countless silken ties of love and thought   10
To everything on earth the compass round,
And only by one's going slightly taut
In the capriciousness of summer air
Is of the slightest bondage made aware.

1942

Spring Pools

These pools that, though in forests, still reflect
The total sky almost without defect,
And like the flowers beside them, chill and shiver,

Will like the flowers beside them soon be gone,
And yet not out by any brook or river,   5
But up by roots to bring dark foliage on.

The trees that have it in their pent-up buds
To darken nature and be summer woods—
Let them think twice before they use their powers
To blot out and drink up and sweep away   10
These flowery waters and these watery flowers
From snow that melted only yesterday.

1927

                                                           1928

'Out, Out—'

The buzz-saw snarled and rattled in the yard
And made dust and dropped stove-length sticks of wood,
Sweet-scented stuff when the breeze drew across it.
And from there those that lifted eyes could count
Five mountain ranges one behind the other   5
Under the sunset far into Vermont.
And the saw snarled and rattled, snarled and rattled,
As it ran light, or had to bear a load.
And nothing happened: day was all but done.
Call it a day, I wish they might have said   10
To please the boy by giving him the half hour
That a boy counts so much when saved from work.
His sister stood beside them in her apron
To tell them 'Supper.' At the word, the saw,
As if to prove saws knew what supper meant,   15
Leaped out at the boy's hand, or seemed to leap—
He must have given the hand. However it was,
Neither refused the meeting. But the hand!
The boy's first outcry was a rueful laugh,
As he swung toward them holding up the hand   20
Half in appeal, but half as if to keep
The life from spilling. Then the boy saw all—
Since he was old enough to know, big boy
Doing a man's work, though a child at heart—
He saw all spoiled. 'Don't let him cut my hand off—   25
The doctor, when he comes. Don't let him, sister!'
So. But the hand was gone already.

The doctor put him in the dark of ether.
He lay and puffed his lips out with his breath.
And then—the watcher at his pulse took fright.   30
No one believed. They listened at his heart.
Little—less—nothing!—and that ended it.
No more to build on there. And they, since they
Were not the one dead, turned to their affairs.

1916

Design

I found a dimpled spider, fat and white,
On a white heal-all, holding up a moth
Like a white piece of rigid satin cloth—
Assorted characters of death and blight
Mixed ready to begin the morning right,   5
Like the ingredients of a witches' broth—
A snow-drop spider, a flower like froth,
And dead wings carried like a paper kite.

What had that flower to do with being white,
The wayside blue and innocent heal-all?   10
What brought the kindred spider to that height,
Then steered the white moth thither in the night?
What but design of darkness to appall?—
If design govern in a thing so small.

1936

A Servant to Servants

I didn't make you know how glad I was
To have you come and camp here on our land.
I promised myself to get down some day
And see the way you lived, but I don't know!
With a houseful of hungry men to feed   5
I guess you'd find. . . . It seems to me
I can't express my feelings any more
Than I can raise my voice or want to lift
My hand (oh, I can lift it when I have to).

Did ever you feel so? I hope you never.   10
It's got so I don't even know for sure
Whether I *am* glad, sorry, or anything.
There's nothing but a voice-like left inside
That seems to tell me how I ought to feel,
And would feel if I wasn't all gone wrong.   15
You take the lake. I look and look at it.
I see it's a fair, pretty sheet of water.
I stand and make myself repeat out loud
The advantages it has, so long and narrow,
Like a deep piece of some old running river   20
Cut short off at both ends. It lies five miles
Straight away through the mountain notch
From the sink window where I wash the plates,
And all our storms come up toward the house,
Drawing the slow waves whiter and whiter and whiter.   25
It took my mind off doughnuts and soda biscuit
To step outdoors and take the water dazzle
A sunny morning, or take the rising wind
About my face and body and through my wrapper,
When a storm threatened from the Dragon's Den,   30
And a cold chill shivered across the lake.
I see it's a fair, pretty sheet of water,
Our Willoughby! How did you hear of it?
I expect, though, everyone's heard of it.
In a book about ferns? Listen to that!   35
You let things more like feathers regulate
Your going and coming. And you like it here?
I can see how you might. But I don't know!
It would be different if more people came,
For then there would be business. As it is,   40
The cottages Len built, sometimes we rent them,
Sometimes we don't. We've a good piece of shore
That ought to be worth something, and may yet.
But I don't count on it as much as Len.
He looks on the bright side of everything,   45
Including me. He thinks I'll be all right
With doctoring. But it's not medicine—
Lowe is the only doctor's dared to say so—
It's rest I want—there, I have said it out—
From cooking meals for hungry hired men   50
And washing dishes after them—from doing
Things over and over that just won't stay done.

By good rights I ought not to have so much
Put on me, but there seems no other way.
Len says one steady pull more ought to do it.   55
He says the best way out is always through.
And I agree to that, or in so far
As that I can see no way out but through—
Leastways for me—and then they'll be convinced.
It's not that Len don't want the best for me.   60
It was his plan our moving over in
Beside the lake from where that day I showed you
We used to live—ten miles from anywhere.
We didn't change without some sacrifice,
But Len went at it to make up the loss.   65
His work's a man's, of course, from sun to sun,
But he works when he works as hard as I do—
Though there's small profit in comparisons.
(Women and men will make them all the same.)
But work ain't all. Len undertakes too much.   70
He's into everything in town. This year
It's highways, and he's got too many men
Around him to look after that make waste.
They take advantage of him shamefully,
And proud, too, of themselves for doing so.   75
We have four here to board, great good-for-nothings,
Sprawling about the kitchen with their talk
While I fry their bacon. Much they care!
No more put out in what they do or say
Than if I wasn't in the room at all.   80
Coming and going all the time, they are:
I don't learn what their names are, let alone
Their characters, or whether they are safe
To have inside the house with doors unlocked.
I'm not afraid of them, though, if they're not   85
Afraid of me. There's two can play at that.
I have my fancies: it runs in the family.
My father's brother wasn't right. They kept him
Locked up for years back there at the old farm.
I've been away once—yes, I've been away.   90
The State Asylum. I was prejudiced;
I wouldn't have sent anyone of mine there;
You know the old idea—the only asylum
Was the poorhouse, and those who could afford,

Rather than send their folks to such a place, 95
Kept them at home; and it does seem more human.
But it's not so: the place is the asylum.
There they have every means proper to do with,
And you aren't darkening other people's lives—
Worse than no good to them, and they no good 100
To you in your condition; you can't know
Affection or the want of it in that state.
I've heard too much of the old-fashioned way.
My father's brother, he went mad quite young.
Some thought he had been bitten by a dog, 105
Because his violence took on the form
Of carrying his pillow in his teeth;
But it's more likely he was crossed in love,
Or so the story goes. It was some girl.
Anyway all he talked about was love 110
They soon saw he would do someone a mischief
If he wa'n't kept strict watch of, and it ended
In father's building him a sort of cage,
Or room within a room, of hickory poles,
Like stanchions in the barn, from floor to ceiling.— 115
A narrow passage all the way around.
Anything they put in for furniture
He'd tear to pieces, even a bed to lie on.
So they made the place comfortable with straw,
Like a beast's stall, to ease their consciences. 120
Of course they had to feed him without dishes.
They tried to keep him clothed, but he paraded
With his clothes on his arm—all of his clothes.
Cruel—it sounds. I'spose they did the best
They knew. And just when he was at the height, 125
Father and mother married, and mother came,
A bride, to help take care of such a creature,
And accommodate her young life to his.
That was what marrying father meant to her.
She had to lie and hear love things made dreadful 130
By his shouts in the night. He'd shout and shout
Until the strength was shouted out of him,
And his voice died down slowly from exhaustion.
He'd pull his bars apart like bow and bowstring,
And let them go and make them twang until 135
His hands had worn them smooth as any oxbow,

1154
ROBERT FROST

And then he'd crow as if he thought that child's play
The only fun he had. I've heard them say, though,
They found a way to put a stop to it.
He was before my time—I never saw him; 140
But the pen stayed exactly as it was
There in the upper chamber in the ell,
A sort of catch-all full of attic clutter.
I often think of the smooth hickory bars.
It got so I would say—you know, half fooling— 145
'It's time I took my turn upstairs in jail'—
Just as you will till it becomes a habit.
No wonder I was glad to get away.
Mind you, I waited till Len said the word.
I didn't want the blame if things went wrong, 150
I was glad though, no end, when we moved out,
And I looked to be happy, and I was;
As I said, for a while—but I don't know!
Somehow the change wore out like a prescription.
And there's more to it than just window-views 155
And living by a lake. I'm past such help—
Unless Len took the notion, which he won't,
And I won't ask him—it's not sure enough.
I'spose I've got to go the road I'm going:
Other folks have to, and why shouldn't I? 160
I almost think if I could do like you,
Drop everything and live out on the ground—
But it might be, come night, I shouldn't like it,
Or a long rain. I should soon get enough,
And be glad of a good roof overhead. 165
I've lain awake thinking of you, I'll warrant,
More than you have yourself, some of these nights.
The wonder was the tents weren't snatched away
From over you as you lay in your beds.
I haven't courage for a risk like that. 170
Bless you, of course, you're keeping me from work,
But the thing of it is, I need to *be* kept.
There's work enough to do—there's always that;
But behind's behind. The worst that you can do
Is set me back a little more behind. 175
I sha'n't catch up in this world, anyway.
I'd *rather* you'd not go unless you must.

1914

Provide Provide

The witch that came (the withered hag)
To wash the steps with pail and rag,
Was once the beauty Abishag,

The picture pride of Hollywood.
Too many fall from great and good   5
For you to doubt the likelihood.

Die early and avoid the fate.
Or if predestined to die late,
Make up your mind to die in state.

Make the whole stock exchange your own!   10
If need be occupy a throne,
Where nobody can call *you* crone.

Some have relied on what they knew;
Others on being simply true.
What worked for them might work for you.   15

No memory of having starred
Atones for later disregard,
Or keeps the end from being hard.

Better to go down dignified
With boughten friendship at your side   20
Than none at all. Provide, provide!

1934

1936

Home Burial

He saw her from the bottom of the stairs
Before she saw him. She was starting down,
Looking back over her shoulder at some fear.
She took a doubtful step and then undid it
To raise herself and look again. He spoke   5
Advancing toward her: 'What is it you see
From up there always—for I want to know.'
She turned and sank upon her skirts at that,
And her face changed from terrified to dull.

He said to gain time: 'What is it you see,'   10
Mounting until she cowered under him.
'I will find out now—you must tell me, dear.'
She, in her place, refused him any help
With the least stiffening of her neck and silence.
She let him look, sure that he wouldn't see.   15
Blind creature; and a while he didn't see.
But at last he murmured, 'Oh,' and again, 'Oh.'

'What is it—what?' she said.

                        'Just that I see.'

'You don't,' she challenged. 'Tell me what it is.'   20

'The wonder is I didn't see at once.
I never noticed it from here before.
I must be wonted to it—that's the reason.
The little graveyard where my people are!
So small the window frames the whole of it.   25
Not so much larger than a bedroom, is it?
There are three stones of slate and one of marble,
Broad-shouldered little slabs there in the sunlight
On the sidehill. We haven't to mind *those*.
But I understand: it is not the stones.   30
But the child's mound—'

               'Don't, don't, don't, don't,' she cried.

She withdrew shrinking from beneath his arm
That rested on the banister, and slid downstairs;
And turned on him with such a daunting look,   35
He said twice over before he knew himself:
'Can't a man speak of his own child he's lost?'

'Not you! Oh, where's my hat? Oh, I don't need it!
I must get out of here. I must get air.
I don't know rightly whether any man can.'   40

'Amy! Don't go to someone else this time.
Listen to me. I won't come down the stairs.'
He sat and fixed his chin between his fists.
'There's something I should like to ask you, dear.'

'You don't know how to ask it.'   45

                   'Help me, then.'

Her fingers moved the latch for all reply.

'My words are nearly always an offence.
I don't know how to speak of anything
So as to please you. But I might be taught   50
I should suppose. I can't say I see how.
A man must partly give up being a man
With women-folk. We could have some arrangement
By which I'd bind myself to keep hands off
Anything special you're a-mind to name.   55
Though I don't like such things 'twixt those that love.
Two that don't love can't live together without them.
But two that do can't live together with them.'
She moved the latch a little. 'Don't—don't go.
Don't carry it to someone else this time.   60
Tell me about it if it's something human.
Let me into your grief. I'm not so much
Unlike other folks as your standing there
Apart would make me out. Give me my chance.
I do think, though, you overdo it a little.   65
What was it brought you up to think it the thing
To take your mother-loss of a first child
So inconsolably—in the face of love.
You'd think his memory might be satisfied—'

'There you go sneering now!'   70

                              'I'm not, I'm not!
You make me angry. I'll come down to you.
God, what a woman! And it's come to this,
A man can't speak of his own child that's dead.'

'You can't because you don't know how to speak.   75
If you had any feelings, you that dug
With your own hand—how could you?—his little grave;
I saw you from that very window there,
Making the gravel leap and leap in air,
Leap up, like that, like that, and land so lightly   80
And roll back down the mound beside the hole.
I thought, Who is that man? I didn't know you.
And I crept down the stairs and up the stairs
To look again, and still your spade kept lifting.
Then you came in. I heard your rumbling voice   85
Out in the kitchen, and I don't know why,
But I went near to see with my own eyes.
You could sit there with the stains on your shoes
Of the fresh earth from your own baby's grave
And talk about your everyday concerns.   90

You had stood the spade up against the wall
Outside there in the entry, for I saw it.'

'I shall laugh the worst laugh I ever laughed.
I'm cursed. God, if I don't believe I'm cursed.'

'I can repeat the very words you were saying.   95
"Three foggy mornings and one rainy day
Will rot the best birch fence a man can build."
Think of it, talk like that at such a time!
What had how long it takes a birch to rot
To do with what was in the darkened parlour.   100
You *couldn't* care! The nearest friends can go
With anyone to death, comes so far short
They might as well not try to go at all.
No, from the time when one is sick to death,
One is alone, and he dies more alone.   105
Friends make pretence of following to the grave,
But before one is in it, their minds are turned
And making the best of their way back to life
And living people, and things they understand.
But the world's evil. I won't have grief so   110
If I can change it. Oh, I won't, I won't!'

'There you have said it all and you feel better.
You won't go now. You're crying. Close the door.
The heart's gone out of it: why keep it up.
Amy! There's someone coming down the road!'   115

'*You*—oh, you think the talk is all. I must go—
Somewhere out of this house. How can I make you—'

'If—you—do!' She was opening the door wider.
'Where do you mean to go? First tell me that.
I'll follow and bring you back by force. I *will!*—'   120

1914

After Apple-Picking

My long two-pointed ladder's sticking through a tree
Toward heaven still,
And there's a barrel that I didn't fill

Beside it, and there may be two or three
Apples I didn't pick upon some bough. 5
But I am done with apple-picking now.
Essence of winter sleep is on the night,
The scent of apples: I am drowsing off.
I cannot rub the strangeness from my sight
I got from looking through a pane of glass 10
I skimmed this morning from the drinking trough
And held against the world of hoary grass.
It melted, and I let it fall and break.
But I was well
Upon my way to sleep before it fell, 15
And I could tell
What form my dreaming was about to take.
Magnified applies appear and disappear,
Stem end and blossom end,
And every fleck of russet showing clear. 20
My instep arch not only keeps the ache,
It keeps the pressure of a ladder-round.
I feel the ladder sway as the boughs bend.
And I keep hearing from the cellar bin
The rumbling sound 25
Of load on load of apples coming in.
For I have had too much
Of apple-picking: I am overtired
Of the great harvest I myself desired.
There were ten thousand thousand fruit to touch, 30
Cherish in hand, lift down, and not let fall.
For all
That struck the earth,
No matter if not bruised or spiked with stubble,
Went surely to the cider-apple heap 35
As of no worth.
One can see what will trouble
This sleep of mine, whatever sleep it is.
Were he not gone,
The woodchuck could say whether it's like his 40
Long sleep, as I describe its coming on,
Or just some human sleep.

1914

Desert Places

Snow falling and night falling fast oh fast
In a field I looked into going past,
And the ground almost covered smooth in snow,
But a few weeds and stubble showing last.

The woods around it have it—it is theirs.   5
All animals are smothered in their lairs.
I am too absent-spirited to count;
The loneliness includes me unawares.

And lonely as it is that loneliness
Will be more lonely ere it will be less—   10
A blanker whiteness of benighted snow
With no expression, nothing to express.

They cannot scare me with their empty spaces
Between stars—on stars where no human race is.
I have it in me so much nearer home   15
To scare myself with my own desert places.

1934

1936

An Old Man's Winter Night

All out of doors looked darkly in at him
Through the thin frost, almost in separate stars,
That gathers on the pane in empty rooms.
What kept his eyes from giving back the gaze
Was the lamp tilted near them in his hand.   5
What kept him from remembering the need
That brought him to that creaking room was age.
He stood with barrels round him—at a loss.
And having scared the cellar under him
In clomping there, he scared it once again   10
In clomping off;—and scared the outer night,
Which has its sounds, familiar, like the roar
Of trees and crack of branches, common things,
But nothing so like beating on a box.
A light he was to no one but himself   15
Where now he sat, concerned with he knew what,

A quiet light, and then not even that.
He consigned to the moon, such as she was,
So late-arising, to the broken moon
As better than the sun in any case   20
For such a charge, his snow upon the roof,
His icicles along the wall to keep;
And slept. The log that shifted with a jolt
Once in the stove, disturbed him and he shifted,
And eased his heavy breathing, but still slept.   25
One aged man—one man—can't keep a house,
A farm, a countryside, or if he can,
It's thus he does it of a winter night.

1916

Come In

As I came to the edge of the woods,
Thrush music—hark!
Now if it was dusk outside,
Inside it was dark.

Too dark in the woods for a bird   5
By sleight of wing
To better its perch for the night,
Though it still could sing.

The last of the light of the sun
That had died in the west   10
Still lived for one song more
In a thrush's breast.

Far in the pillared dark
Thrush music went—
Almost like a call to come in   15
To the dark and lament.

But no, I was out for stars:
I would not come in.
I meant not even if asked,
And I hadn't been.   20

1942

WALLACE STEVENS

(1879–1955)

On its face the life of Wallace Stevens is absolutely bare of romance. Born in Reading, Pennsylvania, Stevens attended Harvard as a special student from 1897 to 1900 (philosopher George Santayana seems to have meant most to him there), then studied law in New York and was admitted to the bar in 1904. In 1916 he joined the legal staff of the Hartford Accident and Indemnity Company (his speciality came to be litigation involving car accidents); in 1934 he became a company vice-president; he stayed with the Hartford Accident until he retired. His first important poems began appearing in literary magazines in 1914, and a major volume, *Harmonium*, was published in 1923. Other books of poetry—the most significant were *The Man with the Blue Guitar* (1937), *Transport to Summer* (1947), and *The Auroras of Autumn* (1950)—followed at a rate of about one to a decade. Stevens also published collections of essays on mainly literary subjects—most notably *The Necessary Angel: Essays on Reality and the Imagination* (1951).

The Collected Poems of Wallace Stevens was published in 1954. Individual volumes of poetry are *Harmonium*, 1923, with subsequent editions in 1931 and 1937; *Ideas of Order*, 1935; *Owl's Clover*, 1936; *The Man with the Blue Guitar*, 1937; *Parts of a World*, 1942, rev., 1951; *Notes Toward a Supreme Fiction*, 1942; *Esthetique du Mal*, 1944; *Transport to Summer*, 1947; *Three Academic Pieces*, 1947; *A Primitive Like an Orb*, 1948; *The Auroras of Autumn*, 1950; *Selected Poems*, 1953; *Opus Posthumous*, 1957, ed. S. F. Morse. *The Necessary Angel*, 1951 is a treatise on poetics. *Letters of Wallace Stevens*, 1966 and *The Palm at the End of the Mind: Selected Poems and a Play*, 1971 were edited by Holly Stevens.

S. F. Morse has published *W. S. A Preliminary Checklist of His Published Writings, 1878–1954*, 1954; this has been reprinted in S. F. Morse, Jackson Bryer, and Joseph Riddle, *Wallace Stevens: Checklist and Bibliography of Stevens' Criticism*, 1964.

A good biography is S. F. Morse, *Wallace Stevens: Poetry as Life*, 1970. Early criticism includes S. F. Morse, *Wallace Stevens*, 1950; W. V. O'Connor, *The Shaping Spirit*, 1950; R. Pack, *Wallace Stevens*, 1958; Frank Kermode, *Wallace Stevens*, 1960; Daniel Fuchs, *The Comic Spirit of Wallace Stevens*, 1963; Eugene P. Nassar, *Wallace Stevens: An Anatomy of Figuration*, 1965; Joseph Riddle, *The Clairvoyant Eye: The Poetry and Poetics of Wallace Stevens*, 1965; Frank Doggett, *Stevens' Poetry of Thought*, 1966; and R. H. Pearce and J. H. Miller, eds., *The Act of the Mind: Essays on the Poetry of Wallace Stevens*.

In addition, see Robert `Buttel, *Wallace Stevens: The Making of Harmonium*, 1967; James Baird, *The Dome and the Rock: Structure in the Poetry of Wallace Stevens*, 1968; Helen Vendler, *On Extended Wings: Wallace Stevens' Longer Poems*, 1969; William Burney, *Wallace Stevens*, 1968; Merle F. Brown, *Wallace Stevens: The Poem as Act*, 1970; Edward Kessler, *Images of Wallace Stevens*, 1972, and A. Walton Litz, *Introspective Voyager: The Poetic Development of Wallace Stevens*, 1972.

Early in 1955 he was awarded the Pulitzer Prize and the National Book Award for his *Collected Poems*, which had appeared the year before; within a few months of these honors he died.

The first point to be made about this poet is that he is not disposed to invite the reader to become his familiar or to endorse common sense versions of things. Stevens is a witty poet, a virtuoso entertainer on occasion, more than once a charming verbal larkster.

> I sang a canto in a canton,
> Cunning-coo, O, cuckoo cock,
> In a canton of Belshazzar . . .
> ("Country Words")

But for companionability he would not be chosen; comfortable socializing is not his thing. The "characters" in his poems—Crispin in "The Comedian as the Letter C"—are, on the whole, unlovingly treated. Tones of irony (suave yet cutting) and strategies of satire are pervasive. Poem after poem begins with a personal address overlaid with condescension.

> Well, nuncle, this plainly won't do.
> ("Floral Decorations for Bananas")

> No more phrases, Swenson . .
> ("Lions in Sweden")

And while the manners are, almost unvaryingly, elegant, the poet keeps his distance from common folk. In a long poem called "Owl's Clover" he forces himself to a direct address to social reality, the mass movements and desperation of a period of economic depression; but in doing so he leans hard on the word squalid ("squalid whole," "squalid cells") and is plainly ill at ease. Often in his essays a turn of argument prompts the writer to an assessment of the public taste of his time, whether in music or education or sculpture, and invariably the tone is scornful. (The "common preference" of the middle class, he notes sniffishly in "The Noble Rider and the Sound of Words," is "for realistic satisfactions.") In one of *his* poems Robert Frost speaks tartly of a scholar who is a democrat, "If not at heart, at least on principle." Neither on principle nor at heart is Wallace Stevens a democrat: in temperament he is far removed from Frost and William Carlos Williams, rather closer to Eliot and Pound.

As with many an artist of comparable temperament, Stevens' detachment from the "mob" bespeaks enthusiasm for the rigor of thought, not simple repugnance at inferior beings. The trouble with vulgarity and grossness is that thinking is anathema to them; they hate pressing beyond appearances and surfaces, they never journey inside the mind, they never overcome the preoccupation with things. Stevens' preoccupations are unabashedly intellectual; where sensations enter—and they enter often—they are dealt with as challenges, pressures to be fully felt but strenuously thought aside. Most of his poems have epistemological conundrums in their margins or at their centers—problems in the theory of knowledge, questions about the relation between (and priorities among) art and reality, imagination and experience. Some poems—including, perhaps, the most widely admired, "Sunday Morning"—are expressions of a post-Christian, quasiheroic mode of aesthetic hedonism. A few—"The Comedian as the Letter C" in the early years and "Credences of Summer" near the end—connect epistemological probings and hedonism with a questing motif—the search for the true Garden—that recurs often in classic American literature.

The essential Stevens may or may not be the ontological wrestler, the arguefier about what is Really Out There; but in many a poem pored over for its bearing on this poet's theory of the imagination there are satisfactions that exist independently of epistemological argument. Stevens is an extraordinary evocator of the sensations of thought itself. Reading "The World as Meditation," you feel the texture of a mind that, by an effort of will, energy, and love, has fixed itself in poised anticipation. "The Snow Man" enacts the mental activity of casting off distraction and irrelevance; "The House was Quiet and the World was Calm" takes the reader inside that moment at which immersion in thinking-imagining draws all externalities to a point of union neither precisely within nor precisely without the self. And these poems are celebrations first and last. The steadiness and clarity of Penelope's evocation of Ulysses (she brings him forth daily into her mind "as an essential exercise"):

She would talk a little to herself as she combed her hair.
Repeating his name with its patient syllables,
Never forgetting him that kept coming constantly so near . . .

and her thought-through resolved preferences concerning the style of his arrival:

She wanted nothing he could not bring her by coming alone.
She wanted no fetchings—

are uncommonly poignant, but they are also a kind of homage to the pacifying power of mind. "The Snow Man" is homage to the condition of true inwardness with a subject—achievement of that objective regard purified of sentiment and of self-regard that is perfect understanding. The unearthly "listener,"

> who listens in the snow,
> And, nothing himself, beholds
> Nothing that is not there and the nothing that is—

is "unreal," and yet, as a dreamable dream, somehow not beyond our range. In "The House was Quiet and the World was Calm" the mind— we may say—arrives at its holy destination: reader, book, the page in the fingers, the summer night are bound into identity as truth.

> The truth in a calm world,
> In which there is no meaning, itself
> Is calm, itself is summer and night, itself
> Is the reader leaning late and reading there.

The climate of thought, another poet once wrote, "has seldom been described." In Wallace Stevens' poetry it is presented, made palpable on the page; if the poet was right to contend that most people like Florida better, he was also right in holding for the beauty of the mind's place. He is the most graceful poet America has yet produced.

Peter Quince at the Clavier[1]

I

Just as my fingers on these keys
Make music, so the self-same sounds
On my spirit make a music, too.

Music is feeling, then, not sound;
And thus it is that what I feel,   5
Here in this room, desiring you,

Thinking of your blue-shadowed silk,
Is music. It is like the strain
Waked in the elders by Susanna.[2]

---

[1] The clavier is probably a harmonium. Peter Quince is the director of a little play in Shakespeare's *A Midsummer Night's Dream*, I, 2.

[2] Susanna was the wife of Joachim, pursued sexually by the Hebrew Elders and finally defended by Daniel. See the History of Susanna, from the Old Testament Apocrypha.

Of a green evening, clear and warm,   10
She bathed in her still garden, while
The red-eyed elders watching, felt

The basses of their beings throb
In witching chords, and their thin blood
Pulse pizzicati of Hosanna.[3]   15
          II
In the green water, clear and warm,
Susanna lay.
She searched
The touch of springs,   20
And found
Concealed imaginings.
She sighed,
For so much melody.

Upon the bank, she stood
In the cool   25
Of spent emotions.
She felt, among the leaves,
The dew
Of old devotions.

She walked upon the grass,   30
Still quavering.
The winds were like her maids,
On timid feet,
Fetching her woven scarves,
Yet wavering.   35

A breath upon her hand
Muted the night.
She turned—
A cymbal crashed,
And roaring horns.   40
          III
Soon, with a noise like tambourines.
Came her attendant Byzantines.[4]

They wondered why Susanna cried
Against the elders by her side;

---

[3] Notes produced by plucking the strings of an instrument. Hosanna is a hymn praising God.

[4] The citizens of Byzantium, a Greek city in the sixth century (the time of Susanna). Byzantium became Constantinople and is now Istanbul.

And as they whispered, the refrain   45
Was like a willow swept by rain.

Anon, their lamps' uplifted flame
Revealed Susanna and her shame.

And then, the simpering Byzantines
Fled, with a noise like tambourines.   50

IV

Beauty is momentary in the mind—
The fitful tracing of a portal;
But in the flesh it is immortal.

The body dies; the body's beauty lives.
So evenings die, in their green going,   55
A wave, interminably flowing.
So gardens die, their meek breath scenting
The cowl of winter, done repenting.
So maidens die, to the auroral
Celebration of a maiden's choral.   60

Susanna's music touched the bawdy strings
Of those white elders; but, escaping,
Left only Death's ironic scraping.
Now, in its immortality, it plays
On the clear viol of her memory,   65
And makes a constant sacrament of praise.

1915

1923

Sunday Morning

I

Complacencies of the peignoir, and late
Coffee and oranges in a sunny chair,
And the green freedom of a cockatoo
Upon a rug mingle to dissipate
The holy hush of ancient sacrifice.   5
She dreams a little, and she feels the dark
Encroachment of that old catastrophe,
As a calm darkens among water-lights.
The pungent oranges and bright, green wings
Seem things in some procession of the dead,   10

Winding across wide water, without sound.
The day is like wide water, without sound,
Stilled for the passing of her dreaming feet
Over the seas, to silent Palestine,
Dominion of the blood and sepulchre.   15

II

Why should she give her bounty to the dead?
What is divinity if it can come
Only in silent shadows and in dreams?
Shall she not find in comforts of the sun,
In pungent fruit and bright, green wings, or else   20
In any balm or beauty of the earth,
Things to be cherished like the thought of heaven?
Divinity must live within herself:
Passions of rain, or moods in falling snow;
Grievings in loneliness, or unsubdued   25
Elations when the forest blooms; gusty
Emotions on wet roads on autumn nights;
All pleasures and all pains, remembering
The bough of summer and the winter branch.
These are the measures destined for her soul.   30

III

Jove[1] in the clouds had his inhuman birth.
No mother suckled him, no sweet land gave
Large-mannered motions to his mythy mind
He moved among us, as a muttering king,
Magnificent, would move among his hinds,   35
Until our blood, commingling, virginal,
With heaven, brought such requital to desire
The very hinds discerned it, in a star.
Shall our blood fail? Or shall it come to be
The blood of paradise? And shall the earth   40
Seem all of paradise that we shall know?
The sky will be much friendlier then than now,
A part of labor and a part of pain,
And next in glory to enduring love,
Not this dividing and indifferent blue.   45

IV

She says, "I am content when wakened birds,
Before they fly, test the reality

---

[1] The god Jupiter

Of misty fields, by their sweet questionings;
But when the birds are gone, and their warm fields
Return no more, where, then, is paradise?"   50
There is not any haunt of prophecy,
Nor any old chimera of the grave,
Neither the golden underground, nor isle
Melodious, where spirits gat them home,
Nor visionary south, nor cloudy palm   55
Remote on heaven's hill, that has endured
As April's green endures; or will endure
Like her remembrance of awakened birds,
Or her desire for June and evening, tipped
By the consummation of the swallow's wings.   60

V

She says, "But in contentment I still feel
The need of some imperishable bliss."
Death is the mother of beauty; hence from her,
Alone, shall come fulfilment to our dreams
And our desires. Although she strews the leaves   65
Of sure obliteration on our paths,
The path sick sorrow took, the many paths
Where triumph rang its brassy phrase, or love
Whispered a little out of tenderness,
She makes the willow shiver in the sun   70
For maidens who were wont to sit and gaze
Upon the grass, relinquished to their feet.
She causes boys to pile new plums and pears
On disregarded plate. The maidens taste
And stray impassioned in the littering leaves   75

VI

Is there no change of death in paradise?
Does ripe fruit never fall? Or do the boughs
Hang always heavy in that perfect sky,
Unchanging, yet so like our perishing earth,
With rivers like our own that seek for seas   80
They never find, the same receding shores
That never touch with inarticulate pang?
Why set the pear upon those river-banks
Or spice the shores with odors of the plum?
Alas, that they should wear our colors there,   85
The silken weavings of our afternoons,
And pick the strings of our insipid lutes!

Death is the mother of beauty, mystical,
Within whose burning bosom we devise
Our earthly mothers waiting, sleeplessly.   90

VII

Supple and turbulent, a ring of men
Shall chant in orgy on a summer morn
Their boisterous devotion to the sun,
Not as a god, but as a god might be,
Naked among them, like a savage source.   95
Their chant shall be a chant of paradise,
Out of their blood, returning to the sky;
And in their chant shall enter, voice by voice,
The windy lake wherein their lord delights,
The trees, like serafin,[2] and echoing hills,   100
That choir among themselves long afterward.
They shall know well the heavenly fellowship
Of men that perish and of summer morn.
And whence they came and whither they shall go
The dew upon their feet shall manifest.   105

VIII

She hears, upon that water without sound,
A voice that cries, "The tomb in Palestine
Is not the porch of spirits lingering.
It is the grave of Jesus, where he lay."
We live in an old chaos of the sun,   110
Or old dependency of day and night,
Or island solitude, unsponsored, free,
Of that wide water, inescapable.
Deer walk upon our mountains, and the quail
Whistle about us their spontaneous cries;   115
Sweet berries ripen in the wilderness;
And, in the isolation of the sky,
At evening, casual flocks of pigeons make
Ambiguous undulations as they sink,
Downward to darkness, on extended wings.   120

1915

1923

[2] Seraphim are celestial beings with three
pairs of wings; they are one of the nine orders of angels.

A High-Toned Old Christian Woman

Poetry is the supreme fiction, madame.
Take the moral law and make a nave[1] of it
And from the nave build haunted heaven. Thus,
The conscience is converted into palms.
Like windy citherns[2] hankering for hymns.   5
We agree in principle. That's clear. But take
The opposing law and make a peristyle,[3]
And from the peristyle project a masque[4]   .
Beyond the planets. Thus, our bawdiness,
Unpurged by epitaph, indulged at last,   10
Is equally converted into palms,
Squiggling like saxophones. And palm for palm,
Madame, we are where we began. Allow,
Therefore, that in the planetary scene
Your disaffected flagellants,[5] well studied,   15
Smacking their muzzy[6] bellies in parade,
Proud of such novelties of the sublime,
Such tink and tank and tunk-a-tunk-tunk,
May, merely may, madame, whip from themselves
A jovial hullabaloo among the spheres.   20
This will make widows wince: But fictive things
Wink as they will. Wink most when widows wince.

1922

1923

[1] The central part of the church, flanked by aisles for the congregation.

[2] A cithern or cittern was a sixteenth-century guitar with a pear-shaped body.

[3] A series of columns surrounding a temple or enclosing a court.

[4] A dramatic entertainment, often a dance.

[5] One who whips or scourges himself by way of religious discipline or public penance.

[6] Muddled.

Anecdote of the Jar

I placed a jar in Tennessee,
And round it was, upon a hill.
It made the slovenly wilderness
Surround that hill.

The wilderness rose up to it,   5
And sprawled around, no longer wild.
The jar was round upon the ground
And tall and of a port in air.

It took dominion everywhere.
The jar was gray and bare.   10
It did not give of bird or bush,
Like nothing else in Tennessee.

1919

1923

A Primitive Like an Orb

I

The essential poem at the centre of things,
The arias that spiritual fiddlings make,
Have gorged the cast-iron of our lives with good
And the cast-iron of our works. But it is, dear sirs,
A difficult apperception, this gorging good,   5
Fetched by such slick-eyed nymphs, this essential gold,
This fortune's finding, disposed and re-disposed
By such slight genii in such pale air.

II

We do not prove the existence of the poem.
It is something seen and known in lesser poems.   10
It is the huge, high harmony that sounds
A little and a little, suddenly,
By means of a separate sense. It is and it
Is not and, therefore, is. In the instant of speech,
The breadth of an accelerando[1] moves,   15
Captives the being, widens—and was there.

III

What milk there is in such captivity,
What wheaten bread and oaten cake and kind,
Green guests and table in the woods and songs
At heart, within an instant's motion, within   20

---

[1] Gradually accelerating in time.

A space grown wide, the inevitable blue
Of secluded thunder, an illusion, as it was,
Oh as, always too heavy for the sense
To seize, the obscurest as, the distant was . . .

IV

One poem proves another and the whole,   25
For the clairvoyant men that need no proof:
The lover, the believer and the poet.
Their words are chosen out of their desire,
The joy of language, when it is themselves.
With these they celebrate the central poem,   30
The fulfillment of fulfillments, in opulent,
Last terms, the largest, bulging still with more,

V

Until the used-to earth and sky, and the tree
And cloud, the used-to tree and used-to cloud,
Lose the old uses that they made of them,   35
And they: these men, and earth and sky, inform
Each other by sharp informations, sharp,
Free knowledges, secreted until then,
Breaches of that which held them fast. It is
As if the central poem became the world,   40

VI

And the world the central poem, each one the mate
Of the other, as if summer was a spouse,
Espoused each morning, each long afternoon,
And the mate of summer: her mirror and her look,
Her only place and person, a self of her   45
That speaks, denouncing separate selves, both one.
The essential poem begets the others. The light
Of it is not a light apart, up-hill.

VII

The central poem is the poem of the whole,
The poem of the composition of the whole,   50
The composition of blue sea and of green,
Of blue light and of green, as lesser poems,

And the miraculous multiplex of lesser poems,
Not merely into a whole, but a poem of
The whole, the essential compact of the parts,   55
The roundness that pulls tight the final ring

VIII

And that which in an altitude would soar,
A vis, a principle or, it may be,
The meditation of a principle,
Or else an inherent order active to be   60
Itself, a nature to its natives all
Beneficence, a repose, utmost repose,
The muscles of a magnet aptly felt,
A giant, on the horizon, glistening,

IX

And in bright excellence adorned, crested   65
With every prodigal, familiar fire,
And unfamiliar escapades: whirroos
And scintillant sizzlings such as children like,
Vested in the serious folds of majesty,
Moving around and behind, a following,   70
A source of trumpeting seraphs in the eye,
A source of pleasant outbursts on the ear.

X

It is a giant, always, that is evolved,
To be in scale, unless virtue cuts him, snips
Both size and solitude or thinks it does,   75
As in a signed photograph on a mantelpiece.
But the virtuoso never leaves his shape,
Still on the horizon elongates his cuts,
And still angelic and still plenteous,
Imposes power by the power of his form.   80

XI

Here, then, is an abstraction given head,
A giant on the horizon, given arms,
A massive body and long legs, stretched out,
A definition with an illustration, not

Too exactly labelled, a large among the smalls   85
Of it, a close, parental magnitude,
At the centre on the horizon, concentrum,[2] grave
And prodigious person, patron of origins.

XII

That's it. The lover writes, the believer hears,
The poet mumbles and the painter sees,   90
Each one, his fated eccentricity,
As a part, but part, but tenacious particle,
Of the skeleton of the ether, the total
Of letters, prophecies, perceptions, clods
Of color, the giant of nothingness, each one   95
And the giant ever changing, living in change.

1948

[2] Having a common center.

Botanist on Alp (No. 2)

The crosses on the convent roofs
Gleam sharply as the sun comes up.

What's down below is in the past
Like last night's crickets, far below.

And what's above is in the past   5
As sure as all the angels are.

Why should the future leap the clouds
The bays of heaven, brighted, blued?

Chant, O ye faithful, in your paths
The poem of long celestial death;   10

For who could tolerate the earth
Without that poem, or without

An earthier one, tum, tum-ti-tum,
As of those crosses, glittering,

And merely of their glittering,   15
A mirror of a mere delight?

1935

The World as Meditation

J'ai passé trop de temps à travailler mon violon, à voyager. Mais l'exercice essentiel du compositeur—la méditation—rien ne l'a jamais suspendu en moi . . . Je vis un rêve permanent, qui ne s'arrête ni nuit ni jour. [1]

GEORGES ENESCO [2]

Is it Ulysses that approaches from the east,
The interminable adventurer? The trees are mended.
That winter is washed away. Someone is moving

On the horizon and lifting himself up above it.
A form of fire approaches the cretonnes [3] of Penelope, [4]   5
Whose mere savage presence awakens the world in which she dwells.

She has composed, so long, a self with which to welcome him,
Companion to his self for her, which she imagined,
Two in a deep-founded sheltering, friend and dear friend.

The trees had been mended, as an essential exercise   10
In an inhuman meditation, larger than her own.
No winds like dogs watched over her at night.

She wanted nothing he could not bring her by coming alone.
She wanted no fetchings. His arms would be her necklace
And her belt, the final fortune of their desire.   15

But was it Ulysses? Or was it only the warmth of the sun
On her pillow? The thought kept beating in her like her heart.
The two kept beating together. It was only day.

It was Ulysses and it was not. Yet they had met,
Friend and dear friend and a planet's encouragement.   20
The barbarous strength within her would never fail.

She would talk a little to herself as she combed her hair,
Repeating his name with its patient syllables,
Never forgetting him that kept coming constantly so near.

1952

1954

<hr>

[1] The epigram is translated, "I have spent too much time working on my violin to travel. But the exercise is essential to composition—the meditation—nothing has ever suspended it in me. . . I have a permanent dream, which stops neither in the night nor the day."

[2] Georges Enesco (1881-1955), Rumanian composer.

[3] A heavy, unglazed cotton used for draperies and slipcovers.

[4] In *The Odyssey*, Penelope was noted for her constancy to Ulysses.

The Idea of Order at Key West

She sang beyond the genius of the sea.
The water never formed to mind or voice,
Like a body wholly body, fluttering
Its empty sleeves; and yet its mimic motion
Made constant cry, caused constantly a cry,   5
That was not ours although we understood,
Inhuman, of the veritable ocean.

The sea was not a mask. No more was she.
The song and water were not medleyed sound
Even if what she sang was what she heard,   10
Since what she sang was uttered word by word.
It may be that in all her phrases stirred.
The grinding water and the gasping wind;
But it was she and not the sea we heard.

For she was the maker of the song she sang.   15
The ever-hooded, tragic-gestured sea
Was merely a place by which she walked to sing.
Whose spirit is this? we said, because we knew
That we should ask this often as she sang.

If it was only the dark voice of the sea   20
That rose, or even colored by many waves;
If it was only the outer voice of sky
And cloud, of the sunken coral water-walled,
However clear, it would have been deep air,
The heaving speech of air, a summer sound   25
Repeated in a summer without end
And sound alone. But it was more than that,
More even than her voice, and ours, among
The meaningless plungings of water and the wind,
Theatrical distances, bronze shadows heaped   30
On high horizons, mountainous atmospheres
Of sky and sea.

        It was her voice that made
The sky acutest at its vanishing.
She measured to the hour its solitude.   35
She was the single artificer of the world

In which she sang. And when she sang, the sea,
Whatever self it had, became the self
That was her song, for she was the maker. Then we,
As we beheld her striding there alone,   40
Knew that there never was a world for her
Except the one she sang and, singing, made.

Ramon Fernandez,[1] tell me, if you know,
Why, when the singing ended and we turned
Toward the town, tell why the glassy lights,   45
The lights in the fishing boats at anchor there,
As the night descended, tilting in the air,
Mastered the night and portioned out the sea,
Fixing emblazoned zones and fiery poles.
Arranging, deepening, enchanting night.   50

Oh! Blessed rage for order, pale Ramon,
The maker's rage to order words of the sea,
Words of the fragrant portals, dimly-starred,
And of ourselves and of our origins,
In ghostlier demarcations, keener sounds.   55

   1934

                                                          1935

[1] Ramon Fernandez (1894-1944), a French literary critic. Stevens says that he invented the name for the poem and later discovered that "it turned out to be an actual name."

The Snow Man

One must have a mind of winter
To regard the frost and the boughs
Of the pine-trees crusted with snow;

And have been cold a long time
To behold the junipers[1] shagged with ice,   5
The spruces rough in the distant glitter

Of the January sun; and not to think
Of any misery in the sound of the wind,
In the sound of a few leaves,

[1] An evergreen tree or shrub with prickly foliage and a berrylike fruit.

Which is the sound of the land   10
Full of the same wind
That is blowing in the same bare place

For the listener, who listens in the snow,
And, nothing himself, beholds
Nothing that is not there and the nothing that is.   15

   1921

                   1923

To the One of Fictive Music

Sister and mother and diviner love,
And of the sisterhood of the living dead
Most near, most clear, and of the clearest bloom,
And of the fragrant mothers the most dear
And queen, and of diviner love the day   5
And flame and summer and sweet fire, no thread
Of cloudy silver sprinkles in your gown
Its venom of renown, and on your head
No crown is simpler than the simple hair.

Now, of the music summoned by the birth   10 •
That separates us from the wind and sea,
Yet leaves us in them, until earth becomes,
By being so much of the things we are,
Gross effigy and simulacrum, none
Gives motion to perfection more serene   15
Than yours, out of our imperfections wrought,
Most rare, or ever of more kindred air
In the laborious weaving that you wear.

For so retentive of themselves are men
That music is intensest which proclaims   20
The near, the clear, and vaunts the clearest bloom,
And of all vigils musing the obscure,
That apprehends the most which sees and names,
As in your name, an image that is sure,
Among the arrant spices of the sun,   25
O bough and bush and scented vine, in whom
We give ourselves our likest issuance.

Yet not too like, yet not so like to be
Too near, too clear, saving a little to endow
Our feigning with the strange unlike, whence springs   30
The difference that heavenly pity brings.
For this, musician, in your girdle fixed
Bear other perfumes. On your pale head wear
A band entwining, set with fatal stones.
Unreal, give back to us what once you gave:
The imagination that we spurned and crave.   35

    1922

                                              1923

The Emperor of Ice-Cream

Call the roller of big cigars,
The muscular one, and bid him whip
In kitchen cups concupiscent[1] curds.
Let the wenches dawdle in such dress
As they are used to wear, and let the boys   5
Bring flowers in last month's newspapers.
Let be be finale of seem.
The only emperor is the emperor of ice-cream.

Take from the dresser of deal,
Lacking the three glass knobs, that sheet   10
On which she embroidered fantails once
And spread it so as to cover her face.
If her horny feet protrude, they come
To show how cold she is, and dumb.
Let the lamp affix its beam.   15
The only emperor is the emperor of ice-cream.

    1922

                                              1923

[1] Lustful

PAINTING
AND MIXED MEDIA

American painters like Pollock
and Rothko were poets of the
visual process—inventors who
reconceived the act of painting
and drew audiences into new
participatorial relationships
with formal works of art. The
emerging schools of "pop art,"
on the other hand, brought a
determinedly objectivizing eye
to bear on American
commercial culture, forcing
fresh awareness of its content
into the public consciousness.

New York Movie, Edward Hopper, 1939.
(Collection, Museum of Modern Art)

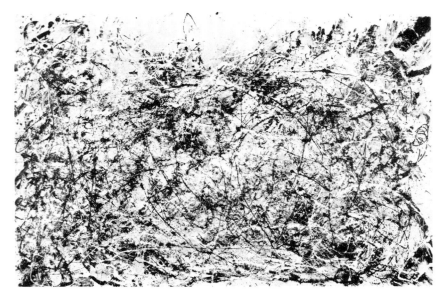

Number 1, Jackson Pollock, 1948.
(Collection, Museum of Modern Art)

Chief, Franz Kline, 1950.
*(Collection, Museum of Modern Art,
Gift of Mr. and Mrs. David M. Solinger)*

Number 10, Mark Rothko, 1950.
*(Collection, Museum of Modern Art,
Gift of Philip Johnson)*

First Landing Jump, Robert Rauschenberg, 1961.
(Collection, Museum of Modern Art, Gift of Philip Johnson)

Gold Marilyn Monroe, Andy Warhol, 1962.
(Collection, Museum of Modern Art, Gift of Philip Johnson)

MARIANNE MOORE

(1887–1972)

Marianne Moore wanted to be, as she says in "Poetry," "a literalist of the imagination" who would produce poems that had "imaginary gardens with real toads in them." She was born in Kirkwood, Missouri, near St. Louis, and studied at Bryn Mawr College, from which she was graduated in 1909, and at a business school in Carlisle, Pennsylvania. She was head of the Commercial Department of the Carlisle Indian School from 1911 to 1915 and then began to publish her poems in *Poetry, The Egoist,* and other journals. Her first volume, *Poems,* was published in 1921; her second, *Observations* (1925), won the *Dial* award; shortly after she became an editor of the *Dial* and remained one until 1929. Her *Collected Poems* (1951) won the Pulitzer Prize, the Bollingen Award, and the National Book Award. In 1967, the *Complete Poems* was published. She has also published *Predilections* (1955), a volume of critical essays, and translations of *The Fables of La Fontaine* (1954).

The poet selected the prose and poetry for *A Marianne Moore Reader,* 1961. Individual volumes of poems include: *Poems,* 1921; *Marriage,* 1923; *The Pangolin and Other Verse,* 1936; *What are Years,* 1941; *Nevertheless,* 1944; *A Face,* 1949; *Like a Bulwark,* 1956; *O To Be a Dragon,* 1959; and *Tell Me, Tell Me: Granite, Steel, and Other Topics,* 1966. Her own criticism appears in *Predilections,* 1955 and *Poetry and Criticism,* 1965. She also has done some translations: *The Fables of La Fontaine,* 1954; and *Selected Fables,* 1955. An early study is B. F. Engel, *Marianne Moore,* 1963. Recent critical studies of the poetry include George W. Nitchie, *Marianne Moore: An Introduction to the Poetry,* 1969; and Donald Hall, *Marianne Moore: The Cage and the Animal,* 1970. Gary Lane edited *A Concordance to the Poems of Marianne Moore,* 1972.

For a full list of essays and reviews written until 1958, see *The Achievement of Marianne Moore: A Bibliography, 1907–1957,* ed. by E. P. Sheehy and A. Lohf, 1958.

Poetry

I, too, dislike it: there are things that are important beyond all this
　　　　fiddle.
　　Reading it, however, with a perfect contempt for it, one discovers
　　　　in
　　it after all, a place for the genuine.
　　　　Hands that can grasp, eyes
　　　　that can dilate, hair that can rise
　　　　　if it must, these things are important not because a　　　　　5

high-sounding interpretation can be put upon them but because they
    are
useful. When they become so derivative as to become
    unintelligible,
the same thing may be said for all of us, that we
    do not admire what   10
    we cannot understand: the bat
        holding on upside down or in quest of something to

eat, elephants pushing, a wild horse taking a roll, a tireless wolf under
a tree, the immovable critic twitching his skin like a horse that feels
    a flea, the base-
ball fan, the statistician—   15
    nor is it valid
        to discriminate against 'business documents and

school-books'; all these phenomena are important. One must make a
    distinction
however: when dragged into prominence by half poets, the result is
    not poetry,
nor till the poets among us can be   20
    'literalists of
    the imagination'—above
        insolence and triviality and can present

for inspection, imaginary gardens with real toads in them, shall we
    have
it. In the meantime, if you demand on the one hand,   25
the raw material of poetry in
    all its rawness and
    that which is on the other hand
        genuine, then you are interested in poetry.

   1919

                        1921

No Swan So Fine

    "No water so still as the
        dead fountains of Versailles." No swan,
    with swart blind look askance
    and gondoliering legs, so fine
        as the chintz china one with fawn-   5
    brown eyes and toothed gold
    collar on to show whose bird it was.

Lodged in the Louis Fifteenth
candelabrum-tree of cockscomb-
tinted buttons, dahlias, 10
sea-urchins, and everlastings,
it perches on the branching foam
of polished sculptured
flowers—at ease and tall. The king is dead.

1932

1935

The Frigate Pelican

Rapidly cruising or lying on the air there is a bird
that realizes Rasselas's friend's project
of wings uniting levity with strength. This
hell-diver, frigate-bird, hurricane-
bird; unless swift is the proper word 5
for him, the storm omen when
he flies close to the waves, should be seen
fishing, although oftener
he appears to prefer
to take, on the wing, from industrious crude-winged 10
species
the fish they have caught, and is seldom successless.
A marvel of grace, no matter how fast his
victim may fly or how often may
turn. The others with similar ease, 15
slowly rising once more
move out to the top
of the circle and stop

and blow back, allowing the wind to reverse their direction— 20
Unlike the more stalwart swan that can ferry the
woodcutter's two children home. Make hay; keep
the shop; I have one sheep; were a less
limber animal's mottoes. This one
finds sticks for the swan's-down-dress 25
of his child to rest upon and would
not know Gretel from Hänsel.
As impassioned Handel—

meant for a lawyer and a masculine German domestic
  career—clandestinely studied the harpsichord   30
  and never was known to have fallen in love,
    the unconfiding frigate-bird hides
in the height and in the majestic
    display of his art. He glides
  a hundred feet or quivers about   35
    as charred paper behaves—full
    of feints; and an eagle

of vigilance. . . . *Festina lente.* Be gay
  civilly? How so? "If I do well I am blessed
  whether any bless me or not, and if I do   40
    ill I am cursed." We watch the moon rise
on the Susequehanna. In his way,
    this most romantic bird flies

to a more mundane place, the mangrove
  swamp to sleep. He wastes the moon.   45
    But he, others, soon
rise from the bough and though flying, are able to foil
    the tired
moment of danger that lays on heart and lungs the
weight of the python that crushes to powder.   50

  1934

                            1935

MELVIN TOLSON

(1900–1960)

Born in Moberly, Missouri, in 1900, Melvin Tolson was educated at
Fisk, Lincoln, and Columbia universities. He received his Master's Degree from Columbia and began to publish his poetry in the early
1940's. His work, collected in three volumes, tends to fuse an intellectual complexity and erudition with a social reality that is earthy and
colloquial. Karl Shapiro called attention to Tolson's significance when

Tolson's poetry is in *Rendezvous with
America*, 1944; *Libretto for the Republic
of Liberia*, 1953; and *Harlem Gallery*, 1965.

he remarked in a review of *Harlem Gallery* that "A great poet has been living in our midst and is almost totally unknown. . . ."
"Dark Symphony" is a forceful, early expression of black pride.

Dark Symphony

1
ALLEGRO MODERATO

Black Crispus Attucks[1] taught
        Us how to die
Before white Patrick Henry's[2] bugle breath
Uttered the vertical
        Transmitting cry: 5
"Yea, give me liberty or give me death."

Waifs of the auction block,
        Men black and strong
The juggernauts of despotism withstood,
Loin-girt with faith that worms   10
        Equate the wrong
And dust is purged to create brotherhood.

No Banquo's ghost can rise
        Against us now,
Aver we hobnailed Man beneath the brute,   15
Squeezed down the thorns of greed
        On Labor's brow,
Garroted lands and carted off the loot.

2
LENTO GRAVE

The centuries-old pathos in our voices
Saddens the great white world,   20
And the wizardry of our dusky rhythms
Conjures up shadow-shapes of ante-bellum years:

[1] Crispus Attucks (1723?-1770), American patriot who was killed by the British at the Boston Massacre. He was believed to be a runaway slave.

[2] Patrick Henry (1736-1799), American Revolutionary leader and orator.

Black slaves singing *One More River to Cross*
In the torture tombs of slave-ships,
Black slaves singing *Steal Away to Jesus*   25
In jungle swamps,
Black slaves singing *The Crucifixion*
In slave-pens at midnight,
Black slaves singing *Swing Low, Sweet Chariot*
In cabins of death,   30
Black slaves singing *Go Down, Moses*
In the canebrakes of the Southern Pharaohs.

3
ANDANTE SOSTENUTO

They tell us to forget
The Golgotha[3] we tread . . .
We who are scourged with hate,   35
A price upon our head.
They who have shackled us
Require of us a song,
They who have wasted us
Bid us condone the wrong.   40

They tell us to forget
Democracy is spurned.
They tell us to forget
The Bill of Rights is burned.
Three hundred years we slaved,   45
We slave and suffer yet:
Though flesh and bone rebel,
They tell us to forget!

Oh, how can we forget
Our human rights denied?   50
Oh, how can we forget
Our manhood crucified?
When Justice is profaned
And plea with curse is met,
When Freedom's gates are barred,   55
Oh, how can we forget?

[3] The hill of Calvary, where Jesus was crucified.

4
TEMPO PRIMO

The New Negro strides upon the continent
In seven-league boots . . .
The New Negro
Who sprang from the vigor-stout loins   60
Of Nat Turner, gallows-martyr for Freedom,
Of Joseph Cinquez, Black Moses of the Amistad Mutiny,
Of Frederick Douglass, oracle of the Catholic Man,
Of Sojourner Truth, eye and ear of Lincoln's legions.
Of Harriet Tubman, Saint Bernard of the Underground Railroad.   65

The New Negro
Breaks the icons of his detractors,
Wipes out the conspiracy of silence,
Speak to *his* America:

"My history-moulding ancestors   70
Planted the first crops of wheat on these shores,
Built ships to conquer the seven seas,
Erected the Cotton Empire,
Flung railroads across a hemisphere,
Disemboweled the earth's iron and coal,   75
Tunneled the mountains and bridged rivers,
Harvested the grain and hewed forests,
Sentineled the Thirteen Colonies,
Unfurled Old Glory at the North Pole,
Fought a hundred battles for the Republic."   80

The New Negro:
His giant hands fling murals upon high chambers,
His drama teaches a world to laugh and weep,
His music leads continents captive,
His voice thunders the Brotherhood of Labor,   85
His science creates seven wonders.
His Republic of Letters challenges the Negro-baiters.

The New Negro,
Hard-muscled, Fascist-hating, Democracy-ensouled,
Strides in seven-league boots   90
Along the Highway of Today
Toward the Promised Land of Tomorrow!

5
LARGHETTO

None in the Land can say
To us black men Today:
You send the tractors on their bloody path,   95
And create Okies for *The Grapes of Wrath.*
You breed the slum that breeds a *Native Son*
To damn the good earth Pilgrim Fathers won.

None in the Land can say
To us black men Today: 100
You dupe the poor with rags-to-riches tales,
And leave the workers empty dinner pails.
You stuff the ballot box, and honest men
Are muzzled by your demagogic din.

None in the Land can say   105
To us black men Today:
You smack stock markets with your coined blitzkriegs,
And make a hundred million guinea pigs.
You counterfeit our Christianity,
And bring contempt upon Democracy.   110

None in the Land can say
To us black men Today:
You prowl when citizens are fast asleep,
And hatch Fifth Column plots to blast the deep
Foundations of the State and leave the Land   115
A vast Sahara with a Fascist brand.

6
TEMPO DI MARCIA

Out of abysses of Illiteracy,
Through labyrinths of Lies,
Across waste lands of Disease . . .
We advance!   120

Out of dead-ends of Poverty,
Through wildernesses of Superstition,
Across barricades of Jim Crowism . . .
We advance!

With the Peoples of the World . . .   125
We advance!

1944

GWENDOLYN BROOKS

(1917–   )

Gwendolyn Brooks established her reputation with the publication of *A Street in Bronzeville* (1945), for which she received a Guggenheim Award, and *Annie Allen* (1949), for which she received the Pulitzer Prize. In these books of poems—as well as in *Bronzeville Boys and Girls* (1956), *The Bean Eaters* (1960), *Selected Poems* (1963), *In the Mecca* (1968), and *Riot* (1969)—Brooks expresses her bittersweet view of human nature with what she has called "the concentration, the crush" of contemporary fact.

Gwendolyn Brooks tends to work in cameo fashion, choosing limited, colloquial subjects and informing them with universal implications. There is a toughness in her early poetry, controlled by the lyrical impulse and modified by a persistent, mocking humor. In recent years, Brooks has become more overtly militant, and the poetry is rougher, more blunt, angrier, and more hostile to the white world.

Brooks has also written a novel, *Maud Martha*, 1953, and an autobiography. An interesting essay is by Arthur P. Davis, "The Black and Tan Motif in the Poetry of Gwendolyn Brooks," *CLA Journal*, VI (December 1962), 90–97.

FROM THE WOMANHOOD

THE CHILDREN OF THE POOR

1

People who have no children can be hard:
Attain a mail of ice and insolence:
Need not pause in the fire, and in no sense
Hesitate in the hurricane to guard.
And when wide world is bitten and bewarred   5
They perish purely, waving their spirits hence
Without a trace of grace or of offense
To laugh or fail, diffident, wonder-starred.
While through a throttling dark we others hear
The little lifting helplessness, the queer   10
Whimper-whine; whose unridiculous
Lost softness softly makes a trap for us.

And makes a curse. And makes a sugar of
The malocclusions, the inconditions of love.

2

What shall I give my children? who are poor,   15
Who are adjudged the leastwise of the land,
Who are my sweetest lepers, who demand
No velvet and no velvety velour;
But who have begged me for a brisk contour,
Crying that they are quasi, contraband   20
Because unfinished, graven by a hand
Less than angelic, admirable or sure.
My hand is stuffed with mode, design, device.
But I lack access to my proper stone.
And plenitude of plan shall not suffice   25
Nor grief nor love shall be enough alone
To ratify my little halves who bear
Across an autumn freezing everywhere.

3

And shall I prime my children, pray, to pray?
Mites, come invade most frugal vestibules   30
Spectered with crusts of penitents' renewals
And all hysterics arrogant for a day.
Instruct yourselves here is no devil to pay.
Children, confine your lights in jellied rules;
Resemble graves; be metaphysical mules;   35
Learn Lord will not distort nor leave the fray.
Behind the scurryings of your neat motif
I shall wait, if you wish: revise the psalm
If that should frighten you: sew up belief
If that should tear: turn, singularly calm   40
At forehead and at fingers rather wise,
Holding the bandage ready for your eyes.

4

First fight. Then fiddle. Ply the slipping string
With feathery sorcery; muzzle the note
With hurting love; the music that they wrote   45
Bewitch, bewilder. Qualify to sing
Threadwise. Devise no salt, no hempen thing
For the dear instrument to bear. Devote
The bow to silks and honey. Be remote

A while from malice and from murdering. 50
But first to arms, to armor. Carry hate
In front of you and harmony behind.
Be deaf to music and to beauty blind.
Win war. Rise bloody, maybe not too late
For having first to civilize a space 55
Wherein to play your violin with grace.

5

When my dears die, the festival-colored brightness
That is their motion and mild repartee
Enchanted, a macabre mockery
Charming the rainbow radiance into tightness 60
And into a remarkable politeness
That is not kind and does not want to be,
May not they in the crisp encounter see
Something to recognize and read as rightness?
I say they may, so granitely discreet, 65
The little crooked questionings inbound,
Concede themselves on most familiar ground,
Cold an old predicament on the breath:
Adroit, the shapely prefaces complete,
Accept the university of death. 70

1949

We Real Cool

THE POOL PLAYERS.
SEVEN AT THE GOLDEN SHOVEL.

We real cool. We
Left school. We

Lurk late. We
Strike straight. We

Sing sin. We 5
Thin gin. We

Jazz June. We
Die soon.

1960

The Chicago Defender Sends a Man to Little Rock

Fall, 1957

In Little Rock the people bear
Babes, and comb and part their hair
And watch the want ads, put repair
To roof and latch. While wheat toast burns
A woman waters multiferns.   5

Time upholds or overturns
The many, tight, and small concerns.

In Little Rock the people sing
Sunday hymns like anything,
Through Sunday pomp and polishing.   10

And after testament and tunes,
Some soften Sunday afternoons
With lemon tea and Lorna Doones.

I forecast
And I believe   15
Come Christmas Little Rock will cleave
To Christmas tree and trifle, weave,
From laugh and tinsel, texture fast.

In Little Rock is baseball; Barcarolle.
That hotness in July . . . the uniformed figures raw and implacable   20
And not intellectual,
Batting the hotness or clawing the suffering dust.
The Open Air Concert, on the special twilight green. . . .
When Beethoven is brutal or whispers to lady-like air.
Blanket-sitters are solemn, as Johann troubles to lean   25
To tell them what to mean. . . .

There is love, too, in Little Rock. Soft women softly
Opening themselves in kindness,
Or, pitying one's blindness,
Awaiting one's pleasure   30
In azure
Glory with anguished rose at the root. . . .
To wash away old semi-discomfitures.
They re-teach purple and unsullen blue.

The wispy soils go. And uncertain   35
Half-havings have they clarified to sures.

In Little Rock they know
Not answering the telephone is a way of rejecting life,
That it is our business to be bothered, is our business
To cherish bores or boredom, be polite   40
To lies and love and many-faceted fuzziness.
I scratch my head, massage the hate-I-had.
I blink across my prim and pencilled pad.
The saga I was sent for is not down.
Because there is a puzzle in this town.   45
The biggest News I do not dare
Telegraph to the Editor's chair:
"They are like people everywhere."

The angry Editor would reply
In hundred harryings of Why.   50

And true, they are hurling spittle, rock,
Garbage and fruit in Little Rock.
And I saw coiling storm a-writhe
On bright madonnas. And a scythe
Of men harassing brownish girls.   55
(The bows and barrettes in the curls
And braids declined away from joy.)

I saw a bleeding brownish boy. . . .

The lariat lynch-wish I deplored.

The loveliest lynchee was our Lord.   60

1960

RANDALL JARRELL

(1914-1965)

A highly affecting volume of tribute to Randall Jarrell appeared shortly after his death, and the point his friends seemed most anxious to make was that he had an instinct for the "exceptional thing," the work of rare quality, in an extraordinary variety of fields. A witty, acerb, virtuoso performer, inexhaustibly knowledgeable (about painting, music, literature, cars, football, cats, you name it), he remarked once what a great pleasure it was to have a conversation with "someone who knows more than I do about a subject I'm interested in." He was an acute critic with a wonderful aptitude for relishing individual poems; in addition to a large body of memorable poetry, he wrote several excellent children's books and the funniest and shrewdest novel of academic life yet produced in this country. And his assumption seemed to be that his own eye for the rare and the perfected was in itself nothing especially unique; he appeared to believe, said Hannah Arendt, that "everybody he came in contact with had his own absolute feeling (like absolute pitch) for quality."

All the more curious, then, that Jarrell's best writing celebrates the *un*exceptional, focuses on life not at the edges of transcendence but at its homely centers. Jarrell is the American poet of dailiness, and the people in his poems are ordinary, middle class, moderately intelligent, moderately sensitive, reasonably neurotic, likeably bare of pretension. ". . . I identify myself, as always," says a voice in one poem,

> With something that there's something wrong with,
> With something human.

And "the human" is most at home in the world of habit and domesticity.

The books of poetry are *The Rage for the Lost Penny*, 1940; *Blood for a Stranger*, 1942; *Little Friend, Little Friend*, 1945; *Losses*, 1948; *The Seven-League Crutches*, 1951; *Selected Poems*, 1st ed. 1955, 2nd ed. including *The Woman at the Washington Zoo*, 1964; *The Woman at the Washington Zoo*, 1960; *The Lost World*, 1965; and *The Collected Poems*, 1969. Jarrell's comic novel is *Pictures from an Institution, A Comedy*, 1954. His criticism is *Poetry and the Age*, 1953; *A Sad Heart at the Supermarket*, 1962; and *The Third Book of Criticism*, 1965.

Two good bibliographies are Charles M. Adams, *Randall Jarrell: A Bibliography*, 1958; and Karl Shapiro, *Randall Jarrell*, 1967. *Randall Jarrell, 1914-1965*, was edited by Robert Lowell, Peter Taylor, and Robert Penn Warren. See also Suzanne Ferguson, *The Poetry of Randall Jarrell*, 1971 and M. L. Rosenthal, *Randall Jarrell*, 1972.

A girl hesitates a moment in mid-air
And settles to the ground a wife, a mother.
Each evening a tired spirit visits
Her full house; wiping his feet upon a mat
Marked *Women and Children First,* the husband looks
At this grown woman. She stands there in slacks
Among the real world's appliances,
Women, and children; kisses him hello
Just as, that morning, she kissed him goodbye,
And he sits down, till dinner, with the paper.
This home of theirs is haunted by a girl's
Ghost. At sunset a woodpecker knocks
At a tree by the window, asking their opinion
Of life. The husband answers, "Life is life,"
And when his wife calls to him from the kitchen
He tells her who it was, and what he wanted.
Beating the whites of seven eggs, the beater
Asks her her own opinion; she says, "Life
Is life." "See how it sounds to say it isn't,"
The beater tempts her. "Life is not life,"
She says. It sounds the same. . . .

The "celebration" of dailiness has its undercurrents of irony. Jarrell observes in another poem that "the ways we miss our lives are life," and the small failures, the dominance of the routine and the undramatic and the downright dull can bring on desperation that cries out, with the "Woman at the Washington Zoo," "Change me, Change me!" But while the poet isn't oblivious to "domestic horror,"—common losses and common pains—he is not obsessed with it. Always alert to the possibility of the irradiation of ordinary life, of small transformations, transcendencies, he makes of that possibility the nerve of tension in poem after poem. Sadly, pityingly, the language registers the pain of being human—and simultaneously lifts itself into perception of joys implicit in that humanness. A hint of human connectedness, an unplanned event, a wayward insight—any or all of these suddenly disclose the "strange ordinariness," the "ordinary strangeness" of the world, surprising consciousness with views of life more magical and spacious than those we are accustomed to. And as you read Jarrell through you begin to sense a larger rhythm, in which the brevity of these openings-out matters less than their steady recurrence. (Adrienne Rich said of Jarrell that he had both a moral and a poetic "realization that virtue exists only in an accretion of particular acts, one of which makes possible the next.") In one of the last poems he wrote, the poet pretends that a woman he sees in the park is a stranger, someone who can change his life, change him, in some wondrous way. But then he drops the joke—the woman is his wife—and the years of shared experience are transformation enough.

> . . . Really I began the day
> Not with a man's wish: "May this day be different,"
> But with the birds' wish: "May this day
> Be the same day, the day of my life."

Jarrell received Bachelor's and Master's Degrees from Vanderbilt University and subsequently taught at various colleges: Kenyon (1937-1939), the University of Texas (1939-1942), Sarah Lawrence (1946-1947), Women's College of the University of North Carolina (1947-1951, 1953-1954), and the University of North Carolina at Greensboro (1961-1965). He was poetry critic for the *Nation, Partisan Review,* and the *Yale Review,* and Consultant in Poetry at the Library of Congress. His volumes of poetry include *Blood for a Stranger* (1942); *Little Friend, Little Friend* (1945); *Losses* (1948); *The Seven League Crutches* (1951); *Selected Poems* (1955); and *The Woman at the Washington Zoo* (1960, for which he won the National Book Award). His critical essays—notably detailed appreciations of contemporaries— were collected in *Poetry and the Age* (1953) and *Sad Heart at the Supermarket* (1962), and his first-rate novel of academic life, *Pictures from an Institution,* appeared in 1954. Jarrell also wrote three highly attractive children's books—*The Gingerbread Rabbit* (1963), *The Bat Poet* (1964), and *The Animal Family* (1965).

A Girl in a Library

An object among dreams, you sit here with your shoes off
And curl your legs up under you; your eyes
Close for a moment, your face moves toward sleep. . .
You are very human.
           But my mind, gone out in tenderness,   5
Shrinks from its object with a thoughtful sigh.
This is a waist the spirit breaks its arm on.
The gods themselves, against you, struggle in vain.
This broad low strong-boned brow; these heavy eyes;
These calves, grown muscular with certainties;   10
This nose, three medium-sized pink strawberries
—But I exaggerate. In a little you will leave:
I'll hear, half squeal, half shriek, your laugh of greeting—
Then, *decrescendo,* bars of that strange speech

In which each sound sets out to seek each other,   15
Murders its own father, marries its own mother,
And ends as one grand transcendental vowel.

(Yet for all I know, the Egyptian Helen[1] spoke so.)
As I look, the world contracts around you:
I see Brünnhilde[2] had brown braids and glasses   20
She used for studying; Salome[3] straight brown bangs,
A calf's brown eyes, and sturdy light-brown limbs
Dusted with cinnamon, an apple-dumplings' . . .
Many a beast has gnawn a leg off and got free,
Many a dolphin curved up from Necessity—   25
The trap has closed about you, and you sleep.
If someone questioned you, *What doest thou here?*
You'd knit your brows like an orangoutang
(But not so sadly; not so thoughtfully)
And answer with a pure heart, guilelessly: 30
I'm studying. . . .
                    If only you were not!
Assignments,
                    recipes,
                    the *Official Rulebook*   35
Of Basketball—ah, let them go; you needn't mind.
The soul has no assignments, neither cooks
Nor referees: it wastes its time.
                    It wastes its time.
Here in this enclave there are centuries   40
For you to waste: the short and narrow stream
Of Life meanders into a thousand valleys
Of all that was, or might have been, or is to be.
The books, just leafed through, whisper endlessly . . .
Yet it is hard. One sees in your blurred eyes   45
The "uneasy half-soul" Kipling[4] saw in dogs'.
One sees it, in the glass, in one's own eyes.
In rooms alone, in galleries, in libraries,
In tears, in searchings of the heart, in staggering joys

[1] In Greek mythology, Helen of Troy was the
daughter of Zeus and Leda, and the wife of
Menelaus. Her abduction by Paris caused the
Trojan War.

[2] Brunnhilde, heroine of Wagner's *Ring of
the Niebelung,* a Valkyrie who is placed in a
circle of fire by Wotan and is eventually released by Siegfried.

[3] Salome was the daughter of Herodias and
niece of Herod Antipas, who granted the
head of John the Baptist in return for her
dancing. See Matthew 14: 6-11.

[4] Rudyard Kipling (1865-1936), English author.

We memorize once more our old creation,
Humanity: with what yawns the unwilling
Flesh puts on its spirit, O my sister!

So many dreams! And not one troubles
Your sleep of life? no self stares shadowly
From these worn hexahedrons,[5] beckoning
With false smiles, tears? . . .
                        Meanwhile Tatyana
Larina (gray eyes nickel with the moonlight
That falls through the willows onto Lensky's tomb;
Now young and shy, now old and cold and sure)
Asks, smiling: "But what is she dreaming of, fat thing?"
I answer: She's not fat. She isn't dreaming.
She purrs or laps or runs, all in her sleep;
Believes, awake, that she is beautiful;
She never dreams.
                        Those sunrise-colored clouds
Around man's head—that inconceivable enchantment
From which, at sunset, we come back to life
To find our graves dug, families dead, selves dying:
Of all this, Tanya, she is innocent.
For nineteen years she's faced reality:
They look alike already.
                        They say, man wouldn't be
The best thing in this world—and isn't he?—
If he were not too good for it. But she
—She's good enough for it.
                        And yet sometimes
Her sturdy form, in its pink strapless formal,
Is as if bathed in moonlight—modulated
Into a form of joy, a Lydian mode;
This Wooden Mean's a kind, furred animal
That speaks, in the Wild of things, delighting riddles
To the soul that listens, trusting . . .
                        Poor senseless Life:
When, in the last light sleep of dawn, the messenger
Comes with his message, you will not awake.
He'll give his feathery whistle, shake you hard,
You'll look with wide eyes at the dewy yard
And dream, with calm slow factuality:
"Today's Commencement. My bachelor's degree

50

55

60

65

70

75

80

85

90

---

[5] A polyhedron with six faces.

In Home Ec., my doctorate of philosophy
In Phys. Ed.
          [Tanya, they won't even *scan*]
Are waiting for me. . . ."
                         Oh, Tatyana,   95
The Angel comes: better to squawk like a chicken
Than to say with truth, "But I'm a *good* girl,"
And Meet his Challenge with a last firm strange
Uncomprehending smile; and—then, then!—see
The blind date that has stood you up: your life.   100
(For all this, if it isn't, perhaps, life,
Has yet, at least, a language of its own
Different from the books'; worse than the books'.)
And yet, the ways we miss our lives are life.
Yet . . . yet . . .   105
          to have one's life add up to *yet!*

You sigh a shuddering sigh. Tatyana murmurs,
"Don't cry, little peasant"; leaves us with a swift
"Good-bye, good-bye . . . Ah, don't think ill of me . . ."
Your eyes open: you sit here thoughtlessly.   110

I love you—and yet—and yet—I love you.

Don't cry, little peasant. Sit and dream.
One comes, a finger's width beneath your skin,
To the braided maidens singing as they spin;
There sound the shepherd's pipe, the watchman's rattle   115
Across the short dark distance of the years.
I am a thought of yours: and yet, you do not think . . .
The firelight of a long, blind, dreaming story
Lingers upon your lips; and I have seen
Firm, fixed forever in your closing eyes,   120
The Corn King beckoning to his Spring Queen.

                                                    1951

THE LOST CHILDREN

Two little girls, one fair, one dark,
One alive, one dead, are running hand in hand
Through a sunny house. The two are dressed
In red and white gingham, with puffed sleeves and sashes.

THE LOST CHILDREN

They run away from me . . . But I am happy;   5
When I wake I feel no sadness, only delight.
I've seen them again, and I am comforted
That, somewhere, they still are.

It is strange
To carry inside you someone else's body;   10
To know it before it's born;
To see at last that it's a boy or girl, and perfect;
To bathe it and dress it; to watch it
Nurse at your breast, till you almost know it
Better than you know yourself—better than it knows itself.   15
You own it as you made it.
You are the authority upon it.

But as the child learns
To take care of herself, you know her less.
Her accidents, adventures are her own,   20
You lose track of them. Still, you know more
About her than anyone *except* her.

Little by little the child in her dies.
You say, "I have lost a child, but gained a friend."
You feel yourself gradually discarded.   25
She argues with you or ignores you
Or is kind to you. She who begged to follow you
Anywhere, just so long as it was you,
Finds follow the leader no more fun.
She makes few demands; you are grateful for the few.   30

The young person who writes once a week
Is the authority upon herself.
She sits in my living room and shows her husband
My albums of her as a child. He enjoys them
And makes fun of them. I look too   35
And I realize the girl in the matching blue
Mother-and-daughter dress, the fair one carrying
The tin lunch box with the half-pint thermos bottle
Or training her pet duck to go down the slide
Is lost just as the dark one, who is dead, is lost.   40
But the world in which the two wear their flared coats
And the hats that match, exists so uncannily
That, after I've seen its picture for an hour,
I believe in it: the bandage coming loose
One has in the picture of the other's birthday,   45
The castles they are building, at the beach for asthma.

I look at them and all the old sure knowledge
Floods over me, when I put the album down
I keep saying inside: *"I did* know those children.
I braided those braids. I was driving the car   50
The day that she stepped in the can of grease
We were taking to the butcher for our ration points.
I *know* those children. I know all about them.
Where are they?"

I stare at her and try to see some sign   55
Of the child she was. I can't believe there isn't any.
I tell her foolishly, pointing at the picture,
That I keep wondering where she is.
She tells me, "Here I am."
                      Yes, and the other   60
Isn't dead, but has everlasting life . . .
The girl from next door, the borrowed child,
Said to me the other day, "You like children so much,
Don't you want to have some of your own?"
I couldn't believe that she could say it.   65
I thought: "Surely you can look at me and see them."

When I see them in my dreams I feel such joy.
If I could dream of them every night!

When I think of my dream of the little girls
It's as if we were playing hide-and-seek.   70
The dark one
Looks at me longingly, and disappears;
The fair one stays in sight, just out of reach
No matter where I reach. I am tired
As a mother who's played all day, some rainy day.   75
I don't want to play it any more, I don't want to,
But the child keeps on playing, so I play.

                                1965

Well Water

What a girl called "the dailiness of life"
(Adding an errand to your errand. Saying,
"Since you're up . . ." Making you a means to
A means to a means to) is well water
Pumped from an old well at the bottom of the world.   5

The pump you pump the water from is rusty
And hard to move and absurd, a squirrel-wheel
A sick squirrel turns slowly, through the sunny
Inexorable hours. And yet sometimes
The wheel turns of its own weight, the rusty   10
Pump pumps over your sweating face the clear
Water, cold, so cold! you cup your hands
And gulp from them the dailiness of life.

1965

Bats

A bat is born
Naked and blind and pale.
His mother makes a pocket of her tail
And catches him. He clings to her long fur
By his thumbs and toes and teeth.   5
And then the mother dances through the night
Doubling and looping, soaring, somersaulting—
Her baby hangs on underneath.
All night, in happiness, she hunts and flies.
Her high sharp cries   10
Like shining needlepoints of sound
Go out into the night and, echoing back,
Tell her what they have touched.
She hears how far it is, how big it is,
Which way it's going: 15
She lives by hearing.
The mother eats the moths and gnats she catches
In full flight; in full flight
The mother drinks the water of the pond
She skims across. Her baby hangs on tight.   20
Her baby drinks the milk she makes him
In moonlight or starlight, in mid-air.
Their single shadow, printed on the moon
Or fluttering across the stars,
Whirls on all night; at daybreak   25
The tired mother flaps home to her rafter.
The others all are there.
They hang themselves up by their toes,
They wrap themselves in their brown wings.
Bunched upside-down, they sleep in air.   30

Their sharp ears, their sharp teeth, their quick sharp faces
Are dull and slow and mild.
All the bright day, as the mother sleeps,
She folds her wings about her sleeping child.

1965

Moving

Some of the sky is grey and some of it is white.
The leaves have lost their heads
And are dancing round the tree in circles, dead;
The cat is in it.
A smeared, banged, tow-headed   5
Girl in a flowered, flour-sack print
Sniffles and holds up her last bite
Of bread and butter and brown sugar to the wind.

Butter the cat's paws
And bread the wind. We are moving.   10
I shall never again sing
Good morning, Dear Teacher, to my own dear teacher.
Never again
Will Augusta be the capital of Maine.
The dew has rusted the catch of the strap of my satchel   15
And the sun has fallen from the place where it was chained
With a blue construction-paper chain. . . .
Someone else must draw the bow
And the blunderbuss, the great gobbler
Upside-down under the stone arrow   20
In the black, bell-brimmed hat—
And the cattycornered bat.
The witch on the blackboard
Says: "Put the Plough into the Wagon
Before it turns into a Bear and sleeps all winter   25
In your play-house under the catalpa."
Never again will Orion
Fall on my speller through the star
Taped on the broken window by my cot.
My knee is ridged like corn   30
And the scab peels off it.

We are going to live in a new pumpkin
Under a gold star.

There is not much else.
The wind blows somewhere else.   35
The brass bed bobs to the van.
The broody hen
Squawks upside-down—her eggs are boiled:
The cat is dragged from the limb.
The little girl   40
Looks over the shoulders of the moving-men
At her own street;
And, yard by lot, it changes.
Never again.
But she feels her tea-set with her elbow   45
And inches closer to her mother;
Then she shuts her eyes, and sits there, and squashed red
Circles and leaves like colored chalk
Come on in her dark head
And are darkened, and float farther   50
And farther and farther from the stretched-out hands
That float out from her in her broody trance:
She hears her own heart and her cat's heart beating.

She holds the cat so close to her he pants.

1948

The Death of the Ball Turret Gunner

From my mother's sleep I fell into the State,
And I hunched in its belly till my wet fur froze.
Six miles from earth, loosed from its dream of life,
I woke to black flak and the nightmare fighters.
When I died they washed me out of the turret with a hose.   5

1945

Eighth Air Force

If, in an odd angle of the hutment,
A puppy laps the water from a can
Of flowers, and the drunk sergeant shaving
Whistles O *Paradiso!*—shall I say that man
Is not as men have said: a wolf to man?   5

The other murderers troop in yawning;
Three of them play Pitch, one sleeps, and one
Lies counting missions, lies there sweating
Till even his heart beats: One; One; One.
O murderers! . . . Still, this is how it's done: 10

This is a war. . . . But since these play, before they die,
Like puppies with their puppy; since, a man,
I did as these have done, but did not die—
I will content the people as I can
And give up these to them: Behold the man!   15

I have suffered, in a dream, because of him,
Many things; for this last saviour, man,
I have lied as I lie now. But what is lying?
Men wash their hands, in blood, as best they can:
I find no fault in this just man.   20

1948

FIGURES OF THE FICTIONIST

ERNEST HEMINGWAY

(1899–1961)

Born in 1899, a doctor's son, thoroughly middle class in background
and origins, Ernest Hemingway wrote and lived in a manner remote
from the respectabilities of his hometown—Oak Park, Illinois. "The

The novels are *The Sun Also Rises*, 1926; *A Farewell to Arms*, 1929; *To Have and Have Not*, 1937; *For Whom the Bell Tolls*, 1940; *Across the River and into the Trees*, 1950; and *The Old Man and the Sea*, 1952. *Islands in the Stream*, 1970 was published posthumously. The stories and a play (Footnote continued next page.)

wonder to me," said one of his teachers after her pupil had won his fame, "is how a boy brought up in Christian and Puritan surroundings should know and write so well of the devil and the underworld." Hemingway may or may not have made a start at learning about "the devil and the underworld" in 1917, when he went to work for the Kansas City *Star.* But it was while he was on this paper that he developed his distinctive style. "Use short sentences," read the paper's style sheet. "Use short first paragraphs. Use vigorous English. Be positive, not negative. Never use old slang. . . . Avoid the use of adjectives, especially such extravagant ones as splendid, gorgeous. . . ." The young reporter simultaneously heeded these injunctions and transformed them by his own sense of rhythm and feeling for the purity of words as objects: a style was born.

Eager to leave the Midwest for adventure or war, Hemingway volunteered to serve in the Red Cross Ambulance Corps in Italy. In July 1918 he was wounded and sent to a hospital in Milan. The experience appears and reappears in his work—in "In Another Country," "The Way You Are," *A Farewell to Arms*, and *Across the River and into the Trees;* it is the locus of Hemingway's preoccupations with stoical courage and death. After the war, Hemingway returned to the United States but found it impossible to accommodate himself to the bland routines of hometown life. He took a job on the *Toronto Star,* married in 1921, and once again left for Europe, this time for Paris and an expatriate colony that included, among other writers, Gertrude Stein and Ezra Pound

have been included in *The Fifth Column and the First Forty-Nine Stories. The Torrents of Spring,* 1926 is, in part, a satire of Sherwood Anderson. Nonfiction includes *Death in the Afternoon,* 1932 and *Green Hills of Africa,* 1935. Recent nonfiction is *The Wild Years,* ed. Gene Z. Hanrahan, 1962, 73 articles Hemingway wrote for *The Toronto Star; A Moveable Feast,* 1964; *By-Line: Ernest Hemingway, Selected Articles and Dispatches of Four Decades,* 1967, ed. William White; *Ernest Hemingway: Cub Reporter. Kansas City Star Stories,* ed. M. Bruccoli, 1970; *Ernest Hemingway's Apprenticeship,* ed. M. Bruccoli, 1971.

A bibliography is Audre Hanneman, *Ernest Hemingway: A Comprehensive Bibliography,* 1973.

The standard biography is Carlos Baker, *Ernest Hemingway: A Life Story,* 1969. Good early criticism is Philip Young, *Er-* *nest Hemingway,* 1952; Carlos Baker, *Hemingway: The Writer as Artist,* 1952, enlarged, 1963; and Charles Fenton, *The Apprenticeship of Ernest Hemingway,* 1954. Recent criticism includes John Killinger, *Hemingway and the Dead Gods,* 1960; Stewart Sanderson, *Hemingway,* 1961; Joseph DeFalco, *The Hero in Hemingway's Short Stories,* 1963; Earl Rovit, *Ernest Hemingway,* 1963; Sheridan Baker, *Ernest Hemingway,* 1967; Robert O. Stephens, *Hemingway's Non-Fiction: The Public Voice,* 1968; Nicholas Joost, *Ernest Hemingway and the Little Magazines,* 1968; Richard B. Hovey, *Hemingway: The Inward Terrain,* 1969; Emily Watts, *Ernest Hemingway and the Arts,* 1968; Delbert Wylder, *Hemingway's Heroes,* 1970; Arthur Waldhorn, *A Reader's Guide to Ernest Hemingway,* 1972; and Sheldon Grebstein, *Hemingway's Craft,* 1973. See also *A Collection of Critical Essays,* ed. Robert W. Weeks, 1962.

(each helped to shape Hemingway's angle of vision), F. Scott Fitzgerald, and Archibald MacLeish. During this period Hemingway produced his richest work. *Three Stories and Ten Poems* appeared in 1923; *In Our Time*, war stories, a year later; *The Sun Also Rises*, still the most affecting account of the "lost generation" in Paris, was published in 1926; and *A Farewell to Arms* three years later.

Hemingway's work is easily parodied and his life is easily caricatured; both are smutched by adolescent posturing and obsession with virility, and by wariness of "refinement," "poetic sensitivity," "elevated taste." Beneath the posturing, however, lay a wholly honorable determination to do what genteel folk all too rarely do: call a spade a spade, grant right names to things. In Hemingway's view half the hells of existence derived from the willful—maybe even loony—impulse to prettify, to decorate disaster, to pretend that all that was needed to bring forth light and order from chaos and murder was some airy moral pronouncement.

> I was always embarrassed by the words sacred, glorious, and sacrifice and the expression in vain. We had heard them, sometimes standing in the rain almost out of earshot, so that only the shouted words came through, and had read them, on proclamations that were slapped up by billposters over other proclamations, now for a long time, and I had seen nothing sacred, and the things that were glorious had no glory and the sacrifices were like the stockyards at Chicago if nothing was done with the meat except to bury it. There were many words that you could not stand to hear and finally only the names of places had dignity . . . . Abstract words such as glory, honor, courage, or hallow were obscene beside the concrete names of villages, the numbers of roads, the names of rivers, the numbers of regiments and the dates. (*A Farewell to Arms*)

As that last sentence suggests, the ground of this writer's repugnance for high-minded literary hogwash was his experience of the first world war.

Faced with a world accustomed to using words as veneer, conventional covering for truths of feeling, what could a writer do? His only decent job of work was that of discovering "truly what you really felt, rather than what you were supposed to feel." On this assumption Hemingway founded his extraordinarily influential style, a spare, speaking idiom absorbed with the "actual thing" and the "actual process"—how to put up a tent, what love is like for a hired girl, the skier's first run down the mountainside, the taste of straight, homely food.

> The beer was very cold and wonderful to drink. The *pommes á l'huile* were firm and marinated and the olive oil delicious. I ground black pepper over the potatoes and moistened the bread in the olive oil. After the first heavy draft of beer I drank and ate very slowly.

In course of doing homage to things, Hemingway does dirt continually on pretension and abstraction. The result, on one page, is an embarrassingly weighted contrast between a European's cultural chitchat and an American's serious discussion of how to track an antelope (*Green Hills of Africa*); on another it's a laconic explanation, by a lieutenant, that he's abandoned the anti-Fascist cause because it's "not my show any more." A more troubling result is the narrowing of sensibility. The author of *The First Forty-Nine Stories* likes simple, even unpromising characters—fishermen, boxers, bullfighters, gangsters, innocent young men—people like the waiters in "A Clean Well-Lighted Place" who do not claim to be complicated, thoughtful, or articulate. For him the distinguished man is distinguished not by cultivation or intricacy of response but, instead, by mastery of craft or discipline—fishing, perhaps, or the perfectly grammatical Italian speech of the Major in "In Another Country." Like the Major, Hemingway's heroes are nearly always losers; their claim is only that they face their losses with stoicism and grace.

And, of course, by that style, by that eschewal of commonality, they rise to a level of life Hemingway understands to be Truly Aristocratic. The best among us are these who have escaped affectation, convention, dead morality, cowardice, solemnity. They cannot be intimidated by riches or rank, not even if they themselves happen by chance to possess both; they have arrived at standards of their own, achieved a release from smothering pieties, whether of money or morality.

Inevitably, Hemingway's values led him toward smugness and self-congratulation. More than once he dismisses, meanly, those who are not initiates (about Fitzgerald, "The mouth worried you until you knew him and then it worried you more"). Figures in his own novels (Robert Cohn in *The Sun Also Rises*) who fail to meet the master's mark, displaying defective self-awareness and discipline, are simply written off. And his capacity to keep alive his standards, through first-rate literary deeds, steadily declines. Hemingway's later work has moments of power and of wit. *Death in the Afternoon* (1932) and *The Green Hills of Africa* (1935), garrulous commentaries on bullfighting, hunting, and letters are intermittently entertaining: "The Snows of Kilimanjaro" (1936) and "The Short Happy Life of Francis Macomber" (1936), stories on heroic themes, are much reprinted; there is some good talk in *To Have and Have Not* (1937), a novel set in Cuba, and a posthumously published memoir of Paris, *A Moveable Feast* (1964), has charm. But other works—*For Whom the Bell Tolls* (1940), *Across the River and into the Trees* (1950), *The Old Man and the Sea* (1952), and the posthumous *Islands in the Stream* (1970)—are cursed by self-parody.

Yet the story is not finally one of limitations or failures. The human gift for idealization is no more remarkable, after all, than the human capacity for facing fact—pain, violence, greed, self-love, death. Hemingway's art was and remains restorative: a powerful reminder of the severity of the common human lot, and of the resources of humor, courage, and style that can be summoned to ease it. The artist won a Nobel Prize in 1954. Severely wounded in World War I, the survivor of two plane crashes and an automobile accident, veteran big game hunter and deep sea fisherman, he died by his own hand in Idaho in 1961.

A Clean, Well-Lighted Place

It was late and every one had left the café except an old man who sat in the shadow the leaves of the tree made against the electric light. In the day time the street was dusty, but at night the dew settled the dust and the old man liked to sit late because he was deaf and now at night it was quiet and he felt the difference. The two waiters inside the café knew that the old man was a little drunk, and while he was a good client they knew that if he became too drunk he would leave without paying, so they kept watch on him.

"Last week he tried to commit suicide," one waiter said.

"Why?"

"He was in despair."

"What about?"

"Nothing."

"How do you know it was nothing?"

"He has plenty of money."

They sat together at a table that was close against the wall near the door of the café and looked at the terrace where the tables were all empty except where the old man sat in the shadow of the leaves of the tree that moved slightly in the wind. A girl and a soldier went by in the street. The street light shone on the brass number on his collar. The girl wore no head covering and hurried beside him.

"The guard will pick him up," one waiter said.

"What does it matter if he gets what he's after?"

"He had better get off the street now. The guard will get him. They went by five minutes ago."

The old man sitting in the shadow rapped on his saucer with his glass. The younger waiter went over to him.

"What do you want?"

The old man looked at him. "Another brandy," he said.

"You'll be drunk," the waiter said. The old man looked at him. The waiter went away.

"He'll stay all night," he said to his colleague. "I'm sleepy now. I never get into bed before three o'clock. He should have killed himself last week."

The waiter took the brandy bottle and another saucer from the counter inside the café and marched out to the old man's table. He put down the saucer and poured the glass full of brandy.

"You should have killed yourself last week," he said to the deaf man. The old man motioned with his finger. "A little more," he said. The waiter poured on into the glass so that the brandy slopped over and ran down the stem into the top saucer of the pile. "Thank you," the old man said. The waiter took the bottle back inside the café. He sat down at the table with his colleague again.

"He's drunk now," he said.

"He's drunk every night."

"What did he want to kill himself for?"

"How should I know."

"How did he do it?"

"He hung himself with a rope."

"Who cut him down?"

"His niece."

"Why did they do it?"

"Fear for his soul."

"How much money has he got?"

"He's got plenty."

"He must be eighty years old."

"Anyway I should say he was eighty."

"I wish he would go home. I never get to bed before three o'clock. What kind of hour is that to go to bed?"

"He stays up because he likes it."

"He's lonely. I'm not lonely. I have a wife waiting in bed for me."

"He had a wife once too."

"A wife would be no good to him now."

"You can't tell. He might be better with a wife."

"His niece looks after him. You said she cut him down."

"I know."

"I wouldn't want to be that old. An old man is a nasty thing."

"Not always. This old man is clean. He drinks without spilling. Even now, drunk. Look at him."

"I don't want to look at him. I wish he would go home. He has no regard for those who must work."

The old man looked from his glass across the square, then over at the waiters.

"Another brandy," he said, pointing to his glass. The waiter who was in a hurry came over.

"Finished," he said, speaking with that omission of syntax stupid people employ when talking to drunken people or foreigners. "No more tonight. Close now."

"Another," said the old man.

"No. Finished." The waiter wiped the edge of the table with a towel and shook his head.

The old man stood up, slowly counted the saucers, took a leather coin purse from his pocket and paid for the drinks, leaving half a peseta tip.

The waiter watched him go down the street, a very old man walking unsteadily but with dignity.

"Why didn't you let him stay and drink?" the unhurried waiter asked. They were putting up the shutters. "It is not half-past two."

"I want to go home to bed."

"What is an hour?"

"More to me than to him."

"An hour is the same."

"You talk like an old man yourself. He can buy a bottle and drink at home."

"It's not the same."

"No, it is not," agreed the waiter with a wife. He did not wish to be unjust. He was only in a hurry.

"And you? You have no fear of going home before your usual hour?"

"Are you trying to insult me?"

"No, hombre, only to make a joke."

"No," the waiter who was in a hurry said, rising from pulling down the metal shutters. "I have confidence. I am all confidence."

"You have youth, confidence, and a job," the older waiter said. "You have everything."

"And what do you lack?"

"Everything but work."

"You have everything I have."

"No. I have never had confidence and I am not young."

"Come on. Stop talking nonsense and lock up."

"I am of those who like to stay late at the café," the older waiter said. "With all those who do not want to go to bed. With all those who need a light for the night."

"I want to go home and into bed."

"We are of two different kinds," the older waiter said. He was now dressed to go home. "It is not only a question of youth and confidence although those things are very beautiful. Each night I am reluctant to close up because there may be some one who needs the café."

"Hombre, there are bodegas open all night long."

"You do not understand. This is a clean and pleasant café. It is well lighted. The light is very good and also, now, there are shadows of the leaves."

"Good night," said the younger waiter.

"Good night," the other said. Turning off the electric light he continued the conversation with himself. It is the light of course but it is necessary that the place be clean and pleasant. You do not want music. Certainly you do not want music. Nor can you stand before a bar with dignity although that is all that is provided for these hours. What did he fear? It was not fear or dread. It was a nothing that he knew too well. It was all a nothing and a man was nothing too. It was only that and light was all it needed and a certain cleanness and order. Some lived in it and never felt it but he knew it all was nada y pues[1] nada y nada y pues nada. Our nada who art in nada, nada be they name thy kingdom nada they will be nada in nada as it is in nada. Give us this nada our daily nada and nada us our nada as we nada our nadas and nada us not into nada but deliver us from nada; pues nada. Hail nothing full of nothing, nothing is with thee. He smiled and stood before a bar with a shining steam pressure coffee machine.

"What's yours?" asked the barman.

"Nada."

"Otro loco mas," said the barman and turned away.

"A little cup," said the waiter.

The barman poured it for him.

"The light is very bright and pleasant but the bar is unpolished," the waiter said.

The barman looked at him but did not answer. It was too late at night for conversation.

"You want another copita?" the barman asked.

"No, thank you," said the waiter and went out. He disliked bars and bodegas. A clean, well-lighted café was a very different thing. Now, without thinking further, he would go home to his room. He would lie in the bed and finally, with daylight, he would go to sleep. After all, he said to himself, it is probably only insomnia. Many must have it.

---

[1] And then nothing, and then nothing.

WILLIAM FAULKNER

(1897–1962)

Faulkner is among those rare writers whose name begs to be wrapped in quotation marks—or accompanied with some other signal answering to the reader's need for a means of sorting out his richness, his contradiction, his variousness. "Faulkner" includes, to begin with, a

Faulkner's two books of poems are *The Marble Faun*, 1924 and *A Green Bough*, 1933. The novels are *Soldier's Pay*, 1926; *Mosquitoes*, 1927; *Sartoris*, 1929; *The Sound and the Fury*, 1929; *As I Lay Dying*, 1930; *Sanctuary*, 1931; *Light in August*, 1932; *Pylon*, 1935; *Absalom, Absalom!*, 1936; *The Unvanquished*, 1938; *The Wild Palms*, 1939; *The Hamlet*, 1940; *Go Down, Moses and Other Stories*, 1942; *Intruder in the Dust*, 1948; *Requiem for a Nun*, 1951; *A Fable*, 1954; *The Town*, 1957; *The Mansion*, 1959; and *The Reivers*, 1962. Collections of stories are *These Thirteen*, 1931; *Doctor Martino and Other Stories*, 1934; *Knight's Gambit*, 1949; and *Big Woods*, 1955. Faulkner's stories have been collected in *Collected Stories of William Faulkner*, 1950. Two good collections of Faulkner's work are *The Portable Faulkner*, ed. Malcolm Cowley, 1946, and *The Faulkner Reader*, ed. Saxe Commins, 1954. Carvel Collins edited *William Faulkner: New Orleans Sketches*, 1958 and *William Faulkner: Early Prose and Poetry*, 1962. Interviews have been collected in *Faulkner at Nagano*, ed. Robert A. Jeliffee, 1956; and *Faulkner in the University*, ed. Frederick L. Gwynn and Joseph L. Blotner, 1959. James Meriwether edited *Essays, Speeches and Public Lectures of William Faulkner*, 1965; Malcolm Cowley edited *The Faulkner-Cowley File: Letters and Memories 1944–1962*, 1966. A bibliography of Faulkner's work is *The Literary Career of William Faulkner: A Bibliographical Study*, ed. James Meriwether, 1961.

The most complete biography is Joseph L. Blotner, *William Faulkner*, 1973. There are interesting reminiscences in John Faulk-

ner, *My Brother Bill: An Affectionate Memoir*, 1963: and Murry C. Falkner, *The Falkners of Mississippi*, 1967. Other biographical information is included in James W. Webb and A. Wigfall Green, *William Faulkner of Oxford*, 1965; and Michael Millgate, *The Achievement of William Faulkner*, 1966.

Early criticism includes Irving Howe, *William Faulkner: A Critical Study*, 1952; William V. O'Connor, *The Tangled Fire of William Faulkner*, 1954; Harry Modean Campbell and Ruel E. Foster, *William Faulkner: A Critical Appraisal*, 1951. See also Frederick J. Hoffman and Olga W. Vickery, eds., *William Faulkner: Two Decades of Criticism*, 1951; and *William Faulkner: Three Decades of Criticism*, 1960.

Other critical studies are Olga W. Vickery, *The Novels of William Faulkner*, 1959, rev., 1964; Hyatt Waggoner, *William Faulkner, From Jefferson to the World*, 1959; Walter J. Slatoff, *Quest for Failure: A Study of William Faulkner*, 1960; John Lewis Longley, Jr., *The Tragic Mask: A Study of Faulkner's Heroes*, 1961; Charles Nilon, *Faulkner and the Negro*, 1962; Peter Swiggart, *The Art of Faulkner's Novels*, 1962; Lawrance Thompson, *William Faulkner: An Introduction and Interpretation*, 1963; Edmond L. Volpe, *A Reader's Guide to William Faulkner*, 1964; Cleanth Brooks, *William Faulkner: The Yoknapatawpha Country*, 1963; R. P. Warren, ed., *Faulkner: A Collection of Critical Essays*, 1966; R. P. Adams, *Faulkner: Myth and Motion*, 1968; Linda Wagner, ed., *William Faulkner: Four Decades of Criticism*, 1973.

poet of the heart's holiest domestic affections: in few places in letters does natural kindness and generosity flow more purely or more glowingly than between Benjy and Caddy in *The Sound and The Fury*. "Faulkner" also includes a mordant folk humorist-black comedian, a chronicler of the fantasies and dementia of a decaying society (genteel, Southern, awash in heroic epic and romance), a somewhat boozy lecturer on the theme of Man's Unconquerable Will, and an explorer out at the boundaries of modern literary form. We are speaking, in other words, of the American writer who is incontestably the greatest in this century.

Born in Oxford, Mississippi, the creator of Flem Snopes was almost ceaselessly preoccupied with his Southern background. A great-grandfather was Colonel William Cuthbert Faulkner, a lawyer, politician, and soldier, well-known in his day, who had traveled from Tennessee to northern Mississippi in 1839 and produced a romantic novel of his own (*The White Rose of Memphis*). A grandfather had been the president of the First National Bank in Oxford. Faulkner's own father (a social descent here) was the owner of a hardware store and later the business manager of the University of Mississippi. In short, Faulkner carried in his bones both the rich tradition and the complex ironies of his region, and his mind was soaked in local legends.

Briefly in Europe, as part of the Royal Flying Company at the end of World War I, Faulkner returned to Oxford in 1918, worked as postmaster of the University of Mississippi for 3 years, and published a book of poems, *The Marble Faun* (1924). Thereafter he began the struggle with fiction, in which he was encouraged by a young lawyer, Phil Stone, an enthusiast of experimentation. Two relatively conventional novels, *Soldier's Pay* (1926) and *Mosquitoes* (1927), were followed by a breakthrough in form and substance—*The Sound and the Fury* (1929), *As I Lay Dying* (1930), and *Light in August* (1932), novels that taken together with *The Hamlet* (1940) and *Go Down, Moses* (1942) represent the core of the artist's achievement.

While Faulkner traveled far on occasion from Oxford, Mississippi—to Europe, Hollywood, New York, and elsewhere—no journey ever laid an imaginative hand on him comparable in force to that of the homeplace. The subject in one phrase was Yoknapatawpha County, Mississippi and its inhabitants—an invented world enriched by remembered realities. More often than not the figures in the Yoknapatawpha fiction are poor, powerless, obsessed, ruined; always they are *local*. "I discovered that my own little postage stamp of native soil was worth writing about and that I would never live long enough to exhaust it . . . so I created a cosmos of my own. I can move these people around like God, not only in space, but in time too."

Who were "these people?" In the early books [*Sartoris* and *The Sound and the Fury* (1929)] they were either members of the old South's crumbling upper classes, or else that class's "enduring" black retainers. More and more, though, Faulkner seemed fascinated with the folk community, the ignorant, dirt-farming people of *The Hamlet* (1940). Few of the latter qualify as heroes or villains in any traditional sense; endurance, shrewdness, bitter energy are as likely to be found in a member of the rapacious, redneck Snopes clan as in the well-placed. A son abandons his vicious father and repudiates his destructive outlawry, yet all at once is briefly enobled by the longing to possess something worthy: "*Father. My father*, he thought. 'He was brave!' he cried suddenly, aloud but not loud, no more than a whisper: 'He was! He was in the war!' " A convict swept away in a Mississippi flood contends with weather, snakes, alligators, hunger, bears the responsibility of caring for a woman and her newborn child, and subsequently turns himself in to the authorities months later with the laconic words: "Yonder's your boat, and here's the woman. But I never did find that bastard on the cottonhouse." Geographically, socially, historically remote, Faulkner's people are tenants of a world almost impossibly bare of deference, grace, surplus; they and it—their world—are lean and mean, necessarily, almost to their core. But the wonder of human response does, indeed, survive. There is a moment in *The Hamlet* at which Mink Snopes, the most wretchedly unlucky of his clan, after committing a murder, drives his miserable wife and his children from his house. Then he witnesses a furtive return.

They were sitting on the floor in the corner, not crouched, not hiding, just sitting there in the dark as they had been sitting doubtless ever since he had watched them scuttle toward the house when he came out of the bottom, looking at him with that same quality which he himself possessed: not abject but just still, with an old tired wisdom, acceptance of the immitigable discrepancy between will and capability due to that handicap of physical size in which none of the three of them had had any choice, turning from him to look without curiosity at the blood on their mother's face and watching quietly as she took a garment from a nail on the wall and spread it on the pallet bed and wrapped the other objects—the other garments, the single pair of half-size shoes which either child wore indiscriminately in cold weather, the cracked hand-glass, the wooden comb, the handleless brush—into it. "Come," she said. He moved aside and they passed him, the children huddled against her skirt and for a moment hidden from him as they emerged from the room, then visible again, moving on up the hallway before her, he following, keeping that same distance, stopping again at the entrance while they crossed the porch and descended the warped and rotting steps. When she paused on the ground beyond the steps he moved again, again with that invincible, that weary implacability, until he saw and stopped also and watched the larger child hurry across the yard, soundless and incorporeal in the dusk which was almost night now, and snatch something from the ground and return, clasping the object—a wooden block with the tops of four snuff tins nailed to it like wheels—to its breast. They went on. He did not follow further. He did not even appear to be looking at them as they passed through the broken gate.

He returned to the house and blew out the lamp, whereupon the dark became complete, as if the puny vanishing flame had carried along with it all that remained of day. . . .

All the mystery of human attachment—and the incapacity of the least of us not somehow to be moved, inexpressibly, at the sight of it—rises from the page.

Faulkner's fondness for high-flown words (ineffaceable, ineluctable) can be jarring; equally so is his "ambition to put everything into one sentence—not only the present but the whole past on which it depends and which keeps overtaking the present." But the prose at its best gathers its reader into the writer's own rushing, vibrant possession of the wholeness of the human lives in which he is involved; the "difficult writing" comes to resemble the pressure of breathing in another body, articulating other limbs. A Nobel Prize winner in 1949, now and then a windy moralist and allegorist, Faulkner was in his best self a highly unpretentious, deeply private man who, as he once claimed, found it unreal that what he wrote would be read by anybody else. He died at home in Oxford, Mississippi, on July 16, 1962.

Mule in the Yard

It was a gray day in late January, though not cold because of the fog. Old Het, just walked in from the poorhouse, ran down the hall toward the kitchen, shouting in a strong, bright, happy voice. She was about seventy probably, though by her own counting, calculated from the ages of various housewives in the town from brides to grandmothers whom she claimed to have nursed in infancy, she would have to be around a hundred and at least triplets. Tall, lean, fog-beaded, in tennis shoes and a long rat-colored cloak trimmed with what forty or fifty years ago had been fur, a modish though not new purple toque set upon her headrag and carrying (time was when she made her weekly rounds from kitchen to kitchen carrying a brocaded carpetbag though since the advent of the ten-cent stores the carpetbag became an endless succession of the convenient paper receptacles with which they supply their customers for a few cents) the shoppingbag, she ran into the kitchen and shouted with strong and childlike pleasure: "Miss Mannie! Mule in de yard!"

Mrs. Hait, stooping to the stove, in the act of drawing from it a scuttle of live ashes, jerked upright; clutching the scuttle, she glared at old Het, then she too spoke at once, strong too, immediate. "Them sons of bitches," she said. She left the kitchen, not running exactly, yet with a kind of outraged celerity, carrying the scuttle—a compact woman of forty-odd, with an air of indomitable yet relieved bereavement, as though that which had relicted her had been a woman and a not particularly valuable one at that. She wore a calico wrapper and a sweater coat, and a man's felt hat which they in the town knew had belonged to her ten years' dead husband. But the man's shoes had not belonged to him. They were high shoes which buttoned, with toes like small tulip bulbs, and in the town they knew that she had bought them new for herself. She and old Het ran down the kitchen steps and into the fog. That's why it was not cold: as though there lay supine and prisoned between earth and mist the long winter night's suspiration of the sleeping town in dark, close rooms—the slumber and the rousing; the stale waking thermostatic, by re-heating heat-engendered: it lay like a scum of cold grease upon the steps and the wooden entrance to the basement and upon the narrow plank walk which led to a shed building in the corner of the yard: upon these planks, running and still carrying the scuttle of live ashes, Mrs. Hait skated viciously.

"Watch out!" old Het, footed securely by her rubber soles, cried happily. "Dey in de front!" Mrs. Hait did not fall. She did not even pause. She took in the immediate scene with one cold glare and was running again when there appeared at the corner of the house and apparently been born before their eyes of the fog itself, a mule. It looked taller than a giraffe. Longheaded, with a flying halter about its scissorlike ears, it rushed down upon them with violent and apparitionlike suddenness.

"Dar hit!" old Het cried, waving the shopping-bag. "Hoo!" Mrs. Hait whirled. Again she skidded savagely on the greasy planks as she and the mule rushed parallel with one another toward the shed building, from whose open doorway there now projected the static and astonished face of a cow. To the cow the fog-born mule doubtless looked taller and more incredibly sudden than a giraffe even, and apparently bent upon charging right through the shed as though it were made of straw or were purely and simply mirage. The cow's head likewise had a quality transient and abrupt and unmundane. It vanished, sucked into invisibility like a match flame, though the mind knew and the reason insisted that she had withdrawn into the shed, from which, as proof's burden, there came an indescribable sound of shock and alarm by shed and beast engendered, analogous to a single note from a profoundly struck lyre or harp. Toward this sound Mrs. Hait sprang, immediately, as if by pure reflex, as though in invulnerable compact of female with female against a world of mule and man. She and the mule converged upon the shed at top speed, the heavy scuttle poised lightly in her hand to hurl. Of course it did not take this long, and likewise it was the mule which refused the gambit. Old Het was still shouting "Dar hit! Dar hit!" when it swerved and rushed at her where she stood tall as a stove pipe, holding the shopping-bag which she swung at the beast as it rushed past her and vanished beyond the other corner of the house as though sucked back into the fog which had produced it, profound and instantaneous and without any sound.

With that unhasteful celerity Mrs. Hait turned and set the scuttle down on the brick coping of the cellar entrance and she and old Het turned the corner of the house in time to see the now wraithlike mule at the moment when its course converged with that of a choleric-looking rooster and eight Rhode Island Red hens emerging from beneath the house. Then for an instant its progress assumed the appearance and trappings of an apotheosis: hell-born and hell-returning, in the act of dissolving completely into the fog, it seemed to rise vanishing into a sunless and dimensionless medium borne upon and enclosed by small winged goblins.

"Dey's mo in de front!" old Het cried.

"Them sons of bitches," Mrs. Hait said, again in that grim, prescient voice without rancor or heat. It was not the mules to which she referred; it was not even the owner of them. It was her whole town-dwelling history as dated from that April dawn ten years ago when what was left of Hait had been gathered from the mangled remains of five mules and several feet of new Manila rope on a blind curve of the railroad just out of town; the geographical hap of her very home; the very components of her bereavement—the mules, the defunct husband, and the owner of them. His name was Snopes; in the town they knew about him too—how he bought his stock at the Memphis market and brought it to Jefferson and sold it to farmers and widows and orphans black and white, for whatever he could contrive— down to a certain figure; and about how (usually in the dead season of winter) teams and even small droves of his stock would escape from the fenced pasture where he kept them and, tied one to another with sometimes quite new hemp rope (and which item Snopes included in the subsequent claim), would be annihilated by freight trains on the same blind curve which was to be the scene of Hait's exit from this world; once a town wag sent him through the mail a printed train schedule for the division. A squat, pasty man perennially tieless and with a strained, harried expression, at stated intervals he passed athwart the peaceful and somnolent life of the town in dust and uproar, his advent heralded by shouts and cries, his passing marked by a yellow cloud filled with tossing jug-shaped heads and clattering hooves and the same forlorn and earnest cries of the drovers; and last of all and well back out of the dust, Snopes himself moving at a harried and panting trot, since it was said in the town that he was deathly afraid of the very beasts in which he cleverly dealt.

The path which he must follow from the railroad station to his pasture crossed the edge of town near Hait's home; Hait and Mrs. Hait had not been in the house a week before they waked one morning to find it surrounded by galloping mules and the air filled with the shouts and cries of the drovers. But it was not until that April dawn some years later, when those who reached the scene first found what might be termed foreign matter among the mangled mules and the savage fragments of new rope, that the town suspected that Hait stood in any closer relationship to Snopes and the mules than that of helping at periodical intervals to drive them out of his front yard. After that they believed that they knew; in a three days' recess of interest, surprise, and curiosity they watched to see if Snopes would try to collect on Hait also.

But they learned only that the adjuster appeared and called upon Mrs. Hait and that a few days later she cashed a check for eight thousand five hundred dollars, since this was back in the old halcyon days when even the companies considered their southern branches and divisions the legitimate prey of all who dwelt beside them. She took the cash: she stood in her sweater coat and the hat which Hait had been wearing on the fatal morning a week ago and listened in cold, grim silence while the teller counted the money and the president and the cashier tried to explain to her the virtues of a bond, then of a savings account, then of a checking account, and departed with the money in a salt sack under her apron; after a time she painted her house: that serviceable and time-defying color which the railroad station was painted, as though out of sentiment or (as some said) gratitude.

The adjuster also summoned Snopes into conference, from which he emerged not only more harried-looking than ever, but with his face stamped with a bewildered dismay which it was to wear from then on, and that was the last time his pasture fence was ever to give inexplicably away at dead of night upon mules coupled in threes and fours by adequate rope even though not always new. And then it seemed as though the mules themselves knew this, as if, even while haltered at the Memphis block at his bid, they sensed it somehow as they sensed that he was afraid of them. Now, three or four times a year and as though by fiendish concord and as soon as they were freed of the box car, the entire uproar—the dust cloud filled with shouts earnest, harried, and dismayed, with plunging demoniac shapes—would become translated in a single burst of perverse and uncontrollable violence, without any intervening contact with time, space, or earth, across the peaceful and astonished town and into Mrs. Hait's yard, where, in a certain hapless despair which abrogated for the moment even physical fear, Snopes ducked and dodged among the thundering shapes about the house (for whose very impervious paint the town believed that he felt he had paid and whose inmate lived within it a life of idle and queen-like ease on money which he considered at least partly his own) while gradually that section and neighborhood gathered to look on from behind adjacent window curtains and porches screened and not, and from the sidewalks and even from halted wagons and cars in the street—housewives in the wrappers and boudoir caps of morning, children on the way to school, casual Negroes and casual whites in static and entertained repose.

They were all there when, followed by old Het and carrying the stub of a worn-out broom, Mrs. Hait ran around the next corner and onto the handkerchief-sized plot of earth which she called her front yard. It was small; any creature with a running stride of three feet could have spanned it in two paces, yet at the moment, due perhaps to the myopic and distortive quality of the fog, it seemed to be as incredibly full of mad life as a drop of water beneath the microscope. Yet again she did not falter. With the broom clutched in her hand and apparently with a kind of sublime faith in her own invulnerability, she rushed on after the haltered mule which was still in that arrested and wraithlike process of vanishing furiously into the fog, its wake indicated by the tossing and dispersing shapes of the nine chickens like so many jagged scraps of paper in the dying air blast of an automobile, and the madly dodging figure of a man. The man was Snopes; beaded too with moisture, his wild face gaped with hoarse shouting and the two heavy lines of shaven beard descending from the corners of it as though in alluvial retrospect of years of tobacco, he screamed at her: "Fore God, Miz Hait! I done everything I could!" She didn't even look at him.

"Ketch that big un with the bridle on," she said in her cold, panting voice. "Git that big un outen here."

"Sho!" Snopes shrieked. "Jest let um take their time. Jest don't git um excited now."

"Watch out!" old Het shouted. "He headin fer de back again!"

"Git the rope," Mrs. Hait said, running again. Snopes glared back at old Het.

"Fore God, where is ere rope?" he shouted.

"In de cellar fo God!" old Het shouted, also without pausing. "Go roun de udder way en head um." Again she and Mrs. Hait turned the corner in time to see again the still-vanishing mule with the halter once more in the act of floating lightly onward in its cloud of chickens with which, they being able to pass under the house and so on the chord of a circle while it had to go around on the arc, it had once more coincided. When they turned the next corner they were in the back yard again.

"Fo God!" old Het cried. "He fixin to misuse de cow!" For they had gained on the mule now, since it had stopped. In fact, they came around the corner on a tableau. The cow now stood in the centre of the yard. She and the mule faced one another a few feet apart. Motionless, with lowered heads and braced forelegs, they looked like two book ends from two distinct pairs of a general pattern which some one of amateurly bucolic leanings might have purchased and which some child had salvaged, brought into idle juxtaposition and then forgotten; and, his head and shoulders projecting above the back-flung slant of the cellar entrance where the scuttle still sat, Snopes standing as though buried to the armpits for a Spanish-Indian-American suttee.[1] Only again it did not take this long. It was less than tableau; it was one of those things which later even memory cannot quite affirm. Now and in turn, man and cow and mule vanished beyond the next corner, Snopes now in the lead, carrying the rope, the cow next with her tail rigid and raked slightly like the stern staff of a boat. Mrs. Hait and old Het ran on, passing the open cellar gaping upon its accumulation of human necessities and widowed womanyears—boxes for kindling wood, old papers and magazines, the broken and outworn furniture and utensils which no woman ever throws away; a pile of coal and another of pitch pine for priming fires—and ran on and turned the next corner to see man and cow and mule all vanishing now in the wild cloud of ubiquitous chickens which had once more crossed beneath the house and emerged. They ran on, Mrs. Hait in grim and unflagging silence, old Het with the eager and happy amazement of a child. But when they gained the front again they saw only Snopes. He lay flat on his stomach, his head and shoulders upreared by his outstretched arms, his coat tail swept forward by its own arrested momentum about his head so that from beneath it his slack-jawed face mused in wild repose like that of a burlesqued nun.

"Whar'd dey go?" old Het shouted at him. He didn't answer.

"Dey tightenin' on de curves!" she cried. "Dey already in de back again!" That's where they were. The cow made a feint at running into her shed, but deciding perhaps that her speed was too great, she whirled in a final desperation of despair-like valor. But they did not see this, nor see the mule, swerving to pass her, crash and blunder for an instant at the open cellar door before going on. When they arrived, the mule was gone. The scuttle was gone too, but they did not notice it; they saw only the cow standing in the centre of the yard as before, panting, rigid, with braced forelegs and lowered head facing nothing, as if the child had returned and removed one of the book ends for some newer purpose or game. They ran on. Mrs. Hait ran heavily now, her mouth too open, her face putty-colored and one hand pressed to her side. So slow was their progress that the mule in its third circuit of the house overtook them from behind and soared past with undiminished speed, with brief demon thunder and a keen ammonia-sweet reek of sweat sudden and sharp as a jeering cry, and was gone. Yet they ran doggedly on around the next corner in time to see it succeed at last in

[1] The practice of a Hindu widow cremating herself on her husband's funeral pyre. It is now forbidden.

vanishing into the fog; they heard its hoofs, brief, staccato, and derisive, on the paved street, dying away.

"Well!" old Het said, stopping. She panted, happily. "Gentlemen, hush! Ain't we had—" Then she became stone still; slowly her head turned, high-nosed, her nostrils pulsing; perhaps for the instant she saw the open cellar door as they had passed it, with no scuttle beside it. "Fo God I smells smoke!" she said. "Chile, run, git yo money."

That was still early, not yet ten o'clock. By noon the house had burned to the ground. There was a farmers' supply store where Snopes could be usually found; more than one had made a point of finding him there by that time. They told him about how when the fire engine and the crowd reached the scene, Mrs. Hait, followed by old Het carrying her shopping-bag in one hand and a framed portrait of Mr. Hait in the other, emerged with an umbrella and wearing a new, dun-colored, mail-order coat, in one pocket of which lay a fruit jar filled with smoothly rolled banknotes and in the other a heavy, nickel-plated pistol, and crossed the street to the house opposite, where with old Het beside her in another rocker, she had been sitting ever since on the veranda, grim, inscrutable, the two of them rocking steadily, while hoarse and tireless men hurled her dishes and furniture and bedding up and down the street.

"What are you telling me for?" Snopes said. "Hit warn't me that set that ere scuttle of live fire where the first thing that passed would knock hit into the cellar."

"It was you that opened the cellar door, though."

"Sho. And for what? To git that rope, her own rope, where she told me to git it."

"To catch your mule with, that was trespassing on her property. You can't get out of it this time, I. O. There ain't a jury in the county that won't find for her."

"Yes. I reckon not. And just because she is a woman. That's why. Because she is a durn woman. All right. Let her go to her durn jury with hit. I can talk too; I reckon hit's a few things I could tell a jury myself about—" He ceased. They were watching him.

"What? Tell a jury about what?"

"Nothing. Because hit ain't going to no jury. A jury between her and me? Me and Mannie Hait? You boys don't know her if you think she's going to make trouble over a pure acci-dent couldn't nobody help. Why, there ain't a fairer finer woman in the county than Miz Mannie Hait. I just wisht I had a opportunity to tell her so." The opportunity came at once. Old Het was behind her, carrying the shopping-bag. Mrs. Hait looked once, quietly, about at the faces, making no response to the murmur of curious salutation, then not again. She didn't look at Snopes long either, nor talk to him long.

"I come to buy that mule," she said.

"What mule?" They looked at one another. "You'd like to own that mule?" She looked at him. "Hit'll cost you a hundred and fifty, Miz Mannie."

"You mean dollars?"

"I don't mean dimes nor nickels neither, Miz Mannie."

"Dollars," she said. "That's more than mules was in Hait's time."

"Lots of things is different since Hait's time. Including you and me."

"I reckon so," she said. Then she went away. She turned without a word, old Het following.

"Maybe one of them others you looked at this morning would suit you," Snopes said. She didn't answer. Then they were gone.

"I don't know as I would have said that last to her," one said.

"What for?" Snopes said. "If she was aiming to law something outen me about that fire, you reckon she would have come and offered to pay me money for hit?" That was about one o'clock. About four o'clock he was shouldering his way through a throng of Negroes before a cheap grocery store when one called his name. It was old Het, the now bulging shopping-bag on her arm, eating bananas from a paper sack.

"Fo God I wuz jest dis minute huntin fer you," she said. She handed the banana to a woman beside her and delved and fumbled in the shopping-bag and extended a greenback. "Miz Mannie gimme dis to give you; I wuz jest on de way to de sto whar you stay at. Here." He took the bill.

"What's this? From Miz Hait?"

"Fer de mule." The bill was for ten dollars. "You don't need to gimme no receipt. I kin be de witness I give hit to you."

"Ten dollars? For that mule? I told her a hundred and fifty dollars."

"You'll have to fix dat up wid her yo'self. She jest gimme dis to give ter you when she sot out to fetch de mule."

"Set out to fetch—She went out there herself and taken my mule outen my pasture?"

"Lawd, chile," old Het said, "Miz Mannie ain't skeered of no mule. Ain't you done foun dat out?"

And then it became late, what with the yet short winter days; when she came in sight of the two gaunt chimneys against the sunset, evening was already finding itself. But she could smell the ham cooking before she came in sight of the cow shed even, though she could not see it until she came around in front where the fire burned beneath an iron skillet set on bricks and where nearby Mrs. Hait was milking the cow. "Well," old Het said, "you is settled down, ain't you?" She looked into the shed, neated and raked and swept even, and floored now with fresh hay. A clean new lantern burned on a box, beside it a pallet bed was spread neatly on the straw and turned neatly back for the night. "Why, you is fixed up," she said with pleased astonishment. Within the door was a kitchen chair. She drew it out and sat down beside the skillet and laid the bulging shopping-bag beside her.

"I'll tend dis meat whilst you milks. I'd offer to strip dat cow fer you ef I wuzn't so wo out wid all dis excitement we been had." She looked around her. "I don't believe I sees yo new mule, dough." Mrs. Hait grunted, her head against the cow's flank. After a moment she said,

"Did you give him that money?"

"I give um ter him. He ack surprise at first, lak maybe he think you didn't aim to trade dat quick. I tole him to settle de details wid you later. He taken de money, dough. So I reckin dat's offen his mine en yo'n bofe." Again Mrs. Hait grunted. Old Het turned the ham in the skillet. Beside it the coffee pot bubbled and steamed. "Cawfee smell good too," she said. "I ain't had no appetite in years now. A bird couldn't live on de vittles I eats. But jest lemme git a whiff er cawfee en seem lak hit always whets me a little. Now, ef you jest had nudder little piece o dis ham, now—Fo God, you got company aready." But Mrs. Hait did not even look up until she had finished. Then she turned without rising from the box on which she sat.

"I reckon you and me better have a little talk," Snopes said. "I reckon I got something that belongs to you and I hear you got something that belongs to me." He looked about, quickly, ceaselessly, while old Het watched him. He turned to her. "You go away, aunty. I don't reckon you want to set here and listen to us."

"Lawd, honey," old Het said. "Don't you mind me. I done already had so much troubles myself dat I kin set en listen to udder folks' widout hit worryin me a-tall. You gawn talk whut you came ter talk; I jest set here en tend de ham." Snopes looked at Mrs. Hait.

"Ain't you going to make her go away?" he said.

"What for?" Mrs. Hait said. "I reckon she ain't the first critter that ever come on this yard when hit wanted and went or stayed when hit liked." Snopes made a gesture, brief, fretted, restrained.

"Well," he said. "All right. So you taken the mule."

"I paid you for it. She give you the money."

"Ten dollars. For a hundred-and-fifty-dollar mule. Ten dollars."

"I don't know anything about hundred-and-fifty-dollar mules. All I know is what the railroad paid." Now Snopes looked at her for a full moment. "What do you mean?"

"Them sixty dollars a head the railroad used to pay you for mules back when you and Hait—"

"Hush," Snopes said; he looked about again, quick, ceaseless. "All right. Even call it sixty dollars. But you just sent me ten."

"Yes. I sent you the difference." He looked at her, perfectly still. "Between that mule and what you owed Hait."

"What I owed—"

"For getting them five mules onto the tr—"

"Hush!" he cried. "Hush!" Her voice went on, cold, grim, level.

"For helping you. You paid him fifty dollars each time, and the railroad paid you sixty dollars a head for the mules. Ain't that right?" He watched her. "The last time you never paid him. So I taken that mule instead. And I sent you the ten dollars difference."

"Yes," he said in a tone of quiet, swift, profound bemusement; then he cried: "But look! Here's where I got you. Hit was our agreement that I wouldn't never owe him nothing until after the mules was—"

"I reckon you better hush yourself," Mrs. Hait said.

"—until hit was over. And this time, when over had come, I never owed nobody no money because the man hit would have been owed to wasn't nobody," he cried triumphantly. "You see?" Sitting on the box, motionless, downlooking, Mrs. Hait seemed to muse. "So you just take your ten dollars back and tell me where my mule is and we'll just go back good friends to where we started at. Fore God, I'm as sorry as ere a living man about that fire—"

"Fo God!" old Het said, "hit was a blaze, wuzn't it?"

"—but likely with all that ere railroad money you still got, you just been wanting a chance to build new, all along. So here. Take hit." He put the money into her hand. "Where's my mule?" But Mrs. Hait didn't move at once.

"You want to give it back to me?" she said.

"Sho. We been friends all the time; now we'll just go back to where we left off being. I don't hold no hard feelings and don't you hold none. Where you got the mule hid?"

"Up at the end of that ravine ditch behind Spilmer's." she said.

"Sho. I know. A good, sheltered place, since you ain't got nere barn. Only if you'd a just left hit in the pasture, hit would a saved us both trouble. But hit ain't no hard feelings though. And so I'll bid you goodnight. You're all fixed up, I see. I reckon you could save some more money by not building no house a-tall."

"I reckon I could," Mrs. Hait said. But he was gone.

"Whut did you leave de mule dar fer?" old Het said.

"I reckon that's far enough," Mrs. Hait said.

"Fer enough?" But Mrs. Hait came and looked into the skillet, and old Het said, "Wuz hit me er you dat mentioned something erbout er nudder piece o dis ham?" So they were both eating when in the not-quite-yet accomplished twilight Snopes returned. He came up quietly and stood, holding his hands to the blaze as if he were quite cold. He did not look at any one now.

"I reckon I'll take that ere ten dollars," he said.

"What ten dollars?" Mrs. Hait said. He seemed to muse upon the fire. Mrs. Hait and old Het chewed quietly, old Het alone watching him.

"You ain't going to give hit back to me?" he said.

"You was the one that said to let's go back to where we started," Mrs. Hait said.

"Fo God you wuz, en dat's de fack," old Het said. Snopes mused upon the fire; he spoke in a tone of musing and amazed despair:

"I go to the worry and the risk and the agoment for years and years and I get sixty dollars. And you, one time, without no trouble and no risk, without even knowing you are going to git it, git eighty-five hundred dollars. I never begrudged hit to you; can't nere a man say I did, even if hit did seem a little strange that you should git it all when he wasn't working for you and you never even knowed where he was at and what doing; that all you done to git it was to be married to him. And now, after all these ten years of not begrudging you hit, you taken the best mule I had and you ain't even going to pay me ten dollars for hit. Hit ain't right. Hit ain't justice."

"You got de mule back, en you ain't satisfied yit," old Het said. "Whut does you want?" Now Snopes looked at Mrs. Hait.

"For the last time I ask hit," he said. "Will you or won't you give hit back?"

"Give what back?" Mrs. Hait said. Snopes turned. He stumbled over something—it was old Het's shopping-bag—and recovered and went on. They could see him in silhouette, as though framed by the two blackened chimneys against the dying west; they saw him fling up both clenched hands in a gesture almost Gallic, of resignation and impotent despair. Then he was gone. Old Het was watching Mrs. Hait.

"Honey," she said. "Whut did you do wid de mule?" Mrs. Hait leaned forward to the fire. On her plate lay a stale biscuit. She lifted the skillet and poured over the biscuit the grease in which the ham had cooked.

"I shot it," she said.

"You which?" old Het said. Mrs. Hait began to eat the biscuit. "Well," old Het said, happily, "de mule burnt de house en you shot de mule. Dat's whut I calls justice." It was getting dark fast now, and before her was still the three-mile walk to the poorhouse. But the dark would last a long time in January, and the poorhouse too would not move at once. She sighed with weary and happy relaxation. "Gentlemen, hush! Ain't we had a day!"

Old Man

Once (it was in Mississippi, in May, in the flood year 1927) there were two convicts. One of them was about twenty-five, tall, lean, flat-stomached, with a sunburned face and Indian-black hair and pale, china-colored outraged eyes—an outrage directed not at the men who had foiled his crime, not even at the lawyers and judges who had sent him here, but at the writers, the uncorporeal names attached to the stories, the paper novels—the Diamond Dicks and Jesse Jameses and such—whom he believed had led him into his present predicament through their own ignorance and gullibility regarding

the medium in which they dealt and took money for, in accepting information on which they placed the stamp of verisimilitude and authenticity (this
so much the more criminal since there was no sworn notarised statement
attached and hence so much quicker would the information be accepted by
one who expected the same unspoken good faith, demanding, asking, expecting no certification, which he extended along with the dime or fifteen cents
to pay for it) and retailed for money and which on actual application proved
to be impractical and (to the convict) criminally false; there would be times
when he would halt his mule and plow in midfurrow (there is no walled
penitentiary in Mississippi; it is a cotton plantation which the convicts work
under the rifles and shotguns of guards and trusties) and muse with a kind of
enraged impotence, fumbling among the rubbish left him by his one and only
experience with courts and law, fumbling until the meaningless and verbose
shibboleth took form at last (himself seeking justice at the same blind fount
where he had met justice and been hurled back and down): Using the mails
to defraud: who felt that he had been defrauded by the third-class mail
system not of crass and stupid money which he did not particularly want
anyway, but of liberty and honor and pride.

He was in for fifteen years (he had arrived shortly after his nineteenth
birthday) for attempted train robbery. He had laid his plans in advance, he
had followed his printed (and false) authority to the letter; he had saved the
paper-backs for two years, reading and re-reading them, memorising them,
comparing and weighing story and method against story and method, taking
the good from each and discarding the dross as his workable plan emerged,
keeping his mind open to make the subtle last-minute changes, without haste
and without impatience, as the newer pamphlets appeared on their appointed days as a conscientious dressmaker makes the subtle alterations in a
court presentation costume as the newer bulletins appear. And then when
the day came, he did not even have a chance to go through the coaches and
collect the watches and the rings, the brooches and the hidden money-belts,
because he had been captured as soon as he entered the express car where
the safe and the gold would be. He had shot no one because the pistol which
they took away from him was not that kind of a pistol although it was loaded;
later he admitted to the District Attorney that he had got it, as well as the
dark lantern in which a candle burned and the black handkerchief to wear
over the face, by peddling among his pinehill neighbors subscriptions to the
Detectives' Gazette. So now from time to time (he had ample leisure for it)
he mused with that raging impotence, because there was something else he
could not tell them at the trial, did not know how to tell them. It was not the
money he had wanted. It was not riches, not the crass loot; that would have
been merely a bangle to wear upon the breast of his pride like the Olympic
runner's amateur medal—a symbol, a badge to show that he too was the best
at his chosen gambit in the living and fluid world of his time. So that at times
as he trod the richly shearing black earth behind his plow or with a hoe

thinned the sprouting cotton and corn or lay on his sullen back in his bunk after supper, he cursed in a harsh steady unrepetitive stream, not at the living men who had put him where he was but at what he did not even know were pen-names, did not even know were not actual men but merely the designations of shades who had written about shades.

The second convict was short and plump. Almost hairless, he was quite white. He looked like something exposed to light by turning over rotting logs or planks and he too carried (though not in his eyes like the first convict) a sense of burning and impotent outrage. So it did not show on him and hence none knew it was there. But then nobody knew very much about him, including the people who had sent him here. His outrage was directed at no printed word but at the paradoxical fact that he had been forced to come here of his own free choice and will. He had been forced to choose between the Mississippi State penal farm and the Federal Penitentiary at Atlanta, and the fact that he, who resembled a hairless and pallid slug, had chosen the out-of-doors and the sunlight was merely another manifestation of the close-guarded and solitary enigma of his character, as something recognisable roils momentarily into view from beneath stagnant and opaque water, then sinks again. None of his fellow prisoners knew what his crime had been, save that he was in for a hundred and ninety-nine years—this incredible and impossible period of punishment or restraint itself carrying a vicious and fabulous quality which indicated that his reason for being here was such that the very men, the paladins and pillars of justice and equity who had sent him here had during that moment become blind apostles not of mere justice but of all human decency, blind instruments not of equity but of all human outrage and vengeance, acting in a savage personal concert, judge, lawyer and jury, which certainly abrogated justice and possibly even law. Possibly only the Federal and State's Attorneys knew what the crime actually was. There had been a woman in it and a stolen automobile transported across a State line, a filling station robbed and the attendant shot to death. There had been a second man in the car at the time and anyone could have looked once at the convict (as the two attorneys did) and known he would not even have had the synthetic courage of alcohol to pull trigger on anyone. But he and the woman and the stolen car had been captured while the second man, doubtless the actual murderer, had escaped, so that, brought to bay at last in the State's Attorney's office, harried, dishevelled and snarling, the two grimly implacable and viciously gleeful attorneys in his front and the now raging woman held by two policemen in the anteroom in his rear, he was given his choice. He could be tried in Federal Court under the Mann Act and for the automobile, that is, by electing to pass through the anteroom where the woman raged he could take his chances on the lesser crime in Federal Court, or by accepting a sentence for manslaughter in the State Court he would be permitted to quit the room by a back entrance, without having to pass the woman. He had chosen; he stood at the bar and heard a judge (who looked down at him as if the District Attorney actually had turned over a rotten plank with his toe and exposed him) sentence him to a hundred and ninety-nine years at the State Farm. Thus (he had ample leisure too; they had tried to teach him to plow and had failed, they had put him in the blacksmith shop and the foreman trusty himself had asked to have him removed: so that now, in a long apron like a woman, he cooked and swept and dusted in the deputy wardens' barracks) he too mused at times with that sense of impotence and outrage though it did not show on him as on the first convict since he leaned on no halted broom to do it and so none knew it was there.

It was this second convict who, toward the end of April, began to read aloud to the others from the daily newspapers when, chained ankle to ankle and herded by armed guards, they had come up from the fields and had eaten supper and were gathered in the bunkhouse. It was the Memphis newspaper which the deputy wardens had read at breakfast; the convict read aloud from it to his companions who could have had but little active interest in the outside world, some of whom could not have read it for themselves at all and did not even know where the Ohio and Missouri river basins were, some of whom had never even seen the Mississippi River although for past periods ranging from a few days to ten and twenty and thirty years (and for future periods ranging from a few months to life) they had plowed and planted and eaten and slept beneath the shadow of the levee itself, knowing only that there was water beyond it from hearsay and because now and then they heard the whistles of steamboats from beyond it and, during that last week or so had seen the stacks and pilot houses moving along the sky sixty feet above their heads.

But they listened, and soon even those who like the taller convict had probably never before seen more water than a horse pond would hold knew what thirty feet on a river gauge at Cairo or Memphis meant and could (and did) talk glibly of sandboils. Perhaps what actually moved them were the accounts of the conscripted levee gangs, mixed blacks and whites working in double shifts against the steadily rising water; stories of men, even though they were negroes, being forced like themselves to do work for which they received no other pay than coarse food and a place in a mudfloored tent to sleep on—stories, pictures, which emerged from the shorter convict's reading voice: the mudsplashed white men with the inevitable shotguns, the antlike lines of negroes carrying sandbags, slipping and crawling up the steep face of the revetment to hurl their futile ammunition into the face of a flood and return for more. Or perhaps it was more than this. Perhaps they watched the approach of the disaster with that same amazed and incredulous hope of the slaves—the lions and bears and elephants, the grooms and bathmen and pastrycooks—who watched the mounting flames of Rome from Ahenobarbus' gardens. But listen they did and presently it was May and the wardens' newspaper began to talk in headlines two inches tall—those black staccato slashes of ink which, it would almost seem, even the illiterate should be able to read: *Crest Passes Memphis at Midnight 4000 Homeless in White River Basin Governor Calls out National Guard Martial Law Declared in Following Counties Red Cross Train with President Hoover Leaves Washington Tonight;* then, three evenings later (It had been raining all day—not the vivid brief thunderous downpours of April and May, but the slow steady gray rain of November and December before a cold north wind. The men had not gone to the fields at all during the day, and the very second-hand optimism of the almost twenty-four-hour-old news seemed to contain its own refutation.): *Crest Now Below Memphis 22,000 Refugees Safe at Vicksburg Army Engineers Say Levees Will Hold.*

"I reckon that means it will bust tonight," one convict said.

"Well, maybe this rain will hold on until the water gets here," a second said. They all agreed to this because what they meant, the living unspoken thought among them, was that if the weather cleared, even though the levees broke and the flood moved in upon the Farm itself, they would have to return to the fields and work, which they would have had to do. There was nothing paradoxical in this, although they could not have expressed the reason for it which they instinctively perceived: that the land they farmed and the substance they produced from it belonged neither to them who worked it nor to those who forced them at guns' point to do so, that as far as either— convicts or guards—were concerned, it could have been pebbles they put into the ground and papiermâché cotton- and corn-sprouts which they thinned. So it was that, what between the sudden wild hoping and the idle day and the evening's headlines, they were sleeping restlessly beneath the sound of the rain on the tin roof when at midnight the sudden glare of the electric bulbs and the guards' voices waked them and they heard the throbbing of the waiting trucks.

"Turn out of there!" the deputy shouted. He was fully dressed—rubber boots, slicker and shotgun. "The levee went out at Mound's Landing an hour ago. Get up out of it!"

When the belated and streaming dawn broke the two convicts, along with twenty others, were in a truck. A trusty drove, two armed guards sat in the cab with him. Inside the high, stall-like topless body the convicts stood, packed like matches in an upright box or like the pencil-shaped ranks of cordite in a shell, shackled by the ankles to a single chain which wove among the motionless feet and swaying legs and a clutter of picks and shovels among which they stood, and was riveted by both ends to the steel body of the truck.

Then and without warning they saw the flood about which the plump convict had been reading and they listening for two weeks or more. The road ran south. It was built on a raised levee, known locally as a dump, about eight feet above the flat surrounding land, bordered on both sides by the barrow pits from which the earth of the levee had been excavated. These barrow pits had held water all winter from the fall rains, not to speak of the rain of yesterday, but now they saw that the pit on either side of the road had vanished and instead there lay a flat still sheet of brown water which extended into the fields beyond the pits, ravelled out into long motionless shreds in the bottom of the plow furrows and gleaming faintly in the gray light like the bars of a prone and enormous grating. And then (the truck was moving at good speed) as they watched quietly (they had not been talking much anyway but now they were all silent and quite grave, shifting and craning as one to look soberly off to the west side of the road) the crests of the furrows vanished too and they now looked at a single perfectly flat and motionless steel-colored sheet in which the telephone poles and the straight hedgerows which marked section lines seemed to be fixed and rigid as though set in concrete.

It was perfectly motionless, perfectly flat. It looked, not innocent, but bland. It looked almost demure. It looked as if you could walk on it. It looked so still that they did not realise it possessed motion until they came to the first bridge. There was a ditch under the bridge, a small stream, but ditch and stream were both invisible now, indicated only by the rows of cypress and bramble which marked its course. Here they both saw and heard movement—the slow profound eastward and upstream ("It's running backward," one convict said quietly.) set of the still rigid surface, from beneath which came a deep faint subaquean rumble which (though none in the truck could have made the comparison) sounded like a subway train passing far beneath the street and which inferred a terrific and secret speed. It was as if the water itself were in three strata, separate and distinct, the bland and unhurried surface bearing a frothy scum and a miniature flotsam of twigs and screening as though by vicious calculation the rush and fury of the flood itself, and beneath this in turn the original stream, trickle, murmuring along in the opposite direction, following undisturbed and unaware its appointed course and serving its Lilliputian end, like a thread of ants between the rails on which an express train passes, they (the ants) as unaware of the power and fury as if it were a cyclone crossing Saturn.

Now there was water on both sides of the road and now, as if once they had become aware of movement in the water the water seemed to have given over deception and concealment, they seemed to be able to watch it rising up the flanks of the dump; trees which a few miles back had stood on tall trunks above the water now seemed to burst from the surface at the level of the lower branches like decorative shrubs on barbered lawns. The truck passed a negro cabin. The water was up to the window ledges. A woman clutching two children squatted on the ridgepole, a man and a halfgrown youth, standing waist-deep, were hoisting a squealing pig onto the slanting roof of a barn, on the ridgepole of which sat a row of chickens and a turkey. Near the barn was a haystack on which a cow stood tied by a rope to the center pole and bawling steadily; a yelling negro boy on a saddleless mule which he flogged steadily, his legs clutching the mule's barrel and his body leaned to the drag of a rope attached to a second mule, approached the haystack, splashing and floundering. The woman on the housetop began to shriek at the passing truck, her voice carrying faint and melodious across the brown water, becoming fainter and fainter as the truck passed and went on, ceasing at last, whether because of distance or because she had stopped screaming those in the truck did not know.

Then the road vanished. There was no perceptible slant to it yet it had slipped abruptly beneath the brown surface with no ripple, no ridgy demarcation, like a flat thin blade slipped obliquely into flesh by a delicate hand, annealed into the water without disturbance, as if it had existed so for years, had been built that way. The truck stopped. The trusty descended from the cab and came back and dragged two shovels from among their feet, the blades clashing against the serpentining of the chain about their ankles. "What is it?" one said. "What are you fixing to do?" The trusty didn't answer. He returned to the cab, from which one of the guards had descended, without his shotgun. He and the trusty, both in hip boots and each carrying a shovel, advanced into the water, gingerly, probing and feeling ahead with the shovel handles. The same convict spoke again. He was a middle-aged man with a wild thatch of iron-gray hair and a slightly mad face. "What the hell are they doing?" he said. Again nobody answered him. The truck moved, on into the water, behind the guard and the trusty, beginning to push ahead of itself a thick slow viscid ridge of chocolate water. Then the gray-haired convict began to scream. "God damn it, unlock the chain!" He began to struggle, thrashing violently about him, striking at the men nearest him until he reached the cab, the roof of which he now hammered on with his fist, screaming. "God damn it, unlock us! Unlock us! Son of a bitch!" he screamed, addressing no one. "They're going to drown us! Unlock the chain!" But for all the answer he got the men within radius of his voice might have been dead. The truck crawled on, the guard and the trusty feeling out the road ahead with the reversed shovels, the second guard at the wheel, the twenty-two convicts packed like sardines into the truck bed and padlocked by the ankles to the body of the truck itself. They crossed another bridge— two delicate and paradoxical iron railings slanting out of the water, travelling parallel to it for a distance, then slanting down into it again with an outrageous quality almost significant yet apparently meaningless like something in a dream not quite nightmare. The truck crawled on.

Along toward noon they came to a town, their destination. The streets were paved; now the wheels of the truck made a sound like tearing silk. Moving faster now, the guard and the trusty in the cab again, the truck even had a slight bone in its teeth, its bow-wave spreading beyond the submerged sidewalks and across the adjacent lawns, lapping against the stoops and porches of houses where people stood among piles of furniture. They passed through the business district; a man in hip boots emerged knee-deep in water from a store, dragging a flat-bottomed skiff containing a steel safe.

At last they reached the railroad. It crossed the street at right angles, cutting the town in two. It was on a dump, a levee, also, eight or ten feet above the town itself; the street ran blankly into it and turned at right angles beside a cotton compress and a loading platform on stilts at the level of a freight car door. On this platform was a khaki army tent and a uniformed National Guard sentry with a rifle and bandolier.

The truck turned and crawled out of the water and up the ramp which cotton wagons used and where trucks and private cars filled with household goods came and unloaded onto the platform. They were unlocked from the chain in the truck and shackled ankle to ankle in pairs they mounted the platform and into an apparently inextricable jumble of beds and trunks, gas and electric stoves, radios and tables and chairs and framed pictures which a chain of negroes under the eye of an unshaven white man in muddy corduroy and hip boots carried piece by piece into the compress, at the door of which another guardsman stood with his rifle, they (the convicts) not stopping here but herded on by the two guards with their shotguns, into the dim and cavernous building where among the piled heterogeneous furniture the ends of cotton bales and the mirrors on dressers and sideboards gleamed with an identical mute and unreflecting concentration of pallid light.

They passed on through, onto the loading platform where the army tent and the first sentry were. They waited here. Nobody told them for what nor why. While the two guards talked with the sentry before the tent the convicts sat in a line along the edge of the platform like buzzards on a fence, their shackled feet dangling above the brown motionless flood out of which the railroad embankment rose, pristine and intact, in a kind of paradoxical denial and repudiation of change and portent, not talking, just looking quietly across the track to where the other half of the amputated town seemed to float, house shrub and tree, ordered and pageantlike and without motion, upon the limitless liquid plain beneath the thick gray sky.

After a while the other four trucks from the Farm arrived. They came up, bunched closely, radiator to tail light, with their four separate sounds of tearing silk and vanished beyond the compress. Presently the ones on the platform heard the feet, the mute clashing of the shackles, the first truckload emerged from the compress, the second, the third; there were more than a hundred of them now in their bed-ticking overalls and jumpers and fifteen or twenty guards with rifles and shotguns. The first lot rose and they mingled, paired, twinned by their clanking and clashing umbilicals; then it began to rain, a slow steady gray drizzle like November instead of May. Yet not one of them made any move toward the open door of the compress. They did not even look toward it, with longing or hope or without it. If they thought at all, they doubtless knew that the available space in it would be needed for furniture, even if it were not already filled. Or perhaps they knew that, even if there were room in it, it would not be for them, not that the guards would wish them to get wet but that the guards would not think about getting them out of the rain. So they just stopped talking and with their jumper collars turned up and shackled in braces like dogs at a field trial they stood, immobile, patient, almost ruminant, their backs turned to the rain as sheep and cattle do.

After another while they became aware that the number of soldiers had increased to a dozen or more, warm and dry beneath rubberised ponchos, there was an officer with a pistol at his belt, then and without making any move toward it, they began to smell food and, turning to look, saw an army field kitchen set up just inside the compress door. But they made no move, they waited until they were herded into line, they inched forward, their heads lowered and patient in the rain, and received each a bowl of stew, a mug of coffee, two slices of bread. They ate this in the rain. They did not sit down because the platform was wet, they squatted on their heels as country men do, hunching forward, trying to shield the bowls and mugs into which nevertheless the rain splashed steadily as into miniature ponds and soaked, invisible and soundless, into the bread.

After they had stood on the platform for three hours, a train came for them. Those nearest the edge saw it, watched it—a passenger coach apparently running under its own power and trailing a cloud of smoke from no visible stack, a cloud which did not rise but instead shifted slowly and heavily aside and lay upon the surface of the aqueous earth with a quality at once weightless and completely spent. It came up and stopped, a single old fashioned open-ended wooden car coupled to the nose of a pushing switch engine considerably smaller. They were herded into it, crowding forward to the other end where there was a small cast iron stove. There was no fire in it, nevertheless they crowded about it—the cold and voiceless lump of iron stained with fading tobacco and hovered about by the ghosts of a thousand Sunday excursions to Memphis or Moorhead and return—the peanuts, the bananas, the soiled garments of infants—huddling, shoving for places near it. "Come on, come on," one of the guards shouted. "Sit down, now." At last three of the guards, laying aside their guns, came among them and broke up the huddle, driving them back and into seats.

There were not enough seats for all. The others stood in the aisle, they stood braced, they heard the air hiss out of the released brakes, the engine whistled four blasts, the car came into motion with a snapping jerk; the platform, the compress fled violently as the train seemed to transpose from immobility to full speed with that same quality of unreality with which it had appeared, running backward now though with the engine in front where before it had moved forward but with the engine behind.

When the railroad in its turn ran beneath the surface of the water, the convicts did not even know it. They felt the train stop, they heard the engine blow a long blast which wailed away unechoed across the waste, wild and forlorn, and they were not even curious; they sat or stood behind the rain-streaming windows as the train crawled on again, feeling its way as the truck had while the brown water swirled between the trucks and among the spokes of the driving wheels and lapped in cloudy steam against the dragging firefilled belly of the engine; again it blew four short harsh blasts filled with the wild triumph and defiance yet also with repudiation and even farewell, as if the articulated steel itself knew it did not dare stop and would not be able to return. Two hours later in the twilight they saw through the streaming windows a burning plantation house. Juxtaposed to nowhere and neighbored by nothing it stood, a clear steady pyre-like flame rigidly fleeing its own reflection, burning in the dusk above the watery desolation with a quality paradoxical, outrageous and bizarre.

Sometime after dark the train stopped. The convicts did not know where they were. They did not ask. They would no more have thought of asking where they were than they would have asked why and what for. They couldn't even see, since the car was unlighted and the windows fogged on the outside by rain and on the inside by the engendered heat of the packed bodies. All they could see was a milky and sourceless flick and glare of flashlights. They could hear shouts and commands, then the guards inside the car began to shout; they were herded to their feet and toward the exit, the ankle chains clashing and clanking. They descended into a fierce hissing of steam, through ragged wisps of it blowing past the car. Laid-to alongside the train and resembling a train itself was a thick blunt motor launch to which was attached a string of skiffs and flat boats. There were more soldiers; the flashlights played on the rifle barrels and bandolier buckles and flicked and glinted on the ankle chains of the convicts as they stepped gingerly down into knee-deep water and entered the boats; now car and engine both vanished completely in steam as the crew began dumping the fire from the firebox.

After another hour they began to see lights ahead—a faint wavering row of red pin-pricks extending along the horizon and apparently hanging low in the sky. But it took almost another hour to reach them while the convicts squatted in the skiffs, huddled into the soaked garments (they no longer felt the rain any more at all as separate drops) and watched the lights draw nearer and nearer until at last the crest of the levee defined itself; now they could discern a row of army tents stretching along it and people squatting about the fires, the wavering reflections from which, stretching across the water, revealed an involved mass of other skiffs tied against the flank of the levee which now stood high and dark overhead. Flashlights glared and winked along the base, among the tethered skiffs; the launch, silent now, drifted in.

When they reached the top of the levee they could see the long line of khaki tents, interspersed with fires about which people—men, women and children, negro and white—crouched or stood among shapeless bales of clothing, their heads turning, their eyeballs glinting in the firelight as they looked quietly at the striped garments and the chains; further down the levee, huddled together too though untethered, was a drove of mules and two or three cows. Then the taller convict became conscious of another sound. He did not begin to hear it all at once, he suddenly became aware that he had been hearing it all the time, a sound so much beyond all his experience and his powers of assimilation that up to this point he had been as oblivious of it as an ant or a flea might be of the sound of the avalanche on which it rides; he had been travelling upon water since early afternoon and for seven years now he had run his plow and harrow and planter within the very shadow of the levee on which he now stood, but this profound deep whisper which came from the further side of it he did not at once recognise. He stopped. The line of convicts behind jolted into him like a line of freight cars stopping, with an iron clashing like cars. "Get on!" a guard shouted.

"What's that?" the convict said. A negro man squatting before the nearest fire answered him:

"Dat's him. Dat's de Ole Man."

"The old man?" the convict said.

"Get on! Get on up there!" the guard shouted. They went on; they passed another huddle of mules, the eyeballs rolling too, the long morose faces turning into and out of the firelight; they passed them and reached a section of empty tents, the light pup tents of a military campaign, made to hold two men. The guard herded the convicts into them, three brace of shackled men to each tent.

They crawled in on all fours, like dogs into cramped kennels, and settled down. Presently the tent became warm from their bodies. Then they became quiet and then all of them could hear it, they lay listening to the bass whisper deep, strong and powerful. "The old man?" the train-robber convict said.

"Yah," another said. "He don't have to brag."

At dawn the guards waked them by kicking the soles of the projecting feet. Opposite the muddy landing and the huddle of skiffs an army field kitchen was set up, already they could smell the coffee. But the taller convict at least, even though he had had but one meal yesterday and that at noon in the rain, did not move at once toward the food. Instead and for the first time he looked at the River within whose shadow he had spent the last seven years of his life but had never seen before; he stood in quiet and amazed surmise and looked at the rigid steel-colored surface not broken into waves but merely slightly undulant. It stretched from the levee on which he stood, further than he could see—a slowly and heavily roiling chocolate-frothy expanse broken only by a thin line a mile away as fragile in appearance as a single hair, which after a moment he recognised. *It's another levee,* he thought quietly. *That's what we look like from there. That's what I am standing on looks like from there.* He was prodded from the rear; a guard's voice carried forward: "Go on! Go on! You'll have plenty of time to look at that!"

They received the same stew and coffee and bread as the day before; they squatted again with their bowls and mugs as yesterday, though it was not raining yet. During the night an intact wooden barn had floated up. It now lay jammed by the current against the levee while a crowd of negroes swarmed over it, ripping off the shingles and planks and carrying them up the bank; eating steadily and without haste, the taller convict watched the barn dissolve rapidly down to the very water-line exactly as a dead fly vanished beneath the moiling industry of a swarm of ants.

They finished eating. Then it began to rain again, as upon a signal, while they stood or squatted in their harsh garments which had not dried out during the night but had become slightly warmer than the air. Presently they were haled to their feet and told off into two groups, one of which was armed from a stack of mud-clogged picks and shovels nearby, and marched away up the levee. A little later the motor launch with its train of skiffs came up across what was, fifteen feet beneath its keel, probably a cotton field, the skiffs loaded to the gunwales with negroes and a scattering of white people nursing bundles on their laps. When the engine shut off the faint plinking of a guitar came across the water. The skiffs warped in and unloaded; the convicts watched the men and women and children struggle up the muddy slope, carrying heavy towsacks and bundles wrapped in quilts. The sound of the guitar had not ceased and now the convicts saw him—a young, black, lean-hipped man, the guitar slung by a piece of cotton plow line about his neck. He mounted the levee, still picking it. He carried nothing else, no food, no change of clothes, not even a coat.

The taller convict was so busy watching this that he did not hear the guard until the guard stood directly beside him shouting his name. "Wake up!" the guard shouted. "Can you fellows paddle a boat?"

"Paddle a boat where?" the taller convict said.

"In the water," the guard said. "Where in hell do you think?"

"I ain't going to paddle no boat nowhere out yonder," the tall convict said, jerking his head toward the invisible river beyond the levee behind him.

"No, it's on this side," the guard said. He stooped swiftly and unlocked the chain which joined the tall convict and the plump hairless one. "It's just down the road a piece." He rose. The two convicts followed him down to the boats. "Follow them telephone poles until you come to a filling station. You can tell it, the roof is still above water. It's on a bayou and you can tell the bayou because the tops of the trees are sticking up. Follow the bayou until you come to a cypress snag with a woman in it. Pick her up and then cut straight back west until you come to a cotton house with a fellow sitting on the ridgepole—" He turned, looking at the two convicts, who stood perfectly still, looking first at the skiff and then at the water with intense sobriety. "Well? What are you waiting for?"

"I cant row a boat," the plump convict said.

"Then it's high time you learned," the guard said. "Get in."

The tall convict shoved the other forward. "Get in," he said. "That water aint going to hurt you. Aint nobody going to make you take a bath."

As, the plump one in the bow and the other in the stern, they shoved away from the levee, they saw other pairs being unshackled and manning the other skiffs. "I wonder how many more of them fellows are seeing this much water for the first time in their lives too," the tall convict said. The other did not answer. He knelt in the bottom of the skiff, pecking gingerly at the water now and then with his paddle. The very shape of his thick soft back seemed to wear that expression of wary and tense concern.

Some time after midnight a rescue boat filled to the guard rail with homeless men and women and children docked at Vicksburg. It was a steamer, shallow of draft; all day long it had poked up and down cypress- and gum-choked bayous and across cotton fields (where at times instead of swimming it waded) gathering its sorry cargo from the tops of houses and barns and even out of trees, and now it warped into that mushroom city of the forlorn and despairing where kerosene flares smoked in the drizzle and hurriedly strung electrics glared upon the bayonets of martial policemen and the Red Cross brassards of doctors and nurses and canteen-workers. The bluff overhead was almost solid with tents, yet still there were more people than shelter for them; they sat or lay, single and by whole families, under what shelter they could find or sometimes under the rain itself, in the little death of profound exhaustion while the doctors and nurses and the soldiers stepped over and around and among them.

Among the first to disembark was one of the penitentiary deputy wardens, followed closely by the plump convict and another white man—a small man with a gaunt unshaven wan face still wearing an expression of incredulous outrage. The deputy warden seemed to know exactly where he wished to go. Followed closely by his two companions he threaded his way swiftly among the piled furniture and the sleeping bodies and stood presently in a fiercely lighted and hastily established temporary office, almost a military post of command in fact, where the Warden of the Penitentiary sat with two army officers wearing majors' leaves. The deputy warden spoke without preamble. "We lost a man," he said. He called the tall convict's name.

"Lost him?" the Warden said.

"Yah. Drowned." Without turning his head he spoke to the plump convict. "Tell him," he said.

"He was the one that said he could row a boat," the plump convict said. "I never. I told him myself—" he indicated the deputy warden with a jerk of his head "—I couldn't. So when we got to the bayou—"

"What's this?" the Warden said.

"The launch brought word in," the deputy warden said. "Woman in a cypress snag on the bayou, then this fellow—" he indicated the third man; the Warden and the two officers looked at the third man "—on a cotton-house. Never had room in the launch to pick them up. Go on."

"So we come to where the bayou was," the plump convict continued in a voice perfectly flat, without any inflection whatever. "Then the boat got away from him. I dont know what happened. I was just sitting there because he was so positive he could row a boat. I never saw any current. Just all of a sudden the boat whirled clean around and begun to run fast backward like it was hitched to a train and it whirled around again and I happened to look up and there was a limb right over my head and I grabbed it just in time and that boat was snatched out from under me like you'd snatch off a sock and I saw it one time more upside down and that fellow that said he knew all about rowing holding to it with one hand and still holding the paddle in the other—" He ceased. There was no dying fall to his voice, it just ceased and the convict stood looking quietly at a half-full quart of whiskey sitting on the table.

"How do you know he's drowned?" the Warden said to the deputy. "How do you know he didn't just see his chance to escape, and took it?"

"Escape where?" the other said. "The whole Delta's flooded. There's fifteen foot of water for fifty miles, clean back to the hills. And that boat was upside down."

"That fellow's drowned," the plump convict said. "You dont need to worry about him. He's got his pardon; it wont cramp nobody's hand signing it, neither."

"And nobody else saw him?" the Warden said. "What about the woman in the tree?"

"I dont know," the deputy said. "I aint found her yet. I reckon some other boat picked her up. But this is the fellow on the cotton house."

Again the Warden and the two officers looked at the third man, at the gaunt, unshaven wild face in which an old terror, an old blending of fear and impotence and rage still lingered. "He never came for you?" the Warden said. "You never saw him?"

"Never nobody came for me," the refugee said. He began to tremble though at first he spoke quietly enough. "I set there on that sonabitching cottonhouse, expecting hit to go any minute. I saw that launch and them boats come up and they never had no room for me. Full of bastard niggers and one of them setting there playing a guitar but there wasn't no room for me. A guitar!" he cried; now he began to scream, trembling, slavering, his face twitching and jerking. "Room for a bastard nigger guitar but not for me—"

"Steady now," the Warden said. "Steady now."

"Give him a drink," one of the officers said. The Warden poured the drink. The deputy handed it to the refugee, who took the glass in both jerking hands and tried to raise it to his mouth. They watched him for perhaps twenty seconds, then the deputy took the glass from him and held it to his lips while he gulped, though even then a thin trickle ran from each corner of his mouth, into the stubble on his chin.

"So we picked him and—" the deputy called the plump convict's name now "—both up just before dark and come on in. But that other fellow is gone."

"Yes," the Warden said. "Well. Here I haven't lost a prisoner in ten years, and now, like this—I'm sending you back to the Farm tomorrow. Have his family notified, and his discharge papers filled out at once."

"All right," the deputy said. "And listen, chief. He wasn't a bad fellow and maybe he never had no business in that boat. Only he did say he could paddle one. Listen. Suppose I write on his discharge, Drowned while trying to save lives in the great flood of nineteen twenty-seven, and send it down for the Governor to sign it. It will be something nice for his folks to have, to hang on the wall when neighbors come in or something. Maybe they will even give his folks a cash bonus because after all they sent him to the Farm to raise cotton, not to fool around in a boat in a flood."

"All right," the Warden said. "I'll see about it. The main thing is to get his name off the books as dead before some politician tries to collect his food allowance."

"All right," the deputy said. He turned and herded his companions out. In the drizzling darkness again he said to the plump convict: "Well, your partner beat you. He's free. He's done served his time out but you've got a right far piece to go yet."

"Yah," the plump convict said. "Free. He can have it."

As the short convict had testified, the tall one, when he returned to the surface, still retained what the short one called the paddle. He clung to it, not instinctively against the time when he would be back inside the boat and would need it, because for a time he did not believe he would ever regain the skiff or anything else that would support him, but because he did not have time to think about turning it loose. Things had moved too fast for him. He had not been warned, he had felt the first snatching tug of the current, he had seen the skiff begin to spin and his companion vanish violently upward like in a translation out of Isaiah, then he himself was in the water, struggling against the drag of the paddle which he did not know he still held each time he fought back to the surface and grasped at the spinning skiff which at one instant was ten feet away and the next poised above his head as though about to brain him, until at last he grasped the stern, the drag of his body becoming a rudder to the skiff, the two of them, man and boat and with the paddle perpendicular above them like a jackstaff, vanishing from the view of the short convict (who had vanished from that of the tall one with the same celerity though in a vertical direction) like a tableau snatched offstage intact with violent and incredible speed.

He was now in the channel of a slough, a bayou, in which until today no current had run probably since the old subterranean outrage which had created the country. There was plenty of current in it now though; from his trough behind the stern he seemed to see the trees and sky rushing past with vertiginous speed, looking down at him between the gouts of cold yellow in lugubrious and mournful amazement. But they were fixed and secure in something; he thought of that, he remembered in an instant of despairing rage the firm earth fixed and founded strong and cemented fast and stable forever by the generations of laborious sweat, somewhere beneath him, beyond the reach of his feet, when, again without warning, the stern of the skiff struck him a stunning blow across the bridge of his nose. The instinct which had caused him to cling to it now caused him to fling the paddle into the boat in order to grasp the gunwale with both hands just as the skiff pivoted and spun away again. With both hands free he now dragged himself over the stern and lay prone on his face, streaming with blood and water and panting, not with exhaustion but with that furious rage which is terror's aftermath.

But he had to get up at once because he believed he had come much faster (and so farther) than he had. So he rose, out of the watery scarlet puddle in which he had lain, streaming, the soaked denim heavy as iron on his limbs, the black hair plastered to his skull, the blood-infused water streaking his jumper, and dragged his forearm gingerly and hurriedly across his lower face and glanced at it then grasped the paddle and began to try to swing the skiff back upstream. It did not even occur to him that he did not know where his companion was, in which tree among all which he had passed or might pass. He did not even speculate on that for the reason that he knew so incontestably that the other was upstream from him, and after his recent experience the mere connotation of the term upstream carried a sense of such violence and force and speed that the conception of it as other than a straight line was something which the intelligence, reason, simply refused to harbor, like the notion of a rifle bullet the width of a cotton field.

The bow began to swing back upstream. It turned readily, it outpaced the aghast and outraged instant in which he realised it was swinging far too easily, it had swung on over the arc and lay broadside to the current and began again that vicious spinning while he sat, his teeth bared in his bloody streaming face while his spent arms flailed the impotent paddle at the water, that innocent-appearing medium which at one time had held him in iron-like and shifting convolutions like an anaconda yet which now seemed to offer no more resistance to the thrust of his urge and need than so much air, like air; the boat which had threatened him and at last actually struck him in the face with the shocking violence of a mule's hoof now seemed to poise weightless upon it like a thistle bloom, spinning like a wind vane while he flailed at the water and thought of, envisioned, his companion safe, inactive and at ease in the tree with nothing to do but wait, musing with impotent and terrified fury upon that arbitrariness of human affairs which had abrogated to the one the secure tree and to the other the hysterical and unmanageable boat for the very reason that it knew that he alone of the two of them would make any attempt to return and rescue his companion.

The skiff had paid off and now ran with the current again. It seemed again to spring from immobility into incredible speed, and he thought he must already be miles away from where his companion had quitted him, though actually he had merely described a big circle since getting back into the skiff, and the object (a clump of cypress trees choked by floating logs and debris) which the skiff was now about to strike was the same one it had careened into before when the stern had struck him. He didn't know this because he had not yet ever looked higher than the bow of the boat. He didn't look higher now, he just saw that he was going to strike; he seemed to feel run through the very insentient fabric of the skiff a current of eager gleeful vicious incorrigible wilfulness; and he who had never ceased to flail at the bland treacherous water with what he had believed to be the limit of his strength now from somewhere, some ultimate absolute reserve, produced a final measure of endurance, will to endure which adumbrated mere muscle and nerves, continuing to flail the paddle right up to the instant of striking, completing one last reach thrust and recover out of pure desperate reflex, as a man slipping on ice reaches for his hat and money-pocket, as the skiff struck and hurled him once more flat on his face in the bottom of it.

This time he did not get up at once. He lay flat on his face, slightly spread-eagled and in an attitude almost peaceful, a kind of abject meditation. He would have to get up sometime, he knew that, just as all life consists of having to get up sooner or later and then having to lie down again sooner or later after a while. And he was not exactly exhausted and he was not particularly without hope and he did not especially dread getting up. It merely seemed to him that he had accidentally been caught in a situation in which time and environment, not himself, was mesmerised; he was being toyed with by a current of water going nowhere, beneath a day which would wane toward no evening; when it was done with him it would spew him back into the comparatively safe world he had been snatched violently out of and in the meantime it did not much matter just what he did or did not do. So he lay on his face, now not only feeling but hearing the strong quiet rustling of the current on the underside of the planks, for a while longer. Then he raised his head and this time touched his palm gingerly to his face and looked at the blood again, then he sat up onto his heels and leaning over the gunwale he pinched his nostrils between thumb and finger and expelled a gout of blood and was in the act of wiping his fingers on his thigh when a voice slightly above his line of sight said quietly, "It's taken you a while," and he who up to this moment had neither reason nor time to raise his eyes higher than the bows looked up and saw, sitting in a tree and looking at him, a woman. She was not ten feet away. She sat on the lowest limb of one of the trees holding the jam he had grounded on, in a calico wrapper and an army private's tunic and a sunbonnet, a woman whom he did not even bother to examine since that first startled glance had been ample to reveal to him all the generations of her life and background, who could have been his sister if he had a sister, his wife if he had not entered the penitentiary at an age scarcely out of adolescence and some years younger than that at which even his prolific and monogamous kind married—a woman who sat clutching the trunk of the tree, her stockingless feet in a pair of man's unlaced brogans less than a yard from the water, who was very probably somebody's sister and quite certainly (or certainly should have been) somebody's wife, though this too he had entered the penitentiary too young to have had more than mere theoretical female experience to discover yet. "I thought for a minute you wasn't aiming to come back."

"Come back?"

"After the first time. After you run into this bush pile the first time and got into the boat and went on." He looked about, touching his face tenderly again; it could very well be the same place where the boat had hit him in the face.

"Yah," he said. "I'm here now though."

"Could you maybe get the boat a little closer? I taken a right sharp strain getting up here; maybe I better . . ." He was not listening; he had just discovered that the paddle was gone; this time when the skiff hurled him forward he had flung the paddle not into it but beyond it. "It's right there in them brush tops," the woman said. "You can get it. Here. Catch a holt of this." It was a grapevine. It had grown up into the tree and the flood had torn the roots loose. She had taken a turn with it about her upper body; she now loosed it and swung it out until he could grasp it. Holding to the end of the vine he warped the skiff around the end of the jam, picking up the paddle, and warped the skiff on beneath the limb and held it and now he watched her move, gather herself heavily and carefully to descend—that heaviness which was not painful but just excruciatingly careful, that profound and almost lethargic awkwardness which added nothing to the sum of that first aghast amazement which had served already for the catafalque of invincible dream since even in durance he had continued (and even with the old avidity, even though they had caused his downfall) to consume the impossible pulp-printed fables carefully censored and as carefully smuggled into the penitentiary; and who to say what Helen, what living Garbo, he had not dreamed of rescuing from what craggy pinnacle or dragoned keep when he and his companion embarked in the skiff. He watched her. He made no further effort to help her beyond holding the skiff savagely steady while she lowered herself from the limb—the entire body, the deformed swell of belly bulging the calico, suspended by its arms, thinking, *And this is what I get.*

This, out of all the female meat that walks, is what I have to be caught in a runaway boat with.

"Where's that cottonhouse?" he said.

"Cottonhouse?"

"With that fellow on it. The other one."

"I don't know. It's a right smart of cottonhouses around here. With folks on them too, I reckon." She was examining him. "You're bloody as a hog," she said. "You look like a convict."

"Yah," he said, snarled. "I feel like I done already been hung. Well, I got to pick up my pardner and then find that cottonhouse." He cast off. That is, he released his hold on the vine. That was all he had to do, for even while the bow of the skiff hung high on the log jam and even while he held it by the vine in the comparatively dead water behind the jam, he felt steadily and constantly the whisper, the strong purring power of the water just one inch beyond the frail planks on which he squatted and which, as soon as he released the vine, took charge of the skiff not with one powerful clutch but in a series of touches light, tentative, and catlike; he realised now that he had entertained a sort of foundationless hope that the added weight might make the skiff more controllable. During the first moment or two he had a wild (and still foundationless) belief that it had; he had got the head upstream and managed to hold it so by terrific exertion continued even after he discovered that they were travelling straight enough but stern-first and continued somehow even after the bow began to wear away and swing: the old irresistible movement which he knew well by now, too well to fight against it, so that he let the bow swing on downstream with the hope of utilising the skiff's own momentum to bring it through the full circle and so upstream again, the skiff travelling broadside then bow-first then broadside again, diagonally across the channel, toward the other wall of submerged trees; it began to flee beneath him with terrific speed, they were in an eddy but did not know it; he had no time to draw conclusions or even wonder; he crouched, his teeth bared in his blood-caked and swollen face, his lungs bursting, flailing at the water while the trees stooped hugely down at him. The skiff struck, spun, struck again; the woman half lay in the bow, clutching the gunwales, as if she were trying to crouch behind her own pregnancy; he banged now not at the water but at the living sapblooded wood with the paddle, his desire now not to go anywhere, reach any destination, but just to keep the skiff from beating itself to fragments against the tree trunks. Then something exploded, this time against the back of his head, and stooping trees and dizzy water, the woman's face and all, fled together and vanished in bright soundless flash and glare.

An hour later the skiff came slowly up an old logging road and so out of the bottom, the forest, and into (or onto) a cottonfield—a gray and limitless desolation now free of turmoil, broken only by a thin line of telephone poles like a wading millipede. The woman was now paddling, steadily and deliberately, with that curious lethargic care, while the convict squatted, his head between his knees, trying to stanch the fresh and apparently inexhaustible flow of blood from his nose with handfuls of water. The woman ceased paddling, the skiff drifted on, slowing, while she looked about. "We're done out," she said.

The convict raised his head and also looked about. "Out where?"

"I thought maybe you might know."

"I dont even know where I used to be. Even if I knowed which way was north, I wouldn't know if that was where I wanted to go." He cupped another handful of water to his face and lowered his hand and regarded the resulting crimson marbling on his palm, not with dejection, not with concern, but with a kind of sardonic and vicious bemusement. The woman watched the back of his head.

"We got to get somewhere."

"Don't I know it? A fellow on a cottonhouse. Another in a tree. And now that thing in your lap."

"It wasn't due yet. Maybe it was having to climb that tree quick yesterday, and having to set in it all night. I'm doing the best I can. But we better get somewhere soon."

"Yah," the convict said. "I thought I wanted to get somewhere too and I ain't had no luck at it. You pick out a place to get to now and we'll try yours. Gimme that oar." The woman passed him the paddle. The boat was a double-ender; he had only to turn around.

"Which way you fixing to go?" the woman said.

"Never you mind that. You just keep on holding on." He began to paddle, on across the cottonfield. It began to rain again, though not hard at first. "Yah," he said. "Ask the boat. I been in it since breakfast and I aint never knowed, where I aimed to go or where I was going either."

That was about one oclock. Toward the end of the afternoon the skiff (they were in a channel of some sort again, they had been in it for some time; they had got into it before they knew it and too late to get out again, granted there had been any reason to get out, as, to the convict anyway, there was certainly none and the fact that their speed had increased again was reason enough to stay in it) shot out upon a broad expanse of debris-filled water which the convict recognised as a river and, from its size, the Yazoo River though it was little enough he had seen of this country which he had not quitted for so much as one single day in the last seven years of his life. What he did not know was that it was now running backward. So as soon as the drift of the skiff indicated the set of the current, he began to paddle in that direction which he believed to be downstream, where he knew there were towns—Yazoo City, and as a last resort, Vicksburg, if his luck was that bad, if not, smaller towns whose names he did not know but where there would be people, houses, something, anything he might reach and surrender his charge to and turn his back on her forever, on all pregnant and female life forever and return to that monastic existence of shotguns and shackles where he would be secure from it. Now, with the imminence of habitations, release from her, he did not even hate her. When he looked upon the swelling and unmanageable body before him it seemed to him that it was not the woman at all but rather a separate demanding threatening inert yet living mass of which both he and she were equally victims; thinking, as he had been for the last three or four hours, of that minute's—nay, second's—aberration of eye or hand which would suffice to precipitate her into the water to be dragged down to death by that senseless millstone which in its turn would not even have to feel agony, he no longer felt any glow of revenge toward her as its custodian, he felt sorry for her as he would for the living timber in a barn which had to be burned to rid itself of vermin.

He paddled on, helping the current, steadily and strongly, with a calculated husbandry of effort, toward what he believed was downstream, towns, people, something to stand upon, while from time to time the woman raised herself to bail the accumulated rain from the skiff. It was raining steadily now though still not hard, still without passion, the sky, the day itself dissolving without grief; the skiff moved in a nimbus, an aura of gray gauze which merged almost without demarcation with the roiling spittle-frothed debris-choked water. Now the day, the light, definitely began to end and the convict permitted himself an extra notch or two of effort because it suddenly seemed to him that the speed of the skiff had lessened. This was actually the case though the convict did not know it. He merely took it as a phenomenon of the increasing obfuscation, or at most as a result of the long day's continuous effort with no food, complicated by the ebbing and fluxing phases of anxiety and impotent rage at his absolutely gratuitous predicament. So he stepped up his stroke a beat or so, not from alarm but on the contrary, since he too had received that lift from the mere presence of a known stream, a river known by its ineradicable name to generations of men who had been drawn to live beside it as man always has been drawn to dwell beside water, even before he had a name for water and fire, drawn to the living water, the course of his destiny and his actual physical appearance rigidly coerced and postulated by it. So he was not alarmed. He paddled on, upstream without knowing it, unaware that all the water which for forty hours now had been pouring through the levee break to the north was somewhere ahead of him, on its way back to the River.

It was full dark now. That is, night had completely come, the gray dissolving sky had vanished, yet as though in perverse ratio surface visibility had sharpened, as though the light which the rain of the afternoon had washed out of the air had gathered upon the water as the rain itself had done, so that the yellow flood spread on before him now with a quality almost phosphorescent, right up to the instant where vision ceased. The darkness in fact had its advantages; he could now stop seeing the rain. He and his garments had been wet for more than twenty-four hours now so he had long since stopped feeling it, and now that he could no longer see it either it had in a certain sense ceased for him. Also, he now had to make no effort even not to see the swell of his passenger's belly. So he was paddling on, strongly and steadily, not alarmed and not concerned but just exasperated because he had not yet begun to see any reflection on the clouds which would indicate the city or cities which he believed he was approaching but which were actually now miles behind him, when he heard a sound. He did not know what it was because he had never heard it before and he would never be expected to hear such again since it is not given to every man to hear such at all and to none to hear it more than once in his life. And he was not alarmed now either because there was not time, for although the visibility ahead, for all its clarity, did not extend very far, yet in the next instant to the hearing he was also seeing something such as he had never seen before. This was that the sharp line where the phosphorescent water met the darkness was now about ten feet higher than it had been an instant before and that it was curled forward upon itself like a sheet of dough being rolled out for a pudding. It reared, stooping; the crest of it swirled like the mane of a galloping horse and, phosphorescent too, fretted and flickered like fire. And while the woman fuddled in the bows, aware or not aware the convict did not know which, he (the convict), his swollen and blood-streaked face gaped in an expression of aghast and incredulous amazement, continued to paddle directly into it. Again he simply had not had time to order his rhythm-hypnotised muscles to cease. He continued to paddle though the skiff had ceased to move forward at all but seemed to be hanging in space while the paddle still reached thrust recovered and reached again; now instead of space the skiff became abruptly surrounded by a welter of fleeing debris—planks, small buildings, the bodies of drowned yet antic animals, entire trees leaping and diving like porpoises above which the skiff seemed to hover in weightless and airy indecision like a bird above a fleeing countryside, undecided where to light or whether to light at all, while the convict squatted in it still going through the motions of paddling, waiting for an opportunity to scream. He never found it. For an instant the skiff seemed to stand erect on its stern and then shoot scrabbling and scrambling up the curling wall of water like a cat, and soared on above the licking crest itself and hung cradled into the high actual air in the limbs of a tree, from which bower of new-leafed boughs and branches the convict, like a bird in its nest and still waiting his chance to scream and still going through the motions of paddling though he no longer even had the paddle now, looked down upon a world turned to furious motion and in incredible retrograde.

Some time about midnight, accompanied by a rolling cannonade of thunder and lightning like a battery going into action, as though some forty hours' constipation of the elements, the firmament itself, were discharging in clapping and glaring salute to the ultimate acquiescence to desperate and furious motion, and still leading its charging welter of dead cows and mules and outhouses and cabins and hencoops, the skiff passed Vicksburg. The convict didn't know it. He wasn't looking high enough above the water; he still squatted, clutching the gunwales and glaring at the yellow turmoil about him out of which entire trees, the sharp gables of houses, the long mournful heads of mules which he fended off with a splintered length of plank snatched from he knew not where in passing (and which seemed to glare reproachfully back at him with sightless eyes, in limber-lipped and incredulous amazement) rolled up and then down again, the skiff now travelling forward now sideways now sternward, sometimes in the water, sometimes riding for yards upon the roofs of houses and trees and even upon the backs of the mules as though even in death they were not to escape that burden-bearing doom with which their eunuch race was cursed. But he didn't see Vicksburg; the skiff, travelling at express speed, was in a seething gut between soaring and dizzy banks with a glare of light above them but he did not see it; he saw the flotsam ahead of him divide violently and begin to climb upon itself, mounting, and he was sucked through the resulting gap too fast to recognise it as the tresling of a railroad bridge; for a horrible moment the skiff seemed to hang in static indecision before the looming flank of a steamboat as though undecided whether to climb over it or dive under it, then a hard icy wind filled with the smell and taste and sense of wet and boundless desolation blew upon him; the skiff made one long bounding lunge as the convict's native state, in a final paroxysm, regurgitated him onto the wild bosom of the Father of Waters.

This is how he told about it seven weeks later, sitting in new bed-ticking garments, shaved and with his hair cut again, on his bunk in the barracks:

During the next three or four hours after the thunder and lightning had spent itself the skiff ran in pitch streaming darkness upon a roiling expanse which, even if he could have seen, apparently had no boundaries. Wild and invisible, it tossed and heaved about and beneath the boat, ridged with dirty phosphorescent foam and filled with a debris of destruction—objects nameless and enormous and invisible which struck and slashed at the skiff and whirled on. He did not know he was now upon the River. At that time he would have refused to believe it, even if he had known. Yesterday he had known he was in a channel by the regularity of the spacing between the bordering trees. Now, since even by daylight he could have seen no boundaries, the last place under the sun (or the streaming sky rather) he would have suspected himself to be would have been a river; if he had pondered at all about his present whereabouts, about the geography beneath him, he would merely have taken himself to be travelling at dizzy and inexplicable speed above the largest cottonfield in the world; if he who yesterday had known he was in a river, had accepted that fact in good faith and earnest, then had seen that river turn without warning and rush back upon him with furious and deadly intent like a frenzied stallion in a lane—if he had suspected for one second that the wild and limitless expanse on which he now

found himself was a river, consciousness would simply have refused; he
would have fainted.

When daylight—a gray and ragged dawn filled with driving scud between
icy rain-squalls—came and he could see again, he knew he was in no cottonfield. He knew that the wild water on which the skiff tossed and fled flowed
above no soil tamely trod by man, behind the straining and surging buttocks
of a mule. That was when it occurred to him that its present condition was
no phenomenon of a decade, but that the intervening years during which it
consented to bear upon its placid and sleepy bosom the frail mechanicals of
man's clumsy contriving was the phenomenon and this the norm and the
river was now doing what it liked to do, had waited patiently the ten years in
order to do, as a mule will work for you ten years for the privilege of kicking
you once. And he also learned something else about fear too, something he
had even failed to discover on that other occasion when he was really
afraid—that three or four seconds of that night in his youth while he looked
down the twice-flashing pistol barrel of the terrified mail clerk before the
clerk could be persuaded that his (the convict's) pistol would not shoot: that
if you just held on long enough a time would come in fear after which it
would no longer be agony at all but merely a kind of horrible outrageous
itching, as after you have been burned bad.

He did not have to paddle now, he just steered (who had been without
food for twenty-four hours now and without any sleep to speak of for fifty)
while the skiff sped on across that boiling desolation where he had long since
begun to not dare believe he could possibly be where he could not doubt he
was, trying with his fragment of splintered plank merely to keep the skiff
intact and afloat among the houses and trees and dead animals (the entire
towns, stores, residences, parks and farmyards, which leaped and played
about him like fish), not trying to reach any destination, just trying to keep
the skiff afloat until he did. He wanted so little. He wanted nothing for
himself. He just wanted to get rid of the woman, the belly, and he was trying
to do that in the right way, not for himself, but for her. He could have put
her back into another tree at anytime—

"Or you could have jumped out of the boat and let her and it drown," the
plump convict said. "Then they could have given you the ten years for
escaping and then hung you for the murder and charged the boat to your
folks."

"Yah," the tall convict said.—But he had not done that. He wanted to do
it the right way, find somebody, anybody he could surrender her to, something solid he could set her down on and then jump back into the river, if
that would please anyone. That was all he wanted—just to come to something, anything. That didn't seem like a great deal to ask. And he couldn't do
it. He told how the skiff fled on—

"Didn't you pass nobody?" the plump convict said. "No steamboat, nothing?"

"I dont know," the tall one said.—while he tried merely to keep it afloat, until the darkness thinned and lifted and revealed—

"Darkness?" the plump convict said. "I thought you said it was already daylight."

"Yah," the tall one said. He was rolling a cigarette, pouring the tobacco carefully from a new sack, into the creased paper. "This was another one. They had several while I was gone."—the skiff to be moving still rapidly up a winding corridor bordered by drowned trees which the convict recognised again to be a river running again in the direction that, until two days ago, had been upstream. He was not exactly warned through instinct that this one, like that of two days ago, was in reverse. He would not say that he now believed himself to be in the same river, though he would not have been surprised to find that he did believe this, existing now, as he did and had and apparently was to continue for an unnamed period, in a state in which he was toy and pawn on a vicious and inflammable geography. He merely realised that he was in a river again, with all the subsequent inferences of a comprehensible, even if not familiar, portion of the earth's surface. Now he believed that all he had to do would be to paddle far enough and he would come to something horizontal and above water even if not dry and perhaps even populated; and, if fast enough, in time, and that his only other crying urgency was to refrain from looking at the woman who, as vision, the incontrovertible and apparently inescapable presence of his passenger, returned with dawn, had ceased to be a human being and (you could add twenty-four more hours to the first twenty-four and the first fifty now, even counting the hen. It was dead, drowned, caught by one wing under a shingle on a roof which rolled momentarily up beside the skiff yesterday and he had eaten some of it raw though the woman would not) had become instead one single inert monstrous sentient womb from which, he now believed, if he could only turn his gaze away and keep it away, would disappear, and if he could only keep his gaze from pausing again at the spot it had occupied, would not return. That's what he was doing this time when he discovered the wave was coming.

He didn't know how he discovered it was coming back. He heard no sound, it was nothing felt nor seen. He did not even believe that finding the skiff to be now in slack water—that is, that the motion of the current which, whether right or wrong, had at least been horizontal, had now stopped that and assumed a vertical direction—was sufficient to warn him. Perhaps it was just an invincible and almost fanatic faith in the inventiveness and innate viciousness of that medium on which his destiny was now cast, apparently forever; a sudden conviction far beyond either horror or suprise that now was none too soon for it to prepare to do whatever it was it intended doing. So he whirled the skiff, spun it on its heel like a running horse, whereupon, reversed, he could not even distinguish the very channel he had come up. He did not know whether he simply could not see it or if it had vanished some time ago and he not aware at the time; whether the river had become lost in a drowned world or if the world had become drowned in one limitless river. So now he could not tell if he were running directly before the wave or quartering across its line of charge; all he could do was keep that sense of swiftly accumulating ferocity behind him and paddle as fast as his spent and now numb muscles could be driven, and try not to look at the woman, to wrench his gaze from her and keep it away until he reached something flat and above water. So, gaunt, hollow-eyed, striving and wrenching almost physically at his eyes as if they were two of those suction-tipped rubber arrows shot from the toy gun of a child, his spent muscles obeying not will now but that attenuation beyond mere exhaustion which, mesmeric, can continue easier than cease, he once more drove the skiff full tilt into something it could not pass and, once more hurled violently forward onto his hands and knees, crouching, he glared with his wild swollen face up at the man with the shotgun and said in a harsh, croaking voice: "Vicksburg? Where's Vicksburg?"

Even when he tried to tell it, even after the seven weeks and he safe, secure, riveted warranted and doubly guaranteed by the ten years they had added to his sentence for attempted escape, something of the old hysteric incredulous outrage came back into his face, his voice, his speech. He never did even get on the other boat. He told how he clung to a strake (it was a dirty unpainted shanty boat with a drunken rake of tin stove pipe, it had been moving when he struck it and apparently it had not even changed course even though the three people on it must have been watching him all the while—a second man, barefoot and with matted hair and beard also at the steering sweep, and then—he did not know how long—a woman leaning in the door, in a filthy assortment of men's garments, watching him too with the same cold speculation) being dragged violently along, trying to state and explain his simple (and to him at least) reasonable desire and need; telling it, trying to tell it, he could feel again the old unforgettable affronting like an ague fit as he watched the abortive tobacco rain steadily and faintly from between his shaking hands and then the paper itself part with a thin dry snapping report:

"Burn my clothes?" the convict cried. "Burn them?"

"How in hell do you expect to escape in them billboards?" the man with the shotgun said. He (the convict) tried to tell it, tried to explain as he had tried to explain not to the three people on the boat alone but to the entire circumambience—desolate water and forlorn trees and sky—not for justification because he needed none and knew that his hearers, the other convicts, required none from him, but rather as, on the point of exhaustion, he might have picked dreamily and incredulously at a suffocation. He told the man with the gun how he and his partner had been given the boat and told to pick up a man and a woman, how he had lost his partner and failed to find the man, and now all in the world he wanted was something flat to leave the woman on until he could find an officer, a sheriff. He thought of home, the place where he had lived almost since childhood, his friends of years whose ways he knew and who knew his ways, the familiar fields where he did work he had learned to do well and to like, the mules with characters he knew and respected as he knew and respected the characters of certain men; he thought of the barracks at night, with screens against the bugs in summer and good stoves in winter and someone to supply the fuel and the food too; the Sunday ball games and the picture shows—things which, with the exception of the ball games, he had never known before. But most of all, his own character (Two years ago they had offered to make a trusty of him. He would no longer need to plow or feed stock, he would only follow those who did with a loaded gun, but he declined. "I reckon I'll stick to plowing," he said, absolutely without humor. "I done already tried to use a gun one time too many.") his good name, his responsibility not only toward those who were responsible toward him but to himself, his own honor of doing what was asked of him, his pride in being able to do it, no matter what it was. He thought of this and listened to the man with the gun talking about escape and it seemed to him that, hanging there, being dragged violently along (it was here he said that he first noticed the goats' beards of moss in the trees, though it could have been there for several days so far as he knew. It just happened that he first noticed it here.) that he would simply burst.

"Cant you get it into your head that the last thing I want to do is run away?" he cried. "You can set there with that gun and watch me; I give you fair lief. All I want is to put this woman—"

"And I told you she could come aboard," the man with the gun said in his level voice. "But there aint no room on no boat of mine for nobody hunting a sheriff in no kind of clothes, let alone a penitentiary suit."

"When he steps aboard, knock him in the head with the gun barrel," the man at the sweep said. "He's drunk."

"He aint coming aboard," the man with the gun said. "He's crazy."

Then the woman spoke. She didn't move, leaning in the door, in a pair of faded and patched and filthy overalls like the two men: "Give them some grub and tell them to get out of here." She moved, she crossed the deck and looked down at the convict's companion with her cold sullen face. "How much more time have you got?"

"It wasn't due till next month," the woman in the boat said. "But I—" The woman in overalls turned to the man with the gun.

"Give them some grub," she said. But the man with the gun was still looking down at the woman in the boat.

"Come on," he said to the convict. "Put her aboard, and beat it."

"And what'll happen to you," the woman in overalls said, "when you try to turn her over to an officer. When you lay alongside a sheriff and the sheriff asks you who you are?" Still the man with the gun didn't even look at her. He hardly even shifted the gun across his arm as he struck the woman across the face with the back of his other hand, hard. "You son of a bitch," she said. Still the man with the gun did not even look at her.

"Well?" he said to the convict.

"Dont you see I cant?" the convict cried. "Cant you see that?"

Now, he said, he gave up. He was doomed. That is, he knew now that he had been doomed from the very start never to get rid of her, just as the ones who sent him out with the skiff knew that he never would actually give up; when he recognised one of the objects which the woman in overalls was hurling into the skiff to be a can of condensed milk, he believed it to be a presage, gratuitous and irrevocable as a death-notice over the telegraph, that he was not even to find a flat stationary surface in time for the child to be born on it. So he told how he held the skiff alongside the shanty boat while the first tentative toying of the second wave made up beneath him, while the woman in overalls passed back and forth between house and rail, flinging the food—the hunk of salt meat, the ragged and filthy quilt, the scorched lumps of cold bread which she poured into the skiff from a heaped dishpan like so much garbage—while he clung to the strake against the mounting pull of the current, the new wave which for the moment he had forgotten because he was still trying to state the incredible simplicity of his desire and need until the man with the gun (the only one of the three who wore shoes) began to stamp at his hands, he snatching his hands away one at a time to avoid the heavy shoes, then grasping the rail again until the man with the gun kicked at his face, he flinging himself sideways to avoid the shoe and so breaking his hold on the rail, his weight canting the skiff off at a tangent on the increasing current so that it began to leave the shanty boat behind and he paddling again now, violently, as a man hurries toward the precipice for which he knows at last he is doomed, looking back at the other boat, the three faces sullen derisive and grim and rapidly diminishing across the widening water and at last, apoplectic, suffocating with the intolerable fact not that he had been refused but that he had been refused so little, had wanted so little, asked for so little, yet there had been demanded of him in return the one price out of all breath which (they must have known) if he could have paid it, he would not have been where he was, asking what he asked, raising the paddle and shaking it and screaming curses back at them even after the shotgun flashed and the charge went scuttering past along the water to one side.

So he hung there, he said, shaking the paddle and howling, when suddenly he remembered that other wave, the second wall of water full of houses and dead mules building up behind him back in the swamp. So he quit yelling then and went back to paddling. He was not trying to outrun it. He just knew from experience that when it overtook him, he would have to travel in the same direction it was moving in anyway, whether he wanted to or not, and when it did overtake him, he would begin to move too fast to stop, no matter what places he might come to where he could leave the woman, land her in time. Time: that was his itch now, so his only chance was to stay ahead of it as long as he could and hope to reach something before it struck. So he went on, driving the skiff with muscles which had been too tired so long they had quit feeling it, as when a man has had bad luck for so long that he ceases to believe it is even bad, let alone luck. Even when he ate—the scorched lumps the size of baseballs and the weight and durability of channel coal even after having lain in the skiff's bilge where the shanty boat woman had thrown them—the iron-like lead-heavy objects which no man would have called bread outside of the crusted and scorched pan in which they had cooked—it was with one hand, begrudging even that from the paddle.

He tried to tell that too—that day while the skiff fled on among the bearded trees while every now and then small quiet tentative exploratory feelers would come up from the wave behind and toy for a moment at the skiff, light and curious, then go on with a faint hissing sighing, almost a chuckling, sound, the skiff going on, driving on with nothing to see but trees and water and solitude: until after a while it no longer seemed to him that he was trying to put space and distance behind him or shorten space and distance ahead but that both he and the wave were now hanging suspended simultaneous and unprogressing in pure time, upon a dreamy desolation in which he paddled on not from any hope even to reach anything at all but merely to keep intact what little of distance the length of the skiff provided between himself and the inert and inescapable mass of female meat before him; then night and the skiff rushing on, fast since any speed over anything unknown and invisible is too fast, with nothing before him and behind him the outrageous idea of a volume of moving water toppling forward, its crest frothed and shredded like fangs, and then dawn again (another of those dreamlike alterations day to dark then back to day again with that quality truncated, anachronic and unreal as the waxing and waning of lights in a theatre scene) and the skiff emerging now with the woman no longer supine beneath the shrunken soaked private's coat but sitting bolt upright, gripping the gunwales with both hands, her closed and her lower lip caught between her teeth and he driving the splintered board furiously now, glaring at her out of his wild swollen sleepless face and crying, croaking, "Hold on! For God's sake hold on!"

"I'm trying to," she said. "But hurry! Hurry!" He told it, the unbelievable: hurry, hasten: the man falling from a cliff being told to catch onto something and save himself; the very telling of it emerging shadowy and burlesque, ludicrous, comic and mad, from the ague of unbearable forgetting with a quality more dreamily furious than any fable behind proscenium lights:

He was in a basin now—"A basin?" the plump convict said. "That's what you wash in."

"All right," the tall one said, harshly, above his hands. "I did." With a
supreme effort he stilled them long enough to release the two bits of cigarette paper and watched them waft in light fluttering indecision to the floor
between his feet, holding his hands motionless even for a moment longer—
a basin, a broad peaceful yellow sea which had an abruptly and curiously
ordered air, giving him, even at that moment, the impression that it was
accustomed to water even if not total submersion; he even remembered the
name of it, told to him two or three weeks later by someone: Atchafalaya—

"Louisiana?" the plump convict said. "You mean you were clean out of
Mississippi? Hell fire." He stared at the tall one. "Shucks," he said. "That
aint but just across from Vicksburg."

"They never named any Vicksburg across from where I was," the tall one
said. "It was Baton Rouge they named." And now he began to talk about a
town, a little neat white portrait town nestling among enormous very green
trees, appearing suddenly in the telling as it probably appeared in actuality,
abrupt and airy and miragelike and incredibly serene before him behind a
scattering of boats moored to a line of freight cars standing flush to the doors
in water. And now he tried to tell that too: how he stood waist-deep in water
for a moment looking back and down at the skiff in which the woman half
lay, her eyes still closed, her knuckles white on the gunwales and a tiny
thread of blood creeping down her chin from her chewed lip, and he looking
down at her in a kind of furious desperation.

"How far will I have to walk?" she said.

"I dont know, I tell you!" he cried. "But it's land somewhere yonder! It's
land, houses."

"If I try to move, it wont even be born inside a boat," she said. "You'll
have to get closer."

"Yes," he cried, wild, desperate, incredulous. "Wait. I'll go and surrender, then they will have—" He didn't finish, wait to finish; he told that too:
himself splashing, stumbling, trying to run, sobbing and gasping; now he saw
it—another loading platform standing above the yellow flood, the khaki figures on it as before, identical, the same; he said how the intervening days
since that first innocent morning telescoped, vanished as if they had never
been, the two contiguous succeeding instants (succeeding? simultaneous) and
he transported across no intervening space but merely turned in his own
footsteps, plunging, splashing, his arms raised, croaking harshly. He heard
the startled shout, "There's one of them!", the command, the clash of equipment, the alarmed cry: "There he goes! There he goes!"

"Yes!" he cried, running, plunging, "here I am! Here! Here!" running on,
into the first scattered volley, stopping among the bullets, waving his arms,
shrieking, "I want to surrender! I want to surrender!" watching not in terror
but in amazed and absolutely unbearable outrage as a squatting clump of the
khaki figures, parted and he saw the machine gun, the blunt thick muzzle
slant and drop and probe toward him and he still screaming in his hoarse

crow's voice, "I want to surrender! Cant you hear me?" continuing to
scream even as he whirled and plunged splashing, ducking, when completely
under and heard the bullets going thuck-thuck-thuck on the water above
him and he scrabbling still on the bottom, still trying to scream even before
he regained his feet and still all submerged save his plunging unmistakable
buttocks, the outraged screaming bubbling from his mouth and about his
face since he merely wanted to surrender. Then he was comparatively
screened, out of range, though not for long. That is (he didn't tell how nor
where) there was a moment in which he paused, breathed for a second
before running again, the course back to the skiff open for the time being
though he could still hear the shouts behind him and now 'and then a shot,
and he panting, sobbing, a long savage tear in the flesh of one hand, got when
and how he did not know, and he wasting precious breath, speaking to no
one now any more than the scream of the dying rabbit is addressed to any
mortal ear but rather an indictment of all breath and its folly and suffering,
its infinite capacity for folly and pain, which seems to be its only immortality:
"All in the world I want is just to surrender."

He returned to the skiff and got in and took up his splintered plank. And
now when he told this, despite the fury of element which climaxed it, it (the
telling) became quite simple; he now even creased another cigarette paper
between fingers which did not tremble at all and filled the paper from the
tobacco sack without spilling a flake, as though he had passed from the
machine gun's barrage into a bourne beyond any more amazement: so that
the subsequent part of his narrative seemed to reach his listeners as though
from beyond a sheet of slightly milky though still transparent glass, as something not heard but seen—a series of shadows, edgeless yet distinct, and
smoothly flowing, logical and unfrantic and making no sound: They were in
the skiff, in the center of the broad placid trough which had no boundaries
and down which the tiny forlorn skiff flew to the irresistible coercion of a
current going once more he knew not where, the neat small liveoak-bowered
towns unattainable and miragelike and apparently attached to nothing upon
the airy and unchanging horizon. He did not believe them, they did not
matter, he was doomed; they were less than the figments of smoke or of
delirium, and he driving his unceasing paddle without destination or even
hope now, looking now and then at the woman sitting with her knees drawn
up and locked and her entire body one terrific clench while the threads of
bloody saliva crept from her teeth-clenched lower lip. He was going nowhere and fleeing from nothing, he merely continued to paddle because he
had paddled so long now that he believed if he stopped his muscles would
scream in agony. So when it happened he was not surprised. He heard the
sound which he knew well (he had heard it but once before, true enough,
but no man needed hear it but once) and he had been expecting it; he
looked back, still driving the paddle, and saw it, curled, crested with its
strawlike flotsam of trees and debris and dead beasts and he glared over his

shoulder at it for a full minute out of that attenuation far beyond the point of outragement where even suffering, the capability of being further affronted, had ceased, from which he now contemplated with savage and invulnerable curiosity the further extent to which his now anesthetised nerves could bear, what next could be invented for them to bear, until the wave actually began to rear above his head into its thunderous climax. Then only did he turn his head. His stroke did not falter, it neither slowed nor increased; still paddling with that spent hypnotic steadiness, he saw the swimming deer. He did not know what it was nor that he had altered the skiff's course to follow it, he just watched the swimming head before him as the wave boiled down and the skiff rose bodily in the old familiar fashion on a welter of tossing trees and houses and bridges and fences, he still paddling even while the paddle found no purchase save air and still paddled even as he and the deer shot forward side by side at arm's length, he watching the deer now, watching the deer begin to rise out of the water bodily until it was actually running along upon the surface, rising still, soaring clear of the water altogether, vanishing upward in a dying crescendo of splashings and snapping branches, its damp scut flashing upward, the entire animal vanishing upward as smoke vanishes. And now the skiff struck and canted and he was out of it too, standing knee-deep, springing out and falling to his knees, scrambling up, glaring after the vanished deer. "Land!" he croaked. "Land! Hold on! Just hold on!" He caught the woman beneath the arms, dragging her out of the boat, plunging and panting after the vanished deer. Now earth actually appeared—an acclivity smooth and swift and steep, bizarre, solid and unbelievable; an Indian mound, and he plunging at the muddy slope, slipping back, the woman struggling in his muddy hands.

"Let me down!" she cried. "Let me down!" But he held her, panting, sobbing, and rushed again at the muddy slope; he had almost reached the flat crest with his now violently unmanageable burden when a stick under his foot gathered itself with thick convulsive speed. *It was a snake,* he thought as his feet fled beneath him and with the indubitable last of his strength he half pushed and half flung the woman up the bank as he shot feet first and face down back into that medium upon which he had lived for more days and nights than he could remember and from which he himself had never completely emerged, as if his own failed and spent flesh were attempting to carry out his furious unflagging will for severance at any price, even that of drowning, from the burden with which, unwitting and without choice, he had been doomed. Later it seemed to him that he had carried back beneath the surface with him the sound of the infant's first mewling cry.

When the woman asked him if he had a knife, standing there in the streaming bedticking garments which had got him shot at, the second time by a machine gun, on the two occasions when he had seen any human life after leaving the levee four days ago, the convict felt exactly as he had in the fleeing skiff when the woman suggested that they had better hurry. He felt the same outrageous affronting of a condition purely moral, the same raging impotence to find any answer to it; so that, standing above her, spent suffocating and inarticulate, it was a full minute before he comprehended that she was now crying. "The can! The can in the boat!" He did not anticipate what she could want with it; he did not even wonder nor stop to ask. He turned running; this time he thought, *It's another mocassin* as the thick body truncated in that awkward reflex which had nothing of alarm in it but only alertness, he not even shifting his stride though he knew his running foot would fall within a yard of the flat head. The bow of the skiff was well up the slope now where the wave had set it and there was another snake just crawling over the stern into it and as he stooped for the bailing can he saw something else swimming toward the mound, he didn't know what—a head, a face at the apex of a vee of ripples. He snatched up the can; by pure juxtaposition of it and water he scooped it full, already turning. He saw the deer again, or another one. That is, he saw a deer—a side glance, the light smoke-colored phantom in a cypress vista then gone, vanished, he not pausing to look after it, galloping back to the woman and kneeling with the can to her lips until she told him better.

It had contained a pint of beans or tomatoes, something, hermetically sealed and opened by four blows of an axe heel, the metal flap turned back, the jagged edges razor-sharp. She told him how, and he used this in lieu of a knife, he removed one of the shoelaces and cut it in two with the sharp tin. Then she wanted warm water—"If I just had a little hot water," she said in a weak serene voice without particular hope; only when he thought of matches it was again a good deal like when she had asked him if he had a knife, until she fumbled in the pocket of the shrunken tunic (it had a darker double vee on one cuff and a darker blotch on the shoulder where service stripes and a divisional emblem had been ripped off but this meant nothing to him) and produced a match-box contrived by telescoping two shotgun shells. So he drew her back a little from the water to hunt wood dry enough to burn, thinking this time, *It's just another snake,* he said, he should have thought *ten thousand other snakes:* and now he knew it was not the same deer because he saw three at one time, does or bucks he did not know which since they were all antlerless in May and besides he had never seen one of any kind anywhere before except on a Christmas card; and then the rabbit, drowned, dead anyway, already torn open, the bird, the hawk, standing upon it—the erected crest, the hard vicious patrician nose, the intolerant omnivorous yellow eye—and he kicking at it, kicking it lurching and broad-winged into the actual air.

When he returned with the wood and the dead rabbit, the baby, wrapped in the tunic, lay wedged between two cypress-knees and the woman was not in sight, though while the convict knelt in the mud, blowing and nursing his meagre flame, she came slowly and weakly from the direction of the water.

Then, the water heated at last and there produced from some where he was never to know, she herself perhaps never to know until the need comes, no woman perhaps ever to know, only no woman will even wonder, that square of something somewhere between sackcloth and silk—squatting, his own wet garments steaming in the fire's heat, he watched her bathe the child with a savage curiosity and interest that became amazed unbelief, so that at last he stood above them both, looking down at the tiny terra-cotta colored creature resembling nothing, and thought, *And this is all. This is what severed me violently from all I ever knew and did not wish to leave and cast me upon a medium I was born to fear, to fetch up at last in a place I never saw before and where I do not even know where I am.*

Then he returned to the water and refilled the bailing can. It was drawing toward sunset now (or what would have been sunset save for the high prevailing overcast) of this day whose beginning he could not even remember; when he returned to where the fire burned in the interlaced gloom of the cypresses, even after this short absence, evening had definitely come, as though darkness too had taken refuge upon that quarter-acre mound, that earthen Ark out of Genesis, that dim wet cypress-choked life-teeming constricted desolation in what direction and how far from what and where he had no more idea than of the day of the month, and had now with the setting of the sun crept forth again to spread upon the waters. He stewed the rabbit in sections while the fire burned redder and redder in the darkness where the shy wild eyes of small animals—once the tall mild almost plate-sized stare of one of the deer—glowed and vanished and glowed again, the broth hot and rank after the four days; he seemed to hear the roar of his own saliva as he watched the woman sip the first canful. Then he drank too; they ate the other fragments which had been charring and scorching on willow twigs; it was full night now. "You and him better sleep in the boat," the convict said. "We want to get an early start tomorrow." He shoved the bow of the skiff off the land so it would lie level, he lengthened the painter with a piece of grapevine and returned to the fire and tied the grapevine about his wrist and lay down. It was mud he lay upon, but it was solid underneath, it was earth, it did not move; if you fell upon it you broke your bones against its incontrovertible passivity sometimes but it did not accept you substanceless and enveloping and suffocating, down and down and down; it was hard at times to drive a plow through, it sent you spent, weary, and cursing its light-long insatiable demands back to your bunk at sunset at times but it did not snatch you violently out of all familiar knowing and sweep you thrall and impotent for days against any returning. *I dont know where I am and I dont reckon I know the way back to where I want to go,* he thought. *But at least the boat has stopped long enough to give me a chance to turn it around.*

He waked at dawn, the light faint, the sky jonquil-colored; the day would be fine. The fire had burned out; on the opposite side of the cold ashes lay three snakes motionless and parallel as underscoring, and in the swiftly making light others seemed to materialise: earth which an instant before had been mere earth broke up into motionless coils and loops, branches which a moment before had been mere branches now become immobile ophidian festoons even as the convict stood thinking about food, about something hot before they started. But he decided against this, against wasting this much time, since there still remained in the skiff quite a few of the rocklike objects which the shanty woman had flung into it, besides (thinking this) no matter how fast nor successfully he hunted, he would never be able to lay up enough food to get them back to where they wanted to go. So he returned to the skiff, paying himself back to it by his vine-spliced painter, back to the water on which a low mist thick as cotton batting (though apparently not very tall, deep) lay, into which the stern of the skiff was already beginning to disappear although it lay with its prow almost touching the mound. The woman waked, stirred. "We fixing to start now?" she said.

"Yah," the convict said. "You aint aiming to have another one this morning, are you?" He got in and shoved the skiff clear of the land, which immediately began to dissolve into the mist. "Hand me the oar," he said over his shoulder, not turning yet.

"The oar?"

He turned his head. "The oar. You're laying on it." But she was not, and for an instant during which the mound, the island continued to fade slowly into the mist which seemed to enclose the skiff in weightless and impalpable wool like a precious or fragile bauble or jewel, the convict squatted not in dismay but in that frantic and astonished outrage of a man who, having just escaped a falling safe, is struck by the following two-ounce paper weight which was sitting on it: this the more unbearable because he knew that never in his life had he less time to give way to it. He did not hesitate. Grasping the grapevine end he sprang into the water, vanishing in the violent action of climbing and reappeared still climbing and (who had never learned to swim) plunged and threshed on toward the almost-vanished mound, moving through the water then upon it as the deer had done yesterday and scrabbled up the muddy slope and lay gasping and panting, still clutching the grapevine end.

Now the first thing he did was to choose what he believed to be the most suitable tree (for an instant in which he knew he was insane he thought of trying to saw it down with the flange of the bailing can) and build a fire against the butt of it. Then he went to seek food. He spent the next six days seeking it while the tree burned through and fell and burned through again at the proper length and he nursing little constant cunning flames along the flanks of the log to make it paddle-shaped, nursing them at night too while the woman and baby (it was eating, nursing now, he turning his back or even returning into the woods each time she prepared to open the faded tunic) slept in the skiff. He learned to watch for stooping hawks and so found more rabbits and twice possums; they ate some drowned fish which gave them both a rash and then a violent flux and one snake which the woman thought was turtle and which did them no harm, and one night it rained and he got up and dragged brush, shaking the snakes (he no longer thought, *It aint nothing but another moccasin,* he just stepped aside for him) out of it with the old former feeling of personal invulnerability and built a shelter and the rain stopped at once and did not recommence and the woman went back to the skiff.

Then one night—the slow tedious charring log was almost a paddle now—one night and he was in bed, in his bed in the bunkhouse and it was cold, he was trying to pull the covers up only his mule wouldn't let him, prodding and bumping heavily at him, trying to get into the narrow bed with him and now the bed was cold too and wet and he was trying to get out of it only the mule would not let him, holding him by his belt in its teeth, jerking and bumping him back into the cold wet bed and, leaning, gave him a long swipe across the face with its cold limber musculated tongue and he waked to no fire, no coal even beneath where the almost-finished paddle had been charring and something else prolonged and coldly limber passed swiftly across his body where he lay in four inches of water while the nose of the skiff alternately tugged at the grapevine tied about his waist and bumped and shoved him back into the water again. Then something else came up and began to nudge at his ankle (the log, the oar, it was) even as he groped frantically for the skiff, hearing the swift rustling going to and fro inside the hull as the woman began to thrash about and scream. "Rats!" she cried. "It's full of rats!"

"Lay still!" he cried. "It's just snakes. Cant you hold still long enough for me to find the boat?" Then he found it, he got into it with the unfinished paddle; again the thick muscular body convulsed under his foot; it did not strike; he would not have cared, glaring astern where he could see a little— the faint outer luminosity of the open water. He poled toward it, thrusting aside the snake-looped branches, the bottom of the skiff resounding faintly to thick solid plops, the woman shrieking steadily. Then the skiff was clear of the trees, the mound, and now he could feel the bodies whipping about his ankles and hear the rasp of them as they went over the gunwale. He drew the log in and scooped it forward along the bottom of the boat and up and out; against the pallid water he could see three more of them in lashing convolutions before they vanished. "Shut up!" he cried. "Hush! I wish I was a snake so I could get out too!"

When once more the pale and heatless wafer disc of the early sun stared down at the skiff (whether they were moving or not the convict did not know) in its nimbus of fine cotton batting, the convict was hearing again that sound which he had heard twice before and would never forget—that sound of deliberate and irresistible and monstrously disturbed water. But this time he could not tell from what direction it came. It seemed to be everywhere, waxing and fading; it was like a phantom behind the mist, at one instant miles away, the next on the point of overwhelming the skiff within the next second; suddenly, in the instant he would believe (his whole weary body would spring and scream) that he was about to drive the skiff point-blank into it and with the unfinished paddle of the color and texture of sooty bricks, like something gnawed out of an old chimney by beavers and weighing twenty-five pounds, he would whirl the skiff frantically and find the sound dead ahead of him again. The something bellowed tremendously above his head, he heard human voices, a bell jangled and the sound ceased and the mist vanished as when you draw your hand across a frosted pane, and the skiff now lay upon a sunny glitter of brown water flank to flank with, and about thirty yards away from, a steamboat. The decks were crowded and packed with men women and children sitting or standing beside and among a homely conglomeration of hurried furniture, who looked mournfully and silently down into the skiff while the convict and the man with a megaphone in the pilot house talked to each other in alternate puny shouts and roars above the chuffing of the reversed engines:

"What in hell are you trying to do? Commit suicide?"

"Which is the way to Vicksburg?"

"Vicksburg? Vicksburg? Lay alongside and come aboard."

"Will you take the boat too?"

"Boat? Boat?" Now the megaphone cursed, the roaring waves of blasphemy and biological supposition empty cavernous and bodiless in turn, as if the water, the air, the mist had spoken it, roaring the words then taking them back to itself and no harm done, no scar, no insult left anywhere. "If I took aboard every floating sardine can you sonabitchin mushrats want me to I wouldn't even have room forrard for a leadsman. Come aboard! Do you expect me to hang here on stern engines till hell freezes?"

"I aint coming without the boat," the convict said. Now another voice spoke, so calm and mild and sensible that for a moment it sounded more foreign and out of place than even the megaphone's bellowing and bodiless profanity:

"Where is it you are trying to go?"

"I aint trying," the convict said. "I'm going. Parchman." The man who had spoken last turned and appeared to converse with a third man in the pilot house. Then he looked down at the skiff again.

"Carnarvon?"

"What?" the convict said. "Parchman?"

"All right. We're going that way. We'll put you off where you can get home. Come aboard."

"The boat too?"

"Yes. yes. Come along. We're burning coal just to talk to you." So the convict came alongside then and watched them help the woman and baby over the rail and he came aboard himself, though he still held to the end of the vine-spliced painter until the skiff was hoisted onto the boiler deck. "My

God," the man, the gentle one, said, "is that what you have been using for a paddle?"

"Yah," the convict said. "I lost the plank."

"The plank, " the mild man (the convict told how he seemed to whisper it), "the plank. Well. Come along and get something to eat. Your boat is all right now."

"I reckon I'll wait here," the convict said. Because now, he told them, he began to notice for the first time that the other people, the other refugees who crowded the deck, who had gathered in a quiet circle about the up-turned skiff on which he and the woman sat, the grapevine painter wrapped several times about his wrist and clutched in his hand, staring at him and the woman with queer hot mournful intensity, were not white people—

"You mean niggers?" the plump convict said.

"No. Not Americans."

"Not Americans? You was clean out of *America* even?"

"I don't know," the tall one said. "They called it Atchafalaya."—Because after a while he said, "What?" to the man and the man did it again, gobble-gobble—

"Gobble-gobble?" the plump convict said.

"That's the way they talked," the tall one said. "Gobble-gobble, whang, caw-caw-to-to."—And he sat there and watched them gobbling at one an-other and then looking at him again, then they fell back and the mild man (he wore a Red Cross brassard) entered, followed by a waiter with a tray of food. The mild man carried two glasses of whiskey.

"Drink this," the mild man said. "This will warm you." The woman took hers and drank it but the convict told how he looked at his and thought, *I aint tasted whiskey in seven years.* He had not tasted it but once before that; it was at the still itself back in a pine hollow; he was seventeen, he had gone there with four companions, two of whom were grown men, one of twenty-two or -three, the other about forty; he remembered it. That is, he remem-bered perhaps a third of that evening—a fierce turmoil in the hell-colored firelight, the shock and shock of blows about his head (and like-wise of his own fists on other hard bone), then the waking to a splitting and blinding sun in a place, a cowshed, he had never seen before and which later turned out to be twenty miles from his home. He said he thought of this and he looked about at the faces watching him and he said,

"I reckon not."

"Come, come," the mild man said. "Drink it."

"I dont want it."

"Nonsense," the mild man said. "I'm a doctor. Here. Then you can eat." So he took the glass and even then he hesitated but again the mild man said, "Come along, down with it; you're still holding us up," in that voice still calm and sensible but a little sharp too—the voice of a man who could keep calm and affable because he wasn't used to being crossed—and he drank the whiskey and even in the second between the sweet full fire in his belly and when it began to happen he was trying to say, "I tried to tell you! I tried to!" But it was too late now in the pallid sun-glare of the tenth day of terror and hopelessness and despair and impotence and rage and outrage and it was himself and the mule, his mule (they had let him name it—John Henry) which no man save he had plowed for five years now and whose ways and habits he knew and respected and who knew his ways and habits so well that each of them could anticipate the other's very movements and intentions; it was himself and the mule, the little gobbling faces flying before them, the familiar hard skull-bones shocking against his fists, his voice shouting, "Come on, John Henry! Plow them down! Gobble them down, boy!" even as the bright hot red wave turned back, meeting it joyously, happily, lifted, poised, then hurling through space, triumphant and yelling, then again the old shocking blow at the back of his head: he lay on the deck, flat on his back and pinned arm and leg and cold sober again, his nostrils gushing again, the mild man stooping over him with behind the thin rimless glasses the coldest eyes the convict had ever seen—eyes which the convict said were not look-ing at him but at the gushing blood with nothing in the world in them but complete impersonal interest.

"Good man," the mild man said. "Plenty of life in the old carcass yet, eh? Plenty of good red blood too. Anyone ever suggested to you that you were hemophilic?" ("What?" the plump convict said. "Hemophilic? You know what that means?" The tall convict had his cigarette going now, his body jackknifed backward into the coffinlike space between the upper and lower bunks, lean, clean, motionless, the blue smoke wreathing across his lean dark, aquiline shaven face. "That's a calf that's a bull and a cow at the same time."

"No, it aint," a third convict said. "It's a calf or a colt that aint neither one."

"Hell fire," the plump one said. "He's got to be one or the other to keep from drounding." He had never ceased to look at the tall one in the bunk; now he spoke to him again: "You let him call you that?") The tall one had done so. He did not answer the doctor (this was where he stopped thinking of him as the mild man) at all. He could not move either, though he felt fine, he felt better than he had in ten days. So they helped him to his feet and steadied him over and lowered him onto the upturned skiff beside the woman, where he sat bent forward, elbows on knees in the immemorial attitude, watching his own bright crimson staining the mud-trodden deck, until the doctor's clean clipped hand appeared under his nose with a phial.

"Smell," the doctor said. "Deep." The convict inhaled, the sharp ammo-niac sensation burned up his nostrils and into his throat. "Again," the doctor said. The convict inhaled obediently. This time he choked and spat a gout of blood, his nose now had no more feeling than a toenail, other than it felt about the size of a ten-inch shovel, and as cold.

"I ask you to excuse me," he said. "I never meant—"

"Why?" the doctor said. "You put up as pretty a scrap against forty or fifty men as I ever saw. You lasted a good two seconds. Now you can eat something. Or do you think that will send you haywire again?"

They both ate, sitting on the skiff, the gobbling faces no longer watching them now, the convict gnawing slowly and painfully at the thick sandwich, hunched, his face laid sideways to the food and parallel to the earth as a dog chews; the steamboat went on. At noon there were bowls of hot soup and bread and more coffee; they ate this too, sitting side by side on the skiff, the grapevine still wrapped about the convict's wrist. The baby waked and nursed and slept again and they talked quietly:

"Was it Parchman he said he was going to take us?"

"That's where I told him I wanted to go."

"It never sounded exactly like Parchman to me. It sounded like he said something else." The convict had thought that too. He had been thinking about that fairly soberly ever since they boarded the steamboat and soberly indeed ever since he had remarked the nature of the other passengers, those men and women definitely a little shorter than he and with skin a little different in pigmentation from any sunburn, even though the eyes were sometimes blue or gray, who talked to one another in a tongue he had never heard before and who apparently did not understand his own, people the like of whom he had never seen about Parchman nor anywhere else and whom he did not believe were going there or beyond there either. But after his hill-billy country fashion and kind he would not ask, because to his raising asking information was asking a favor and you did not ask favors of strangers; if they offered them perhaps you accepted and you expressed gratitude almost tediously recapitulant, but you did not ask. So he would watch and wait, as he had done before, and do or try to do to the best of his ability what the best of his judgment dictated.

So he waited, and in midafternoon the steamboat chuffed and thrust through a willow-choked gorge and emerged from it, and now the convict knew it was the River. He could believe it now—the tremendous reach, yellow and sleepy in the afternoon—("Because it's too big," he told them soberly. "Aint no flood in the world big enough to make it do more than stand a little higher so it can look back and see just where the flea is, just exactly where to scratch. It's the little ones, the little piddling creeks that run backward one day and forward the next and come busting down on a man full of dead mules and hen houses.")—and the steamboat moving up this now (*like a ant crossing a plate*, the convict thought, sitting beside the woman on the upturned skiff, the baby nursing again, apparently looking too out across the water where, a mile away on either hand, the twin lines of levee resembled parallel unbroken floating thread) and then it was nearing sunset and he began to hear, to notice, the voices of the doctor and of the man who had first bawled at him through the megaphone now bawling again from the pilot house overhead:

"Stop? Stop? Am I running a street car?"

"Stop for the novelty then," the doctor's pleasant voice said. "I dont know how many trips back and forth you have made in yonder nor how many of what you call mushrats you have fetched out. But this is the first time you ever had two people—no, three—who not only knew the name of some place they wished to go to but were actually trying to go there." So the convict waited while the sun slanted more and more and the steamboat-ant crawled steadily on across its vacant and gigantic plate turning more and more to copper. But he did not ask, he just waited. *Maybe it was Carrollton he said*, he thought. *It began with a C.* But he did not believe that either. He did not know where he was, but he did know that this was not anywhere near the Carrollton he remembered from that day seven years ago when, shackled wrist to wrist with the deputy sheriff, he had passed through it on the train—the slow spaced repeated shattering banging of trucks where two railroads crossed, a random scattering of white houses tranquil among trees on green hills lush with summer, a pointing spire, the finger of the hand of God. But there was no river there. *And you aint never close to this river without knowing it*, he thought. *I dont care who you are nor where you have been all your life.* Then the head of the steamboat began to swing across the stream, its shadow swinging too, travelling long before it across the water, toward the vacant ridge of willow-massed earth empty of all life. There was nothing there at all, the convict could not even see either earth or water beyond it; it was as though the steamboat were about to crash slowly through the thin low frail willow barrier and embark into space, or lacking this, slow and back and fill and disembark him into space, granted it was about to disembark him, granted this was that place which was not near Parchman and was not Carrollton either, even though it did begin with C. Then he turned his head and saw the doctor stooping over the woman, pushing the baby's eyelid up with his forefinger, peering at it.

"Who else was there when he came?" the doctor said.

"Nobody," the convict said.

"Did it all yourselves, eh?"

"Yes," the convict said. Now the doctor stood up and looked at the convict.

"This is Carnarvon," he said.

"Carnarvon?" the convict said, "That aint—" Then he stopped, ceased. And now he told about that—the intent eyes as dispassionate as ice behind the rimless glasses, the clipped quick-tempered face that was not accustomed to being crossed or lied to either. ("Yes," the plump convict said. "That's what I was aiming to ask. Them clothes. Anybody would know them. How if this doctor was as smart as you claim he was—"

"I had slept in them for ten nights, mostly in the mud," the tall one said. "I had been rowing since midnight with that sapling oar I had tried to burn out that I never had time to scrape the soot off. But it's being scared and worried and then scared and then worried again in clothes for days and days and days that changes the way they look. I dont mean just your pants." He did not laugh. "Your face too. The doctor knowed."

"All right," the plump one said. "Go on.")

"I know it," the doctor said. "I discovered that while you were lying on the deck yonder sobering up again. Now dont lie to me. I dont like lying. This boat is going to New Orleans."

"No," the convict said immediately, quietly, with absolute finality. He could hear them again—the thuck-thuck-thuck on the water where an instant before he had been. But he was not thinking of the bullets. He had forgotten them, forgiven them. He was thinking of himself crouching, sobbing, panting before running again—the voice, the indictment, the cry of final and irrevocable repudiation of the old primal faithless Manipulator of all the lust and folly and injustice: *All in the world I wanted was just to surrender;* thinking of it, remembering it but without heat now, without passion now and briefer than an epitaph: *No. I tried that once. They shot at me.*

"So you dont want to go to New Orleans. And you didn't exactly plan to go to Carnarvon. But you will take Carnarvon in preference to New Orleans." The convict said nothing. The doctor looked at him, the magnified pupils like the heads of two bridge nails. "What were you in for? Hit him harder than you thought, eh?"

"No, I tried to rob a train."

"Say that again." The convict said it again. "Well? Go on. You dont say that in the year 1927 and just stop, man." So the convict told it, dispassionately too—about the magazines, the pistol which would not shoot, the mask and the dark lantern in which no draft had been arranged to keep the candle burning so that it died almost with the match but even then left the metal too hot to carry, won with subscriptions. *Only it aint my eyes or my mouth either he's watching,* he thought. *It's like he is watching the way my hair grows on my head.* "I see," the doctor said. "But something went wrong. But you've had plenty of time to think about it since. To decide what was wrong, what you failed to do."

"Yes," the convict said. "I've thought about it a right smart since."

"So next time you are not going to make that mistake."

"I don't know," the convict said. "There aint going to be a next time."

"Why? If you know what you did wrong, they wont catch you next time."

The convict looked at the doctor steadily. They looked at each other steadily; the two sets of eyes were not so different after all. "I reckon I see what you mean," the convict said presently. "I was eighteen then. I'm twenty-five now."

"Oh," the doctor said. Now (the convict tried to tell it) the doctor did not move, he just simply quit looking at the convict. He produced a pack of cheap cigarettes from his coat. "Smoke?" he said.

"I wouldn't care for none," the convict said.

"Quite," the doctor said in that affable clipped voice. He put the cigarettes away. "There has been conferred upon my race (the Medical race) also the power to bind and to loose, if not by Jehovah perhaps, certainly by the American Medical Association—on which incidentally, in this day of Our Lord, I would put my money, at any odds, at any amount, at any time. I dont know just how far out of bounds I am on this specific occasion but I think we'll put it to the touch." He cupped his hands to his mouth, toward the pilot house overhead. "Captain!" he shouted. "We'll put these three passengers ashore here." He turned to the convict again. "Yes," he said, "I think I shall let your native State lick its own vomit. Here." Again his hand emerged from his pocket, this time with a bill in it.

"No," the convict said.

"Come, come; I dont like to be disputed either."

"No," the convict said. "I aint got any way to pay it back."

"Did I ask you to pay it back?"

"No," the convict said. "I never asked to borrow it either."

So once more he stood on dry land, who had already been toyed with twice by that risible and concentrated power of water, once more than should have fallen to the lot of any one man, any one lifetime, yet for whom there was reserved still another unbelievable recapitulation, he and the woman standing on the empty levee, the sleeping child wrapped in the faded tunic and the grapevine painter still wrapped about the convict's wrist, watching the steamboat back away and turn and once more crawl onward up the platter-like reach of vacant water burnished more and more to copper, its trailing smoke roiling in slow copper-edged gouts, thinning out along the water, fading, stinking away across the vast serene desolation, the boat growing smaller and smaller until it did not seem to crawl at all but to hang stationary in the airy substanceless sunset, dissolving into nothing like a pellet of floating mud.

Then he turned and for the first time looked about him, behind him, recoiling, not through fear but through pure reflex and not physically but the soul, the spirit, that profound sober alert attentiveness of the hillman who will not ask anything of strangers, not even information, thinking quietly, *No. This aint Carrollton neither.* Because he now looked down the almost perpendicular landward slope of the levee through sixty feet of absolute space, upon a surface, a terrain flat as a waffle and of the color of a waffle or perhaps of the summer coat of a claybank horse and possessing that same piled density of a rug or peltry, spreading away without undulation yet with that curious appearance of imponderable solidity like fluid, broken here and there by thick humps of arsenical green which nevertheless still seemed to possess no height and by writhen veins of the color of ink which he began to suspect to be actual water but with judgment reserved, with judgment still reserved even when presently he was walking in it. That's what he said, told: So they went on. He didn't tell how he got the skiff singlehanded up the revetment and across the crown and down the opposite sixty foot drop, he just said he went on, in a swirling cloud of mosquitoes like hot cinders, thrusting and plunging through the saw-edged grass which grew taller than his head and which whipped back at his arms and face like limber knives, dragging by the vine-spliced painter the skiff in which the woman sat, slogging and stumbling knee-deep in something less of earth than water, along one of those black winding channels less of water than earth: and then (he was in the skiff too now, paddling with the charred log, what footing there had been having given away beneath him without warning thirty minutes ago, leaving only the air-filled bubble of his jumper-back ballooning lightly on the twilit water until he rose to the surface and scrambled into the skiff) the house, the cabin a little larger than a horse-box, of cypress boards and an iron roof, rising on ten-foot stilts slender as spiders' legs, like a shabby and death-stricken (and probably poisonous) wading creature which had got that far into that flat waste and died with nothing nowhere in reach or sight to lie down upon, a pirogue[1] tied to the foot of a crude ladder, a man standing in the open door holding a lantern (it was that dark now) above his head, gobbling down at them.

He told it—of the next eight or nine or ten days, he did not remember which, while the four of them—himself and the woman and baby and the little wiry man with rotting teeth and soft wild bright eyes like a rat or a chipmunk, whose language neither of them could understand—lived in the room and a half. He did not tell it that way, just as he apparently did not consider it worth the breath to tell how he had got the hundred-and-sixty-pound skiff singlehanded up and across and down the sixty-foot levee. He just said, "After a while we come to a house and we stayed there eight or nine days then they blew up the levee with dynamite so we had to leave." That was all. But he remembered it, but quietly now, with the cigar now, the good one the Warden had given him (though not lighted yet) in his peaceful and steadfast hand, remembering that first morning when he waked on the thin pallet beside his host (the woman and baby had the one bed) with the fierce sun already latticed through the warped rough planking of the wall, and stood on the rickety porch looking out upon that flat fecund waste neither earth nor water, where even the senses doubted which was which, which rich and massy air and which mazy and impalpable vegetation, and thought quietly, *He must do something here to eat and live. But I dont know what. And until I can go on again, until I can find where I am and how to pass that town without them seeing me I will have to help him do it so we*

---

[1] A canoe made from a hollowed tree trunk.

can eat and live too, and I dont know what. And he had a change of clothing
too, almost at once on that first morning, not telling any more than he had
about the skiff and the levee how he had begged borrowed or bought from
the man whom he had not laid eyes on twelve hours ago and with whom on
the day he saw him for the last time he still could exchange no word, the pair
of dungaree pants which even the Cajan[2] had discarded as no longer wear-
able, filthy, buttonless, the legs slashed and frayed into fringe like that on an
1890 hammock, in which he stood naked from the waist up and holding out
to her the mud-caked and soot-stained jumper and overall when the woman
waked on that first morning in the crude bunk nailed into one corner and
filled with dried grass, saying, "Wash them. Good. I want all them stains out.
All of them."

"But the jumper," she said. "Aint he got ere old shirt too? That sun and
them mosquitoes—" But he did not even answer, and she said no more
either, though when he and the Cajan returned at dark the garments were
clean, stained a little still with the old mud and soot, but clean, resembling
again what they were supposed to resemble as (his arms and back already a
fiery red which would be blisters by tomorrow) he spread the garments out
and examined them and then rolled them up carefully in a six-months-old
New Orleans paper and thrust the bundle behind a rafter, where it remained
while day followed day and the blisters on his back broke and suppurated
and would sit with his face expressionless as a wooden mask beneath the
sweat while the Cajan doped his back with something on a filthy rag from a
filthy saucer, she still saying nothing since she too doubtless knew what his
reason was, not from that rapport of the wedded conferred upon her by the
two weeks during which they had jointly suffered all the crises emotional
social economic and even moral which do not always occur even in the
ordinary fifty married years (the old married: you have seen them, the elec-
troplate reproductions, the thousand identical coupled faces with only a
collarless stud or a fichu out of Louisa Alcott to denote the sex, looking in
pairs like the winning braces of dogs after a field trial, out from among the
packed columns of disaster and alarm and baseless assurance and hope and
incredible insensitivity and insulation from tomorrow propped by a thousand
morning sugar bowls or coffee urns; or singly, rocking on porches or sitting in
the sun beneath the tobacco-stained porticoes of a thousand county court-
houses, as though with the death of the other having inherited a sort of
rejuvenescence, immortality; relict, they take a new lease on breath and
seem to live forever, as though that flesh which the old ceremony or ritual
had morally purified and made legally one had actually become so with long
tedious habit and he or she who entered the ground first took all of it with
him or her, leaving only the old permanent enduring bone, free and tram-

---

[2] A native of Louisiana, believed to be descended from the French exiles of Acadia.

elless)—not because of this but because she too had stemmed at some point from the same dim hill-bred Abraham.

So the bundle remained behind the rafter and day followed day while he and his partner (he was in partnership now with his host, hunting alligators on shares, on the halvers he called it—"Halvers?" the plump convict said. "How could you make a business agreement with a man you claim you couldn't even talk to?"

"I never had to talk to him," the tall one said. "Money aint got but one language.") departed at dawn each day, at first together in the pirogue but later singly, the one in the pirogue and the other in the skiff, the one with the battered and pitted rifle, the other with the knife and a piece of knotted rope and a lightwood club the size and weight and shape of a Thuringian mace, stalking their pleistocene nightmares up and down the secret inky channels which writhed the flat brass-colored land. He remembered that too: that first morning when turning in the sunrise from the rickety platform he saw the hide nailed drying to the wall and stopped dead, looking at it quietly, thinking quietly and soberly, *So that's it. That's what he does in order to eat and live,* knowing it was a hide, a skin, but from what animal, by association, ratiocination or even memory of any picture out of his dead youth, he did not know but knowing that it was the reason, the explanation, for the little lost spider-legged house (which had already begun to die, to rot from the legs upward almost before the roof was nailed on) set in that teeming and myriad desolation, enclosed and lost within the furious embrace of flowing mare earth and stallion sun, divining through pure rapport of kind for kind, hill-billy and bayou-rat, the two one and identical because of the same grudged dispensation and niggard fate of hard and unceasing travail not to gain future security, a balance in the bank or even in a buried soda can for slothful and easy old age, but just permission to endure and endure to buy air to feel and sun to drink for each's little while, thinking (the convict), *Well, anyway I am going to find out what it is sooner than I expected to,* and did so, re-entered the house where the woman was just waking in the one sorry built-in straw-filled bunk which the Cajan had surrendered to her, and ate the breakfast (the rice, a semi-liquid mess violent with pepper and mostly fish considerably high, the chicory-thickened coffee) and, shirtless, followed the little scuttling bobbing bright-eyed rotten-toothed man down the crude ladder and into the pirogue. He had never seen a pirogue either and he believed that it would not remain upright—not that it was light and precariously balanced with its open side upward but that there was inherent in the wood, the very log, some dynamic and unsleeping natural law, almost will, which its present position outraged and violated—yet accepting this too as he had the fact that that hide had belonged to something larger than any calf or hog and that anything which looked like that on the outside would be more than likely to have teeth and claws too, accepting this, squatting in the pirogue, clutching both gunwales, rigidly immobile as though he had an egg filled with nitroglycerin in his mouth and scarcely breathing, thinking, *If that's it, then I can do it too and even if he cant tell me how I reckon I can watch him and find out.* And he did this too, he remembered it, quietly even yet, thinking, *I thought that was how to do it and I reckon I would still think that even if I had it to do again now for the first time*—the brazen day already fierce upon his naked back, the crooked channel like a voluted thread of ink, the pirogue moving steadily to the paddle which both entered and left the water without a sound; then the sudden cessation of the paddle behind him and the fierce hissing gobble of the Cajan at his back and he squatting bate-breathed and with that intense immobility of complete sobriety of a blind man listening while the frail wooden shell stole on at the dying apex of its own parted water. Afterward he remembered the rifle too—the rust-pitted single-shot weapon with a clumsily wired stock and a muzzle you could have driven a whiskey cork into, which the Cajan had brought into the boat—but not now; now he just squatted, crouched, immobile, breathing with infinitesimal care, his sober unceasing gaze going here and there constantly as he thought, *What? What? I not only dont know what I am looking for, I dont even know where to look for it.* Then he felt the motion of the pirogue as the Cajan moved and then the tense gobbling hissing actually, hot rapid and repressed, against his neck and ear, and glancing downward saw projecting between his own arm and body from behind the Cajan's hand holding the knife, and glaring up again saw the flat thick spit of mud which as he looked at it divided and became a thick mud-colored log which in turn seemed, still immobile, to leap suddenly against his retinae in three—no, four—dimensions: volume, solidity, shape, and another: not fear but pure and intense speculation and he looking at the scaled motionless shape, thinking not, *It looks dangerous* but *It looks big*, thinking, *Well, maybe a mule standing in a lot looks big to a man that never walked up to one with a halter before*, thinking, *Only if he could just tell me what to do it would save time*, the pirogue drawing nearer now, creeping now, with no ripple now even and it seemed to him that he could even hear his companion's held breath and he taking the knife from the other's hand now and not even thinking this since it was too fast, a flash; it was not a surrender, not a resignation, it was too calm, it was a part of him, he had drunk it with his mother's milk and lived with it all his life: *After all a man can only do what he has to do, with what he has to do it with, with what he has learned, to the best of his judgment. And I reckon a hog is still a hog, no matter what it looks like. So here goes,* sitting still for an instant longer until the bow of the pirogue grounded lighter than the falling of a leaf and stepped out of it and paused just for one instant while the words *It does look big* stood for just a second, unemphatic and trivial, somewhere where some fragment of his attention could see them and vanished, and stooped straddling, the knife driving even as he grasped the near foreleg, this all in the same instant when the lashing tail struck him a terrific blow upon the back. But the knife was home, he knew that even on his back in the mud, the weight of the thrashing beast longwise upon him, its ridged back clutched to his stomach, his arm about its throat, the hissing head clamped against his jaw, the furious tail lashing and flailing, the knife in his other hand probing for the life and finding it, the hot fierce gush: and now sitting beside the profound upbellied carcass, his head again between his knees in the old attitude while his own blood freshened the other which drenched him, thinking, *It's my durn nose again.*

So he sat there, his head, his streaming face, bowed between his knees in an attitude not of dejection but profoundly bemused, contemplative, while the shrill voice of the Cajan seemed to buzz at him from an enormous distance; after a time he even looked up at the antic wiry figure bouncing hysterically about him, the face wild and grimacing, the voice gobbling and high; while the convict, holding his face carefully slanted so the blood would run free, looked at him with the cold intentness of a curator or custodian paused before one of his own glass cases, the Cajan threw up the rifle, cried "Boom-boom-boom!" flung it down and in pantomime re-enacted the recent scene then whirled his hands again, crying "Magnifique! Magnifique! Cent d'argent! mille d'argent! Tout l'argent sous le ciel de Dieu!"[3] But the convict was already looking down again, cupping the coffee-colored water to his face, watching the constant bright carmine marble, thinking, *It's a little late to be telling me that now,* and not even thinking this long because presently they were in the pirogue again, the convict squatting again with that unbreathing rigidity as though he were trying by holding his breath to decrease his very weight, the bloody skin in the bows before and he looking at it, thinking, *And I cant even ask him how much my half will be.*

But this not for long either, because as he was to tell the plump convict later, money has but one language. He remembered that too (they were at home now, the skin spread on the platform, where for the woman's benefit now the Cajan once more went through the pantomime—the gun which was not used, the hand-to-hand battle; for the second time the invisible alligator was slain amid cries, the victor rose and found this time that not even the woman was watching him. She was looking at the once more swollen and inflamed face of the convict. "You mean it kicked you right in the face?" she said.

"Nah," the convict said harshly, savagely. "It never had to. I done seem to got to where if that boy was to shoot me in the tail with a bean blower my nose would bleed.")—remembered that too but he did not try to tell it. Perhaps he could not have—how two people who could not even talk to one another made an agreement which both not only understood but which each knew the other would hold true and protect (perhaps for this reason) better

---

[3] **Magnificent: Magnificent!** One hundred cents: One thousand cents! All the money under God's heaven!

than any written and witnessed contract. They even discussed and agreed somehow that they should hunt separately, each in his own vessel, to double the chances of finding prey. But this was easy: the convict could almost understand the words in which the Cajan said, "You do not need me and the rifle; we will only hinder you, be in your way." And more than this, they even agreed about the second rifle: that there was someone, it did not matter who—friend, neighbor, perhaps one in business in that line—from whom they could rent a second rifle; in their two patois, the one bastard English, the other bastard French—the one volatile, with his wild bright eyes and his voluble mouth full of stumps of teeth, the other sober, almost grim, swollen-faced and with his naked back blistered and scoriated like so much beef— they discussed this, squatting on either side of the pegged-out hide like two members of a corporation facing each other across a mahogany board table, and decided against it, the convict deciding: "I reckon not," he said. "I reckon if I had knowed enough to wait to start out with a gun, I still would. But since I done already started out without one, I dont reckon I'll change." Because it was a question of the money in terms of time, days. (Strange to say, that was the one thing which the Cajan could not tell him: how much the half would be. But the convict knew it was half.) He had so little of them. He would have to move on soon, thinking (the convict), All this durn foolishness will stop soon and I can get on back, and then suddenly he found that he was thinking, *Will have to get on back*, and he became quite still and looked about at the rich strange desert which surrounded him, in which he was temporarily lost in peace and hope and into which the last seven years had sunk like so many trivial pebbles into a pool, leaving no ripple, and he thought quietly, with a kind of bemused amazement, *Yes. I reckon I had done forgot how good making money was. Being let to make it.*

So he used no gun, his the knotted rope and the Thuringian mace, and each morning he and the Cajan took their separate ways in the two boats to comb and creep the secret channels about the lost land from (or out of) which now and then still other pint-sized dark men appeared gobbling, abruptly and as though by magic from nowhere, in other hollowed logs, to follow quietly and watch him at his single combats—men named Tine and Toto and Theule, who were not much larger than and looked a good deal like the muskrats which the Cajan (the host did this too, supplied the kitchen too, he expressed this too like the rifle business, in his own tongue, the convict comprehending this too as though it had been English: "Do not concern yourself about food, O Hercules. Catch alligators; I will supply the pot.") took now and then from traps as you take a shoat pig at need from a pen, and varied the eternal rice and fish (the convict did tell this: how at night, in the cabin, the door and one sashless window battened against mosquitoes—a form, a ritual, as empty as crossing the fingers or knocking on wood—sitting beside the bug-swirled lantern on the plank table in a temperature close to blood heat he would look down at the swimming segment of meat on his sweating plate and think, *It must be Theule. He was the fat one.*)—day following day, unemphatic and identical, each like the one before the one which would follow while his theoretical half of a sum to be reckoned in pennies, dollars, or tens of dollars he did not know, mounted—the mornings when he set forth to find waiting for him like the *matador* his *aficionados* the small clump of constant and deferential pirogues, the hard noons when ringed half about by little motionless shells he fought his solitary combats, the evenings, the return, the pirogues departing one by one into inlets and passages which during the first few days he could not even distinguish, then the platform in the twilight where before the static woman and the usually nursing infant and the one or two bloody hides of the day's take the Cajan would perform his ritualistic victorious pantomime before the two growing rows of knifemarks in one of the boards of the wall; then the nights when, the woman and child in the single bunk and the Cajan already snoring on the pallet and the reeking lantern set close, he (the convict) would sit on his naked heels, sweating steadily, his face worn and calm, immersed and indomitable, his bowed back raw and savage as beef beneath the suppurant old blisters and the fierce welts of tails, and scrape and chip at the charred sapling which was almost a paddle now, pausing now and then to raise his head while the cloud of mosquitoes about it whined and whirled, to stare at the wall before him until after a while the crude boards themselves must have dissolved away and let his blank unseeing gaze go on and on unhampered, through the rich oblivious darkness, beyond it even perhaps, even perhaps beyond the seven wasted years during which, so he had just realised, he had been permitted to toil but not to work. Then he would retire himself, he would take a last look at the rolled bundle behind the rafter and blow out the lantern and lie down as he was beside his snoring partner, to lie sweating (on his stomach, he could not bear the touch of anything to his back) in the whining ovenlike darkness filled with the forlorn bellowing of alligators, thinking not, *They never gave me time to learn* but *I had forgot how good it is to work.*

Then on the tenth day it happened. It happened for the third time. At first he refused to believe it, not that he felt that now he had served out and discharged his apprenticeship to mischance, had with the birth of the child reached and crossed the crest of his Golgotha and would now be, possibly not permitted so much as ignored, to descend the opposite slope free-wheeling. That was not his feeling at all. What he declined to accept was the fact that a power, a force such as that which had been consistent enough to concentrate upon him with deadly undeviation for weeks, should with all the wealth of cosmic violence and disaster to draw from, have been so barren of invention and imagination, so lacking in pride of artistry and craftsmanship, as to repeat itself twice. Once he had accepted, twice he even forgave, but three times he simply declined to believe, particularly when he was at last persuaded to realise that this third time was to be instigated not by the blind potency of volume and motion but by human direction and hands: that now the cosmic joker, foiled twice, had stooped in its vindictive concentration to the employing of dynamite.

He did not tell that. Doubtless he did not know himself how it happened, what was happening. But he doubtless remembered it (but quietly above the thick rich-colored pristine cigar in his clean steady hand), what he knew, divined of it. It would be evening, the ninth evening, he and the woman on either side of their host's empty place at the evening meal, he hearing the voices from without but not ceasing to eat, still chewing steadily, because it would be the same as though he were seeing them anyway—the two or three or four pirogues floating on the dark water beneath the platform on which the host stood, the voices gobbling and jabbering incomprehensible and filled not with alarm and not exactly with rage or even perhaps absolute surprise but rather just cacophony like those of disturbed marsh fowl, he (the convict) not ceasing to chew but just looking up quietly and maybe without a great deal of interrogation or surprise too as the Cajan burst in and stood before them, wild-faced, glaring, his blackened teeth gaped against the inky orifice of his distended mouth, watching (the convict) while the Cajan went through his violent pantomime of violent evacuation, ejection, scooping something invisible into his arms and hurling it out and downward and in the instant of completing the gesture changing from instigator to victim of that which he had set into pantomimic motion, clasping his head and, bowed over and not otherwise moving, seeming to be swept on and away before it, crying "Boom! Boom! Boom!", the convict watching him, his jaw not chewing now, though for just that moment, thinking, *What? What is it he is trying to tell me?* thinking (this a flash too, since he could not have expressed this, and hence did not even know that he had ever thought it) that though his life had been cast here, circumscribed by this environment, accepted by this environment and accepting it in turn (and he had done well here—this quietly, soberly indeed, if he had been able to phrase it, think it instead of merely knowing it—better than he had ever done, who had not even known until now how good work, making money, could be) yet it was not his life, he still and would ever be no more than the water bug upon the surface of the pond, the plumbless and lurking depths of which he would never know, his only actual contact with it being the instants when on lonely and glaring mudspits under the pitiless sun and amphitheatred by his motionless and riveted semicircle of watching pirogues, he accepted the gambit which he had not elected, entered the lashing radius of the armed tail and beat at the thrashing and hissing head with his lightwood club, or this failing, embraced without hesitation the armored body itself with the frail web of flesh and bone in which he walked and lived and sought the raging life with an eight-inch knife-blade.

So he and the woman merely watched the Cajan as he acted out the whole charade of eviction—the little wiry man gesticulant and wild, his hysterical shadow leaping and falling upon the rough wall as he went through the pantomime of abandoning the cabin, gathering in pantomime his meagre belongings from the walls and corners—objects which no other man would want and only some power or force like blind water or earthquake or fire would ever dispossess him of, the woman watching too, her mouth slightly open upon a mass of chewed food, on her face an expression of placid astonishment, saying, "What? What's he saying?"

"I dont know," the convict said. "But I reckon if it's something we ought to know we will find it out when it's ready for us to." Because he was not alarmed, though by now he had read the other's meaning plainly enough. *He's fixing to leave,* he thought. *He's telling me to leave too*—this later, after they had quitted the table and the Cajan and the woman had gone to bed and the Cajan had risen from the pallet and approached the convict and once more went through the pantomine of abandoning the cabin, this time as one repeats a speech which may have been misunderstood, tediously, carefully repetitional as to a child, seeming to hold the convict with one hand while he gestured, talked, with the other, gesturing as though in single syllables, the convict (squatting, the knife open and the almost-finished paddle across his lap) watching nodding his head, even speaking in English: "Yah; sure. You bet. I got you."—trimming again at the paddle but no faster, with no more haste than on any other night, serene in his belief that when the time came for him to know whatever it was, that would take care of itself, having already and without even knowing it, even before the possibility, the question, ever arose, declined, refused to accept even the thought of moving also, thinking about the hides, thinking, *If there was just some way he could tell me where to carry my share to get the money* but thinking this only for an instant between two delicate strokes of the blade because almost at once he thought, *I reckon as long as I can catch them I wont have no big trouble finding whoever it is that will buy them.*

So the next morning he helped the Cajan load his few belongings—the pitted rifle, a small bundle of clothing (again they traded, who could not even converse with one another, this time the few cooking vessels, a few rusty traps by definite allocation, and something embracing and abstractional which included the stove, the crude bunk, the house or its occupancy— something—in exchange for one alligator hide)—into the pirogue, then, squatting and as two children divide sticks they divided the hides, separating them into two piles, one-for-me-and-one-for-you, two-for-me-and-two-for-you, and the Cajan loaded his share and shoved away from the platform and paused again, though this time he only put the paddle down, gathered something invisibly into his two hands and flung it violently upward, crying "Boom! Boom!" on a rising inflection, nodding violently to the half-naked and savagely scoriated man on the platform who stared with a sort of grim equability back at him and said, "Sure. Boom. Boom." Then the Cajan went on. He did not look back. They watched him, already paddling rapidly, or the woman did; the convict had already turned.

"Maybe he was trying to tell us to leave too," she said.

"Yah," the convict said. "I thought of that last night. Hand me the paddle." She fetched it to him—the sapling, the one he had been trimming at night, not quite finished yet though one more evening would do it (he had been using a spare one of the Cajan's. The other had offered to let him keep it, to include it perhaps with the stove and the bunk and the cabin's freehold, but the convict had declined. Perhaps he had computed it by volume against so much alligator hide, this weighed against one more evening with the tedious and careful blade.) and he departed too with his knotted rope and mace, in the opposite direction, as though not only not content with refusing to quit the place he had been warned against, he must establish and affirm the irrevocable finality of his refusal by penetrating even further and deeper into it. And then and without warning the high fierce drowsing of his solitude gathered itself and struck at him.

He could not have told this if he had tried—this not yet midmorning and he going on, alone for the first time, no pirogue emerging anywhere to fall in behind him, but he had not expected this anyway, he knew that the solitude, his desolation which was now his alone and in full since he had elected to remain; the sudden cessation of the paddle, the skiff shooting on for a moment yet while he thought, *What? What?* Then, *No. No. No,* as the silence and solitude and emptiness roared down upon him in a jeering bellow: and now reversed, the skiff spun violently on its heel, he the betrayed driving furiously back toward the platform where he knew it was already too late, that citadel where the very crux and dear breath of his life—the being allowed to work and earn money, that right and privilege which he believed he had earned to himself unaided, asking no favor of anyone or anything save the right to be let alone to pit his will and strength against the sauric protagonist of a land, a region, which he had not asked to be projected into—was being threatened, driving the home-made paddle in grim fury, coming in sight of the platform at last and seeing the motor launch lying alongside it with no surprise at all but actually with a kind of pleasure as though at a visible justification of his outrage and fear, the privilege of saying *I told you so* to his own affronting, driving on toward it in a dreamlike state in which there seemed to be no progress at all, in which, unimpeded and suffocating, he strove dreamily with a weightless oar, with muscles without strength or resiliency, at a medium without resistance, seeming to watch the skiff creep infinitesimally across the sunny water and up to the platform while a man in the launch (there were five of them in all) gobbled at him in that same tongue he had been hearing constantly now for ten days and still knew no word of, just as a second man, followed by the woman carrying the baby and dressed again for departure in the faded tunic and the sunbonnet, emerged from the house, carrying (the man carried several other things but the convict saw nothing else) the paper-wrapped bundle which the convict had put behind the rafter ten days ago and no other hand had touched since, he (the convict) on the platform too now, holding the skiff's painter in one hand and the bludgeonlike paddle in the other, contriving to speak to the woman at last in a voice dreamy and suffocating and incredibly calm: "Take it away from him and carry it back into the house."

"So you can talk English, can you?" the man in the launch said. "Why didn't you come out like they told you to last night?"

"Out?" the convict said. Again he even looked, glared, at the man in the launch, contriving even again to control his voice: "I aint got time to take trips. I'm busy," already turning to the woman again, his mouth already open to repeat as the dreamy buzzing voice of the man came to him and he turning once more, in a terrific and absolutely unbearable exasperation, crying, "Flood? What flood? Hell a mile, it's done passed me twice months ago! It's gone! What flood?" and then (he did not think this in actual words either but he knew it, suffered that flashing insight into his own character or destiny: how there was a peculiar quality of repetitiveness about his present fate, how not only the almost seminal crises recurred with a certain monotony, but the very physical circumstances followed a stupidly unimaginative pattern) the man in the launch said, "Take him" and he was on his feet for a few minutes yet, lashing and striking in panting fury, then once more on his back on hard unyielding planks while the four men swarmed over him in a fierce wave of hard bones and panting curses and at last the thin dry vicious snapping of handcuffs.

"Damn it, are you mad?" the man in the launch said. "Cant you understand they are going to dynamite that levee at noon today?—Come on," he said to the others. "Get him aboard. Let's get out of here."

"I want my hides and boat," the convict said.

"Damn your hides," the man in the launch said. "If they dont get that levee blowed pretty soon you can hunt plenty more of them on the capitol steps at Baton Rouge. And this is all the boat you will need and you can say your prayers about it."

"I aint going without my boat," the convict said. He said it calmly and with complete finality, so calm, so final that for almost a minute nobody answered him, they just stood looking quietly down at him as he lay, half-naked, blistered and scarred, helpless and manacled hand and foot, on his back, delivering his ultimatum in a voice peaceful and quiet as that in which you talk to your bedfellow before going to sleep. Then the man in the launch moved; he spat quietly over the side and said in a voice as calm and quiet as the convict's:

"All right. Bring his boat." They helped the woman, carrying the baby and the paper-wrapped parcel, into the launch. Then they helped the convict to his feet and into the launch too, the shackles on his wrists and ankles clashing. "I'd unlock you if you'd promise to behave yourself," the man said. The convict did not answer this at all.

"I want to hold the rope," he said.

"The rope?"

"Yes," the convict said. The rope." So they lowered him into the stern and gave him the end of the painter after it had passed the towing cleat, and they went on. The convict did not look back. But then, he did not look forward either, he lay half sprawled, his shackled legs before him, the end of the skiff's painter in one shackled hand. The launch made two other stops; when the hazy wafer of the intolerable sun began to stand once more directly overhead there were fifteen people in the launch; and then the convict, sprawled and motionless, saw the flat brazen land begin to rise and become a greenish-black mass of swamp, bearded and convoluted, this in turn stopping short off and there spread before him an expanse of water embraced by a blue dissolution of shoreline and glittering thinly under the noon, larger than he had ever seen before, the sound of the launch's engine ceasing, the hull sliding on behind its fading bow-wave. "What are you doing?" the leader said.

"It's noon," the helmsman said. "I thought we might hear the dynamite." So they all listened, the launch lost of all forward motion, rocking slightly, the glitter-broken small waves slapping and whispering at the hull, but no sound, no tremble even, came anywhere under the fierce hazy sky; the long moment gathered itself and turned on and noon was past. "All right," the leader said. "Let's go." The engine started again, the hull began to gather speed. The leader came aft and stooped over the convict, key in hand. "I guess you'll have to behave now, whether you want to or not," he said, unlocking the manacles. "Wont you?"

"Yes," the convict said. They went on; after a time the shore vanished completely and a little sea got up. The convict was free now but he lay as before, the end of the skiff's painter in his hand, bent now with three or four turns about his wrist; he turned his head now and then to look back at the towing skiff as it slewed and bounced in the launch's wake, now and then he even looked out over the lake, the eyes alone moving, the face grave and expressionless, thinking, *This is a greater immensity of water, of waste and desolation, than I have ever seen before;* perhaps not; thinking three or four hours later, the shoreline raised again and broken into a clutter of sailing sloops and power cruisers, *These are more boats than I believed existed, a maritime race of which I also had no cognizance* or perhaps not thinking it but just watching as the launch opened the shored gut of the ship canal, the low smoke of the city beyond it, then a wharf, the launch slowing in; a quiet crowd of people watching with that same forlorn passivity he had seen before and whose race he did recognise even though he had not seen Vicksburg when he passed it—the brand, the unmistakable hallmark of the violently homeless, he more so than any, who would have permitted no man to call him one of them.

"All right," the leader said to him. "Here you are."

"The boat," the convict said.

"You've got it. What do you want me to do—give you a receipt for it?"

"No," the convict said. "I just want the boat."

"Take it. Only you ought to have a bookstrap or something to carry it in." ("Carry it in?" the plump convict said. "Carry it where? Where would you have to carry it?")

He (the tall one) told that: how he and the woman disembarked and how one of the men helped him haul the skiff up out of the water and how he stood there with the end of the painter wrapped around his wrist and the man bustled up, saying, "All right. Next load! Next load!" and how he told this man too about the boat and the man cried, "Boat? Boat?" and how he (the convict) went with them when they carried the skiff over and racked, berthed, it with the others and how he lined himself up by a coca-cola sign and the arch of a draw bridge so he could find the skiff again quick when he returned, and how he and the woman (he carrying the paper-wrapped parcel) were herded into a truck and after a while the truck began to run in traffic, between close houses, then there was a big building, an armory—

"Armory?" the plump one said. "You mean a jail."

"No. It was a kind of warehouse, with people with bundles laying on the floor." And how he thought maybe his partner might be there and how he even looked about for the Cajan while waiting for a chance to get back to the door again, where the soldier was and how he got back to the door at last, the woman behind him and his chest actually against the dropped rifle.

"Gwan, gwan," the soldier said. "Get back. They'll give you some clothes in a minute. You cant walk around the streets that way. And something to eat too. Maybe your kinfolks will come for you by that time." And he told that too: how the woman said,

"Maybe if you told him you had some kinfolks here he would let us out." And how he did not; he could not have expressed this either, it too deep, too ingrained; he had never yet had to think it into words through all the long generations of himself—his hillman's sober and jealous respect not for truth but for the power, the strength, of lying—not to be niggard with lying but rather to use it with respect and even care, delicate quick and strong, like a fine and fatal blade. And how they fetched him clothes—a blue jumper and overalls, and then food too (a brisk starched young woman saying, "But the baby must be bathed, cleaned. It will die if you dont" and the woman saying, "Yessum. He might holler some, he aint never been bathed before. But he's a good baby.") and now it was night, the unshaded bulbs harsh and savage and forlorn above the snorers and he rising, gripping the woman awake, and then the window. He told that: how there were doors in plenty, leading he did not know where, but he had a hard time finding a window they could use but he found one at last, he carrying the parcel and the baby too while he climbed through first—"You ought to tore up a sheet and slid down it," the plump convict said. But he needed no sheet, there were cobbles under his feet now, in the rich darkness. The city was there too but he had not seen it yet and would not—the low constant glare; Bienville had stood there too, it had been the figment of an emasculate also calling himself Napoleon but no more, Andrew Jackson had found it one step from Pennsylvania Avenue. But the convict found it considerably further than one step back to the ship canal and the skiff, the coca-cola sign dim now, the draw bridge arching spidery against the jonquil sky at dawn: nor did he tell, any more than about the sixty-foot levee, how he got the skiff back into the water. The lake was behind him now; there was but one direction he could go. When he saw the River again he knew it at once. He should have; it was now ineradicably a part of his past, his life; it would be a part of what he would bequeath, if that were in store for him. But four weeks later it would look different from what it did now, and did: he (the Old Man) had recovered from his debauch, back in banks again, the Old Man, rippling placidly toward the sea, brown and rich as chocolate between levees whose inner faces were wrinkled as though in a frozen and aghast amazement, crowned with the rich green of summer in the willows; beyond them, sixty feet below, slick mules squatted against the broad pull of middle-busters in the richened soil which would not need to be planted, which would need only to be shown a cotton seed to sprout and make; there would be the symmetric miles of strong stalks by July, purple bloom in August, in September the black fields snowed over, spilled, the middles dragged smooth by the long sacks, the long black limber hands plucking, the hot air filled with the whine of gins, the September air then but now June air heavy with locust and (the towns) the smell of new paint and the sour smell of the paste which holds wall paper—the towns, the villages, the little lost wood landings on stilts on the inner face of the levee, the lower storeys bright and rank under the new paint and paper and even the marks on spile and post and tree of May's raging water-height fading beneath each bright silver gust of summer's loud and inconstant rain; there was a store at the levee's lip, a few saddled and rope-bridled mules in the sleepy dust, a few dogs, a handful of negroes sitting on the steps beneath the chewing tobacco and malaria medicine signs, and three white men, one of them a deputy sheriff canvassing for votes to beat his superior (who had given him his job) in the August primary, all pausing to watch the skiff emerge from the glitter-glare of the afternoon water and approach and land, a woman carrying a child stepping out, then a man, a tall man who, approaching proved to be dressed in a faded but recently washed and quite clean suit of penitentiary clothing, stopping in the dust where the mules dozed and watching with pale cold humorless eyes while the deputy sheriff was still making toward his armpit that gesture which everyone present realised was to have produced a pistol in one flashing motion for a considerable time while still nothing came of it. It was apparently enough for the newcomer, however.

"You a officer?" he said.

"You damn right I am," the deputy said. "Just let me get this damn gun—"

"All right," the other said. "Yonder's your boat, and here's the woman. But I never did find that bastard on the cottonhouse."

One of the Governor's young men arrived at the Penitentiary the next morning. That is, he was fairly young (he would not see thirty again though without doubt he did not want to, there being that about him which indicated a character which never had and never would want anything it did not, or was not about to, possess), a Phi Beta Kappa out of an Eastern university, a colonel on the Governor's staff who did not buy it with a campaign contribution, who had stood in his negligent Eastern-cut clothes and his arched nose and lazy contemptuous eyes on the galleries of any number of little lost backwoods stores and told his stories and received the guffaws of his overalled and spitting hearers and with the same look in his eyes fondled infants named in memory of the last administration and in honor (or hope) of the next, and (it was said of him and doubtless not true) by lazy accident the behinds of some who were not infants any longer though still not old enough to vote. He was in the Warden's office with a briefcase, and presently the deputy warden of the levee was there too. He would have been sent for presently though not yet, but he came anyhow, without knocking, with his hat on, calling the Governor's young man loudly by a nickname and striking him with a flat hand on the back and lifted one thigh to the Warden's desk, almost between the Warden and the caller, the emissary. Or the vizier with the command, the knotted cord, as began to appear immediately.

"Well," the Governor's young man said, "you've played the devil, haven't you?" The Warden had a cigar. He had offered the caller one. It had been refused, though presently, while the Warden looked at the back of his neck with hard immobility even a little grim, the deputy leaned and reached back and opened the desk drawer and took one.

"Seems straight enough to me," the Warden said. "He got swept away against his will. He came back as soon as he could and surrendered."

"He even brought that damn boat back," the deputy said. "If he'd a throwed the boat away he could a walked back in three days. But no sir. He's got to bring the boat back. 'Here's your boat and here's the woman but I never found no bastard on no cottonhouse.'" He slapped his knee, guffawing. "Them convicts. A mule's got twice as much sense."

"A mule's got twice as much sense as anything except a rat," the emissary said in his pleasant voice. "But that's not the trouble."

"What is the trouble?" the Warden said.

"This man is dead."

"Hell fire, he aint dead," the deputy said. "He's up yonder in that bunk-house right now, lying his head off probly. I'll take you up there and you can see him." The Warden was looking at the deputy.

"Look," he said. "Bledsoe was trying to tell me something about that Kate mule's leg. You better go up to the stable and—"

"I done tended to it," the deputy said. He didn't even look at the Warden. He was watching, talking to, the emissary. "No sir. He aint—"

"But he has received an official discharge as being dead. Not a pardon nor a parole either: a discharge. He's either dead, or free. In either case he doesn't belong here." Now both the Warden and the deputy looked at the emissary, the deputy's mouth open a little, the cigar poised in his hand to have its tip bitten off. The emissary spoke pleasantly, extremely distinctly: "On a report of death forwarded to the Governor by the Warden of the Penitentiary." The deputy closed his mouth, though otherwise he didn't move. "On the official evidence of the officer delegated at the time to the charge and returning of the body of the prisoner to the Penitentiary." Now the deputy put the cigar into his mouth and got slowly off the desk, the cigar rolling across his lip as he spoke:

"So that's it. I'm to be it, am I?" He laughed shortly, a stage laugh, two notes. "When I done been right three times running through three separate administrations? That's on a book somewhere too. Somebody in Jackson can find that too. And if they cant, I can show—"

"Three administrations?" the emissary said. "Well, well. That's pretty good."

"You damn right it's good," the deputy said. "The woods are full of folks that didn't." The Warden was again watching the back of the deputy's neck.

"Look," he said. "Why dont you step up to my house and get that bottle of whiskey out of the sideboard and bring it down here?"

"All right," the deputy said. "But I think we better settle this first. I'll tell you what we'll do—"

"We can settle it quicker with a drink or two," the Warden said. "You better step on up to your place and get a coat so the bottle—"

"That'll take too long," the deputy said. "I wont need no coat." He moved to the door, where he stopped and turned. "I'll tell you what to do. Just call twelve men in here and tell him it's a jury—he never seen but one before and he wont know no better—and try him over for robbing that train. Hamp can be the judge."

"You cant try a man twice for the same crime," the emissary said. "He might know that even if he doesn't know a jury when he sees one."

"Look," the Warden said.

"All right. Just call it a new train robbery. Tell him it happened yesterday, tell him he robbed another train while he was gone and just forgot it. He couldn't help himself. Besides, he wont care. He'd just as lief be here as out.

He wouldn't have nowhere to go if he was out. None of them do. Turn one loose and be damned if he aint right back here by Christmas like it was a reunion or something for doing the very same thing they caught him at before." He guffawed again. "Them convicts."

"Look," the Warden said. "While you're there, why dont you open the bottle and see if the liquor's any good. Take a drink or two. Give yourself time to feel it. If it's not good, no use in bringing it."

"O.K.," the deputy said. He went out this time.

"Couldn't you lock the door?" the emissary said. The Warden squirmed faintly. That is, he shifted his position in his chair.

"After all, he's right," he said. "He's guessed right three times now. And he's kin to all the folks in Pittman County except the niggers."

"Maybe we can work fast then." The emissary opened the briefcase and took out a sheaf of papers. "So there you are," he said.

"There what are?"

"He escaped."

"But he came back voluntarily and surrendered."

"But he escaped."

"All right," the Warden said. "He escaped. Then what?" Now the emissary said look. That is, he said,

"Listen. I'm on per diem. That's tax-payers, votes. And if there's any possible chance for it to occur to anyone to hold an investigation about this, there'll be ten senators and twenty-five representatives here on a special train maybe. On per diem. And it will be mighty hard to keep some of them from going back to Jackson by way of Memphis or New Orleans—on per diem."

"All right," the Warden said. "What does he say to do?"

"This. The man left here in charge of one specific officer. But he was delivered back here by a different one."

"But he surren—" This time the Warden stopped of his own accord. He looked, stared almost, at the emissary. "All right. Go on."

"In specific charge of an appointed and delegated officer, who returned here and reported that the body of the prisoner was no longer in his possession; that, in fact, he did not know where the prisoner was. That's correct, isn't it?" The Warden said nothing. "Isn't that correct?" the emissary said, pleasantly, insistently.

"But you cant do that to him. I tell you he's kin to half the—"

"That's taken care of. The Chief has made a place for him on the highway patrol."

"Hell," the Warden said. "He cant ride a motorcycle. I dont even let him try to drive a truck."

"He wont have to. Surely an amazed and grateful State can supply the man who guessed right three times in succession in Mississippi general elections with a car to ride in and somebody to run it if necessary. He wont even have to stay in it all the time. Just so he's near enough so when an inspector sees the car and stops and blows the horn of it he can hear it and come out."

"I still dont like it," the Warden said.

"Neither do I. Your man could have saved all of this if he had just gone on and drowned himself, as he seems to have led everybody to believe he had. But he didn't. And the Chief says do. Can you think of anything better?" The Warden sighed.

"No," he said.

"All right." The emissary opened the papers and uncapped a pen and began to write. "Attempted escape from the Penitentiary, ten years' additional sentence," he said. "Deputy Warden Buckworth transferred to Highway Patrol. Call it for meritorious service even if you want to. It wont matter now. Done?"

"Done," the Warden said.

"Then suppose you send for him. Get it over with." So the Warden sent for the tall convict and he arrived presently, saturnine and grave, in his new bed-ticking, his jowls blue and close under the sunburn, his hair recently cut and neatly parted and smelling faintly of the prison barber's (the barber was in for life, for murdering his wife, still a barber) pomade. The Warden called him by name.

"You had bad luck, didn't you?" The convict said nothing. "They are going to have to add ten years to your time."

"All right," the convict said.

"It's hard luck. I'm sorry."

"All right," the convict said. "If that's the rule." So they gave him the ten years more and the Warden gave him the cigar and now he sat, jackknifed backward into the space between the upper and lower bunks, the unlighted cigar in his hand while the plump convict and four others listened to him. Or questioned him, that is, since it was all done, finished, now and he was safe again, so maybe it wasn't even worth talking about any more.

"All right," the plump one said. "So you come back into the River. Then what?"

"Nothing. I rowed."

"Wasn't it pretty hard rowing coming back?"

"The water was still high. It was running pretty hard still. I never made much speed for the first week or two. After that it got better." Then, suddenly and quietly, something—the inarticulateness, the innate and inherited reluctance for speech, dissolved and he found himself, listened to himself, telling it quietly, the words coming not fast but easily to the tongue as he required them: How he paddled on (he found out by trying it that he could make better speed, if you could call it speed, next the bank—this after he had been carried suddenly and violently out to midstream before he could prevent it and found himself, the skiff, traveling back toward the region from which he had just escaped and he spent the better part of the morning getting back inshore and up to the canal again from which he had emerged at dawn) until night came and they tied up to the bank and ate some of the food he had secreted in his jumper before leaving the armory in New Orleans and the woman and the infant slept in the boat as usual and when daylight came they went on and tied up again that night too and the next day the food gave out and he came to a landing, a town, he didn't notice the name of it, and he got a job. It was a cane farm—

"Cane?" one of the other convicts said. "What does anybody want to raise cane for? You cut cane. You have to fight it where I come from. You burn it just to get shut of it."

"It was sorghum," the tall convict said.

"Sorghum?" another said. "A whole farm just raising sorghum? *Sorghum?* What did they do with it?" The tall one didn't know. He didn't ask, he just came up the levee and there was a truck waiting full of niggers and a white man said, "You there. Can you run a shovel plow?" and the convict said, "Yes," and the man said, "Jump in then," and the convict said, "Only I've got a—"

"Yes," the plump one said. "That's what I been aiming to ask. What did—" The tall convict's face was grave, his voice was calm, just a little short:

"They had tents for the folks to live in. They were behind." The plump one blinked at him.

"Did they think she was your wife?"

"I dont know. I reckon so." The plump one blinked at him.

"Wasn't she your wife? Just from time to time kind of, you might say?" The tall one didn't answer this at all. After a moment he raised the cigar and appeared to examine a loosening of the wrapper because after another moment he licked the cigar carefully near the end. "All right," the plump one said. "Then what?" So he worked there four days. He didn't like it. Maybe that was why: that he too could not quite put credence in that much of what he believed to be sorghum. So when they told him it was Saturday and paid him and the white man told him about somebody who was going to Baton Rouge the next day in a motor boat, he went to see the man and took the six dollars he had earned and bought food with it and tied the skiff behind the motor boat and went to Baton Rouge. It didn't take long and even after they left the motor boat at Baton Rouge and he was paddling again it seemed to the convict that the River was lower and the current not so fast, so hard, so they made fair speed, tying up to the bank at night among the willows, the woman and baby sleeping in the skiff as of old. Then the food gave out again. This time it was a wood landing, the wood stacked and waiting, a wagon and team being unladen of another load. The men with the wagon told him about the sawmill and helped him drag the skiff up the levee; they wanted to leave it there but he would not so they loaded it onto the wagon too and he and the woman got on the wagon too and they went to the sawmill. They gave them one room in a house to live in here. They paid two dollars a day and furnish. The work was hard. He liked it. He stayed there eight days.

"If you liked it so well, why did you quit?" the plump one said. The tall convict examined the cigar again, holding it up where the light fell upon the rich chocolate-colored flank.

"I got in trouble," he said.

"What trouble?"

"Woman. It was a fellow's wife."

"You mean you had been toting one piece up and down the country day and night for over a month, and now the first time you have a chance to·stop and catch your breath almost you got to get in trouble over another one?" The tall convict had thought of that. He remembered it: how there were times, seconds, at first when if it had not been for the baby he might have, might have tried. But they were just seconds because in the next instant his whole being would seem to flee the very idea in a kind of savage and horrified revulsion; he would find himself looking from a distance at this millstone which the force and power of blind and risible Motion had fastened upon him, thinking, saying aloud actually, with harsh and savage outrage even though it had been two years since he had had a woman and that a nameless and not young negress, a casual, a straggler whom he had caught more or less by chance on one of the fifth-Sunday visiting days, the man—husband or sweetheart—whom she had come to see having been shot by a trusty a week or so previous and she had not heard about it: "She aint even no good to me for that."

"But you got this one, didn't you?" the plump convict said.

"Yah," the tall one said. The plump one blinked at him.

"Was it good?"

"It's all good," one of the others said. "Well? Go on. How many more did you have on the way back? Sometimes when a fellow starts getting it it looks like he just cant miss even if—" That was all, the convict told them. They left the sawmill fast, he had no time to buy food until they reached the next landing. There he spent the whole sixteen dollars he had earned and they went on. The River was lower now, there was no doubt of it, and sixteen dollars' worth looked like a lot of food and he thought maybe it would do, would be enough. But maybe there was more current in the River still than it looked like. But this time it was Mississippi, it was cotton; the plow handles felt right to his palms again, the strain and squat of the slick buttocks against the middle buster's blade was what he knew, even though they paid but a dollar a day here. But that did it. He told it: they told him it was Saturday again and paid him and he told about it—night, a smoked lantern in a disc of worn and barren earth as smooth as silver, a circle of crouching figures, the importunate murmurs and ejaculations, the meagre piles of worn bills beneath the crouching knees, the dotted cubes clicking and scuttering in the dust; that did it. "How much did you win?" the second convict said.

"Enough," the tall one said.

"But how much?"

"Enough," the tall one said. It was enough exactly; he gave it all to the man who owned the second motor boat (he would not need food now), he and the woman in the launch now and the skiff towing behind, the woman with the baby and the paper-wrapped parcel beneath his peaceful hand, on his lap; almost at once he recognised, not Vicksburg because he had never seen Vicksburg, but the trestle beneath which on his roaring wave of trees and houses and dead animals he had shot, accompanied by thunder and lightning, a month and three weeks ago; he looked at it once without heat, even without interest as the launch went on. But now he began to watch the bank, the levee. He didn't know how he would know but he knew he would, and then it was early afternoon and sure enough the moment came and he said to the launch owner: "I reckon this will do."

"Here?" the launch owner said. "This dont look like anywhere to me."

"I reckon this is it," the convict said. So the launch put inshore, the engine ceased, it drifted up and lay against the levee and the owner cast the skiff loose.

"You better let me take you on until we come to something," he said. "That was what I promised."

"I reckon this will do," the convict said. So they got out and he stood with the grapevine painter in his hand while the launch purred again and drew away, already curving; he did not watch it. He laid the bundle down and made the painter fast to a willow root and picked up the bundle and turned. He said no word, he mounted the levee, passing the mark, the tide-line of the old raging, dry now and lined, traversed by shallow and empty cracks like foolish and deprecatory senile grins, and entered a willow clump and removed the overalls and shirt they had given him in New Orleans and dropped them without even looking to see where they fell and opened the parcel and took out the other, the known, the desired, faded a little, stained and worn, but clean, recognisable, and put them on and returned to the skiff and took up the paddle. The woman was already in it.

The plump convict stood blinking at him. "So you come back," he said. "Well well." Now they all watched the tall convict as he bit the end from the cigar neatly and with complete deliberation and spat it out and licked the bite smooth and damp and took a match from his pocket and examined the match for a moment as though to be sure it was a good one, worthy of the cigar perhaps, and raked it up his thigh with the same deliberation—a motion almost too slow to set fire to it, it would seem—and held it until the flame burned clear and free of sulphur, then put it to the cigar. The plump one watched him, blinking rapidly and steadily. "And they give you ten years more for running. That's bad. A fellow can get used to what they give him at first, to start off with, I dont care how much it is, even a hundred and ninety-nine years. But ten more years. Ten years more, on top of that. When you never expected it. Ten more years to have to do without no society, no female companionship—" He blinked steadily at the tall convict. But he (the tall convict) had thought of that too. He had had a sweetheart. That is, he had gone to church singings and picnics with her—a girl a year or so younger than he, short-legged, with ripe breasts and a heavy mouth and dull eyes like ripe muscadines, who owned a baking-powder can almost full of ear-rings and brooches and rings bought (or presented at suggestion) from ten-cent stores. Presently he had divulged his plan to her, and there were times later when, musing, the thought occurred to him that possibly if it had not been for her he would not actually have attempted it—this a mere feeling, unworded, since he could not have phrased this either: that who to know what Capone's uncandled bridehood she might not have dreamed to be her destiny and fate, what fast car filled with authentic colored glass and machine guns, running traffic lights. But that was all past and done when the notion first occurred to him, and in the third month of his incarceration she came to see him. She wore ear-rings and a bracelet or so which he had never seen before and it never became quite clear how she had got that far from home, and she cried violently for the first three minutes though presently (and without his ever knowing either exactly how they had got separated or how she had made the acquaintance) he saw her in animated conversation with one of the guards. But she kissed him before she left that evening and said she would return the first chance she got, clinging to him, sweating a little, smelling of scent and soft young female flesh, slightly pneumatic. But she didn't come back though he continued to write to her, and seven months later he got an answer. It was a postcard, a colored lithograph of a Birmingham hotel, a childish X inked heavily across one window, the heavy writing on the reverse slanted and primer-like too: *This is where were honnymonning at. Your friend (Mrs.) Vernon Waldrip*

The plump convict stood blinking at the tall one, rapidly and steadily. "Yes, sir," he said. "It's them ten more years that hurt. Ten more years to do without a woman, no woman a tall a fellow wants—" He blinked steadily and rapidly, watching the tall one. The other did not move, jacknifed backward between the two bunks, grave and clean, the cigar burning smoothly and richly in his clean steady hand, the smoke wreathing upward across his face saturnine, humorless, and calm. "Ten more years—"

"Women—!" the tall convict said.

THE MOVIES

The emergence of the movies was by far the most exciting event in the modern history of mass entertainment. The manners of the stars, their appearance, patterns of speech, and tastes profoundly influenced behavior in every sector of domestic life. Hollywood simultaneously created and reflected the dreams of a nation. Great performers like Charlie Chaplin refined new visions of traditional comic genres and movingly criticized the realities of technological society.

Charlie Chaplin in *Modern Times.*
(Museum of Modern Art, Film Stills Archive)

The Marx Brothers in *A Night at the Opera*.
(Museum of Modern Art, Film Stills Archive)

Clark Gable and Vivien Leigh in *Gone with the Wind.*
(Museum of Modern Art, Film Stills Archive)

Marlon Brando and Lee J. Cobb in *On the Waterfront.*
(Museum of Modern Art, Film Stills Archive)

F. SCOTT FITZGERALD

(1896-1941)

F. Scott Fitzgerald spoke of himself as having been "brought up in a family sunk from haute bourgeoisie to petit bourgeoisie, yet expensively educated" and, as this way of speaking suggests, he was remarkable among American novelists of the period for his interest in class relationships and in connections between money and manners. His best books, *The Great Gatsby* (1925) and *Tender is the Night* (1934), are partly about the bearings and consequences of the success myth for American life and, time and again, in nonfiction as well as in novels and stories, he set himself up as an analyst of the habits and morals of the rich.

The novels are *This Side of Paradise,* 1920; *The Beautiful and the Dammed,* 1922; *The Great Gatsby,* 1925; *Tender is the Night,* 1934, a revised edition, ed., Malcolm Cowley, 1951; and *The Last Tycoon,* ed., Edmund Wilson, 1941. The stories have been collected in *Flappers and Philosophers,* 1921; *Tales of the Jazz Age,* 1922; *All the Sad Young Men,* 1926; and *Taps at Reveille,* 1935. *The Stories of F. Scott Fitzgerald,* 1951 contains 28 stories. *The Vegetable, or from President to Postman,* 1923 is a play. Edmund Wilson edited *The Crack-up,* 1945; Arthur Mizener edited *Afternoon of an Author: A Selection of Uncollected Stories and Essays,* 1958; and Andrew Turnbull edited *The Letters of F. Scott Fitzgerald,* 1963 and *Scott Fitzgerald: Letters to His Daughter,* 1965. Other correspondence has been edited by John Kuehl and Jackson Bryer, *Dear Max: The Fitzgerald-Perkins Correspondence,* 1971; and Matthew J. Bruccoli and Jennifer McCabe Atkinson, *As Ever, Scott Fitz—: Letters Between F. Scott Fitzgerald and His Literary Agent, Harold Ober—1919-1940,* 1972. Dorothy Parker edited *The Portable F. Scott Fitzgerald,* 1945 and Arthur Mizener edited *The Fitzgerald Reader,* 1963. Useful bibliographies are Jackson F. Bryer, *The Critical Reputation of F. Scott Fitzgerald: A Bibliographical Study,* 1967; and Matthew J.

Bruccoli, *F. Scott Fitzgerald—A Descriptive Bibliography,* 1972.

The two best biographies are Arthur Mizener, *The Far Side of Paradise,* 1951, rev., 1965; and Andrew Turnbull, *Scott Fitzgerald,* 1970.

Critical appraisals include Alfred Kazin, ed., *F. Scott Fitzgerald: The Man and His Work,* 1951; James E. Miller, *The Fictional Technique of F. Scott Fitzgerald,* 1957 and *F. Scott Fitzgerald, His Art and His Technique,* 1964; Arthur Mizener, ed., *F. Scott Fitzgerald: A Collection of Critical Essays,* 1963; Kenneth Eble, *F. Scott Fitzgerald,* 1963; K. G. W. Cross, *F. Scott Fitzgerald,* 1964; Sergio Perosa, *The Art of F. Scott Fitzgerald,* 1965; Henry D. Piper, *F. Scott Fitzgerald, A Critical Portrait,* 1965; Richard D. Lehan, *F. Scott Fitzgerald and the Craft of Fiction,* 1966; Robert Sklar, *F. Scott Fitzgerald, The Last Laocoon,* 1967; Milton R. Stern, *The Golden Moment: The Novels of F. Scott Fitzgerald,* 1970; John F. Callahan, *The Illusions of a Nation—Myth and History in the Novels of F. Scott Fitzgerald,* 1972; Nancy Milford, *Zelda,* 1970; Aaron Latham, *Crazy Sundays: F. Scott Fitzgerald in Hollywood,* 1971, and Sara Mayfield, *Exiles from Paradise; Zelda and Scott Fitzgerald,* 1971. Sheilah Graham wrote two personal memoirs, *Beloved Infidel,* 1968 and *College of One,* 1967.

The analysis is not, on balance, friendly. Like most writers with an acute sense of style, a developed feeling for rhythm and nuance of language, Fitzgerald relished visual beauty; he found it often in the world of wealth and laid himself under stern obligations to represent it precisely and caringly. The search for the exact phrase that would show forth, freshly, the cut of the rich man's riding breeches or the motion of the rich man's summer curtains swelling suddenly with a noon breeze, seemed to him not a frivolity but a cause: glamour served as an incitement to aesthetic creation, and Fitzgerald respected it for that service. But the rich, in his view, were by no means mere harmless inhabitants of handsome settings, scenes that gave rise, when talent contemplated them, to finely edged phrases; the rich were, at the core, careless and exploitative in human relationships. People unlucky enough to have to associate with them except as equals were likely to suffer bad wounds.

A thousand writers have spoken ill of money; one key to Fitzgerald's claim to distinction is that his critique is finally not of a class studied in isolation, but of a class taken as an index to the quality of a culture. The point painfully made in his pages is that the rage to produce and consume, to rise into the sun of glamour, to behave like the rich, afflicts all classes and kinds, and has fearfully corrupted the values of cooperativeness and joint concern. Not the least extraordinary moment in *The Great Gatsby*, for example, is that in which a garageman's wife, sexually exploited by a man of wealth, herself turns contemptuously on a hotel bellboy, aping the crude arrogance of her betters, and dramatizing the way in which blockages of human feeling can become norms at every level of a money culture.

Fitzgerald's own life records the confusions and chaos of the money culture. Born into a Catholic family in St. Paul, Minnesota, he seems to have seen himself from the start as not quite as securely "good" as they were—they meaning rich, toney Easterners. His parents sent him to an Eastern preparatory school that had little social standing, and then on to Princeton from 1913 to 1917. He left college without a degree to join the Army and, while serving as an Army lieutenant during World War I in the South, he met Zelda Sayre, daughter of a well-off Southern judge. Her grace and beauty were linked, for Fitzgerald, with the glamour of Privilege and Class Style; in pursuing and at length marrying her, he acted out longings that he himself was to subject, before then, to remorseless critical scrutiny. Driven by the dream of success and position, he first labored (after the war) in a New York advertising agency, then he returned to St. Paul, bent on finishing a book that would earn him a quick fortune and enable him to marry Zelda. The book was a novel, *This Side of Paradise* (1920), and it made a sensation. The young author moved to New York, married his dream woman, and began a life of extravagance and glitter that turned the couple into "jazz age" symbols, and thereafter into parts that he himself saw as irreconcilable. To support what we now call his life-style he needed a fortune, which he "earned" partly by borrowing and partly by writing "debutante" stories at high rates for the *Saturday Evening Post.* Three collections of Fitzgerald's stories appeared in the 1920's—*Flappers and Philosophers* (1921), *Tales of the Jazz Age* (1922), and *All the Sad Young Men* (1926). To support that sense of himself that insisted he was a serious mind and a talented artist, he wrote "serious fiction"—works that brought him praise from T. S. Eliot and earned him the regard of the literary men of distinction he knew at Princeton and kept as friends—the poet John Peale Bishop, the critic Edmund Wilson, the teacher Christian Gauss.

It was a life without a center. The Fitzgeralds shuttled between Europe and America. Zelda fell victim to mental illness and was hospitalized in a sanitarium. Fitzgerald turned to Hollywood for writing jobs that would enable him to carry his debts. The book he conceived as his major work, *Tender is the Night,* a version in part of the tortured lives of the Fitzgeralds themselves, was received less enthusiastically than Fitzgerald had hoped. His drinking problem worsened and a period of self-destruction began, during which he was, by his own word, "a bad caretaker" of his talent. (The period was described in a series of pieces written for *Esquire* and published as *The Crack-up,* which was edited after the author's death by his friend and "intellectual conscience," Edmund Wilson.) Toward the end of his life, while working on movie scripts in Hollywood, Fitzgerald launched a novel about the movie industry, *The Last Tycoon,* but he died of a heart attack at the age of 45 before the book was finished.

Many who knew the man in his years of dissipation and swift decline allude to him as someone unworthy of respect—a violator of intimacies, a bully or braggart; certainly it is clear that seriousness and genuine self-knowledge woke in him relatively late. There is a refinement of perception and moral clarity in his best writing, however, that taken together with his generosity to his natural competitors (Hemingway most notable among them) and with his courageous movement toward self-command after "the crackup," continues to lend meaning and moment to his books and to his life story.

The Rich Boy

Begin with an individual, and before you know it you find that you have created a type; begin with a type, and you find that you have created—nothing. That is because we are all queer fish, queerer behind our faces and voices than we want any one to know or than we know ourselves. When I hear a man proclaiming himself an "average, honest, open fellow," I feel pretty sure that he has some definite and perhaps terrible abnormality which he has agreed to conceal—and his protestation of being average and honest and open is his way of reminding himself of his misprision.

There are no types, no plurals. There is a rich boy, and this is his and not his brothers' story. All my life I have lived among his brothers but this one has been my friend. Besides, if I wrote about his brothers I should have to begin by attacking all the lies that the poor have told about the rich and the rich have told about themselves—such a wild structure they have erected that when we pick up a book about the rich, some instinct prepares us for unreality. Even the intelligent and impassioned reporters of life have made the country of the rich as unreal as fairy-land.

Let me tell you about the very rich. They are different from you and me. They possess and enjoy early, and it does something to them, makes them soft where we are hard, and cynical where we are trustful, in a way that, unless you are born rich, it is very difficult to understand. They think, deep in their hearts, that they are better than we are because we had to discover the compensations and refuges of life for ourselves. Even when they enter deep into our world or sink below us, they still think that they are better than we are. They are different. The only way I can describe young Anson Hunter is to approach him as if he were a foreigner and cling stubbornly to my point of view. If I accept his for a moment I am lost—I have nothing to show but a preposterous movie.

II

Anson was the eldest of six children who would some day divide a fortune of fifteen million dollars, and he reached the age of reason—is it seven?—at the beginning of the century when daring young women were already gliding along Fifth Avenue in electric "mobiles." In those days he and his brother had an English governess who spoke the language very clearly and crisply and well, so that the two boys grew to speak as she did—their words and sentences were all crisp and clear and not run together as ours are. They didn't talk exactly like English children but acquired an accent that is peculiar to fashionable people in the city of New York.

In the summer the six children were moved from the house on 71st Street to a big estate in northern Connecticut. It was not a fashionable locality—Anson's father wanted to delay as long as possible his children's knowledge of that side of life. He was a man somewhat superior to his class, which composed New York society, and to his period, which was the snobbish and formalized vulgarity of the Gilded Age, and he wanted his sons to learn habits of concentration and have sound constitutions and grow up into right-living and successful men. He and his wife kept an eye on them as well as they were able until the two older boys went away to school, but in huge establishments this is difficult—it was much simpler in that series of small and medium-sized houses in which my own youth was spent—I was never far out of the reach of my mother's voice, of the sense of her presence, her approval or disapproval.

Anson's first sense of his superiority came to him when he realized the half-grudging American deference that was paid to him in the Connecticut village. The parents of the boys he played with always inquired after his father and mother, and were vaguely excited when their own children were asked to the Hunters' house. He accepted this as the natural state of things, and a sort of impatience with all groups of which he was not the centre—in money, in position, in authority—remained with him for the rest of his life. He disdained to struggle with other boys for precedence—he expected it to be given him freely, and when it wasn't he withdrew into his family. His family was sufficient, for in the East money is still a somewhat feudal thing, a clan-forming thing. In the snobbish West, money separates families to form "sets."

At eighteen, when he went to New Haven, Anson was tall and thick-set, with a clear complexion and a healthy color from the ordered life he had led in school. His hair was yellow and grew in a funny way on his head, his nose was beaked—these two things kept him from being handsome—but he had a confident charm and a certain brusque style, and the upper-class men who passed him on the street knew without being told that he was a rich boy and had gone to one of the best schools. Nevertheless, his very superiority kept him from being a success in college—the independence was mistaken for egotism, and the refusal to accept Yale standards with the proper awe seemed to belittle all those who had. So, long before he graduated, he began to shift the centre of his life to New York.

He was at home in New York—there was his own house with "the kind of servants you can't get any more"—and his own family, of which, because of his good humor and a certain ability to make things go, he was rapidly becoming the centre, and the débutante parties, and the correct manly world of the men's clubs, and the occasional wild spree with the gallant girls whom New Haven only knew from the fifth row. His aspirations were conventional enough—they included even the irreproachable shadow he would some day marry, but they differed from the aspirations of the majority of young men in that there was no mist over them, none of that quality which is variously known as "idealism" or "illusion." Anson accepted without reservation the world of high finance and high extravagance, of divorce and dissipation, of snobbery and of privilege. Most of our lives end as a compromise—it was as a compromise that his life began.

He and I first met in the late summer of 1917 when he was just out of Yale, and, like the rest of us, was swept up into the systematized hysteria of the war. In the blue-green uniform of the naval aviation he came down to Pensacola, where the hotel orchestras played "I'm sorry, dear," and we young officers danced with the girls. Every one liked him, and though he ran with the drinkers and wasn't an especially good pilot, even the instructors treated him with a certain respect. He was always having long talks with them in his confident, logical voice—talks which ended by his getting himself, or, more frequently, another officer, out of some impending trouble. He was convivial, bawdy, robustly avid for pleasure, and we were all surprised when he fell in love with a conservative and rather proper girl.

Her name was Paula Legendre, a dark, serious beauty from somewhere in California. Her family kept a winter residence just outside of town, and in spite of her primness she was enormously popular; there is a large class of men whose egotism can't endure humor in a woman. But Anson wasn't that sort, and I couldn't understand the attraction of her "sincerity"—that was the thing to say about her—for his keen and somewhat sardonic mind.

Nevertheless, they fell in love—and on her terms. He no longer joined the twilight gathering at the De Soto bar, and whenever they were seen together they were engaged in a long, serious dialogue, which must have gone on several weeks. Long afterward he told me that it was not about anything in particular but was composed on both sides of immature and even meaningless statements—the emotional content that gradually came to fill it grew up not out of the words but out of its enormous seriousness. It was a sort of hypnosis. Often it was interrupted, giving way to that emasculated humor we call fun; when they were alone it was resumed again, solemn, low-keyed, and pitched so as to give each other a sense of unity in feeling and thought. They came to resent any interruptions of it, to be unresponsive to facetiousness about life, even to the mild cynicism of their contemporaries. They were only happy when the dialogue was going on, and its seriousness bathed them like the amber glow of an open fire. Toward the end there came an interruption they did not resent—it began to be interrupted by passion.

Oddly enough, Anson was as engrossed in the dialogue as she was and as profoundly affected by it, yet at the same time aware that on his side much was insincere, and on hers much was merely simple. At first, too, he despised her emotional simplicity as well, but with his love her nature deepened and blossomed, and he could despise it no longer. He felt that if he could enter into Paula's warm safe life he would be happy. The long preparation of the dialogue removed any constraint—he taught her some of what he had learned from more adventurous women, and she responded with a rapt holy intensity. One evening after a dance they agreed to marry, and he wrote a long letter about her to his mother. The next day Paula told him that she was rich, that she had a personal fortune of nearly a million dollars.

III

It was exactly as if they could say "Neither of us has anything: we shall be poor together"—just as delightful that they should be rich instead. It gave them the same communion of adventure. Yet when Anson got leave in April, and Paula and her mother accompanied him North, she was impressed with the standing of his family in New York and with the scale on which they lived. Alone with Anson for the first time in the room where he had played as a boy, she was filled with a comfortable emotion, as though she were pre-eminently safe and taken care of. The pictures of Anson in a skull cap at his first school, of Anson on horseback with the sweetheart of a mysterious forgotten summer, of Anson in a gay group of ushers and bridesmaids at a wedding, made her jealous of his life apart from her in the past, and so completely did his authoritative person seem to sum up and typify these possessions of his that she was inspired with the ideas of being married immediately and returning to Pensacola as his wife.

But an immediate marriage wasn't discussed—even the engagement was to be secret until after the war. When she realized that only.two days of his leave remained, her dissatisfaction crystallized in the intention of making him as unwilling to wait as she was. They were driving to the country for dinner and she determined to force the issue that night.

Now a cousin of Paula's was staying with them at the Ritz, a severe, bitter girl who loved Paula but was somewhat jealous of her impressive engagement, and as Paula was late in dressing, the cousin, who wasn't going to the party, received Anson in the parlor of the suite.

Anson had met friends at five o'clock and drunk freely and indiscreetly with them for an hour. He left the Yale Club at a proper time, and his mother's chauffeur drove him to the Ritz, but his usual capacity was not in evidence, and the impact of the steam-heated sitting-room made him suddenly dizzy. He knew it, and he was both amused and sorry.

Paula's cousin was twenty-five, but she was exceptionally naïve, and at first failed to realize what was up. She had never met Anson before, and she was surprised when he mumbled strange information and nearly fell off his chair, but until Paula appeared it didn't occur to her that what she had taken for the odor of a dry-cleaned uniform was really whiskey. But Paula understood as soon as she appeared; her only thought was to get Anson away before her mother saw him, and at the look in her eyes the cousin understood too.

When Paula and Anson descended to the limousine they found two men inside, both asleep; they were the men with whom he had been drinking at the Yale Club, and they were also going to the party. He had entirely forgotten their presence in the car. On the way to Hempstead they awoke and sang. Some of the songs were rough, and though Paula tried to reconcile herself to the fact that Anson had few verbal inhibitions, her lips tightened with shame and distaste.

Back at the hotel the cousin, confused and agitated, considered the incident, and then walked into Mrs. Legendre's bedroom, saying: "Isn't he funny?"

"Who is funny?"

"Why—Mr. Hunter. He seemed so funny."

Mrs. Legendre looked at her sharply.

"How is he funny?"

"Why, he said he was French. I didn't know he was French."

"That's absurd. You must have misunderstood." She smiled: "It was a joke."

The cousin shook her head stubbornly.

"No. He said he was brought up in France. He said he couldn't speak any English, and that's why he couldn't talk to me. And he couldn't!"

Mrs. Legendre looked away with impatience just as the cousin added thoughtfully, "Perhaps it was because he was so drunk," and walked out of the room.

This curious report was true. Anson, finding his voice thick and uncontrollable, had taken the unusual refuge of announcing that he spoke no English. Years afterwards he used to tell that part of the story, and he invariably communicated the uproarious laughter which the memory aroused in him.

Five times in the next hour Mrs. Legendre tried to get Hempstead on the phone. When she succeeded, there was a ten-minute delay before she heard Paula's voice on the wire.

"Cousin Jo told me Anson was intoxicated."

"Oh, no. . . ."

"Oh, yes. Cousin Jo says he was intoxicated. He told her he was French, and fell off his chair and behaved as if he was very intoxicated. I don't want you to come home with him."

"Mother, he's all right! Please don't worry about——"

"But I do worry. I think it's dreadful. I want you to promise me not to come home with him."

"I'll take care of it, mother. . . ."

"I don't want you to come home with him."

"All right, mother. Good-by."

"Be sure now, Paula. Ask some one to bring you."

Deliberately Paula took the receiver from her ear and hung it up. Her face was flushed with helpless annoyance. Anson was stretched asleep out in a bedroom up-stairs, while the dinner-party below was proceeding lamely toward conclusion.

The hour's drive had sobered him somewhat—his arrival was merely hilarious—and Paula hoped that the evening was not spoiled, after all, but two imprudent cocktails before dinner completed the disaster. He talked boisterously and somewhat offensively to the party at large for fifteen minutes, and then slid silently under the table; like a man in an old print—but, unlike an old print, it was rather horrible without being at all quaint. None of the young girls present remarked upon the incident—it seemed to merit only silence. His uncle and two other men carried him up-stairs, and it was just after this that Paula was called to the phone.

An hour later Anson awoke in a fog of nervous agony, through which he perceived after a moment the figure of his uncle Robert standing by the door.

". . . I said are you better?"

"What?"

"Do you feel better, old man?"

"Terrible," said Anson.

"I'm going to try you on another bromo-seltzer. If you can hold it down, it'll do you good to sleep."

With an effort Anson slid his legs from the bed and stood up.

"I'm all right," he said dully.

"Take it easy."

"I thin' if you gave me a glassbrandy I could go down-stairs."

"Oh, no———"

"Yes, that's the only thin'. I'm all right now. . . . I suppose I'm in Dutch dow' there."

"They know you're a little under the weather," said his uncle deprecatingly. "But don't worry about it. Schuyler didn't even get here. He passed away in the locker-room over at the Links."

Indifferent to any opinion, except Paula's, Anson was nevertheless determined to save the débris of the evening, but when after a cold bath he made his appearance most of the party had already left. Paula got up immediately to go home.

In the limousine the old serious dialogue began. She had known that he drank, she admitted, but she had never expected anything like this—it seemed to her that perhaps they were not suited to each other, after all. Their ideas about life were too different, and so forth. When she finished speaking, Anson spoke in turn, very soberly. Then Paula said she'd have to think it over; she wouldn't decide to-night; she was not angry but she was terribly sorry. Nor would she let him come into the hotel with her, but just before she got out of the car she leaned and kissed him unhappily on the cheek.

The next afternoon Anson had a long talk with Mrs. Legendre while Paula sat listening in silence. It was agreed that Paula was to brood over the incident for a proper period and then, if mother and daughter thought it best, they would follow Anson to Pensacola. On his part he apologized with sincerity and dignity—that was all; with every card in her hand Mrs. Legendre was unable to establish any advantage over him. He made no promises, showed no humility, only delivered a few serious comments on life which brought him off with rather a moral superiority at the end. When they came

South three weeks later, neither Anson in his satisfaction nor Paula in her relief at the reunion realized that the psychological moment had passed forever.

IV

He dominated and attracted her, and at the same time filled her with anxiety. Confused by his mixture of solidity and self-indulgence, of sentiment and cynicism—incongruities which her gentle mind was unable to resolve—Paula grew to think of him as two alternating personalities. When she saw him alone, or at a formal party, or with his casual inferiors, she felt a tremendous pride in his strong, attractive presence, the paternal, understanding stature of his mind. In other company she became uneasy when what had been a fine imperviousness to mere gentility showed its other face. The other face was gross, humorous, reckless of everything but pleasure. It startled her mind temporarily away from him, even led her into a short covert experiment with an old beau, but it was no use—after four months of Anson's enveloping vitality there was an anæmic pallor in all other men.

In July he was ordered abroad, and their tenderness and desire reached a crescendo. Paula considered a last-minute marriage—decided against it only because there were always cocktails on his breath now, but the parting itself made her physically ill with grief. After his departure she wrote him long letters of regret for the days of love they had missed by waiting. In August Anson's plane slipped down into the North Sea. He was pulled onto a destroyer after a night in the water and sent to a hospital with pneumonia; the armistice was signed before he was finally sent home.

Then, with every opportunity given back to them, with no material obstacle to overcome, the secret weavings of their temperaments came between them, drying up their kisses and their tears, making their voices less loud to one another, muffling the intimate chatter of their hearts until the old communication was only possible by letters, from far away. One afternoon a society reporter waited for two hours in the Hunters' house for a confirmation of their engagement. Anson denied it; nevertheless an early issue carried the report as a leading paragraph—they were "constantly seen together at Southhampton, Hot Springs, and Tuxedo Park." But the serious dialogue had turned a corner into a long-sustained quarrel, and the affair was almost played out. Anson got drunk flagrantly and missed an engagement with her, whereupon Paula made certain behavioristic demands. His despair was helpless before his pride and his knowledge of himself: the engagement was definitely broken.

"Dearest," said their letters now, "Dearest, Dearest, when I wake up in the middle of the night and realize that after all it was not to be, I feel that I want to die. I can't go on living any more. Perhaps when we meet this summer we may talk things over and decide differently—we were so excited and sad that day, and I don't feel that I can live all my life without you. You speak of other people. Don't you know there are no other people for me, but only you. . . ."

But as Paula drifted here and there around the East she would sometimes mention her gaieties to make him wonder. Anson was too acute to wonder. When he saw a man's name in her letters he felt more sure of her and a little disdainful—he was always superior to such things. But he still hoped that they would some day marry.

Meanwhile he plunged vigorously into all the movement and glitter of post-bellum New York, entering a brokerage house, joining half a dozen clubs, dancing late, and moving in three worlds—his own world, the world of young Yale graduates, and that section of the half-world which rests one end on Broadway. But there was always a thorough and infractible eight hours devoted to his work in Wall Street, where the combination of his influential family connection, his sharp intelligence, and his abundance of sheer physical energy brought him almost immediately forward. He had one of those invaluable minds with partitions in it; sometimes he appeared at his office refreshed by less than an hour's sleep, but such occurrences were rare. So early as 1920 his income in salary and commissions exceeded twelve thousand dollars.

As the Yale tradition slipped into the past he became more and more of a popular figure among his classmates in New York, more popular than he had ever been in college. He lived in a great house, and had the means of introducing young men into other great houses. Moreover, his life already seemed secure, while theirs, for the most part, had arrived again at precarious beginnings. They commenced to turn to him for amusement and escape, and Anson responded readily, taking pleasure in helping people and arranging their affairs.

There were no men in Paula's letters now, but a note of tenderness ran through them that had not been there before. From several sources he heard that she had "a heavy beau," Lowell Thayer, a Bostonian of wealth and position, and though he was sure she still loved him, it made him uneasy to think that he might lose her, after all. Save for one unsatisfactory day she had not been in New York for almost five months, and as the rumors multiplied he became increasingly anxious to see her. In February he took his vacation and went down to Florida.

Palm Beach sprawled plump and opulent between the sparkling sapphire of Lake Worth, flawed here and there by house-boats at anchor, and the great turquoise bar of the Atlantic Ocean. The huge bulks of the Breakers and the Royal Poinciana rose as twin paunches from the bright level of the sand, and around them clustered the Dancing Glade, Bradley's House of Chance, and a dozen modistes and milliners with goods at triple prices from New York. Upon the trellised veranda of the Breakers two hundred women stepped right, stepped left, wheeled, and slid in that then celebrated calisthenic known as the double-shuffle, while in half-time to the music two thousand bracelets clicked up and down on two hundred arms.

At the Everglades Club after dark Paula and Lowell Thayer and Anson and a casual fourth played bridge with hot cards. It seemed to Anson that her kind, serious face was wan and tired—she had been around now for four, five, years. He had known her for three.

"Two spades."

"Cigarette? . . . Oh, I beg your pardon. By me."

"By."

"I'll double three spades."

There were a dozen tables of bridge in the room, which was filling up with smoke. Anson's eyes met Paula's, held them persistently even when Thayer's glance fell between them. . . .

"What was bid?" he asked abstractedly.

"Rose of Washington Square"

sang the young people in the corners:

*"I'm withering there
In basement air——*

The smoke banked like fog, and the opening of a door filled the room with blown swirls of ectoplasm. Little Bright Eyes streaked past the tables seeking Mr. Conan Doyle among the Englishmen who were posing as Englishmen about the lobby.

"You could cut it with a knife."

". . . cut it with a knife."

". . . a knife."

At the end of the rubber Paula suddenly got up and spoke to Anson in a tense, low voice. With scarcely a glance at Lowell Thayer, they walked out the door and descended a long flight of stone steps—in a moment they were walking hand in hand along the moonlit beach.

"Darling, darling. . . ." They embraced recklessly, passionately, in a shadow. . . . Then Paula drew back her face to let his lips say what she wanted to hear—she could feel the words forming as they kissed again. . . . Again she broke away, listening, but as he pulled her close once more she realized that he had said nothing—only *"Darling! Darling!"* in that deep, sad whisper that always made her cry. Humbly, obediently, her emotions yielded to him and the tears streamed down her face, but her heart kept on crying: "Ask me—oh, Anson, dearest, ask me!"

"Paula. . . . *Paula!*"

The words wrung her heart like hands, and Anson, feeling her tremble, knew that emotion was enough. He need say no more, commit their destinies to no practical enigma. Why should he, when he might hold her so, biding his own time, for another year—forever? He was considering them both, her more than himself. For a moment, when she said suddenly that she must go back to her hotel, he hesitated, thinking, fast, "This is the moment, after all," and then: "No, let it wait—she is mine. . . ."

He had forgotten that Paula too was worn away inside with the strain of three years. Her mood passed forever in the night.

He went back to New York next morning filled with a certain restless dissatisfaction. Late in April, without warning, he received a telegram from Bar Harbor in which Paula told him that she was engaged to Lowell Thayer, and that they would be married immediately in Boston. What he never really believed could happen had happened at last.

Anson filled himself with whiskey that morning, and going to the office, carried on his work without a break—rather with a fear of what would happen if he stopped. In the evening he went out as usual, saying nothing of what had occurred; he was cordial, humorous, unabstracted. But one thing he could not help—for three days, in any place, in any company, he would suddenly bend his head into his hands and cry like a child.

V

In 1922 when Anson went abroad with the junior partner to investigate some London loans, the journey intimated that he was to be taken into the firm. He was twenty-seven now, a little heavy without being definitely stout, and with a manner older than his years. Old people and young people liked him and trusted him, and mothers felt safe when their daughters were in his charge, for he had a way, when he came into a room, of putting himself on a footing with the oldest and most conservative people there. "You and I," he seemed to say, "we're solid. We understand."

He had an instinctive and rather charitable knowledge of the weaknesses of men and women, and, like a priest, it made him the more concerned for the maintenance of outward forms. It was typical of him that every Sunday morning he taught in a fashionable Episcopal Sunday school—even though a cold shower and a quick change into a cutaway coat were all that separated him from the wild night before.

After his father's death he was the practical head of his family, and, in effect, guided the destinies of the younger children. Through a complication his authority did not extend to his father's estate, which was administrated by his Uncle Robert, who was the horsey member of the family, a good-natured, hard-drinking member of that set which centres about Wheatley Hills.

Uncle Robert and his wife, Edna, had been great friends of Anson's youth, and the former was disappointed when his nephew's superiority failed to take a horsey form. He backed him for a city club which was the most difficult in America to enter—one could only join if one's family had "helped to build up New York" (or, in other words, were rich before 1880)—and when Anson, after his election, neglected it for the Yale Club, Uncle Robert gave him a little talk on the subject. But when on top of that Anson declined to enter Robert Hunter's own conservative and somewhat neglected brokerage house, his manner grew cooler. Like a primary teacher who has taught all he knew, he slipped out of Anson's life.

There were so many friends in Anson's life—scarcely one for whom he had not done some unusual kindness and scarcely one whom he did not occasionally embarrass by his bursts of rough conversation or his habit of getting drunk whenever and however he liked. It annoyed him when any one else blundered in that regard—about his own lapses he was always humorous. Odd things happened to him and he told them with infectious laughter.

I was working in New York that spring, and I used to lunch with him at the Yale Club, which my university was sharing until the completion of our own. I had read of Paula's marriage, and one afternoon, when I asked him about her, something moved him to tell me the story. After that he frequently invited me to family dinners at his house and behaved as though there was a special relation between us, as though with his confidence a little of that consuming memory had passed into me.

I found that despite the trusting mothers, his attitude toward girls was not indiscriminately protective. It was up to the girl—if she showed an inclination toward looseness, she must take care of herself, even with him.

"Life," he would explain sometimes, "has made a cynic of me."

By life he meant Paula. Sometimes, especially when he was drinking, it became a little twisted in his mind, and he thought that she had callously thrown him over.

This "cynicism," or rather his realization that naturally fast girls were not worth sparing, led to his affair with Dolly Karger. It wasn't his only affair in those years, but it came nearest to touching him deeply, and it had a profound effect upon his attitude toward life.

Dolly was the daughter of a notorious "publicist" who had married into society. She herself grew up into the Junior League, came out at the Plaza, and went to the Assembly; and only a few old families like the Hunters could question whether or not she "belonged," for her picture was often in the papers, and she had more enviable attention than many girls who undoubtedly did. She was dark-haired, with carmine lips and a high, lovely color, which she concealed under pinkish-gray powder all through the first year out, because high color was unfashionable—Victorian-pale was the thing to be. She wore black, severe suits and stood with her hands in her pockets leaning a little forward, with a humorous restraint on her face. She danced exquisitely—better than anything she liked to dance—better than anything except making love. Since she was ten she had always been in love, and, usually, with some boy who didn't respond to her. Those who did—and there were many—bored her after a brief encounter, but for her failures she reserved the warmest spot in her heart. When she met them she would always try once more—sometimes she succeeded, more often she failed.

It never occurred to this gypsy of the unattainable that there was a certain resemblance in those who refused to love her—they shared a hard intuition that saw through to her weakness, not a weakness of emotion but a weakness of rudder. Anson perceived this when he first met her, less than a month after Paula's marriage. He was drinking rather heavily, and he pretended for a week that he was falling in love with her. Then he dropped her abruptly and forgot—immediately he took up the commanding position in her heart.

Like so many girls of that day Dolly was slackly and indiscreetly wild. The unconventionality of a slightly older generation had been simply one facet of a post-war movement to discredit obsolete manners—Dolly's was both older and shabbier, and she saw in Anson the two extremes which the emotionally shiftless woman seeks, an abandon to indulgence alternating with a protective strength. In his character she felt both the sybarite and the solid rock, and these two satisfied every need of her nature.

She felt that it was going to be difficult, but she mistook the reason—she thought that Anson and his family expected a more spectacular marriage, but she guessed immediately that her advantage lay in his tendency to drink.

They met at the large débutante dances, but as her infatuation increased they managed to be more and more together. Like most mothers, Mrs. Karger believed that Anson was exceptionally reliable, so she allowed Dolly to go with him to distant country clubs and suburban houses without inquiring closely into their activities or questioning her explanations when they came in late. At first these explanations might have been accurate, but Dolly's worldly ideas of capturing Anson were soon engulfed in the rising sweep of her emotion. Kisses in the back of taxis and motor-cars were no longer enough; they did a curious thing:

They dropped out of their world for a while and made another world just beneath it where Anson's tippling and Dolly's irregular hours would be less noticed and commented on. It was composed, this world, of varying elements—several of Anson's Yale friends and their wives, two or three young brokers and bond salesmen and a handful of unattached men, fresh from college, with money and a propensity to dissipation. What this world lacked in spaciousness and scale it made up for by allowing them a liberty that it scarcely permitted itself. Moreover, it centred around them and permitted Dolly the pleasure of a faint condescension—a pleasure which Anson, whose whole life was a condescension from the certitudes of his childhood, was unable to share.

He was not in love with her, and in the long feverish winter of their affair he frequently told her so. In the spring he was weary—he wanted to renew his life at some other source—moreover, he saw that either he must break with her now or accept the responsibility of a definite seduction. Her family's encouraging attitude precipitated his decision—one evening when Mr. Karger knocked discreetly at the library door to announce that he had left a bottle of old brandy in the dining-room, Anson felt that life was hemming him in. That night he wrote her a short letter in which he told her that he was going on his vacation, and that in view of all the circumstances they had better meet no more.

It was June. His family had closed up the house and gone to the country, so he was living temporarily at the Yale Club. I had heard about his affair with Dolly as it developed—accounts salted with humor, for he despised unstable women, and granted them no place in the social edifice in which he believed—and when he told me that night that he was definitely breaking with her I was glad. I had seen Dolly here and there, and each time with a feeling of pity at the hopelessness of her struggle, and of shame at knowing so much about her that I had no right to know. She was what is known as "a pretty little thing," but there was a certain recklessness which rather fascinated me. Her dedication to the goddess of waste would have been less obvious had she been less spirited—she would most certainly throw herself away, but I was glad when I heard that the sacrifice would not be consummated in my sight.

Anson was going to leave the letter of farewell at her house next morning. It was one of the few houses left open in the Fifth Avenue district, and he knew that the Kargers, acting upon erroneous information from Dolly, had foregone a trip abroad to give their daughter her chance. As he stepped out the door of the Yale Club into Madison Avenue the postman passed him, and he followed back inside. The first letter that caught his eye was in Dolly's hand.

He knew what it would be—a lonely and tragic monologue, full of the reproaches he knew, the invoked memories, the "I wonder if's"—all the immemorial intimacies that he had communicated to Paula Legendre in what seemed another age. Thumbing over some bills, he brought it on top again and opened it. To his surprise it was a short, somewhat formal note, which said that Dolly would be unable to go to the country with him for the week-end, because Perry Hull from Chicago had unexpectedly come to town. It added that Anson had brought this on himself: "—if I felt that you loved me as I love you I would go at any time, any place, but Perry is *so* nice, and he so much wants me to marry him———"

Anson smiled contemptuously—he had had experience with such decoy epistles. Moreover, he knew how Dolly had labored over this plan, probably sent for the faithful Perry and calculated the time of his arrival—even labored over the note so that it would make him jealous without driving him away. Like most compromises, it had neither force nor vitality but only a timorous despair.

Suddenly he was angry. He sat down in the lobby and read it again. Then he went to the phone, called Dolly and told her in his clear, compelling voice that he had received her note and would call for her at five o'clock as they had previously planned. Scarcely waiting for the pretended uncertainty of her "Perhaps I can see you for an hour," he hung up the receiver and went down to his office. On the way home he tore his own letter into bits and dropped it in the street.

He was not jealous—she meant nothing to him—but at her pathetic ruse everything stubborn and self-indulgent in him came to the surface. It was a presumption from a mental inferior and it could not be overlooked. If she wanted to know to whom she belonged she would see.

He was on the door-step at quarter past five. Dolly was dressed for the street, and he listened in silence to the paragraph of "I can only see you for an hour," which she had begun on the phone.

"Put on your hat, Dolly," he said, "we'll take a walk."

They strolled up Madison Avenue and over to Fifth while Anson's shirt dampened upon his portly body in the deep heat. He talked little, scolding her, making no love to her, but before they had walked six blocks she was his again, apologizing for the note, offering not to see Perry at all as an atonement, offering anything. She thought that he had come because he was beginning to love her.

"I'm hot," he said when they reached 71st Street. "This is a winter suit. If I stop by the house and change, would you mind waiting for me down-stairs? I'll only be a minute."

She was happy; the intimacy of his being hot, of any physical fact about him, thrilled her. When they came to the iron-grated door and Anson took out his key she experienced a sort of delight.

Down-stairs it was dark, and after he ascended in the lift Dolly raised a curtain and looked out through opaque lace at the houses over the way. She head the lift machinery stop, and with the notion of teasing him pressed the button that brought it down. Then on what was more than an impulse she got into it and sent it up to what she guessed was his floor.

"Anson," she called, laughing a little.

"Just a minute," he answered from his bedroom . . . then after a brief delay: "Now you can come in."

He had changed and was buttoning his vest.

"This is my room," he said lightly. "How do you like it?"

She caught sight of Paula's picture on the wall and stared at it in fascination, just as Paula had stared at the pictures of Anson's childish sweethearts five years before. She knew something about Paula—sometimes she tortured herself with fragments of the story.

Suddenly she came close to Anson, raising her arms. They embraced. Outside the area window a soft artificial twilight already hovered, though the sun was still bright on a back roof across the way. In half an hour the room would be quite dark. The uncalculated opportunity overwhelmed them, made them both breathless, and they clung more closely. It was imminent, inevitable. Still holding one another, they raised their heads—their eyes fell together upon Paula's picture, staring down at them from the wall.

Suddenly Anson dropped his arms, and sitting down at his desk tried the drawer with a bunch of keys.

"Like a drink?" he asked in a gruff voice.

"No, Anson."

He poured himself half a tumbler of whiskey, swallowed it, and then opened the door into the hall.

"Come on," he said.

Dolly hesitated.

"Anson—I'm going to the country with you tonight, after all. You understand that, don't you?"

"Of course," he answered brusquely.

In Dolly's car they rode on to Long Island, closer in their emotions than they had ever been before. They knew what would happen—not with Paula's face to remind them that something was lacking, but when they were alone in the still, hot Long Island night they did not care.

The estate in Port Washington where they were to spend the weekend belonged to a cousin of Anson's who had married a Montana copper operator. An interminable drive began at the lodge and twisted under imported poplar saplings toward a huge, pink Spanish house. Anson had often visited there before.

After dinner they danced at the Linx Club. About midnight Anson assured himself that his cousins would not leave before two—then he explained that Dolly was tired; he would take her home and return to the dance later. Trembling a little with excitement, they got into a borrowed car together and drove to Port Washington. As they reached the lodge he stopped and spoke to the night-watchman.

"When are you making a round, Carl?"

"Right away."

"Then you'll be here till everybody's in?"

"Yes, sir."

"All right. Listen: if any automobile, no matter whose it is, turns in at this gate, I want you to phone the house immediately." He put a five-dollar bill into Carl's hand. "Is that clear?"

"Yes, Mr. Anson." Being of the Old World, he neither winked nor smiled. Yet Dolly sat with her face turned slightly away.

Anson had a key. Once inside he poured a drink for both of them—Dolly left hers untouched—then he ascertained definitely the location of the phone, and found that it was within easy hearing distance of their rooms, both of which were on the first floor.

Five minutes later he knocked at the door of Dolly's room. "Anson?" He went in, closing the door behind him. She was in bed, leaning up anxiously with elbows on the pillow; sitting beside her he took her in his arms.

"Anson, darling."

He didn't answer.

"Anson. . . . Anson! I love you. . . . Say you love me. Say it now—can't you say it now? Even if you don't mean it?"

He did not listen. Over her head he perceived that the picture of Paula was hanging here upon this wall.

He got up and went close to it. The frame gleamed faintly with thrice-reflected moonlight—within was a blurred shadow of a face that he saw he did not know. Almost sobbing, he turned around and stared with abomination at the little figure on the bed.

"This is all foolishness," he said thickly. "I don't know what I was thinking about. I don't love you and you'd better wait for somebody that loves you. I don't love you a bit, can't you understand?"

His voice broke, and he went hurriedly out. Back in the salon he was pouring himself a drink with uneasy fingers, when the front door opened suddenly, and his cousin came in.

"Why, Anson, I hear Dolly's sick," she began solicitously. "I hear she's sick. . . ."

"It was nothing," he interrupted, raising his voice so that it would carry into Dolly's room. "She was a little tired. She went to bed."

For a long time afterward Anson believed that a protective God sometimes interfered in human affairs. But Dolly Karger, lying awake and staring at the ceiling, never again believed in anything at all.

VI

When Dolly married during the following autumn, Anson was in London on business. Like Paula's marriage, it was sudden, but it affected him in a different way. At first he felt that it was funny, and had an inclination to laugh when he thought of it. Later it depressed him—it made him feel old.

There was something repetitive about it—why, Paula and Dolly had belonged to different generations. He had a foretaste of the sensation of a man of forty who hears that the daughter of an old flame has married. He wired congratulations and, as was not the case with Paula, they were sincere—he had never really hoped that Paula would be happy.

When he returned to New York, he was made a partner in the firm, and, as his responsibilities increased he had less time on his hands. The refusal of a life-insurance company to issue him a policy made such an impression on him that he stopped drinking for a year, and claimed that he felt better physically, though I think he missed the convivial recounting of those Celliniesque adventures which, in his early twenties, had played such a part in his life. But he never abandoned the Yale Club. He was a figure there, a personality, and the tendency of his class, who were now seven years out of college, to drift away to more sober haunts was checked by his presence.

His day was never too full nor his mind too weary to give any sort of aid to any one who asked it. What had been done at first through pride and superiority had become a habit and a passion. And there was always something—a younger brother in trouble at New Haven, a quarrel to be patched up between a friend and his wife, a position to be found for this man, an investment for that. But his specialty was the solving of problems for young married people. Young married people fascinated him and their apartments were almost sacred to him—he knew the story of their love-affair, advised them where to live and how, and remembered their babies' names. Toward young wives his attitude was circumspect: he never abused the trust which their husbands—strangely enough in view of his unconcealed irregularities— invariably reposed in him.

He came to take a vicarious pleasure in happy marriages, and to be inspired to an almost equally pleasant melancholy by those that went astray. Not a season passed that he did not witness the collapse of an affair that perhaps he himself had fathered. When Paula was divorced and almost immediately remarried to another Bostonian, he talked about her to me all one afternoon. He would never love any one as he had loved Paula, but he insisted that he no longer cared.

"I'll never marry," he came to say; "I've seen too much of it, and I know a happy marriage is a very rare thing. Besides, I'm too old."

But he did believe in marriage. Like all men who spring from a happy and successful marriage, he believed in it passionately—nothing he had seen would change his belief, his cynicism dissolved upon it like air. But he did really believe he was too old. At twenty-eight he began to accept with equanimity the prospect of marrying without romantic love; he resolutely chose a New York girl of his own class, pretty, intelligent, congenial, above reproach—and set about falling in love with her. The things he had said to Paula with sincerity, to other girls with grace, he could no longer say at all without smiling, or with the force necessary to convince.

"When I'm forty," he told his friends, "I'll be ripe. I'll fall for some chorus girl like the rest."

Nevertheless, he persisted in his attempt. His mother wanted to see him married, and he could now afford it—he had a seat on the Stock Exchange, and his earned income came to twenty-five thousand a year. The idea was agreeable: when his friends—he spent most of his time with the set he and Dolly had evolved—closed themselves in behind domestic doors at night, he no longer rejoiced in his freedom. He even wondered if he should have married Dolly. Not even Paula had loved him more, and he was learning the rarity, in a single life, of encountering true emotion.

Just as this mood began to creep over him a disquieting story reached his ear. His Aunt Edna, a woman just this side of forty, was carrying on an open intrigue with a dissolute, hard-drinking young man named Cary Sloane. Every one knew of it except Anson's Uncle Robert, who for fifteen years had talked long in clubs and taken his wife for granted.

Anson heard the story again and again with increasing annoyance. Something of his old feeling for his uncle came back to him, a feeling that was more than personal, a reversion toward that family solidarity on which he had based his pride. His intuition singled out the essential point of the affair, which was that his uncle shouldn't be hurt. It was his first experiment in unsolicited meddling, but with his knowledge of Edna's character he felt that he could handle the matter better than a district judge or his uncle.

His uncle was in Hot Springs. Anson traced down the sources of the scandal so that there should be no possibility of mistake and then he called Edna and asked her to lunch with him at the Plaza next day. Something in his tone must have frightened her, for she was reluctant, but he insisted, putting off the date until she had no excuse for refusing.

She met him at the appointed time in the Plaza lobby, a lovely, faded, gray-eyed blonde in a coat of Russian sable. Five great rings, cold with diamonds and emeralds, sparkled on her slender hands. It occurred to Anson that it was his father's intelligence and not his uncle's that had earned the fur and the stones, the rich brilliance that buoyed up her passing beauty.

Though Edna scented his hostility, she was unprepared for the directness of his approach.

"Edna, I'm astonished at the way you've been acting," he said in a strong, frank voice. "At first I couldn't believe it."

"Believe what?" she demanded sharply.

"You needn't pretend with me, Edna. I'm talking about Cary Sloane. Aside from any other consideration, I didn't think you could treat Uncle Robert——"

"Now look here, Anson——" she began angrily, but his peremptory voice broke through hers:

"——and your children in such a way. You've been married eighteen years, and you're old enough to know better."

"You can't talk to me like that! You——"

"Yes, I can. Uncle Robert has always been my best friend." He was tremendously moved. He felt a real distress about his uncle, about his three young cousins.

Enda stood up, leaving her crab-flake cocktail untasted.

"This is the silliest thing—— "

"Very well, if you won't listen to me I'll go to Uncle Robert and tell him the whole story—he's bound to hear it sooner or later. And afterward I'll go to old Moses Sloane."

Edna faltered back into her chair.

"Don't talk so loud," she begged him. Her eyes blurred with tears. "You have no idea how your voice carries. You might have chosen a less public place to make all these crazy accusations."

He didn't answer.

"Oh, you never liked me, I know," she went on. "You're just taking advantage of some silly gossip to try and break up the only interesting friendship I've ever had. What did I ever do to make you hate me so?"

Still Anson waited. There would be the appeal to his chivalry, then to his pity, finally to his superior sophistication—when he had shouldered his way through all these there would be admissions, and he could come to grips with her. By being silent, by being impervious, by returning constantly to his main weapon, which was his own true emotion, he bullied her into frantic despair as the luncheon hour slipped away. At two o'clock she took out a mirror and a handkerchief, shined away the marks of her tears and powdered the slight hollows where they had lain. She had agreed to meet him at her own house at five.

When he arrived she was stretched on a *chaise-longue* which was covered with cretonne for the summer, and the tears he had called up at luncheon seemed still to be standing in her eyes. Then he was aware of Cary Sloane's dark anxious presence upon the cold hearth.

"What's this idea of yours?" broke out Sloane immediately. "I understand you invited Edna to lunch and then threatened her on the basis of some cheap scandal."

Anson sat down.

"I have no reason to think it's only scandal."

"I hear you're going to take it to Robert Hunter, and to my father."

Anson nodded.

"Either you break it off—or I will," he said.

"What God damned business is it of yours, Hunter?"

"Don't lose your temper, Cary," said Edna nervously. "It's only a question of showing him how absurd——"

"For one thing, it's my name that's being handed around," interrupted Anson. "That's all that concerns you, Cary."

"Edna isn't a member of your family."

"She most certainly is!" His anger mounted. "Why—she owes this house and the rings on her fingers to my father's brains. When Uncle Robert married her she didn't have a penny."

They all looked at the rings as if they had a significant bearing on the situation. Edna made a gesture to take them from her hand.

"I guess they're not the only rings in the world," said Sloane.

"Oh, this is absurd," cried Edna. "Anson, will you listen to me? I've found out how the silly story started. It was a maid I discharged who went right to the Chilicheffs—all these Russians pump things out of their servants and then put a false meaning on them." She brought down her fist angrily on the table: "And after Robert lent them the limousine for a whole month when we were South last winter——"

"Do you see?" demanded Sloane eagerly. "This maid got hold of the wrong end of the thing. She knew that Edna and I were friends, and she carried it to the Chilicheffs. In Russia they assume that if a man and a woman——"

He enlarged the theme to a disquisition upon social relations in the Caucasus.

"If that's the case it better be explained to Uncle Robert," said Anson dryly, "so that when the rumors do reach him he'll know they're not true."

Adopting the method he had followed with Edna at luncheon he let them explain it all away. He knew that they were guilty and that presently they would cross the line from explanation into justification and convict themselves more definitely than he could ever do. By seven they had taken the desperate step of telling him the truth—Robert Hunter's neglect, Edna's empty life, the casual dalliance that had flamed up into passion—but like so many true stories it had the misfortune of being old, and its enfeebled body beat helplessly against the armor of Anson's will. The threat to go to Sloane's father sealed their helplessness, for the latter a retired cotton broker out of Alabama, was a notorious fundamentalist who controlled his son by a rigid allowance and the promise that at his next vagary the allowance would stop forever.

They dined at a small French restaurant, and the discussion continued—at one time Sloane resorted to physical threats, a little later they were both imploring him to give them time. But Anson was obdurate, He saw that Edna was breaking up, and that her spirit must not be refreshed by any renewal of their passion.

At two o'clock in a small night-club on 53d Street, Edna's nerves suddenly collapsed, and she cried to go home. Sloane had been drinking heavily all evening, and he was faintly maudlin, leaning on the table and weeping a little with his face in his hands. Quickly Ason gave them his terms. Sloane was to leave town for six months, and he must be gone within forty-eight hours. When he returned there was to be no resumption of the affair, but at the end of a year Edna might, if she wished, tell Robert Hunter that she wanted a divorce and go about it in the usual way.

He paused, gaining confidence from their faces for his final word.

"Or there's another thing you can do," he said slowly, "if Edna wants to leave her children, there's nothing I can do to prevent your running off together."

"I want to go home!" cried Edna again. "Oh, haven't you done enough to us for one day?"

Outside it was dark, save for a blurred glow from Sixth Avenue down the street. In that light those two who had been lovers looked for the last time into each other's tragic faces, realizing that between them there was not enough youth and strength to avert their eternal parting. Sloane walked suddenly off down the street and Anson tapped a dozing taxi-driver on the arm.

It was almost four; there was a patient flow of cleaning water along the ghostly pavement of Fifth Avenue, and the shadows of two night women flitted over the dark facade of St. Thomas's church. Then the desolate shrubbery of Central Park where Anson had often played as a child, and the mounting numbers, significant as names, of the marching streets. This was his city, he thought, where his name had flourished through five generations. No change could alter the permanence of its place here, for change itself was the essential substratum by which he and those of his name identified themselves with the spirit of New York. Resourcefulness and a powerful will—for his threats in weaker hands would have been less than nothing—had beaten the gathering dust from his uncle's name, from the name of his family, from even this shivering figure that sat beside him in the car.

Cary Sloane's body was found next morning on the lower shelf of a pillar of Queensboro Bridge. In the darkness and in his excitement he had thought that it was the water flowing black beneath him, but in less than a second it made no possible difference—unless he had planned to think one last thought of Edna, and call out her name as he struggled feebly in the water.

VII

Anson never blamed himself for his part in this affair—the situation which brought it about had not been of his making. But the just suffer with the unjust, and he found that his oldest and somehow his most precious friendship was over. He never knew what distorted story Edna told, but he was welcome in his uncle's house no longer.

Just before Christmas Mrs. Hunter retired to a select Episcopal heaven, and Anson became the responsible head of his family. An unmarried aunt who had lived with them for years ran the house, and attempted with helpless inefficiency to chaperone the younger girls. All the children were less self-reliant than Anson, more conventional both in their virtues and in their shortcomings. Mrs. Hunter's death had postponed the début of one daughter and the wedding of another. Also it had taken something deeply material from all of them, for with her passing the quiet, expensive superiority of the Hunters came to an end.

For one thing, the estate, considerably diminished by two inheritance taxes and soon to be divided among six children, was not a notable fortune any more. Anson saw a tendency in his youngest sisters to speak rather respectfully of families that hadn't "existed" twenty years ago. His own feeling of precedence was not echoed in them—sometimes they were conventionally snobbish, that was all. For another thing, this was the last summer they would spend on the Connecticut estate; the clamor against it was too loud: "Who wants to waste the best months of the year shut up in that dead old town?" Reluctantly he yielded—the house would go into the market in the fall, and next summer they would rent a smaller place in Westchester County. It was a step down from the expensive simplicity of his father's idea, and, while he sympathized with the revolt, it also annoyed him; during his mother's lifetime he had gone up there at least every other week-end—even in the gayest summers.

Yet he himself was part of this change, and his strong instinct for life had turned him in his twenties from the hollow obsequies of that abortive leisure class. He did not see this clearly—he still felt that there was a norm, a standard of society. But there was no norm, it was doubtful if there ever had been a true norm in New York. The few who still paid and fought to enter a particular set succeeded only to find that as a society it scarcely functioned—or, what was more alarming, that the Bohemia from which they fled sat above them at table.

At twenty-nine Anson's chief concern was his own growing loneliness. He was sure now that he would never marry. The number of weddings at which he had officiated as best man or usher was past all counting—there was a drawer at home that bulged with the official neckties of this or that wedding-party, neckties standing for romances that had not endured a year, for couples who had passed completely from his life. Scarf-pins, gold pencils, cuff-buttons, presents from a generation of grooms had passed through his jewel-box and been lost—and with every ceremony he was less and less able to imagine himself in the groom's place. Under his hearty good-will toward all those marriages there was despair about his own.

And as he neared thirty he became not a little depressed at the inroads that marriage, especially lately, had made upon his friendships. Groups of people had a disconcerting tendency to dissolve and disappear. The men from his own college—and it was upon them he had expended the most time and affection—were the most elusive of all. Most of them were drawn deep into domesticity, two were dead, one lived abroad, one was in Hollywood writing continuities for pictures that Anson went faithfully to see.

Most of them, however, were permanent commuters with an intricate family life centring around some suburban country club, and it was from these that he felt his estrangement most keenly.

In the early days of their married life they had all needed him; he gave them advice about their slim finances, he exorcised their doubts about the advisability of bringing a baby into two rooms and a bath, especially he stood for the great world outside. But now their financial troubles were in the past and the fearfully expected child had evolved into an absorbing family. They were always glad to see old Anson, but they dressed up for him and tried to impress him with their present importance, and kept their troubles to themselves. They needed him no longer.

A few weeks before his thirtieth birthday the last of his early and intimate friends was married. Anson acted in his usual rôle of best man, gave his usual silver tea-service, and went down to the usual *Homeric* to say good-by. It was a hot Friday afternoon in May, and as he walked from the pier he realized that Saturday closing had begun and he was free until Monday morning.

"Go where?" he asked himself.

The Yale Club, of course; bridge until dinner, then four or five raw cocktails in somebody's room and a pleasant confused evening. He regretted that this afternoon's groom wouldn't be along—they had always been able to cram so much into such nights: they knew how to attach women and how to get rid of them, how much consideration any girl deserved from their intelligent hedonism. A party was an adjusted thing—you took certain girls to certain places and spent just so much on their amusement; you drank a little, not much, more than you ought to drink, and at a certain time in the morning you stood up and said you were going home. You avoided college boys, sponges, future engagements, fights, sentiment, and indiscretions. That was the way it was done. All the rest was dissipation.

In the morning you were never violently sorry—you made no resolutions, but if you had overdone it and your heart was slightly out of order, you went on the wagon for a few days without saying anything about it, and waited until an accumulation of nervous boredom projected you into another party.

The lobby of the Yale Club was unpopulated. In the bar three very young alumni looked up at him, momentarily and without curiosity.

"Hello, there, Oscar," he said to the bartender. "Mr. Cahill been around this afternoon?"

"Mr. Cahill's gone to New Haven."

"Oh . . . that so?"

"Gone to the ball game. Lot of men gone up."

Anson looked once again into the lobby, considered for a moment, and then walked out and over to Fifth Avenue. From the broad window of one of his clubs—one that he had scarcely visited in five years— a gray man with watery eyes stared down at him. Anson looked quickly away—that figure sitting in vacant resignation, in supercilious solitude, depressed him. He stopped and, retracing his steps, started over 47th Street toward Teak Warden's apartment. Teak and his wife had once been his most familiar friends—it was a household where he and Dolly Karger had been used to go in the days of their affair. But Teak had taken to drink, and his wife had remarked publicly that Anson was a bad influence on him. The remark reached Anson in an exaggerated form—when it was finally cleared up, the delicate spell of intimacy was broken, never to be renewed.

"Is Mr. Warden at home?" he inquired.

"They've gone to the country."

The fact unexpectedly cut at him. They were gone to the country and he hadn't known. Two years before he would have known the date, the hour, come up at the last moment for a final drink, and planned his first visit to them. Now they had gone without a word.

Anson looked at his watch and considered a week-end with his family, but the only train was a local that would jolt through the aggressive heat for three hours. And to-morrow in the country, and Sunday—he was in no mood for porch-bridge with polite undergraduates, and dancing after dinner at a rural roadhouse, a diminutive of gaiety which his father had estimated too well.

"Oh, no," he said to himself. . . . "No."

He was a dignified, impressive young man, rather stout now, but otherwise unmarked by dissipation. He could have been cast for a pillar of something—at times you were sure it was not society, at others nothing else—for the law, for the church. He stood for a few minutes motionless on the sidewalk in front of a 47th Street apartment-house; for almost the first time in his life he had nothing whatever to do.

Then he began to walk briskly up Fifth Avenue, as if he had just been reminded of an important engagement there. The necessity of dissimulation is one of the few characteristics that we share with dogs, and I think of Anson on that day as some well-bred specimen who had been disappointed at a familiar back door. He was going to see Nick, once a fashionable bartender in demand at all private dances, and now employed in cooling non-alcoholic champagne among the labyrinthine cellars of the Plaza Hotel.

"Nick," he said, "what's happened to everything?"

"Dead," Nick said.

"Make me a whiskey sour." Anson handed a pint bottle over the counter. "Nick, the girls are different; I had a little girl in Brooklyn and she got married last week without letting me know."

"That a fact? Ha-ha-ha," responded Nick diplomatically. "Slipped it over on you."

"Absolutely," said Anson. "And I was out with her the night before."

"Ha-ha-ha," said Nick, "ha-ha-ha!"

"Do you remember the wedding, Nick, in Hot Springs where I had the waiters and the musicians singing 'God save the King'?"

"Now where was that, Mr. Hunter?" Nick concentrated doubtfully. "Seems to me that was——"

"Next time they were back for more, and I began to wonder how much I'd paid them," continued Anson.

"—seems to me that was at Mr. Trenholm's wedding."

"Don't know him," said Anson decisively. He was offended that a strange name should intrude upon his reminiscences; Nick perceived this.

"Na—aw—" he admitted, "I ought to know that. It was one of *your* crowd—Brakins . . . Baker——"

"Bicker Baker," said Anson responsively. "They put me in a hearse after it was over and covered me up with flowers and drove me away."

"Ha-ha-ha," said Nick. "Ha-ha-ha."

Nick's simulation of the old family servant paled presently and Anson went up-stairs to the lobby. He looked around—his eyes met the glance of an unfamiliar clerk at the desk, then fell upon a flower from the morning's marriage hesitating in the mouth of a brass cuspidor. He went out and walked slowly toward the blood-red sun over Columbus Circle. Suddenly he turned around and, retracing his steps to the Plaza, immured himself in a telephone-booth.

Later he said that he tried to get me three times that afternoon, that he tried every one who might be in New York—men and girls he had not seen for years, an artist's model of his college days whose faded number was still in his address book—Central told him that even the exchange existed no longer. At length his quest roved into the country, and he held brief disappointing conversations with emphatic butlers and maids. So-and-so was out, riding, swimming, playing golf, sailed to Europe last week. Who shall I say phoned?

It was intolerable that he should pass the evening alone—the private reckonings which one plans for a moment of leisure lose every charm when the solitude is enforced. There were always women of a sort, but the ones he knew had temporarily vanished, and to pass a New York evening in the hired company of a stranger never occurred to him—he would have considered that that was something shameful and secret, the diversion of a travelling salesman in a strange town.

Anson paid the telephone bill—the girl tried unsuccessfully to joke with him about its size—and for the second time that afternoon started to leave the Plaza and go he knew not where. Near the revolving door the figure of a woman, obviously with child, stood sideways to the light—a sheer beige cape fluttered at her shoulders when the door turned and, each time, she looked impatiently toward it as if she were weary of waiting. At the first sight of her a strong nervous thrill of familiarity went over him, but not until he was within five feet of her did he realize that it was Paula.

"Why, Anson Hunter!"

His heart turned over.

"Why, Paula——"

"Why, this is wonderful. I can't believe it, *Anson!*"

She took both his hands, and he saw in the freedom of the gesture that the memory of him had lost poignancy to her. But not to him—he felt that old mood that she evoked in him stealing over his brain, that gentleness with which he had always met her optimism as if afraid to mar its surface.

"We're at Rye for the summer. Pete had to come East on business—you know of course I'm Mrs. Peter Hagerty now—so we brought the children and took a house. You've got to come out and see us."

"Can I?" he asked directly. "When?"

"When you like. Here's Pete." The revolving door functioned, giving up a fine tall man of thirty with a tanned face and a trim mustache. His immaculate fitness made a sharp contrast with Anson's increasing bulk, which was obvious under the faintly tight cut-away coat.

"You oughtn't to be standing," said Hagerty to his wife. "Let's sit down here." He indicated lobby chairs, but Paula hesitated.

"I've got to go right home," she said. "Anson, why don't you—why don't you come out and have dinner with us to-night? We're just getting settled, but if you can stand that——"

Hagerty confirmed the invitation cordially.

"Come out for the night."

Their car waited in front of the hotel, and Paula with a tired gesture sank back against silk cushions in the corner.

"There's so much I want to talk to you about," she said, "it seems hopeless."

"I want to hear about you."

"Well"—she smiled at Hagerty—"that would take a long time too. I have three children—by my first marriage. The oldest is five, then four, then three." She smiled again. "I didn't waste much time having them, did I?"

"Boys?"

"A boy and two girls. Then—oh, a lot of things happened, and I got a divorce in Paris a year ago and married Pete. That's all—except that I'm awfully happy."

In Rye they drove up to a large house near the Beach Club, from which there issued presently three dark, slim children who broke from an English governess and approached them with an esoteric cry. Abstractedly and with difficulty Paula took each one into her arms, a caress which they accepted stiffly, as they had evidently been told not to bump into Mummy. Even against their fresh faces Paula's skin showed scarcely any weariness—for all her physical languor she seemed younger than when he had last seen her at Palm Beach seven years ago.

At dinner she was preoccupied, and afterward, during the homage to the radio, she lay with closed eyes on the sofa, until Anson wondered if his presence at this time were not an intrusion. But at nine o'clock, when Hagerty rose and said pleasantly that he was going to leave them by themselves for a while, she began to talk slowly about herself and the past.

"My first baby," she said—"the one we call Darling, the biggest little girl—I wanted to die when I knew I was going to have her, because Lowell was like a stranger to me. It didn't seem as though she could be my own. I wrote you a letter and tore it up. Oh, you were *so* bad to me, Anson."

It was the dialogue again, rising and falling. Anson felt a sudden quickening of memory.

"Weren't you engaged once!" she asked—"a girl named Dolly something?"

"I wasn't ever engaged. I tried to be engaged, but I never loved anybody but you, Paula."

"Oh," she said, Then after a moment: "This baby is the first one I ever really wanted. You see, I'm in love now—at last."

He didn't answer, shocked at the treachery of her remembrance. She must have seen that the "at last" bruised him, for she continued:

"I was infatuated with you, Anson—you could make me do anything you liked. But we wouldn't have been happy. I'm not smart enough for you. I don't like things to be complicated like you do." She paused. "You'll never settle down," she said.

The phrase struck at him from behind—it was an accusation that of all accusations he had never merited.

"I could settle down if women were different," he said, "If I didn't understand so much about them, if women didn't spoil you for other women, if they had only a little pride. If I could go to sleep for a while and wake up into a home that was really mine—why, that's what I'm made for, Paula, that's what women have seen in me and liked in me. It's only that I can't get through the preliminaries any more."

Hagerty came in a little before eleven; after a whiskey Paula stood up and announced that she was going to bed. She went over and stood by her husband.

"Where did you go, dearest?" she demanded.

"I had a drink with Ed Saunders."

"I was worried. I thought maybe you'd run away."

She rested her head against his coat.

"He's sweet, isn't he, Anson?" she demanded.

"Absolutely," said Anson, laughing.

She raised her face to her husband.

"Well, I'm ready," she said. She turned to Anson: "Do you want to see our family gymnastic stunt?"

"Yes," he said in an interested voice.

"All right, Here we go!"

Hagerty picked her up easily in his arms.

"This is called the family acrobatic stunt," said Paula. "He carries me upstairs. Isn't it sweet of him?"

"Yes," said Anson.

Hagerty bent his head slightly until his face touched Paula's.

"And I love him," she said. "I've just been telling you, haven't I, Anson?"

"Yes," he said.

"He's the dearest thing that ever lived in this world; aren't you, darling? . . . Well, good night. Here we go. Isn't he strong?"

"Yes," Anson said.

"You'll find a pair of Pete's pajamas laid out for you. Sweet dreams—see you at breakfast."

"Yes," Anson said.

VIII

The older members of the firm insisted that Anson should go abroad for the summer. He had scarcely had a vacation in seven years, they said, He was stale and needed a change. Anson resisted.

"If I go," he declared, "I won't come back any more."

"That's absurd, old man. You'll be back in three months with all this depression gone. Fit as ever."

"No." He shook his head stubbornly. "If I stop, I won't go back to work. If I stop, that means I've given up—I'm through."

"We'll take a chance on that. Stay six months if you like—we're not afraid you'll leave us. Why, you'd be miserable if you didn't work."

They arranged his passage for him. They liked Anson—every one liked Anson—and the change that had been coming over him cast a sort of pall over the office. The enthusiasm that had invariably signalled up business, the consideration toward his equals and his inferiors, the lift of his vital presence—within the past four months his intense nervousness had melted down these qualities into the fussy pessimism of a man of forty. On every transaction in which he was involved he acted as a drag and a strain.

"If I go I'll never come back," he said.

Three days before he sailed Paula Legendre Hagerty died in childbirth. I was with him a great deal then, for we were crossing together, but for the first time in our friendship he told me not a word of how he felt, nor did I see the slightest sign of emotion. His chief preoccupation was with the fact that he was thirty years old—he would turn the conversation to the point where he could remind you of it and then fall silent, as if he assumed that the statement would start a chain of thought sufficient to itself. Like his partners, I was amazed at the change in him, and I was glad when the *Paris* moved off into the wet space between the worlds, leaving his principality behind.

"How about a drink?" he suggested.

We walked into the bar with that defiant feeling that characterized the day of departure and ordered four Martinis. After one cocktail a change came over him—he suddenly reached across and slapped my knee with the first joviality I had seen him exhibit for months.

"Did you see that girl in the red tam?" he demanded, "the one with the high color who had the two police dogs down to bid her good-by."

"She's pretty," I agreed.

"I looked her up in the purser's office and found out that she's alone. I'm going down to see the steward in a few minutes. We'll have dinner with her to-night."

After a while he left me, and within an hour he was walking up and down the deck with her, talking to her in strong, clear voice. Her red tam was a bright spot of color against the steel-green sea, and from time to time she looked up with a flashing bob of her head, and smiled with amusement and interest, and anticipation. At dinner we had champagne, and were very joyous—afterward Anson ran the pool with infectious gusto, and several people who had seen me with him asked me his name. He and the girl were talking and laughing together on a lounge in the bar when I went to bed.

I saw less of him on the trip than I had hoped. He wanted to arrange a foursome, but there was no one available, so I saw him only at meals. Sometimes, though, he would have a cocktail in the bar, and he told me about the girl in the red tam, and his adventures with her, making them all bizarre and amusing, as he had a way of doing, and I was glad that he was himself again, or at least the self that I knew, and with which I felt at home. I don't think he was ever happy unless some one was in love with him, responding to him like filings to a magnet, helping him to explain himself, promising him something. What it was I do not know. Perhaps they promised that there would always be women in the world who would spend their brightest, freshest, rarest hours to nurse and protect that superiority he cherished in his heart.

JOHN STEINBECK

(1902-1968)

Often cited as evidence that commercial success "spoils" a writer, the works that John Steinbeck published in his forties and fifties were, with few exceptions, poorly received. Two books about World War II—*Bombs Away* (1942) and *The Moon is Down* (1942)—were properly dismissed as jingoistic and superficial; *Cannery Row* (1945), *The Wayward Bus* (1947), and *Sweet Thursday* (1954) are mannered and oversweet; *The Pearl* (1947), a fable, has at best a thin charm, and *East of Eden* (1952), a family chronicle, seems untrimmed, a work lacking in form and in narrative tension.

The most reliable study of Steinbeck is Peter Lisca, *The World of John Steinbeck* 1958. Other critical assessments are the pioneering Harry Thorton Moore, *The Novels of John Steinbeck, A First Study* 1939, rev., 1968; Warren French, *John Steinbeck*, 1961, and F. W. Watt, *John Steinbeck*, 1962.

For a listing of works on Steinbeck, see E. W. Tedlock, Jr. and C. V. Wicker, *Steinbeck and His Critics, A Record of Twenty-Five Years*, 1957, and Richard Astro and Tetscionaro Hayashi, eds., *Steinbeck: The Man and His Work*, 1970.

The earlier Steinbeck is by no means wholly free of sentimentality. *Of Mice and Men* (1937), a huge success as a novel, a play, and a film, traveled the path of pathos on its way toward popularity. And, from the beginning, this novelist diluted his vision with sugary celebrations of the Little People—common working folk whose virtues sometimes seemed to be perceived as inevitable accompaniments of powerlessness. In four books, however—they constitute a record of the ruin visited on ordinary Westerners and Southerners—the novelist's capacity to care about the humble and to represent them believably shows to striking advantage. *Tortilla Flat* (1935), character sketches of California Spanish and Indians—*paisanos* vividly presented as appetitive and uninhibited—is weakened a little by a tendency to romanticize vagabondism. *In Dubious Battle* (1936) is a stronger book—the story of a strike by migratory workers, bitter and chill in tone. Steinbeck's best book, *The Grapes of Wrath,* appeared in 1939; it tells of the catastrophes and the moments of moving familial solidarity experienced by the Joad family on their journey from Oklahoma to California after a dustbowl storm has wiped them out. Something of the same feeling for the elemental dignity of "the folk" is present in *The Long Valley,* a collection of stories also published in 1939. (It is from the best story in this collection, "The Red Pony," that "The Leader of the People" is taken.)

Steinbeck was born in Salinas, Monterey County, California, on February 27, 1902, of parents with German, Irish, and Yankee backgrounds. (His father was a county treasurer and his mother a school teacher.) A restless young man, he entered Stanford University in 1919; he left 6 years later without graduating—to go on the road, to work on ranches, in a sugar-beet factory (a laboratory job), and as a bricklayer constructing the original Madison Square Garden. (He had come to New York to establish himself as a writer, but after a period of frustration—it is recalled in "The Making of a New Yorker"—he returned to the West.) The proper praise of Steinbeck is that he stands forth as the first gifted Anglo writer of this century to grasp the extraordinary resources the nation was losing by excluding migrants, Indians, and Mexican-Americans from its social and cultural mainstream. The novelist was awarded the Nobel Prize for Literature in 1962.

The Leader of the People

On Saturday afternoon Billy Buck, the ranch-hand, raked together the last of the old year's haystack and pitched small forkfuls over the wire fence to a few mildly interested cattle. High in the air small clouds like puffs of cannon smoke were driven eastward by the March wind. The wind could be heard whishing in the brush on the ridge crests, but no breath of it penetrated down into the ranch-cup.

The little boy, Jody, emerged from the house eating a thick piece of buttered bread. He saw Billy working on the last of the haystack. Jody tramped down scuffing his shoes in a way he had been told was destructive to good shoe-leather. A flock of white pigeons flew out of the black cypress tree as Jody passed, and circled the tree and landed again. A half-grown tortoise-shell cat leaped from the bunkhouse porch, galloped on stiff legs across the road, whirled and galloped back again. Jody picked up a stone to help the game along, but he was too late, for the cat was under the porch before the stone could be discharged. He threw the stone into the cypress tree and started the white pigeons on another whirling flight.

Arriving at the used-up haystack, the boy leaned against the barbed wire fence. "Will that be all of it, do you think?" he asked.

The middle-aged ranch-hand stopped his careful raking and stuck his fork into the ground. He took off his black hat and smoothed down his hair. "Nothing left of it that isn't soggy from ground moisture," he said. He replaced his hat and rubbed his dry leathery hands together.

"Ought to be plenty mice," Jody suggested.

"Lousy with them," said Billy. "Just crawling with mice."

"Well, maybe, when you get all through, I could call the dogs and hunt the mice."

"Sure, I guess you could," said Billy Buck. He lifted a forkful of the damp ground-hay and threw it into the air. Instantly three mice leaped out and burrowed frantically under the hay again.

Jody sighed with satisfaction. Those plump. sleek, arrogant mice were doomed. For eight months they had lived and multiplied in the haystack. They had been immune from cats, from traps, from poison and from Jody. They had grown smug in their security, overbearing and fat. Now the time of disaster had come; they would not survive another day.

Billy looked up at the top of the hills that surrounded the ranch. "Maybe you better ask your father before you do it," he suggested.

"Well, where is he? I'll ask him now."

"He rode up to the ridge ranch after dinner. He'll be back pretty soon."

Jody slumped against the fence post. "I don't think he'd care."

As Billy went back to his work he said ominously, "You'd better ask him anyway. You know how he is."

Jody did know. His father, Carl Tiflin, insisted upon giving permission for anything that was done on the ranch, whether it was important or not. Jody sagged farther against the post until he was sitting on the ground. He looked up at the little puffs of wind-driven cloud. "Is it like to rain, Billy?"

"It might. The wind's good for it, but not strong enough."

"Well, I hope it don't rain until after I kill those damn mice." He looked over his shoulder to see whether Billy had noticed the mature profanity. Billy worked on without comment.

Jody turned back and looked at the side-hill where the road from the outside world came down. The hill was washed with lean March sunshine. Silver thistles, blue lupins and a few poppies bloomed among the sage bushes. Halfway up the hill Jody could see Doubletree Mutt, the black dog, digging in a squirrel hole. He paddled for a while and then paused to kick bursts of dirt out between his hind legs, and he dug with an earnestness which belied the knowledge he must have had that no dog had ever caught a squirrel by digging in a hole.

Suddenly, while Jody watched, the black dog stiffened, and backed out of the hole and looked up the hill toward the cleft in the ridge where the road came through. Jody looked up too. For a moment Carl Tiflin on horseback stood out against the pale sky and then he moved down the road toward the house. He carried something white in his hand.

The boy started to his feet. "He's got a letter," Jody cried. He trotted away toward the ranch house, for the letter would probably be read aloud and he wanted to be there. He reached the house before his father did, and ran in. He heard Carl dismount from his creaking saddle and slap the horse on the side to send it to the barn where Billy would unsaddle it and turn it out.

Jody ran into the kitchen. "We got a letter!" he cried.

His mother looked up from a pan of beans. "Who has?"

"Father has. I saw it in his hand."

Carl strode into the kitchen then, and Jody's mother asked, "Who's the letter from, Carl?"

He frowned quickly. "How did you know there was a letter?"

She nodded her head in the boy's direction. "Big-Britches Jody told me."

Jody was embarrassed.

His father looked down at him contemptuously. "He *is* getting to be a Big-Britches," Carl said. "He's minding everybody's business but his own. Got his big nose into everything."

Mrs. Tiflin relented a little. "Well, he hasn't enough to keep him busy. Who's the letter from?"

Carl still frowned on Jody. "I'll keep him busy if he isn't careful." He held out a sealed letter. "I guess it's from your father."

Mrs. Tiflin took a hairpin from her head and slit open the flap. Her lips pursed judiciously. Jody saw her eyes snap back and forth over the lines. "He says," she translated, "he says he's going to drive out Saturday to stay for a little while. Why, this is Saturday. The letter must have been delayed." She looked at the postmark. "This was mailed day before yesterday. It should have been here yesterday." She looked up questioningly at her husband, and then her face darkened angrily. "Now what have you got that look on you for? He doesn't come often."

Carl turned his eyes away from her anger. He could be stern with her most of the time, but when occasionally her temper arose, he could not combat it.

"What's the matter with you?" she demanded again.

In his explanation there was a tone of apology Jody himself might have used. "It's just that he talks," Carl said lamely. "Just talks."

"Well, what of it? You talk yourself."

"Sure I do. But your father only talks about one thing."

"Indians!" Jody broke in excitedly. "Indians and crossing the plains!"

Carl turned fiercely on him. "You get out, Mr. Big-Britches! Go on, now! Get out!"

Jody went miserably out the back door and closed the screen with elaborate quietness. Under the kitchen window his shamed, downcast eyes fell upon a curiously shaped stone, a stone of such fascination that he squatted down and picked it up and turned it over in his hands.

The voices came clearly to him through the open kitchen window. "Jody's damn well right," he heard his father say. "Just Indians and crossing the plains. I've heard that story about how the horses got driven off about a thousand times. He just goes on and on, and he never changes a word in the things he tells."

When Mrs. Tiflin answered her tone was so changed that Jody, outside the window, looked up from his study of the stone. Her voice had become soft and explanatory. Jody knew how her face would have changed to match the tone. She said quietly, "Look at it this way, Carl. That was the big thing in my father's life. He led a wagon train clear across the plains to the coast, and when it was finished, his life was done. It was a big thing to do, but it didn't last long enough. Look!" she continued, "it's as though he was born to do that, and after he finished it, there wasn't anything more for him to do but think about it and talk about it. If there'd been any farther west to go, he'd have gone. He's told me so himself. But at last there was the ocean. He lives right by the ocean where he had to stop."

She had caught Carl, caught him and entangled him in her soft tone.

"I've seen him," he agreed quietly. "He goes down and stares off west over the ocean." His voice sharpened a little. "And then he goes up to the Horseshoe Club in Pacific Grove, and he tells people how the Indians drove off the horses."

She tried to catch him again. "Well, it's everything to him. You might be patient with him and pretend to listen."

Carl turned impatiently away. "Well, if it gets too bad, I can always go down to the bunkhouse and sit with Billy," he said irritably. He walked through the house and slammed the front door after him.

Jody ran to his chores. He dumped the grain to the chickens without chasing any of them. He gathered the eggs from the nest. He trotted into the house with the wood and interlaced it so carefully in the wood-box that two armloads seemed to fill it to overflowing.

His mother had finished the beans by now. She stirred up the fire and brushed off the stove-top with a turkey wing. Jody peered cautiously at her to see whether any rancor toward him remained. "Is he coming today?" Jody asked.

"That's what his letter said."

"Maybe I better walk up the road to meet him."

Mrs. Tiflin clanged the stove-lid shut. "That would be nice," she said. "He'd probably like to be met."

"I guess I'll just do it then."

Outside, Jody whistled shrilly to the dogs. "Come on up the hill," he commanded. The two dogs waved their tails and ran ahead. Along the road-side the sage had tender new tips. Jody tore off some pieces and rubbed them on his hands until the air was filled with the sharp wild smell. With a rush the dogs leaped from the road and yapped into the brush after a rabbit. That was the last Jody saw of them, for when they failed to catch the rabbit, they went back home.

Jody plodded on up the hill toward the ridge top. When he reached the little cleft where the road came through, the afternoon wind struck him and blew up his hair and ruffled his shirt. He looked down on the little hills and ridges below and then out at the huge green Salinas Valley. He could see the white town of Salinas far out in the flat and the flash of its windows under the waning sun. Directly below him, in an oak tree, a crow congress had convened. The tree was black with crows all cawing at once.

Then Jody's eyes followed the wagon road down from the ridge where he stood, and lost it behind a hill, and picked it up again on the other side. On that distant stretch he saw a cart slowly pulled by a bay horse. It disappeared behind the hill. Jody sat down on the ground and watched the place where the cart would reappear again. The wind sang on the hilltops and the puff-ball clouds hurried eastward.

Then the cart came into sight and stopped. A man dressed in black dis-mounted from the seat and walked to the horse's head. Although it was so far away, Jody knew he had unhooked the check-rein, for the horse's head dropped forward. The horse moved on, and the man walked slowly up the hill beside it. Jody gave a glad cry and ran down the road toward them. The squirrels bumped along off the road, and a road-runner flirted its tail and raced over the edge of the hill and sailed out like a glider.

Jody tried to leap into the middle of his shadow at every step. A stone rolled under his foot and he went down. Around a little bend he raced, and there, a short distance ahead, were his grandfather and the cart. The boy dropped from his unseemly running and approached at a dignified walk.

The horse plodded stumble-footedly up the hill and the old man walked beside it. In the lowering sun their giant shadows flickered darkly behind them. The grandfather was dressed in a black broadcloth suit and he wore kid congress gaiters and a black tie on a short, hard collar. He carried his black slouch hat in his hand. His white beard was cropped close and his white eyebrows overhung his eyes like moustaches. The blue eyes were sternly merry. About the whole face and figure there was a granite dignity, so that every motion seemed an impossible thing. Once at rest, it seemed the old man would be stone, would never move again. His steps were slow and certain. Once made, no step could ever be retraced; once headed in a direction, the path would never bend nor the pace increase nor slow.

When Jody appeared around the bend, Grandfather waved his hat slowly in welcome, and he called, "Why, Jody! Come down to meet me, have you?"

Jody sidled near and turned and matched his step to the old man's step and stiffened his body and dragged his heels a little. "Yes, sir," he said. "We got your letter only today."

"Should have been here yesterday," said Grandfather. "It certainly should. How are all the folks?"

"They're fine, sir." He hesitated and then suggested shyly, "Would you like to come on a mouse hunt tomorrow, sir?"

"Mouse hunt, Jody?" Grandfather chuckled. "Have the people of this generation come down to hunting mice? They aren't very strong, the new people, but I hardly thought mice would be game for them."

"No, sir. It's just play. The haystack's gone. I'm going to drive out the mice to the dogs. And you can watch, or even beat the hay a little."

The stern, merry eyes turned down on him. "I see. You don't eat them, then. You haven't come to that yet."

Jody explained, "The dogs eat them, sir. It wouldn't be much like hunting Indians, I guess."

"No, not much—but then later, when the troops were hunting Indians and shooting children and burning teepees, it wasn't much different from your mouse hunt."

They topped the rise and started down into the ranch cup, and they lost the sun from their shoulders. "You've grown," Grandfather said. "Nearly an inch, I should say."

"More," Jody boasted. "Where they mark me on the door, I'm up more than an inch since Thanksgiving even."

Grandfather's rich throaty voice said, "Maybe you're getting too much water and turning to pith and stalk. Wait until you head out, and then we'll see."

Jody looked quickly into the old man's face to see whether his feelings should be hurt, but there was no will to injure, no punishing nor putting-in-your-place light in the keen blue eyes. "We might kill a pig," Jody suggested.

"Oh, no! I couldn't let you do that. You're just humoring me. It isn't the time and you know it."

"You know Riley, the big boar, sir?"

"Yes, I remember Riley well."

"Well, Riley ate a hole into that same haystack, and it fell down on him and smothered him."

"Pigs do that when they can," said Grandfather.

"Riley was a nice pig, for a boar, sir. I rode him sometimes, and he didn't mind."

A door slammed at the house below them, and they saw Jody's mother standing on the porch waving her apron in welcome. And they saw Carl Tiflin walking up from the barn to be at the house for the arrival.

The sun had disappeared from the hills by now. The blue smoke from the house chimney hung in flat layers in the purpling ranch-cup. The puff-ball clouds, dropped by the falling wind, hung listlessly in the sky.

Billy Buck came out of the bunkhouse and flung a wash basin of soapy water on the ground. He had been shaving in mid-week, for Billy held Grandfather in reverence, and Grandfather said that Billy was one of the few men of the new generation who had not gone soft. Although Billy was in middle age, Grandfather considered him a boy. Now Billy was hurrying toward the house too.

When Jody and Grandfather arrived, the three were waiting for them in front of the yard gate.

Carl said, "Hello, sir. We've been looking for you."

Mrs. Tiflin kissed Grandfather on the side of his beard, and stood still while his big hand patted her shoulder. Billy shook hands solemnly, grinning under his straw moustache. "I'll put up your horse," said Billy, and he led the rig away.

Grandfather watched him go, and then, turning back to the group, he said as he had said a hundred times before, "There's a good boy. I knew his father, old Mule-tail Buck. I never knew why they called him Mule-tail except he packed mules."

Mrs. Tiflin turned and led the way into the house. "How long are you going to stay, Father? Your letter didn't say."

"Well, I don't know. I thought I'd stay about two weeks. But I never stay as long as I think I'm going to."

In a short while they were sitting at the white oilcloth table eating their supper. The lamp with the tin reflector hung over the table. Outside the dining-room windows the big moths battered softly against the glass.

Grandfather cut his steak into tiny pieces and chewed slowly. "I'm hungry," he said. "Driving out here got my appetite up. It's like when we were crossing. We all got so hungry every night we could hardly wait to let the meat get done. I could eat about five pounds of buffalo meat every night."

"It's moving around does it," said Billy. "My father was a government packer. I helped him when I was a kid. Just the two of us could about clean up a deer's ham."

"I knew your father, Billy," said Grandfather. "A fine man he was. They called him Mule-tail Buck. I don't know why except he packed mules."

"That was it," Billy agreed. "He packed mules."

Grandfather put down his knife and fork and looked around the table. "I remember one time we ran out of meat—" His voice dropped to a curious low sing-song, dropped into a tonal groove the story had worn for itself. "There was no buffalo, no antelope, not even rabbits. The hunters couldn't even shoot a coyote. That was the time for the leader to be on the watch. I was the leader, and I kept my eyes open. Know why? Well, just the minute the people began to get hungry they'd start slaughtering the team oxen. Do you believe that? I've heard of parties that just ate up their draft cattle. Started from the middle and worked toward the ends. Finally they'd eat the lead pair, and then the wheelers. The leader of a party had to keep them from doing that."

In some manner a big moth got into the room and circled the hanging kerosene lamp. Billy got up and tried to clap it between his hands. Carl struck with a cupped palm and caught the moth and broke it. He walked to the window and dropped it out.

"As I was saying," Grandfather began again, but Carl interrupted him. "You'd better eat some more meat. All the rest of us are ready for our pudding."

Jody saw a flash of anger in his mother's eyes. Grandfather picked up his knife and fork. "I'm pretty hungry, all right," he said. "I'll tell you about that later."

When supper was over, when the family and Billy Buck sat in front of the fireplace in the other room, Jody anxiously watched Grandfather. He saw the signs he knew. The bearded head leaned forward; the eyes lost their sternness and looked wonderingly into the fire; the big lean fingers laced themselves on the black knees. "I wonder," he began, "I just wonder whether I ever told you how those thieving Piutes drove off thirty-five of our horses."

"I think you did," Carl interrupted. "Wasn't it just before you went up into the Tahoe country?"

Grandfather turned quickly toward his son-in-law. "That's right. I guess I must have told you that story."

"Lots of times," Carl said cruelly, and he avoided his wife's eyes. But he felt the angry eyes on him, and he said, " 'Course I'd like to hear it again."

Grandfather looked back at the fire. His fingers unlaced and laced again. Jody knew how he felt, how his insides were collapsed and empty. Hadn't Jody been called a Big-Britches that very afternoon? He arose to heroism and opened himself to the term Big-Britches again, "Tell about Indians," he said softly.

Grandfather's eyes grew stern again. "Boys always want to hear about Indians. It was a job for men, but boys want to hear about it. Well, let's see. Did I ever tell you how I wanted each wagon to carry a long iron plate?"

Everyone but Jody remained silent. Jody said, "No. You didn't."

"Well, when the Indians attacked, we always put the wagons in a circle and fought from between the wheels. I thought that if every wagon carried a long plate with rifle holes, the men could stand the plates on the outside of the wheels when the wagons were in the circle and they would be protected. It would save lives and that would make up for the extra weight of the iron. But of course the party wouldn't do it. No party had done it before and they couldn't see why they should go to the expense. They lived to regret it, too."

Jody looked at his mother, and knew from her expression that she was not listening at all. Carl picked at a callus on his thumb and Billy Buck watched a spider crawling up the wall.

Grandfather's tone dropped into its narrative groove again. Jody knew in advance exactly what words would fall. The story droned on, speeded up for the attack, grew sad over the wounds, struck a dirge at the burials on the great plains. Jody sat quietly watching Grandfather. The stern blue eyes were detached. He looked as though he were not very interested in the story himself.

When it was finished, when the pause had been politely respected as the frontier of the story, Billy Buck stood up and stretched and hitched his trousers. "I guess I'll turn in," he said, Then he faced Grandfather. "I've got an old powder horn and a cap and ball pistol down to the bunkhouse. Did I ever show them to you?"

Grandfather nodded slowly. "Yes, I think you did, Billy. Reminds me of a pistol I had when I was leading the people across." Billy stood politely until the little story was done, and then he said, "Good night," and went out of the house.

Carl Tiflin tried to turn the conversation then. "How's the country between here and Monterey? I've heard it's pretty dry."

"It is dry," said Grandfather. "There's not a drop of water in the Laguna Seca. But it's a long pull from '87. The whole country was powder then, and in '61 I believe all the coyotes starved to death. We had fifteen inches of rain this year."

"Yes, but it all came too early. We could do with some now." Carl's eye fell on Jody. "Hadn't you better be getting to bed?"

Jody stood up obediently. "Can I kill the mice in the old haystack, sir?"

"Mice? Oh! Sure, kill them all off. Billy said there isn't any good hay left."

Jody exchanged a secret and satisfying look with Grandfather. "I'll kill every one tomorrow," he promised.

Jody lay in his bed and thought of the impossible world of Indians and buffaloes, a world that had ceased to be forever. He wished he could have been living in the heroic time, but he knew he was not of heroic timber. No one living now, save possibly Billy Buck, was worthy to do the things that had been done. A race of giants had lived then, fearless men, men of a staunchness unknown in this day. Jody thought of the wide plains and of the wagons moving across like centipedes. He thought of Grandfather on a huge white horse, marshaling the people. Across his mind marched the great phantoms, and they marched off the earth and they were gone.

He came back to the ranch for a moment, then. He heard the dull rushing sound that space and silence make. He heard one of the dogs, out in the doghouse, scratching a flea and bumping his elbow against the floor with every stroke. Then the wind arose again and the black cypress groaned and Jody went to sleep.

He was up half an hour before the triangle sounded for breakfast. His mother was rattling the stove to make the flames roar when Jody went through the kitchen. "You're up early," she said. "Where are you going?"

"Out to get a good stick. We're going to kill the mice today."

"Who is 'we' ?"

"Why, Grandfather and I."

"So you've got him in it. You always like to have someone in with you in case there's blame to share."

"I'll be right back," said Jody. "I just want to have a good stick ready for after breakfast."

He closed the screen door after him and went out into the cool blue morning. The birds were noisy in the dawn and the ranch cats came down from the hill like blunt snakes. They had been hunting gophers in the dark, and although the four cats were full of gopher meat, they sat in a semi-circle at the back door and mewed piteously for milk. Doubletree Mutt and Smasher moved sniffing along the edge of the brush, performing the duty with rigid ceremony, but when Jody whistled, their heads jerked up and their tails waved. They plunged down to him, wriggling their skins and yawning. Jody patted their heads seriously, and moved on to the weathered scrap pile. He selected an old broom handle and a short piece of inch-square scrap wood. From his pocket he took a shoelace and tied the ends of the sticks loosely together to make a flail. He whistled his new weapon through the air and struck the ground experimentally, while the dogs leaped aside and whined with apprehension.

Jody turned and started down past the house toward the old haystack ground to look over the field of slaughter, but Billy Buck, sitting patiently on the back steps, called to him, "You better come back. It's only a couple of minutes till breakfast."

Jody changed his course and moved toward the house. He leaned his flail against the steps. "That's to drive the mice out," he said. "I'll bet they're fat. I'll bet they don't know what's going to happen to them today."

"No, nor you either," Billy remarked philosophically, "nor me, nor anyone."

Jody was staggered by this thought. He knew it was true. His imagination twitched away from the mouse hunt. Then his mother came out on the back porch and struck the triangle, and all thoughts fell in a heap.

Grandfather hadn't appeared at the table when they sat down. Billy nodded at his empty chair. "He's all right? He isn't sick?"

"He takes a long time to dress," said Mrs. Tiflin. "He combs his whiskers and rubs up his shoes and brushes his clothes."

Carl scattered sugar on his mush. "A man that's led a wagon train across the plains has to be pretty careful how he dresses."

Mrs. Tiflin turned on him. "Don't do that, Carl! Please don't!" There was more of threat than of request in her tone. And the threat irritated Carl.

"Well, how many times do I have to listen to the story of the iron plates, and the thirty-five horses? That time's done. Why can't he forget it, now it's done?" He grew angrier while he talked, and his voice rose. "Why does he have to tell them over and over? He came across the plains. All right! Now it's finished. Nobody wants to hear about it over and over."

The door into the kitchen closed softly. The four at the table sat frozen. Carl laid his mush spoon on the table and touched his chin with his fingers.

Then the kitchen door opened and Grandfather walked in. His mouth smiled tightly and his eyes were squinted. "Good morning," he said, and he sat down and looked at his mush dish.

Carl could not leave it there. "Did—did you hear what I said?"

Grandfather jerked a little nod.

"I don't know what got into me, sir. I didn't mean it. I was just being funny."

Jody glanced in shame at his mother, and he saw that she was looking at Carl, and that she wasn't breathing. It was an awful thing that he was doing. He was tearing himself to pieces to talk like that. It was a terrible thing to him to retract a word, but to retract it in shame was infinitely worse.

Grandfather looked sidewise. "I'm trying to get right side up," he said gently. "I'm not being mad. I don't mind what you said, but it might be true, and I would mind that."

"It isn't true," said Carl. "I'm not feeling well this morning. I'm sorry I said it."

"Don't be sorry, Carl. An old man doesn't see things sometimes. Maybe you're right. the crossing is finished. Maybe it should be forgotten, now it's done."

Carl got up from the table. "I've had enough to eat. I'm going to work. Take your time, Billy!" He walked quickly out of the dining-room. Billy gulped the rest of his food and followed soon after. But Jody could not leave his chair.

"Won't you tell any more stories?" Jody asked.

"Why, sure I'll tell them, but only when—I'm sure people want to hear them."

"I like to hear them, sir."

"Oh! Of course you do, but you're a little boy. It was a job for men, but only little boys like to hear about it."

Jody got up from his place. "I'll wait outside for you, sir. I've got a good stick for those mice."

He waited by the gate until the old man came out on the porch. "Let's go down and kill the mice now," Jody called.

"I think I'll just sit in the sun, Jody. You go kill the mice."

"You can use my stick if you like."

"No, I'll just sit here a while."

Jody turned disconsolately away, and walked down toward the old hay-stack. He tried to whip up his enthusiasm with thoughts of the fat juicy mice. He beat the ground with his flail. The dogs coaxed and whined about him, but he could not go. Back at the house he could see Grandfather sitting on the porch, looking small and thin and black.

Jody gave up and went to sit on the steps at the old man's feet.

"Back already? Did you kill the mice?"

"No, sir. I'll kill them some other day."

The morning flies buzzed close to the ground and the ants dashed about in front of the steps. The heavy smell of sage slipped down the hill. The porch boards grew warm in the sunshine.

Jody hardly knew when Grandfather started to talk. "I shouldn't stay here, feeling the way I do." He examined his strong old hands. "I feel as though the crossing wasn't worth doing." His eyes moved up the side-hill and stopped on a motionless hawk perched on a dead limb. "I tell those old stories, but they're not what I want to tell. I only know how I want people to feel when I tell them.

"It wasn't Indians that were important, nor adventures, nor even getting out here. It was a whole bunch of people made into one big crawling beast. And I was the head. It was westering and westering. Every man wanted something for himself, but the big beast that was all of them wanted only westering. I was the leader, but if I hadn't been there, someone else would have been the head. The thing had to have a head.

"Under the little bushes the shadows were black at white noonday. When we saw the mountains at last, we cried—all of us. But it wasn't getting here that mattered, it was movement and westering.

"We carried life out here and set it down the way those ants carry eggs. And I was the leader. The westering was as big as God, and the slow steps that made the movement piled up and piled up until the continent was crossed.

"Then we came down to the sea, and it was done." He stopped and wiped his eyes until the rims were red. "That's what I should be telling instead of stories."

When Jody spoke, Grandfather started and looked down at him. "Maybe I could lead the people some day," Jody said.

The old man smiled. "There's no place to go. There's the ocean to stop you. There's a line of old men along the shore hating the ocean because it stopped them."

"In boats I might, sir."

"No place to go, Jody. Every place is taken. But that's not the worst—no, not the worst. Westering has died out of the people. Westering isn't a hunger any more. It's all done. Your father is right. It is finished." He laced his fingers on his knee and looked at them.

Jody felt very sad. "If you'd like a glass of lemonade I could make it for you."

Grandfather was about to refuse, and then he saw Jody's face. "That would be nice," he said. "Yes, it would be nice to drink a lemonade."

Jody ran into the kitchen where his mother was wiping the last of the breakfast dishes. "Can I have a lemon to make a lemonade for Grandfather?"

His mother mimicked—"And another lemon to make a lemonade for you."

"No, ma'am. I don't want one."

"Jody! You're sick!" Then she stopped suddenly. "Take a lemon out of the cooler," she said softly. "Here, I'll reach the squeezer down to you."

1939

EUDORA WELTY

(1909–   )

"Relationship is a pervading and changing mystery," Eudora Welty has written. "Brutal or lovely, the mystery waits for people wherever they go, whatever extreme they run to." Her many short stories, written over 40 years, focus on individuals who are often isolated, lonely, and suffering, and who seek connections with others; regeneration is achieved through the imagination as a human factor that insists on reasserting itself. Throughout Welty's fiction runs the sense of wonder,

The first two volumes of stories *A Curtain of Green*, 1941 and *The Wide Net*, 1943, are both reprinted in the Modern Library edition, *Selected Stories of Eudora Welty*, 1954.

For criticism, see Ruth M. Vande Kieft, *Eudora Welty*, 1962, Alfred Appel, Jr., *A Season of Dreams: The Fiction of Eudora Welty*, 1965; and J. A. Bryant, Jr., *Eudora Welty*, 1968.

freedom, and humor—life-giving attributes. She delights in the exploration of human differences and eccentricities, but she has an abiding respect for the mystery of their reality, too. The opening words of "First Love" express this respect of mystery, of the dreamlike, uncertain quality of most people's lives: "Whatever happened, it happened in extraordinary times, in a season of dreams."

Welty is one of the most respected craftsmen of the short story, an experimental writer who has ranged in style, point of view, and subject matter, adapting the dream life of characters so that their realistic nature may be intensified. As a writer influenced by photography and painting, she attends to the physical detail not only of character but of landscape, too—she wishes to give sharp focus to whatever she describes. Her talent is limited and she is not, like other Southern writers of her time, deeply involved in tensions that result from a changing South. She lived near Faulkner and was very aware of his work; he was, as she has said, "a big fact. Like living near a mountain." She shares some of Faulkner's comic sensibility, but she is really a writer of detail instead of large historical forces. She is content—unlike Faulkner, Robert Penn Warren, or John Crowe Ransom—to restrict the boundaries of her art.

Welty was born on April 13, 1909, in Jackson, Mississippi. She attended Mississippi State College for Women from 1925 to 1927 and then went to the University of Wisconsin, from which she was graduated in 1929. For a year she studied advertising at the Columbia School of Business, but she returned in 1931 to Jackson, where she has lived ever since. During these years she had a particular interest in photography as well as journalism and fiction and had a photographic show of Mississippi Negroes in a New York gallery. Although she maintained her interest in photography, she began to publish her stories in different magazines and was soon launched on an active literary career. Her period of most intense creativity was from 1937 until the early 1950's when she wrote the fiction for which she has become famous: "Death of a Traveling Salesman," "A Worn Path," "The Petrified Man," "Asphodel," "I Live at the P. O.," "The Wide Net," "Livvie is Back," and "The Burning." Her stories have been collected in *A Curtain of Green* (1941), *The Wide Net* (1943), *The Bride of the Innisfallen* (1945), *Delta Wedding* (1946), and *The Golden Apples* (1949). Her longer fiction includes *The Robber Bridegroom* (1942), *The Ponder Heart* (1954), *Losing Battles* (1970), and *The Optimist's Daughter* (1972). She has also written perceptively on the craft of writing and collected her essays in *Place in Fiction* (1957).—T.G.

A Worn Path

It was December—a bright frozen day in the early morning. Far out in the country there was an old Negro woman with her head tied in a red rag, coming along a path through the pinewoods. Her name was Phoenix Jackson. She was very old and small and she walked slowly in the dark pine shadows, moving a little from side to side in her steps, with the balanced heaviness and lightness of a pendulum in a grandfather clock. She carried a thin, small cane made from an umbrella, and with this she kept tapping the frozen earth in front of her. This made a grave and persistent noise in the still air, that seemed meditative like the chirping of a solitary little bird.

She wore a dark striped dress reaching down to her shoe tops, and an equally long apron of bleached sugar sacks, with a full pocket: all neat and tidy, but every time she took a step she might have fallen over her shoelaces, which dragged from her unlaced shoes. She looked straight ahead. Her eyes were blue with age. Her skin had a pattern all its own of numberless branching wrinkles and as though a whole little tree stood in the middle of her forehead, but a golden color ran underneath, and the two knobs of her cheeks were illumined by a yellow burning under the dark. Under the red rag her hair came down on her neck in the frailest of ringlets, still black, and with an odor like copper.

Now and then there was a quivering in the thicket. Old Phoenix said, "Out of my way, all you foxes, owls, beetles, jack rabbits, coons and wild animals! . . . Keep out from under these feet, little bob-whites. . . . Keep the big wild hogs out of my path. Don't let none of those come running my direction. I got a long way." Under her small black-freckled hand her cane, limber as a buggy whip, would switch at the brush as if to rouse up any hiding things.

On she went. The woods were deep and still. The sun made the pine needles almost too bright to look at, up where the wind rocked. The cones dropped as light as feathers. Down in the hollow was the mourning dove—it was not too late for him.

The path ran up a hill. "Seem like there is chains about my feet, time I get this far," she said, in the voice of argument old people keep to use with themselves. "Something always take a hold of me on this hill—pleads I should stay."

After she got to the top she turned and gave a full, severe look behind her where she had come. "Up through pines," she said at length. "Now down through oaks."

Her eyes opened their widest, and she started down gently. But before she got to the bottom of the hill a bush caught her dress.

Her fingers were busy and intent, but her skirts were full and long, so that before she could pull them free in one place they were caught in another. It was not possible to allow the dress to tear. "I in the thorny bush," she said. "Thorns, you doing your appointed work. Never want to let folks pass, no sir. Old eyes thought you was a pretty little *green* bush."

Finally, trembling all over, she stood free, and after a moment dared to stoop for her cane.

"Sun so high!" she cried, leaning back and looking, while the thick tears went over her eyes. "The time getting all gone here."

At the foot of this hill was a place where a log was laid across the creek. "Now comes the trial," said Phoenix.

Putting her right foot out, she mounted the log and shut her eyes. Lifting her skirt, leveling her cane fiercely before her, like a festival figure in some parade, she began to march across. Then she opened her eyes and she was safe on the other side.

"I wasn't as old as I thought," she said.

But she sat down to rest. She spread her skirts on the bank around her and folded her hands over her knees. Up above her was a tree in a pearly cloud of mistletoe. She did not dare to close her eyes, and when a little boy brought her a plate with a slice of marble-cake on it she spoke to him. "That would be acceptable," she said. But when she went to take it there was just her own hand in the air.

So she left that tree, and had to go through a barbed-wire fence. There she had to creep and crawl, spreading her knees and stretching her fingers like a baby trying to climb the steps. But she talked loudly to herself: she could not let her dress be torn now, so late in the day, and she could not pay for having her arm or her leg sawed off if she got caught fast where she was.

At last she was safe through the fence and risen up out in the clearing. Big dead trees, like black men with one arm, were standing in the purple stalks of the withered cotton field. There sat a buzzard.

"Who you watching?"

In the furrow she made her way along.

"Glad this not the season for bulls," she said looking sideways, "and the good Lord made his snakes to curl up and sleep in the winter. A pleasure I don't see no two-headed snake coming around that tree, where it come once. It took a while to get by him, back in the summer."

She passed through the old cotton and went into a field of dead corn. It whispered and shook and was taller than her head. "Through the maze now," she said, for there was no path.

Then there was something tall, black, and skinny there, moving before her.

At first she took it for a man. It could have been a man dancing in the field. But she stood still and listened, and it did not make a sound. It was as silent as a ghost.

"Ghost," she said sharply, "who be you the ghost of? For I have heard of nary death close by."

But there was no answer—only the ragged dancing in the wind.

She shut her eyes, reached out her hand, and touched a sleeve. She found a coat and inside that an emptiness, cold as ice.

"You scarecrow," she said. Her face`lighted. "I ought to be shut up for good," she said with laughter. "My senses is gone. I too old. I the oldest people I ever know. Dance, old scarecrow," she said, "while I dancing with you."

She kicked her foot over the furrow, and with mouth drawn down, shook her head once or twice in a little strutting way. Some husks blew down and whirled in streamers about her skirts.

Then she went on, parting her way from side to side with the cane, through the whispering field. At last she came to the end, to a wagon track where the silver grass blew between the red ruts. The quail were walking around like pullets, seeming all dainty and unseen.

"Walk pretty," she said. "This the easy place. This the easy going."

She followed the track, swaying through the quiet bare fields, through the little strings of trees silver in their dead leaves, past cabins silver from weather, with the doors and windows boarded shut, all like old women under a spell sitting there. "I walking in their sleep," she said, nodding her head vigorously.

In a ravine she went where a spring was silently flowing through a hollow log. Old Phoenix bent and drank. "Sweet-gum makes the water sweet," she said, and drank more. "Nobody know who made this well, for it was here when I was born."

The track crossed a swampy part where the moss hung as white as lace from every limb. "Sleep on, alligators, and blow your bubbles." Then the track went into the road.

Deep, deep the road went down between the high green-colored banks. Overhead the live-oaks met, and it was as dark as a cave.

A black dog with a lolling tongue came up out of the weeds by the ditch. She was meditating, and not ready, and when he came at her she only hit him a little with her cane. Over she went in the ditch, like a little puff of milkweed.

Down there, her senses drifted away. A dream visited her, and she reached her hand up, but nothing reached down and gave her a pull. So she lay there and presently went to talking. "Old woman," she said to herself, "that black dog come up out of the weeds to stall you off, and now there he sitting on his fine tail, smiling at you."

A white man finally came along and found her—a hunter, a young man, with his dog on a chain.

"Well, Granny!" he laughed. "What are you doing there?"

"Lying on my back like a June-bug waiting to be turned over, mister," she said, reaching up her hand.

He lifted her up, gave her a swing in the air, and set her down. "Anything broken, Granny?"

"No sir, them old dead weeds is springy enough," said Phoenix, when she had got her breath. "I thank you for your trouble."

"Where do you live, Granny?" he asked, while the two dogs were growling at each other.

"Away back yonder, sir, behind the ridge. You can't even see it from here."

"On your way home?"

"No sir, I going to town."

"Why, that's too far! That's as far as I walk when I come out myself, and I get something for my trouble." He patted the stuffed bag he carried, and there hung down a little closed claw. It was one of the bob-whites, with its beak hooked bitterly to show it was dead. "Now you go on home, Granny!"

"I bound to go to town, mister," said Phoenix. "The time come around."

He gave another laugh, filling the whole landscape. "I know you old colored people! Wouldn't miss going to town to see Santa Claus!"

But something held old Phoenix very still. The deep lines in her face went into a fierce and different radiation. Without warning, she had seen with her own eyes a flashing nickel fall out of the man's pocket onto the ground.

"How old are you, Granny?" he was saying.

"There is no telling, mister," she said, "no telling."

Then she gave a little cry and clapped her hands and said, "Git on away from here, dog! Look! Look at that dog!" She laughed as if in admiration. "He ain't scared of nobody. He a big black dog." She whispered, "Sic him!"

"Watch me get rid of that cur," said the man. "Sic him, Pete! Sic him!"

Phoenix heard the dogs fighting, and heard the man running and throwing sticks. She even heard a gunshot. But she was slowly bending forward by that time, further and further forward, the lids stretched down over her eyes, as if she were doing this in her sleep. Her chin was lowered almost to her knees. The yellow palm of her hand came out from the fold of her apron. Her fingers slid down and along the ground under the piece of money with the grace and care they would have in lifting an egg from under a setting hen. Then she slowly straightened up, she stood erect, and the nickel was in her apron pocket. A bird flew by. Her lips moved. "God watching me the whole time. I come to stealing."

The man came back, and his own dog panted about them. "Well, I scared him off that time," he said, and then he laughed and lifted his gun and pointed it at Phoenix.

She stood straight and faced him.

"Doesn't the gun scare you?" he said, still pointing it.

"No, sir, I seen plenty go off closer by, in my day, and for less than what I done," she said, holding utterly still.

He smiled, and shouldered the gun. "Well, Granny," he said, "you must be a hundred years old, and scared of nothing. I'd give you a dime if I had any money with me. But you take my advice and stay home, and nothing will happen to you."

"I bound to go on my way, mister," said Phoenix. She inclined her head in the red rag. Then they went in different directions, but she could hear the gun shooting again and again over the hill.

She walked on. The shadows hung from the oak trees to the road like curtains. Then she smelled wood-smoke, and smelled the river, and she saw a steeple and the cabins on their steep steps. Dozens of little black children whirled around her. There ahead was Natchez shining. Bells were ringing. She walked on.

In the paved city it was Christmas time. There were red and green electric lights strung and criss-crossed everywhere, and all turned on in the daytime. Old Phoenix would have been lost if she had not distrusted her eyesight and depended on her feet to know where to take her.

She paused quietly on the sidewalk where people were passing by. A lady came along in the crowd, carrying an armful of red, green- and sliver-wrapped presents; she gave off perfume like the red roses in hot summer, and Phoenix stopped her.

"Please, missy, will you lace up my shoe?" She held up her foot.

"What do you want, Grandma?"

"See my shoe," said Phoenix. "Do all right for out in the country, but wouldn't look right to go in a big building."

"Stand still then, Grandma," said the lady. She put her packages down on the sidewalk beside her and laced and tied both shoes tightly.

"Can't lace 'em with a cane," said Phoenix. "Thank you, missy. I doesn't mind asking a nice lady to tie up my shoe, when I gets out on the street."

Moving slowly and from side to side, she went into the big building, and into a tower of steps, where she walked up and around and around until her feet knew to stop.

She entered a door, and there she saw nailed up on the wall the document that had been stamped with the gold seal and framed in the gold frame, which matched the dream that was hung up in her head.

"Here I be," she said. There was a fixed and ceremonial stiffness over her body.

"A charity case, I suppose," said an attendant who sat at the desk before her.

But Phoenix only looked above her head. There was sweat on her face, the wrinkles in her skin shone like a bright net.

"Speak up, Grandma," the woman said. "What's your name? We must have your history, you know. Have you been here before? What seems to be the trouble with you?"

Old Phoenix only gave a twitch to her face as if a fly were bothering her.

"Are you deaf?" cried the attendant.

But then the nurse came in.

"Oh, that's just old Aunt Phoenix," she said. "She doesn't come for her-self—she has a little grandson. She makes these trips just as regular as clock-work. She lives away back off the Old Natchez Trace." She bent down. "Well, Aunt Phoenix, why don't you just take a seat? We won't keep you standing after your long trip." She pointed.

The old woman sat down, bolt upright in the chair.

"Now, how is the boy?" asked the nurse.

Old Phoenix did not speak.

"I said, how is the boy?"

But Phoenix only waited and stared straight ahead, her face very solemn and withdrawn into rigidity.

"Is his throat any better?" asked the nurse. "Aunt Phoenix, don't you hear me? Is your grandson's throat any better since the last time you came for the medicine?"

With her hands on her knees, the old woman waited, silent, erect and motionless, just as if she were in armor.

"You mustn't take up our time this way, Aunt Phoenix," the nurse said. "Tell us quickly about your grandson, and get it over. He isn't dead, is he?"

At last there came a flicker and then a flame of comprehension across her face, and she spoke.

"My grandson. It was my memory had left me. There I sat and forgot why I made my long trip."

"Forgot?" The nurse frowned. "After you came so far?"

Then Phoenix was like an old woman begging a dignified forgiveness for waking up frightened in the night. "I never did go to school, I was too old at the Surrender," she said in a soft voice. "I'm an old woman without an education. It was my memory fail me. My little grandson, he is just the same, and I forgot it in the coming."

"Throat never heals, does it?" said the nurse, speaking in a loud, sure voice to old Phoenix. By now she had a card with something written on it, a little list. "Yes. Swallowed lye. When was it?—January—two-three years ago—"

Phoenix spoke unasked now. "No, missy, he not dead, he just the same. Every little while his throat begin to close up again, and he not able to swallow. He not get his breath. He not able to help himself. So the time come around, and I go on another trip for the soothing medicine."

"All right. The doctor said as long as you came to get it, you could have it," said the nurse. "But it's an obstinate case."

"My little grandson, he sit up there in the house all wrapped up, waiting by himself," Phoenix went on. "We is the only two left in the world. He suffer and it don't seem to put him back at all. He got a sweet look. He going to last. He wear a little patch quilt and peep out holding his mouth open like a little bird. I remembers so plain now. I not going to forget him again, no, the whole enduring time. I could tell him from all the others in creation."

"All right." The nurse was trying to hush her now. She brought her a bottle of medicine. "Charity," she said, making a check mark in a book.

Old Phoenix held the bottle close to her eyes, and then carefully put it into her pocket.

"I thank you," she said.

"It's Christmas time, Grandma," said the attendant. "Could I give you a few pennies out of my purse?"

"Five pennies is a nickel," said Phoenix stiffly.

"Here's a nickel," said the attendant.

Phoenix rose carefully and held out her hand. She received the nickel and then fished the other nickel out of her pocket and laid it beside the new one. She stared at her palm closely, with her head on one side.

Then she gave a tap with her cane on the floor.

"This is what come to me to do," she said. "I going to the store and buy my child a little windmill they sells, made out of paper. He going to find it hard to believe there such a thing in the world. I'll march myself back where he waiting, holding it straight up in this hand."

She lifted her free hand, gave a little nod, turned around, and walked out of the doctor's office. Then her slow step began on the stairs, going down.

FLANNERY O'CONNOR

(1925-1964)

Flannery O'Connor was born in Savannah, Georgia, of Roman Catholic parents; she grew up in Milledgeville, Georgia. She was educated in parochial schools, at the Women's College of Georgia, and then in the Writer's Workshop of the University of Iowa, where she was awarded a Master of Fine Arts degree in 1947. In the early 1950's, she discovered that she had inherited an incurable disease related to arthritis—a disease called lupus—that crippled her for the last 10 years of her life. She died at the age of 39 in 1964.

Some of the important critical studies are Melvin J. Friedman and Lewis A. Lawson, eds., *The Added Dimension: The Art and Mind of Flannery O'Connor*, 1966; Joseph Hendin, *The World of Flannery O'Connor*, 1970; and Dorothy Walters, *Flannery O'Connor*, 1973.

During her life Flannery O'Connor published a volume of stories, *A Good Man is Hard to Find* (1955) and two novellas, *Wise Blood* (1952), and *The Violent Bear It Away* (1960). A posthumous collection of stories, *Everything That Rises Must Converge,* was published in 1965, with an introduction by Robert Fitzgerald; *The Complete Stories,* which includes 31 short stories, in 1971; her essays and lectures on the writing of fiction, *Mystery and Manners: Occasional Prose,* edited by Robert and Sally Fitzgerald, in 1969.

Flannery O'Connor's fiction reflects the violence one finds in the fiction of Southern writers like Faulkner, Warren, Styron, and Capote. Like them, she is concerned with the local characters of the Southern landscape; but she does not create myths of the past and present, and she is not driven to explore the interrelationships of social history and human nature. Her vision is tragic, and it sees into the violent tendencies of people; at the same time, she has a keen grip on realism and her characters are generally limited and insensitive, without values or inner complexity. It is no accident that this vision of human nature should project people—whether they are Southern ladies and gentlemen, blacks, farmers, peddlers, or outlaws—as misfits. Flannery O'Connor's vision is without symbols or myths, but it is intense in its rendering of meaningless violence, death, disease, and rage. It is a vision that may repel many readers, since it wishes to remind the reader of the evil in the world—it is rigidly Catholic, even evangelical, in its point of view; but once this vision is experienced, it is rarely forgotten.—T.G.

Parker's Back

Parker's wife was sitting on the front porch floor, snapping beans. Parker was sitting on the step, some distance away, watching her sullenly. She was plain, plain. The skin on her face was thin and drawn as tight as the skin on an onion and her eyes were grey and sharp like the points of two icepicks. Parker understood why he had married her—he couldn't have got her any other way—but he couldn't understand why he stayed with her now. She was pregnant and pregnant women were not his favorite kind. Nevertheless, he stayed as if she had him conjured. He was puzzled and ashamed of himself.

The house they rented sat alone save for a single tall pecan tree on a high embankment overlooking a highway. At intervals a car would shoot past below and his wife's eyes would swerve suspiciously after the sound of it and then come back to rest on the newspaper full of beans in her lap. One of the things she did not approve of was automobiles. In addition to her other bad qualities, she was forever sniffing up sin. She did not smoke or dip, drink whiskey, use bad language or paint her face, and God knew some paint would have improved it, Parker thought. Her being against color, it was the more remarkable she had married him. Sometimes he supposed that she had married him because she meant to save him. At other times he had a suspicion that she actually liked everything she said she didn't. He could account for her one way or another; it was himself he could not understand.

She turned her head in his direction and said, "It's no reason you can't work for a man. It don't have to be a woman."

"Aw shut your mouth for a change," Parker muttered.

If he had been certain she was jealous of the woman he worked for he would have been pleased but more likely she was concerned with the sin that would result if he and the woman took a liking to each other. He had told her that the woman was a hefty young blonde; in fact she was nearly seventy years old and too dried up to have an interest in anything except getting as much work out of him as she could. Not that an old woman didn't sometimes get an interest in a young man, particularly if he was as attractive as Parker felt he was, but this old woman looked at him the same way she looked at her old tractor—as if she had to put up with it because it was all she had. The tractor had broken down the second day Parker was on it and she had set him at once to cutting bushes, saying out of the side of her mouth to the nigger, "Everything he touches, he breaks." She also asked him to wear his shirt when he worked; Parker had removed it even though the day was not sultry; he put it back on reluctantly.

This ugly woman Parker married was his first wife. He had had other women but he had planned never to get himself tied up legally. He had first seen her one morning when his truck broke down on the highway. He had managed to pull it off the road into a neatly swept yard on which sat a peeling two-room house. He got out and opened the hood of the truck and began to study the motor. Parker had an extra sense that told him when there was a woman nearby watching him. After he had leaned over the motor a few minutes, his neck began to prickle. He cast his eye over the empty yard and porch of the house. A woman he could not see was either nearby beyond a clump of honeysuckle or in the house, watching him out the window.

Suddenly Parker began to jump up and down and fling his hand about as if he had mashed it in the machinery. He doubled over and held his hand close to his chest. "God dammit!" he hollered, "Jesus Christ in hell! Jesus God Almighty damm! God dammit to hell!" he went on flinging out the same few oaths over and over as loud as he could.

Without warning a terrible bristly claw slammed the side of his face and he fell backwards on the hood of the truck. "You don't talk no filth here!" a voice close to him shrilled.

Parker's vision was so blurred that for an instant he thought he had been attacked by some creature from above, a giant hawk-eyed angel wielding a hoary weapon. As his sight cleared, he saw before him a tall raw-boned girl with a broom.

"I hurt my hand," he said, "I HURT my hand." He was so incensed that he forgot that he hadn't hurt his hand. "My hand may be broke," he growled although his voice was still unsteady.

"Lemme see it," the girl demanded.

Parker stuck out his hand and she came closer and looked at it. There was no mark on the palm and she took the hand and turned it over. Her own hand was dry and hot and rough and Parker felt himself jolted back to life by her touch. He looked more closely at her. I don't want nothing to do with this one, he thought.

The girl's sharp eyes peered at the back of the stubby reddish hand she held. There emblazoned in red and blue was a tattooed eagle perched on a cannon. Parker's sleeve was rolled to the elbow. Above the eagle a serpent was coiled about a shield and in the spaces between the eagle and the serpent there were hearts, some with arrows through them. Above the serpent there was a spread hand of cards. Every space on the skin of Parker's arm, from wrist to elbow, was covered in some loud design. The girl gazed at this with an almost stupefied smile of shock, as if she had accidentally grasped a poisonous snake; she dropped the hand.

"I got most of my other ones in foreign parts," Parker said. "These here I mostly got in the United States. I got my first one when I was only fifteen year old."

"Don't tell me," the girl said, "I don't like it. I ain't got any use for it."

"You ought to see the ones you can't see," Parker said and winked.

Two circles of red appeared like apples on the girl's cheeks and softened her appearance. Parker was intrigued. He did not for a minute think that she didn't like the tattoos. He had never yet met a woman who was not attracted to them.

Parker was fourteen when he saw a man in a fair, tattooed from head to foot. Except for his loins which were girded with a panther hide, the man's skin was patterned in what seemed from Parker's distance—he was near the back of the tent, standing on a bench—a single intricate design of brilliant color. The man, who was small and sturdy, moved about on the platform, flexing his muscles so that the arabesque of men and beasts and flowers on his skin appeared to have a subtle motion of its own. Parker was filled with emotion, lifted up as some people are when the flag passes. He was a boy whose mouth habitually hung open. He was heavy and earnest, as ordinary as a loaf of bread. When the show was over, he had remained standing on the bench, staring where the tattooed man had been, until the tent was almost empty.

Parker had never before felt the least motion of wonder in himself. Until he saw the man at the fair, it did not enter his head that there was anything out of the ordinary about the fact that he existed. Even then it did not enter his head, but a peculiar unease settled in him. It was as if a blind boy had been turned so gently in a different direction that he did not know his destination had been changed.

He had his first tattoo some time after—the eagle perched on the cannon. It was done by a local artist. It hurt very little, just enough to make it appear to Parker to be worth doing. This was peculiar too for before he had thought that only what did not hurt was worth doing. The next year he quit school because he was sixteen and could. He went to the trade school for a while, then he quit the trade school and worked for six months in a garage. The only reason he worked at all was to pay for more tattoos. His mother worked in a laundry and could support him, but she would not pay for any tattoo except her name on a heart, which he had put on, grumbling. However, her name was Betty Jean and nobody had to know it was his mother. He found out that the tattoos were attractive to the kind of girls he liked but who had never liked him before. He began to drink beer and get in fights. His mother wept over what was becoming of him. One night she dragged him off to a revival with her, not telling him where they were going. When he saw the big lighted church, he jerked out of her grasp and ran. The next day he lied about his age and joined the navy.

Parker was large for the tight sailor's pants but the silly white cap, sitting low on his forehead, made his face by contrast look thoughtful and almost intense. After a month or two in the navy, his mouth ceased to hang open. His features hardened into the features of a man. He stayed in the navy five years and seemed a natural part of the grey mechanical ship, except for his eyes, which were the same pale slate-color as the ocean and reflected the immense spaces around him as if they were a microcosm of the mysterious sea. In port Parker wandered about comparing the run-down places he was in to Birmingham, Alabama. Everywhere he went he picked up more tattoos.

He had stopped having lifeless ones like anchors and crossed rifles. He had a tiger and a panther on each shoulder, a cobra coiled about a torch on his chest, hawks on his thighs, Elizabeth II and Philip over where his stomach and liver were respectively. He did not care much what the subject was so long as it was colorful; on his abdomen he had a few obscenities but only because that seemed the proper place for them. Parker would be satisfied with each tattoo about a month, then something about it that had attracted him would wear off. Whenever a decent-sized mirror was available, he would get in front of it and study his overall look. The effect was not of one intricate arabesque of colors but of something haphazard and botched. A huge dissatisfaction would come over him and he would go off and find another tattooist and have another space filled up. The front of Parker was almost completely covered but there were no tattoos on his back. He had no desire for one anywhere he could not readily see it himself. As the space on the front of him for tattoos decreased, his dissatisfaction grew and became general.

After one of his furloughs, he didn't go back to the navy but remained away without official leave, drunk, in a rooming house in a city he did not know. His dissatisfaction, from being chronic and latent, had suddenly become acute and raged in him. It was as if the panther and the lion and the serpents and the eagles and the hawks had penetrated his skin and lived inside him in a raging warfare. The navy caught up with him, put him in the brig for nine months and then gave him a dishonorable discharge.

After that Parker decided that country air was the only kind fit to breathe. He rented the shack on the embankment and bought the old truck and took various jobs which he kept as long as it suited him. At the time he met his future wife, he was buying apples by the bushel and selling them for the same price by the pound to isolated homesteaders on back country roads.

"All that there," the woman said, pointing to his arm, "is no better than what a fool Indian would do. It's a heap of vanity." She seemed to have found the word she wanted. "Vanity of vanities," she said.

Well what the hell do I care what she thinks of it? Parker asked himself, but he was plainly bewildered. "I reckon you like one of these better than another anyway," he said, dallying until he thought of something that would impress her. He thrust the arm back at her. "Which you like best?"

"None of them," she said, "but the chicken is not as bad as the rest."

"What chicken?" Parker almost yelled.

She pointed to the eagle.

"That's an eagle," Parker said. "What fool would waste their time having a chicken put on themself?"

"What fool would have any of it?" the girl said and turned away. She went slowly back to the house and left him there to get going. Parker remained for almost five minutes, looking agape at the dark door she had entered.

The next day he returned with a bushel of apples. He was not one to be outdone by anything that looked like her. He liked women with meat on them, so you didn't feel their muscles, much less their old bones. When he arrived, she was sitting on the top step and the yard was full of children, all as thin and poor as herself; Parker remembered it was Saturday. He hated to be making up to a woman when there were children around, but it was fortunate he had brought the bushel of apples off the truck. As the children approached him to see what he carried, he gave each child an apple and told it to get lost; in that way he cleared out the whole crowd.

The girl did nothing to acknowledge his presence. He might have been a stray pig or goat that had wandered into the yard and she too tired to take up the broom and send it off. He set the bushel of apples down next to her on the step. He sat down on a lower step.

"Hep yourself," he said, nodding at the basket; then he lapsed into silence.

She took an apple quickly as if the basket might disappear if she didn't make haste. Hungry people made Parker nervous. He had always had plenty to eat himself. He grew very uncomfortable. He reasoned he had nothing to say so why should he say it? He could not think now why he had come or why he didn't go before he wasted another bushel of apples on the crowd of children. He supposed they were her brothers and sisters.

She chewed the apple slowly but with a kind of relish of concentration, bent slightly but looking out ahead. The view from the porch stretched off across a long incline studded with iron weed and across the highway to a vast vista of hills and one small mountain. Long views depressed Parker. You look out into space like that and you begin to feel as if someone were after you, the navy or the government or religion.

"Who them children belong to, you?" he said at length.

"I ain't married yet," she said. "They belong to momma." She said it as if it were only a matter of time before she would be married.

Who in God's name would marry her? Parker thought.

A large barefooted woman with a wide gap-toothed face appeared in the door behind Parker. She had apparently been there for several minutes.

"Good evening," Parker said.

The woman crossed the porch and picked up what was left of the bushel of apples. "We thank you," she said and returned with it into the house.

"That your old woman?" Parker muttered.

The girl nodded. Parker knew a lot of sharp things he could have said like "You got my sympathy," but he was gloomily silent. He just sat there, looking at the view. He thought he must be coming down with something.

"If I pick up some peaches tomorrow I'll bring you some," he said.

"I'll be much obliged to you," the girl said.

Parker had no intention of taking any basket of peaches back there but the next day he found himself doing it. He and the girl had almost nothing to say to each other. One thing he did say was, "I ain't got any tattoo on my back."

"What you got on it?" the girl said.

"My shirt," Parker said. "Haw."

"Haw, haw," the girl said politely.

Parker thought he was losing his mind. He could not believe for a minute that he was attracted to a woman like this. She showed not the least interest in anything but what he brought until he appeared the third time with two cantaloups. "What's your name?" she asked.

"O. E. Parker," he said.

"What does the O. E. stand for?"

"You can just call me O. E.," Parker said. "Or Parker. Don't nobody call me by my name."

"What's it stand for?" she persisted.

"Never mind," Parker said. "What's yours?"

"I'll tell you when you tell me what them letters are the short of," she said. There was just a hint of flirtatiousness in her tone and it went rapidly to Parker's head. He had never revealed the name to any man or woman, only to the files of the navy and the government, and it was on his baptismal record which he got at the age of a month; his mother was a Methodist. When the name leaked out of the navy files, Parker narrowly missed killing the man who used it.

"You'll go blab it around," he said.

"I'll swear I'll never tell nobody," she said "On God's holy word I swear it."

Parker sat for a few minutes in silence. Then he reached for the girl's neck, drew her ear close to his mouth and revealed the name in a low voice.

"Obadiah," she whispered. Her face slowly brightened as if the name came as a sign to her. "Obadiah," she said.

The name still stank in Parker's estimation.

"Obadiah Elihue," she said in a reverent voice.

"If you call me that aloud, I'll bust your head open" Parker said. "What's yours?"

"Sarah Ruth Cates," she said.

"Glad to meet you, Sarah Ruth," Parker said.

Sarah Ruth's father was a Straight Gospel preacher but he was away, spreading it in Florida. Her mother did not seem to mind his attention to the girl so long as he brought a basket of something with him when he came. As for Sarah Ruth herself, it was plain to Parker after he had visited three times that she was crazy about him. She liked him even though she insisted that pictures on the skin were vanity of vanities and even after hearing him curse, and even after she had asked him if he was saved and he replied that he didn't see it was anything in particular to save him from. After that, inspired, Parker had said, "I'd be saved enough if you was to kiss me."

She scowled. "That ain't being saved," she said.

Not long after that she agreed to take a ride in his truck. Parker parked it on a deserted road and suggested to her that they lie down together in the back of it.

"Not until after we're married," she said—just like that.

"Oh that ain't necessary," Parker said and as he reached for her, she thrust him away with such force that the door of the truck came off and he found himself flat on his back on the ground. He made up his mind then and there to have nothing further to do with her.

They were married in the County Ordinary's office because Sarah Ruth thought churches were idolatrous. Parker had no opinion about that one way or the other. The Ordinary's office was lined with cardboard file boxes and record books with dusty yellow slips of paper hanging out of them. The Ordinary was an old woman with red hair who held office for forty years and looked as dusty as her books. She married them from behind the iron-grill of a stand-up desk and when she finished, she said with a flourish, "Three dollars and fifty cents and till death do you part!" and yanked some forms out of a machine.

Marriage did not change Sarah Ruth a jot and it made Parker gloomier than ever. Every morning he decided he had had enough and would not return that night; every night he returned. Whenever Parker couldn't stand the way he felt, he would have another tattoo, but the only surface left on him now was his back. To see a tattoo on his own back he would have to get two mirrors and stand between them in just the correct position and this seemed to Parker a good way to make an idiot of himself. Sarah Ruth who, if she had had better sense, could have enjoyed a tattoo on his back, would not even look at the ones he had elsewhere. When he attempted to point out especial details of them, she would shut her eyes tight and turn her back as well. Except in total darkness, she preferred Parker dressed and with his sleeves rolled down.

"At the judgement seat of God, Jesus is going to say to you, 'What you been doing all your life besides have pictures drawn all over you?' " she said.

"You don't fool me none," Parker said, "you're just afraid that hefty girl I work for'll like me so much she'll say, 'Come on, Mr. Parker, let's you and me . . .' "

"You're tempting sin," she said, "and at the judgement seat of God you'll have to answer for that too. You ought to go back to selling the fruits of the earth."

Parker did nothing much when he was at home but listen to what the judgement seat of God would be like for him if he didn't change his ways. When he could, he broke in with tales of the hefty girl he worked for. " 'Mr. Parker,' " he said she said, 'I hired you for your brains.' " (She had added, "So why don't you use them?")

"And you should have seen her face the first time she saw me without my shirt," he said. " 'Mr. Parker,' she said, 'you're a walking panner-rammer!' " This had, in fact, been her remark but it had been delivered out of one side of her mouth.

Dissatisfaction began to grow so great in Parker that there was no containing it outside of a tattoo. It had to be his back. There was no help for it. A dim half-formed inspiration began to work in his mind. He visualized having a tattoo put there that Sarah Ruth would not be able to resist— a religious subject. He thought of an open book with HOLY BIBLE tattooed under it and an actual verse printed on the page. This seemed just the thing for a while; then he began to hear her say, "Ain't I already got a real Bible? What you think I want to read the same verse over and over for when I can read it all?" He needed something better even than the Bible! He thought about it so much that he began to lose sleep. He was already losing flesh—Sarah Ruth just threw food in the pot and let it boil. Not knowing for certain why he continued to stay with a woman who was both ugly and pregnant and no cook made him generally nervous and irritable, and he developed a little tic in the side of his face.

Once or twice he found himself turning around abruptly as if someone were trailing him. He had had a granddaddy who had ended in the state mental hospital, althought not until he was seventy-five, but as urgent as it might be for him to get a tattoo, it was just as urgent that he get exactly the right one to bring Sarah Ruth to heel. As he continued to worry over it, his eyes took on a hollow preoccupied expression. The old woman he worked for told him that if he couldn't keep his mind on what he was doing, she knew where she could find a fourteen-year-old colored boy who could. Parker was too preoccupied even to be offended. At any time previous, he would have left her then and there, saying drily, "Well, you go ahead on and get him then."

Two or three mornings later he was baling hay with the old woman's sorry baler and her broken down tractor in a large field, cleared save for one enormous old tree standing in the middle of it. The old woman was the kind who would not cut down a large old tree because it was a large old tree. She had pointed it out to Parker as if he didn't have eyes and told him to be careful not to hit it as the machine picked up hay near it. Parker began at the outside of the field and made circles inward toward it. He had to get off the tractor every now and then and untangle the baling cord or kick a rock out of the way. The old woman had told him to carry the rocks to the edge of the field, which he did when she was there watching. When he thought he could make it, he ran over them. As he circled the field his mind was on a suitable design for his back. The sun, the size of a golf ball, began to switch regularly from in front to behind him, but he appeared to see it both places as if he had eyes in the back of his head. All at once he saw the tree reaching out to grasp him. A ferocious thud propelled him into the air, and he heard himself yelling in an unbelievably loud voice, "GOD ABOVE!"

He landed on his back while the tractor crashed upsidedown into the tree and burst into flame. The first thing Parker saw were his shoes, quickly being eaten by the fire; one was caught under the tractor, the other was some distance away, burning by itself. He was not in them. He could feel the hot breath of the burning tree on his face. He scrambled backwards, still sitting, his eyes cavernous, and if he had known how to cross himself he would have done it.

His truck was on a dirt road at the edge of the field. He moved toward it, still sitting, still backwards, but faster and faster; halfway to it he got up and began a kind of forwardbent run from which he collapsed on his knees twice. His legs felt like two old rusted rain gutters. He reached the truck finally and took off in it, zigzagging up the road. He drove past his house on the embankment and straight for the city, fifty miles distant.

Parker did not allow himself to think on the way to the city. He only knew that there had been a great change in his life, a leap forward into a worse unknown, and that there was nothing he could do about it. It was for all intents accomplished.

The artist had two large cluttered rooms over a chiropodist's office on a back street. Parker, still barefooted, burst silently in on him at a little after three in the afternoon. The artist, who was about Parker's own age—twenty-eight—but thin and bald, was behind a small drawing table, tracing a design in green ink. He looked up with an annoyed glare and did not seem to recognize Parker in the holloweyed creature before him.

"Let me see the book you got with all the pictures of God in it," Parker said breathlessly. "The religious one."

The artist continued to look at him with his intellectual, superior stare. "I don't put tattoos on drunks," he said.

"You know me!" Parker cried indignantly. "I'm O. E. Parker! You done work for me before and I always paid!"

The artist looked at him another moment as if he were not altogether sure. "You've fallen off some," he said. "You must have been in jail."

"Married," Parker said.

"Oh," said the artist. With the aid of mirrors the artist had tattooed on the top of his head a miniature owl, perfect in every detail. It was about the size of a half-dollar and served him as a show piece. There were cheaper artists in town but Parker had never wanted anything but the best. The artist went over to a cabinet at the back of the room and began to look over some art books. "Who are you interested in?" he said, "saints, angels, Christs or what?"

"God," Parker said.

"Father, Son or Spirit?"

"Just God," Parker said impatiently. "Christ. I don't care. Just so it's God."

The artist returned with a book. He moved some papers off another table and put the book down on it and told Parker to sit down and see what he liked. "The up-t-date ones are in the back," he said.

Parker sat down with the book and wet his thumb. He began to go through it, beginning at the back where the up-to-date pictures were. Some of them he recognized—The Good Shepherd, Forbid Them Not, The Smiling Jesus, Jesus the Physician's Friend, but he kept turning rapidly backwards and the pictures became less and less reassuring. One showed a gaunt green dead face streaked with blood. One was yellow with sagging purple eyes. Parker's heart began to beat faster and faster until it appeared to be roaring inside him like a great generator. He flipped the pages quickly, feeling that when he reached the one ordained, a sign would come. He continued to flip through until he had almost reached the front of the book. On one of the pages a pair of eyes glanced at him swiftly. Parker sped on, then stopped. His heart too appeared to cut off; there was absolute silence. It said as plainly as if silence were a language itself, GO BACK.

Parker returned to the picture—the haloed head of a flat stern Byzantine Christ with all-demanding eyes. He sat there trembling; his heart began slowly to beat again as if it were being brought to life by a subtle power.

"You found what you want?" the artist asked.

Parker's throat was too dry to speak. He got up and thrust the book at the artist, opened at the picture.

"That'll cost you plenty," the artist said. "You don't want all those little blocks though, just the outline and some better features."

"Just like it is," Parker said, "just like it is or nothing."

"It's your funeral," the artist said, "but I don't do that kind of work for nothing."

"How much?" Parker asked.

"It'll take maybe two days work."

"How much?" Parker said.

"On time or cash?" the artist asked. Parker's other jobs had been on time, but he had paid.

"Ten down and ten for every day it takes," the artist said.

Parker drew ten dollar bills out of his wallet; he had three left in.

"You come back in the morning," the artist said, putting the money in his own pocket. "First I'll have to trace that out of the book."

"No no!" Parker said. "Trace it now or gimme my money back," and his eyes blared as if he were ready for a fight.

The artist agreed. Any one stupid enough to want a Christ on his back, he reasoned, would be just as likely as not to change his mind the next minute, but once the work was begun he could hardly do so.

While he worked on the tracing, he told Parker to go wash his back at the sink with the special soap he used there. Parker did it and returned to pace back and forth across the room, nervously flexing his shoulders. He wanted to go look at the picture again but at the same time he did not want to. The artist got up finally and had Parker lie down on the table. He swabbed his back with ethyl chloride and then began to outline the head on it with his iodine pencil. Another hour passed before he took up his electric instrument. Parker felt no particular pain. In Japan he had had a tattoo of the Buddha done on his upper arm with ivory needles; in Burma, a little brown root of a man had made a peacock on each of his knees using thin pointed sticks, two feet long; amateurs had worked on him with pins and soot. Parker was usually so relaxed and easy under the hand of the artist that he often went to sleep, but this time he remained awake, every muscle taut.

At midnight the artist said he was ready to quit. He propped one mirror, four feet square, on a table by the wall and took a smaller mirror off the lavatory wall and put it in Parker's hands. Parker stood with his back to the one on the table and moved the other until he saw a flashing burst of color reflected from his back. It was almost completely covered with little red and blue and ivory and saffron squares; from them he made out the lineaments of the face—a mouth, the beginning of heavy brows, a straight nose, but the face was empty; the eyes had not yet been put in. The impression for the moment was almost as if the artist had tricked him and done the Physician's Friend.

"It don't have eyes," Parker cried out.

"That'll come," that artist said, "in due time. We have another day to go on it yet."

Parker spent the night on a cot at the Haven of Light Christian Mission. He found these the best places to stay in the city because they were free and included a meal of sorts. He got the last available cot and because he was still barefooted, he accepted a pair of second-hand shoes which, in his confusion, he put on to go to bed; he was still shocked from all that had happened to him. All night he lay awake in the long dormitory of cots with lumpy figures on them. The only light was from a phosphorescent cross glowing at the end of the room. The tree reached out to grasp him again, then burst into flame; the shoe burned quietly by itself; the eyes in the book said to him distinctly GO BACK and at the same time did not utter a sound. He wished that he were not in this city, not in this Haven of Light Mission, not in a bed by himself. He longed miserably for Sarah Ruth. Her sharp tongue and icepick eyes were the only comfort he could bring to mind. He decided he was losing it. Her eyes appeared soft and dilatory compared with the eyes in the book, for even though he could not summon up the exact look of those eyes, he could still feel their penetration. He felt as though, under their gaze, he was as transparent as the wing of a fly.

The tattooist had told him not to come until ten in the morning, but when he arrived at that hour, Parker was sitting in the dark hallway on the floor, waiting for him. He had decided upon getting up that, once the tattoo was on him, he would not look at it, that all his sensations of the day and night before were those of a crazy man and that he would return to doing things according to his own sound judgement.

The artist began where he left off. "One thing I want to know," he said presently as he worked over Parker's back, "why do you want this on you? Have you gone and got religion? Are you saved?" he asked in a mocking voice.

Parker's throat felt salty and dry. "Naw," he said, "I ain't got no use for none of that. A man can't save his self from whatever it is he don't deserve none of my sympathy." These words seemed to leave his mouth like wraiths and to evaporate at once as if he had never uttered them.

"Then why . . ."

"I married this woman that's saved," Parker said. "I never should have done it. I ought to leave her. She's done gone and got pregnant."

"That's too bad," the artist said. "Then it's her making you have this tattoo."

"Naw," Parker said, "she don't know nothing about it. It's a surprise for her."

"You think she'll like it and lay off you a while?"

"She can't hep herself," Parker said. "She can't say she don't like the looks of God." He decided he had told the artist enough of his business. Artists were all right in their place but he didn't like them poking their noses into the affairs of regular people. "I didn't get no sleep last night," he said. "I think I'll get some now."

That closed the mouth of the artist but it did not bring him any sleep. He lay there, imagining how Sarah Ruth would be struck speechless by the face on his back and every now and then this would be interrupted by a vision of the tree of fire and his empty shoe burning beneath it.

The artist worked steadily until nearly four o'clock, not stopping to have lunch, hardly pausing with the electric instrument except to wipe the dripping dye off Parker's back as he went along. Finally he finished. "You can get up and look at it now," he said.

Parker sat up but he remained on the edge of the table.

The artist was pleased with his work and wanted Parker to look at it at once. Instead Parker continued to sit on the edge of the table, bent forward slightly but with a vacant look. "What ails you?" the artist said. "Go look at it."

"Ain't nothing ail me," Parker said in a sudden belligerent voice. "That tattoo ain't going nowhere. It'll be there when I get there." He reached for his shirt and began gingerly to put it on.

The artist took him roughly by the arm and propelled him between the two mirrors. "Now *look*," he said, angry at having his work ignored.

Parker looked, turned white and moved away. The eyes in the reflected face continued to look at him—still, straight, all-demanding, enclosed in silence.

"It was your idea, remember," the artist said. "I would have advised something else."

Parker said nothing. He put on his shirt and went out the door while the artist shouted, "I'll expect all of my money!"

Parker headed toward a package shop on the corner. He bought a pint of whiskey and took it into a nearby alley and drank it all in five minutes. Then he moved on to a pool hall nearby which he frequented when he came to the city. It was a well-lighted barn-like place with a bar up one side and gambling machines on the other and pool tables in the back. As soon as Parker entered, a large man in a red and black checkered shirt hailed him by slapping him on the back and yelling, "Yeyyyyyy boy! O. E. Parker!"

Parker was not yet ready to be struck on the back. "Lay off," he said, "I got a fresh tatto there."

"What you got this time?" the man asked and then yelled to a few at the machines. "O. E.'s got him another tattoo."

"Nothing special this time," Parker said and slunk over to a machine that was not being used.

"Come on," the big man said, "let's have a look at O. E.'s tattoo," and while Parker squirmed in their hands, they pulled up his shirt. Parker felt all the hands drop away instantly and his shirt fell again like a veil over the face. There was a silence in the pool room which seemed to Parker to grow from the circle around him until it extended to the foundations under the building and upward through the beams in the roof.

Finally some one said, "Christ!" Then they all broke into noise at once. Parker turned around, an uncertain grin on his face.

"Leave it to O. E.!" the man in the checkered shirt said. "That boy's a real card!"

"Maybe he's gone and got religion," some one yelled.

"Not on your life," Parker said.

"O. E.'s got religion and is witnessing for Jesus, ain't you, O. E.?" a little man with a piece of cigar in his mouth said wryly. "An o-riginal way to do it if I ever saw one."

"Leave it to Parker to think of a new one!" the fat man said

"Yyeeeeeeyyyyyyy boy!" someone yelled and they all began to whistle and curse in compliment until Parker said, "Aaa shut up."

"What'd you do it for?" somebody asked.

"For laughs," Parker said. "What's it to you?"

"Why ain't you laughing then?" somebody yelled. Parker lunged into the midst of them and like a whirlwind on a summer's day there began a fight that raged amid overturned tables and swinging fists until two of them grabbed him and ran to the door with him and threw him out. Then a calm descended on the pool hall as nerve shattering as if the long barn-like room were the ship from which Jonah had been cast into the sea.

Parker sat for a long time on the ground in the alley behind the pool hall, examining his soul. He saw it as a spider web of facts and lies that was not at all important to him but which appeared to be necessary in spite of his opinion. The eyes that were now forever on his back were eyes to be obeyed. He was as certain of it as he had ever been of anything. Throughout his life, grumbling and sometimes cursing, often afraid, once in rapture, Parker had obeyed whatever instinct of this kind had come to him—in rapture when his spirit had lifted at the sight of the tattooed man at the fair, afraid when he had joined the navy, grumbling when he had married Sarah Ruth.

The thought of her brought him slowly to his feet. She would know what he had to do. She would clear up the rest of it, and she would at least be pleased. It seemed to him that, all along, that was what he wanted, to please her. His truck was still parked in front of the building where the artist had his place, but it was not far away. He got in it and drove out of the city and into the country night. His head was almost clear of liquor and he observed that his dissatisfaction was gone, but he felt not quite like himself. It was as if he were himself but a stranger to himself, driving into a new country though everything he saw was familiar to him, even at night.

He arrived finally at the house on the embankment, pulled the truck under the pecan tree and got out. He made as much noise as possible to assert that he was still in charge here, that his leaving her for a night without word meant nothing except it was the way he did things. He slammed the car door, stamped up the two steps and across the porch and rattled the door knob. It did not respond to his touch. "Sarah Ruth!" he yelled, "let me in."

There was no lock on the door and she had evidently placed the back of a chair against the knob. He began to beat on the door and rattle the knob at the same time.

He heard the bed springs screak and bent down and put his head to the keyhole, but it was stopped up with paper. "Let me in!" he hollered, bamming on the door again. "What you got me locked out for?"

A sharp voice close to the door said, "Who's there?"

"Me," Parker said, "O. E."

He waited a moment.

"Me," he said impatiently, "O. E."

Still no sound from inside.

He tried once more. "O. E.," he said, bamming the door two or three more times. "O. E. Parker. You know me."

There was a silence. Then the voice said slowly, "I don't know no O. E."

"Quit fooling," Parker pleaded. "You ain't got any business doing me this way. It's me, old O. E., I'm back. You ain't afraid of me."

"Who's there?" the same unfeeling voice said.

Parker turned his head as if he expected someone behind him to give him the answer. The sky had lightened slightly and there were two or three streaks of yellow floating above the horizon. Then as he stood there, a tree of light burst over the skyline.

Parker fell back against the door as if he had been pinned there by a lance.

"Who's there?" the voice from inside said and there was a quality about it now that seemed final. The knob rattled and the voice said peremptorily, "Who's there, I ast you?"

Parker bent down and put his mouth near the stuffed keyhole. "Obadiah," he whispered and all at once he felt the light pouring through him, turning his spider web soul into a perfect arabesque of color, a garden of trees and birds and beasts.

"Obadiah Elihue!" he whispered.

The door opened and he stumbled in. Sarah Ruth loomed there, hand on her hips. She began at once, "That was no hefty blonde woman you was working for and you'll have to pay her every penny on her tractor you busted up. She don't keep insurance on it. She came here and her and me had us a long talk and I . . ."

Trembling, Parker set about lighting the kerosene lamp.

"What's the matter with you, wasting that kerosene this near daylight?" she demanded. "I ain't got to look at you."

A yellow glow enveloped them. Parker put the match down and began to unbutton his shirt.

"And you ain't going to have none of me this near morning," she said.

"Shut your mouth," he said quietly. "Look at this and then I don't want to hear no more out of you." He removed the shirt and turned his back to her.

"Another picture," Sarah Ruth growled. "I might have known you was off after putting some more trash on yourself."

Parker's knees went hollow under him. He wheeled around and cried, "Look at it! Don't just say that! *Look* at it!"

"I done looked," she said

"Don't you know who it is?" he cried in anguish.

"No, who is it?" Sarah Ruth said. "It ain't anybody I know."

"It's him," Parker said.

"Him who?"

"God!" Parker cried.

"God? God don't look like that!"

"What do you know how he looks?" Parker moaned. "You ain't seen him."

"He don't *look*," Sarah Ruth said. "He's a spirit. No man shall see his face."

"Aw listen," Parker groaned, "this is just a picture of him."

"Idolatry!" Sarah Ruth screamed. "Idolatry! Enflaming yourself with idols under every green tree! I can put up with lies and vanity but I don't want no idolator in this house!" and she grabbed up the broom and began to thrash him across the shoulders with it.

Parker was too stunned to resist. He sat there and let her beat him until she had nearly knocked him senseless and large welts had formed on the face of the tattooed Christ. Then he staggered up and made for the door.

She stamped the broom two or three times on the floor and went to the window and shook it out to get the taint of him off it. Still gripping it, she looked toward the pecan tree and her eyes hardened still more. There he was—who called himself Obadiah Elihue—leaning against the tree, crying like a baby.

1965

SAUL BELLOW

(1915-)

For three decades, in seven strongly shaped novels and a handful of stories, Saul Bellow has been America's chief "poet of the city" in prose. What this means, to begin with, is that Bellow knows the texture of urban existence, the strangeness of its common sights, the look and feel of its air.

> At the corner he paused to watch the work of the wrecking crew. The great metal ball swung at the walls, passed easily through brick, and entered the rooms, the lazy weight browsing on kitchens and parlors. Everything it touched wavered and burst, spilled down. There rose a white tranquil cloud of plaster dust. The afternoon was ending, and in the widening area of demolition was a fire, fed by the wreckage. Moses heard the air, softly pulled toward the flames, felt the heat. The workmen, heaping the bonfire with wood, threw strips of molding like javelins. Paint and varnish smoked like incense. The old flooring burned gratefully— the funeral of exhausted objects. Scaffolds walled with pink, white, green doors quivered as the six-wheeled trucks carried off fallen brick. The sun, now leaving for New Jersey and the west, was surrounded by a dazzling broth of atmospheric gases.

But being a *true* poet of the city entails much more; the writer must know what it feels like to be a city person—what the conditions of relatedness are.

On this front Bellow is extraordinary. His novels vary in their structure; some are relatively dramatic and objective (*Seize the Day, The Victim*), some are intensely subjective (*Herzog*). Each is concerned, however, with a more or less passive, burdened, solipsistic man who has a clear sense of his sufferings as a mark of distinction. And, partly for that reason, the sensibility of each is urban to its core. The characteristic state of mind is that of Tommy Wilhelm at the moment in *Seize the Day* (1956) when he discovers what seems to be the center of life:

> But at the same time, since there were depths in Wilhelm not unsuspected by himself, he received a suggestion from some re-

Critical studies include Tony Tanner, *Saul Bellow,* 1965; Irving Malin, ed., *Saul Bellow and the Critics,* 1967; Keith M. Opdahl, *The Novels of Saul Bellow,* 1967; Irving Malin, *Saul Bellow's Fiction,* 1969; and Earl H. Rovit, *Saul Bellow,* 1973.

mote element in his thoughts that the business of life, the real business — to carry his particular burden, to feel shame and impotence, to taste these quelled tears — the only important business, the highest business was being done.

The state of mind has terrible limitations; people who share it slip easily into self-pity or edge, perversely, into self-hatred. They often lack force, seem overly accepting of humiliation, short-circuit their own emotion, slide off into "resolutions" without ever generating tension within themselves. Losing father, family, money within the course of a single day, Tommy Wilhelm makes no effort to gain control of events, reacts only in a muffled outrage at these events; tears at the end, "the consummation of his heart's ultimate need," bring no real relief, no transformation of what has been, almost from the beginning, a sustained orgy of the heart.

And then beyond this lies a problem more troubling: some kind of total wipeout of fraternity as a value. In this fiction there is talk but little dialogue. The sufferer is the only reality and the action occurs in his head and heart and, if suffering is distinction, moral significance, those who cause the pain are invariably shown to be of lesser stature. Other people are shadowy, dreamlike to Tommy Wilhelm; to Herzog they are less intelligent, less sensitive than he; to Mr. Sammler, in *Mr. Sammler's Planet*, they are absurd boors. Herzog turns off a talkative cab driver effortlessly—"He answered cheerfully, but by rote. He had stopped listening. Oratorical lechery, momentarily amusing"—not simply ignoring the man but, with patronizing affability, *classifying* him. He does the same, speaking in a voice at once self-congratulatory and dismissive, to a policeman who has apprehended him: "There were labels to fit him, naturally, but a harness cop like this would not be familiar with them."

Not only do these people resist knowing others; they don't want to *be* known, they want somehow to be beyond "known-ness." Herzog, not reluctant to define others as "evildoers," resists categorically the notion that these same others might define him:

> . . . Hard ruthless action taken against a man is the assertion by evildoers that he is fully knowable. They put me down, ergo they claimed final knowledge of Herzog. They *knew* me! And I hold with Spinoza (I hope he won't mind) that to demand what is impossible for any human being, to exercise power where it can't be exercised, is tyranny. Excuse me, therefore, sir and madam, but I reject your definitions of me.

The question arises: what is identity without relationship, without awareness of other minds, and without firm lodging *in* other minds?

Bellow's heroes have little to push against except themselves, and the result is a ceaseless multiplication of perspectives on the person by the person, endless redefinitions, and many a pathetic solitary encounter with self, like Tommy Wilhelm's at the end of *Seize the Day*.

Yet there is genuine feeling in Bellow's pages, and more than one touching movement outward beyond the self—as, for example, when Moses Herzog looks through a window and sees his own child being bathed, lovingly, by the man who's replaced him as her guardian. Once, in a finely rendered moment, Wilhelm is moved in the depths of his being. Asked whether he loves his "old man," he is surprised by his own response:

> Of course I love him. My father. My mother—As he said this there was a great pull at the very center of his soul. When a fish strikes the line you feel the line force in your hand. A mysterious being beneath the water, driven by the hunger, has taken the hook and rushes away and fights, writhing. Wilhelm never identified what struck within him. It did not reveal itself. It got away.

Herzog, immensely more articulate than Wilhelm, cannot make his friends understand his pain at the breakup of his marriage and, for a moment, is aware of the blessed relief it might be to touch the consciousness of another: "If ever Herzog knew the loathsomeness of a *particular* existence, knew that the *whole* was required to redeem every separate spirit, it was then, in his terrible passion, which he tried, impossibly, to share, telling his story."

But these are, to repeat, city men, accustomed to the preservation of distance, and the maintenance of unviolated space; it is not a dream of ordinary human fellowship that haunts them most deeply. Their demon is the prospect of some sort of ultimate understanding, their unshakeable conviction that sooner or later some revelation will make everything clear. Now and then comes an instant of insight, but it quickly recedes, undercut by wry, reductive—urban—mockery or by ensuing events that reveal the momentary clarity or peace to have been illusory, a mode of teasing. Yet the character's confidence that sense can be made by the isolated ego, that perseverance will, finally, pay, that to learn to see clearly is a moral virtue, falters only temporarily. Value and order are hard to discern in these lives, but the heroes themselves assert that seeking is value enough. Conceivably Bellow agrees. Conceivably he could say, with Herzog, "I go after reality with language. Perhaps I'd like to change it all into language. . . . I must be trying to keep tight the tensions without which human beings can no longer be called human." But the groping, ridiculous, ineffectual figures he has produced stand as powerful criticisms of the age: ever on the verge of sobbing, they tell more than a little about the fearful pressure of a nation of equalitarians on fraternal hope.

Born in Lachine, Quebec, Saul Bellow grew up in a Montreal slum. When he was 9 years old, his family moved to Chicago. He attended the University of Chicago and Northwestern University, where he was influenced by the anthropologist Melville Jean Herskovitz, and majored in anthropology and sociology. Bellow went to graduate school at the University of Wisconsin but found that he was more interested in writing than in anthropology. "Every time I worked on my thesis," he later remarked, "it turned out to be a story." (The effect of the anthropological studies is most obvious in *Henderson the Rain King*; much of that novel is set in Africa.) The novelist was closely associated, in the 1940's, with the *Partisan Review* group of intellectuals and academics. He published *Dangling Man* in 1944, and has since published six other novels: *The Victim* (1947), *The Adventures of Augie March* (1953), *Seize the Day* (1956), *Henderson the Rain King* (1959), *Herzog* (1964), and *Mr. Sammler's Planet* (1970). He has also written a play, *The Last Analysis* (1965) and a number of stories (collected as *Mosby's Memoirs* in 1968). Presently Bellow is a professor at the University of Chicago and chairman of its Committee on Social Thought. His novels have won three National Book Awards.

Seize the Day

I

When it came to concealing his troubles, Tommy Wilhelm was not less capable than the next fellow. So at least he thought, and there was a certain amount of evidence to back him up. He had once been an actor—no, not quite, an extra—and he knew what acting should be. Also, he was smoking a cigar, and when a man is smoking a cigar, wearing a hat, he has an advantage; it is harder to find out how he feels. He came from the twenty-third floor down to the lobby on the mezzanine to collect his mail before breakfast, and he believed—he hoped—that he looked passably well: doing all right. It was a matter of sheer hope, because there was not much that he could add to his present effort. On the fourteenth floor he looked for his father to enter the elevator; they often met at this hour, on the way to breakfast. If he worried about his appearance it was mainly for his old father's sake. But there was no stop on the fourteenth, and the elevator sank and sank. Then the smooth door opened and the greak dark red uneven carpet that covered the lobby billowed toward Wilhelm's feet. In the foreground the lobby was dark, sleepy. French drapes like sails kept out the sun, but three high, narrow windows were open, and in the blue air Wilhelm saw a pigeon about to light on the great chain that supported the marquee of the movie house directly underneath the lobby. For one moment he heard the wings beating strongly.

Most of the guests at the Hotel Gloriana were past the age of retirement. Along Broadway in the Seventies, Eighties, and Nineties, a great part of New York's vast population of old men and women lives. Unless the weather is too cold or wet they fill the benches about the tiny railed parks and along the subway gratings from Verdi Square to Columbia University, they crowd the shops and cafeterias, the dime stores, the tea-rooms, the bakeries, the beauty parlors, the reading rooms and club rooms. Among these old people at the Gloriana, Wilhelm felt out of place. He was comparatively young, in his middle forties, large and blond, with big shoulders; his back was heavy and strong, if already a little stooped or thickened. After breakfast the old guests sat down on the green leather armchairs and sofas in the lobby and began to gossip and look into the papers; they had nothing to do but wait out the day. But Wilhelm was used to an active life and liked to go out energetically in the morning. And for several months, because he had no position, he had kept up his morale by rising early; he was shaved and in the lobby by eight o'clock. He bought the paper and some cigars and drank a Coca-Cola or two before he went in to breakfast with his father. After breakfast—out, out, out to attend to business. The getting out had in itself become the chief business. But he had realized that he could not keep this up much longer, and today he was afraid. He was aware that his routine was about to break up and he sensed that a huge trouble long presaged but till now formless was due. Before evening, he'd know.

Nevertheless he followed his daily course and crossed the lobby.

Rubin, the man at the newsstand, had poor eyes. They may not have been actually weak but they were poor in expression, with lacy lids that furled down at the corners. He dressed well. It didn't seem necessary—he was behind the counter most of the time—but he dressed very well. He had on a rich brown suit; the cuffs embarrassed the hairs on his small hands. He wore a Countess Mara painted necktie. As Wilhelm approached, Rubin did not see him; he was looking out dreamily at the Hotel Ansonia, which was visible from his corner, several blocks away. The Ansonia, the neighborhood's great landmark, was built by Stanford White. It looks like a baroque palace from Prague or Munich enlarged a hundred times, with towers, domes, huge swells and bubbles of metal gone green from exposure, iron fretwork and festoons. Black television antennae are densely planted on its round summits. Under the changes of weather it may look like marble or like sea water, black as slate in the fog, white as tufa in sunlight. This morning it looked like the image of itself reflected in deep water, white and cumulous above, with cavernous distortions underneath. Together, the two men gazed at it.

Then Rubin said, "Your dad is in to breakfast already, the old gentleman."

"Oh, yes? Ahead of me today?"

"That's a real knocked-out shirt you got on," said Rubin. "Where's it from, Saks?"

"No, it's a Jack Fagman—Chicago."

Even when his spirits were low, Wilhelm could still wrinkle his forehead in a pleasing way. Some of the slow, silent movements of his face were very attractive. He went back a step, as if to stand away from himself and get a better look at his shirt. His glance was comic, a comment upon his untidiness. He liked to wear good clothes, but once he had put it on each article appeared to go its own way. Wilhelm, laughing, panted a little; his teeth were small; his cheeks when he laughed and puffed grew round, and he looked much younger than his years. In the old days when he was a college freshman and wore a raccoon coat and a beanie on his large blond head his father used to say that, big as he was, he could charm a bird out of a tree. Wilhelm had great charm still.

"I like this dove-gray color," he said in his sociable, good-natured way. "It isn't washable. You have to send it to the cleaner. It never smells as good as washed. But it's a nice shirt. It cost sixteen, eighteen bucks."

This shirt had not been bought by Wilhelm; it was a present from his boss—his former boss, with whom he had had a falling out. But there was no reason why he should tell Rubin the history of it. Although perhaps Rubin knew—Rubin was the kind of man who knew, and knew and knew. Wilhelm also knew many things about Rubin, for that matter, about Rubin's wife and Rubin's business, Rubin's health. None of these could be mentioned, and the great weight of the unspoken left them little to talk about.

"Well, y'lookin' pretty sharp today," Rubin said.

And Wilhelm said gladly, "Am I? Do you really think so?" He could not believe it. He saw his reflection in the glass cupboard full of cigar boxes, among the grand seals and paper damask and the gold-embossed portraits of famous men, García, Edward the Seventh, Cyrus the Great. You had to allow for the darkness and deformations of the glass, but he thought he didn't look too good. A wide wrinkle like a comprehensive bracket sign was written upon his forehead, the point between his brows, and there were patches of brown on his dark blond skin. He began to be half amused at the shadow of his own marveling, troubled, desirous eyes, and his nostrils and his lips. Fair-haired hippopotamus!—that was how he looked to himself. He saw a big round face, a wide, flourishing red mouth, stump teeth. And the hat, too; and the cigar, too. I should have done hard labor all my life, he reflected. Hard honest labor that tires you out and makes you sleep. I'd have worked off my energy and felt better. Instead, I had to distinguish myself—yet.

He had put forth plenty of effort, but that was not the same as working hard, was it? And if as a young man he had got off to a bad start it was due to this very same face. Early in the nineteen-thirties, because of his striking looks, he had been very briefly considered star material, and he had gone to Hollywood. There for seven years, stubbornly, he had tried to become a screen artist. Long before that time his ambition or delusion had ended, but through pride and perhaps also through laziness he had remained in California. At last he turned to other things, but those seven years of persistence and defeat had unfitted him somehow for trades and businesses, and then it was too late to go into one of the professions. He had been slow to mature, and he had lost ground, and so he hadn't been able to get rid of his energy and he was convinced that this energy itself had done him the greatest harm.

"I didn't see you at the gin game last night," said Rubin.

"I had to miss it. How did it go?"

For the last few weeks Wilhelm had played gin almost nightly, but yesterday he had felt that he couldn't afford to lose any more. He had never won. Not once. And while the losses were small they weren't gains, were they? They were losses. He was tired of losing, and tired also of the company, and so he had gone by himself to the movies.

"Oh," said Rubin, "it went okay. Carl made a chump of himself yelling at the guys. This time Doctor Tamkin didn't let him get away with it. He told him the psychological reason why."

"What was the reason?"

Rubin said, "I can't quote him. Who could? You know the way Tamkin talks. Don't ask me. Do you want the *Trib*? Aren't you going to look at the closing quotations?"

"It won't help much to look. I know what they were yesterday at three," said Wilhelm. "But I suppose I better had get the paper." It seemed necessary for him to lift one shoulder in order to put his hand into his jacket pocket. There, among little packets of pills and crushed cigarette butts and strings of cellophane, the red tapes of packages which he sometimes used as dental floss, he recalled that he had dropped some pennies.

"That doesn't sound so good," said Rubin. He meant to be conversationally playful, but his voice had no tone and his eyes, slack and lid-blinded, turned elsewhere. He didn't want to hear. It was all the same to him. Maybe he already knew, being the sort of man who knew and knew.

No, it wasn't good. Wilhelm held three orders of lard in the commodities market. He and Dr. Tamkin had bought this lard together four days ago at 12.96, and the price at once began to fall and was still falling. In the mail this morning there was sure to be a call for additional margin payment. One came every day.

The psychologist, Dr. Tamkin, had got him into this. Tamkin lived at the Gloriana and attended the card game. He had explained to Wilhelm that you could speculate in commodities at one of the uptown branches of a good Wall Street house without making the full deposit of margin legally required. It was up to the branch manager. If he knew you—and all the branch managers knew Tamkin—he would allow you to make short-term purchases. You needed only to open a small account.

"The whole secret of this type of speculation," Tamkin had told him, "is in the alertness. You have to act fast—buy it and sell it; sell it and buy in again. But quick! Get to the window and have them wire Chicago at just the right second. Strike and strike again! Then get out the same day. In no time at all you turn over fifteen, twenty thousand dollars' worth of soy beans, coffee, corn, hides, wheat, cotton." Obviously the doctor understood the market well. Otherwise he could not make it sound so simple. "People lose because they are greedy and can't get out when it starts to go up. They gamble, but I do it scientifically. This is not guesswork. You must take a few points and get out. Why, ye gods!" said Dr. Tamkin with his bulging eyes, his bald head, and his drooping lip. "Have you stopped to think how much dough people are making in the market?"

Wilhelm with a quick shift from gloomy attention to the panting laugh which entirely changed his face, said, "Ho, have I ever! What do you think? Who doesn't know it's way beyond nineteen-twenty-eight—twenty-nine and still on the rise? Who hasn't read the Fulbright investigation? There's money everywhere. Everyone is shoveling it in. Money is—is—"

"And can you rest—can you sit still while this is going on?" said Dr. Tamkin. "I confess to you I can't. I think about people, just because they have a few bucks to invest, making fortunes. They have no sense, they have no talent, they just have the extra dough and it makes them more dough. I get so worked up and tormented and restless, so restless! I haven't even been able to practice my profession. With all this money around you don't want to be a fool while everyone else is making. I know guys who make five, ten thousand a week just by fooling around. I know a guy at the Hotel Pierre. There's nothing to him, but he has a whole case of Mumm's champagne at lunch. I know another guy on Central Park South—But what's the use of talking. They make millions. They have smart lawyers who get them out of taxes by a thousand schemes."

"Whereas I got taken," said Wilhelm. "My wife refused to sign a joint return. One fairly good year and I got into the thirty-two-per-cent bracket and was stripped bare. What of all my bad years?"

"It's a businessmen's government," said Dr. Tamkin. "You can be sure that these men making five thousand a week—"

"I don't need that sort of money," Wilhelm had said. "But oh! if I could only work out a little steady income from this. Not much. I don't ask much."

But how badly I need—! I'd be so grateful if you'd show me how to work it."

"Sure I will. I do it regularly. I'll bring you my receipts if you like. And do you want to know something? I approve of your attitude very much. You want to avoid catching the money fever. This type of activity is filled with hostile feeling and lust. You should see what it does to some of these fellows. They go on the market with murder in their hearts."

"What's that I once heard a guy say?" Wilhelm remarked. "A man is only as good as what he loves."

"That's it—just it," Tamkin said. "You don't have to go about it their way. There's also a calm and rational, a psychological approach."

Wilhelm's father, old Dr. Adler, lived in an entirely different world from his son, but he had warned him once against Dr. Tamkin. Rather casually— he was a very bland old man—he said, "Wilky, perhaps you listen too much to this Tamkin. He's interesting to talk to. I don't doubt it. I think he's pretty common but he's a persuasive man. However, I don't know how reliable he may be."

It made Wilhelm profoundly bitter that his father should speak to him with such detachment about his welfare. Dr. Adler liked to appear affable. Affable! His own son, his one and only son, could not speak his mind or ease his heart to him. I wouldn't turn to Tamkin, he thought, if I could turn to him. At least Tamkin sympathizes with me and tries to give me a hand, whereas Dad doesn't want to be disturbed.

Old Dr. Adler had retired from practice; he had a considerable fortune and could easily have helped his son. Recently Wilhelm had told him, "Father—it so happens that I'm in a bad way now. I hate to have to say it. You realize that I'd rather have good news to bring you. But it's true. And since it's true, Dad—What else am I supposed to say? It's true."

Another father might have appreciated how difficult this confession was— so much bad luck, weariness, weakness, and failure. Wilhelm had tried to copy the old man's tone and made himself sound gentlemanly, low-voiced, tasteful. He didn't allow his voice to tremble; he made no stupid gesture. But the doctor had no answer. He only nodded. You might have told him that Seattle was near Puget Sound, or that the Giants and Dodgers were playing a night game, so little was he moved from his expression of healthy, handsome, good-humored old age. He behaved toward his son as he had formerly done toward his patients, and it was a great grief to Wilhelm; it was almost too much to bear. Couldn't he see—couldn't he feel? Had he lost his family sense?

Greatly hurt, Wilhelm struggled however to be fair. Old people are bound to change, he said. They have hard things to think about. They must prepare for where they are going. They can't live by the old schedule any longer and all their perspectives change, and other people become alike, kin and acquaintances. Dad is no longer the same person, Wilhelm reflected. He was thirty-two when I was born, and now he's going on eighty. Furthermore, it's time I stopped feeling like a kid toward him, a small son.

The handsome old doctor stood well above the other old people in the hotel. He was idolized by everyone. This was what people said: "That's Old Professor Adler, who used to teach internal medicine. He was a diagnostician, one of the best in New York, and had a tremendous practice. Isn't he a wonderful-looking old guy? It's a pleasure to see such a fine old scientist, clean and immaculate. He stands straight and understands every single thing you say. He still has all his buttons. You can discuss any subject with him." The clerks, the elevator operators, the telephone girls and waitresses and chambermaids, the management flattered and pampered him. That was what he wanted. He had always been a vain man. To see how his father loved himself sometimes made Wilhelm madly indignant.

He folded over the *Tribune* with its heavy, black, crashing sensational print and read without recognizing any of the words, for his mind was still on his father's vanity. The doctor had created his own praise. People were primed and did not know it. And what did he need praise for? In a hotel where everyone was busy and contacts were so brief and had such small weight, how could it satisfy him? He could be in people's thoughts here and there for a moment; in and then out. He could never matter much to them. Wilhelm let out a long, hard breath and raised the brows of his round and somewhat circular eyes. He stared beyond the thick borders of the paper.

. . . love that well which thou must leave ere long.

Involuntary memory brought him this line. At first he thought it referred to his father, but then he understood that it was for himself, rather. *He* should love that well. "This thou perceivest, which makes *thy* love more strong." Under Dr. Tamkin's influence Wilhelm had recently begun to remember the poems he used to read. Dr. Tamkin knew, or said he knew, the great English poets and once in a while he mentioned a poem of his own. It was a long time since anyone had spoken to Wilhelm about this sort of thing. He didn't like to think about his college days, but if there was one course that now made sense it was Literature I. The textbook was Lieder and Lovett's *British Poetry and Prose*, a black heavy book with thin pages. Did I read that? he asked himself. Yes, he had read it and there was one accomplishment at least he could recall with pleasure. He had read "Yet once more, O ye laurels." How pure this was to say! It was beautiful.

Sunk though he be beneath the wat'ry floor . . .

Such things had always swayed him, and now the power of such words was far, far greater.

Wilhelm respected the truth, but he could lie and one of the things he lied often about was his education. He said he was an alumnus of Penn State; in fact he had left school before his sophomore year was finished. His sister Catherine had a B.S. degree. Wilhelm's late mother was a graduate of Bryn Mawr. He was the only member of the family who had no education. This was another sore point. His father was ashamed of him.

But he had heard the old man bragging to another old man, saying, "My son is a sales executive. He didn't have the patience to finish school. But he does all right for himself. His income is up to the five figures somewhere."

"What—thirty, forty thousand?" said his stooped old friend.

"Well, he needs at least that much for his style of life. Yes, he needs that."

Despite his troubles, Wilhelm almost laughed. Why that boasting old hypocrite. He knew the sales executive was no more. For many weeks there had been no executive, no sales, no income. But how we love looking fine in the eyes of the world—how beautiful are the old when they are doing a snow job! It's Dad, thought Wilhelm, who is the salesman. He's selling me. *He* should have gone on the road.

But what of the truth? Ah, the truth was that there were problems, and of these problems his father wanted no part. His father was ashamed of him. The truth, Wilhelm thought, was very awkward. He pressed his lips together, and his tongue went soft; it pained him far at the back, in the cords and throat, and a knot of ill formed in his chest. Dad never was a pal to me when I was young, he reflected. He was at the office or the hospital, or lecturing. He expected me to look out for myself and never gave me much thought. Now he looks down on me. And maybe in some respects he's right.

No wonder Wilhelm delayed the moment when he would have to go into the dining room. He had moved to the end of Rubin's counter. He had opened the *Tribune;* the fresh pages drooped from his hands; the cigar was smoked out and the hat did not defend him. He was wrong to suppose that he was more capable than the next fellow when it came to concealing his troubles. They were clearly written out upon his face. He wasn't even aware of it.

There was the matter of the different names, which, in the hotel, came up frequently, "Are you Doctor Adler's son?" "Yes, but my name is Tommy Wilhelm." And the doctor would say, "My son and I use different monickers. I uphold tradition. He's for the new." The Tommy was Wilhelm's own invention. He adopted it when he went to Hollywood, and dropped the Adler. Hollywood was his own idea, too. He used to pretend that it had all been the doing of a certain talent scout named Maurice Venice. But the scout had never made him a definite offer of a studio connection. He had approached him, but the results of the screen tests had not been good. After the test Wilhelm took the initiative and pressed Maurice Venice until he got him to say, "Well, I suppose you might make it out there." On the strength of this Wilhelm had left college and had gone to California.

Someone had said, and Wilhelm agreed with the saying, that in Los Angeles all the loose objects in the country were collected, as if America had been tilted and everything that wasn't tightly screwed down had slid into Southern California. He himself had been one of these loose objects. Sometimes he told people, "I was too mature for college. I was a big boy, you see. Well, I thought, when do you start to become a man?" After he had driven a painted flivver and had worn a yellow slicker with slogans on it, and played illegal poker, and gone out on Coke dates, he had *had* college. He wanted to try something new and quarreled with his parents about his career. And then a letter came from Maurice Venice.

The story of the scout was long and intricate and there were several versions of it. The truth about it was never told. Wilhelm had lied first boastfully and then out of charity to himself. But his memory was good, he could still separate what he had invented from the actual happenings, and this morning he found it necessary as he stood by Rubin's showcase with his *Tribune* to recall the crazy course of the true events.

I didn't seem even to realize that there was a depression. How could I have been such a jerk as not to prepare for anything and just go on luck and inspiration? With round gray eyes expanded and his large shapely lips closed in severity toward himself he forced open all that had been hidden. Dad I couldn't affect one way or another. Mama was the one who tried to stop me, and we carried on and yelled and pleaded. The more I lied the louder I raised my voice, and charged—like a hippopotamus. Poor Mother! How I disappointed her. Rubin heard Wilhelm give a broken sigh as he stood with the forgotten *Tribune* crushed under his arm.

When Wilhelm was aware that Rubin watched him, loitering and idle, apparently not knowing what to do with himself this morning, he turned to the Coca-Cola machine. He swallowed hard at the coke bottle and coughed over it, but he ignored his coughing, for he was still thinking, his eyes upcast and his lips closed behind his hand. By a peculiar twist of habit he wore his coat collar turned up always, as though there were a wind. It never lay flat. But on his broad back, stooped with its own weight, its strength warped almost into deformity, the collar of his sports coat appeared anyway to be no wider than a ribbon.

He was listening to the sound of his own voice as he explained, twenty-five years ago in the living room on West End Avenue, "But Mother, if I don't pan out as an actor I can still go back to school."

But she was afraid he was going to destroy himself. She said, "Wilky, Dad could make it easy for you if you wanted to go into medicine." To remember this stifled him.

"I can't bear hospitals. Besides, I might make a mistake and hurt someone or even kill a patient. I couldn't stand that. Besides, I haven't got that sort of brains."

Then his mother had made the mistake of mentioning her nephew Artie, Wilhelm's cousin, who was an honor student at Columbia in math and languages. That dark little gloomy Artie with his disgusting narrow face, and his moles and self-sniffing ways and his unclear table manners, the boring habit he had of conjugating verbs when you went for a walk with him. "Roumanian is an easy language. You just add a *tl* to everything." He was now a professor, this same Artie with whom Wilhelm had played near the Soldiers' and Sailors' Monument on Riverside Drive. Not that to be a professor was in itself so great. How could anyone bear to know so many languages? And Artie also had to remain Artie, which was a bad deal. But perhaps success had changed him. Now that he had a place in the world perhaps he was better. Did Artie love his languages, and live for them, or was he also, in his heart, cynical? So many people nowadays were. No one seemed satisfied, and Wilhelm was especially horrified by the cynicism of successful people. Cynicism was bread and meat to everyone. And irony, too. Maybe it couldn't be helped. It was probably even necessary. Wilhelm, however, feared it intensely. Whenever at the end of the day he was unusually fatigued he attributed it to cynicism. Too much of the world's business done. Too much falsity. He had various words to express the effect this had on him. Chicken! Unclean! Congestion! he exclaimed in his heart. Rat race! Phony! Murder! Play the Game! Buggers!

At first the letter from the talent scout was nothing but a flattering sort of joke. Wilhelm's picture in the college paper when he was running for class treasurer was seen by Maurice Venice, who wrote to him about a screen test. Wilhelm at once took the train to New York. He found the scout to be huge and oxlike, so stout that his arms seemed caught from beneath in a grip of flesh and fat; it looked as though it must be positively painful. He had little hair. Yet he enjoyed a healthy complexion. His breath was noisy and his voice rather difficult and husky because of the fat in his throat. He had on a doublebreasted suit of the type then known as the pillbox; it was chalk-striped, pink on blue; the trousers hugged his ankles.

They met and shook hands and sat down. Together these two big men dwarfed the tiny Broadway office and made the furnishings look like toys. Wilhelm had the color of a Golden Grimes apple when he was well, and then his thick blond hair had been vigorous and his wide shoulders unwarped; he was leaner in the jaws, his eyes fresher and wider; his legs were then still awkward but he was impressively handsome. And he was about to make his first great mistake. Like, he sometimes thought, I was going to pick up a weapon and strike myself a blow with it.

Looming over the desk in the small office darkened by overbuilt midtown—sheer walls, gray spaces, dry lagoons of tar and pebbles—Maurice Venice proceeded to establish his credentials. He said, "My letter was on the regular stationery, but maybe you want to check on me?"

"Who, *me?*" said Wilhelm. "Why?"

"There's guys who think I'm in a racket and make a charge for the test. I don't ask a cent. I'm no agent. There ain't no commission."

"I never even thought of it," said Wilhelm. Was there perhaps something fishy about this Maurice Venice? He protested too much.

In his husky, fat-weakened voice he finally challenged Wilhelm, "If you're not sure, you can call the distributor and find out who I am, Maurice Venice."

Wilhelm wondered at him. "Why shouldn't I be sure? Of course I am."

"Because I can see the way you size me up, and because this is a dinky office. Like you don't believe me. Go ahead. Call. I won't care if you're cautious. I mean it. There's quite a few people who doubt me at first. They can't really believe that fame and fortune are going to hit 'em."

"But I tell you I do believe you," Wilhelm had said, and bent inward to accommodate the pressure of his warm, panting laugh. It was purely nervous. His neck was ruddy and neatly shaved about the ears—he was fresh from the barbershop; his face anxiously glowed with his desire to make a pleasing impression. It was all wasted on Venice, who was just as concerned about the impression *he* was making.

"If you're surprised, I'll just show you what I mean," Venice had said. "It was about fifteen months ago right in this identical same office when I saw a beautiful thing in the paper. It wasn't even a photo but a drawing, a brassière ad, but I knew right away that this was star material. I called up the paper to ask who the girl was, they gave me the name of the advertising agency; I phoned the agency and they gave me the name of the artist; I got hold of the artist and he gave me the number of the model agency. Finally, finally I got her number and phoned her and said, 'This is Maurice Venice, scout for Kaskaskia Films.' So right away she says, 'Yah, so's your old lady.' Well, when I saw I wasn't getting nowhere with her I said to her, "well, miss. I don't blame you. You're a very beautiful thing and must have a dozen admirers after you all the time, boy friends who like to call and pull your leg and give a tease. But as I happen to be a very busy fellow and don't have the time to horse around or argue, I tell you what to do. Here's my number, and here's the number of the Kaskaskia Distributors, Inc. Ask them who am I, Maurice Venice. The scout.' She did it. A little while later she phoned me back, all apologies and excuses, but I didn't want to embarrass her and get off on the wrong foot with an artist. I know better than to do that. So I told her it was a natural precaution, never mind. I wanted to run a screen test right away. Because I seldom am wrong about talent. If I see it, it's there. Get that, please. And do you know who that little girl is today?"

"No." Wilhelm said eagerly, "Who is she?"

Venice said impressively, "'Nita Christenberry."

Wilhelm sat utterly blank. This was failure. He didn't know the name, and Venice was waiting for his response and would be angry.

And in fact Venice had been offended. He said, "What's the matter with you! Don't you read a magazine? She's a starlet."

"I'm sorry," Wilhelm answered. "I'm at school and don't have time to keep up. If I don't know her, it doesn't mean a thing. She made a big hit, I'll bet."

"You can say that again. Here's a photo of her." He handed Wilhelm some pictures. She was a bathing beauty—short, the usual breasts, hips, and smooth thighs. Yes, quite good, as Wilhelm recalled. She stood on high heels and wore a Spanish comb and mantilla. In her hand was a fan.

He had said, "She looks awfully peppy."

"Isn't she a divine girl? And what personality! Not just another broad in the show business, believe me." He had a surprise for Wilhelm. "I have found happiness with her," he said.

"You have?" said Wilhelm, slow to understand.

"Yes, boy, we're engaged."

Wilhelm saw another photograph, taken on the beach. Venice was dressed in a terry-cloth beach outfit, and he and the girl, cheek to cheek, were looking into the camera. Below, in white ink, was written "Love at Malibu Colony."

"I'm sure you'll be very happy. I wish you—"

"I *know*," said Venice firmly, "I'm going to be happy. When I saw that drawing, the breath of fate breathed on me. I felt it over my entire body."

"Say, it strikes a bell suddenly," Wilhelm had said. "Aren't you related to Martial Venice the producer?"

Venice was either a nephew of the producer or the son of a first cousin. Decidedly he had not made good. It was easy enough for Wilhelm to see this now. The office was so poor, and Venice bragged so nervously and identified himself so scrupulously—the poor guy. He was the obscure failure of an aggressive and powerful clan. As such he had the greatest sympathy from Wilhelm.

Venice had said, "Now I suppose you want to know where you come in. I seen your school paper, by accident. You take quite a remarkable picture."

"It can't be so much," said Wilhelm, more panting than laughing.

"You don't want to tell me my business," Venice said. "Leave it to me. I studied up on this."

"I never imagined— Well, what kind of roles do you think I'd fit?"

"All this time that we've been talking, I've been watching. Don't think I haven't. You remind me of someone. Let's see who it can be—one of the great old-timers. Is it Milton Sills? No, that's not the one. Conway Tearle, Jack Mulhall? George Bancroft? No, his face was ruggeder. One thing I can tell you, though, a George Raft type you're not—those tough, smooth, black little characters."

"No, I wouldn't seem to be."

"No, you're not that flyweight type, with the fists, from a nightclub, and the glamorous sideburns, doing the tango or the bolero. Not Edward G. Robinson, either—I'm thinking aloud. Or the Cagney fly-in-your-face role, a cabbie, with that mouth and those punches."

"I realize that."

"Not suave like William Powell, or a lyric juvenile like Buddy Rogers. I suppose you don't play the sax? No. But—"

"But what?"

"I have you placed as the type that loses the girl to the George Raft type or the William Powell type. You are steady, faithful, you get stood up. The older women would know better. The mothers are on your side. With what they been through, if it was up to them, they'd take you in a minute. You're very sympathetic, even the young girls feel that. You'd make a good provider. But they go more for the other types. It's as clear as anything."

This was not how Wilhelm saw himself. And as he surveyed the old ground he recognized now that he had been not only confused but hurt. Why, he thought, he cast me even then for a loser.

Wilhelm had said, with half a mind to be defiant, "Is that your opinion?"

It never occurred to Venice that a man might object to stardom in such a role. "Here is your chance," he said. "Now you're just in college. What are you studying?" He snapped his fingers. "Stuff." Wilhelm himself felt this way about it. "You may plug along fifty years before you get anywheres. This way, in one jump, the world knows who you are. You become a name like Roosevelt, Swanson. From east to west, out to China, into South America. This is no bunk. You become a lover to the whole world. The world wants it, needs it. One fellow smiles, a billion people also smile. One fellow cries, the other billion sob with him. Listen, bud—" Venice had pulled himself together to make an effort. On his imagination there was some great weight which he could not discharge. He wanted Wilhelm, too, to feel it. He twisted his large, clean, well-meaning, rather foolish features as though he were their unwilling captive, and said in his choked, fat-obstructed voice, "Listen, everywhere there are people trying hard, miserable, in trouble, downcast, tired, trying and trying. They need a break, right? A break through, a help, luck or sympathy."

"That certainly is the truth," said Wilhelm. He had seized the feeling and he waited for Venice to go on. But Venice had no more to say; he had concluded. He gave Wilhelm several pages of blue hectographed script, stapled together, and told him to prepare for the screen test. "Study your lines in front of a mirror," he said. "Let yourself go. The part should take ahold of you. Don't be afraid to make faces and be emotional. Shoot the works. Because when you start to act you're no more an ordinary person, and those things don't apply to you. You don't behave the same way as the average."

And so Wilhelm had never returned to Penn State. His roommate sent his things to New York for him, and the school authorities had to write to Dr. Adler to find out what had happened.

Still, for three months Wilhelm delayed his trip to California. He wanted to start out with the blessings of his family, but they were never given. He quarreled with his parents and his sister. And then, when he was best aware of the risks and knew a hundred reasons against going and had made himself sick with fear, he left home. This was typical of Wilhelm. After much thought and hesitation and debate he invariably took the course he had rejected innumerable times. Ten such decisions made up the history of his life. He had decided that it would be a bad mistake to go to Hollywood, and then he went. He had made up his mind not to marry his wife, but ran off and got married. He had resolved not to invest money with Tamkin, and then had given him a check.

But Wilhelm had been eager for life to start. College was merely another delay. Venice had approached him and said that the world had named Wilhelm to shine before it. He was to be freed from the anxious and narrow life of the average. Moreover, Venice had claimed that he never made a mistake. His instinct for talent was infallible, he said.

But when Venice saw the results of the screen test he did a quick about-face. In those days Wilhelm had had a speech difficulty. It was not a true stammer, it was a thickness of speech which the sound track exaggerated. The film showed that he had many peculiarities, otherwise unnoticeable. When he shrugged, his hands drew up within his sleeves. The vault of his chest was huge, but he really didn't look strong under the lights. Though he called himself a hippopotamus, he more nearly resembled a bear. His walk was bearlike, quick and rather soft, toes turned inward, as though his shoes were an impediment. About one thing Venice had been right. Wilhelm was photogenic and his wavy blond hair (now graying) came out well but after the test Venice refused to encourage him. He tried to get rid of him. He couldn't afford to take a chance on him, he had made too many mistakes already and lived in fear of his powerful relatives.

Wilhelm had told his parents, "Venice says I owe it to myself to go." How ashamed he was now of this lie! He had begged Venice not to give him up. He had said, "Can't you help me out? It would kill me to go back to school now."

Then when he reached the Coast he learned that a recommendation from Maurice Venice was the kiss of death. Venice needed help and charity more than he, Wilhelm, ever had. A few years later when Wilhelm was down on his luck and working as an orderly in a Los Angeles hospital, he saw Venice's picture in the papers. He was under indictment for pandering. Closely following the trial, Wilhelm found out that Venice had indeed been employed by Kaskaskia Films but that he had evidently made use of the connection to organize a ring of call girls. Then what did he want with me? Wilhelm had cried to himself. He was unwilling to believe anything very bad about Venice. Perhaps he was foolish and unlucky, a fall guy, a dupe, a sucker. You didn't give a man fifteen years in prison for that. Wilhelm often thought that he might write him a letter to say how sorry he was. He remembered the

breath of fate and Venice's certainty that he would be happy. 'Nita Christenberry was sentenced to three years. Wilhelm recognized her although she
had changed her name.

By that time Wilhelm too had taken his new name. In California he
became Tommy Wilhelm. Dr. Adler would not accept the change. Today he
still called his son Wilky, as he had done for more than forty years. Well,
now, Wilhelm was thinking, the paper crowded in disarray under his arm,
there's really very little that a man can change at will. He can't change his
lungs, or nerves, or constitution or temperament. They're not under his
control. When he's young and strong and impulsive and dissatisfied with the
way things are he wants to rearrange them to assert his freedom. He can't
overthrow the government or be differently born; he only has a little scope
and maybe a foreboding, too, that essentially you can't change. Nevertheless,
he makes a gesture and becomes Tommy Wilhelm. Wilhelm had always had
a great longing to be Tommy. He had never, however, succeeded in feeling
like Tommy, and in his soul had always remained Wilky. When he was drunk
he reproached himself horribly as Wilky. "You fool, you clunk, you Wilky!"
he called himself. He thought that it was a good thing perhaps that he had
not become a success as Tommy since that would not have been a genuine
success. Wilhelm would have feared that not he but Tommy had brought it
off, cheating Wilky of his birthright. Yes, it had been a stupid thing to do, but
it was his imperfect judgment at the age of twenty which should be blamed.
He had cast off his father's name, and with it his father's opinion of him. It
was, he knew it was, his bid for liberty, Adler being in his mind the title of
the species, Tommy the freedom of the person. But Wilky was his inescapable self.

In middle age you no longer thought such thoughts about free choice.
Then it came over you that from one grandfather you had inherited such and
such a head of hair which looked like honey when it whitens or sugars in the
jar; from another, broad thick shoulders; an oddity of speech from one
uncle, and small teeth from another, and the gray eyes with darkness diffused even into the whites, and a wide-lipped mouth like a statue from Peru.
Wandering races have such looks, the bones of one tribe, the skin of another.
From his mother he had gotten sensitive feelings, a soft heart, a brooding
nature, and a tendency to be confused under pressure.

The changed name was a mistake, and he would admit it as freely as you
liked. But this mistake couldn't be undone now, so why must his father
continually remind him how he had sinned? It was too late. He would have
to go back to the pathetic day when the sin was committed. And where was
that day? Past and dead. Whose humiliating memories were these? His and
not his father's. What had he to think back on that he could call good? Very,
very little. You had to forgive. First, to forgive yourself, and then general
forgiveness. Didn't he suffer from his mistakes far more than his father
could?

"Oh, God," Wilhelm prayed. "Let me out of my trouble. Let me out of my thoughts, and let me do something better with myself. For all the time I have wasted I am very sorry. Let me out of this clutch and into a different life. For I am all balled up. Have mercy."

II

The mail.

The clerk who gave it to him did not care what sort of appearance he made this morning. He only glanced at him from under his brows, upward, as the letters changed hands. Why should the hotel people waste courtesies on him? They had his number. The clerk knew that he was handing him, along with the letters, a bill for his rent. Wilhelm assumed a look that removed him from all such things. But it was bad. To pay the bill he would have to withdraw money from his brokerage account, and the account was being watched because of the drop in lard. According to the *Tribune*'s figures lard was still twenty points below last year's level. There were government price supports. Wilhelm didn't know how these worked but he understood that the farmer was protected and that the SEC kept an eye on the market and therefore he believed that lard would rise again and he wasn't greatly worried as yet. But in the meantime his father might have offered to pick up his hotel tab. Why didn't he? What a selfish old man he was! He saw his son's hardships; he could so easily help him. How little it would mean to him, and how much to Wilhelm! Where was the old man's heart? Maybe, thought Wilhelm, I was sentimental in the past and exaggerated his kindliness—warm family life. It may never have been there.

Not long ago his father had said to him in his usual affable, pleasant way, "Well, Wilky, here we are under the same roof again, after all these years."

Wilhelm was glad for an instant. At last they would talk over old times. But he was also on guard against insinuations. Wasn't his father saying, "Why are you here in a hotel with me and not at home in Brooklyn with your wife and two boys? You're neither a widower nor a bachelor. You have brought me all your confusions. What do you expect me to do with them?"

So Wilhelm studied the remark for a bit, then said, "The roof is twenty-six stories up. But how many years has it been?"

"That's what I was asking you."

"Gosh, Dad, I'm not sure. Wasn't it the year Mother died? What year was that?"

He asked this question with an innocent frown on his Golden Grimes, dark blond face. *What year was it!* As though he didn't know the year, the month, the day, the very hour of his mother's death.

"Wasn't it nineteen-thirty-one?" said Dr. Adler.

"Oh, was it?" said Wilhelm. And in hiding the sadness and the overwhelming irony of the question he gave a nervous shiver and wagged his head and felt the ends of his collar rapidly.

"Do you know?" his father said. "You must realize, an old fellow's memory becomes unreliable. It was in winter, that I'm sure of. Nineteen-thirty-two?"

Yes, it was age. Don't make an issue of it, Wilhelm advised himself. If you were to ask the old doctor in what year he had interned, he'd tell you correctly. All the same, don't make an issue. Don't quarrel with your own father. Have pity on an old man's failings.

"I believe the year was closer to nineteen-thirty-four, Dad," he said.

But Dr. Adler was thinking, Why the devil can't he stand still when we're talking? He's either hoisting his pants up and down by the pockets or jittering with his feet. A regular mountain of tics, he's getting to be. Wilhelm had a habit of moving his feet back and forth as though, hurrying into a house, he had to clean his shoes first on the doormat.

Then Wilhelm had said, "Yes, that was the beginning of the end, wasn't it, Father?"

Wilhelm often astonished Dr. Adler. Beginning of the end? What could he mean—what was he fishing for? Whose end? The end of family life? The old man was puzzled but he would not give Wilhelm an opening to introduce his complaints. He had learned that it was better not to take up Wilhelm's strange challenges. So he merely agreed pleasantly, for he was a master of social behavior, and said, "It was an awful misfortune for us all."

He thought, What business has he to complain to *me* of his mother's death?

Face to face they had stood, each declaring himself silently after his own way. It was: it was not, the beginning of the end—*some* end.

Unaware of anything odd in his doing it, for he did it all the time, Wilhelm had pinched out the coal of his cigarette and dropped the butt in his pocket, where there were many more. And as he gazed at his father the little finger of his right hand began to twitch and tremble; of that he was unconscious, too.

And yet Wilhelm believed that when he put his mind to it he could have perfect and even distinguished manners, outdoing his father. Despite the slight thickness in his speech—it amounted almost to a stammer when he started the same phrase over several times in his effort to eliminate the thick sound—he could be fluent. Otherwise he would never have made a good salesman. He claimed also that he was a good listener. When he listened he made a tight mouth and rolled his eyes thoughtfully. He would soon tire and begin to utter short, loud, impatient breaths, and he would say, "Oh yes . . . yes . . . yes. I couldn't agree more." When he was forced to differ he would declare, "Well, I'm not sure. I don't really see it that way. I'm of two minds about it." He would never willingly hurt any man's feelings.

But in conversation with his father he was apt to lose control of himself. After any talk with Dr. Adler, Wilhelm generally felt dissatisfied, and his dissatisfaction reached its greatest intensity when they discussed family matters. Ostensibly he had been trying to help the old man to remember a date, but in reality he meant to tell him, "You were set free when Ma died. You wanted to forget her. You'd like to get rid of Catherine, too. Me, too. You're not kidding anyone"—Wilhelm striving to put this across, and the old man not having it. In the end he was left struggling, while his father seemed unmoved.

And then once more Wilhelm had said to himself, "But man! you're not a kid. Even then you weren't a kid!" He looked down over the front of his big, indecently big, spoiled body. He was beginning to lose his shape, his gut was fat, and he looked like a hippopotamus. His younger son called him "a hummuspotamus"; that was little Paul. And here he was still struggling with his old dad, filled with ancient grievances. Instead of saying, "Good-by, youth! Oh, good-by those marvelous, foolish wasted days. What a big clunk I was—I *am.*"

Wilhelm was still paying heavily for his mistakes. His wife Margaret would not give him a divorce, and he had to support her and the two children. She would regularly agree to divorce him, and then think things over again and set new and more difficult conditions. No court would have awarded her the amounts he paid. One of today's letters, as he had expected, was from her. For the first time he had sent her a postdated check, and she protested. She also enclosed bills for the boys' educational insurance policies, due next week. Wilhelm's mother-in-law had taken out these policies in Beverly Hills, and since her death two years ago he had to pay the premiums. Why couldn't she have minded her own business! They were his kids, and he took care of them and always would. He had planned to set up a trust fund. But that was on his former expectations. Now he had to rethink the future, because of the money problem. Meanwhile, here were the bills to be paid. When he saw the two sums punched out so neatly on the cards he cursed the company and its IBM equipment. His heart and his head were congested with anger. Everyone was supposed to have money. It was nothing to the company. It published pictures of funerals in the magazines and frightened the suckers, and then punched out little holes, and the customers would lie awake to think out ways to raise the dough. They'd be ashamed not to have it. They couldn't let a great company down, either, and they got the scratch. In the old days a man was put in prison for debt, but there were subtler things now. They made it a shame not to have money and set everybody to work.

Well, and what else had Margaret sent him? He tore the envelope open with his thumb, swearing that he would send any other bills back to her. There was, luckily, nothing more. He put the hole-punched cards in his pocket. Didn't Margaret know that he was nearly at the end of his rope? Of course. Her instinct told her that this was her opportunity, and she was giving him the works.

He went into the dining room, which was under Austro-Hungarian management at the Hotel Gloriana. It was run like a European establishment. The pastries were excellent, especially the strudel. He often had apple strudel and coffee in the afternoon.

As soon as he entered he saw his father's small head in the sunny bay at the farther end, and heard his precise voice. It was with an odd sort of perilous expression that Wilhelm crossed the dining room.

Dr. Adler liked to sit in a corner that looked across Broadway down to the Hudson and New Jersey. On the other side of the street was a supermodern cafeteria with gold and purple mosaic columns. On the second floor a private-eye school, a dental laboratory, a reducing parlor, a veteran's club, and a Hebrew school shared the space. The old man was sprinkling sugar on his strawberries. Small hoops of brilliance were cast by the water glasses on the white tablecloth, despite a faint murkiness in the sunshine. It was early summer, and the long window was turned inward; a moth was on the pane; the putty was broken and the white enamel on the frames was streaming with wrinkles.

"Ha, Wilky," said the old man to his tardy son. "You haven't met our neighbor Mr. Perls, have you? From the fifteenth floor."

"How d'do," Wilhelm said. He did not welcome this stranger; he began at once to find fault with him. Mr. Perls carried a heavy cane with a crutch tip. Dyed hair, a skinny forehead—these were not reasons for bias. Nor was it Mr. Perls's fault that Dr. Adler was using him, not wishing to have breakfast with his son alone. But a gruffer voice within Wilhelm spoke, asking "Who is this damn frazzle-faced herring with his dyed hair and his fish teeth and this drippy mustache? Another one of Dad's German friends. Where does he collect all these guys? What is the stuff on his teeth? I never saw such pointed crowns. Are they stainless steel, or a kind of silver? How can a human face get into this condition. Uch!" Staring with his widely spaced gray eyes, Wilhelm sat, his broad back stooped under the sports jacket. He clasped his hands on the table with an implication of suppliance. Then he began to relent a little toward Mr. Perls, beginning at the teeth. Each of those crowns represented a tooth ground to the quick, and estimating a man's grief with his teeth as two per cent of the total, and adding to that his flight from Germany and the probable origin of his wincing wrinkles, not to be confused with the wrinkles of his smile, it came to a sizable load.

"Mr. Perls was a hosiery wholesaler," said Dr. Adler.

"Is this the son you told me was in the selling line?" said Mr. Perls.

Dr. Adler replied, "I have only this one son. One daughter. She was a medical technician before she got married—anesthetist. At one time she had an important position in Mount Sinai."

He couldn't mention his children without boasting. In Wilhelm's opinion, there was little to boast of. Catherine, like Wilhelm, was big and fair-haired. She had married a court reporter who had a pretty hard time of it. She had taken a professional name, too—Philippa. At forty she was still ambitious to become a painter. Wilhelm didn't venture to criticize her work. It didn't do much to him he said, but then he was no critic. Anyway, he and his sister were generally on the outs and he didn't often see her paintings. She worked very hard, but there were fifty thousand people in New York with paints and brushes, each practically a law unto himself. It was the Tower of Babel in paint. *He* didn't want to go far into this. Things were chaotic all over.

Dr. Adler thought that Wilhelm looked particularly untidy this morning—unrested, too, his eyes red-rimmed from excessive smoking. He was breathing through his mouth and he was evidently much distracted and rolled his red-shot eyes barbarously. As usual, his coat collar was turned up as though he had to go out in the rain. When he went to business he pulled himself together a little; otherwise he let himself go and looked like hell.

"What's the matter, Wilky, didn't you sleep last night?"

"Not very much."

"You take too many pills of every kind—first stimulants and then depressants, anodynes followed by analeptics, until the poor organism doesn't know what's happened. Then the luminal won't put people to sleep, and the Pervitin or Benzedrine won't wake them. God knows! These things get to be as serious as poisons, and yet everyone puts all their faith in them."

"No, Dad, it's not the pills. It's that I'm not used to New York any more. For a native, that's very peculiar, isn't it? It was never so noisy at night as now, and every little thing is a strain. Like the alternate parking. You have to run out at eight to move your car. And where can you put it? If you forget for a minute they tow you away. Then some fool puts advertising leaflets under your windshield wiper and you have heart failure a block away because you think you've got a ticket. When you do get stung with a ticket, you can't argue. You haven't got a chance in court and the city wants the revenue."

"But in your line you have to have a car, eh?" said Mr. Perls.

"Lord knows why any lunatic would want one in the city who didn't need it for his livelihood."

Wilhelm's old Pontiac was parked in the street. Formerly, when on an expense account, he had always put it up in a garage. Now he was afraid to move the car from Riverside Drive lest he lose his space, and he used it only on Saturdays when the Dodgers were playing in Ebbets Field and he took his boys to the game. Last Saturday, when the Dodgers were out of town, he had gone out to visit his mother's grave.

Dr. Adler had refused to go along. He couldn't bear his son's driving. Forgetfully, Wilhelm traveled for miles in second gear; he was seldom in the right lane and he neither gave signals nor watched for lights. The upholstery of his Pontiac was filthy with grease and ashes. One cigarette burned in the ashtray, another in his hand, a third on the floor with maps and other waste paper and Coca-Cola bottles. He dreamed at the wheel or argued and gestured, and therefore the old doctor would not ride with him.

Then Wilhelm had come back from the cemetery angry because the stone bench between his mother's and his grandmother's graves had been overturned and broken by vandals. "Those damn teen-age hoodlums get worse and worse," he said. "Why, they must have used a sledgehammer to break the seat smack in half like that. If I could catch one of them!" He wanted the doctor to pay for a new seat, but his father was cool to the idea. He said he was going to have himself cremated.

Mr. Perls said, "I don't blame you if you get no sleep up where you are." His voice was turned somewhat sharp, as though he were slightly deaf. "Don't you have Parigi the singing teacher there? God, they have some queer elements in this hotel. On which floor is that Estonian woman with all her cats and dogs? They should have made her leave long ago."

"They've moved her down to twelve," said Dr. Adler.

Wilhelm ordered a large Coca-Cola with his breakfast. Working in secret at the small envelopes in his pocket, he found two pills by touch. Much fingering had worn and weakened the paper. Under cover of a napkin he swallowed a Phenaphen sedative and a Unicap, but the doctor was sharp-eyed and said, "Wilky, what are you taking now?"

"Just my vitamin pills." He put his cigar butt in an ashtray on the table behind him, for his father did not like the odor. Then he drank his Coca-Cola.

"That's what you drink for breakfast, and not orange juice?" said Mr. Perls. He seemed to sense that he would not lose Dr. Adler's favor by taking an ironic tone with his son.

"The caffeine stimulates brain activity," said the old doctor. "It does all kinds of things to the respiratory center."

"It's just a habit of the road, that's all," Wilhelm said. "If you drive around long enough it turns your brains, your stomach, and everything else."

His father explained, "Wilky used to be with the Rojax Corporation. He was their northeastern sales representative for a good many years but recently ended the connection."

"Yes," said Wilhelm, "I was with them from the end of the war." He sipped the Coca-Cola and chewed the ice, glancing at one and the other with his attitude of large, shaky, patient dignity. The waitress set two boiled eggs before him.

"What kind of line does this Rojax company manufacture?" said Mr. Perls.

"Kiddies' furniture. Little chairs, rockers, tables, Jungle-Gyms, slides, swings, seesaws."

Wilhelm let his father do the explaining. Large and stiff-backed, he tried to sit patiently, but his feet were abnormally restless. All right! His father had to impress Mr. Perls? He would go along once more, and play his part. Fine! He would play along and help his father maintain his style. Style was the main consideration. That was just fine!

"I was with the Rojax Corporation for almost ten years," he said. "We parted ways because they wanted me to share my territory. They took a son-in-law into the business—a new fellow. It was his idea."

To himself, Wilhelm said, Now God alone can tell why I have to lay my whole life bare to this blasted herring here. I'm sure nobody else does' it. Other people keep their business to themselves. Not me.

He continued, "But the rationalization was that it was too big a territory for one man. I had a monopoly. That wasn't so. The real reason was that they had gotten to the place where they would have to make me an officer of the corporation. Vice presidency. I was in line for it, but instead this son-in-law got in, and—"

Dr. Adler thought Wilhelm was discussing his grievances much too openly and said, "My son's income was up in the five figures."

As soon as money was mentioned, Mr. Perls's voice grew eagerly sharper. "Yes? What, the thirty-two-per-cent bracket? Higher even, I guess?" He asked for a hint, and he named the figures not idly but with a sort of hugging relish. Uch! How they love money, thought Wilhelm. They adore money! Holy money! Beautiful money! It was getting so that people were feeble-minded about everything except money. While if you didn't have it you were a dummy, a dummy! You had to excuse yourself from the face of the earth. Chicken! that's what it was. The world's business. If only he could find a way out of it.

Such thinking brought on the usual congestion. It would grow into a fit of passion if he allowed it to continue. Therefore he stopped talking and began to eat.

Before he struck the egg with his spoon he dried the moisture with his napkin. Then he battered it (in his father's opinion) more than was necessary. A faint grime was left by his fingers on the white of the egg after he had picked away the shell. Dr. Adler saw it with silent repugnance. What a Wilky he had given to the world! Why, he didn't even wash his hands in the morning. He used an electric razor so that he didn't have to touch water. The doctor couldn't bear Wilky's dirty habits. Only once—and never again, he swore—had he visited his room. Wilhelm, in pajamas and stockings had sat on his bed, drinking gin from a coffee mug and rooting for the Dodgers on television. "That's two and two on you, Duke. Come on—hit it, now." He came down on the mattress—bam! The bed looked kicked to pieces. Then he drank the gin as though it were tea, and urged his team on with his fist. The smell of dirty clothes was outrageous. By the bedside lay a quart bottle and foolish magazines and mystery stories for the hours of insomnia. Wilhelm lived in worse filth than a savage. When the doctor spoke to him about this he answered, "Well, I have no wife to look after my things." And who— *who!*—had done the leaving? Not Margaret. The doctor was certain that she wanted him back.

Wilhelm drank his coffee with a trembling hand. In his full face his abused bloodshot gray eyes moved back and forth. Jerkily he set his cup back and put half the length of a cigarette into his mouth; he seemed to hold it with his teeth, as though it were a cigar.

"I can't let them get away with it," he said. "It's also a question of morale."

His father corrected him. "Don't you mean a moral question, Wilky?"

"I mean that, too. I have to do something to protect myself. I was promised executive standing." Correction before a stranger mortified him, and his dark blond face changed color, more pale, and then more dark. He went on talking to Perls but his eyes spied on his father. "I was the one who opened the territory for them. I could go back for one of their competitors and take away their customers. *My* customers. Morale enters into it because they've tried to take away my confidence."

"Would you offer a different line to the same people?" Mr. Perls wondered.

"Why not? I know what's wrong with the Rojax product."

"Nonsense," said his father. "Just nonsense and kid's talk, Wilky. You're only looking for trouble and embarrassment that way. What would you gain by such a silly feud? You have to think about making a living and meeting your obligations."

Hot and bitter, Wilhelm said with pride, while his feet moved angrily under the table, "I don't have to be told about my obligations. I've been meeting them for years. In more than twenty years I've never had a penny of help from anybody. I preferred to dig a ditch on the WPA but never asked anyone to meet my obligations for me."

"Wilky has had all kinds of experiences," said Dr. Adler.

The old doctor's face had a wholesome reddish and almost translucent color, like a ripe apricot. The wrinkles beside his ears were deep because the skin conformed so tightly to his bones. With all his might, he was a healthy and fine small old man. He wore a white vest of a light check pattern. His hearing-aid doodad was in the pocket. An unusual shirt of red and black stripes covered his chest. He bought his clothes in a college shop farther uptown. Wilhelm thought he had no business to get himself up like a jockey, out of respect for his profession.

"Well," said Mr. Perls. "I can understand how you feel. You want to fight it out. By a certain time of life, to have to start all over again can't be a pleasure, though a good man can always do it. But anyway you want to keep on with a business you know already, and not have to meet a whole lot of new contacts."

Wilhelm again thought, Why does it have to be me and my life that's discussed, and not him and his life? He would never allow it. But I am an idiot. I have no reserve. To me it can be done. I talk. I must ask for it. Everybody wants to have intimate conversations, but the smart fellows don't give out, only the fools. The smart fellows talk intimately about the fools, and examine them all over and give them advice. Why do I allow it? The hint about his age had hurt him. No, you can't admit it's as good as ever, he conceded. Things do give out.

"In the meanwhile," Dr. Adler said, "Wilky is taking it easy and considering various propositions. Isn't that so?"

"More or less," said Wilhelm. He suffered his father to increase Mr. Perls's respect for him. The WPA ditch had brought the family into contempt. He was a little tired. The spirit, the peculiar burden of his existence lay upon him like an accretion, a load, a hump. In any moment of quiet, when sheer fatigue prevented him from struggling, he was apt to feel this mysterious weight, this growth or collection of nameless things which it was the business of his life to carry about. That must be what a man was for. This large, odd, excited, fleshy, blond, abrupt personality named Wilhelm, or Tommy, was here, present, in the present—Dr. Tamkin had been putting into his mind many suggestions about the present moment, the here and now—this Wilky, or Tommy Wilhelm, forty-four years old, father of two sons, at present living in the Hotel Gloriana, was assigned to be the carrier of a load which was his own self, his characteristic self. There was no figure or estimate for the value of this load. But it is probably exaggerated by the subject, T. W. Who is a visionary sort of animal. Who has to believe that he can know why he exists. Though he has never seriously tried to find out why.

Mr. Perls said, "If he wants time to think things over and have a rest, why doesn't he run down to Florida for a while? Off season it's cheap and quiet. Fairyland. The mangoes are just coming in. I got two acres down there. You'd think you were in India."

Mr. Perls utterly astonished Wilhelm when he spoke of fairyland with a foreign accent. Mangoes—India? What did he mean, India?

"Once upon a time," said Wilhelm, "I did some public-relations work for a big hotel down in Cuba. If I could get them a notice in Leonard Lyons or one of the other columns it might be good for another holiday there, gratis. I haven't had a vacation for a long time, and I could stand a rest after going so hard. You know that's true, Father." He meant that his father knew how deep the crisis was becoming; how badly he was strapped for money; and that he could not rest but would be crushed if he stumbled; and that his obligations would destroy him. He couldn't falter. He thought. The money! When I had it, I flowed money. They bled it away from me. I hemorrhaged money. But now it's almost all gone, and where am I supposed to turn for more?

He said, "As a matter of fact, Father, I am tired as hell."

But Mr. Perls began to smile and said, "I understand from Doctor Tamkin that you're going into some kind of investment with him, partners."

"You know, he's a very ingenious fellow," said Dr. Adler. "I really enjoy hearing him go on. I wonder if he really is a medical doctor."

"Isn't he?" said Perls. "Everybody thinks he is. He talks about his patients. Doesn't he write prescriptions?"

"I don't really know what he does," said Dr. Adler. "He's a cunning man."

"He's a psychologist, I understand," said Wilhelm.

"I don't know what sort of psychologist or psychiatrist he may be," said his father. "He's a little vague. It's growing into a major industry, and a very expensive one. Fellows have to hold down very big jobs in order to pay those fees. Anyway, this Tamkin is clever. He never said he practiced here, but I believe he was a doctor in California. They don't seem to have much legislation out there to cover these things, and I hear a thousand dollars will get you a degree from a Los Angeles correspondence school. He gives the impression of knowing something about chemistry, and things like hypnotism. I wouldn't trust him, though."

"And why wouldn't you?" Wilhelm demanded.

"Because he's probably a liar. Do you believe he invented all the things he claims?"

Mr. Perls was grinning.

"He was written up in *Fortune*," said Wilhelm. "Yes, in *Fortune* magazine. He showed me the article. I've seen his clippings."

"That doesn't make him legitimate," said Dr. Adler. "It might have been another Tamkin. Make no mistake, he's an operator. Perhaps even crazy."

"Crazy, you say?"

Mr. Perls put in. "He could be both sane and crazy. In these days nobody can tell for sure which is which."

"An electrical device for truck drivers to wear in their caps," said Dr. Adler, describing one of Tamkin's proposed inventions. "To wake them with a shock when they begin to be drowsy at the wheel. It's triggered by the change in blood-pressure when they start to doze."

"It doesn't sound like such an impossible thing to me," said Wilhelm.

Mr. Perls said, "To me he described an underwater suit so a man could walk on the bed of the Hudson in case of an atomic attack. He said he could walk to Albany in it."

"Ha, ha, ha, ha, ha!" cried Dr. Adler in his old man's voice. "Tamkin's Folly. You could go on a camping trip under Niagara Falls."

"This is just his kind of fantasy," said Wilhelm. "It doesn't mean a thing. Inventors are supposed to be like that. I get funny ideas myself. Everybody wants to make something. Any American does."

But his father ignored this and said to Perls, "What other inventions did he describe?"

While the frazzle-faced Mr. Perls and his father in the unseemly, monkey-striped shirt were laughing, Wilhelm could not restrain himself and joined in with his own panting laugh. But he was in despair. They were laughing at the man to whom he had given a power of attorney over his last seven hundred dollars to speculate for him in the commodities market. They had bought all that lard. It had to rise today. By ten o'clock, or half-past ten, trading would be active, and he would see.

III

Between white tablecloths and glassware and glancing silverware, through overfull light, the long figure of Mr. Perls went away into the darkness of the lobby. He thrust with his cane, and dragged a large builtup shoe which Wilhelm had not included in his estimate of troubles. Dr. Adler wanted to talk about him. "There's a poor man," he said, "with a bone condition which is gradually breaking him up."

"One of those progressive diseases?" said Wilhelm.

"Very bad. I've learned," the doctor told him, "to keep my sympathy for the real ailments. This Perls is more to be pitied than any man I know."

Wilhelm understood he was being put on notice and did not express his opinion. He ate and ate. He did not hurry but kept putting food on his plate until he had gone through the muffins and his father's strawberries, and then some pieces of bacon that were left; he had several cups of coffee, and when he was finished he sat gigantically in a state of arrest and didn't seem to know what he should do next.

For a while father and son were uncommonly still. Wilhelm's preparation to please Dr. Adler had failed completely, for the old man kept thinking, You'd never guess he had a clean upbringing, and, What a dirty devil this son of mine is. Why can't he try to sweeten his appearance a little? Why does he want to drag himself like this? And he makes himself look so idealistic.

Wilhelm sat, mountainous. He was not really so slovenly as his father found him to be. In some aspects he even had a certain delicacy. His mouth, though broad, had a fine outline, and his brow and his gradually incurved nose, dignity, and in his blond hair there was white but there were also shades of gold and chestnut. When he was with the Rojax Corporation Wilhelm had kept a small apartment in Roxbury, two rooms in a large house with a small porch and garden, and on mornings of leisure, in late spring weather like this, he used to sit expanded in a wicker chair with the sunlight pouring through the weave, and sunlight through the slug-eaten holes of the young hollyhocks and as deeply as the grass allowed into small flowers. This peace (he forgot that that time had had its troubles, too), this peace was gone. It must not have belonged to him, really, for to be here in New York with his old father was more genuinely like his life. He was well aware that he didn't stand a chance of getting sympathy from his father, who said he kept his for real ailments. Moreover, he advised himself repeatedly not to discuss his vexatious problems with him, for his father, with some justice, wanted to be left in peace. Wilhelm also knew that when he began to talk about these things he made himself feel worse, he became congested with them and worked himself into a clutch. Therefore he warned himself, Lay off, pal. It'll only be an aggravation. From a deeper source, however, came other promptings. If he didn't keep his troubles before him he risked losing them altogether, and he knew by experience that this was worse. And furthermore, he could not succeed in excusing his father on the ground of old age. No. No, he could not. I am his son, he thought. He is my father. He is as much father as I am son—old or not. Affirming this, though in complete silence, he sat, and, sitting, he kept his father at the table with him.

"Wilky," said the old man, "have you gone down to the baths here yet?"

"No, Dad, not yet?"

"Well, you know the Gloriana has one of the finest pools in New York. Eighty feet, blue tile. It's a beauty."

Wilhelm had seen it. On the way to the gin game you passed the stairway to the pool. He did not care for the odor of the wall-locked and chlorinated water.

"You ought to investigate the Russian and Turkish baths, and the sunlamps and massage. I don't hold with sunlamps. But the massage does a world of good, and there's nothing better than hydrotherapy when you come right down to it. Simple water has a calming effect and would do you more good than all the barbiturates and alcohol in the world."

Wilhelm reflected that this advice was as far as his father's help and sympathy would extend.

"I thought," he said, "that the water cure was for lunatics."

The doctor received this as one of his son's jokes and said with a smile, "Well, it won't turn a sane man into a lunatic. It does a great deal for me. I couldn't live without my massages and steam."

"You're probably right. I ought to try it one of these days. Yesterday, late in the afternoon, my head was about to bust and I just had to have a little air, so I walked around the reservoir, and I sat down for a while in a playground. It rests me to watch the kids play potsy and skiprope."

The doctor said with approval, "Well, now, that's more like the idea."

"It's the end of the lilacs," said Wilhelm. "When they burn it's the beginning of the summer. At least, in the city. Around the time of year when the candy stores take down the windows and start to sell sodas on the sidewalk. But even though I was raised here, Dad, I can't take city life any more, and I miss the country. There's too much push here for me. It works me up too much. I take things too hard. I wonder why you never retired to a quieter place."

The doctor opened his small hand on the table in a gesture so old and so typical that Wilhelm felt it like an actual touch upon the foundations of his life. "I am a city boy myself, you must remember," Dr. Adler explained. "But if you find the city so hard on you, you ought to get out."

"I'll do that," said Wilhelm, "as soon as I can make the right connection. Meanwhile—"

His father interrupted, "Meanwhile I suggest you cut down on drugs."

"You exaggerate that, Dad. I don't really—I give myself a little boost against—" He almost pronounced the word "misery" but he kept his resolution not to complain.

The doctor, however, fell into the error of pushing his advice too hard. It was all he had to give his son and he gave it once more. "Water and exercise," he said.

He wants a young, smart, successful son, thought Wilhelm, and he said, "Oh, Father, it's nice of you to give me this medical advice, but steam isn't going to cure what ails me."

The doctor measurably drew back, warned by the sudden weak strain of Wilhelm's voice and all that the droop of his face, the swell of his belly against the restraint of his belt intimated.

"Some new business?" he asked unwillingly.

Wilhelm made a preliminary summary which involved the whole of his body. He drew and held a long breath, and his color changed and his eyes swam. "New?" he said.

"You make too much of your problems," said the doctor. "They ought not to be turned into a career. Concentrate on real troubles—fatal sickness, accidents." The old man's whole manner said, Wilky, don't start this on me. I have a right to be spared.

Wilhelm himself prayed for restraint; he knew this weakness of his and fought it. He knew, also, his father's character. And he began mildly, "As far as the fatal part of it goes, everyone on this side of the grave is the same distance from death. No. I guess my trouble is not exactly new. I've got to pay premiums on two policies for the boys. Margaret sent them to me. She unloads everything on me. Her mother left her an income. She won't even file a joint tax return. I get stuck. Etcetera. But you've heard the whole story before."

"I certainly have," said the old man. "And I've told you to stop giving her so much money."

Wilhelm worked his lips in silence before he could speak. The congestion was growing. "Oh, but my kids, Father. My kids. I love them. I don't want them to lack anything."

The doctor said with a half-deaf benevolence, "Well, naturally. And she, I'll bet, is the beneficiary of that policy."

"Let her be. I'd sooner die myself before I collected a cent of such money."

"Ah yes," The old man sighed. He did not like the mention of death. "Did I tell you that your sister Catherine—Philippa—is after me again."

"What for?"

"She wants to rent a gallery for an exhibition."

Stiffly fair-minded, Wilhelm said, "Well, of course that's up to you, Father."

The round-headed old man with his fine, feather-white, ferny hair said, "No, Wilky. There's not a thing on those canvases. I don't believe it; it's a case of the emperor's clothes. I may be old enough for my second childhood, but at least the first is well behind me. I was glad enough to buy crayons for her when she was four. But now she's a woman of forty and too old to be encouraged in her delusions. She's no painter."

"I wouldn't go so far as to call her a born artist," said Wilhelm, "but you can't blame her for trying something worth while."

"Let her husband pamper her."

Wilhelm had done his best to be just to his sister, and he had sincerely meant to spare his father, but the old man's tight, benevolent deafness had its usual effect on him. He said, "When it comes to women and money, I'm completely in the dark. What makes Margaret act like this?"

"She's showing you that you can't make it without her," said the doctor. "She aims to bring you back by financial force."

"But if she ruins me, Dad, how can she expect me to come back? No, I have a sense of honor. What you don't see is that she's trying to put an end to me."

His father stared. To him this was absurd. And Wilhelm thought, Once a guy starts to slip, he figures he might as well be a clunk. A real big clunk. He even takes pride in it. But there's nothing to be proud of—hey, boy? Nothing. I don't blame Dad for his attitude. And it's no cause for pride.

"I don't understand that. But if you feel like this why don't you settle with her once and for all?"

"What do you mean, Dad?" said Wilhelm, surprised. "I thought I told you. Do you think I'm not willing to settle? Four years ago when we broke up I gave her everything—goods, furniture, savings. I tried to show good will, but I didn't get anywhere. Why when I wanted Scissors, the dog, because the animal and I were so attached to each other—it was bad enough to leave the kids—she absolutely refused me. Not that she cared a damn about the animal. I don't think you've seen him. He's an Australian sheep dog. They usually have one blank or whitish eye which gives a misleading look, but they're the gentlest dogs and have unusual delicacy about eating or talking. Let me at least have the companionship of this animal. Never." Wilhelm was greatly moved. He wiped his face at all corners with his napkin. Dr. Adler felt that his son was indulging himself too much in his emotions.

"Whenever she can hit me, she hits, and she seems to live for that alone. And she demands more and more, and still more. Two years ago she wanted to go back to college and get another degree. It increased my burden but I thought it would be wiser in the end if she got a better job through it. But still she takes as much from me as before. Next thing she'll want to be a Doctor of Philosophy. She says the women in her family live long, and I'll have to pay and pay for the rest of my life."

The doctor said impatiently, "Well, these are details, not principles. Just details which you can leave out. The dog! You're mixing up all kinds of irrelevant things. Go to a good lawyer."

"But I've already told you, Dad, I got a lawyer, and she got one, too, and both of them talk and send me bills, and I eat my heart out. Oh, Dad, Dad,· what a hole I'm in!" said Wilhelm in utter misery. "The lawyers—see?— draw up an agreement, and she says okay on Monday and wants more money on Tuesday. And it begins again."

"I always thought she was a strange kind of woman," said Dr. Adler. He felt that by disliking Margaret from the first and disapproving of the marriage he had done all that he could be expected to do.

"Strange, Father? I'll show you what she's like." Wilhelm took hold of his broad throat with brown-stained fingers and bitten nails and began to choke himself.

"What are you doing?" cried the old man.

"I'm showing you what she does to me."

"Stop that—stop it!" the old man said and tapped the table commandingly.

"Well, Dad, she hates me. I feel that she's strangling me. I can't catch my breath. She just has fixed herself on me to kill me. She can do it at long distance. One of these days I'll be struck down by suffocation or apoplexy because of her. I just can't catch my breath."

"Take your hands off your throat, you foolish man," said his father. "Stop this bunk. Don't expect me to believe in all kinds of voodoo."

"If that's what you want to call it, all right." His face flamed and paled and swelled and his breath was laborious.

"But I'm telling you that from the time I met her I've been a slave. The Emancipation Proclamation was only for colored people. A husband like me is a slave, with an iron collar. The churches go up to Albany and supervise the law. They won't have divorces. The court says, 'You want to be free. Then you have to work twice as hard—twice, at least! Work! you bum.' So then guys kill each other for the buck, and they may be free of a wife who hates them but they are sold to the company. The company knows a guy has got to have his salary, and takes full advantage of him. Don't talk to me about being free. A rich man may be free on an income of a million net. A poor man may be free because nobody cares what he does. But a fellow in my position has to sweat it out until he drops dead."

His father replied to this, "Wilky, it's entirely your own fault. You don't have to allow it."

Stopped in his eloquence, Wilhelm could not speak for a while. Dumb and incompetent, he struggled for breath and frowned with effort into his father's face.

"I dont't understand your problems, " said the old man. "I never had any like them."

By now Wilhelm had lost his head and he waved his hands and said over and over, "Oh, Dad, don't give me that stuff, don't give me that. Please don't give me that sort of thing."

"It's true," said his father. "I come from a different world. Your mother and I led an entirely different life."

"Oh, how can you compare Mother," Wilhelm said. "Mother was a help to you. Did she harm you ever?"

"There's no need to carry on like an opera, Wilky," said the doctor. "This is only your side of things."

"What? It's the truth." said Wilhelm.

The old man could not be persuaded and shook his round head and drew his vest down over the gilded shirt, and leaned back with a completeness of style that made this look, to anyone out of hearing, like an ordinary conversation between a middle-aged man and his respected father. Wilhelm towerd and swayed, big and sloven, with his gray eyes red-shot and his honey-colored hair twisted in flaming shapes upward. Injustice made him angry, made him beg. But he wanted an understanding with his father, and he tried to capitulate to him. He said, "You can't compare Mother and Margaret, and neither can you and I be compared, because you, Dad, were a success. And a success—is a success. I never made a success."

The doctor's old face lost all of its composure and became hard and angry. His small breast rose sharply under the red and black shirt and he said, "Yes. Because of hard work. I was not self-indulgent, not lazy. My old man sold dry goods in Williamsburg. We were nothing, do you understand? I knew I couldn't afford to waste my chances."

"I wouldn't admit for one minute that I was lazy," said Wilhelm. "If anything, I tried too hard. I admit I made many mistakes. Like I thought I shouldn't do things you had done already. Study chemistry. You had done it already. It was in the family."

His father continued, "I didn't run around with fifty women, either. I was not a Hollywood star. I didn't have time to go to Cuba for a vacation. I stayed at home and took care of my children."

Oh, thought Wilhelm, eyes turning upward. Why did I come here in the first place, to live near him? New York is like a gas. The colors are running. My head feels so tight, I don't know what I'm doing. He thinks I want to take away his money or that I envy him. He doesn't see what I want.

"Dad," Wilhelm said aloud, "you're being very unfair. It's true the movies was a false step. But I love my boys. I didn't abandon them. I left Margaret because I had to."

"Why did you have to?"

"Well—" said Wilhelm, struggling to condense his many reasons into a few plain words. "I had to—I had to."

With sudden and surprising bluntness his father said, "Did you have bed-trouble with her? Then you should have stuck it out. Sooner or later everyone has it. Normal people stay with it. It passes. But you wouldn't, so now you pay for your stupid romantic notions. Have I made my view clear?"

It was very clear. Wilhelm seemed to hear it repeated from various sides and inclined his head different ways, and listened and thought. Finally he said, "I guess that's the medical standpoint. You may be right. I just couldn't live with Margaret. I wanted to stick it out, but I was getting very sick. She was one way and I was another. She wouldn't be like me, so I tried to be like her, and I couldn't do it."

"Are you sure she didn't tell *you* to go?" the doctor said.

"I wish she had. I'd be in a better position now. No, it was me. I didn't want to leave, but I couldn't stay. Somebody had to take the initiative. I did. Now I'm the fall guy too."

Pushing aside in advance all the objections that his son would make, the doctor said, "Why did you lose your job with Rojax?"

"I didn't, I've told you."

"You're lying. You wouldn't have ended the connection. You need the money too badly. But you must have got into trouble." The small old man spoke concisely and with great strength. "Since you have to talk and can't let it alone, tell the truth. Was there a scandal—a woman?"

Wilhelm fiercely defended himself. "No, Dad, there wasn't any woman. I told you how it was."

"Maybe it was a man, then," the old man said wickedly.

Shocked, Wilhelm stared at him with burning pallor and dry lips. His skin looked a little yellow. "I don't think you know what you're talking about," he answered after a moment. "You shouldn't let your imagination run so free. Since you've been living here on Broadway you must think you understand life, up to date. You ought to know your own son a little better. Let's drop that, now."

"All right, Wilky, I'll withdraw it. But something must have happened in Roxbury nevertheless. You'll never go back. You're just talking wildly about representing a rival company. You won't. You've done something to spoil your reputation, I think. But you've got girl friends who are expecting you back, isn't that so?"

"I take a lady out now and then while on the road," said Wilhelm. "I'm not a monk."

"No one special? Are you sure you haven't gotten into complications?"

He had tried to unburden himself and instead, Wilhelm thought, he had to undergo an inquisition to prove himself worthy of a sympathetic word. Because his father believed that he did all kinds of gross things.

"There is a woman in Roxbury that I went with. We fell in love and want to marry, but she got tired of waiting for my divorce. Margaret figured that. On top of which the girl was a Catholic and I had to go with her to the priest and make an explanation."

Neither did this last confession touch Dr. Adler's sympathies or sway his calm old head or affect the color of his complexion.

"No, no, no; all wrong," he said.

Again Wilhelm cautioned himself. Remember his age. He is no longer the same person. He can't bear trouble. I'm so choked up and congested anyway I can't see straight. Will I ever get out of the woods, and recover my balance? You're never the same afterward. Trouble rusts out the system.

"You really *want* a divorce?" said the old man.

"For the price I pay I should be getting something."

"In that case," Dr. Adler said, "it seems to me no normal person would stand for such treatment from a woman."

"Ah, Father, Father!" said Wilhelm, "It's always the same thing with you. Look how you lead me on. You always start out to help me with my problems, and be sympathetic and so forth. It gets my hopes up and I begin to be grateful. But before we're through I'm a hundred times more depressed than before. Why is that? You have no sympathy. You want to shift all the blame on to me. Maybe you're wise to do it." Wilhelm was beginning to lose himself. "All you seem to think about is your death. Well, I'm sorry. But I'm going to die too. And I'm your son. It isn't my fault in the first place. There ought to be a right way to do this, and be fair to each other. But what I want to know is, why do you start up with me if you're not going to help me? What do you want to know about my problems for, Father? So you can lay the whole responsibility on me—so that you won't have to help me? D'you want me to comfort you for having such a son?" Wilhelm had a great knot of wrong tied tight within his chest, and tears approached his eyes but he didn't let them out. He looked shabby enough as it was. His voice was thick and hazy, and he was stammering and could not bring his awful feelings forth.

"You have some purpose of your own," said the doctor, "in acting so unreasonable. What do you want from me? What do you expect?"

"What do I expect?" said Wilhelm. He felt as though he were unable to recover something. Like a ball in the surf, washed beyond reach, his self-control was going out. "I expect *help!*" The words escaped him in a loud, wild, frantic cry and startled the old man, and two or three breakfasters within hearing glanced their way. Wilhelm's hair, the color of whitened honey, rose dense and tall with the expansion of his face, and he said, "When I suffer—you aren't even sorry. That's because you have no affection for me, and you don't want any part of me."

"Why must I like the way you behave? No, I don't like it," said Dr. Adler.

"All right. You want me to change myself. But suppose I could do it— what would I become? What could I? Let's suppose that all my life I have had the wrong ideas about myself and wasn't what I thought I was. And wasn't even careful to take a few precautions, as most people do—like a woodchuck has a few exits to his tunnel. But what shall I do now? More than half my life is over. More than half. And now you tell me I'm not even normal."

The old man too had lost his calm. "You cry about being helped," he said. "When you thought you had to go into the service I sent a check to Margaret every month. As a family man you could have had an exemption. But no! The war couldn't be fought without you and you had to get yourself drafted and be an office-boy in the Pacific theater. Any clerk could have done what you did. You could find nothing better to become than a GI."

Wilhelm was going to reply, and half raised his bearish figure from the chair, his fingers spread and whitened by their grip on the table, but the old man would not let him begin. He said, "I see other elderly people here with children who aren't much good, and they keep backing them and holding them up at a great sacrifice. But I'm not going to make that mistake. It doesn't enter your mind that when I die—a year, two years from now—you'll still be here. I do think of it."

He had intended to say that he had a right to be left in peace. Instead he gave Wilhelm the impression that he meant it was not fair for the better man of the two, and the more useful, the more admired, to leave the world first. Perhaps he meant that, too—a little; but he would not under other circumstances have come out with it so flatly.

"Father," said Wilhelm with an unusual openness of appeal. "Don't you think I know how you feel? I have pity. I want you to live on and on. If you outlive me, that's perfectly okay by me." As his father did not answer this avowal and turned away his glance, Wilhelm suddenly burst out, "No, but you hate me. And if I had money you wouldn't. By God, you have to admit it. The money makes the difference. Then we would be a fine father and son, if I was a credit to you—so you could boast and brag about me all over the hotel. But I'm not the right type of son. I'm too old, I'm too old and too unlucky."

His father said, "I can't give you any money. There would be no end to it if I started. You and your sister would take every last buck from me. I'm still alive, not dead. I am still here. Life isn't over yet. I am as much alive as you or anyone. And I want nobody on my back. Get off! And I give you the same advice, Wilky. Carry nobody on your back."

"Just keep your money," said Wilhelm miserably. "Keep it and enjoy it yourself. That's the ticket!"

IV

Ass! Idiot! Wild boar! Dumb mule! Slave! Lousy, wallowing hippopotamus! Wilhelm called himself as his bending legs carried him from the dining room.

His pride! His inflamed feelings! His begging and feebleness! And trading insults with his old father—and spreading confusion over everything. Oh, how poor, contemptible, and ridiculous he was! When he remembered how he had said, with great reproof, "You ought to know your own son"—why, how corny and abominable it was.

He could not get out of the sharply brilliant dining room fast enough. He was horribly worked up; his neck and shoulders, his entire chest ached as though they had been tightly tied with ropes. He smelled the salt odor of tears in his nose.

But at the same time, since there were depths in Wilhelm not unsuspected by himself, he received a suggestion from some remote element in his thoughts that the business of life, the real business—to carry his peculiar burden, to feel shame and impotence, to taste these quelled tears—the only important business, the highest business was being done. Maybe the making of mistakes expressed the very purpose of his life and the essence of his being here. Maybe he was supposed to make them and suffer from them on this earth. And though he had raised himself above Mr. Perls and his father because they adored money, still they were called to act energetically and this was better than to yell and cry, pray and beg, poke and blunder and go by fits and starts and fall upon the thorns of life. And finally sink beneath that watery floor—would that be tough luck, or would it be good riddance?

But he raged once more against his father. Other people with money, while they're still alive, want to see it do some good. Granted, he shouldn't support me. But have I ever asked him to do that? Have I ever asked for dough at all, either for Margaret or for the kids or for myself? It isn't the money, but only the assistance; not even assistance, but just the feeling. But he may be trying to teach me that a grown man should be cured of such feelings. Feeling got me in dutch at Rojax. I had the *feeling* that I belong to the firm, and my *feelings* were hurt when they put Gerber in over me. Dad thinks I'm too simple. But I'm not so simple as he thinks. What about his feelings? He doesn't forget death for one single second, and that's what makes him like this. And not only is death on his mind but through money he forces me to think about it, too. It gives him power over me. He forces me that way, he himself, and then he's sore. If he was poor, I could care for him and show it. The way I *could* care, too, if I only had a chance. He'd see how much love and respect I had in me. It would make him a different man, too. He'd put his hands on me and give me his blessing.

Someone in a gray straw hat with a wide cocoa-colored band spoke to Wilhelm in the lobby. The light was dusky, splotched with red underfoot; green, the leather furniture; yellow, the indirect lighting.

"Hey, Tommy. Say, there."

"Excuse me," said Wilhelm, trying to reach a house phone. But this was Dr. Tamkin, whom he was just about to call.

"You have a very obsessional look on your face," said Dr. Tamkin.

Wilhelm thought, Here he is, Here he is. If I could only figure this guy out.

"Oh," he said to Tamkin. "Have I got such a look? Well, whatever it is, you name it and I'm sure to have it."

The sight of Dr. Tamkin brought his quarrel with his father to a close. He found himself flowing into another channel.

"What are we doing?" he said. "What's going to happen to lard today?"

"Don't worry yourself about that. All we have to do is hold on to it and it's sure to go up. But what's made you so hot under the collar, Wilhelm?"

"Oh, one of those family situations." This was the moment to take a new look at Tamkin, and he viewed him closely but gained nothing by the new effort. It was conceivable that Tamkin was everything that he claimed to be, and all the gossip false. But was he a scientific man, or not? If he was not, this might be a case for the district attorney's office to investigate. Was he a liar? That was a delicate question. Even a liar might be trustworthy in some ways. Could he trust Tamkin—could he? He feverishly, fruitlessly sought an answer.

But the time for this question was past, and he had to trust him now. After a long struggle to come to a decision, he had given him the money. Practical judgment was in abeyance. He had worn himself out, and the decision was no decision. How had this happened? But how had his Hollywood career begun? It was not because of Maurice Venice, who turned out to be a pimp. It was because Wilhelm himself was ripe for the mistake. His marriage, too, had been like that. Through such decisions somehow his life had taken form. And so, from the moment when he tasted the peculiar flavor of fatality in Dr. Tamkin, he could no longer keep back the money.

Five days ago Tamkin had said, "Meet me tomorrow, and we'll go to the market." Wilhelm, therefore, had had to go. At eleven o'clock they had walked to the brokerage office. On the way, Tamkin broke the news to Wilhelm that though this was an equal partnership, he couldn't put up his half of the money just yet; it was tied up for a week or so in one of his patients. Today he would be two hundred dollars short; next week he'd make it up. But neither of them needed an income from the market, of course. This was only a sporting proposition anyhow, Tamkin said. Wilhelm had to answer. "Of course." It was too late to withdraw. What else could he do? Then came the formal part of the transaction, and it was frightening. The very shade of green of Tamkin's check looked wrong; it was a false, disheartening color. His handwriting was peculiar, even monstrous; the e's were like i's, the t's and l's the same, and the h's like wasps' bellies. He wrote like a fourth-grader. Scientists, however, dealt mostly in symbols; they printed. This was Wilhelm's explanation.

Dr. Tamkin had given him his check for three hundred dollars. Willhelm, in a blinded and convulsed aberration, pressed and pressed to try to kill the trembling of his hand as he wrote out his check for a thousand. He set his lips tight, crouched with his huge back over the table, and wrote with crumbling, terrified fingers, knowing that if Tamkin's check bounced his own would not be honored either. His sole cleverness was to set the date ahead by one day to give the green check time to clear.

Next he had signed a power of attorney, allowing Tamkin to speculate with his money, and this was an even more frightening document. Tamkin had never said a word about it but here they were and it had to be done.

After delivering his signatures, the only precaution Wilhelm took was to come back to the manager of the brokerage office and ask privately, "Uh, about Doctor Tamkin. We were in here a few minutes ago, remember?"

That day had been a weeping, smoky one and Wilhelm had gotten away from Tamkin on the pretext of having to run to the post office. Tamkin had gone to lunch alone, and here was Wilhelm, back again, breathless, his hat dripping, needlessly asking the manager if he remembered.

"Yes, sir, I know," the manager had said. He was a cold, mild, lean German who dressed correctly and around his neck wore a pair of opera glasses with which he read the board. He was an extremely correct person except that he never shaved in the morning, not caring, probably, how he looked to the fumblers and the old people and the operators and the gamblers and the idlers of Broadway uptown. The market closed at three. Maybe, Wilhelm guessed, he had a thick beard and took a lady out to dinner and wanted to look fresh-shaven.

"Just a question," said Wilhelm. "A few minutes ago I signed a power of attorney so Doctor Tamkin could invest for me. You gave me the blanks."

"Yes, sir, I remember."

"Now this is what I want to know," Wilhelm had said. "I'm no lawyer and I only gave the paper a glance. Does this give Doctor Tamkin power of attorney over any other assets of mine—money or property?"

The rain had dribbled from Wilhelm's deformed, transparent raincoat; the buttons of his shirt, which always seemed tiny, were partly broken, in pearly quarters of the moon, and some of the dark, thick golden hairs that grew on his belly stood out. It was the manager's business to conceal his opinion of him; he was shrewd, gray, correct (although unshaven) and had little to say except on matters that came to his desk. He must have recognized in Wilhelm a man who reflected long and then made the decision he had rejected twenty separate times. Silvery, cool, level, long-profiled, experienced, indifferent, observant, with unshaven refinement, he scarcely looked at Wilhelm, who trembled with fearful awkwardness. The manager's face, low-colored, long-nostriled, acted as a unit of perception; his eyes merely did their reduced share. Here was a man like Rubin, who knew and knew and knew. He, a foreigner, knew; Wilhelm, in the city of his birth, was ignorant.

The manager had said, "No, sir, it does not give him."

"Only over the funds I deposited with you?"

"Yes, that is right, sir."

"Thank you, that's what I wanted to find out," Wilhelm had said, grateful. The answer comforted him. However, the question had no value. None at all. For Wilhelm had no other assets. He had given Tamkin his last money. There wasn't enough of it to cover his obligations anyway, and Wilhelm had reckoned that he might as well go bankrupt now as next month. "Either broke or rich," was how he had figured, and that formula had encouraged him to make the gamble. Well, not rich; he did not expect that, but perhaps Tamkin might really show him how to earn what he needed in the market. By now, however, he had forgotten his own reckoning and was aware only that he stood to lose his seven hundred dollars to the last cent.

Dr. Tamkin took the attitude that they were a pair of gentlemen experimenting with lard and grain futures. The money, a few hundred dollars, meant nothing much to either of them. He said to Wilhelm, "Watch. You'll get a big kick out of this and wonder why more people don't go into it. You think the Wall Street guys are so smart—geniuses? That's because most of us are psychologically afraid to think about the details. Tell me this. When you're on the road, and you don't understand what goes on under the hood of your car, you'll worry what'll happen if something goes wrong with the engine. Am I wrong?" No, he was right. "Well," said Dr. Tamkin with an expression of quiet triumph about his mouth, almost the suggestion of a jeer. "It's the same psychological principle, Wilhelm. They are rich because you don't understand what goes on. But it's no mystery, and by putting in a little money and applying certain principles of observation, you begin to grasp it. It can't be studied in the abstract. You have to take a specimen risk so that you feel the process, the money-flow, the whole complex. To know how it feels to be a seaweed you have to get in the water. In a very short time we'll take out a hundred-per-cent profit." Thus Wilhelm had had to pretend at the outset that his interest in the market was theoretical.

"Well," said Tamkin when he met him now in the lobby, "what's the problem, what is this family situation? Tell me." He put himself forward as the keen mental scientist. Whenever this happened Wilhelm didn't know what to reply. No matter what he said or did it seemed that Dr. Tamkin saw through him.

"I had some words with my dad."

Dr. Tamkin found nothing extraordinary in this. "It's the eternal same story," he said. "The elemental conflict of parent and child. It won't end, ever. Even with a fine old gentleman like your dad."

"I don't suppose it will. I've never been able to get anywhere with him. He objects to my feelings. He thinks they're sordid. I upset him and he gets mad at me. But maybe all old men are alike."

"Sons, too. Take it from one of them." said Dr. Tamkin. "All the same, you should be proud of such a fine old patriarch of a father. It should give you hope. The longer he lives, the longer your life-expectancy becomes."

Wilhelm answered, brooding, "I guess so. But I think I inherit more from my mother's side, and she died in her fifties."

"A problem arose between a young fellow I'm treating and his dad—I just had a consultation," said Dr. Tamkin as he removed his dark gray hat.

"So early in the morning?" said Wilhelm with suspicion.

"Over the telephone, of course."

What a creature Tamkin was when he took off his hat! The indirect light showed the many complexities of his bald skull, his gull's nose, his rather handsome eyebrows, his vain mustache, his deceiver's brown eyes. His figure was stocky, rigid, short in the neck, so that the large ball of the occiput touched his collar. His bones were peculiarly formed, as though twisted twice where the ordinary human bone was turned only once, and his shoulders rose in two pagoda-like points. At mid-body he was thick. He stood pigeon-toed, a sign perhaps that he was devious or had much to hide. The skin of his hands was aging, and his nails were moonless, concave, clawlike, and they appeared loose. His eyes were as brown as beaver fur and full of strange lines. The two large brown naked balls looked thoughtful—but were they? And honest—but was Dr. Tamkin honest? There was a hypnotic power in his eyes, but this was not always of the same strength, nor was Wilhelm convinced that it was completely natural. He felt that Tamkin tried to make his eyes deliberately conspicuous, with studied art, and that he brought forth his hypnotic effect by an exertion. Occasionally it failed or drooped, and when this happened the sense of his face passed downward to his heavy (possibly foolish?) red underlip.

Wilhelm wanted to talk about the lard holdings, but Dr. Tamkin said, "This father-and-son case of mine would be instructive to you. It's a different psychological type completely than your dad. This man's father thinks that he isn't his son."

"Why not?"

"Because he has found out something about the mother carrying on with a friend of the family for twenty-five years."

"Well, what do you know!" said Wilhelm. His silent thought was, Pure bull. Nothing but bull!

"You must note how interesting the woman is, too. She has two husbands. Whose are the kids? The fellow detected her and she gave a signed confession that two of the four children were not the father's."

"It's amazing," said Wilhelm, but he said it in a rather distant way. He was always hearing such stories from Dr. Tamkin. If you were to believe Tamkin, most of the world was like this. Everybody in the hotel had a mental disorder, a secret history, a concealed disease. The wife of Rubin at the newsstand was supposed to be kept by Carl, the yelling, loud-mouthed gin-rummy player. The wife of Frank in the barbershop had disappeared with a GI while he was waiting for her to disembark at the French Lines' pier. Everyone was like the faces on a playing card, upside down either way.

Every public figure had a character-neurosis. Maddest of all were the businessmen, the heartless, flaunting, boisterous business class who ruled this country with their hard manners and their bold lies and their absurd words that nobody could believe. They were crazier than anyone. They spread the plague. Wilhelm, thinking of the Rojax Corporation, was inclined to agree that many businessmen were insane. And he supposed that Tamkin, for all his peculiarities, spoke a kind of truth and did some people a sort of good. It confirmed Wilhelm's suspicions to hear that there was a plague, and he said, "I couldn't agree with you more. They trade on anything, they steal everything, they're cynical right to the bones."

"You have to realize," said Tamkin, speaking of his patient, or his client, "that the mother's confession isn't good. It's a confession of duress. I try to tell the young fellow he shouldn't worry about a phony confession. But what does it help him if I am rational with him?"

"No?" said Wilhelm, intensely nervous. "I think we ought to go over to the market. It'll be opening pretty soon."

"Oh, come on," said Tamkin. "It isn't even nine o'clock, and there isn't much trading the first hour anyway. Things don't get hot in Chicago until half-past ten, and they're an hour behind us, don't forget. Anyway, I say lard will go up, and it will. Take my word. I've made a study of the guilt-aggression cycle which is behind it. I ought to know *something* about that. Straighten your collar."

"But meantime," said Wilhelm, "we have taken a licking this week. Are you sure your insight is at its best? Maybe when it isn't we should lay off and wait."

"Don't you realize," Dr. Tamkin told him, "you can't march in a straight line to the victory? You fluctuate toward it. From Euclid to Newton there was straight lines. The modern age analyzes the wavers. On my own accounts, I took a licking in hides and coffee. But I have confidence. I'm sure I'll outguess them." He gave Wilhelm a narrow smile, friendly, calming, shrewd, and wizard-like, patronizing, secret, potent. He saw his fears and smiled at them. "It's something," he remarked, "to see how the competition-factor will manifest itself in different individuals."

"So? Let's go over."

"But I haven't had my breakfast yet."

"I've had mine."

"Come, have a cup of coffee."

"I wouldn't want to meet my dad." Looking through the glass doors, Wilhelm saw that his father had left by the other exit. Wilhelm thought, He didn't want to run into me, either. He said to Dr. Tamkin, "Okay, I'll sit with you, but let's hurry it up because I'd like to get to the market while there's still a place to sit. Everybody and his uncle gets in ahead of you."

"I want to tell you about this boy and his dad. It's highly absorbing. The father was a nudist. Everybody went naked in the house. Maybe the woman found men *with* clothes attractive. Her husband didn't believe in cutting his hair, either. He practiced dentistry. In his office he wore riding pants and a pair of boots, and he wore a green eyeshade."

"Oh, come off it," said Wilhelm.

"This is a true case history."

Without warning, Wilhelm began to laugh. He himself had had no premonition of his change of humor. His face became warm and pleasant, and he forgot his father, his anxieties; he panted bearlike, happily, through his teeth. "This sounds like a horse-dentist. He wouldn't have to put on pants to treat a horse. Now what else are you going to tell me? Did the wife play the mandolin? Does the boy join the cavalry? Oh, Tamkin, you really are a killerdiller."

"Oh, you think I'm trying to amuse you," said Tamkin. "That's because you aren't familiar with my outlook. I deal in facts. Facts always are sensational. I'll say that a second time. Facts *always!* are sensational."

Wilhelm was reluctant to part with his good mood. The doctor had little sense of humor. He was looking at him earnestly.

"I'd bet you any amount of money," said Tamkin, "that the facts about you are sensational."

"Oh—ha, ha! You want them? You can sell them to a true confession magazine."

"People forget how sensational things are that they do. They don't see it on themselves. It blends into the background of their daily life."

Wilhelm smiled. "Are you sure this boy tells you the truth?"

"Yes, because I've known the whole family for years."

"And you do psychological work with your own friends? I didn't know that was allowed."

"Well, I'm a radical in the profession. I have to do good wherever I can."

Wilhelm's face became ponderous again and pale. His whitened gold hair lay heavy on his head, and he clasped uneasy fingers on the table. Sensational, but oddly enough, dull, too. Now how do you figure that out? It blends with the background. Funny but unfunny. True but false. Casual but laborious. Tamkin was. Wilhelm was most suspicious of him when he took his driest tone.

"With me," said Dr. Tamkin, "I am at my most efficient when I don't need the fee. When I only love. Without a financial reward. I remove myself from the social influence. Especially money. The spiritual compensation is what I look for. Bringing people into the here-and-now. The real universe. That's the present moment. The past is no good to us. The future is full of anxiety. Only the present is real—the here-and-now. Seize the day."

"Well," said Wilhelm, his earnestness returning. "I know you are a very unusual man. I like what you say about here-and-now. Are all the people who come to see you personal friends and patients too? Like that tall handsome girl, the one who always wears those beautiful broomstick skirts and belts?"

"She was an epileptic, and a most bad and serious pathology, too. I'm curing her successfully. She hasn't had a seizure in six months, and she used to have one every week."

"And that young cameraman, the one who showed us those movies from the jungles of Brazil, isn't he related to her?"

"Her brother. He's under my care, too. He has some terrible tendencies, which are to be expected when you have an epileptic sibling. I came into their lives when they needed help desperately, and took hold of them. A certain man forty years older than she had her in his control and used to give her fits by suggestion whenever she tried to leave him. If you only knew one per cent of what goes on in the City of New York! You see, I understand what it is when the lonely person begins to feel like an animal. When the night comes and he feels like howling from his window like a wolf. I'm taking complete care of that young fellow and his sister. I have to steady him down or he'll go from Brazil to Australia the next day. The way I keep him in the here-and-now is by teaching him Greek."

This was a complete surprise! "What, do you know Greek?"

"A friend of mine taught me when I was in Cairo. I studied Aristotle with him to keep from being idle."

Wilhelm tried to take in these new claims and examine them. Howling from the window like a wolf when night comes sounded genuine to him. That was something really to think about. But the Greek! He realized that Tamkin was watching to see how he took it. More elements were continually being added. A few days ago Tamkin had hinted that he had once been in the underworld, one of the Detroit Purple Gang. He was once head of a mental clinic in Toledo. He had worked with a Polish inventor on an unsinkable ship. He was a technical consultant in the field of television. In the life of a man of genius, all of these things might happen. But had they happened to Tamkin? Was he a genius? He often said that he had attended some of the Egyptian royal family as a psychiatrist. "But everybody is alike, common or aristocrat," he told Wilhelm. "The aristocrat knows less about life."

An Egyptian princess whom he had treated in California, for horrible disorders he had described to Wilhelm, retained him to come back to the old country with her, and there he had had many of her friends and relatives under his care. They turned over a villa on the Nile to him. "For ethical reasons, I can't tell you many of the details about them," he said—but Wilhelm had already heard all these details, and strange and shocking they were, if true. *If* true—he could not be free from doubt. For instance, the general who had to wear ladies' silk stockings and stand otherwise naked before the mirror—and all the rest. Listening to the doctor when he was so strangely factual, Wilhelm had to translate his words into his own language, and he could not translate fast enough or find terms to fit what he heard.

"Those Egyptian big shots invested in the market, too, for the heck of it. What did they need extra money for? By association, I almost became a millionaire myself, and if I had played it smart there's no telling what might have happened. I could have been the ambassador." The American? The Egyptian ambassador? "A friend of mine tipped me off on the cotton. I made a heavy purchase of it. I didn't have that kind of money, but everybody there knew me. It never entered their minds that a person of their social circle didn't have dough. The sale was made on the phone. Then, while the cotton shipment was at sea, the price tripled. When the stuff suddenly became so valuable all hell broke loose on the world cotton market, they looked to me who was the owner of this big shipment. Me! They investigated my credit and found out I was a mere doctor, and they canceled. This was illegal. I sued them. But as I didn't have the money to fight them I sold the suit to a Wall Street lawyer for twenty thousand dollars. He fought it and was winning. They settled with him out of court for more than a million. But on the way back from Cairo, flying, there was a crash. All on board died. I have this guilt on my conscience, of being the murderer of that lawyer. Although he was a crook."

Wilhelm thought, I must be a real jerk to sit and listen to such impossible stories. I guess I am a sucker for people who talk about the deeper things of life, even the way he does.

"We scientific men speak of irrational guilt, Wilhelm," said Dr. Tamkin, as if Wilhelm were a pupil in his class. "But in such a situation, because of the money, I wished him harm. I realize it. This isn't the time to describe all the details, but the money made me guilty. *M*oney and *M*urder both begin with *M*. *M*achinery. *M*ischief."

Wilhelm, his mind thinking for him at random, said, "What about *M*ercy? *M*ilk-of-human-kindness?"

"One fact should be clear to you by now. Moneymaking is aggression. That's the whole thing. The functionalistic explanation is the only one. People come to the market to kill. They say, "I'm going to make a killing." It's not accidental. Only they haven't got the genuine courage to kill, and they erect a symbol of it. The money. They make a killing by a fantasy. Now, counting and number is always a sadistic activity. Like hitting. In the Bible, the Jews wouldn't allow you to count them. They knew it was sadistic."

"I don't understand what you mean," said Wilhelm. A strange uneasiness tore at him. The day was growing too warm and his head felt dim. "What makes them want to kill?"

"By and by, you'll get the drift," Dr. Tamkin assured him. His amazing eyes had some of the rich dryness of a brown fur. Innumerable crystalline hairs or spicules of light glittered in their bold surfaces. "You can't understand without first spending years on the study of the ultimates of human and animal behavior, the deep chemical, organismic, and spirtual secrets of life. I am a psychological poet."

"If you're this kind of poet," said Wilhelm, whose fingers in his pocket were feeling in the little envelopes for the Phenaphen capsules, "what are you doing on the market?"

"That's a good question. Maybe I am better at speculation because I don't care. Basically, I don't wish hard enough for money, and therefore I come with a cool head to it."

Wilhelm thought, Oh, sure! That's an answer, is it? I bet that if I took a strong attitude he'd back down on everything. He'd grovel in front of me. The way he looks at me on the sly, to see if I'm being taken in! He swallowed his Phenaphen pill with a long gulp of water. The rims of his eyes grew red as it went down. And then he felt calmer.

"Let me see if I can give you an answer that will satisfy you," said Dr. Tamkin. His flapjacks were set before him. He spread the butter on them, poured on brown maple syrup, quartered them, and began to eat with hard, active, muscular jaws which sometimes gave a creak at the hinges. He pressed the handle of his knife against his chest and said, "In here, the human bosom—mine, yours, everybody's—there isn't just one soul. There's a lot of souls. But there are two main ones, the real soul and a pretender soul. Now! Every man realizes that he has to love something or somebody. He feels that he must go outward. 'If thou canst not love, what art thou?' Are you with me?"

"Yes, Doc, I think so," said Wilhelm listening:—a little skeptically but nonetheless hard.

" 'What art thou?' Nothing. That's the answer. Nothing. In the heart of hearts—Nothing! So of course you can't stand that and want to be Something, and you try. But instead of being this Something, the man puts it over on everybody instead. You can't be that strict to yourself. You love a *little*. Like you have a dog" (*Scissors!*) "or give some money to a charity drive. Now that isn't love, is it? What is it? Egotism, pure and simple. It's a way to love the pretender soul. Vanity. Only vanity, is what it is. And social control. The interest of the pretender soul is the same as the interest of the social life, the society mechanism. This is the main tragedy of human life. Oh, it is terrible! Terrible! You are not free. Your own betrayer is inside of you and sells you out. You have to obey him like a slave. He makes you work like a horse. And for what? For who?"

"Yes, for what?" The doctor's words caught Wilhelm's heart. "I couldn't agree more," he said. "When do we get free?"

"The purpose is to keep the whole thing going. The true soul is the one that pays the price. It suffers and gets sick, and it realizes that the pretender can't be loved. Because the pretender is a lie. The true soul loves the truth. And when the true soul feels like this, it wants to kill the pretender. The love has turned into hate. Then you become dangerous. A killer. You have to kill the deceiver."

"Does this happen to everybody?"

The doctor answered simply, "Yes, to everybody. Of course, for simplification purposes, I have spoken of the soul; it isn't a scientific term, but it helps you to understand it. Whenever the slayer slays, he wants to slay the soul in him which has gypped and deceived him. Who is his enemy? Him. And his lover? Also. Therefore, all suicide is murder, and all murder is suicide. It's the one identical phenomenon. Biologically, the pretender soul takes away the energy of the true soul and makes it feeble, like a parasite. It happens unconsciously, unawaringly, in the depths of the organism. Ever take up parasitology?"

"No, it's my dad who's the doctor."

"You should read a book about it."

Wilhelm said, "But this means that the world is full of murderers. So it's not the world. It's a kind of hell."

"Sure," the doctor said, "At least a kind of purgatory. You walk on the bodies. They are all around. I can hear them cry *de profundis* and wring their hands. I hear them, poor human beasts. I can't help hearing. And my eyes are open to it. I have to cry, too. This is the human tragedy-comedy."

Wilhelm tried to capture his vision. And again the doctor looked untrustworthy to him, and he doubted him. "Well," he said, "there are also kind, ordinary, helpful people. They're—out in the country. All over. What kind of morbid stuff do you read, anyway?" The doctor's room was full of books.

"I read the best of literature, science and philosophy," Dr. Tamkin said. Wilhelm had observed that in his room even the TV aerial was set upon a pile of volumes. "Korzybski, Aristotle, Freud, W. H. Sheldon, and all the great poets. You answer me like a layman. You haven't applied your mind strictly to this."

"Very interesting," said Wilhelm. He was aware that he hadn't applied his mind strictly to anything. "You don't have to think I'm a dummy, though. I have ideas, too." A glance at the clock told him that the market would soon open. They could spare a few minutes yet. There were still more things he wanted to hear from Tamkin. He realized that Tamkin spoke faultily, but then scientific men were not always strictly literate. It was the description of the two souls that had awed him. In Tommy he saw the pretender. And even Wilky might not be himself. Might the name of his true soul be the one by which his old grandfather had called him—Velvel? The name of a soul, however, must be only that—soul. What did it look like? Does my soul look like me? Is there a soul that looks like Dad? Like Tamkin? Where does the true soul get its strength? Why does it have to love truth? Wilhelm was tormented, but tried to be oblivious to his torment. Secretly, he prayed the doctor would give him some useful advice and transform his life. "Yes, I understand you," he said. "It isn't lost on me."

"I never said you weren't intelligent, but only you just haven't made a study of it all. As a matter of fact you're a profound personality with very profound creative capacities but also disturbances. I've been concerned with you, and for some time I've been treating you."

"Without my knowing it? I haven't felt you doing anything. What do you mean? I don't think I like being treated without my knowledge. I'm of two minds. What's the matter, don't you think I'm normal?" And he really was divided in mind. That the doctor cared about him pleased him. This was what he craved, that someone should care about him, wish him well. Kindness, mercy, he wanted. But—and here he retracted his heavy shoulders in his peculiar way, drawing his hands up into his sleeves; his feet moved uneasily under the table—but he was worried, too, and even somewhat indignant. For what right had Tamkin to meddle without being asked? What kind of privileged life did this man lead? He took other people's money and speculated with it. Everybody came under his care. No one could have secrets from him.

The doctor looked at him with his deadly brown, heavy, impenetrable eyes, his naked shining head, his red hanging underlip, and said, "You have lots of guilt in you."

Wilhelm helplessly admitted, as he felt the heat rise to his wide face, "Yes, I think so too. But personally," he added, "I don't feel like a murderer. I always try to lay off. It's the others who get me. You know—make me feel oppressed. And if you don't mind, and it's all the same to you, I would rather know it when you start to treat me. And now, Tamkin, for Christ's sake, they're putting out the lunch menus already. Will you sign the check, and let's go!"

Tamkin did as he asked, and they rose. They were passing the bookkeeper's desk when he took out a substantial bundle of onionskin papers and said, "These are receipts of the transactions. Duplicates. You'd better keep them as the account is in your name and you'll need them for income taxes. And here is a copy of a poem I wrote yesterday."

"I have to leave something at the desk for my father," Wilhelm said, and he put the hotel bill in an envelope with a note. *Dear Dad, Please carry me this month, Yours, W.*

He watched the clerk with his sullen pug's profile and his stiff-necked look push the envelope into his father's box.

"May I ask you really why you and your dad had words?" said Dr. Tamkin, who had hung back, waiting.

"It was about my future," said Wilhelm. He hurried down the stairs with swift steps, like a tower in motion, his hands in his trousers pockets. He was ashamed to discuss the matter. "He says there's a reason why I can't go back to my old territory, and there is. I told everybody I was going to be an officer of the corporation. And I was supposed to. It was promised. But then they welshed because of the son-in-law. I bragged and made myself look big."

"If you was humble enough, you could go back. But it doesn't make much difference. We'll make you a good living on the market."

They came into the sunshine of upper Broadway, not clear but throbbing through the dust and fumes, a false air of gas visible at eye-level as it spurted from the bursting buses. From old habit, Wilhelm turned up the collar of his jacket.

"Just a technical question," Wilhelm said. "What happens if your losses are bigger than your deposit?"

"Don't worry. They have ultra-modern electronic bookkeeping machinery, and it won't let you get in debt. It puts you out automatically. But I want you to read this poem. You haven't read it yet."

Light as a locust, a helicopter bringing mail from Newark Airport to La Guardia sprang over the city in a long leap.

The paper Wilhelm unfolded had ruled borders in red ink. He read:

MECHANISM VS FUNCTIONALISM
ISM VS HISM

If thee thyself couldst only see
Thy greatness that is and yet to be,
Thou would feel joy-beauty-what ecstasy.
They are at thy feet, earth-moon-sea, the trinity.

Why-forth then dost thou tarry
And partake thee only of the crust
And skim the earth's surface narry
When all creations art thy just?

Seek ye then that which art not there
In thine own glory let thyself rest.
Witness. Thy power is not bare.
Thou art King. Thou art at thy best.

Look then right before thee.
Open thine eyes and see.
At the foot of Mt. Serenity
Is thy cradle to eternity.

Utterly confused, Wilhelm said to himself explosively, What kind of mish-mash, claptrap is this! What does he want from me? Damn him to hell, he might as well hit me on the head, and lay me out, kill me. What does he give me this for? What's the purpose? Is it a deliberate test? Does he want to mix me up? He's already got me mixed up completely. I was never good at riddles. Kiss those seven hundred bucks good-by, and call it one more mistake in a long line of mistakes—Oh, Mama, what a line! He stood near the shining window of a fancy fruit store, holding Tamkin's paper, rather dazed, as though a charge of photographer's flash powder had gone up in his eyes.

But he's waiting for my reaction. I have to say something to him about his poem. It really is no joke. What will I tell him? Who is this King? The poem is written *to* someone. But who? I can't even bring myself to talk. I feel too choked and strangled. With all the books he reads, how come the guy is so illiterate? And why do people just naturally assume that you'll know what they're talking about? No. I don't know, and nobody knows. The planets don't, the stars don't, infinite space doesn't. It doesn't square with Planck's Constant or anything else. So what's the good of it? Where's the need of it? What does he mean here by Mount Serenity? Could it be a figure of speech for Mount Everest? As he says people are all committing suicide, maybe those guys who climbed Everest were only trying to kill themselves, and if we want peace we should stay at the foot of the mountain. In the here-and-now. But it's also here-and-now on the slope, and on the top, where they climbed to seize the day. Surface narry is something he can't mean. I don't believe. I'm about to start foaming at the mouth. "Thy cradle . . ." *Who* is resting in his cradle—in his glory? My thoughts are at an end. I feel the wall. No more. So ——k it all! The money and everything. Take it away! When I have the money they eat me alive, like those piranha fish in the movie about the Brazilian jungle. It was hideous when they ate up that Brahma bull in the river. He turned pale, just like clay, and in five minutes nothing was left except the skeleton still in one piece, floating away. When I haven't got it any more, at least they'll let me alone.

"Well, what do you think of this?" said Dr. Tamkin. He gave a special sort of wise smile, as though Wilhelm must now see what kind of man he was dealing with.

"Nice. Very nice. Have you been writing long?"

"I've been developing this line of thought for years and years. You follow it all the way?"

"I'm trying to figure out who this Thou is."

"Thou? Thou is you."

"Me! Why? This applies to *me?*"

"Why shouldn't it apply to you. You were in my mind when I composed it. Of course, the hero of the poem is sick humanity. If it would open its eyes it would be great."

"Yes, but how do I get into this?"

"The main idea of the poem is *con*struct or *de*struct. There is no ground in between. Mechanism is *de*struct. Money of course is *de*struct. When the last grave is dug, the gravedigger will have to be paid. If you could have confidence in nature you would not have to fear. It would keep you up. Creative is nature. Rapid. Lavish. Inspirational. It shapes leaves. It rolls the waters of the earth. Man is the chief of this. All creations are his just inheritance. You don't know what you've got within you. A person either creates or he destroys. There is not neutrality . . ."

"I realized you were no beginner," said Wilhelm with propriety. "I have only one criticism to make. I think 'why-forth' is wrong. You should write "Wherefore then dost thou . . . ' " And he reflected. So? I took a gamble. It'll have to be a miracle, though, to save me. My money will be gone, then it won't be able to destruct me. He can't just take and lose it, though. He's in it, too. I think he's in a bad way himself. He must be. I'm sure because, come to think of it, he sweated blood when he signed that check. But what have I let myself in for? The waters of the earth are going to roll over me.

V

Patiently, in the window of the fruit store, a man with a scoop spread crushed ice between his rows of vegetables. There were also Persian melons, lilacs, tulips with radiant black at the middle. The many street noises came back after a little while from the caves of the sky. Crossing the tide of Broadway traffic, Wilhelm was saying to himself, The reason Tamkin lectures me is that somebody has lectured him, and the reason for the poem is that he wants to give me good advice. Everybody seems to know something. Even fellows like Tamkin. Many people know what to do, but how many can do it?

He believed that he must, that he could and would recover the good things, the happy things, the easy tranquil things of life. He had made mistakes, but he could overlook these. He had been a fool, but that could be forgiven. The time wasted—must be relinquished. What else could one do about it? Things were too complex, but they might be reduced to simplicity again. Recovery was possible. First he had to get out of the city. No, first he had to pull out his money. . . .

From the carnival of the street—pushcarts, accordion and fiddle, shoeshine, begging, the dust going round like a woman on stilts—they entered the narrow crowded theater of the brokerage office. From front to back it was filled with the Broadway crowd. But how was lard doing this morning? Fom the rear of the hall Wilhelm tried to read the tiny figures. The German manager was looking through his binoculars. Tamkin placed himself on Wilhelm's left and covered his conspicuous bald head. "The guy'll ask me about the margin," he muttered. They passed, however, unobserved. "Look, the lard has held its place," he said.

Tamkin's eyes must be very sharp to read the figures over so many heads and at this distance—another respect in which he was unusual.

The room was always crowded. Everyone talked. Only at the front could you hear the flutter of the wheels within the board. Teletyped news items crossed the illuminated screen above.

"Lard. Now what about rye?" said Tamkin, rising on his toes. Here he was a different man, active and impatient. He parted people who stood in his way. His face turned resolute, and on either side of his mouth odd bulges formed under his mustache. Already he was pointing out to Wilhelm the appearance of a new pattern on the board. "There's something up today," he said.

"Then why'd you take so long with breakfast?" said Wilhelm.

There were no reserved seats in the room, only customary ones. Tamkin always sat in the second row, on the commodities side of the aisle. Some of his acquaintances kept their hats on the chairs for him.

"Thanks. Thanks," said Tamkin, and he told Wilhelm, "I fixed it up yesterday."

"That was a smart thought," said Wilhelm. They sat down.

With folded hands, by the wall, sat an old Chinese businessman in a seersucker coat. Smooth and fat, he wore a white Vandyke. One day Wilhelm had seen him on Riverside Drive pushing two little girls along in a baby carriage—his grandchildren. Then there were two women in their fifties, supposed to be sisters, shrewd and able money-makers, according to Tamkin. They had never a word to say to Wilhelm. But they would chat with Tamkin. Tamkin talked to everyone.

Wilhelm sat between Mr. Rowland, who was elderly, and Mr. Rappaport, who was very old. Yesterday Rowland had told him that in the year 1908, when he was a junior at Harvard, his mother had given him twenty shares of steel for his birthday, and then he had started to read the financial news and had never practiced law but instead followed the market for the rest of his life. Now he speculated only in soy beans, of which he had made a specialty. By his conservative method, said Tamkin, he cleared two hundred a week. Small potatoes, but then he was a bachelor, retired, and didn't need money.

"Without dependents," said Tamkin. "He doesn't have the problems that you and I do."

Did Tamkin have dependents? He had everything that it was possible for a man to have—science, Greek, chemistry, poetry, and now dependents too. That beautiful girl with epilepsy, perhaps. He often said that she was a pure, marvelous, spiritual child who had no knowledge of the world. He protected her, and if he was not lying, adored her. And if you encouraged Tamkin by believing him, or even if you refrained from questioning him, his hints became more daring. Sometimes he said that he paid for her music lessons. Sometimes he seemed to have footed the bill for the brother's camera expedition to Brazil. And he spoke of paying for the support of the orphaned child of a dead sweetheart. These hints, made dully as asides, grew by repetition into sensational claims.

"For myself, I don't need much," said Tamkin. "But a man can't live for himself and I need the money for certain important things. What do you figure you have to have, to get by?"

"Not less than fifteen grand, after taxes. That's for my wife and the two boys."

"Isn't there anybody else?" said Tamkin with a shrewdness almost cruel. But his look grew more sympathetic as Wilhelm stumbled, not willing to recall another grief.

"Well—there was. But it wasn't a money matter."

"I should hope!" said Tamkin. "If love is love, it's free. Fifteen grand, though, isn't too much for a man of your intelligence to ask out of life. Fools, hard-hearted criminals, and murderers have millions to squander. They burn up the world—oil, coal, wood, metal, and soil, and suck even the air and the sky. They consume, and they give back no benefit. A man like you, humble for life, who wants to feel and live, has trouble—not wanting," said Tamkin in his parenthetical fashion, "to exchange an ounce of soul for a pound of social power—he'll never make it without help in a world like this. But don't you worry." Wilhelm grasped at this assurance. "Just you never mind. We'll go easily beyond your figure."

Dr. Tamkin gave Wilhelm comfort. He often said that he had made as much as a thousand a week in commodities. Wilhelm had examined the receipts, but until this moment it had never occurred to him that there must be debit slips too; he had been shown only the credits.

"But fifteen grand is not an ambitious figure," Tamkin was telling him. "For that you don't have to wear yourself out on the road, dealing with narrow-minded people. A lot of them don't like Jews, either, I suppose?"

"I can't afford to notice. I'm lucky when I have my occupation. Tamkin, do you mean you can save our money?"

"Oh, did I forget to mention what I did before closing yesterday? You see, I closed out one of the lard contracts and bought a hedge of December rye. The rye is up three points already and takes some of the sting out. But lard will go up, too."

"Where? God, yes, you're right," said Wilhelm, eager, and got to his feet to look. New hope freshened his heart, "Why didn't you tell me before?"

And Tamkin, smiling like a benevolent magician, said, "You must learn to have trust. The slump in lard can't last. You just take a look at eggs. Didn't I predict they couldn't go any lower? They're rising and rising. If we had taken eggs we'd be far ahead."

"Then why didn't we take them?"

"We were just about to. I had a buying order in at .24, but the tide turned at .26¼ and we barely missed. Never mind. Lard will go back to last year's levels."

Maybe. But when? Wilhelm could not allow his hopes to grow too strong. However, for a little while he could breathe more easily. Late-morning trading was getting active. The shining numbers whirred on the board, which sounded like a huge cage of artificial birds. Lard fluctuated between two points, but rye slowly climbed.

He closed his strained, greatly earnest eyes briefly and nodded his Buddha's head, too large to suffer such uncertainties. For several moments of peace he was removed to his small yard in Roxbury.

He breathed in the sugar of the pure morning.

He heard the long phrases of the birds.

No enemy wanted his life.

Wilhelm thought, I will get out of here. I don't belong in New York any more. And he sighed like a sleeper.

Tamkin said, "Excuse me," and left his seat. He could not sit still in the room but passed back and forth between the stocks and commodities sections. He knew dozens of people and was continually engaging in discussions. Was he giving advice, gathering information, or giving it, or practicing—whatever mysterious profession he practiced? Hypnotism? Perhaps he could put people in a trance while he talked to them. What a rare, peculiar bird he was, with those pointed shoulders, that bare head, his loose nails, almost claws, and those brown, soft, deadly, heavy eyes.

He spoke of things that mattered, and as very few people did this he could take you by surprise, excite you, move you. Maybe he wished to do good, maybe give himself a lift to a higher level, maybe believe his own prophecies, maybe touch his own heart. Who could tell? He had picked up a lot of strange ideas; Wilhelm could only suspect, he could not say with certainty, that Tamkin hadn't made them his own.

Now Tamkin and he were equal partners, but Tamkin had put up only three hundred dollars. Suppose he did this not only once but five times; then an investment of fifteen hundred dollars gave him five thousand to speculate with. If he had power of attorney in every case, he could shift the money from one account to another. No, the German probably kept an eye on him. Nevertheless it was possible. Calculations like this made Wilhelm feel ill. Obviously Tamkin was a plunger. But how did he get by? He must be in his fifties. How did he support himself? Five years in Egypt; Hollywood before that; Michigan; Ohio; Chicago. A man of fifty has supported himself for at least thirty years. You could be sure that Tamkin had never worked in a factory or in an office. How did he make it? His taste in clothes was horrible, but he didn't buy cheap things. He wore corduroy or velvet shirts from Clyde's, painted neckties, striped socks. There was a slightly acid or pasty smell about his person; for a doctor, he didn't bathe much. Also, Dr. Tamkin had a good room at the Gloriana and had had it for about a year. But so was Wilhelm himself a guest, with an unpaid bill at present in his father's box. Did the beautiful girl with the skirts and belts pay him? Was he defrauding his so-called patients? So many questions impossible to answer could not be asked about an honest man. Nor perhaps about a sane man. Was Tamkin a lunatic, then? That sick Mr. Perls at breakfast had said that there was no easy way to tell the sane from the mad, and he was right about that in any big city and especially in New York—the end of the world, with its complexity and machinery, bricks and tubes, wires and stones, holes and heights. And was everybody crazy here? What sort of people did you see? Every other man spoke a language entirely his own, which he had figured out by private thinking; he had his own ideas and peculiar ways. If you wanted to talk about a glass of water, you had to start back with God creating the heavens and earth; the apple; Abraham; Moses and Jesus; Rome; the Middle Ages; gunpowder; the Revolution; back to Newton; up to Einstein; then war and Lenin and Hitler. After reviewing this and getting it all straight again you could proceed to talk about a glass of water. You were lucky even then to make yourself understood. And this happened over and over and over with everyone you met. You had to translate and translate, explain and explain, back and forth, and it was the punishment of hell itself not to understand or be understood, not to know the crazy from the sane, the wise from the fools, the young from the old or the sick from the well. The fathers were no fathers and the sons no sons. You had to talk with yourself in the daytime and reason with yourself at night. Who else was there to talk to in a city like New York?

A queer look came over Wilhelm's face with its eyes turned up and his silent mouth with its high upper lip. He went several degrees further—when you are like this, dreaming that everybody is outcast, you realize that this must be one of the small matters. There is a larger body, and from this you cannot be separated. The glass of water fades out. You do not go from simple a and simple b to the great x and y, nor does it matter whether you agree about the glass but, far beneath such details, what Tamkin would call the real soul says plain and understandable things to everyone. There sons and fathers are themselves, and a glass of water is only an ornament; it makes a hoop of brightness on the cloth; it is an angel's mouth. There truth for everybody may be found, and confusion is only—only temporary, thought Wilhelm.

The idea of this larger body had been planted in him a few days ago beneath Times Square, when he had gone downtown to pick up tickets for the baseball game on Saturday (a doubleheader at the Polo Grounds). He was going through an underground corridor, a place he had always hated and hated more than ever now. On the walls between the advertisements were words in chalk: "Sin No More," and "Do Not Eat the Pig," he had particularly noticed. And in the dark tunnel, in the haste, heat, and darkness which disfigure and make freaks and fragments of nose and eyes and teeth, all of a sudden, unsought, a general love for all these imperfect and lurid-looking people burst out in Wilhelm's breast. He loved them. One and all, he passionately loved them. They were his brothers and his sisters. He was imperfect and disfigured himself, but what difference did that make if he was united with them by this blaze of love! And as he walked he began to say, "Oh my brothers—my brothers and my sisters," blessing them all as well as himself.

So what did it matter how many languages there were, or how hard it was to describe a glass of water? Or matter that a few minutes later he didn't feel anything like a brother toward the man who sold him the tickets?

On that very same afternoon he didn't hold so high an opinion of this same onrush of loving kindness. What did it come to? As they had the capacity and must use it once in a while, people were bound to have such involuntary feelings. It was only another one of those subway things. Like having a hard-on at random. But today, his day of reckoning, he consulted his memory again and thought, I must go back to that. That's the right clue and may do me the most good. Something very big. Truth, like.

The old fellow on the right, Mr. Rappaport, was nearly blind and kept asking Wilhelm, "What's the new figure on November wheat? Give me July soy beans too." When you told him he didn't say thank you. He said, "Okay," instead, or, "Check," and turned away until he needed you again. He was very old, older even than Dr. Adler, and if you believed Tamkin he had once been the Rockefeller of the chicken business and had retired with a large fortune.

Wilhelm had a queer feeling about the chicken industry, that it was sinister. On the road, he frequently passed chicken farms. Those big, rambling, wooden buildings out in the neglected fields; they were like prisons. The lights burned all night in them to cheat the poor hens into laying. Then the slaughter. Pile all the coops of the slaughtered on end, and in one week they'd go higher than Mount Everest or Mount Serenity. The blood filling the Gulf of Mexico. The chicken shit, acid, burning the earth.

How old—old this Mr. Rappaport was! Purple stains were buried in the flesh of his nose, and the cartilage of his ear was twisted like a cabbage heart. Beyond remedy by glasses, his eyes were smoky and faded.

"Read me that soy-bean figure now, boy," he said, and Wilhelm did. He thought perhaps the old man might give him a tip, or some useful advice or information about Tamkin. But no. He only wrote memoranda on a pad, and put the pad in his pocket. He let no one see what he had written. And Wilhelm thought this was the way a man who had grown rich by the murder of millions of animals, little chickens, would act. If there was a life to come he might have to answer for the killing of all those chickens. What if they all were waiting? But if there was a life to come, everybody would have to answer. But if there was a life to come, the chickens themselves would be all right.

Well! What stupid ideas he was having this morning. Phooey!

Finally old Rappaport did address a few remarks to Wilhelm. He asked him whether he had reserved his seat in the synagogue for Yom Kippur.

"No," said Wilhelm.

"Well, you better hurry up if you expect to say *Yiskor* for your parents. I never miss."

And Wilhelm thought, Yes, I suppose I should say a prayer for Mother once in a while. His mother had belonged to the Reform congregation. His father had no religion. At the cemetery Wilhelm had paid a man to say a prayer for her. He was among the tombs and he wanted to be tipped for the *El molai rachamin.* "Thou God of Mercy," Wilhelm thought that meant. *B'gan Aden*—"in Paradise." Singing, they drew it out. *B'gan Ayden.* The broken bench beside the grave made him wish to do something. Wilhelm often prayed in his own manner. He did not go to the synagogue but he would occasionally perform certain devotions, according to his feelings. Now he reflected, In Dad's eyes I am the wrong kind of Jew. He doesn't like the way I act. Only he is the right kind of Jew. Whatever you are, it always turns out to be the wrong kind.

Mr. Rappaport grumbled and whiffed at his long cigar. And the board, like a swarm of electrical bees, whirred.

"Since you were in the chicken business, I thought you'd speculate in eggs, Mr. Rappaport." Wilhelm, with his warm, panting laugh, sought to charm the old man.

"Oh. Yeah. Loyalty, hey?" said old Rappaport. "I should stick to them. I spent a lot of time amongst chickens. I got to be an expert chicken-sexer. When the chick hatches you have to tell the boys from the girls. It's not easy. You need long, long experience. What do you think, it's a joke? A whole industry depends on it. Yes, now and then I buy contract eggs. What have you got today?"

Wilhelm said anxiously, "Lard. Rye."

"Buy? Sell?"

"Bought."

"Uh," said the old man. Wilhelm could not determine what he meant by this. But of course you couldn't expect him to make himself any clearer. It was not in the code to give information to anyone. Sick with desire, Wilhelm waited for Mr. Rappaport to make an exception in his case. Just this once! Because it was critical. Silently, by a sort of telepathic concentration, he begged the old man to speak the single word that would save him, give him the merest sign. "Oh, please—please help," he nearly said. If Rappaport would close one eye, or lay his head to one side, or raise his finger and point to a column in the paper or to a figure on his pad. A hint! A hint!

A long perfect ash formed on the end of the cigar, the white ghost of the leaf with all its veins and its fainter pungency. It was ignored, in its beauty, by the old man. For it was beautiful. Wilhelm he ignored as well.

Then Tamkin said to him, "Wilhelm, look at the jump our rye just took."

December rye climbed three points as they tensely watched; the tumblers raced and the machine's lights buzzed.

"A point and a half more, and we can cover the lard losses," said Tamkin. He showed him his calculations on the margin of the *Times*.

"I think you should put in the selling order now. Let's get out with a small loss."

"Get out now? Nothing doing."

"Why not? Why should we wait?"

"Because," said Tamkin with a smiling, almost openly scoffing look, "you've got to keep your nerve when the market starts to go places. Now's when you can make something."

"I'd get out while the getting's good."

"No, you shouldn't lose your head like this. It's obvious to me what the mechanism is, back in the Chicago market. There's a short supply of December rye. Look, it's just gone up another quarter. We should ride it."

"I'm losing my taste for the gamble," said Wilhelm. "You can't feel safe when it goes up so fast. It's liable to come down just as quick."

Dryly, as though he were dealing with a child, Tamkin told him in a tone of tiring patience, "Now listen, Tommy. I have it diagnosed right. If you wish I should sell I can give the sell order. But this is the difference between healthiness and pathology. One is objective, doesn't change his mind every minute, enjoys the risk element. But that's not the neurotic character. The neurotic character—"

"Damn it, Tamkin!" said Wilhelm roughly. "Cut that out. I don't like it. Leave my character out of consideration. Don't pull any more of that stuff on me. I tell you I don't like it."

Tamkin therefore went no further; he backed down. "I meant," he said, softer, "that as a salesman you are basically an artist type. The seller is in the visionary sphere of the business function. And then you're an actor, too."

"No matter what type I am—" An angry and yet weak sweetness rose into Wilhelm's throat. He coughed as though he had the flu. It was twenty years since he had appeared on the screen as an extra. He blew the bagpipes in a film called *Annie Laurie*. Annie had come to warn the young Laird; he would not believe her and called the bagpipers to drown her out. He made fun of her while she wrung her hands. Wilhelm, in a kilt, barelegged, blew and blew and blew and not a sound came out. Of course all the music was recorded. He fell sick with the flu after that and still suffered sometimes from chest weakness.

"Something stuck in your throat?" said Tamkin. "I think maybe you are too disturbed to think clearly. You should try some of my 'here-and-now' mental exercises. It stops you from thinking so much about the future and the past and cuts down confusion."

"Yes, yes, yes, yes," said Wilhelm, his eyes fixed on December rye.

"Nature only knows one thing, and that's the present. Present, present, eternal present, like a big, huge, giant wave—colossal, bright and beautiful, full of life and death, climbing into the sky, standing in the seas. You must go along with the actual, the Here-and-Now, the glory—"

. . . chest weakness, Wilhelm's recollection went on. Margaret nursed him. They had had two rooms of furniture, which was later seized. She sat on the bed and read to him. He made her read for days, and she read stories, poetry, everything in the house. He felt dizzy, stifled when he tried to smoke. They had him wear a flannel vest.

> Come then, Sorrow!
> Sweetest Sorrow!
> Like an own babe I nurse thee on my breast!

Why did he remember that? Why?

"You have to pick out something that's in the actual, immediate present moment," said Tamkin. "And say to yourself here-and-now, here-and-now, here-and-now. 'Where am I?' 'Here.' 'When is it?' 'Now.' Take an object or a person. Anybody. 'Here and now I see a person.' 'Here and now I see a man.' 'Here and now I see a man sitting on a chair.' Take me, for instance. Don't let your mind wander. 'Here and now I see a man in a brown suit. Here and now I see a corduroy shirt.' You have to narrow it down, one item at a time, and not let your imagination shoot ahead. Be in the present. Grasp the hour, the moment, the instant."

Is he trying to hypnotize or con me? Wilhelm wondered. To take my mind off selling? But even if I'm back at seven hundred bucks, then where am I?

As if in prayer, his lids coming down with raised veins, frayed out, on his significant eyes, Tamkin said, " 'Here and now I see a button. Here and now I see a thread that sews a button. Here and now I see the green thread.' " Inch by inch he contemplated himself in order to show Wilhelm how calm it would make him. But Wilhelm was hearing Margaret's voice as she read, somewhat unwillingly,

> Come then, Sorrow!
>
> .   .   .   .
> I thought to leave thee,
> And deceive thee,
> But now of all the world I love thee best.

Then Mr. Rappaport's old hand pressed his thigh, and he said, "What's my wheat? Those damn guys are blocking the way. I can't see."

VI

Rye was still ahead when they went out to lunch, and lard was holding its own.

They ate in the cafeteria with the gilded front. There was the same art inside as outside. The food looked sumptuous. Whole fishes were framed like pictures with carrots, and the salads were like terraced landscapes or like Mexican pyramids; slices of lemon and onion and radishes were like sun and moon and stars; the cream pies were about a foot thick and the cakes swollen as if sleepers had baked them in their dreams.

"What'll you have?" said Tamkin.

"Not much. I ate a big breakfast. I'll find a table. Bring me some yogurt and crackers and a cup of tea. I don't want to spend much time over lunch."

Tamkin said, "You've got to eat."

Finding an empty place at this hour was not easy. The old people idled and gossiped over their coffee. The elderly ladies were rouged and mascaraed and hennaed and used blue hair rinse and eye shadow and wore costume jewelry, and many of them were proud and stared at you with expressions that did not belong to their age. Were there no longer any respectable old ladies who knitted and cooked and looked after their grandchildren? Wilhelm's grandmother had dressed him in a sailor suit and danced him on her knee, blew on the porridge for him and said, "Admiral, you must eat." But what was the use of remembering this so late in the day?

He managed to find a table, and Dr. Tamkin came along with a tray piled with plates and cups. He had Yankee pot roast, purple cabbage, potatoes, a big slice of watermelon, and two cups of coffee. Wilhelm could not even swallow his yogurt. His chest pained him still.

At once Tamkin involved him in a lengthy discussion. Did he do it to stall Wilhelm and prevent him from selling out the rye—or to recover the ground lost when he had made Wilhelm angry by hints about the neurotic character? Or did he have no purpose except to talk?

"I think you worry a lot too much about what your wife and your father will say. Do they matter so much?"

Wilhelm replied, "A person can become tired of looking himself over and trying to fix himself up. You can spend the entire second half of your life recovering from the mistakes of the first half."

"I believe your dad told me he had some money to leave you."

"He probably does have something."

"A lot?"

"Who can tell," said Wilhelm guardedly.

"You ought to think over what you'll do with it."

"I may be too feeble to do anything by the time I get it. If I get anything."

"A thing like this you ought to plan out carefully. Invest it properly." He began to unfold schemes whereby you bought bonds, and used the bonds as security to buy something else and thereby earned twelve per cent safely on your money. Wilhelm failed to follow the details. Tamkin said, "If he made you a gift now, you wouldn't have to pay the inheritance taxes."

Bitterly, Wilhelm told him, "My father's death blots out all other considerations from his mind. He forces me to think about it, too. Then he hates me because he succeeds. When I get desperate—of course I think about money. But I don't want anything to happen to him. I certainly don't want him to die." Tamkin's brown eyes glittered shrewdly at him. "You don't believe it. Maybe it's not psychological. But on my word of honor. A joke is a joke, but I don't want to joke about stuff like this. When he dies, I'll be robbed, like. I'll have no more father."

"You love your old man?"

Wilhelm grasped at this. "Of course, of course I love him. My father. My mother—" As he said this there was a great pull at the very center of his soul. When a fish strikes the line you feel the live force in your hand. A mysterious being beneath the water, driven by hunger, has taken the hook and rushes away and fights, writhing. Wilhelm never identified what struck within him. It did not reveal itself. It got away.

And Tamkin, the confuser of the imagination, began to tell, or to fabricate, the strange history of *his* father. "He was a great singer," he said. "He left us five kids because he fell in love with an opera soprano. I never held it against him, but admired the way he followed the life-principle. I wanted to do the same. Because of unhappiness, at a certain age, the brain starts to die back." (True, true! thought Wilhelm) "Twenty years later I was doing experiments in Eastman Kodak, Rochester, and I found the old fellow. He had five more children." (False, false!) "He wept; he was ashamed. I had nothing against him. I naturally felt strange."

"My dad is something of a stranger to me, too," said Wilhelm, and he began to muse. Where is the familiar person he used to be? Or I used to be? Catherine—she won't even talk to me any more, my own sister. It may not be so much my trouble that Papa turns his back on as my confusion. It's too much. The ruins of life, and on top of that confusion—chaos and old night. Is it an easier farewell for Dad if we don't part friends? He should maybe do it angrily—"Blast you with my curse!" And why, Wilhelm further asked, should he or anybody else pity me; or why should I be pitied sooner than another fellow? It is my childish mind that thinks people are ready to give it just because you need it.

Then Wilhelm began to think about his own two sons and to wonder how he appeared to them, and what they would think of him. Right now he had an advantage through baseball. When he went to fetch them, to go to Ebbets Field, though, he was not himself. He put on a front but he felt as if he had swallowed a fistful of sand. The strange, familiar house, horribly awkward; the dog, Scissors, rolled over on his back and barked and whined. Wilhelm acted as if there was nothing irregular, but a weary heaviness came over him. On the way to Flatbush he would think up anecdotes about old Pigtown and Charlie Ebbets for the boys and reminiscences of the old stars, but it was very heavy going. They did not know how much he cared for them. No. It hurt him greatly and he blamed Margaret for turning them against him. She wanted to ruin him, while she wore the mask of kindness. Up in Roxbury he had to go and explain to the priest, who was not sympathetic. They don't care about individuals, their rules come first. Olive said she would marry him outside the Church when he was divorced. But Margaret would not let go. Olive's father was a pretty decent old guy, an osteopath, and he understood what it was all about. Finally he said, "See here, I have to advise Olive. She is asking me. I am mostly a free-thinker myself, but the girl has to live in this town." And by now Wilhelm and Olive had had a great many troubles and she was beginning to dread his days in Roxbury, she said. He trembled at offending this small, pretty, dark girl whom he adored. When she would get up late on Sunday morning she would wake him almost in tears at being late for Mass. He would try to help her hitch her garters and smooth out her slip and dress and even put on her hat with shaky hands; then he would rush her to church and drive in second gear in his forgetful way, trying to apologize and to calm her. She got out a block from church to avoid gossip. Even so she loved him, and she would have married him if he had obtained the divorce. But Margaret must have sensed this. Margaret would tell him he did not really want a divorce; he was afraid of it. He cried, "Take everything I've got, Margaret. Let me go to Reno. Don't you want to marry again?" No. She went out with other men, but took his money. She lived in order to punish him.

Dr. Tamkin told Wilhelm, "Your dad is jealous of you."

Wilhelm smiled. "Of *me?* That's rich."

"Sure. People are always jealous of a man who leaves his wife."

"Oh," said Wilhelm scornfully. "When it comes to wives he wouldn't have to envy me."

"Yes, and your wife envies you, too. She thinks, He's free and goes with young women. Is she getting old?"

"Not exactly old," said Wilhelm, whom the mention of his wife made sad. Twenty years ago, in a neat blue wool suit, in a soft hat made of the same cloth—he could plainly see her. He stopped his yellow head and looked under the hat at her clear, simple face, her living eyes moving, her straight small nose, her jaw beautifully, painfully clear in its form. It was a cool day, but he smelled the odor of pines in the sun, in the granite canyon. Just south of Santa Barbara, this was.

"She's forty-some years old," he said.

"I was married to a lush," said Tamkin. "A painful alcoholic. I couldn't take her out to dinner because she'd say she was going to the ladies toilet and disappear into the bar. I'd ask the bartenders they shouldn't serve her. But I loved her deeply. She was the most spiritual woman of my entire experience."

"Where is she now?"

"Drowned," said Tamkin. "At Provincetown, Cape Cod. It must have been a suicide. She was that way—suicidal. I tried everything in my power to cure her. Because," said Tamkin, "my real calling is to be a healer. I get wounded. I suffer from it. I would like to escape from the sicknesses of others, but I can't. I am only on loan to myself, so to speak. I belong to humanity."

Liar! Wilhelm inwardly called him. Nasty lies. He invented a woman and killed her off and then called himself a healer, and made himself so earnest he looked like a bad-natured sheep. He's a puffed-up little bogus and humbug with smelly feet. A doctor! A doctor would wash himself. He believes he's making a terrific impression, and he practically invites you to take off your hat when he talks about himself; and he thinks he has an imagination, but he hasn't; neither is he smart.

Then what am I doing with him here, and why did I give him the seven hundred dollars? thought Wilhelm.

Oh, this was a day of reckoning. It was a day, he thought, on which, willing or not, he would take a good close look at the truth. He breathed hard and his misshapen hat came low upon his congested dark blond face. A rude look. Tamkin was a charlatan, and furthermore he was desperate. And furthermore, Wilhelm had always known this about him. But he appeared to have worked it out at the back of his mind that Tamkin for thirty or forty years had gotten through many a tight place, that he would get through this crisis too and bring him, Wilhelm, to safety also. And Wilhelm realized that he was on Tamkin's back. It made him feel that he had virtually left the ground and was riding upon the other man. He was in the air. It was for Tamkin to take the steps.

The doctor, if he was a doctor, did not look anxious. But then his face did not have much variety. Talking always about spontaneous emotion and open receptors and free impulses, he was about as expressive as a pincushion. When his hypnotic spell failed, his big underlip made him look weak-minded. Fear stared from his eyes, sometimes, so humble as to make you sorry for him. Once or twice Wilhelm had seen that look. Like a dog, he thought. Perhaps he didn't look it now, but he was very nervous. Wilhelm knew, but he could not afford to recognize this too openly. The doctor needed a little room, a little time. He should not be pressed now. So Tamkin went on, telling his tales.

Wilhelm said to himself, I am on his back—his back. I gambled seven hundred bucks, so I must take this ride. I have to go along with him. It's too late. I can't get off.

"You know," Tamkin said. "that blind old man Rappaport—he's pretty close to totally blind—is one of the most interesting personalities around here. If you could only get him to tell his true story. It's fascinating. This is what he told me. You often hear about bigamists with a secret life. But this old man never hid anything from anybody. He's a regular patriarch. Now, I'll tell you what he did. He had two whole families, separate and apart, one in Williamsburg and the other in The Bronx. The two wives knew about each other. The wife in The Bronx was younger; she's close to seventy now. When he got sore at one wife he went to live with the other one. Meanwhile he ran his chicken business in New Jersey. By one wife he had four kids, and by the other six. They're all grown, but they never have met their half-brothers and sisters and don't want to. The whole bunch of them are listed in the telephone book."

"I can't believe it," said Wilhelm.

"He told me this himself. And do you know what else? While he had his eyesight he used to read a lot, but the only books he would read were by Theodore Roosevelt. He had a set in each of the places where he lived, and he brought his kids up on those books."

"Please," said Wilhelm, "don't feed me any more of this stuff, will you? Kindly do not—"

"In telling you this," said Tamkin with one of his hypnotic subtleties, "I do have a motive. I want you to see how some people free themselves from morbid guilt feelings and follow their instincts. Innately, the female knows how to cripple by sickening a man with guilt. It is a very special destruct, and she sends her curse to make a fellow impotent. As if she says, 'Unless I allow it, you will never more be a man.' But men like my old dad or Mr. Rappaport answer, 'Woman, what art thou to me?' You can't do that yet. You're a halfway case. You want to follow your instinct, but you're too worried still. For instance, about your kids—"

"Now look here," said Wilhelm, stamping his feet. "One thing! Don't bring up my boys. Just lay off."

"I was only going to say that they are better off than with conflicts in the home."

"I'm deprived of my children." Wilhelm bit his lip. It was too late to turn away. The anguish struck him. "I pay and pay. I never see them. They grow up without me. She makes them like herself. She'll bring them up to be my enemies. Please let's not talk about this."

But Tamkin said, "Why do you let her make you suffer so? It defeats the original object in leaving her. Don't play her game. Now, Wilhelm, I'm trying to do you some good. I want to tell you, don't marry suffering. Some people do. They get married to it, and sleep and eat together, just as husband and wife. If they go with joy they think it's adultery."

When Wilhelm heard this he had, in spite of himself, to admit that there was a great deal in Tamkin's words. Yes, thought Wilhelm, suffering is the only kind of life they are sure they can have, and if they quit suffering they're afraid they'll have nothing. He knows it. This time the father knows what he's talking about.

Looking at Tamkin he believed he saw all this confessed from his usually barren face. Yes, yes, he too. One hundred falsehoods, but at last one truth. Howling like a wolf from the city window. No one can hear it any more. Everyone is so full of it that at last everybody must proclaim it. It! It!

Then suddenly Wilhem rose and said, "That's enough of this. Tamkin, let's go back to the market."

"I haven't finished my melon."

"Never mind that. You've had enough to eat. I want to go back."

Dr. Tamkin slid the two checks across the table. "Who paid yesterday? It's your turn, I think."

It was not until they were leaving the cafeteria that Wilhelm remembered definitely that he had paid yesterday too. But it wasn't worth arguing about.

Tamkin kept repeating as they walked down the street that there were many who were dedicated to suffering. But he told Wilhelm, "I'm optimistic in your case, and I have seen a world of maladjustment. There's hope for you. You don't really want to destroy yourself. You're trying hard to keep your feelings open, Wilhelm. I can see it. Seven per cent of this country is committing suicide by alcohol. Another three, maybe, narcotics. Another sixty just fading away into dust by boredom. Twenty more who have sold their souls to the Devil. Then there's a small percentage of those who want to live. That's the only significant thing in the whole world of today. Those are the only two classes of people there are. Some want to live, but the great majority don't. This fantastic Tamkin began to surpass himself. "They don't. Or else, why these wars? I'll tell you more," he said. "The love of the dying amounts to one thing; they want you to die with them. It's because they love you. Make no mistake."

True, true! thought Wilhelm, profoundly moved by these revelations. How does he know these things? How can he be such a jerk, and even perhaps an operator, a swindler, and understand so well what gives? I believe what he says. It simplifies much—everything. People are dropping like flies. I am trying to stay alive and work too hard at it. That's what's turning my brains. This working hard defeats its own end. At what point should I start over? Let me go back a ways and try once more.

Only a few hundred yards separated the cafeteria from the broker's, and within that short space Wilhelm turned again, in measurable degrees, from these wide considerations to the problems of the moment. The closer he approached to the market, the more Wilhelm had to think about money.

They passed the newsreel theater where the ragged shoeshine kids called after them. The same old bearded man with his bandaged beggar face and his tiny ragged feet and the old press clipping on his fiddle case to prove he had once been a concert violinist, pointed his bow at Wilhelm, saying, "You!" Wilhelm went by with worried eyes, bent on crossing Seventy-second Street. In full tumult the great afternoon current raced for Columbus Circle, where the mouth of midtown stood open and the skyscrapers gave back the yellow fire of the sun.

As they approached the polished stone front of the new office building, Dr. Tamkin said, "Well, isn't that old Rappaport by the door? I think he should carry a white cane, but he will never admit there's a single thing the matter with his eyes."

Mr. Rappaport did not stand well; his knees were sunk, while his pelvis only half filled his trousers. His suspenders held them, gaping.

He stopped Wilhelm with an extended hand, having somehow recognized him. In his deep voice he commanded him, "Take me to the cigar store."

"You want me—? Tamkin!" Wilhelm whispered, "You take him."

Tamkin shook his head. "He wants you. Don't refuse the old gentleman." Significantly he said in a lower voice, "This minute is another instance of the 'here-and-now.' You have to live in this very minute, and you don't want to. A man asks you for help. Don't think of the market. It won't run away. Show your respect to the old boy. Go ahead. That may be more valuable."

"Take me," said the old chicken merchant again.

Greatly annoyed, Wilhelm wrinkled his face at Tamkin. He took the old man's big but light elbow at the bone. "Well, let's step on it," he said. "Or wait—I want to have a look at the board first to see how we're doing."

But Tamkin had already started Mr. Rappaport forward. He was walking, and he scolded Wilhelm, saying, "Don't leave me standing in the middle of the sidewalk. I'm afraid to get knocked over."

"Let's get a move on. Come." Wilhelm urged him as Tamkin went into the broker's.

The traffic seemed to come down Broadway out of the sky, where the hot spokes of the sun rolled from the south. Hot, stony odors rose from the subway grating in the street.

"These teen-age hoodlums worry me. I'm ascared of these Puerto Rican kids, and these young characters who take dope," said Mr. Rappaport. "They go around all hopped up."

"Hoodlums?" said Wilhelm. "I went to the cemetery and my mother's stone bench was split. I could have broken somebody's neck for that. Which store do you go to?"

"Across Broadway. That La Magnita sign next door to the Automat."

"What's the matter with this store here on this side?"

"They don't carry my brand, that's what's the matter."

Wilhelm cursed, but checked the words.

"What are you talking?"

"Those damn taxis," said Wilhelm. "They want to run everybody down."

They entered the cool, odorous shop. Mr. Rappaport put away his large cigars with great care in various pockets while Wilhelm muttered, "Come on, you old creeper. What a poky old character! The whole world waits on him." Rappaport did not offer Wilhelm a cigar, but, holding one up, he asked, "What do you say at the size of these, huh? They're Churchill-type cigars."

He barely crawls along, thought Wilhelm. His pants are dropping off because he hasn't got enough flesh for them to stick to. He's almost blind, and covered with spots, but this old man still makes money in the market. Is loaded with dough, probably. And I bet he doesn't give his children any. Some of them must be in their fifties. This is what keeps middle-aged men as children. He's master over the dough. Think—just think! Who controls everything? Old men of this type. Without needs. They don't need therefore they have. I need, therefore I don't have. That would be too easy.

"I'm older even than Churchill," said Rappaport.

Now he wanted to talk! But if you asked him a question in the market, he couldn't be bothered to answer.

"I bet you are," said Wilhelm. "Come, let's get going."

"I was a fighter, too, like Churchill," said the old man. "When we licked Spain I went into the Navy. Yes, I was a gob that time. What did I have to lose? Nothing. After the battle of San Juan Hill, Teddy Roosevelt kicked me off the beach."

"Come, watch the curb," said Wilhelm.

"I was curious and wanted to see what went on. I didn't have no business there, but I took a boat and rowed myself to the beach. Two of our guys was dead, layin' under the American flag to keep the flies off. So I says to the guy on duty, there, who was the sentry, 'Let's have a look at these guys. I want to see what went on here,' and he says, 'Naw,' but I talked him into it. So he took off the flag and there were these two tall guys, both gentlemen, lying in their boots. They was very tall. The two of them had long mustaches. They were high-society boys. I think one of them was called Fish, from up the Hudson, a big-shot family. When I looked up, there was Teddy Roosevelt, with his hat off, and he was looking at these fellows, the only ones who got killed there. Then he says to me, 'What's the Navy want here? Have you got orders?' 'No, sir,' I says to him. 'Well, get the hell off the beach, then.' "

Old Rappaport was very proud of this memory. "Everything he said had such snap, such class. Man! I love that Teddy Roosevelt," he said, "I love him!"

Ah, what people are! He is almost not with us, and his life is nearly gone, but T. R. once yelled at him, so he loves him. I guess it is love, too. Wilhelm smiled. So maybe the rest of Tamkin's story was true, about the ten children and the wives and the telephone directory.

He said, "Come on, come on, Mr. Rappaport," and hurried the old man back by the large hollow elbow; he gripped it through the thin cotton cloth. Re-entering the brokerage office where under the lights the tumblers were speeding with the clack of drumsticks upon wooden blocks, more than ever resembling a Chinese theater, Wilhelm strained his eyes to see the board.

The lard figures were unfamiliar. That amount couldn't be lard! They must have put the figures in the wrong slot. He traced the line back to the margin. It was down to .19, and had dropped twenty points since noon. And what about the contract of rye? It had sunk back to its earlier position, and they had lost their chance to sell.

Old Mr. Rappaport said to Wilhelm, "Read me my wheat figure."

"Oh, leave me alone for a minute," he said, and positively hid his face from the old man beside one hand. He looked for Tamkin, Tamkin's bald head, or Tamkin with his gray straw and the cocoa-colored band. He couldn't see him. Where was he? The seats next to Rowland were taken by strangers. He thrust himself over the one on the aisle, Mr. Rappaport's former place, and pushed at the back of the chair until the new occupant, a red-headed man with a thin, determined face, leaned forward to get out of his way but would not surrender the seat. "Where's Tamkin?" Wilhelm asked Rowland.

"Gee, I don't know. Is anything wrong?"

"You must have seen him. He came in a while back."

"No, but I didn't."

Wilhelm fumbled out a pencil from the top pocket of his coat and began to make calculations. His very fingers were numb, and in his agitation he was afraid he made mistakes with the decimal points and went over the subtraction and multiplication like a schoolboy at an exam. His heart, accustomed to many sorts of crisis, was now in a new panic. And, as he had dreaded, he was wiped out. It was unnecessary to ask the German manager. He could see for himself that the electronic bookkeeping device must have closed him out. The manager probably had known that Tamkin wasn't to be trusted, and on that first day he might have warned him. But you couldn't expect him to interfere.

"You get hit?" said Mr. Rowland.

And Wilhelm, quite coolly, said, "Oh, it could have been worse, I guess." He put the piece of paper into his pocket with its cigarette butts and packets of pills. The lie helped him out—although, for a moment, he was afraid he would cry. But he hardened himself. The hardening effort made a violent, vertical pain go through his chest, like that caused by a pocket of air under the collar bones. To the old chicken millionaire, who by this time had become acquainted with the drop in rye and lard, he also denied that anything serious had happened. "It's just one of those temporary slumps. Nothing to be scared about," he said, and remained in possession of himself. His need to cry, like someone in a crowd, pushed and jostled and abused him from behind, and Wilhelm did not dare turn. He said to himself, I will not cry in front of these people. I'll be damned if I'll break down in front of them like a kid, even though I never expect to see them again. No! No! And yet his unshed tears rose and rose and he looked like a man about to drown. But when they talked to him, he answered very distinctly. He tried to speak proudly.

". . . going away?" he heard Rowland ask.

"What?"

"I thought you might be going away too. Tamkin said he was going to Maine this summer for his vacation."

"Oh, going away?"

Wilhelm broke off and went to look for Tamkin in the men's toilet. Across the corridor was the room where the machinery of the board was housed. It hummed and whirred like mechanical birds, and the tubes glittered in the dark. A couple of businessmen with cigarettes in their fingers were having a conversation in the lavatory. At the top of the closet door sat a gray straw hat with a cocoa-colored band. "Tamkin," said Wilhelm. He tried to identify the feet below the door. "Are you in there, Doctor Tamkin?" he said with stifled anger. "Answer me. It's Wilhelm."

The hat was taken down, the latch lifted, and a stranger came out who looked at him with annoyance.

"You waiting?" said one of the businessmen. He was warning Wilhelm that he was out of turn.

"Me? Not me," said Wilhelm. "I'm looking for a fellow."

Bitterly angry, he said to himself that Tamkin would pay him the two hundred dollars at least, his share of the original deposit. "And before he takes the train to Maine, too. Before he spends a penny on vacation—that liar! We went into this as equal partners."

VII

I was the man beneath; Tamkin was on my back, and I thought I was on his. He made me carry him, too, besides Margaret. Like this they ride on me with hoofs and claws. Tear me to pieces, stamp on me and break my bones.

Once more the hoary old fiddler pointed his bow at Wilhelm as he hurried by. Wilhelm rejected his begging and denied the omen. He dodged heavily through traffic and with his quick, small steps ran up the lower stairway of the Gloriana Hotel with its dark-tinted mirrors, kind to people's defects. From the lobby he phoned Tamkin's room, and when no one answered he took the elevator up. A rouged woman in her fifties with a mink stole led three tiny dogs on a leash, high-strung creatures with prominent black eyes, like dwarf deer, and legs like twigs. This was the eccentric Estonian lady who had been moved with her pets to the twelfth floor.

She identified Wilhelm. "You are Doctor Adler's son," she said.

Formally, he nodded.

"I am a dear friend of your father."

He stood in the corner and would not meet her glance, and she thought he was snubbing her and made a mental note to speak of it to the doctor.

The linen-wagon stood at Tamkin's door, and the chambermaid's key with its big brass tongue was in the lock.

"Has Doctor Tamkin been here?" he asked her.

"No, I haven't seen him."

Wilhelm came in, however, to look around. He examined the photos on the desk, trying to connect the faces with the strange people in Tamkin's stories. Big, heavy volumes were stacked under the double-pronged TV aerial. *Science and Sanity*, he read, and there were several books of poetry. The *Wall Street Journal* hung in separate sheets from the bed-table under the weight of the silver jug. A bathrobe with lightning streaks of red and white was laid across the foot of the bed with a pair of expensive batik pajamas. It was a box of a room, but from the windows you saw the river as far uptown as the bridge, as far downtown as Hoboken. What lay between was deep, azure, dirty, complex, crystal, rusty, with the red bones of new apartments rising on the bluffs of New Jersey, and huge liners in their berths, the tugs with matted beards of cordage. Even the brackish tidal river smell rose this high, like the smell of mop water. From every side he heard pianos, and the voices of men and women singing scales and opera, all mixed, and the sounds of pigeons on the ledges.

Again Wilhelm took the phone. "Can you locate Doctor Tamkin in the lobby for me?" he asked. And when the operator reported that she could not, Wilhelm gave the number of his father's room, but Dr. Adler was not in either. "Well, please give me the masseur. I say the massage room. Don't you understand me? The men's health club. Yes, Max Schilper's—how am I supposed to know the name of it?"

There a strange voice said, "Toktor Adler?" It was the old Czech prizefighter with the deformed nose and ears who was attendant down there and gave out soap, sheets, and sandals. He went away. A hollow endless silence followed. Wilhelm flickered the receiver with his nails, whistled into it, but could not summon either the attendant or the operator.

The maid saw him examining the bottles of pills on Tamkin's table and seemed suspicious of him. He was running low on Phenaphen pills and was looking for something else. But he swallowed one of his own tablets and went out and rang again for the elevator. He went down to the health club. Through the steamy windows, when he emerged, he saw the reflection of the swimming pool swirling green at the bottom of the lowest stairway. He went through the locker-room curtains. Two men wrapped in towels were playing Ping-pong. They were awkward and the ball bounded high. The Negro in the toilet was shining shoes. He did not know Dr. Adler by name, and Wilhelm descended to the massage room. On the tables naked men were lying. It was not a brightly lighted place, and it was very hot, and under the white faint moons of the ceiling shone pale skins. Calendar pictures of pretty girls dressed in tiny fringes were pinned on the wall. On the first table, eyes deeply shut in heavy silent luxury lay a man with a full square beard and short legs, stocky and black-haired. He might have been an orthodox Russian. Wrapped in a sheet, waiting, the man beside him was newly shaved and red from the steambath. He had a big happy face and was dreaming. And after him was an athlete, strikingly muscled, powerful and young, with a strong white curve to his genital and a half-angry smile on his mouth. Dr. Adler was on the fourth table, and Wilhelm stood over his father's pale, slight body. His ribs were narrow and small, his belly round, white, and high. It had its own being, like something separate. His thighs were weak, the muscles of his arms had fallen, his throat was creased.

The masseur in his undershirt bent and whispered in his ear, "It's your son," and Dr. Adler opened his eyes into Wilhelm's face. At once he saw the trouble in it, and by an instantaneous reflex he removed himself from the danger of contagion, and he said serenely, "Well, have you taken my advice, Wilky?"

"Oh, Dad," said Wilhelm.

"To take a swim and get a massage?"

"Did you get my note?" said Wilhelm.

SAUL BELLOW

"Yes, but I'm afraid you'll have to ask somebody else, because I can't. I had no idea you were so low on funds. How did you let it happen? Didn't you lay anything aside?"

"Oh, please, Dad," said Wilhelm, almost bringing his hands together in a clasp.

"I'm sorry," said the doctor. "I really am. But I have set up a rule. I've thought about it, I believe it is a good rule, and I don't want to change it. You haven't acted wisely. What's the matter?"

"Everything. Just everything. What isn't? I did have a little, but I haven't been very smart."

"You took some gamble? You lost it? Was it Tamkin? I told you, Wilky, not to build on that Tamkin. Did you? I suspect—"

"Yes, Dad, I'm afraid I trusted him."

Dr. Adler surrendered his arm to the masseur, who was using wintergreen oil.

"Trusted! And got taken?"

"I'm afraid I kind of—" Wilhelm glanced at the masseur but he was absorbed in his work. He probably did not listen to conversations. "I did. I might as well say it. I should have listened to you."

"Well, I won't remind you how often I warned you. It must be very painful."

"Yes, Father, it is."

"I don't know how many times you have to be burned in order to learn something. The same mistakes, over and over."

"I couldn't agree with you more," said Wilhelm with a face of despair. "You're so right, Father. It's the same mistakes, and I get burned again and again. I can't seem to—I'm stupid, Dad, I just can't breathe. My chest is all up—I feel choked. I just simply can't catch my breath."

He stared at his father's nakedness. Presently he became aware that Dr. Adler was making an effort to keep his temper. He was on the verge of an explosion. Wilhelm hung his face and said, "Nobody likes bad luck, eh Dad?"

"So! It's bad luck now. A minute ago it was stupidity."

"It is stupidity—it's some of both. It's true that I can't learn. But I—"

"I don't want to listen to the details," said his father. "And I want you to understand that I'm too old to take on new burdens. I'm just too old to do it. And people who will just wait for help—must *wait* for help. They have got to stop waiting."

"It isn't all a question of money—there are other things a father can give to a son." He lifted up his gray eyes and his nostrils grew wide with a look of suffering appeal that stirred his father even more deeply against him.

He warningly said to him, "Look out, Wilky, you're tiring my patience very much."

"I try not to. But one word from you, just a word, would go a long way. I've never asked you for very much. But you are not a kind man, Father. You don't give the little bit I beg you for."

He recognized that his father was now furiously angry. Dr. Adler started to say something, and then raised himself and gathered the sheet over him as he did so. His mouth opened, wide, dark, twisted, and he said to Wilhelm, "You want to make yourself into my cross. But I am not going to pick up a cross. I'll see you dead, Wilky, by Christ, before I let you do that to me."

"Father, listen! Listen!"

"Go away from me now. It's torture for me to look at you, you slob!" cried Dr. Adler.

Wilhelm's blood rose up madly, in anger equal to his father's, but then it sank down and left him helplessly captive to misery. He said stiffly, and with a strange sort of formality, "Okay, Dad. That'll be enough. That's about all we should say." And he stalked out heavily by the door adjacent to the swimming pool and the steam room, and labored up two long flights from the basement. Once more he took the elevator to the lobby on the mezzanine.

He inquired at the desk for Dr. Tamkin.

The clerk said, "No, I haven't seen him. But I think there's something in the box for you."

"Me? Give it here," said Wilhelm and opened a telephone message from his wife. It read, "Please phone Mrs. Wilhelm on return. Urgent."

Whenever he received an urgent message from his wife he was always thrown into a great fear for the children. He ran to the phone booth, spilled out the change from his pockets onto the little curved steel shelf under the telephone, and dialed the Digby number.

"Yes?" said his wife. Scissors barked in the parlor.

"Margaret?"

"Yes, hello." They never exchanged any other greeting. She instantly knew his voice.

"The boys all right?"

"They're out on their bicycles. Why shouldn't they be all right? Scissors, quiet!"

"Your message scared me," he said. "I wish you wouldn't make 'urgent' so common."

"I had something to tell you."

Her familiar unbending voice awakened in him a kind of hungry longing, not for Margaret but for the peace he had once known.

"You sent me a postdated check," she said. "I can't allow that. It's already five days past the first. You dated your check for the twelfth."

"Well, I have no money. I haven't got it. You can't send me to prison for that. I'll be lucky if I can raise it by the twelfth."

She answered, "You better get it, Tommy."

"Yes? What for?" he said. "Tell me. For the sake of what? To tell lies about me to everyone? You—"

She cut him off. "You know what for. I've got the boys to bring up."

Wilhelm in the narrow booth broke into a heavy sweat. He dropped his head and shrugged while with his fingers he arranged nickels, dimes, and quarters in rows. "I'm doing my best," he said. "I've had some bad luck. As a matter of fact, it's been so bad that I don't know where I am. I couldn't tell you what day of the week this is. I can't think straight. I'd better not even try. This has been one of those days, Margaret. May I never live to go through another like it. I mean that with all my heart. So I'm not going to try to do any thinking today. Tomorrow I'm going to see some guys. One is a sales manager. The other is in television. But not to act," he hastily added. "On the business end."

"That's just some more of your talk, Tommy," she said. "You ought to patch things up with Rojax Corporation. They'd take you back. You've got to stop thinking like a youngster."

"What do you mean?"

"Well," she said, measured and unbending, remorselessly unbending, "you still think like a youngster. But you can't do that any more. Every other day you want to make a new start. But in eighteen years you'll be eligible for retirement. Nobody wants to hire a new man of your age."

"I know. But listen, you don't have to sound so hard. I can't get on my knees to them. And really you don't have to sound so hard. I haven't done you so much harm."

"Tommy, I have to chase you and ask you for money that you owe us, and I hate it."

She hated also to be told that her voice was hard.

"I'm making an effort to control myself," she told him.

He could picture her, her graying bangs cut with strict fixity above her pretty, decisive face. She prided herself on being fair-minded. We could not bear, he thought, to know what we do. Even though blood is spilled. Even though the breath of life is taken from someone's nostrils. This is the way of the weak; quiet and fair. And then smash! They smash!

"Rojax take me back? I'd have to crawl back. They don't need me. After so many years I should have got stock in the firm. How can I support the three of you, and live myself, on half the territory? And why should I even try when you won't lift a finger to help? I sent you back to school, didn't I? At that time you said—"

His voice was rising. She did not like that and intercepted him. "You misunderstood me," she said.

"You must realize you're killing me. You can't be as blind as all that. Thou shalt not kill! Don't you remember that?"

She said, "You're just raving now. When you calm down it'll be different. I have great confidence in your earning ability."

"Margaret, you don't grasp the situation. You'll have to get a job."

"Absolutely not. I'm not going to have two young children running loose."

"They're not babies," Wilhelm said. "Tommy is fourteen. Paulie is going to be ten."

"Look," Margaret said in her deliberate manner. "We can't continue this conversation if you're going to yell so, Tommy. They're at a dangerous age. There are teen-aged gangs—the parents working, or the families broken up."

Once again she was reminding him that it was he who had left her. She had the bringing up of the children as her burden, while he must expect to pay the price of his freedom.

Freedom! he thought with consuming bitterness. Ashes in his mouth, not freedom. Give me my children. For they are mine too.

Can you be the woman I lived with? he started to say. Have you forgotten that we slept so long together? Must you now deal with me like this, and have no mercy?

He would be better off with Margaret again than he was today. This was what she wanted to make him feel, and she drove it home. "Are you in misery?" she was saying. "But you have deserved it." And he could not return to her any more than he could beg Rojax to take him back. If it cost him his life, he could not. Margaret had ruined him with Olive. She hit him and hit him, beat him, battered him, wanted to beat the very life out of him.

"Margaret, I want you please to reconsider about work. You have that degree now. Why did I pay your tuition?"

"Because it seemed practical. But it isn't. Growing boys need parental authority and a home."

He begged her, "Margaret, go easy on me. You ought to. I'm at the end of my rope and feel that I'm suffocating. You don't want to be responsible for a person's destruction. You've got to let up. I feel I'm about to burst." His face had expanded. He struck a blow upon the tin and wood and nails of the wall of the booth. "You've got to let me breathe. If I should keel over, what then? And it's something I can never understand about you. How you can treat someone like this whom you lived with so long. Who gave you the best of himself. Who tried. Who loved you." Merely to pronounce the word "love" made him tremble.

"Ah," she said with a sharp breath. "Now we're coming to it. How did you imagine it was going to be—big shot? Everything made smooth for you? I thought you were leading up to this."

She had not, perhaps, intended to reply as harshly as she did, but she brooded a great deal and now she could not forbear to punish him and make him feel pains like those she had to undergo.

He struck the wall again, this time with his knuckles, and he had scarcely enough air in his lungs to speak in a whisper, because his heart pushed upward with a frightful pressure. He got up and stamped his feet in the narrow enclosure.

"Haven't I always done my best?" he yelled, though his voice sounded weak and thin to his own ears. "Everything comes from me and nothing back again to me. There's no law that'll punish this, but you are committing a crime against me. Before God—and that's no joke. I mean that. Before God! Sooner or later the boys will know it."

In a firm tone, levelly, Margaret said to him, "I won't stand to be howled at. When you can speak normally and have something sensible to say I'll listen. But not to this." She hung up.

Wilhelm tried to tear the apparatus from the wall. He ground his teeth and seized the black box with insane digging fingers and made a stifled cry and pulled. Then he saw an elderly lady staring through the glass door, utterly appalled by him, and he ran from the booth, leaving a large amount of change on the shelf. He hurried down the stairs and into the street.

On Broadway it was still bright afternoon and the gassy air was almost motionless under the leaden spokes of sunlight, and sawdust footprints lay about the doorways of butcher shops and fruit stores. And the great, great crowd, the inexhaustible current of millions of every race and kind pouring out, pressing round, of every age, of every genius, possessors of every human secret, antique and future, in every face the refinement of one particular motive or essence—*I labor, I spend, I strive, I design, I love, I cling, I uphold, I give way, I envy, I long, I scorn, I die, I hide, I want.* Faster, much faster than any man could make the tally. The sidewalks were wider than any causeway; the street itself was immense, and it quaked and gleamed and it seemed to Wilhelm to throb at the last limit of endurance. And although the sunlight appeared like a broad tissue, its actual weight made him feel like a drunkard.

"I'll get a divorce if it's the last thing I do," he swore. "As for Dad—As for Dad—I'll have to sell the car for junk and pay the hotel. I'll have to go on my knees to Olive and say, 'Stand by me a while. Don't let her win. Olive!'" And he thought, I'll try to start again with Olive. In fact, I must. Olive loves me. Olive—

Beside a row of limousines near the curb he thought he saw Dr. Tamkin. Of course he had been mistaken before about the hat with the cocoa-colored band and didn't want to make the same mistake twice. But wasn't that Tamkin who was speaking so earnestly, with pointed shoulders, to someone under the canopy of the funeral parlor? For this was a huge funeral. He looked for the singular face under the dark gray, fashionable hatbrim. There were two open cars filled with flowers, and a policeman tried to keep a path open to pedestrians. Right at the canopy-pole, now wasn't that that damned Tamkin talking away with a solemn face, gesticulating with an open hand?

"Tamkin!" shouted Wilhelm, going forward. But he was pushed to the side by a policeman clutching his nightstick at both ends, like a rolling pin. Wilhelm was even farther from Tamkin now, and swore under his breath at the cop who continued to press him back, back, belly and ribs, saying, "Keep it moving there, please," his face red with impatient sweat, his brows like red fur. Wilhelm said to him haughtily, "You shouldn't push people like this."

The policeman, however, was not really to blame. He had been ordered to keep a way clear. Wilhelm was moved forward by the pressure of the crowd.

He cried, "Tamkin!"

But Tamkin was gone. Or rather, it was he himself who was carried from the street into the chapel. The pressure ended inside, where it was dark and cool. The flow of fan-driven air dried his face, which he wiped hard with his handkerchief to stop the slight salt itch. He gave a sigh when he heard the organ notes that stirred and breathed from the pipes and he saw people in the pews. Men in formal clothes and black homburgs strode softly back and forth on the cork floor, up and down the center aisle. The white of the stained glass was like mother-of-pearl, the blue of the Star of David like velvet ribbon.

Well, thought Wilhelm, if that was Tamkin outside I might as well wait for him here where it's cool. Funny, he never mentioned he had a funeral to go to today. But that's just like the guy.

But within a few minutes he had forgotten Tamkin. He stood along the wall with others and looked toward the coffin and the slow line that was moving past it, gazing at the face of the dead. Presently he too was in this line, and slowly, slowly, foot by foot, the beating of his heart anxious, thick, frightening, but somehow also rich, he neared the coffin and paused for his turn, and gazed down. He caught his breath when he looked at the corpse, and his face swelled, his eyes shone hugely with instant tears.

The dead man was gray-haired. He had two large waves of gray hair at the front. But he was not old. His face was long, and he had a bony nose, slightly, delicately twisted. His brows were raised as though he had sunk into the final thought. Now at last he was with it, after the end of all distractions, and when his flesh was no longer flesh. And by this meditative look Wilhelm was so struck that he could not go away. In spite of the tinge of horror, and then the splash of heartsickness that he felt, he could not go. He stepped out of line and remained beside the coffin; his eyes filled silently and through his still tears he studied the man as the line of visitors moved with veiled looks past the satin coffin toward the standing bank of lilies, lilacs, roses. With great stifling sorrow, almost admiration, Wilhelm nodded and nodded. On the surface, the dead man with his formal shirt and his tie and silk lapels and his powdered skin looked so proper; only a little beneath so—black, Wilhelm thought, so fallen in the eyes.

Standing a little apart, Wilhelm began to cry. He cried at first softly and from sentiment, but soon from deeper feeling. He sobbed loudly and his face grew distorted and hot, and the tears stung his skin. A man—another human creature, was what first went through his thoughts, but other and different things were torn from him. What'll I do? I'm stripped and kicked out . . . Oh, Father, what do I ask of you? What'll I do about the kids—Tommy, Paul? My children. And Olive? My dear! Why, why, why—you must protect me against that devil who wants my life. If you want it, then kill me. Take, take it, take it from me.

Soon he was past words, past reason, coherence. He could not stop. The source of all tears had suddenly sprung open within him, black, deep, and hot, and they were pouring out and convulsed his body, bending his stubborn head, bowing his shoulders, twisting his face, crippling the very hands with which he held the handkerchief. His efforts to collect himself were useless. The great knot of ill and grief in his throat swelled upward and he gave in utterly and held his face and wept. He cried with all his heart.

He, alone of all the people in the chapel, was sobbing. No one knew who he was.

One woman said, "Is that perhaps the cousin from New Orleans they were expecting?"

"It must be somebody real close to carry on so."

"Oh my, oh my! To be mourned like that," said one man and looked at Wilhelm's heavy shaken shoulders, his clutched face and whitened fair hair, with wide, glinting, jealous eyes.

"The man's brother, maybe?"

"Oh, I doubt that very much," said another bystander. "They're not alike at all. Night and day."

The flowers and lights fused ecstatically in Wilhelm's blind, wet eyes; the heavy sea-like music came up to his ears. It poured into him where he had hidden himself in the center of a crowd by the great and happy oblivion of tears. He heard it and sank deeper than sorrow, through torn sobs and cries toward the consummation of his heart's ultimate need.

JOHN UPDIKE

(1932–   )

John Updike was born in a small town, Shillington, Pennsylvania, where his father was a high school teacher. His mother, herself a published storywriter, seems early on to have given her son a sense of his "difference." (The protagonist of more than one Updike story remembers his mother as having "set me moving toward an unseen goal with a vague expectation that in the beginning was more hers than mine. . . . I felt that . . . she was pointing me through these corridors toward a radiant place she had despaired of reaching." And it is said that Updike went to Harvard because his mother decided that more distinguished writers had gone there than anywhere else.) College was a series of triumphs, and Updike graduated *summa cum laude* in English in 1954, selling his first story (to *The New Yorker*) that same year. After a year at the Ruskin School of Drawing and Fine Art in Oxford, England, he returned to America and worked as a staff writer for *The New Yorker*, producing material for a number of that magazine's departments, including "The Talk of the Town." He was shortly able, owing to the success of his stories, to leave the magazine and work full time at his own writing. Among writers of his generation with literary as well as commercial goals, Updike is almost unique in his ability to live exclusively by his pen. He now makes his home, with his wife and four children, in Ipswich, Massachusetts.

As this account suggests, Updike has never been an outsider or a loser. He has produced eight well-ordered novels [*The Poorhouse Fair* (1959), *Rabbit, Run* (1960), *The Centaur* (1963), *Of the Farm* (1966), *Couples* (1968), *Bech: A Book* (1970), *Rabbit Redux* (1971), and *A Month of Sundays* (1975)], three volumes of verse [*The Carpentered Hen* (1958), *Telephone Poles and Other Poems* (1963), and *Midpoint and Other Poems* (1969)], and five collections of short stories [*The Same Door* (1959), *Pigeon Feathers and Other Stories* (1962), *Olinger Stories, A Selection* (1964), *The Music School* (1966), and *Museums and Women* (1972)]. Some essays and reviews were collected in *Assorted Prose* (1965). He has also published a play, *Buchanan Dying* (1974), and several books for children.

Critical studies include Alice and Kenneth Hamilton, *The Elements of John Updike,* 1970; Rachael C. Burchard, *John Updike: Yea Sayings,* 1971; and Larry E. Taylor, *Pastoral and Anti-Pastoral Patterns in John Updike's Fiction,* 1971.

Amidst this profusion of work the outlines of two worlds come reasonably clear, one now lost, the other now all too palpable. The lost world is Shillington, transformed in fiction into Olinger, a place

neither young nor old, poor nor rich, backward nor forward. It is beyond the western edge of Megalopolis, and hangs between its shallow hills enchanted, nowhere, anywhere; there is no place like it.

Updike's Olinger stories are delicate recollections of what it was like to grow up in Protestant, middle-class, smalltown America of the 1940's; they evoke states of mind and expectation no longer easily imaginable except with the aid of props. (Updike has admitted to a weakness for old photograph albums: "I find old photographs powerful. . . . There's a funny thing about the way the flux of time was halted at this particular spot. You just can't get back to it.") In this world commonplace domestic events—wobblings of childhood faith, encounters in adolescence with the smug amorality that calls itself sophistication, adjustments in familial relationships—are treated unembarrassedly as consequential. The social detail and gestures are full and authoritative and the standards of assessment are unambiguous. The nostalgia is pervasive, but its idealizations are subjected to irony; the moment of happiness—rarest of all sights in modern fiction—is allowed to breathe, but there are glimpses of the opposite and many an acknowledgment that if the past could be recaptured, it would no longer be desired. And for a time, as Updike once expressed it, whatever the limits of this world, he had no real choice save to explore and reexplore it.

To transcribe middleness with all its grits, bumps, and anonymities, in its fullness of satisfaction and mystery: is it possible or, in view of the suffering that violently colors the periphery and that at all moments threatens to move into the center, worth doing? Possibly not; but the horse chestnut trees, the telephone poles, the porches, the green hedges recede to a calm point that in my subjective geography is still the center of the world.

In addition to the early short stories about "middleness," there was *The Centaur,* a novel that won the National Book Award in 1964. (Updike saw the tale as a version of "the Protestant kind of goodness going down with all the guns firing—antic, frantic, comic, but goodness nonetheless.") There is also a shapely novella, *Of the Farm,* that takes as its subject a conflict of loyalties, Olinger values under pressure from new currents of self-indulgence. And, as late as the mid-1960's, the earlier material still surfaces—as, for example, in a story about a family clan's annual reunion, in a meadow where the once pure creek is now polluted and unfriendly eyes watch from surrounding ranch-houses ("The Family Meadow" in *The Music School).*

But well before then it had been largely displaced by the claims of a world less easy to characterize but nevertheless, from the Olinger perspective, wholly other. What makes it other is that a confusion of values lies at its center, whether the subject is blue-collar frustration as in *Rabbit, Run,* the "postpill paradise" of *Couples,* social and sexual chaos as in *Rabbit Redux,* or travestied religion as in *A Month of Sundays.* Often the writer steps forth as moralist in these fictions; he retails sins committed against children and sins between husband and wife. But the moralist knows far less on this turf than in his first world. About adultery in *Couples,* for instance, he will remark, sternly, that: "All these goings-on would be purely lyrical, like nymphs and satyrs in a grove, except for the group of distressed and neglected children." About the same book he once said that: "There's a lot of dry talk around about love and sex being somehow the new ground of our morality. . . . I thought I should show the ground and ask, is it entirely to be wished for?" The implication is that the novelist had a rooted opinion of his own—but the texture of the book says otherwise: the writer is more convincing as voluptuary than as assessor of behavior and taste. Updike's other recent novels have been filled with social news about what is happening to middle-class manners and desires on a dozen underreported fronts. But, like *Couples,* they locate no center of worth as deserving as the consciousness that mapped the Olinger world.

They are, however, superior entertainments—and proof that a distinguished craftsman in letters can still create and hold an audience in the so-called "postprint culture." Updike aspired to and has achieved successes beyond those of the wit and the gifted stylist; his brio and energy remain intact, and his powers of interpretation, as of assessment, seem almost certain to increase.

When Everyone Was Pregnant

I'm in securities, but I read a lot, on the train. Read yesterday that the Fifties were coming back. All through the Sixties writers kept knocking them: Eisenhower, Lester Lanin, skirts below the knee, ho-hum. Well, turns out Eisenhower was a great non-war President. Rock is dead. Skirts have dropped to the ankle. But *my* Fifties won't come back.

Kind years to me. Entered them poor and left them comfortable. Entered them chaste and left them a father. Of four and a miscarriage. Those the years when everyone was pregnant. Not only kind but beautiful years.

How they would float across the sand like billowed sails. My wife and the wives of our friends. Shakespeare, Titania to Oberon: "laughed to see the sails conceive, And grow bigbellied with the wanton wind." In their sun-paled plaid maternity bathing suits, the pregnant young women. Tugging behind them the toddlers already born. Dinghies. Moved to a town with a beach in 54: my first promotion. Nancy's second child.

Coming along the water's edge, heads higher than the line of the sea. The horizon blue, sparkling, severe. Proust and the "little band" at Balbec. Yet more fully in flower than those, bellies swollen stately. Faces and limbs freckled in every hollow, burnished on the ball of the shoulder, the tip of the nose. Sunburned nostril-wings, peeling. The light in their eyes stealing sparkle from the far hard edge of the sea. Where a few sails showed, leaning, curling.

They would come up to us, join us. Laughter, aluminum chairs, towels, infant sun hats, baby-food jars, thermoses chuckling in the straw hampers. Above me, edge of maternity skirt lifted by touch of wind, curl of pubic hair high inside thigh showed. Sickening sensation of love. Sand-warmed wind blowing cool out of the future.

They would settle with us, forming a ring. Their heads inward with gossip, their bare legs spokes of a wheel. On the rim, children with sandpails each digging by the feet of his own mother. The shades of sand darkening as they dug. The milk smell of sun lotion. The way our words drifted up and out: sandwich wrappers blowing.

Katharine, Sarah, Liz, Peggy, Angela, June. Notes of a scale, colors of a rainbow. Nancy the seventh. Now in the Seventies two have moved. To Denver, to Birmingham. Two are divorced. Two still among us with their husbands. But all are gone, receding. Can never be revisited, that time when everyone was pregnant guiltlessly.

Guiltlessness. Our fat Fifties cars, how we loved them, revved them: no thought of pollution. Exhaust smoke, cigarette smoke, factory smoke, all romantic. Romance of consumption at its height. Shopping for baby food in the gaudy trash of the supermarkets. Purchasing power: young, newly powerful, born to consume. To procreate greedily. A smug conviction that the world was doomed. Beyond the sparkling horizon, an absolute enemy. Above us, bombs whose flash would fill the scene like a cup to overflowing.

Old slides. June's husband had a Kodak with a flash attachment (nobody owned Japanese cameras then). How young we were. The men scrawny as boys. Laughable military haircuts: the pea-brain look. The women with bangs and lipsticked smiles. We look drunk. Sometimes we were.

Jobs, houses, spouses of our own. Permission to drink and change diapers and operate power mowers and stay up past midnight. At college Nancy had not been allowed to smoke upstairs, made herself do it in our home. Like a sexual practice personally distasteful but recommended by Van der Velde. Dreadful freedom. Phrase fashionable then.

Had we expected to starve in the Depression? Be bayonetted by Japs when they invaded California? Korea seemed the best bargain we could strike: extremities of superpowers tactfully clashing in distant cold mud. The world's skin of fear shivered but held. Then came Eisenhower and gave us a precarious peace and a sluggishly rising market and a (revokable) license to have fun, to make babies. Viewed the world through two lenses since discarded: fear and gratitude. Young people now are many things but they aren't afraid, and aren't grateful.

Those summer parties. Should remember them better. Sunlight in the gin, the sprig of mint wilting. The smell of grass freshly mowed coming in through the evening screens. Children wandering in and out with complaints their mothers brushed away like cigarette smoke. What were we saying? The words we spoke were nonsense except the breath we took to speak them was life—us alive, able.

Katharine's husband Jerry had only one eye, the other frosted by childhood accident. No one felt sorry for him, too healthy, hearty. Born salesman. Him saying across to Sarah Harris, her pregnant in a big-flowered dress, sitting dreaming in a plush wing chair, "Sarah, sitting there you look just like a voluptuous big piece of wallpaper!" I thought, *has only one eye, everything looks flat to him*. Sickening sensation of love.

Years later I said to Sarah "You voluptuous piece of wallpaper you" but she had forgotten and I had to explain.

Another night, my flat tire in the Connellys' newly gravelled driveway. Sharp bluestones. Two in the morning. Ed came up out of his cellar holding high a cruciform lug wrench chanting Veni Creator Spiritus. Shocked me. My own footsteps on the gravel, *unch, unch*. A monster coming closer. Most of us at least sent the kids to Sunday school.

Dancing. Hand squeezes. Moonlight songs, smoke getting in your eyes. All innocent enough. The bump, bump of pregnant bellies against me. Seeing each other's names in the Birth column of the local paper a private joke. Hospital visits, wifeless nights. The time our fourth was born, night after the first storm of winter. Gynecologist swung by for her in his car on the way to the hospital. Just starting up practice, handsome man in ski hat. On the stark white empty street below our window looked like a lover tossing pebbles. Her contractions coming every three minutes, her little suitcase, hurrying from room to room kissing the children in their sleep. Gynecologist waiting, his face turned upward in the moonlight, in the silence. A lover howling.

Nervous of the creaking wind I slept one or two of those nights with a golf club in the bed. I think a seven iron. Figured I could get it around on a burglar quicker than a wood.

The time Sarah was with me. Nancy off in the hospital with varicose veins. Diagnosis: no more babies. Our last baby cried. Sarah rose and mothered it. Child went silent, laughed, knew something was funny, maybe thought Sarah was Nancy making a face, pretending something. Same smell, woman smell, same safety. Mullioned moonlight on Sarah's bare shoulders, bent over crib. Baby gurgled and laughed. "Crazy kid you have here." Too much love. Too many babies, breathing all over the dark house like searchlights that might switch on.

Sarah's lovely wide shoulders, big hips, breasts shallow and firm. First time I saw them it tore at me, exclaimed she had breasts like a Greek statue. She laughed and told me I read too much. But it had been torn out of me.

The ritual of taking out Nancy's hairpins one by one before making love. Rain on the roof. Fifties a house decade, never ventured into the streets. Cuba, Sputnik, Tibet. Rain on the roof.

The brown line on her belly a woman brings back from the hospital, after being pregnant. Nobody had ever told me that line existed. Why hadn't they?

The babies got bigger. The parties got wilder. Time at the beach, after Cancer dance, hot summer, might have been 1960. We took off our clothes and swam. Scary tide, strong moon, could see the women had aged. Slack bellies, knees and faces full of shadow. Used their long gauzy dance dresses as towels, wrapped around them as sarongs. Over the ocean, riots. Assassinations, protests, a decade's overdue bills heaped like surf thunder on the sand bar. We were no longer young. Embarrassed. Groped for our underclothes and shoes. Yet the warm kiss of wind off of sand, even at night.

I make some notes on the train. My hand shakes. My town slides by, the other comfortable small towns, the pastures and glimpses of sea, a single horse galloping, a golf course with a dawn foursome frozen on the green, dew-white, and then the lesser cities, the little one-hotel disgruntled cities, black walls hurled like fists at our windows, broken factory windows, a rusted drawbridge halted forever at almost-down, a gravel yard with bluestones pyramided by size, a dump smoldering, trash gaudy with all the colors of jewels; then the metropolis, the tracks multiplying in lightning calculations, the hazed skyscrapers changing relationship to one another like the steeples in Proust, the tunnels of billboards, the station, vast and derelict; the final stop. This evening, the same thing backwards.

But never get bored with how the train slices straight. Lightly rocking. Through intersections of warning bells tingling, past playgrounds and back yards, warehouses built on a bias to fit the right-of-way. Like time. Cuts sleepwalking through everything.

Notes not come to anything. Lives not come to anything. Life a common stock that fluctuates in value. But you cannot sell, you must hold, hold till it dips to nothing. The big boys sell you out.

Edgar to blinded Gloucester: Ripeness is all. Have never exactly understood. Ripeness is all that is left? Or, deeper and more hopeful, ripeness is all that matters? Encloses all, answers all, justifies all. Ripeness is God.

Now: our babies drive cars, push pot, shave, menstruate, riot for peace, eat macrobiotic. Wonderful in many ways, but not ours, never ours, we see now. Now: we go to a party and see only enemies. Fifteen shared years have made us wary, survival-conscious. Sarah looks away. Spokes of the wheel are missing. Our babies accuse us.

Did the Fifties exist? Voluptuous wallpaper. Crazy kid. Sickening sensation of love. The train slides forward. The decades slide seaward, taking us along. I am still afraid. Still grateful.

THOMAS PYNCHON

(1937–   )

Thomas Pynchon's life story is a closely held secret. The dust jacket of *V.* (1963) revealed that he was born on Long Island, "is a graduate of Cornell University and is now living in Mexico"; nothing has been officially vouchsafed since then. It is said that he went to public high school in Oyster Bay or Glen Cove, Long Island, New York, that his father was employed in the public works department for one or the other of these towns, that his mother was a nurse in a local hospital, that Pynchon as a high school boy seemed to identify his family name with that of the Pyncheons in Nathaniel Hawthorne's *The House of the Seven Gables,* and that, at Cornell, the writer-to-be studied engineering, not literature. But distinguishing shadow from substance in such information is a task that awaits future scholars.

The same can be said about the task of placing and evaluating the novels. A tissue of enigmas, conundrums, unsolved mysteries, popcult allusions and gags, *V., The Crying of Lot 49* (1966) and *Gravity's Rainbow* (1973) are challenging and mystifying books. They resemble here and there certain earlier American fictional explorations of absurdity (Joseph Heller's *Catch-22,* the short stories of John Cheever); they also have something in common with fables composed by such specialists in epistemological highjinks as Donald Barthelme, John Barth, and Robert Coover. Moreover, their cultural and intellectual bearings are reasonably obvious. Pynchon is the child of an age seemingly eager to destroy itself, whether by wars fought for the sake of "preserving" older political values, or by technological "innovation" undertaken for the sake of producing "higher forms" of human life. He is also the inheritor of an extraordinary burden of literary self-consciousness, the result of decades of intense theorizing—in France, South America, and elsewhere—about the nature of fiction; those who share the self-consciousness tend to believe that the obligation of fiction now is to reconstruct itself as antifiction, a medium for criticizing the assumptions that governed the fables of the past.

While these and other contexts for the consideration of Pynchon's books are helpful to a degree, none can prepare a reader for the variety of the man's tones—or for the oddities of his characterizations, or the impenetrabilities of his plots. Without exception Pynchon's stories are densely plotted, with multiple lies disappearing into each other and "characters" disintegrating in midair. Invariably the author steps forth for long stretches as a joker, a relisher of popular culture, an entertainer—but, no less invariably, he sheds his larking self (see the chapel scene with Roger Mexico and Jessica early in *Gravity's Rainbow*), rising to an astonishing, even noble, solemnity. Always there is a quest; always there is a character or characters engaged in putting the world together, explaining a series of events or coincidences that have piqued their minds; always the pursuit leads swiftly into a labyrinth wherein relations are endless and nothing can be cleared up; always there are glimpses of orderly, obscure, and useless bodies of knowledge, historical or scientific, that stand symbol for the emptiness of most achievements of the organizing mind.

Arguably Thomas Pynchon is engaged in creating a world beyond structure in order to dramatize the limits of the existing linguistic, narrative, and social arrangements to which people now give their faith. But he is at once less abstract and wittier from page to page than any such account of him can convey. Who but this writer, for instance, could have imagined, playfully yet ponderably, a Mucho Maas, a *sensitive* used car salesman tormented by the corruption of his kind?

For a couple of years he'd been a used car salesman and so hyperaware of what *that* profession had come to mean that working hours were exquisite torture to him. Mucho shaved his upper lip every morning three times with, three times against the grain to remove any remotest breath of a moustache . . . bought all natural shoulder suits, then went to a tailor to have the lapels made yet more abnormally narrow, on his hair used only water, combing it like Jack Lemmon to throw them further off. The sight of sawdust, even pencil shavings, made him wince, his own kind being known to use it for hushing sick transmissions, and though he dieted he could still not [as his wife did] use honey to sweeten his coffee for like all things viscous it distressed him, recalling too poignantly what is often mixed with motor oil to ooze dishonest into gaps between piston and cylinder wall. He walked out of a party one night because somebody used the word "creampuff," it seemed maliciously, in his hearing. The man was a refugee Hungarian pastry cook talking shop, but there was your Mucho: thinskinned. (*The Crying of Lot 49*)

Gravity's Rainbow shared the National Book Award for fiction in 1974 and was recommended for the Pulitzer Prize by that year's fiction jury. The Pulitzer trustees rejected the recommendation without explanation, awarding no prize that year.

From Gravity's Rainbow

Near her battery one night, driving Somewhere in Kent, Roger and Jessica came upon a church, a hummock in the dark upland, lamplit, growing out of the earth. It was Sunday evening, and shortly before vespers. Men in greatcoats, in oilskins, in dark berets they slipped off at the entrance, American fliers in leather lined with sheep's wool, a few women in clinking boots and wide-shouldered swagger coats, but no children, not a child in sight, just grownups, trudging in from their bomber fields, balloon-bivouacs, pillboxes over the beach, through the Norman doorway shaggy with wintering vines. Jessica said, "Oh, I remember . . ." but didn't go on. She was remembering other Advents, and hedges snowy as sheep from her window, and the Star ready to be pasted up on the sky again.

Roger pulled over, and they watched the scuffed and dun military going in to evensong. The wind smelled of fresh snow.

"We ought to be home," she said, after a bit, "it's late."

"We could just pop in here for a moment."

Well, *that* surprised her, but def, after weeks of his snide comments? His unbeliever's annoyance with the others in Psi Section he thought were out to drive him dotty as they were, and his Scroogery growing as shopping days till Xmas dwindled—"You're not supposed to be the sort," she told him. But she did want to go in, nostalgia was heavy in tonight's snow-sky, her own voice ready to betray her and run to join the waits whose carols we're so apt to hear now in the distances, these days of Advent dropping one by one, voices piping across frozen downs where the sown mines crowd thick as plums in a pudding . . . often above sounds of melting snow, winds that must blow not through Christmas air but through the substance of time would bring her those child-voices, singing for sixpences, and if her heart wasn't ready to take on quite all the stresses of her mortality and theirs, at least there was the fear that she was beginning to lose them—that one winter she would go running to look, out to the gate to find them, run as far as the trees but in vain, their voices fading. . . .

They walked through the tracks of all the others in the snow, she gravely on his arm, wind blowing her hair to snarls, heels slipping once on ice. "To hear the music," he explained.

Tonight's scratch choir was all male, epauletted shoulders visible under the wide necks of the white robes, and many faces nearly as white with the exhaustion of soaked and muddy fields, midwatches, cables strummed by the nervous balloons sunfishing in the clouds, tents whose lights inside shone nuclear at twilight, soullike, through the crosshatched walls, turning canvas to fine gauze, while the wind drummed there. Yet there was one black face, the counter-tenor, a Jamaican corporal, taken from his warm island to this—from singing his childhood along the rum-smoky saloons of High Holborn Street where the sailors throw mammoth red firecrackers, quarter of a stick of dynamite man, over the swinging doors and run across the street giggling, or come walking out with high-skirted girls, girls of the island, Chinese and French girls . . . lemon peels crushed in the gutters of the streets scented the early mornings where he used to sing, O have you seen my darlin' Lola, with a shape like a bottle of Coca-Cola, sailors running up and down in the brown shadows of alleys, flapping at neckerchief and pants-leg, and the girls whispering together and laughing . . . each morning he counted out half a pocket full of coins of all nations. From palmy Kingston, the intricate needs of the Anglo-American Empire (1939–1945) had brought him to this cold field-mouse church, nearly in earshot of a northern sea he'd hardly glimpsed in crossing, to a compline service, a program tonight of plainsong in English, forays now and then into polyphony: Thomas Tallis, Henry Purcell, even a German macronic from the fifteenth century, attributed to Heinrich Suso:

> In dulci jubilo
> Nun singet und seid froh!
> Unsers Herzens Wonne
> Leit in praesipio,
> Leuchtet vor die Sonne
> Matris in gremio.
> Alpha es et O.

With the high voice of the black man riding above the others, no head falsetto here but complete, out of the honest breast, a baritone voice brought over years of woodshedding up to this range . . . he was bringing brown girls to sashay among these nervous Protestants, down the ancient paths the music had set, Big and Little Anita, Stiletto May, Plongette who loves it between her tits and will do it that way for free—not to mention the Latin, the German? in an English church? These are not heresies so much as imperial outcomes, necessary as the black man's presence, from acts of minor surrealism—which, taken in the mass, are an act of suicide, but which in its pathology, in its dreamless version of the real, the Empire commits by the thousands every day, completely unaware of what it's doing. . . . So the pure counter-tenor voice was soaring, finding its way in to buoy Jessica's heart and even Roger's, she guessed, risking glances at his face sideways and up through brown ghosts of her hair, during recitatives or releases. He wasn't looking nihilistic, not even cheaply so. He was . . .

No, Jessica's never seen his face exactly like this, in the light of a few hanging oil lamps, the flames unguttering and very yellow, on the nearest the verger's two long fingerprints in fine, pollen V-for-victory up around the belly of the glass, Roger's skin more child-pink, his eyes more glowing than the lamplight alone can account for—isn't it? or is that how she wants it to be? The church is as cold as the night outside. There's the smell of damp wool, of bitter on the breaths of these professionals, of candle smoke and melting wax, of smothered farting, of hair tonic, of the burning oil itself, folding the other odors in a maternal way, more closely belonging to Earth, to deep strata, other times, and listen . . . listen: this is the War's evensong, the War's canonical hour, and the night is real. Black greatcoats crowd together, empty hoods full of dense, church-interior shadows. Over on the coast the Wrens work late, down inside cold and gutted shells, their blue torches are newborn stars in the tidal evening. Hullplates swing in the sky, like great iron leaves, on cables that creak in splinters of sound. At ease, on standby, the flames of the torches, softened, fill the round glass faces of the gauges with apricot light. In the pipefitters' sheds, icicled, rattling when the gales are in the Straits, here's thousands of old used toothpaste tubes, heaped often to the ceilings, thousands of somber man-mornings made tolerable, transformed to mint fumes and bleak song that left white spots across the quicksilver mirrors from Harrow to Gravesend, thousands of children who pestled foam up out of soft mortars of mouths, who lost easily a thousand times as many words among the chalky bubbles—bed-going complaints, timid announcements of love, news of fat or translucent, fuzzy or gentle beings from the country under the counterpane—uncounted soapy-liquorice moments spat and flushed down to sewers and the slow-scumming gray estuary, the morning mouths growing with the day tobacco and fish-furred, dry with fear, foul with idleness, flooded at thoughts of impossible meals, settling instead for the week's offal in gland pies, Household Milk, broken biscuits at half the usual points, and isn't menthol a marvelous invention to take just enough of it away each morning, down to become dusty oversize bubbles tessellating tough and stagnant among the tar shorelines, the intricate draftsmanship of outlets feeding, multiplying out to sea, as one by one these old toothpaste tubes are emptied and returned to the War, heaps of dimly fragrant metal, phantoms of peppermint in the winter shacks, each tube wrinkled or embossed by the unconscious hands of London, written over in interference-patterns, hand against hand, waiting now—it is true return—to be melted for solder, for plate, alloyed for castings, bearings, gasketry, hidden smokeshriek linings the children of that other domestic incarnation will never see. Yet the continuity, flesh to kindred metals, home to hedgeless sea, has persisted. It is not death that separates these incarnations, but paper: paper specialties, paper routines. The War, the Empire, will expedite such barriers between our lives. The War needs to divide this way, and to subdivide, though its propaganda will always stress unity, alliance, pulling together. The War does not appear to want a folk-consciousness, not even of the sort the Germans have engineered, ein Volk ein Führer—it wants a machine of many separate parts, not oneness, but a complexity. . . . Yet who can presume to say *what* the War wants, so vast and aloof is it . . . so *absentee*. Perhaps the War isn't even an awareness—not a life at all, really. There may only be some cruel, accidental resemblance of life. At "The White Visitation" there's a long-time schiz, you know, who believes that *he* is World War II. He gets no newspapers, refuses to listen to the wireless, but still, the day of the Normandy invasion somehow his temperature shot up to 104°. Now, as the pincers east and west continue their slow reflex contraction, he speaks of darkness invading his mind, of an attrition of self. . . . The Rundstedt offensive perked him up though, gave him a new lease on life—"A beautiful Christmas gift," he confessed to the resident on his ward, "it's the season of birth, of fresh beginnings." Whenever the rockets fall—those which are audible—he smiles, turns out to pace the ward, tears about to splash from the corners of his merry eyes, caught up in a ruddy high tonicity that can't help cheering his fellow patients. His days are numbered. He's to die on V-E Day. If he's not in fact the War then he's its child-surrogate, living high for a certain term but come the ceremonial day, look out. The true king only dies a mock death. Remember. Any number of young men may be selected to die in his place while the real king, foxy old bastard, goes on. Will he show up under the Star, slyly genuflecting with the other kings as this winter solstice draws on us? Bring to the serai gifts of tungsten, cordite, high-octane? Will the child gaze up from his ground of golden straw then, gaze into the eyes of the old king who bends long and unfurling overhead, leans to proffer his gift, will the eyes meet, and what message, what possible greeting or entente will flow between the king and the infant prince? Is the baby smiling, or is it just gas? Which do you want it to be?

Advent blows from the sea, which at sunset tonight shone green and smooth as iron-rich glass: blows daily upon us, all the sky above pregnant with saints and slender heralds' trumpets. Another year of wedding dresses abandoned in the heart of winter, never called for, hanging in quiet satin ranks now, their white-crumpled veils begun to yellow, rippling slightly only at your passing, spectator . . . visitor to the city at all the dead ends. . . . Glimpsing in the gowns your own reflection once or twice, halfway from shadow, only blurred flesh-colors across the peau de soie, urging you in to where you can smell the mildew's first horrible touch, which was really the idea—covering all trace of her own smell, middleclass bride-to-be perspiring, genteel soap and powder. But virgin in her heart, in her hopes. None of your bright-Swiss or crystalline season here, but darkly billowed in the day with cloud and the snow falling like gowns in the country, gowns of the winter, gentle at night, a nearly windless breathing around you. In the stations of the city the prisoners are back from Indo-China, wandering their poor visible bones, light as dreamers or men on the moon, among chrome-sprung prams of black hide resonant as drumheads, blonde wood high-chairs pink and blue with scraped and mush-spattered floral decals, folding-cots and bears with red felt tongues, baby-blankets making bright pastel clouds in the coal and steam smells, the metal spaces, among the queued, the drifting, the warily asleep, come by their hundreds in for the holidays, despite the warnings, the gravity of Mr. Morrison, the tube under the river a German rocket may pierce now, even now as the words are set down, the absences that may be waiting them, the city addresses that surely can no longer exist. The eyes from Burma, from Tonkin, watch these women at their hundred perseverances—stare out of blued orbits, through headaches no Alasils can ease. Italian P/Ws curse underneath the mail sacks that are puffing, echo-clanking in now each hour, in seasonal swell, clogging the snowy trainloads like mushrooms, as if the trains have been all night underground, passing through the country of the dead. If these Eyeties sing now and then you can bet it's not "Giovinezza" but something probably from *Rigoletto* or *La Bohème*—indeed the Post Office is considering issuing a list of Nonacceptable Songs, with ukulele chords as an aid to ready identification. Their cheer and songfulness, this lot, is genuine up to a point—but as the days pile up, as this orgy of Christmas greeting grows daily beyond healthy limits, with no containment in sight before Boxing Day, they settle, themselves, for being more professionally Italian, rolling the odd eye at the lady evacuees, finding techniques of balancing the sack with one hand whilst the other goes playing "dead"—*cioé*, conditionally alive—where the crowds thicken most feminine, directionless . . . well, most promising. Life has to go on. Both kinds of prisoner recognize that, but there's no *mano morto* for the Englishmen back from CBI, no leap from dead to living at mere permission from a likely haunch or thigh—no *play*, for God's sake, about life-and-death! They want no more adventures: only the old dutch fussing over the old stove or warming the old bed, cricketers in the wintertime, they want the semi-detached Sunday dead-leaf somnolence of a dried garden. If the brave new world should also come about, a kind of windfall, why there'll be time to adjust certainly to that. . . .But they want the nearly postwar luxury this week of buying an electric train set for the kid, trying that way each to light his own set of sleek little faces here, calibrating his strangeness, well-known photographs all, brought to life now, oohs and aahs but not yet, not here in the station, any of the moves most necessary: the War has shunted them, earthed them, those heedless destroying signalings of love. The children have unfolded last year's toys and found reincarnated Spam tins, they're hep this may be the other and, who knows, unavoidable side to the Christmas game. In the months between—country springs and summers—they played with real Spam tins—tanks, tank-destroyers, pillboxes, dreadnoughts deploying meat-pink, yellow and blue about the dusty floors of lumber-rooms or butteries, under the cots or couches of their exile. Now it's time again. The plaster baby, the oxen frosted with gold leaf and the human-eyed sheep are turning real again, paint quickens to flesh. To believe is not a price they pay—it happens all by itself. He is the New Baby. On the magic night before, the animals will talk, and the sky will be milk. The grandparents, who've waited each week for the Radio Doctor asking, What Are Piles? What Is Emphysema? What Is A Heart Attack? will wait up beyond insomnia, watching again for the yearly impossible not to occur, but with some mean residue—this *is* the hillside, the sky *can* show us a light—like a thrill, a good time you wanted too much, not a complete loss but still too far short of a miracle . . . keeping their sweatered and shawled vigils, theatrically bitter, but with the residue inside going through a new winter fermentation every year, each time a bit less, but always good for a revival at this season. . . . All but naked now, the shiny suits and gowns of their pubcrawling primes long torn to strips for lagging the hot-water pipes and heaters of landlords, strangers, for holding the houses' identities against the winter. The War needs coal. They have taken the next-to-last steps, attended the Radio Doctor's certifications of what they knew in their bodies, and at Christmas they are naked as geese under this woolen, murky, cheap old-people's swaddling. Their electric clocks run fast, even Big Ben will be fast now until the new spring's run in, all fast, and no one else seems to understand or to care. The War needs electricity. It's a lively game, Electric Monopoly, among the power companies, the Central Electricity Board, and other War agencies, to keep Grid Time synchronized with Greenwich Mean Time. In the night, the deepest concrete wells of night, dynamos whose locations are classified spin faster, and so, responding, the clock-hands next to all the old, sleepless eyes—gathering in their minutes whining, pitching higher toward the vertigo of a siren. It is the Night's Mad Carnival. There is merriment under the shadows of the minute-hands. Hysteria in the pale faces between the numerals. The power companies speak of loads, war-drains so vast the clocks will slow again unless this nightmare march is stolen, but the loads expected daily do not occur, and the Grid runs inching ever faster, and the old faces turn to the clock faces, thinking *plot*, and the numbers go whirling toward the Nativity, a violence, a nova of heart that will turn us all, change us forever to the very forgotten roots of who we are. But over the sea the fog tonight still is quietly scalloped pearl. Up in the city the arc-lamps crackle, furious, in smothered blaze up the centerlines of the streets, too ice-colored for candles, too chill-dropleted for holocaust . . . the tall red busses sway, all the headlamps by regulation newly unmasked now parry, cross, traverse and blind, torn great fistfuls of wetness blow by, desolate as the beaches beneath the nacre fog, whose barbed wire that never knew the inward sting of current, that only lay passive, oxidizing in the night, now weaves like underwater grass, looped, bitter cold, sharp as the scorpion, all the printless sand miles past cruisers abandoned in the last summers of peacetime that once holidayed the old world away, wine and olive-grove and pipe-smoke evenings away the other side of the War, stripped now to rust axles and brackets and smelling inside of the same brine as this beach you cannot really walk, because of the War. Up across the downs, past the spotlights where the migrant birds in autumn choked the beams night after night, fatally held till they dropped exhausted out of the sky, a shower of dead birds, the compline worshipers sit in the unheated church, shivering, voiceless as the choir asks: where are the joys? Where else but there where the Angels sing new songs and the bells ring out in the court of the King. *Eia*—strange thousand-year sigh—*eia, wärn wir da!* were we but there. . . . The tired men and their black bellwether reaching as far as they can, as far from their sheeps' clothing as the year will let them stray. Come then. Leave your war awhile, paper or iron war, petrol or flesh, come in with your love, your fear of losing, your exhaustion with it. All day it's been at you, coercing, jiving, claiming your belief in so much that isn't true. Is that who you are, that vaguely criminal face on your ID card, its soul snatched by the government camera as the guillotine shutter fell—or maybe just left behind with your heart, at the Stage Door Canteen, where they're counting the night's take, the NAAFI girls, the girls named Eileen, carefully sorting into refrigerated compartments the rubbery maroon organs with their yellow garnishes of fat—oh Linda come here feel this one, put your finger down in the ventricle here, isn't it swoony, it's still *going*. . . . Everybody you don't suspect is in on this, everybody but you: the chaplain, the doctor, your mother hoping to hang that Gold Star, the vapid soprano last night on the Home Service programme, let's not forget Mr. Noel Coward so stylish and cute about death and the afterlife, packing them into the Duchess for the fourth year running, the lads in Hollywood telling us how grand it all is over here, how much fun, Walt Disney causing Dumbo the elephant to clutch to that feather like how many carcasses under the snow tonight among the white-painted tanks, how many hands each frozen around a Miraculous Medal, lucky piece of worn bone, half-dollar with the grinning sun peering up under Liberty's wispy gown, clutching, dumb, when the 88 fell—what do you think, it's a children's story? There aren't any. The children are away dreaming, but the Empire has no place for dreams and it's Adults Only in here tonight, here in this refuge with the lamps burning deep, in pre-Cambrian exhalation, savory as food cooking, heavy as soot. And 60 miles up the rockets hanging the measureless instant over the black North Sea before the fall, ever faster, to orange heat, Christmas star, in helpless plunge to Earth. Lower in the sky the flying bombs are out too, roaring like the Adversary, seeking whom they may devour. It's a long walk home tonight. Listen to this mock-angel singing, let your communion be at least in listening, even if they are not spokesmen for your exact hopes, your exact, darkest terror, listen. There must have been evensong here long before the news of Christ. Surely for as long as there have been nights bad as this one—something to raise the possibility of another night that could actually, with love and cockcrows, light the path home, banish the Adversary, destroy the boundaries between our lands, our bodies, our stories, all false, about who we are: for the one night, leaving only the clear way home and the memory of the infant you saw, almost too frail, there's too much shit in these streets, camels and other beasts stir heavily outside, each hoof a chance to wipe him out, make him only another Messiah, and sure somebody's around already taking bets on that one, while here in this town the Jewish collaborators are selling useful gossip to Imperial Intelligence, and the local hookers are keeping the fore-skinned invaders happy, charging whatever the traffic will bear, just like the innkeepers who're naturally delighted with this registration thing, and up in the capital they're wondering should they, maybe, give everybody a *number,* yeah, something to help SPQR Record-keeping . . . and Herod or Hitler, fellas (the chaplains out in the Bulge are manly, haggard, hard drinkers), what kind of a world is it ("You forgot Roosevelt, padre," come the voices from the back, the good father can never see them, they harass him, these tempters, even into his dreams: "Wendell Willkie!" "How about Churchill?" "'Arry Pollitt!'") for a baby to come in tippin' those Toledos at 7 pounds 8 ounces thinkin' he's gonna redeem it, why, he oughta have his head exam-ined. . . .

But on the way home tonight, you wish you'd picked him up, held him a bit. Just held him, very close to your heart, his cheek by the hollow of your shoulder, full of sleep. As if it were you who could, somehow, save him. For the moment not caring who you're supposed to be registered as. For the moment anyway, no longer who the Caesars say you are.

O Jesu parvule,
Nach dir ist mir so weh . . .

So this pickup group, these exiles and horny kids, sullen civilians called up in their middle age, men fattening despite their hunger, flatulent because of it, pre-ulcerous, hoarse, runny-nosed, red-eyed, sore-throated, piss-swollen men suffering from acute lower backs and all-day hangovers, wishing death on officers they truly hate, men you have seen on foot and smileless in the cities but forgot, men who don't remember you either, knowing they ought to be grabbing a little sleep, not out here performing for strangers, give you this evensong, climaxing now with its rising fragment of some ancient scale, voices overlapping three- and fourfold, up, echoing, filling the entire hollow of the church—no counterfeit baby, no announcement of the Kingdom, not even a try at warming or lighting this terrible night, only, damn us, our scruffy obligatory little cry, our maximum reach outward—*praise be to God!*—for you to take back to your war-address, your war-identity, across the snow's footprints and tire tracks finally to the path you must create by yourself, alone in the dark. Whether you want it or not, whatever seas you have crossed, the way home. . . .

FIGURES OF THE DRAMATIST

EUGENE O'NEILL

(1888–1953)

Eugene O'Neill published almost 50 plays, and ranks as the most significant writer in the history of the American stage. The son of a famous
actor, he was at home in the theater from his earliest days, and his first
plays, produced by the Provincetown Players while he was in his twenties, won quick and enthusiastic approval. Some of the applause was
of doubtful worth—a mere endorsement of the playwright's impatience with genteel stage conventions, his contempt for facile American optimism, his overformulaic use of borrowings from theories
about human motivation advanced by the newly fashionable Freud
and Jung. And it cannot be claimed that O'Neill's career as dramatist
represents a steady progression toward mastery of style, whether literary, dramatic, or both. He began with a sort of local color lyricism,
then turned toward expressionism [*The Emperor Jones* (1920), *The
Hairy Ape* (1921)], then experimented with versions of New England
familial disasters elevated by mythical allusions [*Desire Under the Elms*
(1924) and *Mourning Becomes Electra* (1931)]; traces of all the earlier
styles surface amid the flat realism of his best plays—*The Iceman Com-*

Individual plays are readily available. The
closest approach to a standard edition is
The Plays of Eugene O'Neill, 3 vols., 1941,
reissued 1951, with *The Iceman Cometh*.
This edition must be supplemented by *A
Moon for the Misbegotten*, 1952; *A Long
Day's Journey into Night*, 1952; *A Touch
of the Poet*, 1957; "*Hughie*," 1959; and
More Stately Mansions, 1969.

The most complete biography is Arthur
and Barbara Gelb, *O'Neill*, 1962, rev. and
enlarged, 1973; but see also Louis Sheaf-
fer, *O'Neill: Son and Playwright*, 1968 and
O'Neill: Son and Artist, 1973. For bibliographies see Jordan Y. Miller, *Eugene
O'Neill and the American Critic: A Sum-*

mary and Bibliographical Checklist, 1963;
Ralph Sanborn and Barrett Clark, *A Bib-
liography of the Works of Eugene O'Neill
Together with the Collected Poems of Eu-
gene O'Neill*, 1965, and J. Russell Reaver,
An O'Neill Concordance, 3 vols., 1969.

Recent criticism includes Doris Alex-
ander, *The Tempering of Eugene O'Neill*,
1961; Clifford Leech, *Eugene O'Neill*,
1963; Frederic J. Carpenter, *Eugene
O'Neill*, 1964; John Raleigh, *The Plays of
Eugene O'Neill*, 1965; Jordan Y. Miller,
*Playwright's Progress: O'Neill and the
Critics*, 1965, a collection of theater re-
views, and Travis Bogard, *Contour in
Time: The Plays of Eugene O'Neill*, 1972.

eth (1946) and *Long Day's Journey Into Night* (produced after his death)—but neither work is distinguished for structure or verbal elegance.

As a consequence O'Neill has not had an easy time with critics for whom clumsiness and addiction to formula are the unpardonable literary sins. Mary McCarthy charitably attributes this clumsiness to honesty and sincerity, but she asks: "How does one judge the great logical symphonies of a tone-deaf musician?" Another critic, Eric Bentley, objects to the inelegance and schematic plotting, calling the result "jelly in an iron jar." Still another, Hugo von Hofmannsthal, complains that O'Neill's characters

> . . . utter the precise words demanded of them by the logic of the situation; they seem to stand rooted in the situation where for the time being they happen to be placed; they are not sufficiently drenched in the atmosphere of their own individual past [and] . . . the way in which the characters go from one theme to another and return to the central theme is lacking in that seemingly inevitable abandon that creates vitality . . . . The close of *The Hairy Ape,* as well as that of *The Emperor Jones,* seems to me to be too direct, too simple, too expected; it is a little disappointing . . . to see the arrow strike the target toward which [one] . . . has watched it speeding all the while.

And certainly it is undeniable that the progressive checking out of possible "locations" for Yank in *The Hairy Ape* has a depressingly mechanical, predictable quality.

But it also has, intermittently yet overwhelmingly, remarkable moral intensity. O'Neill does not simply insist on the "rights" of the debased and the exploited; he drives himself to create, at levels of life where one hardly believes it can exist, a believably complex human response to exploitation—because it is the reality of such response alone that can stir any profound concern for the whole human situation of which greed and self-enclosure are only parts. The writer casts himself fully and passionately into the events onstage; Yank's fury and frustration possess him wholly; he hurls the shovel at the door, shatters the furnace room with his own rage. There is no ironical distancing, but there is a determination to touch rage and frustration from inside that is at once terrible and noble—and sufficiently powerful as to make most murmurings about the ungainly, overschematic writing seem little better than trivial chic.

This is not a literary career that emerges in affirmation. The movement of all the plays is circular at best. In *The Iceman Cometh* and *Long Day's Journey* the writer turns round and round in his own length, coiling and uncoiling a loneliness that is so unrelieved as to be almost stupefying: the desperate attempts of a group of derelicts to make life bearable, the frustrated efforts of a family to find some way of understanding their past. The plays are an incremental detailing of grief, aging, of how hard it is to forgive and how painful not to forgive; all avenues of possibility are closed off; the prospect of human resiliency barely flickers. But the writing gives significance to human energies—to the human capacity not only to experience frustration, but to know it, to know at least minimally the terms on which life is given. And, in these plays, as wherever such knowledge comes into sight, a hint of the heroic survives. O'Neill three times won the Pulitzer Prize and was chosen Nobel Laureate in 1938.

The Hairy Ape
A Comedy of Ancient and Modern Life in Eight Scenes

CHARACTERS

ROBERT SMITH, "YANK"
PADDY
LONG
MILDRED DOUGLAS
HER AUNT
SECOND ENGINEER
A GUARD
A SECRETARY OF AN
 ORGANIZATION
STOKERS, LADIES,
 GENTLEMEN, ETC.

SCENES

SCENE I: The firemen's forecastle of an ocean liner—an hour after sailing from New York.
SCENE II: Section of promenade deck, two days out—morning.
SCENE III: The stokehole. A few minutes later.
SCENE IV: Same as Scene I. Half an hour later.
SCENE V: Fifth Avenue, New York. Three weeks later.
SCENE VI: An island near the city. The next night.
SCENE VII: In the city. About a month later.
SCENE VIII: In the city. Twilight of the next day.

SCENE ONE

SCENE—*The firemen's forecastle of a transatlantic liner an hour after sailing from New York for the voyage across. Tiers of narrow, steel bunks, three deep, on all sides. An entrance in rear. Benches on the floor before the bunks. The room is crowded with men, shouting, cursing, laughing, sing-ing—a confused, inchoate uproar swelling into a sort of unity, a mean-ing—the bewildered, furious, baffled defiance of a beast in a cage. Nearly all the men are drunk. Many bottles are passed from hand to hand. All are dressed in dungaree pants, heavy ugly shoes. Some wear singlets, but the majority are stripped to the waist.*

The treatment of this scene, or of any other scene in the play, should by no means be naturalistic. The effect sought after is a cramped space in the bowels of a ship, imprisoned by white steel. The lines of bunks, the uprights supporting them, cross each other like the steel framework of a cage. The ceiling crushes down upon the men's heads. They cannot stand upright. This accentuates the natural stooping posture which shoveling coal and the resultant over-development of back and shoulder muscles have given them. The men themselves should resemble those pictures in which the appearance of Neanderthal Man is guessed at. All are hairy-chested, with long arms of tremendous power, and low, receding brows above their small, fierce, resentful eyes. All the civilized white races are represented, but except for the slight differentiation in color of hair, skin, eyes, all these men are alike.

The curtain rises on a tumult of sound. YANK is seated in the fore-ground. He seems broader, fiercer, more truculent, more powerful, more sure of himself than the rest. They respect his superior strength—the grudging respect of fear. Then, too, he represents to them a self-expression, the very last word in what they are, their most highly developed individ-ual.

VOICES. Gif me trink dere, you!
     'Ave a wet!
     Salute!
     Gesundheit!
     Skoal!
     Drunk as a lord, God stiffen you!
     Here's how!
     Luck!
     Pass back that bottle, damn you!
     Pourin' it down his neck!
     Ho, Froggy! Where the devil have you been?
     La Touraine.
     I hit him smash in yaw, py Gott!
     Jenkins—the First—he's a rotten swine——
     And the coppers nabbed him—and I run——

I like peer better. It don't pig head gif you.
A slut, I'm sayin'! She robbed me aslape—
To hell with 'em all!
You're a bloody liar!
Say dot again! [*Commotion. Two men about to fight are pulled apart.*]
No scrappin' now!
Tonight——
See who's the best man!
Bloody Dutchman!
Tonight on the for'ard square.
I'll bet on Dutchy.
He packa da wallop, I tella you!
Shut up, Wop!
No fightin', maties. We're all chums, ain't we?
[*A voice starts bawling a song.*]
"Beer, beer, glorious beer!
Fill yourselves right up to here."

YANK [*For the first time seeming to take notice of the uproar about him, turns around threateningly—in a tone of contemptuous authority*]. Choke off dat noise! Where d'yuh get dat beer stuff? Beer, hell! Beer's for goils —and Dutchmen. Me for somep'n wit a kick to it! Gimme a drink, one of youse guys. [*Several bottles are eagerly offered. He takes a tremendous gulp at one of them; then, keeping the bottle in his hand, glares belligerently at the owner, who hastens to acquiesce in this robbery by saying:*] All righto, Yank. Keep it and have another. [YANK *contemptuously turns his back on the crowd again. For a second there is an embarrassed silence. Then——*]

VOICES. We must be passing the Hook.
See's beginning to roll to it.
Six days in hell—and then Southampton.
Py Yesus, I vish somepody take my first vatch for me!
Gittin' seasick, Square-head?
Drink up and forget it!
What's in your bottle?
Gin.
Dot's nigger trink.
Absinthe? It's doped. You'll go off your chump, Froggy!
Cochon![1]
Whisky, that's the ticket!
Where's Paddy?
Going asleep.
Sing us that whisky song, Paddy.

[1] Dirty pig.

They all turn to an old, wizened Irishman who is dozing, very drunk, on the benches forward. His face is extremely monkey-like with all the sad, patient pathos of that animal in his small eyes.

VOICES. Singa da song, Caruso Pat!
He's gettin' old. The drink is too much for him.
He's too drunk.

PADDY [*Blinking about him, starts to his feet resentfully, swaying, holding on to the edge of a bunk*]. I'm never too drunk to sing. 'Tis only when I'm dead to the world I'd be wishful to sing at all. [*With a sort of sad contempt.*] "Whisky Johnny," ye want? A chanty, ye want? Now that's a queer wish from the ugly like of you, God help you. But no mather. [*He starts to sing in a thin, nasal, doleful tone*]:

Oh, whisky is the life of man!
Whisky! O Johnny! [*They all join in on this.*]
Oh, whisky is the life of man!
Whisky for my Johnny! [*Again chorus.*]
Oh, whisky drove my old man mad!
Whisky! O Johnny!
Oh. whisky drove my old man mad!
Whisky for my Johnny!

YANK [*Again turning around scornfully*]. Aw hell! Nix on dat old sailing ship stuff! All dat bull's dead, see? And you're dead, too, yuh damned old Harp, on'y yuh don't know it. Take it easy, see. Give us a rest. Nix on de loud noise. [*With a cynical grin.*] Can't youse see I'm tryin' to t'ink?

ALL [*Repeating the word after him as one with the same cynical amused mockery*]. Think! [*The chorused word has a brazen metallic quality as if their throats were phonograph horns. It is followed by a general uproar of hard, barking laughter.*]

VOICES. Don't be cracking your head wit ut, Yank.
You gat headache, py yingo!
One thing about it—it rhymes with drink!
Ha, ha, ha!
Drink, don't think!
Drink, don't think!
Drink, don't think! [*A whole chorus of voices has taken up this refrain, stamping on the floor, pounding on the benches with fists.*]

YANK [*Taking a gulp from his bottle—good-naturedly*]. Aw right. Can de noise. I got yuh de foist time. [*The uproar subsides. A very drunken sentimental tenor begins to sing*]:

"Far away in Canada,
Far across the sea,
There's a lass who fondly waits
Making a home for me——"

YANK [*Fiercely contemptuous*].   Shut up, yuh lousy boob! Where d'yuh get dat tripe? Home? Home, hell! I'll make a home for yuh! I'll knock yuh dead. Home! T'hell wit home! Where d'yuh get dat tripe? Dis is home, see? What d'yuh want wit home? [*Proudly.*] I runned away from mine when I was a kid. On'y too glad to beat it, dat was me. Home was lickings for me, dat's all. But yuh can bet your shoit no one ain't never licked me since! Wanter try it, any of youse? Huh! I guess not. [*In a more placated but still contemptuous tone.*] Goils waitin' for yuh, huh? Aw, hell! Dat's all tripe. Dey don't wait for no one. Dey'd double-cross yuh for a nickel. Dey're all tarts, get me? Treat 'em rough, dat's me. To hell wit 'em. Tarts, dat's what, de whole bunch of 'em.

LONG [*Very drunk, jumps on a bench excitedly, gesticulating with a bottle in his hand*].   Listen 'ere, Comrades. Yank 'ere is right. 'E says this 'ere stinkin' ship is our 'ome. And 'e says as 'ome is 'ell. And 'e's right! This is 'ell. We lives in 'ell, Comrades—and right enough we'll die in it. [*Raging.*] And who's ter blame, I arsks yer? We ain't. We wasn't born this rotten way. All men is born free and ekal. That's in the bleedin' Bible, maties. But what d'they care for the Bible—them lazy, bloated swine what travels first cabin? Them's the ones. They dragged us down 'til we're on'y wage slaves in the bowels of a bloody ship, sweatin', burnin' up, eatin' coal dust! Hit's them's ter blame—the damned Capitalist clarss! [*There had been a gradual murmur of contemptuous resentment rising among the men until now he is interrupted by a storm of catcalls, hisses, boos, hard laughter.*]

VOICES. Turn it off!
    Shut up!
    Sit down!
    Closa da face!
    Tamn fool! [*Etc.*]

YANK [*Standing up and glaring at* LONG].   Sit down before I knock yuh down! [LONG *makes haste to efface himself.* YANK *goes on contemptuously.*] De Bible, huh? De Cap'tlist class, huh? Aw nix on dat Salvation Army-Socialist bull. Git a soapbox! Hire a hall! Come and be saved, huh? Jerk us to Jesus, huh? Aw g'wan! I've listened to lots of guys like you, see. Yuh're all wrong. Wanter know what I t'ink? Yuh ain't no good for no one. Yuh're de bunk. Yuh ain't got no noive, get me? Yuh're yellow, dat's what. Yellow, dat's you. Say! What's dem slobs in de foist cabin got to do wit us? We're better men dan dey are, ain't we? Sure! One of us guys could clean up de whole mob wit one mit. Put one of 'em down here for one watch in de stokehole, what'd happen? Dey'd carry him off on a stretcher. Dem boids don't amount to nothin'. Dey're just baggage. Who makes dis old tub run? Ain't it us guys? Well den, we belong, don't we? We belong and dey don't. Dat's all. [*A loud chorus of approval.* YANK *goes on.*] As for dis bein' hell—aw, nuts! Yuh lost your noive, dat's what. Dis is a man's job, get me? It belongs. It runs dis tub. No stiffs need apply. But yuh're a stiff, see? Yuh're yellow, dat's you.

VOICES. [*With a great hard pride in them*].
Righto!
A man's job!
Talk is cheap, Long.
He never could hold up his end.
Divil take him!
Yank's right. We make it go.
Py Gott, Yank say right ting!
We don't need no one cryin' over us.
Makin' speeches.
Throw him out!
Yellow!
Chuck him overboard!
I'll break his jaw for him!
[*They crowd around* LONG *threateningly.*]

YANK [*Half good-natured again—contemptuously*]. Aw, take it easy. Leave him alone. He ain't woith a punch. Drink up. Here's how, whoever owns dis. [*He takes a long swallow from his bottle. All drink with him. In a flash all is hilarious amiability again, back-slapping, loud talk, etc.*]

PADDY [*Who has been sitting in a blinking, melancholy daze—suddenly cries out in a voice full of old sorrow*]. We belong to this, you're saying? We make the ship to go, you're saying? Yerra then, that Almighty God have pity on us! [*His voice runs into the wail of a keen, he rocks back and forth on his bench. The men stare at him, startled and impressed in spite of themselves.*] Oh, to be back in the fine days of my youth, ochone! Oh, there was fine beautiful ships them days—clippers wid tall masts touching the sky—fine strong men in them—men that was sons of the sea as if 'twas the mother that bore them. Oh, the clean skins of them, and the clear eyes, the straight backs and full chests of them! Brave men they was, and bold men surely! We'd be sailing out, bound down round the Horn maybe. We'd be making sail in the dawn, with a fair breeze, singing a chanty song wid no care to it. And astern the land would be sinking low and dying out, but we'd give it no heed but a laugh, and never a look behind. For the day that was, was enough, for we was free men—and I'm thinking 'tis only slaves do be giving heed to the day that's gone or the day to come—until they're old like me. [*With a sort of religious exaltation.*] Oh, to be scudding south again wid the power of the Trade Wind driving her on steady through the nights and the days! Full sail on her! Nights and days! Nights when the foam of the wake would be flaming wid fire, when the sky'd be blazing and winking wid stars. Or the full of the moon maybe. Then you'd see her driving through the gray night, her sails stretching aloft all silver and white, not a sound on the deck, the lot of us dreaming dreams, till you'd believe 'twas no real ship at all you was on but a ghost ship like the *Flying Dutchman* they say does be roaming the seas forevermore widout touching a port. And there was the days, too. A warm sun on the clean decks. Sun warming the blood of you, and wind over the miles of shiny green ocean like strong drink to your lungs. Work—aye, hard work—but who'd mind that at all? Sure, you worked under the sky and 'twas work wid skill and daring to it. And wid the day done, in the dog watch, smoking me pipe at ease, the lookout would be raising land maybe, and we'd see the mountains of South Americy wid the red fire of the setting sun painting their white tops and the clouds floating by them! [*His tone of exaltation ceases. He goes on mournfully.*] Yerra, what's the use of talking? 'Tis a dead man's whisper. [*To* YANK *resentfully.*] 'Twas them days men belonged to ships, not now. 'Twas them days a ship was part of the sea, and a man was part of a ship, and the sea joined all together and made it one. [*Scornfully.*] Is it one wid this you'd be, Yank—black smoke from the funnels smudging the sea, smudging the decks—the bloody engines pounding and throbbing and shaking—wid divil a sight of sun or a breath of clean air—choking our lungs wid coal dust—breaking our backs and hearts in the hell of the stokehole—feeding the bloody furnace—feeding our lives along wid the coal, I'm thinking—caged in by steel from a sight of the sky like bloody apes in the Zoo! [*With a harsh laugh.*] Ho-ho, divil mend you! Is it to belong to that you're wishing? Is it a flesh and blood wheel of the engines you'd be?

YANK [*Who has been listening with a contemptuous sneer, barks out the answer*]. Sure ting! Dat's me. What about it?

PADDY [*As if to himself—with great sorrow*]. Me time is past due. That a great wave wid sun in the heart of it may sweep me over the side sometime I'd be dreaming of the days that's gone!

YANK. Aw, yuh crazy Mick! [*He springs to his feet and advances on Paddy threateningly—then stops, fighting some queer struggle within himself—lets his hands fall to his sides—contemptuously.*] Aw, take it easy. Yuh're aw right, at dat. Yuh're bugs, dat's all—nutty as a cuckoo. All dat tripe yuh been pullin'—Aw, dat's all right. On'y it's dead, get me? Yuh don't belong no more, see. Yuh don't get de stuff. Yuh're too old. [*Disgustedly.*] But aw say, come up for air onct in a while, can't yuh? See what's happened since yuh croaked. [*He suddenly bursts forth vehemently, growing more and more excited.*] Say! Sure! Sure I meant it! What de hell—Say, lemme talk! Hey! Hey, you old Harp! Hey, youse guys! Say, listen to me—wait a moment—I gotta talk, see. I belong and he don't. He's dead but I'm livin'. Listen to me! Sure I'm part of de engines! Why de hell not? Dey move, don't dey? Dey're speed, ain't dey? Dey smash trou, don't dey? Twenty-five knots a hour! Dat's goin some! Dat's new stuff! Dat belongs! But him, he's too old. He gets dizzy. Say, listen. All dat crazy tripe about nights and days; all dat crazy tripe about suns and winds, fresh air and de rest of it—Aw hell, dat's all a dope dream! Hittin' de pipe of de past, dat's what he's doin'. He's old and don't belong no more. But me, I'm young! I'm in de pink! I move wit it!

It, get me! I mean de ting dat's de guts of all dis. It ploughs trou all de tripe he's been sayin'. It blows dat up! It knocks dat dead! It slams dat offen de face of de oith! It, get me! De engines and de coal and de smoke and all de rest of it! He can't breathe and swallow coal dust, but I kin, see? Dat's fresh air for me! Dat's food for me! I'm new, get me? Hell in de stokehole? Sure! It takes a man to work in hell. Hell, sure, dat's my fav'rite climate. I eat it up! I git fat on it! It's me makes it hot! It's me makes it roar! It's me makes it move! Sure, on'y for me everyting stops. It all goes dead, get me? De noise and smoke and all de engines movin' de woild, dey stop. Dere ain't nothin' no more! Dat's what I'm sayin'. Everyting else dat makes de woild move, somep'n makes it move. It can't move witout somep'n else, see? Den yuh get down to me. I'm at de bottom, get me! Dere ain't nothin' foither. I'm de end! I'm de start! I start somep'n and de woild moves! It—dat's me!—de new dat's moiderin' de old! I'm de ting in coal dat makes it boin; I'm steam and oil for de engines; I'm de ting in noise dat makes yuh hear it; I'm smoke and express trains and steamers and factory whistles; I'm de ting in gold dat makes money! And I'm what makes iron into steel! Steel, dat stands for de whole ting! And I'm steel—steel—steel! I'm de muscles in steel, de punch behind it! [*As he says this he pounds with his fist against the steel bunks. All the men, roused to a pitch of frenzied self-glorification by his speech, do likewise. There is a deafening metallic roar, through which* YANK's *voice can be heard bellowing.*] Slaves, hell! We run de whole woiks. All de rich guys dat tink dey're somep'n, dey ain't nothin'! Dey don't belong. But us guys, we're in de move, we're at de bottom, de whole ting is us! [PADDY *from the start of* YANK's *speech has been taking one gulp after another from his bottle, at first frightenedly, as if he were afraid to listen, then desperately, as if to drown his senses, but finally has achieved complete indifferent, even amused, drunkenness.* YANK *sees his lips moving. He quells the uproar with a shout.*] Hey, youse guys, take it easy! Wait a moment! De nutty Harp is sayin' somep'n.

PADDY [*Is heard now—throws his head back with a mocking burst of laughter*]. Ho-ho-ho-ho-ho—

YANK [*Drawing back his fist, with a snarl*]. Aw! Look out who yuh're givin' the bark!

PADDY [*Begins to sing the "Miller of Dee" with enormous good nature*].

> "I care for nobody, no, not I,
> And nobody cares for me."

YANK [*Good-natured himself in a flash, interrupts* PADDY *with a slap on the bare back like a report*]. Dat's de stuff! Now yuh're gettin' wise to somep'n. Care for nobody, dat's de dope! To hell wit 'em all! And nix on nobody else carin'. I kin care for myself, get me! [*Eight bells sound, muffled, vibrating through the steel walls as if some enormous brazen gong were imbedded in the heart of the ship. All the men jump up mechanically, file through the door silently close upon each other's heels in what is very like a prisoners' lockstep.* YANK *slaps* PADDY *on the back.*] Our watch, yuh old Harp! [*Mockingly.*] Come on down in hell. Eat up de coal dust. Drink in de heat. It's it, see! Act like yuh liked it, yuh better—or croak yuhself.

PADDY [*With jovial defiance*]. To the divil wid it! I'll not report this watch. Let thim log me and be damned. I'm no slave the like of you. I'll be sittin' here at me ease, and drinking, and thinking, and dreaming dreams.

YANK [*Contemptuously*]. Tinkin' and dreamin', what'll that get yuh? What's tinkin' got to do wit it? We move, don't we? Speed, ain't it? Fog, dat's all you stand for. But we drive trou dat, don't we? We split dat up and smash trou—twenty-five knots a hour! [*Turns his back on* PADDY *scornfully.*] Aw, yuh make me sick! Yuh don't belong! [*He strides out the door in rear. Paddy hums to himself, blinking drowsily.*]

[*Curtain.*]

SCENE TWO

SCENE—*Two days out. A section of the promenade deck.* MILDRED DOUGLAS *and her aunt are discovered reclining in deck chairs. The former is a girl of twenty, slender, delicate, with a pale, pretty face marred by a self-conscious expression of disdainful superiority. She looks fretful, nervous and discontented, bored by her own anemia. Her aunt is a pompous and proud—and fat—old lady. She is a type even to the point of a double chin and lorgnettes. She is dressed pretentiously, as if afraid her face alone would never indicate her position in life.* MILDRED *is dressed all in white.*

The impression to be conveyed by this scene is one of the beautiful, vivid life of the sea all about—sunshine on the deck in a great flood, the fresh sea wind blowing across it. In the midst of this, these two incongruous, artificial figures, inert and disharmonious, the elder like a gray lump of dough touched up with rouge, the younger looking as if the vitality of her stock had been sapped before she was conceived, so that she is the expression not of its life energy but merely of the artificialities that energy had won for itself in the spending.

MILDRED [*Looking up with affected dreaminess*]. How the black smoke swirls back against the sky! Is it not beautiful?

AUNT [*Without looking up*]. I dislike smoke of any kind.

MILDRED. My great-grandmother smoked a pipe—a clay pipe.

AUNT [*Ruffling*]. Vulgar!

MILDRED. She was too distant a relative to be vulgar. Time mellows pipes.

AUNT [*Pretending boredom but irritated*]. Did the sociology you took up at college teach you that—to play the ghoul on every possible occasion, excavating old bones? Why not let your great-grandmother rest in her grave?

MILDRED [*Dreamily*]. With her pipe beside her—puffing in Paradise.

AUNT [*With spite*]. Yes, you are a natural born ghoul. You are even getting to look like one, my dear.

MILDRED [*In a passionless tone*]. I detest you, Aunt. [*Looking at her critically.*] Do you know what you remind me of? Of a cold pork pudding against a background of linoleum tablecloth in the kitchen of a—but the possibilities are wearisome. [*She closes her eyes.*]

AUNT [*With a bitter laugh*]. Merci for your candor. But since I am and must be your chaperon—in appearance—at least—let us patch up some sort of armed truce. For my part you are quite free to indulge any pose of eccentricity that beguiles you—as long as you observe the amenities——

MILDRED [*Drawling*]. The inanities?

AUNT [*Going on as if she hadn't heard*]. After exhausting the morbid thrills of social service work on New York's East Side—how they must have hated you, by the way, the poor that you made so much poorer in their own eyes!—you are now bent on making your slumming international. Well, I hope Whitechapel will provide the needed nerve tonic. Do not ask me to chaperon you there, however. I told your father I would not. I loathe deformity. We will hire an army of detectives and you may investigate everything—they allow you to see.

MILDRED [*Protesting with a trace of genuine earnestness*]. Please do not mock at my attempts to discover how the other half lives. Give me credit for some sort of groping sincerity in that at least. I would like to help them. I would like to be of some use in the world. Is it my fault I don't know how? I would like to be sincere, to touch life somewhere. [*With weary bitterness.*] But I'm afraid I have neither the vitality nor integrity. All that was burnt out in our stock before I was born. Grandfather's blast furnaces flaming to the sky, melting steel, making millions—then father keeping those home fires burning, making more millions—and little me at the tailend of it all. I'm a waste product in the Bessemer process[2]—like the millions. Or rather, I inherit the acquired trait of the by-product, wealth, but none of the energy, none of the strength of the steel that made it. I am sired by gold and damned by it, as they say at the race track—damned in more ways than one. [*She laughs mirthlessly.*]

AUNT [*Unimpressed—superciliously*]. You seem to be going in for sincerity today. It isn't becoming to you, really—except as an obvious pose. Be as artificial as you are, I advise. There's a sort of sincerity in that, you know. And, after all, you must confess you like that better.

[2] A method for making steel by blasting air through molten iron, burning out excess carbon and other impurities.

MILDRED [*Again affected and bored*]. Yes, I suppose I do. Pardon me for my outburst. When a leopard complains of its spots, it must sound rather grotesque. [*In a mocking tone.*] Purr, little leopard. Purr, scratch, tear, kill, gorge yourself and be happy—only stay in the jungle where your spots are camouflage. In a cage they make you conspicuous.

AUNT. I don't know what you are talking about.

MILDRED. It would be rude to talk about anything to you. Let's just talk. [*She looks at her wrist watch.*] Well, thank goodness, it's about time for them to come for me. That ought to give me a new thrill, Aunt.

AUNT [*Affectedly troubled*]. You don't mean to say you're really going? The dirt—the heat must be frightful——

MILDRED. Grandfather started as a puddler. I should have inherited an immunity to heat that would make a salamander shiver. It will be fun to put it to the test.

AUNT. But don't you have to have the captain's—or someone's—permission to visit the stokehole?

MILDRED [*With a triumphant smile*]. I have it—both his and the chief engineer's. Oh, they didn't want to at first, in spite of my social service credentials. They didn't seem a bit anxious that I should investigate how the other half lives and works on a ship. So I had to tell them that my father, the president of Nazareth Steel, chairman of the board of directors of this line, had told me it would be all right.

AUNT. He didn't.

MILDRED. How naïve age makes one! But I said he did, Aunt. I even said he had given me a letter to them—which I had lost. And they were afraid to take the chance that I might be lying. [*Excitedly.*] So it's ho! for the stokehole. The second engineer is to escort me. [*Looking at her watch again.*] It's time. And here he comes, I think. [*The SECOND ENGINEER enters. He is a husky, fine-looking man of thirty-five or so. He stops before the two and tips his cap, visibly embarrassed and ill-at-ease.*]

SECOND ENGINEER. Miss Douglas?

MILDRED. Yes. [*Throwing off her rugs and getting to her feet.*] Are we all ready to start?

SECOND ENGINEER. In just a second, ma'am. I'm waiting for the Fourth. He's coming along.

MILDRED [*With a scornful smile*]. You don't care to shoulder this responsibility alone, is that it?

SECOND ENGINEER [*Forcing a smile*]. Two are better than one. [*Disturbed by her eyes, glances out to sea—blurts out.*] A fine day we're having.

MILDRED. Is it?

SECOND ENGINEER. A nice warm breeze——

MILDRED. It feels cold to me.

SECOND ENGINEER. But it's hot enough in the sun——

MILDRED. Not hot enough for me. I don't like Nature. I was never athletic.

SECOND ENGINEER [*Forcing a smile*]. Well, you'll find it hot enough where you're going.

MILDRED. Do you mean hell?

SECOND ENGINEER [*Flabbergasted, decides to laugh*]. Ho-ho! No, I mean the stokehole.

MILDRED. My grandfather was a puddler. He played with boiling steel.

SECOND ENGINEER [*All at sea—uneasily*]. Is that so? Hum, you'll excuse me, ma'am, but are you intending to wear that dress?

MILDRED. Why not?

SECOND ENGINEER. You'll likely rub against oil and dirt. It can't be helped.

MILDRED. It doesn't matter. I have lots of white dresses.

SECOND ENGINEER. I have an old coat you might throw over——

MILDRED. I have fifty dresses like this. I will throw this one into the sea when I come back. That ought to wash it clean, don't you think?

SECOND ENGINEER [*Doggedly*]. There's ladders to climb down that are none too clean—and dark alleyways——

MILDRED. I will wear this very dress and none other.

SECOND ENGINEER. No offense meant. It's none of my business. I was only warning you——

MILDRED. Warning? That sounds thrilling.

SECOND ENGINEER [*Looking down the deck—with a sigh of relief*]. There's the Fourth now. He's waiting for us. If you'll come——

MILDRED. Go on. I'll follow you. [*He goes.* MILDRED *turns a mocking smile on her aunt.*] An oaf—but a handsome, virile oaf.

AUNT [*Scornfully*]. Poser!

MILDRED. Take care. He said there were dark alleyways——

AUNT [*In the same tone*]. Poser!

MILDRED [*Biting her lips angrily*]. You are right. But would that my millions were not so anemically chaste!

AUNT. Yes, for a fresh pose I have no doubt you would drag the name of Douglas in the gutter!

MILDRED. From which it sprang. Good-by, Aunt. Don't pray too hard that I may fall into the fiery furnace.

AUNT. Poser!

MILDRED [*Viciously*]. Old hag! [*She slaps her aunt insultingly across the face and walks off, laughing gaily.*]

AUNT [*Screams after her*]. I said poser!

[*Curtain.*]

SCENE THREE

SCENE—*The stokehole. In the rear, the dimly-outlined bulks of the furnaces and boilers. High overhead one hanging electric bulb sheds just enough light through the murky air laden with coal dust to pile up masses of shadows everywhere. A line of men, stripped to the waist, is before the furnace doors. They bend over, looking neither to right nor left, handling their shovels as if they were part of their bodies, with a strange, awkward, swinging rhythm. They use the shovels to throw open the furnace doors. Then from these fiery round holes in the black a flood of terrific light and heat pours full upon the men who are outlined in silhouette in the crouching, inhuman attitudes of chained gorillas. The men shovel with a rhythmic motion, swinging as on a pivot from the coal which lies in heaps on the floor behind to hurl it into the flaming mouths before them. There is a tumult of noise—the brazen clang of the furnace doors as they are flung open or slammed shut, the grating, teeth-gritting grind of steel against steel, of crunching coal. This clash of sounds stuns one's ears with its rending dissonance. But there is order in it, rhythm, a mechanical regulated recurrence, a tempo. And rising above all, making the air hum with the quiver of liberated energy, the roar of leaping flames in the furnaces, the monotonous throbbing beat of the engines.*

As the curtain rises, the furnace doors are shut. The men are taking a breathing spell. One or two are arranging the coal behind them, pulling it into more accessible heaps. The others can be dimly made out leaning on their shovels in relaxed attitudes of exhaustion.

PADDY [*From somewhere in the line—plaintively*].   Yerra, will this divil's own watch nivir end? Me back is broke. I'm destroyed entirely.

YANK [*From the center of the line—with exuberant scorn*].   Aw, yuh make me sick! Lie down and croak, why don't yuh? Always beefin', dat's you! Say, dis is a cinch! Dis was made for me! It's my meat, get me! [*A whistle is blown—a thin, shrill note from somewhere overhead in the darkness.* YANK *curses without resentment.*] Dere's de damn engineer crackin' de whip. He tinks we're loafin'.

PADDY [*Vindictively*].   God stiffen him!

YANK [*In an exultant tone of command*].   Come on, youse guys! Git into de game! She's gittin' hungry! Pile some grub in her. Trow it into her belly! Come on now, all of youse! Open her up! [*At this last all the men, who have followed his movements of getting into position throw open their furnace doors with a deafening clang. The fiery light floods over their shoulders as they bend round for the coal. Rivulets of sooty sweat have traced maps on their backs. The enlarged muscles form bunches of high light and shadow.*]

YANK [*Chanting a count as he shovels without seeming effort*].   One—two—tree——[*His voice rising exultantly in the joy of battle.*] Dat's de stuff!

Let her have it! All togedder now! Sling it into her! Let her ride! Shoot de piece now! Call de toin on her! Drive her into it! Feel her move! Watch her smoke! Speed dat's her middle name! Give her coal, youse guys! Coal, dat's her booze! Drink it up, baby! Let's see yuh sprint! Dig in and gain a lap! Dere she go-o-es. [*This last in the chanting formula of the gallery gods at the six-day bike race. He slams his furnace door shut. The others do likewise with as much unison as their wearied bodies will permit. The effect is of one fiery eye after another being blotted out with a series of accompanying bangs.*]

PADDY [*Groaning*].   Me back is broke. I'm bate out—bate— [*There is a pause. Then the inexorable whistle sounds again from the dim regions above the electric light. There is a growl of cursing rage from all sides.*]

YANK [*Shaking his fist upward—contemptuously*].   Take it easy dere, you! Who d'yuh tinks runnin' dis game, me or you? When I git ready, we move. Not before! When I git ready, get me!

VOICES [*Approvingly*].   That's the stuff!

> Yank tal him, py golly!
>
> Yank ain't afeerd.
>
> Goot poy, Yank!
>
> Give him hell!
>
> Tell 'im 'e's a bloody swine!
>
> Bloody slave-driver!

YANK [*Contemptuously*].   He ain't got no noive. He's yellow, get me? All de engineers is yellow. Dey got streaks a mile wide. Aw, to hell with him! Let's move, youse guys. We had a rest. Come on, she needs it! Give her pep! It ain't for him. Him and his whistle, dey don't belong. But we belong, see! We gotter feed de baby! Come on! [*He turns and flings his furnace door open. They all follow his lead. At this instant the* SECOND *and* FOURTH ENGINEERS *enter from the darkness on the left with* MILDRED *between them. She starts, turns paler, her pose is crumbling, she shivers with fright in spite of the blazing heat, but forces herself to leave the* ENGINEERS *and take a few steps near the men. She is right behind* YANK. *All this happens quickly while the men have their backs turned.*]

YANK.   Come on, youse guys! [*He is turning to get coal when the whistle sounds again in a peremptory, irritating note. This drives* YANK *into a sudden fury. While the other men have turned full around and stopped dumbfounded by the spectacle of* MILDRED *standing there in her white dress,* YANK *does not turn far enough to see her. Besides, his head is thrown back, he blinks upward through the murk trying to find the owner of the whistle, he brandishes his shovel murderously over his head in one hand, pounding on his chest, gorilla-like, with the other, shouting.*] Toin off dat whistle! Come down outa dere, yuh yellow, brass-buttoned, Belfast bum, yuh! Come down and I'll knock yer brains out! Yuh lousy, stinkin', yellow mut of a Catholic-moiderin' bastard! Come down and I'll moider yuh! Pullin' dat whistle on me, huh? I'll show yuh! I'll crash yer skull in! I'll drive yer teet' down yer troat! I'll slam yer nose trou de back of yer head! I'll cut yer guts out for a nickel, yuh lousy boob, yuh dirty, crummy, muck-eatin' son of a—— [*Suddenly he becomes conscious of all the other men staring at something directly behind his back. He whirls defensively with a snarling, murderous growl, crouching to spring, his lips drawn back over his teeth, his small eyes gleaming ferociously. He sees* MILDRED, *like a white apparition in the full light from the open furnace doors. He glares into her eyes, turned to stone. As for her, during his speech she has listened, paralyzed with horror, terror, her whole personality crushed, beaten in, collapsed, by the terrific impact of this unknown, abysmal brutality, naked and shameless. As she looks at his gorilla face, as his eyes bore into hers, she utters a low, choking cry and shrinks away from him, putting both hands up before her eyes to shut out the sight of his face, to protect her own. This startles* YANK *to a reaction. His mouth falls open, his eyes grow bewildered.*]

MILDRED [*About to faint—to the* ENGINEERS, *who now have her one by each arm—whimperingly*]. Take me away! Oh, the filthy beast! [*She faints. They carry her quickly back, disappearing in the darkness at the left, rear. An iron door clangs shut. Rage and bewildered fury rush back on* YANK. *He feels himself insulted in some unknown fashion in the very heart of his pride. He roars.*] God damn yuh! [*And hurls his shovel after them at the door which has just closed. It hits the steel bulkhead with a clang and falls clattering on the steel floor. From overhead the whistle sounds again in a long, angry, insistent command.*]

[*Curtain.*]

SCENE FOUR

SCENE—*The firemen's forecastle.* YANK'S *watch has just come off duty and had dinner. Their faces and bodies shine from a soap and water scrubbing but around their eyes, where a hasty dousing does not touch, the coal dust sticks like black make-up, giving them a queer, sinister expression.* YANK *has not washed either face or body. He stands out in contrast to them, a blackened, brooding figure. He is seated forward on a bench in the exact attitude of Rodin's "The Thinker." The others, most of them smoking pipes, are staring at* YANK *half-apprehensively, as if fearing an outburst; half-amusedly, as if they saw a joke somewhere that tickled them.*

VOICES. He ain't ate nothin'.
    Py golly, a fallar gat to gat grub in him.
    Divil a lie.
    Yank feeda da fire, no feeda da face.
    Ha-ha.
    He ain't even washed hisself.
    He's forgot.
    Hey, Yank, you forgot to wash.

YANK [*Sullenly*].   Forgot nothin'! To hell wit washin'.

VOICES. It'll stick to you.

It'll get under your skin.

Give yer the bleedin' itch, that's wot.

It makes spots on you—like a leopard.

Like a piebald nigger, you mean.

Better wash up, Yank.

You sleep better.

Wash up, Yank.

Wash up! Wash up!

YANK [*Resentfully*].   Aw say, youse guys. Lemme alone. Can't youse see I'm tryin to tink?

ALL [*Repeating the word after him as one with cynical mockery*].   Think! [*The word has a brazen, metallic quality as if their throats were phonograph horns. It is followed by a chorus of hard, barking laughter.*]

YANK [*Springing to his feet and glaring at them belligerently*].   Yes, tink! Tink, dat's what I said! What about it? [*They are silent, puzzled by his sudden resentment at what used to be one of his jokes.* YANK *sits down again in the same attitude of "The Thinker."*]

VOICES. Leave him alone.

He's got a grouch on.

Why wouldn't he?

PADDY [*With a wink at the others*].   Sure I know what's the matter. 'Tis aisy to see. He's fallen in love, I'm telling you.

ALL [*Repeating the word after him as one with cynical mockery*].   Love! [*The word has a brazen, metallic quality as if their throats were phonograph horns. It is followed by a chorus of hard, barking laughter.*]

YANK [*With a contemptuous snort*].   Love, hell! Hate, dat's what. I've fallen in hate, get me?

PADDY [*Philosophically*].   'Twould take a wise man to tell one from the other. [*With a bitter, ironical scorn, increasing as he goes on.*] But I'm telling you it's love that's in it. Sure what else but love for us poor bastes in the stokehole would be bringing a fine lady, dressed like a white quane, down a mile of ladders and steps to be havin' a look at us? [*A growl of anger goes up from all sides.*]

LONG [*Jumping on a bench—hecticly*].   Hinsultin' us! Hinsultin' us, the bloody cow! And them bloody engineers! What right 'as they got to be exhibitin' us 's if we was bleedin' monkeys in a menagerie? Did we sign for hinsults to our dignity as 'onest workers? Is that in the ship's articles? You kin bloody well bet it ain't! But I knows why they done it. I arsked a deck steward 'o she was and 'e told me. 'Er old man's a bleedin' millionaire, a bloody Capitalist! 'E's got enuf bloody gold to sink this bleedin' ship! 'E makes arf the bloody steel in the world! 'E owns this bloody boat! And you and me, Comrades, we're 'is slaves! And the skipper and mates and engineers, they're 'is slaves! And she's 'is bloody daughter and we're all 'er slaves, too! And she gives 'er orders as 'ow she wants to see the bloody animals below decks and down they takes 'er! [*There is a roar of rage from all sides.*]

YANK [*Blinking at him bewilderedly*]. Say! Wait a moment! Is all dat straight goods?

LONG. Straight as string! The bleedin' steward as waits on 'em, 'e told me about 'er. And what're we goin' ter do, I arsks yer? 'Ave we got ter swaller 'er hinsults like dogs? It ain't in the ship's articles. I tell yer we got a case. We kin go to law——

YANK [*With abysmal contempt*]. Hell! Law!

ALL [*Repeating the word after him as one with cynical mockery*]. Law! [*The word has a brazen metallic quality as if their throats were phonograph horns. It is followed by a chorus of hard, barking laughter.*]

LONG [*Feeling the ground slipping from under his feet—desperately*]. As voters and citizens we kin force the bloody governments——

YANK [*With abysmal contempt*]. Hell! Governments!

ALL [*Repeating the word after him as one with cynical mockery*]. Governments! [*The word has a brazen metallic quality as if their throats were phonograph horns. It is followed by a chorus of hard, barking laughter.*]

LONG [*Hysterically*]. We're free and equal in the sight of God——

YANK [*With abysmal contempt*]. Hell! God!

ALL [*Repeating the word after him as one with cynical mockery*]. God! [*The word has a brazen metallic quality as if their throats were phonograph horns. It is followed by a chorus of hard, barking laughter.*]

YANK [*Witheringly*]. Aw, join de Salvation Army!

ALL. Sit down! Shut up! Damn fool! Sealawyer! [LONG *slinks back out of sight.*]

PADDY [*Continuing the trend of his thoughts as if he had never been interrupted—bitterly*]. And there she was standing behind us, and the Second pointing at us like a man you'd hear in a circus would be saying: In this cage is a queerer kind of baboon than ever you'd find in darkest Africy. We roast them in their own sweat—and be damned if you won't hear some of thim saying they like it! [*He glances scornfully at* YANK.]

YANK [*With a bewildered uncertain growl*]. Aw!

PADDY. And there was Yank roarin' curses and turning round wid his shovel to brain her—and she looked at him, and him at her——

YANK [*Slowly*]. She was all white. I tought she was a ghost. Sure.

PADDY [*With heavy, biting sarcasm*]. 'Twas love at first sight, divil a doubt of it! If you'd seen the endearin' look on her pale mug when she shriveled away with her hands over her eyes to shut out the sight of him! Sure, 'twas as if she'd seen a great hairy ape escaped from the Zoo!

YANK [*Stung—with a growl of rage*]. Aw!

PADDY. And the loving way Yank heaved his shovel at the skull of her, only she was out the door! [*A grin breaking over his face.*] 'Twas touching, I'm telling you! It put the touch of home, swate home in the stokehole. [*There is a roar of laughter from all.*]

YANK [*Glaring at* PADDY *menacingly*]. Aw, choke dat off, see!

PADDY [*Not heeding him—to the others*]. And her grabbin' at the Second's arm for protection. [*With a grotesque imitation of a woman's voice.*] Kiss me, Engineer dear, for it's dark down here and me old man's in Wall Street making money! Hug me tight, darlin', for I'm afeerd in the dark and me mother's on deck makin' eyes at the skipper! [*Another roar of laughter.*]

YANK [*Threateningly*]. Say! What yuh tryin' to do, kid me, yuh old Harp?

PADDY. Divil a bit! Ain't I wishin' myself you'd brained her?

YANK [*Fiercely*]. I'll brain her! I'll brain her yet, wait 'n' see! [*Coming over to* PADDY *slowly.*] Say, is dat what she called me—a hairy ape?

PADDY. She looked it at you if she didn't say the word itself.

YANK [*Grinning horribly*]. Hairy ape, huh? Sure! Dat's de way she looked at me, aw right. Hairy ape! So dat's me, huh? [*Bursting into rage—as if she were still in front of him.*] Yuh skinny tart! Yuh white-faced bum, yuh! I'll show yuh who's a ape! [*Turning to the others, bewilderment seizing him again.*] Say, youse guys. I was bawlin' him out for pullin' de whistle on us. You heard me. And den I seen youse lookin' at somep'n and I tought he'd sneaked down to come up in back of me, and I hopped round to knock him dead wit de shovel. And dere she was wit de light on her! Christ, yuh coulda pushed me over with a finger! I was scared, get me? Sure! I tought she was a ghost, see? She was all in white like dey wrap around stiffs. You seen her. Kin yuh blame me? She didn't belong, dat's what. And den when I come to and seen it was a real skoit and seen de way she was lookin' at me—like Paddy said—Christ, I was sore, get me? I don't stand for dat stuff from nobody. And I flung de shovel—on'y she'd beat it. [*Furiously.*] I wished it'd banged her! I wished it'd knocked her block off!

LONG. And be 'anged for murder or 'lectrocuted? She ain't bleedin' well worth it.

YANK. I don't give a damn what! I'd be square wit her, wouldn't I? Tink I wanter let her put somep'n over on me? Tink I'm goin' to let her git away wit dat stuff! Yuh don't know me! No one ain't never put nothin' over on me and got away wit it, see!—not dat kind of stuff—no guy and no skoit neither! I'll fix her! Maybe she'll come down again——

VOICE. No chance, Yank. You scared her out of a year's growth.

YANK. I scared her? Why de hell should I scare her? Who de hell is she? Ain't she de same as me? Hairy ape, Huh? [*With his old confident bravado.*] I'll show her I'm better'n her, if she on'y knew it. I belong and she don't, see! I move and she's dead! Twenty-five knots a hour, dat's me! Dat carries her but I make dat. She's on'y baggage. Sure! [*Again bewilderedly.*] But, Christ, she was funny lookin'! Did yuh pipe her hands? White and skinny. Yuh could see de bones through 'em. And her mush, dat was dead white, too. And her eyes, dey was like dey'd seen a ghost. Me, dat was! Sure! Hairy ape! Ghost, huh? Look at dat arm! [*He extends his right arm, swelling out the great muscles.*] I coulda took her wit dat, wit' just my little finger even, and broke her in two. [*Again bewilderedly.*] Say, who is dat skoit, huh? What is she? What's she come from? Who made her? Who give her de noive to look at me like dat? Dis ting's got my goat right. I don't get her. She's new to me. What does a skoit like her mean, huh? She don't belong, get me! I can't see her. [*With growing anger.*] But one ting I'm wise to, aw right, aw right! Youse all kin bet your shoits I'll git even wit her. I'll show her if she tinks she— She grinds de organ and I'm on de string, huh? I'll fix her! Let her come down again and I'll fling her in de furnace! She'll move den! She won't shiver at nothin', den! Speed, dat'll be her! She'll belong den! [*He grins horribly.*]

PADDY.   She'll never come. She's had her belly-full, I'm telling you. She'll be in bed now, I'm thinking, wid ten doctors and nurses feedin' her salts to clean the fear out of her.

YANK [*Enraged*].   Yuh tink I made her sick, too, do yuh? Just lookin' at me, huh? Hairy ape, huh? [*In a frenzy of rage.*] I'll fix her! I'll tell her where to git off! She'll git down on her knees and take it back or I'll bust de face offen her! [*Shaking one fist upward and beating on his chest with the other.*] I'll find yuh! I'm comin', d'yuh hear? I'll fix yuh, God damn yuh! [*He makes a rush for the door.*]

VOICES.   Stop him!
        He'll get shot!
        He'll murder her!
        Trip him up!
        Hold him!
        He's gone crazy!
        Gott, he's strong!
        Hold him down!
        Look out for a kick!
        Pin his arms!

[*They have all piled on him and, after a fierce struggle, by sheer weight of numbers have borne him to the floor just inside the door.*]

PADDY [*Who has remained detached*].   Kape him down till he's cooled off. [*Scornfully.*] Yerra, Yank, you're a great fool. Is it payin' attention at all you are to the like of that skinny sow widout one drop of rale blood in her?

YANK [*Frenziedly, from the bottom of the heap*].   She done me doit! She done me doit, didn't she? I'll git square wit her! I'll get her some way! Git offen me, youse guys! Lemme up! I'll show her who's a ape!

[*Curtain.*]

SCENE FIVE

SCENE—*Three weeks later. A corner of Fifth Avenue in the Fifties on a fine Sunday morning. A general atmosphere of clean, well-tidied, wide street; a flood of mellow, tempered sunshine; gentle, genteel breezes. In the rear, the show windows of two shops, a jewelry establishment on the corner, a furrier's next to it. Here the adornments of extreme wealth are tantalizingly displayed. The jeweler's window is gaudy with glittering diamonds, emeralds, rubies, pearls, etc., fashioned in ornate tiaras, crowns, necklaces, collars, etc. From each piece hangs an enormous tag from which a dollar sign and numerals in intermittent electric lights wink out the incredible prices. The same in the furrier's. Rich furs of all varieties hang there bathed in a downpour of artificial light. The general effect is of a background of magnificence cheapened and made grotesque by commercialism, a background in tawdry disharmony with the clear light and sunshine on the street itself.*

Up the side street YANK *and* LONG *come swaggering.* LONG *is dressed in shore clothes, wears a black Windsor tie, cloth cap.* YANK *is in his dirty dungarees. A fireman's cap with black peak is cocked defiantly on the side of his head. He has not shaved for days and around his fierce, resentful eyes—as around those of* LONG *to a lesser degree—the black smudge of coal dust still sticks like make-up. They hesitate and stand together at the corner, swaggering, looking about them with a forced, defiant contempt.*

LONG [*Indicating it all with an oratorical gesture*]. Well, 'ere we are. Fif' Avenoo. This 'ere's their bleedin' private lane, as yer might say. [*Bitterly.*] We're trespassers 'ere. Proletarians keep orf the grass!

YANK [*Dully*]. I don't see no grass, yuh boob. [*Staring at the sidewalk.*] Clean, ain't it? Yuh could eat a fried egg offen it. The white wings got some job sweepin' dis up. [*Looking up and down the avenue—surlily.*] Where's all de white-collar stiffs yuh said was here—and de skoits—*her* kind?

LONG. In church, blarst 'em! Arskin' Jesus to give 'em more money.

YANK. Choich, huh? I useter go to choich onct—sure—when I was a kid. Me old man and woman, dey made me. Dey never went demselves, dough. Always got too big a head on Sunday mornin', dat was dem. [*With a grin.*] Dey was scrappers for fair, bot' of dem. On Satiday nights when dey bot' got a skinful dey could put up a bout oughter been staged at de Garden. When dey got trough dere wasn't a chair or table wit a leg under it. Or else dey bot' jumped on me for somep'n. Dat was where I loined to take punishment. [*With a grin and a swagger.*] I'm a chip offen de old block, get me?

LONG. Did yer old man follow the sea?

YANK. Naw. Worked along shore. I runned away when me old lady croaked wit de tremens. I helped at truckin' and in de market. Den I shipped in de stokehole. Dat belongs. De rest was nothin'. [*Looking around him.*] I ain't never seen dis before. De Brooklyn waterfront, dat was where I was dragged up. [*Taking a deep breath.*] Dis ain't so bad at dat, hun?

LONG. Not bad? Well, we pays for it wiv our bloody sweat, if yer wants to know!

YANK [*With sudden angry disgust*]. Aw, hell! I don't see no one, see— like her. All dis gives me a pain. It don't belong. Say, ain't dere a back room around dis dump? Let's go shoot a ball. All dis is too clean and quiet and dolled-up, get me? It gives me a pain.

LONG. Wait and yer'll bloody well see——

YANK. I don't wait for no one. I keep on de move. Say, what yuh drag me up here for, anyway? Tryin' to kid me, yuh simp, yuh?

LONG. Yer wants to get back at 'er, don't yer? That's what yer been sayin' every bloomin' hour since she hinsulted yer.

YANK [*Vehemently*]. Sure ting I do! Didn't I try to get even wit her in Southampton? Didn't I sneak on de dock and wait for her by de gangplank? I was goin' to spit in her pale mug, see! Sure, right in her pop-eyes! Dat woulda made me even, see? But no chanct. Dere was a whole army of plainclothes bulls around. Dey spotted me and gimme de bum's rush. I never seen her. But I'll git square wit her yet, you watch! [*Furiously.*] De lousy tart! She tinks she kin get away with moider—but not wit me! I'll fix her! I'll tink of a way!

LONG [*As disgusted as he dares to be*]. Ain't that why I brought yer up 'ere—to show yer? Yer been lookin' at this 'ere 'ole affair wrong. Yer been actin' an' talkin' 's if it was all a bleedin' personal matter between yer and that bloody cow. I wants to convince yer she was on'y a representative of 'er clarss. I wants to awaken yer bloody clarss consciousness. Then yer'll see it's 'er clarss yer've got to fight, not 'er alone. There's a 'ole mob of 'em like 'er, Gawd blind 'em!

YANK [*Spitting on his hands—belligerently*]. De more de merrier when I gits started. Bring on de gang!

LONG. Yer'll see 'em in arf a mo', when that church lets out. [*He turns and sees the window display in the two stores for the first time.*] Blimey! Look at that, will yer? [*They both walk back and stand looking in the jeweler's. LONG flies into a fury.*] Just look at this 'ere bloomin' mess! Just look at it! Look at the bleedin' prices on 'em—more'n our 'ole bloody stokehole makes in ten voyages sweatin' in 'ell! And they—'er and 'er bloody clarss—buys 'em for toys to dangle on 'em! One of these 'ere would buy scoff for a starvin' family for a year!

YANK. Aw, cut de sob stuff! T'hell wit de starvin' family! Yuh'll be passin' de hat to me next. [*With naïve admiration.*] Say, dem tings is pretty, huh? Bet yuh dey'd hock for a piece of change aw right. [*Then turning away, bored.*] But, aw hell, what good are dey? Let 'er have 'em. Dey don't belong no more'n she does. [*With a gesture of sweeping the jewelers into oblivion.*] All dat don't count, get me?

LONG [*Who has moved to the furrier's—indignantly*].   And I s'pose this 'ere don't count neither—skins of poor, 'armless animals slaughtered so as 'er and 'ers can keep their bleedin' noses warm!

YANK [*Who has been staring at something inside—with queer excitement*]. Take a slant at dat! Give it de once-over! Monkey fur—two t'ousand bucks! [*Bewilderedly.*] Is dat straight goods—monkey fur? What de hell——?

LONG [*Bitterly*].   It's straight enuf. [*With grim humor.*] They wouldn't bloody well pay that for a 'airy ape's skin—no, nor for the 'ole livin' ape with all 'is 'ead, and body, and soul thrown in!

YANK [*Clenching his fists, his face growing pale with rage as if the skin in the window were a personal insult*].   Trowin' it up in my face! Christ! I'll fix her!

LONG [*Excitedly*].   Church is out. 'Ere they come, the bleedin' swine. [*After a glance at* YANK's *lowering face—uneasily.*] Easy goes, Comrade. Keep yer bloomin' temper. Remember force defeats itself. It ain't our weapon. We must impress our demands through peaceful means—the votes of the on-marching proletarians of the bloody world!

YANK [*With abysmal contempt*].   Votes, hell! Votes is a joke, see. Votes for women! Let dem do it!

LONG [*Still more uneasily*].   Calm, now. Treat 'em wiv the proper contempt. Observe the bleedin' parasites but 'old yer 'orses.

YANK [*Angrily*].   Git away from me! Yuh're yellow, dat's what. Force, dat's me! De punch, dat's me every time, see! [*The crowd from church enter from the right, sauntering slowly and affectedly, their heads held stiffly up, looking neither to right nor left, talking in toneless, simpering voices. The women are rouged, calcimined, dyed, overdressed to the nth degree. The men are in Prince Alberts, high hats, spats, canes, etc. A procession of gaudy marionettes, yet with something of the relentless horror of Frankenstein monsters in their detached, mechanical unawareness.*]

VOICES. Dear Doctor Caiaphas! He is so sincere!

What was the sermon? I dozed off.

About the radicals, my dear—and the false doctrines that are being preached.

We must organize a hundred percent American bazaar.

And let everyone contribute one one-hundredth per cent of their income tax.

What an original idea!

We can devote the proceeds to rehabilitating the veil of the temple.

But that has been done so many times.

YANK [*Glaring from one to the other of them—with an insulting snort of scorn*] Huh! Huh! [*Without seeming to see him, they make wide detours to avoid the spot where he stands in the middle of the sidewalk.*]

LONG [*Frightenedly*]. Keep yer bloomin' mouth shut, I tells yer.

YANK [*Viciously*]. G'wan! Tell it to Sweeney! [*He swaggers away and deliberately lurches into a top-hatted gentleman, then glares at him pugnaciously.*] Say, who d'yuh tink yuh're bumpin'? Tink yuh own de oith?

GENTLEMAN [*Coldly and affectedly*]. I beg your pardon. [*He has not looked at* YANK *and passes on without a glance, leaving him bewildered.*]

LONG [*Rushing up and grabbing* YANK'S *arm*]. 'Ere! Come away! This wasn't what I meant. Yer'll 'ave the bloody coppers down on us.

YANK [*Savagely—giving him a push that sends him sprawling*]. G'wan!

LONG [*Picks himself up—hysterically*]. I'll pop orf then. This ain't what I meant. And whatever 'appens, yer can't blame me. [*He slinks off left.*]

YANK. T' hell wit youse! [*He approaches a lady—with a vicious grin and a smirking wink.*] Hello, Kiddo. How's every little ting? Got anyting on for tonight? I know an old boiler down to de docks we kin crawl into. [*The lady stalks by without a look, without a change of pace.* YANK *turns to others—insultingly.*] Holy smokes, what a mug! Go hide yuhself before de horses shy at yuh. Gee, pipe de heine on dat one! Say, youse, yuh look like de stoin of a ferryboat. Paint and powder! All dolled up to kill! Yuh look like stiffs laid out for de boneyard! Aw, g'wan, de lot of youse! Yuh give me de eye-ache. Yuh don't belong, get me! Look at me, why don't youse dare? I belong, dat's me! [*Pointing to a skyscraper across the street which is in process of construction—with bravado.*] See dat building goin' up dere? See de steel work? Steel, dat's me! Youse guys live on it and tink yuh're somep'n. But I'm *in* it, see! I'm de hoistin' engine dat makes it go up! I'm it—de inside and bottom of it! Sure! I'm steel and steam and smoke and de rest of it! It moves—speed—twenty-five stories up—and me at de top and bottom—movin'! Youse simps don't move. Yuh're on'y dolls I winds up to see 'm spin. Yuh're de garbage, get me—de leavins—de ashes we dump over de side! Now, what 'a' yuh gotta say? [*But as they seem neither to see nor hear him, he flies into a fury.*] Bums! Pigs! Tarts! Bitches! [*He turns in a rage on the men, bumping viciously into them but not jarring them the least bit. Rather it is he who recoils after each collision. He keeps growling.*] Git off de oith! G'wan, yuh bum! Look where yuh're goin', can't yuh? Git outa here! Fight, why don't yuh? Put up yer mits! Don't be a dog! Fight or I'll knock yuh dead! [*But, without seeming to see him, they all answer with mechanical affected politeness.*] I beg your pardon. [*Then at a cry from one of the women, they all scurry to the furrier's window.*]

THE WOMAN [*Ecstatically, with a gasp of delight*]. Monkey fur! [*The whole crowd of men and women chorus after her in the same tone of affected delight.*] Monkey fur!

YANK [*With a jerk of his head back on his shoulders, as if he had received a punch full in the face—raging*]. I see yuh, all in white! I see yuh, yuh white-faced tart, yuh! Hairy ape, huh? I'll hairy ape yuh! [*He bends down and grips at the street curbing as if to pluck it out and hurl it. Foiled in this, snarling with passion, he leaps to the lamp-post on the corner and tries to pull it up for a club. Just at that moment a bus is heard rumbling up. A fat, high-hatted, spatted gentleman runs out from the side street. He calls out plaintively.*] Bus! Bus! Stop there! [*And runs full tilt into the bending, straining* YANK, *who is bowled off his balance.*]

YANK [*Seeing a fight—with a roar of joy as he springs to his feet*]. At last! Bus, huh! I'll bust yuh! [*He lets drive a terrific swing, his fist landing full on the fat gentleman's face. But the gentleman stands unmoved as if nothing had happened.*]

GENTLEMAN. I beg your pardon. [*Then irritably.*] You have made me lose my bus. [*He claps his hands and begins to scream.*] Officer! Officer! [*Many police whistles shrill out on the instant and a whole platoon of policemen rush in on* YANK *from all sides. He tries to fight but is clubbed to the pavement and fallen upon. The crowd at the window have not moved or noticed this disturbance. The clanging gong of the patrol wagon approaches with a clamoring din.*]

[*Curtain.*]

SCENE SIX

SCENE—*Night of the following day. A row of cells in the prison on Blackwell's Island. The cells extend back diagonally from right front to left rear. They do not stop, but disappear in the dark background as if they ran on, numberless, into infinity. One electric bulb from the low ceiling of the narrow corridor sheds its light through the heavy steel bars of the cell at the extreme front and reveals part of the interior.* YANK *can be seen within, crouched on the edge of his cot in the attitude of Rodin's "The Thinker." His face is spotted with black and blue bruises. A blood-stained bandage is wrapped around his head.*

YANK [*Suddenly starting as if awakening from a dream, reaches out and shakes the bars—aloud to himself, wonderingly*]. Steel. Dis is de Zoo, huh? [*A burst of hard, barking laughter comes from the unseen occupants of the cells, runs back down the tier, and abruptly ceases.*]

VOICES [*Mockingly*]. The Zoo? That's a new name for this coop—a damn good name!

Steel, eh? You said a mouthful. This is the old iron house.

Who is that boob talkin'?

He's the bloke they brung in out of his head. The bulls had beat him up fierce.

YANK [*Dully*]. I musta been dreamin'. I tought I was in a cage at de Zoo—but de apes don't talk, do dey?

VOICES. [*With mocking laughter*].   You're in a cage aw right.
A coop!
A pen!
A sty!
A kennel! [*Hard laughter — a pause.*]
Say, guy! Who are you? No, never mind lying. What are you?
Yes, tell us your sad story. What's your game?
What did they jug yuh for?

YANK [*Dully*].   I was a fireman—stokin' on de liners. [*Then with sudden rage, rattling his cell bars.*] I'm a hairy ape, get me? And I'll bust youse all in de jaw if yuh don't lay off kiddin' me.

VOICES. Huh! You're a hard boiled duck, ain't you!
When you spit, it bounces! [*Laughter.*]
Aw, can it. He's a regular guy. Ain't you?
What did he say he was—a ape?

YANK [*Defiantly*].   Sure ting! Ain't dat what youse all are—apes? [*A silence. Then a furious rattling of bars from down the corridor.*]

A VOICE [*Thick with rage*].   I'll show yuh who's a ape, yuh bum!

VOICES. Ssshh! Nix!
Can de noise!
Piano!
You'll have the guard down on us!

YANK [*Scornfully*].   De guard? Yuh mean de keeper, don't yuh? [*Angry exclamations from all the cells.*]

VOICE [*Placatingly*].   Aw, don't pay no attention to him. He's off his nut from the beatin'-up he got. Say, you guy! We're waitin' to hear what they landed you for—or ain't yuh tellin'?

YANK.   Sure, I'll tell youse. Sure! Why de hell not? On'y—youse won't get me. Nobody gets me but me, see? I started to tell de Judge and all he says was: "Toity days to tink it over." Tink it over! Christ, dat's all I been doin' for weeks! [*After a pause.*] I was tryin' to git even wit someone, see?—someone dat done me doit.

VOICES [*Cynically*].   De old stuff, I bet. Your goil, huh?
Give yuh the double-cross, huh?
That's them every time!
Did yuh beat up de odder guy?

YANK [*Disgustedly*].   Aw, yuh're all wrong! Sure dere was a skoit in it—but not what youse mean, not dat old tripe. Dis was a new kind of skoit. She was dolled up all in white—in de stokehole. I tought she was a ghost. Sure. [*A pause.*]

VOICES [*Whispering*].   Gee, he's still nutty.
Let him rave. It's fun listenin'.

YANK [*Unheeding — groping in his thoughts*].   Her hands—dey was skinny and white like dey wasn't real but painted on somep'n. Dere was a million miles from me to her—twenty-five knots a hour. She was like some dead ting de cat brung in. Sure, dat's what. She didn't belong. She belonged in de window of a toy store, or on de top of a garbage can, see! Sure! [*He breaks out angrily.*] But would yuh believe it, she had the noive to do me doit. She lamped me like she was seein' somep'n broke loose from de menagerie. Christ, yuh'd oughter seen her eyes! [*He rattles the bars of his cell furiously.*] But I'll get back at her yet, you watch! And if I can't find her I'll take it out on de gang she runs wit. I'm wise to where dey hangs out now. I'll show her who belongs! I'll show her who's in de move and who ain't. You watch my smoke!

VOICES [*Serious and joking*].   Dat's de talkin'!
           Take her for all she's got!
           What was this dame, anyway? Who was she, eh?

YANK.   I dunno. First cabin stiff. Her old man's a millionaire, dey says—name of Douglas.

VOICES.   Douglas? That's the president of the Steel Trust, I bet.
           Sure. I seen his mug in de papers.
           He's filthy. with dough.

VOICE.   Hey, feller, take a tip from me. If you want to get back at that dame, you better join the Wobblies. You'll get some action then.

YANK.   Wobblies? What de hell's dat?

VOICE.   Ain't you ever heard of the I. W. W.?   *Ind Worker Wld* [handwritten]

YANK.   Naw. What is it?

VOICE.   A gang of blokes—a tough gang. I been readin' about 'em today in the paper. The guard give me the *Sunday Times*. There's a long spiel about 'em. It's from a speech made in the Senate by a guy named Senator Queen. [*He is in the cell next to* YANK'S. *There is a rustling of paper.*] Wait'll I see if I got light enough and I'll read you. Listen. [*He reads.*] "There is a menace existing in this country today which threatens the vitals of our fair Republic—as foul a menace aginst the very life-blood of the American Eagle as was the foul conspiracy of Cataline against the eagles of ancient Rome!"

VOICE [*Disgustedly*].   Aw, hell! Tell him to salt de tail of dat eagle!

VOICE [*Reading*].   "I refer to that devil's brew of rascals, jailbirds, murderers and cutthroats who libel all honest working men by calling themselves the Industrial Workers of the World; but in the light of their nefarious plots, I call them the Industrious *Wreckers* of the World!"

YANK [*With vengeful satisfaction*].   Wreckers, dat's de right dope! Dat belongs! Me for dem!

VOICE.   Ssshh! [*Reading.*] "This fiendish organization is a foul ulcer on the fair body of our Democracy——"

VOICE.   Democracy, hell! Give him the boid, fellers—the raspberry! [*They do.*]

VOICE.   Ssshh! [*Reading.*] "Like Cato I say to this Senate, the I. W. W. must be destroyed! For they represent an ever-present dagger pointed at the heart of the greatest nation the world has ever known, where all men are born free and equal, with equal opportunities to all, where the Founding Fathers have guaranteed to each one happiness, where Truth, Honor, Liberty, Justice, and the Brotherhood of Man are a religion absorbed with one's mother's milk, taught at our father's knee, sealed, signed, and stamped upon in the glorious Constitution of these United States!" [*A perfect storm of hisses, catcalls, boos, and hard laughter.*]

VOICES [*Scornfully*].   Hurrah for de Fort' of July!
> Pass de hat!
> Liberty!
> Justice!
> Honor!
> Opportunity!
> Brotherhood!

ALL [*With abysmal scorn*].   Aw, hell!

VOICE.   Give the Queen Senator guy the bark! All togedder now—one—two—tree——[*A terrific chorus of barking and yapping.*]

GUARD [*From a distance*].   Quiet there, youse—or I'll git the hose. [*The noise subsides.*]

YANK [*With growling rage*].   I'd like to catch dat senator guy alone for a second. I'd loin him some trute!

VOICE.   Ssshh! Here's where he gits down to cases on the Wobblies. [*Reads.*] "They plot with fire in one hand and dynamite in the other. They stop not before murder to gain their ends, nor at the outraging of defenseless womanhood. They would tear down society, put the lowest scum in the seats of the mighty, turn Almighty God's revealed plan for the world topsy-turvy, and make of our sweet and lovely civilization a shambles, a desolation where man, God's masterpiece, would soon degenerate back to the ape!"

VOICE [*To* YANK].   Hey, you guy. There's your ape stuff again.

YANK [*With a growl of fury*].   I got him. So dey blow up tings, do dey? Dey turn tings round, do dey? Hey, lend me dat paper, will yuh?

VOICE.   Sure. Give it to him. On'y keep it to yourself, see. We don't wanter listen to no more of that slop.

VOICE.   Here you are. Hide it under your mattress.

YANK [*Reaching out*].   Tanks. I can't read much but I kin manage. [*He sits, the paper in the hand at his side, in the attitude of Rodin's "The Thinker." A pause. Several snores from down the corridor. Suddenly* YANK *jumps to his feet with a furious groan as if some appalling thought had crashed on him—bewilderedly.*] Sure—her old man—president of de Steel Trust—makes half de steel in de world—steel—where I tought I belonged—drivin' trou—movin'—in dat—to make her—and cage me in for her to spit on! Christ [*He shakes the bars of his cell door till the whole tier trembles. Irritated, protesting exclamations from those awakened or trying to get to sleep.*] He made dis—dis cage! Steel! *It* don't belong, dat's what!

Cages, cells, locks, bolts, bars—dat's what it means!—holdin' me down wit him at de top! But I'll drive trou! Fire dat melts it! I'll be fire—under de heap—fire dat never goes out—hot as hell—breakin' out in de night— [*While he has been saying this last he has shaken his cell door to a clanging accompaniment. As he comes to the "breakin' out" he seizes one bar with both hands and, putting his two feet up against the others so that his position is parallel to the floor like a monkey's, he gives a great wrench backwards. The bar bends like a licorice stick under his tremendous strength. Just at this moment the* PRISON GUARD *rushes in, dragging a hose behind him.*]

GUARD [*Angrily*].   I'll loin youse bums to wake me up! [*Sees* YANK.] Hello, it's you, huh? Got the D. Ts., hey? Well, I'll cure 'em. I'll drown your snakes for yuh! [*Noticing the bar.*] Hell, look at dat bar bended! On'y a bug is strong enough for dat!

YANK [*Glaring at him*].   Or a hairy ape, yuh big yellow bum! Look out! Here I come! [*He grabs another bar.*]

GUARD [*Scared now—yelling off left*].   Toin de hose on, Ben!—full pressure! And call de others—and a straitjacket! [*The curtain is falling. As it hides* YANK *from view, there is a splattering smash as the stream of water hits the steel of* YANK's *cell.*]

[*Curtain.*]

SCENE SEVEN

SCENE—*Nearly a month later. An I.W.W. local near the waterfront, showing the interior of a front room on the ground floor, and the street outside. Moonlight on the narrow street, buildings massed in black shadow. The interior of the room, which is general assembly room, office, and reading room, resembles some dingy settlement boys' club. A desk and high stool are in one corner. A table with papers, stacks of pamphlets, chairs about it, is at center. The whole is decidedly cheap, banal, commonplace and unmysterious as a room could well be. The Secretary is perched on the stool making entries in a large ledger. An eye shade casts his face into shadows. Eight or ten men, longshoremen, iron workers, and the like are grouped about the table. Two are playing checkers. One is writing a letter. Most of them are smoking pipes. A big signboard is on the wall at the rear, "Industrial Workers of the World—Local No. 57."*

YANK [*Comes down the street outside. He is dressed as in Scene Five. He moves cautiously, mysteriously. He comes to a point opposite the door; tiptoes softly up to it, listens, is impressed by the silence within, knocks carefully, as if he were guessing at the password to some secret rite. Listens. No answer. Knocks again a bit louder. No answer. Knocks impatiently, much louder.*]

SECRETARY [*Turning around on his stool*].   What the hell is that—someone knocking? [*Shouts.*] Come in, why don't you? [*All the men in the room look up.* YANK *opens the door slowly, gingerly, as if afraid of an ambush. He looks around for secret doors, mystery, is taken aback by the commonplaceness of the room and the men in it, thinks he may have gotten in the wrong place, then sees the signboard on the wall and is reassured.*]

YANK [*Blurts out*].   Hello.

MEN [*Reservedly*].   Hello.

YANK [*More easily*].   I tought I'd bumped into de wrong dump.

SECRETARY [*Scrutinizing him carefully*].   Maybe you have. Are you a member?

YANK.   Naw, not yet. Dat's what I come for—to join.

SECRETARY.   That's easy. What's your job—longshore?

YANK.   Naw. Fireman—stoker on de liners.

SECRETARY [*With satisfaction*].   Welcome to our city. Glad to know you people are waking up at last. We haven't got many members in your line.

YANK.   Naw. Dey're all dead to de woild.

SECRETARY.   Well, you can help to wake 'em. What's your name? I'll make out your card.

YANK [*Confused*].   Name? Lemme tink.

SECRETARY [*Sharply*].   Don't you know your own name?

YANK.   Sure; but I been just Yank for so long—Bob, dat's it—Bob Smith.

SECRETARY [*Writing*].   Robert Smith. [*Fills out the rest of the card.*] Here you are. Cost you half a doller.

YANK.   Is dat all—four bits? Dat's easy. [*Gives the Secretary the money.*]

SECRETARY [*Throwing it in drawer*].   Thanks. Well, make yourself at home. No introductions needed. There's literature on the table. Take some of those pamphlets with you to distribute aboard ship. They may bring results. Sow the seed, only go about it right. Don't get caught and fired. We got plenty out of work. What we need is men who can hold their jobs—and work for us at the same time.

YANK.   Sure. [*But he still stands, embarrassed and uneasy.*]

SECRETARY [*Looking at him—curiously*].   What did you knock for? Think we had a coon in uniform to open doors?

YANK.   Naw. I tought it was locked—and dat yuh'd wanter give me the once-over trou a peep-hole or somep'n to see if I was right.

SECRETARY [*Alert and suspicious but with an easy laugh*].   Think we were running a crap game? That door is never locked. What put that in your nut?

YANK [*With a knowing grin, convinced that this is all camouflage, a part of the secrecy*].   Dis burg is full of bulls, ain't it?

SECRETARY [*Sharply*].   What have the cops got to do with us? We're breaking no laws.

YANK [*With a knowing wink*]. Sure. Youse wouldn't for woilds. Sure. I'm wise to dat.

SECRETARY. You seem to be wise to a lot of stuff none of us knows about.

YANK [*With another wink*]. Aw, dat's aw right, see. [*Then made a bit resentful by the suspicious glances from all sides.*] Aw, can it! Youse needn't put me trou de toid degree. Can't youse see I belong? Sure! I'm reg'lar. I'll stick, get me? I'll shoot de woiks for youse. Dat's why I wanted to join in.

SECRETARY [*Breezily, feeling him out*]. That's the right spirit. Only are you sure you understand what you've joined? It's all plain and aboveboard; still, some guys get a wrong slant on us. [*Sharply.*] What's your notion of the purpose of the I. W. W.?

YANK. Aw, I know all about it.

SECRETARY [*Sarcastically*]. Well, give us some of your valuable information.

YANK [*Cunningly*]. I know enough not to speak outa my toin. [*Then resentfully again.*] Aw, say! I'm reg'lar. I'm wise to de game. I know yuh got to watch your step wit a stranger. For all youse know, I might be a plainclothes dick, or somep'n, dat's what yuh're tinkin', huh? Aw, forget it! I belong, see? Ask any guy down to de docks if I don't.

SECRETARY. Who said you didn't?

YANK. After I'm 'nitiated, I'll show yuh.

SECRETARY [*Astounded*]. Initiated? There's no initiation.

YANK [*Disappointed*]. Ain't there no password—no grip nor nothin'?

SECRETARY. What'd you think this is—the Elks—or the Black Hand?

YANK. De Elks, hell! De Black Hand, dey're a lot of yellow backstickin' Ginees. Naw. Dis is a man's gang, ain't it?

SECRETARY. You said it! That's why we stand on our two feet in the open. We got no secrets.

YANK [*Surprised but admiringly*]. Yuh mean to say yuh always run wide open—like dis?

SECRETARY. Exactly.

YANK. Den yuh sure got your noive wit youse!

SECRETARY [*Sharply*]. Just what was it made you want to join us? Come out with that straight.

YANK. Yuh call me? Well, I got noive, too! Here's my hand. Yuh wanter blow tings up, don't yuh? Well, dat's me! I belong!

SECRETARY [*With pretended carelessness*]. You mean change the unequal conditions of society by legitimate direct action—or with dynamite?

YANK. Dynamite! Blow it offen de oith—steel—all de cages—all de factories, steamers, buildings, jails—de Steel Trust and all dat makes it go.

SECRETARY. So—that's your idea, eh? And did you have any special job in that line you wanted to propose to us? [*He makes a sign to the men, who get up cautiously one by one and group behind* YANK.]

YANK [*Boldly*].   Sure, I'll come out wit it. I'll show youse I'm one of de gang. Dere's dat millionaire guy, Douglas——

SECRETARY.   President of the Steel Trust, you mean? Do you want to assassinate him?

YANK.   Naw, dat don't get yuh nothin'. I mean blow up de factory, de woiks, where he makes de steel. Dat's what I'm after—to blow up de steel, knock all de steel in de woild up to de moon. Dat'll fix tings! [*Eagerly, with a touch of bravado.*] I'll do it by me lonesome! I'll show yuh! Tell me where his woiks is, how to git there, all de dope. Gimme de stuff, de old butter—and watch me do de rest! Watch de smoke and see it move! I don't give a damn if dey nab me—long as it's done! I'll soive life for it—and give 'em de laugh! [*Half to himself.*] And I'll write her a letter and tell her de hairy ape done it. Dat'll square tings.

SECRETARY [*Stepping away from* YANK].   Very interesting. [*He gives a signal. The men, huskies all, throw themselves on* YANK *and before he knows it they have his legs and arms pinioned. But he is too flabbergasted to make a struggle, anyway. They feel him over for weapons.*]

MAN.   No gat, no knife. Shall we give him what's what and put the boots to him?

SECRETARY.   No. He isn't worth the trouble we'd get into. He's too stupid. [*He comes closer and laughs mockingly in* YANK's *face.*] Ho-ho! By God, this is the biggest joke they've put up on us yet. Hey, you Joke! Who sent you—Burns or Pinkerton? No, by God, you're such a bone-head I'll bet you're in the Secret Service! Well, you dirty spy, you rotten agent provocator, you can go back and tell whatever skunk is paying you blood-money for betraying your brothers that he's wasting his coin. You couldn't catch a cold. And tell him that all he'll ever get on us, or ever has got, is just his own sneaking plots that he's framed up to put us in jail. We are what our manifesto says we are, neither more nor less—and we'll give him a copy of that any time he calls. And as for you—— [*He glares scornfully at* YANK, *who is sunk in an oblivious stupor.*] Oh, hell, what's the use of talking? You're a brainless ape.

YANK [*Aroused by the word to fierce but futile struggles*].   What's dat, yuh Sheeny bum, yuh!

SECRETARY.   Throw him out, boys. [*In spite of his struggles, this is done with gusto and éclat. Propelled by several parting kicks,* YANK *lands sprawling in the middle of the narrow cobbled street. With a growl he starts to get up and storm the closed door, but stops bewildered by the confusion in his brain, pathetically impotent. He sits there, brooding, in as near to the attitude of Rodin's "Thinker" as he can get in his position.*]

YANK [*Bitterly*].   So dem boids don't tink I belong, neider. Aw, to hell wit 'em! Dey're in de wrong pew—de same old bull—soapboxes and Salvation Army—no guts! Cut out an hour offen de job a day and make me happy! Gimme a dollar more a day and make me happy! Tree square a day, and cauliflowers in de front yard—ekal rights—a woman and kids—a lousy vote—and I'm all fixed for Jesus, huh? Aw, hell! What does dat get yuh? Dis ting's in your inside, but it ain't your belly. Feedin' your face—sinkers and coffee—dat don't touch it. It's way down—at de bottom. Yuh can't grab it, and yuh can't stop it. It. moves, and everything moves. It stops and de whole woild stops. Dat's me now—I don't tick, see?—I'm a busted Ingersoll, dat's what. Steel was me, and I owned de woild. Now I ain't steel, and de woild owns me. Aw, hell! I can't see—it's all dark, get me? It's all wrong! [*He turns a bitter mocking face up like an ape gibbering at the moon.*] Say, youse up dere, Man in de Moon, yuh look so wise, gimme de answer, huh? Slip me de inside dope, de information right from de stable—where do I get off at, huh?

A POLICEMAN [*Who has come up the street in time to hear this last—with grim humor*]. You'll get off at the station, you boob, if you don't get up out of that and keep movin'.

YANK [*Looking up at him—with a hard, bitter laugh*]. Sure! Lock me up! Put me in a cage! Dat's de on'y answer yuh know. G'wan, lock me up!

POLICEMAN. What you been doin'?

YANK. Enuf to gimme life for! I was born, see? Sure, dat's de charge. Write it in de blotter. I was born; get me!

POLICEMAN [*Jocosely*]. God pity your old woman! [*Then matter-of-fact.*] But I've no time for kidding. You're soused. I'd run you in but it's too long a walk to the station. Come on now, get up, or I'll fan your ears with this club. Beat it now! [*He hauls YANK to his feet.*]

YANK [*In a vague mocking tone*]. Say, where do I go from here?

POLICEMAN [*Giving him a push—with a grin, indifferently*]. Go to hell.

[*Curtain.*]

SCENE EIGHT

SCENE—*Twilight of the next day. The monkey house at the Zoo. One spot of clear gray light falls on the front of one cage so that the interior can be seen. The other cages are vague, shrouded in shadow from which chatterings pitched in a conversational tone can be heard. On the one cage a sign from which the word "gorilla" stands out. The gigantic animal himself is seen squatting on his haunches on a bench in much the same attitude as Rodin's "Thinker." YANK enters from the left. Immediately a chorus of angry chattering and screeching breaks out. The gorilla turns his eyes but makes no sound or move.*

YANK [*With a hard, bitter laugh*]. Welcome to your city, huh? Hail, hail, de gang's all here! [*At the sound of his voice the chattering dies away into an attentive silence. YANK walks up to the gorilla's cage and, leaning over railing, stares in at its occupant, who stares back at him, silent and motionless.*

There is a pause of dead stillness. Then YANK *begins to talk in a friendly confidential tone, half-mockingly, but with a deep undercurrent of sympathy.*] Say, yuh're some hard-lookin' guy, ain't yuh? I seen lots of tough nuts dat de gang called gorillas, but yuh're de foist real one I ever seen. Some chest yuh got, and shoulders, and dem arms and mits! I bet yuh got a punch in eider fist dat'd knock 'em all silly! [*This with genuine admiration. The gorilla, as if he understood, stands upright, swelling out his chest and pounding on it with his fist.* YANK *grins sympathetically.*] Sure, I get yuh. Yuh challenge de whole woild, huh? Yuh got what I was sayin' even if yuh muffed de woids. [*Then bitterness creeping in.*] And why wouldn't yuh get me? Ain't we both members of de same club—de Hairy Ape? [*They stare at each other—a pause—then* YANK *goes on slowly and bitterly.*] So yuh're what she seen when she looked at me, de white-faced tart! I was you to her, get me? On'y outa de cage—broke out—free to moider her, see? Sure! Dat's what she tought. She wasn't wise dat I was in a cage, too—worser'n yours—sure—a damn sight—'cause you got some chanct to bust loose—but me—— [*He grows confused.*] Aw, hell! It's all wrong, ain't it? [*A pause.*] I s'pose yuh wanter know what I'm doin' here, huh? I been warmin' a bench down to de Battery—ever since last night. Sure. I seen de sun come up. Dat was pretty, too—all red and pink and green. I was lookin' at de skyscrapers—steel—and all de ships comin' in, sailin' out, all over de oith—and dey was steel, too. De sun was warm, dey wasn't no clouds, and dere was a breeze blowin'. Sure, it was great stuff. I got it aw right—what Paddy said about dat bein' de right dope—on'y I couldn't get *in* it, see? I couldn't belong in dat. It was over my head. And I kept tinkin'—and den I beat it up here to see what youse was like. And I waited till dey was all gone to git yuh alone. Say, how d'yuh feel sittin' in dat pen all de time, havin' to stand for 'em comin' and starin' at yuh—de white-faced, skinny tarts and de boobs what marry 'em—makin' fun of yuh, laughin' at yuh, gittin' scared of yuh—damn 'em! [*He pounds on the rail with his fist. The gorilla rattles the bars of his cage and snarls. All the other monkeys set up an angry chattering in the darkness.* YANK *goes on excitedly.*] Sure! Dat's de way it hits me, too. On'y yuh're lucky, see? Yuh don't belong wit 'em and yuh know it. But me, I belong wit 'em—but I don't, see? Dey don't belong wit me, dat's what. Get me? Tinkin' is hard—— [*He passes one hand across his forehead with a painful gesture. The gorilla growls impatiently.* YANK *goes on gropingly.*] It's dis way, what I'm drivin' at. Youse can sit and dope dream in de past, green woods, de jungle and de rest of it. Den yuh belong and dey don't. Den yuh kin laugh at 'em, see? Yuh're de champ of de woild. But me—I ain't got no past to tink in, nor nothin' dat's comin', on'y what's now—and dat don't belong. Sure, you're de best off! Yuh can't tink, can yuh? Yuh can't talk neider. But I kin make a bluff at talkin' and tinkin'—a'most git away wit it—a'most!—and dat's where de joker comes in. [*He laughs.*] I ain't on oith and I ain't in heaven, get me? I'm in de middle tryin' to separate 'em, takin' all de woist punches from bot' of 'em. Maybe dat's what dey call hell, huh? But you, yuh're at de bottom. You belong! Sure! Yuh're de on'y one in de woild dat does, yuh lucky stiff! [*The gorilla growls proudly.*] And dat's why dey gotter put yuh in a cage, see? [*The gorilla roars angrily.*] Sure! Yuh get me. It beats it when you try to tink it or talk it—it's way down—deep—behind—you 'n' me we feel it. Sure! Bot' members of dis club! [*He laughs— then in a savage tone.*] What de hell! T' hell wit it! A little action, dat's our meat! Dat belongs! Knock 'em down and keep bustin' 'em till dey croaks yuh wit a gat—wit steel! Sure! Are yuh game? Dey've looked at youse, ain't dey—in a cage? Wanter get even? Wanter wind up like a sport 'stead of croakin' slow in dere? [*The gorilla roars an emphatic affirmative.* YANK *goes on with a sort of furious exaltation.*] Sure! Yuh're reg'lar! Yuh'll stick to de finish! Me 'n' you, huh?—bot' members of this club! We'll put up one last star bout dat'll knock 'em offen deir seats! Dey'll have to make de cages stronger after we're trou! [*The gorilla is straining at his bars, growling, hopping from one foot to the other.* YANK *takes a jimmy from under his coat and forces the lock on the cage door. He throws this open.*] Pardon from de governor! Step out and shake hands! I'll take yuh for a walk down Fif' Avenoo. We'll knock 'em offen de oith and croak wit de band playin'. Come on, Brother. [*The gorilla scrambles gingerly out of his cage. Goes to* YANK *and stands looking at him.* YANK *keeps his mocking tone—holds out his hand*] Shake—de secret grip of our order. [*Something, the tone of mockery, perhaps, suddenly enrages the animal. With a spring he wraps his huge arms around* YANK *in a murderous hug. There is a crackling snap of crushed ribs—a gasping cry, still mocking, from* YANK.] Hey, I didn't say kiss me! [*The gorilla lets the crushed body slip to the floor; stands over it uncertainly, considering; then picks it up, throws it in the cage, shuts the door, and shuffles off menacingly into the darkness at left. A great uproar of frightened chattering and whimpering comes from the other cages. Then* YANK *moves, groaning, opening his eyes, and there is silence. He mutters painfully.*] Say—dey oughter match him—wit Zybazko. He got me, aw right. I'm trou. Even him didn't tink I belonged. [*Then, with sudden passionate despair.*] Christ, where do I get off at? Where do I fit in? [*Checking himself as suddenly.*] Aw, what de hell! No squawkin', see! No quittin', get me! Croak wit your boots on! [*He grabs hold of the bars of the cage and hauls himself painfully to his feet—looks around him bewilderedly—forces a mocking laugh.*] In de cage, huh? [*In the strident tones of a circus barker.*] Ladies and gents, step forward and take a slant at de one and only—[*His voice weakened*]—one and original—Hairy Ape from de wilds of—— [*He slips in a heap on the floor and dies. The monkeys set up a chattering, whimpering wail. And, perhaps, the Hairy Ape at last belongs.*]

[*Curtain.*]

EDWARD ALBEE

(1928-   )

A playwright with thoroughly consistent and serious concerns, Edward Albee describes himself as one who "deals very directly with an audience." The manner of these dealings is that of the moralist; he himself characterized *The American Dream* (1961), for example, as "an examination of the American Scene, an attack on the substitution of artificial for real values in our society, a condemnation of complacency, cruelty, emasculation and vacuity; . . . a stand against the fiction that everything in this slipping land of ours is peachy-keen." And the settings and modes of relationship that preoccupy him are domestic and familial.

Early in his career Albee favored short forms and abstract one-dimensional characters—grotesques especially handy as "evidence" of the pervasiveness in American life of insincerity, euphemism, sentimentality, cliché, and other strategies by which people avoid facing their own poverties of caring and commitment. True maturity does not exist in the world of plays like *Zoo Story* or *The Sandbox* (1960). Grownups are called "kids," no recognizable children appear; wisdom (if any) surfaces as a relic of an earlier, more innocent and vital America, residing, ironically, in such persons as the supposedly senile Grandma of *The American Dream*. Mommy and Daddy in this play are, for some of its length, merely harmless hypocrites, as in their account of their selfless concern for a leaking toilet:

DADDY: I've been trying for two weeks and it isn't so much for my sake; I can always go to the club.
MOMMY: It isn't so much for my sake, either; I can always go shopping.
DADDY: It's really for Grandma's sake.

Edward Albee's plays and the dates of their first American appearance are *The Zoo Story,* 1960; *The Sandbox,* 1960; *Fam and Yam,* 1960; *The Death of Bessie Smith,* 1961; *The American Dream,* 1961; *Who's Afraid of Virginia Woolf,* 1962; *The Ballad of the Sad Cafe,* 1963; *Tiny Alice,* 1964; *Malcolm,* 1966; *A Delicate Balance,* 1966; *Everything in the Garden,* 1967; *Box-Mao-Box,* 1968; *All Over,* 1971, and *Seascape,* 1974. He won the Pulitzer Prize for *A Delicate Balance* and *Seascape.*

A critical study is Michael E. Rutenberg, *Edward Albee: Playwright in Protest,* 1969. See also the appropriate chapters in Gerald Weales, *American Drama Since World War II,* 1962 and George Wellwarth, *The Theater of Protest and Paradox,* 1964.

But there is hatred and violence at their core. Themselves unable to have a child, Mommy and Daddy have adopted "a bumble of joy," and when they do not "get satisfaction" from it, they dismember it and demand what amounts to a refund. At length, at Grandma's suggestion, they get just what they deserve, a handsome young man who is the personification of the American Dream, an incarnation of total emptiness and alienation.

> Once . . . it was as if all at once my heart . . . became numb . . . almost as though I . . . almost as though . . . just like that . . . it had been wrenched from my body . . . and from that time I have been unable to love. Once . . . I was asleep at the time . . . I awoke, and my eyes were burning. And since that time I have been unable to see anything, *anything*, with pity, with affection . . . with anything but . . . cool disinterest. And my groin . . . even there . . . since one time . . . one specific agony . . . since then I have not been able to *love* anyone with my body. And even my hands . . . I cannot touch another person and feel love. And there is more . . . there are more losses, but it all comes down to this: I no longer have the capacity to feel anything. I have no emotions. I have been drained, torn asunder . . . disemboweled. I have, now, only my person . . . my body, my face.

With the production in 1962 of his best play, *Who's Afraid of Virginia Woolf* (when it was denied the Pulitzer Prize two members of the drama committee resigned in protest), Albee moved on from the earlier style to a full-length play about convincingly substantial human beings. The moral problem is still isolation: the inability to respond to life as it is directly and compassionately, the retreat into self-protective postures, illusions, and games that only intensify self-involvement. And the arena is still domestic. Martha, the wife, alternates aggressive sexuality with banal babytalk, ceaselessly assaulting her husband's self-respect. Her husband combines self-pity with preening, oratorical rant, relentlessly ridiculing her age, drinking habits, and "braying" boorishness. In the course of a "Walpurgisnacht," layers of deceit are shed and a central illusion exposed and destroyed; unable to have children (like Mommy and Daddy), George and Martha have created an imaginary son, whom George, maddened and wearied by combat, at last "kills." The play ends without easy optimism, without a suggestion that George and Martha, having rid themselves of fantasy, will experience reconciliation and rebirth. Yet the sense that their loss is mutual is affecting; a moment at the end of the play, during which they offer each other what comfort they can, brief pity, and brief kindness, discloses that the playwright has a natural feeling for true values.

He also has a weakness for fanciness, obfuscation, and brittle chat. In *Tiny Alice* (1964) much play is made about a butler named Butler. In *All Over* (1971) the first words between the mistress and the wife of a dying man are a discussion of the propriety of the phrase "are dead," since "the verb to be [is not] appropriate to a state of . . . non-being." The epigrams are often leaden: ". . . sometimes a person has to go a very long distance out of his way to come back a short distance correctly." And the writer's self-consciousness is painfully distracting.

However, the gift displayed in *Virginia Woolf* (and in *A Delicate Balance*, which *did* win the 1966 Pulitzer Prize) is genuine. Part of a symbolic structure, the characters nevertheless do not turn bloodless; the talk is canny, alert to the bickering tones in which the long-married "get at" each other; and everywhere the control is precise—witness the acerbic practiced ease with which Agnes in *A Delicate Balance* reproves her husband (for giving an alcoholic sister a drink): "My, what an odd glass to put a soft drink in. Tobias, you have a quiet sense of humor, after all. . . . Well, it *can't* be brandy; Tobias is a grown-up, and knows far better than to. . . ." The premise Albee begins with, as he writes in *A Delicate Balance*, is that "We're not a communal nation . . . giving, but not sharing, outgoing, but not friendly," and he often manages to bring his characters to agonized personal recognition of the meaning of that premise as embodied in ordinary relationships.

> Oh, for God's sake, Agnes! It is our friends! What am I supposed to do? Say: "Look, you can't stay here, you two, you've got trouble. You're friends, and all, but you come in here *clean*." Well, I can't do that. No, Agnes, for God's sake, if . . . if that's all Harry and Edna mean to us, then . . . then what about *us*? When we talk to each other . . . what have we meant? Anything? When we touch, when we promise, and say . . . yes, or please . . . with *ourselves?* . . . have we meant, yes, but only if . . . if there's any condition, Agnes! Then it's . . . all been empty.

The playwright appears to lean to the notion that this emptiness is less a necessity than a choice; here and there, in a beacon scene, he offers reminders that other choices, given courage, are possible.

The American Dream

THE PLAYERS:

MOMMY
DADDY
GRANDMA
MRS. BARKER
YOUNG MAN

THE SCENE:

A living room. Two armchairs, one toward either side of the stage, facing each other diagonally out toward the audience. Against the rear wall, a sofa. A door, leading out from the apartment, in the rear wall, far stage-right. An archway, leading to other rooms, in the side wall, stage-left.

At the beginning, MOMMY *and* DADDY *are seated in the armchairs,* DADDY *in the armchair stage-left,* MOMMY *in the other.*

Curtain up. A silence. Then:

MOMMY. I don't know what can be keeping them.

DADDY. They're late, naturally.

MOMMY. Of course, they're late; it never fails.

DADDY. That's the way things are today, and there's nothing you can do about it.

MOMMY. You're quite right.

DADDY. When we took this apartment, they were quick enough to have me sign the lease; they were quick enough to take my check for two months' rent in advance . . .

MOMMY. And one month's security . . .

DADDY. . . . and one month's security. They were quick enough to check my references; they were quick enough about all that. But now! But now, try to get the icebox fixed, try to get the doorbell fixed, try to get the leak in the johnny fixed! Just try it . . . they aren't so quick about *that*.

MOMMY. Of course not; it never fails. People think they can get away with anything these days . . . and, of course they can. I went to buy a new hat yesterday.

(Pause)

I said, I went to buy a new hat yesterday.

DADDY. Oh! Yes . . . yes.

MOMMY. Pay attention.

DADDY. I *am* paying attention, Mommy.

MOMMY. Well, be sure you do.

DADDY. Oh, I am.

MOMMY. All right, Daddy; now listen.

DADDY. I'm listening, Mommy.

MOMMY. You're sure!

DADDY. Yes . . . yes, I'm sure, I'm all ears.

MOMMY (*Giggles at the thought; then*). All right, now. I went to buy a new hat yesterday and I said, "I'd like a new hat, please." And so, they showed me a few hats, green ones and blue ones, and I didn't like any of them, not one bit. What did I say? What did I just say?

DADDY. You didn't like any of them, not one bit.

MOMMY. That's right; you just keep paying attention. And then they showed me one that I did like. It was a lovely little hat, and I said, "Oh, this is a lovely little hat; I'll take this hat; oh my, it's lovely. What color is it?" And they said, "Why, this is beige; isn't it a lovely little beige hat?" And I said, "Oh, it's just lovely." And so, I bought it.

(*Stops, looks at* DADDY)

DADDY (*To show he is paying attention*). And so you bought it.

MOMMY. And so I bought it, and I walked out of the store with the hat right on my head, and I ran spang into the chairman of our woman's club, and she said, "Oh, my dear, isn't that a lovely little hat? Where did you get that lovely little hat? It's the loveliest little hat; I've always wanted a wheat-colored hat *myself*." And, I said, "Why, no, my dear; this hat is beige; beige." And she laughed and said, "Why no, my dear, that's a wheat-colored hat . . . wheat. I know beige from wheat." And I said, "Well, my dear, I know beige from wheat, too." What did I say? What did I just say?

DADDY (*Tonelessly*). Well, my dear, I know beige from wheat, too.

MOMMY. That's right. And she laughed, and she said, "Well, my dear, they certainly put one over on you. That's wheat if I ever saw wheat. But it's lovely, just the same." And then she walked off. She's a dreadful woman, you don't know her; she has dreadful taste, two dreadful children, a dreadful house, and an absolutely adorable husband who sits in a wheel chair all the time. You don't know him. You don't know anybody, do you? She's just a dreadful woman, but she *is* chairman of our woman's club, so naturally I'm terribly fond of her. So, I went right back into the hat shop, and I said, "Look here; what do you mean selling me a hat that you say is beige, when it's wheat all the time . . . wheat! I can tell beige from wheat any day in the week, but not in this artificial light of yours." They have artificial light, Daddy.

DADDY. Have they!

MOMMY. And I said, "The minute I got outside I could tell that it wasn't a beige hat at all; it was a wheat hat." And they said to me, "How could you tell that when you had the hat on the top of your head?" Well, that made me angry, and so I made a scene right there; I screamed as hard as I could; I took my hat off and I threw it down on the counter, and oh, I made a terrible scene. I said, I made a terrible scene.

DADDY (*Snapping to*).   Yes . . . yes . . . good for you!

MOMMY.   And I made an absolutely terrible scene; and they became frightened, and they said, "Oh, madam; oh, madam." But I kept right on, and finally they admitted that they might have made a mistake; so they took my hat into the back, and then they came out again with a hat that looked exactly like it. I took one look at it, and I said, "This hat is wheat-colored; wheat." Well, of course, they said, "Oh, no, madam, this hat is beige; you go outside and see." So, I went outside, and lo and behold, it *was* beige. So I bought it.

DADDY (*Clearing his throat*).   I would imagine that it was the same hat they tried to sell you before.

MOMMY (*With a little laugh*).   Well, of course it was!

DADDY.   That's the way things are today; you just can't get satisfaction; you just try.

MOMMY.   Well, *I* got satisfaction.

DADDY.   That's right, Mommy. *You did* get satisfaction, didn't you?

MOMMY.   Why are they so late? I don't know what can be keeping them.

DADDY.   I've been trying for two weeks to have the leak in the johnny fixed.

MOMMY.   You can't get satisfaction; just try. *I* can get satisfaction, but you can't.

DADDY.   I've been trying for two weeks and it isn't so much for my sake; I can always go to the club.

MOMMY.   It isn't so much for my sake, either; I can always go shopping.

DADDY.   It's really for Grandma's sake.

MOMMY.   Of course it's for Grandma's sake. Grandma cries every time she goes to the johnny as it is; but now that it doesn't work it's even worse, it makes Grandma think she's getting feeble-headed.

DADDY.   Grandma *is* getting feeble-headed.

MOMMY.   Of course Grandma is getting feeble-headed, but not about johnny-do's.

DADDY.   No; that's true. I must have it fixed.

MOMMY.   WHY are they so late? I don't know what can be keeping them.

DADDY.   When they came here the first time, they were ten minutes early; they were quick enough about it then.

(*Enter* GRANDMA *from the archway, stage left. She is loaded down with boxes, large and small, neatly wrapped and tied.*)

MOMMY.   Why Grandma, look at you! What *is* all that you're carrying?

GRANDMA.   They're boxes. What do they look like?

MOMMY.   Daddy! Look at Grandma; look at all the boxes she's carrying!

DADDY.   My goodness, Grandma; look at all those boxes.

GRANDMA.   Where'll I put them?

MOMMY.   Heavens! I don't know. Whatever are they for?

GRANDMA.   That's nobody's damn business.

MOMMY.   Well, in that case, put them down next to Daddy; there.

GRANDMA (*Dumping the boxes down, on and around* DADDY's *feet*).   I sure wish you'd get the john fixed.

DADDY.   Oh, I do wish they'd come and fix it. We hear you . . . for hours . . . whimpering away. . . .

MOMMY.   Daddy! What a terrible thing to say to Grandma!

GRANDMA.   Yeah. For shame, talking to me that way.

DADDY.   I'm sorry, Grandma.

MOMMY.   Daddy's sorry, Grandma.

GRANDMA.   Well, all right. In that case I'll go get the rest of the boxes. I suppose I deserve being talked to that way. I've gotten so old. Most people think that when you get so old, you either freeze to death, or you burn up. But you don't. When you get so old, all that happens is that people talk to you that way.

DADDY (*Contrite*).   I said I'm sorry, Grandma.

MOMMY.   Daddy said he was sorry.

GRANDMA.   Well, that's all that counts. People being sorry. Makes you feel better; gives you a sense of dignity, and that's all that's important . . . a sense of dignity. And it doesn't matter if you don't care, or not, either. You got to have a sense of dignity, even if you don't care, 'cause, if you don't have that, civilization's doomed.

MOMMY.   You've been reading my book club selections again!

DADDY.   How dare you read Mommy's book club selections, Grandma!

GRANDMA.   Because I'm old! When you're old you gotta do something. When you get old, you can't talk to people because people snap at you. When you get old, people talk to you that way. That's why you become deaf, so you won't be able to hear people talking to you that way. And that's why you go and hide under the covers in the big soft bed, so you won't feel the house shaking from people talking to you that way. That's why old people die, eventually. People talk to them that way. I've got to go and get the rest of the boxes.

(GRANDMA *exits*)

DADDY.   Poor Grandma, I didn't mean to hurt her.

MOMMY.   Don't you worry about it; Grandma doesn't know what she means.

DADDY.   She knows what she says, though.

MOMMY.   Don't you worry about it; she won't know that soon. I love Grandma.

DADDY. I love her, too. Look how nicely she wrapped these boxes.

MOMMY. Grandma has always wrapped boxes nicely. When I was a little girl, I was very poor, and Grandma was very poor, too, because Grandpa was in heaven. And every day, when I went to school, Grandma used to wrap a box for me, and I used to take it with me to school; and when it was lunchtime, all the little boys and girls used to take out their boxes of lunch, and they weren't wrapped nicely at all, and they used to open them and eat their chicken legs and chocolate cakes; and I used to say, "Oh, look at my lovely lunch box; it's so nicely wrapped it would break my heart to open it." And so, I wouldn't open it.

DADDY. Because it was empty.

MOMMY. Oh no. Grandma always filled it up, because she never ate the dinner she cooked the evening before; she gave me all her food for my lunch box the next day. After school, I'd take the box back to Grandma, and she'd open it and eat the chicken legs and chocolate cake that was inside. Grandma used to say, "I love day-old cake." That's where the expression day-old cake came from. Grandma always ate everything a day late. I used to eat all the other little boys' and girls' food at school, because they thought my lunch box was empty. They thought my lunch box was empty, and that's why I wouldn't open it. They thought I suffered from the sin of pride, and since that made them better than me, they were very generous.

DADDY. You were a very deceitful little girl.

MOMMY. We were very poor! But then I married you, Daddy, and now we're very rich.

DADDY. Grandma isn't rich.

MOMMY. No, but you've been so good to Grandma she feels rich. She doesn't know you'd like to put her in a nursing home.

DADDY. I wouldn't!

MOMMY. Well, heaven knows, I would! I can't stand it, watching her do the cooking and the housework, polishing the silver, moving the furniture. . . .

DADDY. She likes to do that. She says it's the least she can do to earn her keep.

MOMMY. Well, she's right. You can't live off people. I can live off you, because I married you. And aren't you lucky all I brought with me was Grandma. A lot of women I know would have brought their whole families to live off you. All I brought was Grandma. Grandma is all the family I have.

DADDY. I feel very fortunate.

MOMMY. You should. I have a right to live off of you because I married you, and because I used to let you get on top of me and bump your uglies; and I have a right to all your money when you die. And when you do, Grandma and I can live by ourselves . . . if she's still here. Unless you have her put away in a nursing home.

DADDY. I have no intention of putting her in a nursing home.

MOMMY. Well, I wish somebody would do something with her!

DADDY. At any rate, you're very well provided for.

MOMMY. You're my sweet Daddy; that's very nice.

DADDY. I love my Mommy.

(*Enter* GRANDMA *again, laden with more boxes*)

GRANDMA (*Dumping the boxes on and around* DADDY's *feet*). There; that's the lot of them.

DADDY. They're wrapped so nicely.

GRANDMA (*To* DADDY). You won't get on my sweet side that way . . .

MOMMY. Grandma!

GRANDMA. . . . telling me how nicely I wrap boxes. Not after what you said: how I whimpered for hours. . . .

MOMMY. Grandma!

GRANDMA (*To* MOMMY). Shut up! (*To* DADDY) You don't have any feelings, that's what's wrong with you. Old people make all sorts of noises, half of them they can't help. Old people whimper, and cry, and belch, and make great hollow rumbling sounds at the table; old people wake up in the middle of the night screaming, and find out they haven't even been asleep; and when old people *are* asleep, they try to wake up, and they can't . . . not for the longest time.

MOMMY. Homilies, homilies!

GRANDMA. And there's more, too.

DADDY. I'm really very sorry, Grandma.

GRANDMA. I know you are, Daddy; it's Mommy over there makes all the trouble. If you'd listened to me, you wouldn't have married her in the first place. She was a tramp and a trollop and a trull to boot, and she's no better now.

MOMMY. Grandma!

GRANDMA (*To* MOMMY). Shut up! (*To* DADDY) When she was no more than eight years old she used to climb up on my lap and say, in a sickening little voice, "When I gwo up, I'm going to mahwy a wich old man; I'm going to set my wittle were end right down in a tub o' butter, that's what I'm going to do." And I warned you, Daddy; I told you to stay away from her type. I told you to. I did.

MOMMY. You stop that! You're my mother, not his!

GRANDMA. I am?

DADDY. That's right, Grandma. Mommy's right.

GRANDMA. Well, how would you expect somebody as old as I am to remember a thing like that? You don't make allowances for people. I want an allowance. I want an allowance!

DADDY. All right, Grandma; I'll see to it.

MOMMY. Grandma! I'm ashamed of you.

GRANDMA. Humf! It's a fine time to say that. You should have gotten rid of me a long time ago if that's the way you feel. You should have had Daddy set me up in business somewhere . . . I could have gone into the fur business, or I could have been a singer. But no; not you. You wanted me around so you could sleep in my room when Daddy got fresh. But now it isn't important, because Daddy doesn't want to get fresh with you any more, and I don't blame him. You'd rather sleep with me, wouldn't you, Daddy?

MOMMY. Daddy doesn't want to sleep with anyone. Daddy's been sick.

DADDY. I've been sick. I don't even want to sleep in the apartment.

MOMMY. You see? I told you.

DADDY. I just want to get everything over with.

MOMMY. That's right. Why are they so late? Why can't they get here on time?

GRANDMA (An owl). Who? Who? . . . Who? Who?

MOMMY. You know, Grandma.

GRANDMA. No, I don't.

MOMMY. Well, it doesn't really matter whether you do or not.

DADDY. Is that true?

MOMMY. Oh, more or less. Look how pretty Grandma wrapped these boxes.

GRANDMA. I didn't really like wrapping them; it hurt my fingers, and it frightened me. But it had to be done.

MOMMY. Why, Grandma?

GRANDMA. None of your damn business.

MOMMY. Go to bed.

GRANDMA. I don't want to go to bed. I just got up. I want to stay here and watch. Besides . . .

MOMMY. Go to bed.

DADDY. Let her stay up, Mommy; it isn't noon yet.

GRANDMA. I want to watch; besides . . .

DADDY. Let her watch, Mommy.

MOMMY. Well all right, you can watch; but don't you dare say a word.

GRANDMA. Old people are very good at listening; old people don't like to talk; old people have colitis and lavender perfume. Now I'm going to be quiet.

DADDY. She never mentioned she wanted to be a singer.

MOMMY. Oh, I forgot to tell you, but it was ages ago.

(*The doorbell rings*)

Oh, goodness! Here they are!

GRANDMA. Who? Who?

MOMMY. Oh, just some people.

GRANDMA. The van people? Is it the van people? Have you finally done it? Have you called the van people to come and take me away?

DADDY.   Of course not, Grandma!

GRANDMA.   Oh, don't be too sure. She'd have you carted off too, if she thought she could get away with it.

MOMMY.   Pay no attention to her, Daddy.

(*An aside to* GRANDMA)

My God, you're ungrateful! (*The doorbell rings again*)

DADDY (*Wringing his hands*).   Oh dear; oh dear.

MOMMY (*Still to* GRANDMA).   Just you wait; I'll fix your wagon.

(*Now to* DADDY)

Well, go let them in, Daddy. What are you waiting for?

DADDY.   I think we should talk about it some more. Maybe we've been hasty . . . a little hasty, perhaps.

(*Doorbell rings again*)

I'd like to talk about it some more.

MOMMY.   There's no need. You made up your mind; you were firm; you were masculine and decisive.

DADDY.   We might consider the pros and the . . .

MOMMY.   I won't argue with you; it has to be done; you were right. Open the door.

DADDY.   But I'm not sure that . . .

MOMMY.   Open the door.

DADDY.   Was I firm about it?

MOMMY.   Oh, so firm; so firm.

DADDY.   And was I decisive?

MOMMY.   SO decisive! Oh, I shivered.

DADDY.   And masculine? Was I really masculine?

MOMMY.   Oh, Daddy, you were so masculine; I shivered and fainted.

GRANDMA.   Shivered and fainted, did she? Humf!

MOMMY.   You be quiet.

GRANDMA.   Old people have a right to talk to themselves; it doesn't hurt the gums, and it's comforting.

(*Doorbell rings again*)

DADDY.   I shall now open the door.

MOMMY.   WHAT a masculine Daddy! Isn't he a masculine Daddy?

GRANDMA.   Don't expect me to say anything. Old people are obscene.

MOMMY.   Some of your opinions aren't so bad. You know that?

DADDY (*Backing off from the door*).   Maybe we can send them away.

MOMMY.   Oh, look at you! You're turning into jelly; you're indecisive; you're a woman.

DADDY.   All right. Watch me now; I'm going to open the door. Watch. Watch!

MOMMY.   We're watching; we're watching.
GRANDMA.   *I'm* not.
DADDY.   Watch now; it's opening.

(*He opens the door*)

It's open!

(MRS. BARKER *steps into the room*)

Here they are!
MOMMY.   Here they are!
GRANDMA.   Where?
DADDY.   Come in. You're late. But, of course, we expected you to be late; we were saying that we expected you to be late.
MOMMY.   Daddy, don't be rude! We were saying that you just can't get satisfaction these days, and we were talking about you, of course. Won't you come in?
MRS. BARKER.   Thank you. I don't mind if I do.
MOMMY.   We're very glad that you're here, late as you are. You do remember us, don't you? You were here once before. I'm Mommy, and this is Daddy, and that's Grandma, doddering there in the corner.
MRS. BARKER.   Hello, Mommy; hello, Daddy; and hello there, Grandma.
DADDY.   Now that you're here, I don't suppose you could go away and maybe come back some other time.
MRS. BARKER.   Oh no; we're much too efficient for that. I said, hello there, Grandma.
MOMMY.   Speak to them, Grandma.
GRANDMA.   I don't see them.
DADDY.   For shame, Grandma; they're here.
MRS. BARKER.   Yes, we're here, Grandma. I'm Mrs. Barker. I remember you; don't you remember me?
GRANDMA.   I don't recall. Maybe you were younger, or something.
MOMMY.   Grandma! What a terrible thing to say!
MRS. BARKER.   Oh now, don't scold her, Mommy; for all she knows she may be right.
DADDY.   Uh . . . Mrs. Barker, is it? Won't you sit down?
MRS. BARKER.   I don't mind if I do.
MOMMY.   Would you like a cigarette, and a drink, and would you like to cross your legs?
MRS. BARKER.   You forget yourself, Mommy; I'm a professional woman. But I will cross my legs.
DADDY.   Yes, make yourself comfortable.
MRS. BARKER.   I don't mind if I do.
GRANDMA.   Are they still here?
MOMMY.   Be quiet, Grandma.

MRS. BARKER. Oh, we're still here. My, what an unattractive apartment you have!

MOMMY. Yes, but you don't know what a trouble it is. Let me tell you . . .

DADDY. I was saying to Mommy . . .

MRS. BARKER. Yes, I know. I was listening outside.

DADDY. About the icebox, and . . . the doorbell . . . and the . . .

MRS. BARKER. . . . and the johnny. Yes, we're very efficient; we have to know everything in our work.

DADDY. Exactly what do you do?

MOMMY. Yes, what is your work?

MRS. BARKER. Well, my dear, for one thing, I'm chairman of your woman's club.

MOMMY. Don't be ridiculous. I was talking to the chairman of my woman's club just yester—Why, so you are. You remember, Daddy, the lady I was telling you about? The lady with the husband who sits in the *swing?* Don't you remember?

DADDY. No . . . no . . .

MOMMY. Of course you do. I'm so sorry, Mrs. Barker. I would have known you anywhere, except in this artificial light. And look! You have a hat just like the one I bought yesterday.

MRS. BARKER (*With a little laugh*). No, not really; this hat is cream.

MOMMY. Well, my dear, that may look like a cream hat to you, but I can . . .

MRS. BARKER. Now, now; you seem to forget who I am.

MOMMY. Yes, I do, don't I? Are you sure you're comfortable? Won't you take off your dress?

MRS. BARKER. I don't mind if I do.

(*She removes her dress*)

MOMMY. There. You must feel a great deal more comfortable.

MRS. BARKER. Well, I certainly *look* a great deal more comfortable.

DADDY. I'm going to blush and giggle.

MOMMY. Daddy's going to blush and giggle.

MRS. BARKER (*Pulling the hem of her slip above her knees*). You're lucky to have such a man for a husband.

MOMMY. Oh, don't I know it!

DADDY. I just blushed and giggled and went sticky wet.

MOMMY. Isn't Daddy a caution, Mrs. Barker?

MRS. BARKER. Maybe if I smoked . . .?

MOMMY. Oh, that isn't necessary.

MRS. BARKER. I don't mind if I do.

MOMMY. No; no, don't. Really.

MRS. BARKER. I don't mind . . .

MOMMY. I won't have you smoking in my house, and that's that! You're a professional woman.

DADDY. Grandma drinks AND smokes; don't you, Grandma?

GRANDMA. No.

MOMMY. Well, now, Mrs. Barker; suppose you tell us why you're here.

GRANDMA (*As* MOMMY *walks through the boxes*). The boxes . . . the boxes . . .

MOMMY. Be quiet, Grandma.

DADDY. What did you say, Grandma?

GRANDMA (*As* MOMMY *steps on several of the boxes*). The boxes, damn it!

MRS. BARKER. Boxes; she said boxes. She mentioned the boxes.

DADDY. What about the boxes, Grandma? Maybe Mrs. Barker is here because of the boxes. Is that what you meant, Grandma?

GRANDMA. I don't know if that's what I meant or not. It's certainly not what I *thought* I meant.

DADDY. Grandma is of the opinion that . . .

MRS. BARKER. Can we assume that the boxes are for us? I mean, can we assume that you had us come here for the boxes?

MOMMY. Are you in the habit of receiving boxes?

DADDY. A very good question.

MRS. BARKER. Well, that would depend on the reason we're here. I've got my fingers in so many little pies, you know. Now, I can think of one of my little activities in which we are in the habit of receiving *baskets;* but more in a literary sense than really. We *might* receive boxes, though, under very special circumstances. I'm afraid that's the best answer I can give you.

DADDY. It's a very interesting answer.

MRS. BARKER. I thought so. But, does it help?

MOMMY. No; I'm afraid not.

DADDY. I wonder if it might help us any if I said I feel misgivings, that I have definite qualms.

MOMMY. Where, Daddy?

DADDY. Well, mostly right here, right around where the stitches were.

MOMMY. Daddy had an operation, you know.

MRS. BARKER. Oh, you poor Daddy! I didn't know; but then, how could I?

GRANDMA. You might have asked; it wouldn't have hurt you.

MOMMY. Dry up, Grandma.

GRANDMA. There you go. Letting your true feelings come out. Old people aren't dry enough, I suppose. My sacks are empty, the fluid in my eyeballs is all caked on the inside edges, my spine is made of sugar candy, I breathe ice; but you don't hear me complain. Nobody hears old people complain because people think that's all old people do. And *that's* because old people are gnarled and sagged and twisted into the shape of a complaint.

(*Signs off*)

That's all.

MRS. BARKER. What was wrong, Daddy?

DADDY. Well, you know how it is: the doctors took out something that was there and put in something that wasn't there. An operation.

MRS. BARKER. You're very fortunate, I should say.

MOMMY. Oh, he is; he is. All his life, Daddy wanted to be a United States Senator; but now . . . why now he's changed his mind, and for the rest of his life he's going to want to be Governor . . . it would be nearer the apartment, you know.

MRS. BARKER. You *are* fortunate, Daddy.

DADDY. Yes, indeed; except that I get these qualms now and then, definite ones.

MRS. BARKER. Well, it's just a matter of things settling; you're like an old house.

MOMMY. Why, Daddy, thank Mrs. Barker.

DADDY. Thank you.

MRS. BARKER. Ambition! That's the ticket. I have a brother who's very much like you, Daddy . . . ambitious. Of course, he's a great deal younger than you; he's even younger than I am . . . if such a thing is possible. He runs a little newspaper. Just a little newspaper . . . but he runs it. He's chief cook and bottle washer of that little newspaper, which he calls *The Village Idiot*. He has such a sense of humor; he's so self-deprecating, so modest. And he'd never admit it himself, but he *is* the Village Idiot.

MOMMY. Oh, I think that's just grand. Don't you think so, Daddy?

DADDY. Yes, just grand.

MRS. BARKER. My brother's a dear man, and he has a dear little wife, whom he loves, dearly. He loves her so much he just can't get a sentence out without mentioning her. He wants everybody to know he's married. He's really a stickler on that point; he can't be introduced to anybody and say hello without adding, "Of course, I'm married." As far as I'm concerned, he's the chief exponent of Woman Love in this whole country; he's even been written up in psychiatric journals because of it.

DADDY. Indeed!

MOMMY. Isn't that lovely.

MRS. BARKER. Oh, I think so. There's too much woman hatred in this country, and that's a fact.

GRANDMA. Oh, I don't know.

MOMMY. Oh, I think that's just grand. Don't you think so, Daddy?

DADDY. Yes, just grand.

GRANDMA. In case anybody's interested . . .

MOMMY. Be quiet, Grandma.

GRANDMA. Nuts!

MOMMY. Oh, Mrs. Barker, you *must* forgive Grandma. She's rural.

MRS. BARKER. I don't mind if I do.

DADDY. Maybe Grandma has something to say.

MOMMY. Nonsense. Old people have nothing to say; and if old people *did* have something to say, nobody would listen to them. (*To* GRANDMA) You see? I can pull that stuff just as easy as you can.

GRANDMA. Well, you got the rhythm, but you don't really have the quality. Besides, you're middle-aged.

MOMMY. I'm proud of it!

GRANDMA. Look. I'll show you how it's really done. Middle-aged people think they can do anything, but the truth is that middle-aged people can't do most things as well as they used to. Middle-aged people think they're special because they're like everybody else. We live in the age of deformity. You see? Rhythm *and* content. You'll learn.

DADDY. I do wish I weren't surrounded by women; I'd like some men around here.

MRS. BARKER. You can say that again!

GRANDMA. I don't hardly count as a woman, so can I say my piece?

MOMMY. Go on. Jabber away.

GRANDMA. It's very simple; the fact is, these boxes don't have anything to do with why this good lady is come to call. Now, if you're interested in knowing why these boxes *are* here . . .

DADDY. I'm sure that must be all very true, Grandma, but what does it have to do with why . . . pardon me; what is that name again?

MRS. BARKER. Mrs. Barker.

DADDY. Exactly. What does it have to with why . . . that name again?

MRS. BARKER. Mrs. Barker.

DADDY. Precisely. What does it have to do with why what's-her-name is here?

MOMMY. They're here because we asked them.

MRS. BARKER. Yes. That's why.

GRANDMA. Now if you're interested in knowing why these boxes *are* here . . .

MOMMY. Well, nobody *is* interested!

GRANDMA. You can be as snippety as you like for all the good it'll do you.

DADDY. You two will have to stop arguing.

MOMMY. I don't argue with her.

DADDY. It will just have to stop.

MOMMY. Well, why don't you call a van and have her taken away?

GRANDMA. Don't bother, there's no need.

DADDY. No, now, perhaps I can go away myself . . .

MOMMY. Well, one or the other; the way things are now it's impossible. In the first place, it's too crowded in this apartment. (*To* GRANDMA) And it's you that takes up all the space, with your enema bottles, and your Pekinese, and God-only-knows-what-else . . . and now all these boxes. . . .

GRANDMA. These boxes are . . .

MRS. BARKER. I've never heard of enema *bottles*. . . .

GRANDMA. She means enema bags, but she doesn't know the difference. Mommy comes from extremely bad stock. And besides, when Mommy was born . . . well, it was a difficult delivery, and she had a head shaped like a banana.

MOMMY. You ungrateful—Daddy? Daddy? Daddy, you see how ungrateful she is after all these years, after all the things we've done for her? (*To* GRANDMA) One of these days you're going away in a van; that's what's going to happen to you!

GRANDMA. Do tell!

MRS. BARKER. Like a banana?

GRANDMA. Yup, just like a banana.

MRS. BARKER. My word!

MOMMY. You stop listening to her; she'll say anything. Just the other night she called Daddy a hedgehog.

MRS. BARKER. She didn't!

GRANDMA. That's right, baby; you stick up for me.

MOMMY. I don't know where she gets the words; on the television, maybe.

MRS. BARKER. Did you really call him a hedgehog?

GRANDMA. Oh look; what difference does it make whether I did or not?

DADDY. Grandma's right. Leave Grandma alone.

MOMMY (*To* DADDY). How dare you!

GRANDMA. Oh, leave her alone, Daddy; the kid's all mixed up.

MOMMY. You see? I told you. It's all those television shows. Daddy, you go right into Grandma's room and take her television and shake all the tubes loose.

DADDY. Don't mention tubes to me.

MOMMY. Oh! Mommy forgot! (*To* MRS. BARKER) Daddy has tubes now, where he used to have tracts.

MRS. BARKER. Is that a fact!

GRANDMA. I know why this dear lady is here.

MOMMY. You be still.

MRS. BARKER. Oh, I do wish you'd tell me.

MOMMY. No! No! That wouldn't be fair at all.

DADDY. Besides, she knows why she's here; she's here because we called them.

Mrs. Barker. La! But that still leaves me puzzled. I know I'm here because you called us, but I'm such a busy girl, with this committee and that committee, and the Responsible Citizens Activities I indulge in.

Mommy. Oh my; busy, busy.

Mrs. Barker. Yes, indeed. So I'm afraid you'll have to give me some help.

Mommy. Oh, no. No, you must be mistaken. I can't believe we asked you here to give you any help. With the way taxes are these days, and the way you can't get satisfaction in ANYTHING . . . no, I don't believe so.

Daddy. And if you need help . . . why, I should think you'd apply for a Fulbright Scholarship. . . .

Mommy. And if not that . . . why, then a Guggenheim Fellowship. . . .

Grandma. Oh, come on; why not shoot the works and try for the Prix de Rome. (*Under her breath to* Mommy *and* Daddy) Beasts!

Mrs. Barker. Oh, what a jolly family. But let me think. I'm knee-deep in work these days; there's the Ladies' Auxiliary Air Raid Committee, for one thing; how do you feel about air raids?

Mommy. Oh, I'd say we're hostile.

Daddy. Yes, definitely; we're hostile.

Mrs. Barker. Then, you'll be no help there. There's too much hostility in the world these days as it is; but I'll not badger you! There's a surfeit of badgers as well.

Grandma. While we're at it, there's been a run on old people, too. The Department of Agriculture, or maybe it wasn't the Department of Agriculture—anyway, it was some department that's run by a girl—put on figures showing that ninety per cent of the adult population of the country is over eight years old . . . or eighty per cent is over ninety years old . . .

Mommy. You're such a liar! You just finished saying that everyone is middle-aged.

Grandma. I'm just telling you what the government says . . . that doesn't have anything to do with what . . .

Mommy. It's that television! Daddy, go break her television.

Grandma. You won't find it.

Daddy (*Wearily getting up*). If I must . . . I must.

Mommy. And don't step on the Pekinese; it's blind.

Daddy. It may be blind, but Daddy isn't.

(*He exits, through the archway, stage left*)

Grandma. You won't find *it*, either.

Mommy. Oh, I'm so fortunate to have such a husband. Just think; I could have a husband who was poor, or argumentative, or a husband who sat in a wheel chair all day . . . OOOOHHHH! *What* have I said? What *have* I said?

Grandma. You said you could have a husband who sat in a wheel . . .

MOMMY.   I'm mortified! I could die! I could cut my tongue out! I could
. . .

MRS. BARKER (*Forcing a smile*).   Oh, now . . . now . . . don't think about
it . . .

MOMMY.   I could . . . why, I could . . .

MRS. BARKER.   . . . don't think about it . . . really . . .

MOMMY.   You're quite right. I won't think about it, and that way I'll
forget that I ever said it, and that way it will be all right.

(*Pause*)

There . . . I've forgotten. Well, now, now that Daddy is out of the room
we can have some girl talk.

MRS. BARKER.   I'm not sure that I . . .

MOMMY.   You *do* want to have some girl talk, don't you?

MRS. BARKER.   I was going to say I'm not sure that I wouldn't care for a
glass of water. I feel a little faint.

MOMMY.   Grandma, go get Mrs. Barker a glass of water.

GRANDMA.   Go get it yourself. I quit.

MOMMY.   Grandma loves to do little things around the house; it gives her
a false sense of security.

GRANDMA.   I quit! I'm through!

MOMMY.   Now, you be a good Grandma, or you know what will happen
to you. You'll be taken away in a van.

GRANDMA.   You don't frighten me. I'm too old to be frightened.
Besides . . .

MOMMY.   WELL! I'll tend to you later. I'll hide your teeth . . . I'll . . .

GRANDMA.   Everything's hidden.

MRS. BARKER.   I *am* going to faint. I *am.*

MOMMY.   Good heavens! I'll go myself.

(*As she exits, through the archway, stage-left*)

I'll fix you, Grandma. I'll take care of you later.

(*She exits*)

GRANDMA.   Oh, go soak your head. (*To* MRS. BARKER) Well, dearie, how
do you feel?

MRS. BARKER.   A little better, I think, Yes, much better, thank you,
Grandma.

GRANDMA.   That's good.

MRS. BARKER.   But . . . I feel so lost . . . not knowing why I'm here . . .
and, on top of it, they say I was here before.

GRANDMA.   Well, you were. You weren't *here,* exactly, because we've
moved around a lot, from one apartment to another, up and down the social
ladder like mice, if you like similes.

Mrs. Barker. I don't . . . particularly.

Grandma. Well, then, I'm sorry.

Mrs. Barker (*Suddenly*). Grandma, I feel I can trust you.

Grandma. Don't be too sure; it's every man for himself around this place. . . .

Mrs. Barker. Oh . . . is it? Nonetheless, I really do feel that I can trust you. *Please* tell me why they called and asked us to come. I implore you!

Grandma. Oh my; that feels good. It's been so long since anybody implored me. Do it again. Implore me some more.

Mrs. Barker. You're your daughter's mother, all right!

Grandma. Oh, I don't mean to be hard. If you won't implore me, then beg me, or ask me, or entreat me . . . just anything like that.

Mrs. Barker. You're a dreadful old woman!

Grandma. You'll understand some day. Please!

Mrs. Barker. Oh, for heaven's sake! . . . I implore you . . . I beg you . . . I beseech you!

Grandma. Beseech! Oh, that's the nicest word I've heard in ages. You're a dear, sweet woman. . . . You . . . beseech . . . me. I can't resist that.

Mrs. Barker. Well, then . . . please tell me why they asked us to come.

Grandma. Well, I'll give you a hint. That's the best I can do, because I'm a muddleheaded old woman. Now listen, because it's important. Once upon a time, not too very long ago, but a long enough time ago . . . oh, about twenty years ago . . . there was a man very much like Daddy, and a woman very much like Mommy, who were married to each other, very much like Mommy and Daddy are married to each other; and they lived in an apartment very much like one that's very much like this one, and they lived there with an old woman who was very much like yours truly, only younger, because it was some time ago; in fact, they were all somewhat younger.

Mrs. Barker. How fascinating!

Grandma. Now, at the same time, there was a dear lady very much like you, only younger then, who did all sorts of Good Works. . . . And one of the Good Works this dear lady did was in something very much like a volunteer capacity for an organization very much like the Bye-Bye Adoption Service, which is nearby and which was run by a terribly deaf old lady very much like the Miss Bye-Bye who runs the Bye-Bye Adoption Service nearby.

Mrs. Barker. How enthralling!

Grandma. Well, be that as it may. Nonetheless, one afternoon this man, who was very much like Daddy, and this woman who was very much like Mommy came to see this dear lady who did all the Good Works, who was very much like you, dear, and they were very sad and very hopeful, and they cried and smiled and bit their fingers, and they said all the most intimate things.

Mrs. Barker. How spellbinding! What did they say?

GRANDMA. Well, it was very sweet. The woman, who was very much like Mommy, said that she and the man who was very much like Daddy had never been blessed with anything very much like a bumble of joy.

MRS. BARKER. A what?

GRANDMA. A bumble; a bumble of joy.

MRS. BARKER. Oh, like bundle.

GRANDMA. Well, yes; very much like it. Bundle, bumble; who cares? At any rate, the woman, who was very much like Mommy, said that they wanted a bumble of their own, but that the man, who was very much like Daddy, couldn't have a bumble; and the man, who was very much like Daddy, said that yes, they had wanted a bumble of their own, but that the woman, who was very much like Mommy, couldn't have one, and that now they wanted to buy something very much like a bumble.

MRS. BARKER. How engrossing!

GRANDMA. Yes. And the dear lady, who was very much like you, said something that was very much like, "Oh, what a shame; but take heart . . . I think we have just the bumble *for* you." And, well, the lady, who was very much like Mommy, and the man, who was very much like Daddy, cried and smiled and bit their fingers, and said some more intimate things, which were totally irrelevant but which were pretty hot stuff, and so the dear lady, who was very much like you, and who had something very much like a penchant for pornography, listened with something very much like enthusiasm. "Whee," she said. "Whoooopeeeeee!" But that's beside the point.

MRS. BARKER. I suppose *so*. But how gripping!

GRANDMA. Anyway . . . they *bought* something very much like a bumble, and they took it away with them. But . . . things didn't work out very well.

MRS. BARKER. You mean there was trouble?

GRANDMA. You got it.

(*With a glance through the archway*)

But, I'm going to have to speed up now because I think I'm leaving soon.

MRS. BARKER. Oh. Are you really?

GRANDMA. Yup.

MRS. BARKER. But old people don't go anywhere; they're either taken places, or put places.

GRANDMA. Well, this old person is different. Anyway . . . things started going badly.

MRS. BARKER. Oh yes. Yes.

GRANDMA. Weeeeellll . . . in the first place, it turned out the bumble didn't look like either one of its parents. That was enough of a blow, but things got worse. One night, it cried its heart out, if you can imagine such a thing.

MRS. BARKER. Cried its heart out! Well!

GRANDMA. But that was only the beginning. Then it turned out it only had eyes for its Daddy.

MRS. BARKER. For its Daddy! Why, any self-respecting woman would have gouged those eyes right out of its head.

GRANDMA. Well, she did. That's exactly what she did. But then, it kept its nose up in the air.

MRS. BARKER. Ufggh! How disgusting!

GRANDMA. That's what they thought. But *then,* it began to develop an interest in its you-know-what.

MRS. BARKER. In its you-know-what! Well! I hope they cut its hands off at the wrists.

GRANDMA. Well, yes they did that eventually. But first, they cut off its you-know-what.

MRS. BARKER. A much better idea!

GRANDMA. That's what they thought. But after they cut off its you-know-what, it *still* put its hands under the covers, *looking* for its you-know-what. So, finally, they *had* to cut off its hands at the wrists.

MRS. BARKER. Naturally!

GRANDMA. And it was such a resentful bumble. Why, one day it called its Mommy a dirty name.

MRS. BARKER. Well, I hope they cut its tongue out!

GRANDMA. Of course. And then, as it got bigger, they found out all sorts of terrible things about it, like: it didn't have a head on its shoulders, it had no guts, it was spineless, its feet were made of clay . . . just dreadful things.

MRS. BARKER. Dreadful!

GRANDMA. So you can understand how they became discouraged.

MRS. BARKER. I certainly can! And what did they do?

GRANDMA. What did they do? Well, for the last straw, it finally up and died; and you can imagine how *that* made them feel, their having paid for it, and all. So, they called up the lady who sold them the bumble in the first place and told her to come right over to their apartment. They wanted satisfaction; they wanted their money back. That's what they wanted.

MRS. BARKER. My, my, my.

GRANDMA. How do you like *them* apples?

MRS. BARKER. My, my, my.

DADDY (*Off stage*). Isn't that funny! And I can't find the water.

GRANDMA. Heh, heh, heh. I told them everything was hidden.

MRS. BARKER. Did you hide the water, too?

GRANDMA (*Puzzled*). No. No, I didn't do *that.*

DADDY (*Off stage*). The truth of the matter is, I can't even find Grandma's room.

GRANDMA. Heh, heh, heh.

MRS. BARKER. My! You certainly did hide things, didn't you?

GRANDMA. Sure, kid, sure.

MOMMY (*Sticking her head in the room*).   Did you ever hear of such a thing, Grandma? Daddy can't find your television, and he can't find the Pekinese, and the truth of the matter is he can't even find your room.

GRANDMA.   I told you. I hid everything.

MOMMY.   Nonsense, Grandma! Just wait until I get my hands on you. You're a troublemaker . . . that's what you are.

GRANDMA.   Well, I'll be out of here pretty soon, baby.

MOMMY.   Oh, you don't know how right you are! Daddy's been wanting to send you away for a long time now, but I've been restraining him. I'll tell you one thing, though . . . I'm getting sick and tired of this fighting, and I might just let him have his way. Then you'll see what'll happen. Away you'll go; in a van, too. I'll let Daddy call the van man.

GRANDMA.   I'm way ahead of you.

MOMMY.   How can you be so old and so smug at the same time? You have no sense of proportion.

GRANDMA.   You just answered your own question.

MOMMY.   Mrs. Barker, I'd much rather you came into the kitchen for that glass of water, what with Grandma out here, and all.

MRS. BARKER.   I don't see what Grandma has to do with it; and besides, I don't think you're very polite.

MOMMY.   You seem to forget you're a guest in this house . . .

GRANDMA.   Apartment!

MOMMY.   Apartment! And that you're a professional woman. So, if you'll be so good as to come into the kitchen, I'll be more than happy to show you where the water is, and where the glass is, and then you can put two and two together, if you're clever enough.

(*She vanishes*)

MRS. BARKER (*After a moment's consideration*).   I suppose she's right.

GRANDMA.   Well, that's how it is when people call you up and ask you over to do something for them.

MRS. BARKER.   I suppose you're right, too. Well, Grandma, it's been very nice talking to you.

GRANDMA.   And I've enjoyed listening. Say, don't tell Mommy or Daddy that I gave you that hint, will you?

MRS. BARKER.   Oh, dear me, the hint! I'd forgotten about it, if you can imagine such a thing. No, I won't breathe a word of it to them.

GRANDMA.   I don't know if it helped you any . . .

MRS. BARKER.   I can't tell, yet. I'll have to . . . what *is* the word I want? . . . I'll have to relate it . . . that's it . . . I'll have to relate it to certain things that I *know*, and . . . draw . . . conclusions. . . . What I'll really have to do is to see if it applies to anything. I mean, after all, I *do* do volunteer work for an adoption service, but it isn't very much *like* the Bye-Bye Adoption Service . . . it *is* the Bye-Bye Adoption Service . . . and while I can remember

Mommy and Daddy coming to see me, oh, about twenty years ago, about buying a bumble, I can't quite remember anyone very much *like* Mommy and Daddy coming to see me about buying a bumble. Don't you see? It really presents quite a problem. . . . I'll have to think about it . . . mull it . . . but at any rate, it was truly first-class of you to try to help me. Oh, will you still be here after I've had my drink of water?

GRANDMA.   Probably . . . I'm not as spry as I used to be.

MRS. BARKER.   Oh. Well, I won't say good-by then.

GRANDMA.   No. Don't.

(MRS. BARKER *exits through the archway*)

People don't say good-by to old people because they think they'll frighten them. Lordy! If they only knew how awful "hello" and "my, you're looking chipper" sounded, they wouldn't say those things either. The truth is, there isn't much you *can* say to old people that doesn't sound just terrible.

(*The doorbell rings*)

Come on in!

(*The* YOUNG MAN *enters.* GRANDMA *looks him over*)

Well, now, aren't you a breath of fresh air!

YOUNG MAN.   Hello there.

GRANDMA.   My, my, my. Are you the van man?

YOUNG MAN.   The what?

GRANDMA.   The van man. The van man. Are you come to take me away?

YOUNG MAN.   I don't know what you're talking about.

GRANDMA.   Oh.

(*Pause*)

Well.

(*Pause*)

My, my, aren't you something!

YOUNG MAN.   Hm?

GRANDMA.   I said, my, my, aren't you something.

YOUNG MAN.   Oh. Thank you.

GRANDMA.   You don't sound very enthusiastic.

YOUNG MAN.   Oh, I'm . . . I'm used to it.

GRANDMA.   Yup . . . yup. You know, if I were about a hundred and fifty years younger I could go for you.

YOUNG MAN.   Yes, I imagine so.

GRANDMA.   Unh-hunh . . . will you look at those muscles!

YOUNG MAN (*Flexing his muscles*).   Yes, they're quite good, aren't they?

GRANDMA.   Boy, they sure are. They natural?

YOUNG MAN.   Well the basic structure was there, but I've done some work, too . . . you know, in a gym.

GRANDMA. I'll bet you have. You ought to be in the movies, boy.

YOUNG MAN. I know.

GRANDMA. Yup! Right up there on the old silver screen. But I suppose you've heard that before.

YOUNG MAN. Yes, I have.

GRANDMA. You ought to try out for them . . . the movies.

YOUNG MAN. Well, actually, I may have a career there yet. I've lived out on the West Coast almost all my life . . . and I've met a few people who . . . might be able to help me. I'm not in too much of a hurry, though. I'm almost as young as I look.

GRANDMA. Oh, that's nice. And will you look at that face!

YOUNG MAN. Yes, it's quite good, isn't it? Clean-cut, midwest farm boy type, almost insultingly good-looking in a typically American way. Good profile, straight nose, honest eyes, wonderful smile . . .

GRANDMA. Yup. Boy, you know what you are, don't you? You're the American Dream, that's what you are. All those other people, they don't know what they're talking about. You . . . *you* are the American Dream.

YOUNG MAN. Thanks.

MOMMY (*Off stage*). Who rang the doorbell?

GRANDMA (*Shouting off-stage*). The American Dream!

MOMMY (*Off stage*). What? What was that, Grandma?

GRANDMA (*Shouting*). The American Dream! The American Dream! Damn it!

DADDY (*Off stage*). How's that, Mommy?

MOMMY (*Off stage*). Oh, some gibberish; pay no attention. Did you find Grandma's room?

DADDY (*Off stage*). No. I can't even find Mrs. Barker.

YOUNG MAN. What was all that?

GRANDMA. Oh, that was just the folks, but let's not talk about them, honey; let's talk about you.

YOUNG MAN. All right.

GRANDMA. Well, let's see. If you're not the van man, what are you doing here?

YOUNG MAN. I'm looking for work.

GRANDMA. Are you! Well, what kind of work?

YOUNG MAN. Oh, almost anything . . . almost anything that pays. I'll do almost anything for money.

GRANDMA. Will you . . . will you? Hmmmm. I wonder if there's anything you could do around here?

YOUNG MAN. There might be. It looked to be a likely building.

GRANDMA. It's always looked to be a rather unlikely building to me, but I suppose you'd know better than I.

YOUNG MAN. I can sense these things.

GRANDMA. There *might* be something you could do around here. Stay there! Don't come any closer.

YOUNG MAN. Sorry.

GRANDMA. I don't mean I'd *mind.* I don't know whether I'd mind, or not. . . . But it wouldn't look well; it would look just *awful.*

YOUNG MAN. Yes; I suppose so.

GRANDMA. Now, stay there, let me concentrate. What could you do? The folks have been in something of a quandary around here today, sort of a dilemma, and I wonder if you mightn't be some help.

YOUNG MAN. I hope so . . . if there's money in it. Do you have any money?

GRANDMA. Money! Oh, there's more money around here than you'd know what to do with.

YOUNG MAN. I'm not so sure.

GRANDMA. Well, maybe not. Besides, I've got money of my own.

YOUNG MAN. You have?

GRANDMA. Sure. Old people quite often have lots of money; more often than most people expect. Come here, so I can whisper to you . . . not too close. I might faint.

YOUNG MAN. Oh, I'm sorry.

GRANDMA. It's all right, dear. Anyway . . . have you ever heard of that big baking contest they run? The one where all the ladies get together in a big barn and bake away?

YOUNG MAN. I'm . . . not . . . sure. . . .

GRANDMA. Not so close. Well, it doesn't matter whether you've heard of it or not. The important thing is—and I don't want anybody to hear this . . . the folks think I haven't been out of the house in eight years—the important thing is that I won first prize in that baking contest this year. Oh, it was in all the papers; not under my own name, though. I used a *nom de boulangère;*[1] I called myself Uncle Henry.

YOUNG MAN. Did you?

GRANDMA. Why not? I didn't see any reason not to. I look just as much like an old man as I do like an old woman. And you know what I called it . . . what I won for?

YOUNG MAN. No. What did you call it?

GRANDMA. I called it Uncle Henry's Day-Old Cake.

YOUNG MAN. That's a very nice name.

GRANDMA. And it wasn't any trouble, either. All I did was go out and get a store-bought cake, and keep it around for a while, and then slip it in, unbeknownst to anybody. Simple.

YOUNG MAN. You're a very resourceful person.

GRANDMA. Pioneer stock.

YOUNG MAN. Is all this true? Do you want me to believe all this?

[1] Name of a baker.

GRANDMA. Well, you can believe it or not . . . it doesn't make any difference to me. All *I* know is, Uncle Henry's Day-Old Cake won me twenty-five thousand smackerolas.

YOUNG MAN. Twenty-five thou—

GRANDMA. Right on the old loggerhead. Now . . . how do you like them apples?

YOUNG MAN. Love 'em.

GRANDMA. I thought you'd be impressed.

YOUNG MAN. Money talks.

GRANDMA. Hey! You look familiar.

YOUNG MAN. Hm? Pardon?

GRANDMA. I said, you look familiar.

YOUNG MAN. Well, I've done some modeling.

GRANDMA. No . . . no. I don't mean that. You look familiar.

YOUNG MAN. Well, I'm a type.

GRANDMA. Yup; you sure are. Why do you say you'd do anything for money . . . if you don't mind my being nosy?

YOUNG MAN. No, no. It's part of the interviews. I'll be happy to tell you. It's that I have no talents at all, except what you see . . . my person; my body, my face. In every other way I am incomplete, and I must therefore . . . compensate.

GRANDMA. What do you mean, incomplete? You look pretty complete to me.

YOUNG MAN. I think I can explain it to you, partially because you're very old, and very old people have perceptions they keep to themselves, because if they expose them to other people . . . well, you know what ridicule and neglect are.

GRANDMA. I do, child, I do.

YOUNG MAN. Then listen. My mother died the night that I was born, and I never knew my father; I doubt my mother did. But, I wasn't alone, because lying with me . . . in the placenta . . . there was someone else . . . my brother . . . my twin.

GRANDMA. Oh, my child.

YOUNG MAN. We were identical twins . . . he and I . . . not fraternal . . . identical; we were derived from the same ovum; and in *this*, in that we were twins not from separate ova but from the same one, we had a kinship such as you cannot imagine. We . . . we felt each other breathe . . . his heartbeats thundered in my temples . . . mine in his . . . our stomachs ached and we cried for feeding at the same time . . . are you old enough to understand?

GRANDMA. I think so, child; I think I'm nearly old enough.

YOUNG MAN. I hope so. But we were separated when we were still very young, my brother, my twin and I . . . inasmuch as you can separate one being. We were torn apart . . . thrown to opposite ends of the continent. I don't know what became of my brother . . . to the rest of myself . . . except that, from time to time, in the years that have passed, I have suffered losses . . . that I can't explain. A fall from grace . . . a departure of innocence . . . loss . . . loss. How can I put it to you? All right; like this: Once . . . it was as if all at once my heart . . . became numb . . . almost as though I . . . almost as though . . . just like that . . . it had been wrenched from my body . . . and from that time I have been unable to love. Once . . . I was asleep at the time . . . I awoke, and my eyes were burning. And since that time I have been unable to see anything, *anything*, with pity, with affection . . . with anything but . . . cool disinterest. And my groin . . . even there . . . since one time . . . one specific agony . . . since then I have not been able to *love* anyone with my body. And even my hands . . . I cannot touch another person and feel love. And there is more . . . there are more losses, but it all comes down to this: I no longer have the capacity to feel anything. I have no emotions. I have been drained, torn asunder . . . disemboweled. I have, now, only my person . . . my body, my face. I use what I have . . . I let people love me . . . I accept the syntax around me, for while I know I cannot relate . . . I know I must be related *to*. I let people love me . . . I let people touch me . . . I let them draw pleasure from my groin . . . from my presence . . . from the fact of me . . . but, that is all it comes to. As I told you, I am incomplete . . . I can feel nothing. I can feel nothing. And so . . . here I am . . . as you see me. I am . . . but this . . . what you see. And it will always be thus.

GRANDMA. Oh, my child; my child.

(Long pause; then)

I was mistaken . . . before. I don't know you from somewhere, but I knew . . . once . . . someone very much like you . . . or, very much as perhaps you were.

YOUNG MAN. Be careful; be very careful. What I have told you may not be true. In my profession . . .

GRANDMA. Shhhhhh.

(The YOUNG MAN *bows his head, in acquiescence)*

Someone . . . to be more precise . . . who might have turned out to be very much like you might have turned out to be. And . . . unless I'm terribly mistaken . . . you've found yourself a job.

YOUNG MAN. What are my duties?

MRS. BARKER *(Off stage)*. Yoo-hoo! Yoo-hoo!

GRANDMA. Oh-oh. You'll . . . you'll have to play it by ear, my dear . . . unless I get a chance to talk to you again. I've got to go into my act, now.

YOUNG MAN. But, I . . .

GRANDMA. Yoo-hoo!

MRS. BARKER *(Coming through archway)*. Yoo-hoo . . . oh, there you are, Grandma. I'm glad to see somebody. I can't find Mommy or Daddy.

(Double takes)

Well . . . who's this?

GRANDMA.   This? Well . . . un . . . oh, this is the . . . uh . . . the van man. That's who it is . . . the van man.

MRS. BARKER.   So! It's true! They *did* call the van man. They *are* having you carted away.

GRANDMA (*Shrugging*).   Well, you know. It figures.

MRS. BARKER (*To young man*).   How dare you cart this poor old woman away!

YOUNG MAN (*After a quick look at* GRANDMA, *who nods*).   I do what I'm paid to do. I don't ask any questions.

MRS. BARKER (*After a brief pause*).   Oh.

(*Pause*)

Well, you're quite right, of course, and I shouldn't meddle.

GRANDMA (*To young man*).   Dear, will you take my things out to the van?

(*She points to the boxes*)

YOUNG MAN (*After only the briefest hesitation*).   Why certainly.

GRANDMA (*As the* YOUNG MAN *takes up half the boxes, exits by the front door*).   Isn't that a nice young van man?

MRS. BARKER (*Shaking her head in disbelief, watching the* YOUNG MAN *exit*).   Unh-hunh . . . some things have changed for the better. I remember when I had *my* mother carted off . . . the van man who came for her wasn't anything near as nice as this one.

GRANDMA.   Oh, did you have your mother carted off, too?

MRS. BARKER (*Cheerfully*).   Why certainly! Didn't you?

GRANDMA (*Puzzling*).   No . . . no, I didn't. At least, I can't remember. Listen dear; I got to talk to you for a second.

MRS. BARKER.   Why certainly, Grandma.

GRANDMA.   Now, listen.

MRS. BARKER.   Yes, Grandma. Yes.

GRANDMA.   Now listen carefully. You got this dilemma here with Mommy and Daddy . . .

MRS. BARKER.   Yes! I wonder where they've gone to?

GRANDMA.   They'll be back in. Now, LISTEN!

MRS. BARKER.   Oh, I'm sorry.

GRANDMA.   Now, you got this dilemma here with Mommy and Daddy, and I think I got the way out for you.

(*The* YOUNG MAN *re-enters through the front door*)

Will you take the rest of my things out now, dear?

(*To* MRS. BARKER, *while the* YOUNG MAN *takes the rest of the boxes, exits again by the front door*)

Fine. Now listen, dear.

(*She begins to whisper in* MRS. BARKER's *ear*)

MRS. BARKER.   Oh! Oh! Oh! I don't think I could . . . do you really think I could? Well, why not? What a wonderful idea . . . what an absolutely wonderful idea!

GRANDMA.   Well, yes, I thought it was.

MRS. BARKER.   And you so old!

GRANDMA.   Heh, heh, heh.

MRS. BARKER.   Well, I think it's absolutely marvelous, anyway. I'm going to find Mommy and Daddy right now.

GRANDMA.   Good. You do that.

MRS. BARKER.   Well, now. I think I will say good-by. I can't thank you enough.

(*She starts to exit through the archway*)

GRANDMA.   You're welcome. Say it!

MRS. BARKER.   Huh? What?

GRANDMA.   Say good-by.

MRS. BARKER.   Oh. Good-by.

(*She exits*)

Mommy! I say, Mommy! Daddy!

GRANDMA.   Good-by.

(*By herself now, she looks about*)

Ah me.

(*Shakes her head*)

Ah me.

(*Takes in the room*)

Good-by.

(*The* YOUNG MAN *re-enters*)

GRANDMA.   Oh, hello, there.

YOUNG MAN.   All the boxes are outside.

GRANDMA (*A little sadly*).   I don't know why I bother to take them with me. They don't have much in them . . . some old letters, a couple of regrets . . . Pekinese . . . blind at that . . . the television . . . my Sunday teeth . . . eighty-six years of living . . . some sounds . . . a few images, a little garbled by now . . . and, well . . .

(*She shrugs*)

. . . you know . . . the things one accumulates.

YOUNG MAN.   Can I get you . . . a cab, or something?

GRANDMA.   Oh no, dear . . . thank you just the same. I'll take it from here.

YOUNG MAN.   And what shall I do now?

GRANDMA. Oh, you stay here, dear. It will all become clear to you. It will be explained. You'll understand.

YOUNG MAN. Very well.

GRANDMA (*After one more look about*). Well . . .

YOUNG MAN. Let me see you to the elevator.

GRANDMA. Oh . . . that *would* be nice, dear.

(*They both exit by the front door, slowly*)

(*Enter Mrs. Barker, followed by* MOMMY *and* DADDY)

MRS. BARKER. . . . and I'm happy to tell you that the whole thing's settled. Just like that.

MOMMY. Oh, we're so glad. We were afraid there might be a problem, what with delays, and all.

DADDY. Yes, we're very relieved.

MRS. BARKER. Well, now; that's what professional women are for.

MOMMY. Why . . . where's Grandma? Grandma's not here! Where's Grandma! And look! The boxes are gone, too. Grandma's gone, and so are the boxes. She's taken off, and she's stolen something! Daddy!

MRS. BARKER. Why, Mommy, the van man was here.

MOMMY. The what?

MRS. BARKER. The van man. The van man was here.

(*The lights might dim a little, suddenly*)

MOMMY (*Shakes her head*). No, that's impossible.

MRS. BARKER. Why, I saw him with my own two eyes.

MOMMY (*Near tears*). No, no, that's impossible. No. There's no such thing as the van man. We . . . we made him up. Grandma? Grandma?

DADDY (*Moving to* MOMMY). There, there now.

MOMMY. Oh Daddy . . . where's Grandma?

DADDY. There, there, now.

(*While* DADDY *is comforting* MOMMY, GRANDMA *comes out, stage right, near the footlights*)

GRANDMA (*To the audience*). Shhhhhh! I want to watch this.

(*She motions to* MRS. BARKER *who, with a secret smile, tiptoes to the front door and opens it. The* YOUNG MAN *is framed therein. Lights up full again as he steps into the room*)

MRS. BARKER. Surprise! Surprise! Here we are!

MOMMY. What? What?

DADDY. Hm? What?

MOMMY (*Her tears merely sniffles now*). What surprise?

MRS. BARKER. Why, I told you. The surprise I told you about.

DADDY. You . . . you know, Mommy.

MOMMY. Sur . . . prise?

DADDY (*Urging her to cheerfulness*).   You remember, Mommy; why we asked . . . uh . . . what's-her-name to come here?

MRS. BARKER.   Mrs. Barker, if you don't mind.

DADDY.   Yes. Mommy? You remember now? About the bumble . . . about wanting satisfaction?

MOMMY (*Her sorrow turning into delight*).   Yes. Why yes! Of course! Yes!, Oh, how wonderful!

MRS. BARKER (*To the Young Man*).   This is Mommy.

YOUNG MAN.   How . . . how do you do?

MRS. BARKER (*Stage whisper*).   Her name's Mommy.

YOUNG MAN.   How . . . how do you do, Mommy?

MOMMY.   Well! Hello there!

MRS. BARKER (*To the* YOUNG MAN).   And that is Daddy.

YOUNG MAN.   How do you do, sir?

DADDY.   How do you do?

MOMMY (*Herself again, circling the* YOUNG MAN, *feeling his arm, poking him*).   Yes, sir! Yes, sirree! Now this is more like it. Now this is a great deal more like it! Daddy! Come see. Come see if this isn't a great deal more like it.

DADDY.   I . . . I can see from here, Mommy. It does look a great deal more like it.

MOMMY.   Yes, sir. Yes sirree! Mrs. Barker, I don't know *how* to thank you.

MRS. BARKER.   Oh, **don't** worry about that. I'll send you a bill in the mail.

MOMMY.   What **this really** calls for is a celebration. It calls for a drink.

MRS. BARKER.   Oh, what a nice idea.

MOMMY.   There's some sauterne in the kitchen.

YOUNG MAN.   I'll go.

MOMMY.   Will you? Oh, how nice. The kitchen's through the archway there.

(*As the* YOUNG MAN *exits; to* MRS. BARKER)

He's very nice. Really top notch; much better than the other one.

MRS. BARKER.   I'm glad you're pleased. And I'm glad everything's all straightened out.

MOMMY.   Well, at least we know why we sent for you. We're glad that's cleared up. By the way, what's his name?

MRS. BARKER.   Ha! Call him whatever you like. He's yours. Call him what you called the other one.

MOMMY.   Daddy? What did we call the other one?

DADDY (*Puzzles*).   Why . . .

YOUNG MAN (*Re-entering with a tray on which are a bottle of sauterne and five glasses*).   Here we are!

MOMMY.   Hooray! Hooray!

MRS. BARKER.   Oh, good!

MOMMY (*Moving to the tray*).   So, let's—Five glasses? Why five? There are only four of us. Why five?

YOUNG MAN (*Catches* GRANDMA's *eye;* GRANDMA *indicates she is not there*).   Oh, I'm sorry.

MOMMY.   You must learn to count. We're a wealthy family, and you must learn to count.

YOUNG MAN.   I will.

MOMMY.   Well, everybody take a glass.

(*They do*)

And we'll drink to celebrate. To satisfaction! Who says you can't get satisfaction these days!

MRS. BARKER.   What dreadful sauterne!

MOMMY.   Yes, isn't it?

(*To* YOUNG MAN, *her voice already a little fuzzy from the wine*)

You don't know how happy I am to see you! Yes sirree. Listen, that time we had with . . . with the other one. I'll tell you about it some time.

(*Indicates* MRS. BARKER)

After she's gone. She was responsible for all the trouble in the first place. I'll tell you all about it.

(*Sidles up to him a little*)

Maybe . . . maybe later tonight.

YOUNG MAN (*Not moving away*).   Why yes. That would be very nice.

MOMMY (*Puzzles*).   Something familiar about you . . . you know that? I can't quite place it. . . .

GRANDMA (*Interrupting . . . to audience*).   Well, I guess that just about wraps it up. I mean, for better or worse, this is a comedy, and I don't think we'd better go any further. No, definitely not. So, let's leave things as they are right now . . . while everybody's got what he wants . . . or everybody's got what he thinks he wants. Good night, dears.

Curtain

III
Reportorial Eyes

JOHN DOS PASSOS

(1896–1970)

John Dos Passos was born in Chicago and graduated from Harvard in 1916. After traveling to Spain in pursuit of a career as an architect, he enlisted in the volunteer ambulance corps of the French Army, and his war experiences are reflected in his first two books: *One Man's Initiation—1917* (1920) and *Three Soldiers* (1921). Dos Passos' innovative combination of naturalism, stream-of-consciousness narrative techniques, and radical politics first became visible in *Manhattan Transfer* (1925); it found full expression in *U.S.A.* [*The 42nd Parallel* (1930); *1919* (1932); and *The Big Money* (1936)].

The themes of *U.S.A.* are pointed at in a remark about World War I that Dos Passos made in the *New Masses* in 1930: "It's as if the carnage of the European war and the years following it and the rapid mechanization of life had entirely dulled the imaginative response (putting

The fiction includes *One Man's Initiation—1917*, 1920; *Three Soldiers*, 1921; *Streets of Night*, 1923; *Manhattan Transfer*, 1925; and *Orient Express*, 1927. The three novels included in *U.S.A.* are *The 42nd Parallel*, 1930; *1919*, 1932; and *The Big Money*, 1936; the entire volume appeared in 1937. A later trilogy includes *Adventures of a Young Man*, 1939; *Number One*, 1943; and *The Grand Design*, 1949; this trilogy, entitled *District of Columbia*, was published as a unit in 1953. Other novels include *Most Likely to Succeed*, 1954, *The Great Days*, 1958, and *Mid-Century*, 1961. Dos Passos also wrote journalistic accounts: *In All Countries*, 1934; *Journeys Between Wars*, 1938; *State of the Nation*, 1944; *Tour of Duty*, 1946; *Brazil on the Move*, 1963; *Occasions and Protest*, 1964; *The Portugal Story*, 1969; and *Easter Island*, 1971. His autobiography is *The Best Times: An Informal Memoir*, 1966. Two collections of his work are *World in a Glass: A View of Our Century Selected from the Novels of John Dos Passos*, ed. Kenneth S. Lynn, 1966, and *The Fourteenth Chronicle: Letters and Diaries of John Dos Passos*, 1973, ed. by Townsend Ludington.

Critical studies are John H. Wrenn, *John Dos Passos*, 1961; Allen Belkind, ed., *Dos Passos, The Critics, and the Writer's Intention*, 1971; and Melvin Landsberg, *Dos Passos' Path to U.S.A.*, 1972.

PHOTOGRAPHIC ART

The American "art photographer" reads the face of the nation in human
faces, seeking a special revelatory "American-ness" in characteristic
expressions, and in sometimes remorseless portraits of unique American
places and sights—from the village barber shop to the town dump. The
great names in contemporary nature photography are those of Eliot Porter
and Ansel Adams. A major chronicler of lost rural ways is Wright Morris.
Still the most affecting of American art photographers is Walker Evans.

Billboards and frame houses, Atlanta, Georgia, March 1936.
(F.S.A. photo by Walker Evans, Courtesy of Library of Congress)

**Client whose property has been optioned by the government,
Brown County, Indiana, October 1935.**
(F.S.A. photo by Theo Jung, Courtesy of Library of Congress)

Crossroads store, Sprott, Alabama, July-August 1936.
(F.S.A. photo by Walker Evans,
Courtesy of Library of Congress)

Girl and movie poster, Cincinnati, Ohio, October 1938.
(F.S.A. photo by John Vachon, Courtesy of Library of Congress)

Sunday night in a saloon, Craigsville, Minnesota, September 1937.
(F.S.A. photo by Russell Lee, Courtesy of Library of Congress)

yourself in the other man's place) that's biologically at the bottom of feelings of mercy and compassion." *U.S.A.* was an attempt to renew that response in a context that did not ignore the consequences of either war or mechanization. The task was enormously difficult, partly because of the nature of the postwar, postmechanization culture. Brutal, profit-maddened, bloated, the society cannot produce figures worthy of full sympathy. When men and women have been cheapened by an exploitative culture, stuffed with lies and clichés through the media, cramped and broken by meaningless work, how can they become figures to be cared about, sympathized with, honored?

Dos Passos tackles his problem by developing a structure that will free him from the need of claiming too much humanity, too much interest or complexity, for any single individual caught in this culture. *U.S.A.* is history as well as fiction—an overview of 25 years of public events and private experience focused on 12 Americans. There is a series of narrative accounts of the 12 characters, interspersed with collages of headlines and news items ("Newsreel"); in addition, there are vignettes called "The Camera Eye" that provide impressionistic, personal perspectives, and (often ironic) biographies of prominent Americans of the day. The narratives are invariably tales of defeat, and the novelist repeatedly voices the bitterness of the weak, as in a "Camera Eye" episode following the story of the Sacco-Vanzetti execution:

> they have clubbed us off the streets   they are stronger   they
> are rich   they hire and fire the politicians the newspapereditors
> the old judges the small men with reputations the collegepresi-
> dents the wardheelers (listen businessmen collegepresidents
> judges   America will not forget her betrayers)   they hire the
> men with   guns the uniforms the policecars the patrolwagons
>   all right you have won

While here and there a winning character appears—usually a radical leader or sympathizer—they are allowed no satisfying success, no sustained value and hope.

And Dos Passos is at pains to demonstrate the connections between the imaginative impoverishment of the society overall and the stunting of personal language and response. Not the least of the characters' woes in *U.S.A.* is that they are forced to listen to "mealy voices saying, deceased, bereavement, hereafter," or to speeches praising "Brave Little Belgium," or claiming that "it is the greatest pride of Americans to have demonstrated the immense love of humanity which they bear in their hearts." Fed a diet of clichés, they themselves are helpless to speak any other language. Nobody possesses a distinctive voice, all are trapped in banality.

> She made them cocoa on her gasburner and told him how unhappy she was, it was so tiring being on your feet all day behind the counter and the women who came to buy things were so mean to you, and the floorwalkers were always pinching your seat and expecting you to cuddlecooty with them in the fitting booths. Some day she was going to turn on the gas. It made Charley feel bad having her talk like that and he had to pet her a little to make her stop crying.

And the flatness of their language is an outward sign of inner deprivation. The women are types, either promiscuous and silly or frozen and neurotic; the men are crude workers, tortured intellectuals, or bloated capitalists. Problems and motivations lack nuance; a sympathetic woman, Mary French, helping out during a flu epidemic, is confused by the very different values of her father and mother, but the conflict is defined as between pure selflessness and pure selfishness; all intricacy of response is lost.

> Mary's fingers were cold and she felt trembly all over when she heard the anxious voices, men's, women's, asking for Doc French [her self-sacrificing father]. It was five before she got away from the office. She took the streetcar out to the Broadmoor.
> It gave her quite a turn to hear the band playing in the casino for the teadance and to see the colored lights and feel the quiet warmth of the hotel halls and the air of neat luxury in her mother's room. Mother was pretty peevish and said what was the use of her daughter's coming home if she neglected her like this. "I had to do some things for Daddy," was all Mary said. Mother started talking a blue streak about her campaign to put German women out of the Woman's Tuesday Lunch Club.

This is a book wherein an unfeeling businessman speaks dismissively of the death of one of his workers ("After all . . . he was only a mechanic") and wherein protecting yourself from unwanted advances is itself only another descent into cliché ("She made him keep his hands to himself"). The dominant impression is of dim lights of life, living a pointless length of years.

But, astonishingly, the book does work. The variety of the narratives, the ceaseless interruptions distract the reader from his consciousness of the pallor and depressing tonelessness of individual lives. Intermittently a sense of the vividness of the world and of human experience within it leaps out from the page. A footloose vagabond takes stock of his bare surroundings in Mexico.

When Mac woke up in the morning he was in a small room calsomined bright yellow. The furniture was painted blue and there were red curtains in the window. Between the curtains the long shutters were barred with a vivid violet sunlight that cut a warm path across the bedclothes. A canary was singing somewhere and he could hear the flap pat flap pat of a woman making tortillas. He got up and threw open the shutters. The sky was cloudless above the redtile roofs. The street was empty and full of sunlight.

Or a "Camera Eye" is suddenly appreciative of a striking seascape.

    throat tightens when the redstacked steamer churning the faintlyheaving slatecolored swell swerves shaking in a long green-marbled curve past the red lightship
    spine stiffens with the remembered chill of the off-shore Atlantic
    and the jag of framehouses in the west above the invisible land and spiderweb rollercoasters and the chewinggum towers of Coney and the freighters with their stacks way aft and the blur beyond Sandy Hook
    and the smell of saltmarshes warmclammysweet

And the writer occasionally relaxes his own doctrines, enabling his reader to grasp that, within the stereotyped social and political roles of a mechanized society, wayward, contradictory instincts and reactions somehow survive. Once, indeed, even a standard-form radical is allowed, briefly, to become a doubtful, ambiguous figure of reverie:

    that time you leant from a soapbox over faces avid young opinionated old the middleaged numb with over-work eyes bleared with newspaperreading trying to tell them the straight dope make them laugh tell them what they want to hear wave a flag whispers the internal agitator crazy or succeed

What emerges is an impression of life hurried and harried: numberless souls pushed and nudged through their years, allowed no space, inner or outer, ceaselessly buffeted and driven. Probably most touching when they are young, these people are, to repeat, not themselves distinguished or complex, but they usually see with clear eyes and remember in vivid detail. And a feeling of odd solidarity is deep in the grain of the work, a persuasive belief in the fate of the American as a *common* fate: we are all in the same jam, at one in our origins as in our attitudes. The praise of *U.S.A.* is that it seeks to recover a vital belief in the importance and political dignity of "insignificant" lives. The "materials" are intractable and the defeats are depressing, but the insistence that more can and must be asked of life than these souls have been allowed to ask—this is, in the end, both morally and imaginatively arousing.

Dos Passos undertook a second trilogy—*Adventures of A Young Man* (1939), *Number One* (1943), and *The Grand Design* (1949)—that is at once thinner as fiction and less generous in its political hope. His later novels, the works of an avowed conservative, include *Most Likely to Succeed* (1954), *The Great Days* (1958), and *Mid-Century* (1961). Dos Passos published a number of travel books and historical and biographical works toward the end of his life. He died in Baltimore on September 28, 1970.

From U.S.A.
FROM NINETEEN-NINETEEN

THE CAMERA EYE (41)

arent you coming to the anarchist picnic   there's going to be an anarchist picnic sure you've got to come to the anarchist picnic this afternoon it was way out at Garches in a kind of park it took a long time to get out there we were late there were youngsters and young girls with glasses and old men with their whiskers and long white zits and everybody wore black artist ties some had taken off their shoes and stockings and were wandering around in the long grass   a young man with a black artist tie was reading a poem Voilà said a voice c'est plûtot le geste proletaire[1] it was a nice afternoon we sat on the grass and looked around le geste proletaire

But God damn it they've got all the machineguns in the world all the printingpresses linotypes tickerribbon curling irons plushhorses Ritz and we you   I?   barehands a few songs not very good songs plûtot le geste proletaire

Les bourgeois à la lanterne nom de dieu[2]

et l'humanité la futurité la lutte des classes l'inépuisible angoisse des foules la misère du travailleur tu sais mon vieux sans blague[3]

it was chilly early summer gloaming among the eighteenthcenturyshaped trees when we started home   I sat on the impériale of the third class car

---

[1] It is rather the proletarian gesture.

[2] The enlightened bourgeois, for God's sake.

[3] And humanity, the future, the class struggle, the inextinguishable anxiety of the masses, the misery of the worker—you know, old fellow, no kidding.

with the daughter of the Libertaire (that's Patrick Henry ours after all give me or death) a fine girl her father she said never let her go out alone never let her see young men it was like being in a convent she wanted liberty fraternity equality and a young man to take her out   in the tunnels the coalgas made us cough and she wanted l'Amérique la vie le theatre le feev o'clock le smoking le foxtrot   she was a nice girl we sat side by side on the roof of the car and looked at the banlieue de Paris a desert of little gingerbread brick maisonettes flattening out under the broad gloom of evening she and I tu sais mon ami[4] but what kind of goddam management is this?

NEWSREEL XL

CRIMINAL IN PYJAMAS SAWS BARS; SCALES WALLS; FLEES

Italians! against all and everything remember that the beacon is lighted at Fiume and that all harangues are contained in the words: Fiume or Death.

Criez au quatre vents que je n'accepte aucune transaction. Le reste ici contre tout le monde et je prépare de très mauvais jours.

Criez cela je vous prie a tû-tête[5]

the call for enlistments mentions a chance for gold service stripes, opportunities for big game hunting and thrilling watersports added to the general advantages of travel in foreign countries

> *Chi va piano*
> *Va sano*
> *Chi va forte*
> *Va 'la morte*
> *Evviva la libertá*[6]

EARTHQUAKE IN ITALY DEVASTATES LIKE WAR

only way Y.M.C.A. girls can travel is on troop ships; part of fleet will go seaward to help Wilson

DEMPSEY KNOCKS OUT WILLARD IN THIRD ROUND

Ils sont sourds.
Je vous embrasse.
Le cœur de Fiume est à vous.[7]

---

[4] You know, my friend.
[5] Shout to the four winds that I accept no compromise. The rest here are against everyone, and I am preparing very bad days. Shout that, I beg you, very loudly.
[6] Who goes slowly, goes safely. Who goes hastily, goes toward death. Hurrah for freedom.

[7] They are deaf
   I kiss you
   The heart of Fiume is yours.

JOE HILL

A young Swede named Hillstrom went to sea, got himself calloused hands on sailingships and tramps, learned English in the focastle of the steamers that make the run from Stockholm to Hull, dreamed the Swede's dream of the west;

when he got to America they gave him a job polishing cuspidors in a Bowery saloon.

He moved west to Chicago and worked in a machineshop.

He moved west and followed the harvest, hung around employment agencies, paid out many a dollar for a job in a construction camp, walked out many a mile when the grub was too bum, or the boss too tough, or too many bugs in the bunkhouse;

read Marx and the I.W.W. Preamble and dreamed about forming the structure of the new society within the shell of the old.

He was in California for the S.P. strike (*Casey Jones, two locomotives, Casey Jones*), used to play the concertina outside the bunkhouse door, after supper, evenings (*Longhaired preachers come out every night*), had a knack for setting rebel words to tunes (*And the union makes us strong*).

Along the coast in cookshacks flophouses jungles wobblies hoboes bindlestiffs began singing Joe Hill's songs. They sang 'em in the county jails of the State of Washington, Oregon, California, Nevada, Idaho, in the bullpens in Montana and Arizona, sang 'em in Walla Walla, San Quentin and Leavenworth,

forming the structure of the new society within the jails of the old.

At Bingham, Utah, Joe Hill organized the workers of the Utah Construction Company in the One Big Union, won a new wagescale, shorter hours, better grub. (The angel Moroni didn't like labororganizers any better than the Southern Pacific did.)

The angel Moroni moved the hearts of the Mormons to decide it was Joe Hill shot a grocer named Morrison. The Swedish consul and President Wilson tried to get him a new trial but the angel Moroni moved the hearts of the supreme court of the State of Utah to sustain the verdict of guilty. He was in jail a year, went on making up songs. In November 1915 he was stood up against the wall in the jail yard in Salt Lake City.

"Don't mourn for me organize," was the last word he sent out to the workingstiffs of the I.W.W. Joe Hill stood up against the wall of the jail yard, looked into the muzzles of the guns and gave the word to fire.

They put him in a black suit, put a stiff collar around his neck and a bow tie, shipped him to Chicago for a bangup funeral, and photographed his handsome stony mask staring into the future.

The first of May they scattered his ashes to the wind.

EDMUND WILSON

(1895–1972)

Literary and social criticism, intellectual history, fiction, plays, parodies, and assorted opinions compose the varied stuff of Edmund Wilson's more than 30 books: this was the career of a writer without patience for "a life that aims at nothing beyond itself," and persuaded that his proper work, in whatever genre, was "to give a meaning to our experience." His moral commitments are no less visible in his fiction than in his literary criticism, causing the former to be a shade doctrinaire and the latter to be generous where pure aestheticians tend to be strict. (Wilson once wrote—he deserves admiration for doing so—that even if Dreiser's prose was "always collapsing . . . the man behind it remains sound. His prose has a long and steady rhythm which continues to convey his feelings and ideas even when the words don't quite make sense. . . .") Everywhere the key assumption is that literature and criticism and history matter finally not in and for themselves alone, but as means by which we "break through into the real world."

Wilson's social and literary criticism is included in *Discordant Encounters: Plays and Dialogues*, 1926; *Axel's Castle: A Study in the Imaginative Literature of 1870 to 1930*, 1931; *The American Jitters: A Year of the Slump*, 1932; *Travels in Two Democracies*, 1936; *The Triple Thinkers: Ten Essays on Literature*, 1938; *To the Finland Station: A Study in the Writing and Acting of History*, 1940; *The Boys in the Back Room: Notes on California Novelists*, 1941; *The Wound and The Bow: Seven Studies in Literature*, 1941; *The Shock of Recognition: The Development of Literature in the United States Recorded by the Men Who Made It*, (Ed.) 1943; *Memoirs of Hecate County*, 1946; *Europe Without Baedeker: Sketches Among the Ruins of Italy, Greece, and England*, 1947; *Classics and Commercials: A Literary Chronicle of the Forties*, 1950; *The Shores of Light: A Literary Chronicle of the Twenties and Thirties*, 1952; *Eight Essays*, 1954; *The Scrolls from the Dead Sea*, 1955; *Red, Black, Blond, and Olive: Studies in Four Civilizations: Zuni, Haiti, Soviet Russia, Israel*, 1956; *A Piece of My Mind: Reflections at Sixty*, 1956; *A Literary Chronicle: 1920–1950*, 1956; *The American Earthquake: A Documentary of the Twenties and Thirties*, 1958; *Apologies to the Iroquois*, 1960; *Patriotic Gore: Studies in the Literature of the American Civil War*, 1962; *The Cold War and the Income Tax: A Protest*, 1963; *O Canada: An American's Notes on Canadian Culture*, 1965; and *A Prelude: Landscapes, Characters and Conversations from the Earlier Years of My Life*, 1967.

I Thought of Daisy, 1929, is a novel. Wilson's plays are in *This Room and This Gin and These Sandwiches: Three Plays*, 1937, reprinted and enlarged in *Five Plays*, 1954.

Richard D. Ramsay has compiled *Edmund Wilson: A Bibliography*, 1971. Critical studies include Sherman Paul, *Edmund Wilson, A Study of Literary Vocation in Our Time*, 1965, and Leonard Kriegel, *Edmund Wilson*, 1971.

Edmund Wilson's first "real world" was Red Bank, New Jersey, where he was born; he graduated from Princeton University in 1916 and began his career as a journalist for the *New York Evening Sun;* later he served as editor of *Vanity Fair* (1920–1921) and the *New Republic* (1921–1931) and as book critic for the *New Yorker* (1944–1948). Wilson's major volumes of literary criticism are *Axel's Castle* (1931), *The Triple Thinkers* (1938), *The Wound and the Bow* (1941), *The Shores of Light* (1952), and *Classics and Commercials* (1950). Important historical essays—on the backgrounds of the Russian Revolution and on our own Civil War writers—are *To the Finland Station* (1940) and *Patriotic Gore* (1962). *I Thought of Daisy* (1929) is a novel; *The Shock of Recognition* (1943), an influential collection of literary criticism by Americans; *The Scrolls from the Dead Sea* (1955), an account of discoveries made in the Near East; and *The Fruits of the MLA* (1969), an attack on what Wilson considered to be a scholarly boondoggle involving the production of overpraised, graceless editions of American classics.

Politically this critic could be (and was) at one time described as leftist, at another as reactionary, but if his politics were difficult to classify, his sense of values was never obscure. He was against abuses of power, perversions of wealth, corruptions of taste and morality. He was intolerant of ignorance and smugness, whether in evangelical demogogues, mindless bureaucrats, or greedy politicians. When a candidate droned comfortably in the 1930's that too much prosperity ruins the fiber of the people, Wilson commented that "It is a reassuring thought, in the cold weather, that the emaciated men in the bread lines, the men and women beggars in the streets, and the children dependent on them, are all having their fibre hardened." He was prepared to use the bludgeon—especially on Congressional committees (he said about one House group appointed to investigate Communism that it was simultaneously in "apparent ignorance of everything connected with Communism" yet "intent on doing everything in [its] power to abolish American civil liberties"). And sometimes his frontal attacks are oversimple—one or another enemy is characterized as "pot-gutted and greasy-looking, with small black pig eyes" or as a "blank-eyed vacuous Bashan bull," and heroes are saluted in terms that raise a question whether they may not be too good to be interesting or true; partisanship could lead Wilson away from his feeling for the complexities and contradictions of particulars.

As an observer of American society, though, Wilson was invariably committed and serious. His collected sketches of life during the Depression in *The American Jitters* (1932) are usually intelligent, conscientious, and caring. And his lifelong effort to know his country, including people wholly unlike himself, yielded many affecting works— among the most notable, an inquiry into the survival, in upper New

York state, of a tribe of native Americans, published as *Apologies to the Iroquois* (1960). A proud, tetchy man, Wilson sometimes sounded a snob; the protagonists of his fiction are often intellectuals trying to find a place for themselves in the "real world," hoping to relate to ordinary, even boorish American people, and, clearly, this was among Wilson's hopes for himself. But there were limits to his imagination as to his personal flexibility. He can deal successfully with people in their "otherness"—mountain folk or blue-collar worker when he can be analytical, impersonal, attentive to individuals as part of a social problem.

> . . . the West Virginia miners have been out on strike and starved back again, the operators refusing to meet the union and evicting so many families that there is now quite a large colony of them sheltering in tents along the road, living on pinto beans and black coffee and watching the children die of typhus and malnutrition.

But at putting himself in their places he was uncomfortable, and when he sought to do so his writing turned portentously mythic or struck a postured ironic note. His feeling for the writer's social responsibility was, however, wholly genuine, and it drew him on to apply his gifts to intelligence on every element of American life, congenial or not. In a word, he matters as a moral example, not alone as a writing man.

From The American Jitters

CHAPTER XXVII
THE BEST PEOPLE

Mr. Southworth, whom the union leaders had always rather liked, left the room and left them blank.

It is not hard to imagine Mr. Southworth—(let us call him Mr. X, as the following picture is purely imaginary: I want merely to describe a type.) You can see him as one of those decent, pleasant, well-pressed and well-polished people who mildly ornament country club society. He is, in short, no doubt, one of the best people. Though his satisfactions are more bound up than he realizes with tangible things that money can buy him, he never spends money ostentatiously; and he has a conscience about civic affairs, giving to charitable causes and being opposed to political corruption, especially as practised by crude politicians who have never been to Amherst. His wife, if he is married, feels this even more strongly; she was opposed to Al Smith in the

White House on the ground of his dreadful commonness. She dresses extremely well and usually notices in a Pullman that she is the only really smart woman there. Mr. X plays a pretty good game of something—probably tennis or golf. He collects first editions or etchings—or perhaps even has a taste for pictures or reading. He gets his liquor from the same bootlegger who serves the *very* rich people, but he never drinks to excess.

Yet Mr. X's conviction of his importance has very little basis in fact. He is as helpless, he occupies as cramped a position between the upper and nether millstones of society, as the old detective who as superintendent at Ward has to shortweight the miners at the tipple or as "Hurry Up" Crowe at Boulder Dam.

As Mr. X has to tell a plant committee when they protest against a wage cut, he can make "no promises or recommendations." And precisely because he can make no promises or recommendations, Mr. and Mrs. X's culture and distinction, all that Mr. and Mrs. X regard as the basis of their social position, have no solid or durable value. Such pretensions can only be valid in the case of a real governing class. And Mr. X does not govern. He gets his orders from officials higher up, and they may get their orders from the bankers from whom they borrow. Yet neither bankers nor higher officials constitute a governing class: they are merely people of all sorts of origins, capacities and ideals who come and go in lucrative positions. The system they belong to governs, but they are only individuals on the make. They take no collective responsibility and their power is not hereditary—so they have none of the special training which permanent power and responsibility requires and which may dignify and refine a strongly established owning class.

Yet Mr. and Mrs. X are firmly convinced of their superiority. Let us see what this superiority consists of. If Mr. X derives from some family who have already been property holders for a generation or two during the simpler days of the Republic, he will attach himself to the memory of family habits as if they were in fact the characteristics of such a strongly established class—a high civilization from whose standards the present era is a lamentable lapse. If, say, Mr. X is a Southerner, he will like to talk about the Civil War, will cherish family photographs of the Civil War generation, will dream of retiring from industry altogether and going to live in the country, where he can keep hunting dogs and raise race-horses. If he is a Bostonian, he may still live in a family house, solid and square but rather bleak and Spartan in the taste of his fathers who built it, and decorated with copies of paintings and old brown photographs of Italy brought back by his mother from abroad. If he is a New Yorker or a Philadelphian, the glamor of his ancestral memories will shine from an expensive social life, polo and yachting, brandy and champagne, and historical research or civic reform. If, on the other hand, he is a Middle Westerner, he will have the pride of affluence hard-won, of virtue and distinction maintained amidst the hardships of the wilderness. If he is Californian, he will look back to the days when food and drink were so plentiful and cheap, when people were so hearty and gay, when life was so easy and free. In any case, he will respect his college as the stronghold of good-fellowship and learning, guard his club as the temple of manners and honor, and scrupulously observe in his business and domestic relations the old-fashioned rules of integrity among equals.

This is his morality and thus he manages part at least of the time to live in a world which does not really exist, which has never except briefly and locally existed. The real conditions of Mr. X's life are being determined by quite other public standards, which have been crowding or modifying his private ones more and more every day. For the society that Mr. X lives in is not a society of planters or ranchers or pioneers, nor of provincial importers and exporters not far removed from pioneering: it is an enormous machine for money-making and exploitation which has long ago rendered impossible the advantages enjoyed by those more or less independent communities. The planters have gone down before the industrialists; the capitalists have captured the farmers and ranchers. And the business class, cut off from Europe, with no deep-rooted traditions to sustain it, soon lost what little it had of sound conservatism—the discipline and culture of slowly built-up social institutions which has kept the European nations standing in spite of the fact that capitalism in Europe was worse shaken by the War than over here. In America, by the years after the War, life had become merely a stampede to make and sell things—the question wasn't whether people needed or wanted them but whether by any means they could be induced to buy them. Hence advertising—one of the most fantastic features of capitalistic society. Advertising, as we have it in America, is a sheer waste of money and brains; but if you allow competitive business for private profit, you have to have a whole corps of poets, artists, preachers, blackmailers and flatterers to compete in selling the products. It is a formidable undertaking to persuade people to invest at high prices in a great variety of valueless breakfast foods and toothpastes; in cosmetics that poison the face, lubricants that corrode your car, insecticides that kill your trees; in health builders made of cheese, fat reducers made of cascara, coffee made of dried peas, gelatine made of glue, olive oil made of cotton-seed, straw hats made of wood shavings, sterling silver made of lead and cement, woolen blankets, silk stockings and linen sheets all made out of cotton, sealskin coats made out of muskrat, and mink and sable out of woodchuck hides, mahogany furniture made out of gum-wood which will splinter into bits under use; in foods that do not nourish, disinfectants that do not disinfect, electric irons that burn out in one brief burst as soon as they have been attached to the plug, shock-absorbers that cause you to ride more roughly and gas-logs that asphyxiate—(all articles which have actually been put over with more or less success). And even when the article is both good and what it pretends to be, it has to have its ballyhoo to outshout or underinsinuate the other articles of the same kind. And the cumulative result of all the publicity is that the Americans have come generally to accept an ideal of personal glory and merit based solely on the possession of things: cars, clothes, toilet accessories, electrical appliances; with, transcending them, a patriotic ideal of America as a great market.

The Americans were eager for self-improvement, and the people who had to get rid of the manufacturer's goods for him realized that they could exploit this desire. And as the Americans had also kept a considerable remnant of the feeling of social inferiority of a recently revolted middle class, the advertisement writers and the salesmen saw that they could play on this, too. The mass production of "exclusiveness" became a major racket—with great damage to our comprehension of our real situation. American society, in the technical sense, is largely bourgeois: since the fall of the Southern planters, we have had no such thing as a true aristocracy—that is, a privileged class of hereditary property owners. "Middle class" and "aristocratic," no longer derived from social actualities, are now only descriptive adjectives like "rude" or "polite" indicating such clumsy manners or such sordid and narrow ideas as people get from struggling with small business or such ease and wider range, on the other hand, as they get from security and leisure. We use them a good deal in this sense; but the truth is that security and leisure have been coming and going so quickly in America with the coming and going of the money that makes them possible that we have never had anything other than a bourgeoisie which, though you can find in it many varieties of education and sophistication, is fundamentally homogeneous. Our society, within this bourgeoisie and its sphere of influence among the working people, is so far democratic and its future will certainly be more democratic still. Yet the effect of capitalist advertising has been not only to persuade people that owning things provides the last satisfaction of the spirit but also to mislead them with delusions of aristocratic distinction to be obtained in the same way. You have the cigarettes which are supposed to identify you as a "person of culture and refinement," the apartment hotel which, though as yet uncompleted, will certify the tenants as social successes, the restaurants with "aristocratic" headwaiters who consent to shed a little glamor on the patrons by allowing them to be waited on, the steamship lines which apparently, if you sail on them, equip you with a monocle, a slender figure and an arrogant knife-like profile, and the department stores which are ready to convert a whole city of bourgeois women into snobs by selling them copies of Chanel gowns and which try to popularize silk hats as "a delightful piece of swank." You have superiority sold in cans and packages and with the enamel on mechanical ice-boxes and the paint on motor-cars until every suburban community of brokers, every resort full of idle investors, every group of Tammany grafters and their wives, every "residential street" of well-off village storekeepers, every white-collar set of bridge players in a mill-town, are convinced, like Mr. and Mrs. X, that they are consecrated to the guardianship of certain inestimable values which make its existence a benefit or ornament to the community and which justify the sacrifice of other groups to its interest.

And Mr. and Mrs. X themselves, who think themselves better than all these other kinds of people, end by being "sold" like everybody else. Mr. X's textile company, for example, will find the market for ordinary sheets and towels glutted and it will call upon its sales department to invent some new way of stimulating a demand. The sales department will propose making colored sheets and towels to harmonize with the colors of people's rooms; and Mr. X will find himself involved in the production of green, pink, purple, yellow and blue sheets and towels and in the excitation of an unnatural appetite for them through mendacious and hypnotic methods which disfigure the rural roadsides, interrupt stories in the magazines and razzle-dazzle people on the streets with jumpy signs in public places. If he wants to send his sons to old Amherst or Harvard or Yale, he has got to turn out green and purple towels. If he is the agent for a bathroom-fixture company, he will have to turn out green and purple bathtubs. If he is the agent in a paper-mill, he will have to turn out green and purple toilet-paper. And he will be obliged to view with complaisance the publication of absurd and revolting advertisements threatening the reader with horrible diseases and immediate loss of social prestige unless he uses this particular kind. And poor Mr. X, who has begun by trying to impose on the simple-minded in order to get the means of remaining superior to them, will end by becoming simple-minded himself. He and his wife will become more and more like the men and women in the advertisements, more and more insipid, fatuously cheerful, two-dimensional, spic and span—more and more identified with smart cars, clean shaves, exclusive face lotions, unrippable silk stockings and Louis Quatorze radio sets. They will own all the things people are supposed to own; and Mr. X will fall a victim to his own blackmail: the X's will put in green and purple toilet paper. And without knowing it, they will have become partly dependent for their assurance of superiority on their patronage of this article of luxury. They will in short finally come to be patronized by the imperial paper itself.

I have said that Mr. and Mrs. X end by becoming as simple-minded as the people at whom the advertisements of Mr. X's company are aimed. But the truth is that it is almost impossible for human beings to attain the two-dimensional simple-mindedness of the ideal in the advertisements; and insofar as he falls short of attaining it, Mr. X can only feel uncomfortable. He may never admit it even to himself, but there doesn't seem to be much point to his activities. If he is serious-minded, as I have imagined him, he cannot but feel the lack of harmony between what he believes to be his principles and ideals and the society of which he is part. If he tends to have an inquiring mind and to be interested in ideas, his commerce with political and social ideas must be largely confined to books. In conversation capitalist business has come to play for Mr. X's generation exactly the rôle that religion did for the generation of his grandfathers: it is something that simply must not be discussed. Private enterprise and private profit have taken the place of the book of Genesis and the Divinity of Christ—with the Soviets in the rôle of Darwin, Huxley, Robert Ingersoll, Renan and Strauss.[1] The newspapers won't deal with the matter; even the philosophers try to get around it; and if you introduce it into conversation, you are guilty of an act of bad taste like making jokes about the Scriptures to your great-aunt. The result is that though by the time the world is delivered of the new order with which it is now in labor, most of Mr. X's assumptions will have been knocked sky-high, the chances are that Mr. X's ideas remain dim as to what it is all about. He believes he is free-minded and free-speaking; but really he lends himself to a general conspiracy not to mention, not to recognize, certain facts. He has tried to be satisfied with making money and owning things; but now he can't even make money and it's not permitted seriously to ask what's wrong.

At most, if he is unusually intelligent, he will be in favor of consolidation, stabilization and government control for his industry; but he will not find many of his associates to agree with him. And he will be far from clear how, even if you had this, you would be able to operate at a profit.

If, on the other hand, Mr. X is gay and likes people who drink and are sophisticated and amusing, they will talk about the things they drink, about the new tunes of Cole Porter and Gershwin, about the pictures in *The New Yorker* and the imbecilities in Mencken's Americana, about the plays of Philip Barry and the novels of S. S. Van Dine. They will make jokes about Lesbians and fairies; meet each other in France in the summer, furnish their apartments and houses with silver-glass tulips and chairs on bent pipes. They will suffer from unreciprocated love; they will go abroad to get away or get nearer; they will live for years with unfaithful mates, and their friends will know that liquor, travel and entertaining make but a sorry consolation for their anguish. And they will try to find in sterile love affairs which involve no social or moral responsibility, which at best can only feed in the imagination an ideal of desperate pleasure, the passion and the romance which the world seems no longer to hold. The women, with good brains and independent wills, still cling to the privileges and comforts which they have been brought up as ladies to enjoy and will be neither conventional wives and mothers nor independent economic producers. The men, their skill, their energy and their intelligence exploited by the capitalist enterprises out of which they can get nothing but money for luxuries, have lost the force of male authority. Or provided with money they do not work for and with no relation to its

[1] Charles R. Darwin (1809-1892) British naturalist who expounded the theory of evolution by natural selection in *On the Origin of Species* (1859). Thomas Henry Huxley (1825-1895), British biologist and advocate of Darwinism. Sir Robert G. Ingersoll (1833-1899), American political leader, orator, and agnostic. Ernest Renan (1823-1892), French philosopher. Richard Strauss (1864-1949), German composer.

source that seems real, though they may start out with exceptional abilities they have not even use to keep them bright and can only try to find their way back into life through sport or snobbery or debauchery or art till, baffled at last by their own idleness and dullness, they end as hypochondriacs who can do nothing but nurse themselves, or as tuberculars or alcoholics.

A good many kill themselves. The suicides of workers in this book should be supplemented to make the picture complete with examples of the suicides of bourgeois. The machine is running down and it no longer carries us along with its momentum. We exhaust the pleasures, the emotions, the excitements, of a life which aims at nothing beyond itself, which is a part of no general human effort; and we decide to quit out of sheer futility. Or people suddenly find themselves without money which they have been at great pains to acquire and which is the only thing they have acquired. Brokers find their occupations gone and don't know now what to do with themselves. Bankers realize that they have caused to evaporate the savings of thousands of depositors and that they are now not only poor men but swindlers when they had only been trying to play the game. Artists who have been unsuccessful in supplying the capitalist market or unhappy in spite of success find that they haven't originality or self-sufficiency enough to pursue lines of their own under conditions which make individual revaluations of experience unremunerative, lonely and hard. And to well-off people the lowering of a standard of living which to people less well-off seems luxurious may appear as desperate a disaster as the loss to poor people of their very means of subsistence and eviction from their only shelter. An attorney for the Pennsylvania Railroad, who had formerly been a millionaire, committed suicide last year because he had only $25,000 a year left: he couldn't bear to face the privation.

The people in Mr. X's world who despair thus and kill themselves are not kept up by any sense of solidarity. They feel no obligation to their society to live: they have simply lost out like gamblers at Monte Carlo. Perhaps the poor have more loyalty to life: when John Dravic killed himself and his children, the other working people felt ashamed. The working people are like soldiers in the trenches: they at least have to keep up each other's morale. But the American bourgeoisie to-day feel little individual responsibility—and in fact they haven't much. Capitalistic society in America is a vast system for passing the buck. Lincoln Steffens has just shown from how many years back nobody in America has been what he pretended to be. The politicians and the government are not the civil servants of a governing class: they are people who have a racket in serving business. And business has become daily more impersonal; the relations between the people who have kept it running have become daily more indirect and remote. And that is the reason why most of the business people, no matter how sound or important they seem, say such stupid or feeble things when you talk to them. Mr. X and his inferiors and his superiors will all repeat to you the same banalities—catchphrases which seem to derive from neither insight nor the practice of power, the pale phantoms of the intellectual limbo which lies so deep in the capitalist mind between those areas of the brain that control the motor activities of the right and left hands. You will hear Mr. X and his associates say that we have got to learn new uses for surplus leisure; that we have got to go back and live as our fathers lived (and presumably, if we are workers out of work, to die as our fathers died); that prices are coming down so that money buys more than it did before and that "equilibrium" (a magic word) has got to be established by an "adjustment" (another magic word) of wages—that is, that wages have got to be cut; that American labor has been spoiled, that the working people in the European countries have known very well how to get along with hard work and thrift, and that the American workers can very well stand to do without their radios and cars until "business recovers"; that the American Federation of Labor (regarded as a very radical organization) has got to back down and moderate its demands; that taxation of the big industries would cripple them and that the burden must be distributed more evenly; that we must leave relief to voluntary charity, as otherwise it would be eaten up by graft; that the dole has ruined England; that your guess is as good as mine as to what is going to happen now. Or if they are the younger and more sophisticated kind, they will talk about pulling out for a distant island or enjoying the last twenty-four hours of capitalism; or they will say that after all the only kind of government is a monarchy; or they will even tell you they have a red flag in the attic.

In any case, they do not talk like people who are up to anything in particular. They are barbarians who cannot even collaborate on a plan of self-government for themselves but only pray each to the God of Business to bring their victories back again. The most curious thing of all they say sometimes is that they are waiting for the revolution. Though they assume their own superiority and though they had been assiduously teaching the working people up to yesterday their own shibboleths and ideals, they now pass the buck to labor: they expect labor to take the initiative. But under capitalism in America, no class of people is responsible. Not only are all the business men of high and low degree merely out for their own personal fortunes; not only are the politicians merely out to racketeer the business men; but the working class, too, has been counting on big business as on God to give them work and increase their standard of living. They are wholly unprepared to make a revolution. In this book, I have usually shown them at their most resolute and political-minded, as represented by their radical leaders; but these leaders even in these hard times have a formidable task before them to destroy belief in the Business God.

And as for the professional experts, they have either been so long in the pay of the business men that they have come to share the business man's point of view or they hold academic positions so that, however much they may rail at the irresponsibility of the people who manage affairs, they have no responsibility themselves. And as for the professional ideologues, despite their reiterated discontent, they too have been trusting to the capitalist structure which seemed so solid over their heads and which, provided—what was not very difficult—they were able to make themselves a place in it, gave them a feeling of being well taken care of. It also gave them a feeling of impotence, an assumption of inferiority, in regard to their own ideas. And the result was that they would either dilute their ideas or compromise them by verbal sleight-of-hand tricks without being conscious of what they were doing; or they would resign themselves to wait for the new order with a patience scarcely distinguishable from stagnation. Then when the roof of the big mill suddenly caved in and the walls began to totter, too, and they found themselves like any Indian caciques[2] under a blank sky never built for human shelter, they went on living, if they were stolid, like the business men as if nothing had occurred—really buoyed up by the "prosperity" psychology which in their preachments they had assumed they were discrediting—or, if they were more alert, they went scurrying bewilderedly about like bugs uncovered by the lifting of a stone. They too had been passing the buck—to the management which it was their rôle to criticize. Unlike the Indian caciques, in short, they had not been running the tribe. Our only professional wise men with genuine political power have been the Brieglebs and the Bob Shulers.

And now it turns out that there is nobody running it: it is not run. Least of all does the ambitious promoter whom Mr. X thought he was installing in the White House to take care of his own interests, really control or organize or inspire. When Mr. X expects him to do so, he is again merely passing the buck; and he should not blame Mr. Hoover too harshly. In a recent book about politics it is asserted that the President "can hardly be classed as a member of the human family." This is an exaggeration: Mr. Hoover, though stupid and timid, is a member of the human race. And he is perhaps no worse than his immediate predecessors. If he seems helpless, resourceless, inhuman, it is merely because he is the mask for an impersonal system which has jammed itself and which is no longer able to generate the power to give him the semblance of personal will.

At any rate, poor Mr. X, who had supposed he was playing the part of a gentleman coöperating with his employees, has found out that when the machine is brought up short he is suddenly transformed into an arrogant despot starving subjects back to their tasks. The owning classes under capitalism are probably able to be more kindly and democratic than they were under feudalism, for example; but it is harder for them to understand their own position. Mr. X really does not know about the cold and hunger and fatigue and hopelessness of Lawrence this October; he does not know about

[2] Indian chiefs.

the hatred and suspicion and fear that the company's spies and the efficiency experts bring into the lives of the workers; he does not know that Lawrence during the strike is a filthy, festering disgrace to humanity—with decent people turned into outlaws and sent to jail for trying to insist on a living wage and with other people essentially no different set on to club them, to take their jobs away from them, to kidnap their leaders and break up their meetings. Mr. X does not really see this, let alone see the part he plays in it. So that he and the union leaders do not yet confront each other like Foster and Fish—the avowed champions to the death of two hostile classes.

But in the meantime the Lawrence strike goes from bad to worse. Two days after the big riot in front of the Arlington Mills, Sam Bakely, after a meeting on the Common, sets out to lead a mob of 15,000 strikers in a march on the Monomac Mills, where several hundred have gone back to work. A line of police halts them and a police captain reads them the riot act—the strikers refuse to disperse. The police charge them with clubs—people trampled on, strikers arrested. Sam Bakely is arrested, too.

But Sam Bakely has Muste for a hero and the morality of socialism for a guide—he is neither pained nor surprised to land in jail. Whereas Mr. X, who has no leader to follow and no morality based on anything real, is probably not a little dismayed to find himself behind the policemen's clubs.

In any case, the strike is broken, and even after the other mills have reopened, the Pacific keeps its workers locked out.

TRUMAN CAPOTE

(1924–   )

Truman Capote, equally gifted at marketing his prose and his personality, reached a summit in both lines in 1965 with the publication of *In Cold Blood,* an account of the real-life slaughter of a Kansas family by two men who were later hanged for the crime. Puffed first in the gossip columns months in advance of its appearance, then met by reviews in every major journal, illustrated by the author himself in magazine and talk-show interviews and at Beautiful People parties hosted by himself,

The novels are *Other Voices, Other Rooms,* 1948; *The Grass Harp* 1951; and *Breakfast at Tiffany's* (1958) is the title of a collection: a short novel, "Breakfast at Tiffany's," and 3 stories. Collections of stories are *A Tree of Night and Other Stories,* 1949, and *A Christmas Memory,* 1966. A good compendium is *The Selected*

Writings of Truman Capote, 1963. Nonfiction includes *Local Color,* 1950; *The Muses are Heard,* 1956; *Observations,* 1959; and *In Cold Blood,* 1965.
For a complete bibliography of Capote and most of the important essays written about *In Cold Blood,* see Irving Malin, *In Cold Blood: A Critical Handbook,* 1968.

the book won a mass audience, became a "major motion picture," and aroused enormous interest among critics of culture and literary commentators. The point at issue for most critics was Capote's claim that he'd invented something—a *nonfiction novel.* What on earth did the term mean? If this was a new kind of writing, what were its key features, characteristics, formal requirements?

The noisy public relations about *In Cold Blood* hid the book's achievement and also obscured the connections between it and the author's earlier writing. The stories and novels that Capote wrote in his younger days were as heavy in pathos as this "experimental" venture; they told of eccentric, isolated, loveless folk who march to drums altogether as freaky in beat as those that drove the Clutter murderers, Smith and Hickock.

Born on September 30, 1924, Truman Streckfus Persons was brought up by different relatives after his parents were divorced. His mother's remarriage gave him the name Capote and brought him to New York. His stories began to appear in magazines in 1945, and his first novel, *Other Voices, Other Rooms,* about a Southern boy growing up amid a gothic decadence, was published to much acclaim in 1948. In many of the books that followed—notably *A Tree of Night* (1949), a collection of stories, *The Grass Harp* (1951), a novel, and *Breakfast at Tiffany's* (1958), a short novel and 3 stories—there is a softness, even a sentimentality at the center. But his best and worst alike are distinguished by the precision of ear and the attentiveness to appearance and gesture that are evident in the Clutters' story. In "Breakfast at Tiffany's" Capote tells of fragments of a torn letter: *"Remember* and *miss you* and *rain* and *please write* and *damn* and *goddamn* were the words that recurred most often on those slips; those, and *lonesome* and *love."* The same suggestiveness and authority—the same easy conversancy with ordinary speech and with "the way it is"—figures in *In Cold Blood;* the same aptitude for pathos drew in a readership of millions.

The Clutter story is, at bottom, about a collision between two worlds, one that is insular and innocent and believing in American goodness (Mr. Clutter was an official in the Eisenhower administration), decorated with money and 4-H clubs and "grand" Thanksgiving dinners, and a room and private bath for every kid in the house; the other world is the savage, restless, desperate underside: Hickock's and Smith's America. The "innocent" world somehow assumes that sunrise and stability—the daylight air—are all that's real: familial ruin is impossible. The remarkable success of Capote's book is its showing forth of the way that assumption denudes the opposing reality of substance, makes the disasters of the unlucky register as nearly unreal even to those who suffer them.

I was extradited back to Kansas, [says Smith.] To Phillipsburg. That same cute jail. They nailed me to the cross—larceny, jail-break, car theft. I got five to ten years. In Lansing. After I'd been there awhile, I wrote Dad. Let him know the news. And wrote Barbara, my sister. By now, over the years, that was all I had left me. Jimmy a suicide. Fern out the window. My mother dead. Been dead eight years. Everybody gone but Dad and Barbara.

This is a book about unvoiced interdependencies.

To feel them, to know the intertwinings of luck and unluck, requires exceptional agility. Capote's claim is that "above all, the reporter must be able to empathize with personalities outside his usual imaginative range, mentalities unlike his own, kinds of people he would never have written about. . . ." The demand on the reader is no different. For the central convention of the nonfiction novel is the eschewal of judgment; the reader is confronted with events and people that he knows to be "real"; he is brought close to them by Capote's novelistic resources, but he is left without the comfort of explanation and directive, without an easy path toward "proper" allegiances and conclusions. The effect is to press the audience for "original" response, primary unmediated commitment. A way of saying it is that what this book does to its reader resembles what the pictures of the murder victims do to the jurors in the Clutter case.

> . . . as they were passed from hand to hand, the jurors' expressions reflected the impact the pictures made; one man's cheeks reddened, as if he had been slapped, and a few, after the first distressing glance, obviously had no heart for the task; it was as though the photographs had prised open their minds' eye, and forced them to at last really *see* the true and pitiful thing that had happened to a neighbor and his wife and children.

Capote probably emerged as the closest friend Smith or Hickock ever had—this was a minor part of their pathos. But his book does not become a sentimental plea for "sociological understanding" and discounting of the enormity of this crime. The Clutters were square and naive but also good and decent, and while the reader comes to know and sympathize with the murderers, he is not invited to forego moral judgment. What is special about *In Cold Blood* is its determination that this judgment be made in full context of the imponderables, and that it be made freely and independently, not as a rote performance by viewers of a standardized ballet of heroes and villains. "Civilization begins anew with every child," says an old saying; *In Cold Blood* is written as though its pages might become, for each reader, the commencement of the first serious moral education.

From In Cold Blood

Duntz, not to be diverted, reminds him, "Hickock had the knife. You had the gun. How did you get into the house?"

"The door was unlocked. A side door. It took us into Mr. Clutter's office. Then we waited in the dark. Listening. But the only sound was the wind. There was quite a little wind outside. It made the trees move, and you could hear the leaves. The one window was curtained with Venetian blinds, but moonlight was coming through. I closed the blinds, and Dick turned on his flashlight. We saw the desk. The safe was supposed to be in the wall directly behind the desk, but we couldn't find it. It was a paneled wall, and there were books and framed maps, and I noticed, on a shelf, a terrific pair of binoculars. I decided I was going to take them with me when we left there."

"Did you?" asks Dewey, for the binoculars had not been missed.

Smith nods. "We sold them in Mexico."

"Sorry. Go on."

"Well, when we couldn't find the safe, Dick doused the flashlight and we moved in darkness out of the office and across a parlor, a living room. Dick whispered to me couldn't I walk quieter. But he was just as bad. Every step we took made a racket. We came to a hall and a door, and Dick, remembering the diagram, said it was a bedroom. He shined the flashlight and opened the door. A man said, 'Honey?' He'd been asleep, and he blinked and he said, 'Is that you, honey?' Dick asked him, 'Are you Mr. Clutter?' He was wide awake now; he sat up and said, 'Who is it? What do you want?' Dick told him, very polite, like we were a couple of door-to-door salesmen, 'We want to talk to you, sir. In your office, please.' And Mr. Clutter, barefoot, just wearing pajamas, he went with us to the office and we turned on the office lights.

"Up till then he hadn't been able to see us very good. I think what he saw hit him hard. Dick says, 'Now, sir, all we want you to do is show us where you keep that safe.' But Mr. Clutter says, 'What safe?' He says he don't have any safe. I knew right then it was true. He had that kind of face. You just knew whatever he told you was pretty much the truth. But Dick shouted at him, 'Don't lie to me, you sonofabitch! I know goddam well you got a safe!' My feeling was nobody had ever spoken to Mr. Clutter like that. But he looked Dick straight in the eye and told him, being very mild about it—said, well, he was sorry but he just didn't have any safe. Dick tapped him on the chest with the knife, says, 'Show us where the safe is or you're gonna be a good bit sorrier.' But Mr. Clutter—oh, you could see he was scared, but his voice stayed mild and steady—he went on denying he had a safe.

"Sometime along in there, I fixed the telephone. The one in the office. I ripped out the wires. And I asked Mr. Clutter if there were any other telephones in the house. He said yes, there was one in the kitchen. So I took the flashlight and went to the kitchen—it was quite a distance from the office. When I found the telephone, I removed the receiver and cut the line with a pair of pliers. Then, heading back, I heard a noise. A creaking overhead. I stopped at the foot of the stairs leading to the second floor. It was dark, and I didn't dare use the flashlight. But I could tell there was someone there. At the top of the stairs, silhouetted against a window. A figure. Then it moved away."

Dewey imagines it must have been Nancy. He'd often theorized, on the basis of the gold wristwatch found tucked in the toe of a shoe in her closet, that Nancy had awakened, heard persons in the house, thought they might be thieves, and prudently hidden the watch, her most valuable property.

"For all I knew, maybe it was somebody with a gun. But Dick wouldn't even listen to me. He was so busy playing tough boy. Bossing Mr. Clutter around. Now he'd brought him back to the bedroom. He was counting the money in Mr. Clutter's billfold. There was about thirty dollars. He threw the billfold on the bed and told him, 'you've got more money in this house than that. A rich man like you. Living on a spread like this.' Mr. Clutter said that was all the cash he had, and explained he always did business by check. He offered to write us a check. Dick just blew up—'What kind of Mongolians do you think we are?'—and I thought Dick was ready to smash him, so I said, 'Dick. Listen to me. There's somebody awake upstairs.' Mr. Clutter told us the only people upstairs were his wife and a son and daughter. Dick wanted to know if the wife had any money, and Mr. Clutter said if she did, it would be very little, a few dollars, and he asked us—really kind of broke down—please not to bother her, because she was an invalid, she'd been very ill for a long time. But Dick insisted on going upstairs. He made Mr. Clutter lead the way.

"At the foot of the stairs, Mr. Clutter switched on lights that lighted the hall above, and as we were going up, he said, 'I don't know why you boys want to do this. I've never done you any harm. I never saw you before.' That's when Dick told him, 'Shut up! When we want you to talk, we'll tell you.' Wasn't anybody in the upstairs hall, and all the doors were shut. Mr. Clutter pointed out the rooms where the boy and girl were supposed to be sleeping, then opened his wife's door. He lighted a lamp beside the bed and told her, 'It's all right, sweetheart. Don't be afraid. These men, they want some money.' She was a thin, frail sort of woman in a long white nightgown. The minute she opened her eyes, she started to cry. She says, talking to her husband, 'Sweetheart, I don't have any money.' He was holding her hand, patting it. He said, 'Now, don't cry, honey. It's nothing to be afraid of. It's just I gave these men all the money I had, but they want some more. They believe we have a safe somewhere in the house. I told them we don't. Dick raised his hand, like he was going to crack him across the mouth. Says, 'Didn't I tell you to shut up?' Mrs. Clutter said, 'But my husband's telling you the God's truth. There isn't any safe.' And Dick answers back, 'I know goddam well you got a safe. And I'll find it before I leave here. Needn't worry that I won't.' Then he asked her where she kept her purse. The purse was in a bureau drawer. Dick turned it inside out. Found some change and a dollar or two. I motioned to him to come into the hall. I wanted to discuss the situation. So we stepped outside, and I said—"

Duntz interrupts him to ask if Mr. and Mrs. Clutter could overhear the conversation.

"No. We were just outside the door, where we could keep an eye on them. But we were whispering. I told Dick, 'These people are telling the truth. The one who lied is your friend Floyd Wells. There isn't any safe, so let's get the hell out of here.' But Dick was too ashamed to face it. He said he wouldn't believe it till we searched the whole house. He said the thing to do was tie them up, then take our time looking around. You couldn't argue with him, he was so excited. The glory of having everybody at his mercy, that's what excited him. Well, there was a bathroom next door to Mrs. Clutter's room. The idea was to lock the parents in the bathroom, and wake the kids and put them there, then bring them out one by one and tie them up in different parts of the house. And then, says Dick, after we've found the safe, we'll cut their throats. Can't shoot them, he says—that would make too much noise."

Perry frowns, rubs his knees with his manacled hands. "Let me think a minute. Because along in here things begin to get a little complicated. I remember. Yes. Yes, I took a chair out of the hall and stuck it in the bathroom. So Mrs. Clutter could sit down. Seeing she was said to be an invalid. When we locked them up, Mrs. Clutter was crying and telling us, 'Please don't hurt anybody. Please don't hurt my children.' And her husband had his arms around her, saying, like, 'Sweetheart, these fellows don't mean to hurt anybody. All they want is some money.'

"We went to the boy's room. He was awake. Lying there like he was too scared to move. Dick told him to get up, but he didn't move, or move fast enough, so Dick punched him, pulled him out of bed, and I said, 'You don't have to hit him, Dick.' And I told the boy—he was only wearing a T-shirt—to put on his pants. He put on a pair of blue jeans, and we'd just locked him in the bathroom when the girl appeared—came out of her room. She was all dressed, like she'd been awake some while. I mean, she had on socks and slippers, and a kimono, and her hair was wrapped in a bandanna. She was trying to smile. She said, 'Good grief, what is this? Some kind of joke?' I don't guess she thought it was much of a joke, though. Not after Dick opened the bathroom door and shoved her in . . ."

Dewey envisions them: the captive family, meek and frightened but without any premonition of their destiny. Herb *couldn't* have suspected, or he would have fought. He was a gentle man but strong and no coward. Herb, his friend Alvin Dewey felt certain, would have fought to the death defending Bonnie's life and the lives of his children.

"Dick stood guard outside the bathroom door while I reconnoitered. I frisked the girl's room, and I found a little purse—like a doll's purse. Inside it was a silver dollar. I dropped it somehow, and it rolled across the floor. Rolled under a chair. I had to get down on my knees. And just then it was like I was outside myself. Watching myself in some nutty movie. It made me sick. I was just disgusted. Dick, and all his talk about a rich man's safe, and here I am crawling on my belly to steal a child's silver dollar. One dollar. And I'm crawling on my belly to get it."

Perry squeezes his knees, asks the detectives for aspirin, thanks Duntz for giving him one, chews it, and resumes talking. "But that's what you do. You get what you can. I frisked the boy's room, too. Not a dime. But there was a little portable radio, and I decided to take it. Then I remembered the binoculars I'd seen in Mr. Clutter's office. I went downstairs to get them. I carried the binoculars and the radio out to the car. It was cold, and the wind and the cold felt good. The moon was so bright you could see for miles. And I thought, Why don't I walk off? Walk to the highway, hitch a ride. I sure Jesus didn't want to go back in that house. And yet—How can I explain this? It was like I wasn't part of it. More as though I was reading a story. And I had to know what was going to happen. The end. So I went back upstairs. And now, let's see—uh-huh, that's when we tied them up. Mr. Clutter first. We called him out of the bathroom, and I tied his hands together. Then I marched him all the way down to the basement—"

Dewey says, "Alone and unarmed?"

"I had the knife."

Dewey says, "But Hickock stayed guard upstairs?"

"To keep them quiet. Anyway, I didn't need help. I've worked with rope all my life."

Dewey says, "Were you using the flashlight or did you turn on the basement lights?"

"The lights. The basement was divided into two sections. One part seemed to be a playroom. Took him to the other section, the furnace room. I saw a big cardboard box leaning against the wall. A mattress box. Well, I didn't feel I ought to ask him to stretch out on the cold floor, so I dragged the mattress box over, flattened it, and told him to lie down."

The driver, via the rear-view mirror, glances at his colleague, attracts his eye, and Duntz slightly nods, as if in tribute. All along Dewey had argued that the mattress box had been placed on the floor for the *comfort* of Mr. Clutter, and taking heed of similar hints, other fragmentary indications of ironic, erratic compassion, the detective had conjectured that at least one of the killers was not altogether uncharitable.

"I tied his feet, then tied his hands to his feet. I asked him was it too tight, and he said no, but said would we please leave his wife alone. There was no need to tie her up—she wasn't going to holler or try to run out of the house. He said she'd been sick for years and years, and she was just beginning to get a little better, but an incident like this might cause her to have a setback. I know it's nothing to laugh over, only I couldn't help it—him talking about a 'setback.'

"Next thing, I brought the boy down. First I put him in the room with his dad. Tied his hands to an overhead steampipe. Then I figured that wasn't very safe. He might somehow get loose and undo the old man, or vice versa. So I cut him down and took him to the playroom, where there was a comfortable-looking couch. I roped his feet to the foot of the couch, roped his hands, then carried the rope up and made a loop around his neck, so if he struggled he'd choke himself. Once, while I was working, I put the knife down on this—well, it was a freshly varnished cedar chest; the whole cellar smelled of varnish—and he asked me not to put my knife there. The chest was a wedding present he'd built for somebody. A sister, I believe he said. Just as I was leaving, he had a coughing fit, so I stuffed a pillow under his head. Then I turned off the lights—"

Dewey says, "But you hadn't taped their mouths?"

"No. The taping came later, after I'd tied both the women in their bedrooms. Mrs. Clutter was still crying, at the same time she was asking me about Dick. She didn't trust him, but she felt I was a decent young man. I'm *sure* you are, she says, and made me promise I wouldn't let Dick hurt anybody. I think what she really had in mind was her daughter. I was worried about that myself. I suspected Dick was plotting something, something I wouldn't stand for. When I finished tying Mrs. Clutter, sure enough, I found he'd taken the girl to her bedroom. She was in the bed, and he was sitting on the edge of it talking to her. I stopped that; I told him to go look for the safe while I tied her up. After he'd gone, I roped her feet together and tied her hands behind her back. Then I pulled up the covers, tucked her in till just her head showed. There was a little easy chair near the bed, and I thought I'd rest a minute; my legs were on fire—all that climbing and kneeling. I asked Nancy if she had a boy friend. She said yes, she did. She was trying to act casual and friendly. I really liked her. She was really nice. A very pretty girl, and not spoiled or anything. She told me quite a lot about herself. About school, and how she was going to go to a university to study music and art. Horses. Said next to dancing what she liked best was to gallop a horse, so I mentioned my mother had been a champion rodeo rider.

"And we talked about Dick; I was curious, see, what he'd been saying to her. Seems she'd asked him why he did things like this. Rob people. And, wow, did he toss her a tearjerker—said he'd been raised an orphan in an orphanage, and how nobody had ever loved him, and his only relative was a sister who lived with men without marrying them. All the time we were talking, we could hear the lunatic roaming around below, looking for the safe. Looking behind the pictures. Tapping the walls. Tap tap tap. Like some nutty woodpecker. When he came back, just to be a real bastard I asked had he found it. Course he hadn't, but he said he'd come across another purse in the kitchen. With seven dollars."

Duntz says, "How long now had you been in the house?"

"Maybe an hour."

Duntz says, "And when did you do the taping?"

"Right then. Started with Mrs. Clutter. I made Dick help me—because I didn't want to leave him alone with the girl. I cut the tape in long strips, and Dick wrapped them around Mrs. Clutter's head like you'd wrap a mummy. He asked her, 'How come you keep on crying? Nobody's hurting you,' and he turned off the bedside lamp and said, 'Good night, Mrs. Clutter. Go to sleep.' Then he says to me, as we're heading along the hall toward Nancy's room, 'I'm gonna bust that little girl.' And I said, 'Uh-huh. But you'll have to kill me first.' He looked like he didn't believe he'd heard right. He says, 'What do you care? Hell, you can bust her, too.' Now, that's something I despise. Anybody that can't control themselves sexually. Christ, I hate that kind of stuff. I told him straight, 'Leave her alone. Else you've got a buzzsaw to fight.' That really burned him, but he realized it wasn't the time to have a flat-out free-for-all. So he says, 'O.K., honey. If that's the way you feel.' The end of it was we never even taped her. We switched off the hall light and went down to the basement."

Perry hesitates. He has a question but phrases it as a statement: "I'll bet he never said anything about wanting to rape the girl."

Dewey admits it, but he adds that except for an apparently somewhat expurgated version of his own conduct, Hickock's story supports Smith's. The details vary, the dialogue is not identical, but in substance the two accounts—thus far, at least—corroborate one another.

"Maybe. But I knew he hadn't told about the girl. I'd have bet my shirt."

Duntz says, "Perry, I've been keeping track of the lights. The way I calculate it, when you turned off the upstairs light, that left the house completely dark."

"Did. And we never used the lights again. Except the flashlight. Dick carried the flashlight when we went to tape Mr. Clutter and the boy. Just before I taped him, Mr. Clutter asked me—and these were his last words—wanted to know how his wife was, if she was all right, and I said she was fine, she was ready to go to sleep, and I told him it wasn't long till morning, and how in the morning somebody would find them, and then all of it, me and Dick and all, would seem like something they dreamed. I wasn't kidding him. I didn't want to harm the man. I thought he was a very nice gentleman. Soft-spoken. I thought so right up to the moment I cut his throat.

"Wait. I'm not telling it the way it was." Perry scowls. He rubs his legs; the handcuffs rattle. "After, see, after we'd taped them, Dick and I went off in a corner. To talk it over. Remember, now, there were hard feelings between us. Just then it made my stomach turn to think I'd ever admired him, lapped up all that brag. I said, 'Well, Dick. Any qualms?' He didn't answer me. I said, 'Leave them alive, and this won't be any small rap. Ten years the very least.' He still didn't say anything. He was holding the knife. I asked him for it, and he gave it to me, and I said, 'All right, Dick. Here goes.' But I didn't mean it. I meant to call his bluff, make him argue me out of it, make him admit he was a phony and a coward. See, it was something between me and Dick. I knelt down beside Mr. Clutter, and the pain of kneeling—I thought of that goddam dollar. Silver dollar. The shame. Disgust. And *they'd* told me never to come back to Kansas. But I didn't realize what I'd done till I heard the sound. Like somebody drowning. Screaming under water. I handed the knife to Dick. I said, 'Finish him. You'll feel better.' Dick tried— or pretended to. But the man had the strength of ten men—he was half out of his ropes, his hands were free. Dick panicked. Dick wanted to get the hell out of there. But I wouldn't let him go. The man would have died anyway, I know that, but I couldn't leave him like he was. I told Dick to hold the flashlight, focus it. Then I aimed the gun. The room just exploded. Went blue. Just blazed up. Jesus, I'll never understand why they didn't hear the noise twenty miles around."

Dewey's ears ring with it—a ringing that almost deafens him to the whispery rush of Smith's soft voice. But the voice plunges on, ejecting a fusillade of sounds and images: Hickock hunting the discharged shell; hurrying, hurrying, and Kenyon's head in a circle of light, the murmur of muffled pleadings, then Hickock again scrambling after a used cartridge; Nancy's room, Nancy listening to boots on hardwood stairs, the creak of the steps as they climbed toward her, Nancy's eyes, Nancy watching the flashlight's shine seek the target ("She said, 'Oh, no! Oh, please. No! No! No! No! Don't! Oh, please don't! Please!' I gave the gun to Dick. I told him I'd done all I could do. He took aim, and she turned her face to the wall"); the dark hall, the assassins hastening toward the final door. Perhaps, having heard all she had, Bonnie welcomed their swift approach.

"That last shell was a bitch to locate. Dick wiggled under the bed to get it. Then we closed Mrs. Clutter's door and went downstairs to the office. We waited there, like we had when we first came. Looked through the blinds to see if the hired man was poking around, or anybody else who might have heard the gunfire. But it was just the same—not a sound. Just the wind—and Dick panting like wolves were after him. Right there, in those few seconds before we ran out to the car and drove away, that's when I decided I'd better shoot Dick. He'd said over and over, he'd drummed it into me: *No witnesses.* And I thought, *He's* a witness. I don't know what stopped me. God knows I should've done it. Shot him dead. Got in the car and kept on going till I lost myself in Mexico."

A hush. For ten miles and more, the three men ride without speaking.

Sorrow and profound fatigue are at the heart of Dewey's silence. It had been his ambition to learn "exactly what happened in that house that night." Twice now he'd been told, and the two versions were very much alike, the only serious discrepancy being that Hickock attributed all four deaths to Smith, while Smith contended that Hickock had killed the two women. But the confessions, though they answered questions of how and why, failed to satisfy his sense of meaningful design. The crime was a psychological accident, virtually an impersonal act; the victims might as well have been killed by lightning. Except for one thing: they had experienced prolonged terror, they had suffered. And Dewey could not forget their sufferings. Nonetheless, he found it possible to look at the man beside him without anger—with, rather, a measure of sympathy—for Perry Smith's life had been no bed of roses but pitiful, an ugly and lonely progress toward one mirage and then another. Dewey's sympathy, however, was not deep enought to accommodate either forgiveness or mercy. He hoped to see Perry and his partner hanged—hanged back to back.

Duntz asks Smith, "Added up, how much money did you get from the Clutters?"

"Between forty and fifty dollars."

. . .

IV
Toward the New Society

JANE ADDAMS
(1860–1935)

Born into an upper middle-class family in Cedarville, Illinois, Jane Addams ranks with the broadest-gauged, most comprehensively informed Americans of her time. She graduated from Rockford College in 1881, studied medicine for a short time, and then traveled in Europe. In 1888, after visiting Toynbee Hall, a settlement house in London, she decided to devote herself to improving the lives of the poor. The chief setting for her achievements in social knowledge and social responsibility was Hull-House, a combination school-charitable institution-employment agency-center for radical political action that she founded in the Chicago slums when she was 29 years old. In the course of the decades spent nourishing and administering this settlement house, raising funds for it, and enlarging the scope of its projects and influence, she touched ranges of experience open to virtually no other social thinker of her time, regardless of sex. And in two extraordinary books—*Democracy and Social Ethics* (1902) and *Twenty Years at Hull-House* (1910)—she shaped that experience into a mode of inquiry into American social problems that was at once original, brilliant, and moving.

At the center of Jane Addams' thought three key values can be discerned: alertness to the web of human and social relationships, respect

The principal work, *Twenty Years at Hull-House,* with autobiographical notes, was published in 1910. *Jane Addams: A Centennial Reader,* 1960, contains the important texts. *The Social Thought of Jane Addams,* 1965, was edited by Christopher Lasch.

Biographies include Josephine Blackstock, *Jane Addams,* 1950; Gail Keller, *Jane Addams,* 1971; and Allen F. Davis, *American Heroine: The Life and Legend of Jane Addams,* 1973.

Studies include Clara Judson, *City Neighbor: The Story of Jane Addams,* 1951; Margaret Tims, *Jane Addams of Hull House, 1860–1935,* 1961; John C. Farrell, *Beloved Lady, A History of Jane Addams' Ideas on Reform and Peace,* 1967; Elizabeth C. Mooney, *Jane Addams,* 1968; Helen Stone Peterson, *Jane Addams, Pioneer of Hull House,* 1965.

for human difference, and moral realism. Her sense of the necessity of attending to the whole configuration of a place and time is revealed in her explanation of how she decided on a location for her settlement. The site for Hull-House was chosen, she said, because of "its diversity and the variety of activity for which it presented an opportunity"; her own aim, and that of her "social worker" colleagues, was "to respond to all sides of the neighborhood life: not to the poor people alone, nor to the well-to-do, nor to the young in contradistinction to the old, but to the neighborhood as a whole. . . ."

Jane Addams' feeling for the dignity of what is now called "ethnic identity," the natural and unpretentious pluralism of her own sympathies, is vivid whenever she reports on encounters, in Hull-House meeting rooms, between "home country" civilization and "the new":

> I have seen sons and daughters stand in complete surprise as their mother's knitting-needles softly beat time to the song she was singing, or her worn face turned rosy under the handclapping as she made an old-fashioned courtesy at the end of a German poem. It was easy to fancy a growing touch of respect in her children's manner to her, and a rising enthusiasm for German literature and reminiscence on the part of all the family, an effort to bring together the old life and the new, a respect for the older cultivation, and not quite so much assurance that the new was the best.

And her moral realism led her, time and again, to penetrate facts of feeling that eluded conventional moral analysis. Writing about "Why the Ward Boss Rules" in 1898, she advanced beyond standard-form denunciations of corruption to a grasp of the ward heeler as perceived by the immigrant himself In the Nineteenth Ward, she notes, the Alderman whom Good Society called corrupt appears as nothing of the sort; he is simply a good, friendly, powerful human being who stands by his constituents, bails them out, pays their rent, gets them jobs, gives presents at weddings, and helps out with funerals. And she points the morally realistic lesson as follows:

> If we would hold to our political democracy, some pains must be taken to keep on common ground in our human experiences, and to some solidarity in our ethical conceptions. And if we discover that men of low ideals and corrupt practice are forming popular political standards because such men stand by and for and with the people, then nothing remains but to obtain a like sense of identification before we can hope to modify ethical standards.

Jane Addams campaigned, wrote, worked (even delivered a baby once), and endured vilification; she fought ceaselessly for peace, women's rights, and political reform. Her migration "from one condition of life to another totally unlike it" is reported with an earnestness always gentle yet never beamish or humorless; everywhere in her pages the ruling conviction is that "to allow a large number of persons to remain outside the circle of [community] because they have not been given a sense of participation would at last not only cripple our national life but limit our human possibilities." Her best contemporary critic, Christopher Lasch, has wisely remarked that her effort "aimed not so much at helping the poor as at understanding them; and by understanding them, at bridging the chasm that industrialism had opened between social classes." In 1931, at last respectable, Jane Addams won the Nobel Peace Prize. She died in Chicago of cancer.

The Subjective Necessity for Social Settlements

Hull House, which was Chicago's first Settlement, was established in September, 1889. It represented no association, but was opened by two women, backed by many friends, in the belief that the mere foothold of a house easily accessible, ample in space, hospitable and tolerant in spirit, situated in the midst of the large foreign colonies which so easily isolate themselves in American cities, would be in itself a serviceable thing for Chicago. Hull House endeavors to make social intercourse express the growing sense of the economic unity of society. It is an effort to add the social function to democracy. It was opened on the theory that the dependence of classes on each other is reciprocal; and that as "the social relation is essentially a reciprocal relation, it gave a form of expression that has peculiar value."

This paper is an attempt to treat of the subjective necessity for Social Settlements, to analyze the motives which underlie a movement based not only upon conviction, but genuine emotion. Hull House of Chicago is used as an illustration, but so far as the analysis is faithful, it obtains wherever educated young people are seeking an outlet for that sentiment of universal brotherhood which the best spirit of our times is forcing from an emotion into a motive.

I have divided the motives which constitute the subjective pressure toward Social Settlements into three great lines: the first contains the desire to make the entire social organism democratic, to extend democracy beyond its political expression; the second is the impulse to share the race life, and to bring as much as possible of social energy and the accumulation of civilization to those portions of the race which have little; the third springs from a certain *renaissance* of Christianity, a movement toward its early humanitarian aspects.

It is not difficult to see that although America is pledged to the democratic ideal, the view of democracy has been partial, and that its best achievement thus far has been pushed along the line of the franchise. Democracy has made little attempt to assert itself in social affairs. We have refused to move beyond the position of its eighteenth-century leaders, who believed that political equality alone would secure all good to all men. We conscientiously followed the gift of the ballot hard upon the gift of freedom to the negro, but we are quite unmoved by the fact that he lives among us in a practical social ostracism. We hasten to give the franchise to the immigrant from a sense of justice, from a tradition that he ought to have it, while we dub him with epithets deriding his past life or present occupation, and feel no duty to invite him to our houses. We are forced to acknowledge that it is only in our local and national politics that we try very hard for the ideal so dear to those who were enthusiasts when the century was young. We have almost given it up as our ideal in social intercourse. There are city wards in which many of the votes are sold for drinks and dollars; still there is a remote pretense, at least a fiction current, that a man's vote is his own. The judgment of the voter is consulted and an opportunity for remedy given. There is not even a theory in the social order, not a shadow answering to the polls in politics. The time may come when the politician who sells one by one to the highest bidder all the offices in his grasp, will not be considered more base in his code or morals, more hardened in his practice, than the woman who constantly invites to her receptions those alone who bring her an equal social return, who shares her beautiful surroundings only with those who minister to a liking she has for successful social events. In doing this is she not just as unmindful of the common weal, as unscrupulous in her use of power, as is any city "boss" who consults only the interests of the "ring"?

In politics "bossism" arouses a scandal. It goes on in society constantly and is only beginning to be challenged. Our consciences are becoming tender in regard to the lack of democracy in social affairs. We are perhaps entering upon the second phase of democracy, as the French philosophers entered upon the first, somewhat bewildered by its logical conclusions. The social organism has broken down through large districts of our great cities. Many of the people living there are very poor, the majority of them without leisure or energy for anything but the gain of subsistence. They move often from one wretched lodging to another. They live for the moment side by side, many of them without knowledge of each other, without fellowship, without local tradition or public spirit, without social organization of any kind. Practically nothing is done to remedy this. The people who might do it, who have the social tact and training, the large houses, and the traditions and custom of hospitality, live in other parts of the city. The club-houses, libraries, galleries, and semi-public conveniences for social life are also blocks away. We find working-men organized into armies of producers because men of executive ability and business sagacity have found it to their interests thus to organize them. But these working-men are not organized socially; although living in crowded tenement-houses, they are living without a corresponding social contact. The chaos is as great as it would be were they working in huge factories without foreman or superintendent. Their ideas and resources are cramped. The desire for higher social pleasure is extinct. They have no share in the traditions and social energy which make for progress. Too often their only place of meeting is a saloon, their only host a bartender; a local demagogue forms their public opinion. Men of ability and refinement, of social power and university cultivation, stay away from them. Personally, I believe the men who lose most are those who thus stay away. But the paradox is here; when cultivated people do stay away from a certain portion of the population, when all social advantages are persistently withheld, it may be for years, the result itself is pointed at as a reason, is used as an argument, for the continued withholding.

It is constantly said that because the masses have never had social advantages they do not want them, that they are heavy and dull, and that it will take political or philanthropic machinery to change them. This divides a city into rich and poor; into the favored, who express their sense of the social obligation by gifts of money, and into the unfavored, who express it by clamoring for a "share"—both of them actuated by a vague sense of justice. This division of the city would be more justifiable, however, if the people who thus isolate themselves on certain streets and use their social ability for each other gained enough thereby and added sufficient to the sum total of social progress to justify the withholding of the pleasures and results of that progress from so many people who ought to have them. But they cannot accomplish this. "The social spirit discharges itself in many forms, and no one form is adequate to its total expression." We are all uncomfortable in regard to the sincerity of our best phrases, because we hesitate to translate our philosophy into the deed.

It is inevitable that those who feel most keenly this insincerity and partial living should be our young people, our so-called educated young people who accomplish little toward the solution of this social problem, and who bear the brunt of being cultivated into unnourished, over-sensitive lives. They have been shut off from the common labor by which they live and which is a great source of moral and physical health. They feel a fatal want of harmony between their theory and their lives, a lack of co-ordination between thought and action. I think it is hard for us to realize how seriously many of them are taking to the notion of human brotherhood, how eagerly they long to give tangible expression to the democratic ideal. These young men and women, longing to socialize their democracy, are animated by certain hopes.

These hopes may be loosely formulated thus: that if in a democratic country nothing can be permanently achieved save through the masses of the people, it will be impossible to establish a higher political life than the people themselves crave; that it is difficult to see how the notion of a higher civic life can be fostered save through common intercourse; that the blessings which we associate with a life of refinement and cultivation can be made universal and must be made universal if they are to be permanent; that the good we secure for ourselves is precarious and uncertain, is floating in mid-air, until it is secured for all of us and incorporated into our common life.

These hopes are responsible for results in various directions, pre-eminently in the extension of educational advantages. We find that all educational matters are more democratic in their political than in their social aspects. The public schools in the poorest and most crowded wards of the city are inadequate to the number of children, and many of the teachers are ill-prepared and overworked; but in each ward there is an effort to secure public education. The schoolhouse itself stands as a pledge that the city recognizes and endeavors to fulfil the duty of educating its children. But what becomes of these children when they are no longer in public schools? Many of them never come under the influence of a professional teacher nor a cultivated friend after they are twelve. Society at large does little for their intellectual development. The dream of transcendentalists that each New England village would be a university, that every child taken from the common school would be put into definite lines of study and mental development, had its unfulfilled beginning in the village lyceum and lecture courses, and has its feeble representative now in the multitude of clubs for study which are so sadly restricted to educators, to the leisure class, or only to the advanced and progressive wage-workers.

The University Extension movement—certainly when it is closely identified with Settlements—would not confine learning to those who already want it, or to those who, by making an effort, can gain it, or to those among whom professional educators are already at work, but would take it to the tailors of East London and the dock-laborers of the Thames. It requires tact and training, and the conviction of the justice of its diffusion to give it to people whose intellectual faculties are untrained and disused. But men in England are found who do it successfully, and it is believed there are men and women in America who can do it. I also believe that the best work in University Extension can be done in Settlements, where the teaching will be further socialized, where the teacher will grapple his students, not only by formal lectures, but by every hook possible to the fuller intellectual life which he represents. This teaching requires distinct methods, for it is true of people who have been allowed to remain undeveloped and whose faculties are inert and sterile, that they cannot take their learning heavily. It has to be diffused in a social atmosphere. Information held in solution, a medium of fellowship and goodwill can be assimilated by the dullest.

If education is, as Froebel[1] defined it, "deliverance," deliverance of the forces of the body and mind, then the untrained must first be delivered from all constraint and rigidity before their faculties can be used. Possibly one of the most pitiful periods in the drama of the much-praised young American who attempts to rise in life is the time when his educational requirements seem to have locked him up and made him rigid. He fancies himself shut off from his uneducated family and misunderstood by his friends. He is bowed down by his mental accumulations and often gets no farther than to carry them through life as a great burden. Not once has he had a glimpse of the delights of knowledge. Intellectual life requires for its expansion and manifestation the influence and assimilation of the interests and affections of others. Mazzini,[2] that greatest of all democrats, who broke his heart over the condition of the South European peasantry, said: "Education is not merely a necessity of true life by which the individual renews his vital force in the vital force of humanity; it is a Holy Communion with generations dead and living, by which he fecundates all his faculties. When he is withheld from this Communion for generations, as the Italian peasant has been, we point our finger at him and say, 'He is like a beast of the field; he must be controlled by force.'" Even to this it is sometimes added that it is absurd to educate him, immoral to disturb his content. We stupidly use again the effect as an argument for a continuance of the cause. It is needless to say that a Settlement is a protest against a restricted view of education, and makes it possible for every educated man or woman with a teaching faculty to find out those who are ready to be taught. The social and educational activities of a Settlement are but differing manifestations of the attempt to socialize democracy, as is the existence of the settlement itself.

I find it somewhat difficult to formulate the second line of motives which I believe to constitute the trend of the subjective pressure toward the Settlement. There is something primordial about these motives, but I am perhaps over-bold in designating them as a great desire to share the race life. We all bear traces of the starvation struggle which for so long made up the life of the race. Our very organism holds memories and glimpses of that long life of our ancestors which still goes on among so many of our contemporaries. Nothing so deadens the sympathies and shrivels the power of enjoyment as the persistent keeping away from the great opportunities for helpfulness and a continual ignoring of the starvation struggle which makes up the life of at least half the race. To shut one's self away from that half of the race life is to shut one's self away from the most vital part of it; it is to live out but half the

---

[1] Friedrich Wilhelm August Froebel (1782-1852), a German educational reformer, continued the work of Pestalozzi.

[2] Guiseppe Mazzini (1805-1872), Italian patriot and revolutionary.

humanity which we have been born heir to and to use but half our faculties. We have all had longings for a fuller life which should include the use of these faculties. These longings are the physical complement of the "Intimations of Immortality" on which no ode has yet been written. To portray these would be the work of a poet, and it is hazardous for any but a poet to attempt it.

You may remember the forlorn feeling which occasionally seizes you when you arrive early in the morning a stranger in a great city. The stream of laboring people goes past you as you gaze through the plate-glass window of your hotel. You see hard-working men lifting great burdens; you hear the driving and jostling of huge carts. Your heart sinks with a sudden sense of futility. The door opens behind you and you turn to the man who brings you in your breakfast with a quick sense of human fellowship. You find yourself praying that you may never lose your hold on it at all. A more poetic prayer would be that the great mother breasts of our common humanity, with its labor and suffering and its homely comforts, may never be withheld from you. You turn helplessly to the waiter. You feel that it would be almost grotesque to claim from him the sympathy you crave. Civilization has placed you far apart, but you resent your position with a sudden sense of snobbery. Literature is full of portrayals of these glimpses. They come to shipwrecked men on rafts; they overcome the differences of an incongruous multitude when in the presence of a great danger or when moved by a common enthusiasm. They are not, however, confined to such moments, and if we were in the habit of telling them to each other, the recital would be as long as the tales of children are, when they sit down on the green grass and confide to each other how many times they have remembered that they lived once before. If these tales are the stirring of inherited impressions, just so surely is the other the striving of inherited powers.

"There is nothing after disease, indigence, and a sense of guilt so fatal to health and to life itself as the want of a proper outlet for active faculties." I have seen young girls suffer and grow sensibly lowered in vitality in the first years after they leave school. In our attempt then to give a girl pleasure and freedom from care we succeed, for the most part, in making her pitifully miserable. She finds "life" so different from what she expected it to be. She is besotted with innocent little ambitions, and does not understand this apparent waste of herself, this elaborate preparation, if no work is provided for her. There is a heritage of noble obligation which young people accept and long to perpetuate. The desire for action, the wish to right wrong and alleviate suffering, haunts them daily. Society smiles at it indulgently instead of making it of value to itself. The wrong to them begins even farther back, when we restrain the first childish desires for "doing good" and tell them that they must wait until they are older and better fitted. We intimate that social obligation begins at a fixed date, forgetting that it begins with birth itself. We treat them as children who, with strong-growing limbs, are allowed to use their legs but not their arms, or whose legs are daily carefully exercised that after awhile their arms may be put to high use. We do this in spite of the protest of the best educators, Locke[3] and Pestalozzi.[4] We are fortunate in the mean time if their unused members do not weaken and disappear. They do sometimes. There are a few girls who, by the time they are "educated," forget their old childish desires to help the world and to play with poor little girls "who haven't playthings." Parents are often inconsistent. They deliberately expose their daughters to knowledge of the distress in the world. They send them to hear missionary addresses on famines in India and China; they accompany them to lectures on the suffering in Siberia; they agitate together over the forgotten region of East London. In addition to this, from babyhood the altruistic tendencies of these daughters are persistently cultivated. They are taught to be self-forgetting and self-sacrificing, to consider the good of the Whole before the good of the Ego. But when all this information and culture show results, when the daughter comes back from college and begins to recognize her social claim to the "submerged tenth," and to evince a disposition to fulfil it, the family claim is strenuously asserted; she is told that she is unjustified, ill-advised in her efforts. If she persists the family too often are injured and unhappy, unless the efforts are called missionary, and the religious zeal of the family carry them over their sense of abuse. When this zeal does not exist the result is perplexing. It is a curious violation of what we would fain believe a fundamental law—that the final return of the Deed is upon the head of the Doer. The deed is that of exclusiveness and caution, but the return instead of falling upon the head of the exclusive and cautious, falls upon a young head full of generous and unselfish plans. The girl loses something vital out of her life which she is entitled to. She is restricted and unhappy; her elders, meanwhile, are unconscious of the situation, and we have all the elements of a tragedy.

We have in America a fast-growing number of cultivated young people who have no recognized outlet for their active faculties. They hear constantly of the great social mal-adjustment, but no way is provided for them to change it, and their uselessness hangs about them heavily. Huxley declares that the sense of uselessness is the severest shock which the human system can sustain, and that, if persistently sustained, it results in atrophy of function. These young people have had advantages of college, of European travel and economic study, but they are sustaining this shock of inaction. They have pet phrases, and they tell you that the things that make us all alike are stronger than the things that make us different. They say that all men are united by needs and sympathies far more permanent and radical than anything that temporarily divides them and sets them in opposition to each other. If they affect art, they say that the decay in artistic expression is due to

[3] John Locke (1632-1704), English philosopher.

[4] Johann Heinrich Pestalozzi (1746-1827), Swiss educationalist.

the decay in ethics, that art when shut away from the human interests and from the great mass of humanity, is self-destructive. They tell their elders with all the bitterness of youth that if they expect success from them in business, or politics, or in whatever lines their ambition for them has run, they must let them consult all of humanity; that they must let them find out what the people want and how they want it. It is only the stronger young people, however, who formulate this. Many of them dissipate their energies in so-called enjoyment. Others, not content with that, go on studying and go back to college for their second degrees, not that they are especially fond of study, but because they want something definite to do, and their powers have been trained in the direction of mental accumulation. Many are buried beneath more mental accumulation with lowered vitality and discontent. Walter Besant[5] says that they have had the vision that Peter had when he saw the great sheet let down from heaven, wherein was neither clean nor unclean. He calls it the sense of humanity. It is not philanthrophy nor benevolence. It is a thing fuller and wider than either of these. This young life, so sincere in its emotion and good phrases and yet so undirected, seems to me as pitiful as the other great mass of destitute lives. One is supplementary to the other, and some method of communication can surely be devised. Mr. Barnett,[6] who urged the first Settlement,—Toynbee Hall, in East London,— recognized this need of outlet for the young men of Oxford and Cambridge, and hoped that the Settlement would supply the communication. It is easy to see why the Settlement movement originated in England, where the years of education are more constrained and definite than they are here, where class distinctions are more rigid. The necessity of it was greater there, but we are fast feeling the pressure of the need and meeting the necessity for Settlements in America. Our young people feel nervously the need of putting theory into action, and respond quickly to the Settlement form of activity.

The third division of motives which I believe make toward the Settlement is the result of a certain *renaissance* going forward in Christianity. The impulse to share the lives of the poor, the desire to make social service, irrespective of propaganda, express the spirit of Christ, is as old as Christianity itself. We have no proof from the records themselves that the early Roman Christians, who strained their simple art to the point of grotesqueness in their eagerness to record a "good news" on the walls of the catacombs, considered this "good news" a religion. Jesus had no set of truths labelled "Religious." On the contrary, his doctrine was that all truth is one, that the appropriation of it is freedom. His teaching had no dogma to mark it off from truth and action in general. He himself called it a revelation—a life. These early Roman Christians received the Gospel message, a command to love all

---

[5] Walter Besant (1836-1901), English novelist of social reform.

[6] Samuel Augustus Barnett (1844-1913), an Anglican clergyman and the first warden of the social settlement Toynbee Hall, founded in 1884.

men, with a certain joyous simplicity. The image of the Good Shepherd is blithe and gay beyond the gentlest shepherd of Greek mythology; the hart no longer pants, but rushes to the water brooks. The Christians looked for the continuous revelation, but believed what Jesus said, that this revelation to be held and made manifest must be put into terms of action; that action is the only medium man has for receiving and appropriating truth. "If any man will do His will, he shall know of the doctrine."

That Christianity has to be revealed and embodied in the line of social progress is a corollary to the simple proposition that man's action is found in his social relationships in the way in which he connects with his fellows, that his motives for action are the zeal and affection with which he regards his fellows. By this simple process was created a deep enthusiasm for humanity, which regarded man as at once the organ and object of revelation; and by this process came about that wonderful fellowship, that true democracy of the early Church, that so captivates the imagination. The early Christians were pre-eminently non-resistant. They believed in love as a cosmic force. There was no iconoclasm during the minor peace of the Church. They did not yet denounce, nor tear down temples, nor preach the end of the world. They grew to a mighty number, but it never occurred to them, either in their weakness or their strength, to regard other men for an instant as their foes or as aliens. The spectacle of the Christians loving all men was the most astounding Rome had ever seen. They were eager to sacrifice themselves for the weak, for children and the aged. They identified themselves with slaves and did not avoid the plague. They longed to share the common lot that they might receive the constant revelation. It was a new treasure which the early Christians added to the sum of all treasures, a joy hitherto unknown in the world—the joy of finding the Christ which lieth in each man, but which no man can unfold save in fellowship. A happiness ranging from the heroic to the pastoral enveloped them. They were to possess a revelation as long as life had new meaning to unfold, new action to propose.

I believe that there is a distinct turning among many young men and women toward this simple acceptance of Christ's message. They resent the assumption that Christianity is a set of ideas which belong to the religious consciousness, whatever that may be, that it is a thing to be proclaimed and instituted apart from the social life of the community. They insist that it shall seek a simple and natural expression in the social organism itself. The Settlement movement is only one manifestation of that wider humanitarian movement which throughout Christendom, but pre-eminently in England, is endeavoring to embody itself, not in a sect, but in society itself. Tolstoi has reminded us all very forcibly of Christ's principle of non-resistance. His formulation has been startling and his expression has deviated from the general movement, but there is little doubt that he has many adherents, men and women who are philosophically convinced of the futility of opposition, who believe that evil can be overcome only with good and cannot be opposed. If love is the creative force of the universe, the principle which binds men together, and by their interdependence on each other makes them human, just so surely is anger and the spirit of opposition the destructive principle of the universe, that which tears down, thrusts men apart, and makes them isolated and brutal.

I cannot, of course, speak for other Settlements, but it would, I think, be unfair to Hull House not to emphasize the conviction with which the first residents went there, that it would be a foolish and unwarrantable expenditure of force to oppose or to antagonize any individual or set of people in the neighborhood; that whatever of good the House had to offer should be put into positive terms; that its residents should live with opposition to no man, with recognition of the good in every man, even the meanest. I believe that this turning, this *renaissance* of the early Christian humanitarianism, is going on in America, in Chicago, if you please, without leaders who write or philosophize, without much speaking, but with a bent to express in social service, in terms of action, the spirit of Christ. Certain it is that spiritual force is found in the Settlement movement, and it is also true that this force must be evoked and must be called into play before the success of any Settlement is assured. There must be the overmastering belief that all that is noblest in life is common to men as men, in order to accentuate the likenesses and ignore the differences which are found among the people whom the Settlement constantly brings into juxtaposition. It may be true, as Frederic Harrison[7] insists, that the very religious fervor of man can be turned into love for his race and his desire for a future life into content to live in the echo of his deeds. How far the Positivists' formula of the high ardor for humanity can carry the Settlement movement, Mrs. Humphry Ward's[8] house in London may in course of time illustrate. Paul's formula of seeking for the Christ which lieth in each man and founding our likenesses on him seems a simpler formula to many of us.

If you have heard a thousand voices singing in the Hallelujah Chorus in Handel's "Messiah," you have found that the leading voices could still be distinguished, but that the differences of training and cultivation between them and the voices of the chorus were lost in the unity of purpose and the fact that they were all human voices lifted by a high motive. This is a weak illustration of what a Settlement attempts to do. It aims, in a measure, to lead whatever of social life its neighborhood may afford, to focus and give form to that life, to bring to bear upon it the results of cultivation and training; but it receives in exchange for the music of isolated voices the volume and strength of the chorus. It is quite impossible for me to say in what proportion or degree the subjective necessity which led to the opening of Hull House

[7] Frederic Harrison (1831–1923), English writer and social critic.

[8] Mrs. Humphry Ward (1851–1920), English novelist, author of *Robert Elsmere* (1888), a novel of social reform.

combined the three trends: first the desire to interpret democracy in social terms; secondly, the impulse beating at the very source of our lives urging us to aid in the race progress; and, thirdly, the Christian movement toward Humanitarianism. It is difficult to analyze a living thing; the analysis is at best imperfect. Many more motives may blend with the three trends; possibly the desire for a new form of social success due to the nicety of imagination, which refuses worldly pleasures unmixed with the joys of self-sacrifice; possibly a love of approbation, so vast that it is not content with the treble clapping of delicate hands, but wishes also to hear the bass notes from toughened palms, may mingle with these. . . .

W. E. B. DuBOIS

(1868–1963)

The Souls of Black Folk collects the strongest and keenest observations of one of the most remarkable writers ever to address the issues of race in America. Born in Great Barrington, Massachusetts, W. E. B. DuBois studied at Fisk and Harvard and arrived, by his mid-30's, at the prophetic conviction that "the problem of the twentieth century is the problem of the color line." This became the theme of a life bent on educating the uncultivated black and the narrow and prejudiced white, showing forth worlds that each was either unable or unwilling to know. The man's conviction was clear: blacks must and will have their full human rights. Yet the voice that maintained this principle struggled for evenness of tone and went close to the limits of human generosity and scrupulosity in its attempt to be fair. "I should be the last to withhold sympathy from the white South," DuBois wrote, "in its efforts to solve its intricate social problems." And time and again he interrupts his account of the souls of black folk to probe the feelings of the poor white, outnumbered and threatened by his black neighbors, or the landowner's son whose father lost wealth and family overnight in the Civil War. Excusing ill-conceived or destructive Reconstruction policies, he reminds his reader that the problems were complex and that hindsight is easy.

DuBois' nonfiction also includes *Dusk of Dawn,* 1940. Some of his fiction is *The Quest of the Silver Fleece,* 1911; *Dark Princess,* 1928; *The Black Flame,* 1957. His autobiography is *The Autobiography of W. E. B. DuBois,* 1968.

Criticism includes Francis Broderick, *W. E. B. DuBois, Negro Leader in a Time of Crisis,* 1959, and Elliot M. Rudwick, *W. E. B. DuBois: A Study in Minority Group Leadership,* 1961.

Here at a stroke of the pen was erected a government of millions of men,—and not ordinary men either, but black men emasculated by a peculiarly complete system of slavery, centuries old; and now, suddenly, violently, they come into a new birthright, at a time of war and passion, in the midst of the stricken and embittered population of their former masters. Any man might well have hesitated to assume charge of such a work, with vast responsibilities, indefinite powers, and limited resources.

DuBois' great theme—it is the root of his calm as well as of his anger—is that of the black contribution, the reality of substance of what these people have given their land. More than a dreadfully exploited labor force or an incompletely evolved race, black Americans bestow on the nation ". . . the rich and bitter depth of their experience, the unknown treasures of their inner life, the strange rendings of nature they have seen. . . ." Their gifts outright are priceless, but only when reckoned in their own terms, counted in their separate coin, will the country receive their full benefit.

Actively we have woven ourselves with the very warp and woof of this nation,—we fought their battles, shared their sorrow, mingled our blood with theirs, and generation after generation have pleaded with a headstrong, careless people to despise not Justice, Mercy, and Truth, lest the nation be smitten with a curse. Our song, our toil, our cheer, and warning have been given to this nation in blood-brotherhood. Are not these gifts worth the giving? Is not this work and striving? Would America have been America without her Negro people?

DuBois first achieved prominence as the guiding spirit of the NAACP in 1909 and as the editor of the organization's magazine, *The Crisis,* in 1910. Later he became interested in Pan-Africanism and was responsible for the second and third of the six Pan-African Conferences held between 1900 and 1945. A voluminous writer in almost every genre, his historical studies include *The Philadelphia Negro* (1899), *The Souls of Black Folk* (1903), *The Negro* (1915), *Darkwater* (1920), *The Gift of Black Folk* (1929), *Black Reconstruction* (1935), *Black Folk, Then and Now* (1939), and *Color and Democracy* (1945). But there were also books of poetry, and works of fiction and biography and, in 1968, an autobiography. *The Souls of Black Folk* is among the most widely read books of its time; more than 20 editions have been published.

From The Souls of Black Folk

OF OUR SPIRITUAL STRIVINGS

O water, voice of my heart, crying in the sand,
  All night long crying with a mournful cry,
As I lie and listen, and cannot understand
    The voice of my heart in my side or the voice
      of the sea,
    O water, crying for rest, is it I, is it I?
  All night long the water is crying to me.

Unresting water, there shall never be rest
  Till the last moon droop and the last tide fail,
And the fire of the end begin to burn in the west;
    And the heart shall be weary and wonder and cry
      like the sea,
  All life long crying without avail,
    As the water all night long is crying to me.

ARTHUR SYMONS.[1]

Between me and the other world there is ever an unasked question: unasked by some through feelings of delicacy; by others through the difficulty of rightly framing it. All, nevertheless, flutter round it. They approach me in a half-hesitant sort of way, eye me curiously or compassionately, and then, instead of saying directly, How does it feel to be a problem? they say, I know an excellent colored man in my town; or, I fought at Mechanicsville; or, Do not these Southern outrages make your blood boil? At these I smile, or am interested, or reduce the boiling to a simmer, as the occasion may require. To the real question, How does it feel to be a problem? I answer seldom a word.

And yet, being a problem is a strange experience,—peculiar even for one who has never been anything else, save perhaps in babyhood and in Europe. It is in the early days of rollicking boyhood that the revelation first bursts upon one, all in a day, as it were. I remember well when the shadow swept across me. I was a little thing, away up in the hills of New England, where the dark Housatonic winds between Hoosac and Taghkanic to the sea. In a wee wooden schoolhouse, something put it into the boys' and girls' heads to buy gorgeous visiting-cards—ten cents a package—and exchange. The exchange was merry, till one girl, a tall newcomer, refused my card,—refused it peremptorily, with a glance. Then it dawned upon me with a certain suddenness that I was different from the others; or like, mayhap, in heart and

[1] Arthur Symons (1865-1945), English poet and literary critic.

life and longing, but shut out from their world by a vast veil. I had thereafter no desire to tear down that veil, to creep through; I held all beyond it in common contempt, and lived above it in a region of blue sky and great wandering shadows. That sky was bluest when I could beat my mates at examination-time, or beat them at a foot-race, or even beat their stringy heads. Alas, with the years all this fine contempt began to fade; for the worlds I longed for, and all their dazzling opportunities, were theirs, not mine. But they should not keep these prizes, I said; some, all, I would wrest from them. Just how I would do it I could never decide: by reading law, by healing the sick, by telling the wonderful tales that swam in my head,—some way. With other black boys the strife was not so fiercely sunny: their youth shrunk into tasteless sycophancy, or into silent hatred of the pale world about them and mocking distrust of everything white; or wasted itself in a bitter cry, Why did God make me an outcast and a stranger in mine own house? The shades of the prison-house closed round about us all: walls strait and stubborn to the whitest, but relentlessly narrow, tall, and unscalable to sons of night who must plod darkly on in resignation, or beat unavailing palms against the stone, or steadily, half hopelessly, watch the streak of blue above.

After the Egyptian and Indian, the Greek and Roman, the Teuton and Mongolian, the Negro is a sort of seventh son, born with a veil, and gifted with second-sight in this American world,—a world which yields him no true self-consciousness, but only lets him see himself through the revelation of the other world. It is a peculiar sensation, this double-consciousness, this sense of always looking at one's self through the eyes of others, of measuring one's soul by the tape of a world that looks on in amused contempt and pity. One ever feels his twoness,—an American, a Negro; two souls, two thoughts, two unreconciled strivings; two warring ideals in one dark body, whose dogged strength alone keeps it from being torn asunder.

The history of the American Negro is the history of this strife,—this longing to attain self-conscious manhood, to merge his double self into a better and truer self. In this merging he wishes neither of the older selves to be lost. He would not Africanize America, for America has too much to teach the world and Africa. He would not bleach his Negro soul in a flood of white Americanism, for he knows that Negro blood has a message for the world. He simply wishes to make it possible for a man to be both a Negro and an American, without being cursed and spit upon by his fellows, without having the doors of Opportunity closed roughly in his face.

This, then, is the end of his striving; to be a co-worker in the kingdom of culture, to escape both death and isolation, to husband and use his best powers and his latent genius. These powers of body and mind have in the past been strangely wasted, dispersed, or forgotten. The shadow of a mighty Negro past flits through the tale of Ethiopia the Shadowy and of Egypt the Sphinx. Throughout history, the powers of single black men flash here and there like falling stars, and die sometimes before the world has rightly gauged their brightness. Here in America, in the few days since Emancipation, the black man's turning hither and thither in hesitant and doubtful striving has often made his very strength to lose effectiveness, to seem like absence of power, like weakness. And yet it is not weakness,—it is the contradiction of double aims. The double-aimed struggle of the black artisan—on the one hand to escape white contempt for a nation of mere hewers of wood and drawers of water, and on the other hand to plough and nail and dig for a poverty-stricken horde—could only result in making him a poor craftsman, for he had but half a heart in either cause. By the poverty and ignorance of his people, the Negro minister or doctor was tempted toward quackery and demagogy; and by the criticism of the other world, toward ideals that made him ashamed of his lowly tasks. The would-be black *savant* was confronted by the paradox that the knowledge his people needed was a twice-told tale to his white neighbors, while the knowledge which would teach the white world was Greek to his own flesh and blood. The innate love of harmony and beauty that set the ruder souls of his people a-dancing and a-singing raised but confusion and doubt in the soul of the black artist; for the beauty revealed to him was the soul-beauty of a race which his larger audience despised, and he could not articulate the message of another people. This waste of double aims, this seeking to satisfy two unreconciled ideals, has wrought sad havoc with the courage and faith and deeds of ten thousand thousand people,—has sent them often wooing false gods and invoking false means of salvation, and at times has even seemed about to make them ashamed of themselves.

Away back in the days of bondage they thought to see in one divine event the end of all doubt and disappointment; few men ever worshipped Freedom with half such unquestioning faith as did the American Negro for two centuries. To him, so far as he thought and dreamed, slavery was indeed the sum of all villainies, the cause of all sorrow, the root of all prejudice; Emancipation was the key to a promised land of sweeter beauty than ever stretched before the eyes of wearied Israelites. In song and exhortation swelled one refrain—Liberty; in his tears and curses the God he implored had Freedom in his right hand. At last it came,—suddenly, fearfully, like a dream. With one wild carnival of blood and passion came the message in his own plaintive cadences:—

> "Shout, O children!
> Shout, you're free!
> For God has bought your liberty!"

Years have passed away since then,—ten, twenty, forty; forty years of national life, forty years of renewal and development, and yet the swarthy spectre sits in its accustomed seat at the Nation's feast. In vain do we cry to this our vastest social problem:—

"Take any shape but that, and my firm nerves
Shall never tremble!"

The Nation has not yet found peace from its sins; the freed man has not yet
found in freedom his promised land. Whatever of good may have come in
these years of change, the shadow of a deep disappointment rests upon the
Negro people,—a disappointment all the more bitter because the unattained
ideal was unbounded save by the simple ignorance of a lowly people.

The first decade was merely a prolongation of the vain search for freedom, the boon that seemed ever barely to elude their grasp,—like a tantalizing will-o'-the-wisp, maddening and misleading the headless host. The holocaust of war, the terrors of the Ku-Klux Klan, the lies of carpet-baggers, the
disorganization of industry, and the contradictory advice of friends and foes,
left the bewildered serf with no new watchword beyond the old cry for
freedom. As the time flew, however, he began to grasp a new idea. The ideal
of liberty demanded for its attainment powerful means, and these the Fifteenth Amendment gave him. The ballot, which before he had looked upon
as a visible sign of freedom, he now regarded as the chief means of gaining
and perfecting the liberty with which war had partially endowed him. And
why not? Had not votes made war and emancipated millions? Had not votes
enfranchised the freedmen? Was anything impossible to a power that had
done all this? A million black men started with renewed zeal to vote themselves into the kingdom. So the decade flew away, the revolution of 1876
came, and left the half-free serf weary, wondering but still inspired. Slowly
but steadily, in the following years, a new vision began gradually to replace
the dream of political power,—a powerful movement, the rise of another
ideal to guide the unguided, another pillar of fire by night after a clouded
day. It was the ideal of "book-learning"; the curiosity, born of compulsory
ignorance, to know and test the power of the cabalistic letters of the white
man, the longing to know. Here at last seemed to have been discovered the
mountain path to Canaan; longer than the highway of Emancipation and
law, steep and rugged, but straight, leading to heights high enough to overlook life.

Up the new path the advance guard toiled, slowly, heavily, doggedly;
only those who have watched and guided the faltering feet, the misty minds,
the dull understandings, of the dark pupils of these schools know how faithfully, how piteously, this people strove to learn. It was weary work. The cold
statistician wrote down the inches of progress here and there, noted also
where here and there a foot had slipped or some one had fallen. To the tired
climbers, the horizon was ever dark, the mists were often cold, the Canaan
was always dim and far away. If, however, the vistas disclosed as yet no goal,
no resting-place, little but flattery and criticism, the journey at least gave
leisure for reflection and self-examination; it changed the child of Emancipation to the youth with dawning self-consciousness, self-realization, self-re-

spect. In those sombre forests of his striving his own soul rose before him, and he saw himself,—darkly as through a veil; and yet he saw in himself some faint revelation of his power, of his mission. He began to have a dim feeling that, to attain his place in the world, he must be himself, and not another. For the first time he sought to analyze the burden he bore upon his back, that deadweight of social degradation partially masked behind a half-named Negro problem. He felt his poverty; without a cent, without a home, without land, tools, or savings, he had entered into competition with rich, landed, skilled neighbors. To be a poor man is hard, but to be a poor race in a land of dollars is the very bottom of hardships. He felt the weight of his ignorance,—not simply of letters, but of life, of business, of the humanities; the accumulated sloth and shirking and awkwardness of decades and centuries shackled his hands and feet. Nor was his burden all poverty and ignorance. The red stain of bastardy, which two centuries of systemic legal defilement of Negro women had stamped upon his race, meant not only the loss of ancient African chastity, but also the hereditary weight of a mass of corruption from white adulterers, threatening almost the obliteration of the Negro home.

A people thus handicapped ought not to be asked to race with the world, but rather allowed to give all its time and thought to its own social problems. But alas! while sociologists gleefully count his bastards and his prostitutes, the very soul of the toiling, sweating black man is darkened by the shadow of a vast despair. Men call the shadow prejudice, and learnedly explain it as the natural defense of culture against barbarism, learning against ignorance, purity against crime, the "higher" against the "lower" races. To which the Negro cries Amen! and swears that to so much of this strange prejudice as is founded on just homage to civilization, culture, righteousness, and progress, he humbly bows and meekly does obeisance. But before that nameless prejudice that leaps beyond all this he stands helpless, dismayed, and well-nigh speechless; before that personal disrespect and mockery, the ridicule and systematic humiliation, the distortion of fact and wanton license of fancy, the cynical ignoring of the better and the boisterous welcoming of the worse, the all-pervading desire to inculcate disdain for everything black, from Toussaint to the devil,—before this there rises a sickening despair that would disarm and discourage any nation save that black host to whom "discouragement" is an unwritten word.

But the facing of so vast a prejudice could not but bring the inevitable self-questioning, self-disparagement, and lowering of ideals which ever accompany repression and breed in an atmosphere of contempt and hate. Whispering and portents came borne upon the four winds: Lo! we are diseased and dying, cried the dark hosts; we cannot write, our voting is vain; what need of education, since we must always cook and serve? And the Nation echoed and enforced this self-criticism, saying: Be content to be servants, and nothing more; what need of higher culture for half-men? Away with the black man's ballot, by force or fraud,—and behold the suicide of a race! Nevertheless, out of the evil came something of good,—the more careful adjustment of education to real life, the clearer perception of the Negroes' social responsibilities, and the sobering realization of the meaning of progress.

So dawned the time of *Sturm und Drang:* storm and stress to-day rocks our little boat on the mad waters of the world-sea; there is within and without the sound of conflict, the burning of body and rending of soul; inspiration strives with doubt, and faith with vain questionings. The bright ideals of the past,—physical freedom, political power, the training of brains and the training of hands,—all these in turn have waxed and waned, until even the last grows dim and overcast. Are they all wrong,—all false? No, not that, but each alone was over-simple and incomplete,—the dreams of a credulous race, childhood, or the fond imaginings of the other world which does not know and does not want to know our power. To be really true, all these ideals must be melted and welded into one. The training of the schools we need to-day more than ever,—the training of deft hands, quick eyes and ears, and above all the broader, deeper, higher culture of gifted minds and pure hearts. The power of the ballot we need in sheer self-defence,—else what shall save us from a second slavery? Freedom, too, the long-sought, we still seek,—the freedom of life and limb, the freedom to work and think, the freedom to love and aspire. Work, culture, liberty,—all these we need, not singly but together, not successively but together, each growing and aiding each, and all striving toward that vaster ideal that swims before the Negro people, the ideal of human brotherhood, gained through the unifying ideal of Race; the ideal of fostering and developing the traits and talents of the Negro, not in opposition to or contempt for other races, but rather in large conformity to the greater ideals of the American Republic, in order that some day on American soil two world-races may give each to each those characteristics both so sadly lack. We the darker ones come even now not altogether empty-handed: there are to-day no truer exponents of the pure human spirit of the Declaration of Independence than the American Negroes; there is no true American music but the wild sweet melodies of the Negro slave; the American fairy tales and folk-lore are Indian and African; and, all in all, we black men seem the sole oasis of simple faith and reverence in a dusty desert of dollars and smartness. Will America be poorer if she replace her brutal dyspeptic blundering with light-hearted but determined Negro humility? or her coarse and cruel wit with loving jovial good-humor? or her vulgar music with the soul of the Sorrow Songs?

Merely a concrete test of the underlying principles of the great republic is the Negro Problem, and the spiritual striving of the freedmen's sons is the travail of souls whose burden is almost beyond the measure of their strength, but who bear it in the name of an historic race, in the name of this the land of their fathers' fathers, and in the name of human opportunity.

JOSEPH FREEMAN

(1897-   )

A recurring issue in American literary history concerns right relationships between the poet and the people, the writer and ordinary workers, literature and social justice. And dispute in this area reached its highest intensity, perhaps, in the 1920's and 1930's, when writers on the American left argued ferociously among themselves and against aesthetes and apathetes outside about the revolutionary role and meaning of letters. A continuing focus in the dispute was the Soviet Union and the sometimes ambiguous stages by which socialist revolution was transformed into totalitarianism, wherein individual deviancy on the part of artists was not tolerated, and writers who made the mistake of referring to one or another "enemy of the revolution" as a person rather than as a monster could themselves be branded as criminals.

Among the scores of American poets, novelists, journalists, and critics who entered this argument, Joseph Freeman is particularly notable. The forceful "introduction" he contributed to a collection of left-oriented writing, *Proletarian Literature in the United States* (1935), was exceptional for its grasp of the truth that writing "on the people's side" need not be a mere assemblage of pious political abstraction, and that, depending on its quality, it might become the means by which a whole new continent of experience and feeling became available to contemporary minds. Freeman, the son of Ukrainian-Jewish immigrants, who came to America shortly after the turn of the century, spent his early youth in a poverty-struck Brooklyn ghetto. He graduated from Columbia in 1920, and for nearly twenty years thereafter was in the thick of the radical movement, first as an expatriate in Paris and newspaper correspondent in London and elsewhere, then as writer, reporter, editor, lecturer, and party activist in the Communist movement in America. In 1926, serving as translator for the American delegation to the plenum session of the Communist International's Executive Committee, he heard the last debate between Stalin and Trotsky; by 1939, after a long and tortured effort to maintain an independent stance as a left intellectual, he was denounced and expelled by Communist party leaders. His novel *Never Call Retreat* (1935) is a remarkable probe of two decades of involvement and disillusionment with revolutionary political struggle.

Introduction

Whatever rôle art may have played in epochs preceding ours, whatever may be its function in the classless society of the future, social war today has made it the subject of partisan polemic. The form of polemic varies with the social class for which the critic speaks, as well as with his personal intelligence, integrity, and courage. The Communist says frankly: art, an instrument in the class struggle, must be developed by the proletariat as one of its weapons. The fascist, with equal frankness, says: art must serve the aims of the capitalist state. The liberal, speaking for the middle class which vacillates between monopoly capital and the proletariat, between fascism and communism, poses as the "impartial" arbiter in this, as in all other social disputes. He alone presumes to speak from above the battle, in the "scientific" spirit.

Wrapping himself in linen, donning rubber gloves, and lifting his surgical instruments—all stage props—the Man in White, the "impartial" liberal critic, proceeds to lecture the assembled boys and girls on the anatomy of art in the quiet, disinterested voice of the old trouper playing the rôle of "science." He has barely finished his first sentence, when it becomes clear that his lofty "scientific" spirit drips with the bitter gall of partisan hatred. Long before he approaches the vaguest semblance of an idea, the Man in White assaults personalities and parties. We are reading, it turns out, not a scientific treatise on art but a political pamphlet. To characterize an essay or a book as a political pamphlet is neither to praise nor to condemn it. Such pamphlets have their place in the world. In the case of the liberal critic, however, we have a political pamphlet which pretends to be something else. We have an attack on the theory of art as a political weapon which turns out to be itself a political weapon.

The liberal's quarrel with the Marxists does not spring from the desire to defend a new and original theory. After the ideals are sifted from the abuse, the theories from the polemics, we find nothing more than a series of commonplaces, unhappily wedded to a series of negations. The basic commonplace is that art is something different from action and something different from science. It is hard to understand why anyone should pour out bottles of ink to labor so obvious and elementary a point. No one has ever denied it, least of all the Marxists. We have always recognized that there is a difference between poetry and science, between poetry and action; that life extends beyond statistics, indices, resolutions. To labor that idea with showers of abuse on the heads of the "Marxists-Leninists" is not dispassionate science but polemics, and very dishonest polemics at that.

The problem is: what, in the class society of today, is the relation between art and society, art and science, art and action. It is true that the specific province of art, as distinguished from action or science, is the grasp and transmission of human experience. But is any human experience changeless and universal? Are the humans of the twelfth century the same in their specific experience as the humans of the twentieth? Is life, experience, thought, emotion, the same for the knight of 1300, the young merchant of 1400, the discoverer of 1500, the adventurer of 1600, the scientist of 1700, the factory owner of 1800, the banker of 1900, the worker of 1935? Is there no difference in the "experience" grasped and transmitted by Catholic and Protestant poets, by feudal and bourgeois playwrights, by Broadway and the Theatre Union? Is Heine's social experience the same as Archibald Mac-Leish's? Is the love experience of Pietro Aretino the same as T. S. Eliot's?

We may say that these are all personal differences: experience is an individual affair and individuals differ from age to age. Yet nothing is more obvious than the social, the *class* basis of fundamental differences. Greeks of the slave-owning class, for all their individual differences, had more in common with each other than any of them has with the bourgeois poets of the Romantic school; the Romantics, for all their individual differences and conflicts, had more in common with each other than with individuals of similar temperament in Soviet letters or American fiction.

Art, then, is not same as action; it is not identical with science; it is distinct from party program. It has its own special function, the grasp and transmission of experience. The catch lies in the word "experience." The liberal critic, the Man in White, wants us to believe that when you write about the autumn wind blowing a girl's hair or about "thirsting breasts," you are writing about "experience"; but when you write about the October Revolution, or the Five Year Plan, or the lynching of Negroes in the South, or the San Francisco strike you are not writing about "experience." Hence to say: "bed your desire among the pressing grasses" is *art;* while *Roar China,* Mayakovsky's poems, or the novels of Josephine Herbst and Robert Cantwell are *propaganda.*

Studying the life of their own country, Soviet critics observed that the poet deals with living people, not with abstractions. He conveys the tremendous experience of the revolution through the personal experience of individual beings who participate in it, fight for or against it, help to forward or retard its purposes, are in turn refashioned by it. He describes people who make friends and enemies, love women and are loved by them, work mightily to transform the land. All this the artist—if he is an artist and not an agitator—does with the specific technique of his craft. He does not repeat party theses; he communicates that experience out of which the theses arose. In so far as the artist's deepest thoughts and feelings are bound to the old régime, in so far as he experiences life with the mind and heart of a bourgeois, the experience he conveys will be seen with the eyes of the bourgeois. Such a poet will best understand all those weaknesses of the revolution which have their roots in the old, that is near and dear to him; he will be blind to the greatness of the revolution which springs from the new, that is alien to him. He will create a false picture of Soviet reality; he will discourage people who read and believe him. But whether an artist grasps the true course of the revolution or is blind to it, his work is not divorced from science and action and class.

No party resolution, no government decree can produce art, or transform an agitator into a poet. A party card does not automatically endow a Communist with artistic genius. Whatever it is that makes an artist, as distinguished from a scientist or a man of action, it is something beyond the power of anyone to produce deliberately. But once the artist is here, once there is the man with the specific sensibility, the mind, the emotions, the images, the gift for language which make the creative writer, he is not a creature in a vacuum.

The poet describes a flower differently from a botanist, a war differently from a general. Ernest Hemingway's description of the retreat at Carporetto is different from the Italian general staff's; Tretiakov's stories of China are not the same as the resolution on that country by a Comintern plenum. The poet deals with experience rather than theory or action. But the social class to which the poet is attached conditions the nature and flavor of his experience. A Chinese poet of the proletariat of necessity conveys to us experiences different from those of a poet attached to Chiang Kai Shek or a bourgeois poet who thinks he is above the battle. Moreover, in an era of bitter class war such as ours, party programs, collective actions, class purposes, when they are enacted in life, themselves become experiences—experiences so great, so far-reaching, so all-inclusive that, *as experiences,* they transcend flirtations and autumn winds and stars and nightingales and getting drunk in Paris cafés. It is a petty mind indeed which cannot conceive how men in the Soviet Union, even poets, may be moved more by the vast transformation of an entire people from darkness to light, from poverty to security, from weakness to strength, from bondage to freedom, than by their own personal sensations as loafers or lovers. He is indeed lost in the morass of philistinism who is blind to the *experience,* the *emotion* aroused by the struggle of the workers in all capitalist countries to emancipate themselves and to create a new world.

Here lies the key to the dispute current in American literary circles. No one says the artist should cease being an artist; no one urges him to ignore experience. The question is: what constitutes experience? Only he who is remote from the revolution, if not directly hostile to it, can look upon the poet whose experiences are those of the proletariat as being nothing more than "an adjunct, a servitor, a pedagogue, and faithful illustrator," while the poet who lives the life of the bourgeois, whose experiences are the self-indulgences of the philistine, "asserts with self-dependent force" the sovereignty of art. Art, however it may differ in its specific nature from science and action, is never wholly divorced from them. It is no more self-dependent and sovereign than science and action are self-dependent and sovereign. To speak of art in those terms is to follow the priests who talk of the church, and the politicians who talk of the state, as being self-dependent and sovereign. In all these cases the illusion of self-dependence and sovereignty are propagated in order to conceal the class-nature of society, to cover the propagandist of the ruling class with the mantle of impartiality.

In the name of art and by the vague term experience, accompanied by pages of abuse against the Communists, the ideologues of the ruling class have added another intellectual sanction for the *status quo*. What they are really saying is that only *their* experience is experience. They are ignorant of or hate proletarian experience; hence for them it is not experience at all and not a fit subject for art. But if art is to be divorced from the "development of knowledge" and the "technique of scientific action," if it is to ignore politics and the class struggle—matters of the utmost importance in the life of the workers—what sort of experience is left to art? Only the experience of personal sensation, emotion, and conduct, the experience of the parasitic classes. Such art is produced today by bourgeois writers. Their experience is class-conditioned, but, as has always been the case with the bourgeoisie, they pretend that their values are the values of humanity.

If you were to take a worker gifted with a creative imagination and ask him to set down his experience honestly, it would be an experience so remote from that of the bourgeois that the Man in White would, as usual, raise the cry of "propaganda." Yet the worker's life revolves precisely around those experiences which are alien to the bourgeois aesthete, who loathes them, who cannot believe they are experiences at all. To the Man in White it seems that only a decree from Moscow could force people to write about factories, strikes, political discussions. He knows that only force would compel *him* to write about such things; he would never do it of his own free will, since the themes of proletarian literature are outside his own life. But the worker writes about the very experiences which the bourgeois labels "propaganda," those experiences which reveal the exploitation upon which the prevailing society is based.

Often the writer who describes the contemporary world from the viewpoint of the proletariat is not himself a worker. War, unemployment, a widespread social-economic crisis drive middle-class writers into the ranks of the proletariat. Their experience becomes contiguous to or identical with that of the working class; they see their former life, and the life of everyone around them with new eyes; their grasp of experience is conditioned by the class to which they have now attached themselves; they write from the viewpoint of the revolutionary proletariat; they create what is called proletarian literature.

The class basis of art is most obvious when a poem, play, or novel deals with a political theme. Readers and critics then react to literature, as they do to life, in an unequivocal manner. There is a general assumption, however, that certain "biologic" experiences transcend class factors. Love, anger, hatred, fear, the desire to please, to pose, to mystify, even vanity and self-love, may be universal motives; but the form they take, and above all the factors which arouse them, are conditioned, even determined, by class culture. Consider Proust's superb study of a dying aristocracy and a bourgeoisie in full bloom; note the things which rouse pride, envy, shame in a Charlus or a Madame Verdurin. Can anyone in his senses say that these things—an invitation to a party at a duke's home, a long historical family tree—would stir a worker to the boastful eloquence of a Guermantes or a Verdurin? Charlus might be angry at Charlie Morel for deceiving him with a midinette; could the Baron conceive what it is to be angry with a foreman for being fired?

Art at its best does not deal with abstract anger. When it does it becomes abstract and didactic. The best art deals with specific experience which arouses specific emotion in specific people at a specific moment in a specific locale, in such a way that other people who have had similar experiences in other places and times recognize it as their own. Jack Conroy, to whom a Proustian salon with its snobbish pride, envy, and shame is a closed world, can describe the pride, envy, and shame of a factory. We may recognize analogies between the *feelings* of the salon and those of the factory, but the objects and events which arouse them are different. And since no feeling can exist without an object or event, art must of necessity deal with specific experience, even if only obliquely, by evasion and flight. The liberal critic who concludes that all literature *except proletarian literature* is equally sincere and artistic, that every poet *except the proletarian poet* is animated by "experience," "life," "human values," has abandoned the search before it has really begun. The creative writer's motives, however "human" they may be, however analogous to the motives of the savage, are modified by his social status, his class, or the class to which he is emotionally and intellectually attached, from whose viewpoint he sees the world around him.

Is there any writer, however remote his theme or language may seem at first glance from contemporary reality, however "sincere" and "artistic" his creations may be, whose work is not in some way conditioned by the political state in which he lives, by the knowledge of his time, by the attitudes of his class, by the revolution which he loves, hates, or seeks to ignore? What is the *real* antagonism involved in the fake and academic antagonism between "experience" on the one hand and the state, education, science, revolution on the other? This question is all the more significant since the best literary minds of all times have agreed on some kind of social sanction for art, from Plato and Aristotle to Wordsworth and Shelley, to Voronsky and I. A. Richards. Recent attempts to destroy the "Marxo-Leninist aesthetics" fall into a morass of idealistic gibberish. The term "experience" becomes an abstract, metaphysical concept, like "life" or the "Idea" or the "Absolute." But even the most abstract metaphysical concept, like the most fantastic dream, conceals a reality.

Let us examine one typical example of this metaphysical concept. Recently a bourgeois critic cited the following words by Karl Marx: "At a certain stage of their development, the material forces of production in society come in conflict with the existing relations of production, or, what is but a legal expression for the same thing, with the property relations within which they had been at work before. From forms of development of the forces of production, these relations turn into their fetters. Then comes the period of social revolution. With the change of the economic foundation, the entire immense superstructure is more or less rapidly transformed." The critic commented that this was a *true scientific description of a social law;* in the future some "intellectually inventive" artist might write a poem in which this thought would be "greatly and spontaneously portrayed." But, he added, no man "can get into a position to experience a revolution concretely in those terms." Therefore, the attempt "to convey the conception in concrete images and pictures will be *normally a tour de force.*"

Our author himself underlined the word *normally.* That indeed is the significant word not only in the essay, but in the entire campaign which bourgeois ideologues have been conducting against proletarian literature. If Karl Marx's law is true, as the conservative critic admits, then the process it describes involves every individual in capitalist society, even when he is utterly ignorant of Marx's formulation. The worker may never have heard of Marx, but he knows that the factory is overstocked with goods, that he is unemployed, that he is unable to purchase the goods he has produced. He may not know the phrases about the conflict between the material forces of production and the existing relations of production; he may accept the explanation of demagogues like Roosevelt, General Johnson, Father Coughlin, Huey Long, or Phil La Follette; but he knows the *facts*, his "experience" consists of those facts.

Let us now suppose that a given worker is a gifted story-teller, yet ignorant of Marxian theory. He accurately describes his own specific experiences at the moment when the social revolution breaks out, as many Russian, German, Hungarian, Mexican, and Chinese workers have done. Such a worker would not be writing an *illustration* of the *Communist Manifesto* any more than the bee's conduct is an illustration of Fabre's famous book. The worker's experience, however, would sustain Marx's theory, otherwise the theory would not be true. The worker's poetic rendering of the specific experience would be art, as Marx's summation of that experience is science. Nor would such a story be for the *worker* or the intellectual *writing from the worker's standpoint* a *tour de force:* It would be a "natural," "free" expression of experience.

But is the worker or the intellectual who identifies himself with the worker *normal?* Remember, the conservative critic I cited only said that *normally* the attempt to convey Marx's concept in concrete images and pictures would be a *tour de force*. From the viewpoint of the bourgeois aesthete, the worker is apparently not normal, just as the experience of the worker or of the crushed middle-class is not experience. The "normal" poet is the bourgeois poet; "experience" is bourgeois experience. It is only if we make that false assumption that the *tour de force* becomes inevitable. Only when an aesthete lives the life of a bourgeois and attempts intellectually to be a "Communist" does the dualism here involved arise. For the Man in White art develops out of experience and experience is bourgeois; he can conceive of writing about proletarian life, which Marx has described scientifically, only as an intellectual *tour de force*, only by reading a Communist book and then "with a teacherly intention and a sufficiently deliberate ingenuity" attempt to "show" the Marxian concept, admittedly true, in images and pictures. Such a man, naturally, is compelled to a *tour de force*, to very bad "proletarian art"; he proceeds from the general to the specific instead of from the specific to the general.

We have had such writings in the revolutionary press, nearly always from intellectuals new to the movement. It is well known that American Marxist critics have fought against this tendency. We have maintained for years that to put a Comintern resolution in rhyme does not make proletarian poetry. It is better for the poet honestly to describe his real experiences, his doubts and inner conflicts, and the external circumstances which brought him to the revolutionary movement, than to fake his feelings by rehashing and corrupting political manifestoes which we prefer to read in their original form. But the intellectual who sympathizes with the proletariat in the abstract and continues his bourgeois life in the concrete is bound to resort to a *tour de force*. Such a poet can only write of his bourgeois experience; he must violate his real feelings when he attempts to translate Marxian science into art. It is when the intellectual describes his own conflicts sincerely that he can create revolutionary art; it is when he has transformed his life, when his experience is in the ranks of the advanced proletariat that he begins to create proletarian art.

Art varies with experience; its so-called sanctions vary with experience. The experience of the mass of humanity today is such that social and political themes are more interesting, more significant, more "normal" than the personal themes of other eras. Social themes today correspond to the general experience of men, acutely conscious of the violent and basic transformations through which they are living, which they are helping to bring about. It does not require much imagination to see why workers and intellectuals sympathetic to the working class—and themselves victims of the general social-economic crisis—should be more interested in unemployment, strikes, the fight against war and fascism, revolution and counter-revolution than in nightingales, the stream of the middle-class unconscious, or love in Greenwich Village.

JAMES AGEE

(1909–1955)

Born in Knoxville, Tennessee, James Agee was educated at Philips Exeter and Harvard. He began his career as a poet [*Permit Me Voyage* (1934)] and went on to become a magazine journalist *(Fortune, Time, The Nation)* and a screenwriter, novelist, and playwright. *A Death in the Family,* a novel published posthumously in 1957, won the Pulitzer Prize; his film criticism [collected in *Agee on Film: Review and Comments* (1958)] and a volume of original scripts brought out in 1960 *(Agee on Film, Volume II, Five Film Scripts)* have also been highly praised.

Nothing Agee wrote, however, matters one-tenth as much as *Let Us Now Praise Famous Men* (1941), an account of the 8 weeks in 1936 that he spent in Alabama interviewing, photographing, living with, and coming to cherish three tenant families. And no major book of this period seems on its face more determined to put its reader off. The epigraph echoes King Lear's cry, "Expose thyself to feel as wretches feel," but the author's initial and recurrent manner is of fierce anger and bitterness. The *New York Times'* obituary for Agee described the book as "arrogant, mannered, precious, gross," and parts of it are even harder to take than those labels suggest. Agee attacks his readers as boors, his publishers as corrupt, the purchase of the book as obscene:

> [this book] is written for all those who have a soft place in their hearts for the laughter and tears inherent in poverty viewed at a distance, and especially for those who can afford the retail price; in the hope that the reader will be edified, and may feel kindly disposed toward any well-thought out liberal efforts to rectify the unpleasant situation down South, and will somewhat better and more guiltily appreciate the next good meal he eats; and in the hope, too, that he will recommend this little book to really sym-

Agee's fiction includes *The Morning Watch,* 1951; and *A Death in the Family,* 1957, published posthumously. His poetry is in *Permit Me Voyage,* 1934. Film criticism is in *Agee on Film: Reviews and Comments,* 1958; film scripts appear in *Agee on Film, Vol. II: Five Film Scripts,* 1960. His non-fiction book is *Let Us Now Praise Famous Men,* 1941, with Walker Evans.

An interesting perspective on Agee may be found in *The Letters of James Agee to Father Flye,* 1962. Peter Ohlin has written *Agee,* 1966, and *James Agee: Promise and Fulfillment,* 1968. An assessment is Kenneth Seib, *James Agee,* 1968.

pathetic friends, in order that our publishers may at least cover
their investment and that (just the merest perhaps) some kindly
thought may be turned our way, and a little of your money fall to
poor little us.

This is an outrageous as well as outraged man, and his unfocused fury
launches a dozen choked and gratuitous attacks—on illiterate PhDs,
American architecture, the *Partisan Review,* "state normal schools"—
that are both distracting and functionless.

Nor are these the only problems with the book. At times the author
appears trapped in sentimental self-regard, as when a white landlord
summons his Negro tenants to sing for Agee and his collaborator, the
photographer Walker Evans.

> Meanwhile, and during all this singing, I had been sick in the
> knowledge that they felt they were here at our demand, mine and
> Walker's, and that I could communicate nothing otherwise: and
> now, in a perversion of self-torture, I played my part through. I
> gave their leader fifty cents, trying at the same time, through my
> eyes, to communicate much more. . . .

There are tortured harangues about art and life and the impossibility of
trusting words. The rhetoric is steamily pretentious.

> . . . and in each successive instant of the existence of each exis-
> tence not only human being but in him the tallest and most san-
> guine hope of godhead is in a billionate choiring and drone of
> pain of generations upon generations unceasingly crucified and
> is bringing forth crucifixions into their necessities. . . .

More than once the reader wonders whether Agee does in truth trust
his central assumption, reiterated many times—that these lives and
these places are beautiful, "famous," in and for themselves.

But despite the bad temper, the patronizing sense of superiority to
the audience, and the portentous manner, *Let Us Now Praise Famous
Men* is, in its cumulative effect, an overwhelming work. For the subject—the *activity* of the work—is nothing less than the breaking of the
chains of class and caste, the achievement by a single human being of
a realized sense of human solidarity, and the frustration, thereafter, of
attempting to share that sense with those who cannot, in the nature of
things, know what you are talking about. Agee's bluster, like his earnestness, is a face of his guilt. The man, himself a privileged son of
Exeter and Harvard, sees a vision of interconciliation and interdepen-

dence, desperately flings after it—and after a language capable of showing forth its meaning to others. But how much can be said? How much is expressible? It is frustration with the segmentation of society that drives this writer to his own boorishness and gracelessness and, by a paradox, it is the force of that frustration, binding itself into words, coiling, reaching, longing, falling away again, that ultimately persuades us of the momentousness of the enterprise and of the fundamental integrity of the writer.

And at length, to repeat, he does break free. This is not alone a book about James Agee. It is about tenant families, their homes, work, temperament, about George Gudger and his wife who, awakened in the middle of the night, insist on feeding their unexpected guest.

> . . . people plain enough take a much more profoundly courteous care of one another and of themselves without much if any surprise and no flurry of fussiness and a kind of respect which does not much ask questions. So it was there was neither any fake warmth or heartiness nor any coldness in his saying, Sure, come on in, to my asking could he put me up for the night after all, and he added, Better eat some supper . . . and she sits a little away from the table out of courtesy, trying to hold her head up and her eyes open, until I shall have finished eating, saying at one time how it's an awful poor sort of supper and at another how it's awful plain, mean food. . . .

Agee catalogs contents of their house: "The broom stands in the corner at the foot of the table and above, on nails, hang the round crockery head of the churn, and the dasher." Clothes, schoolbooks, and wall decorations are described with extraordinary intensity, as if the writer were obedient to an iron imperative of completeness. But well before the end the separateness of the observer and the observed burns off, most movingly, and we grasp that this writer, transcending anger and posing, has come to recognize himself as son and brother to the Gudgers, to accept and be accepted with perfect openness, respect, and simplicity.

> Over by the toolshed of fresh pine a negro, harnessing his team, threw back his head and looked into the sun and sang, shouting, a phrase which sprang out of his throat like a wet green branch. Gudger said he was agoin to have to git on to work now. I told him I sure was obliged to him for taking me in last night and he said he was glad to have holp me.

From Let Us Now Praise Famous Men

NEAR A CHURCH

It was a good enough church from the moment the curve opened and we saw it that I slowed a little and we kept our eyes on it. But as we came even with it the light so held it that it shocked us with its goodness straight through the body, so that at the same instant we said *Jesus.* I put on the brakes and backed the car slowly, watching the light on the building, until we were at the same apex, and we sat still for a couple of minutes at least before getting out, studying in arrest what had hit us so hard as we slowed past its perpendicular.

It lost nothing at all in stasis, but even more powerfully strove in through the eyes its paralyzing classicism: stood from scoured clay, a light lift above us, no trees near, and few weeds; every grain, each nailhead, distinct, the subtle almost strangling strong asymmetries of that which has been hand wrought toward symmetry (as if it were an earnest description, better than the intended object): so intensely sprung against so scarcely eccentric a balance that my hands of themselves spread out their bones, trying to regiment on air between their strengths its tensions and their mutual structures as they stood subject to the only scarcely eccentric, almost annihilating stress, of the serene, wild, rigorous light: empty, shut, bolted, of all that was now withdrawn from it upon the fields the utter statement, God's mask and wooden skull and home stood empty in the meditation of the sun: and this light upon it was strengthening still further its imposal and embrace, and in about a quarter of an hour would have trained itself ready, and there would be a triple convergence in the keen historic spasm of the shutter.

I helped get the camera ready and we stood away and I watched what would be trapped, possessed, fertilized, in the leisures and shyness which are a phase of all love for any object: searching out and registering in myself all its lines, planes, stresses of relationship, along diagonals withdrawn and approached, and vertical to the slightly off-centered door, and broadside, and at several distances, and near, examining merely the ways of the wood, and the nails, the three new boards of differing lengths that were let in above the left of the door, the staring small white porcelain knob, the solesmoothed stairlifts, the wrung stance of thick steeple, the hewn wood stoblike spike at sky, the old hasp and new padlock, the randomshuttered windowglass whose panes were like the surfaces of springs, the fat gold fly who sang and botched against a bright pane within, and within, the rigid benches, box organ, bright stops, hung charts, wrecked hymnals, the platform, pine lectern doilied, pressed-glass pitcher, suspended lamp, four funeral chairs, the little stove

with long swan throat aluminum in the hard sober shade, a button in sun, a
flur of lint, a torn card of Jesus among children:

While we were wondering whether to force a window, a young negro
couple came past up the road. Without appearing to look either longer or
less long, or with more or less interest, than a white man might care for, and
without altering their pace, they made thorough observation of us, of the car,
and of the tripod and camera. We spoke and nodded, smiling as if casually;
they spoke and nodded, gravely, as they passed, and glanced back once, not
secretly, nor long, nor in amusement. They made us, in spite of our knowledge of our own meanings, ashamed and insecure in our wish to break into
and possess their church, and after a minute or two I decided to go after
them and speak to them, and ask them if they knew where we might find a
minister or some other person who might let us in, if it would be all right.
They were fifty yards or so up the road, walking leisurely, and following
them, I watched aspects of them which are less easily seen (as surrounding
objects are masked by looking into a light) when one's own eyes and face and
the eyes and face of another are mutually visible and appraising. They were
young, soberly buoyant of the body, and strong, the man not quite thin, the
girl not quite plump, and I remembered their mild and sober faces, hers
softly wide and sensitive to love and to pleasure, and his resourceful and
intelligent without intellect and without guile, and their extreme dignity,
which was as effortless, unvalued, and undefended in them as the assumption
of superiority which suffuses a rich and social adolescent boy; and I was
taking pleasure also in the competence and rhythm of their walking in the
sun, which was incapable of being less than a muted dancing, and in the
beauty in the sunlight of their clothes, which were strange upon them in the
middle of the week. He was in dark trousers, black dress shoes, a new-
laundered white shirt with lights of bluing in it, and a light yellow, soft straw
hat with a broad band of dark flowered cloth and a daisy in the band; she
glossy-legged without stockings, in freshly whited pumps, a flowered pink
cotton dress, and a great sun of straw set far back on her head. Their swung
hands touched gently with their walking, stride by stride, but did not engage.
I was walking more rapidly than they but quietly; before I had gone ten
steps they turned their heads (toward each other) and looked at me briefly
and impersonally, like horses in a field, and faced front again; and this, I am
almost certain, not through having heard sound of me, but through a subtler
sense. By the time I raised my hand, they had looked away, and did not see
me, though nothing in their looking had been quick with abruptness or
surreptition. I walked somewhat faster now, but I was overtaking them a
little slowly for my patience, the light would be right by now or very soon;
I had no doubt Walker would do what he wanted whether we had 'permission' or not, but I wanted to be on hand, and broke into a trot. At the sound
of the twist of my shoe in the gravel, the young woman's whole body was
jerked down tight as a fist into a crouch from which immediately, the rear

foot skidding in the loose stone so that she nearly fell, like a kicked cow scrambling out of a creek, eyes crazy, chin stretched tight, she sprang forward into the first motions of a running not human but that of a suddenly terrified wild animal. In this same instant the young man froze, the emblems of sense in his wild face wide open toward me, his right hand stiff toward the girl who, after a few strides, her consciousness overtaking her reflex, shambled to a stop and stood, not straight but sick, as if hung from a hook in the spine of the will not to fall for weakness, while he hurried to her and put his hand on her flowered shoulder and, inclining his head forward and sidewise as if listening, spoke with her, and they lifted, and watched me while, shaking my head, and raising my hand palm outward, I came up to them (not trotting) and stopped a yard short of where they, closely, not touching now, stood, and said, still shaking my head (*No; no; oh, Jesus, no, no, no!*) and looking into their eyes; at the man, who was not knowing what to do, and at the girl, whose eyes were lined with tears, and who was trying so hard to subdue the shaking in her breath, and whose heart I could feel, though not hear, blasting as if it were my whole body, and I trying in some fool way to keep it somehow relatively light, because I could not bear that they should receive from me any added reflection of the shattering of their grace and dignity, and of the nakedness and depth and meaning of their fear, and of my horror and pity and self-hatred; and so, smiling, and so distressed that I wanted only that they should be restored, and should know I was their friend, and that I might melt from existence: 'I'm *very sorry!* I'm *very* sorry if I scared you! I didn't mean to scare you at all. I wouldn't have done any such thing for anything.'

They just kept looking at me. There was no more for them to say than for me. The least I could have done was to throw myself flat on my face and embrace and kiss their feet. That impulse took hold of me so powerfully, from my whole body, not by thought, that I caught myself from doing it exactly and as scarcely as you snatch yourself from jumping from a sheer height: here, with the realization that it would have frightened them still worse (to say nothing of me) and would have been still less explicable; so that I stood and looked into their eyes and loved them, and wished to God I was dead. After a little the man got back his voice, his eyes grew a little easier, and he said without conviction that that was all right and that I hadn't scared her. She shook her head slowly, her eyes on me; she did not yet trust her voice. Their faces were secret, soft, utterly without trust of me, and utterly without understanding; and they had to stand here now and hear what I was saying, because in that country no negro safely walks away from a white man, or even appears not to listen while he is talking, and because I could not walk away abruptly, and relieve them of me, without still worse a crime against nature than the one I had committed, and the second I was committing by staying, and holding them. And so, and in this horrid grinning of faked casualness, I gave them a better reason why I had followed them than to frighten them, asked what I had followed them to ask; they said the thing it is usually safest for negroes to say, that they did not know; I thanked them very much, and was seized once more and beyond resistance with the wish to clarify and set right, so that again, with my eyes and smile wretched and out of key with all I was able to say, I said I was awfully sorry if I had bothered them; but they only retreated still more profoundly behind their faces, their eyes watching mine as if awaiting any sudden move they must ward, and the young man said again that that was all right, and I nodded, and turned away from them, and walked down the road without looking back.

RICHARD WRIGHT

(1908-1960)

Richard Wright was born in 1908 near Natchez, Mississippi. His father was a sharecropper who soon deserted the family, and his mother a struggling domestic worker until, when Wright was still a child, she became a helpless invalid. He fled this harsh life fast, to Chicago and New York, where he was involved for a dozen years with the Communist Party; during this period he published, in a 1937 anthology of work by members of the Federal Writers' Project, a piece called "The Ethics of Living Jim Crow." A bitterly compressed indictment of the accommodations American blacks must make to survive, the account begins: "My first lesson in how to live as a Negro . . ." The youth learns—through a succession of painful, scarring encounters with the white world, reinforced by admonitions and beatings dealt out "for his own protection" by his family—that in the face of white aggression he must be passive; that if others of his race suffer he must feel only relief at his fortunate escape; that his best protection in the white world is invisi-

Wright's novels are *Native Son* 1940; *The Outsider* 1953; *Savage Holiday,* 1954; *The Long Dream,* 1958; *Lawd Today,* 1963, published posthumously and written in the 1930's. His autobiography is *Black Boy: A Record Of Childhood and Youth,* 1945. Nonfiction includes *12 Million Voices: A Folk History of the Negro in the United States,* 1941; *Black Power,* 1954; *The Color Curtain,* 1956; *Pagan Spain,* 1957; and *White Man, Listen,* 1957.

Collections of short stories are *Uncle Tom's Children,* 1940, and *Eight Men,* 1961.

Biographies and critical studies include Constance Webb, *Richard Wright: A Biography,* 1968; Dan McCall, *The Example of Richard Wright,* 1969; Edward Margolies, *The Art of Richard Wright,* 1969; and Michel Fabre, *The Unfinished Quest of Richard Wright,* 1973.

bility; that sexually he has no rights and must stand by, clownishly, when his women are abused; that whatever aspirations manage, incredibly, to survive in him must be camouflaged; and that the extent of his satisfactions can be only the canny salvaging of pitiful shreds of dignity (managing by ingenious, involuted subterfuge not to remove his hat when a white man enters an elevator).

Wright later fleshed out these sketches into an enormously successful autobiography, *Black Boy* (1945). Violent disillusion is the substance of this book, but even the small, gently registered disappointments are affectingly rendered. (Told that he is to be taken to Memphis on a steamboat, the lad dreams for days about "a huge white boat floating on a vast body of water, but when my mother took me down to the levee on the day of leaving, I saw a tiny, dirty boat that was not at all like the boat I had imagined.") Wherever the black boy looks—home, school, friends, work—he finds only humiliation, deception, brutality; the elements of the life are desertion, hunger, drink (Wright was an alcoholic at age 6), a stint in an orphanage, beatings, lynchings. And the accompanying pain and barrenness are *felt*.

For readers the sense of the dimensions of the impoverishment is carried in the curve of Wright's literary career. As the sequel proved, the story of *Black Boy* was the single story Wright knew. One flawed but important novel, *Native Son* (1940), was a popular success. But after the autobiography Wright's work was almost uniformly disappointing: predictable, overschematic, dry. In 1946 he became a permanent expatriate in Paris, where he was a friend of Gertrude Stein, was visited constantly by distinguished writers, diplomats, and intellectuals, and was closely associated with the circle of Sartre and Simone de Beauvoir. His preoccupation with existential philosophy, his interest in African nationalism, and other factors have been cited in explanation of the declining impact of his writing. Certainly one root of the problem—visible even in his earliest and best writing—was Wright's urgent, self-hating need to separate himself from his own blackness, which expressed itself as contempt for the people closest to him. Even in *Black Boy* he was arguing that common suffering does not unite or make the sufferers kind to one another.

> I used to mull over the strange absence of real kindness in Negroes, how unstable was our tenderness, how lacking in genuine passion we were, how void of great hope, how timid our joy, how bare our traditions, how hollow our memories, how lacking we were in those intangible sentiments that bind man to man, and how shallow was even our despair.

Wright was not oblivious to his own impulse to isolate himself; he felt it as a fearful trap.

> He hated his family because he knew that they were suffering and that he was powerless to help them. He knew that the moment he allowed himself to feel to its fullness how they lived, he would be swept out of himself with fear and despair. So he held toward them an attitude of iron reserve; he lived with them, but behind a wall, a curtain.

Neither did he lack the power to objectify the situation of the loner. About Cross, the chief character of *The Outsider* (1953), he said: "[He] had had no party, no myths, no tradition, no race, no soil, no culture, and no ideas. . . ." But he sought to persuade himself that this abstraction was a clear advantage, because it guaranteed an escape from the blackness he hated. And the delusion cost him heavily. In a brilliant 1951 essay, James Baldwin assessed the cost, while discussing black protest fiction. In these novels, he asserted:

> . . . a necessary dimension has been cut away; this dimension being the relationship that Negroes bear to one another, that depth of involvement and unspoken recognition of shared experience which creates a way of life . . . it is this climate, common to most Negro protest novels, which has led us all to believe that in Negro life there exists no tradition, no field of manners, no possibility of ritual or intercourse, such as may, for example, sustain the Jew even after he has left his father's house. But the fact is not that the Negro has no tradition but that there has as yet arrived no sensibility sufficiently profound and tough to make this tradition articulate.

If Richard Wright's childhood had stunted him less terribly, he might well have grown into the sensibility whose absence Baldwin laments. He did succeed in exploring, in a series of works published in the 1950's, some dimensions of black power and related issues: *Black Power* (1954), *The Color Curtain* (1956), *Pagan Spain* (1957), *White Man, Listen* (1957), and *The Long Dream* (1958). And two posthumously published works of fiction [*Eight Men* (1961), a collection of stories, and a novel, *Lawd Today* (1963), written before *Native Son*] are by no means without interest. Wright died in Paris in 1960 at the age of 52.

The Ethics of Living Jim Crow

AN AUTOBIOGRAPHICAL SKETCH

I

My first lesson in how to live as a Negro came when I was quite small. We were living in Arkansas. Our house stood behind the railroad tracks. Its skimpy yard was paved with black cinders. Nothing green ever grew in that yard. The only touch of green we would see was far away, beyond the tracks, over where the white folks lived. But cinders were good enough for me, and I never missed the green growing things. And anyhow, cinders were fine weapons. You could always have a nice hot war with huge black cinders. All you had to do was crouch behind the brick pillars of a house with your hands full of gritty ammunition. And the first woolly black head you saw pop out from behind another row of pillars was your target. You tried your very best to knock it off. It was great fun.

I never fully realized the appalling disadvantages of a cinder environment till one day the gang to which I belonged found itself engaged in a war with the white boys who lived beyond the tracks. As usual we laid down our cinder barrage, thinking that this would wipe the white boys out. But they replied with a steady bombardment of broken bottles. We doubled our cinder barrage, but they hid behind trees, hedges, and the sloping embankments of their lawns. Having no such fortifications, we retreated to the brick pillars of our homes. During the retreat a broken milk bottle caught me behind the ear, opening a deep gash which bled profusely. The sight of blood pouring over my face completely demoralized our ranks. My fellow-combatants left me standing paralyzed in the center of the yard, and scurried for their homes. A kind neighbor saw me and rushed me to a doctor, who took three stitches in my neck.

I sat brooding on my front steps, nursing my wound and waiting for my mother to come from work. I felt that a grave injustice had been done me. It was all right to throw cinders. The greatest harm a cinder could do was leave a bruise. But broken bottles were dangerous; they left you cut, bleeding, and helpless.

When night fell, my mother came from the white folks' kitchen. I raced down the street to meet her. I could just feel in my bones that she would understand. I knew she would tell me exactly what to do next time. I grabbed her hand and babbled out the whole story. She examined my wound, then slapped me.

"How come yuh didn't hide?" she asked me. "How come yuh awways fightin'?"

I was outraged, and bawled. Between sobs I told her that I didn't have any trees or hedges to hide behind. There wasn't a thing I could have used as a trench. And you couldn't throw very far when you were hiding behind the brick pillars of a house. She grabbed a barrel stave, dragged me home, stripped me naked, and beat me till I had a fever of one hundred and two. She would smack my rump with the stave, and while the skin was still smarting, impart to me gems of Jim Crow wisdom. I was never to throw cinders any more. I was never to fight any more wars. I was never, never, under any conditions, to fight *white* folks again. And they were absolutely right in clouting me with the broken milk bottle. Didn't I know she was working hard every day in the hot kitchens of the white folks to make money to take care of me? When was I ever going to learn to be a good boy? She couldn't be bothered with my fights. She finished by telling me that I ought to be thankful to God as long as I lived that they didn't kill me.

All that night I was delirious and could not sleep. Each time I closed my eyes I saw monstrous white faces suspended from the ceiling, leering at me.

From that time on, the charm of my cinder yard was gone. The green trees, the trimmed hedges, the cropped lawns grew very meaningful, became a symbol. Even today when I think of white folks, the hard, sharp outlines of white houses surrounded by trees, lawns, and hedges are present somewhere in the background of my mind. Through the years they grew into an overreaching symbol of fear.

It was a long time before I came in close contact with white folks again. We moved from Arkansas to Mississippi. Here we had the good fortune not to live behind the railroad tracks, or close to white neighborhoods. We lived in the very heart of the local Black Belt. There were black churches and black preachers; there were black schools and black teachers; black groceries and black clerks. In fact, everything was so solidly black that for a long time I did not even think of white folks, save in remote and vague terms. But this could not last forever. As one grows older one eats more. One's clothing costs more. When I finished grammar school I had to go to work. My mother could no longer feed and clothe me on her cooking job.

There is but one place where a black boy who knows no trade can get a job, and that's where the houses and faces are white, where the trees, lawns, and hedges are green. My first job was with an optical company in Jackson, Mississippi. The morning I applied I stood straight and neat before the boss, answering all his questions with sharp yessirs and nosirs. I was very careful to pronounce my *sirs* distinctly, in order that he might know that I was polite, that I knew where I was, and that I knew he was a *white* man. I wanted that job badly.

He looked me over as though he were examining a prize poodle. He questioned me closely about my schooling, being particularly insistent about how much mathematics I had had. He seemed very pleased when I told him I had had two years of algebra.

"Boy, how would you like to try to learn something around here?" he asked me.

"I'd like it fine, sir," I said, happy. I had visions of "working my way up." Even Negroes have those visions.

"All right," he said. "Come on."

I followed him to the small factory.

"Pease," he said to a white man of about thirty-five, "this is Richard. He's going to work for us."

Pease looked at me and nodded.

I was then taken to a white boy of about seventeen.

"Morrie, this is Richard, who's going to work for us."

"Whut yuh sayin' there, boy!" Morrie boomed at me.

"Fine!" I answered.

The boss instructed these two to help me, teach me, give me jobs to do, and let me learn what I could in my spare time.

My wages were five dollars a week.

I worked hard, trying to please. For the first month I got along O.K. Both Pease and Morrie seemed to like me. But one thing was missing. And I kept thinking about it. I was not learning anything and nobody was volunteering to help me. Thinking they had forgotten that I was to learn something about the mechanics of grinding lenses, I asked Morrie one day to tell me about the work. He grew red.

"Whut yuh tryin' t' do, nigger, get smart?" he asked.

"Naw; I ain' tryin' t' get smart," I said.

"Well, don't, if yuh know whut's good for yuh!"

I was puzzled. Maybe he just doesn't want to help me, I thought. I went to Pease.

"Say, are yuh crazy, you black bastard?" Pease asked me, his gray eyes growing hard.

I spoke out, reminding him that the boss had said I was to be given a chance to learn something.

"Nigger, you think you're *white*, don't you?"

"Naw, sir!"

"Well, you're acting mighty like it!"

"But, Mr. Pease, the boss said . . .

Pease shook his fist in my face.

"This is a *white* man's work around here, and you better watch yourself!"

From then on they changed toward me. They said goodmorning no more. When I was just a bit slow in performing some duty, I was called a lazy black son-of-a-bitch.

Once I thought of reporting all this to the boss. But the mere idea of what would happen to me if Pease and Morrie should learn that I had "snitched" stopped me. And after all the boss was a white man, too. What was the use?

The climax came at noon one summer day. Pease called me to his workbench. To get to him I had to go between two narrow benches and stand with my back against a wall.

"Yes, sir," I said.

"Richard, I want to ask you something," Pease began pleasantly, not looking up from his work.

"Yes, sir," I said again.

Morrie came over, blocking the narrow passage between the benches. He folded his arms, staring at me solemnly.

I looked from one to the other, sensing that something was coming.

"Yes, sir," I said for the third time.

Pease looked up and spoke very slowly.

"Richard, *Mr.* Morrie here tells me you called me *Pease.*"

I stiffened. A void seemed to open up in me. I knew this was the showdown.

He meant that I had failed to call him Mr. Pease. I looked at Morrie. He was gripping a steel bar in his hands. I opened my mouth to speak, to protest, to assure Pease that I had never called him simply *Pease,* and that I had never had any intentions of doing so, when Morrie grabbed me by the collar, ramming my head against the wall.

"Now, be careful, nigger!" snarled Morrie, baring his teeth. "*I* heard yuh call 'im *Pease!* 'N' if yuh say yuh didn't, yuh're callin' me a *lie,* see?" He waved the steel bar threateningly.

If I had said: No, sir, Mr. Pease, I never called you *Pease,* I would have been automatically calling Morrie a liar. And if I had said: Yes, sir, Mr. Pease, I called you *Pease,* I would have been pleading guilty to having uttered the worst insult that a Negro can utter to a southern white man. I stood hesitating, trying to frame a neutral reply.

"Richard, I asked you a question!" said Pease. Anger was creeping into his voice.

"I don't remember called you *Pease,* Mr. Pease," I said cautiously. "And if I did, I sure didn't mean . . ."

"You black son-of-a-bitch! You called me *Pease,* then!" he spat, slapping me till I bent sideways over a bench. Morrie was on top of me, demanding:

"Didn't yuh call 'im *Pease?* If yuh say yuh didn't, I'll rip yo' gut string loose with this bar, yuh black granny dodger! Yuh can't call a white man a lie 'n' get erway with it, you black son-of-a-bitch!"

I wilted. I begged them not to bother me. I knew what they wanted. They wanted me to leave.

"I'll leave," I promised. "I'll leave right *now.*"

They gave me a minute to get out of the factory. I was warned not to show up again, or tell the boss.

I went.

When I told the folks at home what had happened, they called me a fool. They told me that I must never again attempt to exceed my boundaries. When you are working for white folks, they said, you got to "stay in your place" if you want to keep working.

II

My Jim Crow education continued on my next job, which was portering in a clothing store. One morning, while polishing brass out front, the boss and his twenty-year-old son got out of their car and half dragged and half kicked a Negro woman into the store. A policeman standing at the corner looked on, twirling his night-stick. I watched out of the corner of my eye, never slackening the strokes of my chamois upon the brass. After a few minutes, I heard shrill screams coming from the rear of the store. Later the woman stumbled out, bleeding, crying, and holding her stomach. When she reached the end of the block, the policeman grabbed her and accused her of being drunk. Silently, I watched him throw her into a patrol wagon.

When I went to the rear of the store, the boss and his son were washing their hands at the sink. They were chuckling. The floor was bloody and strewn with wisps of hair and clothing. No doubt I must have appeared pretty shocked, for the boss slapped me reassuringly on the back.

"Boy, that's what we do to niggers when they don't want to pay their bills," he said laughing.

His son looked at me and grinned.

"Here, hava cigarette," he said.

Not knowing what to do, I took it. He lit his and held the match for me. This was a gesture of kindness, indicating that even if they had beaten the poor old woman, they would not beat me if I knew enough to keep my mouth shut.

"Yes, sir," I said, and asked no questions.

After they had gone, I sat on the edge of a packing box and stared at the bloody floor till the cigarette went out.

That day at noon, while eating in a hamburger joint, I told my fellow Negro porters what had happened. No one seemed surprised. One fellow, after swallowing a huge bite, turned to me and asked:

"Huh! Is tha' all they did t'her?"

"Yeah. Wasn't tha'enough?" I asked.

"Shucks! Man, she's a lucky bitch!" he said, burying his lips deep into a juicy hamburger. "Hell, it's a wonder they didn't lay her when they got through."

III

I was learning fast, but not quite fast enough. One day, while I was delivering packages in the suburbs, my bicycle tire was punctured. I walked along the hot, dusty road, sweating and leading my bicycle by the handle-bars.

A car slowed at my side.

"What's the matter, boy?" a white man called.

I told him my bicycle was broken and I was walking back to town.

"That's too bad," he said, "Hop on the running board."

He stopped the car. I clutched hard at my bicycle with one hand and clung to the side of the car with the other.

"All set?"

"Yes sir," I answered. The car started.

It was full of young white men. They were drinking. I watched the flask pass from mouth to mouth.

"Wanna drink, boy?" one asked.

I laughed as the wind whipped my face. Instinctively obeying the freshly planted precepts of my mother, I said: "Oh, no!"

The words were hardly out of my mouth before I felt something hard and cold smash me between the eyes. It was an empty whisky bottle. I saw stars, and fell backwards from the speeding car into the dust of the road, my feet becoming entangled in the steel spokes of my bicycle. The white men piled out, and stood over me.

"Nigger, ain'yuh learned no better sense'n tha' yet?" asked the man who hit me. "Ain' yuh learned t' say *sir* t' a white man yet?"

Dazed, I pulled to my feet. My elbows and legs were bleeding. Fists doubled, the white man advanced, kicking my bicycle out of the way.

"Aw, leave the bastard alone. He's got enough," said one.

They stood looking at me. I rubbed my shins, trying to stop the flow of blood. No doubt they felt a sort of contemptuous pity, for one asked:

"Yuh wanna ride t'town now, nigger? Yuh reckon yuh know enough t'ride now?"

"I wanna walk," I said, simply.

Maybe it sounded funny. They laughed.

"Well, walk, yuh black son-of-a-bitch!"

When they left they comforted me with:

"Nigger, yuh sho better be damn glad it wuz us yuh talked t'tha'way. Yuh're a lucky bastard, 'cause if youh'd said tha' t'somebody else, yuh might've been a dead nigger now."

IV

Negroes who have lived South know the dread of being caught alone upon the streets in white neighborhoods after the sun has set. In such a simple situation as this the plight of the Negro in America is graphically symbolized. While white strangers may be in these neighborhoods trying to get home, they can pass unmolested. But the color of a Negro's skin makes him easily recognizable, makes him suspect, converts him into a defenseless target.

Late one Saturday night I made some deliveries in a white neighborhood. I was pedaling my bicycle back to the store as fast as I could, when a police car, swerving toward me, jammed me into the curbing.

"Get down and put up your hands!" the policemen ordered.

I did. They climbed out of the car, guns drawn, faces set, and advanced slowly.

"Keep still!" they ordered.

I reached my hands higher. They searched my pockets and packages. They seemed dissatisfied when they could find nothing incriminating. Finally, one of them said:

"Boy, tell your boss not to send you out in white neighborhoods after sundown."

As usual, I said:

"Yes, sir."

V

My next job was a hall-boy in a hotel. Here my Jim Crow education broadened and deepened. When the bell-boys were busy, I was often called to assist them. As many of the rooms in the hotel were occupied by prostitutes, I was constantly called to carry them liquor and cigarettes. These women were nude most of the time. They did not bother about clothing, even for bell-boys. When you went into their rooms, you were supposed to take their nakedness for granted, as though it startled you no more than a blue vase or a red rug. Your presence awoke in them no sense of shame, for you were not regarded as human. If they were alone, you could steal sidelong glimpses at them. But if they were receiving men, not a flicker of your eyelids could show. I remember one incident vividly. A new woman, a huge, snowy-skinned blonde, took a room on my floor. I was sent to wait upon her. She was in bed with a thick-set man; both were nude and uncovered. She said she wanted some liquor and slid out of bed and waddled across the floor to get her money from a dresser drawer. I watched her.

"Nigger, what in hell you looking at?" the white man asked me, raising himself upon his elbows.

"Nothing," I answered, looking miles deep into the blank wall of the room.

"Keep your eyes where they belong, if you want to be healthy!" he said.

"Yes, sir."

VI

One of the bell-boys I knew in this hotel was keeping steady company with one of the Negro maids. Out of a clear sky the police descended upon his home and arrested him, accusing him of bastardy. The poor boy swore he had had no intimate relations with the girl. Nevertheless, they forced him to marry her. When the child arrived, it was found to be much lighter in complexion than either of the two supposedly legal parents. The white men around the hotel made a great joke of it. They spread the rumor that some white cow must have scared the poor girl while she was carrying the baby. If you were in their presence when this explanation was offered, you were supposed to laugh.

VII

One of the bell-boys was caught in bed with a white prostitute. He was castrated and run out of town. Immediately after this all the bell-boys and hall-boys were called together and warned. We were given to understand that the boy who had been castrated was a "mighty, mighty lucky bastard." We were impressed with the fact that next time the management of the hotel would not be responsible for the lives of "trouble-makin' niggers." We were silent.

VIII

One night, just as I was about to go home, I met one of the Negro maids. She lived in my direction, and we fell in to walk part of the way home together. As we passed the white night-watchman, he slapped the maid on her buttock. I turned around, amazed. The watchman looked at me with a long, hard, fixed-under stare. Suddenly he pulled his gun and asked:

"Nigger, don't yuh like it?"

I hesitated.

"I asked yuh don't yuh like it?" he asked again, stepping forward.

"Yes, sir," I mumbled.

"Talk like it, then!"

"Oh, yes, sir!" I said with as much heartiness as I could muster.

Outside, I walked ahead of the girl, ashamed to face her. She caught up with me and said:

"Don't be a fool! Yuh couldn't help it!"

This watchman boasted of having killed two Negroes in self-defense.

Yet, in spite of all this, the life of the hotel ran with an amazing smoothness. It would have been impossible for a stranger to detect anything. The maids, the hall-boys, and the bell-boys were all smiles. They had to be.

IX

I had learned my Jim Crow lessons so thoroughly that I kept the hotel job till I left Jackson for Memphis. It so happened that while in Memphis I applied for a job at a branch of the optical company. I was hired. And for some reason, as long as I worked there, they never brought my past against me.

Here my Jim Crow education assumed quite a different form. It was no longer brutally cruel, but subtly cruel. Here I learned to lie, to steal, to dissemble. I learned to play that dual role which every Negro must play if he wants to eat and live.

For example, it was almost impossible to get a book to read. It was assumed that after a Negro had imbibed what scanty schooling the state furnished he had no further need for books. I was always borrowing books from men on the job. One day I mustered enough courage to ask one of the men to let me get books from the library in his name. Surprisingly, he consented. I cannot help but think that he consented because he was a Roman Catholic and felt a vague sympathy for Negroes, being himself an object of hatred. Armed with a library card, I obtained books in the following manner: I would write a note to the librarian, saying: "Please let this nigger boy have the following books." I would then sign it with the white man's name.

When I went to the library, I would stand at the desk, hat in hand, looking as unbookish as possible. When I received the books desired I would take them home. If the books listed in the note happened to be out, I would sneak into the lobby and forge a new one. I never took any chances guessing with the white librarian about what the fictitious white man would want to read. No doubt if any of the white patrons had suspected that some of the volumes they enjoyed had been in the home of a Negro, they would not have tolerated it for an instant.

The factory force of the optical company in Memphis was much larger than that in Jackson, and more urbanized. At least they liked to talk, and would engage the Negro help in conversation whenever possible. By this means I found that many subjects were taboo from the white man's point of view. Among the topics they did not like to discuss with Negroes were the following: American white women; the Ku Klux Klan; France, and how Negro soldiers fared while there; French women; Jack Johnson; the entire northern part of the United States; the Civil War; Abraham Lincoln; U.S. Grant; General Sherman; Catholics; the Pope; Jews; the Republican Party; slavery; social equality; Communism; Socialism; the 13th and 14th Amendments to the Constitution; or any topic calling for positive knowledge or manly self assertion on the part of the Negro. The most accepted topics were sex and religion.

There were many times when I had to exercise a great deal of ingenuity to keep out of trouble. It is a southern custom that all men must take off their hats when they enter an elevator. And especially did this apply to us blacks with rigid force. One day I stepped into an elevator with my arms full of packages. I was forced to ride with my hat on. Two white men stared at me coldly. Then one of them very kindly lifted my hat and placed it upon my armful of packages. Now the most accepted response for a Negro to make under such circumstances is to look at the white man out of the corner of his eye and grin. To have said: "Thank you!" would have made the white man *think* that you *thought* you were receiving from him a personal service. For such an act I have seen Negroes take a blow in the mouth. Finding the first alternative distasteful, and the second dangerous, I hit upon an acceptable course of action which fell safely between the two poles. I immediately—no sooner than my hat was lifted—pretended that my packages were about to spill, and appeared deeply distressed with keeping them in my arms. In this fashion I evaded having to acknowledge his service, and, in spite of adverse circumstances, salvaged a slender shred of personal pride.

How do Negroes feel about the way they have to live? How do they discuss it when alone among themselves? I think this question can be answered in a single sentence. A friend of mine who ran an elevator once told me:

"Lawd, man! Ef it wuzn't fer them polices 'n' them ol' lynch-mobs, there wouldn't be nothin' but uproar down here!'"

RALPH ELLISON

(1914-   )

At the time Ralph Ellison was born, his state of birth, Oklahoma, had been a state for only 7 years. "It had no tradition of slavery," Ellison has remarked, "and while it was segregated, relationships between the races were more fluid and thus more human than in the older slave states." As a consequence "I felt no innate sense of inferiority which would keep me from getting those things I desired out of life." Ellison studied at the Tuskegee Institute from 1933 to 1936, went to New York in his junior year to study sculpture and then musical composition and, at length, under Richard Wright's influence, he began writing essays and short stories. The essays, which appeared in *New Challenge,* a magazine Wright was editing, *New Masses,* and *The Negro Quarterly* were politically radical. The stories, most of which appeared at intervals throughout the 1940's and 1950's, were the workshop in which Ellison worked out the themes that shaped *Invisible Man,* which won the National Book Award for fiction in 1953. Since the publication of this novel, Ellison has been showered with honorary degrees and has become the occupant of one of the most distinguished academic posts in America—the Schweitzer professorship at New York University. The speed with which *Invisible Man* attained recognition as a major work was partly a consequence of Ellison's unique ability to take his race's experience for granted, neither to ignore nor preach about it but to use it naturally. The novel investigates a broadly human problem—pattern-

Criticism includes Robert Bone, "Ralph Ellison and the Uses of Imagination," *Triquarterly,* Number Six (1966), Ihab Hassan, *Radical Innocence,* 1961, and Marcus Klein, *After Alienation,* 1965.

ings of life that simultaneously falsify experience and give it order—in terms of a clearly identifiable group. As Ellison put it in an interview:

> Invisibility has to do with the failure of most of us to regard the individual we contact as a human being. We resort to stereotypes. Sometimes they are dramatic. On the other hand you have the failure of the individual to exert himself, to be mature, to run the risk of humanity—and so he contributes to his own invisibility.

Granted the problem has an especially obvious relevance for members of minority groups; the majority culture is dense with stereotypes of black people, as of "Indians," "Mexes," and the rest. Still, Ellison's book is not primarily a protest against a particular form of social abuse or prejudice; in accepting his own blackness he also accepts society and its surfaces; his book does not demand the transformation of society but, instead, the development, within individuals, of knowledge about how to live in it. The Invisible Man has to learn to resist, within himself, the forces that drive him to do to himself, in the name of order, the kind of injury that has been done to him by the slotting mechanisms of the culture:

> I was dominated by the all-embracing idea of Brotherhood. The organization had given the world a new shape, and me a vital role. We recognized no loose ends, everything could be controlled by our science. Life was all pattern and discipline . . .

In a sense, then, race difference becomes, for Ellison, a source of strength. But from this it does not follow that his novel is without moments of bitterness. What the writer resents most is the way in which the exigencies of his struggle, the black man's struggle, have robbed him not of rights but of natural human feelings, of the freedom to indulge an impulse or to enjoy his heritage. In one of the most moving passages in the book, the Invisible Man envies the naturalness with which an old black man is able to break into song:

> It was a song from the past, the past of the campus and the still earlier past of home. And now some of the elder ones in the march were joining it . . .[I] saw a slender black man with his face turned toward the sun, singing through the upturned bells of the horn . . . It was a worn, yellow face and his eyes were closed and I could see a knife welt around his upturned neck as his throat threw out the song. He sang with his whole body, phrasing each verse as naturally as he walked. . . . It was as though the song had

been there all the time and he knew it and aroused it; and I knew that I had known it too and had failed to release it out of a vague, nameless shame or fear.

The moments of self-hatred for his own participation in acts done to and against him are not few; inhibition, or the compulsion to be "politically aware," often forces him, to his own shame, to deny heritage, instinct, love of home and family. Always the hero suffers the strain of knowing he must work for the public good and knowing that that obligation deprives him of a personal life, personal satisfactions. And always the scars of social injustice resurface on this mind. Ellison can write coolly and observantly about, for example, the black man's obsession with technical mastery:

> . . . freedom in America has always centered around the mastery of techniques, and what the Negroes want—the real mark of progress—lies in this ability to master the techniques and to have the full benefits that come from them. . . .

But at times his own self-doubt, his own desire to display his gifts, produce patches of desperate overwriting: "Stale and wilted flowers, rejected downtown, blazed feverishly on a cart, like glamorous rags festering beneath a futile spray from a punctured fruit juice can. The crowd were boiling figures seen through steaming glass from inside a washing machine . . ." And he presses his claims as thinker to an extreme that stimulates resistance. (The critic Alfred Kazin once remarked about *Invisible Man* that "Ellison was working consciously with so many literary symbols and rituals . . . that he clearly thought less about making the hero's character complex than he did about putting into his book his lesson in the symbol-hunting fashionable criticism of the time.")

Yet at its best the book eloquently celebrates both human possibility and existing individual talent. In the realm of imagination, Ellison discovers, human versatility and variousness come together in an encounter that is a true source of wonder; most wondrous is the writer's opportunity to contribute to a survival, to draw on the wholeness and particularity of his experience as a means of saving a richness of response that might otherwise be lost:

> . . . what I have tried to communicate in fiction is that which I believe to be enduring and abiding in our situation, especially those human qualities which the American Negro has developed despite and in rejection of the obstacles and meannesses imposed upon us. If the writer exists for any social good, his role is

that of preserving in art those human values which can endure by confronting change. Our Negro situation is changing rapidly, but so much which we've gleaned through the harsh discipline of Negro American life is simply too precious to be lost.

In *Invisible Man* a good deal of that precious experience is preserved.

Ellison has taught at a score of universities over the last two decades. He published a volume of essays, *Shadow and Act,* in 1964 and has been at work for some years on a new novel.

Invisible Man

PROLOGUE

I am an invisible man. No, I am not a spook like those who haunted Edgar Allan Poe; nor am I one of your Hollywood-movie ectoplasms. I am a man of substance, of flesh and bone, fiber and liquids—and I might even be said to possess a mind. I am invisible, understand, simply because people refuse to see me. Like the bodiless heads you see sometimes in circus sideshows, it is as though I have been surrounded by mirrors of hard, distorting glass. When they approach me they see only my surroundings, themselves, or figments of their imagination—indeed, everything and anything except me.

Nor is my invisibility exactly a matter of a bio-chemical accident to my epidermis. That invisibility to which I refer occurs because of a peculiar disposition of the eyes of those with whom I come in contact. A matter of the construction of their *inner* eyes, those eyes with which they look through their physical eyes upon reality. I am not complaining, nor am I protesting either. It is sometimes advantageous to be unseen, although it is most often rather wearing on the nerves. Then too, you're constantly being bumped against by those of poor vision. Or again, you often doubt if you really exist. You wonder whether you aren't simply a phantom in other people's minds. Say, a figure in a nightmare which the sleeper tries with all his strength to destroy. It's when you feel like this that, out of resentment, you begin to bump people back. And, let me confess, you feel that way most of the time. You ache with the need to convince yourself that you do exist in the real world, that you're a part of all the sound and anguish, and you strike out with your fists, you curse and you swear to make them recognize you. And, alas, it's seldom successful.

One night I accidentally bumped into a man, and perhaps because of the near darkness he saw me and called me an insulting name. I sprang at him, seized his coat lapels and demanded that he apologize. He was a tall blond man, and as my face came close to his he looked insolently out of his blue eyes and cursed me, his breath hot in my face as he struggled. I pulled his chin down sharp upon the crown of my head, butting him as I had seen the West Indians do, and I felt his flesh tear and the blood gush out, and I yelled, "Apologize! Apologize!" But he continued to curse and struggle, and I butted him again and again until he went down heavily, on his knees, profusely bleeding. I kicked him repeatedly, in a frenzy because he still uttered insults though his lips were frothy with blood. Oh yes, I kicked him! And in my outrage I got out my knife and prepared to slit his throat, right there beneath the lamplight in the deserted street, holding him by the collar with one hand, and opening the knife with my teeth—when it occurred to me that the man had not *seen* me, actually; that he, as far as he knew, was in the midst of a walking nightmare! And I stopped the blade, slicing the air as I pushed him away, letting him fall back to the street. I stared at him hard as the lights of a car stabbed through the darkness. He lay there, moaning on the asphalt; a man almost killed by a phantom. It unnerved me. I was both disgusted and ashamed. I was like a drunken man myself, wavering about on weakened legs. Then I was amused. Something in this man's thick head had sprung out and beaten him within an inch of his life. I began to laugh at this crazy discovery. Would he have awakened at the point of death? Would Death himself have freed him for wakeful living? But I didn't linger. I ran away into the dark, laughing so hard I feared I might rupture myself. The next day I saw his picture in the *Daily News*, beneath a caption stating that he had been "mugged." Poor fool, poor blind fool, I thought with sincere compassion, mugged by an invisible man!

Most of the time (although I do not choose as I once did to deny the violence of my days by ignoring it) I am not so overtly violent. I remember that I am invisible and walk softly so as not to awaken the sleeping ones. Sometimes it is best not to awaken them; there are few things in the world as dangerous as sleepwalkers. I learned in time though that it is possible to carry on a fight against them without their realizing it. For instance, I have been carrying on a fight with Monopolated Light & Power for some time now. I use their service and pay them nothing at all, and they don't know it. Oh, they suspect that power is being drained off, but they don't know where. All they know is that according to the master meter back there in their power station a hell of a lot of free current is disappearing somewhere into the jungle of Harlem. The joke, of course, is that I don't live in Harlem but in a border area. Several years ago (before I discovered the advantage of being invisible) I went through the routine process of buying service and paying their outrageous rates. But no more. I gave up all that, along with my apartment, and my old way of life: That way based upon the fallacious assumption that I, like other men, was visible. Now, aware of my invisibility, I live rent-free in a building rented strictly to whites, in a section of the basement that was shut off and forgotten during the nineteenth century, which I discovered when I was trying to escape in the night from Ras the

Destroyer. But that's getting too far ahead of the story, almost to the end, although the end is in the beginning and lies far ahead.

The point now is that I found a home—or a hole in the ground, as you will. Now don't jump to the conclusion that because I call my home a "hole" it is damp and cold like a grave; there are cold holes and warm holes. Mine is a warm hole. And remember, a bear retires to his hole for the winter and lives until spring; then he comes strolling out like the Easter chick breaking from its shell. I say all this to assure you that it is incorrect to assume that, because I'm invisible and live in a hole, I am dead. I am neither dead nor in a state of suspended animation. Call me Jack-the-Bear, for I am in a state of hibernation.

My hole is warm and full of light. Yes, *full* of light. I doubt if there is a brighter spot in all New York than this hole of mine, and I do not exclude Broadway. Or the Empire State Building on a photographer's dream night. But that is taking advantage of you. Those two spots are among the darkest of our whole civilization—pardon me, our whole *culture* (an important distinction, I've heard)—which might sound like a hoax, or a contradiction, but that (by contradiction, I mean) is how the world moves: Not like an arrow, but a boomerang. (Beware of those who speak of the *spiral* of history: they are preparing a boomerang. Keep a steel helmet handy.) I know; I have been boomeranged across my head so much that I now can see the darkness of lightness. And I love light. Perhaps you'll think it strange that an invisible man should need light, desire light, love light. But maybe it is exactly because I *am* invisible. Light confirms my reality, gives birth to my form. A beautiful girl once told me of a recurring nightmare in which she lay in the center of a large dark room and felt her face expand until it filled the whole room, becoming a formless mass while her eyes ran in bilious jelly up the chimney. And so it is with me. Without light I am not only invisible, but formless as well; and to be unaware of one's form is to live a death. I myself, after existing some twenty years, did not become alive until I discovered my invisibility.

That is why I fight my battle with Monopolated Light & Power. The deeper reason, I mean; It allows me to feel my vital aliveness. I also fight them for taking so much of my money before I learned to protect myself. In my hole in the basement there are exactly 1,369 lights. I've wired the entire ceiling, every inch of it. And not with fluorescent bulbs, but with the older, more-expensive-to-operate kind, the filament type. An act of sabotage, you know. I've already begun to wire the wall. A junk man I know, a man of vision, has supplied me with wire and sockets. Nothing, storm or flood, must get in the way of our need for light and ever more and brighter light. The truth is the light and light is the truth. When I finish all four walls, then I'll start on the floor. Just how that will go, I don't know. Yet when you have lived invisible as long as I have you develop a certain ingenuity. I'll solve the problem. And maybe I'll invent a gadget to place my coffeepot on the fire while I lie in bed, and even invent a gadget to warm my bed—like the fellow I saw in one of the picture magazines who made himself a gadget to warm his shoes! Though invisible, I am in the great American tradition of tinkers. That makes me kin to Ford, Edison and Franklin. Call me, since I have a theory and a concept, a "thinker-tinker." Yes, I'll warm my shoes; they need it, they're usually full of holes. I'll do that and more.

Now I have one radio-phonograph; I plan to have five. There is a certain acoustical deadness in my hole, and when I have music I want to *feel* its vibration, not only with my ear but with my whole body. I'd like to hear five recordings of Louis Armstrong playing and singing "What Did I Do to Be so Black and Blue"—all at the same time. Sometimes now I listen to Louis while I have my favorite dessert of vanilla ice cream and sloe gin. I pour the red liquid over the white mound, watching it glisten and the vapor rising as Louis bends that military instrument into a beam of lyrical sound. Perhaps I like Louis Armstrong because he's made poetry out of being invisible. I think it must be because he's unaware that he *is* invisible. And my own grasp of invisibility aids me to understand his music. Once when I asked for a cigarette, some jokers gave me a reefer, which I lighted when I got home and sat listening to my phonograph. It was a strange evening. Invisibility, let me explain, gives one a slightly different sense of time, you're never quite on the beat. Sometimes you're ahead and sometimes behind. Instead of the swift and imperceptible flowing of time, you are aware of its nodes, those points where time stands still or from which it leaps ahead. And you slip into the breaks and look around. That's what you hear vaguely in Louis' music.

Once I saw a prizefighter boxing a yokel. The fighter was swift and amazingly scientific. His body was one violent flow of rapid rhythmic action. He hit the yokel a hundred times while the yokel held up his arms in stunned surprise. But suddenly the yokel, rolling about in the gale of boxing gloves, struck one blow and knocked science, speed and footwork as cold as a well-digger's posterior. The smart money hit the canvas. The long shot got the nod. The yokel had simply stepped inside of his opponent's sense of time. So under the spell of the reefer I discovered a new analytical way of listening to music. The unheard sounds came through, and each melodic line existed of itself, stood out clearly from all the rest, said its piece, and waited patiently for the other voices to speak. That night I found myself hearing not only in time, but in space as well. I not only entered the music but descended, like Dante, into its depths. And *beneath the swiftness of the hot tempo there was a slower tempo and a cave and I entered it and looked around and heard an old woman singing a spiritual as full of Weltschmerz as flamenco, and beneath that lay a still lower level on which I saw a beautiful girl the color of ivory pleading in a voice like my mother's as she stood before a group of slave owners who bid for her naked body, and below that I found a lower level and a more rapid tempo and I heard someone shout:*

"Brothers and sisters, my text this morning is the 'Blackness of Blackness.'"

And a congregation of voices answered: "That blackness is most black, brother, most black . . ."

"In the beginning . . ."

"At the very start," they cried.

". . . there was blackness . . ."

"Preach it . . ."

". . . and the sun . . ."

"The sun, Lawd . . ."

". . . was bloody red . . ."

"Red . . ."

"Now black is . . ." the preacher shouted.

"Bloody . . ."

"I said black is . . ."

"Preach it, brother . . ."

". . . an' black ain't . . ."

"Red, Lawd, red: He said it's red!"

"Amen, brother . . ."

"Black will git you . . ."

"Yes, it will . . ."

". . . an' black won't . . ."

"Naw, it won't!"

"It do. . ."

"It do, Lawd . . ."

". . . an' it don't."

"Halleluiah . . ."

". . . It'll put you, glory, glory, Oh my Lawd, in the WHALE'S BELLY."

"Preach it, dear brother . . ."

". . . an' make you tempt . . ."

"Good God a-mighty!"

"Old Aunt Nelly!"

"Black will make you . . ."

"Black . . ."

". . . or black will un-make you."

"Ain't it the truth, Lawd?"

And at that point a voice of trombone timbre screamed at me, "Git out of here, you fool! Is you ready to commit treason?"

And I tore myself away, hearing the old singer of spirituals moaning, "Go curse your God, boy and die."

I stopped and questioned her, asked her what was wrong.

"I dearly loved my master, son," she said.

"You should have hated him," I said.

"He gave me several sons," she said, *"and because I loved my sons I learned to love their father though I hated him too."*

"I too have become acquainted with ambivalence," I said. *"That's why I'm here."*

"What's that?"

"Nothing, a word that doesn't explain it. Why do you moan?"

"I moan this way ' cause he's dead," she said.

"Then tell me, who is that laughing upstairs?"

"Them's my sons. They glad."

"Yes, I can understand that too," I said.

"I laughs too, but I moans too. He promised to set us free but he never could bring hisself to do it. Still I loved him . . ."

"Loved him? You mean . . ."

"Oh yes, but I loved something else even more."

"What more?"

"Freedom."

"Freedom," I said. *"Maybe freedom lies in hating."*

"Naw, son, it's in loving. I loved him and give him the poison and he withered away like a frost-bit apple. Them boys woulda tore him to pieces with they homemake knives."

"A mistake was made somewhere," I said, *"I'm confused."* And I wished to say other things, but the laughter upstairs became too loud and moan-like for me and I tried to break out of it, but I couldn't. Just as I was leaving I felt an urgent desire to ask her what freedom was and went back. She sat with her head in her hands, moaning softly; her leatherbrown face was filled with sadness.

"Old woman, what is this freedom you love so well?" I asked around a corner of my mind.

She looked surprised, then thoughtful, then baffled. *"I done forgot, son. It's all mixed up. First I think it's one thing, then I think it's another. It gits my head to spinning. I guess now it ain't nothing but knowing how to say what I got up in my head. But it's a hard job, son. Too much is done happen to me in too short a time. Hit's like I have a fever. Ever' time I starts to walk my head gits swirling and I falls down. Or if it ain't that, it's the boys; they gits to laughing and wants to kill up the white folks. They's bitter, that's what they is . . ."*

"But what about freedom?"

"Leave me 'lone, boy; my head aches!"

I left her, feeling dizzy myself. I didn't get far.

Suddenly one of the sons, a big fellow six feet tall, appeared out of nowhere and struck me with his fist.

"What's the matter, man?" I cried.

"You made Ma cry!"

"But how?" I said, dodging a blow.

"Askin' her them questions, that's how. Git outa here and stay, and next time you got questions like that, ask yourself!"

He held me in a grip like cold stone, his fingers fastening upon my windpipe until I thought I would suffocate before he finally allowed me to go. I stumbled about dazed, the music beating hysterically in my ears. It was dark. My head cleared and I wandered down a dark narrow passage, thinking I heard his footsteps hurrying behind me. I was sore, and into my being had come a profound craving for tranquillity, for peace and quiet, a state I felt I could never achieve. For one thing, the trumpet was blaring and the rhythm was too hectic. A tom-tom beating like heart-thuds began drowning out the trumpet, filling my ears, I longed for water and I heard it rushing through the cold mains my fingers touched as I felt my way, but I couldn't stop to search because of the footsteps behind me.

"Hey, Ras," I called. "Is it you, Destroyer? Rinehart?"

No answer, only the rhythmic footsteps behind me. Once I tried crossing the road, but a speeding machine struck me, scraping the skin from my leg as it roared past.

Then somehow I came out of it, ascending hastily from this underworld of sound to hear Louis Armstrong innocently asking,

What did I do
To be so black
And blue?

At first I was afraid; this familiar music had demanded action, the kind of which I was incapable, and yet had I lingered there beneath the surface I might have attempted to act. Nevertheless, I know now that few really listen to this music. I sat on the chair's edge in a soaking sweat, as though each of my 1,369 bulbs had everyone become a klieg light in an individual setting for a third degree with Ras and Rinehart in charge. It was exhausting—as though I had held my breath continuously for an hour under the terrifying serenity that comes from days of intense hunger. And yet, it was a strangely satisfying experience for an invisible man to hear the silence of sound. I had discovered unrecognized compulsions of my being—even though I could not answer "yes" to their promptings. I haven't smoked a reefer since, however; not because they're illegal, but because to *see* around corners is enough (that is not unusual when you are invisible). But to hear around them is too much; it inhibits action. And despite Brother Jack and all that sad, lost period of the Brotherhood, I believe in nothing if not in action.

Please, a definition: A hibernation is a covert preparation for a more overt action.

Besides, the drug destroys one's sense of time completely. If that happened, I might forget to dodge some bright morning and some cluck would run me down with an orange and yellow street car, or a bilious bus! Or I might forget to leave my hole when the moment for action presents itself.

Meanwhile I enjoy my life with the compliments of Monopolated Light & Power. Since you never recognize me even when in closest contact with me, and since, no doubt, you'll hardly believe that I exist, it won't matter if you know that I tapped a power line leading into the building and ran it into my hole in the ground. Before that I lived in the darkness into which I was chased, but now I see. I've illuminated the blackness of my invisibility—and vice versa. And so I play the invisible music of my isolation. The last statement doesn't seem just right, does it? But it is; you hear this music simply because music is heard and seldom seen, except by musicians. Could this compulsion to put invisibility down in black and white be thus an urge to make music of invisibility? But I am an orator, a rabble rouser—Am? I *was*, and perhaps shall be again. Who knows? All sickness is not unto death, neither is invisibility.

I can hear you say, "What a horrible, irresponsible bastard!" And you're right. I leap to agree with you. I am one of the most irresponsible beings that ever lived. Irresponsibility is part of my invisibility; any way you face it, it is a denial. But to whom can I be responsible, and why should I be, when you refuse to see me? And wait until I reveal how truly irresponsible I am. Responsibility rests upon recognition, and recognition is a form of agreement. Take the man whom I almost killed: Who was responsible for that near murder—I? I don't think so, and I refuse it. I won't buy it. You can't give it to me. *He* bumped *me*, *he* insulted *me*. Shouldn't he, for his own personal safety, have recognized my hysteria, my "danger potential"? He, let us say, was lost in a dream world. But didn't *he* control that dream world—which, alas, is only too real!—and didn't *he* rule me out of it? And if he had yelled for a policeman, wouldn't I have been taken for the offending one? Yes, yes, yes! Let me agree with you, I was the irresponsible one; for I should have used my knife to protect the higher interests of society. Some day that kind of foolishness will cause us tragic trouble. All dreamers and sleepwalkers must pay the price, and even the invisible victim is responsible for the fate of all. But I shirked that responsibility; I became too snarled in the incompatible notions that buzzed within my brain. I was a coward.

But what did *I* do to be so blue? Bear with me.

JAMES BALDWIN

(1924-   )

In *Nobody Knows My Name* (1961) James Baldwin, probably this country's most widely read black writer, argued that "The one thing that all Americans have in common is that they have no other identity apart from the identity which is being achieved on this continent." Baldwin's position on racial questions has become edgier with time— hard for a celebrity, a spokesman, to avoid responding to the currents of opinion as they shift—but his sense of the centrality of "Americanness" has remained constant. He sees himself as American first, black second. The protagonists of his novels are, pointedly, both black and white. All his writing attests to a concern not finally with blackness but with humanness.

The Fire Next Time (1963), an apocalyptic cry for social justice, was a key document in the struggle of the 1960's to raise national consciousness of social injustice. Baldwin's voice is both fierce and moving as it lays out a life experience of discrimination and oppression; and it never whines. And the pride at the core has less to do with race than with personal intellect, sense of personal worth.

> Why, for example—especially knowing the family as I do—I should *want* to marry your sister is a great mystery to me. But your sister and I have every right to marry if we wish to, and no one has the right to stop us. If she cannot raise me to her level, perhaps I can raise her to mine.

> Something very sinister happens to the people of a country when they begin to distrust their own reactions as deeply as they do here, and become as joyless as they have become.

Baldwin is uninterested in exchanging blackness for whiteness; his notion is that black culture could become a source of renewal for the nation, and his admiration for his race's history is deep; always the energy is bent on clearing off the muck and lies that have induced self-contempt:

The best criticism appears in essay form: Robert Bone, "The Novels of James Baldwin," *Tri-Quarterly* (Winter 1965), Robert Coles, "Baldwin's Burden," *Partisan Review*, XXXI (Summer 1964), Theodore L. Gross, "The World of James Baldwin," *Critique*, VII (Winter 1964–1965), Marcus Klein, "James Baldwin: A Question of Identity," *After Alienation*, 1962. *The Fire Next Time* originally appeared as *Letter From a Region in my Mind* in *The New Yorker*, 1962.

. . the experience of generations of Negroes. . .helps to explain how they have endured and how they have been able to produce children of kindergarten age who can walk through mobs to get to school. . . .The Negro boys and girls who are facing mobs today come out of a long line of improbable aristocrats—the only genuine aristocrats this country has produced.

Paradoxically, belief in the worth of "his kind" makes Baldwin determined to avoid doing the injustice to others that they have done to him. His resentment at being perceived as less worthy than he knows himself to be drives him to the task of correcting those whose vision is flawed. He draws the battle plan in *Notes of a Native Son* (1955).

The first idea was acceptance, the acceptance, totally without rancor, of life as it is, and men as they are: in the light of this idea, it goes without saying that injustice is a commonplace. But this did not mean that one could be complacent, for the second idea was of equal power: that one must never, in one's own life, accept these injustices as commonplace but must fight them with all one's strength. This fight begins, however, in the heart and it now has been laid to my charge to keep my own heart free of hatred and despair.

He and all other "relatively conscious" and committed blacks and whites must address themselves to awakening the rest of the nation—in fact, to saving it. And if *The Fire Next Time* ends with a threat, the threat is a measure of Baldwin's unreserved, obstinate, thoroughly American hope that a just society and a full life are possible for everyone. Salvation, in a word, is conceivable.

But what is the route that leads to it? Baldwin's name for it is "love," and his dream holds out possibilities of moral transformation that are less than realistic. Partly this is because Baldwin's own feeling for the otherness of "the enemy" has necessarily had to fit itself to stereotypes. Baldwin's own presence is overwhelming; he is there on the page, palpable, a human voice—but the others lack substance. He can write off white liberals as people whose attitudes "have little connection. . .with their perceptions or their lives." Refused a drink in the Chicago airport, he dismisses the bartender and bystanders as "typical," despicable, and, in wholly understandable rage, loses touch with their minds and fears, as though no realities existed except those of moral consciousness. Furious, frustrated, he tries to ask, What are they like, those people who are so dim about me? He has an intuition of the "bafflement and pain and essential decency" of white people, "beneath [their] cruelty and hysteria and apathy. . . ." But the hour at which he spoke permitted no advance into particulars of feeling, solid imaginings of the insides of "the oppressors"; that advance had to wait upon the growth of the consciousness of injustice that this writer did so much to foster.

There are other dimensions, of course, to Baldwin's literary career besides the political one. The first of nine children, he was the son of a minister, and the force of these beginnings—a religious intensity—is felt throughout his work, from *Go Tell It On the Mountain* to *The Fire Next Time*. (Baldwin himself became a minister at the age of 14.) Of equal significance is that Baldwin has lived much of his life as an expatriate. Influenced partly by the example of Richard Wright, whose work "was an immense liberation and revelation" for him, Baldwin took up residence in Paris in 1948, and it was there that he did the writing that made him a spokesman for blacks in the 1950's: *Go Tell It On the Mountain* (1953), a novel of his childhood and black ancestry; *Notes of a Native Son* (1955), and *Nobody Knows My Name* (1961). And, perhaps most significant, Baldwin has considered himself, from the beginning of his writing life to the present, an imaginative artist, not primarily a social commentator. In addition to *Go Tell It On the Mountain,* his novels include *Giovanni's Room* (1955) and *Another Country* (1962), works concerned in part with homosexuality; and the more recent *Tell Me How Long the Train's Been Gone* (1968) and *If Beale Street Could Talk* (1974). There are also plays, *Blues for Mister Charlie* (1964) and *The Amen Corner* (1965), and a collection of stories, *Going to Meet the Man* (1965).

The Fire Next Time

DOWN AT THE CROSS
LETTER FROM A REGION IN MY MIND

> *Take up the White Man's burden—*
> *Ye dare not stoop to less—*
> *Nor call too loud on Freedom*
> *To cloak your weariness;*
> *By all ye cry or whisper,*
> *By all ye leave or do,*
> *The silent, sullen peoples*
> *Shall weigh your Gods and you.*
> —Kipling

> *Down at the cross where my Saviour died,*
> *Down where for cleansing from sin I cried,*
> *There to my heart was the blood applied,*
> *Singing glory to His name!*
> —Hymn

I underwent, during the summer that I became fourteen, a prolonged religious crisis. I use the word "religious" in the common, and arbitrary, sense, meaning that I then discovered God, His saints and angels, and His blazing Hell. And since I had been born in a Christian nation, I accepted this Deity as the only one. I supposed Him to exist only within the walls of a church— in fact, of *our* church—and I also supposed that God and safety were synonymous. The word "safety" brings us to the real meaning of the word "religious" as we use it. Therefore, to state it in another, more accurate way, I became, during my fourteenth year, for the first time in my life, afraid— afraid of the evil within me and afraid of the evil without. What I saw around me that summer in Harlem was what I had always seen; nothing had changed. But now, without any warning, the whores and pimps and racketeers on the Avenue had become a personal menace. It had not before occurred to me that I could become one of them, but now I realized that we had been produced by the same circumstances. Many of my comrades were clearly headed for the Avenue, and my father said that I was headed that way, too. My friends began to drink and smoke, and embarked—at first avid, then groaning—on their sexual careers. Girls, only slightly older than I was, who sang in the choir or taught Sunday school, the children of holy parents, underwent, before my eyes, their incredible metamorphosis, of which the most bewildering aspect was not their budding breasts or their rounding behinds but something deeper and more subtle, in their eyes, their heat, their odor, and the inflection of their voices. Like the strangers on the Avenue, they became, in the twinkling of an eye, unutterably different and fantastically *present*. Owing to the way I had been raised, the abrupt discomfort that all this aroused in me and the fact that I had no idea what my voice or my mind or my body was likely to do next caused me to consider myself one of the most depraved people on earth. Matters were not helped by the fact that these holy girls seemed rather to enjoy my terrified lapses, our grim, guilty, tormented experiments, which were at once as chill and joyless as the Russian steppes and hotter, by far, than all the fires of Hell.

Yet there was something deeper than these changes, and less definable, that frightened me. It was real in both the boys and the girls, but it was, somehow, more vivid in the boys. In the case of the girls, one watched them turning into matrons before they had become women. They began to manifest a curious and really terrifying single-mindedness. It is hard to say exactly how this was conveyed: something implacable in the set of the lips, something farseeing (seeing what?) in the eyes, some new and crushing determination in the walk, something peremptory in the voice. They did not tease us, the boys, any more; they reprimanded us sharply, saying, "You better be thinking about your soul!" For the girls also saw the evidence on the Avenue, knew what the price would be, for them, of one misstep, knew that they had to be protected and that we were the only protection there was. They understood that they must act as God's decoys, saving the souls of the boys for Jesus and binding the bodies of the boys in marriage. For this was the beginning of our burning time, and "It is better," said St. Paul[1]—who elsewhere, with a most unusual and stunning exactness, described himself as a "wretched man"—"to marry than to burn." And I began to feel in the boys a curious, wary, bewildered despair, as though they were now settling in for the long, hard winter of life. I did not know then what it was that I was reacting to; I put it to myself that they were letting themselves go. In the same way that the girls were destined to gain as much weight as their mothers, the boys, it was clear, would rise no higher than their fathers. School began to reveal itself, therefore, as a child's game that one could not win, and the boys dropped out of school and went to work. My father wanted me to do the same. I refused, even though I no longer had any illusions about what an education could do for me; I had already encountered too many college-graduate handymen. My friends were now "downtown," busy, as they put it, "fighting the man." They began to care less about the way they looked, the way they dressed, the things they did; presently, one found them in twos and threes and fours, in a hallway, sharing a jug of wine or a bottle of whiskey, talking cursing, fighting, sometimes weeping: lost, and unable to say what it was that oppressed them, except that they knew it was "the man"—the white man. And there seemed to be no way whatever to remove this cloud that stood between them and the sun, between them and love and life and power, between them and whatever it was that they wanted. One did not have to be very bright to realize how little one could do to change one's situation; one did not have to be abnormally sensitive to be worn down to a cutting edge by the incessant and gratuitous humiliation and danger one encountered every working day, all day long. The humiliation did not apply merely to working days, or workers; I was thirteen and was crossing Fifth Avenue on my way to the Forty-second Street library, and the cop in the middle of the street muttered as I passed him, "Why don't you niggers stay uptown where you belong?" When I was ten, and didn't look, certainly, any older, two policemen amused themselves with me by frisking me, making comic (and terrifying) speculations concerning my ancestry and probable sexual prowess, and for good measure, leaving me flat on my back in one of Harlem's empty lots. Just before and then during the Second World War, many of my friends fled into the service, all to be changed there, and rarely for the better, many to be ruined, and many to die. Others fled to other states and cities—that is, to other ghettos. Some went on wine or whiskey or the needle, and are still on it. And others, like me, fled into the church.

---

[1] St. Paul (AD 5?–67?), originally called "Saul of Tarsus." Paul was the apostle to the Gentiles.

For the wages of sin were visible everywhere, in every wine-stained and urine-splashed hallway, in every clanging ambulance bell, in every scar on the faces of the pimps and their whores, in every helpless, newborn baby being brought into this danger, in every knife and pistol fight on the Avenue, and in every disastrous bulletin: a cousin, mother of six, suddenly gone mad, the children parcelled out here and there; an indestructible aunt rewarded for years of hard labor by a slow, agonizing death in a terrible small room; someone's bright son blown into eternity by his own hand; another turned robber and carried off to jail. It was a summer of dreadful speculations and discoveries, of which these were not the worst. Crime became real, for example—for the first time—not as *a* possibility but as *the* possibility. One would never defeat one's circumstances by working and saving one's pennies; one would never, by working, acquire that many pennies, and, besides, the social treatment accorded even the most successful Negroes proved that one needed, in order to be free, something more than a bank account. One needed a handle, a lever, a means of inspiring fear. It was absolutely clear that the police would whip you and take you in as long as they could get away with it, and that everyone else—housewives, taxi-drivers, elevator boys, dishwashers, bartenders, lawyers, judges, doctors, and grocers—would never, by the operation of any generous human feeling, cease to use you as an outlet for his frustrations and hostilities. Neither civilized reason nor Christian love would cause any of the people to treat you as they presumably wanted to be treated; only the fear of your power to retaliate would cause them to do that, or to seem to do it, which was (and is) good enough. There appears to be the vast amount of confusion on this point, but I do not know many Negroes who are eager to be "accepted" by white people, still less to be loved by them; they, the blacks, simply don't wish to be beaten over the head by the whites every instant of our brief passage on this planet. White people in this country will have quite enough to do in learning how to accept and love themselves and each other, and when they have achieved this—which will not be tomorrow and may very well be never—the Negro problem will no longer exist, for it will no longer be needed.

People more advantageously placed than we in Harlem were, and are, will no doubt find the psychology and the view of human nature sketched above dismal and shocking in the extreme. But the Negro's experience of the white world cannot possibly create in him any respect for the standards by which the white world claims to live. His own condition is overwhelming proof that white people do not live by these standards. Negro servants have been smuggling odds and ends out of white homes for generations and white people have been delighted to have them do it, because it has assuaged a dim guilt and testified to the intrinsic superiority of white people. Even the most doltish and servile Negro could scarcely fail to be impressed by the disparity between his situation and that of the people for whom he worked; Negroes who were neither doltish nor servile did not feel that they were doing anything wrong when they robbed white people. In spite of the Puritan-Yankee equation of virtue with well-being, Negroes had excellent reasons for doubting that money was made or kept by any very striking adherence to the Christian virtues; it certainly did not work that way for black Christians. In any case, white people, who had robbed black people of their liberty and who profited by this theft every hour that they lived, had no moral ground on which to stand. They had the judges, the juries, the shot-guns, the law—in a word, power. But it was a criminal power, to be feared but not respected, and to be outwitted in any way whatever. And those virtues preached but not practiced by the white world were merely another means of holding Negroes in subjection.

It turned out, then, that summer, that the moral barriers that I had sup-posed to exist between me and the dangers of a criminal career were so tenuous as to be nearly nonexistent. I certainly could not discover any prin-cipled reason for not becoming a criminal, and it is not my poor, God-fearing parents who are to be indicted for the lack but this society. I was icily determined—more determined, really, than I then knew—never to make my peace with the ghetto but to die and go to Hell before I would let any white man spit on me, before I would accept my "place" in this republic. I did not intend to allow the white people of this country to tell me who I was, and limit me that way, and polish me off that way. And yet, of course, at the same time, I was being spat on and defined and described and limited, and could have been polished off with no effort whatever. Every Negro boy—in my situation during those years, at least—who reaches this point realizes, at once, profoundly, because he wants to live, that he stands in great peril and must find, with speed, a "thing," a gimmick, to lift him out, to start him on his way. *And it does not matter what the gimmick is.* It was this last realiza-tion that terrified me and—since it revealed that the door opened on so many dangers—helped to hurl me into the church. And, by an unforeseeable paradox, it was my career in the church that turned out, precisely, to be my gimmick.

For when I tried to assess my capabilities, I realized that I had almost none. In order to achieve the life I wanted, I had been dealt, it seemed to me, the worst possible hand. I could not become a prize-fighter—many of us tried but very few succeeded. I could not sing. I could not dance. I had been well conditioned by the world in which I grew up, so I did not yet dare take the idea of becoming a writer seriously. The only other possibility seemed to involve my becoming one of the sordid people on the Avenue, who were not really as sordid as I then imagined but who frightened me terribly, both because I did not want to live that life and because of what they made me feel. Everything inflamed me, and that was bad enough, but I myself had also become a source of fire and temptation. I had been far too well raised, alas, to suppose that any of the extremely explicit overtures made to me that summer, sometimes by boys and girls but also, more alarmingly, by older men and women, had anything to do with my attractiveness. On the contrary, since the Harlem idea of seduction is, to put it mildly, blunt, whatever these people saw in me merely confirmed my sense of my depravity.

It is certainly sad that the awakening of one's senses should lead to such a merciless judgement of oneself—to say nothing of the time and anguish one spends in the effort to arrive at any other—but it is also inevitable that a literal attempt to mortify the flesh should be made among black people like those with whom I grew up. Negroes in this country—and Negroes do not, strictly or legally speaking, exist in any other—are taught really to despise themselves from the moment their eyes open on the world. This world is white and they are black. White people hold the power, which means that they are superior to blacks (intrinsically, that is: God decreed it so), and the world has innumerable ways of making this difference known and felt and feared. Long before the Negro child perceives this difference, and even longer before he understands it, he has begun to react to it, he has begun to be controlled by it. Every effort made by the child's elders to prepare him for a fate from which they cannot protect him causes him secretly, in terror, to begin to await, without knowing that he is doing so, his mysterious and inexorable punishment. He must be "good" not only in order to please his parents and not only to avoid being punished by them; behind their authority stands another, nameless and impersonal, infinitely harder to please, and bottomlessly cruel. And this filters into the child's consciousness through his parents' tone of voice as he is being exhorted, punished, or loved; in the sudden, uncontrollable note of fear heard in his mother's or his father's voice when he has strayed beyond some particular boundary. He does not know what the boundary is, and he can get no explanation of it, which is frightening enough, but the fear he hears in the voices of his elders is more frightening still. The fear that I heard in my father's voice, for example, when he realized that I really *believed* I could do anything a white boy could do, and had every intention of proving it, was not at all like the fear I heard when one of us was ill or had fallen down the stairs or strayed too far from the house. It was another fear, a fear that the child, in challenging the white world's assumptions, was putting himself in the path of destruction. A child cannot, thank Heaven, know how vast and how merciless is the nature of power, with what unbelievable cruelty people treat each other. He reacts to the fear in his parents' voices because his parents hold up the world for him and he has no protection without them. I defended myself, as I imagined, against the fear my father made me feel by remembering that he was very old-fashioned. Also, I prided myself on the fact that I already knew how to outwit him. To defend oneself against a fear is simply to insure that one will, one day, be conquered by it; fears must be faced. As for one's wits, it is just not true that one can live by them—not, that is, if one wishes really to live. That summer, in any case, all the fears with which I had grown up, and which were now a part of me and controlled my vision of the world, rose up like a wall between the world and me, and drove me into the church.

As I look back, everything I did seems curiously deliberate, though it certainly did not seem deliberate then. For example, I did not join the church of which my father was a member and in which he preached. My best friend in school, who attended a different church, had already "surrendered his life to the Lord," and he was very anxious about my soul's salvation. (I wasn't, but any human attention was better than none.) One Saturday afternoon, he took me to his church. There were no services that day, and the church was empty, except for some women cleaning and some other women praying. My friend took me into the back room to meet his pastor— a woman. There she sat, in her robes, smiling, an extremely proud and handsome woman, with Africa, Europe, and the America of the American Indian blended in her face. She was perhaps forty-five or fifty at this time, and in our world she was a very celebrated woman. My friend was about to introduce me when she looked at me and smiled and said, "Whose little boy are you?" Now this, unbelievably, was precisely the phrase used by pimps and racketeers on the Avenue when they suggested, both humorously and intensely, that I "hang out" with them. Perhaps part of the terror they had caused me to feel came from the fact that I unquestionably wanted to be *somebody's* little boy. I was so frightened, and at the mercy of so many conundrums, that inevitably, that summer, *someone* would have taken me over; one doesn't, in Harlem, long remain standing on any auction block. It was my good luck—perhaps—that I found myself in the church racket instead of some other, and surrendered to a spiritual seduction long before I came to any carnal knowledge. For when the pastor asked me, with that marvellous smile, "Whose little boy are you?" my heart replied at once, "Why, yours."

The summer wore on, and things got worse. I became more guilty and more frightened, and kept all this bottled up inside me, and naturally, inescapably, one night, when this woman had finished preaching, everything came roaring, screaming, crying out, and I fell to the ground before the altar. It was the strangest sensation I have ever had in my life—up to that time, or since. I had not known that it was going to happen, or that it could happen. One moment I was on my feet, singing and clapping and, at the same time, working out in my head the plot of a play I was working on then; the next moment, with no transition, no sensation of falling, I was on my back, with the lights beating down into my face and all the vertical saints above me. I did not know what I was doing down so low, or how I had got there. And the anguish that filled me cannot be described. It moved in me like one of those floods that devastate counties, tearing everything down, tearing children from their parents and lovers from each other, and making everything an unrecognizable waste. All I really remember is the pain, the unspeakable pain; it was as though I were yelling up to Heaven and Heaven would not hear me. And if Heaven would not hear me, if love could not descend from Heaven—to wash me, to make me clean—then utter disaster was my portion. Yes, it does indeed mean something—something unspeakable—to be born, in a white country, an Anglo-Teutonic, antisexual country, black. You very soon, without knowing it, give up all hope of communion. Black people, mainly, look down or look up but do not look at each other, not at you, and white people, mainly, look away. And the universe is simply a sounding drum; there is no way, no way whatever, so it seemed then and has sometimes seemed since to get through a life, to love your wife and children, or your friends, or your mother and father, or to be loved. The universe, which is not merely the stars and the moon and the planets, flowers, grass, and trees, but *other* people, has evolved no terms for your existence, has made no room for you, and if love will not swing wide the gates, no other power will or can. And if one despairs—as who has not?—of human love, God's love alone is left. But God—and I felt this even then, so long ago, on that tremendous floor, unwillingly—is white. And if His love was so great, and if He loved all His children, why were we, the blacks, cast down so far? Why? In spite of all I said thereafter, I found no answer on the floor—not *that* answer anyway—and I was on the floor all night. Over me, to bring me "through," the saints sang and rejoiced and prayed. And in the morning, when they raised me, they told me that I was "saved."

Well, indeed I was, in a way, for I was utterly drained and exhausted, and released, for the first time, from all my guilty torment. I was aware then only of my relief. For many years, I could not ask myself why human relief had to be achieved in a fashion at once so pagan and so desperate—in a fashion at once so unspeakably old and so unutterably new. And by the time I was able to ask myself this question, I was also able to see that the principles governing the rites and customs of the churches in which I grew up did not differ from the principles governing the rites and customs of other churches, white. The principles were Blindness, Loneliness, and Terror, the first principle necessarily and actively cultivated in order to deny the two others. I would love to believe that the principles were Faith, Hope, and Charity, but this is clearly not so for most Christians, or for what we call the Christian world.

I was saved. But at the same time, out of a deep adolescent cunning I do not pretend to understand, I realized immediately that I could not remain in the church merely as another worshipper. I would have to give myself something to do, in order not to be too bored and find myself among all the wretched unsaved of the Avenue. And I don't doubt that I also intended to best my father on his own ground. Anyway, very shortly after I joined the church, I became a preacher—a Young Minister—and I remained in the pulpit for more than three years. My youth quickly made me a much bigger drawing card than my father. I pushed this advantage ruthlessly, for it was the most effective means I had found of breaking his hold over me. That was the most frightening time of my life, and quite the most dishonest, and the resulting hysteria lent great passion to my sermons—for a while. I relished the attention and the relative immunity from punishment that my new status gave me, and I relished, above all, the sudden right to privacy. It had to be recognized, after all, that I was still a schoolboy, with my schoolwork to do, and I was also expected to prepare at least one sermon a week. During what we may call my heyday, I preached much more often than that. This meant that there were hours and even whole days when I could not be interrupted—not even by my father. I had immobilized him. It took rather more time for me to realize that I had also immobilized myself, and had escaped from nothing whatever.

The church was very exciting. It took a long time for me to disengage myself from this excitement, and on the blindest, most visceral level, I never really have, and never will. There is no music like that music, no drama like the drama of the saints rejoicing, the sinners moaning, the tambourines racing, and all those voices coming together and crying holy unto the Lord. There is still, for me, no pathos quite like the pathos of those multicolored, worn, somehow triumphant and transfigured faces, speaking from the depths of a visible, tangible, continuing despair of the goodness of the Lord. I have never seen anything to equal the fire and excitement that sometimes, without warning, fill a church, causing the church, as Leadbelly and so many others have testified, to "rock." Nothing that has happened to me since equals the power and the glory that I sometimes felt when, in the middle of a sermon, I knew that I was somehow, by some miracle, really carrying, as they said, "the Word"—when the church and I were one. Their pain and their joy were mine, and mine were theirs—they surrendered their pain and joy to me, I surrendered mine to them—and their cries of "Amen!" and "Hallelujah!" and "Yes, Lord!" and "Praise His name!" and "Preach it, brother!" sustained and whipped on my solos until we all became equal, wringing wet, singing and dancing, in anguish and rejoicing, at the foot of the altar. It was, for a long time, in spite of—or, not inconceivably, because of—the shabbiness of my motives, my only sustenance, my meat and drink. I rushed home from school, to the church, to the altar, to be alone there, to commune with Jesus, my dearest Friend, who would never fail me, who knew all the secrets of my heart. Perhaps He did, but I didn't, and the bargain we struck, actually, down there at the foot of the cross, was that He would never let me find out.

He failed His bargain. He was a much better Man than I took Him for. It happened, as things do, imperceptibly, in many ways at once. I date it—the slow crumbling of my faith, the pulverization of my fortress—from the time, about a year after I had begun to preach, when I began to read again. I justified this desire by the fact that I was still in school, and I began, fatally, with Dostoevski.[2] By this time, I was in a high school that was predominantly Jewish. This meant that I was surrounded by people who were, by definition, beyond any hope of salvation, who laughed at the tracts and leaflets I brought to school, and who pointed out that the Gospels had been written long after the death of Christ. This might not have been so distressing if it had not forced me to read the tracts and leaflets myself, for they were indeed, and unless one believed their message already, impossible to believe. I remember feeling dimly that there was a kind of blackmail in it. People, I felt, ought to love the Lord *because* they loved Him, and not because they were afraid of going to Hell. I was forced, reluctantly, to realize that the Bible itself had been written by men, and translated by men out of languages I could not read, and I was already, without quite admitting it to myself, terribly involved with the effort of putting words on paper. Of course, I had the rebuttal ready: These men had all been operating under divine inspiration. *Had* they? *All* of them? And I also knew by now, alas, far more about divine inspiration that I dared admit, for I knew how I worked myself up into my own visions, and how frequently—indeed, incessantly—the visions God granted to me differed from the visions He granted to my father. I did not understand the dreams I had at night, but I knew that they were not holy. For that matter, I knew that my waking hours were far from holy. I spent most of my time in a state of repentance for things I had vividly desired to do but had not done. The fact that I was dealing with Jews brought the whole question of color, which I had been desperately avoiding, into the terrified center of my mind. I realized that the Bible had been written by white men. I knew that, according to many Christians, I was a descendant of Ham, who had been cursed, and that I was therefore predestined to be a slave. This had nothing to do with anything I was, or contained, or could become; my fate had been sealed forever, from the beginning of time. And it seemed, indeed, when one looked out over Christendom, that this was what Christendom effectively believed. It was certainly the way it behaved. I remembered the Italian priests and bishops blessing Italian boys who were on their way to Ethiopia.

Again, the Jewish boys in high school were troubling because I could find no point of connection between them and the Jewish pawnbrokers and landlords and grocerystore owners in Harlem. I knew that these people were Jews—God knows I was told it often enough—but I thought of them only as white. Jews, as such, until I got to high school, were all incarcerated in the Old Testament, and their names were Abraham, Moses, Daniel, Ezekiel, and Job, and Shadrach, Meshach, and Abednego. It was bewildering to find them so many miles and centuries out of Egypt, and so far from the fiery furnace. My best friend in high school was a Jew. He came to our house once, and

---

[2] Fyodor Dostoevski (1821–1881), Russian novelist, author of *Crime and Punishment* (1866), *The Brothers Karamazov* (1879), and other works.

afterward my father asked, as he asked about everyone, "Is he a Christian?"—by which he meant "Is he saved?" I really do not know whether my answer came out of innocence or venom, but I said coldly. "No. He's Jewish." My father slammed me across the face with his great palm, and in that moment everything flooded back—all the hatred and all the fear, and the depth of a merciless resolve to kill my father rather than allow my father to kill me—and I knew that all those sermons and tears and all that repentance and rejoicing had changed nothing. I wondered if I was expected to be glad that a friend of mine, or anyone, was to be tormented forever in Hell, and I also thought, suddenly, of the Jews in another Christian nation, Germany. They were not so far from the fiery furnace after all, and my best friend might have been one of them. I told my father, "He's a better Christian than you are," and walked out of the house. The battle between us was in the open, but that was all right; it was almost a relief. A more deadly struggle had begun.

Being in the pulpit was like being in the theatre; I was behind the scenes and knew how the illusion was worked. I knew the other ministers and knew the quality of their lives. And I don't mean to suggest by this the "Elmer Gantry"[3] sort of hypocrisy concerning sensuality; it was a deeper, deadlier, and more subtle hypocrisy than that, and a little honest sensuality, or a lot, would have been like water in an extremely bitter desert. I knew how to work on a congregation until the last dime was surrendered—it was not very hard to do—and I knew where the money for "the Lord's work" went. I knew, though I did not wish to know it, that I had no respect for the people with whom I worked. I could not have said it then, but I also knew that if I continued I would soon have no respect for myself. And the fact that I was "the young Brother Baldwin" increased my value with those same pimps and racketeers who had helped to stampede me into the church in the first place. They still saw the little boy they intended to take over. They were waiting for me to come to my senses and realize that I was in a very lucrative business. They knew that I did not yet realize this, and also that I had not yet begun to suspect where my own needs, *coming up* (they were very patient), could drive me. They themselves did know the score, and they knew that the odds were in their favor. And, really, I knew it, too. I was even lonelier and more vulnerable than I had been before. And the blood of the Lamb had not cleansed me in any way whatever. I was just as black as I had been the day that I was born. Therefore, when I faced a congregation, it began to take all the strength I had not to stammer, not to curse, not to tell them to throw away their Bibles and get off their knees and go home and organize, for example, a rent strike. When I watched all the children, their copper, brown, and beige faces staring up at me as I taught Sunday school, I felt that

[3] *Elmer Gantry* (1937), a novel by Sinclair
Lewis in which evangelicalism is satirized.

I was committing a crime in talking about the gentle Jesus, in telling them to reconcile themselves to their misery on earth in order to gain the crown of eternal life. Were only Negroes to gain this crown? Was Heaven, then, to be merely another ghetto? Perhaps I might have been able to reconcile myself even to this if I had been able to believe that there was any loving-kindness to be found in the heaven I represented. But I had been in the pulpit too long and I had seen too many monstrous things. I don't refer merely to the glaring fact that the minister eventually acquires houses and Cadillacs while the faithful continue to scrub floors and drop their dimes and quarters and dollars into the plate. I really mean that there was no love in the church. It was a mask for hatred and self-hatred and despair. The transfiguring power of the Holy Ghost ended when the service ended, and salvation stopped at the church door. When we were told to love everybody, I had thought that that meant *everybody*. But no. It applied only to those who believed as we did, and it did not apply to white people at all. I was told by a minister, for example, that I should never, on any public conveyance, under any circumstances, rise and give my seat to a white woman. White men never rose for Negro women. Well, that was true enough, in the main—I saw his point. But what was the point, the purpose, of *my* salvation if it did not permit me to behave with love toward others, no matter how they behaved toward me? What others did was their responsibility, for which they would answer when the judgment trumpet sounded. But what *I* did was *my* responsibility, and I would have to answer, too—unless, of course, there was also in Heaven a special dispensation for the benighted black, who was not to be judged in the same way as other human beings, or angels. It probably occurred to me around this time that the vision people hold of the world to come is but a reflection, with predictable wishful distortions, of the world in which they live. And this did not apply only to Negroes, who were no more "simple" or "spontaneous" or "Christian" than anybody else—who were merely more oppressed. In the same way that we, for white people, were the descendants of Ham, and were cursed forever, white people were, for us, the descendants of Cain. And the passion with which we loved the Lord was a measure of how deeply we feared and distrusted and, in the end, hated almost all strangers, always, and avoided and despised ourselves.

But I cannot leave it at that; there is more to it than that. In spite of everything, there was in the life I fled a zest and a joy and a capacity for facing and surviving disaster that are very moving and very rare. Perhaps we were, all of us—pimps, whores, racketeers, church members, and children—bound together by the nature of our oppression, the specific and peculiar complex of risks we had to run; if so, within these limits we sometimes achieved with each other a freedom that was close to love. I remember, anyway, church suppers and outings, and later, after I left the church, rent and waistline parties where rage and sorrow sat in the darkness and did not stir, and we ate and drank and talked and laughed and danced and forgot all about "the man." We had the liquor, the chicken, the music, and each other, and had no need to pretend to be what we were not. This is the freedom that one hears in some gospel songs, for example, and in jazz. In all jazz, and especially in the blues, there is something tart and ironic, authoritative and double-edged. White Americans seem to feel that happy songs are *happy* and sad songs are *sad*, and that, God help us, is exactly the way most white Americans sing them—sounding, in both cases, so helplessly, defenselessly fatuous that one dare not speculate on the temperature of the deep freeze from which issue their brave and sexless little voices. Only people who have been "down the line," as the song puts it, know what this music is about. I think it was Big Bill Broonzy who used to sing "I Feel So Good," a really joyful song about a man who is on his way to the railroad station to meet his girl. She's coming home. It is the singer's incredibly moving exuberance that makes one realize how leaden the time must have been while she was gone. There is no guarantee that she will stay this time, either, as the singer clearly knows, and, in fact, she has not yet actually arrived. Tonight, or tomorrow, or within the next five minutes, he may very well be singing "Lonesome in My Bedroom," or insisting, "Ain't we, ain't we, going to make it all right? Well, if we don't today, we will tomorrow night." White Americans do not understand the depths out of which such an ironic tenacity comes, but they suspect that the force is sensual, and they are terrified of sensuality and do not any longer understand it. The word "sensual" is not intended to bring to mind quivering dusky maidens or priapic black studs. I am referring to something much simpler and much less fanciful. To be sensual, I think, is to respect and rejoice in the force of life, of life itself, and to be *present* in all that one does, from the effort of loving to the breaking of bread. It will be a great day for America, incidentally, when we begin to eat bread again, instead of the blasphemous and tasteless foam rubber that we have substituted for it. And I am not being frivolous now, either. Something very sinister happens to the people of a country when they begin to distrust their own reactions as deeply as they do here, and become as joyless as they have become. It is the individual uncertainty on the part of white American men and women, this inability to renew themselves at the fountain of their own lives, that makes the discussion, let alone elucidation, of any conundrum— that is, any reality—so supremely difficult. The person who distrusts himself has no touchstone for reality—for this touchstone can be only oneself. Such a person interposes between himself and reality nothing less than a labyrinth of attitudes. And these attitudes, furthermore, though the person is usually unaware of it (is unaware of so much!), are historical and public attitudes. They do not relate to the present any more than they relate to the person. Therefore, whatever white people do not know about Negroes reveals, precisely and inexorably, what they do not know about themselves.

White Christians have also forgotten several elementary historical details. They have forgotten that the religion that is now identified with their virtue and their power—"God is on our side," says Dr. Verwoerd—came out of a rocky piece of ground in what is now known as the Middle East before color was invented, and that in order for the Christian church to be established, Christ had to be put to death, by Rome, and that the real architect of the Christian church was not the disreputable, sun-baked Hebrew who gave it his name but the mercilessly fanatical and self-righteous St. Paul. The energy that was buried with the rise of the Christian nations must come back into the world; nothing can prevent it. Many of us, I think, both long to see this happen and are terrified of it, for though this transformation contains the hope of liberation, it also imposes a necessity for great change. But in order to deal with the untapped and dormant force of the previously subjugated, in order to survive as a human, moving, moral weight in the world, America and all the Western nations will be forced to reëxamine themselves and release themselves from many things that are now taken to be sacred, and to discard nearly all the assumptions that have been used to justify their lives and their anguish and their crimes so long.

"The white man's Heaven," sings a Black Muslim minister, "is the black man's Hell." One may object—possibly—that this puts the matter somewhat too simply, but the song is true, and it has been true for as long as white men have ruled the world. The Africans put it another way: When the white man came to Africa, the white man had the Bible and the African had the land, but now it is the white man who is being, reluctantly and bloodily, separated from the land, and the African who is still attempting to digest or to vomit up the Bible. The struggle, therefore, that now begins in the world is extremely complex, involving the historical role of Christianity in the realm of power— that is, politics—and in the realm of morals. In the realm of power, Christianity has operated with an unmitigated arrogance and cruelty—necessarily, since a religion ordinarily imposes on those who have discovered the true faith the spiritual duty of liberating the infidels. This particular true faith, moreover, is more deeply concerned about the soul than it is about the body, to which fact the flesh (and the corpses) of countless infidels bears witness. It goes without saying, then, that whoever questions the authority of the true faith also contests the right of the nations that hold this faith to rule over him—contests, in short, their title to his land. The spreading of the Gospel, regardless of the motives or the integrity or the heroism of some of the missionaries, was an absolutely indispensable justification for the planting of the flag. Priests and nuns and schoolteachers helped to protect and sanctify the power that was so ruthlessly being used by people who were indeed seeking a city, but not one in the heavens, and one to be made, very definitely, by captive hands. The Christian church itself—again, as distinguished from some of its ministers—sanctified and rejoiced in the conquests of the flag, and encouraged, if it did not formulate, the belief that conquest, with the resulting relative well-being of the Western populations, was proof of the favor of God. God had come a long way from the desert—but then so had

Allah, though in a very different direction. God, going north, and rising on the wings of power, had become white, and Allah, out of power, and on the dark side of Heaven, had become—for all practical purposes, anyway—black. Thus, in the realm of morals the role of Christianity has been, at best, ambivalent. Even leaving out of account the remarkable arrogance that assumed that the ways and morals of others were inferior to those of Christians, and that they therefore had every right, and could use any means, to change them, the collision between cultures—and the schizophrenia in the mind of Christendom—had rendered the domain of morals as chartless as the sea once was, and as trecherous as the sea still is. It is not too much to say that whoever wishes to become a truly moral human being (and let us not ask whether or not this is possible; I think we must *believe* that it is possible) must first divorce himself from all the prohibitions, crimes, and hypocrisies of the Christian church. If the concept of God has any validity or any use, it can only be to make us larger, freer, and more loving. If God cannot do this, then it is time we got rid of Him.

I had heard a great deal, long before I finally met him, of the Honorable Elijah Muhammad,[4] and of the Nation of Islam movement, of which he is the leader. I paid very little attention to what I heard, because the burden of his message did not strike me as being very original; I had been hearing variations of it all my life. I sometimes found myself in Harlem on Saturday nights, and I stood in the crowds, at 125th Street and Seventh Avenue, and listened to the Muslim speakers. But I had heard hundreds of such speeches—or so it seemed to me at first. Anyway, I have long had a very definite tendency to tune out the moment I come anywhere near either a pulpit or a soapbox. What these men were saying about white people I had often heard before. And I dismissed the Nation of Islam's demand for a separate black economy in America, which I had also heard before, as willful, and even mischievous, nonsense. Then two things caused me to begin to listen to the speeches, and one was the behavior of the police. After all, I had seen men dragged from their platforms on this very corner for saying less virulent things, and I had seen many crowds dispersed by policemen, with clubs or on horseback. But the policemen were doing nothing now. Obviously, this was not because they had become more human but because they were under orders and because they were afraid. And indeed they were, and I was delighted to see it. There they stood, in twos and threes and fours, in their Cub Scout uniforms and with their Cub Scout faces, totally unprepared, as is the way with American he-men, for anything that could not be settled with a club or a fist or a gun. I might have pitied them if I had not found myself in their hands so often and discovered, through ugly experi-

---

[4] Elijah Muhammad (?-1975), leader of the
Black Muslims in America.

ence, what they were like when *they* held the power and what they were like when *you* held the power. The behavior of the crowd, its silent intensity, was the other thing that forced me to reassess the speakers and their message. I sometimes think, with despair, that Americans will swallow whole any political speech whatever—we've been doing very little else, these last, bad years—so it may not mean anything to say that this sense of integrity, after what Harlem, especially, has been through in the way of demagogues, was a very startling change. Still, the speakers had an air of utter dedication, and the people looked toward them with a kind of intelligence of hope on their faces—not as though they were being consoled or drugged but as though they were being jolted.

Power was the subject of the speeches I heard. We were offered, as Nation of Islam doctrine, historical and divine proof that all white people are cursed, and are devils, and are about to be brought down. This has been revealed by Allah Himself to His prophet, the Honorable Elijah Muhammad. The white man's rule will be ended forever in ten or fifteen years (and it must be conceded that all present signs would seem to bear witness to the accuracy of the prophet's statement). The crowd seemed to swallow this theology with no effort—all crowds do swallow theology this way, I gather, in both sides of Jerusalem, in Istanbul, and in Rome—and, as theology goes, it was no more indigestible than the more familiar brand asserting that there is a curse on the sons of Ham. No more, and no less, and it had been designed for the same purpose; namely, the sanctification of power. But very little time was spent on theology, for one did not need to prove to a Harlem audience that all white men were devils. They were merely glad to have, at last, divine corroboration of their experience, to hear—and it was a tremendous thing to hear—that they had been lied to for all these years and generations, and that their captivity was ending, for God was black. Why were they *hearing* it now, since this was not the first time it had been said? I had heard it many times, from various prophets, during all the years that I was growing up. Elijah Muhammad himself has now been carrying the same message for more than thirty years; he is not an overnight sensation, and we owe his ministry, I am told, to the fact that when he was a child of six or so, his father was lynched before his eyes. (So much for states' rights.) And now, suddenly, people who have never before been able to hear this message hear it, and believe it, and are changed. Elijah Muhammad has been able to do what generations of welfare workers and committees and resolutions and reports and housing projects and playgrounds have failed to do: to heal and redeem drunkards and junkies, to convert people who have come out of prison and to keep them out, to make men chaste and women virtuous, and to invest both the male and the female with a pride and a serenity that hang about them like an unfailing light. He has done all these things, which our Christian church has spectacularly failed to do. How has Elijah managed it?

Well, in a way—and I have no wish to minimize his peculiar role and his peculiar achievement—it is not he who has done it but time. Time catches up with kingdoms and crushes them, gets its teeth into doctrines and rends them; time reveals the foundations on which any kingdom rests, and eats at those foundations, and it destroys doctrines by proving them to be untrue. In those days, not so very long ago, when the priests of that church which stands in Rome gave God's blessing to Italian boys being sent out to ravage a defenseless black country—which until that event, incidentally, had not considered itself to be black—it was not possible to believe in a black God. To entertain such a belief would have been to entertain madness. But time has passed, and in that time the Christian world has revealed itself as morally bankrupt and politically unstable. The Tunisians were quite right in 1956— and it was a very significant moment in Western (and African) history— when they countered the French justification for remaining in North Africa with the question "Are the *French* ready for self-government?" Again, the terms "civilized" and "Christian" begin to have a very strange ring, particularly in the ears of those who have been judged to be neither civilized nor Christian, when a Christian nation surrenders to a foul and violent orgy, as Germany did during the Third Reich. For the crime of their ancestry, millions of people in the middle of the twentieth century, and in the heart of Europe—God's citadel—were sent to a death so calculated, so hideous, and so prolonged that no age before this enlightened one had been able to imagine it, much less achieve and record it. Furthermore, those beneath the Western heel, unlike those within the West, are aware that Germany's current role in Europe is to act as a bulwark against the "uncivilized" hordes, and since power is what the powerless want, they understand very well what we of the West want to keep, and are not deluded by our talk of a freedom that we have never been willing to share with them. From my own point of view, the fact of the Third Reich alone makes obsolete forever any question of Christian superiority, except in technological terms. White people were, and are, astounded by the holocaust in Germany. They did not know that they could act that way. But I very much doubt whether black people were astounded—at least, in the same way. For my part, the fate of the Jews, and the world's indifference to it, frightened me very much. I could not but feel, in those sorrowful years, that this human indifference, concerning which I knew so much already, would be my portion on the day that the United States decided to murder its Negroes systematically instead of little by little and catch-as-catch-can. I was, of course, authoritatively assured that what had happened to the Jews in Germany could not happen to the Negroes in America, but I thought, bleakly, that the German Jews had probably believed similar counsellors, and, again, I could not share the white man's vision of himself for the very good reason that white men in America do not behave toward black men the way they behave toward each other. When a white man faces a black man, especially if the black man is helpless, terrible things are revealed. I know. I have been carried into precinct basements often enough, and I have seen and heard and endured the secrets of desperate white men and women, which they knew were safe with me, because even if I should speak, no one would believe me. And they would not believe me precisely because they would know that what I said was true.

The treatment accorded the Negro during the Second World War marks, for me, a turning point in the Negro's relation to America. To put it briefly, and somewhat too simply, a certain hope died, a certain respect for white Americans faded. One began to pity them, or to hate them. You must put yourself in the skin of a man who is wearing the uniform of his country, is a candidate for death in its defense, and who is called a "nigger" by his comrades-in-arms and his officers; who is almost always given the hardest, ugliest, most menial work to do; who knows that the white G.I. has informed the Europeans that he is subhuman (so much for the American male's sexual security); who does not dance at the U.S.O. the night white soldiers dance there, and does not drink in the same bars white soldiers drink in; and who watches German prisoners of war being treated by Americans with more human dignity than he has ever received at their hands. And who, at the same time, as a human being, is far freer in a strange land than he has ever been at home. *Home!* The very word begins to have a despairing and diabolical ring. You must consider what happens to this citizen, after all he has endured, when he returns—home: search, in his shoes, for a job, for a place to live; ride, in his skin, on segregated buses; see, with his eyes, the signs saying "White" and "Colored," and especially the signs that say "White Ladies" and "Colored *Women*"; look into the eyes of his wife; look into the eyes of his son; listen, with his ears, to political speeches, North and South; imagine yourself being told to "wait." And all this is happening in the richest and freest country in the world, and in the middle of the twentieth century. The subtle and deadly change of heart that might occur in you would be involved with the realization that a civilization is not destroyed by wicked people; it is not necessary that people be wicked but only that they be spineless. I and two Negro acquaintances, all of us well past thirty, and looking it, were in the bar of Chicago's O'Hare Airport several months ago, and the bartender refused to serve us, because, he said, we looked too young. It took a vast amount of patience not to strangle him, and great insistence and some luck to get the manager, who defended his bartender on the ground that he was "new" and had not yet, presumably, learned how to distinguish between a Negro boy of twenty and a Negro "boy" of thirty-seven. Well, we were served, finally, of course, but by this time no amount of Scotch would have helped us. The bar was very crowded, and our altercation had been extremely noisy; not one customer in the bar had done anything to help us. When it was over, and the three of us stood at the bar trembling with rage and frustration, and drinking—and trapped, now, in the airport, for we had deliberately come early in order to have a few drinks and to eat—a young white man standing near us asked if we were students. I suppose he thought that this was the only possible explanation for our putting up a fight. I told him that he hadn't wanted to talk to us earlier and we didn't want to talk to him now. The reply visibly hurt his feelings, and this, in turn, caused me to despise him. But when one of us, a Korean War veteran, told this young man that the fight we had been having in the bar had been his fight, too, the young man said, "I lost my conscience a long time ago," and turned and walked out. I know that one would rather not think so, but this young man is typical. So on the basis of the evidence, had everyone else in the bar lost *his* conscience. A few years ago, I would have hated these people with all my heart. Now I pitied them, pitied them in order not to despise them. And this is not the happiest way to feel toward one's countrymen.

But, in the end, it is the threat of universal extinction hanging over all the world today that changes, totally and forever, the nature of reality and brings into devastating question the true meaning of man's history. We human beings now have the power to exterminate ourselves; this seems to be the entire sum of our achievement. We have taken this journey and arrived at this place in God's name. This, then, is the best that God (the white God) can do. If that is so, then it is time to replace Him—replace Him with what? And this void, this despair, this torment is felt everywhere in the West, from the streets of Stockholm to the churches of New Orleans and the sidewalks of Harlem.

God is black. All black men belong to Islam; they have been chosen. And Islam shall rule the world. The dream, the sentiment is old; only the color is new. And it is this dream, this sweet possibility, that thousands of oppressed black men and women in this country now carry away with them after the Muslim minister has spoken, through the dark, noisome ghetto streets, into the hovels where so many have perished. The white God has not delivered them; perhaps the Black God will.

While I was in Chicago last summer, the Honorable Elijah Muhammad invited me to have dinner at his home. This is a stately mansion on Chicago's South Side, and it is the headquarters of the Nation of Islam movement. I had not gone to Chicago to meet Elijah Muhammad—he was not in my thoughts at all—but the moment I received the invitation, it occurred to me that I ought to have expected it. In a way, I owe the invitation to the incredible, abysmal, and really cowardly obtuseness of white liberals. Whether in private debate or in public, any attempt I made to explain how the Black Muslim movement came about, and how it has achieved such force, was met with a blankness that revealed the little connection that the liberals' attitudes have with their perceptions or their lives, or even their knowledge—revealed, in fact, that they could deal with the Negro as a symbol or a victim but had no sense of him as a man. When Malcolm X,[5] who is considered the movement's second-in-command, and heir apparent, points out that the cry of "violence" was not raised, for example, when the Israelis fought to regain Israel, and, indeed, is raised only when black men indicate that they will fight for *their* rights, he is speaking the truth. The conquests of England, every single one of them bloody, are part of what Americans have in mind when they speak of England's glory. In the United States, violence and heroism have been made synonymous except when it comes to blacks, and the only way to defeat Malcolm's point is to concede it and then ask oneself why this is so. Malcolm's statement is *not* answered by references to the triumphs of the N.A.A.C.P., the more particularly since very few liberals have any notion of how long, how costly, and how heart-breaking a task it is to gather the evidence that one can carry into the court, or how long such court battles take. Neither is it answered by references to the student sit-in movement, if only because not all Negroes are students and not all of them live in the South. I, in any case, certainly refuse to be put in the position of denying the truth of Malcolm's statements simply because I disagree with his conclusions, or in order to pacify the liberal conscience. Things are as bad as the Muslims say they are—in fact, they are worse, and the Muslims do not help matters—but there *is* no reason that black men should be expected to be more patient, more forbearing, more farseeing than whites; indeed, quite the contrary. The real reason that nonviolence is con-sidered to be a virtue in Negroes—I am not speaking now of its racial value, another matter altogether—is that white men do not want their lives, their self-image, or their property threatened. One wishes they would say so more often. At the end of a television program on which Malcolm X and I both appeared, Malcolm was stopped by a white member of the audience who said, "I have a thousand dollars and an acre of land. What's going to happen to me?" I admired the directness of the man's question, but I didn't hear Malcolm's reply, because I was trying to explain to someone else that the situation of the Irish a hundred years ago and the situation of the Negro today cannot very usefully be compared. Negroes were brought here in chains long before the Irish ever thought of leaving Ireland; what manner of consolation is it to be told that emigrants arriving here—voluntarily—long after you did have risen far above you? In the hall, as I was waiting for the elevator, someone shook my hand and said, "Goodbye, Mr. James Baldwin. We'll soon be addressing you as Mr. James X." And I thought, for an awful moment, My God, if this goes on much longer, you probably will. Elijah Muhammad had seen this show, I think, or another one, and he had been

[5] Malcolm X (1925–1965), black leader and author of *The Autobiography of Malcolm X.* He was assassinated.

told about me. Therefore, late on a hot Sunday afternoon, I presented myself at his door.

I was frightened, because I had, in effect, been summoned into a royal presence. I was frightened for another reason, too. I knew the tension in me between love and power, between pain and rage, and the curious, the grinding way I remained extended between these poles—perpetually attempting to choose the better rather than the worse. But this choice was a choice in terms of a personal, a private better (I was, after all, a writer); what was its relevance in terms of a social worse? Here was the South Side—a million in captivity—stretching from this doorstep as far as the eye could see. And they didn't even read; depressed populations don't have the time or energy to spare. The affluent populations, which should have been their help, didn't, as far as could be discovered, read, either—they merely bought books and devoured them, but not in order to learn: in order to learn new attitudes. Also, I knew that once I had entered the house, I couldn't smoke or drink, and I felt guilty about the cigarettes in my pocket, as I had felt years ago when my friend first took me into his church. I was half an hour late, having got lost on the way here, and I felt as deserving of a scolding as a schoolboy.

The young man who came to the door—he was about thirty, perhaps, with a handsome, smiling face—didn't seem to find my lateness offensive, and led me into a large room. On one side of the room sat half a dozen women, all in white; they were much occupied with a beautiful baby, who seemed to belong the youngest of the women. On the other side of the room sat seven or eight men, young, dressed in dark suits, very much at ease, and very imposing. The sunlight came into the room with the peacefulness one remembers from rooms in one's early childhood—a sunlight encountered later only in one's dreams. I remember being astounded by the quietness, the ease, the peace, the taste. I was introduced, they greeted me with a genuine cordiality and respect—and the respect increased my fright, for it meant that they expected something of me that I knew in my heart, for their sakes, I could not give—and we sat down. Elijah Muhammad was not in the room. Conversation was slow, but not as stiff as I had feared it would be. They kept it going, for I simply did not know which subjects I could acceptably bring up. They knew more about me, and had read more of what I had written, than I had expected, and I wondered what they made of it all, what they took my usefulness to be. The women were carrying on their own conversation, in low tones; I gathered that they were not expected to take part in male conversations. A few women kept coming in and out of the room, apparently making preparations for dinner. We, the men, did not plunge deeply into any subject, for, clearly, we were all waiting for the appearance of Elijah. Presently, the men, one by one, left the room and returned. Then I was asked if I would like to wash, and I, too, walked down the hall to the bathroom. Shortly after I came back, we stood up, and Elijah entered.

I do not know what I had expected to see. I had read some of his speeches, and had heard fragments of others on the radio and on television, so I associated him with ferocity. But, no—the man who came into the room was small and slender, really very delicately put together, with a thin face, large, warm eyes, and a most winning smile. Something came into the room with him—his disciples' joy at seeing him, his joy at seeing them. It was the kind of encounter one watches with a smile simply because it is so rare that people enjoy one another. He teased the women, like a father, with no hint of that ugly and unctuous flirtatiousness I knew so well from other churches, and they responded like that, with great freedom and yet from a great and loving distance. He had seen me when he came into the room, I knew, though he had not looked my way. I had the feeling, as he talked and laughed with the others, whom I could only think of as his children, that he was sizing me up, deciding something. Now he turned toward me, to welcome me, with that marvellous smile, and carried me back nearly twenty-four years, to that moment when the pastor had smiled at me and said, "Whose little boy are you?" I did not respond now as I had responded then, because there are some things (not many, alas!) that one cannot do twice. But I knew what he made me feel, how I was drawn toward his peculiar authority, how his smile promised to take the burden of my life off my shoulders. *Take your burdens to the Lord and leave them there.* The central quality in Elijah's face is pain, and his smile is a witness to it—pain so old and deep and black that it becomes personal and particular only when he smiles. One wonders what he would sound like if he could sing. He turned to me, with that smile, and said something like "I've got a lot to say to *you*, but we'll wait until we sit *down.*" And I laughed. He made me think of my father and me as we might have been if we had been friends.

In the dining room, there were two long tables; the men sat at one and the women at the other. Elijah was at the head of our table, and I was seated at his left. I can scarcely remember what we ate, except that it was plentiful, sane, and simple—so sane and simple that it made me feel extremely decadent, and I think that I drank, therefore, two glasses of milk. Elijah mentioned having seen me on television and said that it seemed to him that I was not yet brainwashed and was trying to become myself. He said this in a curiously unnerving way, his eyes looking into mine and one hand half hiding his lips, as though he were trying to conceal bad teeth. But his teeth were not bad. Then I remembered hearing that he had spent time in prison. I suppose that I *would* like to become myself, whatever that may mean, but I knew that Elijah's meaning and mine were not the same. I said yes, I was trying to be me, but I did not know how to say more than that, and so I waited.

Whenever Elijah spoke, a kind of chorus arose from the table, saying "Yes, that's right." This began to set my teeth on edge. And Elijah himself had a further, unnerving habit, which was to ricochet his questions and comments off someone else on their way to you. Now, turning to the man on his right, he began to speak of the white devils with whom I had last appeared on TV: What had they made *him* (me) feel? I could not answer this and was not absolutely certain that I was expected to. The people referred to had certainly made me feel exasperated and useless, but I did not think of them as devils. Elijah went on about the crimes of white people, to this endless chorus of "Yes, that's right." Someone at the table said. "The white man sure *is* a devil. He proves that by his own actions." I looked around. It was a very young man who had said this, scarcely more than a boy—very dark and sober, very bitter. Elijah began to speak of the Christian religion, of Christians, in the same soft, joking way. I began to see that Elijah's power came from his single-mindedness. There is nothing calculated about him; he means every word he says. The real reason, according to Elijah, that I failed to realize that the white man was a devil was that I had been too long exposed to white teaching and had never received true instruction. "The so-called American Negro" is the only reason Allah has permitted the United States to endure so long; the white man's time was up in 1913, but it is the will of Allah that this lost black nation, the black men of this country, be redeemed from their white masters and returned to the true faith, which is Islam. Until this is done—and it will be accomplished very soon—the total destruction of the white man is being delayed. Elijah's mission is to return "the so-called Negro" to Islam, to separate the chosen of Allah from this doomed nation. Furthermore, the white man knows his history, knows himself to be a devil, and knows that his time is running out, and all his technology, psychology, science, and "tricknology" are being expended in the effort to prevent black men from hearing the truth. This truth is that at the very beginning of time there was not one white face to be found in all the universe. Black men ruled the earth and the black man was perfect. This is the truth concerning the era that white men now refer to as prehistoric. They want black men to believe that they, like white men, once lived in caves and swung from trees and ate their meat raw and did not have the power of speech. But this is not true. Black men were never in such a condition. Allah allowed the Devil, through his scientists, to carry on informal experiments, which resulted, finally, in the creation of the devil known as the white man, and later, even more disastrously, in the creation of the white woman. And it was decreed that these monstrous creatures should rule the earth for a certain number of years—I forget how many thousand, but, in any case, their rule now is ending, and Allah, who had never approved of the creation of the white man in the first place (who knows him, in fact, to be not a man at all but a devil), is anxious to restore the rule of peace that the rise of the white man totally destroyed. There is thus, by definition, no virtue in white people, and since they are another creation entirely and can no more, by breeding, become black than a cat, by breeding, can become a horse, there is no hope for them.

There is nothing new in this merciless formulation except the explicitness of its symbols and the candor of its hatred. Its emotional tone is as familiar to me as my own skin; it is but another way of saying that *sinners shall be bound in Hell a thousand years.* That sinners have always, for American Negroes, been white is a truth we needn't labor, and every American Negro, therefore, risks having the gates of paranoia close on him. In a society that is entirely hostile, and, by its nature, seems determined to cut you down—that has cut down so many in the past and cuts down so many every day—it begins to be almost impossible to distinguish a real from a fancied injury. One can very quickly cease to attempt this distinction, and, what is worse, one usually ceases to attempt it without realizing that one has done so. All doormen, for example, and all policemen have by now, for me, become exactly the same, and my style with them is designed simply to intimidate them before they can intimidate me. No doubt I am guilty of some injustice here, but it is irreducible, since I cannot risk assuming that the humanity of these people is more real to them than their uniforms. Most Negroes cannot risk assuming that the humanity of white people is more real to them than their color. And this leads, imperceptibly but inevitably, to a state of mind in which, having long ago learned to expect the worst, one finds it very easy to believe the worst. The brutality with which Negroes are treated in this country simply cannot be overstated, however unwilling white men may be to hear it. In the beginning—neither can this be overstated—a Negro just cannot *believe* that white people are treating him as they do; he does not know what he has done to merit it. And when he realizes that the treatment accorded him has nothing to do with anything he has done, that the attempt of white people to destroy him—for that is what it is—is utterly gratuitous, it is not hard for him to think of white people as devils. For the horrors of the American Negro's life there has been almost no language. The privacy of his experience, which is only beginning to be recognized in language, and which is denied or ignored in official and popular speech—hence the Negro idiom—lends credibility to any system that pretends to clarify it. And, in fact, the truth about the black man, as a historical entity and as a human being, *has* been hidden from him deliberately and cruelly; the power of the white world is threatened whenever a black man refuses to accept the white world's definitions. So every attempt is made to cut that black man down—not only was made yesterday but is made today. Who, then, is to say with authority where the root of so much anguish and evil lies? Why, then, is it not possible that all things began with the black man and that he was perfect—especially since this is precisely the claim that white people have put forward for themselves all these years? Furthermore, it is now absolutely clear that white people are a minority in the world—so severe a minority that they now look rather more like an invention—and that they cannot possibly hope to rule it any longer. If this is so, why is it not also possible that they achieved their original dominance by stealth and cunning and bloodshed and in opposition to the will of Heaven, and not, as they claim, by Heaven's will? And if *this* is so, then the sword they have used so long against others, can now, without mercy, be used against them. Heavenly witnesses are a tricky lot, to be used by whoever is closest to Heaven at the time. And legend and theology, which are designed to sanctify our fears, crimes, and aspirations, also reveal them for what they are.

I said, at last, in answer to some other ricocheted questions, "I left the church twenty years ago and I haven't joined anything since." It was my way of saying that I did not intend to join their movement, either.

"And what are you now?" Elijah asked.

I was in something of a bind, for I really could not say—could not allow myself to be stampeded into saying—that I was a Christian. "I? Now? Nothing." This was not enough. "I'm a writer. I like doing things alone." I heard myself saying this. Elijah smiled at me. "I don't, anyway," I said, finally, "think about it a great deal."

Elijah said, to his right, "I think he ought to think about it *all* the deal," and with this the table agreed. But there was nothing malicious or condemnatory in it. I had the stifling feeling that *they* knew I belonged to them but knew that I did not know it yet, that I remained unready, and that they were simply waiting, patiently, and with assurance, for me to discover the truth for myself. For where else, after all, could I go? I was black, and therefore a part of Islam, and would be saved from the holocaust awaiting the white world whether I would or no. My weak, deluded scruples could avail nothing against the iron word of the prophet.

I felt that I was back in my father's house—as, indeed, in a way, I was—and I told Elijah that *I* did not care if white and black people married, and that I had many white friends. I would have no choice, if it came to it, but to perish with them, for (I said to myself, but not to Elijah), "I love a few people and they love me and some of them are white, and isn't love more important than color?"

Elijah looked at me with great kindness and affection, great pity, as though he were reading my heart, and indicated, skeptically, that I *might* have white friends, or think I did, and they *might* be trying to be decent—now—but their time was up. It was almost as though he were saying, "They had their chance, man, and they goofed!"

And I looked around the table. I certainly had no evidence to give them that would outweigh Elijah's authority or the evidence of their own lives or the reality of the streets outside. Yes, I knew two or three people, white, whom I would trust with my life, and I knew a few others, white, who were struggling as hard as they knew how, and with great effort and sweat and risk, to make the world more human. But how could I say this? One cannot argue with anyone's experience or decision or belief. All my evidence would be thrown out of court as irrelevant to the main body of the case, for I could cite only exceptions. The South Side proved the justice of the indictment;

the state of the world proved the justice of the indictment. Everything else, stretching back throughout recorded time, was merely a history of those exceptions who had tried to change the world and had failed. Was this true? *Had* they failed? How much depended on the point of view? For it would seem that a certain category of exceptions never failed to make the world worse—that category, precisely, for whom power is more real than love. And yet power *is* real, and many things, including, very often, love, cannot be achieved without it. In the eeriest way possible, I suddenly had a glimpse of what white people must go through at a dinner table when they are trying to prove that Negroes are not subhuman. I had almost said, after all, "Well, take my friend Mary," and very nearly descended to a catalogue of those virtues that gave Mary the right to be alive. And in what hope? That Elijah and the others would nod their heads solemnly and say, at least, "Well, *she's* all right—but the *others!*"

And I looked again at the young faces around the table, and looked back to Elijah, who was saying that no people in history had ever been respected who had not owned their land. And the table said, "Yes, that's right." I could not deny the truth of this statement. For everyone else has, *is*, a nation, with a specific location and a flag—even, these days, the Jew. It is only "the so-called American Negro" who remains trapped, disinherited, and despised, in a nation that has kept him in bondage for nearly four hundred years and is still unable to recognize him as a human being. And the Black Muslims, along with many people who are not Muslims, no longer wish for a recognition so grudging and (should it ever be achieved) so tardy. Again, it cannot be denied that this point of view is abundantly justified by American Negro history. It is galling indeed to have stood so long, hat in hand, waiting for Americans to grow up enough to realize that you do not threaten them. On the other hand, how is the American Negro now to form himself into a separate nation? For this—and not only from the Muslim point of view— would seem to be his only hope of not perishing in the American backwater and being entirely and forever forgotten as though he had never existed at all and his travail had been for nothing.

Elijah's intensity and the bitter isolation and dissaffection of these young men and the despair of the streets outside had caused me to glimpse dimly what may now seem to be a fantasy, although, in an age so fantastical, I would hesitate to say precisely what a fantasy is. Let us say that the Muslims were to achieve the possession of the six or seven states that they claim are owed to Negroes by the United States as "back payment" for slave labor. Clearly, the United States would never surrender this territory, on any terms whatever, unless it found it impossible, for whatever reason, to hold it— unless, that is, the United States were to be reduced as a world power, exactly the way, and at the same degree of speed, that England has been forced to relinquish her Empire. (It is simply not true—and the state of her ex-colonies proves this—that England "always meant to go.") If the states were Southern states—and the Muslims seem to favor this—then the borders of a hostile Latin America would be raised, in effect, to, say, Maryland. Of the American borders on the sea, one would face toward a powerless Europe and the other toward an untrustworthy and non-white East, and on the North, after Canada, there would be only Alaska, which is a Russian border. The effect of this would be that the white people of the United States and Canada would find themselves marooned on a hostile continent, with the rest of the white world probably unwilling and certainly unable to come to their aid. All this is not, to my mind, the most imminent of possibilities, but if I were a Muslim, this is the possibility that I would find myself holding in the center of my mind, and driving toward. And if I were a Muslim, I would not hesitate to utilize—or, indeed, to exacerbate—the social and spiritual discontent that reigns here, for at the very worst, I would merely have contributed to the destruction of a house I hated, and it would not matter if I perished, too. One has been perishing here so long!

And what were they thinking around the table? "I've come," said Elijah, "to give you something which can never be taken away from you." How solemn the table became then, and how great a light rose in the dark faces! This is the message that has spread through streets and tenements and prisons, through the narcotics wards, and past the filth and sadism of mental hospitals to a people from whom everything has been taken away, including, most crucially, their sense of their own worth. People cannot live without this sense; they will do anything whatever to regain it. This is why the most dangerous creation of any society is that man who has nothing to lose. You do not need ten such men—one will do. And *Elijah*, I should imagine, has had nothing to lose since the day he saw his father's blood rush out—rush down, and splash, so the legend has it, down through the leaves of a tree, on him. But neither did the other men around the table have anything to lose. "Return to your true religion," Elijah has written. "Throw off the chains of the slavemaster, the devil, and return to the fold. Stop drinking his alcohol, using his dope—protect your women—and forsake the filthy swine." I remembered my buddies of years ago, in the hallways, with their wine and their whiskey and their tears; in hallways still, frozen on the needle; and my brother saying to me once, "If Harlem didn't have so many churches and junkies, there'd be blood flowing in the streets." *Protect your women:* a difficult thing to do in a civilization sexually so pathetic that the white man's masculinity depends on a denial of the masculinity of the blacks. *Protect your women:* in a civilization that emasculates the male and abuses the female, and in which, moreover, the male is forced to depend on a female's bread-winning power. *Protect your women:* in the teeth of the white man's boast "We figure we're doing you folks a favor by pumping some white blood into your kids," and while facing the Southern shotgun and the Northern billy. Years ago, we used to say, "*Yes*, I'm black, goddammit, and I'm beautiful!"—in defiance, into the void. But now—now—African kings and heroes have come into the world, out of the past, the past that can now be put to the uses of power. And black has *become* a beautiful color—not because it is loved but because it is feared. And this urgency on the part of American Negroes is *not to be forgotten!* As they watch black men elsewhere rise, the promise held out, at last, that they may walk the earth with the authority with which white men walk, protected by the power that white men shall have no longer, is enough, and more than enough, to empty prisons and pull God down from Heaven. It has happened before, many times, before color was invented, and the hope of Heaven has always been a metaphor for the achievement of this particular state of grace. The song says, "I know my robe's going to fit me well. I tried it on at the gates of Hell."

It was time to leave, and we stood in the large living room, saying good night, with everything curiously and heavily unresolved. I could not help feeling that I had failed a test, in their eyes and in my own, or that I had failed to heed a warning. Elijah and I shook hands, and he asked me where I was going. Wherever it was, I would be driven there—"because, when we invite someone here," he said, "we take the responsibility of protecting him from the white devils until he gets wherever it is he's going." I was, in fact, going to have a drink with several white devils on the other side of town. I confess that for a fraction of a second I hesitated to give the address—the kind of address that in Chicago, as in all American cities, identified itself as a white address by virtue of its location. But I did give it, and Elijah and I walked out onto the steps, and one of the young men vanished to get the car. It was very strange to stand with Elijah for those few moments, facing those vivid, violent, so problematical streets. I felt very close to him, and really wished to be able to love and honor him as a witness, an ally, and a father. I felt that I knew something of his pain and his fury, and, yes, even his beauty. Yet precisely because of the reality and the nature of those streets—because of what he conceived as his responsibility and what I took to be mine—we would always be strangers, and possibly, one day, enemies. The car arrived—a gleaming, metallic, grossly American blue—and Elijah and I shook hands and said good night once more. He walked into his mansion and shut the door.

The driver and I started on our way through dark, murmuring—and, at this hour, strangely beautiful—Chicago, along the lake. We returned to the discussion of the land. How were we—Negroes—to get this land? I asked this of the dark boy who had said earlier, at the table, that the white man's actions proved him to be a devil. He spoke to me first of the Muslim temples that were being built or were about to be built, in various parts of the United States, of the strength of the Muslim following, and of the amount of money that is annually at the disposal of Negroes—something like twenty billion dollars. "That alone shows you how strong we are," he said. But, I persisted, cautiously, and in somewhat different terms, this twenty billion dollars, or whatever it is, depends on the total economy of the United States. What happens when the Negro is no longer a part of this economy? Leaving aside the fact that in order for this to happen the economy of the United States will itself have had to undergo radical and certainly disastrous changes, the American Negro's spending power will obviously no longer be the same. On what, then, will the economy of this separate nation be based? The boy gave me a rather strange look. I said hurriedly, "I'm not saying it *can't* be done— I just want to know *how* it's to be done." I was thinking, in order for this to happen, your entire frame of reference will have to change, and you will be forced to surrender many things that you now scarcely know you have. I didn't feel that the things I had in mind, such as the pseudo-elegant heap of tin in which we were riding, had any very great value. But life would be very different without them, and I wondered if he had thought of this.

How can one, however, dream of power in any other terms than in the symbols of power? The boy could see that freedom depended on the posses-sion of land; he was persuaded that, in one way or another, Negroes must achieve this possession. In the meantime, he could walk the streets and fear nothing, because there were millions like him, coming soon, now, to power. He was held together, in short, by a dream—though it is just as well to remember that some dreams come true—and was united with his "brothers" on the basis of their color. Perhaps one cannot ask for more. People always seem to band together in accordance to a principle that has nothing to do with love, a principle that releases them from responsibility.

Yet I could have hoped that the Muslim movement had been able to inculcate in the demoralized Negro population a truer and more individual sense of its own worth, so that Negroes in the Northern ghettos could begin, in concrete terms, and at whatever price, to change their situation. But in order to change a situation one has first to see it for what it is: in the present case, to accept the fact, whatever one does with it thereafter, that the Negro has been formed by this nation, for better or for worse, and does not belong to any other—not to Africa, and certainly not to Islam. The paradox—and a fearful paradox it is—is that the American Negro can have no future any-where, on any continent, as long as he is unwilling to accept his past. To accept one's past—one's history—is not the same thing as drowning in it; it is learning how to use it. An invented past can never be used; it cracks and crumbles under the pressures of life like clay in a season of drought. How can the American Negro's past be used? The unprecedented price de-manded—and at this embattled hour of the world's history—is the transcen-dence of the realities of color, of nations, and of altars.

"Anyway," the boy said suddenly, after a very long silence, "things won't ever again be the way they used to be. I know *that*."

And so we arrived in enemy territory, and they set me down at the enemy's door.

No one seems to know where the Nation of Islam gets its money. A vast amount, of course, is contributed by Negroes, but there are rumors to the effect that people like Birchites and certain Texas oil millionaires look with favor on the movement. I have no way of knowing whether there is any truth to the rumors, though since these people make such a point of keeping the races separate, I wouldn't be surprised if for this smoke there was some fire. In any case, during a recent Muslim rally, George Lincoln Rockwell, the chief of the American Nazi party, made a point of contributing about twenty dollars to the cause, and he and Malcolm X decided that, racially speaking, anyway, they were in complete agreement. The glorification of one race and the consequent debasement of another—or others—always has been and always will be a recipe for murder. There is no way around this. If one is permitted to treat any group of people with special disfavor because of their race or the color of their skin, there is no limit to what one will force them to endure, and, since the entire race has been mysteriously indicted, no reason not to attempt to destroy it root and branch. This is precisely what the Nazis attempted. Their only originality lay in the means they used. It is scarcely worthwhile to attempt remembering how many times the sun has looked down on the slaughter of the innocents. I am very much concerned that American Negroes achieve their freedom here in the United States. But I am also concerned for their dignity, for the health of their souls, and must oppose any attempt that Negroes may make to do to others what has been done to them. I think I know—we see it around us every day—the spiritual wasteland to which that road leads. It is so simple a fact and one that is so hard, apparently, to grasp: *Whoever debases others is debasing himself.* That is not a mystical statement but a most realistic one, which is proved by the eyes of any Alabama sheriff—and I would not like to see Negroes ever arrive at so wretched a condition.

Now, it is extremely unlikely that Negroes will ever rise to power in the United States, because they are only approximately a ninth of this nation. They are not in the position of the Africans, who are attempting to reclaim their land and break the colonial yoke and recover from the colonial experience. The Negro situation is dangerous in a different way, both for the Negro qua Negro and for the country of which he forms so troubled and troubling a part. The American Negro is a unique creation; he has no counterpart anywhere, and no predecessors. The Muslims react to this fact by referring to the Negro as "the so-called American Negro" and substituting for the names inherited from slavery the letter "X." It is a fact that every American Negro bears a name that originally belonged to the white man whose chattel he was. I am called Baldwin because I was either sold by my African tribe or kidnapped out of it into the hands of a white Christian named Baldwin, who forced me to kneel at the foot of the cross. I am, then, both visibly and legally the descendant of slaves in a white, Protestant country, and this is what it means to be an American Negro, this is who he is—a kidnapped pagan, who was sold like an animal and treated like one, who was once defined by the American Constitution as "three-fifths" of a man, and who, according to the Dred Scott decision, had no rights that a white man was bound to respect. And today, a hundred years after his technical emancipation, he remains—with the possible exception of the American Indian—the most despised creature in his country. Now, there is simply no possibility of a real change in the Negro's situation without the most radical and far-reaching changes in the American political and social structure. And it is clear that white Americans are not simply unwilling to effect these changes; they are, in the main, so slothful have they become, unable even to envision them. It must be added that the Negro himself no longer believes in the good faith of white Americans—if, indeed, he ever could have. What the Negro *has* discovered, and on an international level, is that power to intimidate which he has always had privately but hitherto could manipulate only privately—for private ends often, for limited ends always. And therefore when the country speaks of a "new" Negro, which it has been doing every hour on the hour for decades, it is not really referring to a change in the Negro, which, in any case, it is quite incapable of assessing, but only to a new difficulty in keeping him in his place, to the fact that it encounters him (again! again!) barring yet another door to its spiritual and social ease. This is probably, hard and odd as it may sound, the most important thing that one human being can do for another—it is certainly *one* of the most important things; hence the torment and necessity of love—and this is the enormous contribution that the Negro has made to this otherwise shapeless and undiscovered country. Consequently, white Americans are in nothing more deluded than in supposing that Negroes could ever have imagined that white people would "give" them anything. It is rare indeed that people give. Most people guard and keep; they suppose that it is they themselves and what they identify with themselves that they are guarding and keeping, whereas what they are actually guarding and keeping is their system of reality and what they assume themselves to be. One can give nothing whatever without giving oneself—that is to say, risking oneself. If one cannot risk oneself, then one is simply incapable of giving. And, after all, one can give freedom only by setting someone free. This, in the case of the Negro, the American republic has never become sufficiently mature to do. White Americans have contented themselves with gestures that are now described as "tokenism." For hard example, white Americans congratulate themselves on the 1954 Supreme Court decision outlawing segregation in the schools; they suppose, in spite of the mountain of evidence that has since accumulated to the contrary, that this was proof of a change of heart—or, as they like to say, progress. Perhaps. It all depends on how one reads the word "progress." Most of the Negroes I know do not believe that this immense concession would ever have been made if it had not been for the competition of the Cold War, and the fact that Africa was clearly liberating herself and therefore had, for political reasons, to be wooed by the descendants of her former masters. Had it been a matter of love or justice, the 1954 decision would surely have occurred sooner; were it not for the realities of power in this difficult era, it might very well not have occurred yet. This seems an extremely harsh way of stating the case—ungrateful, as it were—but the evidence that supports this way of stating it is not easily refuted. I myself do not think that it can be refuted at all. In any event, the sloppy and fatuous nature of American good will can never be relied upon to deal with hard problems. These have been dealt with, when they have been dealt with at all, out of necessity—and in political terms, anyway, necessity means concessions made in order to stay on top. I think this is a fact, which it serves no purpose to deny, *but, whether it is a fact or not, this is what the black population of the world, including black Americans, really believe.* The word "independence" in Africa and the word "integration" here are almost equally meaningless; that is, Europe has not yet left Africa, and black men here are not yet free. And both of these last statements are undeniable facts, related facts, containing the gravest implications for us all. The Negroes of this country may never be able to rise to power, but they are very well placed indeed to precipitate chaos and ring down the curtain on the American dream.

This has everything to do, of course, with the nature of that dream and with the fact that we Americans, of whatever color, do not dare examine it and are far from having made it a reality. There are too many things we do not wish to know about ourselves. People are not, for example, terribly anxious to be equal (equal, after all, to what and to whom?) but they love the idea of being superior. And this human truth has an especially grinding force here, where identity is almost impossible to achieve and people are perpetually attempting to find their feet on the shifting sands of status. (Consider the history of labor in a country in which, spiritually speaking, there are no workers, only candidates for the hand of the boss's daughter.) Furthermore, I have met only a very few people—and most of these were not Americans—who had any real desire to be free. Freedom is hard to bear. It can be objected that I am speaking of political freedom in spiritual terms, but the political institutions of any nation are always menaced and are ultimately controlled by the spiritual state of that nation. We are controlled here by our confusion, far more than we know, and the American dream has therefore become something much more closely resembling a nightmare, on the private, domestic, and international levels. Privately, we cannot stand our lives and dare not examine them; domestically, we take no responsibility for (and no pride in) what goes on in our country; and, internationally, for many millions of people, we are an unmitigated disaster. Whoever doubts this last statement has only to open his ears, his heart, his mind, to the testimony of— for example—any Cuban peasant or any Spanish poet, and ask himself what *he* would feel about us if *he* were the victim of our performance in pre-Castro Cuba or in Spain. We defend our curious role in Spain by referring to the Russian menace and the necessity of protecting the free world. It has not occurred to us that we have simply been mesmerized by Russia, and that the only real advantage Russia has in what we think of as a struggle between the East and the West is the moral history of the Western world. Russia's secret weapon is the bewilderment and despair and hunger of millions of people of whose existence we are scarcely aware. The Russian Communists are not in the least concerned about these people. But our ignorance and indecision have had the effect, if not of delivering them into Russian hands, of plunging them very deeply in the Russian shadow, for which effect—and it is hard to blame them—the most articulate among them, and the most oppressed as well, distrust us all the more. Our power and our fear of change help bind these people to their misery and bewilderment, and insofar as they find this state intolerable we are intolerably menaced. For if they find their state intolerable, but are too heavily oppressed to change it, they are simply pawns in the hands of larger powers, which, in such a context, are always unscrupulous, and when, eventually, they do change their situation—as in Cuba—we are menaced more than ever, by the vacuum that succeeds all violent upheavals. We should certainly know by now that it is one thing to overthrow a dictator or repel an invader and quite another thing really to achieve a revolution. Time and time and time again, the people discover that they have merely betrayed themselves into the hands of yet another Pharaoh, who, since he was necessary to put the broken country together, will not let them go. Perhaps, people being the conundrums that they are, and having so little desire to shoulder the burden of their lives, this is what will always happen. But at the bottom of my heart I do not believe this. I think that people can be better than that, and I know that people can be better than they are. We are capable of bearing a great burden, once we discover that the burden is reality and arrive where reality is. Anyway, the point here is that we are living in an age of revolution, whether we will or no, and that America is the only Western nation with both the power and, as I hope to suggest, the experience that may help to make these revolutions real and minimize the human damage. Any attempt we make to oppose these out-bursts of energy is tantamount to signing our death warrant.

Behind what we think of as the Russian menace lies what we do not wish to face, and what white Americans do not face when they regard a Negro: reality—the fact that life is tragic. Life is tragic simply because the earth turns and the sun inexorably rises and sets, and one day, for each of us, the sun will go down for the last, last time. Perhaps the whole root of our trouble, the human trouble, is that we will sacrifice all the beauty of our lives, will imprison ourselves in totems, taboos, crosses, blood sacrifices, stee-ples, mosques, races, armies, flags, nations, in order to deny the fact of death, which is the only fact we have. It seems to me that one ought to rejoice in the *fact* of death—ought to decide, indeed, to *earn* one's death by confront-ing with passion the conundrum of life. One is responsible to life: It is the small beacon in that terrifying darkness from which we come and to which we shall return. One must negotiate this passage as nobly as possible, for the sake of those who are coming after us. But white Americans do not believe in death, and this is why the darkness of my skin so intimidates them. And this is also why the presence of the Negro in this country can bring about its destruction. It is the responsibility of free men to trust and to celebrate what is constant—birth, struggle, and death are constant, and so is love, though we may not always think so—and to apprehend the nature of change, to be able and willing to change. I speak of change not on the surface but in the depths—change in the sense of renewal. But renewal becomes impossible if one supposes things to be constant that are not—safety, for example, or money, or power. One clings then to chimeras, by which one can only be betrayed, and the entire hope—the entire possibility—of freedom disappears. And by destruction I mean precisely the abdication of Americans of any effort really to be free. The Negro can precipitate this abdication because white Americans have never, in all their long history, been able to look on him as a man like themselves. This point need not be labored; it is proved over and over again by the Negro's continuing position here, and his indescribable struggle to defeat the stratagems that white Americans have used, and use, to deny him his humanity. America could have used in other ways the energy that both groups have expended in this conflict. America, of all the Western nations, has been best placed to prove the uselessness and the obsolescence of the concept of color. But it has not dared to accept this opportunity, or even to conceive of it as an opportunity. White Americans have thought of it as their shame, and have envied those more civilized and elegant European nations that were untroubled by the presence of black men on their shores. This is because white Americans have supposed "Europe" and "civilization" to be synonyms—which they are not—and have been distrustful of other standards and other sources of vitality, especially those produced in America itself, and have attempted to behave in all matters as though what was east for Europe was also east for them. What it comes to is that if we, who can scarcely be considered a white nation, persist in thinking of ourselves as one, we condemn ourselves, with the truly white nations, to sterility and decay, whereas if we could accept ourselves *as we are*, we might bring new life to the Western achievements, and transform them. The price of this transformation is the unconditional freedom of the Negro; it is not too much to say that he, who has been so long rejected, must now be embraced, and at no matter what psychic or social risk. He is *the* key figure in his country, and the American future is precisely as bright or as dark as his. And the Negro recognizes this, in a negative way. Hence the question: Do I really *want* to be integrated into a burning house?

White Americans find it as difficult as white people elsewhere do to divest themselves of the notion that they are in possession of some intrinsic value that black people need, or want. And this assumption—which, for example, makes the solution to the Negro problem depend on the speed with which Negroes accept and adopt white standards—is revealed in all kinds of striking ways, from Bobby Kennedy's assurance that a Negro can become President in forty years to the unfortunate tone of warm congratulation with which so many liberals address their Negro equals. It is the Negro, of course, who is presumed to have become equal—an achievement that not only proves the comforting fact that perseverance has no color but also overwhelmingly corroborates the white man's sense of his own value. Alas, this value can scarcely be corroborated in any other way; there is certainly little enough in the white man's public or private life that one should desire to imitate. White men, at the bottom of their hearts, know this. Therefore, a vast amount of the energy that goes into what we call the Negro problem is produced by the white man's profound desire not to be judged by those who are not white, not to be seen as he is, and at the same time a vast amount of the white anguish is rooted in the white man's equally profound need to be seen as he is, to be released from the tyranny of his mirror. All of us know, whether or not we are able to admit it, that mirrors can only lie, that death by drowning is all that awaits one there. It is for this reason that love is so desperately sought and so cunningly avoided. Love takes off the masks that we fear we cannot live without and know we cannot live within. I use the word "love" here not merely in the personal sense but as a state of being, or a state of grace—not in the infantile American sense of being made happy but in the tough and universal sense of quest and daring and growth. And I submit, then, that the racial tensions that menace Americans today have little to do with real antipathy—on the contrary, indeed—and are involved only symbolically with color. These tensions are rooted in the very same depths as those from which love springs, or murder. The white man's unadmitted— and apparently, to him unspeakable—private fears and longings are projected onto the Negro. The only way he can be released from the Negro's tyrannical power over him is to consent, in effect, to become black himself, to become a part of that suffering and dancing country that he now watches wistfully from the heights of his lonely power and, armed with spiritual traveller's checks, visits surreptitiously after dark. How can one respect, let alone adopt, the values of a people who do not, on any level whatever, live the way they say they do, or the way they say they should? I cannot accept the proposition that the four-hundred-year travail of the American Negro should result merely in his attainment of the present level of the American civilization. I am far from convinced that being released from the African witch doctor was worthwhile if I am now—in order to support the moral contradictions and the spiritual aridity of my life—expected to become dependent on the American psychiatrist. It is a bargain I refuse. The only thing white people have that black people need, or should want, is power—and no one holds power forever. White people cannot, in the generality, be taken as models of how to live. Rather, the white man is himself in sore need of new standards, which will release him from his confusion and place him once again in fruitful communion with the depths of his own being. And I repeat: The price of the liberation of the white people is the liberation of the blacks—the total liberation, in the cities, in the towns, before the law, and in the mind. Why, for example—especially knowing the family as I do—I should *want* to marry your sister is a great mystery to me. But your sister and I have every right to marry if we wish to, and no one has the right to stop us. If she cannot raise me to her level, perhaps I can raise her to mine.

In short, we, the black and the white, deeply need each other here if we are really to become a nation—if we are really, that is, to achieve our identity, our maturity, as men and women. To create one nation has proved to be a hideously difficult task; there is certainly no need now to create two, one black and one white. But white men with far more political power than that possessed by the Nation of Islam movement have been advocating exactly this, in effect, for generations. If this sentiment is honored when it falls from the lips of Senator Byrd, then there is no reason it should not be honored when it falls from the lips of Malcolm X. And any Congressional committee wishing to investigate the latter must also be willing to investigate the former. They are espressing exactly the same sentiments and represent exactly the same danger. There is absolutely no reason to suppose that white people are better equipped to frame the laws by which I am to be governed than I am. It is entirely unacceptable that I should have no voice in the political affairs of my own country, for I am not a ward of America; I am one of the first Americans to arrive on these shores.

This past, the Negro's past, of rope, fire, torture, castration, infanticide, rape; death and humiliation; fear by day and night, fear as deep as the marrow of the bone; doubt that he was worthy of life, since everyone around him denied it; sorrow for his women, for his kinfolk, for his children, who needed his protection, and whom he could not protect; rage, hatred, and murder, hatred for white men so deep that it often turned against him and his own, and made all love, all trust, all joy impossible—this past, this endless struggle to achieve and reveal and confirm a human identity, human authority, yet contains, for all its horror, something very beautiful. I do not mean to be sentimental about suffering—enough is certainly as good as a feast—but people who cannot suffer can never grow up, can never discover who they are. That man who is forced each day to snatch his manhood, his identity, out of the fire of human cruelty that rages to destroy it knows, if he survives his effort, and even if he does not survive it, something about himself and human life that no school on earth—and, indeed, no church—can teach. He achieves his own authority, and that is unshakable. This is because, in order to save his life, he is forced to look beneath appearances, to take nothing for granted, to hear the meaning behind the words. If one is continually surviving the worst that life can bring, one eventually ceases to be controlled by a fear of what life can bring; whatever it brings must be borne. And at this level of experience one's bitterness begins to be palatable, and hatred becomes too heavy a sack to carry. The apprehension of life here so briefly and inadequately sketched has been the experience of generations of Negroes, and it helps to explain how they have endured and how they have been able to produce children of kindergarten age who can walk through mobs to get to school. It demands great force and great cunning continually to assault the mighty and indifferent fortress of white supremacy, as Negroes in this country have done so long. It demands great spiritual resilience not to hate the hater whose foot is on your neck, and an even greater miracle of perception and charity not to teach your child to hate. The Negro boys and girls who are facing mobs today come out of a long line of improbable aristocrats—the only genuine aristocrats this country has produced. I say "this country" because their frame of reference was totally American. They were hewing out of the mountain of white supremacy the stone of their individuality. I have great respect for that unsung army of black men and women who trudged down back lanes and entered back doors, saying "Yes, sir" and "No, Ma'am" in order to acquire a new roof for the schoolhouse, new books, a new chemistry lab, more beds for the dormitories, more dormitories. They did not like saying "Yes, sir" and "No, Ma'am," but the country was in no hurry to educate Negroes, these black men and women knew that the job had to be done, and they put their pride in their pockets in order to do it. It is very hard to believe that they were in any way inferior to the white men and women who opened those back doors. It is very hard to believe that those men and women, raising their children, eating their greens, crying their curses, weeping their tears, singing their songs, making their love, as the sun rose, as the sun set, were in any way inferior to the white men and women who crept over to share these splendors after the sun went down. But we must avoid the European error; we must not suppose that, because the situation, the ways, the perceptions of black people so radically differed from those of whites, they were racially superior. I am proud of these people not because of their color but because of their intelligence and their spiritual force and their beauty. The country should be proud of them, too, but, alas, not many people in this country even know of their existence. And the reason for this ignorance is that a knowledge of the role these people played—and play—in American life would reveal more about America to Americans than Americans wish to know.

The American Negro has the great advantage of having never believed that collection of myths to which white Americans cling: that their ancestors were all freedom-loving heroes, that they were born in the greatest country the world has ever seen, or that Americans are invincible in battle and wise in peace, that Americans have always dealt honorably with Mexicans and Indians and all other neighbors or inferiors, that American men are the world's most direct and virile, that American women are pure. Negroes know far more about white Americans than that; it can almost be said, in fact, that they know about white Americans what parents—or, anyway, mothers—know about their children, and that they very often regard white Americans that way. And perhaps this attitude, held in spite of what they know and have endured, helps to explain why Negroes, on the whole, and until lately, have allowed themselves to feel so little hatred. The tendency has really been, insofar as this was possible, to dismiss white people as the slightly mad victims of their own brainwashing. One watched the lives they led. One could not be fooled about that; one watched the things they did and the excuses that they gave themselves, and if a white man was really in trouble, deep trouble, it was to the Negro's door that he came. And one felt that if one had had that white man's worldly advantages, one would never have become as bewildered and as joyless and as thoughtlessly cruel as he. The Negro came to the white man for a roof or for five dollars or for a letter to the judge; the white man came to the Negro for love. But he was not often able to give what he came seeking. The price was too high; he had too much to lose. And the Negro knew this, too. When one knows this about a man, it is impossible for one to hate him, but unless he becomes a man— becomes equal—it is also impossible for one to love him. Ultimately, one tends to avoid him, for the universal characteristic of children is to assume that they have a monopoly on trouble, and therefore, a monopoly on *you*. (Ask any Negro what he knows about the white people with whom he works. And then ask the white people with whom he works what they know about *him*.)

How can the American Negro past be used? It is entirely possible that this dishonored past will rise up soon to smite all of us. There are some wars, for example (if anyone on the globe is still mad enough to go to war) that the American Negro will not support, however many of his people may be coerced—and there is a limit to the number of people any government can put in prison, and a rigid limit indeed to the practicality of such a course. A bill is coming in that I fear America is not prepared to pay. "The problem of the twentieth century," wrote W.E.B. Du Bois[6] around sixty years ago, "is the problem of the color line." A fearful and delicate problem, which compromises, when it does not corrupt, all the American efforts to build a better world—here, there, or anywhere. It is for this reason that everything white Americans think they believe in must now be reëxamined. What one would not like to see again is the consolidation of peoples on the basis of their color. But as long as we in the West place on color the value that we do, we make it impossible for the great unwashed to consolidate themselves according to any other principle. Color is not a human or a personal reality; it is a political reality. But this is a distinction so extremely hard to make that the West has not been able to make it yet. And at the center of this dreadful storm, this

---

[6] W. E. B. DuBois (1868–1963), black writer, editor, and political figure. See p. 1578.

vast confusion, stand the black people of this nation, who must now share the fate of a nation that has never accepted them, to which they were brought in chains. Well, if this is so, one has no choice but to do all in one's power to change that fate, and at no matter what risk—eviction, imprisonment, torture, death. For the sake of one's children, in order to minimize the bill that *they* must pay, one must be careful not to take refuge in any delusion—and the value placed on the color of the skin is always and everywhere and forever a delusion. I know that what I am asking is impossible. But in our time, as in every time, the impossible is the least that one can demand—and one is, after all, emboldened by the spectacle of human history in general, and American Negro history in particular, for it testifies to nothing less than the perpetual achievement of the impossible.

When I was very young, and was dealing with my buddies in those wine- and urine-stained hallways, something in me wondered, *What will happen to all that beauty?* For black people, though I am aware that some of us, black and white, do not know it yet, are very beautiful. And when I sat at Elijah's table and watched the baby, the women, and the men, and we talked about God's—or Allah's—vengeance, I wondered, when that vengeance was achieved, *What will happen to all that beauty then?* I could also see that the intransigence and ignorance of the white world might make that vengeance inevitable—a vengeance that does not really depend on, and cannot really be executed by, any person or organization, and that cannot be prevented by any police force or army: historical vengeance, a cosmic vengeance, based on the law that we recognize when we say, "Whatever goes up must come down." And here we are, at the center of the arc, trapped in the gaudiest, most valuable, and most improbable water wheel the world has ever seen. Everything now, we must assume, is in our hands; we have no right to assume otherwise. If we—and now I mean the relatively conscious whites and the relatively conscious blacks, who must, like lovers, insist on, or create, the consciousness of the others—do not falter in our duty now, we may be able, handful that we are, to end the racial nightmare, and achieve our country, and change the history of the world. If we do not dare everything, the fulfillment of that prophecy, re-created from the Bible in song by a slave, is upon us: *God gave Noah the rainbow sign, No more water, the fire next time!*

ROBERT COLES

(1929-   )

A doctor specializing in child psychiatry, Robert Coles has ranged far from the boundaries of an upper-middle-class, Harvard-based practice, and has spent the better part of the last 15 years listening to and reporting on America—on blacks and on racists, on the reviled "middle American," whom sane political commentators call "Joe Six Pack," on all those who are "still hungry in America." His tools are a tape recorder, drawing materials, and an alertness to the experience of others; the oral histories represented in his work (more than 350 articles and 13 books) contribute invaluably to understanding contemporary American social life. The core enterprise is a three-volume series called *Children of Crisis,* which studies children who helped integrate Southern schools in the 1960's, migrant workers and poor farmers in the South, and blacks who moved North in the last decade in search of a better life. A new volume on Mexican-American, Indian, and Eskimo children is now in progress.

Not the least of Coles' strengths as an observer is that he inclines to eclecticism when "explaining" questions of individual psychology, and seldom hides out in the categories of conventional psychology, Freudian or otherwise. Concerned to uncover the roots of the remarkable strength and courage of a young black during two stressful years in a newly integrated all-white school, Coles at length proposes that they are to be found, by a paradox, in the lad's wholly unpromising family life—an alcoholic, sporadically employed father and a thoroughly neurotic mother diagnosed at one time as a paranoid schizophrenic. The analyst argues that the child took what he needed from each parent and, in the end, the argument sticks:

> John . . . had learned both the melancholy and the strength in [his] mother's personality. She is full of doubt, hesitation, anxiety, vacillation, religious fanaticism. . . . She also can be a stern, tough woman, and a very determined one. She can pray and sing; what is more, she can dissolve many of her tensions in prayer and

Children of Crisis: A Study of Courage and Fear was first published in 1967. See also Coles' study, *Erik H. Erikson* 1970; *Farewell to the South,* 1972, a collection of essays; *The Grass Pyre,* 1969; *The Middle Americans,* 1971; *Migrants, Sharecrop-* *pers, Mountaineers,* 1971; *The Old Ones of New Mexico,* 1973; *Riding Free,* 1973; *Saving Face,* 1972; *The South Goes North,* 1971; *Still Hungry in America,* 1969; and *Uprooted Children, The Early Life of Migrant Farm Workers,* 1970.

song, in faith and in hard work. When John was under pressure he could fall back on her ability to wave aside pain, concentrate hard on the intense moment—and the distant future's promise . . . John drew upon some of his father's capacity to shrug his shoulders at the world, to avoid looking at it too clearly. John shrugged off cannily the useless baggage of anxiety a fear-ridden world gave him.

Much of Coles' strength is that he does not overestimate his capacity to become "one of them"; he knows himself to be, inescapably, an outsider, a Northerner, a psychiatrist. In sum, arriving at "the truth of a particular life" requires something more than rigid adherence to the received dogmas of a profession:

> It must be clear by now that the closer we look at human behavior, the more nonpsychiatric influences must be summoned to "explain" what turns out to be a rather complicated and not always obvious connection between the life of the mind and the life of the world. Those two lives . . . are but convenient abstractions to aid our thinking about an *intensely shared continuity* that actually exists.

Viewed in literary terms, Coles hardly qualifies as an original stylist; he is the plainest of writers, achieves no personal rhythm or accent, and sometimes voices his own frustration with his limits, as when he speaks of searching "desperately for more nouns, more adjectives, more modifying phrases—in the perhaps futile hope that what James Agee called 'human actuality' somehow will come across." Viewed in moral-political terms, he is open to the charge that he tries too hard to be fair, to prove, in David Riesman's words, that all "policemen are not pigs, white Southerners are not rednecks and blacks are not all suffering in exotic misery." Can everything be understood? If dynamiting Freedom Houses and murdering young civil rights workers is not sickness, what is? But often the generosity of his assessment seems wholly just and, as in these sentences on the early leaders of the Movement, not bare of genuine eloquence:

> . . . they have somehow done more than persist, more than endure. They have prevailed in the way that Faulkner knew they would by summoning every bit of their humanity in the face of every effort made to deny any of it to them. In so doing they have become more than they were, more than they themselves thought they were, and perhaps more than anyone watching them can quite put to word: bearers and makers of tradition;

children who in a moment . . . took what they had from the past, in their minds, out of their homes, and made of *all* these possessions something else: a change in the world, and in themselves, too.

The proper praise of Coles' achievement is as a gesture of attentiveness to lives usually hidden. Poor, deprived, hurt, uneducated, Coles' people have spirit and determination; they come alive as possessors of dignity and worth, in something resembling the way their counterparts did earlier—not only in Agee but in Dreiser. What he is saying, as Riesman put it, is that "People are more complicated, more varied, more interesting, have more resiliency and more survivability than you might think. I listen to them! You listen to them!"

From The Children of Crisis

1. FRED

"You know as much as I do how I started becoming a jailbird. Public enemy number one, that's my ambition." It was banter, as good a way as any for him to deal with his anger and hurt. He had just been released from jail, his eighth confinement, and I noticed the sarcasm, the forced gaiety, the boasting, all common in youths like him. Yet, at heart Fred was confused; when he was growing up he never planned to be in and out of jails at age seventeen.

As he said, I did indeed know how it all started. Fred was one of hundreds of youths in Atlanta who in 1961 decided to seek entry to white schools. His father worked in a clothing store, a new and attractive one serving the city's growing Negro middle class. "My dad never even wanted me to go to an integrated school, let alone join the movement. He kept on telling me it would only mean trouble. He was so proud of that job that I think he couldn't see anything jeopardizing it. We had a big fight, because he wouldn't sign the slip, to give me permission to apply for transfer to the white schools. I told him he was hypnotized by those gray flannel suits he was selling, and the silk ties with the 'Made in England' stickers on them. I told him I wasn't going to spend my life fooling myself. My mother was on my side. She always used to say that you can't hide your shame behind clothes. My dad agreed with her, underneath he really did. I can't blame him. It's a good job he has, the best he's ever had, and he was lucky to get it. There must have been a hundred men trying for it. His answer to my mother is that clothes do more than hide things; they make you feel better, more of a person.

"Anyway, my mother said she would sign for me. My dad asked what she would do if he got fired. She said she would go to work again. Then he really exploded. The day she could stop taking that bus across to her white lady-boss was the biggest day in our life. It happened two years before I went to the white school, about a month after the store opened and my dad got his job. He came home one day and said: 'Give those people notice. Tell them you're going to stay home and take care of us. Tell them you've had enough of cleaning other people's homes, so you're going to take care of your own.' A little later he was so sure about the future that he was talking about hiring a maid for *us*. That's what my mother and I couldn't take. My mother asked him how he could talk about the mean whites, then try to be just like them the first chance he gets. He didn't have much to say back to that.

"The next thing you know, though, we were having the same kind of argument, this time over my going to a white school. Dad didn't want to risk anything, or get any bad publicity. Sometimes I think he really wants to be like white folks, only a poor, scared version."

Fred did apply, because his mother gave her consent. More than that, she encouraged him strongly; and when he was chosen, she rejoiced. During his long ordeal as one of three Negro students in a new high school, located in a distinctly well-to-do suburban neighborhood, it was his mother's attitude—as I saw it—that really made the difference. When I asked him where he obtained the will and endurance he displayed, he would shrug his shoulders and shake his head in silence, or say that he didn't know or wasn't sure, but that I might find out if I asked his mother.

An important clue to the source of his stamina came out when we were talking about his childhood, not his racial attitudes. As a child Fred suffered polio, and the muscles of his legs were particularly affected. The disease might have been more crippling were it not for Fred's stubborn character, much encouraged by his mother. Together they did the exercises prescribed by the doctors with a regularity and intensity that earned Fred a bit of fame: "I was taken around the ward. They showed me to all the patients, as an example of what you can do to beat polio. After a while I began to feel like I was on stage."

That was the way he felt at school, the white high school that was his while a senior. It was quite a change for him. The contrasts were everywhere to be seen, heard and experienced. The building was modern, with wide windows and spacious classrooms. The desks were to him like antiques—strong, usable, yet a little forbidding. ("They're so good to look at, I hate to use them; I might mark one up.")

The school was located on a hill. From it one could see fine houses separated by trees and still intact meadowland. Fred had seen the country-side of Georgia before—his grandfather had a farm—but this was different. "Those trees and the land look somehow *pretty* to me. I never used to think of trees being pretty. They were just trees; they were there to be cut or to protect pastureland from the wind. But I catch a glance out the window every once in a while and I think to myself that it's as if they arranged it all, the trees and the brook and the hill we're on, almost as if they gave the school makeup after they built it, lipstick and powder and real shine."

Inside he admired the science laboratories and the "language rooms" with their individual headgear and record machines. The cafeteria had the air and appointments of a first-class white restaurant. The school had a splendid auditorium—to him it was like a theater. Then, there were his classmates, his rich classmates. "That's what I keep thinking. They're rich. They're rich. They're rich. You are sitting beside millions of dollars."

Actually, he went to school that year with the children of his mother's old boss. He went to school for a while in a police car, then on the same bus his mother used to take to work. He and his mother shared stories about the scenery, the talk he heard and the people he saw—and the cars that brought the other students to school. "Those cars, every one of them is new and a lot of them are foreign. I never saw so many cars in all my life, not owned by people my age."

He often joked with his father about the clothing his classmates wore, the expensive yet casual shoes, pants and shirts. "They spend ten dollars on a button-down shirt, then they roll up its sleeves and treat it like it was a sweat shirt, or my old work shirt. They even wear work shirts to school—with ties. You never could get away with that in a Negro school. They would think you'd lost your mind."

Of course, when they wanted to, when the occasion demanded or suggested it, they could—in Fred's words—"dress to kill." In fact Fred once suggested that his father come to school with him as an observer. He could learn a lot about high fashion in men's clothing, then use what he learned in his store.

As the year moved along Fred gradually lost his sense of surprise and awe at what was about him. He had to study hard to keep up with his classmates, and though they were generally but not exclusively polite—in contrast to the behavior of many white students in the city's more modest high schools—they were also increasingly hard for him merely to notice and accept.

"I'm getting tired of them," he told me after the Christmas holidays. He had been away from school for two weeks, and upon his return felt critical and short-tempered. "They think they're God's gift to the human race. For a time I thought how lucky I was, being with them in class and being spared all the trouble other Negroes have gone through during desegregation. I don't think I could take the behavior of white trash. But you know in a way I'm more nervous here than I would be if I had to walk through a howling mob and fight my way down the corridor every hour. It's not even race that's the trouble. It's the fact that my classmates think they're above everyone—white or black."

He became increasingly interested in how other Negro children in Atlanta were faring, not only the handful in white schools but the many thousands still in Negro schools. Though for a long time he had wanted to be a lawyer, by Easter of that year he abandoned all interest in the law, or any other profession. He was developing an interest in violating the law rather than studying it. Just before the end of school he told his parents that he wanted to defer college for a while.

About that time he and I had one of our longest talks. I had been sensing all along his rising dissatisfaction with what he called "rich livers" at school. Unlike his sister, who is two years younger and who at that stage wanted to be a model (later she became interested in commercial art work), he showed less and less interest in "success." He spoke very bluntly to me: "Success, that's what my dad has been talking about all my life. The poor guy, he doesn't see how ridiculous his talk is. He thinks I can be 'successful,' when actually I'll be lucky if I can vote, and be treated better than a dog every time I go register my car, or try for a driving license, or go buy something in a store. They say I'm lucky; I'm going to the best high school in Georgia. Well that's about what success is for a Negro: being alone; being the exception; and knowing every second that the top for you isn't even enough to make you feel safe on the street, because it's the bottom for everyone else."

In addition to his sister, Fred has three younger brothers—at that time they were in elementary school. He didn't want to set the same example for them that their father did for him. It was an example, he felt, of surrender, of acquiescence. Perhaps with a bit of nervousness in my voice I asked him what he *expected* his father to do. "You don't think I don't wonder myself," he replied with some resignation. Then he stared at me. He was suddenly aware that I was willing to extend a good deal more "understanding" to his father then he was, at least then. It wasn't what I said, it was the tone of my voice, the look on my face.

I myself didn't realize how fully I had communicated my thoughts to him until he told me: "You're all for trying to feel sorry for him, I know. So am I sometimes. I say to myself: 'Look, Fred. He's over forty, and he has a family, and he's only trying to do the best he can. So why give him a hard time? Do you want him to join the sit-in movement, and picket the State Capitol, so that the colored man will get a better deal? If he did, what kind of a deal would you get, and your sister and your brothers, and especially your mother? She would have to go back to work, and though she might say that wouldn't bother her, if it had to be done, I don't think it would be fair to push her that far.' That's what I say to myself. But I have an answer, too. My dad has his life. It's not the same as *his* dad's. Unlike my grandfather, my dad was lucky. He came here to Atlanta and stayed with an uncle of his. He got himself a high school education. Then he fought in the war, and so afterward he could pay for some college time through Uncle Sam's help. He still had trouble keeping a job down until lately. But now he's got a good one, and he forgets how lucky and unusual he is. My grandfather used to tell him that he was wasting his time going to college, that Negroes could go to college for twenty years, then be fortunate if they found jobs in the post office or the Pullman trains. That was the truth my grandfather knew. My father proved him wrong. So you see, everyone has to figure out what's right for *him*, and that depends on his age. I'm angry at my father now because he wants me to be like him. He had his ambitions. I have a right to mine."

When he had finished talking it was late, near midnight. Fred still had work to do, study that he himself had decided to put off, study that meant increasingly little to him. As I left he smiled and shook my hand, as always. Then he started talking again. "Your children may not always go along with you, just as I'm not following all my father's advice; but there's a difference, too. You are white and I am Negro. If I don't join the movement and try to change things here, *my* children might just as well not be born. It's that bad." It was the first and last time I would ever hear him explicitly refer to my race.

Fred's disenchantment and his progressive involvement in the student protest movement came precisely at a time when he seemed best in command of himself and his work. He was nearing the successful end of a unique and hard experience. He had every right to be confident, even self-congratulatory. Instead, his mood turned dark, even sour. He became increasingly critical of his classmates, picking out their faults with almost indiscriminate zeal. When I mentioned to him—as gently as I knew how—that everyone had some annoying characteristics, he replied immediately: "Yes; but that's not what bothers me about them. It's the way they treat me as a Negro, regardless of who they are and what they're like otherwise. The nice ones act like royalty out slumming. The unfriendly ones stare, and you can see the hate in their eyes. Sometimes I try to forget it, and just imagine that I'm one of them. I'm not, though. I don't really know whether to blame their attitudes or mine. I know I get upset, too, apart from what they do."

Clearly he distrusted not only his classmates, but himself. It is easy to say that he felt "guilty"; that as a result he could not allow himself to enjoy a triumph that had other implications to him: "I'll graduate, and some people at the ceremony might even forget I'm a Negro. I'll probably never feel whiter than I will that day."

Yet, more was at issue. Yes, he was tempted. Yes, he wanted to disappear, to be reborn. On the other hand, he had personal, only indirectly race-connected reasons to reject a world he finally had seen and experienced. His mother had done that, done it gladly and emphatically. A year after he had graduated from high school I talked with him in Mississippi, where he was working in a voter-registration project. We were by then old friends, and able to relax rather well with one another. Moreover, he was now a man, on his own, working hard in a hard world. He liked beer; when he had it in him he liked to talk and reminisce. I had attended his graduation, and now he wanted to talk about that; about the tuxedo, and the roses the girls carried, and the band, and his parents, sitting there in'the audience: "All my classmates were straining their necks to find their parents; a lot of them couldn't, there were so many people. I was sure lucky then; I could spot mine so fast it wasn't funny."

We lingered on that scene, then in a flash he changed the subject: "You know, no matter how beautiful and nice it was there, I was glad to get out. I felt like my mother did when she came home for the last time. She threw her coat down—I can remember her doing it as if it just happened. Then she said: "They've been squeezing me dry, telling me to do everything, expecting me to smile all the while, and give every ounce of my energy to their kids. I'm so glad to be home to stay. I'm afraid that tomorrow I'll wake up and it won't be true. I'll probably be pinching myself for a few days.' She said more; it was a long speech she made. I've never heard my mother talk so much, before or after. Until she stopped working she never had time to talk. She worked two days every day; one started at five-thirty in the morning and the other at five-thirty in the evening."

He continued to talk about his mother and her routine. He had watched her more closely than even he himself knew. He had seen her leave home strong and come home weak, depart in good spirits and return bitter. It was only now, when he was away from home, that he could look more closely at his mother's life, and at his own shifting emotions during that year of "integrated" education: "Since I've been away from it all I've been able to see that my mother didn't come back in a bad mood just because she was tired. It wasn't only the work she did for white people that got to her. I'm sure that part of her problem was leaving our broken-down apartment to go to that mansion. I never realized what the change was like until I saw those homes myself, and went through the same kind of experience she did. You watch it all on television, the way they live; but you can't really believe it's real until you see it. She must have been glad to get away from us and spend a day in that place, and she must have hated to come back and face it all at home, the mess in the house, with everything old, secondhand or cheap compared to things out there. I guess she couldn't admit how she felt herself, any more than I could. You feel you're a traitor. You feel so low and bad. I realize now that it's inevitable, being so split up, but I sure didn't then."

Like his mother, he reacted only when he safely could; like her own, his was a reaction of both nostalgia and outrage. Both of them, I thought, were as loyal to the white people they knew as they were contemptuous of them. Fred could describe his mother's mixed feelings much more readily than his own: "She was glad to have it over, going to them, but I think she was sad, too. Now all she had to do was be at home, and it wasn't that big home with all those fine things. I could tell. It's like a drug. You get hooked on it, and it won't let you alone, even though you know it hurts you. I began to see how much she missed her work. She would say how handy the money would be that she used to make. She would ask me how the bus ride was, and whether the trees were in bloom. She would try to figure out how near I came to her old boss's home. I could tell. Even Dad could tell, and he's not tuned in to anything but his work. He would tell her to go back to work, because she missed it. I think he knew it wasn't only the work."

For both Fred and his mother, integration, real integration, meant achieving for themselves a life each of them had tasted, but recognized—and guiltily disavowed—as still not theirs. "I'm doing this," Fred told me once shortly after coming out of jail, "because I don't think a few like myself should go into the white world, leaving twenty million Negro people standing outside, scared and hungry as they always have been."

Fred spent two years in Mississippi, the first one when there were very few like him in the state, the second in 1964, when students came from all over the country to assist "field workers" like himself. From the beginning he lived in constant danger of death. He moved into a particularly tense racial district, and set to work encouraging Negroes to secure the vote. Many of them thought him crazy and feared his presence more than that of any white man. Had it not been for the help of two Negro farmers who fed and kept him, he would have been run out of town by his own people as well as the sheriff. For a long time he expected to be killed. He wrote a letter to his mother that told her of his love, that explained his work to her. He put it in the hands of one of his local friends, to be mailed after his death. He lived expecting each day to be his last.

His mere presence in the town was a living symbol of defiance to both whites and Negroes. He lived because the sheriff wanted to outlast him, see him leave. The sheriff told him so several times. Every day he drove by Fred's home, usually waving to him as he did with that mixture of politeness and scorn that certain Southern officials can express toward Negroes. Once or twice a month he would take the youth into custody for what he called "a heart-to-heart talking." I heard about the content of one such encounter from Fred.

" 'What you want here, boy,' the sheriff said. Then he poured me a cup of coffee even though I didn't ask for one. I don't drink coffee, and I certainly didn't want any of his, but I took it. I don't know why; probably I was afraid, and I knew he was testing me so I wanted to show him I *wasn't* afraid—to take it when he offered it, and show him I felt his equal. It even flashed through my mind that they were poisoning me. (I've watched too many television programs.) Anyway, I kept on drinking it. Once I had it I was glad to have it; I had something to do while he talked.

"At first he tried being the kind plantation owner. He wanted to know how I was getting along. Did I like the county? Was I planning to stay long? They always liked tourists. They liked for them to be right at home. 'Now boy, you feel free to come here any time you want, and let me know if there's anything I can do for you.' That's what he said, and he started toward me with his coffeepot. Suddenly I had to go, or see if I *could* go. He asked me whom I was going to see. I didn't answer, because I knew it meant trouble for anyone I mentioned; and besides, I really didn't plan to see a soul that day, just write my weekly report for the Atlanta office, and maybe a few letters. When I didn't reply for a few seconds he blew up. He must have been looking for an excuse. He put the coffeepot down on a table near me, slamming it real hard. Then he moved closer, still holding a cup in his other hand. I didn't know what to expect. I thought to myself: 'This is it. He'll put the cup down, and then he'll reach for his gun.'

"It was a funny thing. He didn't say anything, not a word. He moved closer and closer, until he was practically on top of me. He kept staring at me. I can see his eyes right now; they were light blue, and I think a little watery, as if he had a cold. I couldn't keep looking into them. I was afraid, and I was worried that if I kept staring he would get angrier than he was already. So I looked halfway down. I could see his thick leather belt, loose around his stomach—he had a tire of fat. I was too scared even to look at that. I thought he would resent my noticing his flabbiness. He didn't seem flabby then. In fact, I thought he was going to be the man who killed me.

"It's funny what comes to your mind in moments like that. I pictured my mother sitting with us in church and praying. She was doing the praying and I was just sitting there, watching her lips move and looking at her face, and then the Bible she was holding. For some reason I remember her gloves. She had on a pair of white gloves. She used to wear them every Sunday to church. She called them her church gloves. My sister could play with her shoes or her pocketbook, but not those gloves. Then I went blank. I heard him telling me to 'git.' He repeated it several times: 'Git, boy, git before you become too welcome here, and we decide to make you a trusty. We need one or two, and you look the right man for the job, a smart nigger who knows enough to do what he's told, or else. So git, and I mean from the county.' I especially heard his last words. It was after them that I looked at him, right into his eyes. I didn't say a word and moved toward the door. He turned to his flunky and said, 'Show the goddamn nigger to the street, and let him know that the next time he comes here it'll be for a year or two on bread and water!' "

Fred went through such "visits" repeatedly before he was arrested for the first time—for exceeding a twenty-mile-an-hour speed limit. He denied the charge: "I drove so carefully I was a menace; I kept my eyes on the speedometer all the time." In any event that was the beginning of a series of imprisonments, six of them in a matter of months on similar charges—speeding, being a "public nuisance," talking to high school students and thus "contributing to the delinquency of minors."

Ironically, with the arrival of Northern students for the Summer Project of 1964, he and the sheriff found themselves, for once, in agreement. The sheriff started preparing for an invasion. The town was put on alert; people were encouraged to arm themselves; and the paper talked as if the final moment of truth was at hand: resistance or death. Fred was also fearful, and for his own reasons resentful. Who were these youths, and what would their sudden, naive, white presence do to the hard-won trust he had earned from increasing numbers of Negroes, even from a few white businessmen and the sheriff himself? "I was against this, as well as for it," he told me just after the students started coming into the state, ten of them to his town. "We need help, God knows we do. Maybe the whole country will get to know our problems as a result of this project; but meanwhile I don't know what we're going to do with these volunteers. They don't know a thing about living down here—how to get along with Negroes or whites or anyone. Yesterday I found myself thinking like the sheriff and his police and the white people. I thought to myself: 'Who are these outsiders? Why do they want to come here? Why don't they clean up the mess in their own backyards first?' "

Much later, toward the end of the summer, he learned the value of the project, and the reasons for his fear and suspicion. He had good reason to be afraid that violence would be widespread once the students arrived. He also had reason to be envious of them. In comparison to him they were rich, well educated and influential. It was *their* work in the state that captured the nation's interest and concern—the attention started even before they arrived. When they did arrive, even though he recognized them to be the diverse group they were, all of them roused tension in him: the able and effective workers because he felt their occasional arrogance; the hesitant and fearful ones because he recognized their incompetence and the burden it placed on everyone. Those who got on easily with the Negro families prompted his jealousy. Those who were reticent or embarrassingly ingratiating with Negroes earned his misgivings and scorn.

In the end, though, he was sad to see them leave. "I've come to like them, and I can see now that they probably made me feel insecure. I'm glad that two of them are staying, and especially that it's the two I like best. They've all done a lot, not just for the people here, but for me. It's been like going to college; I've met different people. I've got to leave here myself one day, when this is all over and we've won."

One year later he did leave, to enter college. At this writing he seems solidly directed toward the law as a career. He wants to be a lawyer so that he can continue to work for the rights of his people. He wants to be a lawyer because he will have a profession, be a person respected and called upon for advice. He wants to be a lawyer because he is faithful to his father's lifelong dream that his children will surpass him and attain the favored if still emaciated ranks of the Negro middle class. He wants to be a lawyer—most of all, he thinks—because "my mother used to say to me that if I became one, I could fight for my rights, and it would be legal." He used to think of his mother when he went from home to home in Mississippi urging people to vote who were sometimes even reluctant to listen to him. "I finally would have to tell them about my mother, and it worked if anything was going to work. I'd say my mother felt the way they did. She just followed orders all her life and was glad even to be able to have the orders to obey. Then one day she got tired of it and stopped.

"The next thing that happened was that I was going to school with her old boss's children. Now don't you believe that Georgia and Mississippi are sister states, and the same can happen here? That's how I'd always end, with that question."

Sometimes they wouldn't listen to him. Sometimes they would only listen. Yet sometimes, in his words, he "scored." Most often it would be the young who joined company with him, the young who had the approval of their mothers. "I could see their mothers giving them the silent nod. They must have felt my mother's voice coming through to them, saying just what she always used to say to me: 'It's time; maybe not for everything, but enough to start in the direction of everything. Starting is harder than fighting to get what you want after you've started.' When I left Mississippi I felt that my people had begun. They were trying to register, even before the Congress passed the voting bill. After it was passed, they could really respect themselves for their own work, for starting before Washington had. They got me started, too. When I went back to college, I knew why I was going, and I knew where I was going. I told them I would keep coming back, and one day I'll come back a lawyer. If they need one, I'll be there, or someplace like there."

N. SCOTT MOMADAY

(1934–   )

The Pulitzer Prize for fiction in 1969 startled nearly everybody; it went to a young American Indian named Scott Momaday about whom virtually nothing was known. (Subsequently it became known that Momaday was an Oklahoman, the son of artists, educated at the University of Mexico and at Stanford, and that he worked as professor of English.) The prize-winning book, *House Made of Dawn*, (1968) was about a Kiowa youth who leaves the reservation and then discovers that he cannot adjust to the world beyond it. A work of literature, not a polemic, the novel nevertheless carries a harsh, implicit comment on American society—on a nation that simultaneously calls for assimilation and frustrates it, stifling the native American's own sense of cultural identity yet denying him participation in any other.

Momaday's fiction also includes *The Owl in the Cedar Tree,* 1965.

This is not a theme that can quickly be exhausted, and Momaday has continued to explore it. In *The Way to Rainy Mountain* (1969), he attempts both a celebration of a tribal identity and an account of the processes that brought it into being. The book rides on juxtapositions: first a fragment of Kiowa myth, an "objective" bit of Indian history, then a personal reminiscence. Unpretentiously, suggestively, Momaday clarifies interdependencies among historical, cultural, religious, and individual perspectives, and shows forth, in his own person, a model of cultural variousness and flexibility. Clichés about Indian understanding of natural forces cease to seem clichés as Momaday enters the imaginations of his ancestors, creating a felt sense of connection between nature and man by linking history and myth with fancied remembrance.

> In the winter of 1848–49, the buffalo ranged away from easy reach, and feed was scarce. There was an antelope drive in the vicinity of Bent's Fort, Colorado. According to ancient custom, antelope medicine was made, and the Kiowas set out on foot and on horseback—men, women, and children—after game. . . .
>
> One morning on the high plains of Wyoming I saw several pronghorns in the distance. They were moving very slowly at an angle away from me, and they were almost invisible in the tall brown and yellow grass. They ambled along in their own wilderness dimension of time, as if no notion of flight could ever come upon them. But I remembered once having seen a frightened buck on the run, how the white rosette of its rump seemed to hang for the smallest fraction of time at the top of each frantic bound—like a succession of sunbursts against the purple hills.

At bottom the purpose is to track, through the journey of a people, the birth, maturing, and death of a culture or, as Momaday put it, the history of the life of "man's idea of himself." By probing the origins of his tribe's mythmaking, he reveals freshly the ways in which the stories people tell themselves constitute both a self-image and a purchase on the world. Two hundred years ago the base of a rock called Devil's Tower grew into the foundation of a tribal legend. It spoke of children who played nearby but were killed one day by a bear; the seven sisters were taken up into the sky and became the stars of the Big Dipper.

> From that moment, and so long as the legend lives, the Kiowas have kinsmen in the night sky. Whatever they were in the mountains, they could be no more. However tenuous their well-being, however much they had suffered and would suffer again, they had found a way out of the wilderness.

A few pages later Momaday describes the death of the tribe, the moment at which their assembly for a ritual Sun Dance was abruptly broken up by soldiers.

> Forbidden without cause the essential act of their faith, having seen the wild herds slaughtered and left to rot upon the ground, the Kiowas backed away forever from the medicine tree. That was July 20, 1890, at the great bend of the Washita. My grandmother was there. Without bitterness, and for as long as she lived, she bore a vision of deicide.

In addition to *House Made of Dawn* and *The Way to Rainy Mountain* Momaday has published an edition of *The Complete Poems of Frederick Goddard Tuckerman* (1965) and *The Journey of Tai-me* (1968), a retelling of Kiowa Indian folktales.

A gentle voice, Momaday stands forth nevertheless as a major influence on the contemporary stream of protest against characteristic American attitudes toward racial and ethnic minorities. His comprehension of the national course record encompasses, for the past, the cavalry officer's toast, "Civilization or death to all American savages" and, in the present, those life circumstances that a national magazine recently summarized as follows: "Indians are the poorest of the poor, with the highest unemployment, the lowest standard of living, and the worst health and housing of any American." Yet Scott Momaday is not only a spokesman for conscience: his prose at its best is marked by qualities of sympathy, economy, stillness, and precision that lend it uncommon distinction.

The Way to Rainy Mountain

PROLOGUE

The journey began one day long ago on the edge of the northern Plains. It was carried on over a course of many generations and many hundreds of miles. In the end there were many things to remember, to dwell upon and talk about.

"You know, everything had to begin. . . ." For the Kiowas the beginning was a struggle for existence in the bleak northern mountains. It was there, they say, that they entered the world through a hollow log. The end, too, was a struggle, and it was lost. The young Plains culture of the Kiowas withered and died like grass that is burned in the prairie wind. There came a day like destiny; in every direction, as far as the eye could see, carrion lay out in the land. The buffalo was the animal representation of the sun, the essential and sacrificial victim of the Sun Dance. When the wild herds were destroyed, so too was the will of the Kiowa people; there was nothing to sustain them in spirit. But these are idle recollections, the mean and ordinary agonies of human history. The interim was a time of great adventure and nobility and fulfillment.

Tai-me came to the Kiowas in a vision born of suffering and despair. "Take me with you," Tai-me said, "and I will give you whatever you want." And it was so. The great adventure of the Kiowas was a going forth into the heart of the continent. They began a long migration from the headwaters of the Yellowstone River eastward to the Black Hills and south to the Wichita Mountains. Along the way they acquired horses, the religion of the Plains, a love and possession of the open land. Their nomadic soul was set free. In alliance with the Comanches they held dominion in the southern Plains for a hundred years. In the course of that long migration they had come of age as a people. They had conceived a good idea of themselves; they had dared to imagine and determine who they were.

In one sense, then, the way to Rainy Mountain is preeminently the history of an idea, man's idea of himself, and it has old and essential being in language. The verbal tradition by which it has been preserved has suffered a deterioration in time. What remains is fragmentary: mythology, legend, lore, and hearsay—and of course the idea itself, as crucial and complete as it ever was. That is the miracle.

The journey herein recalled continues to be made anew each time the miracle comes to mind, for that is peculiarly the right and responsibility of the imagination. It is a whole journey, intricate with motion and meaning; and it is made with the whole memory, that experience of the mind which is legendary as well as historical, personal as well as cultural. And the journey is an evocation of three things in particular: a landscape that is incomparable, a time that is gone forever, and the human spirit, which endures. The imaginative experience and the historical express equally the traditions of man's reality. Finally, then, the journey recalled is among other things the revelation of one way in which these traditions are conceived, developed, and interfused in the human mind. There are on the way to Rainy Mountain many landmarks, many journeys in the one. From the beginning the migration of the Kiowas was an expression of the human spirit, and that expression is most truly made in terms of wonder and delight: "There were many people, and oh, it was beautiful. That was the beginning of the Sun Dance. It was all for Tai-me, you know, and it was a long time ago."

I

You know, everything had to begin, and this is how it was: the Kiowas came one by one into the world through a hollow log. They were many more than now, but not all of them got out. There was a woman whose body was swollen up with child, and she got stuck in the log. After that, no one could get through, and that is why the Kiowas are a small tribe in number. They looked all around and saw the world. It made them glad to see so many things. They called themselves *Kwuda*, "coming out."

They called themselves Kwuda and later Tepda, both of which mean "coming out." And later still they took the name Gaigwu, a name which can be taken to indicate something of which the two halves differ from each other in appearance. It was once a custom among Kiowa warriors that they cut their hair on the right side of the head only and on a line level with the lobe of the ear, while on the left they let the hair grow long and wore it in a thick braid wrapped in otter skin. "Kiowa" is indicated in sign language by holding the hand palm up and slightly cupped to the right side of the head and rotating it back and forth from the wrist. "Kiowa" is thought to derive from the softened Comanche form of Gaigwu.

I remember coming out upon the northern Great Plains in the late spring. There were meadows of blue and yellow wildflowers on the slopes, and I could see the still, sunlit plain below, reaching away out of sight. At first there is no discrimination in the eye, nothing but the land itself, whole and impenetrable. But then smallest things begin to stand out of the depths— herds and rivers and groves—and each of these has perfect being in terms of distance and of silence and of age. Yes, I thought, now I see the earth as it really is; never again will I see things as I saw them yesterday or the day before.

IV

They lived at first in the mountains. They did not yet know of Tai-me, but this is what they knew: There was a man and his wife. They had a beautiful child, a little girl whom they would not allow to go out of their sight. But one day a friend of the family came and asked if she might take the child outside to play. The mother guessed that would be all right, but she told the friend to leave the child in its cradle and to place the cradle in a tree. While the child was in the tree, a redbird came among the branches. It was not like any bird that you have seen; it was very beautiful, and it did not fly away. It kept still upon a limb, close to the child. After a while the child got out of its cradle and began to climb after the redbird. And at the same time the tree began to grow taller, and the child was borne up into the sky. She was then a woman, and she found herself in a strange place. Instead of a redbird, there was a young man standing before her. The man spoke to her and said: "I have been watching you for a long time, and I knew that I would find a way to bring you here. I have brought you here to be my wife." The woman looked all around; she saw that he was the only living man there. She saw that he was the sun.

There the land itself ascends into the sky. These mountains lie at the top of the continent, and they cast a long rain shadow on the sea of grasses to the east. They arise out of the last North American wilderness, and they have wilderness names: Wasatch, Bitterroot, Bighorn, Wind River.

I have walked in a mountain meadow bright with Indian paintbrush, lupine, and wild buckwheat, and I have seen high in the branches of a lodgepole pine the male pine grosbeak, round and rose-colored, its dark, striped wings nearly invisible in the soft, mottled light. And the uppermost branches of the tree seemed very slowly to ride across the blue sky.

X

Long ago there were bad times. The Kiowas were hungry and there was no food. There was a man who heard his children cry from hunger, and he went out to look for food. He walked four days and became very weak. On the fourth day he came to a great canyon. Suddenly there was thunder and lightning. A voice spoke to him and said, "Why are you following me? What do you want?" The man was afraid. The thing standing before him had the feet of a deer, and its body was covered with feathers. The man answered that the Kiowas were hungry. "Take me with you," the voice said, "and I will give you whatever you want." From that day Tai-me has belonged to the Kiowas.

The great central figure of the kado, or Sun Dance, ceremony is the taime. *This is a small image, less than 2 feet in length, representing a human figure dressed in a robe of white feathers, with a headdress consisting of a single upright feather and pendants of ermine skin, with numerous strands of blue beads around its neck, and painted upon the face, breast, and back with designs symbolic of the sun and moon. The image itself is of dark-green stone, in form rudely resembling a human head and bust, probably shaped by art like the stone fetishes of the Pueblo tribes. It is preserved in a rawhide box in charge of the hereditary keeper, and is never under any circumstances exposed to view except at the annual Sun Dance, when it is fastened to a short upright stick planted within the medicine lodge, near the western side. It was last exposed in 1888.—Mooney*

Once I went with my father and grandmother to see the Tai-me bundle. It was suspended by means of a strip of ticking from the fork of a small ceremo-

nial tree. I made an offering of bright red cloth, and my grandmother prayed aloud. It seemed a long time that we were there. I had never come into the presence of Tai-me before—nor have I since. There was a great holiness all about in the room, as if an old person had died there or a child had been born.

XXIV

East of my grandmother's house, south of the pecan grove, there is buried a woman in a beautiful dress. Mammedaty used to know where she is buried, but now no one knows. If you stand on the front porch of the house and look eastward towards Carnegie, you know that the woman is buried somewhere within the range of your vision. But her grave is unmarked. She was buried in a cabinet, and she wore a beautiful dress. How beautiful it was! It was one of those fine buckskin dresses, and it was decorated with elk's teeth and beadwork. That dress is still there, under the ground.

Aho's high moccasins are made of softest, cream-colored skins. On each instep there is a bright disc of beadwork—an eight-pointed star, red and pale blue on a white field—and there are bands of beadwork at the soles and ankles. The flaps of the leggings are wide and richly ornamented with blue and red and green and white and lavender beads.

East of my grandmother's house the sun rises out of the plain. Once in his life a man ought to concentrate his mind upon the remembered earth, I believe. He ought to give himself up to a particular landscape in his experience to look at it from as many angles as he can, to wonder about it, to dwell upon it. He ought to imagine that he touches it with his hands at every season and listens to the sounds that are made upon it. He ought to imagine the creatures there and all the faintest motions of the wind. He ought to recollect the glare of noon and all the colors of the dawn and dusk.

EPILOGUE

During the first hours after midnight on the morning of November 13, 1833, it seemed that the world was coming to an end. Suddenly the stillness of the night was broken; there were brilliant flashes of light in the sky, light of such intensity that people were awakened by it. With the speed and density of a driving rain, stars were falling in the universe. Some were brighter than Venus; one was said to be as large as the moon.

That most brilliant shower of Leonid meteors has a special place in the memory of the Kiowa people. It is among the earliest entries in the Kiowa calendars, and it marks the beginning as it were of the historical period in the tribal mind. In the preceding year Tai-me had been stolen by a band of Osages, and although it was later returned, the loss was an almost unimaginable tragedy; and in 1837 the Kiowas made the first of their treaties with the

United States. The falling stars seemed to image the sudden and violent disintegration of an old order.

But indeed the golden age of the Kiowas had been short-lived, ninety or a hundred years, say, from about 1740. The culture would persist for a while in decline, until about 1875, but then it would be gone, and there would be very little material evidence that it had ever been. Yet it is within the reach of memory still, though tenuously now, and moreover it is even defined in a remarkably rich and living verbal tradition which demands to be preserved for its own sake. The living memory and the verbal tradition which transcends it were brought together for me once and for all in the person of Ko-sahn.

A hundred-year-old woman came to my grandmother's house one afternoon in July. Aho was dead; Mammedaty had died before I was born. There were very few Kiowas left who could remember the Sun Dances; Ko-sahn was one of them; she was a grown woman when my grandparents came into the world. Her body was twisted and her face deeply lined with age. Her thin white hair was held in place by a cap of black netting, though she wore braids as well, and she had but one eye. She was dressed in the manner of a Kiowa matron, a dark, full-cut dress that reached nearly to the ankles, full, flowing sleeves, and a wide, apron-like sash. She sat on a bench in the arbor so concentrated in her great age that she seemed extraordinarily small. She was quiet for a time—she might almost have been asleep—and then she began to speak and to sing. She spoke of many things, and once she spoke of the Sun Dance:

My sisters and I were very young; that was a long time ago. Early one morning they came to wake us up. They had brought a great buffalo in from the plain. Everyone went out to see and to pray. We heard a great many voices. One man said that the lodge was almost ready. We were told to go there, and someone gave me a piece of cloth. It was very beautiful. Then I asked what I ought to do with it, and they said that I must tie it to the Tai-me tree. There were other pieces of cloth on the tree, and so I put mine there as well. When the lodge frame was finished, a woman—sometimes a man—began to sing. It was like this:

Everything is ready.
Now the four societies must go out.
They must go out and get the leaves,
the branches for the lodge.

And when the branches were tied in place, again there was singing:

Let the boys go out.
Come on, boys, now we must get the earth.

The boys began to shout. Now they were not just ordinary boys, not all of them; they were those for whom prayers had been made, and they were dressed in different ways. There was an old, old woman. She had something on her back. The boys went out to see. The old woman had a bag full of earth on her back. It was a certain kind of sandy earth. That is what they must have in the lodge. The dancers must dance upon the sandy earth. The old woman held a digging tool in her hand. She turned towards the south and pointed with her lips. It was like a kiss, and she began to sing:

> We have brought the earth.
> Now it is time to play;
> As old as I am, I still have the feeling of play.

That was the beginning of the Sun Dance. The dancers treated themselves with buffalo medicine, and slowly they began to take their steps . . . And all the people were around, and they wore splendid things—beautiful buckskin and beads. The chiefs wore necklaces, and their pendants shone like the sun. There were many people, and oh, it was beautiful! That was the beginning of the Sun Dance. It was all for Taime, you know, and it was a long time ago.

It was—all of this and more—a quest, a going forth upon the way to Rainy Mountain. Probably Ko-sahn too is dead now. At times, in the quiet of evening, I think she must have wondered, dreaming, who she was. Was she become in her sleep that old purveyor of the sacred earth, perhaps, that ancient one who, old as she was, still had the feeling of play? And in her mind, at times, did she see the falling stars?

GENERAL BIBLIOGRAPHY

I. REFERENCE WORKS

Dictionary of American Biography. Allen Johnson, and Dumas Malone, Editors. Twenty volumes plus supplements, 1928-1958.

Gohdes, Clarence. *Bibliographical Guide to the Study of the Literature of the U.S.A.*, 1976.

Handlin, O., A. M. Schlesinger, S. E. Morison, and others, Editors. *Harvard Guide to American History*, 1954.

Hart, J. D. *The Oxford Companion to American Literature*, 4th Edition, 1965.

Kunitz, S. J., and Howard Haycraft, Editors. *American Authors, 1600-1900*, 1944.

———. *Twentieth Century Authors*, 1942. Supplement, 1955.

Leary, Lewis, Editor. *Articles on American Literature, 1900-1950*, 1954; *1950-1967*, 1970.

Millett, F. B. *Contemporary American Authors, A Critical Survey and 219 Bibliographies*, 1940.

Morris, R. B., ed., *Encyclopedia of American History*, 1953.

Mott, F. L. *American Journalism: A History of Newspapers in the United States Through 250 Years, 1690 to 1940*, 1941. Revised, 1951.

———. *A History of American Magazines.* Four volumes, 1938-1957.

Quinn, Arthur Hobson, ed., *The Literature of the American People*, 1951.

Reader's Guide to Periodical Literature. Annual, 1900—.

Spiller, R. E., and others, eds. *Literary History of the United States.* Two-volume edition, 1953. Bibliography Supplement prepared by Richard M. Ludwig, 1959. Supplement II, 1970.

Stovall, Floyd. *Eight American Authors*, 1956.

Trent, W. P., John Erskine, S. P. Sherman, and Carl Van Doren, Editors, *Cambridge History of American Literature.* Four volumes, 1917-1921.

Who's Who in America. Biennial, 1899—.

Woodress, James. *American Literary Scholarship.* Annual, 19—.

———. *Dissertations in American Literature, 1891-1955.* 1957.

II. GENERAL STUDIES

A. LITERARY HISTORY AND CRITICISM

Aaron, Daniel. *Writers on the Left: Episodes in American Literary Communism*, 1961.

———. *American Writers on the Civil War*, 1973.

American Writers Series. H. H. Clark, General Editor, 1934—. Twenty-eight volumes published.

Bercovitch, Sacvan, ed. *The Revaluation of Puritanism*, 1974.

———. *The Puritan Origins of the American Self*, 1975.

Blair, Walter. *Native American Humor (1800–1900)*, 1947.

Brown, Sterling. *Negro Poetry and Drama*, 1937.

Carter, Everett. *The American Idea*, 1977.

Chase, Richard. *The American Novel and Its Tradition*, 1957.

Clark, H. H., Editor. *Transitions in American Literary History*, 1954.

Cowie, Alexander. *The Rise of the American Novel*, 1948.

Cunliffe, Marcus. *The Literature of the United States*, 1954.

Davis, Richard Beale. *Intellectual Life in the Colonial South, 1585–1763*, 1977.

Emerson, Everett, ed. *Major Writers of Early American Literature*, 1972.

Fiedler, Leslie. *Love and Death in the American Novel*, 1960.

Feidelson, Charles. *Symbolism in American Literature*, 1953.

Gelpi, Albert J. *The Tenth Muse*, 1975.

Hoffman, Daniel. *Form and Fable in American Literature*, 1965.

Hoffman, Frederick J. *The Art of Southern Fiction*, 1967.

Hubbell, Jay. *The South in American Literature, 1607–1900*, 1954.

Hughes, Glenn. *A History of the American Theatre, 1700–1950*, 1951.

Kammen, Michael. *People of Paradox*, 1972.

Lawrence, D. H. *Studies in Classic American Literature*, 1923.

Leisy, E. E. *The American Historical Novel*, 1950.

Levin, David. *In Defense of Historical Literature*, 1967.

Lewis, R. W. B. *The American Adam: Innocence, Tragedy, and Tradition in the Nineteenth Century*, 1955.

Loggins, Vernon. *The Negro Author*, 1931.

Marx, Leo. *The Machine in the Garden: Technology and the Pastoral Ideal in America*, 1964.

Matthiessen, F. O. *American Renaissance: Art and Expression in the Age of Emerson and Whitman*, 1941.

May, Henry. *The Enlightenment in America*, 1976.

Mencken, H. L. *The American Language: An Inquiry into the Development of English in the United States*, 1919. Revised, 1936. Supplement I, 1945. Supplement II, 1948.

Meserve, Walter. *An Emerging Entertainment: The Drama of the American People from the Beginnings to 1828*, 1977

Parrington, V. L. *Main Currents in American Thought: An Interpretation of American Literature from the Beginnings to 1920*. Three volumes, 1927–1930.

Pearce, Roy Harvey. *The Continuity of American Poetry*, 1961.

Poirier, Richard. *A World Elsewhere: The Place of Style in American Literature*, 1966.

Pritchard, J. P. *Criticism in America*, 1956.

Quinn, Arthur Hobson. *American Fiction: An Historical and Critical Survey*, 1936.

———. *A History of the American Drama: From the Beginning to the Civil War*, 1923. Revised, 1943.

———. *A History of the American Drama: From the Civil War to the Present Day*. Two volumes, 1927. Reissued in one volume, 1936.

———, Murdock, K. B., Clarence Gohdes, and G. F. Whicher. *The Literature of the American People*, 1951.

Rourke, Constance. *American Humor: A Study of the National Character*, 1931.

Seelye, John. *Prophetic Waters: The River in Early American Life and Literature*, 1977.

Silverman, Kenneth. *A Cultural History of the American Revolution*, 1976.

Smith, Henry Nash. *Virgin Land: The American West as Symbol and Myth*, 1950.

Spencer, B. T. *The Quest of Nationality: An American Literary Campaign*, 1957.

Spengermann, William C. *The Adventurous Muse: The Poetics of American Fiction, 1789-1900*, 1977.

Spiller, R. W. *The Cycle of American Literature: An Essay in Historical Criticism*, 1956.

Stewart, Randall. *American Literature and the Christian Tradition*, 1958.

Taylor, W. F. *The Economic Novel in America*, 1942.

Tyler, M. C. *A History of American Literature During the Colonial Period, 1607-1765*. Two volumes, 1878. Revised edition, 1897. One volume, 1949.

———. *The Literary History of the American Revolution, 1763-1783*. Two volumes, 1897; one volume, 1941.

Waggoner, Hyatt, *American Poets: From the Puritans to the Present*, 1968.

Williams, Stanley T. *The Spanish Background of American Literature*, 1955.

Wilson, Edmund, Editor. *The Shock of Recognition*.

———. *Patriotic Gore: Studies in the Literature of the American Civil War*, 1962.

B. HISTORY

Bailyn, Bernard. *The Ideological Origins of the American Revolution*, 1977.

Bailyn, Bernard, David B. Davis, David H. Donald, et al. *The Great Republic: A History of the American People*, 1977.

Baritz, Loren. *City on a Hill: A History of Ideas and Myths in America*, 1964.

Buck, Paul H. *The Road to Reunion, 1865-1900*, 1937.

Beard, C. A., and M. R. Beard. *The Rise of American Civilization*. Four volumes, 1927-1942.

Billington, R. A. *Westward Expansion: A History of the American Frontier*, 1949.

Burnham, John C., Editor. *Science in America*, 19—.

Butcher, Margaret. *The Negro in American Culture*, 1956.

Cargill, Oscar. *Intellectual America: Ideas on the March*, 1941.

Cash, W. J. *The Mind of the South*, 1941.

Chronicles of America Series. Allen Johnson, General Editor. Fifty volumes, 1918-1921. Six supplementary volumes, Allen Nevins, Editor, 1950-1951.

Commager, Henry S. *The American Mind: An Interpretation of American Thought and Character Since the 1880's*, 1950.

Curti, Merle. *The Growth of American Thought*, 1943.

Dorfman, Joseph. *The Economic Mind in American Civilization.* Three volumes, 1946-1949 (through World War I).

Fish, C. R. *The Rise of the Common Man, 1830-50*, 1927.

Franklin, John Hope. *From Slavery to Freedom: A History of American Negroes*, 3rd edition, revised and enlarged, 1967.

Gabriel, R. H. *The Course of American Thought*, 1943.

Gaustad, Edwin Scott. *A Religious History of America*, 1943.

Hesseltine, W. B. *A History of the South.* Revised, 1943.

Horton, Rod W., and Herbert Edwards. *Backgrounds of American Literary Thought*, 1952.

Howe, Irving. *A World More Attractive: A View of Modern Literature and Politics*, 1963.

Lasch, Christopher. *The New Radicalism in America, 1899-1963: The Intellectual as a Social Type*, 1965.

Lerner, Max. *America as a Civilization*, 19—.

Lomax, Alan. *The Folk Songs of North America*, 1960.

Lynn, Kenneth S., Editor. *The Comic Tradition in America*, 1958.

Miller, Perry. *Errand in the Wilderness*, 1963.

———. *The Life of the Mind in America from the Revolution to the Civil War*, 1965.

———. *The New England Mind: The Seventeenth Century*, 1939.

———. *The New England Mind: From Colony to Province*, 1953.

———. *The Raven and the Whale: The War of the Words and Wits in the Era of Poe and Melville*, 1956.

Morison, Samuel Eliot, and Henry S. Commager. *The Growth of the American Republic.* Two volumes, revised, 1950.

Myrdal, Gunnar. *An American Dilemma: The Negro Problem and Modern Democracy.* Two volumes, 1944.

Nevins, Allan. *The Emergence of Modern America, 1865-1878*, 1927.

Nichols, R. F. *The Disruption of American Democracy*, 1948.

Redding, J. Saunders. *The Lonesome Road: The Story of the Negro's Part in America.*

Reingold, Nathan, Editor. *Science in Nineteenth Century America*, 1946.

Rosenberg, Bernard, and David N. White. *Mass Culture: The Popular Arts in America*, 1957.

Schlesinger, A. M. *The Rise of the City, 1878-1898*, 1933.

———. *The Rise of Modern America, 1865-1951*, 1951.

Schlesinger, A. M., Jr. *The Age of Jackson*, 1945.

Schneider, H. W. *History of American Philosophy*, 1946.

Stampp, Kenneth. *The Peculiar Institution*, 1956.

Washburn, Wilcomb E. and John Aubrey. *The North American Indian Captivity*, 1977.

Stephenson, W. J., and E. M. Coulter, Editors. *A History of the South.* Six volumes, 1948-1953.

Washburn, Wilcomb E. and John Aubrey. *The North American Indian Captivity*, 1977.

Wish, Harvey. *Society and Thought in America.* Two volumes, 1950-1952.

C. ART

Andrews, Wayne. *Architecture in America: A Photographic History,* 1960.

Dunlap, William. *A History of the Rise and Progress of the Arts of Design in the United States.* Two volumes, 1834. Reissued, edited with additions by F. W. Bayley and C. E. Goodspeed. Three volumes. Revised, enlarged edition, edited by Alexander Wyckoff, preface by William P. Campbell. Three volumes, 1965.

Barker, Virgil. *American Painting: History and Interpretation,* 1950.

Burroughs, Alan. *Liners and Likenesses: Three Centuries of American Painting,* 1936.

Eliot, Alexander. *Three Hundred Years of American Painting,* 1957.

Flexner, James Thomas. *First Flowers of our Wilderness: American Painting,* 1947.

———. *The Light of Distant Skies, 1760-1835,* 1954.

———. *That Wilder Image,* 1962.

Jarves, James Jackson. *Art Hints, Architecture, Sculpture, and Painting,* 1855.

———. *The Art-Idea,* 1864; reissued, 1960.

———. *Art Thoughts,*

LaFollette, Suzanne. *Art in America From Colonial Times to the Present Day,* 1929.

Larkin, Oliver W. *Art and Life in America.* New York, 1960.

Richardson, E. P. *Painting in America,* 1956.

———. *A Short History of Painting in America,* 1963.

Whiffen, Marcus. *American Architecture Since 1780: A Guide to the Styles,* 1969.

D. MUSIC

Chase, Gilbert. *America's Music From the Pilgrims to the Present,* 1953.

Howard, J. J., and G. K. Bellows. *A Short History of Music in America,* 1957.

Jackson, G. P. *White and Negro Spirituals: Their Life Span and Kinship,* 1943.

Lomax, Alan. *The Folk Songs of North America,* 1960.

VOLUME II

THE AGE OF REALISM

Brooks, Van Wyck. *New England: Indian Summer, 1865-1915,* 1940.

Cochran, Thomas, and William Miller. *The Age of Enterprise: A Social History of Industrial America,* 1942.

Griswold, A. Whitman. *The American Cult of Success,* 1934.

Hofstadter, Richard. *Social Darwinism in American Thought,* 1943.

Lively, Robert A. *Fiction Fights the Civil War,* 1956.

Martin, Jay. *Harvests of Change: American Literature, 1865-1914,* 1967.

Nevins, Allan. *The Emergence of Modern America, 1860-1878,* 1927.

Odum, Howard W. and Harry E. Moore. *American Regionalism: A Cultural-Historical Approach to National Integration,* 1938.

Pattee, F. L. *A History of American Literature Since 1870,* 1915.

Pizer, Donald. *Realism and Naturalism in Nineteenth-Century American Literature,* 1966.

Wiener, Philip P. *Evolution and the Founders of Pragmatism*, 1949.

Ziff, Larzer. *The American 1890's: Life and Times of a Lost Generation*, 1966.

THE TWENTIETH CENTURY

Ahnbrinker, Lars. *The Beginnings of Naturalism in American Fiction*, 1950.

Baumbach, Jonathan. *Landscape of Nightmare: Studies in the Contemporary American Novel*, 1965.

Berthoff, Warner. *The Ferment of Realism: American Literature, 1884–1919*, 1965.

Bogan, Louise. *Achievement in American Poetry, 1900–1950*, 1951.

Bone, Robert A. *The Negro Novel in America*. Revised Edition, 1965.

Cowley, Malcolm. *After the Genteel Tradition, 1910–1930*. Revised Edition, 1964.

———. *A Second Flowering: Works and Days of the Lost Generation*, 1973.

Edel, Leon. *The Psychological Novel, 1900–1950*, 1955.

Geismar, Maxwell. *American Moderns: From Rebellion to Conformity*, 1958.

———. *The Last of the Provincials*, 1947.

———. *Rebels and Ancestors*, 1890–1915.

Writers in Crisis: The American Novel Between Two Wars, 1942.

Hassan, Ihab. *Radical Innocence: The Contemporary Novel*, 1961.

Hoffman, Frederick J. *The Twenties: American Writing in the Postwar Decade*, 1955.

Howe, Irving. *The World of Our Fathers*, 1976.

Kazin, Alfred. *On Native Grounds: An Interpretation of Modern American Prose Literature*, 1942.

Klein. *After Alienation: American Novels in Mid-Century*, 1962.

Kramer, Dale. *Chicago Renaissance: The Literary Life in the Midwest, 1900–1930*, 1966.

Krutch, J. W. *The American Drama Since 1918: An Informal History*, 1939.

Margolies, Edward. *Native Sons: A Critical Study of Twentieth-Century American Authors*, 1968.

Millgate, Michael. *American Social Fiction: James to Cozzens*, 1967.

O'Connor, W. V. *An Age of Criticism, 1900–1950*, 1952.

Rosenthal, M. L. *The Modern Poets: A Critical Introduction*, 196?.

Vogel, Dan. *The Three Masks of American Tragedy*, 1976.

Walcutt, Charles C. *American Literary Naturalism: A Divided Stream*, 1956.

Weales, Gerald. *American Drama Since World War Two*, 1962.

Winters, Yvor. *In Defense of Reason*, 1947, 1959.

Index

Authors and selection included in these volumes are indicated by bold face type. Page numbers on which main discussion of an author or the page on which an individual selection begins are indicated by bold face type. Titles of works referred to but not included in these volumes are in bold face italic.

CREDITS *(continued)*

Emily Dickinson: From *The Complete Poems of Emily Dickinson:* Poem Numbers 67, 130, 158, 199, 214, 249, 258, 287, 288, 303, 327, 328, 389, 435, 448, 449, 465, 520, 528, 579, 585, 640, 657, 712, 754, 959, 963, 986, 1068, 1129, and 1540 by Emily Dickinson. Reprinted by permission of the publishers and the trustees of Amherst College. Edited by Thomas H. Johnson. Cambridge, Mass.: The Belknap Press of Harvard University Press, Copyright 1951, 1955, by the President and Fellows of Harvard College.

Emily Dickinson: From *The Complete Poems of Emily Dickinson,* Edited by Thomas H. Johnson. Poem numbers 985 and 1071. Copyright 1914, 1942, by Martha Dickinson Bianchi. Poem numbers 341, 448, 657, 754, and 910. Copyright 1929, by Martha Dickinson Bianchi. Copyright 1957, by Mary L. Hampson. Poem numbers 281, 383, and 963. Copyright 1935, by Martha Dickinson Bianchi. Copyright renewed 1963, by Mary L. Hampson. Reprinted by permission of Little, Brown and Co.

Frederick Jackson Turner: From "The Significance of the Frontier in American History," in *The Frontier in American History* by Frederick Jackson Turner. Copyright 1920, by Frederick Jackson Turner. Copyright 1948, by Caroline M.S. Turner. Reprinted by permission of Holt, Rinehart and Winston, Publishers.

Henry Adams: From "The Dynamo and the Virgin," in *The Education of Henry Adams* by Henry Adams. Copyright 1918, by the Massachusetts Historical Society. Copyright 1946, by Charles F. Adams. Reprinted by permission of Houghton Mifflin Company.

Thomas Eakins: From *"Gross Clinic"* by Thomas Eakins. Courtesy of Jefferson Medical College, Thomas Jefferson University, Philadelphia.

Thomas Eakins: From "Will Schuster and Blackman Going Shooting for Rail" by Thomas Eakins. Yale University Art Gallery, Bequest of Stephen Carlton Clark.

Winslow Homer: From "The Morning Bell" by Winslow Homer. Yale University Art Gallery, Bequest of Stephen Carlton Clark.

James Abbott McNeill Whistler: From "The White Girl (Symphony in White, No. 1)" by James Abbott McNeill Whistler. National Gallery of Art, Washington, Harris Whittemore Collection.

Thomas Anshutz: From "Steelworkers' Noontime" by Thomas Anshutz. Courtesy of Kennedy Galleries.

Randolph Bourne: From in "The History of a Literary Radical" in *The History of a Literary Radical & Other Papers* by Randolph Bourne. New York: S.A. Russell, 1956.

Van Wyck Brooks: From *Three Essays on America* by Van Wyck Brooks. Copyright 1934, by E.P. Dutton & Co. renewed in 1962, by Van Wyck Brooks. Reprinted by permission of the publishers, E.P. Dutton & Co.

John Dewey: From *Democracy and Education* by John Dewey. Copyright 1916, by Macmillan Publishing Co. Renewed in 1944 by John Dewey. Reprinted by permission of Macmillan Publishing Co.

John Crowe Ranson: From "Reconstructed but Unregenerate" by John Crowe Ransom in *I'll Take My Stand* by Twelve Southerners. Copyright 1930, by Harper & Brothers. Renewed in 1958 by Donald Davidson.

John Crowe Ransom: From *Introduction to the Torchbook Edition.* Copyright 1962, by Virginia Rock. Reprinted by permission of Harper & Row, Publishers.

Theodore Dreiser: From *An American Tragedy* by Theodore Dreiser. Copyright 1925, by Horace Liveright; renewed in 1926, by Theodore Dreiser; renewed in 1953 by Helen Dreiser. Reprinted by permission of Thomas Y. Crowell Company, Publisher.

Ezra Pound: From *Personae* by Ezra Pound. Copyright 1926, by Ezra Pound. Reprinted by permission of New Directions Publishing Corporation.

T.S. Eliot: From *Collected Poems 1909–1962* by T.S. Eliot. Copyright 1936, by Harcourt Brace Jovanovich. Copyright renewed in 1963, 1964, by T.S. Eliot. Reprinted by permission of the publishers.

T.S. Eliot: From "East Coker," *Four Quarters* by T.S. Eliot. Copyright 1943, by T.S. Eliot. Copyright renewed in 1971, by Esme Valerie Eliot. Reprinted by permission of Harcourt Brace Jovanovich.

William Carlos Williams: From *Collected Earlier Poems* by William Carlos Williams. Copyright 1938, by New Directions Publishing Corporation. Reprinted by permission of New Directions Publishing Corporation.

William Carlos Williams: From "Asphodel: That Greeny Flower," *Pictures From Brueghel and Other Poems* by William Carlos Williams. Copyright 1954, by William Carlos Williams. Reprinted by permission of New Directions Publishing Corporation.

James Weldon Johnson: From "O Black and Unknown Bards," in *St. Peter Relates an Incident* by James Weldon Johnson. Copyright 1917, by James Weldon Johnson. All rights reserved. Reprinted by permission of Viking Penguin.

James Weldon Johnson: From "The Creation" in *God's Trombones* by James Weldon Johnson. Copyright 1927, by the Viking Press. Renewed in 1955 by Grace Neil Johnson. Reprinted by permission of Viking Penguin.

Claude McKay: From "The White House," "If We Must Die," "Harlem Shadows," "Harlem Dancer," in *Selected Poems of Claude McKay.* Copyright 1953, by Twayne Publishers. Reprinted by permission of Twayne Publishers, a division of G.K. Hall & Company.

Jean Toomer: From *Cane* by Jean Toomer. Copyright 1923, by Goni & Liveright. Renewed in 1951, by Jean Toomer. Reprinted by permission of Liveright, Publishers, New York.

Countee Cullen: "Yet Do I Marvell," "For Paul Laurence Dunbar," "Incident" in *On These I Stand* by Countee Cullen. Copyright 1925, by Harper & Row, Publishers. Renewed in 1963, by Ida M. Cullen. Reprinted by permission of the publisher.

Countee Cullen: From "Scottsboro, Too, Is Worth Its Song" in *On These I Stand* by Countee Cullen. Copyright 1935, by Harper & Row, Publishers. Renewed in 1963, by Ida M. Cullen. Reprinted by permission of the publisher.

Langston Hughes: From "Evenin' Air Blues" in *Shakespeare in Harlem*, 1942. Copyright 1942, by Alfred A. Knopf. Renewed. Reprinted by permission of Harold Ober Associates Incorporated.

Langston Hughes: From "Dream Boogie" in *Montage of a Dream Deferred* by Langston Hughes. Copyright 1951, by Langston Hughes. Reprinted by permission of Harold Ober Associates, Incorporated.

Langston Hughes: From "Theme For English B" in *Montage of a Dream Deferred* by Langston Hughes. Copyright 1951, by Langston Hughes. Reprinted by permission of Harold Ober Associates, Incorporated.

Langston Hughes: From "Jazz, Jive and Jam" in *The Best of Simple* by Langston Hughes. Copyright 1961, by Langston Hughes. Reprinted by permission of Farrar, Straus & Giroux. This selection originally appeared in *Simple Stakes a Claim.* Copyright 1953, 1954, 1955, 1956, by Langston Hughes.

Langston Hughes: From "The Negro Speaks of Rivers" in *Selected Poems* by Langston Hughes. Copyright 1926, by Alfred A. Knopf. Renewed in 1954, by Langston Hughes. Reprinted by permission of Alfred A. Knopf.

Norman Mailer: From "The White Negro," in *Advertisements for Myself* by Norman Mailer. Copyright 1959, by Norman Mailer. Reprinted by permission of G.P. Putnam's Sons.

Norman Mailer: From "The Marshal and the Nazi," *Armies of the Night* by Norman Mailer. Reprinted by permission of the New American Library.

Allen Ginsberg: From "Howl for Carl Solomon," "A Supermarket in California," "To Aunt Rose." Copyright 1956, 1959, by Allen Ginsberg. Reprinted by permission of City Lights Books.

Robert Lowell: From *For the Union Dead:* "The Old Flame," "For the Union Dead." From *Life Studies* (1958): "Skunk Hour," "Beyond the Alps," and "91 Revere Street." Reprinted by permission of Farrar, Straus & Giroux. From *Life Studies* by Robert Lowell, copyright 1956, 1959, by Robert Lowell. From *For the Union Dead* by Robert Lowell, copyright 1960, 1962, by Robert Lowell.

Robert Lowell: From "In Memory of Arthur Winslow," in *Lord Weary's Castle* by Robert Lowell, copyright 1946, 1974, by Robert Lowell. Reprinted by permission of Harcourt Brace Jovanovich.

Robert Lowell: From "Mr. Edwards and the Spider," "The Quaker Graveyard in Nantucket" in *Lord Weary's Castle.* Copyright 1946, 1974, by Robert Lowell. Reprinted by permission of Harcourt Brace Jovanovich, Inc.

Adrienne Rich: From "Living In Sin" in *Poems, Selected and New 1950-1974* by Adrienne Rich. Copyright 1975, 1973, 1971, 1969, 1966, by W.W. Norton & Company. Copyright 1967, 1963, 1962, 1961, 1960, 1959, 1957, 1956, 1955, 1954, 1953, 1952, 1951 by Adrienne Rich. Reprinted by permission of W.W. Norton & Company.

Adrienne Rich: From "Peeling Onions" in *Snapshots of a Daughter-In-Law, Poems 1954-1962* by Adrienne Rich. Copyright 1956, 1957, 1958, 1960, 1961, 1962, 1963, 1967, by Adrienne Rich Conrad. Reprinted by permission of W.W. Norton & Company.

Adrienne Rich: From "Rape" *Diving Into the Wreck, Poems 1971-1972* by Adrienne Rich. Copyright 1973, by W.W. Norton & Company. Reprinted by permssion of W.W. Norton & Company.

Adrienne Rich: From "A Valediction Forbidding Mourning" in *The Will To Change, Poems, 1968-1970* by Adrienne Rich. By permission of W.W. Norton & Company, Inc. Copyright 1971, by W.W. Norton & Company. Reprinted by permission of W.W. Norton & Company.

Sylvia Plath: From *Ariel* by Sylvia Plath: "Daddy," "The Applicant," "Lady Lazarus," "Death & Co." Copyright 1963, by Ted Hughes; "Ariel," copyright, 1965 by Ted Hughes. All reprinted by permission of Harper & Row, Publishers.

Imamu Amiri Baraka: From "Preface to a Twenty-Volume Suicide Note" in *Twenty-Volume Suicide Note* by LeRoi Jones (Imamu Amiri Baraka). Copyright 1961 (Totem Press in Association with Cornith Press, 1961); "A Poem for Black Hearts" (reprinted from *Negro Digest;* September 1965). Reprinted by permission of Sterling Lord Agency.

Michael Harper: From "Reuben, Reuben" in Dear John, Dear Coltrane by Michael S. Harper. Copyright 1970, by the University of Pittsburgh Press. Renewed in 1972, by Michael S. Harper. Reprinted by permission of the University of Pittsburgh Press.

Don Lee: From "The New Integrationist," "The Negro" in *Directioncore: Selected and New Poems* by Don Lee. Copyright 1971, by Don L. Lee. Reprinted by permission of Broadside Press.

Edwin Arlington Robinson: From "Mr. Flood's Party" in *Collected Poems* by Edwin Arlington Robinson. Copyright 1921, by Edwin Arlington Robinson. Renewed in 1949 by Ruth Nivison. Reprinted by permission of Macmillan Publishing Co.

Edwin Arlington Robinson: From "Bewick Finzer," "Casandre," "Flammode," "Eros Turannos" in *Collected Poems* by Edwin Arlington Robinson. Copyright 1916, by Edwin Arlington Robinson. Renewed in 1944, by Ruth Nivison. Reprinted by permission of Macmillan Publishing Co.

Edwin Arlington Robinson: From "George Crabbe," "Richard Cory," and "Rueben Bright" in *The Children of the Night* by Edwin Arlington Robinson. Reprinted by permission of Charles Scribner's Sons. "Miniver Cheevy" (copyright 1907, Charles Scribner's Sons) and "Clavering" are reprinted by permission of Charles Scribner's Sons from *The Town Down the River* by Edwin Arlington Robinson. Copyright 1910, Charles Scribner's Sons.

Carl Sandburg: From "Chicago" in *Chicago Poems* by Carl Sandburg. Copyright 1916, by Holt, Rinehart and Winston. Copyright 1944, by Carl Sandburg. Reprinted by permission of Harcourt Brace Jovanovich.

Carl Sandburg: From "Grass," "Washerwoman," "Cool Tombs" in *Cork Huskers* by Carl Sandburg. Copyright 1918, by Holt, Rinehart & Winston. Copyright 1946, by Carl Sandburg. Reprinted by permission of Harcourt Brace Jovanovich.

Carl Sandburg: From "Waiting for the Chariot" in *Complete Poems* by Carl Sandburg. Copyright 1950, by Carl Sandburg. Reprinted by permission of Harcourt Brace Jovanovich.

Hart Crane: From *The Collected Poems and Selected Letters and Prose of Hart Crane* by Hart Crane. Copyright 1933, 1958, 1966, by Liveright Publishing Corporation. Reprinted by permission of Liveright Publishing, New York.

Robert Frost: From *The Poetry of Robert Frost* edited by Edward Connery Lathem. Copyright 1916, 1928, 1930, 1939, 1947, 1969, Holt, Rinehart and Winston. Copyright 1936, 1942, 1944, 1956, 1958, by Robert Frost. Copyright 1964, 1967, 1970, 1975, by Lesley Frost Ballantine. Reprinted by permission of Holt, Rinehart and Winston, Publishers.

Wallace Stevens: From "The Idea of Order at Key West." Copyright 1935, by Wallace Stevens and renewed 1964, by Holly Stevens, "The World as Meditation." Copyright 1952, by Wallace Stevens. "Botanist on Alp (No. 2). Copyright 1936, by Wallace Stevens and renewed 1964, by Holly Stevens. "A Primitive Like and Orb." Copyright 1948, by Wallace Stevens. "Anecdote of the Jar." Copyright 1923 and renewed 1951, by Wallace Stevens. "A High-Toned Old Christian Woman," "Sunday Morning," "Peter Quince at the Clavier," "The Emperor of Ice-Cream," "The Snow Man," "To the One of Fictive Music." Reprinted from *The Collected Poems of Wallace Stevens.* By permission of Alfred A. Knopf.

Marianne Moore: "Poetry," "No Swan so Fine" "The Frigate Pelican" in *Collected Poems* by Marianne Moore. Copyright 1935, by Marianne Moore, renewed 1963, by Marianne Moore and T.S. Eliot. Reprinted by permission of Macmillan Publishing Co.

Melvin Tolson: From "Dark Symphony" in *Rendezvous With America* by Melvin B. Tolson. Copyright 1944, by Dodd, Mead & Company. Copyright renewed in 1972, by Ruth S. Tolson. Reprinted by permission of Dodd, Mead & Company.

Gwendolyn Brooks: From "The Children of the poor, 1 & 4," in *The World of Gwendolyn Brooks* (1971) by Gwendolyn Brooks. Copyright 1949, by Gwendolyn Brooks Blakely.

Gwendolyn Brooks: From "We Real Cool: The Pool Players. Seven at the Golden Shovel" in *The World of Gwendolyn Brooks* (1971).

Gwendolyn Brooks: From "The Chicago Defender Sends a Man to Little Rock" in *The World of Gwendolyn Brooks* (1971). Copyright 1960, by Gwendolyn Brooks.
All reprinted by permission of Harper & Row, Publishers.

Randall Jarrell: From "The Lost Children," "Well Water" in *The Lost World* by Randall Jarrell. Copyright 1965, by Randall Jarrell. Reprinted by permission of Macmillan Publishing Co.

Randall Jarrell: From "Bats" in *The Bat-Poet* by Randall Jarrell. Copyright 1963, 1964, Macmillan Publishing Co. Reprinted by permission of Macmillan Publishing Co.

Randall Jarrell: From "A Girl in the Library," "Moving," "The Death of the Ball Turret Gunner," "Eight Air Force" in *The Complete Poems* by Randall Jarrell. Copyright 1969. Reprinted by permission of Farrar, Straus & Giroux.

Ernest Hemingway: From "A Clean, Well-Lighted Place" in *Winner Take Nothing* by Ernest Hemingway. (Copyright 1933, Charles Scribner's Sons.) Reproduced by permission of Charles Scribner's Sons.

William Faulkner: From "Mule in the Yard," copyright 1934 and renewed 1962, by William Faulkner. "Old Man," copyright 1939 and renewed 1967, by Mrs. William Faulkner and Mrs. Paul D. Summers. Reprinted from *Collected Stories of William Faulkner*, by permission of Random House.

F. Scott Fitzgerald: From "The Rich Boy" in *All the Sad Young Men* by F. Scott Fitzgerald. (Copyright 1925, 1926, Consolidated Magazines Corp.) Reproduced by permission of Charles Scribner's Sons.

John Steinbeck: From "The Leader of the People" in *The Red Pony* by John Steinbeck. Copyright 1938, renewed 1966, by John Steinbeck. Reprinted by permission of Viking Penguin.

Eudora Welty: From "A Worn Path" in *A Curtain of Green and Other Stories* by Eudora Welty. (New York: Harcourt, Brace Jovanovich, Inc., 1969.)

Flannery O'Connor: From "Parker's Back" in *Everything that Rises Must Converge* by Flannery O'Connor. Copyright 1965. Reprinted by permission of Farrar, Straus & Giroux, Publishers.

Saul Bellow: From *Seize the Day* by Saul Bellow. Copyright 1956, by Saul Bellow. Reprinted by permission of Viking Penguin.

John Updike: From "When Everyone Was Pregnant" in *Museums and Women and Other Stories* by John Updike. Copyright 1971, by John Updike. Reprinted by permission of Alfred A. Knopf.

Thomas Pynchon: From *Gravity's Rainbow* by Thomas Pynchon. Copyright 1973, by Thomas Pynchon. Reprinted by permission of The Viking Press.

Eugene O'Neill: From "The Hairy Ape," in Selected Plays of Eugene O'Neill. Copyright 1922 and renewed 1950, by Eugene O'Neill. Reprinted by permission of Random House.

Edward Albee: From *The American Dream* by Edward Albee. Copyright 1960, 1961, by Edward Albee. Reprinted by permission of Coward, McCann, Geoghegan, Inc. *The*

American Dream is the sole property of the author and is fully protected by copyright. It may not be acted either by professionals or amateurs without written consent. Public readings, radio and television broadcasts likewise are forbidden. All inquiries concerning these rights should be addressed to the William Morris Agency, 1350 Avenue of the Americas, New York, New York 10019.

John Dos Passos: From *U.S.A. An Omnibus.* Published by Houghton Mifflin Co. Copyright © 1963, Elizabeth H. Dos Passos. Reprinted by permission of Elizabeth H. Dos Passos.

Edmund Wilson: From *The American Jitters* "Chapter XXVII: The Best People" from *The American Earthquake* by Edmund Wilson. Copyright 1958, by Edmund Wilson. Reprinted by permission of Farrar, Straus & Giroux, Inc.

Truman Capote: From *In Cold Blood* by Truman Capote. Copyright 1965, by Truman Capote. Reprinted by permission of Random House. Originally appeared in *The New Yorker* in slightly different form.

Jane Addams: From "The Subjective Necessity for Social Settlements," in *Philanthropy and Social Progress*, New York: Thomas Y. Crowell, 1893.

Joseph Freeman: From *Proletarian Literature in the United States: An Anthology.* Edited by Joseph Freeman, Joseph North, et al. Copyright 1935. Reprinted by permission of International Publishers, New York.

James Agee: From *Let Us Now Praise Famous Men*, pp. 38–43 and 49–73. (Boston: Houghton Mifflin, 1941.) Copyright © renewed by Mia Fritsch Agee. Reprinted by permission of Houghton Mifflin Company.

Richard Wright: From "The Ethics of Living Jim Crow" in *Uncle Tom's Children* by Richard Wright (pp. 3–15). Copyright 1937, by Richard Wright; renewed 1965, by Ellen Wright. Reprinted by permission of Harper & Row, Publishers.

Ralph Ellison: From "Prologue" in *Invisible Man* by Ralph Ellison. Copyright 1952, by Ralph Ellison. Reprinted by permission of Random House.

James Baldwin: From "Down at the Cross: Letter from a Region in My Mind" excerpted from *The Fire Next Time* by James Baldwin. Copyright © 1962, 1963, by James Baldwin. Reprinted with the permission of The Dial Press.

Robert Coles: From *Children of Crisis: A Study of Courage and Fear* by Robert Coles. Reprinted by permission of Little, Brown and Co., in association with the Atlantic Monthly Press.

N. Scott Momaday: From *The Way to Rainy Mountain* by N. Scott Momaday. Copyright 1969. Reproduced by permission of The University of New Mexico Press.

This book was designed by Suzanne Bennett.
Picture research was done by Abi Gail Solomon.
Debra Schwartz supervised production.

THE EDITORS

Volume 1

David Levin. Commonwealth Professor of English, University of Virginia. Harvard Ph.D. He has also taught at Stanford, University of Strasbourg, University of Toulouse, and the University of Madrid. Chief publications: articles and books on American literature, especially historical literature, including fiction and autobiography. *History as Romantic Art: Bancroft, Prescott, Motley, and Parkman; In Defense of Historical Literature;* and he is now writing a biography of Cotton Mather. Edited books: *What Happened In Salem? Documents Pertaining to the Salem Witchcraft Trials; Bonifacius, An essay Upon The Good by Cotton Mather;* and *The Puritan in the Enlightenment: Franklin and Edwards.*

Theodore L. Gross (General Editor). Vice-President for Institutional Advancement and Professor of English, The City College of The City University of New York. Columbia Ph.D. He has also taught at Barnard College, University of Nancy, and the University of Nice. Author of *The Heroic Ideal in American Literature; Hawthorne, Melville, Crane: A Critical Bibliography* (with S. Wertheim); *Thomas Nelson Page;* and *Albion W. Tourgée.* Edited books: *The Literature of American Jews; A Nation of Nations; Representative Men;* and *Dark Symphony: The Development of Negro Literature in America* (Coeditor, James Emanuel).

Volume 2

Alan Trachtenberg. Professor of American Studies and English, Yale University. Minnesota Ph.D. He has also taught at Pennsylvania State University and the University of New Mexico. Author of *Brooklyn Bridge: Fact and Symbol.* Edited books: *Democratic Vistas, 1865–1880; The City: American Experience* (Coeditors Peter Bunnell and Peter Neil); *Memoirs of Waldo Frank;* and *Critics of Culture.*

Benjamin DeMott. Professor of English, Amherst College. Harvard Ph.D. He has also taught at MIT, Yale, the City University of New York, and Birmingham University (England). He has written two novels, *The Body's Cage* and *A Married Man,* and is the author of numerous works on cultural commentary: *Hells & Benefits; You Don't Say; Supergrow; Surviving the Seventies;* and *Scholarship for Society.* He has been a book critic for *Harper's,* a contributing editor for *Saturday Review,* and is a columnist for *The Atlantic Monthly.*